1999 EDITION

FEDERAL CIVIL JUDICIAL PROCEDURE and RULES

as amended to January 4, 1999

Rules of Civil Procedure
Rules of Judicial Panel on Multidistrict Litigation
Rules—Habeas Corpus Cases
Rules—Motion Attacking Sentence
Rules of Evidence
Rules of Appellate Procedure
Rules of the Supreme Court

Includes laws through the close of the 105th Congress, Second Session (1998)

Title 28, Judiciary and Judicial Procedure
Act June 25, 1948, c. 646, §§ 2 to 39
Appendix:
Judicial Personnel Financial Disclosure Requirements [Repealed]
Development of Mechanisms for Resolving Minor Disputes [Codified]
Constitution of the United States
Title 5, Government Organization and Employees
App. 4—Financial Disclosure Requirements of Federal Personnel
Consolidated Index

WEST'S COMMITMENT TO THE ENVIRONMENT

In 1906, West began recycling materials left over from the production of books. This began a tradition of efficient and responsible use of resources. Today, 100% of our legal bound volumes are printed on acid-free, recycled paper consisting of 50% new fibers. West recycles nearly 27,700,000 pounds of scrap paper annually—the equivalent of 229,300 trees. Since the 1960s, West has devised ways to capture and recycle waste inks, solvents, oils, and vapors created in the printing process. We also recycle plastics of all kinds, wood, glass, corrugated cardboard, and batteries, and have eliminated the use of polystyrene book packaging. We at West are proud of the longevity and the scope of our commitment to the environment.

West pocket parts and advance sheets are printed on recyclable paper and can be collected and recycled with newspapers. Staples do not have to be removed. Bound volumes can be recycled after removing the cover.

ISBN 0–314–23494–2

PRINTED ON 10% POST CONSUMER RECYCLED PAPER

PREFACE

This pamphlet updates the rules and statutes in the 1998 Edition Pamphlet and its 1998 Supplement.

Reference should also be made to Supreme Court Reporter, Federal Reporter, Federal Supplement, and Federal Rules Decisions advance sheets, as well as WESTLAW, for any interim changes affecting the court rules in this Pamphlet.

This convenient reference Pamphlet, in form suitable for courtroom and office use, contains the text of the —

Federal Rules of Civil Procedure.

Supplementary Rules—Admiralty and Maritime Claims.

Rules of Procedure of the Judicial Panel on Multidistrict Litigation.

Rules governing Habeas Corpus Cases and Motions Attacking Sentence.

Federal Rules of Evidence.

Federal Rules of Appellate Procedure.

Rules of the Supreme Court of the United States.

Title 28, Judiciary and Judicial Procedure.

Miscellaneous provisions from sections 2 to 39 of Act June 25, 1948, c. 646, are set out after the text of Title 28. An Appendix follows these miscellaneous provisions and refers to former provisions relating to judicial personnel financial disclosure requirements in Pub.L. 95–521, title III, sections 301 to 309, and to former provisions relating to the development of mechanisms for resolving minor disputes in Pub.L. 96–190. The Constitution of the United States follows the Appendix. Provisions relating to financial disclosure requirements of federal personnel are set out in Title 5 Appendix 4.

The several Committees on Rules of Practice and Procedure of the Judicial Conference of the United States are listed herein for the information of the Bench and Bar.

A combined Time Table for Lawyers under Title 28, Judiciary and Judicial Procedure; the Federal Rules of Civil Procedure; the Federal Rules of Appellate Procedure; and the Revised Rules of the Supreme Court is also included. This Table indicates the time for each of the various procedural steps required by the Rules.

A detailed, consolidated Index appears in the back of this pamphlet.

THE PUBLISHER

February, 1999

*

FEDERAL PRACTICE TOOLS FROM WEST

TEXTBOOKS

Administrative Law and Practice—Koch

Business and Commercial Litigation in Federal Courts—Haig

Constitutional Law: Substance and Procedure, 2nd Edition—Rotunda and Nowak

Courtroom Handbook on Federal Evidence—Goode and Wellborn

Criminal Law Defenses—Robinson

Criminal Procedure—LaFave and Israel

Expert Evidence—Black and Lee

Federal Jury Practice and Instructions
Edward J. Devitt, Charles B. Blackmar, Michael A. Wolff and Kevin F. O'Malley

Federal Grand Jury: A Guide to Law and Practice—Brenner & Lockhart

Federal Civil Rules Handbook—Baicker-McKee, Janssen and Corr

Handbook of Federal Civil Discovery and Disclosure—Grenig and Kinsler

Federal Criminal Practice: Prosecution and Defense—Subin, Mirsky & Weinstein

Federal Practice and Procedure, Revised Edition

Federal Sentencing Law and Practice, 1998 Edition—Hutchison & Yellen

Federal Evidence 3d—Graham

Litigating Civil Rights and Employment Discrimination Cases—Lewis

Modern Scientific Evidence—Faigman, Kaye, Saks and Sanders

Newberg on Class Actions, 3rd—Newberg and Conte

Search and Seizure 3d—LaFave

Social Security Claims and Procedure 4th—McCormick

Substantive Criminal Law—LaFave and Scott

West's Federal Forms

West's Federal Practice Manual 2d

United States Code Annotated

West's Federal Practice Digest 4th

United States Code Congressional and Administrative News

PAMPHLETS

Bankruptcy Code, Rules and Forms

Federal Environmental Laws

TABLE OF CONTENTS

	Page
Committees on Rules of Practice and Procedure of the Judicial Conference of the United States	IX
Federal Rules of Civil Procedure:	
Table of Rules	1
Time Table for Lawyers in Federal Civil Cases	3
Orders of the Supreme Court of the United States Adopting and Amending Rules	24
Text of Rules	35
Appendix of Forms	268
Supplemental Rules for Certain Admiralty and Maritime Claims	284
Rules of Procedure of the Judicial Panel on Multidistrict Litigation	296
Rules Governing Habeas Corpus Cases	305
Rules Governing Motions Attacking Sentences	326
Federal Rules of Evidence:	
Table of Rules	342
Orders of the Supreme Court of the United States Adopting and Amending Rules	343
Text of Rules	345
Federal Rules of Appellate Procedure:	
Table of Rules	439
Orders of the Supreme Court of the United States Adopting and Amending Rules	439
Text of Rules	443
Appendix of Forms	494
Rules of the Supreme Court of the United States	497
Title 28, U.S. Code, Judiciary and Judicial Procedure	520
Act June 25, 1948, c. 646, §§ 2 to 39, 62 Stat. 869, Miscellaneous Provisions	1031
Appendix:	
Judicial Personnel Financial Disclosure Requirements [Repealed]	1036
Development of Mechanisms for Resolving Minor Disputes [Codified]	1037
Constitution of the United States	1038
Title 5, U.S. Code, Government Organization and Employees:	
Appendix 4—Financial Disclosure Requirements of Federal Personnel	1056
Consolidated Index	1083

*

Committees on Rules OF PRACTICE AND PROCEDURE OF THE JUDICIAL CONFERENCE OF THE UNITED STATES

Announcement of the Chief Justice of the United States

SUPREME COURT OF THE UNITED STATES WASHINGTON, D.C.

APRIL 4, 1960

The Chief Justice of the United States announced today the appointment of six nationally–organized committees of judges, lawyers, and legal scholars whose job it will be to study and to recommend to the Supreme Court improvement in the rules of practice and procedure in the Federal courts.

The Committees were appointed pursuant to an Act passed by Congress [P.L. 85–513, 72 Stat. 356] July 11, 1958 [28 U.S.C.A. § 331], authorizing the Judicial Conference of the United States, of which the Chief Justice is Chairman, to make a continuous study of the Federal rules.

"The rules of court" Chief Justice Earl Warren said, "are the most important tools of the courtroom lawyer. So long as we have the inevitable changes in our social, economic and political lives, the demand for amendments in the rules, and also for new rules, by which we resolve conflicts in the courts is equally inevitable."

"It is essential that our rules of court by up–to–date and all amendments should be studied and recommended by committees with as broad an outlook and base as possible. Accordingly these committees include representatives of the bar, the judiciary and the legal scholars and for their ideas they will draw upon the bench and bar of the country as a whole and particularly the Judicial Conferences in all eleven of the Federal circuits.

"Experience has shown that in order to promote simplicity in procedure, the just determination of litigation and the elimination of unjustifiable expense and delay, it is essential that the operation and effect of the Federal rules of practice and procedure should be the subject of continuous study. Such study is the objective of the committees being announced today, and every judge, practicing lawyer, and legal scholar will be afforded the opportunity to participate—to state his views—with assurances that those views will be given consideration."

The Committees, and the Committee Chairmen, are:

COMMITTEES ON RULES

Standing Committee on Rules of Practice and Procedure

ALBERT B. MARIS, *Chairman*

Advisory Committees on Civil Rules

DEAN ACHESON, *Chairman*

Advisory Committee on Criminal Rules

JOHN C. PICKETT, *Chairman*

Advisory Committee on Admiralty Rules

WALTER L. POPE, *Chairman*

Advisory Committee on General Orders in Bankruptcy

PHILLIP FORMAN, *Chairman*

Advisory Committee on Appellate Rules

E. BARRETT PRETTYMAN, *Chairman*

The Advisory Committees will conduct the basic studies and develop reports and recommendations in the respective fields. These will be forwarded to the standing Committees on Rules of Practice and Procedure which, in turn, will report to the Judicial Conference of the United States. If approved, the Judicial Conference will formally forward the report and recommendations to the Supreme Court of the United States. The Supreme Court will approve, modify, or disapprove of the changes in the Federal rules, and those adopted will be transmitted by the Supreme Court to the Congress. In such cases, the rules automatically become law in ninety days unless the Congress acts adversely.

Memberships on the Committees are for 2 and 4 year terms, with each member entitled to one additional term. This will have the effect of bringing new ideas to the Committees and keeping pace with developments in the law.

Headquarters Secretariat for the rules study will be in the Administrative Office of the United States Courts, Supreme Court Building, Washington, D.C. under the direction of Warren Olney III, Director.* * *.

SECRETARIAT

Administrative Office of the United States Courts

Washington, D.C. 20544

L. RALPH MECHAM, Director

CLARENCE A. LEE, JR., Associate Director

Special Notice

Inquiries and correspondence with reference to the Rules of Practice and Procedure may be directed to—

PETER G. MCCABE, Secretary

Committee on Rules of Practice and Procedure
Administrative Office of the United States Courts
Washington, D.C. 20544

*

PROCEDURES FOR THE CONDUCT OF BUSINESS BY THE JUDICIAL CONFERENCE COMMITTEES ON RULES OF PRACTICE AND PROCEDURE

Scope

These procedures govern the operations of the Judicial Conference Committee on Rules of Practice, Procedure, and Evidence (Standing Committee) and the various Judicial Conference Advisory Committees on Rules of Practice and Procedure in drafting and recommending new rules of practice, procedure, and evidence and amendments to existing rules.

Part I—Advisory Committees

1. Functions

   Each Advisory Committee shall carry on "a continuous study of the operation and effect of the general rules of practice and procedure now or hereafter in use" in its particular field, taking into consideration suggestions and recommendations received from any source, new statutes and court decisions affecting the rules, and legal commentary.

2. Suggestions and Recommendations

   Suggestions and recommendations with respect to the rules should be sent to the Secretary, Committee on Rules of Practice and Procedure, Administrative Office of the United States Courts, Washington, D.C. 20544, who shall, to the extent feasible, acknowledge in writing every written suggestion or recommendation so received and shall refer all suggestions and recommendations to the appropriate Advisory Committee. To the extent feasible, the Secretary, in consultation with the Chairman of the Advisory Committee, shall advise the person making a recommendation or suggestion of the action taken thereon by the Advisory Committee.

3. Drafting Rules Changes

   a. An Advisory Committee shall meet at such times and places as the Chairman may authorize. All Advisory Committee meetings shall be open to the public, except when the committee so meeting, in open session and with a majority present, determines that it is in the public interest that all or part of the remainder of the meeting on that day shall be closed to the public and states the reason for closing the meeting. Each meeting shall be preceded by notice of the time and place of the meeting, including publication in the Federal Register, sufficient to permit interested persons to attend.

   b. The reporter assigned to each Advisory Committee shall, under the direction of the Committee or its Chairman, prepare initial draft rules changes, "Committee Notes" explaining their purpose and intent, copies or summaries of all written recommendations and suggestions received by the Advisory Committee, and shall forward them to the Advisory Committee.

   c. The Advisory Committee shall then meet to consider the draft proposed new rules and rules amendments, together with Committee Notes, make revisions therein, and submit them for approval of publication to the Standing Committee, or its Chairman, with a written report explaining the Committee's action, including any minority or other separate views.

4. Publication and Public Hearings

a. When publication is approved by the Standing Committee, the Secretary shall arrange for the printing and circulation of the proposed rules changes to the bench and bar, and to the public generally. Publication shall be as wide as practicable. Notice of the proposed rule shall be published in the Federal Register and copies provided to appropriate legal publishing firms with a request that they be timely included in their publications. The Secretary shall also provide copies to the chief justice of the highest court of each state and, insofar as is practicable, to all individuals and organizations that request them.

b. In order to provide full notice and opportunity for comment on proposed rule changes, a period of at least six months from the time of publication of notice in the Federal Register shall be permitted, unless a shorter period is approved under the provisions of subparagraph d of this paragraph.

c. An Advisory Committee shall conduct public hearings on all proposed rules changes unless elimination of such hearings is approved under the provisions of subparagraph d of this paragraph. The hearings shall be held at such times and places as determined by the chairman of the Advisory Committee and shall be preceded by adequate notice, including publication in the Federal Register. Proceedings shall be recorded and a transcript prepared. Subject to the provisions of paragraph six, such transcript shall be available for public inspection.

d. Exceptions to the time period for public comment and the public hearing requirement may be granted by the Standing Committee or its chairman when the Standing Committee or its chairman determines that the administration of justice requires that a proposed rule change should be expedited and that appropriate public notice and comment may be achieved by a shortened comment period, without public hearings, or both. The Standing Committee may eliminate the public notice and comment requirement if, in the case of a technical or conforming amendment, it determines that notice and comment are not appropriate or necessary. Whenever such an exception is made, the Standing Committee shall advise the Judicial Conference of the exception and the reasons for the exception.

5. Subsequent Procedures

a. At the conclusion of the comment period the reporter shall prepare a summary of the written comments received and the testimony presented at public hearings. The Advisory Committee shall review the proposed rules changes in the light of the comments and testimony. If the Advisory Committee makes any substantial change, an additional period for public notice and comment may be provided.

b. The Advisory Committee shall submit proposed rules changes and Committee Notes, as finally agreed upon, to the Standing Committee. Each submission shall be accompanied by a separate report of the comments received and shall explain any changes made subsequent to the original publication. The submission shall also include minority views of Advisory Committee members who wish to have separate views recorded.

6. Records

   a. The Chairman of the Advisory Committee shall arrange for the preparation of minutes of all Advisory Committee meetings.

   b. The records of an Advisory Committee shall consist of the written suggestions received from the public; the written comments received on drafts of proposed rules, responses thereto, transcripts of public hearings, and summaries prepared by the reporter; all correspondence relating to proposed rules changes; minutes of Advisory Committee meetings; approved drafts of rules changes; and reports to the Standing Committee. The records shall be maintained at the Administrative Office of the United States Courts for a minimum of two years and shall be available for public inspection during reasonable office hours. Thereafter the records may be transferred to a Government Records Center in accordance with applicable Government retention and disposition schedules.

   c. Any portion of minutes, relating to a closed meeting and made available to the public, may contain such deletions as may be necessary to avoid frustrating the purposes of closing the meeting as provided in subparagraph 3a.

   d. Copies of records shall be furnished to any person upon payment of a reasonable fee for the cost of reproduction.

PART II—Standing Committee

7. Functions

   The Standing Committee shall coordinate the work of the several Advisory Committees, make suggestions of proposals to be studied by them, consider proposals recommended by the Advisory Committees, and transmit such proposals with its recommendation to the Judicial Conference, or recommit them to the appropriate Advisory Committee for further study and consideration.

8. Procedures

   a. The Standing Committee shall meet at such times and places as the Chairman may authorize. All Committee meetings shall be open to the public, except when the committee so meeting, in open session and with a majority present, determines that it is in the public interest that all or part of the remainder of the meeting on that day shall be closed to the public and states the reason for closing the meeting. Each meeting shall be preceded by notice of the time and place of the meeting, including publication in the Federal Register, sufficient to permit interested persons to attend.

   b. When an Advisory Committee's final recommendations for rules changes have been submitted, the Chairman and Reporter of the Advisory Committee shall attend the Standing Committee meeting to present the proposed rules changes and Committee Notes.

   c. The Standing Committee may accept, reject, or modify a proposal. If a modification effects a substantial change, the proposal will be returned to the Advisory Committee with appropriate instructions.

   d. The Standing Committee shall transmit to the Judicial Conference the proposed rules changes and Committee Notes approved by it, together with the Advisory Committee report. The Standing Committee's report to the Judicial Conference shall include its recommendations and explain any changes it has made.

9. Records

   a. The Secretary shall prepare minutes of all Standing Committee meetings.

   b. The records of the Standing Committee shall consist of the minutes of Standing and Advisory Committee meetings, reports to the Judicial Conference, and correspondence concerning rules changes including correspondence with Advisory Committee Chairmen. The records shall be maintained at the Administrative Office of the United States Courts for a minimum of two years and shall be available for public inspection during reasonable office hours. Thereafter the records may be transferred to a Government Records Center in accordance with applicable Government retention and disposition schedules.

   c. Copies of records shall be furnished to any person upon payment of a reasonable fee for the cost of reproduction.

STANDING COMMITTEE ON RULES OF PRACTICE AND PROCEDURE

As Constituted December 29, 1998

Chair:

HONORABLE ANTHONY J. SCIRICA

Members:

HONORABLE PHYLLIS A. KRAVITCH
HONORABLE A. WALLACE TASHIMA
HONORABLE WILLIAM R. WILSON, JR.
HONORABLE JAMES A. PARKER
HONORABLE FRANK W. BULLOCK, JR.
HONORABLE MOREY L. SEAR
HONORABLE E. NORMAN VEASEY
PROFESSOR GEOFFREY C. HAZARD, JR.
SOL SCHREIBER, ESQUIRE
GENE W. LAFITTE, ESQUIRE
PATRICK F. MCCARTAN, ESQUIRE
DEPUTY ATTORNEY GENERAL (EX OFFICIO)
HONORABLE ERIC H. HOLDER, JR.

Reporter:

PROF. DANIEL R. COQUILLETTE

Consultants:

JOSEPH F. SPANIOL, JR., ESQUIRE
ASST. PROFESSOR MARY P. SQUIERS
BRYAN A. GARNER, ESQUIRE

Secretary:

PETER G. MCCABE

ADVISORY COMMITTEE ON APPELLATE RULES

As Constituted December 29, 1998

Chair:

HONORABLE WILL L. GARWOOD

Members:

HONORABLE DIANA GRIBBON MOTZ
HONORABLE SAMUEL A. ALITO, JR.
HONORABLE STANWOOD R. DUVAL, JR.
HONORABLE PASCAL F. CALOGERO, JR.
MICHAEL J. MEEHAN, ESQUIRE
HONORABLE JOHN CHARLES THOMAS
PROFESSOR CAROL ANN MOONEY
W. THOMAS MCGOUGH, JR., ESQUIRE
HONORABLE SETH P. WAXMAN
SOLICITOR GENERAL (EX OFFICIO)

Reporter:

ASSOC. PROFESSOR PATRICK J. SCHILTZ

Liaison Member:

HONORABLE PHYLLIS A. KRAVITCH

Secretary:

PETER G. MCCABE

ADVISORY COMMITTEE ON BANKRUPTCY RULES

As Constituted December 29, 1998

Chair:

HONORABLE ADRIAN G. DUPLANTIER

Members:

HONORABLE EDUARDO C. ROBRENO
HONORABLE ROBERT W. GETTLEMAN
HONORABLE BERNICE B. DONALD
HONORABLE NORMAN C. ROETTGER, JR.
HONORABLE ROBERT J. KRESSEL
HONORABLE DONALD E. CORDOVA
HONORABLE A. JAY CRISTOL
HONORABLE A. THOMAS SMALL
PROFESSOR KENNETH N. KLEE
PROFESSOR MARY JO WIGGINS
GERALD K. SMITH, ESQUIRE
LEONARD M. ROSEN, ESQUIRE
NEAL BATSON, ESQUIRE
ERIC L. FRANK, ESQUIRE
DIRECTOR, COMMERCIAL LITIGATION BRANCH, CIVIL DIVISION, U.S. DEPT. OF JUSTICE (EX OFFICIO)
J. CHRISTOPHER KOHN, ESQUIRE

Reporter:

PROFESSOR ALAN N. RESNICK

Liaison Member:

HONORABLE A. WALLACE TASHIMA

Bankruptcy Clerk:

RICHARD G. HELTZEL

Representative from Executive Office for United States Trustees:

JERRY PATCHAN, ESQUIRE

Secretary:

PETER G. MCCABE

ADVISORY COMMITTEE ON CIVIL RULES

As Constituted December 29, 1998

Chair:

HONORABLE PAUL V. NIEMEYER

Members:

HONORABLE C. ROGER VINSON
HONORABLE DAVID F. LEVI
HONORABLE LEE H. ROSENTHAL
HONORABLE RICHARD H. KYLE
HONORABLE SHIRA ANN SCHEINDLIN
HONORABLE JOHN L. CARROLL
HONORABLE CHRISTINE M. DURHAM
PROFESSOR THOMAS D. ROWE, JR.
MARK O. KASANIN, ESQUIRE
SHEILA L. BIRNBAUM, ESQUIRE
ANDREW M. SHERFFIUS, ESQUIRE
MYLES V. LYNK, ESQUIRE
ASSISTANT ATTORNEY GENERAL FOR THE CIVIL DIVISION (EX OFFICIO)
HONORABLE FRANK W. HUNGER

Liaison Members:

HONORABLE ADRIAN G. DUPLANTIER
SOL SCHREIBER, ESQUIRE

Reporter:

PROFESSOR EDWARD H. COOPER

Secretary:

PETER G. MCCABE

ADVISORY COMMITTEE ON CRIMINAL RULES

As Constituted December 29, 1998

Chair:

HONORABLE W. EUGENE DAVIS

Members:

HONORABLE EDWARD E. CARNES
HONORABLE DAVID D. DOWD, JR.
HONORABLE D. BROOKS SMITH
HONORABLE JOHN M. ROLL
HONORABLE SUSAN C. BUCKLEW
HONORABLE TOMMY E. MILLER
HONORABLE DANIEL E. WATHEN
PROFESSOR KATE STITH
ROBERT C. JOSEFSBERG, ESQUIRE
DARRYL W. JACKSON, ESQUIRE
HENRY A. MARTIN, ESQUIRE

ASSISTANT ATTORNEY GENERAL FOR THE CRIMINAL DIVISION (EX OFFICIO)
ROGER A. PAULEY, ESQUIRE

Reporter:

PROFESSOR DAVID A. SCHLUETER

Liaison Member:

HONORABLE WILLIAM R. WILSON, JR.

Secretary:

PETER G. MCCABE

ADVISORY COMMITTEE ON EVIDENCE RULES

As Constituted December 29, 1998

Chair:

HONORABLE FERN M. SMITH

Members:

HONORABLE JERRY E. SMITH
HONORABLE MILTON I. SHADUR
HONORABLE DAVID C. NORTON
HONORABLE JAMES T. TURNER
HONORABLE JEFFREY L. AMESTOY
PROFESSOR KENNETH S. BROUN
GREGORY P. JOSEPH, ESQUIRE
JOHN M. KOBAYASHI, ESQUIRE
DAVID S. MARING, ESQUIRE
FREDERIC F. KAY, ESQUIRE

ASSISTANT ATTORNEY GENERAL FOR THE CRIMINAL DIVISION (EX OFFICIO)
MARY FRANCES HARKENRIDER, ESQUIRE

Liaison Members:

HONORABLE FRANK W. BULLOCK, JR.
HONORABLE RICHARD H. KYLE
HONORABLE DAVID D. DOWD, JR.

Reporter:

PROFESSOR DANIEL J. CAPRA

Secretary:

PETER G. MCCABE

*

FEDERAL
RULES OF CIVIL PROCEDURE
FOR THE
UNITED STATES DISTRICT COURTS

Amendments received to January 4, 1999

TABLE OF RULES

		Rules
I.	SCOPE OF RULES—ONE FORM OF ACTION	1, 2
II.	COMMENCEMENT OF ACTION; SERVICE OF PROCESS, PLEADINGS, MOTIONS, AND ORDERS	3–6
III.	PLEADINGS AND MOTIONS	7–16
IV.	PARTIES	17–25
V.	DEPOSITIONS AND DISCOVERY	26–37
VI.	TRIALS	38–53
VII.	JUDGMENT	54–63
VIII.	PROVISIONAL AND FINAL REMEDIES	64–71
IX.	SPECIAL PROCEEDINGS	71A–76
IX.	APPEALS	72–76
X.	DISTRICT COURTS AND CLERKS	77–80
XI.	GENERAL PROVISIONS	81–86
	APPENDIX OF FORMS	
	SUPPLEMENTAL RULES FOR CERTAIN ADMIRALTY AND MARITIME CLAIMS	

I. SCOPE OF RULES—ONE FORM OF ACTION

Rule

1. Scope and Purpose of Rules.
2. One Form of Action.

II. COMMENCEMENT OF ACTION; SERVICE OF PROCESS, PLEADINGS, MOTIONS, AND ORDERS

3. Commencement of Action.
4. Summons.
4.1. Service of Other Process.
5. Service and Filing of Pleadings and Other Papers.
6. Time.

III. PLEADINGS AND MOTIONS

7. Pleadings Allowed; Form of Motions.
8. General Rules of Pleading.
9. Pleading Special Matters.

Rule

III. PLEADINGS AND MOTIONS—Cont'd

10. Form of Pleadings.
11. Signing of Pleadings, Motions, and Other Papers; Representations to Court; Sanctions.
12. Defenses and Objections—When and How Presented—By Pleading or Motion—Motion for Judgment on Pleadings.
13. Counterclaim and Cross-Claim.
14. Third-Party Practice.
15. Amended and Supplemental Pleadings.
16. Pretrial Conferences; Scheduling; Management.

IV. PARTIES

17. Parties Plaintiff and Defendant; Capacity.
18. Joinder of Claims and Remedies.
19. Joinder of Persons Needed for Just Adjudication.
20. Permissive Joinder of Parties.
21. Misjoinder and Non-Joinder of Parties.
22. Interpleader.
23. Class Actions.
23.1. Derivative Actions by Shareholders.
23.2. Actions Relating to Unincorporated Associations.
24. Intervention.
25. Substitution of Parties.

V. DEPOSITIONS AND DISCOVERY

26. General Provisions Governing Discovery; Duty of Disclosure.
27. Depositions Before Action or Pending Appeal.
28. Persons Before Whom Depositions may be Taken.
29. Stipulations Regarding Discovery Procedure.
30. Depositions Upon Oral Examination.
31. Depositions Upon Written Questions.
32. Use of Depositions in Court Proceedings.
33. Interrogatories to Parties.
34. Production of Documents and Things and Entry Upon Land for Inspection and Other Purposes.
35. Physical and Mental Examinations of Persons.
36. Requests for Admission.
37. Failure to Make Disclosure or Cooperate in Discovery: Sanctions.

Complete Annotation Materials, see Title 28 U.S.C.A.

Rule

VI. TRIALS

38. Jury Trial of Right.
39. Trial by Jury or by the Court.
40. Assignment of Cases for Trial.
41. Dismissal of Actions.
42. Consolidation; Separate Trials.
43. Taking of Testimony.
44. Proof of Official Record.
44.1. Determination of Foreign Law.
45. Subpoena.
46. Exceptions Unnecessary.
47. Selection of Jurors.
48. Number of Jurors—Participation in Verdict.
49. Special Verdicts and Interrogatories.
50. Judgment as a Matter of Law in Jury Trials; Alternative Motion for New Trial; Conditional Rulings.
51. Instructions to Jury: Objection.
52. Findings by the Court; Judgment on Partial Findings.
53. Masters.

VII. JUDGMENT

54. Judgments; Costs.
55. Default.
56. Summary Judgment.
57. Declaratory Judgments.
58. Entry of Judgment.
59. New Trials; Amendment of Judgments.
60. Relief From Judgment or Order.
61. Harmless Error.
62. Stay of Proceedings to Enforce a Judgment.
63. Inability of a Judge to Proceed.

VIII. PROVISIONAL AND FINAL REMEDIES

64. Seizure of Person or Property.
65. Injunctions.
65.1. Security: Proceedings Against Sureties.
66. Receivers Appointed by Federal Courts.
67. Deposit in Court.
68. Offer of Judgment.
69. Execution.
70. Judgment for Specific Acts; Vesting Title.
71. Process in Behalf of and Against Persons not Parties.

IX. SPECIAL PROCEEDINGS

71A. Condemnation of Property.
72. Magistrate Judges; Pretrial Orders.
73. Magistrate Judges; Trial by Consent and Appeal Options.
74. [Abrogated.]
75. [Abrogated.]
76. [Abrogated.]

Rule

X. DISTRICT COURTS AND CLERKS

77. District Courts and Clerks.
78. Motion Day.
79. Books and Records Kept by the Clerk and Entries Therein.
80. Stenographer; Stenographic Report or Transcript as Evidence.

XI. GENERAL PROVISIONS

81. Applicability in General.
82. Jurisdiction and Venue Unaffected.
83. Rules by District Courts; Judge's Directives.
84. Forms.
85. Title.
86. Effective Date.

APPENDIX OF FORMS

Form

1. Summons.
1A. Notice of Lawsuit and Request for Waiver of Service of Summons.
1B. Waiver of Service of Summons.
2. Allegation of Jurisdiction.
3. Complaint on a Promissory Note.
4. Complaint on an Account.
5. Complaint for Goods Sold and Delivered.
6. Complaint for Money Lent.
7. Complaint for Money Paid by Mistake.
8. Complaint for Money Had and Received.
9. Complaint for Negligence.
10. Complaint for Negligence Where Plaintiff is Unable to Determine Definitely Whether the Person Responsible is C. D. or E. F. or Whether Both are Responsible and Where his Evidence may Justify a Finding of Wilfulness or of Recklessness or of Negligence.
11. Complaint for Conversion.
12. Complaint for Specific Performance of Contract to Convey Land.
13. Complaint on Claim for Debt and to Set Aside Fraudulent Conveyance Under Rule 18(b).
14. Complaint for Negligence Under Federal Employer's Liability Act.
15. Complaint for Damages Under Merchant Marine Act.
16. Complaint for Infringement of Patent.
17. Complaint for Infringement of Copyright and Unfair Competition.
18. Complaint for Interpleader and Declaratory Relief.
18–A. [Abrogated].
19. Motion to Dismiss, Presenting Defenses of Failure to State a Claim, of Lack of Service of Process, of Improper Venue, and of Lack of Jurisdiction Under Rule 12(b).
20. Answer Presenting Defenses Under Rule 12(b).
21. Answer to Complaint Set Forth in Form 8, With Counterclaim for Interpleader.
22. Eliminated.

Form	
22–A.	Summons and Complaint Against Third-Party Defendant.
22–B.	Motion to Bring in Third-Party Defendant.
23.	Motion to Intervene as a Defendant Under Rule 24.
24.	Request for Production of Documents, etc., Under Rule 34.
25.	Request for Admission Under Rule 36.
26.	Allegation of Reason for Omitting Party.
27.	[Abrogated.]
28.	Notice: Condemnation.
29.	Complaint: Condemnation.
30.	Suggestion of Death Upon the Record Under Rule 25(a)(1).
31.	Judgment on Jury Verdict.
32.	Judgment on Decision by the Court.
33.	Notice of Availability of Magistrate Judge to Exercise Jurisdiction.
34.	Consent to Exercise of Jurisdiction by a United States Magistrate Judge.
34A.	Order of Reference.
35.	Report of Parties' Planning Meeting.

TIME TABLE FOR LAWYERS IN FEDERAL CIVIL CASES

Amended to January 4, 1999

This Time Table, prepared by the Publisher's editorial staff as a guide to the user, indicates the time for each of the steps of a civil action as provided by the Federal Rules of Civil Procedure and the Federal Rules of Appellate Procedure. Certain steps governed by statute and by the 1997 Revised Rules of the Supreme Court are also listed. The user should always consult the actual text of the rule or statute. Usually the periods permitted for each of these steps may be enlarged by the court in its discretion. In some cases no enlargement is permitted. Citations to supporting authority are in the form "Civ.R. ———" for the Rules of Civil Procedure; "App.R. ———" for the Rules of Appellate Procedure; "28 U.S.C.A. § ———" for statutes; and "Supreme Court Rule ———".

ADMISSIONS

Requests for admissions, service of	On any other party after the parties have conferred pursuant to Civ.R. 26(f). Civ.R. 36(a).
Response to requested admissions	Answers or objections must be served within 30 days after service of the request, or such shorter or longer time as court may allow or as parties may agree to in writing. Civ.R. 36(a).

ALTERNATE jurors — The institution of the alternate juror has been abolished. Civ.R. 47, 1991 Advisory Committee note, subd. (b).

ANSWER — See, also, "Responsive Pleadings", this table.

To complaint	Service within 20 days after being served with summons and complaint unless a different time is prescribed in a federal statute. Civ.R. 12(a)(1)(A). Service within 60 days after date request is sent for waiver of service of summons or within 90 days after that date if defendant was addressed outside any judicial district of the United States unless a different time is prescribed in a federal statute. Civ.R. 12(a)(1)(B). Service within 60 days after service upon the United States Attorney, in action against the United States or an officer or agency thereof. Civ.R. 12(a). The time for responsive pleading is altered by service of Civ.R. 12 motions. See "Responsive Pleadings", this table.

ANSWER

To cross-claim	Service within 20 days after being served with cross-claim. Civ.R. 12(a)(2). 60 days for United States. Civ.R. 12(a). The time for responsive pleading is altered by service of Civ.R. 12(a) motions, see "Responsive Pleadings", this table.
To third-party complaint	Service of reply within 20 days after service of answer or, if reply is ordered by a court, within 20 days after service of order. Civ.R. 12(a)(2). 60 days for United States. Civ.R. 12(a)(3).
To notice of condemnation	Service within 20 days after service of notice. Civ.R. 71A(e).
Removed actions	20 days after receipt of pleading, or within 20 days after service of summons, or within 5 days after filing of removal petition, whichever is longest. Civ.R. 81(c).
Proceedings to cancel certificates of citizenship under 8 U.S.C.A. § 1451	60 days after service of petition. Civ.R. 81(a)(6).
ANSWERS (or objections) to interrogatories to party	Service within 30 days after service of the interrogatories. A shorter or longer time may be directed by the court or agreed to. Civ.R. 33(b)(3).

APPEAL

As of right	30 days from entry of judgment or order. App.R. 4(a)(1)(A). District court may extend for excusable neglect or good cause upon motion filed not later than 30 days after expiration of time prescribed by App.R. 4(a); no extension to exceed 30 days past prescribed time or 10 days from entry of order granting motion, whichever occurs later. App.R. 4(a)(5). 60 days in cases in which the United States or its officers, agencies are parties. App.R. 4(a)(1)(B). If any party files a timely motion of a type specified below, time for appeal for all parties runs from entry of order disposing of last such motion outstanding. App.R. 4(a)(4). (1) motion for judgment under Civ.R. 50(b); (2) Motion under Civ.R. 52(b) to amend or make additional findings of fact, whether or not granting the motion would alter the judgement; (3) motion under Civ.R. 59 to alter or amend judgment; (4) Motion under Civ.R. 54 for attorney's fees if time to appeal extended under Civ.R. 58. (5) Motion under Civ.R. 59 for new trial. (6) Motion for relief under Civ.R. 60 if motion filed no later than 10 days after entry of judgement. App.R. 4(a)(4). By other parties, within 14 days of filing of first notice of appeal, or within the time otherwise prescribed by App.R. 4(a), whichever last expires. App.R. 4(a)(3).

APPEAL

By permission	Petition filed with circuit clerk with proof of service within time specified by statute or rule authorizing the appeal, or if no such time is specified, within the time provided by App.R. 4(a) for filing a notice of appeal. App.R. 5(a).
Bankruptcy	If a motion for rehearing under Bankruptcy Rule 8015 is filed in a district court or in a bankruptcy appellate panel, time for appeal to court of appeals runs from entry of order disposing of motion. App.R. 6(b)(2)(A).
Class actions	Within 10 days after entry of order of district court granting or denying class action certification. Civ.R. 23(f).
Inmates	A notice of appeal is timely filed if deposited in the institution's internal mail system on or before the last day for filing. App.R. 4(c), 25(a).
Representation statement	Within 10 days after filing notice of appeal unless court of appeals designates another time, attorney who filed notice shall file with the circuit clerk a statement naming each party represented on appeal by that attorney. App.R. 12(b).
Entry of judgment or order, notice of	Lack of such notice by clerk does not affect time to appeal or relieve or authorize court to relieve party for failure to appeal within time allowed, except as permitted in App.R. 4(a). Civ.R. 77(d).
Record (Appellant)	Within 10 days after filing notice of appeal or entry of an order disposing of last timely remaining motion specified in App.R. 4(a)(4)(A), whichever is later: Appellant to place written order for transcript and file copy of order with clerk; if none to be ordered, file a certificate to that effect; unless entire transcript to be included, file a statement of issues and serve appellee a copy of order or certificate and of statement. App.R. 10(b).
Record (Appellee)	Within 10 days after service of appellant's order or certificate and statement, appellee to file and serve on appellant a designation of additional parts of transcript to be included. Unless within 10 days after designation appellant has ordered such parts and so notified appellee, appellee may within following 10 days either order the parts or move in district court for order requiring appellant to do so. App.R. 10(b).
Record (costs)	At time of ordering, party to make satisfactory arrangements with reporter for payment of cost of transcript. App.R. 10(b)(4).
Record (Reporter)	If transcript cannot be completed within 30 days of receipt of order, reporter shall request extension of time from circuit clerk. App.R. 11(b).
Stay of proceedings to enforce judgment	Effective when supersedeas bond is approved by court. Civ.R. 62(d). Supersedeas bond may be given at or after time of filing notice of appeal or of procuring the order allowing appeal. Civ.R. 62(d).
Briefs	Appellant must serve and file a brief within 40 days after the record is filed. Appellee must serve and file a brief within 30 days after service of the

APPEAL

appellant's brief. A reply brief may be filed within 14 days after service of appellee's brief and, except for good cause shown, at least 3 days before argument. A court of appeals may shorten the times allowed for briefs either by local rule for all cases or by order for a particular case. App.R. 31(a).

Transcripts — See "RECORD", ante, this heading.

Tax Court decisions — Review must be obtained by filing a notice of appeal with the Tax Court clerk within 90 days after entry of decision. If a timely notice of appeal is filed by one party, any other party may take an appeal by filing a notice of appeal within 120 days after entry of decision by the Tax Court. If timely motion made to vacate or revise decision, time to file notice of appeal runs from entry of order disposing of motion or entry of new decision, whichever is later. App.R. 13(a).

APPEAL from magistrate judge to district judge under 28 U.S.C.A. § 636(c)(4) and Civ.R. 73(d)

Notice of Appeal — [This Rule provided as follows, prior to its abrogation:] Filed with clerk of district court within 30 days of entry of judgment. Within 60 days if United States or officer or agency thereof is a party. Within 15 days after entry of an interlocutory decision or order. Civ.R. 74(a) [Rule 74 abrogated eff. Dec. 1, 1997].

[This Rule provided as follows, prior to its abrogation:] When timely notice is filed by a party, any other party may file notice within 14 days thereafter or within time otherwise prescribed by Civ.R. 74(a), whichever period last expires. Civ.R. 74(a) [Rule 74 abrogated eff. Dec 1, 1997].

[This Rule provided as follows, prior to its abrogation:] Upon showing of excusable neglect, time for filing may be extended on motion filed not later than 20 days from expiration of time for filing. Civ.R. 74(a) [Rule 74 abrogated eff. Dec. 1, 1997].

Running of time for filing terminated as to all parties by timely filing of any of the following motions with the magistrate judge by any party, and the full time for appeal from judgment entered commences to run anew from entry of any of the following orders:

(1) granting or denying motion for judgment under Civ.R. 50(b);

(2) granting or denying motion under Civ.R. 52(b) to amend or make additional findings of fact;

(3) granting or denying motion under Civ.R. 59 to alter or amend judgment;

(4) denying motion for new trial under Civ.R. 59. Civ.R. 74(a) [prior to its abrogation] [Rule 74 abrogated eff. Dec. 1, 1997.]

Joint statement of case — Parties could file in lieu of record within 10 days after filing of notice of appeal, under provisions of

APPEAL from magistrate judge to district judge under 28 U.S.C.A. § 636(c)(4) and Civ.R. 73(d)	this rule prior to its abrogation. Civ.R. 75(b)(1) [Rule 75 abrogated eff. Dec. 1, 1997].
Transcript	Within 10 days after filing notice of appeal appellant to make arrangements for production. Unless entire transcript is to be included, description of parts appellant intends to present must be served on the appellee and filed by the appellant within the 10 day period. If appellee deems transcript of other parts to be necessary, designation of additional parts to be included must be served on the appellant and filed within 10 days after service of appellant's statement. Civ.R. 75(b)(2) [Rule 75 abrogated eff. Dec. 1, 1997].
Statement in lieu of transcript	If no record is available for transcription, parties must file a statement of evidence in lieu of transcript within 10 days after filing of notice of appeal. Civ.R. 75(b)(3) [Rule 75 abrogated eff. Dec. 1, 1997].
Briefs	Appellant to serve and file within 20 days after the filing of transcript, statement of case, or statement of evidence. Civ.R. 75(c)(1) [Rule 75 abrogated eff. Dec. 1, 1997].
	Appellee to serve and file within 20 days after service of appellant's brief. Civ.R. 75(c)(2) [Rule 75 abrogated eff. Dec. 1, 1997].
	Appellant may serve and file reply brief within 10 days after service of appellee's brief. Civ.R. 75(c)(3) [Rule 75 abrogated eff. Dec. 1, 1997].
	If appellee files a cross-appeal, appellee may file a reply brief within 10 days after service of the reply brief of the appellant. Civ.R. 75(c)(4) [Rule 75 abrogated eff. Dec. 1, 1997].
Stay of judgments	Decision of district judge stayed for 10 days during which term a party may petition for rehearing. Civ.R. 76(b) [Rule 76 abrogated eff. Dec. 1, 1997].
APPEAL from magistrate judge under 28 U.S.C.A. § 636(c)(3)	Appeal to court of appeals in identical fashion as appeals from other judgments of district courts. App.R. 3.1. [Rule 3.1 abrogated eff. Dec. 1, 1998].
APPEAL from district court to court of appeals under 28 U.S.C.A. § 636(c)(5)	Petition for leave to appeal filed with clerk of the court of appeals within time provided by App.R. 4(a) for filing notice of appeal, with proof of service on all parties to action in district court. App.R. 5.1(a). [Rule 5.1 abrogated eff. Dec. 1, 1998].
	Within 14 days after service of petition for leave to appeal, a party may file an answer or cross petition in opposition. App.R. 5.1(a). [Rule 5.1 abrogated eff. Dec. 1, 1998].
APPEAL to Supreme Court	
Direct appeals	30 days after entry of interlocutory or final order, decree or judgment holding Act of Congress unconstitutional under circumstances provided by 28 U.S.C.A. §§ 1252, and 1253. 28 U.S.C.A. § 2101(a), as amended by Act May 24, 1949, c. 139, § 106, 63 Stat. 104. [28 U.S.C.A. § 1252 was repealed and 28 U.S.C.A. § 2101(a) was amended by Pub.L. 100–352, §§ 1, 5(b), June 27, 1988, 102 Stat. 662, 663, respectively. For effective date and ap-

APPEAL to Supreme Court	plicability to cases, see section 7 of Pub.L. 100–352, set out as 28 U.S.C.A. § 1254 note.]
	30 days from interlocutory judgment, order, or decree in any other direct appeal authorized by law from decision of district court. 28 U.S.C.A. § 2101(b).
	60 days from final judgment, order, or decree in any other direct appeal authorized by law from decision of district court. 28 U.S.C.A. § 2101(b).
Other appeals and certiorari	90 days after entry of judgment or decree; justice of Supreme Court for good cause shown may extend time for applying for writ of certiorari for period not exceeding 60 days. 28 U.S.C.A. § 2101(c).
Briefs supporting certiorari	No separate brief supporting petition for certiorari shall be filed; See Supreme Court Rule 14.2.
Brief opposing certiorari	30 days after case is placed on the docket unless time is extended by Court or a Justice or by the Clerk; See Supreme Court Rule 15.3.
Brief on merits on appeal or certiorari	By appellant or petitioner, filed within 45 days of the order granting the writ of certiorari or the order noting probable jurisdiction or postponing consideration of jurisdiction; see Supreme Court Rule 25.1.
	By appellee or respondent, filed within 30 days after receipt of the brief filed by the appellant or petitioner; see Supreme Court Rule 25.2.
	Reply brief, if any, filed within 30 days after receipt of brief for appellee or respondent, but any reply brief to be received by Clerk not later than one week before the date of oral argument. See Supreme Court Rule 25.3.
Stay of mandate pending petition for certiorari	A stay of mandate pending a petition to the Supreme Court for certiorari cannot exceed 90 days unless the period is extended for good cause or unless during the period of stay, the party who obtained the stay files a petition for the writ and notifies the circuit clerk in writing in which case the stay will continue until final disposition by the Supreme Court. The court of appeals must issue the mandate immediately when a copy of the Supreme Court order denying the petition for writ of certiorari is filed. App.R. 41(d)(2).
ATTORNEY'S fees	See "Costs", this table.
BILL of particulars	Abolished. See Civ.R. 12(e), as amended in 1948. See, however, "More definite statement", this table.
CLASS actions	As soon as practicable after commencement court is to determine by order whether action is to be so maintained. Civ.R. 23(c)(1).
CLERICAL mistakes in judgments, orders, or record	May be corrected at any time; but during pendency of appeal, may be corrected before appeal is docketed in the appellate court, and thereafter while appeal pending may be corrected with leave of appellate court. Civ.R. 60(a).
COMPLAINT	Filing commences action—must be served with summons. Civ.R. 3.
	Service of summons and complaint within 120 days after filing. Civ.R. 4(m).

COMPUTATION of time	
	Exclude day of the act, event or default from which designated period of time begins to run. Include last day of the period so computed unless it is a Saturday, Sunday, or legal holiday, or, when act to be done is the filing of a paper in court, a day on which weather or other conditions have made the office of the clerk of the district court inaccessible, in which event period runs until end of the next day which is not one of the aforementioned days. Civ.R. 6(a).
	Intermediate Saturdays, Sundays, and legal holidays are excluded if the period is less than 11 days. Civ.R. 6(a).
	Exclude day of the act, event, or default that begins the period. Include last day of the period unless it is a Saturday, Sunday, or legal holiday, or, when the act to be done is filing of paper in court, a day on which weather or other conditions have made office of clerk inaccessible. App.R. 26(a).
	Intermediate Saturdays, Sundays, and legal holidays are excluded if the period is less than 7 days, unless stated in calendar days. App.R. 26(a).
	Service by mail is complete upon mailing. Civ.R. 5(b).
	Service by mail or by commercial carrier is complete upon mailing or delivery to the carrier. App.R. 25(c).
	Service by mail adds three days to a period of time which is computed from such service. Civ.R. 6(e).
	When a party is required or permitted to act within a prescribed period after service of a paper upon that party, three calendar days are added to the period unless the paper is delivered on the date of service stated in the proof of service. App.R. 26(c).
	Legal holidays are defined by Civ.R. 6(a) and App.R. 26(a)(4).
	Supreme Court matters—See Supreme Court Rule 30.
CONDEMNATION of property	
Answer to notice of condemnation	20 days after service of notice. Civ.R. 71A(e).
COSTS	
	Taxation on 1 day's notice. Motion to review taxation of costs 5 days after taxation. Civ.R. 54(d).
	Failure to comply with request for waiver of service of summons and to return waiver within time allowed which must be at least 30 days from date request is sent or 60 days from that date for a defendant addressed outside any judicial district of the United States. Civ.R. 4(d).
Attorney's fees and related nontaxable expenses	Motion filed and served no later than 14 days after entry of judgement. Civ.R. 54(d)(2)(B).
CROSS APPEAL	
Optional appeal from magistrate judge to district judge	Appellee may file reply brief within 10 days after service of reply brief of appellant. Civ.R. 75(c)(4) [Rule 75 abrogated eff. Dec. 1, 1997].

CROSS APPEAL	
Appellate rules	Within 14 days of filing of first notice of appeal or within the time otherwise prescribed by App.R. 4(a), whichever last expires. App.R. 4(a)(3).
Inmates	Within 14 days after date when first notice of appeal was docketed by the district court. The 14 day period runs from date district court receives first notice of appeal. App.R. 4(c).
DEFAULT	
Entry by clerk	No time stated. Civ.R. 55(b).
Entry by court	If party against whom default is sought has appeared, the party shall be served with written notice of application for default judgment at least 3 days prior to hearing on such application. Civ.R. 55(b).
DEFENSES and objections, presentation of	
By pleading	See "Answer", this table.
By motion	Motion shall be made before pleading if further pleading is permitted. Civ.R. 12(b).
At trial	Adverse party may assert at trial any defense in law or fact to claim for relief to which such party is not required to serve responsive pleading. Civ.R. 12(b).
Motion affects time for responsive pleading	Service of motion under Civ.R. 12 alters times for responsive pleading. See "Responsive Pleadings", this table.
DEMURRERS	Abolished. Civ.R. 7(c).
DEPOSITIONS	See, also, "Interrogatories", "Depositions on written questions", this table.
Notice of filing	Promptly. Civ.R. 30(f)(3) and Civ.R. 31(c).
Notice of taking	Reasonable notice to every party. Civ.R. 30(b).
Objections	As to admissibility, objection may be made at trial or hearing, but subject to Civ.R. 28(b) and 32(d)(3). Civ.R. 32(b).
	As to errors or irregularities in the notice, service promptly. Civ.R. 32(d)(1).
	As to disqualification of officer, objection made before deposition begins or as soon thereafter as disqualification becomes known or could be discovered. Civ.R. 32(d)(2).
	As to competency of witness or competency, relevancy, or materiality of testimony—not waived by failure to make such objection before or during deposition unless the ground might have been obviated or removed if presented at that time. Civ.R. 32(d)(3)(A).
	As to errors and irregularities at oral examination in manner of taking deposition, in the form of questions or answers, in the oath or affirmation, or in conduct of parties, and errors which might be obviated, removed, or cured if promptly presented—seasonable objection made at taking of deposition. Civ.R. 32(d)(3)(B).
	As to form of written questions submitted under Civ.R. 31—service within time allowed for serving succeeding cross or other questions and within 5

	days after service of last questions authorized. Civ.R. 32(d)(3)(C).
	As to completion and return (transcription, signing, certification, sealing, etc.)—motion to suppress made with reasonable promptness after defect is or might have been ascertained. Civ.R. 32(d)(4).
Orders of protection	Subsequent to certification that movant has in good faith conferred or attempted to confer with other affected parties to resolve dispute without court action. Civ.R. 26(c).
Motion to terminate or limit examination	Any time during a deposition. Civ.R. 30(d)(3).
Perpetuate testimony pending appeal	Motion in district court upon same notice and service thereof as if action was pending in district court. Civ.R. 27(b).
Perpetuate testimony before action	Service of notice and petition 20 days before date of hearing. Civ.R. 27(a)(2).
Taking	Time specified in the notice of taking. Civ. R. 30(b)(1).
	Prior notice by a party to deponent and other parties to designate another method to record deponent's testimony in addition to method specified by person taking deposition. Civ.R. 30(b)(3).
Review of transcript or recording	Request by a party or deponent before completion of deposition. Deponent has 30 days after notice of availability of transcript or recording to review and to indicate changes. Civ.R. 30(e).
DEPOSITIONS on written questions	See, also, "Depositions", "Interrogatories", this table.
When taken	After parties have met and conferred to discuss their claims, defenses and possibility of settlement and to develop a proposed discovery plan under Civ.R. 26(f). Civ.R. 26(d).
Cross questions	Service within 14 days after service of the notice and question. Court may enlarge or shorten time. Civ.R. 31(a)(4).
Redirect questions	Service within 7 days after being served with cross questions. Court may enlarge or shorten time. Civ.R. 31(a)(4).
Recross questions	Service within 7 days after service of redirect questions. Court may enlarge or shorten time. Civ.R. 31(a)(4).
Notice of filing of deposition	Promptly. Civ.R. 31(c).
Objections to form	Service within the time allowed for serving the succeeding cross or other questions and within 5 days after service of last questions authorized. Civ.R. 32(d)(3)(C).
DISCOVERY	See, also, "Admissions", "Depositions", "Depositions on written questions", "Interrogatories", "Production of documents", this Table.

DISCOVERY	Discovery Conference Except in exempted actions or when otherwise ordered, as soon as practicable and at least 14 days before a scheduling conference is held or a scheduling order is due under Civ.R. 16(b), the parties shall meet to discuss their claims, defenses, and possibility of settlement, to make or arrange for disclosures, and to develop a proposed discovery plan. A written report outlining the plan is to be submitted to the court within 10 days after the meeting. Civ.R. 26(f); See, also, Civ.R. 26(d). Without waiting for a discovery request and within 10 days after the Civ.R. 26(f) meeting of parties, a party must provide information specified in Civ.R. 26(a)(1). Disclosure of expert testimony under Civ.R. 26(a)(2), in absence of court direction or stipulation, is to be made at least 90 days before trial date or date case is ready for trial or if evidence intended as rebuttal of Civ.R. 26(a)(2)(B), within 30 days after disclosure of such evidence. Civ.R. 26(a)(2)(C). All disclosures are to be promptly filed with court. Civ.R. 26(a)(4). Identification of witnesses, documents, exhibits, including summaries of other evidence, and designation of witnesses whose testimony will be by deposition with a transcript of pertinent testimony if deposition is not taken stenographically to be provided to other parties at least 30 days before trial unless otherwise directed by court. Within 14 days thereafter, unless otherwise specified by court, a party may file objections. Civ.R. 26(a)(3).
DISMISSAL for want of subject-matter jurisdiction	Any time. Civ.R. 12(h)(3).
DISMISSAL by plaintiff voluntarily without court order	Any time before service of answer or motion for summary judgment. Civ.R. 41(a)(1).
DISMISSAL of counter-claim, cross-claim or third-party claim, voluntary	Before service of responsive pleading, or if none, before introduction of evidence at trial or hearing. Civ.R. 41(c).
DISMISSAL without prejudice	Service of summons and complaint not made within 120 days after filing of complaint. Civ.R. 4(m).
DOCUMENTS, Production of	See "Production of documents", this Table.
ENLARGEMENT of time generally	
Act required or allowed at or within specified time by Civil Rule, notice thereunder, or court order	Court for cause shown may (1) with or without motion or notice order period enlarged if request therefor is made before expiration of period originally prescribed or as extended by previous order, or (2) upon motion made after expiration of the specified period permit act to be done where failure to act was result of excusable neglect; but court may not extend time for taking any action under Civ.R. 50(b) and (c)(2), 52(b), 59(b), (d) and (e), and 60(b), except to extent and under conditions stated in them. Civ.R. 6(b).
Affidavits in opposition, service	Time may be extended by court. Civ.R. 6(d).
Hearing of motions and defenses	May be deferred until trial. Civ.R. 12(d).

ENLARGEMENT of time generally	
Mail, service by	Adds three days to a period that is computed from time of service. Civ.R. 6(e).
	When a party is required or permitted to act within a prescribed period after service of a paper upon that party, three calendar days are added to the period unless the paper is delivered on the date of service stated in the proof of service. App.R. 26(c).
Injunction—temporary restraining order	May be extended 10 days by order of court or for a longer period by consent of party against whom order is directed. Civ.R. 65(b).
Response to request for admissions	Time may be enlarged or shortened by court or as the parties may agree in writing subject to Civ.R. 29. Civ.R. 36(a).
Optional appeal from magistrate judge to district judge	Upon showing of excusable neglect, time to file notice of appeal may be extended upon motion filed not later than 20 days from expiration of time for filing. Civ.R. 74(a) [Rule 74 abrogated eff. Dec. 1, 1997].
Motion for judgment notwithstanding the verdict	No enlargement of the 10 day period except to the extent and under conditions stated in Civ.R. 50(b). Civ.R. 6(b).
Findings by the court, amendment of additional findings	No enlargement of the 10 day period except to the extent and under conditions stated in Civ.R. 52(b). Civ.R. 6(b).
Motion for new trial	No enlargement of the 10 day period except to the extent and under conditions stated in Civ.R. 59(b), (d), and (e). Civ.R. 6(b).
Motion for relief from judgment or order	No enlargement of the 1 year period except to the extent and under conditions stated in Civ.R. 60(b). Civ.R. 6(b).
Notice of appeal from magistrate judge to district judge	No enlargement of the 30 day period except to the extent and under conditions stated in Civ.R. 74(a). Civ.R. 6(b) [Rule 74 abrogated eff. Dec. 1, 1997.]
Appellate rules	Court for good cause may extend time prescribed by App.Rules or by its order to perform any act or may permit act to be done after expiration of such time; but court may not extend time for filing notice of appeal, or petition for permission to appeal a notice of appeal from or a petition to enjoin, set aside, suspend, modify, enforce or otherwise review an order of an administrative agency, board, commission or officer of the United States, unless specifically authorized by law. App.R. 26(b).
Supreme Court matters	See Supreme Court Rule 30.
EXCEPTIONS for insufficiency of pleadings	Abolished. Civ.R. 7(c).
EXECUTION	
Stay	Automatically: No execution to issue, nor proceedings for enforcement to be taken, until expiration of 10 days after entry of judgment; exceptions—injunctions, receiverships, and patent accountings. Civ.R. 62(a).
	Stay according to state law. Civ.R. 62(f).
	Motion for new trial or for judgment. Civ.R. 62(b).
	Stay in favor of government. Civ.R. 62(e).

EXECUTION

Supersedeas on appeal. Civ.R. 62(d).

Stay of judgment as to multiple claims or multiple parties. Civ.R. 62(h).

Stay of judgment pending appeal from magistrate judge to district judge. Civ.R. 74(c). Stay of decision of district judge for 10 days during which time a party may petition for rehearing. Civ.R. 76(b) [Rules 74 and 76 abrogated eff. Dec. 1, 1997].

FILING papers

Complaint must be filed at commencement of action. Civ.R. 3.

Service of summons and complaint within 120 days after filing of complaint. Civ.R. 4(m).

All papers required to be filed must be filed with clerk unless the judge permits them to be filed with the judge. Civ.R. 5(e).

Local court rules may permit papers to be filed by electronic means if consistent with standards of Judicial Conference of the United States, and clerk shall not refuse for filing any paper solely because it is not presented in proper form under Rules of Civil Procedure or any local rule or practice. Civ.R. 5(e).

All papers after the complaint required to be served upon a party, together with a certificate of service, shall be filed with the court within a reasonable time after service. Civ.R. 5(d).

FINDINGS

Motion to amend — 10 days after entry of judgment. Civ.R. 52(b). Exception from general rule relating to enlargement. Civ.R. 6(b).

FINDINGS of master — See "References and Referees", this table.

FOREIGN law — Reasonable written notice required of party intending to raise an issue concerning the law of a foreign country. Civ.R. 44.1.

HEARING of motions

Unless local conditions make it impracticable, district court shall establish regular times and places for hearing and disposition of motions requiring notice and hearing; but judge may make orders for the advancement, conduct, and hearing of actions. Civ.R. 78.

Service of notice 5 days before time specified for hearing unless otherwise provided by these rules or order of court. Civ.R. 6(d).

Hearing of certain motions and defenses before trial on application of any party unless court orders deferral until trial. Civ.R. 12(d).

HOLIDAYS

New Year's Day, Birthday of Martin Luther King, Jr., Presidents' Day, Memorial Day, Independence Day, Labor Day, Columbus Day, Veterans' Day, Thanksgiving Day, Christmas Day, and any other day declared a holiday by the President, Congress or the state in which is located either the district court that rendered the challenged judgment or order, or the circuit clerk's principal office. Civ.R. 6(a); App.R. 26(a).

HOLIDAYS	Exclusion in computation of time. Civ.R. 6(a); App.R. 26(a).
INJUNCTION (Temporary restraining order granted without notice)	Order shall be indorsed with date and hour of issuance, filed forthwith in clerk's office, and entered of record. Civ.R. 65(b).
	Expiration within such time, not to exceed 10 days, as court fixes, unless within time so fixed the order is extended for like period or, with consent of party against whom order is directed, for longer period. Civ.R. 65(b).
	Motion for preliminary injunction shall be set down for hearing at earliest possible time—takes precedence of all matters except older ones of same character. Civ.R. 65(b).
	Motion for dissolution or modification on 2 days' notice or such shorter notice as court may prescribe; hear and determine motion as expeditiously as ends of justice require. Civ.R. 65(b).
INSTRUCTIONS	
Requests	At close of evidence or such earlier time as court directs. Civ.R. 51.
Objections	Before jury retires to consider verdict. Civ.R. 51.
INTERROGATORIES to parties	See, also, "Depositions", "Depositions on written questions", this table.
	Service after parties have met and conferred pursuant to Civ.R. 26(f). Civ.R. 33(a).
Answers or objections	Service within 30 days after service of the interrogatories. A shorter or longer time may be directed by the court or agreed to. Civ.R. 33(b)(3).
INTERVENTION	Upon timely application. Civ.R. 24(a), (b).
	Person desiring to intervene shall serve a motion to intervene upon the parties as provided in Civil Rule 5. Civ.R. 24(c).
JUDGMENT or order	
Alter or amend judgment, motion to	Shall be filed not later than 10 days after entry of judgment. Civ.R. 59(e). Exception to general rule, relating to enlargement. Civ.R. 6(b).
Clerical mistakes	May be corrected any time; but during pendency of appeal, may be corrected before appeal is docketed in the appellate court, and thereafter while appeal pending may be corrected with leave of appellate court. Civ.R. 60(a).
Default	See "Default", this table.
Renewal of motion for judgment after trial	Not later than 10 days after entry of judgment. Exception from general rule relating to enlargement. Civ.R. 6(b).
Effectiveness	Judgment effective only when set forth on a separate document and when entered as provided in Civ.R. 79(a). Civ.R. 58.
Entry of judgment	Upon general verdict of jury or upon court decision that a party shall recover only a sum certain or

JUDGMENT or order	
	costs or that all relief shall be denied, entry forthwith and without awaiting any direction by court (unless court otherwise orders). Upon court decision granting other relief or upon special verdict or general verdict accompanied by answers to interrogatories, entry upon prompt court approval of form. Entry shall not be delayed for taxing of costs. Civ.R. 58.
Entry, notice of	Immediately upon entry, clerk shall serve notice thereof by mail in manner provided in Civ.R. 5 and make note in docket of the mailing. Any party may in addition serve a notice of such entry in manner provided in Civ.R. 5 for service of papers. Civ.R. 77(d).
	Lack of notice of entry by clerk does not affect time to appeal or relieve or authorize court to relieve party for failure to appeal within time allowed, except as permitted by App.R. 4(a). Civ.R. 77(d).
Offer of judgment	Service more than 10 days before trial begins. Civ.R. 68.
	Acceptance, written notice of—service within 10 days after service of offer. Civ.R. 68.
On pleadings, motion for judgment	After pleadings are closed but within such time as not to delay the trial. Civ.R. 12(c).
Relief from, on grounds stated in Rule 60(b)	Motion within a reasonable time and not more than 1 year after judgment, order, or proceeding entered or taken, for following grounds: (1) mistake, inadvertence, surprise, or excusable neglect; (2) newly discovered evidence; (3) fraud, misrepresentation, or other misconduct. Civ.R. 60(b). Exception from general rule relating to enlargement. Civ.R. 60(b).
	Motion within a reasonable time, for following grounds: (1) judgment void, (2) judgment satisfied, released, or discharged, (3) prior underlying judgment reversed or otherwise vacated, (4) no longer equitable that judgment have prospective application, (5) any other reason justifying relief. Civ.R. 60(b). Exception from general rule relating to enlargement. Civ.R. 6(b).
Stay	See "Execution", this table.
Summary judgment	See "Summary Judgment", this table.
JURORS	The institution of the alternate juror has been abolished. Civ.R. 47, 1991 Advisory Committee note, subd. (b).
JURY trial	
Demand	Service any time after commencement of action and not later than 10 days after service of last pleading directed to the triable issue. Civ.R. 38(b).
	Adverse party may serve demand for jury trial within 10 days after service of first demand or such lesser time as court fixes. Civ.R. 38(c).
Removed actions	If at the time of removal all necessary pleadings have been served, demand for jury trial may be served:
	By petitioner, 10 days after the petition for removal is filed;

JURY trial	
	By any other party, within 10 days after service on party of the notice of filing the petition. Civ.R. 81(c).
	Demand after removal not necessary in either of two instances: (1) prior to removal, party has made express demand in accordance with state law; (2) state law does not require express demands and court does not direct otherwise. Civ.R. 81(c).
LEGAL HOLIDAY	See "Holidays", this table.
MAGISTRATE JUDGES	
Trial by consent	Consent of parties to magistrate judge's authority to be exercised within period specified by local rule. Civ.R. 73(b).
Pretrial matters	Objections of parties to order disposing of matter not dispositive of claim or defense to be served and filed within 10 days after being served with copy of order. Civ.R. 72(a).
	Clerk to forthwith mail copies to all parties of recommendation of magistrate judge for disposition of matter dispositive of claim or defense of a party or prisoner petition. Specific written objections to recommended disposition may be served and filed within 10 days after service. Response to objections may be made within 10 days after being served with copy. Civ.R. 72(b).
MAIL	**Service by mail adds 3 days to a period computed from time of service. Civ.R. 6(e).**
	When a party is required or permitted to act within a prescribed period after service of a paper upon that party, three calendar days are added to the period unless the paper is delivered on the date of service stated in the proof of service. App.R. 26(c).
	A brief or appendix is timely filed if on or before the last day for filing it is mailed First-Class or other class at least as expeditious, postage prepaid, or dispatched for delivery within three calendar days by a third-party commercial carrier. App.R. 25(a)(2)(B).
MASTERS	See "References and Referees", this table.
MORE DEFINITE STATEMENT	
Furnished	Must be furnished within 10 days after notice of order or other time fixed by court or court may strike pleading. Civ.R. 12(e).
Motion for	Must be made before responsive pleading is interposed. Civ.R. 12(e).
MOTIONS, notices, and affidavits	
	See, also, specific headings, this table.
In general	A written motion, supporting affidavits, and notice of hearing thereof—service not later than 5 days before time specified for hearing unless a different time is fixed by rule or by order of court. Civ.R. 6(d).
	Opposing affidavits may be served not later than one day before hearing, unless court permits otherwise. Civ.R. 6(d).
	Pleading, written motion, or other paper not signed by attorney or party shall be stricken unless omis-

MOTIONS, notices, and affidavits

sion of signature is corrected promptly after being called to attention of attorney or party. Civ.R. 11(a).

NEW TRIAL

Motion and affidavits	Motion shall be filed not later than 10 days after entry of judgment. Civ.R. 59(b). Exception from general rule relating to enlargement. Civ.R. 6(b). If motion based on affidavits, they must be filed with motion. Civ.R. 59(c).
Opposing affidavits	Shall be filed within 10 days of service of motion for new trial; period may be extended up to 20 days either by court for good cause shown or by parties by written stipulation. Civ.R. 59(c).
Initiative of court	Not later than 10 days after entry of judgment, court may order new trial for any reason that would justify granting one on a party's motion. Civ.R. 59(d). Exception to general rule relating to enlargement. Civ.R. 6(b).
	After giving parties notice and opportunity to be heard, court may grant a timely motion for new trial, for reason not stated in the motion. Civ.R. 59(d). Exception to general rule relating to enlargement. Civ.R. 6(b).
Judgment as a matter of law	Party against whom judgment as a matter of law is rendered shall file a motion for a new trial under Civ.R. 59 no later than 10 days after entry of the judgment. Civ.R. 50(c)(2).

OBJECTIONS to orders or rulings of court

	At time ruling or order of court is made or sought; if party has no opportunity to object to ruling or order at time it is made, absence of objection does not thereafter prejudice the party. Civ.R. 46.
Pretrial matters referred to magistrate judge	Objections of parties to order disposing of matter not dispositive of claim or defense to be served and filed within 10 days after being served with copy of order. Civ.R. 72(a).
	Specific written objections to recommended disposition of matter dispositive of claim or defense of a party or prisoner petition may be served or filed within 10 days after service. Response to objections may be made within 10 days after being served with copy. Civ.R. 72(b).

OFFER of judgment

	Must be served more than 10 days before trial. Civ.R. 68.
	Acceptance must be served within 10 days after service of offer. Civ.R. 68.
ORDERS	See Judgment or order.
PARTICULARS, Bill of	Abolished. Civ.R. 12(e), as amended in 1948. See, however, "More definite statement", this table.

PLEADINGS

Amendment of	Once as matter of course before responsive pleading served or within 20 days if no response is permitted and action has not been placed on trial calendar. Civ.R. 15(a).

PLEADINGS	
	By leave of court or written consent of adverse parties, at any time. Civ.R. 15(a).
	During trial or after judgment to conform to evidence or to raise issues not raised in pleadings, but tried by express or implied consent of parties. Civ.R. 15(b).
Supplemental	Upon motion of party—court may upon reasonable notice permit service of supplemental pleading setting forth transactions, etc., which have happened since date of pleading sought to be supplemented. Civ.R. 15(d).
	Adverse party plead to supplemental pleading—if court deems advisable, it shall so order, specifying time therefor. Civ.R. 15(d)
Averments of time	Such averments are material and shall be considered like all other averments of material matter. Civ.R. 9(f).
Judgment on, motion for	After pleadings are closed but within such time as not to delay the trial. Civ.R. 12(c).
Striking of matter from	Motion made before responding to a pleading or, if no responsive pleading permitted, within 20 days after service of pleading. Civ.R. 12(f).
	On court's own initiative at any time. Civ.R. 12(f).
Signing of	
	Pleading, written motion, or other paper not signed by attorney or party shall be stricken unless omission of signature is corrected promptly after being called to attention of attorney or party. Civ.R. 11(a).
PLEAS	Abolished. Civ.R. 7(c).
PRETRIAL conferences	
	Scheduling order to issue as soon as practicable but in any event within 90 days after appearance of a defendant and within 120 days after complaint served on defendant. Civ.R. 16(b).
PROCESS	See "Summons", this Table.
PRODUCTION of documents	
Request for, service of	
	Without leave of court or written stipulation, request may not be served before parties have met and conferred pursuant to Civ.R. 26(f). Civ.R. 34(b).
	May accompany notice of taking deposition. Civ.R. 30(b)(5).
Response to request	
	Within 30 days after service of the request. A shorter or longer time may be directed by court or agreed to. Civ.R. 34(b).
Time of inspection	The request shall specify a reasonable time. Civ.R. 34(b).
Subpoena	See "Subpoena", this table.
REFERENCES and Referees	
Order of reference	When reference is made, clerk shall forthwith furnish master with copy of order. Civ.R. 53(d)(1).
Hearings before master	Time for beginning and closing the hearings, as fixed by order of reference. Civ.R. 53(c).

REFERENCES and Referees

Meetings	First meeting of parties or attorneys to be held within 20 days after date of order of reference. Civ.R. 53(d)(1). Upon receipt of the order of reference, unless order otherwise provides, master shall forthwith set time and place for such meeting and notify parties or their attorneys. Civ.R. 53(d)(1).
	Speed—either party, on notice to parties and master, may apply to court for order requiring master to speed the proceedings and make report. Civ.R. 53(d)(1).
	Failure of party to appear at appointed time and place—master may proceed ex parte or adjourn to future day, giving notice to absent party of adjournment. Civ.R. 53(d)(1).
Report of master	Filing of, time as fixed in order of reference. Master shall serve on all parties notice of the filing. Civ.R. 53(e)(1). Master, unless otherwise directed by the order of reference, shall serve a copy of the report on each party. Civ.R. 53(e)(1).
	Objections (in non-jury actions) may be served within 10 days after being served with notice of filing of report. Civ.R. 53(e)(2).
	Court action on report and objections thereto—application (in non-jury actions) for such action shall be by motion and upon notice as prescribed in Civ.R. 6(d). Civ.R. 53(e)(2).
	Speed—either party, on notice to parties and master, may apply to court for order requiring master to speed the proceedings and make report. Civ.R. 53(d)(1).

REHEARING

Petition for panel rehearing	Petitions for panel rehearings may be filed within 14 days after entry of judgement unless the time is shortened or extended by order or local rule. In all civil cases in which the United States or its agency or officer thereof is a party, the time within which any party may seek a rehearing shall be 45 days after entry of judgement unless the time is shortened or extended by order. App.R. 40(a).
Issuance of mandate	The mandate of the court must issue 7 days after the time to file a petition for rehearing expires, or 7 days after entry of an order denying a timely petition for panel rehearing, rehearing en banc, or motion for stay of mandate, whichever is later. The court may shorten or extend the time. The timely filing of a petition for panel rehearing, petition for rehearing en banc, or motion for stay of mandate, stays the mandate until disposition of the petition or motion, unless the court orders otherwise. App.R. 41(b), (d)(1).

REMOVED actions

Answers and defenses	Within 20 days after the receipt through service or otherwise of a copy of the initial pleading setting forth the claim for relief upon which the action or proceeding is based, or within 20 days after the service of summons upon such initial pleading, then filed, or within 5 days after filing of the petition for removal, whichever period is longest. Civ.R. 81(c).
Demand for jury trial	Demand after removal not necessary in either of two instances: (1) prior to removal, party has made

REMOVED actions	
	express demand in accordance with state law; (2) state law does not require express demands and court does not direct otherwise. Civ.R. 81(c).
Notice of removal	Within 30 days after receipt through service or otherwise of a copy of the initial pleading setting forth the claim for relief upon which the action or proceeding is based, or within 30 days after service of summons if such initial pleading has then been filed in court and is not required to be served on defendant, whichever period is shorter. 28 U.S.C.A. § 1446(b).
	If the case stated by the initial pleading is not removable, a notice of removal may be filed within 30 days after receipt by the defendant, through service or otherwise, of a copy of an amended pleading, motion, order or other paper from which it may first be ascertained that the case is one which is or has become removable. 28 U.S.C.A. § 1446(b).
	A case may not be removed on the basis of jurisdiction conferred by 28 U.S.C.A. § 1332 more than one year after action's commencement. 28 U.S.C.A. § 1446(b).
REPLY	
	See, also, "Responsive pleadings", this table.
To answer or third-party answer	Only if ordered by court. Civ.R. 7(a). Service within 20 days after service of order, unless order otherwise directs. Civ.R. 12(a).
To counterclaim	Service within 20 days after service of answer. Civ.R. 12(a).
	United States or agency or officer thereof shall serve reply within 60 days after service upon U.S. attorney. Civ.R. 12(a).
Alteration of time by service of Civ.R. 12 motion	See "Responsive pleadings", this table.
RESPONSIVE PLEADINGS	
	See, also, "Answer", "Reply", this table.
To amend pleading	Within 10 days after service of amended pleading or within time remaining for response to original pleading, whichever is longer, unless court otherwise orders. Civ.R. 15(a).
To supplemental pleading	As ordered by court. Civ.R. 15(d).
Alteration of time by service of Civ.R. 12 motion	Service of motion permitted under Civ.R. 12 alters times for responsive pleadings as follows unless different time fixed by court: (1) if court denies motion, service of responsive pleading within 10 days after notice of denial; (2) if court postpones disposition until trial on merits, service of responsive pleading within 10 days after notice of postponement; (3) if court grants motion for more definite statement, service of responsive pleading within 10 days after service of the more definite statement.
RESTRAINING order, temporary, without notice	See "Injunction", this table.
RETURN	
	The court may allow a summons or proof of service to be amended. Civ.R. 4(a) & (*l*).

	The person effecting service shall make proof thereof to the court. Civ.R. 4(*l*).
SANCTIONS	Presentation to court of a pleading, written motion, or other paper is a certification under Civ.R. 11(b). If after notice and reasonable opportunity to respond, court determines that Civ.R. 11(b) was violated, sanctions may be imposed by a motion for sanctions which shall not be filed or presented to court unless, within 21 days after service of the motion, the challenged matter is not withdrawn or corrected. Civ.R. 11(c). Sanctions are inapplicable to discovery. Civ.R. 11(d).
SATURDAYS AND SUNDAYS	Exclusion in computation of time. Civ.R. 6(a); App.R. 26(a).
STAY or supersedeas	See "Appeal", "Execution", this table.
SUBPOENA	
Objection	Within 14 days after service of the subpoena or before the time specified for compliance if such time is less than 14 days after service, there be served upon the party or attorney designated in the subpoena written objection to inspection or copying of any or all of the designated materials or of the premises. Civ.R. 45(c)(2)(B).
Motion to compel production	If objection has been made, the party serving the subpoena may, upon notice to the person commanded to produce, move at any time for an order to compel the production. Civ.R. 45(c)(2)(B).
Motion to quash	The court by which a subpoena was issued shall quash or modify the subpoena on timely motion. Civ.R. 45(c)(3)(A).
Witnesses, documentary evidence, etc.	Subpoena specifies time for attendance and giving of testimony or to produce and permit inspection and copying of designated books, documents or tangible things in the possession, custody or control of that person, or to permit inspection of premises. Civ.R. 45(a)(1)(C).
SUBSTITUTION of parties	
	In cases of death, incompetency, or transfer of interest—motion for substitution, together with notice of hearing, served on parties as provided in Civ.R. 5 and upon persons not parties in manner provided in Civ.R. 4 for service of a summons. Civ.R. 25(a), (b), (c).
	Dismissal as to deceased party unless motion for substitution is made not later than 90 days after death is suggested upon the record. Civ.R. 25(a).
	Successor of public officer substituted automatically. Order of substitution may be entered at any time. Civ.R. 25(d).
SUMMARY JUDGMENT, motion for	
Claimant	May move at any time after expiration of 20 days from commencement of action or after service of motion for summary judgment by adverse party. Civ.R. 56(a).
Defending party	May move at any time. Civ.R. 56(b).
Service	Service of motion at least 10 days before time fixed for hearing. Civ.R. 56(c).
	Service of opposing affidavits prior to day of hearing. Civ.R. 56(c).

SUMMONS	Served with a copy of complaint. Civ.R. 4(c)(1). If not served within 120 days after filing complaint, court may dismiss action without prejudice, direct service be effected within a specified time, or extend time for service. Civ.R. 4(m).
	The person effecting service shall make proof thereof to the court. Civ.R. 4(*l*).
	Service by any nonparty at least 18, a U.S. marshal, deputy U.S. marshal, or other person or officer specially appointed. Civ.R. 4(c)(2).
SUPPLEMENTAL pleadings	See "Pleadings", this table.
SUPERSEDEAS or stay	See "Appeal", "Execution", this table.
TERM	The district courts deemed always open. Civ.R. 77(a).
	Terms of court have been abolished. 28 U.S.C.A. §§ 138–141, as amended by Act of Oct. 16, 1963, Pub.L. 88–139, 77 Stat. 248.
THIRD–PARTY practice	Third-party plaintiff need not obtain leave if third-party plaintiff files third-party complaint not later than 10 days after serving the original answer. Otherwise, must obtain leave on motion upon notice to all parties to the action. Civ.R. 14(a).
VERDICT	
Renewal of motion for judgment after trial	No later than 10 days after entry of judgment, motion for judgment as a matter of law may be renewed by filing the motion where motion made at the close of all the evidence is denied or for any reason is not granted. Civ.R. 50(b).
	Exception from general rule relating to enlargement. Civ.R. 6(b).
New trial where judgment as a matter of law rendered	Party against whom judgment as a matter of law is rendered shall file a motion for a new trial pursuant to Civ.R. 59 no later than 10 days after entry of the judgment. Civ.R. 50(c)(2).

EQUITY RULES REFERENCE TABLE

The Federal Rules of Civil Procedure supplant the Equity Rules since in general they cover the field now covered by the Equity Rules and the Conformity Act (former section 724 of this title).

This table shows the Equity Rules to which references are made in the notes to the Federal Rules of Civil Procedure.

Equity Rules	Federal Rules of Civil Procedure
1	77
2	77
3	79
4	77
5	77
6	78
7	4, 70
8	6, 70
9	70
10	18, 54
11	71
12	3, 4, 5, 12, 55
13	4
14	4
15	4, 45
16	6, 55
17	55
18	7, 8
19	1, 15, 61
20	12
21	11, 12
22	1
23	1, 39
24	11
25	8, 9, 10, 19
26	18, 20, 82
27	23
28	15
29	7, 12, 42, 55
30	8, 13, 82
31	7, 8, 12, 55
32	15
33	7, 12
34	15
35	15
36	11
37	17, 19, 20, 24
38	23

Equity Rules	Federal Rules of Civil Procedure
39	19
40	20
41	17
42	19, 20
43	12, 21
44	12, 21
45	25
46	43, 61
47	26
48	43
49	53
50	30, 80
51	30, 53
52	45, 53
53	53
54	26
55	30
56	40
57	40
58	26, 33, 34, 36
59	53
60	53
61	53
61½	53
62	53
63	53
64	26
65	53
66	53
67	53
68	53
69	59
70	17
70½	52
71	54
72	60, 61
73	65
74	62
75	75
76	75
77	76
78	43
79	83
80	6
81	86

ORDERS OF THE SUPREME COURT OF THE UNITED STATES ADOPTING AND AMENDING RULES

ORDER OF DECEMBER 20, 1937

It is ordered that Rules of Procedure for the District Courts of the United States be adopted pursuant to Section 2 of the Act of June 19, 1934, Chapter 651 (48 Stat. 1064), and the Chief Justice is authorized and directed to transmit the Rules as adopted to the Attorney General and to request him, as provided in that section, to report these Rules to the Congress at the beginning of the regular session in January next. MR. JUSTICE BRANDEIS states that he does not approve of the adoption of the Rules.

ORDER OF DECEMBER 28, 1939

1. That the first sentence of Rule 81(a)(6) of the Rules of Civil Procedure be amended so as to read as follows:

"(6) These rules do not apply to proceedings under the Act of September 13, 1888, c. 1015, § 13 (25 Stat. 479) as amended, U.S.C., Title 8, § 282, 8 U.S.C.A. § 282, relating to deportation of Chinese; they apply to proceedings for enforcement or review of compensation orders under the Longshoremen's and Harbor Workers' Compensation Act, Act of March 4, 1927, c. 509, §§ 18, 21 (44 Stat. 1434, 1436), U.S.C., Title 33, §§ 918, 921, 33 U.S.C.A. §§ 918, 921, except to the extent that matters of procedure are provided for in that Act".

2. Effective Date. That the foregoing amendment take effect on the day which is three months subsequent to the adjournment of the second regular session of the 76th Congress, but if that day is prior to September 1, 1940, then this amendment shall take effect on September 1, 1940. This amendment governs all proceedings in actions brought after it takes effect and also all further proceedings in actions then pending, except to the extent that in the opinion of the Court its application in a particular action pending when the amendment takes effect would not be feasible or would work injustice, in which event the former procedure applies.

3. That THE CHIEF JUSTICE be authorized to transmit this amendment to the Attorney General with the request that he report it to the Congress at the beginning of the regular session in January, 1940.

MR. JUSTICE BLACK does not approve of the adoption of this amendment.

ORDER OF DECEMBER 27, 1946

1. That subdivisions (a) and (b) of Rule 80 of the Rules of Civil Procedure be, and they hereby are, abrogated.

2. That Rules 6, 7, 12, 13, 14, 17, 24, 26, 27, 28, 33, 34, 36, 41, 45, 52, 54, 56, 58, 59, 60, 62, 65, 66, 68, 73, 75, 77, 79, 81, 84, and 86 of the Rules of Civil Procedure and Forms Nos. 17, 20, 22, and 25, be, and they hereby are, amended as hereinafter set forth.

[See the amendments made thereby under the respective rules and forms, post.]

3. That THE CHIEF JUSTICE be authorized to transmit these amendments to the Attorney General with the request that he report them to the Congress at the beginning of the regular session in January, 1947.

MR. JUSTICE FRANKFURTER joins in approval of the proposed amendments essentially because of his confidence in the informed judgment of the Advisory Committee on Rules of Civil Procedure.

ORDER OF DECEMBER 29, 1948

1. That the title "Rules of Civil Procedure for the District Courts of the United States" be amended to read "Rules of Civil Procedure for the United States District Courts".

2. That Rules 1, 17, 22, 24, 25, 27, 37, 45, 57, 60, 62, 65, 66, 67, 69, 72, 73, 74, 75, 76, 79, 81, 82, and 86 of the Rules of Civil Procedure and Forms Nos. 1, 19, 22, 23, and 27, be, and they hereby are, amended as hereinafter set forth.

[See the amendments made thereby under the respective rules and forms, post.]

3. That THE CHIEF JUSTICE be authorized to transmit these amendments to the Attorney General with the request that he report them to the Congress at the beginning of the regular session in January, 1949.

ORDER OF APRIL 30, 1951

1. That paragraph (7) of Rule 81(a) of the Rules of Civil Procedure, be, and it hereby is, abrogated.

2. That the Rules of Civil Procedure be, and they hereby are, amended by including therein a rule to govern condemnation cases in the United States District Courts, numbered 71A, as follows:

[See text of Rule 71A, post.]

3. Effective Date. That this Rule 71A and the amendment to Rule 81(a) will take effect on August 1, 1951. Rule 71A governs all proceedings in actions brought after it takes effect and also all further proceedings in actions then pending, except to the extent that in the opinion of the court its application in a particular action pending when the rule takes effect would not be feasible or would work injustice, in which event the former procedure applies.

4. That Forms Nos. 28 and 29 be, and they hereby are, approved and added to the Appendix of Forms to the Rules of Civil Procedure. The forms read respectively as follows:

[See text of Forms 28 and 29, post.]

5. That THE CHIEF JUSTICE be authorized to transmit these amendments to the Congress on or before May 1, 1951.

ORDER OF APRIL 17, 1961

1. That Rules 25, 54, 62 and 86 of the Rules of Civil Procedure and Forms Nos. 2 and 19, be, and they hereby are, amended as hereinafter set forth:

[See the amendments made thereby under the respective rules and forms, post.]

2. That THE CHIEF JUSTICE be authorized to transmit these amendments to Congress in accordance with the provisions of Title 28, U.S.C., Sec. 2072.

3. MR. JUSTICE BLACK does not join in approval of the Rules because he believes that it would be better for Congress to act directly by legislation on the matters treated by the Rules.

4. MR. JUSTICE DOUGLAS filed the following statement:

"Most of the proposed changes in the Rules of Civil Procedure are picayune and harmless, yet hardly worth making apart from any overall revision of the Rules. The change in Rule 25 of the Rules of Civil Procedure is, however, a major one; and it seems to me unwise. The policy that a cabinet officer under one administration pursues is often not the policy of the next administration. I would not make the contrary assumption, as does the proposed change. I think the ends served by *Snyder v. Buck*, 340 U.S. 15, 71 S.Ct. 93, 95 L.Ed. 15, are proper ones. The Rule in its present form leaves the burden on the claimant who challenges a particular government policy to re-establish that the controversy he had with a predecessor is a live one as respects the successor. The burden should rest there, not with the newcomer to office.

"The critical language in Rule 25(d) that is changed by the proposed amendment derived from 28 U.S.C. § 780 which the Revised Code dropped in 1949 because it had been incorporated in Rule 25(d). See 28 U.S.C., p. XXIX. The history of § 780 is reviewed in *Snyder v. Buck*, supra, pp. 18–19.

"Congress dealt with the matter beginning with the Act of February 8, 1899, 30 Stat. 822. The care with which it approached the problem is shown in H.R.Rep. No. 960, 55th Cong., 2d Sess., p. 2, where it is said:

" 'A mandamus proceeding against an officer is based upon the claim that he is personally refusing to perform some duty which the law requires of him in his official character, and if decided against him he is properly liable, personally, for all cost of the proceeding, but if he vacates the office before a decision, it might seem harsh to compel his successor to become a party to the suit and to the costs already accrued without having been guilty of any personal neglect of the official duty involved in the proceeding; but to provide against this seeming harshness your committee propose to amend the bill so as to give the succeeding official an opportunity to perform the official act involved in the proceeding and thereby prevent the survival of the action against himself, and if he fails to do so, he can not then complain of being mulct in costs accruing against his predecessor.'

"The provision of § 780 that the action might be continued against the successor in office on the requisite showing within the stated period was added by § 11 of the Judiciary Act of 1925. 43 Stat. 936, 941. The last word Congress spoke on the matter reflected the views in a Report submitted by Chief Justice Taft dated March 11, 1922, which explained § 11 in the following words:

" 'It will be noted ..... that the provision is not mandatory, but leaves it to the sound discretion of the court to determine whether there is a substantial need for continuing the cause and obtaining an adjudication of the questions involved. This will tend to restrict the exercise of the right to cases which have a sound basis.' This language was repeated in the Senate Committee Print, 68th Cong., 1st Sess., of A General Review of H.R. 10479, 67th Cong., p. 16. The language so carefully tailored by Congress is now rejected by the professional group who constitute our advisors in these matters. I do not think we should allow a known and established congressional policy to be so readily abrogated.

"We said in *Snyder v. Buck*, supra, p. 20, that if Rule 25(d) is to be amended in the manner then urged and now adopted 'the amending process is available.' Where we have a matter so heavily encrusted with legislative policy, I think any change should be left to Congress.

"I, therefore, dissent from the submission to Congress of the proposed amendments to Rule 25 of the Rules of Civil Procedure under 28 U.S.C. § 2072. For under that Act the Rules submitted become effective at the expiration of a 90–day period, unless Congress takes contrary action. This machinery seems therefore, inappropriate to me for effecting such a basic change in congressional policy as the proposed Rule 25(d) achieves."

ORDER OF JANUARY 21, 1963

1. That the Rules of Civil Procedure be, and they hereby are, amended by including therein Forms Number 30, 31 and 32, and the amendments to Rules 4, 5, 6, 7, 12, 13, 14, 15, 24, 25, 26, 28, 30, 41, 49, 50, 52, 56, 58, 71A, 77, 79, 81, and 86 and to Forms Number 3, 4, 5, 6, 7, 8, 9, 10, 11, 12, 13, 16, 18, 21, 22–A and 22–B, as hereinafter set forth:

[See additions and amendments made thereby under the respective rules and forms, post.]

2. That THE CHIEF JUSTICE be authorized to transmit these amendments to Congress in accordance with the provisions of Title 28, U.S.C., Sec. 2072.

MR. JUSTICE BLACK and MR. JUSTICE DOUGLAS are opposed to the submission of these rules [1] to the Congress under a statute which permits them to "take effect" and to repeal "all laws in conflict with such rules" without requiring any affirmative consideration, action, or approval of the rules by Congress or by the President.[2] We believe that while some of the Rules of Civil Procedure are simply housekeeping details,[3] many determine matters so substantially affecting the rights of litigants in law suits that in practical effect they are the equivalent of new legislation which, in our judgment, the Constitution requires to be initiated in and enacted by the Congress [4] and approved by the President.[5] The Constitution, as we read it, provides that all laws shall be enacted by the House, the Senate, and the President, not by the mere failure of Congress to reject proposals of an outside agency. Even were there not this constitutional limitation, the authorizing statute itself qualifies this Court's power by imposing upon it a solemn responsibility not to submit rules that "abridge, enlarge or modify any substantive right" and by specifically charging the Court with the duty to "preserve the right to trial by jury as at common law and as declared by the Seventh Amendment to the Constitution." [6] Our chief objections to the rules relate essentially to the fact that many of their provisions do "abridge, enlarge or modify" substantive rights and do not "preserve the right to trial by jury" but actually encroach upon it.

(1)(a) Rule 50(a) is amended by making the order of a judge granting a motion for a directed verdict effective without submitting the question to the jury at all. It was pointed out in *Galloway v. United States,* 319 U.S. 372, 396, 401–407, 63 S.Ct. 1077, 87 L.Ed. 1458 (dissenting opinion), how judges have whittled away or denied the right of trial by jury through the devices of directed verdicts and judgments notwithstanding verdicts. Although the amendment here is not itself a momentous one, it gives formal sanction to the process by which the courts have been wresting from juries the power to render verdicts. Since we do not approve of this sapping of the Seventh Amendment's guarantee of a jury trial, we cannot join even this technical *coup de grace.*

(b) The proposed amendment to 50(c) in practical effect vests appellate courts with more power than they have had to grant or deny new trials. The Court in *Cone v. West Virginia Pulp & Paper Co.,* 330 U.S. 212, 217–218, 67 S.Ct. 752, 91 L.Ed. 849, and *Globe Liquor Co. v. San Roman,* 332 U.S. 571, 68 S.Ct. 246, 92 L.Ed. 177, refused to construe the federal rules then existing to allow Courts of Appeals to interfere with trial judges' discretion to grant new trials. To the extent that jury verdicts are to be set aside and new trials granted, we believe that those who hear the evidence, the trial judges, are the ones who should primarily exercise such discretion.

(c) The proposed amendment to Rule 56(e) imposes additional burdens upon litigants to protect against summary judgments rendered without hearing evidence on the part of witnesses who are confronted by the persons against whom they testify so that these persons can subject the witnesses to cross-examination. The summary judgment procedure, while justified in some cases, is made a handy instrument to let judges rather than juries try law suits and to let those judges try cases not on evidence of witnesses subjected to cross-examination but on ex parte affidavits obtained by parties. Most trial lawyers would agree, we think, that a litigant can frequently obtain in an actual trial favorable testimony which could not have been secured by affidavits or even by depositions.

(d) If there are to be amendments, Rule 49 should be repealed. That rule authorizes judges to require juries to return "only a special verdict in the form of a special written finding upon each issue of fact" or to answer "written interrogatories upon one or more issues of fact the decision of which is necessary to a verdict" in addition to rendering the general verdict. Such devices are used to impair or wholly take away the power of a jury to render a general verdict. One of the ancient, fundamental reasons for having general jury verdicts was to preserve the right of trial by jury as an indispensable part of a free government. Many of the most famous constitutional controversies in England revolved around litigants' insistence, particularly in seditious libel cases, that a jury had the right to render a general verdict without being compelled to return a number of subsidiary findings to support its general verdict. Some English jurors had to go to jail because they insisted upon their right to render general verdicts over the repeated commands of tyrannical judges not to do so. Rule 49 is but another means utilized by courts to weaken the constitutional power of juries and to vest judges with more power to decide cases according to their own judgments. A scrutiny of the special verdict and written interrogatory cases in appellate courts will show the confusion that necessarily results from the employment of these devices and the ease with which judges can use them to take away the right to trial by jury. We believe that Rule 49 be repealed, not amplified.

(2) There is a proposal to amend Rule 41, which provides for dismissal of actions. We believe that, if the Rules are to be changed, a major amendment to this rule is required in the interest of justice. Before dismissing a plaintiff's action for failure of his lawyer to prosecute, the trial judge should be required to have notice served on the plaintiff himself. The hardship that can result from the absence of such requirement is shown by *Link v. Wabash R. Co.,* 370 U.S. 626, 82 S.Ct. 1386, 8 L.Ed.2d 734. Link's lawyer failed to appear in response to a judge's order for a pre-trial conference, and the judge dismissed the case. As pointed out in the dissent, plaintiff had been severely injured, and a fair system of justice should not have penalized him because his lawyer, through neglect or any other reason, failed to appear when ordered. It would do a defendant no injury for the court to refuse to dismiss any apparently bona fide case until the plaintiff has actually had notice that some failure of his lawyer has irked the judge.

(3) MR. JUSTICE BLACK and MR. JUSTICE DOUGLAS object to the changes in Rule 4, which for the first time permit a Federal District Court to obtain jurisdiction over a defendant by service of process outside the state or over his property by garnishment or attachment, under the circumstances and in the manner prescribed by state law. Those changes will apparently have little effect insofar as "federal question" litigation is concerned, since 28 U.S.C. § 1391(b) requires such suits to be brought "only in the judicial district where all defendants reside. . . ." Diversity actions, however, may be greatly increased, for the effect of proposed 4(e) is not limited to suits authorized by such statutes as the Federal Interpleader Act, 28 U.S.C. § 1335. See Advisory Committee Rept., 5–8; 28 U.S.C. § 1391(a); Fed.Rules Civ. Proc. 1. We see no justification for an increase in the number of diversity cases. We also see no reason why the extent of a Federal District Court's personal jurisdiction should depend upon the existence or nonexistence of a state "long-arm" statute. Moreover, at present a state court action commenced by attachment or garnishment can get into a District Court only if a nonresident defendant chooses to appear and remove the case, see 28 U.S.C. § 1441, and there is no good reason, absent a congressional finding, why this should be changed.

Instead of recommending changes to the present Rules, we recommend that the statute authorizing this Court to prescribe Rules of Civil Procedure, if it is to remain a law, be amended to place the responsibility upon the Judicial Conference rather than upon this Court. Since the statute was first enacted in 1934, 48 Stat. 1064, the Judicial Conference has been enlarged and improved and is now very active in its surveillance of the work of the federal courts and in recommending appropriate legislation to Congress. The present Rules produced under 28 U.S.C. § 2072 are not prepared by us but by Committees of the Judicial Conference designated by the Chief Justice, and before coming to us they are approved by the Judicial Conference pursuant to 28 U.S.C. § 331.[7] The Committees and the Conference are composed of able and distinguished members and they render a high public service. It is they, however, who do the work, not we, and the rules have only our imprimatur. The only contribution that we actually make is an occasional exercise of a veto power. If the rule-making for Federal District Courts is to continue under the present plan, we believe that the Supreme Court should not have any part in the task; rather, the statute should be amended to substitute the Judicial Conference. The Judicial Conference can participate more actively in fashioning the rules and affirmatively contribute to their content and design better than we can. Transfer of the function to the Judicial Conference would relieve us of the embarrassment of having to sit in judgment on the constitutionality of rules which we have approved and which as applied in given situations might have to be declared invalid.

1 See our earlier statements in 368 U.S. 1012–1014 and 346 U.S. 946–947.

2 28 U.S.C. § 2072 gives this Court the power to prescribe rules of practice and procedure for Federal District Courts and further provides that such rules

> "shall not take effect until they have been reported to Congress by THE CHIEF JUSTICE at or after the beginning of a regular session thereof but not later than the first day of May, and until the expiration of ninety days after they have been thus reported.

"All laws in conflict with such rules shall be of no further force or effect after such rules have taken effect."

3 See 368 U.S. 1012.

4 "All legislative Powers herein granted shall be vested in a Congress of the United States, which shall consist of a Senate and House of Representatives." U.S. Const., Art. I, § 1.

5 Every Bill which shall have passed the House of Representatives and the Senate, shall, before it becomes a Law, be presented to the President of the United States; . . . ." U.S. Const., Art. I, § 7.

6 28 U.S.C. § 2072.

7 "The Conference shall also carry on a continuous study of the operation and effect of the general rules of practice and procedure now or hereafter in use as prescribed by the Supreme Court for the other courts of the United States pursuant to law. Such changes in and additions to those rules as the Conference may deem desirable to promote simplicity in procedure, fairness in administration, the just determination of litigation, and the elimination of unjustifiable expense and delay shall be recommended by the Conference from time to time to the Supreme Court for its consideration and adoption, modification or rejection, in accordance with law."

ORDER OF FEBRUARY 28, 1966

1. That the Rules of Civil Procedure for the United States District Courts be, and they hereby are, amended by including therein Rules 23.1, 23.2, 44.1 and 65.1, Supplemental Rules A, B, C, D, E and F for Certain Admiralty and Maritime Claims, and amendments to Rules 1, 4, 8, 9, 12, 13, 14, 15, 17, 18, 19, 20, 23, 24, 26, 38, 41, 42, 43, 44, 47, 53, 59, 65, 68, 73, 74, 75, 81 and 82, and to Forms 2 and 15, as hereinafter set forth:

[See added, amended and supplemental Rules and Forms, post.]

2. That the foregoing amendments and additions to the Rules of Civil Procedure shall take effect on July 1, 1966, and shall govern all proceedings in actions brought thereafter and also in all further proceedings in actions then pending, except to the extent that in the opinion of the court their application in a particular action then pending would not be feasible or would work injustice, in which event the former procedure applies.

3. That THE CHIEF JUSTICE be, and he hereby is, authorized to transmit to the Congress the foregoing amendments and additions to the Rules of Civil Procedure in accordance with the provisions of Title 28, U.S.C., §§ 2072 and 2073.

4. That: (a) subdivision (c) of Rule 6 of the Rules of Civil Procedure for the United States District Courts promulgated by this court on December 20, 1937, effective September 16, 1938; (b) Rule 2 of the Rules for Practice and Procedure under section 25 of An Act to amend and consolidate the Acts respecting copyright, approved March 4, 1909, promulgated by this court on June 1, 1909, effective July 1, 1909; and (c) the Rules of Practice in Admiralty and Maritime Cases, promulgated by this court on December 6, 1920, effective March 7, 1921, as revised, amended and supplemented, be, and they hereby are, rescinded, effective July 1, 1966.

MR. JUSTICE BLACK, dissenting.

The Amendments to the Federal Rules of Civil and Criminal Procedure today transmitted to the Congress are the work of very capable advisory committees. Those committees, not the Court, wrote the rules. Whether by this transmittal the individual members of the Court who voted to transmit the rules intended to express approval of the varied policy decisions the rules embody I am not sure. I am reasonably certain, however, that the Court's transmittal does not carry with it a decision that the amended rules are all constitutional. For such a decision would be the equivalent of an advisory opinion which, I assume the Court would unanimously agree, we are without constitutional power to give. And I agree with my Brother DOUGLAS that some of the proposed criminal rules go to the very border line if they do not actually transgress the constitutional right of a defendant not to be compelled to be a witness against himself. This phase of the criminal rules in itself so infects the whole collection of proposals that, without mentioning other objections, I am opposed to transmittal of the proposed amendments to the criminal rules.

I am likewise opposed to transmittal of the proposed revision of the civil rules. In the first place I think the provisions of 28 U.S.C. § 2072 (1964 ed.), under which these rules are transmitted and the corresponding section, 18 U.S.C. § 3771 (1964 ed.), relating to the criminal rules, both of which provide for giving transmitted rules the effect of law as though they had been properly enacted by Congress are unconstitutional for reasons I have previously stated.[1] And in prior dissents I have stated some of the basic reasons for my objections to repeated rules revisions [2] that tend to upset established meanings and need not repeat those grounds of objection here. The confusion created by the adoption of the present rules, over my objection, has been partially dispelled by judicial interpretations of them by this Court and others. New rules and extensive amendments to present rules will mean renewed confusion resulting in new challenges and new reversals and prejudicial "pretrial" dismissals of cases before a trial on the merits for failure of lawyers to understand and comply with new rules of uncertain meaning. Despite my continuing objection to the old rules, it seems to me that since they have at least gained some degree of certainty it would be wiser to "bear those ills we have than fly to others we know not of," unless, of course, we are reasonably sure that the proposed reforms of the old rules are badly needed. But I am not. The new proposals, at least some of them, have, as I view them, objectionable possibilities that cause me to believe our judicial system could get along much better without them.

The momentum given the proposed revision of the old rules by this Court's transmittal makes it practically certain that Congress, just as has this Court, will permit the rules to take effect exactly as they were written by the Advisory Committee on Rules. Nevertheless, I am including here a memorandum I submitted to the Court expressing objections to the Committee's proposals and suggesting changes should they be transmitted. These suggestions chiefly center around rules that grant broad discretion to trial judges with reference to class suits, pretrial procedures, and dismissal of cases with prejudice. Cases coming before the federal courts over the years now filling nearly 40 volumes of Federal Rules Decisions show an accumulation of grievances by lawyers and litigants about the way many trial judges exercise their almost unlimited discretionary powers to use pretrial procedures to dismiss cases without trials. In fact, many of these cases indicate a belief of many judges and legal commentators that the cause of justice is best served in the long run not by trials on the merits but by summary dismissals based on out of court affidavits, pretrial depositions, and other pretrial techniques. My belief is that open court trials on the merits where litigants have the right to prove their case or defense best comports with due process of law.

The proposed rules revisions, instead of introducing changes designed to prevent the continued abuse of pretrial power to dismiss cases summarily without trials, move in the opposite direction. Of course, each such dismissal results in removal of one more case from our congested court dockets, but that factor should not weigh more heavily in our system of justice than assuring a full-fledged due process trial of every bona fide lawsuit brought to vindicate an honest, substantial claim. It is to protect this ancient right of a person to have his case tried rather than summarily thrown out of court that I suggested to the Court that it recommend changes in the Committee's proposals of the nature set out in the following memorandum.

"Dear Brethren:

"I have gone over all the proposed amendments carefully and while there are probably some good suggestions, it is my belief that the bad results that can come from the adoption of these amendments predominate over any good they can bring about. I particularly think that every member of the Court should examine with great care the amendments relating to class suits. It seems to me that they place too much power in the hands of the trial judges and that the rules might almost as well simply provide that 'class suits can be maintained either for or against particular groups whenever in the discretion of a judge he thinks it is wise.' The power given to the judge to dismiss such suits or to divide them up into groups at will subjects members of classes to dangers that could not follow from carefully prescribed legal standards enacted to control class suits.

"In addition, the rules as amended, in my judgment, greatly aggravate the evil of vesting judges with practically uncontrolled power to dismiss with prejudice cases brought by plaintiffs or defenses interposed by defendants. The power to dismiss a plaintiff's case or to render judgments by default against defendants can work great harm to both parties. There are many inherent urges in existence which may subconsciously incline a judge towards disposing of the cases before him without having to go through the burden of a trial. Mr. Chief Justice White, before he became Chief Justice, wrote an opinion in the case of *Hovey v. Elliott*, 167 U.S. 409 [17 S.Ct. 841, 42 L.Ed. 215], which pointed out grave constitutional questions raised by attempting to punish the parties by depriving them of the right to try their law suits or to defend against law suits brought against them by others.

"Rule 41 entitled 'Dismissal of Actions' points up the great power of judges to dismiss actions and provides an automatic method under which a dismissal must be construed as a dismissal 'with prejudice' unless the judge specifically states otherwise. For that reason I suggest to the Conference that if the Rules are accepted, including that one, the last sentence of Rule 41(b) be amended so as to provide that a simple order of dismissal by a judge instead of operating 'as an adjudication upon the merits,' as the amended rule reads, shall provide that such a dismissal 'does not operate as an adjudication upon the merits.'

"As a further guarantee against oppressive dismissals I suggest the addition of the following as subdivision (c) of Rule 41.

" 'No plaintiff's case shall be dismissed or defendant's right to defend be cut off because of the neglect, misfeasance, malfeasance, or failure of their counsel to obey any order of the court, until and unless such plaintiff or defendant shall have been personally served with notice of their counsel's delinquency, and not then unless the parties themselves do or fail to do something on their own part that can legally justify dismissal of the plaintiff's case or of the defendant's defense.'

"This proposed amendment is suggested in order to protect litigants, both plaintiffs and defendants, against being thrown out of court as a penalty for their lawyer's neglect or misconduct. The necessity for such a rule is shown, I think, by the dismissal in the plaintiff's case in *Link v. Wabash R. Co.,* 370 U.S. 626 [82 S.Ct. 1386, 8 L.Ed.2d 734]. The usual argument against this suggestion is that a party to a law suit hires his lawyer and should therefore be responsible for everything his lawyer does in the conduct of his case. This may be a good argument with reference to affluent litigants who not only know the best lawyers but are able to hire them. It is a wholly unrealistic argument, however, to make with reference to individual persons who do not know the ability of various lawyers or who are not financially able to hire those at the top of the bar and who are compelled to rely on the assumption that a lawyer licensed by the State is competent. It seems to me to be an uncivilized practice to punish clients by throwing their cases out of court because of their lawyers' conduct. It may be supportable by good, sound, formal logic but I think has no support whatever in a procedural system supposed to work as far as humanly possible to the end of obtaining equal and exact justice.

"For all the reasons stated above and in my previous objections to the transmittals of rules I dissent from the transmittals here."

1 In a statement accompanying a previous transmittal of the civil rules, MR. JUSTICE DOUGLAS and I said:

"MR. JUSTICE BLACK and MR. JUSTICE DOUGLAS are opposed to the submission of these rules to the Congress under a statute which permits them to 'take effect' and to repeal 'all laws in conflict with such rules' without requiring any affirmative consideration, action, or approval of the rules by Congress or by the President. We believe that while some of the Rules of Civil Procedure are simply housekeeping details, many determine matters so substantially affecting the rights of litigants in lawsuits that in practical effect they are the equivalent of new legislation which, in our judgment, the Constitution requires to be initiated in and enacted by the Congress and approved by the President. The Constitution, as we read it, provides that all laws shall be enacted by the House, the Senate, and the President, not by the mere failure of Congress to reject proposals of an outside agency. * * *" (Footnotes omitted.) 374 U.S. 865–866.

2 346 U.S. 946, 374 U.S. 865. And see 368 U.S. 1011 and 1012.

MR. JUSTICE DOUGLAS, dissenting in part.

I reiterate today what I stated on an earlier occasion (374 U.S. 865, 869–870) (statement of Black and Douglas, JJ.), that the responsibility for promulgating Rules of the kind we send to Congress today should rest with the Judicial Conference and not the Court. It is the Judicial Conference, not the Court, which appoints the Advisory Committee on Criminal Rules which makes the actual recommendations.[1] Members of the Judicial Conference, being in large part judges of the lower courts and attorneys who are using the Rules day in and day out, are in a far better position to make a practical judgment upon their utility or inutility than we.

But since under the statute[2] the Rules go to Congress only on the initiative of the Court, I cannot be only a conduit. I think that placing our imprimatur on the amendments to the Rules entails a large degree of responsibility of judgment concerning them. Some of the criminal Rules which we forward to Congress today are very bothersome—not in the sense that they may be unwieldy or unworkable—but in the sense that they may entrench on important constitutional rights of defendants.

In my judgment, the amendments to Rule 16 dealing with discovery require further reflection. To the extent that they expand the defendant's opportunities for discovery, they accord with the views of a great many commentators who have concluded that a civilized society ought not to tolerate the conduct of a criminal prosecution as a "game."[3] But the proposed changes in the Rule go further. Rule 16(c) would permit a trial judge to condition granting the defendant discovery on the defendant's willingness to permit the prosecution to discover "scientific or medical reports, books, papers, documents, tangible objects, or copies or portions thereof" which (1) are in the defendant's possession; (2) he intends to produce at trial; and (3) are shown to be material to the preparation of the prosecution's case.[4]

The extent to which a court may compel the defendant to disclose information or evidence pertaining to his case without infringing the privilege against self-incrimination is a source of current controversy among judges, prosecutors, defense lawyers, and other legal commentators. A distinguished state court has concluded—although not without a strong dissent—that the privilege is not violated by discovery of the names of expert medical witnesses whose appearance at trial is contemplated by the defense.[5] I mean to imply no views on the point, except to note that a serious constitutional question lurks here.

The prosecution's opportunity to discover evidence in the possession of the defense is somewhat limited in the proposal with which we deal in that it is tied to the exercise by the defense of the right to discover from the prosecution. But *if* discovery, by itself, of information in the possession of the defendant would violate the privilege against self-incrimination, is it any less a violation if conditioned on the defendant's exercise of the opportunity to discover evidence? May benefits be conditioned on the abandonment of constitutional rights? See, e.g., *Sherbert v. Verner,* 374 U.S. 398, 403–406, 83 S.Ct. 1790, 1793–1795, 10 L.Ed.2d 965. To deny a defendant the opportunity to discovery—an opportunity not withheld from defendants who agree to prosecutorial discovery or from whom discovery is not sought—merely because the defendant chooses to exercise the constitutional right to refrain from self-incrimination arguably imposes a penalty upon the exercise of that fundamental privilege. It is said, however, that fairness may require disclosure by a defendant who obtains information from the prosecution.

Perhaps—but the proposed rule establishes no such standards. Its application is mechanical: if the defendant is allowed discovery, so, too, is the prosecution. No requirement is imposed, for example, that the subject matter of the material sought to be discovered by the prosecution be limited to that relating to the subject of the defendant's discovery.

The proposed addition of Rule 17.1 also suggests difficulties, perhaps of constitutional dimension. This rule would establish a pretrial conference procedure. The language of the rule and the Advisory Committee's comments suggest that under some circumstances, the conference might even take place in the absence of the defendant! Cf. *Lewis v. United States,* 146 U.S. 370, 13 S.Ct. 136, 36 L.Ed. 1011; Fed.Rules Crim.Proc. Rule 43.

The proposed amendment to Rule 32(c)(2) states that the trial judge "may" disclose to the defendant or his counsel the contents of a presentence report on which he is relying in fixing sentence. The imposition of sentence is of critical importance to a man convicted of crime. Trial judges need presentence reports so that they may have at their disposal the fullest possible information. See *Williams v. People of State of New York*, 337 U.S. 241, 69 S.Ct. 1079, 93 L.Ed. 1337. But while the formal rules of evidence do not apply to restrict the factors which the sentencing judge may consider, fairness would, in my opinion, require that the defendant be advised of the facts—perhaps very damaging to him—on which the judge intends to rely. The presentence report may be inaccurate, a flaw which may be of constitutional dimension. Cf. *Townsend v. Burke*, 334 U.S. 736, 68 S.Ct. 1252, 92 L.Ed. 1690. It may exaggerate the gravity of the defendant's prior offenses. The investigator may have made an incomplete investigation. See Tappan, Crime, Justice and Correction 556 (1960). There may be countervailing factors not disclosed by the probation report. In many areas we can rely on the sound exercise of discretion by the trial judge; but how can a judge know whether or not the presentence report calls for a reply by the defendant? Its faults may not appear on the face of the document.

Some States require full disclosure of the report to the defense.[6] The proposed Model Penal Code takes the middle-ground and requires the sentencing judge to disclose to the defense the factual contents of the report so that there is an opportunity to reply.[7] Whatever should be the rule for the federal courts, it ought not to be one which permits a judge to impose sentence on the basis of information of which the defendant may be unaware and to which he has not been afforded an opportunity to reply.

I do not think we should approve Rule 16, 17.1, and 32(c)(2). Instead, we should refer them back to the Judicial Conference and the Advisory Committee for further consideration and reflection, where I believe they were approved only by the narrowest majority.

WILLIAM O. DOUGLAS.

1 28 U.S.C. § 331 (1964 ed.) which establishes the Judicial Conference of the United States, provides that the Conference shall "carry on a continuous study of the operation and effect of the general rules of practice and procedure * * * prescribed by the Supreme Court * * *." The Conference has resolved that a standing Committee on Rules of Practice and Procedure be appointed by the Chief Justice and that, in addition, five advisory committees be established to recommend to the Judicial Conference changes in the rules of practice and procedure for the federal courts. See Annual Report of the Proceedings of the Judicial Conference of the United States 6–7 (1958).

2 18 U.S.C. § 3771 (1964 ed.).

3 See, e.g., Brennan, The Criminal Prosecution: Sporting Event or Quest for Truth?, 1963 Wash.U.L.Q. 279; Louisell, Criminal Discovery: Dilemma Real or Apparent?, 49 Calif.L.Rev. 56 (1961); Traynor, Ground Lost and Found in Criminal Discovery, 39 N.Y.U.L.Rev. 228 (1964).

4 The proposed rule explicitly provides that the prosecution may not discover nonmedical documents or reports "made by the defendant, or his attorneys or agents in connection with the investigation or defense of the case, or of statements made by the defendant, or by government or defense witnesses, or by prospective government or defense witnesses, to the defendant, his agents or attorneys."

5 *Jones v. Superior Court of Nevada County*, 58 Cal.2d 56, 22 Cal. Rptr. 879, 372 P.2d 919, 96 A.L.R.2d 1213. See Comment, 51 Calif.L.Rev. 135; Note, 76 Harv.L.Rev. 838 (1963). The case is more extensively treated in Louisell, Criminal Discovery and Self–Incrimination, 53 Calif.L.Rev. 89 (1965).

6 E.g., Calif.Penal Code § 1203.

7 Model Penal Code § 7.07(5) (Proposed Official Draft, 1962). The Code provides that the sources of confidential information need not be disclosed. "Less disclosure than this hardly comports with elementary fairness." Comment to § 7.07 (Tent.Draft No. 2, 1954), at 55. A discarded draft of the amendment to Fed.Rules Crim.Proc.Rule 32 would have allowed disclosure to defense counsel of the report, from which the confidential sources would be removed. A defendant not represented by counsel would be told of the "essential facts" in the report. See 8 Moore's Federal Practice ¶¶ 32.03[4], 32.09 (1965).

ORDER OF DECEMBER 4, 1967

1. That the following rules, to be known as the Federal Rules of Appellate Procedure, be, and they hereby are, prescribed, pursuant to sections 3771 and 3772 of Title 18, United States Code, and sections 2072 and 2075 of Title 28, United States Code, to govern the procedure in appeals to United States courts of appeals from the United States district courts, in the review by United States courts of appeals of decisions of the Tax Court of the United States, in proceedings in the United States courts of appeals for the review or enforcement of orders of administrative agencies, boards, commissions and officers, and in applications for writs or other relief which a United States court of appeals or judge thereof is competent to give:

[See text of Rules of Appellate Procedure, post.]

2. That the foregoing rules shall take effect on July 1, 1968, and shall govern all proceedings in appeals and petitions for review or enforcement of orders thereafter brought and in all such proceedings then pending, except to the extent that in the opinion of the court of appeals their application in a particular proceeding then pending would not be feasible or would work injustice, in which case the former procedure may be followed.

3. That Rules 6, 9, 41, 77 and 81 of the Rules of Civil Procedure for the United States District Courts be, and they hereby are, amended, effective July 1, 1968, as hereinafter set forth:

[See the amendments made thereby under the respective rules, post.]

4. That the chapter heading "IX. APPEALS", all of Rules 72, 73, 74, 75 and 76 of the Rules of Civil Procedure for the United States District Courts, and Form 27 annexed to the said rules, be, and they hereby are, abrogated, effective July 1, 1968.

[Paragraphs 5 and 6 of the order pertain to certain Rules of Criminal Procedure for the United States District Courts and to certain Forms annexed to the said rules. For text, see Pamphlet containing Federal Rules of Criminal Procedure.]

7. That THE CHIEF JUSTICE be, and he hereby is, authorized to transmit to the Congress the foregoing new rules and amendments to and abrogation of existing rules, in accordance with the provisions of Title 18, U.S.C., § 3771, and Title 28, U.S.C., §§ 2072 and 2075.

ORDER OF MARCH 30, 1970

1. That subdivision (a) of Rule 5, subdivision (h) of Rule 9 and Rules 26, 29, 30, 31, 32, 33, 34, 35, 36 and 37, and subdivision (d) of Rule 45, subdivision (a) of Rule 69, and Form 24 of the Rules of Civil Procedure for the United

States District Courts be, and they hereby are, amended to read as follows:

[See the amendments made thereby under the respective rules and forms, post.]

2. That the foregoing amendments to the Rules of Civil Procedure shall take effect on July 1, 1970, and shall govern all proceedings in actions brought thereafter and also in all further proceedings in actions then pending, except to the extent that in the opinion of the court their application in a particular action then pending would not be feasible or would work injustice, in which event the former procedure applies.

3. That THE CHIEF JUSTICE be, and he hereby is, authorized to transmit to the Congress the foregoing amendments to the Rules of Civil Procedure in accordance with the provisions of Title 28, U.S.C. § 2072.

MR. JUSTICE BLACK and MR. JUSTICE DOUGLAS disapprove of the Amendments to the Federal Rules of Civil Procedure relating to Discovery, and dissent from the action of the Court in transmitting them to the Congress.

ORDER OF MARCH 1, 1971

1. That subdivision (a) of Rule 6, paragraph (4) of subdivision (a) of Rule 27, paragraph (6) of subdivision (b) of Rule 30, subdivision (c) of Rule 77, and paragraph (2) of subdivision (a) of Rule 81 of the Federal Rules of Civil Procedure be, and they hereby are, amended, effective July 1, 1971, to read as follows:

[See amendments made thereby under the respective rules, post.]

2. [*Certain Rules of Criminal Procedure for the United States District Courts amended*].

3. That subdivision (a) of Rule 26 and subdivision (a) of Rule 45 of the Federal Rules of Appellate Procedure be, and they hereby are, amended, effective July 1, 1971, to read as follows:

[See amendments made thereby under the respective Rules of Appellate Procedure, post.]

4. That THE CHIEF JUSTICE be, and he hereby is, authorized to transmit to the Congress the foregoing amendments to the Rules of Civil, Criminal and Appellate Procedure, in accordance with the provisions of Title 18 U.S.C. § 3771, and Title 28 U.S.C. §§ 2072 and 2075.

MR. JUSTICE BLACK and MR. JUSTICE DOUGLAS dissent.

ORDER OF NOVEMBER 20, 1972

1. That the rules hereinafter set forth, to be known as the Federal Rules of Evidence, be, and they hereby are, prescribed pursuant to Sections 3402, 3771, and 3772, Title 18, United States Code, and Sections 2072 and 2075, Title 28, United States Code, to govern procedure, in the proceedings and to the extent set forth therein, in the United States courts of appeals, the United States district courts, the District Court for the District of the Canal Zone and the district courts of Guam and the Virgin Islands, and before United States magistrates.

2. That the aforementioned Federal Rules of Evidence shall take effect on July 1, 1973, and shall be applicable to actions and proceedings brought thereafter and also to further procedure in actions and proceedings then pending, except to the extent that in the opinion of the court their application in a particular action or proceeding then pending would not be feasible or would work injustice in which event the former procedure applies.

3. That subdivision (c) of Rule 30 and Rules 43 and 44.1 of the Federal Rules of Civil Procedure be, and they hereby are, amended, effective July 1, 1973, to read as hereinafter set forth:

[See amendments made thereby under the respective rules, post.]

4. That subdivision (c) of Rule 32 of the Federal Rules of Civil Procedure be, and it hereby is, abrogated, effective July 1, 1973.

5. *[Certain Rules of Criminal Procedure for the United States District Courts amended].*

6. That THE CHIEF JUSTICE be, and he hereby is, authorized to transmit the foregoing new rules and amendments to and abrogation of existing rules to the Congress at the beginning of its next regular session, in accordance with the provisions of Title 18 U.S.C. § 3771 and Title 28 U.S.C. §§ 2072 and 2075.

ORDER OF DECEMBER 18, 1972

1. That Rule 43 of the Federal Rules of Civil Procedure, as amended by Order of this Court entered November 20, 1972, be, and it hereby is, further amended, effective July 1, 1973, to read as follows:

[See amendment made thereby under Rule 43 post.]

2. That THE CHIEF JUSTICE be, and he hereby is, authorized to transmit the foregoing amendment of Rule 43 of the Federal Rules of Civil Procedure to the Congress at the beginning of its next regular session in accordance with the provisions of Title 28, U.S.C. § 2072.

CONGRESSIONAL ACTION ON PROPOSED RULES OF EVIDENCE AND 1972 AMENDMENTS TO FEDERAL RULES OF CIVIL PROCEDURE AND FEDERAL RULES OF CRIMINAL PROCEDURE

Pub.L. 93–12, Mar. 30, 1973, 87 Stat. 9, provided: "That notwithstanding any other provisions of law, the Rules of Evidence for United States Courts and Magistrates, the Amendments to the Federal Rules of Civil Procedure, and the Amendments to the Federal Rules of Criminal Procedure, which are embraced by the orders entered by the Supreme Court of the United States on Monday, November 20, 1972, and Monday, December 18, 1972, shall have no force or effect except to the extent, and with such amendments, as they may be expressly approved by Act of Congress."

Pub.L. 93–595, § 3, Jan. 2, 1975, 88 Stat. 1959, provided that: "The Congress expressly approves the amendments to the Federal Rules of Civil Procedure, and the amendments to the Federal Rules of Criminal Procedure, which are embraced by the orders entered by the Supreme Court of the United States on November 20, 1972, and December 18, 1972, and such amendments shall take effect on the one hundred and eightieth day beginning after the date of the enactment of this Act [Jan. 2, 1975]."

ORDER OF APRIL 26, 1976

1. That the rules and forms governing proceedings in the United States District Courts under Section 2254 and Section 2255 of Title 28, United States Code, as approved by the Judicial Conference of the United States be, and they hereby are, prescribed pursuant to Section 2072 of Title 28, United States Code and Sections 3771 and 3772 of Title 18, United States Code.

2. That the aforementioned rules and forms shall take effect August 1, 1976, and shall be applicable to all proceedings then pending except to the extent that in the opinion of the court their application in a particular proceeding would not be feasible or would work injustice.

3. That THE CHIEF JUSTICE be, and he hereby is, authorized to transmit the aforementioned rules and forms governing Section 2254 and Section 2255 proceedings to the Congress in accordance with the provisions of Section 2072 of Title 28 and Sections 3771 and 3772 of Title 18, United States Code.

CONGRESSIONAL ACTION ON PROPOSED RULES AND FORMS GOVERNING PROCEEDINGS UNDER 28 U.S.C. §§ 2254 AND 2255

Pub.L. 94–349, § 2, July 8, 1976, 90 Stat. 822, provided: "That, notwithstanding the provisions of section 2072 of title 28 of the United States Code, the rules and forms governing section 2254 cases in the United States district courts and the rules and forms governing section 2255 proceedings in the United States district courts which are embraced by the order entered by the United States Supreme Court on April 26, 1976, and which were transmitted to the Congress on or about April 26, 1976, shall not take effect until thirty days after the adjournment sine die of the 94th Congress, or until and to the extent approved by Act of Congress, whichever is earlier."

Pub.L. 94–426, § 1, Sept. 28, 1976, 90 Stat. 1334, provided: "That the rules governing section 2254 cases in the United States district courts and the rules governing section 2255 proceedings for the United States district courts, as proposed by the United States Supreme Court, which were delayed by the Act entitled 'An Act to delay the effective date of certain proposed amendments to the Federal Rules of Criminal Procedure and certain other rules promulgated by the United States Supreme Court' (Public Law 94–349), are approved with the amendments set forth in section 2 of this Act and shall take effect as so amended, with respect to petitions under section 2254 and motions under section 2255 of title 28 of the United States Code filed on or after February 1, 1977."

ORDER OF APRIL 29, 1980

1. That the Federal Rules of Civil Procedure be, and they hereby are, amended by including therein amendments to Rules 4, 5, 26, 28, 30, 32, 33, 34, 37 and 45 as hereinafter set forth:

[See amendments made thereby under respective rules, post.]

2. That the foregoing amendments to the Federal Rules of Civil Procedure shall take effect on August 1, 1980, and shall govern all civil proceedings thereafter commenced and, insofar as just and practicable, all proceedings then pending.

3. That subsection (e) of Rule 37 of the Federal Rules of Civil Procedure is hereby abrogated, effective August 1, 1980.

4. That THE CHIEF JUSTICE be, and he hereby is, authorized to transmit to the Congress the foregoing amendments to the Federal Rules of Civil Procedure in accordance with the provisions of Section 2072 of Title 28, United States Code.

MR. JUSTICE POWELL, with whom MR. JUSTICE STEWART and MR. JUSTICE REHNQUIST join, filed a dissenting statement.

I dissent from the Court's adoption of the amendments to Federal Rules of Civil Procedure 26, 33, 34, and 37—the cluster of Rules authorizing and regulating discovery generally, interrogatories, production of documents, and sanctions for failure to make discovery. These amendments are not inherently objectionable. Indeed, they represent the culmination of several years' work by the Judicial Conference's distinguished and conscientious Standing Committee on Rules of Practice and Procedure and Advisory Committee on Civil Rules.[1] But the changes embodied in the amendments fall short of those needed to accomplish reforms in civil litigation that are long overdue.

The American Bar Association proposed significant and substantial reforms.[2] Although the Standing Committee initially favored most of these proposals, it ultimately rejected them in large part. The ABA now accedes to the Standing Committee's amendments because they make some improvements, but the most recent report of the ABA Section of Litigation makes clear that the "serious and widespread abuse of discovery" will remain largely uncontrolled.[3] There are wide differences of opinion within the profession as to the need for reform. The bench and the bar are familiar with the existing Rules, and it often is said that the bar has a vested interest in maintaining the status quo. I imply no criticism of the bar or the Standing Committee when I suggest that the present recommendations reflect a compromise as well as the difficulty of framing satisfactory discovery Rules. But whatever considerations may have prompted the Committee's final decision, I doubt that many judges or lawyers familiar with the proposed amendments believe they will have an appreciable effect on the acute problems associated with discovery. The Court's adoption of these inadequate changes could postpone effective reform for another decade.

When the Federal Rules first appeared in 1938, the discovery provisions properly were viewed as a constructive improvement. But experience under the discovery Rules demonstrates that "not infrequently [they have been] exploited to the disadvantage of justice." *Herbert v. Lando*, 441 U.S. 153, 179 (1979) (POWELL, J., concurring). Properly limited and controlled discovery is necessary in most civil litigation. The present Rules, however, invite discovery of such scope and duration that district judges often cannot keep the practice within reasonable bounds.[4] Even in a relatively simple case, discovery through depositions, interrogatories, and demands for documents may take weeks. In complex litigation, discovery can continue for years. One must doubt whether empirical evidence would demonstrate that untrammeled discovery actually contributes to the just resolution of disputes. If there is disagreement about that, there is none whatever about the effect of discovery practices upon the average citizen's ability to afford legal remedies.

Delay and excessive expense now characterize a large percentage of all civil litigation. The problems arise in significant part, as every judge and litigator knows, from abuse of the discovery procedures available under the Rules.[5] Indeed, the National Conference on the Causes of Popular Dissatisfaction with the Administration of Justice, led by THE CHIEF JUSTICE,[6] identified "Abuse in the use of discovery [as] a major concern" within our legal system.[7] Lawyers devote an enormous number of "chargeable hours" to the practice of discovery. We may assume that discovery usually is conducted in good faith. Yet all too often discovery practices enable the party with greater financial resources to prevail by exhausting the resources of a weaker opponent. The mere threat of delay or unbearable expense denies justice to many actual or prospective litigants. Persons or businesses of comparatively limited means settle unjust claims and relinquish just claims simply because they cannot afford to litigate.[8] Litigation costs have become intolerable, and they cast a lengthening shadow over the basic fairness of our legal system.

I reiterate that I do not dissent because the modest amendments recommended by the Judicial Conference are undesirable. I simply believe that Congress' acceptance of these tinkering changes will delay for years the adoption of genuinely effective reforms. The process of change, as experience teaches, is tortuous and contentious. Favorable congressional action on these amendments will create complacency and encourage inertia. Meanwhile, the discovery Rules will continue to deny justice to those least able to bear the burdens of delay, escalating legal fees, and rising court costs.

The amendments to Rules 26, 33, 34, and 37 recommended by the Judicial Conference should be rejected, and the Conference should be directed to initiate a thorough reexamination of the discovery Rules that have become so central to the conduct of modern civil litigation.

1 This Court's role in the rulemaking process is largely formalistic. Standing and advisory committees of the Judicial Conference make the initial studies, invite comments on their drafts, and prepare the Rules. Both the Judicial Conference and this Court necessarily rely upon the careful work of these committees. Congress should bear in mind that our approval of proposed Rules is more a certification that they are the products of proper procedures than a considered judgment on the merits of the proposals themselves. See generally 409 U.S. 1132, 1133 (1973) (DOUGLAS, J., dissenting from adoption of Federal Rules of Evidence); 383 U.S. 1032 (1966) (BLACK, J., dissenting from adoption of amendment to civil rules); 374 U.S. 865, 869–870 (1963) (statement of BLACK and DOUGLAS, JJ., upon adoption of amendments to Federal Rules of Civil Procedure).

2 American Bar Association, Report of the Section of Litigation Special Committee for the Study of Discovery Abuse (App.Draft 1977).

3 ABA Section of Litigation, Second Report of the Special Committee for the Study of Discovery Abuse, 5 (1980).

4 MR. JUSTICE WHITE, writing for the Court, recently reminded the federal courts that "the discovery provisions . . . are subject to the injunction of Rule 1 that they be 'construed to secure the just, *speedy*, and *inexpensive* determination of every action.'" *Herbert v. Lando,* 441 U.S. 153, 177 (1979).

In his most recent Annual Report on the State of the Judiciary, THE CHIEF JUSTICE declared that "[t]he responsibility for control [of pretrial process] rests on both judges and lawyers. Where existing rules and statutes permit abuse, they must be changed. Where the power lies with judges to prevent or correct abuse and misuse of the system, judges must act." Address to American Bar Association Mid-Year Meeting, 6 (Feb. 3, 1980).

5 Writing from his wide experience as a judge, practicing lawyer, and Attorney General, Griffin B. Bell advised the Standing Committee that "the scope of discovery is far too broad and that excessive discovery has significantly contributed to the delays, complexity and high cost of civil litigation in the federal courts." Letter to The Honorable Roszel C. Thomsen, Chairman of the Committee on Rules of Practice and Procedure of the Judicial Conference, 1 (June 27, 1978).

6 THE CHIEF JUSTICE'S keynote address to this distinguished assembly, popularly known as the Pound Conference, recognized that discovery processes "are being misused and abused." See Burger, Agenda for 2000 A.D.—A Need for Systematic Anticipation, 70 F.R.D. 83, 95–96 (1976).

7 See Erickson, The Pound Conference Recommendations: A Blueprint for the Justice System in the Twenty-first Century, 76 F.R.D. 277, 288 (1978); ABA, Report of Pound Conference Follow-up Task Force, 74 F.R.D. 159, 171–192 (1976).

8 "The principal function of procedural rules," as MR. JUSTICE BLACK observed in another context, "should be to serve as useful guides to help, not hinder, persons who have a legal right to bring their problems before the courts." 346 U.S. 946 (1954) (separate statement upon adoption of revised Supreme Court Rules).

ORDER OF APRIL 28, 1983

1. That the Federal Rules of Civil Procedure be, and they hereby are, amended by including therein new Rules 26(g), 53(f), 72 through 76 and new Official Forms 33 and 34, and amendments to Rules 6(b), 7(b), 11, 16, 26(a) and (b), 52(a), 53(a), (b) and (c) and 67, as hereinafter set forth:

[See additions and amendments made thereby under respective rules and forms, post.]

2. That the foregoing additions and amendments to the Federal Rules of Civil Procedure shall take effect on August 1, 1983 and shall govern all civil proceedings thereafter commenced and, insofar as just and practicable, in proceedings then pending.

3. That THE CHIEF JUSTICE be, and he hereby is, authorized to transmit to the Congress the foregoing additions to and changes in the Federal Rules of Civil Procedure in accordance with the provisions of Section 2072 of Title 28, United States Code.

ORDER OF APRIL 29, 1985

1. That the Federal Rules of Civil Procedure for the United States District Courts be, and they hereby are, amended by including therein a new Rule E(4)(f) to the Supplemental Rules for Certain Admiralty and Maritime Claims; amendments to Rules 6(a), 45(d)(2), 52(a), 71A(h) and 83; amendments to Supplemental Admiralty Rules B(1) and C(3); and amendments to Official Form 18–A, as hereinafter set forth:

[See additions and amendments made thereby under respective rules and forms, post.]

2. That the foregoing addition to and changes in the Federal Rules of Civil Procedure, the Supplemental Rules for Certain Admiralty and Maritime Claims, and the Official Form shall take effect on August 1, 1985 and shall govern all proceedings in civil actions thereafter commenced and, insofar as just and practicable, all proceedings in civil actions then pending.

3. That THE CHIEF JUSTICE be, and he hereby is, authorized to transmit to the Congress the foregoing addition to and changes in the rules of civil procedure in accordance with the provisions of Section 2072 of Title 28, United States Code.

ORDER OF MARCH 2, 1987

1. That the Federal Rules of Civil Procedure and the Supplemental Rules for Certain Admiralty and Maritime Claims be, and they hereby are, amended by including therein amendments to Civil Rules 4, 5, 6, 8, 9, 11, 12, 13, 14, 15, 16, 17, 18, 19, 20, 22, 23, 23.1, 24, 25, 26, 27, 28, 30, 31, 32, 34, 35, 36, 37 38, 41, 43, 44, 44.1, 45, 46, 49, 50, 51, 53, 54, 55, 56, 60, 62, 63, 65, 65.1, 68, 69, 71, 71A, 73, 75, 77, 78, 81, and to the Supplemental Rules for Certain Admiralty and Maritime Claims, Rules B, C, E, and F, as hereinafter set forth:

[See amendments made thereby under respective rules, post.]

2. That the foregoing amendments to the Federal Rules of Civil Procedure and the Supplemental Rules for Certain Admiralty and Maritime Claims shall take effect on August 1, 1987.

3. That THE CHIEF JUSTICE be, and he hereby is, authorized to transmit to the Congress the foregoing amendments in accordance with the provisions of Section 2072 of Title 28, United States Code.

ORDER OF APRIL 25, 1988

1. That the Federal Rules of Civil Procedure be, and they hereby are, amended by including therein amendments to Civil Rules 17 and 71, as hereinafter set forth:

[See amendments made thereby under respective rules, post.]

2. That the foregoing amendments to the Federal Rules of Civil Procedure shall take effect on August 1, 1988.

3. That THE CHIEF JUSTICE be, and he hereby is, authorized to transmit to the Congress the foregoing amendments in accordance with the provisions of Section 2072 of Title 28, United States Code.

ORDER OF APRIL 30, 1991

1. That the Federal Rules of Civil Procedure for the United States District Courts be, and they hereby are, amended by including therein new chapter headings VIII and IX, amendments to Rules C and E of the Supplemental Rules for Certain Admiralty and Maritime Claims, new Forms 1A and 1B to the Appendix of Forms, the abrogation of Form 18A, and amendments to Civil Rules 5, 15, 24, 34, 35, 41, 44, 45, 47, 48, 50, 52, 53, 63, 72, and 77, as hereinafter set forth.

[See additions and amendments made thereby under respective rules and forms, post.]

2. That the foregoing additions to and changes in the Federal Rules of Civil Procedure, the Supplemental Rules for Certain Admiralty and Maritime Claims, and the Civil Forms shall take effect on December 1, 1991, and shall govern all proceedings in civil actions thereafter commenced and, insofar as just and practicable, all proceedings in civil actions then pending.

3. That THE CHIEF JUSTICE be, and hereby is, authorized to transmit to the Congress the foregoing addition to and changes in the Rules of Civil Procedure in accordance with the provisions of Section 2072 of Title 28, United States Code.

[Congress may postpone the proposed rule and form additions and amendments effective December 1, 1991, may decline to approve such additions and amendments, or may make changes to the additions and amendments.]

ORDER OF APRIL 22, 1993

1. That the Federal Rules of Civil Procedure for the United States District Courts be, and they hereby are, amended by including therein amendments to Civil Rules 1, 4, 5, 11, 12, 15, 16, 26, 28, 29, 30, 31, 32, 33, 34, 36, 37, 38, 50, 52, 53, 54, 58, 71A, 72, 73, 74, 75, and 76, and new Rule 4.1, and abrogation of Form 18–A, and amendments to Forms 2, 33, 34, and 34A, and new Forms 1A, 1B, and 35.

[See amendments made thereby under respective rules and forms, post.]

2. That the foregoing amendments to the Federal Rules of Civil Procedure shall take effect on December 1, 1993, and shall govern all proceedings in civil cases thereafter commenced and, insofar as just and practicable, all proceedings in civil cases then pending.

3. That THE CHIEF JUSTICE be, and he hereby is, authorized to transmit to the Congress the foregoing amendments to the Federal Rules of Civil Procedure in accordance with the provisions of Section 2072 of Title 23, United States Code.

ORDER OF APRIL 27, 1995

1. That the Federal Rules of Civil Procedure for the United States District Courts be, and they hereby are, amended by including therein amendments to Civil Rules 50, 52, 59, and 83.

[See amendments made thereby under respective rules, post.]

2. That the foregoing amendments to the Federal Rules of Civil Procedure shall take effect on December 1, 1995, and shall govern all proceedings in civil cases thereafter commenced and, insofar as just and practicable, all proceedings in civil cases then pending.

3. That THE CHIEF JUSTICE be, and hereby is, authorized to transmit to the Congress the foregoing amendments to the Federal Rules of Civil Procedure in accordance with the provisions of Section 2072 of Title 28, United States Code.

ORDER OF APRIL 23, 1996

1. That the Federal Rules of Civil Procedure for the United States District Courts be, and they hereby are, amended by including therein amendments to Civil Rules 5 and 43.

[See amendments made thereby under respective rules, post]

2. That the foregoing amendments to the Federal Rules of Civil Procedure shall take effect on December 1, 1996, and shall govern all proceedings in civil cases thereafter commenced and, insofar as just and practicable, all proceedings in civil cases then pending.

3. That THE CHIEF JUSTICE be, and hereby is, authorized to transmit to the Congress the foregoing amendments to the Federal Rules of Civil Procedure in accordance with the provisions of Section 2072 of Title 28, United States Code.

ORDER OF APRIL 11, 1997

1. That the Federal Rules of Civil Procedure for the United States District Courts be, and they hereby are, amended by including therein amendments to Civil Rules 9 and 73, and abrogation of Rules 74, 75, and 76, and amendments to Forms 33 and 34.

[See amendments made thereby under respective rules, post]

2. That the foregoing amendments to the Federal Rules of Civil Procedure shall take effect on December 1, 1997, and shall govern all proceedings in civil cases thereafter commenced and, insofar as just and practicable, all proceedings in civil cases then pending.

3. That THE CHIEF JUSTICE be, and hereby is, authorized to transmit to the Congress the foregoing amendments to the Federal Rules of Civil Procedure in accordance with the provisions of Section 2072 of Title 28, United States Code.

ORDER OF APRIL 24, 1998

ORDERED:

1. That the Federal Rules of Civil Procedure for the United States District Courts be, and they hereby are, amended by including therein a new Civil Rule 23(f).

[See amendments made thereby under respective rules, post]

2. That the foregoing amendments to the Federal Rules of Civil Procedure shall take effect on December 1, 1998, and shall govern all proceedings in civil cases thereafter commenced and, insofar as just and practicable, all proceedings in civil cases then pending.

3. That THE CHIEF JUSTICE be, and hereby is, authorized to transmit to the Congress the foregoing amendments to the Federal Rules of Civil Procedure in accordance with the provisions of Section 2072 of Title 28, United States Code.

HISTORICAL NOTES

The original Rules of Civil Procedure for the District Courts were adopted by order of the Supreme Court on Dec. 20, 1937, transmitted to Congress by the Attorney General on Jan. 3, 1938, and became effective on Sept. 16, 1938.

The Rules have been amended Dec. 28, 1939, eff. Apr. 3, 1941; Dec. 27, 1946, eff. Mar. 19, 1948; Dec. 29, 1948, eff. Oct. 20, 1949; Apr. 30, 1951, eff. Aug. 1, 1951; Apr. 17, 1961, eff. July 19, 1961; Jan. 21, 1963, eff. July 1, 1963; Feb. 28, 1966, eff. July 1, 1966; Dec. 4, 1967, eff. July 1, 1968; Mar. 30, 1970, eff. July 1, 1970; Mar. 1, 1971, eff. July 1, 1971; Nov. 20, 1972, and Dec. 18, 1972, eff. July 1, 1975; Apr. 29, 1980, eff. Aug. 1, 1980; Oct. 21, 1980, Pub.L. 96–481, Title II, § 205(a), (b), 94 Stat. 2330; Jan. 12, 1983, Pub.L. 97–462, §§ 2–4, 96 Stat. 2527–2530, eff. Feb. 26, 1983; Apr. 28, 1983, eff. Aug. 1, 1983; Apr. 29, 1985, eff. Aug. 1, 1985; Mar. 2, 1987, eff. Aug. 1, 1987; Apr. 25, 1988, eff. Aug. 1, 1988; Nov. 18, 1988, Pub.L. 100–690, Title VII, §§ 7047(b), 7049, 7050, 102 Stat. 4401; Apr. 30, 1991, eff. Dec. 1, 1991; Apr. 22, 1993, eff. Dec. 1, 1993; Apr. 27, 1995, eff. Dec. 1, 1995; Apr. 23, 1996, eff. Dec. 1, 1996; Apr. 11, 1997, eff. Dec. 1, 1997 Apr. 24, 1998, eff. Dec. 1, 1998.

I. SCOPE OF RULES—ONE FORM OF ACTION

Rule 1. Scope and Purpose of Rules

These rules govern the procedure in the United States district courts in all suits of a civil nature whether cognizable as cases at law or in equity or in admiralty, with the exceptions stated in Rule 81. They shall be construed and administered to secure the just, speedy, and inexpensive determination of every action.

(As amended Dec. 29, 1948, eff. Oct. 20, 1949; Feb. 28, 1966, eff. July 1, 1966; Apr. 22, 1993, eff. Dec. 1, 1993.)

ADVISORY COMMITTEE NOTES

1937 Adoption

1. Rule 81 states certain limitations in the application of these rules to enumerated special proceedings.

2. The expression "district courts of the United States" appearing in the statute authorizing the Supreme Court of the United States to promulgate rules of civil procedure does not include the district courts held in the territories and insular possessions. See *Mookini et al. v. United States,* 1938, 58 S.Ct. 543, 303 U.S. 201, 82 L.Ed. 748.

3. These rules are drawn under the authority of the Act of June 19, 1934, U.S.C., Title 28, § 723b [see 2072] (Rules in actions at law; Supreme Court authorized to make), and § 723c [see 2072] (Union of equity and action at law rules; power of Supreme Court) and also other grants of rule making power to the Court. See Clark and Moore, *A New Federal Civil Procedure—I. The Background,* 44 Yale L.J. 387, 391 (1935). Under § 723b after the rules have taken effect all laws in conflict therewith are of no further force or effect. In accordance with § 723c the Court has united the general rules prescribed for cases in equity with those in actions at law so as to secure one form of civil action and procedure for both. See Rule 2 (One Form of Action). For the former practice in equity and at law see U.S.C.A., Title 28, §§ 723 and 730 [see 2071 et seq.] (conferring power on the Supreme Court to make rules of practice in equity) and the [former] Equity Rules promulgated thereunder; U.S.C., Title 28, [former] § 724 (Conformity act); [former] Equity Rule 22 (Action at Law Erroneously Begun as Suit in Equity—Transfer); [former] Equity Rule 23 (Matters Ordinarily Determinable at Law When Arising in Suit in Equity to be Disposed of Therein); U.S.C., Title 28, [former] §§ 397 (Amendments to pleadings when case brought to wrong side

of court), and 398 (Equitable defenses and equitable relief in actions at law).

4. With the second sentence compare U.S.C., Title 28, [former] §§ 777 (Defects of form; amendments), [former] 767 (Amendment of process); [former] Equity Rule 19 (Amendments Generally).

1948 Amendment

The amendment effective Oct. 20, 1949, substituted the words "United States district courts" for the words "district courts of the United States."

1966 Amendment

This is the fundamental change necessary to effect unification of the civil and admiralty procedure. Just as the 1938 rules abolished the distinction between actions at law and suits in equity, this change would abolish the distinction between civil actions and suits in admiralty. See also Rule 81.

1993 Amendments

The purpose of this revision, adding the words "and administered" to the second sentence, is to recognize the affirmative duty of the court to exercise the authority conferred by these rules to ensure that civil litigation is resolved not only fairly, but also without undue cost or delay. As officers of the court, attorneys share this responsibility with the judge to whom the case is assigned.

Rule 2. One Form of Action

There shall be one form of action to be known as "civil action".

ADVISORY COMMITTEE NOTES

1937 Adoption

1. This rule modifies U.S.C., Title 28, [former] § 384 (Suits in equity, when not sustainable). U.S.C., Title 28, §§ 723 and 730 [sec. 2071, et seq.] (conferring power on the Supreme Court to make rules of practice in equity), are unaffected in so far as they relate to the rule making power in admiralty. These sections, together with § 723b [sec. 2072] (Rules in actions at law; Supreme Court authorized to make) are continued in so far as they are not inconsistent with § 2072, formerly § 723c (Union of equity and action at law rules; power of Supreme Court). See Note 3 to Rule 1. U.S.C., Title 28, [former] §§ 724 (Conformity act), 397 (Amendments to pleadings when case brought to wrong side of court) and 398 (Equitable defenses and equitable relief in actions at law) are superseded.

2. Reference to actions at law or suits in equity in all statutes should now be treated as referring to the civil action prescribed in these rules.

3. This rule follows in substance the usual introductory statements to code practices which provide for a single action and mode of procedure, with abolition of forms of action and procedural distinctions. Representative statutes are N.Y. Code 1848 (Laws 1848, ch. 379) § 62; N.Y.C.P.A. (1937) § 8; Calif.Code Civ.Proc. (Deering, 1937) § 307; 2 Minn.Stat.Ann. 1945 § 540.01; 2 Wash.Rev.Stat.Ann. (Remington, 1932) §§ 153, 255.

II. COMMENCEMENT OF ACTION; SERVICE OF PROCESS, PLEADINGS, MOTIONS, AND ORDERS

Rule 3. Commencement of Action

A civil action is commenced by filing a complaint with the court.

ADVISORY COMMITTEE NOTES

1937 Adoption

1. Rule 5(e) defines what constitutes filing with the court.

2. This rule governs the commencement of all actions, including those brought by or against the United States or an officer or agency thereof, regardless of whether service is to be made personally pursuant to Rule 4(d), or otherwise pursuant to Rule 4(e).

3. With this rule compare [former] Equity Rule 12 (Issue of Subpoena—Time for Answer) and the following statutes (and other similar statutes) which provide a similar method for commencing an action:

U.S.C., Title 28:

§ 45 [former] (District courts; practice and procedure in certain cases under interstate commerce laws).

§ 762 [see 1402] (Petition in suit against United States).

§ 766 [see 2409] (Partition suits where United States is tenant in common or joint tenant).

4. This rule provides that the first step in an action is the filing of the complaint. Under Rule 4(a) this is to be followed forthwith by issuance of a summons and its delivery to an officer for service. Other rules providing for dismissal for failure to prosecute suggest a method available to attack unreasonable delay in prosecuting an action after it has been commenced. When a Federal or State statute of limitations is pleaded as a defense, a question may arise under this rule whether the mere filing of the complaint stops the running of the statute, or whether any further step is required, such as, service of the summons and complaint or their delivery to the marshal for service. The answer to this question may depend on whether it is competent for the Supreme Court, exercising the power to make rules of procedure without affecting substantive rights, to vary the operation of statutes of limitations. The requirement of rule 4(a) that the clerk shall forthwith issue the summons and deliver it to the marshal for service will reduce the chances of such a question arising.

COMMENTARIES

See 28 U.S.C.A. Rule 3, Federal Rules of Civil Procedure, for Commentary by David D. Siegel.

Rule 4. Summons

(a) Form. The summons shall be signed by the clerk, bear the seal of the court, identify the court and the parties, be directed to the defendant, and state the name and address of the plaintiff's attorney or, if unrepresented, of the plaintiff. It shall also state the time within which the defendant must appear and defend, and notify the defendant that failure to do so will result in a judgment by default against the defendant for the relief demanded in the complaint. The court may allow a summons to be amended.

(b) Issuance. Upon or after filing the complaint, the plaintiff may present a summons to the clerk for signature and seal. If the summons is in proper form, the clerk shall sign, seal, and issue it to the plaintiff for service on the defendant. A summons, or a copy of the summons if addressed to multiple defendants, shall be issued for each defendant to be served.

(c) Service with Complaint; by Whom Made.

(1) A summons shall be served together with a copy of the complaint. The plaintiff is responsible for service of a summons and complaint within the time allowed under subdivision (m) and shall furnish the person effecting service with the necessary copies of the summons and complaint.

(2) Service may be effected by any person who is not a party and who is at least 18 years of age. At the request of the plaintiff, however, the court may direct that service be effected by a United States marshal, deputy United States marshal, or other person or officer specially appointed by the court for that purpose. Such an appointment must be made when the plaintiff is authorized to proceed in forma pauperis pursuant to 28 U.S.C. § 1915 or is authorized to proceed as a seaman under 28 U.S.C. § 1916.

(d) Waiver of Service; Duty to Save Costs of Service; Request to Waive.

(1) A defendant who waives service of a summons does not thereby waive any objection to the venue or to the jurisdiction of the court over the person of the defendant.

(2) An individual, corporation, or association that is subject to service under subdivision (e), (f), or (h) and that receives notice of an action in the manner provided in this paragraph has a duty to avoid unnecessary costs of serving the summons. To avoid costs, the plaintiff may notify such a defendant of the commencement of the action and request that the defendant waive service of a summons. The notice and request

(A) shall be in writing and shall be addressed directly to the defendant, if an individual, or else to an officer or managing or general agent (or other agent authorized by appointment or law to receive service of process) of a defendant subject to service under subdivision (h);

(B) shall be dispatched through first-class mail or other reliable means;

(C) shall be accompanied by a copy of the complaint and shall identify the court in which it has been filed;

(D) shall inform the defendant, by means of a text prescribed in an official form promulgated pursuant to Rule 84, of the consequences of compliance and of a failure to comply with the request;

(E) shall set forth the date on which the request is sent;

(F) shall allow the defendant a reasonable time to return the waiver, which shall be at least 30 days from the date on which the request is sent, or 60 days from that date if the defendant is addressed outside any judicial district of the United States; and

(G) shall provide the defendant with an extra copy of the notice and request, as well as a prepaid means of compliance in writing.

If a defendant located within the United States fails to comply with a request for waiver made by a plaintiff located within the United States, the court shall impose the costs subsequently incurred in effecting service on the defendant unless good cause for the failure be shown.

(3) A defendant that, before being served with process, timely returns a waiver so requested is not required to serve an answer to the complaint until 60 days after the date on which the request for waiver of service was sent, or 90 days after that date if the defendant was addressed outside any judicial district of the United States.

(4) When the plaintiff files a waiver of service with the court, the action shall proceed, except as provided in paragraph (3), as if a summons and complaint had been served at the time of filing the waiver, and no proof of service shall be required.

(5) The costs to be imposed on a defendant under paragraph (2) for failure to comply with a request to waive service of a summons shall include the costs subsequently incurred in effecting service under subdivision (e), (f), or (h), together with the costs, including a reasonable attorney's fee, of any motion required to collect the costs of service.

(e) Service Upon Individuals Within a Judicial District of the United States. Unless otherwise provided by federal law, service upon an individual from whom a waiver has not been obtained and filed, other than an infant or an incompetent person, may be effected in any judicial district of the United States:

(1) pursuant to the law of the state in which the district court is located, or in which service is effected, for the service of a summons upon the

defendant in an action brought in the courts of general jurisdiction of the State; or

(2) by delivering a copy of the summons and of the complaint to the individual personally or by leaving copies thereof at the individual's dwelling house or usual place of abode with some person of suitable age and discretion then residing therein or by delivering a copy of the summons and of the complaint to an agent authorized by appointment or by law to receive service of process.

(f) Service Upon Individuals in a Foreign Country. Unless otherwise provided by federal law, service upon an individual from whom a waiver has not been obtained and filed, other than an infant or an incompetent person, may be effected in a place not within any judicial district of the United States:

(1) by any internationally agreed means reasonably calculated to give notice, such as those means authorized by the Hague Convention on the Service Abroad of Judicial and Extrajudicial Documents; or

(2) if there is no internationally agreed means of service or the applicable international agreement allows other means of service, provided that service is reasonably calculated to give notice:

(A) in the manner prescribed by the law of the foreign country for service in that country in an action in any of its courts of general jurisdiction; or

(B) as directed by the foreign authority in response to a letter rogatory or letter of request; or

(C) unless prohibited by the law of the foreign country, by

(i) delivery to the individual personally of a copy of the summons and the complaint; or

(ii) any form of mail requiring a signed receipt, to be addressed and dispatched by the clerk of the court to the party to be served; or

(3) by other means not prohibited by international agreement as may be directed by the court.

(g) Service Upon Infants and Incompetent Persons. Service upon an infant or an incompetent person in a judicial district of the United States shall be effected in the manner prescribed by the law of the state in which the service is made for the service of summons or other like process upon any such defendant in an action brought in the courts of general jurisdiction of that state. Service upon an infant or an incompetent person in a place not within any judicial district of the United States shall be effected in the manner prescribed by paragraph (2)(A) or (2)(B) of subdivision (f) or by such means as the court may direct.

(h) Service Upon Corporations and Associations. Unless otherwise provided by federal law, service upon a domestic or foreign corporation or upon a partnership or other unincorporated association that is subject to suit under a common name, and from which a waiver of service has not been obtained and filed, shall be effected:

(1) in a judicial district of the United States in the manner prescribed for individuals by subdivision (e)(1), or by delivering a copy of the summons and of the complaint to an officer, a managing or general agent, or to any other agent authorized by appointment or by law to receive service of process and, if the agent is one authorized by statute to receive service and the statute so requires, by also mailing a copy to the defendant, or

(2) in a place not within any judicial district of the United States in any manner prescribed for individuals by subdivision (f) except personal delivery as provided in paragraph (2)(C)(i) thereof.

(i) Service Upon the United States, and Its Agencies, Corporations, or Officers.

(1) Service upon the United States shall be effected

(A) by delivering a copy of the summons and of the complaint to the United States attorney for the district in which the action is brought or to an assistant United States attorney or clerical employee designated by the United States attorney in a writing filed with the clerk of the court or by sending a copy of the summons and of the complaint by registered or certified mail addressed to the civil process clerk at the office of the United States attorney and

(B) by also sending a copy of the summons and of the complaint by registered or certified mail to the Attorney General of the United States at Washington, District of Columbia, and

(C) in any action attacking the validity of an order of an officer or agency of the United States not made a party, by also sending a copy of the summons and of the complaint by registered or certified mail to the officer or agency.

(2) Service upon an officer, agency, or corporation of the United States, shall be effected by serving the United States in the manner prescribed by paragraph (1) of this subdivision and by also sending a copy of the summons and of the complaint by registered or certified mail to the officer, agency, or corporation.

(3) The court shall allow a reasonable time for service of process under this subdivision for the purpose of curing the failure to serve multiple officers, agencies, or corporations of the United States if the plaintiff has effected service on either the United States attorney or the Attorney General of the United States.

(j) Service Upon Foreign, State, or Local Governments.

(1) Service upon a foreign state or a political subdivision, agency, or instrumentality thereof shall be effected pursuant to 28 U.S.C. § 1608.

(2) Service upon a state, municipal corporation, or other governmental organization subject to suit shall be effected by delivering a copy of the summons and of the complaint to its chief executive officer or by serving the summons and complaint in the manner prescribed by the law of that state for the service of summons or other like process upon any such defendant.

(k) Territorial Limits of Effective Service.

(1) Service of a summons or filing a waiver of service is effective to establish jurisdiction over the person of a defendant

(A) who could be subjected to the jurisdiction of a court of general jurisdiction in the state in which the district court is located, or

(B) who is a party joined under Rule 14 or Rule 19 and is served at a place within a judicial district of the United States and not more than 100 miles from the place from which the summons issues, or

(C) who is subject to the federal interpleader jurisdiction under 28 U.S.C. § 1335, or

(D) when authorized by a statute of the United States.

(2) If the exercise of jurisdiction is consistent with the Constitution and laws of the United States, serving a summons or filing a waiver of service is also effective, with respect to claims arising under federal law, to establish personal jurisdiction over the person of any defendant who is not subject to the jurisdiction of the courts of general jurisdiction of any state.

***(l)* Proof of Service.** If service is not waived, the person effecting service shall make proof thereof to the court. If service is made by a person other than a United States marshal or deputy United States marshal, the person shall make affidavit thereof. Proof of service in a place not within any judicial district of the United States shall, if effected under paragraph (1) of subdivision (f), be made pursuant to the applicable treaty or convention, and shall, if effected under paragraph (2) or (3) thereof, include a receipt signed by the addressee or other evidence of delivery to the addressee satisfactory to the court. Failure to make proof of service does not affect the validity of the service. The court may allow proof of service to be amended.

(m) Time Limit for Service. If service of the summons and complaint is not made upon a defendant within 120 days after the filing of the complaint, the court, upon motion or on its own initiative after notice to the plaintiff, shall dismiss the action without prejudice as to that defendant or direct that service be effected within a specified time; provided that if the plaintiff shows good cause for the failure, the court shall extend the time for service for an appropriate period. This subdivision does not apply to service in a foreign country pursuant to subdivision (f) or (j)(1).

(n) Seizure of Property; Service of Summons Not Feasible.

(1) If a statute of the United States so provides, the court may assert jurisdiction over property. Notice to claimants of the property shall then be sent in the manner provided by the statute or by service of a summons under this rule.

(2) Upon a showing that personal jurisdiction over a defendant cannot, in the district where the action is brought, be obtained with reasonable efforts by service of summons in any manner authorized by this rule, the court may assert jurisdiction over any of the defendant's assets found within the district by seizing the assets under the circumstances and in the manner provided by the law of the state in which the district court is located.

(As amended Jan. 21, 1963, eff. July 1, 1963; Feb. 28, 1966, eff. July 1, 1966; Apr. 29, 1980, eff. Aug. 1, 1980; Jan. 12, 1983, Pub.L. 97–462, § 2, 96 Stat. 2527; Mar. 2, 1987, eff. Aug. 1, 1987; Apr. 22, 1993, eff. Dec. 1, 1993.)

ADVISORY COMMITTEE NOTES

1937 Adoption

Note to Subdivision (a). With the provision permitting additional summons upon request of the plaintiff, compare former Equity Rule 14 (Alias Subpoena) and the last sentence of former Equity Rule 12 (Issue of Subpoena—Time for Answer).

Note to Subdivision (b). This rule prescribes a form of summons which follows substantially the requirements stated in former Equity Rules 12 (Issue of Subpoena—Time for Answer) and 7 (Process, Mesne and Final).

U.S.C., Title 28, § 721 [now 1691] (Sealing and testing of writs) is substantially continued insofar as it applies to a summons, but its requirements as to teste of process are superseded. U.S.C., Title 28, [former] § 722 (Teste of process, day of) is superseded.

See Rule 12(a) for a statement of the time within which the defendant is required to appear and defend.

Note to Subdivision (c). This rule does not affect U.S.C., Title 28, § 503 [see 566], as amended June 15, 1935 (Marshals; duties) and such statutes as the following insofar as they provide for service of process by a marshal, but modifies them in so far as they may imply service by a marshal only:

U.S.C., Title 15:

§ 5 (Bringing in additional parties) (Sherman Act)

§ 10 (Bringing in additional parties)

§ 25 (Restraining violations; procedure)

U.S.C., Title 28:

§ 45 [former] (Practice and procedure in certain cases under the interstate commerce laws)

Compare [former] Equity Rule 15 (Process, by Whom Served).

Note to Subdivision (d). Under this rule the complaint must always be served with the summons.

Paragraph (1). For an example of a statute providing for service upon an agent of an individual see U.S.C., Title 28, § 109 [now 1400, 1694] (Patent cases).

Paragraph (3). This enumerates the officers and agents of a corporation or of a partnership or other unincorporated association upon whom service of process may be made, and permits service of process only upon the officers, managing or general agents, or agents authorized by appointment or by law, of the corporation, partnership or unincorporated association against which the action is brought. See *Christian v. International Ass'n of Machinists,* 7 F.(2d) 481 (D.C.Ky. 1925) and *Singleton v. Order of Railway Conductors of America,* 9 F.Supp. 417 (D.C.Ill.1935). Compare *Operative Plasterers' and Cement Finishers' International Ass'n of the United States and Canada v. Case,* 93 F.(2d) 56 (App.D.C. 1937).

For a statute authorizing service upon a specified agent and requiring mailing to the defendant, see U.S.C., Title 6, § 7 (Surety companies as sureties; appointment of agents; service of process).

Paragraphs (4) and (5) provide a uniform and comprehensive method of service for all actions against the United States or an officer or agency thereof. For statutes providing for such service, see U.S.C., Title 7, §§ 217 (Proceedings for suspension of orders) 499k (Injunctions; application of injunction laws governing orders of Interstate Commerce Commission), 608c(15)(B) (Court review of ruling of Secretary of Agriculture), and 855 (making § 608c(15)(B) applicable to orders of the Secretary of Agriculture as to handlers of anti-hog-cholera serum and hog-cholera virus); U.S.C., Title 26, § 3679, (Bill in chancery to clear title to realty on which the United States has a lien for taxes); U.S.C., Title 28, former §§ 45, (District Courts; practice and procedure in certain cases under the interstate commerce laws), [former] 763 (Petition in suit against the United States; service; appearance by district attorney), 766 [now 2409] (Partition suits where United States is tenant in common or joint tenant), 902 [now 2410] (Foreclosure of mortgages or other liens on property in which the United States has an interest). These and similar statutes are modified in so far as they prescribe a different method of service or dispense with the service of a summons.

For the [former] Equity Rule on service, see [former] Equity Rule 13, Manner of Serving Subpoena.

Note to Subdivision (e). The provisions for the service of a summons or of notice or of an order in lieu of summons contained in U.S.C., Title 8, § 405 (Cancellation of certificates of citizenship fraudulently or illegally procured) (service by publication in accordance with State law); U.S.C., Title 28, § 118 [now 1655] (Absent defendants in suits to enforce liens); U.S.C., Title 35, § 72a [now 146, 291] (Jurisdiction of District Court of United States for the District of Columbia in certain equity suits where adverse parties reside elsewhere) (service by publication against parties residing in foreign countries); U.S.C., Title 38, § 445 [now 784] (Action against the United States on a veteran's contract of insurance) (parties not inhabitants of or not found within the district may be served with an order of the court, personally or by publication) and similar statutes are continued by this rule. Title 24, § 378 [now title 13, § 336] of the Code of the District of Columbia (Publication against non-resident; those absent for six months; unknown heirs or devisees; for divorce or in rem; actual service beyond District) is continued by this rule.

Note to Subdivision (f). This rule enlarges to some extent the present rule as to where service may be made. It does not, however, enlarge the jurisdiction of the district courts.

U.S.C., Title 28, §§ 113 [now 1392] (Suits in States containing more than one district) (where there are two or more defendants residing in different districts), [former] 115 (Suits of a local nature), 116 [now 1392] (Property in different districts in same state), [former] 838 (Executions run in all districts of state); U.S.C., Title 47, § 13 (Action for damages against a railroad or telegraph company whose officer or agent in control of a telegraph line refuses or fails to operate such line in a certain manner—"upon any agent of the company found in such state"); U.S.C., Title 49, § 321(c) [now 10330(b)] (Requiring designation of a process agent by interstate motor carriers and in case of failure so to do, service may be made upon any agent in the state) and similar statutes, allowing the running of process throughout a state, are substantially continued.

U.S.C., Title 15, §§ 5 (Bringing in additional parties) (Sherman Act), 25 (Restraining violations; procedure); U.S.C., Title 28, §§ 44 [now 2321] (Procedure in certain cases under interstate commerce laws; service of processes of court), 117 [now 754, 1692] (Property in different states in same circuit; jurisdiction of receiver), 839 [now 2413] (Executions; run in every State and Territory) and similar statutes, providing for the running of process beyond the territorial limits of a State, are expressly continued.

Note to Subdivision (g). With the second sentence compare [former] Equity Rule 15, (Process, by Whom Served).

Note to Subdivision (h). This rule substantially continues U.S.C., Title 28, [former] § 767 (Amendment of process).

1963 Amendment

Subdivision (b). Under amended subdivision (e) of this rule, an action may be commenced against a nonresident of the State in which the district court is held by complying with State procedures. Frequently the form of the summons or notice required in these cases by State law differs from the Federal form of summons described in present subdivision (b) and exemplified in Form 1. To avoid confusion, the amendment of subdivision (b) states that a form of summons or notice, corresponding "as nearly as may be" to the State form, shall be employed. See also a corresponding amendment of Rule 12(a) with regard to the time to answer.

Subdivision (d)(4). This paragraph, governing service upon the United States, is amended to allow the use of certified mail as an alternative to registered mail for sending copies of the papers to the Attorney General or to a United States officer or agency. Cf. N.J. Rule 4:5–2. See also the amendment of Rule 30(f)(1).

Subdivision (d)(7). Formerly a question was raised whether this paragraph, in the context of the rule as a whole, authorized service in original Federal actions pursuant to State statutes permitting service on a State official as a means of bringing a nonresident motorist defendant into court. It was argued in *McCoy v. Siler,* 205 F.2d 498, 501–2 (3d Cir.) (concurring opinion), cert. denied, 346 U.S. 872, 74 S.Ct. 120, 98 L.Ed. 380 (1953), that the effective service in those cases occurred not when the State official was served but when notice was given to the defendant outside the State, and that subdivision (f) (Territorial limits of effective service), as then worded, did not authorize out-of-State service. This contention found little support. A considerable number of cases held the service to be good, either by fixing upon the service on the official within the State as the effective service, thus satisfying the wording of subdivision (f) as it then stood, see *Holbrook v. Cafiero,* 18 F.R.D. 218 (D.Md. 1955); *Pasternack v. Dalo,* 17 F.R.D. 420 (W.D.Pa.1955); *Super Prods. Corp. v. Parkin,* 20 F.R.D. 377 (S.D.N.Y.1957), or by reading paragraph (7) as not limited by subdivision (f). See *Giffin v. Ensign,* 234 F.2d 307 (3d Cir. 1956); 2 Moore's *Federal Practice,* ¶4.19 (2d ed. 1948); 1 Barron & Holtzoff, *Federal Practice & Procedure* § 182.1 (Wright ed. 1960); Comment, 27 U. of Chi.L.Rev. 751 (1960). See also *Olberding v. Illinois Central R.R.,* 201 F.2d 582 (6th Cir.), rev'd on other grounds, 346 U.S. 338, 74 S.Ct. 83, 98 L.Ed. 39 (1953); *Feinsinger v. Bard,* 195 F.2d 45 (7th Cir. 1952).

An important and growing class of State statutes base personal jurisdiction over nonresidents on the doing of acts or on other contacts within the State, and permit notice to be given the defendant outside the State without any requirement of service on a local State official. See, e.g., Ill.Ann. Stat., c. 110, §§ 16, 17 (Smith–Hurd 1956); Wis.Stat. § 262.06 (1959). This service, employed in original Federal actions pursuant to paragraph (7), has also been held proper. See *Farr & Co. v. Cia. Intercontinental de Nav. de Cuba,* 243 F.2d 342 (2d Cir. 1957); *Kappus v. Western Hills Oil, Inc.,* 24 F.R.D. 123 (E.D.Wis.1959); *Star v. Rogalny,* 162 F.Supp. 181 (E.D.Ill.1957). It has also been held that the clause of paragraph (7) which permits service "in the manner prescribed by the law of the state," etc., is not limited by subdivision (c) requiring that service of all process be made by certain designated persons. See *Farr & Co. v. Cia. Intercontinental de Nav. de Cuba, supra.* But *cf. Sappia v. Lauro Lines,* 130 F.Supp. 810 (S.D.N.Y.1955).

The salutary results of these cases are intended to be preserved. See paragraph (7), with a clarified reference to State law, and amended subdivisions (e) and (f).

Subdivision (e). For the general relation between subdivisions (d) and (e), see 2 Moore, supra, ¶4.32.

The amendment of the first sentence inserting the word "thereunder" supports the original intention that the "order of court" must be authorized by a specific United States statute. See 1 Barron & Holtzoff, supra, at 731. The clause added at the end of the first sentence expressly adopts the view taken by commentators that, if no manner of service is prescribed in the statute or order, the service may be made in a manner stated in Rule 4. See 2 Moore, supra, ¶4.32, at 1004; Smit, *International Aspects of Federal Civil Procedure,* 61 Colum.L.Rev. 1031, 1036–39 (1961). But see Commentary, 5 Fed. Rules Serv. 791 (1942).

Examples of the statutes to which the first sentence relates are 28 U.S.C. § 2361 (Interpleader; process and procedure); 28 U.S.C. § 1655 (Lien enforcement; absent defendants).

The second sentence, added by amendment, expressly allows resort in original Federal actions to the procedures provided by State law for effecting service on nonresident parties (as well as on domiciliaries not found within the State). See, as illustrative, the discussion under amended subdivision (d)(7) of service pursuant to State nonresident motorist statutes and other comparable State statutes. Of particular interest is the change brought about by the reference in this sentence to State procedures for commencing actions against nonresidents by attachment and the like, accompanied by notice. Although an action commenced in a State court by attachment may be removed to the Federal court if ordinary conditions for removal are satisfied, see 28 U.S.C. § 1450; *Rorick v. Devon Syndicate, Ltd.,* 307 U.S. 299, 59 S.Ct. 877, 83 L.Ed. 1303 (1939); *Clark v. Wells,* 203 U.S. 164, 27 S.Ct. 43, 51 L.Ed. 138 (1906), there has heretofore been no provision recognized by the courts for commencing an original Federal civil action by attachment. See Currie, *Attachment and Garnishment in the Federal Courts,* 59 Mich.L.Rev. 337 (1961), arguing that this result came about through historical anomaly. Rule 64, which refers to attachment, garnishment, and similar procedures under State law, furnishes only provisional remedies in actions otherwise validly commenced. See *Big Vein Coal Co. v. Read,* 229 U.S. 31, 33 S.Ct. 694, 57 L.Ed. 1053 (1913); *Davis v. Ensign–Bickford Co.,* 139 F.2d 624 (8th Cir. 1944); 7 Moore's *Federal Practice* ¶64.05 (2d ed. 1954); 3 Barron & Holtzoff, *Federal Practice & Procedure* § 1423 (Wright ed. 1958); but cf. Note, 13 So.Calif.L.Rev. 361 (1940). The amendment will now permit the institution of original Federal actions against nonresidents through the use of familiar State procedures by which property of these defendants is brought within the custody of the court and some appropriate service is made upon them.

The necessity of satisfying subject-matter jurisdictional requirements and requirements of venue will limit the practical utilization of these methods of effecting service. Within those limits, however, there appears to be no reason for denying plaintiffs means of commencing actions in Federal courts which are generally available in the State courts. See 1 Barron & Holtzoff, supra, at 374–80; Nordbye, *Comments on Proposed Amendments to Rules of Civil Procedure for the United States District Courts,* 18 F.R.D. 105, 106 (1956); Note, 34 Corn.L.Q. 103 (1948); Note, 13 So.Calif.L.Rev. 361 (1940).

If the circumstances of a particular case satisfy the applicable Federal law (first sentence of Rule 4(e), as amended) and the applicable State law (second sentence), the party seeking to make the service may proceed under the Federal or the State law, at his option.

See also amended Rule 13(a), and the Advisory Committee's Note thereto.

Subdivision (f). The first sentence is amended to assure the effectiveness of service outside the territorial limits of the State in all the cases in which any of the rules authorize service beyond those boundaries. Besides the preceding provisions of Rule 4, see Rule 71A(d)(3). In addition, the new second sentence of the subdivision permits effective service within a limited area outside the State in certain special situations, namely, to bring in additional parties to a counterclaim or cross-claim (Rule 13 (h)), impleaded parties (Rule 14), and indispensable or conditionally necessary parties to a pending action (Rule 19); and to secure compliance with an order of commitment for civil contempt. In those situations effective service can be made at points not more than 100 miles distant from the courthouse in which the action is commenced, or to which it is assigned or transferred for trial.

The bringing in of parties under the 100-mile provision in the limited situations enumerated is designed to promote the objective of enabling the court to determine entire controversies. In the light of present-day facilities for communication and travel, the territorial range of the service allowed, analogous to that which applies to the service of a subpoena under Rule 45(e)(1), can hardly work hardship on the parties summoned. The provision will be especially useful in metropolitan areas spanning more than one State. Any requirements of subject-matter jurisdiction and venue will still have to be satisfied as to the parties brought in, although these requirements will be eased in some instances when the parties can be regarded as "ancillary." See *Pennsylvania R.R. v. Erie Avenue Warehouse Co.*, 5 F.R.Serv.2d 14a.62, Case 2 (3d Cir.1962); *Dery v. Wyer*, 265 F.2d 804 (2d Cir.1959); *United Artists Corp. v. Masterpiece Productions, Inc.*, 221 F.2d 213 (2d Cir.1955); *Lesnik v. Public Industrials Corp.*, 144 F.2d 968 (2d Cir.1944); *Vaughn v. Terminal Transp. Co.*, 162 F.Supp. 647 (E.D.Tenn.1957); and compare the fifth paragraph of the Advisory Committee's Note to Rule 4(e), as amended. The amendment is but a moderate extension of the territorial reach of Federal process and has ample practical justification. See 2 Moore, supra, § 4.01[13] (Supp. 1960); 1 Barron & Holtzoff, supra, § 184; Note, 51 Nw. U.L.Rev. 354 (1956). But cf. Nordbye, *Comments on Proposed Amendments to Rules of Civil Procedure for the United States District Courts*, 18 F.R.D. 105, 106 (1956).

As to the need for enlarging the territorial area in which orders of commitment for civil contempt may be served, see *Graber v. Graber*, 93 F.Supp. 281 (D.D.C.1950); *Teele Soap Mfg. Co. v. Pine Tree Products Co., Inc.*, 8 F.Supp. 546 (D.N.H.1934); *Mitchell v. Dexter*, 244 Fed. 926 (1st Cir. 1917); *In re Graves*, 29 Fed. 60 (N.D.Iowa 1886).

As to the Court's power to amend subdivisions (e) and (f) as here set forth, see *Mississippi Pub. Corp. v. Murphree*, 326 U.S. 438, 66 S.Ct. 242, 90 L.Ed. 185 (1946).

Subdivision (i). The continual increase of civil litigation having international elements makes it advisable to consolidate, amplify, and clarify the provisions governing service upon parties in foreign countries. See generally Jones, *International Judicial Assistance: Procedural Chaos and a Program for Reform*, 62 Yale L.J. 515 (1953); Longley, *Serving Process, Subpoenas and Other Documents in Foreign Territory*, Proc.A.B.A., Sec.Int'l & Comp.L. 34 (1959); Smit, *International Aspects of Federal Civil Procedure*, 61 Colum.L.Rev. 1031 (1961).

As indicated in the opening lines of new subdivision (i), referring to the provisions of subdivision (e), the authority for effecting foreign service must be found in a statute of the United States or a statute or rule of court of the State in which the district court is held providing in terms or upon proper interpretation for service abroad upon persons not inhabitants of or found within the State. See the Advisory Committee's Note to amended Rule 4(d)(7) and Rule 4(e). For examples of Federal and State statutes expressly authorizing such service, see 8 U.S.C. § 1451(b); 35 U.S.C. §§ 146, 293; Me.Rev.Stat., ch. 22, § 70 (Supp.1961); Minn.Stat.Ann. § 303.13 (1947); N.Y.Veh. & Tfc.Law § 253. Several decisions have construed statutes to permit service in foreign countries, although the matter is not expressly mentioned in the statutes. See, e.g., *Chapman v. Superior Court*, 162 Cal.App.2d 421, 328 P.2d 23 (Dist.Ct.App.1958); *Sperry v. Fliegers*, 194 Misc. 438, 86 N.Y.S.2d 830 (Sup.Ct.1949); *Ewing v. Thompson*, 233 N.C. 564, 65 S.E.2d 17 (1951); *Rushing v. Bush*, 260 S.W.2d 900 (Tex.Ct.Civ.App.1953). Federal and State statutes authorizing service on nonresidents in such terms as to warrant the interpretation that service abroad is permissible include 15 U.S.C. §§ 77v(a), 78aa, 79y; 28 U.S.C. § 1655; 38 U.S.C. § 784(a); Ill.Ann.Stat., c. 110, §§ 16, 17 (Smith–Hurd 1956); Wis.Stat. § 262.06 (1959).

Under subdivisions (e) and (i), when authority to make foreign service is found in a Federal statute or statute or rule of court of a State, it is always sufficient to carry out the service in the manner indicated therein. Subdivision (i) introduces considerable further flexibility by permitting the foreign service and return thereof to be carried out in any of a number of other alternative ways that are also declared to be sufficient. Other aspects of foreign service continue to be governed by the other provisions of Rule 4. Thus, for example, subdivision (i) effects no change in the form of the summons, or the issuance of separate or additional summons, or the amendment of service.

Service of process beyond the territorial limits of the United States may involve difficulties not encountered in the case of domestic service. Service abroad may be considered by a foreign country to require the performance of judicial, and therefore, "sovereign," acts within its territory, which that country may conceive to be offensive to its policy or contrary to its law. See Jones, supra, at 537. For example, a person not qualified to serve process according to the law of the foreign country may find himself subject to sanctions if he attempts service therein. See Inter-American Juridical Committee, *Report on Uniformity of Legislation on International Cooperation in Judicial Procedures* 20 (1952). The enforcement of a judgment in the foreign country in which the service was made may be embarrassed or prevented if the service did not comport with the law of that country. See ibid.

One of the purposes of subdivision (i) is to allow accommodation to the policies and procedures of the foreign country. It is emphasized, however, that the attitudes of foreign countries vary considerably and that the question of recognition of United States judgments abroad is complex. Accordingly, if enforcement is to be sought in the country of service, the foreign law should be examined before a choice is made among the methods of service allowed by subdivision (i).

Subdivision (i)(1). Subparagraph (a) of paragraph (1), permitting service by the method prescribed by the law of the foreign country for service on a person in that country in a civil action in any of its courts of general jurisdiction, provides an alternative that is likely to create least objection in the place of service and also is likely to enhance the possibilities of securing ultimate enforcement of the judgment abroad. See *Report on Uniformity of Legislation on International Cooperation in Judicial Procedures*, supra.

In certain foreign countries service in aid of litigation pending in other countries can lawfully be accomplished only upon request to the foreign courts, which in turn directs the service to be made. In many countries this has long been a customary way of accomplishing the service. See *In re Letters Rogatory out of First Civil Court of City of Mexico*, 261 Fed. 652 (S.D.N.Y.1919); Jones, supra, at 543; Comment, 44 Colum.L.Rev. 72 (1944); Note 58 Yale L.J. 1193 (1949). Subparagraph (B) of paragraph (1), referring to a letter rogatory, validates this method. A proviso, applicable to this subparagraph and the preceding one, requires, as a safeguard, that the service made shall be reasonably calculated to give actual notice of the proceedings to the party. See *Milliken v. Meyer,* 311 U.S. 457, 61 S.Ct. 339, 85 L.Ed. 278 (1940).

Subparagraph (C) of paragraph (1), permitting foreign service by personal delivery on individuals and corporations, partnerships, and associations, provides for a manner of service that is not only traditionally preferred, but also is most likely to lead to actual notice. Explicit provision for this manner of service was thought desirable because a number of Federal and State statutes permitting foreign service do not specifically provide for service by personal delivery abroad, see e.g., 35 U.S.C. §§ 146, 293; 46 U.S.C. § 1292; Calif.Ins.Code § 1612; N.Y.Veh. & Tfc.Law § 253, and it also may be unavailable under the law of the country in which the service is made.

Subparagraph (D) of paragraph (1), permitting service by certain types of mail, affords a manner of service that is inexpensive and expeditious, and requires a minimum of activity within the foreign country. Several statutes specifically provide for service in a foreign country by mail, e.g., Hawaii Rev.Laws §§ 230–31, 230–32 (1955); Minn.Stat.Ann. § 303.13 (1947); N.Y.Civ.Prac.Act, § 229–b; N.Y.Veh. & Tfc. Law § 253, and it has been sanctioned by the courts even in the absence of statutory provision specifying that form of service. *Zurini v. United States,* 189 F.2d 722 (8th Cir. 1951); *United States v. Cardillo,* 135 F.Supp. 798 (W.D.Pa. 1955); *Autogiro Co. v. Kay Gyroplanes, Ltd.,* 55 F.Supp. 919 (D.D.C.1944). Since the reliability of postal service may vary from country to country, service by mail is proper only when it is addressed to the party to be served and a form of mail requiring a signed receipt is used. An additional safeguard is provided by the requirement that the mailing be attended to by the clerk of the court. See also the provisions of paragraph (2) of this subdivision (i) regarding proof of service by mail.

Under the applicable law it may be necessary, when the defendant is an infant or incompetent person, to deliver the summons and complaint to a guardian, committee, or similar fiduciary. In such a case it would be advisable to make service under subparagraph (A), (B), or (E).

Subparagraph (E) of paragraph (1) adds flexibility by permitting the court by order to tailor the manner of service to fit the necessities of a particular case or the peculiar requirements of the law of the country in which the service is to be made. A similar provision appears in a number of statutes, e.g., 35 U.S.C. §§ 146, 293; 38 U.S.C. § 784(a); 46 U.S.C. § 1292.

The next-to-last sentence of paragraph (1) permits service under (C) and (E) to be made by any person who is not a party and is not less than 18 years of age or who is designated by court order or by the foreign court. Cf. Rule 45(c); N.Y.Civ.Prac.Act §§ 233, 235. This alternative increases the possibility that the plaintiff will be able to find a process server who can proceed unimpeded in the foreign country; it also may improve the changes of enforcing the judgment in the country of service. Especially is this alternative valuable when authority for the foreign service is found in a statute or rule of court that limits the group of eligible process servers to designated officials or special appointees who, because directly connected with another "sovereign," may be particularly offensive to the foreign country. See generally Smit, supra, at 1040–41. When recourse is had to subparagraph (A) or (B) the identity of the process server always will be determined by the law of the foreign country in which the service is made.

The last sentence of paragraph (1) sets forth an alternative manner for the issuance and transmission of the summons for service. After obtaining the summons from the clerk, the plaintiff must ascertain the best manner of delivering the summons and complaint to the person, court, or officer who will make the service. Thus the clerk is not burdened with the task of determining who is permitted to serve process under the law of a particular country or the appropriate governmental or nongovernmental channel for forwarding a letter rogatory. Under (D), however, the papers must always be posted by the clerk.

Subdivision (i)(2). When service is made in a foreign country, paragraph (2) permits methods for proof of service in addition to those prescribed by subdivision (g). Proof of service in accordance with the law of the foreign country is permitted because foreign process servers, unaccustomed to the form or the requirement of return of service prevalent in the United States, have on occasion been unwilling to execute the affidavit required by Rule 4(g). See Jones, supra, at 537; Longley, supra, at 35. As a corollary of the alternate manner of service in subdivision (i)(1)(E), proof of service as directed by order of the court is permitted. The special provision for proof of service by mail is intended as an additional safeguard when that method is used. On the type of evidence of delivery that may be satisfactory to a court in lieu of a signed receipt, see *Aero Associates, Inc. v. La Metropolitana,* 183 F.Supp. 357 (S.D.N.Y.1960).

1966 Amendment

The wording of Rule 4(f) is changed to accord with the amendment of Rule 13(h) referring to Rule 19 as amended.

1980 Amendment

Subdivision (a). This is a technical amendment to conform this subdivision with the amendment of subdivision (c).

Subdivision (c). The purpose of this amendment is to authorize service of process to be made by any person who is authorized to make service in actions in the courts of general jurisdiction of the state in which the district court is held or in which service is made.

There is a troublesome ambiguity in Rule 4. Rule 4(c) directs that all process is to be served by the marshal, by his deputy, or by a person specially appointed by the court. But Rule 4(d)(7) authorizes service in certain cases "in the manner prescribed by the law of the state in which the district court is held. . . ." And Rule 4(e), which authorizes service beyond the state and service in quasi in rem cases when state law permits such service, directs that "service may be made . . . under the circumstances and in the manner prescribed in the [state] statute or rule." State statutes and rules of the kind referred to in Rule 4(d)(7) and Rule 4(e) commonly designate the persons who are to make the service provided for, e.g., a sheriff or a plaintiff. When that is so, may the persons so designated by state law make service, or is service in all cases to be made by a marshal or by one specially appointed under present Rule 4(c)? The commentators have noted the ambiguity and have suggested the desirability of an amendment. See 2 Moore's *Federal Practice* ¶4.08 (1974); Wright & Miller, *Federal Practice and Procedure:* Civil § 1092 (1969). And the ambiguity has given rise to unfortunate results. See *United States for the use of Tanos v. St. Paul Mercury Ins. Co.*, 361 F.2d 838 (5th Cir. 1966); *Veeck v. Commodity Enterprises, Inc.*, 487 F.2d 423 (9th Cir.1973).

The ambiguity can be resolved by specific amendments to Rules 4(d)(7) and 4(e), but the Committee is of the view that there is no reason why Rule 4(c) should not generally authorize service of process in all cases by anyone authorized to make service in the courts of general jurisdiction of the state in which the district court is held or in which service is made. The marshal continues to be the obvious, always effective officer for service of process.

1987 Amendment

The amendments are technical. No substantive change is intended.

1993 Amendments

SPECIAL NOTE: Mindful of the constraints of the Rules Enabling Act, the Committee calls the attention of the Supreme Court and Congress to new subdivision (k)(2). Should this limited extension of service be disapproved, the Committee nevertheless recommends adoption of the balance of the rule, with subdivision (k)(1) becoming simply subdivision (k). The Committee Notes would be revised to eliminate references to subdivision (k)(2).

Purposes of Revision. The general purpose of this revision is to facilitate the service of the summons and complaint. The revised rule explicitly authorizes a means for service of the summons and complaint on any defendant. While the methods of service so authorized always provide appropriate notice to persons against whom claims are made, effective service under this rule does not assure that personal jurisdiction has been established over the defendant served.

First, the revised rule authorizes the use of any means of service provided by the law not only of the forum state, but also of the state in which a defendant is served, unless the defendant is a minor or incompetent.

Second, the revised rule clarifies and enhances the cost-saving practice of securing the assent of the defendant to dispense with actual service of the summons and complaint. This practice was introduced to the rule in 1983 by an act of Congress authorizing "service-by-mail," a procedure that effects economic service with cooperation of the defendant. Defendants that magnify costs of service by requiring expensive service not necessary to achieve full notice of an action brought against them are required to bear the wasteful costs. This provision is made available in actions against defendants who cannot be served in the districts in which the actions are brought.

Third, the revision reduces the hazard of commencing an action against the United States or its officers, agencies, and corporations. A party failing to effect service on all the offices of the United States as required by the rule is assured adequate time to cure defects in service.

Fourth, the revision calls attention to the important effect of the Hague Convention and other treaties bearing on service of documents in foreign countries and favors the use of internationally agreed means of service. In some respects, these treaties have facilitated service in foreign countries but are not fully known to the bar.

Finally, the revised rule extends the reach of federal courts to impose jurisdiction over the person of all defendant against whom federal law claims are made and who can be constitutionally subjected to the jurisdiction of the courts of the United States. The present territorial limits on the effectiveness of service to subject a defendant to the jurisdiction of the court over the defendant's person are retained for all actions in which there is a state in which personal jurisdiction can be asserted consistently with state law and the Fourteenth Amendment. A new provision enables district courts to exercise jurisdiction, if permissible under the Constitution and not precluded by statute, when a federal claim is made against a defendant not subject to the jurisdiction of any single state.

The revised rule is reorganized to make its provisions more accessible to those not familiar with all of them. Additional subdivisions in this rule allow for more captions; several overlaps among subdivisions are eliminated; and several disconnected provisions are removed, to be relocated in a new Rule 4.1.

The Caption of the Rule. Prior to this revision, Rule 4 was entitled "Process" and applied to the service of not only the summons but also other process as well, although these are not covered by the revised rule. Service of process in eminent domain proceedings is governed by Rule 71A. Service of a subpoena is governed by Rule 45, and service of papers such as orders, motions, notices, pleadings, and other documents is governed by Rule 5.

The revised rule is entitled "Summons" and applies only to that form of legal process. Unless service of the summons is waived, a summons must be served whenever a person is joined as a party against whom a claim is made. Those few provisions of the former rule which relate specifically to service of process other than a summons are relocated in Rule 4.1 in order to simplify the text of this rule.

Subdivision (a). Revised subdivision (a) contains most of the language of the former subdivision (b). The second sentence of the former subdivision (b) has been stricken, so that the federal court summons will be the same in all cases. Few states now employ, distinctive requirements of form for a summons and the applicability of such a requirement in federal court can only serve as a trap for an unwary party or attorney. A sentence is added to this subdivision authorizing an amendment of a summons. This sentence replaces the rarely used former subdivision 4(h). See 4A Wright & Miller, Federal Practice and Procedure § 1131 (2d ed. 1987).

Subdivision (b). Revised subdivision (b) replaces the former subdivision (a). The revised text makes clear that the responsibility for filling in the summons falls on the plaintiff, not the clerk of the court. If there are multiple defendants, the plaintiff may secure issuance of a summons for each defendant, or may serve copies of a single original bearing the names of multiple defendants if the addressee of the summons is effectively identified.

Subdivision (c). Paragraph (1) of revised subdivision (c) retains language from the former subdivision (d)(1). Paragraph (2) retains language from the former subdivision (a), and adds an appropriate caution regarding the time limit for service set forth in subdivision (m).

The 1983 revision of Rule 4 relieved the marshals' offices of much of the burden of serving the summons. Subdivision (c) eliminates the requirement for service by the marshal's office in actions in which the party seeking service is the United States. The United States, like other civil litigants, is now permitted to designate any person who is 18 years of age and not a party to serve its summons.

The court remains obligated to appoint a marshal, a deputy, or some other person to effect service of a summons in two classes of cases specified by statute: actions brought in forma pauperis or by a seaman. 28 U.S.C. §§ 1915, 1916. The court also retains discretion to appoint a process server on motion of a party. If a law enforcement presence appears to be necessary or advisable to keep the peace, the court should appoint a marshal or deputy or other official person to make the service. The Department of Justice may also call upon the Marshals Service to perform services in actions brought by the United States. 28 U.S.C. § 651.

Subdivision (d). This text is new, but is substantially derived from the former subdivisions (c)(2)(C) and (D), added to the rule by Congress in 1983. The aims of the provision are to eliminate the costs of service of a summons on many parties and to foster cooperation among adversaries and counsel. The rule operates to impose upon the defendant those costs that could have been avoided if the defendant had cooperated reasonably in the manner prescribed. This device is useful in dealing with defendants who are furtive, who reside in places not easily reached by process servers, or who are outside the United States and can be served only at substantial and unnecessary expense. Illustratively, there is no useful purpose achieved by requiring a plaintiff to comply with all the formalities of service in a foreign country, including costs of translation, when suing a defendant manufacturer, fluent in English, whose products are widely distributed in the United States. See Bankston v. Toyota Motor Corp., 889 F.2d 172 (8th Cir.1989).

The former text described this process as service-by-mail. This language misled some plaintiffs into thinking that service could be effected by mail without the affirmative cooperation of the defendant. E.g., Gulley v. Mayo Foundation, 886 F.2d 161 (8th Cir.1989). It is more accurate to describe the communication sent to the defendant as a request for a waiver of formal service.

The request for waiver of service may be sent only to defendants subject to service under subdivision (e), (f), or (h). The United States is not expected to waive service for the reason that its mail receiving facilities are inadequate to assure that the notice is actually received by the correct person in the Department of Justice. The same principle is applied to agencies, corporations, and officers of the United States and to other governments and entities subject to service under subdivision (j). Moreover, there are policy reasons why governmental entities should not be confronted with the potential for bearing costs of service in cases in which they ultimately prevail. Infants or incompetent persons likewise are not called upon to waive service because, due to their presumed inability to understand the request and its consequences, they must generally be served through fiduciaries.

It was unclear whether the former rule authorized, mailing of a request for "acknowledgement of service" to defendants outside the forum state. See 1 R. Casad, Jurisdiction in Civil Actions (2d Ed.) 5–29, 30 (1991) and cases cited. But, as Professor Casad observed, there was no reason not to employ this device in an effort to obtain service outside the state, and there are many instances in which it was in fact so used, with respect both to defendants within the United States and to defendants in other countries.

The opportunity for waiver has distinct advantages to a foreign defendant. By waiving service, the defendant can reduce the costs that may ultimately be taxed against it if unsuccessful in the lawsuit, including the sometimes substantial expense of translation that may be wholly unnecessary for defendants fluent in English. Moreover, a foreign defendant that waives service is afforded substantially more time to defend against the action than if it had been formally served: under Rule 12, a defendant ordinarily has only 20 days after service in which to file its answer or raise objections by motion, but by signing a waiver it is allowed 90 days after the date the request for waiver was mailed in which to submit its defenses. Because of the additional time needed for mailing and the unreliability of some foreign mail services, a period of 60 days (rather than the 30 days required for domestic transmissions) is provided for a return of a waiver sent to a foreign country.

It is hoped that, since transmission of the notice and waiver forms is a private nonjudicial act, does not purport to effect service, and is not accompanied by any summons or directive from a court, use of the procedure will not offend foreign sovereignties, even those that have withheld their assent to formal service by mail or have objected to the "service-by-mail" provisions of the former rule. Unless the addressee consents, receipt of the request under the revised rule does not give rise to any obligation to answer the lawsuit, does not provide a basis for default judgment, and does not suspend the statute of limitations in those states where the period continues to run until service. Nor are there any adverse consequences to a foreign defendant, since the provisions for shifting the expense of service to a defendant that declines to waive service apply only if the plaintiff and defendant are both located in the United States.

With respect to a defendant located in a foreign country like the United Kingdom, which accepts documents in English, whose Central Authority acts promptly in effecting service, and whose policies discourage its residents from waiving formal service, there will be little reason for a plaintiff to send the notice and request under subdivision (d) rather than use convention methods. On the other hand, the procedure offers significant potential benefits to a plaintiff when suing a defendant that, though fluent in English, is located in a country where, as a condition to formal service under a convention, documents must be translated into another language or where formal service will be otherwise costly or time-consuming.

Paragraph (1) is explicit that a timely waiver of service of a summons does not prejudice the right of a defendant to object by means of a motion authorized by Rule 12(b)(2) to the absence of jurisdiction over the defendant's person, or to assert other defenses that may be available. The only issues eliminated are those involving the sufficiency of the summons or the sufficiency of the method by which it is served.

Paragraph (2) states what the present rule implies: the defendant has a duty to avoid costs associated with the service of a summons not needed to inform the defendant regarding the commencement of an action. The text of the rule also sets forth the requirements for a Notice and

Request for Waiver sufficient to put the cost-shifting provision in place. These requirements are illustrated in Forms 1A and 1B, which replace the former Form 18–A.

Paragraph (2)(A) is explicit that a request for waiver of service by a corporate defendant must be addressed to a person qualified to receive service. The general mail rooms of large organizations cannot be required to identify the appropriate individual recipient for an institutional summons.

Paragraph (2)(B) permits the use of alternatives to the United States mails in sending the Notice and Request. While private messenger services or electronic communications may be more expensive than the mail, they may be equally reliable and on occasion more convenient to the parties. Especially with respect to transmissions to foreign countries, alternative means may be desirable, for in some countries facsimile transmission is the most efficient and economical means of communication. If electronic means such as facsimile transmission are employed, the sender should maintain a record of the transmission to assure proof of transmission if receipt is denied, but a party receiving such a transmission has a duty to cooperate and cannot avoid liability for the resulting cost of formal service if the transmission is prevented at the point of receipt.

A defendant failing to comply with a request for waiver shall be given an opportunity to show good cause for the failure, but sufficient cause should be rare. It is not a good cause for failure to waive service that the claim is unjust or that the court lacks jurisdiction. Sufficient cause not to shift the cost of service would exist, however, if the defendant did not receive the request or was insufficiently literate in English to understand it. It should be noted that the provisions for shifting the cost of service apply only if the plaintiff and the defendant are both located in the United States, and accordingly a foreign defendant need not show "good cause" for its failure to waive service.

Paragraph (3) extends the time for answer if, before being served with process, the defendant waives formal service. The extension is intended to serve as an inducement to waive service and to assure that a defendant will not gain any delay be declining to waive service and thereby causing the additional time needed to effect service. By waiving service, a defendant is not called upon to respond to the complaint until 60 days from the date the notice was sent to it—90 days if the notice was sent to a foreign country—rather than within the 20 day period from date of service specified in Rule 12.

Paragraph (4) clarifies the effective date of service when service is waived; the provision is needed to resolve an issue arising when applicable law requires service of process to toll the statute of limitations. E.g., Morse v. Elmira Country Club, 752 F.2d 35 (2d Cir.1984). Cf. Walker v. Armco Steel Corp., 446 U.S. 740 (1980).

The provisions in former subdivision (c)(2)(C)(ii) of this rule may have been misleading to some parties. Some plaintiffs, not reading the rule carefully, supposed that receipt by the defendant of the mailed complaint had the effect both of establishing the jurisdiction of the court over the defendant's person and of tolling the statute of limitations in actions in which service of the summons is required to toll the limitations period. The revised rule is clear that, if the waiver is not returned and filed, the limitations period under such a law is not tolled and the action will not otherwise proceed until formal service of process is effected.

Some state limitations laws may toll an otherwise applicable statute at the time when the defendant receives notice of the action. Nevertheless, the device of requested waiver of service is not suitable if a limitations period which is about to expire is not tolled by filing the action. Unless there is ample time, the plaintiff should proceed directly to the formal methods for service identified in subdivisions (e), (f), or (h).

The procedure of requesting waiver of service should also not be used if the time for service under subdivision (m) will expire before the date on which the waiver must be returned. While a plaintiff has been allowed additional time for service in that situation, e.g., Prather v. Raymond Constr. Co., 570 F.Supp. 278 (N.D.Ga.1983), the court could refuse a request for additional time unless the defendant appears to have evaded service pursuant to subdivision (e) or (h). It may be noted that the presumptive time limit for service under subdivision (m) does not apply to service in a foreign country.

Paragraph (5) is a cost-shifting provision retained from the former rule. The costs that may be imposed on the defendant could include, for example, the cost of the time of a process server required to make contact with a defendant residing in a guarded apartment house or residential development. The paragraph is explicit that the costs of enforcing the cost-shifting provision are themselves recoverable from a defendant who fails to return the waiver. In the absence of such a provision, the purpose of the rule would be frustrated by the cost of its enforcement, which is likely to be high in relation to the small benefit secured by the plaintiff.

Some plaintiffs may send a notice and request for waiver and, without waiting for return of the waiver, also proceed with efforts to effect formal service on the defendant. To discourage this practice, the cost-shifting provisions in paragraphs (2) and (5) are limited to costs of effecting service incurred after the time expires for the defendant to return the waiver. Moreover, by returning the waiver within the time allowed and before being served with process, a defendant receives the benefit of the longer period for responding to the complaint afforded for waivers under paragraph (3).

Subdivision (e). This subdivision replaces former subdivisions (c)(2)(C)(i) and (d)(1). It provides a means for service of summons on individuals within a judicial district of the United States. Together with subdivision (f), it provides for service on persons anywhere, subject to constitutional and statutory constraints.

Service of the summons under this subdivision does not conclusively establish the jurisdiction of the court over the person of the defendant. A defendant may assert the territorial limits of the court's reach set forth in subdivision (k), including the constitutional limitations that may be imposed by the Due Process Clause of the Fifth Amendment.

Paragraph (1) authorizes service in any judicial district in conformity with state law. This paragraph sets forth the language of former subdivision (c)(2)(C)(i), which authorized the use of the law of the state in which the district court sits, but adds as an alternative the use of the law of the state in which the service is effected.

Paragraph (2) retains the text of the former subdivision (d)(1) and authorizes the use of the familiar methods of personal or abode service or service on an authorized agent in any judicial district.

To conform to these provisions, the former subdivision (e) bearing on proceedings against parties not found within the state is stricken. Likewise stricken is the first sentence of the former subdivision (f), which had restricted the authority of the federal process server to the state in which the district court sits.

Subdivision (f). This subdivision provides for service on individuals who are in a foreign country, replacing the former subdivision (i) that was added to Rule 4 in 1963. Reflecting the pattern of Rule 4 in incorporating state law limitations on the exercise of jurisdiction over persons, the former subdivision (i) limited service outside the United States to cases in which extraterritorial service was authorized by state or federal law. The new rule eliminates the requirement of explicit authorization. On occasion, service in a foreign country was held to be improper for lack of statutory authority. E.g., Martens v. Winder, 341 F.2d 197 (9th Cir.), cert. denied, 382 U.S. 937 (1965). This authority, however, was found to exist by implication. E.g., SEC v. VTR, Inc., 39 F.R.D. 19 (S.D.N.Y.1966). Given the substantial increase in the number of international transactions and events that are the subject of litigation in federal courts, it is appropriate to infer a general legislative authority to effect service on defendants in a foreign country.

A secondary effect of this provision for foreign service of a federal summons is to facilitate the use of federal long-arm law in actions brought to enforce the federal law against defendants who cannot be served under any state law but who can be constitutionally subjected to the jurisdiction of the federal court. Such a provision is set forth in paragraph (2) of subdivision (k) of this rule, applicable only to persons not subject to the territorial jurisdiction of any particular state.

Paragraph (1) gives effect to the Hague Convention on the Service Abroad of Judicial and Extrajudicial Documents, which entered into force for the United States on February 10, 1969. See 28 U.S.C.A., Fed.R.Civ.P. 4 (Supp.1986). This Convention is an important means of dealing with problems of service in a foreign country. See generally 1 B. Ristau, International Judicial Assistance §§ 4–1–1 to 4–5–2 (1990). Use of the Convention procedures, when available, is mandatory if documents must be transmitted abroad to effect service. See Volkswagenwerk Aktiengesellschaft v. Schlunk, 486 U.S. 694 (1988) (noting that voluntary use of these procedures may be desirable even when service could constitutionally be effected in another manner); J. Weis, The Federal Rules and the Hague Conventions: Concerns of Conformity and Comity, 50 U.Pitt.L.Rev. 903 (1989). Therefore, this paragraph provides that, when service is to be effected outside a judicial district of the United States, the methods of service appropriate under an applicable treaty shall be employed if available and if the treaty so requires.

The Hague Convention furnishes safeguards against the abridgment of rights of parties through inadequate notice. Article 15 provides for verification of actual notice or a demonstration that process was served by a method prescribed by the internal laws of the foreign state before a default judgment may be entered. Article 16 of the Convention also enables the judge to extend the time for appeal after judgment if the defendant shows a lack of adequate notice either to defend or to appeal the judgment, or has disclosed a prima facie case on the merits.

The Hague Convention does not specify a time within which a foreign country's Central Authority must effect service, but Article 15 does provide that alternate methods may be used if a Central Authority does not respond within six months. Generally, a Central Authority can be expected to respond much more quickly than that limit might permit, but there have been occasions when the signatory state was dilatory or refused to cooperate for substantive reasons. In such cases, resort may be had to the provision set forth in subdivision (f)(3).

Two minor changes in the text reflect the Hague Convention. First, the term "letter of request" has been added. Although these words are synonymous with "letter rogatory," "letter of request" is preferred in modern usage. The provision should not be interpreted to authorize use of a letter of request when there is in fact no treaty obligation on the receiving country to honor such a request from this country or when the United States does not extend diplomatic recognition to the foreign nation. Second, the passage formerly found in subdivision (i)(1)(B), "when service in either case is reasonably calculated to give actual notice," has been relocated.

Paragraph (2) provides alternative methods for use when internationally agreed methods are not intended to be exclusive, or where there is no international agreement applicable. It contains most of the language formerly set forth in subdivision (i) of the rule. Service by methods that would violate foreign law is not generally authorized. Subparagraphs (A) and (B) prescribe the more appropriate methods for conforming to local practice or using a local authority. Subparagraph (C) prescribes other methods authorized by the former rule.

Paragraph (3) authorizes the court to approve other methods of service not prohibited by international agreements. The Hague Convention, for example, authorizes special forms of service in cases of urgency if convention methods will not permit service within the time required by the circumstances. Other circumstances that might justify the use of additional methods include the failure of the foreign country's Central Authority to effect service within the six-month period provided by the Convention, or the refusal of the Central Authority to serve a complaint seeking punitive damages or to enforce the antitrust laws of the United States. In such cases, the court may direct a special method of service not explicitly authorized by international agreement if not prohibited by the agreement. Inasmuch as our Constitution requires that reasonable notice be given, an earnest effort should be made to devise a method of communication that is consistent with due process and minimizes offense to foreign law. A court may in some instances specially authorize use of ordinary mail. Cf. Levin v. Ruby Trading Corp., 248 F.Supp. 537 (S.D.N.Y.1965).

Subdivision (g). This subdivision retains the text of former subdivision (d)(2). Provision is made for service upon an infant or incompetent person in a foreign country.

Subdivision (h). This subdivision retains the text of former subdivision (d)(3), with changes reflecting those made in subdivision (e). It also contains the provisions for service on a corporation or association in a foreign country, as formerly found in subdivision (i).

Frequent use should be made of the Notice and Request procedure set forth in subdivision (d) in actions against corporations. Care must be taken, however, to address the request to an individual officer or authorized agent of the corporation. It is not effective use of the Notice and Request procedure if the mail is sent undirected to the mail room of the organization.

Subdivision (i). This subdivision retains much of the text of former subdivisions (d)(4) and (d)(5). Paragraph (1) provides for service of a summons on the United States; it amends former subdivision (d)(4) to permit the United States attorney to be served by registered or certified mail. The rule does not authorize the use of the Notice and Request procedure of revised subdivision (d) when the United States is the defendant. To assure proper handling of mail in the United States attorney's office, the authorized mail service must be specifically addressed to the civil process clerk of the office of the United States attorney.

Paragraph (2) replaces former subdivision (d)(5). Paragraph (3) saves the plaintiff from the hazard of losing a substantive right because of failure to comply with the complex requirements of multiple service under this subdivision. That risk has proved to be more than nominal. E.g., Whale v. United States, 792 F.2d 951 (9th Cir.1986). This provision should be read in connection with the provisions of subdivision (c) of Rule 15 to preclude the loss of substantive rights against the United States or its agencies, corporations, or officers resulting from a plaintiff's failure to correctly identify and serve all the persons who should be named or served.

Subdivision (j). This subdivision retains the text of former subdivision (d)(6) without material change. The waiver-of-service provision is also inapplicable to actions against governments subject to service pursuant to this subdivision.

The revision adds a new paragraph (1) referring to the statute governing service of a summons on a foreign state and its political subdivisions, agencies, and instrumentalities, the Foreign Sovereign Immunities Act of 1976, 28 U.S.C. § 1608. The caption of the subdivision reflects that change.

Subdivision (k). This subdivision replaces the former subdivision (f), with no change in the title. Paragraph (1) retains the substance of the former rule in explicitly authorizing the exercise of personal jurisdiction over persons who can be reached under state long-arm law, the "100-mile bulge" provision added in 1963, or the federal interpleader act. Paragraph (1)(D) is new, but merely calls attention to federal legislation that may provide for nationwide or even world-wide service of process in cases arising under particular federal laws. Congress has provided for nationwide service of process and full exercise of territorial jurisdiction by all district courts with respect to specified federal actions. See 1 R. Casad, Jurisdiction in Civil Actions (2d Ed.) chap. 5 (1991).

Paragraph (2) is new. It authorizes the exercise of territorial jurisdiction over the person of any defendant against whom is made a claim arising under any federal law if that person is subject to personal jurisdiction in no state. This addition is a companion to the amendments made in revised subdivisions (e) and (f).

This paragraph corrects a gap in the enforcement of federal law. Under the former rule, a problem was presented when the defendant was a non-resident of the United States having contacts with the United States sufficient to justify the application of United States law and to satisfy federal standards of forum selection, but having insufficient contact with any single state to support jurisdiction under state long-arm legislation or meet the requirements of the Fourteenth Amendment limitation on state court territorial jurisdiction. In such cases, the defendant was shielded from the enforcement of federal law by the fortuity of a favorable limitation on the power of state courts, which was incorporated into the federal practice by the former rule. In this respect, the revision responds to the suggestion of the Supreme Court made in Omni Capital Int'l. v. Rudolf Wolff & Co., Ltd., 484 U.S. 97, 111 (1987).

There remain constitutional limitations on the exercise of territorial jurisdiction by federal courts over persons outside the United States. These restrictions arise from the Fifth Amendment rather than from the Fourteenth Amendment, which limits state-court reach and which was incorporated into federal practice by the reference to state law in the text of the former subdivision (e) that is deleted by this revision. The Fifth Amendment requires that any defendant have affiliating contacts with the United States sufficient to justify the exercise of personal jurisdiction over that party. Cf. Wells Fargo & Co. v. Wells Fargo Express Co., 556 F.2d 406, 418 (9th Cir.1977). There also may be a further Fifth Amendment constraint in that a plaintiff's forum selection might be so inconvenient to a defendant that it would be a denial of "fair play and substantial justice" required by the due process clause, even though the defendant had significant affiliating contacts with the United States. See DeJames v. Magnificent Carriers, 654 F.2d 280, 286 n. 3 (3rd Cir.), cert. denied, 454 U.S. 1085 (1981). Compare World-Wide Volkswagen Corp. v. Woodson, 444 U.S. 286, 293–294 (1980); Insurance Corp. of Ireland v. Compagnie des Bauxites de Guinee, 456 U.S. 694, 702–03 (1982); Burger King Corp. v. Rudzewicz, 471 U.S. 462, 476–78 (1985); Asahi Metal Indus. v. Superior Court of Cal., Solano County, 480 U.S. 102, 108–13 (1987). See generally R. Lusardi, Nationwide Service of Process: Due Process Limitations on the Power of the Sovereign, 33 Vill.L.Rev. 1 (1988).

This provision does not affect the operation of federal venue legislation. See generally 28 U.S.C. § 1391. Nor does it affect the operation of federal law providing for the change of venue. 28 U.S.C. §§ 1404, 1406. The availability of transfer for fairness and convenience under § 1404 should preclude most conflicts between the full exercise of territorial jurisdiction permitted by this rule and the Fifth Amendment requirement of "fair play and substantial justice."

The district court should be especially scrupulous to protect aliens who reside in a foreign country from forum selections so onerous that injustice could result. "[G]reat care and reserve should be exercised when extending our notions of personal jurisdiction into the international field." Asahi Metal Indus. v. Superior Court of Cal., Solano County, 480 U.S. 102, 115 (1987), quoting United States v. First Nat'l City Bank, 379 U.S. 378, 404 (1965) (Harlan, J., dissenting).

This narrow extension of the federal reach applies only if a claim is made against the defendant under federal law. It does not establish personal jurisdiction if the only claims are those arising under state law or the law of another country, even though there might be diversity or alienage subject matter jurisdiction as to such claims. If, however, personal jurisdiction is established under this paragraph with respect to a federal claim, then 28 U.S.C. § 1367(a) provides supplemental jurisdiction over related claims against that defendant, subject to the court's discretion to decline exercise of that jurisdiction under 28 U.S.C. § 1367(c).

Subdivision (*l*). This subdivision assembles in one place all the provisions of the present rule bearing on proof of service. No material change in the rule is effected. The provision that proof of service can be amended by leave of court is retained from the former subdivision (h). See generally 4A Wright & Miller, Federal Practice and Procedure § 1132 (2d ed. 1987).

Subdivision (m). This subdivision retains much of the language of the present subdivision (j).

The new subdivision explicitly provides that the court shall allow additional time if there is good cause for the plaintiff's failure to effect service in the prescribed 120 days, and authorizes the court to relieve a plaintiff of the consequences of an application of this subdivision even if there is no good cause shown. Such relief formerly was afforded in some cases, partly in reliance on Rule 6(b). Relief may be justified, for example, if the applicable statute of limitations would bar the refiled action, or if the defendant is evading service or conceals a defect in attempted service. E.g., Ditkof v. Owens–Illinois, Inc., 114 F.R.D. 104 (E.D.Mich. 1987). A specific instance of good cause is set forth in paragraph (3) of this rule, which provides for extensions if necessary to correct oversights in compliance with the requirements of multiple service in actions against the United States or its officers, agencies, and corporations. The district court should also take care to protect pro se plaintiffs from consequences of confusion or delay attending the resolution of an in forma pauperis petition. Robinson v. America's Best Contacts & Eyeglasses, 876 F.2d 596 (7th Cir. 1989).

The 1983 revision of this subdivision referred to the "party on whose behalf such service was required," rather than to the "plaintiff," a term used generically elsewhere in this rule to refer to any party initiating a claim against a person who is not a party to the action. To simplify the text, the revision returns to the usual practice in the rule of referring simply to the plaintiff even though its principles apply with equal force to defendants who may assert claims against nonparties under Rules 13(h), 14, 19, 20, or 21.

Subdivision (n). This subdivision provides for in rem and quasi-in-rem jurisdiction. Paragraph (1) incorporates any requirements of 28 U.S.C. § 1655 or similar provisions bearing on seizures or liens.

Paragraph (2) provides for other uses of quasi-in-rem jurisdiction but limits its use to exigent circumstances. Provisional remedies may be employed as a means to secure jurisdiction over the property of a defendant whose person is not within reach of the court, but occasions for the use of this provision should be rare, as where the defendant is a fugitive or assets are in imminent danger of disappearing. Until 1963, it was not possible under Rule 4 to assert jurisdiction in a federal court over the property of a defendant not personally served. The 1963 amendment to subdivision (e) authorized the use of state law procedures authorizing seizures of assets as a basis for jurisdiction. Given the liberal availability of long-arm jurisdiction, the exercise of power quasi-in-rem has become almost an anachronism. Circumstances too spare to affiliate the defendant to the forum state sufficiently to support long-arm jurisdiction over the defendant's person are also inadequate to support seizure of the defendant's assets fortuitously found within the state. Shaffer v. Heitner, 433 U.S. 186 (1977).

HISTORICAL NOTES

References in Text

Form 18–A, referred to in subsec. (c)(2)(C)(ii), was abrogated effective December 1, 1991, subject to contrary Congressional action.

Effective Dates

1983 Act. Amendment by Pub.L. 97–462 effective 45 days after Jan. 12, 1983, see section 4 of Pub.L. 97–462, set out as a note under section 2071 of this title.

LEGISLATIVE STATEMENT

1983 Amendment

128 Congressional Record H 9848, Dec. 15, 1982. Mr. EDWARDS of California. Mr. Speaker, in July Mr. McClory and I brought before the House a bill to delay the effective date of proposed changes in rule 4 of the Federal Rules of Civil Procedure dealing with service of process. The Congress enacted that legislation and delayed the effective date so that we could cure certain problems in the proposed amendments to rule 4.

Since that time, Mr. McClory and I introduced a bill, H.R. 7154, that cures those problems. It was drafted in consultation with representatives of the Department of Justice, the Judicial Conference of the United States, and others.

The Department of Justice and the Judicial Conference have endorsed the bill and have urged its prompt enactment. Indeed, the Department of Justice has indicated that the changes occasioned by the bill will facilitate its collection of debts owed to the Government.

I have a letter from the Office of Legislative Affairs of the Department of Justice supporting the bill that I will submit for the Record. Also, I am submitting for the Record a section-by-section analysis of the bill.

H.R. 7154 makes much needed changes in rule 4 of the Federal Rules of Civil Procedure and is supported by all interested parties. I urge my colleagues to support it.

U.S. Department of Justice,
Office of Legislative Affairs,
Washington, D.C., December 10, 1982.

Hon. Peter W. Rodino, Jr.

Chairman, Committee on the Judiciary House of Representatives, Washington, D.C.

Dear Mr. Chairman: This is to proffer the views of the Department of Justice on H.R. 7154, the proposed Federal Rules of Civil Procedure Amendments Act of 1982. While the agenda is extremely tight and we appreciate that fact, we do reiterate that this Department strongly endorses the enactment of H.R. 7154. We would greatly appreciate your watching for any possible way to enact this legislation expeditiously.

H.R. 7154 would amend Rule 4 of the Federal Rules of Civil Procedure to relieve effectively the United States Marshals Service of the duty of routinely serving summonses and complaints for private parties in civil actions and would thus achieve a goal this Department has long sought. Experience has shown that the Marshals Service's increasing workload and limited budget require such major relief from the burdens imposed by its role as process-server in all civil actions.

The bill would also amend Rule 4 to permit certain classes of defendants to be served by first class mail with a notice and acknowledgment of receipt form enclosed. We have previously expressed a preference for the service-by-mail provisions of the proposed amendments to Rule 4 which the Supreme Court transmitted to Congress on April 28, 1982.

The amendments proposed by the Supreme Court would permit service by registered or certified mail, return receipt requested. We had regarded the Supreme Court proposal as the more efficient because it would not require an affirmative act of signing and mailing on the part of a defendant. Moreover, the Supreme Court proposal would permit the entry of a default judgment if the record contained a returned receipt showing acceptance by the defendant or a returned envelope showing refusal of the process by the defendant and subsequent service and notice by first class mail. However, critics of that system of mail service have argued that certified mail is not an effective method of providing actual notice to defendants of claims against them because signatures may be illegible or may not match the name of the defendant, or because it may be difficult to determine whether mail has been "unclaimed" or "refused," the latter providing the sole basis for a default judgment.

As you know, in light of these criticisms the Congress enacted Public Law 97–227 (H.R. 6663) postponing the effective date of the proposed amendments to Rule 4 until October 1, 1983, so as to facilitate further review of the problem. This Department opposed the delay in the effective date, primarily because the Supreme Court's proposed amendments also contained urgently needed provisions designed to relieve the United States Marshals of the burden of serving summonses and complaints in private civil actions. In our view, these necessary relief provisions are readily separable from the issues of service by certified mail and the propriety of default judgment after service by certified mail which the Congress felt warranted additional review.

During the floor consideration of H.R. 6663 Congressman Edwards and other proponents of the delayed effective date pledged to expedite the review of the proposed amendments to Rule 4, given the need to provide prompt relief for the Marshals Service in the service of process area. In this spirit Judiciary Committee staff consulted with representatives of this Department, the Judicial Conference, and others who had voiced concern about the proposed amendments.

H.R. 7154 is the product of those consultations and accommodated the concerns of the Department in a very workable and acceptable manner.

Accordingly, we are satisfied that the provisions of H.R. 7154 merit the support of all three branches of the Federal Government and everyone else who has a stake in the fair and efficient service of process in civil actions. We urge prompt consideration of H.R. 7154 by the Committee.[1]

The Office of Management and Budget has advised that there is no objection to the submission of this report from the standpoint of the Administration's program.

Sincerely,

Robert A. McConnell,
Assistant Attorney General

[1] In addition to amending Rule 4, we have previously recommended: (a) amendments to 28 U.S.C. § 569(b) redefining the Marshals traditional role by eliminating the statutory requirement that they serve subpoenas, as well as summonses and complaints, and; (b) amendments to 28 U.S.C. § 1921 changing the manner and level in which marshal fees are charged for serving private civil process. These legislative changes are embodied in Section 10 of S. 2567 and the Department's proposed fiscal year 1983 Appropriations Authorization bill. If, in the Committee's judgment, efforts to incorporate these suggested amendments in H.R. 7154 would in any way impede consideration of the bill during the few remaining legislative days in the 97th Congress, we would urge that they be separately considered early in the 98th Congress.

H.R. 7154—Federal Rules of Civil Procedure Amendments Act of 1982

Background

The Federal Rules of Civil Procedure set forth the procedures to be followed in civil actions and proceedings in United States district courts. These rules are usually amended by a process established by 28 U.S.C. 2072, often referred to as the "Rules Enabling Act". The Rules Enabling Act provides that the Supreme Court can propose new rules of "practice and procedure" and amendments to existing rules by transmitting them to Congress after the start of a regular session but not later than May 1. The rules and amendments so proposed take effect 90 days after transmittal unless legislation to the contrary is enacted.[1]

On April 28, 1982, the Supreme Court transmitted to Congress several proposed amendments to the Federal Rules of Civil Procedure, the Federal Rules of Criminal Procedure (which govern criminal cases and proceedings in Federal courts), and the Rules and Forms Governing Proceedings in the United States District Courts under sections 2254 and 2255 of Title 28, United States Code (which govern habeas corpus proceedings). These amendments were to have taken effect on August 1, 1982.

The amendments to Rule 4 of the Federal Rules of Civil Procedure were intended primarily to relieve United States marshals of the burden of serving summonses and complaints in private civil actions. Appendix II, at 7 (Report of the Committee on Rules of Practice and Procedure), 16 (Advisory Committee Note). The Committee received numerous complaints that the changes not only failed to achieve that goal, but that in the process the changes saddled litigators with flawed mail service, deprived litigants of the use of effective local procedures for service, and created a time limit for service replete with ambiguities that could only be resolved by costly litigation. See House Report No. 97–662, at 2–4 (1982).

In order to consider these criticisms, Congress enacted Public Law 97–227, postponing the effective date of the proposed amendments to Rule 4 until October 1, 1983.[2] Accordingly, in order to help shape the policy behind, and the form of, the proposed amendments, Congress must enact legislation before October 1, 1983.[3]

With that deadline and purpose in mind, consultations were held with representatives of the Judicial Conference, the Department of Justice, and others who had voiced concern about the proposed amendments. H.R. 7154 is the product of those consultations. The bill seeks to effectuate the policy of relieving the Marshals Service of the duty of routinely serving summonses and complaints. It provides a system of service by mail modeled upon a system found to be effective in California, and finally, it makes appropriate stylistic, grammatical, and other changes in Rule 4.

NEED FOR THE LEGISLATION

1. Current Rule 4

Rule 4 of the Federal Rules of Civil Procedure relates to the issuance and service of process. Subsection (c) authorizes service of process by personnel of the Marshals Service, by a person specially appointed by the Court, or "by a person authorized to serve process in an action brought in the courts of general jurisdiction of the state in which the district court is held or in which service is made." Subsection (d) describes how a summons and complaint must be served and designates those persons who must be served in cases involving specified categories of defendants. Mail service is not directly authorized. Subsection (d)(7), however, authorizes service under the law of the state in which the district court sits upon defendants described in subsections (d)(1) (certain individuals) and (d)(3) (organizations). Thus, if state law authorizes service by mail of a summons and complaint upon an individual or organization described in subsections (d)(1) or (3), then subsection (d)(7) authorizes service by mail for United States district courts in that state.[4]

2. Reducing the role of marshals

The Supreme Court's proposed modifications of Rule 4 were designed to alleviate the burden on the Marshals Service of serving summonses and complaints in private civil actions. Appendix II, at 7 (Report of the Committee on Rules of Practice and Procedure), 16 (Advisory Committee Note). While the Committee received no complaints about the goal of reducing the role of the Marshals Service, the Court's proposals simply failed to achieve that goal. See House Report No. 97–662, at 2–3 (1982).

The Court's proposed Rule 4(c)(2)(B) required the Marshals Service to serve summonses and complaints "pursuant to any statutory provision expressly providing for service by a United States Marshal or his deputy." [5] One such statutory provision is 28 U.S.C. 569(b), which compels marshals to "execute *all* lawful writs, process and orders issued under authority of the United States, *including those of the courts* * * *." (emphasis added). Thus, any party could have invoked 28 U.S.C. 569(b) to utilize a marshal for service of a summons and complaint, thereby thwarting the intent of the new subsection to limit the use of marshals. The Justice Department acknowledges that the proposed subsection did not accomplish its objectives.[6]

Had 28 U.S.C. 569(b) been inconsistent with proposed Rule 4(c)(2)(B), the latter would have nullified the former under 28 U.S.C. 2072, which provides that "All laws in conflict with such rules shall be of no further force or effect after such rules have taken effect." Since proposed Rule 4(c)(2)(B) specifically referred to statutes such as 28 U.S.C. 569(b), however, the new subsection did not conflict with 28 U.S.C. 569(b) and did not, therefore, supersede it.

H.R. 7154 cures this problem and achieves the desired reduction in the role of the Marshals Service by authorizing marshals to serve summonses and complaints "on behalf of the United States". By so doing, H.R. 7154 eliminates the loophole in the Court's proposed language and still provides for service by marshals on behalf of the Government.[7]

3. Mail service

The Supreme Court's proposed subsection (d)(7) and (8) authorized, as an alternative to personal service, mail service of summonses and complaints on individuals and organizations described in subsection (d)(1) and (3), but only through registered or certified mail, restricted delivery. Critics of that system of mail service argued that registered and certified mail were not necessarily effective methods of providing actual notice to defendants of claims against them. This was so, they argued, because signatures may be illegible or may not match the name of the defendant, or because it may be difficult to determine whether mail has been "unclaimed" or "refused", the latter apparently providing the sole basis for a default judgment.[8]

H.R. 7154 provides for a system of service by mail similar to the system now used in California. See Cal.Civ.Pro. § 415.30 (West 1973). Service would be by ordinary mail with a notice and acknowledgment of receipt form enclosed. If the defendant returns the acknowledgment form to the sender within 20 days of mailing, the sender files the return and service is complete. If the acknowledgment is not returned within 20 days of mailing, then service must be effected through some other means provided for in the Rules.

This system of mail service avoids the notice problems created by the registered and certified mail procedures proposed by the Supreme Court. If the proper person receives the notice and returns the acknowledgment, service is complete. If the proper person does not receive the mailed form, or if the proper person receives the notice but fails to return the acknowledgment form, another method of service authorized by law is required.[9] In either instance, however, the defendant will receive actual notice of the claim. In order to encourage defendants to return the acknowledgment form, the court can order a defendant who does not return it to pay the costs of service unless the defendant can show good cause for the failure to return it.

4. The local option

The Court's proposed amendments to Rule 4 deleted the provision in current subsection (d)(7) that authorizes service of a summons and complaint upon individuals and organizations "in the manner prescribed by the law of the state in which the district court is held for the service of summons or other like process upon any such defendant in an action brought in the courts of general jurisdiction of that state." The Committee received a variety of complaints about the deletion of this provision. Those in favor of preserving the local option saw no reason to forego systems of service that had been successful in achieving effective notice.[10]

H.R. 7154 carries forward the policy of the current rule and permits a party to serve a summons and complaint upon individuals and organizations described in Rule 4(d)(1) and (3) in accordance with the law of the state in which the district court sits. Thus, the bill authorizes four methods of serving a summons and complaint on such defendants: (1) service by a nonparty adult (Rule 4(c)(2)(A)); (2) service by personnel of the Marshals Service, if the party qualifies, such as because the party is proceeding in forma pauperis (Rule

4(c)(2)(B)); (3) service in any manner authorized by the law of the state in which the district court is held (Rule 4(c)(2)(C)(i)); or (4) service by regular mail with a notice and acknowledgment of receipt form enclosed (Rule 4(c)(2)(C)(ii)).[11]

5. *Time limits*

Rule 4 does not currently provide a time limit within which service must be completed. Primarily because United States marshals currently effect service of process, no time restriction has been deemed necessary, Appendix II, at 18 (Advisory Committee Note). Along with the proposed changes to subdivisions (c) and (d) to reduce the role of the Marshals Service, however, came new subdivision (j), requiring that service of a summons and complaint be made within 120 days of the filing of the complaint. If service were not accomplished within that time, proposed subdivision (j) required that the action "be dismissed as to that defendant without prejudice upon motion or upon the court's own initiative". Service by mail was deemed made for purposes of subdivision (j) "as of the date on which the process was accepted, refused, or returned as unclaimed".[12]

H.R. 7154 adopts a policy of limiting the time to effect service. It provides that if a summons and complaint have not been served within 120 days of the filing of the complaint and the plaintiff fails to show "good cause" for not completing service within that time, then the court must dismiss the action as to the unserved defendant. H.R. 7154 ensures that a plaintiff will be notified of an attempt to dismiss the action. If dismissal for failure to serve is raised by the court upon its own motion, the legislation requires that the court provide notice to the plaintiff. If dismissal is sought by someone else, Rule 5(a) of the Federal Rules of Civil Procedure requires that the motion be served upon the plaintiff.

Like proposed subsection (j), H.R. 7154 provides that a dismissal for failure to serve within 120 days shall be "without prejudice". Proposed subsection (j) was criticized by some for ambiguity because, it was argued, neither the text of subsection (j) nor the Advisory Committee Note indicated whether a dismissal without prejudice would toll a statute of limitation. *See* House Report 97–662, at 3–4 (1982). The problem would arise when a plaintiff files the complaint within the applicable statute of limitation period but does not effect service within 120 days. If the statute of limitation period expires during that period, and if the plaintiff's action is dismissed "without prejudice", can the plaintiff refile the complaint and maintain the action? The answer depends upon how the statute of limitation is tolled.[13]

If the law provides that the statute of limitation is tolled by filing and service of the complaint, then a dismissal under H.R. 7154 for failure to serve within the 120 days would, by the terms of the law controlling the tolling bar the plaintiff from later maintaining the cause of action.[14] If the law provides that the statute of limitation is tolled by filing alone, then the status of the plaintiff's cause of action turns upon the plaintiff's diligence. If the plaintiff has not been diligent, the court will dismiss the complaint for failure to serve within 120 days, and the plaintiff will be barred from later maintaining the cause of action because the statute of limitation has run. A dismissal without prejudice does not confer upon the plaintiff any rights that the plaintiff does otherwise possess and leaves a plaintiff whose action has been dismissed in the same position as if the action had never been filed.[15] If, on the other hand, the plaintiff has made reasonable efforts to effect service, then the plaintiff can move under Rule 6(b) to enlarge the time within which to serve or can oppose dismissal for failure to serve. A court would undoubtedly permit such a plaintiff additional time within which to effect service. Thus, a diligent plaintiff can preserve the cause of action. This result is consistent with the policy behind the time limit for service and with statutes of limitation, both of which are designed to encourage prompt movement of civil actions in the federal courts.

6. *Conforming and clarifying subsections (d)(4) and (5)*

Current subsections (d)(4) and (5) prescribe which persons must be served in cases where an action is brought against the United States or an officer or agency of the United States. Under subsection (d)(4), where the United States is the named defendant, service must be made as follows: (1) personal service upon the United States attorney, an assistant United States attorney, or a designated clerical employee of the United States attorney in the district in which the action is brought; (2) registered or certified mail service to the Attorney General of the United States in Washington, D.C.; and (3) registered or certified mail service to the appropriate officer or agency if the action attacks an order of that officer or agency but does not name the officer or agency as a defendant. Under subsection (d)(5), where an officer or agency of the United States is named as a defendant, service must be made as in subsection (d)(4), except that personal service upon the officer or agency involved is required.[16]

The time limit for effecting service in H.R. 7154 would present significant difficulty to a plaintiff who has to arrange for personal service upon an officer or agency that may be thousands of miles away. There is little reason to require different types of service when the officer or agency is named as a party, and H.R. 7154 therefore conforms the manner of service under subsection (d)(5) to the manner of service under subsection (d)(4).

Section-By-Section Analysis

Section 1

Section 1 provides that the short title of the bill is the "Federal Rules of Civil Procedure Amendments Act of 1982".

Section 2

Section 2 of the bill consists of 7 numbered paragraphs, each amending a different part of Rule 4 of the Federal Rules of Civil Procedure.

Paragraph (1) deletes the requirement in present Rule 4(a) that a summons be delivered for service to the marshal or other person authorized to serve it. As amended by the legislation, Rule 4(a) provides that the summons be delivered to "the plaintiff or the plaintiff's attorney, who shall be responsible for prompt service of the summons and complaint". This change effectuates the policy proposed by the Supreme Court. See Appendix II, at — (Advisory Committee Note).

Paragraph (2) amends current Rule 4(c), which deals with the service of process. New Rule 4(c)(1) requires that all process, other than a subpoena or a summons and complaint, be served by the Marshals Service or by a person especially appointed for that purpose. Thus, the Marshals Service or persons specially appointed will continue to serve all process other than subpoenas and summonses and complaints, a policy identical to that proposed by the Supreme Court. See Appendix II, at 8 (Report of the Judicial Conference Committee on Rules of Practice and Procedure). The service of subpoenas is governed by Rule 45,[17] and the service of summonses and complaints is governed by new Rule 4(c)(2).

New Rule 4(c)(2)(A) sets forth the general rule that summonses and complaints shall be served by someone who is at least 18 years old and not a party to the action or proceeding. This is consistent with the Court's proposal. Appendix II, at 16 (Advisory Committee Note). Subparagraphs (B) and (C) of new Rule 4(c)(2) set forth exceptions to this general rule.

Subparagraph (B) sets forth 3 exceptions to the general rule. First, subparagraph (B)(i) requires the Marshals Service (or someone specially appointed by the court) to serve summonses and complaints on behalf of a party proceeding in forma pauperis or a seaman authorized to proceed under 28 U.S.C. 1916. This is identical to the Supreme Court's proposal. *See* Appendix II, at 3 (text of proposed rule), 16 (Advisory Committee Note). Second, subparagraph (B)(ii) requires the Marshals Service (or someone specially appointed by the court) to serve a summons and complaint when the court orders the marshals to do so in order properly to effect service in that particular action.[18] This, except for nonsubstantive changes in phrasing, is identical to the Supreme Court's proposal. See Appendix II, at 3 (text of proposed rule), 16 (Advisory Committee Note).

Subparagraph (C) of new Rule 4(c)(2) provides 2 exceptions to the general rule of service by a nonparty adult. These exceptions apply only when the summons and complaint is to be served upon persons described in Rule 4(d)(1) (certain individuals) or Rule 4(d)(3) (organizations).[19] First, subparagraph (C)(i) permits service of a summons and complaint in a manner authorized by the law of the state in which the court sits. This restates the option to follow local law currently found in Rule 4(d)(7) and would authorize service by mail if the state law so allowed. The method of mail service in that instance would, of course, be the method permitted by state law.

Second, subparagraph (C)(ii) permits service of a summons and complaint by regular mail. The sender must send to the defendant, by first-class mail, postage prepaid, a copy of the summons and complaint, together with 2 copies of a notice and acknowledgment of receipt of summons and complaint form and a postage prepaid return envelope addressed to the sender. If a copy of the notice and acknowledgment form is not received by the sender within 20 days after the date of mailing, then service must be made under Rule 4(c)(2)(A) or (B) (i.e., by a nonparty adult or, if the person qualifies,[20] by personnel of the Marshals Service or a person specially appointed by the court) in the manner prescribed by Rule 4(d)(1) or (3) (i.e., personal or substituted service).

New Rule 4(c)(2)(D) permits a court to penalize a person who avoids service by mail. It authorizes the court to order a person who does not return the notice and acknowledgment form within 20 days after mailing to pay the costs of service, unless that person can show good cause for failing to return the form. The purpose of this provision is to encourage the prompt return of the form so that the action can move forward without unnecessary delay. Fairness requires that a person who causes another additional and unnecessary expense in effecting service ought to reimburse the party who was forced to bear the additional expense.

Subparagraph (E) of Rule 4(c)(2) requires that the notice and acknowledgment form described in new Rule 4(c)(2)(C)(ii) be executed under oath or affirmation. This provision tracks the language of 28 U.S.C. 1746, which permits the use of unsworn declarations under penalty of perjury whenever an oath or affirmation is required. Statements made under penalty of perjury are subject to 18 U.S.C. 1621(2), which provides felony penalties for someone who "willfully subscribes as true any material matter which he does not believe to be true". The requirement that the form be executed under oath or affirmation is intended to encourage truthful submissions to the court, as the information contained in the form is important to the parties.[21]

New Rule 4(c)(3) authorizes the court freely to make special appointments to serve summonses and complaints under Rule 4(c)(2)(B) and all other process under Rule 4(c)(1). This carries forward the policy of present Rule 4(c).

Paragraph (3) of section 2 of the bill makes a non-substantive change in the caption of Rule 4(d) in order to reflect more accurately the provisions of Rule 4(d). Paragraph (3) also deletes a provision on service of a summons and complaint pursuant to state law. This provision is redundant in view of new Rule 4(c)(2)(C)(i).

Paragraph (4) of section 2 of the bill conforms Rule 4(d)(5) to present Rule 4(d)(4). Rule 4(d)(5) is amended to provide that service upon a named defendant agency or officer of the United States shall be made by "sending" a copy of the summons and complaint "by registered or certified mail" to the defendant.[22] Rule 4(d)(5) currently provides for service by "delivering" the copies to the defendant, but 28 U.S.C. 1391(e) authorizes delivery upon a defendant agency or officer outside of the district in which the action is brought by means of certified mail. Hence, the change is not a marked departure from current practice.

Paragraph (5) of section 2 of the bill amends the caption of Rule 4(e) in order to describe subdivision (e) more accurately.

Paragraph (6) of section 2 of the bill amends Rule 4(g), which deals with return of service. Present rule 4(g) is not changed except to provide that, if service is made pursuant to the new system of mail service (Rule 4(c)(2)(C)(ii)), the plaintiff or the plaintiff's attorney must file the court the signed acknowledgment form returned by the person served.

Paragraph (7) of section 2 of the bill adds new subsection (j) to provide a time limitation for the service of a summons and complaint. New Rule 4(j) retains the Supreme Court's requirement that a summons and complaint be served within 120 days of the filing of the complaint. See Appendix II, at 18 (Advisory Committee Note).[23] The plaintiff must be notified of an effort or intention to dismiss the action. This notification is mandated by subsection (j) if the dismissal is being raised on the court's own initiative and will be provided pursuant to Rule 5 (which requires service of motions upon the adverse party) if the dismissal is sought by someone else.[24] The plaintiff may move under Rule 6(b) to enlarge the time period. See Appendix II, at Id. (Advisory Committee Note). If service is not made within the time period or enlarged time period, however, and if the plaintiff fails to show "good cause" for not completing service, then the court must dismiss the action as to the unserved defendant. The dismissal is "without prejudice". The term "without prejudice" means that the dismissal does not constitute an adjudication of the merits of the complaint. A dismissal "without prejudice" leaves a plaintiff whose action has been dismissed in the position in which that person would have been if the action had never been filed.

Section 3

Section 3 of the bill amends the Appendix of Forms at the end of the Federal Rules of Civil Procedure by adding a new form 18A, "Notice and Acknowledgment for Service by Mail". This new form is required by new Rule 4(c)(2)(C)(ii), which requires that the notice and acknowledgment form used with service by regular mail conform substantially to Form 18A.

Form 18A as set forth in section 3 of the bill is modeled upon a form used in California.[25] It contains 2 parts. The first part is a notice to the person being served that tells that person that the enclosed summons and complaint is being served pursuant to Rule 4(c)(2)(C)(ii); advises that person to sign and date the acknowledgment form and indicate the authority to receive service if the person served is not the party to the action (e.g., the person served is an officer of the organization being served); and warns that failure to return the form to the sender within 20 days may result in the court ordering the party being served to pay the expenses involved in effecting service. The notice also warns that if the complaint is not responded to within 20 days, a default judgment can be entered against the party being served. The notice is dated under penalty of perjury by the plaintiff or the plaintiff's attorney.[26]

The second part of the form contains the acknowledgment of receipt of the summons and complaint. The person served must declare on this part of the form, under penalty of perjury, the date and place of service and the person's authority to receive service.

Section 4

Section 4 of the bill provides that the changes in Rule 4 made by H.R. 7154 will take effect 45 days after enactment, thereby giving the bench and bar, as well as other interested persons and organizations (such as the Marshals Service), an opportunity to prepare to implement the changes made by the legislation. The delayed effective date means that service of process issued before the effective date will be made in accordance with current Rule 4. Accordingly, all process in the hands of the Marshals Service prior to the effective date will be served by the Marshals Service under the present rule.

Section 5

Section 5 of the bill provides that the amendments to Rule 4 proposed by the Supreme Court (whose effective date was postponed by Public Law 97–227) shall not take effect. This is necessary because under Public Law 97–227 the proposed amendments will take effect on October 1, 1983.

1 The drafting of the rules and amendments is actually done by a committee of the Judicial Conference of the United States. In the case of the Federal Rules of Civil Procedure, the initial draft is prepared by the Advisory Committee on Civil Rules. The Advisory Committee's draft is then reviewed by the Committee on Rules of Practice and Procedure, which must give its approval to the draft. Any draft approved by that committee is forwarded to the Judicial Conference. If the Judicial Conference approves the draft, it forwards the draft to the Supreme Court. The Judicial Conference's role in the rule-making process is defined by 28 U.S.C. 331.

For background information about how the Judicial Conference committees operate, see Wright, "Procedural Reform: Its Limitation and Its Future," 1 Ga.L.Rev. 563, 565–66 (1967) (civil rules); statement of United States District Judge Roszel C. Thomsen, Hearings on Proposed Amendments to the Federal Rules of Criminal Procedure Before the Subcommittee on Criminal Justice of the House Committee on the Judiciary, 93d Cong., 2d Sess. at 25 (1974) (criminal rules); statement of United States Circuit Judge J. Edward Lumbard, id. at 203 (criminal rules); J. Weinstein, Reform of Federal Court Rulemaking Procedure (1977); Weinstein, "Reform of Federal Rulemaking Procedures," 76 Colum.L.Rev. 905 (1976).

2 All of the other amendments, including all of the proposed amendments to the Federal Rules of Criminal Procedure and the Rules and Forms Governing Proceedings in the United States District Courts under sections 2254 and 2255 of Title 28, United States Code, took effect on August 1, 1982, as scheduled.

3 The President has urged Congress to act promptly. See President's Statement on Signing H.R. 6663 into Law, 18 Weekly Comp. of Pres. Doc. 982 (August 2, 1982).

4 Where service of a summons is to be made upon a party who is neither an inhabitant of, nor found within, the state where the district court sits, subsection (e) authorizes service under a state statute or rule of court that provides for service upon such a party. This would authorize mail service if the state statute or rule of court provided for service by mail.

5 The Court's proposal authorized service by the Marshals Service in other situations. This authority, however, was not seen as thwarting the underlying policy of limiting the use of marshals. *See* Appendix II, at 16, 17 (Advisory Committee Note).

6 Appendix I, at 2 (letter of Assistant Attorney General Robert A. McConnell).

7 The provisions of H.R. 7154 conflict with 28 U.S.C. 569(b) because the latter is a broader command to marshals to serve all federal court process. As a later statutory enactment, however, H.R. 7154 supersedes 28 U.S.C. 569(b), thereby achieving the goal of reducing the role of marshals.

8 Proposed Rule 4(d)(8) provided that "Service . . . shall not be the basis for the entry of a default or a judgment by default unless the record contains a return receipt showing acceptance by the defendant or a returned envelope showing refusal of the process by the defendant." This provision reflects a desire to preclude default judgments on unclaimed mail. See Appendix II, at 7 (Report of the Committee on Rules of Practice and Procedure).

The interpretation of Rule 4(d)(8) to require a refusal of delivery in order to have a basis for a default judgment, while undoubtedly the interpretation intended and the interpretation that reaches the fairest result, may not be the only possible interpretation. Since a default judgment can be entered for defendant's failure to respond to the complaint once defendant has been served and the time to answer the complaint has run, it can be argued that a default judgment can be obtained where the mail was unclaimed because proposed subsection (j), which authorized dismissal of a complaint not served within 120 days, provided that mail service would be deemed made "on the date on which the process was accepted, refused, or *returned as unclaimed* " (emphasis added).

9 *See* p. 15 infra.

10 Proponents of the California system of mail service, in particular, saw no reason to supplant California's proven method of mail service with a certified mail service that they believed likely to result in default judgments without actual notice to defendants. See House Report No. 97–662, at 3 (1982).

11 The parties may, of course, stipulate to service, as is frequently done now.

12 While return of the letter as unclaimed was deemed service for the purpose of determining whether the plaintiff's action could be dismissed, return of the letter as unclaimed was not service for the

purpose of entry of a default judgment against the defendant. See note 8 supra.

13 The law governing the tolling of a statute of limitation depends upon the type of civil action involved. In a diversity action, state law governs tolling. *Walker v. Armco Steel Corp.*, 446 U.S. 740 (1980). In *Walker*, plaintiff had filed his complaint and thereby commenced the action under Rule 3 of the Federal Rules of Civil Procedure within the statutory period. He did not, however, serve the summons and complaint until after the statutory period had run. The Court held that state law (which required both filing and service within the statutory period) governed, barring plaintiff's action.

In the federal question action, the courts of appeals have generally held that Rule 3 governs, so that the filing of the complaint tolls a statute of limitation. *United States v. Wahl*, 538 F.2d 285 (6th Cir. 1978); *Windbrooke Dev. Co. v. Environmental Enterprises Inc. of Fla.*, 524 F.2d 461 (5th Cir. 1975); *Metropolitan Paving Co. v. International Union of Operating Engineers*, 439 F.2d 300 (10th Cir. 1971); *Moore Co. v. Sid Richardson Carbon & Gasoline Co.*, 347 F.2d 921 (8th Cir.), cert. denied, 383 U.S. 925, reh. denied, 384 U.S. 914 (1965); *Hoffman v. Halden*, 268 F.2d 280 (9th Cir. 1959). The continued validity of this line of cases, however, must be questioned in light of the *Walker* case, even though the Court in that case expressly reserved judgment about federal question actions, *see Walker v. Armco Steel Corp.*, 446 U.S. 741, 751 n.11 (1980).

14 The same result obtains even if service occurs within the 120 day period, if the service occurs after the statute of limitation has run.

15 See p. 19 infra.

16 See p. 17 infra.

17 Rule 45(c) provides that "A subpoena may be served by the marshal, by his deputy, or by any other person who is not a party and is not less than 18 years of age."

18 Some litigators have voiced concern that there may be situations in which personal service by someone other than a member of the Marshals Service may present a risk of injury to the person attempting to make the service. For example, a hostile defendant may have a history of injuring persons attempting to serve process. Federal judges undoubtedly will consider the risk of harm to private persons who would be making personal service when deciding whether to order the Marshals Service to make service under Rule 4(c)(2)(B)(iii).

19 The methods of service authorized by Rule 4(c)(2)(C) may be invoked by any person seeking to effect service. Thus, a nonparty adult who receives the summons and complaint for service under Rule 4(c)(1) may serve them personally or by mail in the manner authorized by Rule 4(c)(2)(C)(ii). Similarly, the Marshals Service may utilize the mail service authorized by Rule 4(c)(2)(C)(ii) when serving a summons and complaint under Rule 4(c)(2)(B)(i)(iii). When serving a summons and complaint under Rule 4(c)(2)(B)(ii), however, the Marshals Service must serve in the manner set forth in the court's order. If no particular manner of service is specified, then the Marshals Service may utilize Rule 4(c)(2)(C)(ii). It would not seem to be appropriate, however, for the Marshals Service to utilize Rule 4(c)(2)(C)(ii) in a situation where a previous attempt to serve by mail failed. Thus, it would not seem to be appropriate for the Marshals Service to attempt service by regular mail when serving a summons and complaint on behalf of a plaintiff who is proceeding in forma pauperis if that plaintiff previously attempted unsuccessfully to serve the defendant by mail.

20 To obtain service by personnel of the Marshals Service or someone specially appointed by the court, a plaintiff who has unsuccessfully attempted mail service under Rule 4(c)(2)(C)(ii) must meet the conditions of Rule 4(c)(2)(B)—for example, the plaintiff must be proceeding *in forma pauperis*.

21 For example, the sender must state the date of mailing on the form. If the form is not returned to the sender within 20 days of that date, then the plaintiff must serve the defendant in another manner and the defendant may be liable for the costs of such service. Thus, a defendant would suffer the consequences of a misstatement about the date of mailing.

22 See p. 12 supra.

23 The 120 day period begins to run upon the filing of each complaint. Thus, where a defendant files a cross-claim against the plaintiff, the 120 day period begins to run upon the filing of the cross-complaint, not upon the filing of the plaintiff's complaint initiating the action.

24 The person who may move to dismiss can be the putative defendant (i.e., the person named as defendant in the complaint filed with the court) or, in multi-party actions, another party to the action. (If the putative defendant moves to dismiss and the failure to effect service is due to that person's evasion of service, a court should not dismiss because the plaintiff has "good cause" for not completing service.)

25 See Cal.Civ.Pro. § 415.30 (West 1973).

26 See p. 16 supra.

CONVENTIONS

CONVENTION ON THE SERVICE ABROAD OF JUDICIAL AND EXTRAJUDICIAL DOCUMENTS IN CIVIL OR COMMERCIAL MATTERS

The States signatory to the present Convention,

Desiring to create appropriate means to ensure that judicial and extrajudicial documents to be served abroad shall be brought to the notice of the addressee in sufficient time,

Desiring to improve the organisation of mutual judicial assistance for that purpose by simplifying and expediting the procedure,

Have resolved to conclude a Convention to this effect and have agreed upon the following provisions:

Article 1

The present Convention shall apply in all cases, in civil or commercial matters, where there is occasion to transmit a judicial or extrajudicial document for service abroad.

This Convention shall not apply where the address of the person to be served with the document is not known.

CHAPTER I—JUDICIAL DOCUMENTS

Article 2

Each contracting State shall designate a Central Authority which will undertake to receive requests for service coming from other contracting States and to proceed in conformity with the provisions of articles 3 to 6.

Each State shall organise the Central Authority in conformity with its own law.

Article 3

The authority or judicial officer competent under the law of the State in which the documents originate shall forward to the Central Authority of the State addressed a request conforming to the model annexed to the present Convention, without any requirement of legalisation or other equivalent formality.

The document to be served or a copy thereof shall be annexed to the request. The request and the document shall both be furnished in duplicate.

Article 4

If the Central Authority considers that the request does not comply with the provisions of the present Convention it shall promptly inform the applicant and specify its objections to the request.

Article 5

The Central Authority of the State addressed shall itself serve the document or shall arrange to have it served by an appropriate agency, either—

(a) by a method prescribed by its internal law for the service of documents in domestic actions upon persons who are within its territory, or

(b) by a particular method requested by the applicant, unless such a method is incompatible with the law of the State addressed.

Subject to sub-paragraph (b) of the first paragraph of this article, the document may always be served by delivery to an addressee who accepts it voluntarily.

If the document is to be served under the first paragraph above, the Central Authority may require the document to be written in, or translated into, the official language or one of the official languages of the State addressed.

That part of the request, in the form attached to the present Convention, which contains a summary of the document to be served, shall be served with the document.

Article 6

The Central Authority of the State addressed or any authority which it may have designated for that purpose, shall complete a certificate in the form of the model annexed to the present Convention.

The certificate shall state that the document has been served and shall include the method, the place and the date of service and the person to whom the document was delivered. If the document has not been served, the certificate shall set out the reasons which have prevented service.

The applicant may require that a certificate not completed by a Central Authority or by a judicial authority shall be countersigned by one of these authorities.

The certificate shall be forwarded directly to the applicant.

Article 7

The standard terms in the model annexed to the present Convention shall in all cases be written either in French or in English. They may also be written in the official language, or in one of the official languages, of the State in which the documents originate.

The corresponding blanks shall be completed either in the language of the State addressed or in French or in English.

Article 8

Each contracting State shall be free to effect service of judicial documents upon persons abroad, without application of any compulsion, directly through its diplomatic or consular agents.

Any State may declare that it is opposed to such service within its territory, unless the document is to be served upon a national of the State in which the documents originate.

Article 9

Each contracting State shall be free, in addition, to use consular channels to forward documents, for the purpose of service, to those authorities of another contracting State which are designated by the latter for this purpose.

Each contracting State may, if exceptional circumstances so require, use diplomatic channels for the same purpose.

Article 10

Provided the State of destination does not object, the present Convention shall not interfere with—

(a) the freedom to send judicial documents, by postal channels, directly to persons abroad,

(b) the freedom of judicial officers, officials or other competent persons of the State of origin to effect service of judicial documents directly through the judicial officers, officials or other competent persons of the State of destination,

(c) the freedom of any person interested in a judicial proceeding to effect service of judicial documents directly through the judicial officers, officials or other competent persons of the State of destination.

Article 11

The present Convention shall not prevent two or more contracting States from agreeing to permit, for the purpose of service of judicial documents, channels of transmission other than those provided for in the preceding articles and, in particular, direct communication between their respective authorities.

Article 12

The service of judicial documents coming from a contracting State shall not give rise to any payment or reimbursement of taxes or costs for the services rendered by the State addressed.

The applicant shall pay or reimburse the costs occasioned by—

(a) the employment of a judicial officer or of a person competent under the law of the State of destination,

(b) the use of a particular method of service.

Article 13

Where a request for service complies with the terms of the present Convention, the State addressed may refuse to comply therewith only if it deems that compliance would infringe its sovereignty or security.

It may not refuse to comply solely on the ground that, under its internal law, it claims exclusive jurisdiction over the subject-matter of the action or that its internal law would not permit the action upon which the application is based.

The Central Authority shall, in case of refusal, promptly inform the applicant and state the reasons for the refusal.

Article 14

Difficulties which may arise in connection with the transmission of judicial documents for service shall be settled through diplomatic channels.

Article 15

Where a writ of summons or an equivalent document had to be transmitted abroad for the purpose of service, under the provisions of the present Convention, and the defendant has not appeared, judgment shall not be given until it is established that—

(a) the document was served by a method prescribed by the internal law of the State addressed for the service of documents in domestic actions upon persons who are within its territory, or

(b) the document was actually delivered to the defendant or to his residence by another method provided for by this Convention,

and that in either of these cases the service or the delivery was effected in sufficient time to enable the defendant to defend.

Each contracting State shall be free to declare that the judge, notwithstanding the provisions of the first paragraph of this article, may give judgment even if no certificate of service or delivery has been received, if all the following conditions are fulfilled—

(a) the document was transmitted by one of the methods provided for in this Convention,

(b) a period of time of not less than six months, considered adequate by the judge in the particular case, has elapsed since the date of the transmission of the document,

(c) no certificate of any kind has been received, even though every reasonable effort has been made to obtain it through the competent authorities of the State addressed.

Notwithstanding the provisions of the preceding paragraphs the judge may order, in case of urgency, any provisional or protective measures.

Article 16

When a writ of summons or an equivalent document had to be transmitted abroad for the purpose of service, under the provisions of the present Convention, and a judgment has been entered against a defendant who has not appeared, the judge shall have the power to relieve the defendant from the effects of the expiration of the time for appeal from the judgment if the following conditions are fulfilled—

(a) the defendant, without any fault on his part, did not have knowledge of the document in sufficient time to defend, or knowledge of the judgment in sufficient time to appeal, and

(b) the defendant has disclosed a *prima facie* defense to the action on the merits.

An application for relief may be filed only within a reasonable time after the defendant has knowledge of the judgment.

Each contracting State may declare that the application will not be entertained if it is filed after the expiration of a time to be stated in the declaration, but which shall in no case be less than one year following the date of the judgment.

This article shall not apply to judgments concerning status or capacity of persons.

CHAPTER II—EXTRAJUDICIAL DOCUMENTS

Article 17

Extrajudicial documents emanating from authorities and judicial officers of a contracting State may be transmitted for the purpose of service in another contracting State by the methods and under the provisions of the present Convention.

CHAPTER III—GENERAL CLAUSES

Article 18

Each contracting State may designate other authorities in addition to the Central Authority and shall determine the extent of their competence.

The applicant shall, however, in all cases, have the right to address a request directly to the Central Authority.

Federal States shall be free to designate more than one Central Authority.

Article 19

To the extent that the internal law of a contracting State permits methods of transmission, other than those provided for in the preceding articles, of documents coming from abroad, for service within its territory, the present Convention shall not affect such provisions.

Article 20

The present Convention shall not prevent an agreement between any two or more contracting States to dispense with—

(a) the necessity for duplicate copies of transmitted documents as required by the second paragraph of article 3,

(b) the language requirements of the third paragraph of article 5 and article 7,

(c) the provisions of the fourth paragraph of article 5,

(d) the provisions of the second paragraph of article 12.

Article 21

Each contracting State shall, at the time of the deposit of its instrument of ratification or accession, or at a later date, inform the Ministry of Foreign Affairs of the Netherlands of the following—

(a) the designation of authorities, pursuant to articles 2 and 18,

(b) the designation of the authority competent to complete the certificate pursuant to article 6,

(c) the designation of the authority competent to receive documents transmitted by consular channels, pursuant to article 9.

Each contracting State shall similarly inform the Ministry, where appropriate, of—

(a) opposition to the use of methods of transmission pursuant to articles 8 and 10,

(b) declarations pursuant to the second paragraph of article 15 and the third paragraph of article 16,

(c) all modifications of the above designations, oppositions and declarations.

Article 22

Where Parties to the present Convention are also Parties to one or both of the Conventions on civil procedure signed at The Hague on 17th July 1905 [99 BFSP 990], and on 1st March 1954 [286 UNTS 265], this Convention shall replace as between them articles 1 to 7 of the earlier Conventions.

Article 23

The present Convention shall not affect the application of article 23 of the Convention on civil procedure signed at The Hague on 17th July 1905, or of article 24 of the Convention on civil procedure signed at The Hague on 1st March 1954.

These articles shall, however, apply only if methods of communication, identical to those provided for in these Conventions, are used.

Article 24

Supplementary agreements between parties to the Conventions of 1905 and 1954 shall be considered as equally applicable to the present Convention, unless the Parties have otherwise agreed.

Article 25

Without prejudice to the provisions of articles 22 and 24, the present Convention shall not derogate from Conventions containing provisions on the matters governed by this Convention to which the contracting States are, or shall become, Parties.

Article 26

The present Convention shall be open for signature by the States represented at the Tenth Session of the Hague Conference on Private International Law.

It shall be ratified, and the instruments of ratification shall be deposited with the Ministry of Foreign Affairs of the Netherlands.

Article 27

The present Convention shall enter into force on the sixtieth day after the deposit of the third instrument of ratification referred to in the second paragraph of article 26.

The Convention shall enter into force for each signatory State which ratifies subsequently on the sixtieth day after the deposit of its instrument of ratification.

Article 28

Any State not represented at the Tenth Session of the Hague Conference on Private International Law may accede to the present Convention after it has entered into force in accordance with the first paragraph of article 27. The instrument of accession shall be deposited with the Ministry of Foreign Affairs of the Netherlands.

The Convention shall enter into force for such a State in the absence of any objection from a State, which has ratified the Convention before such deposit, notified to the Ministry of Foreign Affairs of the Netherlands within a period of six months after the date on which the said Ministry has notified it of such accession.

In the absence of any such objection, the Convention shall enter into force for the acceding State on the first day of the month following the expiration of the last of the periods referred to in the preceding paragraph.

Article 29

Any State may, at the time of signature, ratification or accession, declare that the present Convention shall extend to all the territories for the international relations of which it is responsible, or to one or more of them. Such a declaration shall take effect on the date of entry into force of the Convention for the State concerned.

At any time thereafter, such extensions shall be notified to the Ministry of Foreign Affairs of the Netherlands.

The Convention shall enter into force for the territories mentioned in such an extension on the sixtieth day after the notification referred to in the preceding paragraph.

Article 30

The present Convention shall remain in force for five years from the date of its entry into force in accordance with the first paragraph of article 27, even for States which have ratified it or acceded to it subsequently.

If there has been no denunciation, it shall be renewed tacitly every five years.

Any denunciation shall be notified to the Ministry of Foreign Affairs of the Netherlands at least six months before the end of the five year period.

It may be limited to certain of the territories to which the Convention applies.

The denunciation shall have effect only as regards the State which has notified it. The Convention shall remain in force for the other contracting States.

Article 31

The Ministry of Foreign Affairs of the Netherlands shall give notice to the States referred to in article 26, and to the States which have acceded in accordance with article 28, of the following—

(a) the signatures and ratifications referred to in article 26;

(b) the date on which the present Convention enters into force in accordance with the first paragraph of article 27;

(c) the accessions referred to in article 28 and the dates on which they take effect;

(d) the extensions referred to in article 29 and the dates on which they take effect;

(e) the designations, oppositions and declarations referred to in article 21;

(f) the denunciations referred to in the third paragraph of article 30.

IN WITNESS WHEREOF the undersigned, being duly authorised thereto, have signed the present Convention.

DONE at The Hague, on the 15th day of November, 1965, in the English and French languages, both texts being equally authentic, in a single copy which shall be deposited in the archives of the Government of the Netherlands, and of which a certified copy shall be sent, through the diplomatic channel, to each of The States represented at the Tenth Session of the Hague Conference on Private International Law.

[Signatures omitted.]

Service of Documents Convention

ANNEX TO THE CONVENTION

Forms *

* These forms may be obtained from the Offices of United States Marshals.

REQUEST
FOR SERVICE ABROAD OF JUDICIAL OR EXTRAJUDICIAL DOCUMENTS

Convention on the service abroad of judicial and extra-judicial documents in civil or commercial matters, signed at The Hague, November 15, 1965.

Identity and address of the applicant

Address of receiving authority

The undersigned applicant has the honour to transmit—in duplicate—the documents listed below and, in conformity with article 5 of the above-mentioned Convention, requests prompt service of one copy thereof on the addressee, i.e., (identity and address) ....

....

(*a*) in accordance with the provisions of sub-paragraph (*a*) of the first paragraph of article 5 of the Convention*.

(*b*) in accordance with the following particular method (sub-paragraph (*b*) of the first paragraph of article 5)*: ....

....

....

(*c*) by delivery to the addressee, if he accepts it voluntarily (second paragraph of article 5)*.

The authority is requested to return or to have returned to the applicant a copy of the documents—and of the annexes*—with a certificate as provided on the reverse side.

List of documents

....

....

....

....

....

....

Done at ....,

the ....

....

....

Signature and/or stamp.

* Delete if inappropriate.

Reverse of the request

CERTIFICATE

The undersigned authority has the honour to certify, in conformity with article 6 of the Convention,

1) that the document has been served *

— the (date) ....

— at (place, street, number) ....

....

— in one of the following methods authorised by article 5—

(*a*) in accordance with the provisions of sub-paragraph (*a*) of the first paragraph of article 5 of the Convention*.

(*b*) in accordance with the following particular method *: ....

....

(*c*) by delivery to the addressee, who accepted it voluntarily*.

The documents referred to in the request have been delivered to:

—(identity and description of person) ....

....

—relationship to the addressee (family, business or other) .

....

2) that the document has not been served, by reason of the following facts*:

....

....

....

In conformity with the second paragraph of article 12 of the Convention, the applicant is requested to pay or reimburse the expenses detailed in the attached statement *.

Annexes

Documents returned: ....

....

....

In appropriate cases, documents establishing the service:

....

....

Done at ....,

the ....

Signature and/or stamp.

*Delete if inappropriate.

SUMMARY OF THE DOCUMENT TO BE SERVED

Convention on the service abroad of judicial and extrajudicial documents in civil or commercial matters, signed at The Hague, the 15th of November 1965.

(article 5, fourth paragraph)

Name and address of the requesting authority: ....

....

....

Particulars of the parties*:

....

....

....

JUDICIAL DOCUMENT **

Nature and purpose of the document:

....

....

....

Nature and purpose of the proceedings and, where appropriate, the amount in dispute: ....

Date and place for entering appearance**:

....

....

Court which has given judgment **:

. . . .

. . . .

Date of judgment **: . . . .

Time limits stated in the document **:

. . . .

. . . .

EXTRAJUDICIAL DOCUMENT **

Nature and purpose of the document:

. . . .

. . . .

. . . .

Time limits stated in the document **:

. . . .

. . . .

. . . .

* If appropriate, identity and address of the person interested in the transmission of the document.

** Delete if inappropriate.

Convention on the service abroad of judicial and extrajudicial documents in civil or commercial matters. Done at The Hague November 15, 1965; entered into force for the United States February 10, 1969. 20 UST 361; TIAS 6638; 658 UNTS 163. States which are parties:

Antigua and Barbuda [1]
Barbados [1a]
Belgium [2]
Botswana [2a2]
Canada [3]
China [3a]
Cyprus [3b]
Czech Republic [3c]
Denmark [4]
Egypt [5]
Estonia [5a]
Finland [6]
France [7]
Federal Republic of Germany [7a]
Greece [7b]
Ireland [7c]
Israel [8]
Italy [8a]
Japan [9]
Latvia
Luxembourg [9a]
Malawi [10]
Netherlands [10a]
Norway [11]
Pakistan [11a]
Poland [11b]
Portugal [11c]
Seychelles [11d]
Slovak Republic [11e]
Spain [11f]
Sweden [12]
Switzerland [12a]
Turkey [13]
United Kingdom [14]
United States [15]
Venezuela [16]

1 *Notification in conformity with Article 31 of the Convention*

By note of 1 May 1985, received at the Ministry of Foreign Affairs of the Kingdom of the Netherlands on 17 May 1985, the Government of Antigua and Barbuda informed the Ministry of Foreign Affairs it does consider itself bound by the abovementioned Convention, declared applicable to Antigua by the Government of the United Kingdom of Great Britain and Northern Ireland on 20 May 1970.

Notification in conformity with Article 31, letter e, of the Convention

The Government of Antigua and Barbuda informed the Ministry of Foreign Affairs of the Kingdom of the Netherlands by Note of 2 May 1986 that as the authority referred to in Article 21 has been designated:

The Registrar-Eastern Caribbean Supreme Court.

Notification in conformity with Article 31, letter e, of the Convention

Rectification of the Notifications *Judicial and Extrajudicial Documents Nos. 2 and 3/ 1987* of 14 July 1987 and 28 August 1987.

The competent authorities under Article 21 of the above-mentioned Convention, designated by the Government of Antigua and Barbuda, are:

a) The Governor-General, Antigua and Barbuda;

b) The Registrar of the High Court of Antigua and Barbuda, St. John's, Antigua.

The Hague, 18 November 1987

Notification in conformity with Article 31, paragraph e, of the Convention

Referring to the extension of the Convention in 1970 to Hong Kong and the designation of the Central Authority for Hong Kong the Government of the United Kingdom of Great Britain and Northern Ireland informed the Ministry of Foreign Affairs of the Kingdom of the Netherlands by letter of 3 May 1984 that "the Colonial Secretary of Hong Kong" has been re-designated as "the Chief Secretary of Hong Kong". Requests for documents to be served in Hong Kong should be addressed accordingly.

1a With the following declaration:

"The Government of Barbados has designated the Registrar of the Supreme Court of Barbados as the Central Authority for the purposes of Articles 2 and 18, in accordance with the provisions of Article 21 of the Convention."

2 With the following declaration:

"**1.** In conformity with the first paragraph of Article 2 of the Convention, the Ministry of Justice, Administration de la Législation, Place Poelaert, 4, 1.000 Brussels is designated as the Central Authority;

"**2.** The Ministry of Justice is also designated as the competent authority to receive documents forwarded by the channels provided for in the first paragraph of Article 9 of the Convention;

"**3.** The Belgian Government is opposed to use being made within its territory of the freedom to effect service provided for in the first paragraph of Article 8;

"**4.** The Belgian Government declares that it will avail itself of the provision contained in the second paragraph of Article 15;

"**5.** In conformity with the third paragraph of Article 16, the Belgian Government declares that the applications mentioned in the second paragraph of Article 16 will not be entertained if they are filed after the expiration of a period of one year following the date of the judgment;

"**6.** The Belgian Government believes it should draw attention to the fact that any request for the service of documents made under sections a) or b) of the first paragraph of Article 5 requires the agency of a process-server (huissier de justice) and that the resulting costs should be reimbursed in conformity with Article 12 of the Convention."

2a With the following declaration:

"**1.** Pursuant to the first paragraph of Article 2 of the Convention the Minister of State in the Office of the President of the Republic of

Botswana has been designated the Central Authority to receive requests for service from other contracting states.

"**2.** The Registrar of the High Court of Botswana is designated as the authority competent to complete the certificate in the form of the Model annexed to the Convention pursuant to the first paragraph of Article 6.

"**3.** In accordance with the provisions of Article 9 of the Convention the Minister of State in the Office of the President is designated as the receiver of process sent through Consular channels.

"**4.** It is declared that the Government of Botswana objects to the method of service referred to in sub-paragraphs (b) and (c) of Article 10.

"**5.** It is declared that a judge of the High Court of Botswana may give judgment if all the conditions specified in paragraph 2 of Article 15 are fulfilled."

All documents forwarded for service must be in duplicate and written in or translated into the English language.

3 *Notification in conformity with Article 31, paragraph c, of the Convention*

Canada deposited its instrument of accession to the above-mentioned Convention with the Ministry of Foreign Affairs of the Kingdom of the Netherlands on 26 September 1988 in accordance with Article 28, paragraph 1.

The States which have ratified the Convention were notified by the Dutch Government of the accession on 29 September 1988. Since none of these States raised an objection to the accession within the period of six months specified in Article 28, paragraph 2, the said accession became perfect on 10 April 1989.

In accordance with Article 28, paragraph 3, the provisions of the Convention will enter into force for Canada on 1 May 1989.

A copy of a document transmitted by Canada and containing the designations and declarations referred to in Article 21 of the Convention is attached to this Notification.

CANADA

A. *Transmission and execution of requests for service*

1. Central Authority
(Article 2 and Article 18, paragraph 3)
comment: To save time, requests should be forwarded directly to the Central Authority of the province or territory concerned. They may, however, also be forwarded to the Federal Central Authority which will transmit them to the relevant Central Authority.

Alberta
name: Attorney-General for Alberta
Att: Executive Director—Court Services
address: 9833–109th Street
Edmonton, Alberta
Canada T5K 2E8
telephone: (403) 427–4992

British Columbia
name: Ministry of the Attorney-General
for British Columbia
Office of the Deputy Minister
address: Fifth Floor, 910 Government Street
Victoria, British Columbia
Canada V8V 1X4
telephone: (604) 387–5211

Manitoba
name: Attorney-General for Manitoba
c/o Director—Civil Legal Services
address: Woodsworth Building
6th Floor
405 Broadway
Winnipeg, Manitoba
Canada, R3C 0V8
telephone: (204) 945–2847

New Brunswick
name: Attorney-General for New Brunswick
address: P.O. Box 6000
Fredericton, New Brunswick
Canada, E3B 5H1
telephone: (506) 453–2208

Newfoundland
name: Department of Justice
address: Confederation Building
St. John's, Newfoundland
Canada A1C 5T7
telephone: (709) 576–2869

Nova Scotia
name: Attorney General of Nova Scotia
Legal Services Division
address: P.O. Box 7
Halifax, Nova Scotia
B3J 2L6
telephone: (902) 424–4024

Ontario
name: Ministry of the Attorney General for Ontario
Reciprocity Office: Civil Law Division
address: 18 King Street East
Toronto, Ontario
Canada M5C 1C5
telephone: (416) 965–2570

Prince Edward Island
name: Attorney General of Prince Edward Island
Office of the Deputy Minister
address: P.O. Box 2000
Charlottetown, Prince Edward Island
Canada C1A 7N8
telephone: (902) 368–4570

Québec
name: Ministre de la Justice du Québec
a/s Le service juridique
address: 1200 route de l'Église
5ème étage
Ste-Foy, Québec
Canada G1V 4M1
telephone: (418) 643–1436

Saskatchewan
name: Minister of Justice for Saskatchewan
Att. of Director of Sheriff Services
address: 1874 Scarth St., 10th Floor
Regina, Saskatchewan
Canada S4P 3V7
telephone: (306) 787–5488

Yukon
name: Director of Court Services
address: Department of Justice,
Box 2703
Whitehorse, Yukon Y1A 2C6
telephone: (403) 667–5942

Northwest Territories
name: Deputy Minister of Justice
Government of the Northwest Territories
address: Box 1320
Yellowknife, Northwest Territories
Canada X1A 2L9
telephone: (613) 995–0119

Canada
name: Director, Legal Advisory Division
Department of External Affairs
address: 125 Sussex Drive
Ottawa, Ontario
Canada K1A 0G2
telephone: (613) 995–0119

Payment of Service Costs:

The payment of Service costs should be made to:

Alberta:	Provincial Treasurer of Alberta
British Columbia:	Minister of Finance of British Columbia
Prince Edward Island:	Minister of Finance of Prince Edward Island
Manitoba:	Minister of Finance of Manitoba
New Brunswick:	Minister of Finance of New Brunswick
Nova Scotia:	Minister of Finance of Nova Scotia
Ontario:	Treasurer of Ontario
Quebec:	"Ministre des Finances du Québec"
Saskatchewan:	Department of Justice of Saskatchewan—Sheriff Services
Newfoundland:	Newfoundland Exchequer Account
Yukon:	Territorial Treasurer of the Government of Yukon
Northwest Territories:	Government of the Northwest Territories

2. Methods of service employed by the Central Authority (Article 5)

2.1 Formal service
(Article 5, paragraph 1, sub-paragraph a)
In Canada, service will be effected according to the methods of service prescribed by the laws in force in each province and territory.
The normal procedure that will be used by central authorities in Canada is personal service made by a sheriff or deputy sheriff or a *huissier* in Quebec, on an individual or on a corporation by handing a copy of the document to the defendant in person, wherever he may be, or to the President, Chairman or other Chief Officer of a corporation at the place of business.
Service may also be effected by leaving a copy of the document with a person of a reasonable age at the defendant's domicile or residence.
Where service is made on a corporation, provincial laws usually provide for service on a director or senior officer of the corporation or, in some cases, on a registered agent or on a responsible person at the registered office of the corporation.

2.2 Informal delivery (Article 5, paragraph 2)
The practice of informal delivery ("par simple remise") of judicial or extra-judicial documents is not known in Canada.

2.3 Service by a particular method (Article 5, paragraph 1, sub-paragraph b)
In Alberta, New Brunswick and Ontario, service will be made by certified mail at the option of the requesting party. In Ontario, the Central Authority will serve by any form of mail, at the option of the requesting party.

2.4 Translation requirements (Article 5, paragraph 3)
For both Formal service and Service by a particular method, translation requirements will depend on the province or territory concerned.
For Alberta, British Columbia, Newfoundland, Nova Scotia, Prince Edward Island, Saskatchewan, all documents must be written in or translated into English.
For Ontario, Manitoba, and the Northwest Territories, all documents must be written in or translated into English or French.
For New Brunswick and the Yukon, all documents must be written in or translated into English or French. The Central Authority of New Brunswick or the Yukon may reserve the right to require documents to be translated into English or French depending on the language understood by the addressee.
For Quebec, translation will be required in all cases where the recipient does not understand the language in which the document is written. All documents which commence actions must be translated. Summary translation of all other documents is acceptable if the recipient agrees. Translation is to be done into the French language; however, the Quebec central authority may, upon request, allow a translation in English at the condition that the recipient understands this language.
Costs (Article 12, paragraph 2, sub-paragraph a)
Costs for execution of service will be of $50.-Can.

3. Authority competent to complete the certificate of service (Article 6)
In addition to the Central Authorities, the sheriffs, deputy-sheriffs, sub-sheriffs, clerk of the court or his/her deputy for the judicial district (except in Manitoba where there are no judicial districts) in which the person is to be served or the *huissiers* (only in Quebec) are competent to complete the certificate of service.

B. *Forwarding of requests for service to the Central Authority of another Contracting State*
Forwarding Authorities (Article 3)
Requests for service to Central Authorities of other States may be transmitted by:
— The Attorney General for Canada
— The Attorneys General or the Ministry of Attorney General or Minister of Justice of a province or a territory—as the case may be.
— Clerks of the courts and their deputies for a judicial or a court district
— The members of the law societies of all provinces and territories
— The member of the Board of Notaries of the Province of Quebec (for non-litigious matters only).
— Local registrars
— The huissiers and sheriffs
— The prothonotaries and deputy prothonotaries
— The "Percepteur des pensions alimentaires" in Québec

CANADA

I *Transmission through consular or diplomatic channels (Articles 8 and 9)*

A Acceptance
On accession, Canada has not declared that it objects to service by consular or diplomatic channels on its territory.
Receiving authority (Article 9, paragraph 1)
The Central Authorities in Canada designated in accordance with Articles 2 and 18 of the *Convention* are competent to receive requests for service transmitted by a foreign consul within Canada.

B Forwarding to the Contracting States

Canada does not object to service by consular channels of Canadian documents abroad providing that the recipient accepts this method of service.

II *Transmission through postal channels (Article 10, sub-paragraph a)*

A Acceptance

Canada does not object to service by postal channels.

B Forwarding to other contracting States

Canadian law allows the use of postal channels to serve Canadian documents to persons abroad.

III *Service through judicial officers, notably "huissiers", etc. of the requested State (Article 10, sub-paragraphs b) and c))*

On accession, Canada has not declared to object to methods of service of Article 10, sub-paragraphs b) and c).

IV *Other direct channels (Article 11); special agreements (Articles 24 and 25)*

Canada is party to bilateral conventions on civil procedure with the following States:

Austria	Canada Treaty Series, 1935, n♦ 16
Belgium	Canada Treaty Series, 1928, n♦ 16
Czechoslovakia	Canada Treaty Series, 1928, n♦ 17
Denmark	Canada Treaty Series, 1936, n♦ 4
Finland	Canada Treaty Series, 1936, n♦ 5
France	Canada Treaty Series, 1928, n♦ 15
Germany	Canada Treaty Series, 1935, n♦ 11
Greece	Canada Treaty Series, 1938, n♦ 11
Hungary	Canada Treaty Series, 1939, n♦ 6
Iraq	Canada Treaty Series, 1938, n♦ 12
Italy	Canada Treaty Series, 1938, n♦ 14
Netherlands	Canada Treaty Series, 1936, n♦ 2
Norway	Canada Treaty Series, 1935, n♦ 15
Poland	Canada Treaty Series, 1935, n♦ 18
Portugal	Canada Treaty Series, 1935, n♦ 17
Spain	Canada Treaty Series, 1935, n♦ 12
Sweden	Canada Treaty Series, 1935, n♦ 13
Turkey	Canada Treaty Series, 1935, n♦ 19
Yugoslavia	Canada Treaty Series, 1939, n♦ 4

CANADA
GUARANTEES UNDER THE CONVENTION

Declarations made pursuant to Articles 15, paragraph 1 or 16, paragraph 3.

1. *Stays of entry* (Article 15, paragraph 2)

Canada declares that the judges may give judgment under the conditions stated in Article 15 of the Convention.

2. *Relief from expiration of the period of time for appeal* (Article 16, paragraph 3)

Canada declares that an application filed under Article 16 of the Convention will not be entertained if it is filed after the expiration of one year following the date of the judgment, except in exceptional cases determined by the rules of the Court seized of the matter.

3a The People's Republic of China deposited its instrument of accession with the Ministry of Foreign Affairs of the Kingdom of the Netherlands on May 6, 1991, in accordance with Article 28, paragraph 1, of the Convention.

The instrument of accession contains the following declarations:

"1. to designate according to Article 2 and Article 9 of the Convention the Ministry of Justice of the People's Republic of China as the Central Authority and the authority competent to receive documents transmitted by foreign States through consular channels.

"The communication address is:

Bureau of International Judicial Assistance
Ministry of Justice of the People's Republic of China
10, Chaoyangmen Nandajie, Chaoyang District, Beijing, P.C. 100020
People's Republic of China

"2. to declare according to the second paragraph of Article 8 that the means of service stipulated in the first paragraph of that Article may be used within the territory of the People's Republic of China only when the document is to be served upon a national of the State in which the documents originate.

"3. to oppose the service of documents in the territory of the People's Republic of China by the methods provided by Article l0 of the Convention.

"4. to declare in accordance with the second paragraph of Article 15 of the Convention that if all the conditions provided in that paragraph are fulfilled, the judge, notwithstanding the provisions of the first paragraph of that Article, may give judgment even if no certificate of service or delivery has been received.

"5. to declare in accordance with the third paragraph of Article 16 of the Convention that the application for relief from the effects of the expiration of the time for appeal shall not be entertained except that it is filed within one year following the date of the judgment."

(courtesy translation)

In accordance with the terms of Article 28, paragraph 1, of the Convention any State not represented at the Tenth Session of the Hague Conference on private international law may accede to the present Convention after it has entered into force in accordance with the first paragraph of Article 27 (viz.: 10 February 1969).

In accordance with Article 28, paragraph 2, the Convention shall enter into force for the People's Republic of China in the absence of any objection from a State which has ratified the Convention (at present: Belgium, Denmark, Egypt, Finland, France, the Federal Republic of Germany, Greece, Israel, Italy, Japan, Luxembourg, the Kingdom of the Netherlands, Norway, Portugal, Spain, Sweden, Turkey, the United Kingdom of Great Britain and Northern Ireland and the United States of America) before such deposit, notified to the Ministry of Foreign Affairs of the Kingdom of the Netherlands within a period of six months after the date on which the said Ministry has notified it of such accession. For practical reasons this six months' period in this case is running from 1 June 1991 till 1 December 1991.

Notification in conformity with Article 31 of the Convention

The States which ratified the Convention were notified of the accession by the Dutch Government on 17 May 1991. Since none of these States raised an objection to the accession within the period of six months specified in Article 28, paragraph 2, the said accession became perfect on 1 December 1991.

The provisions of the Convention will enter into force for the People's Republic of China on 1 January 1992 in accordance with Article 28, paragraph 3.

"The Embassy of the People's Republic of China in the Kingdom of the Netherlands

No. He Wai Fa (97)–52 (Translation)

The Hague, June 10, 1997

Your Excellency

In accordance with the Joint Declaration of the Government of the People's Republic of China and the Government of the United Kingdom of Great Britain and Northern Ireland on the Question of Hong Kong signed on 19 December 1984, the People's Republic of China will resume the exercise of sovereignty over Hong Kong with effect from 1 July 1997. Hong Kong will, with effect from that date, become a Special Administrative Region of the People's Republic of China and will enjoy a high degree of autonomy, except in foreign and defence affairs which are the responsibilities of the Central People's Government of the People's Republic of China.

In this connection, I am instructed by the Minister of Foreign Affairs of the People's Republic of China to make the following notification:

The Convention on the Service Abroad of Judicial and Extrajudicial Documents in Civil and Commercial Matters done on 15 November 1965 (hereinafter referred to as the "Convention"), by which the

Government of the Kingdom of the Netherlands is designated as the depository, to which the Government of the People's Republic of China deposited its instrument of accession on 3 May 1991, will apply to the Hong Kong Special Administrative Region with effect from 1 July 1997. The Government of the People's Republic of China also makes the following declarations:

1. In accordance with Paragraph 2 of Article 8 of the Convention, it declares that the means of service referred to in Paragraph 1 of this Article may be used within the Hong Kong Special Administrative Region only when the document is to be served upon a national of the state in which the document originates.

2. In accordance with Article 18 of the Convention, it designates the Administrative Secretary of the Government of the Hong Kong Special Administrative Region as the Other Authority in the Hong Kong Special Administrative Region.

3. It designates the Registrar of the High Court of the Hong Kong Special Administrative Region as the authority for the purpose of Article 6 and 9 of the Convention.

4. With reference to the provisions of Sub-paragraphs (b) and (c) of Article 10 of the Convention, documents for service through official channels will be accepted in the Hong Kong Special Administrative Region only by the Central Authority or Other Authority designated, and only from judicial, consular or diplomatic officers of other Contracting States.

The Government of the People's Republic of China will assume responsibility for the international rights and obligations arising from the application of the Convention to the Hong Kong Special Administrative Region. ..."

3b *Notification in conformity with Article 31, paragraph c, of the Convention.*

The Republic of Cyprus deposited its instrument of accession with the Ministry of Foreign Affairs of the Kingdom of the Netherlands on 26 October 1982 in accordance with Article 28, paragraph 1, of the Convention.

In accordance with Article 28, paragraph 3, the provisions of the Convention will enter into force for the Republic of Cyprus on 1 June 1983.

The States which have ratified the Convention were notified by the Netherlands Government of the accession on 3 November 1982. Since none of these States raised an objection to the accession within the period of six months specified in Article 28, paragraph 2, the said accession became perfect on 15 May 1983.

Referring to the accession of Cyprus to the above-mentioned Convention the Embassy of Turkey at The Hague addressed a Note dated 6 April 1983 to the Ministry of Foreign Affairs of the Kingdom of the Netherlands. [See note 13.]

Notification in conformity with Article 31, paragraph e, of the Convention

In conformity with Article 21 of the Convention the Government of Cyprus informed the Ministry of Foreign Affairs of the Kingdom of the Netherlands by Note dated 5 January 1984 of the designation of the following authorities and made the following declarations:

"**(a)** *Article 2:*

Designation of Central Authority which will undertake to receive requests for service:—Ministry of Justice.

(b) *Article 6:*

Designation of the authority competent to complete the certificate of Service:—Ministry of Justice.

(c) *Article 9:*

Designation of the authority competent to receive documents transmitted by Consular Channels:—Ministry of Justice.

(d) *Articles 8 and 10:*

No opposition to the methods of transmission of documents provided by these articles.

(e) *Article 15:*

Declaration that judgement may be given if all conditions laid down in paragraph 2 are fulfilled.

(f) *Article 16:*

Declaration pursuant to paragraph 3 that the application will not be entertained if it is filed after the expiration of one year from the date of the judgement.

(g) *Article 18:*

Designation of other authorities in addition to the Central Authorities.

The Courts of the Republic. Competence:

Service of documents through their Registries.".

3c *Notification in conformity with Article 31, paragraphs c and e, of the Convention*

By notification dated January 28, 1993 the Czech Republic communicated the following: "In accordance with the valid principles of international law and to the extent defined by it, the Czech Republic, as a successor state created as a result of the division of the Czech and Slovak Federal Republic, considers itself bound, as of January 1, 1993, i.e. the date of the division of the Czechoslovak federation, by multilateral international treaties to which the Czech and Slovak Federal Republic was a party on that date, including reservations and declarations to their provisions made earlier by Czechoslovakia", which are as follow:

Translation

—in accordance with Article 8 of the Convention, within the territory of the Socialist Republic of Czechoslovakia judicial documents may not be served directly through the diplomatic or consular agents of another contracting State unless the document is to be served upon a national of the State in which the documents originate;

—in accordance with Article 10 of the Convention, within the territory of the Socialist Republic of Czechoslovakia judicial documents may not be served by another contracting State through postal channels nor through the judicial officers, officials or other competent persons;

—in accordance with Article 15, paragraph 2 of the Convention, Czechoslovakian judges may give judgement even if the conditions pursuant to Article 15, paragraph 1, have not been fulfilled;

—the provisions of Article 29 of the Convention concerning the extension of the Convention to territories for the international relations of which the contracting States are responsible are at variance with the Declaration of the United Nations General Assembly on the Granting of Independence to Colonial Countries and Peoples of 14 December 1960, and for this reason the Socialist Republic of Czechoslovakia does not consider itself to be bound by these provisions.

A copy of the original text of the declaration is attached.

By Note dated 31 March 1982 and received at the Ministry of Foreign Affairs on 1 April 1982, the Embassy of the Czechoslovak Socialist Republic communicated the following with regard to the above-cited declaration concerning Article 29 of the Convention:

"This declaration cannot be considered a reserve in view of the fact that it does not follow other purposes than a similar declaration made at the ratification of the Convention on the Taking of Evidence Abroad in Civil or Commercial Matters, though a different formulation was used.

"By this declaration the Czechoslovak Socialist Republic expresses its disagreement of principle with the status of colonies and other dependent territories which is in contradiction with the Declaration of the United Nations General Assembly on the Granting of Independence to Colonial Countries and Peoples of December 14, 1960.

"The Czechoslovak Socialist Republic, however, has no intention to exclude the application of the Convention on the relations with the territories on which the use of the Convention has been extended in accordance with its Art. 29.".

The States which have ratified the Convention were notified by the Netherlands Government of the accession on 26 October 1981. Since none of these States raised an objection to the accession within the period of six months specified in Article 28, paragraph 2, the said accession became perfect on 9 May 1982.

The provisions of the Convention will enter into force for the Czechoslovak Socialist Republic on 1 June 1982.

The Czechoslovak Government has designated the following authorities as the authorities referred to in Articles 2, 6 and 9 of the Convention;

competent for the Czech Socialist Republic:

Ministerstvo spravedlnosti České socialistické republiky/Ministry of Justice of the Czech Socialist Republic 128 10 Praha 2, Vyšehradská 16;

competent for the Slovak Socialist Republic:

Ministerstvo spravodlivosti Slovenskej socialistickej republiky/Ministry of Justice of the Slovak Socialist Republic 883 11 Bratislava, Suvorovova 12.

4 With the following declarations:

re Art. 2 and 18

The Ministry of Justice is designated as the Central Authority.

re Art. 6

The Danish court of law that has asked for the service to be made is designated as competent to complete the certificate in accordance with Article 6.

re Art. 9

The local judge of first instance—though, as regards the court of first instance at Copenhagen and the court of first instance of the city and of the canton of Arhus, the president of the court—is designated as competent to receive documents forwarded through consular channels in accordance with Art. 9.

re Art. 10

Denmark is unable to recognize the method of effecting service set out in Art. 10, para. c.

re Art. 15

Denmark avails itself of the power, provided for in Art. 15, second paragraph, to declare that the judge may give judgment in a matter even if the provisions of Art. 15, first paragraph, are not fulfilled.

re Art. 16

Denmark avails itself of the power, provided for in Art. 16, third paragraph, to declare that an application will not be entertained if it is made after the expiration of a period of one year following the date of judgment. The question of the re-hearing of a matter in which a person has been judged by default shall be decided in accordance with the rules of the code of procedure, Art. 373 and Art. 374, cf. Art. 434. According to these rules, any person against whom judgment is given by default in an action, in first instance may apply for a re-hearing of the matter if he can prove that the default cannot be imputed to him. The application for a re-hearing should be filed as soon as possible and may not be submitted after the expiration of a period of one year following the date of judgment.

5 With a declaration that the signing of the Agreement "does not mean in any way a recognition of Israel" by the Arab Republic of Egypt and that "no treaty relation will arise between" the two countries.

The Arab Republic of Egypt also declared that it "opposes the use of the methods of transmitting abroad the judicial and extrajudicial documents according to Articles 8 and 10 of the Convention."

In conformity with article 21 of the Convention the Arab Republic of Egypt has designated the Ministry of Justice as the central authority as provided for in Articles 2 and 18.

First paragraph of declaration withdrawn effective Jan. 25, 1980.

5a *Notification in conformity with Article 31, paragraph c, of the Convention*

The Republic of Estonia deposited its instrument of accession to the above-mentioned Convention with the Ministry of Foreign Affairs of the Kingdom of the Netherlands on 2 February 1996, in accordance with Article 28, paragraph 1, of the Convention.

The instrument of accession of the Republic of Estonia contains the following declarations:

"1) the Republic of Estonia is against the way of forwarding referred to in point c of Article 10;

"2) on the basis of Article 15 the judge may give judgment under the said conditions;

"3) on the basis of paragraph 3 of Article 16 for a period of 3 years;"

In accordance with the terms of Article 28, paragraph 1, of the Convention any State not represented at the Tenth Session of the Hague Conference on Private International Law may accede to the present Convention after it has entered into force in accordance with the first paragraph of Article 27 (viz: 10 February 1969).

In accordance with Article 28, paragraph 2, the Convention shall enter into force for such a State in the absence of any objection from a State, which has ratified the Convention (at present: Belgium, Denmark, Egypt, Germany, Finland, France, Greece, Ireland, Israel, Japan, the Kingdom of the Netherlands, Luxemburg, Norway, Portugal, Spain, Sweden, Switzerland, Turkey, the United Kingdom of Great Britain and Northern Ireland and the United States of America) before such deposit, notified to the Ministry of Foreign Affairs of the Kingdom of the Netherlands within a period of six months after the date on which the said Ministry has notified it of such accession. For practical reasons this six months' period will in this case run from 15 March 1996 to 15 September 1996.

6 With the following declarations:

"**1.** The Ministry of Justice has been designated Central Authority, pursuant to the first paragraph of article 2 of the Convention.

"**2.** The Central Authority (The Ministry of Justice) is acting as the authority presupposed in art. 9 of the Convention.

"**3.** Finnish authorities are not obliged to assist in serving documents transmitted by using any of the methods referred to in subparagraphs (b) and (c) of art. 10 of the Convention."

(Ministry of Justice was substituted for Ministry of Foreign Affairs as Central Authority by Note dated 31 March 1982, effective 1 June 1982.)

7 With the following declarations:

"**1.** In conformity with Articles 2 and 18 of the Convention, the Ministry of Justice, Civil Division of International Judicial Assistance (Ministeàere de la Justice, Service Civil de l'Entraide judiciaire internationale), 13 Place Vendôme, Paris (1er), is designated as the Central Authority to the exclusion of all other authorities.

"**2.** The authority competent to complete the certificate referred to in Article 6 is the Public Prosecutor of the Republic (Procureur de la République) in whose district the addressee of the document to be served resides.

"**3.** The Public Prosecutor of the Republic (Procureur de la République) is likewise authorized to receive documents forwarded through consular channels in accordance with Article 9.

"**4.** The Government of the French Republic declares that it is opposed, as has been provided for in Article 8, to the direct service, through diplomatic and consular agents of the contracting States, of documents upon persons who are not nationals of those States.

"**5.** The Government of the French Republic declares that the provisions of the second paragraph of Article 15 have its approval. It furthermore declares, with reference to Article 16, paragraph 3, that an application for relief from the effects of the expiration of the time for appeal from a judgment will not be entertained if it is filed more than twelve months following the date of the judgment."

7a On October 3, 1990 the German Democratic Republic acceded to the Federal Republic of Germany.

With the following declarations:

"**(1)** Requests for service shall be addressed to the Central Authority of the Land where the request is to be complied with. The Central Authority pursuant to Article 2 and paragraph 3 of Article 18 of the Convention shall be for

Baden-Württemberg	das Justizministerium Baden-Württemberg (The Ministry of Justice of Baden-Württemberg), D 7000 Stuttgart
Bavaria	das Bayerische Staatsministerium der Justiz (The Bavarian State Ministry of Justice), D 8000 München
Berlin	der Senator für Justiz (The Senator of Justice), D 1000 Berlin

By Note of 29 September 1992 the following central authorities were designated pursuant to Articles 2 and 18

in Brandenburg:	Das Ministerium der Justiz des Landes Brandenburg D–O–1561 Potsdam;
Bremen	der Präsident des Landgerichts Bremen (The President of the Regional Court of Bremen), D 2800 Bremen
Hamburg	der Präsident des Amtsgerichts Hamburg (The President of the Local Court of Hamburg), D 2000 Hamburg
Hesse	der Hessische Minister der Justiz (The Hessian Minister of Justice), D 6200 Wiesbaden
Lower Saxony	der Niedersächsische Minister der Justiz (The Minister of Justice of Lower Saxony), D 3000 Hannover

By Note of 29 September 1992 the following central authority was designated in

Mecklenburg-Western Pomerania:	Der Minister für Justiz, Bundes-und Europaangelegenheiten D–O–2754 Schwerin
Northrhine-Westphalia	Pursuant to Article 21 of the Convention, the Government of the Federal Republic of Germany notified the Ministry of Foreign Affairs of the Kingdom of the Netherlands by note dated February 19, 1991, that with effect from April 1, 1991, the designated authority for the Land Northrhine-Westphalia will no longer be "der Justizminister des Landes Nordrhein-Westfalen" but "der Präsident des Oberlandesgerichts Düsseldorf". D 4000 Düsseldorf
Rhineland-Palatinate	das Ministerium der Justiz (The Ministry of Justice), D 6500 Mainz
Saarland	der Minister für Rechtspflege (The Minister of Justice), D 6600 Saarbrücken

By Note of 29 September 1992 the following central authority was designated

in Saxe:	Das Sächsische Staatsministerium der Justiz D–O 8060 Dresden

By Note of 29 September 1992 the following central authority was designated

in Saxe-Anhalt:	Das Ministerium der Justiz des Landes Sachsen-Anhalt D–O 3037 Magdeburg
Schleswig-Holstein	der Justizminister des Landes Schleswig-Holstein (The Minister of Justice of the Land Schleswig-Holstein), D 2300 Kiel

By Note of 29 September 1992 the following central authority was designated

in Thuringe:	Das Justizministerium Thüringen D-O-5082 Erfurt

"The Central Authorities are empowered to have requests for service complied with directly by postal channels if the conditions for service in accordance with paragraph 1(a) of Article 5 of the Convention have been fulfilled. In that case the competent Central Authority will hand over the document to the postal authorities for service. In all other cases the local court (Amtsgericht) in whose district the documents are to be served shall be competent to comply with requests for service. Service shall be effected by the registry of the local court.

"Formal service (paragraph 1 of Article 5 of the Convention) shall be permissible only if the document to be served is written in, or translated into, the German language.

"(2) The Central Authority shall complete the certificate (paragraphs 1 and 2 of Article 6 of the Convention) if it has itself arranged for the request for service to be complied with directly by postal channels; in all other cases this shall be done by the registry of the local court.

"(3) The Central Authority of the Land where the documents are to be served and the authorities competent under Section 1 of the Act of 18th December 1958 implementing the Convention on Civil Procedure, signed at The Hague on 1st March 1954, to receive requests from consuls of foreign States, shall be competent to receive requests for service transmitted by a foreign consul within the Federal Republic of Germany (paragraph 1 of Article 9 of the Convention). Under that Act the president of the regional court (Landgericht) in whose district the documents are to be served shall be competent; in his place the president of the local court shall be competent if the request for service is to be complied with in the district of the local court which is subject to his administrative supervision.

"(4) In accordance with paragraph 2(a) of Article 21 of the Convention, the Government of the Federal Republic of Germany objects to the use of methods of transmission pursuant to Articles 8 and 10. Service through diplomatic or consular agents (Article 8 of the Convention) is therefore only permissible if the document is to be served upon a national of the State sending the document. Service pursuant to Article 10 of the Convention shall not be effected." At the time of the deposit of its instrument of ratification the Federal Republic of Germany declared that the said Convention shall also apply to Land Berlin with effect from the date on which it enters into force for the Federal Republic of Germany.

By a Note dated November 19, 1992 addressed to the Ministry of Foreign Affairs of the Kingdom of the Netherlands, the Government of the Federal Republic of Germany made in conformity with Article 21, second paragraph, letter *b*, of the above mentioned Convention the following declaration:

1. Notwithstanding the provisions of the first paragraph of Article 15, a German judge may give judgement even if no certificate of service or delivery has been received, if all the following conditions are fulfilled:

—the document was transmitted by one of the methods provided for in this Convention,

—a period of time of not less than six months, considered adequate by the judge in the particular case, has elapsed since the date of the transmission of the document,

—no certificate of any kind has been received, even though every reasonable effort has been made to obtain it through the competent authorities of the State addressed.

2. An application for relief in accordance with Article 16 will not be entertained if it is filed after the expiration of one year following the termination of the time-limit which has not been observed.

7b *Notification in conformity with Article 31 of the Convention*

In accordance with Article 26 of the Convention the Ambassador of Greece at The Hague signed on 20 July 1983 for the Hellenic Republic the above-mentioned Convention as follows:

P.ECONOMOU 20 juillet 1983

and deposited on the same date the instrument of ratification by the Hellenic Republic of the Convention.

In conformity with its Article 27, paragraph 2, the Convention will enter into force for the Hellenic Republic on 18 September 1983.

The Greek Government designated the Department of Administrative and Judicial Affairs of the Ministry of Foreign Affairs of the Hellenic Republic as the Central Authority pursuant to Article 2 of the Convention.

The Permanent Bureau of the Hague Conference on private international law presents its compliments to the Diplomatic Missions of the Member States and to the National Organs and has the honour to inform them that, by a Note dated 23 November 1989 addressed to the Ministry of Foreign Affairs of the Kingdom of the Netherlands, the Government of

the *Hellenic Republic*

made in conformity with Article 15, second paragraph, and Article 21, second paragraph, of the above-mentioned Convention the following declaration:

The judges of the Hellenic Republic may give judgment if all the conditions in Article 15, paragraph 2, letters (a), (b), and (c) of the Convention are fulfilled even if no certificate of service or delivery has been received.

[Translation]

7c *Notification in conformity with Article 31*

Ireland deposited, in accordance with Article 26, paragraph 2, of the above-mentioned Convention, its instrument of ratification with the Ministry of Foreign Affairs of the Kingdom of the Netherlands on 5 April 1994.

The instrument of ratification contains the following declarations:

"Article 3

The authority or judicial officer competent under the laws of Ireland for the purpose of Article 3 of the Convention are the Central Authority, a practising Solicitor, a Country Registrar or a District Court Clerk.

Article 15

Pursuant to the Second paragraph of Article 15 a Judge in Ireland may give judgment even if no certificate of service or delivery has been received, if the conditions set out in the second part of Article 15 of the Convention are fulfilled.

and the following objections:

Article 10

In accordance with the provision in Article 10 of the Convention the Government of Ireland objects to

(i) the freedom under Article 10(b) of judicial officers, officials or other competent persons of the State of origin to effect service in Ireland of judicial documents directly to judicial officers, officials or other competent persons and

(ii) the freedom under Article 10(c) of any person interested in a judicial proceeding to effect service in Ireland of judicial documents directly through judicial officers, officials or other competent persons

but this is not intended to preclude any person in another contracting State who is interested in a judicial proceeding (including his lawyer) from effecting service in Ireland directly through a solicitor in Ireland."

The Master of the High Court is designated as the Central Authority for Ireland in accordance with Article 2 and shall be the appropriate authority for completion of certificates on the form of the model annexed to the Convention.

The Convention will enter into force for Ireland on 4 June 1994.

By Note, received at the Ministry of Foreign Affairs of the Kingdom of the Netherlands on 31 March 1994, the Government of the United States of America declared that in accordance with Article 29, paragraph 2, of the above-mentioned Convention, in addition to the territorial extensions made upon deposit of the U.S. instrument of ratification (November 19, 1970), the Government of the United States of America hereby declares that the Convention shall also be extended to the Commonwealth of the Northern Mariana Islands (which became a U.S. Commonwealth on November 3, 1986).

The authorities currently designated by the Government of the United States of America to perform certain functions under the Treaty shall also be the authorities designated to perform those functions for the Commonwealth of the Northern Mariana Islands.

The Convention will enter into force for the Commonwealth of the Northern Mariana Islands on 30 May 1994.

8 With the following declarations and reservations:

"**a)** The Central Authority in Israel within the meaning of Articles 2, 6 and 18 of the Convention is: The Director of Courts, Directorate of Courts, Russian Compound, Jerusalem;

"**b)** The State of Israel, in its quality as State of destination, will, in what concerns Article 10, paragraphs b) and c), of the Convention, effect the service of judicial documents only through the Directorate of Courts, and only where an application for such service emanates from a judicial authority or from the diplomatic or consular representation of a Contracting State;

"**c)** An application to relieve a defendant from the effects of the expiration of the time of appeal from a judgment within the meaning of Article 16 of the Convention will be entertained only if filed within one year from the date of the judgment in question."

8a *Notification in conformity with Article 31, paragraph a and e of the Convention*

In accordance with Article 26, paragraph 2, the Italian Republic deposited its instrument of ratification of the Convention with the Ministry of Foreign Affairs of the Kingdom of the Netherlands on 25 November 1981.

On the occasion of the deposit of the instrument of ratification the Italian Government notified of the following:

Translation

"**a)** pursuant to Articles 2 and 18, 'l'Ufficio unico degli ufficiali giudiziari presso la corte d'appello di Roma' (the registry of the court of appeal in Rome) is designated as the Central Authority for the purpose of Article 5;

"**b)** 'gli uffici unici degli ufficiali giudiziari costituiti presso le corti di appello e i tribunali e gli ufficiali giudiziari addetti alle preture' (the registries of the courts of appeal and other courts, and the bailiffs appointed to the courts of first instance) are competent to issue the certificate pursuant to Article 6;

"**c)** 'gli uffici unici degli ufficiali giudiziari presso le corti di appello e i tribunali e gli ufficiali giudiziari addetti alle preture' (the registries of the courts of appeal and other courts, and the bailiffs appointed to the courts of first instance) are competent to receive for the purpose of service, documents forwarded by consular or diplomatic authorities pursuant to Article 9;

"**d)** the costs proceeding from each request for service in accordance with Article 5, first paragraph, under a and b, which requires the employment of a bailiff, have to be paid in advance in the size of 6,000 lire, except adjustment at the time of restitution of the notified document.

"However, the costs in relation to the notified document pursuant to Article 12, paragraph 2, of the Convention, can be paid after the restitution in a way specifically fixed by the bailiff.

"The Italian State shall not require any advance or repayment of costs for service of documents requested by the Contracting States in so far as those States for their parts shall not require the payment or repayment of costs for documents originated from Italy."

In accordance with Article 27, paragraph 2, the Convention shall enter into force for the Italian Republic on 24 January 1982.

9 With the following declarations and reservations:

"**(1)** The Minister for Foreign Affairs is designated as the Central Authority which receives requests for service from other contracting States, pursuant to the first paragraph of Article 2.

"**(2)** The District Court which has rendered judicial aid with respect to the service is designated as the authority competent to complete the certificate in the form of the model annexed to the Convention, pursuant to the first paragraph of Article 6.

"**(3)** The Minister for Foreign Affairs is designated as the authority competent to receive documents transmitted through consular channels, pursuant to the first paragraph of Article 9.

"**(4)** It is declared that the Government of Japan objects to the use of the methods of service referred to in subparagraphs (b) and (c) of Article 10.

"**(5)** It is declared that Japanese courts may give judgment if all the conditions specified in the second paragraph of Article 15 are fulfilled."

9a With the following declarations:

"**1.** The Public Prosecutor at the Superior Court of Justice has been designated as the Central Authority within the meaning of Article 2 of the Convention. He is also competent to receive the documents forwarded through the channels referred to in Article 9, para. 1, of the Convention.

"**2.** In accordance with Article 8, the Luxembourg Government is opposed to diplomatic and consular agents directly serving within its territory judicial documents on persons other than nationals of their own country.

"**3.** [Withdrawn by Note dated June 2, 1978.]

"**4.** When foreign judicial documents are served, in connection with Articles 5(a) and 10(b) and (c), through the intermediary of a Luxembourg official, they must be drawn up in French or German or accompanied by a translation into one of those languages.

"**5.** The Luxembourg Government declares that notwithstanding the provisions of Article 15, para. 1, of the Convention, its judges can enter judgment if the conditions set out in para. 2 of the said Article are fulfilled.

"**6.** In accordance with Article 16, para. 3, of the Convention, the Luxembourg Government declares that the applications referred to in para. 2 of the said Article will not be entertained if they are filed after the expiration of a period of one year following the date of the judgment."

10 With a declaration designating the Registrar of the High Court of Malawi, P.O. Box 30244, Chichiri, Blantyre 3, Malawi, as the Central Authority referred to in Article 2.

10a With the following declarations:

"**1.** The Public Prosecutor at the District Court of The Hague is designated for the Netherlands as the Central Authority referred to in Article 2 of the Convention.

"The office of the Public Prosecutor is situated at Juliana van Stolberglaan 2–4, The Hague.

"**2.** Pursuant to Article 18, paragraph 1, of the Convention, the Public Prosecutor at a District Court other than that of The Hague is likewise competent to receive requests and serve documents in accordance with Articles 3 to 6 of the Convention within the area of jurisdiction of such other Court.

"**3.** The Public Prosecutor at the District Court in the area of jurisdiction where service of the document has been requested is competent to complete a certificate as referred to under Article 6 of the Convention.

"**4.** The Public Prosecutor at the District Court in the area of jurisdiction where service of the document is requested has been designated for the Netherlands as the authority referred to in Article 9, paragraph 1, of the Convention which is competent to serve documents forwarded through consular channels.

"**5.** Notwithstanding the provisions of Article 15, paragraph 1, of the Convention, the Netherlands Court may give judgment, even if no certificate of service or delivery has been received, if all the following conditions are fulfilled:

"**a)** the document was transmitted by one of the methods provided for in this Convention;

"**b)** a period of time of not less than six months, considered adequate by the judge in the particular case, has elapsed since the date of the transmission of the document;

"**c)** no certificate, either of service or of delivery, has been received even though every reasonable effort has been made to obtain it through the competent authorities.

"**6.** An application for relief from the effects of the expiration of the time for appeal as provided for in Article 16 is only admissible, if it is submitted within a year, to be calculated from the date on which the judgment is given."

In accordance with Article 27, paragraph 2, the Convention shall enter into force for the Kingdom of the Netherlands (for the Kingdom in Europe) on January 2, 1976.

In accordance with Article 29, paragraph 2, the Kingdom of the Netherlands declared on 28 May 1986 that the above-mentioned Convention shall extend to Aruba.

In conformity with Article 29, paragraph 3, the Convention will enter into force for Aruba on 27 July 1986.

Notification in conformity with Article 31, letter e, of the Convention

The Ministry of Foreign Affairs of the Kingdom of the Netherlands notifies hereby the designation of the

Head, Central Office for General
Legal Affairs
L.G. Smith Boulevard 76
Oranjestad
Aruba

as the authority for Aruba referred to in Article 21 of the Convention.

11 With the following declarations:

"**1.** In accordance with Article 2, the Ministry of Justice, Oslo/Dep, is designated as the Central Authority.

"**2.** In accordance with Article 6, the County or Town Court in whose district the document has been served is designated for the purpose of completing the certificate in the form annexed to the Convention.

"**3.** In accordance with Article 9 first paragraph, the County or Town Court in whose district the person to be served is a resident or is staying, is designated as receiver of documents forwarded through consular channels.

"**4.** The Government of Norway is opposed to the use of such methods of service or transmission of documents on its territory as mentioned in Articles 8 and 10 of the Convention.

"**5.** Norwegian courts may give judgment when all the conditions specified in the second paragraph of Article 15 are fulfilled.

"**6.** In accordance with the third paragraph of Article 16, applications for relief according to Article 16 will not be entertained if they are delivered to the competent Norwegian authorities after the expiration of three years following the date of the judgment."

11a *Notification in conformity with Article 31, paragraph c, of the Convention*

Pakistan deposited its instrument of accession to the above-mentioned Convention with the Ministry of Foreign Affairs of the Kingdom of the Netherlands on 7 December 1988 in accordance with Article 28, paragraph 1.

The States which have ratified the Convention were notified by the Dutch Government of the accession on 19 December 1988. Since none of these States raised an objection to the accession within the period of six months specified in Article 28, paragraph 2, the said accession became perfect on 6 July 1989.

The provisions of the Convention will enter into force for Pakistan on 1 August 1989 in accordance with Article 28, paragraph 3.

The Permanent Bureau of the Hague Conference on private international law presents its compliments to the Diplomatic Missions of the Member States and to the National Organs and has the honour to inform them that, by a Note dated 1 February 1990, the Government of

Pakistan

informed the Ministry of Foreign Affairs of the Kingdom of the Netherlands of the designation of authorities, in conformity with Article 21 of the above-mentioned convention, and made declarations. The text of the communication is as follows:

"the Government of Pakistan has designated the Solicitor, Ministry of Law and Justice to the Government of Pakistan in Islamabad, as the central authority, for receiving requests for service coming from other Contracting States and Registrars of Lahore High Court Lahore, Peshawar High Court Peshwar, Baluchistan High Court Quetta, and the High Court of Sind, Karachi, 'other authorities' in addition to the Central Authority, within their respective territorial jurisdictions.

"The certificate prescribed by Article 6 of the Convention if not completed by a judicial authority shall be completed or countersigned by the Registrars of the High Courts.

"For the purposes of Article 8 of the Convention it is hereby declared that the Government of Pakistan is opposed to service of Judicial Documents upon persons, other than nationals of the requesting States, residing in Pakistan, directly through the Diplomatic and Consular

agents of the requesting States. However, it has no objection to such service by postal channels directly to the persons concerned [Article 10(a)] or directly through the judicial officers of Pakistan in terms of Article 10(b) of the Convention if such service is recognised by the law of the requesting State.

"In terms of the second paragraph of Article 15 of the Convention, it is hereby declared that notwithstanding the provision of the first paragraph there-of the judge may give judgement even if no certificate of service or delivery has been received, if the following conditions are fulfilled:—

"a) the document was transmitted by one of the methods provided for in the Convention;

"b) the period of time of not less than 6 months, considered adequate by the Judge in the particular case, has elapsed since the date of transmission of the document; and

"c) no certificate of any kind has been received even though every reasonable effort has been made to obtain it through the competent authorities of the State addressed.

"As regards Article 16, paragraph 3, of the Convention it is hereby declared that in case of ex-parte decisions, an application for setting it aside will not be entertained if it is filed after the expiration of the period of limitation prescribed by law of Pakistan."

11b *Notification in conformity with Article 31,. paragraph c, of the Convention*

The Republic of *Poland* deposited with the Ministry of Foreign Affairs of the Kingdom of the Netherlands its instrument of accession to the above-mentioned Convention on 13 February 1996, in accordance with Article 28, paragraph 1, of the Convention.

The instrument of accession of the Republic of Poland contains a declaration the text of which is attached and the translation of which is as follows:

Translation

—The Republic of Poland has decided to join the Convention, declaring that it is opposed to the modes of service specified in Articles 8 and 10 within its territory;

The instrument of accession was accompanied by a declaration the text of which is also attached and the translation of which is as follows:

In compliance with Article 21, the following actions are undertaken:

Article 2, Paragraph 1—the Central Authority designated to receive requests for service coming from another contracting State shall be the Ministry of Justice.

Article 18—other authorities (in addition to the Central Authority) designated to receive requests for service are Presidents of the voivodship courts.

Article 6—the authority designated to complete a certificate of service in the Republic of Poland shall be the court that has performed such service.

Article 9, Paragraph 1—the authorities designated for that purpose shall be the voivodship courts.

Articles 8 and 10—the Republic of Poland declares that it is opposed to the modes of service specified in Articles 8 and 10 within its territory.

In accordance with the terms of Article 28, paragraph 1, of the Convention any State not represented at the Tenth Session of the Hague Conference on Private International Law may accede to the present Convention after it has entered into force in accordance with the first paragraph of Article 27 (viz: 10 February 1969).

In accordance with Article 28, paragraph 2, the Convention shall enter into force for such a State in the absence of any objection from a State, which has ratified the Convention (at present: Belgium, Denmark, Egypt, Germany, Finland, France, Greece, Ireland, Israel, Japan, the Kingdom of the Netherlands, Luxemburg, Norway, Portugal, Spain, Sweden, Switzerland, Turkey, the United Kingdom of Great Britain and Northern Ireland and the United States of America) before such deposit, notified to the Ministry of Foreign Affairs of the Kingdom of the Netherlands within a period of six months after the date on which the said Ministry has notified it of such accession. For practical reasons this six months' period will in this case run from 29 February 1996 to 29 August 1996.

11c *Declaration of Portugal.*—Legal Affairs Department of Ministry of Justice has been designated as Central Authority, in accordance with Art. 2, paragraph 1, of Convention. Justice Department officials: court clerks (escrivães) and process-servers (officiais de diligências) have been designated as persons competent to prepare certificate referred to in Article 6 of Convention. In accordance with Art. 8, paragraph 2, of Convention, the Portuguese government grants diplomatic and consular agents power to serve documents on their own nationals only. Portuguese government declares that, notwithstanding provisions of first paragraph of Art. 15 of Convention its judges may give judgment if conditions listed in paragraph 2 of said Art. are fulfilled. In accordance with Art. 16, paragraph 3 of Convention, Portuguese government states that applications referred to in Art. 16, paragraph 2, will not be considered if they are made after expiration of a period of one year from date of judgment.

11d *Notification in conformity with Article 31, paragraph e of the Convention*

By Note dated 4 June 1981 and received at The Ministry of Foreign Affairs of the Kingdom of the Netherlands on 14 July 1981 the Republic of Seychelles informed the Ministry in accordance with Article 21 of the Convention of the following:

"Article 2

"The Central Authority designated is:

The Registrar

Supreme Court,

Victoria,

Mahé,

Republic of Seychelles.

"Article 8

"The Government of the Republic of Seychelles declares that it is opposed to service by a contracting state of judicial documents upon persons abroad, without application of any compulsion, directly through the diplomatic or consular agents of that contracting state unless the document is to be served upon a national of the state in which the documents originate.

"Article 10

"The Government of the Republic of Seychelles declares that it objects to paragraph (b) and (c) of this Article, in so far as they permit service of judicial documents through officials or persons *other than* judicial officers.

"Article 15

"The Government of the Republic of Seychelles declares that notwithstanding the provisions of the first paragraph of this Article, the judge may give judgment even if no certificate of service or delivery has been received, if all the following conditions are fulfilled.

"**a)** the document was transmitted by one of the methods provided for in this Convention,

"**b)** a period of time of not less than six months, considered adequate by the judge in the particular case, has elapsed since the date of the transmission of the document,

"**c)** no certificate of any kind has been received, even though every reasonable effort has been made to obtain it through the competent authorities of the State addressed.

"Article 16

"The Government of the Republic of Seychelles declares that it will not entertain an application for relief if filed later than one year following the date of the judgment."

11e By notification dated March 15, 1993 the Slovak Republic communicated the following: "In accordance with relevant principles and norms of international law and to extent defined by it, the Slovak Republic, as a successor State, born from the division of the Czech and Slovak Federal Republic, considers itself bound, as of January 1, 1993, i.e. the date of the division of the Czechoslovak Federation, by multilateral international treaties to which the Czech and Slovak

Federal Republic was a party at that date, including reservations and declarations in respect of provisions made earlier by Czechoslovakia, as well as objections by Czechoslovakia in respect of reservations made by other treaty parties", which are as follows: [Same declarations and reservations, *mutatis mutandis*, under Czech Republic, see footnote 3c].

11f The Permanent Bureau of the Hague Conference on private international law presents its compliments to the Diplomatic Missions of the Member States and to the National Organs and has the honour to inform them that, by instrument deposited on 4 June 1987 with the Ministry of Foreign Affairs of the Kingdom of the Netherlands,

Spain

ratified the above-mentioned Convention.

In accordance with Article 27, paragraph 2, the Convention will enter into force for *Spain on 3 August 1987*.

The instrument of ratification contains the following declarations:

"1) The Spanish State declares that its judges, notwithstanding the provisions of Article 15, may give judgment even if no certificate of service or delivery of documents has been received, if all the conditions enumerated in the said Article 15, paragraph 2, are fulfilled.

"2) The Spanish State declares that the time of expiration, referred to in Article 16, is sixteen months from the date of the judgment.

"3) The Spanish State designates as the Central Authority to issue the certificates in the form of the model annexed to the Convention:

Secretaría General Técnica,
Subdirección de Cooperación Jurídica Internacional,
Ministerio de Justicia,
San Bernardo, 45,
28015 MADRID." (Translation)

12 With the following declarations:

"**a**) The Ministry for Foreign Affairs (address: Utrikesdepartementet, Juridiska bry.an, Box 16121, S–103 23 Stockholm 16, Sweden) has been designated Central Authority.

"**b**) The Central Authority (the Ministry for Foreign Affairs) has been designated to receive documents transmitted through consular channels, pursuant to art. 9.

"**c**) Swedish authorities are not obliged to assist in serving documents transmitted by using any of the methods referred to in subparagraphs (b) and (c) of art. 10.

"By virtue of the third paragraph of art. 5 of the Convention the Central Authority requires that any document to be served under the first paragraph of the same article must be written in or translated into Swedish."

12a The Permanent Bureau of the Hague Conference on private international law presents its compliments to the Diplomatic Missions of the Member States and to the National Organs and has the honour to inform them that, by instrument deposited on 2 November 1994 with the Ministry of Foreign Affairs of the Kingdom of the Netherlands,

Switzerland

ratified the above-mentioned Convention.

In accordance with Article 27, paragraph 2, the Convention will enter into force for *Switzerland* on *1 January 1995*.

The instrument of ratification contains the following reservations and declarations:

Translation:

"Re Article 1

1. With regard to Article 1, Switzerland takes the view that the Convention applies exclusively to the Contracting States. In particular, it believes that documents which are effectively addressed to a person resident abroad cannot be served on a legal entity who is not authorized to receive them in the country in which they were drawn up without derogating from Articles 1 and 15, first paragraph, of the Convention.

Re Articles 2 and 18

2. In accordance with Article 21, first paragraph (a), Switzerland designates the cantonal authorities listed in the annex as Central Authorities as referred to in Articles 2 and 18 of the Convention. Requests for the service of documents may also be addressed to the Federal Justice and Police Department in Bern, which will forward them to the appropriate Central Authority.

Re Article 5, third paragraph

3. Switzerland declares that in cases where the addressee does not voluntarily accept a document, it cannot officially be served on him or her in accordance with Article 5, first paragraph, unless it is in the language of the authority address, *i.e.* German, French or Italian, or accompanied by a translation into one of these languages, depending on the part of Switzerland in which the document is to be served (*cf.* annex).

Re Article 6

4. In accordance with Article 21, first paragraph (b), Switzerland designates the competent cantonal court or the cantonal Central Authority as the body responsible for completing the certificate referred to in Article 6.

Re Articles 8 and 10

5. In accordance with Article 21, second paragraph (a), Switzerland declares that it is opposed to the use in its territory of the methods of transmission provided for in Articles 8 and 10.

Re Article 9

6. In accordance with Article 21, first paragraph (c), Switzerland designates the cantonal Central Authorities as the authorities competent to receive documents transmitted by consular channels pursuant to Article 9 of the Convention."

The list of Central Authorities for the Cantons is attached.

Cantonal Central Authorities *Annex*

Cantons	Official language(s) (G=German) (F=French) (I=Italian)	Addresses	Telephone numbers
Appenzell Ausserrhoden	G	Kantonsgericht Appenzell A.Rh., 9043 Trogen	071/94 24 61
Appenzell Innerrhoden	G	Kantonsgericht Appenzell I.Rh., 9050 Appenzell	071/ 87 95 51
Aargau	G	Obergericht des Kantons Aargau, 5000 Aarau	064/ 21 19 40
Basel-Landschaft	G	Obergericht des Kantons Basel-Landschaft, 4410 Liestal	061/925 51 11
Basel-Stadt	G	Appellationsgericht Basel-Stadt, 4054 Basel	061/267 81 81
Bern	G/F	Justizdirektion des Kantons Bern, 3011 Bern	031/633 76 76

Cantons	Official language(s) (G=German) (F=French) (I=Italian)	Addresses	Telephone numbers
Fribourg	F/G	Tribunal cantonal, 1700 Fribourg	037/ 25 39 10
Genève	F	Parquet du Procureur général, 1211 Genève 3	022/319 21 11
Glarus	G	Obergericht des Kantons Glarus, 8750 Glarus	058/ 61 15 32
Graubünden,	G	Justiz-, Polizei- und Sanitäts-departement Graubünden, 7001 Chur	081/ 21 21 21
Jura	F	Département de la Justice, 2800 Delémont	066/ 21 51 11
Luzern	G	Obergericht des Kantons Luzern, 6002 Luzern	041/ 24 51 11
Neuchâtel	F	Département de Justice, 2001 Neuchâtel	038/ 22 31 11
Nidwalden	G	Kantonsgericht Nidwalden, 6370 Stans	041/ 63 79 50
Obwalden	G	Kantonsgericht des Kantons Obwalden, 6060 Sarnen	041/ 66 92 22
St. Gallen	G	Kantonsgericht St. Gallen, 9001 St. Gallen	071/ 21 31 11
Schaffhausen	G	Obergericht des Kantons Schaffhausen, 8201 Schaffhausen	053/ 82 74 22
Schwyz	G	Kantonsgericht Schwyz, 6430 Schwyz	043/ 24 11 24
Solothurn	G	Obergericht des Kantons Solothurn, 4500 Solothurn	065/ 21 73 11
Tessin	I	Tribunale di appello, 6901 Lugano	091/ 21 51 11
Thurgau	G	Obergericht des Kantons Thurgau, 8500 Frauenfeld	054/ 22 31 21
Uri	G	Gerichtskanzlei Uri, 6460 Altdorf	044/ 4 22 44
Valais	F/G	Tribunal cantonal, 1950 Sion	027/ 22 93 93
Vaud	F	Tribunal cantonal, 1014 Lausanne	021/313 15 11
Zug	G	Obergericht des Kantons Zug, Rechtshilfe, 6300 Zug	042/ 25 33 11
Zürich	G	Obergericht des Kantons Zürich, Rechtshilfe, 8023 Zürich	01/257 91 91

Autorités centrales cantonales *Annexe*

Cantons	Langue(s) officielle(s) (a=allemand) (f=français) (i=italien)	Adresses	Numéros de téléphone
Appenzell Ausserrho-den	a	Kantonsgericht Appenzell A.Rh., 9043 Trogen	071/ 94 24 61
Appenzell Innerrhoden	a	Kantonsgericht Appenzell I.Rh., 9050 Appenzell	071/ 87 95 51
Aargau	a	Obergericht des Kantons Aargau, 5000 Aarau	064/ 21 19 40
Basel-Landschaft	a	Obergericht des Kantons Basel-Landschaft, 4410 Liestal	061/925 51 11
Basel-Stadt	a	Appellationsgericht Basel-Stadt, 4054 Basel	061/267 81 81
Bern	a/f	Justizdirektion des Kantons Bern, 3011 Bern	031/633 76 76
Fribourg	f/a	Tribunal cantonal, 1700 Fribourg	037/25 39 10
Genève	f	Parquet du Procureur général, 1211 Genève 3	022/319 21 11
Glarus	a	Obergericht des Kantons Glarus, 8750 Glarus	058/ 61 15 32
Graubünden	a	Justiz-, Polizei- und Sanitäts-departement	081/ 21 21 21

Cantons	Langue(s) officielle(s) (a=allemand) (f=français) (i=italien)	Adresses	Numéros de téléphone
		Graubünden, 7001 Chur	
Jura	f	Département de la Justice, 2800 Delémont	066/ 21 51 11
Luzern	a	Obergericht des Kantons Luzern, 6002 Luzern	041/ 24 51 11
Neuchâtel	f	Départment de Justice, 2001 Neuchâtel	038/ 22 31 11
Nidwalden	a	Kantonsgericht Nidwalden, 6370 Stans	041/ 63 79 50
Obwalden	a	Kantonsgericht des Kantons Obwalden, 6060 Sarnen	041/ 66 92 22
St. Gallen	a	Kantonsgericht St. Gallen, 9001 St. Gallen	071/ 21 31 11
Schaffhausen	a	Obergericht des Kantons Schaffhausen, 8201 Schaffhausen	053/ 82 74 22
Schwyz	a	Kantonsgericht Schwyz, 6340 Schwyz	043/ 24 11 24
Solothurn	a	Obergericht des Kantons Solothurn, 4500 Solothurn	065/ 21 73 11
Tessin	i	Tribunale di appello, 6901 Lugano	091/ 21 51 11
Thurgau	a	Obergericht des Kantons Thurgau, 8500 Frauenfeld	054/ 22 31 21
Uri	a	Gerichtskanzlei Uri, 6460 Altdorf	044/ 4 22 44
Valais	f/a	Tribunal cantonal, 1950 Sion	027/ 22 93 93
Vaud	f	Tribunal cantonal, 1014 Lausanne	021/313 15 11
Zug	a	Obergericht des Kantons Zug, Rechtshilfe, 6300 Zug	042 25 33 11
Zürich	a	Obergericht des Kantons Zürich, Rechtshilfe, 8023 Zürich	01/257 91 91

13 With the following declaration:

"**1.** Pursuant to Article 2, paragraph 1 of the Convention, the Directorate General of Civil Affairs of the Ministry of Justice (Adalet Bakanliği Hukuk Isleri Genel Müdürlüğü, Ankara) is designated as the Central Authority.

"**2.** The Directorate General of Civil Affairs of the Ministry of Justice is also competent to complete certificates as referred to in Article 6 of the Convention.

"**3.** The Directorate General of Civil Affairs is also designated as the authority competent to receive documents forwarded through the channels specified in Article 9, paragraph 1 of the Convention.

"**4.** Pursuant to Article 8 of the Convention, the Government of the Republic of Turkey acknowledges the freedom of diplomatic and consular agents to serve judicial documents upon their own nationals only.

"**5.** The Government of the Republic of Turkey declares that it is opposed to the use of the methods of serving judicial documents listed in Article 10 of the Convention.

"**6.** The Government of the Republic of Turkey declares that its judges, notwithstanding the provisions of the first paragraph of Article 15, may give judgment if all the conditions set out in the second paragraph of the said Article are fulfilled.

"**7.** Pursuant to Article 16, paragraph 3, the Government of the Republic of Turkey declares that applications for relief as referred to in Article 16, paragraph 2, will not be entertained if they are filed after the expiration of a period of one year following the date of the judgment."

Embassy of the Republic of Turkey [at the Hague]

No. 18313/328–78

The Embassy of Turkey presents its compliments to the Ministry of Foreign Affairs, the depositary of the Convention on the service abroad of judicial and extrajudicial documents in civil or commercial matters, and has the honor to inform it of the text of the declaration of the Turkish Government regarding the accession to the aforementioned Convention by the Greek Cypriot Government:

Quote:

The Republic of Turkey, although not exercising its right of opposition as set forth in Article 28(2) of the Convention, declares that it does not consider itself bound to apply the provisions of the Convention with respect to the Greek Cypriot Government which, in constitutional terms, is not authorized to represent the "Republic of Cyprus" as a whole.

The Embassy of Turkey avails itself of this opportunity to renew to the Ministry of Foreign Affairs the assurances of its highest consideration.

The Hague, April 6, 1983

[Initialed]

[Official stamp]

14 With the following declarations:

(1)"(a) In accordance with the provisions of Articles 2 and 18 of the Convention, Her Majesty's Principal Secretary of State for Foreign Affairs is designated as the Central Authority; and the Senior Master of the Supreme Court, Royal Courts of Justice, Strand, London W.C. 2, the Crown Agent for Scotland, Lord Advocate's Department, Crown Office, 9 Parliament Square, Edinburgh 1, and the [as per letter dated 10 June 1980] the Master (Queen's Bench and Appeals), Royal Courts of Justice, Belfast 1, are designated as additional authorities for England and Wales, Scotland, and Northern Ireland respectively.

"**(b)** The authorities competent under Article 6 of the Convention to complete the Certificate of Service are the authorities designated under Articles 2 and 18.

"**(c)** In accordance with the provisions of Article 9 of the Convention, the United Kingdom designates as receivers of process through consular channels the same authorities as those designated under Articles 2 and 18.

"**(d)** With reference to the provisions of paragraphs (b) and (c) of Article 10 of the Convention, documents for service through official channels will be accepted in the United Kingdom only by the central or additional authorities and only from judicial, consular or diplomatic officers of other Contracting States.

"**(e)** The United Kingdom declares its acceptance of the provisions of the second paragraph of Article 15 of the Convention.

"**(f)** In accordance with the provisions of the third paragraph of Article 16 of the Convention, the United Kingdom declares, in relation to Scotland only, that applications for setting aside judgments on the grounds that the defendant did not have knowledge of the proceedings in sufficient time to defend the action will not be entertained if filed more than one year after the date of judgment.

"The authorities designated by the United Kingdom will require all documents forwarded to them for service under the provisions of the Convention to be in duplicate and, pursuant to the third paragraph of Article 5 of the Convention, will require the documents to be written in, or translated into, the English language.

"A notification under the second and third paragraphs of Article 29 regarding the extension of the Convention to the territories for the international relations of which the United Kingdom is responsible will be addressed to the Royal Netherlands Government in due course."

(2)"(a) In accordance with Article 18 of the Convention the authority shown against the name of each territory in the Annex (hereinafter severally called 'the designated authority') is designated as the authority in that territory competent to receive requests for service in accordance with Article 2 of the Convention.

"**(b)** The authority in each territory competent under Article 6 of the Convention to complete the Certificate of Service is the designated authority.

"**(c)** In accordance with the provisions of Article 9 of the Convention, the designated Authority shall receive process sent through consular channels.

"**(d)** With reference to the provisions of paragraphs (b) and (c) of Article 10 of the Convention, documents sent for service through official channels will be accepted in a territory listed in the Annex by the designated authority and only from judicial, consular or diplomatic officers of other Contracting States.

"**(e)** The acceptance by the United Kingdom of the provisions of the second paragraph of Article 15 of the Convention shall equally apply to the territories named in the Annex.

"The authorities designated in the Annex will require all documents forwarded to them for service under the provisions of the Convention to be in duplicate and, pursuant to the third paragraph of Article 5 of the Convention, will require the documents to be written in, or translated into, the English language."

ANNEX

Antigua and Barbuda*	The Governor General, Antigua and Barbuda.
	The Registrar of the High Court of Antigua and Barbuda, St. John's, Antigua.
Bermuda	The Registrar of the Supreme Court, Bermuda.
British Honduras	The Supreme Court Registry, British Honduras.
British Solomon Islands Protectorate	The Registrar of the High Court, Honiara, British Solomon Islands Protectorate.
British Virgin Islands	The Registrar of the Supreme Court, British Virgin Islands.
Cayman Islands	The Clerk of the Courts, Grand Cayman, Cayman Islands
Central and Southern Line Islands	The Registrar of the High Court, Honiara, British Solomon Islands Protectorate.
Falkland Islands and Dependencies	The Registrar of the Supreme Court, Stanley, Falkland Islands.
Fiji	The Registrar of the Supreme Court, Fiji.
Gibraltar	The Registrar of the Supreme Court, Gibraltar.
Gilbert and Ellice Islands Colony	The Registrar of the High Court, Tarawa, Gilbert and Ellice Islands Colony.
Guernsey	The Bailiff, Bailiff's Office, Royal Court House, Guernsey, Channel Islands.
Isle of Man	The First Deemster and Clerk of the Rolls, Rolls Office, Douglas, Isle of Man.
Jersey	The Attorney General, Jersey, Channel Islands.
Montserrat	The Registrar of the High Court, Montserrat.
Pitcairn	The Governor and Commander-in-Chief, Pitcairn.
St. Helena and Dependencies	The Supreme Court, St. Helena.
St. Lucia	The Registrar of the High Court of Justice, St. Lucia.
St. Vincent	The Registrar of the Supreme Court, St. Vincent.
Seychelles*	The Supreme Court, Seychelles.
Turks and Caicos Islands	The Registrar of the Supreme Court, Turks and Caicos Islands.

* Ed. note—Now independent parties to the Convention. See also country footnote.

Extension to Anguilla.—

Notification in conformity with Article 31, paragraphs d and e, of the Convention

In accordance with Article 29, paragraph 2, of the Convention the Ambassador of the United Kingdom of Great Britain and Northern Ireland at The Hague notified the Minister of Foreign Affairs of the Kingdom of the Netherlands, by a Letter dated 30 July 1982 and received on 3 August 1982, the extension of the Convention to Anguilla.

In accordance with Article 29, paragraph 3, the Convention will enter into force for Anguilla on 28 September 1982.

The extension was accompanied by the following declarations:

(a) in accordance with Article 18 of the Convention the Registrar of the Supreme Court of Anguilla (hereinafter called the designated authority) is designated as the authority competent to receive requests for service in accordance with Article 2 of the Convention.

(b) the authority competent under Article 6 of the Convention to complete the Certificate of Service is the designated authority.

(c) in accordance with the provisions of Article 9 of the Convention the designated authority shall receive process sent through consular channels.

(d) with reference to the provisions of paragraphs (b) and (c) of Article 10 of the Convention, documents sent for service through official channels will be accepted by the designated authority and only from judicial, consular or diplomatic officers of other contracting states.

(e) the acceptance by the United Kingdom of the provisions of the second paragraph of Article 15 of the Convention shall apply to Anguilla.

The designated authority will require all documents forwarded to it for service under the provisions of the Convention to be in duplicate and, pursuant to the third paragraph of Article 5 of the Convention, will require the documents to be written in, or translated into, the English language.

Extension to the Associated State of Saint Christopher and Nevis.

Notification in conformity with Article 31, paragraphs d and e, of the Convention

In accordance with Article 29, paragraph 2, of the Convention the Ambassador of the United Kingdom of Great Britain and Northern Ireland at The Hague notified the Minister of Foreign Affairs of the Kingdom of the Netherlands by Letter dated 1 March 1983 and received on 2 March 1983 of the extension of the Convention to the Associated State of Saint Christopher and Nevis.

In accordance with Article 29, paragraph 3, the Convention will enter into force for Saint Christopher and Nevis on 1 May 1983.

The Letter contains the following declarations:

"a) in accordance with Article 18 of the Convention the Registrar of the West Indies Associated State Supreme Court, Saint Christopher and Nevis circuit (hereinafter called the designated authority) is designated as the authority competent to receive requests for service in accordance with Article 2 of the Convention;

"b) the authority competent under Article 6 of the Convention to complete the Certificate of Service is the designated authority;

"c) in accordance with the provisions of Article 9 of the Convention the designated authority shall receive process sent through consular channels;

"d) with reference to the provisions of paragraphs (b) and (c) of Article 10 of the Convention, documents sent for service through official channels will be accepted by the designated authority and only from judicial, consular or diplomatic officers of other contracting states;

"e) the acceptance by the United Kingdom of the provisions of the second paragraph of Article 15 of the Convention shall apply to Saint Christopher and Nevis.

"The designated authority will require all documents forwarded to it for service under the provisions of the Convention to be in duplicate and, pursuant to the third paragraph of Article 5 of the Convention, will require the documents to be written in, or translated into, the English language."

15 With the following declarations:

"1. In accordance with Article 2, the United States Department of Justice is designated as the Central Authority to receive requests for service from other Contracting States and to proceed in conformity with Articles 3 to 6.

"2. In accordance with Article 6, in addition to the United States Department of Justice, the United States Marshal or Deputy Marshal for the judicial district in which service is made are designated for the purpose of completing the certificate in the form annexed to the Convention.

"3. In accordance with the second paragraph of Article 15, it is declared that the judge may, notwithstanding the provisions of the first paragraph of Article 15, give judgment even if no certificate of service or delivery has been received, if all the conditions specified in subdivisions (a), (b) and (c) of the second paragraph of Article 15 are fulfilled.

"4. In accordance with the third paragraph of Article 16, it is declared that an application under Article 16 will not be entertained if it is filed (a) after the expiration of the period within which the same may be filed under the procedural regulations of the court in which the judgment has been entered, or (b) after the expiration of one year following the date of the judgment, whichever is later.

"5. In accordance with Article 29, it is declared that the Convention shall extend to all the States of the United States, the District of Columbia, Guam, Puerto Rico, and the Virgin Islands.

"6. By Note, received at the Ministry of Foreign Affairs of the Kingdom of the Netherlands on 31 March 1994, the Government of the United States of America declared that in accordance with Article 29, paragraph 2, of the above-mentioned Convention, in addition to the territorial extensions made upon deposit of the U.S. instrument of ratification (November 19, 1970), the Government of the United States of America hereby declares that the Convention shall also be extended to the Commonwealth of the Northern Mariana Islands (which became a U.S. Commonwealth on November 3, 1986).

"The authorities currently designated by the Government of the United States of America to perform certain functions under the Treaty shall also be the authorities designated to perform those functions for the Commonwealth of the Northern Mariana Islands.

"The Convention will enter into force for the Commonwealth of the Northern Mariana Islands on 30 May 1994."

Each request for service should be accompanied by an international money order (not "postal" money order) made payable to the "Treasurer of the United States" in the sum of $15.00. No fee will be charged for a request for service from any State party to the Convention which does not impose a charge for the service of documents sent from the United states for service under the Convention.

(The address of the U.S. Central Authority for purposes of service under the Convention is: Office of International Judicial Assistance, Department of Justice, Washington, D.C. 20530.)

16 The Permanent Bureau of the Hague Conference on private international law presents its compliments to the Diplomatic Missions of the Member States and to the National Organs and has the honour to inform them that, by instrument deposited on 29 October 1993 with the Ministry of Foreign Affairs of the Kingdom of the Netherlands,

the *Republic of Venezuela*

acceded to the above-mentioned Convention.

The instrument of accession contains the following declarations:

Translations

1.— With regard to Article 5, paragraph 3:

"The Republic of Venezuela declares that notices and documents and other items annexed to the notices will be accepted only when they are properly translated into the Spanish language".

2.— With regard to Article 8:

"The Republic of Venezuela does not agree to the exercise of the faculty provided for in the first paragraph of this Article within its territory, in respect of other persons who are not nationals of the country of origin".

3.— With regard to Article 10(a):

"The Republic of Venezuela does not agree to the transmission of documents through postal channels".

4.— With regard to Article 15(a), (b) and (c):

"The Republic of Venezuela declares that 'Venezuelan judges shall be empowered to decide when the conditions contained in sections (a), (b) and (c) of this Article are fulfilled, even though they have not received any communication evidencing either the notice or transfer, or delivery of the document".

5.— With regard to Article 16:

"The Republic of Venezuela declares that the request allowed by the third paragraph of this Article shall not be admissible if it is made after the expiration of the period specified in Venezuelan law".

The States which ratified the Convention were notified of the accession by the Netherlands Government on 30 November 1993. Since none of these States raised an objection to the accession within the period of six months specified in Article 28, paragraph 2, the said accession became perfect on 15 June 1994.

In accordance with Article 28, paragraph 3, the Convention entered into force for the *Republic of Venezuela on 1 July 1994.*

Notification in conformity with Article 31

The Ministry of Foreign Affairs of the Kingdom of the Netherlands, depositary of the Convention on the service abroad of judicial and extrajudicial documents in civil or commercial matters of 15 November 1965, has the honour to inform the Members States of the Hague Conference on Private International and the States having acceded to the Convention that in accordance with Article 2 Venezuela has designated the "Ministry of Foreign Affairs" as the Central Authority.

Notes and Annotations to the Convention

Litigants wishing to serve a person in one of the Convention countries should request copies in duplicate of the three forms prescribed by the Convention: the "Request", the "Certificate" and the "Summary." These forms may be obtained from the offices of the United States Marshals. Upon completion of these forms, the litigants must then transmit them, together with the documents to be served—all in duplicate—to the local process server.

The local process server thereupon mails all these documents to the "Central Authority" abroad. After service has been effected, one copy of the documents served and an executed "Certificate" all be returned to the local process server, who will transmit these documents to the litigant who initiated the request.

—— **Annotations**

"The Effect of the Hague Convention on Service Abroad of Judicial and Extrajudicial Documents in Civil or Commercial Matters", 2 Cornell Int'l L.J. 125 (1969).

Julen v. Larson, 25 Cal.App.3d 325, 101 Cal. 796 (1972).

Shoei Kako Co., Ltd. v. Superior Court, 33 Cal.App.3d 808, 109 Cal. 402 (1973).

COMMENTARIES

See 28 U.S.C.A. Rule 4, Federal Rules of Civil Procedure, for Commentaries by David D. Siegel.

Rule 4.1. Service of Other Process

(a) Generally. Process other than a summons as provided in Rule 4 or subpoena as provided in Rule 45 shall be served by a United States marshal, a deputy United States marshal, or a person specially appointed for that purpose, who shall make proof of service as provided in Rule 4(1). The process may be served anywhere within the territorial limits of the state in which the district court is located, and, when authorized by a statute of the United States, beyond the territorial limits of that state.

(b) Enforcement of Orders: Commitment for Civil Contempt. An order of civil commitment of a person held to be in contempt of a decree or injunction issued to enforce the laws of the United States may be served and enforced in any district. Other orders in civil contempt proceedings shall be served in the state in which the court issuing the order to be enforced is located or elsewhere within the United States if not more than 100 miles from the place at which the order to be enforced was issued.

(Added Apr. 22, 1993, eff. Dec. 1, 1993.)

ADVISORY COMMITTEE NOTES

1993 Adoption

This is a new rule. Its purpose is to separate those few provisions of the former Rule 4 bearing on matters other than service of a summons to allow greater textual clarity in Rule 4. Subdivision (a) contains no new language.

Subdivision (b) replaces the final clause of the penultimate sentence of the former subdivision 4(f), a clause added to the rule in 1963. The new rule provides for nationwide service of orders of civil commitment enforcing decrees of injunctions issued to compel compliance with federal law. The rule makes no change in the practice with respect to the enforcement of injunctions or decrees not involving the enforcement of federally-created rights.

Service of process is not required to notify a party of a decree or injunction, or of an order that the party show cause why that party should not be held in contempt of such an order. With respect to a party who has once been served with a summons, the service of the decree or injunction itself or of an order to show cause can be made pursuant to Rule 5. Thus, for example, an injunction may be served on a party through that person's attorney. *Chagas v. United States,* 369 F.2d 643 (5th Cir.1966). The same is true for service of an order to show cause. *Waffenschmidt v. Mackay,* 763 F.2d 711 (5th Cir.1985).

The new rule does not affect the reach of the court to impose criminal contempt sanctions. Nationwide enforcement of federal decrees and injunctions is already available with respect to criminal contempt: a federal court may effect the arrest of a criminal contemnor anywhere in the United States, 28 U.S.C. § 3041, and a contemnor when arrested may be subject to removal to the district in which punishment may be imposed. Fed.R.Crim.P. 40. Thus, the present law permits criminal contempt enforcement against a contemnor wherever that person may be found.

The effect of the revision is to provide a choice of civil or criminal contempt sanctions in those situations to which it applies. Contempt proceedings, whether civil or criminal, must be brought in the court that was allegedly defied by a contumacious act. *Ex parte Bradley,* 74 U.S. 366 (1869). This is so even if the offensive conduct or inaction occurred outside the district of the court in which the enforcement proceeding must be conducted. *E.g., McCourtney v. United States,* 291 Fed. 497 (8th Cir.), *cert. denied,* 263 U.S. 714 (1923). For this purpose, the rule as before does not distinguish between parties and other persons subject to contempt sanctions by reason of their relation or connection to parties.

Rule 5. Service and Filing of Pleadings and Other Papers

(a) Service: When required. Except as otherwise provided in these rules, every order required by its terms to be served, every pleading subsequent to the original complaint unless the court otherwise orders because of numerous defendants, every paper relating to discovery required to be served upon a party unless the court otherwise orders, every written motion other than one which may be heard ex parte, and every written notice, appearance, demand, offer of judgment, designation of record on appeal, and similar paper shall be served upon each of the parties. No service need be made on parties in default for failure to appear except that pleadings asserting new or additional claims for relief against them shall be served upon them in the manner provided for service of summons in Rule 4.

In an action begun by seizure of property, in which no person need be or is named as defendant, any service required to be made prior to the filing of an answer, claim, or appearance shall be made upon the person having custody or possession of the property at the time of its seizure.

(b) Same: How Made. Whenever under these rules service is required or permitted to be made upon a party represented by an attorney the service shall be made upon the attorney unless service upon the party is ordered by the court. Service upon the attorney or upon a party shall be made by delivering a copy to the attorney or party or by mailing it to the attorney or party at the attorney's or party's last known address or, if no address is known, by leaving it with the clerk of the court. Delivery of a copy within this rule means: handing it to the attorney or to the party; or leaving it at the attorney's or party's office with a clerk or other person in charge thereof; or, if there is no one in charge, leaving it in a conspicuous place therein; or, if the office is closed or the person to be served has no office, leaving it at the person's dwelling house or usual place of abode with some person of suitable age and discretion then residing therein. Service by mail is complete upon mailing.

(c) Same: Numerous Defendants. In any action in which there are unusually large numbers of defendants, the court, upon motion or of its own initiative, may order that service of the pleadings of the defendants and replies thereto need not be made as between the defendants and that any cross-claim, counterclaim, or matter constituting an avoidance or affirmative defense contained therein shall be deemed to be denied or avoided by all other parties and that the filing of any such pleading and service thereof upon the plaintiff constitutes due notice of it to the parties. A copy of every such order shall be served upon the parties in such manner and form as the court directs.

(d) Filing; Certificate of Service. All papers after the complaint required to be served upon a party, together with a certificate of service, shall be filed with the court within a reasonable time after service, but the court may on motion of a party or on its own initiative order that depositions upon oral examination and interrogatories, requests for documents, requests for admission, and answers and responses thereto not be filed unless on order of the court or for use in the proceeding.

(e) Filing with the Court Defined. The filing of papers with the court as required by these rules shall be made by filing them with the clerk of court, except that the judge may permit the papers to be filed with the judge, in which event the judge shall note thereon the filing date and forthwith transmit them to the office of the clerk. A court may by local rule permit papers to be filed, signed, or verified by electronic means that are consistent with technical standards, if any, that the Judicial Conference of the United States establishes. A paper filed by electronic means in compliance with a local rule constitutes a written paper for the purpose of applying these rules. The clerk shall not refuse to accept for filing any paper presented for that purpose solely because it is not presented in proper form as required by these rules or any local rules or practices.

(As amended Jan. 21, 1963, eff. July 1, 1963; Mar. 30, 1970, eff. July 1, 1970; Apr. 29, 1980, eff. Aug. 1, 1980; Mar. 2, 1987, eff. Aug. 1, 1987; Apr. 30, 1991, eff. Dec. 1, 1991; Apr. 22, 1993, eff. Dec. 1, 1993; Apr. 23, 1996, eff. Dec. 1, 1996.)

ADVISORY COMMITTEE NOTES

1937 Adoption

Note to Subdivisions (a) and (b). Compare 2 Minn.Stat. (1927) §§ 9240, 9241, 9242; N.Y.C.P.A. (1937) §§ 163, 164 and N.Y.R.C.P. (1937) Rules 20, 21; 2 Wash.Rev.Stat.Ann. (Remington, 1932) §§ 244 to 249.

Note to Subdivision (d). Compare the present practice under former Equity Rule 12 (Issue of Subpoena—Time for Answer).

1963 Amendment

The words "affected thereby," stricken out by the amendment, introduced a problem of interpretation. See 1 Barron & Holtzoff, *Federal Practice & Procedure* 760–61 (Wright ed. 1960). The amendment eliminates this difficulty and promotes full exchange of information among the parties by requiring service of papers on all the parties to the action, except as otherwise provided in the rules. See also subdivision (c) of Rule 5. So, for example, a third-party defendant is required to serve his answer to the third-party complaint not only upon the defendant but also upon the plaintiff. See amended Form 22–A and the Advisory Committee's Note thereto.

As to the method of serving papers upon a party whose address is unknown, see Rule 5(b).

1970 Amendment

The amendment makes clear that all papers relating to discovery which are required to be served on any party must be served on all parties, unless the court orders otherwise. The present language expressly includes notices and demands, but it is not explicit as to answers or responses as provided in Rules 33, 34, and 36. Discovery papers may be voluminous or the parties numerous, and the court is empowered to vary the requirement if in a given case it proves needlessly onerous.

In actions begun by seizure of property, service will at times have to be made before the absent owner of the property has filed an appearance. For example, a prompt deposition may be needed in a maritime action in rem. See Rules 30(a) and 30(b)(2) and the related notes. A provision is added authorizing service on the person having custody or possession of the property at the time of its seizure.

1980 Amendment

Subdivision (d). By the terms of this rule and Rule 30(f)(1) discovery materials must be promptly filed, although it often happens that no use is made of the materials after they are filed. Because the copies required for filing are an added expense and the large volume of discovery filings presents serious problems of storage in some districts, the Committee in 1978 first proposed that discovery materials not be filed unless on order of the court or for use in the proceedings. But such materials are sometimes of interest to those who may have no access to them except by a requirement of filing, such as members of a class, litigants similarly situated, or the public generally. Accordingly, this amendment and a change in Rule 30(f)(1) continue the requirement of filing but make it subject to an order of the court that discovery materials not be filed unless filing is requested by the court or is effected by parties who wish to use the materials in the proceeding.

1987 Amendment

The amendments are technical. No substantive change is intended.

1991 Amendment

Subdivision (d). This subdivision is amended to require that the person making service under the rule certify that service has been effected. Such a requirement has generally been imposed by local rule.

Having such information on file may be useful for many purposes, including proof of service if an issue arises concerning the effectiveness of the service. The certificate will generally specify the date as well as the manner of service, but parties employing private delivery services may sometimes be unable to specify the date of delivery. In the latter circumstance, a specification of the date of transmission of the paper to the delivery service may be sufficient for the purposes of this rule.

Subdivision (e). The words *"pleading and other"* are stricken as unnecessary. Pleadings are papers within the meaning of the rule. The revision also accommodates the development of the use of facsimile transmission for filing.

Several local district rules have directed the office of the clerk to refuse to accept for filing papers not conforming to certain requirements of form imposed by local rules or practice. This is not a suitable role for the office of the clerk, and the practice exposes litigants to the hazards of time bars; for these reasons, such rules are proscribed by this revision. The enforcement of these rules and of the local rules is a role for a judicial officer. A clerk may of course advise a party or counsel that a particular instrument is not in proper form, and may be directed to so inform the court.

1993 Amendments

This is a technical amendment, using the broader language of Rule 25 of the Federal Rules of Appellate Procedure. The district court—and the bankruptcy court by virtue of a cross-reference in Bankruptcy Rule 7005—can, by local rule, permit filing not only by facsimile transmissions but also by other electronic means, subject to standards approved by the Judicial Conference.

1996 Amendments

The present Rule 5(e) has authorized filing by facsimile or other electronic means on two conditions. The filing must be authorized by local rule. Use of this means of filing must be authorized by the Judicial Conference of the United States and must be consistent with standards established by the Judicial Conference. Attempts to develop Judicial Conference standards have demonstrated the value of several adjustments in the rule.

The most significant change discards the requirement that the Judicial Conference authorize local electronic filing rules. As before, each district may decide for itself whether it has the equipment and personnel required to establish electronic filing, but a district that wishes to establish electronic filing need no longer await Judicial Conference action.

The role of Judicial Conference standards is clarified by specifying that the standards are to govern technical matters. Technical standards can provide nationwide uniformity, enabling ready use of electronic filing without pausing to adjust for the otherwise inevitable variations among local rules. Judicial Conference adoption of technical standards should prove superior to specification in these rules. Electronic technology has advanced with great speed. The process of adopting Judicial Conference standards should prove speedier and more flexible in determining the time for the first uniform standards, in adjusting standards at appropriate intervals, and in sparing the Supreme Court and Congress the need to consider technological details. Until Judicial Conference standards are adopted, however, uniformity will occur only to the extent that local rules deliberately seek to copy other local rules.

It is anticipated that Judicial Conference standards will govern such technical specifications as data formatting, speed of transmission, means to transmit copies of supporting documents, and security of communication. Perhaps more important, standards must be established to assure proper maintenance and integrity of the record and to provide appropriate access and retrieval mechanisms. Local rules must address these issues until Judicial Conference standards are adopted.

The amended rule also makes clear the equality of filing by electronic means with written filings. An electronic filing that complies with the local rule satisfies all requirements for filing on paper, signature, or verification. An electronic filing that otherwise satisfies the requirements of 28 U.S.C. § 1746 need not be separately made in writing. Public access to electronic filings is governed by the same rules as govern written filings.

The separate reference to filing by facsimile transmission is deleted. Facsimile transmission continues to be included as an electronic means.

Rule 6. Time

(a) Computation. In computing any period of time prescribed or allowed by these rules, by the local rules of any district court, by order of court, or by any applicable statute, the day of the act, event, or default from which the designated period of time begins to run shall not be included. The last day of the period so computed shall be included, unless it is a Saturday, a Sunday, or a legal holiday, or, when the act to be done is the filing of a paper in court, a day on which weather or other conditions have made the office of the clerk of the district court inaccessible, in which event the period runs until the end of the next day which is not one of the aforementioned days. When the period of time prescribed or allowed is less than 11 days, intermediate Saturdays, Sundays, and legal holidays shall be excluded in the computation. As used in this rule and in Rule 77(c), "legal holiday" includes New Year's Day, Birthday of Martin Luther King, Jr., Washington's Birthday, Memorial Day, Independence Day, Labor Day, Columbus Day, Veterans Day, Thanksgiving Day, Christmas Day, and any other day appointed as a holiday by the President or the Congress of the United States, or by the state in which the district court is held.

(b) Enlargement. When by these rules or by a notice given thereunder or by order of court an act is required or allowed to be done at or within a specified time, the court for cause shown may at any time in its discretion (1) with or without motion or notice order the period enlarged if request therefor is made before the expiration of the period originally prescribed or as extended by a previous order, or (2) upon motion made after the expiration of the specified period permit the act to be done where the failure to act was the result of excusable neglect; but it may not extend the time for taking any action under Rules 50(b) and (c)(2), 52(b), 59(b), (d) and (e), 60(b), and 74(a), except to the extent and under the conditions stated in them.

[(c) Rescinded Feb. 28, 1966, eff. July 1, 1966]

(d) For Motions—Affidavits. A written motion, other than one which may be heard ex parte, and notice of the hearing thereof shall be served not later than 5 days before the time specified for the hearing, unless a different period is fixed by these rules or by order of the court. Such an order may for cause shown be made on ex parte application. When a motion is supported by affidavit, the affidavit shall be served with the motion; and, except as otherwise provided in Rule 59(c), opposing affidavits may be served not later than 1 day before the hearing, unless the court permits them to be served at some other time.

(e) Additional Time After Service by Mail. Whenever a party has the right or is required to do some act or take some proceedings within a prescribed period after the service of a notice or other paper upon the party and the notice or paper is served upon the party by mail, 3 days shall be added to the prescribed period.

(As amended Dec. 27, 1946, eff. Mar. 19, 1948; Jan. 21, 1963, eff. July 1, 1963; Feb. 28, 1966, eff. July 1, 1966; Dec. 4, 1967, eff. July 1, 1968; Mar. 1, 1971, eff. July 1, 1971; Apr. 28, 1983, eff. Aug. 1, 1983; Apr. 29, 1985, eff. Aug. 1, 1985; Mar. 2, 1987, eff. Aug. 1, 1987.)

ADVISORY COMMITTEE NOTES

1937 Adoption

Note to Subdivisions (a) and (b). These are amplifications along lines common in state practices, of [former] Equity Rule 80 (Computation of Time—Sundays and Holidays) and of the provisions for enlargement of time found in [former] Equity Rules 8 (Enforcement of Final Decrees) and 16 (Defendant to Answer—Default—Decree Pro Confesso). See also Rule XIII, Rules and Forms in Criminal Cases, 1934, 292 U.S. 661, 666. Compare Ala.Code Ann. (Michie, 1928) § 13 and former Law Rule 8 of the Rules of the Supreme Court of the District of Columbia (1924), superseded in 1929 by Law Rule 8, Rules of the District Court of the United States for the District of Columbia (1937).

Note to Subdivision (c). This eliminates the difficulties caused by the expiration of terms of court. Such statutes as U.S.C., Title 28, [former] § 12 (Trials not discontinued by new term) are not affected. Compare Rules of the United States District Court of Minnesota, Rule 25 (Minn.Stat. (Mason, Supp.1936), p. 1089).

Note to Subdivision (d). Compare 2 Minn.Stat. (Mason, 1927) § 9246; N.Y.R.C.P. (1937) Rules 60 and 64.

1946 Amendment

Note to Subdivision (b). The purpose of the amendment is to clarify the finality of judgments. Prior to the advent of the Federal Rules of Civil Procedure, the general rule that a court loses jurisdiction to disturb its judgments, upon the expiration of the term at which they were entered, had long been the classic device which (together with the statutory limits on the time for appeal) gave finality to judgments. See note to rule 73(a). Rule 6(c) abrogates that limit on judicial power. That limit was open to many objections, one of them being inequality of operation because, under it, the time for vacating a judgment rendered early in a term was much longer than for a judgment rendered near the end of the term.

The question to be met under rule 6(b) is: how far should the desire to allow correction of judgments be allowed to postpone their finality? The rules contain a number of provisions permitting the vacation or modification of judgments on various grounds. Each of these rules contains express time limits on the motions for granting of relief.

Rule 6(b) is a rule of general application giving wide discretion to the court to enlarge these time limits or revive them after they have expired, the only exceptions stated in the original rule being a prohibition against enlarging the time specified in Rule 59(b) and (d) for making motions for or granting new trials, and a prohibition against enlarging the time fixed by law for taking an appeal. It should also be noted that Rule 6(b) itself contains no limitation of time within which the court may exercise its discretion, and since the expiration of the term does not end its power, there is now no time limit on the exercise of its discretion under Rule 6(b).

Decisions of lower federal courts suggest that some of the rules containing time limits which may be set aside under Rule 6(b) are Rules 25, 50(b), 52(b), 60(b), and 73(g).

In a number of cases the effect of Rule 6(b) on the time limitations of these rules has been considered. Certainly the rule is susceptible of the interpretation that the court is given the power in its discretion to relieve a party from failure to act within the times specified in any of these other rules, with only the exceptions stated in Rule 6(b), and in some cases the rule has been so construed.

With regard to Rule 25(a) for substitution, it was held in *Anderson v. Brady,* Ky.1941, 1 F.R.D. 589, 4 Fed.Rules Service 25a.1, Case 1, and in *Anderson v. Yungkau,* C.C.A.6, 1946, 153 F.2d 685, certiorari granted 66 S.Ct. 1025, 328 U.S. 829, 90 L.Ed. 1606, that under Rule 6(b) the court had no authority to allow substitution of parties after the expiration of the limit fixed in Rule 25(a).

As to Rules 50(b) for judgments notwithstanding the verdict and 52(b) for amendment of findings and vacation of judgment, it was recognized in *Leishman v. Associated Wholesale Electric Co.,* 1943, 63 S.Ct. 543, 318 U.S. 203, 87 L.Ed. 714, that Rule 6(b) allowed the district court to enlarge the time to make a motion for amended findings and judgment beyond the limit expressly fixed in Rule 52(b). See *Coca-Cola v. Busch,* E.D.Pa.1943, 7 Fed.Rules Service, 59b.2, Case 4. Obviously, if the time limit in Rule 52(b) could be set aside under Rule 6(b), the time limit in Rule 50(b) for granting judgment notwithstanding the verdict (and thus vacating the judgment entered "forthwith" on the verdict) likewise could be set aside.

As to Rule 59 on motions for a new trial, it has been settled that the time limits in Rule 59(b) and (d) for making motions for or granting new trial could not be set aside under Rule 6(b), because Rule 6(b) expressly refers to Rule 59, and forbids it. See *Safeway Stores, Inc. v. Coe,* App.D.C. 1943, 136 F.2d 771, 78 U.S.App.D.C. 19; *Jusino v. Morales & Tio,* C.C.A.1, 1944, 139 F.2d 946; *Coca-Cola Co. v. Busch,* E.D.Pa.1943, 7 Fed.Rules Service 59b.2, Case 4; *Peterson v. Chicago Great Western Ry. Co.,* D.Neb.1943, 3 F.R.D. 346, 7 Fed.Rules Service 59b.2, Case 1; *Leishman v. Associated Wholesale Electric Co.,* 1943, 63 S.Ct. 543, 318 U.S. 203, 87 L.Ed. 714.

As to Rule 60(b) for relief from a judgment, it was held in *Schram v. O'Connor,* Mich.1941, 5 Fed.Rules Serv. 6b.31, Case 1, 2 F.R.D. 192, s.c. 5 Fed.Rules Serv. 6b.31, Case 2, 2 F.R.D. 192, that the six-months time limit in original rule 60(b) for making a motion for relief from a judgment for surprise, mistake, or excusable neglect could be set aside under Rule 6(b). The contrary result was reached in *Wallace v. United States,* C.C.A.2, 1944, 142 F.2d 240, certiorari denied 65 S.Ct. 37, 323 U.S. 712, 89 L.Ed. 573; *Reed v. South Atlantic Steamship Co. of Del.,* Del.1942, 2 F.R.D. 475, 6 Fed.Rules Serv. 60b.31, Case 1.

As to Rule 73(g), fixing the time for docketing an appeal, it was held in *Ains-worth v. Gill Glass & Fixture Co.,* C.C.A.3, 1939, 104 F.2d 83, that under Rule 6(b) the district court, upon motion made after the expiration of the forty-day period, stated in Rule 73(g), but before the expiration of the ninety-day period therein specified, could permit the docketing of the appeal on a showing of excusable neglect. The contrary was held in *Mutual Benefit Health & Accident Ass'n v. Snyder,* C.C.A.6, 1940, 109 F.2d 469 and in *Burke v. Canfield,* 1940, 111 F.2d 526, 72 App.D.C. 127.

The amendment of Rule 6(b) now proposed is based on the view that there should be a definite point where it can be said a judgment is final; that the right method of dealing with the problem is to list in Rule 6(b) the various other rules whose time limits may not be set aside, and then, if the time limit in any of those other rules is too short, to amend that other rule to give a longer time. The further argument is that Rule 6(c) abolished the long standing device to produce finality in judgments through expiration of the term, and since that limitation on the jurisdiction of courts to set aside their own judgments has been removed by Rule 6(c), some other limitation must be substituted or judgments never can be said to be final.

In this connection reference is made to the established rule that if a motion for new trial is seasonably made, the mere making or pendency of the motion destroys the finality of the judgment, and even though the motion is ultimately denied, the full time for appeal starts anew from the date of denial. Also, a motion to amend the findings under Rule 52(b) has the same effect on the time for appeal. *Leishman v. Associated Wholesale Electric Co.,* 1943, 63 S.Ct. 543, 318 U.S. 203, 87 L.Ed. 714. By the same reasoning a motion for judgment under Rule 50(b), involving as it does the vacation of a judgment entered "forthwith" on the verdict (Rule 58), operates to postpone, until an order is made, the running of the time for appeal. The Committee believes that the abolition by Rule 6(c) of the old rule that a court's power over its judgments ends with the term, requires a substitute limitation, and that unless Rule 6(b) is amended to prevent enlargement of the times specified in Rules 50(b), 52(b) and 60(b), and the limitation as to Rule 59(b) and (d) is retained, no one can say when a judgment is final. This is also true with regard to proposed Rule 59(e), which authorizes a motion to alter or amend a judgment, hence that rule is also included in the enumeration in amended Rule 6(b). In consideration of the amendment, however, it should be noted that Rule 60(b) is also to be amended so as to lengthen the six-months period originally prescribed in that rule to one year.

As to Rule 25 on substitution, while finality is not involved, the limit there fixed should be controlling. That rule, as amended, gives the court power, upon showing of a reasonable excuse, to permit substitution after the expiration of the two-year period.

As to Rule 73(g), it is believed that the conflict in decisions should be resolved and not left to further litigation, and that the rule should be listed as one whose limitation may not be set aside under Rule 6(b).

As to Rule 59(c), fixing the time for serving affidavits on motion for new trial, it is believed that the court should have authority under Rule 6(b) to enlarge the time, because, once the motion for new trial is made, the judgment no longer has finality, and the extension of time for affidavits thus does not of itself disturb finality.

Other changes proposed in Rule 6(b) are merely clarifying and conforming. Thus "request" is substituted for "application" in clause (1) because an application is defined as a motion under Rule 7(b). The phrase "extend the time" is substituted for "enlarge the period" because the former is a more suitable expression and relates more clearly to both clauses (1) and (2). The final phrase in Rule 6(b), "or the period for taking an appeal as provided by law", is deleted and a reference to Rule 73(a) inserted, since it is proposed to state in that rule the time for appeal to a circuit court of appeals, which is the only appeal governed by the Federal Rules, and allows an extension of time. See Rule 72.

Subdivision (c). The purpose of this amendment is to prevent reliance upon the continued existence of a term as a source of power to disturb the finality of a judgment upon grounds other than those stated in these rules. See *Hill v. Hawes,* 1944, 64 S.Ct. 334, 320 U.S. 520, 88 L.Ed. 283; *Boaz v. Mutual Life Ins. Co. of New York,* C.C.A.8, 1944, 146 F.2d 321; *Bucy v. Nevada Construction Co.,* C.C.A.9, 1942, 125 F.2d 213.

1963 Amendment

Subdivision (a). This amendment is related to the amendment of Rule 77(c) changing the regulation of the days on which the clerk's office shall be open.

The wording of the first sentence of Rule 6(a) is clarified and the subdivision is made expressly applicable to computing periods of time set forth in local rules.

Saturday is to be treated in the same way as Sunday or a "legal holiday" in that it is not to be included when it falls on the last day of a computed period, nor counted as an intermediate day when the period is less than 7 days. "Legal holiday" is defined for purposes of this subdivision and amended Rule 77(c). Compare the definition of "holiday" in 11 U.S.C. § 1(18); also 5 U.S.C. § 86a; Executive Order No. 10358, *"Observance of Holidays,"* June 9, 1952, 17 Fed.Reg. 5269. In the light of these changes the last sentence of the present subdivision, dealing with half holidays, is eliminated.

With Saturdays and State holidays made "dies non" in certain cases by the amended subdivision, computation of the usual 5-day notice of motion or the 2-day notice to dissolve or modify a temporary restraining order may work out so as to cause embarrassing delay in urgent cases. The delay can be obviated by applying to the court to shorten the time, see Rules 6(d) and 65(b).

Subdivision (b). The prohibition against extending the time for taking action under Rule 25 (Substitution of parties) is eliminated. The only limitation of time provided for in amended Rule 25 is the 90-day period following a suggestion upon the record of the death of a party within which to make a motion to substitute the proper parties for the deceased party. See Rule 25(a)(1), as amended, and the Advisory Committee's Note thereto. It is intended that the court shall have discretion to enlarge that period.

1966 Amendment

P.L. 88–139, § 1, 77 Stat. 248, approved on October 16, 1963, amended 28 U.S.C. § 138 to read as follows: "The district court shall not hold formal terms." Thus Rule 6(c) is rendered unnecessary, and it is rescinded.

1967 Amendment

The amendment eliminates the references to Rule 73, which is to be abrogated.

1971 Amendment

The amendment adds Columbus Day to the list of legal holidays to conform the subdivision to the Act of June 28, 1968, 82 Stat. 250, which constituted Columbus Day a legal holiday effective after January 1, 1971.

The Act, which amended Title 5, U.S.C. § 6103(a), changes the day on which certain holidays are to be observed. Washington's Birthday, Memorial Day and Veterans Day are to be observed on the third Monday in February, the last Monday in May and the fourth Monday in October, respectively, rather than, as heretofore, on February 22, May 30, and November 11, respectively, Columbus Day is to be observed on the second Monday in October. New Year's Day, Independence Day, Thanksgiving Day and Christmas continue to be observed on the traditional days.

1983 Amendment

Subdivision (b). The amendment confers finality upon the judgments of magistrates by foreclosing enlargement of the time for appeal except as provided in new Rule 74(a) (20 day period for demonstration of excusable neglect).

1985 Amendment

Rule 6(a) is amended to acknowledge that weather conditions or other events may render the clerk's office inaccessible one or more days. Parties who are obliged to file something with the court during that period should not be penalized if they cannot do so. The amendment conforms to changes made in Federal Rule of Criminal Procedure 45(a), effective August 1, 1982.

The Rule also is amended to extend the exclusion of intermediate Saturdays, Sundays, and legal holidays to the computation of time periods less than 11 days. Under the current version of the Rule, parties bringing motions under rules with 10-day periods could have as few as 5 working days to prepare their motions. This hardship would be especially acute in the case of Rules 50(b) and (c)(2), 52(b), and 59(b), (d), and (e), which may not be enlarged at the discretion of the court. See Rule 6(b). If the exclusion of Saturdays, Sundays, and legal holidays will operate to cause excessive delay in urgent cases, the delay can be obviated by applying to the court to shorten the time. See Rule 6(b).

The Birthday of Martin Luther King, Jr., which becomes a legal holiday effective in 1986, has been added to the list of legal holidays enumerated in the Rule.

1987 Amendment

The amendments are technical. No substantive change is intended.

HISTORICAL NOTES

Effective Dates

1946 Amendment. Effective date of amendment to this rule, see rule 86(b).

III. PLEADINGS AND MOTIONS

Rule 7. Pleadings Allowed; Form of Motions

(a) Pleadings. There shall be a complaint and an answer; a reply to a counterclaim denominated as such; an answer to a cross-claim, if the answer contains a cross-claim; a third-party complaint, if a person who was not an original party is summoned under the provisions of Rule 14; and a third-party answer, if a third-party complaint is served. No other pleading shall be allowed, except that the court may order a reply to an answer or a third-party answer.

(b) Motions and Other Papers.

(1) An application to the court for an order shall be by motion which, unless made during a hearing or trial, shall be made in writing, shall state with particularity the grounds therefor, and shall set forth the relief or order sought. The requirement of writing is fulfilled if the motion is stated in a written notice of the hearing of the motion.

(2) The rules applicable to captions and other matters of form of pleadings apply to all motions and other papers provided for by these rules.

(3) All motions shall be signed in accordance with Rule 11.

(c) Demurrers, Pleas, etc., Abolished. Demurrers, pleas, and exceptions for insufficiency of a pleading shall not be used.

(As amended Dec. 27, 1946, eff. Mar. 19, 1948; Jan. 21, 1963, eff. July 1, 1963; Apr. 28, 1983, eff. Aug. 1, 1983.)

ADVISORY COMMITTEE NOTES

1937 Adoption

1. A provision designating pleadings and defining a motion is common in the state practice acts. See Smith-Hurd Ill.Stats. ch. 110, § 156 (Designation and order of pleadings); 2 Minn.Stat. (Mason, 1927) § 9246 (Definition of motion); and N.Y.C.P.A. (1937) § 113 (Definition of motion). Former Equity Rules 18 (Pleadings—Technical Forms Abrogated), 29 (Defenses—How Presented), and 33 (Testing Sufficiency of Defense) abolished technical forms of pleading, demurrers and pleas, and exceptions for insufficiency of an answer.

2. Note to Subdivision (a). This preserves the substance of [former] Equity Rule 31 (Reply—When Required—When Cause at Issue). Compare the English practice, *English Rules under the Judicature Act* (The Annual Practice, 1937) O. 23, r.r. 1, 2 (Reply to counterclaim; amended, 1933, to be subject to the rules applicable to defenses, O. 21). See O. 21, r.r. 1–14; O. 27, r. 13 (When pleadings deemed denied and put in issue). Under the codes the pleadings are generally limited. A reply is sometimes required to an affirmative defense in the answer. 1 Colo.Stat.Ann. (1935) § 66; Ore. Code Ann. (1930) §§ 1–614, 1–616. In other jurisdictions no reply is necessary to an affirmative defense in the answer, but a reply may be ordered by the court. N.C.Code Ann. (1935) § 525; 1 S.D.Comp.Laws (1929) § 2357. A reply to a counterclaim is usually required. Ark.Civ.Code (Crawford, 1934) §§ 123 to 125; Wis.Stat. (1935) §§ 263.20, 263.21. U.S.C. Title 28, [former] § 45 (District courts; practice and procedure in certain cases) is modified insofar as it may dispense with a reply to a counterclaim.

For amendment of pleadings, see Rule 15 dealing with amended and supplemental pleadings.

3. All statutes which use the words "petition", "bill of complaint", "plea", "demurrer", and other such terminology are modified in form by this rule.

1946 Amendment

Note. This amendment eliminates any question as to whether the compulsory reply, where a counterclaim is pleaded, is a reply only to the counterclaim or is a general reply to the answer containing the counterclaim. The Commentary, *Scope of Reply where Defendant Has Pleaded Counterclaim,* 1939, 1 Fed.Rules Serv. 672; *Fort Chartres and Ivy Landing Drainage and Levee District No. Five v. Thompson,* Ill.1945, 8 Fed.Rules Serv. 13.32, Case 1.

1963 Amendment

Certain redundant words are eliminated and the subdivision is modified to reflect the amendment of Rule 14(a) which in certain cases eliminates the requirement of obtaining leave to bring in a third-party defendant.

1983 Amendment

One of the reasons sanctions against improper motion practice have been employed infrequently is the lack of clarity of Rule 7. That rule has stated only generally that the pleading requirements relating to captions, signing, and other matters of form also apply to motions and other papers. The addition of Rule 7(b)(3) makes explicit the applicability of the signing requirement and the sanctions of Rule 11, which have been amplified.

HISTORICAL NOTES

Effective Dates

1946 Amendment. Effective date of amendment to this rule, see rule 86(b).

Rule 8. General Rules of Pleading

(a) Claims for Relief. A pleading which sets forth a claim for relief, whether an original claim, counterclaim, cross-claim, or third-party claim, shall contain

(1) a short and plain statement of the grounds upon which the court's jurisdiction depends, unless the court already has jurisdiction and the claim needs no new grounds of jurisdiction to support it, (2) a short and plain statement of the claim showing that the pleader is entitled to relief, and (3) a demand for judgment for the relief the pleader seeks. Relief in the alternative or of several different types may be demanded.

(b) Defenses; Form of Denials. A party shall state in short and plain terms the party's defenses to each claim asserted and shall admit or deny the averments upon which the adverse party relies. If a party is without knowledge or information sufficient to form a belief as to the truth of an averment, the party shall so state and this has the effect of a denial. Denials shall fairly meet the substance of the averments denied. When a pleader intends in good faith to deny only a part or a qualification of an averment, the pleader shall specify so much of it as is true and material and shall deny only the remainder. Unless the pleader intends in good faith to controvert all the averments of the preceding pleading, the pleader may make denials as specific denials of designated averments or paragraphs or may generally deny all the averments except such designated averments or paragraphs as the pleader expressly admits; but, when the pleader does so intend to controvert all its averments, including averments of the grounds upon which the court's jurisdiction depends, the pleader may do so by general denial subject to the obligations set forth in Rule 11.

(c) Affirmative Defenses. In pleading to a preceding pleading, a party shall set forth affirmatively accord and satisfaction, arbitration and award, assumption of risk, contributory negligence, discharge in bankruptcy, duress, estoppel, failure of consideration, fraud, illegality, injury by fellow servant, laches, license, payment, release, res judicata, statute of frauds, statute of limitations, waiver, and any other matter constituting an avoidance or affirmative defense. When a party has mistakenly designated a defense as a counterclaim or a counterclaim as a defense, the court on terms, if justice so requires, shall treat the pleading as if there had been a proper designation.

(d) Effect of Failure to Deny. Averments in a pleading to which a responsive pleading is required, other than those as to the amount of damage, are admitted when not denied in the responsive pleading. Averments in a pleading to which no responsive pleading is required or permitted shall be taken as denied or avoided.

(e) Pleading to be Concise and Direct; Consistency.

(1) Each averment of a pleading shall be simple, concise, and direct. No technical forms of pleading or motions are required.

(2) A party may set forth two or more statements of a claim or defense alternately or hypothetically, either in one count or defense or in separate counts or defenses. When two or more statements are made in the alternative and one of them if made independently would be sufficient, the pleading is not made insufficient by the insufficiency of one or more of the alternative statements. A party may also state as many separate claims or defenses as the party has regardless of consistency and whether based on legal, equitable, or maritime grounds. All statements shall be made subject to the obligations set forth in Rule 11.

(f) Construction of Pleadings. All pleadings shall be so construed as to do substantial justice.

(As amended Feb. 28, 1966, eff. July 1, 1966; Mar. 2, 1987, eff. Aug. 1, 1987.)

ADVISORY COMMITTEE NOTES

1937 Adoption

Note to Subdivision (a). See [former] Equity Rules 25 (Bill of Complaint—Contents), and 30 (Answer—Contents—Counterclaim). Compare 2 Ind.Stat.Ann. (Burns, 1933) §§ 2–1004, 2–1015; 2 Ohio Gen.Code Ann. (Page, 1926) §§ 11305, 11314; Utah Rev.Stat.Ann. (1933) §§ 104–7–2, 104–9–1.

See Rule 19(c) for the requirement of a statement in a claim for relief of the names of persons who ought to be parties and the reason for their omission.

See Rule 23(b) for particular requirements as to the complaint in a secondary action by shareholders.

Note to Subdivision (b). **1.** This rule supersedes the methods of pleading prescribed in U.S.C., Title 19, § 508 (Persons making seizures pleading general issue and proving special matter); U.S.C. Title 35, [former] §§ 40d (Proving under general issue, upon notice, that a statement in application for an extended patent is not true), 69 [now 282] (Pleading and proof in actions for infringement) and similar statutes.

2. This rule is, in part, [former] Equity Rule 30 (Answer—Contents—Counterclaim), with the matter on denials largely from the Connecticut practice. See Conn. Practice Book (1934) §§ 107, 108, and 122; Conn.Gen.Stat. (1930) §§ 5508 to 5514. Compare the English practice, *English Rules Under the Judicature Act* (The Annual Practice, 1937) O. 19, r.r. 17–20.

Note to Subdivision (c). This follows substantially *English Rules Under the Judicature Act* (The Annual Practice, 1937) O. 19, r. 15 and N.Y.C.P.A. (1937) § 242, with "surprise" omitted in this rule.

Note to Subdivision (d). The first sentence is similar to former Equity Rule 30 (Answer—Contents—Counterclaim). For the second sentence see former Equity Rule 31 (Reply—When Required—When Cause at Issue). This is similar to *English Rules Under the Judicature Act* (The Annual Practice, 1937) O. 19, r.r. 13, 18; and to the practice of the States.

Note to Subdivision (e). This rule is an elaboration upon [former] Equity Rule 30 (Answer—Contents—Counterclaim), plus a statement of the actual practice under some codes. Compare also [former] Equity Rule 18 (Pleadings—Technical Forms Abrogated). See Clark, *Code Pleading* (1928), pp. 171–4, 432–5; Hankin, *Alternative and Hypothetical Pleading* (1924), 33 Yale L.J. 365.

Note to Subdivision (f). A provision of like import is of frequent occurrence in the codes. Smith-Hurd Ill.Stats. ch. 110, § 157(3); 2 Minn.Stat. (Mason, 1927) § 9266; N.Y.C.P.A. (1937) § 275; 2 N.D.Comp.Laws Ann. (1913) § 7458.

1966 Amendment

The change here is consistent with the broad purposes of unification.

1987 Amendment

The amendments are technical. No substantive change is intended.

Rule 9. Pleading Special Matters

(a) Capacity. It is not necessary to aver the capacity of a party to sue or be sued or the authority of a party to sue or be sued in a representative capacity or the legal existence of an organized association of persons that is made a party, except to the extent required to show the jurisdiction of the court. When a party desires to raise an issue as to the legal existence of any party or the capacity of any party to sue or be sued or the authority of a party to sue or be sued in a representative capacity, the party desiring to raise the issue shall do so by specific negative averment, which shall include such supporting particulars as are peculiarly within the pleader's knowledge.

(b) Fraud, Mistake, Condition of the Mind. In all averments of fraud or mistake, the circumstances constituting fraud or mistake shall be stated with particularity. Malice, intent, knowledge, and other condition of mind of a person may be averred generally.

(c) Conditions Precedent. In pleading the performance or occurrence of conditions precedent, it is sufficient to aver generally that all conditions precedent have been performed or have occurred. A denial of performance or occurrence shall be made specifically and with particularity.

(d) Official Document or Act. In pleading an official document or official act it is sufficient to aver that the document was issued or the act done in compliance with law.

(e) Judgment. In pleading a judgment or decision of a domestic or foreign court, judicial or quasi-judicial tribunal, or of a board or officer, it is sufficient to aver the judgment or decision without setting forth matter showing jurisdiction to render it.

(f) Time and Place. For the purpose of testing the sufficiency of a pleading, averments of time and place are material and shall be considered like all other averments of material matter.

(g) Special Damage. When items of special damage are claimed, they shall be specifically stated.

(h) Admiralty and Maritime Claims. A pleading or count setting forth a claim for relief within the admiralty and maritime jurisdiction that is also within the jurisdiction of the district court on some other ground may contain a statement identifying the claim as an admiralty or maritime claim for the purposes of Rules 14(c), 38(e), 82, and the Supplemental Rules for Certain Admiralty and Maritime Claims. If the claim is cognizable only in admiralty, it is an admiralty or maritime claim for those purposes whether so identified or not. The amendment of a pleading to add or withdraw an identifying statement is governed by the principles of Rule 15. A case that includes an admiralty or maritime claim within this subdivision is an admiralty case within 28 U.S.C. § 1292(a)(3).

(As amended Feb. 28, 1966, eff. July 1, 1966; Dec. 4, 1967, eff. July 1, 1968; Mar. 30, 1970, eff. July 1, 1970; Mar. 2, 1987, eff. Aug. 1, 1987; April 11, 1997, eff. Dec. 1, 1997.)

ADVISORY COMMITTEE NOTES

1937 Adoption

Note to Subdivision (a). Compare [former] Equity Rule 25 (Bill of Complaint—Contents) requiring disability to be stated; Utah Rev.Stat.Ann. (1933) § 104–13–15, enumerating a number of situations where a general averment of capacity is sufficient. For provisions governing averment of incorporation, see 2 Minn.Stat. (Mason, 1927) § 9271; N.Y.R.C.P. (1937) Rule 93; 2 N.D.Comp.Laws Ann. (1913) § 7981 et seq.

Note to Subdivision (b). See *English Rules Under the Judicature Act* (The Annual Practice, 1937) O. 19, r. 22.

Note to Subdivision (c). The codes generally have this or a similar provision. See *English Rules Under the Judicature Act* (The Annual Practice, 1937) O. 19, r. 14; 2 Minn. Stat. (Mason, 1927) § 9273; N.Y.R.C.P. (1937) Rule 92; 2 N.D.Comp.Laws Ann. (1913) § 7461; 2 Wash.Rev.Stat.Ann. (Remington, 1932) § 288.

Note to Subdivision (e). The rule expands the usual code provisions on pleading a judgment by including judgments or decisions of administrative tribunals and foreign courts. Compare Ark.Civ.Code (Crawford, 1934) § 141; 2 Minn.Stat. (Mason, 1927) § 9269; N.Y.R.C.P. (1937) Rule 95; 2 Wash. Rev.Stat.Ann. (Remington, 1932) § 287.

1966 Amendment

Certain distinctive features of the admiralty practice must be preserved for what are now suits in admiralty. This raises the question: After unification, when a single form of action is established, how will the counterpart of the present suit in admiralty be identifiable? In part the question is easily answered. Some claims for relief can only be suits in admiralty, either because the admiralty jurisdiction is exclusive or because no nonmaritime ground of federal jurisdiction exists. Many claims, however, are cognizable by the district courts whether asserted in admiralty or in a civil action, assuming the existence of a nonmaritime ground of jurisdiction. Thus at present the pleader has power to determine procedural consequences by the way in which he exercises the classic privilege given by the saving-to-suitors clause (28 U.S.C. § 1333) or by equivalent statutory provisions. For example, a longshoreman's claim for personal injuries suffered by reason of the unseaworthiness of a vessel may be asserted in a suit in admiralty or, if diversity of citizenship exists, in a civil action. One of the important procedural consequences is that in the civil action either party may demand a jury trial, while in the suit in admiralty there is no right to jury trial except as provided by statute.

It is no part of the purpose of unification to inject a right to jury trial into those admiralty cases in which that right is not provided by statute. Similarly as will be more specifically noted below, there is no disposition to change the present law as to interlocutory appeals in admiralty, or as to the venue of suits in admiralty; and, of course, there is no disposition to inject into the civil practice as it now is the distinctively maritime remedies (maritime attachment and garnishment, actions in rem, possessory, petitory and partition actions and limitation of liability). The unified rules must therefore provide some device for preserving the present power of the pleader to determine whether these historically maritime procedures shall be applicable to his claim or not; the pleader must be afforded some means of designating his claim as the counterpart of the present suit in admiralty, where its character as such is not clear.

The problem is different from the similar one concerning the identification of claims that were formerly suits in equity. While that problem is not free from complexities, it is broadly true that the modern counterpart of the suit in equity is distinguishable from the former action at law by the character of the relief sought. This mode of identification is possible in only a limited category of admiralty cases. In large numbers of cases the relief sought in admiralty is simple money damages, indistinguishable from the remedy afforded by the common law. This is true, for example, in the case of the longshoreman's action for personal injuries stated above. After unification has abolished the distinction between civil actions and suits in admiralty, the complaint in such an action would be almost completely ambiguous as to the pleader's intentions regarding the procedure invoked. The allegation of diversity of citizenship might be regarded as a clue indicating an intention to proceed as at present under the saving-to-suitors clause; but this, too, would be ambiguous if there were also reference to the admiralty jurisdiction, and the pleader ought not be required to forego mention of all available jurisdictional grounds.

Other methods of solving the problem were carefully explored, but the Advisory Committee concluded that the preferable solution is to allow the pleader who now has power to determine procedural consequences by filing a suit in admiralty to exercise that power under unification, for the limited instances in which procedural differences will remain, by a simple statement in his pleading to the effect that the claim is an admiralty or maritime claim.

The choice made by the pleader in identifying or in failing to identify his claim as an admiralty or maritime claim is not an irrevocable election. The rule provides that the amendment of a pleading to add or withdraw an identifying statement is subject to the principles of Rule 15.

1968 Amendment

The amendment eliminates the reference to Rule 73 which is to be abrogated and transfers to Rule 9(h) the substance of Subsection (h) of Rule 73 which preserved the right to an interlocutory appeal in admiralty cases which is provided by 28 U.S.C. § 1292(a)(3).

1970 Amendment

The reference to Rule 26(a) is deleted, in light of the transfer of that subdivision to Rule 30(a) and the elimination of the de bene esse procedure therefrom. See the Advisory Committee's note to Rule 30(a).

1987 Amendment

The amendment is technical. No substantive change is intended.

1997 Amendment

Section 1292(a)(3) of the Judicial Code provides for appeal from "[i]nterlocutory decrees of * * * district courts * * * determining the rights and liabilities of the parties to admiralty cases in which appeals from final decrees are allowed."

Rule 9(h) was added in 1966 with the unification of civil and admiralty procedure. Civil Rule 73(h) was amended at the same time to provide that the § 1292(a)(3) reference "to admiralty cases shall be construed to mean admiralty and maritime claims within the meaning of Rule 9(h)." This provision was transferred to Rule 9(h) when the Appellate Rules were adopted.

A single case can include both admiralty or maritime claims and nonadmiralty claims or parties. This combination reveals an ambiguity in the statement in present Rule 9(h) that an admiralty "claim" is an admiralty "case." An order "determining the rights and liabilities of the parties" within the meaning of § 1292(a)(3) may resolve only a nonadmiralty claim, or may simultaneously resolve interdependent admiralty and nonadmiralty claims. Can appeal be taken as to the nonadmiralty matter, because it is part of a case that includes an admiralty claim, or is appeal limited to the admiralty claim?

The courts of appeals have not achieved full uniformity in applying the § 1292(a)(3) requirement that an order "determin[e] the rights and liabilities of the parties." It is common to assert that the statute should be construed narrowly, under the general policy that exceptions to the final judgment rule should be construed narrowly. This policy would suggest that the ambiguity should be resolved by limiting the interlocutory appeal right to orders that determine the rights and liabilities of the parties to an admiralty claim.

A broader view is chosen by this amendment for two reasons. The statute applies to admiralty "cases," and may itself provide for appeal from an order that disposes of a nonadmiralty claim that is joined in a single case with an admiralty claim. Although a rule of court may help to clarify and implement a statutory grant of jurisdiction, the line is not always clear between permissible implementation and impermissible withdrawal of jurisdiction. In addition, so long as an order truly disposes of the rights and liabilities of the parties within the meaning of § 1292(a)(3), it may prove important to permit appeal as to the nonadmiralty claim. Disposition of the nonadmiralty claim, for example, may make it unnecessary to consider the admiralty claim and have the same effect on the case and parties as disposition of the admiralty claim. Or the admiralty and nonadmiralty claims may be interdependent. An illustration is provided by Roco Carriers, Ltd. v. M/V Nurnberg Express, 899 F.2d 1292 (2d Cir.1990). Claims for losses of ocean shipments were made against two defendants, one subject to admiralty jurisdiction and the other not. Summary judgment was granted in favor of the admiralty defendant and against the nonadmiralty defendant. The nonadmiralty defendant's appeal was accepted, with the explanation that the determination of its liability was "integrally linked with the determination of non-liability" of the admiralty defendant, and that "section 1292(a)(3) is not limited to admiralty claims; instead, it refers to admiralty cases." 899 F.2d at 1297. The advantages of permitting appeal by the nonadmiralty defendant would be particularly clear if the plaintiff had appealed the summary judgment in favor of the admiralty defendant.

It must be emphasized that this amendment does not rest on any particular assumptions as to the meaning of the § 1292(a)(3) provision that limits interlocutory appeal to orders that determine the rights and liabilities of the parties. It simply reflects the conclusion that so long as the case involves an admiralty claim and an order otherwise meets statutory requirements, the opportunity to appeal should not turn on the circumstance that the order does—or does not—dispose of an admiralty claim. No attempt is made to invoke the authority conferred by 28 U.S.C. § 1292(e) to provide by rule for appeal of an interlocutory decision that is not otherwise provided for by other subsections of § 1292.

GAP Report on Rule 9(h). No changes have been made in the published proposal.

Rule 10. Form of Pleadings

(a) Caption; Names of Parties. Every pleading shall contain a caption setting forth the name of the court, the title of the action, the file number, and a designation as in Rule 7(a). In the complaint the title of the action shall include the names of all the parties, but in other pleadings it is sufficient to state the name of the first party on each side with an appropriate indication of other parties.

(b) Paragraphs; Separate Statements. All averments of claim or defense shall be made in numbered paragraphs, the contents of each of which shall be limited as far as practicable to a statement of a single set of circumstances; and a paragraph may be referred to by number in all succeeding pleadings. Each claim founded upon a separate transaction or occurrence and each defense other than denials shall be stated in a separate count or defense whenever a separation facilitates the clear presentation of the matters set forth.

(c) Adoption by Reference; Exhibits. Statements in a pleading may be adopted by reference in a different part of the same pleading or in another pleading or in any motion. A copy of any written instrument which is an exhibit to a pleading is a part thereof for all purposes.

ADVISORY COMMITTEE NOTES

1937 Adoption

The first sentence is derived in part from the opening statement of former Equity Rule 25 (Bill of Complaint—Contents). The remainder of the rule is an expansion in conformity with usual state provisions. For numbered paragraphs and separate statements, see Conn.Gen.Stat., 1930, § 5513; Smith-Hurd Ill.Stats. ch. 110, § 157(2); N.Y.R.C.P., (1937) Rule 90. For incorporation by reference, see N.Y.R.C.P., (1937) Rule 90. For written instruments as exhibits, see Smith-Hurd Ill.Stats. ch. 110, § 160.

Rule 11. Signing of Pleadings, Motions, and Other Papers; Representations to Court; Sanctions

(a) Signature. Every pleading, written motion, and other paper shall be signed by at least one attorney of record in the attorney's individual name, or, if the party is not represented by an attorney, shall be signed by the party. Each paper shall state the signer's address and telephone number, if any. Except when otherwise specifically provided by rule or statute, pleadings need not be verified or accompanied by affidavit. An unsigned paper shall be stricken unless omission of the signature is corrected promptly after being called to the attention of the attorney or party.

(b) Representations to Court. By presenting to the court (whether by signing, filing, submitting, or later advocating) a pleading, written motion, or other paper, an attorney or unrepresented party is certifying that to the best of the person's knowledge, information, and belief, formed after an inquiry reasonable under the circumstances,—

(1) it is not being presented for any improper purpose, such as to harass or to cause unnecessary delay or needless increase in the cost of litigation;

(2) the claims, defenses, and other legal contentions therein are warranted by existing law or by a nonfrivolous argument for the extension, modification, or reversal of existing law or the establishment of new law;

(3) the allegations and other factual contentions have evidentiary support or, if specifically so identified, are likely to have evidentiary support after a reasonable opportunity for further investigation or discovery; and

(4) the denials of factual contentions are warranted on the evidence or, if specifically so identified, are reasonably based on a lack of information or belief.

(c) Sanctions. If, after notice and a reasonable opportunity to respond, the court determines that subdivision (b) has been violated, the court may, subject to the conditions stated below, impose an appropriate sanction upon the attorneys, law firms, or parties that have violated subdivision (b) or are responsible for the violation.

(1) How Initiated.

(A) By Motion. A motion for sanctions under this rule shall be made separately from other motions or requests and shall describe the specific conduct alleged to violate subdivision (b). It shall be served as provided in Rule 5, but shall not be filed with or presented to the court unless, within 21 days after service of the motion (or such other period as the court may prescribe), the challenged paper, claim, defense, contention, allegation, or denial is not withdrawn or appropriately corrected. If warranted, the court may award to the party prevailing on the motion the reasonable expenses and attorney's fees incurred in presenting or opposing the motion. Absent exceptional circumstances, a law firm shall be held jointly responsible for violations committed by its partners, associates, and employees.

(B) On Court's Initiative. On its own initiative, the court may enter an order describing the specific conduct that appears to violate subdivision (b) and directing an attorney, law firm, or party to show cause why it has not violated subdivision (b) with respect thereto.

(2) Nature of Sanction; Limitations. A sanction imposed for violation of this rule shall be limited to what is sufficient to deter repetition of such conduct or comparable conduct by others similarly situated. Subject to the limitations in subparagraphs (A) and (B), the sanction may consist of, or include, directives of a nonmonetary nature, an order to pay a penalty into court, or, if imposed on motion and warranted for effective deterrence, an order directing payment to the movant of some or all of the reasonable attorneys' fees and other expenses incurred as a direct result of the violation.

(A) Monetary sanctions may not be awarded against a represented party for a violation of subdivision (b)(2).

(B) Monetary sanctions may not be awarded on the court's initiative unless the court issues its order to show cause before a voluntary dismissal or settlement of the claims made by or against the party which is, or whose attorneys are, to be sanctioned.

(3) Order. When imposing sanctions, the court shall describe the conduct determined to constitute a violation of this rule and explain the basis for the sanction imposed.

(d) Inapplicability to Discovery. Subdivisions (a) through (c) of this rule do not apply to disclosures and discovery requests, responses, objections, and motions that are subject to the provisions of Rules 26 through 37.

(As amended Apr. 28, 1983, eff. Aug. 1, 1983; Mar. 2, 1987, eff. Aug. 1, 1987; Apr. 22, 1993, eff. Dec. 1, 1993.)

ADVISORY COMMITTEE NOTES

1937 Adoption

This is substantially the content of [former] Equity Rules 24 (Signature of Counsel) and 21 (Scandal and Impertinence) consolidated and unified. Compare former Equity Rule 36 (Officers Before Whom Pleadings Verified). Compare to similar purposes, *English Rules Under the Judicature Act* (The Annual Practice, 1937) O. 19, r. 4, and *Great Australian Gold Mining Co. v. Martin,* L.R. 5 Ch.Div. 1, 10 (1877). Subscription of pleadings is required in many codes. 2 Minn.Stat. (Mason, 1927) § 9265; N.Y.R.C.P. (1937) Rule 91; 2 N.D.Comp.Laws Ann. (1913) § 7455.

This rule expressly continues any statute which requires a pleading to be verified or accompanied by an affidavit, such as: U.S.C., Title 28:

§ 381 [former] (Preliminary injunctions and temporary restraining orders)

§ 762 [now 1402] (Suit against the United States)

U.S.C., Title 28, § 829 [now 1927] (Costs; attorney liable for, when) is unaffected by this rule.

For complaints which must be verified under these rules, see Rules 23(b) (Secondary Action by Shareholders) and 65 (Injunctions).

For abolition of former rule in equity that the averments of an answer under oath must be overcome by the testimony of two witnesses or of one witness sustained by corroborating circumstances, see 12 P.S.Pa. § 1222; for the rule in equity itself, see *Greenfield v. Blumenthal,* C.C.A.3, 1934, 69 F.2d 294.

1983 Amendment

Since its original promulgation, Rule 11 has provided for the striking of pleadings and the imposition of disciplinary sanctions to check abuses in the signing of pleadings. Its provisions have always applied to motions and other papers by virtue of incorporation by reference in Rule 7(b)(2). The amendment and the addition of Rule 7(b)(3) expressly confirms this applicability.

Experience shows that in practice Rule 11 has not been effective in deterring abuses. See 6 Wright & Miller, *Federal Practice and Procedure: Civil* § 1334 (1971). There has been considerable confusion as to (1) the circumstances that should trigger striking a pleading or motion or taking disciplinary action, (2) the standard of conduct expected of attorneys who sign pleadings and motions, and (3) the range of available and appropriate sanctions. See Rodes, Ripple & Mooney, *Sanctions Imposable for Violations of the Federal Rules of Civil Procedure* 64–65, Federal Judicial Center (1981). The new language is intended to reduce the reluctance of courts to impose sanctions, see Moore, **Federal Practice** ¶ 7.05, at 1547, by emphasizing the responsibilities of the attorney and reenforcing those obligations by the imposition of sanctions.

The amended rule attempts to deal with the problem by building upon and expanding the equitable doctrine permitting the court to award expenses, including attorney's fees, to a litigant whose opponent acts in bad faith in instituting or conducting litigation. See, e.g., *Roadway Express, Inc. v. Piper,* 447 U.S. 752 (1980); *Hall v. Cole,* 412 U.S. 1, 5 (1973). Greater attention by the district courts to pleading and motion abuses and the imposition of sanctions when appropriate, should discourage dilatory or abusive tactics and help to streamline the litigation process by lessening frivolous claims or defenses.

The expanded nature of the lawyer's certification in the fifth sentence of amended Rule 11 recognizes that the litigation process may be abused for purposes other than delay. See, e.g., *Browning Debenture Holders' Committee v. DASA Corp.,* 560 F.2d 1078 (2d Cir.1977).

The words "good ground to support" the pleading in the original rule were interpreted to have both factual and legal elements. See, e.g., *Heart Disease Research Foundation v. General Motors Corp.,* 15 Fed.R.Serv.2d 1517, 1519 (S.D.N.Y.1972). They have been replaced by a standard of conduct that is more focused.

The new language stresses the need for some prefiling inquiry into both the facts and the law to satisfy the affirmative duty imposed by the rule. The standard is one of reasonableness under the circumstances. See *Kinee v. Abraham Lincoln Fed. Sav. & Loan Ass'n,* 365 F.Supp. 975 (E.D.Pa.1973). This standard is more stringent than the original good-faith formula and thus it is expected that a greater range of circumstances will trigger its violation. See *Nemeroff v. Abelson,* 620 F.2d 339 (2d Cir.1980).

The rule is not intended to chill an attorney's enthusiasm or creativity in pursuing factual or legal theories. The court is expected to avoid using the wisdom of hindsight and should test the signer's conduct by inquiring what was reasonable to believe at the time the pleading, motion, or other paper was submitted. Thus, what constitutes a reasonable inquiry may depend on such factors as how much time for investigation was available to the signer; whether he had to rely on a client for information as to the facts underlying the pleading, motion, or other paper; whether the pleading, motion, or other paper was based on a plausible view of the law; or whether he depended on forwarding counsel or another member of the bar.

The rule does not require a party or an attorney to disclose privileged communications or work product in order to show that the signing of the pleading, motion, or other paper is substantially justified. The provisions of Rule 26(c), including appropriate orders after *in camera* inspection by the court, remain available to protect a party claiming privilege or work product protection.

Amended Rule 11 continues to apply to anyone who signs a pleading, motion, or other paper. Although the standard is the same for unrepresented parties, who are obliged themselves to sign the pleadings, the court has sufficient discretion to take account of the special circumstances that often arise in *pro se* situations. See *Haines v. Kerner,* 404 U.S. 519 (1972).

The provision in the original rule for striking pleadings and motions as sham and false has been deleted. The passage has rarely been utilized, and decisions thereunder have tended to confuse the issue of attorney honesty with the merits of the action. See generally Risinger, *Honesty in Pleading and its Enforcement: Some "Striking" Problems with Fed.R.Civ.P. 11,* 61 Minn.L.Rev. 1 (1976). Motions under this provision generally present issues better dealt with under Rules 8, 12, or 56. See *Murchison v. Kirby,* 27 F.R.D. 14 (S.D.N.Y.1961); 5 Wright & Miller, *Federal Practice and Procedure: Civil* § 1334 (1969).

The former reference to the inclusion of scandalous or indecent matter, which is itself strong indication that an improper purpose underlies the pleading, motion, or other paper, also has been deleted as unnecessary. Such matter may be stricken under Rule 12(f) as well as dealt with under the more general language of amended Rule 11.

The text of the amended rule seeks to dispel apprehensions that efforts to obtain enforcement will be fruitless by insuring that the rule will be applied when properly invoked. The word "sanctions" in the caption, for example, stresses a deterrent orientation in dealing with improper pleadings, motions or other papers. This corresponds to the approach in imposing sanctions for discovery abuses. See *National Hockey League v. Metropolitan Hockey Club,* 427 U.S. 639 (1976) (per curiam). And the words "shall impose" in the last sentence focus the court's attention on the need to impose sanctions for pleading and motion abuses. The court, however, retains the necessary flexibility to deal appropriately with violations of the rule. It has discretion to tailor sanctions to the particular facts of the case, with which it should be well acquainted.

The references in the former text to wilfulness as a prerequisite to disciplinary action has been deleted. However, in considering the nature and severity of the sanctions to be imposed, the court should take account of the state of the attorney's or party's actual or presumed knowledge when the pleading or other paper was signed. Thus, for example, when a party is not represented by counsel, the absence of legal advice is an appropriate factor to be considered.

Courts currently appear to believe they may impose sanctions on their own motion. See *North American Trading Corp. v. Zale Corp.,* 73 F.R.D. 293 (S.D.N.Y.1979). Authority to do so has been made explicit in order to overcome the traditional reluctance of courts to intervene unless requested by one of the parties. The detection and punishment of a violation of the signing requirement, encouraged by the amended rule, is part of the court's responsibility for securing the system's effective operation.

If the duty imposed by the rule is violated, the court should have the discretion to impose sanctions on either the attorney, the party the signing attorney represents, or both, or on an unrepresented party who signed the pleading, and the new rule so provides. Although Rule 11 has been silent on the point, courts have claimed the power to impose sanctions on an attorney personally, either by imposing costs or employing the contempt technique. See 5 Wright & Miller, *Federal Practice and Procedure: Civil* § 1334 (1969); 2A Moore, *Federal Practice* ¶ 11.02, at 2104 n. 8. This power has been used infrequently. The amended rule should eliminate any doubt as to the propriety of assessing sanctions against the attorney.

Even though it is the attorney whose signature violates the rule, it may be appropriate under the circumstances of the case to impose a sanction on the client. See *Browning Debenture Holders' Committee v. DASA Corp.,* supra. This modification brings Rule 11 in line with practice under Rule 37, which allows sanctions for abuses during discovery to be imposed upon the party, the attorney, or both.

A party seeking sanctions should give notice to the court and the offending party promptly upon discovering a basis for doing so. The time when sanctions are to be imposed rests in the discretion of the trial judge. However, it is anticipated that in the case of pleadings the sanctions issue under Rule 11 normally will be determined at the end of the litigation, and in the case of motions at the time when the motion is decided or shortly thereafter. The procedure obviously must comport with due process requirements. The particular format to be followed should depend on the circumstances of the situation and the severity of the sanction under consideration. In many situations the judge's participation in the proceedings provides him with full knowledge of the relevant facts and little further inquiry will be necessary.

To assure that the efficiencies achieved through more effective operation of the pleading regimen will not be offset by the cost of satellite litigation over the imposition of sanctions, the court must to the extent possible limit the scope of sanction proceedings to the record. Thus, discovery should be conducted only by leave of the court, and then only in extraordinary circumstances.

Although the encompassing reference to "other papers" in new Rule 11 literally includes discovery papers, the certification requirement in that context is governed by proposed new Rule 26(g). Discovery motions, however, fall within the ambit of Rule 11.

1987 Amendment

The amendments are technical. No substantive change is intended.

1993 Amendments

Purpose of revision. This revision is intended to remedy problems that have arisen in the interpretation and application of the 1983 revision of the rule. For empirical examination of experience under the 1983 rule, see, *e.g.,* New York State Bar Committee on Federal Courts, *Sanctions and Attorneys' Fees* (1987); T. Willging, *The Rule 11 Sanctioning Process* (1989); American Judicature Society, *Report of the Third Circuit Task Force on Federal Rule of Civil Procedure 11* (S. Burbank ed., 1989); E. Wiggins, T. Willging, and D. Stienstra, *Report on Rule 11* (Federal Judicial Center 1991). For book-length analyses of the case law, see G. Joseph, *Sanctions: The Federal Law of Litigation Abuse* (1989); J. Solovy, *The Federal Law of Sanctions* (1991); G. Vairo, *Rule 11 Sanctions: Case Law Perspectives and Preventive Measures* (1991).

The rule retains the principle that attorneys and pro se litigants have an obligation to the court to refrain from conduct that frustrates the aims of Rule 1. The revision broadens the scope of this obligation, but places greater constraints on the imposition of sanctions and should reduce the number of motions for sanctions presented to the court. New subdivision (d) removes from the ambit of this rule all discovery requests, responses, objections, and motions subject to the provisions of Rule 26 through 37.

Subdivision (a). Retained in this subdivision are the provisions requiring signatures on pleadings, written motions, and other papers. Unsigned papers are to be received by the Clerk, but then are to be stricken if the omission of the signature is not corrected promptly after being called to the attention of the attorney or pro se litigant. Correction can be made by signing the paper on file or by submitting a duplicate that contains the signature. A court may require by local rule that papers contain additional identifying information regarding the parties or attorneys, such as telephone numbers to facilitate facsimile transmissions, though, as for omission of a signature, the paper should not be rejected for failure to provide such information.

The sentence in the former rule relating to the effect of answers under oath is no longer needed and has been eliminated. The provision in the former rule that signing a paper constitutes a certificate that it has been read by the signer also has been eliminated as unnecessary. The obligations imposed under subdivision (b) obviously require that a pleading, written motion, or other paper be read before it is filed or submitted to the court.

Subdivisions (b) and (c). These subdivisions restate the provisions requiring attorneys and pro se litigants to conduct a reasonable inquiry into the law and facts before signing pleadings, written motions, and other documents, and prescribing sanctions for violation of these obligations. The revision in part expands the responsibilities of litigants to the court, while providing greater constraints and flexibility in dealing with infractions of the rule. The rule continues to require litigants to "stop-and-think" before initially making legal or factual contentions. It also, however, emphasizes the duty of candor by subjecting litigants to potential sanctions for insisting upon a position after it is no longer tenable and by generally providing protection against sanctions if they withdraw or correct contentions after a potential violation is called to their attention.

The rule applies only to assertions contained in papers filed with or submitted to the court. It does not cover matters arising for the first time during oral presentations to the court, when counsel may make statements that would not have been made if there had been more time for study and reflection. However, a litigant's obligations with respect to the contents of these papers are not measured solely as of the time they are filed with or submitted to the court, but include reaffirming to the court and advocating positions contained in those pleadings and motions after learning that they cease to have any merit. For example, an attorney who during a pretrial conference insists on a claim or defense should be viewed as "presenting to the court" that contention and would be subject to the obligations of subdivision (b) measured as of that time. Similarly, if after a notice of removal is filed, a party urges in federal court the allegations of a pleading filed in state court (whether as claims, defenses, or in disputes regarding removal or remand), it would be viewed as "presenting"—and hence certifying to the district court under Rule 11—those allegations.

The certification with respect to allegations and other factual contentions is revised in recognition that sometimes a litigant may have good reason to believe that a fact is true or false but may need discovery, formal or informal, from opposing parties or third persons to gather and confirm the evidentiary basis for the allegation. Tolerance of factual contentions in initial pleadings by plaintiffs or defendants when specifically identified as made on information and belief does not relieve litigants from the obligation to conduct an appropriate investigation into the facts that is reasonable under the circumstances; it is not a license to join parties, make claims, or present defenses without any factual basis or justification. Moreover, if evidentiary support is not obtained after a reasonable opportunity for further investigation or discovery, the party has a duty under the rule not to persist with that contention. Subdivision (b) does not require a formal amendment to pleadings for which evidentiary support is not obtained, but rather calls upon a litigant not thereafter to advocate such claims or defenses.

The certification is that there is (or likely will be) "evidentiary support" for the allegation, not that the party will prevail with respect to its contention regarding the fact. That summary judgment is rendered against a party does not necessarily mean, for purposes of this certification, that it had no evidentiary support for its position. On the other hand, if a party has evidence with respect to a contention that would suffice to defeat a motion for summary judgment based thereon, it would have sufficient "evidentiary support" for purposes of Rule 11.

Denials of factual contentions involve somewhat different considerations. Often, of course, a denial is premised upon the existence of evidence contradicting the alleged fact. At other times a denial is permissible because, after an appropriate investigation, a party has no information concerning the matter or, indeed, has a reasonable basis for doubting the credibility of the only evidence relevant to the matter. A party should not deny an allegation it knows to be true; but it is not required, simply because it lacks contradictory evidence, to admit an allegation that it believes is not true.

The changes in subdivisions (b)(3) and (b)(4) will serve to equalize the burden of the rule upon plaintiffs and defendants, who under Rule 8(b) are in effect allowed to deny allegations by stating that from their initial investigation they lack sufficient information to form a belief as to the truth of the allegation. If, after further investigation or discovery, a denial is no longer warranted, the defendant should not continue to insist on that denial. While sometimes helpful, formal amendment of the pleadings to withdraw an allegation or denial is not required by subdivision (b).

Arguments for extensions, modifications, or reversals of existing law or for creation of new law do not violate subdivision (b)(2) provided they are "nonfrivolous." This establishes an objective standard, intended to eliminate any "empty-head pure-heart" justification for patently frivolous arguments. However, the extent to which a litigant has researched the issues and found some support for its theories even in minority opinions, in law review articles, or through consultation with other attorneys should certainly be taken into account in determining whether paragraph (2) has been violated. Although arguments for a change of law are not required to be specifically so identified, a contention that is so identified should be viewed with greater tolerance under the rule.

The court has available a variety of possible sanctions to impose for violations, such as striking the offending paper; issuing an admonition, reprimand, or censure; requiring participation in seminars or other educational programs; ordering a fine payable to the court; referring the matter to disciplinary authorities (or, in the case of government attorneys, to the Attorney General, Inspector General, or agency head), etc. *See Manual for Complex Litigation, Second,* § 42.3. The rule does not attempt to enumerate the factors a court should consider in deciding whether to impose a sanction or what sanctions would be appropriate in the circumstances; but, for emphasis, it does specifically note that a sanction may be nonmonetary as well as monetary. Whether the improper conduct was willful, or negligent; whether it was part of a pattern of activity, or an isolated event; whether it infected the entire pleading, or only one particular count or defense; whether the person has engaged in similar conduct in other litigation; whether it was intended to injure; what effect it had on the litigation process in time or expense; whether the responsible person is trained in the law; what amount, given the financial resources of the responsible person, is needed to deter that person from repetition in the same case; what amount is needed to deter similar activity by other litigants: all of these may in a particular case be proper considerations. The court has significant discretion in determining what sanctions, if any, should be imposed for a violation, subject to the principle that the sanctions should not be more severe than reasonably necessary to deter repetition of the conduct by the offending person or comparable conduct by similarly situated persons.

Since the purpose of Rule 11 sanctions is to deter rather than to compensate, the rule provides that, if a monetary sanction is imposed, it should ordinarily be paid into court as a penalty. However, under unusual circumstances, particularly for (b)(1) violations, deterrence may be ineffective unless the sanction not only requires the person violating the rule to make a monetary payment, but also directs that some or all of this payment be made to those injured by the violation. Accordingly, the rule authorizes the court, if requested in a motion and if so warranted, to award attorney's fees to another party. Any such award to another party, however, should not exceed the expenses and attorneys' fees for the services directly and unavoidably caused by the violation of the certification requirement. If, for example, a wholly unsupportable count were included in a multi-count complaint or counterclaim for the purpose of needlessly increasing the cost of litigation to an impecunious adversary, any award of expenses should be limited to those directly caused by inclusion of the improper count, and not those resulting from the filing of the complaint or answer itself. The award should not provide compensation for services that could have been avoided by an earlier disclosure of evidence or an earlier challenge to the groundless claims or defenses. Moreover, partial reimbursement of fees may constitute a sufficient deterrent with respect to violations by persons having modest financial resources. In cases brought under statutes providing for fees to be awarded to prevailing parties, the court should not employ cost-shifting under this rule in a manner that would be inconsistent with the standards that govern the statutory award of fees, such as stated in *Christiansburg Garment Co. v. EEOC,* 434 U.S. 412 (1978).

The sanction should be imposed on the persons—whether attorneys, law firms, or parties—who have violated the rule or who may be determined to be responsible for the violation. The person signing, filing, submitting, or advocating a document has a nondelegable responsibility to the court, and in most situations is the person to be sanctioned for a violation. Absent exceptional circumstances, a law firm is to be held also responsible when, as a result of a motion under subdivision (c)(1)(A), one of its partners, associates, or employees is determined to have violated the rule. Since such a motion may be filed only if the offending paper is not withdrawn or corrected within 21 days after service of the motion, it is appropriate that the law firm ordinarily be viewed as jointly responsible under established principles of agency. This provision is designed to remove the restrictions of the former rule. *Cf. Pavelic & LeFlore v. Marvel Entertainment Group,* 493 U.S. 120 (1989) (1983 version of Rule 11 does not permit sanctions against law firm of attorney signing groundless complaint).

The revision permits the court to consider whether other attorneys in the firm, co-counsel, other law firms, or the party itself should be held accountable for their part in causing a violation. When appropriate, the court can make an additional inquiry in order to determine whether the sanction should be imposed on such persons, firms, or parties either in addition to or, in unusual circumstances, instead of the person actually making the presentation to the court. For example, such an inquiry may be appropriate in cases involving governmental agencies or other institutional parties that frequently impose substantial restrictions on the discretion of individual attorneys employed by it.

Sanctions that involve monetary awards (such as a fine or an award of attorney's fees) may not be imposed on a represented party for causing a violation of subdivision (b)(2), involving frivolous contentions of law. Monetary responsibility for such violations is more properly placed solely on the party's attorneys. With this limitation, the rule should not be subject to attack under the Rules Enabling Act. See *Willy v. Coastal Corp.,* — U.S. — (1992); *Business Guides, Inc. v. Chromatic Communications Enter. Inc.,* — U.S. — (1991). This restriction does not limit the court's power to impose sanctions or remedial orders that may have collateral financial consequences upon a party, such as dismissal of a claim, preclusion of a defense, or preparation of amended pleadings.

Explicit provision is made for litigants to be provided notice of the alleged violation and an opportunity to respond before sanctions are imposed. Whether the matter should be decided solely on the basis of written submissions or should be scheduled for oral argument (or, indeed, for evidentiary presentation) will depend on the circumstances. If the court imposes a sanction, it must, unless waived, indicate its reasons in a written order or on the record; the court should not ordinarily have to explain its denial of a motion for sanctions. Whether a violation has occurred and what sanctions, if any, to impose for a violation are matters committed to the discretion of the trial court; accordingly, as under current law, the standard for appellate review of these decisions will be for abuse of discretion. *See Cooter & Gell v. Hartmarx Corp.,* 496 U.S. 384 (1990) (noting, however, that an abuse would be established if the court based its ruling on an erroneous view of the law or on a clearly erroneous assessment of the evidence).

The revision leaves for resolution on a case-by-case basis, considering the particular circumstances involved, the question as to when a motion for violation of Rule 11 should be served and when, if filed, it should be decided. Ordinarily the motion should be served promptly after the inappropriate paper is filed, and, if delayed too long, may be viewed as untimely. In other circumstances, it should not be served until the other party has had a reasonable opportunity for discovery. Given the "safe harbor" provisions discussed below, a party cannot delay serving its Rule 11 motion until conclusion of the case (or judicial rejection of the offending contention).

Rule 11 motions should not be made or threatened for minor, inconsequential violations of the standards prescribed by subdivision (b). They should not be employed as a discovery device or to test the legal sufficiency or efficacy of allegations in the pleadings; other motions are available for those purposes. Nor should Rule 11 motions be prepared to emphasize the merits of a party's position, to exact an unjust settlement, to intimidate an adversary into withdrawing contentions that are fairly debatable, to increase the costs of litigation, to create a conflict of interest between attorney and client, or to seek disclosure of matters otherwise protected by the attorney-client privilege or the work-product doctrine. As under the prior rule, the court may defer its ruling (or its decision as to the identity of the persons to be sanctioned) until final resolution of the case in order to avoid immediate conflicts of interest and to reduce the disruption created if a disclosure of attorney-client communications is needed to determine whether a violation occurred or to identify the person responsible for the violation.

The rule provides that requests for sanctions must be made as a separate motion, *i.e.,* not simply included as an additional prayer for relief contained in another motion. The motion for sanctions is not, however, to be filed until at least 21 days (or such other period as the court may set) after being served. If, during this period, the alleged violation is corrected, as by withdrawing (whether formally or informally) some allegation or contention, the motion should not be filed with the court. These provisions are intended to provide a type of "safe harbor" against motions under Rule 11 in that a party will not be subject to sanctions on the basis of another party's motion unless, after receiving the motion, it refuses to withdraw that position or to acknowledge candidly that it does not currently have evidence to support a specified allegation. Under the former rule, parties were sometimes reluctant to abandon a questionable contention lest that be viewed as evidence of a violation of Rule 11; under the revision, the timely withdrawal of a contention will protect a party against a motion for sanctions.

To stress the seriousness of a motion for sanctions and to define precisely the conduct claimed to violate the rule, the revision provides that the "safe harbor" period begins to run only upon service of the motion. In most cases, however, counsel should be expected to give informal notice to the other party, whether in person or by a telephone call or letter, of a potential violation before proceeding to prepare and serve a Rule 11 motion.

As under former Rule 11, the filing of a motion for sanctions is itself subject to the requirements of the rule and can lead to sanctions. However, service of a cross motion under Rule 11 should rarely be needed since under the revision the court may award to the person who prevails on a motion under Rule 11—whether the movant or the target of the motion—reasonable expenses, including attorney's fees, incurred in presenting or opposing the motion.

The power of the court to act on its own initiative is retained, but with the condition that this be done through a show cause order. This procedure provides the person with notice and an opportunity to respond. The revision provides that a monetary sanction imposed after a court-initiated show cause order be limited to a penalty payable to the court and that it be imposed only if the show cause order is issued before any voluntary dismissal or an agreement of the parties to settle the claims made by or against the litigant.

Parties settling a case should not be subsequently faced with an unexpected order from the court leading to monetary sanctions that might have affected their willingness to settle or voluntarily dismiss a case. Since show cause orders will ordinarily be issued only in situations that are akin to a contempt of court, the rule does not provide a "safe harbor" to a litigant for withdrawing a claim, defense, etc., after a show cause order has been issued on the court's own initiative. Such corrective action, however, should be taken into account in deciding what—if any—sanction to impose if, after consideration of the litigant's response, the court concludes that a violation has occurred.

Subdivision (d). Rules 26(g) and 37 establish certification standards and sanctions that apply to discovery disclosures, requests, responses, objections, and motions. It is appropriate that Rules 26 through 37, which are specially designed for the discovery process, govern such documents and conduct rather than the more general provisions of Rule 11. Subdivision (d) has been added to accomplish this result.

Rule 11 is not the exclusive source for control of improper presentations of claims, defenses, or contentions. It does not supplant statutes permitting awards of attorney's fees to prevailing parties or alter the principles governing such awards. It does not inhibit the court in punishing for contempt, in exercising its inherent powers, or in imposing sanctions, awarding expenses, or directing remedial action authorized under other rules or under 28 U.S.C. § 1927. *See Chambers v. NASCO,* —— U.S. —— (1991). Chambers cautions, however, against reliance upon inherent powers if appropriate sanctions can be imposed under provisions such as Rule 11, and the procedures specified in Rule 11—notice, opportunity to respond, and findings—should ordinarily be employed when imposing a sanction under the court's inherent powers. Finally, it should be noted that Rule 11 does not preclude a party from initiating an independent action for malicious prosecution or abuse of process.

Rule 12. Defenses and Objections—When and How Presented—By Pleading or Motion—Motion for Judgment on Pleadings

(a) When Presented.

(1) Unless a different time is prescribed in a statute of the United States, a defendant shall serve an answer

(A) within 20 days after being served with the summons and complaint, or

(B) if service of the summons has been timely waived on request under Rule 4(d), within 60 days after the date when the request for waiver was sent, or within 90 days after that date if the defendant was addressed outside any judicial district of the United States.

(2) A party served with a pleading stating a cross-claim against that party shall serve an answer thereto within 20 days after being served. The plaintiff shall serve a reply to a counterclaim in the answer within 20 days after service of the answer, or, if a reply is ordered by the court, within 20 days after service of the order, unless the order otherwise directs.

(3) The United States or an officer or agency thereof shall serve an answer to the complaint or to a cross-claim, or a reply to a counterclaim, within 60 days after the service upon the United States attorney of the pleading in which the claim is asserted.

(4) Unless a different time is fixed by court order, the service of a motion permitted under this rule alters these periods of time as follows:

(A) if the court denies the motion or postpones its disposition until the trial on the merits, the responsive pleading shall be served within 10 days after notice of the court's action; or

(B) if the court grants a motion for a more definite statement, the responsive pleading shall be served within 10 days after the service of the more definite statement.

(b) How Presented. Every defense, in law or fact, to a claim for relief in any pleading, whether a claim, counterclaim, cross-claim, or third-party claim, shall be asserted in the responsive pleading thereto if one is required, except that the following defenses may at the option of the pleader be made by motion: (1) lack of jurisdiction over the subject matter, (2) lack of jurisdiction over the person, (3) improper venue, (4) insufficiency of process, (5) insufficiency of service of process, (6) failure to state a claim upon which relief can be granted, (7) failure to join a party under Rule 19. A motion making any of these defenses shall be made before pleading if a further pleading is permitted. No defense or objection is waived by being joined with one or more other defenses or objections in a responsive pleading or motion. If a pleading sets forth a claim for relief to which the adverse party is not required to serve a responsive pleading, the adverse party may assert at the trial any defense in law or fact to that claim for relief. If, on a motion asserting the defense numbered (6) to dismiss for failure of the pleading to state a claim upon which relief can be granted, matters outside the pleading are presented to and not excluded by the court, the motion shall be treated as one for summary judgment and disposed of as provided in Rule 56, and all parties shall be given reasonable opportunity to present all material made pertinent to such a motion by Rule 56.

(c) Motion for Judgment on the Pleadings. After the pleadings are closed but within such time as not to delay the trial, any party may move for judgment on the pleadings. If, on a motion for judgment on the pleadings, matters outside the pleadings are presented to and not excluded by the court, the motion shall be treated as one for summary judgment and disposed of as provided in Rule 56, and all parties shall be given reasonable opportunity to present all material made pertinent to such a motion by Rule 56.

(d) Preliminary Hearings. The defenses specifically enumerated (1)–(7) in subdivision (b) of this rule, whether made in a pleading or by motion, and the motion for judgment mentioned in subdivision (c) of this rule shall be heard and determined before trial on application of any party, unless the court orders that the hearing and determination thereof be deferred until the trial.

(e) Motion for More Definite Statement. If a pleading to which a responsive pleading is permitted is so vague or ambiguous that a party cannot reasonably be required to frame a responsive pleading, the party may move for a more definite statement before interposing a responsive pleading. The motion shall point out the defects complained of and the details desired. If the motion is granted and the order of the court is not obeyed within 10 days after notice of the order or within such other time as the court may fix, the court may strike the pleading to which the motion was directed or make such order as it deems just.

(f) Motion to Strike. Upon motion made by a party before responding to a pleading or, if no responsive pleading is permitted by these rules, upon motion made by a party within 20 days after the service of the pleading upon the party or upon the court's own initiative at any time, the court may order stricken from any pleading any insufficient defense or any redundant, immaterial, impertinent, or scandalous matter.

(g) Consolidation of Defenses in Motion. A party who makes a motion under this rule may join with it any other motions herein provided for and then available to the party. If a party makes a motion under this rule but omits therefrom any defense or objection then available to the party which this rule permits to be raised by motion, the party shall not thereafter make a motion based on the defense or objection so omitted, except a motion as provided in subdivision (h)(2) hereof on any of the grounds there stated.

(h) Waiver or Preservation of Certain Defenses.

(1) A defense of lack of jurisdiction over the person, improper venue, insufficiency of process, or insufficiency of service of process is waived (A) if omitted from a motion in the circumstances described in subdivision (g), or (B) if it is neither made by motion under this rule nor included in a responsive pleading or an amendment thereof permitted by Rule 15(a) to be made as a matter of course.

(2) A defense of failure to state a claim upon which relief can be granted, a defense of failure to join a party indispensable under Rule 19, and an objection of failure to state a legal defense to a claim may be made in any pleading permitted or ordered under Rule 7(a), or by motion for judgment on the pleadings, or at the trial on the merits.

(3) Whenever it appears by suggestion of the parties or otherwise that the court lacks jurisdiction of the subject matter, the court shall dismiss the action.

(As amended Dec. 27, 1946, eff. Mar. 19, 1948; Jan. 21, 1963, eff. July 1, 1963; Feb. 28, 1966, eff. July 1, 1966; Mar. 2, 1987, eff. Aug. 1, 1987; Apr. 22, 1993, eff. Dec. 1, 1993.)

ADVISORY COMMITTEE NOTES

1937 Adoption

Note to Subdivision (a). **1.** Compare [former] Equity Rules 12 (Issue of Subpoena—Time for Answer) and 31 (Reply—When Required—When Cause at Issue); 4 Mont. Rev.Codes Ann. (1935) §§ 9107, 9158; N.Y.C. P.A. (1937) § 263; N.Y.R.C.P. (1937) Rules 109–111.

2. U.S.C., Title 28, § 763 (now § 547) (Petition in action against United States; service; appearance by district attorney) provides that the United States as a defendant shall have 60 days within which to answer or otherwise defend. This and other statutes which provide 60 days for the United States or an officer or agency thereof to answer or otherwise defend are continued by this rule. In so far as any statutes not excepted in rule 81 provide a different time for a defendant to defend, such statutes are modified. See U.S.C., Title 28, [former] § 45 (District courts; practice and procedure in certain cases under the interstate commerce laws) (30 days).

3. Compare the last sentence of [former] Equity Rule 29 (Defenses—How Presented) and N.Y.C.P.A. (1937) § 283. See Rule 15(a) for time within which to plead to an amended pleading.

Note to Subdivisions (b) and (d). **1.** See generally [former] Equity Rules 29 (Defenses—How Presented), 33 (Testing Sufficiency of Defense), 43 (Defect of Parties—Resisting Objection), and 44 (Defect of Parties—Tardy Objection); N.Y.C.P.A. (1937) §§ 277–280; N.Y.R.C.P. (1937) Rules 106–112; *English Rules Under the Judicature Act* (The Annual Practice, 1937) O. 25, r.r. 1–4; Clark, *Code Pleading,* 1928, pp. 371–381.

2. For provisions authorizing defenses to be made in the answer or reply see *English Rules Under the Judicature Act,* (The Annual Practice, 1937) O. 25, r.r. 1–4; 1 Miss.Code Ann. (1930) §§ 378, 379. Compare Equity Rule 29 (Defenses—How Presented); U.S.C.A., Title 28, [former] § 45 (District Courts; practice and procedure in certain cases under the interstate commerce laws). U.S.C., Title 28, [former] § 45, substantially continued by this rule, provides: "No replication need be filed to the answer, and objections to the sufficiency of the petition or answer as not setting forth a cause of action or defense must be taken at the final hearing or by motion to dismiss the petition based on said grounds, which motion may be made at any time before answer is filed." Compare Calif.Code Civ.Proc., (Deering, 1937) § 433; 4 Nev.Comp.Laws (Hillyer, 1929) § 8600. For provisions that the defendant may demur and answer at the same time, see Calif.Code Civ.Proc. (Deering, 1937) § 431; 4 Nev.Comp. Laws (Hillyer, 1929) § 8598.

3. [Former] Equity Rule 29 (Defenses—How Presented) abolished demurrers and provided that defenses in point of law arising on the face of the bill should be made by motion to dismiss or in the answer, with further provision that every

such point of law going to the whole or material part of the cause or causes stated might be called up and disposed of before final hearing "at the discretion of the court." Likewise many state practices have abolished the demurrer, or retain it only to attack substantial and not formal defects. See 6 Tenn.Code Ann. (Williams, 1934) § 8784; Ala.Code Ann. (Michie, 1928) § 9479; 2 Mass.Gen.Laws (Ter.Ed., 1932) ch. 231, §§ 15–18; Kansas Gen.Stat.Ann. (1935) §§ 60–705, 60–706.

Note to Subdivision (c). Compare [former] Equity Rule 33 (Testing Sufficiency of Defense); N.Y.R.C.P. (1937) Rules 111 and 112.

Note to Subdivisions (e) and (f). Compare [former] Equity Rules 20 (Further and Particular Statement in Pleading May be Required) and 21 (Scandal and Impertinence); *English Rules Under the Judicature Act* (The Annual Practice, 1937) O. 19, r.r. 7, 7a, 7b, 8; 4 Mont.Rev.Codes Ann. (1935) §§ 9166, 9167; N.Y.C.P.A. (1937) § 247; N.Y.C.P.A. (1937) Rules 103, 115, 116, 117; Wyo.Rev.Stat.Ann. (Courtright, 1931) §§ 89–1033, 89–1034.

Note to Subdivision (g). Compare Rules of the District Court of the United States for the District of Columbia (1937) Equity Rule 11; N.M. Rules of Pleading, Practice and Procedure, 38 N.M.Rep. vii. [105–408] (1934); Wash.Gen. Rules of the Superior Courts, 1 Wash.Rev.Stat.Ann. (Remington, 1932) p. 160, Rule VI(e) and (f).

Note to Subdivision (h). Compare Calif.Code Civ.Proc. (Deering, 1937) § 434; 2 Minn.Stat. (Mason, 1927) § 9252; N.Y.C.P.A. (1937) §§ 278 and 279; Wash.Gen.Rules of the Superior Courts, 1 Wash.Rev.Stat.Ann. (Remington, 1932) p. 160, Rule VI(e). This rule continues U.S.C.A., Title 28, former § 80 [now 1359, 1447, 1919] (Dismissal or remand) (of action over which district court lacks jurisdiction), while U.S.C.A., Title 28, § 399 (Amendments to show diverse citizenship) is continued by Rule 15.

1946 Amendment

Note. Subdivision (a). Various minor alterations in language have been made to improve the statement of the rule. All references to bills of particulars have been stricken in accordance with changes made in subdivision (e).

Subdivision (b). The addition of defense (7), "failure to join an indispensable party", cures an omission in the rules which are silent as to the mode of raising such failure. See Commentary, *Manner of Raising Objection of Non-Joinder of Indispensable Party,* 1940, 2 Fed.Rules Serv. 658, and, 1942, 5 Fed.Rules Serv. 820. In one case, *United States v. Metropolitan Life Ins. Co.*, E.D.Pa.1941, 36 F.Supp. 399, the failure to join an indispensable party was raised under Rule 12(c).

Rule 12(b)(6), permitting a motion to dismiss for failure of the complaint to state a claim on which relief can be granted, is substantially the same as the old demurrer for failure of a pleading to state a cause of action. Some courts have held that as the rule by its terms refers to statements in the complaint, extraneous matter on affidavits, depositions or otherwise, may not be introduced in support of the motion, or to resist it. On the other hand, in many cases the district courts have permitted the introduction of such material. When these cases have reached circuit courts of appeals in situations where the extraneous material so received shows that there is no genuine issue as to any material question of fact and that on the undisputed facts as disclosed by the affidavits or depositions, one party or the other is entitled to judgment as a matter of law, the circuit courts, properly enough, have been reluctant to dispose of the case merely on the face of the pleading, and in the interest of prompt disposition of the action have made a final disposition of it. In dealing with such situations the Second Circuit has made the sound suggestion that whatever its label or original basis, the motion may be treated as a motion for summary judgment and disposed of as such. *Samara v. United States*, C.C.A.2, 1942, 129 F.2d 594, certiorari denied 63 S.Ct. 258, 317 U.S. 686, 87 L.Ed. 549; *Boro Hall Corp. v. General Motors Corp.*, C.C.A.2, 1942, 124 F.2d 822, certiorari denied 63 S.Ct. 436, 317 U.S. 695, 87 L.Ed. 556. See, also, *Kithcart v. Metropolitan Life Ins. Co.,* C.C.A.8, 1945, 150 F.2d 997.

It has also been suggested that this practice could be justified on the ground that the federal rules permit "speaking" motions. The Committee entertains the view that on motion under Rule 12(b)(6) to dismiss for failure of the complaint to state a good claim, the trial court should have authority to permit the introduction of extraneous matter, such as may be offered on a motion for summary judgment, and if it does not exclude such matter the motion should then be treated as a motion for summary judgment and disposed of in the manner and on the conditions stated in Rule 56 relating to summary judgments, and, of course, in such a situation, when the case reaches the circuit court of appeals, that court should treat the motion in the same way. The Committee believes that such practice, however, should be tied to the summary judgment rule. The term "speaking motion" is not mentioned in the rules, and if there is such a thing its limitations are undefined. Where extraneous matter is received, by tying further proceedings to the summary judgment rule the courts have a definite basis in the rules for disposing of the motion.

The Committee emphasizes particularly the fact that the summary judgment rule does not permit a case to be disposed of by judgment on the merits on affidavits, which disclose a conflict on a material issue of fact, and unless this practice is tied to the summary judgment, rule, the extent to which a court, on the introduction of such extraneous matter, may resolve questions of fact on conflicting proof would be left uncertain.

The decisions dealing with this general situation may be generally grouped as follows: (1) cases dealing with the use of affidavits and other extraneous material on motions; (2) cases reversing judgments to prevent final determination on mere pleading allegations alone.

Under group (1) are: *Boro Hall Corp. v. General Motors Corp.*, C.C.A.2, 1942, 124 F.2d 822, certiorari denied 1943, 63 S.Ct. 436, 317 U.S. 695, 87 L.Ed. 556; *Gallup v. Caldwell,* C.C.A.3, 1941, 120 F.2d 90; *Central Mexico Light & Power Co. v. Munch,* C.C.A.2, 1940, 116 F.2d 85; *National Labor Relations Board v. Montgomery Ward & Co.*, 1944, 144 F.2d 528, 79 U.S.App.D.C. 200, certiorari denied 1944, 65 S.Ct. 134, 323 U.S. 774, 89 L.Ed. 619; *Urquhart v. American-La France Foamite Corp.*, 1944, 144 F.2d 542, 79 U.S.App.D.C. 219; *Samara v. United States*, C.C.A.2, 1942, 129 F.2d 594; *Cohen v. American Window Glass Co.*, C.C.A.2, 1942, 126 F.2d 111; *Sperry Products Inc. v. Association of American Railroads,* C.C.A.2, 1942, 132 F.2d 408; *Joint Council Dining Car Employees Local 370 v. Delaware, Lackawanna and Western R. Co.*, C.C.A.2, 1946, 157 F.2d 417; *Weeks v.*

Bareco Oil Co., C.C.A.7, 1941, 125 F.2d 84; *Carroll v. Morrison Hotel Corp.*, C.C.A.7, 1945, 149 F.2d 404; *Victory v. Manning*, C.C.A.3, 1942, 128 F.2d 415; *Locals No. 1470, No. 1469, and No. 1512 of International Longshoremen's Association v. Southern Pacific Co.*, C.C.A.5, 1942, 131 F.2d 605; *Lucking v. Delano*, C.C.A.6, 1942, 129 F.2d 283; *San Francisco Lodge No. 68 of International Association of Machinists v. Forrestal*, Cal.1944, 58 F.Supp. 466; *Benson v. Export Equipment Corp.*, 1945, 164 P.2d 380, 49 N.M. 356, construing New Mexico rule identical with Rule 12(b)(6); *F. E. Myers & Bros. Co. v. Gould Pumps, Inc.*, W.D.N.Y.1946, 9 Fed.Rules Serv. 12b.33, Case 2, 5 F.R.D. 132. Cf. *Kohler v. Jacobs*, C.C.A.5, 1943, 138 F.2d 440; *Cohen v. United States*, C.C.A.8, 1942, 129 F.2d 733.

Under group (2) are: *Sparks v. England*, C.C.A.8, 1940, 113 F.2d 579; *Continental Collieries, Inc. v. Shober*, C.C.A.3, 1942, 130 F.2d 631; *Downey v. Palmer*, C.C.A.2, 1940, 114 F.2d 116; *DeLoach v. Crowley's Inc.*, C.C.A.5, 1942, 128 F.2d 378; *Leimer v. State Mutual Life Assurance Co. of Worcester, Mass.*, C.C.A.8, 1940, 108 F.2d 302; *Rossiter v. Vogel*, C.C.A.2, 1943, 134 F.2d 908, compare s.c., C.C.A.2, 1945, 148 F.2d 292; *Karl Kiefer Machine Co. v. United States Bottlers Machinery Co.*, C.C.A.7, 1940, 113 F.2d 356; *Chicago Metallic Mfg. Co. v. Edward Katzinger Co.*, C.C.A.7, 1941, 123 F.2d 518; *Louisiana Farmers' Protective Union, Inc. v. Great Atlantic & Pacific Tea Co. of America, Inc.*, C.C.A.8, 1942, 131 F.2d 419; *Publicity Bldg. Realty Corp. v. Hannegan*, C.C.A.8, 1943, 139 F.2d 583; *Dioguardi v. Durning*, C.C.A.2, 1944, 139 F.2d 774; *Package Closure Corp. v. Sealright Co., Inc.*, C.C.A.2, 1944, 141 F.2d 972; *Tahir Erk v. Glenn L. Martin Co.*, C.C.A.4, 1941, 116 F.2d 865; *Bell v. Preferred Life Assurance Society of Montgomery, Ala.*, 1943, 64 S.Ct. 5, 320 U.S. 238, 88 L.Ed. 15.

The addition at the end of subdivision (b) makes it clear that on a motion under Rule 12(b)(6) extraneous material may not be considered if the court excludes it, but that if the court does not exclude such material the motion shall be treated as a motion for summary judgment and disposed of as provided in Rule 56. It will also be observed that if a motion under Rule 12(b)(6) is thus converted into a summary judgment motion, the amendment insures that both parties shall be given a reasonable opportunity to submit affidavits and extraneous proofs to avoid taking a party by surprise through the conversion of the motion into a motion for summary judgment. In this manner and to this extent the amendment regularizes the practice above described. As the courts are already dealing with cases in this way, the effect of this amendment is really only to define the practice carefully and apply the requirements of the summary judgment rule in the disposition of the motion.

Subdivision (c). The sentence appended to subdivision (c) performs the same function and is grounded on the same reasons as the corresponding sentence added in subdivision (b).

Subdivision (d). The change here was made necessary because of the addition of defense (7) in subdivision (b).

Subdivision (e). References in this subdivision to a bill of particulars have been deleted, and the motion provided for is confined to one for more definite statement to be obtained only in cases where the movant cannot reasonably be required to frame an answer or other responsive pleading to the pleading in question. With respect to preparations for trial, the party is properly relegated to the various methods of examination and discovery provided in the rules for that purpose. *Slusher v. Jones*, E.D.Ky.1943, 7 Fed.Rules Serv. 12e.231, Case 5, 3 F.R.D. 168; *Best Foods, Inc. v. General Mills, Inc.*, D.Del.1943, 7 Fed.Rules Serv. 12e.231, Case 7, 3 F.R.D. 275; *Braden v. Callaway*, E.D.Tenn.1943, 8 Fed. Rules Serv. 12e.231, Case 1 (". . . most courts . . . conclude that the definiteness required is only such as will be sufficient for the party to prepare responsive pleadings"). Accordingly, the reference to the 20 day time limit has also been eliminated, since the purpose of this present provision is to state a time period where the motion for a bill is made for the purpose of preparing for trial.

Rule 12(e) as originally drawn has been the subject of more judicial rulings than any other part of the rules, and has been much criticized by commentators, judges and members of the bar. See general discussion and cases cited in 1 Moore's *Federal Practice*, 1938, Cum.Supplement, § 12.07, under "Page 657"; also, Holtzoff, *New Federal Procedure and the Courts*, 1940, 35–41. And compare vote of Second Circuit Conference of Circuit and District Judges, June 1940, recommending the abolition of the bill of particulars; *Sun Valley Mfg. Co. v. Mylish*, E.D.Pa.1944, 8 Fed.Rules Serv. 12e.231, Case 6 ("Our experience . . . has demonstrated not only that 'the office of the bill of particulars is fast becoming obsolete' . . . but that in view of the adequate discovery procedure available under the Rules, motions for bills of particulars should be abolished altogether."); *Walling v. American Steamship Co.*, W.D.N.Y.1945, 4 F.R.D. 355, 8 Fed.Rules Serv. 12e.244, Case 8 (". . . the adoption of the rule was ill advised. It has led to confusion, duplication and delay.") The tendency of some courts freely to grant extended bills of particulars has served to neutralize any helpful benefits derived from rule 8, and has overlooked the intended use of the rules on depositions and discovery. The words "or to prepare for trial"—eliminated by the proposed amendment—have sometimes been seized upon as grounds for compulsory statement in the opposing pleading of all the details which the movant would have to meet at the trial. On the other hand, many courts have in effect read these words out of the rule. See *Walling v. Alabama Pipe Co.*, W.D.Mo. 1942, 3 F.R.D. 159, 6 Fed.Rules Serv. 12e.244, Case 7; *Fleming v. Mason & Dixon Lines, Inc.*, E.D.Tenn.1941, 42 F.Supp. 230; *Kellogg Co. v. National Biscuit Co.*, D.N.J. 1941, 38 F.Supp. 643; *Brown v. H. L. Green Co.*, S.D.N.Y. 1943, 7 Fed.Rules Serv. 12e.231, Case 6; *Pedersen v. Standard Accident Ins. Co.*, W.D.Mo.1945, 8 Fed.Rules Serv. 12e.231, Case 8; *Bowles v. Ohse*, D.Neb.1945, 4 F.R.D. 403, 9 Fed.Rules Serv. 12e.231, Case 1; *Klages v. Cohen*, E.D.N.Y. 1945, 9 Fed.Rules Serv. 8a.25, Case 4; *Bowles v. Lawrence*, D.Mass.1945, 8 Fed.Rules Serv. 12e.231, Case 19; *McKinney Tool & Mfg. Co. v. Hoyt*, N.D.Ohio 1945, 9 Fed.Rules Serv. 12e.235, Case 1; *Bowles v. Jack*, D.Minn.1945, 5 F.R.D. 1, 9 Fed.Rules Serv. 12e.244, Case 9. And it has been urged from the bench that the phrase be stricken, *Poole v. White*, N.D.W.Va.1941, 5 Fed.Rules Serv. 12e.231, Case 4, 2 F.R.D. 40. See also *Bowles v. Gabel*, W.D.Mo.1946, 9 Fed.Rules Serv. 12e.244, Case 10. ("The courts have never favored that portion of the rules which undertook to justify a motion of this kind for the purpose of aiding counsel in preparing his case for trial.").

Subdivision (f). This amendment affords a specific method of raising the insufficiency of a defense, a matter which has troubled some courts, although attack has been permitted in one way or another. See *Dysart v. Remington-Rand,*

Inc., D.Conn.1939, 31 F.Supp. 296; *Eastman Kodak Co. v. McAuley*, S.D.N.Y.1941, 4 Fed.Rules Serv., 12f.21, Case 8, 2 F.R.D. 21; *Schenley Distillers Corp. v. Renken*, E.D.S.C. 1940, 34 F.Supp. 678; *Yale Transport Corp. v. Yellow Truck & Coach Mfg. Co.*, S.D.N.Y.1944, 3 F.R.D. 440; *United States v. Turner Milk Co.*, N.D.Ill.1941, 4 Fed.Rules Serv. 12b.51, Case 3, 1 F.R.D. 643; *Teiger v. Stephan Oderwald, Inc.*, S.D.N.Y.1940, 31 F.Supp. 626; *Teplitsky v. Pennsylvania R. Co.*, N.D.Ill.1941, 38 F.Supp. 535; *Callagher v. Carroll*, E.D.N.Y.1939, 27 F.Supp. 568; *United States v. Palmer*, S.D.N.Y.1939, 28 F.Supp. 936. And see *Indemnity Ins. Co. of North America v. Pan American Airways, Inc.*, S.D.N.Y. 1944, 58 F.Supp. 338; Commentary, *Modes of Attacking Insufficient Defenses in the Answer*, 901, 1939, 1 Fed.Rules Serv. 669, 1940, 2 Fed.Rules Serv. 640.

Subdivision (g). The change in title conforms with the companion provision in subdivision (h).

The alteration of the "except" clause requires that other than provided in subdivision (h) a party who resorts to a motion to raise defenses specified in the rule, must include in one motion all that are then available to him. Under the original rule defenses which could be raised by motion were divided into two groups which could be the subjects of two successive motions.

Subdivision (h). The addition of the phrase relating to indispensable parties is one of necessity.

1963 Amendment

This amendment conforms to the amendment of Rule 4(e). See also the Advisory Committee's Note to amended Rule 4(b).

1966 Amendment

Subdivision (b)(7). The terminology of this subdivision is changed to accord with the amendment of Rule 19. See the Advisory Committee's Note to Rule 19, as amended, especially the third paragraph therein before the caption "Subdivision (c)."

Subdivision (g). Subdivision (g) has forbidden a defendant who makes a preanswer motion under this rule from making a further motion presenting any defense or objection which was available to him at the time he made the first motion and which he could have included, but did not in fact include therein. Thus if the defendant moves before answer to dismiss the complaint for failure to state a claim, he is barred from making a further motion presenting the defense of improper venue, if that defense was available to him when he made his original motion. Amended subdivision (g) is to the same effect. This required consolidation of defenses and objections in a Rule 12 motion is salutary in that it works against piecemeal consideration of a case. For exceptions to the requirement of consolidation, see the last clause of subdivision (g), referring to new subdivision (h)(2).

Subdivision (h). The question has arisen whether an omitted defense which cannot be made the basis of a second motion may nevertheless be pleaded in the answer. Subdivision (h) called for waiver of "* * * defenses and objections which he [defendant] does not present * * * by motion * * * or, if he has made no motion, in his answer * * *." If the clause "if he has made no motion," was read literally, it seemed that the omitted defense was waived and could not be pleaded in the answer. On the other hand, the clause might be read as adding nothing of substance to the preceding words; in that event it appeared that a defense was not waived by reason of being omitted from the motion and might be set up in the answer. The decisions were divided. Favoring waiver, see *Keef v. Derounian*, 6 F.R.D. 11 (N.D.Ill.1946); *Elbinger v. Precision Metal Workers Corp.*, 18 F.R.D. 467 (E.D.Wis.1956); see also *Rensing v. Turner Aviation Corp.*, 166 F.Supp. 790 (N.D.Ill.1958); *P. Beiersdorf & Co. v. Duke Laboratories, Inc.*, 10 F.R.D. 282 (S.D.N.Y. 1950); *Neset v. Christensen*, 92 F.Supp. 78 (E.D.N.Y.1950). Opposing waiver, see *Phillips v. Baker*, 121 F.2d 752 (9th Cir.1941); *Crum v. Graham*, 32 F.R.D. 173 (D.Mont.1963) (regretfully following the Phillips case); see also *Birnbaum v. Birrell*, 9 F.R.D. 72 (S.D.N.Y.1948); *Johnson v. Joseph Schlitz Brewing Co.*, 33 F.Supp. 176 (E.D.Tenn.1940); cf. *Carter v. American Bus Lines, Inc.*, 22 F.R.D. 323 (D.Neb. 1958).

Amended subdivision (h)(1)(A) eliminates the ambiguity and states that certain specified defenses which were available to a party when he made a preanswer motion, but which he omitted from the motion, are waived. The specified defenses are lack of jurisdiction over the person, improper venue, insufficiency of process, and insufficiency of service of process (see Rule 12(b)(2)–(5)). A party who by motion invites the court to pass upon a threshold defense should bring forward all the specified defenses he then has and thus allow the court to do a reasonably complete job. The waiver reinforces the policy of subdivision (g) forbidding successive motions.

By amended subdivision (h)(1)(B), the specified defenses, even if not waived by the operation of (A), are waived by the failure to raise them by a motion under Rule 12 or in the responsive pleading or any amendment thereof to which the party is entitled as a matter of course. The specified defenses are of such a character that they should not be delayed and brought up for the first time by means of an application to the court to amend the responsive pleading.

Since the language of the subdivisions is made clear, the party is put on fair notice of the effect of his actions and omissions and can guard himself against unintended waiver. It is to be noted that while the defenses specified in subdivision (h)(1) are subject to waiver as there provided, the more substantial defenses of failure to state a claim upon which relief can be granted, failure to join a party indispensable under Rule 19, and failure to state a legal defense to a claim (see Rule 12(b)(6), (7), (f)), as well as the defense of lack of jurisdiction over the subject matter (see Rule 12(b)(1)), are expressly preserved against waiver by amended subdivision (h)(2) and (3).

1987 Amendment

The amendments are technical. No substantive change is intended.

1993 Amendments

Subdivision (a) is divided into paragraphs for greater clarity, and paragraph (1)(B) is added to reflect amendments to Rule 4. Consistent with Rule 4(d)(3), a defendant that timely waives service is allowed 60 days from the date the request was mailed in which to respond to the complaint, with an additional 30 days afforded if the request was sent out of the country. Service is timely waived if the waiver is returned within the time specified in the request (30 days after the request was mailed, or 60 days if mailed out of the country) and before being formally served with process. Sometimes a plaintiff may attempt to serve a defendant with process while also sending the defendant a request for waiver of service; if the defendant executes the waiver of service within the time specified and before being served with process, it should have the longer time to respond afforded by waiving service.

The date of sending the request is to be inserted by the plaintiff on the face of the request for waiver and on the waiver itself. This date is used to measure the return day for the waiver form, so that the plaintiff can know on a day certain whether formal service of process will be necessary; it is also a useful date to measure the time for answer when service is waived. The defendant who returns the waiver is given additional time for answer in order to assure that it loses nothing by waiving service of process.

Rule 13. Counterclaim and Cross-Claim

(a) Compulsory Counterclaims. A pleading shall state as a counterclaim any claim which at the time of serving the pleading the pleader has against any opposing party, if it arises out of the transaction or occurrence that is the subject matter of the opposing party's claim and does not require for its adjudication the presence of third parties of whom the court cannot acquire jurisdiction. But the pleader need not state the claim if (1) at the time the action was commenced the claim was the subject of another pending action, or (2) the opposing party brought suit upon the claim by attachment or other process by which the court did not acquire jurisdiction to render a personal judgment on that claim, and the pleader is not stating any counterclaim under this Rule 13.

(b) Permissive Counterclaims. A pleading may state as a counterclaim any claim against an opposing party not arising out of the transaction or occurrence that is the subject matter of the opposing party's claim.

(c) Counterclaim Exceeding Opposing Claim. A counterclaim may or may not diminish or defeat the recovery sought by the opposing party. It may claim relief exceeding in amount or different in kind from that sought in the pleading of the opposing party.

(d) Counterclaim Against the United States. These rules shall not be construed to enlarge beyond the limits now fixed by law the right to assert counterclaims or to claim credits against the United States or an officer or agency thereof.

(e) Counterclaim Maturing or Acquired After Pleading. A claim which either matured or was acquired by the pleader after serving a pleading may, with the permission of the court, be presented as a counterclaim by supplemental pleading.

(f) Omitted Counterclaim. When a pleader fails to set up a counterclaim through oversight, inadvertence, or excusable neglect, or when justice requires, the pleader may by leave of court set up the counterclaim by amendment.

(g) Cross-Claim Against Co-Party. A pleading may state as a cross-claim any claim by one party against a co-party arising out of the transaction or occurrence that is the subject matter either of the original action or of a counterclaim therein or relating to any property that is the subject matter of the original action. Such cross-claim may include a claim that the party against whom it is asserted is or may be liable to the cross-claimant for all or part of a claim asserted in the action against the cross-claimant.

(h) Joinder of Additional Parties. Persons other than those made parties to the original action may be made parties to a counterclaim or cross-claim in accordance with the provisions of Rules 19 and 20.

(i) Separate Trials; Separate Judgments. If the court orders separate trials as provided in Rule 42(b), judgment on a counterclaim or cross-claim may be rendered in accordance with the terms of Rule 54(b) when the court has jurisdiction so to do, even if the claims of the opposing party have been dismissed or otherwise disposed of.

(As amended Dec. 27, 1946, eff. Mar. 19, 1948; Jan. 21, 1963, eff. July 1, 1963; Feb. 28, 1966, eff. July 1, 1966; Mar. 2, 1987, eff. Aug. 1, 1987.)

ADVISORY COMMITTEE NOTES

1937 Adoption

1. This is substantially [former] Equity Rule 30 (Answer—Contents—Counterclaim), broadened to include legal as well as equitable counterclaims.

2. Compare the English practice, *English Rules Under the Judicature Act* (The Annual Practice, 1937) O. 19, r.r. 2 and 3, and O. 21, r.r. 10–17; *Beddall v. Maitland*, L.R. 17 Ch.Div. 174, 181, 182 (1881).

3. Certain States have also adopted almost unrestricted provisions concerning both the subject matter of and the parties to a counterclaim. This seems to be the modern tendency. Ark.Civ.Code (Crawford, 1934) §§ 117 (as amended) and 118; N.J.Comp.Stat. (2 Cum.Supp. 1911–1924); N.Y.C.P.A. (1937) §§ 262, 266, 267 (all as amended, Laws of 1936, ch. 324), 268, 269, and 271; Wis.Stat. (1935) § 263.14(1)(c).

4. Most codes do not expressly provide for a counterclaim in the reply. Clark, *Code Pleading* (1928), p. 486. Ky.Codes (Carroll, 1932) Civ.Pract. § 98 does provide, however, for such counterclaim.

5. The provisions of this rule respecting counterclaims are subject to Rule 82 (Jurisdiction and Venue Unaffected). For a discussion of Federal jurisdiction and venue in regard to counterclaims and cross-claims, see Shulman and Jaegerman, *Some Jurisdictional Limitations in Federal Procedure* (1936), 45 Yale L.J. 393, 410 et seq.

6. This rule does not affect such statutes of the United States as U.S.C., Title 28, § 41(1) (now §§ 1332, 1345, 1359) (United States as plaintiff; civil suits at common law and in

equity), relating to assigned claims in actions based on diversity of citizenship.

7. If the action proceeds to judgment without the interposition of a counterclaim as required by subdivision (a) of this rule, the counterclaim is barred. See *American Mills Co. v. American Surety Co.*, 260 U.S. 360, 43 S.Ct. 149, 67 L.Ed. 306 (1922); *Marconi Wireless Telegraph Co. v. National Electric Signalling Co.*, 206 Fed. 295 (E.D.N.Y., 1913); Hopkins, *Federal Equity Rules* (8th ed., 1933), p. 213; Simkins, *Federal Practice* (1934), p. 663.

8. For allowance of credits against the United States see U.S.C., Title 26, §§ 1672–1673 [sec. 7442] (Suits for refunds of internal revenue taxes—limitations); U.S.C., Title 28, § 774 (now § 2406) (Suits by United States against individuals; credits), [former] § 775 (Suits under postal laws; credits); U.S.C., Title 31, § 227 [now 3728] (Offsets against judgments and claims against United States).

1946 Amendment

Note. Subdivision (a). The use of the word "filing" was inadvertent. The word "serving" conforms with subdivision (e) and with usage generally throughout the rules.

The removal of the phrase "not the subject of a pending action" and the addition of the new clause at the end of the subdivision is designed to eliminate the ambiguity noted in *Prudential Insurance Co. of America v. Saxe*, App.D.C.1943, 77 U.S.App.D.C. 144, 134 F.2d 16, 33–34, cert. den., 1943, 319 U.S. 745, 63 S.Ct. 1033. The rewording of the subdivision in this respect insures against an undesirable possibility presented under the original rule whereby a party having a claim which would be the subject of a compulsory counterclaim could avoid stating it as such by bringing an independent action in another court after the commencement of the federal action but before serving his pleading in the federal action.

Subdivision (g). The amendment is to care for a situation such as where a second mortgagee is made defendant in a foreclosure proceeding and wishes to file a cross-complaint against the mortgagor in order to secure a personal judgment for the indebtedness and foreclose his lien. A claim of this sort by the second mortgagee may not necessarily arise out of the transaction or occurrence that is the subject matter of the original action under the terms of Rule 13(g).

Subdivision (h). The change clarifies the interdependence of Rules 13(i) and 54(b).

1963 Amendment

When a defendant, if he desires to defend his interest in property, is obliged to come in and litigate in a court to whose jurisdiction he could not ordinarily be subjected, fairness suggests that he should not be required to assert counterclaims, but should rather be permitted to do so at his election. If, however, he does elect to assert a counterclaim, it seems fair to require him to assert any other which is compulsory within the meaning of Rule 13(a). Clause (2), added by amendment to Rule 13(a), carries out this idea. It will apply to various cases described in Rule 4(e), as amended, where service is effected through attachment or other process by which the court does not acquire jurisdiction to render a personal judgment against the defendant. Clause (2) will also apply to actions commenced in State courts jurisdictionally grounded on attachment or the like, and removed to the Federal courts.

1966 Amendment

Rule 13(h), dealing with the joinder of additional parties to a counterclaim or cross-claim, has partaken of some of the textual difficulties of Rule 19 on necessary joinder of parties. See Advisory Committee's Note to Rule 19, as amended; cf. 3 *Moore's Federal Practice,* par. 13.39 (2d ed. 1963), and Supp. thereto; 1A Barron & Holtzoff, *Federal Practice and Procedure* § 399 (Wright ed. 1960). Rule 13(h) has also been inadequate in failing to call attention to the fact that a party pleading a counterclaim or cross-claim may join additional persons when the conditions for permissive joinder of parties under Rule 20 are satisfied.

The amendment of Rule 13(h) supplies the latter omission by expressly referring to Rule 20, as amended, and also incorporates by direct reference the revised criteria and procedures of Rule 19, as amended. Hereafter, for the purpose of determining who must or may be joined as additional parties to a counterclaim or cross-claim, the party pleading the claim is to be regarded as a plaintiff and the additional parties as plaintiffs or defendants as the case may be, and amended Rules 19 and 20 are to be applied in the usual fashion. See also Rules 13(a) (compulsory counterclaims) and 22 (interpleader).

The amendment of Rule 13(h), like the amendment of Rule 19, does not attempt to regulate Federal jurisdiction or venue. See Rule 82. It should be noted, however, that in some situations the decisional law has recognized "ancillary" Federal jurisdiction over counterclaims and cross-claims and "ancillary" venue as to parties to these claims.

1987 Amendment

The amendments are technical. No substantive change is intended.

Rule 14. Third-Party Practice

(a) When Defendant May Bring in Third Party. At any time after commencement of the action a defending party, as a third-party plaintiff, may cause a summons and complaint to be served upon a person not a party to the action who is or may be liable to the third-party plaintiff for all or part of the plaintiff's claim against the third-party plaintiff. The third-party plaintiff need not obtain leave to make the service if the third-party plaintiff files the third-party complaint not later than 10 days after serving the original answer. Otherwise the third-party plaintiff must obtain leave on motion upon notice to all parties to the action. The person served with the summons and third-party complaint, hereinafter called the third-party defendant, shall make any defenses to the third-party plaintiff's claim as provided in Rule 12 and any counterclaims against the third-party plaintiff and cross-claims against other third-party defendants as provided in Rule 13. The third-party defendant may assert against the plaintiff any defenses which the third-party plaintiff has to the plaintiff's claim. The third-party defendant may also assert any claim against the plaintiff arising out of the transaction or occurrence that is the subject matter of the plaintiff's claim against the third-party plaintiff. The plaintiff may assert any claim against the third-party defendant arising out of the transaction or occurrence that is the subject matter of the plaintiff's claim against the third-party plaintiff, and the third-party defendant thereupon shall assert any defenses as provided in Rule 12 and any counterclaims and cross-claims as provided in Rule 13. Any party may move to strike the third-party claim, or for its severance or separate trial. A third-party defendant may proceed under this rule against any person not a party to the action who is or may be liable to the third-party defendant for all or part of the claim made in the action against the third-party defendant. The third-party complaint, if within the admiralty and maritime jurisdiction, may be in rem against a vessel, cargo, or other property subject to admiralty or maritime process in rem, in which case references in this rule to the summons include the warrant of arrest, and references to the third-party plaintiff or defendant include, where appropriate, the claimant of the property arrested.

(b) When Plaintiff May Bring in Third Party. When a counterclaim is asserted against a plaintiff, the plaintiff may cause a third party to be brought in under circumstances which under this rule would entitle a defendant to do so.

(c) Admiralty and Maritime Claims. When a plaintiff asserts an admiralty or maritime claim within the meaning of Rule 9(h), the defendant or claimant, as a third-party plaintiff, may bring in a third-party defendant who may be wholly or partly liable, either to the plaintiff or to the third-party plaintiff, by way of remedy over, contribution, or otherwise on account of the same transaction, occurrence, or series of transactions or occurrences. In such a case the third-party plaintiff may also demand judgment against the third-party defendant in favor of the plaintiff, in which event the third-party defendant shall make any defenses to the claim of the plaintiff as well as to that of the third-party plaintiff in the manner provided in Rule 12 and the action shall proceed as if the plaintiff had commenced it against the third-party defendant as well as the third-party plaintiff.

(As amended Dec. 27, 1946, eff. Mar. 19, 1948; Jan. 21, 1963, eff. July 1, 1963; Feb. 28, 1966, eff. July 1, 1966; Mar. 2, 1987, eff. Aug. 1, 1987.)

ADVISORY COMMITTEE NOTES

1937 Adoption

Third-party impleader is in some aspects a modern innovation in law and equity although well known in admiralty. Because of its many advantages a liberal procedure with respect to it has developed in England, in the federal admiralty courts, and in some American state jurisdictions. See *English Rules Under the Judicature Act* (The Annual Practice, 1937) O. 16A, r.r. 1–13; United States Supreme Court Admiralty Rules (1920), Rule 56 (Right to Bring in Party Jointly Liable); 12 P.S.Pa. § 141; Wis.Stat. (1935) §§ 260.19, 260.20; N.Y.C.P.A. (1937) §§ 193(2), 211(a). Compare La. Code Pract. (Dart, 1932) §§ 378–388. For the practice in Texas as developed by judicial decision, see *Lottman v. Cuilla*, Tex.1926, 288 S.W. 123, 126. For a treatment of this subject see Gregory, *Legislative Loss Distribution in Negligence Actions* (1936); *Shulman and Jaegerman, Some Jurisdictional Limitations on Federal Procedure (1936)*, 45 Yale L.J. 393, 417 et seq.

Third-party impleader under the-conformity act has been applied in actions at law in the Federal courts. *Lowry and Co., Inc. v. National City Bank of New York*, N.Y.1928, 28 F.2d 895; *Yellow Cab Co. of Philadelphia v. Rodgers*, C.C.A.3, 1932, 61 F.2d 729.

1946 Amendment

Note. The provisions in Rule 14(a) which relate to the impleading of a third party who is or may be liable to the plaintiff have been deleted by the proposed amendment. It has been held that under Rule 14(a) the plaintiff need not amend his complaint to state a claim against such third party if he does not wish to do so. *Satink v. Holland Township*, D.N.J.1940, 31 F.Supp. 229, noted, 1940, 88 U.Pa.L.Rev. 751; *Connelly v. Bender*, E.D.Mich.1941, 36 F.Supp. 368; *Whitmire v. Partin (Milton)*, E.D.Tenn.1941, 2 F.R.D. 83, 5 Fed.Rules Serv. 14a.513, Case 2; *Crim v. Lumbermen's Mutual Casualty Co.*, D.D.C.1939, 26 F.Supp. 715; *Carbola Chemical Co., Inc. v. Trundle*, S.D.N.Y.1943, 3 F.R.D. 502, 7 Fed.Rules Serv. 14a.224, Case 1; *Roadway Express, Inc. v. Automobile Ins. Co. of Hartford, Conn., (Providence Washington Ins. Co.)* N.D.Ohio 1945, 8 Fed.Rules Serv. 14a.513, Case 3. In *Delano v. Ives*, E.D.Pa.1941, 40 F.Supp. 672, the court said: ". . . the weight of authority is to the effect that a defendant cannot compel the plaintiff, who has sued him, to sue also a third party whom he does not wish to sue, by tendering in a third party complaint the third party as an additional defendant directly liable to the plaintiff." Thus impleader here amounts to no more than a mere offer of a party to the plaintiff, and if he rejects it, the attempt is a time-consuming futility. See *Satink v. Holland Township, supra; Malkin v. Arundel Corp.*, D.Md.1941, 36 F.Supp. 948; also Koenigsberger, *Suggestions for Changes in the Federal Rules of Civil Procedure*, 1941, 4 Fed.Rules Serv. 1010. But cf. *Atlantic Coast Line R. Co. v. United States Fidelity & Guaranty Co.*, Ga.1943, 52 F.Supp. 177. Moreover, in any case where the plaintiff could not have joined the third party originally because of jurisdictional limitations such as lack of diversity of citizenship, the majority view is that any attempt by the plaintiff to amend his complaint and assert a claim against the impleaded third party would be unavailing. *Hoskie v. Prudential Ins. Co. of America, (Lorrac Real Estate Corp.)*, E.D.N.Y.1941, 39 F.Supp. 305; *Johnson v. G. J. Sherrard Co., (New England Telephone & Telegraph Co.)*, D.Mass.1941, 5 Fed.Rules Serv. 14a.511, Case 1, 2 F.R.D. 164; *Thompson v. Cranston*, W.D.N.Y.1942, 6 Fed.Rules Serv. 14a.511, Case 1, 2 F.R.D. 270, affirmed CCA2d, 1942, 132 F.2d 631, certiorari denied 1945, 63 S.Ct. 1028, 319 U.S. 741, 87 L.Ed. 1698; *Friend v. Middle Atlantic Transportation Co.*, C.C.A.2, 1946, 153 F.2d 778, certiorari denied 1946, 66 S.Ct. 1370, 328 U.S. 865, 90 L.Ed. 1635; *Herrington v.*

Jones, E.D.La.1941, 5 Fed.Rules Serv. 14a.511, Case 2, 2 F.R.D. 108; *Banks v. Employers' Liability Assurance Corp., (Central Surety & Ins. Corp.)* W.D.Mo.1943, 7 Fed.Rules Serv. 14a.11, Case 2; *Saunders v. Baltimore & Ohio R. Co.,* S.D.W.Va.1945, 9 Fed.Rules Serv. 14a.62, Case 2; *Hull v. United States Rubber Co. (Johnson Larsen and Co.),* E.D.Mich.1945, 9 Fed.Rules Serv. 14a.62, Case 3. See also concurring opinion of Circuit Judge Minton in *People of State of Illinois for Use of Trust Co. of Chicago v. Maryland Casualty Co.,* C.C.A.7, 1942, 132 F.2d 850, 853. Contra: *Sklar v. Hayes (Singer),* E.D.Pa.1941, 4 Fed.Rules Serv. 14a.511, Case 2, 1 F.R.D. 594. Discussion of the problem will be found in Commentary, *Amendment of Plaintiff's Pleading to Assert Claim Against Third-Party Defendant,* 1942, 5 Fed.Rules Serv. 811; Commentary, *Federal Jurisdiction in Third-Party Practice,* 1943, 6 Fed.Rules Serv. 766; Holtzoff, *Some Problems Under Federal Third-Party Practice,* 1941, 3 La.L.Rev. 408, 419–420; 1 Moore's *Federal Practice,* 1938, Cum.Supplement § 14.08. For these reasons therefore, the words "or to the plaintiff" in the first sentence of subdivision (a) have been removed by the amendment; and in conformance therewith the words "the plaintiff" in the second sentence of the subdivision, and the words "or to the third-party plaintiff" in the concluding sentence thereof have likewise been eliminated.

The third sentence of rule 14(a) has been expanded to clarify the right of the third-party defendant to assert any defenses which the third-party plaintiff may have to the plaintiff's claim. This protects the impleaded third-party defendant where the third-party plaintiff fails or neglects to assert a proper defense to the plaintiff's action. A new sentence has also been inserted giving the third-party defendant the right to assert directly against the original plaintiff any claim arising out of the transaction or occurrence that is the subject matter of the plaintiff's claim against the third-party plaintiff. This permits all claims arising out of the same transaction or occurrence to be heard and determined in the same action. See *Atlantic Coast Line R. Co. v. United States Fidelity & Guaranty Co.,* Ga.1943, 52 F.Supp. 177. Accordingly, the next to the last sentence of subdivision (a) has also been revised to make clear that the plaintiff may, if he desires, assert directly against the third-party defendant either by amendment or by a new pleading any claim he may have against him arising out of the transaction or occurrence that is the subject matter of the plaintiff's claim against the third-party plaintiff. In such a case, the third-party defendant then is entitled to assert the defenses, counter-claims and cross-claims provided in Rules 12 and 13.

The sentence reading "The third-party defendant is bound by the adjudication of the third-party plaintiff's liability to the plaintiff, as well as of his own to the plaintiff, or to the third-party plaintiff" has been stricken from Rule 14(a), not to change the law, but because the sentence states a rule of substantive law which is not within the scope of a procedural rule. It is not the purpose of the rules to state the effect of a judgment.

The elimination of the words "the third-party plaintiff, or any other party" from the second sentence of rule 14(a), together with the insertion of the new phrases therein, are not changes of substance but are merely for the purpose of clarification.

1963 Amendment

Under the amendment of the initial sentences of the subdivision, a defendant as a third-party plaintiff may freely and without leave of court bring in a third-party defendant if he files the third-party complaint not later than 10 days after he serves his original answer. When the impleader comes so early in the case, there is little value in requiring a preliminary ruling by the court on the propriety of the impleader.

After the third-party defendant is brought in, the court has discretion to strike the third-party claim if it is obviously unmeritorious and can only delay or prejudice the disposition of the plaintiff's claim, or to sever the third-party claim or accord it separate trial if confusion or prejudice would otherwise result. This discretion, applicable not merely to the cases covered by the amendment where the third-party defendant is brought in without leave, but to all impleaders under the rule, is emphasized in the next-to-last sentence of the subdivision, added by amendment.

In dispensing with leave of court for an impleader filed not later than 10 days after serving the answer, but retaining the leave requirement for impleaders sought to be effected thereafter, the amended subdivision takes a moderate position on the lines urged by some commentators, see Note, 43 Minn.L.Rev. 115 (1958); cf. Pa.R.Civ.P. 2252–53 (60 days after service on the defendant; Minn.R.Civ.P. 14.01 (45 days). Other commentators would dispense with the requirement of leave regardless of the time when impleader is effected, and would rely on subsequent action by the court to dismiss the impleader if it would unduly delay or complicate the litigation or would be otherwise objectionable. See 1A Barron & Holtzoff, *Federal Practice & Procedure* 649–50 (Wright ed. 1960); Comment, 58 Colum.L.Rev. 532, 546 (1958); cf. N.Y.Civ.Prac.Act § 193–a; Me.R.Civ.P. 14. The amended subdivision preserves the value of a preliminary screening, through the leave procedure, of impleaders attempted after the 10-day period.

The amendment applies also when an impleader is initiated by a third-party defendant against a person who may be liable to him, as provided in the last sentence of the subdivision.

1966 Amendment

Rule 14 was modeled on Admiralty Rule 56. An important feature of Admiralty Rule 56 was that it allowed impleader not only of a person who might be liable to the defendant by way of remedy over, but also of any person who might be liable to the plaintiff. The importance of this provision was that the defendant was entitled to insist that the plaintiff proceed to judgment against the third-party defendant. In certain cases this was a valuable implementation of a substantive right. For example, in a case of ship collision where a finding of mutual fault is possible, one shipowner, if sued alone, faces the prospect of an absolute judgment for the full amount of the damage suffered by an innocent third party; but if he can implead the owner of the other vessel, and if mutual fault is found, the judgment against the original defendant will be in the first instance only for a moiety of the damages; liability for the remainder will be conditioned on the plaintiff's inability to collect from the third-party defendant.

This feature was originally incorporated in Rule 14, but was eliminated by the amendment of 1946, so that under the amended rule a third party could not be impleaded on the basis that he might be liable to the plaintiff. One of the reasons for the amendment was that the Civil Rule, unlike the Admiralty Rule, did not require the plaintiff to go to judgment against the third-party defendant. Another reason was that where jurisdiction depended on diversity of citizenship the impleader of an adversary having the same citizenship as the plaintiff was not considered possible.

Retention of the admiralty practice in those cases that will be counterparts of a suit in admiralty is clearly desirable.

1987 Amendment

The amendments are technical. No substantive change is intended.

Rule 15. Amended and Supplemental Pleadings

(a) Amendments. A party may amend the party's pleading once as a matter of course at any time before a responsive pleading is served or, if the pleading is one to which no responsive pleading is permitted and the action has not been placed upon the trial calendar, the party may so amend it at any time within 20 days after it is served. Otherwise a party may amend the party's pleading only by leave of court or by written consent of the adverse party; and leave shall be freely given when justice so requires. A party shall plead in response to an amended pleading within the time remaining for response to the original pleading or within 10 days after service of the amended pleading, whichever period may be the longer, unless the court otherwise orders.

(b) Amendments to Conform to the Evidence. When issues not raised by the pleadings are tried by express or implied consent of the parties, they shall be treated in all respects as if they had been raised in the pleadings. Such amendment of the pleadings as may be necessary to cause them to conform to the evidence and to raise these issues may be made upon motion of any party at any time, even after judgment; but failure so to amend does not affect the result of the trial of these issues. If evidence is objected to at the trial on the ground that it is not within the issues made by the pleadings, the court may allow the pleadings to be amended and shall do so freely when the presentation of the merits of the action will be subserved thereby and the objecting party fails to satisfy the court that the admission of such evidence would prejudice the party in maintaining the party's action or defense upon the merits. The court may grant a continuance to enable the objecting party to meet such evidence.

(c) Relation Back of Amendments. An amendment of a pleading relates back to the date of the original pleading when

(1) relation back is permitted by the law that provides the statute of limitations applicable to the action, or

(2) the claim or defense asserted in the amended pleading arose out of the conduct, transaction, or occurrence set forth or attempted to be set forth in the original pleading, or

(3) the amendment changes the party or the naming of the party against whom a claim is asserted if the foregoing provision (2) is satisfied and, within the period provided by Rule 4(m) for service of the summons and complaint, the party to be brought in by amendment (A) has received such notice of the institution of the action that the party will not be prejudiced in maintaining a defense on the merits, and (B) knew or should have known that, but for a mistake concerning the identity of the proper party, the action would have been brought against the party.

The delivery or mailing of process to the United States Attorney, or United States Attorney's designee, or the Attorney General of the United States, or an agency or officer who would have been a proper defendant if named, satisfies the requirement of subparagraphs (A) and (B) of this paragraph (3) with respect to the United States or any agency or officer thereof to be brought into the action as a defendant.

(d) Supplemental Pleadings. Upon motion of a party the court may, upon reasonable notice and upon such terms as are just, permit the party to serve a supplemental pleading setting forth transactions or occurrences or events which have happened since the date of the pleading sought to be supplemented. Permission may be granted even though the original pleading is defective in its statement of a claim for relief or defense. If the court deems it advisable that the adverse party plead to the supplemental pleading, it shall so order, specifying the time therefor.

(As amended Jan. 21, 1963, eff. July 1, 1963; Feb. 28, 1966, eff. July 1, 1966; Mar. 2, 1987, eff. Aug. 1, 1987; Apr. 30, 1991, eff. Dec. 1, 1991; Dec. 9, 1991, Pub.L. 102–198, § 11(a), 105 Stat. 1626; Apr. 22, 1993, eff. Dec. 1, 1993.)

ADVISORY COMMITTEE NOTES

1937 Adoption

See generally for the present federal practice, [former] Equity Rules 19 (Amendments Generally), 28 (Amendment of Bill as of Course), 32 (Answer to Amended Bill), 34 (Supplemental Pleading), and 35 (Bills of Revivor and Supplemental Bills—Form); U.S.C. Title 28, § 399 [now 1653] (Amendments to show diverse citizenship) and [former] 777 (Defects of form; amendments). See *English Rules Under the Judicature Act* (The Annual Practice, 1937) O. 28, r. r. 1–13; O. 20, r. 4; O. 24, r. r. 1–3.

Note to Subdivision (a). The right to serve an amended pleading once as of course is common. 4 Mont.Rev.Codes Ann. (1935) § 9186; 1 Ore.Code Ann. (1930) § 1–904; 1

S.C.Code (Michie, 1932) § 493; *English Rules Under the Judicature Act* (The Annual Practice, 1937) O. 28, r. 2. Provision for amendment of pleading before trial, by leave of court, is in almost every code. If there is no statute the power of the court to grant leave is said to be inherent. Clark, *Code Pleading* (1928), pp. 498, 509.

Note to Subdivision (b). Compare [former] Equity Rule 19 (Amendments Generally) and code provisions which allow an amendment "at any time in furtherance of justice," (e.g., Ark.Civ.Code (Crawford, 1934) § 155) and which allow an amendment of pleadings to conform to the evidence, where the adverse party has not been misled and prejudiced (e.g., N.M.Stat.Ann. (Courtright, 1929) §§ 105–601, 105–602).

Note to Subdivision (c). "Relation back" is a well recognized doctrine of recent and now more frequent application. Compare Ala.Code Ann. (Michie, 1928) § 9513; Smith-Hurd Ill.Stats. ch. 110, § 170(2); 2 Wash.Rev.Stat.Ann. (Remington, 1932) § 308–3(4). See U.S.C., Title 28, § 399 [now 1653] (Amendments to show diverse citizenship) for a provision for "relation back".

Note to Subdivision (d). This is an adaptation of former Equity Rule 34 (Supplemental Pleading).

1963 Amendment

Rule 15(d) is intended to give the court broad discretion in allowing a supplemental pleading. However, some cases, opposed by other cases and criticized by the commentators, have taken the rigid and formalistic view that where the original complaint fails to state a claim upon which relief can be granted, leave to serve a supplemental complaint must be denied. See *Bonner v. Elizabeth Arden, Inc.*, 177 F.2d 703 (2d Cir. 1949); *Bowles v. Senderowitz*, 65 F.Supp. 548 (E.D.Pa.), rev'd on other grounds, 158 F.2d 435 (3d Cir. 1946), cert. denied, *Senderowitz v. Fleming*, 330 U.S. 848, 67 S.Ct. 1091, 91 L.Ed. 1292 (1947); cf. *LaSalle Nat. Bank v. 222 East Chestnut St. Corp.*, 267 F.2d 247 (7th Cir.), cert. denied, 361 U.S. 836, 80 S.Ct. 88, 4 L.Ed.2d 77 (1959). But see *Camilla Cotton Oil Co. v. Spencer Kellogg & Sons*, 257 F.2d 162 (5th Cir. 1958); *Genuth v. National Biscuit Co.*, 81 F.Supp. 213 (S.D.N.Y.1948), app. dism., 177 F.2d 962 (2d Cir. 1949); 3 Moore's *Federal Practice* ¶15.01[5] (Supp.1960); 1A Barron & Holtzoff, *Federal Practice & Procedure* 820–21 (Wright ed. 1960). Thus plaintiffs have sometimes been needlessly remitted to the difficulties of commencing a new action even though events occurring after the commencement of the original action have made clear the right to relief.

Under the amendment the court has discretion to permit a supplemental pleading despite the fact that the original pleading is defective. As in other situations where a supplemental pleading is offered, the court is to determine in the light of the particular circumstances whether filing should be permitted, and if so, upon what terms. The amendment does not attempt to deal with such questions as the relation of the statute of limitations to supplemental pleadings, the operation of the doctrine of laches, or the availability of other defenses. All these questions are for decision in accordance with the principles applicable to supplemental pleadings generally. Cf. *Blau v. Lamb*, 191 F.Supp. 906 (S.D.N.Y.1961); *Lendonsol Amusement Corp. v. B. & Q. Assoc., Inc.*, 23 F.R.Serv. 15d.3, Case 1 (D.Mass.1957).

1966 Amendment

Rule 15(c) is amplified to state more clearly when an amendment of a pleading changing the party against whom a claim is asserted (including an amendment to correct a misnomer or misdescription of a defendant) shall "relate back" to the date of the original pleading.

The problem has arisen most acutely in certain actions by private parties against officers or agencies of the United States. Thus an individual denied social security benefits by the Secretary of Health, Education, and Welfare may secure review of the decision by bringing a civil action against that officer within sixty days. 42 U.S.C. § 405(g) (Supp. III, 1962). In several recent cases the claimants instituted timely action but mistakenly named as defendant the United States, the Department of HEW, the "Federal Security Administration" (a nonexistent agency), and a Secretary who had retired from the office nineteen days before. Discovering their mistakes, the claimants moved to amend their complaints to name the proper defendant; by this time the statutory sixty-day period had expired. The motions were denied on the ground that the amendment "would amount to the commencement of a new proceeding and would not relate back in time so as to avoid the statutory provision * * * that suit be brought within sixty days * * *" *Cohn v. Federal Security Adm.*, 199 F.Supp. 884, 885 (W.D.N.Y.1961); see also *Cunningham v. United States*, 199 F.Supp. 541 (W.D.Mo.1958); *Hall v. Department of HEW*, 199 F.Supp. 833 (S.D.Tex.1960); *Sandridge v. Folsom, Secretary of HEW*, 200 F.Supp. 25 (M.D.Tenn.1959). [The Secretary of Health, Education, and Welfare has approved certain ameliorative regulations under 42 U.S.C. § 405(g). See 29 Fed. Reg. 8209 (June 30, 1964); Jacoby, *The Effect of Recent Changes in the Law of "Nonstatutory" Judicial Review*, 53 Geo.L.J. 19, 42–43 (1964); see also *Simmons v. United States Dept. HEW*, 328 F.2d 86 (3d Cir. 1964).]

Analysis in terms of "new proceeding" is traceable to *Davis v. L. L. Cohen & Co.*, 268 U.S. 638 (1925), and *Mellon v. Arkansas Land & Lumber Co.*, 275 U.S. 460 (1928), but those cases antedate the adoption of the Rules which import different criteria for determining when an amendment is to "relate back". As lower courts have continued to rely on the *Davis* and *Mellon* cases despite the contrary intent of the Rules, clarification of Rule 15(c) is considered advisable.

Relation back is intimately connected with the policy of the statute of limitations. The policy of the statute limiting the time for suit against the Secretary of HEW would not have been offended by allowing relation back in the situations described above. For the government was put on notice of the claim within the stated period—in the particular instances, by means of the initial delivery of process to a responsible government official (see Rule 4(d)(4) and (5)). In these circumstances, characterization of the amendment as a new proceeding is not responsive to the realty [sic], but is merely question-begging; and to deny relation back is to defeat unjustly the claimant's opportunity to prove his case. See the full discussion by Byse, *Suing the "Wrong" Defendant in Judicial Review of Federal Administrative Action: Proposals for Reform*, 77 Harv.L.Rev. 40 (1963); see also Ill.Civ.P. Act § 46(4).

Much the same question arises in other types of actions against the government (see *Byse*, supra, at 45 n. 15). In actions between private parties, the problem of relation back of amendments changing defendants has generally been better handled by the courts, but incorrect criteria have sometimes been applied, leading sporadically to doubtful results. See 1A Barron & Holtzoff, *Federal Practice & Procedure* § 451 (Wright ed. 1960); 1 id. § 186 (1960); 2 id. § 543 (1961); 3 *Moore's Federal Practice,* par. 15.15 (Cum.Supp. 1962); Annot., *Change in Party After Statute of Limitations Has Run,* 8 A.L.R.2d 6 (1949). Rule 15(c) has been amplified to provide a general solution. An amendment changing the party against whom a claim is asserted relates back if the amendment satisfies the usual condition of Rule 15(c) of "arising out of the conduct * * * set forth * * * in the original pleading," and if, within the applicable limitations period, the party brought in by amendment, first, received such notice of the institution of the action—the notice need not be formal—that he would not be prejudiced in defending the action, and, second, knew or should have known that the action would have been brought against him initially had there not been a mistake concerning the identity of the proper party. Revised Rule 15(c) goes on to provide specifically in the government cases that the first and second requirements are satisfied when the government has been notified in the manner there described (see Rule 4(d)(4) and (5)). As applied to the government cases, revised Rule 15(c) further advances the objectives of the 1961 amendment of Rule 25(d) (substitution of public officers).

The relation back of amendments changing plaintiffs is not expressly treated in revised Rule 15(c) since the problem is generally easier. Again the chief consideration of policy is that of the statute of limitations, and the attitude taken in revised Rule 15(c) toward change of defendants extends by analogy to amendments changing plaintiffs. Also relevant is the amendment of Rule 17(a) (real party in interest). To avoid forfeitures of just claims, revised Rule 17(a) would provide that no action shall be dismissed on the ground that it is not prosecuted in the name of the real party in interest until a reasonable time has been allowed for correction of the defect in the manner there stated.

1987 Amendment

The amendments are technical. No substantive change is intended.

1991 Amendment

The rule has been revised to prevent parties against whom claims are made from taking unjust advantage of otherwise inconsequential pleading errors to sustain a limitations defense.

Paragraph (c)(1). This provision is new. It is intended to make it clear that the rule does not apply to preclude any relation back that may be permitted under the applicable limitations law. Generally, the applicable limitations law will be state law. If federal jurisdiction is based on the citizenship of the parties, the primary reference is the law of the state in which the district court sits. *Walker v. Armco Steel Corp.,* 446 U.S. 740 (1980). If federal jurisdiction is based on a federal question, the reference may be to the law of the state governing relations between the parties. *E.g., Board of Regents v. Tomanio,* 446 U.S. 478 (1980). In some circumstances, the controlling limitations law may be federal law. *E.g., West v. Conrail, Inc.,* 107 S.Ct. 1538 (1987). Cf. *Burlington Northern R. Co. v. Woods,* 480 U.S. 1 (1987); *Stewart Organization v. Ricoh,* 108 S.Ct. 2239 (1988). Whatever may be the controlling body of limitations law, if that law affords a more forgiving principle of relation back than the one provided in this rule, it should be available to save the claim. Accord, *Marshall v. Mulrenin,* 508 F.2d 39 (1st cir.1974). If *Schiavone v. Fortune,* 106 S.Ct. 2379 (1986) implies the contrary, this paragraph is intended to make a material change in the rule.

Paragraph (c)(3). This paragraph has been revised to change the result in *Schiavone v. Fortune, supra,* with respect to the problem of a misnamed defendant. An intended defendant who is notified of an action within the period allowed by Rule 4(m) [subdivision (m) in Rule 4 was a proposed subdivision which was withdrawn by the Supreme Court] for service of a summons and complaint may not under the revised rule defeat the action on account of a defect in the pleading with respect to the defendant's name, provided that the requirements of clauses (A) and (B) have been met. If the notice requirement is met within the Rule 4(m) [subdivision (m) in Rule 4 was a proposed subdivision which was withdrawn by the Supreme Court] period, a complaint may be amended at any time to correct a formal defect such as a misnomer or misidentification. On the basis of the text of the former rule, the Court reached a result in *Schiavone v. Fortune* that was inconsistent with the liberal pleading practices secured by Rule 8. See Bauer, Schiavone: *An Un-Fortune-ate Illustration of the Supreme Court's Role as Interpreter of the Federal Rules of Civil Procedure,* 63 Notre Dame L.Rev. 720 (1988); Brussack, *Outrageous Fortune: The Case for Amending Rule 15(c) Again,* 61 S.Cal. L.Rev. 671 (1988); Lewis, *The Excessive History of Federal Rule 15(c) and Its Lessons for Civil Rules Revision,* 86 Mich.L.Rev. 1507 (1987).

In allowing a name-correcting amendment within the time allowed by Rule 4(m), this rule allows not only the 120 days specified in that rule, but also any additional time resulting from any extension ordered by the court pursuant to that rule, as may be granted, for example, if the defendant is a fugitive from service of the summons.

This revision, together with the revision of Rule 4(i) with respect to the failure of a plaintiff in an action against the United States to effect timely service on all the appropriate officials, is intended to produce results contrary to those reached in *Gardner v. Gartman,* 880 F.2d 797 (4th Cir. 1989), *Rys v. U.S. Postal Service,* 886 F.2d 443 (1st Cir. 1989), *Martin's Food & Liquor, Inc. v. U.S. Dept. of Agriculture,* 14 F.R.D.3d 86 (N.D.Ill.1988). *But cf. Montgomery v. United States Postal Service,* 867 F.2d 900 (5th Cir. 1989), *Warren v. Department of the Army,* 867 F.2d 1156 (8th Cir. 1989); *Miles v. Department of the Army,* 881 F.2d 777 (9th Cir. 1989), *Barsten v. Department of the Interior,* 896 F.2d 422 (9th Cir. 1990); *Brown v. Georgia Dept. of Revenue,* 881 F.2d 1018 (11th Cir. 1989).

1993 Amendments

The amendment conforms the cross reference to Rule 4 to the revision of that rule.

HISTORICAL NOTES

Effective Dates

1991 Act. Section 11(a) of Pub.L. 102–198 amended subd. (c)(3) of this rule, as transmitted to the Congress by the

Supreme Court pursuant to section 2074 of title 28, United States Code, to become effective on December 1, 1991.

Rule 16. Pretrial Conferences; Scheduling; Management

(a) Pretrial Conferences; Objectives. In any action, the court may in its discretion direct the attorneys for the parties and any unrepresented parties to appear before it for a conference or conferences before trial for such purposes as

(1) expediting the disposition of the action;

(2) establishing early and continuing control so that the case will not be protracted because of lack of management;

(3) discouraging wasteful pretrial activities;

(4) improving the quality of the trial through more thorough preparation, and;

(5) facilitating the settlement of the case.

(b) Scheduling and Planning. Except in categories of actions exempted by district court rule as inappropriate, the district judge, or a magistrate judge when authorized by district court rule, shall, after receiving the report from the parties under Rule 26(f) or after consulting with the attorneys for the parties and any unrepresented parties by a scheduling conference, telephone, mail, or other suitable means, enter a scheduling order that limits the time

(1) to join other parties and to amend the pleadings;

(2) to file motions; and

(3) to complete discovery.

The scheduling order may also include

(4) modifications of the times for disclosures under Rules 26(a) and 26(e)(1) and of the extent of discovery to be permitted;

(5) the date or dates for conferences before trial, a final pretrial conference, and trial; and

(6) any other matters appropriate in the circumstances of the case.

The order shall issue as soon as practicable but in any event within 90 days after the appearance of a defendant and within 120 days after the complaint has been served on a defendant. A schedule shall not be modified except upon a showing of good cause and by leave of the district judge or, when authorized by local rule, by a magistrate judge.

(c) Subjects for Consideration at Pretrial Conferences. At any conference under this rule consideration may be given, and the court may take appropriate action, with respect to

(1) the formulation and simplification of the issues, including the elimination of frivolous claims or defenses;

(2) the necessity or desirability of amendments to the pleadings;

(3) the possibility of obtaining admissions of fact and of documents which will avoid unnecessary proof, stipulations regarding the authenticity of documents, and advance rulings from the court on the admissibility of evidence;

(4) the avoidance of unnecessary proof and of cumulative evidence, and limitations or restrictions on the use of testimony under Rule 702 of the Federal Rules of Evidence;

(5) the appropriateness and timing of summary adjudication under Rule 56;

(6) the control and scheduling of discovery, including orders affecting disclosures and discovery pursuant to Rule 26 and Rules 29 through 37;

(7) the identification of witnesses and documents, the need and schedule for filing and exchanging pretrial briefs, and the date or dates for further conferences and for trial;

(8) the advisability of referring matters to a magistrate judge or master;

(9) settlement and the use of special procedures to assist in resolving the dispute when authorized by statute or local rule;

(10) the form and substance of the pretrial order;

(11) the disposition of pending motions;

(12) the need for adopting special procedures for managing potentially difficult or protracted actions that may involve complex issues, multiple parties, difficult legal questions, or unusual proof problems;

(13) an order for a separate trial pursuant to Rule 42(b) with respect to a claim, counterclaim, cross-claim, or third-party claim, or with respect to any particular issue in the case;

(14) an order directing a party or parties to present evidence early in the trial with respect to a manageable issue that could, on the evidence, be the basis for a judgment as a matter of law under Rule 50(a) or a judgment on partial findings under Rule 52(c);

(15) an order establishing a reasonable limit on the time allowed for presenting evidence; and

(16) such other matters as may facilitate the just, speedy, and inexpensive disposition of the action.

At least one of the attorneys for each party participating in any conference before trial shall have authority to enter into stipulations and to make admissions regarding all matters that the participants may reasonably anticipate may be discussed. If appropriate, the court may require that a party or its representative be present or reasonably available by telephone in order to consider possible settlement of the dispute.

(d) Final Pretrial Conference. Any final pretrial conference shall be held as close to the time of trial as reasonable under the circumstances. The participants at any such conference shall formulate a plan for trial, including a program for facilitating the admission of evidence. The conference shall be attended by at least one of the attorneys who will conduct the trial for each of the parties and by any unrepresented parties.

(e) Pretrial Orders. After any conference held pursuant to this rule, an order shall be entered reciting the action taken. This order shall control the subsequent course of the action unless modified by a subsequent order. The order following a final pretrial conference shall be modified only to prevent manifest injustice.

(f) Sanctions. If a party or party's attorney fails to obey a scheduling or pretrial order, or if no appearance is made on behalf of a party at a scheduling or pretrial conference, or if a party or party's attorney is substantially unprepared to participate in the conference, or if a party or party's attorney fails to participate in good faith, the judge, upon motion or the judge's own initiative, may make such orders with regard thereto as are just, and among others any of the orders provided in Rule 37(b)(2)(B), (C), (D). In lieu of or in addition to any other sanction, the judge shall require the party or the attorney representing the party or both to pay the reasonable expenses incurred because of any noncompliance with this rule, including attorney's fees, unless the judge finds that the noncompliance was substantially justified or that other circumstances make an award of expenses unjust.

(As amended Apr. 28, 1983, eff. Aug. 1, 1983; Mar. 2, 1987, eff. Aug. 1, 1987; Apr. 22, 1993, eff. Dec. 1, 1993.)

ADVISORY COMMITTEE NOTES

1937 Adoption

1. Similar rules of pre-trial procedure are now in force in Boston, Cleveland, Detroit, and Los Angeles, and a rule substantially like this one has been proposed for the urban centers of New York state. For a discussion of the successful operation of pre-trial procedure in relieving the congested condition of trial calendars of the courts in such cities and for the proposed New York plan, see *A Proposal for Minimizing Calendar Delay in Jury Cases* (Dec. 1936—published by the New York Law Society); *Pre-Trial Procedure and Administration,* Third Annual Report of the Judicial Council of the State of New York (1937), pages 207–243; *Report of the Commission on the Administration of Justice in New York State* (1934), pp. (288) to (290). See also *Pre-Trial Procedure in the Wayne Circuit Court,* Detroit, Michigan, Sixth Annual Report of the Judicial Council of Michigan (1936), pp. 63 to 75; and Sunderland, *The Theory and Practice of Pre-trial Procedure* (Dec. 1937) 36 Mich.L.Rev. 215–226, 21 J.Am.Jud. Soc. 125. Compare the English procedure known as the "summons for directions", *English Rules Under the Judicature Act* (The Annual Practice, 1937) O. 38a; and a similar procedure in New Jersey, N.J.S.A. 2:27–135, 2:27–136, 2:27–160; N.J. Supreme Court Rules, 2 N.J.Misc.Rep. (1924) 1230, Rules 94, 92, 93, 95 (the last three as amended 1933, 11 N.J.Misc.Rep. (1933) 955).

2. Compare the similar procedure under Rule 56(d) (Summary Judgment—Case Not Fully Adjudicated on Motion). Rule 12(g) (Consolidation of Motions), by requiring to some extent the consolidation of motions dealing with matters preliminary to trial, is a step in the same direction. In connection with clause (5) of this rule, see Rules 53(b) (Masters; Reference) and 53(e)(3) (Master's Report; In Jury Actions).

1983 Amendment

Introduction

Rule 16 has not been amended since the Federal Rules were promulgated in 1938. In many respects, the rule has been a success. For example, there is evidence that pretrial conferences may improve the quality of justice rendered in the federal courts by sharpening the preparation and presentation of cases, tending to eliminate trial surprise, and improving, as well as facilitating, the settlement process. See 6 Wright & Miller, *Federal Practice and Procedure:* Civil § 1522 (1971). However, in other respects particularly with regard to case management, the rule has not always been as helpful as it might have been. Thus there has been a widespread feeling that amendment is necessary to encourage pretrial management that meets the needs of modern litigation. See *Report of the National Commission for the Review of Antitrust Laws and Procedures* (1979).

Major criticism of Rule 16 has centered on the fact that its application can result in over-regulation of some cases and under-regulation of others. In simple, run-of-the-mill cases, attorneys have found pretrial requirements burdensome. It is claimed that over-administration leads to a series of mini-trials that result in a waste of an attorney's time and needless expense to a client. Pollack, *Pretrial Procedures More Effectively Handled,* 65 F.R.D. 475 (1974). This is especially likely to be true when pretrial proceedings occur long before trial. At the other end of the spectrum, the discretionary character of Rule 16 and its orientation toward a single conference late in the pretrial process has led to under-administration of complex or protracted cases. Without judicial guidance beginning shortly after institution, these cases often become mired in discovery.

Four sources of criticism of pretrial have been identified. First, conferences often are seen as a mere exchange of legalistic contentions without any real analysis of the particular case. Second, the result frequently is nothing but a formal agreement on minutiae. Third, the conferences are seen as unnecessary and time-consuming in cases that will be settled before trial. Fourth, the meetings can be ceremonial and ritualistic, having little effect on the trial and being of minimal value, particularly when the attorneys attending the sessions are not the ones who will try the case or lack authority to enter into binding stipulations. See generally *McCargo v. Hedrick,* 545 F.2d 393 (4th Cir.1976); Pollack, *Pretrial Procedures More Effectively Handled,* 65 F.R.D. 475 (1974); Rosenberg, *The Pretrial Conference and Effective Justice* 45 (1964).

There also have been difficulties with the pretrial orders that issue following Rule 16 conferences. When an order is entered far in advance of trial, some issues may not be properly formulated. Counsel naturally are cautious and often try to preserve as many options as possible. If the judge who tries the case did not conduct the conference, he could find it difficult to determine exactly what was agreed to at the conference. But any insistence on a detailed order may be too burdensome, depending on the nature or posture of the case.

Given the significant changes in federal civil litigation since 1938 that are not reflected in Rule 16, it has been extensively rewritten and expanded to meet the challenges of modern litigation. Empirical studies reveal that when a trial judge intervenes personally at an early stage to assume judicial control over a case and to schedule dates for completion by the parties of the principal pretrial steps, the case is disposed of by settlement or trial more efficiently and with less cost and delay than when the parties are left to their own devices. Flanders, *Case Management and Court Management in United States District Courts* 17, Federal Judicial Center (1977). Thus, the rule mandates a pretrial scheduling order. However, although scheduling and pretrial conferences are encouraged in appropriate cases, they are not mandated.

Discussion

Subdivision (a); Pretrial Conferences; Objectives. The amended rule makes scheduling and case management an express goal of pretrial procedure. This is done in Rule 16(a) by shifting the emphasis away from a conference focused solely on the trial and toward a process of judicial management that embraces the entire pretrial phase, especially motions and discovery. In addition, the amendment explicitly recognizes some of the objectives of pretrial conferences and the powers that many courts already have assumed. Rule 16 thus will be a more accurate reflection of actual practice.

Subdivision (b); Scheduling and Planning. The most significant change in Rule 16 is the mandatory scheduling order described in Rule 16(b), which is based in part on Wisconsin Civil Procedure Rule 802.10. The idea of scheduling orders is not new. It has been used by many federal courts. See, *e.g.*, Southern District of Indiana, Local Rule 19.

Although a mandatory scheduling order encourages the court to become involved in case management early in the litigation, it represents a degree of judicial involvement that is not warranted in many cases. Thus, subdivision (b) permits each district court to promulgate a local rule under Rule 83 exempting certain categories of cases in which the burdens of scheduling orders exceed the administrative efficiencies that would be gained. See Eastern District of Virginia, Local Rule 12(1). Logical candidates for this treatment include social security disability matters, habeas corpus petitions, forfeitures, and reviews of certain administrative actions.

A scheduling conference may be requested either by the judge, a magistrate when authorized by district court rule, or a party within 120 days after the summons and complaint are filed. If a scheduling conference is not arranged within that time and the case is not exempted by local rule, a scheduling order must be issued under Rule 16(b), after some communication with the parties, which may be by telephone or mail rather than in person. The use of the term "judge" in subdivision (b) reflects the Advisory Committee's judgment that it is preferable that this task should be handled by a district judge rather than a magistrate, except when the magistrate is acting under 28 U.S.C. § 636(c). While personal supervision by the trial judge is preferred, the rule, in recognition of the impracticality or difficulty of complying with such a requirement in some districts, authorizes a district by local rule to delegate the duties to a magistrate. In order to formulate a practicable scheduling order, the judge, or a magistrate when authorized by district court rule, and attorneys are required to develop a timetable for the matters listed in Rule 16(b)(1)–(3). As indicated in Rule 16(b)(4)–(5), the order may also deal with a wide range of other matters. The rule is phrased permissively as to clauses (4) and (5), however, because scheduling these items at an early point may not be feasible or appropriate. Even though subdivision (b) relates only to scheduling, there is no reason why some of the procedural matters listed in Rule 16(c) cannot be addressed at the same time, at least when a scheduling conference is held.

Item (1) assures that at some point both the parties and the pleadings will be fixed, by setting a time within which joinder of parties shall be completed and the pleadings amended.

Item (2) requires setting time limits for interposing various motions that otherwise might be used as stalling techniques.

Item (3) deals with the problem of procrastination and delay by attorneys in a context in which scheduling is especially important-discovery. Scheduling the completion of discovery can serve some of the same functions as the conference described in Rule 26(f).

Item (4) refers to setting dates for conferences and for trial. Scheduling multiple pretrial conferences may well be desirable if the case is complex and the court believes that a more elaborate pretrial structure, such as that described in the *Manual for Complex Litigation*, should be employed. On the other hand, only one pretrial conference may be necessary in an uncomplicated case.

As long as the case is not exempted by local rule, the court must issue a written scheduling order even if no scheduling conference is called. The order, like pretrial orders under the former rule and those under new Rule 16(c), normally will "control the subsequent course of the action." See Rule 16(e). After consultation with the attorneys for the parties and any unrepresented parties-a formal motion is not necessary-the court may modify the schedule on a showing of good cause if it cannot reasonably be met despite the diligence of the party seeking the extension. Since the scheduling order is entered early in the litigation, this standard seems more appropriate than a "manifest injustice" or "substantial hardship" test. Otherwise, a fear that extensions will not be granted may encourage counsel to request the longest possible periods for completing pleading, joinder, and discovery. Moreover, changes in the court's calendar sometimes will oblige the judge or magistrate when authorized by district court rule to modify the scheduling order.

The district courts undoubtedly will develop several prototype scheduling orders for different types of cases. In addition, when no formal conference is held, the court may obtain scheduling information by telephone, mail, or otherwise. In many instances this will result in a scheduling order better suited to the individual case than a standard order, without taking the time that would be required by a formal conference.

Rule 16(b) assures that the judge will take some early control over the litigation, even when its character does not warrant holding a scheduling conference. Despite the fact that the process of preparing a scheduling order does not always bring the attorneys and judge together, the fixing of time limits serves

> to stimulate litigants to narrow the areas of inquiry and advocacy to those they believe are truly relevant and material. Time limits not only compress the amount of time for litigation, they should also reduce the amount of resources invested in litigation. Litigants are forced to establish discovery priorities and thus to do the most important work first.

Report of the National Commission for the Review of Antitrust Laws and Procedures 28 (1979).

Thus, except in exempted cases, the judge or a magistrate when authorized by district court rule will have taken some action in every case within 120 days after the complaint is filed that notifies the attorneys that the case will be moving toward trial. Subdivision (b) is reenforced by subdivision (f), which makes it clear that the sanctions for violating a scheduling order are the same as those for violating a pretrial order.

Subdivision (c); Subjects to be Discussed at Pretrial Conferences. This subdivision expands upon the list of things that may be discussed at a pretrial conference that appeared in original Rule 16. The intention is to encourage better planning and management of litigation. Increased judicial control during the pretrial process accelerates the processing and termination of cases. Flanders, *Case Management and Court Management in United States District Courts,* 39 Federal Judicial Center (1977). See also *Report of the National Commission for the Review of Antitrust Laws and Procedures* (1979).

The reference in Rule 16(c)(1) to "formulation" is intended to clarify and confirm the court's power to identify the litigable issues. It has been added in the hope of promoting efficiency and conserving judicial resources by identifying the real issues prior to trial, thereby saving time and expense for everyone. See generally *Meadow Gold Prods. Co. v. Wright,* 278 F.2d 867 (D.C.Cir.1960). The notion is emphasized by expressly authorizing the elimination of frivolous claims or defenses at a pretrial conference. There is no reason to require that this await a formal motion for summary judgment. Nor is there any reason for the court to wait for the parties to initiate the process called for in Rule 16(c)(1).

The timing of any attempt at issue formulation is a matter of judicial discretion. In relatively simple cases it may not be necessary or may take the form of a stipulation between counsel or a request by the court that counsel work together to draft a proposed order.

Counsel bear a substantial responsibility for assisting the court in identifying the factual issues worthy of trial. If counsel fail to identify an issue for the court, the right to have the issue tried is waived. Although an order specifying the issues is intended to be binding, it may be amended at trial to avoid manifest injustice. See Rule 16(e). However, the rule's effectiveness depends on the court employing its discretion sparingly.

Clause (6) acknowledges the widespread availability and use of magistrates. The corresponding provision in the original rule referred only to masters and limited the function of the reference to the making of "findings to be used as evidence" in a case to be tried to a jury. The new text is not limited and broadens the potential use of a magistrate to that permitted by the Magistrate's Act.

Clause (7) explicitly recognizes that it has become commonplace to discuss settlement at pretrial conferences. Since it obviously eases crowded court dockets and results in savings to the litigants and the judicial system, settlement should be facilitated at as early a stage of the litigation as possible. Although it is not the purpose of Rule 16(b)(7) to impose settlement negotiations on unwilling litigants, it is believed that providing a neutral forum for discussing the subject might foster it. See Moore's *Federal Practice* ¶ 16.17; 6 Wright & Miller, *Federal Practice and Procedure: Civil* § 1522 (1971). For instance, a judge to whom a case has been assigned may arrange, on his own motion or at a party's request, to have settlement conferences handled by another member of the court or by a magistrate. The rule does not make settlement conferences mandatory because they would be a waste of time in many cases. See Flanders, *Case Management and Court Management in the United States District Courts,* 39 Federal Judicial Center (1977). Requests for a conference from a party indicating a willingness to talk settlement normally should be honored, unless thought to be frivolous or dilatory.

A settlement conference is appropriate at any time. It may be held in conjunction with a pretrial or discovery conference, although various objectives of pretrial management, such as moving the case toward trial, may not always be compatible with settlement negotiations, and thus a separate settlement conference may be desirable. See 6 Wright & Miller, *Federal Practice and Procedure: Civil* § 1522, at p. 571 (1971).

In addition to settlement, Rule 16(c)(7) refers to exploring the use of procedures other than litigation to resolve the dispute. This includes urging the litigants to employ adjudicatory techniques outside the courthouse. See, for example, the experiment described in *Green, Marks & Olson, Settling Large Case Litigation: An Alternative Approach,* 11 Loyola of L.A.L.Rev. 493 (1978).

Rule 16(c)(10) authorizes the use of special pretrial procedures to expedite the adjudication of potentially difficult or protracted cases. Some district courts obviously have done so for many years. See Rubin, *The Managed Calendar: Some Pragmatic Suggestions About Achieving the Just, Speedy and Inexpensive Determination of Civil Cases in Federal Courts,* 4 Just.Sys.J. 135 (1976). Clause 10 provides an explicit authorization for such procedures and encourages their use. No particular techniques have been described; the Committee felt that flexibility and experience are the keys to efficient management of complex cases. Extensive guidance is offered in such documents as the *Manual for Complex Litigation.*

The rule simply identifies characteristics that make a case a strong candidate for special treatment. The four mentioned are illustrative, not exhaustive, and overlap to some degree. But experience has shown that one or more of them will be present in every protracted or difficult case and it seems desirable to set them out. See Kendig, *Procedures for Management of Non-Routine Cases,* 3 Hofstra L.Rev. 701 (1975).

The last sentence of subdivision (c) is new. See Wisconsin Civil Procedure Rule 802.11(2). It has been added to meet one of the criticisms of the present practice described earlier and insure proper preconference preparation so that the meeting is more than a ceremonial or ritualistic event. The reference to "authority" is not intended to insist upon the ability to settle the litigation. Nor should the rule be read to encourage the judge conducting the conference to compel attorneys to enter into stipulations or to make admissions that they consider to be unreasonable, that touch on matters that could not normally have been anticipated to arise at the conference, or on subjects of a dimension that normally require prior consultation with and approval from the client.

Subdivision (d); Final Pretrial Conference. This provision has been added to make it clear that the time between any final pretrial conference (which in a simple case may be the **only** pretrial conference) and trial should be as short as possible to be certain that the litigants make substantial progress with the case and avoid the inefficiency of having that preparation repeated when there is a delay between the last pretrial conference and trial. An optimum time of 10 days to two weeks has been suggested by one federal judge. Rubin, *The Managed Calendar: Some Pragmatic Suggestions About Achieving the Just, Speedy and Inexpensive Determination of Civil Cases in Federal Courts,* 4 Just. Sys.J. 135, 141 (1976). The Committee, however, concluded that it would be inappropriate to fix a precise time in the rule, given the numerous variables that could bear on the matter. Thus the timing has been left to the court's discretion.

At least one of the attorneys who will conduct the trial for each party must be present at the final pretrial conference. At this late date there should be no doubt as to which attorney or attorneys this will be. Since the agreements and stipulations made at this final conference will control the trial, the presence of lawyers who will be involved in it is especially useful to assist the judge in structuring the case, and to lead to a more effective trial.

Subdivision (e); Pretrial Orders. Rule 16(e) does not substantially change the portion of the original rule dealing with pretrial orders. The purpose of an order is to guide the course of the litigation and the language of the original rule making that clear has been retained. No compelling reason has been found for major revision, especially since this portion of the rule has been interpreted and clarified by over forty years of judicial decisions with comparatively little difficulty. See 6 Wright & Miller, *Federal Practice and Procedure: Civil* §§ 1521–30 (1971). Changes in language therefore have been kept to a minimum to avoid confusion.

Since the amended rule encourages more extensive pretrial management than did the original, two or more conferences may be held in many cases. The language of Rule 16(e) recognizes this possibility and the corresponding need to issue more than one pretrial order in a single case.

Once formulated, pretrial orders should not be changed lightly; but total inflexibility is undesirable. See, *e.g., Clark v. Pennsylvania R.R. Co.,* 328 F.2d 591 (2d Cir.1964). The exact words used to describe the standard for amending the pretrial order probably are less important than the meaning given them in practice. By not imposing any limitation on the ability to modify a pretrial order, the rule reflects the reality that in any process of continuous management, what is done at one conference may have to be altered at the next. In the case of the final pretrial order, however, a more stringent standard is called for and the words "to prevent manifest injustice," which appeared in the original rule, have been retained. They have the virtue of familiarity and adequately describe the restraint the trial judge should exercise.

Many local rules make the plaintiff's attorney responsible for drafting a proposed pretrial order, either before or after the conference. Others allow the court to appoint any of the attorneys to perform the task, and others leave it to the court. See Note, *Pretrial Conference: A Critical Examination of Local Rules Adopted by Federal District Courts,* 64 Va.L.Rev. 467 (1978). Rule 16 has never addressed this matter. Since there is no consensus about which method of drafting the order works best and there is no reason to believe that nationwide uniformity is needed, the rule has been left silent on the point. See *Handbook for Effective Pretrial Procedure,* 37 F.R.D. 225 (1964).

Subdivision (f); Sanctions. Original Rule 16 did not mention the sanctions that might be imposed for failing to comply with the rule. However, courts have not hesitated to enforce it by appropriate measures. See, e.g., *Link v. Wabash R. Co.,* 370 U.S. 628 (1962) (district court's dismissal under Rule 41(b) after plaintiff's attorney failed to appear at a pretrial conference upheld); *Admiral Theatre Corp. v. Douglas Theatre,* 585 F.2d 877 (8th Cir.1978) (district court has discretion to exclude exhibits or refuse to permit the testimony of a witness not listed prior to trial in contravention of its pretrial order).

To reflect that existing practice, and to obviate dependence upon Rule 41(b) or the court's inherent power to regulate litigation, *cf. Societe Internationale Pour Participations Industrielles et Commerciales, S.A. v. Rogers,* 357 U.S. 197 (1958), Rule 16(f) expressly provides for imposing sanctions on disobedient or recalcitrant parties, their attorneys, or both in four types of situations. Rodes, Ripple & Mooney, *Sanctions Imposable for Violations of the Federal Rules of Civil Procedure* 65–67, 80–84, Federal Judicial Center (1981). Furthermore, explicit reference to sanctions reenforces the rule's intention to encourage forceful judicial management.

Rule 16(f) incorporates portions of Rule 37(b)(2), which prescribes sanctions for failing to make discovery. This should facilitate application of Rule 16(f), since courts and lawyers already are familiar with the Rule 37 standards. Among the sanctions authorized by the new subdivision are: preclusion order, striking a pleading, staying the proceeding, default judgment, contempt, and charging a party, his attorney, or both with the expenses, including attorney's fees, caused by noncompliance. The contempt sanction, however, is only available for a violation of a court order. The references in Rule 16(f) are not exhaustive.

As is true under Rule 37(b)(2), the imposition of sanctions may be sought by either the court or a party. In addition, the court has discretion to impose whichever sanction it feels is appropriate under the circumstances. Its action is reviewable under the abuse-of-discretion standard. See *National Hockey League v. Metropolitan Hockey Club, Inc.,* 427 U.S. 639 (1976).

1987 Amendment

The amendments are technical. No substantive change is intended.

1993 Amendments

Subdivision (b). One purpose of this amendment is to provide a more appropriate deadline for the initial scheduling order required by the rule. The former rule directed that the order be entered within 120 days from the filing of the complaint. This requirement has created problems because Rule 4(m) allows 120 days for service and ordinarily at least one defendant should be available to participate in the process of formulating the scheduling order. The revision provides that the order is to be entered within 90 days after the date a defendant first appears (whether by answer or by a motion under Rule 12) or, if earlier (as may occur in some actions against the United States or if service is waived under Rule 4), within 120 days after service of the complaint on a defendant. The longer time provided by the revision is not intended to encourage unnecessary delays in entering the scheduling order. Indeed, in most cases the order can and should be entered at a much earlier date. Rather, the additional time is intended to alleviate problems in multi-defendant cases and should ordinarily be adequate to enable participation by all defendants initially named in the action.

In many cases the scheduling order can and should be entered before this deadline. However, when setting a scheduling conference, the court should take into account the effect this setting will have in establishing deadlines for the parties to meet under revised Rule 26(f) and to exchange information under revised Rule 26(a)(1). While the parties are expected to stipulate to additional time for making their disclosures when warranted by the circumstances, a scheduling conference held before defendants have had time to learn much about the case may result in diminishing the value of the Rule 26(f) meeting, the parties' proposed discovery plan, and indeed the conference itself.

New paragraph (4) has been added to highlight that it will frequently be desirable for the scheduling order to include provisions relating to the timing of disclosures under Rule 26(a). While the initial disclosures required by Rule 26(a)(1) will ordinarily have been made before entry of the scheduling order, the timing and sequence for disclosure of expert testimony and of the witnesses and exhibits to be used at trial should be tailored to the circumstances of the case and is a matter that should be considered at the initial scheduling conference. Similarly, the scheduling order might contain provisions modifying the extent of discovery (*e.g.,* number and length of depositions) otherwise permitted under these rules or by a local rule.

The report from the attorneys concerning their meeting and proposed discovery plan, as required by revised Rule 26(f), should be submitted to the court before the scheduling order is entered. Their proposals, particularly regarding matters on which they agree, should be of substantial value to the court in setting the timing and limitations on discovery and should reduce the time of the court needed to conduct a meaningful conference under Rule 16(b). As under the prior rule, while a scheduling order is mandated, a scheduling conference is not. However, in view of the benefits to be derived from the litigants and a judicial officer meeting in person, a Rule 16(b) conference should, to the extent practicable, be held in all cases that will involve discovery.

This subdivision, as well as subdivision (c)(8), also is revised to reflect the new title of United States Magistrate Judges pursuant to the Judicial Improvements Act of 1990.

Subdivision (c). The primary purposes of the changes in subdivision (c) are to call attention to the opportunities for structuring of trial under Rules 42, 50, and 52 and to eliminate questions that have occasionally been raised regarding the authority of the court to make appropriate orders designed either to facilitate settlement or to provide for an efficient and economical trial. The prefatory language of this subdivision is revised to clarify the court's power to enter appropriate orders at a conference notwithstanding the objection of a party. Of course settlement is dependent upon agreement by the parties and, indeed, a conference is most effective and productive when the parties participate in a spirit of cooperation and mindful of their responsibilities under Rule 1.

Paragraph (4) is revised to clarify that in advance of trial the court may address the need for, and possible limitations on, the use of expert testimony under Rule 702 of the Federal Rules of Evidence. Even when proposed expert testimony might be admissible under the standards of Rules 403 and 702 of the evidence rules, the court may preclude or limit such testimony if the cost to the litigants—which may include the cost to adversaries of securing testimony on the same subjects by other experts—would be unduly expensive given the needs of the case and the other evidence available at trial.

Paragraph (5) is added (and the remaining paragraphs renumbered) in recognition that use of Rule 56 to avoid or reduce the scope of trial is a topic that can, and often should, be considered at a pretrial conference. Renumbered paragraph (11) enables the court to rule on pending motions for summary adjudication that are ripe for decision at the time of the conference. Often, however, the potential use of Rule 56 is a matter that arises from discussions during a conference. The court may then call for motions to be filed.

Paragraph (6) is added to emphasize that a major objective of pretrial conferences should be to consider appropriate controls on the extent and timing of discovery. In many cases the court should also specify the times and sequence for disclosure of written reports from experts under revised Rule 26(a)(2)(B) and perhaps direct changes in the types of experts from whom written reports are required. Consideration should also be given to possible changes in the timing or form of the disclosure of trial witnesses and documents under Rule 26(a)(3).

Paragraph (9) is revised to describe more accurately the various procedures that, in addition to traditional settlement conferences, may be helpful in settling litigation. Even if a case cannot immediately be settled, the judge and attorneys can explore possible use of alternative procedures such as mini-trials, summary jury trials, mediation, neutral evaluation, and nonbinding arbitration that can lead to consensual resolution of the dispute without a full trial on the merits. The rule acknowledges the presence of statutes and local rules or plans that may authorize use of some of these procedures even when not agreed to by the parties. See 28 U.S.C. §§ 473(a)(6), 473(b)(4), 651–58; Section 104(b)(2), Pub.L. 101–650. The rule does not attempt to resolve questions as to the extent a court would be authorized to require such proceedings as an exercise of its inherent powers.

The amendment of paragraph (9) should be read in conjunction with the sentence added to the end of subdivision (c), authorizing the court to direct that, in appropriate cases, a responsible representative of the parties be present or available by telephone during a conference in order to discuss possible settlement of the case. The sentence refers to participation by a party or its representative. Whether this would be the individual party, an officer of a corporate party, a representative from an insurance carrier, or someone else would depend on the circumstances. Particularly in litigation in which governmental agencies or large amounts of money are involved, there may be no one with on-the-spot settlement authority, and the most that should be expected is access to a person who would have a major role in submitting a recommendation to the body or board with ultimate decision-making responsibility. The selection of the appropriate representative should ordinarily be left to the party and its counsel. Finally, it should be noted that the unwillingness of a party to be available, even by telephone, for a settlement conference may be a clear signal that the time and expense involved in pursuing settlement is likely to be unproductive and that personal participation by the parties should not be required.

The explicit authorization in the rule to require personal participation in the manner stated is not intended to limit the reasonable exercise of the court's inherent powers, *e.g., G. Heileman Brewing Co. v. Joseph Oat Corp.*, 871 F.2d 648 (7th Cir.1989), or its power to require party participation under the Civil Justice Reform Act of 1990. See 28 U.S.C. § 473(b)(5) (civil justice expense and delay reduction plans adopted by district courts may include requirement that representatives "with authority to bind [parties] in settlement discussions" be available during settlement conferences).

New paragraphs (13) and (14) are added to call attention to the opportunities for structuring of trial under Rule 42 and under revised Rules 50 and 52.

Paragraph (15) is also new. It supplements the power of the court to limit the extent of evidence under Rules 403 and 611(a) of the Federal Rules of Evidence, which typically would be invoked as a result of developments during trial. Limits on the length of trial established at a conference in advance of trial can provide the parties with a better opportunity to determine priorities and exercise selectivity in presenting evidence than when limits are imposed during trial. Any such limits must be reasonable under the circumstances, and ordinarily the court should impose them only after receiving appropriate submissions from the parties outlining the nature of the testimony expected to be presented through various witnesses, and the expected duration of direct and cross-examination.

HISTORICAL NOTES

Change of Name

Reference to United States magistrate or to magistrate deemed to refer to United States magistrate judge pursuant to section 321 of Pub.L. 101–650, set out as a note under section 631 of this title.

IV. PARTIES

Rule 17. Parties Plaintiff and Defendant; Capacity

(a) Real Party in Interest. Every action shall be prosecuted in the name of the real party in interest. An executor, administrator, guardian, bailee, trustee of an express trust, a party with whom or in whose name a contract has been made for the benefit of another, or a party authorized by statute may sue in that person's own name without joining the party for whose benefit the action is brought; and when a statute of the United States so provides, an action for the use or benefit of another shall be brought in the name of the United States. No action shall be dismissed on the ground that it is not prosecuted in the name of the real party in interest until a reasonable time has been allowed after objection for ratification of commencement of the action by, or joinder or substitution of, the real party in interest; and such ratification, joinder, or substitution shall have the same effect as if the action had been commenced in the name of the real party in interest.

(b) Capacity to Sue or be Sued. The capacity of an individual, other than one acting in a representative capacity, to sue or be sued shall be determined by the law of the individual's domicile. The capacity of a corporation to sue or be sued shall be determined by the law under which it was organized. In all other cases capacity to sue or be sued shall be determined by the law of the state in which the district court is held, except (1) that a partnership or other unincorporated association, which has no such capacity by the law of such state, may sue or be sued in its common name for the purpose of enforcing for or against it a substantive right existing under the Constitution or laws of the United States, and (2) that the capacity of a receiver appointed by a court of the United States to sue or be sued in a court of the United States is governed by Title 28, U.S.C., Sections 754 and 959(a).

(c) Infants or Incompetent Persons. Whenever an infant or incompetent person has a representative, such as a general guardian, committee, conservator, or other like fiduciary, the representative may sue or defend on behalf of the infant or incompetent person. An infant or incompetent person who does not have a duly appointed representative may sue by a next friend or by a guardian ad litem. The court shall appoint a guardian ad litem for an infant or incompetent person not otherwise represented in an action or shall make such other order as it deems proper for the protection of the infant or incompetent person.

(As amended Dec. 27, 1946, eff. Mar. 19, 1948; Dec. 29, 1948, eff. Oct. 20, 1949; Feb. 28, 1966, eff. July 1, 1966; Mar. 2, 1987, eff. Aug. 1, 1987; Apr. 25, 1988, eff. Aug. 1, 1988; Nov. 18, 1988, Pub.L. 100–690, Title VII, § 7049, 102 Stat. 4401.)

ADVISORY COMMITTEE NOTES

1937 Adoption

Note to Subdivision (a). The real party in interest provision, except for the last clause which is new, is taken verbatim from [former] Equity Rule 37 (Parties Generally—Intervention), except that the word "expressly" has been omitted. For similar provisions see N.Y.C.P.A., (1937) § 210; Wyo.Rev.Stat.Ann. (1931) §§ 89–501, 89–502, 89–503; *English Rules Under the Judicature Act* (The Annual Practice, 1937) O. 16, r. 8. See, also Equity Rule 41 (Suit to Execute Trusts of Will—Heir as Party). For examples of statutes of the United States providing particularly for an action for the use or benefit of another in the name of the United States, see U.S.C., Title 40, § 270b (Suit by persons furnishing labor and material for work on public building contracts * * * may sue on a payment bond, "in the name of the United States for the use of the person suing"); and U.S.C., Title 25, § 201 (Penalties under laws relating to Indians—how recovered). Compare U.S.C., Title 26, Int. Rev.Code [1939], § 3745(c) [former § 1645(c)] (Suits for penalties, fines, and forfeitures, under this title, where not otherwise provided for, to be in name of United States).

Note to Subdivision (b). For capacity see generally Clark and Moore, *New Federal Civil Procedure*—II. Pleadings and Parties, 44 Yale L.J. 1291, 1312–1317 (1935) and specifically *Coppedge v. Clinton*, 72 F.2d 531 (C.C.A.10th, 1934) (natural person); *David Lupton's Sons Co. v. Automobile Club of America*, 225 U.S. 489, 32 S.Ct. 711, 56 L.Ed. 1177, Ann.Cas.1914A, 699 (1912) (corporation); *Puerto Rico v. Russell & Co.*, 288 U.S. 476, 53 S.Ct. 447, 77 L.Ed. 903 (1933) (unincorporated assn.); *United Mine Workers of America v. Coronado Coal Co.*, 259 U.S. 344, 42 S.Ct. 570, 66 L.Ed. 975, 27 A.L.R. 762 (1922) (federal substantive right enforced against unincorporated association by suit against the association in its common name without naming all its members as parties). This rule follows the existing law as to such associations, as declared in the case last cited above. Compare *Moffat Tunnel League v. United States*, 289 U.S. 113, 53 S.Ct. 543, 77 L.Ed. 1069 (1933). See note to Rule 23, clause (1).

Note to Subdivision (c). The provision for infants and incompetent persons is substantially former Equity Rule 70 (Suits by or Against Incompetents) with slight additions. Compare the more detailed English provisions, *English Rules Under the Judicature Act* (The Annual Practice, 1937) O. 16, r.r. 16–21.

1946 Amendment

Note. The new matter [in subdivision (b)] makes clear the controlling character of Rule 66 regarding suits by or against a federal receiver in a federal court.

1948 Amendment

The amendment effective October 20, 1949, deleted the words "Rule 66" at the end of subdivision (b) and substituted the words "Title 28, U.S.C., §§ 754 and 959(a)".

1966 Amendment

The minor change in the text of the rule is designed to make it clear that the specific instances enumerated are not exceptions to, but illustrations of, the rule. These illustrations, of course, carry no negative implication to the effect that there are not other instances of recognition as the real party in interest of one whose standing as such may be in doubt. The enumeration is simply of cases in which there might be substantial doubt as to the issue but for the specific enumeration. There are other potentially arguable cases that are not excluded by the enumeration. For example, the enumeration states that the promisee in a contract for the benefit of a third party may sue as real party in interest; it does not say, because it is obvious, that the third-party beneficiary may sue (when the applicable law gives him that right.)

The rule adds to the illustrative list of real parties in interest a bailee—meaning, of course, a bailee suing on behalf of the bailor with respect to the property bailed. (When the possessor of property other than the owner sues for an invasion of the possessory interest he is the real party in interest.) The word "bailee" is added primarily to preserve the admiralty practice whereby the owner of a vessel as bailee of the cargo, or the master of the vessel as bailee of both vessel and cargo, sues for damage to either property interest or both. But there is no reason to limit such a provision to maritime situations. The owner of a warehouse in which household furniture is stored is equally entitled to sue on behalf of the numerous owners of the furniture stored. Cf. *Gulf Oil Corp. v. Gilbert*, 330 U.S. 501 (1947).

The provision that no action shall be dismissed on the ground that it is not prosecuted in the name of the real party in interest until a reasonable time has been allowed, after the objection has been raised, for ratification, substitution, etc., is added simply in the interests of justice. In its origin the rule concerning the real party in interest was permissive in purpose: it was designed to allow an assignee to sue in his own name. That having been accomplished, the modern function of the rule in its negative aspect is simply to protect the defendant against a subsequent action by the party actually entitled to recover, and to insure generally that the judgment will have its proper effect as res judicata.

This provision keeps pace with the law as it is actually developing. Modern decisions are inclined to be lenient when an honest mistake has been made in choosing the party in whose name the action is to be filed—in both maritime and nonmaritime cases. See *Levinson v. Deupree*, 345 U.S. 648 (1953); *Link Aviation, Inc. v. Downs*, 325 F.2d 613 (D.C.Cir. 1963). The provision should not be misunderstood or distorted. It is intended to prevent forfeiture when determination of the proper party to sue is difficult or when an understandable mistake has been made. It does not mean, for example, that, following an airplane crash in which all aboard were killed, an action may be filed in the name of John Doe (a fictitious person), as personal representative of Richard Roe (another fictitious person), in the hope that at a later time the attorney filing the action may substitute the real name of the real personal representative of a real victim, and have the benefit of suspension of the limitation period. It does not even mean, when an action is filed by the personal representative of John Smith, of Buffalo, in the good faith belief that he was aboard the flight, that upon discovery that Smith is alive and well, having missed the fatal flight, the representative of James Brown, of San Francisco, an actual victim, can be substituted to take advantage of the suspension of the limitation period. It is, in cases of this sort, intended to insure against forfeiture and injustice—in short, to codify in broad terms the salutary principle of *Levinson v. Deupree,* 345 U.S. 648 (1953), and *Link Aviation, Inc. v. Downs,* 325 F.2d 613 (D.C.Cir. 1963).

1987 Amendment

The amendments are technical. No substantive change is intended.

1988 Amendment

The amendment is technical. No substantive change is intended.

Rule 18. Joinder of Claims and Remedies

(a) Joinder of Claims. A party asserting a claim to relief as an original claim, counterclaim, cross-claim, or third-party claim, may join, either as independent or as alternate claims, as many claims, legal, equitable, or maritime, as the party has against an opposing party.

(b) Joinder of Remedies; Fraudulent Conveyances. Whenever a claim is one heretofore cognizable only after another claim has been prosecuted to a conclusion, the two claims may be joined in a single action; but the court shall grant relief in that action only in accordance with the relative substantive rights of the parties. In particular, a plaintiff may state a claim for money and a claim to have set aside a conveyance fraudulent as to that plaintiff, without first having obtained a judgment establishing the claim for money.

(As amended Feb. 28, 1966, eff. July 1, 1966; Mar. 2, 1987, eff. Aug. 1, 1987.)

ADVISORY COMMITTEE NOTES

1937 Adoption

Note to Subdivision (a). 1. Recent development, both in code and common law states, has been toward unlimited joinder of actions. See Ill.Rev.Stat. (1937) ch. 110, § 168; N.J.S.A. 2:27–37, as modified by N.J.Sup.Ct.Rules, Rule 21, 2 N.J.Misc. 1208 (1924); N.Y.C.P.A. (1937) § 258 as amended by Laws of 1935, ch. 339.

2. This provision for joinder of actions has been patterned upon [former] Equity Rule 26 (Joinder of Causes of Action) and broadened to include multiple parties. Compare the English practice, *English Rules Under the Judicature Act* (The Annual Practice, 1937) O. 18, r.r. 1–9 (noting rules 1 and 6). The earlier American codes set forth classes of joinder, following the now abandoned New York rule. See N.Y.C.P.A. § 258 before amended in 1935; Compare Kan. Gen.Stat.Ann. (1935) § 60–601; Wis.Stat.(1935) § 263.04 for the more liberal practice.

3. The provisions of this rule for the joinder of claims are subject to Rule 82 (Jurisdiction and Venue Unaffected). For the jurisdictional aspects of joinder of claims, see Shulman and Jaegerman, *Some Jurisdictional Limitations on Federal Procedure* (1936), 45 Yale L.J. 393, 397–410. For separate trials of joined claims, see Rule 42(b).

Note to Subdivision (b). This rule is inserted to make it clear that in a single action a party should be accorded all the relief to which he is entitled regardless of whether it is legal or equitable or both. This necessarily includes a deficiency judgment in foreclosure actions formerly provided for in [former] Equity Rule 10 (Decree for Deficiency in Foreclosures, Etc.). In respect to fraudulent conveyances the rule changes the former rule requiring a prior judgment against the owner (*Braun v. American Laundry Mach. Co.,* 56 F.2d 197 (S.D.N.Y. 1932)) to conform to the provisions of the Uniform Fraudulent Conveyance Act, §§ 9 and 10. See McLaughlin, *Application of the Uniform Fraudulent Conveyance Act,* 46 Harv.L.Rev. 404, 444 (1933).

1966 Amendment

The Rules "proceed upon the theory that no inconvenience can result from the joinder of any two or more matters in the pleadings, but only from trying two or more matters together which have little or nothing in common." Sunderland, *The New Federal Rules,* 45 W.Va.L.Q. 5, 13 (1938); see Clark, Code Pleading 58 (2d ed. 1947). Accordingly, Rule 18(a) has permitted a party to plead multiple claims of all types against an opposing party, subject to the court's power to direct an appropriate procedure for trying the claims. See Rules 42(b), 20(b), 21.

The liberal policy regarding joinder of claims in the pleadings extends to cases with multiple parties. However, the language used in the second sentence of Rule 18(a)—"if the requirements of Rules 19 [necessary joinder of parties], 20 [permissive joinder of parties], and 22 [interpleader] are satisfied"—has led some courts to infer that the rules regulating joinder of parties are intended to carry back to Rule 18(a) and to impose some special limits on joinder of claims in multiparty cases. In particular, Rule 20(a) has been read as restricting the operation of Rule 18(a) in certain situations in which a number of parties have been permissively joined in an action. In *Federal Housing Admr. v. Christianson,* 26 F.Supp. 419 (D.Conn.1939), the indorsee of two notes sued the three comakers of one note, and sought to join in the action a count on a second note which had been made by two of the three defendants. There was no doubt about the propriety of the joinder of the three parties defendant, for a right to relief was being asserted against all three defendants which arose out of a single "transaction" (the first note) and a question of fact or law "common" to all three defendants would arise in the action. See the text of Rule 20(a). The court, however, refused to allow the joinder of the count on the second note, on the ground that this right to relief, assumed to arise from a distinct transaction, did not involve a question common to all the defendants but only two of them. For analysis of the *Christianson* case and other authorities, see 2 Barron & Holtzoff, *Federal Practice & Procedure,* § 533.1 (Wright ed. 1961); 3 Moore's *Federal Practice,* par. 18.04[3] (2d ed. 1963).

If the court's view is followed, it becomes necessary to enter at the pleading stage into speculations about the exact relation between the claim sought to be joined against fewer than all the defendants properly joined in the action, and the claims asserted against all the defendants. Cf. Wright, *Joinder of Claims and Parties Under Modern Pleading Rules,* 36 Minn.L.Rev. 580, 605–06 (1952). Thus if it could be found in the Christianson situation that the claim on the second note arose out of the same transaction as the claim on the first or out of a transaction forming part of a "series," and that any question of fact or law with respect to the second note also arose with regard to the first, it would be held that the claim on the second note could be joined in the complaint. See 2 Barron & Holtzoff, supra, at 109; see also id. at 198 n. 60.4; cf. 3 Moore's *Federal Practice,* supra, at 1811. Such pleading niceties provide a basis for delaying and wasteful maneuver. It is more compatible with the design of the Rules to allow the claim to be joined in the pleading, leaving the question of possible separate trial of that claim to be later decided. See 2 Barron & Holtzoff, supra, § 533.1; Wright, supra, 36 Minn.L.Rev. at 604–11; *Developments in the Law—Multiparty Litigation in the Federal Courts,* 71 Harv. 874, 970–71 (1958); Commentary, *Relation Between Joinder of Parties and Joinder of Claims,* 5 F.R.Serv. 822 (1942). It is instructive to note that the court in the *Christianson* case, while holding that the claim on the second note could not be joined as a matter of pleading, held open the possibility that both claims would later be consolidated for trial under Rule 42(a). See 26 F.Supp. 419.

Rule 18(a) is now amended not only to overcome the *Christianson* decision and similar authority, but also to state clearly as a comprehensive proposition, that a party asserting a claim (an original claim, counterclaim, cross-claim, or third-party claim) may join as many claims as he has against an opposing party. See *Noland Co., Inc. v. Graver Tank & Mfg. Co.,* 301 F.2d 43, 49–51 (4th Cir.1962); but cf. *C. W. Humphrey Co. v. Security Alum. Co.,* 31 F.R.D. 41 (E.D.Mich.1962). This permitted joinder of claims is not affected by the fact that there are multiple parties in the action. The joinder of parties is governed by other rules operating independently.

It is emphasized that amended Rule 18(a) deals only with pleading. As already indicated, a claim properly joined as a matter of pleading need not be proceeded with together with the other claims if fairness or convenience justifies separate treatment.

Amended Rule 18(a), like the rule prior to amendment, does not purport to deal with questions of jurisdiction or venue which may arise with respect to claims properly joined as a matter of pleading. See Rule 82.

See also the amendment of Rule 20(a) and the Advisory Committee's Note thereto.

Free joinder of claims and remedies is one of the basic purposes of unification of the admiralty and civil procedure. The amendment accordingly provides for the inclusion in the rule of maritime claims as well as those which are legal and equitable in character.

1987 Amendment

The amendments are technical. No substantive change is intended.

Rule 19. Joinder of Persons Needed for Just Adjudication

(a) Persons to be Joined if Feasible. A person who is subject to service of process and whose joinder will not deprive the court of jurisdiction over the subject matter of the action shall be joined as a party in the action if (1) in the person's absence complete relief cannot be accorded among those already parties, or (2) the person claims an interest relating to the subject of the action and is so situated that the disposition of the action in the person's absence may (i) as a practical matter impair or impede the person's ability to protect that interest or (ii) leave any of the persons already parties subject to a substantial risk of incurring double, multiple, or otherwise inconsistent obligations by reason of the claimed interest. If the person has not been so joined, the court shall order that the person be made a party. If the person should join as a plaintiff but refuses to do so, the person may be made a defendant, or, in a proper case, an involuntary plaintiff. If the joined party objects to venue and joinder of that party would render the venue of the action improper, that party shall be dismissed from the action.

(b) Determination by Court Whenever Joinder not Feasible. If a person as described in subdivision (a)(1)–(2) hereof cannot be made a party, the court shall determine whether in equity and good conscience the action should proceed among the parties before it, or should be dismissed, the absent person being thus regarded as indispensable. The factors to be considered by the court include: first, to what extent a judgment rendered in the person's absence might be prejudicial to the person or those already parties; second, the extent to which, by protective provisions in the judgment, by the shaping of relief, or other measures, the prejudice can be lessened or avoided; third, whether a judgment rendered in the person's absence will be adequate; fourth, whether the plaintiff will have an adequate remedy if the action is dismissed for nonjoinder.

(c) Pleading Reasons for Nonjoinder. A pleading asserting a claim for relief shall state the names, if known to the pleader, of any persons as prescribed in subdivision (a)(1)–(2) hereof who are not joined, and the reasons why they are not joined.

(d) Exception of Class Actions. This rule is subject to the provisions of Rule 23.

(As amended Feb. 28, 1966, eff. July 1, 1966; Mar. 2, 1987, eff. Aug. 1, 1987.)

ADVISORY COMMITTEE NOTES

1937 Adoption

Note to Subdivision (a). The first sentence with verbal differences (e.g., "united" interest for "joint" interest) is to be found in [former] Equity Rule 37 (Parties Generally—Intervention). Such compulsory joinder provisions are common. Compare Alaska Comp.Laws (1933) § 3392 (containing in same sentence a "class suit" provision); Wyo.Rev.Stat. Ann. (Courtright, 1931) § 89–515 (immediately followed by "class suit" provisions, § 89–516). See also former Equity Rule 42 (Joint and Several Demands). For example of a proper case for involuntary plaintiff, see *Independent Wireless Telegraph Co. v. Radio Corp. of America,* 269 U.S. 459, 46 S.Ct. 166, 70 L.Ed. 357 (1926).

The joinder provisions of this rule are subject to Rule 82 (Jurisdiction and Venue Unaffected).

Note to Subdivision (b). For the substance of this rule see [former] Equity Rule 39 (Absence of Persons Who Would be Proper Parties) and U.S.C., Title 28, § 111 [now § 1391] (When part of several defendants cannot be served); *Camp v. Gress,* 250 U.S. 308, 39 S.Ct. 478, 63 L.Ed. 997 (1919). See also the second and third sentences of [former] Equity Rule 37 (Parties Generally—Intervention).

Note to Subdivision (c). For the substance of this rule see the fourth subdivision of [former] Equity Rule 25 (Bill of Complaint—Contents).

1966 Amendment

General Considerations

Whenever feasible, the persons materially interested in the subject of an action—see the more detailed description of these persons in the discussion of new subdivision (a) below—should be joined as parties so that they may be heard and a complete disposition made. When this comprehensive joinder cannot be accomplished—a situation which may be encountered in Federal courts because of limitations on service of process, subject matter jurisdiction, and venue—the case should be examined pragmatically and a choice made between the alternatives of proceeding with the action in the absence of particular interested persons, and dismissing the action.

Even if the court is mistaken in its decision to proceed in the absence of an interested person, it does not by that token deprive itself of the power to adjudicate as between the parties already before it through proper service of process. But the court can make a legally binding adjudication only between the parties actually joined in the action. It is true that an adjudication between the parties before the court may on occasion adversely affect the absent person as a practical matter, or leave a party exposed to a later inconsistent recovery by the absent person. These are factors which should be considered in deciding whether the action should proceed, or should rather be dismissed; but they do not themselves negate the court's power to adjudicate as between the parties who have been joined.

Defects in the Original Rule

The foregoing propositions were well understood in the older equity practice, see Hazard, *Indispensable Party: The Historical Origin of a Procedural Phantom,* 61 Colum.L.Rev. 1254 (1961), and Rule 19 could be and often was applied in consonance with them. But experience showed that the rule was defective in its phrasing and did not point clearly to the proper basis of decision.

Textual defects.—(1) The expression "persons * * * who ought to be parties if complete relief is to be accorded between those already parties," appearing in original subdivision (b), was apparently intended as a description of the persons whom it would be desirable to join in the action, all questions of feasibility of joinder being put to one side; but it was not adequately descriptive of those persons.

(2) The word "indispensable," appearing in original subdivision (b), was apparently intended as an inclusive reference to the interested persons in whose absence it would be advisable, all factors having been considered, to dismiss the action. Yet the sentence implied that there might be interested persons, not "indispensable," in whose absence the action ought also to be dismissed. Further, it seemed at least superficially plausible to equate the word "indispensable" with the expression "having a joint interest," appearing in subdivision (a). See *United States v. Washington Inst. of Tech., Inc.,* 138 F.2d 25, 26 (3d Cir. 1943); cf. *Chidester v. City of Newark,* 162 F.2d 598 (3d Cir. 1947). But persons holding an interest technically "joint" are not always so related to an action that it would be unwise to proceed without joining all of them, whereas persons holding an interest not technically "joint" may have this relation to an action. See Reed, *Compulsory Joinder of Parties in Civil Actions,* 55 Mich.L.Rev. 327, 356 ff., 483 (1957).

(3) The use of "indispensable" and "joint interest" in the context of original Rule 19 directed attention to the technical or abstract character of the rights or obligations of the persons whose joinder was in question, and correspondingly distracted attention from the pragmatic considerations which should be controlling.

(4) The original rule, in dealing with the feasibility of joining a person as a party to the action, besides referring to whether the person was "subject to the jurisdiction of the court as to both service of process and venue," spoke of whether the person could be made a party "without depriving the court of jurisdiction of the parties before it." The second quoted expression used "jurisdiction" in the sense of the competence of the court over the subject matter of the action, and in this sense the expression was apt. However, by a familiar confusion, the expression seems to have suggested to some that the absence from the lawsuit of a person who was "indispensable" or "who ought to be [a] part[y]" itself deprived the court of the power to adjudicate as between the parties already joined. See *Samuel Goldwyn, Inc. v. United Artists Corp.,* 113 F.2d 703, 707 (3d Cir. 1940); *McArthur v. Rosenbaum Co. of Pittsburgh,* 180 F.2d 617, 621 (3d Cir. 1949); cf. *Calcote v. Texas Pac. Coal & Oil Co.,* 157 F.2d 216 (5th Cir. 1946), cert. denied, 329 U.S. 782 (1946), noted in 56 Yale L.J. 1088 (1947); Reed, supra, 55 Mich. L.Rev. at 332–34.

Failure to point to correct basis of decision. The original rule did not state affirmatively what factors were relevant in deciding whether the action should proceed or be dismissed when joinder of interested persons was infeasible. In some instances courts did not undertake the relevant inquiry or were misled by the "jurisdiction" fallacy. In other instances there was undue preoccupation with abstract classifications of rights or obligations, as against consideration of the particular consequences of proceeding with the action and the ways by which these consequences might be ameliorated by the shaping of final relief or other precautions.

Although these difficulties cannot be said to have been general analysis of the cases showed that there was good reason for attempting to strengthen the rule. The literature also indicated how the rule should be reformed. See Reed, supra (discussion of the important case of *Shields v. Barrow,* 17 How. (58 U.S.) 130 (1854), appears at 55 Mich.L.Rev., p. 340 ff.); Hazard, supra; N.Y. Temporary Comm. on Courts, First Preliminary Report, Legis.Doc.1957, No. 6(b), pp. 28, 233; N.Y. Judicial Council, Twelfth Ann.Rep., Legis.Doc.1946, No. 17, p. 163; Joint Comm. on Michigan Procedural Revision, Final Report, Pt. III, p. 69 (1960); Note, *Indispensable Parties in the Federal Courts,* 65 Harv.L.Rev.

1050 (1952); *Developments in the Law—Multiparty Litigation in the Federal Courts,* 71 Harv.L.Rev. 874, 879 (1958); Mich.Gen.Court Rules, R. 205 (effective Jan. 1, 1963); N.Y.Civ.Prac.Law & Rules, § 1001 (effective Sept. 1, 1963).

The Amended Rule

New subdivision (a) defines the persons whose joinder in the action is desirable. Clause (1) stresses the desirability of joining those persons in whose absence the court would be obliged to grant partial or "hollow" rather than complete relief to the parties before the court. The interests that are being furthered here are not only those of the parties, but also that of the public in avoiding repeated lawsuits on the same essential subject matter. Clause (2)(i) recognizes the importance of protecting the person whose joinder is in question against the practical prejudice to him which may arise through a disposition of the action in his absence. Clause (2)(ii) recognizes the need for considering whether a party may be left, after the adjudication, in a position where a person not joined can subject him to a double or otherwise inconsistent liability. See Reed, supra, 55 Mich.L.Rev. at 330, 338; Note, supra, 65 Harv.L.Rev. at 1052–57; *Developments in the Law,* supra, 71 Harv.L.Rev. at 881–85.

The subdivision (a) definition of persons to be joined is not couched in terms of the abstract nature of their interests—"joint," "united," "separable," or the like. See N.Y. Temporary Comm. on Courts, First Preliminary Report, supra; Developments in the Law, supra, at 880. It should be noted particularly, however, that the description is not at variance with the settled authorities holding that a tortfeasor with the usual "joint-and-several" liability is merely a permissive party to an action against another with like liability. See 3 Moore's *Federal Practice* 2153 (2d ed. 1963); 2 Barron & Holtzoff, *Federal Practice & Procedure* § 513.8 (Wright ed. 1961). Joinder of these tortfeasors continues to be regulated by Rule 20; compare Rule 14 on third-party practice.

If a person as described in subdivision (a)(1)(2) is amenable to service of process and his joinder would not deprive the court of jurisdiction in the sense of competence over the action, he should be joined as a party; and if he has not been joined, the court should order him to be brought into the action. If a party joined has a valid objection to the venue and chooses to assert it, he will be dismissed from the action.

Subdivision (b).—When a person as described in subdivision (a)(1)–(2) cannot be made a party, the court is to determine whether in equity and good conscience the action should proceed among the parties already before it, or should be dismissed. That this decision is to be made in the light of pragmatic considerations has often been acknowledged by the courts. See *Roos v. Texas Co.,* 23 F.2d 171 (2d Cir. 1927), cert. denied 277 U.S. 587 (1928); *Niles-Bement-Pond Co. v. Iron Moulders' Union,* 254 U.S. 77, 80 (1920). The subdivision sets out four relevant considerations drawn from the experience revealed in the decided cases. The factors are to a certain extent overlapping, and they are not intended to exclude other considerations which may be applicable in particular situations.

The first factor brings in a consideration of what a judgment in the action would mean to the absentee. Would the absentee be adversely affected in a practical sense, and if so, would the prejudice be immediate and serious, or remote and minor? The possible collateral consequences of the judgment upon the parties already joined are also to be appraised. Would any party be exposed to a fresh action by the absentee, and if so, how serious is the threat? See the elaborate discussion in Reed, supra; cf. *A. L. Smith Iron Co. v. Dickson,* 141 F.2d 3 (2d Cir. 1944); *Caldwell Mfg. Co. v. Unique Balance Co.,* 18 F.R.D. 258 (S.D.N.Y.1955).

The second factor calls attention to the measures by which prejudice may be averted or lessened. The "shaping of relief" is a familiar expedient to this end. See, e.g., the award of money damages in lieu of specific relief where the latter might affect an absentee adversely. *Ward v. Deavers,* 203 F.2d 72 (D.C.Cir.1953); *Miller & Lux, Inc. v. Nickel,* 141 F.Supp. 41 (N.D.Calif.1956). On the use of "protective provisions," see *Roos v. Texas Co.,* supra; *Atwood v. Rhode Island Hosp. Trust Co.,* 275 Fed. 513, 519 (1st Cir. 1921), cert. denied, 257 U.S. 661 (1922); cf. *Stumpf v. Fidelity Gas Co.,* 294 F.2d 886 (9th Cir. 1961); and the general statement in *National Licorice Co. v. Labor Board,* 309 U.S. 350, 363 (1940).

Sometimes the party is himself able to take measures to avoid prejudice. Thus a defendant faced with a prospect of a second suit by an absentee may be in a position to bring the latter into the action by defensive interpleader. See *Hudson v. Newell,* 172 F.2d 848, 852 mod., 176 F.2d 546 (5th Cir. 1949); *Gauss v. Kirk,* 198 F.2d 83, 86 (D.C.Cir. 1952); *Abel v. Brayton Flying Service, Inc.,* 248 F.2d 713, 716 (5th Cir. 1957) (suggestion of possibility of counter-claim under Rule 13(h)); cf. *Parker Rust-Proof Co. v. Western Union Tel. Co.,* 105 F.2d 976 (2d Cir. 1939), cert. denied, 308 U.S. 597 (1939). So also the absentee may sometimes be able to avert prejudice to himself by voluntarily appearing in the action or intervening on an ancillary basis. See *Developments in the Law,* supra, 71 Harv.L.Rev. at 882; Annot., *Intervention or Subsequent Joinder of Parties as Affecting Jurisdiction of Federal Court Based on Diversity of Citizenship,* 134 A.L.R. 335 (1941); *Johnson v. Middleton,* 175 F.2d 535 (7th Cir. 1949); *Kentucky Nat. Gas Corp. v. Duggins,* 165 F.2d 1011 (6th Cir. 1948); *McComb v. McCormack,* 159 F.2d 219 (5th Cir. 1947). The court should consider whether this, in turn, would impose undue hardship on the absentee. (For the possibility of the court's informing an absentee of the pendency of the action, see comment under subdivision (c) below.)

The third factor—whether an "adequate" judgment can be rendered in the absence of a given person—calls attention to the extent of the relief that can be accorded among the parties joined. It meshes with the other factors, especially the "shaping of relief" mentioned under the second factor. Cf. *Kroese v. General Steel Castings Corp.,* 179 F.2d 760 (3d Cir. 1949), cert. denied, 339 U.S. 983 (1950).

The fourth factor, looking to the practical effects of a dismissal, indicates that the court should consider whether there is any assurance that the plaintiff, if dismissed, could sue effectively in another forum where better joinder would be possible. See *Fitzgerald v. Haynes,* 241 F.2d 417, 420 (3d Cir. 1957); *Fouke v. Schenewerk,* 197 F.2d 234, 236 (5th Cir. 1952); cf. *Warfield v. Marks,* 190 F.2d 178 (5th Cir. 1951).

The subdivision uses the word "indispensable" only in a conclusory sense, that is, a person is "regarded as indispensable" when he cannot be made a party and, upon consideration of the factors above mentioned, it is determined that in his absence it would be preferable to dismiss the action, rather than to retain it.

A person may be added as a party at any stage of the action on motion or on the court's initiative (see Rule 21); and a motion to dismiss, on the ground that a person has not been joined and justice requires that the action should not proceed in his absence, may be made as late as the trial on the merits (see Rule 12(h)(2), as amended; cf. Rule 12(b)(7), as amended). However, when the moving party is seeking dismissal in order to protect himself against a later suit by the absent person (subdivision (a)(2)(ii)), and is not seeking vicariously to protect the absent person against a prejudicial judgment (subdivision (a)(2)(i)), his undue delay in making the motion can properly be counted against him as a reason for denying the motion. A joinder question should be decided with reasonable promptness, but decision may properly be deferred if adequate information is not available at the time. Thus the relationship of an absent person to the action, and the practical effects of an adjudication upon him and others, may not be sufficiently revealed at the pleading stage; in such a case it would be appropriate to defer decision until the action was further advanced. Cf. Rule 12(d).

The amended rule makes no special provision for the problem arising in suits against subordinate Federal officials where it has often been set up as a defense that some superior officer must be joined. Frequently this defense has been accompanied by or intermingled with defenses of sovereign community or lack of consent of the United States to suit. So far as the issue of joinder can be isolated from the rest, the new subdivision seems better adapted to handle it than the predecessor provision. See the discussion in *Johnson v. Kirkland,* 290 F.2d 440, 446–47 (5th Cir. 1961) (stressing the practical orientation of the decisions); *Shaughnessy v. Pedreiro,* 349 U.S. 48, 54 (1955). Recent legislation, P.L. 87–748, 76 Stat. 744, approved October 5, 1962, adding §§ 1361, 1391(e) to Title 28, U.S.C., vests original jurisdiction in the District Courts over actions in the nature of mandamus to compel officials of the United States to perform their legal duties, and extends the range of service of process and liberalizes venue in these actions. If, then, it is found that a particular official should be joined in the action, the legislation will make it easy to bring him in.

Subdivision (c) parallels the predecessor subdivision (c) of Rule 19. In some situations it may be desirable to advise a person who has not been joined of the fact that the action is pending, and in particular cases the court in its discretion may itself convey this information by directing a letter or other informal notice to the absentee.

Subdivision (d) repeats the exception contained in the first clause of the predecessor subdivision (a).

1987 Amendment

The amendments are technical. No substantive change is intended.

Rule 20. Permissive Joinder of Parties

(a) Permissive Joinder. All persons may join in one action as plaintiffs if they assert any right to relief jointly, severally, or in the alternative in respect of or arising out of the same transaction, occurrence, or series of transactions or occurrences and if any question of law or fact common to all these persons will arise in the action. All persons (and any vessel, cargo or other property subject to admiralty process in rem) may be joined in one action as defendants if there is asserted against them jointly, severally, or in the alternative, any right to relief in respect of or arising out of the same transaction, occurrence, or series of transactions or occurrences and if any question of law or fact common to all defendants will arise in the action. A plaintiff or defendant need not be interested in obtaining or defending against all the relief demanded. Judgment may be given for one or more of the plaintiffs according to their respective rights to relief, and against one or more defendants according to their respective liabilities.

(b) Separate Trials. The court may make such orders as will prevent a party from being embarrassed, delayed, or put to expense by the inclusion of a party against whom the party asserts no claim and who asserts no claim against the party, and may order separate trials or make other orders to prevent delay or prejudice.

(As amended Feb. 28, 1966, eff. July 1, 1966; Mar. 2, 1987, eff. Aug. 1, 1987.)

ADVISORY COMMITTEE NOTES

1937 Adoption

The provisions for joinder here stated are in substance the provisions found in England, California, Illinois, New Jersey, and New York. They represent only a moderate expansion of the present federal equity practice to cover both law and equity actions.

With this rule compare also [former] Equity Rules 26 (Joinder of Causes of Action), 37 (Parties Generally—Intervention), 40 (Nominal Parties), and 42 (Joint and Several Demands).

The provisions of this rule for the joinder of parties are subject to Rule 82 (Jurisdiction and Venue Unaffected).

Note to Subdivision (a). The first sentence is derived from *English Rules Under the Judicature Act* (The Annual Practice, 1937) O. 16, r. 1. Compare Calif.Code Civ.Proc. (Deering, 1937) §§ 378, 379a; Ill.Rev.Stat. (1937) ch. 110, § 147–148; N.J.Comp.Stat. (2 Cum.Supp., 1911–1924), N.Y.C.P.A. (1937) §§ 209, 211. The second sentence is derived from *English Rules Under the Judicature Act* (The Annual Practice, 1937) O. 16, r. 4. The third sentence is derived from O. 16, r. 5, and the fourth from O. 16, r.r. 1 and 4.

Note to Subdivision (b). This is derived from *English Rules Under the Judicature Act* (The Annual Practice, 1937) O. 16, r.r. 1 and 5.

1966 Amendment

See the amendment of Rule 18(a) and the Advisory Committee's Note thereto. It has been thought that a lack of clarity in the antecedent of the word "them," as it appeared in two places in Rule 20(a), contributed to the view, taken by some courts, that this rule limited the joinder of claims in certain situations of permissive party joinder. Although the amendment of Rule 18(a) should make clear that this view is untenable, it has been considered advisable to amend Rule

20(a) to eliminate any ambiguity. See 2 Barron & Holtzoff, *Federal Practice & Procedure* 202 (Wright Ed. 1961).

A basic purpose of unification of admiralty and civil procedure is to reduce barriers to joinder; hence the reference to "any vessel," etc.

1987 Amendment

The amendments are technical. No substantive change is intended.

Rule 21. Misjoinder and Non-Joinder of Parties

Misjoinder of parties is not ground for dismissal of an action. Parties may be dropped or added by order of the court on motion of any party or of its own initiative at any stage of the action and on such terms as are just. Any claim against a party may be severed and proceeded with separately.

ADVISORY COMMITTEE NOTES

1937 Adoption

See *English Rules Under the Judicature Act* (The Annual Practice, 1937) O. 16, r. 11. See also [former] Equity Rules 43 (Defect of Parties—Resisting Objection) and 44 (Defect of Parties—Tardy Objection).

For separate trials see Rules 13(i) (Counterclaims and Cross-Claims: Separate Trials; Separate Judgments), 20(b) (Permissive Joinder of Parties: Separate Trials), and 42(b) (Separate Trials, generally) and the note to the latter rule.

Rule 22. Interpleader

(1) Persons having claims against the plaintiff may be joined as defendants and required to interplead when their claims are such that the plaintiff is or may be exposed to double or multiple liability. It is not ground for objection to the joinder that the claims of the several claimants or the titles on which their claims depend do not have a common origin or are not identical but are adverse to and independent of one another, or that the plaintiff avers that the plaintiff is not liable in whole or in part to any or all of the claimants. A defendant exposed to similar liability may obtain such interpleader by way of cross-claim or counterclaim. The provisions of this rule supplement and do not in any way limit the joinder of parties permitted in Rule 20.

(2) The remedy herein provided is in addition to and in no way supersedes or limits the remedy provided by Title 28, U.S.C., §§ 1335, 1397, and 2361. Actions under those provisions shall be conducted in accordance with these rules.

(As amended Dec. 29, 1948, eff. Oct. 20, 1949; Mar. 2, 1987, eff. Aug. 1, 1987.)

ADVISORY COMMITTEE NOTES

1937 Adoption

The first paragraph provides for interpleader relief along the newer and more liberal lines of joinder in the alternative. It avoids the confusion and restrictions that developed around actions of strict interpleader and actions in the nature of interpleader. Compare *John Hancock Mutual Life Insurance Co. v. Kegan et al.,* 22 F.Supp. 326 (D.C.Md.1938). It does not change the rules on service of process, jurisdiction, and venue, as established by judicial decision.

The second paragraph allows an action to be brought under the recent interpleader statute when applicable. By this paragraph all remedies under the statute are continued, but the manner of obtaining them is in accordance with these rules. For temporary restraining orders and preliminary injunctions under this statute, see Rule 65(e).

This rule substantially continues such statutory provisions as U.S.C., Title 38, § 445 [now 784] (Actions on claims; jurisdiction; parties; procedure; limitation; witnesses; definitions) (actions upon veterans' contracts of insurance with the United States), providing for interpleader by the United States where it acknowledges indebtedness under a contract of insurance with the United States; U.S.C., Title 49, § 97 (Interpleader of conflicting claimants) (by carrier which has issued bill of lading). See Chaffee, *The Federal Interpleader Act of 1936: I and II* (1936), 45 Yale L.J. 963, 1161.

1948 Amendment

The amendment effective October 20, 1949, substituted the reference to "Title 28, U.S.C., §§ 1335, 1397, and 2361," at the end of the first sentence of paragraph (2), for the reference to "Section 24(26) of the Judicial Code, as amended, U.S.C., Title 28, § 41(26)." The amendment also substituted the words "those provisions" in the second sentence of paragraph (2) for the words "that section."

1987 Amendment

The amendment is technical. No substantive change is intended.

Rule 23. Class Actions

(a) Prerequisites to a Class Action. One or more members of a class may sue or be sued as representative parties on behalf of all only if (1) the class is so numerous that joinder of all members is impracticable, (2) there are questions of law or fact common to the class, (3) the claims or defenses of the representative parties are typical of the claims or defenses of the class, and (4) the representative parties will fairly and adequately protect the interests of the class.

(b) Class Actions Maintainable. An action may be maintained as a class action if the prerequisites of subdivision (a) are satisfied, and in addition:

(1) the prosecution of separate actions by or against individual members of the class would create a risk of

(A) inconsistent or varying adjudications with respect to individual members of the class which would establish incompatible standards of conduct for the party opposing the class, or

(B) adjudications with respect to individual members of the class which would as a practical matter be dispositive of the interests of the other members not parties to the adjudications or substantially impair or impede their ability to protect their interests; or

(2) the party opposing the class has acted or refused to act on grounds generally applicable to the class, thereby making appropriate final injunctive relief or corresponding declaratory relief with respect to the class as a whole; or

(3) the court finds that the questions of law or fact common to the members of the class predominate over any questions affecting only individual members, and that a class action is superior to other available methods for the fair and efficient adjudication of the controversy. The matters pertinent to the findings include: (A) the interest of members of the class in individually controlling the prosecution or defense of separate actions; (B) the extent and nature of any litigation concerning the controversy already commenced by or against members of the class; (C) the desirability or undesirability of concentrating the litigation of the claims in the particular forum; (D) the difficulties likely to be encountered in the management of a class action.

(c) Determination by Order Whether Class Action to be Maintained; Notice; Judgment; Actions Conducted Partially as Class Actions.

(1) As soon as practicable after the commencement of an action brought as a class action, the court shall determine by order whether it is to be so maintained. An order under this subdivision may be conditional, and may be altered or amended before the decision on the merits.

(2) In any class action maintained under subdivision (b)(3), the court shall direct to the members of the class the best notice practicable under the circumstances, including individual notice to all members who can be identified through reasonable effort. The notice shall advise each member that (A) the court will exclude the member from the class if the member so requests by a specified date; (B) the judgment, whether favorable or not, will include all members who do not request exclusion; and (C) any member who does not request exclusion may, if the member desires, enter an appearance through counsel.

(3) The judgment in an action maintained as a class action under subdivision (b)(1) or (b)(2), whether or not favorable to the class, shall include and describe those whom the court finds to be members of the class. The judgment in an action maintained as a class action under subdivision (b)(3), whether or not favorable to the class, shall include and specify or describe those to whom the notice provided in subdivision (c)(2) was directed, and who have not requested exclusion, and whom the court finds to be members of the class.

(4) When appropriate (A) an action may be brought or maintained as a class action with respect to particular issues, or (B) a class may be divided into subclasses and each subclass treated as a class, and the provisions of this rule shall then be construed and applied accordingly.

(d) Orders in Conduct of Actions. In the conduct of actions to which this rule applies, the court may make appropriate orders: (1) determining the course of proceedings or prescribing measures to prevent undue repetition or complication in the presentation of evidence or argument; (2) requiring, for the protection of the members of the class or otherwise for the fair conduct of the action, that notice be given in such manner as the court may direct to some or all of the members of any step in the action, or of the proposed extent of the judgment, or of the opportunity of members to signify whether they consider the representation fair and adequate, to intervene and present claims or defenses, or otherwise to come into the action; (3) imposing conditions on the representative parties or on intervenors; (4) requiring that the pleadings be amended to eliminate therefrom allegations as to representation of absent persons, and that the action proceed accordingly; (5) dealing with similar procedural matters. The orders may be combined with an order under Rule 16, and may be altered or amended as may be desirable from time to time.

(e) Dismissal or Compromise. A class action shall not be dismissed or compromised without the approval of the court, and notice of the proposed dismissal or compromise shall be given to all members of the class in such manner as the court directs.

(f) Appeals. A court of appeals may in its discretion permit an appeal from an order of a district court granting or denying class action certification under this rule if application is made to it within ten days after entry of the order. An appeal does not stay proceedings in the district court unless the district judge or the court of appeals so orders.

(As amended Feb. 28, 1966, eff. July 1, 1966; Mar. 2, 1987, eff. Aug. 1, 1987; Apr. 24, 1998, eff. Dec. 1, 1998.)

ADVISORY COMMITTEE NOTES

1937 Adoption

Note to Subdivision (a). This is a substantial restatement of [former] Equity Rule 38 (Representatives of Class) as that rule has been construed. It applies to all actions, whether formerly denominated legal or equitable. For a general analysis of class actions, effect of judgment, and requisites of jurisdiction see Moore, *Federal Rules of Civil Procedure: Some Problems Raised by the Preliminary*

Draft, 25 Georgetown L.J. 551, 570 et seq. (1937); Moore and Cohn, *Federal Class Actions,* 32 Ill.L.Rev. 307 (1937); Moore and Cohn, *Federal Class Actions—Jurisdiction and Effect of Judgment,* 32 Ill.L.Rev. 555–567 (1938); Lesar, *Class Suits and the Federal Rules,* 22 Minn.L.Rev. 34 (1937); cf. Arnold and James, *Cases on Trials, Judgments and Appeals* (1936) 175; and see Blume, *Jurisdictional Amount in Representative Suits,* 15 Minn.L.Rev. 501 (1931).

The general test of [former] Equity Rule 38 (Representatives of Class) that the question should be "one of common or general interest to many persons constituting a class so numerous as to make it impracticable to bring them all before the court," is a common test. For states which require the two elements of a common or general interest and numerous persons, as provided for in [former] Equity Rule 38, see Del.Ch. Rule 113; Fla.Comp.Gen.Laws Ann. (Supp., 1936) § 4918(7); Georgia Code (1933) § 37–1002, and see *English Rules Under the Judicature Act* (The Annual Practice, 1937) O. 16, r. 9. For statutory provisions providing for class actions when the question is one of common or general interest or when the parties are numerous, see Ala.Code Ann. (Michie, 1928) § 5701; 2 Ind.Stat.Ann. (Burns, 1933) § 2–220; N.Y.C.P.A. (1937) 195; Wis.Stat. (1935) § 260.12. These statutes have, however, been uniformly construed as though phrased in the conjunctive. See *Garfein v. Stiglitz,* 260 Ky. 430, 86 S.W.2d 155 (1935). The rule adopts the test of [former] Equity Rule 38, but defines what constitutes a "common or general interest". Compare with code provisions which make the action dependent upon the propriety of joinder of the parties. See Blume, *The "Common Questions" Principle in the Code Provision for Representative Suits,* 30 Mich.L.Rev. 878 (1932). For discussion of what constitutes "numerous persons" see Wheaton, *Representative Suits Involving Numerous Litigants,* 19 Corn.L.Q. 399 (1934); Note, 36 Harv.L.Rev. 89 (1922).

Clause (1), Joint, Common, or Secondary Right. This clause is illustrated in actions brought by or against representatives of an unincorporated association. See *Oster v. Brotherhood of Locomotive Firemen and Enginemen,* 271 Pa. 419, 114 Atl. 377 (1921); *Pickett v. Walsh,* 192 Mass. 572, 78 N.E. 753, 6 L.R.A., N.S., 1067 (1906); *Colt v. Hicks,* 97 Ind.App. 177, 179 N.E. 335 (1932). Compare Rule 17(b) as to when an unincorporated association has capacity to sue or be sued in its common name; *United Mine Workers of America v. Coronado Coal Co.,* 42 S.Ct. 570, 259 U.S. 344, 66 L.Ed. 975, 27 A.L.R. 762 (1922) (an unincorporated association was sued as an entity for the purpose of enforcing against it a federal substantive right); Moore, *Federal Rules of Civil Procedure: Some Problems Raised by the Preliminary Draft,* 25 Georgetown L.J. 551, 566 (for discussion of jurisdictional requisites when an unincorporated association sues or is sued in its common name and jurisdiction is founded upon diversity of citizenship). For an action brought by representatives of one group against representatives of another group for distribution of a fund held by an unincorporated association, see *Smith v. Swormstedt,* 16 How. 288, 14 L.Ed. 942 (U.S. 1853). Compare *Christopher, et al. v. Brusselback,* 1938, 58 S.Ct. 350, 302 U.S. 500, 82 L.Ed. 388.

For an action to enforce rights held in common by policyholders against the corporate issuer of the policies, see *Supreme Tribe of Ben Hur v. Cauble,* 255 U.S. 356, 41 S.Ct. 338, 65 L.Ed. 673 (1921). See also *Terry v. Little,* 101 U.S. 216, 25 L.Ed. 864 (1880); *John A. Roebling's Sons Co. v. Kinnicutt,* 248 Fed. 596 (D.C.N.Y., 1917) dealing with the right held in common by creditors to enforce the statutory liability of stockholders.

Typical of a secondary action is a suit by stockholders to enforce a corporate right. For discussion of the general nature of these actions see *Ashwander v. Tennessee Valley Authority,* 297 U.S. 288, 56 S.Ct. 466, 80 L.Ed. 688 (1936); Glenn, *The Stockholder's Suit—Corporate and Individual Grievances,* 33 Yale L.J. 580 (1924); McLaughlin, *Capacity of Plaintiff-Stockholder to Terminate a Stockholder's Suit,* 46 Yale L.J. 421 (1937). See also Subdivision (b) of this rule which deals with Shareholder's Action; Note, 15 Minn.L.Rev. 453 (1931).

Clause (2). A creditor's action for liquidation or reorganization of a corporation is illustrative of this clause. An action by a stockholder against certain named defendants as representatives of numerous claimants presents a situation converse to the creditor's action.

Clause (3). See *Everglades Drainage League v. Napoleon Broward Drainage Dist.,* 253 Fed. 246 (D.C.Fla., 1918); *Gramling v. Maxwell,* 52 F.2d 256 (D.C.N.C., 1931), approved in 30 Mich.L.Rev. 624 (1932); *Skinner v. Mitchell,* 108 Kan. 861, 197 Pac. 569 (1921); *Duke of Bedford v. Ellis* (1901) A.C. 1, for class actions when there were numerous persons and there was only a question of law or fact common to them; and see Blume, *The "Common Questions" Principle in the Code Provision for Representative Suits,* 30 Mich. L.Rev. 878 (1932).

Note to Subdivision (b). This is [former] Equity Rule 27 (Stockholder's Bill) with verbal changes. See also *Hawes v. Oakland,* 104 U.S. 450, 26 L.Ed. 827 (1882) and former Equity Rule 94, promulgated January 23, 1882, 104 U.S. IX.

Note to Subdivision (c). See McLaughlin, Capacity of Plaintiff-Stockholder to Terminate a Stockholder's Suit, 46 Yale L.J. 421 (1937).

Supplementary Note

Note. Subdivision (b), relating to secondary actions by shareholders, provides among other things, that in such an action the complainant "shall aver (1) that the plaintiff was a shareholder at the time of the transaction of which he complains or that his share thereafter devolved on him by operation of law * * *".

As a result of the decision in *Erie R. Co. v. Tompkins,* 1938, 304 U.S. 64, 58 S.Ct. 817 (decided April 25, 1938, after this rule was promulgated by the Supreme Court, though before it took effect) a question has arisen as to whether the provision above quoted deals with a matter of substantive right or is a matter of procedure. If it is a matter of substantive law or right, then under *Erie R. Co. v. Tompkins* clause (1) may not be validly applied in cases pending in states whose local law permits a shareholder to maintain such actions, although not a shareholder at the time of the transactions complained of. The Advisory Committee, believing the question should be settled in the courts, proposes no change in Rule 23 but thinks rather that the situation should be explained in an appropriate note.

The rule has a long history. In *Hawes v. Oakland,* 1882, 104 U.S. 450, the Court held that a shareholder could not maintain such an action unless he owned shares at the time of the transactions complained of, or unless they devolved on him by operation of law. At that time the decision in *Swift v.*

Tyson, 1842, 16 Peters 1, was the law, and the federal courts considered themselves free to establish their own principles of equity jurisprudence, so the Court was not in 1882 and has not been, until *Erie R. Co. v. Tompkins* in 1938, concerned with the question whether *Hawes v. Oakland* dealt with substantive right or procedure.

Following the decision in *Hawes v. Oakland,* and at the same term, the Court, to implement its decision, adopted [former] Equity Rule 94, which contained the same provision above quoted from Rule 23 F.R.C.P. The provision in [former] Equity Rule 94 was later embodied in [former] Equity Rule 27, of which the present Rule 23 is substantially a copy.

In *City of Quincy v. Steel,* 1887, 120 U.S. 241, 245, 7 S.Ct. 520, the Court referring to *Hawes v. Oakland* said: "In order to give effect to the principles there laid down, this Court at that term adopted Rule 94 of the rules of practice for courts of equity of the United States."

Some other cases dealing with [former] Equity Rules 94 or 27 prior to the decision in *Erie R. Co. v. Tompkins* are *Dimpfel v. Ohio & Miss. R.R.,* 1884, 3 S.Ct. 573, 110 U.S. 209, 28 L.Ed. 121; *Illinois Central R. Co. v. Adams,* 1901, 21 S.Ct. 251, 180 U.S. 28, 34, 45L.Ed. 410; *Venner v. Great Northern Ry.,* 1908, 28 S.Ct. 328, 209 U.S. 24, 30, 52 L.Ed. 666; *Jacobson v. General Motors Corp.,* S.D.N.Y.1938, 22 F.Supp. 255, 257. These cases generally treat *Hawes v. Oakland* as establishing a "principle" of equity, or as dealing not with jurisdiction but with the "right" to maintain an action, or have said that the defense under the equity rule is analogous to the defense that the plaintiff has no "title" and results in a dismissal "for want of equity."

Those state decisions which held that a shareholder acquiring stock after the event may maintain a derivative action are founded on the view that it is a right belonging to the shareholder at the time of the transaction and which passes as a right to the subsequent purchaser. See *Pollitz v. Gould,* 1911, 202 N.Y. 11, 94 N.E. 1088.

The first case arising after the decision in *Erie R. Co. v. Tompkins,* in which this problem was involved, was *Summers v. Hearst,* S.D.N.Y.1938, 23 F.Supp. 986. It concerned [former] Equity Rule 27, as Federal Rule 23 was not then in effect. In a well considered opinion Judge Leibell reviewed the decisions and said: "The federal cases that discuss this section of [former] Rule 27 support the view that it states a principle of substantive law." He quoted *Pollitz v. Gould,* 1911, 202 N.Y. 11, 94 N.E. 1088, as saying that the United States Supreme Court "seems to have been more concerned with establishing this rule as one of practice than of substantive law" but that "whether it be regarded as establishing a principle of law or a rule of practice, this authority has been subsequently followed in the United States courts."

He then concluded that, although the federal decisions treat the equity rule as "stating a principle of substantive law", if "[former] Equity Rule 27 is to be modified or revoked in view of *Erie R. Co. v. Tompkins,* it is not the province of this Court to suggest it, much less impliedly to follow that course by disregarding the mandatory provisions of the Rule."

In *Piccard v. Sperry Corporation,* S.D.N.Y.1941, 36 F.Supp. 1006, 1009–10, affirmed without opinion, C.C.A.2d 1941, 120 F.2d 328, a shareholder, not such at the time of the transactions complained of, sought to intervene. The court held an intervenor was as much subject to Rule 23 as an original plaintiff; and that the requirement of Rule 23(b) was "a matter of practice," not substance, and applied in New York where the state law was otherwise, despite *Erie R. Co. v. Tompkins.* In *New York v. Guaranty Trust Co. of New York,* C.C.A.2, 1944, 143 F.2d 503, rev'd on other grounds, 1945, 65 S.Ct. 1464, the court said: "Restrictions on the bringing of stockholders' actions, such as those imposed by F.R.C.P. 23(b) or other state statutes are procedural," citing the *Piccard* and other cases.

Some other federal decisions since 1938 touch the question.

In *Gallup v. Caldwell,* C.C.A.3, 1941, 120 F.2d 90, 95 arising in New Jersey, the point was raised but not decided, the court saying that it was not satisfied that the then New Jersey rule differed from Rule 23(b), and that "under the circumstances the proper course was to follow Rule 23(b)."

In *Mullins v. DeSoto Securities Co.,* W.D.La.1942, 45 F.Supp. 871, 878, the point was not decided, because the court found the Louisiana rule to be the same as that stated in Rule 23(b).

In *Toebelman v. Missouri-Kansas Pipe Line Co.,* D.Del. 1941, 41 F.Supp. 334, 340, the court dealt only with another part of Rule 23(b), relating to prior demands on the stockholders and did not discuss *Erie R. Co. v. Tompkins,* or its effect on the rule.

In *Perrott v. United States Banking Corp.,* D.Del.1944, 53 F.Supp. 953, it appeared that the Delaware law does not require the plaintiff to have owned shares at the time of the transaction complained of. The court sustained Rule 23(b), after discussion of the authorities, saying:

"It seems to me the rule does not go beyond procedure. * * * Simply because a particular plaintiff cannot qualify as a proper party to maintain such an action does not destroy or even whittle at the cause of action. The cause of action exists until a qualified plaintiff can get it started in a federal court."

In *Bankers Nat. Corp. v. Barr,* S.D.N.Y.1945, 9 Fed.Rules Serv. 23b.11, Case 1, the court held Rule 23(b) to be one of procedure, but that whether the plaintiff was a stockholder was a substantive question to be settled by state law.

The New York rule, as stated in *Pollitz v. Gould,* supra, has been altered by an act of the New York Legislature, Chapter 667, Laws of 1944, effective April 9, 1944, General Corporation Law, § 61, which provides that "in any action brought by a shareholder in the right of a * * * corporation, it must appear that the plaintiff was a stockholder at the time of the transaction of which he complains, or that his stock thereafter devolved upon him by operation of law." At the same time a further and separate provision was enacted, requiring under certain circumstances the giving of security for reasonable expenses and attorney's fees, to which security the corporation in whose right the action is brought and the defendants therein may have recourse. (Chapter 668, Laws of 1944, effective April 9, 1944, General Corporation Law, § 61–b.) These provisions are aimed at so-called "strike" stockholders' suits and their attendant abuses. *Shielcrawt v. Moffett,* Ct.App.1945, 294 N.Y. 180, 61 N.E.2d 435, rev'g 51 N.Y.S.2d 188, aff'g 49 N.Y.S.2d 64; *Noel Associates, Inc. v. Merrill,* Sup.Ct.1944, 184 Misc. 646, 63 N.Y.S.2d 143.

Insofar as § 61 is concerned, it has been held that the section is procedural in nature. *Klum v. Clinton Trust Co.,* Sup.Ct.1944, 183 Misc. 340, 48 N.Y.S.2d 267; *Noel Associates, Inc. v. Merrill,* supra. In the latter case the court pointed out that "The 1944 amendment to Section 61 rejected the rule laid down in the Pollitz case and substituted, in place thereof, in its precise language, the rule which has long prevailed in the Federal Courts and which is now Rule 23(b) * * *". There is, nevertheless, a difference of opinion regarding the application of the statute to pending actions. See *Klum v. Clinton Trust Co.*, supra (applicable); *Noel Associates, Inc. v. Merrill*, supra (inapplicable).

With respect to § 61–b, which may be regarded as a separate problem, *Noel Associates, Inc. v. Merrill*, supra, it has been held that even though the statute is procedural in nature—a matter not definitely decided—the Legislature evinced no intent that the provisions should apply to actions pending when it became effective. *Shielcrawt v. Moffett*, supra. As to actions instituted after the effective date of the legislation, the constitutionality of § 61–b is in dispute. See *Wolf v. Atkinson*, Sup.Ct.1944, 182 Misc. 675, 49 N.Y.S.2d 703 (constitutional); *Citron v. Mangel Stores Corp.*, Sup.Ct. 1944, 50 N.Y.S.2d 416 (unconstitutional); Zlinkoff, *The American Investor and the Constitutionality of § 61–b of the New York General Corporation Law*, 1945, 54 Yale L.J. 352.

New Jersey also enacted a statute, similar to Chapters 667 and 668 of the New York law. See P.L.1945, Ch. 131, R.S.Cum.Supp. 14:3–15. The New Jersey provision similar to Chapter 668, § 61–b, differs, however, in that it specifically applies retroactively. It has been held that this provision is procedural and hence will not govern a pending action brought against a New Jersey corporation in the New York courts. *Shielcrawt v. Moffett*, Sup.Ct.N.Y.1945, 184 Misc. 1074, 56 N.Y.S.2d 134.

See, also generally, 2 Moore's *Federal Practice*, 1938, 2250–2253, and Cum.Supplement § 23.05.

The decisions here discussed show that the question is a debatable one, and that there is respectable authority for either view, with a recent trend towards the view that Rule 23(b)(1) is procedural. There is reason to say that the question is one which should not be decided by the Supreme Court ex parte, but left to await a judicial decision in a litigated case, and that in the light of the material in this note, the only inference to be drawn from a failure to amend Rule 23(b) would be that the question is postponed to await a litigated case.

The Advisory Committee is unanimously of the opinion that this course should be followed.

If, however, the final conclusion is that the rule deals with a matter of substantive right, then the rule should be amended by adding a provision that Rule 23(b)(1) does not apply in jurisdictions where state law permits a shareholder to maintain a secondary action, although he was not a shareholder at the time of the transactions of which he complains.

1966 Amendment

Difficulties with the original rule. The categories of class actions in the original rule were defined in terms of the abstract nature of the rights involved: the so-called "true" category was defined as involving "joint, common, or secondary rights"; the "hybrid" category, as involving "several" rights related to "specific property"; the "spurious" category, as involving "several" rights affected by a common question and related to common relief. It was thought that the definitions accurately described the situations amenable to the class-suit device, and also would indicate the proper extent of the judgment in each category, which would in turn help to determine the res judicata effect of the judgment if questioned in a later action. Thus the judgments in "true" and "hybrid" class actions would extend to the class (although in somewhat different ways); the judgment in a "spurious" class action would extend only to the parties including intervenors. See Moore, *Federal Rules of Civil Procedure: Some Problems Raised by the Preliminary Draft*, 25 Geo.L.J. 551, 570–76 (1937).

In practice the terms "joint," "common," etc., which were used as the basis of the Rule 23 classification proved obscure and uncertain. See Chafee, *Some Problems of Equity* 245–46, 256–57 (1950); Kalven & Rosenfield, *The Contemporary Function of the Class Suit*, 8 U. of Chi.L.Rev. 684, 707 & n. 73 (1941); Keeffe, Levy & Donovan, *Lee Defeats Ben Hur*, 33 Corn.L.Q. 327, 329–36 (1948); *Developments in the Law: Multiparty Litigation in the Federal Courts*, 71 Harv. L.Rev. 874, 931 (1958); Advisory Committee's Note to Rule 19, as amended. The courts had considerable difficulty with these terms. See, e.g., *Gullo v. Veterans' Coop. H. Assn.*, 13 F.R.D. 11 (D.D.C.1952); *Shipley v. Pittsburgh & L.E.R. Co.*, 70 F.Supp. 870 (W.D.Pa.1947); *Deckert v. Independence Shares Corp.*, 27 F.Supp. 763 (E.D.Pa.1939), rev'd 108 F.2d 51 (3d Cir. 1939), rev'd, 311 U.S. 282 (1940), on remand, 39 F.Supp. 592 (E.D.Pa.1941), rev'd sub nom. *Pennsylvania Co. for Ins. on Lives v. Deckert*, 123 F.2d 979 (3d Cir.1941) (see Chafee, supra, at 264–65).

Nor did the rule provide an adequate guide to the proper extent of the judgments in class actions. First, we find instances of the courts classifying actions as "true" or intimating that the judgments would be decisive for the class where these results seemed appropriate but were reached by dint of depriving the word "several" of coherent meaning. See, e.g., *System Federation No. 91 v. Reed*, 180 F.2d 991 (6th Cir.1950); *Wilson v. City of Paducah*, 100 F.Supp. 116 (W.D.Ky.1951); *Citizens Banking Co. v. Monticello State Bank*, 143 F.2d 261 (8th Cir.1944); *Redmond v. Commerce Trust Co.*, 144 F.2d 140 (8th Cir.1944), cert. denied, 323 U.S. 776 (1944); *United States v. American Optical Co.*, 97 F.Supp. 66 (N.D.Ill.1951); *National Hairdressers' & C. Assn. v. Philad Co.*, 34 F.Supp. 264 (D.Del.1940); 41 F.Supp. 701 (D.Del.1940), aff'd mem., 129 F.2d 1020 (3d Cir.1942). Second, we find cases classified by the courts as "spurious" in which, on a realistic view, it would seem fitting for the judgments to extend to the class. See, e.g., *Knapp v. Bankers Sec. Corp.*, 17 F.R.D. 245 (E.D.Pa.1954), aff'd 230 F.2d 717 (3d Cir.1956); *Giesecke v. Denver Tramway Corp.*, 81 F.Supp. 957 (D.Del.1949); *York v. Guaranty Trust Co.*, 143 F.2d 503 (2d Cir.1944), rev'd on grounds not here relevant, 326 U.S. 99 (1945) (see Chafee, supra, at 208); cf. *Webster Eisenlohr, Inc. v. Kalodner*, 145 F.2d 316, 320 (3d Cir.1944), cert. denied, 325 U.S. 867 (1945). But cf. the early decisions, *Duke of Bedford v. Ellis*, [1901] A.C. 1; *Sheffield Waterworks v. Yeomans*, L.R. 2 Ch.App. 8 (1866); *Brown v. Vermuden*, 1 Ch.Cas. 272, 22 Eng.Rep. 796 (1676).

The "spurious" action envisaged by original Rule 23 was in any event an anomaly because, although denominated a "class" action and pleaded as such, it was supposed not to adjudicate the rights or liabilities of any person not a party. It was believed to be an advantage of the "spurious" category that it would invite decisions that a member of the "class" could, like a member of the class in a "true" or "hybrid" action, intervene on an ancillary basis without being required to show an independent basis of Federal jurisdiction, and have the benefit of the date of the commencement of the action for purposes of the statute of limitations. See 3 Moore's *Federal Practice,* pars. 23.10[1], 23.12 (2d ed.1963). These results were attained in some instances but not in others. On the statute of limitations, see *Union Carbide & Carbon Corp. v. Nisley,* 300 F.2d 561 (10th Cir.1961), pet. cert. dism., 371 U.S. 801 (1963); but cf. *P. W. Husserl, Inc. v. Newman,* 25 F.R.D. 264 (S.D.N.Y.1960); *Athas v. Day,* 161 F.Supp. 916 (D.Colo.1958). On ancillary intervention, see *Amen v. Black,* 234 F.2d 12 (10th Cir.1956), cert. granted, 352 U.S. 888 (1956), dism. on stip., 355 U.S. 600 (1958); but cf. *Wagner v. Kemper,* 13 F.R.D. 128 (W.D.Mo.1952). The results, however, can hardly depend upon the mere appearance of a "spurious" category in the rule; they should turn on more basic considerations. See discussion of subdivision (c)(1) below.

Finally, the original rule did not squarely address itself to the question of the measures that might be taken during the course of the action to assure procedural fairness, particularly giving notice to members of the class, which may in turn be related in some instances to the extension of the judgment to the class. See Chafee, supra, at 230–31; Keeffe, Levy & Donovan, supra; *Developments in the law,* supra, 71 Harv. L.Rev. at 937–38; Note, *Binding Effect of Class Actions,* 67 Harv.L.Rev. 1059, 1062–65 (1954); Note, *Federal Class Actions: A Suggested Revision of Rule 23,* 46 Colum.L.Rev. 818, 833–36 (1946); Mich.Gen.Court R. 208.4 (effective Jan. 1, 1963); Idaho R.Civ.P. 23(d); Minn.R.Civ.P. 23.04; N.Dak.R.Civ.P. 23(d).

The amended rule describes in more practical terms the occasions for maintaining class actions; provides that all class actions maintained to the end as such will result in judgments including those whom the court finds to be members of the class, whether or not the judgment is favorable to the class; and refers to the measures which can be taken to assure the fair conduct of these actions.

Subdivision (a) states the prerequisites for maintaining any class action in terms of the numerousness of the class making joinder of the members impracticable, the existence of questions common to the class, and the desired qualifications of the representative parties. See Weinstein, *Revision of Procedure: Some Problems in Class Actions,* 9 Buffalo L.Rev. 433, 458–59 (1960); 2 Barron & Holtzoff, *Federal Practice & Procedure* § 562, at 265, § 572, at 351–52 (Wright ed. 1961). These are necessary but not sufficient conditions for a class action. See, e.g., *Giordano v. Radio Corp. of Am.,* 183 F.2d 558, 560 (3d Cir.1950); *Zachman v. Erwin,* 186 F.Supp. 681 (S.D.Tex.1959); *Baim & Blank, Inc. v. Warren-Connelly Co., Inc.,* 19 F.R.D. 108 (S.D.N.Y.1956). Subdivision (b) describes the additional elements which in varying situations justify the use of a class action.

Subdivision (b)(1). The difficulties which would be likely to arise if resort were had to separate actions by or against the individual members of the class here furnish the reasons for, and the principal key to, the propriety and value of utilizing the class-action device. The considerations stated under clauses (A) and (B) are comparable to certain of the elements which define the persons whose joinder in an action is desirable as stated in Rule 19(a), as amended. See amended Rule 19(a)(2)(i) and (ii), and the Advisory Committee's Note thereto; Hazard, *Indispensable Party: The Historical Origin of a Procedural Phantom,* 61 Colum.L.Rev. 1254, 1259–60 (1961); cf. 3 Moore, supra, par. 23.08, at 3435.

Clause (A): One person may have rights against, or be under duties toward, numerous persons constituting a class, and be so positioned that conflicting or varying adjudications in lawsuits with individual members of the class might establish incompatible standards to govern his conduct. The class action device can be used effectively to obviate the actual or virtual dilemma which would thus confront the party opposing the class. The matter has been stated thus: "The felt necessity for a class action is greatest when the courts are called upon to order or sanction the alteration of the status quo in circumstances such that a large number of persons are in a position to call on a single person to alter the status quo, or to complain if it is altered, and the possibility exists that [the] actor might be called upon to act in inconsistent ways." Louisell & Hazard, *Pleading and Procedure: State and Federal* 719 (1962); see *Supreme Tribe of Ben-Hur v. Cauble,* 255 U.S. 356, 366–67 (1921). To illustrate: Separate actions by individuals against a municipality to declare a bond issue invalid or condition or limit it, to prevent or limit the making of a particular appropriation or to compel or invalidate an assessment, might create a risk of inconsistent or varying determinations. In the same way, individual litigations of the rights and duties of riparian owners, or of landowners' rights and duties respecting a claimed nuisance, could create a possibility of incompatible adjudications. Actions by or against a class provide a ready and fair means of achieving unitary adjudication. See *Maricopa County Mun. Water Con. Dist. v. Looney,* 219 F.2d 529 (9th Cir.1955); *Rank v. Krug,* 142 F.Supp. 1, 154–59 (S.D.Calif.1956), on app., *State of California v. Rank,* 293 F.2d 340, 348 (9th Cir.1961); *Gart v. Cole,* 263 F.2d 244 (2d Cir.1959), cert. denied 359 U.S. 978 (1959); cf. *Martinez v. Maverick Cty. Water Con. & Imp. Dist.,* 219 F.2d 666 (5th Cir.1955); 3 Moore, supra, par. 23.11[2], at 3458–59.

Clause (B): This clause takes in situations where the judgment in a nonclass action by or against an individual member of the class, while not technically concluding the other members, might do so as a practical matter. The vice of an individual action would lie in the fact that the other members of the class, thus practically concluded, would have had no representation in the lawsuit. In an action by policy holders against a fraternal benefit association attacking a financial reorganization of the society, it would hardly have been practical, if indeed it would have been possible, to confine the effects of a validation of the reorganization to the individual plaintiffs. Consequently a class action was called for with adequate representation of all members of the class. See *Supreme Tribe of Ben-Hur v. Cauble,* 255 U.S. 356 (1921); *Waybright v. Columbian Mut. Life Ins. Co.,* 30 F.Supp. 885 (W.D.Tenn.1939); cf. *Smith v. Swormstedt,* 16 How. (57 U.S.) 288 (1853). For much the same reason actions by shareholders to compel the declaration of a dividend[,] the proper recognition and handling of redemption or pre-emption rights, or the like (or actions by the corporation for corresponding declarations of rights), should ordinarily be conducted as class actions, although the matter has been much obscured by the insistence that each shareholder has an individual claim. See *Knapp v. Bankers Securities Corp.,* 17 F.R.D. 245 (E.D.Pa.1954), aff'd, 230 F.2d 717 (3d Cir. 1956); *Giesecke v. Denver Tramway Corp.,* 81 F.Supp. 957 (D.Del.1949); *Zahn v. Transamerica Corp.,* 162 F.2d 36 (3d Cir.1947); *Speed v. Transamerica Corp.,* 100 F.Supp. 461

(D.Del.1951); *Sobel v. Whittier Corp.,* 95 F.Supp. 643 (E.D.Mich.1951), app. dism., 195 F.2d 361 (6th Cir.1952); *Goldberg v. Whittier Corp.,* 111 F.Supp. 382 (E.D.Mich.1953); *Dann v. Studebaker-Packard Corp.,* 288 F.2d 201 (6th Cir. 1961); *Edgerton v. Armour & Co.,* 94 F.Supp. 549 (S.D.Calif.1950); *Ames v. Mengel Co.,* 190 F.2d 344 (2d Cir.1951). (These shareholders' actions are to be distinguished from derivative actions by shareholders dealt with in new Rule 23.1). The same reasoning applies to an action which charges a breach of trust by an indenture trustee or other fiduciary similarly affecting the members of a large class of security holders or other beneficiaries, and which requires an accounting or like measures to restore the subject of the trust. See *Boesenberg v. Chicago T. & T. Co.,* 128 F.2d 245 (7th Cir.1942); *Citizens Banking Co. v. Monticello State Bank,* 143 F.2d 261 (8th Cir.1944); *Redmond v. Commerce Trust Co.,* 144 F.2d 140 (8th Cir.1944), cert. denied, 323 U.S. 776 (1944); cf. *York v. Guaranty Trust Co.,* 143 F.2d 503 (2d Cir.1944), rev'd on grounds not here relevant, 326 U.S. 99 (1945).

In various situations an adjudication as to one or more members of the class will necessarily or probably have an adverse practical effect on the interests of other members who should therefore be represented in the lawsuit. This is plainly the case when claims are made by numerous persons against a fund insufficient to satisfy all claims. A class action by or against representative members to settle the validity of the claims as a whole, or in groups, followed by separate proof of the amount of each valid claim and proportionate distribution of the fund, meets the problem. Cf. *Dickinson v. Burnham,* 197 F.2d 973 (2d Cir.1952), cert. denied, 344 U.S. 875 (1952); 3 Moore, supra, at par. 23.09. The same reasoning applies to an action by a creditor to set aside a fraudulent conveyance by the debtor and to appropriate the property to his claim, when the debtor's assets are insufficient to pay all creditors' claims. See *Heffernan v. Bennett & Armour,* 110 Cal.App.2d 564, 243 P.2d 846 (1952); cf. *City & County of San Francisco v. Market Street Ry.,* 95 Cal.App.2d 648, 213 P.2d 780 (1950). Similar problems, however, can arise in the absence of a fund either present or potential. A negative or mandatory injunction secured by one of a numerous class may disable the opposing party from performing claimed duties toward the other members of the class or materially affect his ability to do so. An adjudication as to movie "clearances and runs" nominally affecting only one exhibitor would often have practical effects on all the exhibitors in the same territorial area. Cf. *United States v. Paramount Pictures, Inc.,* 66 F.Supp. 323, 341–46 (S.D.N.Y. 1946); 334 U.S. 131, 144–48 (1948). Assuming a sufficiently numerous class of exhibitors, a class action would be advisable. (Here representation of subclasses of exhibitors could become necessary; see subdivision (c)(3)(B).)

Subdivision (b)(2). This subdivision is intended to reach situations where a party has taken action or refused to take action with respect to a class, and final relief of an injunctive nature or of a corresponding declaratory nature, settling the legality of the behavior with respect to the class as a whole, is appropriate. Declaratory relief "corresponds" to injunctive relief when as a practical matter it affords injunctive relief or serves as a basis for later injunctive relief. The subdivision does not extend to cases in which the appropriate final relief relates exclusively or predominantly to money damages. Action or inaction is directed to a class within the meaning of this subdivision even if it has taken effect or is threatened only as to one or a few members of the class, provided it is based on grounds which have general application to the class.

Illustrative are various actions in the civil-rights field where a party is charged with discriminating unlawfully against a class, usually one whose members are incapable of specific enumeration. See *Potts v. Flax,* 313 F.2d 284 (5th Cir. 1963); *Bailey v. Patterson,* 323 F.2d 201 (5th Cir. 1963), cert. denied, 376 U.S. 910, (1964); *Brunson v. Board of Trustees of School District No. 1, Clarendon Cty., S.C.,* 311 F.2d 107 (4th Cir. 1962), cert. denied, 373 U.S. 933 (1963); *Green v. School Bd. of Roanoke, Va.,* 304 F.2d 118 (4th Cir. 1962); *Orleans Parish School Bd. v. Bush,* 242 F.2d 156 (5th Cir. 1957), cert. denied, 354 U.S. 921 (1957); *Mannings v. Board of Public Inst. of Hillsborough County, Fla.,* 277 F.2d 370 (5th Cir. 1960); *Northcross v. Board of Ed. of City of Memphis,* 302 F.2d 818 (6th Cir. 1962), cert. denied, 370 U.S. 944 (1962); *Frasier v. Board of Trustees of Univ. of N.C.,* 134 F.Supp. 589 (M.D.N.C.1955, 3-judge court), aff'd 350 U.S. 979 (1956). Subdivision (b)(2) is not limited to civil-rights cases. Thus an action looking to specific or declaratory relief could be brought by a numerous class of purchasers, say retailers of a given description, against a seller alleged to have undertaken to sell to that class at prices higher than those set for other purchasers, say retailers of another description, when the applicable law forbids such a pricing differential. So also a patentee of a machine, charged with selling or licensing the machine on condition that purchasers or licensees also purchase or obtain licenses to use an ancillary unpatented machine, could be sued on a class basis by a numerous group of purchasers or licensees, or by a numerous group of competing sellers or licensors of the unpatented machine, to test the legality of the "tying" condition.

Subdivision (b)(3). In the situations to which this subdivision relates, class-action treatment is not as clearly called for as in those described above, but it may nevertheless be convenient and desirable depending upon the particular facts. Subdivision (b)(3) encompasses those cases in which a class action would achieve economies of time, effort, and expense, and promote uniformity of decision as to persons similarly situated, without sacrificing procedural fairness or bringing about other undesirable results. Cf. Chafee, supra, at 201.

The court is required to find, as a condition of holding that a class action may be maintained under this subdivision, that the questions common to the class predominate over the questions affecting individual members. It is only where this predominance exists that economies can be achieved by means of the class-action device. In this view, a fraud perpetrated on numerous persons by the use of similar misrepresentations may be an appealing situation for a class action, and it may remain so despite the need, if liability is found, for separate determination of the damages suffered by individuals within the class. On the other hand, although having some common core, a fraud case may be unsuited for treatment as a class action if there was material variation in the representations made or in the kinds or degrees of reliance by the persons to whom they were addressed. See *Oppenheimer v. F. J. Young & Co., Inc.,* 144 F.2d 387 (2d Cir. 1944); *Miller v. National City Bank of N.Y.,* 166 F.2d 723 (2d Cir. 1948); and for like problems in other contexts, see *Hughes v. Encyclopaedia Britannica,* 199 F.2d 295 (7th Cir. 1952); *Sturgeon v. Great Lakes Steel Corp.,* 143 F.2d 819

(6th Cir. 1944). A "mass accident" resulting in injuries to numerous persons is ordinarily not appropriate for a class action because of the likelihood that significant questions, not only of damages but of liability and defenses of liability, would be present, affecting the individuals in different ways. In these circumstances an action conducted nominally as a class action would degenerate in practice into multiple lawsuits separately tried. See *Pennsylvania R.R. v. United States,* 111 F.Supp. 80 (D.N.J.1953); cf. Weinstein, supra, 9 Buffalo L.Rev. at 469. Private damage claims by numerous individuals arising out of concerted antitrust violations may or may not involve predominating common questions. See *Union Carbide & Carbon Corp. v. Nisley,* 300 F.2d 561 (10th Cir. 1961), pet. cert. dism., 371 U.S. 801 (1963); cf. *Weeks v. Bareco Oil Co.,* 125 F.2d 84 (7th Cir. 1941); *Kainz v. Anheuser-Busch, Inc.,* 194 F.2d 737 (7th Cir. 1952); *Hess v. Anderson, Clayton & Co.,* 20 F.R.D. 466 (S.D.Calif.1957).

That common questions predominate is not itself sufficient to justify a class action under subdivision (b)(3), for another method of handling the litigious situation may be available which has greater practical advantages. Thus one or more actions agreed to by the parties as test or model actions may be preferable to a class action; or it may prove feasible and preferable to consolidate actions. Cf. Weinstein, supra, 9 Buffalo L.Rev. at 438–54. Even when a number of separate actions are proceeding simultaneously, experience shows that the burdens on the parties and the courts can sometimes be reduced by arrangements for avoiding repetitious discovery or the like. Currently the Coordinating Committee on Multiple Litigation in the United States District Courts (a subcommittee of the Committee on Trial Practice and Technique of the Judicial Conference of the United States) is charged with developing methods for expediting such massive litigation. To reinforce the point that the court with the aid of the parties ought to assess the relative advantages of alternative procedures for handling the total controversy, subdivision (b)(3) requires, as a further condition of maintaining the class action, that the court shall find that that procedure is "superior" to the others in the particular circumstances.

Factors (A)–(D) are listed, non-exhaustively, as pertinent to the findings. The court is to consider the interests of individual members of the class in controlling their own litigations and carrying them on as they see fit. See *Weeks v. Bareco Oil Co.,* 125 F.2d 84, 88–90, 93–94 (7th Cir. 1941) (anti-trust action); see also *Pentland v. Dravo Corp.,* 152 F.2d 851 (3d Cir. 1945), and Chafee, supra, at 273–75, regarding policy of Fair Labor Standards Act of 1938, § 16(b), 29 U.S.C. § 216(b), prior to amendment by Portal-to-Portal Act of 1947, § 5(a). [The present provisions of 29 U.S.C. § 216(b) are not intended to be affected by Rule 23, as amended.]

In this connection the court should inform itself of any litigation actually pending by or against the individuals. The interests of individuals in conducting separate lawsuits may be so strong as to call for denial of a class action. On the other hand, these interests may be theoretic rather than practical; the class may have a high degree of cohesion and prosecution of the action through representatives would be quite unobjectionable, or the amounts at stake for individuals may be so small that separate suits would be impracticable. The burden that separate suits would impose on the party opposing the class, or upon the court calendars, may also fairly be considered. (See the discussion, under subdivision (c)(2) below, of the right of members to be excluded from the class upon their request.)

Also pertinent is the question of the desirability of concentrating the trial of the claims in the particular forum by means of a class action, in contrast to allowing the claims to be litigated separately in forums to which they would ordinarily be brought. Finally, the court should consider the problems of management which are likely to arise in the conduct of a class action.

Subdivision (c)(1). In order to give clear definition to the action, this provision requires the court to determine, as early in the proceedings as may be practicable, whether an action brought as a class action is to be so maintained. The determination depends in each case on satisfaction of the terms of subdivision (a) and the relevant provisions of subdivision (b).

An order embodying a determination can be conditional; the court may rule, for example, that a class action may be maintained only if the representation is improved through intervention of additional parties of a stated type. A determination once made can be altered or amended before the decision on the merits if, upon fuller development of the facts, the original determination appears unsound. A negative determination means that the action should be stripped of its character as a class action. See subdivision (d)(4). Although an action thus becomes a nonclass action, the court may still be receptive to interventions before the decision on the merits so that the litigation may cover as many interests as can be conveniently handled; the questions whether the intervenors in the nonclass action shall be permitted to claim "ancillary" jurisdiction or the benefit of the date of the commencement of the action for purposes of the statute of limitations are to be decided by reference to the laws governing jurisdiction and limitations as they apply in particular contexts.

Whether the court should require notice to be given to members of the class of its intention to make a determination, or of the order embodying it, is left to the court's discretion under subdivision (d)(2).

Subdivision (c)(2) makes special provision for class actions maintained under subdivision (b)(3). As noted in the discussion of the latter subdivision, the interests of the individuals in pursing their own litigations may be so strong here as to warrant denial of a class action altogether. Even when a class action is maintained under subdivision (b)(3), this individual interest is respected. Thus the court is required to direct notice to the members of the class of the right of each member to be excluded from the class upon his request. A member who does not request exclusion may, if he wishes, enter an appearance in the action through his counsel; whether or not he does so, the judgment in the action will embrace him.

The notice[,] setting forth the alternatives open to the members of the class, is to be the best practicable under the circumstances, and shall include individual notice to the members who can be identified through reasonable effort. (For further discussion of this notice, see the statement under subdivision (d)(2) below.)

Subdivision (c)(3). The judgment in a class action maintained as such to the end will embrace the class, that is, in a class action under subdivision (b)(1) or (b)(2), those found by the court to be class members; in a class action under subdivision (b)(3), those to whom the notice prescribed by subdivision (c)(2) was directed, excepting those who requested exclusion or who are ultimately found by the court not to be members of the class. The judgment has this scope whether it is favorable or unfavorable to the class. In a (b)(1) or (b)(2) action the judgment "describes" the members of the class, but need not specify the individual members; in a (b)(3) action the judgment "specifies" the individual members who have been identified and described the others.

Compare subdivision (c)(4) as to actions conducted as class actions only with respect to particular issues. Where the class-action character of the lawsuit is based solely on the existence of a "limited fund," the judgment, while extending to all claims of class members against the fund, has ordinarily left unaffected the personal claims of nonappearing members against the debtor. See 3 Moore, supra, par. 23.11[4].

Hitherto, in a few actions conducted as "spurious" class actions and thus nominally designed to extend only to parties and others intervening before the determination of liability, courts have held or intimated that class members might be permitted to intervene after a decision on the merits favorable to their interests, in order to secure the benefits of the decision for themselves, although they would presumably be unaffected by an unfavorable decision. See, as to the propriety of this so-called "one-way" intervention in "spurious" actions, the conflicting views expressed in *Union Carbide & Carbon Corp. v. Nisley,* 300 F.2d 561 (10th Cir. 1961), pet. cert. dism., 371 U.S. 801 (1963); *York v. Guaranty Trust Co.,* 143 F.2d 503, 529 (2d Cir. 1944), rev'd on grounds not here relevant, 326 U.S. 99 (1945); *Pentland v. Dravo Corp.,* 152 F.2d 851, 856 (3d Cir. 1945); *Speed v. Transamerica Corp.,* 100 F.Supp. 461, 463 (D.Del.1951); *State Wholesale Grocers v. Great Atl. & Pac. Tea Co.,* 24 F.R.D. 510 (N.D.Ill.1959); *Alabama Ind. Serv. Stat. Assn. v. Shell Pet. Corp.,* 28 F.Supp. 386, 390 (N.D.Ala.1939); *Tolliver v. Cudahy Packing Co.,* 39 F.Supp. 337, 339 (E.D.Tenn.1941); Kalven & Rosenfield, supra, 8 U. of Chi.L.Rev. 684 (1941); Comment, 53 Nw.U.L.Rev. 627, 632–33 (1958); *Developments in the Law,* supra, 71 Harv.L.Rev. at 935; 2 Barron & Holtzoff, supra, § 568; but cf. *Lockwood v. Hercules Powder Co.,* 7 F.R.D. 24, 28–29 (W.D.Mo.1947); *Abram v. San Joaquin Cotton Oil Co.,* 46 F.Supp. 969, 976–77 (S.D.Calif.1942); Chafee, supra, at 280, 285; 3 Moore, supra, par. 23.12, at 3476. Under proposed subdivision (c)(3), one-way intervention is excluded; the action will have been early determined to be a class or nonclass action, and in the former case the judgment, whether or not favorable, will include the class, as above stated.

Although thus declaring that the judgment in a class action includes the class, as defined, subdivision (c)(3) does not disturb the recognized principle that the court conducting the action cannot predetermine the *res judicata* effect of the judgment; this can be tested only in a subsequent action. See Restatement, Judgments § 86, comment (h), § 116 (1942). The court, however, in framing the judgment in any suit brought as a class action, must decide what its extent or coverage shall be, and if the matter is carefully considered, questions of *res judicata* are less likely to be raised at a later time and if raised will be more satisfactorily answered. See Chafee, supra, at 294; Weinstein, supra, 9 Buffalo L.Rev. at 460.

Subdivision (c)(4). This provision recognizes that an action may be maintained as a class action as to particular issues only. For example, in a fraud or similar case the action may retain its "class" character only through the adjudication of liability to the class; the members of the class may thereafter be required to come in individually and prove the amounts of their respective claims.

Two or more classes may be represented in a single action. Where a class is found to include subclasses divergent in interest, the class may be divided correspondingly, and each subclass treated as a class.

Subdivision (d) is concerned with the fair and efficient conduct of the action and lists some types of orders which may be appropriate.

The court should consider how the proceedings are to be arranged in sequence, and what measures should be taken to simplify the proof and argument. See subdivision (d)(1). The orders resulting from this consideration, like the others referred to in subdivision (d), may be combined with a pretrial order under Rule 16, and are subject to modification as the case proceeds.

Subdivision (d)(2) sets out a non-exhaustive list of possible occasions for orders requiring notice to the class. Such notice is not a novel conception. For example, in "limited fund" cases, members of the class have been notified to present individual claims after the basic class decision. Notice has gone to members of a class so that they might express any opposition to the representation, see *United States v. American Optical Co.,* 97 F.Supp. 66 (N.D.Ill.1951), and 1950–51 CCH Trade Cases 64573–74 (par. 62869); cf. *Weeks v. Bareco Oil Co.,* 125 F.2d 84, 94 (7th Cir. 1941), and notice may encourage interventions to improve the representation of the class. Cf. *Oppenheimer v. F. J. Young & Co.,* 144 F.2d 387 (2d Cir. 1944). Notice has been used to poll members on a proposed modification of a consent decree. See record in *Sam Fox Publishing Co. v. United States,* 366 U.S. 683 (1961).

Subdivision (d)(2) does not require notice at any stage, but rather calls attention to its availability and invokes the court's discretion. In the degree that there is cohesiveness or unity in the class and the representation is effective, the need for notice to the class will tend toward a minimum. These indicators suggest that notice under subdivision (d)(2) may be particularly useful and advisable in certain class actions maintained under subdivision (b)(3), for example, to permit members of the class to object to the representation. Indeed, under subdivision (c)(2), notice must be ordered, and is not merely discretionary, to give the members in a subdivision (b)(3) class action an opportunity to secure exclusion from the class. This mandatory notice pursuant to subdivision (c)(2), together with any discretionary notice which the court may find it advisable to give under subdivision (d)(2), is designed to fulfill requirements of due process to which the class action procedure is of course subject. See *Hansberry v. Lee,* 311 U.S. 32 (1940); *Mullane v. Central Hanover Bank & Trust Co.,* 339 U.S. 306 (1950); cf. *Dickinson v. Burnham,* 197 F.2d 973, 979 (2d Cir. 1952), and studies cited at 979 in 4; see also *All American Airways, Inc. v. Elderd,* 209 F.2d 247, 249 (2d Cir. 1954); *Gart v. Cole,* 263 F.2d 244, 248–49 (2d Cir. 1959), cert. denied, 359 U.S. 978 (1959).

Notice to members of the class, whenever employed under amended Rule 23, should be accommodated to the particular purpose but need not comply with the formalities for service of process. See Chafee, supra, at 230–31; *Brendle v. Smith,* 7 F.R.D. 119 (S.D.N.Y.1946). The fact that notice is given at one stage of the action does not mean that it must be given at subsequent stages. Notice is available fundamentally "for the protection of the members of the class or otherwise for the fair conduct of the action" and should not be used merely as a device for the undesirable solicitation of claims. See the discussion in *Cherner v. Transitron Electronic Corp.,* 201 F.Supp. 934 (D.Mass.1962); *Hormel v. United States,* 17 F.R.D. 303 (S.D.N.Y.1955).

In appropriate cases the court should notify interested government agencies of the pendency of the action or of particular steps therein.

Subdivision (d)(3) reflects the possibility of conditioning the maintenance of a class action, e.g., on the strengthening of the representation, see subdivision (c)(1) above; and recognizes that the imposition of conditions on intervenors may be required for the proper and efficient conduct of the action.

As to orders under subdivision (d)(4), see subdivision (c)(1) above.

Subdivision (e) requires approval of the court, after notice, for the dismissal or compromise of any class action.

1987 Amendment

The amendments are technical. No substantive change is intended.

Rule 23.1. Derivative Actions by Shareholders

In a derivative action brought by one or more shareholders or members to enforce a right of a corporation or of an unincorporated association, the corporation or association having failed to enforce a right which may properly be asserted by it, the complaint shall be verified and shall allege (1) that the plaintiff was a shareholder or member at the time of the transaction of which the plaintiff complains or that the plaintiff's share or membership thereafter devolved on the plaintiff by operation of law, and (2) that the action is not a collusive one to confer jurisdiction on a court of the United States which it would not otherwise have. The complaint shall also allege with particularity the efforts, if any, made by the plaintiff to obtain the action the plaintiff desires from the directors or comparable authority and, if necessary, from the shareholders or members, and the reasons for the plaintiff's failure to obtain the action or for not making the effort. The derivative action may not be maintained if it appears that the plaintiff does not fairly and adequately represent the interests of the shareholders or members similarly situated in enforcing the right of the corporation or association. The action shall not be dismissed or compromised without the approval of the court, and notice of the proposed dismissal or compromise shall be given to shareholders or members in such manner as the court directs.

(Added Feb. 28, 1966, eff. July 1, 1966, and amended Mar. 2, 1987, eff. Aug. 1, 1987.)

ADVISORY COMMITTEE NOTES

1966 Addition

A derivative action by a shareholder of a corporation or by a member of an unincorporated association has distinctive aspects which require the special provisions set forth in the new rule. The next-to-the-last sentence recognizes that the question of adequacy of representation may arise when the plaintiff is one of a group of shareholders or members. Cf. 3 Moore's *Federal Practice,* par. 23.08 (2d ed. 1963).

The court has inherent power to provide for the conduct of the proceedings in a derivative action, including the power to determine the course of the proceedings and require that any appropriate notice be given to shareholders or members.

1987 Amendment

The amendments are technical. No substantive change is intended.

Rule 23.2. Actions Relating to Unincorporated Associations

An action brought by or against the members of an unincorporated association as a class by naming certain members as representative parties may be maintained only if it appears that the representative parties will fairly and adequately protect the interests of the association and its members. In the conduct of the action the court may make appropriate orders corresponding with those described in Rule 23(d), and the procedure for dismissal or compromise of the action shall correspond with that provided in Rule 23(e).

(Added Feb. 28, 1966, eff. July 1, 1966.)

ADVISORY COMMITTEE NOTES

1966 Addition

Although an action by or against representatives of the membership of an unincorporated association has often been viewed as a class action, the real or main purpose of this characterization has been to give "entity treatment" to the association when for formal reasons it cannot sue or be sued as a jural person under Rule 17(b). See Louisell & Hazard, *Pleading and Procedure: State and Federal* 718 (1962); 3 Moore's *Federal Practice,* par. 23.08 (2d ed. 1963); Story, J. in *West v. Randall,* 29 Fed.Cas. 718, 722–23, No. 17,424 (C.C.D.R.I.1820); and, for examples, *Gibbs v. Buck,* 307 U.S. 66 (1939); *Tunstall v. Brotherhood of Locomotive F. & E.,* 148 F.2d 403 (4th Cir. 1945); *Oskoian v. Canuel,* 269 F.2d 311 (1st Cir. 1959). Rule 23.2 deals separately with these actions, referring where appropriate to Rule 23.

Rule 24. Intervention

(a) Intervention of Right. Upon timely application anyone shall be permitted to intervene in an action: (1) when a statute of the United States confers an unconditional right to intervene; or (2) when the applicant claims an interest relating to the property or transaction which is the subject of the action and the applicant is so situated that the disposition of the action may as a practical matter impair or impede the applicant's ability to protect that interest, unless the applicant's interest is adequately represented by existing parties.

(b) Permissive Intervention. Upon timely application anyone may be permitted to intervene in an action: (1) when a statute of the United States confers a conditional right to intervene; or (2) when an applicant's claim or defense and the main action have a question of law or fact in common. When a party to an action relies for ground of claim or defense upon any statute or executive order administered by a federal or state governmental officer or agency or upon any regulation, order, requirement, or agreement issued or made pursuant to the statute or executive order, the officer or agency upon timely application may be permitted to intervene in the action. In exercising its discretion the court shall consider whether the intervention will unduly delay or prejudice the adjudication of the rights of the original parties.

(c) Procedure. A person desiring to intervene shall serve a motion to intervene upon the parties as provided in Rule 5. The motion shall state the grounds therefor and shall be accompanied by a pleading setting forth the claim or defense for which intervention is sought. The same procedure shall be followed when a statute of the United States gives a right to intervene. When the constitutionality of an act of Congress affecting the public interest is drawn in question in any action in which the United States or an officer, agency, or employee thereof is not a party, the court shall notify the Attorney General of the United States as provided in Title 28, U.S.C. § 2403. When the constitutionality of any statute of a State affecting the public interest is drawn in question in any action in which that State or any agency, officer, or employee thereof is not a party, the court shall notify the attorney general of the State as provided in Title 28, U.S.C. § 2403. A party challenging the constitutionality of legislation should call the attention of the court to its consequential duty, but failure to do so is not a waiver of any constitutional right otherwise timely asserted.

(As amended Dec. 27, 1946, eff. Mar. 19, 1948; Dec. 29, 1948, eff. Oct. 20, 1949; Jan. 21, 1963, eff. July 1, 1963; Feb. 28, 1966, eff. July 1, 1966; Mar. 2, 1987, eff. Aug. 1, 1987; Apr. 30, 1991, eff. Dec. 1, 1991.)

ADVISORY COMMITTEE NOTES

1937 Adoption

The right to intervene given by the following and similar statutes is preserved, but the procedure for its assertion is governed by this rule:

U.S.C., Title 28 former sections:

45a [now 2323] (Special attorneys; participation by Interstate Commerce Commission; intervention) (in certain cases under interstate commerce laws)

48 [now 2322] (Suits to be against United States; intervention by United States)

401 [now 2403] (Intervention by United States; constitutionality of Federal statute)

U.S.C., Title 40:

276a–2(b) (Bonds of contractors for public buildings or works; rights of persons furnishing labor and materials).

Compare with the last sentence of [former] Equity Rule 37 (Parties Generally—Intervention). This rule amplifies and restates the present federal practice at law and in equity. For the practice in admiralty see Admiralty Rules 34 (How Third Party May Intervene) and 42 (Claims Against Proceeds in Registry). See generally Moore and Levi, *Federal Intervention: I The Right to Intervene and Reorganization* (1936), 45 Yale L.J. 565. Under the codes two types of intervention are provided, one for the recovery of specific real or personal property (2 Ohio Gen.Code Ann. (Page, 1926) § 11263; Wyo.Rev.Stat.Ann. (Courtright, 1931) § 89–522), and the other allowing intervention generally when the applicant has an interest in the matter in litigation (1 Colo.Stat.Ann. (1935) Code Civ.Proc. § 22; La.Code Pract. (Dart, 1932) Arts. 389–394; Utah Rev.Stat.Ann. (1933) § 104–3–24). The English intervention practice is based upon various rules and decisions and falls into the two categories of absolute right and discretionary right. For the absolute right see *English Rules Under the Judicature Act* (The Annual Practice, 1937) O. 12, r. 24 (admiralty), r. 25 (land), r. 23 (probate); O. 57, r. 12 (execution); J.A. (1925) §§ 181, 182, 183(2) (divorce); *In re Metropolitan Amalgamated Estates, Ltd.*, (1912) 2 Ch. 497 (receivership); *Wilson v. Church*, 9 Ch.D. 552 (1878) (representative action). For the discretionary right see O. 16, r. 11 (non-joinder) and *Re Fowler*, 142 L.T.Jo. 94 (Ch.1916), *Vavasseur v. Krupp*, 9 Ch.D. 351 (1878) (persons out of the jurisdiction).

1946 Amendment

Note. Subdivision (a). The addition to subdivision (a)(3) covers the situation where property may be in the actual custody of some other officer or agency—such as the Secretary of the Treasury—but the control and disposition of the property is lodged in the court wherein the action is pending.

Subdivision (b). The addition in subdivision (b) permits the intervention of governmental officers or agencies in proper cases and thus avoids exclusionary constructions of the rule. For an example of the latter, see *Matter of Bender Body Co.*, Ref. Ohio 1941, 47 F.Supp. 224, holding that the Administrator of the Office of Price Administration, then acting under the authority of an Executive Order of the President, could not intervene in a bankruptcy proceeding to protest the sale of assets above ceiling prices. Compare, however, *Securities and Exchange Commission v. United States Realty & Improvement Co.*, 1940, 310 U.S. 434, 60 S.Ct. 1044, where permissive intervention of the Commission to protect the public interest in an arrangement proceeding under Chapter XI of the Bankruptcy Act was upheld. See also dissenting opinion in *Securities and Exchange Commission v. Long Island Lighting Co.*, C.C.A.2d 1945, 148 F.2d 252, judgment vacated as moot and case remanded with direction to dismiss complaint, 1945, 325 U.S. 833, 65 S.Ct. 1085. For discussion see Commentary, *Nature of Permissive Intervention Under Rule 24b*, 1940, 3 Fed.Rules Serv. 704; Berger, *Intervention by Public Agencies in Private Litigation in the Federal Courts*, 1940, 50 Yale L.J. 65.

Regarding the construction of subdivision (b)(2), see *Allen Calculators, Inc. v. National Cash Register Co.,* 1944, 64 S.Ct. 905, 322 U.S. 137, 88 L.Ed. 1188.

1948 Amendment

The amendment effective Oct. 20, 1949, substituted the reference to "Title 28, U.S.C.A. § 2403" at the end of subdivision (c) for the reference to "the Act of August 24, 1937, c. 754, § 1."

1963 Amendment

This amendment conforms to the amendment of Rule 5(a). See the Advisory Committee's Note to that amendment.

1966 Amendment

In attempting to overcome certain difficulties which have arisen in the application of present Rule 24(a)(2) and (3), this amendment draws upon the revision of the related Rules 19 (joinder of persons needed for just adjudication) and 23 (class actions), and the reasoning underlying that revision.

Rule 24(a)(3) as amended in 1948 provided for intervention of right where the applicant established that he would be adversely affected by the distribution or disposition of property involved in an action to which he had not been made a party. Significantly, some decided cases virtually disregarded the language of this provision. Thus Professor Moore states: "The concept of a fund has been applied so loosely that it is possible for a court to find a fund in almost any in personam action." 4 Moore's *Federal Practice,* par. 24.09[3], at 55 (2d ed. 1962), and see, e.g., *Formulabs, Inc. v. Hartley Pen Co.,* 275 F.2d 52 (9th Cir.1960). This development was quite natural, for Rule 24(a)(3) was unduly restricted. If an absentee would be substantially affected in a practical sense by the determination made in an action, he should, as a general rule, be entitled to intervene, and his right to do so should not depend on whether there is a fund to be distributed or otherwise disposed of. Intervention of right is here seen to be a kind of counterpart to Rule 19(a)(2)(i) on joinder of persons needed for a just adjudication: where, upon motion of a party in an action, an absentee should be joined so that he may protect his interest which as a practical matter may be substantially impaired by the disposition of the action, he ought to have a right to intervene in the action on his own motion. See Louisell & Hazard, *Pleading and Procedure: State and Federal* 749–50 (1962).

The general purpose of original Rule 24(a)(2) was to entitle an absentee, purportedly represented by a party, to intervene in the action if he could establish with fair probability that the representation was inadequate. Thus, where an action is being prosecuted or defended by a trustee, a beneficiary of the trust should have a right to intervene if he can show that the trustee's representation of his interest probably is inadequate; similarly a member of a class should have the right to intervene in a class action if he can show the inadequacy of the representation of his interest by the representative parties before the court.

Original Rule 24(a)(2), however, made it a condition of intervention that "the applicant is or may be bound by a judgment in the action," and this created difficulties with intervention in class actions. If the "bound" language was read literally in the sense of res judicata, it could defeat intervention in some meritorious cases. A member of a class to whom a judgment in a class action extended by its terms (see Rule 23(c)(3), as amended) might be entitled to show in a later action, when the judgment in the class action was claimed to operate as res judicata against him, that the "representative" in the class action had not in fact adequately represented him. If he could make this showing, the class-action judgment might be held not to bind him. See *Hansberry v. Lee,* 311 U.S. 32 (1940). If a class member sought to intervene in the class action proper, while it was still pending, on grounds of inadequacy of representation, he could be met with the argument: if the representation was in fact inadequate, he would not be "bound" by the judgment when it was subsequently asserted against him as res judicata, hence he was not entitled to intervene; if the representation was in fact adequate, there was no occasion or ground for intervention. See *Sam Fox Publishing Co. v. United States,* 366 U.S. 683 (1961); cf. *Sutphen Estates, Inc. v. United States,* 342 U.S. 19 (1951). This reasoning might be linguistically justified by original Rule 24(a)(2); but it could lead to poor results. Compare the discussion in *International M. & I. Corp. v. Von Clemm,* 301 F.2d 857 (2d Cir.1962); *Atlantic Refining Co. v. Standard Oil Co.,* 304 F.2d 387 (D.C.Cir. 1962). A class member who claims that his "representative" does not adequately represent him, and is able to establish that proposition with sufficient probability, should not be put to the risk of having a judgment entered in the action which by its terms extends to him, and be obliged to test the validity of the judgment as applied to his interest by a later collateral attack. Rather he should, as a general rule, be entitled to intervene in the action.

The amendment provides that an applicant is entitled to intervene in an action when his position is comparable to that of a person under Rule 19(a)(2)(i), as amended, unless his interest is already adequately represented in the action by existing parties. The Rule 19(a)(2)(i) criterion imports practical considerations, and the deletion of the "bound" language similarly frees the rule from undue preoccupation with strict considerations of res judicata.

The representation whose adequacy comes into question under the amended rule is not confined to formal representation like that provided by a trustee for his beneficiary or a representative party in a class action for a member of the class. A party to an action may provide practical representation to the absentee seeking intervention although no such formal relationship exists between them, and the adequacy of this practical representation will then have to be weighed. See *International M. & I. Crop. v. Von Clemm,* and *Atlantic Refining Co. v. Standard Oil Co.,* both supra; *Wolpe v. Poretsky,* 144 F.2d 505 (D.C.Cir.1944), cert. denied, 323 U.S. 777 (1944); cf. *Ford Motor Co. v. Bisanz Bros.,* 249 F.2d 22 (8th Cir.1957); and generally, Annot., 84 A.L.R.2d 1412 (1961).

An intervention of right under the amended rule may be subject to appropriate conditions or restrictions responsive among other things to the requirements of efficient conduct of the proceedings.

1987 Amendment

The amendments are technical. No substantive change is intended.

1991 Amendment

Language is added to bring Rule 24(c) into conformity with the statute cited, resolving some confusion reflected in district court rules. As the text provides, counsel challenging the constitutionality of legislation in an action in which the appropriate government is not a party should call the attention of the court to its duty to notify the appropriate governmental officers. The statute imposes the burden of notification on the court, not the party making the constitutional challenge, partly in order to protect against any possible waiver of constitutional rights by parties inattentive to the need for notice. For this reason, the failure of a party to call the court's attention to the matter cannot be treated as a waiver.

Rule 25. Substitution of Parties

(a) Death.

(1) If a party dies and the claim is not thereby extinguished, the court may order substitution of the proper parties. The motion for substitution may be made by any party or by the successors or representatives of the deceased party and, together with the notice of hearing, shall be served on the parties as provided in Rule 5 and upon persons not parties in the manner provided in Rule 4 for the service of a summons, and may be served in any judicial district. Unless the motion for substitution is made not later than 90 days after the death is suggested upon the record by service of a statement of the fact of the death as provided herein for the service of the motion, the action shall be dismissed as to the deceased party.

(2) In the event of the death of one or more of the plaintiffs or of one or more of the defendants in an action in which the right sought to be enforced survives only to the surviving plaintiffs or only against the surviving defendants, the action does not abate. The death shall be suggested upon the record and the action shall proceed in favor of or against the surviving parties.

(b) Incompetency. If a party becomes incompetent, the court upon motion served as provided in subdivision (a) of this rule may allow the action to be continued by or against the party's representative.

(c) Transfer of Interest. In case of any transfer of interest, the action may be continued by or against the original party, unless the court upon motion directs the person to whom the interest is transferred to be substituted in the action or joined with the original party. Service of the motion shall be made as provided in subdivision (a) of this rule.

(d) Public Officers; Death or Separation from Office.

(1) When a public officer is a party to an action in his official capacity and during its pendency dies, resigns, or otherwise ceases to hold office, the action does not abate and the officer's successor is automatically substituted as a party. Proceedings following the substitution shall be in the name of the substituted party, but any misnomer not affecting the substantial rights of the parties shall be disregarded. An order of substitution may be entered at any time, but the omission to enter such an order shall not affect the substitution.

(2) A public officer who sues or is sued in an official capacity may be described as a party by the officer's official title rather than by name; but the court may require the officer's name to be added.

(As amended Dec. 29, 1948, eff. Oct. 20, 1949; Apr. 17, 1961, eff. July 19, 1961; Jan. 21, 1963, eff. July 1, 1963; Mar. 2, 1987, eff. Aug. 1, 1987.)

ADVISORY COMMITTEE NOTES

1937 Adoption

Note to Subdivision (a). 1. The first paragraph of this rule is based upon [former] Equity Rule 45 (Death of Party—Revivor) and U.S.C., Title 28, former § 778 (Death of parties; substitution of executor or administrator). The *scire facias* procedure provided for in the statute cited is superseded and the writ is abolished by Rule 81(b). Paragraph two states the content of U.S.C., Title 28, former § 779 (Death of one of several plaintiffs or defendants). With these two paragraphs compare generally *English Rules Under the Judicature Act* (The Annual Practice, 1937) O. 17, r.r. 1–10.

2. This rule modifies U.S.C., Title 28, [former] §§ 778 (Death of parties; substitution of executor or administrator), 779 (Death of one of several plaintiffs or defendants), and 780 (Survival of actions, suits, or proceedings, etc.), in so far as they differ from it.

Note to Subdivisions (b) and (c). These are a combination and adaptation of N.Y.C.P.A. (1937) § 83 and Calif.Code Civ.Proc. (1937) § 385; see also 4 Nev.Comp.Laws (Hillyer, 1929) § 8561.

Note to Subdivision (d). With the first and last sentences compare U.S.C.A., Title 28, former § 780 (Survival of actions, suits, or proceedings, etc.). With the second sentence of this subdivision compare *Ex parte La Prade,* 1933, 53 S.Ct. 682, 289 U.S. 444, 77 L.Ed. 1311.

1948 Amendment

The amendment effective October 19, 1949, inserted the words, "the Canal Zone, a territory, an insular possession," in the first sentence of subdivision (d), and, in the same sentence, after the phrase "or other governmental agency," deleted the words, "or any other officer specified in the Act of February 13, 1925, c. 229, § 11 (43 Stat. 941), formerly section 780 of this title."

1961 Amendment

Subdivision (d)(1). Present Rule 25(d) is generally considered to be unsatisfactory. 4 Moore's *Federal Practice* ¶25.01[7] (2d ed. 1950); Wright, *Amendments to the Federal Rules: The Function of a Continuing Rules Committee,* 7 Vand.L.Rev. 521, 529 (1954); *Developments in the Law—Remedies Against the United States and Its Officials,* 70 Harv.L.Rev. 827, 931–34 (1957). To require, as a condition of substituting a successor public officer as a party to a pending action, that an application be made with a showing that there is substantial need for continuing the litigation, can rarely serve any useful purpose and fosters a burdensome formality. And to prescribe a short, fixed time period for substitution which cannot be extended even by agreement, see *Snyder v. Buck*, 340 U.S. 15, 19 (1950), with the penalty of dismissal of the action, "makes a trap for unsuspecting litigants which seems unworthy of a great government." *Vibra Brush Corp. v. Schaffer*, 256 F.2d 681, 684 (2d Cir. 1958). Although courts have on occasion found means of undercutting the rule, e.g. *Acheson v. Furusho*, 212 F.2d 284 (9th Cir.1954) (substitution of defendant officer unnecessary on theory that only a declaration of status was sought), it has operated harshly in many instances, e.g. *Snyder v. Buck*, supra; *Poindexter v. Folsom*, 242 F.2d 516 (3d Cir.1957).

Under the amendment, the successor is automatically substituted as a party without an application or showing of need to continue the action. An order of substitution is not required, but may be entered at any time if a party desires or the court thinks fit.

The general term "public officer" is used in preference to the enumeration which appears in the present rule. It comprises Federal, State, and local officers.

The expression "in his official capacity" is to be interpreted in its context as part of a simple procedural rule for substitution; care should be taken not to distort its meaning by mistaken analogies to the doctrine of sovereign immunity from suit or the Eleventh Amendment. The amended rule will apply to all actions brought by public officers for the government, and to any action brought in form against a named officer, but intrinsically against the government or the office or the incumbent thereof whoever he may be from time to time during the action. Thus the amended rule will apply to actions against officers to compel performance of official duties or to obtain judicial review of their orders. It will also apply to actions to prevent officers from acting in excess of their authority or under authority not validly conferred, cf. *Philadelphia Co. v. Stimson*, 223 U.S. 605 (1912), or from enforcing unconstitutional enactments, cf. *Ex parte Young*, 209 U.S. 123 (1908); *Ex parte La Prade*, 289 U.S. 444 (1933). In general it will apply whenever effective relief would call for corrective behavior by the one then having official status and power, rather than one who has lost that status and power through ceasing to hold office. Cf. *Land v. Dollar*, 330 U.S. 731 (1947); *Larson v. Domestic & Foreign Commerce Corp.*, 337 U.S. 682 (1949). Excluded from the operation of the amended rule will be the relatively infrequent actions which are directed to securing money judgments against the named officers enforceable against their personal assets; in these cases Rule 25(a)(1), not Rule 25(d), applies to the question of substitution. Examples are actions against officers seeking to make them pay damages out of their own pockets for defamatory utterances or other misconduct in some way related to the office, see *Barr v. Matteo*, 360 U.S. 564 (1959); *Howard v. Lyons*, 360 U.S. 593 (1959); *Gregoire v. Biddle*, 177 F.2d 579 (2d Cir.1949). cert. denied, 339 U.S. 949 (1950). Another example is the anomalous action for a tax refund against a collector of internal revenue, see *Ignelzi v. Granger*, 16 F.R.D. 517 (W.D.Pa.1955), 28 U.S.C. § 2006, 4 Moore, supra, ¶25.05, p. 531; but see 28 U.S.C. § 1346(a)(1), authorizing the bringing of such suits against the United States rather than the officer.

Automatic substitution under the amended rule, being merely a procedural device for substituting a successor for a past officeholder as a party, is distinct from and does not affect any substantive issues which may be involved in the action. Thus a defense of immunity from suit will remain in the case despite a substitution.

Where the successor does not intend to pursue the policy of his predecessor which gave rise to the lawsuit, it will be open to him, after substitution, as plaintiff to seek voluntary dismissal of the action, or as defendant to seek to have the action dismissed as moot or to take other appropriate steps to avert a judgment or decree. Contrast *Ex parte La Prade*, supra; *Allen v. Regents of the University System*, 304 U.S. 439 (1938); *McGrath v. National Assn. of Mfgrs.*, 344 U.S. 804 (1952); *Danenberg v. Cohen*, 213 F.2d 944 (7th Cir.1954).

As the present amendment of Rule 25(d)(1) eliminates a specified time period to secure substitution of public officers, the reference in Rule 6(b) (regarding enlargement of time) to Rule 25 will no longer apply to these public-officer substitutions.

As to substitution on appeal, the rules of the appellate courts should be consulted.

Subdivision (d)(2). This provision, applicable in "official capacity" cases as described above, will encourage the use of the official title without any mention of the officer individually, thereby recognizing the intrinsic character of the action and helping to eliminate concern with the problem of substitution. If for any reason it seems desirable to add the individual's name, this may be done upon motion or on the court's initiative; thereafter the procedure of amended Rule 25(d)(1) will apply if the individual named ceases to hold office.

For examples of naming the officer or title rather than the officeholder, see *Annot.*, 102 A.L.R. 943, 948–52; *Comment*, 50 Mich.L.Rev. 443, 450 (1952); cf. 26 U.S.C. § 7484. Where an action is brought by or against a board or agency with continuity of existence, it has been often decided that there is no need to name the individual members and substitution is unnecessary when the personnel changes. 4 Moore, supra, ¶25.09, p. 536. The practice encouraged by amended Rule 25(d)(2) is similar.

1963 Amendment

Present Rule 25(a)(1), together with present Rule 6(b), results in an inflexible requirement that an action be dismissed as to a deceased party if substitution is not carried out within a fixed period measured from the time of the death. The hardships and inequities of this unyielding requirement plainly appear from the cases. See, e.g., *Anderson v. Yungkau*, 329 U.S. 482, 67 S.Ct. 428, 91 L.Ed. 436 (1947); *Iovino v. Waterson*, 274 F.2d 41 (1959), cert. denied, *Carlin v. Sovino*, 362 U.S. 949, 80 S.Ct. 860, 4 L.Ed.2d 867 (1960); *Perry v. Allen*, 239 F.2d 107 (5th Cir.1956); *Starnes v. Pennsylvania R.R.*, 26 F.R.D. 625 (E.D.N.Y.), aff'd per curiam, 295 F.2d 704 (2d Cir.1961), cert. denied, 369 U.S. 813, 82 S.Ct. 688, 7 L.Ed.2d 612 (1962); *Zdanok v. Glidden Co.*, 28 F.R.D. 346 (S.D.N.Y.1961). See also 4 Moore's *Federal Practice* ¶25.01[9] (Supp.1960); 2 Barron & Holtzoff, *Federal Practice & Procedure* § 621, at 420–21 (Wright ed.1961).

The amended rule establishes a time limit for the motion to substitute based not upon the time of the death, but rather upon the time information of the death is provided by means of a suggestion of death upon the record, i.e. service of a statement of the fact of the death. Cf. Ill.Ann.Stat., c. 110, § 54(2) (Smith-Hurd 1956). The motion may not be made later than 90 days after the service of the statement unless the period is extended pursuant to Rule 6(b), as amended. See the Advisory Committee's Note to amended Rule 6(b). See also the new Official Form 30.

A motion to substitute may be made by any party or by the representative of the deceased party without awaiting the suggestion of death. Indeed, the motion will usually be so made. If a party or the representative of the deceased party desires to limit the time within which another may make the motion, he may do so by suggesting the death upon the record.

A motion to substitute made within the prescribed time will ordinarily be granted, but under the permissive language of the first sentence of the amended rule ("the court may order") it may be denied by the court in the exercise of a sound discretion if made long after the death—as can occur if the suggestion of death is not made or is delayed—and circumstances have arisen rendering it unfair to allow substitution. Cf. *Anderson v. Yungkau,* supra, 329 U.S. at 485, 486, 67 S.Ct. at 430, 431, 91 L.Ed. 436, where it was noted under the present rule that settlement and distribution of the estate of a deceased defendant might be so far advanced as to warrant denial of a motion for substitution even though made within the time limit prescribed by that rule. Accordingly, a party interested in securing substitution under the amended rule should not assume that he can rest indefinitely awaiting the suggestion of death before he makes his motion to substitute.

1987 Amendment

The amendments are technical. No substantive change is intended.

HISTORICAL NOTES

Effective Dates

1961 Amendment. Amendment adopted on Apr. 17, 1961, effective July 19, 1961, see rule 86(d).

V. DEPOSITIONS AND DISCOVERY

ADVISORY COMMITTEE'S EXPLANATORY STATEMENT CONCERNING 1970 AMENDMENTS TO DISCOVERY RULES

This statement is intended to serve as a general introduction to the amendments of Rules 26–37, concerning discovery, as well as related amendments of other rules. A separate note of customary scope is appended to amendments proposed for each rule. This statement provides a framework for the consideration of individual rule changes.

Changes in the Discovery Rules

The discovery rules, as adopted in 1938, were a striking and imaginative departure from tradition. It was expected from the outset that they would be important, but experience has shown them to play an even larger role than was initially foreseen. Although the discovery rules have been amended since 1938, the changes were relatively few and narrowly focused, made in order to remedy specific defects. The amendments now proposed reflect the first comprehensive review of the discovery rules undertaken since 1938. These amendments make substantial changes in the discovery rules. Those summarized here are among the more important changes.

Scope of Discovery. New provisions are made and existing provisions changed affecting the scope of discovery: (1) The contents of insurance policies are made discoverable (Rule 26(b)(2)). (2) A showing of good cause is no longer required for discovery of documents and things and entry upon land (Rule 34). However, a showing of need is required for discovery of "trial preparation" materials other than a party's discovery of his own statement and a witness' discovery of his own statement; and protection is afforded against disclosure in such documents of mental impressions, conclusions, opinions, or legal theories concerning the litigation. (Rule 26(b)(3)). (3) Provision is made for discovery with respect to experts retained for trial preparation, and particularly those experts who will be called to testify at trial (Rule 26(b)(4)). (4) It is provided that interrogatories and requests for admission are not objectionable simply because they relate to matters of opinion or contention, subject of course to the supervisory power of the court (Rules 33(b), 36(a)). (5) Medical examination is made available as to certain nonparties. (Rule 35(a)).

Mechanics of Discovery. A variety of changes are made in the mechanics of the discovery process, affecting the sequence and timing of discovery, the respective obligations of the parties with respect to requests, responses, and motions for court orders, and the related powers of the court to enforce discovery requests and to protect against their abusive use. A new provision eliminates the automatic grant of priority in discovery to one side (Rule 26(d)). Another provides that a party is not under a duty to supplement his responses to requests for discovery, except as specified (Rule 26(e)).

Other changes in the mechanics of discovery are designed to encourage extrajudicial discovery with a minimum of court intervention. Among these are the following: (1) The requirement that a plaintiff seek leave of court for early discovery requests is eliminated or reduced, and motions for a court order under Rule 34 are made unnecessary. Motions under Rule 35 are continued. (2) Answers and objections are to be served together and an enlargement of the time for response is provided. (3) The party seeking discovery, rather than the objecting party, is made responsible for invoking judicial determination of discovery disputes not resolved by the parties. (4) Judicial sanctions are tightened with respect to unjustified insistence upon or objection to discovery. These changes bring Rules 33, 34, and 36 substantially into line with the procedure now provided for depositions.

Failure to amend Rule 35 in the same way is based upon two considerations. First, the Columbia Survey (described below) finds that only about 5 percent of medical examinations require court motions, of which about half result in court orders. Second and of greater importance, the interest of the person to be examined in the privacy of his person was recently stressed by the Supreme Court in *Schlagenhauf v. Holder*, 379 U.S. 104 (1964). The court emphasized the trial judge's responsibility to assure that the medical examination was justified, particularly as to its scope.

Rearrangement of Rules. A limited rearrangement of the discovery rules has been made, whereby certain provisions are transferred from one rule to another. The reasons for this rearrangement are discussed below in a separate section of this statement and the details are set out in a table at the end of this statement.

Optional Procedures. In two instances, new optional procedures have been made available. A new procedure is provided to a party seeking to take the deposition of a corporation or other organization (Rule 30(b)(6)). A party on whom interrogatories have been served requesting information derivable from his business records may under specified circumstances produce the records rather than give answers (Rule 33(c)).

Other Changes. This summary of changes is by no means exhaustive. Various changes have been made in order to improve, tighten, or clarify particular provisions, to resolve conflicts in the case law, and to improve language. All changes, whether mentioned here or not, are discussed in the appropriate note for each rule.

A Field Survey of Discovery Practice

Despite widespread acceptance of discovery as an essential part of litigation, disputes have inevitably arisen concerning the values claimed for discovery and abuses alleged to exist. Many disputes about discovery relate to particular rule provisions or court decisions and can be studied in traditional fashion with a view to specific amendment. Since discovery is in large measure extra-judicial, however, even these disputes may be enlightened by a study of discovery "in the field." And some of the larger questions concerning discovery can be pursued only by a study of its operation at the law office level and in unreported cases.

The Committee, therefore, invited the Project for Effective Justice of Columbia Law School to conduct a field survey of discovery. Funds were obtained from the Ford Foundation and the Walter E. Meyer Research Institute of Law, Inc. The survey was carried on under the direction of Prof. Maurice Rosenberg of Columbia Law School. The Project for Effective Justice has submitted a report to the Committee entitled "Field Survey of Federal Pretrial Discovery" (hereafter referred to as the Columbia Survey). The Committee is deeply grateful for the benefit of this extensive undertaking and is most appreciative of the cooperation of the Project and the funding organizations. The Committee is particularly grateful to Professor Rosenberg who not only directed the survey but has given much time in order to assist the Committee in assessing the results.

The Columbia Survey concludes, in general, that there is no empirical evidence to warrant a fundamental change in the philosophy of the discovery rules. No widespread or profound failings are disclosed in the scope or availability of discovery. The costs of discovery do not appear to be oppressive, as a general matter, either in relation to ability to pay or to the stakes of the litigation. Discovery frequently provides evidence that would not otherwise be available to the parties and thereby makes for a fairer trial or settlement. On the other hand, no positive evidence is found that discovery promotes settlement.

More specific findings of the Columbia Survey are described in other Committee notes, in relation to particular rule provisions and amendments. Those interested in more detailed information may obtain it from the Project for Effective Justice.

Rearrangement of the Discovery Rules

The present discovery rules are structured entirely in terms of individual discovery devices, except for Rule 27 which deals with perpetuation of testimony, and Rule 37 which provides sanctions to enforce discovery. Thus, Rules 26 and 28 to 32 are in terms addressed only to the taking of a deposition of a party or third person. Rules 33 to 36 then deal in succession with four additional discovery devices: Written interrogatories to parties, production for inspection of documents and things, physical or mental examination and requests for admission.

Under the rules as promulgated in 1938, therefore, each of the discovery devices was separate and self-contained. A defect of this arrangement is that there is no natural location in the discovery rules for provisions generally applicable to all discovery or to several discovery devices. From 1938 until the present, a few amendments have applied a discovery provision to several rules. For example, in 1948, the scope of deposition discovery in Rule 26(b) and the provision for protective orders in Rule 30(b) were incorporated by reference in Rules 33 and 34. The arrangement was adequate so long as there were few provisions governing discovery generally and these provisions were relatively simple.

As will be seen, however, a series of amendments are now proposed which govern most or all of the discovery devices. Proposals of a similar nature will probably be made in the future. Under these circumstances, it is very desirable, even necessary, that the discovery rules contain one rule addressing itself to discovery generally.

Rule 26 is obviously the most appropriate rule for this purpose. One of its subdivisions, Rule 26(b), in terms governs only scope of deposition discovery, but it has been expressly incorporated by reference in Rules 33 and 34 and is treated by courts as setting a general standard. By means of a transfer to Rule 26 of the provisions for protective orders now contained in Rule 30(b), and a transfer from Rule 26 of provisions addressed exclusively to depositions, Rule 26 is converted into a rule concerned with discovery generally. It becomes a convenient vehicle for the inclusion of new provisions dealing with the scope, timing, and regulation of discovery. Few additional transfers are needed. See table showing rearrangement of rules, set out following this statement.

There are, to be sure, disadvantages in transferring any provision from one rule to another. Familiarity with the present pattern, reinforced by the references made by prior court decisions and the various secondary writings about the rules, is not lightly to be sacrificed. Revision of treatises and other reference works is burdensome and costly. Moreover, many States have adopted the existing pattern as a model for their rules.

On the other hand, the amendments now proposed will in any event require revision of texts and reference works as well as reconsideration by States following the Federal model. If these amendments are to be incorporated in an understandable way, a rule with general discovery provisions is needed. As will be seen, the proposed rearrangement produces a more coherent and intelligible pattern for the discovery rules taken as a whole. The difficulties described are those encountered whenever statutes are reexamined and revised. Failure to rearrange the discovery rules now would freeze the present scheme, making future change even more difficult.

Table Showing Rearrangement of Rules

Existing Rule No.	New Rule No.
26(a)	30(a), 31(a)
26(c)	30(c)
26(d)	32(a)
26(e)	32(b)
26(f)	32(c)
30(a)	30(b)
30(b)	26(c)
32	32(d)

Rule 26. General Provisions Governing Discovery; Duty of Disclosure

(a) Required Disclosures; Methods to Discover Additional Matter.

(1) Initial Disclosures. Except to the extent otherwise stipulated or directed by order or local rule, a party shall, without awaiting a discovery request, provide to other parties:

(A) the name and, if known, the address and telephone number of each individual likely to have discoverable information relevant to disputed facts alleged with particularity in the pleadings, identifying the subjects of the information;

(B) a copy of, or a description by category and location of, all documents, data compilations, and tangible things in the possession, custody, or control of the party that are relevant to disputed facts alleged with particularity in the pleadings;

(C) a computation of any category of damages claimed by the disclosing party, making available for inspection and copying as under Rule 34 the documents or other evidentiary material, not privileged or protected from disclosure, on which such computation is based, including materials bearing on the nature and extent of injuries suffered; and

(D) for inspection and copying as under Rule 34 any insurance agreement under which any person carrying on an insurance business may be liable to satisfy part or all of a judgment which may be entered in the action or to indemnify or reimburse for payments made to satisfy the judgment.

Unless otherwise stipulated or directed by the court, these disclosures shall be made at or within 10 days after the meeting of the parties under subdivision (f). A party shall make its initial disclosures based on the information then reasonably available to it and is not excused from making its disclosures because it has not fully completed its investigation of the case or because it challenges the sufficiency of another party's disclosures or because another party has not made its disclosures.

(2) Disclosure of Expert Testimony.

(A) In addition to the disclosures required by paragraph (1), a party shall disclose to other parties the identity of any person who may be used at trial to present evidence under Rules 702, 703, or 705 of the Federal Rules of Evidence.

(B) Except as otherwise stipulated or directed by the court, this disclosure shall, with respect to a witness who is retained or specially employed to provide expert testimony in the case or whose duties as an employee of the party regularly involve giving expert testimony, be accompanied by a written report prepared and signed by the witness. The report shall contain a complete statement of all opinions to be expressed and the basis and reasons therefor; the data or other information considered by the witness in forming the opinions; any exhibits to be used as a summary of or support for the opinions; the qualifications of the witness, including a list of all publications authored by the witness within the preceding ten years; the compensation to be paid for the study and testimony; and a listing of any other cases in which the witness has testified as an expert at trial or by deposition within the preceding four years.

(C) These disclosures shall be made at the times and in the sequence directed by the court. In the absence of other directions from the court or stipulation by the parties, the disclosures shall be made at least 90 days before the trial date or the date the case is to be ready for trial or, if the evidence is intended solely to contradict or rebut evidence on the same subject matter identified by another party under paragraph (2)(B), within 30 days after the disclosure made by the other party. The parties shall supplement these disclosures when required under subdivision (e)(1).

(3) Pretrial Disclosures. In addition to the disclosures required in the preceding paragraphs, a party shall provide to other parties the following information regarding the evidence that it may present at trial other than solely for impeachment purposes:

(A) the name and, if not previously provided, the address and telephone number of each witness, separately identifying those whom the party expects to present and those whom the party may call if the need arises;

(B) the designation of those witnesses whose testimony is expected to be presented by means of a deposition and, if not taken stenographically, a transcript of the pertinent portions of the deposition testimony; and

(C) an appropriate identification of each document or other exhibit, including summaries of other evidence, separately identifying those which the party expects to offer and those which the party may offer if the need arises.

Unless otherwise directed by the court, these disclosures shall be made at least 30 days before trial. Within 14 days thereafter, unless a different time is specified by the court, a party may serve and file a list disclosing (i) any objections to the use under Rule 32(a) of a deposition designated by another party under subparagraph (B) and (ii) any objection, together with the grounds therefor, that may be made to the admissibility of materials identified under subparagraph (C). Objections not so disclosed, other than objections under Rules 402 and 403 of the Federal Rules of Evidence, shall be deemed waived unless excused by the court for good cause shown.

(4) Form of Disclosures; Filing. Unless otherwise directed by order or local rule, all disclosures under paragraphs (1) through (3) shall be made in writing, signed, served, and promptly filed with the court.

(5) Methods to Discover Additional Matter. Parties may obtain discovery by one or more of the following methods: depositions upon oral examination or written questions; written interrogatories; production of documents or things or permission to enter upon land or other property under Rule 34 or 45(a)(1)(C), for inspection and other purposes; physical and mental examinations; and requests for admission.

(b) Discovery Scope and Limits. Unless otherwise limited by order of the court in accordance with these rules, the scope of discovery is as follows:

(1) In General. Parties may obtain discovery regarding any matter, not privileged, which is relevant to the subject matter involved in the pending action, whether it relates to the claim or defense of the party seeking discovery or to the claim or defense of any other party, including the existence, description, nature, custody, condition, and location of any books, documents, or other tangible things and the identity and location of persons having knowledge of any discoverable matter. The information sought need not be admissible at the trial if the information sought appears reasonably calculated to lead to the discovery of admissible evidence.

(2) Limitations. By order or by local rule, the court may alter the limits in these rules on the number of depositions and interrogatories and may also limit the length of depositions under Rule 30 and the number of requests under Rule 36. The frequency or extent of use of the discovery methods otherwise permitted under these rules and by any local rule shall be limited by the court if it determines that: (i) the discovery sought is unreasonably cumulative or duplicative, or is obtainable from some other source that is more convenient, less burdensome, or less expensive; (ii) the party seeking discovery has had ample opportunity by discovery in the action to obtain the information sought; or (iii) the burden or expense of the proposed discovery outweighs its likely benefit, taking into account the needs of the case, the amount in controversy, the parties' resources, the importance of the issues at stake in the litigation, and the importance of the proposed discovery in resolving the issues. The court may act upon its own initiative after reasonable notice or pursuant to a motion under subdivision (c).

(3) Trial Preparation: Materials. Subject to the provisions of subdivision (b)(4) of this rule, a party may obtain discovery of documents and tangible things otherwise discoverable under subdivision (b)(1) of this rule and prepared in anticipation of litigation or for trial by or for another party or by or for that other party's representative (including the other party's attorney, consultant, surety, indemnitor, insurer, or agent) only upon a showing that the party seeking discovery has substantial need of the materials in the preparation of the party's case and that the party is unable without undue hardship to obtain the substantial equivalent of the materials by other means. In ordering discovery of such materials when the required showing has been made, the court shall protect against disclosure of the mental impressions, conclusions, opinions, or legal theories of an attorney or other representative of a party concerning the litigation.

A party may obtain without the required showing a statement concerning the action or its subject matter previously made by that party. Upon request, a person not a party may obtain without the required showing a statement concerning the action or its subject matter previously made by that person. If the request is refused, the person may move for a court order. The provisions of Rule 37(a)(4) apply to the award of expenses incurred in relation to the motion. For purposes of this paragraph, a statement previously made is (A) a written statement signed or otherwise adopted or approved by the person making it, or (B) a stenographic, mechanical, electrical, or other recording, or a transcription thereof, which is a substantially verbatim recital of an oral statement by the person making it and contemporaneously recorded.

(4) Trial Preparation: Experts.

(A) A party may depose any person who has been identified as an expert whose opinions may be presented at trial. If a report from the expert is required under subdivision (a)(2)(B), the deposition shall not be conducted until after the report is provided.

(B) A party may, through interrogatories or by deposition, discover facts known or opinions held by an expert who has been retained or specially employed by another party in anticipation of litigation or preparation for trial and who is not expected to be called as a witness at trial, only as provided in Rule 35(b) or upon a showing of exceptional circumstances under which it is impracticable for the party seeking discovery to obtain facts or opinions on the same subject by other means.

(C) Unless manifest injustice would result, (i) the court shall require that the party seeking discovery pay the expert a reasonable fee for time spent in responding to discovery under this subdivision; and (ii) with respect to discovery obtained under subdivision (b)(4)(B) of this rule the court shall require the party seeking discovery to pay the other party a fair portion of the fees and expenses reasonably incurred by the latter party in obtaining facts and opinions from the expert.

(5) Claims of Privilege or Protection of Trial Preparation Materials. When a party withholds information otherwise discoverable under these rules by claiming that it is privileged or subject to protection as trial preparation material, the party shall make the claim expressly and shall describe the nature of the documents, communications, or things not produced or disclosed in a manner that, without revealing information itself privileged or protected, will enable other parties to assess the applicability of the privilege or protection.

(c) Protective Orders. Upon motion by a party or by the person from whom discovery is sought, accompanied by a certification that the movant has in good faith conferred or attempted to confer with other affected parties in an effort to resolve the dispute without court action, and for good cause shown, the court in which the action is pending or alternatively, on matters relating to a deposition, the court in the district where the deposition is to be taken may make any order which justice requires to protect a party or person from annoyance, embarrassment, oppression, or undue burden or expense, including one or more of the following:

(1) that the disclosure or discovery not be had;

(2) that the disclosure or discovery may be had only on specified terms and conditions, including a designation of the time or place;

(3) that the discovery may be had only by a method of discovery other than that selected by the party seeking discovery;

(4) that certain matters not be inquired into, or that the scope of the disclosure or discovery be limited to certain matters;

(5) that discovery be conducted with no one present except persons designated by the court;

(6) that a deposition, after being sealed, be opened only by order of the court;

(7) that a trade secret or other confidential research, development, or commercial information not be revealed or be revealed only in a designated way; and

(8) that the parties simultaneously file specified documents or information enclosed in sealed envelopes to be opened as directed by the court.

If the motion for a protective order is denied in whole or in part, the court may, on such terms and conditions as are just, order that any party or other person provide or permit discovery. The provisions of Rule 37(a)(4) apply to the award of expenses incurred in relation to the motion.

(d) Timing and Sequence of Discovery. Except when authorized under these rules or by local rule, order, or agreement of the parties, a party may not seek discovery from any source before the parties have met and conferred as required by subdivision (f). Unless the court upon motion, for the convenience of parties and witnesses and in the interests of justice, orders otherwise, methods of discovery may be used in any sequence, and the fact that a party is conducting discovery, whether by deposition or otherwise, shall not operate to delay any other party's discovery.

(e) Supplementation of Disclosures and Responses. A party who has made a disclosure under subdivision (a) or responded to a request for discovery with a disclosure or response is under a duty to supplement or correct the disclosure or response to include information thereafter acquired if ordered by the court or in the following circumstances:

(1) A party is under a duty to supplement at appropriate intervals its disclosures under subdivision (a) if the party learns that in some material respect the information disclosed is incomplete or incorrect and if the additional or corrective information has not otherwise been made known to the other parties during the discovery process or in writing. With respect to testimony of an expert from whom a report is required under subdivision (a)(2)(B) the duty extends both to information contained in the report and to information provided through a deposition of the expert, and any additions or other changes to this information shall be disclosed by the time the party's disclosures under Rule 26(a)(3) are due.

(2) A party is under a duty seasonably to amend a prior response to an interrogatory, request for

production, or request for admission if the party learns that the response is in some material respect incomplete or incorrect and if the additional or corrective information has not otherwise been made known to the other parties during the discovery process or in writing.

(f) Meeting of Parties; Planning for Discovery. Except in actions exempted by local rule or when otherwise ordered, the parties shall, as soon as practicable and in any event at least 14 days before a scheduling conference is held or a scheduling order is due under Rule 16(b), meet to discuss the nature and basis of their claims and defenses and the possibilities for a prompt settlement or resolution of the case, to make or arrange for the disclosures required by subdivision (a)(1), and to develop a proposed discovery plan. The plan shall indicate the parties' views and proposals concerning:

(1) what changes should be made in the timing, form, or requirement for disclosures under subdivision (a) or local rule, including a statement as to when disclosures under subdivision (a)(1) were made or will be made;

(2) the subjects on which discovery may be needed, when discovery should be completed, and whether discovery should be conducted in phases or be limited to or focused upon particular issues;

(3) what changes should be made in the limitations on discovery imposed under these rules or by local rule, and what other limitations should be imposed; and

(4) any other orders that should be entered by the court under subdivision (c) or under Rule 16(b) and (c).

The attorneys of record and all unrepresented parties that have appeared in the case are jointly responsible for arranging and being present or represented at the meeting, for attempting in good faith to agree on the proposed discovery plan, and for submitting to the court within 10 days after the meeting a written report outlining the plan.

(g) Signing of Disclosures, Discovery Requests, Responses, and Objections.

(1) Every disclosure made pursuant to subdivision (a)(1) or subdivision (a)(3) shall be signed by at least one attorney of record in the attorney's individual name, whose address shall be stated. An unrepresented party shall sign the disclosure and state the party's address. The signature of the attorney or party constitutes a certification that to the best of the signer's knowledge, information, and belief, formed after a reasonable inquiry, the disclosure is complete and correct as of the time it is made.

(2) Every discovery request, response, or objection made by a party represented by an attorney shall be signed by at least one attorney of record in the attorney's individual name, whose address shall be stated. An unrepresented party shall sign the request, response, or objection and state the party's address. The signature of the attorney or party constitutes a certification that to the best of the signer's knowledge, information, and belief, formed after a reasonable inquiry, the request, response, or objection is:

(A) consistent with these rules and warranted by existing law or a good faith argument for the extension, modification, or reversal of existing law;

(B) not interposed for any improper purpose, such as to harass or to cause unnecessary delay or needless increase in the cost of litigation; and

(C) not unreasonable or unduly burdensome or expensive, given the needs of the case, the discovery already had in the case, the amount in controversy, and the importance of the issues at stake in the litigation.

If a request, response, or objection is not signed, it shall be stricken unless it is signed promptly after the omission is called to the attention of the party making the request, response, or objection, and a party shall not be obligated to take any action with respect to it until it is signed.

(3) If without substantial justification a certification is made in violation of the rule, the court, upon motion or upon its own initiative, shall impose upon the person who made the certification, the party on whose behalf the disclosure, request, response, or objection is made, or both, an appropriate sanction, which may include an order to pay the amount of the reasonable expenses incurred because of the violation, including a reasonable attorney's fee.

(As amended Dec. 27, 1946, eff. Mar. 19, 1948; Jan. 21, 1963, eff. July 1, 1963; Feb. 28, 1966, eff. July 1, 1966; Mar. 30, 1970, eff. July 1, 1970; Apr. 29, 1980, eff. Aug. 1, 1980; Apr. 28, 1983, eff. Aug. 1, 1983; Mar. 2, 1987, eff. Aug. 1, 1987; Apr. 22, 1993, eff. Dec. 1, 1993.)

ADVISORY COMMITTEE NOTES

1937 Adoption

Note to Subdivision (a). This rule freely authorizes the taking of depositions under the same circumstances and by the same methods whether for the purpose of discovery or for the purpose of obtaining evidence. Many states have adopted this practice on account of its simplicity and effectiveness, safeguarding it by imposing such restrictions upon the subsequent use of the deposition at the trial or hearing as are deemed advisable. See Ark.Civ.Code (Crawford, 1934) §§ 606 to 607; Calif.Code Civ.Proc. (Deering, 1937) § 2021; 1 Colo.Stat.Ann. (1935) Code Civ.Proc. § 376; Idaho Code Ann. (1932) § 16–906; Ill.Rules of Pract.Rule 19 (Smith-Hurd Ill.Stats. c. 110, § 259.19); Smith-Hurd Ill.Stats. c. 51, § 24; 2 Ind.Stat.Ann. (Burns, 1933) §§ 2–1501, 2–1506; Ky.

Codes (Carroll, 1932) Civ.Pract. § 557; 1 Mo.Rev.Stat. (1929) § 1753; 4 Mont.Rev.Codes Ann. (1935) § 10645; Neb.Comp. Stat. (1929) ch. 20, §§ 1246–7; 4 Nev.Comp.Laws (Hillyer, 1929) § 9001; 2 N.H.Pub.Laws (1926) ch. 337, § 1; N.C.Code Ann. (1935) § 1809; 2 N.D.Comp.Laws Ann. (1913) §§ 7889 to 7897; 2 Ohio Gen.Code Ann. (Page, 1926) §§ 11525–6; 1 Ore.Code Ann. (1930) Tit. 9, § 1503; 1 S.D.Comp.Laws (1929) §§ 2713–16; Vernon's Ann.Civ.Stats. Tex. arts. 3738, 3752, 3769; Utah Rev.Stat.Ann. (1933) § 104–51–7; Wash.Rules of Practice adopted by the Supreme Ct., Rule 8, 2 Wash.Rev.Stat.Ann. (Remington, 1932) § 308–8; W.Va.Code (1931) ch. 57, art. 4, § 1. Compare [former] Equity Rules 47 (Depositions—To be Taken in Exceptional Instances); 54 (Depositions Under Revised Statutes, §§ 863, 865, 866, 867—Cross Examination); 58 (Discovery—Interrogatories—Inspection and Production of Documents—Admission of Execution or Genuineness).

This and subsequent rules incorporate, modify, and broaden the provisions for depositions under U.S.C., Title 28, [former] §§ 639 (Depositions *de bene esse;* when and where taken; notice), 640 (Same; mode of taking), 641 (Same; transmission to court), 644 (Depositions under *dedimus potestatem* and *in perpetuam*), 646 (Deposition under *dedimus potestatem*; how taken). These statutes are superseded in so far as they differ from this and subsequent rules. U.S.C. Title 28, [former] § 643 (Depositions; taken in mode prescribed by State laws) is superseded by the third sentence of Subdivision (a).

While a number of states permit discovery only from parties or their agents, others either make no distinction between parties or agents of parties and ordinary witnesses, or authorize the taking of ordinary depositions, without restriction, from any persons who have knowledge of relevant facts. See Ark.Civ.Code (Crawford, 1934) §§ 606 to 607; 1 Idaho Code Ann. (1932) § 16–906; Ill.Rules of Pract., Rule 19 (Smith-Hurd Ill.Stats. c. 110, § 259.19); Smith-Hurd Ill.Stats. c. 51, § 24; 2 Ind.Stat.Ann. (Burns, 1933) § 2–1501; Ky.Codes (Carroll, 1932) Civ.Pract. §§ 554 to 558; 2 Md. Ann.Code (Bagby, 1924) Art. 35, § 21; 2 Minn.Stat. (Mason, 1927) § 9820; Mo.St.Ann. §§ 1753, 1759, pp. 4023, 4026; Neb.Comp.Stat. (1929) ch. 20, §§ 1246–7; 2 N.H.Pub.Laws (1926) ch. 337, § 1; 2 N.D.Comp.Laws Ann. (1913) § 7897; 2 Ohio Gen.Code Ann. (Page, 1926) §§ 11525–6; 1 S.D.Comp. Laws (1929) §§ 2713–16; Vernon's Ann.Civil Stats.Tex. arts. 3738, 3752, 3769; Utah Rev.Stat.Ann. (1933) § 104–51–7; Wash.Rules of Practice adopted by Supreme Ct., Rule 8, 2 Wash.Rev.Stat.Ann. (Remington, 1932) § 308–8; W.Va.Code (1931) ch. 57, art. 4, § 1.

The more common practice in the United States is to take depositions on notice by the party desiring them, without any order from the court, and this has been followed in these rules. See Calif.Code Civ.Proc. (Deering, 1937) § 2031; 2 Fla.Comp.Gen.Laws Ann. (1927) §§ 4405–7; 1 Idaho Code Ann. (1932) § 16–902; Ill.Rules of Pract., Rule 19 (Smith-Hurd Ill.Stats. c. 110, § 259.19); Smith-Hurd Ill.Stats. c. 51, § 24; 2 Ind.Stat.Ann. (Burns, 1933) § 2–1502; Kan.Gen.Stat. Ann. (1935) § 60–2827; Ky.Codes (Carroll, 1932) Civ.Pract. § 565; 2 Minn.Stat. (Mason, 1927) § 9820; Mo.St.Ann. § 1761, p. 4029; 4 Mont.Rev.Codes Ann. (1935) § 10651; Nev.Comp.Laws (Hillyer, 1929) § 9002; N.C.Code Ann. (1935) § 1809; 2 N.D.Comp.Laws Ann. (1913) § 7895; Utah Rev.Stat.Ann. (1933) § 104–51–8.

Note to Subdivision (b). While the old chancery practice limited discovery to facts supporting the case of the party seeking it, this limitation has been largely abandoned by modern legislation. See Ala.Code Ann. (Michie, 1928) §§ 7764 to 7773; 2 Ind.Stat.Ann. (Burns, 1933) §§ 2–1028, 2–1506, 2–1728–2–1732; Iowa Code (1935) § 11185; Ky. Codes (Carroll, 1932) Civ.Pract. §§ 557, 606(8); La.Code Pract. (Dart, 1932) arts. 347–356; 2 Mass.Gen.Laws (Ter.Ed., 1932) ch. 231, §§ 61 to 67; Mo.St.Ann. §§ 1753, 1759, pp. 4023, 4026; Neb.Comp.Stat. (1929) §§ 20–1246, 20–1247; 2 N.H.Pub.Laws (1926) ch. 337, § 1; 2 Ohio Gen.Code Ann. (Page, 1926) §§ 11497, 11526; Vernon's Ann.Civ.Stats.Tex. arts. 3738, 3753, 3769; Wis.Stat. (1935) § 326.12; Ontario Consol.Rules of Pract. (1928) Rules 237–347; Quebec Code of Civ.Proc. (Curran, 1922) §§ 286 to 290.

Note to Subdivisions (d), (e), and (f). The restrictions here placed upon the use of depositions at the trial or hearing are substantially the same as those provided in U.S.C., Title 28, [former] § 641, for depositions taken, *de bene esse,* with the additional provision that any deposition may be used when the court finds the existence of exceptional circumstances. Compare English Rules Under the Judicature Act (The Annual Practice, 1937) O. 37, r. 18 (with additional provision permitting use of deposition by consent of the parties). See also [former] Equity Rule 64 (Former Depositions, Etc. May be Used Before Master); and 2 Minn. Stat. (Mason, 1927) § 9835 (Use in a subsequent action of a deposition filed in a previously dismissed action between the same parties and involving the same subject matter).

1946 Amendment

Note. Subdivision (a). The amendment eliminates the requirement of leave of court for the taking of a deposition except where a plaintiff seeks to take a deposition within 20 days after the commencement of the action. The retention of the requirement where a deposition is sought by a plaintiff within 20 days of the commencement of the action protects a defendant who has not had an opportunity to retain counsel and inform himself as to the nature of the suit; the plaintiff, of course, needs no such protection. The present rule forbids the plaintiff to take a deposition, without leave of court, before the answer is served. Sometimes the defendant delays the serving of an answer for more than 20 days, but as 20 days are sufficient time for him to obtain a lawyer, there is no reason to forbid the plaintiff to take a deposition without leave merely because the answer has not been served. In all cases, Rule 30(a) empowers the court, for cause shown, to alter the time of the taking of a deposition, and Rule 30(b) contains provisions giving ample protection to persons who are unreasonably pressed. The modified practice here adopted is along the line of that followed in various states. See e.g., 8 Mo.Rev.Stat.Ann.1939, § 1917; 2 Burns' Ind.Stat.Ann.1933, § 2–1506.

Subdivision (b). The amendments to subdivision (b) make clear the broad scope of examination and that it may cover not only evidence for use at the trial but also inquiry into matters in themselves inadmissible as evidence but which will lead to the discovery of such evidence. The purpose of discovery is to allow a broad search for facts, the names of witnesses, or any other matters which may aid a party in the preparation or presentation of his case. *Engl v. Aetna Life Ins. Co.*, C.C.A.2, 1943, 139 F.2d 469; *Mahler v. Pennsylvania R. Co.*, E.D.N.Y.1945, 8 Fed.Rules Serv.

33.351, Case 1. In such a preliminary inquiry admissibility at trial should not be the test as to whether the information sought is within the scope of proper examination. Such a standard unnecessarily curtails the utility of discovery practice. Of course, matters entirely without bearing either as direct evidence or as leads to evidence are not within the scope of inquiry, but to the extent that the examination develops useful information, it functions successfully as an instrument of discovery, even if it produces no testimony directly admissible. *Lewis v. United Air Lines Transportation Corp.*, D.Conn.1939, 27 F.Supp. 946; *Engl v. Aetna Life Ins. Co.*, supra; *Mahler v. Pennsylvania R. Co.*, supra; *Bloomer v. Sirian Lamp Co.*, D.Del.1944, 8 Fed.Rules Serv. 26b.31, Case 3; *Rosseau v. Langley*, N.Y.1945, 9 Fed.Rules Serv. 34.41, Case 1 (Rule 26 contemplates "examinations not merely for the narrow purpose of adducing testimony which may be offered in evidence but also for the broad discovery of information which may be useful in preparation for trial."); *Olson Transportation Co. v. Socony-Vacuum Co.*, E.D.Wis. 1944, 8 Fed.Rules Serv. 34.41, Case 2 (". . . the Rules . . . permit 'fishing' for evidence as they should."); Note, 1945, 45 Col.L.Rev. 482. Thus hearsay, while inadmissible itself, may suggest testimony which properly may be proved. Under Rule 26(b) several cases, however, have erroneously limited discovery on the basis of admissibility, holding that the word "relevant" in effect meant "material and competent under the rules of evidence". *Poppino v. Jones Store Co.*, W.D.Mo.1940, 1 F.R.D. 215, 3 Fed.Rules Serv. 26b.5, Case 1; *Benevento v. A. & P. Food Stores, Inc.*, E.D.N.Y.1939, 26 F.Supp. 424. Thus it has been said that inquiry might not be made into statements or other matters which, when disclosed, amounted only to hearsay. *See Maryland for use of Montvila v. Pan-American Bus Lines, Inc.*, D.Md.1940, 1 F.R.D. 213, 3 Fed.Rules Serv. 26b.211, Case 3; *Gitto v. "Italia," Societa Anonima Di Navigazione*, E.D.N.Y.1940, 31 F.Supp. 567; *Rose Silk Mills, Inc. v. Insurance Co. of North America*, S.D.N.Y.1939, 29 F.Supp. 504; *Colpak v. Hetterick*, E.D.N.Y.1941, 40 F.Supp. 350; *Matthies v. Peter F. Connolly Co.*, E.D.N.Y.1941, 6 Fed.Rules Serv. 30a.22, Case 1, 2 F.R.D. 277; *Matter of Examination of Citizens Casualty Co. of New York*, S.D.N.Y.1942, 3 F.R.D. 171, 7 Fed.Rules Serv. 26b.211, Case 1; *United States v. Silliman*, D.C.N.J.1944, 8 Fed.Rules Serv. 26b.52, Case 1. The contrary and better view, however, has often been stated. See, e.g., *Engl v. Aetna Life Ins. Co.*, supra; *Stevenson v. Melady*, S.D.N.Y. 1940, 3 Fed.Rules Serv. 26b.31, Case 1, 1 F.R.D. 329; *Lewis v. United Air Lines Transport Corp.*, supra; *Application of Zenith Radio Corp.*, E.D.Pa.1941, 4 Fed.Rules Serv. 30b.21, Case 1, 1 F.R.D. 627; *Steingut v. Guaranty Trust Co. of New York*, S.D.N.Y.1941, 1 F.R.D. 723, 4 Fed.Rules Serv. 26b.5, Case 2; *DeSeversky v. Republic Aviation Corp.*, E.D.N.Y.1941, 2 F.R.D. 183, 5 Fed.Rules Serv. 26b.31, Case 5; *Moore v. George A. Hormel & Co.*, S.D.N.Y.1942, 6 Fed.Rules Serv. 30b.41, Case 1, 2 F.R.D. 340; *Hercules Powder Co. v. Rohm & Haas Co.*, D.Del.1943, 7 Fed.Rules Serv. 45b.311, Case 2, 3 F.R.D. 302; *Bloomer v. Sirian Lamp Co.*, supra; *Crosby Steam Gage & Valve Co. v. Manning, Maxwell & Moore, Inc.*, D.Mass.1944, 8 Fed.Rules Serv. 26b.31, Case 1; *Patterson Oil Terminals, Inc. v. Charles Kurz & Co., Inc.*, E.D.Pa.1945, 9 Fed.Rules Serv. 33.321, Case 2; *Pueblo Trading Co. v. Reclamation Dist. No. 1500*, N.D.Cal.1945, 9 Fed.Rules Serv. 33.321, Case 4, 4 F.R.D. 471. See also discussion as to the broad scope of discovery in *Hoffman v. Palmer*, C.C.A.2, 1942, 129 F.2d 976, 995–997, affirmed 63 S.Ct. 477, 318 U.S. 109, 87 L.Ed. 645; Note, 1945, 45 Col.L.Rev. 482.

1963 Amendment

This amendment conforms to the amendment of Rule 28(b). See the next-to-last paragraph of the Advisory Committee's Note to that amendment.

1966 Amendment

The requirement that the plaintiff obtain leave of court in order to serve notice of taking of a deposition within 20 days after commencement of the action gives rise to difficulties when the prospective deponent is about to become unavailable for examination. The problem is not confined to admiralty, but has been of special concern in that context because of the mobility of vessels and their personnel. When Rule 26 was adopted as Admiralty Rule 30A in 1961, the problem was alleviated by permitting depositions *de bene esse*, for which leave of court is not required. See Advisory Committee's Note to Admiralty Rule 30A (1961).

A continuing study is being made in the effort to devise a modification of the 20-day rule appropriate to both the civil and admiralty practice to the end that Rule 26(a) shall state a uniform rule applicable alike to what are now civil actions and suits in admiralty. Meanwhile, the exigencies of maritime litigation require preservation, for the time being at least, of the traditional *de bene esse* procedure for the post-unification counterpart of the present suit in admiralty. Accordingly, the amendment provides for continued availability of that procedure in admiralty and maritime claims within the meaning of Rule 9(h).

1970 Amendment

A limited rearrangement of the discovery rules is made, whereby certain rule provisions are transferred, as follows: Existing Rule 26(a) is transferred to Rules 30(a) and 31(a). Existing Rule 26(c) is transferred to Rule 30(c). Existing Rules 26(d), (e), and (f) are transferred to Rule 32. Revisions of the transferred provisions, if any, are discussed in the notes appended to Rules 30, 31, and 32. In addition, Rule 30(b) is transferred to Rule 26(c). The purpose of this rearrangement is to establish Rule 26 as a rule governing discovery in general. (The reasons are set out in the Advisory Committee's explanatory statement.)

Subdivision (a)—Discovery Devices. This is a new subdivision listing all of the discovery devices provided in the discovery rules and establishing the relationship between the general provisions of Rule 26 and the specific rules for particular discovery devices. The provision that the frequency of use of these methods is not limited confirms existing law. It incorporates in general form a provision now found in Rule 33.

Subdivision (b)—Scope of Discovery. This subdivision is recast to cover the scope of discovery generally. It regulates the discovery obtainable through any of the discovery devices listed in Rule 26(a).

All provisions as to scope of discovery are subject to the initial qualification that the court may limit discovery in accordance with these rules. Rule 26(c) (transferred from 30(b)) confers broad powers on the courts to regulate or prevent discovery even though the materials sought are within the scope of 26(b), and these powers have always been freely exercised. For example, a party's income tax return is generally held not privileged, 2A Barron & Holtzoff, *Federal Practice and Procedure,* § 651.2 (Wright ed. 1961), and yet courts have recognized that interests in privacy may call for a measure of extra protection. E.g., *Wiesenberger v. W. E. Hutton & Co.,* 35 F.R.D. 556 (S.D.N.Y.1964). Similarly, the courts have in appropriate circumstances protected materials that are primarily of an impeaching character. These two types of materials merely illustrate the many situations, not capable of governance by precise rule, in which courts must exercise judgment. The new subsections in Rule 26(b) do not change existing law with respect to such situations.

Subdivision (b)(1)—In General. The language is changed to provide for the scope of discovery in general terms. The existing subdivision, although in terms applicable only to depositions, is incorporated by reference in existing Rules 33 and 34. Since decisions as to relevance to the subject matter of the action are made for discovery purposes well in advance of trial, a flexible treatment of relevance is required and the making of discovery, whether voluntary or under court order, is not a concession or determination of relevance for purposes of trial. *Cf.* 4 *Moore's Federal Practice* ¶26–16[1] (2d ed. 1966).

Subdivision (b)(2)—Insurance Policies. Both the cases and commentators are sharply in conflict on the question whether defendant's liability insurance coverage is subject to discovery in the usual situation when the insurance coverage is not itself admissible and does not bear on another issue in the case. Examples of Federal cases requiring disclosure and supporting comments: *Cook v. Welty,* 253 F.Supp. 875 (D.D.C.1966) (cases cited); *Johanek v. Aberle,* 27 F.R.D. 272 (D.Mont.1961); Williams, *Discovery of Dollar Limits in Liability Policies in Automobile Tort Cases,* 10 Ala.L.Rev. 355 (1958); Thode, *Some Reflections on the 1957 Amendments to the Texas Rules,* 37 Tex.L.Rev. 33, 40–42 (1958). Examples of Federal cases refusing disclosure and supporting comments: *Bisserier v. Manning,* 207 F.Supp. 476 (D.N.J.1962); *Cooper v. Stender,* 30 F.R.D. 389 (E.D.Tenn.1962); Frank, *Discovery and Insurance, Coverage,* 1959 Ins.L.J. 281; Fournier, *Pre-trial Discovery of Insurance Coverage and Limits,* 28 Ford.L.Rev. 215 (1959).

The division in reported cases is close. State decisions based on provisions similar to the federal rules are similarly divided. See cases collected in 2A Barron & Holtzoff, *Federal Practice and Procedure* § 647.1, nn. 45.5, 45.6 (Wright ed. 1961). It appears to be difficult if not impossible to obtain appellate review of the issue. Resolution by rule amendment is indicated. The question is essentially procedural in that it bears upon preparation for trial and settlement before trial, and courts confronting the question, however they have decided it, have generally treated it as procedural and governed by the rules.

The amendment resolves this issue in favor of disclosure. Most of the decisions denying discovery, some explicitly, reason from the text of Rule 26(b) that it permits discovery only of matters which will be admissible in evidence or appear reasonably calculated to lead to such evidence; they avoid considerations of policy, regarding them as foreclosed. See *Bisserier v. Manning, supra.* Some note also that facts about a defendant's financial status are not discoverable as such, prior to judgment with execution unsatisfied, and fear that, if courts hold insurance coverage discoverable, they must extend the principle to other aspects of the defendant's financial status. The cases favoring disclosure rely heavily on the practical significance of insurance in the decisions lawyers make about settlement and trial preparation. In *Clauss v. Danker,* 264 F.Supp. 246 (S.D.N.Y.1967), the court held that the rules forbid disclosure but called for an amendment to permit it.

Disclosure of insurance coverage will enable counsel for both sides to make the same realistic appraisal of the case, so that settlement and litigation strategy are based on knowledge and not speculation. It will conduce to settlement and avoid protracted litigation in some cases, though in others it may have an opposite effect. The amendment is limited to insurance coverage, which should be distinguished from any other facts concerning defendant's financial status (1) because insurance is an asset created specifically to satisfy the claim; (2) because the insurance company ordinarily controls the litigation; (3) because information about coverage is available only from defendant or his insurer; and (4) because disclosure does not involve a significant invasion of privacy.

Disclosure is required when the insurer "may be liable" on part or all of the judgment. Thus, an insurance company must disclose even when it contests liability under the policy, and such disclosure does not constitute a waiver of its claim. It is immaterial whether the liability is to satisfy the judgment directly or merely to indemnify or reimburse another after he pays the judgment.

The provision applies only to persons "carrying on an insurance business" and thus covers insurance companies and not the ordinary business concern that enters into a contract of indemnification. *Cf.* N.Y.Ins.Law § 41. Thus, the provision makes no change in existing law on discovery of indemnity agreements other than insurance agreements by persons carrying on an insurance business. Similarly, the provision does not cover the business concern that creates a reserve fund for purposes of self-insurance.

For some purposes other than discovery, an application for insurance is treated as a part of the insurance agreement. The provision makes clear that, for discovery purposes, the application is not to be so treated. The insurance application may contain personal and financial information concerning the insured, discovery of which is beyond the purpose of this provision.

In no instance does disclosure make the facts concerning insurance coverage admissible in evidence.

Subdivision (b)(3)—Trial Preparation: Materials. Some of the most controversial and vexing problems to emerge from the discovery rules have arisen out of requests for the production of documents or things prepared in anticipation of litigation or for trial. The existing rules make no explicit provision for such materials. Yet, two verbally distinct doctrines have developed, each conferring a qualified immunity on these materials—the "good cause" requirement in Rule 34 (now generally held applicable to discovery of documents via deposition under Rule 45 and interrogatories under Rule 33) and the work-product doctrine of *Hickman v. Taylor,* 329 U.S. 495 (1947). Both demand a showing of justification before production can be had, the one of "good cause" and the other variously described in the *Hickman* case: "necessity or justification," "denial * * * would unduly prejudice the preparation of petitioner's case," or "cause hardship or injustice" 329 U.S. at 509–510.

In deciding the *Hickman* case, the Supreme Court appears to have expressed a preference in 1947 for an approach to the problem of trial preparation materials by judicial decision rather than by rule. Sufficient experience has accumulated, however, with lower court applications of the *Hickman* decision to warrant a reappraisal.

The major difficulties visible in the existing case law are (1) confusion and disagreement as to whether "good cause" is made out by a showing of relevance and lack of privilege, or requires an additional showing of necessity, (2) confusion and disagreement as to the scope of the *Hickman* work-product doctrine, particularly whether it extends beyond work actually performed by lawyers, and (3) the resulting difficulty of relating the "good cause" required by Rule 34 and the "necessity or justification" of the work-product doctrine, so that their respective roles and the distinctions between them are understood.

Basic Standard.—Since Rule 34 in terms requires a showing of "good cause" for the production of all documents and things, whether or not trial preparation is involved, courts have felt that a single formula is called for and have differed over whether a showing of relevance and lack of privilege is enough or whether more must be shown. When the facts of the cases are studied, however, a distinction emerges based upon the type of materials. With respect to documents not obtained or prepared with an eye to litigation, the decisions, while not uniform, reflect a strong and increasing tendency to relate "good cause" to a showing that the documents are relevant to the subject matter of the action. *E.g., Connecticut Mutual Life Ins. Co. v. Shields,* 17 F.R.D. 273 (S.D.N.Y. 1959), with cases cited; *Houdry Process Corp. v. Commonwealth Oil Refining Co.,* 24 F.R.D. 58 (S.D.N.Y.1955); see *Bell v. Commercial Ins. Co.,* 280 F.2d 514, 517 (3d Cir. 1960). When the party whose documents are sought shows that the request for production is unduly burdensome or oppressive, courts have denied discovery for lack of "good cause", although they might just as easily have based their decision on the protective provisions of existing Rule 30(b) (new Rule 26(c)). *E.g., Lauer v. Tankrederi,* 39 F.R.D. 334 (E.D.Pa. 1966).

As to trial-preparation materials, however, the courts are increasingly interpreting "good cause" as requiring more than relevance. When lawyers have prepared or obtained the materials for trial, all courts require more than relevance; so much is clearly commanded by *Hickman.* But even as to the preparatory work of nonlawyers, while some courts ignore work-product and equate "good cause" with relevance, *e.g., Brown v. New York, N.H. & H.R.R.,* 17 F.R.D. 324 (S.D.N.Y.1955), the more recent trend is to read "good cause" as requiring inquiry into the importance of and need for the materials as well as into alternative sources for securing the same information. In *Guilford Nat'l Bank v. Southern Ry.,* 297 F.2d 921 (4th Cir. 1962), statements of witnesses obtained by claim agents were held not discoverable because both parties had had equal access to the witnesses at about the same time, shortly after the collision in question. The decision was based solely on Rule 34 and "good cause"; the court declined to rule on whether the statements were work-products. The court's treatment of "good cause" is quoted at length and with approval in *Schlagenhauf v. Holder,* 379 U.S. 104, 117–118 (1964). See also *Mitchell v. Bass,* 252 F.2d 513 (8th Cir. 1958); *Hauger v. Chicago, R.I. & Pac. R.R.,* 216 F.2d 501 (7th Cir. 1954); *Burke v. United States,* 32 F.R.D. 213 (E.D.N.Y.1963). While the opinions dealing with "good cause" do not often draw an explicit distinction between trial preparation materials and other materials, in fact an overwhelming proportion of the cases in which a special showing is required are cases involving trial preparation materials.

The rules are amended by eliminating the general requirement of "good cause" from Rule 34 but retaining a requirement of a special showing for trial preparation materials in this subdivision. The required showing is expressed, not in terms of "good cause" whose generality has tended to encourage confusion and controversy, but in terms of the elements of the special showing to be made: substantial need of the materials in the preparation of the case and inability without undue hardship to obtain the substantial equivalent of the materials by other means.

These changes conform to the holdings of the cases, when viewed in light of their facts. Apart from trial preparation, the fact that the materials sought are documentary does not in and of itself require a special showing beyond relevance and absence of privilege. The protective provisions are of course available, and if the party from whom production is sought raises a special issue of privacy (as with respect to income tax returns or grand jury minutes) or points to evidence primarily impeaching, or can show serious burden or expense, the court will exercise its traditional power to decide whether to issue a protective order. On the other hand, the requirement of a special showing for discovery of trial preparation materials reflects the view that each side's informal evaluation of its case should be protected, that each side should be encouraged to prepare independently, and that one side should not automatically have the benefit of the detailed preparatory work of the other side. See Field and McKusick, *Maine Civil Practice* 264 (1959).

Elimination of a "good cause" requirement from Rule 34 and the establishment of a requirement of a special showing in this subdivision will eliminate the confusion caused by having two verbally distinct requirements of justification that the courts have been unable to distinguish clearly. Moreover, the language of the subdivision suggests the factors which the courts should consider in determining whether the requisite showing has been made. The importance of the materials sought to the party seeking them in preparation of his case and the difficulty he will have obtaining them by other means are factors noted in the *Hickman* case. The courts should also consider the likelihood that the party, even if he obtains the information by independent means, will not have the substantial equivalent of the documents the production of which he seeks.

Consideration of these factors may well lead the court to distinguish between witness statements taken by an investigator, on the one hand, and other parts of the investigative file, on the other. The court in *Southern Ry. v. Lanham,* 403 F.2d 119 (5th Cir. 1968), while it naturally addressed itself to the "good cause" requirements of Rule 34, set forth as controlling considerations the factors contained in the language of this subdivision. The analysis of the court suggests circumstances under which witness statements will be discoverable. The witness may have given a fresh and contemporaneous account in a written statement while he is available to the party seeking discovery only a substantial time thereafter. *Lanham, supra* at 127–128; *Guilford, supra* at 926. Or he may be reluctant or hostile. *Lanham, supra* at 128–129; *Brookshire v. Pennsylvania RR,* 14 F.R.D. 154 (N.D.Ohio 1953); *Diamond v. Mohawk Rubber Co.,* 33 F.R.D. 264 (D.Colo.1963). Or he may have a lapse of memory. *Tannenbaum v. Walker,* 16 F.R.D. 570 (E.D.Pa. 1954). Or he may probably be deviating from his prior statement. *Cf. Hauger v. Chicago, R.I. & Pac. RR,* 216 F.2d 501 (7th Cir. 1954). On the other hand, a much stronger showing is needed to obtain evaluative materials in an investigator's reports. *Lanham, supra* at 131–133; *Pickett v. L. R. Ryan, Inc.,* 237 F.Supp. 198 (E.D.S.C.1965).

Materials assembled in the ordinary course of business, or pursuant to public requirements unrelated to litigation, or for other nonlitigation purposes are not under the qualified immunity provided by this subdivision. *Goosman v. A. Duie Pyle, Inc.,* 320 F.2d 45 (4th Cir. 1963); cf. *United States v. New York Foreign Trade Zone Operators, Inc.,* 304 F.2d 792 (2d Cir. 1962). No change is made in the existing doctrine, noted in the *Hickman* case, that one party may discover relevant facts known or available to the other party, even though such facts are contained in a document which is not itself discoverable.

Treatment of Lawyers; Special Protection of Mental Impressions, Conclusions, Opinions, and Legal Theories Concerning the Litigation.—The courts are divided as to whether the work-product doctrine extends to the preparatory work only of lawyers. The *Hickman* case left this issue open since the statements in that case were taken by a lawyer. As to courts of appeals compare *Alltmont v. United States,* 177 F.2d 971, 976 (3d Cir. 1949), cert. denied, 339 U.S. 967 (1950) (*Hickman* applied to statements obtained by FBI agents on theory it should apply to "all statements of prospective witnesses which a party has obtained for his trial counsel's use"), with *Southern Ry. v. Campbell,* 309 F.2d 569 (5th Cir. 1962) (Statements taken by claim agents not work-product), and *Guilford Nat'l Bank v. Southern Ry.,* 297 F.2d 921 (4th Cir. 1962) (avoiding issue of work-product as to claim agents, deciding case instead under Rule 34 "good cause"). Similarly, the district courts are divided on statements obtained by claim agents, compare, e.g., *Brown v. New York, N.H. & H.R.R.,* 17 F.R.D. 324 (S.D.N.Y.1955) with *Hanke v. Milwaukee Electric Ry. & Transp. Co.,* 7 F.R.D. 540 (E.D.Wis.1947); investigators, compare *Burke v. United States,* 32 F.R.D. 213 (E.D.N.Y.1963) with *Snyder v. United States,* 20 F.R.D. 7 (E.D.N.Y.1956); and insurers, compare *Gottlieb v. Bresler,* 24 F.R.D. 371 (D.D.C.1959) with *Burns v. Mulder,* 20 F.R.D. 605 (E.D.Pa.1957). See 4 Moore's *Federal Practice* ¶26.23[8.1] (2d ed. 1966); 2A Barron & Holtzoff, *Federal Practice and Procedure* § 652.2 (Wright ed. 1961).

A complication is introduced by the use made by courts of the "good cause" requirement of Rule 34, as described above. A court may conclude that trial preparation materials are not work-product because not the result of lawyer's work and yet hold that they are not producible because "good cause" has not been shown. *Cf. Guilford Nat'l Bank v. Southern Ry.,* 297 F.2d 921 (4th Cir. 1962), cited and described above. When the decisions on "good cause" are taken into account, the weight of authority affords protection of the preparatory work of both lawyers and nonlawyers (though not necessarily to the same extent) by requiring more than a showing of relevance to secure production.

Subdivision (b)(3) reflects the trend of the cases by requiring a special showing, not merely as to materials prepared by an attorney, but also as to materials prepared in anticipation of litigation or preparation for trial by or for a party or any representative acting on his behalf. The subdivision then goes on to protect against disclosure the mental impressions, conclusions, opinions, or legal theories concerning the litigation of an attorney or other representative of a party. The *Hickman* opinion drew special attention to the need for protecting an attorney against discovery of memoranda prepared from recollection of oral interviews. The courts have steadfastly safeguarded against disclosure of lawyers' mental impressions and legal theories, as well as mental impressions and subjective evaluations of investigators and claim-agents. In enforcing this provision of the subdivision, the courts will sometimes find it necessary to order disclosure of a document but with portions deleted.

Rules 33 and 36 have been revised in order to permit discovery calling for opinions, contentions, and admissions relating not only to fact but also to the application of law to fact. Under those rules, a party and his attorney or other representative may be required to disclose, to some extent, mental impressions, opinions, or conclusions. But documents or parts of documents containing these matters are protected against discovery by this subdivision. Even though a party may ultimately have to disclose in response to interrogatories or requests to admit, he is entitled to keep confidential documents containing such matters prepared for internal use.

Party's Right to Own Statement—An exception to the requirement of this subdivision enables a party to secure production of his own statement without any special showing. The cases are divided. Compare, *e.g., Safeway Stores, Inc. v. Reynolds,* 176 F.2d 476 (D.C. Cir.1949); *Shupe v. Pennsylvania R.R.,* 19 F.R.D. 144 (W.D.Pa.1956); with *e.g., New York Central R.R. v. Carr,* 251 F.2d 433 (4th Cir. 1957); *Belback v. Wilson Freight Forwarding Co.,* 40 F.R.D. 16 (W.D.Pa.1966).

Courts which treat a party's statement as though it were that of any witness overlook the fact that the party's statement is, without more, admissible in evidence. Ordinarily, a party gives a statement without insisting on a copy because he does not yet have a lawyer and does not understand the legal consequences of his actions. Thus, the statement is given at a time when he functions at a disadvantage. Discrepancies between his trial testimony and earlier statement may result from lapse of memory or ordinary inaccuracy; a written statement produced for the first time at trial may give such discrepancies a prominence which they do not deserve. In appropriate cases the court may order a party to be deposed before his statement is produced. *E.g., Smith v. Central Linen Service Co.,* 39 F.R.D. 15 (D.Md.1966); *McCoy v. General Motors Corp.,* 33 F.R.D. 354 (W.D.Pa. 1963).

Commentators strongly support the view that a party be able to secure his statement without a showing. 4 *Moore's Federal Practice* ¶26.23[8.4] (2d ed. 1966); 2A Barron & Holtzoff, *Federal Practice and Procedure* § 652.3 (Wright ed. 1961); see also Note, *Developments in the Law—Discovery,* 74 Harv.L.Rev. 940, 1039 (1961). The following states have by statute or rule taken the same position: *Statutes:* Fla.Stat.Ann. § 92.33; Ga.Code Ann. § 38–2109(b); La.Stat. Ann.R.S. 13:3732; Mass.Gen.Laws Ann. c. 271, § 44; Minn. Stat.Ann. § 602.01; N.Y.C.P.L.R. § 3101(e); *Rules:* Mo. R.C.P. 56.01(a); N.Dak.R.C.P. 34(b); Wyo.R.C.P. 34(b); *cf.* Mich.G.C.R. 306.2.

In order to clarify and tighten the provision on statements by a party, the term "statement" is defined. The definition is adapted from 18 U.S.C. § 3500(e) (Jencks Act). The statement of a party may of course be that of plaintiff or defendant, and it may be that of an individual or of a corporation or other organization.

Witness' Right to Own Statement.—A second exception to the requirement of this subdivision permits a non-party witness to obtain a copy of his own statement without any special showing. Many, though not all, of the considerations supporting a party's right to obtain his statement apply also to the non-party witness. Insurance companies are increasingly recognizing that a witness is entitled to a copy of his statement and are modifying their regular practice accordingly.

Subdivision (b)(4)—Trial Preparation: Experts. This is a new provision dealing with discovery of information (including facts and opinions) obtained by a party from an expert retained by that party in relation to litigation or obtained by the expert and not yet transmitted to the party. The subdivision deals separately with those experts whom the party expects to call as trial witnesses and with those experts who have been retained or specially employed by the party but who are not expected to be witnesses. It should be noted that the subdivision does not address itself to the expert whose information was not acquired in preparation for trial but rather because he was an actor or viewer with respect to transactions or occurrences that are part of the subject matter of the lawsuit. Such an expert should be treated as an ordinary witness.

Subsection (b)(4)(A) deals with discovery of information obtained by or through experts who will be called as witnesses at trial. The provision is responsive to problems suggested by a relatively recent line of authorities. Many of these cases present intricate and difficult issues as to which expert testimony is likely to be determinative. Prominent among them are food and drug, patent, and condemnation cases. See, *e.g., United States v. Nysco Laboratories, Inc.*, 26 F.R.D. 159, 162 (E.D.N.Y.1960) (food and drug); *E. I. du Pont de Nemours & Co. v. Phillips Petroleum Co.*, 24 F.R.D. 416, 421 (D.Del.1959) (patent); *Cold Metal Process Co. v. Aluminum Co. of America*, 7 F.R.D. 425 (N.D.Ohio 1947), aff'd, *Sachs v. Aluminum Co. of America*, 167 F.2d 570 (6th Cir. 1948) (same); *United States v. 50.34 Acres of Land*, 13 F.R.D. 19 (E.D.N.Y.1952) (condemnation).

In cases of this character, a prohibition against discovery of information held by expert witnesses produces in acute form the very evils that discovery has been created to prevent. Effective cross-examination of an expert witness requires advance preparation. The lawyer even with the help of his own experts frequently cannot anticipate the particular approach his adversary's expert will take or the data on which he will base his judgment on the stand. McGlothlin, *Some Practical Problems in Proof of Economic, Scientific, and Technical Facts*, 23 F.R.D. 467, 478 (1958). A California study of discovery and pretrial in condemnation cases notes that the only substitute for discovery of experts' valuation materials is "lengthy—and often fruitless—cross-examination during trial," and recommends pretrial exchange of such material. Calif.Law Rev.Comm'n, Discovery in Eminent Domain Proceedings 707–710 (Jan. 1963). Similarly, effective rebuttal requires advance knowledge of the line of testimony of the other side. If the latter is foreclosed by a rule against discovery, then the narrowing of issues and elimination of surprise which discovery normally produces are frustrated.

These considerations appear to account for the broadening of discovery against experts in the cases cited where expert testimony was central to the case. In some instances, the opinions are explicit in relating expanded discovery to improved cross-examination and rebuttal at trial. *Franks v. National Dairy Products Corp.*, 41 F.R.D. 234 (W.D.Tex. 1966); *United States v. 23.76 Acres*, 32 F.R.D. 593 (D.Md. 1963); see also an unpublished opinion of Judge Hincks, quoted in *United States v. 48 Jars, etc.*, 23 F.R.D. 192, 198 (D.D.C.1958). On the other hand, the need for a new provision is shown by the many cases in which discovery of expert trial witnesses is needed for effective cross-examination and rebuttal, and yet courts apply the traditional doctrine and refuse disclosure. *E.g., United States v. Certain Parcels of Land*, 25 F.R.D. 192 (N.D.Cal.1959); *United States v. Certain Acres*, 18 F.R.D. 98 (M.D.Ga.1955).

Although the trial problems flowing from lack of discovery of expert witnesses are most acute and noteworthy when the case turns largely on experts, the same problems are encountered when a single expert testifies. Thus, subdivision (b)(4)(A) draws no line between complex and simple cases, or between cases with many experts and those with but one. It establishes by rule substantially the procedure adopted by decision of the court in *Knighton v. Villian & Fassio*, 39 F.R.D. 11 (D.Md.1965). For a full analysis of the problem and strong recommendations to the same effect, see Friedenthal, *Discovery and Use of an Adverse Party's Expert Information*, 14 Stan.L.Rev. 455, 485–488 (1962); Long, *Discovery and Experts under the Federal Rules of Civil Procedure*, 38 F.R.D. 111 (1965).

Past judicial restrictions on discovery of an adversary's expert, particularly as to his opinions, reflect the fear that one side will benefit unduly from the other's better preparation. The procedure established in subsection (b)(4)(A) holds the risk to a minimum. Discovery is limited to trial witnesses, and may be obtained only at a time when the parties know who their expert witnesses will be. A party must as a practical matter prepare his own case in advance of that time, for he can hardly hope to build his case out of his opponent's experts.

Subdivision (b)(4)(A) provides for discovery of an expert who is to testify at the trial. A party can require one who intends to use the expert to state the substance of the testimony that the expert is expected to give. The court may order further discovery, and it has ample power to regulate its timing and scope and to prevent abuse. Ordinarily, the order for further discovery shall compensate the expert for his time, and may compensate the party who intends to use the expert for past expenses reasonably incurred in obtaining facts or opinions from the expert. Those provisions are likely to discourage abusive practices.

Subdivision (b)(4)(B) deals with an expert who has been retained or specially employed by the party in anticipation of litigation or preparation for trial (thus excluding an expert who is simply a general employee of the party not specially employed on the case), but who is not expected to be called as a witness. Under its provisions, a party may discover facts known or opinions held by such an expert only on a showing of exceptional circumstances under which it is impracticable for the party seeking discovery to obtain facts or opinions on the same subject by other means.

Subdivision (b)(4)(B) is concerned only with experts retained or specially consulted in relation to trial preparation. Thus the subdivision precludes discovery against experts who were informally consulted in preparation for trial, but not retained or specially employed. As an ancillary procedure, a party may on a proper showing require the other party to name experts retained or specially employed, but not those informally consulted.

These new provisions of subdivision (b)(4) repudiate the few decisions that have held an expert's information privileged simply because of his status as an expert, *e.g., American Oil Co. v. Pennsylvania Petroleum Products Co.,* 23 F.R.D. 680, 685–686 (D.R.I.1959). See *Louisell, Modern California Discovery* 315–316 (1963). They also reject as ill-considered the decisions which have sought to bring expert information within the work-product doctrine. See *United States v. McKay,* 372 F.2d 174, 176–177 (5th Cir. 1967). The provisions adopt a form of the more recently developed doctrine of "unfairness". See *e.g., United States v. 23.76 Acres of Land,* 32 F.R.D. 593, 597 (D.Md.1963); Louisell, *supra,* at 317–318; 4 *Moore's Federal Practice* 26.24 (2d ed. 1966).

Under subdivision (b)(4)(C), the court is directed or authorized to issue protective orders, including an order that the expert be paid a reasonable fee for time spent in responding to discovery, and that the party whose expert is made subject to discovery be paid a fair portion of the fees and expenses that the party incurred in obtaining information from the expert. The court may issue the latter order as a condition of discovery, or it may delay the order until after discovery is completed. These provisions for fees and expenses meet the objection that it is unfair to permit one side to obtain without cost the benefit of an expert's work for which the other side has paid, often a substantial sum. E.g., *Lewis v. United Air Lines Transp. Corp.,* 32 F.Supp. 21 (W.D.Pa.1940); *Walsh v. Reynolds Metal Co.,* 15 F.R.D. 376 (D.N.J.1954). On the other hand, a party may not obtain discovery simply by offering to pay fees and expenses. Cf. *Boynton v. R. J. Reynolds Tobacco Co.,* 36 F.Supp. 593 (D.Mass.1941).

In instances of discovery under subdivision (b)(4)(B), the court is directed to award fees and expenses to the other party, since the information is of direct value to the discovering party's preparation of his case. In ordering discovery under (b)(4)(A)(ii), the court has discretion whether to award fees and expenses to the other party; its decision should depend upon whether the discovering party is simply learning about the other party's case or is going beyond this to develop his own case. Even in cases where the court is directed to issue a protective order, it may decline to do so if it finds that manifest injustice would result. Thus, the court can protect, when necessary and appropriate, the interests of an indigent party.

Subdivision (c)—Protective Orders. The provisions of existing Rule 30(b) are transferred to this subdivision (c), as part of the rearrangement of Rule 26. The language has been changed to give it application to discovery generally. The subdivision recognizes the power of the court in the district where a deposition is being taken to make protective orders. Such power is needed when the deposition is being taken far from the court where the action is pending. The court in the district where the deposition is being taken may, and frequently will, remit the deponent or party to the court where the action is pending.

In addition, drafting changes are made to carry out and clarify the sense of the rule. Insertions are made to avoid any possible implication that a protective order does not extend to "time" as well as to "place" or may not safeguard against "undue burden or expense."

The new reference to trade secrets and other confidential commercial information reflects existing law. The courts have not given trade secrets automatic and complete immunity against disclosure, but have in each case weighed their claim to privacy against the need for disclosure. Frequently, they have been afforded a limited protection. See, *e.g., Covey Oil Co. v. Continental Oil Co.,* 340 F.2d 993 (10th Cir. 1965); *Julius M. Ames Co. v. Bostitch, Inc.,* 235 F.Supp. 856 (S.D.N.Y.1964).

The subdivision contains new matter relating to sanctions. When a motion for a protective order is made and the court is disposed to deny it, the court may go a step further and issue an order to provide or permit discovery. This will bring the sanctions of Rule 37(b) directly into play. Since the court has heard the contentions of all interested persons, an affirmative order is justified. See *Rosenberg, Sanctions to Effectuate Pretrial Discovery,* 58 Col.L.Rev. 480, 492–493 (1958). In addition, the court may require the payment of expenses incurred in relation to the motion.

Subdivision (d)—Sequence and Priority. This new provision is concerned with the sequence in which parties may proceed with discovery and with related problems of timing. The principal effects of the new provision are first, to eliminate any fixed priority in the sequence of discovery, and second, to make clear and explicit the court's power to establish priority by an order issued in a particular case.

A priority rule developed by some courts, which confers priority on the party who first serves notice of taking a deposition, is unsatisfactory in several important respects:

First, this priority rule permits a party to establish a priority running to all depositions as to which he has given earlier notice. Since he can on a given day serve notice of taking many depositions he is in a position to delay his adversary's taking of depositions for an inordinate time. Some courts have ruled that deposition priority also permits a party to delay his answers to interrogatories and production of documents. *E.g., E. I. du Pont de Nemours & Co. v. Phillips Petroleum Co.,* 23 F.R.D. 237 (D.Del.1959); *but cf. Sturdevant v. Sears, Roebuck & Co.,* 32 F.R.D. 426 (W.D.Mo. 1963).

Second, since notice is the key to priority, if both parties wish to take depositions first a race results. See *Caldwell-Clements, Inc. v. McGraw-Hill Pub. Co.,* 11 F.R.D. 156 (S.D.N.Y.1951) (description of tactics used by parties). But the existing rules on notice of deposition create a race with runners starting from different positions. The plaintiff may not give notice without leave of court until 20 days after commencement of the action, whereas the defendant may serve notice at any time after commencement. Thus, a careful and prompt defendant can almost always secure priority. This advantage of defendants is fortuitous, because the purpose of requiring plaintiff to wait 20 days is to afford defendant an opportunity to obtain counsel, not to confer priority.

Third, although courts have ordered a change in the normal sequence of discovery on a number of occasions, *e.g., Kaeppler v. James H. Matthews & Co.,* 200 F.Supp. 229 (E.D.Pa.1961); *Park & Tilford Distillers Corp. v. Distillers Co.,* 19 F.R.D. 169 (S.D.N.Y.1956), and have at all times avowed discretion to vary the usual priority, most commentators are agreed that courts in fact grant relief only for "the most obviously compelling reasons." 2A Barron & Holtzoff, *Federal Practice and Procedure* 44–47 (Wright ed. 1961); see also Younger, *Priority of Pretrial Examination in the Federal Courts—A Comment,* 34 N.Y.U.L.Rev. 1271 (1959); Freund, *The Pleading and Pretrial of an Antitrust Claim,* 46 Corn.L.Q. 555, 564 (1964). Discontent with the fairness of actual practice has been evinced by other observers. Comments, 59 Yale L.J. 117, 134–136 (1949); Yudkin, *Some Refinements in Federal Discovery Procedure,* 11 Fed.B.J. 289, 296–297 (1951); *Developments in the Law-Discovery,* 74 Harv.L.Rev. 940, 954–958 (1961).

Despite these difficulties, some courts have adhered to the priority rule, presumably because it provides a test which is easily understood and applied by the parties without much court intervention. It thus permits deposition discovery to function extradjudicially, which the rules provide for and the courts desire. For these same reasons, courts are reluctant to make numerous exceptions to the rule.

The Columbia Survey makes clear that the problem of priority does not affect litigants generally. It found that most litigants do not move quickly to obtain discovery. In over half of the cases, both parties waited at least 50 days. During the first 20 days after commencement of the action—the period when defendant might assure his priority by noticing depositions—16 percent of the defendants acted to obtain discovery. A race could not have occurred in more than 16 percent of the cases and it undoubtedly occurred in fewer. On the other hand, five times as many defendants as plaintiffs served notice of deposition during the first 19 days. To the same effect, see Comment, *Tactical Use and Abuse of Depositions Under the Federal Rules,* 59 Yale L.J. 117, 134 (1949).

These findings do not mean, however, that the priority rule is satisfactory or that a problem of priority does not exist. The court decisions show that parties do battle on this issue and carry their disputes to court. The statistics show that these court cases are not typical. By the same token, they reveal that more extensive exercise of judicial discretion to vary the priority will not bring a flood of litigation, and that a change in the priority rule will in fact affect only a small fraction of the cases.

It is contended by some that there is no need to alter the existing priority practice. In support, it is urged that there is no evidence that injustices in fact result from present practice and that, in any event, the courts can and do promulgate local rules, as in New York, to deal with local situations and issue orders to avoid possible injustice in particular cases.

Subdivision (d) is based on the contrary view that the rule of priority based on notice is unsatisfactory and unfair in its operation. Subdivision (d) follows an approach adapted from Civil Rule 4 of the District Court for the Southern District of New York. That rule provides that starting 40 days after commencement of the action, unless otherwise ordered by the court, the fact that one party is taking a deposition shall not prevent another party from doing so "concurrently." In practice, the depositions are not usually taken simultaneously; rather, the parties work out arrangements for alternation in the taking of depositions. One party may take a complete deposition and then the other, or, if the depositions are extensive, one party deposes for a set time, and then the other. See *Caldwell-Clements, Inc. v. McCraw-Hill Pub. Co.,* 11 F.R.D. 156 (S.D.N.Y.1951).

In principle, one party's initiation of discovery should not wait upon the other's completion, unless delay is dictated by special considerations. Clearly the principle is feasible with respect to all methods of discovery other than depositions. And the experience of the Southern District of New York shows that the principle can be applied to depositions as well. The courts have not had an increase in motion business on this matter. Once it is clear to lawyers that they bargain on an equal footing, they are usually able to arrange for an orderly succession of depositions without judicial intervention. Professor Moore has called attention to Civil Rule 4 and suggested that it may usefully be extended to other areas. 4 *Moore's Federal Practice* 1154 (2d ed. 1966).

The court may upon motion and by order grant priority in a particular case. But a local court rule purporting to confer priority in certain classes of cases would be inconsistent with this subdivision and thus void.

Subdivision (e)—Supplementation of Responses. The rules do not now state whether interrogatories (and questions at deposition as well as requests for inspection and admissions) impose a "continuing burden" on the responding party to supplement his answers if he obtains new information. The issue is acute when new information renders substantially incomplete or inaccurate an answer which was complete and accurate when made. It is essential that the rules provide an answer to this question. The parties can adjust to a rule either way, once they know what it is. See 4 *Moore's Federal Practice* ¶33.25[4] (2d ed. 1966).

Arguments can be made both ways. Imposition of a continuing burden reduces the proliferation of additional sets of interrogatories. Some courts have adopted local rules establishing such a burden. *E.g.,* E.D.Pa.R. 20(f), quoted in *Taggart v. Vermont Transp. Co.,* 32 F.R.D. 587 (E.D.Pa. 1963); D.Me.R. 15(c). Others have imposed the burden by decision. *E.g., Chenault v. Nebraska Farm Products, Inc.,* 9 F.R.D. 529, 533 (D.Nebr.1949). On the other hand, there are serious objections to the burden, especially in protracted cases. Although the party signs the answers, it is his lawyer who understands their significance and bears the responsibility to bring answers up to date. In a complex case all sorts of information reaches the party, who little understands its bearing on answers previously given to interrogatories. In practice, therefore, the lawyer under a continuing burden must periodically recheck all interrogatories and canvass all new information. But a full set of new answers may no longer be needed by the interrogating party. Some issues will have been dropped from the case, some questions are now seen as unimportant, and other questions must in any event be reformulated. See *Novick v. Pennsylvania R.R.,* 18 F.R.D. 296, 298 (W.D.Pa.1955).

Subdivision (e) provides that a party is not under a continuing burden except as expressly provided. Cf. Note, 68 Harv.L.Rev. 673, 677 (1955). An exception is made as to the identity of persons having knowledge of discoverable matters, because of the obvious importance to each side of knowing all witnesses and because information about witnesses routinely comes to each lawyer's attention. Many of the decisions on the issue of a continuing burden have in fact concerned the identity of witnesses. An exception is also made as to expert trial witnesses in order to carry out the provisions of Rule 26(b)(4). See *Diversified Products Corp. v. Sports Center Co.*, 42 F.R.D. 3 (D.Md.1967).

Another exception is made for the situation in which a party, or more frequently his lawyer, obtains actual knowledge that a prior response is incorrect. This exception does not impose a duty to check the accuracy of prior responses, but it prevents knowing concealment by a party or attorney. Finally, a duty to supplement may be imposed by order of the court in a particular case (including an order resulting from a pretrial conference) or by agreement of the parties. A party may of course make a new discovery request which requires supplementation of prior responses.

The duty will normally be enforced, in those limited instances where it is imposed, through sanctions imposed by the trial court, including exclusion of evidence, continuance, or other action, as the court may deem appropriate.

1980 Amendment

Subdivision (f). This subdivision is new. There has been widespread criticism of abuse of discovery. The Committee has considered a number of proposals to eliminate abuse, including a change in Rule 26(b)(1) with respect to the scope of discovery and a change in Rule 33(a) to limit the number of questions that can be asked by interrogatories to parties.

The Committee believes that abuse of discovery, while very serious in certain cases, is not so general as to require such basic changes in the rules that govern discovery in all cases. A very recent study of discovery in selected metropolitan districts tends to support its belief. P. Connolly, E. Holleman, & M. Kuhlman, *Judicial Controls and the Civil Litigative Process: Discovery* (Federal Judicial Center, 1978). In the judgment of the Committee abuse can best be prevented by intervention by the court as soon as abuse is threatened.

To this end this subdivision provides that counsel who has attempted without success to effect with opposing counsel a reasonable program or plan for discovery is entitled to the assistance of the court.

It is not contemplated that requests for discovery conferences will be made routinely. A relatively narrow discovery dispute should be resolved by resort to Rules 26(c) or 37(a), and if it appears that a request for a conference is in fact grounded in such a dispute, the court may refer counsel to those rules. If the court is persuaded that a request is frivolous or vexatious, it can strike it. See Rules 11 and 7(b)(2).

A number of courts routinely consider discovery matters in preliminary pretrial conferences held shortly after the pleadings are closed. This subdivision does not interfere with such a practice. It authorizes the court to combine a discovery conference with a pretrial conference under Rule 16 if a pretrial conference is held sufficiently early to prevent or curb abuse.

1983 Amendment

Excessive discovery and evasion or resistance to reasonable discovery requests pose significant problems. Recent studies have made some attempt to determine the sources and extent of the difficulties. See Brazil, *Civil Discovery: Lawyers' Views of its Effectiveness, Principal Problems and Abuses*, American Bar Foundation (1980); Connolly, Holleman & Kuhlman, *Judicial Controls and the Civil Litigative Process: Discovery*, Federal Judicial Center (1978); Ellington, *A Study of Sanctions for Discovery Abuse*, Department of Justice (1979); Schroeder & Frank, *The Proposed Changes in the Discovery Rules*, 1978 Ariz.St.L.J. 475.

The purpose of discovery is to provide a mechanism for making relevant information available to the litigants. "Mutual knowledge of all the relevant facts gathered by both parties is essential to proper litigation." *Hickman v. Taylor*, 329 U.S. 495, 507 (1947). Thus the spirit of the rules is violated when advocates attempt to use discovery tools as tactical weapons rather than to expose the facts and illuminate the issues by overuse of discovery or unnecessary use of defensive weapons or evasive responses. All of this results in excessively costly and time-consuming activities that are disproportionate to the nature of the case, the amount involved, or the issues or values at stake.

Given our adversary tradition and the current discovery rules, it is not surprising that there are many opportunities, if not incentives, for attorneys to engage in discovery that, although authorized by the broad, permissive terms of the rules, nevertheless results in delay. See Brazil, *The Adversary Character of Civil Discovery: A Critique and Proposals for Change*, 31 Vand.L.Rev. 1259 (1978). As a result, it has been said that the rules have "not infrequently [been] exploited to the disadvantage of justice." *Herbert v. Lando*, 441 U.S. 153, 179 (1979) (Powell, J., concurring). These practices impose costs on an already overburdened system and impede the fundamental goal of the "just, speedy, and inexpensive determination of every action." Fed.R.Civ.P. 1.

Subdivision (a); Discovery Methods. The deletion of the last sentence of Rule 26(a)(1), which provided that unless the court ordered otherwise under Rule 26(c) "the frequency of use" of the various discovery methods was not to be limited, is an attempt to address the problem of duplicative, redundant, and excessive discovery and to reduce it. The amendment, in conjunction with the changes in Rule 26(b)(1), is designed to encourage district judges to identify instances of needless discovery and to limit the use of the various discovery devices accordingly. The question may be raised by one of the parties, typically on a motion for a protective order, or by the court on its own initiative. It is entirely appropriate to consider a limitation on the frequency of use of discovery at a discovery conference under Rule 26(f) or at any other pretrial conference authorized by these rules. In considering the discovery needs of a particular case, the court should consider the factors described in Rule 26(b)(1).

Subdivision (b); Discovery Scope and Limits. Rule 26(b)(1) has been amended to add a sentence to deal with the problem of over-discovery. The objective is to guard against redundant or disproportionate discovery by giving the court authority to reduce the amount of discovery that may be directed to matters that are otherwise proper subjects of inquiry. The new sentence is intended to encourage judges to be more aggressive in identifying and discouraging discovery overuse. The grounds mentioned in the amended rule for limiting discovery reflect the existing practice of many courts in issuing protective orders under Rule 26(c). See, e.g., *Carlson Cos. v. Sperry & Hutchinson Co.*, 374 F.Supp.

1080 (D.Minn.1974); *Dolgow v. Anderson,* 53 F.R.D. 661 (E.D.N.Y.1971); *Mitchell v. American Tobacco Co.,* 33 F.R.D. 262 (M.D.Pa.1963); *Welty v. Clute,* 1 F.R.D. 446 (W.D.N.Y.1941). On the whole, however, district judges have been reluctant to limit the use of the discovery devices. See, *e.g., Apco Oil Co. v. Certified Transp., Inc.,* 46 F.R.D. 428 (W.D.Mo.1969). See generally 8 Wright & Miller, *Federal Practice and Procedure: Civil* §§ 2036, 2037, 2039, 2040 (1970).

The first element of the standard, Rule 26(b)(1)(i), is designed to minimize redundancy in discovery and encourage attorneys to be sensitive to the comparative costs of different methods of securing information. Subdivision (b)(1)(ii) also seeks to reduce repetitiveness and to oblige lawyers to think through their discovery activities in advance so that full utilization is made of each deposition, document request, or set of interrogatories. The elements of Rule 26(b)(1)(iii) address the problem of discovery that is disproportionate to the individual lawsuit as measured by such matters as its nature and complexity, the importance of the issues at stake in a case seeking damages, the limitations on a financially weak litigant to withstand extensive opposition to a discovery program or to respond to discovery requests, and the significance of the substantive issues, as measured in philosophic, social, or institutional terms. Thus the rule recognizes that many cases in public policy spheres, such as employment practices, free speech, and other matters, may have importance far beyond the monetary amount involved. The court must apply the standards in an even-handed manner that will prevent use of discovery to wage a war of attrition or as a device to coerce a party, whether financially weak or affluent.

The rule contemplates greater judicial involvement in the discovery process and thus acknowledges the reality that it cannot always operate on a self-regulating basis. See Connolly, Holleman & Kuhlman, *Judicial Controls and the Civil Litigative Process: Discovery* 77, Federal Judicial Center (1978). In an appropriate case the court could restrict the number of depositions, interrogatories, or the scope of a production request. But the court must be careful not to deprive a party of discovery that is reasonably necessary to afford a fair opportunity to develop and prepare the case.

The court may act on motion, or its own initiative. It is entirely appropriate to resort to the amended rule in conjunction with a discovery conference under Rule 26(f) or one of the other pretrial conferences authorized by the rules.

Subdivision (g); Signing of Discovery Requests, Responses, and Objections. Rule 26(g) imposes an affirmative duty to engage in pretrial discovery in a responsible manner that is consistent with the spirit and purposes of Rules 26 through 37. In addition, Rule 26(g) is designed to curb discovery abuse by explicitly encouraging the imposition of sanctions. The subdivision provides a deterrent to both excessive discovery and evasion by imposing a certification requirement that obliges each attorney to stop and think about the legitimacy of a discovery request, a response thereto, or an objection. The term "response" includes answers to interrogatories and to requests to admit as well as responses to production requests.

If primary responsibility for conducting discovery is to continue to rest with the litigants, they must be obliged to act responsibly and avoid abuse. With this in mind, Rule 26(g), which parallels the amendments to Rule 11, requires an attorney or unrepresented party to sign each discovery request, response, or objection. Motions relating to discovery are governed by Rule 11. However, since a discovery request, response, or objection usually deals with more specific subject matter than motions or papers, the elements that must be certified in connection with the former are spelled out more completely. The signature is a certification of the elements set forth in Rule 26(g).

Although the certification duty requires the lawyer to pause and consider the reasonableness of his request, response, or objection, it is not meant to discourage or restrict necessary and legitimate discovery. The rule simply requires that the attorney make a reasonable inquiry into the factual basis of his response, request, or objection.

The duty to make a "reasonable inquiry" is satisfied if the investigation undertaken by the attorney and the conclusions drawn therefrom are reasonable under the circumstances. It is an objective standard similar to the one imposed by Rule 11. See the Advisory Committee Note to Rule 11. See also *Kinee v. Abraham Lincoln Fed. Sav. & Loan Ass'n,* 365 F.Supp. 975 (E.D.Pa.1973). In making the inquiry, the attorney may rely on assertions by the client and on communications with other counsel in the case as long as that reliance is appropriate under the circumstances. Ultimately, what is reasonable is a matter for the court to decide on the totality of the circumstances.

Rule 26(g) does not require the signing attorney to certify the truthfulness of the client's factual responses to a discovery request. Rather, the signature certifies that the lawyer has made a reasonable effort to assure that the client has provided all the information and documents available to him that are responsive to the discovery demand. Thus, the lawyer's certification under Rule 26(g) should be distinguished from other signature requirements in the rules, such as those in Rules 30(e) and 33.

Nor does the rule require a party or an attorney to disclose privileged communications or work product in order to show that a discovery request, response, or objection is substantially justified. The provisions of Rule 26(c), including appropriate orders after *in camera* inspection by the court, remain available to protect a party claiming privilege or work product protection.

The signing requirement means that every discovery request, response, or objection should be grounded on a theory that is reasonable under the precedents or a good faith belief as to what should be the law. This standard is heavily dependent on the circumstances of each case. The certification speaks as of the time it is made. The duty to supplement discovery responses continues to be governed by Rule 26(e).

Concern about discovery abuse has led to widespread recognition that there is a need for more aggressive judicial control and supervision. *ACF Industries, Inc. v. EEOC,* 439 U.S. 1081 (1979) (certiorari denied) (Powell, J., dissenting). Sanctions to deter discovery abuse would be more effective if they were diligently applied "not merely to penalize those whose conduct may be deemed to warrant such a sanction, but to deter those who might be tempted to such conduct in the absence of such a deterrent." *National Hockey League v. Metropolitan Hockey Club,* 427 U.S. 639, 643 (1976). See also Note, *The Emerging Deterrence Orientation in the Imposition of Discovery Sanctions,* 91 Harv.L.Rev. 1033 (1978). Thus the premise of Rule 26(g) is that imposing sanctions on attorneys who fail to meet the rule's standards will significantly reduce abuse by imposing disadvantages therefor.

Because of the asserted reluctance to impose sanctions on attorneys who abuse the discovery rules, see Brazil, *Civil Discovery: Lawyers' Views of its Effectiveness, Principal Problems and Abuses,* American Bar Foundation (1980); Ellington, *A Study of Sanctions for Discovery Abuse,* Department of Justice (1979), Rule 26(g) makes explicit the authority judges now have to impose appropriate sanctions and requires them to use it. This authority derives from Rule 37, 28 U.S.C. § 1927, and the court's inherent power. See *Roadway Express, Inc. v. Piper,* 447 U.S. 752 (1980); *Martin v. Bell Helicopter Co.,* 85 F.R.D. 654, 661–62 (D.Col. 1980); Note, *Sanctions Imposed by Courts on Attorneys Who Abuse the Judicial Process,* 44 U.Chi.L.Rev. 619 (1977). The new rule mandates that sanctions be imposed on attorneys who fail to meet the standards established in the first portion of Rule 26(g). The nature of the sanction is a matter of judicial discretion to be exercised in light of the particular circumstances. The court may take into account any failure by the party seeking sanctions to invoke protection under Rule 26(c) at an early stage in the litigation.

The sanctioning process must comport with due process requirements. The kind of notice and hearing required will depend on the facts of the case and the severity of the sanction being considered. To prevent the proliferation of the sanction procedure and to avoid multiple hearings, discovery in any sanction proceeding normally should be permitted only when it is clearly required by the interests of justice. In most cases the court will be aware of the circumstances and only a brief hearing should be necessary.

1987 Amendment

The amendments are technical. No substantive change is intended.

1993 Amendments

Subdivision (a). Through the addition of paragraphs (1)–(4), this subdivision imposes on parties a duty to disclose, without awaiting formal discovery requests, certain basic information that is needed in most cases to prepare for trial or make an informed decision about settlement. The rule requires all parties (1) early in the case to exchange information regarding potential witnesses, documentary evidence, damages, and insurance, (2) at an appropriate time during the discovery period to identify expert witnesses and provide a detailed written statement of the testimony that may be offered at trial through specially retained experts, and (3) as the trial date approaches to identify the particular evidence that may be offered at trial. The enumeration in Rule 26(a) of items to be disclosed does not prevent a court from requiring by order or local rule that the parties disclose additional information without a discovery request. Nor are parties precluded from using traditional discovery methods to obtain further information regarding these matters, as for example asking an expert during a deposition about testimony given in other litigation beyond the four-year period specified in Rule 26(a)(2)(B).

A major purpose of the revision is to accelerate the exchange of basic information about the case and to eliminate the paper work involved in requesting such information, and the rule should be applied in a manner to achieve those objectives. The concepts of imposing a duty of disclosure were set forth in Brazil, *The Adversary Character of Civil Discovery: A Critique and Proposals for Change,* 31 *Vand. L.Rev.* 1348 (1978), and Schwarzer, *The Federal Rules, the Adversary Process, and Discovery Reform,* 50 *U.Pitt.L.Rev. 703, 721–23 (1989).*

The rule is based upon the experience of district courts that have required disclosure of some of this information through local rules, court-approved standard interrogatories, and standing orders. Most have required pretrial disclosure of the kind of information described in Rule 26(a)(3). Many have required written reports from experts containing information like that specified in Rule 26(a)(2)(B). While far more limited, the experience of the few state and federal courts that have required pre-discovery exchange of core information such as is contemplated in Rule 26(a)(1) indicates that savings in time and expense can be achieved, particularly if the litigants meet and discuss the issues in the case as a predicate for this exchange and if a judge supports the process, as by using the results to guide further proceedings in the case. Courts in Canada and the United Kingdom have for many years required disclosure of certain information without awaiting a request from an adversary.

Paragraph (1). As the functional equivalent of court-ordered interrogatories, this paragraph requires early disclosure, without need for any request, of four types of information that have been customarily secured early in litigation through formal discovery. The introductory clause permits the court, by local rule, to exempt all or particular types of cases from these disclosure requirement *[sic]* or to modify the nature of the information to be disclosed. It is expected that courts would, for example, exempt cases like Social Security reviews and government collection cases in which discovery would not be appropriate or would be unlikely. By order the court may eliminate or modify the disclosure requirements in a particular case, and similarly the parties, unless precluded by order or local rule, can stipulate to elimination or modification of the requirements for that case. The disclosure obligations specified in paragraph (1) will not be appropriate for all cases, and it is expected that changes in these obligations will be made by the court or parties when the circumstances warrant.

Authorization of these local variations is, in large measure, included in order to accommodate the Civil Justice Reform Act of 1990, which implicitly directs districts to experiment during the study period with differing procedures to reduce the time and expense of civil litigation. The civil justice delay and expense reduction plans adopted by the courts under the Act differ as to the type, form, and timing of disclosures required. Section 105(c)(1) of the Act calls for a report by the Judicial Conference to Congress by December 31, 1995, comparing experience in twenty of these courts; and section 105(c)(2)(B) contemplates that some changes in the Rules may then be needed. While these studies may indicate the desirability of further changes in Rule 26(a)(1), these changes probably could not become effective before December 1998 at the earliest. In the meantime, the present revision puts in place a series of disclosure obligations that, unless a court acts affirmatively to impose other requirements or indeed to reject all such requirements for the present, are designed to eliminate certain discovery, help focus the discovery that is needed, and facilitate preparation for trial or settlement.

Subparagraph (A) requires identification of all persons who, based on the investigation conducted thus far, are likely to have discoverable information relevant to the factual disputes between the parties. All persons with such information should be disclosed, whether or not their testimony will be supportive of the position of the disclosing party. As officers of the court, counsel are expected to disclose the identity of those persons who may be used by them as witnesses or who, if their potential testimony were known, might reasonably be expected to be deposed or called as a witness by any of the other parties. Indicating briefly the general topics on which such persons have information should not be burdensome, and will assist other parties in deciding which depositions will actually be needed.

Subparagraph (B) is included as a substitute for the inquiries routinely made about the existence and location of documents and other tangible things in the possession, custody, or control of the disclosing party. Although, unlike subdivision (a)(3)(C), an itemized listing of each exhibit is not required, the disclosure should describe and categorize, to the extent identified during the initial investigation, the nature and location of potentially relevant documents and records, including computerized data and other electronically-recorded information, sufficiently to enable opposing parties (1) to make an informed decision concerning which documents might need to be examined, at least initially, and (2) to frame their document requests in a manner likely to avoid squabbles resulting from the wording of the requests. As with potential witnesses, the requirement for disclosure of documents applies to all potentially relevant items then known to the party, whether or not supportive of its contentions in the case.

Unlike subparagraphs (C) and (D), subparagraph (B) does not require production of any documents. Of course, in cases involving few documents a disclosing party may prefer to provide copies of the documents rather than describe them, and the rule is written to afford this option to the disclosing party. If, as will be more typical, only the description is provided, the other parties are expected to obtain the documents desired by proceeding under Rule 34 or through informal requests. The disclosing party does not, by describing documents under subparagraph (B), waive its right to object to production on the basis of privilege or work product protection, or to assert that the documents are not sufficiently relevant to justify the burden or expense of production.

The initial disclosure requirements of subparagraphs (A) and (B) are limited to identification of potential evidence "relevant to disputed facts alleged with particularity in the pleadings." There is no need for a party to identify potential evidence with respect to allegations that are admitted. Broad, vague, and conclusory allegations sometimes tolerated in notice pleading—for example, the assertion that a product with many component parts is defective in some unspecified manner—should not impose upon responding parties the obligation at that point to search for and identify all persons possibly involved in, or all documents affecting, the design, manufacture, and assembly of the product. The greater the specificity and clarity of the allegations in the pleadings, the more complete should be the listing of potential witnesses and types of documentary evidence. Although paragraphs (1)(A) and (1)(B) by their terms refer to the factual disputes defined in the pleadings, the rule contemplates that these issues would be informally refined and clarified during the meeting of the parties under subdivision (f) and that the disclosure obligations would be adjusted in the light of these discussions. The disclosure requirements should, in short, be applied with common sense in light of the principles of Rule 1, keeping in mind the salutary purposes that the rule is intended to accomplish. The litigants should not indulge in gamesmanship with respect to the disclosure obligations.

Subparagraph (C) imposes a burden of disclosure that includes the functional equivalent of a standing Request for Production under Rule 34. A party claiming damages or other monetary relief must, in addition to disclosing the calculation of such damages, make available the supporting documents for inspection and copying as if a request for such materials had been made under Rule 34. This obligation applies only with respect to documents then reasonably available to it and not privileged or protected as work product. Likewise, a party would not be expected to provide a calculation of damages which, as in many patent infringement actions, depends on information in the possession of another party or person.

Subparagraph (D) replaces subdivision (b)(2) of Rule 26, and provides that liability insurance policies be made available for inspection and copying. The last two sentences of that subdivision have been omitted as unnecessary, not to signify any change of law. The disclosure of insurance information does not thereby render such information admissible in evidence. See Rule 411, Federal Rules of Evidence. Nor does subparagraph (D) require disclosure of applications for insurance, though in particular cases such information may be discoverable in accordance with revised subdivision (a)(5).

Unless the court directs a different time, the disclosures required by subdivision (a)(1) are to be made at or within 10 days after the meeting of the parties under subdivision (f). One of the purposes of this meeting is to refine the factual disputes with respect to which disclosures should be made under paragraphs (1)(A) and (1)(B), particularly if an answer has not been filed by a defendant, or, indeed, to afford the parties an opportunity to modify by stipulation the timing or scope of these obligations. The time of this meeting is generally left to the parties provided it is held at least 14 days before a scheduling conference is held or before a scheduling order is due under Rule 16(b). In cases in which no scheduling conference is held, this will mean that the meeting must ordinarily be held within 75 days after a defendant has first appeared in the case and hence that the initial disclosures would be due no later than 85 days after the first appearance of a defendant.

Before making its disclosures, a party has the obligation under subdivision (g)(1) to make a reasonable inquiry into the facts of the case. The rule does not demand an exhaustive investigation at this stage of the case, but one that is reasonable under the circumstances, focusing on the facts that are alleged with particularity in the pleadings. The type of investigation that can be expected at this point will vary based upon such factors as the number and complexity of the issues; the location, nature, number, and availability of potentially relevant witnesses and documents; the extent of past working relationships between the attorney and the client, particularly in handling related or similar litigation; and of course how long the party has to conduct an investigation, either before or after filing of the case. As provided in the last sentence of subdivision (a)(1), a party is not excused from the duty of disclosure merely because its investigation is incomplete. The party should make its initial disclosures based on the pleadings and the information then reasonably available to it. As its investigation continues and as the issues in the pleadings are clarified, it should supplement its disclosures as required by subdivision (e)(1). A party is not relieved from its obligation of disclosure merely because another party has not made its disclosures or has made an inadequate disclosure.

It will often be desirable, particularly if the claims made in the complaint are broadly stated, for the parties to have their Rule 26(f) meeting early in the case, perhaps before a defendant has answered the complaint or had time to conduct other than a cursory investigation. In such circumstances, in order to facilitate more meaningful and useful initial disclosures, they can and should stipulate to a period of more than 10 days after the meeting in which to make these disclosures, at least for defendants who had no advance notice of the potential litigation. A stipulation at an early meeting affording such a defendant at least 60 days after receiving the complaint in which to make its disclosures under subdivision (a)(1)—a period that is two weeks longer than the time formerly specified for responding to interrogatories served with a complaint—should be adequate and appropriate in most cases.

Paragraph (2). This paragraph imposes an additional duty to disclose information regarding expert testimony sufficiently in advance of trial that opposing parties have a reasonable opportunity to prepare for effective cross examination and perhaps arrange for expert testimony from other witnesses. Normally the court should prescribe a time for these disclosures in a scheduling order under Rule 16(b), and in most cases the party with the burden of proof on an issue should disclose its expert testimony on that issue before other parties are required to make their disclosures with respect to that issue. In the absence of such a direction, the disclosures are to be made by all parties at least 90 days before the trial date or the date by which the case is to be ready for trial, except that an additional 30 days is allowed (unless the court specifies another time) for disclosure of expert testimony to be used solely to contradict or rebut the testimony that may be presented by another party's expert. For a discussion of procedures that have been used to enhance the reliability of expert testimony, see M. Graham, *Expert Witness Testimony and the Federal Rules of Evidence: Insuring Adequate Assurance of Trustworthiness,* 1986 U.Ill.L.Rev. 90.

Paragraph (2)(B) requires that persons retained or specially employed to provide expert testimony, or whose duties as an employee of the party regularly involve the giving of expert testimony, must prepare a detailed and complete written report, stating the testimony the witness is expected to present during direct examination, together with the reasons therefor. The information disclosed under the former rule in answering interrogatories about the "substance" of expert testimony was frequently so sketchy and vague that it rarely dispensed with the need to depose the expert and often was even of little help in preparing for a deposition of the witness. Revised Rule 37(c)(1) provides an incentive for full disclosure; namely, that a party will not ordinarily be permitted to use on direct examination any expert testimony not so disclosed. Rule 26(a)(2)(B) does not preclude counsel from providing assistance to experts in preparing the reports, and indeed, with experts such as automobile mechanics, this assistance may be needed. Nevertheless, the report, which is intended to set forth the substance of the direct examination, should be written in a manner that reflects the testimony to be given by the witness and it must be signed by the witness.

The report is to disclose the data and other information considered by the expert and any exhibits or charts that summarize or support the expert's opinions. Given this obligation of disclosure, litigants should no longer be able to argue that materials furnished to their experts to be used in forming their opinions—whether or not ultimately relied upon by the expert—are privileged or otherwise protected from disclosure when such persons are testifying or being deposed.

Revised subdivision (b)(4)(A) authorizes the deposition of expert witnesses. Since depositions of experts required to prepare a written report may be taken only after the report has been served, the length of the deposition of such experts should be reduced, and in many cases the report may eliminate the need for a deposition. Revised subdivision (e)(1) requires disclosure of any material changes made in the opinions of an expert from whom a report is required, whether the changes are in the written report or in testimony given at a deposition.

For convenience, this rule and revised Rule 30 continue to use the term "expert" to refer to those persons who will testify under Rule 702 of the Federal Rules of Evidence with respect to scientific, technical, and other specialized matters. The requirement of a written report in paragraph (2)(B), however, applies only to those experts who are retained or specially employed to provide such testimony in the case or whose duties as an employee of a party regularly involve the giving of such testimony. A treating physician, for example, can be deposed or called to testify at trial without any requirement for a written report. By local rule, order, or written stipulation, the requirement of a written report may be waived for particular experts or imposed upon additional persons who will provide opinions under Rule 702.

Paragraph (3). This paragraph imposes an additional duty to disclose, without any request, information customarily needed in final preparation for trial. These disclosures are to be made in accordance with schedules adopted by the court under Rule 16(b) or by special order. If no such schedule is directed by the court, the disclosures are to be made at least 30 days before commencement of the trial. By its terms, rule 26(a)(3) does not require disclosure of evidence to be used solely for impeachment purposes; however, disclosure of such evidence—as well as other items relating to conduct of trial—may be required by local rule or a pretrial order.

Subparagraph (A) requires the parties to designate the persons whose testimony they may present as substantive evidence at trial, whether in person or by deposition. Those who will probably be called as witnesses should be listed separately from those who are not likely to be called but who are being listed in order to preserve the right to do so if needed because of developments during trial. Revised Rule 37(c)(1) provides that only persons so listed may be used at trial to present substantive evidence. This restriction does not apply unless the omission was "without substantial justification" and hence would not bar an unlisted witness if the need for such testimony is based upon developments during trial that could not reasonably have been anticipated—*e.g.*, a change of testimony.

Listing a witness does not obligate the party to secure the attendance of the person at trial, but should preclude the party from objecting if the person is called to testify by another party who did not list the person as a witness.

Subparagraph (B) requires the party to indicate which of these potential witnesses will be presented by deposition at trial. A party expecting to use at trial a deposition not recorded by stenographic means is required by revised Rule 32 to provide the court with a transcript of the pertinent portions of such depositions. This rule requires that copies of the transcript of a nonstenographic deposition be provided to other parties in advance of trial for verification, an obvious concern since counsel often utilize their own personnel to prepare transcripts from audio or video tapes. By order or local rule, the court may require that parties designate the particular portions of stenographic depositions to be used at trial.

Subparagraph (C) requires disclosure of exhibits, including summaries (whether to be offered in lieu of other documentary evidence or to be used as an aid in understanding such evidence), that may be offered as substantive evidence. The rule requires a separate listing of each such exhibit, though it should permit voluminous items of a similar or standardized character to be described by meaningful categories. For example, unless the court has otherwise directed, a series of vouchers might be shown collectively as a single exhibit with their starting and ending dates. As with witnesses, the exhibits that will probably be offered are to be listed separately from those which are unlikely to be offered but which are listed in order to preserve the right to do so if needed because of developments during trial. Under revised Rule 37(c)(1) the court can permit use of unlisted documents the need for which could not reasonably have been anticipated in advance of trial.

Upon receipt of these final pretrial disclosures, other parties have 14 days (unless a different time is specified by the court) to disclose any objections they wish to preserve to the usability of the deposition testimony or to the admissibility of the documentary evidence (other than under Rules 402 and 403 of the Federal Rules of Evidence). Similar provisions have become commonplace either in pretrial orders or by local rules, and significantly expedite the presentation of evidence at trial, as well as eliminate the need to have available witnesses to provide "foundation" testimony for most items of documentary evidence. The listing of a potential objection does not constitute the making of that objection or require the court to rule on the objection; rather, it preserves the right of the party to make the objection when and as appropriate during trial. The court may, however, elect to treat the listing as a motion "in limine" and rule upon the objections in advance of trial to the extent appropriate.

The time specified in the rule for the final pretrial disclosures is relatively close to the trial date. The objective is to eliminate the time and expense in making these disclosures of evidence and objections in those cases that settle shortly before trial, while affording a reasonable time for final preparation for trial in those cases that do not settle. In many cases, it will be desirable for the court in a scheduling or pretrial order to set an earlier time for disclosures of evidence and provide more time for disclosing potential objections.

Paragraph (4). This paragraph prescribes the form of disclosures. A signed written statement is required, reminding the parties and counsel of the solemnity of the obligations imposed; and the signature on the initial or pretrial disclosure is a certification under subdivision (g)(1) that it is complete and correct as of the time when made. Consistent with Rule 5(d), these disclosures are to be filed with the court unless otherwise directed. It is anticipated that many courts will direct that expert reports required under paragraph (2)(B) not be filed until needed in connection with a motion or for trial.

Paragraph (5). This paragraph is revised to take note of the availability of revised Rule 45 for inspection from nonparties of documents and premises without the need for a deposition.

Subdivision (b). This subdivision is revised in several respects. First, former paragraph (1) is subdivided into two paragraphs for ease of reference and to avoid renumbering of paragraphs (3) and (4). Textual changes are then made in new paragraph (2) to enable the court to keep tighter rein on the extent of discovery. The information explosion of recent decades has greatly increased both the potential cost of wide-ranging discovery and the potential for discovery to be used as an instrument for delay or oppression. Amendments to Rules 30, 31, and 33 place presumptive limits on the number of depositions and interrogatories, subject to leave of court to pursue additional discovery. The revisions in Rule 26(b)(2) are intended to provide the court with broader discretion to impose additional restrictions on the scope and extent of discovery and to authorize courts that develop case tracking systems based on the complexity of cases to increase or decrease by local rule the presumptive number of depositions and interrogatories allowed in particular types or classifications of cases. The revision also dispels any doubt as to the power of the court to impose limitations on the length of depositions under Rule 30 or on the number of requests for admission under Rule 36.

Second, former paragraph (2), relating to insurance, has been relocated as part of the required initial disclosures under subdivision (a)(1)(D), and revised to provide for disclosure of the policy itself.

Third, paragraph (4)(A) is revised to provide that experts who are expected to be witnesses will be subject to deposition prior to trial, conforming the norm stated in the rule to the actual practice followed in most courts, in which depositions of experts have become standard. Concerns regarding the expense of such depositions should be mitigated by the fact that the expert's fees for the deposition will ordinarily be borne by the party taking the deposition. The requirement under subdivision (a)(2)(B) of a complete and detailed report of the expected testimony of certain forensic experts may, moreover, eliminate the need for some such depositions or at least reduce the length of the depositions. Accordingly, the deposition of an expert required by subdivision (a)(2)(B) to provide a written report may be taken only after the report has been served.

Paragraph (4)(C), bearing on compensation of experts, is revised to take account of the changes in paragraph (4)(A).

Paragraph (5) is a new provision. A party must notify other parties if it is withholding materials otherwise subject to disclosure under the rule or pursuant to a discovery request because it is asserting a claim of privilege or work product protection. To withhold materials without such notice is contrary to the rule, subjects the party to sanctions under Rule 37(b)(2), and may be viewed as a waiver of the privilege or protection.

The party must also provide sufficient information to enable other parties to evaluate the applicability of the claimed privilege or protection. Although the person from whom the discovery is sought decides whether to claim a privilege or protection, the court ultimately decides whether, if this claim is challenged, the privilege or protection applies. Providing information pertinent to the applicability of the privilege or protection should reduce the need for in camera examination of the documents.

The rule does not attempt to define for each case what information must be provided when a party asserts a claim of privilege or work product protection. Details concerning time, persons, general subject matter, etc., may be appropriate if only a few items are withheld, but may be unduly burdensome when voluminous documents are claimed to be privileged or protected, particularly if the items can be described by categories. A party can seek relief through a protective order under subdivision (c) if compliance with the requirement for providing this information would be an unreasonable burden. In rare circumstances some of the pertinent information affecting applicability of the claim, such as the identity of the client, may itself be privileged; the rule provides that such information need not be disclosed.

The obligation to provide pertinent information concerning withheld privileged materials applies only to items "otherwise discoverable." If a broad discovery request is made—for example, for all documents of a particular type during a twenty year period—and the responding party believes in good faith that production of documents for more than the past three years would be unduly burdensome, it should make its objection to the breadth of the request and, with respect to the documents generated in that three year period, produce the unprivileged documents and describe those withheld under the claim of privilege. If the court later rules that documents for a seven year period are properly discoverable, the documents for the additional four years should then be either produced (if not privileged) or described (if claimed to be privileged).

Subdivision (c). The revision requires that before filing a motion for a protective order the movant must confer—either in person or by telephone—with the other affected parties in a good faith effort to resolve the discovery dispute without the need for court intervention. If the movant is unable to get opposing parties even to discuss the matter, the efforts in attempting to arrange such a conference should be indicated in the certificate.

Subdivision (d). This subdivision is revised to provide that formal discovery—as distinguished from interviews of potential witnesses and other informal discovery—not commence until the parties have met and conferred as required by subdivision (f). Discovery can begin earlier if authorized under Rule 30(a)(2)(C) (deposition of person about to leave the country) or by local rule, order, or stipulation. This will be appropriate in some cases, such as those involving requests for a preliminary injunction or motions challenging personal jurisdiction. If a local rule exempts any types of cases in which discovery may be needed from the requirement of a meeting under Rule 26(f), it should specify when discovery may commence in those cases.

The meeting of counsel is to take place as soon as practicable and in any event at least 14 days before the date of the scheduling conference under Rule 16(b) or the date a scheduling order is due under Rule 16(b). The court can assure that discovery is not unduly delayed either by entering a special order or by setting the case for a scheduling conference.

Subdivision (e). This subdivision is revised to provide that the requirement for supplementation applies to all disclosures required by subdivisions (a)(1)–(3). Like the former rule, the duty, while imposed on a "party," applies whether the corrective information is learned by the client or by the attorney. Supplementations need not be made as each new item of information is learned but should be made at appropriate intervals during the discovery period, and with special promptness as the trial date approaches. It may be useful for the scheduling order to specify the time or times when supplementations should be made.

The revision also clarifies that the obligation to supplement responses to formal discovery requests applies to interrogatories, requests for production, and requests for admissions, but not ordinarily to deposition testimony. However, with respect to experts from whom a written report is required under subdivision (a)(2)(B), changes in the opinions expressed by the expert whether in the report or at a subsequent deposition are subject to a duty of supplemental disclosure under subdivision (e)(1).

The obligation to supplement disclosures and discovery responses applies whenever a party learns that its prior disclosures or responses are in some material respect incomplete or incorrect. There is, however, no obligation to provide supplemental or corrective information that has been otherwise made known to the parties in writing or during the discovery process, as when a witness not previously disclosed is identified during the taking of a deposition or when an expert during a deposition corrects information contained in an earlier report.

Subdivision (f). This subdivision was added in 1980 to provide a party threatened with abusive discovery with a special means for obtaining judicial intervention other than through discrete motions under Rules 26(c) and 37(a). The amendment envisioned a two-step process: first, the parties would attempt to frame a mutually agreeable plan; second, the court would hold a "discovery conference" and then enter an order establishing a schedule and limitations for the conduct of discovery. It was contemplated that the procedure, an elective one triggered on request of a party, would be used in special cases rather than as a routine matter. As expected, the device has been used only sparingly in most courts, and judicial controls over the discovery process have ordinarily been imposed through scheduling orders under Rule 16(b) or through rulings on discovery motions.

The provisions relating to a conference with the court are removed from subdivision (f). This change does not signal any lessening of the importance of judicial supervision. Indeed, there is a greater need for early judicial involvement to consider the scope and timing of the disclosure requirements of Rule 26(a) and the presumptive limits on discovery imposed under these rules or by local rules. Rather, the change is made because the provisions addressing the use of conferences with the court to control discovery are more properly included in Rule 16, which is being revised to highlight the court's powers regarding the discovery process.

The desirability of some judicial control of discovery can hardly be doubted. Rule 16, as revised, requires that the court set a time for completion of discovery and authorizes various other orders affecting the scope, timing, and extent of discovery and disclosures. Before entering such orders, the court should consider the views of the parties, preferably by means of a conference, but at the least through written submissions. Moreover, it is desirable that the parties' proposals regarding discovery be developed through a process where they meet in person, informally explore the nature and basis of the issues, and discuss how discovery can be conducted most efficiently and economically.

As noted above, former subdivision (f) envisioned the development of proposed discovery plans as an optional procedure to be used in relatively few cases. The revised rule directs that in all cases not exempted by local rule or special order the litigants must meet in person and plan for discovery. Following this meeting, the parties submit to the court their proposals for a discovery plan and can begin formal discovery. Their report will assist the court in seeing that the timing and scope of disclosures under revised Rule 26(a) and the limitations on the extent of discovery under these rules and local rules are tailored to the circumstances of the particular case.

To assure that the court has the litigants' proposals before deciding on a scheduling order and that the commencement of discovery is not delayed unduly, the rule provides that the meeting of the parties take place as soon as practicable and in any event at least 14 days before a scheduling conference is held or before a scheduling order is due under Rule 16(b). (Rule 16(b) requires that a scheduling order be entered within 90 days after the first appearance of a defendant or, if earlier, within 120 days after the complaint has been served on any defendant.) The obligation to participate in the planning process is imposed on all parties that have appeared in the case, including defendants who, because of a pending Rule 12 motion, may not have yet filed an answer in the case. Each such party should attend the meeting, either through one of its attorneys or in person if unrepresented. If more parties are joined or appear after the initial meeting, an additional meeting may be desirable.

Subdivision (f) describes certain matters that should be accomplished at the meeting and included in the proposed discovery plan. This listing does not exclude consideration of other subjects, such as the time when any dispositive motions should be filed and when the case should be ready for trial.

The parties are directed under subdivision (a)(1) to make the disclosures required by that subdivision at or within 10 days after this meeting. In many cases the parties should use the meeting to exchange, discuss, and clarify their respective disclosures. In other cases, it may be more useful if the disclosures are delayed until after the parties have discussed at the meeting the claims and defenses in order to define the issues with respect to which the initial disclosures should be made. As discussed in the Notes to subdivision (a)(1), the parties may also need to consider whether a stipulation extending this 10–day period would be appropriate, as when a defendant would otherwise have less than 60 days after being served in which to make its initial disclosure. The parties should also discuss at the meeting what additional information, although not subject to the disclosure requirements, can be made available informally without the necessity for formal discovery requests.

The report is to be submitted to the court within 10 days after the meeting and should not be difficult to prepare. In most cases counsel should be able to agree that one of them will be responsible for its preparation and submission to the court. Form 35 has been added in the Appendix to the Rules, both to illustrate the type of report that is contemplated and to serve as a checklist for the meeting.

The litigants are expected to attempt in good faith to agree on the contents of the proposed discovery plan. If they cannot agree on all aspects of the plan, their report to the court should indicate the competing proposals of the parties on those items, as well as the matters on which they agree. Unfortunately, there may be cases in which, because of disagreements about time or place or for other reasons, the meeting is not attended by all parties or, indeed, no meeting takes place. In such situations, the report—or reports—should describe the circumstances and the court may need to consider sanctions under Rule 37(g).

By local rule or special order, the court can exempt particular cases or types of cases from the meet-and-confer requirement of subdivision (f). In general this should include any types of cases which are exempted by local rule from the requirement for a scheduling order under Rule 16(b), such as cases in which there will be no discovery (*e.g.*, bankruptcy appeals and reviews of social security determinations). In addition, the court may want to exempt cases in which discovery is rarely needed (*e.g.*, government collection cases and proceedings to enforce administrative summonses) or in which a meeting of the parties might be impracticable (*e.g.*, actions by unrepresented prisoners). Note that if a court exempts from the requirements for a meeting any types of cases in which discovery may be needed, it should indicate when discovery may commence in those cases.

Subdivision (g). Paragraph (1) is added to require signatures on disclosures, a requirement that parallels the provisions of paragraph (2) with respect to discovery requests, responses, and objections. The provisions of paragraph (3) have been modified to be consistent with Rules 37(a)(4) and 37(c)(1); in combination, these rules establish sanctions for violation of the rules regarding disclosures and discovery matters. Amended Rule 11 no longer applies to such violations.

Rule 27. Depositions Before Action or Pending Appeal

(a) Before Action.

(1) Petition. A person who desires to perpetuate testimony regarding any matter that may be cognizable in any court of the United States may file a verified petition in the United States district court in the district of the residence of any expected adverse party. The petition shall be entitled in the name of the petitioner and shall show: 1, that the petitioner expects to be a party to an action cognizable in a court of the United States but is presently unable to bring it or cause it to be brought, 2, the subject matter of the expected action and the petitioner's interest therein, 3, the facts which the petitioner desires to establish by the proposed testimony and the reasons for desiring to perpetuate it, 4, the names or a description of the persons the petitioner expects will be adverse parties and their addresses so far as known, and 5, the names and addresses of the persons to be examined and the substance of the testimony which the petitioner expects to elicit from each, and shall ask for an order authorizing the petitioner to take the depositions of the persons to be examined named in the petition, for the purpose of perpetuating their testimony.

(2) Notice and Service. The petitioner shall thereafter serve a notice upon each person named in the petition as an expected adverse party, together with a copy of the petition, stating that the petitioner will apply to the court, at a time and place named therein, for the order described in the petition. At least 20 days before the date of hearing the notice shall be served either within or without the district or state in the manner provided in Rule 4(d) for service of summons; but if such service cannot with due diligence be made upon any expected adverse party named in the petition, the court may make such order as is just for service by publication or otherwise, and shall appoint, for persons not served in the manner provided in Rule 4(d), an attorney who shall represent them, and, in case they are not otherwise represented, shall cross-examine the deponent. If any expected adverse party is a minor or incompetent the provisions of Rule 17(c) apply.

(3) Order and Examination. If the court is satisfied that the perpetuation of the testimony may prevent a failure or delay of justice, it shall make an order designating or describing the persons whose depositions may be taken and specifying the subject matter of the examination and whether the depositions shall be taken upon oral examination or written interrogatories. The depositions may then be taken in accordance with these rules; and the court may make orders of the character provided for by Rules 34 and 35. For the purpose of applying these rules to depositions for perpetuating testimony, each reference therein to the court in which the action is pending shall be deemed to refer to the court in which the petition for such deposition was filed.

(4) Use of Deposition. If a deposition to perpetuate testimony is taken under these rules or if, although not so taken, it would be admissible in evidence in the courts of the state in which it is taken, it may be used in any action involving the same subject matter subsequently brought in a United States district court, in accordance with the provisions of Rule 32(a).

(b) Pending Appeal. If an appeal has been taken from a judgment of a district court or before the taking of an appeal if the time therefor has not expired, the district court in which the judgment was rendered may allow the taking of the depositions of witnesses to perpetuate their testimony for use in the event of further proceedings in the district court. In such case the party who desires to perpetuate the testimony may make a motion in the district court for leave to take the depositions, upon the same notice and service thereof as if the action was pending in the district court. The motion shall show (1) the names and addresses of persons to be examined and the substance of the testimony which the party expects to elicit from each; (2) the reasons for perpetuating their testimony. If the court finds that the perpetuation of the testimony is proper to avoid a failure or delay of justice, it may make an order allowing the depositions to be taken and may make orders of the character provided for by Rules 34 and 35, and thereupon the depositions may be taken and used in the same manner and under the same conditions as are prescribed in these rules for depositions taken in actions pending in the district court.

(c) Perpetuation by Action. This rule does not limit the power of a court to entertain an action to perpetuate testimony.

(As amended Dec. 27, 1946, eff. Mar. 19, 1948; Dec. 29, 1948, eff. Oct. 20, 1949; Mar. 1, 1971, eff. July 1, 1971; Mar. 2, 1987, eff. Aug. 1, 1987.)

ADVISORY COMMITTEE NOTES

1937 Adoption

Note to Subdivision (a). This rule offers a simple method of perpetuating testimony in cases where it is usually allowed under equity practice or under modern statutes. See *Arizona v. California*, 1934, 54 S.Ct. 735, 292 U.S. 341, 78 L.Ed. 1298; *Todd Engineering Dry Dock and Repair Co. v. United States*, C.C.A.5, 1929, 32 F.2d 734; *Hall v. Stout*, 4 Del.Ch. 269 (1871). For comparable state statutes see Ark.Civ.Code (Crawford, 1934) §§ 666 to 670; Calif.Code Civ.Proc. (Deering, 1937) 2083–2089; Smith-Hurd Ill.Stats. c. 51, §§ 39 to 46; Iowa Code (1935) §§ 11400 to 11407; 2 Mass.Gen.Laws (Ter.Ed., 1932) ch. 233, §§ 46 to 63; N.Y.C.P.A. (1937) § 295; Ohio Gen.Code Ann. (Throckmorton, 1936) §§ 12216 to 12222; Va.Code Ann. (Michie, 1936) § 6235; Wis.Stat. (1935) §§ 326.27 to 326.29. The appointment of an attorney to represent absent parties or parties not personally notified, or a guardian ad litem to represent minors and incompetents, is provided for in several of the above statutes.

Note to Subdivision (b). This follows the practice approved in *Richter v. Union Trust Co.*, 1885, 5 S.Ct. 1162, 115 U.S. 55, 29 L.Ed. 345, by extending the right to perpetuate testimony to cases pending an appeal.

Note to Subdivision (c). This preserves the right to employ a separate action to perpetuate testimony under U.S.C., Title 28, [former] § 644 (Depositions under *dedimus potestatem* and *in perpetuam*) as an alternate method.

1946 Amendment

Note. Since the second sentence in subdivision (a)(3) refers only to depositions, it is arguable that Rules 34 and 35 are inapplicable in proceedings to perpetuate testimony. The new matter [in subdivisions (a)(3) and (b)] clarifies. A conforming change is also made in subdivision (b).

1948 Amendment

The amendment effective October 1949, substituted the words "United States district court" in subdivision (a)(1) and (4) for "district court of the United States."

1971 Amendment

The reference intended in this subdivision is to the rule governing the use of depositions in court proceedings. Formerly Rule 26(d), that rule is now Rule 32(a). The subdivision is amended accordingly.

1987 Amendment

The amendments are technical. No substantive change is intended.

HISTORICAL NOTES

References in Text

"Rule 4(d)", referred to in subd. (a)(2), is Rule 4(d) prior to amendment by Supreme Court of the United States order dated Apr. 22, 1993, which failed to make conforming amendments to subd. (a)(2) of this rule. Rule 4(d) does not relate to manner of service which is provided for in Rule 4(e)(2) and (g) to (j).

Rule 28. Persons Before Whom Depositions may be Taken

(a) Within the United States. Within the United States or within a territory or insular possession subject to the jurisdiction of the United States, depositions shall be taken before an officer authorized to administer oaths by the laws of the United States or of the place where the examination is held, or before a person appointed by the court in which the action is pending. A person so appointed has power to administer oaths and take testimony. The term officer as used in Rules 30, 31 and 32 includes a person appointed by the court or designated by the parties under Rule 29.

(b) In Foreign Countries. Depositions may be taken in a foreign country (1) pursuant to any applicable treaty or convention, or (2) pursuant to a letter of request (whether or not captioned a letter rogatory), or (3) on notice before a person authorized to administer oaths in the place where the examination is held, either by the law thereof or by the law of the United States, or (4) before a person commissioned by the court, and a person so commissioned shall have the power by virtue of the commission to administer any necessary oath and take testimony. A commission or a letter of request shall be issued on application and notice and on terms that are just and appropriate. It is not requisite to the issuance of a commission or a letter of request that the taking of the deposition in any other manner is impracticable or inconvenient; and both a commission and a letter of request may be issued in proper cases. A notice or commission may designate the person before whom the deposition is to be taken either by name or descriptive title. A letter of request may be addressed "To the Appropriate Authority in [here name the country]." When a letter of request or any other device is used pursuant to any applicable treaty or convention, it shall be captioned in the form prescribed by that treaty or convention. Evidence obtained in response to a letter of request need not be excluded merely because it is not a verbatim transcript, because the testimony was not taken under oath, or because of any similar departure from the requirements for depositions taken within the United States under these rules.

(c) Disqualification for Interest. No deposition shall be taken before a person who is a relative or employee or attorney or counsel of any of the parties, or is a relative or employee of such attorney or counsel, or is financially interested in the action.

(As amended Dec. 27, 1946, eff. Mar. 19, 1948; Jan. 21, 1963, eff. July 1, 1963; Apr. 29, 1980, eff. Aug. 1, 1980; Mar. 2, 1987, eff. Aug. 1, 1987; Apr. 22, 1993, eff. Dec. 1, 1993.)

ADVISORY COMMITTEE NOTES

1937 Adoption

In effect this rule is substantially the same as U.S.C., Title 28, [former] § 639 (Depositions *de bene esse*; when and where taken; notice). U.S.C., Title 28, [former] § 642 (Depositions, acknowledgments, and affidavits taken by notaries public) does not conflict with subdivision (a).

1946 Amendments

Note. The added language [in subdivision (a)] provides for the situation, occasionally arising, when depositions must be taken in an isolated place where there is no one readily available who has the power to administer oaths and take testimony according to the terms of the rule as originally stated. In addition, the amendment affords a more convenient method of securing depositions in the case where state lines intervene between the location of various witnesses otherwise rather closely grouped. The amendment insures that the person appointed shall have adequate power to perform his duties. It has been held that a person authorized to act in the premises, as, for example, a master, may take testimony outside the district of his appointment. *Consolidated Fastener Co. v. Columbian Button & Fastener Co.*, C.C.N.D.N.Y.1898, 85 Fed. 54; *Mathieson Alkali Works v. Arnold, Hoffman & Co.*, C.C.A.1, 1929, 31 F.2d 1.

1963 Amendments

The amendment of clause (1) is designed to facilitate depositions in foreign countries by enlarging the class of persons before whom the depositions may be taken on notice. The class is no longer confined, as at present, to a secretary of embassy or legation, consul general, consul, vice consul, or consular agent of the United States. In a country that regards the taking of testimony by a foreign official in aid of litigation pending in a court of another country as an infringement upon its sovereignty, it will be expedient to notice depositions before officers of the country in which the examination is taken. See generally *Symposium, Letters Rogatory* (Grossman ed. 1956); Doyle, *Taking Evidence by Deposition and Letters Rogatory and Obtaining Documents in Foreign Territory,* Proc.A.B.A., Sec.Int'l & Comp.L. 37 (1959); Heilpern, *Procuring Evidence Abroad,* 14 Tul.L.Rev. 29 (1939); Jones, *International Judicial Assistance: Procedural Chaos and a Program for Reform,* 62 Yale L.J. 515, 526–29 (1953); Smit, *International Aspects of Federal Civil Procedure,* 61 Colum.L.Rev. 1031, 1056–58 (1961).

Clause (2) of amended subdivision (b), like the corresponding provision of subdivision (a) dealing with depositions taken in the United States, makes it clear that the appointment of a person by commission in itself confers power upon him to administer any necessary oath.

It has been held that a letter rogatory will not be issued unless the use of a notice or commission is shown to be impossible or impractical. See, e.g., *United States v. Matles,* 154 F.Supp. 574 (E.D.N.Y.1957); *The Edmund Fanning,* 89 F.Supp. 282 (E.D.N.Y.1950); *Branyan v. Koninklijke Luchtvaart Maatschappij,* 13 F.R.D. 425 (S.D.N.Y.1953). See also *Ali Akber Kiachif v. Philco International Corp.,* 10 F.R.D. 277 (S.D.N.Y.1950). The intent of the fourth sentence of the amended subdivision is to overcome this judicial antipathy and to permit a sound choice between depositions under a letter rogatory and on notice or by commission in the light of all the circumstances. In a case in which the foreign country will compel a witness to attend or testify in aid of a letter rogatory but not in aid of a commission, a letter rogatory may be preferred on the ground that it is less expensive to execute, even if there is plainly no need for compulsive process. A letter rogatory may also be preferred when it cannot be demonstrated that a witness will be recalcitrant or when the witness states that he is willing to testify voluntarily, but the contingency exists that he will change his mind at the last moment. In the latter case, it may be advisable to issue both a commission and a letter rogatory, the latter to be executed if the former fails. The choice between a letter rogatory and a commission may be conditioned by other factors, including the nature and extent of the assistance that the foreign country will give to the execution of either.

In executing a letter rogatory the courts of other countries may be expected to follow their customary procedure for taking testimony. See *United States v. Paraffin Wax, 2255 Bags,* 23 F.R.D. 289 (E.D.N.Y.1959). In many noncommon-law countries the judge questions the witness, sometimes without first administering an oath, the attorneys put any supplemental questions either to the witness or through the judge, and the judge dictates a summary of the testimony, which the witness acknowledges as correct. See *Jones, supra,* at 530–32; *Doyle, supra,* at 39–41. The last sentence of the amended subdivision provides, contrary to the implications of some authority, that evidence recorded in such a fashion need not be excluded on that account. See *The Mandu,* 11 F.Supp. 845 (E.D.N.Y.1935). But *cf. Nelson v. United States,* 17 Fed.Cas. 1340 (No. 10,116) (C.C.D.Pa. 1816); *Winthrop v. Union Ins. Co.,* 30 Fed.Cas. 376 (No. 17901) (C.C.D.Pa.1807). The specific reference to the lack of an oath or a verbatim transcript is intended to be illustrative. Whether or to what degree the value or weight of the evidence may be affected by the method of taking or recording the testimony is left for determination according to the circumstances of the particular case, *cf. Uebersee Finanz-Korporation, A.G. v. Brownell,* 121 F.Supp. 420 (D.D.C. 1954); *Danisch v. Guardian Life Ins. Co.,* 19 F.R.D. 235 (S.D.N.Y.1956); the testimony may indeed be so devoid of substance or probative value as to warrant its exclusion altogether.

Some foreign countries are hostile to allowing a deposition to be taken in their country, especially by notice or commission, or to lending assistance in the taking of a deposition. Thus compliance with the terms of amended subdivision (b) may not in all cases ensure completion of a deposition abroad. Examination of the law and policy of the particular foreign country in advance of attempting a deposition is therefore advisable. See 4 *Moore's Federal Practice* ¶¶28.05–28.08 (2d ed. 1950).

1980 Amendments

The amendments are clarifying.

1987 Amendments

The amendment is technical. No substantive change is intended.

1993 Amendments

This revision is intended to make effective use of the Hague Convention on the Taking of Evidence Abroad in Civil or Commercial Matters, and of any similar treaties that the United States may enter into in the future which provide procedures for taking depositions abroad. The party taking the deposition is ordinarily obliged to conform to an applicable treaty or convention if an effective deposition can be taken by such internationally approved means, even though a verbatim transcript is not available or testimony cannot be taken under oath. For a discussion of the impact of such treaties upon the discovery process, and of the application of principles of comity upon discovery in countries not signatories to a convention, see *Société Nationale Industrielle Aérospatiale v. United States District Court,* 482 U.S. 522 (1987).

The term "letter of request" has been substituted in the rule for the term "letter rogatory" because it is the primary method provided by the Hague Convention. A letter rogatory is essentially a form of letter of request. There are several other minor changes that are designed merely to carry out the intent of the other alterations.

Rule 29. Stipulations Regarding Discovery Procedure

Unless otherwise directed by the court, the parties may by written stipulation (1) provide that depositions may be taken before any person, at any time or place, upon any notice, and in any manner and when so taken may be used like other depositions, and (2) modify other procedures governing or limitations placed upon discovery, except that stipulations extending the time provided in Rules 33, 34, and 36 for responses to discovery may, if they would interfere with any time set for completion of discovery, for hearing of a motion, or for trial, be made only with the approval of the court.

(As amended Mar. 30, 1970, eff. July 1, 1970; Apr. 22, 1993, eff. Dec. 1, 1993.)

ADVISORY COMMITTEE NOTES

1970 Amendment

There is no provision for stipulations varying the procedures by which methods of discovery other than depositions are governed. It is common practice for parties to agree on such variations, and the amendment recognizes such agreements and provides a formal mechanism in the rules for giving them effect. Any stipulation varying the procedures may be superseded by court order, and stipulations extending the time for response to discovery under Rules 33, 34, and 36 require court approval.

1993 Amendments

This rule is revised to give greater opportunity for litigants to agree upon modifications to the procedures governing discovery or to limitations upon discovery. Counsel are encouraged to agree on less expensive and time-consuming methods to obtain information, as through voluntary exchange of documents, use of interviews in lieu of depositions, etc. Likewise, when more depositions or interrogatories are needed than allowed under these rules or when more time is needed to complete a deposition than allowed under a local rule, they can, by agreeing to the additional discovery, eliminate the need for a special motion addressed to the court.

Under the revised rule, the litigants ordinarily are not required to obtain the court's approval of these stipulations. By order or local rule, the court can, however, direct that its approval be obtained for particular types of stipulations; and, in any event, approval must be obtained if a stipulation to extend the 30–day period for responding to interrogatories, requests for production, or requests for admissions would interfere with dates set by the court for completing discovery, for hearing of a motion, or for trial.

Rule 30. Depositions Upon Oral Examination

(a) When Depositions May Be Taken; When Leave Required.

(1) A Party may take the testimony of any person, including a party, by deposition upon oral examination without leave of court except as provided in paragraph (2). The attendance of witnesses may be compelled by subpoena as provided in Rule 45.

(2) A party must obtain leave of court, which shall be granted to the extent consistent with the principles stated in Rule 26(b)(2), if the person to be examined is confined in prison or if, without the written stipulation of the parties.

(A) a proposed deposition would result in more than ten depositions being taken under this rule or Rule 31 by the plaintiffs, or by the defendants, or by third-party defendants;

(B) the person to be examined already has been deposed in the case; or

(C) a party seeks to take a deposition before the time specified in Rule 26(d) unless the notice contains a certification, with supporting facts, that the person to be examined is expected to leave the United States and be unavailable for examination in this country unless deposed before that time.

(b) Notice of Examination: General Requirements; Method of Recording; Production of Documents and Things; Deposition of Organization; Deposition by Telephone.

(1) A party desiring to take the deposition of any person upon oral examination shall give reasonable notice in writing to every other party to the action. The notice shall state the time and place for taking the deposition and the name and address of each person to be examined, if known, and, if the name is not known, a general description sufficient to identify the person or the particular class or group to which the person belongs. If a subpoena duces tecum is to be served on the person to be examined, the designation of the materials to be produced as set forth in the subpoena shall be attached to, or included in, the notice.

(2) The party taking the deposition shall state in the notice the method by which the testimony shall be recorded. Unless the court orders otherwise, it may be recorded by sound, sound-and-visual, or stenographic means, and the party taking the deposition shall bear the cost of the recording. Any party may arrange for a transcription to be made from the recording of a deposition taken by nonstenographic means.

(3) With prior notice to the deponent and other parties, any party may designate another method to record the deponent's testimony in addition to the method specified by the person taking the deposition. The additional record or transcript shall be made at that party's expense unless the court otherwise orders.

(4) Unless otherwise agreed by the parties, a deposition shall be conducted before an officer appointed or designated under Rule 28 and shall begin with a statement on the record by the officer that includes (A) the officer's name and business address; (B) the date, time, and place of the deposition; (C) the name of the deponent; (D) the administration of the oath or affirmation to the deponent; and (E) an identification of all persons present. If the deposition is recorded other than stenographically, the officer shall repeat items (A) through (C) at the beginning of each unit of recorded tape or other recording medium. The appearance or demeanor of deponents or attorneys shall not be dis-

torted through camera or sound-recording techniques. At the end of the deposition, the officer shall state on the record that the deposition is complete and shall set forth any stipulations made by counsel concerning the custody of the transcript or recording and the exhibits, or concerning other pertinent matters.

(5) The notice to a party deponent may be accompanied by a request made in compliance with Rule 34 for the production of documents and tangible things at the taking of the deposition. The procedure of Rule 34 shall apply to the request.

(6) A party may in the party's notice and in a subpoena name as the deponent a public or private corporation or a partnership or association or governmental agency and describe with reasonable particularity the matters on which examination is requested. In that event, the organization so named shall designate one or more officers, directors, or managing agents, or other persons who consent to testify on its behalf, and may set forth, for each person designated, the matters on which the person will testify. A subpoena shall advise a non-party organization of its duty to make such a designation. The persons so designated shall testify as to matters known or reasonably available to the organization. This subdivision (b)(6) does not preclude taking a deposition by any other procedure authorized in these rules.

(7) The parties may stipulate in writing or the court may upon motion order that a deposition be taken by telephone or other remote electronic means. For the purposes of this rule and Rules 28(a), 37(a)(1), and 37(b)(1), a deposition taken by such means is taken in the district and at the place where the deponent is to answer questions.

(c) Examination and Cross–Examination; Record of Examination; Oath; Objections.

Examination and cross-examination of witnesses may proceed as permitted at the trial under the provisions of the Federal Rules of Evidence except Rules 103 and 615. The officer before whom the deposition is to be taken shall put the witness on oath or affirmation and shall personally, or by someone acting under the officer's direction and in the officer's presence, record the testimony of the witness. The testimony shall be taken stenographically or recorded by any other method authorized by subdivision (b)(2) of this rule. All objections made at the time of the examination to the qualifications of the officer taking the deposition, to the manner of taking it, to the evidence presented, to the conduct of any party, or to any other aspect of the proceedings shall be noted by the officer upon the record of the deposition; but the examination shall proceed, with the testimony being taken subject to the objections. In lieu of participating in the oral examination, parties may serve written questions in a sealed envelope on the party taking the deposition and the party taking the deposition shall transmit them to the officer, who shall propound them to the witness and record the answers verbatim.

(d) Schedule and Duration; Motion to Terminate or Limit Examination.

(1) Any objection to evidence during a deposition shall be stated concisely and in a non-argumentative and non-suggestive manner. A party may instruct a deponent not to answer only when necessary to preserve a privilege, to enforce a limitation on evidence directed by the court, or to present a motion under paragraph (3).

(2) By order or local rule, the court may limit the time permitted for the conduct of a deposition, but shall allow additional time consistent with Rule 26(b)(2) if needed for a fair examination of the deponent or if the deponent or another party impedes or delays the examination. If the court finds such an impediment, delay, or other conduct that has frustrated the fair examination of the deponent, it may impose upon the persons responsible an appropriate sanction, including the reasonable costs and attorney's fees incurred by any parties as a result thereof.

(3) At any time during a deposition, on motion of a party or of the deponent and upon a showing that the examination is being conducted in bad faith or in such manner as unreasonably to annoy, embarrass, or oppress the deponent or party, the court in which the action is pending or the court in the district where the deposition is being taken may order the officer conducting the examination to cease forthwith from taking the deposition, or may limit the scope and manner of the taking of the deposition as provided in Rule 26(c). If the order made terminates the examination, it shall be resumed thereafter only upon the order of the court in which the action is pending. Upon demand of the objecting party or deponent, the taking of the deposition shall be suspended for the time necessary to make a motion for an order. The provisions of Rule 37(a)(4) apply to the award of expenses incurred in relation to the motion.

(e) Review by Witness; Changes; Signing.

If requested by the deponent or a party before completion of the deposition, the deponent shall have 30 days after being notified by the officer that the transcript or recording is available in which to review the transcript or recording and, if there are changes in form or substance, to sign a statement reciting such changes and the reasons given by the deponent for making them. The officer shall indicate in the certificate prescribed by subdivision (f)(1) whether any review was requested and, if so, shall append any changes made by the deponent during the period allowed.

(f) Certification and Filing by Officer; Exhibits; Copies; Notice of Filing.

(1) The officer shall certify that the witness was duly sworn by the officer and that the deposition is a true record of the testimony given by the witness. This certificate shall be in writing and accompany the record of the deposition. Unless otherwise ordered by the court, the officer shall securely seal the deposition in an envelope or package indorsed with the title of the action and marked "Deposition of [here insert name of witness]" and shall promptly file it with the court in which the action is pending or send it to the attorney who arranged for the transcript or recording, who shall store it under conditions that will protect it against loss, destruction, tampering, or deterioration. Documents and things produced for inspection during the examination of the witness, shall, upon the request of a party, be marked for identification and annexed to the deposition and may be inspected and copied by any party, except that if the person producing the materials desires to retain them the person may (A) offer copies to be marked for identification and annexed to the deposition and to serve thereafter as originals if the person affords to all parties fair opportunity to verify the copies by comparison with the originals, or (B) offer the originals to be marked for identification, after giving to each party an opportunity to inspect and copy them, in which event the materials may then be used in the same manner as if annexed to the deposition. Any party may move for an order that the original be annexed to and returned with the deposition to the court, pending final disposition of the case.

(2) Unless otherwise ordered by the court or agreed by the parties, the officer shall retain stenographic notes of any deposition taken stenographically or a copy of the recording of any deposition taken by another method. Upon payment of reasonable charges therefor, the officer shall furnish a copy of the transcript or other recording of the deposition to any party or to the deponent.

(3) The party taking the deposition shall give prompt notice of its filing to all other parties.

(g) Failure to Attend or to Serve Subpoena; Expenses.

(1) If the party giving the notice of the taking of a deposition fails to attend and proceed therewith and another party attends in person or by attorney pursuant to the notice, the court may order the party giving the notice to pay to such other party the reasonable expenses incurred by that party and that party's attorney in attending, including reasonable attorney's fees.

(2) If the party giving the notice of the taking of a deposition of a witness fails to serve a subpoena upon the witness and the witness because of such failure does not attend, and if another party attends in person or by attorney because that party expects the deposition of that witness to be taken, the court may order the party giving the notice to pay to such other party the reasonable expenses incurred by that party and that party's attorney in attending, including reasonable attorney's fees.

(As amended Jan. 21, 1963, eff. July 1, 1963; Mar. 30, 1970, eff. July 1, 1970; Mar. 1, 1971, eff. July 1, 1971; Nov. 20, 1972, eff. July 1, 1975; Apr. 29, 1980, eff. Aug. 1, 1980; Mar. 2, 1987, eff. Aug. 1, 1987; Apr. 22, 1993, eff. Dec. 1, 1993.)

ADVISORY COMMITTEE NOTES

1937 Adoption

Note to Subdivision (a). This is in accordance with common practice. See U.S.C., Title 28, [former] § 639 (Depositions *de bene esse*; when and where taken; notice), the relevant provisions of which are incorporated in this rule; West's Ann.Code Civ.Proc. § 2031; and statutes cited in respect to notice in the Note to Rule 26(a). The provision for enlarging or shortening the time of notice has been added to give flexibility to the rule.

Note to Subdivisions (b) and (d). These are introduced as a safeguard for the protection of parties and deponents on account of the unlimited right of discovery given by Rule 26.

Note to Subdivisions (c) and (e). These follow the general plan of [former] Equity Rule 51 (Evidence Taken Before Examiners, Etc.) and U.S.C., Title 28, [former] §§ 640 (Depositions *de bene esse*; mode of taking), and [former] 641 (Same; transmission to court), but are more specific. They also permit the deponent to require the officer to make changes in the deposition if the deponent is not satisfied with it. See also [former] Equity Rule 50 (Stenographer—Appointment—Fees.)

Note to Subdivision (f). Compare [former] Equity Rule 55 (Depositions Deemed Published When Filed.)

Note to Subdivision (g). This is similar to 2 Minn.Stat. (Mason, 1927) § 9833, but is more extensive.

1963 Amendments

This amendment corresponds to the change in Rule 4(d)(4). See Advisory Committee's Note to that amendment.

1970 Amendments

Subdivision (a). This subdivision contains the provisions of existing Rule 26(a), transferred here as part of the rearrangement relating to Rule 26. Existing Rule 30(a) is transferred to 30(b). Changes in language have been made to conform to the new arrangement.

This subdivision is further revised in regard to the requirement of leave of court for taking a deposition. The present procedure, requiring a plaintiff to obtain leave of court if he serves notice of taking a deposition within 20 days after commencement of the action, is changed in several respects.

First, leave is required by reference to the time the deposition is to be taken rather than the date of serving notice of taking. Second, the 20-day period is extended to 30 days and runs from the service of summons and complaint on any defendant, rather than the commencement of the action. *Cf.* Ill.S.Ct.R. 19–1 S-H Ill.Ann.Stat. § 101.19–1. Third, leave is not required beyond the time that defendant initiates discovery, thus showing that he has retained counsel. As under the present practice, a party not afforded a reasonable opportunity to appear at a deposition, because he has not yet been served with process, is protected against use of the deposition at trial against him. See Rule 32(a), transferred from 26(d). Moreover, he can later redepose the witness if he so desires.

The purpose of requiring the plaintiff to obtain leave of court is, as stated by the Advisory Committee that proposed the present language of Rule 26(a), to protect "a defendant who has not had an opportunity to retain counsel and inform himself as to the nature of the suit." Note to 1948 amendment of Rule 26(a), quoted in 3A Barron & Holtzoff, *Federal Practice and Procedure* 455–456 (Wright ed. 1958). In order to assure defendant of this opportunity, the period is lengthened to 30 days. This protection, however, is relevant to the time of taking the deposition, not to the time that notice is served. Similarly, the protective period should run from the service of process rather than the filing of the complaint with the court. As stated in the note to Rule 26(d), the courts have used the service of notice as a convenient reference point for assigning priority in taking depositions, but with the elimination of priority in new Rule 26(d) the reference point is no longer needed. The new procedure is consistent in principle with the provisions of Rules 33, 34, and 36 as revised.

Plaintiff is excused from obtaining leave even during the initial 30-day period if he gives the special notice provided in subdivision (b)(2). The required notice must state that the person to be examined is about to go out of the district where the action is pending and more than 100 miles from the place of trial, or out of the United States, or on a voyage to sea, and will be unavailable for examination unless deposed within the 30-day period. These events occur most often in maritime litigation, when seamen are transferred from one port to another or are about to go to sea. Yet, there are analogous situations in nonmaritime litigation, and although the maritime problems are more common, a rule limited to claims in the admiralty and maritime jurisdiction is not justified.

In the recent unification of the civil and admiralty rules, this problem was temporarily met through addition in Rule 26(a) of a provision that depositions *de bene esse* may continue to be taken as to admiralty and maritime claims within the meaning of Rule 9(h). It was recognized at the time that "a uniform rule applicable alike to what are now civil actions and suits in admiralty" was clearly preferable, but the de bene esse procedure was adopted "for the time being at least." See Advisory Committee's Note in Report of the Judicial Conference: Proposed Amendments to Rules of Civil Procedure 43–44 (1966).

The changes in Rule 30(a) and the new Rule 30(b)(2) provide a formula applicable to ordinary civil as well as maritime claims. They replace the provision for depositions *de bene esse*. They authorize an early deposition without leave of court where the witness is about to depart and, unless his deposition is promptly taken, (1) it will be impossible or very difficult to depose him before trial or (2) his deposition can later be taken but only with substantially increased effort and expense. *Cf. S.S. Hai Chang,* 1966 A.M.C. 2239 (S.D.N.Y.1966), in which the deposing party is required to prepay expenses and counsel fees of the other party's lawyer when the action is pending in New York and depositions are to be taken on the West Coast. Defendant is protected by a provision that the deposition cannot be used against him if he was unable through exercise of diligence to obtain counsel to represent him.

The distance of 100 miles from place of trial is derived from the *de bene esse* provision and also conforms to the reach of a subpoena of the trial court, as provided in Rule 45(e). See also S.D.N.Y. Civ.R. 5(a). Some parts of the *de bene esse* provision are omitted from Rule 30(b)(2). Modern deposition practice adequately covers the witness who lives more than 100 miles away from place of trial. If a witness is aged or infirm, leave of court can be obtained.

Subdivision (b). Existing Rule 30(b) on protective orders has been transferred to Rule 26(c), and existing Rule 30(a) relating to the notice of taking deposition has been transferred to this subdivision. Because new material has been added, subsection numbers have been inserted.

Subdivision (b)(1). If a subpoena duces tecum is to be served, a copy thereof or a designation of the materials to be produced must accompany the notice. Each party is thereby enabled to prepare for the deposition more effectively.

Subdivision (b)(2). This subdivision is discussed in the note to subdivision (a), to which it relates.

Subdivision (b)(3). This provision is derived from existing Rule 30(a), with a minor change of language.

Subdivision (b)(4). In order to facilitate less expensive procedures, provision is made for the recording of testimony by other than stenographic means—*e.g.*, by mechanical, electronic, or photographic means. Because these methods give rise to problems of accuracy and trustworthiness, the party taking the deposition is required to apply for a court order. The order is to specify how the testimony is to be recorded, preserved, and filed, and it may contain whatever additional safeguards the court deems necessary.

Subdivision (b)(5). A provision is added to enable a party, through service of notice, to require another party to produce documents or things at the taking of his deposition. This may now be done as to a nonparty deponent through use of a subpoena duces tecum as authorized by Rule 45, but some courts have held that documents may be secured from a party only under Rule 34. See 2A Barron & Holtzoff, *Federal Practice and Procedure* § 644.1 n. 83.2, § 792 n. 16 (Wright ed. 1961). With the elimination of "good cause" from Rule 34, the reason for this restrictive doctrine has disappeared. *Cf.* N.Y.C.P.L.R. § 3111.

Whether production of documents or things should be obtained directly under Rule 34 or at the deposition under this rule will depend on the nature and volume of the documents or things. Both methods are made available. When the documents are few and simple, and closely related to the oral examination, ability to proceed via this rule will facilitate discovery. If the discovering party insists on examining many and complex documents at the taking of the deposition, thereby causing undue burdens on others, the latter may, under Rules 26(c) or 30(d), apply for a court order that the examining party proceed via Rule 34 alone.

Subdivision (b)(6). A new provision is added, whereby a party may name a corporation, partnership, association, or governmental agency as the deponent and designate the matters on which he requests examination, and the organization shall then name one or more of its officers, directors, or managing agents, or other persons consenting to appear and testify on its behalf with respect to matters known or reasonably available to the organization. *Cf.* Alberta Sup.Ct.R. 255. The organization may designate persons other than officers, directors, and managing agents, but only with their consent. Thus, an employee or agent who has an independent or conflicting interest in the litigation—for example, in a personal injury case—can refuse to testify on behalf of the organization.

This procedure supplements the existing practice whereby the examining party designates the corporate official to be deposed. Thus, if the examining party believes that certain officials who have not testified pursuant to this subdivision have added information, he may depose them. On the other hand, a court's decision whether to issue a protective order may take account of the availability and use made of the procedures provided in this subdivision.

The new procedure should be viewed as an added facility for discovery, one which may be advantageous to both sides as well as an improvement in the deposition process. It will reduce the difficulties now encountered in determining, prior to the taking of a deposition, whether a particular employee or agent is a "managing agent." See Note, *Discovery Against Corporations Under the Federal Rules*, 47 Iowa L.Rev. 1006–1016 (1962). It will curb the "bandying" by which officers or managing agents of a corporation are deposed in turn but each disclaims knowledge of facts that are clearly known to persons in the organization and thereby to it. *Cf. Haney v. Woodward & Lothrop, Inc.*, 330 F.2d 940, 944 (4th Cir. 1964). The provision should also assist organizations which find that an unnecessarily large number of their officers and agents are being deposed by a party uncertain of who in the organization has knowledge. Some courts have held that under the existing rules a corporation should not be burdened with choosing which person is to appear for it. E.g., *United States v. Gahagan Dredging Corp.*, 24 F.R.D. 328, 329 (S.D.N.Y.1958). This burden is not essentially different from that of answering interrogatories under Rule 33, and is in any case lighter than that of an examining party ignorant of who in the corporation has knowledge.

Subdivision (c). A new sentence is inserted at the beginning, representing the transfer of existing Rule 26(c) to this subdivision. Another addition conforms to the new provision in subdivision (b)(4).

The present rule provides that transcription shall be carried out unless all parties waive it. In view of the many depositions taken from which nothing useful is discovered, the revised language provides that transcription is to be performed if any party requests it. The fact of the request is relevant to the exercise of the court's discretion in determining who shall pay for transcription.

Parties choosing to serve written questions rather than participate personally in an oral deposition are directed to serve their questions on the party taking the deposition, since the officer is often not identified in advance. Confidentiality is preserved, since the questions may be served in a sealed envelope.

Subdivision (d). The assessment of expenses incurred in relation to motions made under this subdivision (d) is made subject to the provisions of Rule 37(a). The standards for assessment of expenses are more fully set out in Rule 37(a), and these standards should apply to the essentially similar motions of this subdivision.

Subdivision (e). The provision relating to the refusal of a witness to sign his deposition is tightened through insertion of a 30-day time period.

Subdivision (f)(1). A provision is added which codifies in a flexible way the procedure for handling exhibits related to the deposition and at the same time assures each party that he may inspect and copy documents and things produced by a nonparty witness in response to a subpoena duces tecum. As a general rule and in the absence of agreement to the contrary or order of the court, exhibits produced without objection are to be annexed to and returned with the deposition, but a witness may substitute copies for purposes of marking and he may obtain return of the exhibits. The right of the parties to inspect exhibits for identification and to make copies is assured. *Cf.* N.Y.C.P.L.R. § 3116(c).

1971 Amendments

The subdivision permits a party to name a corporation or other form of organization as a deponent in the notice of examination and to describe in the notice the matters about which discovery is desired. The organization is then obliged to designate natural persons to testify on its behalf. The amendment clarifies the procedure to be followed if a party desires to examine a non-party organization through persons designated by the organization. Under the rules, a subpoena rather than a notice of examination is served on a non-party to compel attendance at the taking of a deposition. The amendment provides that a subpoena may name a non-party organization as the deponent and may indicate the matters about which discovery is desired. In that event, the non-party organization must respond by designating natural persons, who are then obliged to testify as to matters known or reasonably available to the organization. To insure that a non-party organization that is not represented by counsel has knowledge of its duty to designate, the amendment directs the party seeking discovery to advise of the duty in the body of the subpoena.

1972 Amendments

Subdivision (c). Existing Rule 43(b), which is to be abrogated, deals with the use of leading questions, the calling, interrogation, impeachment, and scope of cross-examination of adverse parties, officers, etc. These topics are dealt with in many places in the Rules of Evidence. Moreover, many pertinent topics included in the Rules of Evidence are not mentioned in Rule 43(b), e.g. privilege. A reference to the Rules of Evidence generally is therefore made in subdivision (c) of Rule 30.

1980 Amendments

Subdivision (b)(4). It has been proposed that electronic recording of depositions be authorized as a matter of course, subject to the right of a party to seek an order that a deposition be recorded by stenographic means. The Committee is not satisfied that a case has been made for a reversal of present practice. The amendment is made to encourage parties to agree to the use of electronic recording of depositions so that conflicting claims with respect to the potential of electronic recording for reducing costs of depositions can be appraised in the light of greater experience. The provision that the parties may stipulate that depositions may be recorded by other than stenographic means seems implicit in Rule 29. The amendment makes it explicit. The provision that the stipulation or order shall designate the person before whom the deposition is to be taken is added to encourage the naming of the recording technician as that person, eliminating the necessity of the presence of one whose only function is to administer the oath. See Rules 28(a) and 29.

Subdivision (b)(7). Depositions by telephone are now authorized by Rule 29 upon stipulation of the parties. The amendment authorizes that method by order of the court. The final sentence is added to make it clear that when a deposition is taken by telephone it is taken in the district and at the place where the witness is to answer the questions rather than that where the questions are propounded.

Subdivision (f)(1). For the reasons set out in the Note following the amendment of Rule 5(d), the court may wish to permit the parties to retain depositions unless they are to be used in the action. The amendment of the first paragraph permits the court to so order.

The amendment of the second paragraph is clarifying. The purpose of the paragraph is to permit a person who produces materials at a deposition to offer copies for marking and annexation to the deposition. Such copies are a "substitute" for the originals, which are not to be marked and which can thereafter be used or even disposed of by the person who produces them. In the light of that purpose, the former language of the paragraph had been justly termed "opaque." Wright & Miller, *Federal Practice and Procedure: Civil* § 2114.

1987 Amendments

The amendments are technical. No substantive change is intended.

1993 Amendments

Subdivision (a). Paragraph (1) retains the first and third sentences from the former subdivision (a) without significant modification. The second and fourth sentences are relocated.

Paragraph (2) collects all provisions bearing on requirements of leave of court to take a deposition.

Paragraph (2)(A) is new. It provides a limit on the number of depositions the parties may take, absent leave of court or stipulation with the other parties. One aim of this revision is to assure judicial review under the standards stated in Rule 26(b)(2) before any side will be allowed to take more than ten depositions in a case without agreement of the other parties. A second objective is to emphasize that counsel have a professional obligation to develop a mutual cost-effective plan for discovery in the case. Leave to take additional depositions should be granted when consistent with the principles of Rule 26(b)(2), and in some cases the ten-per-side limit should be reduced in accordance with those same principles. Consideration should ordinarily be given at the planning meeting of the parties under Rule 26(f) and at the time of a scheduling conference under Rule 16(b) as to enlargements or reductions in the number of depositions, eliminating the need for special motions.

A deposition under Rule 30(b)(6) should, for purposes of this limit, be treated as a single deposition even though more than one person may be designated to testify.

In multi-party cases, the parties on any side are expected to confer and agree as to which depositions are most needed, given the presumptive limit on the number of depositions they can take without leave of court. If these disputes cannot be amicably resolved, the court can be requested to resolve the dispute or permit additional depositions.

Paragraph (2)(B) is new. It requires leave of court if any witness is to be deposed in the action more than once. This requirement does not apply when a deposition is temporarily recessed for convenience of counsel or the deponent or to enable additional materials to be gathered before resuming the deposition. If significant travel costs would be incurred to resume the deposition, the parties should consider the feasibility of conducting the balance of the examination by telephonic means.

Paragraph (2)(C) revises the second sentence of the former subdivision (a) as to when depositions may be taken. Consistent with the changes made in Rule 26(d), providing that formal discovery ordinarily not commence until after the litigants have met and conferred as directed in revised Rule 26(f), the rule requires leave of court or agreement of the parties if a deposition is to be taken before that time (except when a witness is about to leave the country).

Subdivision (b). The primary change in subdivision (b) is that parties will be authorized to record deposition testimony by nonstenographic means without first having to obtain permission of the court or agreement from other counsel.

Former subdivision (b)(2) is partly relocated in subdivision (a)(2)(C) of this rule. The latter two sentences of the first paragraph are deleted, in part because they are redundant to Rule 26(g) and in part because Rule 11 no longer applies to discovery requests. The second paragraph of the former subdivision (b)(2), relating to use of depositions at trial where a party was unable to obtain counsel in time for an accelerated deposition, is relocated in Rule 32.

New paragraph (2) confers on the party taking the deposition the choice of the method of recording, without the need to obtain prior court approval for one taken other than stenographically. A party choosing to record a deposition only by videotape or audiotape should understand that a transcript will be required by Rule 26(a)(3)(B) and Rule 32(c) if the deposition is later to be offered as evidence at trial or on a dispositive motion under Rule 56. Objections to the nonstenographic recording of a deposition, when warranted by the circumstances, can be presented to the court under Rule 26(c).

Paragraph (3) provides that other parties may arrange, at their own expense, for the recording of a deposition by a means (stenographic, visual, or sound) in addition to the method designated by the person noticing the deposition. The former provisions of this paragraph, relating to the court's power to change the date of a deposition, have been eliminated as redundant in view of Rule 26(c)(2).

Revised paragraph (4) requires that all depositions be recorded by an officer designated or appointed under Rule 28 and contains special provisions designed to provide basic safeguards to assure the utility and integrity of recordings taken other than stenographically.

Paragraph (7) is revised to authorize the taking of a deposition not only by telephone but also by other remote electronic means, such as satellite television, when agreed to by the parties or authorized by the court.

Subdivision (c). Minor changes are made in this subdivision to reflect those made in subdivision (b) and to complement the new provisions of subdivision (d)(1), aimed at reducing the number of interruptions during depositions.

In addition, the revision addresses a recurring problem as to whether other potential deponents can attend a deposition. Courts have disagreed, some holding that witnesses should be excluded through invocation of Rule 615 of the evidence rules, and others holding that witnesses may attend unless excluded by an order under Rule 26(c)(5). The revision provides that other witnesses are not automatically excluded from a deposition simply by the request of a party. Exclusion, however, can be ordered under Rule 26(c)(5) when appropriate; and, if exclusion is ordered, consideration should be given as to whether the excluded witnesses likewise should be precluded from reading, or being otherwise informed about, the testimony given in the earlier depositions. The revision addresses only the matter of attendance by potential deponents, and does not attempt to resolve issues concerning attendance by others, such as members of the public or press.

Subdivision (d). The first sentence of new paragraph (1) provides that any objections during a deposition must be made concisely and in a non-argumentative and non-suggestive manner. Depositions frequently have been unduly prolonged, if not unfairly frustrated, by lengthy objections and colloquy, often suggesting how the deponent should respond. While objections may, under the revised rule, be made during a deposition, they ordinarily should be limited to those that under Rule 32(d)(3) might be waived if not made at that time, *i.e.*, objections on grounds that might be immediately obviated, removed, or cured, such as to the form of a question or the responsiveness of an answer. Under Rule 32(b), other objections can, even without the so-called "usual stipulation" preserving objections, be raised for the first time at trial and therefore should be kept to a minimum during a deposition.

Directions to a deponent not to answer a question can be even more disruptive than objections. The second sentence of new paragraph (1) prohibits such directions except in the three circumstances indicated: to claim a privilege or protection against disclosure (*e.g.*, as work product), to enforce a court directive limiting the scope or length of permissible discovery, or to suspend a deposition to enable presentation of a motion under paragraph (3).

Paragraph (2) is added to this subdivision to dispel any doubts regarding the power of the court by order or local rule to establish limits on the length of depositions. The rule also explicitly authorizes the court to impose the cost resulting from obstructive tactics that unreasonably prolong a deposition on the person engaged in such obstruction. This sanction may be imposed on a non-party witness as well as a party or attorney, but is otherwise congruent with Rule 26(g).

It is anticipated that limits on the length of depositions prescribed by local rules would be presumptive only, subject to modification by the court or by agreement of the parties. Such modifications typically should be discussed by the parties in their meeting under Rule 26(f) and included in the scheduling order required by Rule 16(b). Additional time, moreover, should be allowed under the revised rule when justified under the principles stated in Rule 26(b)(2). To reduce the number of special motions, local rules should ordinarily permit—and indeed encourage—the parties to agree to additional time, as when, during the taking of a deposition, it becomes clear that some additional examination is needed.

Paragraph (3) authorizes appropriate sanctions not only when a deposition is unreasonably prolonged, but also when an attorney engages in other practices that improperly frustrate the fair examination of the deponent, such as making improper objections or giving directions not to answer prohibited by paragraph (1). In general, counsel should not engage in any conduct during a deposition that would not be allowed in the presence of a judicial officer. The making of an excessive number of unnecessary objections may itself constitute sanctionable conduct, as may the refusal of an attorney to agree with other counsel on a fair apportionment of the time allowed for examination of a deponent or a refusal to agree to a reasonable request for some additional time to complete a deposition, when that is permitted by the local rule or order.

Subdivision (e). Various changes are made in this subdivision to reduce problems sometimes encountered when depositions are taken stenographically. Reporters frequently have difficulties obtaining signatures—and the return of depositions—from deponents. Under the revision pre-filing review by the deponent is required only if requested before the deposition is completed. If review is requested, the deponent will be allowed 30 days to review the transcript or recording and to indicate any changes in form or substance. Signature of the deponent will be required only if review is requested and changes are made.

Subdivision (f). Minor changes are made in this subdivision to reflect those made in subdivision (b). In courts which direct that depositions not be automatically filed, the reporter can transmit the transcript or recording to the attorney taking the deposition (or ordering the transcript or record), who then becomes custodian for the court of the original record of the deposition. Pursuant to subdivision (f)(2), as under the prior rule, any other party is entitled to secure a copy of the deposition from the officer designated to take the deposition; accordingly, unless ordered or agreed, the officer must retain a copy of the recording or the stenographic notes.

HISTORICAL NOTES

Effective Date of Amendment Proposed November 20, 1972

Amendment of this rule embraced by the order entered by the Supreme Court of the United States on November 20, 1972, effective on the 180th day beginning after January 2, 1975, see section 3 of Pub.L. 93–595, Jan. 2, 1975, 88 Stat. 1959, set out as a note under section 2071 of Title 28.

Rule 31. Depositions Upon Written Questions

(a) Serving Questions; Notice.

(1) A party may take the testimony of any person, including a party, by deposition upon written questions without leave of court except as provided in paragraph (2). The attendance of witnesses may be compelled by the use of subpoena as provided in Rule 45.

(2) A party must obtain leave of court, which shall be granted to the extent consistent with the principles stated in Rule 26(b)(2), if the person to be examined is confined in prison or if, without the written stipulation of the parties.

(A) a proposed deposition would result in more than ten depositions being taken under this rule or Rule 30 by the plaintiffs, or by the defendants, or by third-party defendants;

(B) the person to be examined has already been deposed in the case; or

(C) a party seeks to take a deposition before the time specified in Rule 26(d).

(3) A party desiring to take a deposition upon written questions shall serve them upon every other party with a notice stating (1) the name and address of the person who is to answer them, if known, and if the name is not known, a general description sufficient to identify the person or the particular class or group to which the person belongs, and (2) the name or descriptive title and address of the officer before whom the deposition is to be taken. A deposition upon written questions may be taken of a public or private corporation or a partnership or association or governmental agency in accordance with the provisions of Rule 30(b)(6).

(4) Within 14 days after the notice and written questions are served, a party may serve cross questions upon all other parties. Within 7 days after being served with cross questions, a party may serve redirect questions upon all other parties. Within 7 days after being served with redirect questions, a party may serve recross questions upon all other parties. The court may for cause shown enlarge or shorten the time.

(b) Officer to Take Responses and Prepare Record. A copy of the notice and copies of all questions served shall be delivered by the party taking the deposition to the officer designated in the notice, who shall proceed promptly, in the manner provided by Rule 30(c), (e), and (f), to take the testimony of the witness in response to the questions and to prepare, certify, and file or mail the deposition, attaching thereto the copy of the notice and the questions received by the officer.

(c) Notice of Filing. When the deposition is filed the party taking it shall promptly give notice thereof to all other parties.

(As amended Mar. 30, 1970, eff. July 1, 1970; Mar. 2, 1987, eff. Aug. 1, 1987; Apr. 22, 1993, eff. Dec. 1, 1993.)

ADVISORY COMMITTEE NOTES

1937 Adoption

This rule is in accordance with common practice. In most of the states listed in the Note to Rule 26(a), provisions similar to this rule will be found in the statutes which in their respective statutory compilations follow those cited in the Note to Rule 26(a).

1970 Amendment

Confusion is created by the use of the same terminology to describe both the taking of a deposition upon "written interrogatories" pursuant to this rule and the serving of "written interrogatories" upon parties pursuant to Rule 33. The distinction between these two modes of discovery will be more readily and clearly grasped through substitution of the word "questions" for "interrogatories" throughout this rule.

Subdivision (a). A new paragraph is inserted at the beginning of this subdivision to conform to the rearrangement of provisions in Rules 26(a), 30(a), and 30(b).

The revised subdivision permits designation of the deponent by general description or by class or group. This conforms to the practice for depositions on oral examination.

The new procedure provided in Rule 30(b)(6) for taking the deposition of a corporation or other organization through persons designated by the organization is incorporated by reference.

The service of all questions, including cross, redirect, and recross, is to be made on all parties. This will inform the parties and enable them to participate fully in the procedure.

The time allowed for service of cross, redirect, and recross questions has been extended. Experience with the existing time limits shows them to be unrealistically short. No special restriction is placed on the time for serving the notice of taking the deposition and the first set of questions. Since no party is required to serve cross questions less than 30 days after the notice and questions are served, the defendant has sufficient time to obtain counsel. The court may for cause shown enlarge or shorten the time.

Subdivision (d). Since new Rule 26(c) provides for protective orders with respect to all discovery, and expressly provides that the court may order that one discovery device be used in place of another, subdivision (d) is eliminated as unnecessary.

1987 Amendment

The amendments are technical. No substantive change is intended.

1993 Amendments

Subdivision (a). The first paragraph of subdivision (a) is divided into two subparagraphs, with provisions comparable to those made in the revision of Rule 30. Changes are made in the former third paragraph, numbered in the revision as paragraph (4), to reduce the total time for developing cross-examination, redirect, and recross questions from 50 days to 28 days.

Rule 32. Use of Depositions in Court Proceedings

(a) Use of Depositions. At the trial or upon the hearing of a motion or an interlocutory proceeding, any part or all of a deposition, so far as admissible under the rules of evidence applied as though the witness were then present and testifying, may be used against any party who was present or represented at the taking of the deposition or who had reasonable notice thereof, in accordance with any of the following provisions:

(1) Any deposition may be used by any party for the purpose of contradicting or impeaching the testimony of deponent as a witness, or for any other purpose permitted by the Federal Rules of Evidence.

(2) The deposition of a party or of anyone who at the time of taking the deposition was an officer, director, or managing agent, or a person designated under Rule 30(b)(6) or 31(a) to testify on behalf of a public or private corporation, partnership or association or governmental agency which is a party may be used by an adverse party for any purpose.

(3) The deposition of a witness, whether or not a party, may be used by any party for any purpose if the court finds:

(A) that the witness is dead; or

(B) that the witness is at a greater distance than 100 miles from the place of trial or hearing, or is out of the United States, unless it appears that the absence of the witness was procured by the party offering the deposition; or

(C) that the witness is unable to attend or testify because of age, illness, infirmity, or imprisonment; or

(D) that the party offering the deposition has been unable to procure the attendance of the witness by subpoena; or

(E) upon application and notice, that such exceptional circumstances exist as to make it desirable, in the interest of justice and with due regard to the importance of presenting the testimony of witnesses orally in open court, to allow the deposition to be used.

A deposition taken without leave of court pursuant to a notice under Rule 30(a)(2)(C) shall not be used against a party who demonstrates that, when served with the notice, it was unable through the exercise of diligence to obtain counsel to represent it at the taking of the deposition; nor shall a deposition be used against a party who, having received less than 11 days notice of a deposition, has promptly upon receiving such notice filed a motion for a protective order under Rule 26(c)(2) requesting that the deposition not be held or be held at a different time or place and such motion is pending at the time the deposition is held.

(4) If only part of a deposition is offered in evidence by a party, an adverse party may require the offeror to introduce any other part which ought in fairness to be considered with the part introduced, and any party may introduce any other parts.

Substitution of parties pursuant to Rule 25 does not affect the right to use depositions previously taken; and, when an action has been brought in any court of the United States or of any State and another action involving the same subject matter is afterward brought between the same parties or their representatives or successors in interest, all depositions lawfully taken and duly filed in the former action may be used in the latter as if originally taken therefor. A deposition previously taken may also be used as permitted by the Federal Rules of Evidence.

(b) Objections to Admissibility. Subject to the provisions of Rule 28(b) and subdivision (d)(3) of this rule, objection may be made at the trial or hearing to receiving in evidence any deposition or part thereof for any reason which would require the exclusion of the evidence if the witness were then present and testifying.

(c) Form of Presentation. Except as otherwise directed by the court, a party offering deposition testimony pursuant to this rule may offer it in stenographic or nonstenographic form, but, if in nonstenographic form, the party shall also provide the court with a transcript of the portions so offered. On request of any party in a case tried before a jury, deposition testimony offered other than for impeachment purposes shall be presented in nonstenographic form, if available, unless the court for good cause orders otherwise.

(d) Effect of Errors and Irregularities in Depositions.

(1) As to Notice. All errors and irregularities in the notice for taking a deposition are waived unless written objection is promptly served upon the party giving the notice.

(2) As to Disqualification of Officer. Objection to taking a deposition because of disqualification of the officer before whom it is to be taken is waived unless made before the taking of the deposition begins or as soon thereafter as the disqualification becomes known or could be discovered with reasonable diligence.

(3) As to Taking of Deposition.

(A) Objections to the competency of a witness or to the competency, relevancy, or materiality of testimony are not waived by failure to make them before or during the taking of the deposition, unless the ground of the objection is one which might have been obviated or removed if presented at that time.

(B) Errors and irregularities occurring at the oral examination in the manner of taking the deposition, in the form of the questions or answers, in the oath or affirmation, or in the conduct of parties, and errors of any kind which might be obviated, removed, or cured if promptly presented, are waived unless seasonable objection thereto is made at the taking of the deposition.

(C) Objections to the form of written questions submitted under Rule 31 are waived unless served in writing upon the party propounding them within the time allowed for serving the succeeding cross or other questions and within 5 days after service of the last questions authorized.

(4) As to Completion and Return of Deposition. Errors and irregularities in the manner in which the testimony is transcribed or the deposition is prepared, signed, certified, sealed, indorsed, transmitted, filed, or otherwise dealt with by the officer under Rules 30 and 31 are waived unless a motion to suppress the deposition or some part thereof is made with reasonable promptness after such defect is, or with due diligence might have been, ascertained.

(As amended Mar. 30, 1970, eff. July 1, 1970; Nov. 20, 1972, eff. July 1, 1975; Apr. 29, 1980, eff. Aug. 1, 1980; Mar. 2, 1987, eff. Aug. 1, 1987; Apr. 22, 1993, eff. Dec. 1, 1993.)

ADVISORY COMMITTEE NOTES

1937 Adoption

This rule is in accordance with common practice. In most of the states listed in the note to rule 26, provisions similar to this rule will be found in the statutes which in their respective statutory compilations follow those cited in the Note to Rule 26.

1970 Amendment

As part of the rearrangement of the discovery rules, existing subdivisions (d), (e), and (f) of Rule 26 are transferred to Rule 32 as new subdivisions (a), (b), and (c). The provisions of Rule 32 are retained as subdivision (d) of Rule 32 with appropriate changes in the lettering and numbering of subheadings. The new rule is given a suitable new title. A beneficial byproduct of the rearrangement is that provisions which are naturally related to one another are placed in one rule.

A change is made in new Rule 32(a), whereby it is made clear that the rules of evidence are to be applied to depositions offered at trial as though the deponent were then present and testifying at trial. This eliminates the possibility of certain technical hearsay objections which are based, not on the contents of deponent's testimony, but on his absence from court. The language of present Rule 26(d) does not appear to authorize these technical objections, but it is not entirely clear. Note present Rule 26(e), transferred to Rule 32(b); see 2A Barron & Holtzoff, *Federal Practice and Procedure* 164–166 (Wright ed. 1961).

An addition in Rule 32(a)(2) provides for use of a deposition of a person designated by a corporation or other organization, which is a party, to testify on its behalf. This complements the new procedure for taking the deposition of a corporation or other organization provided in Rules 30(b)(6) and 31(a). The addition is appropriate, since the deposition is in substance and effect that of the corporation or other organization which is a party.

A change is made in the standard under which a party offering part of a deposition in evidence may be required to introduce additional parts of the deposition. The new standard is contained in a proposal made by the Advisory Committee on Rules of Evidence. See Rule 1–07 and accompanying Note, *Preliminary Draft of Proposed Rules of Evidence for the United States District Courts and Magistrates* 21–22 (March, 1969).

References to other rules are changed to conform to the rearrangement, and minor verbal changes have been made for clarification. The time for objecting to written questions served under Rule 31 is slightly extended.

1972 Amendment

Subdivision (c). The concept of "making a person one's own witness" appears to have had significance principally in two respects: impeachment and waiver of incompetency. Neither retains any vitality under the Rules of Evidence. The old prohibition against impeaching one's own witness is eliminated by Evidence Rule 607. The lack of recognition in the Rules of Evidence of state rules of incompetency in the Dead Man's area renders it unnecessary to consider aspects of waiver arising from calling the incompetent party-witness. Subdivision (c) is deleted because it appears to be no longer necessary in the light of the Rules of Evidence.

1980 Amendment

Subdivision (a)(1). Rule 801(d) of the Federal Rules of Evidence permits a prior inconsistent statement of a witness in a deposition to be used as substantive evidence. And Rule 801(d)(2) makes the statement of an agent or servant admissible against the principal under the circumstances described in the Rule. The language of the present subdivision is, therefore, too narrow.

Subdivision (a)(4). The requirement that a prior action must have been dismissed before depositions taken for use in it can be used in a subsequent action was doubtless an oversight, and the courts have ignored it. See Wright & Miller, *Federal Practice and Procedure: Civil* § 2150. The final sentence is added to reflect the fact that the Federal Rules of Evidence permit a broader use of depositions previously taken under certain circumstances. For example, Rule 804(b)(1) of the Federal Rules of Evidence provides that if a witness is unavailable, as that term is defined by the rule, his deposition in any earlier proceeding can be used against a party to the prior proceeding who had an opportunity and similar motive to develop the testimony of the witness.

1987 Amendment

The amendment is technical. No substantive change is intended.

1993 Amendments

Subdivision (a). The last sentence of revised subdivision (a) not only includes the substance of the provisions formerly contained in the second paragraph of Rule 30(b)(2), but adds a provision to deal with the situation when a party, receiving minimal notice of a proposed deposition, is unable to obtain a court ruling on its motion for a protective order seeking to delay or change the place of the deposition. Ordinarily a party does not obtain protection merely by the filing of a motion for a protective order under Rule 26(c); any protection is dependent upon the court's ruling. Under the revision, a party receiving less than 11 days notice of a deposition can, provided its motion for a protective order is filed promptly, be spared the risks resulting from nonattendance at the deposition held before its motion is ruled upon. Although the revision of Rule 32(a) covers only the risk that the deposition could be used against the non-appearing movant, it should also follow that, when the proposed deponent is the movant, the deponent would have "just cause" for failing to appear for purposes of Rule 37(d)(1). Inclusion of this provision is not intended to signify that 11 days' notice is the minimum advance notice for all depositions or that greater than 10 days should necessarily be deemed sufficient in all situations.

Subdivision (c). This new subdivision, inserted at the location of a subdivision previously abrogated, is included in view of the increased opportunities for video-recording and audio-recording of depositions under revised Rule 30(b). Under this rule a party may offer deposition testimony in any of the forms authorized under Rule 30(b) but, if offering it in a nonstenographic form, must provide the court with a transcript of the portions so offered. On request of any party in a jury trial, deposition testimony offered other than for impeachment purposes is to be presented in a nonstenographic form if available, unless the court directs otherwise. Note that under Rule 26(a)(3)(B) a party expecting to use nonstenographic deposition testimony as substantive evidence is required to provide other parties with a transcript in advance of trial.

HISTORICAL NOTES

Effective Date of Amendment Proposed November 20, 1972

Amendment of this rule embraced by the order entered by the Supreme Court of the United States on November 20, 1972, effective on the 180th day beginning after January 2, 1975, see section 3 of Pub.L. 93–595, Jan. 2, 1975, 88 Stat. 1959, set out as a note under section 2071 of Title 28.

Rule 33. Interrogatories to Parties

(a) Availability. Without leave of court or written stipulation, any party may serve upon any other party written interrogatories, not exceeding 25 in number including all discrete subparts, to be answered by the party served or, if the party served is a public or private corporation or a partnership or association or governmental agency, by any officer or agent, who shall furnish such information as is available to the party. Leave to serve additional interrogatories shall be granted to the extent consistent with the principles of Rule 26(b)(2). Without leave of court or written stipulation, interrogatories may not be served before the time specified in Rule 26(d).

(b) Answers and Objections.

(1) Each interrogatory shall be answered separately and fully in writing under oath, unless it is objected to, in which event the objecting party shall state the reasons for objection and shall answer to the extent the interrogatory is not objectionable.

(2) The answers are to be signed by the person making them, and the objections signed by the attorney making them.

(3) The party upon whom the interrogatories have been served shall serve a copy of the answers, and objections if any, within 30 days after the service of the interrogatories. A shorter or longer time may be directed by the court or, in the absence of such an order, agreed to in writing by the parties subject to Rule 29.

(4) All grounds for an objection to an interrogatory shall be stated with specificity. Any ground not stated in a timely objection is waived unless the party's failure to object is excused by the court for good cause shown.

(5) The party submitting the interrogatories may move for an order under Rule 37(a) with respect to any objection to or other failure to answer an interrogatory.

(c) Scope; Use at Trial. Interrogatories may relate to any matters which can be inquired into under Rule 26(b)(1), and the answers may be used to the extent permitted by the rules of evidence.

An interrogatory otherwise proper is not necessarily objectionable merely because an answer to the interrogatory involves an opinion or contention that relates to fact or the application of law to fact, but the court may order that such an interrogatory need not be answered until after designated discovery has been completed or until a pre-trial conference or other later time.

(d) Option to Produce Business Records.

Where the answer to an interrogatory may be derived or ascertained from the business records of the party upon whom the interrogatory has been served or from an examination, audit or inspection of such business records, including a compilation, abstract or summary thereof, and the burden of deriving or ascertaining the answer is substantially the same for the party serving the interrogatory as for the party served, it is a sufficient answer to such interrogatory to specify the records from which the answer may be derived or ascertained and to afford to the party serving the interrogatory reasonable opportunity to examine, audit or inspect such records and to make copies, compilations, abstracts or summaries. A specification shall be in sufficient detail to permit the interrogating party to locate and to identify, as readily as can the party served, the records from which the answer may be ascertained.

(As amended Dec. 27, 1946, eff. Mar. 19, 1948; Mar. 30, 1970, eff. July 1, 1970; Apr. 29, 1980, eff. Aug. 1, 1980; Apr. 22, 1993, eff. Dec. 1, 1993.)

ADVISORY COMMITTEE NOTES

1937 Adoption

This rule restates the substance of [former] Equity Rule 58 (Discovery—Interrogatories—Inspection and Production of Documents—Admission of Execution or Genuineness), with modifications to conform to these rules.

1946 Amendment

Note. The added second sentence in the first paragraph of Rule 33 conforms with a similar change in Rule 26(a) and will avoid litigation as to when the interrogatories may be served. Original Rule 33 does not state the times at which parties may serve written interrogatories upon each other. It has been the accepted view, however, that the times were the same in Rule 33 as those stated in Rule 26(a). *United States v. American Solvents & Chemical Corp. of California*, D.Del.1939, 30 F.Supp. 107; *Sheldon v. Great Lakes Transit Corp.*, W.D.N.Y.1942, 2 F.R.D. 272, 5 Fed.Rules Serv. 33.11, Case 3; *Musher Foundation, Inc., v. Alba Trading Co.*, S.D.N.Y.1941, 42 F.Supp. 281; 2 *Moore's Federal Practice*, 1938, 2621. The time within which leave of court must be secured by a plaintiff has been fixed at 10 days, in view of the fact that a defendant has 10 days within which to make objections in any case, which should give him ample time to engage counsel and prepare.

Further in the first paragraph of Rule 33, the word "service" is substituted for "delivery" in conformance with the use of the word "serve" elsewhere in the rule and generally throughout the rules. See also Note to Rule 13(a) herein. The portion of the rule dealing with practice on objections has been revised so as to afford a clearer statement of the procedure. The addition of the words "to interrogatories to which objection is made" insures that only the answers to the objectionable interrogatories may be deferred, and that the answers to interrogatories not objectionable shall be forthcoming within the time prescribed in the rule. Under the original wording, answers to all interrogatories may be withheld until objections, sometimes to but a few interrogatories, are determined. The amendment expedites the procedure of the rule and serves to eliminate the strike value of objections to minor interrogatories. The elimination of the last sentence of the original rule is in line with the policy stated subsequently in this note.

The added second paragraph in Rule 33 contributes clarity and specificity as to the use and scope of interrogatories to the parties. The field of inquiry will be as broad as the scope of examination under Rule 26(b). There is no reason why interrogatories should be more limited than depositions, particularly when the former represent an inexpensive means of securing useful information. See *Hoffman v. Wilson Line, Inc.*, E.D.Pa.1946, 9 Fed.Rules Serv. 33.514, Case 2; *Brewster v. Technicolor, Inc.*, N.Y.1941, 2 F.R.D. 186, 5 Fed.Rules Serv. 33.319, Case 3; *Kingsway Press, Inc. v. Farrell Publishing Corp.*, S.D.N.Y.1939, 30 F.Supp. 775. Under present Rule 33 some courts have unnecessarily restricted the breadth of inquiry on various grounds. See *Auer v. Hershey Creamery Co.*, D.N.J.1939, 2 Fed.Rules Serv. 33.31, Case 2, 1 F.R.D. 14; *Tudor v. Leslie*, D.Mass.1940, 1 F.R.D. 448, 4 Fed.Rules Serv. 33.324, Case 1. Other courts have read into the rule the requirement that interrogation should be directed only towards "important facts", and have tended to fix a more or less arbitrary limit as to the number of interrogatories which could be asked in any case. See *Knox v. Alter*, W.D.Pa.1942, 2 F.R.D. 337, 6 Fed.Rules Serv. 33.352, Case 1; *Byers Theaters, Inc. v. Murphy*, W.D.Va.1940, 3 Fed.Rules Serv. 33.31, Case 3, 1 F.R.D. 286; *Coca-Cola Co. v. Dixi-Cola Laboratories, Inc.*, D.Md.1939, 30 F.Supp. 275. See also comment on these restrictions in Holtzoff, *Instruments of Discovery under Federal Rules of Civil Procedure*, 1942, 41 Mich.L.Rev. 205, 216–217. Under amended Rule 33, the party interrogated is given the right to invoke such protective orders under Rule 30(b) as are appropriate to the situation. At the same time, it is provided that the number of or number of sets of interrogatories to be served may not be limited arbitrarily or as a general policy to any particular number, but that a limit may be fixed only as justice requires to avoid annoyance, expense, embarrassment or oppression in individual cases. The party interrogated, therefore, must show the necessity for limitation on that basis. It will be noted that in accord with this change the last sentence of the present rule, restricting the sets of interrogatories to be served, has been stricken. In *J. Schoeneman, Inc. v. Brauer*, W.D.Mo.1940, 1 F.R.D. 292, 3 Fed.Rules Serv. 33.31, Case 2, the court said: "Rule 33 * * * has been interpreted * * * as being just as broad in its implications as in the case of depositions * * * It makes no difference therefore, how many interrogatories are propounded. If the inquiries are pertinent the opposing party cannot complain." To the same effect, see *Canuso v. City of Niagara Falls*, W.D.N.Y.1945, 8 Fed.Rules Serv. 33.352, Case 1; *Hoffman v. Wilson Line, Inc.*, supra.

By virtue of express language in the added second paragraph of Rule 33, as amended, any uncertainty as to the use of the answers to interrogatories is removed. The omission of a provision on this score in the original rule has caused some difficulty. See, e.g., *Bailey v. New England Mutual Life Ins. Co.*, S.D.Cal.1940, 1 F.R.D. 494, 4 Fed.Rules Serv. 33.46, Case 1.

The second sentence of the second paragraph in Rule 33, as amended, concerns the situation where a party wishes to serve interrogatories on a party after having taken his deposition, or vice versa. It has been held that an oral examination of a party, after the submission to him and answer of interrogatories, would be permitted. *Howard v. State Marine Corp.*, S.D.N.Y.1940, 4 Fed.Rules Serv. 33.62, Case 1, 1 F.R.D. 499; *Stevens v. Minder Construction Co.*, S.D.N.Y.1943, 3 F.R.D. 498, 7 Fed.Rules Serv. 30b.31, Case 2. But objections have been sustained to interrogatories served after the oral deposition of a party had been taken. *McNally v. Simons*, S.D.N.Y.1940, 3 Fed.Rules Serv. 33.61, Case 1, 1 F.R.D. 254; *Currier v. Currier*, S.D.N.Y.1942, 3 F.R.D. 21, 6 Fed.Rules Serv. 33.61, Case 1. Rule 33, as amended, permits either interrogatories after a deposition or a deposition after interrogatories. It may be quite desirable or necessary to elicit additional information by the inexpensive method of interrogatories where a deposition has already been taken. The party to be interrogated, however, may seek a protective order from the court under Rule 30(b) where the additional deposition or interrogation works a hardship or injustice on the party from whom it is sought.

1970 Amendment

Subdivision (a). The mechanics of the operation of Rule 33 are substantially revised by the proposed amendment, with a view to reducing court intervention. There is general agreement that interrogatories spawn a greater percentage of objections and motions than any other discovery device. The Columbia Survey shows that, although half of the litigants resorted to depositions and about one-third used interrogatories, about 65 percent of the objections were made with respect to interrogatories and 26 percent related to depositions. See also Speck, *The Use of Discovery in United States District Courts,* 60 Yale L.J. 1132, 1144, 1151 (1951); Note, 36 Minn.L.Rev. 364, 379 (1952).

The procedures now provided in Rule 33 seem calculated to encourage objections and court motions. The time periods now allowed for responding to interrogatories—15 days for answers and 10 days for objections—are too short. The Columbia Survey shows that tardy response to interrogatories is common, virtually expected. The same was reported in Speck, *supra,* 60 Yale L.J. 1132, 1144. The time pressures tend to encourage objections as a means of gaining time to answer.

The time for objections is even shorter than for answers, and the party runs the risk that if he fails to object in time he may have waived his objections. *E.g., Cleminshaw v. Beech Aircraft Corp.,* 21 F.R.D. 300 (D.Del.1957); See 4 *Moore's Federal Practice,* ¶33.27 (2d ed. 1966); 2A Barron & Holtzoff, *Federal Practice and Procedure* 372–373 (Wright ed. 1961). It often seems easier to object than to seek an extension of time. Unlike Rules 30(d) and 37(a), Rule 33 imposes no sanction of expenses on a party whose objections are clearly unjustified.

Rule 33 assures that the objections will lead directly to court, through its requirement that they be served with a notice of hearing. Although this procedure does not preclude an out-of-court resolution of the dispute, the procedure tends to discourage informal negotiations. If answers are served and they are thought inadequate, the interrogating party may move under Rule 37(a) for an order compelling adequate answers. There is no assurance that the hearing on objections and that on inadequate answers will be heard together.

The amendment improves the procedure of Rule 33 in the following respects:

(1) The time allowed for response is increased to 30 days and this time period applies to both answers and objections, but a defendant need not respond in less than 45 days after service of the summons and complaint upon him. As is true under existing law, the responding party who believes that some parts or all of the interrogatories are objectionable may choose to seek a protective order under new Rule 26(c) or may serve objections under this rule. Unless he applies for a protective order, he is required to serve answers or objections in response to the interrogatories, subject to the sanctions provided in Rule 37(d). Answers and objections are served together, so that a response to each interrogatory is encouraged, and any failure to respond is easily noted.

(2) In view of the enlarged time permitted for response, it is no longer necessary to require leave of court for service of interrogatories. The purpose of this requirement—that defendant have time to obtain counsel before a response must be made—is adequately fulfilled by the requirement that interrogatories be served upon a party with or after service of the summons and complaint upon him.

Some would urge that the plaintiff nevertheless not be permitted to serve interrogatories with the complaint. They fear that a routine practice might be invited, whereby form interrogatories would accompany most complaints. More fundamentally, they feel that, since very general complaints are permitted in present-day pleading, it is fair that the defendant have a right to take the lead in serving interrogatories. (These views apply also to Rule 36.) The amendment of Rule 33 rejects these views, in favor of allowing both parties to go forward with discovery, each free to obtain the information he needs respecting the case.

(3) If objections are made, the burden is on the interrogating party to move under Rule 37(a) for a court order compelling answers, in the course of which the court will pass on the objections. The change in the burden of going forward does not alter the existing obligation of an objecting party to justify his objections. *E.g., Pressley v. Bochlke,* 33 F.R.D. 316 (W.D.N.C. 1963). If the discovering party asserts that an answer is incomplete or evasive, again he may look to Rule 37(a) for relief, and he should add this assertion to his motion to overrule objections. There is no requirement that the parties consult informally concerning their differences, but the new procedure should encourage consultation, and the court may by local rule require it.

The proposed changes are similar in approach to those adopted by California in 1961. See Calif.Code Civ.Proc. § 2030(a). The experience of the Los Angeles Superior Court is informally reported as showing that the California amendment resulted in a significant reduction in court motions concerning interrogatories. Rhode Island takes a similar approach. See R. 33, *R.I.R. Civ.Proc. Official Draft,* p. 74 (Boston Law Book Co.).

A change is made in subdivision (a) which is not related to the sequence of procedures. The restriction to "adverse" parties is eliminated. The courts have generally construed this restriction as precluding interrogatories unless an issue between the parties is disclosed by the pleadings—even though the parties may have conflicting interests. E.g., *Mozeika v. Kaufman Construction Co.,* 25 F.R.D. 233 (E.D.Pa.1960) (plaintiff and third-party defendant); *Biddle v. Hutchinson,* 24 F.R.D. 256 (M.D.Pa.1959) (codefendants). The resulting distinctions have often been highly technical. In *Schlagenhauf v. Holder,* 379 U.S. 104 (1964), the Supreme Court rejected a contention that examination under Rule 35 could be had only against an "opposing" party, as not in keeping "with the aims of a liberal, nontechnical application of the Federal Rules." 379 U.S. at 116. Eliminating the requirement of "adverse" parties from Rule 33 brings it into line with all other discovery rules.

A second change in subdivision (a) is the addition of the term "governmental agency" to the listing of organizations whose answers are to be made by any officer or agent of the organization. This does not involve any change in existing law. Compare the similar listing in Rule 30(b)(6).

The duty of a party to supplement his answers to interrogatories is governed by a new provision in Rule 26(e).

Subdivision (b). There are numerous and conflicting decisions on the question whether and to what extent interrogatories are limited to matters "of fact," or may elicit opinions, contentions, and legal conclusions. Compare, e.g., *Payer, Hewitt & Co. v. Bellanca Corp.*, 26 F.R.D. 219 (D.Del.1960) (opinions bad); *Zinsky v. New York Central R.R.*, 36 F.R.D. 680 (N.D.Ohio 1964) (factual opinion or contention good, but legal theory bad); *United States v. Carter Products, Inc.*, 28 F.R.D. 373 (S.D.N.Y.1961) (factual contentions and legal theories bad) with *Taylor v. Sound Steamship Lines, Inc.*, 100 F.Supp. 388 (D.Conn.1951) (opinions good); *Bynum v. United States*, 36 F.R.D. 14 (E.D.La.1964) (contentions as to facts constituting negligence good). For lists of the many conflicting authorities, see 4 *Moore's Federal Practice* ¶33.17 (2d ed. 1966); 2A Barron & Holtzoff, *Federal Practice and Procedure* § 768 (Wright ed. 1961).

Rule 33 is amended to provide that an interrogatory is not objectionable merely because it calls for an opinion or contention that relates to fact or the application of law to fact. Efforts to draw sharp lines between facts and opinions have invariably been unsuccessful, and the clear trend of the cases is to permit "factual" opinions. As to requests for opinions or contentions that call for the application of law to fact, they can be most useful in narrowing and sharpening the issues, which is a major purpose of discovery. See *Diversified Products Corp. v. Sports Center Co.*, 42 F.R.D. 3 (D.Md. 1967); Moore, *supra*; Field & McKusick, *Maine Civil Practice* § 26.18 (1959). On the other hand, under the new language interrogatories may not extend to issues of "pure law," *i.e.*, legal issues unrelated to the facts of the case. *Cf. United States v. Maryland & Va. Milk Producers Assn., Inc.*, 22 F.R.D. 300 (D.D.C.1958).

Since interrogatories involving mixed questions of law and fact may create disputes between the parties which are best resolved after much or all of the other discovery has been completed, the court is expressly authorized to defer an answer. Likewise, the court may delay determination until pretrial conference, if it believes that the dispute is best resolved in the presence of the judge.

The principal question raised with respect to the cases permitting such interrogatories is whether they reintroduce undesirable aspects of the prior pleading practice, whereby parties were chained to misconceived contentions or theories, and ultimate determination on the merits was frustrated. See James, *The Revival of Bills of Particulars under the Federal Rules*, 71 Harv.L.Rev. 1473 (1958). But there are few if any instances in the recorded cases demonstrating that such frustration has occurred. The general rule governing the use of answers to interrogatories is that under ordinary circumstances they do not limit proof. See, *e.g.*, *McElroy v. United Air Lines, Inc.*, 21 F.R.D. 100 (W.D.Mo.1967); *Pressley v. Boehlke*, 33 F.R.D. 316, 317 (W.D.N.C.1963). Although in exceptional circumstances reliance on an answer may cause such prejudice that the court will hold the answering party bound to his answer, *e.g.*, *Zielinski v. Philadelphia Piers, Inc.*, 139 F.Supp. 408 (E.D.Pa.1956), the interrogating party will ordinarily not be entitled to rely on the unchanging character of the answers he receives and cannot base prejudice on such reliance. The rule does not affect the power of a court to permit withdrawal or amendment of answers to interrogatories.

The use of answers to interrogatories at trial is made subject to the rules of evidence. The provisions governing use of depositions, to which Rule 33 presently refers, are not entirely apposite to answers to interrogatories, since deposition practice contemplates that all parties will ordinarily participate through cross-examination. See 4 *Moore's Federal Practice* ¶33.29[1] (2d ed. 1966).

Certain provisions are deleted from subdivision (b) because they are fully covered by new Rule 26(c) providing for protective orders and Rules 26(a) and 26(d). The language of the subdivision is thus simplified without any change of substance.

Subdivision (c). This is a new subdivision, adapted from Calif.Code Civ.Proc. § 2030(c), relating especially to interrogatories which require a party to engage in burdensome or expensive research into his own business records in order to give an answer. The subdivision gives the party an option to make the records available and place the burden of research of the party who seeks the information. "This provision, without undermining the liberal scope of interrogatory discovery, places the burden of discovery upon its potential benefittee," Louisell, *Modern California Discovery*, 124–125 (1963), and alleviates a problem which in the past has troubled Federal courts. See Speck, *The Use of Discovery in United States District Courts*, 60 Yale L.J. 1132, 1142–1144 (1951). The interrogating party is protected against abusive use of this provision through the requirement that the burden of ascertaining the answer be substantially the same for both sides. A respondent may not impose on an interrogating party a mass of records as to which research is feasible only for one familiar with the records. At the same time, the respondent unable to invoke this subdivision does not on that account lose the protection available to him under new Rule 26(c) against oppressive or unduly burdensome or expensive interrogatories. And even when the respondent successfully invokes the subdivision, the court is not deprived of its usual power, in appropriate cases, to require that the interrogating party reimburse the respondent for the expense of assembling his records and making them intelligible.

1980 Amendment

Subdivision (c). The Committee is advised that parties upon whom interrogatories are served have occasionally responded by directing the interrogating party to a mass of business records or by offering to make all of their records available, justifying the response by the option provided by this subdivision. Such practices are an abuse of the option. A party who is permitted by the terms of this subdivision to offer records for inspection in lieu of answering an interrogatory should offer them in a manner than permits the same direct and economical access that is available to the party. If the information sought exists in the form of compilations, abstracts or summaries then available to the responding party, those should be made available to the interrogating party. The final sentence is added to make it clear that a responding party has the duty to specify, by category and location, the records from which answers to interrogatories can be derived.

1993 Amendments

Purpose of Revision. The purpose of this revision is to reduce the frequency and increase the efficiency of interrogatory practice. The revision is based on experience with local rules. For ease of reference, subdivision (a) is divided into two subdivisions and the remaining subdivisions renumbered.

Subdivision (a). Revision of this subdivision limits interrogatory practice. Because Rule 26(a)(1)–(3) requires disclosure of much of the information previously obtained by this form of discovery, there should be less occasion to use it. Experience in over half of the district courts has confirmed that limitations on the number of interrogatories are useful and manageable. Moreover, because the device can be costly and may be used as a means of harassment, it is desirable to subject its use to the control of the court consistent with the principles stated in Rule 26(b)(2), particularly in multi-party cases where it has not been unusual for the same interrogatory to be propounded to a party by more than one of its adversaries.

Each party is allowed to serve 25 interrogatories upon any other party, but must secure leave of court (or a stipulation from the opposing party) to serve a larger number. Parties cannot evade this presumptive limitation through the device of joining as "subparts" questions that seek information about discrete separate subjects. However, a question asking about communications of a particular type should be treated as a single interrogatory even though it requests that the time, place, persons present, and contents be stated separately for each such communication.

As with the number of depositions authorized by Rule 30, leave to serve additional interrogatories is to be allowed when consistent with Rule 26(b)(2). The aim is not to prevent needed discovery, but to provide judicial scrutiny before parties make potentially excessive use of this discovery device. In many cases it will be appropriate for the court to permit a larger number of interrogatories in the scheduling order entered under Rule 16(b).

Unless leave of court is obtained, interrogatories may not be served prior to the meeting of the parties under Rule 26(f).

When a case with outstanding interrogatories exceeding the number permitted by this rule is removed to federal court, the interrogating party must seek leave allowing the additional interrogatories, specify which twenty-five are to be answered, or resubmit interrogatories that comply with the rule. Moreover, under Rule 26(d), the time for response would be measured from the date of the parties' meeting under Rule 26(f). See Rule 81(c), providing that these rules govern procedures after removal.

Subdivision (b). A separate subdivision is made of the former second paragraph of subdivision (a). Language is added to paragraph (1) of this subdivision to emphasize the duty of the responding party to provide full answers to the extent not objectionable. If, for example, an interrogatory seeking information about numerous facilities or products is deemed objectionable, but an interrogatory seeking information about a lesser number of facilities or products would not have been objectionable, the interrogatory should be answered with respect to the latter even though an objection is raised as to the balance of the facilities or products. Similarly, the fact that additional time may be needed to respond to some questions (or to some aspects of questions) should not justify a delay in responding to those questions (or other aspects of questions) that can be answered within the prescribed time.

Paragraph (4) is added to make clear that objections must be specifically justified, and that unstated or untimely grounds for objection ordinarily are waived. Note also the provisions of revised Rule 26(b)(5), which require a responding party to indicate when it is withholding information under a claim of privilege or as trial preparation materials.

These provisions should be read in light of Rule 26(g), authorizing the court to impose sanctions on a party and attorney making an unfounded objection to an interrogatory.

Subdivisions (c) and (d). The provisions of former subdivisions (b) and (c) are renumbered.

Rule 34. Production of Documents and Things and Entry Upon Land for Inspection and Other Purposes

(a) Scope. Any party may serve on any other party a request (1) to produce and permit the party making the request, or someone acting on the requestor's behalf, to inspect and copy, any designated documents (including writings, drawings, graphs, charts, photographs, phonorecords, and other data compilations from which information can be obtained, translated, if necessary, by the respondent through detection devices into reasonably usable form), or to inspect and copy, test, or sample any tangible things which constitute or contain matters within the scope of Rule 26(b) and which are in the possession, custody or control of the party upon whom the request is served; or (2) to permit entry upon designated land or other property in the possession or control of the party upon whom the request is served for the purpose of inspection and measuring, surveying, photographing, testing, or sampling the property or any designated object or operation thereon, within the scope of Rule 26(b).

(b) Procedure. The request shall set forth, either by individual item or by category, the items to be inspected and describe each with reasonable particularity. The request shall specify a reasonable time, place, and manner of making the inspection and performing the related acts. Without leave of court or written stipulation, a request may not be served before the time specified in Rule 26(d).

The party upon whom the request is served shall serve a written response within 30 days after the service of the request. A shorter or longer time may be directed by the court or, in the absence of such an order, agreed to in writing by the parties, subject to Rule 29. The response shall state, with respect to each item or category, that inspection and related activities will be permitted as requested, unless the request is objected to, in which event the reasons for the objection shall be stated. If objection is made to part of an item or category, the part shall be specified and inspection permitted of the remaining parts. The party submitting the request may move for an order under Rule 37(a) with respect to any objection to or other failure to respond to the request or any part thereof, or any failure to permit inspection as requested.

A party who produces documents for inspection shall produce them as they are kept in the usual course of business or shall organize and label them to correspond with the categories in the request.

(c) Persons Not Parties. A person not a party to the action may be compelled to produce documents and things or to submit to an inspection as provided in Rule 45.

(As amended Dec. 27, 1946, effective March 19, 1948; Mar. 30, 1970, eff. July 1, 1970; Apr. 29, 1980, eff. Aug. 1, 1980; Mar. 2, 1987, eff. Aug. 1, 1987; Apr. 30, 1991, eff. Dec. 1, 1991; Apr. 22, 1993, eff. Dec. 1, 1993.)

ADVISORY COMMITTEE NOTES

1937 Adoption

In England orders are made for the inspection of documents, *English Rules Under the Judicature Act (The Annual Practice,* 1937) O. 31, r.r. 14, et seq., or for the inspection of tangible property or for entry upon land, O. 50, r. 3. Michigan provides for inspection of damaged property when such damage is the ground of the action. Mich.Court Rules Ann. (Searl, 1933) Rule 41, § 2.

Practically all states have statutes authorizing the court to order parties in possession or control of documents to permit other parties to inspect and copy them before trial. See Ragland, *Discovery Before Trial* (1932) Appendix, p. 267, setting out the statutes.

Compare [former] Equity Rule 58 (Discovery—Interrogatories—Inspection and Production of Documents—Admission of Execution or Genuineness) (fifth paragraph).

1946 Amendment

Note. The changes in clauses (1) and (2) correlate the scope of inquiry permitted under Rule 34 with that provided in Rule 26(b), and thus remove any ambiguity created by the former differences in language. As stated in *Olson Transportation Co. v. Socony-Vacuum Oil Co.,* E.D.Wis.1944, 8 Fed.Rules Serv. 34.41, Case 2, "* * * Rule 34 is a direct and simple method of discovery." At the same time the addition of the words following the term "parties" makes certain that the person in whose custody, possession, or control the evidence reposes may have the benefit of the applicable protective orders stated in Rule 30(b). This change should be considered in the light of the proposed expansion of Rule 30(b).

An objection has been made that the word "designated" in Rule 34 has been construed with undue strictness in some district court cases so as to require great and impracticable specificity in the description of documents, papers, books, etc., sought to be inspected. The Committee, however, believes that no amendment is needed, and that the proper meaning of "designated" as requiring specificity has already been delineated by the Supreme Court. *See Brown v. United States,* 1928, 48 S.Ct. 288, 276 U.S. 134, 143, 72 L.Ed. 500 ("The subpoena * * * specifies * * * with reasonable particularity the subjects to which the documents called for related."); *Consolidated Rendering Co. v. Vermont,* 1908, 28 S.Ct. 178, 207 U.S. 541, 543–544, 52 L.Ed. 327 ("We see no reason why all such books, papers and correspondence which related to the subject of inquiry, and were described with reasonable detail, should not be called for and the company directed to produce them. Otherwise, the State would be compelled to designate each particular paper which it desired, which presupposes an accurate knowledge of such papers, which the tribunal desiring the papers would probably rarely, if ever, have.").

1970 Amendment

Rule 34 is revised to accomplish the following major changes in the existing rule: (1) to eliminate the requirement of good cause; (2) to have the rule operate extrajudicially; (3) to include testing and sampling as well as inspecting or photographing tangible things; and (4) to make clear that the rule does not preclude an independent action for analogous discovery against persons not parties.

Subdivision (a). Good cause is eliminated because it has furnished an uncertain and erratic protection to the parties from whom production is sought and is now rendered unnecessary by virtue of the more specific provisions added to Rule 26(b) relating to materials assembled in preparation for trial and to experts retained or consulted by parties.

The good cause requirement was originally inserted in Rule 34 as a general protective provision in the absence of experience with the specific problems that would arise thereunder. As the note to Rule 26(b)(3) on trial preparation materials makes clear, good cause has been applied differently to varying classes of documents, though not without confusion. It has often been said in court opinions that good cause requires a consideration of need for the materials and of alternative means of obtaining them, i.e., something more than relevance and lack of privilege. But the overwhelming proportion of the cases in which the formula of good cause has been applied to require a special showing are those involving trial preparation. In practice, the courts have not treated documents as having a special immunity to discovery simply because of their being documents. Protection may be afforded to claims of privacy or secrecy or of undue burden or expense under what is now Rule 26(c) (previously Rule 30(b)). To be sure, an appraisal of "undue" burden inevitably entails consideration of the needs of the party seeking discovery. With special provisions added to govern trial preparation materials and experts, there is no longer any occasion to retain the requirement of good cause.

The revision of Rule 34 to have it operate extrajudicially, rather than by court order, is to a large extent a reflection of existing law office practice. The Columbia Survey shows that of the litigants seeking inspection of documents or things, only about 25 percent filed motions for court orders. This minor fraction nevertheless accounted for a significant number of motions. About half of these motions were uncontested and in almost all instances the party seeking production ultimately prevailed. Although an extrajudicial procedure will not drastically alter existing practice under Rule 34—it will conform to it in most cases—it has the potential of saving court time in a substantial though proportionately small number of cases tried annually.

The inclusion of testing and sampling of tangible things and objects or operations on land reflects a need frequently encountered by parties in preparation for trial. If the operation of a particular machine is the basis of a claim for negligent injury, it will often be necessary to test its operating parts or to sample and test the products it is producing. *Cf.* Mich.Gen.Ct.R. 310.1(1) (1963) (testing authorized).

The inclusive description of "documents" is revised to accord with changing technology. It makes clear that Rule 34 applies to electronics data compilations from which information can be obtained only with the use of detection devices, and that when the data can as a practical matter be made usable by the discovering party only through respondent's devices, respondent may be required to use his devices to translate the data into usable form. In many instances, this means that respondent will have to supply a print-out of computer data. The burden thus placed on respondent will vary from case to case, and the courts have ample power under Rule 26(c) to protect respondent against undue burden or expense, either by restricting discovery or requiring that the discovering party pay costs. Similarly, if the discovering party needs to check the electronic source itself, the court may protect respondent with respect to preservation of his records, confidentiality of nondiscoverable matters, and costs.

Subdivision (b). The procedure provided in Rule 34 is essentially the same as that in Rule 33, as amended, and the discussion in the note appended to that rule is relevant to Rule 34 as well. Problems peculiar to Rule 34 relate to the specific arrangements that must be worked out for inspection and related acts of copying, photographing, testing, or sampling. The rule provides that a request for inspection shall set forth the items to be inspected either by item or category, describing each with reasonable particularity, and shall specify a reasonable time, place, and manner of making the inspection.

Subdivision (c). Rule 34 as revised continues to apply only to parties. Comments from the bar make clear that in the preparation of cases for trial it is occasionally necessary to enter land or inspect large tangible things in the possession of a person not a party, and that some courts have dismissed independent actions in the nature of bills in equity for such discovery on the ground that Rule 34 is preemptive. While an ideal solution to this problem is to provide for discovery against persons not parties in Rule 34, both the jurisdictional and procedural problems are very complex. For the present, this subdivision makes clear that Rule 34 does not preclude independent actions for discovery against persons not parties.

1980 Amendment

Subdivision (b). The Committee is advised that, "It is apparently not rare for parties deliberately to mix critical documents with others in the hope of obscuring significance." *Report of the Special Committee for the Study of Discovery Abuse, Section of Litigation of the American Bar Association* (1977) 22. The sentence added by this subdivision follows the recommendation of the *Report.*

1987 Amendment

The amendment is technical. No substantive change is intended.

1991 Amendment

This amendment reflects the change effected by revision of Rule 45 to provide for subpoenas to compel non-parties to produce documents and things and to submit to inspections of premises. The deletion of the text of the former paragraph is not intended to preclude an independent action for production of documents or things or for permission to enter upon land, but such actions may no longer be necessary in light of this revision.

1993 Amendments

The rule is revised to reflect the change made by Rule 26(d), preventing a party from seeking formal discovery prior to the meeting of the parties required by Rule 26(f). Also, like a change made in Rule 33, the rule is modified to make clear that, if a request for production is objectionable only in part, production should be afforded with respect to the unobjectionable portions.

When a case with outstanding requests for production is removed to federal court, the time for response would be measured from the date of the parties' meeting. See Rule 81(c), providing that these rules govern procedures after removal.

Rule 35. Physical and Mental Examinations of Persons

(a) Order for Examination. When the mental or physical condition (including the blood group) of a party or of a person in the custody or under the legal control of a party, is in controversy, the court in which the action is pending may order the party to submit to a physical or mental examination by a suitably licensed or certified examiner or to produce for examination the person in the party's custody or legal control. The order may be made only on motion for good cause shown and upon notice to the person to be examined and to all parties and shall specify the time, place, manner, conditions, and scope of the examination and the person or persons by whom it is to be made.

(b) Report of Examiner.

(1) If requested by the party against whom an order is made under Rule 35(a) or the person examined, the party causing the examination to be made shall deliver to the requesting party a copy of the detailed written report of the examiner setting out the examiner's findings, including results of all tests made, diagnoses and conclusions, together with like reports of all earlier examinations of the same condition. After delivery the party causing the examination shall be entitled upon request to receive from the party against whom the order is made a like report of any examination, previously or thereafter made, of the same condition, unless, in the case of a report of examination of a person not a party, the party shows that the party is unable to obtain it. The court on motion may make an order against a party requiring delivery of a report on such terms as are just, and if an examiner fails or refuses to make a report the court may exclude the examiner's testimony if offered at trial.

(2) By requesting and obtaining a report of the examination so ordered or by taking the deposition of the examiner, the party examined waives any privilege the party may have in that action or any other involving the same controversy, regarding the testimony of every other person who has examined or may thereafter examine the party in respect of the same mental or physical condition.

(3) This subdivision applies to examinations made by agreement of the parties, unless the agreement expressly provides otherwise. This subdivision does not preclude discovery of a report of an examiner or the taking of a deposition of the examiner in accordance with the provisions of any other rule.

(As amended Mar. 30, 1970, eff. July 1, 1970; Mar. 2, 1987, eff. Aug. 1, 1987; Nov. 18, 1988, Pub.L. 100–690, Title VII, § 7047(b), 102 Stat. 4401; Apr. 30, 1991, eff. Dec. 1, 1991.)

ADVISORY COMMITTEE NOTES

1937 Adoption

Physical examination of parties before trial is authorized by statute or rule in a number of states. See Ariz.Rev. Code Ann. (Struckmeyer, 1928) § 4468; Mich. Court Rules Ann. (Searl, 1933) Rule 41, § 2; 2 N.J.Comp.Stat. (1910); N.Y.C.P.A. (1937) § 306; 1 S.D.Comp.Laws (1929) § 2716A; 3 Wash.Rev.Stat.Ann. (Remington, 1932) § 1230–1.

Mental examination of parties is authorized in Iowa. Iowa Code (1935) ch. 491–F1. See McCash, *The Evolution of the Doctrine of Discovery and Its Present Status in Iowa,* 20 Ia.L.Rev. 68 (1934).

The constitutionality of legislation providing for physical examination of parties was sustained in *Lyon v. Manhattan Railway Co.,* 1894, 37 N.E. 113, 142 N.Y. 298, and *McGovern v. Hope,* 1899, 42 A. 830, 63 N.J.L. 76. In *Union Pacific Ry. Co. v. Botsford,* 1891, 11 S.Ct. 1000, 141 U.S. 250, 35 L.Ed. 734, it was held that the court could not order the physical examination of a party in the absence of statutory authority. But in *Camden and Suburban Ry. Co. v. Stetson,* 1900, 20 S.Ct. 617, 177 U.S. 172, 44 L.Ed. 721 where there was statutory authority for such examination, derived from a state statute made operative by the conformity act, the practice was sustained. Such authority is now found in the present rule made operative by the Act of June 19, 1934, c. 651, U.S.C., Title 28, § 2072, formerly §§ 723b (Rules in actions at law; Supreme Court authorized to make) and 723c (Union of equity and action at law rules; power of Supreme Court).

1970 Amendment

Subdivision (a). Rule 35(a) has hitherto provided only for an order requiring a party to submit to an examination. It is desirable to extend the rule to provide for an order against the party for examination of a person in his custody or under his legal control. As appears from the provisions of amended Rule 37(b)(2) and the comment under that rule, an order to "produce" the third person imposes only an obligation to use good faith efforts to produce the person.

The amendment will settle beyond doubt that a parent or guardian suing to recover for injuries to a minor may be ordered to produce the minor for examination. Further, the amendment expressly includes blood examination within the kinds of examinations that can be ordered under the rule. See *Beach v. Beach,* 114 F.2d 479 (D.C. Cir. 1940). Provisions similar to the amendment have been adopted in at least 10 States: Calif. Code Civ.Proc. § 2032; Ida.R.Civ.P. 35; Ill. S–H Ann. c. 110A, § 215; Md.R.P. 420; Mich.Gen.Ct.R. 311; Minn.R.Civ.P. 35; Mo.Vern.Ann.R.Civ.p. 60.01; N.Dak.R.Civ.P. 35; N.Y.C.P.L. § 3121; Wyo.R.Civ.P. 35.

The amendment makes no change in the requirements of Rule 35 that, before a court order may issue, the relevant physical or mental condition must be shown to be "in controversy" and "good cause" must be shown for the examination. Thus, the amendment has no effect on the recent decision of the Supreme Court in *Schlagenhauf v. Holder,* 379 U.S. 104 (1964), stressing the importance of these requirements and applying them to the facts of the case. The amendment makes no reference to employees of a party. Provisions relating to employees in the State statutes and rules cited above appear to have been virtually unused.

Subdivision (b)(1). This subdivision is amended to correct an imbalance in Rule 35(b)(1) as heretofore written. Under that text, a party causing a Rule 35(a) examination to be made is required to furnish to the party examined, on request, a copy of the examining physician's report. If he delivers this copy, he is in turn entitled to receive from the party examined reports of all examinations of the same condition previously or later made. But the rule has not in terms entitled the examined party to receive from the party causing the Rule 35(a) examination any reports of earlier examinations of the same condition to which the latter may have access. The amendment cures this defect. See La. Stat.Ann., Civ.Proc. art 1495 (1960); Utah R.Civ.P. 35(c).

The amendment specifies that the written report of the examining physician includes results of all tests made, such as results of X-rays and cardiograms. It also embodies changes required by the broadening of Rule 35(a) to take in persons who are not parties.

Subdivision (b)(3). This new subdivision removes any possible doubt that reports of examination may be obtained although no order for examination has been made under Rule 35(a). Examinations are very frequently made by agreement, and sometimes before the party examined has an attorney. The courts have uniformly ordered that reports be supplied, see 4 *Moore's Federal Practice* ¶35.06, n. 1 (2d ed. 1966); 2A Barron & Holtzoff, *Federal Practice and Procedure* § 823, n. 22 (Wright ed. 1961), and it appears best to fill the technical gap in the present rule.

The subdivision also makes clear that reports of examining physicians are discoverable not only under Rule 35(b), but under other rules as well. To be sure, if the report is privileged, then discovery is not permissible under any rule other than Rule 35(b) and it is permissible under Rule 35(b) only if the party requests a copy of the report of examination made by the other party's doctor. *Sher v. De Haven,* 199 F.2d 777 (D.C. Cir. 1952), *cert. denied* 345 U.S. 936 (1953). But if the report is unprivileged and is subject to discovery under the provisions of rules other than Rule 35(b)—such as Rules 34 or 26(b)(3) or (4)—discovery should not depend upon whether the person examined demands a copy of the report. Although a few cases have suggested the contrary, *e.g., Galloway v. National Dairy Products Corp.,* 24 F.R.D. 362 (E.D.Pa.1959), the better considered district court decisions hold that Rule 35(b) is not preemptive. *E.g., Leszynski v. Russ*, 29 F.R.D. 10, 12 (D.Md.1961) and cases cited. The question was recently given full consideration in *Buffington v. Wood*, 351 F.2d 292 (3d Cir. 1965), holding that Rule 35(b) is not preemptive.

1987 Amendment

The amendments are technical. No substantive change is intended.

1991 Amendment

The revision authorizes the court to require physical or mental examinations conducted by any person who is suitably licensed or certified.

The rule was revised in 1988 by Congressional enactment to authorize mental examinations by licensed clinical psychologists. This revision extends that amendment to include other certified or licensed professionals, such as dentists or occupational therapists, who are not physicians or clinical psychologists, but who may be well-qualified to give valuable testimony about the physical or mental condition that is the subject of dispute.

The requirement that the examiner be *suitably* licensed or certified is a new requirement. The court is thus expressly authorized to assess the credentials of the examiner to assure that no person is subjected to a court-ordered examination by an examiner whose testimony would be of such limited value that it would be unjust to require the person to undergo the invasion of privacy associated with the examination. This authority is not wholly new, for under the former rule, the court retained discretion to refuse to order an examination, or to restrict an examination. 8 WRIGHT & MILLER, FEDERAL PRACTICE & PROCEDURE § 2234 (1986 Supp.). The revision is intended to encourage the exercise of this discretion, especially with respect to examinations by persons having narrow qualifications.

The court's responsibility to determine the suitability of the examiner's qualifications applies even to a proposed examination by a physician. If the proposed examination and testimony calls for an expertise that the proposed examiner does not have, it should not be ordered, even if the proposed examiner is a physician. The rule does not, however, require that the license or certificate be conferred by the jurisdiction in which the examination is conducted.

Rule 36. Requests for Admission

(a) Request for Admission. A party may serve upon any other party a written request for the admission, for purposes of the pending action only, of the truth of any matters within the scope of Rule 26(b)(1) set forth in the request that relate to statements or opinions of fact or of the application of law to fact, including the genuineness of any documents described in the request. Copies of documents shall be served with the request unless they have been or are otherwise furnished or made available for inspection and copying. Without leave of court or written stipulation, requests for admission may not be served before the time specified in Rule 26(d).

Each matter of which an admission is requested shall be separately set forth. The matter is admitted unless, within 30 days after service of the request, or within such shorter or longer time as the court may allow or as the parties may agree to in writing, subject to Rule 29, the party to whom the request is directed serves upon the party requesting the admission a written answer or objection addressed to the matter, signed by the party or by the party's attorney. If objection is made, the reasons therefor shall be stated. The answer shall specifically deny the matter or set forth in detail the reasons why the answering party cannot truthfully admit or deny the matter. A denial shall fairly meet the substance of the requested admission, and when good faith requires that a party qualify an answer or deny only a part of the matter of which an admission is requested, the party shall specify so much of it as is true and qualify or deny the remainder. An answering party may not give lack of information or knowledge as a reason for failure to admit or deny unless the party states that the party has made reasonable inquiry and that the information known or readily obtainable by the party is insufficient to enable the party to admit or deny. A party who considers that a matter of which an admission has been requested presents a genuine issue for trial may not, on that ground alone, object to the request; the party may, subject to the provisions of Rule 37(c), deny the matter or set forth reasons why the party cannot admit or deny it.

The party who has requested the admissions may move to determine the sufficiency of the answers or objections. Unless the court determines that an objection is justified, it shall order that an answer be served. If the court determines that an answer does not comply with the requirements of this rule, it may order either that the matter is admitted or that an amended answer be served. The court may, in lieu of these orders, determine that final disposition of the request be made at a pre-trial conference or at a designated time prior to trial. The provisions of Rule 37(a)(4) apply to the award of expenses incurred in relation to the motion.

(b) Effect of Admission. Any matter admitted under this rule is conclusively established unless the court on motion permits withdrawal or amendment of the admission. Subject to the provision of Rule 16 governing amendment of a pre-trial order, the court may permit withdrawal or amendment when the presentation of the merits of the action will be subserved thereby and the party who obtained the admission fails to satisfy the court that withdrawal or amendment will prejudice that party in maintaining the action or defense on the merits. Any admission made by a party under this rule is for the purpose of the pending action only and is not an admission for any other purpose nor may it be used against the party in any other proceeding.

(As amended Dec. 27, 1946, effective Mar. 19, 1948; Mar. 30, 1970, eff. July 1, 1970; Mar. 2, 1987, eff. Aug. 1, 1987; Apr. 22, 1993, eff. Dec. 1, 1993.)

ADVISORY COMMITTEE NOTES

1937 Adoption

Compare similar rules: [Former] Equity Rule 58 (last paragraph, which provides for the admission of the execution and genuineness of documents); *English Rules Under the Judicature Act* (The Annual Practice, 1937) O. 32; Ill.Rev. Stat. (1937) ch. 110, § 182 and Rule 18 (Ill.Rev.Stat. (1937) ch. 110, § 259.18); 2 Mass.Gen.Laws (Ter.Ed., 1932) ch. 231, § 69; Mich. Court Rules Ann. (Searl, 1933) Rule 42; N.J. Comp.Stat. (2 Cum.Supp. 1911–1924); N.Y.C.P.A. (1937) §§ 322, 323; Wis.Stat. (1935) § 327.22.

1946 Amendment

Note. The first change in the first sentence of Rule 36(a) and the addition of the new second sentence, specifying when requests for admissions may be served, bring Rule 36 in line with amended Rules 26(a) and 33. There is no reason why these rules should not be treated alike. Other provisions of Rule 36(a) give the party whose admissions are requested adequate protection.

The second change in the first sentence of the rule [subdivision (a)] removes any uncertainty as to whether a party can be called upon to admit matters of fact other than those set forth in relevant documents described in and exhibited with the request. In *Smyth v. Kaufman*, C.C.A.2, 1940, 114 F.2d 40, it was held that the word "therein", now stricken from the rule [said subdivision] referred to the request and that a matter of fact not related to any document could be presented to the other party for admission or denial. The rule of this case is now clearly stated.

The substitution of the word "served" for "delivered" in the third sentence of the amended rule [said subdivision] is in conformance with the use of the word "serve" elsewhere in the rule and generally throughout the rules. See also Notes to Rules 13(a) and 33 herein. The substitution [in said subdivision] of "shorter or longer" for "further" will enable a court to designate a lesser period than 10 days for answer. This conforms with a similar provision already contained in Rule 33.

The addition of clause (1) [in said subdivision] specifies the method by which a party may challenge the propriety of a request to admit. There has been considerable difference of judicial opinion as to the correct method, if any, available to secure relief from an allegedly improper request. See Commentary, *Methods of Objecting to Notice to Admit*, 1942, 5 Fed.Rules Serv. 835; *International Carbonic Engineering Co. v. Natural Carbonic Products, Inc.*, S.D.Cal.1944, 57 F.Supp. 248. The changes in clause (1) are merely of a clarifying and conforming nature.

The first of the added last two sentences [in said subdivision] prevents an objection to a part of a request from holding up the answer, if any, to the remainder. See similar proposed change in Rule 33. The last sentence strengthens the rule by making the denial accurately reflect the party's position. It is taken, with necessary changes, from Rule 8(b).

1970 Amendment

Rule 36 serves two vital purposes, both of which are designed to reduce trial time. Admissions are sought, first to facilitate proof with respect to issues that cannot be eliminated from the case, and secondly, to narrow the issues by eliminating those that can be. The changes made in the rule are designed to serve these purposes more effectively. Certain disagreements in the courts about the proper scope of the rule are resolved. In addition, the procedural operation of the rule is brought into line with other discovery procedures, and the binding effect of an admission is clarified. See generally Finman, *The Request for Admissions in Federal Civil Procedure*, 71 Yale L.J. 371 (1962).

Subdivision (a). As revised, the subdivision provides that a request may be made to admit any matters within the scope of Rule 26(b) that relate to statements or opinions of fact or of the application of law to fact. It thereby eliminates the requirement that the matters be "of fact." This change resolves conflicts in the court decisions as to whether a request to admit matters of "opinion" and matters involving "mixed law and fact" is proper under the rule. As to "opinion," compare, *e.g., Jackson Buff Corp. v. Marcelle*, 20 F.R.D. 139 (E.D.N.Y.1957); *California v. The S. S. Jules Fribourg*, 19 F.R.D. 432 (N.D.Calif.1955), with *e.g., Photon, Inc. v. Harris Intertype, Inc.*, 28 F.R.D. 327 (D.Mass.1961); *Hise v. Lockwood Grader Corp.*, 153 F.Supp. 276 (D.Nebr.1957). As to "mixed law and fact" the majority of courts sustain objections, *e.g., Minnesota Mining and Mfg. Co. v. Norton Co.*, 36 F.R.D. 1 (N.D.Ohio 1964), but *McSparran v. Hanigan*, 225 F.Supp. 628 (E.D.Pa.1963) is to the contrary.

Not only is it difficult as a practical matter to separate "fact" from "opinion," see 4 *Moore's Federal Practice* ¶36.04 (2d ed. 1966); cf. 2A Barron & Holtzoff, *Federal Practice and Procedure* 317 (Wright ed. 1961), but an admission on a matter of opinion may facilitate proof or narrow the issues or both. An admission of a matter involving the application of law to fact may, in a given case, even more clearly narrow the issues. For example, an admission that an employee acted in the scope of his employment may remove a major issue from the trial. In *McSparran v. Hanigan, supra*, plaintiff admitted that "the premises on which said accident occurred, were occupied or under the control" of one of the defendants, 225 F.Supp. at 636. This admission, involving law as well as fact, removed one of the issues from the lawsuit and thereby reduced the proof required at trial. The amended provision does not authorize requests for admissions of law unrelated to the facts of the case.

Requests for admission involving the application of law to fact may create disputes between the parties which are best resolved in the presence of the judge after much or all of the other discovery has been completed. Power is therefore expressly conferred upon the court to defer decision until a pretrial conference is held or until a designated time prior to trial. On the other hand, the court should not automatically defer decision; in many instances, the importance of the admission lies in enabling the requesting party to avoid the burdensome accumulation of proof prior to the pretrial conference.

Courts have also divided on whether an answering party may properly object to request for admission as to matters which that party regards as "in dispute." Compare, *e.g., Syracuse Broadcasting Corp. v. Newhouse,* 271 F.2d 910, 917 (2d Cir. 1959); *Driver v. Gindy Mfg. Corp.,* 24 F.R.D. 473 (E.D.Pa.1959); with, *e.g., McGonigle v. Baxter,* 27 F.R.D. 504 (E.D.Pa.1961); *United States v. Ehbauer,* 13 F.R.D. 462 (W.D.Mo.1952). The proper response in such cases is an answer. The very purpose of the request is to ascertain whether the answering party is prepared to admit or regards the matter as presenting a genuine issue for trial. In his answer, the party may deny, or he may give as his reason for inability to admit or deny the existence of a genuine issue. The party runs no risk of sanctions if the matter is genuinely in issue, since Rule 37(c) provides a sanction of costs only when there are no good reasons for a failure to admit.

On the other hand, requests to admit may be so voluminous and so framed that the answering party finds the task of identifying what is in dispute and what is not unduly burdensome. If so, the responding party may obtain a protective order under Rule 26(c). Some of the decisions sustaining objections on "disputability" grounds could have been justified by the burdensome character of the requests. See, *e.g., Syracuse Broadcasting Corp. v. Newhouse, supra.*

Another sharp split of authority exists on the question whether a party may base his answer on lack of information or knowledge without seeking out additional information. One line of cases has held that a party may answer on the basis of such knowledge as he has at the time he answers. *E.g., Jackson Buff Corp. v. Marcelle,* 20 F.R.D. 139 (E.D.N.Y.1957); *Sladek v. General Motors Corp.,* 16 F.R.D. 104 (S.D.Iowa 1954). A larger group of cases, supported by commentators, has taken the view that if the responding party lacks knowledge, he must inform himself in reasonable fashion. *E.g., Hise v. Lockwood Grader Corp.,* 153 F.Supp. 276 (D.Nebr. 1957); *E. H. Tate Co. v. Jiffy Enterprises, Inc.,* 16 F.R.D. 571 (E.D.Pa.1954); Finman, *supra,* 71 Yale L.J. 371, 404–409; 4 *Moore's Federal Practice* ¶36.04 (2d ed. 1966); 2A Barron & Holtzoff, *Federal Practice and Procedure* 509 (Wright ed. 1961).

The rule as revised adopts the majority view, as in keeping with a basic principle of the discovery rules that a reasonable burden may be imposed on the parties when its discharge will facilitate preparation for trial and ease the trial process. It has been argued against this view that one side should not have the burden of "proving" the other side's case. The revised rule requires only that the answering party make reasonable inquiry and secure such knowledge and information as are readily obtainable by him. In most instances, the investigation will be necessary either to his own case or to preparation for rebuttal. Even when it is not, the information may be close enough at hand to be "readily obtainable." Rule 36 requires only that the party state that he has taken these steps. The sanction for failure of a party to inform himself before he answers lies in the award of costs after trial, as provided in Rule 37(c).

The requirement that the answer to a request for admission be sworn is deleted, in favor of a provision that the answer be signed by the party or by his attorney. The provisions of Rule 36 make it clear that admissions function very much as pleadings do. Thus, when a party admits in part and denies in part, his admission is for purposes of the pending action only and may not be used against him in any other proceeding. The broadening of the rule to encompass mixed questions of law and fact reinforces this feature. Rule 36 does not lack a sanction for false answers; Rule 37(c) furnishes an appropriate deterrent.

The existing language describing the available grounds for objection to a request for admission is eliminated as neither necessary nor helpful. The statement that objection may be made to any request which is "improper" adds nothing to the provisions that the party serve an answer or objection addressed to each matter and that he state his reasons for any objection. None of the other discovery rules sets forth grounds for objection, except so far as all are subject to the general provisions of Rule 26.

Changes are made in the sequence of procedures in Rule 36 so that they conform to the new procedures in Rules 33 and 34. The major changes are as follows:

(1) The normal time for response to a request for admissions is lengthened from 10 to 30 days, conforming more closely to prevailing practice. A defendant need not respond, however, in less than 45 days after service of the summons and complaint upon him. The court may lengthen or shorten the time when special situations require it.

(2) The present requirement that the plaintiff wait 10 days to serve requests without leave of court is eliminated. The revised provision accords with those in Rules 33 and 34.

(3) The requirement that the objecting party move automatically for a hearing on his objection is eliminated, and the burden is on the requesting party to move for an order. The change in the burden of going forward does not modify present law on burden of persuasion. The award of expenses incurred in relation to the motion is made subject to the comprehensive provisions of Rule 37(a)(4).

(4) A problem peculiar to Rule 36 arises if the responding party serves answers that are not in conformity with the requirements of the rule—for example, a denial is not "specific," or the explanation of inability to admit or deny is not "in detail." Rule 36 now makes no provision for court scrutiny of such answers before trial, and it seems to contemplate that defective answers bring about admissions just as effectively as if no answer had been served. Some cases have so held. *E.g., Southern Ry. Co. v. Crosby,* 201 F.2d 878 (4th Cir. 1953); *United States v. Laney,* 96 F.Supp. 482 (E.D.S.C.1951).

Giving a defective answer the automatic effect of an admission may cause unfair surprise. A responding party who purported to deny or to be unable to admit or deny will for the first time at trial confront the contention that he has made a binding admission. Since it is not always easy to know whether a denial is "specific" or an explanation is "in detail," neither party can know how the court will rule at trial and whether proof must be prepared. Some courts, therefore, have entertained motions to rule on defective answers. They have at times ordered that amended answers be served, when the defects were technical, and at other times have declared that the matter was admitted. *E.g., Woods v. Stewart,* 171 F.2d 544 (5th Cir. 1948); *SEC v. Kaye, Real & Co.,* 122 F.Supp. 639 (S.D.N.Y.1954); *Sieb's Hatcheries, Inc. v. Lindley,* 13 F.R.D. 113 (W.D.Ark.1952). The rule as revised conforms to the latter practice.

Subdivision (b). The rule does not how indicate the extent to which a party is bound by his admission. Some courts view admissions as the equivalent of sworn testimony.

E.g., Ark–Tenn Distributing Corp. v. Breidt, 209 F.2d 359 (3d Cir. 1954); *United States v. Lemons,* 125 F.Supp. 686 (W.D.Ark.1954); 4 *Moore's Federal Practice* ¶36.08 (2d ed. 1966 Supp.). At least in some jurisdictions a party may rebut his own testimony, *e.g., Alamo v. Del Rosario,* 98 F.2d 328 (D.C.Cir.1938), and by analogy an admission made pursuant to Rule 36 may likewise be thought rebuttable. The courts in *Ark–Tenn* and *Lemons, supra,* reasoned in this way, although the results reached may be supported on different grounds. In *McSparran v. Hanigan,* 225 F.Supp. 628, 636–637 (E.D.Pa.1963), the court held that an admission is conclusively binding, though noting the confusion created by prior decisions.

The new provisions give an admission a conclusively binding effect, for purposes only of the pending action, unless the admission is withdrawn or amended. In form and substance a Rule 36 admission is comparable to an admission in pleadings or a stipulation drafted by counsel for use at trial, rather than to an evidentiary admission of a party. Louisell, *Modern California Discovery* § 8.07 (1963); 2A Barron & Holtzoff, *Federal Practice and Procedure* § 838 (Wright ed. 1961). Unless the party securing an admission can depend on its binding effect, he cannot safely avoid the expense of preparing to prove the very matters on which he has secured the admission, and the purpose of the rule is defeated. Field v. McKusick, *Maine Civil Practice* § 36.4 (1959); Finman, *supra,* 71 Yale L.J. 371, 418–426; Comment, 56 Nw.U.L.Rev. 679, 682–683 (1961).

Provision is made for withdrawal or amendment of an admission. This provision emphasizes the importance of having the action resolved on the merits, while at the same time assuring each party that justified reliance on an admission in preparation for trial will not operate to his prejudice. *Cf. Moosman v. Joseph P. Blitz, Inc.,* 358 F.2d 686 (2d Cir. 1966).

1987 Amendment

The amendments are technical. No substantive change is intended.

1993 Amendments

The rule is revised to reflect the change made by Rule 26(d), preventing a party from seeking formal discovery until after the meeting of the parties required by Rule 26(f).

Rule 37. Failure to Make Disclosure or Cooperate in Discovery: Sanctions

(a) Motion For Order Compelling Disclosure or Discovery. A party, upon reasonable notice to other parties and all persons affected thereby, may apply for an order compelling disclosure or discovery as follows:

(1) Appropriate Court. An application for an order to a party shall be made to the court in which the action is pending. An application for an order to a person who is not a party shall be made to the court in the district where the discovery is being, or is to be, taken.

(2) Motion.

(A) If a party fails to make a disclosure required by Rule 26(a), any other party may move to compel disclosure and for appropriate sanctions. The motion must include a certification that the movant has in good faith conferred or attempted to confer with the party not making the disclosure in an effort to secure the disclosure without court action.

(B) If a deponent fails to answer a question propounded or submitted under Rules 30 or 31, or a corporation or other entity fails to make a designation under Rule 30(b)(6) or 31(a), or a party fails to answer an interrogatory submitted under Rule 33, or if a party, in response to a request for inspection submitted under Rule 34, fails to respond that inspection will be permitted as requested or fails to permit inspection as requested, the discovering party may move for an order compelling an answer, or a designation, or an order compelling inspection in accordance with the request. The motion must include a certification that the movant has in good faith conferred or attempted to confer with the person or party failing to make the discovery in an effort to secure the information or material without court action. When taking a deposition on oral examination, the proponent of the question may complete or adjourn the examination before applying for an order.

(3) Evasive or Incomplete Disclosure, Answer, or Response. For purposes of this subdivision an evasive or incomplete disclosure, answer, or response is to be treated as a failure to disclose, answer, or respond.

(4) Expenses and Sanctions.

(A) If the motion is granted or if the disclosure or requested discovery is provided after the motion was filed, the court shall, after affording an opportunity to be heard, require the party or deponent whose conduct necessitated the motion or the party or attorney advising such conduct or both of them to pay to the moving party the reasonable expenses incurred in making the motion, including attorney's fees, unless the court finds that the motion was filed without the movant's first making a good faith effort to obtain the disclosure or discovery without court action, or that the opposing party's nondisclosure, response, or objection was substantially justified, or that other circumstances make an award of expenses unjust.

(B) If the motion is denied, the court may enter any protective order authorized under Rule 26(c) and shall, after affording an opportunity to be heard, require the moving party or the attorney filing the motion or both of them to pay to the party or deponent who opposed the motion the reasonable expenses incurred in opposing the motion, including attorney's fees, unless the court finds that the making of the motion was substantially justified or that other circumstances make an award of expenses unjust.

(C) If the motion is granted in part and denied in part, the court may enter any protective order authorized under Rule 26(c) and may, after affording an opportunity to be heard, apportion the reasonable expenses incurred in relation to the motion among the parties and persons in a just manner.

(b) Failure to Comply With Order.

(1) Sanctions by Court in District Where Deposition is Taken. If a deponent fails to be sworn or to answer a question after being directed to do so by the court in the district in which the deposition is being taken, the failure may be considered a contempt of that court.

(2) Sanctions by Court in Which Action is Pending. If a party or an officer, director, or managing agent of a party or a person designated under Rule 30(b)(6) or 31(a) to testify on behalf of a party fails to obey an order to provide or permit discovery, including an order made under subdivision (a) of this rule or Rule 35, or if a party fails to obey an order entered under Rule 26(f), the court in which the action is pending may make such orders in regard to the failure as are just, and among others the following:

(A) An order that the matters regarding which the order was made or any other designated facts shall be taken to be established for the purposes of the action in accordance with the claim of the party obtaining the order;

(B) An order refusing to allow the disobedient party to support or oppose designated claims or defenses, or prohibiting that party from introducing designated matters in evidence;

(C) An order striking out pleadings or parts thereof, or staying further proceedings until the order is obeyed, or dismissing the action or proceeding or any part thereof, or rendering a judgment by default against the disobedient party;

(D) In lieu of any of the foregoing orders or in addition thereto, an order treating as a contempt of court the failure to obey any orders except an order to submit to a physical or mental examination;

(E) Where a party has failed to comply with an order under Rule 35(a) requiring that party to produce another for examination, such orders as are listed in paragraphs (A), (B), and (C) of this subdivision, unless the party failing to comply shows that that party is unable to produce such person for examination.

In lieu of any of the foregoing orders or in addition thereto, the court shall require the party failing to obey the order or the attorney advising that party or both to pay the reasonable expenses, including attorney's fees, caused by the failure, unless the court finds that the failure was substantially justified or that other circumstances make an award of expenses unjust.

(c) Failure to Disclose; False or Misleading Disclosure; Refusal to Admit.

(1) A party that without substantial justification fails to disclose information required by Rule 26(a) or 26(e)(1) shall not, unless such failure is harmless, be permitted to use as evidence at a trial, at a hearing, or on a motion any witness or information not so disclosed. In addition to or in lieu of this sanction, the court, on motion and after affording an opportunity to be heard, may impose other appropriate sanctions. In addition to requiring payment of reasonable expenses, including attorney's fees, caused by the failure, these sanctions may include any of the actions authorized under subparagraphs (A), (B), and (C) of subdivision (b)(2) of this rule and may include informing the jury of the failure to make the disclosure.

(2) If a party fails to admit the genuineness of any document or the truth of any matter as requested under Rule 36, and if the party requesting the admissions thereafter proves the genuineness of the document or the truth of the matter, the requesting party may apply to the court for an order requiring the other party to pay the reasonable expenses incurred in making that proof, including reasonable attorney's fees. The court shall make the order unless it finds that (A) the request was held objectionable pursuant to Rule 36(a), or (B) the admission sought was of no substantial importance, or (C) the party failing to admit had reasonable ground to believe that the party might prevail on the matter, or (D) there was other good reason for the failure to admit.

(d) Failure of Party to Attend at Own Deposition or Serve Answers to Interrogatories or Respond to Request for Inspection. If a party or an officer, director, or managing agent of a party or a person designated under Rule 30(b)(6) or 31(a) to testify on behalf of a party fails (1) to appear before the officer who is to take the deposition, after being served with a proper notice, or (2) to serve answers or objections to interrogatories submitted under Rule 33, after proper service of the interrogatories, or (3) to serve a written response to a request for inspection submitted under Rule 34, after proper service of the request, the court in which the action is pending on motion may make such orders in regard to the failure as are just, and among others it may take any action authorized under subparagraphs (A), (B), and (C) of subdivision (b)(2) of this rule. Any motion specifying a failure under clause (2) or (3) of this subdivision shall include a certification that the movant has in good faith conferred or attempted to confer with the party failing to answer or respond in an effort to obtain such answer or response without court action. In lieu of any order or in addition thereto, the court shall require the party failing to act or the attorney advising that party or both to pay the reasonable expenses, including attorney's fees, caused by the failure unless the court finds that the failure was substantially justified or that other circumstances make an award of expenses unjust.

The failure to act described in this subdivision may not be excused on the ground that the discovery sought is objectionable unless the party failing to act has a pending motion for a protective order as provided by Rule 26(c).

(e) [Abrogated]

(f) [Repealed. Pub.L. 96–481, Title II, § 205(a), Oct. 21, 1980, 94 Stat. 2330]

(g) Failure to Participate in the Framing of a Discovery Plan. If a party or a party's attorney fails to participate in good faith in the development and submission of a proposed discovery plan as required by Rule 26(f), the court may, after opportunity for hearing, require such party or attorney to pay to any other party the reasonable expenses, including attorney's fees, caused by the failure.

(As amended Dec. 29, 1948, eff. Oct. 20, 1949; Mar. 30, 1970, eff. July 1, 1970; Apr. 29, 1980, eff. Aug. 1, 1980; Pub.L. 96–481, Title II, § 205(a), Oct. 21, 1980, 94 Stat. 2330; Mar. 2, 1987, eff. Aug. 1, 1987; Apr. 22, 1993, eff. Dec. 1, 1993.)

ADVISORY COMMITTEE NOTES

1937 Adoption

The provisions of this rule authorizing orders establishing facts or excluding evidence or striking pleadings, or authorizing judgments of dismissal or default, for refusal to answer questions or permit inspection or otherwise make discovery, are in accord with *Hammond Packing Co. v. Arkansas,* 1909, 29 S.Ct. 370, 212 U.S. 322, 53 L.Ed. 530, 15 Ann.Cas. 645, which distinguishes between the justifiable use of such measures as a means of compelling the production of evidence, and their unjustifiable use, as in *Hovey v. Elliott,* 1897, 17 S.Ct. 841, 167 U.S. 409, 42 L.Ed. 215, for the mere purpose of punishing for contempt.

1948 Amendment

The amendment effective October 1949, substituted the reference to "Title 28, U.S.C., § 1783" in subdivision (e) for the reference to "the Act of July 3, 1926, c. 762, § 1 (44 Stat. 835), U.S.C., Title 28, § 711."

1970 Amendment

Rule 37 provides generally for sanctions against parties or persons unjustifiably resisting discovery. Experience has brought to light a number of defects in the language of the rule as well as instances in which it is not serving the purposes for which it was designed. See Rosenberg, *Sanctions to Effectuate Pretrial Discovery,* 58 Col.L.Rev. 480 (1958). In addition, changes being made in other discovery rules require conforming amendments to Rule 37.

Rule 37 sometimes refers to a "failure" to afford discovery and at other times to a "refusal" to do so. Taking note of this dual terminology, courts have imported into "refusal" a requirement of "wilfullness." See *Roth v. Paramount Pictures Corp.,* 8 F.R.D. 31 (W.D.Pa.1948); *Campbell v. Johnson,* 101 F.Supp. 705, 707 (S.D.N.Y.1951). In *Societe Internationale v. Rogers,* 357 U.S. 197 (1958), the Supreme Court concluded that the rather random use of these two terms in Rule 37 showed no design to use them with consistently distinctive meanings, that "refused" in Rule 37(b)(2) meant simply a failure to comply, and that wilfullness was relevant only to the selection of sanctions, if any, to be imposed. Nevertheless, after the decision in *Societe,* the court in *Hinson v. Michigan Mutual Liability Co.,* 275 F.2d 537 (5th Cir. 1960) once again ruled that "refusal" required wilfullness. Substitution of "failure" for "refusal" throughout Rule 37 should eliminate this confusion and bring the rule into harmony with the *Societe Internationale* decision. See Rosenberg, *supra,* 58 Col.L.Rev. 480, 489–490 (1958).

Subdivision (a). Rule 37(a) provides relief to a party seeking discovery against one who, with or without stated objections, fails to afford the discovery sought. It has always fully served this function in relation to depositions, but the amendments being made to Rules 33 and 34 give Rule 37(a) added scope and importance. Under existing Rule 33, a party objecting to interrogatories must make a motion for court hearing on his objections. The changes now made in Rules 33 and 37(a) make it clear that the interrogating party must move to compel answers, and the motion is provided for in Rule 37(a). Existing Rule 34, since it requires a court order prior to production of documents or things or permission to enter on land, has no relation to Rule 37(a). Amendments of Rules 34 and 37(a) create a procedure similar to that provided for Rule 33.

Subdivision (a)(1). This is a new provision making clear to which court a party may apply for an order compelling discovery. Existing Rule 37(a) refers only to the court in which the deposition is being taken; nevertheless, it has been held that the court where the action is pending has "inherent power" to compel a party deponent to answer. *Lincoln Laboratories, Inc. v. Savage Laboratories, Inc.,* 27 F.R.D. 476 (D.Del.1961). In relation to Rule 33 interrogatories and Rule 34 requests for inspection, the court where the action is pending is the appropriate enforcing tribunal. The new provision eliminates the need to resort to inherent power by spelling out the respective roles of the court where the action is pending and the court where the deposition is taken. In some instances, two courts are available to a party seeking to compel answers from a party deponent. The party seeking discovery may choose the court to which he will apply, but the court has power to remit the party to the other court as a more appropriate forum.

Subdivision (a)(2). This subdivision contains the substance of existing provisions of Rule 37(a) authorizing motions to compel answers to questions put at depositions and to interrogatories. New provisions authorize motions for orders compelling designation under Rules 30(b)(6) and 31(a) and compelling inspection in accordance with a request made under Rule 34. If the court denies a motion, in whole or part, it may accompany the denial with issuance of a protective order. Compare the converse provision in Rule 26(c).

Subdivision (a)(3). This new provision makes clear that an evasive or incomplete answer is to be considered, for purposes of subdivision (a), a failure to answer. The courts have consistently held that they have the power to compel adequate answers. *E.g., Cone Mills Corp. v. Joseph Bancroft & Sons Co.*, 33 F.R.D. 318 (D.Del.1963). This power is recognized and incorporated into the rule.

Subdivision (a)(4). This subdivision amends the provisions for award of expenses, including reasonable attorney's fees, to the prevailing party or person when a motion is made for an order compelling discovery. At present, an award of expenses is made only if the losing party or person is found to have acted without substantial justification. The change requires that expenses be awarded unless the conduct of the losing party or person is found to have been substantially justified. The test of "substantial justification" remains, but the change in language is intended to encourage judges to be more alert to abuses occurring in the discovery process.

On many occasions, to be sure, the dispute over discovery between the parties is genuine, though ultimately resolved one way or the other by the court. In such cases, the losing party is substantially justified in carrying the matter to court. But the rules should deter the abuse implicit in carrying or forcing a discovery dispute to court when no genuine dispute exists. And the potential or actual imposition of expenses is virtually the sole formal sanction in the rules to deter a party from pressing to a court hearing frivolous requests for or objections to discovery.

The present provision of Rule 37(a) that the court shall require payment if it finds that the defeated party acted without "substantial justification" may appear adequate, but in fact it has been little used. Only a handful of reported cases include an award of expenses, and the Columbia Survey found that in only one instance out of about 50 motions decided under Rule 37(a) did the court award expenses. It appears that the courts do not utilize the most important available sanction to deter abusive resort to the judiciary.

The proposed change provides in effect that expenses should ordinarily be awarded unless a court finds that the losing party acted justifiably in carrying his point to court. At the same time, a necessary flexibility is maintained, since the court retains the power to find that other circumstances make an award of expenses unjust—as where the prevailing party also acted unjustifiably. The amendment does not significantly narrow the discretion of the court, but rather presses the court to address itself to abusive practices. The present provision that expenses may be imposed upon either the party or his attorney or both is unchanged. But it is not contemplated that expenses will be imposed upon the attorney merely because the party is indigent.

Subdivision (b). This subdivision deals with sanctions for failure to comply with a court order. The present captions for subsections (1) and (2) entitled, "Contempt" and "Other Consequences," respectively, are confusing. One of the consequences listed in (2) is the arrest of the party, representing the exercise of the contempt power. The contents of the subsections show that the first authorizes the sanction of contempt (and no other) by the court in which the deposition is taken, whereas the second subsection authorizes a variety of sanctions, including contempt, which may be imposed by the court in which the action is pending. The captions of the subsections are changed to reflect their contents.

The scope of Rule 37(b)(2) is broadened by extending it to include any order "to provide or permit discovery," including orders issued under Rules 37(a) and 35. Various rules authorize orders for discovery—*e.g.*, Rule 35(b)(1), Rule 26(c) as revised, Rule 37(d). See Rosenberg, *supra*, 58 Col.L.Rev. 480, 484–486. Rule 37(b)(2) should provide comprehensively for enforcement of all these orders. *Cf. Societe Internationale v. Rogers*, 357 U.S. 197, 207 (1958). On the other hand, the reference to Rule 34 is deleted to conform to the changed procedure in that rule.

A new subsection (E) provides that sanctions which have been available against a party for failure to comply with an order under Rule 35(a) to submit to examination will now be available against him for his failure to comply with a Rule 35(a) order to produce a third person for examination, unless he shows that he is unable to produce the person. In this context, "unable" means in effect "unable in good faith." See *Societe Internationale v. Rogers*, 357 U.S. 197 (1958).

Subdivision (b)(2) is amplified to provide for payment of reasonable expenses caused by the failure to obey the order. Although Rules 37(b)(2) and 37(d) have been silent as to award of expenses, courts have nevertheless ordered them on occasion. *E.g., United Sheeplined Clothing Co. v. Arctic Fur Cap Corp.*, 165 F.Supp. 193 (S.D.N.Y.1958); *Austin Theatre, Inc. v. Warner Bros. Pictures, Inc.*, 22 F.R.D. 302 (S.D.N.Y. 1958). The provision places the burden on the disobedient party to avoid expenses by showing that his failure is justified or that special circumstances make an award of expenses unjust. Allocating the burden in this way conforms to the changed provisions as to expenses in Rule 37(a), and is particularly appropriate when a court order is disobeyed.

An added reference to directors of a party is similar to a change made in subdivision (d) and is explained in the note to that subdivision. The added reference to persons designated by a party under Rules 30(b)(6) or 31(a) to testify on behalf of the party carries out the new procedure in those rules for taking a deposition of a corporation or other organization.

Subdivision (c). Rule 37(c) provides a sanction for the enforcement of Rule 36 dealing with requests for admission. Rule 36 provides the mechanism whereby a party may obtain from another party in appropriate instances either (1) an admission, or (2) a sworn and specific denial or (3) a sworn statement "setting forth in detail the reasons why he cannot truthfully admit or deny." If the party obtains the second or third of these responses, in proper form, Rule 36 does not provide for a pretrial hearing on whether the response is warranted by the evidence thus far accumulated. Instead, Rule 37(c) is intended to provide posttrial relief in the form of a requirement that the party improperly refusing the admission pay the expenses of the other side in making the necessary proof at trial.

Rule 37(c), as now written, addresses itself in terms only to the sworn denial and is silent with respect to the statement of reasons for an inability to admit or deny. There is no apparent basis for this distinction, since the sanction provided in Rule 37(c) should deter all unjustified failures to admit.

This omission in the rule has caused confused and diverse treatment in the courts. One court has held that if a party give inadequate reasons, he should be treated before trial as having denied the request, so that Rule 37(c) may apply. *Bertha Bldg. Corp. v. National Theatres Corp.*, 15 F.R.D. 339 (E.D.N.Y.1954). Another has held that the party should be treated as having admitted the request. *Heng Hsin Co. v. Stern, Morgenthau & Co.*, 20 Fed.Rules Serv. 36a.52, Case 1 (S.D.N.Y. Dec. 10, 1954). Still another has ordered a new response, without indicating what the outcome should be if the new response were inadequate. *United States Plywood Corp. v. Hudson Lumber Co.*, 127 F.Supp. 489, 497–498 (S.D.N.Y.1954). See generally Finman, *The Request for Admissions in Federal Civil Procedure*, 71 Yale L.J. 371, 426–430 (1962). The amendment eliminates this defect in Rule 37(c) by bringing within its scope all failures to admit.

Additional provisions in Rule 37(c) protect a party from having to pay expenses if the request for admission was held objectionable under Rule 36(a) or if the party failing to admit had reasonable ground to believe that he might prevail on the matter. The latter provision emphasizes that the true test under Rule 37(c) is not whether a party prevailed at trial but whether he acted reasonably in believing that he might prevail.

Subdivision (d). The scope of subdivision (d) is broadened to include responses to requests for inspection under Rule 34, thereby conforming to the new procedures of Rule 34.

Two related changes are made in subdivision (d): the permissible sanctions are broadened to include such orders "as are just"; and the requirement that the failure to appear or respond be "wilful" is eliminated. Although Rule 37(d) in terms provides for only three sanctions, all rather severe, the courts have interpreted it as permitting softer sanctions than those which it sets forth. E.g., *Gill v. Stolow*, 240 F.2d 669 (2d Cir.1957); *Saltzman v. Birrell*, 156 F.Supp. 538 (S.D.N.Y.1957); 2A Barron & Holtzoff, *Federal Practice and Procedure* 554–557 (Wright ed. 1961). The rule is changed to provide the greater flexibility as to sanctions which the cases show is needed.

The resulting flexibility as to sanctions eliminates any need to retain the requirement that the failure to appear or respond be "wilful." The concept of "wilful failure" is at best subtle and difficult, and the cases do not supply a bright line. Many courts have imposed sanctions without referring to wilfullness. E.g., *Milewski v. Schneider Transportation Co.*, 238 F.2d 397 (6th Cir.1956); *Dictograph Products, Inc. v. Kentworth Corp.*, 7 F.R.D. 543 (W.D.Ky.1947). In addition, in view of the possibility of light sanctions, even a negligent failure should come within Rule 37(d). If default is caused by counsel's ignorance of Federal practice, cf. *Dunn v. Pa. R.R.*, 96 F.Supp. 597 (N.D.Ohio 1951), or by his preoccupation with another aspect of the case, *cf. Maurer–Neuer, Inc. v. United Packinghouse Workers*, 26 F.R.D. 139 (D.Kans.1960), dismissal of the action and default judgment are not justified, but the imposition of expenses and fees may well be. "Wilfullness" continues to play a role, along with various other factors, in the choice of sanctions. Thus, the scheme conforms to Rule 37(b) as construed by the Supreme Court in *Societe Internationale v. Rogers*, 357 U.S. 197, 208 (1958).

A provision is added to make clear that a party may not properly remain completely silent even when he regards a notice to take his deposition or a set of interrogatories or requests to inspect as improper and objectionable. If he desires not to appear or not to respond, he must apply for a protective order. The cases are divided on whether a protective order must be sought. Compare *Collins v. Wayland*, 139 F.2d 677 (9th Cir. 1944), *cert. den.* 322 U.S. 744; *Bourgeois v. El Paso Natural Gas Co.*, 20 F.R.D. 358 (S.D.N.Y. 1957); *Loosley v. Stone*, 15 F.R.D. 373 (S.D.Ill.1954), with *Scarlatos v. Kulukundis*, 21 F.R.D. 185 (S.D.N.Y.1957); *Ross v. True Temper Corp.*, 11 F.R.D. 307 (N.D.Ohio 1951). Compare also Rosenberg, *supra*, 58 Col.L.Rev. 480, 496 (1958) with 2A Barron & Holtzoff, *Federal Practice and Procedure* 530–531 (Wright ed. 1961). The party from whom discovery is sought is afforded, through Rule 26(c), a fair and effective procedure whereby he can challenge the request made. At the same time, the total noncompliance with which Rule 37(d) is concerned may impose severe inconvenience or hardship on the discovering party and substantially delay the discovery process. Cf. 2B Barron & Holtzoff, *Federal Practice and Procedure* 306–307 (Wright ed. 1961) (response to a subpoena).

The failure of an officer or managing agent of a party to make discovery as required by present Rule 37(d) is treated as the failure of the party. The rule as revised provides similar treatment for a director of a party. There is slight warrant for the present distinction between officers and managing agents on the one hand and directors on the other. Although the legal power over a director to compel his making discovery may not be as great as over officers or managing agents, *Campbell v. General Motors Corp.*, 13 F.R.D. 331 (S.D.N.Y.1952), the practical differences are negligible. That a director's interests are normally aligned with those of his corporation is shown by the provisions of old Rule 26(d)(2), transferred to 32(a)(2) (deposition of director of party may be used at trial by an adverse party for any purpose) and of Rule 43(b) (director of party may be treated at trial as a hostile witness on direct examination by any adverse party). Moreover, in those rare instances when a corporation is unable through good faith efforts to compel a director to make discovery, it is unlikely that the court will impose sanctions. Cf. *Societe Internationale v. Rogers*, 357 U.S. 197 (1958).

Subdivision (e). The change in the caption conforms to the language of 28 U.S.C. § 1783, as amended in 1964.

Subdivision (f). Until recently, costs of a civil action could be awarded against the United States only when expressly provided by Act of Congress, and such provision was rarely made. See H.R.Rep.No. 1535, 89th Cong., 2d Sess., 2–3 (1966). To avoid any conflict with this doctrine, Rule 37(f) has provided that expenses and attorney's fees may not be imposed upon the United States under Rule 37. See 2A Barron & Holtzoff, *Federal Practice and Procedure* 857 (Wright ed. 1961).

A major change in the law was made in 1966, 80 Stat. 308, 28 U.S.C. § 2412 (1966), whereby a judgment for costs may ordinarily be awarded to the prevailing party in any civil action brought by or against the United States. Costs are not to include the fees and expenses of attorneys. In light of this legislative development, Rule 37(f) is amended to permit the award of expenses and fees against the United States under Rule 37, but only to the extent permitted by statute. The amendment brings Rule 37(f) into line with present and future statutory provisions.

1980 Amendment

Subdivision (b)(2). New Rule 26(f) provides that if a discovery conference is held, at its close the court shall enter an order respecting the subsequent conduct of discovery. The amendment provides that the sanctions available for violation of other court orders respecting discovery are available for violation of the discovery conference order.

Subdivision (e). Subdivision (e) is stricken. Title 28, U.S.C. § 1783 no longer refers to sanctions. The subdivision otherwise duplicates Rule 45(e)(2).

Subdivision (g). New Rule 26(f) imposes a duty on parties to participate in good faith in the framing of a discovery plan by agreement upon the request of any party. This subdivision authorizes the court to award to parties who participate in good faith in an attempt to frame a discovery plan the expenses incurred in the attempt if any party or his attorney fails to participate in good faith and thereby causes additional expense.

Failure of United States to Participate in Good Faith in Discovery. Rule 37 authorizes the court to direct that parties or attorneys who fail to participate in good faith in the discovery process pay the expenses, including attorneys' fees, incurred by other parties as a result of that failure. Since attorneys' fees cannot ordinarily be awarded against the United States (28 U.S.C. § 2412), there is often no practical remedy for the misconduct of its officers and attorneys. However, in the case of a government attorney who fails to participate in good faith in discovery, nothing prevents a court in an appropriate case from giving written notification of that fact to the Attorney General of the United States and other appropriate heads of offices or agencies thereof.

1987 Amendment

The amendments are technical. No substantive change is intended.

1993 Amendments

Subdivision (a). This subdivision is revised to reflect the revision of Rule 26(a), requiring disclosure of matters without a discovery request.

Pursuant to new subdivision (a)(2)(A), a party dissatisfied with the disclosure made by an opposing party may under this rule move for an order to compel disclosure. In providing for such a motion, the revised rule parallels the provisions of the former rule dealing with failures to answer particular interrogatories. Such a motion may be needed when the information to be disclosed might be helpful to the party seeking the disclosure but not to the party required to make the disclosure. If the party required to make the disclosure would need the material to support its own contentions, the more effective enforcement of the disclosure requirement will be to exclude the evidence not disclosed, as provided in subdivision (c)(1) of this revised rule.

Language is included in the new paragraph and added to the subparagraph (B) that requires litigants to seek to resolve discovery disputes by informal means before filing a motion with the court. This requirement is based on successful experience with similar local rules of court promulgated pursuant to Rule 83.

The last sentence of paragraph (2) is moved into paragraph (4).

Under revised paragraph (3), evasive or incomplete disclosures and responses to interrogatories and production requests are treated as failures to disclose or respond. Interrogatories and requests for production should not be read or interpreted in an artificially restrictive or hypertechnical manner to avoid disclosure of information fairly covered by the discovery request, and to do so is subject to appropriate sanctions under subdivision (a).

Revised paragraph (4) is divided into three subparagraphs for ease of reference, and in each the phrase "after opportunity for hearing" is changed to "after affording an opportunity to be heard" to make clear that the court can consider such questions on written submissions as well as on oral hearings.

Subparagraph (A) is revised to cover the situation where information that should have been produced without a motion to compel is produced after the motion is filed but before it is brought on for hearing. The rule also is revised to provide that a party should not be awarded its expenses for filing a motion that could have been avoided by conferring with opposing counsel.

Subparagraph (C) is revised to include the provision that formerly was contained in subdivision (a)(2) and to include the same requirement of an opportunity to be heard that is specified in subparagraphs (A) and (B).

Subdivision (c). The revision provides a self-executing sanction for failure to make a disclosure required by Rule 26(a), without need for a motion under subdivision (a)(2)(A).

Paragraph (1) prevents a party from using as evidence any witnesses or information that, without substantial justification, has not been disclosed as required by Rules 26(a) and 26(e)(1). This automatic sanction provides a strong inducement for disclosure of material that the disclosing party would expect to use as evidence, whether at a trial, at a hearing, or on a motion, such as one under Rule 56. As disclosure of evidence offered solely for impeachment purposes is not required under those rules, this preclusion sanction likewise does not apply to that evidence.

Limiting the automatic sanction to violations "without substantial justification," coupled with the exception for violations that are "harmless," is needed to avoid unduly harsh penalties in a variety of situations: *e.g.*, the inadvertent omission from a Rule 26(a)(1)(A) disclosure of the name of a potential witness known to all parties; the failure to list as a trial witness a person so listed by another party; or the lack of knowledge of a pro se litigant of the requirement to make disclosures. In the latter situation, however, exclusion would be proper if the requirement for disclosure had been called to the litigant's attention by either the court or another party.

Preclusion of evidence is not an effective incentive to compel disclosure of information that, being supportive of the position of the opposing party, might advantageously be concealed by the disclosing party. However, the rule provides the court with a wide range of other sanctions—such as declaring specified facts to be established, preventing contradictory evidence, or, like spoliation of evidence, allowing the jury to be informed of the fact of nondisclosure—that, though not self-executing, can be imposed when found to be warranted after a hearing. The failure to identify a witness or document in a disclosure statement would be admissible under the Federal Rules of Evidence under the same principles that allow a party's interrogatory answers to be offered against it.

Subdivision (d). This subdivision is revised to require that, where a party fails to file any response to interrogatories or a Rule 34 request, the discovering party should informally seek to obtain such responses before filing a motion for sanctions.

The last sentence of this subdivision is revised to clarify that it is the pendency of a motion for protective order that may be urged as an excuse for a violation of subdivision (d). If a party's motion has been denied, the party cannot argue that its subsequent failure to comply would be justified. In this connection, it should be noted that the filing of a motion under Rule 26(c) is not self-executing—the relief authorized under that rule depends on obtaining the court's order to that effect.

Subdivision (g). This subdivision is modified to conform to the revision of Rule 26(f).

HISTORICAL NOTES

Effective Dates

1980 Act. Amendment by Pub.L. 96–481 effective Oct. 1, 1981, and applicable to adversary adjudication defined in section 504(b)(1)(C) of Title 5, and to civil actions and adversary adjudications described in section 2412 of Title 28, Judiciary and Judicial Procedure, which are pending on, or commenced on or after Oct. 1, 1981, see section 208 of Pub.L. 96–481, set out as an Effective Date note under section 504 of Title 5, Government Organization and Employees.

VI. TRIALS

Rule 38. Jury Trial of Right

(a) Right Preserved. The right of trial by jury as declared by the Seventh Amendment to the Constitution or as given by a statute of the United States shall be preserved to the parties inviolate.

(b) Demand. Any party may demand a trial by jury of any issue triable of right by a jury by (1) serving upon the other parties a demand therefor in writing at any time after the commencement of the action and not later than 10 days after the service of the last pleading directed to such issue, and (2) filing the demand as required by Rule 5(d). Such demand may be indorsed upon a pleading of the party.

(c) Same: Specification of Issues. In the demand a party may specify the issues which the party wishes so tried; otherwise the party shall be deemed to have demanded trial by jury for all the issues so triable. If the party has demanded trial by jury for only some of the issues, any other party within 10 days after service of the demand or such lesser time as the court may order, may serve a demand for trial by jury of any other or all of the issues of fact in the action.

(d) Waiver. The failure of a party to serve and file a demand as required by this rule constitutes a waiver by the party of trial by jury. A demand for trial by jury made as herein provided may not be withdrawn without the consent of the parties.

(e) Admiralty and Maritime Claims. These rules shall not be construed to create a right to trial by jury of the issues in an admiralty or maritime claim within the meaning of Rule 9(h).

(As amended Feb. 28, 1966, eff. July 1, 1966; Mar. 2, 1987, eff. Aug. 1, 1987; Apr. 22, 1993, eff. Dec. 1, 1993.)

ADVISORY COMMITTEE NOTES

1937 Adoption

This rule provides for the preservation of the constitutional right of trial by jury as directed in the enabling act (act of June 19, 1934, 48 Stat. 1064, U.S.C., Title 28, § 723c [sec. 2072]), and it and the next rule make definite provision for claim and waiver of jury trial, following the method used in many American states and in England and the British Dominions. Thus the claim must be made at once on initial pleading or appearance under Ill.Rev.Stat. (1937) ch. 110, § 188; 6 Tenn.Code Ann. (Williams, 1934) § 8734; compare Wyo.Rev.Stat.Ann. (1931) § 89–1320 (with answer or reply); within 10 days after the pleadings are completed or the case is at issue under 2 Conn.Gen.Stat. (1930) § 5624; Hawaii Rev.Laws (1935) § 4101; 2 Mass.Gen.Laws (Ter.Ed.1932) ch. 231, § 60; 3 Mich.Comp.Laws (1929) § 14263; Mich. Court Rules Ann. (Searl, 1933) Rule 33 (15 days); England (until 1933) O. 36, r.r. 2 and 6; and Ontario Jud. Act (1927) § 57(1) (4 days, or, where prior notice of trial, 2 days from such notice); or at a definite time varying under different codes, from 10 days before notice of trial to 10 days after notice, or, as in many, when the case is called for assignment, Ariz.Rev. Code Ann. (Struckmeyer, 1928) § 3802; Calif. Code Civ.Proc. (Deering, 1937) § 631, par. 4; Iowa Code (1935) § 10724; 4 Nev.Comp.Laws (Hillyer, 1929) § 8782; N.M. Stat.Ann. (Courtright, 1929) § 105–814; N.Y.C.P.A. (1937) § 426, subdivision 5 (applying to New York, Bronx, Richmond, Kings, and Queens Counties); R.I. Pub. Laws (1929), ch. 1327, amending R.I. Gen.Laws (1923) ch. 337, § 6; Utah Rev.Stat. Ann. (1933) § 104–23–6; 2 Wash.Rev.Stat.Ann. (Remington, 1932) § 316; England (4 days after notice of trial), Administration of Justice Act (1933) § 6 and amended rule under the Judicature Act (The Annual Practice, 1937), O. 36, r. 1; Australia High Court Procedure Act (1921) § 12, Rules, O. 33, r. 2; Alberta Rules of Ct. (1914) 172, 183, 184; British Columbia Sup.Ct.Rules (1925) O. 36, r.r. 2, 6, 11, and 16; New Brunswick Jud. Act (1927) O. 36, r.r. 2 and 5. See James, Trial by Jury and the New Federal Rules of Procedure (1936), 45 Yale L.J. 1022.

Rule 81(c) provides for claim for jury trial in removed actions.

The right to trial by jury as declared in U.S.C., Title 28, § 770 (Trial of issues of fact; by jury; exceptions), and similar statutes, is unaffected by this rule. This rule modifies U.S.C., Title 28, [former] § 773 (Trial of issues of fact; by court).

1966 Amendments

See Note to Rule 9(h), supra.

1987 Amendments

The amendments are technical. No substantive change is intended.

1993 Amendments

Language requiring the filing of a jury demand as provided in subdivision (d) is added to subdivision (b) to eliminate an apparent ambiguity between the two subdivisions. For proper scheduling of cases, it is important that jury demands not only be served on other parties, but also be filed with the court.

Rule 39. Trial by Jury or by the Court

(a) By Jury. When trial by jury has been demanded as provided in Rule 38, the action shall be designated upon the docket as a jury action. The trial of all issues so demanded shall be by jury, unless (1) the parties or their attorneys of record, by written stipulation filed with the court or by an oral stipulation made in open court and entered in the record, consent to trial by the court sitting without a jury or (2) the court upon motion or of its own initiative finds that a right of trial by jury of some or all of those issues does not exist under the Constitution or statutes of the United States.

(b) By the Court. Issues not demanded for trial by jury as provided in Rule 38 shall be tried by the court; but, notwithstanding the failure of a party to demand a jury in an action in which such a demand might have been made of right, the court in its discretion upon motion may order a trial by a jury of any or all issues.

(c) Advisory Jury and Trial by Consent. In all actions not triable of right by a jury the court upon motion or of its own initiative may try any issue with an advisory jury or, except in actions against the United States when a statute of the United States provides for trial without a jury, the court, with the consent of both parties, may order a trial with a jury whose verdict has the same effect as if trial by jury had been a matter of right.

ADVISORY COMMITTEE NOTES

1937 Adoption

The provisions for express waiver of jury trial found in U.S.C., Title 28, [former] § 773 (Trial of issues of fact; by court) are incorporated in this rule. See Rule 38, however, which extends the provisions for waiver of jury. U.S.C., Title 28, [former] § 772 (Trial of issues of fact; in equity in patent causes) is unaffected by this rule. When certain of the issues are to be tried by jury and others by the court, the court may determine the sequence in which such issues shall be tried. *See Liberty Oil Co. v. Condon Nat. Bank*, 260 U.S. 235, 43 S.Ct. 118, 67 L.Ed. 232 (1922).

A discretionary power in the courts to send issues of fact to the jury is common in state procedure. Compare Calif. Code Civ.Proc. (Deering, 1937) § 592; 1 Colo.Stat.Ann. (1935) Code Civ.Proc., ch. 12, § 191; Conn.Gen.Stat. (1930) § 5625; 2 Minn.Stat. (Mason, 1927) § 9288; 4 Mont.Rev. Codes Ann. (1935) § 9327; N.Y.C.P.A. (1937) § 430; 2 Ohio Gen.Code Ann. (Page, 1926) § 11380; 1 Okla.Stat.Ann. (Harlow, 1931) § 351 [12 Okl.St.Ann. § 557]; Utah Rev.Stat.Ann. (1933) § 104–23–5; 2 Wash.Rev.Stat.Ann. (Remington, 1932) § 315; Wis.Stat. (1935) § 270.07. See [former] Equity Rule 23 (Matters Ordinarily Determinable at Law When Arising in Suit in Equity to be Disposed of Therein) and U.S.C., Title 28 [former] § 772 (Trial of issues of fact; in equity in patent causes); *Colleton Merc. Mfg. Co. v. Savannah River Lumber Co.*, C.C.A.4, 1922, 280 F. 358; *Fed. Res. Bk. of San Francisco v. Idaho Grimm Alfalfa Seed Growers' Ass'n*, C.C.A.9, 1925, 8 F.2d 922, certiorari denied 46 S.Ct. 347, 270 U.S. 646, 70 L.Ed. 778 (1926); *Watt v. Starke*, 1879, 101 U.S. 247, 25 L.Ed. 826.

Rule 40. Assignment of Cases for Trial

The district courts shall provide by rule for the placing of actions upon the trial calendar (1) without request of the parties or (2) upon request of a party and notice to the other parties or (3) in such other manner as the courts deem expedient. Precedence shall be given to actions entitled thereto by any statute of the United States.

ADVISORY COMMITTEE NOTES

1937 Adoption

U.S.C., Title 28, [former] § 769 (Notice of case for trial) is modified. See former Equity Rule 56 (On Expiration of Time for Depositions, Case Goes on Trial Calendar). See also [former] Equity Rule 57 (Continuances).

For examples of statutes giving precedence, see U.S.C., Title 28, § 47 (now §§ 1253, 2101, 2325) (Injunctions as to orders of Interstate Commerce Commission); § 380 (now §§ 1253, 2101, 2284) (Injunctions; alleged unconstitutionality of state statutes); § 380a (now §§ 1253, 2101, 2284) (Same; Constitutionality of federal statute); [former] § 768 (Priority of cases where a state is party); Title 15, § 28 (Antitrust laws; suits against monopolies expedited); Title 22, § 240 (Petition for restoration of property seized as munitions of war, etc.); and Title 49, [former] § 44 (Proceedings in equity under interstate commerce laws; expedition of suits).

Rule 41. Dismissal of Actions

(a) Voluntary Dismissal: Effect Thereof.

(1) By Plaintiff; by Stipulation. Subject to the provisions of Rule 23(e), of Rule 66, and of any statute of the United States, an action may be dismissed by the plaintiff without order of court (i) by filing a notice of dismissal at any time before service by the adverse party of an answer or of a motion for summary judgment, whichever first occurs, or (ii) by filing a stipulation of dismissal signed by all parties who have appeared in the action. Unless otherwise stated in the notice of dismissal or stipulation, the dismissal is without prejudice, except that a notice of dismissal operates as an adjudication upon the merits when filed by a plaintiff who has once dismissed in any court of the United States or of any state an action based on or including the same claim.

(2) By Order of Court. Except as provided in paragraph (1) of this subdivision of this rule, an action shall not be dismissed at the plaintiff's instance save upon order of the court and upon such terms and conditions as the court deems proper. If a counterclaim has been pleaded by a defendant prior to the service upon the defendant of the plaintiff's motion to dismiss, the action shall not be dismissed against the defendant's objection unless the counterclaim can remain pending for independent adjudication by the court. Unless otherwise specified in the order, a dismissal under this paragraph is without prejudice.

(b) Involuntary Dismissal: Effect Thereof. For failure of the plaintiff to prosecute or to comply with these rules or any order of court, a defendant may move for dismissal of an action or of any claim against the defendant. Unless the court in its order for dismissal otherwise specifies, a dismissal under this subdivision and any dismissal not provided for in this rule, other than a dismissal for lack of jurisdiction, for improper venue, or for failure to join a party under Rule 19, operates as an adjudication upon the merits.

(c) Dismissal of Counterclaim, Cross-Claim, or Third-Party Claim. The provisions of this rule apply to the dismissal of any counterclaim, cross-claim, or third-party claim. A voluntary dismissal by the claimant alone pursuant to paragraph (1) of subdivision (a) of this rule shall be made before a responsive pleading is served or, if there is none, before the introduction of evidence at the trial or hearing.

(d) Costs of Previously-Dismissed Action. If a plaintiff who has once dismissed an action in any court commences an action based upon or including the same claim against the same defendant, the court may make such order for the payment of costs of the action previously dismissed as it may deem proper and may stay the proceedings in the action until the plaintiff has complied with the order.

(As amended Dec. 27, 1946, eff. Mar. 19, 1948; Jan. 21, 1963, eff. July 1, 1963; Feb. 28, 1966, eff. July 1, 1966; Dec. 4, 1967, eff. July 1, 1968; Mar. 2, 1987, eff. Aug. 1, 1987; Apr. 30, 1991, eff. Dec. 1, 1991.)

ADVISORY COMMITTEE NOTES

1937 Adoption

Note to Subdivision (a). Compare Ill.Rev.Stat. (1937) c. 110, § 176, and *English Rules Under the Judicature Act* (The Annual Practice, 1937) O. 26.

Provisions regarding dismissal in such statutes as U.S.C., Title 8, § 164 [see 1329] (Jurisdiction of district courts in immigration cases) and U.S.C., Title 31, § 232 [now 3730] (Liability of persons making false claims against United States; suits) are preserved by paragraph (1).

Note to Subdivision (b). This provides for the equivalent of a nonsuit on motion by the defendant after the completion of the presentation of evidence by the plaintiff. Also, for actions tried without a jury, it provides the equivalent of the directed verdict practice for jury actions which is regulated by Rule 50.

1946 Amendment

Note. Subdivision (a). The insertion of the reference to Rule 66 correlates Rule 41(a)(1) with the express provisions concerning dismissal set forth in amended Rule 66 on receivers.

The change in Rule 41(a)(1)(i) gives the service of a motion for summary judgment by the adverse party the same effect in preventing unlimited dismissal as was originally given only to the service of an answer. The omission of reference to a motion for summary judgment in the original rule was subject to criticism. 3 *Moore's Federal Practice,* 1938, 3037–3038, n. 12. A motion for summary judgment may be forthcoming prior to answer, and if well taken will eliminate the necessity for an answer. Since such a motion may require even more research and preparation than the answer itself, there is good reason why the service of the motion, like that of the answer, should prevent a voluntary dismissal by the adversary without court approval.

The word "generally" has been stricken from Rule 41(a)(1)(ii) in order to avoid confusion and to conform with the elimination of the necessity for special appearance by original Rule 12(b).

Subdivision (b). In some cases tried without a jury, where at the close of plaintiff's evidence the defendant moves for dismissal under Rule 41(b) on the ground that plaintiff's evidence is insufficient for recovery, the plaintiff's own evidence may be conflicting or present questions of credibility. In ruling on the defendant's motion, questions arise as to the function of the judge in evaluating the testimony and whether findings should be made if the motion is sustained. Three circuits hold that as the judge is the trier of the facts in such a situation his function is not the same as on a motion to direct a verdict, where the jury is the trier of the facts, and that the judge in deciding such a motion in a non-jury case may pass on conflicts of evidence and credibility, and if he performs that function of evaluating the testimony and grants the motion on the merits, findings are required. *Young v. United States,* C.C.A.9, 1940, 111 F.2d 823; *Gary Theatre Co. v. Columbia Pictures Corporation,* C.C.A.7, 1941, 120 F.2d 891; *Bach v. Friden Calculating Machine Co., Inc.,* C.C.A.6, 1945, 148 F.2d 407. Cf. *Mateas v. Fred Harvey, a Corporation,* C.C.A.9, 1945, 146 F.2d 989. The Third Circuit has held that on such a motion the function of the court is the same as on a motion to direct in a jury case, and that the court should only decide whether there is evidence which would support a judgment for the plaintiff, and therefore, findings are not required by Rule 52. *Federal Deposit Insurance Corp. v. Mason,* C.C.A.3, 1940, 115 F.2d 548; *Schad v. Twentieth Century-Fox Film Corp.,* C.C.A.3, 1943, 136 F.2d 991. The added sentence in Rule 41(b) incorporates the view of the Sixth, Seventh and Ninth Circuits. See also 3 *Moore's Federal Practice,* 1938, Cum.Supplement § 41.03, under "Page 3045"; Commentary, *The Mo-*

tion to Dismiss in Non-Jury Cases, 1946, 9 Fed.Rules Serv., Comm.Pg. 41b.14.

1963 Amendment

Under the present text of the second sentence of this subdivision, the motion for dismissal at the close of the plaintiff's evidence may be made in a case tried to a jury as well as in a case tried without a jury. But, when made in a jury-tried case, this motion overlaps the motion for a directed verdict under Rule 50(a), which is also available in the same situation. It has been held that the standard to be applied in deciding the Rule 41(b) motion at the close of the plaintiff's evidence in a jury-tried case is the same as that used upon a motion for a directed verdict made at the same stage; and, just as the court need not make findings pursuant to Rule 52(a) when it directs a verdict, so in a jury-tried case it may omit these findings in granting the Rule 41(b) motion. See generally *O'Brien v. Westinghouse Electric Corp.,* 293 F.2d 1, 5–10 (3d Cir. 1961).

As indicated by the discussion in the *O'Brien* case, the overlap has caused confusion. Accordingly, the second and third sentences of Rule 41(b) are amended to provide that the motion for dismissal at the close of the plaintiff's evidence shall apply only to nonjury cases (including cases tried with an advisory jury). Hereafter the correct motion in jury-tried cases will be the motion for a directed verdict. This involves no change of substance. It should be noted that the court upon a motion for a directed verdict may in appropriate circumstances deny that motion and grant instead a new trial, or a voluntary dismissal without prejudice under Rule 41(a)(2). See 6 *Moore's Federal Practice* ¶59.08[5] (2d ed. 1954); *cf. Cone v. West Virginia Pulp & Paper Co.,* 330 U.S. 212, 217, 67 S.Ct. 752, 91 L.Ed. 849 (1947).

The first sentence of Rule 41(b), providing for dismissal for failure to prosecute or to comply with the Rules or any order of court, and the general provisions of the last sentence remain applicable in jury as well as nonjury cases.

The amendment of the last sentence of Rule 41(b) indicates that a dismissal for lack of an indispensable party does not operate as an adjudication on the merits. Such a dismissal does not bar a new action, for it is based merely "on a plaintiff's failure to comply with a precondition requisite to the Court's going forward to determine the merits of his substantive claim." See *Costello v. United States,* 365 U.S. 265, 284–288, 81 S.Ct. 534, 5 L.Ed.2d 551 & n. 5 (1961); *Mallow v. Hinde,* 12 Wheat. (25 U.S.) 193, 6 L.Ed. 599 (1827); Clark, *Code Pleading* 602 (2d ed. 1947); *Restatement of Judgments* § 49, comm. a, b (1942). This amendment corrects an omission from the rule and is consistent with an earlier amendment, effective in 1948, adding "the defense of failure to join an indispensable party" to clause (1) of Rule 12(h).

1966 Amendment

The terminology is changed to accord with the amendment of Rule 19. See that amended rule and the Advisory Committee's Note thereto.

1968 Amendment

The amendment corrects an inadvertent error in the reference to amended Rule 23.

1987 Amendment

The amendment is technical. No substantive change is intended.

1991 Amendment

Language is deleted that authorized the use of this rule as a means of terminating a non-jury action on the merits when the plaintiff has failed to carry a burden of proof in presenting the plaintiff's case. The device is replaced by the new provisions of Rule 52(c), which authorize entry of judgment against the defendant as well as the plaintiff, and earlier than the close of the case of the party against whom judgment is rendered. A motion to dismiss under Rule 41 on the ground that a plaintiff's evidence is legally insufficient should now be treated as a motion for judgment on partial findings as provided in Rule 52(c).

Rule 42. Consolidation; Separate Trials

(a) Consolidation. When actions involving a common question of law or fact are pending before the court, it may order a joint hearing or trial of any or all the matters in issue in the actions; it may order all the actions consolidated; and it may make such orders concerning proceedings therein as may tend to avoid unnecessary costs or delay.

(b) Separate Trials. The court, in furtherance of convenience or to avoid prejudice, or when separate trials will be conducive to expedition and economy, may order a separate trial of any claim, cross-claim, counterclaim, or third-party claim, or of any separate issue or of any number of claims, cross-claims, counterclaims, third-party claims, or issues, always preserving inviolate the right of trial by jury as declared by the Seventh Amendment to the Constitution or as given by a statute of the United States.

(As amended Feb. 28, 1966, eff. July 1, 1966.)

ADVISORY COMMITTEE NOTES

1937 Adoption

Subdivision (a) is based upon U.S.C., Title 28, [former] § 734 (Orders to save costs; consolidation of causes of like nature) but in so far as the statute differs from this rule, it is modified.

For comparable statutes dealing with consolidation see Ark.Dig.Stat. (Crawford & Moses, 1921) § 1081; Calif.Code Civ.Proc. (Deering, 1937) § 1048; N.M.Stat.Ann. (Courtright, 1929) § 105–828; N.Y.C.P.A. (1937) §§ 96, 96a, and 97; American Judicature Society, Bulletin XIV, (1919) Art. 26.

For severance or separate trials see Calif.Code Civ.Proc. (Deering, 1937) § 1048; N.Y.C.P.A. (1937) § 96; American Judicature Society, Bulletin XIV (1919) Art. 3, § 2 and Art. 10, § 10. See also the third sentence of Equity Rule 29 (Defenses—How Presented) providing for discretionary separate hearing and disposition before trial of pleas in bar or abatement, and see also Rule 12(d) of these rules for preliminary hearings of defenses and objections.

For the entry of separate judgments, see Rule 54(b) (Judgment at Various Stages).

1966 Amendment

In certain suits in admiralty separation for trial of the issues of liability and damages (or of the extent of liability other than damages, such as salvage and general average) has been conducive to expedition and economy, especially because of the statutory right to interlocutory appeal in admiralty cases (which is of course preserved by these Rules). While separation of issues for trial is not to be routinely ordered, it is important that it be encouraged where experience has demonstrated its worth. Cf. Weinstein, *Routine Bifurcation of Negligence Trials,* 14 Vand. L.Rev. 831 (1961).

In cases (including some cases within the admiralty and maritime jurisdiction) in which the parties have a constitutional or statutory right of trial by jury, separation of issues may give rise to problems. See *e.g., United Air Lines, Inc. v. Wiener,* 286 F.2d 302 (9th Cir.1961). Accordingly, the proposed change in Rule 42 reiterates the mandate of Rule 38 respecting preservation of the right to jury trial.

Rule 43. Taking of Testimony

(a) Form. In every trial, the testimony of witnesses shall be taken in open court, unless a federal law, these rules, the Federal Rules of Evidence, or other rules adopted by the Supreme Court provide otherwise. The court may, for good cause shown in compelling circumstances and upon appropriate safeguards, permit presentation of testimony in open court by contemporaneous transmission from a different location.

[(b), (c) Abrogated]

(d) Affirmation in Lieu of Oath. Whenever under these rules an oath is required to be taken, a solemn affirmation may be accepted in lieu thereof.

(e) Evidence on Motions. When a motion is based on facts not appearing of record the court may hear the matter on affidavits presented by the respective parties, but the court may direct that the matter be heard wholly or partly on oral testimony or deposition.

(f) Interpreters. The court may appoint an interpreter of its own selection and may fix the interpreter's reasonable compensation. The compensation shall be paid out of funds provided by law or by one or more of the parties as the court may direct, and may be taxed ultimately as costs, in the discretion of the court.

(As amended Feb. 28, 1966, eff. July 1, 1966; Nov. 20, 1972, and Dec. 18, 1972, eff. July 1, 1975; Mar. 2, 1987, eff. Aug. 1, 1987; Apr. 23, 1996, eff. Dec. 1, 1996.)

ADVISORY COMMITTEE NOTES

1937 Adoption

Note to Subdivision (a). The first sentence is a restatement of the substance of U.S.C., Title 28, § 635 (Proof in common-law actions), [former] § 637 (see §§ 2072, 2073) (Proof in equity and admiralty), and [former] Equity Rule 46 (Trial—Testimony Usually Taken in Open Court—Rulings on Objections to Evidence). This rule abolishes in patent and trademark actions, the practice under [former] Equity Rule 48 of setting forth in affidavits the testimony in chief of expert witnesses whose testimony is directed to matters of opinion. The second and third sentences on admissibility of evidence and Subdivision (b) on contradiction and cross-examination modify U.S.C., Title 28, § 725 (now 1652) (Laws of states as rules of decision) insofar as that statute has been construed to prescribe conformity to state rules of evidence. Compare Callahan and Ferguson, *Evidence and the New Federal Rules of Civil Procedure,* 45 Yale L.J. 622 (1936), and *Same: 2,* 47 Yale L.J. 195 (1937). The last sentence modifies to the extent indicated U.S.C., Title 28, [former] § 631 (Competency of witnesses governed by State laws).

Note to Subdivision (b). See 4 *Wigmore on Evidence* (2d ed., 1923) § 1885 et seq.

Note to Subdivision (c). See [former] Equity Rule 46 (Trial—Testimony Usually Taken in Open Court-Rulings on Objections to Evidence). With the last sentence compare *Dowagiac v. Lochren,* 143 Fed. 211 (C.C.A. 8th, 1906). See also *Blease v. Garlington,* 92 U.S. 1, 23 L.Ed. 521 (1876); *Nelson v. United States,* 201 U.S. 92, 114, 26 S.Ct. 358, 50 L.Ed. 673 (1906); *Unkle v. Wills,* 281 Fed. 29 (C.C.A. 8th, 1922).

See Rule 61 for harmless error in either the admission or exclusion of evidence.

Note to Subdivision (d). See [former] Equity Rule 78 (Affirmation in Lieu of Oath) and U.S.C., Title 1, § 1 (Words importing singular number, masculine gender, etc.; extended application), providing for affirmation in lieu of oath.

Supplementary Note on Advisory Committee Regarding Rules 43 and 44

Note. These rules have been criticized and suggested improvements offered by commentators. 1 *Wigmore on Evidence,* 3d ed. 1940, 200–204; Green, *The Admissibility of Evidence Under the Federal Rules,* 1941, 55 Harv.L.Rev. 197. Cases indicate, however, that the rule is working better than these commentators had expected. *Boerner v. United States,* C.C.A.2d, 1941, 117 F.2d 387, cert. den., 1941, 313 U.S. 587, 61 S.Ct. 1120; *Mosson v. Liberty Fast Freight Co.,* C.C.A.2d, 1942, 124 F.2d, 448; *Hartford Accident & Indemnity Co. v. Olivier,* C.C.A. 5th, 1941, 123 F.2d 709; *Anzano v. Metropolitan Life Ins. Co. of New York,* C.C.A.3d, 1941, 118 F.2d 430; *Franzen v. E. I. DuPont De Nemours & Co.,* C.C.A.3d, 1944, 146 F.2d 837; *Fakouri v. Cadais,* C.C.A. 5th, 1945, 147 F.2d 667; *In re C. & P. Co.,* S.D.Cal.1945, 63 F.Supp. 400, 408. But cf. *United States v. Aluminum Co. of America,* S.D.N.Y.1938, 1 Fed.Rules Serv. 43a.3, Case 1; Note, 1946, 46 Col.L.Rev. 267. While consideration of a comprehensive and detailed set of rules of evidence seems very desirable, it has not been feasible for the Committee so far to undertake this important task. Such consideration should include the adaptability to federal practice of all or parts of the proposed Code of Evidence of the American Law Institute. See Armstrong, *Proposed Amendments to Federal Rules of Civil Procedure,* 4 F.R.D. 124, 137–138.

1966 Amendment

Note to Subdivision (f). This new subdivision [subdivision (f)] authorizes the court to appoint interpreters (including interpreters for the deaf), to provide for their compensation, and to tax the compensation as costs. Compare proposed subdivision (b) of Rule 28 of the Federal Rules of Criminal Procedure.

1972 Amendment

Rule 43, entitled Evidence, has heretofore served as the basic rule of evidence for civil cases in federal courts. Its very general provisions are superseded by the detailed provisions of the new Rules of Evidence. The original title and many of the provisions of the rule are, therefore, no longer appropriate.

Subdivision (a). The provision for taking testimony in open court is not duplicated in the Rules of Evidence and is retained. Those dealing with admissibility of evidence and competency of witnesses, however, are no longer needed or appropriate since those topics are covered at large in the Rules of Evidence. They are accordingly deleted. The language is broadened, however, to take account of acts of Congress dealing with the taking of testimony, as well as of the Rules of Evidence and any other rules adopted by the Supreme Court.

Subdivision (b). The subdivision is no longer needed or appropriate since the matters with which it deals are treated in the Rules of Evidence. The use of leading questions, both generally and in the interrogation of an adverse party or witness identified with him, is the subject of Evidence Rule 611(c). Who may impeach is treated in Evidence Rule 601 [sic; probably means 607], and scope of cross-examination is covered in Evidence Rule 611(b). The subdivision is accordingly deleted.

Subdivision (c). Offers of proof and making a record of excluded evidence are treated in Evidence Rule 103. The subdivision is no longer needed or appropriate and is deleted.

1987 Amendment

The amendment is technical. No substantive change is intended.

1996 Amendment

Rule 43(a) is revised to conform to the style conventions adopted for simplifying the present Civil Rules. The only intended changes of meaning are described below.

The requirement that testimony be taken "orally" is deleted. The deletion makes it clear that testimony of a witness may be given in open court by other means if the witness is not able to communicate orally. Writing or sign language are common examples. The development of advanced technology may enable testimony to be given by other means. A witness unable to sign or write by hand may be able to communicate through a computer or similar device.

Contemporaneous transmission of testimony from a different location is permitted only on showing good cause in compelling circumstances. The importance of presenting live testimony in court cannot be forgotten. The very ceremony of trial and the presence of the factfinder may exert a powerful force for truthtelling. The opportunity to judge the demeanor of a witness face-to-face is accorded great value in our tradition. Transmission cannot be justified merely by showing that it is inconvenient for the witness to attend the trial.

The most persuasive showings of good cause and compelling circumstances are likely to arise when a witness is unable to attend trial for unexpected reasons, such as accident or illness, but remains able to testify from a different place. Contemporaneous transmission may be better than an attempt to reschedule the trial, particularly if there is a risk that other—and perhaps more important—witnesses might not be available at a later time.

Other possible justifications for remote transmission must be approached cautiously. Ordinarily depositions, including video depositions, provide a superior means of securing the testimony of a witness who is beyond the reach of a trial subpoena, or of resolving difficulties in scheduling a trial that can be attended by all witnesses. Deposition procedures ensure the opportunity of all parties to be represented while the witness is testifying. An unforeseen need for the testimony of a remote witness that arises during trial, however, may establish good cause and compelling circumstances. Justification is particularly likely if the need arises from the interjection of new issues during trial or from the unexpected inability to present testimony as planned from a different witness.

Good cause and compelling circumstances may be established with relative ease if all parties agree that testimony should be presented by transmission. The court is not bound by a stipulation, however, and can insist on live testimony. Rejection of the parties' agreement will be influenced, among other factors, by the apparent importance of the testimony in the full context of the trial.

A party who could reasonably foresee the circumstances offered to justify transmission of testimony will have special difficulty in showing good cause and the compelling nature of the circumstances. Notice of a desire to transmit testimony from a different location should be given as soon as the reasons are known, to enable other parties to arrange a deposition, or to secure an advance ruling on transmission so as to know whether to prepare to be present with the witness while testifying.

No attempt is made to specify the means of transmission that may be used. Audio transmission without video images may be sufficient in some circumstances, particularly as to less important testimony. Video transmission ordinarily should be preferred when the cost is reasonable in relation to the matters in dispute, the means of the parties, and the circumstances that justify transmission. Transmission that merely produces the equivalent of a written statement ordinarily should not be used.

Safeguards must be adopted that ensure accurate identification of the witness and that protect against influence by persons present with the witness. Accurate transmission likewise must be assured.

Other safeguards should be employed to ensure that advance notice is given to all parties of foreseeable circumstances that may lead the proponent to offer testimony by transmission. Advance notice is important to protect the opportunity to argue for attendance of the witness at trial. Advance notice also ensures an opportunity to depose the witness, perhaps by video record, as a means of supplementing transmitted testimony.

HISTORICAL NOTES

Effective Date of Amendments Proposed November 20, 1972, and December 18, 1972

Amendments of this rule embraced by orders entered by the Supreme Court of the United States on November 20, 1972, and December 18, 1972, effective on the 180th day beginning after January 2, 1975, see section 3 of Pub.L. 93–595, Jan. 2, 1975, 88 Stat. 1959, set out as a note under section 2071 of Title 28.

Rule 44. Proof of Official Record

(a) Authentication.

(1) Domestic. An official record kept within the United States, or any state, district, or commonwealth, or within a territory subject to the administrative or judicial jurisdiction of the United States, or an entry therein, when admissible for any purpose, may be evidenced by an official publication thereof or by a copy attested by the officer having the legal custody of the record, or by the officer's deputy, and accompanied by a certificate that such officer has the custody. The certificate may be made by a judge of a court of record of the district or political subdivision in which the record is kept, authenticated by the seal of the court, or may be made by any public officer having a seal of office and having official duties in the district or political subdivision in which the record is kept, authenticated by the seal of the officer's office.

(2) Foreign. A foreign official record, or an entry therein, when admissible for any purpose, may be evidenced by an official publication thereof; or a copy thereof, attested by a person authorized to make the attestation, and accompanied by a final certification as to the genuineness of the signature and official position (i) of the attesting person, or (ii) of any foreign official whose certificate of genuineness of signature and official position relates to the attestation or is in a chain of certificates of genuineness of signature and official position relating to the attestation. A final certification may be made by a secretary of embassy or legation, consul general, vice consul, or consular agent of the United States, or a diplomatic or consular official of the foreign country assigned or accredited to the United States. If reasonable opportunity has been given to all parties to investigate the authenticity and accuracy of the documents, the court may, for good cause shown, (i) admit an attested copy without final certification or (ii) permit the foreign official record to be evidenced by an attested summary with or without a final certification. The final certification is unnecessary if the record and the attestation are certified as provided in a treaty or convention to which the United States and the foreign country in which the official record is located are parties.

(b) Lack of Record. A written statement that after diligent search no record or entry of a specified tenor is found to exist in the records designated by the statement, authenticated as provided in subdivision (a)(1) of this rule in the case of a domestic record, or complying with the requirements of subdivision (a)(2) of this rule for a summary in the case of a foreign record, is admissible as evidence that the records contain no such record or entry.

(c) Other Proof. This rule does not prevent the proof of official records or of entry or lack of entry therein by any other method authorized by law.

(As amended Feb. 28, 1966, eff. July 1, 1966; Mar. 2, 1987, eff. Aug. 1, 1987; Apr. 30, 1991, eff. Dec. 1, 1991.)

ADVISORY COMMITTEE NOTES

1937 Adoption

This rule provides a simple and uniform method of proving public records, and entry or lack of entry therein, in all cases including those specifically provided for by statutes of the United States. Such statutes are not superseded, however, and proof may also be made according to their provisions whenever they differ from this rule. Some of those statutes are:

U.S.C., Title 28 [former sections]:

§ 661[now 1733] (Copies of department or corporation records and papers; admissibility; seal)

§ 662[now 1733] (Same; in office of General Counsel of the Treasury)

§ 663[now 1733] (Instruments and papers of Comptroller of Currency; admissibility)

§ 664[now 1733] (Organization certificates of national banks; admissibility)

§ 665[now 1733] (Transcripts from books of Treasury in suits against delinquents; admissibility)

§ 666[now 1733] (Same; certificate by Secretary or Assistant Secretary)

§ 670[now 1743] (Admissibility of copies of statements of demands by Post Office Department)

§ 671[now 1733] (Admissibility of copies of post office records and statement of accounts)

§ 672[former] (Admissibility of copies of records in General Land Office)

§ 673[now 1744] (Admissibility of copies of records, and so forth, of Patent Office)

§ 674[now 1745] (Copies of foreign letters patent as prima facie evidence)

§ 675[former] (Copies of specifications and drawings of patents admissible)

§ 676[now 1736] (Extracts from Journals of Congress admissible when injunction of secrecy removed)

§ 677[now 1740] (Copies of records in offices of United States consuls admissible)

§ 678[former] (Books and papers in certain district courts)

§ 679[former] (Records in clerks' offices, western district of North Carolina)

§ 680[former] (Records in clerks' offices of former district of California)

§ 681[now 1734] (Original records lost or destroyed; certified copy admissible)

§ 682[now 1734] (Same; when certified copy not obtainable)

§ 685[now 1735] (Same; certified copy of official papers)

§ 687[now 1738] (Authentication of legislative acts; proof of judicial proceedings of State)

§ 688[now 1739] (Proofs of records in offices not pertaining to courts)

§ 689[now 1742] (Copies of foreign records relating to land titles)

§ 695[now 1732] (Writings and records made in regular course of business; admissibility)

§ 695e[now 1741] (Foreign documents on record in public offices; certification)

U.S.C., Title 1:

§ 30[now 112] (Statutes at large; contents; admissibility in evidence)

§ 30a[now 113] ("Little and Brown's" edition of laws and treaties competent evidence of Acts of Congress)

§ 54[now 204] (Codes and supplements as establishing prima facie the laws of United States and District of Columbia, etc.)

§ 55[now 208] (Copies of supplements to Code of Laws of United States and of District of Columbia Code and supplements; conclusive evidence of original)

U.S.C., Title 5:

§ 490[former] (Records of Department of Interior; authenticated copies as evidence)

U.S.C., Title 6:

§ 7[now Title 31, § 9306] (Surety Companies as sureties; appointment of agents; service of process)

U.S.C., Title 8:

§ 9a[see 1435(c)] (Citizenship of children of persons naturalized under certain laws; repatriation of native-born women married to aliens prior to September 22, 1922; copies of proceedings)

§ 356[see 1443] (Regulations for execution of naturalization laws; certified copies of papers as evidence)

§ 399b(d)[see 1443] (Certifications of naturalization records; authorization; admissibility as evidence)

U.S.C., Title 11:

§ 44(d), (e), (f), (g)[former] (Bankruptcy court proceedings and orders as evidence)

§ 204[former] (Extensions extended, etc.; evidence of confirmation)

§ 207(j)[former] (Corporate reorganizations; certified copy of decree as evidence)

U.S.C., Title 15:

§ 127 (Trade-mark records in Patent Office; copies as evidence)

U.S.C., Title 20:

§ 52 (Smithsonian Institution; evidence of title to site and buildings)

U.S.C., Title 25:

§ 6 (Bureau of Indian Affairs; seal; authenticated and certified documents; evidence)

U.S.C., Title 31:

§ 46[now 704] (Laws governing General Accounting Office; copies of books, records, etc., thereof as evidence)

U.S.C., Title 38:

§ 11g[see 202] (Seal of Veterans' Administration; authentication of copies of records)

U.S.C., Title 40:

§ 238 (National Archives; seal; reproduction of archives; fee; admissibility in evidence of reproductions)

§ 270c (Bonds of contractors for public works; right of person furnishing labor or material to copy of bond)

U.S.C., Title 43:

§§ 57–59 (Copies of land surveys, etc., in certain states and districts admissible as evidence)

§ 83 (General Land Office registers and receivers; transcripts of records as evidence)

U.S.C., Title 46:

§ 823 (Records of Maritime Commission; copies; publication of reports; evidence)

U.S.C., Title 47:

§ 154(m) (Federal Communications Commission; copies of reports and decisions as evidence)

§ 412 (Documents filed with Federal Communications Commission as public records; prima facie evidence; confidential records)

U.S.C., Title 49:

§ 14(3)[now 10310] (Interstate Commerce Commission reports and decisions; printing and distribution of copies)

§ 16(13)[now 10303(b)] (Copies of schedules, tariffs, etc. filed with Interstate Commerce Commission as evidence)

§ 19a(i)[now 10785(c)] (Valuation of property of carriers by Interstate Commerce Commission; final published valuations as evidence)

Supplementary Note of Advisory Committee Regarding Rules 43 and 44.

For supplementary note of Advisory Committee on this rule, see note under Rule 43.

1966 Amendment

Note to Subdivision (a)(1). These provisions on proof of official records kept within the United States are similar in substance to those heretofore appearing in Rule 44. There is a more exact description of the geographical areas covered. An official record kept in one of the areas enumerated qualifies for proof under subdivision (a)(1) even though it is not a United States official record. For example, an official record kept in one of these areas by a government in exile falls within subdivision (a)(1). It also falls within subdivision (a)(2) which may be availed of alternatively. Cf. *Banco de Espana v. Federal Reserve Bank,* 114 F.2d 438 (2d Cir. 1940).

Note to Subdivision (a)(2). Foreign official records may be proved, as heretofore, by means of official publications thereof. See *United States v. Aluminum Co. of America,* 1 F.R.D. 71 (S.D.N.Y.1939). Under this rule, a document that, on its face, appears to be an official publication, is admissible, unless a party opposing its admission into evidence shows that it lacks that character.

The rest of subdivision (a)(2) aims to provide greater clarity, efficiency, and flexibility in the procedure for authenticating copies of foreign official records.

The reference to attestation by "the officer having the legal custody of the record," hitherto appearing in Rule 44, has been found inappropriate for official records kept in foreign countries where the assumed relation between custody and the authority to attest does not obtain. See 2B Barron & Holtzoff, Federal Practice & Procedure § 992 (Wright ed. 1961). Accordingly it is provided that an attested copy may be obtained from any person authorized by the law of the foreign country to make the attestation without regard to whether he is charged with responsibility for maintaining the record or keeping it in his custody.

Under Rule 44 a United States foreign service officer has been called on to certify to the authority of the foreign official attesting the copy as well as the genuineness of his signature and his official position. See Schlesinger, *Comparative Law* 57 (2d ed. 1959); Smit. *International Aspects of Federal Civil Procedure*, 61 Colum.L.Rev. 1031, 1063 (1961); 22 C.F.R. § 92.41(a), (e) (1958). This has created practical difficulties. For example, the question of the authority of the foreign officer might raise issues of foreign law which were beyond the knowledge of the United States officer. The difficulties are met under the amended rule by eliminating the element of the authority of the attesting foreign official from the scope of the certifying process, and by specifically permitting use of the chain-certificate method. Under this method, it is sufficient if the original attestation purports to have been issued by an authorized person and is accompanied by a certificate of another foreign official whose certificate may in turn be followed by that of a foreign official of higher rank. The process continues until a foreign official is reached as to whom the United States foreign service official (or a diplomatic or consular officer of the foreign country assigned or accredited to the United States) has adequate information upon which to base a "final certification." See *New York Life Ins. Co. v. Aronson*, 38 F.Supp. 687 (W.D.Pa.1941); 22 C.F.R. § 92.37 (1958).

The final certification (a term used in contradistinction to the certificates prepared by the foreign officials in a chain) relates to the incumbency and genuineness of signature of the foreign official who attested the copy of the record or, where the chain-certificate method is used, of a foreign official whose certificate appears in the chain, whether that certificate is the last in the chain or not. A final certification may be prepared on the basis of material on file in the consulate or any other satisfactory information.

Although the amended rule will generally facilitate proof of foreign official records, it is recognized that in some situations it may be difficult or even impossible to satisfy the basic requirements of the rule. There may be no United States consul in a particular foreign country; the foreign officials may not cooperate, peculiarities may exist or arise hereafter in the law or practice of a foreign country. See *United States v. Grabina*, 119 F.2d 863 (2d Cir. 1941); and, generally, Jones, *International Judicial Assistance: Procedural Chaos and a Program for Reform*, 62 Yale L.J. 515, 548–49 (1953). Therefore the final sentence of subdivision (a)(2) provides the court with discretion to admit an attested copy of a record without a final certification, or an attested summary of a record with or without a final certification. See Rep. of Comm. on Comparative Civ.Proc. & Prac., Proc. A.B.A., Sec. Int'l & Comp.L. 123, 130–31 (1952); Model Code of Evidence §§ 517, 519 (1942). This relaxation should be permitted only when it is shown that the party has been unable to satisfy the basic requirements of the amended rule despite his reasonable efforts. Moreover it is specially provided that the parties must be given a reasonable opportunity in these cases to examine into the authenticity and accuracy of the copy or summary.

Note to Subdivision (b). This provision relating to proof of lack of record is accommodated to the changes made in subdivision (a).

Note to Subdivision (c). The amendment insures that international agreements of the United States are unaffected by the rule. Several consular conventions contain provisions for reception of copies or summaries of foreign official records. See, e.g., Consular Conv. with Italy, May 8, 1878, art. X, 20 Stat. 725, T.S. No. 178 (Dept. State 1878). See also 28 U.S.C. §§ 1740–42, 1745; *Fakouri v. Cadais*, 149 F.2d 321 (5th Cir.1945), cert. denied 326 U.S. 742 (1945); 5 *Moore's Federal Practice*, par. 44.05 (2d ed. 1951).

1987 Amendment

The amendments are technical. No substantive change is intended.

1991 Amendment

The amendment to paragraph (a)(1) strikes the references to specific territories, two of which are no longer subject to the jurisdiction of the United States, and adds a generic term to describe governments having a relationship with the United States such that their official records should be treated as domestic records.

The amendment to paragraph (a)(2) adds a sentence to dispense with the final certification by diplomatic officers when the United States and the foreign country where the record is located are parties to a treaty or convention that abolishes or displaces the requirement. In that event the treaty or convention is to be followed. This changes the former procedure for authenticating foreign official records only with respect to records from countries that are parties to the Hague Convention Abolishing the Requirement of Legalization for Foreign Public Documents. Moreover, it does not affect the former practice of attesting the records, but only changes the method of certifying the attestation.

The Hague Public Documents Convention provides that the requirement of a final certification is abolished and replaced with a model *apostille*, which is to be issued by officials of the country where the records are located. See Hague Public Documents Convention, Arts. 2–4. The *apostille* certifies the signature, official position, and seal of the attesting officer. The authority who issues the *apostille* must maintain a register or card index showing the serial number of the *apostille* and other relevant information recorded on it. A foreign court can then check the serial number and information on the *apostille* with the issuing authority in order to guard against the use of fraudulent *apostilles*. This system provides a reliable method for maintaining the integrity of the authentication process, and the *apostille* can be accorded greater weight than the normal authentication procedure because foreign officials are more likely to know the precise capacity under their law of the attesting officer than would an American official. See generally Comment, *The United States and the Hague Convention Abolishing the Requirement of Legalization for Foreign Public Documents,* 11 HARV. INT'L L.J. 476, 482, 488 (1970).

CONVENTIONS

Convention Abolishing the Requirement of Legalisation for Foreign Public Documents

The States signatory to the present Convention,

Desiring to abolish the requirement of diplomatic or consular legalisation for foreign public documents,

Have resolved to conclude a Convention to this effect and have agreed upon the following provisions:

ARTICLE 1

The present Convention shall apply to public documents which have been executed in the territory of one contracting State and which have to be produced in the territory of another contracting State.

For the purposes of the present Convention, the following are deemed to be public documents:

(a) Documents emanating from an authority or an official connected with the courts or tribunals of the State, including those emanating from a public prosecutor, a clerk of a court or a process server ("huissier de justice");

(b) Administrative documents;

(c) Notarial acts;

(d) Official certificates which are placed on documents signed by persons in their private capacity, such as official certificates recording the registration of a document or the fact that it was in existence on a certain date and official and notarial authentications of signatures.

However, the present Convention shall not apply:

(a) To documents executed by diplomatic or consular agents;

(b) To administrative documents dealing directly with commercial or customs operations.

ARTICLE 2

Each contracting State shall exempt from legalisation documents to which the present Convention applies and which have to be produced in its territory. For the purposes of the present Convention, legalisation means only the formality by which the diplomatic or consular agents of the country in which the document has to be produced certify the authenticity of the signature, the capacity in which the person signing the document has acted and, where appropriate, the identity of the seal or stamp which it bears.

ARTICLE 3

The only formality that may be required in order to certify the authenticity of the signature, the capacity in which the person signing the document has acted and, where appropriate, the identity of the seal or stamp which it bears, is the addition of the certificate described in Article 4, issued by the competent authority of the State from which the document emanates.

However, the formality mentioned in the preceding paragraph cannot be required when either the laws, regulations, or practice in force in the State where the document is produced or an agreement between two or more contracting States have abolished or simplified it, or exempt the document itself from legalisation.

ARTICLE 4

The certificate referred to in the first paragraph of Article 3 shall be placed on the document itself or on an "allonge"; it shall be in the form of the model annexed to the present Convention.

It may, however, be drawn up in the official language of the authority which issues it. The standard terms appearing therein may be in a second language also. The title "Apostille (Convention de La Haye du 5 octobre 1961)" shall be in the French language.

ARTICLE 5

The certificate shall be issued at the request of the person who has signed the document or of any bearer.

When properly filled in, it will certify the authenticity of the signature, the capacity in which the person signing the document has acted and, where appropriate, the identity of the seal or stamp which the document bears.

The signature, seal and stamp on the certificate are exempt from all certification.

ARTICLE 6

Each contracting State shall designate by reference to their official function, the authorities who are competent to issue the certificate referred to in the first paragraph of Article 3.

It shall give notice of such designation to the Ministry of Foreign Affairs of the Netherlands at the time it deposits its instrument of ratification or of accession or its declaration of extension. It shall also give notice of any change in the designated authorities.

ARTICLE 7

Each of the authorities designated in accordance with Article 6 shall keep a register or card index in which it shall record the certificates issued, specifying:

(a) The number and date of the certificate,

(b) The name of the person signing the public document and the capacity in which he has acted, or in the case of unsigned documents, the name of the authority which has affixed the seal or stamp.

At the request of any interested person, the authority which has issued the certificate shall verify whether the particulars in the certificate correspond with those in the register or card index.

ARTICLE 8

When a treaty, convention or agreement between two or more contracting States contains provisions which subject the certification of a signature, seal or stamp to certain formalities, the present Convention will only override such provisions if those formalities are more rigorous than the formality referred to in Articles 3 and 4.

ARTICLE 9

Each contracting State shall take the necessary steps to prevent the performance of legalisations by its diplomatic or consular agents in cases where the present Convention provides for exemption.

ARTICLE 10

The present Convention shall be open for signature by the States represented at the Ninth session of the Hague Conference on Private International Law and Iceland, Ireland, Liechtenstein and Turkey.

It shall be ratified, and the instruments of ratification shall be deposited with the Ministry of Foreign Affairs of the Netherlands.

ARTICLE 11

The present Convention shall enter into force on the sixtieth day after the deposit of the third instrument of ratification referred to in the second paragraph of Article 10.

The Convention shall enter into force for each signatory State which ratifies subsequently on the sixtieth day after the deposit of its instrument of ratification.

ARTICLE 12

Any State not referred to in Article 10 may accede to the present Convention after it has entered into force in accordance with the first paragraph of Article 11. The instrument of accession shall be deposited with the Ministry of Foreign Affairs of the Netherlands.

Such accession shall have effect only as regards the relations between the acceding State and those contracting States which have not raised an objection to its accession in the six months after the receipt of the notification referred to in sub-paragraph (d) of Article 15. Any such objection shall be notified to the Ministry of Foreign Affairs of the Netherlands.

The Convention shall enter into force as between the acceding State and the States which have raised no objection to its accession on the sixtieth day after the expiry of the period of six months mentioned in the preceding paragraph.

ARTICLE 13

Any State may, at the time of signature, ratification or accession, declare that the present Convention shall extend to all the territories for the international relations of which it is responsible, or to one or more of them. Such a declaration shall take effect on the date of entry into force of the Convention for the State concerned.

At any time thereafter, such extension shall be notified to the Ministry of Foreign Affairs of the Netherlands.

When the declaration of extension is made by a State which has signed and ratified, the Convention shall enter into force for the territories concerned in accordance with Article 11. When the declaration of extension is made by a State which has acceded, the Convention shall enter into force for the territories concerned in accordance with Article 12.

ARTICLE 14

The present Convention shall remain in force for five years from the date of its entry into force in accordance with the first paragraph of Article 11, even for States which have ratified it or acceded to it subsequently.

If there has been no denunciation, the Convention shall be renewed tacitly every five years.

Any denunciation shall be notified to the Ministry of Foreign Affairs of the Netherlands at least six months before the end of the five year period.

It may be limited to certain of the territories to which the Convention applies.

The denunciation will only have effect as regards the State which has notified it. The Convention shall remain in force for the other contracting States.

ARTICLE 15

The Ministry of Foreign Affairs of the Netherlands shall give notice to the States referred to in Article 10, and to the States which have acceded in accordance with Article 12, of the following:

(a) The notifications referred to in the second paragraph of Article 6;

(b) The signatures and ratifications referred to in Article 10;

(c) The date on which the present Convention enters into force in accordance with the first paragraph of Article 11;

(d) The accessions and objections referred to in Article 12 and the date on which such accessions take effect;

(e) The extensions referred to in Article 13 and the date on which they take effect;

(f) The denunciations referred to in the third paragraph of Article 14.

In witness whereof the undersigned, being duly authorised thereto, have signed the present Convention.

Done at The Hague the 5th October 1961, in French and in English, the French text prevailing in case of divergence between the two texts, in a single copy which shall be deposited in the archives of the Government of the Netherlands, and of which a certified copy shall be sent, through the diplomatic channel, to each of the States represented at the Ninth session of the Hague Conference on Private International Law and also to Iceland, Ireland, Liechtenstein and Turkey.

[Signatures omitted.]

ANNEX TO THE CONVENTION

Model of certificate

The certificate will be in the form of a square with sides at least 9 centimetres long

APOSTILLE

(Convention de La Haye du 5 octobre 1961)

1. Country: ....

This public document

2. has been signed by ....
3. acting in the capacity of ....
4. bears the seal/stamp of ....
....

Certified

5. at .... 6. the ....
7. by ....
8. N♦ ....
9. Seal/stamp: 10. Signature:
....

Convention abolishing the requirement of legalization for foreign public documents, with annex. Done at The Hague October 5, 1961; entered into force for the United States October 15, 1981. (TIAS 10072; 527 UNTS 189).

Parties to the Convention

In addition to the United States, the following are parties to the Convention:

Contracting State	Territories to which Extended
Andorra [1]	
Antigua and Barbuda	
Argentina [1a]	
Armenia	
Australia [1b]	All the territories for the international relations of which it is responsible
Austria	
Bahamas	
Barbados	
Belarus [1c]	
Belgium	
Belize [1d]	
Bosnia-Herzegovina	
Botswana	
Brunei	
China, Hong Kong Special Administrative Region only [1e]	
Croatia	
Cyprus	
El Salvador	
Fiji	
Finland	
France	Entire territory of the French Republic Anglo-French Condominium of the New Hebrides (Vanuatu)*
Germany, Federal Republic of [1f]	
Greece	
Hungary	
Israel	
Italy	
Japan	
Latvia	
Lesotho	
Liberia [1g]	
Liechtenstein	
Lithuania	
Luxembourg	
Macedonia, former Yugoslav Republic of	
Malawi	
Malta	
Marshall Islands [2]	
Mauritius	
Mexico	
Netherlands	the Kingdom in Europe Netherlands Antilles and Aruba

Contracting State	Territories to which Extended
Norway	
Panama	
Portugal	Angola* Mozambique* and other overseas departments
Russian Federation [3]	
San Marino	
Seychelles	
Slovenia	
South Africa	
Spain	
St. Kitts & Nevis	
Suriname	
Swaziland	
Switzerland	
Tonga	
Turkey	
United Kingdom of Great Britain and Northern Ireland	Anguilla the Bailiwick of Guernsey Barbados* Bermuda British Antarctic Territory British Guiana (Guyana)* British Solomon Islands Protectorate (Solomon Islands)* Cayman Islands Dominica* Falkland Islands Gibraltar Gilbert and Ellice Islands (Kiribati/Tuvalu)* Grenada* the Isle of Man Jersey Montserrat New Hebrides (Vanuatu)* St. Helena Saint Christopher and Nevis* Saint Lucia* Saint Vincent* Southern Rhodesia (Zimbabwe)* Turks and Caicos Islands British Virgin Islands
United States	Those territories for the foreign relations of which the United States is responsible

Yugoslavia [4]

* Now independent and no confirmation issued by the newly independent country that the Convention is deemed to apply.

[1] *Notification in conformity with Article 15 of the Convention*

On 15 April 1996 the Ministry of Foreign Affairs of the Kingdom of the Netherlands received the instrument of accession of the Principality of Andorra to the above-mentioned Convention in accordance with Article 12, first paragraph, of the Convention.

In accordance with the terms of Article 12, paragraph 1, of the Convention any State not mentioned in Article 10 may accede to this Convention. In accordance with Article 12, paragraph 2, such accession shall have effect only as regards the relations between the Principality of Andorra and those contracting States (at present: Anitgua and Barbuda, Argentina, Armenia, Australia, Austria, Bahamas, Barbados, Belgium, Belize, Byelorus, Bosnia and Herzegovina, Botswana, Brunei, Darussalam, Croatia, Cyprus, El Salvador, Fiji, Finland, France, Germany, Greece, Hungary, Israel, Italy, Japan, the Kingdom of the Netherlands, Lesotho, Liechtenstein, Luxembourg, the former Yugoslav Republic of Macedonia, Malawi, Malta, Marshall Islands, Mauritius, Mexico, Norway, Panama, Portugal, Russia, Saint Kitts and Nevis, San Marino, Seychelles, Slovenia, South Africa, Spain, Surinam, Swaziland, Switerland, Tonga, Turkey, the United Kingdom of Great Britain and Northern Ireland and the United States of America) which have not raised an objection to its accession in the six months after receipt of this notification. For practical reasons this six months' period will run from 1 May 1996 till 1 November 1996.

[1a] In accordance with Article 12, paragraph 1, the instrument of accession by the Argentine Republic to the above-mentioned Convention was deposited with the Ministry of Foreign Affairs of the Kingdom of the Netherlands on 8 May 1987. The instrument of accession contains the declaration annexed to this notification.

"In accordance with the terms of Article 12, paragraph 1, of the Convention any State not mentioned in Article 10 may accede to this Convention. In accordance with Article 12, paragraph 2, such accession shall have effect only as regards the relations between the Argentine Republic and those contracting States (at present: Antigua and Barbuda, Austria, Bahamas, Belgium, Botswana, Brunei Darussalam, Cyprus, Fiji, Finland, France, the Federal Republic of Germany, Greece, Hungary, Israel, Italy, Japan, Lesotho, Liechtenstein, Luxembourg, Malawi, Malta, Mauritius, the Kingdom of the Netherlands, Norway, Portugal, Seychelles, Spain, Surinam, Swaziland, Switzerland, Tonga, Turkey, the United Kingdom of Great Britain and Northern Ireland, the United States of America and Yugoslavia) which have not raised an objection to its accession in the six months after the receipt of this notification. For practical reasons this six months' period will extend from 20 June 1987 till 20 December 1987."

"The Argentine Republic rejects the extension of the application of the Convention Abolishing the Requirement of Legalization for Foreign Public Documents, concluded at The Hague on October 5, 1961, to the Malvinas, South Georgia, and South Sandwich Islands, as notified by the United Kingdom of Great Britain and Northern Ireland to the Ministry of Foreign Affairs of the Kingdom of the Netherlands on February 24, 1965, and reaffirms its sovereign rights over the Malvinas, South Georgia, and South Sandwich Islands, which form an integral part of its national territory.

"The United Nations General Assembly has adopted resolutions 2065(XX), 3160(XXVIII), 31/49, 37/9, 38/12, 39/6, 40/21, and 41/40, acknowledging the existence of a sovereignty dispute with respect to the question of the Malvinas Islands, and urging the Argentine Republic and the United Kingdom of Great Britain and Northern Ireland to continue negotiating in order to reach a peaceful and definitive solution to the dispute as soon as possible, through the good offices of the United Nations Secretary General, who is to inform the General Assembly of the progress achieved.

"The Argentine Republic also rejects the extension of the Convention, notified on the same date as above, to the so-called "British Antarctic Territory," and thereby reaffirms the rights of the Republic to the Argentine Antarctic Sector, including those relating to its corresponding maritime sovereignty or jurisdiction. It further recalls the safeguards on claims of territorial sovereignty in Antarctica set forth in Article IV of the Antarctic Treaty, done at Washington on December 1, 1959, to which the Argentine Republic and the United Kingdom of Great Britain and Northern Ireland are parties." (Translation provided by the Division of Language Services, Department of State)

[1b] *Notification in conformity with Article 15 of the Convention*

On 11 July 1994 Australia deposited its instrument of accession at the Ministry of Foreign Affairs of the Kingdom of the Netherlands to the above-mentioned Convention in accordance with Article 12, first paragraph, of the Convention. Australia made the following declarations:

"—pursuant to the second paragraph of Article 6, the Secretary to the Department of Foreign Affairs and Trade of the Commonwealth will be its competent authority for the purpose of that Article; and

—pursuant to Article 13, the Convention shall extend to all the territories for the international relations of which it is responsible."

In accordance with the terms of Article 12, paragraph 1, of the Convention any State not mentioned in Article 10 may accede to this Convention. In accordance with Article 12, paragraph 2, such accession shall have effect only as regards the relations between Australia and those contracting States (at present: Antigua and Barbuda, Argentina, Armenia, Austria, Bahamas, Belgium, Belize, Byelorus, Bosnia and Herzegovina, Botswana, Brunei Darussalam, Croatia, Cyprus, Fiji, Finland, France, Germany, Greece, Hungary, Israel, Italy, Japan, the Kingdom of the Netherlands, Lesotho, Liechtenstein, Luxemburg, The former Yugoslav Republic of Macedonia, Malawi, Malta, Marshall Islands, Mauritius, Norway, Panama, Portugal, Russia, Seychelles, Slovenia, Spain, Surinam, Swaziland, Switzerland, Tonga, Turkey, the United Kingdom of Great Britain and Northern Ireland and the United States of America) which have not raised an objection to its accession in the six months after receipt of this notification. For practical reasons this six months' period will run from 15 July 1994 till 15 January 1995.

[1c] The Ministry of Foreign Affairs of the Byelorussian Republic communicated the following by Note of 8 February 1993:

Translation

. . . .the Ministry would advise that in accordance with Article 6 of the Convention and in accordance with the Decree issued by the Government of the Byelorussian Republic on 1 January 1993, official documents issued by the government agencies of the Byelorussian Republic for use in the territories of contracting States of the Hague Convention, repealing the necessity of legalisation of foreign official documents, are now authorised only by an apostille written on these documents.

[1d] *Notification in conformity with Article 15 of the Convention*

On 17 July 1992 the Ministry of Foreign Affairs of the Kingdom of the Netherlands received the instrument of accession by Belize to the above–mentioned Convention in accordance with Article 12, first paragraph, of the Convention.

In accordance with the terms of Article 12, paragraph 1, of the Convention any State not mentioned in Article 10 may accede to this Convention. In accordance with Article 12, paragraph 2, such accession shall have effect only as regards the relations between Belize and those contracting States (at present Antigua and Barbuda, Argentina, Austria, Bahamas, Belgium, Botswana, Brunei Darussalam, Cyprus, Fiji, Finland, France, the Federal Republic of Germany, Greece, Hungary, Israel, Italy, Japan, Lesotho, Liechtenstein, Luxembourg, Malawi, Malta, Marshall Islands, Mauritius, the Kingdom of the Netherlands, Norway, Panama, Portugal, Russia, Seychelles, Spain, Surinam, Swaziland, Switzerland, Tonga, Turkey, the United Kingdom of Great Britain and Northern Ireland, the United States of America and Yugoslavia) which have not raised an objection to its accession in the six months after the receipt of this notification. For practical reasons this six months' period will extend from 10 August 1992 till 10 February 1993.

The Contracting States were notified by the depositary of the accession on 10 August 1992. None of these States raised an objection to the accession within the period of six months specified in Article 12, paragraph 2, which period expired on 10 February 1993.

The provisions of the Convention will enter into force between Belize and the Contracting States on 11 April 1993.

[1e] "The Embassy of the People's Republic of China in the Kingdom of the Netherlands

No. He Wai Fa (97)–54è(Translation)

The Hague, June 3, 1997

Your Excellency,

In accordance with the Joint Declaration of the Government of the People's Republic of China and the Government of the United Kingdom of Great Britain and Northern Ireland on the Question of Hong Kong signed on 19 December 1984 (hereinafter referred to as the "Joint Declaration"), the People's Republic of China will resume the exercise of sovereignty over Hong Kong with effect from 1 July 1997. Hong Kong will, with effect from that date, become a Special Administrative Region of the People's Republic of China and will enjoy a high degree of autonomy, except in foreign and defence affairs which are the responsibilities of the Central People's Government of the People's Republic of China.

It is provided both in Section XI of Annex I to the Joint Declaration, "Elaboration by the Government of the People's Republic of China of its Basic Policies Regarding Hong Kong", and Article 153 of the Basic Law of the Hong Kong Special Administrative Region of the People's Republic of China, which was adopted on 4 April 1990 by the National People's Congress of the People's Republic of China, that international agreements to which the People's Republic of China is not a party but which are implemented in Hong Kong may continue to be implemented in the Hong Kong Special Administrative Region.

In accordance with the above provisions, I am instructed by the Minister of Foreign Affairs of the People's Republic of China to make the following notification:

The Convention Abolishing the Requirement of Legalization for Foreign Public Documents done at the Hague on 5 October 1961 (hereinafter referred to as the "Convention"), by which the Government of the Kingdom of the Netherlands is designated as the depository, which applies to Hong Kong at present, will continue to apply to the Hong Kong Special Administrative Region with effect from 1 July 1997. The Government of the People's Republic of China also makes the following declaration:

In accordance with Article 6 of the Convention, it designates each of the following as the competent authorities in the Hong Kong Special Administrative Region to issue the certificates referred to in Paragraph 1 of Article 3 of the Convention for the Hong Kong Special Administrative Region: the Administrative Secretary, the Registrar of the High Court, the Deputy Registrar of the High Court and the Assistant Registrar of the High Court.

Within the above ambit, responsibility for the international rights and obligations of a party to the Convention will be assumed by the Government of the People's Republic of China. ..."

[1f] On October 3, 1990 the German Democratic Republic acceded to the Federal Republic of Germany.

[1g] *Ed. Note*—The Government of the United States of America does not accept the accession of the Government of Liberia to the Convention. The Convention is not in force between the Government of the United States of America and the Government of Liberia.

[2] *Notification in conformity with Article 15 of the Convention*

The Government of the Marshall Islands deposited its instrument of accession to the Convention with the Ministry of Foreign Affairs of the Kingdom of the Netherlands on 18 November 1991 in accordance with Article 12, first paragraph, of the Convention.

The Contracting States were notified by the depositary of the accession on 25 November 1991. None of these States raised an objection to the accession within the period of six months specified in Article 12, paragraph 2, which period expired on 15 June 1992.

The provisions of the Convention entered into force between the Marshall Islands and the Contracting States on 14 August 1992.

[3] . . . the Convention entered into force between the Russian Federation and the Contracting States on 31 May 1992. The status of the Republics with respect to this Convention is under review by the Depositary.

[4] [Ed. Note—The U.S. view is that the Socialist Federal Republic of Yugoslavia has dissolved and no successor state represents its continuation.]

Authorities in the United States of America Competent to Issue the Certificate Referred to in Article 3 of the Convention

I. Authentication Officer and Acting Authentication Officer, United States Department of State

II. Clerks and deputy clerks of the following: The Supreme Court of the United States, the Courts of Appeals for the First through the Eleventh Circuits, the District of Columbia Circuit and the Federal Circuit; the United States District Courts; the United States Court of International Trade; the United States Claims Court; the District Court of Guam, the District Court of the Virgin Islands, and the District Court for the Northern Mariana Islands.

The District Court for the District of the Canal Zone ceased to exist on Mar. 31, 1982. Its records have been transferred to the National Archives which will certify those records.

III. Officers of the individual States and other subdivisions as indicated:

States:

Alabama: Secretary of State

Alaska: Lieutenant Governor; Attorney General; Clerk of the Appellate Court

Arizona: Secretary of State; Assistant Secretary of State

Arkansas: Secretary of State; Chief Deputy Secretary of State

California: Secretary of State; any Assistant Secretary of State; any Deputy Secretary of State

Colorado: Secretary of State; Deputy Secretary of State

Connecticut: Secretary of the State; Deputy Secretary of the State

Delaware: Secretary of State; Acting Secretary of State

Florida: Secretary of State

Georgia: Georgia Superior Court Clerks' Cooperative Authority

Hawaii: Lieutenant Governor of the State of Hawaii

Idaho: Secretary of State; Chief Deputy Secretary of State; Deputy Secretary of State; Notary Public Clerk

Illinois: Secretary of State; Assistant Secretary of State; Deputy Secretary of State

Indiana: Secretary of State; Deputy Secretary of State

Iowa: Secretary of State; Deputy Secretary of State

Kansas: Secretary of State; Assistant Secretary of State; any Deputy Assistant Secretary of State

Kentucky: Secretary of State; Assistant Secretary of State

Louisiana: Secretary of State

Maine: Secretary of State; Deputy Secretary of State

Maryland: Secretary of State

Massachusetts: Deputy Secretary of the Commonwealth of Massachusetts for Public Records (beginning in 1981 through January 13, 1995); Deputy Secretary of State of the Commonwealth of Massachusetts (beginning January 16, 1995, through November 16, 1995); Secretary of the Commonwealth of Massachusetts (from November 17, 1995)

Michigan: Secretary of State; Deputy Secretary of State

Minnesota: Secretary of State; Deputy Secretary of State

Mississippi: Secretary of State; any Assistant Secretary of State

Missouri: Secretary of State; Deputy Secretary of State

Montana: Secretary of State; Chief Deputy Secretary of State; Government Affairs Bureau Chief

Nebraska: Secretary of State; Deputy Secretary of State

Nevada: Secretary of State; Chief Deputy Secretary of State; Deputy Secretary of State

New Hampshire: Secretary of State; Deputy Secretary of State

New Jersey: Secretary of State; Assistant Secretary of State

New Mexico: Secretary of State

New York: Secretary of State; Executive Deputy Secretary of State; any Deputy Secretary of State; any Special Deputy Secretary of State

North Carolina: Secretary of State; Deputy Secretary of State

North Dakota: Secretary of State; Deputy Secretary of State

Ohio: Secretary of State; Assistant Secretary of State

Oklahoma: Secretary of State; Assistant Secretary of State; Budget Officer of the Secretary of State

Oregon: Secretary of State; Deputy Secretary of State; Acting Secretary of State; Assistant to the Secretary of State

Pennsylvania: Secretary of the Commonwealth; any Deputy Secretary of the Commonwealth

Rhode Island: Secretary of State; First Deputy Secretary of State; Second Deputy Secretary of State

South Carolina: Secretary of State

South Dakota: Secretary of State; Deputy Secretary of State

Tennessee: Secretary of State

Texas: Secretary of State; Assistant Secretary of State

Utah: Lieutenant Governor; Deputy Lieutenant Governor; Administrative Assistant

Vermont: Secretary of State; Deputy Secretary of State

Virginia: Secretary of the Commonwealth; Chief Clerk, Office of the Secretary of the Commonwealth

Washington (State): Secretary of State; Assistant Secretary of State; Director, Department of Licensing

West Virginia: Secretary of State; Under Secretary of State; any Deputy Secretary of State

Wisconsin: Secretary of State; Assistant Secretary of State

Wyoming: Secretary of State; Deputy Secretary of State

Other Subdivisions:

American Samoa: Secretary of American Samoa; Attorney General of American Samoa

District of Columbia (Washington, D.C.): Executive Secretary; Assistant Executive Secretary; Mayor's Special Assistant and Assistant to the Executive Secretary; Secretary of the District of Columbia

Guam (Territory of): Director, Department of Administration; Acting Director, Department of Administration; Deputy Director, Department of Administration; Acting Deputy Director, Department of Administration

Northern Mariana Islands (Commonwealth of the): Attorney General; Acting Attorney General; Clerk of the Court, Commonwealth Trial Court; Deputy Clerk, Commonwealth Trial Court

Puerto Rico (Commonwealth of): Under Secretary of State; Assistant Secretary of State for External Affairs; Assistant Secretary of State; Chief, Certifications Office; Director, Office of Protocol; Assistant Secretary of State for International Affairs; Chief Certification Office

Virgin Islands of the United States: no authority designated

Rule 44.1. Determination of Foreign Law

A party who intends to raise an issue concerning the law of a foreign country shall give notice by pleadings or other reasonable written notice. The court, in determining foreign law, may consider any relevant material or source, including testimony, whether or not submitted by a party or admissible under the Federal Rules of Evidence. The court's determination shall be treated as a ruling on a question of law.

(Added Feb. 28, 1966, eff. July 1, 1966, and amended Nov. 20, 1972, eff. July 1, 1975; Mar. 2, 1987, eff. Aug. 1, 1987.)

ADVISORY COMMITTEE NOTES

1966 Adoption

Rule 44.1 is added by amendment to furnish Federal courts with a uniform and effective procedure for raising and determining an issue concerning the law of a foreign country.

To avoid unfair surprise, the *first sentence* of the new rule requires that a party who intends to raise an issue of foreign law shall give notice thereof. The uncertainty under Rule 8(a) about whether foreign law must be pleaded—compare *Siegelman v. Cunard White Star, Ltd.*, 221 F.2d 189 (2d Cir.1955), and *Pedersen v. United States*, 191 F.Supp. 95 (D. Guam 1961), with *Harrison v. United Fruit Co.*, 143 F.Supp. 598 (S.D.N.Y.1956)—is eliminated by the provision that the notice shall be "written" and "reasonable." It may, but need not be, incorporated in the pleadings. In some situations the pertinence of foreign law is apparent from the outset; accordingly the necessary investigation of that law will have been accomplished by the party at the pleading stage, and the notice can be given conveniently in the pleadings. In other situations the pertinence of foreign law may remain doubtful until the case is further developed. A requirement that notice of foreign law be given only through the medium of the pleadings would tend in the latter instances to force the party to engage in a peculiarly burdensome type of investigation which might turn out to be unnecessary; and correspondingly the adversary would be forced into a possible wasteful investigation. The liberal provisions for amendment of the pleadings afford help if the pleadings are used as the medium of giving notice of the foreign law; but it seems best to permit a written notice to be given outside of and later than the pleadings, provided the notice is reasonable.

The new rule does not attempt to set any definite limit on the party's time for giving the notice of an issue of foreign law; in some cases the issue may not become apparent until the trial and notice then given may still be reasonable. The stage which the case had reached at the time of the notice, the reason proffered by the party for his failure to give earlier notice, and the importance to the case as a whole of the issue of foreign law sought to be raised, are among the factors which the court should consider in deciding a question of the reasonableness of a notice. If notice is given by one party it need not be repeated by any other and serves as a basis for presentation of material on the foreign law by all parties.

The *second sentence* of the new rule describes the materials to which the court may resort in determining an issue of foreign law. Heretofore the district courts, applying Rule 43(a), have looked in certain cases to State law to find the rules of evidence by which the content of foreign-country law is to be established. The State laws vary; some embody procedures which are inefficient, time consuming and expensive. See, generally, Nussbaum, *Proving the Law of Foreign Countries*, 3 Am. J. Comp. L. 60 (1954). In all events the ordinary rules of evidence are often inapposite to the problem of determining foreign law and have in the past prevented examination of material which could have provided a proper basis for the determination. The new rule permits consideration by the court of any relevant material, including testimony, without regard to its admissibility under Rule 43. Cf. N.Y. Civ. Prac. Law & Rules, R. 4511 (effective Sept. 1, 1963); 2 Va. Code Ann. tit. 8, § 8–273; 2 W. Va. Code Ann. § 5711.

In further recognition of the peculiar nature of the issue of foreign law, the new rule provides that in determining this law the court is not limited by material presented by the parties; it may engage in its own research and consider any relevant material thus found. The court may have at its disposal better foreign law materials than counsel have presented, or may wish to reexamine and amplify material that has been presented by counsel in partisan fashion or in insufficient detail. On the other hand, the court is free to insist on a complete presentation by counsel.

There is no requirement that the court give formal notice to the parties of its intention to engage in its own research on an issue of foreign law which has been raised by them, or of its intention to raise and determine independently an issue not raised by them. Ordinarily the court should inform the parties of material it has found diverging substantially from the material which they have presented; and in general the court should give the parties an opportunity to analyze and counter new points upon which it proposes to rely. See Schlesinger, *Comparative Law* 142 (2d ed. 1959); Wyzanski, *A Trial Judge's Freedom and Responsibility*, 65 Harv. L.Rev. 1281, 1296 (1952); cf. *Siegelman v. Cunard White Star, Ltd.*, supra, 221 F.2d at 197. To require, however, that the court give formal notice from time to time as it proceeds with its study of the foreign law would add an element of undesirable rigidity to the procedure for determining issues of foreign law.

The new rule refrains from imposing an obligation on the court to take "judicial notice" of foreign law because this would put an extreme burden on the court in many cases; and it avoids use of the concept of "judicial notice" in any form because of the uncertain meaning of that concept as applied to foreign law. See, e.g., Stern, *Foreign Law in the Courts: Judicial Notice and Proof,* 45 Calif.L.Rev. 23, 43 (1957). Rather the rule provides flexible procedures for presenting and utilizing material on issues of foreign law by which a sound result can be achieved with fairness to the parties.

Under the *third sentence,* the court's determination of an issue of foreign law is to be treated as a ruling on a question of "law," not "fact," so that appellate review will not be narrowly confined by the "clearly erroneous" standard of Rule 52(a). *Cf. Uniform Judicial Notice of Foreign Law Act* § 3; Note, 72 Harv.L.Rev. 318 (1958).

The new rule parallels Article IV of the Uniform Interstate and International Procedure Act, approved by the Commissioners on Uniform State Laws in 1962, except that § 4.03 of Article IV states that "[t]he court, not the jury" shall determine foreign law. The new rule does not address itself to this problem, since the Rules refrain from allocating functions as between the court and the jury. See Rule 38(a). It has long been thought, however, that the jury is not the appropriate body to determine issues of foreign law. See, e.g., Story, *Conflict of Laws,* § 638 (1st ed. 1834, 8th ed. 1883); 1 Greenleaf, *Evidence,* § 486 (1st ed. 1842, 16th ed. 1899); 4 Wigmore, *Evidence* § 2558 (1st ed. 1905); 9 id. § 2558 (3d ed. 1940). The majority of the States have committed such issues to determination by the court. See Article 5 of the Uniform Judicial Notice of Foreign Law Act, adopted by twenty-six states, 9A U.L.A. 318 (1957) (Suppl.1961, at 134); N.Y.Civ.Prac.Law & Rules, R. 4511 (effective Sept. 1, 1963); Wigmore, loc. cit. And Federal courts that have considered the problem in recent years have reached the same conclusion without reliance on statute. See *Jansson v. Swedish American Line,* 185 F.2d 212, 216 (1st Cir.1950); *Bank of Nova Scotia v. San Miguel,* 196 F.2d 950, 957, n. 6 (1st Cir.1952); *Liechti v. Roche,* 198 F.2d 174 (5th Cir.1952); *Daniel Lumber Co. v. Empresas Hondureñas, S.A.,* 215 F.2d 465 (5th Cir.1954).

1972 Amendment

Since the purpose of the provision is to free the judge, in determining foreign law, from any restrictions imposed by evidence rules, a general reference to the Rules of Evidence is appropriate and is made.

1987 Amendment

The amendment is technical. No substantive change is intended.

HISTORICAL NOTES

Effective Date of Amendment Proposed November 20, 1972

Amendment of this rule embraced by the order entered by the Supreme Court of the United States on November 20, 1972, effective on the 180th day beginning after January 2, 1975, see section 3 of Pub.L. 93–595, Jan. 2, 1975, 88 Stat. 1959, set out as a note under section 2071 of Title 28.

Rule 45. Subpoena

(a) Form; Issuance.

(1) Every subpoena shall

(A) state the name of the court from which it is issued; and

(B) state the title of the action, the name of the court in which it is pending, and its civil action number; and

(C) command each person to whom it is directed to attend and give testimony or to produce and permit inspection and copying of designated books, documents or tangible things in the possession, custody or control of that person, or to permit inspection of premises, at a time and place therein specified; and

(D) set forth the text of subdivisions (c) and (d) of this rule.

A command to produce evidence or to permit inspection may be joined with a command to appear at trial or hearing or at deposition, or may be issued separately.

(2) A subpoena commanding attendance at a trial or hearing shall issue from the court for the district in which the hearing or trial is to be held. A subpoena for attendance at a deposition shall issue from the court for the district designated by the notice of deposition as the district in which the deposition is to be taken. If separate from a subpoena commanding the attendance of a person, a subpoena for production or inspection shall issue from the court for the district in which the production or inspection is to be made.

(3) The clerk shall issue a subpoena, signed but otherwise in blank, to a party requesting it, who shall complete it before service. An attorney as officer of the court may also issue and sign a subpoena on behalf of

(A) a court in which the attorney is authorized to practice; or

(B) a court for a district in which a deposition or production is compelled by the subpoena, if the deposition or production pertains to an action pending in a court in which the attorney is authorized to practice.

(b) Service.

(1) A subpoena may be served by any person who is not a party and is not less than 18 years of age. Service of a subpoena upon a person named therein shall be made by delivering a copy thereof to such person and, if the person's attendance is commanded, by tendering to that person the fees for one day's attendance and the mileage allowed by law. When the subpoena is issued on behalf of the

United States or an officer or agency thereof, fees and mileage need not be tendered. Prior notice of any commanded production of documents and things or inspection of premises before trial shall be served on each party in the manner prescribed by Rule 5(b).

(2) Subject to the provisions of clause (ii) of subparagraph (c)(3)(A) of this rule, a subpoena may be served at any place within the district of the court by which it is issued, or at any place without the district that is within 100 miles of the place of the deposition, hearing, trial, production, or inspection specified in the subpoena or at any place within the state where a state statute or rule of court permits service of a subpoena issued by a state court of general jurisdiction sitting in the place of the deposition, hearing, trial, production, or inspection specified in the subpoena. When a statute of the United States provides therefor, the court upon proper application and cause shown may authorize the service of a subpoena at any other place. A subpoena directed to a witness in a foreign country who is a national or resident of the United States shall issue under the circumstances and in the manner and be served as provided in Title 28, U.S.C. § 1783.

(3) Proof of service when necessary shall be made by filing with the clerk of the court by which the subpoena is issued a statement of the date and manner of service and of the names of the persons served, certified by the person who made the service.

(c) Protection of Persons Subject to Subpoenas.

(1) A party or an attorney responsible for the issuance and service of a subpoena shall take reasonable steps to avoid imposing undue burden or expense on a person subject to that subpoena. The court on behalf of which the subpoena was issued shall enforce this duty and impose upon the party or attorney in breach of this duty an appropriate sanction, which may include, but is not limited to, lost earnings and a reasonable attorney's fee.

(2)(A) A person commanded to produce and permit inspection and copying of designated books, papers, documents or tangible things, or inspection of premises need not appear in person at the place of production or inspection unless commanded to appear for deposition, hearing or trial.

(B) Subject to paragraph (d)(2) of this rule, a person commanded to produce and permit inspection and copying may, within 14 days after service of the subpoena or before the time specified for compliance if such time is less than 14 days after service, serve upon the party or attorney designated in the subpoena written objection to inspection or copying of any or all of the designated materials or of the premises. If objection is made, the party serving the subpoena shall not be entitled to inspect and copy the materials or inspect the premises except pursuant to an order of the court by which the subpoena was issued. If objection has been made, the party serving the subpoena may, upon notice to the person commanded to produce, move at any time for an order to compel the production. Such an order to compel production shall protect any person who is not a party or an officer of a party from significant expense resulting from the inspection and copying commanded.

(3)(A) On timely motion, the court by which a subpoena was issued shall quash or modify the subpoena if it

(i) fails to allow reasonable time for compliance;

(ii) requires a person who is not a party or an officer of a party to travel to a place more than 100 miles from the place where that person resides, is employed or regularly transacts business in person, except that, subject to the provisions of clause (c)(3)(B)(iii) of this rule, such a person may in order to attend trial be commanded to travel from any such place within the state in which the trial is held, or

(iii) requires disclosure of privileged or other protected matter and no exception or waiver applies, or

(iv) subjects a person to undue burden.

(B) If a subpoena

(i) requires disclosure of a trade secret or other confidential research, development, or commercial information, or

(ii) requires disclosure of an unretained expert's opinion or information not describing specific events or occurrences in dispute and resulting from the expert's study made not at the request of any party, or

(iii) requires a person who is not a party or an officer of a party to incur substantial expense to travel more than 100 miles to attend trial,

the court may, to protect a person subject to or affected by the subpoena, quash or modify the subpoena or, if the party in whose behalf the subpoena is issued shows a substantial need for the testimony or material that cannot be otherwise met without undue hardship and assures that the person to whom the subpoena is addressed will be reasonably compensated, the court may order appearance or production only upon specified conditions.

(d) Duties in Responding to Subpoena.

(1) A person responding to a subpoena to produce documents shall produce them as they are kept in the usual course of business or shall orga-

nize and label them to correspond with the categories in the demand.

(2) When information subject to a subpoena is withheld on a claim that it is privileged or subject to protection as trial preparation materials, the claim shall be made expressly and shall be supported by a description of the nature of the documents, communications, or things not produced that is sufficient to enable the demanding party to contest the claim.

(e) Contempt. Failure by any person without adequate excuse to obey a subpoena served upon that person may be deemed a contempt of the court from which the subpoena issued. An adequate cause for failure to obey exists when a subpoena purports to require a non-party to attend or produce at a place not within the limits provided by clause (ii) of subparagraph (c)(3)(A).

(As amended Dec. 27, 1946, eff. Mar. 19, 1948; Dec. 29, 1948, eff. Oct. 20, 1949; Mar. 30, 1970, eff. July 1, 1970; Apr. 29, 1980, eff. Aug. 1, 1980; Apr. 29, 1985, eff. Aug. 1, 1985; Mar. 2, 1987, eff. Aug. 1, 1987; Apr. 30, 1991, eff. Dec. 1, 1991.)

ADVISORY COMMITTEE NOTES

1937 Adoption

This rule applies to subpoenas ad testificandum and duces tecum issued by the district courts for attendance at a hearing or a trial, or to take depositions. It does not apply to the enforcement of subpoenas issued by administrative officers and commissions pursuant to statutory authority. The enforcement of such subpoenas by the district courts is regulated by appropriate statutes. Many of these statutes do not place any territorial limits on the validity of subpoenas so issued, but provide that they may be served anywhere within the United States. Among such statutes are the following:

U.S.C., Title 7, §§ 222 and 511n (Secretary of Agriculture)

U.S.C., Title 15, § 49 (Federal Trade Commission)

U.S.C., Title 15, §§ 77v(b), 78u(c), 79r(d) (Securities and Exchange Commission)

U.S.C., Title 16, §§ 797(g) and 825f (Federal Power Commission)

U.S.C., Title 19, § 1333(b) (Tariff Commission)

U.S.C., Title 22, §§ 268, 270d and 270e (International Commissions, etc.)

U.S.C., Title 26, §§ 614, 619(b) [see 7456] (Board of Tax Appeals)

U.S.C., Title 26, § 1523(a) [see 7608] (Internal Revenue Officers)

U.S.C., Title 29, § 161 (Labor Relations Board)

U.S.C., Title 33, § 506 (Secretary of Army)

U.S.C., Title 35, §§ 54 to 56 [now 24] (Patent Office proceedings)

U.S.C., Title 38, [former] § 133 (Veterans' Administration)

U.S.C., Title 41, § 39 (Secretary of Labor)

U.S.C., Title 45, § 157 Third. (h) (Board of Arbitration under Railway Labor Act)

U.S.C., Title 45, § 222(b) (Investigation Commission under Railroad Retirement Act of 1935)

U.S.C., Title 46, § 1124(b) (Maritime Commission)

U.S.C., Title 47, § 409(c) and (d) (Federal Communications Commission)

U.S.C., Title 49, § 12(2) and (3) [now 10321] (Interstate Commerce Commission)

U.S.C., Title 49, § 173a [see 1484] (Secretary of Commerce)

Note to Subdivisions (a) and (b). These simplify the form of subpoena as provided in U.S.C., Title 28, [former] § 655 (Witnesses; subpoena; form; attendance under); and broaden U.S.C, Title 28, [former] § 636 (Production for books and writings) to include all actions, and to extend to any person. With the provision for relief from an oppressive or unreasonable subpoena duces tecum, compare N.Y.C.P.A. (1937) § 411.

Note to Subdivision (c). This provides for the simple and convenient method of service permitted under many state codes; e.g., N.Y.C.P.A. (1937) §§ 220, 404, J.Ct.Act, § 191; 3 Wash.Rev.Stat.Ann. (Remington, 1932) § 1218. Compare former Equity Rule 15 (Process, by Whom Served).

For statutes governing fees and mileage of witnesses see:

U.S.C., Title 28 former sections:

600a[now 1871] (Per diem; mileage)

600c[now 1821, 1823] (Amount per diem and mileage for witnesses; subsistence)

600d[former] (Fees and mileage in certain states)

601[former] (Witnesses' fees; enumeration)

602[now 1824] (Fees and mileage of jurors and witnesses)

603[see Title 5, §§ 5515, 5537] (No officer of court to have witness fees)

Note to Subdivision (d). The method provided in paragraph (1) for the authorization of the issuance of subpoenas has been employed in some districts. See *Henning v. Boyle*, S.D.N.Y.1901, 112 F. 397. The requirement of an order for the issuance of a subpoena duces tecum is in accordance with U.S.C., Title 28, [former] § 647 (Deposition under dedimus potestatem; subpoena duces tecum). The provisions of paragraph (2) are in accordance with common practice. See U.S.C., Title 28, former § 648 (Deposition under dedimus potestatem; witnesses, when required to attend); N.Y.C.P.A. (1937) § 300; 1 N.J.Rev.Stat. (1937) 2:27–174.

Note to Subdivision (e). The first paragraph continues the substance of U.S.C., Title 28, [former] § 654 (Witnesses; subpoenas; may run into another district). Compare U.S.C., Title 11, [former] § 69 (Referees in bankruptcy; contempts before) (production of books and writings) which is not affected by this rule. For examples of statutes which allow the court, upon proper application and cause shown, to authorize the clerk of the court to issue a subpoena for a witness who lives in another district and at a greater distance than 100 miles from the place of the hearing or trial, see:

U.S.C., Title 15:

§ 23 (Suits by United States; subpoenas for witnesses) (under antitrust laws).

U.S.C., Title 38:

§ 445[now 784] (Actions on claims; jurisdiction; parties; procedure; limitation; witnesses; definitions) (Veterans' insurance contracts).

The second paragraph continues the present procedure applicable to certain witnesses who are in foreign countries. See U.S.C., Title 28, §§ 711 [now 1783] (Letters rogatory to take testimony of witness, addressed to court of foreign country; failure of witness to appear; subpoena) and 713 [now 1783] (Service of Subpoena on witness in foreign country).

Note to Subdivision (f). Compare [former] Equity Rule 52 (Attendance of Witnesses Before Commissioner, Master, or Examiner).

1946 Amendment

Note to Subdivision (b). The added words, "or tangible things" in subdivision (b) merely make the rule for the subpoena duces tecum at the trial conform to that of subdivision (d) for the subpoena at the taking of depositions. The insertion of the words "or modify" in clause (1) affords desirable flexibility.

Subdivision (d). The added last sentence of amended subdivision (d)(1) properly gives the subpoena for documents or tangible things the same scope as provided in Rule 26(b), thus promoting uniformity. The requirement in the last sentence of original Rule 45(d)(1)—to the effect that leave of court should be obtained for the issuance of such a subpoena—has been omitted. This requirement is unnecessary and oppressive on both counsel and court, and it had been criticized by district judges. There is no satisfactory reason for a differentiation between a subpoena for the production of documentary evidence by a witness at a trial (Rule 45(a)) and for the production of the same evidence at the taking of a deposition. Under this amendment, the person subpoenaed may obtain the protection afforded by any of the orders permitted under Rule 30(b) or Rule 45(b). See *Application of Zenith Radio Corp.*, E.D.Pa.1941, 4 F.Rules Serv. 30b.21. Case 1, 1 F.R.D. 627; *Fox v. House*, Okla.1939, 29 F.Supp. 673; *United States of America for the Use of Tilo Roofing Co., Inc. v. J. Slotnik Co.*, Conn.1944, 3 F.R.D. 408.

The changes in subdivisions (d)(2) give the court the same power in the case of residents of the district as is conferred in the case of non-residents, and permit the court to fix a place for attendance which may be more convenient and accessible for the parties than that specified in the rule.

1948 Amendment

The amendment effective October 1949, substituted the reference to "Title 28, U.S.C., § 1783" at the end of subdivision (e)(2) for the reference to "the Act of July 3, 1926, c. 762, §§ 1, 3 (44 Stat. 835), U.S.C., Title 28, § 713."

1970 Amendment

At present, when a subpoena duces tecum is issued to a deponent, he is required to produce the listed materials at the deposition, but is under no clear compulsion to permit their inspection and copying. This results in confusion and uncertainty before the time the deposition is taken, with no mechanism provided whereby the court can resolve the matter. Rule 45(d)(1), as revised, makes clear that the subpoena authorizes inspection and copying of the materials produced. The deponent is afforded full protection since he can object, thereby forcing the party serving the subpoena to obtain a court order if he wishes to inspect and copy. The procedure is thus analogous to that provided in Rule 34.

The changed references to other rules conform to changes made in those rules. The deletion of words in the clause describing the proper scope of the subpoena conforms to a change made in the language of Rule 34. The reference to Rule 26(b) is unchanged but encompasses new matter in that subdivision. The changes make it clear that the scope of discovery through a subpoena is the same as that applicable to Rule 34 and the other discovery rules.

1980 Amendment

Subdivision (d)(1). The amendment defines the term "proof of service" as used in the first sentence of the present subdivision. For want of a definition, the district court clerks have been obliged to fashion their own, with results that vary from district to district. All that seems required is a simple certification on a copy of the notice to take a deposition that the notice has been served on every other party to the action. That is the proof of service required by Rule 25(d) of both the Federal Rules of Appellate Procedure and the Supreme Court Rules.

Subdivision (e)(1). The amendment makes the reach of a subpoena of a district court at least as extensive as that of the state courts of general jurisdiction in the state in which the district court is held. Under the present rule the reach of a district court subpoena is often greater, since it extends throughout the district. No reason appears why it should be less, as it sometimes is because of the accident of district lines. Restrictions upon the reach of subpoenas are imposed to prevent undue inconvenience to witnesses. State statutes and rules of court are quite likely to reflect the varying degrees of difficulty and expense attendant upon local travel.

1985 Amendment

Present Rule 45(d)(2) has two sentences setting forth the territorial scope of deposition subpoenas. The first sentence is directed to depositions taken in the judicial district in which the deponent resides; the second sentence addresses situations in which the deponent is not a resident of the district in which the deposition is to take place. The Rule, as currently constituted, creates anomalous situations that often cause logistical problems in conducting litigation.

The first sentence of the present Rule states that a deponent may be required to attend only in the *county* wherein that person resides or is employed or transacts business in person, that is, where the person lives or works. Under this provision a deponent can be compelled, without court order, to travel from one end of that person's home county to the other, no matter how far that may be. The second sentence of the Rule is somewhat more flexible, stating that someone who does not reside in the district in which the deposition is to be taken can be required to attend in the county where the person is served with the subpoena, *or* within 40 miles from the place of service.

Under today's conditions there is no sound reason for distinguishing between residents of the district or county in which a deposition is to be taken and nonresidents, and the Rule is amended to provide that any person may be subpoenaed to attend a deposition within a specified radius from that person's residence, place of business, or where the person was served. The 40-mile radius has been increased to 100 miles.

1987 Amendment

The amendments are technical. No substantive change is intended.

1991 Amendment

Purposes of Revision. The purposes of this revision are (1) to clarify and enlarge the protections afforded persons who are required to assist the court by giving information or evidence; (2) to facilitate access outside the deposition procedure provided by Rule 30 to documents and other information in the possession of persons who are not parties; (3) to facilitate service of subpoenas for depositions or productions of evidence at places distant from the district in which an action is proceeding; (4) to enable the court to compel a witness found within the state in which the court sits to attend trial; (5) to clarify the organization of the text of the rule.

Subdivision (a). This subdivision is amended in seven significant respects.

First, Paragraph (a)(3) modifies the requirement that a subpoena be issued by the clerk of court. Provision is made for the issuance of subpoenas by attorneys as officers of the court. This revision perhaps culminates an evolution. Subpoenas were long issued by specific order of the court. As this became a burden to the court, general orders were made authorizing clerks to issue subpoenas on request. Since 1948, they have been issued in blank by the clerk of any federal court to any lawyer, the clerk serving as stationer to the bar. In allowing counsel to issue the subpoena, the rule is merely a recognition of present reality.

Although the subpoena is in a sense the command of the attorney who completes the form, defiance of a subpoena is nevertheless an act in defiance of a court order and exposes the defiant witness to contempt sanctions. In *ICC v. Brimson*, 154 U.S. 447 (1894), the Court upheld a statute directing federal courts to issue subpoenas to compel testimony before the ICC. In *CAB v. Hermann*, 353 U.S. 322 (1957), the Court approved as established practice the issuance of administrative subpoenas as a matter of absolute agency right. And in *NLRB v. Warren Co.*, 350 U.S. 107 (1955), the Court held that the lower court had no discretion to withhold sanctions against a contemnor who violated such subpoenas. The 1948 revision of Rule 45 put the attorney in a position similar to that of the administrative agency, as a public officer entitled to use the court's contempt power to investigate facts in dispute. Two courts of appeals have touched on the issue and have described lawyer-issued subpoenas as mandates of the court. *Waste Conversion, Inc. v. Rollins Environmental Services (NJ), Inc.*, 893 F.2d 605 (3d cir., 1990); *Fisher v. Marubent Cotton Corp.*, 526 F.2d 1338, 1340 (8th cir., 1975). Cf. *Young v. United States ex rel Vuitton et Fils S.A.*, 481 U.S. 787, 821 (1987) (Scalia, J., concurring). This revision makes the rule explicit that the attorney acts as an officer of the court in issuing and signing subpoenas.

Necessarily accompanying the evolution of this power of the lawyer as officer of the court is the development of increased responsibility and liability for the misuse of this power. The latter development is reflected in the provisions of subdivision (c) of this rule, and also in the requirement imposed by paragraph (3) of this subdivision that the attorney issuing a subpoena must sign it.

Second, Paragraph (a)(3) authorizes attorneys in distant districts to serve as officers authorized to issue commands in the name of the court. Any attorney permitted to represent a client in a federal court, even one admitted pro haec vice, has the same authority as a clerk to issue a subpoena from any federal court for the district in which the subpoena is served and enforced. In authorizing attorneys to issue subpoenas from distant courts, the amended rule effectively authorizes service of a subpoena anywhere in the United States by an attorney representing any party. This change is intended to ease the administrative burdens of inter-district law practice. The former rule resulted in delay and expense caused by the need to secure forms from clerks' offices some distance from the place at which the action proceeds. This change does not enlarge the burden on the witness.

Pursuant to Paragraph (a)(2), a subpoena for a deposition must still issue from the court in which the deposition or production would be compelled. Accordingly, a motion to quash such a subpoena if it overbears the limits of the subpoena power must, as under the previous rule, be presented to the court for the district in which the deposition would occur. Likewise, the court in whose name the subpoena is issued is responsible for its enforcement.

Third, in order to relieve attorneys of the need to secure an appropriate seal to affix to a subpoena issued as an officer of a distant court, the requirement that a subpoena be under seal is abolished by the provisions of Paragraph (a)(1).

Fourth, Paragraph (a)(1) authorizes the issuance of a subpoena to compel a non-party to produce evidence independent of any deposition. This revision spares the necessity of a deposition of the custodian of evidentiary material required to be produced. A party seeking additional production from a person subject to such a subpoena may serve an additional subpoena requiring additional production at the same time and place.

Fifth, Paragraph (a)(2) makes clear that the person subject to the subpoena is required to produce materials in that person's control whether or not the materials are located within the district or within the territory within which the subpoena can be served. The non-party witness is subject to the same scope of discovery under this rule as that person would be as a party to whom a request is addressed pursuant to Rule 34.

Sixth, Paragraph (a)(1) requires that the subpoena include a statement of the rights and duties of witnesses by setting forth in full the text of the new subdivisions (c) and (d).

Seventh, the revised rule authorizes the issuance of a subpoena to compel the inspection of premises in the possession of a non-party. Rule 34 has authorized such inspections of premises in the possession of a party as discovery compelled under Rule 37, but prior practice required an independent proceeding to secure such relief ancillary to the federal proceeding when the premises were not in the possession of a party. Practice in some states has long authorized such use of a subpoena for this purpose without apparent adverse consequence.

Subdivision (b). Paragraph (b)(1) retains the text of the former subdivision (c) with minor changes.

The reference to the United States marshal and deputy marshal is deleted because of the infrequency of the use of these officers for this purpose. Inasmuch as these officers meet the age requirement, they may still be used if available.

A provision requiring service of prior notice pursuant to Rule 5 of compulsory pretrial production or inspection has been added to paragraph (b)(1). The purpose of such notice is to afford other parties an opportunity to object to the production or inspection, or to serve a demand for additional documents or things. Such additional notice is not needed with respect to a deposition because of the requirement of notice imposed by Rule 30 or 31. But when production or inspection is sought independently of a deposition, other parties may need notice in order to monitor the discovery and in order to pursue access to any information that may or should be produced.

Paragraph (b)(2) retains language formerly set forth in subdivision (e) and extends its application to subpoenas for depositions or production.

Paragraph (b)(3) retains language formerly set forth in paragraph (d)(1) and extends its applications to subpoenas for trial or hearing or production.

Subdivision (c). This provision is new and states the rights of witnesses. It is not intended to diminish rights conferred by Rules 26–37 or any other authority.

Paragraph (c)(1) gives specific application to the principle stated in Rule 26(g) and specifies liability for earnings lost by a non-party witness as a result of a misuse of the subpoena. No change in existing law is thereby effected. Abuse of a subpoena is an actionable tort, *Board of Ed. v. Farmingdale Classroom Teach. Ass'n*, 38 N.Y.2d 397, 380 N.Y.S.2d 635, 343 N.E.2d 278 (1975), and the duty of the attorney to the non-party is also embodied in Model Rule of Professional Conduct 4.4. The liability of the attorney is correlative to the expanded power of the attorney to issue subpoenas. The liability may include the cost of fees to collect attorneys' fees owed as a result of a breach of this duty.

Paragraph (c)(2) retains language from the former subdivision (b) and paragraph (d)(1). The 10–day period for response to a subpoena is extended to 14 days to avoid the complex calculations associated with short time periods under Rule 6 and to allow a bit more time for such objections to be made.

A non-party required to produce documents or materials is protected against significant expense resulting from involuntary assistance to the court. This provision applies, for example, to a non-party required to provide a list of class members. The court is not required to fix the costs in advance of production, although this will often be the most satisfactory accommodation to protect the party seeking discovery from excessive costs. In some instances, it may be preferable to leave uncertain costs to be determined after the materials have been produced, provided that the risk of uncertainty is fully disclosed to the discovering party. See, *e.g., United States v. Columbia Broadcasting Systems, Inc.*, 666 F.2d 364 (9th Cir.1982).

Paragraph (c)(3) explicitly authorizes the quashing of a subpoena as a means of protecting a witness from misuse of the subpoena power. It replaces and enlarges on the former subdivision (b) of this rule and tracks the provisions of Rule 26(c). While largely repetitious, this rule is addressed to the witness who may read it on the subpoena, where it is required to be printed by the revised paragraph (a)(1) of this rule.

Subparagraph (c)(3)(A) identifies those circumstances in which a subpoena must be quashed or modified. It restates the former provisions with respect to the limits of mandatory travel that are set forth in the former paragraphs (d)(2) and (e)(1), with one important change. Under the revised rule, a federal court can compel a witness to come from any place in the state to attend trial, whether or not the local state law so provides. This extension is subject to the qualification provided in the next paragraph, which authorizes the court to condition enforcement of a subpoena compelling a non-party witness to bear substantial expense to attend trial. The traveling non-party witness may be entitled to reasonable compensation for the time and effort entailed.

Clause (c)(3)(A)(iv) requires the court to protect all persons from undue burden imposed by the use of the subpoena power. Illustratively, it might be unduly burdensome to compel an adversary to attend trial as a witness if the adversary is known to have no personal knowledge of matters in dispute, especially so if the adversary would be required to incur substantial travel burdens.

Subparagraph (c)(3)(B) identifies circumstances in which a subpoena should be quashed unless the party serving the subpoena shows a substantial need and the court can devise an appropriate accommodation to protect the interests of the witness. An additional circumstance in which such action is required is a request for costly production of documents; that situation is expressly governed by subparagraph (b)(2)(B)[1].

Clause (c)(3)(B)(i) authorizes the court to quash, modify, or condition a subpoena to protect the person subject to or affected by the subpoena from unnecessary or unduly harmful disclosures of confidential information. It corresponds to Rule 26(c)(7).

Clause (c)(3)(B)(ii) provides appropriate protection for the intellectual property of the non-party witness; it does not apply to the expert retained by a party, whose information is subject to the provisions of Rule 26(b)(4). A growing problem has been the use of subpoenas to compel the giving of evidence and information by unretained experts. Experts are not exempt from the duty to give evidence, even if they cannot be compelled to prepare themselves to give effective testimony, *e.g., Carter–Wallace, Inc. v. Otte*, 474 F.2d 529 (2d Cir.1972), but compulsion to give evidence may threaten the intellectual property of experts denied the opportunity to bargain for the value of their services. See generally Maurer, *Compelling the Expert Witness: Fairness and Utility Under the Federal Rules of Civil Procedure*, 19 GA.L.REV. 71 (1984); Note, *Discovery and Testimony of Unretained Experts*, 1987 DUKE L.J. 140. Arguably the compulsion to testify can be regarded as a "taking" of intellectual property. The rule establishes the right of such persons to withhold their expertise, at least unless the party seeking it makes the kind of showing required for a conditional denial of a motion to quash as provided in the final sentence of subparagraph (c)(3)(B); that requirement is the same as that necessary to secure work product under Rule 26(b)(3) and gives assurance of reasonable compensation. The Rule thus approves the accommodation of competing interests exemplified in *United States v. Columbia Broadcasting Systems Inc.*, 666 F.2d 364 (9th Cir.1982). See also *Wright v. Jeep Corporation*, 547 F.Supp. 871 (E.D.Mich.1982).

As stated in *Kaufman v. Edelstein,* 539 F.2d 811, 822 (2d Cir.1976), the district court's discretion in these matters should be informed by "the degree to which the expert is being called because of his knowledge of facts relevant to the case rather than in order to give opinion testimony; the difference between testifying to a previously formed or expressed opinion and forming a new one; the possibility that, for other reasons, the witness is a unique expert; the extent to which the calling party is able to show the unlikelihood that any comparable witness will willingly testify; and the degree to which the witness is able to show that he has been oppressed by having continually to testify. . . ."

Clause (c)(3)(B)(iii) protects non-party witnesses who may be burdened to perform the duty to travel in order to provide testimony at trial. The provision requires the court to condition a subpoena requiring travel of more than 100 miles on reasonable compensation.

Subdivision (d). This provision is new. Paragraph (d)(1) extends to non-parties the duty imposed on parties by the last paragraph of Rule 34(b), which was added in 1980.

Paragraph (d)(2) is new and corresponds to the new Rule 26(b)(5) [paragraph (5) in Rule 26(b) was a proposed paragraph which was withdrawn by the Supreme Court]. Its purpose is to provide a party whose discovery is constrained by a claim of privilege or work product protection with information sufficient to evaluate such a claim and to resist if it seems unjustified. The person claiming a privilege or protection cannot decide the limits of that party's own entitlement.

A party receiving a discovery request who asserts a privilege or protection but fails to disclose that claim is at risk of waiving the privilege or protection. A person claiming a privilege or protection who fails to provide adequate information about the privilege or protection claim to the party seeking the information is subject to an order to show cause why the person should not be held in contempt under subdivision (e). Motions for such orders and responses to motions are subject to the sanctions provisions of Rules 7 and 11.

A person served a subpoena that is too broad may be faced with a burdensome task to provide full information regarding all that person's claims to privilege or work product protection. Such a person is entitled to protection that may be secured through an objection made pursuant to paragraph (c)(2).

Subdivision (e). This provision retains most of the language of the former subdivision (f).

"Adequate cause" for a failure to obey a subpoena remains undefined. In at least some circumstances, a non-party might be guilty of contempt for refusing to obey a subpoena even though the subpoena manifestly overreaches the appropriate limits of the subpoena power. *E.g., Walker v. City of Birmingham,* 388 U.S. 307 (1967). But, because the command of the subpoena is not in fact one uttered by a judicial officer, contempt should be very sparingly applied when the non-party witness has been overborne by a party or attorney. The language added to subdivision (f) is intended to assure that result where a non-party has been commanded, on the signature of an attorney, to travel greater distances than can be compelled pursuant to this rule.

1 So in original. Probably should be "subparagraph (c)(2)(B)".

COMMENTARIES

See 28 U.S.C.A. Rule 45, Federal Rules of Civil Procedure, for Commentary by David D. Siegel.

Rule 46. Exceptions Unnecessary

Formal exceptions to rulings or orders of the court are unnecessary; but for all purposes for which an exception has heretofore been necessary it is sufficient that a party, at the time the ruling or order of the court is made or sought, makes known to the court the action which the party desires the court to take or the party's objection to the action of the court and the grounds therefor; and, if a party has no opportunity to object to a ruling or order at the time it is made, the absence of an objection does not thereafter prejudice the party.

(As amended Mar. 2, 1987, eff. Aug. 1, 1987.)

ADVISORY COMMITTEE NOTES

1937 Adoption

Abolition of formal exceptions is often provided by statute. See Ill.Rev.Stat. (1937), ch. 110, § 204; Neb.Comp.Stat. (1929) § 20–1139; N.M.Stat.Ann. (Courtright, 1929) § 105–830; 2 N.D.Comp.Laws Ann. (1913) § 7653; Ohio Code Ann. (Throckmorton, 1936) § 11560; 1 S.D.Comp.Laws (1929) § 2542; Utah Rev.Stat.Ann. (1933) §§ 104–39–2, 104–24–18; Va.Rules of Court, Rule 22, 163 Va. v. xii (1935); Wis.Stat. (1935) § 270.39. Compare N.Y.C.P.A. (1937) §§ 583, 445, and 446, all as amended by L.1936, ch. 915. Rule 51 deals with objections to the court's instructions to the jury.

U.S.C., Title 28, [former] § 776 (Bill of exceptions; authentication; signing of by judge) and [former] § 875 (Review of findings in cases tried without a jury) are superseded insofar as they provide for formal exceptions, and a bill of exceptions.

1987 Amendment

The amendments are technical. No substantive change is intended.

Rule 47. Selection of Jurors

(a) Examination of Jurors. The court may permit the parties or their attorneys to conduct the examination of prospective jurors or may itself conduct the examination. In the latter event, the court shall permit the parties or their attorneys to supplement the examination by such further inquiry as it deems proper or shall itself submit to the prospective jurors such additional questions of the parties or their attorneys as it deems proper.

(b) Peremptory Challenges. The court shall allow the number of peremptory challenges provided by 28 U.S.C. § 1870.

(c) Excuse. The court may for good cause excuse a juror from service during trial or deliberation.

(As amended Feb. 28, 1966, eff. July 1, 1966; Apr. 30, 1991, eff. Dec. 1, 1991.)

ADVISORY COMMITTEE NOTES

1937 Adoption

Note to Subdivision (a). This permits a practice found very useful by Federal trial judges. For an example of a state practice in which the examination by the court is supplemented by further inquiry by counsel, see Rule 27 of the Code of Rules for the District Courts of Minnesota, 186 Minn. xxxiii (1932), 3 Minn.Stat. (Mason, Supp.1936) Appendix 4, p. 1062.

Note to Subdivision (b). The provision for an alternate juror is one often found in modern state codes. See N.C.Code (1935) § 2330(a); Ohio Gen.Code Ann. (Page, Supp.1926–1935) § 11419–47; Pa.Stat.Ann. (Purdon, Supp. 1936) Title 17, § 1153; compare U.S.C., Title 28, [former] § 417a (Alternate jurors in criminal trials); 1 N.J.Rev.Stat. (1937) 2:91A–1, 2:91A–2, 2:91A–3.

Provisions for qualifying, drawing, and challenging of jurors are found in U.S.C., Title 28:

§ 411 [now 1861] (Qualifications and exemptions)

§ 412 [now 1864] (Manner of drawing)

§ 413 [now 1865] (Apportioned in district)

§ 415 [see 1862] (Not disqualified because of race or color)

§ 416 [now 1867] (Venire; service and return)

§ 417 [now 1866] (Talesmen for petit jurors)

§ 418 [now 1866] (Special juries)

§ 423 [now 1869] (Jurors not to serve more than once a year)

§ 424 [now 1870] (Challenges)

and D.C.Code (1930) Title 18, §§ 341 to 360 (Juries and Jury Commission) and Title 6, § 366 (Peremptory challenges).

1966 Amendment

The revision of this subdivision brings it into line with the amendment of Rule 24(c) of this Federal Rules of Criminal Procedure. That rule previously allowed four alternate jurors, as contrasted with the two allowed in civil cases, and the amendments increase the number to a maximum of six in all cases. The Advisory Committee's Note to amended Criminal Rule 24(c) points to experience demonstrating that four alternates may not be enough in some lengthy criminal trials; and the same may be said of civil trials. The Note adds:

"The words 'or are found to be' are added to the second sentence to make clear that an alternate juror may be called in the situation where it is first discovered during the trial that a juror was unable or disqualified to perform his duties at the time he was sworn."

1991 Amendment

Subdivision (b). The former provision for alternate jurors is stricken and the institution of the alternate juror abolished.

The former rule reflected the long-standing assumption that a jury would consist of exactly twelve members. It provided for additional jurors to be used as substitutes for jurors who are for any reason excused or disqualified from service after the commencement of the trial. Additional jurors were traditionally designated at the outset of the trial, and excused at the close of the evidence if they had not been promoted to full service on account of the elimination of one of the original jurors.

The use of alternate jurors has been a source of dissatisfaction with the jury system because of the burden it places on alternates who are required to listen to the evidence but denied the satisfaction of participating in its evaluation.

Subdivision (c). This provision makes it clear that the court may in appropriate circumstances excuse a juror during the jury deliberations without causing a mistrial. Sickness, family emergency or juror misconduct that might occasion a mistrial are examples of appropriate grounds for excusing a juror. It is not grounds for the dismissal of a juror that the juror refuses to join with fellow jurors in reaching a unanimous verdict.

Rule 48. Number of Jurors—Participation in Verdict

The court shall seat a jury of not fewer than six and not more than twelve members and all jurors shall participate in the verdict unless excused from service by the court pursuant to Rule 47(c). Unless the parties otherwise stipulate, (1) the verdict shall be unanimous and (2) no verdict shall be taken from a jury reduced in size to fewer than six members.

(As amended Apr. 30, 1991, eff. Dec. 1, 1991.)

ADVISORY COMMITTEE NOTES

1937 Adoption

For provisions in state codes, compare Utah Rev.Stat.Ann. (1933) § 48–0–5 (In civil cases parties may agree in open court on lesser number of jurors); 2 Wash.Rev.Stat.Ann. (Remington, 1932) § 323 (Parties may consent to any number of jurors not less than three).

1991 Amendment

The former rule was rendered obsolete by the adoption in many districts of local rules establishing six as the standard size for a civil jury.

It appears that the minimum size of a jury consistent with the Seventh Amendment is six. *Cf. Ballew v. Georgia*, 435 U.S. 223 (1978) (holding that a conviction based on a jury of less than six is a denial of due process of law). If the parties agree to trial before a smaller jury, a verdict can be taken, but the parties should not other than in exceptional circumstances be encouraged to waive the right to a jury of six, not only because of the constitutional stature of the right, but also because smaller juries are more erratic and less effective in serving to distribute responsibility for the exercise of judicial power.

Because the institution of the alternate juror has been abolished by the proposed revision of Rule 47, it will ordinarily be prudent and necessary, in order to provide for sickness or disability among jurors, to seat more than six jurors. The use of jurors in excess of six increases the representativeness of the jury and harms no interest of a party. *Ray v. Parkside Surgery Center*, 13 F.R.Serv. 585 (6th Cir.1989).

If the court takes the precaution of seating a jury larger than six, an illness occurring during the deliberation period will not result in a mistrial, as it did formerly, because all seated jurors will participate in the verdict and a sufficient number will remain to render a unanimous verdict of six or more.

In exceptional circumstances, as where a jury suffers depletions during trial and deliberation that are greater than can reasonably be expected, the parties may agree to be bound by a verdict rendered by fewer than six jurors. The court should not, however, rely upon the availability of such an agreement, for the use of juries smaller than six is problematic for reasons fully explained in *Ballew v. Georgia*, supra.

Rule 49. Special Verdicts and Interrogatories

(a) Special Verdicts. The court may require a jury to return only a special verdict in the form of a special written finding upon each issue of fact. In that event the court may submit to the jury written questions susceptible of categorical or other brief answer or may submit written forms of the several special findings which might properly be made under the pleadings and evidence; or it may use such other method of submitting the issues and requiring the written findings thereon as it deems most appropriate. The court shall give to the jury such explanation and instruction concerning the matter thus submitted as may be necessary to enable the jury to make its findings upon each issue. If in so doing the court omits any issue of fact raised by the pleadings or by the evidence, each party waives the right to a trial by jury of the issue so omitted unless before the jury retires the party demands its submission to the jury. As to an issue omitted without such demand the court may make a finding; or, if it fails to do so, it shall be deemed to have made a finding in accord with the judgment on the special verdict.

(b) General Verdict Accompanied by Answer to Interrogatories. The court may submit to the jury, together with appropriate forms for a general verdict, written interrogatories upon one or more issues of fact the decision of which is necessary to a verdict. The court shall give such explanation or instruction as may be necessary to enable the jury both to make answers to the interrogatories and to render a general verdict, and the court shall direct the jury both to make written answers and to render a general verdict. When the general verdict and the answers are harmonious, the appropriate judgment upon the verdict and answers shall be entered pursuant to Rule 58. When the answers are consistent with each other but one or more is inconsistent with the general verdict, judgment may be entered pursuant to Rule 58 in accordance with the answers, notwithstanding the general verdict, or the court may return the jury for further consideration of its answers and verdict or may order a new trial. When the answers are inconsistent with each other and one or more is likewise inconsistent with the general verdict, judgment shall not be entered, but the court shall return the jury for further consideration of its answers and verdict or shall order a new trial.

(As amended Jan. 21, 1963, eff. July 1, 1963; Mar. 2, 1987, eff. Aug. 1, 1987.)

ADVISORY COMMITTEE NOTES

1937 Adoption

The Federal courts are not bound to follow state statutes authorizing or requiring the court to ask a jury to find a special verdict or to answer interrogatories. *Victor American Fuel Co. v. Peccarich*, 209 Fed. 568 (C.C.A.8th, 1913), cert. den. 232 U.S. 727, 34 S.Ct. 603, 58 L.Ed. 817 (1914); *Spokane and I.E.R. Co. v. Campbell*, 217 Fed. 518 (C.C.A.9th, 1914), affd. 241 U.S. 497, 36 S.Ct. 683, 60 L.Ed. 1125 (1916); Simkins, *Federal Practice* (1934) § 186. The power of a territory to adopt by statute the practice under Subdivision (b) has been sustained. *Walker v. New Mexico and Southern Pacific R.R.*, 165 U.S. 593, 17 S.Ct. 421, 41 L.Ed. 837 (1897); *Southwestern Brewery and Ice Co. v. Schmidt*, 226 U.S. 162, 33 S.Ct. 68, 57 L.Ed. 170 (1912).

Compare Wis.Stat. (1935) §§ 270.27, 270.28 and 270.30; Green, *A New Development in Jury Trial* (1927), 13 A.B.A.J. 715; *Morgan, A Brief History of Special Verdicts and Special Interrogatories*, 1923, 32 Yale L.J. 575.

The provisions of U.S.C., Title 28, [former] § 400(3) (now §§ 2201, 2202) (Declaratory judgments authorized; procedure) permitting the submission of issues of fact to a jury are covered by this rule.

1963 Amendment

This amendment conforms to the amendment of Rule 58. See the Advisory Committee's Note to Rule 58, as amended.

1987 Amendment

The amendments are technical. No substantive change is intended.

Rule 50. Judgment as a Matter of Law in Jury Trials; Alternative Motion for New Trial; Conditional Rulings

(a) Judgment as a Matter of Law.

(1) If during a trial by jury a party has been fully heard on an issue and there is no legally sufficient evidentiary basis for a reasonable jury to find for that party on that issue, the court may determine the issue against that party and may grant a motion for judgment as a matter of law against that party with respect to a claim or defense that cannot under the controlling law be maintained or defeated without a favorable finding on that issue.

(2) Motions for judgment as a matter of law may be made at any time before submission of the case to the jury. Such a motion shall specify the judgment sought and the law and the facts on which the moving party is entitled to the judgment.

(b) Renewing Motion for Judgment After Trial; Alternative Motion for New Trial. If, for any reason, the court does not grant a motion for judgment as a matter of law made at the close of all the evidence, the court is considered to have submitted the action to the jury subject to the court's later deciding the legal questions raised by the motion. The movant may renew its request for judgment as a matter of law by filing a motion no later than 10 days after entry of judgment— and may alternatively request a new trial or join a motion for a new trial under Rule 59. In ruling on a renewed motion, the court may:

(1) if a verdict was returned:

(A) allow the judgment to stand,

(B) order a new trial, or

(C) direct entry of judgment as a matter of law; or

(2) if no verdict was returned;

(A) order a new trial, or

(B) direct entry of judgment as a matter of law.

(c) Granting Renewed Motion for Judgment as a Matter of Law; Conditional Rulings; New Trial Motion

(1) If the renewed motion for judgment as a matter of law is granted, the court shall also rule on the motion for a new trial, if any, by determining whether it should be granted if the judgment is thereafter vacated or reversed, and shall specify the grounds for granting or denying the motion for the new trial. If the motion for a new trial is thus conditionally granted, the order thereon does not affect the finality of the judgment. In case the motion for a new trial has been conditionally granted and the judgment is reversed on appeal, the new trial shall proceed unless the appellate court has otherwise ordered. In case the motion for a new trial has been conditionally denied, the appellee on appeal may assert error in that denial; and if the judgment is reversed on appeal, subsequent proceedings shall be in accordance with the order of the appellate court.

(2) Any motion for a new trial under Rule 59 by a party against whom judgment as a matter of law is rendered shall be filed no later than 10 days after entry of the judgment.

(d) Same: Denial of Motion for Judgment as a Matter of Law. If the motion for judgment as a matter of law is denied, the party who prevailed on that motion may, as appellee, assert grounds entitling the party to a new trial in the event the appellate court concludes that the trial court erred in denying the motion for judgment. If the appellate court reverses the judgment, nothing in this rule precludes it from determining that the appellee is entitled to a new trial, or from directing the trial court to determine whether a new trial shall be granted.

(As amended Jan. 21, 1963, eff. July 1, 1963; Mar. 2, 1987, eff. Aug. 1, 1987; Apr. 30, 1991, eff. Dec. 1, 1991; Apr. 22, 1993, eff. Dec. 1, 1993; Apr. 27, 1995, eff. Dec. 1, 1995.)

ADVISORY COMMITTEE NOTES

1937 Adoption

Note to Subdivision (a). The present federal rule is changed to the extent that the formality of an express reservation of rights against waiver is no longer necessary. See *Sampliner v. Motion Picture Patents Co.,* 41 S.Ct. 79, 254 U.S. 233, 65 L.Ed. 240 (1920); *Union Indemnity Co. v. United States,* 74 F.2d 645 (C.C.A. 6th, 1935). The requirement that specific grounds for the motion for a directed verdict must be stated settles a conflict in the federal cases. See Simkins, *Federal Practice* (1934) § 189.

Note to Subdivision (b). For comparable state practice upheld under the conformity act, see *Baltimore and Carolina Line v. Redman,* 55 S.Ct. 890, 295 U.S. 654, 79 L.Ed. 1636 (1935); compare *Slocum v. New York Life Ins. Co.,* 33 S.Ct. 523, 228 U.S. 364, 57 L.Ed. 879, Ann.Cas.1914D, 1029 (1913).

See *Northern Ry. Co. v. Page,* 47 S.Ct. 491, 274 U.S. 65, 71 L.Ed. 929 (1927), following the Massachusetts practice of alternative verdicts, explained in Thorndike, *Trial by Jury in United States Courts,* 26 Harv.L.Rev. 732 (1913). See also Thayer, *Judicial Administration,* 63 U. of Pa.L.Rev. 585, 600–601, and note 32 (1915); Scott, *Trial by Jury and the Reform of Civil Procedure,* 31 Harv.L.Rev. 669, 685 (1918); Comment, 34 Mich.L.Rev. 93, 98 (1935).

1963 Amendment

Subdivision (a). The practice, after the court has granted a motion for a directed verdict, of requiring the jury to express assent to a verdict they did not reach by their own deliberations serves no useful purpose and may give offense to the members of the jury. See 2B Barron & Holtzoff, *Federal Practice & Procedure* § 1072, at 367 (Wright ed. 1961); Blume, *Origin and Development of the Directed Verdict,* 48 Mich.L.Rev. 555, 582–85, 589–90 (1950). The final sentence of the subdivision, added by amendment, provides that the court's order granting a motion for a directed verdict is effective in itself, and that no action need be taken by the foreman or other members of the jury. See Ariz. R.Civ.P. 50(c); cf. Fed.R.Crim.P. 29(a). No change is intended in the standard to be applied in deciding the motion. To assure this interpretation, and in the interest of simplicity, the traditional term, "directed verdict," is retained.

Subdivision (b). A motion for judgment notwithstanding the verdict will not lie unless it was preceded by a motion for a directed verdict made at the close of all the evidence.

The amendment of the second sentence of this subdivision sets the time limit for making the motion for judgment n.o.v. at 10 days after the entry of judgment, rather than 10 days after the reception of the verdict. Thus the time provision is made consistent with that contained in Rule 59(b) (time for motion for new trial) and Rule 52(b) (time for motion to amend findings by the court).

Subdivision (c) deals with the situation where a party joins a motion for a new trial with his motion for judgment n.o.v., or prays for a new trial in the alternative, and the motion for judgment n.o.v. is granted. The procedure to be followed in making rulings on the motion for the new trial, and the consequences of the rulings thereon, were partly set out in *Montgomery Ward & Co. v. Duncan,* 311 U.S. 243, 253, 61 S.Ct. 189, 85 L.Ed. 147 (1940), and have been further elaborated in later cases. See *Cone v. West Virginia Pulp & Paper Co.,* 330 U.S. 212, 67 S.Ct. 752, 91 L.Ed. 849 (1947); *Globe Liquor Co., Inc. v. San Roman,* 332 U.S. 571, 68 S.Ct. 246, 92 L.Ed. 177 (1948); *Fountain v. Filson,* 336 U.S. 681, 69 S.Ct. 754, 93 L.Ed. 971 (1949); *Johnson v. New York, N.H. & H.R.R. Co.,* 344 U.S. 48, 73 S.Ct. 125, 97 L.Ed. 77 (1952). However, courts as well as counsel have often misunderstood the procedure, and it will be helpful to summarize the proper practice in the text of the rule. The amendments do not alter the effects of a jury verdict or the scope of appellate review.

In the situation mentioned, subdivision (c)(1) requires that the court make a "conditional" ruling on the new-trial motion, i.e., a ruling which goes on the assumption that the motion for judgment n.o.v. was erroneously granted and will be reversed or vacated; and the court is required to state its grounds for the conditional ruling. Subdivision (c)(1) then spells out the consequences of a reversal of the judgment in the light of the conditional ruling on the new-trial motion.

If the motion for new trial has been conditionally granted, and the judgment is reversed, "the new trial shall proceed unless the appellate court has otherwise ordered." The party against whom the judgment n.o.v. was entered below may, as appellant, besides seeking to overthrow that judgment, also attack the conditional grant of the new trial. And the appellate court, if it reverses the judgment n.o.v., may in an appropriate case also reverse the conditional grant of the new trial and direct that judgment be entered on the verdict. See *Bailey v. Slentz,* 189 F.2d 406 (10th Cir. 1951); *Moist Cold Refrigerator Co. v. Lou Johnson Co.,* 249 F.2d 246 (9th Cir. 1957), cert. denied, 356 U.S. 968, 78 S.Ct. 1008, 2 L.Ed.2d 1074 (1958); *Peters v. Smith,* 221 F.2d 721 (3d Cir. 1955); *Dailey v. Timmer,* 292 F.2d 824 (3d Cir. 1961), explaining *Lind v. Schenley Industries, Inc.,* 278 F.2d 79 (3d Cir.), cert. denied, 364 U.S. 835, 81 S.Ct. 58, 5 L.Ed.2d 60 (1960); *Cox v. Pennsylvania R.R.,* 120 A.2d 214 (D.C.Mun. Ct.App.1956); 3 Barron & Holtzoff, *Federal Practice & Procedure* § 1302.1 at 346–47 (Wright ed. 1958); 6 *Moore's Federal Practice* ¶59.16 at 3915 n. 8a (2d ed. 1954).

If the motion for a new trial has been conditionally denied, and the judgment is reversed, "subsequent proceedings shall be in accordance with the order of the appellate court." The party in whose favor judgment n.o.v. was entered below may, as appellee, besides seeking to uphold that judgment, also urge on the appellate court that the trial court committed error in conditionally denying the new trial. The appellee may assert this error in his brief, without taking a cross-appeal. *Cf. Patterson v. Pennsylvania R.R.,* 238 F.2d 645, 650 (6th Cir. 1956); *Hughes v. St. Louis Nat. L. Baseball Club, Inc.,* 359 Mo. 993, 997, 224 S.W.2d 989, 992 (1949). If the appellate court concludes that the judgment cannot stand, but accepts the appellee's contention that there was error in the conditional denial of the new trial, it may order a new trial in lieu of directing the entry of judgment upon the verdict.

Subdivision (c)(2), which also deals with the situation where the trial court has granted the motion for judgment n.o.v., states that the verdict-winner may apply to the trial court for a new trial pursuant to Rule 59 after the judgment n.o.v. has been entered against him. In arguing to the trial court in opposition to the motion for judgment n.o.v., the verdict-winner may, and often will, contend that he is entitled, at the least, to a new trial, and the court has a range of discretion to grant a new trial or (where plaintiff won the verdict) to order a dismissal of the action without prejudice instead of granting judgment n.o.v. See *Cone v. West Virginia Pulp & Paper Co.,* supra, 330 U.S. at 217, 218, 67 S.Ct. at 755, 756, 91 L.Ed. 849. Subdivision (c)(2) is a reminder that the verdict-winner is entitled, even after entry of judgment n.o.v. against him, to move for a new trial in the usual course. If in these circumstances the motion is granted, the judgment is superseded.

In some unusual circumstances, however, the grant of the new-trial motion may be only conditional, and the judgment will not be superseded. See the situation in *Tribble v. Bruin,* 279 F.2d 424 (4th Cir. 1960) (upon a verdict for plaintiff, defendant moves for and obtains judgment n.o.v.; plaintiff moves for a new trial on the ground of inadequate damages; trial court might properly have granted plaintiff's motion, conditional upon reversal of the judgment n.o.v.).

Even if the verdict-winner makes no motion for a new trial, he is entitled upon his appeal from the judgment n.o.v. not only to urge that that judgment should be reversed and judgment entered upon the verdict, but that errors were committed during the trial which at the least entitle him to a new trial.

Subdivision (d) deals with the situation where judgment has been entered on the jury verdict, the motion for judgment n.o.v. and any motion for a new trial having been denied by the trial court. The verdict-winner, as appellee, besides seeking to uphold the judgment may urge upon the appellate court that in case the trial court is found to have erred in entering judgment on the verdict, there are grounds for granting him a new trial instead of directing the entry of judgment for his opponent. In appropriate cases the appellate court is not precluded from itself directing that a new trial be had. See *Weade v. Dichmann, Wright & Pugh, Inc.,* 337 U.S. 801, 69 S.Ct. 1326, 93 L.Ed. 1704 (1949). Nor is it precluded in proper cases from remanding the case for a determination by the trial court as to whether a new trial should be granted. The latter course is advisable where the grounds urged are suitable for the exercise of trial court discretion.

Subdivision (d) does not attempt a regulation of all aspects of the procedure where the motion for judgment n.o.v. and any accompanying motion for a new trial are denied, since the problems have not been fully canvassed in the decisions and the procedure is in some respects still in a formative stage. It is, however, designed to give guidance on certain important features of the practice.

1987 Amendment

The amendments are technical. No substantive change is intended.

1991 Amendment

Subdivision (a). The revision of this subdivision aims to facilitate the exercise by the court of its responsibility to assure the fidelity of its judgment to the controlling law, a responsibility imposed by the Due Process Clause of the Fifth Amendment. *Cf. Galloway v. United States,* 319 U.S. 372 (1943).

The revision abandons the familiar terminology of *direction of verdict* for several reasons. The term is misleading as a description of the relationship between judge and jury. It is also freighted with anachronisms some of which are the subject of the text of former subdivision (a) of this rule that is deleted in this revision. Thus, it should not be necessary to state in the text of this rule that a motion made pursuant to it is not a waiver of the right to jury trial, and only the antiquities of directed verdict practice suggest that it might have been. The term "judgment as a matter of law" is an almost equally familiar term and appears in the text of Rule 56; its use in Rule 50 calls attention to the relationship between the two rules. Finally, the change enables the rule to refer to preverdict and post-verdict motions with a terminology that does not conceal the common identity of two motions made at different times in the proceeding.

If a motion is denominated a motion for directed verdict or for judgment notwithstanding the verdict, the party's error is merely formal. Such a motion should be treated as a motion for judgment as a matter of law in accordance with this rule.

Paragraph (a)(1) articulates the standard for the granting of a motion for judgment as a matter of law. It effects no change in the existing standard. That existing standard was not expressed in the former rule, but was articulated in long-standing case law. *See generally* Cooper, *Directions for Directed Verdicts: A Compass for Federal Courts,* 55 MINN.L.REV. 903 (1971). The expressed standard makes clear that action taken under the rule is a performance of the court's duty to assure enforcement of the controlling law and is not an intrusion on any responsibility for factual determinations conferred on the jury by the Seventh Amendment or any other provision of federal law. Because this standard is also used as a reference point for entry of summary judgment under 56(a), it serves to link the two related provisions.

The revision authorizes the court to perform its duty to enter judgment as a matter of law at any time during the trial, as soon as it is apparent that either party is unable to carry a burden of proof that is essential to that party's case. Thus, the second sentence of paragraph (a)(1) authorizes the court to consider a motion for judgment as a matter of law as soon as a party has completed a presentation on a fact essential to that party's case. Such early action is appropriate when economy and expedition will be served. In no event, however, should the court enter judgment against a party who has not been apprised of the materiality of the dispositive fact and been afforded an opportunity to present any available evidence bearing on that fact. In order further to facilitate the exercise of the authority provided by this rule, Rule 16 is also revised to encourage the court to schedule an order of trial that proceeds first with a presentation on an issue that is likely to be dispositive, if such an issue is identified in the course of pretrial. Such scheduling can be appropriate where the court is uncertain whether favorable action should be taken under Rule 56. Thus, the revision affords the court the alternative of denying a motion for summary judgment while scheduling a separate trial of the issue under Rule 42(b) or scheduling the trial to begin with a presentation on that essential fact which the opposing party seems unlikely to be able to maintain.

Paragraph (a)(2) retains the requirement that a motion for judgment be made prior to the close of the trial, subject to renewal after a jury verdict has been rendered. The purpose of this requirement is to assure the responding party an opportunity to cure any deficiency in that party's proof that may have been overlooked until called to the party's attention by a late motion for judgment. Cf. *Farley Transp. Co. v. Santa Fe Trail Transp. Co.,* 786 F.2d 1342 (9th Cir.1986) ("If the moving party is then permitted to make a later attack on the evidence through a motion for judgment notwithstanding the verdict or an appeal, the opposing party may be prejudiced by having lost the opportunity to present additional evidence before the case was submitted to the jury"); *Benson v. Allphin,* 786 F.2d 268 (7th Cir.1986) ("the motion for directed verdict at the close of all the evidence provides the nonmovant an opportunity to do what he can to remedy the deficiencies in his case . . .); *McLaughlin v. The Fellows Gear Shaper Co.,* 4 F.R.Serv.3d 607 (3d Cir.1986) (per Adams, J., dissenting: "This Rule serves important practical purposes in ensuring that neither party is precluded from presenting the most persuasive case possible and in preventing unfair surprise after a matter has been submitted to the jury"). At one time, this requirement was held to be of constitutional stature, being compelled by the Seventh Amendment. Cf. *Slocum v. New York Insurance Co.,* 228 U.S. 364 (1913). But cf. *Baltimore & Carolina Line v. Redman,* 295 U.S. 654 (1935).

The second sentence of paragraph (a)(2) does impose a requirement that the moving party articulate the basis on which a judgment as a matter of law might be rendered. The articulation is necessary to achieve the purpose of the requirement that the motion be made before the case is submitted to the jury, so that the responding party may seek to correct any overlooked deficiencies in the proof. The revision thus alters the result in cases in which courts have used various techniques to avoid the requirement that a motion for a directed verdict be made as a predicate to a motion for judgment notwithstanding the verdict. E.g., *Benson v. Allphin,* 788 F.2d 268 (7th Cir.1986) ("this circuit has allowed something less than a formal motion for directed verdict to preserve a party's right to move for judgment notwithstanding the verdict"). *See generally* 9 WRIGHT & MILLER, FEDERAL PRACTICE AND PROCEDURE § 2537 (1971 and Supp.). The information required with the motion may be supplied by explicit reference to materials and argument previously supplied to the court.

This subdivision deals only with the entry of judgment and not with the resolution of particular factual issues as a matter of law. The court may, as before, properly refuse to instruct a jury to decide an issue if a reasonable jury could on the evidence presented decide that issue in only one way.

Subdivision (b). This provision retains the concept of the former rule that the post-verdict motion is a renewal of an earlier motion made at the close of the evidence. One purpose of this concept was to avoid any question arising under the Seventh Amendment. *Montgomery Ward & Co. v. Duncan,* 311 U.S. 243 (1940). It remains useful as a means of defining the appropriate issue posed by the post-verdict motion. A post-trial motion for judgment can be granted only on grounds advanced in the pre-verdict motion. *E.g.,*

Kutner Buick, Inc. v. American Motors Corp., 848 F.2d 614 (3d Cir.1989).

Often it appears to the court or to the moving party that a motion for judgment as a matter of law made at the close of the evidence should be reserved for a post-verdict decision. This is so because a jury verdict for the moving party moots the issue and because a preverdict ruling gambles that a reversal may result in a new trial that might have been avoided. For these reasons, the court may often wisely decline to rule on a motion for judgment as a matter of law made at the close of the evidence, and it is not inappropriate for the moving party to suggest such a postponement of the ruling until after the verdict has been rendered.

In ruling on such a motion, the court should disregard any jury determination for which there is no legally sufficient evidentiary basis enabling a reasonable jury to make it. The court may then decide such issues as a matter of law and enter judgment if all other material issues have been decided by the jury on the basis of legally sufficient evidence, or by the court as a matter of law.

The revised rule is intended for use in this manner with Rule 49. Thus, the court may combine facts established as a matter of law either before trial under Rule 56 or at trial on the basis of the evidence presented with other facts determined by the jury under instructions provided under Rule 49 to support a proper judgment under this rule.

This provision also retains the former requirement that a post-trial motion under the rule must be made within 10 days after entry of a contrary judgment. The renewed motion must be served and filed as provided by Rule 5. A purpose of this requirement is to meet the requirements of F.R.App.P. 4(a)(4).

Subdivision (c). Revision of this subdivision conforms the language to the change in diction set forth in subdivision (a) of this revised rule.

Subdivision (d). Revision of this subdivision conforms the language to that of the previous subdivisions.

1993 Amendments

This technical amendment corrects an ambiguity in the text of the 1991 revision of the rule, which, as indicated in the Notes, was not intended to change the existing standards under which "directed verdicts" could be granted. This amendment makes clear that judgments as a matter of law in jury trials may be entered against both plaintiffs and defendants and with respect to issues or defenses that may not be wholly dispositive of a claim or defense.

1995 Amendments

The only change, other than stylistic, intended by this revision is to prescribe a uniform explicit time for filing of post-judgment motions under this rule—no later than 10 days after entry of the judgment. Previously, there was an inconsistency in the wording of Rules 50, 52, and 59 with respect to whether certain post-judgment motions had to be filed, or merely served, during that period. This inconsistency caused special problems when motions for a new trial were joined with other post-judgment motions. These motions affect the finality of the judgment, a matter often of importance to third persons as well as the parties and the court. The Committee believes that each of these rules should be revised to require filing before end of the 10-day period. Filing is an event that can be determined with certainty from court records. The phrase "no later than" is used—rather than "within"—to include post-judgment motions that sometimes are filed before actual entry of the judgment by the clerk. It should be noted that under Rule 6(a) Saturdays, Sundays, and legal holidays are excluded in measuring the 10-day period, and that under Rule 5 the motions when filed are to contain a certificate of service on other parties.

Rule 51. Instructions to Jury: Objection

At the close of the evidence or at such earlier time during the trial as the court reasonably directs, any party may file written requests that the court instruct the jury on the law as set forth in the requests. The court shall inform counsel of its proposed action upon the requests prior to their arguments to the jury. The court, at its election, may instruct the jury before or after argument, or both. No party may assign as error the giving or the failure to give an instruction unless that party objects thereto before the jury retires to consider its verdict, stating distinctly the matter objected to and the grounds of the objection. Opportunity shall be given to make the objection out of the hearing of the jury.

(As amended Mar. 2, 1987, eff. Aug. 1, 1987.)

ADVISORY COMMITTEE NOTES

1937 Adoption

Supreme Court Rule 8 requires exceptions to the charge of the court to the jury which shall distinctly state the several matters of law in the charge to which exception is taken. Similar provisions appear in the rules of the various Circuit Courts of Appeals.

1987 Amendment

Although Rule 51 in its present form specifies that the court shall instruct the jury only after the arguments of the parties are completed, in some districts (typically those in states where the practice is otherwise) it is common for the parties to stipulate to instruction before the arguments. The purpose of the amendment is to give the court discretion to instruct the jury either before or after argument. Thus, the rule as revised will permit resort to the long-standing federal practice or to an alternative procedure, which has been praised because it gives counsel the opportunity to explain the instructions, argue their application to the facts and thereby give the jury the maximum assistance in determining the issues and arriving at a good verdict on the law and the evidence. As an ancillary benefit, this approach aids counsel by supplying a natural outline so that arguments may be directed to the essential fact issues which the jury must decide. See generally Raymond, *Merits and Demerits of the Missouri System of Instructing Juries*, 5 St. Louis U.L.J. 317 (1959). Moreover, if the court instructs before an argument, counsel then know the precise words the court has chosen and need not speculate as to the words the court will later use in its instructions. Finally, by instructing ahead of argument the court has the attention of the jurors when they are fresh and can give their full attention to the court's instructions. It is more difficult to hold the attention of jurors after lengthy arguments.

Rule 52. Findings by the Court; Judgment on Partial Findings

(a) Effect. In all actions tried upon the facts without a jury or with an advisory jury, the court shall find the facts specially and state separately its conclusions of law thereon, and judgment shall be entered pursuant to Rule 58; and in granting or refusing interlocutory injunctions the court shall similarly set forth the findings of fact and conclusions of law which constitute the grounds of its action. Requests for findings are not necessary for purposes of review. Findings of fact, whether based on oral or documentary evidence, shall not be set aside unless clearly erroneous, and due regard shall be given to the opportunity of the trial court to judge of the credibility of the witnesses. The findings of a master, to the extent that the court adopts them, shall be considered as the findings of the court. It will be sufficient if the findings of fact and conclusions of law are stated orally and recorded in open court following the close of the evidence or appear in an opinion or memorandum of decision filed by the court. Findings of fact and conclusions of law are unnecessary on decisions of motions under Rule 12 or 56 or any other motion except as provided in subdivision (c) of this rule.

(b) Amendment. On a party's motion filed no later than 10 days after entry of judgment, the court may amend its findings—or make additional findings—and may amend the judgment accordingly. The motion may accompany a motion for a new trial under Rule 59. When findings of fact are made in actions tried without a jury, the sufficiency of the evidence supporting the findings may be later questioned whether or not in the district court the party raising the question objected to the findings, moved to amend them, or moved for partial findings.

(c) Judgment on Partial Findings. If during a trial without a jury a party has been fully heard on an issue and the court finds against the party on that issue, the court may enter judgment as a matter of law against that party with respect to a claim or defense that cannot under the controlling law be maintained or defeated without a favorable finding on that issue, or the court may decline to render any judgment until the close of all the evidence. Such a judgment shall be supported by findings of fact and conclusions of law as required by subdivision (a) of this rule.

(As amended Dec. 27, 1946, eff. Mar. 19, 1948; Jan. 21, 1963, eff. July 1, 1963; Apr. 28, 1983, eff. Aug. 1, 1983; Apr. 29, 1985, eff. Aug. 1, 1985; Apr. 30, 1991, eff. Dec. 1, 1991; Apr. 22, 1993, eff. Dec. 1, 1993; Apr. 27, 1995, eff. Dec. 1, 1995.)

ADVISORY COMMITTEE NOTES

1937 Adoption

See [former] Equity Rule 70½, as amended Nov. 25, 1935, (Findings of Fact and Conclusions of Law) and U.S.C., Title 28, [former] § 764 (Opinion, findings, and conclusions in action against United States) which are substantially continued in this rule. The provisions of U.S.C., Title 28, [former] §§ 773 (Trial of issues of fact; by court) and [former] 875 (Review in cases tried without a jury) are superseded in so far as they provide a different method of finding facts and a different method of appellate review. The rule stated in the third sentence of Subdivision (a) accords with the decisions on the scope of the review in modern federal equity practice. It is applicable to all classes of findings in cases tried without a jury whether the finding is of a fact concerning which there was conflict of testimony, or of a fact deduced or inferred from uncontradicted testimony. See *Silver King Coalition Mines Co. v. Silver King Consolidated Mining Co.*, C.C.A.8, 1913, 204 F. 166, certiorari denied 33 S.Ct. 1051, 229 U.S. 624, 57 L.Ed. 1356; *Warren v. Keep*, 1894, 15 S.Ct. 83, 155 U.S. 265, 39 L.Ed. 144; *Furrer v. Ferris*, 1892, 12 S.Ct. 821, 145 U.S. 132, 36 L.Ed. 649; *Tilghman v. Proctor*, 1888, 8 S.Ct. 894, 125 U.S. 136, 149, 31 L.Ed. 664; *Kimberly v. Arms*, 1889, 9 S.Ct. 355, 129 U.S. 512, 524, 32 L.Ed. 764. Compare *Kaeser & Blair Inc. v. Merchants' Ass'n*, C.C.A.6, 1933, 64 F.2d 575, 576; *Dunn v. Trefry*, C.C.A.1, 1919, 260 F. 147.

In the following states findings of fact are required in all cases tried without a jury (waiver by the parties being permitted as indicated at the end of the listing): Arkansas, Civ.Code (Crawford, 1934) § 364; California, Code Civ.Proc. (Deering, 1937) §§ 632, 634; Colorado, 1 Stat.Ann. (1935) Code Civ.Proc. §§ 232, 291 (in actions before referees or for possession of and damages to land); Connecticut, Gen.Stats. §§ 5660, 5664; Idaho, 1 Code Ann. (1932) §§ 7–302 through 7–305; Massachusetts (equity cases), 2 Gen.Laws (Ter.Ed., 1932) ch. 214, § 23; Minnesota, 2 Stat. (Mason, 1927) § 9311; Nevada, 4 Comp.Laws (Hillyer, 1929) §§ 8783–8784; New Jersey, Sup.Ct.Rule 113, 2 N.J.Misc. 1197, 1239 (1924); New Mexico, Stat.Ann. (Courtright, 1929) §§ 105–813; North Carolina, Code (1935) § 569; North Dakota, 2 Comp.Laws Ann. (1913) § 7641; Oregon, 2 Code Ann. (1930) §§ 2–502; South Carolina, Code (Michie, 1932) § 649; South Dakota, 1 Comp. Laws (1929) §§ 2525–2526; Utah, Rev.Stat.Ann. (1933) §§ 104–26–2, 104–26–3; Vermont (where jury trial waived), Pub.Laws (1933) § 2069; Washington, 2 Rev.Stat.Ann. (Remington, 1932) § 367; Wisconsin, Stat. (1935) § 270.33. The parties may waive this requirement for findings in California, Idaho, North Dakota, Nevada, New Mexico, Utah, and South Dakota.

In the following states the review of findings of fact in all non-jury cases, including jury waived cases, is assimilated to the equity review: Alabama, Code Ann. (Michie, 1928) §§ 9498, 8599; California, Code Civ.Proc. (Derring, 1937) § 956a; but see 20 Calif.Law Rev. 171 (1932); Colorado, *Johnson v. Kountze*, 1895, 43 P. 445, 21 Colo. 486, semble; Illinois, *Baker v. Hinricks*, 1934, 194 N.E. 284, 359 Ill. 138; *Weininger v. Metropolitan Fire Ins. Co.*, 1935, 195 N.E. 420, 359 Ill. 584, 98 A.L.R. 169; Minnesota, *State Bank of Gibbon v. Walter*, 1926, 208 N.W. 423, 167 Minn. 37; *Waldron v. Page*, 1934, 253 N.W. 894, 191 Minn. 302; New Jersey N.J.S.A. 2:27–241, 2:27–363, as interpreted in *Bussy v. Hatch*, 1920, 111 A. 546, 95 N.J.L. 56; New York, *York*

Mortgage Corporation v. Clotar Const. Corp., 1930, 172 N.E. 265, 254 N.Y. 128; North Dakota, Comp.Laws Ann. (1913) § 7846, as amended by N.D.Laws 1933, c. 208; *Milnor Holding Co. v. Holt*, 1933, 248 N.W. 315, 63 N.D. 362, 370; Oklahoma, *Wichita Mining and Improvement Co. v. Hale*, 1908, 94 P. 530, 20 Okl. 159; South Dakota, *Randall v. Burk Township*, 4 S.D. 337, 57 N.W. 4 (1893); Texas, *Custard v. Flowers*, 1929, 14 S.W.2d 109; Utah, Rev.Stat.Ann. (1933) § 104–41–5; Vermont, *Roberge v. Troy*, 1933, 163 A. 770, 105 Vt. 134; Washington, 2 Rev.Stat.Ann. (Remington, 1932) §§ 309–316; *McCullough v. Puget Sound Realty Associates*, 1913, 136 Pac. 1146, 76 Wash. 700, but see *Cornwall v. Anderson*, 1915, 148 P. 1, 85 Wash. 369; West Virginia, *Kinsey v. Carr*, 1906, 55 S.E. 1004, 60 W.Va. 449, semble; Wisconsin, Stat. (1935) § 251.09; *Campbell v. Sutliff*, 1927, 214 N.W. 374, 193 Wis. 370; *Gessler v. Erwin Co.*, 1924, 193 N.W. 303, 182 Wis. 315.

For examples of an assimilation of the review of findings of fact in cases tried without a jury to the review at law as made in several states, see Clark and Stone, *Review of Findings of Fact*, 4 U. of Chi.L.Rev. 190, 215 (1937).

1946 Amendment

Note to Subdivision (a). The amended rule makes clear that the requirement for findings of fact and conclusions of law thereon applies in a case with an advisory jury. This removes an ambiguity in the rule as originally stated, but carries into effect what has been considered its intent. 3 *Moore's Federal Practice*, 1938, 3119. *Hurwitz v. Hurwitz*, 1943, 136 F.2d 796, 78 U.S.App.D.C. 66.

The two sentences added at the end of Rule 52(a) eliminate certain difficulties which have arisen concerning findings and conclusions. The first of the two sentences permits findings of fact and conclusions of law to appear in an opinion or memorandum of decision. See, e.g., *United States v. One 1941 Ford Sedan*, S.D.Tex.1946, 65 F.Supp. 84. Under original Rule 52(a) some courts have expressed the view that findings and conclusions could not be incorporated in an opinion. *Detective Comics, Inc. v. Bruns Publications*, S.D.N.Y.1939, 28 F.Supp. 399; *Pennsylvania Co. for Insurance on Lives & Granting Annuities v. Cincinnati & L.E.R. Co.*, S.D.Ohio 1941, 43 F.Supp. 5; *United States v. Aluminum Co. of America*, S.D.N.Y.1941, 2 F.R.D. 224, 5 Fed. Rules Serv. 52a.11, Case 3; see also s.c., 44 F.Supp. 97. But, to the contrary, see *Wellman v. United States*, D.Mass.1938, 25 F.Supp. 868; *Cook v. United States*, D.Mass.1939, 26 F.Supp. 253; *Proctor v. White*, D.Mass.1939, 28 F.Supp. 161; *Green Valley Creamery, Inc. v. United States*, C.C.A.1, 1939, 108 F.2d 342. See also *Matton Oil Transfer Corp. v. The Dynamic*, C.C.A.2, 1941, 123 F.2d 999; *Carter Coal Co. v. Litz*, C.C.A.4, 1944, 140 F.2d 934; *Woodruff v. Heiser*, C.C.A.10, 1945, 150 F.2d 869; *Coca Cola Co. v. Busch*, Pa.1943, 7 Fed. Rules Serv. 59b.2, Case 4; Oglebay, *Some Developments in Bankruptcy Law*, 1944, 18 J. of Nat'l Ass'n of Ref. 68, 69. Findings of fact aid in the process of judgment and in defining for future cases the precise limitations of the issues and the determination thereon. Thus they not only aid the appellate court on review, *Hurwitz v. Hurwitz*, App.D.C.1943, 136 F.2d 796, 78 U.S.App.D.C. 66, but they are an important factor in the proper application of the doctrines of res judicata and estoppel by judgment. Nordbye, *Improvements in Statement of Findings of Fact and Conclusions of Law*, 1 F.R.D. 25, 26–27; *United States v. Forness*, C.C.A.2, 1942, 125 F.2d 928, certiorari denied 1942, 62 S.Ct. 1293, 316 U.S. 694, 86 L.Ed. 1764. These findings should represent the judge's own determination and not the long, often argumentative statements of successful counsel. *United States v. Forness*, supra; *United States v. Crescent Amusement Co.*, 1944, 1945, 65 S.Ct. 254, 323 U.S. 173, 89 L.Ed. 160. Consequently, they should be a part of the judge's opinion and decision, either stated therein or stated separately. *Matton Oil Transfer Corp. v. The Dynamic*, supra. But the judge need only make brief, definite, pertinent findings and conclusions upon the contested matters; there is no necessity for over-elaboration of detail or particularization of facts. *United States v. Forness*, supra; *United States v. Crescent Amusement Co.*, supra. See also *Petterson Lighterage & Towing Corp. v. New York Central R. Co.*, C.C.A.2, 1942, 126 F.2d 992; *Brown Paper Mill Co., Inc. v. Irwin*, C.C.A.8, 1943, 134 F.2d 337; *Allen Bradley Co. v. Local Union No. 3, I.B.E.W.*, C.C.A.2, 1944, 145 F.2d 215, reversed on other grounds 65 S.Ct. 1533, 325 U.S. 797; *Young v. Murphy, Ohio* 1946, 9 Fed.Rules Serv. 52a.11, Case 2.

The last sentence of Rule 52(a) as amended will remove any doubt that findings and conclusions are unnecessary upon decision of a motion, particularly one under Rule 12 or Rule 56, except as provided in amended Rule 41(b). As so holding, see *Thomas v. Peyser*, App.D.C.1941, 118 F.2d 369; *Schad v. Twentieth Century-Fox Corp.*, C.C.A.3, 1943, 136 F.2d 991; *Prudential Ins. Co. of America v. Goldstein*, N.Y.1942, 43 F.Supp. 767; *Somers Coal Co. v. United States*, N.D.Ohio 1942, 2 F.R.D. 532, 6 Fed.Rules Serv. 52a.1, Case 1; *Pen-Ken Oil & Gas Corp. v. Warfield Natural Gas Co.*, E.D.Ky.1942, 2 F.R.D. 355, 5 Fed. Rules Serv. 52a.1, Case 3; also Commentary, *Necessity of Findings of Fact*, 1941, 4 Fed. Rules Serv. 936.

1963 Amendment

This amendment conforms to the amendment of Rule 58. See the Advisory Committee's Note to Rule 58, as amended.

1983 Amendment

Rule 52(a) has been amended to revise its penultimate sentence to provide explicitly that the district judge may make the findings of fact and conclusions of law required in nonjury cases orally. Nothing in the prior text of the rule forbids this practice, which is widely utilized by district judges. See Christensen, *A Modest Proposal for Immeasurable Improvement*, 64 A.B.A.J. 693 (1978). The objective is to lighten the burden on the trial court in preparing findings in nonjury cases. In addition, the amendment should reduce the number of published district court opinions that embrace written findings.

1985 Amendment

Rule 52(a) has been amended (1) to avoid continued confusion and conflicts among the circuits as to the standard of appellate review of findings of fact by the court, (2) to eliminate the disparity between the standard of review as literally stated in Rule 52(a) and the practice of some courts of appeals, and (3) to promote nationwide uniformity. See Note, *Rule 52(a): Appellate Review of Findings of Fact Based on Documentary or Undisputed Evidence*, 49 Va. L.Rev. 506, 536 (1963).

Some courts of appeal have stated that when a trial court's findings do not rest on demeanor evidence and evaluation of a witness' credibility, there is no reason to defer to the trial court's findings and the appellate court more readily can find them to be clearly erroneous. See, e.g., *Marcum v. United States,* 621 F.2d 142, 144–45 (5th Cir.1980). Others go further, holding that appellate review may be had without application of the "clearly erroneous" test since the appellate court is in as good a position as the trial court to review a purely documentary record. See, *e.g., Atari, Inc. v. North American Philips Consumer Electronics Corp.,* 672 F.2d 607, 614 (7th Cir.), cert. denied, 459 U.S. 880 (1982); *Lydle v. United States,* 635 F.2d 763, 765 n. 1 (6th Cir.1981); *Swanson v. Baker Indus., Inc.,* 615 F.2d 479, 483 (8th Cir.1980); *Taylor v. Lombard,* 606 F.2d 371, 372 (2d Cir.1979), cert. denied, 445 U.S. 946 (1980); *Jack Kahn Music Co. v. Baldwin Piano & Organ Co.,* 604 F.2d 755, 758 (2d Cir.1979); *John R. Thompson Co. v. United States,* 477 F.2d 164, 167 (7th Cir.1973).

A third group has adopted the view that the "clearly erroneous" rule applies in all nonjury cases even when findings are based solely on documentary evidence or on inferences from undisputed facts. See, *e.g., Maxwell v. Sumner,* 673 F.2d 1031, 1036 (9th Cir.), *cert. denied,* 459 U.S. 976 (1982); *United States v. Texas Education Agency,* 647 F.2d 504, 506–07 (5th Cir.1981), *cert. denied,* 454 U.S. 1143 (1982); *Constructora Maza, Inc. v. Banco de Ponce,* 616 F.2d 573, 576 (1st Cir.1980); *In re Sierra Trading Corp.,* 482 F.2d 333, 337 (10th Cir.1973); *Case v. Morrisette,* 475 F.2d 1300, 1306–07 (D.C.Cir.1973).

The commentators also disagree as to the proper interpretation of the Rule. *Compare* Wright, *The Doubtful Omniscience of Appellate Courts,* 41 Minn.L.Rev. 751, 769–70 (1957) (language and intent of Rule support view that "clearly erroneous" test should apply to all forms of evidence), *and* 9 C. Wright & A. Miller, *Federal Practice and Procedure: Civil § 2587,* at 740 (1971) (language of the Rule is clear), *with* 5A J. Moore, *Federal Practice* ¶ 52.04, 2687–88 (2d ed. 1982) (Rule as written supports broader review of findings based on non-demeanor testimony).

The Supreme Court has not clearly resolved the issue. See, *Bose Corp. v. Consumers Union of United States, Inc.,* 466 U.S. 485, 104 S.Ct. 1949, 1958 (1984); *Pullman Standard v. Swint,* 456 U.S. 273, 293 (1982); *United States v. General Motors Corp.,* 384 U.S. 127, 141 n. 16 (1966); *United States v. United States Gypsum Co.,* 333 U.S. 364, 394–96 (1948).

The principal argument advanced in favor of a more searching appellate review of findings by the district court based solely on documentary evidence is that the rationale of Rule 52(a) does not apply when the findings do not rest on the trial court's assessment of credibility of the witnesses but on an evaluation of documentary proof and the drawing of inferences from it, thus eliminating the need for any special deference to the trial court's findings. These considerations are outweighed by the public interest in the stability and judicial economy that would be promoted by recognizing that the trial court, not the appellate tribunal, should be the finder of the facts. To permit courts of appeals to share more actively in the fact-finding function would tend to undermine the legitimacy of the district courts in the eyes of litigants, multiply appeals by encouraging appellate retrial of some factual issues, and needlessly reallocate judicial authority.

1991 Amendment

Subdivision (c) is added. It parallels the revised Rule 50(a), but is applicable to non-jury trials. It authorizes the court to enter judgment at any time that it can appropriately make a dispositive finding of fact on the evidence.

The new subdivision replaces part of Rule 41(b), which formerly authorized a dismissal at the close of the plaintiff's case if the plaintiff had failed to carry an essential burden of proof. Accordingly, the reference to Rule 41 formerly made in subdivision (a) of this rule is deleted.

As under the former Rule 41(b), the court retains discretion to enter no judgment prior to the close of the evidence.

Judgment entered under this rule differs from a summary judgment under Rule 56 in the nature of the evaluation made by the court. A judgment on partial findings is made after the court has heard all the evidence bearing on the crucial issue of fact, and the finding is reversible only if the appellate court finds it to be "clearly erroneous." A summary judgment, in contrast, is made on the basis of facts established on account of the absence of contrary evidence or presumptions; such establishments of fact are rulings on questions of law as provided in Rule 56(a) and are not shielded by the "clear error" standard of review.

1993 Amendments

This technical amendment corrects an ambiguity in the text of the 1991 revision of the rule, similar to the revision being made to Rule 50. This amendment makes clear that judgments as a matter of law in nonjury trials may be entered against both plaintiffs and defendants and with respect to issues or defenses that may not be wholly dispositive of a claim or defense.

1995 Amendments

The only change, other than stylistic, intended by this revision is to require that any motion to amend or add findings after a nonjury trial must be filed no later than 10 days after entry of the judgment. Previously, there was an inconsistency in the wording of Rules 50, 52, and 59 with respect to whether certain post-judgment motions had to be filed, or merely served, during that period. This inconsistency caused special problems when motions for a new trial were joined with other post-judgment motions. These motions affect the finality of the judgment, a matter often of importance to third persons as well as the parties and the court. The Committee believes that each of these rules should be revised to require filing before end of the 10–day period. Filing is an event that can be determined with certainty from court records. The phrase "no later than" is used—rather than "within"—to include post-judgment motions that sometimes are filed before actual entry of the judgment by the clerk. It should be noted that under Rule 6(a) Saturdays, Sundays, and legal holidays are excluded in measuring the 10–day period, and that under Rule 5 the motions when filed are to contain a certificate of service on other parties.

Rule 53. Masters

(a) Appointment and Compensation. The court in which any action is pending may appoint a special master therein. As used in these rules, the word "master" includes a referee, an auditor, an examiner, and an assessor. The compensation to be allowed to a master shall be fixed by the court, and shall be charged upon such of the parties or paid out of any fund or subject matter of the action, which is in the custody and control of the court as the court may direct; provided that this provision for compensation shall not apply when a United States magistrate judge is designated to serve as a master. The master shall not retain the master's report as security for the master's compensation; but when the party ordered to pay the compensation allowed by the court does not pay it after notice and within the time prescribed by the court, the master is entitled to a writ of execution against the delinquent party.

(b) Reference. A reference to a master shall be the exception and not the rule. In actions to be tried by a jury, a reference shall be made only when the issues are complicated; in actions to be tried without a jury, save in matters of account and of difficult computation of damages, a reference shall be made only upon a showing that some exceptional condition requires it. Upon the consent of the parties, a magistrate judge may be designated to serve as a special master without regard to the provisions of this subdivision.

(c) Powers. The order of reference to the master may specify or limit the master's powers and may direct the master to report only upon particular issues or to do or perform particular acts or to receive and report evidence only and may fix the time and place for beginning and closing the hearings and for the filing of the master's report. Subject to the specifications and limitations stated in the order, the master has and shall exercise the power to regulate all proceedings in every hearing before the master and to do all acts and take all measures necessary or proper for the efficient performance of the master's duties under the order. The master may require the production before the master of evidence upon all matters embraced in the reference, including the production of all books, papers, vouchers, documents, and writings applicable thereto. The master may rule upon the admissibility of evidence unless otherwise directed by the order of reference and has the authority to put witnesses on oath and may examine them and may call the parties to the action and examine them upon oath. When a party so requests, the master shall make a record of the evidence offered and excluded in the same manner and subject to the same limitations as provided in the Federal Rules of Evidence for a court sitting without a jury.

(d) Proceedings.

(1) Meetings. When a reference is made, the clerk shall forthwith furnish the master with a copy of the order of reference. Upon receipt thereof unless the order of reference otherwise provides, the master shall forthwith set a time and place for the first meeting of the parties or their attorneys to be held within 20 days after the date of the order of reference and shall notify the parties or their attorneys. It is the duty of the master to proceed with all reasonable diligence. Either party, on notice to the parties and master, may apply to the court for an order requiring the master to speed the proceedings and to make the report. If a party fails to appear at the time and place appointed, the master may proceed ex parte or, in the master's discretion, adjourn the proceedings to a future day, giving notice to the absent party of the adjournment.

(2) Witnesses. The parties may procure the attendance of witnesses before the master by the issuance and service of subpoenas as provided in Rule 45. If without adequate excuse a witness fails to appear or give evidence, the witness may be punished as for a contempt and be subjected to the consequences, penalties, and remedies provided in Rules 37 and 45.

(3) Statement of Accounts. When matters of accounting are in issue before the master, the master may prescribe the form in which the accounts shall be submitted and in any proper case may require or receive in evidence a statement by a certified public accountant who is called as a witness. Upon objection of a party to any of the items thus submitted or upon a showing that the form of statement is insufficient, the master may require a different form of statement to be furnished, or the accounts or specific items thereof to be proved by oral examination of the accounting parties or upon written interrogatories or in such other manner as the master directs.

(e) Report.

(1) Contents and Filing. The master shall prepare a report upon the matters submitted to the master by the order of reference and, if required to make findings of fact and conclusions of law, the master shall set them forth in the report. The master shall file the report with the clerk of the court and serve on all parties notice of the filing. In an action to be tried without a jury, unless otherwise directed by the order of reference, the master shall file with the report a transcript of the proceedings and of the evidence and the original exhibits. Unless otherwise directed by the order of reference, the master shall serve a copy of the report on each party.

(2) In Non-Jury Actions. In an action to be tried without a jury the court shall accept the master's findings of fact unless clearly erroneous. Within 10 days after being served with notice of the filing of the report any party may serve written objections thereto upon the other parties. Application to the court for action upon the report and upon objections thereto shall be by motion and upon notice as prescribed in Rule 6(d). The court after hearing may adopt the report or may modify it or may reject it in whole or in part or may receive further evidence or may recommit it with instructions.

(3) In Jury Actions. In an action to be tried by a jury the master shall not be directed to report the evidence. The master's findings upon the issues submitted to the master are admissible as evidence of the matters found and may be read to the jury, subject to the ruling of the court upon any objections in point of law which may be made to the report.

(4) Stipulation as to Findings. The effect of a master's report is the same whether or not the parties have consented to the reference; but, when the parties stipulate that a master's findings of fact shall be final, only questions of law arising upon the report shall thereafter be considered.

(5) Draft Report. Before filing the master's report a master may submit a draft thereof to counsel for all parties for the purpose of receiving their suggestions.

(f) Application to Magistrate Judge. A magistrate judge is subject to this rule only when the order referring a matter to the magistrate judge expressly provides that the reference is made under this rule.
(As amended Feb. 28, 1966, eff. July 1, 1966; Apr. 28, 1983, eff. Aug. 1, 1983; Mar. 2, 1987, eff. Aug. 1, 1987; Apr. 30, 1991, eff. Dec. 1, 1991; Apr. 22, 1993, eff. Dec. 1, 1993.)

ADVISORY COMMITTEE NOTES

1937 Adoption

Note to Subdivision (a). This is a modification of former Equity Rule 68 (Appointment and Compensation of Masters).

Note to Subdivision (b). This is substantially the first sentence of [former] Equity Rule 59 (Reference to Master—Exceptional, Not Usual) extended to actions formerly legal. See *Ex parte Peterson,* 1920, 40 S.Ct. 543, 253 U.S. 300, 64 L.Ed. 919.

Note to Subdivision (c). This is [former] Equity Rules 62 (Powers of Master) and 65 (Claimants Before Master Examinable by Him) with slight modifications. Compare [former] Equity Rules 49 (Evidence Taken Before Examiners, Etc.) and 51 (Evidence Taken Before Examiners, Etc.).

Note to Subdivision (d). (1) This is substantially a combination of the second sentence of [former] Equity Rule 59 (Reference to Master—Exceptional, Not Usual) and [former] Equity Rule 60 (Proceedings Before Master). Compare [former] Equity Rule 53 (Notice of Taking Testimony Before Examiner, Etc.).

(2) This is substantially [former] Equity Rule 52 (Attendance of Witnesses Before Commissioner, Master, or Examiner).

(3) This is substantially [former] Equity Rule 63 (Form of Accounts Before Master).

Note to Subdivision (e). This contains the substance of [former] Equity Rules 61 (Master's Report—Documents Identified but not Set Forth), 61½ (Master's Report—Presumption as to Correctness—Review), and 66 (Return of Master's Report—Exceptions—Hearing), with modifications as to the form and effect of the report and for inclusion of reports by auditors, referees, and examiners, and references in actions formerly legal. Compare [former] Equity Rules 49 (Evidence Taken Before Examiners, Etc.) and 67 (Costs on Exceptions to Master's Report). See *Camden v. Stuart,* 144 U.S. 104, 12 S.Ct. 585, 36 L.Ed. 363 (1892); *Ex parte Peterson,* 253 U.S. 300, 40 S.Ct. 543, 64 L.Ed. 919 (1920).

1966 Amendment

These changes are designed to preserve the admiralty practice whereby difficult computations are referred to a commissioner or assessor, especially after an interlocutory judgment determining liability. As to separation of issues for trial see Rule 42(b).

1983 Amendment

Subdivision (a). The creation of full-time magistrates, who serve at government expense and have no nonjudicial duties competing for their time, eliminates the need to appoint standing masters. Thus the prior provision in Rule 53(a) authorizing the appointment of standing masters is deleted. Additionally, the definition of "master" in subdivision (a) now eliminates the superseded office of commissioner.

The term "special master" is retained in Rule 53 in order to maintain conformity with 28 U.S.C. § 636(b)(2), authorizing a judge to designate a magistrate "to serve as a special master pursuant to the applicable provisions of this title and the Federal Rules of Civil Procedure for the United States District Courts." Obviously, when a magistrate serves as a special master, the provisions for compensation of masters are inapplicable, and the amendment to subdivision (a) so provides.

Although the existence of magistrates may make the appointment of outside masters unnecessary in many instances, see, e.g., *Gautreaux v. Chicago Housing Authority,* 384 F.Supp. 37 (N.D.Ill.1974), mandamus denied *sub nom., Chicago Housing Authority v. Austin,* 511 F.2d 82 (7th Cir. 1975); *Avco Corp. v. American Tel. & Tel. Co.,* 68 F.R.D. 532 (S.D.Ohio 1975), such masters may prove useful when some special expertise is desired or when a magistrate is unavailable for lengthy and detailed supervision of a case.

Subdivision (b). The provisions of 28 U.S.C. § 636(b)(2) not only permit magistrates to serve as masters under Rule 53(b) but also eliminate the exceptional condition requirement of Rule 53(b) when the reference is made with the consent of the parties. The amendment to subdivision (b) brings Rule 53 into harmony with the statute by exempting magistrates, appointed with the consent of the parties, from the general requirement that some exceptional condition requires the reference. It should be noted that subdivision (b) does not address the question, raised in recent decisional law and commentary, as to whether the exceptional condition requirement is applicable when *private masters* who are not magistrates are appointed with the consent of the parties. See Silberman, *Masters and Magistrates Part II: The American Analogue,* 50 N.Y.U.L.Rev. 1297, 1354 (1975).

Subdivision (c). The amendment recognizes the abrogation of Federal Rule 43(c) by the Federal Rules of Evidence.

Subdivision (f). The new subdivision responds to confusion flowing from the dual authority for references of pretrial matters to magistrates. Such references can be made, with or without the consent of the parties, pursuant to Rule 53 or under 28 U.S.C. § 636(b)(1)(A) and (b)(1)(B). There are a number of distinctions between references made under the statute and under the rule. For example, under the statute nondispositive pretrial matters may be referred to a magistrate, without consent, for final determination with reconsideration by the district judge if the magistrate's order is clearly erroneous or contrary to law. Under the rule, however, the appointment of a master, without consent of the parties, to supervise discovery would require some exceptional condition (Rule 53(b)) and would subject the proceedings to the report procedures of Rule 53(e). If an order of reference does not clearly articulate the source of the court's authority the resulting proceedings could be subject to attack on grounds of the magistrate's noncompliance with the provisions of Rule 53. This subdivision therefore establishes a presumption that the limitations of Rule 53 are not applicable unless the reference is specifically made subject to Rule 53.

A magistrate serving as a special master under 28 U.S.C. § 636(b)(2) is governed by the provisions of Rule 53, with the exceptional condition requirement lifted in the case of a consensual reference.

1987 Amendment

The amendments are technical. No substantive change is intended.

1991 Amendment

The purpose of the revision is to expedite proceedings before a master. The former rule required only a filing of the master's report, with the clerk then notifying the parties of the filing. To receive a copy, a party would then be required to secure it from the clerk. By transmitting directly to the parties, the master can save some efforts of counsel. Some local rules have previously required such action by the master.

1993 Amendments

This revision is made to conform the rule to changes made by the Judicial Improvements Act of 1990.

HISTORICAL NOTES

References in Text

The Federal Rules of Evidence, referred to in subd. (d), are set out in this title.

Change of Name

United States magistrate appointed under section 631 of Title 28, Judiciary and Judicial Procedure, to be known as United States magistrate judge after Dec. 1, 1990, with any reference to United States magistrate or magistrate in Title 28, in any other Federal statute, etc., deemed a reference to United States magistrate judge appointed under section 631 of Title 28, see section 321 of Pub.L. 101–650, set out as a note under section 631 of Title 28.

VII. JUDGMENT

Rule 54. Judgments; Costs

(a) Definition; Form. "Judgment" as used in these rules includes a decree and any order from which an appeal lies. A judgment shall not contain a recital of pleadings, the report of a master, or the record of prior proceedings.

(b) Judgment Upon Multiple Claims or Involving Multiple Parties. When more than one claim for relief is presented in an action, whether as a claim, counterclaim, cross-claim, or third-party claim, or when multiple parties are involved, the court may direct the entry of a final judgment as to one or more but fewer than all of the claims or parties only upon an express determination that there is no just reason for delay and upon an express direction for the entry of judgment. In the absence of such determination and direction, any order or other form of decision, however designated, which adjudicates fewer than all the claims or the rights and liabilities of fewer than all the parties shall not terminate the action as to any of the claims or parties, and the order or other form of decision is subject to revision at any time before the entry of judgment adjudicating all the claims and the rights and liabilities of all the parties.

(c) Demand for Judgment. A judgment by default shall not be different in kind from or exceed in amount that prayed for in the demand for judgment. Except as to a party against whom a judgment is entered by default, every final judgment shall grant the relief to which the party in whose favor it is rendered is entitled, even if the party has not demanded such relief in the party's pleadings.

(d) Costs; Attorneys' Fees.

(1) Costs Other than Attorneys' Fees. Except when express provision therefor is made either in a statute of the United States or in these rules, costs other than attorneys' fees shall be allowed as of course to the prevailing party unless the court otherwise directs; but costs against the United States, its officers, and agencies shall be imposed only to the extent permitted by law. Such costs may be taxed by the clerk on one day's notice. On motion served within 5 days thereafter, the action of the clerk may be reviewed by the court.

(2) Attorneys' Fees.

(A) Claims for attorneys' fees and related nontaxable expenses shall be made by motion unless the substantive law governing the action provides for the recovery of such fees as an element of damages to be proved at trial.

(B) Unless otherwise provided by statute or order of the court, the motion must be filed and served no later than 14 days after entry of judgment; must specify the judgment and the statute, rule, or other grounds entitling the moving party to the award; and must state the amount or provide a fair estimate of the amount sought. If directed by the court, the motion shall also disclose the terms of any agreement with respect to fees to be paid for the services for which claim is made.

(C) On request of a party or class member, the court shall afford an opportunity for adversary submissions with respect to the motion in accordance with Rule 43(e) or Rule 78. The court may determine issues of liability for fees before receiving submissions bearing on issues of evaluation of services for which liability is imposed by the court. The court shall find the facts and state its conclusions of law as provided in Rule 52(a), and a judgment shall be set forth in a separate document as provided in Rule 58.

(D) By local rule the court may establish special procedures by which issues relating to such fees may be resolved without extensive evidentiary hearings. In addition, the court may refer issues relating to the value of services to a special master under Rule 53 without regard to the provisions of subdivision (b) thereof and may refer a motion for attorneys' fees to a magistrate judge under Rule 72(b) as if it were a dispositive pretrial matter.

(E) The provisions of subparagraphs (A) through (D) do not apply to claims for fees and expenses as sanctions for violations of these rules or under 28 U.S.C. § 1927.

(As amended Dec. 27, 1946, eff. Mar. 19, 1948; Apr. 17, 1961, eff. July 19, 1961; Mar. 2, 1987, eff. Aug. 1, 1987; Apr. 22, 1993, eff. Dec. 1, 1993.)

ADVISORY COMMITTEE NOTES

1937 Adoption

Note to Subdivision (a). The second sentence is derived substantially from [former] Equity Rule 71 (Form of Decree).

Note to Subdivision (b). This provides for the separate judgment of equity and code practice. See Wis.Stat. (1935) § 270.54; Compare N.Y.C.P.A. (1937) § 476.

Note to Subdivision (c). For the limitation on default contained in the first sentence, see 2 N.D.Comp.Laws Ann. (1913) § 7680; N.Y.C.P.A. (1937) § 479. Compare *English Rules Under the Judicature Act* (The Annual Practice, 1937) O. 13, r.r. 3–12. The remainder is a usual code provision. It makes clear that a judgment should give the relief to which a party is entitled, regardless of whether it is legal or equitable or both. This necessarily includes the deficiency judgment in foreclosure cases formerly provided for by Equity Rule 10 (Decree for Deficiency in Foreclosures, Etc.).

Note to Subdivision (d). For the present rule in common law actions, see *Ex parte Peterson,* 253 U.S. 300, 40 S.Ct. 543, 64 L.Ed. 919 (1920); Payne, *Costs in Common Law Actions in the Federal Courts* (1935), 21 Va.L.Rev. 397.

The provisions as to costs in actions in forma pauperis contained in U.S.C., Title 28, former §§ 832–836 [now 1915] are unaffected by this rule. Other sections of U.S.C., Title 28, which are unaffected by this rule are: [former] §§ 815 (Costs; plaintiff not entitled to, when), 821 [now 1928] (Costs; infringement of patent; disclaimer), 825 (Costs; several actions), 829 [now 1927] (Costs; attorney liable for, when), and 830 [now 1920] (Costs; bill of; taxation).

The provisions of the following and similar statutes as to costs against the United States and its officers and agencies are specifically continued:

U.S.C., Title 15, §§ 77v(a), 78aa, 79y (Securities and Exchange Commission)

U.S.C., Title 16, § 825p (Federal Power Commission)

U.S.C., Title 26, [former] §§ 3679(d) and 3745(d) (Internal revenue actions)

U.S.C., Title 26, [former] § 3770(b)(2) (Reimbursement of costs of recovery against revenue officers)

U.S.C., Title 28, [former] § 817 (Internal revenue actions)

U.S.C., Title 28, § 836 [now 1915] (United States—actions in *forma pauperis*)

U.S.C., Title 28, § 842 [now 2006] (Actions against revenue officers)

U.S.C., Title 28, § 870 [now 2408] (United States—in certain cases)

U.S.C., Title 28, [former] § 906 (United States—foreclosure actions)

U.S.C., Title 47, § 401 (Communications Commission)

The provisions of the following and similar statutes as to costs are unaffected:

U.S.C., Title 7, § 210(f) (Actions for damages based on an order of the Secretary of Agriculture under Stockyards Act)

U.S.C., Title 7, § 499g(c) (Appeals from reparations orders of Secretary of Agriculture under Perishable Commodities Act)

U.S.C., Title 8, [former] § 45 (Action against district attorneys in certain cases)

U.S.C., Title 15, § 15 (Actions for injuries due to violation of antitrust laws)

U.S.C., Title 15, § 72 (Actions for violation of law forbidding importation or sale of articles at less than market value or wholesale prices)

U.S.C., Title 15, § 77k (Actions by persons acquiring securities registered with untrue statements under Securities Act of 1933)

U.S.C., Title 15, § 78i(e) (Certain actions under the Securities Exchange Act of 1934)

U.S.C., Title 15, § 78r (Similar to 78i(e))

U.S.C., Title 15, § 96 (Infringement of trade-mark—damages)

U.S.C., Title 15, § 99 (Infringement of trade-mark—injunctions)

U.S.C., Title 15, § 124 (Infringement of trade-mark—damages)

U.S.C., Title 19, § 274 (Certain actions under customs law)
U.S.C., Title 30, § 32 (Action to determine right to possession of mineral lands in certain cases)
U.S.C., Title 31, §§ 232 [now 3730] and 234 [former] (Action for making false claims upon United States)
U.S.C., Title 33, § 926 (Actions under Harbor Workers' Compensation Act)
U.S.C., Title 35, § 67 [now 281, 284] (Infringement of patent—damages)
U.S.C., Title 35, § 69 [now 282] (Infringement of patent—pleading and proof)
U.S.C., Title 35, § 71 [now 288] (Infringement of patent—when specification too broad)
U.S.C., Title 45, § 153p (Actions for non-compliance with an order of National R.R. Adjustment Board for payment of money)
U.S.C., Title 46, [former] § 38 (Action for penalty for failure to register vessel)
U.S.C., Title 46, § 829 (Action based on non-compliance with an order of Maritime Commission for payment of money)
U.S.C., Title 46, § 941 (Certain actions under Ship Mortgage Act)
U.S.C., Title 46, § 1227 (Actions for damages for violation of certain provisions of the Merchant Marine Act, 1936)
U.S.C., Title 47, § 206 (Actions for certain violations of Communications Act of 1934)
U.S.C., Title 49, § 16(2) [now 11705] (Action based on non-compliance with an order of I.C.C. for payment of money)

1946 Amendment

Note. The historic rule in the federal courts has always prohibited piecemeal disposal of litigation and permitted appeals only from final judgments except in those special instances covered by statute. *Hohorst v. Hamburg—American Packet Co.*, 1893, 13 S.Ct. 590, 148 U.S. 262, 37 L.Ed. 443; *Rexford v. Brunswick-Balke-Collender Co.*, 1913, 33 S.Ct. 515, 228 U.S. 339, 57 L.Ed. 864; *Collins v. Miller*, 1920, 40 S.Ct. 347, 252 U.S. 364, 64 L.Ed. 616. Rule 54(b) was originally adopted in view of the wide scope and possible content of the newly created "civil action" in order to avoid the possible injustice of a delay in judgment of a distinctly separate claim to await adjudication of the entire case. It was not designed to overturn the settled federal rule stated above, which, indeed, has more recently been reiterated in *Catlin v. United States*, 1945, 65 S.Ct. 631, 324 U.S. 229, 89 L.Ed. 911. See also *United States v. Florian*, 1941, 61 S.Ct. 713, 312 U.S. 656, 85 L.Ed. 1105; *Reeves v. Beardall*, 1942, 62 S.Ct. 1085, 316 U.S. 283, 86 L.Ed. 1478.

Unfortunately, this was not always understood, and some confusion ensued. Hence situations arose where district courts made a piecemeal disposition of an action and entered what the parties thought amounted to a judgment, although a trial remained to be had on other claims similar or identical with those disposed of. In the interim the parties did not know their ultimate rights, and accordingly took an appeal, thus putting the finality of the partial judgment in question. While most appellate courts have reached a result generally in accord with the intent of the rule, yet there have been divergent precedents and division of views which have served to render the issues more clouded to the parties appellant. It hardly seems a case where multiplicity of precedents will tend to remove the problem from debate. The problem is presented and discussed in the following cases: *Atwater v. North American Coal Corp.*, C.C.A.2, 1940, 111 F.2d 125; *Rosenblum v. Dingfelder*, C.C.A.2, 1940, 111 F.2d 406; *Audi-Vision, Inc. v. RCA Mfg. Co., Inc.*, C.C.A.2, 1943, 136 F.2d 621; *Zalkind v. Scheinman*, C.C.A.2, 1943, 139 F.2d 895; *Oppenheimer v. F. J. Young & Co., Inc.*, C.C.A.2, 1944, 144 F.2d 387; *Libbey-Owens-Ford Glass Co. v. Sylvania Industrial Corp.*, C.C.A.2, 1946, 154 F.2d 814, certiorari denied 1946, 66 S.Ct. 1353, 328 U.S. 859, 90 L.Ed. 1630; *Zarati Steamship Co. v. Park Bridge Corp.*, C.C.A.2, 1946, 154 F.2d 377; *Baltimore and Ohio R. Co. v. United Fuel Gas Co.*, C.C.A.4, 1946, 154 F.2d 545; *Jefferson Electric Co. v. Sola Electric Co.*, C.C.A.7, 1941, 122 F.2d 124; *Leonard v. Socony-Vacuum Oil Co.*, C.C.A.7, 1942, 130 F.2d 535; *Markham v. Kasper*, C.C.A.7, 1945, 152 F.2d 270; *Hanney v. Franklin Fire Ins. Co. of Philadelphia*, C.C.A.9, 1944, 142 F.2d 864; *Toomey v. Toomey*, App.D.C.1945, 149 F.2d 19, 80 U.S.App. D.C. 77.

In view of the difficulty thus disclosed, the Advisory Committee in its two preliminary drafts of proposed amendments attempted to redefine the original rule with particular stress upon the interlocutory nature of partial judgments which did not adjudicate all claims arising out of a single transaction or occurrence. This attempt appeared to meet with almost universal approval from those of the profession commenting upon it, although there were, of course, helpful suggestions for additional changes in language or clarification of detail. But cf. Circuit Judge Frank's dissenting opinion in *Libbey-Owens-Ford Glass Co. v. Sylvania Industrial Corp.*, supra, n. 21 of the dissenting opinion. The Committee, however, became convinced on careful study of its own proposals that the seeds of ambiguity still remained, and that it had not completely solved the problem of piecemeal appeals. After extended consideration, it concluded that a retention of the older federal rule was desirable, and that this rule needed only the exercise of a discretionary power to afford a remedy in the infrequent harsh case to provide a simple, definite, workable rule. This is afforded by amended Rule 54(b). It re-establishes an ancient policy with clarity and precision. For the possibility of staying execution where not all claims are disposed of under Rule 54(b), see amended Rule 62(h).

1961 Amendment

This rule permitting appeal, upon the trial court's determination of "no just reason for delay," from a judgment upon one or more but less than all the claims in an action, has generally been given a sympathetic construction by the courts and its validity is settled. *Reeves v. Beardall*, 316 U.S. 283 (1942); *Sears, Roebuck & Co. v. Mackey*, 351 U.S. 427 (1956); *Cold Metal Process Co. v. United Engineering & Foundry Co.*, 351 U.S. 445 (1956).

A serious difficulty has, however, arisen because the rule speaks of claims but nowhere mentions parties. A line of cases has developed in the circuits consistently holding the rule to be inapplicable to the dismissal, even with the requisite trial court determination, of one or more but less than all defendants jointly charged in an action, i.e. charged with various forms of concerted or related wrongdoing or related liability. See *Mull v. Ackerman*, 279 F.2d 25 (2d Cir. 1960); *Richards v. Smith*, 276 F.2d 652 (5th Cir. 1960); *Hardy v. Bankers Life & Cas. Co.*, 222 F.2d 827 (7th Cir. 1955);

Steiner v. 20th Century-Fox Film Corp., 220 F.2d 105 (9th Cir. 1955). For purposes of Rule 54(b) it was arguable that there were as many "claims" as there were parties defendant and that the rule in its present text applied where less than all of the parties were dismissed, cf. *United Artists Corp. v. Masterpiece Productions, Inc.*, 221 F.2d 213, 215 (2d Cir. 1955); *Bowling Machines, Inc. v. First Nat. Bank*, 283 F.2d 39 (1st Cir. 1960); but the Courts of Appeals are now committed to an opposite view.

The danger of hardship through delay of appeal until the whole action is concluded may be at least as serious in the multiple-parties situations as in multiple-claims cases, see *Pabellon v. Grace Line, Inc.*, 191 F.2d 169, 179 (2d Cir. 1951), cert. denied, 342 U.S. 893 (1951), and courts and commentators have urged that Rule 54(b) be changed to take in the former. See *Reagan v. Traders & General Ins. Co.*, 255 F.2d 845 (5th Cir. 1958); *Meadows v. Greyhound Corp.*, 235 F.2d 233 (5th Cir. 1956); *Steiner v. 20th Century-Fox Film Corp.*, supra; 6 Moore's Federal Practice ¶54.34[2] (2d ed. 1953); 3 Barron & Holtzoff, *Federal Practice & Procedure* § 1193.2 (Wright ed. 1958); *Developments in the Law—Multiparty Litigation*, 71 Harv.L.Rev. 874, 981 (1958); Note, 62 Yale L.J. 263, 271 (1953); Ill.Ann.Stat. ch. 110, § 50(2) (Smith-Hurd 1956). The amendment accomplishes this purpose by referring explicitly to parties.

There has been some recent indication that interlocutory appeal under the provisions of 28 U.S.C. § 1292(b), added in 1958, may now be available for the multiple-parties cases here considered. See *Jaftex Corp. v. Randolph Mills, Inc.*, 282 F.2d 508 (2d Cir. 1960). The Rule 54(b) procedure seems preferable for those cases, and § 1292(b) should be held inapplicable to them when the rule is enlarged as here proposed. See *Luckenbach Steamship Co., Inc., v. H. Muehlstein & Co., Inc.*, 280 F.2d 755, 757 (2d Cir. 1960); 1 Barron & Holtzoff, supra, § 58.1, p. 321 (Wright ed. 1960).

1987 Amendment

The amendment is technical. No substantive change is intended.

1993 Amendments

Subdivision (d). This revision adds paragraph (2) to this subdivision to provide for a frequently recurring form of litigation not initially contemplated by the rules—disputes over the amount of attorneys' fees to be awarded in the large number of actions in which prevailing parties may be entitled to such awards or in which the court must determine the fees to be paid from a common fund. This revision seeks to harmonize and clarify procedures that have been developed through case law and local rules.

Paragraph (1). Former subdivision (d), providing for taxation of costs by the clerk, is renumbered as paragraph (1) and revised to exclude applications for attorneys' fees.

Paragraph (2). This new paragraph establishes a procedure for presenting claims for attorneys' fees, whether or not denominated as "costs." It applies also to requests for reimbursement of expenses, not taxable as costs, when recoverable under governing law incident to the award of fees. *Cf. West Virginia Univ. Hosp. v. Casey,* — U.S. — (1991), holding, prior to the Civil Rights Act of 1991, that expert witness fees were not recoverable under 42 U.S.C. § 1988. As noted in subparagraph (A), it does not, however, apply to fees recoverable as an element of damages, as when sought under the terms of a contract; such damages typically are to be claimed in a pleading and may involve issues to be resolved by a jury. Nor, as provided in subparagraph (E), does it apply to awards of fees as sanctions authorized or mandated under these rules or under 28 U.S.C. § 1927.

Subparagraph (B) provides a deadline for motions for attorneys' fees—14 days after final judgment unless the court or a statute specifies some other time. One purpose of this provision is to assure that the opposing party is informed of the claim before the time for appeal has elapsed. Prior law did not prescribe any specific time limit on claims for attorneys' fees. White v. New Hampshire Dep't of Employment Sec., 455 U.S. 445 (1982). In many nonjury cases the court will want to consider attorneys' fee issues immediately after rendering its judgment on the merits of the case. Note that the time for making claims is specifically stated in some legislation, such as the Equal Access to Justice Act, 28 U.S.C. § 2412(d)(1)(B) (30–day filing period).

Prompt filing affords an opportunity for the court to resolve fee disputes shortly after trial, while the services performed are freshly in mind. It also enables the court in appropriate circumstances to make its ruling on a fee request in time for any appellate review of a dispute over fees to proceed at the same time as review on the merits of the case.

Filing a motion for fees under this subdivision does not affect the finality or the appealability of a judgment, though revised Rule 58 provides a mechanism by which prior to appeal the court can suspend the finality to resolve a motion for fees. If an appeal on the merits of the case is taken, the court may rule on the claim for fees, may defer its ruling on the motion, or may deny the motion without prejudice, directing under subdivision (d)(2)(B) a new period for filing after the appeal has been resolved. A notice of appeal does not extend the time for filing a fee claim based on the initial judgment, but the court under subdivision (d)(2)(B) may effectively extend the period by permitting claims to be filed after resolution of the appeal. A new period for filing will automatically begin if a new judgment is entered following a reversal or remand by the appellate court or the granting of a motion under Rule 59.

The rule does not require that the motion be supported at the time of filing with the evidentiary material bearing on the fees. This material must of course be submitted in due course, according to such schedule as the court may direct in light of the circumstances of the case. What is required is the filing of a motion sufficient to alert the adversary and the court that there is a claim for fees, and the amount of such fees (or a fair estimate).

If directed by the court, the moving party is also required to disclose any fee agreement, including those between attorney and client, between attorneys sharing a fee to be awarded, and between adversaries made in partial settlement of a dispute where the settlement must be implemented by court action as may be required by Rules 23(e) and 23.1 or other like provisions. With respect to the fee arrangements requiring court approval, the court may also by local rule require disclosure immediately after such arrangements are agreed to. *E.g.,* Rule 5 of United States District Court for the Eastern District of New York; *cf. In re "Agent Orange" Product Liability Litigation (MDL 381),* 611 F.Supp. 1452, 1464 (E.D.N.Y.1985).

In the settlement of class actions resulting in a common fund from which fees will be sought, courts frequently have required that claims for fees be presented in advance of hearings to consider approval of the proposed settlement. The rule does not affect this practice, as it permits the court to require submissions of fee claims in advance of entry of judgment.

Subparagraph (C) assures the parties of an opportunity to make an appropriate presentation with respect to issues involving the evaluation of legal services. In some cases, an evidentiary hearing may be needed, but this is not required in every case. The amount of time to be allowed for the preparation of submissions both in support of and in opposition to awards should be tailored to the particular case.

The court is explicitly authorized to make a determination of the liability for fees before receiving submissions by the parties bearing on the amount of an award. This option may be appropriate in actions in which the liability issue is doubtful and the evaluation issues are numerous and complex.

The court may order disclosure of additional information, such as that bearing on prevailing local rates or on the appropriateness of particular services for which compensation is sought.

On rare occasion, the court may determine that discovery under Rules 26–37 would be useful to the parties. *Compare* Rules Governing Section 2254 Cases in the U.S. District Courts, Rule 6. *See* Note, *Determining the Reasonableness of Attorneys' Fees—the Discoverability of Billing Records*, 64 *B.U.L.Rev.* 241 (1984). In complex fee disputes, the court may use case management techniques to limit the scope of the dispute or to facilitate the settlement of fee award disputes.

Fee awards should be made in the form of a separate judgment under Rule 58 since such awards are subject to review in the court of appeals. To facilitate review, the paragraph provides that the court set forth its findings and conclusions as under Rule 52(a), though in most cases this explanation could be quite brief.

Subparagraph (D) explicitly authorizes the court to establish procedures facilitating the efficient and fair resolution of fee claims. A local rule, for example, might call for matters to be presented through affidavits, or might provide for issuance of proposed findings by the court, which would be treated as accepted by the parties unless objected to within a specified time. A court might also consider establishing a schedule reflecting customary fees or factors affecting fees within the community, as implicitly suggested by Justice O'Connor in *Pennsylvania v. Delaware Valley Citizens' Council*, 483 U.S. 711, 733 (1987) (O'Connor, J., concurring) (how particular markets compensate for contingency). *Cf. Thompson v. Kennickell*, 710 F.Supp. 1 (D.D.C.1989) (use of findings in other cases to promote consistency). The parties, of course, should be permitted to show that in the circumstances of the case such a schedule should not be applied or that different hourly rates would be appropriate.

The rule also explicitly permits, without need for a local rule, the court to refer issues regarding the amount of a fee award in a particular case to a master under Rule 53. The district judge may designate a magistrate judge to act as a master for this purpose or may refer a motion for attorneys' fees to a magistrate judge for proposed findings and recommendations under Rule 72(b). This authorization eliminates any controversy as to whether such references are permitted under Rule 53(b) as "matters of account and of difficult computation of damages" and whether motions for attorneys' fees can be treated as the equivalent of a dispositive pretrial matter that can be referred to a magistrate judge. For consistency and efficiency, all such matters might be referred to the same magistrate judge.

Subparagraph (E) excludes from this rule the award of fees as sanctions under these rules or under 28 U.S.C. § 1927.

HISTORICAL NOTES

Effective Dates

1961 Amendments. Amendment adopted on Apr. 17, 1961, effective July 19, 1961, see Rule 86(d).

Rule 55. Default

(a) Entry. When a party against whom a judgment for affirmative relief is sought has failed to plead or otherwise defend as provided by these rules and that fact is made to appear by affidavit or otherwise, the clerk shall enter the party's default.

(b) Judgment. Judgment by default may be entered as follows:

(1) By the Clerk. When the plaintiff's claim against a defendant is for a sum certain or for a sum which can by computation be made certain, the clerk upon request of the plaintiff and upon affidavit of the amount due shall enter judgment for that amount and costs against the defendant, if the defendant has been defaulted for failure to appear and is not an infant or incompetent person.

(2) By the Court. In all other cases the party entitled to a judgment by default shall apply to the court therefor; but no judgment by default shall be entered against an infant or incompetent person unless represented in the action by a general guardian, committee, conservator, or other such representative who has appeared therein. If the party against whom judgment by default is sought has appeared in the action, the party (or, if appearing by representative, the party's representative) shall be served with written notice of the application for judgment at least 3 days prior to the hearing on such application. If, in order to enable the court to enter judgment or to carry it into effect, it is necessary to take an account or to determine the amount of damages or to establish the truth of any averment by evidence or to make an investigation of any other matter, the court may conduct such hearings or order such references as it deems necessary and proper and shall accord a right of trial by jury to the parties when and as required by any statute of the United States.

(c) Setting Aside Default. For good cause shown the court may set aside an entry of default and, if a judgment by default has been entered, may likewise set it aside in accordance with Rule 60(b).

(d) Plaintiffs, Counterclaimants, Cross-Claimants. The provisions of this rule apply whether the party entitled to the judgment by default is a plaintiff, a third-party plaintiff, or a party who has pleaded a cross-claim or counterclaim. In all cases a judgment by default is subject to the limitations of Rule 54(c).

(e) Judgment Against the United States. No judgment by default shall be entered against the United States or an officer or agency thereof unless the claimant establishes a claim or right to relief by evidence satisfactory to the court.

(As amended Mar. 2, 1987, eff. Aug. 1, 1987.)

ADVISORY COMMITTEE NOTES

1937 Adoption

This represents the joining of the equity decree *pro confesso* (former Equity Rules 12 (Issue of Subpoena—Time for Answer), 16 (Defendant to Answer—Default—Decree *Pro Confesso*), 17 (Decree *Pro Confesso* to be Followed by Final Decree—Setting Aside Default), 29 (Defenses—How Presented), 31 (Reply—When Required—When Cause at Issue)) and the judgment by default now governed by U.S.C., Title 28, [former] § 724 (Conformity act). For dismissal of an action for failure to comply with these rules or any order of the court, see Rule 41(b).

Note to Subdivision (a). The provision for the entry of default comes from the Massachusetts practice, 2 Mass.Gen. Laws (Ter.Ed., 1932) ch. 231, § 57. For affidavit of default, see 2 Minn.Stat. (Mason, 1927) § 9256.

Note to Subdivision (b). The provision in paragraph (1) for the entry of judgment by the clerk when plaintiff claims a sum certain is found in the N.Y.C.P.A. (1937) § 485, in Calif.Code Civ.Proc. (Deering, 1937) § 585(1), and in Conn.Practice Book (1934) § 47. For provisions similar to paragraph (2), compare Calif.Code, *supra*, § 585(2); N.Y.C.P.A. (1937) § 490; 2 Minn.Stat. (Mason, 1927) § 9256(3); 2 Wash.Rev.Stat.Ann. (Remington, 1932) § 411(2). U.S.C., Title 28, § 1874, formerly § 785 (Action to recover forfeiture in bond) and similar statutes are preserved by the last clause of paragraph (2).

Note to Subdivision (e). This restates substantially the last clause of U.S.C., Title 28, [former] § 763 (Action against the United States under the Tucker Act). As this rule governs in all actions against the United States, U.S.C., Title 28, [former] § 45 (Practice and procedure in certain cases under the interstate commerce laws) and similar statutes are modified insofar as they contain anything inconsistent therewith.

Supplementary Note

Note. The operation of Rule 55(b) (Judgment) is directly affected by the Soldiers' and Sailors' Civil Relief Act of 1940, 50 U.S.C. Appendix, § 501 et seq. Section 200 of the Act [50 U.S.C. Appendix, § 520] imposes specific requirements which must be fulfilled before a default judgment can be entered, e.g., *Ledwith v. Storkan,* D.Neb.1942, 6 Fed.Rules Serv. 60b.24, Case 2, 2 F.R.D. 539, and also provides for the vacation of a judgment in certain circumstances. See discussion in Commentary, Effect of Conscription Legislation on the Federal Rules, 1940, 3 Fed.Rules Serv. 725; 3 *Moore's Federal Practice,* 1938, Cum.Supplement § 55.02.

1987 Amendment

The amendments are technical. No substantive change is intended.

Rule 56. Summary Judgment

(a) For Claimant. A party seeking to recover upon a claim, counterclaim, or cross-claim or to obtain a declaratory judgment may, at any time after the expiration of 20 days from the commencement of the action or after service of a motion for summary judgment by the adverse party, move with or without supporting affidavits for a summary judgment in the party's favor upon all or any part thereof.

(b) For Defending Party. A party against whom a claim, counterclaim, or cross-claim is asserted or a declaratory judgment is sought may, at any time, move with or without supporting affidavits for a summary judgment in the party's favor as to all or any part thereof.

(c) Motion and Proceedings Thereon. The motion shall be served at least 10 days before the time fixed for the hearing. The adverse party prior to the day of hearing may serve opposing affidavits. The judgment sought shall be rendered forthwith if the pleadings, depositions, answers to interrogatories, and admissions on file, together with the affidavits, if any, show that there is no genuine issue as to any material fact and that the moving party is entitled to a judgment as a matter of law. A summary judgment, interlocutory in character, may be rendered on the issue of liability alone although there is a genuine issue as to the amount of damages.

(d) Case Not Fully Adjudicated on Motion. If on motion under this rule judgment is not rendered upon the whole case or for all the relief asked and a trial is necessary, the court at the hearing of the motion, by examining the pleadings and the evidence before it and by interrogating counsel, shall if practicable ascertain what material facts exist without substantial controversy and what material facts are actually and in good faith controverted. It shall thereupon make an order specifying the facts that appear without substantial controversy, including the extent to which the amount of damages or other relief is not in controversy, and directing such further proceedings in the action as are just. Upon the trial of the action the facts so specified shall be deemed established, and the trial shall be conducted accordingly.

(e) Form of Affidavits; Further Testimony; Defense Required. Supporting and opposing affidavits shall be made on personal knowledge, shall set forth such facts as would be admissible in evidence, and shall show affirmatively that the affiant is competent to testify to the matters stated therein. Sworn or certified copies of all papers or parts thereof referred to in an affidavit shall be attached thereto or served therewith. The court may permit affidavits to be supplemented or opposed by depositions, answers to interrogatories, or further affidavits. When a motion for summary judgment is made and supported as provided in this rule, an adverse party may not rest upon the mere allegations or denials of the adverse party's pleading, but the adverse party's response, by affidavits or as otherwise provided in this rule, must set forth specific facts showing that there is a genuine issue for trial. If the adverse party does not so respond, summary judgment, if appropriate, shall be entered against the adverse party.

(f) When Affidavits are Unavailable. Should it appear from the affidavits of a party opposing the motion that the party cannot for reasons stated present by affidavit facts essential to justify the party's opposition, the court may refuse the application for judgment or may order a continuance to permit affidavits to be obtained or depositions to be taken or discovery to be had or may make such other order as is just.

(g) Affidavits Made in Bad Faith. Should it appear to the satisfaction of the court at any time that any of the affidavits presented pursuant to this rule are presented in bad faith or solely for the purpose of delay, the court shall forthwith order the party employing them to pay to the other party the amount of the reasonable expenses which the filing of the affidavits caused the other party to incur, including reasonable attorney's fees, and any offending party or attorney may be adjudged guilty of contempt.

(As amended Dec. 27, 1946, eff. Mar. 19, 1948; Jan. 21, 1963, eff. July 1, 1963; Mar. 2, 1987, eff. Aug. 1, 1987.)

ADVISORY COMMITTEE NOTES

1937 Adoption

This rule is applicable to all actions, including those against the United States or an officer or agency thereof.

Summary judgment procedure is a method for promptly disposing of actions in which there is no genuine issue as to any material fact. It has been extensively used in England for more than 50 years and has been adopted in a number of American states. New York, for example, has made great use of it. During the first nine years after its adoption there, the records of New York county alone show 5,600 applications for summary judgments. Report of the Commission on the Administration of Justice in New York State (1934), p. 383. See also *Third Annual Report of the Judicial Council of the State of New York* (1937), p. 30.

In England it was first employed only in cases of liquidated claims, but there has been a steady enlargement of the scope of the remedy until it is now used in actions to recover land or chattels and in all other actions at law, for liquidated or unliquidated claims, except for a few designated torts and breach of promise of marriage. *English Rules Under the Judicature Act* (The Annual Practice, 1937) O. 3, r. 6; Orders 14, 14A, and 15; see also O. 32, r. 6, authorizing an application for judgment at any time upon admissions. In Michigan (3 Comp.Laws (1929) § 14260) and Illinois (Smith-Hurd Ill.Stats. c. 110, §§ 181, 259.15, 259.16), it is not limited to liquidated demands. New York (N.Y.R.C.P. (1937) Rule 113; see also Rule 107) has brought so many classes of actions under the operation of the rule that the Commission on Administration of Justice in New York State (1934) recommend that all restrictions be removed and that the remedy be available "in any action" (p. 287). For the history and nature of the summary judgment procedure and citations of state statutes, see Clark and Samenow, *The Summary Judgment* (1929), 38 Yale L.J. 423.

Note to Subdivision (d). See Rule 16 (Pre-Trial Procedure; Formulating Issues) and the Note thereto.

Note to Subdivisions (e) and (f). These are similar to rules in Michigan. Mich.Court Rules Ann. (Searl, 1933) Rule 30.

1946 Amendment

Note to Subdivision (a). The amendment allows a claimant to move for a summary judgment at any time after the expiration of 20 days from the commencement of the action or after service of a motion for summary judgment by the adverse party. This will normally operate to permit an earlier motion by the claimant than under the original rule, where the phrase "at any time after the pleading in answer thereto has been served" operates to prevent a claimant from moving for summary judgment, even in a case clearly proper for its exercise, until a formal answer has been filed. Thus in *Peoples Bank v. Federal Reserve Bank of San Francisco*, N.D.Cal.1944, 58 F.Supp. 25, the plaintiff's countermotion for a summary judgment was stricken as premature, because the defendant had not filed an answer. Since Rule 12(a) allows at least 20 days for an answer, that time plus the 10 days required in Rule 56(c) means that under original Rule 56(a) a minimum period of 30 days necessarily has to elapse in every case before the claimant can be heard on his right to a summary judgment. An extension of time by the court or the service of preliminary motions of any kind will prolong that period even further. In many cases this merely represents unnecessary delay. See *United States v. Adler's Creamery, Inc.*, C.C.A.2, 1939, 107 F.2d 987. The changes are in the interest of more expeditious litigation. The 20-day period, as provided, gives the defendant an opportunity to secure counsel and determine a course of action. But in a case where the defendant himself makes a motion for summary judgment within that time, there is no reason to restrict the plaintiff and the amended rule so provides.

Subdivision (c). The amendment of Rule 56(c), by the addition of the final sentence, resolves a doubt expressed in *Sartor v. Arkansas Natural Gas Corp.*, 1944, 64 S.Ct. 724, 321 U.S. 620, 88 L.Ed. 967. See also Commentary, Summary Judgment as to Damages, 1944, 7 Fed.Rules Serv. 974; *Madeirense Do Brasil S/A v. Stulman-Emrick Lumber Co.*, C.C.A.2d, 1945, 147 F.2d 399, certiorari denied 1945, 65 S.Ct. 1201, 325 U.S. 861, 89 L.Ed. 1982. It makes clear that although the question of recovery depends on the amount of damages, the summary judgment rule is applicable and summary judgment may be granted in a proper case. If the case is not fully adjudicated it may be dealt with as provided in subdivision (d) of Rule 56, and the right to summary recovery determined by a preliminary order, interlocutory in character, and the precise amount of recovery left for trial.

Subdivision (d). Rule 54(a) defines "judgment" as including a decree and "any order from which an appeal lies." Subdivision (d) of Rule 56 indicates clearly, however, that a partial summary "judgment" is not a final judgment, and, therefore, that it is not appealable, unless in the particular case some statute allows an appeal from the interlocutory order involved. The partial summary judgment is merely a pretrial adjudication that certain issues shall be deemed established for the trial of the case. This adjudication is more nearly akin to the preliminary order under Rule 16, and likewise serves the purpose of speeding up litigation by eliminating before trial matters wherein there is no genuine issue of fact. See *Leonard v. Socony-Vacuum Oil Co.*, C.C.A.7, 1942, 130 F.2d 535; *Biggins v. Oltmer Iron Works*, C.C.A.7, 1946, 154 F.2d 214; 3 *Moore's Federal Practice*, 1938, 3190–3192. Since interlocutory appeals are not allowed, except where specifically provided by statute, see 3 Moore, op. cit. supra, 3155–3156, this interpretation is in line with that policy, *Leonard v. Socony-Vacuum Oil Co.*, supra. See also *Audi Vision Inc. v. RCA Mfg. Co.*, C.C.A.2, 1943, 136 F.2d 621; *Toomey v. Toomey*, 1945, 149 F.2d 19, 80 U.S.App.D.C. 77; *Biggins v. Oltmer Iron Works*, supra; *Catlin v. United States*, 1945, 65 S.Ct. 631, 324 U.S. 229, 89 L.Ed. 911.

1963 Amendment

Subdivision (c). By the amendment "answers to interrogatories" are included among the materials which may be considered on motion for summary judgment. The phrase was inadvertently omitted from the rule, see 3 Barron & Holtzoff, *Federal Practice & Procedure* 159–60 (Wright ed. 1958), and the courts have generally reached by interpretation the result which will hereafter be required by the text of the amended rule. See Annot., 74 A.L.R.2d 984 (1960).

Subdivision (e). The words "answers to interrogatories" are added in the third sentence of this subdivision to conform to the amendment of subdivision (c).

The last two sentences are added to overcome a line of cases, chiefly in the Third Circuit, which has impaired the utility of the summary judgment device. A typical case is as follows: A party supports his motion for summary judgment by affidavits or other evidentiary matter sufficient to show that there is no genuine issue as to a material fact. The adverse party, in opposing the motion, does not produce any evidentiary matter, or produces some but not enough to establish that there is a genuine issue for trial. Instead, the adverse party rests on averments of his pleadings which on their face present an issue. In this situation Third Circuit cases have taken the view that summary judgment must be denied, at least if the averments are "well-pleaded," and not suppositious, conclusory, or ultimate. See *Frederick Hart & Co., Inc. v. Recordgraph Corp.*, 169 F.2d 580 (3d Cir. 1948); *United States ex rel. Kolton v. Halpern*, 260 F.2d 590 (3d Cir. 1958); *United States ex rel. Nobles v. Ivey Bros. Constr. Co., Inc.*, 191 F.Supp. 383 (D.Del.1961); *Jamison v. Pennsylvania Salt Mfg. Co.*, 22 F.R.D. 238 (W.D.Pa.1958); *Bunny Bear, Inc. v. Dennis Mitchell Industries*, 139 F.Supp. 542 (E.D.Pa.1956); *Levy v. Equitable Life Assur. Society*, 18 F.R.D. 164 (E.D.Pa.1955).

The very mission of the summary judgment procedure is to pierce the pleadings and to assess the proof in order to see whether there is a genuine need for trial. The Third Circuit doctrine, which permits the pleadings themselves to stand in the way of granting an otherwise justified summary judgment, is incompatible with the basic purpose of the rule. See 6 *Moore's Federal Practice* 2069 (2d ed. 1953); 3 Barron & Holtzoff, supra, § 1235.1.

It is hoped that the amendment will contribute to the more effective utilization of the salutary device of summary judgment.

The amendment is not intended to derogate from the solemnity of the pleadings. Rather it recognizes that, despite the best efforts of counsel to make his pleadings accurate, they may be overwhelmingly contradicted by the proof available to his adversary.

Nor is the amendment designed to affect the ordinary standards applicable to the summary judgment motion. So, for example: Where an issue as to a material fact cannot be resolved without observation of the demeanor of witnesses in order to evaluate their credibility, summary judgment is not appropriate. Where the evidentiary matter in support of the motion does not establish the absence of a genuine issue, summary judgment must be denied even if no opposing evidentiary matter is presented. And summary judgment may be inappropriate where the party opposing it shows under subdivision (f) that he cannot at the time present facts essential to justify his opposition.

1987 Amendment

The amendments are technical. No substantive change is intended.

Rule 57. Declaratory Judgments

The procedure for obtaining a declaratory judgment pursuant to Title 28, U.S.C., § 2201, shall be in accordance with these rules, and the right to trial by jury may be demanded under the circumstances and in the manner provided in Rules 38 and 39. The existence of another adequate remedy does not preclude a judgment for declaratory relief in cases where it is appropriate. The court may order a speedy hearing of an action for a declaratory judgment and may advance it on the calendar.

(As amended Dec. 29, 1948, eff. Oct. 20, 1949.)

ADVISORY COMMITTEE NOTES

1937 Adoption

The fact that a declaratory judgment may be granted "whether or not further relief is or could be prayed" indicates that declaratory relief is alternative or cumulative and not exclusive or extraordinary. A declaratory judgment is appropriate when it will "terminate the controversy" giving rise to the proceeding. Inasmuch as it often involves only an issue of law on undisputed or relatively undisputed facts, it operates frequently as a summary proceeding, justifying docketing the case for early hearing as on a motion, as provided for in California (Code Civ.Proc. (Deering, 1937) § 1062a), Michigan (3 Comp.Laws (1929) § 13904), and Kentucky (Codes (Carroll, 1932) Civ.Pract. § 639a–3).

The "controversy" must necessarily be "of a justiciable nature, thus excluding an advisory decree upon a hypothetical state of facts." *Ashwander v. Tennessee Valley Authority,* 1936, 56 S.Ct. 466, 473, 297 U.S. 288, 80 L.Ed. 688. The existence or non-existence of any right, duty, power, liability, privilege, disability, or immunity or of any fact upon which such legal relations depend, or of a status, may be declared. The petitioner must have a practical interest in the declaration sought and all parties having an interest therein or adversely affected must be made parties or be cited. A declaration may not be rendered if a special statutory proceeding has been provided for the adjudication of some special type of case, but general ordinary or extraordinary legal remedies, whether regulated by statute or not, are not deemed special statutory proceedings.

When declaratory relief will not be effective in settling the controversy, the court may decline to grant it. But the fact that another remedy would be equally effective affords no ground for declining declaratory relief. The demand for relief shall state with precision the declaratory judgment desired, to which may be joined a demand for coercive relief, cumulatively or in the alternative; but when coercive relief only is sought but is deemed ungrantable, or inappropriate, the court may *sua sponte*, if it serves a useful purpose, grant instead a declaration of rights. *Hasselbring v. Koepke,* 1933, 248 N.W. 869, 263 Mich. 466, 93 A.L.R. 1170. Written instruments, including ordinances and statutes, may be construed before or after breach at the petition of a properly interested party, process being served on the private parties or public officials interested. In other respects the Uniform Declaratory Judgment Act affords a guide to the scope and function of the Federal act. Compare *Aetna Life Insurance Co. v. Haworth,* 1937, 57 S.Ct. 461, 300 U.S. 227, 81 L.Ed. 617, 108 A.L.R. 1000; *Nashville, Chattanooga & St. Louis Ry. v. Wallace,* 1933, 53 S.Ct. 345, 288 U.S. 249, 77 L.Ed. 730, 87 A.L.R. 1191; *Gully, Tax Collector v. Interstate Natural Gas Co.,* 82 F.2d 145 (C.C.A.5, 1936); *Ohio Casualty Ins. Co. v. Plummer,* Tex.1935, 13 F.Supp. 169; Borchard, Declaratory Judgments (1934), *passim.*

1948 Amendment

The amendment effective October 1949, substituted the reference to "Title 28, U.S.C., § 2201" in the first sentence for the reference to "Section 274(d) of the Judicial Code, as amended, U.S.C., Title 28, § 400".

Rule 58. Entry of Judgment

Subject to the provisions of Rule 54(b): (1) upon a general verdict of a jury, or upon a decision by the court that a party shall recover only a sum certain or costs or that all relief shall be denied, the clerk, unless the court otherwise orders, shall forthwith prepare, sign, and enter the judgment without awaiting any direction by the court; (2) upon a decision by the court granting other relief, or upon a special verdict or a general verdict accompanied by answers to interrogatories, the court shall promptly approve the form of the judgment, and the clerk shall thereupon enter it. Every judgment shall be set forth on a separate document. A judgment is effective only when so set forth and when entered as provided in Rule 79(a). Entry of the judgment shall not be delayed, nor the time for appeal extended, in order to tax costs or award fees, except that, when a timely motion for attorneys' fees is made under Rule 54(d)(2), the court, before a notice of appeal has been filed and has become effective, may order that the motion have the same effect under Rule 4(a)(4) of the Federal Rules of Appellate Procedure as a timely motion under Rule 59. Attorneys shall not submit forms of judgment except upon direction of the court, and these directions shall not be given as a matter of course.

(As amended Dec. 27, 1946, eff. Mar. 19, 1948; Jan. 21, 1963, eff. July 1, 1963; Apr. 22, 1993, eff. Dec. 1, 1993.)

ADVISORY COMMITTEE NOTES

1937 Adoption

See Wis.Stat. (1935) § 270.31 (judgment entered forthwith on verdict of jury unless otherwise ordered), § 270.65 (where trial is by the court, entered by direction of the court), § 270.63 (entered by clerk on judgment on admitted claim for money). Compare 1 Idaho Code Ann. (1932) § 7–1101, and 4 Mont.Rev.Codes Ann. (1935) § 9403, which provide that judgment in jury cases be entered by clerk within 24 hours after verdict unless court otherwise directs. Conn.Practice Book (1934), § 200, provides that all judgments shall be entered within one week after rendition. In some States such as Washington, 2 Rev.Stat.Ann. (Remington, 1932), § 431, in jury cases the judgment is entered two days after the return of verdict to give time for making motion for new trial; § 435 (*ibid.*), provides that all judgments shall be entered by the clerk, subject to the court's direction.

1946 Amendment

Note. The reference to Rule 54(b) is made necessary by the amendment of that rule.

Two changes have been made in Rule 58 in order to clarify the practice. The substitution of the more inclusive phrase "all relief be denied" for the words "there be no recovery", makes it clear that the clerk shall enter the judgment forthwith in the situations specified without awaiting the filing of a formal judgment approved by the court. The phrase "all relief be denied" covers cases such as the denial of a bankrupt's discharge and similar situations where the relief sought is refused but there is literally no denial of a "recovery".

The addition of the last sentence in the rule emphasizes that judgments are to be entered promptly by the clerk without waiting for the taxing of costs. Certain district court rules, for example, Civil Rule 22 of the Southern District of New York—until its annulment Oct. 1, 1945, for conflict with this rule—and the like rule of the Eastern District of New York, are expressly in conflict with this provision, although the federal law is of long standing and well settled. *Fowler v. Hamill,* 1891, 11 S.Ct. 663, 139 U.S. 549, 35 L.Ed. 266; *Craig v. The Hartford,* C.C.Cal.1856, Fed.Cas. No. 3,333; *Tuttle v. Claflin,* C.C.A.2, 1895, 60 F. 7, certiorari denied 1897; 17 S.Ct. 992, 166 U.S. 721, 41 L.Ed. 1188; *Prescott & A.C. Ry. Co. v. Atchison, T. & S.F.R. Co.,* C.C.A.2, 1897, 84 F. 213; *Stallo v. Wagner,* C.C.A.2, 1917, 245 F. 636, 639–40; *Brown v. Parker,* C.C.A.8, 1899, 97 F. 446; *Allis-Chalmers v.*

United States, C.C.A.7, 1908, 162 F. 679. And this applies even though state law is to the contrary. *United States v. Nordbye,* C.C.A.8, 1935, 75 F.2d 744, certiorari denied 56 S.Ct. 103, 296 U.S. 572, 80 L.Ed. 404. Inasmuch as it has been held that failure of the clerk thus to enter judgment is a "misprision" "not to be excused", *The Washington,* C.C.A.2, 1926, 16 F.2d 206, such a district court rule may have serious consequences for a district court clerk. Rules of this sort also provide for delay in entry of the judgment contrary to Rule 58. See *Commissioner of Internal Revenue v. Bedford's Estate,* 1945, 65 S.Ct. 1157, 325 U.S. 283, 91 L.Ed. 1611.

1963 Amendment

Under the present rule a distinction has sometimes been made between judgments on general jury verdicts, on the one hand, and, on the other, judgments upon decisions of the court that a party shall recover only money or costs or that all relief shall be denied. In the first situation, it is clear that the clerk should enter the judgment without awaiting a direction by the court unless the court otherwise orders. In the second situation it was intended that the clerk should similarly enter the judgment forthwith upon the court's decision; but because of the separate listing in the rule, and the use of the phrase "upon receipt . . . of the direction," the rule has sometimes been interpreted as requiring the clerk to await a separate direction of the court. All these judgments are usually uncomplicated, and should be handled in the same way. The amended rule accordingly deals with them as a single group in clause (1) (substituting the expression "only a sum certain" for the present expression "only money"), and requires the clerk to prepare, sign and enter them forthwith, without awaiting court direction, unless the court makes a contrary order. (The clerk's duty is ministerial and may be performed by a deputy clerk in the name of the clerk. See 28 U.S.C. § 956; cf. *Gilbertson v. United States,* 168 Fed. 672 (7th Cir. 1909).) The more complicated judgments described in clause (2) must be approved by the court before they are entered.

Rule 58 is designed to encourage all reasonable speed in formulating and entering the judgment when the case has been decided. Participation by the attorneys through the submission of forms of judgment involves needless expenditure of time and effort and promotes delay, except in special cases where counsel's assistance can be of real value. See *Matteson v. United States,* 240 F.2d 517, 518–19 (2d Cir. 1956). Accordingly, the amended rule provides that attorneys shall not submit forms of judgment unless directed to do so by the court. This applies to the judgments mentioned in clause (2) as well as clause (1).

Hitherto some difficulty has arisen, chiefly where the court has written an opinion or memorandum containing some apparently directive or dispositive words, e.g., "the plaintiff's motion [for summary judgment] is granted," see *United States v. F. & M. Schaefer Brewing Co.,* 356 U.S. 227, 229, 78 S.Ct. 674, 2 L.Ed.2d 721 (1958). Clerks on occasion have viewed these opinions or memoranda as being in themselves a sufficient basis for entering judgment in the civil docket as provided by Rule 79(a). However, where the opinion or memorandum has not contained all the elements of a judgment, or where the judge has later signed a formal judgment, it has become a matter of doubt whether the purported entry of judgment was effective, starting the time running for post-verdict motions and for the purpose of appeal. See id.; and compare *Blanchard v. Commonwealth Oil Co.,* 294 F.2d 834 (5th Cir. 1961); *United States v. Higginson,* 238 F.2d 439 (1st Cir. 1956); *Danzig v. Virgin Isle Hotel, Inc.,* 278 F.2d 580 (3d Cir. 1960); *Sears v. Austin,* 282 F.2d 340 (9th Cir. 1960), with *Matteson v. United States,* supra; *Erstling v. Southern Bell Tel. & Tel. Co.,* 255 F.2d 93 (5th Cir. 1958); *Barta v. Oglala Sioux Tribe,* 259 F.2d 553 (8th Cir. 1958) cert. denied, 358 U.S. 932, 79 S.Ct. 320, 3 L.Ed.2d 304 (1959); *Beacon Fed. S. & L. Assn. v. Federal Home L. Bank Bd.,* 266 F.2d 246 (7th Cir.), cert. denied, 361 U.S. 823, 80 S.Ct. 70, 4 L.Ed.2d 67 (1959); *Ram v. Paramount Film D. Corp.,* 278 F.2d 191 (4th Cir. 1960).

The amended rule eliminates these uncertainties by requiring that there be a judgment set out on a separate document—distinct from any opinion or memorandum—which provides the basis for the entry of judgment. That judgment shall be on separate documents is also indicated in Rule 79(b); and see General Rule 10 of the U.S. District Courts for the Eastern and Southern Districts of New York; *Ram v. Paramount Film D. Corp.*, supra, at 194.

See the amendment of Rule 79(a) and the new specimen forms of judgment, Forms 31 and 32.

See also Rule 55(b)(1) and (2) covering the subject of judgments by default.

1993 Amendments

Ordinarily the pendency or post-judgment filing of a claim for attorney's fees will not affect the time for appeal from the underlying judgment. See Budinich v. Becton Dickinson & Co., 486 U.S. 196 (1988). Particularly if the claim for fees involves substantial issues or is likely to be affected by the appellate decision, the district court may prefer to defer consideration of the claim for fees until after the appeal is resolved. However, in many cases it may be more efficient to decide fee questions before an appeal is taken so that appeals relating to the fee award can be heard at the same time as appeals relating to the merits of the case. This revision permits, but does not require, the court to delay the finality of the judgment for appellate purposes under revised Fed.R.App.P. 4(a) until the fee dispute is decided. To accomplish this result requires entry of an order by the district court before the time a notice of appeal becomes effective for appellate purposes. If the order is entered, the motion for attorney's fees is treated in the same manner as a timely motion under Rule 59.

Rule 59. New Trials; Amendment of Judgments

(a) Grounds. A new trial may be granted to all or any of the parties and on all or part of the issues (1) in an action in which there has been a trial by jury, for any of the reasons for which new trials have heretofore been granted in actions at law in the courts of the United States; and (2) in an action tried without a jury, for any of the reasons for which rehearings have heretofore been granted in suits in equity in the courts of the United States. On a motion for a new trial in an action tried without a jury, the court may open the judgment if one has been entered, take additional testimony, amend findings of fact and conclusions of law or make new findings and conclusions, and direct the entry of a new judgment.

(b) Time for Motion. Any motion for a new trial shall be filed no later than 10 days after entry of the judgment.

(c) Time for Serving Affidavits. When a motion for new trial is based on affidavits, they shall be filed with the motion. The opposing party has 10 days after service to file opposing affidavits, but that period may be extended for up to 20 days, either by the court for good cause or by the parties' written stipulation. The court may permit reply affidavits.

(d) On Court's Initiative; Notice; Specifying Grounds. No later than 10 days after entry of judgment the court, on its own, may order a new trial for any reason that would justify granting one on a party's motion. After giving the parties notice and an opportunity to be heard, the court may grant a timely motion for a new trial for a reason not stated in the motion. When granting a new trial on its own initiative or for a reason not stated in a motion, the court shall specify the grounds in its order.

(e) Motion to Alter or Amend Judgment. Any motion to alter or amend a judgment shall be filed no later than 10 days after entry of the judgment.

(As amended Dec. 27, 1946, eff. Mar. 19, 1948; Feb. 28, 1966, eff. July 1, 1966; Apr. 27, 1995, eff. Dec. 1, 1995.)

ADVISORY COMMITTEE NOTES

1937 Adoption

This rule represents an amalgamation of the petition for rehearing of [former] Equity Rule 69 (Petition for Rehearing) and the motion for new trial of 28 U.S.C., § 2111, formerly § 391 (New trials; harmless error), made in the light of the experience and provision of the code States. Compare Calif.Code Civ.Proc., Deering, 1937, §§ 656 to 663a, 28 U.S.C., § 2111, formerly § 391 (New trials; harmless error) is thus substantially continued in this rule. U.S.C., Title 28, [former] § 840 (Executions; stay on conditions) is modified insofar as it contains time provisions inconsistent with Subdivision (b). For the effect of the motion for new trial upon the time for taking an appeal see *Morse v. United States*, 1926, 46 S.Ct. 241, 270 U.S. 151, 70 L.Ed. 518; *Aspen Mining and Smelting Co. v. Billings*, 1893, 14 S.Ct. 4, 150 U.S. 31, 37 L.Ed. 986.

For partial new trials which are permissible under Subdivision (a), see *Gasoline Products Co., Inc. v. Champlin Refining Co.*, 1931, 51 S.Ct. 513, 283 U.S. 494, 75 L.Ed. 1188; *Schuerholz v. Roach*, C.C.A.4, 1932, 58 F.2d 32; *Simmons v. Fish*, 1912, 97 N.E. 102, 210 Mass. 563, Ann.Cas.1912D, 588 (sustaining and recommending the practice and citing federal cases and cases in accord from about sixteen States and contra from three States). The procedure in several States provides specifically for partial new trials. Ariz.Rev.Code Ann., Struckmeyer, 1928, § 3852; Calif.Code Civ.Proc., Deering, 1937, §§ 657, 662; Smith-Hurd Ill.Stats., 1937, c. 110, § 216 (Par. (f)); Md.Ann.Code, Bagby, 1924, Art. 5, §§ 25, 26; Mich.Court Rules Ann., Searl, 1933, Rule 47, § 2; Miss.Sup.Ct.Rule 12, 161 Miss. 903, 905, 1931; N.J.Sup.Ct. Rules 131, 132, 147, 2 N.J.Misc. 1197, 1246–1251, 1255, 1924; 2 N.D.Comp.Laws Ann., 1913, § 7844, as amended by N.D.Laws 1927, ch. 214.

1946 Amendment

Note. Subdivision (b). With the time for appeal to a circuit court of appeals reduced in general to 30 days by the proposed amendment of Rule 73(a), the utility of the original "except" clause, which permits a motion for a new trial on the ground of newly discovered evidence to be made before the expiration of the time for appeal, would have been seriously restricted. It was thought advisable, therefore, to take care of this matter in another way. By amendment of Rule 60(b), newly discovered evidence is made the basis for relief from a judgment, and the maximum time limit has been extended to one year. Accordingly the amendment of Rule 59(b) eliminates the "except" clause and its specific treatment of newly discovered evidence as a ground for a motion for new trial. This ground remains, however, as a basis for a motion for new trial served not later than 10 days after the entry of judgment. See also Rule 60(b).

As to the effect of a motion under subdivision (b) upon the running of appeal time, see amended Rule 73(a) and Note.

Note to Subdivision (e). This subdivision has been added to care for a situation such as that arising in *Boaz v. Mutual Life Ins. Co. of New York*, C.C.A.8, 1944, 146 F.2d 321, and makes clear that the district court possesses the power asserted in that case to alter or amend a judgment after its entry. The subdivision deals only with alteration or amendment of the original judgment in a case and does not relate to a judgment upon motion as provided in Rule 50(b). As to the effect of a motion under subdivision (e) upon the running of appeal time, see amended Rule 73(a) and Note.

The title of Rule 59 has been expanded to indicate the inclusion of this subdivision.

1966 Amendment

By narrow interpretation of Rule 59(b) and (d), it has been held that the trial court is without power to grant a motion for a new trial, timely served, by an order made more than 10 days after the entry of judgment, based upon a ground not stated in the motion but perceived and relied on by the trial court sua sponte. *Freid v. McGrath*, 133 F.2d 350 (D.C.Cir. 1942); *National Farmers Union Auto. & Cas. Co. v. Wood*, 207 F.2d 659 (10th Cir. 1953); *Bailey v. Slentz*, 189 F.2d 406 (10th Cir. 1951); *Marshall's U.S. Auto Supply, Inc. v. Cashman*, 111 F.2d 140 (10th Cir. 1940), cert. denied, 311 U.S. 667 (1940); but see *Steinberg v. Indemnity Ins. Co.*, 36 F.R.D. 253 (E.D.La.1964).

The result is undesirable. Just as the court has power under Rule 59(d) to grant a new trial of its own initiative within the 10 days, so it should have power, when an effective new trial motion has been made and is pending, to decide it on grounds thought meritorious by the court although not advanced in the motion. The second sentence added by amendment to Rule 59(d) confirms the court's power in the latter situation, with provision that the parties be afforded a hearing before the power is exercised. See 6 *Moore's Federal Practice*, par. 59.09[2] (2d ed. 1953).

In considering whether a given ground has or has not been advanced in the motion made by the party, it should be borne in mind that the particularity called for in stating the grounds for a new trial motion is the same as that required for all motions by Rule 7(b)(1). The latter rule does not require ritualistic detail but rather a fair indication to court and counsel of the substance of the grounds relied on. See *Lebeck v. William A. Jarvis Co.*, 250 F.2d 285 (3d Cir. 1957); *Tsai v. Rosenthal*, 297 F.2d 614 (8th Cir. 1961); *General Motors Corp. v. Perry*, 303 F.2d 544 (7th Cir. 1962); cf. *Grimm v. California Spray-Chemical Corp.*, 264 F.2d 145 (9th Cir. 1959); *Cooper v. Midwest Feed Products Co.*, 271 F.2d 177 (8th Cir. 1959).

1995 Amendments

The only change, other than stylistic, intended by this revision is to add explicit time limits for filing motions for a new trial, motions to alter or amend a judgment, and affidavits opposing a new trial motion. Previously, there was an inconsistency in the wording of Rules 50, 52, and 59 with respect to whether certain post-judgment motions had to be filed, or merely served, during the prescribed period. This inconsistency caused special problems when motions for a new trial were joined with other post-judgment motions. These motions affect the finality of the judgment, a matter often of importance to third persons as well as the parties and the court. The Committee believes that each of these rules should be revised to require filing before end of the 10–day period. Filing is an event that can be determined with certainty from court records. The phrase "no later than" is used—rather than "within"—to include post-judgment motions that sometimes are filed before actual entry of the judgment by the clerk. It should be noted that under Rule 5 the motions when filed are to contain a certificate of service on other parties. It also should be noted that under Rule 6(a) Saturdays, Sundays, and legal holidays are excluded in measuring the 10–day period, but that Bankruptcy Rule 9006(a) excludes intermediate Saturdays, Sundays, and legal holidays only in computing periods less than 8 days.

Rule 60. Relief From Judgment or Order

(a) Clerical Mistakes. Clerical mistakes in judgments, orders or other parts of the record and errors therein arising from oversight or omission may be corrected by the court at any time of its own initiative or on the motion of any party and after such notice, if any, as the court orders. During the pendency of an appeal, such mistakes may be so corrected before the appeal is docketed in the appellate court, and thereafter while the appeal is pending may be so corrected with leave of the appellate court.

(b) Mistakes; Inadvertence; Excusable Neglect; Newly Discovered Evidence; Fraud, Etc. On motion and upon such terms as are just, the court may relieve a party or a party's legal representative from a final judgment, order, or proceeding for the following reasons: (1) mistake, inadvertence, surprise, or excusable neglect; (2) newly discovered evidence which by due diligence could not have been discovered in time to move for a new trial under Rule 59(b); (3) fraud (whether heretofore denominated intrinsic or extrinsic), misrepresentation, or other misconduct of an adverse party; (4) the judgment is void; (5) the judgment has been satisfied, released, or discharged, or a prior judgment upon which it is based has been reversed or otherwise vacated, or it is no longer equitable that the judgment should have prospective application; or (6) any other reason justifying relief from the operation of the judgment. The motion shall be made within a reasonable time, and for reasons (1), (2), and (3) not more than one year after the judgment, order, or proceeding was entered or taken. A motion under this subdivision (b) does not affect the finality of a judgment or suspend its operation. This rule does not limit the power of a court to entertain an independent action to relieve a party from a judgment, order, or proceeding, or to grant relief to a defendant not actually personally notified as provided in Title 28, U.S.C., § 1655, or to set aside a judgment for fraud upon the court. Writs of coram nobis, coram vobis, audita querela, and bills of review and bills in the nature of a bill of review, are abolished, and the procedure for obtaining any relief from a judgment shall be by motion as prescribed in these rules or by an independent action.

(As amended Dec. 27, 1946, eff. Mar. 19, 1948; Dec. 29, 1948, eff. Oct. 20, 1949; Mar. 2, 1987, eff. Aug. 1, 1987.)

ADVISORY COMMITTEE NOTES

1937 Adoption

Note to Subdivision (a). See [former] Equity Rule 72 (Correction of Clerical Mistakes in Orders and Decrees); Mich.Court Rules Ann. (Searl, 1933) Rule 48, § 3; 2 Wash. Rev.Stat.Ann. (Remington, 1932) § 464(3); Wyo.Rev.Stat. Ann. (Courtright, 1931) § 89–2301(3). For an example of a very liberal provision for the correction of clerical errors and for amendment after judgment, see Va.Code Ann. (Michie, 1936) §§ 6329, 6333.

Note to Subdivision (b). Application to the court under this subdivision does not extend the time for taking an appeal, as distinguished from the motion for new trial. This section is based upon Calif.Code Civ.Proc. (Deering, 1937) § 473. See also N.Y.C.P.A. (1937) § 108; 2 Minn.Stat. (Mason, 1927) § 9283.

For the independent action to relieve against mistake, etc., see Dobie, *Federal Procedure*, pages 760 to 765, compare 639; and Simkins, *Federal Practice*, ch. CXXI (pp. 820 to 830) and ch. CXXII (pp. 831 to 834), compare § 214.

1946 Amendment

Note. Subdivision (a). The amendment incorporates the view expressed in *Perlman v. 322 West Seventy-Second Street, Co., Inc.*, C.C.A.2d, 1942, 127 F.2d 716; 3 *Moore's Federal Practice*, 1938, 3276, and further permits correction after docketing, with leave of the appellate court. Some courts have thought that upon the taking of an appeal the district court lost its power to act. See *Schram v. Safety Investment Co.*, E.D.Mich.1942, 45 F.Supp. 636; also *Miller v. United States*, C.C.A.7th, 1940, 114 F.2d 267.

Subdivision (b). When promulgated, the rules contained a number of provisions, including those found in Rule 60(b), describing the practice by a motion to obtain relief from judgments, and these rules, coupled with the reservation in Rule 60(b) of the right to entertain a new action to relieve a party from a judgment, were generally supposed to cover the field. Since the rules have been in force, decisions have been rendered that the use of bills of review, coram nobis, or audita querela, to obtain relief from final judgments is still proper, and that various remedies of this kind still exist although they are not mentioned in the rules and the practice is not prescribed in the rules. It is obvious that the rules should be complete in this respect and define the practice with respect to any existing rights or remedies to obtain relief from final judgments. For extended discussion of the old common law writs and equitable remedies, the interpretation of Rule 60, and proposals for change, see Moore and Rogers, *Federal Relief from Civil Judgments,* 1946, 55 Yale L.J. 623. See also 3 *Moore's Federal Practice,* 1938, 3254 et seq.; Commentary, *Effect of Rule 60b on Other Methods of Relief From Judgment,* 1941, 4 Fed.Rules Serv. 942, 945; *Wallace v. United States,* C.C.A.2d, 1944, 142 F.2d 240, certiorari denied 65 S.Ct. 37, 323 U.S. 712, 89 L.Ed. 573.

The reconstruction of Rule 60(b) has for one of its purposes a clarification of this situation. Two types of procedure to obtain relief from judgments are specified in the rules as it is proposed to amend them. One procedure is by motion in the court and in the action in which the judgment was rendered. The other procedure is by a new or independent action to obtain relief from a judgment, which action may or may not be begun in the court which rendered the judgment. Various rules, such as the one dealing with a motion for new trial and for amendment of judgments, Rule 59, one for amended findings, Rule 52, and one for judgment notwithstanding the verdict, Rule 50(b), and including the provisions of Rule 60(b) as amended, prescribe the various types of cases in which the practice by motion is permitted. In each case there is a limit upon the time within which resort to a motion is permitted, and this time limit may not be enlarged under Rule 6(b). If the right to make a motion is lost by the expiration of the time limits fixed in these rules, the only other procedural remedy is by a new or independent action to set aside a judgment upon those principles which have heretofore been applied in such an action. Where the independent action is resorted to, the limitations of time are those of laches or statutes of limitations. The Committee has endeavored to ascertain all the remedies and types of relief heretofore available by coram nobis, coram vobis, audita querela, bill of review, or bill in the nature of a bill of review. See Moore and Rogers, *Federal Relief from Civil Judgments,* 1946, 55 Yale L.J. 623, 659 to 682. It endeavored then to amend the rules to permit, either by motion or by independent action, the granting of various kinds of relief from judgments which were permitted in the federal courts prior to the adoption of these rules, and the amendment concludes with a provision abolishing the use of bills of review and the other common law writs referred to, and requiring the practice to be by motion or by independent action.

To illustrate the operation of the amendment, it will be noted that under Rule 59(b) as it now stands, without amendment, a motion for new trial on the ground of newly discovered evidence is permitted within ten days after the entry of the judgment, or after that time upon leave of the court. It is proposed to amend Rule 59(b) by providing that under that rule a motion for new trial shall be served not later than ten days after the entry of the judgment, whatever the ground be for the motion, whether error by the court or newly discovered evidence. On the other hand, one of the purposes of the bill of review in equity was to afford relief on the ground of newly discovered evidence long after the entry of the judgment. Therefore, to permit relief by a motion similar to that heretofore obtained on bill of review, Rule 60(b) as amended permits an application for relief to be made by motion, on the ground of newly discovered evidence, within one year after judgment. Such a motion under Rule 60(b) does not affect the finality of the judgment, but a motion under Rule 59, made within 10 days, does affect finality and the running of the time for appeal.

If these various amendments, including principally those to Rule 60(b), accomplish the purpose for which they are intended, the federal rules will deal with the practice in every sort of case in which relief from final judgments is asked, and prescribe the practice. With reference to the question whether, as the rules now exist, relief by coram nobis, bills of review, and so forth, is permissible, the generally accepted view is that the remedies are still available, although the precise relief obtained in a particular case by use of these ancillary remedies is shrouded in ancient lore and mystery. See *Wallace v. United States,* C.C.A.2d, 1944, 142 F.2d 240, certiorari denied 65 S.Ct. 37, 323 U.S. 712, 89 L.Ed. 573; *Fraser v. Doing,* App.D.C.1942, 130 F.2d 617; *Jones v. Watts,* C.C.A.5th, 1944, 142 F.2d 575; *Preveden v. Hahn,* S.D.N.Y.1941, 36 F.Supp. 952; *Cavallo v. Agwilines, Inc.,* S.D.N.Y.1942, 6 Fed.Rules Serv. 60b.31, Case 2, 2 F.R.D. 526; *McGinn v. United States,* D.C.Mass.1942, 6 Fed.Rules Serv. 60b.51, Case 3, 2 F.R.D. 562; *City of Shattuck, Oklahoma ex rel. Versluis v. Oliver,* W.D.Okl.1945, 8 Fed.Rules Serv. 60b.31, Case 3; Moore and Rogers, *Federal Relief from Civil Judgments,* 1946, 55 Yale L.J. 623, 631 to 653; 3 *Moore's Federal Practice,* 1938, 3254 et seq.; Commentary, *Effect of Rule 60b on Other Methods of Relief From Judgment,* op. cit. supra. Cf. *Norris v. Camp,* C.C.A.10th, 1944, 144 F.2d 1; Reed v. South Atlantic Steamship Co. of Delaware, *D.Del.1942, 2 F.R.D. 475, 6 Fed.Rules Serv. 60b.31, Case 1;* Laughlin v. Berens, *D.D.C.1945, 8 Fed.Rules Serv. 60b.51, Case 1, 73 W.L.R. 209.*

The transposition of the words "the court" and the addition of the word "and" at the beginning of the first sentence are merely verbal changes. The addition of the qualifying word "final" emphasizes the character of the judgments, orders or proceedings from which Rule 60(b) affords relief; and hence interlocutory judgments are not brought within the restrictions of the rule, but rather they are left subject to the complete power of the court rendering them to afford such relief from them as justice requires.

The qualifying pronoun "his" has been eliminated on the basis that it is too restrictive, and that the subdivision should include the mistake or neglect of others which may be just as material and call just as much for supervisory jurisdiction as where the judgment is taken against the party through *his* mistake, inadvertence, etc.

Fraud, whether intrinsic or extrinsic, misrepresentation, or other misconduct of an adverse party are express grounds for relief by motion under amended subdivision (b). There is no sound reason for their exclusion. The incorporation of fraud and the like within the scope of the rule also removes confusion as to the proper procedure. It has been held that relief from a judgment obtained by extrinsic fraud could be secured by motion within a "reasonable time," which might be after the time stated in the rule had run. *Fiske v. Buder*, C.C.A.8th, 1942, 125 F.2d 841; see also inferentially *Bucy v. Nevada Construction Co.*, C.C.A.9th, 1942, 125 F.2d 213. On the other hand, it has been suggested that in view of the fact that fraud was omitted from original Rule 60(b) as a ground for relief, an independent action was the only proper remedy. Commentary, *Effect of Rule 60b on Other Methods of Relief From Judgment*, 1941, 4 Fed.Rules Serv. 942, 945. The amendment settles this problem by making fraud an express ground for relief by motion; and under the saving clause, fraud may be urged as a basis for relief by independent action insofar as established doctrine permits. See Moore and Rogers, *Federal Relief from Civil Judgments*, 1946, 55 Yale L.J. 623, 653 to 659; 3 Moore's Federal Practice, 1938, 3267 et seq. And the rule expressly does not limit the power of the court, when fraud has been perpetrated upon it, to give relief under the saving clause. As an illustration of this situation, see *Hazel-Atlas Glass Co. v. Hartford Empire Co.*, 1944, 64 S.Ct. 997, 322 U.S. 238, 88 L.Ed. 1250.

The time limit for relief by motion in the court and in the action in which the judgment was rendered has been enlarged from six months to one year.

It should be noted that Rule 60(b) does not assume to define the substantive law as to the grounds for vacating judgments, but merely prescribes the practice in proceedings to obtain relief. It should also be noted that under § 200(4) of the Soldiers' and Sailors' Civil Relief Act of 1940, § 501 et seq. [§ 520(4)] of the Appendix to Title 50, a judgment rendered in any action or proceeding governed by the section may be vacated under certain specified circumstances upon proper application to the court.

1948 Amendment

The amendment effective October, 1949 substituted the reference to "Title 28, U.S.C. § 1655," in the next to the last sentence of subdivision (b), for the reference to "Section 57 of the Judicial Code, U.S.C., Title 28, § 118".

1987 Amendment

The amendment is technical. No substantive change is intended.

Rule 61. Harmless Error

No error in either the admission or the exclusion of evidence and no error or defect in any ruling or order or in anything done or omitted by the court or by any of the parties is ground for granting a new trial or for setting aside a verdict or for vacating, modifying, or otherwise disturbing a judgment or order, unless refusal to take such action appears to the court inconsistent with substantial justice. The court at every stage of the proceeding must disregard any error or defect in the proceeding which does not affect the substantial rights of the parties.

ADVISORY COMMITTEE NOTES

1937 Adoption

A combination of U.S.C., Title 28, § 2111, [former] § 391 (New trials; harmless error) and [former] § 777 (Defects of form; amendments) with modifications. See *McCandless v. United States*, 1936, 56 S.Ct. 764, 298 U.S. 342, 80 L.Ed. 1205. Compare [former] Equity Rule 72 (Correction of Clerical Mistakes in Orders and Decrees); and last sentence of [former] Equity Rule 46 (Trial—Testimony Usually Taken in Open Court—Rulings on Objections to Evidence). For the last sentence see the last sentence of [former] Equity Rule 19 (Amendments Generally).

Rule 62. Stay of Proceedings to Enforce a Judgment

(a) Automatic Stay; Exceptions—Injunctions, Receiverships, and Patent Accountings. Except as stated herein, no execution shall issue upon a judgment nor shall proceedings be taken for its enforcement until the expiration of 10 days after its entry. Unless otherwise ordered by the court, an interlocutory or final judgment in an action for an injunction or in a receivership action, or a judgment or order directing an accounting in an action for infringement of letters patent, shall not be stayed during the period after its entry and until an appeal is taken or during the pendency of an appeal. The provisions of subdivision (c) of this rule govern the suspending, modifying, restoring, or granting of an injunction during the pendency of an appeal.

(b) Stay on Motion for New Trial or for Judgment. In its discretion and on such conditions for the security of the adverse party as are proper, the court may stay the execution of or any proceedings to enforce a judgment pending the disposition of a motion for a new trial or to alter or amend a judgment made pursuant to Rule 59, or of a motion for relief from a judgment or order made pursuant to Rule 60, or of a motion for judgment in accordance with a motion for a directed verdict made pursuant to Rule 50, or of a motion for amendment to the findings or for additional findings made pursuant to Rule 52(b).

(c) Injunction Pending Appeal. When an appeal is taken from an interlocutory or final judgment granting, dissolving, or denying an injunction, the court in its discretion may suspend, modify, restore, or grant an injunction during the pendency of the appeal upon such terms as to bond or otherwise as it considers proper for the security of the rights of the adverse party. If the judgment appealed from is rendered by a district court of three judges specially constituted pursuant to a statute of the United States, no such order shall be made except (1) by such court sitting in open court or (2) by the assent of all the judges of such court evidenced by their signatures to the order.

(d) Stay Upon Appeal. When an appeal is taken the appellant by giving a supersedeas bond may obtain a stay subject to the exceptions contained in subdivision (a) of this rule. The bond may be given at or after the time of filing the notice of appeal or of procuring the order allowing the appeal, as the case may be. The stay is effective when the supersedeas bond is approved by the court.

(e) Stay in Favor of the United States or Agency Thereof. When an appeal is taken by the United States or an officer or agency thereof or by direction of any department of the Government of the United States and the operation or enforcement of the judgment is stayed, no bond, obligation, or other security shall be required from the appellant.

(f) Stay According to State Law. In any state in which a judgment is a lien upon the property of the judgment debtor and in which the judgment debtor is entitled to a stay of execution, a judgment debtor is entitled, in the district court held therein, to such stay as would be accorded the judgment debtor had the action been maintained in the courts of that state.

(g) Power of Appellate Court Not Limited. The provisions in this rule do not limit any power of an appellate court or of a judge or justice thereof to stay proceedings during the pendency of an appeal or to suspend, modify, restore, or grant an injunction during the pendency of an appeal or to make any order appropriate to preserve the status quo or the effectiveness of the judgment subsequently to be entered.

(h) Stay of Judgment as to Multiple Claims or Multiple Parties. When a court has ordered a final judgment under the conditions stated in Rule 54(b), the court may stay enforcement of that judgment until the entering of a subsequent judgment or judgments and may prescribe such conditions as are necessary to secure the benefit thereof to the party in whose favor the judgment is entered.

(As amended Dec. 27, 1946, eff. Mar. 19, 1948; Dec. 29, 1948, eff. Oct. 20, 1949; Apr. 17, 1961, eff. July 19, 1961; Mar. 2, 1987, eff. Aug. 1, 1987.)

ADVISORY COMMITTEE NOTES

1937 Adoption

Note to Subdivision (a). The first sentence states the substance of the last sentence of U.S.C., Title 28, [former] § 874 (Supersedeas). The remainder of the subdivision states the substance of the last clause of U.S.C., Title 28, § 1292, [formerly] § 227 (Appeals in proceedings for injunctions; receivers; and admiralty), and of §§ 1292, 2107, [formerly] § 227a (Appeals in suits in equity for infringement of letters patent for inventions; stay of proceedings for accounting), but extended to include final as well as interlocutory judgments.

Note to Subdivision (b). This modifies U.S.C., Title 28, [former] § 840 (Executions; stay on conditions).

Note to Subdivision (c). Compare [former] Equity Rule 74 (Injunction Pending Appeal); and *Cumberland Telephone and Telegraph Co. v. Louisiana Public Service Commission*, 1922, 43 S.Ct. 75, 260 U.S. 212, 67 L.Ed. 217. See Simkins, Federal Practice (1934), § 916, in regard to the effect of appeal on injunctions and the giving of bonds. See U.S.C., [former] Title 6 (Official and Penal Bonds) for bonds by surety companies. For statutes providing for a specially constituted district court of three judges, see:

U.S.C., Title 7:

§ 217 (Proceedings for suspension of orders of Secretary of Agriculture under Stockyards Act)—by reference.

§ 499k (Injunctions; application of injunction laws governing orders of Interstate Commerce Commission to orders of Secretary of Agriculture under Perishable Commodities Act)—by reference.

U.S.C., Title 15:

§ 28 (Antitrust laws; suits against monopolies expedited)

U.S.C., Title 28, former:

§ 47 [now 2325 (repealed)] (Injunctions as to orders of Interstate Commerce Commission, etc.)

§ 380 [now 2284] (Injunctions; alleged unconstitutionality of State statutes)

§ 380a [now 2284] (Same; constitutionality of federal statute)

U.S.C., Title 49:

§ 44 [former] (Suits in equity under interstate commerce laws; expedition of suits)

Note to Subdivision (d). This modifies U.S.C., Title 28, [former] § 874 (Supersedeas). See Rule 36(2), Rules of the Supreme Court of the United States, which governs supersedeas bonds on direct appeals to the Supreme Court, and Rule 73(d), of these rules, which governs supersedeas bonds on appeals to a circuit court of appeals. The provisions governing supersedeas bonds in both kinds of appeals are substantially the same.

Note to Subdivision (e). This states the substance of U.S.C., Title 28, § 2408, formerly § 870 (Bond; not required of the United States).

Note to Subdivision (f). This states the substance of U.S.C., Title 28, [former] § 841 (Executions; stay of one term) with appropriate modification to conform to the provisions of Rule 6(c) as to terms of court.

1946 Amendment

Note. Subdivision (a). [This subdivision not amended]. Sections 203 and 204 of the Soldiers' and Sailors' Civil Relief Act of 1940, 50 U.S.C., Appendix, § 501 et seq. [§§ 523, 524], provide under certain circumstances for the issuance and continuance of a stay of execution of any judgment or order entered against a person in military service. See *Bowsman v. Peterson*, D.Neb.1942, 45 F.Supp. 741. Section 201 of the Act [50 U.S.C. App. § 521] permits under certain circumstances the issuance of a stay of any action or proceeding at any stage thereof, where either the plaintiff or defendant is a person in military service. See also note to Rule 64 herein.

Subdivision (b). This change was necessary because of the proposed addition to Rule 59 of subdivision (e).

Subdivision (h). In proposing to revise Rule 54(b), the Committee thought it advisable to include a separate provision in Rule 62 for stay of enforcement of a final judgment in cases involving multiple claims.

1948 Amendment

The amendment effective October 1949 deleted at the end of subdivision (g) the following language which originally appeared after the word "entered": "and these rules do not supersede the provisions of Section 210 of the Judicial Code, as amended, U.S.C., Title 28, [former] § 47a, or of other statutes of the United States to the effect that stays pending appeals to the Supreme Court may be granted only by that court or a justice thereof."

1961 Amendment

The amendment adopted Apr. 17, 1961, effective July 19, 1961, eliminated words "on some but not all of the claims presented in the action" which followed "final judgment".

1987 Amendment

The amendment is technical. No substantive change is intended.

Rule 63. Inability of a Judge to Proceed

If a trial or hearing has been commenced and the judge is unable to proceed, any other judge may proceed with it upon certifying familiarity with the record and determining that the proceedings in the case may be completed without prejudice to the parties. In a hearing or trial without a jury, the successor judge shall at the request of a party recall any witness whose testimony is material and disputed and who is available to testify again without undue burden. The successor judge may also recall any other witness.

(As amended Mar. 2, 1987, eff. Aug. 1, 1987; Apr. 30, 1991, eff. Dec. 1, 1991.)

ADVISORY COMMITTEE NOTES

1937 Adoption

This rule adapts and extends the provisions of U.S.C., Title 28, [former] § 776 (Bill of exceptions; authentication; signing of by judge) to include all duties to be performed by the judge after verdict or judgment. The statute is therefore superseded.

1987 Amendment

The amendments are technical. No substantive change is intended.

1991 Amendment

The revision substantially displaces the former rule. The former rule was limited to the disability of the judge, and made no provision for disqualification or possible other reasons for the withdrawal of the judge during proceedings. In making provision for other circumstances, the revision is not intended to encourage judges to discontinue participation in a trial for any but compelling reasons. Cf. *United States v. Lane,* 708 F.2d 1394, 1395–1397 (9th Cir.1983). Manifestly, a substitution should not be made for the personal convenience of the court, and the reasons for a substitution should be stated on the record.

The former rule made no provision for the withdrawal of the judge during the trial, but was limited to disqualification after trial. Several courts concluded that the text of the former rule prohibited substitution of a new judge prior to the points described in the rule, thus requiring a new trial, whether or not a fair disposition was within reach of a substitute judge. *E.g., Whalen v. Ford Motor Credit Co.,* 684 F.2d 272 (4th Cir.1982, en banc) *cert. denied,* 459 U.S. 910 (1982) (jury trial); *Arrow–Hart, Inc. v. Philip Carey Co.,* 552 F.2d 711 (6th Cir.1977) (non-jury trial). *See generally* Comment, *The Case of the Dead Judge: Fed.R.Civ.P. 63: Whalen v. Ford Motor Credit Co.,* 67 MINN.L.REV. 827 (1983).

The increasing length of federal trials has made it likely that the number of trials interrupted by the disability of the judge will increase. An efficient mechanism for completing these cases without unfairness is needed to prevent unnecessary expense and delay. To avoid the injustice that may result if the substitute judge proceeds despite unfamiliarity with the action, the new Rule provides, in language similar to Federal Rule of Criminal Procedure 25(a), that the successor judge must certify familiarity with the record and determine that the case may be completed before that judge without prejudice to the parties. This will necessarily require that there be available a transcript or a videotape of the proceedings prior to substitution. If there has been a long but incomplete jury trial, the prompt availability of the transcript or videotape is crucial to the effective use of this rule, for the jury cannot long be held while an extensive transcript is prepared without prejudice to one or all parties.

The revised text authorizes the substitute judge to make a finding of fact at a bench trial based on evidence heard by a different judge. This may be appropriate in limited circumstances. First, if a witness has become unavailable, the testimony recorded at trial can be considered by the successor judge pursuant to F.R.Ev. 804, being equivalent to a recorded deposition available for use at trial pursuant to Rule 32. For this purpose, a witness who is no longer subject to a subpoena to compel testimony at trial is unavailable. Secondly, the successor judge may determine that particular testimony is not material or is not disputed, and so need not be reheard. The propriety of proceeding in this manner may be marginally affected by the availability of a videotape record; a judge who has reviewed a trial on videotape may be entitled to greater confidence in his or her ability to proceed.

The court would, however, risk error to determine the credibility of a witness not seen or heard who is available to be recalled. Cf. *Anderson v. City of Bessemer City NC,* 470 U.S. 564, 575 (1985); *Marshall v. Jerrico Inc.,* 446 U.S. 238, 242 (1980). See also *United States v. Radatz,* 447 U.S. 667 (1980).

VIII. PROVISIONAL AND FINAL REMEDIES

ADVISORY COMMITTEE NOTES

1991 Amendment

The purpose of the revision is to divide this chapter of the Rules into two. No substantive change is effected.

Rule 64. Seizure of Person or Property

At the commencement of and during the course of an action, all remedies providing for seizure of person or property for the purpose of securing satisfaction of the judgment ultimately to be entered in the action are available under the circumstances and in the manner provided by the law of the state in which the district court is held, existing at the time the remedy is sought, subject to the following qualifications: (1) any existing statute of the United States governs to the extent to which it is applicable; (2) the action in which any of the foregoing remedies is used shall be commenced and prosecuted or, if removed from a state court, shall be prosecuted after removal, pursuant to these rules. The remedies thus available include arrest, attachment, garnishment, replevin, sequestration, and other corresponding or equivalent remedies, however designated and regardless of whether by state procedure the remedy is ancillary to an action or must be obtained by an independent action.

ADVISORY COMMITTEE NOTES

1937 Adoption

This rule adopts the existing Federal law, except that it specifies the applicable State law to be that of the time when the remedy is sought. Under U.S.C., Title 28, [former] § 726 (Attachments as provided by State laws) the plaintiff was entitled to remedies by attachment or other process which were on June 1, 1872, provided by the applicable State law, and the district courts might, from time to time, by general rules, adopt such State laws as might be in force. This statute is superseded as are district court rules which are rendered unnecessary by the rule.

Lis pendens. No rule concerning lis pendens is stated, for this would appear to be a matter of substantive law affecting State laws of property. It has been held that in the absence of a State statute expressly providing for the recordation of notice of the pendency of Federal actions, the commencement of a Federal action is notice to all persons affected. *King v. Davis*, 137 F. 198 (W.D.Va., 1903). It has been held, however, that when a state statute does so provide expressly, its provisions are binding. *United States v. Calcasieu Timber Co.*, 236 F. 196 (C.C.A.5th, 1916).

For statutes of the United States on attachment, see, e.g.: U.S.C., Title 28 former:

§ 737 [now 2710] (Attachment in postal suits)
§ 738 [now 2711] (Attachment; application for warrant)
§ 739 [now 2712] (Attachment; issue of warrant)
§ 740 [now 2713] (Attachment; trial of ownership of property)
§ 741 [now 2714] (Attachment; investment of proceeds of attached property)
§ 742 [now 2715] (Attachment; publication of attachment)
§ 743 [now 2716] (Attachment; personal notice of attachment)
§ 744 [now 2717] (Attachment; discharge; bond)
§ 745 [former] (Attachment; accrued rights not affected)
§ 746 (Attachments dissolved in conformity with State laws)

For statutes of the United States on garnishment, see, e.g.: U.S.C., Title 28, former:

§ 748 [now 2405] (Garnishees in suits by United States against a corporation)
§ 749 [now 2405] (Same; issue tendered on denial of indebtedness)
§ 750 [now 2405] (Same; garnishee failing to appear)

For statutes of the United States on arrest, see, e.g.: U.S.C., Title 28 former:

§ 376 [now 1651] (Writs of ne exeat)
§ 755 [former] (Special bail in suits for duties and penalties)
§ 756 [former] (Defendant giving bail in one district and committed in another)
§ 757 [former] (Defendant giving bail in one district and committed in another; defendant held until judgment in first suit)
§ 758 [former] (Bail and affidavits; taking by commissioners)
§ 759 [former] (Calling of bail in Kentucky)
§ 760 [former] (Clerks may take bail de bene esse)
§ 843 [now 2007] (Imprisonment for debt)
§ 844 [now 2007] (Imprisonment for debt; discharge according to State laws)
§ 845 [now 2007] (Imprisonment for debt; jail limits)

For statutes of the United States on replevin, see, e.g.: U.S.C., Title 28:

§ 2463, formerly § 747 (Replevy of property taken under revenue laws).

Supplementary Note

Note. Sections 203 and 204 of the Soldiers' and Sailors' Civil Relief Act of 1940, 50 U.S.C.Appendix, § 501 et seq. [§§ 523 and 524], provide under certain circumstances for the issuance and continuance of a stay of the execution of any judgment entered against a person in military service, or the vacation or stay of any attachment or garnishment directed against such person's property, money, or debts in the hands of another. See also Note to Rule 62 herein.

Rule 65. Injunctions

(a) Preliminary Injunction.

(1) *Notice.* No preliminary injunction shall be issued without notice to the adverse party.

(2) *Consolidation of Hearing With Trial on Merits.* Before or after the commencement of the hearing of an application for a preliminary injunction, the court may order the trial of the action on the merits to be advanced and consolidated with the hearing of the application. Even when this consolidation is not ordered, any evidence received upon an application for a preliminary injunction which would be admissible upon the trial on the merits becomes part of the record on the trial and need not be repeated upon the trial. This subdivision (a)(2) shall be so construed and applied as to save to the parties any rights they may have to trial by jury.

(b) Temporary Restraining Order; Notice; Hearing; Duration. A temporary restraining order may be granted without written or oral notice to the adverse party or that party's attorney only if (1) it clearly appears from specific facts shown by affidavit or by the verified complaint that immediate and irreparable injury, loss, or damage will result to the applicant before the adverse party or that party's attorney can be heard in opposition, and (2) the applicant's attorney certifies to the court in writing the efforts, if any, which have been made to give the notice and the reasons supporting the claim that notice should not be required. Every temporary restraining order granted without notice shall be indorsed with the date and hour of issuance; shall be filed forthwith in the clerk's office and entered of record; shall define the injury and state why it is irreparable and why the order was granted without notice; and shall expire by its terms within such time after entry, not to exceed 10 days, as the court fixes, unless within the time so fixed the order, for good cause shown, is extended for a like period or unless the party against whom the order is directed consents that it may be extended for a longer period. The reasons for the extension shall be entered of record. In case a temporary restraining order is granted without notice, the motion for a preliminary injunction shall be set down for hearing at the earliest possible time and takes precedence of all matters except older matters of the same character; and when the motion comes on for hearing the party who obtained the temporary restraining order shall proceed with the application for a preliminary injunction and, if the party does not do so, the court shall dissolve the temporary restraining order. On 2 days' notice to the party who obtained the temporary restraining order without notice or on such shorter notice to that party as the court may prescribe, the adverse party may appear and move its dissolution or modification and in that event the court shall proceed to hear and determine such motion as expeditiously as the ends of justice require.

(c) Security. No restraining order or preliminary injunction shall issue except upon the giving of security by the applicant, in such sum as the court deems proper, for the payment of such costs and damages as may be incurred or suffered by any party who is found to have been wrongfully enjoined or restrained. No such security shall be required of the United States or of an officer or agency thereof.

The provisions of Rule 65.1 apply to a surety upon a bond or undertaking under this rule.

(d) Form and Scope of Injunction or Restraining Order. Every order granting an injunction and every restraining order shall set forth the reasons for its issuance; shall be specific in terms; shall describe in reasonable detail, and not by reference to the complaint or other document, the act or acts sought to be restrained; and is binding only upon the parties to the action, their officers, agents, servants, employees, and attorneys, and upon those persons in active concert or participation with them who receive actual notice of the order by personal service or otherwise.

(e) Employer and Employee; Interpleader; Constitutional Cases. These rules do not modify any statute of the United States relating to temporary restraining orders and preliminary injunctions in actions affecting employer and employee; or the provisions of Title 28, U.S.C., § 2361, relating to preliminary injunctions in actions of interpleader or in the nature of interpleader; or Title 28, U.S.C., § 2284, relating to actions required by Act of Congress to be heard and determined by a district court of three judges.

(As amended Dec. 27, 1946, eff. Mar. 19, 1948; Dec. 29, 1948, eff. Oct. 20, 1949; Feb. 28, 1966, eff. July 1, 1966; Mar. 2, 1987, eff. Aug. 1, 1987.)

ADVISORY COMMITTEE NOTES

1937 Adoption

Note to Subdivisions (a) and (b). These are taken from U.S.C., Title 28, [former] § 381 (Injunctions; preliminary injunctions and temporary restraining orders).

Note to Subdivision (c). Except for the last sentence, this is substantially U.S.C., Title 28, [former] § 382 (Injunctions; security on issuance of). The last sentence continues the following and similar statutes which expressly except the United States or an officer or agency thereof from such security requirements: U.S.C. Title 15, §§ 77t(b), 78u(e), and 79r(f) (Securities and Exchange Commission). It also excepts the United States or an officer or agency thereof from such security requirements in any action in which a restraining order or interlocutory judgment of injunction issues in its favor whether there is an express statutory exception from such security requirements or not.

See U.S.C., [former] Title 6 (Official and Penal Bonds) for bonds by surety companies.

Note to Subdivision (d). This is substantially U.S.C., Title 28, [former] § 383 (Injunctions; requisites of order; binding effect).

Note to Subdivision (e). The words "relating to temporary restraining orders and preliminary injunctions in actions affecting employer and employee" are words of description and not of limitation.

Compare [former] Equity Rule 73 (Preliminary Injunctions and Temporary Restraining Orders) which is substantially equivalent to the statutes.

For other statutes dealing with injunctions which are continued, see e.g.:

U.S.C., Title 28 former:

- § 46 [now 2324] (Suits to enjoin orders of Interstate Commerce Commission to be against United States)
- § 47 [now 2325] (Injunctions as to orders of Interstate Commerce Commission; appeal to Supreme Court; time for taking)
- § 378 [former] (Injunctions; when granted)
- § 379 [now 2283] (Injunctions; stay in State courts)
- § 380 [now 1253, 2101, 2281, 2284] (Injunctions; alleged unconstitutionality of State statutes; appeal to Supreme Court)
- § 380a [now 1253, 2101, 2281, 2284] (Injunctions; constitutionality of Federal statute; application for hearing; appeal to Supreme Court)

U.S.C., Title 7:

- § 216 (Court proceedings to enforce orders; injunction)
- § 217 (Proceedings for suspension of orders)

U.S.C., Title 15:

- § 4 (Jurisdiction of courts; duty of district attorney; procedure)
- § 25 (Restraining violations; procedure)
- § 26 (Injunctive relief for private parties; exceptions)
- § 77t(b) (Injunctions and prosecution of offenses)

1946 Amendment

Note. It has been held that in actions on preliminary injunction bonds the district court has discretion to grant relief in the same proceeding or to require the institution of a new action on the bond. *Russell v. Farley,* 1881, 105 U.S. 433, 466. It is believed, however, that in all cases the litigant should have a right to proceed on the bond in the same proceeding, in the manner provided in Rule 73(f) for a similar situation. The paragraph added to Rule 65(c) insures this result and is in the interest of efficiency. There is no reason why Rules 65(c) and 73(f) should operate differently. Compare § 50, sub. n of the Bankruptcy Act, 11 U.S.C. § 78, sub. n, under which actions on all bonds furnished pursuant to the Act may be proceeded upon summarily in the bankruptcy court. See 2 *Collier on Bankruptcy,* 14th ed. by Moore and Oglebay, 1853–1854.

1948 Amendment

The amendment effective October 1949, changed subdivision (e) in the following respects: in the first clause the amendment substituted the words "any statute of the United States" for the words "the Act of October 15, 1914, c. 323, §§ 1 and 20 (38 Stat. 730), U.S.C., Title 29, §§ 52 and 53, or the Act of March 23, 1932, c. 90 (47 Stat. 70), U.S.C., Title 29, c. 6"; in the second clause of subdivision (e) the amendment substituted the reference to "Title 28, U.S.C., § 2361" for the reference to "Section 24(26) of the Judicial Code as amended, U.S.C., Title 28, § 41(26)"; and the third clause was amended to read "Title 28, U.S.C., § 2284," etc., as at present, instead of "the Act of August 24, 1937, c. 754, § 3, relating to actions to enjoin the enforcement of acts of Congress."

1966 Amendment

Subdivision (a)(2). This new subdivision provides express authority for consolidating the hearing of an application for a preliminary injunction with the trial on the merits. The authority can be exercised with particular profit when it appears that a substantial part of the evidence offered on the application will be relevant to the merits and will be presented in such form as to qualify for admission on the trial proper. Repetition of evidence is thereby avoided. The fact that the proceedings have been consolidated should cause no delay in the disposition of the application for the preliminary injunction, for the evidence will be directed in the first instance to that relief, and the preliminary injunction, if justified by the proof, may be issued in the course of the consolidated proceedings. Furthermore, to consolidate the proceedings will tend to expedite the final disposition of the action. It is believed that consolidation can be usefully availed of in many cases.

The subdivision further provides that even when consolidation is not ordered, evidence received in connection with an application for a preliminary injunction which would be admissible on the trial on the merits forms part of the trial record. This evidence need not be repeated on the trial. On the other hand, repetition is not altogether prohibited. That would be impractical and unwise. For example, a witness testifying comprehensively on the trial who has previously testified upon the application for a preliminary injunction might sometimes be hamstrung in telling his story if he could not go over some part of his prior testimony to connect it with his present testimony. So also, some repetition of testimony may be called for where the trial is conducted by a judge who did not hear the application for the preliminary injunction. In general, however, repetition can be avoided with an increase of efficiency in the conduct of the case and without any distortion of the presentation of evidence by the parties.

Since an application for a preliminary injunction may be made in an action in which, with respect to all or part of the merits, there is a right to trial by jury, it is appropriate to add the caution appearing in the last sentence of the subdivision. In such a case the jury will have to hear all the evidence bearing on its verdict, even if some part of the evidence has already been heard by the judge alone on the application for the preliminary injunction.

The subdivision is believed to reflect the substance of the best current practice and introduces no novel conception.

Subdivision (b). In view of the possibly drastic consequences of a temporary restraining order, the opposition should be heard, if feasible, before the order is granted. Many judges have properly insisted that, when time does not permit of formal notice of the application to the adverse party, some expedient, such as telephonic notice to the attorney for the adverse party, be resorted to if this can reasonably be done. On occasion, however, temporary restraining orders have been issued without any notice when it was feasible for some fair, although informal, notice to be given. See the emphatic criticisms in *Pennsylvania Rd. Co. v. Transport Workers Union,* 278 F.2d 693, 694 (3d Cir. 1960); *Arvida Corp. v. Sugarman,* 259 F.2d 428, 429 (2d Cir. 1958); *Lummus Co. v. Commonwealth Oil Ref. Co., Inc.,* 297 F.2d 80, 83 (2d Cir. 1961), cert. denied, 368 U.S. 986 (1962).

Heretofore the first sentence of subdivision (b), in referring to a notice "served" on the "adverse party" on which a "hearing" could be held, perhaps invited the interpretation that the order might be granted without notice if the circumstances did not permit of a formal hearing on the basis of a formal notice. The subdivision is amended to make it plain that informal notice, which may be communicated to the attorney rather than the adverse party, is to be preferred to no notice at all.

Before notice can be dispensed with, the applicant's counsel must give his certificate as to any efforts made to give notice and the reasons why notice should not be required. This certificate is in addition to the requirement of an affidavit or verified complaint setting forth the facts as to the irreparable injury which would result before the opposition could be heard.

The amended subdivision continues to recognize that a temporary restraining order may be issued without any notice when the circumstances warrant.

Subdivision (c). Original Rules 65 and 73 contained substantially identical provisions for summary proceedings against sureties on bonds required or permitted by the rules. There was fragmentary coverage of the same subject in the Admiralty Rules. Clearly, a single comprehensive rule is required, and is incorporated as Rule 65.1.

1987 Amendment

The amendments are technical. No substantive change is intended.

Rule 65.1. Security: Proceedings Against Sureties

Whenever these rules, including the Supplemental Rules for Certain Admiralty and Maritime Claims, require or permit the giving of security by a party, and security is given in the form of a bond or stipulation or other undertaking with one or more sureties, each surety submits to the jurisdiction of the court and irrevocably appoints the clerk of the court as the surety's agent upon whom any papers affecting the surety's liability on the bond or undertaking may be served. The surety's liability may be enforced on motion without the necessity of an independent action. The motion and such notice of the motion as the court prescribes may be served on the clerk of the court, who shall forthwith mail copies to the sureties if their addresses are known.

(Added Feb. 28, 1966, eff. July 1, 1966, and amended Mar. 2, 1987, eff. Aug. 1, 1987.)

ADVISORY COMMITTEE NOTES

1966 Addition

See Note to Rule 65.

1987 Amendment

The amendments are technical. No substantive change is intended.

Rule 66. Receivers Appointed by Federal Courts

An action wherein a receiver has been appointed shall not be dismissed except by order of the court. The practice in the administration of estates by receivers or by other similar officers appointed by the court shall be in accordance with the practice heretofore followed in the courts of the United States or as provided in rules promulgated by the district courts. In all other respects the action in which the appointment of a receiver is sought or which is brought by or against a receiver is governed by these rules.

(As amended Dec. 27, 1946, eff. Mar. 19, 1948; Dec. 29, 1948, eff. Oct. 20, 1949.)

ADVISORY COMMITTEE NOTES

1946 Amendment

Note. The title of Rule 66 has been expanded to make clear the subject of the rule, i.e., federal equity receivers.

The first sentence added to Rule 66 prevents a dismissal by any party, after a federal equity receiver has been appointed, except upon leave of court. A party should not be permitted to oust the court and its officer without the consent of that court. See Civil Rule 31(e), Eastern District of Washington.

The second sentence added at the beginning of the rule deals with suits by or against a federal equity receiver. The first clause thereof eliminates the formal ceremony of an ancillary appointment before suit can be brought by a receiver, and is in accord with the more modern state practice, and with more expeditious and less expensive judicial administration. 2 *Moore's Federal Practice*, 1938, 2088–2091. For the rule necessitating ancillary appointment, see *Sterrett v. Second Nat. Bank*, 1918, 39 S.Ct. 27, 248 U.S. 73, 63 L.Ed. 135; *Kelley v. Queeney*, W.D.N.Y.1941, 41 F.Supp. 1015; see also *McCandless v. Furlaud*, 1934, 55 S.Ct. 42, 293 U.S. 67, 79 L.Ed. 202. This rule has been extensively criticized. First, *Extraterritorial Powers of Receivers*, 1932, 27 Ill.L.Rev. 271; Rose, *Extraterritorial Actions by Receivers*, 1933, 17 Minn. L.Rev. 704; Laughlin, *The Extraterritorial Powers of Receivers*, 1932, 45 Harv.L.Rev. 429; Clark and Moore, *A New Federal Civil Procedure—II, Pleadings and Parties*, 1935, 44 Yale L.J. 1291, 1312–1315; Note, 1932, 30 Mich.L.Rev. 1322. See also comment in *Bicknell v. Lloyd-Smith*, C.C.A.2d, 1940, 109 F.2d 527, certiorari denied 61 S.Ct. 15, 311 U.S. 650, 85 L.Ed. 416. The second clause of the sentence merely incorporates the well-known and general rule that, absent statutory authorization, a federal receiver cannot be sued without leave of the court which appointed him, applied in the federal courts since *Barton v. Barbour*, 1881, 104 U.S. 126. See also 1 *Clark on Receivers*, 2d ed., § 549. Under [§ 959 of this title, formerly] 28 U.S.C. § 125 leave of court is unnecessary when a receiver is sued "in respect of any act or transaction of his in carrying on the business" connected with the receivership property, but such suit is subject to the general equity jurisdiction of the court in which the receiver was appointed, so far as justice necessitates.

Capacity of a state court receiver to sue or be sued in Federal court is governed by Rule 17(b).

The last sentence added to Rule 66 assures the application of the rules in all matters except actual administration of the receivership estate itself. Since this implicitly carries with it the applicability of those rules relating to appellate procedure, the express reference thereto contained in Rule 66 has been stricken as superfluous. Under Rule 81(a)(1) the rules do not apply to bankruptcy proceedings except as they may be made applicable by order of the Supreme Court. Rule 66 is applicable to what is commonly known as a federal "chancery" or "equity" receiver, or similar type of court officer. It is not designed to regulate or affect receivers in bankruptcy, which are governed by the Bankruptcy Act and the General Orders. Since the Federal Rules are applicable in bankruptcy by virtue of General Orders in Bankruptcy 36 and 37 [see Appendix II following Rules of Bankruptcy Procedure, Title 11] only to the extent that they are not inconsistent with the Bankruptcy Act or the General Orders, Rule 66 is not applicable to bankruptcy receivers. See 1 *Collier on Bankruptcy,* 14th ed. by Moore and Oglebay, ¶¶2.23–2.36.

1948 Amendment

The amendment effective October 1949 deleted a sentence which formerly appeared immediately following the first sentence and which read as follows: "A receiver shall have the capacity to sue in any district court without ancillary appointment; but actions against a receiver may not be commenced without leave of the court appointing him except when authorized by a statute of the United States."

Rule 67. Deposit in Court

In an action in which any part of the relief sought is a judgment for a sum of money or the disposition of a sum of money or the disposition of any other thing capable of delivery, a party, upon notice to every other party, and by leave of court, may deposit with the court all or any part of such sum or thing, whether or not that party claims all or any part of the sum or thing. The party making the deposit shall serve the order permitting deposit on the clerk of the court. Money paid into court under this rule shall be deposited and withdrawn in accordance with the provisions of Title 28, U.S.C., §§ 2041, and 2042; the Act of June 26, 1934, c. 756, § 23, as amended (48 Stat. 1236, 58 Stat. 845), U.S.C., Title 31, § 725v; or any like statute. The fund shall be deposited in an interest-bearing account or invested in an interest-bearing instrument approved by the court.

(As amended Dec. 29, 1948, eff. Oct. 20, 1949; Apr. 28, 1983, eff. Aug. 1, 1983.)

ADVISORY COMMITTEE NOTES

1937 Adoption

This rule provides for deposit in court generally, continuing similar special provisions contained in such statutes as U.S.C., Title 28, [§§ 1335, 1397, 2361, formerly] § 41(26) (Original jurisdiction of bills of interpleader, and of bills in the nature of interpleader). See generally *Howard v. United States,* 1902, 22 S.Ct. 543, 184 U.S. 676, 46 L.Ed. 754; United States Supreme Court Admiralty Rules (1920), Rules 37 (Bringing Funds into Court), 41 (Funds in Court Registry), and 42 (Claims Against Proceeds in Registry). With the first sentence, compare *English Rules Under the Judicature Act* (The Annual Practice, 1937) O. 22, r. 1(1).

1948 Amendment

The amendment effective October 1949 substituted the reference to "Title 28, U.S.C.A., §§ 2041, and 2042" for the reference to "Sections 995 and 996, Revised Statutes, as amended, U.S.C.A., Title 28, §§ 851, 852." The amendment also added the words "as amended" following the citation of the Act of June 26, 1934, c. 756, § 23, and, in the parenthetical citation immediately following, added the reference to "58 Stat. 845".

1983 Amendment

Rule 67 has been amended in three ways. The first change is the addition of the clause in the first sentence. Some courts have construed the present rule to permit deposit only when the party making it claims no interest in the fund or thing deposited. E.g., *Blasin-Stern v. Beech-Nut Life Savers Corp.,* 429 F.Supp. 533 (D. Puerto Rico 1975); *Dinkins v. General Aniline & Film Corp.,* 214 F.Supp. 281 (S.D.N.Y.1963). However, there are situations in which a litigant may wish to be relieved of responsibility for a sum or thing, but continue to claim an interest in all or part of it. In these cases the deposit-in-court procedure should be available; in addition to the advantages to the party making the deposit, the procedure gives other litigants assurance that any judgment will be collectable. The amendment is intended to accomplish that.

The second change is the addition of a requirement that the order of deposit be served on the clerk of the court in which the sum or thing is to be deposited. This is simply to assure that the clerk knows what is being deposited and what his responsibilities are with respect to the deposit. The latter point is particularly important since the rule as amended contemplates that deposits will be placed in interest-bearing accounts; the clerk must know what treatment has been ordered for the particular deposit.

The third change is to require that any money be deposited in an interest-bearing account or instrument approved by the court.

HISTORICAL NOTES

References in Text

The Act of June 26, 1934, c. 756, § 23, as amended (48 Stat. 1236, 58 Stat. 845), 31 U.S.C. § 725v, referred to in text, was repealed by Pub.L. 97–258, § 5(b), Sept. 13, 1982, 96 Stat. 1074, the first section of which enacted Title 31, Money and Finance. Insofar as not superseded by sections 2041 and 2042 of Title 28, Judiciary and Judicial Procedure, the Act of June 26, 1934, § 23, as amended (31 U.S.C. 725v) was reenacted as sections 572a and 2043 of Title 28 by Pub.L. 97–258, § 2(g)(3), (4).

Rule 68. Offer of Judgment

At any time more than 10 days before the trial begins, a party defending against a claim may serve upon the adverse party an offer to allow judgment to be taken against the defending party for the money or property or to the effect specified in the offer, with costs then accrued. If within 10 days after the service of the offer the adverse party serves written notice that the offer is accepted, either party may then file the offer and notice of acceptance together with proof of service thereof and thereupon the clerk shall enter judgment. An offer not accepted shall be deemed withdrawn and evidence thereof is not admissible except in a proceeding to determine costs. If the judgment finally obtained by the offeree is not more favorable than the offer, the offeree must pay the costs incurred after the making of the offer. The fact that an offer is made but not accepted does not preclude a subsequent offer. When the liability of one party to another has been determined by verdict or order or judgment, but the amount or extent of the liability remains to be determined by further proceedings, the party adjudged liable may make an offer of judgment, which shall have the same effect as an offer made before trial if it is served within a reasonable time not less than 10 days prior to the commencement of hearings to determine the amount or extent of liability.

(As amended Dec. 27, 1946, eff. Mar. 19, 1948; Feb. 28, 1966, eff. July 1, 1966; Mar. 2, 1987, eff. Aug. 1, 1987.)

ADVISORY COMMITTEE NOTES

1937 Adoption

See 2 Minn.Stat. (Mason, 1927) § 9323; 4 Mont.Rev.Codes Ann. (1935) § 9770; N.Y.C.P.A. (1937) § 177.

For the recovery of costs against the United States, see Rule 54(d).

1946 Amendment

Note. The third sentence of Rule 68 has been altered to make clear that evidence of an unaccepted offer is admissible in a proceeding to determine the costs of the action but is not otherwise admissible.

The two sentences substituted for the deleted last sentence of the rule assure a party the right to make a second offer where the situation permits—as, for example, where a prior offer was not accepted but the plaintiff's judgment is nullified and a new trial ordered, whereupon the defendant desires to make a second offer. It is implicit, however, that as long as the case continues—whether there be a first, second or third trial—and the defendant makes no further offer, his first and only offer will operate to save him the costs from the time of that offer if the plaintiff ultimately obtains a judgment less than the sum offered. In the case of successive offers not accepted, the offeror is saved the costs incurred after the making of the offer which was equal to or greater than the judgment ultimately obtained. These provisions should serve to encourage settlements and avoid protracted litigation.

The phrase "before the trial begins", in the first sentence of the rule, has been construed in *Cover v. Chicago Eye Shield Co.,* C.C.A.7th, 1943, 136 F.2d 374, certiorari denied 64 S.Ct. 53, 320 U.S. 749, 88 L.Ed. 445.

1966 Amendment

This logical extension of the concept of offer of judgment is suggested by the common admiralty practice of determining liability before the amount of liability is determined.

1987 Amendment

The amendments are technical. No substantive change is intended.

Rule 69. Execution

(a) In General. Process to enforce a judgment for the payment of money shall be a writ of execution, unless the court directs otherwise. The procedure on execution, in proceedings supplementary to and in aid of a judgment, and in proceedings on and in aid of execution shall be in accordance with the practice and procedure of the state in which the district court is held, existing at the time the remedy is sought, except that any statute of the United States governs to the extent that it is applicable. In aid of the judgment or execution, the judgment creditor or a successor in interest when that interest appears of record, may obtain discovery from any person, including the judgment debtor, in the manner provided in these rules or in the manner provided by the practice of the state in which the district court is held.

(b) Against Certain Public Officers. When a judgment has been entered against a collector or other officer of revenue under the circumstances stated in Title 28, U.S.C., § 2006, or against an officer of Congress in an action mentioned in the Act of March 3, 1875, ch. 130, § 8 (18 Stat. 401), U.S.C., Title 2, § 118, and when the court has given the certificate of probable cause for the officer's act as provided in those statutes, execution shall not issue against the officer or the officer's property but the final judgment shall be satisfied as provided in such statutes.

(As amended Dec. 29, 1948, eff. Oct. 20, 1949; Mar. 30, 1970, eff. July 1, 1970; Mar. 2, 1987, eff. Aug. 1, 1987.)

ADVISORY COMMITTEE NOTES

1937 Adoption

Note to Subdivision (a). This follows in substance U.S.C. Title 28, [former] §§ 727 (Executions as provided by State laws) and [former 729] [now Title 42, § 1988] (Proceedings in vindication of civil rights), except that, as in the similar case of attachments (see note to Rule 64), the rule specifies the applicable state law to be that of the time when the remedy is sought, and thus renders unnecessary, as well as supersedeas, local district court rules.

Statutes of the United States on execution, when applicable, govern under this rule. Among these are:

U.S.C., Title 12:

§ 91 (Transfers by bank and other acts in contemplation of insolvency)

§ 632 (Jurisdiction of United States district courts in cases arising out of foreign banking jurisdiction where Federal reserve bank a party)

U.S.C., Title 19:
- § 199 (Judgments for customs duties, how payable)

U.S.C., Title 26 [I.R.C.1939]:
- § 1610(a) [former] (Surrender of property subject to distraint)

U.S.C., Title 28 former:
- § 122 [now 1656] (Creation of new district or transfer of territory; lien)
- § 350 [now 2101] (Time for making application for appeal or certiorari; stay pending application for certiorari)
- § 489 [now 547] (District Attorneys; reports to Department of Justice)
- § 574 [now 1921] (Marshals, fees enumerated)
- § 786 [former] (Judgments for duties; collected in coin)
- § 811 [now 1961] (Interest on judgments)
- § 838 [former] (Executions; run in all districts of State)
- § 839 [now 2413] (Executions; run in every State and Territory)
- § 840 [former] (Executions; stay on conditions), as modified by Rule 62(b)
- § 841 [former] (Executions; stay of one term), as modified by Rule 62(f)
- § 842 [now 2006] (Executions; against officers of revenue in cases of probable cause), as incorporated in Subdivision (b) of this rule
- § 843 [now 2007] (Imprisonment for debt)
- § 844 [now 2007] (Imprisonment for debt; discharge according to State laws)
- § 845 [now 2007] (Imprisonment for debt; jail limits)
- § 846 [now 2005] (Fieri Facias; appraisal of goods; appraisers)
- § 847 [now 2001] (Sales; real property under order or decree)
- § 848 [now 2004] (Sales; personal property under order or decree)
- § 849 [now 2002] (Sales; necessity of notice)
- § 850 [now 2003] (Sales; death of marshall after levy or after sale)
- § 869 [former] (Bond in former error and on appeal), as incorporated in Rule 73(c)
- § 874 [former] (Supersedeas), as modified by Rules 62(d) and 73(d)

U.S.C., Title 31:
- § 195 [now 3715] (Purchase on execution)

U.S.C., Title 33:
- § 918 (Collection of defaulted payments)

U.S.C., Title 49:
- § 74(g) [former] (Causes of action arising out of Federal control of railroads; execution and other process)

Special statutes of the United States on exemption from execution are also continued. Among these are:

U.S.C., Title 2:
- § 118 (Actions against officers of Congress for official acts)

U.S.C., Title 5 former:
- § 729 [see 8346, 8470] (Federal employees retirement annuities not subject to assignment, execution, levy or other legal process)

U.S.C., Title 10 former:
- § 610 [now 3690, 8690] (Exemption of enlisted men from arrest on civil process)

U.S.C., Title 22 former:
- § 21(h) [see 4060] (Foreign service retirement and disability system; establishment; rules and regulations; annuities; nonassignable; exemption from legal process)

U.S.C., Title 33:
- § 916 (Assignment and exemption from claims of creditors) (Longshoremen's and Harborworkers' Compensation Act)

U.S.C., Title 38 former:
- § 54 [see 3101] (Attachment, levy or seizure of moneys due pensioners prohibited)
- § 393 [former] (Army and Navy Medal of Honor Roll; pensions additional to other pensions; liability to attachment, etc.) Compare [former] Title 34, § 365(c) (Medal of Honor Roll; special pension to persons enrolled)
- § 618 [see 3101] (Benefits exempt from seizure under process and taxation; no deductions for indebtedness to United States)

U.S.C., Title 43:
- § 175 (Exemption from execution of homestead land)

U.S.C., Title 48 former:
- § 1371*o* (Panama canal and railroad retirement annuities, exemption from execution and so forth.)

Supplementary Note

Note. With respect to the provisions of the Soldiers' and Sailors' Civil Relief Act of 1940, 50 U.S.C. Appendix, § 501 et seq., see notes to Rules 62 and 64 herein.

1948 Amendment

The amendment effective October 1949, substituted the citation of "Title 28, U.S.C., § 2006" in subdivision (b) in place of the citation to "Section 989, Revised Statutes, U.S.C., Title 28, § 842".

1970 Amendment

The amendment assures that, in aid of execution on a judgment, all discovery procedures provided in the rules are available and not just discovery via the taking of a deposition. Under the present language, one court had held that Rule 34 discovery is unavailable to the judgment creditor. *M. Lowenstein & Sons, Inc. v. American Underwear Mfg. Co.*, 11 F.R.D. 172 (E.D.Pa.1951). Notwithstanding the language, and relying heavily on legislative history referring to Rule 33, the Fifth Circuit has held that a judgment creditor may invoke Rule 33 interrogatories. *United States v. McWhirter*, 376 F.2d 102 (5th Cir. 1967). But the court's reasoning does not extend to discovery except as provided in Rules 26–33. One commentator suggests that the existing language might properly be stretched to all discovery, 7 *Moore's Federal Practice* ¶69.05[1] (2d ed. 1966), but another believes that a rules amendment is needed. 3 Barron & Holtzoff, *Federal Practice and Procedure* 1484 (Wright ed. 1958). Both commentators and the court in *McWhirter* are clear that, as a matter of policy, Rule 69 should authorize the use of all discovery devices provided in the rules.

1987 Amendment

The amendments are technical. No substantive change is intended.

Rule 70. Judgment for Specific Acts; Vesting Title

If a judgment directs a party to execute a conveyance of land or to deliver deeds or other documents or to perform any other specific act and the party fails to comply within the time specified, the court may direct the act to be done at the cost of the disobedient party by some other person appointed by the court and the act when so done has like effect as if done by the party. On application of the party entitled to performance, the clerk shall issue a writ of attachment or sequestration against the property of the disobedient party to compel obedience to the judgment. The court may also in proper cases adjudge the party in contempt. If real or personal property is within the district, the court in lieu of directing a conveyance thereof may enter a judgment divesting the title of any party and vesting it in others and such judgment has the effect of a conveyance executed in due form of law. When any order or judgment is for the delivery of possession, the party in whose favor it is entered is entitled to a writ of execution or assistance upon application to the clerk.

ADVISORY COMMITTEE NOTES

1937 Adoption

Compare [former] Equity Rules 7 (Process, Mesne and Final), 8 (Enforcement of Final Decrees), and 9 (Writ of Assistance). To avoid possible confusion, both old and new denominations for attachment (sequestration) and execution (assistance) are used in this rule. Compare with the provision in this rule that the judgment may itself vest title, 6 Tenn.Ann.Code (Williams, 1934), § 10594; 2 Conn.Gen.Stat. (1930), § 5455; N.M.Stat.Ann. (Courtright, 1929), § 117–117; 2 Ohio Gen.Code Ann. (Page, 1926), § 11590; and England, Supreme Court of Judicature Act (1925), § 47.

Rule 71. Process in Behalf of and Against Persons not Parties

When an order is made in favor of a person who is not a party to the action, that person may enforce obedience to the order by the same process as if a party; and, when obedience to an order may be lawfully enforced against a person who is not a party, that person is liable to the same process for enforcing obedience to the order as if a party.

(As amended Mar. 2, 1987, eff. Aug. 1, 1987.)

ADVISORY COMMITTEE NOTES

1937 Adoption

Compare [former] Equity Rule 11 (Process in Behalf of and Against Persons Not Parties). Compare also *Terrell v. Allison*, 1875, 21 Wall. 289, 22 L.Ed. 634; *Farmers' Loan and Trust Co. v. Chicago and A. Ry. Co.*, C.C.Ind.1890, 44 F. 653; *Robert Findlay Mfg. Co. v. Hygrade Lighting Fixture Corp.*, E.D.N.Y.1923, 288 F. 80; *Thompson v. Smith*, C.C.Minn.1870, Fed.Cas. No. 13,977.

1987 Amendment

The amendments are technical. No substantive change is intended.

IX. SPECIAL PROCEEDINGS [1]

[1] Another Chapter IX which was set out post has been abrogated.

ADVISORY COMMITTEE NOTES

1991 Addition

This chapter heading is to be inserted between Rule 71 and Rule 71A.

Rule 71A. Condemnation of Property

(a) Applicability of Other Rules. The Rules of Civil Procedure for the United States District Courts govern the procedure for the condemnation of real and personal property under the power of eminent domain, except as otherwise provided in this rule.

(b) Joinder of Properties. The plaintiff may join in the same action one or more separate pieces of property, whether in the same or different ownership and whether or not sought for the same use.

(c) Complaint.

(1) Caption. The complaint shall contain a caption as provided in Rule 10(a), except that the plaintiff shall name as defendants the property, designated generally by kind, quantity, and location, and at least one of the owners of some part of or interest in the property.

(2) Contents. The complaint shall contain a short and plain statement of the authority for the taking, the use for which the property is to be taken, a description of the property sufficient for its identification, the interests to be acquired, and as to each separate piece of property a designation of the defendants who have been joined as owners thereof or of some interest therein. Upon the commencement of the action, the plaintiff need join as defendants only the persons having or claiming an interest in the property whose names are then known, but prior to any hearing involving the compensation to be paid for a piece of property, the plaintiff shall add as defendants all persons having or claiming an interest in that property whose names can be ascertained by a reasonably diligent search of the records, considering the character and value of the property involved and the interests to be acquired, and also those whose names have otherwise been learned. All others may be made defendants under the designation "Unknown Owners." Process shall be served as provided in subdivision (d) of this rule upon all defendants, whether named as defendants at the time of the commencement of the action or subsequently added, and a defendant may answer as provided in subdivision (e) of this rule. The court meanwhile may order such distribution of a deposit as the facts warrant.

(3) Filing. In addition to filing the complaint with the court, the plaintiff shall furnish to the clerk at least one copy thereof for the use of the defendants and additional copies at the request of the clerk or of a defendant.

(d) Process.

(1) Notice; Delivery. Upon the filing of the complaint the plaintiff shall forthwith deliver to the clerk joint or several notices directed to the defendants named or designated in the complaint. Additional notices directed to defendants subsequently added shall be so delivered. The delivery of the notice and its service have the same effect as the delivery and service of the summons under Rule 4.

(2) Same; Form. Each notice shall state the court, the title of the action, the name of the defendant to whom it is directed, that the action is to condemn property, a description of the defendant's property sufficient for its identification, the interest to be taken, the authority for the taking, the uses for which the property is to be taken, that the defendant may serve upon the plaintiff's attorney an answer within 20 days after service of the notice, and that the failure so to serve an answer constitutes a consent to the taking and to the authority of the court to proceed to hear the action and to fix the compensation. The notice shall conclude with the name of the plaintiff's attorney and an address within the district in which action is brought where the attorney may be served. The notice need contain a description of no other property than that to be taken from the defendants to whom it is directed.

(3) Service of Notice.

(A) Personal Service. Personal service of the notice (but without copies of the complaint) shall be made in accordance with Rule 4 upon a defendant whose residence is known and who resides within the United States or a territory subject to the administrative or judicial jurisdiction of the United States.

(B) Service by Publication. Upon the filing of a certificate of the plaintiff's attorney stating that the attorney believes a defendant cannot be personally served, because after diligent inquiry within the state in which the complaint is filed the attorney's[1] place of residence cannot be ascertained by the plaintiff or, if ascertained, that it is beyond the territorial limits of personal service as provided in this rule, service of the notice shall be made on this defendant by publication in a newspaper published in the county where the property is located, or if there is no such newspaper, then in a newspaper having a general circulation where the property is located, once a week for not less than three successive weeks. Prior to the last publication, a copy of the notice shall also be mailed to a defendant who cannot be personally served as provided in this rule but whose place of residence is then known. Unknown owners may be served by publication in like manner by a notice addressed to "Unknown Owners."

Service by publication is complete upon the date of the last publication. Proof of publication and mailing shall be made by certificate of the plaintiff's attorney, to which shall be attached a printed copy of the published notice with the name and dates of the newspaper marked thereon.

(4) Return; Amendment. Proof of service of the notice shall be made and amendment of the notice or proof of its service allowed in the manner provided for the return and amendment of the summons under Rule 4.

(e) Appearance or Answer. If a defendant has no objection or defense to the taking of the defendant's property, the defendant may serve a notice of appearance designating the property in which the defendant claims to be interested. Thereafter, the defendant shall receive notice of all proceedings affecting it. If a defendant has any objection or defense to the taking of the property, the defendant shall serve an answer within 20 days after the service of notice upon the defendant. The answer shall identify the property in which the defendant claims to have an interest, state the nature and extent of the interest claimed, and state all the defendant's objections and defenses to the taking of the property. A defendant waives all defenses and objections not so presented, but at the trial of the issue of just compensation, whether or not the defendant has previously appeared or answered, the defendant may present evidence as to the amount of the compensation to be paid for the property, and the defendant may share in the distribution of the award. No other pleading or motion asserting any additional defense or objection shall be allowed.

(f) Amendment of Pleadings. Without leave of court, the plaintiff may amend the complaint at any time before the trial of the issue of compensation and as many times as desired, but no amendment shall be made which will result in a dismissal forbidden by subdivision (i) of this rule. The plaintiff need not serve a copy of an amendment, but shall serve notice of the filing, as provided in Rule 5(b), upon any party affected thereby who has appeared and, in the manner provided in subdivision (d) of this rule, upon any party affected thereby who has not appeared. The plaintiff shall furnish to the clerk of the court for the use of the defendants at least one copy of each amendment and shall furnish additional copies on the request of the clerk or of a defendant. Within the time allowed by subdivision (e) of this rule a defendant may serve an answer to the amended pleading, in the form and manner and with the same effect as there provided.

(g) Substitution of Parties. If a defendant dies or becomes incompetent or transfers an interest after the defendant's joinder, the court may order substitution of the proper party upon motion and notice of hearing. If the motion and notice of hearing are to be served upon a person not already a party, service shall be made as provided in subdivision (d)(3) of this rule.

(h) Trial. If the action involves the exercise of the power of eminent domain under the law of the United States, any tribunal specially constituted by an Act of Congress governing the case for the trial of the issue of just compensation shall be the tribunal for the determination of that issue; but if there is no such specially constituted tribunal any party may have a trial by jury of the issue of just compensation by filing a demand therefor within the time allowed for answer or within such further time as the court may fix, unless the court in its discretion orders that, because of the character, location, or quantity of the property to be condemned, or for other reasons in the interest of justice, the issue of compensation shall be determined by a commission of three persons appointed by it.

In the event that a commission is appointed the court may direct that not more than two additional persons serve as alternate commissioners to hear the case and replace commissioners who, prior to the time when a decision is filed, are found by the court to be unable or disqualified to perform their duties. An alternate who does not replace a regular commissioner shall be discharged after the commission renders its final decision. Before appointing the members of the commission and alternates the court shall advise the parties of the identity and qualifications of each prospective commissioner and alternate and may permit the parties to examine each such designee. The parties shall not be permitted or required by the court to suggest nominees. Each party shall have the right to object for valid cause to the appointment of any person as a commissioner or alternate. If a commission is appointed it shall have the powers of a master provided in subdivision (c) of Rule 53 and proceedings before it shall be governed by the provisions of paragraphs (1) and (2) of subdivision (d) of Rule 53. Its action and report shall be determined by a majority and its findings and report shall have the effect, and be dealt with by the court in accordance with the practice, prescribed in paragraph (2) of subdivision (e) of Rule 53. Trial of all issues shall otherwise be by the court.

(i) Dismissal of Action.

(1) As of Right. If no hearing has begun to determine the compensation to be paid for a piece of property and the plaintiff has not acquired the title or a lesser interest in or taken possession, the plaintiff may dismiss the action as to that property, without an order of the court, by filing a notice of dismissal setting forth a brief description of the property as to which the action is dismissed.

(2) By Stipulation. Before the entry of any judgment vesting the plaintiff with title or a lesser interest in or possession of property, the action may be dismissed in whole or in part, without an order of the court, as to any property by filing a stipulation of dismissal by the plaintiff and the defendant affected thereby; and, if the parties so stipulate, the court may vacate any judgment that has been entered.

(3) By Order of the Court. At any time before compensation for a piece of property has been determined and paid and after motion and hearing, the court may dismiss the action as to that property, except that it shall not dismiss the action as to any part of the property of which the plaintiff has taken possession or in which the plaintiff has taken title or a lesser interest, but shall award just compensation for the possession, title or lesser interest so taken. The court at any time may drop a defendant unnecessarily or improperly joined.

(4) Effect. Except as otherwise provided in the notice, or stipulation of dismissal, or order of the court, any dismissal is without prejudice.

(j) Deposit and its Distribution. The plaintiff shall deposit with the court any money required by law as a condition to the exercise of the power of eminent domain; and, although not so required, may make a deposit when permitted by statute. In such cases the court and attorneys shall expedite the proceedings for the distribution of the money so deposited and for the ascertainment and payment of just compensation. If the compensation finally awarded to any defendant exceeds the amount which has been paid to that defendant on distribution of the deposit, the court shall enter judgment against the plaintiff and in favor of that defendant for the deficiency. If the compensation finally awarded to any defendant is less than the amount which has been paid to that defendant, the court shall enter judgment against that defendant and in favor of the plaintiff for the overpayment.

(k) Condemnation Under a State's Power of Eminent Domain. The practice as herein prescribed governs in actions involving the exercise of the power of eminent domain under the law of a state, provided that if the state law makes provision for trial of any issue by jury, or for trial of the issue of compensation by jury or commission or both, that provision shall be followed.

(*l*) Costs. Costs are not subject to Rule 54(d).

(Added Apr. 30, 1951, eff. Aug. 1, 1951, and amended Jan. 21, 1963, eff. July 1, 1963; Apr. 29, 1985, eff. Aug. 1, 1985; Mar. 2, 1987, eff. Aug. 1, 1987; Apr. 25, 1988, eff. Aug. 1, 1988; Nov. 18, 1988, Pub.L. 100–690, Title VII, § 7050, 102 Stat. 4401; Apr. 22, 1993, eff. Dec. 1, 1993.)

1 So in original. Probably should be "defendant's".

ADVISORY COMMITTEE NOTES

1951 Addition

Supplementary Report

The Court will remember that at its conference on December 2, 1948, the discussion was confined to subdivision (h) of the rule (* * *), the particular question being whether the tribunal to award compensation should be a commission or a jury in cases where the Congress has not made specific provision on the subject. The Advisory Committee was agreed from the outset that a rule should not be promulgated which would overturn the decision of the Congress as to the kind of tribunal to fix compensation, provided that the system established by Congress was found to be working well. We found two instances where the Congress had specified the kind of tribunal to fix compensation. One case was the District of Columbia ([former] §§ 361 to 386 of Title 40 [now D.C. Code, Title 16, § 1301 et seq.]) where a rather unique system exists under which the court is required in all cases to order the selection of a "jury" of five from among not less than twenty names drawn from "the special box provided by law." They must have the usual qualifications of jurors and in addition must be freeholders of the District and not in the service of the United States or the District. That system has been in effect for many years, and our inquiry revealed that it works well under the conditions prevailing in the District, and is satisfactory to the courts of the District, the legal profession and to property owners.

The other instance is that of the Tennessee Valley Authority, where the act of Congress (section 831x of Title 16) provides that compensation is fixed by three disinterested commissioners appointed by the court, whose award goes before the District Court for confirmation or modification. The Advisory Committee made a thorough inquiry into the practical operation of the TVA commission system. We obtained from counsel for the TVA the results of their experience, which afforded convincing proof that the commission system is preferable under the conditions affecting TVA and that the jury system would not work satisfactorily. We then, under date of February 6, 1947, wrote every Federal judge who had ever sat in a TVA condemnation case, asking his views as to whether the commission system is satisfactory and whether a jury system should be preferred. Of 21 responses from the judges 17 approved the commission system and opposed the substitution of a jury system for the TVA. Many of the judges went further and opposed the use of juries in any condemnation cases. Three of the judges preferred the jury system, and one dealt only with the TVA provision for a three judge district court. The Advisory Committee has not considered abolition of the three judge requirement of the TVA Act, because it seemed to raise a question of jurisdiction, which cannot be altered by rule. Nevertheless the Department of Justice continued its advocacy of the jury system for its asserted expedition and economy; and others favored a uniform procedure. In consequence of these divided counsels the Advisory Committee was itself divided, but in its May 1948 Report to the Court recommended the following rule as approved by a majority (* * *):

(h) Trial. If the action involves the exercise of the power of eminent domain under the law of the United States, any tribunal especially constituted by an Act of Congress governing the case for the trial of the issue of just compensation shall be the tribunal for the determination of that issue; but if there is no such specially constituted tribunal any party may have a trial by jury of the issue of just compensation by filing a demand therefor within the time allowed for answer or within such further time as the court may fix. Trial of all issues shall otherwise be by the court.

The effect of this was to preserve the existing systems in the District of Columbia and in TVA cases, but to provide for a jury to fix compensation in all other cases.

Before the Court's conference of December 2, 1948, the Chief Justice informed the Committee that the Court was particularly interested in the views expressed by Judge John Paul, Judge of the United States District Court for the Western District of Virginia, in a letter from him to the chairman of the Advisory Committee, dated February 13, 1947. Copies of all the letters from judges who had sat in TVA cases had been made available to the Court, and this letter from Judge Paul is one of them. Judge Paul strongly opposed jury trials and recommended the commission system in large projects like the TVA, and his views seemed to have impressed the Court and to have been the occasion for the conference.

The reasons which convinced the Advisory Committee that the use of commissioners instead of juries is desirable in TVA cases were these:

1. The TVA condemns large areas of land of similar kind, involving many owners. Uniformity in awards is essential. The commission system tends to prevent discrimination and provide for uniformity in compensation. The jury system tends to lack of uniformity. Once a reasonable and uniform standard of values for the area has been settled by a commission, litigation ends and settlements result.

2. Where large areas are involved many small landowners reside at great distances from the place where a court sits. It is a great hardship on humble people to have to travel long distances to attend a jury trial. A commission may travel around and receive the evidence of the owner near his home.

3. It is impracticable to take juries long distances to view the premises.

4. If the cases are tried by juries the burden on the time of the courts is excessive.

These considerations are the very ones Judge Paul stressed in his letter. He pointed out that they applied not only to the TVA but to other large governmental projects, such as flood control, hydroelectric power, reclamation, national forests, and others. So when the representatives of the Advisory Committee appeared at the Court's conference December 2, 1948, they found it difficult to justify the proposed provision in subdivision (h) of the rule that a jury should be used to fix compensation in all cases where Congress had not specified the tribunal. If our reasons for preserving the TVA system were sound, provision for a jury in similar projects of like magnitude seemed unsound.

Aware of the apparent inconsistency between the acceptance of the TVA system and the provision for a jury in all other cases, the members of the Committee attending the conference of December 2, 1948, then suggested that in the other cases the choice of jury or commission be left to the discretion of the District Court, going back to a suggestion previously made by Committee members and reported at page 15 of the Preliminary Draft of June 1947. They called the attention of the Court to the fact that the entire Advisory Committee had not been consulted about this suggestion and proposed that the draft be returned to the Committee for further consideration, and that was done.

The proposal we now make for subdivision (h) is as follows:

(h) Trial. If the action involves the exercise of the power of eminent domain under the law of the United States, any tribunal specially constituted by an Act of Congress governing the case for the trial of the issue of just compensation shall be the tribunal for the determination of that issue; but if there is no such specially constituted tribunal any party may have a trial by jury of the issue of just compensation by filing a demand therefor within the time allowed for answer or within such further time as the court may fix, unless the court in its discretion orders that, because of the character, location, or quantity of the property to be condemned, or for other reasons in the interest of justice, the issue of compensation shall be determined by a commission of three persons appointed by it. If a commission is appointed it shall have the powers of a master provided in subdivision (c) of Rule 53 and proceedings before it shall be governed by the provisions of paragraphs (1) and (2) of subdivision (d) of Rule 53. Its action and report shall be determined by a majority and its findings and report shall have the effect, and be dealt with by the court in accordance with the practice, prescribed in paragraph (2) of subdivision (e) of Rule 53. Trial of all issues shall otherwise be by the court.

In the 1948 draft the Committee had been almost evenly divided as between jury or commission and that made it easy for us to agree on the present draft. It would be difficult to state in a rule the various conditions to control the District Court in its choice and we have merely stated generally the matters which should be considered by the District Court.

The rule as now drafted seems to meet Judge Paul's objection. In large projects like the TVA the court may decide to use a commission. In a great number of cases involving only sites for buildings or other small areas, where use of a jury is appropriate, a jury may be chosen. The District Court's discretion may also be influenced by local preference or habit, and the preference of the Department of Justice and the reasons for its preference will doubtless be given weight. The Committee is convinced that there are some types of cases in which use of a commission is preferable and others in which a jury may be appropriately used, and that it would be a mistake to provide that the same kind of tribunal should be used in all cases. We think the available evidence clearly leads to that conclusion.

When this suggestion was made at the conference of December 2, 1948, representatives of the Department of Justice opposed it, expressing opposition to the use of a commission in any case. Their principal ground for opposition to commissions was then based on the assertion that the commission system is too expensive because courts allow commissioners too large compensation. The obvious answer to that is that the compensation of commissioners ought to be fixed or limited by law, as was done in the TVA Act, and the agency dealing with appropriations—either the Administrative Office or some other interested department of the government—should correct that evil, if evil there be, by obtaining such legislation. Authority to promulgate rules of procedure does not include power to fix compensation of government employees. The Advisory Committee is not convinced that even without such legislation the commission system is more expensive than the jury system. The expense of jury trials includes not only the per diem and mileage of the jurors impaneled for a case but like items for the entire venire. In computing cost of jury trials, the salaries of court officials, judges, clerks, marshals and deputies must be considered. No figures have been given to the Committee to establish that the cost of the commission system is the greater.

We earnestly recommend the rule as now drafted for promulgation by the Court, in the public interest.

The Advisory Committee have given more time to this rule, including time required for conferences with the Department of Justice to hear statements of its representatives, than has been required by any other rule. The rule may not be perfect but if faults develop in practice they may be promptly cured. Certainly the present conformity system is atrocious.

Under state practices, just compensation is normally determined by one of three methods: by commissioners; by commissioners with a right of appeal to and trial de novo before a jury; and by a jury, without a commission. A trial to the court or to the court including a master are, however, other methods that are occasionally used. Approximately 5 states use only commissioners; 23 states use commissioners with a trial de novo before a jury; and 18 states use only the jury. This classification is advisedly stated in approximate terms, since the same state may utilize diverse methods, depending upon different types of condemnations or upon the locality of the property, and since the methods used in a few states do not permit of a categorical classification. To reject the proposed rule and leave the situation as it is would not satisfy the views of the Department of Justice. The Department and the Advisory Committee agree that the use of a commission, with appeal to a jury, is a wasteful system.

The Department of Justice has a voluminous "Manual on Federal Eminent Domain," the 1940 edition of which has 948 pages with an appendix of 73 more pages. The title page informs us the preparation of the manual was begun during the incumbency of Attorney General Cummings, was continued under Attorney General Murphy, and completed during the incumbency of Attorney General Jackson. The preface contains the following statement:

It should also be mentioned that the research incorporated in the manual would be of invaluable assistance in the drafting of a new uniform code, or rules of court, for federal condemnation proceedings, which are now greatly confused, not only by the existence of over seventy federal statutes governing condemnations for different purposes—statutes which sometimes conflict with one another—but also by the countless problems occasioned by the requirements of conformity to state law. Progress of the work has already demonstrated that the need for such reform exists.

It is not surprising that more than once Attorneys General have asked the Advisory Committee to prepare a federal rule and rescue the government from this morass.

The Department of Justice has twice tried and failed to persuade the Congress to provide that juries shall be used in all condemnation cases. The debates in Congress show that part of the opposition to the Department of Justice's bills came from representatives opposed to jury trials in all cases, and in part from a preference for the conformity system. Our present proposal opens the door for district judges to yield to local preferences on the subject. It does much for the Department's points of view. It is a great improvement over the present so-called conformity system. It does away with the wasteful "double" system prevailing in 23 states where awards by commissions are followed by jury trials.

Aside from the question as to the choice of a tribunal to award compensation, the proposed rule would afford a simple and improved procedure.

We turn now to an itemized explanation of the other changes we have made in the 1948 draft. Some of these result from recent amendments to the Judicial Code. Others result from a reconsideration by the Advisory Committee of provisions which we thought could be improved.

1. In the amended Judicial Code, the district courts are designated as "United States District Courts" instead of "District Courts of the United States," and a corresponding change has been made in the rule.

2. After the 1948 draft was referred back to the committee, the provision in subdivision (c)(2), relating to naming defendants, * * * which provided that the plaintiff shall add as defendants all persons having or claiming an interest in that property whose names can be ascertained by a search of the records to the extent commonly made by competent searchers of title in the vicinity "in light of the type and value of the property involved," the phrase in quotation marks was changed to read "in the light of the character and value of the property involved and the interests to be acquired."

The Department of Justice made a counter proposal * * * that there be substituted the words "reasonably diligent search of the records, considering the type." When the American Bar Association thereafter considered the draft, it approved the Advisory Committee's draft of this subdivision, but said that it had no objection to the Department's suggestion. Thereafter, in an effort to eliminate controversy, the Advisory Committee accepted the Department's suggestion as to (c)(2), using the word "character" instead of the word "type."

The Department of Justice also suggested that in subdivision (d)(3)(ii) relating to service by publication, the search for a defendant's residence as a preliminary to publication be limited to the state in which the complaint is filed. Here again the American Bar Association's report expressed the view that the Department's suggestion was unobjectionable and the Advisory Committee thereupon adopted it.

3. Subdivision (k) of the 1948 draft is as follows:

(k) Condemnation Under a State's Power of Eminent Domain. If the action involves the exercise of the power of eminent domain under the law of a state, the practice herein prescribed may be altered to the extent necessary to observe and enforce any condition affecting the substantial rights of a litigant attached by the state law to the exercise of the state's power of eminent domain.

Occasionally condemnation cases under a state's power of eminent domain reach a United States District Court because of diversity of citizenship. Such cases are rare, but provision should be made for them.

The 1948 draft of (k) required a district court to decide whether a provision of state law specifying the tribunal to award compensation is or is not a "condition" attached to the exercise of the state's power. On reconsideration we concluded that it would be wise to redraft (k) so as to avoid that troublesome question. As to conditions in state laws which affect the substantial rights of a litigant, the district courts would be bound to give them effect without any rule on the subject. Accordingly we present two alternative revisions. One suggestion supported by a majority of the Advisory Committee is as follows:

(k) Condemnation Under a State's Power of Eminent Domain. The practice herein prescribed governs in actions involving the exercise of the power of eminent domain under the law of a state, provided that if the state law makes provision for trial of any issue by jury, or for trial of the issue of compensation by jury or commission or both, that provision shall be followed.

The other is as follows:

(k) Condemnation Under a State's Power of Eminent Domain. The practice herein prescribed governs in actions involving the exercise of the power of eminent domain under the law of a state, provided that if the state law gives a right to a trial by jury such a trial shall in any case be allowed to the party demanding it within the time permitted by these rules, and in that event no hearing before a commission shall be had.

The first proposal accepts the state law as to the tribunals to fix compensation, and in that respect leaves the parties in precisely the same situation as if the case were pending in a state court, including the use of a commission with appeal to a jury, if the state law so provides. It has the effect of avoiding any question as to whether the decisions in *Erie R. Co. v. Tompkins* and later cases have application to a situation of this kind.

The second proposal gives the parties a right to a jury trial if that is provided for by state law, but prevents the use of both commission and jury. Those members of the Committee who favor the second proposal do so because of the obvious objections to the double trial, with a commission and appeal to a jury. As the decisions in *Erie R. Co. v. Tompkins* and later cases may have a bearing on this point, and the Committee is divided, we think both proposals should be placed before the Court.

4. The provision * * * of the 1948 draft * * * prescribing the effective date of the rule was drafted before the recent amendment of the Judicial Code on that subject. On May 10, 1950, the President approved an act which amended section 2072 of Title 28, United States Code, to read as follows:

> Such rules shall not take effect until they have been reported to Congress by the Chief Justice at or after the beginning of a regular session thereof but not later than the first day of May, and until the expiration of ninety days after they have been thus reported.

To conform to the statute now in force, we suggest a provision as follows:

> **Effective Date.** This Rule 71A and the amendment to Rule 81(a) will take effect on August 1, 1951. Rule 71A governs all proceedings in actions brought after it takes effect and also all further proceedings in actions then pending, except to the extent that in the opinion of the court its application in a particular action pending when the rule takes effect would not be feasible or would work injustice, in which event the former procedure applies.

If the rule is not reported to Congress by May 1, 1951, this provision must be altered.

[Par. 3 of Supreme Court Order adopted Apr. 30, 1951, setting out this rule and providing for the abrogation of par. (7) of Rule 81(a), and providing for the Effective Date, as stated herein, was transmitted to Congress on May 1, 1951 by the Chief Justice of the United States (House Document No. 121, May 1, 1951, 82nd Cong., 1st Sess.), in conformity with § 2072 of this title. As no action was taken by Congress within the 90-day period required by that section, this rule and the abrogation of par. (7) of Rule 81(a) took effect on Aug. 1, 1951, as provided in said order.]

5. We call attention to the fact that the proposed rule does not contain a provision for the procedure to be followed in order to exercise the right of the United States to take immediate possession or title, when the condemnation proceeding is begun. There are several statutes conferring such a right which are cited in the original notes to the May 1948 draft * * *. The existence of this right is taken into account in the rule. In subdivision (c)(2), * * * it is stated: "Upon the commencement of the action, the plaintiff need join as defendants only the persons having or claiming an interest in the property whose names are then known." That is to enable the United States to exercise the right to immediate title or possession without the delay involved in ascertaining the names of all interested parties. The right is also taken into account in the provision relating to dismissal (paragraph (i), subdivisions (1), (2), and (3), * * *); also in paragraph (j) relating to deposits and their distribution.

The Advisory Committee considered whether the procedure for exercising the right should be specified in the rule and decided against it, as the procedure now being followed seems to be giving no trouble, and to draft a rule to fit all the statutes on the subject might create confusion.

The American Bar Association has taken an active interest in a rule for condemnation cases. In 1944 its House of Delegates adopted a resolution which among other things resolved:

> That before adoption by the Supreme Court of the United States of any redraft of the proposed rule, time and opportunity should be afforded to the bar to consider and make recommendations concerning any such redraft.

Accordingly, in 1950 the revised draft was submitted to the American Bar Association and its section of real property, probate and trust law appointed a committee to consider it. That committee was supplied with copies of the written statement from the Department of Justice giving the reasons relied on by the Department for preferring a rule to use juries in all cases. The Advisory Committee's report was approved at a meeting of the section of real property law, and by the House of Delegates at the annual meeting of September 1950. The American Bar Association report gave particular attention to the question whether juries or commissions should be used to fix compensation, approved the Advisory Committee's solution appearing in their latest draft designed to allow use of commissions in projects comparable to the TVA, and rejected the proposal for use of juries in all cases.

In November 1950 a committee of the Federal Bar Association, the chairman of which was a Special Assistant to the Attorney General, made a report which reflected the attitude of the Department of Justice on the condemnation rule.

Aside from subdivision (h) about the tribunal to award compensation the final draft of the condemnation rule here presented has the approval of the American Bar Association and, we understand, the Department of Justice, and we do not know of any opposition to it. Subdivision (h) has the unanimous approval of the Advisory Committee and has been approved by the American Bar Association. The use of commissions in TVA cases, and, by fair inference, in cases comparable to the TVA, is supported by 17 out of 20 judges who up to 1947 had sat in TVA cases. The legal staff of the TVA has vigorously objected to the substitution of juries for commissions in TVA cases. We regret to report that the Department of Justice still asks that subdivision (h) be altered to provide for jury trials in an cases where Congress has not specified the tribunal. We understand that the Department approves the proposal that the system prevailing in 23 states for the "double" trial, by commission with appeal to and trial de novo before a jury, should be abolished, and also asks that on demand a jury should be substituted for a commission, in those states where use of a commission alone is now required. The Advisory Committee has no evidence that commissions do not operate satisfactorily in the case of projects comparable to the TVA.

Original Report

General Statement. 1. Background. When the Advisory Committee was formulating its recommendations to the Court concerning rules of procedure, which subsequently became the Federal Rules of 1938, the Committee concluded at an early stage not to fix the procedure in condemnation cases. This is a matter principally involving the exercise of the federal power of eminent domain, as very few condemnation cases involving the state's power reach the United States District Courts. The Committee's reasons at that time were that inasmuch as condemnation proceedings by the United States are governed by statutes of the United States, prescribing different procedure for various agencies and departments of the government, or, in the absence of such statutes, by local state practice under the Conformity Act (former § 258 of Title 40), it would be extremely difficult to draft a uniform rule satisfactory to the various agencies and departments of the government and to private parties; and that there was no general demand for a uniform rule. The Committee continued in that belief until shortly before the preparation of the April 1937 Draft of the Rules, when the officials of the Department of Justice having to do with condemnation cases urgently requested the Committee to propose rules on this subject. The Committee undertook the task and drafted a Condemnation Rule which appeared for the first time as Rule 74 of the April 1937 Draft. After the publication and distribution of this initial draft many objections were urged against it by counsel for various governmental agencies, whose procedure in condemnation cases was prescribed by federal statutes. Some of these agencies wanted to be excepted in whole or in part from the operation of the uniform rule proposed in April 1937. And the Department of Justice changed its position and stated that it preferred to have government condemnations conducted by local attorneys familiar with the state practice, which was applied under the Conformity Act where the Acts of Congress do not prescribe the practice; that it preferred to work under the Conformity Act without a uniform rule of procedure. The profession generally showed little interest in the proposed uniform rule. For these reasons the Advisory Committee in its Final Report to the Court in November 1937 proposed that all of Rule 74 be stricken and that the Federal Rules be made applicable only to appeals in condemnation cases. See note to Rule 74 of the Final Report.

Some of six or seven years later when the Advisory Committee was considering the subject of amendments to the Federal Rules both government officials and the profession generally urged the adoption of some uniform procedure. This demand grew out of the volume of condemnation proceedings instituted during the war, and the general feeling of dissatisfaction with the diverse condemnation procedures that were applicable in the federal courts. A strongly held belief was that both the sovereign's power to condemn and the property owner's right to compensation could be promoted by a simplified rule. As a consequence the Committee proposed a Rule 71A on the subject of condemnation in its Preliminary Draft of May 1944. In the Second Preliminary Draft of May 1945 this earlier proposed Rule 71A was, however, omitted. The Committee did not then feel that it had sufficient time to prepare a revised draft satisfactorily to it which would meet legitimate objections made to the draft of May 1944. To avoid unduly delaying the proposed amendments to existing rules the Committee concluded to proceed in the regular way with the preparation of the amendments to these rules and deal with the question of a condemnation rule as an independent matter. As a consequence it made no recommendations to the Court on condemnation in its Final Report of Proposed Amendments of June 1946; and the amendments which the Court adopted in December 1946 did not deal with condemnation. After concluding its task relative to amendments, the Committee returned to a consideration of eminent domain, its proposed Rule 71A of May 1944, the suggestions and criticisms that had been presented in the interim, and in June 1947 prepared and distributed to the profession another draft of a proposed condemnation rule. This draft contained several alternative provisions, specifically called attention to and asked for opinion relative to these matters, and in particular as to the constitution of the tribunal to award compensation. The present draft was based on the June 1947 formulation, in light of the advice of the profession on both matters of substance and form.

2. Statutory Provisions. The need for a uniform condemnation rule in the federal courts arises from the fact that by various statutes Congress has prescribed diverse procedures for certain condemnation proceedings, and, in the absence of such statutes, has prescribed conformity to local state practice under former § 258 of Title 40. This general conformity adds to the diversity of procedure since in the United States there are multifarious methods of procedure in existence. Thus in 1931 it was said that there were 269 different methods of judicial procedure in different classes of condemnation cases and 56 methods of nonjudicial or administrative procedure. First Report of Judicial Council of Michigan, 1931, § 46, pp. 55 to 56. These numbers have not decreased. Consequently, the general requirement of conformity to state practice and procedure, particularly where the condemnor is the United States, leads to expense, delay and uncertainty. In advocacy of a uniform federal rule, see Armstrong, *Proposed Amendments to Federal Rules for Civil Procedure,* 1944, 4 F.R.D. 124, 134; id., *Report of the Advisory Committee on Federal Rules of Civil Procedure Recommending Amendments,* 1946, 5 F.R.D. 339, 357.

There are a great variety of Acts of Congress authorizing the exercise of the power of eminent domain by the United States and its officers and agencies. These statutes for the most part do not specify the exact procedure to be followed, but where procedure is prescribed, it is by no means uniform.

The following are instances of Acts which merely authorize the exercise of the power without specific declaration as to the procedure:

U.S.C., Title 16:

§ 404c–11 (Mammoth Cave National Park; acquisition of lands, interests in lands or other property for park by the Secretary of the Interior).

§ 426d (Stones River National Park; acquisition of land for parks by the Secretary of the Army).

§ 450aa (George Washington Carver National Monument; acquisition of land by the Secretary of the Interior).

§ 517 (National forest reservation; title to lands to be acquired by the Secretary of Agriculture).

U.S.C., Title 42:

§§ 1805(b)(5), 1813(b) [now §§ 2061 and 2112, and §§ 2221 to 2224, respectively, of Title 42] (Atomic Energy Act).

The following are instances of Acts which authorized condemnation and declare that the procedure is to conform what that of similar actions in state courts:

U.S.C., Title 16:

§ 423k (Richmond National Battlefield Park; acquisition of lands by the Secretary of the Interior).

§ 814 (Exercise by water power licensee of power of eminent domain).

U.S.C., Title 24:

§ 78 [Repealed] (Condemnation of land for the former National Home for Disabled Volunteer Soldiers).

U.S.C., Title 33:

§ 591 (Condemnation of lands and materials for river and harbor improvement by the Secretary of the Army).

U.S.C., Title 40:

§ 257 (Condemnation of realty for sites for public building and for other public uses by the Secretary of the Treasury authorized).

§ 258 [Omitted as superseded by this rule] (Same procedure).

U.S.C., Title 50:

§ 171 [Repealed and is now covered by § 2663 of Title 10] (Acquisition of land by the Secretary of the Army for national defense).

§ 172 [Repealed and is now covered by §§ 2664 and 2665 of Title 10] (Acquisition of property by the Secretary of the Army, etc., for production of lumber).

§ 632 App. [Omitted as terminated by § 645 of the Appendix to Title 50] (Second War Powers Act, 1942; acquisition of real property for war purposes by the Secretary of Army, the Secretary of the Navy and others).

The following are Acts in which a more or less complete code of procedure is set forth in connection with the taking:

U.S.C., Title 16:

§ 831x (Condemnation by Tennessee Valley Authority).

U.S.C., Title 40:

§ 361–386 [Repealed] [now D.C.Code, Title 16, § 1301 et seq.] (Acquisition of lands in District of Columbia for use of United States; condemnation).

3. Adjustment of Rule to Statutory Provisions. While it was apparent that the principle of uniformity should be the basis for a rule to replace the multiple diverse procedures set out above, there remained a serious question as to whether an exception could properly be made relative to the method of determining compensation. Where Congress had provided for conformity to state law the following were the general methods in use: an initial determination by commissioners, with appeal to a judge; an initial award, likewise made by commissioners, but with the appeal to a jury; and determination by a jury without a previous award by commissioners. In two situations Congress had specified the tribunal to determine the issue of compensation: condemnation by the Tennessee Valley Authority; and condemnation in the District of Columbia. Under the TVA procedure the initial determination of value is by three disinterested commissioners, appointed by the court, from a locality other than the one in which the land lies. Either party may except to the award of the commission; in that case the exceptions are to be heard by three district judges (unless the parties stipulate for a lesser number), with a right of appeal to the circuit court of appeals. The TVA is a regional agency. It is faced with the necessity of acquiring a very substantial acreage within a relatively small area, and charged with the task of carrying on within the Tennessee Valley and in cooperation with the local people a permanent program involving navigation and flood control, electric power, soil conservation, and general regional development. The success of this program is partially dependent upon the good will and cooperation of the people of the Tennessee Valley, and this in turn partially depends upon the land acquisition program. Disproportionate awards among landowners would create dissatisfaction and ill will. To secure uniformity in treatment Congress provided the rather unique procedure of the three-judge court to review de novo the initial award of the commissioners. This procedure has worked to the satisfaction of the property owners and the TVA. A full statement of the TVA position and experience is set forth in Preliminary Draft of Proposed Rule to Govern Condemnation Cases (June, 1947) 15–19. A large majority of the district judges with experience under this procedure approve it, subject to some objection to the requirement for a three-judge district court to review commissioners' awards. A statutory three-judge requirement is, however, jurisdictional and must be strictly followed. *Stratton v. St. Louis, Southwestern Ry. Co.,* 1930, 51 S.Ct. 8, 282 U.S. 10, 75 L.Ed. 135; *Ayrshire Collieries Corp. v. United States,* 1947, 67 S.Ct. 1168, 331 U.S. 132, 91 L.Ed. 1391. Hence except insofar as the TVA statute itself authorizes the parties to stipulate for a court of less than three judges, the requirement must be followed, and would seem to be beyond alteration by court rule even if change were thought desirable. Accordingly the TVA procedure is retained for the determination of compensation in TVA condemnation cases. It was also thought desirable to retain the specific method Congress had prescribed for the District of Columbia, which is a so-called jury of five appointed by the court. This is a local matter and the specific treatment accorded by Congress has given local satisfaction.

Aside from the foregoing limited exceptions dealing with the TVA and the District of Columbia, the question was whether a uniform method for determining compensation should be a commission with appeal to a district judge, or a commission with appeal to a jury, or a jury without a commission. Experience with the commission on a nationwide basis, and in particular with the utilization of a commission followed by an appeal to a jury, has been that the commission is time consuming and expensive. Furthermore, it is largely a futile procedure where it is preparatory to jury trial. Since in the bulk of states a land owner is entitled eventually to a jury trial, since the jury is a traditional tribunal for the determination of questions of value, and since experience with juries has proved satisfactory to both government and land owner, the right to jury trial is adopted as the general rule. Condemnation involving the TVA and the District of Columbia are the two exceptions. See Note to Subdivision (h), infra.

Note to Subdivision (a). As originally promulgated the Federal Rules governed appeals in condemnation proceedings but were not otherwise applicable. Rule 81(a)(7). Preappeal procedure, in the main, conformed to state procedure. See statutes and discussion, supra. The purpose of Rule 71A is to provide a uniform procedure for condemnation in the federal district courts, including the District of Columbia. To achieve this purpose Rule 71A prescribes such specialized procedure as is required by condemnation proceedings, otherwise it utilizes the general framework of the Federal Rules where specific detail is unnecessary. The adoption of Rule 71A, of course, renders paragraph (7) of Rule 81(a) unnecessary.

The promulgation of a rule for condemnation procedure is within the rulemaking power. The Enabling Act [Act of June 19, 1934, c. 651, §§ 1, 2 (48 Stat. 1064), former §§ 723b, 723c, now § 2072, of this title] gives the Supreme Court "the power to prescribe, by general rules * * * the forms of process, writs, pleadings, and motions, and the practice and procedure in civil actions at law." Such rules, however, must not abridge, enlarge, or modify substantive rights. In *Kohl v. United States,* 1875, 91 U.S. 367, 23 L.Ed. 449, a proceeding instituted by the United States to appropriate land for a postoffice site under a statute enacted for such purpose, the Supreme Court held that "a proceeding to take land in virtue of the government's eminent domain, and determining the compensation to be made for it, is * * * a suit at common law, when initiated in a court." See, also, *Madisonville Traction Co. v. Saint Bernard Mining Co.*, 1905, 25 S.Ct. 251, 196 U.S. 239, 49 L.Ed. 462, infra, under subdivision (k). And the Conformity Act [former § 258 of Title 40], which is superseded by Rule 71A, deals only with "practice, pleadings, forms and proceedings and not with matters of substantive laws." *United States v. 243.22 Acres of Land in Village of Farmingdale, Town of Babylon, Suffolk County, N.Y.*, D.C.N.Y.1942, 43 F.Supp. 561, affirmed 129 F.2d 678, certiorari denied 63 S.Ct. 441, 317 U.S. 698, 87 L.Ed. 558.

Rule 71A affords a uniform procedure for all cases of condemnation invoking the national power of eminent domain, and, to the extent stated in subdivision (k), for cases invoking a state's power of eminent domain; and supplants all statutes prescribing a different procedure. While the almost exclusive utility of the rule is for the condemnation of real property, it also applies to the condemnation of personal property, either as an incident to real property or as the sole object of the proceeding, when permitted or required by statute. See former § 438j [now § 5001] of Title 38 (World War Veterans' Relief Act); former §§ 1805, 1811, and 1813 of Title 42 (Atomic Energy Act); former § 79 [now § 100] of Title 50 (Nitrates Act); former §§ 161 to 165 and § 166, of Title 50 (Helium Gas Act). Requisitioning of personal property with the right in the owner to sue the United States, where the compensation cannot be agreed upon (see former § 1813 [now §§ 2221 to 2224] of Title 42, for example) will continue to be the normal method of acquiring personal property and Rule 71A in no way interferes with or restricts any such right. Only where the law requires or permits the formal procedure of condemnation to be utilized will the rule have any applicability to the acquisition of personal property.

Rule 71A is not intended to and does not supersede the Act of February 26, 1931, c. 307, §§ 1 to 5 (46 Stat. 1421), §§ 258a to 258e of Title 40, which is a supplementary condemnation statute, permissive in its nature and designed to permit the prompt acquisition of title by the United States, pending the condemnation proceeding, upon a deposit in court. See *United States v. 76,800 Acres, More or Less, of Land, in Bryan and Liberty Counties, Ga.*, D.C.Ga.1942, 44 F.Supp. 653; *United States v. 17,280 Acres of Land, More or Less, Situated in Saunders County, Neb.*, D.C.Neb.1942, 47 F.Supp. 267. The same is true insofar as the following or any other statutes authorize the acquisition of title or the taking of immediate possession:

U.S.C., Title 33:

§ 594 (When immediate possession of land may be taken; for a work of river and harbor improvements.)

U.S.C., Title 42:

§ 1813(b) [now §§ 2221 to 2224 of Title 42] (When immediate possession may be taken under Atomic Energy Act).

U.S.C., Title 50:

§ 171 [Repealed and is now covered by § 2663 of Title 10] (Acquisition of land by the Secretary of the Army for national defense).

§ 632 App. [Omitted as terminated by § 645 of the Appendix to Title 50] (Second War Powers Act, 1942; acquisition of real property for war purposes by the Secretary of the Army, the Secretary of the Navy, and others).

Note to Subdivision (b). This subdivision provides for broad joinder in accordance with the tenor of other rules such as Rule 18. To require separate condemnation proceedings for each piece of property separately owned would be unduly burdensome and would serve no useful purpose. And a restriction that only properties may be joined which are to be acquired for the same public use would also cause difficulty. For example, a unified project to widen a street, construct a bridge across a navigable river, and for the construction of approaches to the level of the bridge on both sides of the river might involve acquiring property for different public uses. Yet it is eminently desirable that the plaintiff may in one proceeding condemn all the property interests and rights necessary to carry out this project. Rule 21 which allows the court to sever and proceed separately with any claim against a party, and Rule 42(b) giving the court broad discretion to order separate trials give adequate protection to all defendants in condemnation proceedings.

Note to Subdivision (c). Since a condemnation proceeding is in rem and since a great many property owners are often involved, paragraph (1) requires the property to be named and only one of the owners. In other respects and caption will contain the name of the court, the title of the action, file number, and a designation of the pleading as a complaint in accordance with Rule 10(a).

Since the general standards of pleading are stated in other rules, paragraph (2) prescribes only the necessary detail for condemnation proceedings. Certain statutes allow the United States to acquire title or possession immediately upon commencement of an action. See the Act of February 26, 1931, c. 307, §§ 1 to 5 (46 Stat. 1421), §§ 258a to 258e of Title 40; and § 594 of Title 33, former § 1813(b) of Title 42, former § 171 of Title 50, former § 632 of the Appendix to Title 50, supra. To carry out the purpose of such statutes and to aid the condemnor in instituting the action even where title is not acquired at the outset, the plaintiff is initially required to join as defendants only the persons having or claiming an interest in the property whose names are then known. This is no way prejudices the property owner, who must eventually be joined as a defendant, served with process, and allowed to answer before there can be any hearing involving the compensation to be paid for his piece of property. The rule requires the plaintiff to name all persons having or claiming an interest in the property of whom the plaintiff has learned and, more importantly, those appearing of record. By charging the plaintiff with the necessity to make "a search of the records of the extent commonly made by competent searches of title in the vicinity in light of the type and value of the property involved" both the plaintiff and property owner are protected. Where a short term interest in property of little value is involved, as a two or three year easement over a vacant land for purposes of ingress and egress to other property, a search of the records covering a long period of time is not required. Where on the other hand fee simple title in valuable property is being condemned the search must necessarily cover a much longer period of time and be commensurate with the interests involved. But even here the search is related to the type made by competent title searchers in the vicinity. A search that extends back to the original patent may be feasible in some midwestern and western states and be proper under certain circumstances. In the Atlantic seaboard states such a search is normally not feasible nor desirable. There is a common sense business accommodation of what title searchers can and should do. For state statutes requiring persons appearing as owners or otherwise interested in the property to be named as defendants, see 3 Colo.Stat.Ann., 1935, c. 61, § 2; Ill.Ann.Stat. (Smith-Hurd) c. 47, § 2; 1 Iowa Code, 1946, § 472.3; Kans.Stat.Ann., 1935, § 26–101; 2 Mass.Laws Ann., 1932, c. 80A, § 4; 7 Mich.Stat.Ann., 1936, § 8.2; 2 Minn.Stat., Mason 1927, § 6541; 20 N.J.Stat.Ann., 1939, § 1–2; 3 Wash.Revised Stat., Remington, 1932, Title 6, § 891. For state provisions allowing persons whose names are not known to be designated under the descriptive term of "unknown owner", see Hawaii Revised Laws, 1945, c. 8, § 310 ("such [unknown] defendant may be joined in the petition under a fictitious name."); Ill.Ann.Stat. (Smith-Hurd) c. 47, § 2 ("Persons interested, whose names are unknown, may be made parties defendant by the description of the unknown owners; * * *"); Maryland Code Ann., 1939, Art. 33A, § 1 ("In case any owner or owners is or are not known, he or they may be described in such petition as the unknown owner or owners, or the unknown heir or heirs of a deceased owner."); 2 Mass.Laws Ann., 1932, c. 80A, § 4 ("Persons not in being, unascertained or unknown who may have an interest in any of such land shall be made parties respondent by such description as seems appropriate, * * *"); New Mex.Stat.Ann., 1941, § 25–901 ("the owners * * * shall be parties defendant, by name, if the names are known, and by description of the unknown owners of the land therein described, if their names are unknown."); Utah Code Ann., 1943, § 104–61–7 ("The names of all owners and claimants of the property, if known, or a statement that they are unknown, who must be styled defendants").

The last sentence of paragraph (2) enables the court to expedite the distribution of a deposit, in whole or in part, as soon as pertinent facts of ownership, value and the like are established. See also subdivision (j).

The signing of the complaint is governed by Rule 11.

Note to Subdivision (d). In lieu of a summons, which is the initial process in other civil actions under Rule 4(a), subdivision (d) provides for a notice which is to contain sufficient information so that the defendant in effect obtains the plaintiff's statement of his claim against the defendant to whom the notice is directed. Since the plaintiff's attorney is an officer of the court and to prevent unduly burdening the clerk of the court, paragraph (1) of subdivision (d) provides that plaintiff's attorney shall prepare and deliver a notice or notices to the clerk. Flexibility is provided by the provision for joint or several notices, and for additional notices. Where there are only a few defendants it may be convenient to prepare but one notice directed to all the defendants. In other cases where there are many defendants it will be more convenient to prepare two or more notices; but in any event a notice must be directed to each named defendant. Paragraph (2) provides that the notice is to be signed by the plaintiff's attorney. Since the notice is to be delivered to the clerk, the issuance of the notice will appear of record in the court. The clerk should forthwith deliver the notice or notices for service to the marshal or to a person specially appointed to serve the notice. Rule 4(a). The form of the notice is such that, in addition to informing the defendant of the plaintiff's statement of claim, it tells the defendant precisely what his rights are. Failure on the part of the defendant to serve an answer constitutes a consent to the taking and to the authority of the court to proceed to fix compensation therefor, but it does not preclude the defendant from presenting evidence as to the amount of compensation due him or in sharing the award of distribution. See subdivision (e); Form 28.

While under Rule 4(f) the territorial limits of a summons are normally the territorial limits of the state in which the district court is held, the territorial limits for personal service of a notice under Rule 71A(d)(3) are those of the nation. This extension of process is here proper since the aim of the condemnation proceeding is not to enforce any personal liability and the property owner is helped, not imposed upon, by the best type of service possible. If personal service cannot be made either because the defendant's whereabouts cannot be ascertained, or, if ascertained, the defendant cannot be personally served, as where he resides in a foreign country such as Canada or Mexico, then service by publication is proper. The provisions for this type of service are set forth in the rule and are in no way governed by § 118 [now § 1655] of this title.

Note to Subdivision (e). Departing from the scheme of Rule 12, subdivision (e) requires all defenses and objections to be presented in an answer and does not authorize a preliminary motion. There is little need for the latter in condemnation proceedings. The general standard of pleading is governed by other rules, particularly Rule 8, and this subdivision (e) merely prescribes what matters the answer should set forth. Merely by appearing in the action a defendant can receive notice of all proceedings affecting him. And without the necessity of answering a defendant may present evidence as to the amount of compensation due him, and he may share in the distribution of the award. See also subdivision (d)(2); Form 28.

Note to Subdivision (f). Due to the number of persons who may be interested in the property to be condemned, there is a likelihood that the plaintiff will need to amend his complaint, perhaps many times, to add new parties or state new issues. This subdivision recognizes that fact and does not burden the court with applications by the plaintiff for leave to amend. At the same time all defendants are adequately protected; and their need to amend the answer is adequately protected by Rule 15, which is applicable by virtue of subdivision (a) of this Rule 71A.

Note to Subdivision (g). A condemnation action is a proceeding in rem. Commencement of the action as against a defendant by virtue of his joinder pursuant to subdivision (c)(2) is the point of cut-off and there is no mandatory requirement for substitution because of a subsequent change of interest, although the court is given ample power to require substitution. Rule 25 is inconsistent with subdivision (g) and hence inapplicable. Accordingly, the time periods of Rule 25 do not govern to require dismissal nor to prevent substitution.

Note to Subdivision (h). This subdivision prescribes the method for determining the issue of just compensation in cases involving the federal power of eminent domain. The method of jury trial provided by subdivision (h) will normally apply in cases involving the state power by virtue of subdivision (k).

Congress has specially constituted a tribunal for the trial of the issue of just compensation in two instances: condemnation under the Tennessee Valley Authority Act; and condemnation in the District of Columbia. These tribunals are retained for reasons set forth in the General Statement: 3. Adjustment of Rule to Statutory Provisions, supra. Subdivision (h) also has prospective application so that if Congress should create another special tribunal, that tribunal will determine the issue of just compensation. Subject to these exceptions the general method of trial of that issue is to be by jury if any party demands it, otherwise that issue, as well as all other issues, are to be tried by the court.

As to the TVA procedure that is continued, § 831x of Title 16 requires that three commissioners be appointed to fix the compensation; that exceptions to their award are to be heard by three district judges (unless the parties stipulate for a lesser number) and that the district judges try the question de novo; that an appeal to the circuit court of appeals may be taken within 30 days from the filing of the decision of the district judges; and that the circuit court of appeals shall on the record fix compensation "without regard to the awards of findings theretofore made by the commissioners or the district judges." The mode of fixing compensation in the District of Columbia, which is also continued, is prescribed in former §§ 361 to 386 of Title 40. Under former § 371 the court is required in all cases to order the selection of a jury of five from among not less than 20 names, drawn "from the special box provided by law." They must have the usual qualifications of jurors and in addition must be freeholders of the District, and not in the service of the United States or the District. A special oath is administered to the chosen jurors. The trial proceeds in the ordinary way, except that the jury is allowed to separate after they have begun to consider their verdict.

There is no constitutional right to jury trial in a condemnation proceeding. *Bauman v. Ross,* 1897, 17 S.Ct. 966, 167 U.S. 548, 42 L.Ed. 270. See, also, Hines, *Does the Seventh Amendment to the Constitution of the United States Require Jury Trials in all Condemnation Proceedings?,* 1925, 11 Va.L.Rev. 505; Blair, *Federal Condemnation Proceedings and the Seventh Amendment,* 1927, 41 Harv.L.Rev. 29; 3 *Moore's Federal Practice,* 1938, 3007. Prior to Rule 71A, jury trial in federal condemnation proceedings was, however, enjoyed under the general conformity statute, former § 258 of Title 40, in states which provided for jury trial. See generally, 2 Lewis, *Eminent Domain,* 3d ed. 1909, §§ 509, 510; 3 Moore, op. cit. supra. Since the general conformity statute is superseded by Rule 71A, see supra under subdivision (a), and since it was believed that the rule to be substituted should likewise give a right to jury trial, subdivision (h) establishes that method as the general one for determining the issue of just compensation.

Note to Subdivision (i). Both the right of the plaintiff to dismiss by filing a notice of dismissal and the right of the court to permit a dismissal are circumscribed to the extent that where the plaintiff has acquired the title or a lesser interest or possession, viz., any property interest for which just compensation should be paid, the action may not be dismissed, without the defendant's consent, and the property owner remitted to another court, such as the Court of Claims, to recover just compensation for the property right taken. Circuity of action is thus prevented without increasing the liability of the plaintiff to pay just compensation for any interest that is taken. Freedom of dismissal is accorded, where both the condemnor and condemnee agree, up to the time of the entry of judgment vesting plaintiff with title. And power is given to the court, where the parties agree, to vacate the judgment and thus revest title in the property owner. In line with Rule 21, the court may at any time drop a defendant who has been unnecessarily or improperly joined as where it develops that he has no interest.

Note to Subdivision (j). Whatever the substantive law is concerning the necessity of making a deposit will continue to govern. For statutory provisions concerning deposit in court in condemnation proceedings by the United States, see § 258a of Title 40; § 594 of Title 33; acquisition of title and possession statutes referred to in note to subdivision (a), supra. If the plaintiff is invoking the state's power of eminent domain the necessity of deposit will be governed by the state law. For discussion of such law, see 1 Nichols, Eminent Domain, 2d ed. 1917, §§ 209 to 216. For discussion of the function of deposit and the power of the court to enter judgment in cases both of deficiency and overpayment, see *United States v. Miller,* 1943, 63 S.Ct. 276, 317 U.S. 369, 87 L.Ed. 336, 147 A.L.R. 55, rehearing denied 63 S.Ct. 557, 318 U.S. 798, 87 L.Ed. 1162 (judgment in favor of plaintiff for overpayment ordered).

The court is to make distribution of the deposit as promptly as the facts of the case warrant. See also subdivision (c)(2).

Note to Subdivision (k). While the overwhelming number of cases that will be brought in the federal courts under this rule will be actions involving the federal power of eminent domain, a small percentage of cases may be instituted in the federal court or removed thereto on the basis of diversity or alienage which will involve the power of eminent domain under the law of a state. See *Boom Co. v. Patterson,* 1878, 98 U.S. 403, 25 L.Ed. 206; *Searl v. School District No. 2,* 1888, 8 S.Ct. 460, 124 U.S. 197, 31 L.Ed. 415; *Madisonville Traction Co. v. Saint Bernard Mining Co.,* 1905, 25 S.Ct. 251, 196 U.S. 239, 49 L.Ed. 462. In the Madisonville case, and in cases cited therein, it has been held that condemnation actions brought by state corporations in the exercise of a power delegated by the state might be governed by procedure prescribed by the laws of the United States, whether the cases were begun in or removed to the federal court. See, also, *Franzen v. Chicago, M. & St. P. Ry. Co.,* C.C.A.7th, 1921, 278 F. 370, 372.

Any condition affecting the substantial right of a litigant attached by state law is to be observed and enforced, such as making a deposit in court where the power of eminent domain is conditioned upon so doing. (See also subdivision (j). Subject to this qualification, subdivision (k) provides that in cases involving the state power of eminent domain, the practice prescribed by other subdivisions of Rule 71A shall govern.

Note to Subdivision (*l*). Since the condemnor will normally be the prevailing party and since he should not recover his costs against the property owner, Rule 54(d), which provides generally that costs shall go to the prevailing party, is made inapplicable. Without attempting to state what the rule on costs is, the effect of subdivision (*l*) is that costs shall be awarded in accordance with the law that has developed in condemnation cases. This has been summarized as follows: "Costs of condemnation proceedings are not assessable against the condemnee, unless by stipulation he agrees to assume some or all of them. Such normal expenses of the proceeding as bills for publication of notice, commissioners' fees, the cost of transporting commissioners and jurors to take a view, fees for attorneys to represent defendants who have failed to answer, and witness' fees, are properly charged to the government, though not taxed as costs. Similarly, if it is necessary that a conveyance be executed by a commissioner, the United States pay his fees and those for recording the deed. However, the distribution of the award is a matter in which the United States has no legal interest. Expenses incurred in ascertaining the identity of distributees and deciding between conflicting claimants are properly chargeable against the award, not against the United States, although United States attorneys are expected to aid the court in such matters as amici curiae." Lands Division Manual 861. For other discussion and citation, see *Grand River Dam Authority v. Jarvis*, C.C.A.10th, 1942, 124 F.2d 914. Costs may not be taxed against the United States except to the extent permitted by law. *United States v. 125.71 Acres of Land in Loyalhanna Tp., Westmoreland County, Pa.*, D.C.Pa.1944, 54 F.Supp. 193; Lands Division Manual 859. Even if it were thought desirable to allow the property owner's costs to be taxed against the United States, this is a matter for legislation and not court rule.

1963 Amendment

This amendment conforms to the amendment of Rule 4(f).

1985 Amendment

Rule 71A(h) provides that except when Congress has provided otherwise, the issue of just compensation in a condemnation case may be tried by a jury if one of the parties so demands, unless the court in its discretion orders the issue determined by a commission of three persons. In 1980, the Comptroller General of the United States in a Report to Congress recommended that use of the commission procedure should be encouraged in order to improve and expedite the trial of condemnation cases. The Report noted that long delays were being caused in many districts by such factors as crowded dockets, the precedence given criminal cases, the low priority accorded condemnation matters, and the high turnover of Assistant United States Attorneys. The Report concluded that revising Rule 71A to make the use of the commission procedure more attractive might alleviate the situation.

Accordingly, Rule 71A(h) is being amended in a number of respects designed to assure the quality and utility of a Rule 71A commission. First, the amended Rule will give the court discretion to appoint, in addition to the three members of a commission, up to two additional persons as alternate commissioners who would hear the case and be available, at any time up to the filing of the decision by the three-member commission, to replace any commissioner who becomes unable or disqualified to continue. The discretion to appoint alternate commissioners can be particularly useful in protracted cases, avoiding expensive retrials that have been required in some cases because of the death or disability of a commissioner. Prior to replacing a commissioner an alternate would not be present at, or participate in, the commission's deliberations.

Second, the amended Rule requires the court, before appointment, to advise the parties of the identity and qualifications of each prospective commissioner and alternate. The court then may authorize the examination of prospective appointees by the parties and each party has the right to challenge for cause. The objective is to insure that unbiased and competent commissioners are appointed.

The amended Rule does not prescribe a qualification standard for appointment to a commission, although it is understood that only persons possessing background and ability to appraise real estate valuation testimony and to award fair and just compensation on the basis thereof would be appointed. In most situations the chairperson should be a lawyer and all members should have some background qualifying them to weigh proof of value in the real estate field and, when possible, in the particular real estate market embracing the land in question.

The amended Rule should give litigants greater confidence in the commission procedure by affording them certain rights to participate in the appointment of commission members that are roughly comparable to the practice with regard to jury selection. This is accomplished by giving the court permission to allow the parties to examine prospective commissioners and by recognizing the right of each party to object to the appointment of any person for cause.

1987 Amendment

The amendments are technical. No substantive change is intended.

1988 Amendment

The amendment is technical. No substantive change is intended.

1993 Amendments

The references to the subdivisions of Rule 4 are deleted in light of the revision of that rule.

Rule 72. Magistrate Judges; Pretrial Orders

(a) Nondispositive Matters. A magistrate judge to whom a pretrial matter not dispositive of a claim or defense of a party is referred to hear and determine shall promptly conduct such proceedings as are required and when appropriate enter into the record a written order setting forth the disposition of the matter. Within 10 days after being served with a copy of the magistrate judge's order, a party may serve and file objections to the order; a party may not thereafter assign as error a defect in the magistrate judge's order to which objection was not timely made. The district judge to whom the case is assigned shall consider such objections and shall modify or set aside any portion of the magistrate judge's order found to be clearly erroneous or contrary to law.

(b) Dispositive Motions and Prisoner Petitions. A magistrate judge assigned without consent of the parties to hear a pretrial matter dispositive of a claim or defense of a party or a prisoner petition challenging the conditions of confinement shall promptly conduct such proceedings as are required. A record shall be made of all evidentiary proceedings before the magistrate judge, and a record may be made of such other proceedings as the magistrate judge deems necessary. The magistrate judge shall enter into the record a recommendation for disposition of the matter, including proposed findings of fact when appropriate. The clerk shall forthwith mail copies to all parties.

A party objecting to the recommended disposition of the matter shall promptly arrange for the transcription of the record, or portions of it as all parties may agree upon or the magistrate judge deems sufficient, unless the district judge otherwise directs. Within 10 days after being served with a copy of the recommended disposition, a party may serve and file specific, written objections to the proposed findings and recommendations. A party may respond to another party's objections within 10 days after being served with a copy thereof. The district judge to whom the case is assigned shall make a de novo determination upon the record, or after additional evidence, of any portion of the magistrate judge's disposition to which specific written objection has been made in accordance with this rule. The district judge may accept, reject, or modify the recommended decision, receive further evidence, or recommit the matter to the magistrate judge with instructions.

(Added Apr. 28, 1983, eff. Aug. 1, 1983, and amended Apr. 30, 1991, eff. Dec. 1, 1991; Apr. 22, 1993, eff. Dec. 1, 1993.)

ADVISORY COMMITTEE NOTES

1983 Addition

Subdivision (a). This subdivision addresses court-ordered referrals of nondispositive matters under 28 U.S.C. § 636(b)(1)(A). The rule calls for a written order of the magistrate's disposition to preserve the record and facilitate review. An oral order read into the record by the magistrate will satisfy this requirement.

No specific procedures or timetables for raising objections to the magistrate's rulings on nondispositive matters are set forth in the Magistrates Act. The rule fixes a 10-day period in order to avoid uncertainty and provide uniformity that will eliminate the confusion that might arise if different periods were prescribed by local rule in different districts. It also is contemplated that a party who is successful before the magistrate will be afforded an opportunity to respond to objections raised to the magistrate's ruling.

The last sentence of subdivision (a) specifies that reconsideration of a magistrate's order, as provided for in the Magistrates Act, shall be by the district judge to whom the case is assigned. This rule does not restrict experimentation by the district courts under 28 U.S.C. § 636(b)(3) involving references of matters other than pretrial matters, such as appointment of counsel, taking of default judgments, and acceptance of jury verdicts when the judge is unavailable.

Subdivision (b). This subdivision governs court-ordered referrals of dispositive pretrial matters and prisoner petitions challenging conditions of confinement, pursuant to statutory authorization in 28 U.S.C. § 636(b)(1)(B). This rule does not extend to habeas corpus petitions, which are covered by the specific rules relating to proceedings under Sections 2254 and 2255 of Title 28.

This rule implements the statutory procedures for making objections to the magistrate's proposed findings and recommendations. The 10–day period, as specified in the statute, is subject to Rule 6(e) which provides for an additional 3–day period when service is made by mail. Although no specific provision appears in the Magistrates Act, the rule specifies a 10–day period for a party to respond to objections to the magistrate's recommendation.

Implementing the statutory requirements, the rule requires the district judge to whom the case is assigned to make a de novo determination of those portions of the report, findings, or recommendations to which timely objection is made. The term "de novo" signifies that the magistrate's findings are not protected by the clearly erroneous doctrine, but does not indicate that a second evidentiary hearing is required. See *United States v. Raddatz,* 417 [447] U.S. 667 (1980). See also Silberman, *Masters and Magistrates Part II: The American Analogue,* 50 N.Y.U. L.Rev. 1297, 1367 (1975). When no timely objection is filed, the court need only satisfy itself that there is no clear error on the face of the record in order to accept the recommendation. See *Campbell v. United States Dist. Court,* 501 F.2d 196, 206 (9th Cir.1974), cert. denied, 419 U.S. 879, quoted in House Report No. 94–1609, 94th Cong.2d Sess. (1976) at 3. Compare *Park Motor Mart, Inc. v. Ford Motor Co.,* 616 F.2d 603 (1st Cir.1980). Failure to make timely objection to the magistrate's report prior to its adoption by the district judge may constitute a waiver of appellate review of the district judge's order. *See United States v. Walters,* 638 F.2d 947 (6th Cir.1981).

1991 Amendment

This amendment is intended to eliminate a discrepancy in measuring the 10 days for serving and filing objections to a magistrate's action under subdivisions (a) and (b) of this Rule. The rule as promulgated in 1983 required objections to the magistrate's handling of nondispositive matters to be served and filed within 10 days of entry of the order, but required objections to dispositive motions to be made within 10 days of being served with a copy of the recommended disposition. Subdivision (a) is here amended to conform to subdivision (b) to avoid any confusion or technical defaults, particularly in connection with magistrate orders that rule on both dispositive and nondispositive matters.

The amendment is also intended to assure that objections to magistrate's orders that are not timely made shall not be considered. *Compare* Rule 51.

1993 Amendments

This revision is made to conform the rule to changes made by the Judicial Improvements Act of 1990.

Rule 73. Magistrate Judges; Trial by Consent and Appeal Options

(a) Powers; Procedure. When specially designated to exercise such jurisdiction by local rule or order of the district court and when all parties consent thereto, a magistrate judge may exercise the authority provided by Title 28, U.S.C. § 636(c) and may conduct any or all proceedings, including a jury or nonjury trial, in a civil case. A record of the proceedings shall be made in accordance with the requirements of Title 28, U.S.C. § 636(c)(5).

(b) Consent. When a magistrate judge has been designated to exercise civil trial jurisdiction, the clerk shall give written notice to the parties of their opportunity to consent to the exercise by a magistrate judge of civil jurisdiction over the case, as authorized by Title 28, U.S.C. § 636(c). If, within the period specified by local rule, the parties agree to a magistrate judge's exercise of such authority, they shall execute and file a joint form of consent or separate forms of consent setting forth such election.

A district judge, magistrate judge, or other court official may again advise the parties of the availability of the magistrate judge, but, in so doing, shall also advise the parties that they are free to withhold consent without adverse substantive consequences. A district judge or magistrate judge shall not be informed of a party's response to the clerk's notification, unless all parties have consented to the referral of the matter to a magistrate judge.

The district judge, for good cause shown on the judge's own initiative, or under extraordinary circumstances shown by a party, may vacate a reference of a civil matter to a magistrate judge under this subdivision.

(c) Appeal. In accordance with Title 28, U.S.C. § 636(c)(3), appeal from a judgment entered upon direction of a magistrate judge in proceedings under this rule will lie to the court of appeals as it would from a judgment of the district court.

[(d) Optional Appeal Route.] (Abrogated, April 11, 1997, eff. Dec. 1, 1997)

(Added Apr. 28, 1983, eff. Aug. 1, 1983, and amended Mar. 2, 1987, eff. Aug. 1, 1987; Apr. 22, 1993, eff. Dec. 1, 1993; Apr. 11, 1997, eff. Dec. 1, 1997.)

ADVISORY COMMITTEE NOTES

1983 Addition

Subdivision (a). This subdivision implements the broad authority of the 1979 amendments to the Magistrates Act, 28 U.S.C. § 636(c), which permit a magistrate to sit in lieu of a district judge and exercise civil jurisdiction over a case, when the parties consent. See McCabe, *The Federal Magistrate Act of 1979,* 16 Harv.J.Legis. 343, 364–79 (1979). In order to exercise this jurisdiction, a magistrate must be specially designated under 28 U.S.C. § 636(c)(1) by the district court or courts he serves. The only exception to a magistrate's exercise of civil jurisdiction, which includes the power to conduct jury and nonjury trials and decide dispositive motions, is the contempt power. A hearing on contempt is to be conducted by the district judge upon certification of the facts and an order to show cause by the magistrate. See 28 U.S.C. § 639(e). In view of 28 U.S.C. § 636(c)(1) and this rule, it is unnecessary to amend Rule 58 to provide that the decision of a magistrate is a "decision by the court" for the purposes of that rule and a "final decision of the district court" for purposes of 28 U.S.C. § 1291 governing appeals.

Subdivision (b). This subdivision implements the blind consent provision of 28 U.S.C. § 636(c)(2) and is designed to ensure that neither the judge nor the magistrate attempts to induce a party to consent to reference of a civil matter under this rule to a magistrate. See House Rep. No. 96–444, 96th Cong. 1st Sess. 8 (1979).

The rule opts for a uniform approach in implementing the consent provision by directing the clerk to notify the parties of their opportunity to elect to proceed before a magistrate and by requiring the execution and filing of a consent form or forms setting forth the election. However, flexibility at the local level is preserved in that local rules will determine how notice shall be communicated to the parties, and local rules will specify the time period within which an election must be made.

The last paragraph of subdivision (b) reiterates the provision in 28 U.S.C. § 636(c)(6) for vacating a reference to the magistrate.

Subdivision (c). Under 28 U.S.C. § 636(c)(3), the normal route of appeal from the judgment of a magistrate—the only route that will be available unless the parties otherwise agree in advance—is an appeal by the aggrieved party "directly to the appropriate United States court of appeals from the judgment of the magistrate in the same manner as an appeal from any other judgment of a district court." The quoted statutory language indicates Congress' intent that the same procedures and standards of appealability that govern appeals from district court judgments govern appeals from magistrates' judgments.

Subdivision (d). 28 U.S.C. § 636(c)(4) offers parties who consent to the exercise of civil jurisdiction by a magistrate an alternative appeal route to that provided in subdivision (c) of this rule. This optional appellate route was provided by Congress in recognition of the fact that not all civil cases warrant the same appellate treatment. In cases where the amount in controversy is not great and there are no difficult questions of law to be resolved, the parties may desire to avoid the expense and delay of appeal to the court of appeals by electing an appeal to the district judge. See McCabe, *The Federal Magistrate Act of 1979,* 16 Harv.J.Legis, 343, 388 (1979). This subdivision provides that the parties may elect the optional appeal route at the time of reference to a magistrate. To this end, the notice by the clerk under subdivision (b) of this rule shall explain the appeal option and the corollary restriction on review by the court of appeals. This approach will avoid later claims of lack of consent to the avenue of appeal. The choice of the alternative appeal route to the judge of the district court should be made by the parties in their forms of consent. Special appellate rules to govern appeals from a magistrate to a district judge appear in new Rules 74 through 76.

1987 Amendment

The amendment is technical. No substantive change is intended.

1993 Amendments

This revision is made to conform the rule to changes made by the Judicial Improvements Act of 1990. The Act requires that, when being reminded of the availability of a magistrate judge, the parties be advised that withholding of consent will have no "adverse substantive consequences." They may, however, be advised if the withholding of consent will have the adverse procedural consequence of a potential delay in trial.

1997 Amendment

The Federal Courts Improvement Act of 1996 repealed the former provisions of 28 U.S.C. § 636(c)(4) and (5) that enabled parties that had agreed to trial before a magistrate judge to agree also that appeal should be taken to the district court. Rule 73 is amended to conform to this change. Rules 74, 75, and 76 are abrogated for the same reason. The portions of Form 33 and Form 34 that referred to appeals to the district court also are deleted.

HISTORICAL NOTES

Change of Name

Reference to United States magistrate or to magistrate deemed to refer to United States magistrate judge pursuant to section 321 of Pub.L. 101–650, set out as a note under section 631 of this title.

[Rule 74. Method of Appeal From Magistrate Judge to District Judge Under Title 28, U.S.C. § 636(c)(4) and Rule 73(d)] (Abrogated April 11, 1997, eff. Dec. 1, 1997)

ADVISORY COMMITTEE NOTES

1997 Amendment

Rule 74 is abrogated for the reasons described in the Note to Rule 73.

[Rule 75. Proceedings on Appeal From Magistrate Judge to District Judge Under Rule 73(d)] (Abrogated April 11, 1997, eff. Dec. 1, 1997)

ADVISORY COMMITTEE NOTES

1997 Amendment

Rule 75 is abrogated for the reasons described in the Note to Rule 73.

[Rule 76. Judgment of the District Judge on the Appeal Under Rule 73(d) and Costs] (Abrogated April 11, 1997, eff. Dec. 1, 1997)

ADVISORY COMMITTEE NOTES

1997 Amendment

Rule 76 is abrogated for the reasons described in the Note to Rule 73.

[IX. APPEALS [1] (Abrogated)]

[1] Another chapter IX is set out ante.

HISTORICAL NOTES

Prior Provisions

The heading "IX. APPEALS" and Rules 72 to 76, formerly constituting the provisions of IX, were abrogated Dec. 4, 1967, effective July 1, 1968. Former Rules 72 to 76 were the civil rules relating to appeals, the provisions of which, except for Rule 73(h), were transferred to and covered by the Federal Rules of Appellate Procedure and (in the case of Rule 72) the Rules of the Supreme Court. The substance of Rule 73(h) was transferred to Rule 9(h) of these Rules.

X. DISTRICT COURTS AND CLERKS

Rule 77. District Courts and Clerks

(a) District Courts Always Open. The district courts shall be deemed always open for the purpose of filing any pleading or other proper paper, of issuing and returning mesne and final process, and of making and directing all interlocutory motions, orders, and rules.

(b) Trials and Hearings; Orders in Chambers. All trials upon the merits shall be conducted in open court and so far as convenient in a regular court room. All other acts or proceedings may be done or conducted by a judge in chambers, without the attendance of the clerk or other court officials and at any place either within or without the district; but no hearing, other than one ex parte, shall be conducted outside the district without the consent of all parties affected thereby.

(c) Clerk's Office and Orders by Clerk. The clerk's office with the clerk or a deputy in attendance shall be open during business hours on all days except Saturdays, Sundays, and legal holidays, but a district court may provide by local rule or order that its clerk's office shall be open for specified hours on Saturdays or particular legal holidays other than New Year's Day, Birthday of Martin Luther King, Jr., Washington's Birthday, Memorial Day, Independence Day, Labor Day, Columbus Day, Veterans Day, Thanksgiving Day, and Christmas Day. All motions and applications in the clerk's office for issuing mesne process, for issuing final process to enforce and execute judgments, for entering defaults or judgments by default, and for other proceedings which do not require allowance or order of the court are grantable of course by the clerk; but the clerk's action may be suspended or altered or rescinded by the court upon cause shown.

(d) Notice of Orders or Judgments. Immediately upon the entry of an order or judgment the clerk shall serve a notice of the entry by mail in the manner provided for in Rule 5 upon each party who is not in default for failure to appear, and shall make a note in the docket of the mailing. Any party may in addition serve a notice of such entry in the manner provided in Rule 5 for the service of papers. Lack of notice of the entry by the clerk does not affect the time to appeal or relieve or authorize the court to relieve a party for failure to appeal within the time allowed, except as permitted in Rule 4(a) of the Federal Rules of Appellate Procedure.

(As amended Dec. 27, 1946, eff. Mar. 19, 1948; Jan. 21, 1963, eff. July 1, 1963; Dec. 4, 1967, eff. July 1, 1968; Mar. 1, 1971, eff. July 1, 1971; Mar. 2, 1987, eff. Aug. 1, 1987; Apr. 30, 1991, eff. Dec. 1, 1991.)

ADVISORY COMMITTEE NOTES

1937 Adoption

This rule states the substance of U.S.C., Title 28, § 452, formerly § 13 (Courts open as courts of admiralty and equity). Compare [former] Equity Rules 1 (District Court Always Open For Certain Purposes—Orders at Chambers), 2 (Clerk's Office Always Open, Except, Etc.), 4 (Notice of Orders), and 5 (Motions Grantable of Course by Clerk).

1946 Amendment

Note. Rule 77(d) has been amended to avoid such situations as the one arising in *Hill v. Hawes,* 1944, 64 S.Ct. 334, 320 U.S. 520, 88 L.Ed. 283. In that case, an action instituted in the District Court for the District of Columbia, the clerk failed to give notice of the entry of a judgment for defendant as required by Rule 77(d). The time for taking an appeal then was 20 days under Rule 10 of the Court of Appeals (later enlarged by amendment to thirty days), and due to lack of notice of the entry of judgment the plaintiff failed to file his notice of appeal within the prescribed time. On this basis the trial court vacated the original judgment and then re-entered it, whereupon notice of appeal was filed. The Court of Appeals dismissed the appeal as taken too late. The Supreme Court, however, held that although rule 77(d) did not purport to attach any consequence to the clerk's failure to give notice as specified, the terms of the rule were such that the appellant was entitled to rely on it, and the trial court in such a case, in the exercise of a sound discretion, could vacate the former judgment and enter a new one, so that the appeal would be within the allowed time.

Because of Rule 6(c), which abolished the old rule that the expiration of the term ends a court's power over its judgment, the effect of the decision in *Hill v. Hawes* is to give the district court power, in its discretion and without time limit, and long after the term may have expired, to vacate a judgment and reenter it for the purpose of reviving the right of appeal. This seriously affects the finality of judgments. See also proposed Rule 6(c) and Note; proposed Rule 60(b) and Note; and proposed Rule 73(a) and Note.

Rule 77(d) as amended makes it clear that notification by the clerk of the entry of a judgment has nothing to do with the starting of the time for appeal; that time starts to run from the date of entry of judgment and not from the date of notice of the entry. Notification by the clerk is merely for the convenience of litigants. And lack of such notification in itself has no effect upon the time for appeal; but in considering an application for extension of time for appeal as provided in Rule 73(a), the court may take into account, as one of the factors affecting its decision, whether the clerk failed to give notice as provided in Rule 77(d) or the party failed to receive the clerk's notice. It need not, however, extend the time for appeal merely because the clerk's notice was not sent or received. It would, therefore, be entirely unsafe for a party to rely on absence of notice from the clerk of the entry of a judgment, or to rely on the adverse party's failure to serve notice of the entry of a judgment. Any party may, of course, serve timely notice of the entry of a judgment upon the adverse party and thus preclude a successful application, under Rule 73(a), for the extension of the time for appeal.

1963 Amendment

Subdivision (c). The amendment authorizes closing of the clerk's office on Saturday as far as civil business is concerned. However, a district court may require its clerk's office to remain open for specified hours on Saturdays or "legal holidays" other than those enumerated ("Legal holiday" is defined in Rule 6(a), as amended.) The clerk's offices of many district courts have customarily remained open on some of the days appointed as holidays by State law. This practice could be continued by local rule or order.

Subdivision (d). This amendment conforms to the amendment of Rule 5(a). See the Advisory Committee's Note to that amendment.

1968 Amendment

The provisions of Rule 73(a) are incorporated in Rule 4(a) of the Federal Rules of Appellate Procedure.

1971 Amendment

The amendment adds Columbus Day to the list of legal holidays. See the Note accompanying the amendment of Rule 6(a).

1987 Amendment

The amendments are technical. No substantive change is intended. The Birthday of Martin Luther King, Jr. is added to the list of national holidays in Rule 77.

1991 Amendment

This revision is a companion to the concurrent amendment to Rule 4 of the Federal Rules of Appellate Procedure. The purpose of the revisions is to permit district courts to ease strict sanctions now imposed on appellants whose notices of appeal are filed late because of their failure to receive notice of entry of a judgment. See, e.g. *Tucker v. Commonwealth Land Title Ins. Co.*, 800 F.2d 1054 (11th Cir.1986); *Ashby Enterprises, Ltd. v. Weitzman, Dym & Associates*, 780 F.2d 1043 (D.C.Cir.1986); *In re OPM Leasing Services, Inc.*, 769 F.2d 911 (2d Cir.1985); *Spika v. Village of Lombard, Ill.*, 763 F.2d 282 (7th Cir.1985); *Hall v. Community Mental Health Center of Beaver County*, 772 F.2d 42 (3d Cir.1985); *Wilson v. Atwood v. Stark*, 725 F.2d 255 (5th Cir. en banc), cert. dismissed, 105 S.Ct. 17 (1984); *Case v. BASF Wyandotte*, 727 F.2d 1034 (Fed.Cir.1984), cert. denied, 105 S.Ct. 386 (1984); *Hensley v. Chesapeake & Ohio R.R. Co.*, 651 F.2d 226 (4th

Cir.1981); *Buckeye Cellulose Corp. v. Electric Construction Co.*, 569 F.2d 1036 (8th Cir.1978).

Failure to receive notice may have increased in frequency with the growth in the caseload in the clerks' offices. The present strict rule imposes a duty on counsel to maintain contact with the court while a case is under submission. Such contact is more difficult to maintain if counsel is outside the district, as is increasingly common, and can be a burden to the court as well as counsel.

The effect of the revisions is to place a burden on prevailing parties who desire certainty that the time for appeal is running. Such parties can take the initiative to assure that their adversaries receive effective notice. An appropriate procedure for such notice is provided in Rule 5.

The revised rule lightens the responsibility but not the workload of the clerk's offices, for the duty of that office to give notice of entry of judgment must be maintained.

Rule 78. Motion Day

Unless local conditions make it impracticable, each district court shall establish regular times and places, at intervals sufficiently frequent for the prompt dispatch of business, at which motions requiring notice and hearing may be heard and disposed of; but the judge at any time or place and on such notice, if any, as the judge considers reasonable may make orders for the advancement, conduct, and hearing of actions.

To expedite its business, the court may make provision by rule or order for the submission and determination of motions without oral hearing upon brief written statements of reasons in support and opposition.

(As amended Mar. 2, 1987, eff. Aug. 1, 1987.)

ADVISORY COMMITTEE NOTES

1937 Adoption

Compare [former] Equity Rule 6 (Motion Day) with the first paragraph of this rule. The second paragraph authorizes a procedure found helpful for the expedition of business in some of the Federal and State courts. See Rule 43(e) of these rules dealing with evidence on motions. Compare *Civil Practice Rules of the Municipal Court of Chicago* (1935), Rules 269, 270, 271.

1987 Amendment

The amendment is technical. No substantive change is intended.

Rule 79. Books and Records Kept by the Clerk and Entries Therein

(a) Civil Docket. The clerk shall keep a book known as "civil docket" of such form and style as may be prescribed by the Director of the Administrative Office of the United States Courts with the approval of the Judicial Conference of the United States, and shall enter therein each civil action to which these rules are made applicable. Actions shall be assigned consecutive file numbers. The file number of each action shall be noted on the folio of the docket whereon the first entry of the action is made. All papers filed with the clerk, all process issued and returns made thereon, all appearances, orders, verdicts, and judgments shall be entered chronologically in the civil docket on the folio assigned to the action and shall be marked with its file number. These entries shall be brief but shall show the nature of each paper filed or writ issued and the substance of each order or judgment of the court and of the returns showing execution of process. The entry of an order or judgment shall show the date the entry is made. When in an action trial by jury has been properly demanded or ordered the clerk shall enter the word "jury" on the folio assigned to that action.

(b) Civil Judgments and Orders. The clerk shall keep, in such form and manner as the Director of the Administrative Office of the United States Courts with the approval of the Judicial Conference of the United States may prescribe, a correct copy of every final judgment or appealable order, or order affecting title to or lien upon real or personal property, and any other order which the court may direct to be kept.

(c) Indices; Calendars. Suitable indices of the civil docket and of every civil judgment and order referred to in subdivision (b) of this rule shall be kept by the clerk under the direction of the court. There shall be prepared under the direction of the court calendars of all actions ready for trial, which shall distinguish "jury actions" from "court actions."

(d) Other Books and Records of the Clerk. The clerk shall also keep such other books and records as may be required from time to time by the Director of the Administrative Office of the United States Courts with the approval of the Judicial Conference of the United States.

(As amended Dec. 27, 1946, eff. Mar. 19, 1948; Dec. 29, 1948, eff. Oct. 20, 1949; Jan. 21, 1963, eff. July 1, 1963.)

ADVISORY COMMITTEE NOTES

1937 Adoption

Compare [former] Equity Rule 3 (Books Kept by Clerk and Entries Therein). In connection with this rule, see also the following statutes of the United States:

U.S.C., Title 5 former:

- § 301 [See Title 28, § 526] (Officials for investigation of official acts, records and accounts of marshals, attorneys, clerks of courts, United States commissioners, referees and trustees)
- § 318 [former] (Accounts of district attorneys)

U.S.C., Title 28 former:

- § 556 [former] (Clerks of district courts; books open to inspection)
- § 567 [now 751] (Same; accounts)
- § 568 [now 751] (Same; reports and accounts of moneys received; dockets)

§ 813 [former] (Indices of judgment debtors to be kept by clerks)

And see "Instructions to United States Attorneys, Marshals, Clerks and Commissioners" issued by the Attorney General of the United States.

1946 Amendment

Note. Subdivision (a). The amendment substitutes the Director of the Administrative Office of the United States Courts, acting subject to the approval of the Judicial Conference of Senior Circuit Judges, in the place of the Attorney General as a consequence of and in accordance with the provisions of the act establishing the Administrative Office and transferring functions thereto. Act of August 7, 1939, c. 501, §§ 1 to 7, 53 Stat. 1223, 28 U.S.C.A. §§ 601 to 610, formerly §§ 444 to 450.

Subdivision (b). The change in this subdivision does not alter the nature of the judgments and orders to be recorded in permanent form but it does away with the express requirement that they be recorded in a book. This merely gives latitude for the preservation of court records in other than book form, if that shall seem advisable, and permits with the approval of the Judicial Conference the adoption of such modern, space-saving methods as microphotography. See *Proposed Improvements in the Administration of the Offices of Clerks of United States District Courts,* prepared by the Bureau of the Budget, 1941, 38–42. See also Rule 55, Federal Rules of Criminal Procedure.

Subdivision (c). The words "Separate and" have been deleted as unduly rigid. There is no sufficient reason for requiring that the indices in all cases be separate; on the contrary, the requirement frequently increases the labor of persons searching the records as well as the labor of the clerk's force preparing them. The matter should be left to administrative discretion.

The other changes in the subdivision merely conform with those made in subdivision (b) of the rule.

Subdivision (d). Subdivision (d) is a new provision enabling the Administrative Office, with the approval of the Judicial Conference, to carry out any improvements in clerical procedure with respect to books and records which may be deemed advisable. See report cited in Note to subdivision (b), supra.

1948 Amendment

The amendment effective October 1949, substituted the name, "Judicial Conference of the United States," for "Judicial Conference of Senior Circuit Judges," in the first sentence of subdivision (a), and in subdivisions (b) and (d).

1963 Amendment

The terminology is clarified without any change of the prescribed practice. See amended Rule 58, and the Advisory Committee's Note thereto.

Rule 80. Stenographer; Stenographic Report or Transcript as Evidence

[(a) Abrogated (Dec. 27, 1946, eff. Mar. 19, 1948)].

[(b) Abrogated (Dec. 27, 1946, eff. Mar. 19, 1948)].

(c) Stenographic Report or Transcript as Evidence. Whenever the testimony of a witness at a trial or hearing which was stenographically reported is admissible in evidence at a later trial, it may be proved by the transcript thereof duly certified by the person who reported the testimony.

(As amended Dec. 27, 1946, eff. Mar. 19, 1948.)

ADVISORY COMMITTEE NOTES

1937 Adoption

Note to Subdivision (a). This follows substantially [former] Equity Rule 50 (Stenographer—Appointment—Fees). [This subdivision was abrogated. See amendment note of Advisory Committee below.]

Note to Subdivision (b). See *Reports of Conferences of Senior Circuit Judges with the Chief Justice of the United States* (1936), 22 A.B.A.J. 818, 819; (1937), 24 A.B.A.J. 75, 77. [This subdivision was abrogated. See amendment note of Advisory Committee below.]

Note to Subdivision (c). Compare Iowa Code (1935) § 11353.

1946 Amendment

Note. Subdivisions (a) and (b) of Rule 80 have been abrogated because of Public Law 222, 78th Cong., c. 3, 2d Sess., approved Jan. 20, 1944, 28 U.S.C. §§ 550, 604, 753, 1915, 1920, formerly § 9a, providing for the appointment of official stenographers for each district court, prescribing their duties, providing for the furnishing of transcripts, the taxation of the fees therefor as costs, and other related matters. This statute has now been implemented by Congressional appropriation available for the fiscal year beginning July 1, 1945.

Subdivision (c) of Rule 80 (Stenographic Report or Transcript as Evidence) has been retained unchanged.

XI. GENERAL PROVISIONS

Rule 81. Applicability in General

(a) To What Proceedings Applicable

(1) These rules do not apply to prize proceedings in admiralty governed by Title 10, U.S.C., §§ 7651–7681. They do not apply to proceedings in bankruptcy or proceedings in copyright under Title 17, U.S.C., except in so far as they may be made applicable thereto by rules promulgated by the Supreme Court of the United States. They do not apply to mental health proceedings in the United States District Court for the District of Columbia.

(2) These rules are applicable to proceedings for admission to citizenship, habeas corpus, and quo warranto, to the extent that the practice in such proceedings is not set forth in statutes of the United States and has heretofore conformed to the practice in civil actions. The writ of habeas corpus, or order to show cause, shall be directed to the person having custody of the person detained. It shall be returned within 3 days unless for good cause shown additional time is allowed which in cases brought under 28 U.S.C. § 2254 shall not exceed 40 days, and in all other cases shall not exceed 20 days.

(3) In proceedings under Title 9, U.S.C., relating to arbitration, or under the Act of May 20, 1926, ch. 347, § 9 (44 Stat. 585), U.S.C., Title 45, § 159, relating to boards of arbitration of railway labor disputes, these rules apply only to the extent that matters of procedure are not provided for in those statutes. These rules apply to proceedings to compel the giving of testimony or production of documents in accordance with a subpoena issued by an officer or agency of the United States under any statute of the United States except as otherwise provided by statute or by rules of the district court or by order of the court in the proceedings.

(4) These rules do not alter the method prescribed by the Act of February 18, 1922, ch. 57, § 2 (42 Stat. 388), U.S.C., Title 7, § 292; or by the Act of June 10, 1930, ch. 436, § 7 (46 Stat. 534), as amended, U.S.C., Title 7, § 499g(c), for instituting proceedings in the United States district courts to review orders of the Secretary of Agriculture; or prescribed by the Act of June 25, 1934, ch. 742, § 2 (48 Stat. 1214), U.S.C., Title 15, § 522, for instituting proceedings to review orders of the Secretary of the Interior; or prescribed by the Act of February 22, 1935, ch. 18, § 5 (49 Stat. 31), U.S.C., Title 15, § 715d(c), as extended, for instituting proceedings to review orders of petroleum control boards; but the conduct of such proceedings in the district courts shall be made to conform to these rules so far as applicable.

(5) These rules do not alter the practice in the United States district courts prescribed in the Act of July 5, 1935, ch. 372, §§ 9 and 10 (49 Stat. 453), as amended, U.S.C., Title 29, §§ 159 and 160, for beginning and conducting proceedings to enforce orders of the National Labor Relations Board; and in respects not covered by those statutes, the practice in the district courts shall conform to these rules so far as applicable.

(6) These rules apply to proceedings for enforcement or review of compensation orders under the Longshoremen's and Harbor Workers' Compensation Act, Act of March 4, 1927, c. 509, §§ 18, 21 (44 Stat. 1434, 1436), as amended, U.S.C., Title 33, §§ 918, 921, except to the extent that matters of procedure are provided for in that Act. The provisions for service by publication and for answer in proceedings to cancel certificates of citizenship under the Act of June 27, 1952, c. 477, Title III, c. 2, § 340 (66 Stat. 260), U.S.C., Title 8, § 1451, remain in effect.

[(7) Abrogated, effective Aug. 1, 1951. (Supreme Court Order, Apr. 30, 1951.)]

(b) Scire Facias and Mandamus. The writs of scire facias and mandamus are abolished. Relief heretofore available by mandamus or scire facias may be obtained by appropriate action or by appropriate motion under the practice prescribed in these rules.

(c) Removed Actions. These rules apply to civil actions removed to the United States district courts from the state courts and govern procedure after removal. Repleading is not necessary unless the court so orders. In a removed action in which the defendant has not answered, the defendant shall answer or present the other defenses or objections available under these rules within 20 days after the receipt through service or otherwise of a copy of the initial pleading setting forth the claim for relief upon which the action or proceeding is based, or within 20 days after the service of summons upon such initial pleading, then filed, or within 5 days after the filing of the petition for removal, whichever period is longest. If at the time of removal all necessary pleadings have been served, a party entitled to trial by jury under Rule 38 shall be accorded it, if the party's demand therefor is served within 10 days after the petition for removal is filed if the party is the petitioner, or if not the petitioner within 10 days after service on the party of the notice of filing the petition. A party who, prior to removal, has made an express demand for trial by jury in accordance with state law, need not make a demand after removal. If state law applicable in the court from which the case is removed does not require the parties to make express demands in order to claim trial by jury, they need not make demands after removal unless the court directs that they do so within a specified time if they desire to claim trial by jury. The court may make this direction on its own motion and shall do so as a matter of course at the request of any party. The failure of a party to make demand as directed constitutes a waiver by that party of trial by jury.

[(d) Abrogated, effective Oct. 20, 1949. (Supreme Court Order, Dec. 29, 1948)].

(e) Law Applicable. Whenever in these rules the law of the state in which the district court is held is made applicable, the law applied in the District of Columbia governs proceedings in the United States District Court for the District of Columbia. When the word "state" is used, it includes, if appropriate, the District of Columbia. When the term "statute of the United States" is used, it includes, so far as concerns proceedings in the United States District Court for the District of Columbia, any Act of Congress locally applicable to and in force in the District of Columbia. When the law of a state is referred to, the word "law" includes the statutes of that state and the state judicial decisions construing them.

(f) References to Officer of the United States. Under any rule in which reference is made to an officer or agency of the United States, the term "officer" includes a district director of internal revenue, a former district director or collector of internal revenue, or the personal representative of a deceased district director or collector of internal revenue.

(As amended Dec. 28, 1939, eff. Apr. 3, 1941; Dec. 27, 1946, eff. Mar. 19, 1948; Dec. 29, 1948, eff. Oct. 20, 1949; Apr. 30, 1951, eff. Aug. 1, 1951; Jan. 21, 1963, eff. July 1, 1963; Feb. 28, 1966, eff. July 1, 1966; Dec. 4, 1967, eff. July 1, 1968; Mar. 1, 1971, eff. July 1, 1971; Mar. 2, 1987, eff. Aug. 1, 1987.)

ADVISORY COMMITTEE NOTES

1937 Adoption

Note to Subdivision (a). Paragraph (1): Compare the enabling act, Act of June 19, 1934, U.S.C., Title 28, § 2072, formerly § 723b (Rules in actions at law; Supreme Court authorized to make) and § 2072, formerly § 723c (Union of equity and action at law rules; power of Supreme Court). For the application of these rules in bankruptcy and copyright proceedings, see Orders xxxvi and xxxvii in Bankruptcy and Rule 1 of Rules of Practice and Procedure under § 25 of the copyright act, Act of March 4, 1909, U.S.C., Title 17, former § 25 [see 412, 501 et seq.] (Infringement and rules of procedure).

For examples of statutes which are preserved by paragraph (2) see: U.S.C., Title 8, [former] ch. 9 (Naturalization); Title 28, former ch. 14 [now 153] (Habeas corpus); Title 28, former §§ 377a to 377c [now D.C.Code, Title 16 § 3501 et seq.] (Quo warranto); and such forfeiture statutes as U.S.C., Title 7, former § 116 (Misbranded seeds, confiscation), and Title 21, § 334(b), formerly § 14 (Pure Food and Drug Act—condemnation of adulterated or misbranded Food; procedure). See also *443 Cans of Frozen Eggs Product v. U.S.*, 1912, 33 S.Ct. 50, 226 U.S. 172, 57 L.Ed. 174.

For examples of statutes which under paragraph (7) will continue to govern procedure in condemnation cases, see U.S.C. Title 40, [former] § 258 (Condemnation of realty for sites for public building, etc., procedure); U.S.C., Title 16, § 831x (Condemnation by Tennessee Valley Authority); U.S.C., Title 40, § 120 (Acquisition of lands for public use in District of Columbia); Title 40, ch. 7 [now D.C.Code, Title 16, § 1301 et seq.] (Acquisition of lands in District of Columbia for use of United States; condemnation).

Note to Subdivision (b). Some statutes which will be affected by this subdivision are;

U.S.C., Title 7:
- § 222 (Federal Trade Commission powers adopted for enforcement of Stockyards Act) (By reference to Title 15, § 49)

U.S.C., Title 15:
- § 49 (Enforcement of Federal Trade Commission orders and antitrust laws)
- § 77t(c) (Enforcement of Securities and Exchange Commission orders and Securities Act of 1933)
- § 78u(f) (Same; Securities Exchange Act of 1934)
- § 79r(g) (Same; Public Utility Holding Company Act of 1935)

U.S.C., Title 16:
- § 820 (Proceedings in equity for revocation or to prevent violations of license of Federal Power Commission licensee)
- § 825m(b) (Mandamus to compel compliance with Federal Water Power Act, etc.)

U.S.C., Title 19:
- § 1333(c) (Mandamus to compel compliance with orders of Tariff Commission, etc.)

U.S.C., Title 28, former:
- § 377 [now 1651] (Power to issue writs)
- § 572 [now 1923] (Fees, attorneys, solicitors and proctors)
- § 778 [former] (Death of parties; substitution of executor or administrator). Compare Rule 25(a) (Substitution of parties; death), and the note thereto.

U.S.C., Title 33:
- § 495 (Removal of bridges over navigable waters)

U.S.C., Title 45:
- § 88 (Mandamus against Union Pacific Railroad Company)
- § 153(p) (Mandamus to enforce orders of Adjustment Board under Railway Labor Act)
- § 185 (Same; National Air Transport Adjustment Board) (By reference to § 153)

U.S.C., Title 47:
- § 11 (Powers of Federal Communications Commission)
- § 401(a) (Enforcement of Federal Communications Act and orders of Commission)
- § 406 (Same; Compelling furnishing of facilities; mandamus)

U.S.C., Title 49:
- § 19a(*l*) [now 11703] (Mandamus to compel compliance with Interstate Commerce Act)
- § 20(9) [now 11703] (Jurisdiction to compel compliance with interstate commerce laws by mandamus)

For comparable provisions in state practice see Smith-Hurd Ill.Stats.c. 110, § 179 (1937); Calif.Code Civ.Proc. (Deering, 1937) § 802.

Note to Subdivision (c). Such statutes as the following dealing with the removal of actions are substantially continued and made subject to these rules:

U.S.C., Title 28 former:
- § 71 [now 1441, 1445, 1447] (Removal of suits from state courts)
- § 72 [now 1446, 1447] (Same; procedure)
- § 73 [former] (Same; suits under grants of land from different states)
- § 74 [now 1443, 1446, 1447] (Same; causes against persons denied civil rights)
- § 75 [now 1446] (Same; petitioner in actual custody of state court)
- § 76 [now 1442, 1446, 1447] (Same; suits and prosecutions against revenue officers)
- § 77 [now 1442] (Same; suits by aliens)

§ 78 [now 1449] (Same; copies of records refused by clerk of state court)

§ 79 [now 1450] (Same; previous attachment bonds or orders)

§ 80 [now 1359, 1447, 1919] (Same; dismissal or remand)

§ 81 [now 1447] (Same; proceedings in suits removed)

§ 82 [former] (Same; record; filing and return)

§ 83 [now 1447, 1448] (Service of process after removal)

U.S.C., Title 28, §§ 1446, 1447, formerly § 72, supra, however, is modified by shortening the time for pleading in removed actions.

Note to Subdivision (e). The last sentence of this subdivision modifies U.S.C., Title 28, § 1652, formerly § 725 (Laws of States as rules of decision) in so far as that statute has been construed to govern matters of procedure and to exclude state judicial decisions relative thereto.

1946 Amendment

Note to Subdivision (a). Despite certain dicta to the contrary, *Lynn v. United States,* C.C.A.5th, 1940, 110 F.2d 586; *Mount Tivy Winery, Inc. v. Lewis,* N.D.Cal.1942, 42 F.Supp. 636, it is manifest that the rules apply to actions against the United States under the Tucker Act [28 U.S.C., §§ 41(20), 250, 251, 254, 257, 258, 287, 289, 292, 761–765 [now 791, 1346, 1401, 1402, 1491, 1493, 1496, 1501, 1503, 2071, 2072, 2411, 2412, 2501, 2506, 2509, 2510]]. See United States to use of *Foster Wheeler Corp. v. American Surety Co. of New York,* E.D.N.Y.1939, 25 F.Supp. 700; *Boerner v. United States,* E.D.N.Y.1939, 26 F.Supp. 769; *United States v. Gallagher,* C.C.A.9th, 1945, 151 F.2d 556. Rules 1 and 81 provide that the rules shall apply to all suits of a civil nature, whether cognizable as cases at law or in equity except those specifically excepted; and the character of the various proceedings excepted by express statement in Rule 81, as well as the language of the rules generally, shows that the term "civil action" [Rule 2] includes actions against the United States. Moreover, the rules in many places expressly make provision for the situation wherein the United States is a party as either plaintiff or defendant. See Rules 4(d)(4), 12(a), 13(d), 25(d), 37(f), 39(c), 45(c), 54(d), 55(e), 62(e), and 65(c). In *United States v. Sherwood,* 1941, 61 S.Ct. 767, 312 U.S. 584, 85 L.Ed. 1058, the Solicitor General expressly conceded in his brief for the United States that the rules apply to Tucker Act cases. The Solicitor General stated: "The Government, of course, recognizes that the Federal Rules of Civil Procedure apply to cases brought under the Tucker Act." (Brief for the United States, p. 31). Regarding *Lynn v. United States,* supra, the Solicitor General said: "In *Lynn v. United States* . . . the Circuit Court of Appeals for the Fifth Circuit went beyond the Government's contention there, and held that an action under the Tucker Act is neither an action at law nor a suit in equity and, seemingly, that the Federal Rules of Civil Procedure are, therefore, inapplicable. We think the suggestion is erroneous. Rules 4(d), 12(a), 39(c), and 55(e) expressly contemplate suits against the United States, and nothing in the enabling Act (48 Stat. 1064, 28 U.S.C. §§ 723b, 723c [see 2072]) suggests that the Rules are inapplicable to Tucker Act proceedings, which in terms are to accord with court rules and their subsequent modifications (Sec. 4, Act of March 3, 1887, 24 Stat. 505, 28 U.S.C. § 761 [see 2071, 2072])." (Brief for the United States, p. 31, n. 17.)

United States v. Sherwood, supra, emphasizes, however, that the application of the rules in Tucker Act cases affects only matters of procedure and does not operate to extend jurisdiction. See also Rule 82. In the Sherwood case, the New York Supreme Court, acting under § 795 of the New York Civil Practice Act, made an order, authorizing Sherwood, as a judgment creditor, to maintain a suit under the Tucker Act to recover damages from the United States for breach of its contract with the judgment debtor, Kaiser, for construction of a post office building. Sherwood brought suit against the United States and Kaiser in the District Court for the Eastern District of New York. The question before the United States Supreme Court was whether a United States District Court had jurisdiction to entertain a suit against the United States wherein private parties were joined as parties defendant. It was contended that either the Federal Rules of Civil Procedure or the Tucker Act, or both, embodied the consent of the United States to be sued in litigations in which issues between the plaintiff and third persons were to be adjudicated. Regarding the effect of the Federal Rules, the Court declared that nothing in the rules, so far as they may be applicable in Tucker Act cases, authorized the maintenance of any suit against the United States to which it had not otherwise consented. The matter involved was not one of procedure but of jurisdiction, the limits of which were marked by the consent of the United States to be sued. The jurisdiction thus limited is unaffected by the Federal Rules of Civil Procedure.

Subdivision (a)(2). The added sentence makes it clear that the rules have not superseded the requirements of U.S.C., Title 28, § 2253, formerly § 466. *Schenk v. Plummer,* C.C.A.9, 1940, 113 F.2d 726.

For correct application of the rules in proceedings for forfeiture of property for violation of a statute of the United States, such as under U.S.C., Title 22, § 405 (seizure of war materials intended for unlawful export) or U.S.C., Title 21, § 334(b) (Federal Food, Drug, and Cosmetic Act; formerly Title 21, U.S.C. § 14, Pure Food and Drug Act), see *Reynal v. United States,* C.C.A.5, 1945, 153 F.2d 929; *United States v. 108 Boxes of Cheddar Cheese,* S.D.Iowa 1943, 3 F.R.D. 40.

Subdivision (a)(3). The added sentence makes it clear that the rules apply to appeals from proceedings to enforce administrative subpoenas. See *Perkins v. Endicott Johnson Corp.,* C.C.A.2d 1942, 128 F.2d 208, affirmed on other grounds 63 S.Ct. 339, 317 U.S. 501, 87 L.Ed. 424; *Walling v. News Printing Inc.,* C.C.A.3, 1945, 148 F.2d 57; *McCrone v. United States,* 1939, 59 S.Ct. 685, 307 U.S. 61, 83 L.Ed. 1108. And, although the provision allows full recognition of the fact that the rigid application of the rules in the proceedings themselves may conflict with the summary determination desired, *Goodyear Tire & Rubber Co. v. National Relations Board,* C.C.A.6, 1941, 122 F.2d 450; *Cudahy Packing Co. v. National Labor Relations Board,* C.C.A.10, 1941, 117 F.2d 692, it is drawn so as to permit application of any of the rules in the proceedings whenever the district court deems them helpful. See, e.g., *Peoples Natural Gas Co. v. Federal Power Commission,* App.D.C.1942, 127 F.2d 153, certiorari denied 62 S.Ct. 1298, 316 U.S. 700, 86 L.Ed. 1769; *Martin v. Chandis Securities Co.,* C.C.A.9th, 1942, 128 F.2d 731. Compare the application of the rules in summary proceedings in bankruptcy under General Order 37. See 1 *Collier on Bankruptcy,* 14th ed. by Moore and Oglebay, 326–327; 2

Collier, op.cit.supra, 1401–1402; 3 Collier, op.cit.supra, 228–231; 4 Collier, op.cit.supra, 1199–1202.

Subdivision (a)(6). Section 405 of U.S.C., Title 8 originally referred to in the last sentence of paragraph (6), has been repealed and § 738 [now 1451], U.S.C., Title 8, has been enacted in its stead. The last sentence of paragraph (6) has, therefore, been amended in accordance with this change. The sentence has also been amended so as to refer directly to the statute regarding the provision of time for answer, thus avoiding any confusion attendant upon a change in the statute.

That portion of subdivision (a)(6) making the rules applicable to proceedings for enforcement or review of compensation orders under the Longshoremen's and Harbor Workers' Compensation Act [33 U.S.C. § 901 et seq.] was added by an amendment made pursuant to order of the Court, December 28, 1939, effective three months subsequent to the adjournment of the 76th Congress, January 3, 1941.

Subdivision (c). The change in subdivision (c) effects more speedy trials in removed actions. In some states many of the courts have only two terms a year. A case, if filed 20 days before a term, is returnable to that term, but if filed less than 20 days before a term, is returnable to the following term, which convenes six months later. Hence, under the original wording of Rule 81(c), where a case is filed less than 20 days before the term and is removed within a few days but before answer, it is possible for the defendant to delay interposing his answer or presenting his defenses by motion for six months or more. The rule as amended prevents this result.

Subdivision (f). The use of the phrase "the United States or an officer or agency thereof" in the rules (as e.g., in Rule 12(a) and amended Rule 73(a)) could raise the question of whether "officer" includes a collector of internal revenue, a former collector, or the personal representative of a deceased collector, against whom suits for tax refunds are frequently instituted. Difficulty might ensue for the reason that a suit against a collector or his representative has been held to be a personal action. *Sage v. United States,* 1919, 39 S.Ct. 415, 250 U.S. 33, 63 L.Ed. 828; *Smietanka v. Indiana Steel Co.,* 1921, 42 S.Ct. 1, 257 U.S. 1, 66 L.Ed. 99; *United States v. Nunnally Investment Co.,* 1942, 62 S.Ct. 1064, 316 U.S. 258, 86 L.Ed. 1455. The addition of subdivision (f) to Rule 81 dispels any doubts on the matter and avoids further litigation.

1948 Amendment

The amendment effective October 1949, substituted the words "United States District Court" for the words "District Court of the United States" in the last sentence of subdivision (a)(1) and in the first and third sentences of subdivision (e). The amendment substituted the words "United States district courts" in lieu of "district courts of the United States" in subdivision (a)(4) and (5) and in the first sentence of subdivision (c).

The amendment effective October 20, 1949, also made the following changes:

In subdivision (a)(1), the reference to "Title 17, U.S.C." was substituted for the reference to "the Act of March 4, 1909, c. 320, § 25 (35 Stat. 1081), as amended, U.S.C., Title 17, § 25."

In subdivision (a)(2), the reference to "Title 28, U.S.C., § 2253" was substituted for "U.S.C., Title 28, § 466."

In subdivision (a)(3), the reference in the first sentence to "Title 9, U.S.C.," was substituted for "the Act of February 12, 1925, c. 213 (43 Stat. 883), U.S.C., Title 9".

In subdivision (a)(5), the words "as amended" were inserted after the parenthetical citation of "(49 Stat. 453)," and after the citations of "Title 29, §§ 159 and 160," former references to subdivisions "(e), (g), and (i)" were deleted.

In subdivision (a)(6), after the words "These rules" at the beginning of the first sentence, the following words were deleted: "do not apply to proceedings under the Act of September 13, 1888, c. 1015, § 13 (25 Stat. 479), as amended, U.S.C., Title 8, [former] § 282, relating to deportation of Chinese; they". Also in the first sentence, after the parenthetical citation of "(44 Stat. 1434, 1436)," the words "as amended" were added. In the last sentence, the words "October 14, 1940, c. 876, § 338 (54 Stat. 1158)" were inserted in lieu of the words "June 29, 1906, c. 3592, § 15 (34 Stat. 601), as amended."

In subdivision (c), the word "all" originally appearing in the first sentence between the words "govern" and "procedure" was deleted. In the third sentence, the portion beginning with the words "20 days after the receipt" and including all the remainder of that sentence was substituted for the following language: "the time allowed for answer by the law of the state or within 5 days after the filing of the transcript of the record in the district court of the United States, whichever period is longer, but in any event within 20 days after the filing of the transcript". In the fourth or last sentence, after the words at the beginning of the sentence, "If at the time of removal all necessary pleadings have been," the word "served" was inserted in lieu of the word "filed," and the concluding words of the sentence, "petition for removal is filed if he is the petitioner," together with the final clause immediately following, were substituted for the words "record of the action is filed in the district court of the United States."

1963 Amendment

Subdivision (a)(4). This change reflects the transfer of functions from the Secretary of Commerce to the Secretary of the Interior made by 1939 Reorganization Plan No. II, § 4(e), 53 Stat. 1433.

Subdivision (a)(6). The proper current reference is to the 1952 statute superseding the 1940 statute.

Subdivision (c). Most of the cases have held that a party who has made a proper express demand for jury trial in the State court is not required to renew the demand after removal of the action. *Zakoscielny v. Waterman Steamship Corp.,* 16 F.R.D. 314 (D.Md.1954); *Talley v. American Bakeries Co.,* 15 F.R.D. 391 (E.D.Tenn.1954); *Rehrer v. Service Trucking Co.,* 15 F.R.D. 113 (D.Del.1953); 5 *Moore's Federal Practice* ¶38.39[3] (2d ed. 1951); 1 Barron & Holtzoff, *Federal Practice & Procedure* § 132 (Wright ed. 1960). But there is some authority to the contrary. *Petsel v. Chicago, B. & Q.R. Co.,* 101 F.Supp. 1006 (S.D.Iowa 1951); *Nelson v. American Nat. Bank & Trust Co.,* 9 F.R.D. 680 (E.D.Tenn. 1950). The amendment adopts the preponderant view.

In order still further to avoid unintended waivers of jury trial, the amendment provides that where by State law applicable in the court from which the case is removed a party is entitled to jury trial without making an express demand, he need not make a demand after removal. However, the district court for calendar or other purposes may on its own motion direct the parties to state whether they demand a jury, and the court must make such a direction upon the request of any party. Under the amendment a district court may find it convenient to establish a routine practice of giving these directions to the parties in appropriate cases.

Subdivision (f). The amendment recognizes the change of nomenclature made by Treasury Dept. Order 150–26(2), 18 Fed.Reg. 3499 (1953).

As to a special problem arising under Rule 25 (Substitution of parties) in actions for refund of taxes, see the Advisory Committee's Note to the amendment of Rule 25(d), effective July 19, 1961; and 4 *Moore's Federal Practice* ¶25.09 at 531 (2d ed. 1950).

1966 Amendment

See Note to Rule 1, supra.

Statutory proceedings to forfeit property for violation of the laws of the United States, formerly governed by the admiralty rules, will be governed by the unified and supplemental rules. See Supplemental Rule A.

Upon the recommendation of the judges of the United States District Court for the District of Columbia, the Federal Rules of Civil Procedure are made applicable to probate proceedings in that court. The exception with regard to adoption proceedings is removed because the court no longer has jurisdiction of those matters; and the words "mental health" are substituted for "lunacy" to conform to the current characterization in the District.

The purpose of the amendment to paragraph (3) is to permit the deletion from Rule 73(a) of the clause "unless a shorter time is provided by law." The 10 day period fixed for an appeal under 45 U.S.C. § 159 is the only instance of a shorter time provided for appeals in civil cases. Apart from the unsettling effect of the clause, it is eliminated because its retention would preserve the 15 day period heretofore allowed by 28 U.S.C. § 2107 for appeals from interlocutory decrees in admiralty, it being one of the purposes of the amendment to make the time for appeals in civil and admiralty cases uniform under the unified rules. See Advisory Committee's Note to subdivision (a) of Rule 73.

1968 Amendment

The amendments eliminate inappropriate references to appellate procedure.

1971 Amendment

Title 28, U.S.C., § 2243 now requires that the custodian of a person detained must respond to an application for a writ of habeas corpus "within three days unless for good cause additional time, not exceeding twenty days, is allowed." The amendment increases to forty days the additional time that the district court may allow in habeas corpus proceedings involving persons in custody pursuant to a judgment of a state court. The substantial increase in the number of such proceedings in recent years has placed a considerable burden on state authorities. Twenty days has proved in practice too short a time in which to prepare and file the return in many such cases. Allowance of additional time should, of course, be granted only for good cause.

While the time allowed in such a case for the return of the writ may not exceed forty days, this does not mean that the state must necessarily be limited to that period of time to provide for the federal court the transcript of the proceedings of a state trial or plenary hearing if the transcript must be prepared after the habeas corpus proceeding has begun in the federal court.

1987 Amendment

The amendments are technical. No substantive change is intended.

HISTORICAL NOTES

Pending Actions

For applicability of Supreme Court amendments to pending cases, see Orders of the Supreme Court of the United States Adopting and Amending Rules set out preceding Rule 1 of these rules.

Rule 82. Jurisdiction and Venue Unaffected

These rules shall not be construed to extend or limit the jurisdiction of the United States district courts or the venue of actions therein. An admiralty or maritime claim within the meaning of Rule 9(h) shall not be treated as a civil action for the purposes of Title 28, U.S.C., §§ 1391–93.

(As amended Dec. 29, 1948, eff. Oct. 20, 1949; Feb. 28, 1966, eff. July 1, 1966.)

ADVISORY COMMITTEE NOTES

1937 Adoption

These rules grant extensive power of joining claims and counterclaims in one action, but, as this rule states, such grant does not extend federal jurisdiction. The rule is declaratory of existing practice under the [former] Federal Equity Rules with regard to such provisions as [former] Equity Rule 26 on Joinder of Causes of Action and [former] Equity Rule 30 on Counterclaims. Compare Shulman and Jaegerman, *Some Jurisdictional Limitations on Federal Procedure,* 45 Yale L.J. 393 (1936).

1948 Amendment

The amendment effective October 1949, substituted the words "United States district courts" for "district courts of the United States."

1966 Amendment

Title 28, U.S.C., § 1391(b) provides: "A civil action wherein jurisdiction is not founded solely on diversity of citizenship may be brought only in the judicial district where all defendants reside, except as otherwise provided by law." This provision cannot appropriately be applied to what were formerly suits in admiralty. The rationale of decisions holding it inapplicable rests largely on the use of the term "civil action": i.e., a suit in admiralty is not a "civil action" within the statute. By virtue of the amendment to Rule 1, the provisions of Rule 2 convert suits in admiralty into civil actions. The added sentence is necessary to avoid an undesirable change in existing law with respect to venue.

Rule 83. Rules by District Courts; Judge's Directives

(a) Local Rules

(1) Each district court, acting by a majority of its district judges, may, after giving appropriate public notice and an opportunity for comment, make and amend rules governing its practice. A local rule shall be consistent with—but not duplicative of—Acts of Congress and rules adopted under 28 U.S.C. §§ 2072 and 2075, and shall conform to any uniform numbering system prescribed by the Judicial Conference of the United States. A local rule takes effect on the date specified by the district court and remains in effect unless amended by the court or abrogated by the judicial council of the circuit. Copies of rules and amendments shall, upon their promulgation, be furnished to the judicial council and the Administrative Office of the United States Courts and be made available to the public.

(2) A local rule imposing a requirement of form shall not be enforced in a manner that causes a party to lose rights because of a nonwillful failure to comply with the requirement.

(b) Procedures When There is No Controlling Law. A judge may regulate practice in any manner consistent with federal law, rules adopted under 28 U.S.C. §§ 2072 and 2075, and local rules of the district. No sanction or other disadvantage may be imposed for noncompliance with any requirement not in federal law, federal rules, or the local district rules unless the alleged violator has been furnished in the particular case with actual notice of the requirement.

(As amended Apr. 29, 1985, eff. Aug. 1, 1985; Apr. 27, 1995, eff. Dec. 1, 1995.)

ADVISORY COMMITTEE NOTES

1937 Adoption

This rule substantially continues U.S.C., Title 28, § 2071, formerly § 731 (Rules of practice in district courts) with the additional requirement that copies of such rules and amendments be furnished to the Supreme Court of the United States. See [former] Equity Rule 79 (Additional Rules by District Court). With the last sentence compare United States Supreme Court Admiralty Rules, 1920, Rule 44 (Right of Trial Courts to Make Rules of Practice) (originally promulgated in 1842).

1985 Amendment

Rule 83, which has not been amended since the Federal Rules were promulgated in 1938, permits each district to adopt local rules not inconsistent with the Federal Rules by a majority of the judges. The only other requirement is that copies be furnished to the Supreme Court.

The widespread adoption of local rules and the modest procedural prerequisites for their promulgation have led many commentators to question the soundness of the process as well as the validity of some rules. See 12 C. Wright & A. Miller, *Federal Practice and Procedure: Civil* § 3152, at 217 (1973); Caballero, *Is There an Over-Exercise of Local Rule-Making Powers by the United States District Courts?*, 24 Fed.Bar News 325 (1977). Although the desirability of local rules for promoting uniform practice within a district is widely accepted, several commentators also have suggested reforms to increase the quality, simplicity, and uniformity of the local rules. See Note, *Rule 83 and the Local Federal Rules*, 67 Colum.L.Rev. 1251 (1967), and Comment, *The Local Rules of Civil Procedure in the Federal District Courts—A Survey*, 1966 Duke L.J. 1011.

The amended Rule attempts, without impairing the procedural validity of existing local rules, to enhance the local rulemaking process by requiring appropriate public notice of proposed rules and an opportunity to comment on them. Although some district courts apparently consult the local bar before promulgating rules, many do not, which has led to criticism of a process that has district judges consulting only with each other. See 12 C. Wright & A. Miller, *supra*, § 3152, at 217; Blair, *The New Local Rules for Federal Practice in Iowa*, 23 Drake L.Rev. 517 (1974). The new language subjects local rulemaking to scrutiny similar to that accompanying the Federal Rules, administrative rulemaking, and legislation. It attempts to assure that the expert advice of practitioners and scholars is made available to the district court before local rules are promulgated. See Weinstein, *Reform of Court Rule-Making Procedures* 84–87, 127–37, 151 (1977).

The amended Rule does not detail the procedure for giving notice and an opportunity to be heard since conditions vary from district to district. Thus, there is no explicit requirement for a public hearing, although a district may consider that procedure appropriate in all or some rulemaking situations. See generally, Weinstein, *supra*, at 117–37, 151. The new Rule does not foreclose any other form of consultation. For example, it can be accomplished through the mechanism of an "Advisory Committee" similar to that employed by the Supreme Court in connection with the Federal Rules themselves.

The amended Rule provides that a local rule will take effect upon the date specified by the district court and will remain in effect unless amended by the district court or abrogated by the judicial council. The effectiveness of a local rule should not be deferred until approved by the judicial council because that might unduly delay promulgation of a local rule that should become effective immediately, especially since some councils do not meet frequently. Similarly, it was thought that to delay a local rule's effectiveness for a fixed period of time would be arbitrary and that to require the judicial council to abrogate a local rule within a specified time would be inconsistent with its power under 28 U.S.C. § 332 (1976) to nullify a local rule at any time. The expectation is that the judicial council will examine all local rules, including those currently in effect, with an eye toward determining whether they are valid and consistent with the Federal Rules, promote inter-district uniformity and efficiency, and do not undermine the basic objectives of the Federal Rules.

The amended Rule requires copies of local rules to be sent upon their promulgation to the judicial council and the Administrative Office of the United States Courts rather than to the Supreme Court. The Supreme Court was the appropriate filing place in 1938, when Rule 83 originally was promulgated, but the establishment of the Administrative Office makes it a more logical place to develop a centralized file of local rules. This procedure is consistent with both the Criminal and the Appellate Rules. See Fed.R.Crim.P. 57(a); Fed.R.App.P. 47. The Administrative Office also will be able to provide improved utilization of the file because of its recent development of a Local Rules Index.

The practice pursued by some judges of issuing standing orders has been controversial, particularly among members of the practicing bar. The last sentence in Rule 83 has been amended to make certain that standing orders are not inconsistent with the Federal Rules or any local district court rules. Beyond that, it is hoped that each district will adopt procedures, perhaps by local rule, for promulgating and reviewing single-judge standing orders.

1995 Amendments

Subdivision (a). This rule is amended to reflect the requirement that local rules be consistent not only with the national rules but also with Acts of Congress. The amendment also states that local rules should not repeat Acts of Congress or national rules.

The amendment also requires that the numbering of local rules conform with any uniform numbering system that may be prescribed by the Judicial Conference. Lack of uniform numbering might create unnecessary traps for counsel and litigants. A uniform numbering system would make it easier for an increasingly national bar and for litigants to locate a local rule that applies to a particular procedural issue.

Paragraph (2) is new. Its aim is to protect against loss of rights in the enforcement of local rules relating to matters of form. For example, a party should not be deprived of a right to a jury trial because its attorney, unaware of—or forgetting—a local rule directing that jury demands be noted in the caption of the case, includes a jury demand only in the body of the pleading. The proscription of paragraph (2) is narrowly drawn—covering only violations attributable to nonwillful failure to comply and only those involving local rules directed to matters of form. It does not limit the court's power to impose substantive penalties upon a party if it or its attorney contumaciously or willfully violates a local rule, even one involving merely a matter of form. Nor does it affect the court's power to enforce local rules that involve more than mere matters of form—for example, a local rule requiring parties to identify evidentiary matters relied upon to support or oppose motions for summary judgment.

Subdivision (b). This rule provides flexibility to the court in regulating practice when there is no controlling law. Specifically, it permits the court to regulate practice in any manner consistent with Acts of Congress, with rules adopted under 28 U.S.C. §§ 2072 and 2075, and with the district local rules.

This rule recognizes that courts rely on multiple directives to control practice. Some courts regulate practice through the published Federal Rules and the local rules of the court. Some courts also have used internal operating procedures, standing orders, and other internal directives. Although such directives continue to be authorized, they can lead to problems. Counsel or litigants may be unaware of various directives. In addition, the sheer volume of directives may impose an unreasonable barrier. For example, it may be difficult to obtain copies of the directives. Finally, counsel or litigants may be unfairly sanctioned for failing to comply with a directive. For these reasons, the amendment to this rule disapproves imposing any sanction or other disadvantage on a person for noncompliance with such an internal directive, unless the alleged violator has been furnished actual notice of the requirement in a particular case.

There should be no adverse consequence to a party or attorney for violating special requirements relating to practice before a particular court unless the party or attorney has actual notice of those requirements. Furnishing litigants with a copy outlining the judge's practices—or attaching instructions to a notice setting a case for conference or trial—would suffice to give actual notice, as would an order in a case specifically adopting by reference a judge's standing order and indicating how copies can be obtained.

Rule 84. Forms

The forms contained in the Appendix of Forms are sufficient under the rules and are intended to indicate the simplicity and brevity of statement which the rules contemplate.

(As amended Dec. 27, 1946, eff. Mar. 19, 1948.)

ADVISORY COMMITTEE NOTES

1937 Adoption

In accordance with the practice found useful in many codes, provision is here made for a limited number of official forms which may serve as guides in pleading. Compare 2 Mass.Gen.Laws (Ter.Ed., 1932) ch. 231, § 147, Forms 1–47; *English Annual Practice* (1937) Appendix A to M, inclusive; *Conn.Practice Book* (1934) Rules, 47–68, pp. 123 to 427.

1946 Amendment

Note. The amendment serves to emphasize that the forms contained in the Appendix of Forms are sufficient to withstand attack under the rules under which they are drawn, and that the practitioner using them may rely on them to that extent. The circuit courts of appeals generally have upheld the use of the forms as promoting desirable simplicity and brevity of statement. *Sierocinski v. E. I. DuPont DeNemours & Co.*, C.C.A.3, 1939, 103 F.2d 843; *Swift & Co. v. Young*, C.C.A.4, 1939, 107 F.2d 170; *Sparks v. England*, C.C.A.8, 1940, 113 F.2d 579; *Ramsouer v. Midland Valley R. Co.*, C.C.A.8, 1943, 135 F.2d 101. And the forms as a whole have met with widespread approval in the courts. See cases cited in 1 Moore's Federal Practice, 1938, Cum. Supplement § 8.07, under "Page 554"; see also Commentary, The Official Forms, 1941, 4 Fed.Rules Serv. 954. In Cook, "Facts" and "Statements of Fact", 1937, 4 U.Chi.L.Rev. 233, 245–246, it is said with reference to what is now Rule 84: ". . . pleaders in the federal courts are not to be left to guess as to the meaning of [the] language" in Rule 8(a) regarding the form of the complaint. "All of which is as it should be. In no other way can useless litigation be avoided." Ibid. The amended rule will operate to discourage isolated results such as those found in *Washburn v. Moorman Mfg. Co.*, S.D.Cal.

1938, 25 F.Supp. 546; *Employers Mutual Liability Ins. Co. of Wisconsin v. Blue Line Transfer Co.,* W.D.Mo.1941, 2 F.R.D. 121, 5 Fed.Rules Serv. 12e.235, Case 2.

Rule 85. Title

These rules may be known and cited as the Federal Rules of Civil Procedure.

Rule 86. Effective Date

(a) [Effective Date of Original Rules].[1] These rules will take effect on the day which is 3 months subsequent to the adjournment of the second regular session of the 75th Congress, but if that day is prior to September 1, 1938, then these rules will take effect on September 1, 1938. They govern all proceedings in actions brought after they take effect and also all further proceedings in actions then pending, except to the extent that in the opinion of the court their application in a particular action pending when the rules take effect would not be feasible or would work injustice, in which event the former procedure applies.

(b) Effective Date of Amendments. The amendments adopted by the Supreme Court on December 27, 1946, and transmitted to the Attorney General on January 2, 1947, shall take effect on the day which is three months subsequent to the adjournment of the first regular session of the 80th Congress, but, if that day is prior to September 1, 1947, then these amendments shall take effect on September 1, 1947. They govern all proceedings in actions brought after they take effect and also all further proceedings in actions then pending, except to the extent that in the opinion of the court their application in a particular action pending when the amendments take effect would not be feasible or would work injustice, in which event the former procedure applies.

(c) Effective Date of Amendments. The amendments adopted by the Supreme Court on December 29, 1948, and transmitted to the Attorney General on December 31, 1948, shall take effect on the day following the adjournment of the first regular session of the 81st Congress.

(d) Effective Date of Amendments. The amendments adopted by the Supreme Court on April 17, 1961, and transmitted to the Congress on April 18, 1961, shall take effect on July 19, 1961. They govern all proceedings in actions brought after they take effect and also all further proceedings in actions then pending, except to the extent that in the opinion of the court their application in a particular action pending when the amendments take effect would not be feasible or would work injustice, in which event the former procedure applies.

(e) Effective Date of Amendments. The amendments adopted by the Supreme Court on January 21, 1963, and transmitted to the Congress on January 21, 1963, shall take effect on July 1, 1963. They govern all proceedings in actions brought after they take effect and also all further proceedings in actions then pending, except to the extent that in the opinion of the court their application in a particular action pending when the amendments take effect would not be feasible or would work injustice, in which event the former procedure applies.

(As amended Dec. 27, 1946, eff. Mar. 19, 1948; Dec. 29, 1948, eff. Oct. 20, 1949; Apr. 17, 1961, eff. July 19, 1961; Jan. 21 and Mar. 18, 1963, eff. July 1, 1963.)

[1] Subdivision heading supplied editorially.

ADVISORY COMMITTEE NOTES

1937 Adoption

See former Equity Rule 81 (These Rules Effective February 1, 1913—Old Rules Abrogated).

HISTORICAL NOTES

Effective Dates

1948 Amendments. The first regular session of the 81st Congress adjourned sine die on Oct. 19, 1949, therefore the amendments to Rules 1, 17, 22, 24, 25, 27, 37, 45, 57, 60, 65, 66, 67, 69, 72–76, 79, 81, 82, and 86 and to forms 1, 19, 22, 23, and 27 became effective on Oct. 20, 1949, following the adjournment as provided for in subsection (c) of this rule.

1946 Amendments. The first regular session of the 80th Congress adjourned sine die on Friday, Dec. 19, 1947, therefore the amendments to Rules 6, 7, 12, 13, 14, 17, 24, 26, 27, 28, 33, 34, 36, 41, 45, 52, 54, 56, 58, 59, 60, 62, 65, 66, 68, 73, 75, 77, 79, 80, 81, 84, and 86, became effective Mar. 19, 1948 as provided for in subsection (b) of this rule.

Effective Date of 1970 Amendments; Transmission to Congress

Sections 2 and 3 of the Order of the Supreme Court, dated Mar. 30, 1970, provided:

"**2.** That the foregoing amendments to the Rules of Civil Procedure shall take effect on July 1, 1970, and shall govern all proceedings in actions brought thereafter and also in all further proceedings in actions then pending, except to the extent that in the opinion of the court their application in a particular action then pending would not be feasible or would work injustice, in which event the former procedure applies.

"**3.** That the Chief Justice be, and he hereby is, authorized to transmit to the Congress the foregoing amendments to the Rules of Civil Procedure in accordance with the provisions of Title 28, U.S.C. § 2072."

Effective Date of 1966 Amendment; Transmission to Congress; Rescission

Sections 2 to 4 of the Order of the Supreme Court, dated Feb. 28, 1966, 383 U.S. 1031, provided:

"**2.** That the foregoing amendments and additions to the Rules of Civil Procedure shall take effect on July 1, 1966, and shall govern all proceedings in actions brought thereafter and also in all further proceedings in actions then pending, except to the extent that in the opinion of the court their application in a particular action then pending would not be feasible or would work injustice, in which event the former procedure applies.

"3. That the Chief Justice be, and he hereby is, authorized to transmit to the Congress the foregoing amendments and additions to the Rules of Civil Procedure in accordance with the provisions of Title 28, U.S.C., §§ 2072 and 2073.

"4. That: (a) subdivision (c) of Rule 6 of the Rules of Civil Procedure for the United States District Courts promulgated by this court on December 20, 1937, effective September 16, 1938; (b) Rule 2 of the Rules for Practice and Procedure under section 25 of An Act To amend and consolidate the Acts respecting copyright, approved March 4, 1909, promulgated by this court on June 1, 1909, effective July 1, 1909; and (c) the Rules of Practice in Admiralty and Maritime Cases, promulgated by this court on December 6, 1920, effective March 7, 1921, as revised, amended and supplemented, be, and they hereby are, rescinded, effective July 1, 1966."

APPENDIX OF FORMS

(See Rule 84)

INTRODUCTORY STATEMENT

1. The following forms are intended for illustration only. They are limited in number. No attempt is made to furnish a manual of forms. Each form assumes the action to be brought in the Southern District of New York. If the district in which an action is brought has divisions, the division should be indicated in the caption.

2. Except where otherwise indicated each pleading, motion, and other paper should have a caption similar to that of the summons, with the designation of the particular paper substituted for the word "Summons." In the caption of the summons and in the caption of the complaint all parties must be named but in other pleadings and papers, it is sufficient to state the name of the first party on either side, with an appropriate indication of other parties. See Rules 4(b), 7(b)(2), and 10(a).

3. In Form 3 and the forms following, the words, "Allegation of jurisdiction," are used to indicate the appropriate allegation in Form 2.

4. Each pleading, motion, and other paper is to be signed in his individual name by at least one attorney of record (Rule 11). The attorney's name is to be followed by his address as indicated in Form 3. In forms following Form 3 the signature and address are not indicated.

5. If a party is not represented by an attorney, the signature and address of the party are required in place of those of the attorney.

Form 1. Summons

United States District Court for the
Southern District of New York

Civil Action, File Number ________

A. B., Plaintiff)
v.) *Summons*
C. D., Defendant)

To the above-named Defendant:

You are hereby summoned and required to serve upon ______, plaintiff's attorney, whose address is ______, an answer to the complaint which is herewith served upon you, within 20 [1] days after service of this summons upon you, exclusive of the day of service. If you fail to do so, judgment by default will be taken against you for the relief demanded in the complaint.

____________________,

Clerk of Court.

[Seal of the U.S. District Court]

Dated ________

(This summons is issued pursuant to Rule 4 of the Federal Rules of Civil Procedure)

(As amended Dec. 29, 1948, eff. Oct. 20, 1949.)

1 If the United States or an officer or agency there of is a defendant, the time to be inserted as to it is 60 days.

Form 1A. Notice of Lawsuit and Request for Waiver of Service of Summons

TO: (A)

[as (B) of (C)]

A lawsuit has been commenced against you (or the entity on whose behalf you are addressed). A copy of the complaint is attached to this notice. It has been filed in the United States District Court for the (D) and has been assigned docket number (E).

This is not a formal summons or notification from the court, but rather my request that you sign and return the enclosed waiver of service in order to save the cost of serving you with a judicial summons and an additional copy of the complaint. The cost of service will be avoided if I receive a signed copy of the waiver within (F) days after the date designated below as the date on which this Notice and Request is sent. I enclose a stamped and addressed envelope (or other means of cost-free return) for your use. An extra copy of the waiver is also attached for your records.

If you comply with this request and return the signed waiver, it will be filed with the court and no summons will be served on you. The action will then proceed as if you had been served on the date the waiver is filed, except that you will not be obligated to answer the complaint before 60 days from the date designated below as the date on which this notice is sent (or before 90 days from that date if your address is not in any judicial district of the United States).

If you do not return the signed waiver within the time indicated, I will take appropriate steps to effect formal service in a manner authorized by the Federal Rules of Civil Procedure and will then, to the extent authorized by those Rules, ask the court to require you (or the party on whose behalf you are addressed) to pay the full costs of such service. In that connection, please read the statement concerning the duty of parties to waive the service of the summons, which is set forth on the reverse side (or at the foot) of the waiver form.

I affirm that this request is being sent to you on behalf of the plaintiff, this ___ day of _____, _____.

Signature of Plaintiff's Attorney
or Unrepresented Plaintiff

Notes:

A—Name of individual defendant (or name of officer or agent of corporate defendant)

B—Title, or other relationship of individual to corporate defendant

C—Name of corporate defendants, if any

D—District

E—Docket number of action

F—Addresses must be given at least 30 days (60 days if located in foreign country) in which to return waiver

(Added Apr. 22, 1993, eff. Dec. 1, 1993.)

ADVISORY COMMITTEE NOTES

1993 Adoption

Forms 1A and 1B reflect the revision of Rule 4. They replace Form 18–A.

HISTORICAL NOTES

Effective Dates of Enactment and Abrogation

1991 Acts. Amendments by Supreme Court Order dated Apr. 30, 1991, adding Form 1A "Notice of Lawsuit and Request for Waiver of Service of Summons" and Form 1B "Waiver of Service of Summons" became effective Dec. 1, 1991. Pub.L. 102–198, § 11(b), Dec. 9, 1991, 105 Stat. 1626, set out as a note under section 2074 of Title 28, Judiciary and Judicial Procedure, provided that, effective Dec. 9, 1991, Forms 1A and 1B are not to be effective.

Form 1B. Waiver of Service of Summons

TO: (name of plaintiff's attorney or unrepresented plaintiff)

I acknowledge receipt of your request that I waive service of a summons in the action of (caption of action), which is case number (docket number) in the United States District Court for the (district). I have also received a copy of the complaint in the action, two copies of this instrument, and a means by which I can return the signed waiver to you without cost to me.

I agree to save the cost of service of a summons and an additional copy of the complaint in this lawsuit by not requiring that I (or the entity on whose behalf I am acting) be served with judicial process in the manner provided by Rule 4.

I (or the entity on whose behalf I am acting) will retain all defenses or objections to the lawsuit or to the jurisdiction or venue of the court except for objections based on a defect in the summons or in the service of the summons.

I understand that a judgment may be entered against me (or the party on whose behalf I am acting) if an answer or motion under Rule 12 is not served upon you within 60 days after (date request was sent), or within 90 days after that date if the request was sent outside the United States.

_____________ _____________________

Date Signature

Printed/typed name: _______________

[as _______________]

[of _______________]

To be printed on reverse side of the waiver form or set forth at the foot of the form:

Duty to Avoid Unnecessary Costs of Service of Summons

Rule 4 of the Federal Rules of Civil Procedure requires certain parties to cooperate in saving unnecessary costs of service of the summons and complaint. A defendant located in the United States who, after being notified of an action and asked by a plaintiff located in the United States to waive service of a summons, fails to do so will be required to bear the cost of such service unless good cause be shown for its failure to sign and return the waiver.

It is not good cause for a failure to waive service that a party believes that the complaint is unfounded, or that the action has been brought in an improper place or in a court that lacks jurisdiction over the subject matter of the action or over its person or property. A party who waives service of the summons retains all defenses and objections (except any relating to the summons or the service of the summons), and may later object to the jurisdiction of the court or to the place where the action has been brought.

A defendant who waives service must within the time specified on the waiver form serve on the plaintiff's attorney (or unrepresented plaintiff) a response to the complaint and must also file a signed copy of the response with the court. If the answer or motion is not served within this time, a default judgment may be taken against that defendant. By waiving service, a defendant is allowed more time to answer than if the summons had been actually served when the request for waiver of service was received.

(Added Apr. 22, 1993, eff. Dec. 1, 1993.)

ADVISORY COMMITTEE NOTES

1993 Adoption

Forms 1A and 1B reflect the revision of Rule 4. They replace Form 18–A.

HISTORICAL NOTES

Congressional Action Contrary to Supreme Court Enactment of Form

Enactment of Form 1–B, relating to waiver of service of summons, as transmitted to Congress by the Supreme Court pursuant to section 2074 of this title, which was to take effect Dec. 1, 1991, was nullified by Congress, see section 11 of Pub.L. 102–198, set out as a note under section 2074 of this title.

Form 2. Allegation of Jurisdiction

(a) Jurisdiction founded on diversity of citizenship and amount.

Plaintiff is a [citizen of the State of Connecticut] [1] [corporation incorporated under the laws of the State of Connecticut having its principal place of business in the State of Connecticut] and defendant is a corporation incorporated under the laws of the State of New York having its principal place of business in a State other than the State of Connecticut. The matter in controversy exceeds, exclusive of interest and costs, the sum of fifty thousand dollars.

(b) Jurisdiction founded on the existence of a Federal question.

The action arises under [the Constitution of the United States, Article ___, Section ___]; [the ___ Amendment to the Constitution of the United States, Section ___]; [the Act of ___, ___ Stat. ___; U.S.C., Title ___, § ___]; [the Treaty of the United States (here describe the treaty)] [2] as hereinafter more fully appears.

(c) Jurisdiction founded on the existence of a question arising under particular statutes.

The action arises under the Act of ___, ___ Stat. ___; U.S.C., Title ___, § ___, as hereinafter more fully appears.

(d) Jurisdiction founded on the admiralty or maritime character of the claim.

This is a case of admiralty and maritime jurisdiction, as hereinafter more fully appears. [If the pleader wishes to invoke the distinctively maritime procedures referred to in Rule 9(h), add the following or its substantial equivalent: This is an admiralty or maritime claim within the meaning of Rule 9(h).]

1 Form for natural person.

2 Use the appropriate phrase or phrases. The general allegation of the existence of a Federal question is ineffective unless the matters constituting the claim for relief as set forth in the complaint raise a Federal question.

Notes

1. **Diversity of citizenship.** U.S.C., Title 28, § 1332 (Diversity of citizenship; amount in controversy; costs), as amended by PL 85–554, 72 Stat. 415, July 25, 1958, states in subsection (c) that "For the purposes of this section and section 1441 of this title [removable actions], a corporation shall be deemed a citizen of any State by which it has been incorporated and of the State where it has its principal place of business." Thus if the defendant corporation in Form 2(a) had its principal place of business in Connecticut, diversity of citizenship would not exist. An allegation regarding the principal place of business of each corporate party must be made in addition to an allegation regarding its place of incorporation.

2. **Jurisdictional amount.** U.S.C., Title 28, § 1331 (Federal question; amount in controversy; costs) and § 1332 (Diversity of citizenship; amount in controversy; costs), as amended by PL 85–554, 72 Stat. 415, July 25, 1958, require that the amount in controversy, exclusive of interest and costs, be in excess of $10,000. The allegation as to the amount in controversy may be omitted in any case where by law no jurisdictional amount is required. See, for example, U.S.C., Title 28, § 1338 (Patents, copyrights, trade-marks, and unfair competition), § 1343 (Civil rights and elective franchise).

3. **Pleading venue.** Since improper venue is a matter of defense, it is not necessary for plaintiff to include allegations showing the venue to be proper. See 1 *Moore's Federal Practice*, par. 0.140[1–4] (2d ed. 1959).

(As amended Apr. 17, 1961, eff. July 19, 1961; Feb. 28, 1966, eff. July 1, 1966; Apr. 22, 1993, eff. Dec. 1, 1993.)

ADVISORY COMMITTEE NOTES

1966 Amendment

Since the Civil Rules have not heretofore been applicable to proceedings in Admiralty (Rule 81(a)(1)), Form 2 naturally has not contained a provision for invoking the admiralty jurisdiction. The form has never purported to be comprehensive, as making provision for all possible grounds of jurisdiction; but a provision for invoking the admiralty jurisdiction is particularly appropriate as an incident of unification.

Certain distinctive features of the admiralty practice must be preserved in unification, just as certain distinctive characteristics of equity were preserved in the merger of law and equity in 1938. Rule 9(h) provides the device whereby, after unification, with its abolition of the distinction between civil actions and suits in admiralty, the pleader may indicate his choice of the distinctively maritime procedures, and designates those features that are preserved. This form illustrates an appropriate way in which the pleader may invoke those procedures. Use of this device is not necessary if the claim is cognizable only by virtue of the admiralty and maritime jurisdiction, nor if the claim is within the exclusive admiralty jurisdiction of the district court.

Omission of a statement such as this from the pleading indicates the pleader's choice that the action proceed as a conventional civil action, if this is jurisdictionally possible, without the distinctive maritime remedies and procedures. It should be remembered, however, that Rule 9(h) provides that a pleading may be amended to add or withdraw such an identifying statement subject to the principles stated in Rule 15.

1993 Amendments

This form is revised to reflect amendments to 28 U.S.C. §§ 1331 and 1332 providing jurisdiction for federal questions without regard to the amount in controversy and raising the amount required to be in controversy in diversity cases to fifty thousand dollars.

HISTORICAL NOTES

Effective Dates

1961 Amendments. Amendment adopted on Apr. 17, 1961, effective July 19, 1961, see Rule 86(d).

Form 3. Complaint on a Promissory Note

1. Allegation of jurisdiction.

2. Defendant on or about June 1, 1935, executed and delivered to plaintiff a promissory note [in the following words and figures: (here set out the note verbatim)]; [a copy of which is hereto annexed as Exhibit A]; [whereby defendant promised to pay to plaintiff or order [1] on June 1, 1936 the sum of _____ dollars with interest thereon at the rate of six percent. per annum].

3. Defendant owes to plaintiff the amount of said note and interest.

Wherefore plaintiff demands judgment against defendant for the sum of _____ dollars, interest, and costs.

Signed: _______________
Attorney for Plaintiff.
Address: _______________

NOTES

1. The pleader may use the material in one of the three sets of brackets. His choice will depend upon whether he desires to plead the document verbatim, or by exhibit, or according to its legal effect.

2. Under the rules free joinder of claims is permitted. See rules 8(e) and 18. Consequently the claims set forth in each and all of the following forms may be joined with this complaint or with each other. Ordinarily each claim should be stated in a separate division of the complaint, and the divisions should be designated as counts successively numbered. In particular the rules permit alternative and inconsistent pleading. See Form 10.

(As amended Jan. 21, 1963, eff. July 1, 1963.)

[1] So in original.

ADVISORY COMMITTEE NOTES

1963 Amendment

At various places, these Forms [Forms 3, 4, 5, 6, 7, 8, 9, 10, 11, 12, 13, 18, 21] allege or refer to damages of "ten thousand dollars, interest, and costs," or the like. The Forms were written at a time when the jurisdictional amount in ordinary "diversity" and "Federal question" cases was an amount in excess of $3,000, exclusive of interest and costs, so the illustrative amounts set out in the Forms were adequate for jurisdictional purposes. However, U.S.C. Title 28, § 1331 (Federal question; amount in controversy; costs) and § 1332 (Diversity of citizenship; amount in controversy; costs), as amended by Pub.L. 85–554, 72 Stat. 415, July 25, 1958, now require that the amount in controversy, exclusive of interest and costs, be in excess of $10,000. Accordingly the Forms are misleading. They are amended at appropriate places by deleting the stated dollar amount and substituting a blank, to be properly filled in by the pleader.

Form 4. Complaint on an Account

1. Allegation of jurisdiction.

2. Defendant owes plaintiff _____ dollars according to the account hereto annexed as Exhibit A.

Wherefore (etc. as in Form 3).

(As amended Jan. 21, 1963, eff. July 1, 1963.)

ADVISORY COMMITTEE NOTES

1963 Amendment

This form was amended in 1963 by deleting the stated dollar amount and substituting a blank, to be properly filled in by the pleader. See Note of Advisory Committee under Form 3.

Form 5. Complaint for Goods Sold and Delivered

1. Allegation of jurisdiction.

2. Defendant owes plaintiff _____ dollars for goods sold and delivered by plaintiff to defendant between June 1, 1936 and December 1, 1936.

Wherefore (etc. as in Form 3).

NOTE

This form may be used where the action is for an agreed price or for the reasonable value of the goods.

(As amended Jan. 21, 1963, eff. July 1, 1963.)

ADVISORY COMMITTEE NOTES

1963 Amendment

This form was amended in 1963 by deleting the stated dollar amount and substituting a blank, to be properly filled in by the pleader. See Note of Advisory Committee under Form 3.

Form 6. Complaint for Money Lent

1. Allegation of jurisdiction.

2. Defendant owes plaintiff _____ dollars for money lent by plaintiff to defendant on June 1, 1936.

Wherefore (etc. as in Form 3).

(As amended Jan. 21, 1963, eff. July 1, 1963.)

ADVISORY COMMITTEE NOTES

1963 Amendment

This form was amended in 1963 by deleting the stated dollar amount and substituting a blank, to be properly filled in by the pleader. See Note of Advisory Committee under Form 3.

Form 7. Complaint for Money Paid by Mistake

1. Allegation of jurisdiction.

2. Defendant owes plaintiff _____ dollars for money paid by plaintiff to defendant by mistake on June 1,

1936, under the following circumstances: [here state the circumstances with particularity—see Rule 9(b)].

Wherefore (etc. as in Form 3).

(As amended Jan. 21, 1963, eff. July 1, 1963.)

ADVISORY COMMITTEE NOTES

1963 Amendment

This form was amended in 1963 by deleting the stated dollar amount and substituting a blank, to be properly filled in by the pleader. See Note of Advisory Committee under Form 3.

Form 8. Complaint for Money Had and Received

1. Allegation of jurisdiction.

2. Defendant owes plaintiff _____ dollars for money had and received from one G. H. on June 1, 1936, to be paid by defendant to plaintiff.

Wherefore (etc. as in Form 3).

(As amended Jan. 21, 1963, eff. July 1, 1963.)

ADVISORY COMMITTEE NOTES

1963 Amendment

This form was amended in 1963 by deleting the stated dollar amount and substituting a blank, to be properly filled in by the pleader. See Note of Advisory Committee under Form 3.

Form 9. Complaint for Negligence

1. Allegation of jurisdiction.

2. On June 1, 1936, in a public highway called Boylston Street in Boston, Massachusetts, defendant negligently drove a motor vehicle against plaintiff who was then crossing said highway.

3. As a result plaintiff was thrown down and had his leg broken and was otherwise injured, was prevented from transacting his business, suffered great pain of body and mind, and incurred expenses for medical attention and hospitalization in the sum of one thousand dollars.

Wherefore plaintiff demands judgment against defendant in the sum of _____ dollars and costs.

NOTE

Since contributory negligence is an affirmative defense, the complaint need contain no allegation of due care of plaintiff.

(As amended Jan. 21, 1963, eff. July 1, 1963.)

ADVISORY COMMITTEE NOTES

1963 Amendment

This form was amended in 1963 by deleting the stated dollar amount and substituting a blank, to be properly filled in by the pleader. See Note of Advisory Committee under Form 3.

Form 10. Complaint for Negligence Where Plaintiff is Unable to Determine Definitely Whether the Person Responsible is C. D. or E. F. or Whether Both are Responsible and Where his Evidence may Justify a Finding of Wilfulness or of Recklessness or of Negligence

A. B., Plaintiff)
v.) *Complaint*
C. D. and E. F., Defendants)

1. Allegation of jurisdiction.

2. On June 1, 1936, in a public highway called Boylston Street in Boston, Massachusetts, defendant C. D. or defendant E. F., or both defendants C. D. and E. F. wilfully or recklessly or negligently drove or caused to be driven a motor vehicle against plaintiff who was then crossing said highway.

3. As a result plaintiff was thrown down and had his leg broken and was otherwise injured, was prevented from transacting his business, suffered great pain of body and mind, and incurred expenses for medical attention and hospitalization in the sum of one thousand dollars.

Wherefore plaintiff demands judgment against C. D. or against E. F. or against both in the sum of _____ dollars and costs.

(As amended Jan. 21, 1963, eff. July 1, 1963.)

ADVISORY COMMITTEE NOTES

1963 Amendment

This form was amended in 1963 by deleting the stated dollar amount and substituting a blank, to be properly filled in by the pleader. See Note of Advisory Committee under Form 3.

Form 11. Complaint for Conversion

1. Allegation of jurisdiction.

2. On or about December 1, 1936, defendant converted to his own use ten bonds of the _____ Company (here insert brief identification as by number and issue) of the value of _____ dollars, the property of plaintiff.

Wherefore plaintiff demands judgment against defendant in the sum of _____ dollars, interest, and costs.

(As amended Jan. 21, 1963, eff. July 1, 1963.)

ADVISORY COMMITTEE NOTES

1963 Amendment

This form was amended in 1963 by deleting the stated dollar amount and substituting a blank, to be properly filled in by the pleader. See Note of Advisory Committee under Form 3.

Form 12. Complaint for Specific Performance of Contract to Convey Land

1. Allegation of jurisdiction.

2. On or about December 1, 1936, plaintiff and defendant entered into an agreement in writing a copy of which is hereto annexed as Exhibit A.

3. In accord with the provisions of said agreement plaintiff tendered to defendant the purchase price and requested a conveyance of the land, but defendant refused to accept the tender and refused to make the conveyance.

4. Plaintiff now offers to pay the purchase price.

Wherefore plaintiff demands (1) that defendant be required specifically to perform said agreement, (2) damages in the sum of one thousand dollars, and (3) that if specific performance is not granted plaintiff have judgment against defendant in the sum of _____ dollars.

NOTE

Here, as in Form 3, plaintiff may set forth the contract verbatim in the complaint or plead it, as indicated, by exhibit, or plead it according to its legal effect. Furthermore, plaintiff may seek legal or equitable relief or both even though this was impossible under the system in operation before these rules.

(As amended Jan. 21, 1963, eff. July 1, 1963.)

ADVISORY COMMITTEE NOTES

1963 Amendment

This form was amended in 1963 by deleting the stated dollar amount and substituting a blank, to be properly filled in by the pleader. See Note of Advisory Committee under Form 3.

Form 13. Complaint on Claim for Debt and to Set Aside Fraudulent Conveyance Under Rule 18(b)

A. B., Plaintiff)
v.) *Complaint*
C. D. and E. F., Defendants)

1. Allegation of jurisdiction.

2. Defendant C. D. on or about _____ executed and delivered to plaintiff a promissory note [in the following words and figures: (here set out the note verbatim)]; [a copy of which is hereto annexed as Exhibit A]; [whereby defendant C. D. promised to pay to plaintiff or order [1] on _____ the sum of five thousand dollars with interest thereon at the rate of _____ percent. per annum].

3. Defendant C. D. owes to plaintiff the amount of said note and interest.

4. Defendant C. D. on or about _____ conveyed all his property, real and personal [or specify and describe] to defendant E. F. for the purpose of defrauding plaintiff and hindering and delaying the collection of the indebtedness evidenced by the note above referred to.

Wherefore plaintiff demands:

(1) That plaintiff have judgment against defendant C. D. for _____ dollars and interest; (2) that the aforesaid conveyance to defendant E. F. be declared void and the judgment herein be declared a lien on said property; (3) that plaintiff have judgment against the defendants for costs.

(As amended Jan. 21, 1963, eff. July 1, 1963.)

[1] So in original.

ADVISORY COMMITTEE NOTES

1963 Amendment

This form was amended in 1963 by deleting the stated dollar amount and substituting a blank, to be properly filled in by the pleader. See Note of Advisory Committee under Form 3.

Form 14. Complaint for Negligence Under Federal Employer's Liability Act

1. Allegation of jurisdiction.

2. During all the times herein mentioned defendant owned and operated in interstate commerce a railroad which passed through a tunnel located at _____ and known as Tunnel No. ___.

3. On or about June 1, 1936, defendant was repairing and enlarging the tunnel in order to protect interstate trains and passengers and freight from injury and in order to make the tunnel more conveniently usable for interstate commerce.

4. In the course of thus repairing and enlarging the tunnel on said day defendant employed plaintiff as one of its workmen, and negligently put plaintiff to work in a portion of the tunnel which defendant had left unprotected and unsupported.

5. By reason of defendant's negligence in thus putting plaintiff to work in that portion of the tunnel, plaintiff was, while so working pursuant to defendant's orders, struck and crushed by a rock, which fell from the unsupported portion of the tunnel, and was (here describe plaintiff's injuries).

6. Prior to these injuries, plaintiff was a strong, able-bodied man, capable of earning and actually earning _____ dollars per day. By these injuries he has been made incapable of any gainful activity, has suffered great physical and mental pain, and has incurred expense in the amount of _____ dollars for medicine, medical attendance, and hospitalization.

Wherefore plaintiff demands judgment against defendant in the sum of _____ dollars and costs.

Form 15. Complaint for Damages Under Merchant Marine Act

1. Allegation of jurisdiction. [If the pleader wishes to invoke the distinctively maritime procedures referred to in Rule 9(h), add the following or its substantial equivalent: This is an admiralty or maritime claim within the meaning of Rule 9(h).]

2. During all the times herein mentioned defendant was the owner of the steamship ____ and used it in the transportation of freight for hire by water in interstate and foreign commerce.

3. During the first part of (month and year) at ____ plaintiff entered the employ of defendant as an able seaman on said steamship under seamen's articles of customary form for a voyage from ____ ports to the Orient and return at a wage of ____ dollars per month and found, which is equal to a wage of ____ dollars per month as a shore worker.

4. On June 1, 1936, said steamship was about __ days out of the port of ____ and was being navigated by the master and crew on the return voyage to ____ ports. (Here describe weather conditions and the condition of the ship and state as in an ordinary complaint for personal injuries the negligent conduct of defendant.)

5. By reason of defendant's negligence in thus (brief statement of defendant's negligent conduct) and the unseaworthiness of said steamship, plaintiff was (here describe plaintiff's injuries).

6. Prior to these injuries, plaintiff was a strong, able-bodied man, capable of earning and actually earning ____ dollars per day. By these injuries he has been made incapable of any gainful activity; has suffered great physical and mental pain, and has incurred expense in the amount of ____ dollars for medicine, medical attendance, and hospitalization.

Wherefore plaintiff demands judgment against defendant in the sum of ____ dollars and costs.

(As amended Feb. 28, 1966, eff. July 1, 1966.)

ADVISORY COMMITTEE NOTES

1966 Amendment

See Advisory Committee's Note to Form 2.

Form 16. Complaint for Infringement of Patent

1. Allegation of jurisdiction.

2. On May 16, 1934, United States Letters Patent No. ___ were duly and legally issued to plaintiff for an invention in an electric motor; and since that date plaintiff has been and still is the owner of those Letters Patent.

3. Defendant has for a long time past been and still is infringing those Letters Patent by making, selling, and using electric motors embodying the patented invention, and will continue to do so unless enjoined by this court.

4. Plaintiff has placed the required statutory notice on all electric motors manufactured and sold by him under said Letters Patent, and has given written notice to defendant of his said infringement.

Wherefore plaintiff demands a preliminary and final injunction against continued infringement, an accounting for damages, and an assessment of interest and costs against defendant.

(As amended Jan. 21, 1963, eff. July 1, 1963.)

ADVISORY COMMITTEE NOTES

1963 Amendment

The prayer for relief is amended to reflect the language of the present patent statute, Title 35, U.S.C., § 284 (Damages).

Form 17. Complaint for Infringement of Copyright and Unfair Competition

1. Allegation of jurisdiction.

2. Prior to March, 1936, plaintiff, who then was and ever since has been a citizen of the United States, created and wrote an original book, entitled ____.

3. This book contains a large amount of material wholly original with plaintiff and is copyrightable subject matter under the laws of the United States.

4. Between March 2, 1936, and March 10, 1936, plaintiff complied in all respects with the Act of (give citation) and all other laws governing copyright, and secured the exclusive rights and privileges in and to the copyright of said book, and received from the Register of Copyrights a certificate of registration, dated and identified as follows: "March 10, 1936, Class ___, No. ___."

5. Since March 10, 1936, said book has been published by plaintiff and all copies of it made by plaintiff or under his authority or license have been printed, bound, and published in strict conformity with the provisions of the Act of ____ and all other laws governing copyright.

6. Since March 10, 1936, plaintiff has been and still is the sole proprietor of all rights, title, and interest in and to the copyright in said book.

7. After March 10, 1936, defendant infringed said copyright by publishing and placing upon the market a book entitled ____, which was copied largely from plaintiff's copyrighted book, entitled ____.

8. A copy of plaintiff's copyrighted book is hereto attached as "Exhibit 1"; and a copy of defendant's infringing book is hereto attached as "Exhibit 2."

9. Plaintiff has notified defendant that defendant has infringed the copyright of plaintiff, and defendant has continued to infringe the copyright.

10. After March 10, 1936, and continuously since about _____, defendant has been publishing, selling and otherwise marketing the book entitled _____, and has thereby been engaging in unfair trade practices and unfair competition against plaintiff to plaintiff's irreparable damage.

Wherefore plaintiff demands:

(1) That defendant, his agents, and servants be enjoined during the pendency of this action and permanently from infringing said copyright of said plaintiff in any manner, and from publishing, selling, marketing or otherwise disposing of any copies of the book entitled _____.

(2) That defendant be required to pay to plaintiff such damages as plaintiff has sustained in consequence of defendant's infringement of said copyright and said unfair trade practices and unfair competition and to account for

(a) all gains, profits and advantages derived by defendant by said trade practices and unfair competition and

(b) all gains, profits, and advantages derived by defendant by his infringement of plaintiff's copyright or such damages as to the court shall appear proper within the provisions of the copyright statutes, but not less than two hundred and fifty dollars.

(3) That defendant be required to deliver up to be impounded during the pendency of this action all copies of said book entitled _____ in his possession or under his control and to deliver up for destruction all infringing copies and all plates, molds, and other matter for making such infringing copies.

(4) That defendant pay to plaintiff the costs of this action and reasonable attorney's fees to be allowed to the plaintiff by the court.

(5) That plaintiff have such other and further relief as is just.

(As amended Dec. 27, 1946, eff. Mar. 19, 1948.)

ADVISORY COMMITTEE NOTES

1946 Amendment

This form, as set out, incorporates amendments made at the same time certain rules of the Federal Rules of Civil Procedure were amended. See Rule 86(b) of such rules.

Form 18. Complaint for Interpleader and Declaratory Relief

1. Allegation of jurisdiction.

2. On or about June 1, 1935, plaintiff issued to G. H. a policy of life insurance whereby plaintiff promised to pay to K. L. as beneficiary the sum of _____ dollars upon the death of G. H. The policy required the payment by G. H. of a stipulated premium on June 1, 1936, and annually thereafter as a condition precedent to its continuance in force.

3. No part of the premium due June 1, 1936, was ever paid and the policy ceased to have any force or effect on July 1, 1936.

4. Thereafter, on September 1, 1936, G. H. and K. L. died as the result of a collision between a locomotive and the automobile in which G. H. and K. L. were riding.

5. Defendant C. D. is the duly appointed and acting executor of the will of G. H.; defendant E. F. is the duly appointed and acting executor of the will of K. L.; defendant X. Y. claims to have been duly designated as beneficiary of said policy in place of K. L.

6. Each of defendants, C. D., E. F., and X. Y. is claiming that the above-mentioned policy was in full force and effect at the time of the death of G. H.; each of them is claiming to be the only person entitled to receive payment of the amount of the policy and has made demand for payment thereof.

7. By reason of these conflicting claims of the defendants, plaintiff is in great doubt as to which defendant is entitled to be paid the amount of the policy, if it was in force at the death of G. H.

Wherefore plaintiff demands that the court adjudge:

(1) That none of the defendants is entitled to recover from plaintiff the amount of said policy or any part thereof.

(2) That each of the defendants be restrained from instituting any action against plaintiff for the recovery of the amount of said policy or any part thereof.

(3) That, if the court shall determine that said policy was in force at the death of G. H., the defendants be required to interplead and settle between themselves their rights to the money due under said policy, and that plaintiff be discharged from all liability in the premises except to the person whom the court shall adjudge entitled to the amount of said policy.

(4) That plaintiff recover its costs.

(As amended Jan. 21, 1963, eff. July 1, 1963.)

ADVISORY COMMITTEE NOTES

1963 Amendment

This form was amended in 1963 by deleting the stated dollar amount and substituting a blank, to be properly filled in by the pleader. See Note of Advisory Committee under Form 3.

Form 18–A. [Abrogated]

ADVISORY COMMITTEE NOTES

This form is superseded by Forms 1A and 1B in view of the revision of Rule 4.

Form 19. Motion to Dismiss, Presenting Defenses of Failure to State a Claim, of Lack of Service of Process, of Improper Venue, and of Lack of Jurisdiction Under Rule 12(b)

The defendant moves the court as follows:

1. To dismiss the action because the complaint fails to state a claim against defendant upon which relief can be granted.

2. To dismiss the action or in lieu thereof to quash the return of service of summons on the grounds (a) that the defendant is a corporation organized under the laws of Delaware and was not and is not subject to service of process within the Southern District of New York, and (b) that the defendant has not been properly served with process in this action, all of which more clearly appears in the affidavits of M. N. and X. Y. hereto annexed as Exhibit A and Exhibit B respectively.

3. To dismiss the action on the ground that it is in the wrong district because (a) the jurisdiction of this court is invoked solely on the ground that the action arises under the Constitution and laws of the United States and (b) the defendant is a corporation incorporated under the laws of the State of Delaware and is not licensed to do or doing business in the Southern District of New York, all of which more clearly appears in the affidavits of K. L. and V. W. hereto annexed as Exhibits C and D, respectively.

4. To dismiss the action on the ground that the court lacks jurisdiction because the amount actually in controversy is less than ten thousand dollars exclusive of interest and costs.

Signed: ____________
Attorney for Defendant.
Address: ____________

Notice of Motion

To: ____________
Attorney for Plaintiff.

Please take notice, that the undersigned will bring the above motion on for hearing before this Court at Room ___, United States Court House, Foley Square, City of New York, on the ___ day of _____, 19___, at 10 o'clock in the forenoon of that day or as soon thereafter as counsel can be heard.

Signed: ____________
Attorney for Defendant.
Address: ____________

NOTES

1. The above motion and notice of motion may be combined and denominated Notice of Motion. See Rule 7(b).

2. As to paragraph 3, see U.S.C., Title 28, § 1391 (Venue generally), subsections (b) and (c).

3. As to paragraph 4, see U.S.C., Title 28, § 1331 (Federal question; amount in controversy; costs), as amended by P.L. 85–554, 72 Stat. 415, July 25, 1958, requiring that the amount in controversy, exclusive of interest and costs, be in excess of $10,000. [Editor's note: This Note reflects U.S.C., Title 28, § 1331, prior to the 1976 and 1980 amendments eliminating the $10,000 jurisdictional amount. See U.S.C., Title 28, § 1332.]

(As amended Dec. 29, 1948, eff. Oct. 20, 1949; Apr. 17, 1961, eff. July 19, 1961.)

Form 20. Answer Presenting Defenses Under Rule 12(b)

First Defense

The complaint fails to state a claim against defendant upon which relief can be granted.

Second Defense

If defendant is indebted to plaintiffs for the goods mentioned in the complaint, he is indebted to them jointly with G. H. G. H. is alive; is a citizen of the State of New York and a resident of this district, is subject to the jurisdiction of this court, as to both service of process and venue; can be made a party without depriving this court of jurisdiction of the present parties, and has not been made a party.

Third Defense

Defendant admits the allegation contained in paragraphs 1 and 4 of the complaint; alleges that he is without knowledge or information sufficient to form a belief as to the truth of the allegations contained in paragraph 2 of the complaint; and denies each and every other allegation contained in the complaint.

Fourth Defense

The right of action set forth in the complaint did not accrue within six years next before the commencement of this action.

Counterclaim

(Here set forth any claim as a counterclaim in the manner in which a claim is pleaded in a complaint. No statement of the grounds on which the court's jurisdiction depends need be made unless the counterclaim requires independent grounds of jurisdiction.)

Cross-Claim Against Defendant M. N.

(Here set forth the claim constituting a cross-claim against defendant M. N. in the manner in which a claim is pleaded in a complaint. The statement of grounds upon which the court's jurisdiction depends need not be made unless the cross-claim requires independent grounds of jurisdiction.)

NOTE

The above form contains examples of certain defenses provided for in Rule 12(b). The first defense challenges the legal sufficiency of the complaint. It is a substitute for a general demurrer or a motion to dismiss.

The second defense embodies the old plea in abatement; the decision thereon, however, may well provide under Rules 19 and 21 for the citing in of the party rather than an abatement of the action.

The third defense is an answer on the merits.

The fourth defense is one of the affirmative defenses provided for in Rule 8(c).

The answer also includes a counterclaim and a cross-claim.

ADVISORY COMMITTEE NOTES

1946 Amendment

The explanatory note incorporates revisions made by the Advisory Committee at the same time amendments to certain rules of the Federal Rules of Civil Procedure were made. See also Rule 12(b) as amended.

Form 21. Answer to Complaint Set Forth in Form 8, With Counterclaim for Interpleader

Defense

Defendant admits the allegations stated in paragraph 1 of the complaint; and denies the allegations stated in paragraph 2 to the extent set forth in the counterclaim herein.

Counterclaim for Interpleader

1. Defendant received the sum of ____ dollars as a deposit from E. F.

2. Plaintiff has demanded the payment of such deposit to him by virtue of an assignment of it which he claims to have received from E. F.

3. E. F. has notified the defendant that he claims such deposit, that the purported assignment is not valid, and that he holds the defendant responsible for the deposit.

Wherefore defendant demands:

(1) That the court order E. F. to be made a party defendant to respond to the complaint and to this counterclaim.[1]

(2) That the court order the plaintiff and E. F. to interplead their respective claims.

(3) That the court adjudge whether the plaintiff or E. F. is entitled to the sum of money.

(4) That the court discharge defendant from all liability in the premises except to the person it shall adjudge entitled to the sum of money.

(5) That the court award to the defendant its costs and attorney's fees.

(As amended Jan. 21, 1963, eff. July 1, 1963.)

[1] Rule 13(h) provides for the court ordering parties to a counterclaim, but who are not parties to the original action, to be brought in as defendants.

ADVISORY COMMITTEE NOTES

1963 Amendment

This form was amended in 1963 by deleting the stated dollar amount and substituting a blank, to be properly filled in by the pleader. See Note of Advisory Committee under Form 3.

[Form 22. Eliminated, eff. July 1, 1963]

HISTORICAL NOTES

Codifications

Form 22 for motion to bring in third-party defendant, setting out as an exhibit summons and third-party complaint, and for notice of motion, was superseded by Forms 22–A and 22–B, setting out summons and complaint against third-party defendant, and motion to bring in third-party defendant, effective July 1, 1963. See Advisory Committee notes under Forms 22–A and 22–B.

Form 22–A. Summons and Complaint Against Third-Party Defendant

United States District Court for the
Southern District of New York

Civil Action, File Number ____

A. B., Plaintiff)
v.)
C. D., Defendant and)
Third–Party Plaintiff) *Summons*
v.)
E. F., Third-Party Defendant)

To the above-named Third-Party Defendant:

You are hereby summoned and required to serve upon ____, plaintiff's attorney whose address is ____, and upon ____, who is attorney for C. D., defendant and third-party plaintiff, and whose address is ____, an answer to the third-party complaint which is herewith served upon you within 20 days after the service of this summons upon you exclusive of the day of service. If you fail to do so, judgment by default will be taken against you for the relief demanded in the third-party complaint. There is also served upon you herewith a copy of the complaint of the plaintiff which you may but are not required to answer.

____________________,
Clerk of Court.

[Seal of District Court]

Dated ____

United States District Court for the
Southern District of New York

Civil Action, File Number ___

A. B., Plaintiff)
v.)
C. D., Defendant and)
Third-Party Plaintiff) *Third-Party Complaint*
v.)
E. F., Third-Party Defendant)

1. Plaintiff A. B. has filed against defendant C. D. a complaint, a copy of which is hereto attached as "Exhibit A."

2. (Here state the grounds upon which C. D. is entitled to recover from E. F., all or part of what A. B. may recover from C. D. The statement should be framed as in an original complaint.)

Wherefore C. D. demands judgment against third-party defendant E. F. for all sums[1] that may be adjudged against defendant C. D. in favor of plaintiff A. B.

Signed: ___________
Attorney for C. D., Third-Party Plaintiff
Address: ___________

(Added Jan. 21, 1963, eff. July 1, 1963.)

1 Make appropriate change where C. D. is entitled to only partial recovery-over against E. F.

ADVISORY COMMITTEE NOTES

1963 Adoption

Under the amendment of Rule 14(a), a defendant who files a third-party complaint not later than 10 days after serving his original answer need not obtain leave of court to bring in the third-party defendant by service under Rule 4. Form 22–A is intended for use in these cases.

The changes in the form of summons reflect an earlier amendment of Rule 14(a), effective in 1948, making it permissive, rather than mandatory, for the third-party defendant to answer the plaintiff's complaint. See *Cooper v. D/S A/S Progress,* 188 F.Supp. 578 (E.D.Pa.1960); 1A Barron & Holtzoff, *Federal Practice & Procedure* 696 (Wright ed. 1960).

Under the amendment of Rule 5(a) requiring, with certain exceptions, that papers be served upon all the parties to the action, the third-party defendant, even if he makes no answer to the plaintiff's complaint, is obliged to serve upon the plaintiff a copy of his answer to the third-party complaint. Similarly, the defendant is obliged to serve upon the plaintiff a copy of the summons and complaint against the third-party defendant.

Form 22–B. Motion to Bring in Third-Party Defendant

Defendant moves for leave, as third-party plaintiff, to cause to be served upon E. F. a summons and third-party complaint, copies of which are hereto attached as Exhibit X.

Signed: ___________,
Attorney for Defendant C. D.
Address: ___________

Notice of Motion

(Contents the same as in Form 19. The notice should be addressed to all parties to the action.)

Exhibit X

(Contents the same as in Form 22–A.)

(Added Jan. 21, 1963, eff. July 1, 1963.)

ADVISORY COMMITTEE NOTES

1963 Adoption

Form 22–B is intended for use when, under amended Rule 14(a), leave of court is required to bring in a third-party defendant.

Form 23. Motion to Intervene as a Defendant Under Rule 24

(Based upon the complaint, Form 16)

United States District Court for the
Southern District of New York

Civil Action, File Number ___

A. B., plaintiff)
v.) *Motion to intervene*
) *as a defendant*
C. D., defendant)
E. F., applicant)
for intervention)

E. F. moves for leave to intervene as a defendant in this action, in order to assert the defenses set forth in his proposed answer, of which a copy is hereto attached, on the ground that he is the manufacturer and vendor to the defendant, as well as to others, of the articles alleged in the complaint to be an infringement of plaintiff's patent, and as such has a defense to plaintiff's claim presenting both questions of law and of fact which are common to the main action.[1]

Signed: ___________,
Attorney for E. F., Applicant for Intervention.
Address: ___________

Notice of Motion

(Contents the same as in Form 19)

United States District Court for the
Southern District of New York

Civil Action, File Number ___

A. B., plaintiff)
v.) *Intervener's Answer*
C. D., defendant)
E. F., intervener)

First Defense

Intervener admits the allegations stated in paragraphs 1 and 4 of the complaint; denies the allegations in paragraph 3, and denies the allegations in paragraph 2 in so far as they assert the legality of the issuance of the Letters Patent to plaintiff.

Second Defense

Plaintiff is not the first inventor of the articles covered by the Letters Patent specified in his complaint, since articles substantially identical in character were previously patented in Letters Patent granted to intervener on January 5, 1920.

Signed: ______________,
Attorney for E. F., Intervener.
Address: ______________

(As amended Dec. 29, 1948, eff. Oct. 20, 1949.)

[1] For other grounds of intervention, either of right or in the discretion of the court, see Rule 24(a) and (b).

Form 24. Request for Production of Documents, etc., Under Rule 34

Plaintiff A. B. requests defendant C. D. to respond within ______ days to the following requests:

(1) That defendant produce and permit plaintiff to inspect and to copy each of the following documents:

(Here list the documents either individually or by category and describe each of them.)

(Here state the time, place, and manner of making the inspection and performance of any related acts.)

(2) That defendant produce and permit plaintiff to inspect and to copy, test, or sample each of the following objects:

(Here list the objects either individually or by category and describe each of them.)

(Here state the time, place, and manner of making the inspection and performance of any related acts.)

(3) That defendant permit plaintiff to enter (here describe property to be entered) and to inspect and to photograph, test or sample (here describe the portion of the real property and the objects to be inspected).

(Here state the time, place, and manner of making the inspection and performance of any related acts.)

Signed: ______________,
Attorney for Plaintiff.
Address: ______________

(As amended Mar. 30, 1970, eff. July 1, 1970.)

ADVISORY COMMITTEE NOTES

1970 Amendment

Form 24 is revised to accord with the changes made in Rule 34.

Form 25. Request for Admission Under Rule 36

Plaintiff A. B. requests defendant C. D. within ___ days after service of this request to make the following admissions for the purpose of this action only and subject to all pertinent objections to admissibility which may be interposed at the trial:

1. That each of the following documents, exhibited with this request, is genuine.

(Here list the documents and describe each document.)

2. That each of the following statements is true.

(Here list the statements.)

Signed: ______________,
Attorney for Plaintiff.
Address: ______________

(As amended Dec. 27, 1946, eff. Mar. 19, 1948.)

Form 26. Allegation of Reason for Omitting Party

When it is necessary, under Rule 19(c), for the pleader to set forth in his pleading the names of persons who ought to be made parties, but who are not so made, there should be an allegation such as the one set out below:

John Doe named in this complaint is not made a party to this action [because he is not subject to the jurisdiction of this court]; [because he cannot be made a party to this action without depriving this court of jurisdiction].

Form 27. [Abrogated. Dec. 4, 1967, eff. July 1, 1968]

Form 28. Notice: Condemnation

United States District Court for the
Southern District of New York

Civil Action, File Number ___

United States of America, plaintiff	)	
v.	)	
1,000 Acres of Land in [here insert a	)	*Notice*
general location as "City of ____"	)	
or "County of ____"], John Doe et	)	
al., and Unknown Owners, Defendants	)	

To (here insert the names of the defendants to whom the notice is directed):

You are hereby notified that a complaint in condemnation has heretofore been filed in the office of the clerk of the United States District Court for the Southern District of New York, in the United States Court House in New York City, New York, for the taking (here state the interest to be acquired, as "an estate in fee simple") for use (here state briefly the use, "as a site for a post-office building") of the following described property in which you have or claim an interest.

(Here insert brief description of the property in which the defendants, to whom the notice is directed, have or claim an interest.)

The authority for the taking is (here state briefly, as "the Act of ____, ____ Stat. ____, U.S.C., Title ____, § ___".) [1]

You are further notified that if you desire to present any objection or defense to the taking of your property you are required to serve your answer on the plaintiff's attorney at the address herein designated within twenty days after ________________. [2]

Your answer shall identify the property in which you claim to have an interest, state the nature and extent of the interest you claim, and state all of your objections and defenses to the taking of your property. All defenses and objections not so presented are waived. And in case of your failure so to answer the complaint, judgment of condemnation of that part of the above-described property in which you have or claim an interest will be rendered.

But without answering, you may serve on the plaintiff's attorney a notice of appearance designating the property in which you claim to be interested. Thereafter you will receive notice of all proceedings affecting it. At the trial of the issue of just compensation, whether or not you have previously appeared or answered, you may present evidence as to the amount of the compensation to be paid for your property, and you may share in the distribution of the award.

____
United States Attorney.
Address ________________

(Here state an address within the district where the United States Attorney may be served as "United States Court House, New York, N.Y.".)

Dated ________

(Added May 1, 1951, eff. Aug. 1, 1951.)

1 And where appropriate add a citation to any applicable Executive Order.

2 Here insert the words "personal service of this notice upon you," if personal service is to be made pursuant to subdivision (d)(3)(i) of this rule [Rule 71A]; or, insert the date of the last publication of notice, if service by publication is to be made pursuant to subdivision (d)(3)(ii) of this rule.

Form 29. Complaint: Condemnation

United States District Court for the
Southern District of New York

Civil Action, File Number ___

United States of America, Plaintiff	)	
v.	)	
1,000 Acres of Land in [here insert a	)	*Complaint*
general location as "City of ____"	)	
or "County of ____"], John Doe, et	)	
al., and Unknown Owners, Defendants	)	

1. This is an action of a civil nature brought by the United States of America for the taking of property under the power of eminent domain and for the ascertainment and award of just compensation to the owners and parties in interest.[1]

2. The authority for the taking is (here state briefly, as "the Act of ____, ____ Stat. ____, U.S.C., Title ____, § ___").[2]

3. The use for which the property is to be taken is (here state briefly the use, "as a site for a post-office building").

4. The interest to be acquired in the property is (here state the interest as "an estate in fee simple").

5. The property so to be taken is (here set forth a description of the property sufficient for its identification) or (described in Exhibit A hereto attached and made a part hereof).

6. The persons known to the plaintiff to have or claim an interest in the property [3] are:

(Here set forth the names of such persons and the interests claimed.) [4]

7. In addition to the persons named, there are or may be others who have or may claim some interest in the property to be taken, whose names are unknown to the plaintiff and on diligent inquiry have not been ascertained. They are made parties to the action under the designation "Unknown Owners."

Wherefore the plaintiff demands judgment that the property be condemned and that just compensation for the taking be ascertained and awarded and for such other relief as may be lawful and proper.

____
United States Attorney.
Address ________________

(Here state an address within the district where the United States Attorney may be served, as "United States Court House, New York, N.Y.".)

(Added May 1, 1951, eff. Aug. 1, 1951.)

1 If the plaintiff is not the United States, but is, for example, a corporation invoking the power of eminent domain delegated to it by the state, then this paragraph 1 of the complaint should be appropriately modified and should be preceded by a paragraph appropriately alleging federal jurisdiction for the action, such as diversity. See Form 2.

2 And where appropriate add a citation to any applicable Executive Order.

3 At the commencement of the action the plaintiff need name as defendants only the persons having or claiming an interest in the property whose names are then known, but prior to any hearing involving the compensation to be paid for a particular piece of property the plaintiff must add as defendants all persons having or claiming an interest in that property whose names can be ascertained by an appropriate search of the records and also those whose names have otherwise been learned. See Rule 71A(c)(2).

4 The plaintiff should designate, as to each separate piece of property, the defendants who have been joined as owners thereof or of some interest therein. See Rule 71A(c)(2).

Form 30. Suggestion of Death Upon the Record Under Rule 25(a)(1)

A. B. [describe as a party, or as executor, administrator, or other representative or successor of C. D., the deceased party] suggests upon the record, pursuant to Rule 25(a)(1), the death of C. D. [describe as party] during the pendency of this action.

(Added Jan. 21, 1963, eff. July 1, 1963.)

Form 31. Judgment on Jury Verdict

United States District Court for the
Southern District of New York

Civil Action, File Number ___

A. B., Plaintiff)
v.) *Judgment*
C. D., Defendant)

This action came on for trial before the Court and a jury, Honorable John Marshall, District Judge, presiding, and the issues having been duly tried and the jury having duly rendered its verdict,

It is Ordered and Adjudged

[that the plaintiff A. B. recover of the defendant C. D. the sum of _____, with interest thereon at the rate of _____ percent as provided by law, and his costs of action.]

[that the plaintiff take nothing, that the action be dismissed on the merits, and that the defendant C. D. recover of the plaintiff A. B. his costs of action.]

Dated at New York, New York, this ___ day of _____, 19__.

_______________________,
Clerk of Court.

NOTE

1. This Form is illustrative of the judgment to be entered upon the general verdict of a jury. It deals with the cases where there is a general jury verdict awarding the plaintiff money damages or finding for the defendant, but is adaptable to other situations of jury verdicts.

2. The clerk, unless the court otherwise orders, is required forthwith to prepare, sign, and enter the judgment upon a general jury verdict without awaiting any direction by the court. The form of the judgment upon a special verdict or a general verdict accompanied by answers to interrogatories shall be promptly approved by the court, and the clerk shall thereupon enter it. See Rule 58, as amended.

3. The Rules contemplate a simple judgment promptly entered. See Rule 54(a). Every judgment shall be set forth on a separate document. See Rule 58, as amended.

4. Attorneys are not to submit forms of judgment unless directed in exceptional cases to do so by the court. See Rule 58, as amended.

(Added Jan. 21, 1963, eff. July 1, 1963.)

Form 32. Judgment on Decision by the Court

United States District Court for the
Southern District of New York

Civil Action, File Number ___

A. B., Plaintiff)
v.) *Judgment*
C. D., Defendant)

This action came on for [trial] [hearing] before the Court, Honorable John Marshall, District Judge, presiding, and the issues having been duly [tried] [heard] and a decision having been duly rendered,

It is Ordered and Adjudged

[that the plaintiff A. B. recover of the defendant C. D. the sum of _____, with interest thereon at the rate of _____ percent as provided by law, and his costs of action.]

[that the plaintiff take nothing, that the action be dismissed on the merits, and that the defendant C. D. recover of the plaintiff A. B. his costs of action.]

Dated at New York, New York, this ___ day of _____, 19__.

_______________________,
Clerk of Court.

NOTES

1. This Form is illustrative of the judgment to be entered upon a decision of the court. It deals with the cases of decisions by the court awarding a party only money damages or costs, but is adaptable to other decisions by the court.

2. The clerk, unless the court otherwise orders, is required forthwith, without awaiting any direction by the court, to prepare, sign, and enter the judgment upon a decision by the court that a party shall recover only a sum certain or costs or that all relief shall be denied. The form of the judgment upon a decision by the court granting other relief shall be promptly approved by the court, and the clerk shall thereupon enter it. See Rule 58, as amended.

3. See also paragraphs 3–4 of the Explanatory Note to Form 31.

(Added Jan. 21, 1963, eff. July 1, 1963.)

Form 33. Notice of Availability of Magistrate Judge to Exercise Jurisdiction

In accordance with the provisions of Title 28, U.S.C. § 636(c), you are hereby notified that a United States magistrate judge of this district court is available to exercise the court's jurisdiction and to conduct any or all proceedings in this case including a jury or nonjury trial, and entry of a final judgment. Exercise of this jurisdiction by a magistrate judge is, however, permitted only if all parties voluntarily consent.

You may, without adverse substantive consequences, withhold your consent, but this will prevent the court's jurisdiction from being exercised by a magistrate judge. If any party withholds consent, the identity of the parties consenting or withholding consent will not be communicated to any magistrate judge or to the district judge to whom the case has been assigned.

An appeal from a judgment entered by a magistrate judge may be taken directly to the United States court of appeals for this judicial circuit in the same manner as an appeal from any other judgment of a district court.

Copies of the Form for the "Consent to Jurisdiction by a United States Magistrate Judge" are available from the clerk of the court.

(Added Apr. 28, 1983, eff. Aug. 1, 1983, and amended Apr. 22, 1993, eff. Dec. 1, 1993; April 11, 1997, eff. Dec. 1, 1997.)

ADVISORY COMMITTEE NOTES

1993 Amendments

This form, together with Form 34, is revised in light of the Judicial Improvements Act of 1990. Section 308 modified 28 U.S.C. § 636(c)(2) to enhance the potential of parties consenting to trial before a magistrate judge. While the exercise of jurisdiction by a magistrate judge remains dependent on the voluntary consent of the parties, the statute provides that the parties should be advised, and may be reminded, of the availability of this option and eliminates the proscription against judicial suggestions of the potential benefits of referral provided the parties are also advised that they "are free to withhold consent without adverse substantive consequences." The parties may be advised if the withholding of consent will result in a potential delay in trial.

HISTORICAL NOTES

Change of Name

United States magistrate appointed under section 631 of Title 28, Judiciary and Judicial Procedure, to be known as United States magistrate judge after Dec. 1, 1990, with any reference to United States magistrate or magistrate in Title 28, in any other Federal statute, etc., deemed a reference to United States magistrate judge appointed under section 631 of Title 28, see section 321 of Pub.L. 101–650, set out as a note under section 631 of Title 28.

Form 34. Consent to Exercise of Jurisdiction by a United States Magistrate Judge

UNITED STATES DISTRICT COURT

_____ DISTRICT OF _____

)
Plaintiff,)
)
vs.) Docket No. _________
)
Defendant.)

CONSENT TO JURISDICTION BY A UNITED STATES MAGISTRATE JUDGE

In accordance with the provisions of Title 28, U.S.C. § 636(c), the undersigned party or parties to the above-captioned civil matter hereby voluntarily consent to have a United States magistrate judge conduct any and all further proceedings in the case, including trial, and order the entry of a final judgment.

_______________ _______________
Date Signature

Note: Return this form to the Clerk of the Court if you consent to jurisdiction by a magistrate judge. Do not send a copy of this form to any district judge or magistrate judge.

(Added Apr. 28, 1983, eff. Aug. 1, 1983, and amended Apr. 22, 1993, eff. Dec. 1, 1993; April 11, 1997, eff. Dec. 1, 1997.)

HISTORICAL NOTES

Change of Name

United States magistrate appointed under section 631 of Title 28, Judiciary and Judicial Procedure, to be known as United States magistrate judge after Dec. 1, 1990, with any reference to United States magistrate or magistrate in Title 28, in any other Federal statute, etc., deemed a reference to United States magistrate judge appointed under section 631 of Title 28, see section 321 of Pub.L. 101–650, set out as a note under section 631 of Title 28.

Form 34A. Order of Reference

UNITED STATES DISTRICT COURT

_____ DISTRICT OF _____

)
Plaintiff,)
)
vs.) Docket No. _________
)
Defendant.)

ORDER OF REFERENCE

IT IS HEREBY ORDERED that the above-captioned matter be referred to United States Magistrate Judge for all further proceedings and entry of judgment in accordance with Title 28, U.S.C. § 636(c) and the consent of the parties.

____
U.S. District Judge

(Added Apr. 22, 1993, eff. Dec. 1, 1993.)

Form 35. Report of Parties' Planning Meeting

[Caption and Names of Parties]

1. Pursuant to Fed.R.Civ.P. 26(f), a meeting was held on (date) at (place) and was attended by:

(name) for plaintiff(s)

(name) for defendant(s) (party name)

(name) for defendant(s) (party name)

2. Pre–Discovery Disclosures. The parties [have exchanged] [will exchange by (date)] the information required by [Fed.R.Civ.P. 26(a)(1)] [local rule ___].

3. Discovery Plan. The parties jointly propose to the court the following discovery plan: [Use separate paragraphs or subparagraphs as necessary if parties disagree.]

Discovery will be needed on the following subjects: (brief description of subjects on which discovery will be needed)

All discovery commenced in time to be completed by (date). [Discovery on (issue for early discovery) to be completed by (date).]

Maximum of ___ interrogatories by each party to any other party. [Responses due ___ days after service.]

Maximum of ___ requests for admission by each party to any other party. [Responses due ___ days after service.]

Maximum of ___ depositions by plaintiff(s) and ___ by defendant(s).

Each deposition [other than of ______] limited to maximum of ___ hours unless extended by agreement of parties.

Reports from retained experts under Rule 26(a)(2) due:

from plaintiff(s) by (date)

from defendant(s) by (date)

Supplementations under Rule 26(e) due (time(s) or interval(s)).

4. Other Items. [Use separate paragraphs or subparagraphs as necessary if parties disagree.]

The parties [request] [do not request] a conference with the court before entry of the scheduling order.

The parties request a pretrial conference in (month and year).

Plaintiff(s) should be allowed until (date) to join additional parties and until (date) to amend the pleadings.

Defendant(s) should be allowed until (date) to join additional parties and until (date) to amend the pleadings.

All potentially dispositive motions should be filed by (date).

Settlement [is likely] [is unlikely] [cannot be evaluated prior to (date)] [may be enhanced by use of the following alternative dispute resolution procedure: [______].

Final lists of witnesses and exhibits under Rule 26(a)(3) should be due

from plaintiff(s) by (date)

from defendant(s) by (date)

Parties should have ___ days after service of final lists of witnesses and exhibits to list objections under Rule 26(a)(3).

The case should be ready for trial by (date) [and at this time is expected to take approximately (length of time)].

[Other matters.]

Date: ______

(Added Apr. 22, 1993, eff. Dec. 1, 1993.)

ADVISORY COMMITTEE NOTES

1993 Adoption

This form illustrates the type of report the parties are expected to submit to the court under revised Rule 26(f) and may be useful as a checklist of items to be discussed at the meeting.

SUPPLEMENTAL RULES FOR CERTAIN ADMIRALTY AND MARITIME CLAIMS

Adopted February 28, 1966, effective July 1, 1966
Amendments received to January 4, 1999

The former Rules of Practice in Admiralty and Maritime Cases, promulgated by the Supreme Court on December 6, 1920, effective March 7, 1921, as revised, amended and supplemented, were rescinded, effective July 1, 1966.

Rule A. Scope of Rules

These Supplemental Rules apply to the procedure in admiralty and maritime claims within the meaning of Rule 9(h) with respect to the following remedies:

(1) Maritime attachment and garnishment;

(2) Actions in rem;

(3) Possessory, petitory, and partition actions;

(4) Actions for exoneration from or limitation of liability.

These rules also apply to the procedure in statutory condemnation proceedings analogous to maritime actions in rem, whether within the admiralty and maritime jurisdiction or not. Except as otherwise provided, references in these Supplemental Rules to actions in rem include such analogous statutory condemnation proceedings.

The general Rules of Civil Procedure for the United States District Courts are also applicable to the foregoing proceedings except to the extent that they are inconsistent with these Supplemental Rules.

(Added Feb. 28, 1966, eff. July 1, 1966.)

ADVISORY COMMITTEE NOTES

1966 Adoption

Certain distinctively maritime remedies must be preserved in unified rules. The commencement of an action by attachment or garnishment has heretofore been practically unknown in federal jurisprudence except in admiralty, although the amendment of Rule 4(e) effective July 1, 1963, makes available that procedure in accordance with state law. The maritime proceeding in rem is unique, except as it has been emulated by statute, and is closely related to the substantive maritime law relating to liens. Arrest of the vessel or other maritime property is an historic remedy in controversies over title or right to possession, and in disputes among co-owners over the vessel's employment. The statutory right to limit liability is limited to owners of vessels, and has its own complexities. While the unified federal rules are generally applicable to these distinctive proceedings, certain special rules dealing with them are needed.

Arrest of the person and imprisonment for debt are not included because there remedies are not peculiarly maritime. The practice is not uniform but conforms to state law. See 2 Benedict § 286 [Note: reference is to the 6th Edition of Benedict on Admiralty and not to the current 7th Edition]; 28 U.S.C., § 2007; FRCP 64, 69. The relevant provisions of Admiralty Rules 2, 3, and 4 are unnecessary or obsolete.

No attempt is here made to compile a complete and self-contained code governing these distinctively maritime remedies. The more limited objective is to carry forward the relevant provisions of the former Rules of Practice for Admiralty and Maritime Cases, modernized and revised to some extent but still in the context of history and precedent. Accordingly, these Rules are not to be construed as limiting or impairing the traditional power of a district court, exercising the admiralty and maritime jurisdiction, to adapt its procedures and its remedies in the individual case, consistently with these rules, to secure the just, speedy, and inexpensive determination of every action. (See *Swift & Co., Packers v. Compania Columbiana Del Caribe, S/A*, 339 U.S. 684, (1950); Rule 1). In addition, of course, the district courts retain the power to make local rules not inconsistent with these rules. See Rule 83; cf. Admiralty Rule 44.

Rule B. Attachment and Garnishment: Special Provisions

(1) When Available; Complaint, Affidavit, Judicial Authorization, and Process. With respect to any admiralty or maritime claim in personam a verified complaint may contain a prayer for process to attach the defendant's goods and chattels, or credits and effects in the hands of garnishees to be named in the process to the amount sued for, if the defendant shall not be found within the district. Such a complaint shall be accompanied by an affidavit signed by the plaintiff or the plaintiff's attorney that, to the affiant's knowledge, or to the best of the affiant's information and belief, the defendant cannot be found within the district. The verified complaint and affidavit shall be reviewed by the court and, if the conditions set forth in this rule appear to exist, an order so stating and authorizing process of attachment and garnishment shall issue. Supplemental process enforcing the court's order may be issued by the clerk upon application without further order of the court. If the plaintiff or the plaintiff's attorney certifies that exigent circumstances make review by the court impracticable, the clerk shall issue a summons and process of attachment and garnishment and the plaintiff shall have the burden on a post-attachment hearing under Rule E(4)(f) to show that exigent circumstances existed. In addition, or in the alternative, the plaintiff may, pursuant to Rule 4(e), invoke the remedies provided by state law for attachment and garnishment or similar seizure of the defendant's property. Except for Rule E(8) these Supplemental Rules do not apply to state remedies so invoked.

(2) Notice to Defendant. No judgment by default shall be entered except upon proof, which may be by affidavit, (a) that the plaintiff or the garnishee has given notice of the action to the defendant by mailing to the defendant a copy of the complaint, summons, and process of attachment or garnishment, using any form of mail requiring a return receipt, or (b) that the complaint, summons, and process of attachment or garnishment have been served on the defendant in a manner authorized by Rule 4(d) or (i), or (c) that the plaintiff or the garnishee has made diligent efforts to give notice of the action to the defendant and has been unable to do so.

(3) Answer.

(a) By Garnishee. The garnishee shall serve an answer, together with answers to any interrogatories served with the complaint, within 20 days after service of process upon the garnishee. Interrogatories to the garnishee may be served with the complaint without leave of court. If the garnishee refuses or neglects to answer on oath as to the debts, credits, or effects of the defendant in the garnishee's hands, or any interrogatories concerning such debts, credits, and effects that may be propounded by the plaintiff, the court may award compulsory process against the garnishee. If the garnishee admits any debts, credits, or effects, they shall be held in the garnishee's hands or paid into the registry of the court, and shall be held in either case subject to the further order of the court.

(b) By Defendant. The defendant shall serve an answer within 30 days after process has been executed, whether by attachment of property or service on the garnishee.

(Added Feb. 28, 1966, eff. July 1, 1966, and amended Apr. 29, 1985, eff. Aug. 1, 1985; Mar. 2, 1987, eff. Aug. 1, 1987.)

ADVISORY COMMITTEE NOTES

1966 Adoption

Subdivision (1)

This preserves the traditional maritime remedy of attachment and garnishment, and carries forward the relevant substance of Admiralty Rule 2. In addition, or in the alternative, provision is made for the use of similar state remedies made available by the amendment of Rule 4(e) effective July 1, 1963. On the effect of appearance to defend against attachment see Rule E(8).

The rule follows closely the language of Admiralty Rule 2. No change is made with respect to the property subject to attachment. No change is made in the condition that makes the remedy available. The rules have never defined the clause, "if the defendant shall not be found within the district," and no definition is attempted here. The subject seems one best left for the time being to development on a case-by-case basis. The proposal does shift from the marshal (on whom it now rests in theory) to the plaintiff the burden of establishing that the defendant cannot be found in the district.

A change in the context of the practice is brought about by Rule 4(f), which will enable summons to be served throughout the state instead of, as heretofore, only within the district. The Advisory Committee considered whether the rule on attachment and garnishment should be correspondingly changed to permit those remedies only when the defendant cannot be found within the state and concluded that the remedy should not be so limited.

The effect is to enlarge the class of cases in which the plaintiff may proceed by attachment or garnishment although jurisdiction of the person of the defendant may be independently obtained. This is possible at the present time where, for example, a corporate defendant has appointed an agent within the district to accept service of process but is not carrying on activities there sufficient to subject it to jurisdiction. (*Seawind Compania, S.A. v. Crescent Line, Inc.*, 320 F.2d 580 (2d Cir.1963)), or where, though the foreign corporation's activities in the district are sufficient to subject it personally to the jurisdiction, there is in the district no officer on whom process can be served (*United States v. Cia. Naviera Continental, S.A.*, 178 F.Supp. 561, (S.D.N.Y.1959)).

Process of attachment or garnishment will be limited to the district. See Rule E(3)(a).

Subdivision (2)

The former Admiralty Rules did not provide for notice to the defendant in attachment and garnishment proceedings. None is required by the principles of due process, since it is assumed that the garnishee or custodian of the property attached will either notify the defendant or be deprived of the right to plead the judgment as a defense in an action against him by the defendant. *Harris v. Balk*, 198 U.S. 215 (1905); *Pennoyer v. Neff*, 95 U.S. 714 (1878). Modern conceptions of fairness, however, dictate that actual notice be given to persons known to claim an interest in the property that is the subject of the action where that is reasonably practicable. In attachment and garnishment proceedings the persons whose interests will be affected by the judgment are identified by the complaint. No substantial burden is imposed on the plaintiff by a simple requirement that he notify the defendant of the action by mail.

In the usual case the defendant is notified of the pendency of the proceedings by the garnishee or otherwise, and appears to claim the property and to make his answer. Hence notice by mail is not routinely required in all cases, but only in those in which the defendant has not appeared prior to the time when a default judgment is demanded. The rule therefore provides only that no default judgment shall be entered except upon proof of notice, or of inability to give notice despite diligent efforts to do so. Thus the burden of giving notice is further minimized.

In some cases the plaintiff may prefer to give notice by serving process in the usual way instead of simply by mail. (Rule 4(d).) In particular, if the defendant is in a foreign country the plaintiff may wish to utilize the modes of notice recently provided to facilitate compliance with foreign laws and procedures (Rule 4(i)). The rule provides for these alternatives.

The rule does not provide for notice by publication because there is no problem concerning unknown claimants, and publication has little utility in proportion to its expense where the identity of the defendant is known.

Subdivision (3)

Subdivision (a) incorporates the substance of Admiralty Rule 36.

The Admiralty Rules were silent as to when the garnishee and the defendant were to answer. See also 2 Benedict ch. XXIV [Reference is to the 6th Edition of Benedict on Admiralty and not to the current 7th Edition].

The rule proceeds on the assumption that uniform and definite periods of time for responsive pleadings should be substituted for return days (see the discussion under Rule C(6), below). Twenty days seems sufficient time for the garnishee to answer (cf. FRCP 12(a)), and an additional 10 days should suffice for the defendant. When allowance is made for the time required for notice to reach the defendant this gives the defendant in attachment and garnishment approximately the same time that defendants have to answer when personally served.

1985 Amendment

Rule B(1) has been amended to provide for judicial scrutiny before the issuance of any attachment or garnishment process. Its purpose is to eliminate doubts as to whether the Rule is consistent with the principles of procedural due process enunciated by the Supreme Court in *Sniadach v. Family Finance Corp.*, 395 U.S. 337 (1969); and later developed in *Fuentes v. Shevin*, 407 U.S. 67 (1972); *Mitchell v. W.T. Grant Co.*, 416 U.S. 600 (1974); and *North Georgia Finishing, Inc. v. Di-Chem, Inc.*, 419 U.S. 601 (1975). Such doubts were raised in *Grand Bahama Petroleum Co. v. Canadian Transportation Agencies, Ltd.*, 450 F.Supp. 447 (W.D.Wash.1978); and *Schiffahartsgesellschaft Leonhardt & Co. v. A. Bottacchi S.A. de Navegacion*, 552 F.Supp. 771 (S.D.Ga.1982), which was reversed, 732 F.2d 1543 (11th Cir. 1984). But compare *Polar Shipping Ltd. v. Oriental Shipping Corp.*, 680 F.2d 627 (9th Cir.1982), in which a majority of the panel upheld the constitutionality of Rule B because of the unique commercial context in which it is invoked. The practice described in Rule B(1) has been adopted in some districts by local rule. E.g., N.D. Calif. Local Rule 603.3; W.D.Wash. Local Admiralty Rule 15(d).

The rule envisions that the order will issue when the plaintiff makes a prima facie showing that he has a maritime claim against the defendant in the amount sued for and the defendant is not present in the district. A simple order with conclusory findings is contemplated. The reference to review by the "court" is broad enough to embrace review by a magistrate as well as by a district judge.

The new provision recognizes that in some situations, such as when the judge is unavailable and the ship is about to depart from the jurisdiction, it will be impracticable, if not impossible, to secure the judicial review contemplated by Rule B(1). When "exigent circumstances" exist, the rule enables the plaintiff to secure the issuance of the summons and process of attachment and garnishment, subject to a later showing that the necessary circumstances actually existed. This provision is intended to provide a safety valve without undermining the requirement of preattachment scrutiny. Thus, every effort to secure judicial review, including conducting a hearing by telephone, should be pursued before resorting to the exigent-circumstances procedure.

Rule B(1) also has been amended so that the garnishee shall be named in the "process" rather than in the "complaint." This should solve the problem presented in *Filia Compania Naviera, S.A. v. Petroship, S.A.*, 1983 A.M.C. 1 (S.D.N.Y.1982), and eliminate any need for an additional judicial review of the complaint and affidavit when a garnishee is added.

1987 Amendment

The amendments are technical. No substantive change is intended.

Rule C. Actions in Rem: Special Provisions

(1) When Available. An action in rem may be brought:

(a) To enforce any maritime lien;

(b) Whenever a statute of the United States provides for a maritime action in rem or a proceeding analogous thereto.

Except as otherwise provided by law a party who may proceed in rem may also, or in the alternative, proceed in personam against any person who may be liable.

Statutory provisions exempting vessels or other property owned or possessed by or operated by or for the United States from arrest or seizure are not affected by this rule. When a statute so provides, an action against the United States or an instrumentality thereof may proceed on in rem principles.

(2) Complaint. In actions in rem the complaint shall be verified on oath or solemn affirmation. It shall describe with reasonable particularity the property that is the subject of the action and state that it is within the district or will be during the pendency of the action. In actions for the enforcement of forfeitures for violation of any statute of the United States the complaint shall state the place of seizure and whether it was on land or on navigable waters, and shall contain such allegations as may be required by the statute pursuant to which the action is brought.

(3) Judicial Authorization and Process. Except in actions by the United States for forfeitures for federal statutory violations, the verified complaint and any supporting papers shall be reviewed by the court and, if the conditions for an action in rem appear to exist, an order so stating and authorizing a warrant for the arrest of the vessel or other property that is the subject of the action shall issue and be delivered to the clerk who shall prepare the warrant. If the property is a vessel or a vessel and tangible property on board the vessel, the warrant shall be delivered to the marshal for service. If other property, tangible or intangible is the subject of the action, the warrant shall be delivered by the clerk to a person or organization authorized to enforce it, who may be a marshal, a person or organization contracted with by the United States, a person specially appointed by the court for that purpose, or, if the action is brought by the United States, any officer or employee of the United States. If the property that is the subject of the action consists in whole or in part of freight, or the proceeds of property sold, or other intangible property, the clerk shall issue a summons directing any person having control of the funds to show cause why they should not be paid into court to abide the judgment. Supplemental process enforcing the court's order may be issued by the clerk upon application without further order of the court. If the plaintiff or the plaintiff's attorney certifies that exigent circumstances make review by the court impracticable, the clerk shall issue a summons and warrant for the arrest and the plaintiff shall have the burden on a post-arrest hearing under Rule E(4)(f) to show that exigent circumstances existed. In actions by the United States for forfeitures for federal statutory violations, the clerk, upon filing of the complaint, shall forthwith issue a summons and warrant for the arrest of the vessel or other property without requiring a certification of exigent circumstances.

(4) Notice. No notice other than the execution of the process is required when the property that is the subject of the action has been released in accordance with Rule E(5). If the property is not released within 10 days after execution of process, the plaintiff shall promptly or within such time as may be allowed by the court cause public notice of the action and arrest to be given in a newspaper of general circulation in the district, designated by order of the court. Such notice shall specify the time within which the answer is required to be filed as provided by subdivision (6) of this rule. This rule does not affect the requirements of notice in actions to foreclose a preferred ship mortgage pursuant to the Act of June 5, 1920, ch. 250, § 30, as amended.

(5) Ancillary Process. In any action in rem in which process has been served as provided by this rule, if any part of the property that is the subject of the action has not been brought within the control of the court because it has been removed or sold, or because it is intangible property in the hands of a person who has not been served with process, the court may, on motion, order any person having possession or control of such property or its proceeds to show cause why it should not be delivered into the custody of the marshal or other person or organization having a warrant for the arrest of the property, or paid into court to abide the judgment; and, after hearing, the court may enter such judgment as law and justice may require.

(6) Claim and Answer; Interrogatories. The claimant of property that is the subject of an action in rem shall file a claim within 10 days after process has been executed, or within such additional time as may be allowed by the court, and shall serve an answer within 20 days after the filing of the claim. The claim shall be verified on oath or solemn affirmation, and shall state the interest in the property by virtue of which the claimant demands its restitution and the right to defend the action. If the claim is made on behalf of the person entitled to possession by an agent, bailee, or attorney, it shall state that the agent, bailee, or attorney is duly authorized to make the claim. At the time of answering the claimant shall also serve answers to any interrogatories served with the complaint. In actions in rem interrogatories may be so served without leave of court.

(Added Feb. 28, 1966, eff. July 1, 1966, and amended Apr. 29, 1985, eff. Aug. 1, 1985; Mar. 2, 1987, eff. Aug. 1, 1987; Apr. 30, 1991, eff. Dec. 1, 1991.)

ADVISORY COMMITTEE NOTES

1966 Adoption

Subdivision (1).

This rule is designed not only to preserve the proceeding in rem as it now exists in admiralty cases, but to preserve the substance of Admiralty Rules 13–18. The general reference to enforcement of any maritime lien is believed to state the existing law, and is an improvement over the enumeration in the former Admiralty Rules, which is repetitious and incomplete (e.g., there was no reference to general average). The reference to any maritime lien is intended to include liens created by state law which are enforceable in admiralty.

The main concern of Admiralty Rules 13–18 was with the question whether certain actions might be brought in rem or also, or in the alternative, in personam. Essentially, therefore, these rules deal with questions of substantive law, for in general an action in rem may be brought to enforce any maritime lien, and no action in personam may be brought when the substantive law imposes no personal liability.

These rules may be summarized as follows:

1. Cases in which the plaintiff may proceed in rem and/or in personam:

- **a.** Suits for seamen's wages;
- **b.** Suits by materialmen for supplies, repairs, etc.;
- **c.** Suits for pilotage;
- **d.** Suits for collision damages;
- **e.** Suits founded on mere maritime hypothecation;
- **f.** Suits for salvage.

2. Cases in which the plaintiff may proceed only in personam:

- **a.** Suits for assault and beating.

3. Cases in which the plaintiff may proceed only in rem:

- **a.** Suits on bottomry bonds.

The coverage is incomplete, since the rules omit mention of many cases in which the plaintiff may proceed in rem or in personam. This revision proceeds on the principle that it is preferable to make a general statement as to the availability of the remedies, leaving out conclusions on matters of substantive law. Clearly it is not necessary to enumerate the cases listed under Item 1, above, nor to try to complete the list.

The rule eliminates the provision of Admiralty Rule 15 that actions for assault and beating may be brought only in personam. A preliminary study fails to disclose any reason for the rule. It is subject to so many exceptions that it is calculated to deceive rather than to inform. A seaman may sue in rem when he has been beaten by a fellow member of the crew so vicious as to render the vessel unseaworthy, *The Rolph*, 293 Fed. 269, aff'd 299 Fed. 52 (9th Cir. 1923), or where the theory of the action is that a beating by the master is a breach of the obligation under the shipping articles to treat the seaman with proper kindness, *The David Evans*, 187 Fed. 775 (D.Hawaii 1911); and a passenger may sue in rem on the theory that the assault is a breach of the contract of passage, *The Western States*, 159 Fed. 354 (2d Cir. 1908). To say that an action for money damages may be brought only in personam seems equivalent to saying that a maritime lien shall not exist; and that, in turn, seems equivalent to announcing a rule of substantive law rather than a rule of procedure. Dropping the rule will leave it to the courts to determine whether a lien exists as a matter of substantive law.

The specific reference to bottomry bonds is omitted because, as a matter of hornbook substantive law, there is no personal liability on such bonds.

Subdivision (2).

This incorporates the substance of Admiralty Rules 21 and 22.

Subdivision (3).

Derived from Admiralty Rules 10 and 37. The provision that the warrant is to be issued by the clerk is new, but is assumed to state existing law.

There is remarkably little authority bearing on Rule 37, although the subject would seem to be an important one. The rule appears on its face to have provided for a sort of ancillary process, and this may well be the case when tangible property, such as a vessel, is arrested, and intangible property such as freight is incidentally involved. It can easily happen, however, that the only property against which the action may be brought is intangible, as where the owner of a vessel under charter has a lien on subfreights. See 2 Benedict § 299 and cases cited. [Reference is to the 6th Edition of Benedict on Admiralty and not to the current 7th Edition]. In such cases it would seem that the order to the person holding the fund is equivalent to original process, taking the place of the warrant for arrest. That being so, it would also seem that (1) there should be some provision for notice, comparable to that given when tangible property is arrested, and (2) it should not be necessary, as Rule 37 provided, to petition the court for issuance of the process, but that it should issue as of course. Accordingly the substance of Rule 37 is included in the rule covering ordinary process, and notice will be required by Rule C(4). Presumably the rules omit any requirement of notice in these cases because the holder of the funds (e.g., the cargo owner) would be required on general principles (cf. *Harris v. Balk*, 198 U.S. 215 (1905)) to notify his obligee (e.g., the charterer); but in actions in rem such notice seems plainly inadequate because there may be adverse claims to the fund (e.g., there may be liens against the subfreights for seamen's wages, etc.). Compare Admiralty Rule 9.

Subdivision (4).

This carries forward the notice provision of Admiralty Rule 10, with one modification. Notice by publication is too expensive and ineffective a formality to be routinely required. When, as usually happens, the vessel or other property is released on bond or otherwise there is no point in publishing notice; the vessel is freed from the claim of the plaintiff and no other interest in the vessel can be affected by the proceedings. If, however, the vessel is not released, general notice is required in order that all persons, including unknown claimants, may appear and be heard, and in order that the judgment in rem shall be binding on all the world.

Subdivision (5).

This incorporates the substance of Admiralty Rule 9.

There are remarkably few cases dealing directly with the rule. In The *George Prescott*, 10 Fed.Cas. 222 (No. 5,339) (E.D.N.Y.1865), the master and crew of a vessel libeled her for wages, and other lienors also filed libels. One of the lienors suggested to the court that prior to the arrest of the vessel the master had removed the sails, and asked that he be ordered to produce them. He admitted removing the sails and selling them, justifying on the ground that he held a mortgage on the vessel. He was ordered to pay the proceeds into court. Cf. *United States v. The Zarko*, 187 F.Supp. 371 (S.D.Cal.1960), where an armature belonging to a vessel subject to a preferred ship mortgage was in possession of a repairman claiming a lien.

It is evident that, though the rule has had a limited career in the reported cases, it is a potentially important one. It is also evident that the rule is framed in terms narrower than the principle that supports it. There is no apparent reason for limiting it to ships and their appurtenances (2 Benedict § 299) [Reference is to the 6th Edition of Benedict on Admiralty and not to the current 7th Edition]. Also, the reference to "third parties" in the existing rule seems unfortunate. In *The George Prescott*, the person who removed and sold the sails was a plaintiff in the action, and relief against him was just as necessary as if he had been a stranger.

Another situation in which process of this kind would seem to be useful is that in which the principal property that is the subject of the action is a vessel, but her pending freight is incidentally involved. The warrant of arrest, and notice of its service, should be all that is required by way of original process and notice; ancillary process without notice should suffice as to the incidental intangibles.

The distinction between Admiralty Rules 9 and 37 is not at once apparent, but seems to be this: Where the action was against property that could not be seized by the marshal because it was intangible, the original process was required to be similar to that issued against a garnishee, and general notice was required (though not provided for by the present rule; cf. Advisory Committee's Note to Rule C(3)). Under Admiralty Rule 9 property had been arrested and general notice had been given, but some of the property had been removed or for some other reason could not be arrested. Here no further notice was necessary.

The rule also makes provision for this kind of situation: The proceeding is against a vessel's pending freight only; summons has been served on the person supposedly holding the funds, and general notice has been given; it develops that another person holds all or part of the funds. Ancillary process should be available here without further notice.

Subdivision (6).

Adherence to the practice of return days seems unsatisfactory. The practice varies significantly from district to district. A uniform rule should be provided so that any claimant or defendant can readily determine when he is required to file or serve a claim or answer.

A virtue of the return-day practice is that it requires claimants to come forward and identify themselves at an early stage of the proceedings—before they could fairly be required to answer. The draft is designed to preserve this feature of the present practice by requiring early filing of the claim. The time schedule contemplated in the draft is closely comparable to the present practice in the Southern District of New York, where the claimant has a minimum of 8 days to claim and three weeks thereafter to answer.

This rule also incorporates the substance of Admiralty Rule 25. The present rule's emphasis on "the true and bona fide owner" is omitted, since anyone having the right to possession can claim (2 Benedict § 324) [Reference is to the 6th Edition of Benedict on Admiralty and not to the current 7th Edition].

1985 Amendment

Rule C(3) has been amended to provide for judicial scrutiny before the issuance of any warrant of arrest. Its purpose is to eliminate any doubt as to the rule's constitutionality under the *Sniadach* line of cases. *Sniadach v. Family Finance Corp.,* 395 U.S. 337 (1969); *Fuentes v. Shevin,* 407 U.S. 67 (1972); *Mitchell v. W.T. Grant Co.,* 416 U.S. 600 (1974); and *North Georgia Finishing, Inc. v. Di-Chem, Inc.,* 419 U.S. 601 (1975). This was thought desirable even though both the Fourth and the Fifth Circuits have upheld the existing rule. *Amstar Corp. v. S/S Alexandros T.,* 664 F.2d 904 (4th Cir.1981); *Merchants National Bank of Mobile v. The Dredge General G.L. Gillespie,* 663 F.2d 1338 (5th Cir.1981), *cert. dismissed,* 456 U.S. 966 (1982). A contrary view was taken by Judge Tate in the *Merchants National Bank* case and by the district court in *Alyeska Pipeline Service Co. v. The Vessel Bay Ridge,* 509 F.Supp. 1115 (D.Alaska 1981), *appeal dismissed,* 703 F.2d 381 (9th Cir. 1983).

The rule envisions that the order will issue upon a prima facie showing that the plaintiff has an action in rem against the defendant in the amount sued for and that the property is within the district. A simple order with conclusory findings is contemplated. The reference to review by the "court" is broad enough to embrace a magistrate as well as a district judge.

The new provision recognizes that in some situations, such as when a judge is unavailable and the vessel is about to depart from the jurisdiction, it will be impracticable, if not impossible, to secure the judicial review contemplated by Rule C(3). When "exigent circumstances" exist, the rule enables the plaintiff to secure the issuance of the summons and warrant of arrest, subject to a later showing that the necessary circumstances actually existed. This provision is intended to provide a safety valve without undermining the requirement of pre-arrest scrutiny. Thus, every effort to secure judicial review, including conducting a hearing by telephone, should be pursued before invoking the exigent-circumstances procedure.

The foregoing requirements for prior court review or proof of exigent circumstances do not apply to actions by the United States for forfeitures for federal statutory violations. In such actions a prompt hearing is not constitutionally required, *United States v. Eight Thousand Eight Hundred and Fifty Dollars,* 103 S.Ct. 2005 (1983); *Calero-Toledo v. Pearson Yacht Leasing Co.,* 416 U.S. 663 (1974), and could prejudice the government in its prosecution of the claimants as defendants in parallel criminal proceedings since the forfeiture hearing could be misused by the defendants to obtain by way of civil discovery information to which they would not otherwise be entitled and subject the government and the courts to the unnecessary burden and expense of two hearings rather than one.

1987 Amendment

The amendments are technical. No substantive change is intended.

1991 Amendment

These amendments are designed to conform the rule to Fed.R.Civ.P. 4, as amended. As with recent amendments to Rule 4, it is intended to relieve the Marshals Service of the burden of using its limited personnel and facilities for execution of process in routine circumstances. Doing so may involve a contractual arrangement with a person or organization retained by the government to perform these services, or the use of other government officers and employees, or the special appointment by the court of persons available to perform suitably.

The seizure of a vessel, with or without cargo, remains a task assigned to the Marshal. Successful arrest of a vessel frequently requires the enforcement presence of an armed government official and the cooperation of the United States Coast Guard and other governmental authorities. If the marshal is called upon to seize the vessel, it is expected that the same officer will also be responsible for the seizure of any property on board the vessel at the time of seizure that is to be the object of arrest or attachment.

HISTORICAL NOTES

References in Text

The Act of June 5, 1920, c. 250, § 30, referred to in subd. (4), is section 30 of Act June 5, 1920, c. 250, 41 Stat. 988, as amended, known as the "Ship Mortgage Act, 1920", which was classified generally to chapter 25 (section 911 et seq.) of the Appendix to Title 46, Shipping, prior to the repeal of that chapter by Pub.L. 100–710, Title I, § 106(b)(2), Nov. 23, 1988, 102 Stat. 4752. Successor provisions were enacted by Pub.L. 100–710, Title I, § 102(c), Nov. 23, 1988, 102 Stat. 4738, and are set out in chapters 301 (section 30101 et seq.) and 313 (section 31301 seq.) of Subtitle III of Title 46, Shipping (other chapters in that Subtitle being reserved for future legislation). For complete classification of former provisions of Act June 5, 1920, c. 250, § 30, 41 Stat. 988, as amended, see Disposition Table preceding the first section of revised Title 46, Shipping.

Rule D. Possessory, Petitory, and Partition Actions

In all actions for possession, partition, and to try title maintainable according to the course of the admiralty practice with respect to a vessel, in all actions so maintainable with respect to the possession of cargo or other maritime property, and in all actions by one or more part owners against the others to obtain security for the return of the vessel from any voyage undertaken without their consent, or by one or more part owners against the others to obtain possession of the vessel for any voyage on giving security for its safe return, the process shall be by a warrant of arrest of the vessel, cargo, or other property, and by notice in the manner provided by Rule B(2) to the adverse party or parties.

(Added Feb. 28, 1966, eff. July 1, 1966.)

ADVISORY COMMITTEE NOTES

1966 Adoption

This carries forward the substance of Admiralty Rule 19.

Rule 19 provided the remedy of arrest in controversies involving title and possession in general. See *The Tilton,* 23 Fed.Cas.1277 (No. 14,054) (C.C.D.Mass.1830). In addition it provided that remedy in controversies between co-owners respecting the employment of a vessel. It did not deal comprehensively with controversies between co-owners, omitting the remedy of partition. Presumably the omission is traceable to the fact that, when the rules were originally promulgated, concepts of substantive law (sometimes stated as concepts of jurisdiction) denied the remedy of partition except where the parties in disagreement were the owners of equal shares. See *The Steamboat Orleans,* 36 U.S. (11 Pet.) 175 (1837). The Supreme Court has now removed any doubt as to the jurisdiction of the district courts to partition a vessel, and has held in addition that no fixed principle of federal admiralty law limits the remedy to the case of equal shares. *Madruga v. Superior Court,* 346 U.S. 556 (1954). It is therefore appropriate to include a reference to partition in the rule.

Rule E. Actions in Rem and Quasi in Rem: General Provisions

(1) Applicability. Except as otherwise provided, this rule applies to actions in personam with process of maritime attachment and garnishment, actions in rem, and petitory, possessory, and partition actions, supplementing Rules B, C, and D.

(2) Complaint; Security.

(a) *Complaint.* In actions to which this rule is applicable the complaint shall state the circumstances from which the claim arises with such particularity that the defendant or claimant will be able, without moving for a more definite statement, to commence an investigation of the facts and to frame a responsive pleading.

(b) *Security for Costs.* Subject to the provisions of Rule 54(d) and of relevant statutes, the court may, on the filing of the complaint or on the appearance of any defendant, claimant, or any other party, or at any later time, require the plaintiff, defendant, claimant, or other party to give security, or additional security, in such sum as the court shall direct to pay all costs and expenses that shall be awarded against the party by any interlocutory order or by the final judgment, or on appeal by any appellate court.

(3) Process.

(a) *Territorial Limits of Effective Service.* Process in rem and of maritime attachment and garnishment shall be served only within the district.

(b) *Issuance and Delivery.* Issuance and delivery of process in rem, or of maritime attachment and garnishment, shall be held in abeyance if the plaintiff so requests.

(4) Execution of Process; Marshal's Return; Custody of Property; Procedures for Release.

(a) *In General.* Upon issuance and delivery of the process, or, in the case of summons with process of attachment and garnishment, when it appears that the defendant cannot be found within the district, the marshal or other person or organization having a warrant shall forthwith execute the process in accordance with this subdivision (4), making due and prompt return.

(b) *Tangible Property.* If tangible property is to be attached or arrested, the marshal or other person or organization having the warrant shall take it into the marshal's possession for safe custody. If the character or situation of the property is such that the taking of actual possession is impracticable, the marshal or other person executing the process shall affix a copy thereof to the property in a conspicuous place and leave a copy of the complaint and process with the person having possession or the person's agent. In furtherance of the marshal's custody of any vessel the marshal is authorized to make a written request to the collector of customs not to grant clearance to such vessel until notified by the marshal or deputy marshal or by the clerk that the vessel has been released in accordance with these rules.

(c) *Intangible Property.* If intangible property is to be attached or arrested the marshal or other person or organization having the warrant shall execute the process by leaving with the garnishee or other obligor a copy of the complaint and process requiring the garnishee or other obligor to answer as provided in Rules B(3)(a) and C(6); or the marshal may accept for payment into the registry of the court the amount owed to the extent of the amount claimed by the plaintiff with interest and costs, in which event the garnishee or other obligor shall not be required to answer unless alias process shall be served.

(d) *Directions With Respect to Property in Custody.* The marshal or other person or organization having the warrant may at any time apply to the court for directions with respect to property that has been attached or arrested, and shall give notice of such application to any or all of the parties as the court may direct.

(e) *Expenses of Seizing and Keeping Property; Deposit.* These rules do not alter the provisions of Title 28, U.S.C., § 1921, as amended, relative to the expenses of seizing and keeping property attached or arrested and to the requirement of deposits to cover such expenses.

(f) *Procedure for Release From Arrest or Attachment.* Whenever property is arrested or attached, any person claiming an interest in it shall be entitled to a prompt hearing at which the plaintiff shall be required to show why the arrest or attachment should not be vacated or other relief granted consistent with these rules. This subdivision shall have no application to suits for seamen's wages when process is issued upon a certification of sufficient cause filed pursuant to Title 46, U.S.C. §§ 603 and 604 or to actions by the United States for forfeitures for violation of any statute of the United States.

(5) Release of Property.

(a) *Special Bond.* Except in cases of seizures for forfeiture under any law of the United States, whenever process of maritime attachment and garnishment or process in rem is issued the execution of such process shall be stayed, or the property released, on the giving of security, to be approved by the court or clerk, or by stipulation of the parties, conditioned to answer the judgment of the court or of any appellate court. The parties may stipulate the amount and nature of such security. In the event of the inability or refusal of the parties so to stipulate the court shall fix the principal sum of the bond or stipulation at an amount sufficient to cover the amount of the plaintiff's claim fairly stated with accrued interest and costs; but the principal sum shall in no event exceed (i) twice the amount of the plaintiff's claim or (ii) the value of the property on due appraisement, whichever is smaller. The bond or stipulation shall be conditioned for the payment of the principal sum and interest thereon at 6 per cent per annum.

(b) *General Bond.* The owner of any vessel may file a general bond or stipulation, with sufficient surety, to be approved by the court, conditioned to answer the judgment of such court in all or any actions that may be brought thereafter in such court in which the vessel is attached or arrested. Thereupon the execution of all such process against such vessel shall be stayed so long as the amount secured by such bond or stipulation is at least double the aggregate amount claimed by plaintiffs in all actions begun and pending in which such vessel has been attached or arrested. Judgments and remedies may be had on such bond or stipulation as if a special bond or stipulation had been filed in each of such actions. The district court may make necessary orders to carry this rule into effect, particularly as to the giving of proper notice of any action against or attachment of a vessel for which a general bond has been filed. Such bond or stipulation shall be indorsed by the clerk with a minute of the actions wherein process is so stayed. Further security may be required by the court at any time.

If a special bond or stipulation is given in a particular case, the liability on the general bond or stipulation shall cease as to that case.

(c) *Release by Consent or Stipulation; Order of Court or Clerk; Costs.* Any vessel, cargo, or other property in the custody of the marshal or other person or organization having the warrant may be released forthwith upon the marshal's acceptance and approval of a stipulation, bond, or other security, signed by the party on whose behalf the property is detained or the party's attorney and expressly authorizing such release, if all costs and charges of the court and its officers shall have first been paid. Otherwise no property in the custody of the marshal, other person or organization having the warrant, or other officer of the court shall be released without an order of the court; but such order may be entered as of course by the clerk, upon the giving of approved security as provided by law and these rules, or upon the dismissal or discontinuance of the action; but the marshal or other person or organization having the warrant shall not deliver any property so released until the costs and charges of the officers of the court shall first have been paid.

(d) *Possessory, Petitory, and Partition Actions.* The foregoing provisions of this subdivision (5) do not apply to petitory, possessory, and partition actions. In such cases the property arrested shall be released only by order of the court, on such terms and conditions and on the giving of such security as the court may require.

(6) Reduction or Impairment of Security. Whenever security is taken the court may, on motion and hearing, for good cause shown, reduce the amount of security given; and if the surety shall be or become insufficient, new or additional sureties may be required on motion and hearing.

(7) Security on Counterclaim. Whenever there is asserted a counterclaim arising out of the same transaction or occurrence with respect to which the action was originally filed, and the defendant or claimant in the original action has given security to respond in damages, any plaintiff for whose benefit such security has been given shall give security in the usual amount and form to respond in damages to the claims set forth in such counterclaim, unless the court, for cause shown, shall otherwise direct; and proceedings on the original claim shall be stayed until such security is given, unless the court otherwise directs. When the United States or a corporate instrumentality thereof as defendant is relieved by law of the requirement of giving security to respond in damages it shall nevertheless be treated for the purposes of this subdivision E(7) as if it had given such security if a private person so situated would have been required to give it.

(8) Restricted Appearance. An appearance to defend against an admiralty and maritime claim with respect to which there has issued process in rem, or process of attachment and garnishment whether pursuant to these Supplemental Rules or to Rule 4(e), may be expressly restricted to the defense of such claim, and in that event shall not constitute an appearance for the purposes of any other claim with respect to which such process is not available or has not been served.

(9) Disposition of Property; Sales.

(a) *Actions for Forfeitures.* In any action in rem to enforce a forfeiture for violation of a statute of the United States the property shall be disposed of as provided by statute.

(b) *Interlocutory Sales.* If property that has been attached or arrested is perishable, or liable to deterioration, decay, or injury by being detained in custody pending the action, or if the expense of keeping the property is excessive or disproportionate, or if there is unreasonable delay in securing the release of property, the court, on application of any party or of the marshal, or other person or organization having the warrant, may order the property or any portion thereof to be sold; and the proceeds, or so much thereof as shall be adequate to satisfy any judgment, may be ordered brought into court to abide the event of the action; or the court may, upon motion of the defendant or claimant, order delivery of the property to the defendant or claimant, upon the giving of security in accordance with these rules.

(c) *Sales; Proceeds.* All sales of property shall be made by the marshal or a deputy marshal, or by other person or organization having the warrant, or by any other person assigned by the court where the marshal or other person or organization having the warrant is a party in interest; and the proceeds of sale shall be forthwith paid into the registry of the court to be disposed of according to law.

(Added Feb. 28, 1966, eff. July 1, 1966, and amended Apr. 29, 1985, eff. Aug. 1, 1985; Mar. 2, 1987, eff. Aug. 1, 1987; Apr. 30, 1991, eff. Dec. 1, 1991.)

ADVISORY COMMITTEE NOTES

1966 Adoption

Subdivisions (1), (2).

Adapted from Admiralty Rule 24. The rule is based on the assumption that there is no more need for security for costs in maritime personal actions than in civil cases generally, but that there is reason to retain the requirement for actions in which property is seized. As to proceedings for limitation of liability see Rule F(1).

Subdivision (3).

The Advisory Committee has concluded for practical reasons that process requiring seizure of property should continue to be served only within the geographical limits of the district. Compare Rule B(1), continuing the condition that process of attachment and garnishment may be served only if the defendant is not found within the district.

The provisions of Admiralty Rule 1 concerning the persons by whom process is to be served will be superseded by FRCP 4(c).

Subdivision (4).

This rule is intended to preserve the provisions of Admiralty Rules 10 and 36 relating to execution of process, custody of property seized by the marshal, and the marshal's return. It is also designed to make express provision for matters not heretofore covered.

The provision relating to clearance in subdivision (b) is suggested by Admiralty Rule 44 of the District of Maryland.

Subdivision (d) is suggested by English Rule 12, Order 75.

28 U.S.C., § 1921 as amended in 1962 contains detailed provisions relating to the expenses of seizing and preserving property attached or arrested.

Subdivision (5).

In addition to Admiralty Rule 11 (see Rule E(9)), the release of property seized on process of attachment or in rem was dealt with by Admiralty Rules 5, 6, 12, and 57, and 28 U.S.C., § 2464 (formerly Rev.Stat. § 941). The rule consolidates these provisions and makes them uniformly applicable to attachment and garnishment and actions in rem.

The rule restates the substance of Admiralty Rule 5. Admiralty Rule 12 dealt only with ships arrested on in rem process. Since the same ground appears to be covered more generally by 28 U.S.C., § 2464, the subject matter of Rule 12 is omitted. The substance of Admiralty Rule 57 is retained. 28 U.S.C., § 2464 is incorporated with changes of terminology, and with a substantial change as to the amount of the bond. See 2 Benedict 395 n. 1a [Reference is to the 6th Edition of Benedict on Admiralty and not to the current 7th Edition.] *The Lotosland,* 2 F.Supp. 42 (S.D.N.Y.1933). The provision for general bond is enlarged to include the contingency of attachment as well as arrest of the vessel.

Subdivision (6).

Adapted from Admiralty Rule 8.

Subdivision (7).

Derived from Admiralty Rule 50.

Title 46, U.S.C., § 783 extends the principle of Rule 50 to the Government when sued under the Public Vessels Act, presumably on the theory that the credit of the Government is the equivalent of the best security. The rule adopts this principle and extends it to all cases in which the Government is defendant although the Suits in Admiralty Act contains no parallel provisions.

Subdivision (8).

Under the liberal joinder provisions of unified rules the plaintiff will be enabled to join with maritime actions in rem, or maritime actions in personam with process of attachment and garnishment, claims with respect to which such process is not available, including nonmaritime claims. Unification should not, however, have the result that, in order to defend against an admiralty and maritime claim with respect to which process in rem or quasi in rem has been served, the claimant or defendant must subject himself personally to the jurisdiction of the court with reference to other claims with respect to which such process is not available or has not been served, especially when such other claims are nonmaritime. So far as attachment and garnishment are concerned this principle holds true whether process is issued according to admiralty tradition and the Supplemental Rules or according to Rule 4(e) as incorporated by Rule B(1).

A similar problem may arise with respect to civil actions other than admiralty and maritime claims within the meaning of Rule 9(h). That is to say, in an ordinary civil action, whether maritime or not, there may be joined in one action claims with respect to which process of attachment and garnishment is available under state law and Rule 4(e) and claims with respect to which such process is not available or has not been served. The general Rules of Civil Procedure do not specify whether an appearance in such cases to defend the claim with respect to which process of attachment and garnishment has issued is an appearance for the purposes of the other claims. In that context the question has been considered best left to case-by-case development. Where admiralty and maritime claims within the meaning of Rule 9(h) are concerned, however, it seems important to include a specific provision to avoid an unfortunate and unintended effect of unification. No inferences whatever as to the effect of such an appearance in an ordinary civil action should be drawn from the specific provision here and the absence of such a provision in the general Rules.

Subdivision (9).

Adapted from Admiralty Rules 11, 12, and 40. Subdivision (a) is necessary because of various provisions as to disposition of property in forfeiture proceedings. In addition to particular statutes, note the provisions of 28 U.S.C., §§ 2461–65.

The provision of Admiralty Rule 12 relating to unreasonable delay was limited to ships but should have broader application. See 2 Benedict 404 [Reference is to the 6th Edition of Benedict on Admiralty and not to the current 7th Edition]. Similarly, both Rules 11 and 12 were limited to actions in rem, but should equally apply to attached property.

1985 Amendment

Rule E(4)(f) makes available the type of prompt post-seizure hearing in proceedings under Supplemental Rules B and C that the Supreme Court has called for in a number of cases arising in other contexts. See *North Georgia Finishing, Inc. v. Di-Chem, Inc.*, 419 U.S. 601 (1975); *Mitchell v. W.T. Grant Co.*, 416 U.S. 600 (1974). Although post-attachment and post-arrest hearings always have been available on motion, an explicit statement emphasizing promptness and elaborating the procedure has been lacking in the Supplemental Rules. Rule E(4)(f) is designed to satisfy the constitutional requirement of due process by guaranteeing to the shipowner a prompt post-seizure hearing at which he can attack the complaint, the arrest, the security demanded, or any other alleged deficiency in the proceedings. The amendment also is intended to eliminate the previously disparate treatment under local rules of defendants whose property has been seized pursuant to Supplemental Rules B and C.

The new Rule E(4)(f) is based on a proposal by the Maritime Law Association of the United States and on local admiralty rules in the Eastern, Northern, and Southern Districts of New York. E.D.N.Y. Local Rule 13; N.D.N.Y. Local Rule 13; S.D.N.Y. Local Rule 12. Similar provisions have been adopted by other maritime districts. E.g., N.D.Calif. Local Rule 603.4; W.D.La. Local Admiralty Rule 21. Rule E(4)(f) will provide uniformity in practice and reduce constitutional uncertainties.

Rule E(4)(f) is triggered by the defendant or any other person with an interest in the property seized. Upon an oral or written application similar to that used in seeking a temporary restraining order, see Rule 65(b), the court is required to hold a hearing as promptly as possible to determine whether to allow the arrest or attachment to stand. The plaintiff has the burden of showing why the seizure should not be vacated. The hearing also may determine the amount of security to be granted or the propriety of imposing counter-security to protect the defendant from an improper seizure.

The foregoing requirements for prior court review or proof of exigent circumstances do not apply to actions by the United States for forfeitures for federal statutory violations. In such actions a prompt hearing is not constitutionally required, *United States v. Eight Thousand Eight Hundred and Fifty Dollars*, 103 S.Ct. 2005 (1983); *Calero-Toledo v. Pearson Yacht Leasing Co.*, 416 U.S. 663 (1974), and could prejudice the government in its prosecution of the claimants as defendants in parallel criminal proceedings since the forfeiture hearing could be misused by the defendants to obtain by way of civil discovery information to which they would not otherwise be entitled and subject the government and the courts to the unnecessary burden and expense of two hearings rather than one.

1987 Amendment

The amendments are technical. No substantive change is intended.

1991 Amendment

These amendments are designed to conform this rule to Fed.R.Civ.P. 4, as amended. They are intended to relieve the Marshals Service of the burden of using its limited personnel and facilities for execution of process in routine circumstances. Doing so may involve a contractual arrangement with a person or organization retained by the government to perform these services, or the use of other government officers and employees, or the special appointment by the court of persons available to perform suitably.

HISTORICAL NOTES

References in Text

Sections 603 and 604 of Title 46, referred to in subd. (4)(f), were repealed by Pub.L. 98–89, § 4(b), Aug. 26, 1983, 97 Stat. 600, section 1 of which enacted Title 46, Shipping.

Rule F. Limitation of Liability

(1) Time for Filing Complaint; Security. Not later than six months after receipt of a claim in writing, any vessel owner may file a complaint in the appropriate district court, as provided in subdivision (9) of this rule, for limitation of liability pursuant to statute. The owner (a) shall deposit with the court, for the benefit of claimants, a sum equal to the amount or value of the owner's interest in the vessel and pending freight, or approved security therefor, and in addition such sums, or approved security therefor, as the court may from time to time fix as necessary to carry out the provisions of the statutes as amended; or (b) at the owner's option shall transfer to a trustee to be appointed by the court, for the benefit of claimants, the owner's interest in the vessel and pending freight, together with such sums, or approved security therefor, as the court may from time to time fix as necessary to carry out the provisions of the statutes as amended. The plaintiff shall also give security for costs and, if the plaintiff elects to give security, for interest at the rate of 6 percent per annum from the date of the security.

(2) Complaint. The complaint shall set forth the facts on the basis of which the right to limit liability is asserted and all facts necessary to enable the court to determine the amount to which the owner's liability shall be limited. The complaint may demand exoneration from as well as limitation of liability. It shall state the voyage if any, on which the demands sought to be limited arose, with the date and place of its termination; the amount of all demands including all unsatisfied liens or claims of lien, in contract or in tort or otherwise, arising on that voyage, so far as known to the plaintiff, and what actions and proceedings, if any, are pending thereon; whether the vessel was damaged, lost, or abandoned, and, if so, when and where; the value of the vessel at the close of the voyage or, in case of wreck, the value of her wreckage, strippings, or proceeds, if any, and where and in whose possession they are; and the amount of any pending freight recovered or recoverable. If the plaintiff elects to transfer the plaintiff's interest in the vessel to a trustee, the complaint must further show any prior paramount liens thereon, and what voyages or trips, if any, she has made since the voyage or trip on which the claims sought to be limited arose, and any existing liens arising upon any such subsequent voyage or trip, with the amounts and causes thereof, and the names and addresses of the lienors, so far as known; and whether the vessel sustained any injury upon or by reason of such subsequent voyage or trip.

(3) Claims Against Owner; Injunction. Upon compliance by the owner with the requirements of subdivision (1) of this rule all claims and proceedings against the owner or the owner's property with respect to the matter in question shall cease. On application of the plaintiff the court shall enjoin the further prosecution of any action or proceeding against the plaintiff or the plaintiff's property with respect to any claim subject to limitation in the action.

(4) Notice to Claimants. Upon the owner's compliance with subdivision (1) of this rule the court shall issue a notice to all persons asserting claims with respect to which the complaint seeks limitation, admonishing them to file their respective claims with the clerk of the court and to serve on the attorneys for the plaintiff a copy thereof on or before a date to be named in the notice. The date so fixed shall not be less than 30 days after issuance of the notice. For cause shown, the court may enlarge the time within which claims may be filed. The notice shall be published in such newspaper or newspapers as the court may direct once a week for four successive weeks prior to the date fixed for the filing of claims. The plaintiff not later than the day of second publication shall also mail a copy of the notice to every person known to have made any claim against the vessel or the plaintiff arising out of the voyage or trip on which the claims sought to be limited arose. In cases involving death a copy of such notice shall be mailed to the decedent at the decedent's last known address, and also to any person who shall be known to have made any claim on account of such death.

(5) Claims and Answer. Claims shall be filed and served on or before the date specified in the notice provided for in subdivision (4) of this rule. Each claim shall specify the facts upon which the claimant relies in support of the claim, the items thereof, and the dates on which the same accrued. If a claimant desires to contest either the right to exoneration from or the right to limitation of liability the claimant shall file and serve an answer to the complaint unless the claim has included an answer.

(6) Information to be Given Claimants. Within 30 days after the date specified in the notice for filing claims, or within such time as the court thereafter may allow, the plaintiff shall mail to the attorney for each claimant (or if the claimant has no attorney to the claimant) a list setting forth (a) the name of each claimant, (b) the name and address of the claimant's attorney (if the claimant is known to have one), (c) the nature of the claim, i.e., whether property loss, property damage, death, personal injury etc., and (d) the amount thereof.

(7) Insufficiency of Fund or Security. Any claimant may by motion demand that the funds deposited in court or the security given by the plaintiff be increased on the ground that they are less than the value of the plaintiff's interest in the vessel and pending freight. Thereupon the court shall cause due appraisement to be made of the value of the plaintiff's interest in the vessel and pending freight; and if the court finds that the deposit or security is either insufficient or excessive it shall order its increase or reduction. In like manner any claimant may demand that the deposit or security be increased on the ground that it is insufficient to carry out the provisions of the statutes relating to claims in respect of loss of life or bodily injury; and, after notice and hearing, the court may similarly order that the deposit or security be increased or reduced.

(8) Objections to Claims: Distribution of Fund. Any interested party may question or controvert any claim without filing an objection thereto. Upon determination of liability the fund deposited or secured, or the proceeds of the vessel and pending freight, shall be divided pro rata, subject to all relevant provisions of law, among the several claimants in proportion to the amounts of their respective claims, duly proved, saving, however, to all parties any priority to which they may be legally entitled.

(9) Venue; Transfer. The complaint shall be filed in any district in which the vessel has been attached or arrested to answer for any claim with respect to which the plaintiff seeks to limit liability; or, if the vessel has not been attached or arrested, then in any district in which the owner has been sued with respect to any such claim. When the vessel has not been attached or arrested to answer the matters aforesaid, and suit has not been commenced against the owner, the proceedings may be had in the district in which the vessel may be, but if the vessel is not within any district and no suit has been commenced in any district, then the complaint may be filed in any district. For the convenience of parties and witnesses, in the interest of justice, the court may transfer the action to any district; if venue is wrongly laid the court shall dismiss or, if it be in the interest of justice, transfer the action to any district in which it could have been brought. If the vessel shall have been sold, the proceeds shall represent the vessel for the purposes of these rules.

(Added Feb. 28, 1966, eff. July 1, 1966, and amended Mar. 2, 1987, eff. Aug. 1, 1987.)

ADVISORY COMMITTEE NOTES

1966 Adoption

Subdivision (1).

The amendments of 1936 to the Limitation Act superseded to some extent the provisions of Admiralty Rule 51, especially with respect to the time of filing the complaint and with respect to security. The rule here incorporates in substance the 1936 amendment of the Act (46 U.S.C., § 185) with a slight modification to make it clear that the complaint may be filed at any time not later than six months after a claim has been lodged with the owner.

Subdivision (2).

Derived from Admiralty Rules 51 and 53.

Subdivision (3).

This is derived from the last sentence of 46 U.S.C. § 185 and the last paragraph of Admiralty Rule 51.

Subdivision (4).

Derived from Admiralty Rule 51.

Subdivision (5).

Derived from Admiralty Rules 52 and 53.

Subdivision (6).

Derived from Admiralty Rule 52.

Subdivision (7).

Derived from Admiralty Rule 52 and 46 U.S.C., § 185.

Subdivision (8).

Derived from Admiralty Rule 52.

Subdivision (9).

Derived from Admiralty Rule 54. The provision for transfer is revised to conform closely to the language of 28 U.S.C. §§ 1404(a) and 1406(a), though it retains the existing rule's provision for transfer to any district for convenience. The revision also makes clear what has been doubted: that the court may transfer if venue is wrongly laid.

1987 Amendment

The amendments are technical. No substantive change is intended.

RULES OF PROCEDURE OF THE JUDICIAL PANEL ON MULTIDISTRICT LITIGATION

Adopted September 1, 1998

Effective November 2, 1998

Amendments received to December 11, 1998

I. GENERAL RULES/RULE FOR MULTIDISTRICT LITIGATION UNDER 28 U.S.C. § 1407

Rule
1.1. Definitions.
1.2. Practice.
1.3. Failure to Comply with Rules.
1.4. Admission to Practice Before the Panel and Representation in Transferred Actions.
1.5. Effect of the Pendency of an Action Before the Panel.
1.6. Transfer of Files.
5.1. Keeping Records and Files.
5.11. Place of Filing of Papers.
5.12. Manner of Filing Papers.
5.2 Service of Papers Filed.
6.2. Applications for Extensions of Time.

Rule
7.1. Form of Papers Filed.
7.2. Motion Practice.
7.3. Show Cause Orders.
7.4. Conditional Transfer Orders for "Tag–Along Actions".
7.5. Miscellaneous Provisions Concerning "Tag–Along Actions".
7.6. Termination and Remand.
16.1. Hearings.
16.2. Notice of Presentation or Waiver of Oral Argument, and Matters Submitted on the Briefs.

II. RULES FOR MULTICIRCUIT PETITIONS FOR REVIEW UNDER 28 U.S.C. § 2112(a)(3)

17.1 Random Selection.
25.1. Filing of Notices.
25.2. Accompaniments to Notices.
25.3. Service of Notices.
25.4. Form of Notices.
25.5. Service of Panel Consolidation Order.

I. GENERAL RULES/RULES FOR MULTIDISTRICT LITIGATION UNDER 28 U.S.C. § 1407

Rule 1.1. Definitions

As used in these Rules "Panel" means the members of the Judicial Panel on Multidistrict Litigation appointed by the Chief Justice of the United States pursuant to Section 1407, Title 28, United States Code.

"Clerk of the Panel" means the official appointed by the Panel to act as Clerk of the Panel and shall include those deputized by the clerk of the Panel to perform or assist in the performance of the duties of the clerk of the Panel.

"Chairman" means the Chairman of the Judicial Panel on Multidistrict Litigation appointed by the Chief Justice of the United States pursuant to Section 1407, or the member of the Panel designated by the Panel to act as Chairman in the absence or inability of the appointed Chairman.

A "tag-along action" refers to a civil action pending in a district court and involving common questions of fact with actions previously transferred under Section 1407.

(Added May 3, 1993, eff. July 1, 1993, and amended Sept. 1, 1998, eff. Nov. 2, 1998.)

Rule 1.2. Practice

Where not fixed by statute or rule, the practice shall be that heretofore customarily followed by the Panel.

(Added May 3, 1993, eff. July 1, 1993, and amended Sept. 1, 1998, eff. Nov. 2, 1998.)

Rule 1.3. Failure to Comply with Rules

The Clerk of the Panel may, when a paper submitted for filing is not in compliance with the provisions of these Rules, advise counsel of the deficiencies and a date for full compliance. If full compliance is not accomplished within the established time, the non-complying paper shall nonetheless be filed by the Clerk of the Panel but it may be stricken by order of the Chairman of the Panel.

(Added May 3, 1993, eff. July 1, 1993, and amended Sept. 1, 1998, eff. Nov. 2, 1998.)

Rule 1.4. Admission to Practice Before the Panel and Representation in Transferred Actions

Every member in good standing of the Bar of any district court of the United States is entitled without condition to practice before the Judicial Panel on Multidistrict Litigation. Any attorney of record in any action transferred under Section 1407 may continue to represent his or her client in any district court of the United States to which such action is transferred. Parties to any action transferred under Section 1407 are not required to obtain local counsel in the district to which such action is transferred.

(Added May 3, 1993, eff. July 1, 1993, and amended Sept. 1, 1998, eff. Nov. 2, 1998.)

Rule 1.5. Effect of the Pendency of an Action Before the Panel

The pendency of a motion, order to show cause, conditional transfer order or conditional remand order before the Panel concerning transfer or remand of an action pursuant to 28 U.S.C. § 1407 does not affect or suspend orders and pretrial proceedings in the district court in which the action is pending and does not in any way limit the pretrial jurisdiction of that court. A transfer or remand pursuant to 28 U.S.C. § 1407 shall be effective when the transfer or remand order is filed in the office of the clerk of the district court of the transferee district.

(Added May 3, 1993, eff. July 1, 1993, and amended Sept. 1, 1998, eff. Nov. 2, 1998.)

Rule 1.6. Transfer of Files

(a) Upon receipt of a certified copy of a transfer order from the clerk of the transferee district court, the clerk of the transferor district court shall forward to the clerk of the transferee district court the complete original file and a certified copy of the docket sheet for each transferred action.

(b) If an appeal is pending, or a notice of appeal has been filed, or leave to appeal has been sought under 28 U.S.C. § 1292(b) or a petition for an extraordinary writ is pending, in any action included in an order of transfer under 28 U.S.C. § 1407, and the original file or parts thereof have been forwarded to the court of appeals, the clerk of the transferor district court shall notify the clerk of the court of appeals of the order of transfer and secure the original file long enough to prepare and transmit to the clerk of the transferee district court a certified copy of all papers contained in the original file and a certified copy of the docket sheet.

(c) If the transfer order provides for the separation and simultaneous remand of any claim, cross-claim, counterclaim, or third-party claim, the clerk of the transferor district court shall retain the original file and shall prepare and transmit to the clerk of the transferee district court a certified copy of the docket sheet and copies of all papers except those relating exclusively to separated and remanded claims.

(d) Upon receipt of an order to remand from the Clerk of the Panel, the transferee district court shall prepare and send to the clerk of the transferor district court the following:

(i) a certified copy of the individual docket sheet for each action being remanded;

(ii) a certified copy of the master docket sheet, if applicable;

(iii) the entire file for each action being remanded, as originally received from the transferor district court and augmented as set out in this rule;

(iv) a certified copy of the final pretrial order, if applicable; and

(v) a "record on remand" to be composed of those parts of the files and records produced during coordinated or consolidated pretrial proceedings which have been stipulated to or designated by counsel as being necessary for any or all proceedings to be conducted following remand. It shall be the responsibility of counsel originally preparing or filing any document to be included in the "record on remand" to furnish on request sufficient copies to the clerk of the transferee district court.

(e) The Clerk of the Panel shall be notified when any files have been transmitted pursuant to this Rule.

(Added May 3, 1993, eff. July 1, 1993, and amended Sept. 1, 1998, eff. Nov. 2, 1998.)

Rule 5.1. Keeping Records and Files

(a) The records and files of the Panel shall be kept by the Clerk of the Panel at the offices of the Panel. Records and files may be temporarily or permanently removed to such places at such times as the Panel or the Chairman of the Panel shall direct. The Clerk of the Panel may charge fees, as prescribed by the Judicial Conference of the United States, for duplicating records and files Records and files may be transferred whenever appropriate to the Federal Records Center.

(b) In order to assist the Panel in carrying out: its functions, the Clerk of the Panel shall obtain the complaints and docket sheets in all actions under consideration for transfer under 28 U.S.C. § 1407 from the clerk of each district court wherein such actions are pending. The Clerk of the Panel shall similarly obtain any Other Pleadings and orders that could affect the Panel's decision under 28 U.S.C. § 1407.

(Added May 3, 1993, eff. July 1, 1993, and amended Sept. 1, 1998, eff. Nov. 2, 1998.)

Rule 5.11. Place of Filing of Papers

All papers for consideration by the Panel shall be submitted for filing to the Clerk of the Panel by mailing or delivering to:

Clerk of the Panel
Judicial Panel on Multidistrict Litigation
Thurgood Marshall Federal Judiciary Building
One Columbus Circle, N.E., Room G–255, North Lobby
Washington, D.C. 20002–8004

No papers shall be left with or mailed to a Judge of the panel.

(Added May 3, 1993, eff. July 1, 1993, and amended Sept. 1, 1998, eff. Nov. 2, 1998.)

Rule 5.12. Manner of Filing of Papers

(a) An original of the following papers shall be submitted for filing to the Clerk of the Panel: a proof of service pursuant to Rule 5.2(a) and (b) of these Rules, a notice of appearance pursuant to Rule 5.2(c) and (d) of these Rules, a status notice pursuant to Rules 7.2(e), 7.3(e) and 7.4(b) of these Rules, a notice of opposition pursuant to Rules 7.4(c) and 7.6(f)(ii) of these Rules, a notice of related action pursuant to Rule 7.5(e) of these Rules, an application for extension of time pursuant to Rule 6.2 of these Rules, or a notice of Presentation or waiver of oral argument pursuant to Rule 16.2(a) of these Rules. An original and eleven copies of all other papers shall be submitted for filing to the Clerk of the Panel. The Clerk of the Panel may require that additional copies also be submitted for filing.

(b) When, papers are submitted for filing, the Clerk of the Panel shall endorse thereon the date for filing.

(c) Copies of motions for transfer of an action or actions pursuant to 28 U.S.C. § 1407 shall be filed in each district court in which an action is pending that will be affected by the motion. Copies of a motion for remand pursuant to 28 U.S.C. § 1407 shall be filed in the Section 1407 transferee district court in which any action affected by the motion is pending.

(d) Papers requiring only an original may be faxed to the Panel office with prior approval of the Clerk of the Panel. No papers requiring multiple copies shall be accepted via fax.

(Added May 3, 1993, eff. July 1, 1993, and amended Sept. 1, 1998, eff. Nov. 2, 1998.)

Rule 5.2. Service of Papers Filed

(a) All papers filed with the Clerk of the Panel shall be accompanied by proof of previous or simultaneous service on all other parties in all actions involved in the litigation. Service and Proof of service shall be made as provided in Rules 5 and 6 of the Federal Rules of Civil Procedure. The proof of service shall indicate the name and complete address of each person served and shall indicate the party represented by each. If a party is not represented by counsel, the proof of service shall indicate the name of the party and the party's last known address. The proof of service shall indicate why any person named as a party in a constituent complaint was not served with the Section 1407 pleading. The original proof of service shall be filed with the Clerk of the Panel and copies thereof shall be sent to each person included within the proof of service. After the "Panel Service List" described in subsection (d) of this Rule has been received from the Clerk of the Panel, the "Panel Service List" shall be utilized for service of responses to motions and all other filings. In such instances, the "Panel Service List" shall be attached to the proof of service and shall be supplemented in the proof of service in the event of the presence of additional parties or subsequent corrections relating to any party, counsel or address already on the "Panel Service List."

(b) The proof of service pertaining to motions for transfer of actions pursuant to 28 U.S.C. § 1407 shall certify that copies of the motions have been mailed or otherwise delivered for filing to the clerk of each district court in which an action is pending that will be affected by the motion. The proof of service pertaining to a motion for remand pursuant to 28 U.S.C. § 1407 shall certify that a copy of the motion has been mailed or otherwise delivered for filing to the clerk of the Section 1407 transferee district court in which any action affected by the motion is pending.

(c) Within eleven days of filing of a motion to transfer, an order to show cause or a conditional transfer order, each party or designated attorney shall notify the Clerk of the Panel, in writing, of the name and address of the attorney designated to receive service of all pleadings, notices, orders and other papers relating to practice before the Judicial Panel on Multidistrict Litigation. Only one attorney shall be designated for each party. Any party not represented by counsel shall be served by mailing such pleadings to the party's last known address. Requests for an extension of time to file the designation of attorney shall not be granted except in extraordinary circumstances.

(d) In order to facilitate compliance with subsection (a) of this Rule, the Clerk of the Panel shall prepare and serve on all counsel and parties not represented by counsel, a "Panel Service List" containing the names and addresses of the designated attorneys and the party or parties they represent in the actions under consideration by the Panel and the names and addresses of the parties not represented by counsel in the actions under consideration by the Panel. After the "Panel Service List" has been received from the clerk of the Panel, notice of subsequent corrections relating to any party, counsel or address on the "Panel Service List" shall be served on all other parties in all actions involved in the litigation.

(e) If following transfer of any group of multidistrict litigation, the transferee district court appoints liaison counsel, this Rule shall be satisfied by serving each party in each affected action and all liaison counsel. Liaison counsel designated by the transferee district court shall receive copies of all Panel orders concerning their particular litigation and shall be responsible for distribution to the parties for whom he or she serves as liaison counsel.

(Added May 3, 1993, eff. July 1, 1993, and amended Sept. 1, 1998, eff. Nov. 2, 1998.)

Rule 6.2. Applications for Extensions of Time

Any application for an extension of time to file a pleading or perform an act required by these Rules must be in writing, must request a specific number of additional days and may be acted upon by the Clerk of the Panel. Such an application will be evaluated in relation to the impact on the Panel's calendar as well as on the basis of the reasons set forth in support of the application. Any party aggrieved by the Clerk of the Panel's action on such application may submit its objections to the Panel for consideration. Absent exceptional circumstances, no extensions of time shall be granted to file a notice of opposition to either a conditional transfer order or a conditional remand order. All applications for extensions of time shall be filed and served in conformity with Rules 5.12, 5.2 and 7.1 of these Rules.

(Added May 3, 1993, eff. July 1, 1993, and amended Sept. 1, 1998, eff. Nov. 2, 1998.)

Rule 7.1. Form of Papers Filed

(a) Averments in any motion seeking action by the Panel shall be made in numbered paragraphs, each of which shall be limited, as far as practicable, to a statement of a single factual averment.

(b) Responses to averments in motions shall be made in numbered paragraphs, each of which shall correspond to the number of the paragraph of the motion to which the responsive paragraph is directed. Each responsive paragraph shall admit or deny wholly or in part he averment of the motion, and shall contain the respondent's version of the subject matter when the averment or the motion is not wholly admitted.

(c) Each pleading filed shall be:

(i) flat and unfolded;

(ii) plainly written, typed in double space, printed or prepared by means of a duplicating process, without erasures or interlineations which materially deface it;

(iii) on opaque, unglazed, white paper (not onionskin);

(iv) approximately 8–1/2 x 11 inches in size; and

(v) fastened at the top-left corner without side binding or front or back covers.

(d) The heading on the first page of each pleading shall, commence not less than three inches from the top of the page. Each pleading shall bear the heading "Before the Judicial Panel on Multidistrict Litigation," the identification "MDL Docket No. ____" and the descriptive title designated by the Panel for the litigation involved. If the Panel has not yet designated a title, an appropriate descriptive title shall be used.

(e) The final page of each pleading shall contain the name, address and telephone number of the attorney or party in active charge of the case.

(f) Except with the approval of the Panel, each brief submitted for filing with the Panel shall be limited to twenty pages, exclusive of exhibits. Absent exceptional circumstances, motions to exceed page limits shall not be granted.

(g) Exhibits exceeding a cumulative total of 50 pages shall be fastened separately from the accompanying pleading.

(h) Proposed Panel orders shall not be submitted with papers for filing.

(Added May 3, 1993, eff. July 1, 1993, and amended Sept. 1, 1998, eff. Nov. 2, 1998.)

Rule 7.2. Motion Practice

(a) All requests for action by the Panel under 28 U.S.C. § 1407 shall be made by written motion. Every motion shall be accompanied by:

(i) a brief in support thereof in which the background of the litigation and factual and legal contentions of the movant shall be concisely stated in separate portions of the brief with citation of applicable authorities; and

(ii) a schedule giving

(A) the complete name of each action involved, not shortened by the use of references such as "et al." or "etc.";

(B) the district court, and division in which each action is pending;

(C) the civil action number of each action; and

(D) the name of the judge assigned each action, if known.

(b) The Clerk of the Panel shall notify recipients of a motion of the filing date, caption, MDL docket number, briefing schedule and pertinent Panel policies.

(c) Within twenty days after filing of a motion, all other parties shall file a response thereto. Failure of a party to respond to a motion shall be treated as that party's acquiescence to the action requested in the motion.

(d) The movant may, within five days after the lapse of the time period for filing responsive briefs, file a single brief in reply to any opposition.

(e) Motions, their accompaniments, responses, and replies shall also be governed by Rules 5.12, 5.2 and 7.1 of these Rules.

(f) With respect to any action that is the subject of panel consideration, counsel shall promptly notify the Clerk of the panel of any development that would partially or completely moot the matter before the Panel.

(g) A joinder in a motion shall not add any action to the previous motion.

(h) Once a motion is filed, any responsive pleading that purports to be a "motion" in the docket shall be filed by the Clerk of the Panel as a response unless the "Motion" adds an action. The Clerk of the Panel, upon designating such a pleading as a motion, shall acknowledge that designation by the distribution of a briefing schedule to all parties in the docket. Response time resulting from an additional motion shall ordinarily be extended only to those parties directly affected by the additional motion. An accelerated briefing schedule for the additional motion may be set by the Clerk of the Panel to conform with the hearing schedule established by the Chairman.

(Added May 3, 1993, eff. July 1, 1993, and amended Sept. 1, 1998, eff. Nov. 2, 1998.)

Rule 7.3. Show Cause Orders

(a) When transfer of multidistrict litigation is being considered on the initiative of the Panel pursuant to 28 U.S.C. § 1407(c)(i), an order shall be filed by the Clerk of the Panel directing the parties to show cause why the action or actions should not be transferred for coordinated or consolidated pretrial proceedings. Any party or counsel in such actions shall promptly notify the Clerk of the Panel of any other federal district court actions related to the litigation encompassed by the show cause order. Such notification shall be made for additional actions pending at the time of the issuance of the show cause order and whenever new actions are filed.

(b) Any party may file a response to the show cause order within twenty days of the filing of said order unless otherwise provided for in the order. Failure of a party to respond to a show cause order shall be treated as that party's acquiescence to the panel action contemplated in the order.

(c) Within five days after the lapse of the time period for filing a response, any party may file a reply limited to new matters.

(d) Responses and replies shall be filed and served in conformity with Rules 5.12, 5.2 and 7.1 of these Rules.

(e) With respect to any action that is the subject of Panel consideration, counsel shall promptly notify the Clerk of the Panel of any development that would partially or completely moot the matter before the Panel.

(Added May 3, 1993, eff. July 1, 1993, and amended Sept. 1, 1998, eff. Nov. 2, 1998.)

Rule 7.4. Conditional Transfer Orders for "Tag–Along Actions"

(a) Upon learning of the pendency of a potential "tag-along action," as defined in Rule 1.1 of these Rules, an order may be entered by the Clerk of the Panel transferring that action to the previously designated transferee district court on the basis of the prior hearing or hearings and for the reasons expressed in previous opinions and orders of the Panel in the litigation. The Clerk of the Panel shall serve this order on each party to the litigation but, in order to afford all parties the opportunity to oppose transfer, shall not send the order to the clerk, of the transferee district court for fifteen days from the entry thereof.

(b) Parties to an action subject to a conditional transfer order shall notify the Clerk of the Panel within the fifteen-day period if that action is no longer pending in its transferor district court.

(c) Any party opposing the transfer shall file a notice of opposition with the Clerk of The Panel within the fifteen-day period. If a notice of opposition is received by the Clerk of the Panel within this fifteen-day period, the Clerk of the Panel shall not transmit said order to the clerk of the transferee district court until further order of the Panel. The Clerk of the panel notify the parties of the briefing schedule.

(d) Within fifteen days of the filing of its notice of opposition, the party opposing transfer shall file a motion to vacate the conditional transfer order and brief in support thereof. The Clerk of the Panel shall set the motion for hearing at the next appropriate session of Panel. Failure to file and serve a motion and brief shall be treated as withdrawal of the opposition and the Clerk of the Panel shall forthwith transmit the order to the clerk of the transferee district court.

(e) Conditional transfer orders do not become effective unless and until they are filed with the clerk of the transferee district court.

(f) Notices of opposition and motions to vacate such orders of the Panel and responses thereto shall be governed by Rules 5.12, 5.2, 7.1 and 7.2 of these Rules.

(Added May 3, 1993, eff. July 1, 1993, and amended Sept. 1, 1998, eff. Nov. 2, 1998.)

Rule 7.5. Miscellaneous Provisions Concerning "Tag–Along Actions"

(a) Potential "tag-along actions" filed in the transferee district require no action on the part of the Panel and requests for assignment of such actions to the Section 1407 transferee judge should be made in accordance with local rules for the assignment of related actions.

(b) Upon learning of the pendency of a potential "tag-along action" and having reasonable anticipation of opposition to transfer of that action, the Panel may direct the Clerk of the Panel to file a show cause order, in accordance with Rule 7.3 of these Rules, instead of a conditional transfer order.

(c) Failure to serve one or more of the defendants in a potential "tag-along action" with the complaint and summons as required by Rule 4 of the Federal Rules of Civil procedure does not preclude transfer of such action under Section 1407. Such failure, however, may be submitted by such a defendant as a basis for opposing the proposed transfer if prejudice can be shown. The inability of the Clerk of the Panel to serve a conditional transfer order on all plaintiffs or defendants or their counsel shall not render the transfer of the action void but can be submitted by such a party as a basis for moving to remand as to such party if prejudice can be shown.

(d) A civil action apparently involving common questions of fact with actions under consideration by the Panel for transfer under Section 1407, which was filed or came to the attention of the Panel either after the initial hearing before it or too late to be included in the initial hearing, will be treated by the Panel as a potential "tag-along action.

(e) Any party or counsel in actions previously transferred under Section 1407 or under consideration by the Panel for transfer under Section 1407 shall promptly notify the Clerk of the Panel of any potential "tag-along actions" in which that party is also named or in which that counsel appears.

(Added May 3, 1993, eff. July 1, 1993, and amended Sept. 1, 1998, eff. Nov. 2, 1998.)

Rule 7.6. Termination and Remand

In the absence of unusual circumstances—

(a) Actions terminated in the transferee district court by valid judgment, including but not limited to summary judgment, judgment of dismissal and judgment upon stipulation, shall not be remanded by the Panel and shall be dismissed by the transferee district court. The clerk of the transferee district court shall send a copy of the order terminating the action to the Clerk of the Panel but shall retain the original files and records unless otherwise directed by the transferee judge or by the Panel.

(b) Each action transferred only for coordinated or consolidated pretrial proceedings that has not been terminated in the transferee district court shall be remanded by the Panel to the transferor district for trial. Actions that were originally filed in the transferee district require no action by the Panel to be reassigned to another Judge in the transferee district at the conclusion of the coordinated or consolidated pretrial proceedings affecting those actions.

(c) The Panel shall consider remand of each transferred action or any separable claim, cross-claim, counterclaim, or third-party claim at or before the conclusion of coordinated or consolidated pretrial proceedings on

(i) motion of any party,

(ii) suggestion of the transferee district court, or

(iii) the Panel's own initiative, by entry of an order to show cause, a conditional remand order or other appropriate order.

(d) The Panel is reluctant to order remand absent a suggestion of remand from the transferee district court. If remand is sought by motion of a party, the motion shall be accompanied by:

(i) an affidavit reciting

(A) whether the movant has requested a suggestion of remand from the transferee district court, how the court responded to any request, and, if no such request was made, why;

(B) whether all common discovery and other pretrial proceedings have been completed in the action sought to be remanded, and if not, what remains to be done; and

(C) whether all orders of the transferee district court have been satisfactorily complied with, and if not, what remains to be done; and

(ii) a copy of the transferee district court's final pretrial order, where such order has been entered.

Motions to remand and responses thereto shall be governed by Rules 5.12, 5.2, 7.1 and 7.2 of these Rules.

(e) When an Order to show cause why an action or actions should not be remanded is entered pursuant to subsection (c), paragraph (iii) of this Rule, any party may file a response within twenty days of the filing of said order unless otherwise provided for in the order. Within five days of filing of a party's response, any party may file a reply brief limited to new matters. Failure of a party to respond to a show cause order regarding remand shall be treated as that party's acquiescence to the remand. Responses and replies shall be filed and served in conformity with Rules 5.12, 5.2 and 7.1 of these Rules.

(f) Conditional Remand Orders.

(i) When the Panel has been advised by the transferee district judge, or otherwise has reason to believe, that pretrial proceedings in the litigation assigned to the transferee district judge are concluded or that remand of an action or actions is otherwise appropriate, an order may be entered by the Clerk of the Panel remanding the action or actions to the transferor district court. The Clerk of the Panel shall serve this order on each party to the litigation but, in order to afford all parties the opportunity to oppose remand, shall not send the order to the clerk of the transferee district court for fifteen days from the entry thereof.

(ii) Any party opposing the remand shall file a notice Of opposition with the Clerk of the Panel within the fifteen-day period. If a notice of opposition is received by the Clerk of the Panel within this fifteen-day period, the Clerk of the Panel shall not transmit said order to the clerk of the transferee district court until further order of the Panel. The Clerk of the Panel shall notify the parties of the briefing schedule.

(iii) Within fifteen days of the filing of its notice of opposition, the party opposing remand shall file a motion to vacate the conditional remand order and brief in support thereof. The Clerk of the Panel shall set the motion for hearing at the next appropriate session of the Panel. Failure to file and serve a motion and brief shall be treated as a withdrawal of the opposition and the Clerk of the Panel shall forthwith transmit the order to the clerk of the transferee district court.

(iv) Conditional remand orders do not become effective unless and until they are filed with the clerk of the transferee district court.

(v) Notices of opposition and motions to vacate such orders of the panel and responses thereto shall be governed by Rules 5.12, 5.2, 7.1 and 7.2 of these Rules.

(g) Upon receipt of an order to remand from the Clerk of the Panel, the parties shall furnish forthwith to the transferee district clerk a stipulation or designation of the contents of the record or pan thereof to be remanded and furnish the transferee district clerk all necessary copies of any pleading or other matter filed so as to enable the transferee district clerk to comply with the order of remand.

(Added May 3, 1993, eff. July 1, 1993, and amended Sept. 1, 1998, eff. Nov. 2, 1998.)

Rule 16.1. Hearings

(a) Hearings shall be held as ordered by the Panel. The Panel shall convene whenever and wherever desirable or necessary in the judgment of the Chairman. The Chairman shall determine which matters shall be set for hearing at each session and the Clerk of the Panel shall give notice to counsel for all parties involved in the litigation of the time, place and subject matter of such hearing.

(b) No transfer or remand determination regarding any action pending in district court shall be made by the Panel when any party timely opposes such transfer or remand unless a hearing has been held or unless the matter has been submitted on the briefs in accordance with Rule 16.2 of these Rules. Unless otherwise ordered by the Panel, all other matters before the Panel, such as a motion for reconsideration, shall be considered and determined upon the basis of the papers filed.

(c) Except for leave of the Panel on a showing of good cause, only those parties to actions scheduled for hearing who have filed a motion or written response to a motion or order shall be permitted to appear before the Panel and present oral argument.

(d) Counsel for those supporting transfer or remand under Section 1407 and counsel for those opposing such transfer or remand are to confer separately prior to the hearing for the purpose of organizing their arguments and selecting representatives to present all views without duplication.

(e) Unless otherwise ordered by the Panel, a maximum of thirty minutes shall be allotted for argument in each new group of actions being considered for Section 1407 treatment and a maximum of twenty minutes shall be allotted for arguments in all other matters. The time shall be divided equally among those with varying viewpoints. Counsel for the moving party or parties shall generally be heard first.

(f) So far as practicable and consistent with the purposes of Section 1407, the offering of oral testimony before the Panel shall be avoided. Accordingly, oral testimony shall not be received except upon notice, motion and order of the Panel expressly providing for it.

(g) After an action or group of actions has been set for hearing, the hearing may be continued only by order of the Panel on good cause shown.

(Added May 3, 1998, eff. July 1, 1993, and amended Sept. 1, 1998, eff. Nov. 2, 1998.)

Rule 16.2. Notice of Presentation or Waiver of Oral Argument, and Matters Submitted on the Briefs

(a) At such, time in advance of the date of the hearing as required by the Clerk of the Panel in the notice of hearing, counsel shall notify the Clerk of the Panel in writing of one of the following: (1) counsel will waive oral argument, if all other counsel in the matter set for hearing waive oral argument; (2) counsel will present oral argument, regardless of whether any other counsel in the matter set for hearing presents oral argument; or (3) counsel waives oral argument. All notices of presentation or waiver of oral argument shall be filed and served in conformity with Rules 5.12 and 5.2 of these Rules.

(b) If all parties to a matter set for hearing waive oral argument, the matter shall be submitted for decision by the Panel on the basis of the papers filed. If a party is not present when a matter to be heard is called at the hearing, the matter shall not be rescheduled and that party's position shall be treated as submitted for decision by the Panel on the basis of the papers filed, unless otherwise ordered by the Panel.

(Added May 3, 1993, eff. July 1, 1993, and amended Sept. 1, 1998, eff. Nov. 2, 1998.)

II. RULES FOR MULTICIRCUIT PETITIONS FOR REVIEW UNDER 28 U.S.C. § 2112(a)(3)

Rule 17.1. Random Selection

(a) Upon filing a notice of multicircuit petitions for review, the Clerk of the Panel or designated deputy shall randomly select a circuit court of appeals from a drum containing an entry for each circuit wherein a constituent petition for review is pending. Multiple petitions for review pending in a single circuit shall be allotted only a single entry in the drum. This random selection shall be witnessed by the Clerk of the Panel or a designated deputy other than the random selector. Thereafter, an order on behalf of the Panel shall be issued, signed by the random selector and the witness,

(i) consolidating the petitions for review in the court of appeals for the circuit that was randomly selected; and

(ii) designating that circuit as the one in winch the record is to be filed pursuant to Rules 16 and 17 of the Federal Rules of Appellate Procedure.

(b) A consolidation of petitions for review shall be effective when the Panel's consolidation order is filed at the offices of the Panel by the Clerk of the Panel.

(Added May 3, 1993, eff. July 1, 1993, and amended Sept. 1, 1998, eff. Nov. 2, 1998.)

Rule 25.1. Filing of Notices

(a) An original of a notice of multicircuit petitions for review pursuant to 28 U.S.C. § 2112(a)(3) shall be submitted for filing to the Clerk of the Panel by the affected agency, board, commission or officer. The term "agency" as used in Section II of these Rules shall include agency, board, commission or officer.

(b) All notices of multicircuit petitions for review submitted by the affected agency for filing with the Clerk of the Panel shall embrace exclusively petitions for review filed in the courts of appeals within ten days after issuance of an agency order and received by the affected agency from the petitioners within that ten-day period.

(c) When a notice of multicircuit petitions for review is submitted for filing to the Clerk of the Panel, the Clerk of the Panel shall file the notice and endorse thereon the date of filing.

(d) Copies of notices of multicircuit petitions for review shall be filed by the affected agency with the clerk of each circuit court of appeals in which a petition for review is pending that is included in the notice.

(Added May 3, 1993, eff. July 1, 1993, and amended Sept. 1, 1998, eff. Nov. 2, 1998.)

Rule 25.2. Accompaniments to Notices

(a) All notices of multicircuit petitions for review shall be accompanied by:

(i) a copy of each involved petition for review as the petition for review is defined in 28 U.S.C. § 2112(a)(2); and

(ii) a schedule giving

(A) the date of the relevant agency order;

(B) the case name of each petition for review involved;

(C) the circuit court of appeals in which each petition for review is pending;

(D) the appellate docket number of each petition for review;

(E) the date of filing by the court of appeals of each petition for review; and

(F) the date of receipt by the agency of each petition for review.

(b) The schedule in Subsection (a)(ii) of this Rule shall also be governed by Rule 25.1, 25.3 and 25.4(a) of these Rules.

(Added May 3, 1993, eff. July 1, 1993, and amended Sept. 1, 1998, eff. Nov. 2, 1998.)

Rule 25.3. Service of Notices

(a) All notices of multicircuit petitions for review shall be accompanied by proof of service by the affected agency on all other parties in all petitions for review included in the notice. Service and proof of service shall be made as provided in Rule 25 of the Federal Rules of Appellate Procedure. The proof of service shall state the name and address of each person served and shall indicate the party represented by each. If a party is not represented by counsel, the proof of service shall indicate the name of the party and his or her last known address. The original proof of service shall be submitted by the affected agency for filing with the Clerk of the Panel and copies thereof shall be sent by the affected agency to each person included within the proof of service.

(b) The proof of service pertaining to notices of multicircuit petitions for review shall certify that copies of the notices have been mailed or otherwise delivered by the affected agency for filing to the clerk of each circuit court of appeals in which a petition for review is pending that is included in the notice.

(Added May 3, 1993, eff. July 1, 1993, and amended Sept. 1, 1998, eff. Nov. 2, 1998.)

Rule 25.4. Form of Notices

(a) Each notice of multicircuit petitions for review shall be

(i) flat and unfolded;

(ii) plainly written, typed in double space, printed or prepared by means of a duplicating process, without erasures or interlineations which materially deface it;

(iii) on opaque, unglazed white paper (not onionskin);

(iv) approximately 8–1/2 x 11 inches in size; and

(v) fastened at the top-left corner without side binding or front or back covers.

(b) The heading on the first page of each notice of multicircuit petitions for review shall commence not less that three inches from the top of the page. Each notice shall bear the heading "Notice to the Judicial Panel on Multidistrict Litigation of Multicircuit Petitions for Review," followed by a brief caption identifying the involved agency, the relevant agency order, and the date of the order.

(c) The final page of each notice of multicircuit petitions for review shall contain the name, address and telephone number of the individual or individuals who submitted the notice on behalf of the agency.

(Added May 3, 1993, eff. July 1, 1993, and amended Sept. 1, 1998, eff. Nov. 2, 1998.)

Rule 25.5. Service of Panel Consolidation Order

(a) The Clerk of the Panel shall serve the Panel's consolidation order on the affected agency through the individual or individuals, as identified in Rule 25.4(c) of these Rules, who submitted the notice of multicircuit petitions for review on behalf of the agency.

(b) That individual or individuals, or anyone else designated by the agency, shall promptly serve the Panel's consolidation order on all other parties in all petitions for review included in the Panel's consolidation order, and shall promptly submit a proof of that service to the Clerk of the Panel. Service and proof of that service shall also be governed by Rule 25.3 of these Rules.

(c) The Clerk of the Panel shall serve the Panel's consolidation order on the clerks of all circuit courts of appeals that were among the candidates for the Panel's random selection.

(Added May 3, 1993, eff. July 1, 1993, and amended Sept. 1, 1998, eff. Nov. 2, 1998.)

RULES GOVERNING SECTION 2254 CASES IN THE UNITED STATES DISTRICT COURTS

Effective February 1, 1977
Amendments received to January 4, 1999

Rule
1. Scope of Rules.
2. Petition.
3. Filing Petition.
4. Preliminary Consideration by Judge.
5. Answer; Contents.
6. Discovery.
7. Expansion of Record.
8. Evidentiary Hearing.
9. Delayed or Successive Petitions.
10. Powers of Magistrates.
11. Federal Rules of Civil Procedure; Extent of Applicability.

APPENDIX OF FORMS

Model form for use in applications for habeas corpus under 28 U.S.C. § 2254.
Model form for use in 28 U.S.C. § 2254 cases involving a Rule 9 issue.

ORDERS OF THE SUPREME COURT OF THE UNITED STATES ADOPTING AND AMENDING RULES GOVERNING SECTION 2254 PROCEEDINGS IN THE UNITED STATES DISTRICT COURTS

ORDER OF APRIL 26, 1976

1. That the rules and forms governing proceedings in the United States District Courts under Section 2254 and Section 2255 of Title 28, United States Code, as approved by the Judicial Conference of the United States be, and they hereby are, prescribed pursuant to Section 2072 of Title 28, United States Code and Sections 3771 and 3772 of Title 18, United States Code.

2. That the aforementioned rules and forms shall take effect August 1, 1976, and shall be applicable to all proceedings then pending except to the extent that in the opinion of the court their application in a particular proceeding would not be feasible or would work injustice.

3. That THE CHIEF JUSTICE be, and he hereby is, authorized to transmit the aforementioned rules and forms governing Section 2254 and Section 2255 proceedings to the Congress in accordance with the provisions of Section 2072 of Title 28 and Sections 3771 and 3772 of Title 18, United States Code.

CONGRESSIONAL ACTION ON PROPOSED RULES AND FORMS GOVERNING PROCEEDING UNDER 28 U.S.C. §§ 2254 AND 2255

Pub.L. 94–349, § 2, July 8, 1976, 90 Stat. 822, provided: "That, notwithstanding the provisions of section 2072 of title 28 of the United States Code, the rules and forms governing section 2254 cases in the United States district courts and the rules and forms governing section 2255 proceedings in the United States district courts which are embraced by the order entered by the United States Supreme Court on April 26, 1976, and which were transmitted to the Congress on or about April 26, 1976, shall not take effect until thirty days after the adjournment sine die of the 94th Congress, or until and to the extent approved by Act of Congress, whichever is earlier."

Pub.L. 94–426, § 1, Sept. 28, 1976, 90 Stat. 1334, provided: "That the rules governing section 2254 cases in the United States district courts and the rules governing section 2255 proceedings for the United States Supreme Court, which were delayed by the Act entitled 'An Act to delay the effective date of certain proposed amendments to the Federal Rules of Criminal Procedure and certain other rules promulgated by the United States Supreme Court' (Public Law 94–349), are approved with the amendments set forth in section 2 of this Act and shall take effect as so amended, with respect to petitions under section 2254 and motions under section 2255 of title 28 of the United States Code filed on or after February 1, 1977."

ORDER OF APRIL 30, 1979

1. That Rule 10 of the Rules Governing Proceedings in the United States District Courts on application under Section 2254 of Title 28, United States Code, be, and hereby is, amended to read as follows:

[See amendment made thereby under Rule 10, post.]

2. That Rules 10 and 11 of the Rules Governing Proceedings in the United States District Courts on a motion under Section 2255 of Title 28, United States Code, be, and they hereby are, amended to read as follows:

[See amendments made hereby under Rules 10 and 11 set out following section 2255.]

3. That the foregoing amendments to the Rules Governing Proceedings in the United States District Courts under Section 2254 and Section 2255 of Title 28, United States Code, shall take effect on August 1, 1979, and shall be applicable to all proceedings then pending except to the extent that in the opinion of the court their application in a particular proceeding would not be feasible or would work injustice.

4. That THE CHIEF JUSTICE be, and he hereby is, authorized to transmit the aforementioned amendments to the Rules Governing Section 2254 and Section 2255 Proceedings to the Congress in accordance with the provisions of

Section 2072 of Title 28, United States Code, and Sections 3771 and 3772 of Title 18, United States Code.

ORDER OF APRIL 28, 1982

1. That the rules and forms governing proceedings in the United States district courts under Section 2254 and Section 2255 of Title 28, United States Code, be, and they hereby are, amended by including therein an amendment to Rule 2(c) of the rules for Section 2254 cases, an amendment to Rule 2(b) of the rules for Section 2255 proceedings, and amendments to the model forms for use in applications under Section 2254 and motions under Section 2255, as hereinafter set forth:

[See amendments made thereby under respective rules and forms post and following section 2255.]

2. That the aforementioned amendments shall take effect August 1, 1982, and shall be applicable to all proceedings thereafter commenced and, insofar as just and practicable, all proceedings then pending.

3. That THE CHIEF JUSTICE be, and he hereby is, authorized to transmit the aforementioned amendments to the Congress in accordance with Section 2072 of Title 28 and Sections 3771 and 3772 of Title 18, United States Code.

HISTORICAL NOTES

Effective Date of Rules; 1976 Act

Rules governing section 2254 cases, and the amendments thereto by Pub.L. 94–426, Sept. 28, 1976, 90 Stat. 1334, effective with respect to petitions under section 2254 of this title and motions under section 2255 of this title filed on or after Feb. 1, 1977, see section 1 of Pub.L. 94–426, set out as a note under section 2254 of this title.

Rule 1. Scope of Rules

(a) Applicable to cases involving custody pursuant to a judgment of a state court. These rules govern the procedure in the United States district courts on applications under 28 U.S.C. § 2254:

(1) by a person in custody pursuant to a judgment of a state court, for a determination that such custody is in violation of the Constitution, laws, or treaties of the United States; and

(2) by a person in custody pursuant to a judgment of either a state or a federal court, who makes application for a determination that custody to which he may be subject in the future under a judgment of a state court will be in violation of the Constitution, laws, or treaties of the United States.

(b) Other situations. In applications for habeas corpus in cases not covered by subdivision (a), these rules may be applied at the discretion of the United States district court.

ADVISORY COMMITTEE NOTES

1976 Adoption

Rule 1 provides that the habeas corpus rules are applicable to petitions by persons in custody pursuant to a judgment of a state court. See *Preiser v. Rodriguez,* 411 U.S. 475, 484 (1973). Whether the rules ought to apply to other situations (*e.g.*, person in active military service, *Glazier v. Hackel,* 440 F.2d 592 (9th Cir. 1971); or a reservist called to active duty but not reported, *Hammond v. Lenfest,* 398 F.2d 705 (2d Cir. 1968)) is left to the discretion of the court.

The basic scope of habeas corpus is prescribed by statute. 28 U.S.C. § 2241(c) provides that the "writ of habeas corpus shall not extend to a prisoner unless * * * (h)e is *in custody* in violation of the Constitution." 28 U.S.C. § 2254 deals specifically with state custody, providing that habeas corpus shall apply only "in behalf of a person in custody pursuant to a judgment of a state court * * *."

In *Preiser v. Rodriguez, supra,* the court said: "It is clear . . . that the essence of habeas corpus is an attack by a person in custody upon the legality of that custody, and that the traditional function of the writ is to secure release from illegal custody." 411 U.S. at 484.

Initially the Supreme Court held that habeas corpus was appropriate only in those situations in which petitioner's claim would, if upheld, result in an immediate release from a present custody. *McNally v. Hill,* 293 U.S. 131 (1934). This was changed in *Peyton v. Rowe,* 391 U.S. 54 (1968), in which the court held that habeas corpus was a proper way to attack a consecutive sentence to be served in the future, expressing the view that consecutive sentences resulted in present custody under both judgments, not merely the one imposing the first sentence. This view was expanded in *Carafas v. LaVallee,* 391 U.S. 234 (1968), to recognize the propriety of habeas corpus in a case in which petitioner was in custody when the petition had been originally filed but had since been unconditionally released from custody.

See also *Preiser v. Rodriguez,* 411 U.S. at 486 et seq.

Since *Carafas,* custody has been construed more liberally by the courts so as to make a § 2255 motion or habeas corpus petition proper in more situations. "In custody" now includes a person who is: on parole, *Jones v. Cunningham,* 371 U.S. 236 (1963); at large on his own recognizance but subject to several conditions pending execution of his sentence, *Hensley v. Municipal Court,* 411 U.S. 345 (1973); or released on bail after conviction pending final disposition of his case, *Lefkowitz v. Newsome,* 95 S.Ct. 886 (1975). See also *United States v. Re,* 372 F.2d 641 (2d Cir.), cert. denied, 388 U.S. 912 (1967) (on probation); *Walker v. North Carolina,* 262 F.Supp. 102 (W.D.N.C.1966), aff'd per curiam, 372 F.2d 129 (4th Cir.), cert. denied, 388 U.S. 917 (1967) (recipient of a conditionally suspended sentence); *Burris v. Ryan,* 397 F.2d 553 (7th Cir. 1968); *Marden v. Purdy,* 409 F.2d 784 (5th Cir. 1969) (free on bail); *United States ex rel. Smith v. Dibella,* 314 F.Supp. 446 (D.Conn.1970) (release on own recognizance); *Choung v. California,* 320 F.Supp. 625 (E.D.Cal.1970) (federal stay of state court sentence); *United States ex rel. Meadows v. New York,* 426 F.2d 1176 (2d Cir. 1970), cert. denied, 401 U.S. 941 (1971) (subject to parole detainer warrant); *Capler v. City of Greenville,* 422 F.2d 299 (5th Cir. 1970) (released on appeal bond); *Glover v. North Carolina,* 301 F.Supp. 364 (E.D.N.C.1969) (sentence served, but as convicted felon disqualified from engaging in several activities).

The courts are not unanimous in dealing with the above situations, and the boundaries of custody remain somewhat unclear. In *Morgan v. Thomas*, 321 F.Supp. 565 (S.D.Miss. 1970), the court noted:

> It is axiomatic that actual physical custody or restraint is not required to confer habeas jurisdiction. Rather, the term is synonymous with restraint of liberty. The real question is how much restraint of one's liberty is necessary before the right to apply for the writ comes into play. * * *
>
> It is clear however, that something more than moral restraint is necessary to make a case for habeas corpus.

321 F.Supp. at 573

Hammond v. Lenfest, 398 F.2d 705 (2d Cir. 1968), reviewed prior "custody" doctrine and reaffirmed a generalized flexible approach to the issue. In speaking about 28 U.S.C. § 2241, the first section in the habeas corpus statutes, the court said:

> While the language of the Act indicates that a writ of habeas corpus is appropriate only when a petitioner is "in custody" * * * the Act "does not attempt to mark the boundaries of 'custody' nor in any way other than by use of that word attempt to limit the situations in which the writ can be used." * * * And, recent Supreme Court decisions have made clear that "[i]t [habeas corpus] is not now and never has been a static, narrow, formalistic remedy; its scope has grown to achieve its grand purpose—the protection of individuals against erosion of their right to be free from wrongful restraints upon their liberty." * * * "[B]esides physical imprisonment, there are other restraints on a man's liberty, restraints not shared by the public generally, which have been thought sufficient in the English-speaking world to support the issuance of habeas corpus."

398 F.2d at 710–711

There is, as of now, no final list of the situations which are appropriate for habeas corpus relief. It is not the intent of these rules or notes to define or limit "custody."

It is, however, the view of the Advisory Committee that claims of improper conditions of custody or confinement (not related to the propriety of the custody itself), can better be handled by other means such as 42 U.S.C. § 1983 and other related statutes. In *Wilwording v. Swanson*, 404 U.S. 249 (1971), the court treated a habeas corpus petition by a state prisoner challenging the conditions of confinement as a claim for relief under 42 U.S.C. § 1983, the Civil Rights Act. Compare *Johnson v. Avery*, 393 U.S. 483 (1969).

The distinction between duration of confinement and conditions of confinement may be difficult to draw. Compare *Preiser v. Rodriguez*, 411 U.S. 475 (1973), with *Clutchette v. Procunier*, 497 F.2d 809 (9th Cir. 1974), modified, 510 F.2d 613 (1975).

Rule 2. Petition

(a) Applicants in present custody. If the applicant is presently in custody pursuant to the state judgment in question, the application shall be in the form of a petition for a writ of habeas corpus in which the state officer having custody of the applicant shall be named as respondent.

(b) Applicants subject to future custody. If the applicant is not presently in custody pursuant to the state judgment against which he seeks relief but may be subject to such custody in the future, the application shall be in the form of a petition for a writ of habeas corpus with an added prayer for appropriate relief against the judgment which he seeks to attack. In such a case the officer having present custody of the applicant and the attorney general of the state in which the judgment which he seeks to attack was entered shall each be named as respondents.

(c) Form of Petition. The petition shall be in substantially the form annexed to these rules, except that any district court may by local rule require that petitions filed with it shall be in a form prescribed by the local rule. Blank petitions in the prescribed form shall be made available without charge by the clerk of the district court to applicants upon their request. It shall specify all the grounds for relief which are available to the petitioner and of which he has or by the exercise of reasonable diligence should have knowledge and shall set forth in summary form the facts supporting each of the grounds thus specified. It shall also state the relief requested. The petition shall be typewritten or legibly handwritten and shall be signed under penalty of perjury by the petitioner.

(d) Petition to be directed to judgments of one court only. A petition shall be limited to the assertion of a claim for relief against the judgment or judgments of a single state court (sitting in a county or other appropriate political subdivision). If a petitioner desires to attack the validity of the judgments of two or more state courts under which he is in custody or may be subject to future custody, as the case may be, he shall do so by separate petitions.

(e) Return of insufficient petition. If a petition received by the clerk of a district court does not substantially comply with the requirements of rule 2 or rule 3, it may be returned to the petitioner, if a judge of the court so directs, together with a statement of the reason for its return. The clerk shall retain a copy of the petition.

(As amended Pub.L. 94–426, § 2(1), (2), Sept. 28, 1976, 90 Stat. 1334; Apr. 28, 1982, eff. Aug. 1, 1982.)

ADVISORY COMMITTEE NOTES

1976 Adoption

Rule 2 describes the requirements of the actual petition, including matters relating to its form, contents, scope, and sufficiency. The rule provides more specific guidance for a petitioner and the court than 28 U.S.C. § 2242, after which it is patterned.

Subdivision (a) provides that an applicant challenging a state judgment, pursuant to which he is presently in custody, must make his application in the form of a petition for a writ of habeas corpus. It also requires that the state officer having custody of the applicant be named as respondent. This is consistent with 28 U.S.C. § 2242, which says in part, [Application for a writ of habeas corpus] shall allege * * * the name of the person who has custody over [the applicant] * * *." The proper person to be served in the usual case is either the warden of the institution in which the petitioner is incarcerated (*Sanders v. Bennett,* 148 F.2d 19 (D.C.Cir. 1945)) or the chief officer in charge of state penal institutions.

Subdivision (b) prescribes the procedure to be used for a petition challenging a judgment under which the petitioner will be subject to custody in the future. In this event the relief sought will usually not be released from present custody, but rather for a declaration that the judgment being attacked is invalid. Subdivision (b) thus provides for a prayer for "appropriate relief." It is also provided that the attorney general of the state of the judgment as well as the state officer having actual custody of the petitioner shall be named as respondents. This is appropriate because no one will have custody of the petitioner in the state of the judgment being attacked, and the habeas corpus action will usually be defended by the attorney general. The attorney general is in the best position to inform the court as to who the proper party respondent is. If it is not the attorney general, he can move for a substitution of party.

Since the concept of "custody" requisite to the consideration of a petition for habeas corpus has been enlarged significantly in recent years, it may be worthwhile to spell out the various situations which might arise and who should be named as respondent(s) for each situation.

(1) The applicant is in jail, prison, or other actual physical restraint due to the state action he is attacking. The named respondent shall be the state officer who has official custody of the petitioner (for example, the warden of the prison).

(2) The applicant is on probation or parole due to the state judgment he is attacking. The named respondents shall be the particular probation or parole officer responsible for supervising the applicant, and the official in charge of the parole or probation agency, or the state correctional agency, as appropriate.

(3) The applicant is in custody in any other manner differing from (1) and (2) above due to the effects of the state action he seeks relief from. The named respondent should be the attorney general of the state wherein such action was taken.

(4) The applicant is in jail, prison, or other actual physical restraint but is attacking a state action which will cause him to be kept in custody in the future rather than the government action under which he is presently confined. The named respondents shall be the state or federal officer who has official custody of him at the time the petition is filed and the attorney general of the state whose action subjects the petitioner to future custody.

(5) The applicant is in custody, although not physically restrained, and is attacking a state action which will result in his future custody rather than the government action out of which his present custody arises. The named respondent(s) shall be the attorney general of the state whose action subjects the petitioner to future custody, as well as the government officer who has present official custody of the petitioner if there is such an officer and his identity is ascertainable.

In any of the above situations the judge may require or allow the petitioner to join an additional or different party as a respondent if to do so would serve the ends of justice.

As seen in rule 1 and paragraphs (4) and (5) above, these rules contemplate that a petitioner currently in federal custody will be permitted to apply for habeas relief from a state restraint which is to go into effect in the future. There has been disagreement in the courts as to whether they have jurisdiction of the habeas application under these circumstances (compare *Piper v. United States,* 306 F.Supp. 1259 (D.Conn.1969), with *United States ex rel. Meadows v. New York,* 426 F.2d 1176 (2d Cir. 1970), cert. denied, 401 U.S. 941 (1971)). This rule seeks to make clear that they do have such jurisdiction.

Subdivision (c) provides that unless a district court requires otherwise by local rule, the petition must be in the form annexed to these rules. Having a standard prescribed form has several advantages. In the past, petitions have frequently contained mere conclusions of law, unsupported by any facts. Since it is the relationship of the facts to the claim asserted that is important, these petitions were obviously deficient. In addition, lengthy and often illegible petitions, arranged in no logical order, were submitted to judges who have had to spend hours deciphering them. For example, in *Passic v. Michigan,* 98 F.Supp. 1015, 1016 (E.D.Mich. 1951), the court dismissed a petition for habeas corpus, describing it as "two thousand pages of irrational, prolix and redundant pleadings * * *."

Administrative convenience, of benefit to both the court and the petitioner, results from the use of a prescribed form. Judge Hubert L. Will briefly described the experience with the use of a standard form in the Northern District of Illinois:

> Our own experience, though somewhat limited, has been quite satisfactory. * * *
>
> In addition, [petitions] almost always contain the necessary basic information * * *. Very rarely do we get the kind of hybrid federal-state habeas corpus petition with civil rights allegations thrown in which were not uncommon in the past. * * * [W]hen a real constitutional issue is raised it is quickly apparent * * *.

33 F.R.D. 363, 384

Approximately 65 to 70% of all districts have adopted forms or local rules which require answers to essentially the same questions as contained in the standard form annexed to these rules. All courts using forms have indicated the petitions are time-saving and more legible. The form is particularly helpful in getting information about whether there has been an exhaustion of state remedies or, at least, where that information can be obtained.

The requirement of a standard form benefits the petitioner as well. His assertions are more readily apparent, and a meritorious claim is more likely to be properly raised and supported. The inclusion in the form of the ten most frequently raised grounds in habeas corpus petitions is intended to encourage the applicant to raise all his asserted grounds in one petition. It may better enable him to recognize if an issue he seeks to raise is cognizable under habeas corpus and hopefully inform him of those issues as to which he must first exhaust his state remedies.

Some commentators have suggested that the use of forms is of little help because the questions usually are too general, amounting to little more than a restatement of the statute. They contend the blanks permit a prisoner to fill in the same ambiguous answers he would have offered without the aid of a form. See Comment, Developments in the Law—Federal Habeas Corpus, 83 Harv.L.Rev. 1038, 1177–1178 (1970). Certainly, as long as the statute requires factual pleading, the adequacy of a petition will continue to be affected largely by the petitioner's intelligence and the legal advice available to him. On balance, however, the use of forms has contributed enough to warrant mandating their use.

Giving the petitioner a list of often—raised grounds may, it is said, encourage perjury. See Comment, Developments in the Law—Federal Habeas Corpus, 83 Harv.L.Rev. 1038, 1178 (1970). Most inmates are aware of, or have access to, some common constitutional grounds for relief. Thus, the risk of perjury is not likely to be substantially increased and the benefit of the list for some inmates seems sufficient to outweigh any slight risk that perjury will increase. There is a penalty for perjury, and this would seem the most appropriate way to try to discourage it.

Legal assistance is increasingly available to inmates either through paraprofessional programs involving law students or special programs staffed by members of the bar. See Jacob and Sharma, Justice After Trial: Prisoners' Need for Legal Services in the Criminal-Correctional Process, 18 Kan.L.Rev. 493 (1970). In these situations, the prescribed form can be filled out more competently, and it does serve to ensure a degree of uniformity in the manner in which habeas corpus claims are presented.

Subdivision (c) directs the clerk of the district court to make available to applicants upon request, without charge, blank petitions in the prescribed form.

Subdivision (c) also requires that all available grounds for relief be presented in the petition, including those grounds of which, by the exercise of reasonable diligence, the petitioner should be aware. This is reinforced by rule 9(b), which allows dismissal of a second petition which fails to allege new grounds or, if new grounds are alleged, the judge finds an inexcusable failure to assert the ground in the prior petition.

Both subdivision (c) and the annexed form require a legibly handwritten or typewritten petition. As required by 28 U.S.C. § 2242, the petition must be signed and sworn to by the petitioner (or someone acting in his behalf).

Subdivision (d) provides that a single petition may assert a claim only against the judgment or judgments of a single state court (*i.e.*, a court of the same county or judicial district or circuit). This permits, but does not require, an attack in a single petition on judgments based upon separate indictments or on separate counts even though sentences were imposed on separate days by the same court. A claim against a judgment of a court of a different political subdivision must be raised by means of a separate petition.

Subdivision (e) allows the clerk to return an insufficient petition to the petitioner, and it must be returned if the clerk is so directed by a judge of the court. Any failure to comply with the requirements of rule 2 or 3 is grounds for insufficiency. In situations where there may be arguable noncompliance with another rule, such as rule 9, the judge, not the clerk, must make the decision. If the petition is returned it must be accompanied by a statement of the reason for its return. No petitioner should be left to speculate as to why or in what manner his petition failed to conform to these rules.

Subdivision (e) also provides that the clerk shall retain one copy of the insufficient petition. If the prisoner files another petition, the clerk will be in a better position to determine the sufficiency of the new petition. If the new petition is insufficient, comparison with the prior petition may indicate whether the prisoner has failed to understand the clerk's prior explanation for its insufficiency, so that the clerk can make another, hopefully successful, attempt at transmitting this information to the petitioner. If the petitioner insists that the original petition was in compliance with the rules, a copy of the original petition is available for the consideration of the judge. It is probably better practice to make a photocopy of a petition which can be corrected by the petitioner, thus saving the petitioner the task of completing an additional copy.

1982 Amendment

Subdivision (c). The amendment takes into account 28 U.S.C. § 1746, enacted after adoption of the § 2254 rules. Section 1746 provides that in lieu of an affidavit an unsworn statement may be given under penalty of perjury in substantially the following form if executed within the United States, its territories, possessions or commonwealths: "I declare (or certify, verify, or state) under penalty of perjury that the foregoing is true and correct. Executed on (date). (Signature)." The statute is "intended to encompass prisoner litigation," and the statutory alternative is especially appropriate in such cases because a notary might not be readily available. *Carter v. Clark*, 616 F.2d 228 (5th Cir. 1980). The § 2254 forms have been revised accordingly.

Rule 3. Filing Petition

(a) Place of filing; copies; filing fee. A petition shall be filed in the office of the clerk of the district court. It shall be accompanied by two conformed copies thereof. It shall also be accompanied by the filing fee prescribed by law unless the petitioner applies for and is given leave to prosecute the petition in forma pauperis. If the petitioner desires to prosecute the petition in forma pauperis, he shall file the affidavit required by 28 U.S.C. § 1915. In all such cases the petition shall also be accompanied by a certificate of the warden or other appropriate officer of the institution in which the petitioner is confined as to the amount of money or securities on deposit to the petitioner's credit in any account in the institution, which certificate may be considered by the court in acting upon his application for leave to proceed in forma pauperis.

(b) Filing and service. Upon receipt of the petition and the filing fee, or an order granting leave to the petitioner to proceed in forma pauperis, and having ascertained that the petition appears on its face to comply with rules 2 and 3, the clerk of the district court shall file the petition and enter it on the docket in his office. The filing of the petition shall not require the respondent to answer the petition or otherwise move with respect to it unless so ordered by the court.

ADVISORY COMMITTEE NOTES

1976 Adoption

Rule 3 sets out the procedures to be followed by the petitioner and the court in filing the petition. Some of its provisions are currently dealt with by local rule or practice, while others are innovations. Subdivision (a) specifies the petitioner's responsibilities. It requires that the petition, which must be accompanied by two conformed copies thereof, be filed in the office of the clerk of the district court. The petition must be accompanied by the filing fee prescribed by law (presently $5; see 28 U.S.C. § 1914(a)), unless leave to prosecute the petition in forma pauperis is applied for and granted. In the event the petitioner desires to prosecute the petition in forma pauperis, he must file the affidavit required by 28 U.S.C. § 1915, together with a certificate showing the amount of funds in his institutional account.

Requiring that the petition be filed in the office of the clerk of the district court provides an efficient and uniform system of filing habeas corpus petitions.

Subdivision (b) requires the clerk to file the petition. If the filing fee accompanies the petition, it may be filed immediately, and, if not, it is contemplated that prompt attention will be given to the request to proceed in forma pauperis. The court may delegate the issuance of the order to the clerk in those cases in which it is clear from the petition that there is full compliance with the requirements to proceed in forma pauperis.

Requiring the copies of the petition to be filed with the clerk will have an impact not only upon administrative matters, but upon more basic problems as well. In districts with more than one judge, a petitioner under present circumstances may send a petition to more than one judge. If no central filing system exists for each district, two judges may independently take different action on the same petition. Even if the action taken is consistent, there may be needless duplication of effort.

The requirement of an additional two copies of the form of the petition is a current practice in many courts. An efficient filing system requires one copy for use by the court (central file), one for the respondent (under 3(b), the respondent receives a copy of the petition whether an answer is required or not), and one for petitioner's counsel, if appointed. Since rule 2 provides that blank copies of the petition in the prescribed form are to be furnished to the applicant free of charge, there should be no undue burden created by this requirement.

Attached to copies of the petition supplied in accordance with rule 2 is an affidavit form for the use of petitioners desiring to proceed in forma pauperis. The form requires information concerning the petitioner's financial resources.

In forma pauperis cases, the petition must also be accompanied by a certificate indicating the amount of funds in the petitioner's institution account. Usually the certificate will be from the warden. If the petitioner is on probation or parole, the court might want to require a certificate from the supervising officer. Petitions by persons on probation or parole are not numerous enough, however, to justify making special provision for this situation in the text of the rule.

The certificate will verify the amount of funds credited to the petitioner in an institution account. The district court may by local rule require that any amount credited to the petitioner, in excess of a stated maximum, must be used for the payment of the filing fee. Since prosecuting an action in forma pauperis is a privilege (see *Smart v. Heinze,* 347 F.2d 114, 116 (9th Cir. 1965), it is not to be granted when the petitioner has sufficient resources.

Subdivision (b) details the clerk's duties with regard to filing the petition. If the petition does not appear on its face to comply with the requirements of rules 2 and 3, it may be returned in accordance with rule 2(e). If it appears to comply, it must be filed and entered on the docket in the clerk's office. However, under this subdivision the respondent is not required to answer or otherwise move with respect to the petition unless so ordered by the court.

Rule 4. Preliminary Consideration by Judge

The original petition shall be presented promptly to a judge of the district court in accordance with the procedure of the court for the assignment of its business. The petition shall be examined promptly by the judge to whom it is assigned. If it plainly appears from the face of the petition and any exhibits annexed to it that the petitioner is not entitled to relief in the district court, the judge shall make an order for its summary dismissal and cause the petitioner to be notified. Otherwise the judge shall order the respondent to file an answer or other pleading within the period of time fixed by the court or to take such other action as the judge deems appropriate. In every case a copy of the petition and any order shall be served by certified mail on the respondent and the attorney general of the state involved.

ADVISORY COMMITTEE NOTES

1976 Adoption

Rule 4 outlines the options available to the court after the petition is properly filed. The petition must be promptly presented to and examined by the judge to whom it is assigned. If it plainly appears from the face of the petition and any exhibits attached thereto that the petitioner is not entitled to relief in the district court, the judge must enter an order summarily dismissing the petition and cause the petitioner to be notified. If summary dismissal is not ordered, the judge must order the respondent to file an answer or to otherwise plead to the petition within a time period to be fixed in the order.

28 U.S.C. § 2243 requires that the writ shall be awarded, or an order to show cause issued, "unless it appears from the application that the applicant or person detained is not entitled thereto." Such consideration may properly encompass any exhibits attached to the petition, including, but not limited to, transcripts, sentencing records, and copies of state court opinions. The judge may order any of these items for his consideration if they are not yet included with the petition. See 28 U.S.C. § 753(f) which authorizes payment for transcripts in habeas corpus cases.

It has been suggested that an answer should be required in every habeas proceeding, taking into account the usual petitioner's lack of legal expertise and the important functions served by the return. See Developments in the Law—Federal Habeas Corpus, 83 Harv.L.Rev. 1038, 1178 (1970). However, under § 2243 it is the duty of the court to screen out frivolous applications and eliminate the burden that would be placed on the respondent by ordering an unnecessary answer. *Allen v. Perini*, 424 F.2d 134, 141 (6th Cir. 1970). In addition, "notice" pleading is not sufficient, for the petition is expected to state facts that point to a "real possibility of constitutional error." See *Aubut v. State of Maine*, 431 F.2d 688, 689 (1st Cir. 1970).

In the event an answer is ordered under rule 4, the court is accorded greater flexibility than under § 2243 in determining within what time period an answer must be made. Under § 2243, the respondent must make a return within three days after being so ordered, with additional time of up to forty days allowed under the Federal Rules of Civil Procedure, Rule 81(a)(2), for good cause. In view of the widespread state of work overload in prosecutors' offices (see, *e.g., Allen*, 424 F.2d at 141), additional time is granted in some jurisdictions as a matter of course. Rule 4, which contains no fixed time requirement, gives the court the discretion to take into account various factors such as the respondent's workload and the availability of transcripts before determining a time within which an answer must be made.

Rule 4 authorizes the judge to "take such other action as the judge deems appropriate." This is designed to afford the judge flexibility in a case where either dismissal or an order to answer may be inappropriate. For example, the judge may want to authorize the respondent to make a motion to dismiss based upon information furnished by respondent, which may show that petitioner's claims have already been decided on the merits in a federal court; that petitioner has failed to exhaust state remedies; that the petitioner is not in custody within the meaning of 28 U.S.C. § 2254; or that a decision in the matter is pending in state court. In these situations, a dismissal may be called for on procedural grounds, which may avoid burdening the respondent with the necessity of filing an answer on the substantive merits of the petition. In other situations, the judge may want to consider a motion from respondent to make the petition more certain. Or the judge may want to dismiss some allegations in the petition, requiring the respondent to answer only those claims which appear to have some arguable merit.

Rule 4 requires that a copy of the petition and any order be served by certified mail on the respondent and the attorney general of the state involved. See 28 U.S.C. § 2252. Presently, the respondent often does not receive a copy of the petition unless the court directs an answer under 28 U.S.C. § 2243. Although the attorney general is served, he is not required to answer if it is more appropriate for some other agency to do so. Although the rule does not specifically so provide, it is assumed that copies of the court orders to respondent will be mailed to petitioner by the court.

Rule 5. Answer; Contents

The answer shall respond to the allegations of the petition. In addition it shall state whether the petitioner has exhausted his state remedies including any post-conviction remedies available to him under the statutes or procedural rules of the state and including also his right of appeal both from the judgment of conviction and from any adverse judgment or order in the post-conviction proceeding. The answer shall indicate what transcripts (of pretrial, trial, sentencing, and post-conviction proceedings) are available, when they can be furnished, and also what proceedings have been recorded and not transcribed. There shall be attached to the answer such portions of the transcripts as the answering party deems relevant. The court on its own motion or upon request of the petitioner may order that further portions of the existing transcripts be furnished or that certain portions of the non-transcribed proceedings be transcribed and furnished. If a transcript is neither available nor procurable, a narrative summary of the evidence may be submitted. If the petitioner appealed from the judgment of conviction or from an adverse judgment or order in a post-conviction proceeding, a copy of the petitioner's brief on appeal and of the opinion of the appellate court, if any, shall also be filed by the respondent with the answer.

ADVISORY COMMITTEE NOTES

1976 Adoption

Rule 5 details the contents of the "answer". (This is a change in terminology from "return," which is still used below when referring to prior practice.) The answer plays an obviously important role in a habeas proceeding:

> The return serves several important functions: it permits the court and the parties to uncover quickly the disputed issues; it may reveal to the petitioner's attorney grounds for release that the petitioner did not know; and it may demonstrate that the petitioner's claim is wholly without merit.
>
> Developments in the Law—Federal Habeas Corpus, 83 Harv.L.Rev. 1083, 1178 (1970).

The answer must respond to the allegations of the petition. While some districts require this by local rule (see, *e.g.*, E.D.N.C.R. 17(B)), under 28 U.S.C. § 2243 little specificity is demanded. As a result, courts occasionally receive answers which contain only a statement certifying the true cause of detention, or a series of delaying motions such as motions to dismiss. The requirement of the proposed rule that the "answer shall respond to the allegations of the petition" is intended to ensure that a responsive pleading will be filed and thus the functions of the answer fully served.

The answer must also state whether the petitioner has exhausted his state remedies. This is a prerequisite to eligibility for the writ under 28 U.S.C. § 2254(b) and applies to every ground the petitioner raises. Most form petitions now in use contain questions requiring information relevant to whether the petitioner has exhausted his remedies. However, the exhaustion requirement is often not understood by the unrepresented petitioner. The attorney general has both the legal expertise and access to the record and thus is in a much better position to inform the court on the matter of exhaustion of state remedies. An alleged failure to exhaust state remedies as to any ground in the petition may be raised by a motion by the attorney general, thus avoiding the necessity of a formal answer as to that ground.

The rule requires the answer to indicate what transcripts are available, when they can be furnished, and also what proceedings have been recorded and not transcribed. This will serve to inform the court and petitioner as to what factual allegations can be checked against the actual transcripts. The transcripts include pretrial transcripts relating, for example, to pretrial motions to suppress; transcripts of the trial or guilty plea proceeding; and transcripts of any post-conviction proceedings which may have taken place. The respondent is required to furnish those portions of the transcripts which he believes relevant. The court may order the furnishing of additional portions of the transcripts upon the request of petitioner or upon the court's own motion.

Where transcripts are unavailable, the rule provides that a narrative summary of the evidence may be submitted.

Rule 5 (and the general procedure set up by this entire set of rules) does not contemplate a traverse to the answer, except under special circumstances. See advisory committee note to rule 9. Therefore, the old common law assumption of verity of the allegations of a return until impeached, as codified in 28 U.S.C. § 2248, is no longer applicable. The meaning of the section, with its exception to the assumption "to the extent that the judge finds from the evidence that they (the allegations) are not true," has given attorneys and courts a great deal of difficulty. It seems that when the petition and return pose an issue of fact, no traverse is required; *Stewart v. Overholser*, 186 F.2d 339 (D.C.Cir. 1950).

> We read § 2248 of the Judicial Code as not requiring a traverse when a factual issue has been clearly framed by the petition and the return or answer. This section provides that the allegations of a return or answer to an order to show cause shall be accepted as true if not traversed, except to the extent the judge finds from the evidence that they are not true. This contemplates that where the petition and return or answer do present an issue of fact material to the legality of detention, evidence is required to resolve that issue despite the absence of a traverse. This reference to evidence assumes a hearing on issues raised by the allegations of the petition and the return or answer to the order to show cause.

186 F.2d at 342, n. 5

In actual practice, the traverse tends to be a mere pro forma refutation of the return, serving little if any expository function. In the interests of a more streamlined and manageable habeas corpus procedure, it is not required except in those instances where it will serve a truly useful purpose. Also, under rule 11 the court is given the discretion to incorporate Federal Rules of Civil Procedure when appropriate, so civil rule 15(a) may be used to allow the petitioner to amend his petition when the court feels this is called for by the contents of the answer.

Rule 5 does not indicate who the answer is to be served upon, but it necessarily implies that it will be mailed to the petitioner (or to his attorney if he has one). The number of copies of the answer required is left to the court's discretion. Although the rule requires only a copy of petitioner's brief on appeal, respondent is free also to file a copy of respondent's brief. In practice, courts have found it helpful to have a copy of respondent's brief.

Rule 6. Discovery

(a) Leave of court required. A party shall be entitled to invoke the processes of discovery available under the Federal Rules of Civil Procedure if, and to the extent that, the judge in the exercise of his discretion and for good cause shown grants leave to do so, but not otherwise. If necessary for effective utilization of discovery procedures, counsel shall be appointed by the judge for a petitioner who qualifies for the appointment of counsel under 18 U.S.C. § 3006A(g).

(b) Requests for discovery. Requests for discovery shall be accompanied by a statement of the interrogatories or requests for admission and a list of the documents, if any, sought to be produced.

(c) Expenses. If the respondent is granted leave to take the deposition of the petitioner or any other person the judge may as a condition of taking it direct that the respondent pay the expenses of travel and subsistence and fees of counsel for the petitioner to attend the taking of the deposition.

ADVISORY COMMITTEE NOTES

1976 Adoption

This rule prescribes the procedures governing discovery in habeas corpus cases. Subdivision (a) provides that any party may utilize the processes of discovery available under the Federal Rules of Civil Procedure (rules 26–37) if, and to the extent that, the judge allows. It also provides for the appointment of counsel for a petitioner who qualifies for this when counsel is necessary for effective utilization of discovery procedures permitted by the judge.

Subdivision (a) is consistent with *Harris v. Nelson*, 394 U.S. 286 (1969). In that case the court noted,

> [I]t is clear that there was no intention to extend to habeas corpus, as a matter of right, the broad discovery provisions * * * of the new [Federal Rules of Civil Procedure].

394 U.S. at 295

However, citing the lack of methods for securing information in habeas proceedings, the court pointed to an alternative.

> Clearly, in these circumstances * * * the courts may fashion appropriate modes of procedure, by analogy to existing rules or otherwise in conformity with judicial usage. * * * Their authority is expressly confirmed in the All Writs Act, 28 U.S.C. § 1651.

394 U.S. at 299

The court concluded that the issue of discovery in habeas corpus cases could best be dealt with as part of an effort to provide general rules of practice for habeas corpus cases:

> In fact, it is our view that the rulemaking machinery should be invoked to formulate rules of practice with respect to federal habeas corpus and § 2255 proceedings, on a comprehensive basis and not merely one confined to discovery. The problems presented by these proceedings are materially different from those dealt with in the Federal Rules of Civil Procedure and the Federal Rules of

Criminal Procedure, and reliance upon usage and the opaque language of Civil Rule 81(a)(2) is transparently inadequate. In our view the results of a meticulous formulation and adoption of special rules for federal habeas corpus and § 2255 proceedings would promise much benefit.

394 U.S. at 301 n. 7

Discovery may, in appropriate cases, aid in developing facts necessary to decide whether to order an evidentiary hearing or to grant the writ following an evidentiary hearing:

We are award that confinement sometimes induces fantasy which has its basis in the paranoia of prison rather than in fact. But where specific allegations before the court show reason to believe that the petitioner may, if the facts are fully developed, be able to demonstrate that he is confined illegally and is therefore entitled to relief, it is the duty of the court to provide the necessary facilities and procedures for an adequate inquiry. Obviously, in exercising this power, the court may utilize familiar procedures, as appropriate, whether these are found in the civil or criminal rules or elsewhere in the "usages and principles."

Granting discovery is left to the discretion of the court, discretion to be exercised where there is a showing of good cause why discovery should be allowed. Several commentators have suggested that at least some discovery should be permitted without leave of court. It is argued that the courts will be burdened with weighing the propriety of requests to which the discovered party has no objection. Additionally, the availability of protective orders under Fed. R.Civ.R., Rules 30(b) and 31(d) will provide the necessary safeguards. See Developments in the Law—Federal Habeas Corpus, 83 Harv.L.Rev. 1038, 1186–87 (1970); Civil Discovery in Habeas Corpus, 67 Colum.L.Rev. 1296, 1310 (1967).

Nonetheless, it is felt the requirement of prior court approval of all discovery is necessary to prevent abuse, so this requirement is specifically mandated in the rule.

While requests for discovery in habeas proceedings normally follow the granting of an evidentiary hearing, there may be instances in which discovery would be appropriate beforehand. Such an approach was advocated in *Wagner v. United States*, 418 F.2d 618, 621 (9th Cir.1969), where the opinion stated the trial court could permit interrogatories, provide for deposing witnesses, "and take such other prehearing steps as may be appropriate." While this was an action under § 2255, the reasoning would apply equally well to petitions by state prisoners. Such pre-hearing discovery may show an evidentiary hearing to be unnecessary, as when there are "no disputed issues of law or fact." 83 Harv.L.Rev. 1038, 1181 (1970). The court in Harris alluded to such a possibility when it said "the court may * * * authorize such proceedings with respect to development, *before or in conjunction with the hearing* of the facts * * *." [emphasis added] 394 U.S. at 300. Such pre-hearing discovery, like all discovery under rule 6, requires leave of court. In addition, the provisions in rule 7 for the use of an expanded record may eliminate much of the need for this type of discovery. While probably not as frequently sought or granted as discovery in conjunction with a hearing, it may nonetheless serve a valuable function.

In order to make pre-hearing discovery meaningful, subdivision (a) provides that the judge should appoint counsel for a petitioner who is without counsel and qualifies for appointment when this is necessary for the proper utilization of discovery procedures. Rule 8 provides for the appointment of counsel at the evidentiary hearing stage (see rule 8(b) and advisory committee note), but this would not assist the petitioner who seeks to utilize discovery to stave off dismissal of his petition (see rule 9 and advisory committee note) or to demonstrate that an evidentiary hearing is necessary. Thus, if the judge grants a petitioner's request for discovery prior to making a decision as to the necessity for an evidentiary hearing, he should determine whether counsel is necessary for the effective utilization of such discovery and, if so, appoint counsel for the petitioner if the petitioner qualifies for such appointment.

This rule contains very little specificity as to what types and methods of discovery should be made available to the parties in a habeas proceeding, or how, once made available, these discovery procedures should be administered. The purpose of this rule is to get some experience in how discovery would work in actual practice by letting district court judges fashion their own rules in the context of individual cases. When the results of such experience are available it would be desirable to consider whether further, more specific codification should take place.

Subdivision (b) provides for judicial consideration of all matters subject to discovery. A statement of the interrogatories, or requests for admission sought to be answered, and a list of any documents sought to be produced, must accompany a request for discovery. This is to advise the judge of the necessity for discovery and enable him to make certain that the inquiry is relevant and appropriately narrow.

Subdivision (c) refers to the situation where the respondent is granted leave to take the deposition of the petitioner or any other person. In such a case the judge may direct the respondent to pay the expenses and fees of counsel for the petitioner to attend the taking of the deposition, as a condition granting the respondent such leave. While the judge is not required to impose this condition subdivision (c) will give the court the means to do so. Such a provision affords some protection to the indigent petitioner who may be prejudiced by his inability to have counsel, often court-appointed, present at the taking of a deposition. It is recognized that under 18 U.S.C. § 3006A(g), court-appointed counsel in a § 2254 proceeding is entitled to receive up to $250 and reimbursement for expenses reasonably incurred. (Compare Fed.R.Crim.P. 15(c).) Typically, however, this does not adequately reimburse counsel if he must attend the taking of depositions or be involved in other pre-hearing proceedings. Subdivision (c) is intended to provide additional funds, if necessary, to be paid by the state government (respondent) to petitioner's counsel.

Although the rule does not specifically so provide, it is assumed that a petitioner who qualifies for the appointment of counsel under 18 U.S.C. § 3006A(g) and is granted leave to take a deposition will be allowed witness costs. This will include recording and transcription of the witness's statement. Such costs are payable pursuant to 28 U.S.C. § 1825. See Opinion of Comptroller General, February 28, 1974.

Subdivision (c) specifically recognizes the right of the respondent to take the deposition of the petitioner. Although the petitioner could not be called to testify against his will in a criminal trial, it is felt the nature of the habeas proceeding, along with the safeguards accorded by the Fifth

Amendment and the presence of counsel, justify this provision. See 83 Harv.L.Rev. 1038, 1183–84 (1970).

Rule 7. Expansion of Record

(a) Direction for expansion. If the petition is not dismissed summarily the judge may direct that the record be expanded by the parties by the inclusion of additional materials relevant to the determination of the merits of the petition.

(b) Materials to be added. The expanded record may include, without limitation, letters predating the filing of the petition in the district court, documents, exhibits, and answers under oath, if so directed, to written interrogatories propounded by the judge. Affidavits may be submitted and considered as a part of the record.

(c) Submission to opposing party. In any case in which an expanded record is directed, copies of the letters, documents, exhibits, and affidavits proposed to be included shall be submitted to the party against whom they are to be offered, and he shall be afforded an opportunity to admit or deny their correctness.

(d) Authentication. The court may require the authentication of any material under subdivision (b) or (c).

ADVISORY COMMITTEE NOTES

1976 Adoption

This rule provides that the judge may direct that the record be expanded. The purpose is to enable the judge to dispose of some habeas petitions not dismissed on the pleadings, without the time and expense required for an evidentiary hearing. An expanded record may also be helpful when an evidentiary hearing is ordered.

The record may be expanded to include additional material relevant to the merits of the petition. While most petitions are dismissed either summarily or after a response has been made, of those that remain, by far the majority require an evidentiary hearing. In the fiscal year ending June 30, 1970, for example, of 8,423 § 2254 cases terminated, 8,231 required court action. Of these, 7,812 were dismissed before a prehearing conference and 469 merited further court action (*e.g.*, expansion of the record, prehearing conference, or an evidentiary hearing). Of the remaining 469 cases, 403 required an evidentiary hearing, often time-consuming, costly, and, at least occasionally, unnecessary. See Director of the Administrative Office of the United States Courts, Annual Report, 245a–245c (table C4) (1970). In some instances these hearings were necessitated by slight omissions in the state record which might have been cured by the use of an expanded record.

Authorizing expansion of the record will, hopefully, eliminate some unnecessary hearings. The value of this approach was articulated in *Raines v. United States*, 423 F.2d 526, 529–530 (4th Cir. 1970):

> Unless it is clear from the pleadings and the files and records that the prisoner is entitled to no relief, the statute makes a hearing mandatory. We think there is a permissible intermediate step that may avoid the necessity for an expensive and time consuming evidentiary hearing in every Section 2255 case. It may instead be perfectly appropriate, depending upon the nature of the allegations, for the district court to proceed by requiring that the record be expanded to include letters, documentary evidence, and, in an appropriate case, even affidavits. *United States v. Carlino*, 400 F.2d 56 (2nd Cir. 1968); *Mirra v. United States*, 379 F.2d 782 (2nd Cir. 1967); *Accardi v. United States*, 379 F.2d 312 (2nd Cir. 1967). When the issue is one of credibility, resolution on the basis of affidavits can rarely be conclusive, but that is not to say they may not be helpful.

In *Harris v. Nelson*, 394 U.S. 286, 300 (1969), the court said:

> At any time in the proceedings * * * *either on [the court's] own motion* or upon cause shown by the petitioner, it may issue such writs and take or authorize such proceedings * * * *before* or in conjunction with the hearing of the facts * * *. [emphasis added]

Subdivision (b) specifies the materials which may be added to the record. These include, without limitation, letters predating the filing of the petition in the district court, documents, exhibits, and answers under oath directed to written interrogatories propounded by the judge. Under this subdivision affidavits may be submitted and considered part of the record. Subdivision (b) is consistent with 28 U.S.C. §§ 2246 and 2247 and the decision in *Raines* with regard to types of material that may be considered upon application for a writ of habeas corpus. See *United States v. Carlino*, 400 F.2d 56, 58 (2d Cir. 1968), and *Machibroda v. United States*, 368 U.S. 487 (1962).

Under subdivision (c) all materials proposed to be included in the record must be submitted to the party against whom they are to be offered.

Under subdivision (d) the judge can require authentication if he believes it desirable to do so.

Rule 8. Evidentiary Hearing

(a) Determination by court. If the petition is not dismissed at a previous stage in the proceeding, the judge, after the answer and the transcript and record of state court proceedings are filed, shall, upon a review of those proceedings and of the expanded record, if any, determine whether an evidentiary hearing is required. If it appears that an evidentiary hearing is not required, the judge shall make such disposition of the petition as justice shall require.

(b) Function of the magistrate.

(1) When designated to do so in accordance with 28 U.S.C. § 636(b), a magistrate may conduct hearings, including evidentiary hearings, on the petition, and submit to a judge of the court proposed findings of fact and recommendations for disposition.

(2) The magistrate shall file proposed findings and recommendations with the court and a copy shall forthwith be mailed to all parties.

(3) Within ten days after being served with a copy, any party may serve and file written objections to such proposed findings and recommendations as provided by rules of court.

(4) A judge of the court shall make a de novo determination of those portions of the report or specified proposed findings or recommendations to which objection is made. A judge of the court may accept, reject, or modify in whole or in part any findings or recommendations made by the magistrate.

(c) Appointment of counsel; time for hearing. If an evidentiary hearing is required the judge shall appoint counsel for a petitioner who qualifies for the appointment of counsel under 18 U.S.C. § 3006A(g) and the hearing shall be conducted as promptly as practicable, having regard for the need of counsel for both parties for adequate time for investigation and preparation. These rules do not limit the appointment of counsel under 18 U.S.C. § 3006A at any stage of the case if the interest of justice so requires. (As amended Pub.L. 94–426, § 2(5), Sept. 28, 1976, 90 Stat. 1334; Pub.L. 94–577, § 2(a)(1), (b)(1), Oct. 21, 1976, 90 Stat. 2730, 2731.)

ADVISORY COMMITTEE NOTES

1976 Adoption

This rule outlines the procedure to be followed by the court immediately prior to and after the determination of whether to hold an evidentiary hearing.

The provisions are applicable if the petition has not been dismissed at a previous stage in the proceeding [including a summary dismissal under Rule 4; a dismissal pursuant to a motion by the respondent; a dismissal after the answer and petition are considered; or a dismissal after consideration of the pleadings and an expanded record].

If dismissal has not been ordered, the court must determine whether an evidentiary hearing is required. This determination is to be made upon a review of the answer, the transcript and record of state court proceedings, and if there is one, the expanded record. As the United States Supreme Court noted in *Townsend v. Sam,* 372 U.S. 293, 319 (1963):

> Ordinarily [the complete state-court] record—including the transcript of testimony (or if unavailable some adequate substitute, such as a narrative record), the pleadings, court opinions, and other pertinent documents—is indispensable to determining whether the habeas applicant received a full and fair state-court evidentiary hearing resulting in reliable findings.

Subdivision (a) contemplates that all of these materials, if available, will be taken into account. This is especially important in view of the standard set down in *Townsend* for determining *when* a hearing in the federal habeas proceeding is mandatory.

> The appropriate standard * * * is this: Where the facts are in dispute, the federal court in habeas corpus must hold an evidentiary hearing if the habeas applicant did not receive a full and fair evidentiary hearing in a state court, either at the time of the trial or in a collateral proceeding.

372 U.S. at 312

The circumstances under with a federal hearing is mandatory are now specified in 28 U.S.C. § 2254(d). The 1966 amendment clearly places the burden on the petitioner, when there has already been a state hearing, to show that it was not a fair or adequate hearing for one or more of the specifically enumerated reasons, in order to force a federal evidentiary hearing. Since the function of an evidentiary hearing is to try issues of fact (372 U.S. at 309), such a hearing is unnecessary when only issues of law are raised. See, *e.g., Yeaman v. United States,* 326 F.2d 293 (9th Cir. 1963).

In situations in which an evidentiary hearing is not mandatory, the judge may nonetheless decide that an evidentiary hearing is desirable:

> The purpose of the test is to indicate the situations in which the holding of an evidentiary hearing is mandatory. In all other cases where the material facts are in dispute, the holding of such a hearing is in the discretion of the district judge.

372 U.S. at 318

If the judge decides that an evidentiary hearing is neither required nor desirable, he shall make such a disposition of the petition "as justice shall require." Most habeas petitions are dismissed before the prehearing conference stage (see Director of the Administrative Office of the United States Courts, Annual Report 245–245c (table C4) (1970)) and of those not dismissed, the majority raise factual issues that necessitate an evidentiary hearing. If no hearing is required, most petitions are dismissed, but in unusual cases the court may grant the relief sought without a hearing. This includes immediate release from custody or nullification of a judgment under which the sentence is to be served in the future.

Subdivision (b) provides that a magistrate, when so empowered by rule of the district court, may recommend to the district judge that an evidentiary hearing be held or that the petition be dismissed, provided he gives the district judge a sufficiently detailed description of the facts so that the judge may decide whether or not to hold an evidentiary hearing. This provision is not inconsistent with the holding in *Wingo v. Wedding,* 418 U.S. 461 (1974), that the Federal Magistrates Act did not change the requirement of the habeas corpus statute that federal judges personally conduct habeas evidentiary hearings, and that consequently a local district court rule was invalid insofar as it authorized a magistrate to hold such hearings. 28 U.S.C. § 636(b) provides that a district court may by rule authorize any magistrate to perform certain additional duties, including preliminary review of applications for posttrial relief made by individuals convicted of criminal offenses, and submission of a report and recommendations to facilitate the decision of the district judge having jurisdiction over the case as to whether there should be a hearing.

As noted in *Wingo,* review "by Magistrates of applications for post-trial relief is thus limited to review for the purpose of proposing, not holding, evidentiary hearings."

Utilization of the magistrate as specified in subdivision (b) will aid in the expeditious and fair handling of habeas petitions.

> A qualified, experienced magistrate will, it is hoped, acquire an expertise in examining these [postconviction

review] applications and summarizing their important contents for the district judge, thereby facilitating his decisions. Law clerks are presently charged with this responsibility by many judges, but judges have noted that the normal 1-year clerkship does not afford law clerks the time or experience necessary to attain real efficiency in handling such applications.

S.Rep. No. 371, 90th Cong., 1st Sess., 26 (1967).

Under subdivision (c) there are two provisions that differ from the procedure set forth in 28 U.S.C. § 2243. These are the appointment of counsel and standard for determining how soon the hearing will be held.

If an evidentiary hearing is required the judge must appoint counsel for a petitioner who qualified [sic] for appointment under the Criminal Justice Act. Currently, the appointment of counsel is not recognized as a right at any stage of a habeas proceeding. See, *e.g., United States ex rel. Marshall v. Wilkins,* 338 F.2d 404 (2d Cir. 1964). Some district courts have, however, by local rule, required that counsel must be provided for indigent petitioners in cases requiring a hearing. See, *e.g., D.N.M.R. 21(f), E.D.N.Y.R. 26(d).* Appointment of counsel at this stage is mandatory under subdivision (c). This requirement will not limit the authority of the court to provide counsel at an earlier stage if it is thought desirable to do so as is done in some courts under current practice. At the evidentiary hearing stage, however, an indigent petitioner's access to counsel should not depend on local practice and, for this reason, the furnishing of counsel is made mandatory.

Counsel can perform a valuable function benefiting both the court and the petitioner. The issues raised can be more clearly identified if both sides have the benefit of trained legal personnel. The presence of counsel at the prehearing conference may help to expedite the evidentiary hearing or make it unnecessary, and counsel will be able to make better use of available prehearing discovery procedures. Compare ABA Project on Standards for Criminal Justice, Standards Relating to Post-Conviction Remedies § 4.4, p. 66 (Approved Draft 1968). At a hearing, the petitioner's claims are more likely to be effectively and properly presented by counsel.

Under 18 U.S.C. § 3006A(g), payment is allowed counsel up to $250, plus reimbursement for expenses reasonably incurred. The standards of indigency under this section are less strict than those regarding eligibility to prosecute a petition in forma pauperis, and thus many who cannot qualify to proceed under 28 U.S.C. § 1915 will be entitled to the benefits of counsel under 18 U.S.C. § 3006A(g). Under Rule 6(c), the court may order the respondent to reimburse counsel from state funds for fees and expenses incurred as the result of the utilization of discovery procedures by the respondent.

Subdivision (c) provides that the hearing shall be conducted as promptly as possible, taking into account "the need of counsel for both parties for adequate time for investigation and preparation." This differs from the language of 28 U.S.C. § 2243, which requires that the day for the hearing be set "not more than five days after the return unless for good cause additional time is allowed." This time limit fails to take into account the function that may be served by a prehearing conference and the time required to prepare adequately for an evidentiary hearing. Although "additional time" is often allowed under § 2243, subdivision (c) provides more flexibility to take account of the complexity of the case, the availability of important materials, the workload of the attorney general, and the time required by appointed counsel to prepare.

While the rule does not make specific provision for a prehearing conference, the omission is not intended to cast doubt upon the value of such a conference:

> The conference may limit the questions to be resolved, identify areas of agreement and dispute, and explore evidentiary problems that may be expected to arise. * * * [S]uch conferences may also disclose that a hearing is unnecessary * * *.

ABA Project on Standards for Criminal Justice, Standards Relating to Post-Conviction Remedies § 4.6, commentary pp. 74–75. (Approved Draft, 1968.)

See also Developments in the Law—Federal Habeas Corpus, 83 Harv.L.Rev. 1038, 1188 (1970).

The rule does not contain a specific provision on the subpoenaing of witnesses. It is left to local practice to determine the method for doing this. The implementation of 28 U.S.C. § 1825 on the payment of witness fees is dealt with in an opinion of the Comptroller General, February 28, 1974.

HISTORICAL NOTES

Effective Dates

1976 Acts. Section 2(c) of Pub.L. 94–577 provided that: "The amendments made by this section [amending subdivs. (b) and (c) of this rule and Rule 8(b), (c) of the Rules Governing Proceedings Under Section 2255 of this title] shall take effect with respect to petitions under section 2254 and motions under section 2255 of title 28 of the United States Code filed on or after February 1, 1977."

Rule 9. Delayed or Successive Petitions

(a) Delayed petitions. A petition may be dismissed if it appears that the state of which the respondent is an officer has been prejudiced in its ability to respond to the petition by delay in its filing unless the petitioner shows that it is based on grounds of which he could not have had knowledge by the exercise of reasonable diligence before the circumstances prejudicial to the state occurred.

(b) Successive petitions. A second or successive petition may be dismissed if the judge finds that it fails to allege new or different grounds for relief and the prior determination was on the merits or, if new and different grounds are alleged, the judge finds that the failure of the petitioner to assert those grounds in a prior petition constituted an abuse of the writ. (As amended Pub.L. 94–426, § 2(7), (8), Sept. 28, 1976, 90 Stat. 1335.)

ADVISORY COMMITTEE NOTES

1976 Adoption

This rule is intended to minimize abuse of the writ of habeas corpus by limiting the right to assert stale claims and to file multiple petitions. Subdivision (a) deals with the delayed petition. Subdivision (b) deals with the second or successive petition.

Subdivision (a) provides that a petition attacking the judgment of a state court may be dismissed on the grounds of delay if the petitioner knew or should have known of the existence of the grounds he is presently asserting in the petition and the delay has resulted in the state being prejudiced in its ability to respond to the petition. If the delay is more than five years after the judgment of conviction, prejudice is presumed, although this presumption is rebuttable by the petitioner. Otherwise, the state has the burden of showing such prejudice.

The assertion of stale claims is a problem which is not likely to decrease in frequency. Following the decisions in *Jones v. Cunningham,* 371 U.S. 236 (1963), and *Benson v. California,* 328 F.2d 159 (9th Cir. 1964), the concept of custody expanded greatly, lengthening the time period during which a habeas corpus petition may be filed. The petitioner who is not unconditionally discharged may be on parole or probation for many years. He may at some date, perhaps ten or fifteen years after conviction, decide to challenge the state court judgment. The grounds most often troublesome to the courts are ineffective counsel, denial of right of appeal, plea of guilty unlawfully induced, use of a coerced confession, and illegally constituted jury. The latter four grounds are often interlocked with the allegation of ineffective counsel. When they are asserted after the passage of many years, both the attorney for the defendant and the state have difficulty in ascertaining what the facts are. It often develops that the defense attorney has little or no recollection as to what took place and that many of the participants in the trial are dead or their whereabouts unknown. The court reporter's notes may have been lost or destroyed, thus eliminating any exact record of what transpired. If the case was decided on a guilty plea, even if the record is intact, it may not satisfactorily reveal the extent of the defense attorney's efforts in behalf of the petitioner. As a consequence, there is obvious difficulty in investigating petitioner's allegations.

The interest of both the petitioner and the government can best be served if claims are raised while the evidence is still fresh. The American Bar Association has recognized the interest of the state in protecting itself against stale claims by limiting the right to raise such claims after completion of service of a sentence imposed pursuant to a challenged judgment. See ABA Standards Relating to Post-Conviction Remedies § 2.4(c), p. 45 (Approved Draft, 1968). Subdivision (a) is not limited to those who have completed their sentence. Its reach is broader, extending to all instances where delay by the petitioner has prejudiced the state, subject to the qualifications and conditions contained in the subdivision.

In *McMann v. Richardson,* 397 U.S. 759 (1970), the court made reference to the issue of the stale claim:

> What is at stake in this phase of the case is not the integrity of the state convictions obtained on guilty pleas, *but whether, years later,* defendants must be permitted to withdraw their pleas, which were perfectly valid when made, and be given another choice between admitting their guilt and putting the State to its proof. [Emphasis added.]

397 U.S. at 773

The court refused to allow this, intimating its dislike of collateral attacks on sentences long since imposed which disrupt the state's interest in finality of convictions which were constitutionally valid when obtained.

Subdivision (a) is not a statute of limitations. Rather, the limitation is based on the equitable doctrine of laches. "Laches is such delay in enforcing one's rights as works disadvantage to another." 30A C.J.S. Equity § 112, p. 19. Also, the language of the subdivision, "a petition *may* be dismissed" [emphasis added], is permissive rather than mandatory. This clearly allows the court which is considering the petition to use discretion in assessing the equities of the particular situation.

The use of a flexible rule analogous to laches to bar the assertion of stale claims is suggested in ABA Standards Relating to Post-Conviction Remedies § 2.4, commentary at 48 (Approved Draft, 1968). Additionally, in *Fay v. Noia,* 372 U.S. 391 (1963), the Supreme Court noted:

> Furthermore, habeas corpus has traditionally been regarded as governed by equitable principles. *United States ex rel. Smith v. Baldi,* 344 U.S. 561, 573 (dissenting opinion). Among them is the principle that a suitor's conduct in relation to the matter at hand may disentitle him to the relief he seeks.

372 U.S. at 438

Finally, the doctrine of laches has been applied with reference to another postconviction remedy, the writ of coram nobis. See 24 C.J.S. Criminal Law § 1606(25), p. 779.

The standard used for determining if the petitioner shall be barred from asserting his claim is consistent with that used in laches provisions generally. The petitioner is held to a standard of reasonable diligence. Any inference or presumption arising by reason of the failure to attack collaterally a conviction may be disregarded where (1) there has been a change of law or fact (new evidence) or (2) where the court, in the interest of justice, feels that the collateral attack should be entertained and the prisoner makes a proper showing as to why he has not asserted a particular ground for relief.

Subdivision (a) establishes the presumption that the passage of more than five years from the time of the judgment of conviction to the time of filing a habeas petition is prejudicial to the state. "Presumption" has the meaning given it by Fed.R.Evid. 301. The prisoner has "the burden of going forward with evidence to rebut or meet the presumption" that the state has not been prejudiced by the passage of a substantial period of time. This does not impose too heavy a burden on the petitioner. He usually knows what persons are important to the issue of whether the state has been prejudiced. Rule 6 can be used by the court to allow petitioner liberal discovery to learn whether witnesses have died or whether other circumstances prejudicial to the state have occurred. Even if the petitioner should fail to overcome the presumption of prejudice to the state, he is not automatically barred from asserting his claim. As discussed previously, he may proceed if he neither knew nor, by the exercise of reasonable diligence, could have known of the grounds for relief.

The presumption of prejudice does not come into play if the time lag is not more than five years.

The time limitation should have a positive effect in encouraging petitioners who have knowledge of it to assert all their claims as soon after conviction as possible. The implementation of this rule can be substantially furthered by the development of greater legal resources for prisoners. See ABA

Standards Relating to Post-Conviction Remedies § 3.1, pp. 49–50 (Approved Draft, 1968).

Subdivision (a) does not constitute an abridgement or modification of a substantive right under 28 U.S.C. § 2072. There are safeguards for the hardship case. The rule provides a flexible standard for determining when a petition will be barred.

Subdivision (b) deals with the problem of successive habeas petitions. It provides that the judge may dismiss a second or successive petition (1) if it fails to allege new or different grounds for relief or (2) if new or different grounds for relief are alleged and the judge finds the failure of the petitioner to assert those grounds in a prior petition is inexcusable.

In *Sanders v. United States,* 373 U.S. 1 (1963), the court, in dealing with the problem of successive applications, stated:

> Controlling weight *may* be given to denial of a prior application for federal habeas corpus or § 2255 relief only if (1) the same ground presented in the subsequent application was determined adversely to the applicant on the prior application, (2) the prior determination was on the merits, and (3) the ends of justice would not be served by reaching the merits of the subsequent application. [Emphasis added.]

373 U.S. at 15

The requirement is that the prior determination of the same ground has been on the merits. This requirement is in 28 U.S.C. § 2244(b) and has been reiterated in many cases since *Sanders.* See *Gains v. Allgood,* 391 F.2d 692 (5th Cir. 1968); *Hutchinson v. Craven,* 415 F.2d 278 (9th Cir. 1969); *Brown v. Peyton,* 435 F.2d 1352 (4th Cir. 1970).

With reference to a successive application asserting a new ground or one not previously decided on the merits, the court in *Sanders* noted:

> In either case, full consideration of the merits of the new application can be avoided only if there has been an abuse of the writ * * * and this the Government has the burden of pleading. * * *
>
> Thus, for example, if a prisoner deliberately withholds one of two grounds for federal collateral relief at the time of filing his first application, * * * he may be deemed to have waived his right to a hearing on a second application presenting the withheld ground.

373 U.S. at 17–18

Subdivision (b) has incorporated this principle and requires that the judge find petitioner's failure to have asserted the new grounds in the prior petition to be inexcusable.

Sanders, 18 [sic] U.S.C. § 2244, and subdivision (b) make it clear that the court has discretion to entertain a successive application.

The burden is on the government to plead abuse of the writ. See *Sanders v. United States,* 373 U.S. 1, 10 (1963); *Dixon v. Jacobs,* 427 F.2d 589, 596 (D.C.Cir.1970); cf. *Johnson v. Copinger,* 420 F.2d 395 (4th Cir. 1969). Once the government has done this, the petitioner has the burden of proving that he has not abused the writ. In *Price v. Johnston,* 334 U.S. 266, 292 (1948), the court said:

> [I]f the Government chooses * * * to claim that the prisoner has abused the writ of *habeas corpus*, it rests with the Government to make that claim with clarity and particularity in its return to the order to show cause. That is not an intolerable burden. The Government is usually well acquainted with the facts that are necessary to make such a claim. Once a particular abuse has been alleged, the prisoner has the burden of answering that allegation and of proving that he has not abused the writ.

Subdivision (b) is consistent with the important and well established purpose of habeas corpus. It does not eliminate a remedy to which the petitioner is rightfully entitled. However, in *Sanders*, the court pointed out:

> Nothing in the traditions of habeas corpus requires the federal courts to tolerate needless piecemeal litigation, or to entertain collateral proceedings whose only purpose is to vex, harass, or delay.

373 U.S. at 18

There are instances in which petitioner's failure to assert a ground in a prior petition is excusable. A retroactive change in the law and newly discovered evidence are examples. In rare instances, the court may feel a need to entertain a petition alleging grounds that have already been decided on the merits. *Sanders*, 373 U.S. at 1, 16. However, abusive use of the writ should be discouraged, and instances of abuse are frequent enough to require a means of dealing with them. For example, a successive application, already decided on the merits, may be submitted in the hope of getting before a different judge in multijudge courts. A known ground may be deliberately withheld in the hope of getting two or more hearings or in the hope that delay will result in witnesses and records being lost. There are instances in which a petitioner will have three or four petitions pending at the same time in the same court. There are many hundreds of cases where the application is at least the second one by the petitioner. This subdivision is aimed at screening out the abusive petitions from this large volume, so that the more meritorious petitions can get quicker and fuller consideration.

The form petition, supplied in accordance with Rule 2(c), encourages the petitioner to raise all of his available grounds in one petition. It sets out the most common grounds asserted so that these may be brought to his attention.

Some commentators contend that the problem of abuse of the writ of habeas corpus is greatly overstated:

> Most prisoners, of course, are interested in being released as soon as possible; only rarely will one inexcusably neglect to raise all available issues in his first federal application. The purpose of the "abuse" bar is apparently to deter repetitious applications from those few bored or vindictive prisoners * * *.

83 Harv.L.Rev. at 1153–1154

See also ABA Standards Relating to Post-Conviction Remedies § 6.2, commentary at 92 (Approved Draft, 1968), which states: "The occasional, highly litigious prisoner stands out as the rarest exception." While no recent systematic study of repetitious applications exists, there is no reason to believe that the problem has decreased in significance in relation to the total number of § 2254 petitions filed. That number has increased from 584 in 1949 to 12,088 in 1971. See Director of the Administrative Office of the United States Courts, Annual Report, table 16 (1971). It is appropriate that action be taken by rule to allow the courts to deal with this problem, whatever its specific magnitude. The bar set up by subdivision (b) is not one of rigid application, but rather is within the discretion of the courts on a case-by-case basis.

If it appears to the court after examining the petition and answer (where appropriate) that there is a high probability that the petition will be barred under either subdivision of Rule 9, the court ought to afford petitioner an opportunity to explain his apparent abuse. One way of doing this is by the use of the form annexed hereto. The use of a form will ensure a full airing of the issue so that the court is in a better position to decide whether the petition should be barred. This conforms with *Johnson v. Copinger*, 420 F.2d 395 (4th Cir. 1969), where the court stated:

> [T]he petitioner is obligated to present facts demonstrating that his earlier failure to raise his claims is excusable and does not amount to an abuse of the writ. However, it is inherent in this obligation placed upon the petitioner that he must be given an opportunity to make his explanation, if he has one. If he is not afforded such an opportunity, the requirement that he satisfy the court that he has not abused the writ is meaningless. Nor do we think that a procedure which allows the imposition of a forfeiture for abuse of the writ, without allowing the petitioner an opportunity to be heard on the issue, comports with the minimum requirements of fairness.
>
> **420 F.2d at 399**

Use of the recommended form will contribute to an orderly handling of habeas petitions and will contribute to the ability of the court to distinguish the excusable from the inexcusable delay or failure to assert a ground for relief in a prior petition.

Rule 10. Powers of Magistrates

The duties imposed upon the judge of the district court by these rules may be performed by a United States magistrate pursuant to 28 U.S.C. § 636.

(As amended Pub.L. 94–426, § 2(11), Sept. 28, 1976, 90 Stat. 1335; Apr. 30, 1979, eff. Aug. 1, 1979.)

ADVISORY COMMITTEE NOTES

1976 Adoption

Under this rule the duties imposed upon the judge of the district court by rules 2, 3, 4, 6, and 7 may be performed by a magistrate if and to the extent he is empowered to do so by a rule of the district court. However, when such duties involve the making of an order under rule 4 disposing of the petition, that order must be made by the court. The magistrate in such instances must submit to the court his report as to the facts and his recommendation with respect to the order.

The Federal Magistrates Act allows magistrates, when empowered by local rule, to perform certain functions in proceedings for post-trial relief. See 28 U.S.C. § 636(b)(3). The performance of such functions, when authorized, is intended to "afford some degree of relief to district judges and their law clerks, who are presently burdened with burgeoning numbers of habeas corpus petitions and applications under 28 U.S.C. § 2255." Committee on the Judiciary, The Federal Magistrates Act, S.Rep. No. 371, 90th Cong., 1st sess., 26 (1967).

Under 28 U.S.C. § 636(b), any district court,

> by the concurrence of a majority of all the judges of such district court, may establish rules pursuant to which any full-time United States magistrate * * * may be assigned within the territorial jurisdiction of such court such additional duties as are not inconsistent with the Constitution and laws of the United States.

The proposed rule recognizes the limitations imposed by 28 U.S.C. § 636(b) upon the powers of magistrates to act in federal postconviction proceedings. These limitations are: (1) that the magistrate may act only pursuant to a rule passed by the majority of the judges in the district court in which the magistrate serves, and (2) that the duties performed by the magistrate pursuant to such rule be consistent with the Constitution and laws of the United States.

It has been suggested magistrates be empowered by law to hold hearings and make final decisions in habeas proceedings. See Proposed Reformation of Federal Habeas Corpus Procedure: Use of Federal Magistrates, 54 Iowa L.Rev. 1147, 1158 (1969). However, the Federal Magistrates Act does not authorize such use of magistrates. *Wingo v. Wedding,* 418 U.S. 461 (1974). See advisory committee note to Rule 8. While the use of magistrates can help alleviate the strain imposed on the district courts by the large number of unmeritorious habeas petitions, neither 28 U.S.C. § 636(b) nor this rule contemplate the abdication by the court of its decision-making responsibility. See also Developments in the Law—Federal Habeas Corpus, 83 Harv.L.Rev. 1038, 1188 (1970).

Where a full-time magistrate is not available, the duties contemplated by this rule may be assigned to a part-time magistrate.

HISTORICAL NOTES

Change of Name

United States magistrate appointed under section 631 of Title 28, Judiciary and Judicial Procedure, to be known as United States magistrate judge after Dec. 1, 1990, with any reference to United States magistrate or magistrate in Title 28, in any other Federal statute, etc., deemed a reference to United States magistrate judge appointed under section 631 of Title 28, see section 321 of Pub.L. 101–650, set out as a note under section 631 of Title 28.

Rule 11. Federal Rules of Civil Procedure; Extent of Applicability

The Federal Rules of Civil Procedure, to the extent that they are not inconsistent with these rules, may be applied, when appropriate, to petitions filed under these rules.

ADVISORY COMMITTEE NOTES

1976 Adoption

Habeas corpus proceedings are characterized as civil in nature. See, *e.g., Fisher v. Baker,* 203 U.S. 174, 181 (1906). However, under Fed.R.Civ.P. 81(a)(2), the applicability of the civil rules to habeas corpus actions has been limited, although the various courts which have considered this problem have had difficulty in setting out the boundaries of this limitation. See *Harris v. Nelson,* 394 U.S. 286 (1969) at 289, footnote 1. Rule 11 is intended to conform with the Supreme Court's approach in the *Harris* case. There the court was dealing with the petitioner's contention that Civil Rule 33 granting the right to discovery via written interrogatories is wholly applicable to habeas corpus proceedings. The court held:

> We agree with the Ninth Circuit that Rule 33 of the Federal Rules of Civil Procedure is not applicable to habeas corpus proceedings and that 28 U.S.C. § 2246 does not authorize interrogatories except in limited circumstances not applicable to this case; but we conclude that, in appropriate circumstances, a district court, confronted by a petition for habeas corpus which establishes a prima facie case for relief, may use or authorize the use of suitable discovery procedures, including interrogatories, reasonably fashioned to elicit facts necessary to help the court to "dispose of the matter as law and justice require" 28 U.S.C. § 2243.

394 U.S. at 290

The court then went on to consider the contention that the "conformity" provision of Rule 81(a)(2) should be rigidly applied so that the civil rules would be applicable only to the extent that habeas corpus practice had conformed to the practice in civil actions at the time of the adoption of the Federal Rules of Civil Procedure on September 16, 1938. The court said:

> Although there is little direct evidence, relevant to the present problem, of the purpose of the "conformity" provision of Rule 81(a)(2), the concern of the draftsmen, as a general matter, seems to have been to provide for the continuing applicability of the "civil" rules in their new form to those areas of practice in habeas corpus and other enumerated proceedings in which the "specified" proceedings had theretofore utilized the modes of civil practice. Otherwise, those proceedings were to be considered outside of the scope of the rules without prejudice, of course, to the use of particular rules by analogy or otherwise, where appropriate.

394 U.S. at 294

The court then reiterated its commitment to judicial discretion in formulating rules and procedures for habeas corpus proceedings by stating:

> [T]he habeas corpus jurisdiction and the duty to exercise it being present, the courts may fashion appropriate modes of procedure, by analogy to existing rules or otherwise in conformity with judicial usage.

Where their duties require it, this is the inescapable obligation of the courts. Their authority is expressly confirmed in the All Writs Act, 28 U.S.C. § 1651.

394 U.S. at 299

Rule 6 of these proposed rules deals specifically with the issue of discovery in habeas actions in a manner consistent with *Harris*. Rule 11 extends this approach to allow the court considering the petition to use any of the rules of civil procedure (unless inconsistent with these rules of habeas corpus) when in its discretion the court decides they are appropriate under the circumstances of the particular case. The court does not have to rigidly apply rules which would be inconsistent or inequitable in the overall framework of habeas corpus. Rule 11 merely recognizes and affirms their discretionary power to use their judgment in promoting the ends of justice.

Rule 11 permits application of the civil rules only when it would be appropriate to do so. Illustrative of an inappropriate application is that rejected by the Supreme Court in *Pitchess v. Davis,* 95 S.Ct. 1748 (1975), holding that Fed. R.Civ.P. 60(b) should not be applied in a habeas case when it would have the effect of altering the statutory exhaustion requirement of 28 U.S.C. § 2254.

APPENDIX OF FORMS

MODEL FORM FOR USE IN APPLICATIONS FOR HABEAS CORPUS UNDER 28 U.S.C. § 2254

Name ______________________________
Prison number ______________________
Place of confinement _________________

____

United States District Court _______ District of ______________________________________

Case No. ______________________________
(To be supplied by Clerk of U.S. District Court)

______________________________________,
PETITIONER
(Full name)

v.

______________________________________,
RESPONDENT
(Name of Warden, Superintendent, Jailor, or authorized person having custody of petitioner)

and

THE ATTORNEY GENERAL OF THE STATE OF ______________________________________
______________________________, ADDITIONAL RESPONDENT.

(If petitioner is attacking a judgment which imposed a sentence to be served in the *future,* petitioner must fill in the name of the state where the judgment was entered. If petitioner has a sentence to be served in the *future* under a federal judgment which he wishes to attack, he should file a motion under 28 U.S.C. § 2255, in the federal court which entered the judgment.)

PETITION FOR WRIT OF HABEAS CORPUS BY A PERSON IN STATE CUSTODY

Instructions—Read Carefully

(1) This petition must be legibly handwritten or typewritten, and signed by the petitioner under penalty of perjury. Any false statement of a material fact may serve as the basis for prosecution and conviction for perjury. All questions must be answered concisely in the proper space on the form.

(2) Additional pages are not permitted except with respect to the *facts* which you rely upon to support your grounds for relief. No citation of authorities need be furnished. If briefs or arguments are submitted, they should be submitted in the form of a separate memorandum.

(3) Upon receipt of a fee of $5 your petition will be filed if it is in proper order.

(4) If you do not have the necessary filing fee, you may request permission to proceed *in forma pauperis,* in which event you must execute the declaration on the last page, setting forth information establishing your inability to prepay the fees and costs or give security therefor. If you wish to proceed *in forma pauperis,* you must have an authorized officer at the penal institution complete the certificate as to the amount of money and securities on deposit to your credit in any account in the institution. If your prison account exceeds $________, you must pay the filing fee as required by the rule of the district court.

(5) Only judgments entered by one court may be challenged in a single petition. If you seek to challenge judgments entered by different courts either in the same state or in different states, you must file separate petitions as to each court.

(6) Your attention is directed to the fact that you must include all grounds for relief and all facts supporting such grounds for relief in the petition you file seeking relief from any judgment of conviction.

(7) When the petition is fully completed, *the original and two copies* must be mailed to the Clerk of the United States District Court whose address is ______________________________________

____

(8) Petitions which do not conform to these instructions will be returned with a notation as to the deficiency.

PETITION

1. Name and location of court which entered the judgment of conviction under attack ____________________
____
2. Date of judgment of conviction ____________________
3. Length of sentence ____________________
4. Nature of offense involved (all counts) ____________________
____
____
____

5. What was your plea? (Check one)
(a) Not guilty ☐
(b) Guilty ☐
(c) Nolo contendere ☐
If you entered a guilty plea to one count or indictment, and a not guilty plea to another count or indictment, give details:
____

6. Kind of trial: (Check one)
   (a) Jury ☐
   (b) Judge only ☐
7. Did you testify at the trial?
   Yes ☐ No ☐
8. Did you appeal from the judgment of conviction?
   Yes ☐ No ☐
9. If you did appeal, answer the following:
   (a) Name of court ______
   (b) Result ______
   (c) Date of result ______
10. Other than a direct appeal from the judgment of conviction and sentence, have you previously filed any petitions, applications, or motions with respect to this judgment in any court, state or federal?
    Yes ☐ No ☐
11. If your answer to 10 was "yes," give the following information:
    (a) (1) Name of court ______
    (2) Nature of proceeding ______
    (3) Grounds raised ______
    (4) Did you receive an evidentiary hearing on your petition, application or motion?
    Yes ☐ No ☐
    (5) Result ______
    (6) Date of result ______
    (b) As to any second petition, application or motion give the same information:
    (1) Name of court ______
    (2) Nature of proceeding ______
    (3) Grounds raised ______
    (4) Did you receive an evidentiary hearing on your petition, application or motion?
    Yes ☐ No ☐
    (5) Result ______
    (6) Date of result ______
    (c) As to any third petition, application or motion, give the same information:
    (1) Name of court ______
    (2) Nature of proceeding ______
    (3) Grounds raised ______
    (4) Did you receive an evidentiary hearing on your petition, application or motion?
    Yes ☐ No ☐
    (5) Result ______
    (6) Date of result ______
    (d) Did you appeal to the highest state court having jurisdiction the result of action taken on any petition, application or motion?
    (1) First petition, etc. Yes ☐ No ☐
    (2) Second petition, etc. Yes ☐ No ☐
    (3) Third petition, etc. Yes ☐ No ☐
    (e) If you did *not* appeal from the adverse action on any petition, application or motion, explain briefly why you did not:
    ______
12. State *concisely* every ground on which you claim that you are being held unlawfully. Summarize *briefly* the *facts* supporting each ground. If necessary, you may attach pages stating additional grounds and *facts* supporting same.

Caution: In order to proceed in the federal court, you must ordinarily first exhaust your state court remedies as to each ground on which you request action by the federal court. If you fail to set forth all grounds in this petition, you may be barred from presenting additional grounds at a later date.

For your information, the following is a list of the most frequently raised grounds for relief in habeas corpus proceedings. Each statement preceded by a letter constitutes a separate ground for possible relief. You may raise any grounds which you may have other than those listed if you have exhausted your state court remedies with respect to them. However, *you should raise in this petition all available grounds* (relating to this conviction) on which you base your allegations that you are being held in custody unlawfully.

Do not check any of these listed grounds. If you select one or more of these grounds for relief, you must allege facts. The petition will be returned to you if you merely check (a) through (j) or any one of these grounds.

(a) Conviction obtained by plea of guilty which was unlawfully induced or not made voluntarily with understanding of the nature of the charge and the consequences of the plea.
(b) Conviction obtained by use of coerced confession.
(c) Conviction obtained by use of evidence gained pursuant to an unconstitutional search and seizure.
(d) Conviction obtained by use of evidence obtained pursuant an unlawful arrest.
(e) Conviction obtained by a violation of the privilege against self-incrimination.
(f) Conviction obtained by the unconstitutional failure of the prosecution to disclose to the defendant evidence favorable to the defendant.
(g) Conviction obtained by a violation of the protection against double jeopardy.
(h) Conviction obtained by action of a grand or petit jury which was unconstitutionally selected and impaneled.
(i) Denial of effective assistance of counsel.
(j) Denial of right of appeal.

A. Ground one: ______

Supporting FACTS (tell your story *briefly* without citing cases or law): ______

____

____

B. Ground two: ______________________________

Supporting FACTS (tell your story *briefly* without citing cases or law): ______________________________

____

____

____

____

C. Ground three: ______________________________

Supporting FACTS (tell your story *briefly* without citing cases or law): ______________________________

____

____

____

____

D. Ground four: ______________________________

Supporting FACTS (tell your story *briefly* without citing cases or law): ______________________________

____

____

____

13. If any of the grounds listed in 12A, B, C, and D were not previously presented in any other court, state or federal, state *briefly* what grounds were not so presented, and give your reasons for not presenting them: ______________________________

____

14. Do you have any petition or appeal now pending in any court, either state or federal, as to the judgment under attack?
Yes ☐ No ☐
15. Give the name and address, if known, of each attorney who represented you in the following stages of the judgment attacked herein:
(a) At preliminary hearing ______________________________
(b) At arraignment and plea ______________________________
(c) At trial ______________________________
(d) At sentencing ______________________________
(e) On appeal ______________________________
(f) In any post-conviction proceeding ______________________________
(g) On appeal from any adverse ruling in a post-conviction proceeding ______________________________
16. Were you sentenced on more than one count of an indictment, or on more than one indictment, in the same court and at the same time?
Yes ☐ No ☐
17. Do you have any future sentence to serve after you complete the sentence imposed by the judgment under attack?
Yes ☐ No ☐
(a) If so, give name and location of court which imposed sentence to be served in the future: ______________________________
(b) And give date and length of sentence to be served in the future: ______________________________
(c) Have you filed, or do you contemplate filing, any petition attacking the judgment which imposed the sentence to be served in the future?
Yes ☐ No ☐

Wherefore, petitioner prays that the Court grant petitioner relief to which he may be entitled in this proceeding.

____
Signature of Attorney (if any)

I declare (or certify, verify, or state) under penalty of perjury that the foregoing is true and correct. Executed on ______________.
(date)

____
Signature of Petitioner

IN FORMA PAUPERIS DECLARATION

____
[Insert appropriate court]

____
(Petitioner)
v.
____
(Respondent(s))

DECLARATION IN SUPPORT OF REQUEST TO PROCEED *IN FORMA PAUPERIS*

I, ______________, declare that I am the petitioner in the above entitled case; that in support of my motion to proceed without being required to prepay fees, costs or give security therefor, I state that because of my poverty I am unable to pay the costs of said proceeding or to give security therefor; that I believe I am entitled to relief.

1. Are you presently employed? Yes ☐ No ☐
   a. If the answer is "yes," state the amount of your salary or wages per month, and give the name and address of your employer.
   ____
   b. If the answer is "no," state the date of last employment and the amount of the salary and wages per month which you received.
   ____

2. Have you received within the past twelve months any money from any of the following sources?
   a. Business, profession or form of self-employment? Yes ☐ No ☐
   b. Rent payments, interest or dividends? Yes ☐ No ☐
   c. Pensions, annuities or life insurance payments? Yes ☐ No ☐
   d. Gifts or inheritances? Yes ☐ No ☐
   e. Any other sources? Yes ☐ No ☐

   If the answer to any of the above is "yes," describe each source of money and state the amount received from each during the past twelve months. ____________________
   ____
   ____
   ____
   ____

3. Do you own cash, or do you have money in a checking or savings account?
   Yes ☐ No ☐ (include any funds in prison accounts.)

   If the answer is "yes," state the total value of the items owned. ____________________
   ____
   ____

4. Do you own any real estate, stocks, bonds, notes, automobiles, or other valuable property (excluding ordinary household furnishings and clothing)?
   Yes ☐ No ☐

   If the answer is "yes," describe the property and state its approximate value. ____________________
   ____
   ____

5. List the persons who are dependent upon you for support, state your relationship to those persons, and indicate how much you contribute toward their support.
   ____
   ____
   ____

I declare (or certify, verify, or state) under penalty of perjury that the foregoing is true and correct. Executed on ____________.
(date)

____
Signature of Petitioner

Certificate

I hereby certify that the petitioner herein has the sum of $________ on account to his credit at the ____________ institution where he is confined. I further certify that petitioner likewise has the following securities to his credit according to the records of said ____________ institution: ____________
____
____
____

____
Authorized Officer of Institution

(As amended Apr. 28, 1982, eff. Aug. 1, 1982.)

MODEL FORM FOR USE IN 28 U.S.C. § 2254 CASES INVOLVING A RULE 9 ISSUE

Form No. 9

United States District Court,
____________ District of ____________
Case No. ____________
____________, PETITIONER
v.
____________, RESPONDENT
and
____________, ADDITIONAL RESPONDENT

Petitioner's Response as to Why His Petition Should Not Be Barred Under Rule 9

Explanation and Instructions—Read Carefully

(I) Rule 9. Delayed or successive petitions.

(a) Delayed petitions. A petition may be dismissed if it appears that the state of which the respondent is an officer has been prejudiced in its ability to respond to the petition by delay in its filing unless the petitioner shows that it is based on grounds of which he could not have had knowledge by the exercise of reasonable diligence before the circumstances prejudicial to the state occurred.

(b) Successive petitions. A second or successive petition may be dismissed if the judge finds that it fails to allege new or different grounds for relief and the prior determination was on the merits or, if new and different grounds are alleged, the judge finds that the failure of the petitioner to assert those grounds in a prior petition constituted an abuse of the writ.

(II) Your petition for habeas corpus has been found to be subject to dismissal under rule 9( ) for the following reasons(s):
____
____
____
____

(III) This form has been sent so that you may explain why your petition contains the defect(s) noted in (II) above. It is required that you fill out this form and send it back to the court within ________ days. Failure to do so will result in the automatic dismissal of your petition.

(IV) When you have fully completed this form, the original and two copies must be mailed to the Clerk of the United States District Court whose address is ______

______

(V) This response must be legibly handwritten or typewritten, and signed by the petitioner under penalty of perjury. Any false statement of a material fact may serve as the basis for prosecution and conviction for perjury. All questions must be answered concisely in the proper space on the form.

(VI) Additional pages are not permitted except with respect to the *facts* which you rely upon in item 4 or 5 in the response. Any citation of authorities should be kept to an absolute minimum and is only appropriate if there has been a change in the law since the judgment you are attacking was rendered.

(VII) Respond to 4 *or* 5 below, not to both, unless (II) above indicates that you must answer both sections.

RESPONSE

1. Have you had the assistance of an attorney, other law-trained personnel, or writ writers since the conviction your petition is attacking was entered?

   Yes ☐ No ☐

2. If you checked "yes" above, specify as precisely as you can the period(s) of time during which you received such assistance, up to and including the present.

   ______
   ______

3. Describe the nature of the assistance, including the names of those who rendered it to you. ______

   ______
   ______
   ______
   ______

4. If your petition is in jeopardy because of delay prejudicial to the state under rule 9(a), explain why you feel the delay has not been prejudicial and/or why the delay is excusable under the terms of 9(a). This should be done by relying upon FACTS, not your opinions or conclusions.

   ______
   ______
   ______
   ______
   ______
   ______

5. If your petition is in jeopardy under rule 9(b) because it asserts the same grounds as a previous petition, explain why you feel it deserves a reconsideration. If its fault under rule 9(b) is that it asserts new grounds which should have been included in a prior petition, explain why you are raising these grounds now rather than previously. Your explanation should rely on FACTS, not your opinions or conclusions. ______

   ______
   ______
   ______
   ______
   ______
   ______
   ______
   ______

I declare (or certify, verify, or state) under penalty of perjury that the foregoing is true and correct. Executed on ______

(date)

______

Signature of Petitioner

(As amended Apr. 28, 1982, eff. Aug. 1, 1982.)

RULES GOVERNING SECTION 2255 PROCEEDINGS FOR THE UNITED STATES DISTRICT COURTS

Effective February 1, 1977
Amendments received to January 4, 1999

Rule
1. Scope of Rules.
2. Motion.
3. Filing Motion.
4. Preliminary Consideration by Judge.
5. Answers; Contents.
6. Discovery.
7. Expansion of Record.
8. Evidentiary Hearing.
9. Delayed or Successive Motions.
10. Powers of Magistrates.
11. Time for Appeal.
12. Federal Rules of Criminal and Civil Procedure; Extent of Applicability.

APPENDIX OF FORMS

Model Form for Motions under 28 U.S.C. § 2255.
Model Form for Use in 28 U.S.C. § 2255 Cases Involving a Rule 9 Issue.

ORDERS OF THE SUPREME COURT OF THE UNITED STATES ADOPTING AND AMENDING RULES GOVERNING SECTION 2255 PROCEEDINGS

ORDER OF APRIL 26, 1976

1. That the rules and forms governing proceedings in the United States District Courts under Section 2254 and Section 2255 of Title 28, United States Code, as approved by the Judicial Conference of the United States be, and they hereby are, prescribed pursuant to Section 2072 of Title 28, United States Code and Sections 3771 and 3772 of Title 18, United States Code.

2. That the aforementioned rules and forms shall take effect August 1, 1976, and shall be applicable to all proceedings then pending except to the extent that in the opinion of the court their application in a particular proceeding would not be feasible or would work injustice.

3. That THE CHIEF JUSTICE be, and he hereby is, authorized to transmit the aforementioned rules and forms governing Section 2254 and Section 2255 proceedings to the Congress in accordance with the provisions of Section 2072 of Title 28 and Sections 3771 and 3772 of Title 18, United States Code.

CONGRESSIONAL ACTION ON PROPOSED RULES AND FORMS GOVERNING PROCEEDING UNDER 28 U.S.C. §§ 2254 AND 2255

Pub.L. 94–349, § 2, July 8, 1976, 90 Stat. 822, provided: "That, notwithstanding the provisions of section 2072 of title 28 of the United States Code, the rules and forms governing section 2254 cases in the United States district courts and the rules and forms governing section 2255 proceedings in the United States district courts which are embraced by the order entered by the United States Supreme Court on April 26, 1976, and which were transmitted to the Congress on or about April 26, 1976, shall not take effect until thirty days after the adjournment sine die of the 94th Congress, or until and to the extent approved by Act of Congress, whichever is earlier."

Pub.L. 94–426, § 1, Sept. 28, 1976, 90 Stat. 1334, provided: "That the rules governing section 2254 cases in the United States district courts and the rules governing section 2255 proceedings for the United States district courts, as proposed by the United States Supreme Court, which were delayed by the Act entitled 'An Act to delay the effective date of certain proposed amendments to the Federal Rules of Criminal Procedure and certain other rules promulgated by the United States Supreme Court' (Public Law 94–349), are approved with the amendments set forth in section 2 of this Act and shall take effect as so amended, with respect to petitions under section 2254 and motions under section 2255 of title 28 of the United States Code filed on or after February 1, 1977."

ORDER OF APRIL 30, 1979

1. That Rule 10 of the Rules Governing Proceedings in the United States District Courts on application under Section 2254 of Title 28, United States Code, be, and hereby is, amended to read as follows:

[See amendment made thereby under Rule 10 set out following section 2254.]

2. That Rules 10 and 11 of the Rules Governing Proceedings in the United States District Courts on a motion under Section 2255 of Title 28, United States Code, be, and they hereby are, amended to read as follows:

[See amendments made thereby under the respective rules, post.]

3. That the foregoing amendments to the Rules Governing Proceedings in the United States District Courts under Section 2254 and Section 2255 of Title 28, United States Code, shall take effect on August 1, 1979, and shall be applicable to all proceedings then pending except to the extent that in the opinion of the court their application in a particular proceeding would not be feasible or would work injustice.

4. That THE CHIEF JUSTICE be, and he hereby is, authorized to transmit the aforementioned amendments to the Rules Governing Section 2254 and Section 2255 Proceedings to the Congress in accordance with the provisions of Section 2072 of Title 28, United States Code, and Sections 3771 and 3772 of Title 18, United States Code.

ORDER OF APRIL 28, 1982

1. That the rules and forms governing proceedings in the United States district courts under Section 2254 and Section 2255 of Title 28, United States Code, be, and they hereby are, amended by including therein an amendment to Rule 2(c) of the rules for Section 2254 cases, an amendment to Rule 2(b) of the rules for Section 2255 proceedings, and amendments to the model forms for use in applications under Section 2254 and motions under Section 2255, as hereinafter set forth:

[See amendments made thereby under respective rules and forms post and following section 2254.]

2. That the aforementioned amendments shall take effect August 1, 1982, and shall be applicable to all proceedings thereafter commenced and, insofar as just and practicable, all proceedings then pending.

3. That THE CHIEF JUSTICE be, and he hereby is, authorized to transmit the aforementioned amendments to the Congress in accordance with Section 2072 of Title 28 and Sections 3771 and 3772 of Title 18, United States Code.

ORDER OF APRIL 22, 1993

1. That the Federal Rules of Criminal Procedure for the United States District Courts be, and they hereby are, amended by including therein amendments to Criminal Rules 1, 3, 4, 5, 5.1, 6, 9, 12, 16, 17, 26.2, 32, 32.1, 40, 41, 44, 46, 49, 50, 54, 55, 57, and 58, and new Rule 26.3, and an amendment to Rule 8 of the Rules Governing Section 2255 Proceedings.

[See amendments made thereby under the respective rules set out in the Federal Criminal Code and Rules and under Rule 8, post.]

2. That the foregoing amendments to the Federal Rules of Criminal Procedure shall take effect on December 1, 1993, and shall govern all proceedings in criminal cases thereafter commenced and, insofar as just and practicable, all proceedings in criminal cases then pending.

3. That THE CHIEF JUSTICE be, and he hereby is, authorized to transmit to the Congress the foregoing amendments to the Federal Rules of Criminal Procedure in accordance with the provisions of Section 2072 of Title 28, United States Code.

HISTORICAL NOTES

Effective Date of Rules; 1976 Act

Rules, and the amendments thereto by Pub.L. 94–426, Sept. 28, 1976, 90 Stat. 1334, effective with respect to petitions under section 2254 of this title and motions under section 2255 of this title filed on or after Feb. 1, 1977, see section 1 of Pub.L. 94–426, set out as a note under section 2255 of this title.

Rule 1. Scope of Rules

These rules govern the procedure in the district court on a motion under 28 U.S.C. § 2255:

(1) by a person in custody pursuant to a judgment of that court for a determination that the judgment was imposed in violation of the Constitution or laws of the United States, or that the court was without jurisdiction to impose such judgment, or that the sentence was in excess of the maximum authorized by law, or is otherwise subject to collateral attack; and

(2) by a person in custody pursuant to a judgment of a state or other federal court and subject to future custody under a judgment of the district court for a determination that such future custody will be in violation of the Constitution or laws of the United States, or that the district court was without jurisdiction to impose such judgment, or that the sentence was in excess of the maximum authorized by law, or is otherwise subject to collateral attack.

ADVISORY COMMITTEE NOTES

1976 Adoption

The basic scope of this postconviction remedy is prescribed by 28 U.S.C. § 2255. Under these rules the person seeking relief from federal custody files a motion to vacate, set aside, or correct sentence, rather than a petition for habeas corpus. This is consistent with the terminology used in section 2255 and indicates the difference between this remedy and federal habeas for a state prisoner. Also, habeas corpus is available to the person in federal custody if his "remedy by motion is inadequate or ineffective to test the legality of his detention."

Whereas sections 2241–2254 (dealing with federal habeas corpus for those in state custody) speak of the district court judge "issuing the writ" as the operative remedy, section 2255 provides that, if the judge finds the movant's assertions to be meritorious, he "shall discharge the prisoner or resentence him or grant a new trial or correct the sentence as may appear appropriate." This is possible because a motion under § 2255 is a further step in the movant's criminal case and not a separate civil action, as appears from the legislative history of section 2 of S. 20, 80th Congress, the provisions of which were incorporated by the same Congress in title 28 U.S.C. as § 2255. In reporting S. 20 favorably the Senate Judiciary Committee said (Sen.Rep. 1526, 80th Cong.2d Sess., p. 2):

The two main advantages of such motion remedy over the present habeas corpus are as follows:

First, habeas corpus is a separate civil action and not a further step in the criminal case in which petitioner is sentenced (Ex parte *Tom Tong,* 108 U.S. 556, 559 (1883)). It is not a determination of guilt or innocence of the charge upon which petitioner was sentenced. Where a prisoner sustains his right to discharge in habeas corpus, it is usually because some right—such as lack of counsel—has been denied which reflects no determination of his guilt or innocence but affects solely the fairness of his earlier criminal trial. Even under the broad power in the statute "to dispose of the party as law and justice require" (28 U.S.C.A., sec. 461), the court or judge is by no means in the same advantageous position in habeas corpus to do justice as would be so if the matter were determined in the criminal proceeding (see *Medley,* petitioner, 134 U.S. 160, 174 (1890)). For instance, the judge (by habeas corpus) cannot grant a new trial in the criminal case. Since the motion remedy is in the criminal proceeding, this section 2 affords the opportunity and expressly gives the broad powers to set aside the judgment and to "discharge the prisoner or resentence him or grant a new trial or correct the sentence as may appear appropriate."

The fact that a motion under § 2255 is a further step in the movant's criminal case rather than a separate civil action has significance at several points in these rules. See, *e.g.*, advisory committee note to Rule 3 (re no filing fee), advisory committee note to Rule 4 (re availability of files, etc., relating to the judgment), advisory committee note to Rule 6 (re availability of discovery under criminal procedure rules), advisory committee note to Rule 11 (re no extension of time for appeal), and advisory committee note to Rule 12 (re applicability of federal criminal rules). However, the fact that Congress has characterized the motion as a further step in the criminal proceedings does *not* mean that proceedings upon such a motion are of necessity governed by the legal principles which are applicable at a criminal trial regarding such matters as counsel, presence, confrontation, self-incrimination, and burden of proof.

The challenge of decisions such as the revocation of probation or parole are not appropriately dealt with under 28 U.S.C. § 2255, which is a continuation of the original criminal action. Other remedies, such as habeas corpus, are available in such situations.

Although Rule 1 indicates that these rules apply to a motion for a determination that the judgment was imposed "in violation of the . . . laws of the United States," the language of 28 U.S.C. § 2255, it is not the intent of these rules to define or limit what is encompassed within that phrase. See *Davis v. United States,* 417 U.S. 333 (1974), holding that it is not true "that every asserted error of law can be raised on a § 2255 motion," and that the appropriate inquiry is "whether the claimed error of law was 'a fundamental defect which inherently results in a complete miscarriage of justice,' and whether '[i]t . . . present[s] exceptional circumstances where the need for the remedy afforded by the writ of habeas corpus is apparent.' "

For a discussion of the "custody" requirement and the intended limited scope of this remedy, see advisory committee note to § 2254 Rule 1.

Rule 2. Motion

(a) Nature of application for relief. If the person is presently in custody pursuant to the federal judgment in question, or if not presently in custody may be subject to such custody in the future pursuant to such judgment, the application for relief shall be in the form of a motion to vacate, set aside, or correct the sentence.

(b) Form of Motion. The motion shall be in substantially the form annexed to these rules, except that any district court may by local rule require that motions filed with it shall be in a form prescribed by the local rule. Blank motions in the prescribed form shall be made available without charge by the clerk of the district court to applicants upon their request. It shall specify all the grounds for relief which are available to the movant and of which he has or, by the exercise of reasonable diligence, should have knowledge and shall set forth in summary form the facts supporting each of the grounds thus specified. It shall also state the relief requested. The motion shall be typewritten or legibly handwritten and shall be signed under penalty of perjury by the petitioner.

(c) Motion to be directed to one judgment only. A motion shall be limited to the assertion of a claim for relief against one judgment only of the district court. If a movant desires to attack the validity of other judgments of that or any other district court under which he is in custody or may be subject to future custody, as the case may be, he shall do so by separate motions.

(d) Return of insufficient motion. If a motion received by the clerk of a district court does not substantially comply with the requirements of rule 2 or rule 3, it may be returned to the movant, if a judge of the court so directs, together with a statement of the reason for its return. The clerk shall retain a copy of the motion.

(As amended Pub.L. 94–426, § 2(3), (4), Sept. 28, 1976, 90 Stat. 1334; Apr. 28, 1982, eff. Aug. 1, 1982.)

ADVISORY COMMITTEE NOTES

1976 Adoption

Under these rules the application for relief is in the form of a motion rather than a petition (see Rule 1 and advisory committee note). Therefore, there is no requirement that the movant name a respondent. This is consistent with 28 U.S.C. § 2255. The United States Attorney for the district in which the judgment under attack was entered is the proper party to oppose the motion since the federal government is the movant's adversary of record.

If the movant is attacking a federal judgment which will subject him to future custody, he must be in present custody (see Rule 1 and advisory committee note) as the result of a state or federal governmental action. He need not alter the nature of the motion by trying to include the government officer who presently has official custody of him as a pseudo-respondent, or third-party plaintiff, or other fabrication. The court hearing his motion attacking the future custody can exercise jurisdiction over those having him in present custody without the use of artificial pleading devices.

There is presently a split among the courts as to whether a person currently in state custody may use a § 2255 motion to obtain relief from a federal judgment under which he will be subjected to custody in the future. Negative, see *Newton v. United States,* 329 F.Supp. 90 (S.D. Texas 1971); affirmative, see *Desmond v. The United States Board of Parole,* 397 F.2d 386 (1st Cir.1968), *cert. denied,* 393 U.S. 919 (1968); and *Paalino v. United States,* 314 F.Supp. 875 (C.D.Cal.1970). It is intended that these rules settle the matter in favor of the prisoner's being able to file a § 2255 motion for relief under those circumstances. The proper district in which to file such a motion is the one in which is situated the court which rendered the sentence under attack.

Under Rule 35, Federal Rules of Criminal Procedure, the court may correct an illegal sentence or a sentence imposed in an illegal manner, or may reduce the sentence. This remedy should be used, rather than a motion under these § 2255 rules, whenever applicable, but there is some overlap between the two proceedings which has caused the courts difficulty.

The movant should not be barred from an appropriate remedy because he has misstyled his motion. See *United States v. Morgan,* 346 U.S. 502, 505 (1954). The court should construe it as whichever one is proper under the circumstances and decide it on its merits. For a § 2255 motion construed as a Rule 35 motion, see *Heflin v. United States,* 358 U.S. 415 (1959); and *United States v. Coke,* 404 F.2d 836 (2d Cir.1968). For writ of error coram nobis treated as a Rule 35 motion, see *Hawkins v. United States,* 324 F.Supp. 223 (E.D. Texas, Tyler Division 1971). For a Rule 35 motion treated as a § 2255 motion, see *Moss v. United States,* 263 F.2d 615 (5th Cir.1959); *Jones v. United States,* 400 F.2d 892 (8th Cir.1968), cert. denied 394 U.S. 991 (1969); and *United States v. Brown,* 413 F.2d 878 (9th Cir.1969), cert. denied, 397 U.S. 947 (1970).

One area of difference between § 2255 and Rule 35 motions is that for the latter there is no requirement that the movant be "in custody." *Heflin v. United States,* 358 U.S. 415, 418, 422 (1959); *Duggins v. United States,* 240 F.2d 479, 483 (6th Cir.1957). Compare with Rule 1 and advisory committee note for § 2255 motions. The importance of this distinction has decreased since *Peyton v. Rowe,* 391 U.S. 54 (1968), but it might still make a difference in particular situations.

A Rule 35 motion is used to attack the sentence imposed, not the basis for the sentence. The court in *Gilinsky v. United States,* 335 F.2d 914, 916 (9th Cir.1964), stated, "a Rule 35 motion presupposes a valid conviction. * * * [C]ollateral attack on errors allegedly committed at trial is not permissible under Rule 35." By illustration the court noted at page 917: "a Rule 35 proceeding contemplates the correction of a sentence of a court having jurisdiction. * * * [J]urisdictional defects * * * involve a collateral attack, they must ordinarily be presented under 28 U.S.C. § 2255." In *United States v. Semet,* 295 F.Supp. 1084 (E.D.Okla.1968), the prisoner moved under Rule 35 and § 2255 to invalidate the sentence he was serving on the grounds of his failure to understand the charge to which he pleaded guilty. The court said:

> As regards Defendant's Motion under Rule 35, said Motion must be denied as its [sic] presupposes a valid conviction of the offense with which he was charged and may be used only to attack the sentence. It may not be used to examine errors occurring prior to the imposition of sentence.

295 F.Supp. at 1085

See also: *Moss v. United States,* 263 F.2d at 616; *Duggins v. United States,* 240 F.2d at 484; *Migdal v. United States,* 298 F.2d 513, 514 (9th Cir.1961); *Jones v. United States,* 400 F.2d at 894; *United States v. Coke,* 404 F.2d at 847; and *United States v. Brown,* 413 F.2d at 879.

A major difficulty in deciding whether Rule 35 or § 2255 is the proper remedy is the uncertainty as to what is meant by an "illegal sentence." The Supreme Court dealt with this issue in *Hill v. United States,* 368 U.S. 424 (1962). The prisoner brought a § 2255 motion to vacate sentence on the ground that he had not been given a Fed.R.Crim.P. 32(a) opportunity to make a statement in his own behalf at the time of sentencing. The majority held this was not an error subject to collateral attack under § 2255. The five-member majority considered the motion as one brought pursuant to Rule 35, but denied relief, stating:

> [T]he narrow function of Rule 35 is to permit correction at any time of an illegal *sentence,* not to re-examine errors occurring at the trial or other proceedings prior to the imposition of sentence. The sentence in this case was not illegal. The punishment meted out was not in excess of that prescribed by the relevant statutes, multiple terms were not imposed for the same offense, nor were the terms of the sentence itself legally or constitutionally invalid in any other respect.

368 U.S. at 430

The four dissenters felt the majority definition of "illegal" was too narrow.

> [Rule 35] provides for the correction of an "illegal sentence" without regard to the reasons why that sentence is illegal and contains not a single word to support the Court's conclusion that only a sentence illegal by reason of the punishment it imposes is "illegal" within the meaning of the Rule. I would have thought that a sentence imposed in an illegal manner—whether the amount or form of the punishment meted out constitutes an additional violation of law or not—would be recognized as an "illegal sentence" under any normal reading of the English language.

368 U.S. at 431–432

The 1966 amendment of Rule 35 added language permitting correction of a sentence imposed in an "illegal manner." However, there is a 120-day time limit on a motion to do this, and the added language does not clarify the intent of the rule or its relation to § 2255.

The courts have been flexible in considering motions under circumstances in which relief might appear to be precluded by *Hill v. United States.* In *Peterson v. United States,* 432 F.2d 545 (8th Cir.1970), the court was confronted with a motion for reduction of sentence by a prisoner claiming to have received a harsher sentence than his codefendants because he stood trial rather than plead guilty. He alleged that this violated his constitutional right to a jury trial. The court ruled that, even though it was past the 120-day time period for a motion to reduce sentence, the claim was still cognizable under Rule 35 as a motion to correct an illegal sentence.

The courts have made even greater use of § 2255 in these types of situations. In *United States v. Lewis,* 392 F.2d 440 (4th Cir.1968), the prisoner moved under § 2255 and Rule 35 for relief from a sentence he claimed was the result of the judge's misunderstanding of the relevant sentencing law. The court held that he could not get relief under Rule 35 because it was past the 120 days for correction of a sentence imposed in an illegal manner and under *Hill v. United States* it was not an illegal sentence. However, § 2255 was applicable because of its "otherwise subject to collateral attack" language. The flaw was not a mere trial error relating to the finding of guilt, but a rare and unusual error which amounted to "exceptional circumstances" embraced in § 2255's words "collateral attack." See 368 U.S. at 444 for discussion of other cases allowing use of § 2255 to attack the sentence itself in similar circumstances, especially where the judge has sentenced out of a misapprehension of the law.

In *United States v. McCarthy,* 433 F.2d 591, 592 (1st Cir.1970), the court allowed a prisoner who was past the time limit for a proper Rule 35 motion to use § 2255 to attack the sentence which he received upon a plea of guilty on the ground that it was induced by an unfulfilled promise of the prosecutor to recommend leniency. The court specifically noted that under § 2255 this was a proper collateral attack on the sentence and there was no need to attack the conviction as well.

The court in *United States v. Malcolm,* 432 F.2d 809, 814, 818 (2d Cir.1970), allowed a prisoner to challenge his sentence under § 2255 without attacking the conviction. It held Rule 35 inapplicable because the sentence was not illegal on its face, but the manner in which the sentence was imposed raised a question of the denial of due process in the sentencing itself which was cognizable under § 2255.

The flexible approach taken by the courts in the above cases seems to be the reasonable way to handle these situations in which Rule 35 and § 2255 appear to overlap. For a further discussion of this problem, see C. Wright, Federal Practice and Procedure: Criminal §§ 581–587 (1969, Supp. 1975).

See the advisory committee note to Rule 2 of the § 2254 rules for further discussion of the purposes and intent of Rule 2 of these § 2255 rules.

1982 Amendment

Subdivision (b). The amendment takes into account 28 U.S.C. § 1746, enacted after adoption of the § 2255 rules. Section 1746 provides that in lieu of an affidavit an unsworn statement may be given under penalty of perjury in substantially the following form if executed within the United States, its territories, possessions or commonwealths: "I declare (or certify, verify, or state) under penalty of perjury that the foregoing is true and correct. Executed on (date). (Signature)." The statute is "intended to encompass prisoner litigation," and the statutory alternative is especially appropriate in such cases because a notary might not be readily available. *Carter v. Clark,* 616 F.2d 228 (5th Cir.1980). The § 2255 forms have been revised accordingly.

Rule 3. Filing Motion

(a) Place of filing; copies. A motion under these rules shall be filed in the office of the clerk of the district court. It shall be accompanied by two conformed copies thereof.

(b) Filing and service. Upon receipt of the motion and having ascertained that it appears on its face to comply with rules 2 and 3, the clerk of the district court shall file the motion and enter it on the docket in his office in the criminal action in which was entered the judgment to which it is directed. He shall thereupon deliver or serve a copy of the motion together with a notice of its filing on the United States Attorney of the district in which the judgment under attack was entered. The filing of the motion shall not require said United States Attorney to answer the motion or otherwise move with respect to it unless so ordered by the court.

ADVISORY COMMITTEE NOTES

1976 Adoption

There is no filing fee required of a movant under these rules. This is a change from the practice of charging $15 and is done to recognize specifically the nature of a § 2255 motion as being a continuation of the criminal case whose judgment is under attack.

The long-standing practice of requiring a $15 filing fee has followed from 28 U.S.C. § 1914(a) whereby "parties instituting any civil action * * * pay a filing fee of $15, except that on an application for a writ of habeas corpus the filing fee shall be $5." This has been held to apply to a proceeding under § 2255 despite the rationale that such a proceeding is a motion and thus a continuation of the criminal action. (See note to Rule 1.)

> A motion under Section 2255 is a civil action and the clerk has no choice but to charge a $15.00 filing fee unless by leave of court it is filed in forma pauperis.

McCune v. United States, 406 F.2d 417, 419 (6th Cir.1969).

Although the motion has been considered to be a new civil action in the nature of habeas corpus for filing purposes, the reduced fee for habeas has been held not applicable. The Tenth Circuit considered the specific issue in *Martin v. United States,* 273 F.2d 775 (10th Cir.1960), cert. denied, 365 U.S. 853 (1961), holding that the reduced fee was exclusive to habeas petitions.

> Counsel for Martin insists that, if a docket fee must be paid, the amount is $5 rather than $15 and bases his contention on the exception contained in 28 U.S.C. § 1914 that in habeas corpus the fee is $5. This reads into § 1914 language which is not there. While an application under § 2255 may afford the same relief as that previously obtainable by habeas corpus, it is not a petition for a writ of habeas corpus. A change in § 1914 must come from Congress.

273 F.2d at 778

Although for most situations § 2255 is intended to provide to the federal prisoner a remedy equivalent to habeas corpus as used by state prisoners, there is a major distinction between the two. Calling a § 2255 request for relief a motion rather than a petition militates toward charging no new filing fee, not an increased one. In the absence of convincing evidence to the contrary, there is no reason to suppose that Congress did not mean what it said in making a § 2255 action a motion. Therefore, as in other motions filed in a criminal action, there is no requirement of a filing fee. It is appropriate that the present situation of docketing a § 2255 motion as a new action and charging a $15 filing fee be remedied by rule when the whole question of § 2255 motions is thoroughly thought through and organized.

Even though there is no need to have a forma pauperis affidavit to proceed with the action since there is no requirement of a fee for filing the motion the affidavit remains attached to the form to be supplied potential movants. Most such movants are indigent, and this is a convenient way of getting this into the official record so that the judge may appoint counsel, order the government to pay witness fees, allow docketing of an appeal, and grant any other rights to which an indigent is entitled in the course of a § 2255 motion, when appropriate to the particular situation, without the need for an indigency petition and adjudication at such later point in the proceeding. This should result in a streamlining of the process to allow quicker disposition of these motions.

For further discussion of this rule, see the advisory committee note to Rule 3 of the § 2254 rules.

Rule 4. Preliminary Consideration by Judge

(a) Reference to judge; dismissal or order to answer. The original motion shall be presented promptly to the judge of the district court who presided at the movant's trial and sentenced him, or, if the judge who imposed sentence was not the trial judge, then it shall go to the judge who was in charge of that part of the proceedings being attacked by the movant. If the appropriate judge is unavailable to consider the motion, it shall be presented to another judge of the district in accordance with the procedure of the court for the assignment of its business.

(b) Initial consideration by judge. The motion, together with all the files, records, transcripts, and correspondence relating to the judgment under attack, shall be examined promptly by the judge to whom it is assigned. If it plainly appears from the face of the motion and any annexed exhibits and the prior proceedings in the case that the movant is not entitled to relief in the district court, the judge shall make an order for its summary dismissal and cause the movant to be notified. Otherwise, the judge shall order the United States Attorney to file an answer or other pleading within the period of time fixed by the court or to take such other action as the judge deems appropriate.

ADVISORY COMMITTEE NOTES

1976 Adoption

Rule 4 outlines the procedure for assigning the motion to a specific judge of the district court and the options available to the judge and the government after the motion is properly filed.

The long-standing majority practice in assigning motions made pursuant to § 2255 has been for the trial judge to determine the merits of the motion. In cases where the § 2255 motion is directed against the sentence, the merits have traditionally been decided by the judge who imposed sentence. The reasoning for this was first noted in *Carvell v. United States,* 173 F.2d 348–349 (4th Cir.1949):

> Complaint is made that the judge who tried the case passed upon the motion. Not only was there no impropriety in this, but it is highly desirable in such cases that the motions be passed on by the judge who is familiar with the facts and circumstances surrounding the trial, and is consequently not likely to be misled by false allegations as to what occurred.

This case, and its reasoning, has been almost unanimously endorsed by other courts dealing with the issue.

Commentators have been critical of having the motion decided by the trial judge. See Developments in the Law—Federal Habeas Corpus, 83 Harv.L.Rev. 1038, 1206–1208 (1970).

> [T]he trial judge may have become so involved with the decision that it will be difficult for him to review it objectively. Nothing in the legislative history suggests that "court" refers to a specific judge, and the procedural advantages of section 2255 are available whether or not the trial judge presides at the hearing.
>
> The theory that Congress intended the trial judge to preside at a section 2255 hearing apparently originated in *Carvell v. United States,* 173 F.2d 348 (4th Cir.1949) (per curiam), where the panel of judges included Chief Judge Parker of the Fourth Circuit, chairman of the Judicial Conference committee which drafted section 2255. But the legislative history does not indicate that Congress wanted the trial judge to preside. Indeed the advantages of section 2255 can all be achieved if the case is heard in the sentencing district, regardless of which judge hears it. According to the Senate committee report the purpose of the bill was to make the proceeding a part of the criminal action so the court could resentence the applicant, or grant him a new trial. (A judge presiding over a habeas corpus action does not have these powers.) In addition, Congress did not want the cases heard in the district of confinement because that tended to concentrate the burden on a few districts, and made it difficult for witnesses and records to be produced.

83 Harv.L.Rev. at 1207–1208

The Court of Appeals for the First Circuit has held that a judge other than the trial judge should rule on the 2255 motion. See *Halliday v. United States,* 380 F.2d 270 (1st Cir.1967).

There is a procedure by which the movant can have a judge other than the trial judge decide his motion in courts adhering to the majority rule. He can file an affidavit alleging bias in order to disqualify the trial judge. And there are circumstances in which the trial judge will, on his own, disqualify himself. See, *e.g., Webster v. United States,* 330 F.Supp. 1080 (1972). However, there has been some questioning of the effectiveness of this procedure. See Developments in the Law—Federal Habeas Corpus, 83 Harv.L.Rev. 1038, 1200–1207 (1970).

Subdivision (a) adopts the majority rule and provides that the trial judge, or sentencing judge if different and appropriate for the particular motion, will decide the motion made pursuant to these rules, recognizing that, under some circumstances, he may want to disqualify himself. A movant is not without remedy if he feels this is unfair to him. He can file an affidavit of bias. And there is the right to appellate review if the trial judge refuses to grant his motion. Because the trial judge is thoroughly familiar with the case, there is obvious administrative advantage in giving him the first opportunity to decide whether there are grounds for granting the motion.

Since the motion is part of the criminal action in which was entered the judgment to which it is directed, the files, records, transcripts, and correspondence relating to that judgment are automatically available to the judge in his consideration of the motion. He no longer need order them incorporated for that purpose.

Rule 4 has its basis in § 2255 (rather than 28 U.S.C. § 2243 in the corresponding habeas corpus rule) which does not have a specific time limitation as to when the answer must be made. Also, under § 2255, the United States Attorney for the district is the party served with the notice and a copy of the motion and required to answer (when appropriate). Subdivision (b) continues this practice since there is no respondent involved in the motion (unlike habeas) and the United States Attorney, as prosecutor in the case in question, is the most appropriate one to defend the judgment and oppose the motion.

The judge has discretion to require an answer or other appropriate response from the United States Attorney. See advisory committee note to Rule 4 of the § 2254 rules.

Rule 5. Answer; Contents

(a) Contents of answer. The answer shall respond to the allegations of the motion. In addition it shall state whether the movant has used any other available federal remedies including any prior post-conviction motions under these rules or those existing previous to the adoption of the present rules. The answer shall also state whether an evidentiary hearing was accorded the movant in a federal court.

(b) Supplementing the answer. The court shall examine its files and records to determine whether it has available copies of transcripts and briefs whose existence the answer has indicated. If any of these items should be absent, the government shall be ordered to supplement its answer by filing the needed records. The court shall allow the government an appropriate period of time in which to do so, without unduly delaying the consideration of the motion.

ADVISORY COMMITTEE NOTES

1976 Adoption

Unlike the habeas corpus statutes (see 28 U.S.C. §§ 2243, 2248) § 2255 does not specifically call for a return or answer by the United States Attorney or set any time limits as to when one must be submitted. The general practice, however, if the motion is not summarily dismissed, is for the government to file an answer to the motion as well as counter-affidavits, when appropriate. Rule 4 provides for an answer to the motion by the United States Attorney, and Rule 5 indicates what its contents should be.

There is no requirement that the movant exhaust his remedies prior to seeking relief under § 2255. However, the courts have held that such a motion is inappropriate if the movant is simultaneously appealing the decision.

> We are of the view that there is no jurisdictional bar to the District Court's entertaining a Section 2255 motion during the pendency of a direct appeal but that the orderly administration of criminal law precludes considering such a motion absent extraordinary circumstances.

***Womack v. United States,* 395 F.2d 630, 631 (D.C.Cir.1968)**

Also see *Masters v. Eide,* 353 F.2d 517 (8th Cir.1965). The answer may thus cut short consideration of the motion if it discloses the taking of an appeal which was omitted from the form motion filed by the movant.

There is nothing in § 2255 which corresponds to the § 2248 requirement of a traverse to the answer. Numerous cases have held that the government's answer and affidavits are not conclusive against the movant, and if they raise disputed issues of fact a hearing must be held. *Machibroda v. United States,* 368 U.S. 487, 494, 495 (1962); *United States v. Salerno,* 290 F.2d 105, 106 (2d Cir.1961); *Romero v. United States,* 327 F.2d 711, 712 (5th Cir.1964); *Scott v. United States,* 349 F.2d 641, 642, 643 (6th Cir.1965); *Schiebelhut v. United States,* 357 F.2d 743, 745 (6th Cir.1966); and *Del Piano v. United States,* 362 F.2d 931, 932, 933 (3d Cir.1966). None of these cases make any mention of a traverse by the movant to the government's answer. As under Rule 5 of the § 2254 rules, there is no intention here that such a traverse be required, except under special circumstances. See advisory committee note to Rule 9.

Subdivision (b) provides for the government to supplement its answers with appropriate copies of transcripts or briefs if for some reason the judge does not already have them under his control. This is because the government will in all probability have easier access to such papers than the movant, and it will conserve the court's time to have the government produce them rather than the movant, who would in most instances have to apply in forma pauperis for the government to supply them for him anyway.

For further discussion, see the advisory committee note to Rule 5 of the § 2254 rules.

Rule 6. Discovery

(a) Leave of court required. A party may invoke the processes of discovery available under the Federal Rules of Criminal Procedure or the Federal Rules of Civil Procedure or elsewhere in the usages and principles of law if, and to the extent that, the judge in the exercise of his discretion and for good cause shown grants leave to do so, but not otherwise. If necessary for effective utilization of discovery procedures, counsel shall be appointed by the judge for a movant who qualifies for appointment of counsel under 18 U.S.C. § 3006A(g).

(b) Requests for discovery. Requests for discovery shall be accompanied by a statement of the interrogatories or requests for admission and a list of the documents, if any, sought to be produced.

(c) Expenses. If the government is granted leave to take the deposition of the movant or any other person, the judge may as a condition of taking it direct that the government pay the expenses of travel and subsistence and fees of counsel for the movant to attend the taking of the deposition.

ADVISORY COMMITTEE NOTES

1976 Adoption

This rule differs from the corresponding discovery rule under the § 2254 rules in that it includes the processes of discovery available under the Federal Rules of Criminal Procedure as well as the civil. This is because of the nature of a § 2255 motion as a continuing part of the criminal proceeding (see advisory committee note to Rule 1) as well as a remedy analogous to habeas corpus by state prisoners.

See the advisory committee note to rule 6 of the § 2254 rules. The discussion there is fully applicable to discovery under these rules for § 2255 motions.

Rule 7. Expansion of Record

(a) Direction for expansion. If the motion is not dismissed summarily, the judge may direct that the record be expanded by the parties by the inclusion of additional materials relevant to the determination of the merits of the motion.

(b) Materials to be added. The expanded record may include, without limitation, letters predating the filing of the motion in the district court, documents, exhibits, and answers under oath, if so directed, to written interrogatories propounded by the judge. Affidavits may be submitted and considered as a part of the record.

(c) Submission to opposing party. In any case in which an expanded record is directed, copies of the letters, documents, exhibits, and affidavits proposed to be included shall be submitted to the party against whom they are to be offered, and he shall be afforded an opportunity to admit or deny their correctness.

(d) Authentication. The court may require the authentication of any material under subdivision (b) or (c).

ADVISORY COMMITTEE NOTES

1976 Adoption

It is less likely that the court will feel the need to expand the record in a § 2255 proceeding than in a habeas corpus proceeding, because the trial (or sentencing) judge is the one hearing the motion (see Rule 4) and should already have a complete file on the case in his possession. However, Rule 7 provides a convenient method for supplementing his file if the case warrants it.

See the advisory committee note to Rule 7 of the § 2254 rules for a full discussion of reasons and procedures for expanding the record.

Rule 8. Evidentiary Hearing

(a) Determination by court. If the motion has not been dismissed at a previous stage in the proceeding, the judge, after the answer is filed and any transcripts or records of prior court actions in the matter are in his possession, shall, upon a review of those proceedings and of the expanded record, if any, determine whether an evidentiary hearing is required. If it appears that an evidentiary hearing is not required, the judge shall make such disposition of the motion as justice dictates.

(b) Function of the magistrate.

(1) When designated to do so in accordance with 28 U.S.C. § 636(b), a magistrate may conduct hearings, including evidentiary hearings, on the motion, and submit to a judge of the court proposed findings and recommendations for disposition.

(2) The magistrate shall file proposed findings and recommendations with the court and a copy shall forthwith be mailed to all parties.

(3) Within ten days after being served with a copy, any party may serve and file written objections to such proposed findings and recommendations as provided by rules of court.

(4) A judge of the court shall make a de novo determination of those portions of the report or specified proposed findings or recommendations to which objection is made. A judge of the court may accept, reject, or modify in whole or in part any findings or recommendations made by the magistrate.

(c) Appointment of counsel; time for hearing. If an evidentiary hearing is required, the judge shall appoint counsel for a movant who qualifies for the appointment of counsel under 18 U.S.C. § 3006A(g) and the hearing shall be conducted as promptly as practicable, having regard for the need of counsel for both parties for adequate time for investigation and preparation. These rules do not limit the appointment of counsel under 18 U.S.C. § 3006A at any stage of the proceeding if the interest of justice so requires.

(d) Production of statements at evidentiary hearing.

(1) **In General.** Federal Rule of Criminal Procedure 26.2(a)–(d), and (f) applies at an evidentiary hearing under these rules.

(2) **Sanctions for Failure to Produce Statement.** If a party elects not to comply with an order under Federal Rule of Criminal Procedure 26.2(a) to deliver a statement to the moving party, at the evidentiary hearing the court may not consider the testimony of the witness whose statement is withheld.

(As amended Pub.L. 94–426, § 2(6), Sept. 28, 1976, 90 Stat. 1335; Pub.L. 94–577, § 2(a) (2), (b) (2), Oct. 21, 1976, 90 Stat. 2730, 2731; Apr. 22, 1993, eff. Dec. 1, 1993.)

ADVISORY COMMITTEE NOTES

1976 Adoption

The standards for § 2255 hearings are essentially the same as for evidentiary hearings under a habeas petition, except that the previous federal fact-finding proceeding is in issue rather than the state's. Also § 2255 does not set specific time limits for holding the hearing, as does § 2243 for a habeas action. With these minor differences in mind, see the advisory committee note to Rule 8 of § 2254 rules, which is applicable to Rule 8 of these § 2255 rules.

1993 Amendment

The amendment to Rule 8 is one of a series of parallel amendments to Federal Rules of Criminal Procedure 32, 32.1, and 46 which extend the scope of Rule 26.2 (Production of Witness Statements) to proceedings other than the trial itself. The amendments are grounded on the compelling need for accurate and credible information in making decisions concerning the defendant's liberty. *See* the Advisory Committee Note to Rule 26.2(g). A few courts have recognized the authority of a judicial officer to order production of prior statements by a witness at a Section 2255 hearing, see, e.g., *United States v. White,* 342 F.2d 379, 382, n. 4 (4th Cir.1959). The amendment to Rule 8 grants explicit authority to do so. The amendment is not intended to require production of a witness's statement before the witness actually presents oral testimony.

HISTORICAL NOTES

Effective Dates

1976 Acts. Amendments made by Pub.L. 94–577 effective with respect to motions under section 2255 of this title filed on or after Feb. 1, 1977, see section 2(c) of Pub.L. 94–577, set out as a note under Rule 8 of the Rules Governing Cases Under Section 2254 of this title.

Rule 9. Delayed or Successive Motions

(a) Delayed motions. A motion for relief made pursuant to these rules may be dismissed if it appears that the government has been prejudiced in its ability to respond to the motion by delay in its filing unless the movant shows that it is based on grounds of which he could not have had knowledge by the exercise of reasonable diligence before the circumstances prejudicial to the government occurred.

(b) Successive motions. A second or successive motion may be dismissed if the judge finds that it fails to allege new or different grounds for relief and the prior determination was on the merits or, if new and different grounds are alleged, the judge finds that the failure of the movant to assert those grounds in a prior motion constituted an abuse of the procedure governed by these rules.

(As amended Pub.L. 94–426, § 2(9), (10), Sept. 28, 1976, 90 Stat. 1335.)

ADVISORY COMMITTEE NOTES

1976 Adoption

Unlike the statutory provisions on habeas corpus (28 U.S.C. §§ 2241–2254), § 2255 specifically provides that "a motion for such relief may be made *at any time.*" [Emphasis added.] Subdivision (a) provides that delayed motions may be barred from consideration if the government has been prejudiced in its ability to respond to the motion by the delay and the movant's failure to seek relief earlier is not excusable within the terms of the rule. Case law, dealing with this issue, is in conflict.

Some courts have held that the literal language of § 2255 precludes any possible time bar to a motion brought under it. In *Heflin v. United States,* 358 U.S. 415 (1959), the concurring opinion noted:

> The statute [28 U.S.C. § 2255] further provides: "A motion * * * may be made at any time." This * * * simply means that, as in habeas corpus, there is no statute of limitations, no *res judicata,* and that the doctrine of laches is inapplicable.

358 U.S. at 420

McKinney v. United States, 208 F.2d 844 (D.C.Cir.1953) reversed the district court's dismissal of a § 2255 motion for being too late, the court stating:

> McKinney's present application for relief comes late in the day: he has served some fifteen years in prison. But tardiness is irrelevant where a constitutional issue is raised and where the prisoner is still confined.

208 F.2d at 846, 847

In accord, see; *Juelich v. United States,* 300 F.2d 381, 383 (5th Cir.1962); *Conners v. United States,* 431 F.2d 1207, 1208 (9th Cir.1970); *Sturrup v. United States,* 218 F.Supp. 279, 281 (E.D.N.Car.1963); and *Banks v. United States,* 319 F.Supp. 649, 652 (S.D.N.Y.1970).

It has also been held that delay in filing a § 2255 motion does not bar the movant because of lack of reasonable diligence in pressing the claim.

> The statute [28 U.S.C. § 2255], when it states that the motion may be made at any time, excludes the addition of a showing of diligence in delayed filings. A number of courts have considered contentions similar to those made here and have concluded that there are no time limitations. This result excludes the requirement of diligence which is in reality a time limitation.

***Haier v. United States,* 334 F.2d 441, 442 (10th Cir.1964)**

Other courts have recognized that delay may have a negative effect on the movant. In *Raines v. United States,* 423 F.2d 526 (4th Cir.1970), the court stated:

> [B]oth petitioners' silence for extended periods, one for 28 months and the other for nine years, serves to render their allegations less believable. "Although a delay in filing a section 2255 motion is not a controlling element * * * it may merit some consideration * * *."

423 F.2d at 531

In *Aiken v. United States,* 191 F.Supp. 43, 50 (M.D.N.Car. 1961), aff'd 296 F.2d 604 (4th Cir.1961), the court said: "While motions under 28 U.S.C. § 2255 may be made at any time, the lapse of time affects the good faith and credibility of the moving party." For similar conclusions, see: *Parker v. United States,* 358 F.2d 50, 54 n. 4 (7th Cir.1965), cert. denied, 386 U.S. 916 (1967); *Le Clair v. United States,* 241 F.Supp. 819, 824 (N.D.Ind.1965); *Malone v. United States,* 299 F.2d 254, 256 (6th Cir.1962), cert. denied, 371 U.S. 863 (1962); *Howell v. United States,* 442 F.2d 265, 274 (7th Cir.1971); and *United States v. Wiggins,* 184 F.Supp. 673, 676 (D.C.Cir.1960).

There have been holdings by some courts that a delay in filing a § 2255 motion operates to increase the burden of proof which the movant must meet to obtain relief. The reasons for this, as expressed in *United States v. Bostic*, 206 F.Supp. 855 (D.C.Cir.1962), are equitable in nature.

> Obviously, the burden of proof on a motion to vacate a sentence under 28 U.S.C. § 2255 is on the moving party. . . . The burden is particularly heavy if the issue is one of fact and a long time has elapsed since the trial of the case. While neither the statute of limitations nor laches can bar the assertion of a constitutional right, nevertheless, the passage of time may make it impracticable to retry a case if the motion is granted and a new trial is ordered. No doubt, at times such a motion is a product of an afterthought. Long delay may raise a question of good faith.

206 F.Supp. at 856–857

See also *United States v. Wiggins*, 184 F.Supp. at 676.

A requirement that the movant display reasonable diligence in filing a § 2255 motion has been adopted by some courts dealing with delayed motions. The court in *United States v. Moore*, 166 F.2d 102 (7th Cir.1948), cert. denied, 334 U.S. 849 (1948), did this, again for equitable reasons.

> [W]e agree with the District Court that the petitioner has too long slept upon his rights. * * * [A]pparently there is no limitation of time within which * * * a motion to vacate may be filed, except that an applicant must show reasonable diligence in presenting his claim. * * *
>
> The reasons which support the rule requiring diligence seem obvious. * * * Law enforcement officials change, witnesses die, memories grow dim. The prosecuting tribunal is put to a disadvantage if an unexpected retrial should be necessary after long passage of time.

166 F.2d at 105

In accord see *Desmond v. United States*, 333 F.2d 378, 381 (1st Cir.1964), on remand, 345 F.2d 225 (1st Cir.1965).

One of the major arguments advanced by the courts which would penalize a movant who waits an unduly long time before filing a § 2255 motion is that such delay is highly prejudicial to the prosecution. In *Desmond v. United States*, writing of a § 2255 motion alleging denial of effective appeal because of deception by movant's own counsel, the court said:

> [A]pplications for relief such as this must be made promptly. It will not do for a prisoner to wait until government witnesses have become unavailable as by death, serious illness or absence from the country, or until the memory of available government witnesses has faded. It will not even do for a prisoner to wait any longer than is reasonably necessary to prepare appropriate moving papers, however inartistic, after discovery of the deception practiced upon him by his attorney.

333 F.2d at 381

In a similar vein are *United States v. Moore* and *United States v. Bostic*, supra, and *United States v. Wiggins*, 184 F.Supp. at 676.

Subdivision (a) provides a flexible, equitable time limitation based on laches to prevent movants from withholding their claims so as to prejudice the government both in meeting the allegations of the motion and in any possible retrial. It includes a reasonable diligence requirement for ascertaining possible grounds for relief. If the delay is found to be excusable, or nonprejudicial to the government, the time bar is inoperative.

Subdivision (b) is consistent with the language of § 2255 and relevant case law.

The annexed form is intended to serve the same purpose as the comparable one included in the § 2254 rules.

For further discussion applicable to this rule, see the advisory committee note to Rule 9 of the § 2254 rules.

Rule 10. Powers of Magistrates

The duties imposed upon the judge of the district court by these rules may be performed by a United States magistrate pursuant to 28 U.S.C. § 636.

(As amended Pub.L. 94–426, § 2(12), Sept. 28, 1976, 90 Stat. 1335; Apr. 30, 1979, eff. Aug. 1, 1979.)

ADVISORY COMMITTEE NOTES

1976 Adoption

See the advisory committee note to Rule 10 of the § 2254 rules for a discussion fully applicable here as well.

1979 Amendment

This amendment conforms the rule to 18 U.S.C. § 636. See Advisory Committee Note to Rule 10 of the Rules Governing Section 2254 Cases in the United States District Courts.

HISTORICAL NOTES

Change of Name

United States magistrate appointed under section 631 of Title 28, Judiciary and Judicial Procedure, to be known as United States magistrate judge after Dec. 1, 1990, with any reference to United States magistrate or magistrate in Title 28, in any other Federal statute, etc., deemed a reference to United States magistrate judge appointed under section 631 of Title 28, see section 321 of Pub.L. 101–650, set out as a note under section 631 of Title 28.

Rule 11. Time for Appeal

The time for appeal from an order entered on a motion for relief made pursuant to these rules is as provided in Rule 4(a) of the Federal Rules of Appellate Procedure. Nothing in these rules shall be construed as extending the time to appeal from the original judgment of conviction in the district court.

(As amended Apr. 30, 1979, eff. Aug. 1, 1979.)

ADVISORY COMMITTEE NOTES

1976 Adoption

Rule 11 is intended to make clear that, although a § 2255 action is a continuation of the criminal case, the bringing of a § 2255 action does not extend the time.

1979 Amendment

Prior to the promulgation of the Rules Governing Section 2255 Proceedings, the courts consistently held that the time for appeal in a section 2255 case is as provided in Fed. R.App.P. 4(a), that is, 60 days when the government is a party, rather than as provided in appellate rule 4(b), which says that the time is 10 days in criminal cases. This result has often been explained on the ground that rule 4(a) has to do with civil cases and that "proceedings under section 2255 are civil in nature." E.g., *Rothman v. United States,* 508 F.2d 648 (3d Cir.1975). Because the new section 2255 rules are based upon the premise "that a motion under § 2255 is a further step in the movant's criminal case rather than a separate civil action," see Advisory Committee Note to Rule 1, the question has arisen whether the new rules have the effect of shortening the time for appeal to that provided in appellate rule 4(b). A sentence has been added to Rule 11 in order to make it clear that this is not the case.

Even though section 2255 proceedings are a further step in the criminal case, the added sentence correctly states current law. In *United States v. Hayman,* 342 U.S. 205 (1952), the Supreme Court noted that such appeals "are governed by the civil rules applicable to appeals from final judgments in habeas corpus actions." In support, the Court cited *Mercado v. United States,* 183 F.2d 486 (1st Cir.1950), a case rejecting the argument that because § 2255 proceedings are criminal in nature the time for appeal is only 10 days. The *Mercado* court concluded that the situation was governed by that part of 28 U.S.C. § 2255 which reads: "An appeal may be taken to the court of appeals from the order entered on the motion as from a final judgment on application for a writ of habeas corpus." Thus, because appellate rule 4(a) is applicable in habeas cases, it likewise governs in § 2255 cases even though they are criminal in nature.

Rule 12. Federal Rules of Criminal and Civil Procedure; Extent of Applicability

If no procedure is specifically prescribed by these rules, the district court may proceed in any lawful manner not inconsistent with these rules, or any applicable statute, and may apply the Federal Rules of Criminal Procedure or the Federal Rules of Civil Procedure, whichever it deems most appropriate, to motions filed under these rules.

ADVISORY COMMITTEE NOTES

1976 Adoption

This rule differs from rule 11 of the § 2254 rules in that it includes the Federal Rules of Criminal Procedure as well as the civil. This is because of the nature of a § 2255 motion as a continuing part of the criminal proceeding (see advisory committee note to Rule 1) as well as a remedy analogous to habeas corpus by state prisoners.

Since § 2255 has been considered analogous to habeas as respects the restrictions in Fed.R.Civ.P. 81(a) (2) (see *Sullivan v. United States,* 198 F.Supp. 624 (S.D.N.Y.1961)), Rule 12 is needed. For discussion, see the advisory committee note to Rule 11 of the § 2254 rules.

APPENDIX OF FORMS

MODEL FORM FOR MOTIONS UNDER 28 U.S.C. § 2255

Name ______________________________

Prison Number ______________________________

Place of Confinement ______________________________

United States District Court ____________ District of ______________________________

Case No. ________ (to be supplied by Clerk of U.S. District Court) United States,

v.

____

(full name of movant)

(If movant has a sentence to be served in the *future* under a federal judgment which he wishes to attack, he should file a motion in the federal court which entered the judgment.)

MOTION TO VACATE, SET ASIDE, OR CORRECT SENTENCE BY A PERSON IN FEDERAL CUSTODY

(1) This motion must be legibly handwritten or typewritten, and signed by the movant under penalty of perjury. Any false statement of a material fact may serve as the basis for prosecution and conviction for perjury. All questions must be answered concisely in the proper space on the form.

(2) Additional pages are not permitted except with respect to the *facts* which you rely upon to support your grounds for relief. No citation of authorities need be furnished. If briefs or arguments are submitted, they should be submitted in the form of a separate memorandum.

(3) Upon receipt, your motion will be filed if it is in proper order. No fee is required with this motion.

(4) If you do not have the necessary funds for transcripts, counsel, appeal, and other costs connected with a motion of this type, you may request permission to proceed *in forma pauperis,* in which event you must execute the declaration on the last page, setting forth information establishing your inability to pay the costs. If you wish to proceed *in forma pauperis,* you must have an authorized officer at the penal institution complete the certificate as to the amount of money and securities on deposit to your credit in any account in the institution.

(5) Only judgments entered by one court may be challenged in a single motion. If you seek to challenge judgments entered by different judges or divisions either in the same district or in different districts, you must file separate motions as to each such judgment.

(6) Your attention is directed to the fact that you must include all grounds for relief and all facts supporting such grounds for relief in the motion you file seeking relief from any judgment of conviction.

(7) When the motion is fully completed, the *original and two copies* must be mailed to the Clerk of the United States District Court whose address is ______________________________

(8) Motions which do not conform to these instructions will be returned with a notation as to the deficiency.

MOTION

1. Name and location of court which entered the judgment of conviction under attack ______________
2. Date of judgment of conviction ______________
3. Length of sentence ______________
4. Nature of offense involved (all counts) ______________
____
____
____
5. What was your plea? (Check one)
(a) Not guilty ☐
(b) Guilty ☐
(c) Nolo contendere ☐
If you entered a guilty plea to one count or indictment, and a not guilty plea to another count or indictment, give details:
____
____
____
6. Kind of trial: (Check one)
(a) Jury ☐
(b) Judge only ☐
7. Did you testify at the trial?
Yes ☐ No ☐
8. Did you appeal from the judgment of conviction?
Yes ☐ No ☐
9. If you did appeal, answer the following:
(a) Name of court ______________
(b) Result ______________
(c) Date of result ______________
10. Other than a direct appeal from the judgment of conviction and sentence, have you previously filed any petitions, applications or motions with respect to this judgment in any federal court?
Yes ☐ No ☐
11. If your answer to 10 was "yes," give the following information:
(a) (1) Name of court ______________

(2) Nature of proceeding ______

(3) Grounds raised ______

(4) Did you receive an evidentiary hearing on your petition, application or motion?
Yes ☐ No ☐

(5) Result ______

(6) Date of result ______

(b) As to any second petition, application or motion give the same information:

(1) Name of court ______

(2) Nature of proceeding ______

(3) Grounds raised ______

(4) Did you receive an evidentiary hearing on your petition, application or motion?
Yes ☐ No ☐

(5) Result ______

(6) Date of result ______

(c) As to any third petition, application or motion, give the same information:

(1) Name of court ______

(2) Nature of proceeding ______

(3) Grounds raised ______

(4) Did you receive an evidentiary hearing on your petition, application or motion?
Yes ☐ No ☐

(d) Did you appeal, to an appellate federal court having jurisdiction, the result of action taken on any petition, application or motion?

(1) First petition, etc.
Yes ☐ No ☐

(2) Second petition, etc.
Yes ☐ No ☐

(3) Third petition, etc.
Yes ☐ No ☐

(e) If you did *not* appeal from the adverse action on any petition, application or motion, explain briefly why you did not: ______

12. State *concisely* every ground on which you claim that you are being held unlawfully. Summarize *briefly* the fact supporting each ground. If necessary, you may attach pages stating additional grounds and *facts* supporting same.

CAUTION: If you fail to set forth all grounds in this motion, you may be barred from presenting additional grounds at a later date.

For your information, the following is a list of the most frequently raised grounds for relief in these proceedings. Each statement preceded by a letter constitutes a separate ground for possible relief. You may raise any grounds which you have other than those listed. However, *you should raise in this motion all available grounds* (relating to this conviction) on which you based your allegations that you are being held in custody unlawfully.

Do not check any of these listed grounds. If you select one or more of these grounds for relief, you must allege facts. The motion will be returned to you if you merely check (a) through (j) or any one of the grounds.

(a) Conviction obtained by plea of guilty which was unlawfully induced or not made voluntarily or with understanding of the nature of the charge and the consequences of the plea.

(b) Conviction obtained by use of coerced confession.

(c) Conviction obtained by use of evidence gained pursuant to an unconstitutional search and seizure.

(d) Conviction obtained by use of evidence obtained pursuant to an unlawful arrest.

(e) Conviction obtained by a violation of the privilege against self-incrimination.

(f) Conviction obtained by the unconstitutional failure of the prosecution to disclose to the defendant evidence favorable to the defendant.

(g) Conviction obtained by a violation of the protection against double jeopardy.

(h) Conviction obtained by action of a grand or petit jury which was unconstitutionally selected and impanelled.

(i) Denial of effective assistance of counsel.

(j) Denial of right of appeal.

A. Ground one: ______

Supporting FACTS (tell your story *briefly* without citing cases or law): ______

B. Ground two: ______

Supporting FACTS (tell your story *briefly* without citing cases or law): ______

C. Ground three: ______

Supporting FACTS (tell your story *briefly* without citing cases or law): ______

D. Ground four: ______

Supporting FACTS (tell your story *briefly* without citing cases or law): ______

13. If any of the grounds listed in 12A, B, C, and D were not previously presented, state *briefly* what grounds were not so presented, and give your reasons for not presenting them: ____

14. Do you have any petition or appeal now pending in any court as to the judgment under attack?
Yes ☐ No ☐

15. Give the name and address, if known, of each attorney who represented you in the following stages of the judgment attacked herein:
(a) At preliminary hearing ____
(b) At arraignment and plea ____
(c) At trial ____
(d) At sentencing ____
(e) On appeal ____
(f) In any post-conviction proceeding ____
(g) On appeal from any adverse ruling in a post-conviction proceeding ____

16. Were you sentenced on more than one count of an indictment, or on more than one indictment, in the same court and at approximately the same time?
Yes ☐ No ☐

17. Do you have any future sentence to serve after you complete the sentence imposed by the judgment under attack?
Yes ☐ No ☐
(a) If so, give name and location of court which imposed sentence to be served in the future: ____
(b) And give date and length of sentence to be served in the future: ____
(c) Have you filed, or do you contemplate filing, any petition attacking the judgment which imposed the sentence to be served in the future?
Yes ☐ No ☐

Wherefore, movant prays that the Court grant him all relief to which he may be entitled in this proceeding.

____
Signature of Attorney (if any)

I declare (or certify, verify, or state) under penalty of perjury that the foregoing is true and correct. Executed on ____.

(date)

____
Signature of Movant

IN FORMA PAUPERIS DECLARATION

____
[Insert appropriate court]

United States
v.
____
(Movant)

DECLARATION IN SUPPORT OF REQUEST TO PROCEED *IN FORMA PAUPERIS*

I, ____, declare that I am the movant in the above entitled case; that in support of my motion to proceed without being required to prepay fees, costs or give security therefor, I state that because of my poverty, I am unable to pay the costs of said proceeding or to give security therefor; that I believe I am entitled to relief.

1. Are you presently employed?
Yes ☐ No ☐
a. If the answer is "yes," state the amount of your salary or wages per month, and give the name and address of your employer.
____
b. If the answer is "no," state the date of last employment and the amount of the salary and wages per month which you received.
____

2. Have you received within the past twelve months any money from any of the following sources?
a. Business, profession or form of self-employment? Yes ☐ No ☐
b. Rent payments, interest or dividends? Yes ☐ No ☐
c. Pensions, annuities or life insurance payments? Yes ☐ No ☐
d. Gifts or inheritances? Yes ☐ No ☐
e. Any other sources? Yes ☐ No ☐
If the answer to any of the above is "yes," describe each source of money and state the amount received from each during the past twelve months. ____

3. Do you own any cash, or do you have money in a checking or savings account?
Yes ☐ No ☐ (Include any funds in prison accounts)
If the answer is "yes," state the total value of the items owned. ____

4. Do you own real estate, stocks, bonds, notes, automobiles, or other valuable property (excluding ordinary household furnishings and clothing)?
Yes ☐ No ☐

If the answer is "yes," describe the property and state its approximate value. ____________
____
____

5. List the persons who are dependent upon you for support, state your relationship to those persons, and indicate how much you contribute toward their support.
____
____
____

I declare (or certify, verify, or state) under penalty of perjury that the foregoing is true and correct. Executed on ____________.

(date)

____
Signature of Movant

CERTIFICATE

I hereby certify that the movant herein has the sum of $______ on account to his credit at the ______ institution where he is confined.

I further certify that movant likewise has the following securities to his credit according to the records of said ______ institution: ____________
____
____
____
____

____
Authorized Officer of Institution

(As amended Apr. 28, 1982, eff. Aug. 1, 1982.)

MODEL FORM FOR USE IN 28 U.S.C. § 2255 CASES INVOLVING A RULE 9 ISSUE

Form No. 9

United States District Court

____________ District of ____________

Case No. ____________

United States

v.

____

(Name of Movant)

Movant's Response as to Why His Motion Should Not be Barred Under Rule 9

Explanation and Instructions—Read Carefully

(I) Rule 9. Delayed or Successive Motions.

(a) Delayed motions. A motion for relief made pursuant to these rules may be dismissed if it appears that the government has been prejudiced in its ability to respond to the motion by delay in its filing unless the movant shows that it is based on grounds of which he could not have had knowledge by the exercise of reasonable diligence before the circumstances prejudicial to the government occurred.

(b) Successive motions. A second or successive motion may be dismissed if the judge finds that it fails to allege new or different grounds for relief and the prior determination was on the merits or, if new and different grounds are alleged, the judge finds that the failure of the movant to assert those grounds in a prior motion constituted an abuse of the procedure governed by these rules.

(II) Your motion to vacate, set aside, or correct sentence has been found to be subject to dismissal under Rule 9( ) for the following reason(s):
____
____
____
____
____

(III) This form has been sent so that you may explain why your motion contains the defect(s) noted in (II) above. It is required that you fill out this form and send it back to the court within ______ days. Failure to do so will result in the automatic dismissal of your motion.

(IV) When you have fully completed this form, the original and two copies must be mailed to the Clerk of the United States District Court whose address is
____
____

(V) This response must be legibly handwritten or typewritten, and signed by the movant under penalty of perjury. Any false statement of a material fact may serve as the basis for prosecution and conviction for perjury. All questions must be answered concisely in the proper space on the form.

(VI) Additional pages are not permitted except with respect to the *facts* which you rely upon in item 4 or 5 in the response. Any citation of authorities should be kept to an absolute minimum and is only appropriate if there has been a change in the law since the judgment you are attacking was rendered.

(VII) Respond to 4 *or* 5, not to both, unless (II) above indicates that you must answer both sections.

RESPONSE

1. Have you had the assistance of an attorney, other law-trained personnel, or writ writers since the conviction your motion is attacking was entered?

   Yes ☐ No ☐

2. If you checked "Yes" above, specify as precisely as you can the period(s) of time during which you received such assistance, up to and including the present.

   ____
   ____

3. Describe the nature of the assistance, including the names of those who rendered it to you. ______

   ____
   ____
   ____

4. If your motion is in jeopardy because of delay prejudicial to the government under Rule 9(a), explain why you feel the delay has not been prejudicial and/or why the delay is excusable under the terms of 9(a). This should be done by relying upon FACTS, not your opinions or conclusions. ______________

   ____
   ____
   ____

   ____
   ____

5. If your motion is in jeopardy under Rule 9(b) because it asserts the same grounds as a previous motion, explain why you feel it deserves a reconsideration. If its fault under Rule 9(b) is that it asserts new grounds which should have been included in a prior motion, explain why you are raising these grounds now rather than previously. Your explanation should rely on FACTS, not your opinions or conclusions. ______

   ____
   ____
   ____
   ____
   ____
   ____
   ____
   ____

I declare (or certify, verify, or state) under penalty of perjury that the foregoing is true and correct. Executed on ______________

(date) .

____

Signature of Movant

(As amended Apr. 28, 1982, eff. Aug. 1, 1982.)

RULES OF EVIDENCE FOR UNITED STATES COURTS AND MAGISTRATES

Pub.L. 93–595, § 1, January 2, 1975, 88 Stat. 1926
Amendments received to January 4, 1999

ARTICLE I. GENERAL PROVISIONS

Rule
101. Scope.
102. Purpose and Construction.
103. Rulings on Evidence.
104. Preliminary Questions.
105. Limited Admissibility.
106. Remainder of or Related Writings or Recorded Statements.

ARTICLE II. JUDICIAL NOTICE

201. Judicial Notice of Adjudicative Facts.

ARTICLE III. PRESUMPTIONS IN CIVIL ACTIONS AND PROCEEDINGS

301. Presumptions in General in Civil Actions and Proceedings.
302. Applicability of State Law in Civil Actions and Proceedings.

ARTICLE IV. RELEVANCY AND ITS LIMITS

401. Definition of "Relevant Evidence".
402. Relevant Evidence Generally Admissible; Irrelevant Evidence Inadmissible.
403. Exclusion of Relevant Evidence on Grounds of Prejudice, Confusion, or Waste of Time.
404. Character Evidence Not Admissible To Prove Conduct; Exceptions; Other Crimes.
405. Methods of Proving Character.
406. Habit; Routine Practice.
407. Subsequent Remedial Measures.
408. Compromise and Offers to Compromise.
409. Payment of Medical and Similar Expenses.
410. Inadmissibility of Pleas, Plea Discussions, and Related Statements.
411. Liability Insurance.
412. Sex Offense Cases; Relevance of Alleged Victim's Past Sexual Behavior or Alleged Sexual Predisposition.
413. Evidence of Similar Crimes in Sexual Assault Cases.
414. Evidence of Similar Crimes in Child Molestation Cases.
415. Evidence of Similar Acts in Civil Cases Concerning Sexual Assault or Child Molestation.

ARTICLE V. PRIVILEGES

501. General Rule.

Rule

ARTICLE VI. WITNESSES

601. General Rule of Competency.
602. Lack of Personal Knowledge.
603. Oath or Affirmation.
604. Interpreters.
605. Competency of Judge as Witness.
606. Competency of Juror as Witness.
607. Who May Impeach.
608. Evidence of Character and Conduct of Witness.
609. Impeachment by Evidence of Conviction of Crime.
610. Religious Beliefs or Opinions.
611. Mode and Order of Interrogation and Presentation.
612. Writing Used to Refresh Memory.
613. Prior Statements of Witnesses.
614. Calling and Interrogation of Witnesses by Court.
615. Exclusion of Witnesses.

ARTICLE VII. OPINIONS AND EXPERT TESTIMONY

701. Opinion Testimony by Lay Witnesses.
702. Testimony by Experts.
703. Bases of Opinion Testimony by Experts.
704. Opinion on Ultimate Issue.
705. Disclosure of Facts or Data Underlying Expert Opinion.
706. Court Appointed Experts.

ARTICLE VIII. HEARSAY

801. Definitions.
802. Hearsay Rule.
803. Hearsay Exceptions; Availability of Declarant Immaterial.
804. Hearsay Exceptions; Declarant Unavailable.
805. Hearsay Within Hearsay.
806. Attacking and Supporting Credibility of Declarant.
807. Residual Exception.

ARTICLE IX. AUTHENTICATION AND IDENTIFICATION

901. Requirement of Authentication or Identification.
902. Self-authentication.
903. Subscribing Witness' Testimony Unnecessary.

ARTICLE X. CONTENTS OF WRITINGS, RECORDINGS AND PHOTOGRAPHS

1001. Definitions.
1002. Requirement of Original.
1003. Admissibility of Duplicates.

Rule

ARTICLE X. CONTENTS OF WRITINGS, RECORDINGS AND PHOTOGRAPHS —Cont'd

1004. Admissibility of Other Evidence of Contents.
1005. Public Records.
1006. Summaries.
1007. Testimony or Written Admission of Party.
1008. Functions of Court and Jury.

ARTICLE XI. MISCELLANEOUS RULES

1101. Applicability of Rules.
1102. Amendments.
1103. Title.

ORDERS OF THE SUPREME COURT OF THE UNITED STATES ADOPTING AND AMENDING RULES

ORDER OF NOVEMBER 20, 1972

1. That the rules hereinafter set forth, to be known as the Federal Rules of Evidence, be, and they hereby are, prescribed pursuant to Sections 3402, 3771, and 3772, Title 18, United States Code, and Sections 2072 and 2075, Title 28, United States Code, to govern procedure, in the proceedings and to the extent set forth therein, in the United States courts of appeals, the United States district courts, the District Court for the District of the Canal Zone and the district courts of Guam and the Virgin Islands, and before United States magistrates.

2. That the aforementioned Federal Rules of Evidence shall take effect on July 1, 1973, and shall be applicable to actions and proceedings brought thereafter and also to further procedure in actions and proceedings then pending, except to the extent that in the opinion of the court their application in a particular action or proceeding then pending would not be feasible or would work injustice in which event the former procedure applies.

3. That subdivision (c) of Rule 30 and Rules 43 and 44.1 of the Federal Rules of Civil Procedure be, and they hereby are, amended, effective July 1, 1973, to read as hereinafter set forth:

[See amendments made thereby under the respective Rules of Civil Procedure, ante.]

4. That subdivision (c) of Rule 32 of the Federal Rules of Civil Procedure be, and it hereby is, abrogated, effective July 1, 1973.

5. That Rules 26, 26.1 and 28 of the Federal Rules of Criminal Procedure be, and they hereby are, amended effective July 1, 1973, to read as hereinafter set forth.

[For text of amendments, see pamphlet containing Federal Rules of Criminal Procedure.]

6. That the Chief Justice be, and he hereby is, authorized to transmit the foregoing new rules and amendments to and abrogation of existing rules to the Congress at the beginning of its next regular session, in accordance with the provisions of Title 18 U.S.C. § 3771 and Title 28 U.S.C. §§ 2072 and 2075.

CONGRESSIONAL ACTION ON PROPOSED RULES OF EVIDENCE AND 1972 AMENDMENTS TO FEDERAL RULES OF CIVIL PROCEDURE AND FEDERAL RULES OF CRIMINAL PROCEDURE

Pub.L. 93–12, Mar. 30, 1973, 87 Stat. 9, provided: "That notwithstanding any other provisions of law, the Rules of Evidence for United States Courts and Magistrates, the Amendments to the Federal Rules of Civil Procedure, and the Amendments to the Federal Rules of Criminal Procedure, which are embraced by the orders entered by the Supreme Court of the United States on Monday, November 20, 1972, and Monday, December 18, 1972, shall have no force or effect except to the extent, and with such amendments, as they may be expressly approved by Act of Congress."

Pub.L. 93–595, § 3, Jan. 2, 1975, 88 Stat. 1959, provided that: "The Congress expressly approves the amendments to the Federal Rules of Civil Procedure, and the amendments to the Federal Rules of Criminal Procedure, which are embraced by the orders entered by the Supreme Court of the United States on November 20, 1972, and December 18, 1972, and such amendments shall take effect on the one hundred and eightieth day beginning after the date of the enactment of this Act [Jan. 2, 1975]."

ORDER OF APRIL 30, 1979

1. That Rule 410 of the Federal Rules of Evidence be, and it hereby is, amended to read as follows:

[See amendment made thereby following Rule 410, post.]

2. That the foregoing amendment to the Federal Rules of Evidence shall take effect on November 1, 1979, and shall be applicable to all proceedings then pending except to the extent that in the opinion of the court the application of the amended rule in a particular proceeding would not be feasible or would work injustice.

3. That THE CHIEF JUSTICE be, and he hereby is, authorized to transmit to the Congress the foregoing amendment to the Federal Rules of Evidence in accordance with the provisions of 28 U.S.C. § 2076.

CONGRESSIONAL ACTION ON AMENDMENT PROPOSED APRIL 30, 1979

Pub.L. 96–42, July 31, 1979, 93 Stat. 326, provided that the amendment proposed and transmitted to the Federal Rules of Evidence affecting rule 410, shall not take effect until Dec. 1, 1980, or until and then only to the extent approved by Act of Congress, whichever is earlier.

ORDER OF MARCH 2, 1987

1. That the Federal Rules of Evidence be, and they hereby are, amended by including therein amendments to Rules 101, 104, 106, 404, 405, 411, 602, 603, 604, 606, 607, 608, 609, 610, 611, 612, 613, 615, 701, 703, 705, 706, 801, 803, 804, 806, 902, 1004, 1007 and 1101, as hereinafter set forth:

[See amendments made thereby under respective rules, post.]

2. That the foregoing changes in the Federal Rules of Evidence shall take effect on October 1, 1987.

3. That THE CHIEF JUSTICE be, and he hereby is, authorized to transmit to the Congress the foregoing changes

in the rules of evidence in accordance with the provisions of Section 2076 of Title 28, United States Code.

ORDER OF APRIL 25, 1988

1. That the Federal Rules of Evidence be, and they hereby are, amended by including therein amendments to Rules 101, 602, 608, 613, 615, 902, and 1101, as hereinafter set forth:

[See amendments made thereby under respective rules, post.]

2. That the foregoing changes in the Federal Rules of Evidence shall take effect on November 1, 1988.

3. That THE CHIEF JUSTICE be, and he hereby is, authorized to transmit to the Congress the foregoing changes in the rules of evidence in accordance with the provisions of Section 2076 of Title 28, United States Code.

ORDER OF JANUARY 26, 1990

1. That the Federal Rules of Evidence be, and they hereby are, amended by including therein amendments to Rule 609(a)(1) and (2), as hereinafter set forth:

[See amendment made thereby, post].

2. That the foregoing changes in the Federal Rules of Evidence shall take effect on December 1, 1990.

3. That THE CHIEF JUSTICE be, and he hereby is, authorized to transmit to the Congress the foregoing changes in the rules of evidence in accordance with the provisions of Section 2074 of Title 28, United States Code.

ORDER OF APRIL 30, 1991

1. That the Federal Rules of Evidence for the United States District Courts be, and they hereby are, amended by including therein amendments to Evidence Rules 404(b) and 1102.

[See amendments made thereby under respective rules, post.]

2. That the foregoing amendments to the Federal Rules of Evidence shall take effect on December 1, 1991, and shall govern in all proceedings thereafter commenced and, insofar as just and practicable, all proceedings then pending.

3. That THE CHIEF JUSTICE be, and he hereby is, authorized to transmit to the Congress the foregoing amendments to the Federal Rules of Evidence in accordance with the provisions of Section 2072 of Title 28, United States Code.

ORDER OF APRIL 22, 1993

1. That the Federal Rules of Evidence for the United States District Courts be, and they hereby are, amended by including therein amendments to Evidence Rules 101, 705, and 1101.

[See amendments made thereby under respective rules, post.]

2. That the foregoing amendments to the Federal Rules of Evidence shall take effect on December 1, 1993, and shall govern in all proceedings thereafter commenced and, insofar as just and practicable, all proceedings then pending.

3. That THE CHIEF JUSTICE be, and he hereby is, authorized to transmit to the Congress the foregoing amendments to the Federal Rules of Evidence in accordance with the provisions of Section 2072 of Title 28, United States Code.

ORDER OF APRIL 29, 1994

ORDERED:

1. That the Federal Rules of Evidence for the United States District Courts be, and they hereby are, amended by including therein an amendment to Evidence Rule 412.

[See amendment made hereby under Rule 412, post.]

2. That the foregoing amendment to the Federal Rules of Evidence shall take effect on December 1, 1994, and shall govern in all proceedings thereafter commenced and, insofar as just and practicable, all proceedings then pending.

3. That THE CHIEF JUSTICE be, and he hereby is, authorized to transmit to the Congress the foregoing amendment to the Federal Rules of Evidence in accordance with the provisions of Section 2072 of Title 28, United States Code.

ORDER OF APRIL 11, 1997

ORDERED:

1. That the Federal Rules of Evidence be, and they hereby are, amended by including therein amendments to Evidence Rules 407, 801, 803(24), 804(b)(5), and 806, and new Rules 804(b)(6) and 807.

[See amendments made thereby under respective rules, post.]

2. That the foregoing amendments to the Federal Rules of Evidence shall take effect on December 1, 1997, and shall govern in all proceedings thereafter commenced and, insofar as just and practicable, all proceedings then pending.

3. That THE CHIEF JUSTICE be, and hereby is, authorized to transmit to the Congress the foregoing amendments to the Federal Rules of Evidence in accordance with the provisions of Section 2072 of Title 28, United States Code.

ORDER OF APRIL 24, 1998

ORDERED:

1. That the Federal Rules of Evidence be, and they hereby are, amended by including therein amendments to Evidence Rule 615.

[See amendments made thereby under respective rules, post.]

2. That the foregoing amendments to the Federal Rules of Evidence shall take effect on December 1, 1998, and shall govern in all proceedings thereafter commenced and, insofar as just and practicable, all proceedings then pending.

3. That THE CHIEF JUSTICE be, and hereby is, authorized to transmit to the Congress the foregoing amendments to the Federal Rules of Evidence in

accordance with the provisions of Section 2072 of Title 28, United States Code.

HISTORICAL NOTES

Effective Date and Application of Rules

The Federal Rules of Evidence were adopted by order of the Supreme Court on Nov. 20, 1972, transmitted to Congress by the Chief Justice on Feb. 5, 1973, and to have become effective on July 1, 1973. Pub.L. 93–12, Mar. 30, 1973, 87 Stat. 9, provided that the proposed rules "shall have no force or effect except to the extent, and with such amendments, as they may be expressly approved by Act of Congress". Pub.L. 93–595, Jan. 2, 1975, 88 Stat. 1926, enacted the Federal Rules of Evidence proposed by the Supreme Court, with amendments made by Congress, to take effect on July 1, 1975.

The Rules have been amended Oct. 16, 1975, Pub.L. 94–113, § 1, 89 Stat. 576, eff. Oct. 31, 1975; Dec. 12, 1975, Pub.L. 94–149, § 1, 89 Stat. 805; Oct. 28, 1978, Pub.L. 95–540, § 2, 92 Stat. 2046; Nov. 6, 1978, Pub.L. 95–598, Title II, § 251, 92 Stat. 2673, eff. Oct. 1, 1979; Apr. 30, 1979, eff. Dec. 1, 1980; Apr. 2, 1982, Pub.L. 97–164, Title I, § 142, Title IV, § 402, 96 Stat. 45, 57, eff. Oct. 1, 1982; Oct. 12, 1984, Pub.L. 98–473, Title IV, § 406, 98 Stat. 2067; Mar. 2, 1987, eff. Oct. 1, 1987; Apr. 25, 1988, eff. Nov. 1, 1988; Nov. 18, 1988, Pub.L. 100–690, Title VII, §§ 7046, 7075, 102 Stat. 4400, 4405; Jan. 26, 1990, eff. Dec. 1, 1990; Apr. 30, 1991, eff. Dec. 1, 1991; Apr. 22, 1993, eff. Dec. 1, 1993; Apr. 29, 1994, eff. Dec. 1, 1994; Apr. 24, 1998, eff. Dec. 1, 1998.

ARTICLE I. GENERAL PROVISIONS

HISTORICAL NOTES

Change of Name

United States magistrate appointed under section 631 of Title 28, Judiciary and Judicial Procedure, to be known as United States magistrate judge after Dec. 1, 1990, with any reference to United States magistrate or magistrate in Title 28, in any other Federal statute, etc., deemed a reference to United States magistrate judge appointed under section 631 of Title 28, see section 321 of Pub.L. 101–650, set out as a note under section 631 of Title 28.

Rule 101. Scope

These rules govern proceedings in the courts of the United States and before the United States bankruptcy judges and United States magistrate judges, to the extent and with the exceptions stated in rule 1101.

(Pub.L. 93–595, § 1, Jan. 2, 1975, 88 Stat. 1929; Mar. 2, 1987, eff. Oct. 1, 1987; Apr. 25, 1988, eff. Nov. 1, 1988; Apr. 22, 1993, eff. Dec. 1, 1993.)

ADVISORY COMMITTEE NOTES

1972 Proposed Rules

Rule 1101 specifies in detail the courts, proceedings, questions, and stages of proceedings to which the rules apply in whole or in part.

1987 Amendment

United States bankruptcy judges are added to conform this rule with Rule 1101(b) and Bankruptcy Rule 9017.

1988 Amendment

The amendment is technical. No substantive change is intended.

1993 Amendment

This revision is made to conform the rule to changes made by the Judicial Improvements Act of 1990.

HISTORICAL NOTES

Change of Name

United States magistrate appointed under section 631 of Title 28, Judiciary and Judicial Procedure, to be known as United States magistrate judge after Dec. 1, 1990, with any reference to United States magistrate or magistrate in Title 28, in any other Federal statute, etc., deemed a reference to United States magistrate judge appointed under section 631 of Title 28, see section 321 of Pub.L. 101–650, set out as a note under section 631 of Title 28.

Rule 102. Purpose and Construction

These rules shall be construed to secure fairness in administration, elimination of unjustifiable expense and delay, and promotion of growth and development of the law of evidence to the end that the truth may be ascertained and proceedings justly determined.

(Pub.L. 93–595, § 1, Jan. 2, 1975, 88 Stat.1929.)

ADVISORY COMMITTEE NOTES

1972 Proposed Rules

For similar provisions see Rule 2 of the Federal Rules of Criminal Procedure, Rule 1 of the Federal Rules of Civil Procedure, California Evidence Code § 2, and New Jersey Evidence Rule 5.

Rule 103. Rulings on Evidence

(a) Effect of erroneous ruling. Error may not be predicated upon a ruling which admits or excludes evidence unless a substantial right of the party is affected, and

(1) Objection. In case the ruling is one admitting evidence, a timely objection or motion to strike appears of record, stating the specific ground of objection, if the specific ground was not apparent from the context; or

(2) Offer of proof. In case the ruling is one excluding evidence, the substance of the evidence was made known to the court by offer or was apparent from the context within which questions were asked.

(b) Record of offer and ruling. The court may add any other or further statement which shows the character of the evidence, the form in which it was offered, the objection made, and the ruling thereon. It may direct the making of an offer in question and answer form.

(c) Hearing of jury. In jury cases, proceedings shall be conducted, to the extent practicable, so as to prevent inadmissible evidence from being suggested to the jury by any means, such as making statements or offers of proof or asking questions in the hearing of the jury.

(d) Plain error. Nothing in this rule precludes taking notice of plain errors affecting substantial rights although they were not brought to the attention of the court.

(Pub.L. 93–595, § 1, Jan. 2, 1975, 88 Stat. 1929.)

ADVISORY COMMITTEE NOTES

1972 Proposed Rules

Note to Subdivision (a). Subdivision (a) states the law as generally accepted today. Rulings on evidence cannot be assigned as error unless (1) a substantial right is affected, and (2) the nature of the error was called to the attention of the judge, so as to alert him to the proper course of action and enable opposing counsel to take proper corrective measures. The objection and the offer of proof are the techniques for accomplishing these objectives. For similar provisions see Uniform Rules 4 and 5; California Evidence Code §§ 353 and 354; Kansas Code of Civil Procedure §§ 60–404 and 60–405. The rule does not purport to change the law with respect to harmless error. See 28 USC § 2111, F.R.Civ.P. 61, F.R.Crim.P. 52, and decisions construing them. The status of constitutional error as harmless or not is treated in Chapman v. California, 386 U.S. 18, 87 S.Ct. 824, 17 L.Ed.2d 705 (1967), reh. denied id. 987, 87 S.Ct. 1283, 18 L.Ed.2d 241.

Note to Subdivision (b). The first sentence is the third sentence of Rule 43(c) of the Federal Rules of Civil Procedure virtually verbatim. Its purpose is to reproduce for an appellate court, insofar as possible, a true reflection of what occurred in the trial court. The second sentence is in part derived from the final sentence of Rule 43(c). It is designed to resolve doubts as to what testimony the witness would have in fact given, and, in nonjury cases, to provide the appellate court with material for a possible final disposition of the case in the event of reversal of a ruling which excluded evidence. See 5 Moore's Federal Practice § 43.11 (2d ed. 1968). Application is made discretionary in view of the practical impossibility of formulating a satisfactory rule in mandatory terms.

Note to Subdivision (c). This subdivision proceeds on the supposition that a ruling which excludes evidence in a jury case is likely to be a pointless procedure if the excluded evidence nevertheless comes to the attention of the jury. *Bruton v. United States,* 389 U.S. 818, 88 S.Ct. 126, 19 L.Ed.2d 70 (1968). Rule 43(c) of the Federal Rules of Civil Procedure provides: "The court may require the offer to be made out of the hearing of the jury." *In re McConnell,* 370 U.S. 230, 82 S.Ct. 1288, 8 L.Ed.2d 434 (1962), left some doubt whether questions on which an offer is based must first be asked in the presence of the jury. The subdivision answers in the negative. The judge can foreclose a particular line of testimony and counsel can protect his record without a series of questions before the jury, designed at best to waste time and at worst "to waft into the jury box" the very matter sought to be excluded.

Note to Subdivision (d). This wording of the plain error principle is from Rule 52(b) of the Federal Rules of Criminal Procedure. While judicial unwillingness to be constructed by mechanical breakdowns of the adversary system has been more pronounced in criminal cases, there is no scarcity of decisions to the same effect in civil cases. In general, see Campbell, Extent to Which Courts of Review Will Consider Questions Not Properly Raised and Preserved, 7 Wis.L.Rev. 91, 160 (1932); Vestal, Sua Sponte Consideration in Appellate Review, 27 Fordham L.Rev. 477 (1958–59); 64 Harv.L.Rev. 652 (1951). In the nature of things the application of the plain error rule will be more likely with respect to the admission of evidence than to exclusion, since failure to comply with normal requirements of offers of proof is likely to produce a record which simply does not disclose the error.

HISTORICAL NOTES

Conference Committee Notes, House Report No. 93–1597

The House bill contains the word "judge". The Senate amendment substitutes the word "court" in order to conform with usage elsewhere in the House bill.

The Conference adopts the Senate amendment.

Rule 104. Preliminary Questions

(a) Questions of admissibility generally. Preliminary questions concerning the qualification of a person to be a witness, the existence of a privilege, or the admissibility of evidence shall be determined by the court, subject to the provisions of subdivision (b). In making its determination it is not bound by the rules of evidence except those with respect to privileges.

(b) Relevancy conditioned on fact. When the relevancy of evidence depends upon the fulfillment of a condition of fact, the court shall admit it upon, or subject to, the introduction of evidence sufficient to support a finding of the fulfillment of the condition.

(c) Hearing of jury. Hearings on the admissibility of confessions shall in all cases be conducted out of the hearing of the jury. Hearings on other preliminary matters shall be so conducted when the interests of justice require, or when an accused is a witness and so requests.

(d) Testimony by accused. The accused does not, by testifying upon a preliminary matter, become subject to cross-examination as to other issues in the case.

Complete Annotation Materials, see Title 28 U.S.C.A.

(e) Weight and credibility. This rule does not limit the right of a party to introduce before the jury evidence relevant to weight or credibility.

(Pub.L. 93–595, § 1, Jan. 2, 1975, 88 Stat.1930; Mar. 2, 1987, eff. Oct. 1, 1987.)

ADVISORY COMMITTEE NOTES

1972 Proposed Rule

Note to Subdivision (a). The applicability of a particular rule of evidence often depends upon the existence of a condition. Is the alleged expert a qualified physician? Is a witness whose former testimony is offered unavailable? Was a stranger present during a conversation between attorney and client? In each instance the admissibility of evidence will turn upon the answer to the question of the existence of the condition. Accepted practice, incorporated in the rule, places on the judge the responsibility for these determinations. McCormick § 53; Morgan, Basic Problems of Evidence 45–50 (1962).

To the extent that these inquiries are factual, the judge acts as a trier of fact. Often, however, rulings on evidence call for an evaluation in terms of a legally set standard. Thus when a hearsay statement is offered as a declaration against interest, a decision must be made whether it possesses the required against-interest characteristics. These decisions, too, are made by the judge.

In view of these considerations, this subdivision refers to preliminary requirements generally by the broad term "questions," without attempt at specification.

This subdivision is of general application. It must, however, be read as subject to the special provisions for "conditional relevancy" in subdivision (b) and those for confessions in subdivision (d).

If the question is factual in nature, the judge will of necessity receive evidence pro and con on the issue. The rule provides that the rules of evidence in general do not apply to this process. McCormick § 53, p. 123, n. 8, points out that the authorities are "scattered and inconclusive," and observes:

"Should the exclusionary law of evidence, 'the child of the jury system' in Thayer's phrase, be applied to this hearing before the judge? Sound sense backs the view that it should not, and that the judge should be empowered to hear any relevant evidence, such as affidavits or other reliable hearsay."

This view is reinforced by practical necessity in certain situations. An item, offered and objected to, may itself be considered in ruling on admissibility, though not yet admitted in evidence. Thus, the content of an asserted declaration against interest must be considered in ruling whether it is against interest. Again, common practice calls for considering the testimony of a witness, particularly a child, in determining competency. Another example is the requirement of Rule 602 dealing with personal knowledge. In the case of hearsay, it is enough, if the declarant "so far as appears [has] had an opportunity to observe the fact declared." McCormick, § 10, p. 19.

If concern is felt over the use of affidavits by the judge in preliminary hearings on admissibility, attention is directed to the many important judicial determinations made on the basis of affidavits. Rule 47 of the Federal Rules of Criminal Procedure provides:

"An application to the court for an order shall be by motion. * * * It may be supported by affidavit."

The Rules of Civil Procedure are more detailed. Rule 43(e), dealing with motions generally, provides:

"When a motion is based on facts not appearing of record the court may hear the matter on affidavits presented by the respective parties, but the court may direct that the matter be heard wholly or partly on oral testimony or depositions."

Rule 4(g) provides for proof of service by affidavit. Rule 56 provides in detail for the entry of summary judgment based on affidavits. Affidavits may supply the foundation for temporary restraining orders under Rule 65(b).

The study made for the California Law Revision Commission recommended an amendment to Uniform Rule 2 as follows:

"In the determination of the issue aforesaid [preliminary determination], exclusionary rules shall not apply, subject, however, to Rule 45 and any valid claim of privilege." Tentative Recommendation and a Study Relating to the Uniform Rules of Evidence (Article VIII, Hearsay), Cal.Law Revision Comm'n, Rep., Rec. & Studies, 470 (1962). The proposal was not adopted in the California Evidence Code. The Uniform Rules are likewise silent on the subject. However, New Jersey Evidence Rule 8(1), dealing with preliminary inquiry by the judge, provides:

"In his determination the rules of evidence shall not apply except for Rule 4 [exclusion on grounds of confusion, etc.] or a valid claim of privilege."

Note to Subdivision (b). In some situations, the relevancy of an item of evidence, in the large sense, depends upon the existence of a particular preliminary fact. Thus when a spoken statement is relied upon to prove notice to X, it is without probative value unless X heard it. Or if a letter purporting to be from Y is relied upon to establish an admission by him, it has no probative value unless Y wrote or authorized it. Relevance in this sense has been labelled "conditional relevancy." Morgan, Basic Problems of Evidence 45–46 (1962). Problems arising in connection with it are to be distinguished from problems of logical relevancy, e.g., evidence in a murder case that accused on the day before purchased a weapon of the kind used in the killing, treated in Rule 401.

If preliminary questions of conditional relevancy were determined solely by the judge, as provided in subdivision (a), the functioning of the jury as a trier of fact would be greatly restricted and in some cases virtually destroyed. These are appropriate questions for juries. Accepted treatment, as provided in the rule, is consistent with that given fact questions generally. The judge makes a preliminary determination whether the foundation evidence is sufficient to support a finding of fulfillment of the condition. If so, the item is admitted. If after all the evidence on the issue is in, pro and con, the jury could reasonably conclude that fulfillment of the condition is not established, the issue is for them. If the evidence is not such as to allow a finding, the judge withdraws the matter from their consideration. Morgan, *supra;* California Evidence Code § 403; New Jersey Rule 8(2). See also Uniform Rules 19 and 67.

The order of proof here, as generally, is subject to the control of the judge.

Note to Subdivision (c). Preliminary hearings on the admissibility of confessions must be conducted outside the hearing of the jury. See *Jackson v. Denno,* 378 U.S. 368, 84 S.Ct. 1774, 12 L.Ed.2d 908 (1964). Otherwise, detailed treatment of when preliminary matters should be heard outside the hearing of the jury is not feasible. The procedure is time consuming. Not infrequently the same evidence which is relevant to the issue of establishment of fulfillment of a condition precedent to admissibility is also relevant to weight or credibility, and time is saved by taking foundation proof in the presence of the jury. Much evidence on preliminary questions, though not relevant to jury issues, may be heard by the jury with no adverse effect. A great deal must be left to the discretion of the judge who will act as the interests of justice require.

Note to Subdivision (d). The limitation upon cross-examination is designed to encourage participation by the accused in the determination of preliminary matters. He may testify concerning them without exposing himself to cross-examination generally. The provision is necessary because of the breadth of cross-examination under Rule 611(b).

The rule does not address itself to questions of the subsequent use of testimony given by an accused at a hearing on a preliminary matter. See *Walder v. United States,* 347 U.S. 62 (1954); *Simmons v. United States,* 390 U.S. 377 (1968); *Harris v. New York,* 401 U.S. 222 (1971).

Note to Subdivision (e). For similar provisions see Uniform Rule 8; California Evidence Code § 406; Kansas Code of Civil Procedure § 60–408; New Jersey Evidence Rule 8(1).

1974 Enactment

Rule 104(c) as submitted to the Congress provided that hearings on the admissibility of confessions shall be conducted outside the presence of the jury and hearings on all other preliminary matters should be so conducted when the interests of justice require. The Committee amended the Rule to provide that where an accused is a witness as to a preliminary matter, he has the right, upon his request, to be heard outside the jury's presence. Although recognizing that in some cases duplication of evidence would occur and that the procedure could be subject to abuse, the Committee believed that a proper regard for the right of an accused not to testify generally in the case dictates that he be given an option to testify out of the presence of the jury on preliminary matters.

The Committee construes the second sentence of subdivision (c) as applying to civil actions and proceedings as well as to criminal cases, and on this assumption has left the sentence unamended. House Report No. 93–650.

Under rule 104(c) the hearing on a preliminary matter may at times be conducted in front of the jury. Should an accused testify in such a hearing, waiving his privilege against self-incrimination as to the preliminary issue, rule 104(d) provides that he will not generally be subject to cross-examination as to any other issue. This rule is not, however, intended to immunize the accused from cross-examination where, in testifying about a preliminary issue, he injects other issues into the hearing. If he could not be cross-examined about any issues gratuitously raised by him beyond the scope of the preliminary matters, injustice might result. Accordingly, in order to prevent any such unjust result, the committee intends the rule to be construed to provide that the accused may subject himself to cross-examination as to issues raised by his own testimony upon a preliminary matter before a jury. Senate Report No. 93–1277.

1987 Amendment

The amendments are technical. No substantive change is intended.

Rule 105. Limited Admissibility

When evidence which is admissible as to one party or for one purpose but not admissible as to another party or for another purpose is admitted, the court, upon request, shall restrict the evidence to its proper scope and instruct the jury accordingly.

(Pub.L. 93–595, § 1, Jan. 2, 1975, 88 Stat. 1930.)

ADVISORY COMMITTEE NOTES

1972 Proposed Rules

A close relationship exists between this rule and Rule 403 which requires exclusion when "probative value is substantially outweighed by the danger of unfair prejudice, confusion of the issues, or misleading the jury." The present rule recognizes the practice of admitting evidence for a limited purpose and instructing the jury accordingly. The availability and effectiveness of this practice must be taken into consideration in reaching a decision whether to exclude for unfair prejudice under Rule 403. In *Bruton v. United States,* 389 U.S. 818, 88 S.Ct. 126, 19 L.Ed.2d 70 (1968), the Court ruled that a limiting instruction did not effectively protect the accused against the prejudicial effect of admitting in evidence the confession of a codefendant which implicated him. The decision does not, however, bar the use of limited admissibility with an instruction where the risk of prejudice is less serious.

Similar provisions are found in Uniform Rule 6; California Evidence Code § 355; Kansas Code of Civil Procedure § 60–406; New Jersey Evidence Rule 6. The wording of the present rule differs, however, in repelling any implication that limiting or curative instructions are sufficient in all situations.

1974 Enactment

Rule 106 as submitted by the Supreme Court (now Rule 105 in the bill) dealt with the subject of evidence which is admissible as to one party or for one purpose but is not admissible against another party or for another purpose. The Committee adopted this Rule without change on the understanding that it does not affect the authority of a court to order a severance in a multi-defendant case. House Report No. 93–650.

Rule 106. Remainder of or Related Writings or Recorded Statements

When a writing or recorded statement or part thereof is introduced by a party, an adverse party may require the introduction at that time of any other part or any other writing or recorded statement which ought in fairness to be considered contemporaneously with it.

(Pub.L. 93–595, § 1, Jan. 2, 1975, 88 Stat. 1930; Mar. 2, 1987, eff. Oct. 1, 1987.)

ADVISORY COMMITTEE NOTES

1972 Proposed Rules

The rule is an expression of the rule of completeness. McCormick § 56. It is manifested as to depositions in Rule 32(a)(4) of the Federal Rules of Civil Procedure, of which the proposed rule is substantially a restatement.

The rule is based on two considerations. The first is the misleading impression created by taking matters out of context. The second is the inadequacy of repair work when delayed to a point later in the trial. See McCormick § 56; California Evidence Code § 356. The rule does not in any way circumscribe the right of the adversary to develop the matter on cross-examination or as part of his own case.

For practical reasons, the rule is limited to writings and recorded statements and does not apply to conversations.

1987 Amendment

The amendments are technical. No substantive change is intended.

ARTICLE II. JUDICIAL NOTICE

Rule 201. Judicial Notice of Adjudicative Facts

(a) Scope of rule. This rule governs only judicial notice of adjudicative facts.

(b) Kinds of facts. A judicially noticed fact must be one not subject to reasonable dispute in that it is either (1) generally known within the territorial jurisdiction of the trial court or (2) capable of accurate and ready determination by resort to sources whose accuracy cannot reasonably be questioned.

(c) When discretionary. A court may take judicial notice, whether requested or not.

(d) When mandatory. A court shall take judicial notice if requested by a party and supplied with the necessary information.

(e) Opportunity to be heard. A party is entitled upon timely request to an opportunity to be heard as to the propriety of taking judicial notice and the tenor of the matter noticed. In the absence of prior notification, the request may be made after judicial notice has been taken.

(f) Time of taking notice. Judicial notice may be taken at any stage of the proceeding.

(g) Instructing jury. In a civil action or proceeding, the court shall instruct the jury to accept as conclusive any fact judicially noticed. In a criminal case, the court shall instruct the jury that it may, but is not required to, accept as conclusive any fact judicially noticed.

(Pub.L. 93–595, § 1, Jan. 2, 1975, 88 Stat. 1930.)

ADVISORY COMMITTEE NOTES

1972 Proposed Rules

Note to Subdivision (a). This is the only evidence rule on the subject of judicial notice. It deals only with judicial notice of "adjudicative" facts. No rule deals with judicial notice of "legislative" facts. Judicial notice of matters of foreign law is treated in Rule 44.1 of the Federal Rules of Civil Procedure and Rule 26.1 of the Federal Rules of Criminal Procedure.

The omission of any treatment of legislative facts results from fundamental differences between adjudicative facts and legislative facts. Adjudicative facts are simply the facts of the particular case. Legislative facts, on the other hand, are those which have relevance to legal reasoning and the law-making process, whether in the formulation of a legal principle or ruling by a judge or court or in the enactment of a legislative body. The terminology was coined by Professor Kenneth Davis in his article An Approach to Problems of Evidence in the Administrative Process, 55 Harv.L.Rev. 364, 404–407 (1942). The following discussion draws extensively upon his writings. In addition, see the same author's Judicial Notice, 55 Colum.L.Rev. 945 (1955); Administrative Law Treatise, ch. 15 (1958); A System of Judicial Notice Based on Fairness and Convenience, in Perspectives of Law 69 (1964).

The usual method of establishing adjudicative facts is through the introduction of evidence, ordinarily consisting of the testimony of witnesses. If particular facts are outside the area of reasonable controversy, this process is dispensed with as unnecessary. A high degree of indisputability is the essential prerequisite.

Legislative facts are quite different. As Professor Davis says:

"My opinion is that judge-made law would stop growing if judges, in thinking about questions of law and policy, were forbidden to take into account the facts they believe, as distinguished from facts which are 'clearly * * * within the domain of the indisputable.' Facts most needed in thinking about difficult problems of law and policy have a way of being outside the domain of the clearly indisputable." A System of Judicial Notice Based on Fairness and Convenience, *supra*, at 82.

An illustration is *Hawkins v. United States*, 358 U.S. 74, 79 S.Ct. 136, 3 L.Ed.2d 125 (1958), in which the Court refused to discard the common law rule that one spouse could not testify against the other, saying, "Adverse testimony given in criminal proceedings would, we think, be likely to destroy almost any marriage." This conclusion has a large intermixture of fact, but the factual aspect is scarcely "indisputable." See Hutchins and Slesinger, Some Observations on the Law of Evidence—Family Relations, 13 Minn.L.Rev. 675 (1929). If the destructive effect of the giving of adverse testimony by a spouse is not indisputable, should the Court have refrained from considering it in the absence of supporting evidence?

"If the Model Code or the Uniform Rules had been applicable, the Court would have been barred from thinking about the essential factual ingredient of the problems before it, and such a result would be obviously intolerable. What the law needs at its growing points is more, not less, judicial thinking about the factual ingredients of problems of what the law ought to be, and the needed facts are seldom 'clearly' indisputable." Davis, *supra*, at 83.

Professor Morgan gave the following description of the methodology of determining domestic law:

"In determining the content or applicability of a rule of domestic law, the judge is unrestricted in his investigation and conclusion. He may reject the propositions of either party or of both parties. He may consult the sources of pertinent data to which they refer, or he may refuse to do so. He may make an independent search for persuasive data or rest content with what he has or what the parties present. * * * [T]he parties do no more than to assist; they control no part of the process." Morgan, Judicial Notice, 57 Harv. L.Rev. 269, 270–271 (1944).

This is the view which should govern judicial access to legislative facts. It renders inappropriate any limitation in the form of indisputability, any formal requirements of notice other than those already inherent in affording opportunity to hear and be heard and exchanging briefs, and any requirement of formal findings at any level. It should, however leave open the possibility of introducing evidence through regular channels in appropriate situations. See *Borden's Farm Products Co. v. Baldwin*, 293 U.S. 194, 55 S.Ct. 187, 79 L.Ed. 281 (1934), where the cause was remanded for the taking of evidence as to the economic conditions and trade practices underlying the New York Milk Control Law.

Similar considerations govern the judicial use of non-adjudicative facts in ways other than formulating laws and rules. Thayer described them as a part of the judicial reasoning process.

"In conducting a process of judicial reasoning, as of other reasoning, not a step can be taken without assuming something which has not been proved; and the capacity to do this with competent judgment and efficiency, is imputed to judges and juries as part of their necessary mental outfit." Thayer, Preliminary Treatise on Evidence 279–280 (1898).

As Professor Davis points out, A System of Judicial Notice Based on Fairness and Convenience, in Perspectives of Law 69, 73 (1964), every case involves the use of hundreds or thousands of non-evidence facts. When a witness in an automobile accident case says "car," everyone, judge and jury included, furnishes, from non-evidence sources within himself, the supplementing information that the "car" is an automobile, not a railroad car, that it is self-propelled, probably by an internal combustion engine, that it may be assumed to have four wheels with pneumatic rubber tires, and so on. The judicial process cannot construct every case from scratch, like Descartes creating a world based on the postulate *Cogito, ergo sum.* These items could not possibly be introduced into evidence, and no one suggests that they be. Nor are they appropriate subjects for any formalized treatment of judicial notice of facts. See Levin and Levy, Persuading the Jury with Facts Not in Evidence: The Fiction-Science Spectrum, 105 U.Pa.L.Rev. 139 (1956).

Another aspect of what Thayer had in mind is the use of non-evidence facts to appraise or assess the adjudicative facts of the case. Pairs of cases from two jurisdictions illustrate this use and also the difference between non-evidence facts thus used and adjudicative facts. In People v. Strook, 347 Ill. 460, 179 N.E. 821 (1932), venue in Cook County had been held not established by testimony that the crime was committed at 7956 South Chicago Avenue, since judicial notice would not be taken that the address was in Chicago. However, the same court subsequently ruled that venue in Cook County was established by testimony that a crime occurred at 8900 South Anthony Avenue, since notice would be taken of the common practice of omitting the name of the city when speaking of local addresses, and the witness was testifying in Chicago. *People v. Pride*, 16 Ill.2d 82, 156 N.E.2d 551 (1951). And in *Hughes v. Vestal*, 264 N.C. 500, 142 S.E.2d 361 (1965), the Supreme Court of North Carolina disapproved the trial judge's admission in evidence of a state-published table of automobile stopping distances on the basis of judicial notice, though the court itself had referred to the same table in an earlier case in a "rhetorical and illustrative" way in determining that the defendant could not have stopped her car in time to avoid striking a child who suddenly appeared in the highway and that a nonsuit was properly granted. *Ennis v. Dupree*, 262 N.C. 224, 136 S.E.2d 702 (1964). See also *Brown v. Hale*, 263 N.C. 176, 139 S.E.2d 210 (1964); *Clayton v. Rimmer*, 262 N.C. 302, 136 S.E.2d 562 (1964). It is apparent that this use of non-evidence facts in evaluating the adjudicative facts of the case is not an appropriate subject for a formalized judicial notice treatment.

In view of these considerations, the regulation of judicial notice of facts by the present rule extends only to adjudicative facts.

What, then, are "adjudicative" facts? Davis refers to them as those "which relate to the parties," or more fully:

"When a court or an agency finds facts concerning the immediate parties—who did what, where, when, how, and with what motive or intent—the court or agency is performing an adjudicative function, and the facts are conveniently called adjudicative facts. * * *

"Stated in other terms, the adjudicative facts are those to which the law is applied in the process of adjudication. They are the facts that normally go to the jury in a jury case. They relate to the parties, their activities, their properties, their businesses." 2 Administrative Law Treatise 353.

Note to Subdivision (b). With respect to judicial notice of adjudicative facts, the tradition has been one of caution in requiring that the matter be beyond reasonable controversy. This tradition of circumspection appears to be soundly based, and no reason to depart from it is apparent. As Professor Davis says:

"The reason we use trial-type procedure, I think, is that we make the practical judgment, on the basis of experience, that taking evidence, subject to cross-examination and rebuttal, is the best way to resolve controversies involving disputes of adjudicative facts, that is, facts pertaining to the parties. The reason we require a determination on the record is that we think fair procedure in resolving disputes of adjudicative facts calls for giving each party a chance to meet in the appropriate fashion the facts that come to the tribunal's attention, and the appropriate fashion for meeting disputed adjudicative facts includes rebuttal evidence, cross-examination, usually confrontation, and argument (either written or oral or both). The key to a fair trial is opportunity to use the appropriate weapons (rebuttal evidence, cross-examination, and argument) to meet adverse materials that come to the tribunal's attention." A System of Judicial Notice Based on Fairness and Convenience, in Perspectives of Law 69, 93 (1964).

The rule proceeds upon the theory that these considerations call for dispensing with traditional methods of proof only in clear cases. Compare Professor Davis' conclusion that judicial notice should be a matter of convenience, subject to requirements of procedural fairness. *Id.*, 94.

This rule is consistent with Uniform Rule 9(1) and (2) which limit judicial notice of facts to those "so universally known that they cannot reasonably be the subject of dispute," those "so generally known or of such common notoriety within the territorial jurisdiction of the court that they cannot reasonably be the subject of dispute," and those "capable of immediate and accurate determination by resort to easily accessible sources of indisputable accuracy." The traditional textbook treatment has included these general categories (matters of common knowledge, facts capable of verification), McCormick §§ 324, 325, and then has passed on into detailed treatment of such specific topics as facts relating to the personnel and records of the court, *Id.* § 327, and other governmental facts, *Id.* § 328. The California draftsmen, with a background of detailed statutory regulation of judicial notice, followed a somewhat similar pattern. California Evidence Code §§ 451, 452. The Uniform Rules, however, were drafted on the theory that these particular matters are included within the general categories and need no specific mention. This approach is followed in the present rule.

The phrase "propositions of generalized knowledge," found in Uniform Rule 9(1) and (2) is not included in the present rule. It was, it is believed, originally included in Model Code Rules 801 and 802 primarily in order to afford some minimum recognition to the right of the judge in his "legislative" capacity (not acting as the trier of fact) to take judicial notice of very limited categories of generalized knowledge. The limitations thus imposed have been discarded herein as undesirable, unworkable, and contrary to existing practice. What is left, then, to be considered, is the status of a "proposition of generalized knowledge" as an "adjudicative" fact to be noticed judicially and communicated by the judge to the jury. Thus viewed, it is considered to be lacking practical significance. While judges use judicial notice of "propositions of generalized knowledge" in a variety of situations: determining the validity and meaning of statutes, formulating common law rules, deciding whether evidence should be admitted, assessing the sufficiency and effect of evidence, all are essentially nonadjudicative in nature. When judicial notice is seen as a significant vehicle for progress in the law, these are the areas involved, particularly in developing fields of scientific knowledge. See McCormick 712. It is not believed that judges now instruct juries as to "propositions of generalized knowledge" derived from encyclopedias or other sources, or that they are likely to do so, or, indeed, that it is desirable that they do so. There is a vast difference between ruling on the basis of judicial notice that radar evidence of speed is admissible and explaining to the jury its principles and degree of accuracy, or between using a table of stopping distances of automobiles at various speeds in a judicial evaluation of testimony and telling the jury its precise application in the case. For cases raising doubt as to the propriety of the use of medical texts by lay triers of fact in passing on disability claims in administrative proceedings, see *Sayers v. Gardner*, 380 F.2d 940 (6th Cir.1967); *Ross v. Gardner*, 365 F.2d 554 (6th Cir.1966); *Sosna v. Celebrezze*, 234 F.Supp. 289 (E.D.Pa.1964); *Glendenning v. Ribicoff*, 213 F.Supp. 301 (W.D.Mo.1962).

Notes to Subdivisions (c) and (d). Under subdivision (c) the judge has a discretionary authority to take judicial notice, regardless of whether he is so requested by a party. The taking of judicial notice is mandatory, under subdivision (d), only when a party requests it and the necessary information is supplied. This scheme is believed to reflect existing practice. It is simple and workable. It avoids troublesome distinctions in the many situations in which the process of taking judicial notice is not recognized as such.

Compare Uniform Rule 9 making judicial notice of facts universally known mandatory without request, and making judicial notice of facts generally known in the jurisdiction or capable of determination by resort to accurate sources discretionary in the absence of request but mandatory if request is made and the information furnished. But see Uniform Rule 10(3), which directs the judge to decline to take judicial notice if available information fails to convince him that the matter falls clearly within Uniform Rule 9 or is insufficient to enable him to notice it judicially. Substantially the same approach is found in California Evidence Code §§ 451–453 and in New Jersey Evidence Rule 9. In contrast, the present rule treats alike all adjudicative facts which are subject to judicial notice.

Note to Subdivision (e). Basic considerations of procedural fairness demand an opportunity to be heard on the propriety of taking judicial notice and the tenor of the matter noticed. The rule requires the granting of that opportunity upon request. No formal scheme of giving notice is provided. An adversely affected party may learn in advance that judicial notice is in contemplation, either by virtue of being served with a copy of a request by another party under subdivision (d) that judicial notice be taken, or through an advance indication by the judge. Or he may have no advance notice at all. The likelihood of the latter is enhanced by the frequent failure to recognize judicial notice as such. And in the absence of advance notice, a request made after the fact could not in fairness be considered untimely. See the provision for hearing on timely request in the Administrative Procedure Act, 5 U.S.C. § 556(e). See also Revised Model State Administrative Procedure Act (1961), 9C U.L.A. § 10(4) (Supp.1967).

Note to Subdivision (f). In accord with the usual view, judicial notice may be taken at any stage of the proceedings, whether in the trial court or on appeal. Uniform Rule 12; California Evidence Code § 459; Kansas Rules of Evidence § 60–412; New Jersey Evidence Rule 12; McCormick § 330, p. 712.

Note to Subdivision (g). Much of the controversy about judicial notice has centered upon the question whether evidence should be admitted in disproof of facts of which judicial notice is taken.

The writers have been divided. Favoring admissibility are Thayer, Preliminary Treatise on Evidence 308 (1898); 9 Wigmore § 2567; Davis, A System of Judicial Notice Based on Fairness and Convenience, in Perspectives of Law, 69, 76–77 (1964). Opposing admissibility are Keeffe, Landis and Shaad, Sense and Nonsense about Judicial Notice, 2 Stan. L.Rev. 664, 668 (1950); McNaughton, Judicial Notice—Excerpts Relating to the Morgan–Whitmore Controversy, 14 Vand.L.Rev. 779 (1961); Morgan, Judicial Notice, 57 Harv.

L.Rev. 269, 279 (1944); McCormick 710–711. The Model Code and the Uniform Rules are predicated upon indisputability of judicially noticed facts.

The proponents of admitting evidence in disproof have concentrated largely upon legislative facts. Since the present rule deals only with judicial notice of adjudicative facts, arguments directed to legislative facts lose their relevancy.

Within its relatively narrow area of adjudicative facts, the rule contemplates there is to be no evidence before the jury in disproof. The judge instructs the jury to take judicially noticed facts as established. This position is justified by the undesirable effects of the opposite rule in limiting the rebutting party, though not his opponent, to admissible evidence, in defeating the reasons for judicial notice, and in affecting the substantive law to an extent and in ways largely unforeseeable. Ample protection and flexibility are afforded by the broad provision for opportunity to be heard on request, set forth in subdivision (e).

Authority upon the propriety of taking judicial notice against an accused in a criminal case with respect to matters other than venue is relatively meager. Proceeding upon the theory that the right of jury trial does not extend to matters which are beyond reasonable dispute, the rule does not distinguish between criminal and civil cases. *People v. Mayes,* 113 Cal. 618, 45 P. 860 (1896); *Ross v. United States,* 374 F.2d 97 (8th Cir.1967). Cf. *State v. Main,* 94 R.I. 338, 180 A.2d 814 (1962); *State v. Lawrence,* 120 Utah 323, 234 P.2d 600 (1951).

Note on Judicial Notice of Law. By rules effective July 1, 1966, the method of invoking the law of a foreign country is covered elsewhere. Rule 44.1 of the Federal Rules of Civil Procedure; Rule 26.1 of the Federal Rules of Criminal Procedure. These two new admirably designed rules are founded upon the assumption that the manner in which law is fed into the judicial process is never a proper concern of the rules of evidence but rather of the rules of procedure. The Advisory Committee on Evidence, believing that this assumption is entirely correct, proposes no evidence rule with respect to judicial notice of law, and suggests that those matters of law which, in addition to foreign-country law, have traditionally been treated as requiring pleading and proof and more recently as the subject of judicial notice be left to the Rules of Civil and Criminal Procedure.

1974 Enactment

Rule 201(g) as received from the Supreme Court provided that when judicial notice of a fact is taken, the court shall instruct the jury to accept that fact as established. Being of the view that mandatory instruction to a jury in a criminal case to accept as conclusive any fact judicially noticed is inappropriate because contrary to the spirit of the Sixth Amendment right to a jury trial, the Committee adopted the 1969 Advisory Committee draft of this subsection, allowing a mandatory instruction in civil actions and proceedings and a discretionary instruction in criminal cases. House Report No. 93–650.

ARTICLE III. PRESUMPTIONS IN CIVIL ACTIONS AND PROCEEDINGS

Rule 301. Presumptions in General in Civil Actions and Proceedings

In all civil actions and proceedings not otherwise provided for by Act of Congress or by these rules, a presumption imposes on the party against whom it is directed the burden of going forward with evidence to rebut or meet the presumption, but does not shift to such party the burden of proof in the sense of the risk of nonpersuasion, which remains throughout the trial upon the party on whom it was originally cast.

(Pub.L. 93–595, § 1, Jan. 2, 1975, 88 Stat. 1931.)

ADVISORY COMMITTEE NOTES

1972 Proposed Rules

This rule governs presumptions generally. See Rule 302 for presumptions controlled by state law and Rule 303 [deleted] for those against an accused in a criminal case.

Presumptions governed by this rule are given the effect of placing upon the opposing party the burden of establishing the nonexistence of the presumed fact, once the party invoking the presumption establishes the basic facts giving rise to it. The same considerations of fairness, policy, and probability which dictate the allocation of the burden of the various elements of a case as between the prima facie case of a plaintiff and affirmative defenses also underlie the creation of presumptions. These considerations are not satisfied by giving a lesser effect to presumptions. Morgan and Maguire, Looking Backward and Forward at Evidence, 50 Harv. L.Rev. 909, 913 (1937); Morgan, Instructing the Jury upon Presumptions and Burden of Proof, 47 Harv.L.Rev. 59, 82 (1933); Cleary, Presuming and Pleading: An Essay on Juristic Immaturity, 12 Stan.L.Rev. 5 (1959).

The so-called "bursting bubble" theory, under which a presumption vanishes upon the introduction of evidence which would support a finding of the nonexistence of the presumed fact, even though not believed, is rejected as according presumptions too "slight and evanescent" an effect. Morgan and Maguire, *supra,* at p. 913.

In the opinion of the Advisory Committee, no constitutional infirmity attends this view of presumptions. In *Mobile, J. & K. C. R. Co. v. Turnipseed,* 219 U.S. 35, 31 S.Ct. 136, 55 L.Ed. 78 (1910), the Court upheld a Mississippi statute which provided that in actions against railroads proof of injury inflicted by the running of trains should be prima facie evidence of negligence by the railroad. The injury in the case had resulted from a derailment. The opinion made the points (1) that the only effect of the statute was to impose on the railroad the duty of producing some evidence to the contrary, (2) that an inference may be supplied by law if there is a rational connection between the fact proved and the fact presumed, as long as the opposite party is not precluded from presenting his evidence to the contrary, and (3) that considerations of public policy arising from the character of the business justified the application in question. Nineteen years later, in *Western & Atlantic R. Co. v. Henderson,* 279 U.S. 639, 49 S.Ct. 445, 73 L.Ed. 884 (1929), the Court overturned a Georgia statute making railroads liable for damages done by trains, unless the railroad made it appear that reasonable care had been used, the presumption being against the railroad. The declaration alleged the death of plaintiff's husband from a grade crossing collision, due to specified acts of negligence by defendant. The jury were instructed that proof of the injury raised a presumption of negligence; the burden shifted to the railroad to prove ordinary care; and unless it did so, they should find for plaintiff. The instruction was held erroneous in an opinion stating (1) that there was no rational connection between the mere fact of collision and negligence on the part of anyone, and (2) that the statute was different from that in *Turnipseed* in imposing a burden upon the railroad. The reader is left in a state of some confusion. Is the difference between a derailment and a grade crossing collision of no significance? Would the *Turnipseed* presumption have been bad if it had imposed a burden of persuasion on defendant, although that would in nowise have impaired its "rational connection"? If *Henderson* forbids imposing a burden of persuasion on defendants, what happens to affirmative defenses?

Two factors serve to explain *Henderson.* The first was that it was common ground that negligence was indispensable to liability. Plaintiff thought so, drafted her complaint accordingly, and relied upon the presumption. But how in logic could the same presumption establish her alternative grounds of negligence that the engineer was so blind he could not see decedent's truck and that he failed to stop after he saw it? Second, take away the basic assumption of no liability without fault, as *Turnipseed* intimated might be done ("considerations of public policy arising out of the character of the business"), and the structure of the decision in *Henderson* fails. No question of logic would have arisen if the statute had simply said: a prima facie case of liability is made by proof of injury by a train; lack of negligence is an affirmative defense, to be pleaded and proved as other affirmative defenses. The problem would be one of economic due process only. While it seems likely that the Supreme Court of 1929 would have voted that due process was denied, that result today would be unlikely. See, for example, the shift in the direction of absolute liability in the consumer cases. Prosser, The Assault upon the Citadel (Strict Liability to the Consumer), 69 Yale L.J. 1099 (1960).

Any doubt as to the constitutional permissibility of a presumption imposing a burden of persuasion of the nonexistence of the presumed fact in civil cases is laid at rest by *Dick v. New York Life Ins. Co.,* 359 U.S. 437, 79 S.Ct. 921, 3 L.Ed.2d 935 (1959). The Court unhesitatingly applied the North Dakota rule that the presumption against suicide imposed on defendant the burden of proving that the death of insured, under an accidental death clause, was due to suicide.

"Proof of coverage and of death by gunshot wound shifts the burden to the insurer to establish that the death of the insured was due to his suicide." 359 U.S. at 443, 79 S.Ct. at 925.

"In a case like this one, North Dakota presumes that death was accidental and places on the insurer the burden of proving that death resulted from suicide." *Id.* at 446, 79 S.Ct. at 927.

The rational connection requirement survives in criminal cases, *Tot v. United States,* 319 U.S. 463, 63 S.Ct. 1241, 87 L.Ed. 1519 (1943), because the Court has been unwilling to extend into that area the greater-includes-the-lesser theory of *Ferry v. Ramsey,* 277 U.S. 88, 48 S.Ct. 443, 72 L.Ed. 796 (1928). In that case the Court sustained a Kansas statute under which bank directors were personally liable for deposits made with their assent and with knowledge of insolvency, and the fact of insolvency was prima facie evidence of assent and knowledge of insolvency. Mr. Justice Holmes pointed out that the state legislature could have made the directors personally liable to depositors in every case. Since the statute imposed a less stringent liability, "the thing to be considered is the result reached, not the possibly inartificial or clumsy way of reaching it." *Id.* at 94, 48 S.Ct. at 444. Mr. Justice Sutherland dissented: though the state could have created an absolute liability, it did not purport to do so; a rational connection was necessary, but lacking, between the liability created and the prima facie evidence of it; the result might be different if the basis of the presumption were being open for business.

The Sutherland view has prevailed in criminal cases by virtue of the higher standard of notice there required. The fiction that everyone is presumed to know the law is applied to the substantive law of crimes as an alternative to complete unenforceability. But the need does not extend to criminal evidence and procedure, and the fiction does not encompass them. "Rational connection" is not fictional or artificial, and so it is reasonable to suppose that Gainey should have known that his presence at the site of an illicit still could convict him of being connected with (carrying on) the business, *United States v. Gainey,* 380 U.S. 63, 85 S.Ct. 754, 13 L.Ed.2d 658 (1965), but not that Romano should have known that his presence at a still could convict him of possessing it, *United States v. Romano,* 382 U.S. 136, 86 S.Ct. 279, 15 L.Ed.2d 210 (1965).

In his dissent in Gainey, Mr. Justice Black put it more artistically:

"It might be argued, although the Court does not so argue or hold, that Congress if it wished could make presence at a still a crime in itself, and so Congress should be free to create crimes which are called 'possession' and 'carrying on an illegal distillery business' but which are defined in such a way that unexplained presence is sufficient and indisputable evidence in all cases to support conviction for those offenses. See *Ferry v. Ramsey,* 277 U.S. 88, 48 S.Ct. 443, 72 L.Ed. 796. Assuming for the sake of argument that Congress could make unexplained presence a criminal act, and ignoring also the refusal of this Court in other cases to uphold a statutory presumption on such a theory, see *Heiner v. Donnan,* 285 U.S. 312, 52 S.Ct. 358, 76 L.Ed. 772, there is no indication here that Congress intended to adopt such a misleading method of draftsmanship, nor in my judgment could the statutory provisions if so construed escape condemnation for vagueness, under the principles applied in *Lanzetta v. New Jersey,* 306 U.S. 451, 59 S.Ct. 618, 83 L.Ed. 888, and many other cases." 380 U.S. at 84, n. 12, 85 S.Ct. at 766.

And the majority opinion in *Romano* agreed with him:

"It may be, of course, that Congress has the power to make presence at an illegal still a punishable crime, but we find no clear indication that it intended to so exercise this power. The crime remains possession, not presence, and with all due deference to the judgment of Congress, the former may not constitutionally be inferred from the latter." 382 U.S. at 144, 86 S.Ct. at 284.

The rule does not spell out the procedural aspects of its application. Questions as to when the evidence warrants submission of a presumption and what instructions are proper under varying states of fact are believed to present no particular difficulties.

1974 Enactment

Rule 301 as submitted by the Supreme Court provided that in all cases a presumption imposes on the party against whom it is directed the burden of proving that the nonexistence of the presumed fact is more probable than its existence. The Committee limited the scope of Rule 301 to "civil actions and proceedings" to effectuate its decision not to deal with the question of presumptions in criminal cases. (See note on [proposed] Rule 303 in discussion of Rules deleted). With respect to the weight to be given a presumption in a civil case, the Committee agreed with the judgment implicit in the Court's version that the so-called "bursting bubble" theory of presumptions, whereby a presumption vanishes upon the appearance of any contradicting evidence by the other party, gives to presumptions too slight an effect. On the other hand, the Committee believed that the Rule proposed by the Court, whereby a presumption permanently alters the burden of persuasion, no matter how much contradicting evidence is introduced—a view shared by only a few courts—lends too great a force to presumptions. Accordingly, the Committee amended the Rule to adopt an intermediate position under which a presumption does not vanish upon the introduction of contradicting evidence, and does not change the burden of persuasion; instead it is merely deemed sufficient evidence of the fact presumed, to be considered by the jury or other finder of fact. House Report No. 93–650.

The rule governs presumptions in civil cases generally. Rule 302 provides for presumptions in cases controlled by State law.

As submitted by the Supreme Court, presumptions governed by this rule were given the effect of placing upon the opposing party the burden of establishing the nonexistence of the presumed fact, once the party invoking the presumption established the basic facts giving rise to it.

Instead of imposing a burden of persuasion on the party against whom the presumption is directed, the House adopted a provision which shifted the burden of going forward with the evidence. They further provided that "even though met with contradicting evidence, a presumption is sufficient evidence of the fact presumed, to be considered by the trier of fact." The effect of the amendment is that presumptions are to be treated as evidence.

The committee feels the House amendment is ill-advised. As the joint committees (the Standing Committee on Practice and Procedure of the Judicial Conference and the Advisory Committee on the Rules of Evidence) stated: "Presumptions are not evidence, but ways of dealing with evidence." This treatment requires juries to perform the task of considering "as evidence" facts upon which they have no direct evidence and which may confuse them in performance of their duties. California had a rule much like that contained in the House amendment. It was sharply criticized by Justice Traynor in *Speck v. Sarver* [20 Cal.2d 585, 128 P.2d 16, 21 (1942)] and was repealed after 93 troublesome years [Cal.Ev.Code 1965 § 600].

Professor McCormick gives a concise and compelling critique of the presumption as evidence rule:

* * * * * * *

Another solution, formerly more popular than now, is to instruct the jury that the presumption is "evidence", to be weighed and considered with the testimony in the case. This avoids the danger that the jury may infer that the presumption is conclusive, but it probably means little to the jury, and certainly runs counter to accepted theories of the nature of evidence. [McCormick, Evidence, 669 (1954); *Id.* 825 (2d ed. 1972)].

For these reasons the committee has deleted that provision of the House-passed rule that treats presumptions as evidence. The effect of the rule as adopted by the committee is to make clear that while evidence of facts giving rise to a presumption shifts the burden of coming forward with evidence to rebut or meet the presumption, it does not shift the burden of persuasion on the existence of the presumed facts. The burden of persuasion remains on the party to whom it is allocated under the rules governing the allocation in the first instance.

The court may instruct the jury that they may infer the existence of the presumed fact from proof of the basic facts giving rise to the presumption. However, it would be inappropriate under this rule to instruct the jury that the inference they are to draw is conclusive. Senate Report 93–1277.

The House bill provides that a presumption in civil actions and proceedings shifts to the party against whom it is directed the burden of going forward with evidence to meet or rebut it. Even though evidence contradicting the presumption is offered, a presumption is considered sufficient evidence of the presumed fact to be considered by the jury. The Senate amendment provides that a presumption shifts to the party against whom it is directed the burden of going forward with evidence to meet or rebut the presumption, but it does not shift to that party the burden of persuasion on the existence of the presumed fact.

Under the Senate amendment, a presumption is sufficient to get a party past an adverse party's motion to dismiss made at the end of his case-in-chief. If the adverse party offers no evidence contradicting the presumed fact, the court will instruct the jury that if it finds the basic facts, it may presume the existence of the presumed fact. If the adverse party does offer evidence contradicting the presumed fact, the court cannot instruct the jury that it may *presume* the existence of the presumed fact from proof of the basic facts. The court may, however, instruct the jury that it may infer the existence of the presumed fact from proof of the basic facts.

The conference adopts the Senate amendment. House Conference Report No. 93–1597.

Rule 302. Applicability of State Law in Civil Actions and Proceedings

In civil actions and proceedings, the effect of a presumption respecting a fact which is an element of a claim or defense as to which State law supplies the rule of decision is determined in accordance with State law.

(Pub.L. 93–595, § 1, Jan. 2, 1975, 88 Stat. 1931.)

ADVISORY COMMITTEE NOTES

1972 Proposed Rules

A series of Supreme Court decisions in diversity cases leaves no doubt of the relevance of *Erie Railroad Co. v. Tompkins,* 304 U.S. 64, 58 S.Ct. 817, 82 L.Ed. 1188 (1938), to questions of burden of proof. These decisions are *Cities Service Oil Co. v. Dunlap,* 308 U.S. 208, 60 S.Ct. 201, 84 L.Ed. 196 (1939), *Palmer v. Hoffman,* 318 U.S. 109, 63 S.Ct. 477, 87 L.Ed. 645 (1943), and *Dick v. New York Life Ins. Co.,* 359 U.S. 437, 79 S.Ct. 921, 3 L.Ed.2d 935 (1959). They involved burden of proof, respectively, as to status as bona fide purchaser, contributory negligence, and nonaccidental death (suicide) of an insured. In each instance the state rule was held to be applicable. It does not follow, however, that all presumptions in diversity cases are governed by state law. In each case cited, the burden of proof question had to do with a substantive element of the claim or defense. Application of the state law is called for only when the presumption operates upon such an element. Accordingly the rule does not apply state law when the presumption operates upon a lesser aspect of the case, i.e. "tactical" presumptions.

The situations in which the state law is applied have been tagged for convenience in the preceding discussion as "diversity cases." The designation is not a completely accurate one since *Erie* applies to any claim or issue having its source in state law, regardless of the basis of federal jurisdiction, and does not apply to a federal claim or issue, even though jurisdiction is based on diversity. *Vestal, Erie R.R. v. Tompkins:* A Projection, 48 Iowa L.Rev. 248, 257 (1963); Hart and Wechsler, The Federal Courts and the Federal System, 697 (1953); 1A Moore, Federal Practice ¶ 0.305[3] (2d ed. 1965); Wright, Federal Courts, 217–218 (1963). Hence the rule employs, as appropriately descriptive, the phrase "as to which state law supplies the rule of decision." See A.L.I. Study of the Division of Jurisdiction Between State and Federal Courts, § 2344(c), p. 40, P.F.D. No. 1 (1965).

ARTICLE IV. RELEVANCY AND ITS LIMITS

Rule 401. Definition of "Relevant Evidence"

"Relevant evidence" means evidence having any tendency to make the existence of any fact that is of consequence to the determination of the action more probable or less probable than it would be without the evidence.

(Pub.L. 93–595, § 1, Jan. 2, 1975, 88 Stat.1931.)

ADVISORY COMMITTEE NOTES

1972 Proposed Rules

Problems of relevancy call for an answer to the question whether an item of evidence, when tested by the processes of legal reasoning, possesses sufficient probative value to justify receiving it in evidence. Thus, assessment of the probative value of evidence that a person purchased a revolver shortly prior to a fatal shooting with which he is charged is a matter of analysis and reasoning.

The variety of relevancy problems is coextensive with the ingenuity of counsel in using circumstantial evidence as a means of proof. An enormous number of cases fall in no set pattern, and this rule is designed as a guide for handling them. On the other hand, some situations recur with sufficient frequency to create patterns susceptible of treatment by specific rules. Rule 404 and those following it are of that variety; they also serve as illustrations of the application of the present rule as limited by the exclusionary principles of Rule 403.

Passing mention should be made of so-called "conditional" relevancy. Morgan, Basic Problems of Evidence 45–46 (1962). In this situation, probative value depends not only upon satisfying the basic requirement of relevancy as described above but also upon the existence of some matter of fact. For example, if evidence of a spoken statement is relied upon to prove notice, probative value is lacking unless the person sought to be charged heard the statement. The problem is one of fact, and the only rules needed are for the purpose of determining the respective functions of judge and jury. See Rules 104(b) and 901. The discussion which follows in the present note is concerned with relevancy generally, not with any particular problem of conditional relevancy.

Relevancy is not an inherent characteristic of any item of evidence but exists only as a relation between an item of evidence and a matter properly provable in the case. Does the item of evidence tend to prove the matter sought to be proved? Whether the relationship exists depends upon principles evolved by experience or science, applied logically to the situation at hand. James, Relevancy, Probability and the Law, 29 Calif.L.Rev. 689, 696, n. 15 (1941), in Selected Writings on Evidence and Trial 610, 615, n. 15 (Fryer ed. 1957). The rule summarizes this relationship as a "tendency to make the existence" of the fact to be proved "more probable or less probable." Compare Uniform Rule 1(2) which states the crux of relevancy as "a tendency in reason," thus perhaps emphasizing unduly the logical process and ignoring the need to draw upon experience or science to validate the general principle upon which relevancy in a particular situation depends.

The standard of probability under the rule is "more * * * probable than it would be without the evidence." Any more stringent requirement is unworkable and unrealistic. As McCormick § 152, p. 317, says, "A brick is not a wall," or, as Falknor, Extrinsic Policies Affecting Admissibility, 10 Rutgers L.Rev. 574, 576 (1956), quotes Professor McBaine, "* * * [I]t is not to be supposed that every witness can make a home run." Dealing with probability in the language of the rule has the added virtue of avoiding confusion between questions of admissibility and questions of the sufficiency of the evidence.

The rule uses the phrase "fact that is of consequence to the determination of the action" to describe the kind of fact to which proof may properly be directed. The language is that of California Evidence Code § 210; it has the advantage of avoiding the loosely used and ambiguous word "material." Tentative Recommendation and a Study Relating to the Uniform Rules of Evidence (Art. I. General Provisions), Cal.Law Revision Comm'n, Rep., Rec. & Studies, 10–11 (1964). The fact to be proved may be ultimate, intermediate, or evidentiary; it matters not, so long as it is of consequence in the determination of the action. Cf. Uniform Rule 1(2) which requires that the evidence relate to a "material" fact.

The fact to which the evidence is directed need not be in dispute. While situations will arise which call for the exclusion of evidence offered to prove a point conceded by the opponent, the ruling should be made on the basis of such considerations as waste of time and undue prejudice (see Rule 403), rather than under any general requirement that evidence is admissible only if directed to matters in dispute. Evidence which is essentially background in nature can scarcely be said to involve disputed matter, yet it is universally offered and admitted as an aid to understanding. Charts, photographs, views of real estate, murder weapons, and many other items of evidence fall in this category. A rule limiting admissibility to evidence directed to a controversial point would invite the exclusion of this helpful evidence, or at least the raising of endless questions over its admission. Cf. California Evidence Code § 210, defining relevant evidence in terms of tendency to prove a disputed fact.

Rule 402. Relevant Evidence Generally Admissible; Irrelevant Evidence Inadmissible

All relevant evidence is admissible, except as otherwise provided by the Constitution of the United States, by Act of Congress, by these rules, or by other rules prescribed by the Supreme Court pursuant to statutory authority. Evidence which is not relevant is not admissible.

(Pub.L. 93–595, § 1, Jan. 2, 1975, 88 Stat. 1931.)

ADVISORY COMMITTEE NOTES

1972 Proposed Rules

The provisions that all relevant evidence is admissible, with certain exceptions, and that evidence which is not relevant is not admissible are "a presupposition involved in the very conception of a rational system of evidence." Thayer, Preliminary Treatise on Evidence 264 (1898). They constitute the foundation upon which the structure of admission and exclusion rests. For similar provisions see California Evidence Code §§ 350, 351. Provisions that all relevant evidence is admissible are found in Uniform Rule 7(f); Kansas Code of Civil Procedure § 60–407(f); and New Jersey Evidence Rule 7(f); but the exclusion of evidence which is not relevant is left to implication.

Not all relevant evidence is admissible. The exclusion of relevant evidence occurs in a variety of situations and may be called for by these rules, by the Rules of Civil and Criminal Procedure, by Bankruptcy Rules, by Act of Congress, or by constitutional considerations.

Succeeding rules in the present article, in response to the demands of particular policies, require the exclusion of evidence despite its relevancy. In addition, Article V recognizes a number of privileges; Article VI imposes limitations upon witnesses and the manner of dealing with them; Article VII specifies requirements with respect to opinions and expert testimony; Article VIII excludes hearsay not falling within an exception; Article IX spells out the handling of authentication and identification; and Article X restricts the manner of proving the contents of writings and recordings.

The Rules of Civil and Criminal Procedure in some instances require the exclusion of relevant evidence. For example, Rules 30(b) and 32(a)(3) of the Rules of Civil Procedure, by imposing requirements of notice and unavailability of the deponent, place limits on the use of relevant depositions. Similarly, Rule 15 of the Rules of Criminal Procedure restricts the use of depositions in criminal cases, even though relevant. And the effective enforcement of the command, originally statutory and now found in Rule 5(a) of the Rules of Criminal Procedure, that an arrested person be taken without unnecessary delay before a commissioner or other similar officer is held to require the exclusion of statements elicited during detention in violation thereof. *Mallory v. United States,* 354 U.S. 449, 77 S.Ct. 1356, 1 L.Ed.2d 1479 (1957); 18 U.S.C. § 3501(c).

While congressional enactments in the field of evidence have generally tended to expand admissibility beyond the scope of the common law rules, in some particular situations they have restricted the admissibility of relevant evidence. Most of this legislation has consisted of the formulation of a privilege or of a prohibition against disclosure. 8 U.S.C. § 1202(f), records of refusal of visas or permits to enter United States confidential, subject to discretion of Secretary of State to make available to court upon certification of need; 10 U.S.C. § 3693, replacement certificate of honorable discharge from Army not admissible in evidence; 10 U.S.C. § 8693, same as to Air Force; 11 U.S.C. § 25(a)(10), testimony given by bankrupt on his examination not admissible in criminal proceedings against him, except that given in hearing upon objection to discharge; 11 U.S.C. § 205(a), railroad reorganization petition, if dismissed, not admissible in evidence; 11 U.S.C. § 403(a), list of creditors filed with municipal composition plan not an admission; 13 U.S.C. § 9(a), census information confidential, retained copies of reports privileged; 47 U.S.C. § 605, interception and divulgence of wire or radio communications prohibited unless authorized by sender. These statutory provisions would remain undisturbed by the rules.

The rule recognizes but makes no attempt to spell out the constitutional considerations which impose basic limitations upon the admissibility of relevant evidence. Examples are evidence obtained by unlawful search and seizure. *Weeks v. United States,* 232 U.S. 383, 34 S.Ct. 341, 58 L.Ed. 652 (1914); *Katz v. United States,* 389 U.S. 347, 88 S.Ct. 507, 19 L.Ed.2d 576 (1967); incriminating statement elicited from an accused in violation of right to counsel. *Massiah v. United States,* 377 U.S. 201, 84 S.Ct. 1199, 12 L.Ed.2d 246 (1964).

1974 Enactment

Rule 402 as submitted to the Congress contained the phrase "or by other rules adopted by the Supreme Court". To accommodate the view that the Congress should not appear to acquiesce in the Court's judgment that it has authority under the existing Rules Enabling Acts to promulgate Rules of Evidence, the Committee amended the above phrase to read "or by other rules prescribed by the Supreme Court pursuant to statutory authority" in this and other Rules where the reference appears. House Report No. 93–650.

Rule 403. Exclusion of Relevant Evidence on Grounds of Prejudice, Confusion, or Waste of Time

Although relevant, evidence may be excluded if its probative value is substantially outweighed by the danger of unfair prejudice, confusion of the issues, or misleading the jury, or by considerations of undue delay, waste of time, or needless presentation of cumulative evidence.

(Pub.L. 93–595, § 1, Jan. 2, 1975, 88 Stat. 1932.)

ADVISORY COMMITTEE NOTES

1972 Proposed Rules

The case law recognizes that certain circumstances call for the exclusion of evidence which is of unquestioned relevance. These circumstances entail risks which range all the way from inducing decision on a purely emotional basis, at one extreme, to nothing more harmful than merely wasting time, at the other extreme. Situations in this area call for balancing the probative value of and need for the evidence against the harm likely to result from its admission. Slough, Relevancy Unraveled, 5 Kan.L.Rev. 1, 12–15 (1956); Trautman, Logical or Legal Relevancy—A Conflict in Theory, 5 Van. L.Rev. 385, 392 (1952); McCormick § 152, pp. 319–321. The rules which follow in this Article are concrete applications evolved for particular situations. However, they reflect the policies underlying the present rule, which is designed as a guide for the handling of situations for which no specific rules have been formulated.

Exclusion for risk of unfair prejudice, confusion of issues, misleading the jury, or waste of time, all find ample support in the authorities. "Unfair prejudice" within its context means an undue tendency to suggest decision on an improper basis, commonly, though not necessarily, an emotional one.

The rule does not enumerate surprise as a ground for exclusion, in this respect following Wigmore's view of the common law. 6 Wigmore § 1849. Cf. McCormick § 152, p. 320, n. 29, listing unfair surprise as a ground for exclusion but stating that it is usually "coupled with the danger of prejudice and confusion of issues." While Uniform Rule 45 incorporates surprise as a ground and is followed in Kansas Code of Civil Procedure § 60–445, surprise is not included in California Evidence Code § 352 or New Jersey Rule 4, though both the latter otherwise substantially embody Uniform Rule 45. While it can scarcely be doubted that claims of unfair surprise may still be justified despite procedural requirements of notice and instrumentalities of discovery, the granting of a continuance is a more appropriate remedy than exclusion of the evidence. Tentative Recommendation and a Study Relating to the Uniform Rules of Evidence (Art. VI. Extrinsic Policies Affecting Admissibility), Cal.Law Revision Comm'n, Rep., Rec. & Studies, 612 (1964). Moreover, the impact of a rule excluding evidence on the ground of surprise would be difficult to estimate.

In reaching a decision whether to exclude on grounds of unfair prejudice, consideration should be given to the probable effectiveness or lack of effectiveness of a limiting instruction. See Rule 106 [now 105] and Advisory Committee's Note thereunder. The availability of other means of proof may also be an appropriate factor.

Rule 404. Character Evidence Not Admissible To Prove Conduct; Exceptions; Other Crimes

(a) Character evidence generally. Evidence of a person's character or a trait of character is not admissible for the purpose of proving action in conformity therewith on a particular occasion, except:

(1) Character of accused. Evidence of a pertinent trait of character offered by an accused, or by the prosecution to rebut the same;

(2) Character of victim. Evidence of a pertinent trait of character of the victim of the crime offered by an accused, or by the prosecution to rebut the same, or evidence of a character trait of peacefulness of the victim offered by the prosecution in a homicide case to rebut evidence that the victim was the first aggressor;

(3) Character of witness. Evidence of the character of a witness, as provided in rules 607, 608, and 609.

(b) Other crimes, wrongs, or acts. Evidence of other crimes, wrongs, or acts is not admissible to prove the character of a person in order to show action in conformity therewith. It may, however, be admissible for other purposes, such as proof of motive, opportunity, intent, preparation, plan, knowledge, identity, or absence of mistake or accident, provided that upon request by the accused, the prosecution in a criminal case shall provide reasonable notice in advance of trial, or during trial if the court excuses pretrial notice on good cause shown, of the general nature of any such evidence it intends to introduce at trial.

(Pub.L. 93–595, § 1, Jan. 2, 1975, 88 Stat.1932; Mar. 2, 1987, eff. Oct. 1, 1987; Apr. 30, 1991, eff. Dec. 1, 1991.)

ADVISORY COMMITTEE NOTES

1972 Proposed Rules

Note to Subdivision (a). This subdivision deals with the basic question whether character evidence should be admitted. Once the admissibility of character evidence in some form is established under this rule, reference must then be made to Rule 405, which follows, in order to determine the appropriate method of proof. If the character is that of a witness, see Rules 608 and 610 for methods of proof.

Character questions arise in two fundamentally different ways. (1) Character may itself be an element of a crime, claim, or defense. A situation of this kind is commonly referred to as "character in issue." Illustrations are: the chastity of the victim under a statute specifying her chastity as an element of the crime of seduction, or the competency of the driver in an action for negligently entrusting a motor vehicle to an incompetent driver. No problem of the general relevancy of character evidence is involved, and the present rule therefore has no provision on the subject. The only question relates to allowable methods of proof, as to which see Rule 405, immediately following. (2) Character evidence is susceptible of being used for the purpose of suggesting an inference that the person acted on the occasion in question consistently with his character. This use of character is often described as "circumstantial." Illustrations are: evidence of a violent disposition to prove that the person was the aggressor in an affray, or evidence of honesty in disproof of a charge of theft. This circumstantial use of character evidence raises questions of relevancy as well as questions of allowable methods of proof.

In most jurisdictions today, the circumstantial use of character is rejected but with important exceptions: (1) an accused may introduce pertinent evidence of good character (often misleadingly described as "putting his character in issue"), in which event the prosecution may rebut with evidence of bad character; (2) an accused may introduce pertinent evidence of the character of the victim, as in support of a claim of self-defense to a charge of homicide or consent in a case of rape, and the prosecution may introduce similar evidence in rebuttal of the character evidence, or, in a homicide case, to rebut a claim that deceased was the first aggressor, however proved; and (3) the character of a witness may be gone into as bearing on his credibility. McCormick §§ 155–161. This pattern is incorporated in the rule. While its basis lies more in history and experience than in logic an underlying justification can fairly be found in terms of the relative presence and absence of prejudice in the various situations. Falknor, Extrinsic Policies Affecting Admissibility, 10 Rutgers L.Rev. 574, 584 (1956); McCormick § 157. In any event, the criminal rule is so deeply imbedded in our jurisprudence as to assume almost constitutional proportions and to override doubts of the basic relevancy of the evidence.

The limitation to pertinent traits of character, rather than character generally, in paragraphs (1) and (2) is in accordance with the prevailing view. McCormick § 158, p. 334. A similar provision in Rule 608, to which reference is made in paragraph (3), limits character evidence respecting witnesses to the trait of truthfulness or untruthfulness.

The argument is made that circumstantial use of character ought to be allowed in civil cases to the same extent as in criminal cases, i.e. evidence of good (nonprejudicial) character would be admissible in the first instance, subject to rebuttal by evidence of bad character. Falknor, Extrinsic Policies Affecting Admissibility, 10 Rutgers L.Rev. 574, 581–583 (1956); Tentative Recommendation and a Study Relating to the Uniform Rules of Evidence (Art. VI. Extrinsic Policies Affecting Admissibility), Cal.Law Revision Comm'n, Rep., Rec. & Studies, 657–658 (1964). Uniform Rule 47 goes farther, in that it assumes that character evidence in general satisfies the conditions of relevancy, except as provided in Uniform Rule 48. The difficulty with expanding the use of character evidence in civil cases is set forth by the California Law Revision Commission in its ultimate rejection of Uniform Rule 47, *id.*, 615:

"Character evidence is of slight probative value and may be very prejudicial. It tends to distract the trier of fact from the main question of what actually happened on the particular occasion. It subtly permits the trier of fact to reward the good man and to punish the bad man because of their respective characters despite what the evidence in the case shows actually happened."

Much of the force of the position of those favoring greater use of character evidence in civil cases is dissipated by their support of Uniform Rule 48 which excludes the evidence in negligence cases, where it could be expected to achieve its maximum usefulness. Moreover, expanding concepts of "character," which seem of necessity to extend into such areas as psychiatric evaluation and psychological testing, coupled with expanded admissibility, would open up such vistas of mental examinations as caused the Court concern in *Schlagenhauf v. Holder*, 379 U.S. 104, 85 S.Ct. 234, 13 L.Ed.2d 152 (1964). It is believed that those espousing change have not met the burden of persuasion.

Note to Subdivision (b). Subdivision (b) deals with a specialized but important application of the general rule excluding circumstantial use of character evidence. Consistently with that rule, evidence of other crimes, wrongs, or acts is not admissible to prove character as a basis for suggesting the inference that conduct on a particular occasion was in conformity with it. However, the evidence may be offered for another purpose, such as proof of motive, opportunity, and so on, which does not fall within the prohibition. In this situation the rule does not require that the evidence be excluded. No mechanical solution is offered. The determination must be made whether the danger of undue prejudice outweighs the probative value of the evidence in view of the availability of other means of proof and other facts appropriate for making decision of this kind under Rule 403. Slough and Knightly, Other Vices, Other Crimes, 41 Iowa L.Rev. 325 (1956).

1974 Enactment

Note to Subdivision (b). The second sentence of Rule 404(b) as submitted to the Congress began with the words "This subdivision does not exclude the evidence when offered". The Committee amended this language to read "It may, however, be admissible", the words used in the 1971 Advisory Committee draft, on the ground that this formulation properly placed greater emphasis on admissibility than did the final Court version. House Report No. 93–650.

Note to Subdivision (b). This rule provides that evidence of other crimes, wrongs, or acts is not admissible to prove character but may be admissible for other specified purposes such as proof of motive.

Although your committee sees no necessity in amending the rule itself, it anticipates that the use of the discretionary word "may" with respect to the admissibility of evidence of crimes, wrongs, or acts is not intended to confer any arbitrary discretion on the trial judge. Rather, it is anticipated that with respect to permissible uses for such evidence, the trial judge may exclude it only on the basis of those considerations set forth in Rule 403, i.e., prejudice, confusion or waste of time. Senate Report No. 93–1277.

1987 Amendment

The amendments are technical. No substantive change is intended.

1991 Amendment

Rule 404(b) has emerged as one of the most cited Rules in the Rules of Evidence. And in many criminal cases evidence of an accused's extrinsic acts is viewed as an important asset in the prosecution's case against an accused. Although there are a few reported decisions on use of such evidence by the defense, *see, e.g., United States v. McClure*, 546 F.2d 670 (5th Cir.1990) (acts of informant offered in entrapment defense), the overwhelming number of cases involve introduction of that evidence by the prosecution.

The amendment to Rule 404(b) adds a pretrial notice requirement in criminal cases and is intended to reduce surprise and promote early resolution on the issue of admissibility. The notice requirement thus places Rule 404(b) in the mainstream with notice and disclosure provisions in other rules of evidence. *See, e.g.,* Rule 412 (written motion of intent to offer evidence under rule), Rule 609 (written notice of intent to offer conviction older than 10 years), Rule 803(24) and 804(b)(5) (notice of intent to use residual hearsay exceptions).

The Rule expects that counsel for both the defense and the prosecution will submit the necessary request and information in a reasonable and timely fashion. Other than requiring pretrial notice, no specific time limits are stated in recognition that what constitutes a reasonable request or disclosure will depend largely on the circumstances of each case. *Compare* Fla.Stat.Ann. § 90.404(2)(b) (notice must be given at least 10 days before trial) *with* Tex.R.Evid. 404(b) (no time limit).

Likewise, no specific form of notice is required. The Committee considered and rejected a requirement that the notice satisfy the particularity requirements normally required of language used in a charging instrument. *Cf.* Fla.Stat.Ann. § 90.404(2)(b) (written disclosure must describe uncharged misconduct with particularity required of an indictment or information). Instead, the Committee opted for a generalized notice provision which requires the prosecution to apprise the defense of the general nature of the evidence of extrinsic acts. The Committee does not intend that the amendment will supercede other rules of admissibility or disclosure, such as the Jencks Act, 18 U.S.C. § 3500, et. seq. nor require the prosecution to disclose directly or indirectly the names and addresses of its witnesses, something it is currently not required to do under Federal Rule of Criminal Procedure 16.

The amendment requires the prosecution to provide notice, regardless of how it intends to use the extrinsic act evidence at trial, i.e., during its case-in-chief, for impeachment, or for possible rebuttal. The court in its discretion may, under the facts, decide that the particular request or notice was not reasonable, either because of the lack of timeliness or completeness. Because the notice requirement serves as condition precedent to admissibility of 404(b) evidence, the offered evidence is inadmissible if the court decides that the notice requirement has not been met.

Nothing in the amendment precludes the court from requiring the government to provide it with an opportunity to rule *in limine* on 404(b) evidence before it is offered or even mentioned during trial. When ruling *in limine,* the court may require the government to disclose to it the specifics of such evidence which the court must consider in determining admissibility.

The amendment does not extend to evidence of acts which are "intrinsic" to the charged offense, *see United States v. Williams,* 900 F.2d 823 (5th Cir.1990) (noting distinction between 404(b) evidence and intrinsic offense evidence). Nor is the amendment intended to redefine what evidence would otherwise be admissible under Rule 404(b). Finally, the Committee does not intend through the amendment to affect the role of the court and the jury in considering such evidence. *See United States v. Huddleston,* 485 U.S. 681, 108 S.Ct. 1496 (1988).

Rule 405. Methods of Proving Character

(a) Reputation or opinion. In all cases in which evidence of character or a trait of character of a person is admissible, proof may be made by testimony as to reputation or by testimony in the form of an opinion. On cross-examination, inquiry is allowable into relevant specific instances of conduct.

(b) Specific instances of conduct. In cases in which character or a trait of character of a person is an essential element of a charge, claim, or defense, proof may also be made of specific instances of that person's conduct.

(Pub.L. 93–595, § 1, Jan. 2, 1975, 88 Stat. 1932; Mar. 2, 1987, eff. Oct. 1, 1987.)

ADVISORY COMMITTEE NOTES

1972 Proposed Rules

The rule deals only with allowable methods of proving character, not with the admissibility of character evidence, which is covered in Rule 404.

Of the three methods of proving character provided by the rule, evidence of specific instances of conduct is the most convincing. At the same time it possesses the greatest capacity to arouse prejudice, to confuse, to surprise, and to consume time. Consequently the rule confines the use of evidence of this kind to cases in which character is, in the strict sense, in issue and hence deserving of a searching inquiry. When character is used circumstantially and hence occupies a lesser status in the case, proof may be only by reputation and opinion. These latter methods are also available when character is in issue. This treatment is, with respect to specific instances of conduct and reputation, conventional contemporary common law doctrine. McCormick § 153.

In recognizing opinion as a means of proving character, the rule departs from usual contemporary practice in favor of that of an earlier day. See 7 Wigmore § 1986, pointing out that the earlier practice permitted opinion and arguing strongly for evidence based on personal knowledge and belief as contrasted with "the secondhand, irresponsible product of multiplied guesses and gossip which we term 'reputation'." It seems likely that the persistence of reputation evidence is due to its largely being opinion in disguise. Traditionally character has been regarded primarily in moral overtones of good and bad: chaste, peaceable, truthful, honest. Nevertheless, on occasion nonmoral considerations crop up, as in the case of the incompetent driver, and this seems bound to happen increasingly. If character is defined as the kind of person one is, then account must be taken of varying ways of arriving at the estimate. These may range from the opinion of the employer who has found the man honest to the opinion of the psychiatrist based upon examination and testing. No effective dividing line exists between character and mental capacity, and the latter traditionally has been provable by opinion.

According to the great majority of cases, on cross-examination inquiry is allowable as to whether the reputation witness has heard of particular instances of conduct pertinent to the trait in question. *Michelson v. United States*, 335 U.S. 469, 69 S.Ct. 213, 93 L.Ed. 168 (1948); Annot., 47 A.L.R.2d 1258. The theory is that, since the reputation witness relates what he has heard, the inquiry tends to shed light on the accuracy of his hearing and reporting. Accordingly, the opinion witness would be asked whether he knew, as well as whether he had heard. The fact is, of course, that these distinctions are of slight if any practical significance, and the second sentence of subdivision (a) eliminates them as a factor in formulating questions. This recognition of the propriety of inquiring into specific instances of conduct does not circumscribe inquiry otherwise into the bases of opinion and reputation testimony.

The express allowance of inquiry into specific instances of conduct on cross-examination in subdivision (a) and the express allowance of it as part of a case in chief when character is actually in issue in subdivision (b) contemplate that testimony of specific instances is not generally permissible on the direct examination of an ordinary opinion witness to character. Similarly as to witnesses to the character of witnesses under Rule 608(b). Opinion testimony on direct in these situations ought in general to correspond to reputation testimony as now given, *i.e.*, be confined to the nature and extent of observation and acquaintance upon which the opinion is based. See Rule 701.

1974 Enactment

Note to Subdivision (a). Rule 405(a) as submitted proposed to change existing law by allowing evidence of character in the form of opinion as well as reputation testimony. Fearing, among other reasons, that wholesale allowance of opinion testimony might tend to turn a trial into a swearing contest between conflicting character witnesses, the Committee decided to delete from this Rule, as well as from Rule 608(a) which involves a related problem, reference to opinion testimony. House Report No. 93–650.

The Senate makes two language changes in the nature of conforming amendments. The Conference adopts the Senate amendments. House Report No. 93–1597.

1987 Amendment

The amendment is technical. No substantive change is intended.

Rule 406. Habit; Routine Practice

Evidence of the habit of a person or of the routine practice of an organization, whether corroborated or not and regardless of the presence of eyewitnesses, is relevant to prove that the conduct of the person or organization on a particular occasion was in conformity with the habit or routine practice.

(Pub.L. 93–595, § 1, Jan. 2, 1975, 88 Stat. 1932.)

ADVISORY COMMITTEE NOTES

1972 Proposed Rules

An oft-quoted paragraph, McCormick, § 162, p. 340, describes habit in terms effectively contrasting it with character:

"Character and habit are close akin. Character is a generalized description of one's disposition, or of one's disposition in respect to a general trait, such as honesty, temperance, or peacefulness. 'Habit,' in modern usage, both lay and psychological, is more specific. It describes one's regular response to a repeated specific situation. If we speak of character for care, we think of the person's tendency to act prudently in all the varying situations of life, in business, family life, in handling automobiles and in walking across the street. A habit, on the other hand, is the person's regular practice of meeting a particular kind of situation with a specific type of conduct, such as the habit of going down a particular stairway two stairs at a time, or of giving the hand-signal for a left turn, or of alighting from railway cars while they are moving. The doing of the habitual acts may become semi-automatic."

Equivalent behavior on the part of a group is designated "routine practice of an organization" in the rule.

Agreement is general that habit evidence is highly persuasive as proof of conduct on a particular occasion. Again quoting McCormick § 162, p. 341:

"Character may be thought of as the sum of one's habits though doubtless it is more than this. But unquestionably the uniformity of one's response to habit is far greater than the consistency with which one's conduct conforms to character or disposition. Even though character comes in only exceptionally as evidence of an act, surely any sensible man in investigating whether X did a particular act would be greatly helped in his inquiry by evidence as to whether he was in the habit of doing it."

When disagreement has appeared, its focus has been upon the question what constitutes habit, and the reason for this is readily apparent. The extent to which instances must be multiplied and consistency of behavior maintained in order to rise to the status of habit inevitably gives rise to differences of opinion. Lewan, Rationale of Habit Evidence, 16 Syracuse L.Rev. 39, 49 (1964). While adequacy of sampling and uniformity of response are key factors, precise standards for measuring their sufficiency for evidence purposes cannot be formulated.

The rule is consistent with prevailing views. Much evidence is excluded simply because of failure to achieve the status of habit. Thus, evidence of intemperate "habits" is generally excluded when offered as proof of drunkenness in accident cases, Annot., 46 A.L.R.2d 103, and evidence of other assaults is inadmissible to prove the instant one in a civil assault action, Annot., 66 A.L.R.2d 806. In *Levin v. United States*, 119 U.S.App.D.C. 156, 338 F.2d 265 (1964), testimony as to the religious "habits" of the accused, offered as tending to prove that he was at home observing the Sabbath rather than out obtaining money through larceny by trick, was held properly excluded:

"It seems apparent to us that an individual's religious practices would not be the type of activities which would lend themselves to the characterization of 'invariable regularity.' [1 Wigmore 520.] Certainly the very volitional basis of the activity raises serious questions as to its invariable nature, and hence its probative value." *Id.* at 272.

These rulings are not inconsistent with the trend towards admitting evidence of business transactions between one of the parties and a third person as tending to prove that he made the same bargain or proposal in the litigated situation.

Slough, Relevancy Unraveled, 6 Kan.L.Rev. 38–41 (1957). Nor are they inconsistent with such cases as *Whittemore v. Lockheed Aircraft Corp.*, 65 Cal.App.2d 737, 151 P.2d 670 (1944), upholding the admission of evidence that plaintiff's intestate had on four other occasions flown planes from defendant's factory for delivery to his employer airline, offered to prove that he was piloting rather than a guest on a plane which crashed and killed all on board while en route for delivery.

A considerable body of authority has required that evidence of the routine practice of an organization be corroborated as a condition precedent to its admission in evidence. Slough, Relevancy Unraveled, 5 Kan.L.Rev. 404, 449 (1957). This requirement is specifically rejected by the rule on the ground that it relates to the sufficiency of the evidence rather than admissibility. A similar position is taken in New Jersey Rule 49. The rule also rejects the requirement of the absence of eyewitnesses, sometimes encountered with respect to admitting habit evidence to prove freedom from contributory negligence in wrongful death cases. For comment critical of the requirements see Frank, J., in *Cereste v. New York*, N.H. & H.R. Co., 231 F.2d 50 (2d Cir.1956), cert. denied 351 U.S. 951, 76 S.Ct. 848, 100 L.Ed. 1475, 10 Vand.L.Rev. 447 (1957); McCormick § 162, p. 342. The omission of the requirement from the California Evidence Code is said to have effected its elimination. Comment, Cal.Ev.Code § 1105.

Rule 407. Subsequent Remedial Measures

When, after an injury or harm allegedly caused by an event, measures are taken that, if taken previously, would have made the injury or harm less likely to occur, evidence of the subsequent measures is not admissible to prove negligence, culpable conduct, a defect in a product, a defect in a product's design, or a need for a warning or instruction. This rule does not require the exclusion of evidence of subsequent measures when offered for another purpose, such as proving ownership, control, or feasibility of precautionary measures, if controverted, or impeachment.

(Pub.L. 93–595, § 1, Jan. 2, 1975, 88 Stat. 1932; Apr. 11, 1997, eff. Dec. 1, 1997.)

ADVISORY COMMITTEE NOTES

1972 Proposed Rules

The rule incorporates conventional doctrine which excludes evidence of subsequent remedial measures as proof of an admission of fault. The rule rests on two grounds. (1) The conduct is not in fact an admission, since the conduct is equally consistent with injury by mere accident or through contributory negligence. Or, as Baron Bramwell put it, the rule rejects the notion that "because the world gets wiser as it gets older, therefore it was foolish before." *Hart v. Lancashire & Yorkshire Ry. Co.*, 21 L.T.R. N.S. 261, 263 (1869). Under a liberal theory of relevancy this ground alone would not support exclusion as the inference is still a possible one. (2) The other, and more impressive, ground for exclusion rests on a social policy of encouraging people to take, or at least not discouraging them from taking, steps in furtherance of added safety. The courts have applied this principle to exclude evidence of subsequent repairs, installation of safety devices, changes in company rules, and discharge of employees, and the language of the present rule is broad enough to encompass all of them. See Falknor, Extrinsic Policies Affecting Admissibility, 10 Rutgers L.Rev. 574, 590 (1956).

The second sentence of the rule directs attention to the limitations of the rule. Exclusion is called for only when the evidence of subsequent remedial measures is offered as proof of negligence or culpable conduct. In effect it rejects the suggested inference that fault is admitted. Other purposes are, however, allowable, including ownership or control, existence of duty, and feasibility of precautionary measures, if controverted, and impeachment. 2 Wigmore § 283; Annot., 64 A.L.R.2d 1296. Two recent federal cases are illustrative. *Boeing Airplane Co. v. Brown*, 291 F.2d 310 (9th Cir.1961), an action against an airplane manufacturer for using an allegedly defectively designed alternator shaft which caused a plane crash, upheld the admission of evidence of subsequent design modification for the purpose of showing that design changes and safeguards were feasible. And *Powers v. J.B. Michael & Co.*, 329 F.2d 674 (6th Cir.1964), an action against a road contractor for negligent failure to put out warning signs, sustained the admission of evidence that defendant subsequently put out signs to show that the portion of the road in question was under defendant's control. The requirement that the other purpose be controverted calls for automatic exclusion unless a genuine issue be present and allows the opposing party to lay the groundwork for exclusion by making an admission. Otherwise the factors of undue prejudice, confusion of issues, misleading the jury, and waste of time remain for consideration under Rule 403.

For comparable rules, see Uniform Rule 51; California Evidence Code § 1151; Kansas Code of Civil Procedure § 60–451; New Jersey Evidence Rule 51.

1997 Amendment

The amendment to Rule 407 makes two changes in the rule. First, the words "an injury or harm allegedly caused by" were added to clarify that the rule applies only to changes made after the occurrence that produced the damages giving rise to the action. Evidence of measures taken by the defendant prior to the "event" causing "injury or harm" do not fall within the exclusionary scope of Rule 407 even if they occurred after the manufacture or design of the product. See *Chase v. General Motors Corp.*, 856 F.2d 17, 21–22 (4th Cir. 1988).

Second, Rule 407 has been amended to provide that evidence of subsequent remedial measures may not be used to prove "a defect in a product or its design, or that a warning or instruction should have accompanied a product." This amendment adopts the view of a majority of the circuits that have interpreted Rule 407 to apply to products liability actions. See *Raymond v. Raymond Corp., 938 F.2d 1518, 1522 (1st Cir. 1991); In re Joint Eastern District and Southern District Asbestos Litigation v. Armstrong World industries, Inc.*, 995 F.2d 343 (2d Cir. 1993); *Cann v. Ford Motor Co.*, 658 F.2d 54, 60 (2d Cir. 1981), *cert. denied*, 456 U.S. 960 (1982); *Kelly v. Crown Equipment Co.*, 970 F.2d 1273, 1275 (3d Cir. 1992); *Werner v. Upjohn, Inc.*, 628 F.2d 848 (4th Cir. 1980); *cert. denied*, 449 U.S. 1080 (1981); *Grenada Steel Industries, Inc. v. Alabama Oxygen Co., Inc.*, 695 F.2d 883 (5th Cir. 1983); *Bauman v. Volkswagenwerk Aktiengesellschaft*, 621 F.2d 230, 232 (6th Cir. 1980); *Flami-*

nio v. Honda Motor Company, Ltd., 733 F.2d 463, 469 (7th Cir. 1984); *Gauthier v. AMF, Inc.*, 788 F.2d 634, 636–37 (9th Cir. 1986).

Although this amendment adopts a uniform federal rule, it should be noted that evidence of subsequent remedial measures may be admissible pursuant to the second sentence of Rule 407. Evidence of subsequent measures that is not barred by Rule 407 may still be subject to exclusion on Rule 403 grounds when the dangers of prejudice or confusion substantially outweigh the probative value of the evidence.

GAP Report on Rule 407. The words "injury or harm" were substituted for the word "event " in line 3. The stylization changes in the second sentence of the rule were eliminated. The words "causing 'injury or harm' " were added to the Committee Note.

Rule 408. Compromise and Offers to Compromise

Evidence of (1) furnishing or offering or promising to furnish, or (2) accepting or offering or promising to accept, a valuable consideration in compromising or attempting to compromise a claim which was disputed as to either validity or amount, is not admissible to prove liability for or invalidity of the claim or its amount. Evidence of conduct or statements made in compromise negotiations is likewise not admissible. This rule does not require the exclusion of any evidence otherwise discoverable merely because it is presented in the course of compromise negotiations. This rule also does not require exclusion when the evidence is offered for another purpose, such as proving bias or prejudice of a witness, negativing a contention of undue delay, or proving an effort to obstruct a criminal investigation or prosecution.

(Pub.L. 93–595, § 1, Jan. 2, 1975, 88 Stat. 1933.)

ADVISORY COMMITTEE NOTES

1972 Proposed Rules

As a matter of general agreement, evidence of an offer to compromise a claim is not receivable in evidence as an admission of, as the case may be, the validity or invalidity of the claim. As with evidence of subsequent remedial measures, dealt with in Rule 407, exclusion may be based on two grounds. (1) The evidence is irrelevant, since the offer may be motivated by a desire for peace rather than from any concession of weakness of position. The validity of this position will vary as the amount of the offer varies in relation to the size of the claim and may also be influenced by other circumstances. (2) A more consistently impressive ground is promotion of the public policy favoring the compromise and settlement of disputes. McCormick §§ 76, 251. While the rule is ordinarily phrased in terms of offers of compromise, it is apparent that a similar attitude must be taken with respect to completed compromises when offered against a party thereto. This latter situation will not, of course, ordinarily occur except when a party to the present litigation has compromised with a third person.

The same policy underlies the provision of Rule 68 of the Federal Rules of Civil Procedure that evidence of an unaccepted offer of judgment is not admissible except in a proceeding to determine costs.

The practical value of the common law rule has been greatly diminished by its inapplicability to admissions of fact, even though made in the course of compromise negotiations, unless hypothetical, stated to be "without prejudice," or so connected with the offer as to be inseparable from it. McCormick § 251, pp. 540–541. An inevitable effect is to inhibit freedom of communication with respect to compromise, even among lawyers. Another effect is the generation of controversy over whether a given statement falls within or without the protected area. These considerations account for the expansion of the rule herewith to include evidence of conduct or statements made in compromise negotiations, as well as the offer or completed compromise itself. For similar provisions see California Evidence Code §§ 1152, 1154.

The policy considerations which underlie the rule do not come into play when the effort is to induce a creditor to settle an admittedly due amount for a lesser sum. McCormick § 251, p. 540. Hence the rule requires that the claim be disputed as to either validity or amount.

The final sentence of the rule serves to point out some limitations upon its applicability. Since the rule excludes only when the purpose is proving the validity or invalidity of the claim or its amount, an offer for another purpose is not within the rule. The illustrative situations mentioned in the rule are supported by the authorities. As to proving bias or prejudice of a witness, see Annot., 161 A.L.R. 395, *contra*, *Fenberg v. Rosenthal*, 348 Ill.App. 510, 109 N.E.2d 402 (1952), and negativing a contention of lack of due diligence in presenting a claim, 4 Wigmore § 1061. An effort to "buy off" the prosecution or a prosecuting witness in a criminal case is not within the policy of the rule of exclusion. McCormick § 251, p. 542.

For other rules of similar import, see Uniform Rules 52 and 53; California Evidence Code §§ 1152, 1154; Kansas Code of Civil Procedure §§ 60–452, 60–453; New Jersey Evidence Rules 52 and 53.

1974 Enactment

Under existing federal law evidence of conduct and statements made in compromise negotiations is admissible in subsequent litigation between the parties. The second sentence of Rule 408 as submitted by the Supreme Court proposed to reverse that doctrine in the interest of further promoting non-judicial settlement of disputes. Some agencies of government expressed the view that the Court formulation was likely to impede rather than assist efforts to achieve settlement of disputes. For one thing, it is not always easy to tell when compromise negotiations begin, and informal dealings end. Also, parties dealing with government agencies would be reluctant to furnish factual information at preliminary meetings; they would wait until "compromise negotiations" began and thus hopefully effect an immunity for themselves with respect to the evidence supplied. In light of these considerations, the Committee recast the Rule so that admissions of liability or opinions given during compromise negotiations continue inadmissible, but evidence of unqualified factual assertions is admissible. The latter aspect of the Rule is drafted, however, so as to preserve other possible objections to the introduction of such evidence. The Committee intends no modification of current law whereby a party may protect himself from future use of his statements by couching them in hypothetical conditional form. House Report No. 93–650.

This rule as reported makes evidence of settlement or attempted settlement of a disputed claim inadmissible when offered as an admission of liability or the amount of liability. The purpose of this rule is to encourage settlements which would be discouraged if such evidence were admissible.

Under present law, in most jurisdictions, statements of fact made during settlement negotiations, however, are excepted from this ban and are admissible. The only escape from admissibility of statements of fact made in a settlement negotiation is if the declarant or his representative expressly states that the statement is hypothetical in nature or is made without prejudice. Rule 408 as submitted by the Court reversed the traditional rule. It would have brought statements of fact within the ban and made them, as well as an offer of settlement, inadmissible.

The House amended the rule and would continue to make evidence of facts disclosed during compromise negotiations admissible. It thus reverted to the traditional rule. The House committee report states that the committee intends to preserve current law under which a party may protect himself by couching his statements in hypothetical form [See House Report No. 93–650 above]. The real impact of this amendment, however, is to deprive the rule of much of its salutary effect. The exception for factual admissions was believed by the Advisory Committee to hamper free communication between parties and thus to constitute an unjustifiable restraint upon efforts to negotiate settlements—the encouragement of which is the purpose of the rule. Further, by protecting hypothetically phrased statements, it constituted a preference for the sophisticated, and a trap for the unwary.

Three States which had adopted rules of evidence patterned after the proposed rules prescribed by the Supreme Court opted for versions of rule 408 identical with the Supreme Court draft with respect to the inadmissibility of conduct or statements made in compromise negotiations [Nev.Rev.Stats. § 48.105; N.Mex.Stats.Anno. (1973 Supp.) § 20–4–408; West's Wis.Stats.Anno. (1973 Supp.) § 904.08].

For these reasons, the committee has deleted the House amendment and restored the rule to the version submitted by the Supreme Court with one additional amendment. This amendment adds a sentence to insure that evidence, such as documents, is not rendered inadmissible merely because it is presented in the course of compromise negotiations if the evidence is otherwise discoverable. A party should not be able to immunize from admissibility documents otherwise discoverable merely by offering them in a compromise negotiation. Senate Report No. 93–1277.

The House bill provides that evidence of admissions of liability or opinions given during compromise negotiations is not admissible, but that evidence of facts disclosed during compromise negotiations is not inadmissible by virtue of having been first disclosed in the compromise negotiations. The Senate amendment provides that evidence of conduct or statements made in compromise negotiations is not admissible. The Senate amendment also provides that the rule does not require the exclusion of any evidence otherwise discoverable merely because it is presented in the course of compromise negotiations.

The House bill was drafted to meet the objection of executive agencies that under the rule as proposed by the Supreme Court, a party could present a fact during compromise negotiations and thereby prevent an opposing party from offering evidence of that fact at trial even though such evidence was obtained from independent sources. The Senate amendment expressly precludes this result.

The Conference adopts the Senate amendment. House Report No. 93–1597.

Rule 409. Payment of Medical and Similar Expenses

Evidence of furnishing or offering or promising to pay medical, hospital, or similar expenses occasioned by an injury is not admissible to prove liability for the injury.

(Pub.L. 93–595, § 1, Jan. 2, 1975, 88 Stat.1933.)

ADVISORY COMMITTEE NOTES

1972 Proposed Rules

The considerations underlying this rule parallel those underlying Rules 407 and 408, which deal respectively with subsequent remedial measures and offers of compromise. As stated in Annot., 20 A.L.R.2d 291, 293:

"[G]enerally, evidence of payment of medical, hospital, or similar expenses of an injured party by the opposing party, is not admissible, the reason often given being that such payment or offer is usually made from humane impulses and not from an admission of liability, and that to hold otherwise would tend to discourage assistance to the injured person."

Contrary to Rule 408, dealing with offers of compromise, the present rule does not extend to conduct or statements not a part of the act of furnishing or offering or promising to pay. This difference in treatment arises from fundamental differences in nature. Communication is essential if compromises are to be effected, and consequently broad protection of statements is needed. This is not so in cases of payments or offers or promises to pay medical expenses, where factual statements may be expected to be incidental in nature.

For rules on the same subject, but phrased in terms of "humanitarian motives," see Uniform Rule 52; California Evidence Code § 1152; Kansas Code of Civil Procedure § 60–452; New Jersey Evidence Rule 52.

Rule 410. Inadmissibility of Pleas, Plea Discussions, and Related Statements

Except as otherwise provided in this rule, evidence of the following is not, in any civil or criminal proceeding, admissible against the defendant who made the plea or was a participant in the plea discussions:

(1) a plea of guilty which was later withdrawn;

(2) a plea of nolo contendere;

(3) any statement made in the course of any proceedings under Rule 11 of the Federal Rules of Criminal Procedure or comparable state procedure regarding either of the foregoing pleas; or

(4) any statement made in the course of plea discussions with an attorney for the prosecuting

authority which do not result in a plea of guilty or which result in a plea of guilty later withdrawn. However, such a statement is admissible (i) in any proceeding wherein another statement made in the course of the same plea or plea discussions has been introduced and the statement ought in fairness be considered contemporaneously with it, or (ii) in a criminal proceeding for perjury or false statement if the statement was made by the defendant under oath, on the record and in the presence of counsel.

(Pub.L. 93–595, § 1, Jan. 2, 1975, 88 Stat. 1933; Pub.L. 94–149, § 1(9), Dec. 12, 1975, 89 Stat. 805; Apr. 30, 1979, eff. Dec. 1, 1980.)

ADVISORY COMMITTEE NOTES

1972 Proposed Rules

Withdrawn pleas of guilty were held inadmissible in federal prosecutions in *Kercheval v. United States,* 274 U.S. 220, 47 S.Ct. 582, 71 L.Ed. 1009 (1927). The Court pointed out that to admit the withdrawn plea would effectively set at naught the allowance of withdrawal and place the accused in a dilemma utterly inconsistent with the decision to award him a trial. The New York Court of Appeals, in *People v. Spitaleri,* 9 N.Y.2d 168, 212 N.Y.S.2d 53, 173 N.E.2d 35 (1961), reexamined and overturned its earlier decisions which had allowed admission. In addition to the reasons set forth in Kercheval, which was quoted at length, the court pointed out that the effect of admitting the plea was to compel defendant to take the stand by way of explanation and to open the way for the prosecution to call the lawyer who had represented him at the time of entering the plea. State court decisions for and against admissibility are collected in Annot., 86 A.L.R.2d 326.

Pleas of *nolo contendere* are recognized by Rule 11 of the Rules of Criminal Procedure, although the law of numerous States is to the contrary. The present rule gives effect to the principal traditional characteristic of the *nolo* plea, i.e. avoiding the admission of guilt which is inherent in pleas of guilty. This position is consistent with the construction of Section 5 of the Clayton Act, 15 U.S.C. § 16(a), recognizing the inconclusive and compromise nature of judgments based on *nolo* pleas. *General Electric Co. v. City of San Antonio,* 334 F.2d 480 (5th Cir.1964); *Commonwealth Edison Co. v. Allis–Chalmers Mfg. Co.,* 323 F.2d 412 (7th Cir.1963), cert. denied 376 U.S. 939, 84 S.Ct. 794, 11 L.Ed.2d 659; *Armco Steel Corp. v. North Dakota,* 376 F.2d 206 (8th Cir.1967); *City of Burbank v. General Electric Co.,* 329 F.2d 825 (9th Cir.1964). See also state court decisions in Annot., 18 A.L.R.2d 1287, 1314.

Exclusion of offers to plead guilty or *nolo* has as its purpose the promotion of disposition of criminal cases by compromise. As pointed out in McCormick § 251, p. 543.

"Effective criminal law administration in many localities would hardly be possible if a large proportion of the charges were not disposed of by such compromises."

See also *People v. Hamilton,* 60 Cal.2d 105, 32 Cal.Rptr. 4, 383 P.2d 412 (1963), discussing legislation designed to achieve this result. As with compromise offers generally, Rule 408, free communication is needed, and security against having an offer of compromise or related statement admitted in evidence effectively encourages it.

Limiting the exclusionary rule to use against the accused is consistent with the purpose of the rule, since the possibility of use for or against other persons will not impair the effectiveness of withdrawing pleas or the freedom of discussion which the rule is designed to foster. See A.B.A. Standards Relating to Pleas of Guilty § 2.2 (1968). See also the narrower provisions of New Jersey Evidence Rule 52(2) and the unlimited exclusion provided in California Evidence Code § 1153.

1974 Enactment

The Committee added the phrase "Except as otherwise provided by Act of Congress" to Rule 410 as submitted by the Court in order to preserve particular congressional policy judgments as to the effect of a plea of guilty or of nolo contendere. See 15 U.S.C. 16(a). The Committee intends that its amendment refers to both present statutes and statutes subsequently enacted. House Report No. 93–650.

As adopted by the House, rule 410 would make inadmissible pleas of guilty or nolo contendere subsequently withdrawn as well as offers to make such pleas. Such a rule is clearly justified as a means of encouraging pleading. However, the House rule would then go on to render inadmissible for any purpose statements made in connection with these pleas or offers as well.

The committee finds this aspect of the House rule unjustified. Of course, in certain circumstances such statements should be excluded. If, for example, a plea is vitiated because of coercion, statements made in connection with the plea may also have been coerced and should be inadmissible on that basis. In other cases, however, voluntary statements of an accused made in court on the record, in connection with a plea, and determined by a court to be reliable should be admissible even though the plea is subsequently withdrawn. This is particularly true in those cases where, if the House rule were in effect, a defendant would be able to contradict his previous statements and thereby lie with impunity [See *Harris v. New York,* 401 U.S. 222 (1971)]. To prevent such an injustice, the rule has been modified to permit the use of such statements for the limited purposes of impeachment and in subsequent perjury or false statement prosecutions. Senate Report No. 93–1277.

The House bill provides that evidence of a guilty or nolo contendere plea, of an offer of either plea, or of statements made in connection with such pleas or offers of such pleas, is inadmissible in any civil or criminal action, case or proceeding against the person making such plea or offer. The Senate amendment makes the rule inapplicable to a voluntary and reliable statement made in court on the record where the statement is offered in a subsequent prosecution of the declarant for perjury or false statement.

The issues raised by Rule 410 are also raised by proposed Rule 11(e)(6) of the Federal Rules of Criminal Procedure presently pending before Congress. This proposed rule, which deals with the admissibility of pleas of guilty or nolo contendere, offers to make such pleas, and statements made in connection with such pleas, was promulgated by the Supreme Court on April 22, 1974, and in the absence of congressional action will become effective on August 1, 1975. The conferees intend to make no change in the presently-existing case law until that date, leaving the courts free to develop rules in this area on a case-by-case basis.

The Conferees further determined that the issues presented by the use of guilty and nolo contendere pleas, offers of such pleas, and statements made in connection with such pleas or offers, can be explored in greater detail during Congressional consideration of Rule 11(e)(6) of the Federal Rules of Criminal Procedure. The Conferees believe, therefore, that it is best to defer its effective date until August 1, 1975. The Conferees intend that Rule 410 would be superseded by any subsequent Federal Rule of Criminal Procedure or act of Congress with which it is inconsistent, if the Federal Rule of Criminal Procedure or Act of Congress takes effect or becomes law after the date of the enactment of the act establishing the rules of evidence.

The conference adopts the Senate amendment with an amendment that expresses the above intentions. House Report No. 93–1597.

1979 Amendment

Present rule 410 conforms to rule 11(e)(6) of the Federal Rules of Criminal Procedure. A proposed amendment to rule 11(e)(6) would clarify the circumstances in which pleas, plea discussions and related statements are inadmissible in evidence: see Advisory Committee Note thereto. The amendment proposed above would make comparable changes in rule 410.

HISTORICAL NOTES

References in Text

Rule 11 of the Federal Rules of Criminal Procedure, referred to in par. (3), is classified to Title 18, Federal Rules of Criminal Procedure.

Rule 411. Liability Insurance

Evidence that a person was or was not insured against liability is not admissible upon the issue whether the person acted negligently or otherwise wrongfully. This rule does not require the exclusion of evidence of insurance against liability when offered for another purpose, such as proof of agency, ownership, or control, or bias or prejudice of a witness.

(Pub.L. 93–595, § 1, Jan. 2, 1975, 88 Stat.1933; Mar. 2, 1987, eff. Oct. 1, 1987.)

ADVISORY COMMITTEE NOTES

1972 Proposed Rules

The courts have with substantial unanimity rejected evidence of liability insurance for the purpose of proving fault, and absence of liability insurance as proof of lack of fault. At best the inference of fault from the fact of insurance coverage is a tenuous one, as is its converse. More important, no doubt, has been the feeling that knowledge of the presence or absence of liability insurance would induce juries to decide cases on improper grounds. McCormick § 168; Annot., 4 A.L.R.2d 761. The rule is drafted in broad terms so as to include contributory negligence or other fault of a plaintiff as well as fault of a defendant.

The second sentence points out the limits of the rule, using well established illustrations. *Id.*

For similar rules see Uniform Rule 54; California Evidence Code § 1155; Kansas Code of Civil Procedure § 60–454; New Jersey Evidence Rule 54.

1987 Amendment

The amendment is technical. No substantive change is intended.

Rule 412. Sex Offense Cases; Relevance of Alleged Victim's Past Sexual Behavior or Alleged Sexual Predisposition

(a) Evidence generally inadmissible.—The following evidence is not admissible in any civil or criminal proceeding involving alleged sexual misconduct except as provided in subdivisions (b) and (c):

(1) Evidence offered to prove that any alleged victim engaged in other sexual behavior.

(2) Evidence offered to prove any alleged victim's sexual predisposition.

(b) Exceptions.—

(1) In a criminal case, the following evidence is admissible, if otherwise admissible under these rules:

(A) evidence of specific instances of sexual behavior by the alleged victim offered to prove that a person other than the accused was the source of semen, injury or other physical evidence;

(B) evidence of specific instances of sexual behavior by the alleged victim with respect to the person accused of the sexual misconduct offered by the accused to prove consent or by the prosecution; and

(C) evidence the exclusion of which would violate the constitutional rights of the defendant.

(2) In a civil case, evidence offered to prove the sexual behavior or sexual predisposition of any alleged victim is admissible if it is otherwise admissible under these rules and its probative value substantially outweighs the danger of harm to any victim and of unfair prejudice to any party. Evidence of an alleged victim's reputation is admissible only if it has been placed in controversy by the alleged victim.

(c) Procedure to determine admissibility.—

(1) A party intending to offer evidence under subdivision (b) must—

(A) file a written motion at least 14 days before trial specifically describing the evidence and stating the purpose for which it is offered unless the court, for good cause requires a different time for filing or permits filing during trial; and

(B) serve the motion on all parties and notify the alleged victim or, when appropriate, the alleged victim's guardian or representative.

(2) Before admitting evidence under this rule the court must conduct a hearing in camera and afford the victim and parties a right to attend and be heard. The motion, related papers, and the record of the hearing must be sealed and remain under seal unless the court orders otherwise.

(Added Pub.L. 95–540, § 2(a), Oct. 28, 1978, 92 Stat. 2046, and amended Pub.L. 100–690, Title VII, § 7046(a), Nov. 18, 1988, 102 Stat. 4400; Apr. 29, 1994, eff. Dec. 1, 1994; Pub.L. 103–322, Title IV, § 40141(b), Sept. 13, 1994, 108 Stat. 1919.)

ADVISORY COMMITTEE NOTES

1994 Amendments

Rule 412 has been revised to diminish some of the confusion engendered by the original rule and to expand the protection afforded alleged victims of sexual misconduct. Rule 412 applies to both civil and criminal proceedings. The rule aims to safeguard the alleged victim against the invasion of privacy, potential embarrassment and sexual stereotyping that is associated with public disclosure of intimate sexual details and the infusion of sexual innuendo into the factfinding process. By affording victims protection in most instances, the rule also encourages victims of sexual misconduct to institute and to participate in legal proceedings against alleged offenders

Rule 412 seeks to achieve these objectives by barring evidence relating to the alleged victim's sexual behavior or alleged sexual predisposition, whether offered as substantive evidence of for impeachment, except in designated circumstances in which the probative value of the evidence significantly outweighs possible harm to the victim.

The revised rule applies in all cases involving sexual misconduct without regard to whether the alleged victim or person accused is a party to the litigation. Rule 412 extends to "pattern" witnesses in both criminal and civil cases whose testimony about other instances of sexual misconduct by the person accused is otherwise admissible. When the case does not involve alleged sexual misconduct, evidence relating to a third-party witness' alleged sexual activities is not within the ambit of Rule 412. The witness will, however, be protected by other rules such as Rules 404 and 608, as well as Rule 403.

The terminology "alleged victim" is used because there will frequently be a factual dispute as to whether sexual misconduct occurred. It does not connote any requirement that the misconduct be alleged in the pleadings. Rule 412 does not, however, apply unless the person against whom the evidence is offered can reasonably be characterized as a "victim of alleged sexual misconduct." When this is not the case, as for instance in a defamation action involving statements concerning sexual misconduct in which the evidence is offered to show that the alleged defamatory statements were true or did not damage the plaintiff's reputation, neither Rule 404 nor this rule will operate to bar the evidence; Rule 401 and 403 will continue to control. Rule 412 will, however, apply in a Title VII action in which the plaintiff has alleged sexual harassment.

The reference to a person "accused" is also used in a non-technical sense. There is no requirement that there be a criminal charge pending against the person or even that the misconduct would constitute a criminal offense. Evidence offered to prove allegedly false prior claims by the victim is not barred by Rule 412. However, the evidence is subject to the requirements of Rule 404.

Subdivision (a). As amended, Rule 412 bars evidence offered to prove the victim's sexual behavior and alleged sexual predisposition. Evidence, which might otherwise be admissible under Rules 402, 404(b), 405, 607, 608, 609 of some other evidence rule, must be excluded if Rule 412 so requires. The word "other" is used to suggest some flexibility in admitting evidence "intrinsic" to the alleged sexual misconduct. *Cf.* Committee Note to 1991 amendment to Rule 404(b)

Past sexual behavior connotes all activities that involve actual physical conduct, i.e. sexual intercourse or sexual contact. *See, e.g., United States v. Galloway*, 937 F.2d 542 (10th Cir. 1991), *cert. denied*, 113 S.Ct. 418 (1992) (use of contraceptives inadmissible since use implies sexual activity); *United States v. One Feather*, 702 F.2d 736 (8th Cir. 1983) (birth of an illegitimate child inadmissible); *State v. Carmichael*, 727 P.2d 918, 925 (Kan. 1986) (evidence of venereal disease inadmissible). In addition, the word "behavior" should be construed to include activities of the mind, such as fantasies of dreams. *See* 23 C. Wright and K. Graham, Jr., *Federal Practice and Procedure*, § 5384 at p. 548 (1980) ("While there may be some doubt under statutes that require 'conduct,' it would seem that the language of Rule 412 is broad enough to encompass the behavior of the mind.").

The rule has been amended to also exclude all other evidence relating to an alleged victim of sexual misconduct that is offered to prove a sexual predisposition. This amendment is designed to exclude evidence that does not directly refer to sexual activities or thoughts but that the proponent believes may have a sexual connotation for the factfinder. Admission of such evidence would contravene Rule 412's objectives of shielding the alleged victim from potential embarrassment and safeguarding the victim against stereotypical thinking. Consequently, unless the (b)(2) exception is satisfied, evidence such as that relating to the alleged victim's mode of dress, speech, or life-style will not be admissible.

The introductory phrase in subdivision (a) was deleted because it lacked clarity and contained no explicit reference to the other provisions of the law that were intended to be overridden. The conditional clause, "except as provided in subdivisions (b) and (c)" is intended to make clear that evidence of the types described in subdivision (a) is admissible only under the strictures of those sections.

The reason for extending the rule to all criminal cases is obvious. The strong social policy of protecting a victim's privacy and encouraging victims to come forward to report criminal acts is not confined to cases that involve a charge of sexual assault. The need to protect the victim is equally great when a defendant is charged with kidnapping, and evidence is offered, either to prove motive or as background, that the defendant sexually assaulted the victim.

The reason for extending Rule 412 to civil cases is equally obvious. The need to protect alleged victims against invasions of privacy, potential embarrassment, and unwarranted sexual stereotyping, and the wish to encourage victims to come forward when they have been sexually molested do not disappear because the context has shifted from a criminal prosecution to a claim for damages or injunctive relief. There is a strong social policy in not only punishing those who engage in sexual misconduct, but in also providing relief to the victim. Thus, Rule 412 applies in any civil case in which a person claims to be the victim of sexual misconduct, such as actions for sexual battery or sexual harassment.

Subdivision (b). Subdivision (b) spells out the specific circumstances in which some evidence may be admissible that would otherwise be barred by the general rule expressed in subdivision (a). As amended, Rule 412 will be virtually unchanged in criminal cases, but will provide protection to any person alleged to be a victim of sexual misconduct regardless of the charge actually brought against an accused. A new exception has been added for civil cases.

In a criminal case, evidence may be admitted under subdivision (b)(1) pursuant to three possible exceptions, provided the evidence also satisfies other requirements for admissibility specified in the Federal Rules of Evidence, including Rule 403. Subdivisions (b)(1)(A) and (b)(1)(B) require proof in the form of specific instances of sexual behavior in recognition of the limited probative value and dubious reliability of evidence of reputation or evidence in the form of an opinion.

Under subdivision (b)(1)(A), evidence of specific instances of sexual behavior with persons other than the person whose sexual misconduct is alleged may be admissible if it is offered to prove that another person was the source of semen, injury or other physical evidence. Where the prosecution has directly or indirectly asserted that the physical evidence originated with the accused, the defendant must be afforded an opportunity to prove that another person was responsible. See *United States v. Begay*, 937 F.2d 515, 523 n. 10 (10th Cir. 1991). Evidence offered for the specific purpose identified in this subdivision may still be excluded if it does not satisfy Rules 401 or 403. *See, e.g., United States v. Azure*, 845 F.2d 1503, 1505-06 (8th Cir. 1988) (10 year old victim's injuries indicated recent use of force; court excluded evidence of consensual sexual activities with witness who testified at in camera hearing that he had never hurt victim and failed to establish recent activities).

Under the exception in subdivision (b)(1)(B), evidence of specific instances of sexual behavior with respect to the person whose sexual misconduct is alleged is admissible if offered to prove consent, or offered by the prosecution. Admissible pursuant to this exception might be evidence of prior instances of sexual activities between the alleged victim and the accused, as well as statements in which the alleged victim expresses an intent to engage in sexual intercourse with the accused, or voiced sexual fantasies involving that specific accused. In a prosecution for child sexual abuse, for example, evidence of uncharged sexual activity between the accused and the alleged victim offered by the prosecution may be admissible pursuant to Rule 404(b) to show a pattern of behavior. Evidence relating to the victim's alleged sexual predisposition is not admissible pursuant to this exception.

Under subdivision (b)(1)(C), evidence of specific instances of conduct may not be excluded if the result would be to deny a criminal defendant the protections afforded by the Constitution. For example, statements in which the victim has expressed an intent to have sex with the first person encountered on a particular occasion might not be excluded without violating the due process right of a rape defendant seeking to prove consent. Recognition of this basic principle was expressed on subdivision (b)(1) of the original rule. The United States Supreme Court has recognized that in various circumstances a defendant may have a right to introduce evidence otherwise precluded by an evidence rule under the Confrontation Clause. *See, e.g., Olden v. Kentucky*, 488 U.S. 227 (1988) (defendant in rape cases had right to inquire into alleged victim's cohabitation with another man to show bias).

Subdivision (b)(2) governs the admissibility of otherwise proscribed evidence in civil cases. It employs a balancing test rather than the specific exceptions stated in subdivision (b)(1) in recognition of the difficulty of foreseeing future developments in the law. Greater flexibility is needed to accommodate evolving causes of action such as claims for sexual harassment.

The balancing test requires the proponent of the evidence, whether plaintiff or defendant, to convince the court that the probative value of the proffered evidence "substantially outweighs the danger of harm to any victim and of unfair prejudice of any party." This test for admitting evidence offered to prove sexual behavior or sexual propensity in civil cases differs in three respects from the general rule governing admissibility set forth in Rule 403. First, it Reverses that usual procedure spelled out in Rule 403 by shifting the burden to the proponent to demonstrate admissibility rather than making the opponent justify exclusion of the evidence. Second, the standard expressed in subdivision (b)(2) is more stringent than in the original rule; it raises the threshold for admission by requiring that the probative value of the evidence *substantially* outweigh the specified dangers. Finally, the Rule 412 test puts "harm to the victim" on the scale in addition to prejudice to the parties.

Evidence of reputation may be received in a civil case only if the alleged victim has put his or her reputation into controversy. The victim may do so without making a specific allegation in a pleading. *Cf.* Fed.R.Civ.P. 35(a).

Subdivision (c). Amended subdivision (c) is more concise and understandable than the subdivision it replaces. The requirement of a motion before trial is continued in the amended rule, as is the provision that a late motion may be permitted for good cause shown. In deciding whether to permit late filing, the court may take into account the conditions previously included in the rule: namely whether the evidence is newly discovered and could not have been obtained earlier through the existence of due diligence, and whether the issue to which such evidence relates has newly arisen in the case. The rule recognizes that in some instances the circumstances that justify an application to introduce evidence otherwise barred by Rule 412 will not become apparent until trial.

The amended rule provides that before admitting evidence that falls within that prohibition of Rule 412(a), the court must hold a hearing in camera at which the alleged victim and any party must be afforded the right to be present and an opportunity to be heard. All papers connected with the motion must be kept and remain under seal during the course of trial and appellate proceedings unless otherwise ordered. This is to assure that the privacy of the alleged victim is preserved in all cases in which the court rules that proffered evidence is not admissible, and in which the hearing refers to matters that are not received, or are received in another form.

The procedures set forth in subdivision (c) do not apply to discovery of a victim's past sexual conduct or predisposition in civil cases, which will be continued to be governed by Fed. R. Civ. P. 26. In order not to undermine the rationale of Rule 412, however, courts should enter appropriate orders pursuant to Fed. R. Civ. P. 26 (c) to protect the victim against unwarranted inquiries and to ensure confidentiality. Courts should presumptively issue protective orders barring discovery unless the party seeking discovery makes a showing that the evidence sought to be discovered would be relevant under the facts and theories of the particular case, and cannot be obtained except through discovery. In an action for sexual harassment, for instance, while some evidence of the alleged victim's sexual behavior and/or predisposition in the workplace may perhaps be relevant, non-work place conduct will usually be irrelevant. *Cf. Burns v. McGregor Electronic Industries, Inc.*, 989 F.2d 959, 962-63 (8th Cir. 1993) (posing for a nude magazine outside work hours is irrelevant to issue of unwelcomeness of sexual advances at work). Confidentiality orders should be presumptively granted as well.

One substantive change made in subdivision (c) is the elimination of the following sentence: "Notwithstanding subdivision (b) of Rule 104, if the relevancy of the evidence which the accused seeks to offer in trial depends upon the fulfillment of a condition of fact, the court, at the hearing in chambers or at a subsequent hearing in chambers scheduled for such purpose, shall accept evidence on the issue of whether such condition of fact is fulfilled and shall determine such issue." On its face, this language would appear to authorize a trial judge to exclude evidence of past sexual conduct between alleged victim and an accused or a defendant in a civil case based upon the judge's belief that such past acts did not occur. Such an authorization raises questions of invasion of the right to a jury trial under the Sixth and Seventh Amendments. *See* 1 S. Saltzburg & M. Martin, *Federal Rules of Evidence Manual*, 396-97 (5th ed. 1990).

The Advisory Committee concluded that the amended rule provided adequate protection for all persons claiming to be the victims of sexual misconduct, and that it was inadvisable to continue to include a provision in the rule that has been confusing and that raises substantial constitutional issues. [Advisory Committee Note adopted by Congressional Conference Report accompanying Pub.L. 103–322. See H.R. Conf. Rep. No. 103–711, 103rd Cong., 2nd Sess., 383 (1994).]

Congressional Discussion

The following discussion in the House of Representatives of October 10, 1978, preceded passage of H.R. 4727, which enacted Rule 412. The discussion appears in 124 Cong.Record, at page H. 11944.

Mr. MANN. Mr. Speaker, I yield myself such time as I may consume.

Mr. Speaker, for many years in this country, evidentiary rules have permitted the introduction of evidence about a rape victim's prior sexual conduct. Defense lawyers were permitted great latitude in bringing out intimate details about a rape victim's life. Such evidence quite often serves no real purpose and only results in embarrassment to the rape victim and unwarranted public intrusion into her private life.

The evidentiary rules that permit such inquiry have in recent years come under question; and the States have taken the lead to change and modernize their evidentiary rules about evidence of a rape victim's prior sexual behavior. The bill before us similarly seeks to modernize the Federal Evidentiary rules.

The present Federal Rules of Evidence reflect the traditional approach. If a defendant in a rape case raises the defense of consent, that defendant may then offer evidence about the victim's prior sexual behavior. Such evidence may be in the form of opinion evidence, evidence of reputation, or evidence of specific instances of behavior. Rule 404(a)(2) of the Federal Rules of Evidence permits the introduction of evidence of a "pertinent character trait." The advisory committee note to that rule cites, as an example of what the rule covers, the character of a rape victim when the issue is consent. Rule 405 of the Federal Rules of Evidence permits the use of opinion or reputation evidence or the use of evidence of specific behavior to show a character trait.

Thus, Federal evidentiary rules permit a wide ranging inquiry into the private conduct of a rape victim, even though that conduct may have at best a tenuous connection to the offense for which the defendant is being tried.

H.R. 4727 amends the Federal Rules of Evidence to add a new rule, applicable only in criminal cases, to spell out when, and under what conditions, evidence of a rape victim's prior sexual behavior can be admitted. The new rule provides that reputation or opinion evidence about a rape victim's prior sexual behavior is not admissible. The new rule also provides that a court cannot admit evidence of specific instances of a rape victim's prior sexual conduct except in three circumstances.

The first circumstance is where the Constitution requires that the evidence be admitted. This exception is intended to cover those infrequent instances where, because of an unusual chain of circumstances, the general rule of inadmissibility, if followed, would result in denying the defendant a constitutional right.

The second circumstance in which the defendant can offer evidence of specific instances of a rape victim's prior sexual behavior is where the defendant raises the issue of consent and the evidence is of sexual behavior with the defendant. To admit such evidence, however, the court must find that the evidence is relevant and that its probative value outweighs the danger of unfair prejudice.

The third circumstance in which a court can admit evidence of specific instances of a rape victim's prior sexual behavior is where the evidence is of behavior with someone other than the defendant and is offered by the defendant on the issue of whether or not he was the source of semen or injury. Again, such evidence will be admitted only if the court finds that the evidence is relevant and that its probative value outweighs the danger of unfair prejudice.

The new rule further provides that before evidence is admitted under any of these exceptions, there must be an in camera hearing—that is, a proceeding that takes place in the judge's chambers out of the presence of the jury and the general public. At this hearing, the defendant will present the evidence he intends to offer and be able to argue why it should be admitted. The prosecution, of course, will be able to argue against that evidence being admitted.

The purpose of the in camera hearing is twofold. It gives the defendant an opportunity to demonstrate to the court why certain evidence is admissible and ought to be presented to the jury. At the same time, it protects the privacy of the rape victim in those instances when the court finds that evidence is inadmissible. Of course, if the court finds the evidence to be admissible, the evidence will be presented to the jury in open court.

The effect of this legislation, therefore, is to preclude the routine use of evidence of specific instances of a rape victim's prior sexual behavior. Such evidence will be admitted only in clearly and narrowly defined circumstances and only after an in camera hearing. In determining the admissibility of such evidence, the court will consider all of the facts and circumstances surrounding the evidence, such as the amount of time that lapsed between the alleged prior act and the rape charged in the prosecution. The greater the lapse of time, of course, the less likely it is that such evidence will be admitted.

Mr. Speaker, the principal purpose of this legislation is to protect rape victims from the degrading and embarrassing disclosure of intimate details about their private lives. It does so by narrowly circumscribing when such evidence may be admitted. It does not do so, however, by sacrificing any constitutional right possessed by the defendant. The bill before us fairly balances the interests involved—the rape victim's interest in protecting her private life from unwarranted public exposure; the defendant's interest in being able adequately to present a defense by offering relevant and probative evidence; and society's interest in a fair trial, one where unduly prejudicial evidence is not permitted to becloud the issues before the jury.

I urge support of the bill.

Mr. WIGGINS. Mr. Speaker, I yield myself such time as I may consume.

(Mr. WIGGINS asked and was given permission to revise and extend his remarks.)

Mr. WIGGINS. Mr. Speaker, this legislation addresses itself to a subject that is certainly a proper one for our consideration. Many of us have been troubled for years about the indiscriminate and prejudicial use of testimony with respect to a victim's prior sexual behavior in rape and similar cases. This bill deals with that problem. It is not, in my opinion, Mr. Speaker, a perfect bill in the manner in which it deals with the problem, but my objections are not so fundamental as would lead me to oppose the bill.

I think, Mr. Speaker, that it is unwise to adopt a per se rule absolutely excluding evidence of reputation and opinion with respect to the victim—and this bill does that—but it is difficult for me to foresee the specific case in which such evidence might be admissible. The trouble is this, Mr. Speaker: None of us can foresee perfectly all of the various circumstances under which the propriety of evidence might be before the court. If this bill has a defect, in my view it is because it adopts a per se rule with respect to opinion and reputation evidence.

Alternatively we might have permitted that evidence to be considered in camera as we do other evidence under the bill.

I should note, however, in fairness, having expressed minor reservations, that the bill before the House at this time does improve significantly upon the bill which was presented to our committee.

I will not detail all of those improvements but simply observe that the bill upon which we shall soon vote is a superior product to that which was initially considered by our subcommittee.

Mr. Speaker, I ask my colleagues to vote for this legislation as being, on balance, worthy of their support, and urge its adoption.

I reserve the balance of my time.

Mr. MANN. Mr. Speaker, this legislation has more than 100 cosponsors, but its principal sponsor, as well as its architect is the gentlewoman from New York (Ms. Holtzman). As the drafter of the legislation she will be able to provide additional information about the probable scope and effect of the legislation.

I yield such time as she may consume to the gentlewoman from New York (Ms. Holtzman).

(Ms. HOLTZMAN asked and was given permission to revise and extend her remarks.)

Ms. HOLTZMAN. Mr. Speaker, I would like to begin first by complimenting the distinguished gentleman from South Carolina (Mr. Mann), the chairman of the subcommittee, for his understanding of the need for corrective legislation in this area and for the fairness with which he has conducted the subcommittee hearings. I would like also to compliment the other members of the subcommittee, including the gentleman from California (Mr. Wiggins).

Too often in this country victims of rape are humiliated and harassed when they report and prosecute the rape. Bullied and cross-examined about their prior sexual experiences, many find the trial almost as degrading as the rape itself. Since rape trials become inquisitions into the victim's morality, not trials of the defendant's innocence or guilt, it is not surprising that it is the least reported crime. It is estimated that as few as one in ten rapes is ever reported.

Mr. Speaker, over 30 States have taken some action to limit the vulnerability of rape victims to such humiliating cross-examination of their past sexual experiences and intimate personal histories. In federal courts, however, it is permissible still to subject rape victims to brutal cross-examination about their past sexual histories. H.R. 4727 would rectify this problem in Federal courts and I hope, also serve as a model to suggest to the remaining states that reform of existing rape laws is important to the equity of our criminal justice system.

H.R. 4727 applies only to criminal rape cases in Federal courts. The bill provides that neither the prosecution nor the defense can introduce any reputation or opinion evidence about the victim's past sexual conduct. It does permit, however, the introduction of specific evidence about the victim's past sexual conduct in three very limited circumstances.

First, this evidence can be introduced if it deals with the victim's past sexual relations with the defendant and is relevant to the issue of whether she consented. Second, when the defendant claims he had no relations with the victim, he can use evidence of the victim's past sexual relations with others if the evidence rebuts the victim's claim that the rape caused certain physical consequences, such as semen or injury. Finally, the evidence can be introduced if it is constitutionally required. This last exception, added in subcommittee, will insure that the defendant's constitutional rights are protected.

Before any such evidence can be introduced, however, the court must determine at a hearing in chambers that the evidence falls within one of the exceptions.

Furthermore, unless constitutionally required, the evidence of specific instances of prior sexual conduct cannot be introduced at all it if would be more prejudicial and inflammatory that probative.

Mr. Speaker, I urge adoption of this bill. It will protect women from both injustice and indignity.

Mr. MANN. Mr. Speaker, I have no further requests for time, and I yield back the balance of my time.

Mr. WIGGINS. Mr. Speaker, I have no further requests for time, and yield back the balance of my time.

The SPEAKER pro tempore. The question is on the motion offered by the gentleman from South Carolina (Mr. Mann) that the House suspend the rules and pass the bill H.R. 4727, as amended.

The question was taken; and (two-thirds having voted in favor thereof) the rules were suspended and the bill, as amended, was passed.

A motion to reconsider was laid on the table.

HISTORICAL NOTES

Effective Date

Section 3 of Pub.L. 95–540 provided that: "The amendments made by this Act [enacting this rule] shall apply to trials which begin more than thirty days after the date of the enactment of this Act [Oct. 28, 1978]."

Rule 413. Evidence of Similar Crimes in Sexual Assault Cases

(a) In a criminal case in which the defendant is accused of an offense of sexual assault, evidence of the defendant's commission of another offense or offenses of sexual assault is admissible, and may be considered for its bearing on any matter to which it is relevant.

(b) In a case in which the Government intends to offer evidence under this rule, the attorney for the Government shall disclose the evidence to the defendant, including statements of witnesses or a summary of the substance of any testimony that is expected to be offered, at least fifteen days before the scheduled date of trial or at such later time as the court may allow for good cause.

(c) This rule shall not be construed to limit the admission or consideration of evidence under any other rule.

(d) For purposes of this rule and Rule 415, "offense of sexual assault" means a crime under Federal law or the law of a State (as defined in section 513 of title 18, United States Code) that involved—

(1) any conduct proscribed by chapter 109A of title 18, United States Code;

(2) contact, without consent, between any part of the defendant's body or an object and the genitals or anus of another person;

(3) contact, without consent, between the genitals or anus of the defendant and any part of another person's body;

(4) deriving sexual pleasure or gratification from the infliction of death, bodily injury, or physical pain on another person; or

(5) an attempt or conspiracy to engage in conduct described in paragraphs (1)–(4).

(Added Pub.L. 103–322, Title XXXII, § 320935(a), Sept. 13, 1994, 108 Stat. 2136.)

HISTORICAL NOTES

Effective Dates

Section 320935(b) to (e) of Pub.L. 103–322, as amended Pub.L. 104–208, Div. A, Title I, § 101(a), [Title I, § 120], Sept. 30, 1996, 110 Stat. 3009–25, provided that:

"**(b) Implementation.**—The amendments made by subsection (a) [enacting Federal Rules of Evidence 413, 414, and 415] shall become effective pursuant to subsection (d).

"**(c) Recommendations by Judicial Conference.**—Not later than 150 days after the date of enactment of this Act [Sept. 13, 1994], the Judicial Conference of the United States shall transmit to Congress a report containing recommendations for amending the Federal Rules of Evidence as they affect the admission of evidence of a defendant's prior sexual assault or child molestation crimes in cases involving sexual assault and child molestation. The Rules Enabling Act [28 U.S.C.A. § 2072] shall not apply to the recommendations made by the Judicial Conference pursuant to this section.

"**(d) Congressional action.**—

"(1) If the recommendations described in subsection (c) are the same as the amendment made by subsection (a) [enacting Federal Rules of Evidence 413, 414, and 415], then the amendments made by subsection (a) shall become effective 30 days after the transmittal of the recommendations.

"(2) If the recommendations described in subsection (c) are different than the amendments made by subsection (a) [enacting Federal Rules of Evidence 413, 414, and 415], the amendments made by subsection (a) shall become effective 150 days after the transmittal of the recommendations unless otherwise provided by law.

"(3) If the Judicial Conference fails to comply with subsection (c), the amendments made by subsection (a) [enacting Federal of Evidence 413, 414, and 415] shall become effective 150 days after the date the recommendations were due under subsection (c) unless otherwise provided by law.

"**(e) Application.**—The amendments made by subsection (a) [enacting Federal Rules of Evidence 413, 414, and 415] shall apply to proceedings commenced on or after the effective date of such amendments, including all trials commenced on or after the effective date of such amendments."

[The Judicial Conference transmitted a report to Congress on Feb. 9, 1995, containing recommendations described in subsec. (c) different than the amendments made by section 320935(a) of Pub.L. 103–322. Congress did not follow the recommendations submitted or provide otherwise by law. Accordingly, Rules 413, 414, and 415, as added by section 320935(a) of Pub.L. 103–322, became effective on July 9, 1995.]

Submitted to the Congress in accordance with section 320935 of the Violent Crime Control and Law Enforcement Act of 1994 (Pub.L. No. 103–322)

I. INTRODUCTION

This report is transmitted to Congress in accordance with the Violent Crime Control and Law Enforcement Act of 1994, Pub.L. No. 103–322 (September 13, 1994). Section 320935 of the Act invited the Judicial Conference of the United States within 150 days (February 10, 1995) to submit "a report containing recommendations for amending the Federal Rules of Evidence as they affect the admission of evidence of a defendant's prior sexual assault or child molestation crimes in cases involving sexual assault or child molestation."

Under the Act, new Rules 413, 414, and 415 would be added to the Federal Rules of Evidence. These Rules would admit evidence of a defendant's past similar acts in criminal and civil cases involving a sexual assault or child molestation offense for its bearing on any matter to which it is relevant. The effective date of new Rules 413–415 is contingent in part upon the nature of the recommendations submitted by the Judicial Conference.

After careful study, the Judicial Conference urges Congress to reconsider its decision on the policy questions underlying the new rules for reasons set out in Part III below.

If Congress does not reconsider its decision on the underlying policy questions, the Judicial Conference recommends incorporation of the provisions of new Rules 413–415 as amendments to Rules 404 and 405 of the Federal Rules of Evidence. The amendments would not change the substance of the congressional enactment but would clarify drafting ambiguities and eliminate possible constitutional infirmities.

II. BACKGROUND

Under the Act, the Judicial Conference was provided 150 days within which to make and submit to Congress alternative recommendations to new Evidence Rules 413–415. Consideration of Rules 413–415 by the Judicial Conference was specifically excepted from the exacting review procedures set forth in the Rules Enabling Act (codified at 28 U.S.C. §§ 2071–2077). Although the Conference acted on these new rules on an expedited basis to meet the Act's deadlines, the review process was thorough.

The new rules would apply to both civil and criminal cases. Accordingly, the Judicial Conference's Advisory Committee on Criminal Rules and the Advisory Committee on Civil Rules reviewed the rules at separate meetings in October 1994. At the same time and in preparation for its consideration of the new rules, the Advisory Committee on Evidence Rules sent out a notice soliciting comment on new Evidence Rules 413, 414, and 415. The notice was sent to the courts, including all federal judges, about 900 evidence law professors, 40 women's rights organizations, and 1,000 other individuals and interested organizations.

III. DISCUSSION

On October 17–18, 1994, the Advisory Committee on Evidence Rules met in Washington, D.C. It considered the public responses, which included 84 written comments, representing 112 individuals, 8 local and 8 national legal organizations. The overwhelming majority of judges, lawyers, law professors, and legal organizations who responded opposed new Evidence Rules 413, 414, and 415. The principal objections expressed were that the rules would permit the admission of unfairly prejudicial evidence and contained numerous drafting problems not intended by their authors.

The Advisory Committee on Evidence Rules submitted its report to the Judicial Conference Committee on Rules of Practice and Procedure (Standing Committee) for review at its January 11–13, 1995 meeting. The committee's report was unanimous except for a dissenting vote by the representative of the Department of Justice. The advisory committee believed that the concerns expressed by Congress and embodied in new Evidence Rules 413, 414, and 415 are already adequately addressed in the existing Federal Rules of Evidence. In particular, Evidence Rule 404(b) now allows the admission of evidence against a criminal defendant of the commission of prior crimes, wrongs, or acts for specified purposes, including to show intent, plan, motive, preparation, identity, knowledge, or absence of mistake or accident.

Furthermore, the new rules, which are not supported by empirical evidence, could diminish significantly the protections that have safeguarded persons accused in criminal cases and parties in civil cases against undue prejudice. These protections form a fundamental part of American jurisprudence and have evolved under long-standing rules and case law. A significant concern identified by the committee was the danger of convicting a criminal defendant for past, as opposed to charged, behavior or for being a bad person.

In addition, the advisory committee concluded that, because prior bad acts would be admissible even though not the subject of a conviction, mini-trials within trials concerning those acts would result when a defendant seeks to rebut such evidence. The committee also noticed that many of the comments received had concluded that the Rules, as drafted, were mandatory—that is, such evidence had to be admitted regardless of other rules of evidence such as the hearsay rule or the Rule 403 balancing test. The committee believed that this position was arguable because Rules 413–415 declare without qualification that such evidence "is admissible." In contrast, the new Rule 412, passed as part of the same legislation, provided that certain evidence "is admissible if it is otherwise admissible under these Rules." Fed.R.Evid. 412(b)(2). If the critics are right, Rules 413–415 free the prosecution from rules that apply to the defendant—including the hearsay rule and Rule 403. If so, serious constitutional questions would arise.

The Advisory Committees on Criminal and Civil Rules unanimously, except for representatives of the Department of Justice, also opposed the new rules. Those committees also concluded that the new rules would permit the introduction of unreliable but highly prejudicial evidence and would complicate trials by causing mini-trials of other alleged wrongs. After the advisory committees reported, the Standing Committee unanimously, again except for the representative of the Department of Justice, agreed with the view of the advisory committees.

It is important to note the highly unusual unanimity of the members of the Standing and Advisory Committees, composed of over 40 judges, practicing lawyers, and academicians, in taking the view that Rules 413–415 are undesirable. Indeed, the only supporters of the Rules were representatives of the Department of Justice.

For these reasons, the Standing Committee recommended that Congress reconsider its decision on the policy questions embodied in new Evidence Rules 413, 414, and 415.

However, if Congress will not reconsider its decision on the policy questions, the Standing Committee recommended that Congress consider an alternative draft recommended by the Advisory Committee on Evidence Rules. That Committee drafted proposed amendments to existing Evidence Rules 404 and 405 that would both correct ambiguities and possible constitutional infirmities identified in new Evidence Rules 413, 414, and 415 yet still effectuate Congressional intent. In particular, the proposed amendments:

(1) expressly apply the other rules of evidence to evidence offered under the new rules;

(2) expressly allow the party against whom such evidence is offered to use similar evidence in rebuttal;

(3) expressly enumerate the factors to be weighed by a court in making its Rule 403 determination;

(4) render the notice provisions consistent with the provisions in existing Rule 404 regarding criminal cases;

(5) eliminate the special notice provisions of Rules 413–415 in civil cases so that notice will be required as provided in the Federal Rules of Civil Procedure; and

(6) permit reputation or opinion evidence after such evidence is offered by the accused or defendant.

The Standing Committee reviewed the new rules and the alternative recommendations. It concurred with the views of the Evidence Rules Committee and recommended that the Judicial Conference adopt them.

IV. RECOMMENDATIONS

The Judicial Conference concurs with the views of the Standing Committee and urges that Congress reconsider its policy determinations underlying Evidence Rules 413–415. In the alternative, the attached amendments to Evidence Rules 404 and 405 are recommended, in lieu of new Evidence Rules 413, 414, and 415. The alternative amendments to Evidence Rules 404 and 405 are accompanied by the Advisory Committee Notes, which explain them in detail.

RULE 404. CHARACTER EVIDENCE NOT ADMISSIBLE TO PROVE CONDUCT; EXCEPTIONS; OTHER CRIMES

* * * * * * *

(4) Character in sexual misconduct cases. Evidence of another act of sexual assault or child molestation, or evidence to rebut such proof or an inference therefrom, if that evidence is otherwise admissible under these rules, in a criminal case in which the accused is charged with sexual assault or child molestation, or in a civil case in which a claim is predicated on a party's alleged commission of sexual assault or child molestation.

(A) In weighing the probative value of such evidence, the court may, as part of its rule 403 determination, consider:

(i) proximity in time to the charged or predicate misconduct;

(ii) similarity to the charged or predicate misconduct;

(iii) frequency of the other acts;

(iv) surrounding circumstances;

(v) relevant intervening events; and

(vi) other relevant similarities or differences.

(B) In a criminal case in which the prosecution intends to offer evidence under this subdivision, it must disclose the evidence, including statements of witnesses or a summary of the substance of any testimony, at a reasonable time in advance of trial, or during trial if the court excuses pretrial notice on good cause shown.

(C) For purposes of this subdivision.

(i) "sexual assault" means conduct—or an attempt or conspiracy to engage in conduct—of the type proscribed by chapter 109A of title 18, United States Code, or conduct that involved deriving sexual pleasure or gratification from inflicting death, bodily injury, or physical pain on another person irrespective of the age of the victim—regardless of whether that conduct would have subjected the actor to federal jurisdiction.

(ii) "child molestation" means conduct—or an attempt or conspiracy to engage in conduct—of the type proscribed by chapter 110 of title 18, United States Code, or conduct, committed in relation to a child below the age of 14 years, either of the type proscribed by chapter 109A of title 18, United States Code, or that involved deriving sexual pleasure or gratification from inflicting death, bodily injury, or physical pain on another person—regardless of whether that conduct would have subjected the actor to federal jurisdiction.

(b) Other crimes, wrongs, or acts. Evidence of other crimes, wrongs, or acts is not admissible to prove the character of a person in order to show action in conformity therewith except as provided in subdivision (a). . . .

Note to Rule 404(a)(4)

The Committee has redrafted Rules 413, 414 and 415 which the Violent Crime Control and Law Enforcement Act of 1994 conditionally added to the Federal Rules of Evidence.[1] These modifications do not change the substance of the congressional enactment. The changes were made in order to integrate the provisions both substantively and stylistically with the existing Rules of Evidence; to illuminate the intent expressed by the principal drafters of the measure; to clarify drafting ambiguities that might necessitate considerable judicial attention if they remained unresolved; and to eliminate possible constitutional infirmities.

The Committee placed the new provisions in Rule 404 because this rule governs the admissibility of character evidence. The congressional enactment constitutes a new exception to the general rule stated in subdivision (a). The Committee also combined the three separate rules proposed by Congress into one subdivision (a)(4) in accordance with the rules' customary practice of treating criminal and civil issues jointly. An amendment to Rule 405 has been added because the authorization of a new form of character evidence in this rule has an impact on methods of proving character that were not explicitly addressed by Congress. The stylistic changes are self-evident. They are particularly noticeable in the definition section in subdivision (a)(4)(C) in which the Committee eliminated, without any change in meaning, graphic details of sexual acts.

The Committee added language that explicitly provides that evidence under this subdivision must satisfy other rules of evidence such as the hearsay rules in Article VIII and the expert testimony rules in Article VII. Although principal sponsors of the legislation had stated that they intended other evidentiary rules to apply, the Committee believes that the opening phrase of the new subdivision 'if otherwise admissible under these rules' is needed to clarify the relationship between subdivision (a)(4) and other evidentiary provisions.

The Committee also expressly made subdivision (a)(4) subject to Rule 403 balancing in accordance with the repeatedly stated objectives of the legislation's sponsors with which representatives of the Justice Department expressed agreement. Many commentators on Rules 413–415 had objected that Rule 403's applicability was obscured by the actual language employed.

In addition to clarifying the drafters' intent, an explicit reference to Rule 403 may be essential to insulate the rule against constitutional challenge. Constitutional concerns also led the Committee to acknowledge specifically the opposing party's right to offer in rebuttal character evidence that the rules would otherwise bar, including evidence of a third person's prior acts of sexual misconduct offered to prove that the third person rather than the party committed the acts in issue.

In order to minimize the need for extensive and time-consuming judicial interpretation, the Committee listed factors that a court may consider in discharging Rule 403 balancing. Proximity in time is taken into account in a related rule. See Rule 609(b). Similarity, frequency and surrounding circumstances have long been considered by courts in handling other crimes evidence pursuant to Rule 404(b). Relevant intervening events, such as extensive medical treatment of the accused between the time of the prior proffered act and the charged act, may affect the strength of the propensity inference for which the evidence is offered. The final factor—'other relevant similarities or differences'—is added in recognition of the endless variety of circumstances that confront a trial court in rulings on admissibility. Although subdivision (4)(A) explicitly refers to factors that bear on probative value, this enumeration does not eliminate a judge's responsibility to take into account the other factors mentioned in Rule 403 itself—'the danger of unfair prejudice, confusion of the issues, ... misleading the jury, ... undue delay, waste of time, or needless presentation of cumulative evidence.' In addition, the Advisory Committee Note to Rule 403 reminds judges that 'The availability of other means of proof may also be an appropriate factor.'

The Committee altered slightly the notice provision in criminal cases. Providing the trial court with some discretion to excuse pretrial notice was thought preferable to the inflexible 15-day rule provided in Rules 414 and 415. Furthermore, the formulation is identical to that contained in the 1991 amendment to Rule 404(b) so that no confusion will result from having two somewhat different notice provisions in the same rule. The Committee eliminated the notice provision for civil cases stated in Rule 415 because it did not believe that Congress intended to alter the usual time table for disclosure and discovery provided by the Federal Rules of Civil Procedure.

The definition section was simplified with no change in meaning. The reference to 'the law of a State' was eliminated as unnecessarily confusing and restrictive. Conduct committed outside the United States ought equally to be eligible for admission. Evidence offered pursuant to subdivision (a)(4) must relate to a form of conduct proscribed by either chapter 109A or 110 of title 18, United States Code, regardless of whether the actor was subject to federal jurisdiction.

RULE 405. METHODS OF PROVING CHARACTER

(a) Reputation or opinion. In all cases in which evidence of character or a trait of character of a person is admissible, proof may be made by testimony as to reputation or by testimony in the form of an opinion except as provided in subdivision (c) of this rule. On cross-examination, inquiry is allowable into relevant specific instances of conduct.

* * * * * * *

(c) Proof in sexual misconduct cases. In a case in which evidence is offered under rule 404(a)(4), proof may be made by specific instances of conduct, testimony as to reputation, or testimony in the form of an opinion, except that the prosecution or claimant may offer reputation or opinion testimony only after the opposing party has offered such testimony.

Note to Rule 405(c)

The addition of a new subdivision (a)(4) to Rule 404 necessitates adding a new subdivision (c) to Rule 405 to govern methods of proof. Congress clearly intended no change in the preexisting law that precludes the prosecution or a claimant from offering reputation or opinion testimony in its case in chief to prove that the opposing party acted in conformity with character. When evidence is admissible pursuant to Rule 404(a)(4), the proponents proof must consist of specific instances of conduct. The opposing party, however, is free to respond with reputation or opinion testimony (including expert testimony if otherwise admissible) as well as evidence of specific instances. In a criminal case, the admissibility of reputation or opinion testimony would, in any event, be authorized by Rule 404(a)(1). The extension to civil cases is essential in order to provide the opponent with an adequate opportunity to refute allegations about a character for sexual misconduct. Once the opposing party offers reputation or opinion testimony, however, the prosecution or claimant may counter using such methods of proof.

[1] Congress provided that the rules would take effect unless within a specified time period the Judicial Conference made recommendations to amend the rules that Congress enacted.

Congressional Discussion

Floor Statement of the Principal House Sponsor, Representative Susan Molinari, Concerning the Prior Crimes Evidence Rules for Sexual Assault and Child Molestation Cases (Cong.Rec. H8991–92, Aug. 21, 1994):

Mr. Speaker, the revised conference bill contains a critical reform that I have long sought to protect the public from crimes of sexual violence—general rules of admissibility in sexual assault and child molestation cases for evidence that the defendant has committed offenses of the same type on other occasions. The enactment of this reform is first and foremost a triumph for the public—for the women who will not be raped and the children who will not be molested because we have strengthened the legal system's tools for bringing the perpetrators of these atrocious crimes to justice.

Senator Dole and I initially proposed this reform in February of 1991 in the Women's Equal Opportunity Act bill, and we later re-introduced it in the Sexual Assault Prevention Act bills of the 102d and 103d Congresses. The proposal also enjoyed the strong support of the Administration in the 102d Congress, and was included in President Bush's violent crime bill of that Congress, S. 635. The Senate passed the proposed rules on Nov. 5, 1993, by a vote of 75 to 19, in a crime bill amendment offered by Senate Dole. This Chamber endorsed the same rules on June 29, 1994, by a vote of

348 to 62, through a motion to instruct conferees that I offered.

The rules in the revised conference bill are substantially identical to our earlier proposals. We have agreed to a temporary deferral of the effective date of the new rules, pending a report by the Judicial Conference, in order to accommodate procedural objections raised by opponents of the reform. However, regardless of what the Judicial Conference may recommend, the new rules will take effect within at most 300 days of the enactment of this legislation, unless repealed or modified by subsequent legislation.

The need for these rules, their precedential support, their interpretation, and the issues and policy questions they raise have been analyzed at length in the legislative history of this proposal. I would direct the Members' attention particularly to two earlier statements:

The first is the portion of the section-by-section analysis accompanying these rules in section 801 of S. 635, which President Bush transmitted to Congress in 1991. That statement appears on pages S 3238 [to] S 3242 of the daily edition of the Congressional Record for March 13, 1991.

The second is the prepared text of an address—entitled "Evidence of Propensity and Probability in Sex Offense Cases and Other Cases"—by Senior Counsel David J. Karp of the Office of Policy Development of the U.S. Department of Justice. Mr. Karp, who is the author of the new evidence rules, presented this statement on behalf of the Justice Department to the Evidence Section of the Association of American Law Schools on January 9, 1993. The statement provided a detailed account of the views of the legislative sponsors and the Administration concerning the proposed reform, and should also be considered an authoritative part of its legislative history.

These earlier statements address the issues raised by this reform in considerable detail. In my present remarks, I will simply emphasize the following essential points:

The new rules will supersede in sex offense cases the restrictive aspects of Federal Rule of Evidence 404(b). In contrast to Rule 404(b)'s general prohibition of evidence of character or propensity, the new rules for sex offense cases authorize admission and consideration of evidence of an uncharged offense for its bearing "on any matter to which it is relevant." This includes the defendant's propensity to commit sexual assault or child molestation offenses, and assessment of the probability or improbability that the defendant has been falsely or mistakenly accused of such an offense.

In other respects, the general standards of the rules of evidence will continue to apply, including the restrictions on hearsay evidence and the court's authority under Evidence Rule 403 to exclude evidence whose probative value is substantially outweighed by its prejudicial effect. Also, the government (or the plaintiff in a civil case) will generally have to disclose to the defendant any evidence that is to be offered under the new rules at least 15 days before trial.

The proposed reform is critical to the protection of the public from rapists and child molesters, and is justified by the distinctive characteristics of the cases it will affect. In child molestation cases, for example, a history of similar acts tends to be exceptionally probative because it shows an unusual disposition of the defendant—a sexual or sadosexual interest in children—that simply does not exist in ordinary people. Moreover, such cases require reliance on child victims whose credibility can readily be attacked in the absence of substantial corroboration. In such cases, there is a compelling public interest in admitting all significant evidence that will illumine the credibility of the charge and any denial by the defense.

Similarly, adult-victim sexual assault cases are distinctive, and often turn on difficult credibility determinations. Alleged consent by the victim is rarely an issue in prosecutions for other violent crimes—the accused mugger does not claim that the victim freely handed over [his] wallet as a gift—but the defendant in a rape case often contends that the victim engaged in consensual sex and then falsely accused him. Knowledge that the defendant has committed rapes on other occasions is frequently critical in assessing the relative plausibility of these claims and accurately deciding cases that would otherwise become unresolvable swearing matches.

The practical effect of the new rules is to put evidence of uncharged offenses in sexual assault and child molestation cases on the same footing as other types of relevant evidence that are not subject to a special exclusionary rule. The presumption is in favor of admission. The underlying legislative judgment is that the evidence admissible pursuant to the proposed rules is typically relevant and probative, and that its probative value is normally not outweighed by any risk of prejudice or other adverse effects.

In line with this judgment, the rules do not impose arbitrary or artificial restrictions on the admissibility of evidence. Evidence of offenses for which the defendant has not previously been prosecuted or convicted will be admissible, as well as evidence of prior convictions. No time limit is imposed on the uncharged offenses for which evidence may be admitted; as a practical matter, evidence of other sex offenses by the defendant is often probative and properly admitted, notwithstanding very substantial lapses of time in relation to the charged offense or offenses. *See, e.g., United States v. Hadley*, 918 F.2d 848, 850–51 (9th Cir. 1990), *cert. dismissed*, 113 S.Ct. 486 (1992) (evidence of offenses occurring up to 15 years earlier admitted); *State v. Plymate*, 345 N.W.2d 327 (Neb.1984) (evidence of defendant's commission of other child molestations more than 20 years earlier admitted).

Finally, the practical efficacy of these rules will depend on faithful execution by judges of the will of Congress in adopting this critical reform. To implement the legislative intent, the courts must liberally construe these rules to provide the basis for a fully informed decision of sexual assault and child molestation cases, including assessment of the defendant's propensities and questions of probability in light of the defendant's past conduct.

Rule 414. Evidence of Similar Crimes in Child Molestation Cases

(a) In a criminal case in which the defendant is accused of an offense of child molestation, evidence of the defendant's commission of another offense or offenses of child molestation is admissible, and may be considered for its bearing on any matter to which it is relevant.

(b) In a case in which the Government intends to offer evidence under this rule, the attorney for the Government shall disclose the evidence to the defendant, including statements of witnesses or a summary of the substance of any testimony that is expected to be offered, at least fifteen days before the scheduled date of trial or at such later time as the court may allow for good cause.

(c) This rule shall not be construed to limit the admission or consideration of evidence under any other rule.

(d) For purposes of this rule and Rule 415, "child" means a person below the age of fourteen, and "offense of child molestation" means a crime under Federal law or the law of a State (as defined in section 513 of title 18, United States Code) that involved—

(1) any conduct proscribed by chapter 109A of title 18, United States Code, that was committed in relation to a child;

(2) any conduct proscribed by chapter 110 of title 18, United States Code;

(3) contact between any part of the defendant's body or an object and the genitals or anus of a child;

(4) contact between the genitals or anus of the defendant and any part of the body of a child;

(5) deriving sexual pleasure or gratification from the infliction of death, bodily injury, or physical pain on a child; or

(6) an attempt or conspiracy to engage in conduct described in paragraphs (1)–(5).

(Added Pub.L. 103–322, Title XXXII, § 320935(a), Sept. 13, 1994, 108 Stat. 2135.)

HISTORICAL NOTES

Effective Dates

Rule effective July 9, 1995, see section 320935(b) to (e) of Pub.L. 103–322, set out as a note under rule 413 of these rules.

Congressional Discussion

See Floor Statement following Rule 413.

Rule 415. Evidence of Similar Acts in Civil Cases Concerning Sexual Assault or Child Molestation

(a) In a civil case in which a claim for damages or other relief is predicated on a party's alleged commission of conduct constituting an offense of sexual assault or child molestation, evidence of that party's commission of another offense or offenses of sexual assault or child molestation is admissible and may be considered as provided in Rule 413 and Rule 414 of these rules.

(b) A party who intends to offer evidence under this Rule shall disclose the evidence to the party against whom it will be offered, including statements of witnesses or a summary of the substance of any testimony that is expected to be offered, at least fifteen days before the scheduled date of trial or at such later time as the court may allow for good cause.

(c) This rule shall not be construed to limit the admission or consideration of evidence under any other rule.

(Added Pub.L. 103–322, Title XXXII, § 320935(a), Sept. 13, 1994, 108 Stat. 2137.)

HISTORICAL NOTES

Effective Dates

Rule effective July 9, 1995, see section 320935(b) to (e) of Pub.L. 103–322, set out as a note under rule 413 of these rules.

Congressional Discussion

See Floor Statement following Rule 413.

ARTICLE V. PRIVILEGES

Rule 501. General Rule

Except as otherwise required by the Constitution of the United States or provided by Act of Congress or in rules prescribed by the Supreme Court pursuant to statutory authority, the privilege of a witness, person, government, State, or political subdivision thereof shall be governed by the principles of the common law as they may be interpreted by the courts of the United States in the light of reason and experience. However, in civil actions and proceedings, with respect to an element of a claim or defense as to which State law supplies the rule of decision, the privilege of a witness, person, government, State, or political subdivision thereof shall be determined in accordance with State law.

(Pub.L. 93–595, § 1, Jan. 2, 1975, 88 Stat. 1933.)

ADVISORY COMMITTEE NOTES

1974 Enactment

Article V as submitted to Congress contained thirteen Rules. Nine of those Rules defined specific non-constitutional privileges which the federal courts must recognize (i.e. required reports, lawyer-client, psychotherapist-patient, husband-wife, communications to clergymen, political vote, trade secrets, secrets of state and other official information, and identity of informer.) Another Rule provided that only those privileges set forth in Article V or in some other Act of Congress could be recognized by the federal courts. The three remaining Rules addressed collateral problems as to waiver of privilege by voluntary disclosure, privileged matter disclosed under compulsion or without opportunity to claim privilege, comment upon or inference from a claim of privilege, and jury instruction with regard thereto.

The Committee amended Article V to eliminate all of the Court's specific Rules on privileges. Instead, the Committee, through a single Rule, 501, left the law of privileges in its present state and further provided that privileges shall continue to be developed by the courts of the United States under a uniform standard applicable both in civil and criminal cases. That standard, derived from Rule 26 of the Federal Rules of Criminal Procedure, mandates the application of the principles of the common law as interpreted by the courts of the United States in the light of reason and experience. The words "person, government, State, or political subdivision thereof" were added by the Committee to the lone term "witnesses" used in Rule 26 to make clear that, as under present law, not only witnesses may have privileges. The Committee also included in its amendment a proviso modeled after Rule 302 and similar to language added by the Committee to Rule 601 relating to the competency of witnesses. The proviso is designed to require the application of State privilege law in civil actions and proceedings governed by *Erie R. Co. v. Tompkins,* 304 U.S. 64 (1938), a result in accord with current federal court decisions. See *Republic Gear Co. v. Borg–Warner Corp.,* 381 F.2d 551, 555–556 n. 2 (2nd Cir.1967). The Committee deemed the proviso to be necessary in the light of the Advisory Committee's view (see its note to Court [proposed] Rule 501) that this result is not mandated under *Erie.*

The rationale underlying the proviso is that federal law should not supersede that of the States in substantive areas such as privilege absent a compelling reason. The Committee believes that in civil cases in the federal courts where an element of a claim or defense is not grounded upon a federal question, there is no federal interest strong enough to justify departure from State policy. In addition, the Committee considered that the Court's proposed Article V would have promoted forum shopping in some civil actions, depending upon differences in the privilege law applied as among the State and federal courts. The Committee's proviso, on the other hand, under which the federal courts are bound to apply the State's privilege law in actions founded upon a State-created right or defense, removes the incentive to "shop". House Report No. 93–650.

Article V as submitted to Congress contained 13 rules. Nine of those rules defined specific nonconstitutional privileges which the Federal courts must recognize (i.e., required reports, lawyer-client, psychotherapist-patient, husband-wife, communications to clergymen, political vote, trade secrets, secrets of state and other official information, and identity of informer). Many of these rules contained controversial modifications or restrictions upon common law privileges. As noted supra, the House amended article V to eliminate all of the Court's specific rules on privileges. Through a single rule, 501, the House provided that privileges shall be governed by the principles of the common law as interpreted by the courts of the United States in the light of reason and experience (a standard derived from rule 26 of the Federal Rules of Criminal Procedure) except in the case of an element of a civil claim or defense as to which State law supplies the rule of decision, in which event state privilege law was to govern.

The committee agrees with the main thrust of the House amendment: that a federally developed common law based on modern reason and experience shall apply except where the State nature of the issues renders deference to State privilege law the wiser course, as in the usual diversity case. The committee understands that thrust of the House amendment to require that State privilege law be applied in "diversity" cases (actions on questions of State law between citizens of different States arising under 28 U.S.C. § 1332). The language of the House amendment, however, goes beyond this in some respects, and falls short of it in others: State privilege law applies even in nondiversity, Federal question civil cases, where an issue governed by State substantive law is the object of the evidence (such issues do sometimes arise in such cases); and, in all instances where State privilege law is to be applied, e.g., on proof of a State issue in a diversity case, a close reading reveals that State privilege law is not to be applied unless the matter to be proved is an element of that state claim or defense, as distinguished from a step along the way in the proof of it.

The committee is concerned that the language used in the House amendment could be difficult to apply. It provides that "in civil actions * * * with respect to an element of a claim or defense as to which State law supplies the rule of decision," State law on privilege applies. The question of what is an element of a claim or defense is likely to engender considerable litigation. If the matter in question constitutes an element of a claim, State law supplies the privilege rule; whereas if it is a mere item of proof with respect to a claim, then, even though State law might supply the rule of decision, Federal law on the privilege would apply. Further, disputes will arise as to how the rule should be applied in an antitrust action or in a tax case where the Federal statute is silent as to a particular aspect of the substantive law in question, but Federal cases had incorporated State law by reference to State law. [For a discussion of reference to State substantive law, see note on Federal Incorporation by Reference of State Law, Hart & Wechsler, The Federal Courts and the Federal System, pp. 491–494 (2d ed. 1973).] Is a claim (or defense) based on such a reference a claim or defense as to which federal or State law supplies the rule of decision?

Another problem not entirely avoidable is the complexity or difficulty the rule introduces into the trial of a Federal case containing a combination of Federal and State claims and defenses, e.g. an action involving Federal antitrust and State unfair competition claims. Two different bodies of privilege law would need to be consulted. It may even develop that the same witness-testimony might be relevant on both counts and privileged as to one but not the other. [The problems with the House formulation are discussed in Rothstein, The Proposed Amendments to the Federal Rules of Evidence, 62 Georgetown University Law Journal 125 (1973) at notes 25, 26 and 70–74 and accompanying text.]

The formulation adopted by the House is pregnant with litigious mischief. The committee has, therefore, adopted what we believe will be a clearer and more practical guideline for determining when courts should respect State rules of privilege. Basically, it provides that in criminal and Federal question civil cases, federally evolved rules on privilege should apply since it is Federal policy which is being enforced. [It is also intended that the Federal law of privileges should be applied with respect to pendent State law claims when they arise in a Federal question case.] Conversely, in diversity cases where the litigation in question turns on a substantive question of State law, and is brought in the Federal courts because the parties reside in different States, the committee believes it is clear that State rules of privilege should apply unless the proof is directed at a claim or defense for which Federal law supplies the rule of decision (a situation which would not commonly arise.) [While such a situation might require use of two bodies of privilege law, federal and state, in the same case, nevertheless the occasions on which this would be required are considerably reduced as compared with the House version, and confined to situations where the Federal and State interests are such as to justify application of neither privilege law to the case as a whole. If the rule proposed here results in two conflicting bodies of privilege law applying to the same piece of evidence in the same case, it is contemplated that the rule favoring reception of the evidence should be applied. This policy is based on the present rule 43(a) of the Federal Rules of Civil Procedure which provides: In any case, the statute or rule which favors the reception of the evidence governs and the evidence shall be presented according to the most convenient method prescribed in any of the statutes or rules to which reference is herein made.] It is intended that the State rules of privilege should apply equally in original diversity actions and diversity actions removed under 28 U.S.C. § 1441(b).

Two other comments on the privilege rule should be made. The committee has received a considerable volume of correspondence from psychiatric organizations and psychiatrists concerning the deletion of rule 504 of the rule submitted by the Supreme Court. It should be clearly understood that, in approving this general rule as to privileges, the action of Congress should not be understood as disapproving any recognition of a psychiatrist-patient, or husband-wife, or any other of the enumerated privileges contained in the Supreme Court rules. Rather, our action should be understood as reflecting the view that the recognition of a privilege based on a confidential relationship and other privileges should be determined on a case-by-case basis.

Further, we would understand that the prohibition against spouses testifying against each other is considered a rule of privilege and covered by this rule and not by rule 601 of the competency of witnesses. Senate Report No. 93–1277.

Rule 501 deals with the privilege of a witness not to testify. Both the House and Senate bills provide that federal privilege law applies in criminal cases. In civil actions and proceedings, the House bill provides that state privilege law applies "to an element of a claim or defense as to which State law supplies the rule of decision." The Senate bill provides that "in civil actions and proceedings arising under 28 U.S.C. § 1332 or 28 U.S.C. § 1335, or between citizens of different States and removed under 28 U.S.C. § 1441(b) the privilege of a witness, person, government, State or political subdivision thereof is determined in accordance with State law, unless with respect to the particular claim or defense, Federal law supplies the rule of decision."

The wording of the House and Senate bills differs in the treatment of civil actions and proceedings. The rule in the House bill applies to evidence that relates to "an element of a claim or defense." If an item of proof tends to support or defeat a claim or defense, or an element of a claim or defense, and if state law supplies the rule of decision for that claim or defense, then state privilege law applies to that item of proof.

Under the provision in the House bill, therefore, state privilege law will usually apply in diversity cases. There may be diversity cases, however, where a claim or defense is based upon federal law. In such instances, federal privilege law will apply to evidence relevant to the federal claim or defense. See *Sola Electric Co. v. Jefferson Electric Co.,* 317 U.S. 173 (1942).

In nondiversity jurisdiction civil cases, federal privilege law will generally apply. In those situations where a federal court adopts or incorporates state law to fill interstices or gaps in federal statutory phrases, the court generally will apply federal privilege law. As Justice Jackson has said:

> A federal court sitting in a non-diversity case such as this does not sit as a local tribunal. In some cases it may see fit for special reasons to give the law of a particular state highly persuasive or even controlling effect, but in the last analysis its decision turns upon the law of the United States, not that of any state.

D'Oench, Duhme & Co. v. Federal Deposit Insurance Corp., 315 U.S. 447, 471 (1942) (Jackson, J., concurring). When a federal court chooses to absorb state law, it is applying the state law as a matter of federal common law. Thus, state law does not supply the rule of decision (even though the federal court may apply a rule derived from state decisions), and state privilege law would not apply. See C.A. Wright, Federal Courts 251–252 (2d ed. 1970); *Holmberg v. Armbrecht,* 327 U.S. 392 (1946); *DeSylva v. Ballentine,* 351 U.S. 570, 581 (1956); 9 Wright & Miller, Federal Rules and Procedure § 2408.

In civil actions and proceedings, where the rule of decision as to a claim or defense or as to an element of a claim or defense is supplied by state law, the House provision requires that state privilege law apply.

The Conference adopts the House provision. House Report No. 93–1597.

ARTICLE VI. WITNESSES

Rule 601. General Rule of Competency

Every person is competent to be a witness except as otherwise provided in these rules. However, in civil actions and proceedings, with respect to an element of a claim or defense as to which State law supplies the rule of decision, the competency of a witness shall be determined in accordance with State law.

(Pub.L. 93–595, § 1, Jan. 2, 1975, 88 Stat.1934.)

ADVISORY COMMITTEE NOTES

1972 Proposed Rules

This general ground-clearing eliminates all grounds of incompetency not specifically recognized in the succeeding rules of this Article. Included among the grounds thus abolished are religious belief, conviction of crime, and connection with the litigation as a party or interested person or spouse of a party or interested person. With the exception of the so-called Dead Man's Acts, American jurisdictions generally have ceased to recognize these grounds.

The Dead Man's Acts are surviving traces of the common law disqualification of parties and interested persons. They exist in variety too great to convey conviction of their wisdom and effectiveness. These rules contain no provision of this kind. For the reasoning underlying the decision not to give effect to state statutes in diversity cases, see the Advisory Committee's Note to Rule 501.

No mental or moral qualifications for testifying as a witness are specified. Standards of mental capacity have proved elusive in actual application. A leading commentator observes that few witnesses are disqualified on that ground. Weihofen, Testimonial Competence and Credibility, 34 Geo. Wash.L.Rev. 53 (1965). Discretion is regularly exercised in favor of allowing the testimony. A witness wholly without capacity is difficult to imagine. The question is one particularly suited to the jury as one of weight and credibility, subject to judicial authority to review the sufficiency of the evidence. 2 Wigmore §§ 501, 509. Standards of moral qualification in practice consist essentially of evaluating a person's truthfulness in terms of his own answers about it. Their principal utility is in affording an opportunity on voir dire examination to impress upon the witness his moral duty. This result may, however, be accomplished more directly, and without haggling in terms of legal standards, by the manner of administering the oath or affirmation under Rule 603.

Admissibility of religious belief as a ground of impeachment is treated in Rule 610. Conviction of crime as a ground of impeachment is the subject of Rule 609. Marital relationship is the basis for privilege under Rule 505. Interest in the outcome of litigation and mental capacity are, of course, highly relevant to credibility and require no special treatment to render them admissible along with other matters bearing upon the perception, memory, and narration of witnesses.

1974 Enactment

Rule 601 as submitted to the Congress provided that "Every person is competent to be a witness except as otherwise provided in these rules." One effect of the Rule as proposed would have been to abolish age, mental capacity, and other grounds recognized in some State jurisdictions as making a person incompetent as a witness. The greatest controversy centered around the Rule's rendering inapplicable in the federal courts the so-called Dead Man's Statutes which exist in some States. Acknowledging that there is substantial disagreement as to the merit of Dead Man's Statutes, the Committee nevertheless believed that where such statutes have been enacted they represent State policy which should not be overturned in the absence of a compelling federal interest. The Committee therefore amended the Rule to make competency in civil actions determinable in accordance with State law with respect to elements of claims or defenses as to which State law supplies the rule of decision. Cf. *Courtland v. Walston & Co., Inc.*, 340 F.Supp. 1076, 1087–1092 (S.D.N.Y.1972). House Report No. 93–650.

The amendment to rule 601 parallels the treatment accorded Rule 501 discussed immediately above. Senate Report No. 93–1277.

Rule 601 deals with competency of witnesses. Both the House and Senate bills provide that federal competency law applies in criminal cases. In civil actions and proceedings, the House bill provides that state competency law applies "to an element of a claim or defense as to which State law supplies the rule of decision." The Senate bill provides that "in civil actions and proceedings arising under 28 U.S.C. § 1332 or 28 U.S.C. § 1335, or between citizens of different States and removed under 28 U.S.C. § 1441(b) the competency of a witness, person, government, State or political subdivision thereof is determined in accordance with State law, unless with respect to the particular claim or defense, Federal law supplies the rule of decision."

The wording of the House and Senate bills differs in the treatment of civil actions and proceedings. The rule in the House bill applies to evidence that relates to "an element of a claim or defense." If an item of proof tends to support or defeat a claim or defense, or an element of a claim or defense, and if state law supplies the rule of decision for that claim or defense, then state competency law applies to that item of proof.

For reasons similar to those underlying its action on Rule 501, the Conference adopts the House provision. House Report No. 93–1597.

Rule 602. Lack of Personal Knowledge

A witness may not testify to a matter unless evidence is introduced sufficient to support a finding that the witness has personal knowledge of the matter. Evidence to prove personal knowledge may, but need not, consist of the witness' own testimony. This rule is subject to the provisions of rule 703, relating to opinion testimony by expert witnesses.

(Pub.L. 93–595, § 1, Jan. 2, 1975, 88 Stat. 1934; Mar. 2, 1987, eff. Oct. 1, 1987; Apr. 25, 1988, eff. Nov. 1, 1988.)

ADVISORY COMMITTEE NOTES

1972 Proposed Rules

"* * * [T]he rule requiring that a witness who testifies to a fact which can be perceived by the senses must have had an opportunity to observe, and must have actually observed the fact" is a "most pervasive manifestation" of the common law insistence upon "the most reliable sources of information." McCormick § 10, p. 19. These foundation requirements may, of course, be furnished by the testimony of the witness himself; hence personal knowledge is not an absolute but may consist of what the witness thinks he knows from personal perception. 2 Wigmore § 650. It will be observed that the rule is in fact a specialized application of the provisions of Rule 104(b) on conditional relevancy.

This rule does not govern the situation of a witness who testifies to a hearsay statement as such, if he has personal knowledge of the making of the statement. Rules 801 and 805 would be applicable. This rule would, however, prevent him from testifying to the subject matter of the hearsay statement, as he has no personal knowledge of it.

The reference to Rule 703 is designed to avoid any question of conflict between the present rule and the provisions of that rule allowing an expert to express opinions based on facts of which he does not have personal knowledge.

1987 Amendment

The amendments are technical. No substantive change is intended.

1988 Amendment

The amendment is technical. No substantive change is intended.

Rule 603. Oath or Affirmation

Before testifying, every witness shall be required to declare that the witness will testify truthfully, by oath or affirmation administered in a form calculated to awaken the witness' conscience and impress the witness' mind with the duty to do so.

(Pub.L. 93–595, § 1, Jan. 2, 1975, 88 Stat. 1934; Mar. 2, 1987, eff. Oct. 1, 1987.)

ADVISORY COMMITTEE NOTES

1972 Proposed Rules

The rule is designed to afford the flexibility required in dealing with religious adults, atheists, conscientious objectors, mental defectives, and children. Affirmation is simply a solemn undertaking to tell the truth; no special verbal formula is required. As is true generally, affirmation is recognized by federal law. "Oath" includes affirmation, 1 U.S.C. § 1; judges and clerks may administer oaths and affirmations, 28 U.S.C. §§ 459, 953; and affirmations are acceptable in lieu of oaths under Rule 43(d) of the Federal Rules of Civil Procedure. Perjury by a witness is a crime, 18 U.S.C. § 1621.

1987 Amendment

The amendments are technical. No substantive change is intended.

Rule 604. Interpreters

An interpreter is subject to the provisions of these rules relating to qualification as an expert and the administration of an oath or affirmation to make a true translation.

(Pub.L. 93–595, § 1, Jan. 2, 1975, 88 Stat. 1934; Mar. 2, 1987, eff. Oct. 1, 1987.)

ADVISORY COMMITTEE NOTES

1972 Proposed Rules

The rule implements Rule 43(f) of the Federal Rules of Civil Procedure and Rule 28(b) of the Federal Rules of Criminal Procedure, both of which contain provisions for the appointment and compensation of interpreters.

1987 Amendment

The amendment is technical. No substantive change is intended.

Rule 605. Competency of Judge as Witness

The judge presiding at the trial may not testify in that trial as a witness. No objection need be made in order to preserve the point.

(Pub.L. 93–595, § 1, Jan. 2, 1975, 88 Stat. 1934.)

ADVISORY COMMITTEE NOTES

1972 Proposed Rules

In view of the mandate of 28 U.S.C. § 455 that a judge disqualify himself in "any case in which he * * * is or has been a material witness," the likelihood that the presiding judge in a federal court might be called to testify in the trial over which he is presiding is slight. Nevertheless the possibility is not totally eliminated.

The solution here presented is a broad rule of incompetency, rather than such alternatives as incompetency only as to material matters, leaving the matter to the discretion of the judge, or recognizing no incompetency. The choice is the result of inability to evolve satisfactory answers to questions which arise when the judge abandons the bench for the witness stand. Who rules on objections? Who compels him to answer? Can he rule impartially on the weight and admissibility of his own testimony? Can he be impeached or cross-examined effectively? Can he, in a jury trial, avoid conferring his seal of approval on one side in the eyes of the jury? Can he, in a bench trial, avoid an involvement destructive of impartiality? The rule of general incompetency has substantial support. See Report of the Special Committee on the Propriety of Judges Appearing as Witnesses, 36 A.B.A.J. 630 (1950); cases collected in Annot. 157 A.L.R. 311; McCormick § 68, p. 147; Uniform Rule 42; California Evidence Code § 703; Kansas Code of Civil Procedure § 60–442; New Jersey Evidence Rule 42. Cf. 6 Wigmore § 1909, which advocates leaving the matter to the discretion of the judge, and statutes to that effect collected in Annot. 157 A.L.R. 311.

The rule provides an "automatic" objection. To require an actual objection would confront the opponent with a choice between not objecting, with the result of allowing the testimony, and objecting, with the probable result of excluding the testimony but at the price of continuing the trial before a judge likely to feel that his integrity had been attacked by the objector.

Rule 606. Competency of Juror as Witness

(a) At the trial. A member of the jury may not testify as a witness before that jury in the trial of the case in which the juror is sitting. If the juror is called so to testify, the opposing party shall be afforded an opportunity to object out of the presence of the jury.

(b) Inquiry into validity of verdict or indictment. Upon an inquiry into the validity of a verdict or indictment, a juror may not testify as to any matter or statement occurring during the course of the jury's deliberations or to the effect of anything upon that or any other juror's mind or emotions as influencing the juror to assent to or dissent from the verdict or indictment or concerning the juror's mental processes in connection therewith, except that a juror may testify on the question whether extraneous prejudicial information was improperly brought to the jury's attention or whether any outside influence was improperly brought to bear upon any juror. Nor may a juror's affidavit or evidence of any statement by the juror concerning a matter about which the juror would be precluded from testifying be received for these purposes.

(Pub.L. 93–595, § 1, Jan. 2, 1975, 88 Stat. 1934; Pub.L. 94–149, § 1(10), Dec. 12, 1975, 89 Stat. 805; Mar. 2, 1987, eff. Oct. 1, 1987.)

ADVISORY COMMITTEE NOTES

1972 Proposed Rules

Note to Subdivision (a). The considerations which bear upon the permissibility of testimony by a juror in the trial in which he is sitting as juror bear an obvious similarity to those evoked when the judge is called as a witness. See Advisory Committee's Note to Rule 605. The judge is not, however in this instance so involved as to call for departure from usual principles requiring objection to be made; hence the only provision on objection is that opportunity be afforded for its making out of the presence of the jury. Compare Rule 605.

Note to Subdivision (b). Whether testimony, affidavits, or statements of jurors should be received for the purpose of invalidating or supporting a verdict or indictment, and if so, under what circumstances, has given rise to substantial differences of opinion. The familiar rubric that a juror may not impeach his own verdict, dating from Lord Mansfield's time, is a gross oversimplification. The values sought to be promoted by excluding the evidence include freedom of deliberation, stability and finality of verdicts, and protection of jurors against annoyance and embarrassment. *McDonald v. Pless*, 238 U.S. 264, 35 S.Ct. 783, 59 L.Ed. 1300 (1915). On the other hand, simply putting verdicts beyond effective reach can only promote irregularity and injustice. The rule offers an accommodation between these competing considerations.

The mental operations and emotional reactions of jurors in arriving at a given result would, if allowed as a subject of inquiry, place every verdict at the mercy of jurors and invite tampering and harassment. See *Grenz v. Werre*, 129 N.W.2d 681 (N.D.1964). The authorities are in virtually complete accord in excluding the evidence. Fryer, Note on Disqualification of Witnesses, Selected Writings on Evidence and Trial 345, 347 (Fryer ed. 1957); Maguire, Weinstein, et al., Cases on Evidence 887 (5th ed. 1965); 8 Wigmore § 2349 (McNaughton Rev.1961). As to matters other than mental operations and emotional reactions of jurors, substantial authority refuses to allow a juror to disclose irregularities which occur in the jury room, but allows his testimony as to irregularities occurring outside and allows outsiders to testify as to occurrences both inside and out. 8 Wigmore § 2354 (McNaughton Rev.1961). However, the door of the jury room is not necessarily a satisfactory dividing point, and the Supreme Court has refused to accept it for every situation. *Mattox v. United States*, 146 U.S. 140, 13 S.Ct. 50, 36 L.Ed. 917 (1892).

Under the federal decisions the central focus has been upon insulation of the manner in which the jury reached its verdict, and this protection extends to each of the components of deliberation, including arguments, statements, discussions, mental and emotional reactions, votes, and any other feature of the process. Thus testimony or affidavits of jurors have been held incompetent to show a compromise verdict. *Hyde v. United States*, 225 U.S. 347, 382 (1912); a quotient verdict, *McDonald v. Pless*, 238 U.S. 264 (1915); speculation as to insurance coverage. *Holden v. Porter*, 405 F.2d 878 (10th Cir.1969); *Farmers Coop. Elev. Ass'n v. Strand*, 382 F.2d 224, 230 (8th Cir.1967), cert. denied 389 U.S. 1014; misinterpretation of instructions, *Farmers Coop. Elev. Ass'n v. Strand*, supra; mistake in returning verdict, *United States v. Chereton*, 309 F.2d 197 (6th Cir.1962); interpretation of guilty plea by one defendant as implicating others, *United States v. Crosby*, 294 F.2d 928, 949 (2d Cir.1961). The policy does not, however, foreclose testimony by jurors as to prejudicial extraneous information or influences injected into or brought to bear upon the deliberative process. Thus a juror is recognized as competent to testify to statements by the bailiff or the introduction of a prejudicial newspaper account into the jury room, *Mattox v. United States*, 146 U.S. 140 (1892). See also *Parker v. Gladden*, 385 U.S. 363 (1966).

This rule does not purport to specify the substantive grounds for setting aside verdicts for irregularity; it deals only with the competency of jurors to testify concerning those grounds. Allowing them to testify as to matters other than their own inner reactions involves no particular hazard to the values sought to be protected. The rule is based upon this conclusion. It makes no attempt to specify the substantive grounds for setting aside verdicts for irregularity.

See also Rule 6(e) of the Federal Rules of Criminal Procedure and 18 U.S.C. § 3500, governing the secrecy of grand jury proceedings. The present rule does not relate to secrecy and disclosure but to the competency of certain witnesses and evidence.

1974 Enactment

Note to Subdivision (b). As proposed by the Court, Rule 606(b) limited testimony by a juror in the course of an inquiry into the validity of a verdict or indictment. He could testify as to the influence of extraneous prejudicial information brought to the jury's attention (e.g. a radio newscast or a newspaper account) or an outside influence which improperly had been brought to bear upon a juror (e.g. a threat to the safety of a member of his family), but he could not testify as to other irregularities which occurred in the jury room. Under this formulation a quotient verdict could not be attacked through the testimony of a juror, nor could a juror testify to the drunken condition of a fellow juror which so disabled him that he could not participate in the jury's deliberations.

The 1969 and 1971 Advisory Committee drafts would have permitted a member of the jury to testify concerning these kinds of irregularities in the jury room. The Advisory Committee note in the 1971 draft stated that "* * * the door of the jury room is not a satisfactory dividing point, and the Supreme Court has refused to accept it." The Advisory Committee further commented that—

> The trend has been to draw the dividing line between testimony as to mental processes, on the one hand, and as to the existence of conditions or occurrences of events calculated improperly to influence the verdict on the other hand, without regard to whether the happening is within

or without the jury room. * * * The jurors are the persons who know what really happened. Allowing them to testify as to matters other than their own reactions involves no particular hazard to the values sought to be protected. The rule is based upon this conclusion. It makes no attempt to specify the substantive grounds for setting aside verdicts for irregularity.

Objective jury misconduct may be testified to in California, Florida, Iowa, Kansas, Nebraska, New Jersey, North Dakota, Ohio, Oregon, Tennessee, Texas, and Washington.

Persuaded that the better practice is that provided for in the earlier drafts, the Committee amended subdivision (b) to read in the text of those drafts. House Report No. 93–650.

Note to Subdivision (b). As adopted by the House, this rule would permit the impeachment of verdicts by inquiry into, not the mental processes of the jurors, but what happened in terms of conduct in the jury room. This extension of the ability to impeach a verdict is felt to be unwarranted and ill-advised.

The rule passed by the House embodies a suggestion by the Advisory Committee of the Judicial Conference that is considerably broader than the final version adopted by the Supreme Court, which embodied long-accepted Federal law. Although forbidding the impeachment of verdicts by inquiry into the jurors' mental processes, it deletes from the Supreme Court version the proscription against testimony "as to any matter or statement occurring during the course of the jury's deliberations." This deletion would have the effect of opening verdicts up to challenge on the basis of what happened during the jury's internal deliberations, for example, where a juror alleged that the jury refused to follow the trial judge's instructions or that some of the jurors did not take part in deliberations.

Permitting an individual to attack a jury verdict based upon the jury's internal deliberations has long been recognized as unwise by the Supreme Court. In *McDonald v. Pless,* the Court stated:

* * * * * * *

[L]et it once be established that verdicts solemnly made and publicly returned into court can be attacked and set aside on the testimony of those who took part in their publication and all verdicts could be, and many would be, followed by an inquiry in the hope of discovering something which might invalidate the finding. Jurors would be harassed and beset by the defeated party in an effort to secure from them evidence of facts which might establish misconduct sufficient to set aside a verdict. If evidence thus secured could be thus used, the result would be to make what was intended to be a private deliberation, the constant subject of public investigation—to the destruction of all frankness and freedom of discussion and conference [238 U.S. 264, at 267 (1914)].

* * * * * * *

As it stands then, the rule would permit the harassment of former jurors by losing parties as well as the possible exploitation of disgruntled or otherwise badly-motivated ex-jurors.

Public policy requires a finality to litigation. And common fairness requires that absolute privacy be preserved for jurors to engage in the full and free debate necessary to the attainment of just verdicts. Jurors will not be able to function effectively if their deliberations are to be scrutinized in post-trial litigation. In the interest of protecting the jury system and the citizens who make it work, rule 606 should not permit any inquiry into the internal deliberations of the jurors. Senate Report No. 93–1277.

Note to Subdivision (b). Rule 606(b) deals with juror testimony in an inquiry into the validity of a verdict or indictment. The House bill provides that a juror cannot testify about his mental processes or about the effect of anything upon his or another juror's mind as influencing him to assent to or dissent from a verdict or indictment. Thus, the House bill allows a juror to testify about objective matters occurring during the jury's deliberation, such as the misconduct of another juror or the reaching of a quotient verdict. The Senate bill does not permit juror testimony about any matter or statement occurring during the course of the jury's deliberations. The Senate bill does provide, however, that a juror may testify on the question whether extraneous prejudicial information was improperly brought to the jury's attention and on the question whether any outside influence was improperly brought to bear on any juror.

The Conference adopts the Senate amendment. The Conferees believe that jurors should be encouraged to be conscientious in promptly reporting to the court misconduct that occurs during jury deliberations. House Report No. 93–1597.

1987 Amendment

The amendments are technical. No substantive change is intended.

Rule 607. Who May Impeach

The credibility of a witness may be attacked by any party, including the party calling the witness.

(Pub.L. 93–595, § 1, Jan. 2, 1975, 88 Stat.1934; Mar. 2, 1987, eff. Oct. 1, 1987.)

ADVISORY COMMITTEE NOTES

1972 Proposed Rules

The traditional rule against impeaching one's own witness is abandoned as based on false premises. A party does not hold out his witnesses as worthy of belief, since he rarely has a free choice in selecting them. Denial of the right leaves the party at the mercy of the witness and the adversary. If the impeachment is by a prior statement, it is free from hearsay dangers and is excluded from the category of hearsay under Rule 801(d)(1). Ladd, Impeachment of One's Own Witness—New Developments, 4 U.Chi.L.Rev. 69 (1936); McCormick § 38; 3 Wigmore §§ 896–918. The substantial inroads into the old rule made over the years by decisions, rules, and statutes are evidence of doubts as to its basic soundness and workability. Cases are collected in 3 Wigmore § 905. Revised Rule 32(a)(1) of the Federal Rules of Civil Procedure allows any party to impeach a witness by means of his deposition, and Rule 43(b) has allowed the calling and impeachment of an adverse party or person identified with him. Illustrative statutes allowing a party to impeach his own witness under varying circumstances are

Ill.Rev.Stats.1967, c. 110, § 60; Mass.Laws Annot. 1959, c. 233, § 23; 20 N.M.Stats.Annot. 1953, § 20–2–4; N.Y. CPLR § 4514 (McKinney 1963); 12 Vt.Stats.Annot.1959, §§ 1641a, 1642. Complete judicial rejection of the old rule is found in *United States v. Freeman,* 302 F.2d 347 (2d Cir.1962). The same result is reached in Uniform Rule 20; California Evidence Code § 785; Kansas Code of Civil Procedure § 60–420. See also New Jersey Evidence Rule 20.

1987 Amendment

The amendment is technical. No substantive change is intended.

Rule 608. Evidence of Character and Conduct of Witness

(a) Opinion and reputation evidence of character. The credibility of a witness may be attacked or supported by evidence in the form of opinion or reputation, but subject to these limitations: (1) the evidence may refer only to character for truthfulness or untruthfulness, and (2) evidence of truthful character is admissible only after the character of the witness for truthfulness has been attacked by opinion or reputation evidence or otherwise.

(b) Specific instances of conduct. Specific instances of the conduct of a witness, for the purpose of attacking or supporting the witness' credibility, other than conviction of crime as provided in rule 609, may not be proved by extrinsic evidence. They may, however, in the discretion of the court, if probative of truthfulness or untruthfulness, be inquired into on cross-examination of the witness (1) concerning the witness' character for truthfulness or untruthfulness, or (2) concerning the character for truthfulness or untruthfulness of another witness as to which character the witness being cross-examined has testified.

The giving of testimony, whether by an accused or by any other witness, does not operate as a waiver of the accused's or the witness' privilege against self-incrimination when examined with respect to matters which relate only to credibility.

(Pub.L. 93–595, § 1, Jan. 2, 1975, 88 Stat.1935; Mar. 2, 1987, eff. Oct. 1, 1987; Apr. 25, 1988, eff. Nov. 1, 1988.)

ADVISORY COMMITTEE NOTES

1972 Proposed Rules

Note to Subdivision (a). In Rule 404(a) the general position is taken that character evidence is not admissible for the purpose of proving that the person acted in conformity therewith, subject, however, to several exceptions, one of which is character evidence of a witness as bearing upon his credibility. The present rule develops that exception.

In accordance with the bulk of judicial authority, the inquiry is strictly limited to character for veracity, rather than allowing evidence as to character generally. The result is to sharpen relevancy, to reduce surprise, waste of time, and confusion, and to make the lot of the witness somewhat less unattractive. McCormick § 44.

The use of opinion and reputation evidence as means of proving the character of witnesses is consistent with Rule 405(a). While the modern practice has purported to exclude opinion, witnesses who testify to reputation seem in fact often to be giving their opinions, disguised somewhat misleadingly as reputation. See McCormick § 44. And even under the modern practice, a common relaxation has allowed inquiry as to whether the witnesses would believe the principal witness under oath. *United States v. Walker,* 313 F.2d 236 (6th Cir.1963), and cases cited therein; McCormick § 44, pp. 94–95, n. 3.

Character evidence in support of credibility is admissible under the rule only after the witness' character has first been attacked, as has been the case at common law. Maguire, Weinstein, et al., Cases on Evidence 295 (5th ed. 1965); McCormick § 49, p. 105; 4 Wigmore § 1104. The enormous needless consumption of time which a contrary practice would entail justifies the limitation. Opinion or reputation that the witness is untruthful specifically qualifies as an attack under the rule, and evidence of misconduct, including conviction of crime, and of corruption also fall within this category. Evidence of bias or interest does not. McCormick § 49; 4 Wigmore §§ 1106, 1107. Whether evidence in the form of contradiction is an attack upon the character of the witness must depend upon the circumstances. McCormick § 49. Cf. 4 Wigmore §§ 1108, 1109.

As to the use of specific instances on direct by an opinion witness, see the Advisory Committee's Note to Rule 405, *supra.*

Note to Subdivision (b). In conformity with Rule 405, which forecloses use of evidence of specific incidents as proof in chief of character unless character is an issue in the case, the present rule generally bars evidence of specific instances of conduct of a witness for the purpose of attacking or supporting his credibility. There are, however, two exceptions: (1) specific instances are provable when they have been the subject of criminal conviction, and (2) specific instances may be inquired into on cross-examination of the principal witness or of a witness giving an opinion of his character for truthfulness.

(1) Conviction of crime as a technique of impeachment is treated in detail in Rule 609, and here is merely recognized as an exception to the general rule excluding evidence of specific incidents for impeachment purposes.

(2) Particular instances of conduct, though not the subject of criminal conviction, may be inquired into on cross-examination of the principal witness himself or of a witness who testifies concerning his character for truthfulness. Effective cross-examination demands that some allowance be made for going into matters of this kind, but the possibilities of abuse are substantial. Consequently safeguards are erected in the form of specific requirements that the instances inquired into be probative of truthfulness or its opposite and not remote in time. Also, the overriding protection of Rule 403 requires that probative value not be outweighed by danger of unfair prejudice, confusion of issues, or misleading the jury, and that of Rule 611 bars harassment and undue embarrassment.

The final sentence constitutes a rejection of the doctrine of such cases as *People v. Sorge,* 301 N.Y. 198, 93 N.E.2d 637 (1950), that any past criminal act relevant to credibility may be inquired into on cross-examination, in apparent disregard of the privilege against self-incrimination. While it is clear that an ordinary witness cannot make a partial disclosure of incriminating matter and then invoke the privilege on cross-examination, no tenable contention can be made that merely by testifying he waives his right to foreclose inquiry on cross-examination into criminal activities for the purpose of attacking his credibility. So to hold would reduce the privilege to a nullity. While it is true that an accused, unlike an ordinary witness, has an option whether to testify, if the option can be exercised only at the price of opening up inquiry as to any and all criminal acts committed during his lifetime, the right to testify could scarcely be said to possess much vitality. In *Griffin v. California*, 380 U.S. 609, 85 S.Ct. 1229, 14 L.Ed.2d 106 (1965), the Court held that allowing comment on the election of an accused not to testify exacted a constitutionally impermissible price, and so here. While no specific provision in terms confers constitutional status on the right of an accused to take the stand in his own defense, the existence of the right is so completely recognized that a denial of it or substantial infringement upon it would surely be of due process dimensions. See *Ferguson v. Georgia*, 365 U.S. 570, 81 S.Ct. 756, 5 L.Ed.2d 783 (1961); McCormick § 131; 8 Wigmore § 2276 (McNaughton Rev.1961). In any event, wholly aside from constitutional considerations, the provision represents a sound policy.

1974 Enactment

Note to Subdivision (a). Rule 608(a) as submitted by the Court permitted attack to be made upon the character for truthfulness or untruthfulness of a witness either by reputation or opinion testimony. For the same reason underlying its decision to eliminate the admissibility of opinion testimony in Rule 405(a), the Committee amended Rule 608(a) to delete the reference to opinion testimony.

Note to Subdivision (b). The second sentence of Rule 608(b) as submitted by the Court permitted specific instances of misconduct of a witness to be inquired into on cross-examination for the purpose of attacking his credibility, if probative of truthfulness or untruthfulness, "and not remote in time". Such cross-examination could be of the witness himself or of another witness who testifies as to "his" character for truthfulness or untruthfulness.

The Committee amended the Rule to emphasize the discretionary power of the court in permitting such testimony and deleted the reference to remoteness in time as being unnecessary and confusing (remoteness from time of trial or remoteness from the incident involved?). As recast, the Committee amendment also makes clear the antecedent of "his" in the original Court proposal. House Report No. 93–650.

The Senate amendment adds the words "opinion or" to conform the first sentence of the rule with the remainder of the rule.

The Conference adopts the Senate amendment. House Report No. 93–1597.

1987 Amendment

The amendments are technical. No substantive change is intended.

1988 Amendment

The amendment is technical. No substantive change is intended.

Rule 609. Impeachment by Evidence of Conviction of Crime

(a) General rule. For the purpose of attacking the credibility of a witness,

(1) evidence that a witness other than an accused has been convicted of a crime shall be admitted, subject to Rule 403, if the crime was punishable by death or imprisonment in excess of one year under the law under which the witness was convicted, and evidence that an accused has been convicted of such a crime shall be admitted if the court determines that the probative value of admitting this evidence outweighs its prejudicial effect to the accused; and

(2) evidence that any witness has been convicted of a crime shall be admitted if it involved dishonesty or false statement, regardless of the punishment.

(b) Time limit. Evidence of a conviction under this rule is not admissible if a period of more than ten years has elapsed since the date of the conviction or of the release of the witness from the confinement imposed for that conviction, whichever is the later date, unless the court determines, in the interests of justice, that the probative value of the conviction supported by specific facts and circumstances substantially outweighs its prejudicial effect. However, evidence of a conviction more than 10 years old as calculated herein, is not admissible unless the proponent gives to the adverse party sufficient advance written notice of intent to use such evidence to provide the adverse party with a fair opportunity to contest the use of such evidence.

(c) Effect of pardon, annulment, or certificate of rehabilitation. Evidence of a conviction is not admissible under this rule if (1) the conviction has been the subject of a pardon, annulment, certificate of rehabilitation, or other equivalent procedure based on a finding of the rehabilitation of the person convicted, and that person has not been convicted of a subsequent crime which was punishable by death or imprisonment in excess of one year, or (2) the conviction has been the subject of a pardon, annulment, or other equivalent procedure based on a finding of innocence.

(d) Juvenile adjudications. Evidence of juvenile adjudications is generally not admissible under this rule. The court may, however, in a criminal case allow evidence of a juvenile adjudication of a witness other than the accused if conviction of the offense would be admissible to attack the credibility of an adult and the court is satisfied that admission in evidence is necessary for a fair determination of the issue of guilt or innocence.

(e) Pendency of appeal. The pendency of an appeal therefrom does not render evidence of a conviction inadmissible. Evidence of the pendency of an appeal is admissible.

(Pub.L. 93–595, § 1, Jan. 2, 1975, 88 Stat.1935; Mar. 2, 1987, eff. Oct. 1, 1987; Jan. 26, 1990, eff. Dec. 1, 1990.)

ADVISORY COMMITTEE NOTES

1972 Proposed Rules

As a means of impeachment, evidence of conviction of crime is significant only because it stands as proof of the commission of the underlying criminal act. There is little dissent from the general proposition that at least some crimes are relevant to credibility but much disagreement among the cases and commentators about which crimes are usable for this purpose. See McCormick § 43; 2 Wright, Federal Practice and Procedure: Criminal § 416 (1969). The weight of traditional authority has been to allow use of felonies generally, without regard to the nature of the particular offense, and of *crimen falsi* without regard to the grade of the offense. This is the view accepted by Congress in the 1970 amendment of § 14–305 of the District of Columbia Code, P.L. 91–358, 84 Stat. 473. Uniform Rule 21 and Model Code Rule 106 permit only crimes involving "dishonesty or false statement." Others have thought that the trial judge should have discretion to exclude convictions if the probative value of the evidence of the crime is substantially outweighed by the danger of unfair prejudice. *Luck v. United States,* 121 U.S.App.D.C. 151, 348 F.2d 763 (1965); McGowan, Impeachment of Criminal Defendants by Prior Convictions, 1970 Law & Soc.Order 1. Whatever may be the merits of those views, this rule is drafted to accord with the Congressional policy manifested in the 1970 legislation.

The proposed rule incorporates certain basic safeguards, in terms applicable to all witnesses but of particular significance to an accused who elects to testify. These protections include the imposition of definite time limitations, giving effect to demonstrated rehabilitation, and generally excluding juvenile adjudications.

Note to Subdivision (a). For purposes of impeachment, crimes are divided into two categories by the rule: (1) those of what is generally regarded as felony grade, without particular regard to the nature of the offense, and (2) those involving dishonesty or false statement, without regard to the grade of the offense. Probable convictions are not limited to violations of federal law. By reason of our constitutional structure, the federal catalog of crimes is far from being a complete one, and resort must be had to the laws of the states for the specification of many crimes. For example, simple theft as compared with theft from interstate commerce. Other instances of borrowing are the Assimilative Crimes Act, making the state law of crimes applicable to the special territorial and maritime jurisdiction of the United States, 18 U.S.C. § 13, and the provision of the Judicial Code disqualifying persons as jurors on the grounds of state as well as federal convictions, 28 U.S.C. § 1865. For evaluation of the crime in terms of seriousness, reference is made to the congressional measurement of felony (subject to imprisonment in excess of one year) rather than adopting state definitions which vary considerably. See 28 U.S.C. § 1865, *supra,* disqualifying jurors for conviction in state or federal court of crime punishable by imprisonment for more than one year.

Note to Subdivision (b). Few statutes recognize a time limit on impeachment by evidence of conviction. However, practical considerations of fairness and relevancy demand that some boundary be recognized. See Ladd, Credibility Tests—Current Trends, 89 U.Pa.L.Rev. 166, 176–177 (1940). This portion of the rule is derived from the proposal advanced in Recommendation Proposing in Evidence Code, § 788(5), p. 142, Cal.Law Rev.Comm'n (1965), though not adopted. See California Evidence Code § 788.

Note to Subdivision (c). A pardon or its equivalent granted solely for the purpose of restoring civil rights lost by virtue of a conviction has no relevance to an inquiry into character. If, however, the pardon or other proceeding is hinged upon a showing of rehabilitation the situation is otherwise. The result under the rule is to render the conviction inadmissible. The alternative of allowing in evidence both the conviction and the rehabilitation has not been adopted for reasons of policy, economy of time, and difficulties of evaluation.

A similar provision is contained in California Evidence Code § 788. Cf. A.L.I. Model Penal Code, Proposed Official Draft § 306.6(3)(e) (1962), and discussion in A.L.I. Proceedings 310 (1961).

Pardons based on innocence have the effect, of course, of nullifying the conviction *ab initio.*

Note to Subdivision (d). The prevailing view has been that a juvenile adjudication is not usable for impeachment. *Thomas v. United States,* 74 App.D.C. 167, 121 F.2d 905 (1941); *Cotton v. United States,* 355 F.2d 480 (10th Cir.1966). This conclusion was based upon a variety of circumstances. By virtue of its informality, frequently diminished quantum of required proof, and other departures from accepted standards for criminal trials under the theory of *parens patriae,* the juvenile adjudication was considered to lack the precision and general probative value of the criminal conviction. While *In re Gault,* 387 U.S. 1, 87 S.Ct. 1428, 18 L.Ed.2d 527 (1967), no doubt eliminates these characteristics insofar as objectionable, other obstacles remain. Practical problems of administration are raised by the common provisions in juvenile legislation that records be kept confidential and that they be destroyed after a short time. While *Gault* was skeptical as to the realities of confidentiality of juvenile records, it also saw no constitutional obstacles to improvement. 387 U.S. at 25, 87 S.Ct. 1428. See also Note, Rights and Rehabilitation in the Juvenile Courts, 67 Colum.L.Rev. 281, 289 (1967). In addition, policy considerations much akin to those which dictate exclusion of adult convictions after rehabilitation has been established strongly suggest a rule of excluding juvenile adjudications. Admittedly, however, the rehabilitative process may in a given case be a demonstrated failure, or the strategic importance of a given witness may be so great as to require the overriding of general policy in the interests of particular justice. See *Giles v. Maryland,* 386 U.S. 66, 87 S.Ct. 793, 17 L.Ed.2d 737 (1967). Wigmore was outspoken in his condemnation of the disallowance of juvenile adjudications to impeach, especially when the witness is the complainant in a case of molesting a minor. 1 Wigmore § 196; 3 *Id.* §§ 924a, 980. The rule recognizes discretion in the judge to effect an accommodation among these various factors by departing from the general principle of exclusion. In deference to the general pattern and policy of juvenile statutes, however, no discretion is accorded when the witness is the accused in a criminal case.

Note to Subdivision (e). The presumption of correctness which ought to attend judicial proceedings supports the position that pendency of an appeal does not preclude use of a conviction for impeachment. *United States v. Empire Packing Co.,* 174 F.2d 16 (7th Cir.1949), cert. denied 337 U.S. 959, 69 S.Ct. 1534, 93 L.Ed. 1758; *Bloch v. United States,* 226 F.2d 185 (9th Cir.1955), cert. denied 350 U.S. 948, 76 S.Ct. 323, 100 L.Ed. 826 and 353 U.S. 959, 77 S.Ct. 868, 1 L.Ed.2d 910; and see *Newman v. United States,* 331 F.2d 968 (8th Cir.1964). *Contra, Campbell v. United States,* 85 U.S.App.D.C. 133, 176 F.2d 45 (1949). The pendency of an appeal is, however, a qualifying circumstance properly considerable.

1974 Enactment

Note to Subdivision (a). Rule 609(a) as submitted by the Court was modeled after Section 133(a) of Public Law 91–358, 14 D.C.Code 305(b)(1), enacted in 1970. The Rule provided that:

> For the purpose of attacking the credibility of a witness, evidence that he has been convicted of a crime is admissible but only if the crime (1) was punishable by death or imprisonment in excess of one year under the law under which he was convicted or (2) involved dishonesty or false statement regardless of the punishment.

As reported to the Committee by the Subcommittee, Rule 609(a) was amended to read as follows:

> For the purpose of attacking the credibility of a witness, evidence that he has been convicted of a crime is admissible only if the crime (1) was punishable by death or imprisonment in excess of one year, unless the court determines that the danger of unfair prejudice outweighs the probative value of the evidence of the conviction, or (2) involved dishonesty or false statement.

In full committee, the provision was amended to permit attack upon the credibility of a witness by prior conviction only if the prior crime involved dishonesty or false statement. While recognizing that the prevailing doctrine in the federal courts and in most States allows a witness to be impeached by evidence of prior felony convictions without restriction as to type, the Committee was of the view that, because of the danger of unfair prejudice in such practice and the deterrent effect upon an accused who might wish to testify, and even upon a witness who was not the accused, cross-examination by evidence of prior conviction should be limited to those kinds of convictions bearing directly on credibility, *i.e.,* crimes involving dishonesty or false statement.

Note to Subdivision (b). Rule 609(b) as submitted by the Court was modeled after Section 133(a) of Public Law 91–358, 14 D.C.Code 305(b)(2)(B), enacted in 1970. The Rule provided:

> Evidence of a conviction under this rule is not admissible if a period of more than ten years has elapsed since the date of the release of the witness from confinement imposed for his most recent conviction, or the expiration of the period of his parole, probation, or sentence granted or imposed with respect to his most recent conviction, whichever is the later date.

Under this formulation, a witness' entire past record of criminal convictions could be used for impeachment (provided the conviction met the standard of subdivision (a)), if the witness had been most recently released from confinement, or the period of his parole or probation had expired, within ten years of the conviction.

The Committee amended the Rule to read in the text of the 1971 Advisory Committee version to provide that upon the expiration of ten years from the date of a conviction of a witness, or of his release from confinement for that offense, that conviction may no longer be used for impeachment. The Committee was of the view that after ten years following a person's release from confinement (or from the date of his conviction) the probative value of the conviction with respect to that person's credibility diminished to a point where it should no longer be admissible.

Note to Subdivision (c). Rule 609(c) as submitted by the Court provided in part that evidence of a witness' prior conviction is not admissible to attack his credibility if the conviction was the subject of a pardon, annulment, or other equivalent procedure, based on a showing of rehabilitation, and the witness has not been convicted of a subsequent crime. The Committee amended the Rule to provide that the "subsequent crime" must have been "punishable by death or imprisonment in excess of one year", on the ground that a subsequent conviction of an offense not a felony is insufficient to rebut the finding that the witness has been rehabilitated. The Committee also intends that the words "based on a finding of the rehabilitation of the person convicted" apply not only to "certificate of rehabilitation, or other equivalent procedure", but also to "pardon" and "annulment.". House Report No. 93–650.

Note to Subdivision (a). As proposed by the Supreme Court, the rule would allow the use of prior convictions to impeach if the crime was a felony or a misdemeanor if the misdemeanor involved dishonesty or false statement. As modified by the House, the rule would admit prior convictions for impeachment purposes only if the offense, whether felony or misdemeanor, involved dishonesty or false statement.

The committee has adopted a modified version of the House-passed rule. In your committee's view, the danger of unfair prejudice is far greater when the accused, as opposed to other witnesses, testifies, because the jury may be prejudiced not merely on the question of credibility but also on the ultimate question of guilt or innocence. Therefore, with respect to defendants, the committee agreed with the House limitation that only offenses involved false statement or dishonesty may be used. By that phrase, the committee means crimes such as perjury or subornation of perjury, false statement, criminal fraud, embezzlement or false pretense, or any other offense, in the nature of *crimen falsi* the commission of which involves some element of untruthfulness, deceit or falsification bearing on the accused's propensity to testify truthfully.

With respect to other witnesses, in addition to any prior conviction involving false statement or dishonesty, any other felony may be used to impeach if, and only if, the court finds that the probative value of such evidence outweighs its prejudicial effect against the party offering that witness.

Notwithstanding this provision, proof of any prior offense otherwise admissible under Rule 404 could still be offered for the purposes sanctioned by that rule. Furthermore, the committee intends that notwithstanding this rule, a defendant's misrepresentation regarding the existence or nature of prior convictions may be met by rebuttal evidence, including the record of such prior convictions. Similarly, such records may be offered to rebut representations made by the defendant regarding his attitude toward or willingness to commit a general category of offense, although denials or other representations by the defendant regarding the specific conduct which forms the basis of the charge against him shall not make prior convictions admissible to rebut such statement.

In regard to either type of representation, of course, prior convictions may be offered in rebuttal only if the defendant's statement is made in response to defense counsel's questions or is made gratuitously in the course of cross-examination. Prior convictions may not be offered as rebuttal evidence if the prosecution has sought to circumvent the purpose of this rule by asking questions which elicit such representations from the defendant.

One other clarifying amendment has been added to this subsection, that is, to provide that the admissibility of evidence of a prior conviction is permitted only upon cross-examination of a witness. It is not admissible if a person does not testify. It is to be understood, however, that a court record of a prior conviction is admissible to prove that conviction if the witness has forgotten or denies its existence.

Note to Subdivision (b). Although convictions over ten years old generally do not have much probative value, there may be exceptional circumstances under which the conviction substantially bears on the credibility of the witness. Rather than exclude all convictions over 10 years old, the committee adopted an amendment in the form of a final clause to the section granting the court discretion to admit convictions over 10 years old, but only upon a determination by the court that the probative value of the conviction supported by specific facts and circumstances, substantially outweighs its prejudicial effect.

It is intended that convictions over 10 years old will be admitted very rarely and only in exceptional circumstances. The rules provide that the decision be supported by specific facts and circumstances thus requiring the court to make specific findings on the record as to the particular facts and circumstances it has considered in determining that the probative value of the conviction substantially outweighs its prejudicial impact. It is expected that, in fairness, the court will give the party against whom the conviction is introduced a full and adequate opportunity to contest its admission. Senate Report No. 93–1277.

Rule 609 defines when a party may use evidence of a prior conviction in order to impeach a witness. The Senate amendments make changes in two subsections of Rule 609.

Note to Subdivision (a). The House bill provides that the credibility of a witness can be attacked by proof of prior conviction of a crime only if the crime involves dishonesty or false statement. The Senate amendment provides that a witness' credibility may be attacked if the crime (1) was punishable by death or imprisonment in excess of one year under the law under which he was convicted or (2) involves dishonesty or false statement, regardless of the punishment.

The Conference adopts the Senate amendment with an amendment. The Conference amendment provides that the credibility of a witness, whether a defendant or someone else, may be attacked by proof of a prior conviction but only if the crime: (1) was punishable by death or imprisonment in excess of one year under the law under which he was convicted and the court determines that the probative value of the conviction outweighs its prejudicial effect to the defendant; or (2) involved dishonesty or false statement regardless of the punishment.

By the phrase "dishonesty and false statement" the Conference means crimes such as perjury or subornation of perjury, false statement, criminal fraud, embezzlement, or false pretense, or any other offense in the nature of *crimen falsi,* the commission of which involves some element of deceit, untruthfulness, or falsification bearing on the accused's propensity to testify truthfully.

The admission of prior convictions involving dishonesty and false statement is not within the discretion of the Court. Such convictions are peculiarly probative of credibility and, under this rule, are always to be admitted. Thus, judicial discretion granted with respect to the admissibility of other prior convictions is not applicable to those involving dishonesty or false statement.

With regard to the discretionary standard established by paragraph (1) of Rule 609(a), the Conference determined that the prejudicial effect to be weighed against the probative value of the conviction is specifically the prejudicial effect *to the defendant.* The danger of prejudice to a witness other than the defendant (such as injury to the witness' reputation in his community) was considered and rejected by the Conference as an element to be weighed in determining admissibility. It was the judgment of the Conference that the danger of prejudice to a nondefendant witness is outweighed by the need for the trier of fact to have as much relevant evidence on the issue of credibility as possible. Such evidence should only be excluded where it presents a danger of improperly influencing the outcome of the trial by persuading the trier of fact to convict the defendant on the basis of his prior criminal record.

Note to Subdivision (b). The House bill provides in subsection (b) that evidence of conviction of a crime may not be used for impeachment purposes under subsection (a) if more than ten years have elapsed since the date of the conviction or the date the witness was released from confinement imposed for the conviction, whichever is later. The Senate amendment permits the use of convictions older than ten years, if the court determines, in the interests of justice, that the probative value of the conviction, supported by specific facts and circumstances, substantially outweighs its prejudicial effect.

The Conference adopts the Senate amendment with an amendment requiring notice by a party that he intends to request that the court allow him to use a conviction older than ten years. The Conferees anticipate that a written notice, in order to give the adversary a fair opportunity to contest the use of the evidence, will ordinarily include such information as the date of the conviction, the jurisdiction, and the offense or statute involved. In order to eliminate the possibility that the flexibility of this provision may impair the ability of a party-opponent to prepare for trial, the Conferees intend that the notice provision operate to avoid surprise. House Report No. 93–1597.

1987 Amendment

The amendments are technical. No substantive change is intended.

1990 Amendment

The amendment to Rule 609(a) makes two changes in the rule. The first change removes from the rule the limitation that the conviction may only be elicited during cross-examination, a limitation that virtually every circuit has found to be inapplicable. It is common for witnesses to reveal on direct examination their convictions to "remove the sting" of the impeachment. *See e.g., United States v. Bad Cob,* 560 F.2d 877 (8th Cir.1977). The amendment does not contemplate that a court will necessarily permit proof of prior convictions through testimony, which might be time-consuming and more prejudicial than proof through a written record. Rules 403 and 611(a) provide sufficient authority for the court to protect against unfair or disruptive methods of proof.

The second change effected by the amendment resolves an ambiguity as to the relationship of Rules 609 and 403 with respect to impeachment of witnesses other than the criminal defendant. *See, Green v. Bock Laundry Machine Co.,* 109 S.Ct. 1981, 490 U.S. 504 (1989). The amendment does not disturb the special balancing test for the criminal defendant who chooses to testify. Thus, the rule recognizes that, in virtually every case in which prior convictions are used to impeach the testifying defendant, the defendant faces a unique risk of prejudice—*i.e.,* the danger that convictions that would be excluded under Fed.R.Evid. 404 will be misused by a jury as propensity evidence despite their introduction solely for impeachment purposes. Although the rule does not forbid all use of convictions to impeach a defendant, it requires that the government show that the probative value of convictions as impeachment evidence outweighs their prejudicial effect.

Prior to the amendment, the rule appeared to give the defendant the benefit of the special balancing test when defense witnesses other than the defendant were called to testify. In practice, however, the concern about unfairness to the defendant is most acute when the defendant's own convictions are offered as evidence. Almost all of the decided cases concern this type of impeachment, and the amendment does not deprive the defendant of any meaningful protection, since Rule 403 now clearly protects against unfair impeachment of any defense witness other than the defendant. There are cases in which a defendant might be prejudiced when a defense witness is impeached. Such cases may arise, for example, when the witness bears a special relationship to the defendant such that the defendant is likely to suffer some spill-over effect from impeachment of the witness.

The amendment also protects other litigants from unfair impeachment of their witnesses. The danger of prejudice from the use of prior convictions is not confined to criminal defendants. Although the danger that prior convictions will be misused as character evidence is particularly acute when the defendant is impeached, the danger exists in other situations as well. The amendment reflects the view that it is desirable to protect all litigants from the unfair use of prior convictions, and that the ordinary balancing test of Rule 403, which provides that evidence shall not be excluded unless its prejudicial effect substantially outweighs its probative value, is appropriate for assessing the admissibility of prior convictions for impeachment of any witness other than a criminal defendant.

The amendment reflects a judgment that decisions interpreting Rule 609(a) as requiring a trial court to admit convictions in civil cases that have little, if anything, to do with credibility reach undesirable results. *See, e.g., Diggs v. Lyons,* 741 F.2d 577 (3d Cir.1984), *cert. denied,* 105 S.Ct. 2157 (1985). The amendment provides the same protection against unfair prejudice arising from prior convictions used for impeachment purposes as the rules provide for other evidence. The amendment finds support in decided cases. *See, e.g., Petty v. Ideco,* 761 F.2d 1146 (5th Cir.1985); *Czaka v. Hickman,* 703 F.2d 317 (8th Cir.1983).

Fewer decided cases address the question whether Rule 609(a) provides any protection against unduly prejudicial prior convictions used to impeach government witnesses. Some courts have read Rule 609(a) as giving the government no protection for its witnesses. *See, e.g., United States v. Thorne,* 547 F.2d 56 (8th Cir.1976); *United States v. Nevitt,* 563 F.2d 406 (9th Cir.1977), *cert. denied,* 444 U.S. 847 (1979). This approach also is rejected by the amendment. There are cases in which impeachment of government witnesses with prior convictions that have little, if anything, to do with credibility may result in unfair prejudice to the government's interest in a fair trial and unnecessary embarrassment to a witness. Fed.R.Evid. 412 already recognizes this and excluded certain evidence of past sexual behavior in the context of prosecutions for sexual assaults.

The amendment applies the general balancing test of Rule 403 to protect all litigants against unfair impeachment of witnesses. The balancing test protects civil litigants, the government in criminal cases, and the defendant in a criminal case who calls other witnesses. The amendment addresses prior convictions offered under Rule 609, not for other purposes, and does not run afoul, therefore, of *Davis v. Alaska,* 415 U.S. 308 (1974). *Davis* involved the use of a prior juvenile adjudication not to prove a past law violation, but to prove bias. The defendant in a criminal case has the right to demonstrate the bias of a witness and to be assured a fair trial, but not to unduly prejudice a trier of fact. *See generally* Rule 412. In any case in which the trial court believes that confrontation rights require admission of impeachment evidence, obviously the Constitution would take precedence over the rule.

The probability that prior convictions of an ordinary government witness will be unduly prejudicial is low in most criminal cases. Since the behavior of the witness is not the issue in dispute in most cases, there is little chance that the trier of fact will misuse the convictions offered as impeachment evidence as propensity evidence. Thus, trial courts will be skeptical when the government objects to impeachment of its witnesses with prior convictions. Only when the government is able to point to a real danger of prejudice that is sufficient to outweigh substantially the probative value of the conviction for impeachment purposes will the conviction be excluded.

The amendment continues to divide subdivision (a) into subsections (1) and (2) thus facilitating retrieval under current computerized research programs which distinguish the two provisions. The Committee recommended no substantive change in subdivision (a)(2), even though some cases raise a concern about the proper interpretation of the words "dishonesty or false statement." These words were used but not explained in the original Advisory Committee Note accompanying Rule 609. Congress extensively debated the rule, and the Report of the House and Senate Conference Committee states that "[b]y the phrase 'dishonesty and false statement,' the Conference means crimes such as perjury, subornation of perjury, false statement, criminal fraud, embezzlement, or false pretense, or any other offense in the nature of *crimen falsi*, commission of which involves some element of deceit, untruthfulness, or falsification bearing on the accused's propensity to testify truthfully." The Advisory Committee concluded that the Conference Report provides sufficient guidance to trial courts and that no amendment is necessary, notwithstanding some decisions that take an unduly broad view of "dishonesty," admitting convictions such as for bank robbery or bank larceny. Subsection (a)(2) continues to apply to any witness, including a criminal defendant.

Finally, the Committee determined that it was unnecessary to add to the rule language stating that, when a prior conviction is offered under Rule 609, the trial court is to consider the probative value of the prior conviction *for impeachment*, not for other purposes. The Committee concluded that the title of the rule, its first sentence, and its placement among the impeachment rules clearly establish that evidence offered under Rule 609 is offered only for purposes of impeachment.

Rule 610. Religious Beliefs or Opinions

Evidence of the beliefs or opinions of a witness on matters of religion is not admissible for the purpose of showing that by reason of their nature the witness' credibility is impaired or enhanced.

(Pub.L. 93–595, § 1, Jan. 2, 1975, 88 Stat.1936; Mar. 2, 1987, eff. Oct. 1, 1987.)

ADVISORY COMMITTEE NOTES

1972 Proposed Rules

While the rule forecloses inquiry into the religious beliefs or opinions of a witness for the purpose of showing that his character for truthfulness is affected by their nature, an inquiry for the purpose of showing interest or bias because of them is not within the prohibition. Thus disclosure of affiliation with a church which is a party to the litigation would be allowable under the rule. Cf. Tucker v. Reil, 51 Ariz. 357, 77 P.2d 203 (1938). To the same effect, though less specifically worded, is California Evidence Code § 789. See 3 Wigmore § 936.

1987 Amendment

The amendment is technical. No substantive change is intended.

Rule 611. Mode and Order of Interrogation and Presentation

(a) Control by court. The court shall exercise reasonable control over the mode and order of interrogating witnesses and presenting evidence so as to (1) make the interrogation and presentation effective for the ascertainment of the truth, (2) avoid needless consumption of time, and (3) protect witnesses from harassment or undue embarrassment.

(b) Scope of cross-examination. Cross-examination should be limited to the subject matter of the direct examination and matters affecting the credibility of the witness. The court may, in the exercise of discretion, permit inquiry into additional matters as if on direct examination.

(c) Leading questions. Leading questions should not be used on the direct examination of a witness except as may be necessary to develop the witness' testimony. Ordinarily leading questions should be permitted on cross-examination. When a party calls a hostile witness, an adverse party, or a witness identified with an adverse party, interrogation may be by leading questions.

(Pub.L. 93–595, § 1, Jan. 2, 1975, 88 Stat. 1936; Mar. 2, 1987, eff. Oct. 1, 1987.)

ADVISORY COMMITTEE NOTES

1972 Proposed Rules

Note to Subdivision (a). Spelling out detailed rules to govern the mode and order of interrogating witnesses and presenting evidence is neither desirable nor feasible. The ultimate responsibility for the effective working of the adversary system rests with the judge. The rule sets forth the objectives which he should seek to attain.

Item (1) restates in broad terms the power and obligation of the judge as developed under common law principles. It covers such concerns as whether testimony shall be in the form of a free narrative or responses to specific questions, McCormick § 5, the order of calling witnesses and presenting evidence, 6 Wigmore § 1867, the use of demonstrative evidence, McCormick § 179, and the many other questions arising during the course of a trial which can be solved only by the judge's common sense and fairness in view of the particular circumstances.

Item (2) is addressed to avoidance of needless consumption of time, a matter of daily concern in the disposition of cases. A companion piece is found in the discretion vested in the judge to exclude evidence as a waste of time in Rule 403(b).

Item (3) calls for a judgment under the particular circumstances whether interrogation tactics entail harassment or undue embarrassment. Pertinent circumstances include the importance of the testimony, the nature of the inquiry, its relevance to credibility, waste of time, and confusion. McCormick § 42. In *Alford v. United States,* 282 U.S. 687, 694, 51 S.Ct. 218, 75 L.Ed. 624 (1931), the Court pointed out that, while the trial judge should protect the witness from questions which "go beyond the bounds of proper cross-examination merely to harass, annoy or humiliate," this protection by no means forecloses efforts to discredit the witness. Reference to the transcript of the prosecutor's cross-examination in *Berger v. United States,* 295 U.S. 78, 55 S.Ct. 629, 79 L.Ed. 1314 (1935), serves to lay at rest any doubts as to the need for judicial control in this area.

The inquiry into specific instances of conduct of a witness allowed under Rule 608(b) is, of course, subject to this rule.

Note to Subdivision (b). The tradition in the federal courts and in numerous state courts has been to limit the scope of cross-examination to matters testified to on direct, plus matters bearing upon the credibility of the witness.

Various reasons have been advanced to justify the rule of limited cross-examination. (1) A party vouches for his own witness but only to the extent of matters elicited on direct. *Resurrection Gold Mining Co. v. Fortune Gold Mining Co.*, 129 F. 668, 675 (8th Cir.1904), quoted in Maguire, Weinstein, et al., Cases on Evidence 277, n. 38 (5th ed. 1965). But the concept of vouching is discredited, and Rule 607 rejects it. (2) A party cannot ask his own witness leading questions. This is a problem properly solved in terms of what is necessary for a proper development of the testimony rather than by a mechanistic formula similar to the vouching concept. See discussion under subdivision (c). (3) A practice of limited cross-examination promotes orderly presentation of the case. *Finch v. Weiner*, 109 Conn. 616, 145 A. 31 (1929). While this latter reason has merit, the matter is essentially one of the order of presentation and not one in which involvement at the appellate level is likely to prove fruitful. See, for example, *Moyer v. Aetna Life Ins. Co.*, 126 F.2d 141 (3rd Cir.1942); *Butler v. New York Central R. Co.*, 253 F.2d 281 (7th Cir.1958); *United States v. Johnson*, 285 F.2d 35 (9th Cir.1960); *Union Automobile Indemnity Ass'n v. Capitol Indemnity Ins. Co.*, 310 F.2d 318 (7th Cir.1962). In evaluating these considerations, McCormick says:

"The foregoing considerations favoring the wide-open or restrictive rules may well be thought to be fairly evenly balanced. There is another factor, however, which seems to swing the balance overwhelmingly in favor of the wide-open rule. This is the consideration of economy of time and energy. Obviously, the wide-open rule presents little or no opportunity for dispute in its application. The restrictive practice in all its forms, on the other hand, is productive in many court rooms, of continual bickering over the choice of the numerous variations of the 'scope of the direct' criterion, and of their application to particular cross-questions. These controversies are often reventilated on appeal, and reversals for error in their determination are frequent. Observance of these vague and ambiguous restrictions is a matter of constant and hampering concern to the cross-examiner. If these efforts, delays and misprisions were the necessary incidents to the guarding of substantive rights or the fundamentals of fair trial, they might be worth the cost. As the price of the choice of an obviously debatable regulation of the order of evidence, the sacrifice seems misguided. The American Bar Association's Committee for the Improvement of the Law of Evidence for the year 1937–38 said this:

'The rule limiting cross-examination to the precise subject of the direct examination is probably the most frequent rule (except the Opinion rule) leading in the trial practice today to refined and technical quibbles which obstruct the progress of the trial, confuse the jury, and give rise to appeal on technical grounds only. Some of the instances in which Supreme Courts have ordered new trials for the mere transgression of this rule about the order of evidence have been astounding.

'We recommend that the rule allowing questions upon any part of the issue known to the witness * * * be adopted. * * *'" McCormick, § 27, p. 51. See also 5 Moore's Federal Practice ¶ 43.10 (2nd ed. 1964).

The provision of the second sentence, that the judge may in the interests of justice limit inquiry into new matters on cross-examination, is designed for those situations in which the result otherwise would be confusion, complication, or protraction of the case, not as a matter of rule but as demonstrable in the actual development of the particular case.

The rule does not purport to determine the extent to which an accused who elects to testify thereby waives his privilege against self-incrimination. The question is a constitutional one, rather than a mere matter of administering the trial. Under *Simmons v. United States*, 390 U.S. 377, 88 S.Ct. 967, 19 L.Ed.2d 1247 (1968), no general waiver occurs when the accused testifies on such preliminary matters as the validity of a search and seizure or the admissibility of a confession. Rule 104(d), *supra*. When he testifies on the merits, however, can he foreclose inquiry into an aspect or element of the crime by avoiding it on direct? The affirmative answer given in *Tucker v. United States*, 5 F.2d 818 (8th Cir.1925), is inconsistent with the description of the waiver as extending to "all other relevant facts" in *Johnson v. United States*, 318 U.S. 189, 195, 63 S.Ct. 549, 87 L.Ed. 704 (1943). See also *Brown v. United States*, 356 U.S. 148, 78 S.Ct. 622, 2 L.Ed.2d 589 (1958). The situation of an accused who desires to testify on some but not all counts of a multiple-count indictment is one to be approached, in the first instance at least, as a problem of severance under Rule 14 of the Federal Rules of Criminal Procedure. *Cross v. United States*, 118 U.S.App. D.C. 324, 335 F.2d 987 (1964). Cf. *United States v. Baker*, 262 F.Supp. 657, 686 (D.D.C.1966). In all events, the extent of the waiver of the privilege against self-incrimination ought not to be determined as a by-product of a rule on scope of cross-examination.

Note to Subdivision (c). The rule continues the traditional view that the suggestive powers of the leading question are as a general proposition undesirable. Within this tradition, however, numerous exceptions have achieved recognition: The witness who is hostile, unwilling, or biased; the child witness or the adult with communication problems; the witness whose recollection is exhausted; and undisputed preliminary matters. 3 Wigmore §§ 774–778. An almost total unwillingness to reverse for infractions has been manifested by appellate courts. See cases cited in 3 Wigmore § 770. The matter clearly falls within the area of control by the judge over the mode and order of interrogation and presentation and accordingly is phrased in words of suggestion rather than command.

The rule also conforms to tradition in making the use of leading questions on cross-examination a matter of right. The purpose of the qualification "ordinarily" is to furnish a basis for denying the use of leading questions when the cross-examination is cross-examination in form only and not in fact, as for example the "cross-examination" of a party by his own counsel after being called by the opponent (savoring more of re-direct) or of an insured defendant who proves to be friendly to the plaintiff.

The final sentence deals with categories of witnesses automatically regarded and treated as hostile. Rule 43(b) of the Federal Rules of Civil Procedure has included only "an adverse party or an officer, director, or managing agent of a public or private corporation or of a partnership or association which is an adverse party." This limitation virtually to persons whose statements would stand as admissions is believed to be an unduly narrow concept of those who may safely be regarded as hostile without further demonstration. See, for example, *Maryland Casualty Co. v. Kador*, 225 F.2d 120 (5th Cir.1955), and *Degelos v. Fidelity and Casualty Co.*, 313 F.2d 809 (5th Cir.1963), holding despite the language of

Rule 43(b) that an insured fell within it, though not a party in an action under the Louisiana direct action statute. The phrase of the rule, "witness identified with" an adverse party, is designed to enlarge the category of persons thus callable.

1974 Enactment

Note to Subdivision (b). As submitted by the Court, Rule 611(b) provided:

> A witness may be cross-examined on any matter relevant to any issue in the case, including credibility. In the interests of justice, the judge may limit cross-examination with respect to matters not testified to on direct examination.

The Committee amended this provision to return to the rule which prevails in the federal courts and thirty-nine State jurisdictions. As amended, the Rule is in the text of the 1969 Advisory Committee draft. It limits cross-examination to credibility and to matters testified to on direct examination, unless the judge permits more, in which event the cross-examiner must proceed as if on direct examination. This traditional rule facilitates orderly presentation by each party at trial. Further, in light of existing discovery procedures, there appears to be no need to abandon the traditional rule.

Note to Subdivision (c). The third sentence of Rule 611(c) as submitted by the Court provided that:

> In civil cases, a party is entitled to call an adverse party or witness identified with him and interrogate by leading questions.

The Committee amended this Rule to permit leading questions to be used with respect to any hostile witness, not only an adverse party or person identified with such adverse party. The Committee also substituted the word "When" for the phrase "In civil cases" to reflect the possibility that in criminal cases a defendant may be entitled to call witnesses identified with the government, in which event the Committee believed the defendant should be permitted to inquire with leading questions. House Report No. 93–650.

Note to Subdivision (b). Rule 611(b) as submitted by the Supreme Court permitted a broad scope of cross-examination: "cross-examination on any matter relevant to any issue in the case" unless the judge, in the interests of justice, limited the scope of cross-examination.

The House narrowed the Rule to the more traditional practice of limiting cross-examination to the subject matter of direct examination (and credibility), but with discretion in the judge to permit inquiry into additional matters in situations where that would aid in the development of the evidence or otherwise facilitate the conduct of the trial.

The committee agrees with the House amendment. Although there are good arguments in support of broad cross-examination from prospectives of developing all relevant evidence, we believe the factors of insuring an orderly and predictable development of the evidence weigh in favor of the narrower rule, especially when discretion is given to the trial judge to permit inquiry into additional matters. The committee expressly approves this discretion and believes it will permit sufficient flexibility allowing a broader scope of cross-examination whenever appropriate.

The House amendment providing broader discretionary cross-examination permitted inquiry into additional matters only as if on direct examination. As a general rule, we concur with this limitation, however, we would understand that this limitation would not preclude the utilization of leading questions if the conditions of subsection (c) of this rule were met, bearing in mind the judge's discretion in any case to limit the scope of cross-examination [see McCormick on Evidence, §§ 24–26 (especially 24) (2d ed. 1972)].

Further, the committee has received correspondence from Federal judges commenting on the applicability of this rule to section 1407 of title 28. It is the committee's judgment that this rule as reported by the House is flexible enough to provide sufficiently broad cross-examination in appropriate situations in multidistrict litigation.

Note to Subdivision (c). As submitted by the Supreme Court, the rule provided: "In civil cases, a party is entitled to call an adverse party or witness identified with him and interrogate by leading questions."

The final sentence of subsection (c) was amended by the House for the purpose of clarifying the fact that a "hostile witness"—that is a witness who is hostile in fact—could be subject to interrogation by leading questions. The rule as submitted by the Supreme Court declared certain witnesses hostile as a matter of law and thus subject to interrogation by leading questions without any showing of hostility in fact. These were adverse parties or witnesses identified with adverse parties. However, the wording of the first sentence of subsection (c) while generally prohibiting the use of leading questions on direct examination, also provides "except as may be necessary to develop his testimony." Further, the first paragraph of the Advisory Committee note explaining the subsection makes clear that they intended that leading questions could be asked of a hostile witness or a witness who was unwilling or biased and even though that witness was not associated with an adverse party. Thus, we question whether the House amendment was necessary.

However, concluding that it was not intended to affect the meaning of the first sentence of the subsection and was intended solely to clarify the fact that leading questions are permissible in the interrogation of a witness, who is hostile in fact, the committee accepts that House amendment.

The final sentence of this subsection was also amended by the House to cover criminal as well as civil cases. The committee accepts this amendment, but notes that it may be difficult in criminal cases to determine when a witness is "identified with an adverse party," and thus the rule should be applied with caution. Senate Report No. 93–1277.

1987 Amendment

The amendment is technical. No substantive change is intended.

Rule 612. Writing Used to Refresh Memory

Except as otherwise provided in criminal proceedings by section 3500 of title 18, United States Code, if a witness uses a writing to refresh memory for the purpose of testifying, either—

(1) while testifying, or

(2) before testifying, if the court in its discretion determines it is necessary in the interests of justice,

an adverse party is entitled to have the writing produced at the hearing, to inspect it, to cross-examine the witness thereon, and to introduce in evidence

those portions which relate to the testimony of the witness. If it is claimed that the writing contains matters not related to the subject matter of the testimony the court shall examine the writing in camera, excise any portions not so related, and order delivery of the remainder to the party entitled thereto. Any portion withheld over objections shall be preserved and made available to the appellate court in the event of an appeal. If a writing is not produced or delivered pursuant to order under this rule, the court shall make any order justice requires, except that in criminal cases when the prosecution elects not to comply, the order shall be one striking the testimony or, if the court in its discretion determines that the interests of justice so require, declaring a mistrial.
(Pub.L. 93–595, § 1, Jan. 2, 1975, 88 Stat. 1936; Mar. 2, 1987, eff. Oct. 1, 1987.)

ADVISORY COMMITTEE NOTES

1972 Proposed Rules

The treatment of writings used to refresh recollection while on the stand is in accord with settled doctrine. McCormick § 9, p. 15. The bulk of the case law has, however, denied the existence of any right to access by the opponent when the writing is used prior to taking the stand, though the judge may have discretion in the matter. *Goldman v. United States,* 316 U.S. 129, 62 S.Ct. 993, 86 L.Ed. 1322 (1942); *Needelman v. United States,* 261 F.2d 802 (5th Cir.1958), cert. dismissed 362 U.S. 600, 80 S.Ct. 960, 4 L.Ed.2d 980, rehearing denied 363 U.S. 858, 80 S.Ct. 1606, 4 L.Ed.2d 1739, Annot., 82 A.L.R.2d 473, 562 and 7 A.L.R.3d 181, 247. An increasing group of cases has repudiated the distinction. *People v. Scott,* 29 Ill.2d 97, 193 N.E.2d 814 (1963); *State v. Mucci,* 25 N.J. 423, 136 A.2d 761 (1957); *State v. Hunt,* 25 N.J. 514, 138 A.2d 1 (1958); *State v. Deslovers,* 40 R.I. 89, 100 A. 64 (1917), and this position is believed to be correct. As Wigmore put it, "the risk of imposition and the need of safeguard is just as great" in both situations. 3 Wigmore § 762, p. 111. To the same effect is McCormick, § 9, p. 17.

The purpose of the phrase "for the purpose of testifying" is to safeguard against using the rule as a pretext for wholesale exploration of an opposing party's files and to insure that access is limited only to those writings which may fairly be said in fact to have an impact upon the testimony of the witness.

The purpose of the rule is the same as that of the *Jencks* statute, 18 U.S.C. § 3500: to promote the search of credibility and memory. The same sensitivity to disclosure of government files may be involved; hence the rule is expressly made subject to the statute, subdivision (a) of which provides: "In any criminal prosecution brought by the United States, no statement or report in the possession of the United States which was made by a Government witness or prospective Government witness (other than the defendant) shall be the subject of subpena, discovery, or inspection until said witness has testified on direct examination in the trial of the case." Items falling within the purview of the statute are producible only as provided by its terms, *Palermo v. United States,* 360 U.S. 343, 351 (1959), and disclosure under the rule is limited similarly by the statutory conditions. With this limitation in mind, some differences of application may be noted. The *Jencks* statute applies only to statements of witnesses; the rule is not so limited. The statute applies only to criminal cases; the rule applies to all cases. The statute applies only to government witnesses; the rule applies to all witnesses. The statute contains no requirement that the statement be consulted for purposes of refreshment before or while testifying; the rule so requires. Since many writings would qualify under either statute or rule, a substantial overlap exists, but the identity of procedures makes this of no importance.

The consequences of nonproduction by the government in a criminal case are those of the *Jencks* statute, striking the testimony or in exceptional cases a mistrial. 18 U.S.C. § 3500(d). In other cases these alternatives are unduly limited, and such possibilities as contempt, dismissal, finding issues against the offender, and the like are available. See Rule 16(g) of the Federal Rules of Criminal Procedure and Rule 37(b) of the Federal Rules of Civil Procedure for appropriate sanctions.

1974 Enactment

As submitted to Congress, Rule 612 provided that except as set forth in 18 U.S.C. 3500, if a witness uses a writing to refresh his memory for the purpose of testifying, "either before or while testifying," an adverse party is entitled to have the writing produced at the hearing, to inspect it, to cross-examine the witness on it, and to introduce in evidence those portions relating to the witness' testimony. The Committee amended the Rule so as still to require the production of writings used by a witness while testifying, but to render the production of writings used by a witness to refresh his memory before testifying discretionary with the court in the interests of justice, as is the case under existing federal law. See Goldman v. United States, 316 U.S. 129 (1942). The Committee considered that permitting an adverse party to require the production of writings used before testifying could result in fishing expeditions among a multitude of papers which a witness may have used in preparing for trial.

The Committee intends that nothing in the Rule be construed as barring the assertion of a privilege with respect to writings used by a witness to refresh his memory. House Report No. 93–650.

1987 Amendment

The amendment is technical. No substantive change is intended.

Rule 613. Prior Statements of Witnesses

(a) Examining witness concerning prior statement. In examining a witness concerning a prior statement made by the witness, whether written or not, the statement need not be shown nor its contents disclosed to the witness at that time, but on request the same shall be shown or disclosed to opposing counsel.

(b) Extrinsic evidence of prior inconsistent statement of witness. Extrinsic evidence of a prior inconsistent statement by a witness is not admissible unless the witness is afforded an opportunity to explain or deny the same and the opposite party is afforded an opportunity to interrogate the witness thereon, or the interests of justice otherwise require. This provision does not apply to admissions of a party-opponent as defined in rule 801(d)(2).

(Pub.L. 93–595, § 1, Jan. 2, 1975, 88 Stat.1936; Mar. 2, 1987, eff. Oct. 1, 1987; Apr. 25, 1988, eff. Nov. 1, 1988.)

ADVISORY COMMITTEE NOTES

1972 Proposed Rules

Note to Subdivision (a). The Queen's Case, 2 Br. & B. 284, 129 Eng.Rep. 976 (1820), laid down the requirement that a cross-examiner, prior to questioning the witness about his own prior statement in writing, must first show it to the witness. Abolished by statute in the country of its origin, the requirement nevertheless gained currency in the United States. The rule abolishes this useless impediment, to cross-examination. Ladd, Some Observations on Credibility: Impeachment of Witnesses, 52 Cornell L.Q. 239, 246–247 (1967); McCormick § 28; 4 Wigmore §§ 1259–1260. Both oral and written statements are included.

The provision for disclosure to counsel is designed to protect against unwarranted insinuations that a statement has been made when the fact is to the contrary.

The rule does not defeat the application of Rule 1002 relating to production of the original when the contents of a writing are sought to be proved. Nor does it defeat the application of Rule 26(b)(3) of the Rules of Civil Procedure, as revised, entitling a person on request to a copy of his own statement, though the operation of the latter may be suspended temporarily.

Note to Subdivision (b). The familiar foundation requirement that an impeaching statement first be shown to the witness before it can be proved by extrinsic evidence is preserved but with some modifications. See Ladd, Some Observations on Credibility: Impeachment of Witnesses, 52 Cornell L.Q. 239, 247 (1967). The traditional insistence that the attendance of the witness be directed to the statement on cross-examination is relaxed in favor of simply providing the witness an opportunity to explain and the opposite party an opportunity to examine on the statement, with no specification of any particular time or sequence. Under this procedure, several collusive witnesses can be examined before disclosure of a joint prior inconsistent statement. See Comment to California Evidence Code § 770. Also, dangers of oversight are reduced. See McCormick § 37, p. 68.

In order to allow for such eventualities as the witness becoming unavailable by the time the statement is discovered, a measure of discretion is conferred upon the judge. Similar provisions are found in California Evidence Code § 770 and New Jersey Evidence Rule 22(b).

Under principles of *expression unius* the rule does not apply to impeachment by evidence of prior inconsistent conduct. The use of inconsistent statements to impeach a hearsay declaration is treated in Rule 806.

1987 Amendment

The amendments are technical. No substantive change is intended.

1988 Amendment

The amendment is technical. No substantive change is intended.

Rule 614. Calling and Interrogation of Witnesses by Court

(a) Calling by court. The court may, on its own motion or at the suggestion of a party, call witnesses, and all parties are entitled to cross-examine witnesses thus called.

(b) Interrogation by court. The court may interrogate witnesses, whether called by itself or by a party.

(c) Objections. Objections to the calling of witnesses by the court or to interrogation by it may be made at the time or at the next available opportunity when the jury is not present.

(Pub.L. 93–595, § 1, Jan. 2, 1975, 88 Stat.1937.)

ADVISORY COMMITTEE NOTES

1972 Proposed Rules

Note to Subdivision (a). While exercised more frequently in criminal than in civil cases, the authority of the judge to call witnesses is well established. McCormick § 8, p. 14; Maguire, Weinstein, et al., Cases on Evidence 303–304 (5th ed. 1965); 9 Wigmore § 2484. One reason for the practice, the old rule against impeaching one's own witness, no longer exists by virtue of Rule 607, *supra*. Other reasons remain, however, to justify the continuation of the practice of calling court's witnesses. The right to cross-examine, with all it implies, is assured. The tendency of juries to associate a witness with the party calling him, regardless of technical aspects of vouching, is avoided. And the judge is not imprisoned within the case as made by the parties.

Note to Subdivision (b). The authority of the judge to question witnesses is also well established. McCormick § 8, pp. 12–13; Maguire, Weinstein, et al., Cases on Evidence 737–739 (5th ed. 1965); 3 Wigmore § 784. The authority is, of course, abused when the judge abandons his proper role and assumes that of advocate, but the manner in which interrogation should be conducted and the proper extent of its exercise are not susceptible of formulation in a rule. The omission in no sense precludes courts of review from continuing to reverse for abuse.

Note to Subdivision (c). The provision relating to objections is designed to relieve counsel of the embarrassment attendant upon objecting to questions by the judge in the presence of the jury, while at the same time assuring that objections are made in apt time to afford the opportunity to take possible corrective measures. Compare the "automatic" objection feature of Rule 605 when the judge is called as a witness.

Rule 615. Exclusion of Witnesses

At the request of a party the court shall order witnesses excluded so that they cannot hear the testimony of other witnesses, and it may make the order of its own motion. This rule does not authorize exclusion of (1) a party who is a natural person, or (2) an officer or employee of a party which is not a natural person designated as its representative by its attorney, or (3) a person whose presence is shown by a party to be essential to the presentation of the party's cause, or (4) a person authorized by statute to be present.

(Pub.L. 93–595, § 1, Jan. 2, 1975, 88 Stat.1937; Mar. 2, 1987, eff. Oct. 1, 1987; Apr. 25, 1988, eff. Nov. 1, 1988; Pub.L. 100–690, Nov. 18, 1988, Title VII, § 7075(a), 102 Stat. 4405; Apr. 24, 1998, eff. Dec. 1, 1998.)

ADVISORY COMMITTEE NOTES

1972 Proposed Rules

The efficacy of excluding or sequestering witnesses has long been recognized as a means of discouraging and exposing fabrication, inaccuracy, and collusion. 6 Wigmore §§ 1837–1838. The authority of the judge is admitted, the only question being whether the matter is committed to his discretion or one of right. The rule takes the latter position. No time is specified for making the request.

Several categories of persons are excepted. (1) Exclusion of persons who are parties would raise serious problems of confrontation and due process. Under accepted practice they are not subject to exclusion. 6 Wigmore § 1841. (2) As the equivalent of the right of a natural-person party to be present, a party which is not a natural person is entitled to have a representative present. Most of the cases have involved allowing a police officer who has been in charge of an investigation to remain in court despite the fact that he will be a witness. United States v. Infanzon, 235 F.2d 318, (2d Cir.1956); *Portomene v. United States,* 221 F.2d 582 (5th Cir.1955); *Powell v. United States,* 208 F.2d 618 (6th Cir. 1953); *Jones v. United States,* 252 F.Supp. 781 (W.D.Okl. 1966). Designation of the representative by the attorney rather than by the client may at first glance appear to be an inversion of the attorney-client relationship, but it may be assumed that the attorney will follow the wishes of the client, and the solution is simple and workable. See California Evidence Code § 777. (3) The category contemplates such persons as an agent who handled the transaction being litigated or an expert needed to advise counsel in the management of the litigation. See 6 Wigmore § 1841, n. 4.

1974 Enactment

Many district courts permit government counsel to have an investigative agent at counsel table throughout the trial although the agent is or may be a witness. The practice is permitted as an exception to the rule of exclusion and compares with the situation defense counsel finds himself in—he always has the client with him to consult during the trial. The investigative agent's presence may be extremely important to government counsel, especially when the case is complex or involves some specialized subject matter. The agent, too, having lived with the case for a long time, may be able to assist in meeting trial surprises where the best-prepared counsel would otherwise have difficulty. Yet, it would not seem the Government could often meet the burden under rule 615 of showing that the agent's presence is essential. Furthermore, it could be dangerous to use the agent as a witness as early in the case as possible, so that he might then help counsel as a nonwitness, since the agent's testimony could be needed in rebuttal. Using another, nonwitness agent from the same investigative agency would not generally meet government counsel's needs.

This problem is solved if it is clear that investigative agents are within the group specified under the second exception made in the rule, for "an officer or employee of a party which is not a natural person designated as its representative by its attorney." It is our understanding that this was the intention of the House committee. It is certainly this committee's construction of the rule. Senate Report No. 93–1277.

1987 Amendment

The amendment is technical. No substantive change is intended.

1988 Amendment

The amendment is technical. No substantive change is intended.

ARTICLE VII. OPINIONS AND EXPERT TESTIMONY

Rule 701. Opinion Testimony by Lay Witnesses

If the witness is not testifying as an expert, the witness' testimony in the form of opinions or inferences is limited to those opinions or inferences which are (a) rationally based on the perception of the witness and (b) helpful to a clear understanding of the witness' testimony or the determination of a fact in issue.

(Pub.L. 93–595, § 1, Jan. 2, 1975, 88 Stat.1937; Mar. 2, 1987, eff. Oct. 1, 1987.)

ADVISORY COMMITTEE NOTES

1972 Proposed Rules

The rule retains the traditional objective of putting the trier of fact in possession of an accurate reproduction of the event.

Limitation (a) is the familiar requirement of first-hand knowledge or observation.

Limitation (b) is phrased in terms of requiring testimony to be helpful in resolving issues. Witnesses often find difficulty in expressing themselves in language which is not that of an opinion or conclusion. While the courts have made concessions in certain recurring situations, necessity as a standard for permitting opinions and conclusions has proved too elusive and too unadaptable to particular situations for purposes of satisfactory judicial administration. McCormick § 11. Moreover, the practical impossibility of determining by rule what is a "fact," demonstrated by a century of litigation of the question of what is a fact for purposes of pleading under the Field Code, extends into evidence also. 7 Wigmore § 1919. The rule assumes that the natural characteristics of the adversary system will generally lead to an acceptable result, since the detailed account carries more conviction than the broad assertion, and a lawyer can be expected to display his witness to the best advantage. If he fails to do so, cross-examination and argument will point up the weakness. See Ladd, Expert Testimony, 5 Vand.L.Rev. 414, 415–417 (1952). If, despite these considerations, attempts are made to introduce meaningless assertions which amount to little more than choosing up sides, exclusion for lack of helpfulness is called for by the rule.

The language of the rule is substantially that of Uniform Rule 56(1). Similar provisions are California Evidence Code § 800; Kansas Code of Civil Procedure § 60–456(a); New Jersey Evidence Rule 56(1).

1987 Amendment

The amendments are technical. No substantive change is intended.

Rule 702. Testimony by Experts

If scientific, technical, or other specialized knowledge will assist the trier of fact to understand the evidence or to determine a fact in issue, a witness qualified as an expert by knowledge, skill, experience, training, or education, may testify thereto in the form of an opinion or otherwise.

(Pub.L. 93–595, § 1, Jan. 2, 1975, 88 Stat. 1937.)

ADVISORY COMMITTEE NOTES

1972 Proposed Rules

An intelligent evaluation of facts is often difficult or impossible without the application of some scientific, technical, or other specialized knowledge. The most common source of this knowledge is the expert witness, although there are other techniques for supplying it.

Most of the literature assumes that experts testify only in the form of opinions. The assumption is logically unfounded. The rule accordingly recognizes that an expert on the stand may give a dissertation or exposition of scientific or other principles relevant to the case, leaving the trier of fact to apply them to the facts. Since much of the criticism of expert testimony has centered upon the hypothetical question, it seems wise to recognize that opinions are not indispensable and to encourage the use of expert testimony in non-opinion form when counsel believes the trier can itself draw the requisite inference. The use of opinions is not abolished by the rule, however. It will continue to be permissible for the experts to take the further step of suggesting the inference which should be drawn from applying the specialized knowledge to the facts. See Rules 703 to 705.

Whether the situation is a proper one for the use of expert testimony is to be determined on the basis of assisting the trier. "There is no more certain test for determining when experts may be used than the common sense inquiry whether the untrained layman would be qualified to determine intelligently and to the best possible degree the particular issue without enlightenment from those having a specialized understanding of the subject involved in the dispute." Ladd, Expert Testimony, 5 Vand.L.Rev. 414, 418 (1952). When opinions are excluded, it is because they are unhelpful and therefore superfluous and a waste of time. 7 Wigmore § 1918.

The rule is broadly phrased. The fields of knowledge which may be drawn upon are not limited merely to the "scientific" and "technical" but extend to all "specialized" knowledge. Similarly, the expert is viewed, not in a narrow sense, but as a person qualified by "knowledge, skill, experience, training or education." Thus within the scope of the rule are not only experts in the strictest sense of the word, e.g., physicians, physicists, and architects, but also the large group sometimes called "skilled" witnesses, such as bankers or landowners testifying to land values.

Rule 703. Bases of Opinion Testimony by Experts

The facts or data in the particular case upon which an expert bases an opinion or inference may be those perceived by or made known to the expert at or before the hearing. If of a type reasonably relied upon by experts in the particular field in forming opinions or inferences upon the subject, the facts or data need not be admissible in evidence.

(Pub.L. 93–595, § 1, Jan. 2, 1975, 88 Stat.1937; Mar. 2, 1987, eff. Oct. 1, 1987.)

ADVISORY COMMITTEE NOTES

1972 Proposed Rules

Facts or data upon which expert opinions are based may, under the rule, be derived from three possible sources. The first is the firsthand observation of the witness with opinions based thereon traditionally allowed. A treating physician affords an example. Rheingold, The Basis of Medical Testimony, 15 Vand.L.Rev. 473, 489 (1962). Whether he must first relate his observations is treated in Rule 705. The second source, presentation at the trial, also reflects existing practice. The technique may be the familiar hypothetical question or having the expert attend the trial and hear the testimony establishing the facts. Problems of determining what testimony the expert relied upon, when the latter technique is employed and the testimony is in conflict, may be resolved by resort to Rule 705. The third source contemplated by the rule consists of presentation of data to the expert outside of court and other than by his own perception. In this respect the rule is designed to broaden the basis for expert opinions beyond that current in many jurisdictions and to bring the judicial practice into line with the practice of the experts themselves when not in court. Thus a physician in his own practice bases his diagnosis on information from numerous sources and of considerable variety, including statements by patients and relatives, reports and opinions from nurses, technicians and other doctors, hospital records, and X rays. Most of them are admissible in evidence, but only with the expenditure of substantial time in producing and examining various authenticating witnesses. The physician makes life-and-death decisions in reliance upon them. His validation, expertly performed and subject to cross-examination, ought to suffice for judicial purposes. Rheingold, *supra,* at 531; McCormick § 15. A similar provision is California Evidence Code § 801(b).

The rule also offers a more satisfactory basis for ruling upon the admissibility of public opinion poll evidence. Attention is directed to the validity of the techniques employed rather than to relatively fruitless inquiries whether hearsay is involved. See Judge Feinberg's careful analysis in Zippo Mfg. Co. v. Rogers Imports, Inc., 216 F.Supp. 670 (S.D.N.Y. 1963). See also Blum et al., The Art of Opinion Research: A Lawyer's Appraisal of an Emerging Service, 24 U.Chi.L.Rev. 1 (1956); Bonynge Trademark Surveys and Techniques and Their Use in Litigation, 48 A.B.A.J. 329 (1962); Zeisel, The Uniqueness of Survey Evidence, 45 Cornell L.Q. 322 (1960); Annot., 76 A.L.R.2d 919.

If it be feared that enlargement of permissible data may tend to break down the rules of exclusion unduly, notice should be taken that the rule requires that the facts or data "be of a type reasonably relied upon by experts in the particular field." The language would not warrant admitting in evidence the opinion of an "accidentologist" as to the point of impact in an automobile collision based on statements of bystanders since this requirement is not satisfied. See Comment, Cal.Law Rev.Comm'n, Recommendation Proposing an Evidence Code 148–150 (1965).

1987 Amendment

The amendment is technical. No substantive change is intended.

Rule 704. Opinion on Ultimate Issue

(a) Except as provided in subdivision (b), testimony in the form of an opinion or inference otherwise admissible is not objectionable because it embraces an ultimate issue to be decided by the trier of fact.

(b) No expert witness testifying with respect to the mental state or condition of a defendant in a criminal case may state an opinion or inference as to whether the defendant did or did not have the mental state or condition constituting an element of the crime charged or of a defense thereto. Such ultimate issues are matters for the trier of fact alone.

(Pub.L. 93–595, § 1, Jan. 2, 1975, 88 Stat. 1937; Pub.L. 98–473, Title IV, § 406, Oct. 12, 1984, 98 Stat. 2067.)

ADVISORY COMMITTEE NOTES

1972 Proposed Rules

The basic approach to opinions, lay and expert, in these rules is to admit them when helpful to the trier of fact. In order to render this approach fully effective and to allay any doubt on the subject, the so-called "ultimate issue" rule is specifically abolished by the instant rule.

The older cases often contained strictures against allowing witnesses to express opinions upon ultimate issues, as a particular aspect of the rule against opinions. The rule was unduly restrictive, difficult of application, and generally served only to deprive the trier of fact of useful information. 7 Wigmore §§ 1920, 1921; McCormick § 12. The basis usually assigned for the rule, to prevent the witness from "usurping the province of the jury," is aptly characterized as "empty rhetoric." 7 Wigmore § 1920, p. 17. Efforts to meet the felt needs of particular situations led to odd verbal circumlocutions which were said not to violate the rule. Thus a witness could express his estimate of the criminal responsibility of an accused in terms of sanity or insanity, but not in terms of ability to tell right from wrong or other more modern standard. And in cases of medical causation, witnesses were sometimes required to couch their opinions in cautious phrases of "might or could," rather than "did," though the result was to deprive many opinions of the positiveness to which they were entitled, accompanied by the hazard of a ruling of insufficiency to support a verdict. In other instances the rule was simply disregarded, and, as concessions to need, opinions were allowed upon such matters as intoxication, speed, handwriting, and value, although more precise coincidence with an ultimate issue would scarcely be possible.

Many modern decisions illustrate the trend to abandon the rule completely. People v. Wilson, 25 Cal.2d 341, 153 P.2d 720 (1944), whether abortion necessary to save life of patient; *Clifford–Jacobs Forging Co. v. Industrial Comm.,* 19 Ill.2d 236, 166 N.E.2d 582 (1960), medical causation; *Dowling v. L. H. Shattuck,* Inc., 91 N.H. 234, 17 A.2d 529 (1941), proper method of shoring ditch; *Schweiger v. Solbeck,* 191 Or. 454, 230 P.2d 195 (1951), cause of landslide. In each instance the opinion was allowed.

The abolition of the ultimate issue rule does not lower the bars so as to admit all opinions. Under Rules 701 and 702, opinions must be helpful to the trier of fact, and Rule 403 provides for exclusion of evidence which wastes time. These provisions afford ample assurances against the admission of opinions which would merely tell the jury what result to reach, somewhat in the manner of the oath-helpers of an earlier day. They also stand ready to exclude opinions phrased in terms of inadequately explored legal criteria. Thus the question, "Did T have capacity to make a will?" would be excluded, while the question, "Did T have sufficient mental capacity to know the nature and extent of his property and the natural objects of his bounty and to formulate a rational scheme of distribution?" would be allowed. McCormick § 12.

For similar provisions see Uniform Rule 56(4); California Evidence Code § 805; Kansas Code of Civil Procedure § 60–456(d); New Jersey Evidence Rule 56(3).

Rule 705. Disclosure of Facts or Data Underlying Expert Opinion

The expert may testify in terms of opinion or inference and give reasons therefor without first testifying to the underlying facts or data, unless the court requires otherwise. The expert may in any event be required to disclose the underlying facts or data on cross-examination.

(Pub.L. 93–595, § 1, Jan. 2, 1975, 88 Stat. 1938; Mar. 2, 1987, eff. Oct. 1, 1987; Apr. 22, 1993, eff. Dec. 1, 1993.)

ADVISORY COMMITTEE NOTES

1972 Proposed Rules

The hypothetical question has been the target of a great deal of criticism as encouraging partisan bias, affording an opportunity for summing up in the middle of the case, and as complex and time consuming. Ladd, Expert Testimony, 5

Vand.L.Rev. 414, 426–427 (1952). While the rule allows counsel to make disclosure of the underlying facts or data as a preliminary to the giving of an expert opinion, if he chooses, the instances in which he is required to do so are reduced. This is true whether the expert bases his opinion on data furnished him at secondhand or observed by him at firsthand.

The elimination of the requirement of preliminary disclosure at the trial of underlying facts or data has a long background of support. In 1937 the Commissioners on Uniform State Laws incorporated a provision to this effect in their Model Expert Testimony Act, which furnished the basis for Uniform Rules 57 and 58. Rule 4515, N.Y. CPLR (McKinney 1963), provides:

"Unless the court orders otherwise, questions calling for the opinion of an expert witness need not be hypothetical in form, and the witness may state his opinion and reasons without first specifying the data upon which it is based. Upon cross-examination, he may be required to specify the data * * *."

See also California Evidence Code § 802; Kansas Code of Civil Procedure §§ 60–456, 60–457; New Jersey Evidence Rules 57, 58.

If the objection is made that leaving it to the cross-examiner to bring out the supporting data is essentially unfair, the answer is that he is under no compulsion to bring out any facts or data except those unfavorable to the opinion. The answer assumes that the cross-examiner has the advance knowledge which is essential for effective cross-examination. This advance knowledge has been afforded, though imperfectly, by the traditional foundation requirement. Rule 26(b)(4) of the Rules of Civil Procedure, as revised, provides for substantial discovery in this area, obviating in large measure the obstacles which have been raised in some instances to discovery of findings, underlying data, and even the identity of the experts. Friedenthal Discovery and Use of an Adverse Party's Expert Information, 14 Stan.L.Rev. 455 (1962).

These safeguards are reinforced by the discretionary power of the judge to require preliminary disclosure in any event.

1987 Amendment

The amendment is technical. No substantive change is intended.

1993 Amendment

This rule, which relates to the manner of presenting testimony at trial, is revised to avoid an arguable conflict with revised Rules 26(a)(2)(B) and 26(e)(1) of the Federal Rules of Civil Procedure or with revised Rule 16 of the Federal Rules of Criminal Procedure, which require disclosure in advance of trial of the basis and reasons for an expert's opinions.

If a serious question is raised under Rule 702 or 703 as to the admissibility of expert testimony, disclosure of the underlying facts or data on which opinions are based may, of course, be needed by the court before deciding whether, and to what extent, the person should be allowed to testify. This rule does not preclude such an inquiry.

Rule 706. Court Appointed Experts

(a) Appointment. The court may on its own motion or on the motion of any party enter an order to show cause why expert witnesses should not be appointed, and may request the parties to submit nominations. The court may appoint any expert witnesses agreed upon by the parties, and may appoint expert witnesses of its own selection. An expert witness shall not be appointed by the court unless the witness consents to act. A witness so appointed shall be informed of the witness' duties by the court in writing, a copy of which shall be filed with the clerk, or at a conference in which the parties shall have opportunity to participate. A witness so appointed shall advise the parties of the witness' findings, if any; the witness' deposition may be taken by any party; and the witness may be called to testify by the court or any party. The witness shall be subject to cross-examination by each party, including a party calling the witness.

(b) Compensation. Expert witnesses so appointed are entitled to reasonable compensation in whatever sum the court may allow. The compensation thus fixed is payable from funds which may be provided by law in criminal cases and civil actions and proceedings involving just compensation under the fifth amendment. In other civil actions and proceedings the compensation shall be paid by the parties in such proportion and at such time as the court directs, and thereafter charged in like manner as other costs.

(c) Disclosure of appointment. In the exercise of its discretion, the court may authorize disclosure to the jury of the fact that the court appointed the expert witness.

(d) Parties' experts of own selection. Nothing in this rule limits the parties in calling expert witnesses of their own selection.

(Pub.L. 93–595, § 1, Jan. 2, 1975, 88 Stat.1938; Mar. 2, 1987, eff. Oct. 1, 1987.)

ADVISORY COMMITTEE NOTES

1972 Proposed Rules

The practice of shopping for experts, the venality of some experts, and the reluctance of many reputable experts to involve themselves in litigation, have been matters of deep concern. Though the contention is made that court appointed experts acquire an aura of infallibility to which they are not entitled, Levy, Impartial Medical Testimony—Revisited, 34 Temple L.Q. 416 (1961), the trend is increasingly to provide for their use. While experience indicates that actual appointment is a relatively infrequent occurrence, the assumption may be made that the availability of the procedure in itself decreases the need for resorting to it. The ever-present possibility that the judge may appoint an expert in a given case must inevitably exert a sobering effect on the expert witness of a party and upon the person utilizing his services.

The inherent power of a trial judge to appoint an expert of his own choosing is virtually unquestioned. *Scott v. Spanjer Bros., Inc.*, 298 F.2d 928 (2d Cir.1962); *Danville Tobacco Assn. v. Bryant–Buckner Associates*, Inc., 333 F.2d 202 (4th Cir.1964); Sink, The Unused Power of a Federal Judge to Call His Own Expert Witnesses, 29 S.Cal.L.Rev. 195 (1956); 2 Wigmore § 563, 9 *id.* § 2484; Annot., 95 A.L.R.2d 383. Hence the problem becomes largely one of detail.

The New York plan is well known and is described in Report by Special Committee of the Association of the Bar of the City of New York: Impartial Medical Testimony (1956). On recommendation of the Section of Judicial Administration, local adoption of an impartial medical plan was endorsed by the American Bar Association. 82 A.B.A.Rep. 184–185 (1957). Descriptions and analyses of plans in effect in various parts of the country are found in Van Dusen, A United States District Judge's View of the Impartial Medical Expert System, 32 F.R.D. 498 (1963); Wick and Kightlinger, Impartial Medical Testimony Under the Federal Civil Rules: A Tale of Three Doctors, 34 Ins. Counsel J. 115 (1967); and numerous articles collected in Klein, Judicial Administration and the Legal Profession 393 (1963). Statutes and rules include California Evidence Code §§ 730–733; Illinois Supreme Court Rule 215(d), Ill.Rev.Stat.1969, c. 110A, § 215(d); Burns Indiana Stats.1956, § 9–1702; Wisconsin Stats.Annot.1958, § 957.27.

In the federal practice, a comprehensive scheme for court appointed experts was initiated with the adoption of Rule 28 of the Federal Rules of Criminal Procedure in 1946. The Judicial Conference of the United States in 1953 considered court appointed experts in civil cases, but only with respect to whether they should be compensated from public funds, a proposal which was rejected. Report of the Judicial Conference of the United States 23 (1953). The present rule expands the practice to include civil cases.

Note to Subdivision (a). Subdivision (a) is based on Rule 28 of the Federal Rules of Criminal Procedure, with a few changes, mainly in the interest of clarity. Language has been added to provide specifically for the appointment either on motion of a party or on the judge's own motion. A provision subjecting the court appointed expert to deposition procedures has been incorporated. The rule has been revised to make definite the right of any party, including the party calling him, to cross-examine.

Note to Subdivision (b). Subdivision (b) combines the present provision for compensation in criminal cases with what seems to be a fair and feasible handling of civil cases, originally found in the Model Act and carried from there into Uniform Rule 60. See also California Evidence Code §§ 730–731. The special provision for Fifth Amendment compensation cases is designed to guard against reducing constitutionally guaranteed just compensation by requiring the recipient to pay costs. See Rule 71A(*l*) of the Rules of Civil Procedure.

Note to Subdivision (c). Subdivision (c) seems to be essential if the use of court appointed experts is to be fully effective. Uniform Rule 61 so provides.

Note to Subdivision (d). Subdivision (d) is in essence the last sentence of Rule 28(a) of the Federal Rules of Criminal Procedure.

1987 Amendment

The amendments are technical. No substantive change is intended.

ARTICLE VIII. HEARSAY

ADVISORY COMMITTEE NOTES

1972 Proposed Rules

Introductory Note; The Hearsay Problem. The factors to be considered in evaluating the testimony of a witness are perception, memory, and narration. Morgan, Hearsay Dangers and the Application of the Hearsay Concept, 62 Harv. L.Rev. 177 (1948), Selected Writings on Evidence and Trial 764, 765 (Fryer ed. 1957); Shientag, Cross–Examination—A Judge's Viewpoint, 3 Record 12 (1948); Strahorn, A Reconsideration of the Hearsay Rule and Admissions, 85 U.Pa. L.Rev. 484, 485 (1937), Selected Writings, *supra*, 756, 757; Weinstein, Probative Force of Hearsay, 46 Iowa L.Rev. 331 (1961). Sometimes a fourth is added, sincerity, but in fact it seems merely to be an aspect of the three already mentioned.

In order to encourage the witness to do his best with respect to each of these factors, and to expose any inaccuracies which may enter in, the Anglo–American tradition has evolved three conditions under which witnesses will ideally be required to testify: (1) under oath, (2) in the personal presence of the trier of fact, (3) subject to cross-examination.

(1) Standard procedure calls for the swearing of witnesses. While the practice is perhaps less effective than in an earlier time, no disposition to relax the requirement is apparent, other than to allow affirmation by persons with scruples against taking oaths.

(2) The demeanor of the witness traditionally has been believed to furnish trier and opponent with valuable clues. *Universal Camera Corp. v. N.L.R.B.*, 340 U.S. 474, 495–496, 71 S.Ct. 456, 95 L.Ed. 456 (1951); Sahm, Demeanor Evidence: Elusive and Intangible Imponderables, 47 A.B.A.J. 580 (1961), quoting numerous authorities. The witness himself will probably be impressed with the solemnity of the occasion and the possibility of public disgrace. Willingness to falsify may reasonably become more difficult in the presence of the person against whom directed. Rules 26 and 43(a) of the Federal Rules of Criminal and Civil Procedure, respectively, include the general requirement that testimony be taken orally in open court. The Sixth Amendment right of confrontation is a manifestation of these beliefs and attitudes.

(3) Emphasis on the basis of the hearsay rule today tends to center upon the condition of cross-examination. All may not agree with Wigmore that cross-examination is "beyond doubt the greatest legal engine ever invented for the discovery of truth," but all will agree with his statement that it has become a "vital feature" of the Anglo–American system. 5 Wigmore § 1367, p. 29. The belief, or perhaps hope, that cross-examination is effective in exposing imperfections of perception, memory, and narration is fundamental. Morgan, Foreword to Model Code of Evidence 37 (1942).

The logic of the preceding discussion might suggest that no testimony be received unless in full compliance with the three ideal conditions. No one advocates this position. Common sense tells that much evidence which is not given under the three conditions may be inherently superior to much that is. Moreover, when the choice is between evidence which is less than best and no evidence at all, only clear folly would dictate an across-the-board policy of doing without. The problem thus resolves itself into effecting a sensible accommodation between these considerations and the desirability of giving testimony under the ideal conditions.

The solution evolved by the common law has been a general rule excluding hearsay but subject to numerous exceptions under circumstances supposed to furnish guarantees of trustworthiness. Criticisms of this scheme are that it is bulky and complex, fails to screen good from bad hearsay realistically, and inhibits the growth of the law of evidence.

Since no one advocates excluding all hearsay, three possible solutions may be considered: (1) abolish the rule against hearsay and admit all hearsay; (2) admit hearsay possessing sufficient probative force, but with procedural safeguards; (3) revise the present system of class exceptions.

(1) Abolition of the hearsay rule would be the simplest solution. The effect would not be automatically to abolish the giving of testimony under ideal conditions. If the declarant were available, compliance with the ideal conditions would be optional with either party. Thus the proponent could call the declarant as a witness as a form of presentation more impressive than his hearsay statement. Or the opponent could call the declarant to be cross-examined upon his statement. This is the tenor of Uniform Rule 63(1), admitting the hearsay declaration of a person "who is present at the hearing and available for cross-examination." Compare the treatment of declarations of available declarants in Rule 801(d)(1) of the instant rules. If the declarant were unavailable, a rule of free admissibility would make no distinctions in terms of degrees of noncompliance with the ideal conditions and would exact no quid pro quo in the form of assurances of trustworthiness. Rule 503 of the Model Code did exactly that, providing for the admissibility of any hearsay declaration by an unavailable declarant, finding support in the Massachusetts act of 1898, enacted at the instance of Thayer, Mass.Gen.L.1932, c. 233, § 65, and in the English act of 1938, St.1938, c. 28, Evidence. Both are limited to civil cases. The draftsmen of the Uniform Rules chose a less advanced and more conventional position. Comment, Uniform Rule 63. The present Advisory Committee has been unconvinced of the wisdom of abandoning the traditional requirement of some particular assurance of credibility as a condition precedent to admitting the hearsay declaration of an unavailable declarant.

In criminal cases, the Sixth Amendment requirement of confrontation would no doubt move into a large part of the area presently occupied by the hearsay rule in the event of the abolition of the latter. The resultant split between civil and criminal evidence is regarded as an undesirable development.

(2) Abandonment of the system of class exceptions in favor of individual treatment in the setting of the particular case, accompanied by procedural safeguards, has been impressively advocated. Weinstein, The Probative Force of Hearsay, 46 Iowa L.Rev. 331 (1961). Admissibility would be determined by weighing the probative force of the evidence against the possibility of prejudice, waste of time, and the availability of more satisfactory evidence. The bases of the traditional hearsay exceptions would be helpful in assessing probative force. Ladd, The Relationship of the Principles of Exclusionary Rules of Evidence to the Problem of Proof, 18 Minn.L.Rev. 506 (1934). Procedural safeguards would consist of notice of intention to use hearsay, free comment by the judge on the weight of the evidence, and a greater measure of authority in both trial and appellate judges to deal with evidence on the basis of weight. The Advisory Committee has rejected this approach to hearsay as involving too great a measure of judicial discretion, minimizing the predictability of rulings, enhancing the difficulties of preparation for trial, adding a further element to the already overcomplicated congeries of pretrial procedures, and requiring substantially different rules for civil and criminal cases. The only way in which the probative force of hearsay differs from the probative force of other testimony is in the absence of oath, demeanor, and cross-examination as aids in determining credibility. For a judge to exclude evidence because he does not believe it has been described as "altogether atypical, extraordinary. * * *" Chadbourn, Bentham and the Hearsay Rule—A Benthamic View of Rule 63(4)(c) of the Uniform Rules of Evidence, 75 Harv.L.Rev. 932, 947 (1962).

(3) The approach to hearsay in these rules is that of the common law, i.e., a general rule excluding hearsay, with exceptions under which evidence is not required to be excluded even though hearsay. The traditional hearsay exceptions are drawn upon for the exceptions, collected under two rules, one dealing with situations where availability of the declarant is regarded as immaterial and the other with those where unavailability is made a condition to the admission of the hearsay statement. Each of the two rules concludes with a provision for hearsay statements not within one of the specified exceptions "but having comparable circumstantial guarantees of trustworthiness." Rules 803(24) and 804(b)(6). This plan is submitted as calculated to encourage growth and development in this area of the law, while conserving the values and experience of the past as a guide to the future.

Confrontation and Due Process. Until very recently, decisions invoking the confrontation clause of the Sixth Amendment were surprisingly few, a fact probably explainable by the former inapplicability of the clause to the states and by the hearsay rule's occupancy of much the same ground. The pattern which emerges from the earlier cases invoking the clause is substantially that of the hearsay rule, applied to criminal cases: an accused is entitled to have the witnesses against him testify under oath, in the presence of himself and trier, subject to cross-examination; yet considerations of public policy and necessity require the recognition of such exceptions as dying declarations and former testimony of unavailable witnesses. *Mattox v. United States,* 156 U.S. 237, 15 S.Ct. 337, 39 L.Ed. 409 (1895); *Motes v. United States,* 178 U.S. 458, 20 S.Ct. 993, 44 L.Ed. 1150 (1900); *Delaney v. United States,* 263 U.S. 586, 44 S.Ct. 206, 68 L.Ed. 462 (1924). Beginning with *Snyder v. Massachusetts,* 291 U.S. 97, 54 S.Ct. 330, 78 L.Ed. 674 (1934), the Court began to speak of confrontation as an aspect of procedural due process, thus extending its applicability to state cases and to federal cases other than criminal. The language of *Snyder* was that of an elastic concept of hearsay. The deportation case of *Bridges v. Wixon,* 326 U.S. 135, 65 S.Ct. 1443, 89 L.Ed. 2103 (1945), may be read broadly as imposing a strictly construed right of confrontation in all kinds of cases or narrowly as the product of a failure of the Immigration and Naturalization Service to follow its own rules. *In re Oliver,* 333 U.S. 257, 68 S.Ct. 499, 92 L.Ed. 682 (1948), ruled that cross-examination was essential to due process in a state contempt proceeding, but in *United States v. Nugent,* 346 U.S. 1, 73 S.Ct. 991, 97 L.Ed. 1417 (1953), the court held that it was not an essential aspect of a "hearing" for a conscientious objector under the Selective Service Act. *Stein v. New York,* 346 U.S. 156, 196, 73 S.Ct. 1077, 97 L.Ed. 1522 (1953), disclaimed any purpose to read the hearsay rule into the Fourteenth Amendment, but in *Greene v. McElroy,* 360 U.S. 474, 79 S.Ct. 1400, 3 L.Ed.2d 1377 (1959), revocation of security clearance without confrontation and cross-examination was held unauthorized, and a similar result was reached in *Willner v. Committee on Character,* 373 U.S. 96, 83 S.Ct. 1175, 10 L.Ed.2d 224 (1963). Ascertaining the constitutional dimensions of the confrontation-hearsay aggregate against the background of these cases is a matter of some difficulty, yet the general pattern is at least not inconsistent with that of the hearsay rule.

In 1965 the confrontation clause was held applicable to the states. *Pointer v. Texas,* 380 U.S. 400, 85 S.Ct. 1065, 13 L.Ed.2d 923 (1965). Prosecution use of former testimony given at a preliminary hearing where petitioner was not represented by counsel was a violation of the clause. The same result would have followed under conventional hearsay doctrine read in the light of a constitutional right to counsel, and nothing in the opinion suggests any difference in essential outline between the hearsay rule and the right of confrontation. In the companion case of *Douglas v. Alabama,* 380 U.S. 415, 85 S.Ct. 1074, 13 L.Ed.2d 934 (1965), however, the result reached by applying the confrontation clause is one reached less readily via the hearsay rule. A confession implicating petitioner was put before the jury by reading it to the witness in portions and asking if he made that statement. The witness refused to answer on grounds of self-incrimination. The result, said the Court, was to deny cross-examination, and hence confrontation. True, it could broadly be said that the confession was a hearsay statement which for all practical purposes was put in evidence. Yet a more easily accepted explanation of the opinion is that its real thrust was in the direction of curbing undesirable prosecutorial behavior, rather than merely applying rules of exclusion, and that the confrontation clause was the means selected to achieve this end. Comparable facts and a like result appeared in *Brookhart v. Janis,* 384 U.S. 1, 86 S.Ct. 1245, 16 L.Ed.2d 314 (1966).

The pattern suggested in *Douglas* was developed further and more distinctly in a pair of cases at the end of the 1966 term. *United States v. Wade,* 388 U.S. 218, 87 S.Ct. 1926, 18 L.Ed.2d 1149 (1967), and *Gilbert v. California,* 388 U.S. 263, 87 S.Ct. 1951, 18 L.Ed.2d 1178 (1967), hinged upon practices followed in identifying accused persons before trial. This pretrial identification was said to be so decisive an aspect of the case that accused was entitled to have counsel present; a pretrial identification made in the absence of counsel was not itself receivable in evidence and, in addition, might fatally infect a courtroom identification. The presence of counsel at the earlier identification was described as a necessary prerequisite for "a meaningful confrontation at trial." *United States v. Wade, supra,* 388 U.S. at p. 236, 87 S.Ct. at p. 1937. *Wade* involved no evidence of the fact of a prior identification and hence was not susceptible of being decided on hearsay grounds. In *Gilbert,* witnesses did testify to an earlier identification, readily classifiable as hearsay under a fairly strict view of what constitutes hearsay. The Court, however, carefully avoided basing the decision on the hearsay ground, choosing confrontation instead. 388 U.S. 263, 272, n. 3, 87 S.Ct. 1951. See also *Parker v. Gladden,* 385 U.S. 363, 87 S.Ct. 468, 17 L.Ed.2d 420 (1966), holding that the right of confrontation was violated when the bailiff made prejudicial statements to jurors, and Note, 75 Yale L.J. 1434 (1966).

Under the earlier cases, the confrontation clause may have been little more than a constitutional embodiment of the hearsay rule, even including traditional exceptions but with some room for expanding them along similar lines. But under the recent cases the impact of the clause clearly extends beyond the confines of the hearsay rule. These considerations have led the Advisory Committee to conclude that a hearsay rule can function usefully as an adjunct to the confrontation right in constitutional areas and independently in nonconstitutional areas. In recognition of the separateness of the confrontation clause and the hearsay rule, and to avoid inviting collisions between them or between the hearsay rule and other exclusionary principles, the exceptions set forth in Rules 803 and 804 are stated in terms of exemption from the general exclusionary mandate of the hearsay rule, rather than in positive terms of admissibility. See Uniform Rule 63(1) to (31) and California Evidence Code §§ 1200–1340.

Rule 801. Definitions

The following definitions apply under this article:

(a) Statement. A "statement" is (1) an oral or written assertion or (2) nonverbal conduct of a person, if it is intended by the person as an assertion.

(b) Declarant. A "declarant" is a person who makes a statement.

(c) Hearsay. "Hearsay" is a statement, other than one made by the declarant while testifying at the trial or hearing, offered in evidence to prove the truth of the matter asserted.

(d) Statements which are not hearsay. A statement is not hearsay if—

(1) Prior statement by witness. The declarant testifies at the trial or hearing and is subject to cross-examination concerning the statement, and the statement is (A) inconsistent with the declarant's testimony, and was given under oath subject to the penalty of perjury at a trial, hearing, or other proceeding, or in a deposition, or (B) consistent with the declarant's testimony and is offered to rebut an express or implied charge against the declarant of recent fabrication or improper influence or motive, or (C) one of identification of a person made after perceiving the person; or

(2) Admission by party-opponent. The statement is offered against a party and is (A) the party's own statement, in either an individual or a representative capacity or (B) a statement of which the party has manifested an adoption or belief in its truth, or (C) a statement by a person authorized by the party to make a statement concerning the subject, or (D) a statement by the party's agent or servant concerning a matter within the scope of the agency or employment, made during the existence of the relationship, or (E) a statement by a coconspirator of a party during the course and in furtherance of the conspiracy. The contents of the statement shall be considered but are not alone sufficient to establish the declarant's authority under subdivision (C), the agency or employment relationship and scope thereof under subdivision (D), or the existence of the conspiracy and the participation therein of the declarant and the party against whom the statement is offered under subdivision (E).

(Pub.L. 93–595, § 1, Jan. 2, 1975, 88 Stat.1938; Pub.L. 94–113, § 1, Oct. 16, 1975, 89 Stat. 576; Mar. 2, 1987, eff. Oct. 1, 1987; Apr. 11, 1997, eff. Dec. 1, 1997.)

ADVISORY COMMITTEE NOTES

1972 Proposed Rules

Note to Subdivision (a). The definition of "statement" assumes importance because the term is used in the definition of hearsay in subdivision (c). The effect of the definition of "statement" is to exclude from the operation of the hearsay rule all evidence of conduct, verbal or nonverbal, not intended as an assertion. The key to the definition is that nothing is an assertion unless intended to be one.

It can scarcely be doubted that an assertion made in words is intended by the declarant to be an assertion. Hence verbal assertions readily fall into the category of "statement." Whether nonverbal conduct should be regarded as a statement for purposes of defining hearsay requires further consideration. Some nonverbal conduct, such as the act of pointing to identify a suspect in a lineup, is clearly the equivalent of words, assertive in nature, and to be regarded as a statement. Other nonverbal conduct, however, may be offered as evidence that the person acted as he did because of his belief in the existence of the condition sought to be proved, from which belief the existence of the condition may be inferred. This sequence is, arguably, in effect an assertion of the existence of the condition and hence properly includable within the hearsay concept. See Morgan, Hearsay Dangers and the Application of the Hearsay Concept, 62 Harv.L.Rev. 177, 214, 217 (1948), and the elaboration in Finman, Implied Assertions as Hearsay: Some Criticisms of the Uniform Rules of Evidence, 14 Stan.L.Rev. 682 (1962). Admittedly evidence of this character is untested with respect to the perception, memory, and narration (or their equivalents) of the actor, but the Advisory Committee is of the view that these dangers are minimal in the absence of an intent to assert and do not justify the loss of the evidence on hearsay grounds. No class of evidence is free of the possibility of fabrication, but the likelihood is less with nonverbal than with assertive verbal conduct. The situations giving rise to the nonverbal conduct are such as virtually to eliminate questions of sincerity. Motivation, the nature of the conduct, and the presence or absence of reliance will bear heavily upon the weight to be given the evidence. Falknor, The "Hear-Say" Rule as a "See-Do" Rule: Evidence of Conduct, 33 Rocky Mt.L.Rev. 133 (1961). Similar considerations govern nonassertive verbal conduct and verbal conduct which is assertive but offered as a basis for inferring something other than the matter asserted, also excluded from the definition of hearsay by the language of subdivision (c).

When evidence of conduct is offered on the theory that it is not a statement, and hence not hearsay, a preliminary determination will be required to determine whether an assertion is intended. The rule is so worded as to place the burden upon the party claiming that the intention existed; ambiguous and doubtful cases will be resolved against him and in favor of admissibility. The determination involves no greater difficulty than many other preliminary questions of fact. Maguire, The Hearsay System: Around and Through the Thicket, 14 Vand.L.Rev. 741, 765–767 (1961).

For similar approaches, see Uniform Rule 62(1); California Evidence Code §§ 225, 1200; Kansas Code of Civil Procedure § 60–459(a); New Jersey Evidence Rule 62(1).

Note to Subdivision (c). The definition follows along familiar lines in including only statements offered to prove the truth of the matter asserted. McCormick § 225; 5 Wigmore § 1361, 6 *id.* § 1766. If the significance of an offered statement lies solely in the fact that it was made, no issue is raised as to the truth of anything asserted, and the statement is not hearsay. *Emich Motors Corp. v. General Motors Corp.*, 181 F.2d 70 (7th Cir.1950), rev'd on other grounds 340 U.S. 558, 71 S.Ct. 408, 95 L.Ed. 534, letters of complaint from customers offered as a reason for cancellation of dealer's franchise, to rebut contention that franchise was revoked for refusal to finance sales through affiliated finance company. The effect is to exclude from hearsay the entire category of "verbal acts" and "verbal parts of an act," in which the statement itself affects the legal rights of the parties or is a circumstance bearing on conduct affecting their rights.

The definition of hearsay must, of course, be read with reference to the definition of statement set forth in subdivision (a).

Testimony given by a witness in the course of court proceedings is excluded since there is compliance with all the ideal conditions for testifying.

Note to Subdivision (d). Several types of statements which would otherwise literally fall within the definition are expressly excluded from it:

(1) *Prior statement by witness.* Considerable controversy has attended the question whether a prior out-of-court statement by a person now available for cross-examination concerning it, under oath and in the presence of the trier of fact, should be classed as hearsay. If the witness admits on the stand that he made the statement and that it was true, he adopts the statement and there is no hearsay problem. The hearsay problem arises when the witness on the stand denies having made the statement or admits having made it but denies its truth. The argument in favor of treating these latter statements as hearsay is based upon the ground that the conditions of oath, cross-examination, and demeanor observation did not prevail at the time the statement was made and cannot adequately be supplied by the later examination. The logic of the situation is troublesome. So far as concerns the oath, its mere presence has never been regarded as sufficient to remove a statement from the hearsay category, and it receives much less emphasis than cross-examination as a truth-compelling device. While strong expressions are

found to the effect that no conviction can be had or important right taken away on the basis of statements not made under fear of prosecution for perjury, *Bridges v. Wixon*, 326 U.S. 135, 65 S.Ct. 1443, 89 L.Ed. 2103 (1945), the fact is that, of the many common law exceptions to the hearsay rule, only that for reported testimony has required the statement to have been made under oath. Nor is it satisfactorily explained why cross-examination cannot be conducted subsequently with success. The decisions contending most vigorously for its inadequacy in fact demonstrate quite thorough exploration of the weaknesses and doubts attending the earlier statement. *State v. Saporen*, 205 Minn. 358, 285 N.W. 898 (1939); *Ruhala v. Roby*, 379 Mich. 102, 150 N.W.2d 146 (1967); *People v. Johnson*, 68 Cal.2d 646, 68 Cal.Rptr. 599, 441 P.2d 111 (1968). In respect to demeanor, as Judge Learned Hand observed in *Di Carlo v. United States*, 6 F.2d 364 (2d Cir.1925), when the jury decides that the truth is not what the witness says now, but what he said before, they are still deciding from what they see and hear in court. The bulk of the case law nevertheless has been against allowing prior statements of witnesses to be used generally as substantive evidence. Most of the writers and Uniform Rule 63(1) have taken the opposite position.

The position taken by the Advisory Committee in formulating this part of the rule is funded upon an unwillingness to countenance the general use of prior prepared statements as substantive evidence, but with a recognition that particular circumstances call for a contrary result. The judgment is one more of experience than of logic. The rule requires in each instance, as a general safeguard, that the declarant actually testify as a witness, and it then enumerates three situations in which the statement is excepted from the category of hearsay. Compare Uniform Rule 63(1) which allows any out-of-court statement of a declarant who is present at the trial and available for cross-examination.

(A) Prior inconsistent statements traditionally have been admissible to impeach but not as substantive evidence. Under the rule they are substantive evidence. As has been said by the California Law Revision Commission with respect to a similar provision:

"Section 1235 admits inconsistent statements of witnesses because the dangers against which the hearsay rule is designed to protect are largely nonexistent. The declarant is in court and may be examined and cross-examined in regard to his statements and their subject matter. In many cases, the inconsistent statement is more likely to be true than the testimony of the witness at the trial because it was made nearer in time to the matter to which it relates and is less likely to be influenced by the controversy that gave rise to the litigation. The trier of fact has the declarant before it and can observe his demeanor and the nature of his testimony as he denies or tries to explain away the inconsistency. Hence, it is in as good a position to determine the truth or falsity of the prior statement as it is to determine the truth or falsity of the inconsistent testimony given in court. Moreover, Section 1235 will provide a party with desirable protection against the 'turncoat' witness who changes his story on the stand and deprives the party calling him of evidence essential to his case." Comment, California Evidence Code § 1235. See also McCormick § 39. The Advisory Committee finds these views more convincing than those expressed in *People v. Johnson*, 68 Cal.2d 646, 68 Cal.Rptr. 599, 441 P.2d 111 (1968). The constitutionality of the Advisory Committee's view was upheld in *California v. Green*, 399 U.S. 149, 90 S.Ct. 1930, 26 L.Ed.2d 489 (1970). Moreover, the requirement that the statement be inconsistent with the testimony given assures a thorough exploration of both versions while the witness is on the stand and bars any general and indiscriminate use of previously prepared statements.

(B) Prior consistent statements traditionally have been admissible to rebut charges of recent fabrication or improper influence or motive but not as substantive evidence. Under the rule they are substantive evidence. The prior statement is consistent with the testimony given on the stand, and, if the opposite party wishes to open the door for its admission in evidence, no sound reason is apparent why it should not be received generally.

(C) The admission of evidence of identification finds substantial support, although it falls beyond a doubt in the category of prior out-of-court statements. Illustrative are *People v. Gould*, 54 Cal.2d 621, 7 Cal.Rptr. 273, 354 P.2d 865 (1960); *Judy v. State*, 218 Md. 168, 146 A.2d 29 (1958); *State v. Simmons*, 63 Wash.2d 17, 385 P.2d 389 (1963); California Evidence Code § 1238; New Jersey Evidence Rule 63(1)(c); N.Y.Code of Criminal Procedure § 393–b. Further cases are found in 4 Wigmore § 1130. The basis is the generally unsatisfactory and inconclusive nature of courtroom identifications as compared with those made at an earlier time under less suggestive conditions. The Supreme Court considered the admissibility of evidence of prior identification in *Gilbert v. California*, 388 U.S. 263, 87 S.Ct. 1951, 18 L.Ed.2d 1178 (1967). Exclusion of lineup identification was held to be required because the accused did not then have the assistance of counsel. Significantly, the Court carefully refrained from placing its decision on the ground that testimony as to the making of a prior out-of-court identification ("That's the man") violated either the hearsay rule or the right of confrontation because not made under oath, subject to immediate cross-examination, in the presence of the trier. Instead the Court observed:

"There is a split among the States concerning the admissibility of prior extra-judicial identifications, as independent evidence of identity, both by the witness and third parties present at the prior identification. See 71 ALR2d 449. It has been held that the prior identification is hearsay, and, when admitted through the testimony of the identifier, is merely a prior consistent statement. The recent trend, however, is to admit the prior identification under the exception that admits as substantive evidence a prior communication by a witness who is available for cross-examination at the trial. See 5 ALR2d Later Case Service 1225–1228. * * *" 388 U.S. at 272, n. 3, 87 S.Ct. at 1956.

(2) *Admissions.* Admissions by a party-opponent are excluded from the category of hearsay on the theory that their admissibility in evidence is the result of the adversary system rather than satisfaction of the conditions of the hearsay rule. Strahorn, A Reconsideration of the Hearsay Rule and Admissions, 85 U.Pa.L.Rev. 484, 564 (1937); Morgan, Basic Problems of Evidence 265 (1962); 4 Wigmore § 1048. No guarantee of trustworthiness is required in the case of an admission. The freedom which admissions have enjoyed from technical demands of searching for an assurance of truthworthiness in some against-interest circumstance, and from the restrictive influences of the opinion rule and the rule requiring firsthand knowledge, when taken with the apparently prevalent satisfaction with the results, calls for generous treatment of this avenue to admissibility.

The rule specifies five categories of statements for which the responsibility of a party is considered sufficient to justify reception in evidence against him:

(A) A party's own statement is the classic example of an admission. If he has a representative capacity and the statement is offered against him in that capacity, no inquiry whether he was acting in the representative capacity in making the statement is required; the statement need only be relevant to represent affairs. To the same effect in California Evidence Code § 1220. Compare Uniform Rule 63(7), requiring a statement to be made in a representative capacity to be admissible against a party in a representative capacity.

(B) Under established principles an admission may be made by adopting or acquiescing in the statement of another. While knowledge of contents would ordinarily be essential, this is not inevitably so: "X is a reliable person and knows what he is talking about." See McCormick § 246, p. 527, n. 15. Adoption or acquiescence may be manifested in any appropriate manner. When silence is relied upon, the theory is that the person would, under the circumstances, protest the statement made in his presence, if untrue. The decision in each case calls for an evaluation in terms of probable human behavior. In civil cases, the results have generally been satisfactory. In criminal cases, however, troublesome questions have been raised by decisions holding that failure to deny is an admission: the inference is a fairly weak one, to begin with; silence may be motivated by advice of counsel or realization that "anything you say may be used against you"; unusual opportunity is afforded to manufacture evidence; and encroachment upon the privilege against self-incrimination seems inescapably to be involved. However, recent decisions of the Supreme Court relating to custodial interrogation and the right to counsel appear to resolve these difficulties. Hence the rule contains no special provisions concerning failure to deny in criminal cases.

(C) No authority is required for the general proposition that a statement authorized by a party to be made should have the status of an admission by the party. However, the question arises whether only statements to third persons should be so regarded, to the exclusion of statements by the agent to the principal. The rule is phrased broadly so as to encompass both. While it may be argued that the agent authorized to make statements to his principal does not speak for him, Morgan, Basic Problems of Evidence 273 (1962), communication to an outsider has not generally been thought to be an essential characteristic of an admission. Thus a party's books or records are usable against him, without regard to any intent to disclose to third persons. 5 Wigmore § 1557. See also McCormick § 78, pp. 159–161. In accord is New Jersey Evidence Rule 63(8)(a). Cf. Uniform Rule 63(8)(a) and California Evidence Code § 1222 which limit status as an admission in this regard to statements authorized by the party to be made "for" him, which is perhaps an ambiguous limitation to statements to third persons. Falknor, Vicarious Admissions and the Uniform Rules, 14 Vand.L.Rev. 855, 860–861 (1961).

(D) The tradition has been to test the admissibility of statements by agents, as admissions, by applying the usual test of agency. Was the admission made by the agent acting in the scope of his employment? Since few principals employ agents for the purpose of making damaging statements, the usual result was exclusion of the statement. Dissatisfaction with this loss of valuable and helpful evidence has been increasing. A substantial trend favors admitting statements related to a matter within the scope of the agency or employment. *Grayson v. Williams,* 256 F.2d 61 (10th Cir. 1958); *Koninklijke Luchtvaart Maatschappij N.V. KLM Royal Dutch Airlines v. Tuller,* 110 U.S.App.D.C. 282, 292 F.2d 775, 784 (1961); *Martin v. Savage Truck Lines,* Inc., 121 F.Supp. 417 (D.D.C.1954), and numerous state court decisions collected in 4 Wigmore, 1964 Supp. pp. 66–73, with comments by the editor that the statements should have been excluded as not within scope of agency. For the traditional view see *Northern Oil Co. v. Socony Mobil Oil Co.,* 347 F.2d 81, 85 (2d Cir.1965) and cases cited therein. Similar provisions are found in Uniform Rule 63(9)(a), Kansas Code of Civil Procedure § 60–460(i)(1), and New Jersey Evidence Rule 63(9)(a).

(E) The limitation upon the admissibility of statements of co-conspirators to those made "during the course and in furtherance of the conspiracy" is in the accepted pattern. While the broadened view of agency taken in item (iv) might suggest wider admissibility of statements of co-conspirators, the agency theory of conspiracy is at best a fiction and ought not to serve as a basis for admissibility beyond that already established. See Levie, Hearsay and Conspiracy, 52 Mich. L.Rev. 1159 (1954); Comment, 25 U.Chi.L.Rev. 530 (1958). The rule is consistent with the position of the Supreme Court in denying admissibility to statements made after the objectives of the conspiracy have either failed or been achieved. *Krulewitch v. United States,* 336 U.S. 440, 69 S.Ct. 716, 93 L.Ed. 790 (1949); *Wong Sun v. United States,* 371 U.S. 471, 490, 83 S.Ct. 407, 9 L.Ed.2d 441 (1963). For similarly limited provisions see California Evidence Code § 1223 and New Jersey Rule 63(9)(b). Cf. Uniform Rule 63(9)(b).

1974 Enactment

Note to Subdivision (d)(1). Present federal law, except in the Second Circuit, permits the use of prior inconsistent statements of a witness for impeachment only. Rule 801(d)(1) as proposed by the Court would have permitted all such statements to be admissible as substantive evidence, an approach followed by a small but growing number of State jurisdictions and recently held constitutional in California v. Green, 399 U.S. 149 (1970). Although there was some support expressed for the Court Rule, based largely on the need to counteract the effect of witness intimidation in criminal cases, the Committee decided to adopt a compromise version of the Rule similar to the position of the Second Circuit. The Rule as amended draws a distinction between types of prior inconsistent statements (other than statements of identification of a person made after perceiving him which are currently admissible, see United States v. Anderson, 406 F.2d 719, 720 (4th Cir.), cert. denied, 395 U.S. 967 (1969)) and allows only those made while the declarant was subject to cross-examination at a trial or hearing or in a deposition, to be admissible for their truth. Compare United States v. DeSisto, 329 F.2d 929 (2nd Cir.), cert. denied, 377 U.S. 979 (1964); United States v. Cunningham, 446 F.2d 194 (2nd Cir.1971) (restricting the admissibility of prior inconsistent statements as substantive evidence to those made under oath in a formal proceeding, but not requiring that there have been an opportunity for cross-examination). The rationale for the Committee's decision is that (1) unlike in most other situations involving unsworn or oral statements, there can be no dispute as to whether the prior statement was made; and (2) the context of a formal proceeding, an oath, and the opportunity for cross-examination provide firm additional assurances of the reliability of the prior statement. House Report No. 93–650.

Note to Subdivision (d)(1)(A). Rule 801 defines what is and what is not hearsay for the purpose of admitting a prior statement as substantive evidence. A prior statement of a witness at a trial or hearing which is inconsistent with his testimony is, of course, always admissible for the purpose of impeaching the witness' credibility.

As submitted by the Supreme Court, subdivision (d)(1)(A) made admissible as substantive evidence the prior statement of a witness inconsistent with his present testimony.

The House severely limited the admissibility of prior inconsistent statements by adding a requirement that the prior statement must have been subject to cross-examination, thus precluding even the use of grand jury statements. The requirement that the prior statement must have been subject to cross-examination appears unnecessary since this rule comes into play only when the witness testifies in the present trial. At that time, he is on the stand and can explain an earlier position and be cross-examined as to both.

The requirement that the statement be under oath also appears unnecessary. Notwithstanding the absence of an oath contemporaneous with the statement, the witness, when on the stand, qualifying or denying the prior statement, is under oath. In any event, of all the many recognized exceptions to the hearsay rule, only one (former testimony) requires that the out-of-court statement have been made under oath. With respect to the lack of evidence of the demeanor of the witness at the time of the prior statement, it would be difficult to improve upon Judge Learned Hand's observation that when the jury decides that the truth is not what the witness says now but what he said before, they are still deciding from what they see and hear in court. [*Di Carlo v. U.S.*, 6 F.2d 364 (2d Cir.1925)].

The rule as submitted by the Court has positive advantages. The prior statement was made nearer in time to the events, when memory was fresher and intervening influences had not been brought into play. A realistic method is provided for dealing with the turncoat witness who changes his story on the stand [see Comment, California Evidence Code § 1235; McCormick, Evidence, § 38 (2nd ed. 1972)].

New Jersey, California, and Utah have adopted a rule similar to this one; and Nevada, New Mexico, and Wisconsin have adopted the identical Federal rule.

For all of these reasons, we think the House amendment should be rejected and the rule as submitted by the Supreme Court reinstated. [It would appear that some of the opposition to this Rule is based on a concern that a person could be convicted solely upon evidence admissible under this Rule. The Rule, however, is not addressed to the question of the sufficiency of evidence to send a case to the jury, but merely as to its admissibility. Factual circumstances could well arise where, if this were the sole evidence, dismissal would be appropriate.]

Note to Subdivision (d)(1)(C). As submitted by the Supreme Court and as passed by the House, subdivision (d)(1)(C) of rule 801 made admissible the prior statement identifying a person made after perceiving him. The committee decided to delete this provision because of the concern that a person could be convicted solely upon evidence admissible under this subdivision.

Note to Subdivision 801(d)(2)(E). The House approved the long-accepted rule that "a statement by a coconspirator of a party during the course and in furtherance of the conspiracy" is not hearsay as it was submitted by the Supreme Court. While the rule refers to a coconspirator, it is this committee's understanding that the rule is meant to carry forward the universally accepted doctrine that a joint venturer is considered as a coconspirator for the purposes of this rule even though no conspiracy has been charged. *United States v. Rinaldi*, 393 F.2d 97, 99 (2d Cir.), cert. denied 393 U.S. 913 (1968); *United States v. Spencer*, 415 F.2d 1301, 1304 (7th Cir., 1969). Senate Report No. 93–1277.

Rule 801 supplies some basic definitions for the rules of evidence that deal with hearsay. Rule 801(d)(1) defines certain statements as not hearsay. The Senate amendments make two changes in it.

Note to Subdivision (d)(1)(A). The House bill provides that a statement is not hearsay if the declarant testifies and is subject to cross-examination concerning the statement and if the statement is inconsistent with his testimony and was given under oath subject to cross-examination and subject to the penalty of perjury at a trial or hearing or in a deposition. The Senate amendment drops the requirement that the prior statement be given under oath subject to cross-examination and subject to the penalty of perjury at a trial or hearing or in a deposition.

The Conference adopts the Senate amendment with an amendment, so that the rule now requires that the prior inconsistent statement be given under oath subject to the penalty of perjury at a trial, hearing, or other proceeding, or in a deposition. The rule as adopted covers statements before a grand jury. Prior inconsistent statements may, of course, be used for impeaching the credibility of a witness. When the prior inconsistent statement is one made by a defendant in a criminal case, it is covered by Rule 801(d)(2).

Note to Subdivision (d)(1)(C). The House bill provides that a statement is not hearsay if the declarant testifies and is subject to cross-examination concerning the statement and the statement is one of identification of a person made after perceiving him. The Senate amendment eliminated this provision.

The Conference adopts the Senate amendment. House Report No. 93–1597.

1987 Amendment

The amendments are technical. No substantive change is intended.

1997 Amendment

Rule 801(d)(2) has been amended in order to respond to three issues raised by *Bourjaily v. United States*, 483 U.S. 171 (1987). First, the amendment codifies the holding in *Bourjaily* by stating expressly that a court shall consider the contents of a coconspirator's statement in determining "the existence of the conspiracy and the participation therein of the declarant and the party against whom the statement is offered." According to *Bourjaily*, Rule 104(a) requires these preliminary questions to be established by a preponderance of the evidence.

Second, the amendment resolves an issue on which the Court had reserved decision. It provides that the contents of the declarant's statement do not alone suffice to establish a conspiracy in which the declarant and the defendant participated. The court must consider in addition the circumstances surrounding the statement, such as the identity of the speaker, the context in which the statement was made, or evidence corroborating the contents of the statement in making its determination as to each preliminary question. This amendment is in accordance with existing practice. Every court of appeals that has resolved this issue requires some evidence in addition to the contents of the statement. *See, e.g., United States v. Beckham*, 968 F.2d 47, 51 (D.C.Cir. 1992); *United States v. Sepulveda*, 15 F.3d 1161, 1181–82 (1st Cir.1993), *cert. denied*, 114 S.Ct. 2714 (1994); *United States v. Daly*, 842 F.2d 1380, 1386 (2d Cir.), *cert. denied*, 488 U.S. 821 (1988); *United States v. Clark*, 18 F.3d 1337, 1341–42 (6th Cir.), *cert. denied*, 115 S.Ct. 152 (1994); *United States v. Zambrana*, 841 F.2d 1320, 1344–45 (7th Cir.1988); *United States v. Silverman*, 861 F.2d 571, 577 (9th Cir.1988); *United States v. Gordon*, 844 F.2d 1397, 1402 (9th Cir.1988); *United States v. Hernandez*, 829 F.2d 988, 993 (10th Cir. 1987), *cert. denied*, 485 U.S. 1013 (1988); *United States v. Byrom*, 910 F.2d 725, 736 (11th Cir.1990).

Third, the amendment extends the reasoning of Bourjaily to statements offered under subdivisions (C) and (D) of Rule 801(d)(2). In Bourjaily, the Court rejected treating foundational facts pursuant to the law of agency in favor of an evidentiary approach governed by Rule 104(a). The Advisory Committee believes it appropriate to treat analogously preliminary questions relating to the declarant's authority under subdivision (C), and the agency or employment relationship and scope thereof under subdivision (D).

GAP Report on Rule 801. The word "shall" was substituted for the word "may" in line 19. The second sentence of the committee note was changed accordingly.

HISTORICAL NOTES

Effective Date of 1975 Amendment

Section 2 of Pub.L. 94–113 provided that: "This Act [enacting cl. (c) of subd. (d)] shall become effective on the fifteenth day after the date of the enactment of this Act [Oct. 16, 1975]."

Rule 802. Hearsay Rule

Hearsay is not admissible except as provided by these rules or by other rules prescribed by the Supreme Court pursuant to statutory authority or by Act of Congress.

(Pub.L. 93–595, § 1, Jan. 2, 1975, 88 Stat. 1939.)

ADVISORY COMMITTEE NOTES

1972 Proposed Rules

The provision excepting from the operation of the rule hearsay which is made admissible by other rules adopted by the Supreme Court or by Act of Congress continues the admissibility thereunder of hearsay which would not qualify under these Evidence Rules. The following examples illustrate the working of the exception:

Federal Rules of Civil Procedure

Rule 4(g): proof of service by affidavit.

Rule 32: admissibility of depositions.

Rule 43(e): affidavits when motion based on facts not appearing of record.

Rule 56: affidavits in summary judgment proceedings.

Rule 65(b): showing by affidavit for temporary restraining order.

Federal Rules of Criminal Procedure

Rule 4(a): affidavits to show grounds for issuing warrants.

Rule 12(b)(4): affidavits to determine issues of fact in connection with motions.

Acts of Congress

10 U.S.C. § 7730: affidavits of unavailable witnesses in actions for damages caused by vessel in naval service, or towage or salvage of same, when taking of testimony or bringing of action delayed or stayed on security grounds.

29 U.S.C. § 161(4): affidavit as proof of service in NLRB proceedings.

38 U.S.C. § 5206: affidavit as proof of posting notice of sale of unclaimed property by Veterans Administration.

Rule 803. Hearsay Exceptions; Availability of Declarant Immaterial

The following are not excluded by the hearsay rule, even though the declarant is available as a witness:

(1) Present sense impression. A statement describing or explaining an event or condition made while the declarant was perceiving the event or condition, or immediately thereafter.

(2) Excited utterance. A statement relating to a startling event or condition made while the declarant was under the stress of excitement caused by the event or condition.

(3) Then existing mental, emotional, or physical condition. A statement of the declarant's then existing state of mind, emotion, sensation, or physical condition (such as intent, plan, motive, design, mental feeling, pain, and bodily health), but not including a statement of memory or belief to prove the fact remembered or believed unless it relates to the execution, revocation, identification, or terms of declarant's will.

(4) Statements for purposes of medical diagnosis or treatment. Statements made for purposes of medical diagnosis or treatment and describing medical history, or past or present symptoms, pain, or sensations, or the inception or general character of the cause or external source thereof insofar as reasonably pertinent to diagnosis or treatment.

(5) Recorded recollection. A memorandum or record concerning a matter about which a witness once had knowledge but now has insufficient recollection to enable the witness to testify fully and accurately, shown to have been made or adopted by the witness when the matter was fresh in the witness' memory and to reflect that knowledge correctly. If admitted, the memorandum or record may be read into evidence but may not itself be received as an exhibit unless offered by an adverse party.

(6) Records of regularly conducted activity. A memorandum, report, record, or data compilation, in any form, of acts, events, conditions, opinions, or diagnoses, made at or near the time by, or from information transmitted by, a person with knowledge, if kept in the course of a regularly conducted business activity, and if it was the regular practice of that business activity to make the memorandum, report, record, or data compilation, all as shown by the testimony of the custodian or other qualified witness, unless the source of information or the method or circumstances of preparation indicate lack of trustworthiness. The term "business" as used in this paragraph includes business, institution, association, profession, occupation, and calling of every kind, whether or not conducted for profit.

(7) Absence of entry in records kept in accordance with the provisions of paragraph (6). Evidence that a matter is not included in the memoranda reports, records, or data compilations, in any form, kept in accordance with the provisions of paragraph (6), to prove the nonoccurrence or nonexistence of the matter, if the matter was of a kind of which a memorandum, report, record, or data compilation was regularly made and preserved, unless the sources of information or other circumstances indicate lack of trustworthiness.

(8) Public records and reports. Records, reports, statements, or data compilations, in any form, of public offices or agencies, setting forth (A) the activities of the office or agency, or (B) matters observed pursuant to duty imposed by law as to which matters there was a duty to report, excluding, however, in criminal cases matters observed by police officers and other law enforcement personnel, or (C) in civil actions and proceedings and against the Government in criminal cases, factual findings resulting from an investigation made pursuant to authority granted by law, unless the sources of information or other circumstances indicate lack of trustworthiness.

(9) Records of vital statistics. Records or data compilations, in any form, of births, fetal deaths, deaths, or marriages, if the report thereof was made to a public office pursuant to requirements of law.

(10) Absence of public record or entry. To prove the absence of a record, report, statement, or data compilation, in any form, or the nonoccurrence or nonexistence of a matter of which a record, report, statement, or data compilation, in any form, was regularly made and preserved by a public office or agency, evidence in the form of a certification in accordance with rule 902, or testimony, that diligent search failed to disclose the record, report, statement, or data compilation, or entry.

(11) Records of religious organizations. Statements of births, marriages, divorces, deaths, legitimacy, ancestry, relationship by blood or marriage, or other similar facts of personal or family history, contained in a regularly kept record of a religious organization.

(12) Marriage, baptismal, and similar certificates. Statements of fact contained in a certificate that the maker performed a marriage or other ceremony or administered a sacrament, made by a clergyman, public official, or other person authorized by the rules or practices of a religious organization or by law to perform the act certified, and purporting to have been issued at the time of the act or within a reasonable time thereafter.

(13) Family records. Statements of fact concerning personal or family history contained in family Bibles, genealogies, charts, engravings on rings, inscriptions on family portraits, engravings on urns, crypts, or tombstones, or the like.

(14) Records of documents affecting an interest in property. The record of a document purporting to establish or affect an interest in property, as proof of the content of the original recorded document and its execution and delivery by each person by whom it purports to have been executed, if the record is a record of a public office and an applicable statute authorizes the recording of documents of that kind in that office.

(15) Statements in documents affecting an interest in property. A statement contained in a document purporting to establish or affect an interest in property if the matter stated was relevant to the purpose of the document, unless dealings with the property since the document was made have been inconsistent with the truth of the statement or the purport of the document.

(16) Statements in ancient documents. Statements in a document in existence twenty years or more the authenticity of which is established.

(17) Market reports, commercial publications. Market quotations, tabulations, lists, directories, or other published compilations, generally used and relied upon by the public or by persons in particular occupations.

(18) Learned treatises. To the extent called to the attention of an expert witness upon cross-examination or relied upon by the expert witness in direct examination, statements contained in published treatises, periodicals, or pamphlets on a subject of history, medicine, or other science or art, established as a reliable authority by the testimony or admission of the witness or by other expert testimony or by judicial notice. If admitted, the statements may be read into evidence but may not be received as exhibits.

(19) Reputation concerning personal or family history. Reputation among members of a person's family by blood, adoption, or marriage, or among a person's associates, or in the community, concerning a person's birth, adoption, marriage, divorce, death, legitimacy, relationship by blood, adoption, or marriage, ancestry, or other similar fact of personal or family history.

(20) Reputation concerning boundaries or general history. Reputation in a community, arising before the controversy, as to boundaries of or customs affecting lands in the community, and reputation as to events of general history important to the community or State or nation in which located.

(21) Reputation as to character. Reputation of a person's character among associates or in the community.

(22) Judgment of previous conviction. Evidence of a final judgment, entered after a trial or upon a plea of guilty (but not upon a plea of nolo contendere), adjudging a person guilty of a crime punishable by death or imprisonment in excess of one year, to prove any fact essential to sustain the judgment, but not including, when offered by the Government in a criminal prosecution for purposes other than impeachment, judgments against persons other than the accused. The pendency of an appeal may be shown but does not affect admissibility.

(23) Judgment as to personal, family, or general history, or boundaries. Judgments as proof of matters of personal, family or general history, or boundaries, essential to the judgment, if the same would be provable by evidence of reputation.

(24) [Transferred to Rule 807]

(Pub.L. 93–595, § 1, Jan. 2, 1975, 88 Stat. 1939; Pub.L. 94–149, § 1(11), Dec. 12, 1975, 89 Stat. 805; Mar. 2, 1987, eff. Oct. 1, 1987; Apr. 11, 1997, eff. Dec. 1, 1997.)

ADVISORY COMMITTEE NOTES

1972 Proposed Rules

The exceptions are phrased in terms of nonapplication of the hearsay rule, rather than in positive terms of admissibility, in order to repel any implication that other possible grounds for exclusion are eliminated from consideration.

The present rule proceeds upon the theory that under appropriate circumstances a hearsay statement may possess circumstantial guarantees of trustworthiness sufficient to justify nonproduction of the declarant in person at the trial even though he may be available. The theory finds vast support in the many exceptions to the hearsay rule developed by the common law in which unavailability of the declarant is not a relevant factor. The present rule is a synthesis of them, with revision where modern developments and conditions are believed to make that course appropriate.

In a hearsay situation, the declarant is, of course, a witness, and neither this rule nor Rule 804 dispenses with the requirement of firsthand knowledge. It may appear from his statement or be inferable from circumstances. See Rule 602.

Note to Paragraphs (1) and (2). In considerable measure these two examples overlap, though based on somewhat different theories. The most significant practical difference will lie in the time lapse allowable between event and statement.

The underlying theory of Exception [paragraph] (1) is that substantial contemporaneity of event and statement negate the likelihood of deliberate or conscious misrepresentation. Moreover, if the witness is the declarant, he may be examined on the statement. If the witness is not the declarant, he may be examined as to the circumstances as an aid in evaluating the statement. Morgan, Basic Problems of Evidence 340–341 (1962).

The theory of Exception [paragraph] (2) is simply that circumstances may produce a condition of excitement which temporarily stills the capacity of reflection and produces utterances free of conscious fabrication. 6 Wigmore § 1747, p. 135. Spontaneity is the key factor in each instance, though arrived at by somewhat different routes. Both are needed in order to avoid needless niggling.

While the theory of Exception [paragraph] (2) has been criticized on the ground that excitement impairs accuracy of observation as well as eliminating conscious fabrication, Hutchins and Slesinger, Some Observations on the Law of Evidence: Spontaneous Exclamations, 28 Colum.L.Rev. 432 (1928), it finds support in cases without number. See cases in 6 Wigmore § 1750; Annot. 53 A.L.R.2d 1245 (statements as to cause of or responsibility for motor vehicle accident); Annot., 4 A.L.R.3d 149 (accusatory statements by homicide victims). Since unexciting events are less likely to evoke comment, decisions involving Exception [paragraph] (1) are far less numerous. Illustrative are *Tampa Elec. Co. v. Getrost,* 151 Fla. 558, 10 So.2d 83 (1942); *Houston Oxygen Co. v. Davis,* 139 Tex. 1, 161 S.W.2d 474 (1942); and cases cited in McCormick § 273, p. 585, n. 4.

With respect to the *time element,* Exception [paragraph] (1) recognizes that in many, if not most, instances precise contemporaneity is not possible and hence a slight lapse is allowable. Under Exception [paragraph] (2) the standard of measurement is the duration of the state of excitement. "How long can excitement prevail? Obviously there are no pat answers and the character of the transaction or event will largely determine the significance of the time factor." Slough, Spontaneous Statements and State of Mind, 46 Iowa L.Rev. 224, 243 (1961); McCormick § 272, p. 580.

Participation by the declarant is not required: a nonparticipant may be moved to describe what he perceives, and one may be startled by an event in which he is not an actor. Slough, *supra;* McCormick, *supra;* 6 Wigmore § 1755; Annot. 78 A.L.R.2d 300.

Whether *proof of the startling event* may be made by the statement itself is largely an academic question, since in most cases there is present at least circumstantial evidence that something of a startling nature must have occurred. For cases in which the evidence consists of the condition of the declarant (injuries, state of shock), see *Insurance Co. v. Mosely,* 75 U.S. (8 Wall.) 397, 19 L.Ed. 437 (1869); *Wheeler v. United States,* 93 U.S. App.D.C. 159, 211 F.2d 19 (1953), cert. denied 347 U.S. 1019, 74 S.Ct. 876, 98 L.Ed. 1140; *Wetherbee v. Safety Casualty Co.,* 219 F.2d 274 (5th Cir. 1955); *Lampe v. United States,* 97 U.S.App.D.C. 160, 229 F.2d 43 (1956). Nevertheless, on occasion the only evidence may be the content of the statement itself, and rulings that it may be sufficient are described as "increasing," Slough, *supra* at 246, and as the "prevailing practice," McCormick § 272, p. 579. Illustrative are *Armour & Co. v. Industrial Commission,* 78 Colo. 569, 243 P. 546 (1926); *Young v. Stewart,* 191 N.C. 297, 131 S.E. 735 (1926). Moreover, under Rule 104(a) the judge is not limited by the hearsay rule in passing upon preliminary questions of fact.

Proof of declarant's perception by his statement presents similar considerations when declarant is identified. *People v. Poland,* 22 Ill.2d 175, 174 N.E.2d 804 (1961). However, when declarant is an unidentified bystander, the cases indicate hesitancy in upholding the statement alone as sufficient, *Garrett v. Howden,* 73 N.M. 307, 387 P.2d 874 (1963); *Beck v. Dye,* 200 Wash. 1, 92 P.2d 1113 (1939), a result which would under appropriate circumstances be consistent with the rule.

Permissible *subject matter* of the statement is limited under Exception [paragraph] (1) to description or explanation of the event or condition, the assumption being that spontaneity, in the absence of a startling event, may extend no farther. In Exception [paragraph] (2), however, the statement need only "relate" to the startling event or condition, thus affording a broader scope of subject matter coverage. 6 Wigmore §§ 1750, 1754. See *Sanitary Grocery Co. v. Snead,* 67 App.D.C. 129, 90 F.2d 374 (1937), slip-and-fall case sustaining admissibility of clerk's statement. "That has been on the floor for a couple of hours," and *Murphy Auto Parts Co., Inc. v. Ball,* 101 U.S.App.D.C. 416, 249 F.2d 508 (1957), upholding admission, on issue of driver's agency, of his statement that he had to call on a customer and was in a hurry to get home. Quick, Hearsay, Excitement, Necessity and the Uniform Rules: A Reappraisal of Rule 63(4), 6 Wayne L.Rev. 204, 206–209 (1960).

Similar provisions are found in Uniform Rule 63(4)(a) and (b); California Evidence Code § 1240 (as to Exception (2) only); Kansas Code of Civil Procedure § 60–460(d)(1) and (2); New Jersey Evidence Rule 63(4).

Note to Paragraph (3). Exception [paragraph] (3) is essentially a specialized application of Exception [paragraph] (1), presented separately to enhance its usefulness and accessibility. See McCormick §§ 265, 268.

The exclusion of "statements of memory or belief to prove the fact remembered or believed" is necessary to avoid the virtual destruction of the hearsay rule which would otherwise result from allowing state of mind, provable by a hearsay statement, to serve as the basis for an inference of the happening of the event which produced the state of mind. *Shepard v. United States,* 290 U.S. 96, 54 S.Ct. 22, 78 L.Ed. 196 (1933); Maguire, The Hillmon Case—Thirty-three Years After, 38 Harv.L.Rev. 709, 719–731 (1925); Hinton, States of Mind and the Hearsay Rule, 1 U.Chi.L.Rev. 394, 421–423 (1934). The rule of *Mutual Life Ins. Co. v. Hillmon,* 145 U.S. 285, 12 S.Ct. 909, 36 L.Ed. 706 (1892), allowing evidence of intention as tending to prove the doing of the act intended, is, of course, left undisturbed.

The carving out, from the exclusion mentioned in the preceding paragraph, of declarations relating to the execution, revocation, identification, or terms of declarant's will represents and *ad hoc* judgment which finds ample reinforcement in the decisions, resting on practical grounds of necessity and expediency rather than logic. McCormick § 271, pp. 577–578; Annot. 34 A.L.R.2d 588, 62 A.L.R.2d 855. A similar recognition of the need for and practical value of this kind of evidence is found in California Evidence Code § 1260.

Note to Paragraph (4). Even those few jurisdictions which have shied away from generally admitting statements of present condition have allowed them if made to a physician for purposes of diagnosis and treatment in view of the patient's strong motivation to be truthful. McCormick § 266, p. 563. The same guarantee of trustworthiness extends to statements of past conditions and medical history, made for purposes of diagnosis or treatment. It also extends to statements as to causation, reasonably pertinent to the same purposes, in accord with the current trend. *Shell Oil Co. v. Industrial Commission,* 2 Ill.2d 590, 119 N.E.2d 224 (1954); McCormick § 266, p. 564; New Jersey Evidence Rule 63(12)(c). Statements as to fault would not ordinarily qualify under this latter language. Thus a patient's statement that he was struck by an automobile would qualify but not his statement that the car was driven through a red light. Under the exception the statement need not have been made to a physician. Statements to hospital attendants, ambulance drivers, or even members of the family might be included.

Conventional doctrine has excluded from the hearsay exception, as not within its guarantee of truthfulness, statements to a physician consulted only for the purpose of enabling him to testify. While these statements were not admissible as substantive evidence, the expert was allowed to state the basis of his opinion, including statements of this kind. The distinction thus called for was one most unlikely to be made by juries. The rule accordingly rejects the limitation. This position is consistent with the provision of Rule 703 that the facts on which expert testimony is based need not be admissible in evidence if of a kind ordinarily relied upon by experts in the field.

Note to Paragraph (5). A hearsay exception for recorded recollection is generally recognized and has been described as having "long been favored by the federal and practically all the state courts that have had occasion to decide the question." *United States v. Kelly,* 349 F.2d 720, 770 (2d Cir.1965), citing numerous cases and sustaining the exception against a claimed denial of the right of confrontation. Many additional cases are cited in Annot., 82 A.L.R.2d 473, 520. The guarantee of trustworthiness is found in the reliability inherent in a record made while events were still fresh in mind and accurately reflecting them. *Owens v. State,* 67 Md. 307, 316, 10 A. 210, 212 (1887).

The principal controversy attending the exception has centered, not upon the propriety of the exception itself, but upon the question whether a preliminary requirement of impaired memory on the part of the witness should be imposed. The authorities are divided. If regard be had only to the accuracy of the evidence, admittedly impairment of the memory of the witness adds nothing to it and should not be required. McCormick § 277, p. 593; 3 Wigmore § 738, p. 76; *Jordan v. People,* 151 Colo. 133, 376 P.2d 699 (1962), cert. denied 373 U.S. 944, 83 S.Ct. 1553, 10 L.Ed.2d 699;

Hall v. State, 223 Md. 158, 162 A.2d 751 (1960); *State v. Bindhammer,* 44 N.J. 372, 209 A.2d 124 (1965). Nevertheless, the absence of the requirement, it is believed, would encourage the use of statements carefully prepared for purposes of litigation under the supervision of attorneys, investigators, or claim adjusters. Hence the example includes a requirement that the witness not have "sufficient recollection to enable him to testify fully and accurately." To the same effect are California Evidence Code § 1237 and New Jersey Rule 63(1)(b), and this has been the position of the federal courts. *Vicksburg & Meridian R.R. v. O'Brien,* 119 U.S. 99, 7 S.Ct. 118, 30 L.Ed. 299 (1886); Ahern v. Webb, 268 F.2d 45 (10th Cir.1959); and see *N.L.R.B. v. Hudson Pulp and Paper Corp.,* 273 F.2d 660, 665 (5th Cir.1960); *N.L.R.B. v. Federal Dairy Co.,* 297 F.2d 487 (1st Cir.1962). But cf. *United States v. Adams,* 385 F.2d 548 (2d Cir.1967).

No attempt is made in the exception to spell out the method of establishing the initial knowledge or the contemporaneity and accuracy of the record, leaving them to be dealt with as the circumstances of the particular case might indicate. Multiple person involvement in the process of observing and recording, as in *Rathbun v. Brancatella,* 93 N.J.L. 222, 107 A. 279 (1919), is entirely consistent with the exception.

Locating the exception at this place in the scheme of the rules is a matter of choice. There were two other possibilities. The first was to regard the statement as one of the group of prior statements of a testifying witness which are excluded entirely from the category of hearsay by Rule 801(d)(1). That category, however, requires that declarant be "subject to cross-examination," as to which the impaired memory aspect of the exception raises doubts. The other possibility was to include the exception among those covered by Rule 804. Since unavailability is required by that rule and lack of memory is listed as a species of unavailability by the definition of the term in Rule 804(a)(3), that treatment at first impression would seem appropriate. The fact is, however, that the unavailability requirement of the exception is of a limited and peculiar nature. Accordingly, the exception is located at this point rather than in the context of a rule where unavailability is conceived of more broadly.

Note to Paragraph (6). Exception [paragraph] (6) represents an area which has received much attention from those seeking to improve the law of evidence. The Commonwealth Fund Act was the result of a study completed in 1927 by a distinguished committee under the chairmanship of Professor Morgan. Morgan et al., The Law of Evidence: Some Proposals for its Reform 63 (1927). With changes too minor to mention, it was adopted by Congress in 1936 as the rule for federal courts. 28 U.S.C. § 1732. A number of states took similar action. The Commissioners on Uniform State Laws in 1936 promulgated the Uniform Business Records as Evidence Act, 9A U.L.A. 506, which has acquired a substantial following in the states. Model Code Rule 514 and Uniform Rule 63(13) also deal with the subject. Difference of varying degrees of importance exist among these various treatments.

These reform efforts were largely within the context of business and commercial records, as the kind usually encountered, and concentrated considerable attention upon relaxing the requirement of producing as witnesses, or accounting for the nonproduction of, all participants in the process of gathering, transmitting, and recording information which the common law had evolved as a burdensome and crippling aspect of using records of this type. In their areas of primary emphasis on witnesses to be called and the general admissibility of ordinary business and commercial records, the Commonwealth Fund Act and the Uniform Act appear to have worked well. The exception seeks to preserve their advantages.

On the subject of what witnesses must be called, the Commonwealth Fund Act eliminated the common law requirement of calling or accounting for all participants by failing to mention it. *United States v. Mortimer,* 118 F.2d 266 (2d Cir.1941); *La Porte v. United States,* 300 F.2d 878 (9th Cir.1962); McCormick § 290, p. 608. Model Code Rule 514 and Uniform Rule 63(13) did likewise. The Uniform Act, however, abolished the common law requirement in express terms, providing that the requisite foundation testimony might be furnished by "the custodian or other qualified witness." Uniform Business Records as Evidence Act, § 2; 9A U.L.A. 506. The exception follows the Uniform Act in this respect.

The element of unusual reliability of business records is said variously to be supplied by systematic checking, by regularity and continuity which produce habits of precision, by actual experience of business in relying upon them, or by a duty to make an accurate record as part of a continuing job or occupation. McCormick §§ 281, 286, 287; Laughlin, Business Entries and the Like, 46 Iowa L.Rev. 276 (1961). The model statutes and rules have sought to capture these factors and to extend their impact by employing the phrase "regular course of business," in conjunction with a definition of "business" far broader than its ordinarily accepted meaning. The result is a tendency unduly to emphasize a requirement of routineness and repetitiveness and an insistence that other types of records be squeezed into the fact patterns which give rise to traditional business records. The rule therefore adopts the phrase "the course of a regularly conducted activity" as capturing the essential basis of the hearsay exception as it has evolved and the essential element which can be abstracted from the various specifications of what is a "business."

Amplification of the kinds of activities producing admissible records has given rise to problems which conventional business records by their nature avoid. They are problems of the source of the recorded information, of entries in opinion form, of motivation, and of involvement as participant in the matters recorded.

Sources of information presented no substantial problem with ordinary business records. All participants, including the observer or participant furnishing the information to be recorded, were acting routinely, under a duty of accuracy, with employer reliance on the result, or in short "in the regular course of business." If, however, the supplier of the information does not act in the regular course, an essential link is broken; the assurance of accuracy does not extend to the information itself, and the fact that it may be recorded with scrupulous accuracy is of no avail. An illustration is the police report incorporating information obtained from a bystander: the officer qualifies as acting in the regular course but the informant does not. The leading case, *Johnson v. Lutz,* 253 N.Y. 124, 170 N.E. 517 (1930), held that a report thus prepared was inadmissible. Most of the authorities have agreed with the decision. Gencarella v. Fyfe, 171 F.2d 419 (1st Cir.1948); *Gordon v. Robinson,* 210 F.2d 192 (3d Cir.1954); *Standard Oil Co. of California v. Moore,* 251 F.2d

188, 214 (9th Cir.1957), cert. denied 356 U.S. 975, 78 S.Ct. 1139, 2 L.Ed.2d 1148; *Yates v. Bair Transport*, Inc., 249 F.Supp. 681 (S.D.N.Y.1965); Annot., 69 A.L.R.2d 1148. Cf. *Hawkins v. Gorea Motor Express, Inc.*, 360 F.2d 933 (2d Cir.1966); *Contra*, 5 Wigmore § 1530a, n. 1, pp. 391–392. The point is not dealt with specifically in the Commonwealth Fund Act, the Uniform Act, or Uniform Rule 63(13). However, Model Code Rule 514 contains the requirement "that it was the regular course of that business for one with personal knowledge * * * to make such a memorandum or record or to transmit information thereof to be included in such a memorandum or record * * *." The rule follows this lead in requiring an informant with knowledge acting in the course of the regularly conducted activity.

Entries in the form of opinions were not encountered in traditional business records in view of the purely factual nature of the items recorded, but they are now commonly encountered with respect to medical diagnoses, prognoses, and test results, as well as occasionally in other areas. The Commonwealth Fund Act provided only for records of an "act, transaction, occurrence, or event," while the Uniform Act, Model Code Rule 514, and Uniform Rule 63(13) merely added the ambiguous term "condition." The limited phrasing of the Commonwealth Fund Act, 28 U.S.C. § 1732, may account for the reluctance of some federal decisions to admit diagnostic entries. *New York Life Ins. Co. v. Taylor*, 79 U.S.App.D.C. 66, 147 F.2d 297 (1945); *Lyles v. United States*, 103 U.S.App.D.C. 22, 254 F.2d 725 (1957), cert. denied 356 U.S. 961, 78 S.Ct. 997, 2 L.Ed.2d 1067; *England v. United States*, 174 F.2d 466 (5th Cir.1949); *Skogen v. Dow Chemical Co.*, 375 F.2d 692 (8th Cir.1967). Other federal decisions, however, experienced no difficulty in freely admitting diagnostic entries. *Reed v. Order of United Commercial Travelers*, 123 F.2d 252 (2d Cir.1941); *Buckminster's Estate v. Commissioner of Internal Revenue*, 147 F.2d 331 (2d Cir.1944); *Medina v. Erickson*, 226 F.2d 475 (9th Cir. 1955); *Thomas v. Hogan*, 308 F.2d 355 (4th Cir.1962); *Glawe v. Rulon*, 284 F.2d 495 (8th Cir.1960). In the state courts, the trend favors admissibility. Borucki v. MacKenzie Bros. Co., 125 Conn. 92, 3 A.2d 224 (1938); *Allen v. St. Louis Public Service Co.*, 365 Mo. 677, 285 S.W.2d 663, 55 A.L.R.2d 1022 (1956); *People v. Kohlmeyer*, 284 N.Y. 366, 31 N.E.2d 490 (1940); *Weis v. Weis*, 147 Ohio St. 416, 72 N.E.2d 245 (1947). In order to make clear its adherence to the latter position, the rule specifically includes both diagnoses and opinions, in addition to acts, events, and conditions, as proper subjects of admissible entries.

Problems of the motivation of the informant have been a source of difficulty and disagreement. In *Palmer v. Hoffman*, 318 U.S. 109, 63 S.Ct. 477, 87 L.Ed. 645 (1943), exclusion of an accident report made by the since deceased engineer, offered by defendant railroad trustees in a grade crossing collision case, was upheld. The report was not "in the regular course of business," not a record of the systematic conduct of the business as a business, said the Court. The report was prepared for use in litigating, not railroading. While the opinion mentions the motivation of the engineer only obliquely, the emphasis on records of routine operations is significant only by virtue of impact on motivation to be accurate. Absence of routineness raises lack of motivation to be accurate. The opinion of the Court of Appeals had gone beyond mere lack of motive to be accurate: the engineer's statement was "dripping with motivations to misrepresent." *Hoffman v. Palmer*, 129 F.2d 976, 991 (2d Cir.1942). The direct introduction of motivation is a disturbing factor, since absence of motive to misrepresent has not traditionally been a requirement of the rule; that records might be self-serving has not been a ground for exclusion. Laughlin, Business Records and the Like, 46 Iowa L.Rev. 276, 285 (1961). As Judge Clark said in his dissent, "I submit that there is hardly a grocer's account book which could not be excluded on that basis." 129 F.2d at 1002. A physician's evaluation report of a personal injury litigant would appear to be in the routine of his business. If the report is offered by the party at whose instance it was made, however, it has been held inadmissible, *Yates v. Bair Transport, Inc.*, 249 F.Supp. 681 (S.D.N.Y.1965), otherwise if offered by the opposite party, *Korte v. New York, N.H. & H.R. Co.*, 191 F.2d 86 (2d Cir.1951), cert. denied 342 U.S. 868, 72 S.Ct. 108, 96 L.Ed. 652.

The decisions hinge on motivation and which party is entitled to be concerned about it. Professor McCormick believed that the doctor's report or the accident report were sufficiently routine to justify admissibility. McCormick § 287, p. 604. Yet hesitation must be experienced in admitting everything which is observed and recorded in the course of a regularly conducted activity. Efforts to set a limit are illustrated by *Hartzog v. United States*, 217 F.2d 706 (4th Cir.1954), error to admit worksheets made by since deceased deputy collector in preparation for the instant income tax evasion prosecution, and *United States v. Ware*, 247 F.2d 698 (7th Cir.1957), error to admit narcotics agents' records of purchases. See also Exception [paragraph] (8), *infra*, as to the public record aspects of records of this nature. Some decisions have been satisfied as to motivation of an accident report if made pursuant to statutory duty, United States v. New York Foreign Trade Zone Operators, 304 F.2d 792 (2d Cir.1962); Taylor v. Baltimore & O.R. Co., 344 F.2d 281 (2d Cir.1965), since the report was oriented in a direction other than the litigation which ensued. Cf. Matthews v. United States, 217 F.2d 409 (5th Cir.1954). The formulation of specific terms which would assure satisfactory results in all cases is not possible. Consequently the rule proceeds from the base that records made in the course of a regularly conducted activity will be taken as admissible but subject to authority to exclude if "the sources of information or other circumstances indicate lack of trustworthiness."

Occasional decisions have reached for enhanced accuracy by requiring involvement as a participant in matters reported. *Clainos v. United States*, 82 U.S.App.D.C. 278, 163 F.2d 593 (1947), error to admit police records of convictions; *Standard Oil Co. of California v. Moore*, 251 F.2d 188 (9th Cir.1957), cert. denied 356 U.S. 975, 78 S.Ct. 1139, 2 L.Ed.2d 1148, error to admit employees' records of observed business practices of others. The rule includes no requirement of this nature. Wholly acceptable records may involve matters merely observed, e.g. the weather.

The form which the "record" may assume under the rule is described broadly as a "memorandum, report, record, or data compilation, in any form." The expression "data compilation" is used as broadly descriptive of any means of storing information other than the conventional words and figures in written or documentary form. It includes, but is by no means limited to, electronic computer storage. The term is borrowed from revised Rule 34(a) of the Rules of Civil Procedure.

Note to Paragraph (7). Failure of a record to mention a matter which would ordinarily be mentioned is satisfactory evidence of its nonexistence. Uniform Rule 63(14), Comment. While probably not hearsay as defined in Rule 801, *supra,* decisions may be found which class the evidence not only as hearsay but also as not within any exception. In order to set the question at rest in favor of admissibility, it is specifically treated here. McCormick § 289, p. 609; Morgan, Basic Problems of Evidence 314 (1962); 5 Wigmore § 1531; Uniform Rule 63(14); California Evidence Code § 1272; Kansas Code of Civil Procedure § 60–460(n); New Jersey Evidence Rule 63(14).

Note to Paragraph (8). Public records are a recognized hearsay exception at common law and have been the subject of statutes without number. McCormick § 291. See, for example, 28 U.S.C. § 1733, the relative narrowness of which is illustrated by its nonapplicability to nonfederal public agencies, thus necessitating resort to the less appropriate business record exception to the hearsay rule. *Kay v. United States,* 255 F.2d 476 (4th Cir.1958). The rule makes no distinction between federal and nonfederal offices and agencies.

Justification for the exception is the assumption that a public official will perform his duty properly and the unlikelihood that he will remember details independently of the record. *Wong Wing Foo v. McGrath,* 196 F.2d 120 (9th Cir.1952), and see *Chesapeake & Delaware Canal Co. v. United States,* 250 U.S. 123, 39 S.Ct. 407, 63 L.Ed. 889 (1919). As to items (a) and (b), further support is found in the reliability factors underlying records of regularly conducted activities generally. See Exception [paragraph] (6), supra.

(a) Cases illustrating the admissibility of records of the office's or agency's own activities are numerous. *Chesapeake & Delaware Canal Co. v. United States,* 250 U.S. 123, 39 S.Ct. 407, 63 L.Ed. 889 (1919), Treasury records of miscellaneous receipts and disbursements; *Howard v. Perrin,* 200 U.S. 71, 26 S.Ct. 195, 50 L.Ed. 374 (1906), General Land Office records; *Ballew v. United States,* 160 U.S. 187, 16 S.Ct. 263, 40 L.Ed. 388 (1895). Pension Office records.

(b) Cases sustaining admissibility of records of matters observed are also numerous. *United States v. Van Hook,* 284 F.2d 489 (7th Cir.1960), remanded for resentencing 365 U.S. 609, 81 S.Ct. 823, 5 L.Ed.2d 821, letter from induction officer to District Attorney, pursuant to army regulations, stating fact and circumstances of refusal to be inducted; *T'Kach v. United States,* 242 F.2d 937 (5th Cir.1957), affidavit of White House personnel officer that search of records showed no employment of accused, charged with fraudulently representing himself as an envoy of the President; *Minnehaha County v. Kelley,* 150 F.2d 356 (8th Cir.1945); Weather Bureau records of rainfall; *United States v. Meyer,* 113 F.2d 387 (7th Cir.1940), cert. denied 311 U.S. 706, 61 S.Ct. 174, 85 L.Ed. 459, map prepared by government engineer from information furnished by men working under his supervision.

(c) The more controversial area of public records is that of the so-called "evaluative" report. The disagreement among the decisions has been due in part, no doubt, to the variety of situations encountered, as well as to differences in principle. Sustaining admissibility are such cases as *United States v. Dumas,* 149 U.S. 278, 13 S.Ct. 872, 37 L.Ed. 734 (1893), statement of account certified by Postmaster General in action against postmaster; *McCarty v. United States,* 185 F.2d 520 (5th Cir.1950), reh. denied 187 F.2d 234, Certificate of Settlement of General Accounting Office showing indebtedness and letter from Army official stating Government had performed, in action on contract to purchase and remove waste food from Army camp; *Moran v. Pittsburgh–Des Moines Steel Co.,* 183 F.2d 467 (3d Cir.1950), report of Bureau of Mines as to cause of gas tank explosion; Petition of W___, 164 F.Supp. 659 (E.D.Pa.1958), report by Immigration and Naturalization Service investigator that petitioner was known in community as wife of man to whom she was not married. To the opposite effect and denying admissibility are *Franklin v. Skelly Oil Co.,* 141 F.2d 568 (10th Cir. 1944), State Fire Marshal's report of cause of gas explosion; *Lomax Transp. Co. v. United States,* 183 F.2d 331 (9th Cir.1950), Certificate of Settlement from General Accounting Office in action for naval supplies lost in warehouse fire; *Yung Jin Teung v. Dulles,* 229 F.2d 244 (2d Cir.1956), "Status Reports" offered to justify delay in processing passport applications. Police reports have generally been excluded except to the extent to which they incorporate firsthand observations of the officer. Annot., 69 A.L.R.2d 1148. Various kinds of evaluative reports are admissible under federal statutes: 7 U.S.C. § 78, findings of Secretary of Agriculture prima facie evidence of true grade of grain; 7 U.S.C. § 210(f), findings of Secretary of Agriculture prima facie evidence in action for damages against stockyard owner; 7 U.S.C. § 292, order by Secretary of Agriculture prima facie evidence in judicial enforcement proceedings against producers association monopoly; 7 U.S.C. § 1622(h), Department of Agriculture inspection certificates of products shipped in interstate commerce prima facie evidence; 8 U.S.C. § 1440(c), separation of alien from military service on conditions other than honorable provable by certificate from department in proceedings to revoke citizenship; 18 U.S.C. § 4245, certificate of Director of Prisons that convicted person has been examined and found probably incompetent at time of trial prima facie evidence in court hearing on competency; 42 U.S.C. § 269(b), bill of health by appropriate official prima facie evidence of vessel's sanitary history and condition and compliance with regulations; 46 U.S.C. § 679, certificate of consul presumptive evidence of refusal of master to transport destitute seamen to United States. While these statutory exceptions to the hearsay rule are left undisturbed, Rule 802, the willingness of Congress to recognize a substantial measure of admissibility for evaluative reports is a helpful guide.

Factors which may be of assistance in passing upon the admissibility of evaluative reports include: (1) the timeliness of the investigation, McCormick, Can the Courts Make Wider Use of Reports of Official Investigations? 42 Iowa L.Rev. 363 (1957); (2) the special skill or experience of the official, *id.,* (3) whether a hearing was held and the level at which conducted, Franklin v. Skelly Oil Co., 141 F.2d 568 (10th Cir.1944); (4) possible motivation problems suggested by Palmer v. Hoffman, 318 U.S. 109, 63 S.Ct. 477, 87 L.Ed. 645 (1943). Others no doubt could be added.

The formulation of an approach which would give appropriate weight to all possible factors in every situation is an obvious impossibility. Hence the rule, as in Exception [paragraph] (6), assumes admissibility in the first instance but with ample provision for escape if sufficient negative factors are present. In one respect, however, the rule with respect to evaluative reports under item (c) is very specific: they are admissible only in civil cases and against the government in criminal cases in view of the almost certain collision with confrontation rights which would result from their use against the accused in a criminal case.

Note to Paragraph (9). Records of vital statistics are commonly the subject of particular statutes making them admissible in evidence, Uniform Vital Statistics Act, 9C U.L.A. 350 (1957). The rule is in principle narrower than Uniform Rule 63(16) which includes reports required of persons performing functions authorized by statute, yet in practical effect the two are substantially the same. Comment Uniform Rule 63(16). The exception as drafted is in the pattern of California Evidence Code § 1281.

Note to Paragraph (10). The principle of proving nonoccurrence of an event by evidence of the absence of a record which would regularly be made of its occurrence, developed in Exception [paragraph] (7) with respect to regularly conducted activities, is here extended to public records of the kind mentioned in Exceptions [paragraphs] (8) and (9). 5 Wigmore § 1633(6), p. 519. Some harmless duplication no doubt exists with Exception [paragraph] (7). For instances of federal statutes recognizing this method of proof, see 8 U.S.C. § 1284(b), proof of absence of alien crewman's name from outgoing manifest prima facie evidence of failure to detain or deport, and 42 U.S.C. § 405(c)(3), (4)(B), (4)(C), absence of HEW [Department of Health, Education, and Welfare] record prima facie evidence of no wages or self-employment income.

The rule includes situations in which absence of a record may itself be the ultimate focal point of inquiry, e.g. People v. Love, 310 Ill. 558, 142 N.E. 204 (1923), certificate of Secretary of State admitted to show failure to file documents required by Securities Law, as well as cases where the absence of a record is offered as proof of the nonoccurrence of an event ordinarily recorded.

The refusal of the common law to allow proof by certificate of the lack of a record or entry has no apparent justification, 5 Wigmore § 1678(7), p. 752. The rule takes the opposite position, as to Uniform Rule 63(17); California Evidence Code § 1284; Kansas Code of Civil Procedure § 60–460(c); New Jersey Evidence Rule 63(17). Congress has recognized certification as evidence of the lack of a record. 8 U.S.C. § 1360(d), certificate of Attorney General or other designated officer that no record of Immigration and Naturalization Service of specified nature or entry therein is found, admissible in alien cases.

Note to Paragraph (11). Records of activities of religious organizations are currently recognized as admissible at least to the extent of the business records exception to the hearsay rule, 5 Wigmore § 1523, p. 371, and Exception [paragraph] (6) would be applicable. However, both the business record doctrine and Exception [paragraph] (6) require that the person furnishing the information be one in the business or activity. The result is such decisions as Daily v. Grand Lodge, 311 Ill. 184, 142 N.E. 478 (1924), holding a church record admissible to prove fact, date, and place of baptism, but not age of child except that he had at least been born at the time. In view of the unlikelihood that false information would be furnished on occasions of this kind, the rule contains no requirement that the informant be in the course of the activity. See California Evidence Code § 1315 and Comment.

Note to Paragraph (12). The principle of proof by certification is recognized as to public officials in Exceptions [paragraphs] (8) and (10), and with respect to authentication in Rule 902. The present exception is a duplication to the extent that it deals with a certificate by a public official, as in the case of a judge who performs a marriage ceremony. The area covered by the rule is, however, substantially larger and extends the certification procedure to clergymen and the like who perform marriages and other ceremonies or administer sacraments. Thus certificates of such matters as baptism or confirmation, as well as marriage, are included. In principle they are as acceptable evidence as certificates of public officers. See 5 Wigmore § 1645, as to marriage certificates. When the person executing the certificate is not a public official, the self-authenticating character of documents purporting to emanate from public officials, see Rule 902, is lacking and proof is required that the person was authorized and did make the certificate. The time element, however, may safely be taken as supplied by the certificate, once authority and authenticity are established, particularly in view of the presumption that a document was executed on the date it bears.

For similar rules, some limited to certificates of marriage, with variations in foundation requirements, see Uniform Rule 63(18); California Evidence Code § 1316; Kansas Code of Civil Procedure § 60–460(p); New Jersey Evidence Rule 63(18).

Note to Paragraph (13). Records of family history kept in family Bibles have by long tradition been received in evidence. 5 Wigmore §§ 1495, 1496, citing numerous statutes and decisions. See also Regulations, Social Security Administration, 20 C.F.R. § 404.703(c), recognizing family Bible entries as proof of age in the absence of public or church records. Opinions in the area also include inscriptions on tombstones, publicly displayed pedigrees, and engravings on rings. Wigmore, *supra*. The rule is substantially identical in coverage with California Evidence Code § 1312.

Note to Paragraph (14). The recording of title documents is a purely statutory development. Under any theory of the admissibility of public records, the records would be receivable as evidence of the contents of the recorded document, else the recording process would be reduced to a nullity. When, however, the record is offered for the further purpose of proving execution and delivery, a problem of lack of firsthand knowledge by the recorder, not present as to contents, is presented. This problem is solved, seemingly in all jurisdictions, by qualifying for recording only those documents shown by a specified procedure, either acknowledgement or a form of probate, to have been executed and delivered. 5 Wigmore §§ 1647–1651. Thus what may appear in the rule, at first glance, as endowing the record with an effect independently of local law and inviting difficulties of an *Erie* nature under *Cities Service Oil Co. v. Dunlap,* 308 U.S. 208, 60 S.Ct. 201, 84 L.Ed. 196 (1939), is not present, since the local law in fact governs under the example.

Note to Paragraph (15). Dispositive documents often contain recitals of fact. Thus a deed purporting to have been executed by an attorney in fact may recite the existence of the power of attorney, or a deed may recite that the grantors are all the heirs of the last record owner. Under the rule, these recitals are exempted from the hearsay rule. The circumstances under which dispositive documents are executed and the requirement that the recital be germane to the purpose of the document are believed to be adequate guarantees of trustworthiness, particularly in view of the nonapplicability of the rule if dealings with the property have been inconsistent with the document. The age of the document is of no significance, though in practical application the document will most often be an ancient one. See Uniform Rule 63(29), Comment.

Similar provisions are contained in Uniform Rule 63(29); California Evidence Code § 1330; Kansas Code of Civil Procedure § 60–460(aa); New Jersey Evidence Rule 63(29).

Note to Paragraph (16). Authenticating a document as ancient, essentially in the pattern of the common law, as provided in Rule 901(b)(8), leaves open as a separate question the admissibility of assertive statements contained therein as against a hearsay objection. 7 Wigmore § 2145a. Wigmore further states that the ancient document technique of authentication is universally conceded to apply to all sorts of documents, including letters, records, contracts, maps, and certificates, in addition to title documents, citing numerous decisions. *Id.* § 2145. Since most of these items are significant evidentially only insofar as they are assertive, their admission in evidence must be as a hearsay exception. But see 5 *id.* § 1573, p. 429, referring to recitals in ancient deeds as a "limited" hearsay exception. The former position is believed to be the correct one in reason and authority. As pointed out in McCormick § 298, danger of mistake is minimized by authentication requirements, and age affords assurance that the writing antedates the present controversy. See *Dallas County v. Commercial Union Assurance Co.*, 286 F.2d 388 (5th Cir.1961), upholding admissibility of 58–year-old newspaper story. Cf. Morgan, Basic Problems of Evidence 364 (1962), but see *id.* 254.

For a similar provision, but with the added requirement that "the statement has since generally been acted upon as true by persons having an interest in the matter," see California Evidence Code § 1331.

Note to Paragraph (17). Ample authority at common law supported the admission in evidence of items falling in this category. While Wigmore's text is narrowly oriented to lists, etc., prepared for the use of a trade or profession, 6 Wigmore § 1702, authorities are cited which include other kinds of publications, for example, newspaper market reports, telephone directories, and city directories. *Id.* §§ 1702–1706. The basis of trustworthiness is general reliance by the public or by a particular segment of it, and the motivation of the compiler to foster reliance by being accurate.

For similar provisions, see Uniform Rule 63(30); California Evidence Code § 1340; Kansas Code of Civil Procedure § 60–460(bb); New Jersey Evidence Rule 63(30). Uniform Commercial Code § 2–724 provides for admissibility in evidence of "reports in official publications or trade journals or in newspapers or periodicals of general circulation published as the reports of such [established commodity] market."

Note to Paragraph (18). The writers have generally favored the admissibility of learned treatises, McCormick § 296, p. 621; Morgan, Basic Problems of Evidence 366 (1962); 6 Wigmore § 1692, with the support of occasional decisions and rules, *City of Dothan v. Hardy*, 237 Ala. 603, 188 So. 264 (1939); *Lewandowski v. Preferred Risk Mut. Ins. Co.*, 33 Wis.2d 69, 146 N.W.2d 505 (1966), 66 Mich.L.Rev. 183 (1967); Uniform Rule 63(31); Kansas Code of Civil Procedure § 60–460(cc), but the great weight of authority has been that learned treatises are not admissible as substantive evidence though usable in the cross-examination of experts. The foundation of the minority view is that the hearsay objection must be regarded as unimpressive when directed against treatises since a high standard of accuracy is engendered by various factors: the treatise is written primarily and impartially for professionals, subject to scrutiny and exposure for inaccuracy, with the reputation of the writer at stake. 6 Wigmore § 1692. Sound as this position may be with respect to trustworthiness, there is, nevertheless, an additional difficulty in the likelihood that the treatise will be misunderstood and misapplied without expert assistance and supervision. This difficulty is recognized in the cases demonstrating unwillingness to sustain findings relative to disability on the basis of judicially noticed medical texts. *Ross v. Gardner*, 365 F.2d 554 (6th Cir.1966); *Sayers v. Gardner*, 380 F.2d 940 (6th Cir.1967); *Colwell v. Gardner*, 386 F.2d 56 (6th Cir.1967); *Glendenning v. Ribicoff*, 213 F.Supp. 301 (W.D.Mo.1962); *Cook v. Celebrezze*, 217 F.Supp. 366 (W.D.Mo.1963); *Sosna v. Celebrezze*, 234 F.Supp. 289 (E.D.Pa.1964); and see *McDaniel v. Celebrezze*, 331 F.2d 426 (4th Cir.1964). The rule avoids the danger of misunderstanding and misapplication by limiting the use of treatises as substantive evidence to situations in which an expert is on the stand and available to explain and assist in the application of the treatise if desired. The limitation upon receiving the publication itself physically in evidence, contained in the last sentence, is designed, to further this policy.

The relevance of the use of treatises on cross-examination is evident. This use of treatises has been the subject of varied views. The most restrictive position is that the witness must have stated expressly on direct his reliance upon the treatise. A slightly more liberal approach still insists upon reliance but allows it to be developed on cross-examination. Further relaxation dispenses with reliance but requires recognition as an authority by the witness, developable on cross-examination. The greatest liberality is found in decisions allowing use of the treatise on cross-examination when its status as an authority is established by any means. Annot., 60 A.L.R.2d 77. The exception is hinged upon this last position, which is that of the Supreme Court, *Reilly v. Pinkus*, 338 U.S. 269, 70 S.Ct. 110, 94 L.Ed. 63 (1949), and of recent well considered state court decisions, *City of St. Petersburg v. Ferguson*, 193 So.2d 648 (Fla.App.1967), cert. denied Fla., 201 So.2d 556; *Darling v. Charleston Memorial Community Hospital*, 33 Ill.2d 326, 211 N.E.2d 253 (1965); *Dabroe v. Rhodes Co.*, 64 Wash.2d 431, 392 P.2d 317 (1964).

In Reilly v. Pinkus, *supra*, the Court pointed out that testing of professional knowledge was incomplete without exploration of the witness' knowledge of and attitude toward established treatises in the field. The process works equally well in reverse and furnishes the basis of the rule.

The rule does not require that the witness rely upon or recognize the treatise as authoritative, thus avoiding the possibility that the expert may at the outset block cross-examination by refusing to concede reliance or authoritativeness. Dabroe v. Rhodes Co., *supra*. Moreover, the rule avoids the unreality of admitting evidence for the purpose of impeachment only, with an instruction to the jury not to consider it otherwise. The parallel to the treatment of prior inconsistent statements will be apparent. See Rules 613(b) and 801(d)(1).

Note to Paragraphs (19), (20) and (21). Trustworthiness in reputation evidence is found "when the topic is such that the facts are likely to have been inquired about and that persons having personal knowledge have disclosed facts which have thus been discussed in the community; and thus the community's conclusion, if any has been formed, is likely to be a trustworthy one." 5 Wigmore § 1580, p. 444, and see also § 1583. On this common foundation, reputation as to land boundaries, customs, general history, character, and marriage have come to be regarded as admissible. The breadth of the underlying principle suggests the formulation of an equally broad exception, but tradition has in fact been much narrower and more particularized, and this is the pattern of these exceptions in the rule.

Exception [paragraph] (19) is concerned with matters of personal and family history. Marriage is universally conceded to be a proper subject of proof by evidence of reputation in the community. 5 Wigmore § 1602. As to such items as legitimacy, relationship, adoption, birth, and death, the decisions are divided. *Id.* § 1605. All seem to be susceptible to being the subject of well founded repute. The "world" in which the reputation may exist may be family, associates, or community. This world has proved capable of expanding with changing times from the single uncomplicated neighborhood, in which all activities take place, to the multiple and unrelated worlds of work, religious affiliation, and social activity, in each of which a reputation may be generated. *People v. Reeves,* 360 Ill. 55, 195 N.E. 443 (1935); *State v. Axilrod,* 248 Minn. 204, 79 N.W.2d 677 (1956); Mass.Stat. 1947, c. 410, M.G.L.A. c. 233 § 21A; 5 Wigmore § 1616. The family has often served as the point of beginning for allowing community reputation. 5 Wigmore § 1488. For comparable provisions see Uniform Rule 63(26), (27)(c); California Evidence Code §§ 1313, 1314; Kansas Code of Civil Procedure § 60–460(x), (y)(3); New Jersey Evidence Rule 63(26), (27)(c).

The first portion of Exception [paragraph] (20) is based upon the general admissibility of evidence of reputation as to land boundaries and land customs, expanded in this country to include private as well as public boundaries. McCormick § 299, p. 625. The reputation is required to antedate the controversy, though not to be ancient. The second portion is likewise supported by authority, *id.,* and is designed to facilitate proof of events when judicial notice is not available. The historical character of the subject matter dispenses with any need that the reputation antedate the controversy with respect to which it is offered. For similar provisions see Uniform Rule 63(27)(a), (b); California Evidence Code §§ 1320–1322; Kansas Code of Civil Procedure § 60–460(y), (1), (2); New Jersey Evidence Rule 63(27)(a), (b).

Exception [paragraph] (21) recognizes the traditional acceptance of reputation evidence as a means of proving human character. McCormick §§ 44, 158. The exception deals only with the hearsay aspect of this kind of evidence. Limitations upon admissibility based on other grounds will be found in Rules 404, relevancy of character evidence generally, and 608, character of witness. The exception is in effect a reiteration, in the context of hearsay, of Rule 405(a). Similar provisions are contained in Uniform Rule 63(28); California Evidence Code § 1324; Kansas Code of Civil Procedure § 60–460(z); New Jersey Evidence Rule 63(28).

Note to Paragraph (22). When the status of a former judgment is under consideration in subsequent litigation, three possibilities must be noted: (1) the former judgment is conclusive under the doctrine of res judicata, either as a bar or a collateral estoppel; or (2) it is admissible in evidence for what it is worth; or (3) it may be of no effect at all. The first situation does not involve any problem of evidence except in the way that principles of substantive law generally bear upon the relevancy and materiality of evidence. The rule does not deal with the substantive effect of the judgment as a bar or collateral estoppel. When, however, the doctrine of res judicata does not apply to make the judgment either a bar or a collateral estoppel, a choice is presented between the second and third alternatives. The rule adopts the second for judgments of criminal conviction of felony grade. This is the direction of the decisions, Annot., 18 A.L.R.2d 1287, 1299, which manifest an increasing reluctance to reject *in toto* the validity of the law's factfinding processes outside the confines of res judicata and collateral estoppel. While this may leave a jury with the evidence of conviction but without means to evaluate it, as suggested by Judge Hinton, Note 27 Ill.L.Rev. 195 (1932), it seems safe to assume that the jury will give it substantial effect unless defendant offers a satisfactory explanation, a possibility not foreclosed by the provision. But see *North River Ins. Co. v. Militello,* 104 Colo. 28, 88 P.2d 567 (1939), in which the jury found for plaintiff on a fire policy despite the introduction of his conviction for arson. For supporting federal decisions see Clark, J., in *New York & Cuba Mail S.S. Co. v. Continental Cas. Co.,* 117 F.2d 404, 411 (2d Cir.1941); *Connecticut Fire Ins. Co. v. Farrara,* 277 F.2d 388 (8th Cir.1960).

Practical considerations require exclusion of convictions of minor offenses, not because the administration of justice in its lower echelons must be inferior, but because motivation to defend at this level is often minimal or nonexistent. *Cope v. Goble,* 39 Cal.App.2d 448, 103 P.2d 598 (1940); *Jones v. Talbot,* 87 Idaho 498, 394 P.2d 316 (1964); *Warren v. Marsh,* 215 Minn. 615, 11 N.W.2d 528 (1943); Annot., 18 A.L.R.2d 1287, 1295–1297; 16 Brooklyn L.Rev. 286 (1950); 50 Colum.L.Rev. 529 (1950); 35 Cornell L.Q. 872 (1950). Hence the rule includes only convictions of felony grade, measured by federal standards.

Judgments of conviction based upon pleas of *nolo contendere* are not included. This position is consistent with the treatment of *nolo* pleas in Rule 410 and the authorities cited in the Advisory Committee's Note in support thereof.

While these rules do not in general purport to resolve constitutional issues, they have in general been drafted with a view to avoiding collision with constitutional principles. Consequently the exception does not include evidence of the conviction of a third person, offered against the accused in a criminal prosecution to prove any fact essential to sustain the judgment of conviction. A contrary position would seem clearly to violate the right of confrontation. *Kirby v. United States,* 174 U.S. 47, 19 S.Ct. 574, 43 L.Ed. 890 (1899), error to convict of possessing stolen postage stamps with the only evidence of theft being the record of conviction of the thieves. The situation is to be distinguished from cases in which conviction of another person is an element of the crime, e.g. 15 U.S.C. § 902(d), interstate shipment of firearms to a known convicted felon, and, as specifically provided, from impeachment.

For comparable provisions see Uniform Rule 63(20); California Evidence Code § 1300; Kansas Code of Civil Procedure § 60–460(r); New Jersey Evidence Rule 63(20).

Note to Paragraph (23). A hearsay exception in this area was originally justified on the ground that verdicts were evidence of reputation. As trial by jury graduated from the category of neighborhood inquests, this theory lost its validity. It was never valid as to chancery decrees. Nevertheless the rule persisted, though the judges and writers shifted ground and began saying that the judgment or decree was as good evidence as reputation. See *City of London v. Clerke,* Carth. 181, 90 Eng.Rep. 710 (K.B. 1691); *Neill v. Duke of Devonshire,* 8 App.Cas. 135 (1882). The shift appears to be correct, since the process of inquiry, sifting, and scrutiny which is relied upon to render reputation reliable is present in perhaps greater measure in the process of litigation. While this might suggest a broader area of application, the affinity to reputation is strong, and paragraph [paragraph] (23) goes no further, not even including character.

The leading case in the *United States, Patterson v. Gaines,* 47 U.S. (6 How.) 550, 599, 12 L.Ed. 553 (1847), follows in the pattern of the English decisions, mentioning as illustrative matters thus provable: manorial rights, public rights of way, immemorial custom, disputed boundary, and pedigree. More recent recognition of the principle is found in *Grant Bros. Construction Co. v. United States,* 232 U.S. 647, 34 S.Ct. 452, 58 L.Ed. 776 (1914), in action for penalties under Alien Contract Labor Law, decision of board of inquiry of Immigration Service admissible to prove alienage of laborers, as a matter of pedigree; *United States v. Mid–Continent Petroleum Corp.,* 67 F.2d 37 (10th Cir.1933), records of commission enrolling Indians admissible on pedigree; *Jung Yen Loy v. Cahill,* 81 F.2d 809 (9th Cir.1936), board decisions as to citizenship of plaintiff's father admissible in proceeding for declaration of citizenship. *Contra,* In re Estate of Cunha, 49 Haw. 273, 414 P.2d 925 (1966).

1974 Enactment

Note to Paragraph (3). Rule 803(3) was approved in the form submitted by the Court to Congress. However, the Committee intends that the Rule be construed to limit the doctrine of *Mutual Life Insurance Co. v. Hillmon,* 145 U.S. 285, 295–300 (1892), so as to render statements of intent by a declarant admissible only to prove his future conduct, not the future conduct of another person.

Note to Paragraph (4). After giving particular attention to the question of physical examination made solely to enable a physician to testify, the Committee approved Rule 803(4) as submitted to Congress, with the understanding that it is not intended in any way to adversely affect present privilege rules or those subsequently adopted.

Note to Paragraph (5). Rule 803(5) as submitted by the Court permitted the reading into evidence of a memorandum or record concerning a matter about which a witness once had knowledge but now has insufficient recollection to enable him to testify accurately and fully, "shown to have been made when the matter was fresh in his memory and to reflect that knowledge correctly." The Committee amended this Rule to add the words "or adopted by the witness" after the phrase "shown to have been made", a treatment consistent with the definition of "statement" in the Jencks Act, 18 U.S.C. 3500. Moreover, it is the Committee's understanding that a memorandum or report, although barred under this Rule, would nonetheless be admissible if it came within another hearsay exception. This last stated principle is deemed applicable to all the hearsay rules.

Note to Paragraph (6). Rule 803(6) as submitted by the Court permitted a record made "in the course of a regularly conducted activity" to be admissible in certain circumstances. The Committee believed there were insufficient guarantees of reliability in records made in the course of activities falling outside the scope of "business" activities as that term is broadly defined in 28 U.S.C. 1732. Moreover, the Committee concluded that the additional requirement of Section 1732 that it must have been the regular practice of a business to make the record is a necessary further assurance of its trustworthiness. The Committee accordingly amended the Rule to incorporate these limitations.

Note to Paragraph (7). Rule 803(7) as submitted by the Court concerned the *absence* of entry in the records of a "regularly conducted activity." The Committee amended this Rule to conform with its action with respect to Rule 803(6).

Note to Paragraph (8). The Committee approved Rule 803(8) without substantive change from the form in which it was submitted by the Court. The Committee intends that the phrase "factual findings" be strictly construed and that evaluations or opinions contained in public reports shall not be admissible under this Rule.

Note to Paragraph (13). The Committee approved this Rule in the form submitted by the Court, intending that the phrase "Statements of fact concerning personal or family history" be read to include the specific types of such statements enumerated in Rule 803(11). House Report No. 93–650.

Note to Paragraph (4). The House approved this rule as it was submitted by the Supreme Court "with the understanding that it is not intended in any way to adversely affect present privilege rules." We also approve this rule, and we would point out with respect to the question of its relation to privileges, it must be read in conjunction with rule 35 of the Federal Rules of Civil Procedure which provides that whenever the physical or mental condition of a party (plaintiff or defendant) is in controversy, the court may require him to submit to an examination by a physician. It is these examinations which will normally be admitted under this exception.

Note to Paragraph (5). Rule 803(5) as submitted by the Court permitted the reading into evidence of a memorandum or record concerning a matter about which a witness once had knowledge but now has insufficient recollection to enable him to testify accurately and fully, "shown to have been made when the matter was fresh in his memory and to reflect that knowledge correctly." The House amended the rule to add the words "or adopted by the witness" after the phrase "shown to have been made," language parallel to the Jencks Act [18 U.S.C. § 3500].

The committee accepts the House amendment with the understanding and belief that it was not intended to narrow the scope of applicability of the rule. In fact, we understand it to clarify the rule's applicability to a memorandum adopted by the witness as well as one made by him. While the rule as submitted by the Court was silent on the question of who made the memorandum, we view the House amendment as a helpful clarification, noting, however, that the Advisory Committee's note to this rule suggests that the important thing is the accuracy of the memorandum rather than who made it.

The committee does not view the House amendment as precluding admissibility in situations in which multiple participants were involved.

When the verifying witness has not prepared the report, but merely examined it and found it accurate, he has adopted the report, and it is therefore admissible. The rule should also be interpreted to cover other situations involving multiple participants, e.g., employer dictating to secretary, secretary making memorandum at direction of employer, or information being passed along a chain of persons, as in *Curtis v. Bradley* [65 Conn. 99, 31 Atl. 591 (1894); see, also, *Rathbun v. Brancatella*, 93 N.J.L. 222, 107 Atl. 279 (1919); see, also, McCormick on Evidence, § 303 (2d ed. 1972)].

The committee also accepts the understanding of the House that a memorandum or report, although barred under this rule, would nonetheless be admissible if it came within another hearsay exception. We consider this principle to be applicable to all the hearsay rules.

Note to Paragraph (6). Rule 803(6) as submitted by the Supreme Court permitted a record made in the course of a regularly conducted activity to be admissible in certain circumstances. This rule constituted a broadening of the traditional business records hearsay exception which has been long advocated by scholars and judges active in the law of evidence.

The House felt there were insufficient guarantees of reliability of records not within a broadly defined business records exception. We disagree. Even under the House definition of "business" including profession, occupation, and "calling of every kind," the records of many regularly conducted activities will, or may be, excluded from evidence. Under the principle of ejusdem generis, the intent of "calling of every kind" would seem to be related to work-related endeavors—e.g., butcher, baker, artist, etc.

Thus, it appears that the records of many institutions or groups might not be admissible under the House amendments. For example, schools, churches, and hospitals will not normally be considered businesses within the definition. Yet, these are groups which keep financial and other records on a regular basis in a manner similar to business enterprises. We believe these records are of equivalent trustworthiness and should be admitted into evidence.

Three states, which have recently codified their evidence rules, have adopted the Supreme Court version of rule 803(6), providing for admission of memoranda of a "regularly conducted activity." None adopted the words "business activity" used in the House amendment. [See Nev.Rev.Stats. § 15.135; N.Mex.Stats. (1973 Supp.) § 20–4–803(6); West's Wis.Stats.Anno. (1973 Supp.) § 908.03(6).]

Therefore, the committee deleted the word "business" as it appears before the word "activity". The last sentence then is unnecessary and was also deleted.

It is the understanding of the committee that the use of the phrase "person with knowledge" is not intended to imply that the party seeking to introduce the memorandum, report, record, or data compilation must be able to produce, or even identify, the specific individual upon whose first-hand knowledge the memorandum, report, record or data compilation was based. A sufficient foundation for the introduction of such evidence will be laid if the party seeking to introduce the evidence is able to show that it was the regular practice of the activity to base such memorandums, reports, records, or data compilations upon a transmission from a person with knowledge, e.g., in the case of the content of a shipment of goods, upon a report from the company's receiving agent or in the case of a computer printout, upon a report from the company's computer programmer or one who has knowledge of the particular record system. In short, the scope of the phrase "person with knowledge" is meant to be coterminous with the custodian of the evidence or other qualified witness. The committee believes this represents the desired rule in light of the complex nature of modern business organizations.

Note to Paragraph (8). The House approved rule 803(8), as submitted by the Supreme Court, with one substantive change. It excluded from the hearsay exception reports containing matters observed by police officers and other law enforcement personnel in criminal cases. Ostensibly, the reason for this exclusion is that observations by police officers at the scene of the crime or the apprehension of the defendant are not as reliable as observations by public officials in other cases because of the adversarial nature of the confrontation between the police and the defendant in criminal cases.

The committee accepts the House's decision to exclude such recorded observations where the police officer is available to testify in court about his observation. However, where he is unavailable as unavailability is defined in rule 804(a)(4) and (a)(5), the report should be admitted as the best available evidence. Accordingly, the committee has amended rule 803(8) to refer to the provision of [proposed] rule 804(b)(5) [deleted], which allows the admission of such reports, records or other statements where the police officer or other law enforcement officer is unavailable because of death, then existing physical or mental illness or infirmity, or not being successfully subject to legal process.

The House Judiciary Committee report contained a statement of intent that "the phrase 'factual findings' in subdivision (c) be strictly construed and that evaluations or opinions contained in public reports shall not be admissible under this rule." The committee takes strong exception to this limiting understanding of the application of the rule. We do not think it reflects an understanding of the intended operation of the rule as explained in the Advisory Committee notes to this subsection. The Advisory Committee notes on subsection (c) of this subdivision point out that various kinds of evaluative reports are now admissible under Federal statutes. 7 U.S.C. § 78, findings of Secretary of Agriculture prima facie evidence of true grade of grain; 42 U.S.C. § 269(b), bill of health by appropriate official prima facie evidence of vessel's sanitary history and condition and compliance with regulations. These statutory exceptions to the hearsay rule are preserved. Rule 802. The willingness of Congress to recognize these and other such evaluative reports provides a helpful guide in determining the kind of reports which are intended to be admissible under this rule. We think the restrictive interpretation of the House overlooks the fact that while the Advisory Committee assumes admissibility in the first instance of evaluative reports, they are not admissible if, as the rule states, "the sources of information or other circumstances indicate lack of trustworthiness."

The Advisory Committee explains the factors to be considered:

* * * * * *

> Factors which may be assistance in passing upon the admissibility of evaluative reports include: (1) the timeliness of the investigation, McCormick, Can the Courts Make Wider Use of Reports of Official Investigations? 42

Iowa L.Rev. 363 (1957); (2) the special skill or experience of the official, id.; (3) whether a hearing was held and the level at which conducted, *Franklin v. Skelly Oil Co.,* 141 F.2d 568 (19th Cir.1944); (4) possible motivation problems suggested by *Palmer v. Hoffman,* 318 U.S. 109, 63 S.Ct. 477, 87 L.Ed. 645 (1943). Others no doubt could be added.

* * * * * * *

The committee concludes that the language of the rule together with the explanation provided by the Advisory Committee furnish sufficient guidance on the admissibility of evaluative reports.

Note to Paragraph (24). The proposed Rules of Evidence submitted to Congress contained identical provisions in rules 803 and 804 (which set forth the various hearsay exceptions), admitting any hearsay statement not specifically covered by any of the stated exceptions, if the hearsay statement was found to have "comparable circumstantial guarantees of trustworthiness." The House deleted these provisions (proposed rules 803(24) and 804(b)(6)[(5)]) as injecting "too much uncertainty" into the law of evidence and impairing the ability of practitioners to prepare for trial. The House felt that rule 102, which directs the courts to construe the Rules of Evidence so as to promote growth and development, would permit sufficient flexibility to admit hearsay evidence in appropriate cases under various factual situations that might arise.

We disagree with the total rejection of a residual hearsay exception. While we view rule 102 as being intended to provide for a broader construction and interpretation of these rules, we feel that, without a separate residual provision, the specifically enumerated exceptions could become tortured beyond any reasonable circumstances which they were intended to include (even if broadly construed). Moreover, these exceptions, while they reflect the most typical and well recognized exceptions to the hearsay rule, may not encompass every situation in which the reliability and appropriateness of a particular piece of hearsay evidence make clear that it should be heard and considered by the trier of fact.

The committee believes that there are certain exceptional circumstances where evidence which is found by a court to have guarantees of trustworthiness equivalent to or exceeding the guarantees reflected by the presently listed exceptions, and to have a high degree of prolativeness and necessity could properly be admissible.

The case of *Dallas County v. Commercial Union Assoc. Co., Ltd.,* 286 F.2d 388 (5th Cir.1961) illustrates the point. The issue in that case was whether the tower of the county courthouse collapsed because it was struck by lightning (covered by insurance) or because of structural weakness and deterioration of the structure (not covered). Investigation of the structure revealed the presence of charcoal and charred timbers. In order to show that lightning may not have been the cause of the charring, the insurer offered a copy of a local newspaper published over 50 years earlier containing an unsigned article describing a fire in the courthouse while it was under construction. The court found that the newspaper did not qualify for admission as a business record or an ancient document and did not fit within any other recognized hearsay exception. The court concluded, however, that the article was trustworthy because it was inconceivable that a newspaper reporter in a small town would report a fire in the courthouse if none had occurred. See also *United States v. Barbati,* 284 F.Supp. 409 (E.D.N.Y.1968).

Because exceptional cases like the *Dallas County* case may arise in the future, the committee has decided to reinstate a residual exception for rules 803 and 804(b).

The committee, however, also agrees with those supporters of the House version who felt that an overly broad residual hearsay exception could emasculate the hearsay rule and the recognized exceptions or vitiate the rationale behind codification of the rules.

Therefore, the committee has adopted a residual exception for rules 803 and 804(b) of much narrower scope and applicability than the Supreme Court version. In order to qualify for admission, a hearsay statement not falling within one of the recognized exceptions would have to satisfy at least four conditions. First, it must have "equivalent circumstantial guarantees of trustworthiness." Second, it must be offered as evidence of a material fact. Third, the court must determine that the statement "is more probative on the point for which it is offered than any other evidence which the proponent can procure through reasonable efforts." This requirement is intended to insure that only statements which have high probative value and necessity may qualify for admission under the residual exceptions. Fourth, the court must determine that "the general purposes of these rules and the interests of justice will best be served by admission of the statement into evidence."

It is intended that the residual hearsay exceptions will be used very rarely, and only in exceptional circumstances. The committee does not intend to establish a broad license for trial judges to admit hearsay statements that do not fall within one of the other exceptions contained in rules 803 and 804(b). The residual exceptions are not meant to authorize major judicial revisions of the hearsay rule, including its present exceptions. Such major revisions are best accomplished by legislative action. It is intended that in any case in which evidence is sought to be admitted under these subsections, the trial judge will exercise no less care, reflection and caution than the courts did under the common law in establishing the now-recognized exceptions to the hearsay rule.

In order to establish a well-defined jurisprudence, the special facts and circumstances which, in the court's judgment, indicates that the statement has a sufficiently high degree of trustworthiness and necessity to justify its admission should be stated on the record. It is expected that the court will give the opposing party a full and adequate opportunity to contest the admission of any statement sought to be introduced under these subsections. Senate Report No. 93–1277.

Rule 803 defines when hearsay statements are admissible in evidence even though the declarant is available as a witness. The Senate amendments make three changes in this rule.

Note to Paragraph (6). The House bill provides in subsection (6) that records of a regularly conducted "business" activity qualify for admission into evidence as an exception to the hearsay rule. "Business" is defined as including "business, profession, occupation and calling of every kind." The Senate amendment drops the requirement that the records be those of a "business" activity and eliminates the definition of "business." The Senate amendment provides that records are admissible if they are records of a regularly conducted "activity."

The Conference adopts the House provision that the records must be those of a regularly conducted "business" activity. The Conferees changed the definition of "business" contained in the House provision in order to make it clear that the records of institutions and associations like schools, churches and hospitals are admissible under this provision. The records of public schools and hospitals are also covered by Rule 803(8), which deals with public records and reports.

Note to Paragraph (8). The Senate amendment adds language, not contained in the House bill, that refers to another rule that was added by the Senate in another amendment ([proposed] Rule 804(b)(5)—Criminal law enforcement records and reports [deleted]).

In view of its action on [proposed] Rule 804(b)(5) (Criminal law enforcement records and reports) [deleted], the Conference does not adopt the Senate amendment and restores the bill to the House version.

Note to Paragraph (24). The Senate amendment adds a new subsection, (24), which makes admissible a hearsay statement not specifically covered by any of the previous twenty-three subsections, if the statement has equivalent circumstantial guarantees of trustworthiness and if the court determines that (A) the statement is offered as evidence of a material fact; (B) the statement is more probative on the point for which it is offered than any other evidence the proponent can procure through reasonable efforts; and (C) the general purposes of these rules and the interests of justice will best be served by admission of the statement into evidence.

The House bill eliminated a similar, but broader, provision because of the conviction that such a provision injected too much uncertainty into the law of evidence regarding hearsay and impaired the ability of a litigant to prepare adequately for trial.

The Conference adopts the Senate amendment with an amendment that provides that a party intending to request the court to use a statement under this provision must notify any adverse party of this intention as well as of the particulars of the statement, including the name and address of the declarant. This notice must be given sufficiently in advance of the trial or hearing to provide any adverse party with a fair opportunity to prepare to contest the use of the statement. House Report No. 93–1597.

1987 Amendment

The amendments are technical. No substantive change is intended.

1997 Amendment

The contents of Rule 803(24) and Rule 804(b)(5) have been combined and transferred to a new Rule 807. This was done to facilitate additions to Rules 803 and 804. No change in meaning is intended.

GAP Report on Rule 803. The words "Transferred to Rule 807" were substituted for "Abrogated."

Rule 804. Hearsay Exceptions; Declarant Unavailable

(a) Definition of unavailability. "Unavailability as a witness" includes situations in which the declarant—

(1) is exempted by ruling of the court on the ground of privilege from testifying concerning the subject matter of the declarant's statement; or

(2) persists in refusing to testify concerning the subject matter of the declarant's statement despite an order of the court to do so; or

(3) testifies to a lack of memory of the subject matter of the declarant's statement; or

(4) is unable to be present or to testify at the hearing because of death or then existing physical or mental illness or infirmity; or

(5) is absent from the hearing and the proponent of a statement has been unable to procure the declarant's attendance (or in the case of a hearsay exception under subdivision (b)(2), (3), or (4), the declarant's attendance or testimony) by process or other reasonable means.

A declarant is not unavailable as a witness if exemption, refusal, claim of lack of memory, inability, or absence is due to the procurement or wrongdoing of the proponent of a statement for the purpose of preventing the witness from attending or testifying.

(b) Hearsay exceptions. The following are not excluded by the hearsay rule if the declarant is unavailable as a witness:

(1) **Former testimony.** Testimony given as a witness at another hearing of the same or a different proceeding, or in a deposition taken in compliance with law in the course of the same or another proceeding, if the party against whom the testimony is now offered, or, in a civil action or proceeding, a predecessor in interest, had an opportunity and similar motive to develop the testimony by direct, cross, or redirect examination.

(2) **Statement under belief of impending death.** In a prosecution for homicide or in a civil action or proceeding, a statement made by a declarant while believing that the declarant's death was imminent, concerning the cause or circumstances of what the declarant believed to be impending death.

(3) **Statement against interest.** A statement which was at the time of its making so far contrary to the declarant's pecuniary or proprietary interest, or so far tended to subject the declarant to civil or criminal liability, or to render invalid a claim by the declarant against another, that a reasonable person in the declarant's position would not have made the statement unless believing it to be true. A statement tending to expose the declarant to criminal

liability and offered to exculpate the accused is not admissible unless corroborating circumstances clearly indicate the trustworthiness of the statement.

(4) Statement of personal or family history. (A) A statement concerning the declarant's own birth, adoption, marriage, divorce, legitimacy, relationship by blood, adoption, or marriage, ancestry, or other similar fact of personal or family history, even though declarant had no means of acquiring personal knowledge of the matter stated; or (B) a statement concerning the foregoing matters, and death also, of another person, if the declarant was related to the other by blood, adoption, or marriage or was so intimately associated with the other's family as to be likely to have accurate information concerning the matter declared.

(5) [Transferred to Rule 807]

(6) Forfeiture by wrongdoing. A statement offered against a party that has engaged or acquiesced in wrongdoing that was intended to, and did, procure the unavailability of the declarant as a witness.

(Pub.L. 93–595, § 1, Jan. 2, 1975, 88 Stat. 1942; Pub.L. 94–149, § 1(12), (13), Dec. 12, 1975, 89 Stat. 806; Mar. 2, 1987, eff. Oct. 1, 1987; Pub.L. 100–690, Title VII, § 7075(b), Nov. 18, 1988, 102 Stat. 4405; Apr. 11, 1997, eff. Dec. 1, 1997.)

ADVISORY COMMITTEE NOTES

1972 Proposed Rules

As to firsthand knowledge on the part of hearsay declarants, see the introductory portion of the Advisory Committee's Note to Rule 803.

Note to Subdivision (a). The definition of unavailability implements the division of hearsay exceptions into two categories by Rules 803 and 804(b).

At common law the unavailability requirement was evolved in connection with particular hearsay exceptions rather than along general lines. For example, see the separate explications of unavailability in relation to former testimony, declarations against interest, and statements of pedigree, separately developed in McCormick §§ 234, 257, and 297. However, no reason is apparent for making distinctions as to what satisfies unavailability for the different exceptions. The treatment in the rule is therefore uniform although differences in the range of process for witnesses between civil and criminal cases will lead to a less exacting requirement under item (5). See Rule 45(e) of the Federal Rules of Civil Procedure and Rule 17(e) of the Federal Rules of Criminal Procedure.

Five instances of unavailability are specified:

(1) Substantial authority supports the position that exercise of a claim of privilege by the declarant satisfies the requirement of unavailability (usually in connection with former testimony). *Wyatt v. State,* 35 Ala.App. 147, 46 So.2d 837 (1950); *State v. Stewart,* 85 Kan. 404, 116 P. 489 (1911); Annot., 45 A.L.R.2d 1354; Uniform Rule 62(7)(a); California Evidence Code § 240(a)(1); Kansas Code of Civil Procedure § 60–459(g)(1). A ruling by the judge is required, which clearly implies that an actual claim of privilege must be made.

(2) A witness is rendered unavailable if he simply refuses to testify concerning the subject matter of his statement despite judicial pressures to do so, a position supported by similar considerations of practicality. *Johnson v. People,* 152 Colo. 586, 384 P.2d 454 (1963); *People v. Pickett,* 339 Mich. 294, 63 N.W.2d 681, 45 A.L.R.2d 1341 (1954). *Contra, Pleau v. State,* 255 Wis. 362, 38 N.W.2d 496 (1949).

(3) The position that a claimed lack of memory by the witness of the subject matter of his statement constitutes unavailability likewise finds support in the cases, though not without dissent. McCormick § 234, p. 494. If the claim is successful, the practical effect is to put the testimony beyond reach, as in the other instances. In this instance, however, it will be noted that the lack of memory must be established by the testimony of the witness himself, which clearly contemplates his production and subjection to cross-examination.

(4) Death and infirmity find general recognition as grounds. McCormick §§ 234, 257, 297; Uniform Rule 62(7)(c); California Evidence Code § 240(a)(3); Kansas Code of Civil Procedure § 60–459(g)(3); New Jersey Evidence Rule 62(6)(c). See also the provisions on use of depositions in Rule 32(a)(3) of the Federal Rules of Civil Procedure and Rule 15(e) of the Federal Rules of Criminal Procedure.

(5) Absence from the hearing coupled with inability to compel attendance by process or other reasonable means also satisfies the requirement. McCormick § 234; Uniform Rule 62(7)(d) and (e); California Evidence Code § 240(a)(4) and (5); Kansas Code of Civil Procedure § 60–459(g)(4) and (5); New Jersey Rule 62(6)(b) and (d). See the discussion of procuring attendance of witnesses who are nonresidents or in custody in *Barber v. Page,* 390 U.S. 719, 88 S.Ct. 1318, 20 L.Ed.2d 255 (1968).

If the conditions otherwise constituting unavailability result from the procurement or wrongdoing of the proponent of the statement, the requirement is not satisfied. The rule contains no requirement that an attempt be made to take the deposition of a declarant.

Note to Subdivision (b). Rule 803, *supra,* is based upon the assumption that a hearsay statement falling within one of its exceptions possesses qualities which justify the conclusion that whether the declarant is available or unavailable is not a relevant factor in determining admissibility. The instant rule proceeds upon a different theory: hearsay which admittedly is not equal in quality to testimony of the declarant on the stand may nevertheless be admitted if the declarant is unavailable and if his statement meets a specified standard. The rule expresses preferences: testimony given on the stand in person is preferred over hearsay, and hearsay, if of the specified quality, is preferred over complete loss of the evidence of the declarant. The exceptions evolved at common law with respect to declarations of unavailable declarants furnish the basis for the exceptions enumerated in the proposal. The term "unavailable" is defined in subdivision (a).

Exception (1). Former testimony does not rely upon some set of circumstances to substitute for oath and cross-examination, since both oath and opportunity to cross-examine were present in fact. The only missing one of the ideal conditions for the giving of testimony is the presence of trier and opponent ("demeanor evidence"). This is lacking with all hearsay exceptions. Hence it may be argued that former testimony is the strongest hearsay and should be included under Rule 803, supra. However, opportunity to observe demeanor is what in a large measure confers depth and meaning upon oath and cross-examination. Thus in cases under Rule 803 demeanor lacks the significance which it possesses with respect to testimony. In any event, the tradition, founded in experience, uniformly favors production of the witness if he is available. The exception indicates continuation of the policy. This preference for the presence of the witness is apparent also in rules and statutes on the use of depositions, which deal with substantially the same problem.

Under the exception, the testimony may be offered (1) against the party *against* whom it was previously offered or (2) against the party *by* whom it was previously offered. In each instance the question resolves itself into whether fairness allows imposing, upon the party against whom now offered, the handling of the witness of the earlier occasion. (1) If the party against whom now offered is the one against whom the testimony was offered previously, no unfairness is apparent in requiring him to accept his own prior conduct of cross-examination or decision not to cross-examine. Only demeanor has been lost, and that is inherent in the situation. (2) If the party against whom now offered is the one *by* whom the testimony was offered previously, a satisfactory answer becomes somewhat more difficult. One possibility is to proceed somewhat along the line of an adoptive admission, i.e. by offering the testimony proponent in effect adopts it. However, this theory savors of discarded concepts of witnesses' belonging to a party, of litigants' ability to pick and choose witnesses, and of vouching for one's own witnesses. Cf. McCormick § 246, pp. 526–527; 4 Wigmore § 1075. A more direct and acceptable approach is simply to recognize direct and redirect examination of one's own witness as the equivalent of cross-examining an opponent's witness. Falknor, Former Testimony and the Uniform Rules: A Comment, 38 N.Y.U.L.Rev. 651, n. 1 (1963); McCormick § 231, p. 483. See also 5 Wigmore § 1389. Allowable techniques for dealing with hostile, double-crossing, forgetful, and mentally deficient witnesses leave no substance to a claim that one could not adequately develop his own witness at the former hearing. An even less appealing argument is presented when failure to develop fully was the result of a deliberate choice.

The common law did not limit the admissibility of former testimony to that given in an earlier trial of the same case, although it did require identity of issues as a means of insuring that the former handling of the witness was the equivalent of what would now be done if the opportunity were presented. Modern decisions reduce the requirement to "substantial" identity. McCormick § 233. Since identity of issues is significant only in that it bears on motive and interest in developing fully the testimony of the witness, expressing the matter in the latter terms is preferable. *Id.* Testimony given at a preliminary hearing was held in *California v. Green,* 399 U.S. 149, 90 S.Ct. 1930, 26 L.Ed.2d 489 (1970), to satisfy confrontation requirements in this respect.

As a further assurance of fairness in thrusting upon a party the prior handling of the witness, the common law also insisted upon identity of parties, deviating only to the extent of allowing substitution of successors in a narrowly construed privity. Mutuality as an aspect of identity is now generally discredited, and the requirement of identity of the offering party disappears except as it might affect motive to develop the testimony. Falknor, *supra,* at 652; McCormick § 232, pp. 487–488. The question remains whether strict identity, or privity, should continue as a requirement with respect to the party against whom offered. The rule departs to the extent of allowing substitution of one with the right and opportunity to develop the testimony with similar motive and interest. This position is supported by modern decisions. McCormick § 232, pp. 489–490; 5 Wigmore § 1388.

Provisions of the same tenor will be found in Uniform Rule 63(3)(b); California Evidence Code §§ 1290–1292; Kansas Code of Civil Procedure § 60–460(c)(2); New Jersey Evidence Rule 63(3). Unlike the rule, the latter three provide either that former testimony is not admissible if the right of confrontation is denied or that it is not admissible if the accused was not a party to the prior hearing. The genesis of these limitations is a caveat in Uniform Rule 63(3) Comment that use of former testimony against an accused may violate his right of confrontation. *Mattox v. United States,* 156 U.S. 237, 15 S.Ct. 337, 39 L.Ed. 409 (1895), held that the right was not violated by the Government's use, on a retrial of the same case, of testimony given at the first trial by two witnesses since deceased. The decision leaves open the questions (1) whether direct and redirect are equivalent to cross-examination for purposes of confrontation, (2) whether testimony given in a different proceeding is acceptable, and (3) whether the accused must himself have been a party to the earlier proceeding or whether a similarly situated person will serve the purpose. Professor Falknor concluded that, if a dying declaration untested by cross-examination is constitutionally admissible, former testimony tested by the cross-examination of one similarly situated does not offend against confrontation. Falknor, *supra,* at 659–660. The constitutional acceptability of dying declarations has often been conceded. *Mattox v. United States,* 156 U.S. 237, 243, 15 S.Ct. 337, 39 L.Ed. 409 (1895); *Kirby v. United States,* 174 U.S. 47, 61, 19 S.Ct. 574, 43 L.Ed. 890 (1899); *Pointer v. Texas,* 380 U.S. 400, 407, 85 S.Ct. 1065, 13 L.Ed.2d 923 (1965).

Exception (2). The exception is the familiar dying declaration of the common law, expanded somewhat beyond its traditionally narrow limits. While the original religious justification for the exception may have lost its conviction for some persons over the years, it can scarcely be doubted that powerful psychological pressures are present. See 5 Wigmore § 1443 and the classic statement of Chief Baron Eyre in Rex v. Woodcock, 1 Leach 500, 502, 168 Eng.Rep. 352, 353 (K.B.1789).

The common law required that the statement be that of the victim, offered in a prosecution for criminal homicide. Thus declarations by victims in prosecutions for other crimes, e.g. a declaration by a rape victim who dies in childbirth, and all declarations in civil cases were outside the scope of the exception. An occasional statute has removed these restrictions, as in Colo.R.S. § 52–1–20, or has expanded the area of offenses to include abortions, 5 Wigmore § 1432, p. 224, n. 4. Kansas by decision extended the exception to civil cases. *Thurston v. Fritz,* 91 Kan. 468, 138 P. 625 (1914). While the common law exception no doubt originated as a result of the exceptional need for the evidence in homicide cases, the theory of admissibility applies equally in civil cases and in prosecutions for crimes other than homicide. The same considerations suggest abandonment of the limitation to circumstances attending the event in question, yet when the statement deals with matters other than the supposed death, its influence is believed to be sufficiently attenuated to justify the limitation. Unavailability is not limited to death. See subdivision (a) of this rule. Any problem as to declarations phrased in terms of opinion is laid at rest by Rule 701, and continuation of a requirement of firsthand knowledge is assured by Rule 602.

Comparable provisions are found in Uniform Rule 63(5); California Evidence Code § 1242; Kansas Code of Civil Procedure § 60–460(e); New Jersey Evidence Rule 63(5).

Exception (3). The circumstantial guaranty of reliability for declarations against interest is the assumption that persons do not make statements which are damaging to themselves unless satisfied for good reason that they are true. *Hileman v. Northwest Engineering Co.,* 346 F.2d 668 (6th Cir.1965). If the statement is that of a party, offered by his opponent, it comes in as an admission, Rule 803(d)(2), and there is no occasion to inquire whether it is against interest, this not being a condition precedent to admissibility of admissions by opponents.

The common law required that the interest declared against be pecuniary or proprietary but within this limitation demonstrated striking ingenuity in discovering an against-interest aspect. Higham v. Ridgway, 10 East 109, 103 Eng.Rep. 717 (K.B.1808); Reg. v. Overseers of Birmingham, 1 B. & S. 763, 121 Eng.Rep. 897 (Q.B.1861); McCormick, § 256, p. 551, nn. 2 and 3.

The exception discards the common law limitation and expands to the full logical limit. One result is to remove doubt as to the admissibility of declarations tending to establish a tort liability against the declarant or to extinguish one which might be asserted by him, in accordance with the trend of the decisions in this country. McCormick § 254, pp. 548–549. Another is to allow statements tending to expose declarant to hatred, ridicule, or disgrace, the motivation here being considered to be as strong as when financial interests are at stake. McCormick § 255, p. 551. And finally, exposure to criminal liability satisfies the against-interest requirement. The refusal of the common law to concede the adequacy of a penal interest was no doubt indefensible in logic, see the dissent of Mr. Justice Holmes in *Donnelly v. United States,* 228 U.S. 243, 33 S.Ct. 449, 57 L.Ed. 820 (1913), but one senses in the decisions a distrust of evidence of confessions by third persons offered to exculpate the accused arising from suspicions of fabrication either of the fact of the making of the confession or in its contents, enhanced in either instance by the required unavailability of the declarant. Nevertheless, an increasing amount of decisional law recognizes exposure to punishment for crime as a sufficient stake. *People v. Spriggs,* 60 Cal.2d 868, 36 Cal.Rptr. 841, 389 P.2d 377 (1964); *Sutter v. Easterly,* 354 Mo. 282, 189 S.W.2d 284 (1945); Band's Refuse Removal, Inc. v. Fairlawn Borough, 62 N.J.Super. 522, 163 A.2d 465 (1960); *Newberry v. Commonwealth,* 191 Va. 445, 61 S.E.2d 318 (1950); Annot., 162 A.L.R. 446. The requirement of corroboration is included in the rule in order to effect an accommodation between these competing considerations. When the statement is offered by the accused by way of exculpation, the resulting situation is not adapted to control by rulings as to the weight of the evidence, and hence the provision is cast in terms of a requirement preliminary to admissibility. Cf. Rule 406(a). The requirement of corroboration should be construed in such a manner as to effectuate its purpose of circumventing fabrication.

Ordinarily the third-party confession is thought of in terms of exculpating the accused, but this is by no means always or necessarily the case: it may include statements implicating him, and under the general theory of declarations against interest they would be admissible as related statements. Douglas v. Alabama, 380 U.S. 415, 85 S.Ct. 1074, 13 L.Ed.2d 934 (1965), and Bruton v. United States, 389 U.S. 818, 88 S.Ct. 126, 19 L.Ed.2d 70 (1968), both involved confessions by codefendants which implicated the accused. While the confession was not actually offered in evidence in *Douglas,* the procedure followed effectively put it before the jury, which the Court ruled to be error. Whether the confession might have been admissible as a declaration against penal interest was not considered or discussed. *Bruton* assumed the inadmissibility, as against the accused, of the implicating confession of his codefendant, and centered upon the question of the effectiveness of a limiting instruction. These decisions, however, by no means require that all statements implicating another person be excluded from the category of declarations against interest. Whether a statement is in fact against interest must be determined from the circumstances of each case. Thus a statement admitting guilt and implicating another person, made while in custody, may well be motivated by a desire to curry favor with the authorities and hence fail to qualify as against interest. See the dissenting opinion of Mr. Justice White in *Bruton.* On the other hand, the same words spoken under different circumstances, e.g., to an acquaintance, would have no difficulty in qualifying. The rule does not purport to deal with questions of the right of confrontation.

The balancing of self-serving against dissenting aspects of a declaration is discussed in McCormick § 256.

For comparable provisions, see Uniform Rule 63(10); California Evidence Code § 1230; Kansas Code of Civil Procedure § 60–460(j); New Jersey Evidence Rule 63(10).

Exception (4). The general common law requirement that a declaration in this area must have been made *ante litem motam* has been dropped, as bearing more appropriately on weight than admissibility. See 5 Wigmore § 1483. Item (i)[(A)] specifically disclaims any need of firsthand knowledge respecting declarant's own personal history. In some instances it is self-evident (marriage) and in others impossible and traditionally not required (date of birth). Item (ii)[(B)] deals with declarations concerning the history of another person. As at common law, declarant is qualified if related by blood or marriage. 5 Wigmore § 1489. In addition, and contrary to the common law, declarant qualifies by virtue of intimate association with the family. *Id.,* § 1487. The requirement sometimes encountered that when the subject of the statement is the relationship between two other persons the declarant must qualify as to both is omitted. Relationship is reciprocal. *Id.,* § 1491.

For comparable provisions, see Uniform Rule 63(23), (24), (25); California Evidence Code §§ 1310, 1311; Kansas Code of Civil Procedure § 60–460(u), (v), (w); New Jersey Evidence Rules 63–23), 63(24), 63(25).

1974 Enactment

Note to Subdivision (a)(3). Rule 804(a)(3) was approved in the form submitted by the Court. However, the Committee intends no change in existing federal law under which the court may choose to disbelieve the declarant's testimony as to his lack of memory. See *United States v. Insana,* 423 F.2d 1165, 1169–1170 (2nd Cir.), cert. denied, 400 U.S. 841 (1970).

Note to Subdivision (a)(5). Rule 804(a)(5) as submitted to the Congress provided, as one type of situation in which a declarant would be deemed "unavailable", that he be "absent from the hearing and the proponent of his statement has been unable to procure his attendance by process or other reasonable means." The Committee amended the Rule to insert after the word "attendance" the parenthetical expression "(or, in the case of a hearsay exception under subdivision (b)(2), (3), or (4), his attendance or testimony)". The amendment is designed primarily to require that an attempt be made to depose a witness (as well as to seek his attendance) as a precondition to the witness being deemed unavailable. The Committee, however, recognized the propriety of an exception to this additional requirement when it is the declarant's former testimony that is sought to be admitted under subdivision (b)(1).

Note to Subdivision (b)(1). Rule 804(b)(1) as submitted by the Court allowed prior testimony of an unavailable witness to be admissible if the party against whom it is offered or a person "with motive and interest similar" to his had an opportunity to examine the witness. The Committee considered that it is generally unfair to impose upon the party against whom the hearsay evidence is being offered responsibility for the manner in which the witness was previously handled by another party. The sole exception to this, in the Committee's view, is when a party's predecessor in interest in a civil action or proceeding had an opportunity and similar motive to examine the witness. The Committee amended the Rule to reflect these policy determinations.

Note to Subdivision (b)(2). Rule 804(b)(3) as submitted by the Court (now Rule 804(b)(2) in the bill) proposed to expand the traditional scope of the dying declaration exception (i.e. a statement of the victim in a homicide case as to the cause or circumstances of his believed imminent death) to allow such statements in all criminal and civil cases. The Committee did not consider dying declarations as among the most reliable forms of hearsay. Consequently, it amended the provision to limit their admissibility in criminal cases to homicide prosecutions, where exceptional need for the evidence is present. This is existing law. At the same time, the Committee approved the expansion to civil actions and proceedings where the stakes do not involve possible imprisonment, although noting that this could lead to forum shopping in some instances.

Note to Subdivision (b)(3). Rule 804(b)(4) as submitted by the Court (now Rule 804(b)(3) in the bill) provided as follows:

Statement against interest.—A statement which was at the time of its making so far contrary to the declarant's pecuniary or proprietary interest or so far tended to subject him to civil or criminal liability or to render invalid a claim by him against another or to make him an object of hatred, ridicule, or disgrace, that a reasonable man in his position would not have made the statement unless he believed it to be true. A statement tending to exculpate the accused is not admissible unless corroborated.

The Committee determined to retain the traditional hearsay exception for statements against pecuniary or proprietary interest. However, it deemed the Court's additional references to statements tending to subject a declarant to civil liability or to render invalid a claim by him against another to be redundant as included within the scope of the reference to statements against pecuniary or proprietary interest. See *Gichner v. Antonio Triano Tile and Marble Co.,* 410 F.2d 238 (D.C.Cir.1968). Those additional references were accordingly deleted.

The Court's Rule also proposed to expand the hearsay limitation from its present federal limitation to include statements subjecting the declarant to criminal liability and statements tending to make him an object of hatred, ridicule, or disgrace. The Committee eliminated the latter category from the subdivision as lacking sufficient guarantees of reliability. See *United States v. Dovico,* 380 F.2d 325, 327 nn. 2, 4 (2nd Cir.), cert. denied, 389 U.S. 944 (1967). As for statements against penal interest, the Committee shared the view of the Court that some such statements do possess adequate assurances of reliability and should be admissible. It believed, however, as did the Court, that statements of this type tending to exculpate the accused are more suspect and so should have their admissibility conditioned upon some further provision insuring trustworthiness. The proposal in the Court Rule to add a requirement of simple corroboration was, however, deemed ineffective to accomplish this purpose since the accused's own testimony might suffice while not necessarily increasing the reliability of the hearsay statement. The Committee settled upon the language "unless corroborating circumstances clearly indicate the trustworthiness of the statement" as affording a proper standard and degree of discretion. It was contemplated that the result in such cases as *Donnelly v. United States,* 228 U.S. 243 (1912), where the circumstances plainly indicated reliability, would be changed. The Committee also added to the Rule the final sentence from the 1971 Advisory Committee draft, designed to codify the doctrine of *Bruton v. United States,* 391 U.S. 123 (1968). The Committee does not intend to affect the existing exception to the *Bruton* principle where the codefendant takes the stand and is subject to cross-examination, but believed there was no need to make specific provision for this situation in the Rule, since in that event the declarant would not be "unavailable". House Report No. 93–650.

Note to Subdivision (a)(5). Subdivision (a) of rule 804 as submitted by the Supreme Court defined the conditions under which a witness was considered to be unavailable. It was amended in the House.

The purpose of the amendment, according to the report of the House Committee on the Judiciary, is "primarily to require that an attempt be made to depose a witness (as well as to seek his attendance) as a precondition to the witness being unavailable."

Under the House amendment, before a witness is declared unavailable, a party must try to depose a witness (declarant) with respect to dying declarations, declarations against interest, and declarations of pedigree. None of these situations would seem to warrant this needless, impractical and highly restrictive complication. A good case can be made for eliminating the unavailability requirement entirely for declarations against interest cases. [Uniform rule 63(10); Kan. Stat.Anno. 60–460(j); 2A N.J.Stats.Anno. 84–63(10).]

In dying declaration cases, the declarant will usually, though not necessarily, be deceased at the time of trial. Pedigree statements which are admittedly and necessarily based largely on word of mouth are not greatly fortified by a deposition requirement.

Depositions are expensive and time-consuming. In any event, deposition procedures are available to those who wish to resort to them. Moreover, the deposition procedures of the Civil Rules and Criminal Rules are only imperfectly adapted to implementing the amendment. No purpose is served unless the deposition, if taken, may be used in evidence. Under Civil Rule (a)(3) the Criminal Rule 15(e), a deposition, though taken, may not be admissible, and under Criminal Rule 15(a) substantial obstacles exist in the way of even taking a deposition.

For these reasons, the committee deleted the House amendment.

The committee understands that the rule as to unavailability, as explained by the Advisory Committee "contains no requirement that an attempt be made to take the deposition of a declarant." In reflecting the committee's judgment, the statement is accurate insofar as it goes. Where, however, the proponent of the statement, with knowledge of the existence of the statement, fails to confront the declarant with the statement at the taking of the deposition, then the proponent should not, in fairness, be permitted to treat the declarant as "unavailable" simply because the declarant was not amenable to process compelling his attendance at trial. The committee does not consider it necessary to amend the rule to this effect because such a situation abuses, not conforms to, the rule. Fairness would preclude a person from introducing a hearsay statement on a particular issue if the person taking the deposition was aware of the issue at the time of the deposition but failed to depose the unavailable witness on that issue.

Note to Subdivision (b)(1). Former testimony.—Rule 804(b)(1) as submitted by the Court allowed prior testimony of an unavailable witness to be admissible if the party against whom it is offered or a person "with motive and interest similar" to his had an opportunity to examine the witness.

The House amended the rule to apply only to a party's predecessor in interest. Although the committee recognizes considerable merit to the rule submitted by the Supreme Court, a position which has been advocated by many scholars and judges, we have concluded that the difference between the two versions is not great and we accept the House amendment.

Note to Subdivision (b)(3). The rule defines those statements which are considered to be against interest and thus of sufficient trustworthiness to be admissible even though hearsay. With regard to the type of interest declared against, the version submitted by the Supreme Court included inter alia, statements tending to subject a declarant to civil liability or to invalidate a claim by him against another. The House struck these provisions as redundant. In view of the conflicting case law construing pecuniary or proprietary interests narrowly so as to exclude, e.g., tort cases, this deletion could be misconstrued.

Three States which have recently codified their rules of evidence have followed the Supreme Court's version of this rule, i.e., that a statement is against interest if it tends to subject a declarant to civil liability. [Nev.Rev.Stats. § 51.345; N.Mex.Stats. (1973 Supp.) § 20–4–804(4); West's Wis.Stats.Anno. (1973 Supp.) § 908.045(4).]

The committee believes that the reference to statements tending to subject a person to civil liability constitutes a desirable clarification of the scope of the rule. Therefore, we have reinstated the Supreme Court language on this matter.

The Court rule also proposed to expand the hearsay limitation from its present federal limitation to include statements subjecting the declarant to statements tending to make him an object of hatred, ridicule, or disgrace. The House eliminated the latter category from the subdivision as lacking sufficient guarantees of reliability. Although there is considerable support for the admissibility of such statements (all three of the State rules referred to supra, would admit such statements), we accept the deletion by the House.

The House amended this exception to add a sentence making inadmissible a statement or confession offered against the accused in a criminal case, made by a codefendant or other person implicating both himself and the accused. The sentence was added to codify the constitutional principle announced in *Bruton v. United States,* 391 U.S. 123 (1968). Bruton held that the admission of the extrajudicial hearsay statement of one codefendant inculpating a second codefendant violated the confrontation clause of the sixth amendment.

The committee decided to delete this provision because the basic approach of the rules is to avoid codifying, or attempting to codify, constitutional evidentiary principles, such as the fifth amendment's right against self-incrimination and, here, the sixth amendment's right of confrontation. Codification of a constitutional principle is unnecessary and, where the principle is under development, often unwise. Furthermore, the House provision does not appear to recognize the exceptions to the *Bruton* rule, e.g. where the codefendant takes the stand and is subject to cross examination; where the accused confessed, see *United States v. Mancusi,* 404 F.2d 296 (2d Cir.1968), cert. denied 397 U.S. 942 (1907); where the accused was placed at the scene of the crime, see *United States v. Zelker,* 452 F.2d 1009 (2d Cir.1971). For these reasons, the committee decided to delete this provision.

Note to Subdivision (b)(5). See Note to Paragraph (24), Notes of Committee on the Judiciary, Senate Report No. 93–1277, set out as a note under rule 803 of these rules. Senate Report No. 93–1277.

Rule 804 defines what hearsay statements are admissible in evidence if the declarant is unavailable as a witness. The Senate amendments make four changes in the rule.

Note to Subdivision (a)(5). Subsection (a) defines the term "unavailability as a witness". The House bill provides in subsection (a)(5) that the party who desires to use the statement must be unable to procure the declarant's attendance by process or other reasonable means. In the case of dying declarations, statements against interest and statements of personal or family history, the House bill requires that the proponent must also be unable to procure the declarant's *testimony* (such as by deposition or interrogatories) by process or other reasonable means. The Senate amendment eliminates this latter provision.

The Conference adopts the provision contained in the House bill.

Note to Subdivision (b)(3). The Senate amendment to subsection (b)(3) provides that a statement is against interest and not excluded by the hearsay rule when the declarant is unavailable as a witness, if the statement tends to subject a person to civil or criminal liability or renders invalid a claim by him against another. The House bill did not refer specifically to civil liability and to rendering invalid a claim against another. The Senate amendment also deletes from the House bill the provision that subsection (b)(3) does not apply to a statement or confession, made by a codefendant or another, which implicates the accused and the person who made the statement, when that statement or confession is offered against the accused in a criminal case.

The Conference adopts the Senate amendment. The Conferees intend to include within the purview of this rule, statements subjecting a person to civil liability and statements rendering claims invalid. The Conferees agree to delete the provision regarding statements by a codefendant, thereby reflecting the general approach in the Rules of Evidence to avoid attempting to codify constitutional evidentiary principles.

Note to Subdivision (b)(5). The Senate amendment adds a new subsection, (b)(6) [now (b)(5)], which makes admissible a hearsay statement not specifically covered by any of the five previous subsections, if the statement has equivalent circumstantial guarantees of trustworthiness and if the court determines that (A) the statement is offered as evidence of a material fact; (B) the statement is more probative on the point for which it is offered than any other evidence the proponent can procure through reasonable efforts; and (C) the general purposes of these rules and the interests of justice will best be served by admission of the statement into evidence.

The House bill eliminated a similar, but broader, provision because of the conviction that such a provision injected too much uncertainty into the law of evidence regarding hearsay and impaired the ability of a litigant to prepare adequately for trial.

The Conference adopts the Senate amendment with an amendment that renumbers this subsection and provides that a party intending to request the court to use a statement under this provision must notify any adverse party of this intention as well as of the particulars of the statement, including the name and address of the declarant. This notice must be given sufficiently in advance of the trial or hearing to provide any adverse party with a fair opportunity to prepare to contest the use of the statement. House Report No. 93–1597.

1987 Amendment

The amendments are technical. No substantive change is intended.

1997 Amendment

Subdivision (b)(5). The contents of Rule 803(24) and Rule 804(b)(5) have been combined and transferred to a new Rule 807. This was done to facilitate additions to Rules 803 and 804. No change in meaning is intended.

Subdivision (b)(6). Rule 804(b)(6) has been added to provide that a party forfeits the right to object on hearsay grounds to the admission of a declarant's prior statement when the party's deliberate wrongdoing or acquiescence therein procured the unavailability of the declarant as a witness. This recognizes the need for a prophylactic rule to deal with abhorrent behavior "which strikes at the heart of the system of justice itself." United States v. Mastrangelo, 693 F.2d 269, 273 (2d Cir.1982), cert. denied, 467 U.S. 1204 (1984). The wrongdoing need not consist of a criminal act. The rule applies to all parties, including the government.

Every circuit that has resolved the question has recognized the principle of forfeiture by misconduct, although the tests for determining whether there is a forfeiture have varied. *See, e.g., United States v. Aguiar*, 975 F.2d 45, 47 (2d Cir.1992); *United States v. Potamitis*, 739 F.2d 784, 789 (2d Cir.), *cert. denied*, 469 U.S. 918 (1984); *Steele v. Taylor*, 684 F.2d 1193, 1199 (6th Cir.1982), *cert. denied*, 460 U.S. 1053 (1983); United States v. Balano, 618 F.2d 624, 629 (10th Cir.1979), *cert. denied*, 449 U.S. 840 (1980); *United States v. Carlson*, 547 F.2d 1346, 1358–59 (8th Cir.), *cert. denied*, 431 U.S. 914 (1977). The foregoing cases apply a preponderance of the evidence standard. *Contra United States v. Thevis*, 665 F.2d 616, 631 (5th Cir.) (clear and convincing standard), *cert. denied*, 459 U.S. 825 (1982). The usual Rule 104(a) preponderance of the evidence standard has been adopted in light of the behavior the new Rule 804(b)(6) seeks to discourage.

GAP Report on Rule 804(b)(5). The words "Transferred to Rule 807" were substituted for "Abrogated".

GAP Report on Rule 804(b)(6). The title of the rule was changed to "Forfeiture by wrongdoing." The word "who" in line 24 was changed to "that" to indicate that the rule is potentially applicable against the government. Two sentences were added to the first paragraph of the committee note to clarify that the wrongdoing need not be criminal in nature, and to indicate the rule's potential applicability to the government. The word "forfeiture" was substituted for "waiver" in the note.

Rule 805. Hearsay Within Hearsay

Hearsay included within hearsay is not excluded under the hearsay rule if each part of the combined statements conforms with an exception to the hearsay rule provided in these rules.

(Pub.L. 93–595, § 1, Jan. 2, 1975, 88 Stat. 1943.)

ADVISORY COMMITTEE NOTES

1972 Proposed Rules

On principle it scarcely seems open to doubt that the hearsay rule should not call for exclusion of a hearsay statement which includes a further hearsay statement when both conform to the requirements of a hearsay exception. Thus a hospital record might contain an entry of the patient's age based on information furnished by his wife. The hospital record would qualify as a regular entry except that the person who furnished the information was not acting in the routine of the business. However, her statement independently qualifies as a statement of pedigree (if she is unavailable) or as a statement made for purposes of diagnosis or treatment, and hence each link in the chain falls under sufficient assurances. Or, further to illustrate, a dying declaration may incorporate a declaration against interest by another declarant. See McCormick § 290, p. 611.

Rule 806. Attacking and Supporting Credibility of Declarant

When a hearsay statement, or a statement defined in Rule 801(d)(2)(C), (D), or (E), has been admitted in evidence, the credibility of the declarant may be attacked, and if attacked may be supported, by any evidence which would be admissible for those purposes if declarant had testified as a witness. Evidence of a statement or conduct by the declarant at any time, inconsistent with the declarant's hearsay statement, is not subject to any requirement that the declarant may have been afforded an opportunity to deny or explain. If the party against whom a hearsay statement has been admitted calls the declarant as a witness, the party is entitled to examine the declarant on the statement as if under cross-examination.

(Pub.L. 93–595, § 1, Jan. 2, 1975, 88 Stat. 1943; Mar. 2, 1987, eff. Oct. 1, 1987; Apr. 11, 1997, eff. Dec. 1, 1997.)

ADVISORY COMMITTEE NOTES

1972 Proposed Rules

The declarant of a hearsay statement which is admitted in evidence is in effect a witness. His credibility should in fairness be subject to impeachment and support as though he had in fact testified. See Rules 608 and 609. There are however, some special aspects of the impeaching of a hearsay declarant which require consideration. These special aspects center upon impeachment by inconsistent statement, arise from factual differences which exist between the use of hearsay and an actual witness and also between various kinds of hearsay, and involve the question of applying to declarants the general rule disallowing evidence of an inconsistent statement to impeach a witness unless he is afforded an opportunity to deny or explain. See Rule 613(b).

The principal difference between using hearsay and an actual witness is that the inconsistent statement will in the case of the witness almost inevitably of necessity in the nature of things be a *prior* statement, which it is entirely possible and feasible to call to his attention, while in the case of hearsay the inconsistent statement may well be a *subsequent* one, which practically precludes calling it to the attention of the declarant. The result of insisting upon observation of this impossible requirement in the hearsay situation is to deny the opponent, already barred from cross-examination, any benefit of this important technique of impeachment. The writers favor allowing the subsequent statement. McCormick § 37, p. 69; 3 Wigmore § 1033. The cases, however, are divided. Cases allowing the impeachment include *People v. Collup,* 27 Cal.2d 829, 167 P.2d 714 (1946); *People v. Rosoto,* 58 Cal.2d 304, 23 Cal.Rptr. 779, 373 P.2d 867 (1962); *Carver v. United States,* 164 U.S. 694, 17 S.Ct. 228, 41 L.Ed. 602 (1897). *Contra, Mattox v. United States,* 156 U.S. 237, 15 S.Ct. 337, 39 L.Ed. 409 (1895); *People v. Hines,* 284 N.Y. 93, 29 N.E.2d 483 (1940). The force of *Mattox,* where the hearsay was the former testimony of a deceased witness and the denial of use of a subsequent inconsistent statement was upheld, is much diminished by *Carver,* where the hearsay was a dying declaration and denial of use of a subsequent inconsistent statement resulted in reversal. The difference in the particular brand of hearsay seems unimportant when the inconsistent statement is a *subsequent* one. True, the opponent is not totally deprived of cross-examination when the hearsay is former testimony or a deposition but he is deprived of cross-examining on the statement or along lines suggested by it. Mr. Justice Shiras, with two justices joining him, dissented vigorously in *Mattox.*

When the impeaching statement was made prior to the hearsay statement, differences in the kinds of hearsay appear which arguably may justify differences in treatment. If the hearsay consisted of a simple statement by the witness, e.g. a dying declaration or a declaration against interest, the feasibility of affording him an opportunity to deny or explain encounters the same practical impossibility as where the statement is a subsequent one, just discussed, although here the impossibility arises from the total absence of anything resembling a hearing at which the matter could be put to him. The courts by a large majority have ruled in favor of allowing the statement to be used under these circumstances. McCormick § 37, p. 69; 3 Wigmore § 1033. If, however, the hearsay consists of former testimony or a deposition, the possibility of calling the prior statement to the attention of the witness or deponent is not ruled out, since the opportunity to cross-examine was available. It might thus be concluded that with former testimony or depositions the conventional foundation should be insisted upon. Most of the cases involve depositions, and Wigmore describes them as divided. 3 Wigmore § 1031. Deposition procedures at best are cumbersome and expensive, and to require the laying of the foundation may impose an undue burden. Under the federal practice, there is no way of knowing with certainty at the time of taking a deposition whether it is merely for discovery or will ultimately end up in evidence. With respect to both former testimony and depositions the possibility exists that knowledge of the statement might not be acquired until after the time of the cross-examination. Moreover, the expanded admissibility of former testimony and depositions under Rule 804(b)(1) calls for a correspondingly expanded approach to impeachment. The rule dispenses with the requirement in all hearsay situations, which is readily administered and best calculated to lead to fair results.

Notice should be taken that Rule 26(f) of the Federal Rules of Civil Procedure, as originally submitted by the Advisory Committee, ended with the following:

"* * * and, without having first called them to the deponent's attention, may show statements contradictory thereto made at any time by the deponent."

This language did not appear in the rule as promulgated in December, 1937. See 4 Moore's Federal Practice ¶¶ 26.01[9], 26.35 (2d ed.1967). In 1951, Nebraska adopted a provision strongly resembling the one stricken from the federal rule:

"Any party may impeach any adverse deponent by self-contradiction without having laid foundation for such impeachment at the time such deposition was taken." R.S.Neb. § 25–1267.07.

For similar provisions, see Uniform Rule 65; California Evidence Code § 1202; Kansas Code of Civil Procedure § 60–462; New Jersey Evidence Rule 65.

The provision for cross-examination of a declarant upon his hearsay statement is a corollary of general principles of cross-examination. A similar provision is found in California Evidence Code § 1203.

1974 Enactment

Rule 906, as passed by the House and as proposed by the Supreme Court provides that whenever a hearsay statement is admitted, the credibility of the declarant of the statement may be attacked, and if attacked may be supported, by any evidence which would be admissible for those purposes if the declarant had testified as a witness. Rule 801 defines what is a hearsay statement. While statements by a person authorized by a party-opponent to make a statement concerning the subject, by the party-opponent's agent or by a coconspirator of a party—see rule 801(d)(2)(c), (d) and (e)—are traditionally defined as exceptions to the hearsay rule, rule 801 defines such admission by a party-opponent as statements which are not hearsay. Consequently, rule 806 by referring exclusively to the admission of hearsay statements, does not appear to allow the credibility of the declarant to be attacked when the declarant is a coconspirator, agent or authorized spokesman. The committee is of the view that such statements should open the declarant to attacks on his credibility. Indeed, the reason such statements are excluded from the operation of rule 806 is likely attributable to the drafting technique used to codify the hearsay rule, viz. some statements, instead of being referred to as exceptions to the hearsay rule, are defined as statements which are not hearsay. The phrase "or a statement defined in rule 801(d)(2)(c), (d) and (e)" is added to the rule in order to subject the declarant of such statements, like the declarant of hearsay statements, to attacks on his credibility. [The committee considered it unnecessary to include statements contained in rule 801(d)(2)(A) and (B)—the statement by the party-opponent himself or the statement of which he has manifested his adoption—because the credibility of the party-opponent is always subject to an attack on his credibility]. Senate Report No. 93–1277.

The Senate amendment permits an attack upon the credibility of the declarant of a statement if the statement is one by a person authorized by a party-opponent to make a statement concerning the subject, one by an agent of a party-opponent, or one by a coconspirator of the party-opponent, as these statements are defined in Rules 801(d)(2)(C), (D) and (E). The House bill has no such provision.

The Conference adopts the Senate amendment. The Senate amendment conforms the rule to present practice. House Report No. 93–1597.

1987 Amendment

The amendments are technical. No substantive change is intended.

1997 Amendment

The amendment is technical. No substantive change is intended.

GAP Report. Restylization changes in the rule were eliminated.

Rule 807. Residual Exception

A statement not specifically covered by Rule 803 or 804 but having equivalent circumstantial guarantees of trustworthiness, is not excluded by the hearsay rule, if the court determines that (A) the statement is offered as evidence of a material fact; (B) the statement is more probative on the point for which it is offered than any other evidence which the proponent can procure through reasonable efforts; and (C) the general purposes of these rules and the interests of justice will best be served by admission of the statement into evidence. However, a statement may not be admitted under this exception unless the proponent of it makes known to the adverse party sufficiently in advance of the trial or hearing to provide the adverse party with a fair opportunity to prepare to meet it, the proponent's intention to offer the statement and the particulars of it, including the name and address of the declarant.

(Added Apr. 11, 1997, eff. Dec. 1, 1997.)

ADVISORY COMMITTEE NOTES

1997 Amendment

The contents of Rule 803(24) and Rule 804(b)(5) have been combined and transferred to a new Rule 807. This was done to facilitate additions to Rules 803 and 804. No change in meaning is intended.

GAP Report on Rule 807. Restylization changes in the rule were eliminated.

ARTICLE IX. AUTHENTICATION AND IDENTIFICATION

Rule 901. Requirement of Authentication or Identification

(a) General provision. The requirement of authentication or identification as a condition precedent to admissibility is satisfied by evidence sufficient to support a finding that the matter in question is what its proponent claims.

(b) Illustrations. By way of illustration only, and not by way of limitation, the following are examples of authentication or identification conforming with the requirements of this rule:

(1) Testimony of witness with knowledge. Testimony that a matter is what it is claimed to be.

(2) Nonexpert opinion on handwriting. Nonexpert opinion as to the genuineness of handwriting, based upon familiarity not acquired for purposes of the litigation.

(3) Comparison by trier or expert witness. Comparison by the trier of fact or by expert witnesses with specimens which have been authenticated.

(4) Distinctive characteristics and the like. Appearance, contents, substance, internal patterns, or other distinctive characteristics, taken in conjunction with circumstances.

(5) Voice identification. Identification of a voice, whether heard firsthand or through mechanical or electronic transmission or recording, by opinion based upon hearing the voice at any time under circumstances connecting it with the alleged speaker.

(6) Telephone conversations. Telephone conversations, by evidence that a call was made to the number assigned at the time by the telephone company to a particular person or business, if (A) in the case of a person, circumstances, including self-identification, show the person answering to be the one called, or (B) in the case of a business, the call was made to a place of business and the conversation related to business reasonably transacted over the telephone.

(7) Public records or reports. Evidence that a writing authorized by law to be recorded or filed and in fact recorded or filed in a public office, or a purported public record, report, statement, or data compilation, in any form, is from the public office where items of this nature are kept.

(8) Ancient documents or data compilation. Evidence that a document or data compilation, in any form, (A) is in such condition as to create no suspicion concerning its authenticity, (B) was in a place where it, if authentic, would likely be, and (C) has been in existence 20 years or more at the time it is offered.

(9) Process or system. Evidence describing a process or system used to produce a result and showing that the process or system produces an accurate result.

(10) Methods provided by statute or rule. Any method of authentication or identification provided by Act of Congress or by other rules prescribed by the Supreme Court pursuant to statutory authority.

(Pub.L. 93–595, § 1, Jan. 2, 1975, 88 Stat.1943.)

ADVISORY COMMITTEE NOTES

1972 Proposed Rules

Note to Subdivision (a). Authentication and identification represent a special aspect of relevancy. Michael and Adler, Real Proof, 5 Vand.L.Rev. 344, 362 (1952); McCormick §§ 179, 185; Morgan, Basic Problems of Evidence 378 (1962). Thus a telephone conversation may be irrelevant because on an unrelated topic or because the speaker is not identified. The latter aspect is the one here involved. Wigmore describes the need for authentication as "an inherent logical necessity." 7 Wigmore § 2129, p. 564.

This requirement of showing authenticity or identity falls in the category of relevancy dependent upon fulfillment of a condition of fact and is governed by the procedure set forth in Rule 104(b).

The common law approach to authentication of documents has been criticized as an "attitude of agnosticism," McCormick, Cases on Evidence 388, n. 4 (3rd ed. 1956), as one which "departs sharply from men's customs in ordinary affairs," and as presenting only a slight obstacle to the introduction of forgeries in comparison to the time and expense devoted to proving genuine writings which correctly show their origin on their face, McCormick § 185, pp. 395, 396. Today, such available procedures as requests to admit and pretrial conference afford the means of eliminating much of the need for authentication or identification. Also, significant inroads upon the traditional insistence on authentication and identification have been made by accepting as at least prima facie genuine items of the kind treated in Rule 902, *infra*. However, the need for suitable methods of proof still remains, since criminal cases pose their own obstacles to the use of preliminary procedures, unforeseen contingencies may arise, and cases of genuine controversy will still occur.

Note to Subdivision (b). The treatment of authentication and identification draws largely upon the experience embodied in the common law and in statutes to furnish illustrative applications of the general principle set forth in subdivision (a). The examples are not intended as an exclusive enumeration of allowable methods but are meant to guide and suggest, leaving room for growth and development in this area of the law.

The examples relate for the most part to documents, with some attention given to voice communications and computer printouts. As Wigmore noted, no special rules have been developed for authenticating chattels. Wigmore, Code of Evidence § 2086 (3rd ed. 1942).

It should be observed that compliance with requirements of authentication or identification by no means assures admission of an item into evidence, as other bars, hearsay for example, may remain.

Example (1). Example (1) contemplates a broad spectrum ranging from testimony of a witness who was present at the signing of a document to testimony establishing narcotics as taken from an accused and accounting for custody through the period until trial, including laboratory analysis. See California Evidence Code § 1413, eyewitness to signing.

Example (2). Example (2) states conventional doctrine as to lay identification of handwriting, which recognizes that a sufficient familiarity with the handwriting of another person may be acquired by seeing him write, by exchanging correspondence, or by other means, to afford a basis for identifying it on subsequent occasions. McCormick § 189. See also California Evidence Code § 1416. Testimony based upon familiarity acquired for purposes of the litigation is reserved to the expert under the example which follows.

Example (3). The history of common law restrictions upon the technique of proving or disproving the genuineness of a disputed specimen of handwriting through comparison with a genuine specimen, by either the testimony of expert witnesses or direct viewing by the triers themselves, is detailed in 7 Wigmore §§ 1991–1994. In breaking away, the English Common Law Procedure Act of 1854, 17 and 18 Vict., c. 125, § 27, cautiously allowed expert or trier to use exemplars "proved to the satisfaction of the judge to be genuine" for purposes of comparison. The language found its way into numerous statutes in this country, e.g., California Evidence Code §§ 1417, 1418. While explainable as a measure of prudence in the process of breaking with precedent in the handwriting situation, the reservation to the judge of the question of the genuineness of exemplars and the imposition of an unusually high standard of persuasion are at variance with the general treatment of relevancy which depends upon fulfillment of a condition of fact. Rule 104(b). No similar attitude is found in other comparison situations, e.g., ballistics comparison by jury, as in *Evans v. Commonwealth*, 230 Ky. 411, 19 S.W.2d 1091 (1929), or by experts, Annot., 26 A.L.R.2d 892, and no reason appears for its continued existence in handwriting cases. Consequently Example (3) sets no higher standard for handwriting specimens and treats all comparison situations alike, to be governed by Rule 104(b). This approach is consistent with 28 U.S.C. § 1731: "The admitted or proved handwriting of any person shall be admissible, for purposes of comparison, to determine genuineness of other handwriting attributed to such person."

Precedent supports the acceptance of visual comparison as sufficiently satisfying preliminary authentication requirements for admission in evidence. *Brandon v. Collins*, 267 F.2d 731 (2d Cir.1959); *Wausau Sulphate Fibre Co. v. Commissioner of Internal Revenue*, 61 F.2d 879 (7th Cir. 1932); *Desimone v. United States*, 227 F.2d 864 (9th Cir. 1955).

Example (4). The characteristics of the offered item itself, considered in the light of circumstances, afford authentication techniques in great variety. Thus a document or telephone conversation may be shown to have emanated from a particular person by virtue of its disclosing knowledge of facts known peculiarly to him; *Globe Automatic Sprinkler Co. v. Braniff*, 89 Okl. 105, 214 P. 127 (1923); California Evidence Code § 1421; similarly, a letter may be authenticated by content and circumstances indicating it was in reply to a duly authenticated one. McCormick § 192; California Evidence Code § 1420. Language patterns may indicate authenticity or its opposite. *Magnuson v. State*, 187 Wis. 122, 203 N.W. 749 (1925); Arens and Meadow, Psycholinguistics and the Confession Dilemma, 56 Colum.L.Rev. 19 (1956).

Example (5). Since aural voice identification is not a subject of expert testimony, the requisite familiarity may be acquired either before or after the particular speaking which is the subject of the identification, in this respect resembling visual identification of a person rather than identification of handwriting. Cf. Example (2), *supra*, *People v. Nichols*, 378 Ill. 487, 38 N.E.2d 766 (1942); *McGuire v. State*, 200 Md. 601, 92 A.2d 582 (1952); *State v. McGee*, 336 Mo. 1082, 83 S.W.2d 98 (1935).

Example (6). The cases are in agreement that a mere assertion of his identity by a person talking on the telephone is not sufficient evidence of the authenticity of the conversation and that additional evidence of his identity is required. The additional evidence need not fall in any set pattern. Thus the content of his statements or the reply technique, under Example (4), *supra*, or voice identification under Example (5), may furnish the necessary foundation. Outgoing calls made by the witness involve additional factors bearing upon authenticity. The calling of a number assigned by the telephone company reasonably supports the assumption that the listing is correct and that the number is the one reached. If the number is that of a place of business, the mass of authority allows an ensuing conversation if it relates to business reasonably transacted over the telephone, on the theory that the maintenance of the telephone connection is an invitation to do business without further identification. *Matton v. Hoover Co.*, 350 Mo. 506, 166 S.W.2d 557 (1942); *City of Pawhuska v. Crutchfield*, 147 Okl. 4, 293 P. 1095 (1930); *Zurich General Acc. & Liability Ins. Co. v. Baum*, 159 Va. 404, 165 S.E. 518 (1932). Otherwise, some additional circumstance of identification of the speaker is required. The authorities divide on the question whether the self-identifying statement of the person answering suffices. Example (6) answers in the affirmative on the assumption that usual conduct respecting telephone calls furnish adequate assurances of regularity, bearing in mind that the entire matter is open to exploration before the trier of fact. In general, see McCormick § 193; 7 Wigmore § 2155; Annot., 71 A.L.R. 5, 105 id. 326.

Example (7). Public records are regularly authenticated by proof of custody, without more. McCormick § 191; 7 Wigmore §§ 2158, 2159. The example extends the principle to include data stored in computers and similar methods, of which increasing use in the public records area may be expected. See California Evidence Code §§ 1532, 1600.

Example (8). The familiar ancient document rule of the common law is extended to include data stored electronically or by other similar means. Since the importance of appearance diminishes in this situation, the importance of custody or place where found increases correspondingly. This expansion is necessary in view of the widespread use of methods of storing data in forms other than conventional written records.

Any time period selected is bound to be arbitrary. The common law period of 30 years is here reduced to 20 years, with some shift of emphasis from the probable unavailability of witnesses to the unlikeliness of a still viable fraud after the lapse of time. The shorter period is specified in the English Evidence Act of 1938, 1 & 2 Geo. 6, c. 28, and in Oregon R.S.1963, § 41.360(34). See also the numerous statutes prescribing periods of less than 30 years in the case of recorded documents. 7 Wigmore § 2143.

The application of Example (8) is not subject to any limitation to title documents or to any requirement that possession, in the case of a title document, has been consistent with the document. See McCormick § 190.

Example (9). Example (9) is designed for situations in which the accuracy of a result is dependent upon a process or system which produces it. X rays afford a familiar instance. Among more recent developments is the computer, as to which see Transport Indemnity Co. v. Seib, 178 Neb. 253, 132 N.W.2d 871 (1965); *State v. Veres*, 7 Ariz.App. 117, 436 P.2d 629 (1968); *Merrick v. United States Rubber Co.*, 7 Ariz.App. 433, 440 P.2d 314 (1968); Freed, Computer Print–Outs as Evidence, 16 Am.Jur.Proof of Facts 273; Symposium, Law and Computers in the Mid–Sixties, ALI–ABA (1966); 37 Albany L.Rev. 61 (1967). Example (9) does not, of course, foreclose taking judicial notice of the accuracy of the process or system.

Example (10). The example makes clear that methods of authentication provided by Act of Congress and by the Rules of Civil and Criminal Procedure or by Bankruptcy Rules are not intended to be superseded. Illustrative are the provisions for authentication of official records in Civil Procedure Rule 44 and Criminal Procedure Rule 27, for authentication of records of proceedings by court reporters in 28 U.S.C. § 753(b) and Civil Procedure Rule 80(c), and for authentication of depositions in Civil Procedure Rule 30(f).

Rule 902. Self-authentication

Extrinsic evidence of authenticity as a condition precedent to admissibility is not required with respect to the following:

(1) Domestic public documents under seal. A document bearing a seal purporting to be that of the United States, or of any State, district, Commonwealth, territory, or insular possession thereof, or the Panama Canal Zone, or the Trust Territory of the Pacific Islands, or of a political subdivision, department, officer, or agency thereof, and a signature purporting to be an attestation or execution.

(2) Domestic public documents not under seal. A document purporting to bear the signature in the official capacity of an officer or employee of any entity included in paragraph (1) hereof, having no seal, if a public officer having a seal and having official duties in the district or political subdivision of the officer or employee certifies under seal that the signer has the official capacity and that the signature is genuine.

(3) Foreign public documents. A document purporting to be executed or attested in an official capacity by a person authorized by the laws of a foreign country to make the execution or attestation, and accompanied by a final certification as to the genuineness of the signature and official position (A) of the executing or attesting person, or (B) of any foreign official whose certificate of genuineness of signature and official position relates to the execution or attestation or is in a chain of certificates of genuineness of signature and official position relating to the execution or attestation. A final certification may be made by a secretary of an embassy or legation, consul general, consul, vice consul, or consular agent of the United States, or a diplomatic or consular official of the foreign country assigned or accredited to the United States. If reasonable opportunity has been given to all parties to investigate the authenticity and accuracy of official documents, the court may, for good cause shown, order that they be treated as presumptively authentic without final certification or permit them to be evidenced by an attested summary with or without final certification.

(4) Certified copies of public records. A copy of an official record or report or entry therein, or of a document authorized by law to be recorded or filed and actually recorded or filed in a public office, including data compilations in any form, certified as correct by the custodian or other person authorized to make the certification, by certificate complying with paragraph (1), (2), or (3) of this rule or complying with any Act of Congress or rule prescribed by the Supreme Court pursuant to statutory authority.

(5) Official publications. Books, pamphlets, or other publications purporting to be issued by public authority.

(6) Newspapers and periodicals. Printed materials purporting to be newspapers or periodicals.

(7) Trade inscriptions and the like. Inscriptions, signs, tags, or labels purporting to have been affixed in the course of business and indicating ownership, control, or origin.

(8) Acknowledged documents. Documents accompanied by a certificate of acknowledgment executed in the manner provided by law by a notary public or other officer authorized by law to take acknowledgments.

(9) Commercial paper and related documents. Commercial paper, signatures thereon, and documents relating thereto to the extent provided by general commercial law.

(10) Presumptions under Acts of Congress. Any signature, document, or other matter declared by Act of Congress to be presumptively or prima facie genuine or authentic.

(Pub.L. 93–595, § 1, Jan. 2, 1975, 88 Stat. 1944; Mar. 2, 1987, eff. Oct. 1, 1987; Apr. 25, 1988, eff. Nov. 1, 1988.)

ADVISORY COMMITTEE NOTES

1972 Proposed Rules

Case law and statutes have, over the years, developed a substantial body of instances in which authenticity is taken as sufficiently established for purposes of admissibility without extrinsic evidence to that effect, sometimes for reasons of policy but perhaps more often because practical considerations reduce the possibility of unauthenticity to a very small dimension. The present rule collects and incorporates these situations, in some instances expanding them to occupy a larger area which their underlying considerations justify. In no instance is the opposite party foreclosed from disputing authenticity.

Note to Paragraph (1). The acceptance of documents bearing a public seal and signature, most often encountered in practice in the form of acknowledgments or certificates authenticating copies of public records, is actually of broad application. Whether theoretically based in whole or in part upon judicial notice, the practical underlying considerations are that forgery is a crime and detection is fairly easy and certain. 7 Wigmore § 2161, p. 638; California Evidence Code § 1452. More than 50 provisions for judicial notice of official seals are contained in the United States Code.

Note to Paragraph (2). While statutes are found which raise a presumption of genuineness of purported official signatures in the absence of an official seal, 7 Wigmore § 2167; California Evidence Code § 1453, the greater ease of effecting a forgery under these circumstances is apparent. Hence this paragraph of the rule calls for authentication by an officer who has a seal. Notarial acts by members of the armed forces and other special situations are covered in paragraph (10).

Note to Paragraph (3). Paragraph (3) provides a method for extending the presumption of authenticity to foreign official documents by a procedure of certification. It is derived from Rule 44(a)(2) of the Rules of Civil Procedure but is broader in applying to public documents rather than being limited to public records.

Note to Paragraph (4). The common law and innumerable statutes have recognized the procedure of authenticating copies of public records by certificate. The certificate qualifies as a public document, receivable as authentic when in conformity with paragraph (1), (2), or (3). Rule 44(a) of the Rules of Civil Procedure and Rule 27 of the Rules of Criminal Procedure have provided authentication procedures of this nature for both domestic and foreign public records. It will be observed that the certification procedure here provided extends only to public records, reports, and recorded documents, all including data compilations, and does not apply to public documents generally. Hence documents provable when presented in original form under paragraphs (1), (2), or (3) may not be provable by certified copy under paragraph (4).

Note to Paragraph (5). Dispensing with preliminary proof of the genuineness of purportedly official publications, most commonly encountered in connection with statutes, court reports, rules, and regulations, has been greatly enlarged by statutes and decisions. 5 Wigmore § 1684. Paragraph (5), it will be noted, does not confer admissibility upon all official publications; it merely provides a means whereby their authenticity may be taken as established for purposes of admissibility. Rule 44(a) of the Rules of Civil Procedure has been to the same effect.

Note to Paragraph (6). The likelihood of forgery of newspapers or periodicals is slight indeed. Hence no danger is apparent in receiving them. Establishing the authenticity of the publication may, of course, leave still open questions of authority and responsibility for items therein contained. See 7 Wigmore § 2150. Cf. 39 U.S.C. § 4005(b), public advertisement prima facie evidence of agency of person named, in postal fraud order proceeding; Canadian Uniform Evidence Act, Draft of 1936, printed copy of newspaper prima facie evidence that notices or advertisements were authorized.

Note to Paragraph (7). Several factors justify dispensing with preliminary proof of genuineness of commercial and mercantile labels and the like. The risk of forgery is minimal. Trademark infringement involves serious penalties. Great efforts are devoted to inducing the public to buy in reliance on brand names, and substantial protection is given them. Hence the fairness of this treatment finds recognition in the cases. *Curtiss Candy Co. v. Johnson,* 163 Miss. 426, 141 So. 762 (1932), Baby Ruth candy bar; *Doyle v. Continental Baking Co.,* 262 Mass. 516, 160 N.E. 325 (1928), loaf of bread; *Weiner v. Mager & Throne, Inc.,* 167 Misc. 338, 3 N.Y.S.2d 918 (1938), same. And see W.Va.Code 1966, § 47–3–5, trademark on bottle prima facie evidence of ownership. *Contra, Keegan v. Green Giant Co.,* 150 Me. 283, 110 A.2d 599 (1954); *Murphy v. Campbell Soup Co.,* 62 F.2d 564 (1st Cir.1933). Cattle brands have received similar acceptance in the western states. Rev.Code Mont.1947, § 46–606, *State v. Wolfley,* 75 Kan. 406, 89 P. 1046 (1907); Annot., 11 L.R.A.(N.S.) 87. Inscriptions on trains and vehicles are held to be prima facie evidence of ownership or control. *Pittsburgh, Ft. W. & C. Ry. v. Callaghan,* 157 Ill. 406, 41 N.E. 909 (1895); 9 Wigmore § 2510a. See also the provision of 19 U.S.C. § 1615(2) that marks, labels, brands, or stamps indicating foreign origin are prima facie evidence of foreign origin of merchandise.

Note to Paragraph (8). In virtually every state, acknowledged title documents are receivable in evidence without further proof. Statutes are collected in 5 Wigmore § 1676. If this authentication suffices for documents of the importance of those affecting titles, logic scarcely permits denying this method when other kinds of documents are involved. Instances of broadly inclusive statutes are California Evidence Code § 1451 and N.Y.CPLR 4538, McKinney's Consol.Laws 1963.

Note to Paragraph (9). Issues of the authenticity of commercial paper in federal courts will usually arise in diversity cases, will involve an element of a cause of action or defense, and with respect to presumptions and burden of proof will be controlled by *Erie Railroad Co. v. Tompkins,* 304 U.S. 64, 58 S.Ct. 817, 82 L.Ed. 1188 (1938). Rule 302, *supra.* There may, however, be questions of authenticity involving lesser segments of a case or the case may be one governed by federal common law. *Clearfield Trust Co. v. United States,* 318 U.S. 363, 63 S.Ct. 573, 87 L.Ed. 838 (1943). Cf. *United States v. Yazell,* 382 U.S. 341, 86 S.Ct. 500, 15 L.Ed.2d 404 (1966). In these situations, resort to the useful authentication provisions of the Uniform Commercial Code is provided for. While the phrasing is in terms of "general commercial law," in order to avoid the potential complications inherent in borrowing local statutes, today one would have difficulty in determining the general commercial law without referring to the Code. See *Williams v. Walker–Thomas Furniture Co.,* 121 U.S.App.D.C. 315, 350 F.2d 445 (1965). Pertinent Code provisions are sections 1–202, 3–307, and 3–510, dealing with third-party documents, signatures on negotiable instruments, protests, and statements of dishonor.

Note to Paragraph (10). The paragraph continues in effect dispensations with preliminary proof of genuineness provided in various Acts of Congress. See, for example, 10 U.S.C. § 936, signature, without seal, together with title, prima facie evidence of authenticity of acts of certain military personnel who are given notarial powers; 15 U.S.C. § 77f(a), signature on SEC registration presumed genuine; 26 U.S.C. § 6064, signature to tax return prima facie genuine.

1974 Enactment

Note to Paragraph (8). Rule 902(8) as submitted by the Court referred to certificates of acknowledgment "under the hand and seal of" a notary public or other officer authorized by law to take acknowledgments. The Committee amended the Rule to eliminate the requirement, believed to be inconsistent with the law in some States, that a notary public must affix a seal to a document acknowledged before him. As amended the Rule merely requires that the document be executed in the manner prescribed by State law.

Note to Paragraph (9). The Committee approved Rule 902(9) as submitted by the Court. With respect to the meaning of the phrase "general commercial law", the Committee intends that the Uniform Commercial Code, which has been adopted in virtually every State, will be followed generally, but that federal commercial law will apply where federal commercial paper is involved. See Clearfield Trust Co. v. United States, 318 U.S. 363 (1943). Further, in those instances in which the issues are governed by Erie R. Co. v. Tompkins, 304 U.S. 64 (1938), State law will apply irrespective of whether it is the Uniform Commercial Code. House Report No. 93–650.

1987 Amendment

The amendments are technical. No substantive change is intended.

1988 Amendment

These two sentences were inadvertently eliminated from the 1987 amendments. The amendment is technical. No substantive change is intended.

Rule 903. Subscribing Witness' Testimony Unnecessary

The testimony of a subscribing witness is not necessary to authenticate a writing unless required by the laws of the jurisdiction whose laws govern the validity of the writing.

(Pub.L. 93–595, § 1, Jan. 2, 1975, 88 Stat.1945.)

ADVISORY COMMITTEE NOTES

1972 Proposed Rules

The common law required that attesting witnesses be produced or accounted for. Today the requirement has generally been abolished except with respect to documents which must be attested to be valid, e.g. wills in some states. McCormick § 188. Uniform Rule 71; California Evidence Code § 1411; Kansas Code of Civil Procedure § 60–468; New Jersey Evidence Rule 71; New York CPLR Rule 4537.

ARTICLE X. CONTENTS OF WRITINGS, RECORDINGS AND PHOTOGRAPHS

Rule 1001. Definitions

For purposes of this article the following definitions are applicable:

(1) **Writings and recordings.** "Writings" and "recordings" consist of letters, words, or numbers, or their equivalent, set down by handwriting, typewriting, printing, photostating, photographing, magnetic impulse, mechanical or electronic recording, or other form of data compilation.

(2) **Photographs.** "Photographs" include still photographs, X-ray films, video tapes, and motion pictures.

(3) **Original.** An "original" of a writing or recording is the writing or recording itself or any counterpart intended to have the same effect by a person executing or issuing it. An "original" of a photograph includes the negative or any print therefrom. If data are stored in a computer or similar device, any printout or other output readable by sight, shown to reflect the data accurately, is an "original".

(4) **Duplicate.** A "duplicate" is a counterpart produced by the same impression as the original, or from the same matrix, or by means of photography, including enlargements and miniatures, or by mechanical or electronic re-recording, or by chemical reproduction, or by other equivalent techniques which accurately reproduces the original.

(Pub.L. 93–595, § 1, Jan. 2, 1975, 88 Stat. 1945.)

ADVISORY COMMITTEE NOTES

1972 Proposed Rules

In an earlier day, when discovery and other related procedures were strictly limited, the misleading named "best evidence rule" afforded substantial guarantees against inaccuracies and fraud by its insistence upon production or original documents. The great enlargement of the scope of discovery and related procedures in recent times has measurably reduced the need for the rule. Nevertheless important areas of usefulness persist: discovery of documents outside the jurisdiction may require substantial outlay of time and money; the unanticipated document may not practically be discoverable; criminal cases have built-in limitations on discovery. Cleary and Strong, The Best Evidence Rule: An Evaluation in Context, 51 Iowa L.Rev. 825 (1966).

Note to Paragraph (1). Traditionally the rule requiring the original centered upon accumulations of data and expressions affecting legal relations set forth in words and figures. this meant that the rule was one essentially related to writings. Present day techniques have expanded methods of storing data, yet the essential form which the information ultimately assumes for usable purposes is words and figures. Hence the considerations underlying the rule dictate its expansion to include computers, photographic systems, and other modern developments.

Note to Paragraph (3). In most instances, what is an original will be self-evident and further refinement will be unnecessary. However, in some instances particularized definition is required. A carbon copy of a contract executed in duplicate becomes an original, as does a sales ticket carbon copy given to a customer. While strictly speaking the original of a photograph might be thought to be only the negative, practicality and common usage require that any print from the negative be regarded as an original. Similarly, practicality and usage confer the status of original upon any computer printout. *Transport Indemnity Co. v. Seib*, 178 Neb. 253, 132 N.W.2d 871 (1965).

Note to Paragraph (4). The definition describes "copies" produced by methods possessing an accuracy which virtually eliminates the possibility of error. Copies thus produced are given the status of originals in large measure by Rule 1003, *infra.* Copies subsequently produced manually, whether handwritten or typed, are not within the definition. It should be noted that what is an original for some purposes may be a duplicate for others. Thus a bank's microfilm record of checks cleared is the original as a record. However, a print offered as a copy of a check whose contents are in controversy is a duplicate. This result is substantially consistent with 28 U.S.C. § 1732(b). Compare 26 U.S.C. § 7513(c), giving full status as originals to photographic reproductions of tax returns and other documents, made by authority of the Secretary of the Treasury, and 44 U.S.C.

§ 399(a), giving original status to photographic copies in the National Archives.

1974 Enactment

Note to Paragraph (2). The Committee amended this Rule expressly to include "video tapes" in the definition of "photographs." House Report No. 93–650.

Rule 1002. Requirement of Original

To prove the content of a writing, recording, or photograph, the original writing, recording, or photograph is required, except as otherwise provided in these rules or by Act of Congress.

(Pub.L. 93–595, § 1, Jan. 2, 1975, 88 Stat. 1946.)

ADVISORY COMMITTEE NOTES

1972 Proposed Rules

The rule is the familiar one requiring production of the original of a document to prove its contents, expanded to include writings, recordings, and photographs, as defined in Rule 1001(1) and (2), *supra.*

Application of the rule requires a resolution of the question whether contents are sought to be proved. Thus an event may be proved by nondocumentary evidence, even though a written record of it was made. If, however, the event is sought to be proved by the written record, the rule applies. For example, payment may be proved without producing the written receipt which was given. Earnings may be proved without producing books of account in which they are entered. McCormick § 198; 4 Wigmore § 1245. Nor does the rule apply to testimony that books or records have been examined and found not to contain any reference to a designated matter.

The assumption should not be made that the rule will come into operation on every occasion when use is made of a photograph in evidence. On the contrary, the rule will seldom apply to ordinary photographs. In most instances a party *wishes* to introduce the item and the question raised is the propriety of receiving it in evidence. Cases in which an offer is made of the testimony of a witness as to what he saw in a photograph or motion picture, without producing the same, are most unusual. The usual course is for a witness on the stand to identify the photograph or motion picture as a correct representation of events which he saw or of a scene with which he is familiar. In fact he adopts the picture as his testimony, or, in common parlance, uses the picture to illustrate his testimony. Under these circumstances, no effort is made to prove the contents of the picture, and the rule is inapplicable. Paradis, The Celluloid Witness, 37 U.Colo. L.Rev. 235, 249–251 (1965).

On occasion, however, situations arise in which contents are sought to be proved. Copyright, defamation, and invasion of privacy by photograph or motion picture falls in this category. Similarly as to situations in which the picture is offered as having independent probative value, e.g. automatic photograph of bank robber. See *People v. Doggett,* 83 Cal.App.2d 405, 188 P.2d 792 (1948), photograph of defendants engaged in indecent act; Mouser and Philbin, Photographic Evidence—Is There a Recognized Basis for Admissibility? 8 Hastings L.J. 310 (1957). the most commonly encountered of this latter group is of course, the X ray, with substantial authority calling for production of the original. *Daniels v. Iowa City,* 191 Iowa 811, 183 N.W. 415 (1921); *Cellamare v. Third Acc. Transit Corp.,* 273 App.Div. 260, 77 N.Y.S.2d 91 (1948); *Patrick & Tilman v. Matkin,* 154 Okl. 232, 7 P.2d 414 (1932); *Mendoza v. Rivera,* 78 P.R.R. 569 (1955).

It should be noted, however, that Rule 703, *supra,* allows an expert to give an opinion based on matters not in evidence, and the present rule must be read as being limited accordingly in its application. Hospital records which may be admitted as business records under Rule 803(6) commonly contain reports interpreting X-rays by the staff radiologist, who qualifies as an expert, and these reports need not be excluded from the records by the instant rule.

The reference to Acts of Congress is made in view of such statutory provisions as 26 U.S.C. § 7513, photographic reproductions of tax returns and documents, made by authority of the Secretary of the Treasury, treated as originals, and 44 U.S.C. § 399(a), photographic copies in National Archives treated as originals.

Rule 1003. Admissibility of Duplicates

A duplicate is admissible to the same extent as an original unless (1) a genuine question is raised as to the authenticity of the original or (2) in the circumstances it would be unfair to admit the duplicate in lieu of the original.

(Pub.L. 93–595, § 1, Jan. 2, 1975, 88 Stat. 1946.)

ADVISORY COMMITTEE NOTES

1972 Proposed Rules

When the only concern is with getting the words or other contents before the court with accuracy and precision, then a counterpart serves equally as well as the original, if the counterpart is the product of a method which insures accuracy and genuineness. By definition in Rule 1001(4), *supra,* a "duplicate" possesses this character.

Therefore, if no genuine issue exists as to authenticity and no other reason exists for requiring the original, a duplicate is admissible under the rule. This position finds support in the decisions, *Myrick v. United States,* 332 F.2d 279 (5th Cir.1964), no error in admitting photostatic copies of checks instead of original microfilm in absence of suggestion to trial judge that photostats were incorrect; *Johns v. United States,* 323 F.2d 421 (5th Cir.1963), not error to admit concededly accurate tape recording made from original wire recording; *Sauget v. Johnston,* 315 F.2d 816 (9th Cir.1963), not error to admit copy of agreement when opponent had original and did not on appeal claim any discrepancy. Other reasons for acquiring the original may be present when only a part of the original is reproduced and the remainder is needed for cross-examination or may disclose matters qualifying the part offered or otherwise useful to the opposing party. *United States v. Alexander,* 326 F.2d 736 (4th Cir. 1964). And see *Toho Bussan Kaisha, Ltd. v. American President Lines, Ltd.,* 265 F.2d 418, 76 A.L.R.2d 1344 (2d Cir.1959).

1974 Enactment

The Committee approved this Rule in the form submitted by the Court, with the expectation that the courts would be liberal in deciding that a "genuine question is raised as to the authenticity of the original." House Report No. 93–650.

Rule 1004. Admissibility of Other Evidence of Contents

The original is not required, and other evidence of the contents of a writing, recording, or photograph is admissible if—

(1) **Originals lost or destroyed.** All originals are lost or have been destroyed, unless the proponent lost or destroyed them in bad faith; or

(2) **Original not obtainable.** No original can be obtained by any available judicial process or procedure; or

(3) **Original in possession of opponent.** At a time when an original was under the control of the party against whom offered, that party was put on notice, by the pleadings or otherwise, that the contents would be a subject of proof at the hearing, and that party does not produce the original at the hearing; or

(4) **Collateral matters.** The writing, recording, or photograph is not closely related to a controlling issue.

(Pub.L. 93–595, § 1, Jan. 2, 1975, 88 Stat. 1946; Mar. 2, 1987, eff. Oct. 1, 1987.)

ADVISORY COMMITTEE NOTES

1972 Proposed Rules

Basically the rule requiring the production of the original as proof of contents has developed as a rule of preference: if failure to produce the original is satisfactorily explained, secondary evidence is admissible. The instant rule specifies the circumstances under which production of the original is excused.

The rule recognizes no "degrees" of secondary evidence. While strict logic might call for extending the principle of preference beyond simply preferring the original, the formulation of a hierarchy of preferences and a procedure for making it effective is believed to involve unwarranted complexities. Most, if not all, that would be accomplished by an extended scheme of preferences will, in any event, be achieved through the normal motivation of a party to present the most convincing evidence possible and the arguments and procedures available to his opponent if he does not. Compare McCormick § 207.

Note to Paragraph (1). Loss or destruction of the original, unless due to bad faith of the proponent, is a satisfactory explanation of nonproduction. McCormick § 201.

Note to Paragraph (2). When the original is in the possession of a third person, inability to procure it from him by resort to process or other judicial procedure is a sufficient explanation of nonproduction. Judicial procedure includes subpoena duces tecum as an incident to the taking of a deposition in another jurisdiction. No further showing is required. See McCormick § 202.

Note to Paragraph (3). A party who has an original in his control has no need for the protection of the rule if put on notice that proof of contents will be made. He can ward off secondary evidence by offering the original. The notice procedure here provided is not to be confused with orders to produce or other discovery procedures, as the purpose of the procedure under this rule is to afford the opposite party an opportunity to produce the original, not to compel him to do so. McCormick § 203.

Note to Paragraph (4). While difficult to define with precision, situations arise in which no good purpose is served by production of the original. Examples are the newspaper in an action for the price of publishing defendant's advertisement, *Foster–Holcomb Investment Co. v. Little Rock Publishing Co.,* 151 Ark. 449, 236 S.W. 597 (1922), and the streetcar transfer of plaintiff claiming status as a passenger, *Chicago City Ry. Co. v. Carroll,* 206 Ill. 318, 68 N.E. 1087 (1903). Numerous cases are collected in McCormick § 200, p. 412, n. 1.

1974 Enactment

Note to Paragraph (1). The Committee approved Rule 1004(1) in the form submitted to Congress. However, the Committee intends that loss or destruction of an original by another person at the instigation of the proponent should be considered as tantamount to loss or destruction in bad faith by the proponent himself. House Report No. 93–650.

1987 Amendment

The amendments are technical. No substantive change is intended.

Rule 1005. Public Records

The contents of an official record, or of a document authorized to be recorded or filed and actually recorded or filed, including data compilations in any form, if otherwise admissible, may be proved by copy, certified as correct in accordance with rule 902 or testified to be correct by a witness who has compared it with the original. If a copy which complies with the foregoing cannot be obtained by the exercise of reasonable diligence, then other evidence of the contents may be given.

(Pub.L. 93–595, § 1, Jan. 2, 1975, 88 Stat. 1946.)

ADVISORY COMMITTEE NOTES

1972 Proposed Rules

Public records call for somewhat different treatment. Removing them from their usual place of keeping would be attended by serious inconvenience to the public and to the custodian. As a consequence judicial decisions and statutes commonly hold that no explanation need be given for failure to produce the original of a public record. McCormick § 204; 4 Wigmore §§ 1215–1228. This blanket dispensation from producing or accounting for the original would open the door to the introduction of every kind of secondary evidence of contents of public records were it not for the preference given certified or compared copies. Recognition of degrees of secondary evidence in this situation is an appropriate *quid pro quo* for not applying the requirement of producing the original.

The provisions of 28 U.S.C. § 1733(b) apply only to departments or agencies of the United States. The rule, however, applies to public records generally and is comparable in scope in this respect to Rule 44(a) of the Rules of Civil Procedure.

Rule 1006. Summaries

The contents of voluminous writings, recordings, or photographs which cannot conveniently be examined in court may be presented in the form of a chart, summary, or calculation. The originals, or duplicates, shall be made available for examination or copying, or both, by other parties at reasonable time and place. The court may order that they be produced in court.

(Pub.L. 93–595, § 1, Jan. 2, 1975, 88 Stat. 1946.)

ADVISORY COMMITTEE NOTES

1972 Proposed Rules

The admission of summaries of voluminous books, records, or documents offers the only practicable means of making their contents available to judge and jury. The rule recognizes this practice, with appropriate safeguards. 4 Wigmore § 1230.

Rule 1007. Testimony or Written Admission of Party

Contents of writings, recordings, or photographs may be proved by the testimony or deposition of the party against whom offered or by that party's written admission, without accounting for the nonproduction of the original.

(Pub.L. 93–595, § 1, Jan. 2, 1975, 88 Stat. 1947; Mar. 2, 1987, eff. Oct. 1, 1987.)

ADVISORY COMMITTEE NOTES

1972 Proposed Rules

While the parent case, *Slatterie v. Pooley*, 6 M. & W. 664, 151 Eng.Rep. 579 (Exch.1840), allows proof of contents by evidence of an oral admission by the party against whom offered, without accounting for nonproduction of the original, the risk of inaccuracy is substantial and the decision is at odds with the purpose of the rule giving preference to the original. See 4 Wigmore § 1255. The instant rule follows Professor McCormick's suggestion of limiting this use of admissions to those made in the course of giving testimony or in writing. McCormick § 208, p. 424. The limitation, of course, does not call for excluding evidence of an oral admission when nonproduction of the original has been accounted for and secondary evidence generally has become admissible. Rule 1004, supra.

A similar provision is contained in New Jersey Evidence Rule 70(1)(h).

1987 Amendment

The amendment is technical. No substantive change is intended.

Rule 1008. Functions of Court and Jury

When the admissibility of other evidence of contents of writings, recordings, or photographs under these rules depends upon the fulfillment of a condition of fact, the question whether the condition has been fulfilled is ordinarily for the court to determine in accordance with the provisions of rule 104. However, when an issue is raised (a) whether the asserted writing ever existed, or (b) whether another writing, recording, or photograph produced at the trial is the original, or (c) whether other evidence of contents correctly reflects the contents, the issue is for the trier of fact to determine as in the case of other issues of fact.

(Pub.L. 93–595, § 1, Jan. 2, 1975, 88 Stat. 1947.)

ADVISORY COMMITTEE NOTES

1972 Proposed Rules

Most preliminary questions of fact in connection with applying the rule preferring the original as evidence of contents are for the judge, under the general principles announced in Rule 104, *supra*. Thus, the question whether the loss of the originals has been established, or of the fulfillment of other conditions specified in Rule 1004, supra, is for the judge. However, questions may arise which go beyond the mere administration of the rule preferring the original and into the merits of the controversy. For example, plaintiff offers secondary evidence of the contents of an alleged contract, after first introducing evidence of loss of the original, and defendant counters with evidence that no such contract was ever executed. If the judge decides that the contract was never executed and excludes the secondary evidence, the case is at an end without ever going to the jury on a central issue. Levin, Authentication and Content of Writings, 10 Rutgers L.Rev. 632, 644 (1956). The latter portion of the instant rule is designed to insure treatment of these situations as raising jury questions. The decision is not one for uncontrolled discretion of the jury but is subject to the control exercised generally by the judge over jury determinations. See Rule 104(b), *supra*.

For similar provisions, see Uniform Rule 70(2); Kansas Code of Civil Procedure § 60–467(b); New Jersey Evidence Rule 70(2), (3).

ARTICLE XI. MISCELLANEOUS RULES

Rule 1101. Applicability of Rules

(a) Courts and judges. These rules apply to the United States district courts, the District Court of Guam, the District Court of the Virgin Islands, the District Court for the Northern Mariana Islands, the United States courts of appeals, the United States Claims Court, and to United States bankruptcy judges and United States magistrate judges, in the actions, cases, and proceedings and to the extent hereinafter set forth. The terms "judge" and "court" in these rules include United States bankruptcy judges and United States magistrate judges.

(b) Proceedings generally. These rules apply generally to civil actions and proceedings, including admiralty and maritime cases, to criminal cases and proceedings, to contempt proceedings except those in which the court may act summarily, and to proceedings and cases under title 11, United States Code.

(c) Rule of privilege. The rule with respect to privileges applies at all stages of all actions, cases, and proceedings.

(d) Rules inapplicable. The rules (other than with respect to privileges) do not apply in the following situations:

(1) Preliminary questions of fact. The determination of questions of fact preliminary to admissibility of evidence when the issue is to be determined by the court under rule 104.

(2) Grand jury. Proceedings before grand juries.

(3) Miscellaneous proceedings. Proceedings for extradition or rendition; preliminary examinations in criminal cases; sentencing, or granting or revoking probation; issuance of warrants for arrest, criminal summonses, and search warrants; and proceedings with respect to release on bail or otherwise.

(e) Rules applicable in part. In the following proceedings these rules apply to the extent that matters of evidence are not provided for in the statutes which govern procedure therein or in other rules prescribed by the Supreme Court pursuant to statutory authority: the trial of misdemeanors and other petty offenses before United States magistrate judges; review of agency actions when the facts are subject to trial de novo under section 706(2)(F) of title 5, United States Code; review of orders of the Secretary of Agriculture under section 2 of the Act entitled "An Act to authorize association of producers of agricultural products" approved February 18, 1922 (7 U.S.C. 292), and under sections 6 and 7(c) of the Perishable Agricultural Commodities Act, 1930 (7 U.S.C. 499f, 499g(c)); naturalization and revocation of naturalization under sections 310–318 of the Immigration and Nationality Act (8 U.S.C. 1421–1429); prize proceedings in admiralty under sections 7651–7681 of title 10, United States Code; review of orders of the Secretary of the Interior under section 2 of the Act entitled "An Act authorizing associations of producers of aquatic products" approved June 25, 1934 (15 U.S.C. 522); review of orders of petroleum control boards under section 5 of the Act entitled "An Act to regulate interstate and foreign commerce in petroleum and its products by prohibiting the shipment in such commerce of petroleum and its products produced in violation of State law, and for other purposes", approved February 22, 1935 (15 U.S.C. 715d); actions for fines, penalties, or forfeitures under part V of title IV of the Tariff Act of 1930 (19 U.S.C. 1581–1624), or under the Anti–Smuggling Act (19 U.S.C. 1701–1711); criminal libel for condemnation, exclusion of imports, or other proceedings under the Federal Food, Drug, and Cosmetic Act (21 U.S.C. 301–392); disputes between seamen under sections 4079, 4080, and 4081 of the Revised Statutes (22 U.S.C. 256–258); habeas corpus under sections 2241–2254 of title 28, United States Code; motions to vacate, set aside or correct sentence under section 2255 of title 28, United States Code; actions for penalties for refusal to transport destitute seamen under section 4578 of the Revised Statutes (46 U.S.C. 679); actions against the United States under the Act entitled "An Act authorizing suits against the United States in admiralty for damage caused by and salvage service rendered to public vessels belonging to the United States, and for other purposes", approved March 3, 1925 (46 U.S.C. 781–790), as implemented by section 7730 of title 10, United States Code.

(Pub.L. 93–595, § 1, Jan. 2, 1975, 88 Stat. 1947; Pub.L. 94–149, § 1(14), Dec. 12, 1975, 89 Stat. 806; Pub.L. 95–598, Title II, § 251, Nov. 6, 1978, 92 Stat. 2673; Pub.L. 97–164, Title I, § 142, Apr. 2, 1982, 96 Stat. 45; Mar. 2, 1987, eff. Oct. 1, 1987; Apr. 25, 1988, eff. Nov. 1, 1988; Pub.L. 100–690, Title VII, § 7075(c), Nov. 18, 1988, 102 Stat. 4405; Apr. 22, 1993, eff. Dec. 1, 1993.)

ADVISORY COMMITTEE NOTES

1972 Proposed Rules

Note to Subdivision (a). The various enabling acts contain differences in phraseology in their descriptions of the courts over which the Supreme Court's power to make rules of practice and procedure extends. The act concerning civil actions, as amended in 1966, refers to "the district courts * * * of the United States in civil actions, including admiralty and maritime cases. * * *" 28 U.S.C. § 2072, Pub.L. 89–773, § 1, 80 Stat. 1323. The bankruptcy authorization is for rules of practice and procedure "under the Bankruptcy Act." 28 U.S.C. § 2075, Pub.L. 88–623, § 1, 78 Stat. 1001. The Bankruptcy Act in turn creates bankruptcy courts of "the United States district courts and the district courts of the Territories and possessions to which this title is or may hereafter be applicable." 11 U.S.C. §§ 1(10), 11(a). The provision as to criminal rules up to and including verdicts applies to "criminal cases and proceedings to punish for criminal contempt of court in the United States district courts, in the district courts for the districts of the Canal Zone and Virgin Islands, in the Supreme Court of Puerto Rico, and in proceedings before United States magistrates." 18 U.S.C. § 3771.

These various provisions do not in terms describe the same courts. In congressional usage the phrase "district courts of the United States," without further qualification, traditionally has included the district courts established by Congress in the states under Article III of the Constitution, which are "constitutional" courts, and has not included the territorial courts created under Article IV, Section 3, clause 2, which are "legislative" courts. *Hornbuckle v. Toombs,* 85 U.S. 648, 21 L.Ed. 966 (1873). However, any doubt as to the inclusion of the District Court for the District of Columbia in the phrase is laid at rest by the provisions of the Judicial Code constituting the judicial districts, 28 U.S.C. § 81 et seq., creating district courts therein, id. § 132, and specifically providing that the term "district court of the United States" means the court so constituted. *Id.* § 451. The District of Columbia is included. *Id.* § 88. Moreover, when these provisions were enacted, reference to the District of Columbia was deleted from the original civil rules enabling act. 28 U.S.C. § 2072. Likewise Puerto Rico is made a district, with a district court, and included in the term. *Id.* § 119. The question is simply one of the extent of the authority conferred by Congress. With respect to civil rules it seems clearly to include the district courts in the states, the District Court for the District of Columbia, and the District Court for the District of Puerto Rico.

The bankruptcy coverage is broader. The bankruptcy courts include "the United States district courts," which includes those enumerated above. Bankruptcy courts also include "the district courts of the Territories and possessions to which this title is or may hereafter be applicable." 11 U.S.C. §§ 1(10), 11(a). These courts include the district courts of Guam and the Virgin Islands. 48 U.S.C. §§ 1424(b), 1615. Professor Moore points out that whether the District Court for the District of the Canal Zone is a court of bankruptcy "is not free from doubt in view of the fact that no other statute expressly or inferentially provides for the applicability of the Bankruptcy Act in the Zone." He further observes that while there seems to be little doubt that the Zone is a territory or possession within the meaning of the Bankruptcy Act, 11 U.S.C. § 1(10), it must be noted that the appendix to the Canal Zone Code of 1934 did not list the Act among the laws of the United States applicable to the Zone. 1 Moore's Collier on Bankruptcy ¶ 1.10, pp. 67, 72, n. 25 (14th ed. 1967). The Code of 1962 confers on the district court jurisdiction of:

"(4) actions and proceedings involving laws of the United States applicable to the Canal Zone; and

"(5) other matters and proceedings wherein jurisdiction is conferred by this Code or any other law." Canal Zone Code, 1962, Title 3, § 141.

Admiralty jurisdiction is expressly conferred. *Id.* § 142. General powers are conferred on the district court, "if the course of proceeding is not specifically prescribed by this Code, by the statute, or by applicable rule of the Supreme Court of the United States * * *" *Id.* § 279. Neither these provisions nor § 1(10) of the Bankruptcy Act ("district courts of the Territories and possessions to which this title is or may hereafter be applicable") furnishes a satisfactory answer as to the status of the District Court for the District of the Canal Zone as a court of bankruptcy. However, the fact is that this court exercises no bankruptcy jurisdiction in practice.

The criminal rules enabling act specified United States district courts, district courts for the districts of the Canal Zone and the Virgin Islands, the Supreme Court of the Commonwealth of Puerto Rico, and proceedings before United States commissioners. Aside from the addition of commissioners, now magistrates, this scheme differs from the bankruptcy pattern in that it makes no mention of the District Court of Guam but by specific mention removes the Canal Zone from the doubtful list.

The further difference in including the Supreme Court of the Commonwealth of Puerto Rico seems not to be significant for present purposes, since the Supreme Court of the Commonwealth of Puerto Rico is an appellate court. The Rules of Criminal Procedure have not been made applicable to it, as being unneeded and inappropriate, Rule 54(a) of the Federal Rules of Criminal Procedure, and the same approach is indicated with respect to rules of evidence.

If one were to stop at this point and frame a rule governing the applicability of the proposed rules of evidence in terms of the authority conferred by the three enabling acts, an irregular pattern would emerge as follows:

Civil actions, including admiralty and maritime cases—district courts in the states, District of Columbia, and Puerto Rico.

Bankruptcy—same as civil actions, plus Guam and Virgin Islands.

Criminal cases—same as civil actions, plus Canal Zone and Virgin Islands (but not Guam).

This irregular pattern need not, however, be accepted. Originally the Advisory Committee on the Rules of Civil Procedure took the position that, although the phrase "district courts of the United States" did not include territorial courts, provisions in the organic laws of Puerto Rico and Hawaii would make the rules applicable to the district courts thereof, though this would not be so as to Alaska, the Virgin Islands, or the Canal Zone, whose organic acts contained no corresponding provisions. At the suggestion of the Court, however, the Advisory Committee struck from its notes a statement to the above effect. 2 Moore's Federal Practice ¶ 1.07 (2nd ed. 1967); 1 Barron and Holtzoff, Federal Practice and Procedure § 121 (Wright ed. 1960). Congress thereafter by various enactments provided that the rules and future amendments thereto should apply to the district courts of Hawaii, 53 Stat. 841 (1939), Puerto Rico, 54 Stat. 22 (1940), Alaska, 63 Stat. 445 (1949), Guam, 64 Stat. 384–390 (1950), and the Virgin Islands, 68 Stat. 497, 507 (1954). The original enabling act for rules of criminal procedure specifically mentioned the district courts of the Canal Zone and the Virgin Islands. The Commonwealth of Puerto Rico was blanketed in by creating its court a "district court of the United States" as previously described. Although Guam is not mentioned in either the enabling act or in the expanded definition of "district court of the United States," the Supreme Court in 1956 amended Rule 54(a) to state that the Rules of Criminal Procedure are applicable in Guam. The Court took this step following the enactment of legislation by Congress in 1950 that rules theretofore or thereafter promulgated by the Court in civil cases, admiralty, criminal cases and bankruptcy should apply to the District Court of Guam, 48 U.S.C. § 1424(b), and two Ninth Circuit decisions upholding the applicability of the Rules of Criminal Procedure to Guam. *Pugh v. United States,* 212 F.2d 761 (9th Cir.1954); *Hatchett v. Guam,* 212 F.2d 767 (9th Cir.1954); Orfield, The Scope of the Federal Rules of Criminal Procedure, 38 U. of Det.L.J. 173, 187 (1960).

From this history, the reasonable conclusion is that Congressional enactment of a provision that rules and future amendments shall apply in the courts of a territory or possession is the equivalent of mention in an enabling act and that a rule on scope and applicability may properly be drafted accordingly. Therefore the pattern set by Rule 54 of the Federal Rules of Criminal Procedure is here followed.

The substitution of magistrates in lieu of commissioners is made in pursuance of the Federal Magistrates Act, P.L. 90–578, approved October 17, 1968, 82 Stat. 1107.

Note to Subdivision (b). Subdivision (b) is a combination of the language of the enabling acts, supra, with respect to the kinds of proceedings in which the making of rules is authorized. It is subject to the qualifications expressed in the subdivisions which follow.

Note to Subdivision (c). Subdivision (c) singling out the rules of privilege for special treatment, is made necessary by the limited applicability of the remaining rules.

Note to Subdivision (d). The rule is not intended as an expression as to when due process or other constitutional provisions may require an evidentiary hearing. Paragraph (1) restates, for convenience, the provisions of the second sentence of Rule 104(a), *supra.* See Advisory Committee's Note to that rule.

(2) While some states have statutory requirements that indictments be based on "legal evidence," and there is some case law to the effect that the rules of evidence apply to grand jury proceedings, 1 Wigmore § 4(5), the Supreme Court has not accepted this view. In *Costello v. United States,* 350 U.S. 359, 76 S.Ct. 406, 100 L.Ed. 397 (1965), the Court refused to allow an indictment to be attacked, for either constitutional or policy reasons, on the ground that only hearsay evidence was presented.

"It would run counter to the whole history of the grand jury institution, in which laymen conduct their inquiries unfettered by technical rules. Neither justice nor the concept of a fair trial requires such a change." *Id.* at 364. The rule as drafted does not deal with the evidence required to support an indictment.

(3) The rule exempts preliminary examinations in criminal cases. Authority as to the applicability of the rules of evidence to preliminary examinations has been meagre and conflicting. Goldstein, The State and the Accused: Balance of Advantage in Criminal Procedure, 69 Yale L.J. 1149, 1168, n. 53 (1960); Comment, Preliminary Hearings on Indictable Offenses in Philadelphia, 106 U. of Pa.L.Rev. 589, 592–593 (1958). Hearsay testimony is, however, customarily received in such examinations. Thus in a Dyer Act case, for example, an affidavit may properly be used in a preliminary examination to prove ownership of the stolen vehicle, thus saving the victim of the crime the hardship of having to travel twice to a distant district for the sole purpose of testifying as to ownership. It is believed that the extent of the applicability of the Rules of Evidence to preliminary examinations should be appropriately dealt with by the Federal Rules of Criminal Procedure which regulate those proceedings.

Extradition and rendition proceedings are governed in detail by statute. 18 U.S.C. §§ 3181–3195. They are essentially administrative in character. Traditionally the rules of evidence have not applied. 1 Wigmore § 4(6). Extradition proceedings are accepted from the operation of the Rules of Criminal Procedure. Rule 54(b)(5) of Federal Rules of Criminal Procedure.

The rules of evidence have not been regarded as applicable to sentencing or probation proceedings, where great reliance is placed upon the presentence investigation and report. Rule 32(c) of the Federal Rules of Criminal Procedure requires a presentence investigation and report in every case unless the court otherwise directs. In *Williams v. New York,* 337 U.S. 241, 69 S.Ct. 1079, 93 L.Ed. 1337 (1949), in which the judge overruled a jury recommendation of life imprisonment and imposed a death sentence, the Court said that due process does not require confrontation or cross-examination in sentencing or passing on probation, and that the judge has broad discretion as to the sources and types of information relied upon. Compare the recommendation that the substance of all derogatory information be disclosed to the defendant, in A.B.A. Project on Minimum Standards for Criminal Justice, Sentencing Alternatives and Procedures § 4.4, Tentative Draft (1967, Sobeloff, Chm.). Williams was adhered to in *Specht v. Patterson,* 386 U.S. 605, 87 S.Ct. 1209, 18 L.Ed.2d 326 (1967), but not extended to a proceeding under the Colorado Sex Offenders Act, which was said to be a new charge leading in effect to punishment, more like the recidivist statutes where opportunity must be given to be heard on the habitual criminal issue.

Warrants for arrest, criminal summonses, and search warrants are issued upon complaint or affidavit showing probable cause. Rules 4(a) and 41(c) of the Federal Rules of Criminal Procedure. The nature of the proceedings makes application of the formal rules of evidence inappropriate and impracticable.

Criminal contempts are punishable summarily if the judge certifies that he saw or heard the contempt and that it was committed in the presence of the court. Rule 42(a) of the Federal Rules of Criminal Procedure. The circumstances which preclude application of the rules of evidence in this situation are not present, however, in other cases of criminal contempt.

Proceedings with respect to release on bail or otherwise do not call for application of the rules of evidence. The governing statute specifically provides:

"Information stated in, or offered in connection with, any order entered pursuant to this section need not conform to the rules pertaining to the admissibility of evidence in a court of law." 18 U.S.C.A. § 3146(f). This provision is consistent with the type of inquiry contemplated in A.B.A. Project on Minimum Standards for Criminal Justice, Standards Relating to Pretrial Release, § 4.5(b), (c), p. 16 (1968). The references to the weight of the evidence against the accused, in Rule 46(a)(1), (c) of the Federal Rules of Criminal Procedure and in 18 U.S.C.A. § 3146(b), as a factor to be considered, clearly do not have in view evidence introduced at a hearing under the rules of evidence.

The rule does not exempt habeas corpus proceedings. The Supreme Court held in *Walker v. Johnston,* 312 U.S. 275, 61 S.Ct. 574, 85 L.Ed. 830 (1941), that the practice of disposing of matters of fact on affidavit, which prevailed in some circuits, did not "satisfy the command of the statute that the judge shall proceed 'to determine the facts of the case, by hearing the testimony and arguments.'" This view accords with the emphasis in *Townsend v. Sain,* 372 U.S. 293, 83 S.Ct. 745, 9 L.Ed.2d 770 (1963), upon trial-type proceedings, *id.* 311, 83 S.Ct. 745, with demeanor evidence as a significant factor, *id.* 322, 83 S.Ct. 745, in applications by state prisoners aggrieved by unconstitutional detentions. Hence subdivision (3) applies the rules to habeas corpus proceedings to the extent not inconsistent with the statute.

Note to Subdivision (e). In a substantial number of special proceedings, *ad hoc* evaluation has resulted in the promulgation of particularized evidentiary provisions, by Act of Congress or by rule adopted by the Supreme Court. Well adapted to the particular proceedings, though not apt candidates for inclusion in a set of general rules, they are left undisturbed. Otherwise, however, the rules of evidence are applicable to the proceedings enumerated in the subdivision.

1974 Enactment

Note to Subdivision (a). Subdivision (a) as submitted to the Congress, in stating the courts and judges to which the Rules of Evidence apply, omitted the Court of Claims and commissioners of that Court. At the request of the Court of Claims, the Committee amended the Rule to include the Court and its commissioners within the purview of the Rules.

Note to Subdivision (b). Subdivision (b) was amended merely to substitute positive law citations for those which were not. House Report No. 93–650.

1987 Amendment

Subdivision (a) is amended to delete the reference to the District Court for the District of the Canal Zone, which no longer exists, and to add the District Court for the Northern Mariana Islands. The United States bankruptcy judges are added to conform the subdivision with Rule 1101(b) and Bankruptcy Rule 9017.

1988 Amendment

The amendments are technical. No substantive change is intended.

1993 Amendment

This revision is made to conform the rule to changes in terminology made by Rule 58 of the Federal Rules of Criminal Procedure and to the changes in the title of United States magistrates made by the Judicial Improvements Act of 1990.

HISTORICAL NOTES

References in Text

The Tariff Act of 1930, referred to in subsec. (e), is Act June 17, 1930, c. 497, 46 Stat. 590, as amended, which is classified principally to chapter 4 (section 1202 et seq.) of Title 19, Customs Duties. Part V of Title IV of the Tariff Act of 1930 enacted part V (section 1581 et seq.) of subtitle III of chapter 4 of Title 19. For complete classification of this Act to the Code, see section 1654 of Title 19 and Tables.

The Anti–Smuggling Act (19 U.S.C. 1701–1711), referred to in subsec. (e), is Act Aug. 5, 1935, c. 438, 49 Stat. 517, as amended, which is classified principally to chapter 5 (section 1701 et seq.) of Title 19, Customs Duties. For complete classification of this Act to the Code, see section 1711 of Title 19 and Tables.

The Federal Food, Drug, and Cosmetic Act (21 U.S.C. 301–392), referred to in subsec. (e), is Act June 25, 1938, c. 675, 52 Stat. 1040, as amended, which is classified generally to chapter 9 (section 301 et seq.) of Title 21, Food and Drugs. For complete classification of this Act to the Code, see section 301 of Title 21 and Tables.

"An Act authorizing suits against the United States in admirality [sic] for damage caused by and salvage service rendered to public vessels belonging to the United States, and for other purposes," approved Mar. 3, 1925 (46 U.S.C. 781–790), referred to in subsec. (e), is Act Mar. 3, 1925, c. 428, 43 Stat. 1112, as amended, known as the "Public Vessels Act", which is classified generally to chapter 22 (section 781 et seq.) of Title 46, Shipping. For complete classification of this Act to the Code, see Short Title note set out under section 781 of Title 46 and Tables.

Effective Date of 1982 Amendment

Amendment by Pub.L. 97–164 effective Oct. 1, 1982, see section 402 of Pub.L. 97–164, set out as a note under section 171 of this title.

Effective Date of 1978 Amendment

Amendment of subds. (a) and (b) of this rule by section 251 of Pub.L. 95–598 effective Oct. 1, 1979, see section 402(c) of Pub.L. 95–598, set out as a note preceding section 101 of Title 11, Bankruptcy.

Change of Name

United States magistrate appointed under section 631 of Title 28, Judiciary and Judicial Procedure, to be known as United States magistrate judge after Dec. 1, 1990, with any reference to United States magistrate or magistrate in Title 28, in any other Federal statute, etc., deemed a reference to United States magistrate judge appointed under section 631 of Title 28, see section 321 of Pub.L. 101–650, set out as a note under section 631 of Title 28.

Pending Actions

Amendments of Supreme Court to the Federal Rules of Evidence effective December 1, 1993, applicable, insofar as just and practicable, in all proceedings then pending, pursuant to the Order of April 22, 1993.

Rule 1102. Amendments

Amendments to the Federal Rules of Evidence may be made as provided in section 2072 of title 28 of the United States Code.

(Pub.L. 93–595, § 1, Jan. 2, 1975, 88 Stat.1948); Apr. 30, 1991, eff. Dec. 1, 1991.)

ADVISORY COMMITTEE NOTES

1991 Amendment

The amendment is technical. No substantive change is intended.

Rule 1103. Title

These rules may be known and cited as the Federal Rules of Evidence.

(Pub.L. 93–595, § 1, Jan. 2, 1975, 88 Stat.1948.)

HISTORICAL NOTES

Short Title of 1978 Amendment

Pub.L. 95–540, § 1, Oct. 28, 1978, 92 Stat. 2046, provided: "That this Act [enacting rule 412 of these rules and a provision set out as a note under rule 412 of these rules] may be cited as the 'Privacy Protection for Rape Victims Act of 1978'."

FEDERAL RULES OF APPELLATE PROCEDURE

Amendments received to January 4, 1999

TITLE I. APPLICABILITY OF RULES

Rule

1. Scope of Rules; Title.
2. Suspension of Rules.

TITLE II. APPEAL FROM A JUDGMENT OR ORDER OF A DISTRICT COURT

3. Appeal as of Right—How Taken.
3.1. Abrogated.
4. Appeal as of Right—When Taken.
5. Appeal by Permission.
5.1. [Abrogated.]
6. Appeal in a Bankruptcy Case From a Final Judgment, Order, or Decree of a District Court or Bankruptcy Appellate Panel.
7. Bond for Costs on Appeal in a Civil Case.
8. Stay or Injunction Pending Appeal.
9. Release in a Criminal Case.
10. The Record on Appeal.
11. Forwarding the Record.
12. Docketing the Appeal; Filing a Representation Statement; Filing the Record.

TITLE III. REVIEW OF A DECISION OF THE UNITED STATES TAX COURT

13. Review of a Decision of the Tax Court.
14. Applicability of Other Rules to the Review of a Tax Court Decision.

TITLE IV. REVIEW OR ENFORCEMENT OF AN ORDER OF AN ADMINISTRATIVE AGENCY, BOARD, COMMISSION, OR OFFICER

15. Review or Enforcement of an Agency Order—How Obtained; Intervention.
15.1. Briefs and Oral Argument in a National Labor Relations Board Proceeding.
16. The Record on Review or Enforcement.
17. Filing the Record.
18. Stay Pending Review.
19. Settlement of a Judgment Enforcing an Agency Order in Part.
20. Applicability of Rules to the Review or Enforcement of an Agency Order.

TITLE V. EXTRAORDINARY WRITS

21. Writs of Mandamus and Prohibition, and Other Extraordinary Writs.

TITLE VI. HABEAS CORPUS; PROCEEDINGS IN FORMA PAUPERIS

22. Habeas Corpus and Section 2255 Proceedings.

Rule

TITLE VI. HABEAS CORPUS; PROCEEDINGS IN FORMA PAUPERIS—Cont'd

23. Custody or Release of a Prisoner in a Habeas Corpus Proceeding.
24. Proceeding in Forma Pauperis.

TITLE VII. GENERAL PROVISIONS

25. Filing and Service.
26. Computing and Extending Time.
26.1. Corporate Disclosure Statement.
27. Motions.
28. Briefs.
29. Brief of an Amicus Curiae.
30. Appendix to the Briefs.
31. Serving and Filing Briefs.
32. Form of Briefs, Appendices, and Other Papers.
33. Appeal Conferences.
34. Oral Argument.
35. En Banc Determination.
36. Entry of Judgment; Notice.
37. Interest on Judgment.
38. Frivolous Appeal—Damages and Costs.
39. Costs.
40. Petition for Panel Rehearing.
41. Mandate: Contents; Issuance and Effective Date; Stay.
42. Voluntary Dismissal.
43. Substitution of Parties.
44. Case Involving a Constitutional Question When the United States Is Not a Party.
45. Clerk's Duties.
46. Attorneys.
47. Local Rules by Courts of Appeals.
48. Masters.

APPENDIX OF FORMS

Form

1. Notice of Appeal to a Court of Appeals From a Judgment or Order of a District Court.
2. Notice of Appeal to a Court of Appeals From a Decision of the United States Tax Court.
3. Petition for Review of Order of an Agency, Board, Commission or Officer.

ORDERS OF THE SUPREME COURT OF THE UNITED STATES ADOPTING AND AMENDING RULES

ORDER OF DECEMBER 4, 1967

ORDERED:

1. That the following rules, to be known as the Federal Rules of Appellate Procedure, be, and they hereby are, prescribed, pursuant to sections 3771 and 3772 of Title 18,

United States Code, and sections 2072 and 2075 of Title 28, United States Code, to govern the procedure in appeals to United States courts of appeals from the United States district courts, in the review by United States courts of appeals of decisions of the Tax Court of the United States, in proceedings in the United States courts of appeals for the review or enforcement of orders of administrative agencies, boards, commissions and officers, and in applications for writs or other relief which a United States court of appeals or judge thereof is competent to give:

[See text of Rules of Appellate Procedure, post]

2. That the foregoing rules shall take effect on July 1, 1968, and shall govern all proceedings in appeals and petitions for review or enforcement of orders thereafter brought and in all such proceedings then pending, except to the extent that in the opinion of the court of appeals their application in a particular proceeding then pending would not be feasible or would work injustice, in which case the former procedure may be followed.

3. That Rules 6, 9, 41, 77 and 81 of the Rules of Civil Procedure for the United States District Courts be, and they hereby are, amended, effective July 1, 1968, as hereinafter set forth:

[See amendments made thereby under the Rules of Civil Procedure, ante]

4. That the chapter heading "IX. APPEALS", all of Rules 72, 73, 74, 75 and 76 of the Rules of Civil Procedure for the United States District Courts, and Form 27 annexed to the said rules, be, and they hereby are, abrogated, effective July 1, 1968.

5. That Rules 45, 49, 56 and 57 of the Rules of Criminal Procedure for the United States District Courts be, and they hereby are, amended, effective July 1, 1968, as hereinafter set forth:

[For text of amendments, see pamphlet containing Federal Rules of Criminal Procedure]

6. That the chapter heading "VIII. APPEAL", all of Rules 37 and 39, and subdivisions (b) and (c) of Rule 38, of the Rules of Criminal Procedure for the United States District Courts, and Forms 26 and 27 annexed to the said rules, be, and they hereby are, abrogated, effective July 1, 1968.

7. That the Chief Justice be, and he hereby is, authorized to transmit to the Congress the foregoing new rules and amendments to and abrogation of existing rules, in accordance with the provisions of Title 18, U.S.C., § 3771, and Title 28, U.S.C., §§ 2072 and 2075.

ORDER OF MARCH 30, 1970

1. That subdivisions (a) and (c) of Rule 30 and subdivision (a) of Rule 31 of the Federal Rules of Appellate Procedure be, and they hereby are, amended as follows:

[See the amendments made thereby under the respective rules, post]

2. That the foregoing amendments to the Federal Rules of Appellate Procedure shall take effect on July 1, 1970, and shall govern all proceedings in actions brought thereafter and also in all further proceedings in actions then pending, except to the extent that in the opinion of the court their application in a particular action then pending would not be feasible or would work injustice, in which event the former procedure applies.

3. That the Chief Justice be, and he hereby is, authorized to transmit to the Congress the foregoing amendments to existing rules, in accordance with the provisions of Title 18, U.S.C., § 3772, and Title 28, U.S.C., §§ 2072 and 2075.

ORDER OF MARCH 1, 1971

1. That subdivision (a) of Rule 6, paragraph (4) of subdivision (a) of Rule 27, paragraph (6) of subdivision (b) of Rule 30, subdivision (c) of Rule 77, and paragraph (2) of subdivision (a) of Rule 81 of the Federal Rules of Civil Procedure be, and hereby are, amended, effective July 1, 1971, to read as follows:

[See amendments made thereby under the Rules of Civil Procedure, ante]

2. That subdivision (a) of Rule 45 and all of Rule 56 of the Federal Rules of Criminal Procedure be, and they hereby are, amended, effective July 1, 1971, to read as follows:

[For text of amendments, see pamphlet containing Federal Rules of Criminal Procedure]

3. That subdivision (a) of Rule 26 and subdivision (a) of Rule 45 of the Federal Rules of Appellate Procedure be, and they hereby are, amended, effective July 1, 1971, to read as follows:

[See amendments made thereby under the respective rules, post]

4. That THE CHIEF JUSTICE be, and he hereby is, authorized to transmit to the Congress the foregoing amendments to the Rules of Civil, Criminal and Appellate Procedure, in accordance with the provisions of Title 18, U.S.C., § 3771, and Title 28, U.S.C., §§ 2072 and 2075.

MR. JUSTICE BLACK and MR. JUSTICE DOUGLAS dissent.

ORDER OF APRIL 24, 1972

1. That Rules 1, 3, 4(b) & (c), 5, 5.1, 6(b), 7(c), 9(b), (c) & (d), 17(a) & (g), 31(e), 32(b), 38(a), 40, 41, 44, 46, 50, 54 and 55 of the Federal Rules of Criminal Procedure be, and they hereby are, amended effective October 1, 1972, to read as follows:

[For text of amendments, see pamphlet containing Federal Rules of Criminal Procedure]

2. That Rule 9(c) of the Federal Rules of Appellate Procedure be, and hereby is amended, effective October 1, 1972, to read as follows:

[See amendments made thereby under the respective rules, post]

3. That THE CHIEF JUSTICE be, and he hereby is, authorized to transmit to the Congress the foregoing amendments to Rules of Criminal and Appellate Procedure, in accordance with the provisions of Title 18, U.S.Code, §§ 3771 and 3772.

MR. JUSTICE DOUGLAS dissented to adoption of Rule 50(b) of the Federal Rules of Criminal Procedure.

ORDER OF APRIL 30, 1979

1. That the Federal Rules of Appellate Procedure be, and they hereby are, amended by including therein amendments to Rules 1(a), 3(c), (d) and (e), 4(a), 5(d), 6(d), 7, 10(b), 11(a), (b), (c) and (d), 12, 13(a), 24(b), 27(b), 28(g) and (j), 34(a) and (b), 35(b) and (c), 39(c) and (d), and 40 as hereinafter set forth:

[See amendments made thereby under the respective rules, post]

2. That the foregoing amendments to the Federal Rules of Appellate Procedure shall take effect on August 1, 1979, and shall govern all appellate proceedings thereafter commenced and, insofar as just and practicable, all proceedings then pending.

3. That THE CHIEF JUSTICE be, and he hereby is, authorized to transmit to the Congress the foregoing amendments to the Federal Rules of Appellate Procedure in accordance with the provisions of Section 3772 of Title 18, United States Code, and Sections 2072 and 2075 of Title 28, United States Code.

ORDER OF MARCH 10, 1986

1. That the Federal Rules of Appellate Procedure be, and they hereby are, amended by including therein new Appellate Rules 3.1, 5.1 and 15.1 and amendments to Appellate Rules 3(d), 8(b), 10(b) and (c), 11(b), 12(a), 19, 23(b) and (c), 24(a), 25(a) and (b), 26(a) and (c), 28(c) and (j), 30(a), (b) and (c), 31(a) and (c), 34(a) and (e), 39(c) and (d), 43(a) and (c), 45(a), (b), and (d), and 46(a) and (b), as hereinafter set forth:

[See amendments made thereby under the respective rules, post]

2. That the foregoing additions to and changes in the Federal Rules of Appellate Procedure, shall take effect on July 1, 1986 and shall govern all proceedings in appellate actions thereafter commenced and, insofar as just and practicable, all proceedings in appellate actions then pending.

3. That THE CHIEF JUSTICE be, and he hereby is, authorized to transmit to the Congress the foregoing additions to and changes in the rules of appellate procedure in accordance with the provisions of Section 3772 of Title 18 and Section 2072 of Title 28, United States Code.

ORDER OF APRIL 25, 1989

1. That the Federal Rules of Appellate Procedure be, and they hereby are, amended by including therein amendments to Appellate Rules 1(a), 3(a), 26(a), 27(a), 28(g) and new Rules 6 and 26.1, and a new Form 5 as hereinafter set forth:

[See amendments made thereby under the respective rules, post]

2. That the foregoing additions to and changes in the Federal Rules of Appellate Procedure, shall take effect on December 1, 1989 and shall govern all proceedings in appellate actions thereafter commenced and, insofar as just and practicable, all proceedings in appellate actions then pending.

3. That THE CHIEF JUSTICE be, and he hereby is, authorized to transmit to the Congress the foregoing additions to and changes in the rules of appellate procedure in accordance with the provisions of Section 2072 of Title 28, United States Code.

ORDER OF APRIL 30, 1991

1. That the Federal Rules of Appellate Procedure be, and they hereby are, amended by including therein amendments to Appellate Rules 4(a), 6, 10(c), 25(a), 26(a), 26.1, 28(a), (b), and (h), 30(b), and 34(d).

[See amendments made thereby under the respective rules, post]

2. That the foregoing amendments to the Federal Rules of Appellate Procedure shall take effect on December 1, 1991, and shall govern all proceedings in appellate cases thereafter commenced and, insofar as just and practicable, all proceedings in appellate cases then pending.

3. That THE CHIEF JUSTICE be, and he hereby is, authorized to transmit to the Congress the foregoing amendments to the Federal Rules of Appellate Procedure in accordance with the provisions of Section 2072 of Title 28, United States Code.

ORDER OF APRIL 22, 1993

1. That the Federal Rules of Appellate Procedure be, and they hereby are, amended by including therein amendments to Appellate Rules 3, 3.1, 4, 5.1, 6, 10, 12, 15, 25, 28, and 34, and to Forms 1, 2, and 3.

[See amendments made thereby under the respective rules and forms, post.]

2. That the foregoing amendments to the Federal Rules of Appellate Procedure shall take effect on December 1, 1993, and shall govern all proceedings in appellate cases thereafter commenced and, insofar as just and practicable, all proceedings in appellate cases then pending.

3. That THE CHIEF JUSTICE be, and he hereby is, authorized to transmit to the Congress the foregoing amendments to the Federal Rules of Appellate Procedure in accordance with the provisions of Section 2072 of Title 28, United States Code.

ORDER OF APRIL 29, 1994

1. That the Federal Rules of Appellate Procedure be, and they hereby are, amended by including therein amendments to Appellate Rules 1, 3, 5, 5.1, 9, 13, 21, 25, 26.1, 27, 28, 30, 31, 33, 35, 38, 40, 41, and 48.

[See amendments made hereby under respective rules, post]

2. That the foregoing amendments to the Federal Rules of Appellate Procedure shall take effect on December 1, 1994, and shall govern all proceedings in appellate cases thereafter commenced and, insofar as just and practicable, all proceedings in appellate cases then pending.

3. That THE CHIEF JUSTICE be, and he hereby is, authorized to transmit to the Congress the foregoing amendments to the Federal Rules of Appellate Procedure in accordance with the provisions of Section 2072 of Title 28, United States Code.

ORDER OF APRIL 27, 1995

1. That the Federal Rules of Appellate Procedure be, and they hereby are, amended by including therein amendments to Appellate Rules 4, 8, 10, and 47.

[See amendments made thereby under the respective rules, post.]

2. That the foregoing amendments to the Federal Rules of Appellate Procedure shall take effect on December 1, 1995, and shall govern all proceedings in appellate cases thereafter commenced and, insofar as just and practicable, all proceedings in appellate cases then pending.

3. That THE CHIEF JUSTICE be, and he hereby is, authorized to transmit to the Congress the foregoing amendments to the Federal Rules of Appellate Procedure in accordance with the provisions of Section 2072 of Title 28, United States Code.

ORDER OF APRIL 23, 1996

1. That the Federal Rules of Appellate Procedure be, and they hereby are, amended by including therein amendments to Appellate Rules 21, 25, and 26.

[See amendments made thereby under respective rules, post]

2. That the foregoing amendments to the Federal Rules of Appellate Procedure shall take effect on December 1, 1996, and shall govern all proceedings in appellate cases thereafter commenced and, insofar as just and practicable, all proceedings in appellate cases then pending.

3. That THE CHIEF JUSTICE be, and hereby is, authorized to transmit to the Congress the foregoing amendments to the Federal Rules of Appellate Procedure in accordance with the provisions of Section 2072 of Title 28, United States Code.

ORDER OF APRIL 24, 1998

ORDERED:

1. That the Federal Rules of Civil Procedure for the United States District Courts be, and they hereby are, amended by including therein a new Civil Rule 23(f).

[See amendments made thereby under respective rules, post]

2. That the foregoing amendments to the Federal Rules of Civil Procedure shall take effect on December 1, 1998, and shall govern all proceedings in civil cases thereafter commenced and, insofar as just and practicable, all proceedings in civil cases then pending.

3. That THE CHIEF JUSTICE be, and hereby is, authorized to transmit to the Congress the foregoing amendments to the Federal Rules of Civil Procedure in accordance with the provisions of Section 2072 of Title 28, United States Code.

HISTORICAL NOTES

Effective Dates; Application; Transmission to Congress

The Federal Rules of Appellate Procedure were adopted by order of the Supreme Court on Dec. 4, 1967, transmitted to Congress by the Chief Justice on Jan. 15, 1968, and became effective on July 1, 1968.

The Rules have been amended Mar. 30, 1970, eff. July 1, 1970; Mar. 1, 1971, eff. July 1, 1971; Apr. 24, 1972, eff. Oct. 1, 1972; Apr. 30, 1979, eff. Aug. 1, 1979; Oct. 12, 1984, Pub.L. 98–473, Title II, § 210, 98 Stat. 1987; Mar. 10, 1986, eff. July 1, 1986; Nov. 18, 1988, Pub.L. 100–690, Title VII, § 7111, 102 Stat. 4419; Apr. 25, 1989, eff. Dec. 1, 1989; Apr. 30, 1991, eff. Dec. 1, 1991; Apr. 22, 1993, eff. Dec. 1, 1993; Apr. 29, 1994, eff. Dec. 1, 1994; Apr. 27, 1995, eff. Dec. 1, 1995; Apr. 23, 1996, eff. Dec. 1, 1996; Apr. 24, 1998, eff. Dec. 1, 1998.

TITLE I. APPLICABILITY OF RULES

Rule 1. Scope of Rules; Title

(a) Scope of Rules.

(1) These rules govern procedure in the United States courts of appeals.

(2) When these rules provide for filing a motion or other document in the district court, the procedure must comply with the practice of the district court.

(b) Rules Do Not Affect Jurisdiction. These rules do not extend or limit the jurisdiction of the courts of appeals.

(c) Title. These rules are to be known as the Federal Rules of Appellate Procedure.

(As amended Apr. 30, 1979, eff. Aug. 1, 1979; Apr. 25, 1989, eff. Dec. 1, 1989; Apr. 29, 1994, eff. Dec. 1, 1994; Apr. 24, 1998, eff. Dec. 1, 1998.)

ADVISORY COMMITTEE NOTES

1967 Adoption

These rules are drawn under the authority of 28 U.S.C. § 2072 as amended by the Act of November 6, 1966, 80 Stat. 1323 (1 U.S.Code Cong. & Ad.News, p. 1546 (1966)) (Rules of Civil Procedure); 28 U.S.C. § 2075 (Bankruptcy Rules); and 18 U.S.C. §§ 3771 [§ 3771 of Title 18, Crimes and Criminal Procedure] (Procedure to and including verdict) and 3772 [§ 3772 of Title 18] (Procedure after verdict). Those statutes combine to give to the Supreme Court power to make rules of practice and procedure for all cases within the jurisdiction of the courts of appeals. By the terms of the statutes, after the rules have taken effect all laws in conflict with them are of no further force or effect. Practice and procedure in the eleven courts of appeals are now regulated by rules promulgated by each court under the authority of 28 U.S.C. § 2071. Rule 47 expressly authorizes the courts of appeals to make rules of practice not inconsistent with these rules.

As indicated by the titles under which they are found, the following rules are of special application: Rules 3 through 12 apply to appeals from judgments and orders of the district courts; Rules 13 and 14 apply to appeals from decisions of the Tax Court (Rule 13 establishes an appeal as the mode of review of decisions of the Tax Court in place of the present petition for review); Rules 15 through 20 apply to proceedings for review or enforcement of orders of administrative agencies, boards, commissions and officers. Rules 22 through 24 regulate habeas corpus proceedings and appeals in forma pauperis. All other rules apply to all proceedings in the courts of appeals.

1979 Amendment

The Federal Rules of Appellate Procedure were designed as an integrated set of rules to be followed in appeals to the courts of appeals, covering all steps in the appellate process, whether they take place in the district court or in the court of appeals, and with their adoption Rules 72 to 76 of the F.R.C.P. [rules 72 to 76, Federal Rules of Civil Procedure] were abrogated. In some instances, however, the F.R.A.P. provide that a motion or application for relief may, or must, be made in the district court. See Rules 4(a), 10(b) and 24. The proposed amendment would make it clear that when this is so the motion or application is to be made in the form and manner prescribed by the F.R.C.P. or F.R.Cr.P. [Federal Rules Criminal Procedure] and local rules relating to the form and presentation of motions and is not governed by Rule 27 of the F.R.A.P. See Rule 7(b) of the F.R.C.P. [rule 7(b), Federal Rules of Civil Procedure] and Rule 47 of the F.R.Cr.P. [rule 47, Federal Rules of Criminal Procedure].

1989 Amendment

The amendment is technical. No substantive change is intended.

1994 Amendment

Subdivision (c). A new subdivision is added to the rule. The text of new subdivision (c) has been moved from Rule 48 to Rule 1 to allow the addition of new rules at the end of the existing set of appellate rules without burying the title provision among other rules. In a similar fashion the Bankruptcy Rules combine the provisions governing the scope of the rules and the title in the first rule.

HISTORICAL NOTES

Pending Actions

Amendments of Supreme Court to Federal Rules of Appellate Procedure effective December 1, 1993, applicable, insofar as just and practicable, in all proceedings then pending, pursuant to the Order of April 22, 1993.

Rule 2. Suspension of Rules

On its own or a party's motion, a court of appeals may—to expedite its decision or for other good cause—suspend any provision of these rules in a particular case and order proceedings as it directs, except as otherwise provided in Rule 26(b).

(As amended Apr. 24, 1998, eff. Dec. 1, 1998.)

ADVISORY COMMITTEE NOTES

1967 Adoption

The primary purpose of this rule is to make clear the power of the courts of appeals to expedite the determination of cases of pressing concern to the public or to the litigants by prescribing a time schedule other than that provided by the rules. The rule also contains a general authorization to the courts to relieve litigants of the consequences of default where manifest injustice would otherwise result. Rule 26(b) prohibits a court of appeals from extending the time for taking appeal or seeking review.

TITLE II. APPEAL FROM A JUDGMENT OR ORDER OF A DISTRICT COURT

Rule 3. Appeal as of Right—How Taken

(a) Filing the Notice of Appeal.

(1) An appeal permitted by law as of right from a district court to a court of appeals may be taken only by filing a notice of appeal with the district clerk within the time allowed by Rule 4. At the time of filing, the appellant must furnish the clerk with enough copies of the notice to enable the clerk to comply with Rule 3(d).

(2) An appellant's failure to take any step other than the timely filing of a notice of appeal does not affect the validity of the appeal, but is ground only for the court of appeals to act as it considers appropriate, including dismissing the appeal.

(3) An appeal from a judgment by a magistrate judge in a civil case is taken in the same way as an appeal from any other district court judgment.

(4) An appeal by permission under 28 U.S.C. § 1292(b) or an appeal in a bankruptcy case may be taken only in the manner prescribed by Rules 5 and 6, respectively.

(b) Joint or Consolidated Appeals.

(1) When two or more parties are entitled to appeal from a district-court judgment or order, and their interests make joinder practicable, they may file a joint notice of appeal. They may then proceed on appeal as a single appellant.

(2) When the parties have filed separate timely notices of appeal, the appeals may be joined or consolidated by the court of appeals.

(c) Contents of the Notice of Appeal.

(1) The notice of appeal must:

(A) specify the party or parties taking the appeal by naming each one in the caption or body of the notice, but an attorney representing more than one party may describe those parties with such terms as "all plaintiffs," "the defendants," "the plaintiffs A, B, et al.," or "all defendants except X";

(B) designate the judgment, order, or part thereof being appealed; and

(C) name the court to which the appeal is taken.

(2) A pro se notice of appeal is considered filed on behalf of the signer and the signer's spouse and minor children (if they are parties), unless the notice clearly indicates otherwise.

(3) In a class action, whether or not the class has been certified, the notice of appeal is sufficient if it names one person qualified to bring the appeal as representative of the class.

(4) An appeal must not be dismissed for informality of form or title of the notice of appeal, or for failure to name a party whose intent to appeal is otherwise clear from the notice.

(5) Form 1 in the Appendix of Forms is a suggested form of a notice of appeal.

(d) Serving the Notice of Appeal.

(1) The district clerk must serve notice of the filing of a notice of appeal by mailing a copy to each party's counsel of record—excluding the appellant's—or, if a party is proceeding pro se, to the party's last known address. When a defendant in a criminal case appeals, the clerk must also serve a copy of the notice of appeal on the defendant, either by personal service or by mail addressed to the defendant. The clerk must promptly send a copy of the notice of appeal and of the docket entries—and any later docket entries—to the clerk of the court of appeals named in the notice. The district clerk must note, on each copy, the date when the notice of appeal was filed.

(2) If an inmate confined in an institution files a notice of appeal in the manner provided by Rule 4(c), the district clerk must also note the date when the clerk docketed the notice.

(3) The district clerk's failure to serve notice does not affect the validity of the appeal. The clerk must note on the docket the names of the parties to whom the clerk mails copies, with the date of mailing. Service is sufficient despite the death of a party or the party's counsel.

(e) Payment of Fees. Upon filing a notice of appeal, the appellant must pay the district clerk all required fees. The district clerk receives the appellate docket fee on behalf of the court of appeals.

(As amended Apr. 30, 1979, eff. Aug. 1, 1979; Mar. 10, 1986, eff. July 1, 1986; Apr. 25, 1989, eff. Dec. 1, 1989; Apr. 22, 1993, eff. Dec. 1, 1993; Apr. 29, 1994, eff. Dec. 1, 1994; Apr. 24, 1998, eff. Dec. 1, 1998.)

ADVISORY COMMITTEE NOTES

1967 Adoption

General Note. Rule 3 and Rule 4 combine to require that a notice of appeal be filed with the clerk of the district court within the time prescribed for taking an appeal. Because the timely filing of a notice of appeal is "mandatory and jurisdictional," *United States v. Robinson*, 361 U.S. 220, 224, 80 S.Ct. 282, 4 L.Ed.2d 259 (1960), compliance with the provisions of those rules is of the utmost importance. But the proposed rules merely restate, in modified form, provisions now found in the civil and criminal rules (FRCP 5(e), 73 [Rules 5(e) and 73, Federal Rules of Civil Procedure]; FRCrP 37 [rule 37, Federal Rules of Criminal Procedure], and decisions under the present rules which dispense with literal compliance in cases in which it cannot fairly be exacted should control interpretation of these rules. Illustrative decisions are: *Fallen v. United States*, 378 U.S. 139, 84 S.Ct. 1689, 12 L.Ed.2d 760 (1964) (notice of appeal by a prisoner, in the form of a letter delivered, well within the time fixed for appeal, to prison authorities for mailing to the clerk of the district court held timely filed notwithstanding that it was received by the clerk after expiration of the time for appeal; the appellant "did all he could" to effect timely filing); *Richey v. Wilkins*, 335 F.2d 1 (2d Cir. 1964) (notice filed in the court of appeals by a prisoner without assistance of counsel held sufficient); *Halfen v. United States*, 324 F.2d 52 (10th Cir. 1963) (notice mailed to district judge in time to have been received by him in normal course held sufficient); *Riffle v. United States*, 299 F.2d 802 (5th Cir. 1962) (letter of prisoner to judge of court of appeals held sufficient). Earlier cases evidencing "a liberal view of papers filed by indigent and incarcerated defendants" are listed in *Coppedge v. United States*, 369 U.S. 438, 442, n. 5, 82 S.Ct. 917, 8 L.Ed.2d 21 (1962).

Subdivision (a). The substance of this subdivision is derived from FRCP 73(a) [rule 73(a), Federal Rules of Civil Procedure] and FRCrP 37(a)(1) [rule 37(a)(1), Federal Rules of Criminal Procedure]. The proposed rule follows those rules in requiring nothing other than the filing of a notice of appeal in the district court for the perfection of the appeal. The petition for allowance (except for appeals governed by Rules 5 and 6), citations, assignments of error, summons and severance—all specifically abolished by earlier modern rules—are assumed to be sufficiently obsolete as no longer to require pointed abolition.

Subdivision (b). The first sentence is derived from FRCP 74 [rule 74, Federal Rules of Civil Procedure]. The second sentence is added to encourage consolidation of appeals whenever feasible.

Subdivision (c). This subdivision is identical with corresponding provisions in FRCP 73(b) [rule 73(b), Federal Rules of Civil Procedure] and FRCrP 37(a)(1) [rule 37(a)(1), Federal Rules of Criminal Procedure].

Subdivision (d). This subdivision is derived from FRCP 73(b) [rule 73(b), Federal Rules of Civil Procedure] and FRCrP 37(a)(1) [rule 37(a)(1), Federal Rules of Criminal Procedure]. The duty of the clerk to forward a copy of the notice of appeal and of the docket entries to the court of appeals in a criminal case is extended to habeas corpus and 28 U.S.C. § 2255 proceedings.

1979 Amendments

Subdivision (c). The proposed amendment would add the last sentence. Because of the fact that the timely filing of the notice of appeal has been characterized as jurisdictional (see, e.g., Brainerd v. Real (C.A. 7th, 1974) 498 F.2d 901, in which the filing of a notice of appeal one day late was fatal), it is important that the right to appeal not be lost by mistakes of mere form. In a number of decided cases it has been held that so long as the function of notice is met by the filing of a paper indicating an intention to appeal, the substance of the rule has been complied with. See, e.g., Cobb v. Lewis (C.A. 5th, 1974), 488 F.2d 41; *Holley v. Capps* (C.A. 5th, 1972) 468 F.2d 1366. The proposed amendment would give recognition to this practice.

When a notice of appeal is filed, the clerk should ascertain whether any judgment designated therein has been entered in compliance with Rules 58 and 79(a) of the F.R.C.P. [rules 58 and 79(a), Federal Rules of Civil Procedure]. See Note to Rule 4(a)(6), *infra*.

Subdivision (d). The proposed amendment would extend to civil cases the present provision applicable to criminal cases, habeas corpus cases, and proceedings under 28 U.S.C. § 2255, requiring the clerk of the district court to transmit to the clerk of the court of appeals a copy of the notice of appeal and of the docket entries, which should include reference to compliance with the requirements for payment of fees. See Note to (e), *infra*.

This requirement is the initial step in proposed changes in the rules to place in the court of appeals an increased practical control over the early steps in the appeal.

Subdivision (e). Proposed new Rule 3(e) represents the second step in shifting to the court of appeals the control of the early stages of an appeal. See Note to Rule 3(d) above. Under the present rules the payment of the fee prescribed by 28 U.S.C. 1917 is not covered. Under the statute, however, this fee is paid to the clerk of the district court at the time the notice of appeal is filed. Under present Rule 12, the "docket fee" fixed by the Judicial Conference of the United States under 28 U.S.C. § 1913 must be paid to the clerk of the court of appeals within the time fixed for transmission of the record, ". . . and the clerk shall thereupon enter the appeal upon the docket."

Under the proposed new Rule 3(e) both fees would be paid to the clerk of the district court at the time the notice of appeal is filed, the clerk of the district court receiving the docket fee on behalf of the court of appeals.

In view of the provision in Rule 3(a) that "[f]ailure of an appellant to take any step other than the timely filing of a notice of appeal does not affect the validity of the appeal, but is ground only for such action as the court of appeals deems appropriate, which may include dismissal of the appeal," the case law indicates that the failure to prepay the statutory filing fee does not constitute a jurisdictional defect. See *Parissi v. Telechron*, 349 U.S. 46 (1955); *Gould v. Members of N.J. Division of Water Policy & Supply*, 555 F.2d 340 (3d Cir. 1977). Similarly, under present Rule 12, failure to pay the docket fee within the time prescribed may be excused by the court of appeals. See, e.g., *Walker v. Mathews*, 546 F.2d 814 (9th Cir. 1976). Proposed new Rule 3(e) adopts the view of these cases, requiring that both fees be paid at the time the notice of appeal is filed, but subject to the provisions of Rule 26(b) preserving the authority of the court of appeals to permit late payment.

1986 Amendments

The amendments to Rule 3(d) are technical. No substantive change is intended.

1989 Amendments

The amendment is technical. No substantive change is intended.

1993 Amendments

Note to subdivision (c). The amendment is intended to reduce the amount of satellite litigation spawned by the Supreme Court's decision in Torres v. Oakland Scavenger Co., 487 U.S. 312 (1988). In Torres the Supreme Court held that the language in Rule 3(c) requiring a notice of appeal to "specify the party or parties taking the appeal" is a jurisdictional requirement and that naming the first named party and adding "et al.," without any further specificity is insufficient to identify the appellants. Since the Torres decision, there has been a great deal of litigation regarding whether a notice of appeal that contains some indication of the appellants' identities but does not name the appellants is sufficiently specific.

The amendment states a general rule that specifying the parties should be done by naming them. Naming an appellant in an otherwise timely and proper notice of appeal ensures that the appellant has perfected an appeal. However, in order to prevent the loss of a right to appeal through inadvertent omission of a party's name or continued use of such terms as "et al.," which are sufficient in all district court filings after the complaint, the amendment allows an attorney representing more than one party the flexibility to indicate which parties are appealing without naming them individually. The test established by the rule for determining whether such designations are sufficient is whether it is objectively clear that a party intended to appeal. A notice of appeal filed by a party proceeding pro se is filed on behalf of the party signing the notice and the signer's spouse and minor children, if they are parties, unless the notice clearly indicates a contrary intent.

In class actions, naming each member of a class as an appellant may be extraordinarily burdensome or even impossible. In class actions if class certification has been denied, named plaintiffs may appeal the order denying the class certification on their own behalf and on behalf of putative class members, *United States Parole Comm'n v. Geraghty*, 445 U.S. 388 (1980); or if the named plaintiffs choose not to appeal the order denying the class certification, putative class members may appeal, *United Airlines, Inc. v. McDonald*, 432 U.S. 385 (1977). If no class has been certified, naming each of the putative class members as an appellant would often be impossible. Therefore the amendment provides that in class actions, whether or not the class has been certified, it is sufficient for the notice to name one person qualified to bring the appeal as a representative of the class.

Finally, the rule makes it clear that dismissal of an appeal should not occur when it is otherwise clear from the notice that the party intended to appeal. If a court determines it is objectively clear that a party intended to appeal, there are neither administrative concerns nor fairness concerns that should prevent the appeal from going forward.

Note to subdivision (d). The amendment requires the district court clerk to send to the clerk of the court of appeals a copy of every docket entry in a case after the filing of a notice of appeal. This amendment accompanies the amendment to Rule 4(a)(4), which provides that when one of the posttrial motions enumerated in Rule 4(a)(4) is filed, a notice of appeal filed before the disposition of the motion becomes effective upon disposition of the motion. The court of appeals needs to be advised that the filing of a posttrial motion has suspended a notice of appeal. The court of appeals also needs to know when the district court has ruled on the motion. Sending copies of all docket entries after the filing of a notice of appeal should provide the courts of appeals with the necessary information.

1994 Amendments

Subdivision (a). The amendment requires a party filing a notice of appeal to provide the court with sufficient copies of the notice for service on all other parties.

[Rule 3.1. Abrogated Apr. 24, 1998, eff. Dec. 1, 1998]

HISTORICAL NOTES

The abrogated rule provided that: "When the parties consent to a trial before a magistrate judge under 28 U.S.C. § 636(c)(1), any appeal from the judgment must be heard by the court of appeals in accordance with 28 U.S.C. § 636(c)(3), unless the parties consent to an appeal on the record to a district judge and thereafter, by petition only, to the court of appeals, in accordance with 28 U.S.C. § 636(c)(4). An appeal under 28 U.S.C. § 636(c)(3) must be taken in identical fashion as an appeal from any other judgment of the district court."

Rule 4. Appeal as of Right—When Taken

(a) Appeal in a Civil Case.

(1) Time for Filing a Notice of Appeal.

(A) In a civil case, except as provided in Rules 4(a)(1)(B), 4(a)(4), and 4(c), the notice of appeal required by Rule 3 must be filed with the district clerk within 30 days after the judgment or order appealed from is entered.

(B) When the United States or its officer or agency is a party, the notice of appeal may be filed by any party within 60 days after the judgment or order appealed from is entered.

(2) Filing Before Entry of Judgment. A notice of appeal filed after the court announces a decision or order—but before the entry of the judgment or order—is treated as filed on the date of and after the entry.

(3) Multiple Appeals. If one party timely files a notice of appeal, any other party may file a notice of appeal within 14 days after the date when the first notice was filed, or within the time otherwise prescribed by this Rule 4(a), whichever period ends later.

(4) Effect of a Motion on a Notice of Appeal.

(A) If a party timely files in the district court any of the following motions under the Federal Rules of Civil Procedure, the time to file an appeal runs for all parties from the entry of the order disposing of the last such remaining motion:

(i) for judgment under Rule 50(b);

(ii) to amend or make additional factual findings under Rule 52(b), whether or not granting the motion would alter the judgment;

(iii) for attorney's fees under Rule 54 if the district court extends the time to appeal under Rule 58;

(iv) to alter or amend the judgment under Rule 59;

(v) for a new trial under Rule 59; or

(vi) for relief under Rule 60 if the motion is filed no later than 10 days (computed using Federal Rule of Civil Procedure 6(a)) after the judgment is entered.

(B)(i) If a party files a notice of appeal after the court announces or enters a judgment—but before it disposes of any motion listed in Rule 4(a)(4)(A)—the notice becomes effective to appeal a judgment or order, in whole or in part, when the order disposing of the last such remaining motion is entered.

(ii) A party intending to challenge an order disposing of any motion listed in Rule 4(a)(4)(A), or a judgment altered or amended upon such a motion, must file a notice of appeal, or an amended notice of appeal—in compliance with Rule 3(c)—within the time prescribed by this Rule measured from the entry of the order disposing of the last such remaining motion.

(iii) No additional fee is required to file an amended notice.

(5) Motion for Extension of Time.

(A) The district court may extend the time to file a notice of appeal if:

(i) a party so moves no later than 30 days after the time prescribed by this Rule 4(a) expires; and

(ii) that party shows excusable neglect or good cause.

(B) A motion filed before the expiration of the time prescribed in Rule 4(a)(1) or (3) may be ex parte unless the court requires otherwise. If the motion is filed after the expiration of the prescribed time, notice must be given to the other parties in accordance with local rules.

(C) No extension under this Rule 4(a)(5) may exceed 30 days after the prescribed time or 10 days after the date when the order granting the motion is entered, whichever is later.

(6) Reopening the Time to File an Appeal. The district court may reopen the time to file an appeal for a period of 14 days after the date when its order to reopen is entered, but only if all the following conditions are satisfied:

(A) the motion is filed within 180 days after the judgment or order is entered or within 7 days after the moving party receives notice of the entry, whichever is earlier;

(B) the court finds that the moving party was entitled to notice of the entry of the judgment or order sought to be appealed but did not receive the notice from the district court or any party within 21 days after entry; and

(C) the court finds that no party would be prejudiced.

(7) Entry Defined. A judgment or order is entered for purposes of this Rule 4(a) when it is entered in compliance with Rules 58 and 79(a) of the Federal Rules of Civil Procedure.

(b) Appeal in a Criminal Case.

(1) Time for Filing a Notice of Appeal.

(A) In a criminal case, a defendant's notice of appeal must be filed in the district court within 10 days after the later of:

(i) the entry of either the judgment or the order being appealed; or

(ii) the filing of the government's notice of appeal.

(B) When the government is entitled to appeal, its notice of appeal must be filed in the district court within 30 days after the later of:

(i) the entry of the judgment or order being appealed; or

(ii) the filing of a notice of appeal by any defendant.

(2) Filing Before Entry of Judgment. A notice of appeal filed after the court announces a decision, sentence, or order—but before the entry of the judgment or order—is treated as filed on the date of and after the entry.

(3) Effect of a Motion on a Notice of Appeal.

(A) If a defendant timely makes any of the following motions under the Federal Rules of Criminal Procedure, the notice of appeal from a judgment of conviction must be filed within 10 days after the entry of the order disposing of the last such remaining motion, or within 10 days after the entry of the judgment of conviction, whichever period ends later. This provision applies to a timely motion:

(i) for judgment of acquittal under Rule 29;

(ii) for a new trial under Rule 33, but if based on newly discovered evidence, only if the motion is made no later than 10 days after the entry of the judgment; or

(iii) for arrest of judgment under Rule 34.

(B) A notice of appeal filed after the court announces a decision, sentence, or order—but before it disposes of any of the motions referred to in Rule 4(b)(3)(A)—becomes effective upon the later of the following:

(i) the entry of the order disposing of the last such remaining motion; or

(ii) the entry of the judgment of conviction.

(C) A valid notice of appeal is effective—without amendment—to appeal from an order disposing of any of the motions referred to in Rule 4(b)(3)(A).

(4) Motion for Extension of Time. Upon a finding of excusable neglect or good cause, the district court may—before or after the time has expired, with or without motion and notice—extend the time to file a notice of appeal for a period not to exceed 30 days from the expiration of the time otherwise prescribed by this Rule 4(b).

(5) Jurisdiction. The filing of a notice of appeal under this Rule 4(b) does not divest a district court of jurisdiction to correct a sentence under Federal Rule of Criminal Procedure 35(c), nor does the filing of a motion under 35(c) affect the validity of a notice of appeal filed before entry of the order disposing of the motion.

(6) Entry Defined. A judgment or order is entered for purposes of this Rule 4(b) when it is entered on the criminal docket.

(c) Appeal by an Inmate Confined in an Institution.

(1) If an inmate confined in an institution files a notice of appeal in either a civil or a criminal case, the notice is timely if it is deposited in the institution's internal mail system on or before the last day for filing. If an institution has a system designed for legal mail, the inmate must use that system to receive the benefit of this rule. Timely filing may be shown by a declaration in compliance with 28 U.S.C. § 1746 or by a notarized statement, either of which must set forth the date of deposit and state that first-class postage has been prepaid.

(2) If an inmate files the first notice of appeal in a civil case under this Rule 4(c), the 14–day period provided in Rule 4(a)(3) for another party to file a notice of appeal runs from the date when the district court dockets the first notice.

(3) When a defendant in a criminal case files a notice of appeal under this Rule 4(c), the 30–day period for the government to file its notice of appeal runs from the entry of the judgment or order appealed from or from the district court's docketing of the defendant's notice of appeal, whichever is later.

(d) Mistaken Filing in the Court of Appeals. If a notice of appeal in either a civil or a criminal case is mistakenly filed in the court of appeals, the clerk of that court must note on the notice the date when it was received and send it to the district clerk. The notice is then considered filed in the district court on the date so noted.

(As amended Apr. 30, 1979, eff. Aug. 1, 1979; Nov. 18, 1988, Pub.L. 100–690, Title VII, § 7111, 102 Stat. 4419; Apr. 30, 1991, eff. Dec. 1, 1991; Apr. 22, 1993, eff. Dec. 1, 1993; Apr. 27, 1995, eff. Dec. 1, 1995; Apr. 24, 1998, eff. Dec. 1, 1998.)

ADVISORY COMMITTEE NOTES

1967 Adoption

Subdivision (a). This subdivision is derived from FRCP 73(a) [rule 73(a), Federal Rules of Civil Procedure, this title] without any change of substance. The requirement that a request for an extension of time for filing the notice of appeal made after expiration of the time be made by motion and on notice codifies the result reached under the present provisions of FRCP 73(a) and 6(b) [rules 73(a) and 6(b), Federal Rules of Civil Procedure]. *North Umberland Mining Co. v. Standard Accident Ins. Co.*, 193 F.2d 951 (9th Cir., 1952); *Cohen v. Plateau Natural Gas Co.*, 303 F.2d 273 (10th Cir., 1962); *Plant Economy, Inc. v. Mirror Insulation Co.*, 308 F.2d 275 (3d Cir., 1962).

Since this subdivision governs appeals in all civil cases, it supersedes the provisions of § 25 of the Bankruptcy Act (11 U.S.C. § 48). Except in cases to which the United States or an officer or agency thereof is a party, the change is a minor one, since a successful litigant in a bankruptcy proceeding may, under § 25, oblige an aggrieved party to appeal within 30 days after entry of judgment—the time fixed by this subdivision in cases involving private parties only—by serving him with notice of entry on the day thereof, and by the terms of § 25 and aggrieved party must in any event appeal within 40 days after entry of judgment. No reason appears why the time for appeal in bankruptcy should not be the same as that in civil cases generally. Furthermore, § 25 is a potential trap for the uninitiated. The time for appeal which it provides is not applicable to all appeals which may fairly be termed appeals in bankruptcy. Section 25 governs only those cause referred to in § 24 as "proceedings in bankruptcy" and "controversies arising in proceedings in bankruptcy." *Lowenstein v. Reikes*, 54 F.2d 481 (2d Cir., 1931), cert. den., 285 U.S. 539, 52 S.Ct. 311, 76 L.Ed. 932 (1932). The distinction between such cases and other cases which arise out of bankruptcy is often difficult to determine. See 2 Moore's Collier on Bankruptcy ¶24.12 through ¶24.36 (1962). As a result it is not always clear whether an appeal is governed by § 25 or by FRCP 73(a) [rule 73(a), Federal Rules of Civil Procedure, this title], which is applicable to such appeals in bankruptcy as are not governed by § 25.

In view of the unification of the civil and admiralty procedure accomplished by the amendments of the Federal Rules of Civil Procedure effective July 1, 1966, this subdivision governs appeals in those civil actions which involve admiralty or maritime claims and which prior to that date were known as suits in admiralty.

The only other change possibly effected by this subdivision is in the time for appeal from a decision of a district court on a petition for impeachment of an award of a board of arbitration under the Act of May 20, 1926, c. 347, § 9 (44 Stat. 585), 45 U.S.C. § 159. The act provides that a notice of appeal from such a decision shall be filed within 10 days of the decision. This singular provision was apparently repealed by the enactment in 1948 of 28 U.S.C. § 2107, which fixed 30 days from the date of entry of judgment as the time for appeal in all actions a civil nature except actions in admiralty or bankruptcy matters or those in which the United States is a party. But it was not expressly repealed, and its status is in doubt. See 7 Moore's Federal Practice ¶73.09[2] (1966). The doubt should be resolved, and no reason appears why appeals in such cases should not be taken within the time provided for civil cases generally.

Subdivision (b). This subdivision is derived from FRCrP 37(a)(2) [rule 37(a)(2), Federal Rules of Criminal Procedure] without change of substance.

1979 Amendment

Subdivision (a)(1). The words "(including a civil action which involves an admiralty or maritime claim and a proceeding in bankruptcy or a controversy arising therein)," which appear in the present rule are struck out as unnecessary and perhaps misleading in suggesting that there may be other categories that are not either civil or criminal within the meaning of Rule 4(a) and (b).

The phrases "within 30 days of such entry" and "within 60 days of such entry" have been changed to read "after" instead of "or." The change is for clarity only, since the word "of" in the present rule appears to be used to mean "after." Since the proposed amended rule deals directly with the premature filing of a notice of appeal, it was thought useful to emphasize the fact that except as provided, the period during which a notice of appeal may be filed is the 30 days, or 60 days as the case may be, following the entry of the judgment or order appealed from. See Notes to Rule 4(a)(2) and (4), below.

Subdivision (a)(2). The proposed amendment to Rule 4(a)(2) would extend to civil cases the provisions of Rule 4(b), dealing with criminal cases, designed to avoid the loss of the right to appeal by filing the notice of appeal prematurely. Despite the absence of such a provision in Rule 4(a) the courts of appeals quite generally have held premature appeals effective. See, e.g., *Matter of Grand Jury Empanelled Jan. 21, 1975*, 541 F.2d 373 (3d Cir. 1976); *Hodge v. Hodge*, 507 F.2d 87 (3d Cir. 1976); *Song Jook Suh v. Rosenberg*, 437 F.2d 1098 (9th Cir. 1971); *Ruby v. Secretary of the Navy*, 365 F.2d 385 (9th Cir. 1966); *Firchau v. Diamond Nat'l Corp.*, 345 F.2d 269 (9th Cir. 1965).

The proposed amended rule would recognize this practice but make an exception in cases in which a post trial motion has destroyed the finality of the judgment. See Note to Rule 4(a)(4) below.

Subdivision (a)(4). The proposed amendment would make it clear that after the filing of the specified post trial motions, a notice of appeal should await disposition of the motion. Since the proposed amendments to Rules 3, 10, and 12 contemplate that immediately upon the filing of the notice of appeal the fees will be paid and the case docketed in the court of appeals, and the steps toward its disposition set in motion, it would be undesirable to proceed with the appeal while the district court has before it a motion the granting of which would vacate or alter the judgment appealed from. See, e.g., *Keith v. Newcourt*, 530 F.2d 826 (8th Cir. 1976). Under the present rule, since docketing may not take place until the record is transmitted, premature filing is much less likely to involve waste effort. See, e.g. *Stockes v. Peyton's Inc.*, 508 F.2d 1287 (5th Cir. 1975). Further, since a notice of appeal filed before the disposition of a post trial motion, even if it were treated as valid for purposes of jurisdiction, would not embrace objections to the denial of the motion, it is obviously preferable to postpone the notice of appeal until after the motion is disposed of.

The present rule, since it provides for the "termination" of the "running" of the appeal time, is ambiguous in its application to a notice of appeal filed prior to a post trial motion filed within the 10 day limit. The amendment would make it clear that in such circumstances the appellant should not proceed with the appeal during pendency of the motion but should file a new notice of appeal after the motion is disposed of.

Subdivision (a)(5). Under the present rule it is provided that upon a showing of excusable neglect the district court at any time may extend the time for the filing of a notice of appeal for a period not to exceed 30 days from the expiration of the time otherwise prescribed by the rule, but that if the application is made after the original time has run, the order may be made only on motion with such notice as the court deems appropriate.

A literal reading of this provision would require that the extension be ordered and the notice of appeal filed within the 30 day period, but despite the surface clarity of the rule, it has produced considerable confusion. See the discussion by Judge Friendly in In re Orbitek, 520 F.2d 358 (2d Cir. 1975). The proposed amendment would make it clear that a motion to extend the time must be filed no later than 30 days after the expiration of the original appeal time, and that if the motion is timely filed the district court may act upon the motion at a later date, and may extend the time not in excess of 10 days measured from the date on which the order granting the motion is entered.

Under the present rule there is a possible implication that prior to the time the initial appeal time has run, the district court may extend the time on the basis of an informal application. The amendment would require that the application must be made by motion, though the motion may be made *ex parte*. After the expiration of the initial time a motion for the extension of the time must be made in compliance with the F.R.C.P. [Federal Rules of Civil Procedure] and local rules of the district court. See Note to proposed amended Rule 1, *supra*. And see Rules 6(d), 7(b) of the F.R.C.P. [rules 6(d) and 7(b), Federal Rules of Civil Procedure].

The proposed amended rule expands to some extent the standard for the grant of an extension of time. The present rule requires a "showing of excusable neglect." While this was an appropriate standard in cases in which the motion is made after the time for filing the notice of appeal has run, and remains so, it has never fit exactly the situation in which the appellant seeks an extension before the expiration of the initial time. In such a case "good cause," which is the standard that is applied in the granting of other extensions of time under Rule 26(b) seems to be more appropriate.

Subdivision (a)(6). The proposed amendment would call attention to the requirement of Rule 58 of the F.R.C.P. [Federal Rules of Civil Procedure] that the judgment constitute a separate document. See *United States v. Indrelunas*, 411 U.S. 216 (1973). When a notice of appeal is filed, the clerk should ascertain whether any judgment designated therein has been entered in compliance with Rules 58 and 79(a) and if not, so advise all parties and the district judge. While the requirement of Rule 48 is not jurisdictional, (see *Bankers Trust Co. v. Mallis*, 431 U.S. 928 (1977)), compliance is important since the time for the filing of a notice of appeal by other parties is measured by the time at which the judgment is properly entered.

1991 Amendment

The amendment provides a limited opportunity for relief in circumstances where the notice of entry of a judgment or order, required to be mailed by the clerk of the district court pursuant to Rule 77(d) of the Federal Rules of Civil Procedure, is either not received by a party or is received so late as to impair the opportunity to file a timely notice of appeal. The amendment adds a new subdivision (6) allowing a district court to reopen for a brief period the time for appeal upon a finding that notice of entry of a judgment or order was not received from the clerk or a party within 21 days of its entry and that no party would be prejudiced. By "prejudice" the Committee means some adverse consequence other than the cost of having to oppose the appeal and encounter the risk of reversal, consequences that are present in every appeal. Prejudice might arise, for example, if the appellee had taken some action in reliance on the expiration of the normal time period for filing a notice of appeal.

Reopening may be ordered only upon a motion filed within 180 days of the entry of a judgment or order or within 7 days of receipt of notice of such entry, whichever is earlier. This provision establishes an outer time limit of 180 days for a party who fails to receive timely notice of entry of a judgment to seek additional time to appeal and enables any winning party to shorten the 180–day period by sending (and establishing proof of receipt of) its own notice of entry of a judgment, as authorized by Fed.R.Civ.P. 77(d). Winning parties are encouraged to send their own notice in order to lessen the chance that a judge will accept a claim of non-receipt in the face of evidence that notices were sent by both the clerk and the winning party. Receipt of a winning party's notice will shorten only the time for reopening the time for appeal under this subdivision, leaving the normal time periods for appeal unaffected.

If the motion is granted, the district court may reopen the time for filing a notice of appeal only for a period of 14 days from the date of entry of the order reopening the time for appeal.

Transmittal Note: Upon transmittal of this rule to Congress, the Advisory Committee recommends that the attention of Congress be called to the fact that language in the fourth paragraph of 28 U.S.C. § 2107 might appropriately be revised in light of this proposed rule.

1993 Amendment

Note to Paragraph (a)(1). The amendment is intended to alert readers to the fact that paragraph (a)(4) extends the time for filing an appeal when certain posttrial motions are filed. The Committee hopes that awareness of the provisions of paragraph (a)(4) will prevent the filing of a notice of appeal when a posttrial tolling motion is pending.

Note to Paragraph (a)(2). The amendment treats a notice of appeal filed after the announcement of a decision or order, but before its formal entry, as if the notice had been filed after entry. The amendment deletes the language that made paragraph (a)(2) inapplicable to a notice of appeal filed after announcement of the disposition of a posttrial motion enumerated in paragraph (a)(4) but before the entry of the order, see *Acosta v. Louisiana Dep't of Health & Human Resources*, 478 U.S. 251 (1986) (per curiam); *Alerte v. McGinnis*, 898 F.2d 69 (7th Cir.1990). Because the amendment of paragraph (a)(4) recognizes all notices of appeal filed after announcement or entry of judgment—even those that are filed while the posttrial motions enumerated in paragraph (a)(4) are pending—the amendment of this paragraph is consistent with the amendment of paragraph (a)(4).

Note to Paragraph (a)(3). The amendment is technical in nature; no substantive change is intended.

Note to Paragraph (a)(4). The 1979 amendment of this paragraph created a trap for an unsuspecting litigant who files a notice of appeal before a posttrial motion, or while a posttrial motion is pending. The 1979 amendment requires a party to file a new notice of appeal after the motion's disposition. Unless a new notice is filed, the court of appeals lacks jurisdiction to hear the appeal. *Griggs v. Provident Consumer Discount Co.*, 459 U.S. 56 (1982). Many litigants, especially pro se litigants, fail to file the second notice of appeal, and several courts have expressed dissatisfaction with the rule. See, e.g., *Averhart v. Arrendondo*, 773 F.2d 919 (7th Cir.1985); *Harcon Barge Co. v. D & G Boat Rentals, Inc.*, 746 F.2d 278 (5th Cir.1984), cert. denied, 479 U.S. 930 (1986).

The amendment provides that a notice of appeal filed before the disposition of a specified posttrial motion will become effective upon disposition of the motion. A notice filed before the filing of one of the specified motions or after the filing of a motion but before disposition of the motion is, in effect, suspended until the motion is disposed of, whereupon, the previously filed notice effectively places jurisdiction in the court of appeals.

Because a notice of appeal will ripen into an effective appeal upon disposition of a posttrial motion, in some instances there will be an appeal from a judgment that has been altered substantially because the motion was granted in whole or in part. Many such appeals will be dismissed for want of prosecution when the appellant fails to meet the briefing schedule. But, the appellee may also move to strike the appeal. When responding to such a motion, the appellant would have an opportunity to state that, even though some relief sought in a posttrial motion was granted, the appellant still plans to pursue the appeal. Because the appellant's response would provide the appellee with sufficient notice of the appellant's intentions, the Committee does not believe that an additional notice of appeal is needed.

The amendment provides that a notice of appeal filed before the disposition of a posttrial tolling motion is sufficient to bring the underlying case, as well as any orders specified in the original notice, to the court of appeals. If the judgment is altered upon disposition of a posttrial motion, however, and if a party wishes to appeal from the disposition of the motion, the party must amend the notice to so indicate. When a party files an amended notice, no additional fees are required because the notice is an amendment of the original and not a new notice of appeal.

Paragraph (a)(4) is also amended to include, among motions that extend the time for filing a notice of appeal, a Rule 60 motion that is served within 10 days after entry of judgment. This eliminates the difficulty of determining whether a posttrial motion made within 10 days after entry of a judgment is a Rule 59(e) motion, which tolls the time for filing an appeal, or a Rule 60 motion, which historically has not tolled the time. The amendment comports with the practice in several circuits of treating all motions to alter or amend judgments that are made within 10 days after entry of judgment as Rule 59(e) motions for purposes of Rule 4(a)(4). See, e.g., *Finch v. City of Vernon*, 845 F.2d 256 (11th Cir.1988); *Rados v. Celotex Corp.*, 809 F.2d 170 (2d Cir.1986); *Skagerberg v. Oklahoma*, 797 F.2d 881 (10th Cir. 1986). To conform to a recent Supreme Court decision, however—*Budinich v. Becton Dickinson and Co.*, 486 U.S. 196 (1988)—the amendment excludes motions for attorney's fees from the class of motions that extend the filing time unless a district court, acting under Rule 58, enters an order extending the time for appeal. This amendment is to be read in conjunction with the amendment of Fed.R.Civ.P. 58.

Note to subdivision (b). The amendment grammatically restructures the portion of this subdivision that lists the types of motions that toll the time for filing an appeal. This restructuring is intended to make the rule easier to read. No substantive change is intended other than to add a motion for judgment of acquittal under Criminal Rule 29 to the list of tolling motions. Such a motion is the equivalent of a Fed.R.Civ.P. 50(b) motion for judgment notwithstanding the verdict, which tolls the running of time for an appeal in a civil case.

The proposed amendment also eliminates an ambiguity from the third sentence of this subdivision. Prior to this amendment, the third sentence provided that if one of the specified motions was filed, the time for filing an appeal would run from the entry of an order denying the motion. That sentence, like the parallel provision in Rule 4(a)(4), was intended to toll the running of time for appeal if one of the posttrial motions is timely filed. In a criminal case, however, the time for filing the motions runs not from entry of judgment (as it does in civil cases), but from the verdict or finding of guilt. Thus, in a criminal case, a posttrial motion may be disposed of more than 10 days before sentence is imposed, i.e. before the entry of judgment. *United States v. Hashagen*, 816 F.2d 899, 902 n. 5 (3d Cir.1987). To make it clear that a notice of appeal need not be filed before entry of judgment, the amendment states that an appeal may be taken within 10 days after the entry of an order disposing of the motion, or within 10 days after the entry of judgment, whichever is later. The amendment also changes the language in the third sentence providing that an appeal may be taken within 10 days after the entry of an order *denying* the motion; the amendment says instead that an appeal may be taken within 10 days after the entry of an order *disposing* of the last such motion outstanding. (Emphasis added) The change recognizes that there may be multiple posttrial motions filed and that, although one or more motions may be granted in whole or in part, a defendant may still wish to pursue an appeal.

The amendment also states that a notice of appeal filed before the disposition of any of the posttrial tolling motions becomes effective upon disposition of the motions. In most circuits this language simply restates the current practice. See *United States v. Cortes*, 895 F.2d 1245 (9th Cir.), cert. denied, 495 U.S. 939 (1990). Two circuits, however, have questioned that practice in light of the language of the rule, see *United States v. Gargano*, 826 F.2d 610 (7th Cir.1987), and *United States v. Jones*, 669 F.2d 559 (8th Cir.1982), and the Committee wishes to clarify the rule. The amendment is consistent with the proposed amendment of Rule 4(a)(4).

Subdivision (b) is further amended in light of new Fed. R.Crim.P. 35(c), which authorizes a sentencing court to correct any arithmetical, technical, or other clear errors in sentencing within 7 days after imposing the sentence. The Committee believes that a sentencing court should be able to act under Criminal Rule 35(c) even if a notice of appeal has already been filed; and that a notice of appeal should not be affected by the filing of a Rule 35(c) motion or by correction of a sentence under Rule 35(c).

Note to subdivision (c). In *Houston v. Lack*, 487 U.S. 266 (1988), the Supreme Court held that a *pro se* prisoner's notice of appeal is "filed" at the moment of delivery to prison authorities for forwarding to the district court. The amendment reflects that decision. The language of the amendment is similar to that in Supreme Court Rule 29.2.

Permitting an inmate to file a notice of appeal by depositing it in an institutional mail system requires adjustment of the rules governing the filing of cross-appeals. In a civil case, the time for filing a cross-appeal ordinarily runs from the date when the first notice of appeal is filed. If an inmate's notice of appeal is filed by depositing it in an institution's mail system, it is possible that the notice of appeal will not arrive in the district court until several days after the "filing" date and perhaps even after the time for filing a cross-appeal has expired. To avoid that problem, subdivision (c) provides that in a civil case when an institutionalized person files a notice of appeal by depositing it in the institution's mail system, the time for filing a cross-appeal runs from the district court's receipt of the notice. The amendment makes a parallel change regarding the time for the government to appeal in a criminal case.

1995 Amendment

Subdivision (a). Fed.R.Civ.P. 50, 52, and 59 were previously inconsistent with respect to whether certain postjudgment motions had to be filed or merely served no later than 10 days after entry of judgment. As a consequence Rule 4(a)(4) spoke of making or serving such motions rather than filing them. Civil Rules 50, 52, and 59, are being revised to require filing before the end of the 10–day period. As a consequence, this rule is being amended to provide that 'filing' must occur within the 10 day period in order to affect the finality of the judgment and extend the period for filing a notice of appeal.

The Civil Rules require the filing of postjudgment motions 'no later than 10 days after entry of judgment'—rather than 'within' 10 days—to include postjudgment motions that are filed before actual entry of the judgment by the clerk. This rule is amended, therefore, to use the same terminology.

The rule is further amended to clarify the fact that a party who wants to obtain review of an alteration or amendment of a judgment must file a notice of appeal or amend a previously filed notice to indicate intent to appeal from the altered judgment.

Rule 5. Appeal by Permission

(a) Petition for Permission to Appeal.

(1) To request permission to appeal when an appeal is within the court of appeals' discretion, a party must file a petition for permission to appeal. The petition must be filed with the circuit clerk with proof of service on all other parties to the district-court action.

(2) The petition must be filed within the time specified by the statute or rule authorizing the appeal or, if no such time is specified, within the time provided by Rule 4(a) for filing a notice of appeal.

(3) If a party cannot petition for appeal unless the district court first enters an order granting permission to do so or stating that the necessary conditions are met, the district court may amend its order, either on its own or in response to a party's motion, to include the required permission or statement. In that event, the time to petition runs from entry of the amended order.

(b) Contents of the Petition; Answer or Cross–Petition; Oral Argument.

(1) The petition must include the following:

(A) the facts necessary to understand the question presented;

(B) the question itself;

(C) the relief sought;

(D) the reasons why the appeal should be allowed and is authorized by a statute or rule; and

(E) an attached copy of:

(i) the order, decree, or judgment complained of and any related opinion or memorandum, and

(ii) any order stating the district court's permission to appeal or finding that the necessary conditions are met.

(2) A party may file an answer in opposition or a cross-petition within 7 days after the petition is served.

(3) The petition and answer will be submitted without oral argument unless the court of appeals orders otherwise.

(c) Form of Papers; Number of Copies. All papers must conform to Rule 32(a)(1). An original and 3 copies must be filed unless the court requires a different number by local rule or by order in a particular case.

(d) Grant of Permission; Fees; Cost Bond; Filing the Record.

(1) Within 10 days after the entry of the order granting permission to appeal, the appellant must:

(A) pay the district clerk all required fees; and

(B) file a cost bond if required under Rule 7.

(2) A notice of appeal need not be filed. The date when the order granting permission to appeal is entered serves as the date of the notice of appeal for calculating time under these rules.

(3) The district clerk must notify the circuit clerk once the petitioner has paid the fees. Upon receiving this notice, the circuit clerk must enter the appeal on the docket. The record must be forwarded and filed in accordance with Rules 11 and 12(c).

(As amended Apr. 30, 1979, eff. Aug. 1, 1979; Apr. 29, 1994, eff. Dec. 1, 1994; Apr. 24, 1998, eff. Dec. 1, 1998.)

ADVISORY COMMITTEE NOTES

1967 Adoption

This rule is derived in the main from Third Circuit Rule 11(2), which is similar to the rule governing appeals under 28 U.S.C. § 1292(b) in a majority of the circuits. The second sentence of subdivision (a) resolves a conflict over the question of whether the district court can amend an order by supplying the statement required by § 1292(b) at any time after entry of the order, with the result that the time fixed by the statute commences to run on the date of entry of the order as amended. Compare *Milbert v. Bison Laboratories*, 260 F.2d 431 (3d Cir., 1958) with *Sperry Rand Corporation v. Bell Telephone Laboratories*, 272 F.2d 29 (2d Cir., 1959), *Hadjipateras v. Pacifica, S.A.*, 290 F.2d 697 (5th Cir., 1961) and *Houston Fearless Corporation v. Teter*, 313 F.2d 91 (10th Cir., 1962). The view taken by the Second, Fifth and Tenth Circuits seems theoretically and practically sound, and the rule adopts it. Although a majority of the circuits now require the filing of a notice of appeal following the grant of permission to appeal, filing of the notice serves no function other than to provide a time from which the time for transmitting the record and docketing the appeal begins to run.

1979 Amendment

The proposed amendment [to subdivision (d)] adapts to the practice in appeals from interlocutory orders under 28 U.S.C. § 1292(b) the provisions of proposed Rule 3(e) above, requiring payment of all fees in the district court upon the filing of the notice of appeal. See Note to proposed amended Rule 3(e), *supra*.

1994 Amendments

Subdivision (c). The amendment makes it clear that a court may require a different number of copies either by rule or by order in an individual case. The number of copies of any document that a court of appeals needs varies depending upon the way in which the court conducts business. The internal operation of the courts of appeals necessarily varies from circuit to circuit because of differences in the number of judges, the geographic area included within the circuit, and other such factors. Uniformity could be achieved only by setting the number of copies artificially high so that parties in all circuits file enough copies to satisfy the needs of the court requiring the greatest number. Rather than do that, the Committee decided to make it clear that local rules may require a greater or lesser number of copies and that, if the circumstances of a particular case indicate the need for a different number of copies in that case, the court may so order.

[Rule 5.1. Appeal by Permission Under 28 U.S.C. § 636(c)(5)] (Abrogated Apr. 24, 1998, eff. Dec. 1, 1998)

HISTORICAL NOTES

The abrogated rule provided that:

"**(a) Petition for Leave to Appeal; Answer or Cross Petition.** An appeal from a district court judgment, entered after an appeal under 28 U.S.C. § 636(c)(4) to a district judge from a judgment entered upon direction of a magistrate judge in a civil case, may be sought by filing a petition for leave to appeal. An appeal on petition for leave to appeal is not a matter of right, but its allowance is a matter of sound judicial discretion. The petition shall be filed with the clerk of the court of appeals within the time provided by Rule 4(a) for filing a notice of appeal, with proof of service on all parties to the action in the district court. A notice of appeal need not be filed. Within 14 days after service of the petition, a party may file an answer in opposition or a cross petition.

"**(b) Content of Petition; Answer.** The petition for leave to appeal shall contain a statement of the facts necessary to an understanding of the questions to be presented by the appeal; a statement of those questions and of the relief sought; a statement of the reasons why in the opinion of the petitioner the appeal should be allowed; and a copy of the order, decree or judgment complained of and any opinion or memorandum relating thereto. The petition and answer shall be submitted to a panel of judges of the court of appeals without oral argument unless otherwise ordered.

"**(c) Form of Papers; Number of Copies.** All papers may be typewritten. An original and three copies must be filed unless the court requires the filing of a different number by local rule or by order in a particular case.

"**(d) Allowance of the Appeal; Fees; Cost Bond; Filing of Record.** Within 10 days after the entry of an order granting the appeal, the appellant shall (1) pay to the clerk of the district court the fees established by statute and the docket fee prescribed by the Judicial Conference of the United States and (2) file a bond for costs if required pursuant to Rule 7. The clerk of the district court shall notify the clerk of the court of appeals of the payment of the fees. Upon receipt of such notice, the clerk of the court of appeals shall enter the appeal upon the docket. The record shall be transmitted and filed in accordance with Rules 11 and 12(b)."

Rule 6. Appeal in a Bankruptcy Case From a Final Judgment, Order, or Decree of a District Court or Bankruptcy Appellate Panel

(a) Appeal From a Judgment, Order, or Decree of a District Court Exercising Original Jurisdiction in a Bankruptcy Case. An appeal to a court of appeals from a final judgment, order, or decree of a district court exercising jurisdiction under 28 U.S.C. § 1334 is taken as any other civil appeal under these rules.

(b) Appeal From a Judgment, Order, or Decree of a District Court or Bankruptcy Appellate Panel Exercising Appellate Jurisdiction in a Bankruptcy Case.

(1) Applicability of Other Rules. These rules apply to an appeal to a court of appeals under 28 U.S.C. § 158(d) from a final judgment, order, or decree of a district court or bankruptcy appellate panel exercising appellate jurisdiction under 28 U.S.C. § 158(a) or (b). But there are 3 exceptions:

(A) Rules 4(a)(4), 4(b), 9, 10, 11, 12(b), 13–20, 22–23, and 24(b) do not apply;

(B) the reference in Rule 3(c) to 'Form 1 in the Appendix of Forms' must be read as a reference to Form 5; and

(C) when the appeal is from a bankruptcy appellate panel, the term 'district court,' as used in any applicable rule, means 'appellate panel.'

(2) Additional Rules. In addition to the rules made applicable by Rule 6(b)(1), the following rules apply:

(A) Motion for rehearing.

(i) If a timely motion for rehearing under Bankruptcy Rule 8015 is filed, the time to appeal for all parties runs from the entry of the order disposing of the motion. A notice of appeal filed after the district court or bankruptcy appellate panel announces or enters a judgment, order, or decree—but before disposition of the motion for rehearing—becomes effective when the order disposing of the motion for rehearing is entered.

(ii) Appellate review of the order disposing of the motion requires the party, in compliance with Rules 3(c) and 6(b)(1)(B), to amend a previously filed notice of appeal. A party intending to challenge an altered or amended judgment, order, or decree must file a notice of appeal or amended notice of appeal within the time prescribed by Rule 4—excluding Rules 4(a)(4) and 4(b)—measured from the entry of the order disposing of the motion.

(iii) No additional fee is required to file an amended notice.

(B) The record on appeal.

(i) Within 10 days after filing the notice of appeal, the appellant must file with the clerk possessing the record assembled in accordance with Bankruptcy Rule 8006—and serve on the appellee—a statement of the issues to be presented on appeal and a designation of the record to be certified and sent to the circuit clerk.

(ii) An appellee who believes that other parts of the record are necessary must, within 10 days after being served with the appellant's designation, file with the clerk and serve on the appellant a designation of additional parts to be included.

(iii) The record on appeal consists of:

- the redesignated record as provided above;
- the proceedings in the district court or bankruptcy appellate panel; and
- a certified copy of the docket entries prepared by the clerk under Rule 3(d).

(C) Forwarding the record.

(i) When the record is complete, the district clerk or bankruptcy appellate panel clerk must number the documents constituting the record and send them promptly to the circuit clerk together with a list of the documents correspondingly numbered and reasonably identified. Unless directed to do so by a party or the circuit clerk, the clerk will not send to the court of appeals documents of unusual bulk or weight, physical exhibits other than documents, or other parts of the record designated for omission by local rule of the court of appeals. If the exhibits are unusually bulky or heavy, a party must arrange with the clerks in advance for their transportation and receipt.

(ii) All parties must do whatever else is necessary to enable the clerk to assemble and forward the record. The court of appeals may provide by rule or order that a certified copy of the docket entries be sent in place of the redesignated record, but any party may request at any time during the pendency of the appeal that the redesignated record be sent.

(D) Filing the record. Upon receiving the record—or a certified copy of the docket entries sent in place of the redesignated record—the circuit clerk must file it and immediately notify all parties of the filing date.

(Added Apr. 25, 1989, eff. Dec. 1, 1989, and amended Apr. 30, 1991, eff. Dec. 1, 1991; Apr. 22, 1993, eff. Dec. 1, 1993; Apr. 24, 1998, eff. Dec. 1, 1998.)

ADVISORY COMMITTEE NOTES

1989 Addition

A new Rule 6 is proposed. The Bankruptcy Reform Act of 1978, Pub.L. No. 95–598, 92 Stat. 2549, the Supreme Court decision in *Northern Pipeline Construction Co. v. Marathon Pipe Line Co.,* 458 U.S. 50 (1982), and the Bankruptcy Amendments and Federal Judgeship Act of 1984, Pub.L. No. 98–353, 98 Stat. 333, have made the existing Rule 6 obsolete.

Subdivision (a). Subdivision (a) provides that when a district court exercises original jurisdiction in a bankruptcy matter, rather than referring it to a bankruptcy judge for a final determination, the appeal should be taken in identical fashion as appeals from district court decisions in other civil actions. A district court exercises original jurisdiction and this subdivision applies when the district court enters a final order or judgment upon consideration of a bankruptcy judge's proposed findings of fact and conclusions of law in a non-core proceeding pursuant to 28 U.S.C. § 157(c)(1) or when a district court withdraws a proceeding pursuant to 28 U.S.C. § 157(d). This subdivision is included to avoid uncertainty arising from the question of whether a bankruptcy case is a civil case. The rules refer at various points to the procedure "in a civil case", *see,* e.g. Rule 4(a)(1). Subdivision (a) makes it clear that such rules apply to an appeal from a district court bankruptcy decision.

Subdivision (b). Subdivision (b) governs appeals that follow intermediate review of a bankruptcy judge's decision by a district court or a bankruptcy appellate panel.

Subdivision (b)(1). Subdivision (b)(1) provides for the general applicability of the Federal Rules of Appellate Procedure, with specified exceptions, to appeals covered by subdivision (b) and makes necessary word adjustments.

Subdivision (b)(2). Paragraph (i) provides that the time for filing a notice of appeal shall begin to run anew from the entry of an order denying a rehearing or from the entry of a subsequent judgment. The Committee deliberately omitted from the rule any provision governing the validity of a notice of appeal filed prior to the entry of an order denying a rehearing; the Committee intended to leave undisturbed the current state of the law on that issue. Paragraph (ii) calls for a redesignation of the appellate record assembled in the bankruptcy court pursuant to Rule 8006 of the Rules of Bankruptcy Procedure. After an intermediate appeal, a party may well narrow the focus of its efforts on the second appeal and a redesignation of the record may eliminate unnecessary material. The proceedings during the first appeal are included to cover the possibility that independent error in the intermediate appeal, for example failure to follow appropriate procedures, may be assigned in the court of appeals. Paragraph (iii) provides for the transmission of the record and tracks the appropriate subsections of Rule 11. Paragraph (iv) provides for the filing of the record and notices to the parties. Paragraph (ii) and Paragraph (iv) both refer to "a certified copy of the docket entries". The "docket entries" referred to are the docket entries in the district court or the bankruptcy appellate panel, not the entire docket in the bankruptcy court.

1993 Amendments

Note to Subparagraph (b)(2)(i). The amendment accompanies concurrent changes to Rule 4(a)(4). Although Rule 6 never included language such as that being changed in Rule 4(a)(4), language that made a notice of appeal void if it was filed before, or during the pendency of, certain posttrial motions, courts have found that a notice of appeal is premature if it is filed before the court disposes of a motion for rehearing. See, e.g., *In re X–Cel, Inc.*, 823 F.2d 192 (7th Cir.1987); *In re Shah*, 859 F.2d 1463 (10th Cir.1988). The Committee wants to achieve the same result here as in Rule 4, the elimination of a procedural trap.

Rule 7. Bond for Costs on Appeal in a Civil Case

In a civil case, the district court may require an appellant to file a bond or provide other security in any form and amount necessary to ensure payment of costs on appeal. Rule 8(b) applies to a surety on a bond given under this rule.

(As amended Apr. 30, 1979, eff. Aug. 1, 1979; Apr. 24, 1998, eff. Dec. 1, 1998.)

ADVISORY COMMITTEE NOTES

1967 Adoption

This rule is derived from FRCP 73(c) [rule 73(c), Federal Rules of Civil Procedure, this title] without change in substance.

1979 Amendment

The amendment would eliminate the provision of the present rule that requires the appellant to file a $250 bond for costs on appeal at the time of filing his notice of appeal. The $250 provision was carried forward in the F.R.App.P. [these rules] from former Rule 73(c) of the F.R.Civ.P. [rule 73(c), Federal Rules of Civil Procedure], and the $250 figure has remained unchanged since the adoption of that rule in 1937. Today it bears no relationship to actual costs. The amended rule would leave the question of the need for a bond for costs and its amount in the discretion of the court.

Rule 8. Stay or Injunction Pending Appeal

(a) Motion for Stay.

(1) Initial Motion in the District Court. A party must ordinarily move first in the district court for the following relief:

(A) a stay of the judgment or order of a district court pending appeal;

(B) approval of a supersedeas bond; or

(C) an order suspending, modifying, restoring, or granting an injunction while an appeal is pending.

(2) Motion in the Court of Appeals; Conditions on Relief. A motion for the relief mentioned in Rule 8(a)(1) may be made to the court of appeals or to one of its judges.

(A) The motion must:

(i) show that moving first in the district court would be impracticable; or

(ii) state that, a motion having been made, the district court denied the motion or failed to afford the relief requested and state any reasons given by the district court for its action.

(B) The motion must also include:

(i) the reasons for granting the relief requested and the facts relied on;

(ii) originals or copies of affidavits or other sworn statements supporting facts subject to dispute; and

(iii) relevant parts of the record.

(C) The moving party must give reasonable notice of the motion to all parties.

(D) A motion under this Rule 8(a)(2) must be filed with the circuit clerk and normally will be considered by a panel of the court. But in an exceptional case in which time requirements make that procedure impracticable, the motion may be made to and considered by a single judge.

(E) The court may condition relief on a party's filing a bond or other appropriate security in the district court.

(b) Proceeding Against a Surety. If a party gives security in the form of a bond or stipulation or other undertaking with one or more sureties, each surety submits to the jurisdiction of the district court and irrevocably appoints the district clerk as the surety's agent on whom any papers affecting the surety's liability on the bond or undertaking may be served. On motion, a surety's liability may be enforced in the district court without the necessity of an independent action. The motion and any notice that the district court prescribes may be served on the district clerk, who must promptly mail a copy to each surety whose address is known.

(c) Stay in a Criminal Case. Rule 38 of the Federal Rules of Criminal Procedure governs a stay in a criminal case.

(As amended Mar. 10, 1986, eff. July 1, 1986; Apr. 27, 1995, eff. Dec. 1, 1995; Apr. 24, 1998, eff. Dec. 1, 1998.)

ADVISORY COMMITTEE NOTES

1967 Adoption

Subdivision (a). While the power of a court of appeals to stay proceedings in the district court during the pendency of an appeal is not explicitly conferred by statute, it exists by virtue of the all writs statute, 28 U.S.C. § 1651. *Eastern Greyhound Lines v. Fusco*, 310 F.2d 632 (6th Cir., 1962); *United States v. Lynd*, 301 F.2d 818 (5th Cir., 1962); *Public Utilities Commission of Dist. of Col. v. Capital Transit Co.*, 94 U.S.App.D.C. 140, 214 F.2d 242 (1954). And the Supreme Court has termed the power "inherent" (*In re McKenzie*, 180 U.S. 536, 551, 21 S.Ct. 468, 45 L.Ed. 657 (1901)) and "part of its (the court of appeals') traditional equipment for the administration of justice." (*Scripps-Howard Radio v. F.C.C.*, 316 U.S. 4, 9–10, 62 S.Ct. 875, 86 L.Ed. 1229 (1942)). The power of a single judge of the court of appeals to grant a stay pending appeal was recognized in *In re McKenzie, supra*. *Alexander v. United States*, 173 F.2d 865 (9th Cir., 1949) held that a single judge could not stay the judgment of a district court, but it noted the absence of a rule of court authorizing the practice. FRCP 62(g) [rule 62(g), Federal Rules of Civil Procedure] adverts to the grant of a stay by a single judge of the appellate court. The requirement that application be first made to the district court is the case law rule. *Cumberland Tel. & Tel. Co. v. Louisiana Public Service Commission*, 260 U.S. 212, 219, 43 S.Ct. 75, 67 L.Ed. 217 (1922); *United States v. El-O-Pathic Pharmacy*, 192 F.2d 62 (9th Cir., 1951); *United States v. Hansell*, 109 F.2d 613 (2d Cir., 1940). The requirement is explicitly stated in FRCrP 38(c) [rule 38(c), Federal Rules of Criminal Procedure] and in the rules of the First, Third, Fourth and Tenth Circuits. See also Supreme Court Rules 18 and 27.

The statement of the requirement in the proposed rule would work a minor change in present practice. FRCP 73(e) [rule 73(e), Federal Rules of Civil Procedure] requires that if a bond for costs on appeal or a supersedeas bond is offered after the appeal is docketed, leave to file the bond must be obtained from the court of appeals. There appears to be no reason why matters relating to supersedeas and cost bonds should not be initially presented to the district court whenever they arise prior to the disposition of the appeal. The requirement of FRCP 73(e) appears to be a concession of the view that once an appeal is perfected, the district court loses all power over its judgment. See *In re Federal Facilities Realty Trust*, 227 F.2d 651 (7th Cir., 1955) and cases cited at 654–655. No reason appears why all questions related to supersedeas or the bond for costs on appeal should not be presented in the first instance to the district court in the ordinary case.

Subdivision (b). The provisions respecting a surety upon a bond or other undertaking are based upon FRCP 65.1 [rule 65.1, Federal Rules of Civil Procedure].

1986 Amendment

The amendments to Rule 8(b) are technical. No substantive change is intended.

1995 Amendment

Subdivision (c). The amendment conforms subdivision (c) to previous amendments to Fed.R.Crim.P. 38. This amendment strikes the reference to subdivision (a) of Fed. R.Crim.P. 38 so that Fed.R.App.P. 8(c) refers instead to all of Criminal Rule 38. When Rule 8(c) was adopted Fed. R.Crim.P. 38(a) included the procedures for obtaining a stay of execution when the sentence in question was death, imprisonment, a fine, or probation. Criminal Rule 38 was later amended and now addresses those topics in separate subdivisions. Subdivision 38(a) now addresses only stays of death sentences. The proper cross reference is to all of Criminal Rule 38.

Rule 9. Release in a Criminal Case

(a) Release Before Judgment of Conviction.

(1) The district court must state in writing, or orally on the record, the reasons for an order regarding the release or detention of a defendant in a criminal case. A party appealing from the order must file with the court of appeals a copy of the district court's order and the court's statement of reasons as soon as practicable after filing the notice of appeal. An appellant who questions the factual basis for the district court's order must file a transcript of the release proceedings or an explanation of why a transcript was not obtained.

(2) After reasonable notice to the appellee, the court of appeals must promptly determine the appeal on the basis of the papers, affidavits, and parts of the record that the parties present or the court requires. Unless the court so orders, briefs need not be filed.

(3) The court of appeals or one of its judges may order the defendant's release pending the disposition of the appeal.

(b) Release After Judgment of Conviction. A party entitled to do so may obtain review of a district-court order regarding release after a judgment of conviction by filing a notice of appeal from that order in the district court, or by filing a motion in the court of appeals if the party has already filed a notice of appeal from the judgment of conviction. Both the order and the review are subject to Rule 9(a). The papers filed by the party seeking review must include a copy of the judgment of conviction.

(c) Criteria for Release. The court must make its decision regarding release in accordance with the applicable provisions of 18 U.S.C. §§ 3142, 3143, and 3145(c).

(As amended Apr. 24, 1972, eff. Oct. 1, 1972; Oct. 12, 1984, Pub.L. 98–473, Title II, § 210, 98 Stat. 1987; Apr. 29, 1994, eff. Dec. 1, 1994; Apr. 24, 1998, eff. Dec. 1, 1998.)

ADVISORY COMMITTEE NOTES

1967 Adoption

Subdivision (a). The appealability of release orders entered prior to a judgment of conviction is determined by the provisions of 18 U.S.C. § 3147, as qualified by 18 U.S.C. § 3148, and by the rule announced in *Stack v. Boyle*, 342 U.S. 1, 72 S.Ct. 1, 96 L.Ed. 3 (1951), holding certain orders respecting release appealable as final orders under 28 U.S.C. § 1291. The language of the rule, "(a)n appeal authorized by law from an order refusing or imposing conditions of release," is intentionally broader than that used in 18 U.S.C. § 3147 in describing orders made appealable by that section. The summary procedure ordained by the rule is intended to apply to all appeals from orders respecting release, and it would appear that at least some orders not made appealable by 18 U.S.C. § 3147 are nevertheless appealable under the *Stack v. Boyle* rationale. See, for example, *United States v. Foster*, 278 F.2d 567 (2d Cir., 1960), holding appealable an order refusing to extend bail limits. Note also the provisions of 18 U.S.C. § 3148, which after withdrawing from persons charged with an offense punishable by death and from those who have been convicted of an offense the right of appeal granted by 18 U.S.C. § 3147, expressly preserves "other rights to judicial review of conditions of release or orders of detention."

The purpose of the subdivision is to insure the expeditious determination of appeals respecting release orders, an expedition commanded by 18 U.S.C. § 3147 and by the Court in *Stack v. Boyle*, supra. It permits such appeals to be heard on an informal record without the necessity of briefs and on reasonable notice. Equally important to the just and speedy disposition of these appeals is the requirement that the district court state the reasons for its decision. See *Jones v. United States*, 358 F.2d 543 (D.C.Cir., 1966); *Rhodes v. United States*, 275 F.2d 78 (4th Cir., 1960); *United States v. Williams*, 253 F.2d 144 (7th Cir., 1958).

Subdivision (b). This subdivision regulates procedure for review of an order respecting release at a time when the jurisdiction of the court of appeals has already attached by virtue of an appeal from the judgment of conviction. Notwithstanding the fact that jurisdiction has passed to the court of appeals, both 18 U.S.C. § 3148 and FRCrP 38(c) [rule 38(c), Federal Rules of Criminal Procedure] contemplate that the initial determination of whether a convicted defendant is to be released pending the appeal is to be made by the district court. But at this point there is obviously no need for a separate appeal from the order of the district court respecting release. The court of appeals or a judge thereof has power to effect release on motion as an incident to the pending appeal. See FRCrP 38(c) and 46(a)(2) [rules 38(c) and 46(a)(2), Federal Rules of Criminal Procedure. But the motion is functionally identical with the appeal regulated by subdivision (a) and requires the same speedy determination if relief is to be effective. Hence the similarity of the procedure outlined in the two subdivisions.

1972 Amendment

Subdivision (c) is intended to bring the rule into conformity with 18 U.S.C. § 3148 and to allocate to the defendant the burden of establishing that he will not flee and that he poses no danger to pay other person or to the community. The burden is placed upon the defendant in the view that the fact of his conviction justifies retention in custody in situations where doubt exists as to whether he can be safely released pending disposition of his appeal. Release pending appeal may also be denied if "it appears that an appeal is frivolous or taken for delay." 18 U.S.C. § 3148. The burden of establishing the existence of these criteria remains with the government.

1994 Amendments

Rule 9 has been entirely rewritten. The basic structure of the rule has been retained. Subdivision (a) governs appeals from bail decisions made before the judgment of conviction is entered at the time of sentencing. Subdivision (b) governs review of bail decisions made after sentencing and pending appeal.

Subdivision (a). The subdivision applies to appeals from "an order regarding release or detention" of a criminal defendant before judgment of conviction, *i.e.,* before sentencing. *See* Fed. R. Crim. P. 32. The old rule applied only to a defendant's appeal from an order "refusing or imposing conditions of release." The new broader language is needed because the government is now permitted to appeal bail decisions in certain circumstances. 18 U.S.C. §§ 3145 and 3731. For the same reason, the rule now requires a district court to state reasons for its decision in all instances, not only when it refuses release or imposes conditions on release.

The rule requires a party appealing from a district court's decision to supply the court of appeals with a copy of the district court's order and its statement of reasons. In addition, an appellant who questions the factual basis for the district court's decision must file a transcript of the release proceedings, if possible. The rule also permits a court to require additional papers. A court must act promptly to decide these appeals; lack of pertinent information can cause delays. The old rule left the determination of what should be filed entirely within the party's, discretion; it stated that the court of appeals would hear the appeal "upon such papers, affidavits, and portions of the record as the parties shall present."

Subdivision (b). This subdivision applies to review of a district court's decision regarding release made after judgment of conviction. As in subdivision (a), the language has been changed to accommodate the government's ability to seek review.

The word "review" is used in this subdivision, rather than "appeal" because review may be obtained, in some instances, upon motion. Review may be obtained by motion if the party has already filed a notice of appeal from the judgment of conviction. If the party desiring review of the release decision has not filed such a notice of appeal, review may be obtained only by filing a notice of appeal from the order regarding release.

The requirements of subdivision (a) apply to both the order and the review. That is, the district court must state its reasons for the order. The party seeking review must supply the court of appeals with the same information required by subdivision (a). In addition, the party seeking review must also supply the court with information about the conviction and the sentence.

Subdivision (c). This subdivision has been amended to include references to the correct statutory provisions.

Rule 10. The Record on Appeal

(a) Composition of the Record on Appeal. The following items constitute the record on appeal:

(1) the original papers and exhibits filed in the district court;

(2) the transcript of proceedings, if any; and

(3) a certified copy of the docket entries prepared by the district clerk.

(b) The Transcript of Proceedings.

(1) Appellant's Duty to Order. Within 10 days after filing the notice of appeal or entry of an order disposing of the last timely remaining motion of a type specified in Rule 4(a)(4)(A), whichever is later, the appellant must do either of the following:

(A) order from the reporter a transcript of such parts of the proceedings not already on file as the appellant considers necessary, subject to a local rule of the court of appeals and with the following qualifications:

(i) the order must be in writing;

(ii) if the cost of the transcript is to be paid by the United States under the Criminal Justice Act, the order must so state; and

(iii) the appellant must, within the same period, file a copy of the order with the district clerk; or

(B) file a certificate stating that no transcript will be ordered.

(2) Unsupported Finding or Conclusion. If the appellant intends to urge on appeal that a finding or conclusion is unsupported by the evidence or is contrary to the evidence, the appellant must include in the record a transcript of all evidence relevant to that finding or conclusion.

(3) Partial Transcript. Unless the entire transcript is ordered:

(A) the appellant must—within the 10 days provided in Rule 10(b)(1)—file a statement of the issues that the appellant intends to present on the appeal and must serve on the appellee a copy of both the order or certificate and the statement;

(B) if the appellee considers it necessary to have a transcript of other parts of the proceedings, the appellee must, within 10 days after the service of the order or certificate and the statement of the issues, file and serve on the appellant a designation of additional parts to be ordered; and

(C) unless within 10 days after service of that designation the appellant has ordered all such parts, and has so notified the appellee, the appellee may within the following 10 days either order the parts or move in the district court for an order requiring the appellant to do so.

(4) Payment. At the time of ordering, a party must make satisfactory arrangements with the reporter for paying the cost of the transcript.

(c) Statement of the Evidence When the Proceedings Were Not Recorded or When a Transcript Is Unavailable. If the transcript of a hearing or trial is unavailable, the appellant may prepare a statement of the evidence or proceedings from the best available means, including the appellant's recollection. The statement must be served on the appellee, who may serve objections or proposed amendments within 10 days after being served. The statement and any objections or proposed amendments must then be submitted to the district court for settlement and approval. As settled and approved, the statement must be included by the district clerk in the record on appeal.

(d) Agreed Statement as the Record on Appeal. In place of the record on appeal as defined in Rule 10(a), the parties may prepare, sign, and submit to the district court a statement of the case showing how the issues presented by the appeal arose and were decided in the district court. The statement must set forth only those facts averred and proved or sought to be proved that are essential to the court's resolution of the issues. If the statement is truthful, it—together with any additions that the district court may consider necessary to a full presentation of the issues on appeal—must be approved by the district court and must then be certified to the court of appeals as the record on appeal. The district clerk must then send it to the circuit clerk within the time provided by Rule 11. A copy of the agreed statement may be filed in place of the appendix required by Rule 30.

(e) Correction or Modification of the Record.

(1) If any difference arises about whether the record truly discloses what occurred in the district court, the difference must be submitted to and settled by that court and the record conformed accordingly.

(2) If anything material to either party is omitted from or misstated in the record by error or accident, the omission or misstatement may be corrected and a supplemental record may be certified and forwarded:

(A) on stipulation of the parties;

(B) by the district court before or after the record has been forwarded; or

(C) by the court of appeals.

(3) All other questions as to the form and content of the record must be presented to the court of appeals.

(As amended Apr. 30, 1979, eff. Aug. 1, 1979; Mar. 10, 1986, eff. July 1, 1986; Apr. 30, 1991, eff. Dec. 1, 1991; Apr. 22, 1993, eff. Dec. 1, 1993; Apr. 27, 1995, eff. Dec. 1, 1995; Apr. 24, 1998, eff. Dec. 1, 1998.)

ADVISORY COMMITTEE NOTES

1967 Adoption

This rule is derived from FRCP 75(a), (b), (c) and (d) and FRCP 76 [rule 75(a), (b), (c) and (d) and rule 76, Federal Rules of Civil Procedure], without change in substance.

1979 Amendment

The proposed amendments to Rule 10(b) would require the appellant to place with the reporter a written order for the transcript of proceedings and file a copy with the clerk, and to indicate on the order if the transcript is to be provided under the Criminal Justice Act. If the appellant does not plan to order a transcript of any of the proceedings, he must file a certificate to that effect. These requirements make the appellant's steps in readying the appeal a matter of record and give the district court notice of requests for transcripts at the expense of the United States under the Criminal Justice Act. They are also the third step in giving the court of appeals some control over the production and transmission of the record. See Note to Rules 3(d)(e) above and Rule 11 below.

In the event the appellant orders no transcript, or orders a transcript of less than all the proceedings, the procedure under the proposed amended rule remains substantially as before. The appellant must serve on the appellee a copy of his order or in the event no order is placed, of the certificate to that effect, and a statement of the issues he intends to present on appeal, and the appellee may thereupon designate additional parts of the transcript to be included, and upon appellant's refusal to order the additional parts, may either order them himself or seek an order requiring the appellant to order them. The only change proposed in this procedure is to place a 10 day time limit on motions to require the appellant to order the additional portions.

Rule 10(b) is made subject to local rules of the courts of appeals in recognition of the practice in some circuits in some classes of cases, e.g., appeals by indigents in criminal cases after a short trial, of ordering immediate preparation of a complete transcript, thus making compliance with the rule unnecessary.

1986 Amendment

The amendments to Rules 10(b) and (c) are technical. No substantive change is intended.

1993 Amendment

The amendment is technical and no substantive change is intended.

1995 Amendment

Subdivision (b)(1). The amendment conforms this rule to amendments made in Rule 4(a)(4) in 1993. The amendments to Rule 4(a)(4) provide that certain postjudgment motions have the effect of suspending a filed notice of appeal until the disposition of the last of such motions. The purpose of this amendment is to suspend the 10–day period for ordering a transcript if a timely postjudgment motion is made and a notice of appeal is suspended under Rule 4(a)(4). The 10–day period set forth in the first sentence of this rule begins to run when the order disposing of the last of such postjudgment motions outstanding is entered.

HISTORICAL NOTES

References in Text

The Criminal Justice Act, referred to in subd. (b)(1), probably means the Criminal Justice Act of 1964, Pub.L. 88–455, Aug. 20, 1964, 78 Stat. 552, which is classified to § 3006A of Title 18, Crimes and Criminal Procedure.

Rule 11. Forwarding the Record

(a) Appellant's Duty. An appellant filing a notice of appeal must comply with Rule 10(b) and must do whatever else is necessary to enable the clerk to assemble and forward the record. If there are multiple appeals from a judgment or order, the clerk must forward a single record.

(b) Duties of Reporter and District Clerk.

(1) Reporter's Duty to Prepare and File a Transcript. The reporter must prepare and file a transcript as follows:

(A) Upon receiving an order for a transcript, the reporter must enter at the foot of the order the date of its receipt and the expected completion date and send a copy, so endorsed, to the circuit clerk.

(B) If the transcript cannot be completed within 30 days of the reporter's receipt of the order, the reporter may request the circuit clerk to grant additional time to complete it. The clerk must note on the docket the action taken and notify the parties.

(C) When a transcript is complete, the reporter must file it with the district clerk and notify the circuit clerk of the filing.

(D) If the reporter fails to file the transcript on time, the circuit clerk must notify the district judge and do whatever else the court of appeals directs.

(2) District Clerk's Duty to Forward. When the record is complete, the district clerk must number the documents constituting the record and send them promptly to the circuit clerk together with a list of the documents correspondingly numbered and reasonably identified. Unless directed to do so by a party or the circuit clerk, the district clerk will not send to the court of appeals documents of unusual bulk or weight, physical exhibits other than documents, or other parts of the record designated for omission by local rule of the court of appeals. If the exhibits are unusually bulky or heavy, a party must arrange with the clerks in advance for their transportation and receipt.

(c) Retaining the Record Temporarily in the District Court for Use in Preparing the Appeal. The parties may stipulate, or the district court on motion may order, that the district clerk retain the record temporarily for the parties to use in preparing the papers on appeal. In that event the district clerk must certify to the circuit clerk that the record on appeal is complete. Upon receipt of the appellee's brief, or earlier if the court orders or the parties agree, the appellant must request the district clerk to forward the record.

(d) [Abrogated.]

(e) Retaining the Record by Court Order.

(1) The court of appeals may, by order or local rule, provide that a certified copy of the docket entries be forwarded instead of the entire record. But a party may at any time during the appeal request that designated parts of the record be forwarded.

(2) The district court may order the record or some part of it retained if the court needs it while the appeal is pending, subject, however, to call by the court of appeals.

(3) If part or all of the record is ordered retained, the district clerk must send to the court of appeals a copy of the order and the docket entries together with the parts of the original record allowed by the district court and copies of any parts of the record designated by the parties.

(f) Retaining Parts of the Record in the District Court by Stipulation of the Parties. The parties may agree by written stipulation filed in the district court that designated parts of the record be retained in the district court subject to call by the court of appeals or request by a party. The parts of the record so designated remain a part of the record on appeal.

(g) Record for a Preliminary Motion in the Court of Appeals. If, before the record is forwarded, a party makes any of the following motions in the court of appeals:

- for dismissal;
- for release;
- for a stay pending appeal;
- for additional security on the bond on appeal or on a supersedeas bond; or
- for any other intermediate order—

the district clerk must send the court of appeals any parts of the record designated by any party.

(As amended Apr. 30, 1979, eff. Aug. 1, 1979; Mar. 10, 1986, eff. July 1, 1986; Apr. 24, 1998, eff. Dec. 1, 1998.)

ADVISORY COMMITTEE NOTES

1967 Adoption

Subdivisions (a) and (b). These subdivisions are derived from FRCP 73(g) and FRCP 75(e) [rules 73(g) and 75(e), Federal Rules of Civil Procedure]. FRCP 75(e) presently directs the clerk of the district court to transmit the record within the time allowed or fixed for its filing, which, under the provisions of FRCP 73(g) is within 40 days from the date of filing the notice of appeal, unless an extension is obtained from the district court. The precise time at which the record must be transmitted thus depends upon the time required for delivery of the record from the district court to the court of appeals, since, to permit its timely filing, it must reach the court of appeals before expiration of the 40-day period or an extension thereof. Subdivision (a) of this rule provides that the record is to be transmitted within the 40-day period, or any extension thereof; subdivision (b) provides that transmission is effected when the clerk of the district court mails or otherwise forwards the record to the clerk of the court of appeals; Rule 12(b) directs the clerk of the court of appeals to file the record upon its receipt following timely docketing and transmittal. It can thus be determined with certainty precisely when the clerk of the district court must forward the record to the clerk of the court of appeals in order to effect timely filing: the final day of the 40-day period or of any extension thereof.

Subdivision (c). This subdivision is derived from FRCP 75(e) [rule 75(e), Federal Rules of Civil Procedure] without change of substance.

Subdivision (d). This subdivision is derived from FRCP 73(g) [rule 73(g), Federal Rules of Civil Procedure] and FRCrP 39(c) [rule 39(c), Federal Rules of Criminal Procedure]. Under present rules the district court is empowered to extend the time for filing the record and docketing the appeal. Since under the proposed rule timely transmission now insures timely filing (see note to subdivisions (a) and (b) above) the power of the district court is expressed in terms of its power to extend the time for transmitting the record. Restriction of that power to a period of 90 days after the filing of the notice of appeal represents a change in the rule with respect to appeals in criminal cases. FRCrP 39(c) now permits the district court to extend the time for filing and docketing without restriction. No good reason appears for a difference between the civil and criminal rule in this regard, and subdivision (d) limits the power of the district court to extend the time for transmitting the record in all cases to 90 days from the date of filing the notice of appeal, just as its power is now limited with respect to docketing and filing in civil cases. Subdivision (d) makes explicit the power of the court of appeals to permit the record to be filed at any time. See *Pyramid Motor Freight Corporation v. Ispass*, 330 U.S. 695, 67 S.Ct. 954, 91 L.Ed. 1184 (1947).

Subdivisions (e), (f) and (g). These subdivisions are derived from FRCP 75(f) [rule 75(f), Federal Rules of Civil Procedure], (a) and (g), respectively, without change of substance.

1979 Amendment

Under present Rule 11(a) it is provided that the record shall be transmitted to the court of appeals within 40 days after the filing of the notice of appeal. Under present Rule 11(d) the district court, on request made during the initial time or any extension thereof, and cause shown, may extend the time for the transmission of the record to a point not more than 90 days after the filing of the first notice of appeal. If the district court is without authority to grant a request to extend the time, or denies a request for extension, the appellant may make a motion for extension of time in the court of appeals. Thus the duty to see that the record is transmitted is placed on the appellant. Aside from ordering the transcript within the time prescribed the appellant has no control over the time at which the record is transmitted, since all steps beyond this point are in the hands of the reporter and the clerk. The proposed amendments recognize this fact and place the duty directly on the reporter and the clerk. After receiving the written order for the transcript (See Note to Rule 10(b) above), the reporter must acknowledge its receipt, indicate when he expects to have it completed, and mail the order so endorsed to the clerk of the court of appeals. Requests for extensions of time must be made by the reporter to the clerk of the court of appeals and action on such requests is entered on the docket. Thus from the point at which the transcript is ordered the clerk of the court of appeals is made aware of any delays. If the transcript is not filed on time, the clerk of the court of appeals will notify the district judge.

Present Rule 11(b) provides that the record shall be transmitted when it is "complete for the purposes of the appeal." The proposed amended rule continues this requirement. The record is complete for the purposes of the appeal when it contains the original papers on file in the clerk's office, all necessary exhibits, and the transcript, if one is to be included. Cf. present Rule 11(c). The original papers will be in the custody of the clerk of the district court at the time the notice of appeal is filed. See Rule 5(e) of the F.R.C.P. [rule 5(e), Federal Rules of Civil Procedure]. The custody of exhibits is often the subject of local rules. Some of them require that documentary exhibits must be deposited with the clerk. See Local Rule 13 of the Eastern District of Virginia. Others leave exhibits with counsel, subject to order of the court. See Local Rule 33 of the Northern District of Illinois. If under local rules the custody of exhibits is left with counsel, the district court should make adequate provision for their preservation during the time during which an appeal may be taken, the prompt deposit with the clerk of such as under Rule 11(b) are to be transmitted to the court of appeals, and the availability of others in the event that the court of appeals should require their transmission. Cf. Local Rule 11 of the Second Circuit [rule 11, U.S.Ct. of App. 2d Cir.].

Usually the record will be complete with the filing of the transcript. While the proposed amendment requires transmission "forthwith" when the record is complete, it was not designed to preclude a local requirement by the court of appeals that the original papers and exhibits be transmitted when complete without awaiting the filing of the transcript.

The proposed amendments continue the provision in the present rule that documents of unusual bulk or weight and physical exhibits other than documents shall not be transmitted without direction by the parties or by the court of appeals, and the requirement that the parties make special arrangements for transmission and receipt of exhibits of unusual bulk or weight. In addition, they give recognition to local rules that make transmission of other record items subject to order of the court of appeals. See Local Rule 4 of the Seventh Circuit [rule 4, U.S.Ct. of App. 7th Cir., this title].

1986 Amendment

The amendments to Rule 11(b) are technical. No substantive change is intended.

Rule 12. Docketing the Appeal; Filing a Representation Statement; Filing the Record

(a) Docketing the Appeal. Upon receiving the copy of the notice of appeal and the docket entries from the district clerk under Rule 3(d), the circuit clerk must docket the appeal under the title of the district-court action and must identify the appellant, adding the appellant's name if necessary.

(b) Filing a Representation Statement. Unless the court of appeals designates another time, the attorney who filed the notice of appeal must, within 10 days after filing the notice, file a statement with the circuit clerk naming the parties that the attorney represents on appeal.

(c) Filing the Record, Partial Record, or Certificate. Upon receiving the record, partial record, or district clerk's certificate as provided in Rule 11, the circuit clerk must file it and immediately notify all parties of the filing date.

(As amended Apr. 30, 1979, eff. Aug. 1, 1979; Mar. 10, 1986, eff. July 1, 1986; Apr. 22, 1993, eff. Dec. 1, 1993; Apr. 24, 1998, eff. Dec. 1, 1998.)

ADVISORY COMMITTEE NOTES

1967 Adoption

Subdivision (a). All that is involved in the docketing of an appeal is the payment of the docket fee. In practice, after the clerk of the court of appeals receives the record from the clerk of the district court he notifies the appellant of its receipt and requests payment of the fee. Upon receipt of the fee, the clerk enters the appeal upon the docket and files the record. The appellant is allowed to pay the fee at any time within the time allowed or fixed for transmission of the record and thereby to discharge his responsibility for docketing. The final sentence is added in the interest of facilitating future reference and citation and location of cases in indexes. Compare 3d Cir.Rule 10(2) [rule 10(2), U.S.Ct. of App. 3d Cir.]; 4th Cir.Rule 9(8) [rule 9(8), U.S.Ct. of App. 4th Cir.]; 6th Cir.Rule 14(1) [rule 14(1), U.S.Ct. of App. 6th Cir.].

Subdivision (c). The rules of the circuits generally permit the appellee to move for dismissal in the event the appellant fails to effect timely filing of the record. See 1st Cir.Rule 21(3) [rule 21(3), U.S.Ct. of App. 1st Cir.]; 3d Cir.Rule 21(4) [rule 21(4), U.S.Ct. of App. 3d Cir.]; 5th Cir.Rule 16(1) [rule 16(1), U.S.Ct. of App. 5th Cir.]; 8th Cir.Rule 7(d) [rule 7(d), U.S.Ct. of App. 8th Cir.].

1979 Amendments

Subdivision (a). Under present Rule 12(a) the appellant must pay the docket fee within the time fixed for the transmission of the record, and upon timely payment of the fee, the appeal is docketed. The proposed amendment takes the docketing out of the hands of the appellant. The fee is paid at the time the notice of appeal is filed and the appeal is entered on the docket upon receipt of a copy of the notice of appeal and of the docket entries, which are sent to the court of appeals under the provisions of Rule 3(d). This is designed to give the court of appeals control of its docket at the earliest possible time so that within the limits of its facilities and personnel it can screen cases for appropriately different treatment, expedite the proceedings through prehearing conferences or otherwise, and in general plan more effectively for the prompt disposition of cases.

Subdivision (b). The proposed amendment conforms the provision to the changes in Rule 11.

1986 Amendments

The amendment to Rule 12(a) is technical. No substantive change is intended.

1993 Amendments

Note to new subdivision (b). This amendment is a companion to the amendment of Rule 3(c). The Rule 3(c) amendment allows an attorney who represents more than one party on appeal to "specify" the appellants by general description rather than by naming them individually. The requirement added here is that whenever an attorney files a notice of appeal, the attorney must soon thereafter file a statement indicating all parties represented on the appeal by that attorney. Although the notice of appeal is the jurisdictional document and it must clearly indicate who is bringing the appeal, the representation statement will be helpful especially to the court of appeals in identifying the individual appellants.

The rule allows a court of appeals to require the filing of the representation statement at some time other than specified in the rule so that if a court of appeals requires a docketing statement or appearance form the representation statement may be combined with it.

TITLE III. REVIEW OF A DECISION OF THE UNITED STATES TAX COURT

Rule 13. Review of a Decision of the Tax Court

(a) How Obtained; Time for Filing Notice of Appeal.

(1) Review of a decision of the United States Tax Court is commenced by filing a notice of appeal with the Tax Court clerk within 90 days after the entry

of the Tax Court's decision. At the time of filing, the appellant must furnish the clerk with enough copies of the notice to enable the clerk to comply with Rule 3(d). If one party files a timely notice of appeal, any other party may file a notice of appeal within 120 days after the Tax Court's decision is entered.

(2) If, under Tax Court rules, a party makes a timely motion to vacate or revise the Tax Court's decision, the time to file a notice of appeal runs from the entry of the order disposing of the motion or from the entry of a new decision, whichever is later.

(b) Notice of Appeal; How Filed. The notice of appeal may be filed either at the Tax Court clerk's office in the District of Columbia or by mail addressed to the clerk. If sent by mail the notice is considered filed on the postmark date, subject to § 7502 of the Internal Revenue Code, as amended, and the applicable regulations.

(c) Contents of the Notice of Appeal; Service; Effect of Filing and Service. Rule 3 prescribes the contents of a notice of appeal, the manner of service, and the effect of its filing and service. Form 2 in the Appendix of Forms is a suggested form of a notice of appeal.

(d) The Record on Appeal; Forwarding; Filing.

(1) An appeal from the Tax Court is governed by the parts of Rules 10, 11, and 12 regarding the record on appeal from a district court, the time and manner of forwarding and filing, and the docketing in the court of appeals. References in those rules and in Rule 3 to the district court and district clerk are to be read as referring to the Tax Court and its clerk.

(2) If an appeal from a Tax Court decision is taken to more than one court of appeals, the original record must be sent to the court named in the first notice of appeal filed. In an appeal to any other court of appeals, the appellant must apply to that other court to make provision for the record.

(As amended Apr. 30, 1979, eff. Aug. 1, 1979; Apr. 29, 1994, eff. Dec. 1, 1994; Apr. 24, 1998, eff. Dec. 1, 1998.)

ADVISORY COMMITTEE NOTES

1967 Adoption

Subdivision (a). This subdivision effects two changes in practice respecting review of Tax Court decisions: (1) § 7483 of the Internal Revenue Code, 68A Stat. 891, 26 U.S.C. § 7483, provides that review of a Tax Court decision may be obtained by filing a petition for review. The subdivision provides for review by the filing of the simple and familiar notice of appeal used to obtain review of district court judgments; (2) § 7483, supra, requires that a petition for review be filed within 3 months after a decision is rendered, and provides that if a petition is so filed by one party, any other party may file a petition for review within 4 months after the decision is rendered. In the interest of fixing the time for review with precision, the proposed rule substitutes "90 days" and "120 days" for the statutory "3 months" and "4 months", respectively. The power of the Court to regulate these details of practice is clear. Title 28 U.S.C. § 2072, as amended by the Act of November 6, 1966, 80 Stat. 1323 (1 U.S.Code Cong. & Ad. News, p. 1546 (1966)), authorizes the Court to regulate ". . . practice and procedure in proceedings for the review by the courts of appeals of decisions of the Tax Court of the United States. . . ."

The second paragraph states the settled teaching of the case law. See *Robert Louis Stevenson Apartments, Inc. v. C.I.R.*, 337 F.2d 681, 10 A.L.R.3d 112 (8th Cir., 1964); *Denholm & McKay Co. v. C.I.R.*, 132 F.2d 243 (1st Cir., 1942); *Helvering v. Continental Oil Co.*, 63 App.D.C. 5, 68 F.2d 750 (1934); *Burnet v. Lexington Ice & Coal Co.*, 62 F.2d 906 (4th Cir.1933); *Griffiths v. C.I.R.*, 50 F.2d 782 (7th Cir., 1931).

Subdivision (b). The subdivision incorporates the statutory provision (Title 26, U.S.C., § 7502) that timely mailing is to be treated as timely filing. The statute contains special provisions respecting other than ordinary mailing. If the notice of appeal is sent by registered mail, registration is deemed prima facie evidence that the notice was delivered to the clerk of the Tax Court, and the date of registration is deemed the postmark date. If the notice of appeal is sent by certified mail, the effect of certification with respect to prima facie evidence of delivery and the postmark date depends upon regulations of the Secretary of the Treasury. The effect of a postmark made other than by the United States Post Office likewise depends upon regulations of the Secretary. Current regulations are found in 26 CFR § 301.7502–1.

1979 Amendments

The proposed amendment reflects the change in the title of the Tax Court to "United States Tax Court." See 26 U.S.C. § 7441.

1994 Amendments

Subdivision (a). The amendment requires a party filing a notice of appeal to provide the court with sufficient copies of the notice for service on all other parties.

Rule 14. Applicability of Other Rules to the Review of a Tax Court Decision

All provisions of these rules, except Rules 4–9, 15–20, and 22–23, apply to the review of a Tax Court decision.

(As amended Apr. 24, 1998, eff. Dec. 1, 1998.)

ADVISORY COMMITTEE NOTES

1967 Adoption

The proposed rule continues the present uniform practice of the circuits of regulating review of decisions of the Tax Court by the general rules applicable to appeals from judgments of the district courts.

TITLE IV. REVIEW OR ENFORCEMENT OF AN ORDER OF AN ADMINISTRATIVE AGENCY, BOARD, COMMISSION, OR OFFICER

Rule 15. Review or Enforcement of an Agency Order—How Obtained; Intervention

(a) Petition for Review; Joint Petition.

(1) Review of an agency order is commenced by filing, within the time prescribed by law, a petition for review with the clerk of a court of appeals authorized to review the agency order. If their interests make joinder practicable, two or more persons may join in a petition to the same court to review the same order.

(2) The petition must:

(A) name each party seeking review either in the caption or the body of the petition—using such terms as 'et al.,' 'petitioners,' or 'respondents' does not effectively name the parties;

(B) name the agency as a respondent (even though not named in the petition, the United States is a respondent if required by statute); and

(C) specify the order or part thereof to be reviewed.

(3) Form 3 in the Appendix of Forms is a suggested form of a petition for review.

(4) In this rule 'agency' includes an agency, board, commission, or officer; 'petition for review' includes a petition to enjoin, suspend, modify, or otherwise review, or a notice of appeal, whichever form is indicated by the applicable statute.

(b) Application or Cross–Application to Enforce an Order; Answer; Default.

(1) An application to enforce an agency order must be filed with the clerk of a court of appeals authorized to enforce the order. If a petition is filed to review an agency order that the court may enforce, a party opposing the petition may file a cross-application for enforcement.

(2) Within 20 days after the application for enforcement is filed, the respondent must serve on the applicant an answer to the application and file it with the clerk. If the respondent fails to answer in time, the court will enter judgment for the relief requested.

(3) The application must contain a concise statement of the proceedings in which the order was entered, the facts upon which venue is based, and the relief requested.

(c) Service of the Petition or Application. The circuit clerk must serve a copy of the petition for review, or an application or cross-application to enforce an agency order, on each respondent as prescribed by Rule 3(d), unless a different manner of service is prescribed by statute. At the time of filing, the petitioner must:

(1) serve, or have served, a copy on each party admitted to participate in the agency proceedings, except for the respondents;

(2) file with the clerk a list of those so served; and

(3) give the clerk enough copies of the petition or application to serve each respondent.

(d) Intervention. Unless a statute provides another method, a person who wants to intervene in a proceeding under this rule must file a motion for leave to intervene with the circuit clerk and serve a copy on all parties. The motion—or other notice of intervention authorized by statute—must be filed within 30 days after the petition for review is filed and must contain a concise statement of the interest of the moving party and the grounds for intervention.

(e) Payment of Fees. When filing any separate or joint petition for review in a court of appeals, the petitioner must pay the circuit clerk all required fees.

(As amended Apr. 22, 1993, eff. Dec. 1, 1993; Apr. 24, 1998, eff. Dec. 1, 1998.)

ADVISORY COMMITTEE NOTES

1967 Adoption

General Note. The power of the Supreme Court to prescribe rules of practice and procedure for the judicial review or enforcement of orders of administrative agencies, boards, commissions, and officers is conferred by 28 U.S.C. § 2072, as amended by the Act of November 6, 1966, § 1, 80 Stat. 1323 (1 U.S.Code Cong. & Ad. News, p. 1546 (1966). Section 11 of the Hobbs Administrative Orders Review Act of 1950, 64 Stat. 1132, reenacted as 28 U.S.C. § 2352 (28 U.S.C.A. § 2352 (Supp.1966)), repealed by the Act of November 6, 1966, § 4, supra, directed the courts of appeals to adopt and promulgate, subject to approval by the Judicial Conference rules governing practice and procedure in proceedings to review the orders of boards, commissions and officers whose orders were made reviewable in the courts of appeals by the Act. Thereafter, the Judicial Conference approved a uniform rule, and that rule, with minor variations, is now in effect in all circuits. Third Circuit Rule 18 [rule 18, U.S.Ct. of App. 3rd Cir.] is a typical circuit rule, and for convenience it is referred to as the uniform rule in the notes which accompany rules under this Title.

Subdivision (a). The uniform rule (see General Note above) requires that the petition for review contain "a concise statement, in barest outline, of the nature of the proceedings as to which relief is sought, the facts upon which venue is based, the grounds upon which relief is sought, and the relief prayed." That language is derived from § 4 of the Hobbs Administrative Orders Review Act of 1950, 64 Stat. 1130, reenacted as 28 U.S.C. § 2344 (28 U.S.C.A. § 2344 (Supp.

1966)). A few other statutes also prescribe the content of the petition, but the great majority are silent on the point. The proposed rule supersedes 28 U.S.C. § 2344 and other statutory provisions prescribing the form of the petition for review and permits review to be initiated by the filing of a simple petition similar in form to the notice of appeal used in appeals from judgments of district courts. The more elaborate form of petition for review now required is rarely useful either to the litigants or to the courts. There is no effective, reasonable way of obliging petitioners to come to the real issues before those issues are formulated in the briefs. Other provisions of this subdivision are derived from §§ 1 and 2 of the uniform rule.

Subdivision (b). This subdivision is derived from §§ 3, 4 and 5 of the uniform rule.

Subdivision (c). This subdivision is derived from § 1 of the uniform rule.

Subdivision (d). This subdivision is based upon § 6 of the uniform rule. Statutes occasionally permit intervention by the filing of a notice of intention to intervene. The uniform rule does not fix a time limit for intervention, and the only time limits fixed by statute are the 30-day periods found in the Communications Act Amendments, 1952, § 402(e), 66 Stat. 719, 47 U.S.C. § 402(e), and the Sugar Act of 1948, § 205(d), 61 Stat. 927, 7 U.S.C. § 1115(d).

1993 Amendments

Subdivision (a). The amendment is a companion to the amendment of Rule 3(c). Both Rule 3(c) and Rule 15(a) state that a notice of appeal or petition for review must name the parties seeking appellate review. Rule 3(c), however, provides an attorney who represents more than one party on appeal the flexibility to describe the parties in general terms rather than naming them individually. Rule 15(a) does not allow that flexibility; each petitioner must be named. A petition for review of an agency decision is the first filing in any court and, therefore, is analogous to a complaint in which all parties must be named.

Subdivision (e). The amendment adds subdivision (e). Subdivision (e) parallels Rule 3(e) that requires the payment of fees when filing a notice of appeal. The omission of such a requirement from Rule 15 is an apparent oversight. Five circuits have local rules requiring the payment of such fees, see, e.g., Fifth Cir.Loc.R. 15.1, and Fed.Cir.Loc.R. 15(a)(2).

Rule 15.1. Briefs and Oral Argument in a National Labor Relations Board Proceeding

In either an enforcement or a review proceeding, a party adverse to the National Labor Relations Board proceeds first on briefing and at oral argument, unless the court orders otherwise.

(Added Mar. 10, 1986, eff. July 1, 1986, and amended Apr. 24, 1998, eff. Dec. 1, 1998.)

ADVISORY COMMITTEE NOTES

1986 Addition

This rule simply confirms the existing practice in most circuits.

Rule 16. The Record on Review or Enforcement

(a) Composition of the Record. The record on review or enforcement of an agency order consists of:

(1) the order involved;

(2) any findings or report on which it is based; and

(3) the pleadings, evidence, and other parts of the proceedings before the agency.

(b) Omissions From or Misstatements in the Record. The parties may at any time, by stipulation, supply any omission from the record or correct a misstatement, or the court may so direct. If necessary, the court may direct that a supplemental record be prepared and filed.

(As amended Apr. 24, 1998, eff. Dec. 1, 1998.)

ADVISORY COMMITTEE NOTES

1967 Adoption

Subdivision (a) is based upon 28 U.S.C § 2112(b). There is no distinction between the record compiled in the agency proceeding and the record on review; they are one and the same. The record in agency cases is thus the same as that in appeals from the district court—the original papers, transcripts and exhibits in the proceeding below. Subdivision (b) is based upon § 8 of the uniform rule (see General Note following Rule 15).

Rule 17. Filing the Record

(a) Agency to File; Time for Filing; Notice of Filing. The agency must file the record with the circuit clerk within 40 days after being served with a petition for review, unless the statute authorizing review provides otherwise, or within 40 days after it files an application for enforcement unless the respondent fails to answer or the court orders otherwise. The court may shorten or extend the time to file the record. The clerk must notify all parties of the date when the record is filed.

(b) Filing—What Constitutes.

(1) The agency must file:

(A) the original or a certified copy of the entire record or parts designated by the parties; or

(B) a certified list adequately describing all documents, transcripts of testimony, exhibits, and other material constituting the record, or describing those parts designated by the parties.

(2) The parties may stipulate in writing that no record or certified list be filed. The date when the stipulation is filed with the circuit clerk is treated as the date when the record is filed.

(3) The agency must retain any portion of the record not filed with the clerk. All parts of the record retained by the agency are a part of the record on review for all purposes and, if the court or

a party so requests, must be sent to the court regardless of any prior stipulation.

(As amended Apr. 24, 1998, eff. Dec. 1, 1998.)

ADVISORY COMMITTEE NOTES

1967 Adoption

Subdivision (a). This subdivision is based upon § 7 of the uniform rule (see General Note following Rule 15). That rule does not prescribe a time for filing the record in enforcement cases. Forty days are allowed in order to avoid useless preparation of the record or certified list in cases where the application for enforcement is not contested.

Subdivision (b). This subdivision is based upon 28 U.S.C. § 2112 and § 7 of the uniform rule. It permits the agency to file either the record itself or a certified list of its contents. It also permits the parties to stipulate against transmission of designated parts of the record without the fear that an inadvertent stipulation may "diminish" the record. Finally, the parties may, in cases where consultation of the record is unnecessary, stipulate that neither the record nor a certified list of its contents be filed.

Rule 18. Stay Pending Review

(a) Motion for a Stay.

(1) Initial Motion Before the Agency. A petitioner must ordinarily move first before the agency for a stay pending review of its decision or order.

(2) Motion in the Court of Appeals. A motion for a stay may be made to the court of appeals or one of its judges.

(A) The motion must:

(i) show that moving first before the agency would be impracticable; or

(ii) state that, a motion having been made, the agency denied the motion or failed to afford the relief requested and state any reasons given by the agency for its action.

(B) The motion must also include:

(i) the reasons for granting the relief requested and the facts relied on;

(ii) originals or copies of affidavits or other sworn statements supporting facts subject to dispute; and

(iii) relevant parts of the record.

(C) The moving party must give reasonable notice of the motion to all parties.

(D) The motion must be filed with the circuit clerk and normally will be considered by a panel of the court. But in an exceptional case in which time requirements make that procedure impracticable, the motion may be made to and considered by a single judge.

(b) Bond. The court may condition relief on the filing of a bond or other appropriate security.

(As amended Apr. 24, 1998, eff. Dec. 1, 1998.)

ADVISORY COMMITTEE NOTES

1967 Adoption

While this rule has no counterpart in present rules regulating review of agency proceedings, it merely assimilates the procedure for obtaining stays in agency proceedings with that for obtaining stays in appeals from the district courts. The same considerations which justify the requirement of an initial application to the district court for a stay pending appeal support the requirement of an initial application to the agency pending review. See Note accompanying Rule 8. Title 5, U.S.C. § 705 (5 U.S.C.A. § 705 (1966 Pamphlet)), confers general authority on both agencies and reviewing courts to stay agency action pending review. Many of the statutes authorizing review of agency action by the courts of appeals deal with the question of stays, and at least one, the Act of June 15, 1936, 49 Stat. 1499 (7 U.S.C. § 10a), prohibits a stay pending review. The proposed rule in nowise affects such statutory provisions respecting stays. By its terms, it simply indicates the procedure to be followed when a stay is sought.

Rule 19. Settlement of a Judgment Enforcing an Agency Order in Part

When the court files an opinion directing entry of judgment enforcing the agency's order in part, the agency must within 14 days file with the clerk and serve on each other party a proposed judgment conforming to the opinion. A party who disagrees with the agency's proposed judgment must within 7 days file with the clerk and serve the agency with a proposed judgment that the party believes conforms to the opinion. The court will settle the judgment and direct entry without further hearing or argument.

(As amended Mar. 10, 1986, eff. July 1, 1986; Apr. 24, 1998, eff. Dec. 1, 1998.)

ADVISORY COMMITTEE NOTES

1967 Adoption

This is § 12 of the uniform rule (see General Note following Rule 15) with changes in phraseology.

1986 Amendment

The deletion of the words "in whole or" is designed to eliminate delay in the issuance of a judgment when the court of appeals has either enforced completely the order of an agency or denied completely such enforcement. In such a clear-cut situation, it serves no useful purpose to delay the issuance of the judgment until a proposed judgment is submitted by the agency and reviewed by the respondent. This change conforms the Rule to the existing practice in most circuits. Other amendments are technical and no substantive change is intended.

Rule 20. Applicability of Rules to the Review or Enforcement of an Agency Order

All provisions of these rules, except Rules 3–14 and 22–23, apply to the review or enforcement of an agency order. In these rules, 'appellant' includes a petitioner or applicant, and 'appellee' includes a respondent.

(As amended Apr. 24, 1998, eff. Dec. 1, 1998.)

ADVISORY COMMITTEE NOTES

1967 Adoption

The proposed rule continues the present uniform practice of the circuits of regulating agency review or enforcement proceedings by the general rules applicable to appeals from judgments of the district courts.

TITLE V. EXTRAORDINARY WRITS

Rule 21. Writs of Mandamus and Prohibition, and Other Extraordinary Writs

(a) Mandamus or Prohibition to a Court: Petition, Filing, Service, and Docketing.

(1) A party petitioning for a writ of mandamus or prohibition directed to a court must file a petition with the circuit clerk with proof of service on all parties to the proceeding in the trial court. The party must also provide a copy to the trial-court judge. All parties to the proceeding in the trial court other than the petitioner are respondents for all purposes.

(2)(A) The petition must be titled 'In re [name of petitioner].'

(B) The petition must state:

(i) the relief sought;

(ii) the issues presented;

(iii) the facts necessary to understand the issue presented by the petition; and

(iv) the reasons why the writ should issue.

(C) The petition must include a copy of any order or opinion or parts of the record that may be essential to understand the matters set forth in the petition.

(3) Upon receiving the prescribed docket fee, the clerk must docket the petition and submit it to the court.

(b) Denial; Order Directing Answer; Briefs; Precedence.

(1) The court may deny the petition without an answer. Otherwise, it must order the respondent, if any, to answer within a fixed time.

(2) The clerk must serve the order to respond on all persons directed to respond.

(3) Two or more respondents may answer jointly.

(4) The court of appeals may invite or order the trial-court judge to address the petition or may invite an amicus curiae to do so. The trial-court judge may request permission to address the petition but may not do so unless invited or ordered to do so by the court of appeals.

(5) If briefing or oral argument is required, the clerk must advise the parties, and when appropriate, the trial-court judge or amicus curiae.

(6) The proceeding must be given preference over ordinary civil cases.

(7) The circuit clerk must send a copy of the final disposition to the trial-court judge.

(c) Other Extraordinary Writs. An application for an extraordinary writ other than one provided for in Rule 21(a) must be made by filing a petition with the circuit clerk with proof of service on the respondents. Proceedings on the application must conform, so far as is practicable, to the procedures prescribed in Rule 21(a) and (b).

(d) Form of Papers; Number of Copies. All papers must conform to Rule 32(a)(1). An original and 3 copies must be filed unless the court requires the filing of a different number by local rule or by order in a particular case.

(As amended Apr. 29, 1994, eff. Dec. 1, 1994; Apr. 23, 1996, eff. Dec. 1, 1996; Apr. 24, 1998, eff. Dec. 1, 1998.)

ADVISORY COMMITTEE NOTES

1967 Adoption

The authority of courts of appeals to issue extraordinary writs is derived from 28 U.S.C. § 1651. Subdivisions (a) and (b) regulate in detail the procedure surrounding the writs most commonly sought—mandamus or prohibition directed to a judge or judges. Those subdivisions are based upon Supreme Court Rule 31, with certain changes which reflect the uniform practice among the circuits (Seventh Circuit Rule 19 is a typical circuit rule). Subdivision (c) sets out a very general procedure to be followed in applications for the variety of other writs which may be issued under the authority of 28 U.S.C. § 1651.

1994 Amendments

Subdivision (d). The amendment makes it clear that a court may require a different number of copies either by rule or by order in an individual case. The number of copies of any document that a court of appeals needs varies depending upon the way in which the court conducts business. The internal operation of the courts of appeals necessarily varies from circuit to circuit because of differences in the number of judges, the geographic area included within the circuit, and other such factors. Uniformity could be achieved only by setting the number of copies artificially high so that parties in all circuits file enough copies to satisfy the needs of the courts requiring the greatest number. Rather than do that, the Committee decided to make it clear that local rules may require a greater or lesser number of copies and that, if the circumstances of a particular case indicate the need for a different number of copies in that case, the court may so order.

1996 Amendments

In most instances, a writ of mandamus or prohibition is not actually directed to a judge in any more personal way than is an order reversing a court's judgment. Most often a petition for a writ of mandamus seeks review of the intrinsic merits of a judge's action and is in reality an adversary proceeding between the parties. See, *e.g.*, *Walker v. Columbia Broadcasting System, Inc.*, 443 F.2d 33 (7th Cir.1971). In order to change the tone of the rule and of mandamus proceedings generally, the rule is amended so that the judge is not treated as a respondent. The caption and subdivision (a) are amended by deleting the reference to the writs as being "directed to a judge or judges."

Subdivision (a). Subdivision (a) applies to writs of mandamus or prohibition directed to a court, but it is amended so that a petition for a writ of mandamus or prohibition does not bear the name of the judge. The amendments to subdivision (a) speak, however, about mandamus or prohibition "directed to a court." This language is inserted to distinguish subdivision (a) from subdivision (c). Subdivision (c) governs all other extraordinary writs, including a writ of mandamus or prohibition directed to an administrative agency rather than to a court and a writ of habeas corpus.

The amendments require the petitioner to provide a copy of the petition to the trial court judge. This will alert the judge to the filing of the petition. This is necessary because the trial court judge is not treated as a respondent and, as a result, is not served. A companion amendment is made in subdivision (b). It requires the circuit clerk to send a copy of the disposition of the petition to the trial court judge.

Subdivision (b). The amendment provides that even if relief is requested of a particular judge, although the judge may request permission to respond, the judge may not do so unless the court invites or orders a response.

The court of appeals ordinarily will be adequately informed not only by the opinions or statements made by the trial court judge contemporaneously with the entry of the challenged order but also by the arguments made on behalf of the party opposing the relief. The latter does not create an attorney-client relationship between the party's attorney and the judge whose action is challenged, nor does it give rise to any right to compensation from the judge.

If the court of appeals desires to hear from the trial court judge, however, the court may invite or order the judge to respond. In some instances, especially those involving court administration or the failure of a judge to act, it may be that no one other than the judge can provide a thorough explanation of the matters at issue. Because it is ordinarily undesirable to place the trial court judge, even temporarily, in an adversarial posture with a litigant, the rule permits a court of appeals to invite an *amicus curiae* to provide a response to the petition. In those instances in which the respondent does not oppose issuance of the writ or does not have sufficient perspective on the issue to provide an adequate response, participation of an *amicus* may avoid the need for the trial judge to participate.

Subdivision (c). The changes are stylistic only. No substantive changes are intended.

TITLE VI. HABEAS CORPUS; PROCEEDINGS IN FORMA PAUPERIS

Rule 22. Habeas Corpus and Section 2255 Proceedings

(a) Application for the Original Writ. An application for a writ of habeas corpus must be made to the appropriate district court. If made to a circuit judge, the application must be transferred to the appropriate district court. If a district court denies an application made or transferred to it, renewal of the application before a circuit judge is not permitted. The applicant may, under 28 U.S.C. § 2253, appeal to the court of appeals from the district court's order denying the application.

(b) Certificate of Appealability.

(1) In a habeas corpus proceeding in which the detention complained of arises from process issued by a state court, or in a 28 U.S.C. § 2255 proceeding, the applicant cannot take an appeal unless a circuit justice or a circuit or district judge issues a certificate of appealability under 28 U.S.C. § 2253(c). If an applicant files a notice of appeal, the district judge who rendered the judgment must either issue a certificate of appealability or state why a certificate should not issue. The district clerk must send the certificate or statement to the court of appeals with the notice of appeal and the file of the district-court proceedings. If the district judge has denied the certificate, the applicant may request a circuit judge to issue the certificate.

(2) A request addressed to the court of appeals may be considered by a circuit judge or judges, as the court prescribes. If no express request for a certificate is filed, the notice of appeal constitutes a request addressed to the judges of the court of appeals.

(3) A certificate of appealability is not required when a state or its representative or the United States or its representative appeals.

(As amended Pub.L. 104–132, Title I, § 103, Apr. 24, 1996, 110 Stat. 1218; Apr. 24, 1998, eff. Dec. 1, 1998.)

ADVISORY COMMITTEE NOTES

1967 Adoption

Subdivision (a). Title 28 U.S.C. § 2241(a) authorizes circuit judges to issue the writ of habeas corpus. Section 2241(b) [§ 2241(b) of this title], however, authorizes a circuit judge to decline to entertain an application and to transfer it to the appropriate district court, and this is the usual practice. The first two sentences merely make present practice explicit. Title 28 U.S.C. § 2253 seems clearly to contemplate that once an application is presented to a district judge and is denied by him, the remedy is an appeal from the order of denial. But the language of 28 U.S.C. § 2241 seems to authorize a second original application to a circuit judge following a denial by a district judge. *In re Gersing*, 79 U.S.App.D. 245, 145 F.2d 481 (D.C.Cir., 1944) and *Chapman v. Teets*, 241 F.2d 186 (9th Cir., 1957) acknowledge the availability of such a procedure. But the procedure is ordinarily a waste of time for all involved, and the final sentence attempts to discourage it.

A court of appeals has no jurisdiction as a court to grant an original writ of habeas corpus, and courts of appeals have dismissed applications addressed to them. *Loum v. Alvis*, 263 F.2d 836 (6th Cir., 1959); *In re Berry*, 221 F.2d 798 (9th Cir., 1955); *Posey v. Dowd*, 134 F.2d 613 (7th Cir., 1943). The fairer and more expeditious practice is for the court of appeals to regard an application addressed to it as being addressed to one of its members, and to transfer the application to the appropriate district court in accordance with the provisions of this rule. Perhaps such a disposition is required by the rationale of *In re Burwell*, 350 U.S. 521, 76 S.Ct. 539, 100 L.Ed. 666 (1956).

Subdivision (b). Title 28 U.S.C. § 2253 provides that an appeal may not be taken in a habeas corpus proceeding where confinement is under a judgment of a state court unless the judge who rendered the order in the habeas corpus proceeding, or a circuit justice or judge, issues a certificate of probable cause. In the interest of insuring that the matter of the certificate will not be overlooked and that, if the certificate is denied, the reasons for denial in the first instance will be available on any subsequent application, the proposed rule requires the district judge to issue the certificate or to state reasons for its denial.

While 28 U.S.C. § 2253 does not authorize the court of appeals as a court to grant a certificate of probable cause, *In re Burwell*, 350 U.S. 521, 76 S.Ct. 539, 100 L.Ed. 666 (1956) makes it clear that a court of appeals may not decline to consider a request for the certificate addressed to it as a court but must regard the request as made to the judges thereof. The fourth sentence incorporates the Burwell rule.

Although 28 U.S.C. § 2253 appears to require a certificate of probable cause even when an appeal is taken by a state or its representative, the legislative history strongly suggests that the intention of Congress was to require a certificate only in the case in which an appeal is taken by an applicant for the writ. See *United States ex rel. Tillery v. Cavell*, 294 F.2d 12 (3d Cir., 1960). Four of the five circuits which have ruled on the point have so interpreted § 2253. *United States ex rel. Tillery v. Cavell*, supra; *Buder v. Bell*, 306 F.2d 71 (6th Cir., 1962); *United States ex rel. Calhoun v. Pate*, 341 F.2d 885 (7th Cir., 1965); *State of Texas v. Graves*, 352 F.2d 514 (5th Cir., 1965). Cf. *United States ex rel. Carrol v. LaVallee*, 342 F.2d 641 (2d Cir., 1965). The final sentence makes it clear that a certificate of probable cause is not required of a state or its representative.

Rule 23. Custody or Release of a Prisoner in a Habeas Corpus Proceeding

(a) Transfer of Custody Pending Review. Pending review of a decision in a habeas corpus proceeding commenced before a court, justice, or judge of the United States for the release of a prisoner, the person having custody of the prisoner must not transfer custody to another unless a transfer is directed in accordance with this rule. When, upon application, a custodian shows the need for a transfer, the court, justice, or judge rendering the decision under review may authorize the transfer and substitute the successor custodian as a party.

(b) Detention or Release Pending Review of Decision Not to Release. While a decision not to release a prisoner is under review, the court or judge rendering the decision, or the court of appeals, or the Supreme Court, or a judge or justice of either court, may order that the prisoner be:

(1) detained in the custody from which release is sought;

(2) detained in other appropriate custody; or

(3) released on personal recognizance, with or without surety.

(c) Release Pending Review of Decision Ordering Release. While a decision ordering the release of a prisoner is under review, the prisoner must—unless the court or judge rendering the decision, or the court of appeals, or the Supreme Court, or a judge or justice of either court orders otherwise—be released on personal recognizance, with or without surety.

(d) Modification of the Initial Order on Custody. An initial order governing the prisoner's custody or release, including any recognizance or surety, continues in effect pending review unless for special reasons shown to the court of appeals or the Supreme Court, or to a judge or justice of either court, the order is modified or an independent order regarding custody, release, or surety is issued.

(As amended Mar. 10, 1986, eff. July 1, 1986; Apr. 24, 1998, eff. Dec. 1, 1998.)

ADVISORY COMMITTEE NOTES

1967 Adoption

The rule is the same as Supreme Court Rule 49 as amended on June 12, 1967, effective October 2, 1967.

1986 Amendment

The amendments to Rules 23(b) and (c) are technical. No substantive change is intended.

Rule 24. Proceeding in Forma Pauperis

(a) Leave to Proceed in Forma Pauperis.

(1) Motion in the District Court. Except as stated in Rule 24(a)(3), a party to a district-court action who desires to appeal in forma pauperis must file a motion in the district court. The party must attach an affidavit that:

(A) shows in the detail prescribed by Form 4 of the Appendix of Forms, the party's inability to pay or to give security for fees and costs;

(B) claims an entitlement to redress; and

(C) states the issues that the party intends to present on appeal.

(2) Action on the Motion. If the district court grants the motion, the party may proceed on appeal without prepaying or giving security for fees and costs. If the district court denies the motion, it must state its reasons in writing.

(3) Prior Approval. A party who was permitted to proceed in forma pauperis in the district-court action, or who was determined to be financially unable to obtain an adequate defense in a criminal case, may proceed on appeal in forma pauperis without further authorization, unless the district court—before or after the notice of appeal is filed—certifies that the appeal is not taken in good faith or finds that the party is not otherwise entitled to proceed in forma pauperis. In that event, the district court must state in writing its reasons for the certification or finding.

(4) Notice of District Court's Denial. The district clerk must immediately notify the parties and the court of appeals when the district court does any of the following:

(A) denies a motion to proceed on appeal in forma pauperis;

(B) certifies that the appeal is not taken in good faith; or

(C) finds that the party is not otherwise entitled to proceed in forma pauperis.

(5) Motion in the Court of Appeals. A party may file a motion to proceed on appeal in forma pauperis in the court of appeals within 30 days after service of the notice prescribed in Rule 24(a)(4). The motion must include a copy of the affidavit filed in the district court and the district court's statement of reasons for its action. If no affidavit was filed in the district court, the party must include the affidavit prescribed by Rule 24(a)(1).

(b) Leave to Proceed in Forma Pauperis on Appeal or Review of an Administrative–Agency Proceeding. When an appeal or review of a proceeding before an administrative agency, board, commission, or officer (including for the purpose of this rule the United States Tax Court) proceeds directly in a court of appeals, a party may file in the court of appeals a motion for leave to proceed on appeal in forma pauperis with an affidavit prescribed by Rule 24(a)(1).

(c) Leave to Use Original Record. A party allowed to proceed on appeal in forma pauperis may request that the appeal be heard on the original record without reproducing any part.

(As amended Apr. 30, 1979, eff. Aug. 1, 1979; Mar. 10, 1986, eff. July 1, 1986; Apr. 24, 1998, eff. Dec. 1, 1998.)

ADVISORY COMMITTEE NOTES

1967 Adoption

Subdivision (a). Authority to allow prosecution of an appeal in forma pauperis is vested in "[a]ny court of the United States" by 28 U.S.C. § 1915(a). The second paragraph of § 1915(a) seems to contemplate initial application to the district court for permission to proceed in forma pauperis, and although the circuit rules are generally silent on the question, the case law requires initial application to the district court. *Hayes v. United States*, 258 F.2d 400 (5th Cir., 1958), cert. den. 358 U.S. 856, 79 S.Ct. 87, 3 L.Ed.2d 89 (1958); *Elkins v. United States*, 250 F.2d 145 (9th Cir., 1957) see 364 U.S. 206, 80 S.Ct. 1437, 4 L.Ed.2d 1669 (1960); *United States v. Farley*, 238 F.2d 575 (2d Cir., 1956) see 354 U.S. 521, 77 S.Ct. 1371, 1 L.Ed.2d 1529 (1957). D.C.Cir. Rule 41(a) requires initial application to the district court. The content of the affidavit follows the language of the statute; the requirement of a statement of the issues comprehends the statutory requirement of a statement of "the nature of the . . . appeal. . . ." The second sentence is in accord with the decision in *McGann v. United States*, 362 U.S. 309, 80 S.Ct. 725, 4 L.Ed.2d 734 (1960). The requirement contained in the third sentence has no counterpart in present circuit rules, but it has been imposed by decision in at least two circuits. *Ragan v. Cox*, 305 F.2d 58 (10th Cir., 1962); *United States ex rel. Breedlove v. Dowd*, 269 F.2d 693 (7th Cir., 1959).

The second paragraph permits one whose indigency has been previously determined by the district court to proceed on appeal in forma pauperis without the necessity of a redetermination of indigency, while reserving to the district court its statutory authority to certify that the appeal is not taken in good faith, 28 U.S.C. § 1915(a), and permitting an inquiry into whether the circumstances of the party who was originally entitled to proceed in forma pauperis have changed during the course of the litigation. Cf. Sixth Circuit Rule 26 [rule 26, U.S.Ct. of App. 6th Cir.].

The final paragraph establishes a subsequent motion in the court of appeals, rather than an appeal from the order of denial or from the certification of lack of good faith, as the proper procedure for calling in question the correctness of the action of the district court. The simple and expeditious motion procedure seems clearly preferable to an appeal. This paragraph applies only to applications for leave to appeal in forma pauperis. The order of a district court refusing leave to initiate an action in the district court in forma pauperis is reviewable on appeal. See *Roberts v. United States District Court*, 339 U.S. 844, 70 S.Ct. 954, 94 L.Ed. 1326 (1950).

Subdivision (b). Authority to allow prosecution in forma pauperis is vested only in a "court of the United States" (see Note to subdivision (a), above). Thus in proceedings brought directly in a court of appeals to review decisions of agencies or of the Tax Court, authority to proceed in forma pauperis should be sought in the court of appeals. If initial review of agency action is had in a district court, an application to appeal to a court of appeals in forma pauperis from the judgment of the district court is governed by the provisions of subdivision (a).

1979 Amendment

The proposed amendment reflects the change in the title of the Tax Court to "United States Tax Court." See 26 U.S.C. § 7441.

1986 Amendment

The amendments to Rule 24(a) are technical. No substantive change is intended.

TITLE VII. GENERAL PROVISIONS

Rule 25. Filing and Service

(a) Filing.

(1) Filing with the Clerk. A paper required or permitted to be filed in a court of appeals must be filed with the clerk.

(2) Filing: Method and Timeliness.

(A) In general. Filing may be accomplished by mail addressed to the clerk, but filing is not timely unless the clerk receives the papers within the time fixed for filing.

(B) A brief or appendix. A brief or appendix is timely filed, however, if on or before the last day for filing, it is:

(i) mailed to the clerk by First–Class Mail, or other class of mail that is at least as expeditious, postage prepaid; or

(ii) dispatched to a third-party commercial carrier for delivery to the clerk within 3 calendar days.

(C) Inmate filing. A paper filed by an inmate confined in an institution is timely if deposited in the institution's internal mailing system on or before the last day for filing. If an institution has a system designed for legal mail, the inmate must use that system to receive the benefit of this rule. Timely filing may be shown by a declaration in compliance with 28 U.S.C. § 1746 or by a notarized statement, either of which must set forth the date of deposit and state that first-class postage has been prepaid.

(D) Electronic filing. A court of appeals may by local rule permit papers to be filed, signed, or verified by electronic means that are consistent with technical standards, if any, that the Judicial Conference of the United States establishes. A paper filed by electronic means in compliance with a local rule constitutes a written paper for the purpose of applying these rules.

(3) Filing a Motion with a Judge. If a motion requests relief that may be granted by a single judge, the judge may permit the motion to be filed with the judge; the judge must note the filing date on the motion and give it to the clerk.

(4) Clerk's Refusal of Documents. The clerk must not refuse to accept for filing any paper presented for that purpose solely because it is not presented in proper form as required by these rules or by any local rule or practice.

(b) Service of All Papers Required. Unless a rule requires service by the clerk, a party must, at or before the time of filing a paper, serve a copy on the other parties to the appeal or review. Service on a party represented by counsel must be made on the party's counsel.

(c) Manner of Service. Service may be personal, by mail, or by third-party commercial carrier for delivery within 3 calendar days. When reasonable considering such factors as the immediacy of the relief sought, distance, and cost, service on a party must be by a manner at least as expeditious as the manner used to file the paper with the court. Personal service includes delivery of the copy to a responsible person at the office of counsel. Service by mail or by commercial carrier is complete on mailing or delivery to the carrier.

(d) Proof of Service.

(1) A paper presented for filing must contain either of the following:

(A) an acknowledgment of service by the person served; or

(B) proof of service consisting of a statement by the person who made service certifying:

(i) the date and manner of service;

(ii) the names of the persons served; and

(iii) their mailing addresses or the addresses of the places of delivery.

(2) When a brief or appendix is filed by mailing or dispatch in accordance with Rule 25(a)(2)(B), the proof of service must also state the date and manner by which the document was mailed or dispatched to the clerk.

(3) Proof of service may appear on or be affixed to the papers filed.

(e) Number of Copies. When these rules require the filing or furnishing of a number of copies, a court may require a different number by local rule or by order in a particular case.

(As amended Mar. 10, 1986, eff. July 1, 1986; Apr. 30, 1991, eff. Dec. 1, 1991; Apr. 22, 1993, eff. Dec. 1, 1993; Apr. 29, 1994, eff. Dec. 1, 1994; Apr. 23, 1996, eff. Dec. 1, 1996; Apr. 24, 1998, eff. Dec. 1, 1998.)

ADVISORY COMMITTEE NOTES

1967 Adoption

The rule that filing is not timely unless the papers filed are received within the time allowed is the familiar one. *Ward v.*

Atlantic Coast Line R.R. Co., 265 F.2d 75 (5th Cir., 1959), rev'd on other grounds 362 U.S. 396, 80 S.Ct. 789, 4 L.Ed.2d 820 (1960); *Kahler-Ellis Co. v. Ohio Turnpike Commission*, 225 F.2d 922 (6th Cir., 1955). An exception is made in the case of briefs and appendices in order to afford the parties the maximum time for their preparation. By the terms of the exception, air mail delivery must be used whenever it is the most expeditious manner of delivery.

A majority of the circuits now require service of all papers filed with the clerk. The usual provision in present rules is for service on "adverse" parties. In view of the extreme simplicity of service by mail, there seems to be no reason why a party who files a paper should not be required to serve all parties to the proceeding in the court of appeals, whether or not they may be deemed adverse. The common requirement of proof of service is retained, but the rule permits it to be made by simple certification, which may be endorsed on the copy which is filed.

1986 Amendment

The amendments to Rules 25(a) and (b) are technical. No substantive change is intended.

1991 Amendment

Subdivision (a). The amendment permits, but does not require, courts of appeals to adopt local rules that allow filing of papers by electronic means. However, courts of appeals cannot adopt such local rules until the Judicial Conference of the United States authorizes filing by facsimile or other electronic means.

1993 Amendment

The amendment accompanies new subdivision (c) of Rule 4 and extends the holding in *Houston v. Lack*, 487 U.S. 266 (1988), to all papers filed in the courts of appeals by persons confined in institutions.

1994 Amendment

Subdivision (a). Several circuits have local rules that authorize the office of the clerk to refuse to accept for filing papers that are not in the form required by these rules or by local rules. This is not a suitable role for the office of the clerk and the practice exposes litigants to the hazards of time bars; for these reasons, such rules are proscribed by this rule. This provision is similar to Fed.R.Civ.P. 5(e) and Fed.R.Bankr.P. 5005.

The Committee wishes to make it clear that the provision prohibiting a clerk from refusing a document does not mean that a clerk's office may no longer screen documents to determine whether they comply with the rules. A court may delegate to the clerk authority to inform a party about any noncompliance with the rules and, if the party is willing to correct the document, to determine a date by which the corrected document must be resubmitted. If a party refuses to take the steps recommended by the clerk or if in the clerk's judgment the party fails to correct the noncompliance, the clerk must refer the matter to the court for a ruling.

Subdivision (d). Two changes have been made in this subdivision. Subdivision (d) provides that a paper presented for filing must contain proof of service.

The last sentence of subdivision (d) has been deleted as unnecessary. That sentence stated that a clerk could permit papers to be filed without the acknowledgment or proof of service but must require that it be filed promptly thereafter. In light of the change made in subdivision (a) which states that a clerk may not refuse to accept for filing a document because it is not in the proper form, there is no further need for a provision stating that a clerk may accept a paper lacking a proof of service. The clerk must accept such a paper. That portion of the deleted sentence stating that the clerk must require that proof of service be filed promptly after the filing of the document if the proof is not filed concurrently with the document is also unnecessary.

The second amendment requires that the certificate of service must state the addresses to which the papers were mailed or at which they were delivered. The Federal Circuit has a similar local rule, Fed.Cir.R. 25.

Subdivision (e). Subdivision (e) is a new subdivision. It makes it clear that whenever these rules require a party to file or furnish a number of copies a court may require a different number of copies either by rule or by order in an individual case. The number of copies of any document that a court of appeals needs varies depending upon the way in which the court conducts business. The internal operation of the courts of appeals necessarily varies from circuit to circuit because of differences in the number of judges, the geographic area included within the circuit, and other such factors. Uniformity could be achieved only by setting the number of copies artificially high so that parties in all circuits file enough copies to satisfy the needs of the court requiring the greatest number. Rather than do that, the Committee decided to make it clear that local rules may require a greater or lesser number of copies and that, if the circumstances of a particular case indicate the need for a different number of copies in that case, the court may so order.

A party must consult local rules to determine whether the court requires a different number than that specified in these national rules. The Committee believes it would be helpful if each circuit either: 1) included a chart at the beginning of its local rules showing the number of copies of each document required to be filed with the court along with citation to the controlling rule; or 2) made available such a chart to each party upon commencement of an appeal; or both. If a party fails to file the required number of copies, the failure does not create a jurisdictional defect. Rule 3(a) states: "Failure of an appellant to take any step other than the timely filing of a notice of appeal does not affect the validity of the appeal, but is ground only for such action as the court of appeals deems appropriate...."

1996 Amendments

Subdivision (a). The amendment deletes the language requiring a party to use "the most expeditious form of delivery by mail, except special delivery" in order to file a brief using the mailbox rule. That language was adopted before the Postal Service offered Express Mail and other expedited delivery services. The amendment makes it clear that it is sufficient to use First–Class Mail. Other equally or more expeditious classes of mail service, such as Express Mail, also may be used. In addition, the amendment permits the use of commercial carriers. The use of private, overnight courier services has become commonplace in law practice. Expedited services offered by commercial carriers often provide faster delivery than First-Class Mail; therefore, there should be no objection to the use of commercial carriers as long as they are reliable. In order to make use of the mailbox rule when using a commercial carrier, the amendment requires that the filer employ a carrier who undertakes to deliver the document in no more than three calendar days. The three-calendar-day period coordinates with the three-day extension provided by Rule 26(c).

Subdivision (c). The amendment permits service by commercial carrier if the carrier is to deliver the paper to the party being served within three days of the carrier's receipt of the paper. The amendment also expresses a desire that when reasonable, service on a party be accomplished by a manner as expeditious as the manner used to file the paper with the court. When a brief or motion is filed with the court by hand delivering the paper to the clerk's office, or by overnight courier, the copies should be served on the other parties by an equally expeditious manner—meaning either by personal service, if distance permits, or by overnight courier, if mail delivery to the party is not ordinarily accomplished overnight. The reasonableness standard is included so that if a paper is hand delivered to the clerk's office for filing but the other parties must be served in a different city, state, or region, personal service on them ordinarily will not be expected. If use of an equally expeditious manner of service is not reasonable, use of the next most expeditious manner may be. For example, if the paper is filed by hand delivery to the clerk's office but the other parties reside in distant cities, service on them need not be personal but in most instances should be by overnight courier. Even that may not be required, however, if the number of parties that must be served would make the use of overnight service too costly. A factor that bears upon the reasonableness of serving parties expeditiously is the immediacy of the relief requested.

Subdivision (d). The amendment adds a requirement that when a brief or appendix is filed by mail or commercial carrier, the certificate of service state the date and manner by which the document was mailed or dispatched to the clerk. Including that information in the certificate of service avoids the necessity for a separate certificate concerning the date and manner of filing.

Rule 26. Computing and Extending Time

(a) Computing Time. The following rules apply in computing any period of time specified in these rules or in any local rule, court order, or applicable statute:

(1) Exclude the day of the act, event, or default that begins the period.

(2) Exclude intermediate Saturdays, Sundays, and legal holidays when the period is less than 7 days, unless stated in calendar days.

(3) Include the last day of the period unless it is a Saturday, Sunday, legal holiday, or—if the act to be done is filing a paper in court—a day on which the weather or other conditions make the clerk's office inaccessible.

(4) As used in this rule, "legal holiday" means New Year's Day, Martin Luther King, Jr.'s Birthday, Presidents' Day, Memorial Day, Independence Day, Labor Day, Columbus Day, Veterans' Day, Thanksgiving Day, Christmas Day, and any other day declared a holiday by the President, Congress, or the state in which is located either the district court that rendered the challenged judgment or order, or the circuit clerk's principal office.

(b) Extending Time. For good cause, the court may extend the time prescribed by these rules or by its order to perform any act, or may permit an act to be done after that time expires. But the court may not extend the time to file:

(1) a notice of appeal (except as authorized in Rule 4) or a petition for permission to appeal; or

(2) a notice of appeal from or a petition to enjoin, set aside, suspend, modify, enforce, or otherwise review an order of an administrative agency, board, commission, or officer of the United States, unless specifically authorized by law.

(c) Additional Time after Service. When a party is required or permitted to act within a prescribed period after a paper is served on that party, 3 calendar days are added to the prescribed period unless the paper is delivered on the date of service stated in the proof of service.

(As amended Mar. 1, 1971, eff. July 1, 1971; Mar. 10, 1986, eff. July 1, 1986; Apr. 25, 1989, eff. Dec. 1, 1989; Apr. 30, 1991, eff. Dec. 1, 1991; Apr. 23, 1996, eff. Dec. 1, 1996; Apr. 24, 1998, eff. Dec. 1, 1998.)

ADVISORY COMMITTEE NOTES

1967 Adoption

The provisions of this rule are based upon FRCP 6(a), (b) and (e) [rule 6(a), (b) and (e), Federal Rules of Civil Procedure]. See also Supreme Court Rule 34 and FRCrP 45 [rule 45, Federal Rules of Criminal Procedure]. Unlike FRCP 6(b), this rule, read with Rule 27, requires that every request for enlargement of time be made by motion, with proof of service on all parties. This is the simplest, most convenient way of keeping all parties advised of developments. By the terms of Rule 27(b) a motion for enlargement of time under Rule 26(b) may be entertained and acted upon immediately, subject to the right of any party to seek reconsideration. Thus the requirement of motion and notice will not delay the granting of relief of a kind which a court is inclined to grant as of course. Specifically, if a court is of the view that an extension of time sought before expiration of the period originally prescribed or as extended by a previous order ought to be granted in effect ex parte, as FRCP 6(b) permits, it may grant motions seeking such relief without delay.

1971 Amendments

The amendment adds Columbus Day to the list of legal holidays to conform the subdivision to the Act of June 28, 1968, 82 Stat. 250, which constituted Columbus Day a legal holiday effective after January 1, 1971.

The Act, which amended Title 5, U.S.C. § 6103(a), changes the day on which certain holidays are to be observed. Washington's Birthday, Memorial Day and Veterans Day are to be observed on the third Monday in February, the last Monday in May and the fourth Monday in October, respectively, rather than, as heretofore, on February 22, May 30, and November 11, respectively. Columbus Day is to be observed on the second Monday in October. New Year's Day, Independence Day, Thanksgiving Day and Christmas continue to be observed on the traditional days.

1986 Amendments

The Birthday of Martin Luther King, Jr. is added to the list of national holidays in Rule 26(a). The amendment to Rule 26(c) is technical. No substantive change is intended.

1989 Amendments

The proposed amendment brings Rule 26(a) into conformity with the provisions of Rule 6(a) of the Rules of Civil Procedure, Rule 45(a) of the Rules of Criminal Procedure, and Rule 9006(a) of the Rules of Bankruptcy Procedure which allow additional time for filing whenever a clerk's office is inaccessible on the last day for filing due to weather or other conditions.

1996 Amendments

The amendment is a companion to the proposed amendments to Rule 25 that permit service on a party by commercial carrier. The amendments to subdivision (c) of this rule make the three-day extension applicable not only when service is accomplished by mail, but whenever delivery to the party being served occurs later than the date of service stated in the proof of service. When service is by mail or commercial carrier, the proof of service recites the date of mailing or delivery to the commercial carrier. If the party being served receives the paper on a later date, the three-day extension applies. If the party being served receives the paper on the same date as the date of service recited in the proof of service, the three-day extension is not available.

The amendment also states that the three-day extension is three calendar days. Rule 26(a) states that when a period prescribed or allowed by the rules is less than seven days, intermediate Saturdays, Sundays, and legal holidays do not count. Whether the three-day extension in Rule 26(c) is such a period, meaning that three-days could actually be five or even six days, is unclear. The D.C. Circuit recently held that the parallel three-day extension provided in the Civil Rules is not such a period and that weekends and legal holidays do count. *CNPq v. Inter-Trade, 50 F.3d 56 (D.C.Cir.1995).* The Committee believes that is the right result and that the issue should be resolved. Providing that the extension is three calendar days means that if a period would otherwise end on Thursday but the three-day extension applies, the paper must be filed on Monday. Friday, Saturday, and Sunday are the extension days. Because the last day of the period as extended is Sunday, the paper must be filed the next day, Monday.

Rule 26.1. Corporate Disclosure Statement

(a) Who Must File. Any nongovernmental corporate party to a proceeding in a court of appeals must file a statement identifying all its parent corporations and listing any publicly held company that owns 10% or more of the party's stock.

(b) Time for Filing. A party must file the statement with the principal brief or upon filing a motion, response, petition, or answer in the court of appeals, whichever occurs first, unless a local rule requires earlier filing. Even if the statement has already been filed, the party's principal brief must include the statement before the table of contents.

(c) Number of Copies. If the statement is filed before the principal brief, the party must file an original and 3 copies unless the court requires a different number by local rule or by order in a particular case.

(Added Apr. 25, 1989, eff. Dec. 1, 1989, and amended Apr. 30, 1991, eff. Dec. 1, 1991; Apr. 29, 1994, eff. Dec. 1, 1994; Apr. 24, 1998, eff. Dec. 1, 1998.)

ADVISORY COMMITTEE NOTES

1989 Addition

The purpose of this rule is to assist judges in making a determination of whether they have any interests in any of a party's related corporate entities that would disqualify the judges from hearing the appeal. The committee believes that this rule represents minimum disclosure requirements. If a Court of Appeals wishes to require additional information, a court is free to do so by local rule. However, the committee requests the courts to consider the desirability of uniformity and the burden that varying circuit rules creates on attorneys who practice in many circuits.

1994 Amendment

The amendment requires a party to file three copies of the disclosure statement whenever the statement is filed before the party's principle brief. Because the statement is included in each copy of the party's brief, there is no need to require the filing of additional copies at that time. A court of appeals may require the filing of a different number of copies by local rule or by order in a particular case.

Rule 27. Motions

(a) In General.

(1) Application for Relief. An application for an order or other relief is made by motion unless these rules prescribe another form. A motion must be in writing unless the court permits otherwise.

(2) Contents of a Motion.

(A) Grounds and relief sought. A motion must state with particularity the grounds for the motion, the relief sought, and the legal argument necessary to support it.

(B) Accompanying documents.

(i) Any affidavit or other paper necessary to support a motion must be served and filed with the motion.

(ii) An affidavit must contain only factual information, not legal argument.

(iii) A motion seeking substantive relief must include a copy of the trial court's opinion or agency's decision as a separate exhibit.

(C) **Documents barred or not required.**

(i) A separate brief supporting or responding to a motion must not be filed.

(ii) A notice of motion is not required.

(iii) A proposed order is not required.

(3) **Response.**

(A) **Time to file.** Any party may file a response to a motion; Rule 27(a)(2) governs its contents. The response must be filed within 10 days after service of the motion unless the court shortens or extends the time. A motion authorized by Rules 8, 9, 18, or 41 may be granted before the 10–day period runs only if the court gives reasonable notice to the parties that it intends to act sooner.

(B) **Request for affirmative relief.** A response may include a motion for affirmative relief. The time to respond to the new motion, and to reply to that response, are governed by Rule 27(a)(3)(A) and (a)(4). The title of the response must alert the court to the request for relief.

(4) **Reply to Response.** Any reply to a response must be filed within 7 days after service of the response. A reply must not present matters that do not relate to the response.

(b) Disposition of a Motion for a Procedural Order. The court may act on a motion for a procedural order—including a motion under Rule 26(b)—at any time without awaiting a response, and may, by rule or by order in a particular case, authorize its clerk to act on specified types of procedural motions. A party adversely affected by the court's, or the clerk's, action may file a motion to reconsider, vacate, or modify that action. Timely opposition filed after the motion is granted in whole or in part does not constitute a request to reconsider, vacate, or modify the disposition; a motion requesting that relief must be filed.

(c) Power of a Single Judge to Entertain a Motion. A circuit judge may act alone on any motion, but may not dismiss or otherwise determine an appeal or other proceeding. A court of appeals may provide by rule or by order in a particular case that only the court may act on any motion or class of motions. The court may review the action of a single judge.

(d) Form of Papers; Page Limits; and Number of Copies.

(1) **Format.**

(A) **Reproduction.** A motion, response, or reply may be reproduced by any process that yields a clear black image on light paper. The paper must be opaque and unglazed. Only one side of the paper may be used.

(B) **Cover.** A cover is not required but there must be a caption that includes the case number, the name of the court, the title of the case, and a brief descriptive title indicating the purpose of the motion and identifying the party or parties for whom it is filed.

(C) **Binding.** The document must be bound in any manner that is secure, does not obscure the text, and permits the document to lie reasonably flat when open.

(D) **Paper size, line spacing, and margins.** The document must be on 8½ by 11 inch paper. The text must be double-spaced, but quotations more than two lines long may be indented and single-spaced. Headings and footnotes may be single-spaced. Margins must be at least one inch on all four sides. Page numbers may be placed in the margins, but no text may appear there.

(2) **Page Limits.** A motion or a response to a motion must not exceed 20 pages, exclusive of the corporate disclosure statement and accompanying documents authorized by Rule 27(a)(2)(B), unless the court permits or directs otherwise. A reply to a response must not exceed 10 pages.

(3) **Number of Copies.** An original and 3 copies must be filed unless the court requires a different number by local rule or by order in a particular case.

(e) Oral Argument. A motion will be decided without oral argument unless the court orders otherwise.

(As amended Apr. 30, 1979, eff. Aug. 1, 1979; Apr. 25, 1989, eff. Dec. 1, 1989; Apr. 29, 1994, eff. Dec. 1, 1994; Apr. 24, 1998, eff. Dec. 1, 1998.)

ADVISORY COMMITTEE NOTES

1967 Adoption

Subdivisions (a) and (b). Many motions seek relief of a sort which is ordinarily unopposed or which is granted as of course. The provision of subdivision (a) which permits any party to file a response in opposition to a motion within 7 days after its service upon him assumes that the motion is one of substance which ought not be acted upon without affording affected parties an opportunity to reply. A motion to dismiss or otherwise determine an appeal is clearly such a motion. Motions authorized by Rules 8, 9, 18 and 41 are likewise motions of substance; but in the nature of the relief sought, to afford an adversary an automatic delay of at least 7 days is undesirable, thus such motions may be acted upon after notice which is reasonable under the circumstances.

The term "motions for procedural orders" is used in subdivision (b) to describe motions which do not substantially affect the rights of the parties or the ultimate disposition of the appeal. To prevent delay in the disposition of such motions, subdivision (b) provides that they may be acted upon immediately without awaiting a response, subject to the right of any party who is adversely affected by the action to seek reconsideration.

Subdivision (c). Within the general consideration of procedure on motions is the problem of the power of a single circuit judge. Certain powers are granted to a single judge of a court of appeals by statute. Thus, under 28 U.S.C. § 2101(f) a single judge may stay execution and enforcement of a judgment to enable a party aggrieved to obtain certiorari; under 28 U.S.C. § 2251 a judge before whom a habeas corpus proceeding involving a person detained by state authority is pending may stay any proceeding against the person; under 28 U.S.C. § 2253 a single judge may issue a certificate of probably cause. In addition, certain of these rules expressly grant power to a single judge. See Rules 8, 9 and 18.

This subdivision empowers a single circuit judge to act upon virtually all requests for intermediate relief which may be made during the course of an appeal or other proceeding. By its terms he may entertain and act upon any motion other than a motion to dismiss or otherwise determine an appeal or other proceeding. But the relief sought must be "relief which under these rules may properly be sought by motion."

Examples of the power conferred on a single judge by this subdivision are: to extend the time for transmitting the record or docketing the appeal (Rules 11 and 12); to permit intervention in agency cases (Rule 15), or substitution in any case (Rule 43); to permit an appeal in forma pauperis (Rule 24); to enlarge any time period fixed by the rules other than that for initiating a proceeding in the court of appeals (Rule 26(b)); to permit the filing of a brief by amicus curiae (Rule 29); to authorize the filing of a deferred appendix (Rule 30(c)), or dispense with the requirement of an appendix in a specific case (Rule 30(f)), or permit carbon copies of briefs or appendices to be used (Rule 32(a)); to permit the filing of additional briefs (Rule 28(c)), or the filing of briefs of extraordinary length (Rule 28(g)); to postpone oral argument (Rule 34(a)), or grant additional time therefor (Rule 34(b)).

Certain rules require that application for the relief or orders which they authorize be made by petition. Since relief under those rules may not properly be sought by motion, a single judge may not entertain requests for such relief. Thus a single judge may not act upon requests for permission to appeal (see Rules 5 and 6); or for mandamus or other extraordinary writs (see Rule 21), other than for stays or injunctions *pendente lite*, authority to grant which is "expressly conferred by these rules" on a single judge under certain circumstances (see Rules 8 and 18); or upon petitions for rehearing (see Rule 40).

A court of appeals may by order or rule abridge the power of a single judge if it is of the view that a motion or a class of motions should be disposed of by a panel. Exercise of any power granted a single judge is discretionary with the judge. The final sentence in this subdivision makes the disposition of any matter by a single judge subject to review by the court.

1979 Amendment

The proposed amendment would give sanction to local rules in a number of circuits permitting the clerk to dispose of specified types of procedural motions.

1989 Amendment

The amendment is technical. No substantive change is intended.

1994 Amendments

Subdivision (d). The amendment makes it clear that a court may require a different number of copies either by rule or by order in an individual case. The number of copies of any document that a court of appeals needs varies depending upon the way in which the court conducts business. The internal operation of the courts of appeals necessarily varies from circuit to circuit because of differences in the number of judges, the geographic area included within the circuit, and other such factors. Uniformity could be achieved only by setting the number of copies artificially high so that parties in all circuits file enough copies to satisfy the needs of the court requiring the greatest number. Rather than do that, the Committee decided to make it clear that local rules may require a greater or lesser number of copies and that, if the circumstances of a particular case indicate the need for a different number of copies in that case, the court may so order.

Rule 28. Briefs

(a) Appellant's Brief. The appellant's brief must contain, under appropriate headings and in the order indicated:

(1) a corporate disclosure statement if required by Rule 26.1;

(2) a table of contents, with page references;

(3) a table of authorities—cases (alphabetically arranged), statutes, and other authorities—with references to the pages of the brief where they are cited;

(4) a jurisdictional statement, including:

(A) the basis for the district court's or agency's subject-matter jurisdiction, with citations to applicable statutory provisions and stating relevant facts establishing jurisdiction;

(B) the basis for the court of appeals' jurisdiction, with citations to applicable statutory provisions and stating relevant facts establishing jurisdiction;

(C) the filing dates establishing the timeliness of the appeal or petition for review; and

(D) an assertion that the appeal is from a final order or judgment that disposes of all parties' claims, or information establishing the court of appeals' jurisdiction on some other basis;

(5) a statement of the issues presented for review;

(6) a statement of the case briefly indicating the nature of the case, the course of proceedings, and the disposition below;

(7) a statement of facts relevant to the issues submitted for review with appropriate references to the record (see Rule 28(e));

(8) a summary of the argument, which must contain a succinct, clear, and accurate statement of the arguments made in the body of the brief, and which must not merely repeat the argument headings;

(9) the argument, which must contain:

(A) appellant's contentions and the reasons for them, with citations to the authorities and parts of the record on which the appellant relies; and

(B) for each issue, a concise statement of the applicable standard of review (which may appear in the discussion of the issue or under a separate heading placed before the discussion of the issues);

(10) a short conclusion stating the precise relief sought; and

(11) the certificate of compliance, if required by Rule 32(a)(7).

(b) Appellee's Brief. The appellee's brief must conform to the requirements of Rule 28(a)(1)–(9) and (11), except that none of the following need appear unless the appellee is dissatisfied with the appellant's statement:

(1) the jurisdictional statement;

(2) the statement of the issues;

(3) the statement of the case;

(4) the statement of the facts; and

(5) the statement of the standard of review.

(c) Reply Brief. The appellant may file a brief in reply to the appellee's brief. An appellee who has cross-appealed may file a brief in reply to the appellant's response to the issues presented by the cross-appeal. Unless the court permits, no further briefs may be filed. A reply brief must contain a table of contents, with page references, and a table of authorities—cases (alphabetically arranged), statutes, and other authorities—with references to the pages of the reply brief where they are cited.

(d) References to Parties. In briefs and at oral argument, counsel should minimize use of the terms "appellant" and "appellee." To make briefs clear, counsel should use the parties' actual names or the designations used in the lower court or agency proceeding, or such descriptive terms as "the employee," "the injured person," "the taxpayer," "the ship," "the stevedore."

(e) References to the Record. References to the parts of the record contained in the appendix filed with the appellant's brief must be to the pages of the appendix. If the appendix is prepared after the briefs are filed, a party referring to the record must follow one of the methods detailed in Rule 30(c). If the original record is used under Rule 30(f) and is not consecutively paginated, or if the brief refers to an unreproduced part of the record, any reference must be to the page of the original document. For example:

- Answer p. 7;
- Motion for Judgment p. 2;
- Transcript p. 231.

Only clear abbreviations may be used. A party referring to evidence whose admissibility is in controversy must cite the pages of the appendix or of the transcript at which the evidence was identified, offered, and received or rejected.

(f) Reproduction of Statutes, Rules, Regulations, etc. If the court's determination of the issues presented requires the study of statutes, rules, regulations, etc., the relevant parts must be set out in the brief or in an addendum at the end, or may be supplied to the court in pamphlet form.

(g) [Reserved]

(h) Briefs in a Case Involving a Cross-Appeal. If a cross-appeal is filed, the party who files a notice of appeal first is the appellant for the purposes of this rule and Rules 30, 31, and 34. If notices are filed on the same day, the plaintiff in the proceeding below is the appellant. These designations may be modified by agreement of the parties or by court order. With respect to appellee's cross-appeal and response to appellant's brief, appellee's brief must conform to the requirements of Rule 28(a)(1)–(11). But an appellee who is satisfied with appellant's statement need not include a statement of the case or of the facts.

(i) Briefs in a Case Involving Multiple Appellants or Appellees. In a case involving more than one appellant or appellee, including consolidated cases, any number of appellants or appellees may join in a brief, and any party may adopt by reference a part of another's brief. Parties may also join in reply briefs.

(j) Citation of Supplemental Authorities. If pertinent and significant authorities come to a party's attention after the party's brief has been filed—or after oral argument but before decision—a party may promptly advise the circuit clerk by letter, with a copy to all other parties, setting forth the citations. The letter must state without argument the reasons for the supplemental citations, referring either to the page of the brief or to a point argued orally. Any response must be made promptly and must be similarly limited.

(As amended Apr. 30, 1979, eff. Aug. 1, 1979; Mar. 10, 1986, eff. July 1, 1986; Apr. 25, 1989, eff. Dec. 1, 1989; Apr. 30, 1991, eff. Dec. 1, 1991; Apr. 22, 1993, eff. Dec. 1, 1993; Apr. 29, 1994, eff. Dec. 1, 1994; Apr. 24, 1998, eff. Dec. 1, 1998.)

ADVISORY COMMITTEE NOTES

1967 Adoption

This rule is based upon Supreme Court Rule 40. For variations in present circuit rules on briefs see 2d Cir. Rule

17 [rule 17, U.S.Ct. of App. 2d Cir.], 3d Cir. Rule 24 [rule 24, U.S.Ct. of App. 3d Cir.], 5th Cir. Rule 24 [rule 24, U.S.Ct. of App. 5th Cir.], and 7th Cir. Rule 17 [rule 17, U.S.Ct. of App. 7th Cir.]. All circuits now limit the number of pages of briefs, a majority limiting the brief to 50 pages of standard typographic printing. Fifty pages of standard typographic printing is the approximate equivalent of 70 pages of typewritten text, given the page sizes required by Rule 32 and the requirement set out there that text produced by a method other than standard typographic must be double spaced.

1979 Amendments

Subdivision (g). The proposed amendment eliminates the distinction appearing in the present rule between the permissible length in pages of printed and typewritten briefs, investigation of the matter having disclosed that the number of words on the printed page is little if any larger than the number on a page typed in standard elite type.

The provision is made subject to local rule to permit the court of appeals to require that typewritten briefs be typed in larger type and permit a correspondingly larger number of pages.

Subdivision (j). Proposed new Rule 28(j) makes provision for calling the court's attention to authorities that come to the party's attention after the brief has been filed. It is patterned after the practice under local rule in some of the circuits.

1986 Amendments

While Rule 28(g) can be read as requiring that tables of authorities be included in a reply brief, such tables are often not included. Their absence impedes efficient use of the reply brief to ascertain the appellant's response to a particular argument of the appellee or to the appellee's use of a particular authority. The amendment to Rule 28(c) is intended to make it clear that such tables are required in reply briefs.

The amendment to Rule 28(j) is technical. No substantive change is intended.

1989 Amendments

The amendment provides that the corporate disclosure statement required by new Rule 26.1 shall be treated similarly to tables of contents and tables of citations and shall not be counted for purposes of the number of pages allowed in a brief.

1991 Amendments

Subdivision (a). The amendment adds a new subparagraph (2) that requires an appellant to include a specific jurisdictional statement in the appellant's brief to aid the court of appeals in determining whether it has both federal subject matter and appellate jurisdiction.

Subdivision (b). The amendment requires the appellee to include a jurisdictional statement in the appellee's brief except that the appellee need not include the statement if the appellee is satisfied with the appellant's jurisdictional statement.

Subdivision (h). The amendment provides that when more than one party appeals from a judgment or order, the party filing the first appeal is normally treated as the appellant for purposes of this rule and Rules 30 and 31. The party who first files an appeal usually is the principal appellant and should be treated as such. Parties who file a notice of appeal after the first notice often bring protective appeals and they should be treated as cross appellants. Local rules in the Fourth and Federal Circuits now take that approach. If notices of appeal are filed on the same day, the rule follows the old approach of treating the plaintiff below as the appellant. For purposes of this rule, in criminal cases "the plaintiff" means the United States. In those instances where the designations provided by the rule are inappropriate, they may be altered by agreement of the parties or by an order of the court.

1993 Amendments

Note to paragraph (a)(5). The amendment requires an appellant's brief to state the standard of review applicable to each issue on appeal. Five circuits currently require these statements. Experience in those circuits indicates that requiring a statement of the standard of review generally results in arguments that are properly shaped in light of the standard.

1994 Amendments

Subdivision (a). The amendment adds a requirement that an appellant's brief contain a summary of the argument. A number of circuits have local rules requiring a summary and the courts report that they find the summary useful. See, D.C. Cir.R. 11(a)(5); 5th Cir.R. 28.2.2; 8th Cir.R. 28A(i)(6); 11th Cir.R. 28–2(i); and Fed. Cir.R. 28.

Subdivision (b). The amendment adds a requirement that an appellee's brief contain a summary of the argument.

Subdivision (g). The amendment adds proof of service to the list of items in a brief that do not count for purposes of the page limitation. The concurrent amendment to Rule 25(d) requires a certificate of service to list the addresses to which a paper was mailed or at which it was delivered. When a number of parties must be served, the listing of addresses may run to several pages and those pages should not count for purposes of the page limitation.

Rule 29. Brief of an Amicus Curiae

(a) When Permitted. The United States or its officer or agency, or a State, Territory, Commonwealth, or the District of Columbia may file an amicus-curiae brief without the consent of the parties or leave of court. Any other amicus curiae may file a brief only by leave of court or if the brief states that all parties have consented to its filing.

(b) Motion for Leave to File. The motion must be accompanied by the proposed brief and state:

(1) the movant's interest; and

(2) the reason why an amicus brief is desirable and why the matters asserted are relevant to the disposition of the case.

(c) Contents and Form. An amicus brief must comply with Rule 32. In addition to the requirements of Rule 32, the cover must identify the party or parties supported and indicate whether the brief supports affirmance or reversal. If an amicus curiae is a corporation, the brief must include a disclosure statement like that required of parties by Rule 26.1. An amicus brief need not comply with Rule 28, but must include the following:

(1) a table of contents, with page references;

(2) a table of authorities—cases (alphabetically arranged), statutes and other authorities—with references to the pages of the brief where they are cited;

(3) a concise statement of the identity of the amicus curiae, its interest in the case, and the source of its authority to file;

(4) an argument, which may be preceded by a summary and which need not include a statement of the applicable standard of review; and

(5) a certificate of compliance, if required by Rule 32(a)(7).

(d) Length. Except by the court's permission, an amicus brief may be no more than one-half the maximum length authorized by these rules for a party's principal brief. If the court grants a party permission to file a longer brief, that extension does not affect the length of an amicus brief.

(e) Time for Filing. An amicus curiae must file its brief, accompanied by a motion for filing when necessary, no later than 7 days after the principal brief of the party being supported is filed. An amicus curiae that does not support either party must file its brief no later than 7 days after the appellant's or petitioner's principal brief is filed. A court may grant leave for later filing, specifying the time within which an opposing party may answer.

(f) Reply Brief. Except by the court's permission, an amicus curiae may not file a reply brief.

(g) Oral Argument. An amicus curiae may participate in oral argument only with the court's permission.

(As amended Apr. 24, 1998, eff. Dec. 1, 1998.)

ADVISORY COMMITTEE NOTES

1967 Adoption

Only five circuits presently regulate the filing of the brief of an amicus curiae. See D.C.Cir. Rule 18(j) [rule 18(j), U.S.Ct. of App.Dist. of Col.Cir., this title]; 1st Cir. Rule 23(10) [rule 23(10), U.S.Ct. of App. 1st Cir.]; 6th Cir. Rule 17(4) [rule 17(4), U.S.Ct. of App. 6th Cir.]; 9th Cir. Rule 18(9) [rule 18(9), U.S.Ct. of App. 9th Cir.]; 10th Cir. Rule 20 [rule 20, U.S.Ct. of App. 10th Cir.]. This rule follows the practice of a majority of circuits in requiring leave of court to file an amicus brief except under the circumstances stated therein. Compare Supreme Court Rule 42.

Rule 30. Appendix to the Briefs

(a) Appellant's Responsibility.

(1) Contents of the Appendix. The appellant must prepare and file an appendix to the briefs containing:

(A) the relevant docket entries in the proceeding below;

(B) the relevant portions of the pleadings, charge, findings, or opinion;

(C) the judgment, order, or decision in question; and

(D) other parts of the record to which the parties wish to direct the court's attention.

(2) Excluded Material. Memoranda of law in the district court should not be included in the appendix unless they have independent relevance. Parts of the record may be relied on by the court or the parties even though not included in the appendix.

(3) Time to File; Number of Copies. Unless filing is deferred under Rule 30(c), the appellant must file 10 copies of the appendix with the brief and must serve one copy on counsel for each party separately represented. An unrepresented party proceeding in forma pauperis must file 4 legible copies with the clerk, and one copy must be served on counsel for each separately represented party. The court may by local rule or by order in a particular case require the filing or service of a different number.

(b) All Parties' Responsibilities.

(1) Determining the Contents of the Appendix. The parties are encouraged to agree on the contents of the appendix. In the absence of an agreement, the appellant must, within 10 days after the record is filed, serve on the appellee a designation of the parts of the record the appellant intends to include in the appendix and a statement of the issues the appellant intends to present for review. The appellee may, within 10 days after receiving the designation, serve on the appellant a designation of additional parts to which it wishes to direct the court's attention. The appellant must include the designated parts in the appendix. The parties must not engage in unnecessary designation of parts of the record, because the entire record is available to the court. This paragraph applies also to a cross-appellant and a cross-appellee.

(2) Costs of Appendix. Unless the parties agree otherwise, the appellant must pay the cost of the appendix. If the appellant considers parts of the record designated by the appellee to be unnecessary, the appellant may advise the appellee, who must then advance the cost of including those parts. The cost of the appendix is a taxable cost. But if any party causes unnecessary parts of the record to be included in the appendix, the court may impose the cost of those parts on that party. Each circuit must, by local rule, provide for sanctions against attorneys who unreasonably and vexatiously increase litigation costs by including unnecessary material in the appendix.

(c) Deferred Appendix.

(1) Deferral Until After Briefs Are Filed. The court may provide by rule for classes of cases or by order in a particular case that preparation of the appendix may be deferred until after the briefs have been filed and that the appendix may be filed 21 days after the appellee's brief is served. Even though the filing of the appendix may be deferred, Rule 30(b) applies; except that a party must designate the parts of the record it wants included in the appendix when it serves its brief, and need not include a statement of the issues presented.

(2) References to the Record.

(A) If the deferred appendix is used, the parties may cite in their briefs the pertinent pages of the record. When the appendix is prepared, the record pages cited in the briefs must be indicated by inserting record page numbers, in brackets, at places in the appendix where those pages of the record appear.

(B) A party who wants to refer directly to pages of the appendix may serve and file copies of the brief within the time required by Rule 31(a), containing appropriate references to pertinent pages of the record. In that event, within 14 days after the appendix is filed, the party must serve and file copies of the brief, containing references to the pages of the appendix in place of or in addition to the references to the pertinent pages of the record. Except for the correction of typographical errors, no other changes may be made to the brief.

(d) Format of the Appendix. The appendix must begin with a table of contents identifying the page at which each part begins. The relevant docket entries must follow the table of contents. Other parts of the record must follow chronologically. When pages from the transcript of proceedings are placed in the appendix, the transcript page numbers must be shown in brackets immediately before the included pages. Omissions in the text of papers or of the transcript must be indicated by asterisks. Immaterial formal matters (captions, subscriptions, acknowledgments, etc.) should be omitted.

(e) Reproduction of Exhibits. Exhibits designated for inclusion in the appendix may be reproduced in a separate volume, or volumes, suitably indexed. Four copies must be filed with the appendix, and one copy must be served on counsel for each separately represented party. If a transcript of a proceeding before an administrative agency, board, commission, or officer was used in a district-court action and has been designated for inclusion in the appendix, the transcript must be placed in the appendix as an exhibit.

(f) Appeal on the Original Record Without an Appendix. The court may, either by rule for all cases or classes of cases or by order in a particular case, dispense with the appendix and permit an appeal to proceed on the original record with any copies of the record, or relevant parts, that the court may order the parties to file.

(As amended Mar. 30, 1970, eff. July 1, 1970; Mar. 10, 1986, eff. July 1, 1986; Apr. 30, 1991, eff. Dec. 1, 1991; Apr. 29, 1994, eff. Dec. 1, 1994; Apr. 24, 1998. eff. Dec. 1, 1998.)

ADVISORY COMMITTEE NOTES

1967 Adoption

Subdivision (a). Only two circuits presently require a printed record (5th Cir. Rule 23(a) [rule 23(a), U.S.Ct. of App. 5th Cir.]; 8th Cir. Rule 10 [rule 10, U.S.Ct. of App. 8th Cir.] (in civil appeals only)), and the rules and practice in those circuits combine to make the difference between a printed record and the appendix, which is now used in eight circuits and in the Supreme Court in lieu of the printed record, largely nominal. The essential characteristics of the appendix method are: (1) the entire record may not be reproduced; (2) instead, the parties are to set out in an appendix to the briefs those parts of the record which in their judgment the judges must consult in order to determine the issues presented by the appeal; (3) the appendix is not the record but merely a selection therefrom for the convenience of the judges of the court of appeals; the record is the actual trial court record, and the record itself is always available to supply inadvertent omissions from the appendix. These essentials are incorporated, either by rule or by practice, in the circuits that continue to require the printed record rather than the appendix. See 5th Cir. Rule 23(a)(9) [23(a)(9), U.S.Ct. of App. 5th Cir.] and 8th Cir. Rule 10(a)–(d) [rule 10(a)–(d), U.S.Ct. of App. 8th Cir.].

Subdivision (b). Under the practice in six of the eight circuits which now use the appendix method, unless the parties agree to use a single appendix, the appellant files with his brief an appendix containing the parts of the record which he deems it essential that the court read in order to determine the questions presented. If the appellee deems additional parts of the record necessary he must include such parts as an appendix to his brief. The proposed rule differs from that practice. By the new rule a single appendix is to be filed. It is to be prepared by the appellant, who must include therein those parts which he deems essential and those which the appellee designates as essential.

Under the practice by which each party files his own appendix the resulting reproduction of essential parts of the record is often fragmentary; it is not infrequently necessary to piece several appendices together to arrive at a usable reproduction. Too, there seems to be a tendency on the part of some appellants to reproduce less than what is necessary for a determination of the issues presented (see *Moran Towing Corp. v. M. A. Gammino Construction Co.*, 363 F.2d 108 (1st Cir. 1966); *Walters v. Shari Music Publishing*

Corp., 298 F.2d 206 (2d Cir. 1962) and cases cited therein; *Morrison v. Texas Co.*, 289 F.2d 382 (7th Cir. 1961) and cases cited therein), a tendency which is doubtless encouraged by the requirement in present rules that the appellee reproduce in his separately prepared appendix such necessary parts of the record as are not included by the appellant.

Under the proposed rule responsibility for the preparation of the appendix is placed on the appellant. If the appellee feels that the appellant has omitted essential portions of the record, he may require the appellant to include such portions in the appendix. The appellant is protected against a demand that he reproduce parts which he considers unnecessary by the provisions entitling him to require the appellee to advance the costs of reproducing such parts and authorizing denial of costs for matter unnecessarily reproduced.

Subdivision (c). This subdivision permits the appellant to elect to defer the production of the appendix to the briefs until the briefs of both sides are written, and authorizes a court of appeals to require such deferred filing by rule or order. The advantage of this method of preparing the appendix is that it permits the parties to determine what parts of the record need to be reproduced in the light of the issues actually presented by the briefs. Often neither side is in a position to say precisely what is needed until the briefs are completed. Once the argument on both sides is known, it should be possible to confine the matter reproduced in the appendix to that which is essential to a determination of the appeal or review. This method of preparing the appendix is presently in use in the Tenth Circuit (Rule 17) [rule 17, U.S.Ct. of App. 10th Cir.] and in other circuits in review of agency proceedings, and it has proven its value in reducing the volume required to be reproduced. When the record is long, use of this method is likely to result in substantial economy to the parties.

Subdivision (e). The purpose of this subdivision is to reduce the cost of reproducing exhibits. While subdivision (a) requires that 10 copies of the appendix be filed, unless the court requires a lesser number, subdivision (e) permits exhibits necessary for the determination of an appeal to be bound separately, and requires only 4 copies of such a separate volume or volumes to be filed and a single copy to be served on counsel.

Subdivision (f). The subdivision authorizes a court of appeals to dispense with the appendix method of reproducing parts of the record and to hear appeals on the original record and such copies of it as the court may require.

Since 1962 the Ninth Circuit has permitted all appeals to be heard on the original record and a very limited number of copies. Under the practice as adopted in 1962, any party to an appeal could elect to have the appeal heard on the original record and two copies thereof rather than on the printed record theretofore required. The resulting substantial saving of printing costs led to the election of the new practice in virtually all cases, and by 1967 the use of printed records had ceased. By a recent amendment, the Ninth Circuit has abolished the printed record altogether. Its rules now provide that all appeals are to be heard on the original record, and it has reduced the number of copies required to two sets of copies of the transmitted original papers (excluding copies of exhibits, which need not be filed unless specifically ordered). See 9 Cir. Rule 10 [rule 10 U.S.Ct. of App. 9th Cir.], as amended June 2, 1967, effective September 1, 1967. The Eighth Circuit permits appeals in criminal cases and in habeas corpus and 28 U.S.C. § 2255 proceedings to be heard on the original record and two copies thereof. See 8 Cir. Rule 8(i)–(j) [rule 8(i)–(j), U.S.Ct. of App. 8th Cir.]. The Tenth Circuit permits appeals in all cases to be heard on the original record and four copies thereof whenever the record consists of two hundred pages or less. See 10 Cir. Rule 17(a) [rule 17(a), U.S.Ct. of App. 10th Cir.]. This subdivision expressly authorizes the continuation of the practices in the Eighth, Ninth and Tenth Circuits.

The judges of the Court of Appeals for the Ninth Circuit have expressed complete satisfaction with the practice there in use and have suggested that attention be called to the advantages which it offers in terms of reducing cost.

1970 Amendments

Subdivision (a). The amendment of subdivision (a) is related to the amendment of Rule 31(a), which authorizes a court of appeals to shorten the time for filing briefs. By virtue of this amendment, if the time for filing the brief of the appellant is shortened the time for filing the appendix is likewise shortened.

Subdivision (c). As originally written, subdivision (c) permitted the appellant to elect to defer filing of the appendix until 21 days after service of the brief of the appellee. As amended, subdivision (c) requires that an order of court be obtained before filing of the appendix can be deferred, unless a court permits deferred filing by local rule. The amendment should not cause use of the deferred appendix to be viewed with disfavor. In cases involving lengthy records, permission to defer filing of the appendix should be freely granted as an inducement to the parties to include in the appendix only matter that the briefs show to be necessary for consideration by the judges. But the Committee is advised that appellants have elected to defer filing of the appendix in cases involving brief records merely to obtain the 21 day delay. The subdivision is amended to prevent that practice.

1986 Amendments

Subdivision (a). During its study of the separate appendix [see Report of the Advisory Committee on the Federal Appellate Rules on the Operation of Rule 30, FRD (1985)], the Advisory Committee found that this document was frequently encumbered with memoranda submitted to the trial court. *United States v. Noall,* 587 F.2d 123, 125 n. 1 (2nd Cir.1978). See generally *Drewett v. Aetna Cas. & Sur. Co.,* 539 F.2d 496, 500 (5th Cir.1976); *Volkswagenwerk Aktiengesellschaft v. Church,* 413 F.2d 1126, 1128 (9th Cir.1969). Inclusion of such material makes the appendix more bulky and therefore less useful to the appellate panel. It also can increase significantly the costs of litigation.

There are occasions when such trial court memoranda have independent relevance in the appellate litigation. For instance, there may be a dispute as to whether a particular point was raised or whether a concession was made in the district court. In such circumstances, it is appropriate to include pertinent sections of such memoranda in the appendix.

Subdivision (b). The amendment to subdivision (b) is designed to require the circuits, by local rule, to establish a procedural mechanism for the imposition of sanctions against those attorneys who conduct appellate litigation in bad faith.

Both 28 U.S.C. § 1927 and the inherent power of the court authorize such sanctions. See *Brennan v. Local 357, International Brotherhood of Teamsters*, 709 F.2d 611 (9th Cir. 1983). See generally *Roadway Express, Inc. v. Piper*, 447 U.S. 752 (1980). While considerations of uniformity are important and doubtless will be taken into account by the judges of the respective circuits, the Advisory Committee believes that, at this time, the circuits need the flexibility to tailor their approach to the conditions of local practice. The local rule shall provide for notice and opportunity to respond before the imposition of any sanction.

Technical amendments also are made to subdivisions (a), (b) and (c) which are not intended to be substantive changes.

1991 Amendments

Subdivision (b). The amendment requires a cross appellant to serve the appellant with a statement of the issues that the cross appellant intends to pursue on appeal. No later than ten days after the record is filed, the appellant and cross appellant must serve each other with a statement of the issues each intends to present for review and with a designation of the parts of the record that each wants included in the appendix. Within the next ten days, both the appellee and the cross appellee may designate additional materials for inclusion in the appendix. The appellant must then include in the appendix the parts thus designated for both the appeal and any cross appeals. The Committee expects that simultaneous compliance with this subdivision by an appellant and a cross appellant will be feasible in most cases. If a cross appellant cannot fairly be expected to comply until receipt of the appellant's statement of issues, relief may be sought by motion in the court of appeals.

1994 Amendments

Subdivision (a). The only substantive change is to allow a court to require the filing of a greater number of copies of an appendix as well as a lesser number.

HISTORICAL NOTES

Taxation of Fees in Appeals in Which Requirement of Appendix is Dispensed With

See item (6) in the Judicial Conference Schedule of Fees note under 28 U.S.C.A. § 1913.

Rule 31. Serving and Filing Briefs

(a) Time to Serve and File a Brief.

(1) The appellant must serve and file a brief within 40 days after the record is filed. The appellee must serve and file a brief within 30 days after the appellant's brief is served. The appellant may serve and file a reply brief within 14 days after service of the appellee's brief but a reply brief must be filed at least 3 days before argument, unless the court, for good cause, allows a later filing.

(2) A court of appeals that routinely considers cases on the merits promptly after the briefs are filed may shorten the time to serve and file briefs, either by local rule or by order in a particular case.

(b) Number of Copies. Twenty-five copies of each brief must be filed with the clerk and 2 copies must be served on counsel for each separately represented party. An unrepresented party proceeding in forma pauperis must file 4 legible copies with the clerk, and one copy must be served on counsel for each separately represented party. The court may by local rule or by order in a particular case require the filing or service of a different number.

(c) Consequence of Failure to File. If an appellant fails to file a brief within the time provided by this rule, or within an extended time, an appellee may move to dismiss the appeal. An appellee who fails to file a brief will not be heard at oral argument unless the court grants permission.

(As amended Mar. 30, 1970, eff. July 1, 1970; Mar. 10, 1986, eff. July 1, 1986; Apr. 29, 1994, eff. Dec. 1, 1994; Apr. 24, 1998, eff. Dec. 1, 1998.)

ADVISORY COMMITTEE NOTES

1967 Adoption

A majority of the circuits now require the brief of the appellant to be filed within 30 days from the date on which the record is filed. But in those circuits an exchange of designations is unnecessary in the preparation of the appendix. The appellant files with his brief an appendix containing the parts of the record which he deems essential. If the appellee considers other parts essential, he includes those parts in his own appendix. Since the proposed rule requires the appellant to file with his brief an appendix containing necessary parts of the record as designated by both parties, the rule allows the appellant 40 days in order to provide time for the exchange of designations respecting the content of the appendix (see Rule 30(b)).

1970 Amendment

The time prescribed by Rule 31(a) for preparing briefs—40 days to the appellant, 30 days to the appellee—is well within the time that must ordinarily elapse in most circuits before an appeal can be reached for consideration. In those circuits, the time prescribed by the Rule should not be disturbed. But if a court of appeals maintains a current calendar, that is, if an appeal can be heard as soon as the briefs have been filed, or if the practice of the court permits the submission of appeals for preliminary consideration as soon as the briefs have been filed, the court should be free to prescribe shorter periods in the interest of expediting decision.

1986 Amendment

The amendments to Rules 31(a) and (c) are technical. No substantive change is intended.

1994 Amendments

Subdivision (b). The amendment allows a court of appeals to require the filing of a greater, as well as a lesser, number of copies of briefs. The amendment also allows the required number to be prescribed by local rule as well as by order in a particular case.

Rule 32. Form of Briefs, Appendices, and Other Papers

(a) Form of a Brief.

(1) Reproduction.

(A) A brief may be reproduced by any process that yields a clear black image on light paper. The paper must be opaque and unglazed. Only one side of the paper may be used.

(B) Text must be reproduced with a clarity that equals or exceeds the output of a laser printer.

(C) Photographs, illustrations, and tables may be reproduced by any method that results in a good copy of the original; a glossy finish is acceptable if the original is glossy.

(2) Cover. Except for filings by unrepresented parties, the cover of the appellant's brief must be blue; the appellee's, red; an intervenor's or amicus curiae's, green; and any reply brief, gray. The front cover of a brief must contain:

(A) the number of the case centered at the top;

(B) the name of the court;

(C) the title of the case (see Rule 12(a));

(D) the nature of the proceeding (e.g., Appeal, Petition for Review) and the name of the court, agency, or board below;

(E) the title of the brief, identifying the party or parties for whom the brief is filed; and

(F) the name, office address, and telephone number of counsel representing the party for whom the brief is filed.

(3) Binding. The brief must be bound in any manner that is secure, does not obscure the text, and permits the brief to lie reasonably flat when open.

(4) Paper Size, Line Spacing, and Margins. The brief must be on 8½ by 11 inch paper. The text must be double-spaced, but quotations more than two lines long may be indented and single-spaced. Headings and footnotes may be single-spaced. Margins must be at least one inch on all four sides. Page numbers may be placed in the margins, but no text may appear there.

(5) Typeface. Either a proportionally spaced or a monospaced face may be used.

(A) A proportionally spaced face must include serifs, but sans-serif type may be used in headings and captions. A proportionally spaced face must be 14–point or larger.

(B) A monospaced face may not contain more than 10½ characters per inch.

(6) Type Styles. A brief must be set in a plain, roman style, although italics or boldface may be used for emphasis. Case names must be italicized or underlined.

(7) Length.

(A) Page limitation. A principal brief may not exceed 30 pages, or a reply brief 15 pages, unless it complies with Rule 32(a)(7)(B) and (C).

(B) Type-volume limitation.

(i) A principal brief is acceptable if:

- it contains no more than 14,000 words; or
- it uses a monospaced face and contains no more than 1,300 lines of text.

(ii) A reply brief is acceptable if it contains no more than half of the type volume specified in Rule 32(a)(7)(B)(i).

(iii) Headings, footnotes, and quotations count toward the word and line limitations. The corporate disclosure statement, table of contents, table of citations, statement with respect to oral argument, any addendum containing statutes, rules or regulations, and any certificates of counsel do not count toward the limitation.

(C) Certificate of compliance. A brief submitted under Rule 32(a)(7)(B) must include a certificate by the attorney, or an unrepresented party, that the brief complies with the type-volume limitation. The person preparing the certificate may rely on the word or line count of the word-processing system used to prepare the brief. The certificate must state either:

(i) the number of words in the brief; or

(ii) the number of lines of monospaced type in the brief.

(b) Form of an Appendix. An appendix must comply with Rule 32(a)(1), (2), (3), and (4), with the following exceptions:

(1) The cover of a separately bound appendix must be white.

(2) An appendix may include a legible photocopy of any document found in the record or of a printed judicial or agency decision.

(3) When necessary to facilitate inclusion of odd-sized documents such as technical drawings, an appendix may be a size other than 8½ by 11 inches, and need not lie reasonably flat when opened.

(c) Form of Other Papers.

(1) Motion. The form of a motion is governed by Rule 27(d).

(2) Other Papers. Any other paper, including a petition for rehearing and a petition for rehearing en banc, and any response to such a petition, must be reproduced in the manner prescribed by Rule 32(a), with the following exceptions:

(A) a cover is not necessary if the caption and signature page of the paper together contain the information required by Rule 32(a)(2); and

(B) Rule 32(a)(7) does not apply.

(d) Local Variation. Every court of appeals must accept documents that comply with the form requirements of this rule. By local rule or order in a particular case a court of appeals may accept documents that do not meet all of the form requirements of this rule.

(As amended Apr. 24, 1998, eff. Dec. 1, 1988.)

ADVISORY COMMITTEE NOTES

1967 Adoption

Only two methods of printing are now generally recognized by the circuits—standard typographic printing and the offset duplicating process (multilith). A third, mimeographing, is permitted in the Fifth Circuit. The District of Columbia, Ninth, and Tenth Circuits permit records to be reproduced by copying processes. The Committee feels that recent and impending advances in the arts of duplicating and copying warrant experimentation with less costly forms of reproduction than those now generally authorized. The proposed rule permits, in effect, the use of any process other than the carbon copy process which produces a clean, readable page. What constitutes such is left in first instance to the parties and ultimately to the court to determine. The final sentence of the first paragraph of subdivision (a) is added to allow the use of multilith, mimeograph, or other forms of copies of the reporter's original transcript whenever such are available.

Rule 33. Appeal Conferences

The court may direct the attorneys—and, when appropriate, the parties—to participate in one or more conferences to address any matter that may aid in disposing of the proceedings, including simplifying the issues and discussing settlement. A judge or other person designated by the court may preside over the conference, which may be conducted in person or by telephone. Before a settlement conference, the attorneys must consult with their clients and obtain as much authority as feasible to settle the case. The court may, as a result of the conference, enter an order controlling the course of the proceedings or implementing any settlement agreement.

(As amended Apr. 29, 1994, eff. Dec. 1, 1994; Apr. 24, 1998, eff. Dec. 1, 1998.)

ADVISORY COMMITTEE NOTES

1967 Adoption

The uniform rule for review or enforcement of orders of administrative agencies, boards, commissions or officers (see the general note following Rule 15) authorizes a prehearing conference in agency review proceedings. The same considerations which make a prehearing conference desirable in such proceedings may be present in certain cases on appeal from the district courts. The proposed rule is based upon subdivision 11 of the present uniform rule for review of agency orders.

1994 Amendment

Rule 33 has been entirely rewritten. The new rule makes several changes.

The caption of the rule has been changed from "Prehearing Conference" to "Appeal Conferences" to reflect the fact that occasionally a conference is held after oral argument.

The rule permits the court to require the parties to attend the conference in appropriate cases. The Committee does not contemplate that attendance of the parties will become routine, but in certain instances the parties' presence can be useful. The language of the rule is broad enough to allow a court to determine that an executive or an employee (other than the general counsel) of a corporation or government agency with authority regarding the matter at issue, constitutes "the party."

The rule includes the possibility of settlement among the possible conference topics.

The rule recognizes that conferences are often held by telephone.

The rule allows a judge or other person designated by the court to preside over a conference. A number of local rules permit persons other than judges to preside over conferences. 1st Cir. R. 47.5; 6th Cir. R. 18; 8th Cir. R. 33A; 9th Cir. R. 33–1; and 10th Cir. R. 33.

The rule requires an attorney to consult with his or her client before a settlement conference and obtain as much authority as feasible to settle the case. An attorney can never settle a case without his or her client's consent. Certain entities, especially government entities, have particular difficulty obtaining authority to settle a case. The rule requires counsel to obtain only as much authority "as feasible."

Rule 34. Oral Argument

(a) In General.

(1) Party's Statement. Any party may file, or a court may require by local rule, a statement explaining why oral argument should, or need not, be permitted.

(2) Standards. Oral argument must be allowed in every case unless a panel of three judges who have examined the briefs and record unanimously agrees that oral argument is unnecessary for any of the following reasons:

(A) the appeal is frivolous;

(B) the dispositive issue or issues have been authoritatively decided; or

(C) the facts and legal arguments are adequately presented in the briefs and record, and the decisional process would not be significantly aided by oral argument.

(b) Notice of Argument; Postponement. The clerk must advise all parties whether oral argument will be scheduled, and, if so, the date, time, and place for it, and the time allowed for each side. A motion to postpone the argument or to allow longer argument must be filed reasonably in advance of the hearing date.

(c) Order and Contents of Argument. The appellant opens and concludes the argument. Counsel must not read at length from briefs, records, or authorities.

(d) Cross–Appeals and Separate Appeals. If there is a cross-appeal, Rule 28(h) determines which party is the appellant and which is the appellee for purposes of oral argument. Unless the court directs otherwise, a cross-appeal or separate appeal must be argued when the initial appeal is argued. Separate parties should avoid duplicative argument.

(e) Nonappearance of a Party. If the appellee fails to appear for argument, the court must hear appellant's argument. If the appellant fails to appear for argument, the court may hear the appellee's argument. If neither party appears, the case will be decided on the briefs, unless the court orders otherwise.

(f) Submission on Briefs. The parties may agree to submit a case for decision on the briefs, but the court may direct that the case be argued.

(g) Use of Physical Exhibits at Argument; Removal. Counsel intending to use physical exhibits other than documents at the argument must arrange to place them in the courtroom on the day of the argument before the court convenes. After the argument, counsel must remove the exhibits from the courtroom, unless the court directs otherwise. The clerk may destroy or dispose of the exhibits if counsel does not reclaim them within a reasonable time after the clerk gives notice to remove them.

(As amended Apr. 30, 1979, eff. Aug. 1, 1979; Mar. 10, 1986, eff. July 1, 1986; Apr. 30, 1991, eff. Dec. 1, 1991; Apr. 22, 1993, eff. Dec. 1, 1993; Apr. 24, 1998, eff. Dec. 1, 1998.)

ADVISORY COMMITTEE NOTES

1967 Adoption

A majority of circuits now limit oral argument to thirty minutes for each side, with the provision that additional time may be made available upon request. The Committee is of the view that thirty minutes to each side is sufficient in most cases, but that where additional time is necessary it should be freely granted on a proper showing of cause therefor. It further feels that the matter of time should be left ultimately to each court of appeals, subject to the spirit of the rule that a reasonable time should be allowed for argument. The term "side" is used to indicate that the time allowed by the rule is afforded to opposing interests rather than to individual parties. Thus if multiple appellants or appellees have a common interest, they constitute only a single side. If counsel for multiple parties who constitute a single side feel that additional time is necessary, they may request it. In other particulars this rule follows the usual practice among the circuits. See 3d Cir. Rule 31 [rule 31, U.S.Ct. of App.3rd Cir.]; 6th Cir. Rule 20 [rule 20, U.S.Ct. of App.6th Cir.]; 10th Cir. Rule 23 [rule 23, U.S.Ct. of App.10th Cir.].

1979 Amendment

The proposed amendment, patterned after the recommendations in the Report of the Commission on Revision of the Federal Court Appellate System, *Structure and Internal Procedures: Recommendations for Change*, 1975, created by Public Law 489 of the 92nd Cong.2nd Sess., 86 Stat. 807, sets forth general principles and minimum standards to be observed in formulating any local rule.

1986 Amendment

The amendments to Rules 34(a) and (e) are technical. No substantive change is intended.

1991 Amendment

Subdivision (d). The amendment of subdivision (d) conforms this rule with the amendment of Rule 28(h).

1993 Amendment

Subdivision (c). The amendment deletes the requirement that the opening argument must include a fair statement of the case. The Committee proposed the change because in some circuits the court does not want appellants to give such statements. In those circuits, the rule is not followed and is misleading. Nevertheless, the Committee does not want the deletion of the requirement to indicate disapproval of the practice. Those circuits that desire a statement of the case may continue the practice.

Rule 35. En Banc Determination

(a) When Hearing or Rehearing En Banc May Be Ordered. A majority of the circuit judges who are in regular active service may order that an appeal or other proceeding be heard or reheard by the court of appeals en banc. An en banc hearing or rehearing is not favored and ordinarily will not be ordered unless:

(1) en banc consideration is necessary to secure or maintain uniformity of the court's decisions; or

(2) the proceeding involves a question of exceptional importance.

(b) Petition for Hearing or Rehearing En Banc. A party may petition for a hearing or rehearing en banc.

(1) The petition must begin with a statement that either:

(A) the panel decision conflicts with a decision of the United States Supreme Court or of the court to which the petition is addressed (with citation to the conflicting case or cases) and consideration by the full court is therefore necessary to secure and maintain uniformity of the court's decisions; or

(B) the proceeding involves one or more questions of exceptional importance, each of which must be concisely stated; for example, a petition may assert that a proceeding presents a question of exceptional importance if it involves an issue on which the panel decision conflicts with the authoritative decisions of other United States Courts of Appeals that have addressed the issue.

(2) Except by the court's permission, a petition for an en banc hearing or rehearing must not exceed 15 pages, excluding material not counted under Rule 32.

(3) For purposes of the page limit in Rule 35(b)(2), if a party files both a petition for panel rehearing and a petition for rehearing en banc, they are considered a single document even if they are filed separately, unless separate filing is required by local rule.

(c) Time for Petition for Hearing or Rehearing En Banc. A petition that an appeal be heard initially en banc must be filed by the date when the appellee's brief is due. A petition for a rehearing en banc must be filed within the time prescribed by Rule 40 for filing a petition for rehearing.

(d) Number of Copies. The number of copies to be filed must be prescribed by local rule and may be altered by order in a particular case.

(e) Response. No response may be filed to a petition for an en banc consideration unless the court orders a response.

(f) Call for a Vote. A vote need not be taken to determine whether the case will be heard or reheard en banc unless a judge calls for a vote.

(As amended Apr. 30, 1979, eff. Aug. 1, 1979; Apr. 29, 1994, eff. Dec. 1, 1994; Apr. 24, 1998, eff. Dec. 1, 1998.)

ADVISORY COMMITTEE NOTES

1967 Adoption

Statutory authority for in banc hearings is found in 28 U.S.C. § 46(c). The proposed rule is responsive to the Supreme Court's view in *Western Pacific Ry. Corp. v. Western Pacific Ry. Co.*, 345 U.S. 247, 73 S.Ct. 656, 97 L.Ed. 986 (1953), that litigants should be free to suggest that a particular case is appropriate for consideration by all the judges of a court of appeals. The rule is addressed to the procedure whereby a party may suggest the appropriateness of convening the court in banc. It does not affect the power of a court of appeals to initiate in banc hearings *sua sponte*.

The provision that a vote will not be taken as a result of the suggestion of the party unless requested by a judge of the court in regular active service or by a judge who was a member of the panel that rendered a decision sought to be reheard is intended to make it clear that a suggestion of a party as such does not require any action by the court. See *Western Pacific Ry. Corp. v. Western Pacific Ry. Co.*, supra, 345 U.S. at 262, 73 S.Ct. 656. The rule merely authorizes a suggestion, imposes a time limit on suggestions for rehearings in banc, and provides that suggestions will be directed to the judges of the court in regular active service.

In practice, the suggestion of a party that a case be reheard in banc is frequently contained in a petition for rehearing, commonly styled "petition for rehearing in banc." Such a petition is in fact merely a petition for a rehearing, with a suggestion that the case be reheard in banc. Since no response to the suggestion, as distinguished from the petition for rehearing, is required, the panel which heard the case may quite properly dispose of the petition without reference to the suggestion. In such a case the fact that no response has been made to the suggestion does not affect the finality of the judgment or the issuance of the mandate, and the final sentence of the rule expressly so provides.

1979 Amendment

Under the present rule there is no specific provision for a response to a suggestion that an appeal be heard in banc. This has led to some uncertainty as to whether such a response may be filed. The proposed amendment would resolve this uncertainty.

While the present rule provides a time limit for suggestions for rehearing in banc, it does not deal with the timing of a request that the appeal be heard in banc initially. The proposed amendment fills this gap as well, providing that the suggestion must be made by the date of which the appellee's brief is filed.

Provision is made for circulating the suggestions to members of the panel despite the fact that senior judges on the panel would not be entitled to vote on whether a suggestion will be granted.

1994 Amendment

Subdivision (d). Subdivision (d) is added; it authorizes the courts of appeals to prescribe the number of copies of suggestions for hearing or rehearing in banc that must be filed. Because the number of copies needed depends directly upon the number of judges in the circuit, local rules are the best vehicle for setting the required number of copies.

Rule 36. Entry of Judgment; Notice

(a) Entry. A judgment is entered when it is noted on the docket. The clerk must prepare, sign, and enter the judgment:

(1) after receiving the court's opinion—but if settlement of the judgment's form is required, after final settlement; or

(2) if a judgment is rendered without an opinion, as the court instructs.

(b) Notice. On the date when judgment is entered, the clerk must mail to all parties a copy of the opinion—or the judgment, if no opinion was written—and a notice of the date when the judgment was entered.

(As amended Apr. 24, 1998, eff. Dec. 1, 1998.)

ADVISORY COMMITTEE NOTES

1967 Adoption

This is the typical rule. See 1st Cir. Rule 29 [rule 29, U.S.Ct. of App. 1st Cir.]; 3d Cir. Rule 32 [rule 32, U.S.Ct. of App. 3rd Cir.]; 6th Cir. Rule 21 [rule 21, U.S.Ct. of App. 6th Cir.]. At present, uncertainty exists as to the date of entry of judgment when the opinion directs subsequent settlement of the precise terms of the judgment, a common practice in cases involving enforcement of agency orders. See Stern and Gressman, Supreme Court Practice, p. 203 (3d Ed., 1962). The principle of finality suggests that in such cases entry of judgment should be delayed until approval of the judgment in final form.

Rule 37. Interest on Judgment

(a) When the Court Affirms. Unless the law provides otherwise, if a money judgment in a civil case is affirmed, whatever interest is allowed by law is payable from the date when the district court's judgment was entered.

(b) When the Court Reverses. If the court modifies or reverses a judgment with a direction that a money judgment be entered in the district court, the mandate must contain instructions about the allowance of interest.

(As amended Apr. 24, 1998, eff. Dec. 1, 1998.)

ADVISORY COMMITTEE NOTES

1967 Adoption

The first sentence makes it clear that if a money judgment is affirmed in the court of appeals, the interest which attaches to money judgments by force of law (see 28 U.S.C. § 1961 and § 2411) upon their initial entry is payable as if no appeal had been taken, whether or not the mandate makes mention of interest. There has been some confusion on this point. *See Blair v. Durham*, 139 F.2d 260 (6th Cir., 1943) and cases cited therein.

In reversing or modifying the judgment of the district court, the court of appeals may direct the entry of a money judgment, as, for example, when the court of appeals reverses a judgment notwithstanding the verdict and directs entry of judgment on the verdict. In such a case the question may arise as to whether interest is to run from the date of entry of the judgment directed by the court of appeals or from the date on which the judgment would have been entered in the district court except for the erroneous ruling corrected on appeal. In *Briggs v. Pennsylvania R. Co.*, 334 U.S. 304, 68 S.Ct. 1039, 92 L.Ed. 1403 (1948), the Court held that where the mandate of the court of appeals directed entry of judgment upon a verdict but made no mention of interest from the date of the verdict to the date of the entry of the judgment directed by the mandate, the district court was powerless to add such interest. The second sentence of the proposed rule is a reminder to the court, the clerk and counsel of the *Briggs* rule. Since the rule directs that the matter of interest be disposed of by the mandate, in cases where interest is simply overlooked, a party who conceives himself entitled to interest from a date other than the date of entry of judgment in accordance with the mandate should be entitled to seek recall of the mandate for determination of the question.

Rule 38. Frivolous Appeal—Damages and Costs

If a court of appeals determines that an appeal is frivolous, it may, after a separately filed motion or notice from the court and reasonable opportunity to respond, award just damages and single or double costs to the appellee.

(As amended Apr. 29, 1994, eff. Dec. 1, 1994; Apr. 24, 1998, eff. Dec. 1, 1998.)

ADVISORY COMMITTEE NOTES

1967 Adoption

Compare 28 U.S.C. § 1912. While both the statute and the usual rule on the subject by courts of appeals (Fourth Circuit Rule 20 [rule 20, U.S.Ct. of App. 4th Cir.] is a typical rule) speak of "damages for delay," the courts of appeals quite properly allow damages, attorney's fees and other expenses incurred by an appellee if the appeal is frivolous without requiring a showing that the appeal resulted in delay. See *Dunscombe v. Sayle*, 340 F.2d 311 (5th Cir., 1965), cert. den., 382 U.S. 814, 86 S.Ct. 32, 15 L.Ed.2d 62 (1965); *Lowe v. Willacy*, 239 F.2d 179 (9th Cir., 1956); *Griffin Wellpoint Corp. v. Munro-Langstroth, Inc.*, 269 F.2d 64 (1st Cir., 1959); *Ginsburg v. Stern*, 295 F.2d 698 (3d Cir., 1961). The subjects of interest and damages are separately regulated, contrary to the present practice of combining the two (see Fourth Circuit Rule 20) to make it clear that the awards are distinct and independent. Interest is provided for by law; damages are awarded by the court in its discretion in the case of a frivolous appeal as a matter of justice to the appellee and as a penalty against the appellant.

1994 Amendments

The amendment requires that before a court of appeals may impose sanctions, the person to be sanctioned must have notice and an opportunity to respond. The amendment reflects the basic principle enunciated in the Supreme Court's opinion in *Roadway Express, Inc. v. Piper*, 447 U.S. 752, 767 (1980), that notice and opportunity to respond must precede the imposition of sanctions. A separately filed motion requesting sanctions constitutes notice. A statement inserted in a party's brief that the party moves for sanctions is not sufficient notice. Requests in briefs for sanctions have become so commonplace that it is unrealistic to expect careful responses to such requests without any indication that the court is actually contemplating such measures. Only a motion, the purpose of which is to request sanctions, is sufficient. If there is no such motion filed, notice must come from the court. The form of notice from the court and of the opportunity for comment purposely are left to the court's discretion.

Rule 39. Costs

(a) Against Whom Assessed. The following rules apply unless the law provides or the court orders otherwise:

(1) if an appeal is dismissed, costs are taxed against the appellant, unless the parties agree otherwise;

(2) if a judgment is affirmed, costs are taxed against the appellant;

(3) if a judgment is reversed, costs are taxed against the appellee;

(4) if a judgment is affirmed in part, reversed in part, modified, or vacated, costs are taxed only as the court orders.

(b) Costs For and Against the United States. Costs for or against the United States, its agency, or officer will be assessed under Rule 39(a) only if authorized by law.

(c) Costs of Copies. Each court of appeals must, by local rule, fix the maximum rate for taxing the cost of producing necessary copies of a brief or appendix, or copies of records authorized by Rule 30(f). The rate must not exceed that generally charged for such work in the area where the clerk's office is located and should encourage economical methods of copying.

(d) Bill of Costs: Objections; Insertion in Mandate.

(1) A party who wants costs taxed must—within 14 days after entry of judgment—file with the circuit clerk, with proof of service, an itemized and verified bill of costs.

(2) Objections must be filed within 10 days after service of the bill of costs, unless the court extends the time.

(3) The clerk must prepare and certify an itemized statement of costs for insertion in the mandate, but issuance of the mandate must not be delayed for taxing costs. If the mandate issues before costs are finally determined, the district clerk must—upon the circuit clerk's request—add the statement of costs, or any amendment of it, to the mandate.

(e) Costs on Appeal Taxable in the District Court. The following costs on appeal are taxable in the district court for the benefit of the party entitled to costs under this rule:

(1) the preparation and transmission of the record;

(2) the reporter's transcript, if needed to determine the appeal;

(3) premiums paid for a supersedeas bond or other bond to preserve rights pending appeal; and

(4) the fee for filing the notice of appeal.

(As amended Apr. 30, 1979, eff. Aug. 1, 1979; Mar. 10, 1986, eff. July 1, 1986; Apr. 24, 1998, eff. Dec. 1, 1998.)

ADVISORY COMMITTEE NOTES

1967 Adoption

Subdivision (a). Statutory authorization for taxation of costs is found in 28 U.S.C. § 1920. The provisions of this subdivision follow the usual practice in the circuits. A few statutes contain specific provisions in derogation of these general provisions. (See 28 U.S.C. § 1928, which forbids the award of costs to a successful plaintiff in a patent infringement action under the circumstances described by the statute). These statutes are controlling in cases to which they apply.

Subdivision (b). The rules of the courts of appeals at present commonly deny costs to the United States except as allowance may be directed by statute. Those rules were promulgated at a time when the United States was generally invulnerable to an award of costs against it, and they appear to be based on the view that if the United States is not subject to costs if it loses, it ought not be entitled to recover costs if it wins.

The number of cases affected by such rules has been greatly reduced by the Act of July 18, 1966, 80 Stat. 308 (1 U.S.Code Cong. & Ad.News, p. 349 (1966), 89th Cong., 2d Sess., which amended 28 U.S.C. § 2412, the former general bar to the award of costs against the United States. Section 2412 as amended generally places the United States on the same footing as private parties with respect to the award of costs in civil cases. But the United States continues to enjoy immunity from costs in certain cases. By its terms amended § 2412 authorizes an award of costs against the United States only in civil actions, and it excepts from its general authorization of an award of costs against the United States cases which are "otherwise specifically provided (for) by statute." Furthermore, the Act of July 18, 1966, *supra*, provides that the amendments of § 2412 which it effects shall apply only to actions filed subsequent to the date of its enactment. The second clause continues in effect, for these and all other cases in which the United States enjoys immunity from costs, the presently prevailing rule that the United States may recover costs as the prevailing party only if it would have suffered them as the losing party.

Subdivision (c). While only five circuits (D.C.Cir. Rule 20(d) [rule 20(d), U.S.Ct. of App. Dist. of Col.]; 1st Cir. Rule 31(4) [rule 31(4), U.S.Ct. of App. 1st Cir.]; 3d Cir. Rule 35(4) [rule 35(4), U.S.Ct. of App. 3rd Cir.]; 4th Cir. Rule 21(4) [rule 21(4) U.S.Ct. of App. 4th Cir.]; 9th Cir. Rule 25 [rule 25, U.S.Ct. of App.9th Cir.], as amended June 2, 1967) presently tax the cost of printing briefs, the proposed rule makes the cost taxable in keeping with the principle of this rule that all cost items expended in the prosecution of a proceeding should be borne by the unsuccessful party.

Subdivision (e). The costs described in this subdivision are costs of the appeal and, as such, are within the undertaking of the appeal bond. They are made taxable in the district court for general convenience. Taxation of the cost of the reporter's transcript is specifically authorized by 28 U.S.C. § 1920, but in the absence of a rule some district courts have held themselves without authority to tax the cost (*Perlman v. Feldmann*, 116 F.Supp. 102 (D. Conn., 1953); *Firtag v. Gendleman*, 152 F.Supp. 226 (D.D.C., 1957); *Todd Atlantic Shipyards Corp. v. The Southport*, 100 F.Supp. 763 (E.D.S.C., 1951). Provision for taxation of the cost of premiums paid for supersedeas bonds is common in the local rules of district courts and the practice is established in the Second, Seventh, and Ninth Circuits. *Berner v. British Commonwealth Pacific Air Lines, Ltd.*, 362 F.2d 799 (2d Cir. 1966); *Land Oberoesterreich v. Gude*, 93 F.2d 292 (2d Cir., 1937); *In re Northern Ind. Oil Co.*, 192 F.2d 139 (7th Cir., 1951); *Lunn v. F. W. Woolworth*, 210 F.2d 159 (9th Cir., 1954).

1979 Amendment

Subdivision (c). The proposed amendment would permit variations among the circuits in regulating the maximum rates taxable as costs for printing or otherwise reproducing briefs, appendices, and copies of records authorized by Rule 30(f). The present rule has had a different effect in different circuits depending upon the size of the circuit, the location of the clerk's office, and the location of other cities. As a consequence there was a growing sense that strict adherence to the rule produces some unfairness in some of the circuits and the matter should be made subject to local rule.

Subdivision (d). The present rule makes no provision for objections to a bill of costs. The proposed amendment would allow 10 days for such objections. Cf. Rule 54(d) of the F.R.C.P. [rule 54(d), Federal Rules of Civil Procedure]. It provides further that the mandate shall not be delayed for taxation of costs.

1986 Amendment

The amendment to subdivision (c) is intended to increase the degree of control exercised by the courts of appeals over rates for printing and copying recoverable as costs. It further requires the courts of appeals to encourage cost-consciousness by requiring that, in fixing the rate, the court consider the most economical methods of printing and copying.

The amendment to subdivision (d) is technical. No substantive change is intended.

Rule 40. Petition for Panel Rehearing

(a) Time to File; Contents; Answer; Action by the Court if Granted.

(1) Time. Unless the time is shortened or extended by order or local rule, a petition for panel rehearing may be filed within 14 days after entry of judgment. But in a civil case, if the United States or its officer or agency is a party, the time within which any party may seek rehearing is 45 days after entry of judgment, unless an order shortens or extends the time.

(2) Contents. The petition must state with particularity each point of law or fact that the petitioner believes the court has overlooked or misapprehended and must argue in support of the petition. Oral argument is not permitted.

(3) Answer. Unless the court requests, no answer to a petition for panel rehearing is permitted. But ordinarily rehearing will not be granted in the absence of such a request.

(4) Action by the Court. If a petition for panel rehearing is granted, the court may do any of the following:

(A) make a final disposition of the case without reargument;

(B) restore the case to the calendar for reargument or resubmission; or

(C) issue any other appropriate order.

(b) Form of Petition; Length. The petition must comply in form with Rule 32. Copies must be served and filed as Rule 31 prescribes. Unless the court permits or a local rule provides otherwise, a petition for panel rehearing must not exceed 15 pages.

(As amended Apr. 30, 1979, eff. Aug. 1, 1979; Apr. 29, 1994, eff. Dec. 1, 1994; Apr. 24, 1998, eff. Dec. 1, 1998.)

ADVISORY COMMITTEE NOTES

1967 Adoption

This is the usual rule among the circuits, except that the express prohibition against filing a reply to the petition is found only in the rules of the Fourth, Sixth and Eighth Circuits (it is also contained in Supreme Court Rule 58(3) [rule 58(3), U.S.Sup.Ct.Rules). It is included to save time and expense to the party victorious on appeal. In the very rare instances in which a reply is useful, the court will ask for it.

1979 Amendment

Subdivision (a). The Standing Committee added to the first sentence of Rule 40(a) the words "or by local rule," to conform to current practice in the circuits. The Standing Committee believes the change noncontroversial.

Subdivision (b). The proposed amendment would eliminate the distinction drawn in the present rule between printed briefs and those duplicated from typewritten pages in fixing their maximum length. See Note to Rule 28. Since petitions for rehearing must be prepared in a short time, making typographic printing less likely, the maximum number of pages is fixed at 15, the figure used in the present rule for petitions duplicated by means other than typographic printing.

1994 Amendment

Subdivision (a). The amendment lengthens the time for filing a petition for rehearing from 14 to 45 days in civil cases involving the United States or its agencies or officers. It has no effect upon the time for filing in criminal cases. The amendment makes nation-wide the current practice in the District of Columbia and the Tenth Circuits, *see* D.C. Cir. R. 15 (a), 10th Cir. R. 40.3. This amendment, analogous to the provision in Rule 4(a) extending the time for filing a notice of appeal in cases involving the United States, recognizes that the Solicitor General needs time to conduct a thorough review of the merits of a case before requesting a rehearing. In a case in which a court of appeals believes it necessary to restrict the time for filing a rehearing petition, the amendment provides that the court may do so by order. Although the first sentence of Rule 40 permits a court of appeals to shorten or lengthen the usual 14 day filing period by order or by local rule, the sentence governing appeals in civil cases involving the United States purposely limits a court's power to alter the 45 day period to orders in specific cases. If a court of appeals could adopt a local rule shortening the time for filing a petition for rehearing in all cases involving the United States, the purpose of the amendment would be defeated.

Rule 41. Mandate: Contents; Issuance and Effective Date; Stay

(a) Contents. Unless the court directs that a formal mandate issue, the mandate consists of a certified copy of the judgment, a copy of the court's opinion, if any, and any direction about costs.

(b) When Issued. The court's mandate must issue 7 days after the time to file a petition for rehearing expires, or 7 days after entry of an order denying a timely petition for panel rehearing, rehearing en banc, or motion for stay of mandate, whichever is later. The court may shorten or extend the time.

(c) Effective Date. The mandate is effective when issued.

(d) Staying the Mandate.

(1) On Petition for Rehearing or Motion. The timely filing of a petition for panel rehearing, petition for rehearing en banc, or motion for stay of mandate, stays the mandate until disposition of the petition or motion, unless the court orders otherwise.

(2) Pending Petition for Certiorari.

(A) A party may move to stay the mandate pending the filing of a petition for a writ of certiorari in the Supreme Court. The motion must be served on all parties and must show that the certiorari petition would present a substantial question and that there is good cause for a stay.

(B) The stay must not exceed 90 days, unless the period is extended for good cause or unless the party who obtained the stay files a petition for the writ and so notifies the circuit clerk in writing within the period of the stay. In that case, the stay continues until the Supreme Court's final disposition.

(C) The court may require a bond or other security as a condition to granting or continuing a stay of the mandate.

(D) The court of appeals must issue the mandate immediately when a copy of a Supreme Court order denying the petition for writ of certiorari is filed.

(As amended Apr. 29, 1994, eff. Dec. 1, 1994; Apr. 24, 1998, eff. Dec. 1, 1998.)

ADVISORY COMMITTEE NOTES

1967 Adoption

The proposed rule follows the rule or practice in a majority of circuits by which copies of the opinion and the judgment serve in lieu of a formal mandate in the ordinary case. Compare Supreme Court Rule 59. Although 28 U.S.C. § 2101(c) permits a writ of certiorari to be filed within 90 days after entry of judgment, seven of the eight circuits which now regulate the matter of stays pending application for certiorari limit the initial stay of the mandate to the 30-day period provided in the proposed rule. Compare D.C.Cir. Rule 27(e) [rule 27(e), U.S.Ct. of App. Dist. of Col.].

1994 Amendment

Subdivision (a). The amendment conforms Rule 41(a) to the amendment made to Rule 40(a). The amendment keys the time for issuance of the mandate to the expiration of the time for filing a petition for rehearing, unless such a petition is filed in which case the mandate issues 7 days after the entry of the order denying the petition. Because the amendment to Rule 40(a) lengthens the time for filing a petition for rehearing in civil cases involving the United States from 14 to 45 days, the rule requiring the mandate to issue 21 days after the entry of judgment would cause the mandate to issue while the government is still considering requesting a rehearing. Therefore, the amendment generally requires the mandate to issue 7 days after the expiration of the time for filing a petition for rehearing.

Subdivision (b). The amendment requires a party who files a motion requesting a stay of mandate to file, at the same time, proof of service on all other parties. The old rule required the party to give notice to the other parties; the amendment merely requires the party to provide the court with evidence of having done so.

The amendment also states that the motion must show that a petition for certiorari would present a substantial question and that there is good cause for a stay. The amendment is intended to alert the parties to the fact that a stay of mandate is not granted automatically and to the type of showing that needs to be made. The Supreme Court has established conditions that must be met before it will stay a mandate. *See* Robert L. Stern et al., Supreme Court Practice § 17.19 (6th ed. 1986).

Rule 42. Voluntary Dismissal

(a) Dismissal in the District Court. Before an appeal has been docketed by the circuit clerk, the district court may dismiss the appeal on the filing of a stipulation signed by all parties or on the appellant's motion with notice to all parties.

(b) Dismissal in the Court of Appeals. The circuit clerk may dismiss a docketed appeal if the parties file a signed dismissal agreement specifying how costs are to be paid and pay any fees that are due. But no mandate or other process may issue without a court order. An appeal may be dismissed on the appellant's motion on terms agreed to by the parties or fixed by the court.

(As amended Apr. 24, 1998, eff. Dec. 1, 1998.)

ADVISORY COMMITTEE NOTES

1967 Adoption

Subdivision (a). This subdivision is derived from FRCP 73(a) [rule 73(a), Federal Rules of Civil Procedure] without change of substance.

Subdivision (b). The first sentence is a common provision in present circuit rules. The second sentence is added. Compare Supreme Court Rule 60.

Rule 43. Substitution of Parties

(a) Death of a Party.

(1) After Notice of Appeal Is Filed. If a party dies after a notice of appeal has been filed or while a proceeding is pending in the court of appeals, the decedent's personal representative may be substituted as a party on motion filed with the circuit clerk by the representative or by any party. A party's motion must be served on the representative in accordance with Rule 25. If the decedent has no representative, any party may suggest the death on the record, and the court of appeals may then direct appropriate proceedings.

(2) Before Notice of Appeal Is Filed—Potential Appellant. If a party entitled to appeal dies before filing a notice of appeal, the decedent's personal representative—or, if there is no personal representative, the decedent's attorney of record—may file a notice of appeal within the time prescribed by these rules. After the notice of appeal is filed, substitution must be in accordance with Rule 43(a)(1).

(3) Before Notice of Appeal Is Filed—Potential Appellee. If a party against whom an appeal may be taken dies after entry of a judgment or order in the district court, but before a notice of appeal is filed, an appellant may proceed as if the death had not occurred. After the notice of appeal is filed, substitution must be in accordance with Rule 43(a)(1).

(b) Substitution for a Reason Other Than Death. If a party needs to be substituted for any reason other than death, the procedure prescribed in Rule 43(a) applies.

(c) Public Officer: Identification; Substitution.

(1) Identification of Party. A public officer who is a party to an appeal or other proceeding in an official capacity may be described as a party by the public officer's official title rather than by name. But the court may require the public officer's name to be added.

(2) Automatic Substitution of Officeholder. When a public officer who is a party to an appeal or other proceeding in an official capacity dies, resigns, or otherwise ceases to hold office, the action does not abate. The public officer's successor is automatically substituted as a party. Proceedings following the substitution are to be in the name of the substituted party, but any misnomer that does not affect the substantial rights of the parties may be disregarded. An order of substitution may be entered at any time, but failure to enter an order does not affect the substitution.

(As amended Mar. 10, 1986, eff. July 1, 1986; Apr. 24, 1998, eff. Dec. 1, 1998.)

ADVISORY COMMITTEE NOTES

1967 Adoption

Subdivision (a). The first three sentences describe a procedure similar to the rule on substitution in civil actions in the district court. See FRCP 25(a) [rule 25(a), Federal Rules of Civil Procedure]. The fourth sentence expressly authorizes an appeal to be taken against one who has died after the entry of judgment. Compare FRCP 73(b) [rule 73(b), Federal Rules of Civil Procedure], which impliedly authorizes such an appeal.

The sixth sentence authorizes an attorney of record for the deceased to take an appeal on behalf of successors in interest if the deceased has no representative. At present, if a party entitled to appeal dies before the notice of appeal is filed, the appeal can presumably be taken only by his legal representative and must be taken within the time ordinarily prescribed. 13 Cyclopedia of Federal Procedure (3d Ed.) § 63.21. The states commonly make special provision for the even of the death of a party entitled to appeal, usually by extending the time otherwise prescribed. Rules of Civil Procedure for Superior Courts of Arizona, Rule 73(t), 16 A.R.S.; New Jersey Rev.Rules 1:3–3; New York Civil Practice Law and Rules, § 1022; Wisconsin Statutes Ann. 274.01(2). The Provision in the proposed rule is derived from California Code of Civil Procedure, § 941.

Subdivision (c). This subdivision is derived from FRCP 25(d) [rule 25(d), Federal Rules of Civil Procedure] and Supreme Court Rule 48, with appropriate changes.

1986 Amendment

The amendments to Rules 43(a) and (c) are technical. No substantive change is intended.

Rule 44. Case Involving a Constitutional Question When the United States Is Not a Party

If a party questions the constitutionality of an Act of Congress in a proceeding in which the United States or its agency, officer, or employee is not a party in an official capacity, the questioning party must give written notice to the circuit clerk immediately upon the filing of the record or as soon as the question is raised in the court of appeals. The clerk must then certify that fact to the Attorney General.

(As amended Apr. 24, 1998, eff. Dec. 1, 1998.)

ADVISORY COMMITTEE NOTES

1967 Adoption

This rule is now found in the rules of a majority of the circuits. It is in response to the Act of August 24, 1937 (28 U.S.C. § 2403), which requires all courts of the United States to advise the Attorney General of the existence of an action or proceeding of the kind described in the rule.

Rule 45. Clerk's Duties

(a) General Provisions.

(1) Qualifications. The circuit clerk must take the oath and post any bond required by law. Neither the clerk nor any deputy clerk may practice as an attorney or counselor in any court while in office.

(2) When Court Is Open. The court of appeals is always open for filing any paper, issuing and returning process, making a motion, and entering an order. The clerk's office with the clerk or a deputy in attendance must be open during business hours on all days except Saturdays, Sundays, and legal holidays. A court may provide by local rule or by order that the clerk's office be open for specified hours on Saturdays or on legal holidays other than New Year's Day, Martin Luther King, Jr.'s Birthday, Presidents' Day, Memorial Day, Independence Day, Labor Day, Columbus Day, Veterans' Day, Thanksgiving Day, and Christmas Day.

(b) Records.

(1) The Docket. The circuit clerk must maintain a docket and an index of all docketed cases in the manner prescribed by the Director of the Administrative Office of the United States Courts. The clerk must record all papers filed with the clerk and all process, orders, and judgments.

(2) Calendar. Under the court's direction, the clerk must prepare a calendar of cases awaiting argument. In placing cases on the calendar for argument, the clerk must give preference to appeals in criminal cases and to other proceedings and appeals entitled to preference by law.

(3) Other Records. The clerk must keep other books and records required by the Director of the Administrative Office of the United States Courts, with the approval of the Judicial Conference of the United States, or by the court.

(c) Notice of an Order or Judgment. Upon the entry of an order or judgment, the circuit clerk must immediately serve by mail a notice of entry on each party to the proceeding, with a copy of any opinion, and must note the mailing on the docket. Service on a party represented by counsel must be made on counsel.

(d) Custody of Records and Papers. The circuit clerk has custody of the court's records and papers. Unless the court orders or instructs otherwise, the clerk must not permit an original record or paper to be taken from the clerk's office. Upon disposition of the case, original papers constituting the record on appeal or review must be returned to the court or agency from which they were received. The clerk must preserve a copy of any brief, appendix, or other paper that has been filed.

(As amended Mar. 1, 1971, eff. July 1, 1971; Mar. 10, 1986, eff. July 1, 1986; Apr. 24, 1998, eff. Dec. 1, 1998.)

ADVISORY COMMITTEE NOTES

1967 Adoption

The duties imposed upon clerks of the courts of appeals by this rule are those imposed by rule or practice in a majority of the circuits. The second sentence of subdivision (a) authorizing the closing of the clerk's office on Saturday and non-national legal holidays follows a similar provision respecting the district court clerk's office found in FRCP 77(c) [rule 77(c), Federal Rules of Civil Procedure] and in FRCrP 56 [rule 56, Federal Rules of Criminal Procedure].

1971 Amendment

The amendment adds Columbus Day to the list of legal holidays. See the Note accompanying the amendment of Rule 26(a).

1986 Amendment

The amendment to Rule 45(b) permits the courts of appeals to maintain computerized dockets. The Committee believes that the Administrative Office of the United States Courts ought to have maximum flexibility in prescribing the format of this docket in order to ensure a smooth transition from manual to automated systems and subsequent adaptation to technological improvements.

The amendments to Rules 45(a) and (d) are technical. No substantive change is intended. The Birthday of Martin Luther King, Jr. has been added to the list of national holidays.

Rule 46. Attorneys

(a) Admission to the Bar.

(1) Eligibility. An attorney is eligible for admission to the bar of a court of appeals if that attorney is of good moral and professional character and is admitted to practice before the Supreme Court of the United States, the highest court of a state, another United States court of appeals, or a United States district court (including the district courts for Guam, the Northern Mariana Islands, and the Virgin Islands).

(2) Application. An applicant must file an application for admission, on a form approved by the court that contains the applicant's personal statement showing eligibility for membership. The applicant must subscribe to the following oath or affirmation:

"I, ________________, do solemnly swear [or affirm] that I will conduct myself as an attorney and counselor of this court, uprightly and according to law; and that I will support the Constitution of the United States."

(3) Admission Procedures. On written or oral motion of a member of the court's bar, the court will act on the application. An applicant may be admitted by oral motion in open court. But, unless the court orders otherwise, an applicant need not appear before the court to be admitted. Upon admission, an applicant must pay the clerk the fee prescribed by local rule or court order.

(b) Suspension or Disbarment.

(1) Standard. A member of the court's bar is subject to suspension or disbarment by the court if the member:

(A) has been suspended or disbarred from practice in any other court; or

(B) is guilty of conduct unbecoming a member of the court's bar.

(2) Procedure. The member must be given an opportunity to show good cause, within the time prescribed by the court, why the member should not be suspended or disbarred.

(3) Order. The court must enter an appropriate order after the member responds and a hearing is held, if requested, or after the time prescribed for a response expires, if no response is made.

(c) Discipline. A court of appeals may discipline an attorney who practices before it for conduct unbecoming a member of the bar or for failure to comply with any court rule. First, however, the court must afford the attorney reasonable notice, an opportunity to show cause to the contrary, and, if requested, a hearing.

(As amended Mar. 10, 1986, eff. July 1, 1986; Apr. 24, 1998, eff. Dec. 1, 1998.)

ADVISORY COMMITTEE NOTES

1967 Adoption

Subdivision (a). The basic requirement of membership in the bar of the Supreme Court, or of the highest court of a state, or in another court of appeals or a district court is found, with minor variations, in the rules of ten circuits. The only other requirement in those circuits is that the applicant be of good moral and professional character. In the District of Columbia Circuit applicants other than members of the District of Columbia District bar or the Supreme Court bar must claim membership in the bar of the highest court of a state, territory or possession for three years prior to application for admission (D.C.Cir. Rule 7 [rule 7, U.S.Ct. of App. Dist. of Col.]). Members of the District of Columbia District bar and the Supreme Court bar again excepted, applicants for admission to the District of Columbia Circuit bar must meet precisely defined prelaw and law school study requirements (D.C.Cir. Rule 7½ [rule 7½, U.S.Ct. of App.Dist. of Col.]).

A few circuits now require that application for admission be made by oral motion by a sponsor member in open court. The proposed rule permits both the application and the motion by the sponsor member to be in writing, and permits action on the motion without the appearance of the applicant or the sponsor, unless the court otherwise orders.

Subdivision (b). The provision respecting suspension or disbarment is uniform. Third Circuit Rule 8(3) [rule 8(3), U.S.Ct. of App. 3rd Cir.] is typical.

Subdivision (c). At present only Fourth Circuit Rule 36 [rule 36, U.S.Ct. of App. 4th Cir.] contains an equivalent provision. The purpose of this provision is to make explicit the power of a court of appeals to impose sanctions less serious than suspension or disbarment for the breach of rules. It also affords some measure of control over attorneys who are not members of the bar of the court. Several circuits permit a non-member attorney to file briefs and motions, membership being required only at the time of oral argument. And several circuits permit argument pro hac vice by non-member attorneys.

1986 Amendments

The amendments to Rules 46(a) and (b) are technical. No substantive change is intended.

HISTORICAL NOTES

Termination of United States District Court for the District of the Canal Zone

For termination of the United States District Court for the District of the Canal Zone at end of the "transition period", being the 30–month period beginning Oct. 1, 1979, and ending midnight Mar. 31, 1982, see Paragraph 5 of Article XI of the Panama Canal Treaty of 1977 and sections 3831 and 3841 to 3843 of Title 22, Foreign Relations and Intercourse.

Rule 47. Local Rules by Courts of Appeals

(a) Local Rules.

(1) Each court of appeals acting by a majority of its judges in regular active service may, after giving appropriate public notice and opportunity for comment, make and amend rules governing its practice. A generally applicable direction to parties or lawyers regarding practice before a court must be in a local rule rather than an internal operating procedure or standing order. A local rule must be consistent with—but not duplicative of—Acts of Congress and rules adopted under 28 U.S.C. § 2072 and must conform to any uniform numbering system prescribed by the Judicial Conference of the United States. Each circuit clerk must send the Administrative Office of the United States Courts a copy of each local rule and internal operating procedure when it is promulgated or amended.

(2) A local rule imposing a requirement of form must not be enforced in a manner that causes a party to lose rights because of a nonwillful failure to comply with the requirement.

(b) Procedure When There Is No Controlling Law. A court of appeals may regulate practice in a particular case in any manner consistent with federal law, these rules, and local rules of the circuit. No sanction or other disadvantage may be imposed for noncompliance with any requirement not in federal law, federal rules, or the local circuit rules unless the alleged violator has been furnished in the particular case with actual notice of the requirement.

(As amended Apr. 27, 1995, eff. Dec. 1, 1995; Apr. 24, 1998, eff. Dec. 1, 1998.)

ADVISORY COMMITTEE NOTES

1967 Adoption

This rule continues the authority now vested in individual courts of appeals by 28 U.S.C. § 2071 to make rules consistent with rules of practice and procedure promulgated by the Supreme Court.

1995 Amendments

Subdivision (a). This rule is amended to require that a generally applicable direction regarding practice before a court of appeals must be in a local rule rather than an internal operating procedure or some other general directive. It is the intent of this rule that a local rule may not bar any practice that these rules explicitly or implicitly permit. Subdivision (b) allows a court of appeals to regulate practice in an individual case by entry of an order in the case. The amendment also reflects the requirement that local rules be consistent not only with the national rules but also with Acts of Congress. The amendment also states that local rules should not repeat national rules and Acts of Congress.

The amendment also requires that the numbering of local rules conform with any uniform numbering system that may be prescribed by the Judicial Conference. Lack of uniform numbering might create unnecessary traps for counsel and litigants. A uniform numbering system would make it easier for an increasingly national bar and for litigants to locate a local rule that applies to a particular procedural issue.

Paragraph (2) is new. Its aim is to protect against loss of rights in the enforcement of local rules relating to matters of form. The proscription of paragraph (2) is narrowly drawn—covering only violations that are not willful and only those involving local rules directed to matters of form. It does not limit the court's power to impose substantive penalties upon a party if it or its attorney stubbornly or repeatedly violates a local rule, even one involving merely a matter of form. Nor does it affect the court's power to enforce local rules that involve more than mere matters of form.

Subdivision (b). This rule provides flexibility to the court in regulating practice in a particular case when there is no controlling law. Specifically, it permits the court to regulate practice in any manner consistent with Acts of Congress, with rules adopted under 28 U.S.C. § 2072, and with the circuit's local rules.

The amendment to this rule disapproves imposing any sanction or other disadvantage on a person for noncompliance with such a directive, unless the alleged violator has been furnished in a particular case with actual notice of the requirement. There should be no adverse consequence to a party or attorney for violating special requirements relating to practice before a particular court unless the party or attorney has actual notice of those requirements.

Rule 48. Masters

(a) Appointment; Powers. A court of appeals may appoint a special master to hold hearings, if necessary, and to recommend factual findings and disposition in matters ancillary to proceedings in the court. Unless the order referring a matter to a master specifies or limits the master's powers, those powers include, but are not limited to, the following:

(1) regulating all aspects of a hearing;

(2) taking all appropriate action for the efficient performance of the master's duties under the order;

(3) requiring the production of evidence on all matters embraced in the reference; and

(4) administering oaths and examining witnesses and parties.

(b) Compensation. If the master is not a judge or court employee, the court must determine the master's compensation and whether the cost is to be charged to any party.

(As amended Apr. 29, 1994, eff. Dec. 1, 1994; Apr. 24, 1998, eff. Dec. 1, 1998.)

ADVISORY COMMITTEE NOTES

1994 Amendments

The text of the existing Rule 48 concerning the title was moved to Rule 1.

This new Rule 48 authorizes a court of appeals to appoint a special master to make recommendations concerning ancillary matters. The courts of appeals have long used masters in contempt proceedings where the issue is compliance with an enforcement order. See *Polish National Alliance v. NLRB*, 159 F.2d 38 (7th Cir. 1946); *NLRB v. Arcade-Sunshine Co.*, 132 F.2d 8 (D.C. Cir. 1942); *NLRB v. Remington Rand, Inc.*, 130 F.2d 919 (2d Cir. 1942). There are other instances when the question before a court of appeals requires a factual determination. An application for fees or eligibility for Criminal Justice Act status on appeal are examples.

Ordinarily when a factual issue is unresolved, a court of appeals remands the case to the district court or agency that originally heard the case. It is not the Committee's intent to alter that practice. However, when factual issues arise in the first instance in the court of appeals, such as fees for representation on appeal, it would be useful to have authority to refer such determinations to a master for a recommendation.

APPENDIX OF FORMS

Form 1. Notice of Appeal to a Court of Appeals From a Judgment or Order of a District Court

United States District Court for the ______
District of ______
File Number ______

A.B., Plaintiff)
)
v.) *Notice of Appeal*
)
C.D., Defendant)

Notice is hereby given that [(here name all parties taking the appeal) , (plaintiffs) (defendants) in the above named case,[1]] hereby appeal to the United States Court of Appeals for the ______ Circuit (from the final judgment) (from an order (describing it)) entered in this action on the ______ day of ______, 19___.

(s) ______________
Attorney for [______]
[Address:______]

(As amended Apr. 22, 1993, eff. Dec. 1, 1993.)

1 See Rule 3(c) for permissible ways of identifying appellants.

Form 2. Notice of Appeal to a Court of Appeals From a Decision of the United States Tax Court

UNITED STATES TAX COURT
Washington, D.C.

A.B., Petitioner)
)
v.) Docket No. ______
)
Commissioner of Internal)
Revenue, Respondent)

Notice of Appeal

Notice is hereby given that [here name all parties taking the appeal [1]], hereby appeals to the United States Court of Appeals for the ______ Circuit from (that part of) the decision of this court entered in the above captioned proceeding on the ______ day of ______, 19___ (relating to ______).

(s) ______________
Counsel for [______]
[Address:______]

(As amended Apr. 22, 1993, eff. Dec. 1, 1993.)

1 See Rule 3(c) for permissible ways of identifying appellants.

Form 3. Petition for Review of Order of an Agency, Board, Commission or Officer

United States Court of Appeals
for the ______ Circuit

A.B., Petitioner)
)
v.) Petition for Review
XYZ Commission, Respondent)

[(here name all parties bringing the petition[1])] hereby petitions the court for review of the Order of the XYZ Commission (describe the order) entered on ______, 19___.

[(s)] ______________
Attorney for Petitioners
Address:______

(As amended Apr. 22, 1993, eff. Dec. 1, 1993.)

1 See Rule 15.

Form 4. Affidavit Accompanying Motion for Permission to Appeal In Forma Pauperis

United States District Court for the ______ District of ______

A.B., Plaintiff
v. Case No. ______
C.D., Defendant

Affidavit in Support of Motion	**Instructions**
I swear or affirm under penalty of perjury that, because of my poverty, I cannot prepay the docket fees of my appeal or post a bond for them. I believe I am entitled to redress. I swear or affirm under penalty of perjury under United States laws that my answers on this form are true and correct. (28 U.S.C. § 1746; 18 U.S.C. § 1621.)	Complete all questions in this application and then sign it. Do not leave any blanks: if the answer to a question is "0," "none," or "not applicable (N/A)," write in that response. If you need more space to answer a question or to explain your answer, attach a separate sheet of paper identified with your name, your case's docket number, and the question number.
Signed: ______	Date: ______

My issues on appeal are:

1. For both you and your spouse estimate the average amount of money received from each of the following sources during the past 12 months. Adjust any amount that was

received weekly, biweekly, quarterly, semiannually, or annually to show the monthly rate. Use gross amounts, that is, amounts before any deductions for taxes or otherwise.

Income source	**Average monthly amount during the past 12 months**	**Amount expected next month**
	You	**You**
Employment	$______	$______
Self-employment	$______	$______
Income from real property (such as rental income)	$______	$______
Interest and dividends	$______	$______
Gifts	$______	$______
Alimony	$______	$______
Child support	$______	$______
Retirement (such as social security, pensions, annuities, insurance)	$______	$______
Disability (such as social security, insurance payments)	$______	$______
Unemployment payments	$______	$______
Public-assistance (such as welfare)	$______	$______
Other (specify): __	$______	$______
Total monthly income:	$______	$______

2. List your employment history, most recent employer first. (Gross monthly pay is before taxes or other deductions.)

Employer	**Address**	**Dates of employment**	**Gross monthly pay**
______	______	______	______
______	______	______	______
______	______	______	______

3. List your spouse's employment history, most recent employer first. (Gross monthly pay is before taxes or other deductions.)

Employer	**Address**	**Dates of employment**	**Gross monthly pay**
______	______	______	______
______	______	______	______
______	______	______	______

4. How much cash do you and your spouse have? $______

Below, state any money you or your spouse have in bank accounts or in any other financial institution.

Financial institution	**Type of account**	**Amount you have**	**Amount your spouse has**
______	______	$______	$______
______	______	$______	$______
______	______	$______	$______

If you are a prisoner, you must attach a statement certified by the appropriate institutional officer showing all receipts, expenditures, and balances during the last six months in your institutional accounts. If you have multiple accounts, perhaps because you have been in multiple institutions, attach one certified statement of each account.

5. List the assets, and their values, which you own or your spouse owns. Do not list clothing and ordinary household furnishings.

Home (Value)	**Other real estate** (Value)	**Motor vehicle #1** (Value)
______	______	Make & year: ______
______	______	Model: ______
______	______	Registration #: ______

	Motor vehicle #2 (Value)	**Other assets** (Value)	**Other assets** (Value)
Make & year:	______	______	______
Model:	______	______	______
Registration #:	______	______	______

6. State every person, business, or organization owing you or your spouse money, and the amount owed.

Person owing you or your spouse money	**Amount owed to you**	**Amount owed to your spouse**
______	______	______
______	______	______
______	______	______

7. State the persons who rely on you or your spouse for support.

Name	**Relationship**	**Age**
______	______	______
______	______	______
______	______	______

8. Estimate the average monthly expenses of you and your family. Show separately the amounts paid by your spouse. Adjust any payments that are made weekly, biweekly, quarterly, semiannually, or annually to show the monthly rate.

	You	**Your Spouse**
Rent or home-mortgage payment (include lot rented for mobile home)	$______	$______
Are real-estate taxes included? ☐ Yes ☐ No		
Is property insurance included? ☐ Yes ☐ No		
Utilities (electricity, heating fuel, water, sewer, and Telephone)	$______	$______
Home maintenance (repairs and upkeep)	$______	$______
Food	$______	$______
Clothing	$______	$______
Laundry and dry-cleaning	$______	$______

Medical and dental expenses	$____	$____
Transportation (not including motor vehicle payments)	$____	$____
Recreation, entertainment, newspapers, magazines, etc.	$____	$____
Insurance (not deducted from wages or included in Mortgage payments)	$____	$____
Homeowner's or renter's	$____	$____
Life	$____	$____
Health	$____	$____
Motor Vehicle	$____	$____
Other: ____	$____	$____
Taxes (not deducted from wages or included in Mortgage payments) (specify): ____	$____	$____
Installment payments	$____	$____
Motor Vehicle	$____	$____
Credit card (name): ____	$____	$____
Department store (name): ____	$____	$____
Other: ____	$____	$____
Alimony, maintenance, and support paid to others	$____	$____
Regular expenses for operation of business, profession, or farm (attach detailed statement)	$____	$____
Other (specify): ____	$____	$____
Total monthly expenses:	$____	$____

9. Do you expect any major changes to your monthly income or expenses or in your assets or liabilities during the next 12 months?

☐ Yes ☐ No If yes, describe on an attached sheet.

10. Have you paid—or will you be paying—an attorney any money for services in connection with this case, including the completion of this form? Yes No

If yes, how much? $________

If yes, state the attorney's name, address, and telephone number:

____

____

____

11. Have you paid—or will you be paying—anyone other than an attorney (such as a paralegal or a typist) any money for services in connection with this case, including the completion of this form?

☐ Yes ☐ No

If yes, how much? $________

If yes, state the person's name, address, and telephone number:

____

____

____

12. Provide any other information that will help explain why you cannot pay the docket fees for your appeal.

13. State the address of your legal residence.

____

____

Your daytime phone number: ________

Your age: ______ Your years of schooling: ______

Your social-security number: ________

(As amended Apr. 24, 1998, eff. Dec. 1, 1998.)

Form 5. Notice of Appeal to a Court of Appeals from a Judgment or Order of a District Court or a Bankruptcy Appellate Panel

United States District Court for the ....
District of ....

In re)
..........................,)
Debtor)
) File No...........
..........................,)
Plaintiff)
v.)
..........................,)
Defendant)

Notice of Appeal to
United States Court of Appeals
for the .... Circuit

.........................., the plaintiff [or defendant or other party] appeals to the United States Court of Appeals for the .... Circuit from the final judgment [or order or decree] of the district court for the district of .... [or bankruptcy appellate panel of the .... circuit], entered in this case on ...., 19.... [here describe the judgment, order, or decree] ....

The parties to the judgment [or order or decree] appealed from and the names and addresses of their respective attorneys are as follows:

Dated ....
Signed ....
Attorney for Appellant

Address: ....
....

(Added Apr. 25, 1989, eff. Dec. 1, 1989.)

RULES OF THE SUPREME COURT OF THE UNITED STATES[1]

1 For rules effective until April 30, 1997, see 1997 Pocket Part.

Adopted January 16, 1997
Effective May 1, 1997

Amendments received to January 4, 1999

PART I. THE COURT

Rule

1. Clerk.
2. Library.
3. Term.
4. Sessions and Quorum.

PART II. ATTORNEYS AND COUNSELORS

5. Admission to the Bar.
6. Argument Pro Hac Vice.
7. Prohibition Against Practice.
8. Disbarment and Disciplinary Action.
9. Appearance of Counsel.

PART III. JURISDICTION ON WRIT OF CERTIORARI

10. Considerations Governing Review on Certiorari.
11. Certiorari to a United States Court of Appeals Before Judgment.
12. Review on Certiorari: How Sought; Parties.
13. Review on Certiorari: Time for Petitioning.
14. Content of a Petition for a Writ of Certiorari.
15. Briefs in Opposition; Reply Briefs; Supplemental Briefs.
16. Disposition of a Petition for a Writ of Certiorari.

PART IV. OTHER JURISDICTION

17. Procedure in an Original Action.
18. Appeal from a United States District Court.
19. Procedure on a Certified Question.
20. Procedure on a Petition for an Extraordinary Writ.

PART V. MOTIONS AND APPLICATIONS

21. Motions to the Court.
22. Applications to Individual Justices.
23. Stays.

Rule

PART VI. BRIEFS ON THE MERITS AND ORAL ARGUMENT

24. Briefs on the Merits: In General.
25. Briefs on the Merits: Number of Copies and Time to File.
26. Joint Appendix.
27. Calendar.
28. Oral Argument.

PART VII. PRACTICE AND PROCEDURE

29. Filing and Service of Documents; Special Notifications; Corporate Listing.
30. Computation and Extension of Time.
31. Translations.
32. Models, Diagrams, and Exhibits.
33. Document Preparation: Booklet Format; 8½- by 11-inch Paper Format.
34. Document Preparation: General Requirements.
35. Death, Substitution, and Revivor; Public Officers.
36. Custody of Prisoners in Habeas Corpus Proceedings.
37. Brief for an Amicus Curiae.
38. Fees.
39. Proceedings in Forma Pauperis.
40. Veterans, Seamen, and Military Cases.

PART VIII. DISPOSITION OF CASES

41. Opinions of the Court.
42. Interest and Damages.
43. Costs.
44. Rehearing.
45. Process; Mandates.
46. Dismissing Cases.

PART IX. DEFINITIONS AND EFFECTIVE DATE

47. Reference to "State Court" and "State Law".
48. Effective Date of Rules.

Complete Annotation Materials, see Title 28 U.S.C.A.

PART I. THE COURT

Rule 1. Clerk

1. The Clerk receives documents for filing with the Court and has authority to reject any submitted filing that does not comply with these Rules.

2. The Clerk maintains the Court's records and will not permit any of them to be removed from the Court building except as authorized by the Court. Any document filed with the Clerk and made a part of the Court's records may not thereafter be withdrawn from the official Court files. After the conclusion of proceedings in this Court, original records and documents transmitted to this Court by any other court will be returned to the court from which they were received.

3. Unless the Court or the Chief Justice orders otherwise, the Clerk's office is open from 9 a.m. to 5 p.m., Monday through Friday, except on federal legal holidays listed in 5 U.S.C. § 6103.

Rule 2. Library

1. The Court's library is available for use by appropriate personnel of this Court, members of the Bar of this Court, Members of Congress and their legal staffs, and attorneys for the United States and for federal departments and agencies.

2. The library's hours are governed by regulations made by the Librarian with the approval of the Chief Justice or the Court.

3. Library books may not be removed from the Court building, except by a Justice or a member of a Justice's staff.

Rule 3. Term

The Court holds a continuous annual Term commencing on the first Monday in October and ending on the day before the first Monday in October of the following year. See 28 U.S.C. § 2. At the end of each Term, all cases pending on the docket are continued to the next Term.

Rule 4. Sessions and Quorum

1. Open sessions of the Court are held beginning at 10 a.m. on the first Monday in October of each year, and thereafter as announced by the Court. Unless it orders otherwise, the Court sits to hear arguments from 10 a.m. until noon and from 1 p.m. until 3 p.m.

2. Six Members of the Court constitute a quorum. See 28 U.S.C. § 1. In the absence of a quorum on any day appointed for holding a session of the Court, the Justices attending—or if no Justice is present, the Clerk or a Deputy Clerk—may announce that the Court will not meet until there is a quorum.

3. When appropriate, the Court will direct the Clerk or the Marshal to announce recesses.

PART II. ATTORNEYS AND COUNSELORS

Rule 5. Admission to the Bar

1. To qualify for admission to the Bar of this Court, an applicant must have been admitted to practice in the highest court of a State, Commonwealth, Territory or Possession, or the District of Columbia for a period of at least three years immediately before the date of application; must not have been the subject of any adverse disciplinary action pronounced or in effect during that 3–year period; and must appear to the Court to be of good moral and professional character.

2. Each applicant shall file with the Clerk (1) a certificate from the presiding judge, clerk, or other authorized official of that court evidencing the applicant's admission to practice there and the applicant's current good standing, and (2) a completely executed copy of the form approved by this Court and furnished by the Clerk containing (a) the applicant's personal statement, and (b) the statement of two sponsors endorsing the correctness of the applicant's statement, stating that the applicant possesses all the qualifications required for admission, and affirming that the applicant is of good moral and professional character. Both sponsors must be members of the Bar of this Court who personally know, but are not related to, the applicant.

3. If the documents submitted demonstrate that the applicant possesses the necessary qualifications, and if the applicant has signed the oath or affirmation and paid the required fee, the Clerk will notify the applicant of acceptance by the Court as a member of the Bar and issue a certificate of admission. An applicant who so wishes may be admitted in open court on oral motion by a member of the Bar of this Court, provided that all other requirements for admission have been satisfied.

4. Each applicant shall sign the following oath or affirmation: I, ..., do solemnly swear (or affirm) that as an attorney and as a counselor of this Court, I will conduct myself uprightly and according to law, and that I will support the Constitution of the United States.

5. The fee for admission to the Bar and a certificate bearing the seal of the Court is $100, payable to the United States Supreme Court. The Marshal will deposit such fees in a separate fund to be disbursed by the Marshal at the direction of the Chief Justice for the costs of admissions, for the benefit of the Court and its Bar, and for related purposes.

6. The fee for a duplicate certificate of admission to the Bar bearing the seal of the Court is $15, payable to the United States Supreme Court. The proceeds will be maintained by the Marshal as provided in paragraph 5 of this Rule.

Rule 6. Argument *Pro Hac Vice*

1. An attorney not admitted to practice in the highest court of a State, Commonwealth, Territory or Possession, or the District of Columbia for the requisite three years, but otherwise eligible for admission to practice in this Court under Rule 5.1, may be permitted to argue *pro hac vice.*

2. An attorney qualified to practice in the courts of a foreign state may be permitted to argue *pro hac vice.*

3. Oral argument *pro hac vice* is allowed only on motion of the counsel of record for the party on whose behalf leave is requested. The motion shall state concisely the qualifications of the attorney who is to argue *pro hac vice.* It shall be filed with the Clerk, in the form required by Rule 21, no later than the date on which the respondent's or appellee's brief on the merits is due to be filed, and it shall be accompanied by proof of service as required by Rule 29.

Rule 7. Prohibition Against Practice

No employee of this Court shall practice as an attorney or counselor in any court or before any agency of government while employed by the Court; nor shall any person after leaving such employment participate in any professional capacity in any case pending before this Court or in any case being considered for filing in this Court, until two years have elapsed after separation; nor shall a former employee ever participate in any professional capacity in any case that was pending in this Court during the employee's tenure.

Rule 8. Disbarment and Disciplinary Action

1. Whenever a member of the Bar of this Court has been disbarred or suspended from practice in any court of record, or has engaged in conduct unbecoming a member of the Bar of this Court, the Court will enter an order suspending that member from practice before this Court and affording the member an opportunity to show cause, within 40 days, why a disbarment order should not be entered. Upon response, or if no response is timely filed, the Court will enter an appropriate order.

2. After reasonable notice and an opportunity to show cause why disciplinary action should not be taken, and after a hearing if material facts are in dispute, the Court may take any appropriate disciplinary action against any attorney who is admitted to practice before it for conduct unbecoming a member of the Bar or for failure to comply with these Rules or any Rule or order of the Court.

Rule 9. Appearance of Counsel

1. An attorney seeking to file a document in this Court in a representative capacity must first be admitted to practice before this Court as provided in Rule 5, except that admission to the Bar of this Court is not required for an attorney appointed under the Criminal Justice Act of 1964, see 18 U.S.C. § 3006A(d)(6), or under any other applicable federal statute. The attorney whose name, address, and telephone number appear on the cover of a document presented for filing is considered counsel of record, and a separate notice of appearance need not be filed. If the name of more than one attorney is shown on the cover of the document, the attorney who is counsel of record shall be clearly identified.

2. An attorney representing a party who will not be filing a document shall enter a separate notice of appearance as counsel of record indicating the name of the party represented. A separate notice of appearance shall also be entered whenever an attorney is substituted as counsel of record in a particular case.

PART III. JURISDICTION ON WRIT OF CERTIORARI

Rule 10. Considerations Governing Review on Certiorari

Review on a writ of certiorari is not a matter of right, but of judicial discretion. A petition for a writ of certiorari will be granted only for compelling reasons. The following, although neither controlling nor fully measuring the Court's discretion, indicate the character of the reasons the Court considers:

(a) a United States court of appeals has entered a decision in conflict with the decision of another United States court of appeals on the same important matter; has decided an important federal question in a way that conflicts with a decision by a state court of last resort; or has so far departed from the accepted and usual course of judicial proceedings, or sanctioned such a departure by a lower court, as to call for an exercise of this Court's supervisory power;

(b) a state court of last resort has decided an important federal question in a way that conflicts with the decision of another state court of last resort or of a United States court of appeals;

(c) a state court or a United States court of appeals has decided an important question of federal law that has not been, but should be, settled by this Court, or has decided an important federal question in a way that conflicts with relevant decisions of this Court.

A petition for a writ of certiorari is rarely granted when the asserted error consists of erroneous factual findings or the misapplication of a properly stated rule of law.

Rule 11. Certiorari to a United States Court of Appeals Before Judgment

A petition for a writ of certiorari to review a case pending in a United States court of appeals, before judgment is entered in that court, will be granted only upon a showing that the case is of such imperative public importance as to justify deviation from normal appellate practice and to require immediate determination in this Court. See 28 U.S.C. § 2101(e).

Rule 12. Review on Certiorari: How Sought; Parties

1. Except as provided in paragraph 2 of this Rule, the petitioner shall file 40 copies of a petition for a writ of certiorari, prepared as required by Rule 33.1, and shall pay the Rule 38(a) docket fee.

2. A petitioner proceeding *in forma pauperis* under Rule 39 shall file an original and 10 copies of a petition for a writ of certiorari prepared as required by Rule 33.2, together with an original and 10 copies of the motion for leave to proceed *in forma pauperis.* A copy of the motion shall precede and be attached to each copy of the petition. An inmate confined in an institution, if proceeding *in forma pauperis* and not represented by counsel, need file only an original petition and motion.

3. Whether prepared under Rule 33.1 or Rule 33.2, the petition shall comply in all respects with Rule 14 and shall be submitted with proof of service as required by Rule 29. The case then will be placed on the docket. It is the petitioner's duty to notify all respondents promptly, on a form supplied by the Clerk, of the date of filing, the date the case was placed on the docket, and the docket number of the case. The notice shall be served as required by Rule 29.

4. Parties interested jointly, severally, or otherwise in a judgment may petition separately for a writ of certiorari; or any two or more may join in a petition. A party not shown on the petition as joined therein at the time the petition is filed may not later join in that petition. When two or more judgments are sought to be reviewed on a writ of certiorari to the same court and involve identical or closely related questions, a single petition for a writ of certiorari covering all the judgments suffices. A petition for a writ of certiorari may not be joined with any other pleading, except that any motion for leave to proceed *in forma pauperis* shall be attached.

5. No more than 30 days after a case has been placed on the docket, a respondent seeking to file a conditional cross-petition (*i.e.,* a cross-petition that otherwise would be untimely) shall file, with proof of service as required by Rule 29, 40 copies of the cross-petition prepared as required by Rule 33.1, except that a cross-petitioner proceeding *in forma pauperis* under Rule 39 shall comply with Rule 12.2. The cross-petition shall comply in all respects with this Rule and Rule 14, except that material already reproduced in the appendix to the opening petition need not be reproduced again. A cross-petitioning respondent shall pay the Rule 38(a) docket fee or submit a motion for leave to proceed *in forma pauperis.* The cover of the cross-petition shall indicate clearly that it is a conditional cross-petition. The cross-petition then will be placed on the docket, subject to the provisions of Rule 13.4. It is the cross-petitioner's duty to notify all cross-respondents promptly, on a form supplied by the Clerk, of the date of filing, the date the cross-petition was placed on the docket, and the docket number of the cross-petition. The notice shall be served as required by Rule 29. A cross-petition for a writ of certiorari may not be joined with any other pleading, except that any motion for leave to proceed *in forma pauperis* shall be attached. The time to file a conditional cross-petition will not be extended.

6. All parties to the proceeding in the court whose judgment is sought to be reviewed are deemed parties entitled to file documents in this Court, unless the petitioner notifies the Clerk of this Court in writing of the petitioner's belief that one or more of the parties below have no interest in the outcome of the petition. A copy of such notice shall be served as required by Rule 29 on all parties to the proceeding below. A party noted as no longer interested may remain a party by notifying the Clerk promptly, with service on the other parties, of an intention to remain a party. All parties other than the petitioner are considered respondents, but any respondent who supports the position of a petitioner shall meet the petitioner's time schedule for filing documents, except that a response supporting the petition shall be filed within 20 days after the case is placed on the docket, and that time will not be extended. Parties who file no document will not qualify for any relief from this Court.

7. The clerk of the court having possession of the record shall keep it until notified by the Clerk of this Court to certify and transmit it. In any document filed with this Court, a party may cite or quote from the record, even if it has not been transmitted to this Court. When requested by the Clerk of this Court to certify and transmit the record, or any part of it, the clerk of the court having possession of the record shall number the documents to be certified and shall transmit therewith a numbered list specifically identifying each document transmitted. If the record, or stipulated portions, have been printed for the use of the court below, that printed record, plus the proceedings in the court below, may be certified as the record unless one of the parties or the Clerk of this Court requests otherwise. The record may consist of certified copies, but if the lower court is of the view that original documents of any kind should be seen by this Court, that court may provide by order for the transport, safekeeping, and return of such originals.

Rule 13. Review on Certiorari: Time for Petitioning

1. Unless otherwise provided by law, a petition for a writ of certiorari to review a judgment in any case, civil or criminal, entered by a state court of last resort or a United States court of appeals (including the United States Court of Appeals for the Armed Forces) is timely when it is filed with the Clerk of this Court within 90 days after entry of the judgment. A petition for a writ of certiorari seeking review of a judgment of a lower state court that is subject to discretionary review by the state court of last resort is timely when it is filed with the Clerk within 90 days after entry of the order denying discretionary review.

2. The Clerk will not file any petition for a writ of certiorari that is jurisdictionally out of time. See, *e.g.*, 28 U.S.C. § 2101(c).

3. The time to file a petition for a writ of certiorari runs from the date of entry of the judgment or order sought to be reviewed, and not from the issuance date of the mandate (or its equivalent under local practice). But if a petition for rehearing is timely filed in the lower court by any party, the time to file the petition for a writ of certiorari for all parties (whether or not they requested rehearing or joined in the petition for rehearing) runs from the date of the denial of the petition for rehearing or, if the petition for rehearing is granted, the subsequent entry of judgment. A suggestion made to a United States court of appeals for a rehearing en banc is not a petition for rehearing within the meaning of this Rule unless so treated by the United States court of appeals.

4. A cross-petition for a writ of certiorari is timely when it is filed with the Clerk as provided in paragraphs 1, 3, and 5 of this Rule, or in Rule 12.5. However, a conditional cross-petition (which except for Rule 12.5 would be untimely) will not be granted unless another party's timely petition for a writ of certiorari is granted.

5. For good cause, a Justice may extend the time to file a petition for a writ of certiorari for a period not exceeding 60 days. An application to extend the time to file shall set out the basis for jurisdiction in this Court, identify the judgment sought to be reviewed, include a copy of the opinion and any order respecting rehearing, and set out specific reasons why an extension of time is justified. The application must be received by the Clerk at least 10 days before the date the petition is due, except in extraordinary circumstances. For the time and manner of presenting the application, see Rules 21, 22, 30, and 33.2. An application to extend the time to file a petition for a writ of certiorari is not favored.

Rule 14. Content of a Petition for a Writ of Certiorari

1. A petition for a writ of certiorari shall contain, in the order indicated:

(a) The questions presented for review, expressed concisely in relation to the circumstances of the case, without unnecessary detail. The questions should be short and should not be argumentative or repetitive. If the petitioner or respondent is under a death sentence that may be affected by the disposition of the petition, the notation "capital case" shall precede the questions presented. The questions shall be set out on the first page following the cover, and no other information may appear on that page. The statement of any question presented is deemed to comprise every subsidiary question fairly included therein. Only the questions set out in the petition, or fairly included therein, will be considered by the Court.

(b) A list of all parties to the proceeding in the court whose judgment is sought to be reviewed (unless the caption of the case contains the names of all the parties), and a list of parent companies and nonwholly owned subsidiaries as required by Rule 29.6.

(c) If the petition exceeds five pages, a table of contents and a table of cited authorities.

(d) Citations of the official and unofficial reports of the opinions and orders entered in the case by courts or administrative agencies.

(e) A concise statement of the basis for jurisdiction in this Court, showing:

(i) the date the judgment or order sought to be reviewed was entered (and, if applicable, a statement that the petition is filed under this Court's Rule 11);

(ii) the date of any order respecting rehearing, and the date and terms of any order granting an extension of time to file the petition for a writ of certiorari;

(iii) express reliance on Rule 12.5, when a cross-petition for a writ of certiorari is filed under that Rule, and the date of docketing of the petition for a writ of certiorari in connection with which the cross-petition is filed;

(iv) the statutory provision believed to confer on this Court jurisdiction to review on a writ of certiorari the judgment or order in question; and

(v) if applicable, a statement that the notifications required by Rule 29.4(b) or (c) have been made.

(f) The constitutional provisions, treaties, statutes, ordinances, and regulations involved in the case, set out verbatim with appropriate citation. If the provisions involved are lengthy, their citation alone suffices at this point, and their pertinent text shall be set out in the appendix referred to in subparagraph 1(i).

(g) A concise statement of the case setting out the facts material to consideration of the questions presented, and also containing the following:

(i) If review of a state-court judgment is sought, specification of the stage in the proceedings, both in the court of first instance and in the appellate courts, when the federal questions sought to be reviewed were raised; the method or manner of raising them and the way in which they were passed on by those courts; and pertinent quotations of specific portions of the record or summary thereof, with specific reference to the places in the record where the matter appears (*e.g.*, court opinion, ruling on exception, portion of court's charge and exception thereto, assignment of error), so as to show that the federal question was timely and properly raised and that this Court has jurisdiction to review the judgment on a writ of certiorari. When the portions of the record relied on under this subparagraph are voluminous, they shall be included in the appendix referred to in subparagraph 1(i).

(ii) If review of a judgment of a United States court of appeals is sought, the basis for federal jurisdiction in the court of first instance.

(h) A direct and concise argument amplifying the reasons relied on for allowance of the writ. See Rule 10.

(i) An appendix containing, in the order indicated:

(i) the opinions, orders, findings of fact, and conclusions of law, whether written or orally given and transcribed, entered in conjunction with the judgment sought to be reviewed;

(ii) [A]ny other relevant opinions, orders, findings of fact, and conclusions of law entered in the case by courts or administrative agencies, and, if reference thereto is necessary to ascertain the grounds of the judgment, of those in companion cases (each document shall include the caption showing the name of the issuing court or agency, the title and number of the case, and the date of entry);

(iii) any order on rehearing, including the caption showing the name of the issuing court, the title and number of the case, and the date of entry;

(iv) the judgment sought to be reviewed if the date of its entry is different from the date of the opinion or order required in sub-subparagraph (i) of this subparagraph;

(v) material required by subparagraphs 1(f) or 1(g)(i); and

(vi) any other material the petitioner believes essential to understand the petition.

If the material required by this subparagraph is voluminous, it may be presented in a separate volume or volumes with appropriate covers.

2. All contentions in support of a petition for a writ of certiorari shall be set out in the body of the petition, as provided in subparagraph 1(h) of this Rule. No separate brief in support of a petition for a writ of certiorari may be filed, and the Clerk will not file any petition for a writ of certiorari to which any supporting brief is annexed or appended.

3. A petition for a writ of certiorari should be stated briefly and in plain terms and may not exceed the page limitations specified in Rule 33.

4. The failure of a petitioner to present with accuracy, brevity, and clarity whatever is essential to ready and adequate understanding of the points requiring consideration is sufficient reason for the Court to deny a petition.

5. If the Clerk determines that a petition submitted timely and in good faith is in a form that does not comply with this Rule or with Rule 33 or Rule 34, the Clerk will return it with a letter indicating the deficiency. A corrected petition received no more than 60 days after the date of the Clerk's letter will be deemed timely.

Rule 15. Briefs in Opposition; Reply Briefs; Supplemental Briefs

1. A brief in opposition to a petition for a writ of certiorari may be filed by the respondent in any case, but is not mandatory except in a capital case, see Rule 14.1(a), or when ordered by the Court.

2. A brief in opposition should be stated briefly and in plain terms and may not exceed the page limitations specified in Rule 33. In addition to presenting other arguments for denying the petition, the brief in opposition should address any perceived misstatement of fact or law in the petition that bears on what issues properly would be before the Court if certiorari were granted. Counsel are admonished that they have an obligation to the Court to point out in the brief in opposition, and not later, any perceived misstatement made in the petition. Any objection to consideration of a question presented based on what occurred in the proceedings below, if the objection does not go to jurisdiction, may be deemed waived unless called to the Court's attention in the brief in opposition.

3. Any brief in opposition shall be filed within 30 days after the case is placed on the docket, unless the time is extended by the Court or a Justice, or by the Clerk under Rule 30.4. Forty copies shall be filed, except that a respondent proceeding *in forma pauperis* under Rule 39, including an inmate of an institution, shall file the number of copies required for a petition by such a person under Rule 12.2, together with a motion for leave to proceed *in forma pauperis,* a copy of which shall precede and be attached to each copy of the brief in opposition. If the petitioner is proceeding *in forma pauperis,* the respondent may file an original and 10 copies of a brief in opposition prepared as required by Rule 33.2. Whether prepared under Rule 33.1 or Rule 33.2, the brief in opposition shall comply with the requirements of Rule 24 governing a respondent's brief, except that no summary of the argument is required. A brief in opposition may not be joined with any other pleading, except that any motion for leave to proceed *in forma pauperis* shall be attached. The brief in opposition shall be served as required by Rule 29.

4. No motion by a respondent to dismiss a petition for a writ of certiorari may be filed. Any objections to the jurisdiction of the Court to grant a petition for a writ of certiorari shall be included in the brief in opposition.

5. The Clerk will distribute the petition to the Court for its consideration upon receiving an express waiver of the right to file a brief in opposition, or, if no waiver or brief in opposition is filed, upon the expiration of the time allowed for filing. If a brief in opposition is timely filed, the Clerk will distribute the petition, brief in opposition, and any reply brief to the Court for its consideration no less than 10 days after the brief in opposition is filed.

6. Any petitioner may file a reply brief addressed to new points raised in the brief in opposition, but distribution and consideration by the Court under paragraph 5 of this Rule will not be deferred pending its receipt. Forty copies shall be filed, except that petitioner proceeding *in forma pauperis* under Rule 39, including an inmate of an institution, shall file the number of copies required for a petition by such a person under Rule 12.2. The reply brief shall be served as required by Rule 29.

7. If a cross-petition for a writ of certiorari has been docketed, distribution of both petitions will be deferred until the cross-petition is due for distribution under this Rule.

8. Any party may file a supplemental brief at any time while a petition for a writ of certiorari is pending, calling attention to new cases, new legislation, or other intervening matter not available at the time of the party's last filing. A supplemental brief shall be restricted to new matter and shall follow, insofar as applicable, the form for a brief in opposition prescribed by this Rule. Forty copies shall be filed, except that a party proceeding *in forma pauperis* under Rule 39, including an inmate of an institution, shall file the number of copies required for a petition by such a person under Rule 12.2. The supplemental brief shall be served as required by Rule 29.

Rule 16. Disposition of a Petition for a Writ of Certiorari

1. After considering the documents distributed under Rule 15, the Court will enter an appropriate order. The order may be a summary disposition on the merits.

2. Whenever the Court grants a petition for a writ of certiorari, the Clerk will prepare, sign, and enter an order to that effect and will notify forthwith counsel of record and the court whose judgment is to be reviewed. The case then will be scheduled for briefing and oral argument. If the record has not previously been filed in this Court, the Clerk will request the clerk of the court having possession of the record to certify and transmit it. A formal writ will not issue unless specially directed.

3. Whenever the Court denies a petition for a writ of certiorari, the Clerk will prepare, sign, and enter an order to that effect and will notify forthwith counsel of record and the court whose judgment was sought to be reviewed. The order of denial will not be suspended pending disposition of a petition for rehearing except by order of the Court or a Justice.

PART IV. OTHER JURISDICTION

Rule 17. Procedure in an Original Action

1. This Rule applies only to an action invoking the Court's original jurisdiction under Article III of the Constitution of the United States. See also 28 U.S.C. § 1251 and U.S. Const., Amdt. 11. A petition for an extraordinary writ in aid of the Court's appellate jurisdiction shall be filed as provided in Rule 20.

2. The form of pleadings and motions prescribed by the Federal Rules of Civil Procedure is followed. In other respects, those Rules and the Federal Rules of Evidence may be taken as guides.

3. The initial pleading shall be preceded by a motion for leave to file, and may be accompanied by a brief in support of the motion. Forty copies of each document shall be filed, with proof of service. Service shall be as required by Rule 29, except that when an adverse party is a State, service shall be made on both the Governor and the Attorney General of that State.

4. The case will be placed on the docket when the motion for leave to file and the initial pleading are filed with the Clerk. The Rule 38(a) docket fee shall be paid at that time.

5. No more than 60 days after receiving the motion for leave to file and the initial pleading, an adverse party shall file 40 copies of any brief in opposition to the motion, with proof of service as required by Rule 29. The Clerk will distribute the filed documents to the Court for its consideration upon receiving an express waiver of the right to file a brief in opposition, or, if no waiver or brief is filed, upon the expiration of the time allowed for filing. If a brief in opposition is timely filed, the Clerk will distribute the filed documents to the Court for its consideration no less than 10 days after the brief in opposition is filed. A reply brief may be filed, but consideration of the case will not be deferred pending its receipt. The Court thereafter may grant or deny the motion, set it for oral argument, direct that additional documents be filed, or require that other proceedings be conducted.

6. A summons issued out of this Court shall be served on the defendant 60 days before the return day specified therein. If the defendant does not respond by the return day, the plaintiff may proceed *ex parte.*

7. Process against a State issued out of this Court shall be served on both the Governor and the Attorney General of that State.

Rule 18. Appeal from a United States District Court

1. When a direct appeal from a decision of a United States district court is authorized by law, the appeal is commenced by filing a notice of appeal with the clerk of the district court within the time provided by law after entry of the judgment sought to be reviewed. The time to file may not be extended. The notice of appeal shall specify the parties taking the appeal, designate the judgment, or part thereof, appealed from and the date of its entry, and specify the statute or statutes under which the appeal is taken. A copy of the notice of appeal shall be served on all parties to the proceeding as required by Rule 29, and proof of service shall be filed in the district court together with the notice of appeal.

2. All parties to the proceeding in the district court are deemed parties entitled to file documents in this Court, but a party having no interest in the outcome of the appeal may so notify the Clerk of this Court and shall serve a copy of the notice on all other parties. Parties interested jointly, severally, or otherwise in the judgment may appeal separately, or any two or more may join in an appeal. When two or more judgments involving identical or closely related questions are sought to be reviewed on appeal from the same court, a notice of appeal for each judgment shall be filed with the clerk of the district court, but a single jurisdictional statement covering all the judgments suffices. Parties who file no document will not qualify for any relief from this Court.

3. No more than 60 days after filing the notice of appeal in the district court, the appellant shall file 40 copies of a jurisdictional statement and shall pay the Rule 38 docket fee, except that an appellant proceeding *in forma pauperis* under Rule 39, including an inmate of an institution, shall file the number of copies required for a petition by such a person under Rule 12.2, together with a motion for leave to proceed *in forma pauperis,* a copy of which shall precede and be attached to each copy of the jurisdictional statement. The jurisdictional statement shall follow, insofar as applicable, the form for a petition for a writ of certiorari prescribed by Rule 14, and shall be served as required by Rule 29. The case will then be placed on the docket. It is the appellant's duty to notify all appellees promptly, on a form supplied by the Clerk, of the date of filing, the date the case was placed on the docket, and the docket number of the case. The notice shall be served as required by Rule 29. The appendix shall include a copy of the notice of appeal showing the date it was filed in the district court. For good cause, a Justice may extend the time to file a jurisdictional statement for a period not exceeding 60 days. An application to extend the time to file a jurisdictional statement shall set out the basis for jurisdiction in this Court; identify the judgment sought to be reviewed; include a copy of the opinion, any order respecting rehearing, and the notice of appeal; and set out specific reasons why an extension of time is justified. For the time and manner of presenting the application, see Rules 21, 22, and 30. An application to extend the time to file a jurisdictional statement is not favored.

4. No more than 30 days after a case has been placed on the docket, an appellee seeking to file a conditional cross-appeal (*i.e.,* a cross-appeal that otherwise would be untimely) shall file, with proof of service as required by Rule 29, a jurisdictional statement that complies in all respects (including number of copies filed) with paragraph 3 of this Rule, except that material already reproduced in the appendix to the opening jurisdictional statement need not be reproduced again. A cross-appealing appellee shall pay the Rule 38 docket fee or submit a motion for leave to proceed *in forma pauperis.* The cover of the cross-appeal shall indicate clearly that it is a conditional cross-appeal. The cross-appeal then will be placed on the docket. It is the cross-appellant's duty to notify all cross-appellees promptly, on a form supplied by the Clerk, of the date of filing, the date the cross-appeal was placed on the docket, and the docket number of the cross-appeal. The notice shall be served as required by Rule 29. A cross-appeal may not be joined with any other pleading, except that any motion for leave to proceed *in forma pauperis* shall be attached. The time to file a cross-appeal will not be extended.

5. After a notice of appeal has been filed in the district court, but before the case is placed on this Court's docket, the parties may dismiss the appeal by stipulation filed in the district court, or the district court may dismiss the appeal on the appellant's motion, with notice to all parties. If a notice of appeal has been filed, but the case has not been placed on this Court's docket within the time prescribed for docketing, the district court may dismiss the appeal on the appellee's motion, with notice to all parties, and may make any just order with respect to costs. If the district court has denied the appellee's motion to dismiss the appeal, the appellee may move this Court to docket and dismiss the appeal by filing an original and 10 copies of a motion presented in conformity with Rules 21 and 33.2. The motion shall be accompanied by proof of service as required by Rule 29, and by a certificate from the clerk of the district court, certifying that a notice of appeal was filed and that the appellee's motion to dismiss was denied. The appellant may not thereafter file a jurisdictional statement without special leave of the Court, and the Court may allow costs against the appellant.

6. Within 30 days after the case is placed on this Court's docket, the appellee may file a motion to dismiss, to affirm, or in the alternative to affirm or dismiss. Forty copies of the motion shall be filed, except that an appellee proceeding *in forma pauperis* under Rule 39, including an inmate of an institution, shall file the number of copies required for a petition by such a person under Rule 12.2, together with a motion for leave to proceed *in forma pauperis,* a copy of which shall precede and be attached to each copy of the motion to dismiss, to affirm, or in the alternative to affirm or dismiss. The motion shall follow, insofar as applicable, the form for a brief in opposition prescribed by Rule 15, and shall comply in all respects with Rule 21.

7. The Clerk will distribute the jurisdictional statement to the Court for its consideration upon receiving an express waiver of the right to file a motion to dismiss or to affirm or, if no waiver or motion is filed, upon the expiration of the time allowed for filing. If a motion to dismiss or to affirm is timely filed, the Clerk will distribute the jurisdictional statement, motion, and any brief opposing the motion to the Court for its consideration no less than 10 days after the motion is filed.

8. Any appellant may file a brief opposing a motion to dismiss or to affirm, but distribution and consideration by the Court under paragraph 7 of this Rule will not be deferred pending its receipt. Forty copies shall be filed, except that an appellant proceeding *in forma pauperis* under Rule 39, including an inmate of an institution, shall file the number of copies required for a petition by such a person under Rule 12.2. The brief shall be served as required by Rule 29.

9. If a cross-appeal has been docketed, distribution of both jurisdictional statements will be deferred until the cross-appeal is due for distribution under this Rule.

10. Any party may file a supplemental brief at any time while a jurisdictional statement is pending, calling attention to new cases, new legislation, or other intervening matter not available at the time of the party's last filing. A supplemental brief shall be restricted to new matter and shall follow, insofar as applicable, the form for a brief in opposition prescribed by Rule 15. Forty copies shall be filed, except that a party proceeding *in forma pauperis* under Rule 39, including an inmate of an institution, shall file the number of copies required for a petition by such a person under Rule 12.2. The supplemental brief shall be served as required by Rule 29.

11. The clerk of the district court shall retain possession of the record until notified by the Clerk of this Court to certify and transmit it. See Rule 12.7.

12. After considering the documents distributed under this Rule, the Court may dispose summarily of the appeal on the merits, note probable jurisdiction, or postpone consideration of jurisdiction until a hearing of the case on the merits. If not disposed of summarily, the case stands for briefing and oral argument on the merits. If consideration of jurisdiction is postponed, counsel, at the outset of their briefs and at oral argument, shall address the question of jurisdiction. If the record has not previously been filed in this Court, the Clerk of this Court will request the clerk of the court in possession of the record to certify and transmit it.

13. If the Clerk determines that a jurisdictional statement submitted timely and in good faith is in a form that does not comply with this Rule or with Rule 33 or Rule 34, the Clerk will return it with a letter indicating the deficiency. If a corrected jurisdictional statement is received no more than 60 days after the date of the Clerk's letter, its filing will be deemed timely.

Rule 19. Procedure on a Certified Question

1. A United States court of appeals may certify to this Court a question or proposition of law on which it seeks instruction for the proper decision of a case. The certificate shall contain a statement of the nature of the case and the facts on which the question or proposition of law arises. Only questions or propositions of law may be certified, and they shall be stated separately and with precision. The certificate shall be prepared as required by Rule 33.2 and shall be signed by the clerk of the court of appeals.

2. When a question is certified by a United States court of appeals, this Court, on its own motion or that of a party, may consider and decide the entire matter in controversy. See 28 U.S.C. § 1254(2).

3. When a question is certified, the Clerk will notify the parties and docket the case. Counsel shall then enter their appearances. After docketing, the Clerk will submit the certificate to the Court for a preliminary examination to determine whether the case should be briefed, set for argument, or dismissed. No brief may be filed until the preliminary examination of the certificate is completed.

4. If the Court orders the case briefed or set for argument, the parties will be notified and permitted to file briefs. The Clerk of this Court then will request the clerk of the court in possession of the record to certify and transmit it. Any portion of the record to which the parties wish to direct the Court's particular attention should be printed in a joint appendix, prepared in conformity with Rule 26 by the appellant or petitioner in the court of appeals, but the fact that any part of the record has not been printed does not prevent the parties or the Court from relying on it.

5. A brief on the merits in a case involving a certified question shall comply with Rules 24, 25, and 33.1, except that the brief for the party who is the appellant or petitioner below shall be filed within 45 days of the order requiring briefs or setting the case for argument.

Rule 20. Procedure on a Petition for an Extraordinary Writ

1. Issuance by the Court of an extraordinary writ authorized by 28 U.S.C. § 1651(a) is not a matter of right, but of discretion sparingly exercised. To justify the granting of any such writ, the petition must show that the writ will be in aid of the Court's appellate jurisdiction, that exceptional circumstances warrant the exercise of the Court's discretionary powers, and that adequate relief cannot be obtained in any other form or from any other court.

2. A petition seeking a writ authorized by 28 U.S.C. § 1651(a), § 2241, or § 2254(a) shall be prepared in all respects as required by Rules 33 and 34. The petition shall be captioned "*In re* [name of petitioner]" and shall follow, insofar as applicable, the form of a petition for a writ of certiorari prescribed by Rule 14. All contentions in support of the petition shall be included in the petition. The case will be placed on the docket when 40 copies of the petition are filed with the Clerk and the docket fee is paid, except that a petitioner proceeding *in forma pauperis* under Rule 39, including an inmate of an institution, shall file the number of copies required for a petition by such a person under Rule 12.2, together with a motion for leave to proceed *in forma pauperis,* a copy of which shall precede and be attached to each copy of the petition. The petition shall be served as required by Rule 29 (subject to subparagraph 4(b) of this Rule).

3. **(a)** A petition seeking a writ of prohibition, a writ of mandamus, or both in the alternative shall state the name and office or function of every person against whom relief is sought and shall set out with particularity why the relief sought is not available in any other court. A copy of the judgment with respect to which the writ is sought, including any related opinion, shall be appended to the petition together with any other document essential to understanding the petition.

(b) The petition shall be served on every party to the proceeding with respect to which relief is sought. Within 30 days after the petition is placed on the docket, a party shall file 40 copies of any brief or briefs in opposition thereto, which shall comply fully with Rule 15. If a party named as a respondent does not wish to respond to the petition, that party may so advise the Clerk and all other parties by letter. All persons served are deemed respondents for all purposes in the proceedings in this Court.

4. **(a)** A petition seeking a writ of habeas corpus shall comply with the requirements of 28 U.S.C. §§ 2241 and 2242, and in particular with the provision in the last paragraph of § 2242, which requires a statement of the "reasons for not making application to the district court of the district in which the applicant is held." If the relief sought is from the judgment of a state court, the petition shall set out specifically how and where the petitioner has exhausted available remedies in the state courts or otherwise comes within the provisions of 28 U.S.C. § 2254(b). To justify the granting of a writ of habeas corpus, the petitioner must show that exceptional circumstances warrant the exercise of the Court's discretionary powers, and that adequate relief cannot be obtained in any other form or from any other court. This writ is rarely granted.

(b) Habeas corpus proceedings, except in capital cases, are *ex parte,* unless the Court requires the respondent to show cause why the petition for a writ of habeas corpus should not be granted. A response, if ordered, or in a capital case, shall comply fully with Rule 15. Neither the denial of the petition, without more, nor an order of transfer to a district court under the authority of 28 U.S.C. § 2241(b), is an adjudication on the merits, and therefore does not preclude further application to another court for the relief sought.

5. The Clerk will distribute the documents to the Court for its consideration when a brief in opposition under subparagraph 3(b) of this Rule has been filed, when a response under subparagraph 4(b) has been ordered and filed, when the time to file has expired, or when the right to file has been expressly waived.

6. If the Court orders the case set for argument, the Clerk will notify the parties whether additional briefs are required, when they shall be filed, and, if the case involves a petition for a common-law writ of certiorari, that the parties shall prepare a joint appendix in accordance with Rule 26.

PART V. MOTIONS AND APPLICATIONS

Rule 21. Motions to the Court

1. Every motion to the Court shall clearly state its purpose and the facts on which it is based and may present legal argument in support thereof. No separate brief may be filed. A motion should be concise and shall comply with any applicable page limits. Rule 22 governs an application addressed to a single Justice.

2. **(a)** A motion in any action within the Court's original jurisdiction shall comply with Rule 17.3.

(b) A motion to dismiss as moot (or a suggestion of mootness), a motion for leave to file a brief as *amicus curiae,* and any motion the granting of which would dispose of the entire case or would affect the final judgment to be entered (other than a motion to docket and dismiss under Rule 18.5 or a motion for voluntary dismissal under Rule 46) shall be prepared as required by Rule 33.1, and 40 copies shall be filed, except that a movant proceeding *in forma pauperis* under Rule 39, including an inmate of an institution, shall file a motion prepared as required by Rule 33.2, and shall file the number of copies required for a petition by such a person under Rule 12.2. The motion shall be served as required by Rule 29.

(c) Any other motion to the Court shall be prepared as required by Rule 33.2; the moving party shall file an original and 10 copies. The Court subsequently may order the moving party to prepare the motion as required by Rule 33.1; in that event, the party shall file 40 copies.

3. A motion to the Court shall be filed with the Clerk and shall be accompanied by proof of service as required by Rule 29. No motion may be presented in open Court, other than a motion for admission to the Bar, except when the proceeding to which it refers is being argued. Oral argument on a motion will not be permitted unless the Court so directs.

4. Any response to a motion shall be filed as promptly as possible considering the nature of the relief sought and any asserted need for emergency action, and, in any event, within 10 days of receipt, unless the Court or a Justice, or the Clerk under Rule 30.4, orders otherwise. A response to a motion prepared as required by Rule 33.1, except a response to a motion for leave to file an *amicus curiae* brief (see Rule 37.5), shall be prepared in the same manner if time permits. In an appropriate case, the Court may act on a motion without waiting for a response.

Rule 22. Applications to Individual Justices

1. An application addressed to an individual Justice shall be filed with the Clerk, who will transmit it promptly to the Justice concerned if an individual Justice has authority to grant the sought relief.

2. The original and two copies of any application addressed to an individual Justice shall be prepared as required by Rule 33.2, and shall be accompanied by proof of service as required by Rule 29.

3. An application shall be addressed to the Justice allotted to the Circuit from which the case arises. When the Circuit Justice is unavailable for any reason, the application addressed to that Justice will be distributed to the Justice then available who is next junior to the Circuit Justice; the turn of the Chief Justice follows that of the most junior Justice.

4. A Justice denying an application will note the denial thereon. Thereafter, unless action thereon is restricted by law to the Circuit Justice or is untimely under Rule 30.2, the party making an application, except in the case of an application for an extension of time, may renew it to any other Justice, subject to the provisions of this Rule. Except when the denial is without prejudice, a renewed application is not favored. Renewed application is made by a letter to the Clerk, designating the Justice to whom the application is to be directed, and accompanied by 10 copies of the original application and proof of service as required by Rule 29.

5. A Justice to whom an application for a stay or for bail is submitted may refer it to the Court for determination.

6. The Clerk will advise all parties concerned, by appropriately speedy means, of the disposition made of an application.

Rule 23. Stays

1. A stay may be granted by a Justice as permitted by law.

2. A party to a judgment sought to be reviewed may present to a Justice an application to stay the enforcement of that judgement See 28 U.S.C. § 2101(f).

3. An application for a stay shall set out with particularity why the relief sought is not available from any other court or judge. Except in the most extraordinary circumstances, an application for a stay will not be entertained unless the relief requested was first sought in the appropriate court or courts below or from a judge or judges thereof. An application for a stay shall identify the judgment sought to be reviewed and have appended thereto a copy of the order and opinion, if any, and a copy of the order, if any, of the court or judge below denying the relief sought, and shall set out specific reasons why a stay is justified. The form and content of an application for a stay are governed by Rules 22 and 33.2.

4. A judge, court, or Justice granting an application for a stay pending review by this Court may condition the stay on the filing of a supersedeas bond having an approved surety or sureties. The bond will be conditioned on the satisfaction of the judgment in full, together with any costs, interest, and damages for delay that may awarded. If a part of the judgment sought to be reviewed has already been satisfied, or is otherwise secured, the bond may be conditioned on the satisfaction of the part of the judgment not otherwise secured or satisfied, together with costs, interest, and damages.

PART VI. BRIEFS ON THE MERITS AND ORAL ARGUMENT

Rule 24. Briefs on the Merits: In General

1. A brief on the merits for a petitioner or an appellant shall comply in all respects with Rule 33.1 and 34 and shall contain in the order here indicated:

(a) The questions presented for review under Rule 14.1(a). The questions shall be set out on the first page following the cover, and no other information may appear on that page. The phrasing of the questions presented need not be identical with that in the petition for a writ of certiorari or the jurisdictional statement, but the brief may not raise additional questions or change the substance of the questions already presented in those documents. At its option, however, the Court may consider a plain error not among the questions presented but evident from the record and otherwise within its jurisdiction to decide.

(b) A list of all parties to the proceeding in the court whose judgment is under review (unless the caption of the case in this Court contains the names of all parties). Any amended list of parent companies and nonwholly owned subsidiaries as required by Rule 29.6 shall be placed here.

(c) If the brief exceeds five pages, a table of contents and a table of cited authorities.

(d) Citations of the official and unofficial reports of the opinions and orders entered in the case by courts and administrative agencies.

(e) A concise statement of the basis for jurisdiction in this Court, including the statutory provisions and time factors on which jurisdiction rests.

(f) The constitutional provisions, treaties, statutes, ordinances, and regulations involved in the case, set out verbatim with appropriate citation. If the provisions involved are lengthy, their citation alone suffices at this point, and their pertinent text, if not already set out in the petition for a writ of certiorari, jurisdictional statement, or an appendix to either document, shall be set out in an appendix to the brief.

(g) A concise statement of the case, setting out the facts material to the consideration of the questions presented, with appropriate references to the joint appendix, *e.g.,* App. 12, or to the record, *e.g.,* Record 12.

(h) A summary of the argument, suitably paragraphed. The summary should be a clear and concise condensation of the argument made in the body of the brief; mere repetition of the headings under which the argument is arranged is not sufficient.

(i) The argument, exhibiting clearly the points of fact and of law presented and citing the authorities and statutes relied on.

(j) A conclusion specifying with particularity the relief the party seeks.

2. A brief on the merits for a respondent or an appellee shall conform to the foregoing requirements, except that items required by subparagraphs 1(a), (b), (d), (e), (f), and (g) of this Rule need not be included unless the respondent or appellee is dissatisfied with their presentation by the opposing party.

3. A brief on the merits may not exceed the page limitations specified in Rule 33.1(g). An appendix to a brief may include only relevant material, and counsel are cautioned not to include in an appendix arguments or citations that properly belong in the body of the brief.

4. A reply brief shall conform to those portions of this Rule applicable to the brief for a respondent or an appellee, but, if appropriately divided by topical headings, need not contain a summary of the argument.

5. A reference to the joint appendix or to the record set out in any brief shall indicate the appropriate page number. If the reference is to an exhibit, the page numbers at which the exhibit appears, at which it was offered in evidence, and at which it was ruled on by the judge shall be indicated, *e.g.*, Pl.Exh. 14, Record 199, 2134.

6. A brief shall be concise, logically arranged with proper headings, and free of irrelevant, immaterial, or scandalous matter. The Court may disregard or strike a brief that does not comply with this paragraph.

Rule 25. Briefs on the Merits: Number of Copies and Time to File

1. The petitioner or appellant shall file 40 copies of the brief on the merits within 45 days of the order granting the writ of certiorari, noting probable jurisdiction, or postponing consideration of jurisdiction.

2. The respondent or appellee shall file 40 copies of the brief on the merits within 30 days after receiving the brief for the petitioner or appellant.

3. The petitioner or appellant shall file 40 copies of the reply brief, if any, within 30 days after receiving the brief for the respondent or appellee, but any reply brief must actually be received by the Clerk not later than one week before the date of oral argument.

4. The time periods stated in paragraphs 1 and 2 of this Rule may be extended as provided in Rule 30. An application to extend the time to file a brief on the merits is not favored. If a case is advanced for hearing, the time to file briefs on the merits may be abridged as circumstances require pursuant to an order of the Court on its own motion or that of a party.

5. A party wishing to present late authorities, newly enacted legislation, or other intervening matter that was not available in time to be included in a brief may file 40 copies of a supplemental brief, restricted to such new matter and otherwise presented in conformity with these Rules, up to the time the case is called for oral argument or by leave of the Court thereafter.

6. After a case has been argued or submitted, the Clerk will not file any brief, except that of a party filed by leave of the Court.

7. The Clerk will not file any brief that is not accompanied by proof of service as required by Rule 29.

Rule 26. Joint Appendix

1. Unless the Clerk has allowed the parties to use the deferred method described in paragraph 4 of this Rule, the petitioner or appellant, within 45 days after entry of the order granting the writ of certiorari, noting probable jurisdiction, or postponing consideration of jurisdiction, shall file 40 copies of a joint appendix, prepared as required by Rule 33.1. The joint appendix shall contain: (1) the relevant docket entries in all the courts below; (2) any relevant pleadings, jury instructions, findings, conclusions, or opinions; (3) the judgment, order, or decision under review; and (4) any other parts of the record that the parties particularly wish to bring to the Court's attention. Any of the foregoing items already reproduced in a petition for a writ of certiorari, jurisdictional statement, brief in opposition to a petition for a writ of certiorari, motion to dismiss or affirm, or any appendix to the foregoing, that was prepared as required by Rule 33.1, need not be reproduced again in the joint appendix. The petitioner or appellant shall serve three copies of the joint appendix on each of the other parties to the proceeding as required by Rule 29.

2. The parties are encouraged to agree on the contents of the joint appendix. In the absence of agreement, the petitioner or appellant, within 10 days after entry of the order granting the writ of certiorari, noting probable jurisdiction, or postponing consideration of jurisdiction, shall serve on the respondent or appellee a designation of parts of the record to be included in the joint appendix. Within 10 days after receiving the designation, a respondent or appellee who considers the parts of the record so designated insufficient shall serve on the petitioner or appellant a designation of additional parts to be included in the joint appendix, and the petitioner or appellant shall include the parts so designated. If the Court has permitted the respondent or appellee to proceed *in forma pauperis,* the petitioner or appellant may seek by motion to be excused from printing portions of the record the petitioner or appellant considers unnecessary. In making these designations, counsel should include only those materials the Court should examine; unnecessary designations should be avoided. The record is on file with the Clerk and available to the Justices, and counsel may refer in briefs and in oral argument to relevant portions of the record not included in the joint appendix.

3. When the joint appendix is filed, the petitioner or appellant immediately shall file with the Clerk a statement of the cost of printing 50 copies and shall serve a copy of the statement on each of the other parties as required by Rule 29. Unless the parties agree otherwise, the cost of producing the joint appendix shall be paid initially by the petitioner or appellant; but a petitioner or appellant who considers that parts of the record designated by the respondent or appellee are unnecessary for the determination of the issues presented may so advise the respondent or appellee, who then shall advance the cost of printing the additional parts, unless the Court or a Justice otherwise fixes the initial allocation of the costs. The cost of printing the joint appendix is taxed as a cost in the case, but if a party unnecessarily causes matter to be included in the joint appendix or prints excessive copies, the Court may impose these costs on that party.

4. **(a)** On the parties' request, the Clerk may allow preparation of the joint appendix to be deferred until after the briefs have been filed. In that event, the petitioner or appellant shall file the joint appendix no more than 14 days after receiving the brief for the respondent or appellee. The provisions of paragraphs 1, 2, and 3 of this Rule shall be followed, except that the designations referred to therein shall be made by each party when that party's brief is served. Deferral of the joint appendix is not favored.

(b) If the deferred method is used, the briefs on the merits may refer to the pages of the record. In that event, the joint appendix shall include in brackets on each page thereof the page number of the record where that material may be found. A party wishing to refer directly to the pages of the joint appendix may serve and file copies of its brief prepared as required by Rule 33.2 within the time provided by Rule 25, with appropriate references to the pages of the record. In that event, within 10 days after the joint appendix is filed, copies of the brief prepared as required by Rule 33.1 containing references to the pages of the joint appendix in place of, or in addition to, the initial references to the pages of the record, shall be served and filed. No other change may be made in the brief as initially served and filed, except that typographical errors may be corrected.

5. The joint appendix shall be prefaced by a table of contents showing the parts of the record that it contains, in the order in which the parts are set out, with references to the pages of the joint appendix at which each part begins. The relevant docket entries shall be set out after the table of contents, followed by the other parts of the record in chronological order. When testimony contained in the reporter's transcript of proceedings is set out in the joint appendix, the page of the transcript at which the testimony appears shall be indicated in brackets immediately before the statement that is set out. Omissions in the transcript or in any other document printed in the joint appendix shall be indicated by asterisks. Immaterial formal matters (*e.g.*, captions, subscriptions, acknowledgments) shall be omitted. A question and its answer may be contained in a single paragraph.

6. Exhibits designated for inclusion in the joint appendix may be contained in a separate volume or volumes suitably indexed. The transcript of a proceeding before an administrative agency, board, commission, or officer used in an action in a district court or court of appeals is regarded as an exhibit for the purposes of this paragraph.

7. The Court, on its own motion or that of a party, may dispense with the requirement of a joint appendix and may permit a case to be heard on the original record (with such copies of the record, or relevant parts thereof, as the Court may require) or on the appendix used in the court below, if it conforms to the requirements of this Rule.

8. For good cause, the time limits specified in this Rule may be shortened or extended by the Court or a Justice, or by the Clerk under Rule 30.4.

Rule 27. Calendar

1. From time to time, the Clerk will prepare a calendar of cases ready for argument. A case ordinarily will not be called for argument less than two weeks after the brief on the merits for the respondent or appellee is due.

2. The Clerk will advise counsel when they are required to appear for oral argument and will publish a hearing list in advance of each argument session for the convenience of counsel and the information of the public.

3. The Court, on its own motion or that of a party, may order that two or more cases involving the same or related questions be argued together as one case or on such other terms as the Court may prescribe.

Rule 28. Oral Argument

1. Oral argument should emphasize and clarify the written arguments in the briefs on the merits. Counsel should assume that all Justices have read the briefs before oral argument. Oral argument read from a prepared text is not favored.

2. The petitioner or appellant shall open and may conclude the argument. A cross-writ of certiorari or cross-appeal will be argued with the initial writ of certiorari or appeal as one case in the time allowed for that one case, and the Court will advise the parties who shall open and close.

3. Unless the Court directs otherwise, each side is allowed one-half hour for argument. Counsel is not required to use all the allotted time. Any request for additional time to argue shall be presented by motion under Rule 21 no more than 15 days after the petitioner's or appellant's brief on the merits is filed, and shall set out specifically and concisely why the case cannot be presented within the half-hour limitation. Additional time is rarely accorded.

4. Only one attorney will be heard for each side, except by leave of the Court on motion filed no more than 15 days after the respondent's or appellee's brief on the merits is filed. Any request for divided argument shall be presented by motion under Rule 21 and shall set out specifically and concisely why more than one attorney should be allowed to argue. Divided argument is not favored.

5. Regardless of the number of counsel participating in oral argument, counsel making the opening argument shall present the case fairly and completely and not reserve points of substance for rebuttal.

6. Oral argument will not be allowed on behalf of any party for whom a brief has not been filed.

7. By leave of the Court, and subject to paragraph 4 of this Rule, counsel for an *amicus curiae* whose brief has been filed as provided in Rule 37 may argue orally on the side of a party, with the consent of that party. In the absence of consent, counsel for an *amicus curiae* may seek leave of the Court to argue orally by a motion setting out specifically and concisely why oral argument would provide assistance to the Court not otherwise available. Such a motion will be granted only in the most extraordinary circumstances.

PART VII. PRACTICE AND PROCEDURE

Rule 29. Filing and Service of Documents; Special Notifications; Corporate Listing

1. Any document required or permitted to be presented to the Court or to a Justice shall be filed with the Clerk.

2. A document is timely filed if it is received by the Clerk within the time specified for filing; or if it is sent to the Clerk through the United States Postal Service by first-class mail (including express or priority mail), postage prepaid, and bears a postmark showing that the document was mailed on or before the last day for filing. Commercial postage meter labels alone are not acceptable. If submitted by an inmate confined in an institution, a document is timely filed if it is deposited in the institution's internal mail system on or before the last day for filing and is accompanied by a notarized statement or declaration in compliance with 28 U.S.C. § 1746 setting out the date of deposit and stating that first-class postage has been prepaid. If the postmark is missing or not legible, the Clerk will require the person who mailed the document to submit a notarized statement or declaration in compliance with 28 U.S.C. § 1746 setting out the details of the mailing and stating that the mailing took place on a particular date within the permitted time. A document also is timely filed if it is forwarded through a private delivery or courier service and is actually received by the Clerk within the time permitted for filing.

3. Any document required by these Rules to be served may be served personally or by mail on each party to the proceeding at or before the time of filing. If the document has been prepared as required by Rule 33.1, three copies shall be served on each other party separately represented in the proceeding. If the document has been prepared as required by Rule 33.2, service of a single copy on each other separately represented party suffices. If personal service is made, it shall consist of delivery at the office of the counsel of record, either to counsel or to an employee therein. If service is by mail, it shall consist of depositing the document with the United States Postal Service, with no less than first-class postage prepaid, addressed to counsel of record at the proper post office address. When a party is not represented by counsel, service shall be made on the party, personally or by mail.

4. **(a)** If the United States or any federal department, office, agency, officer, or employee is a party to be served, service shall be made on the Solicitor General of the United States, Room 5614, Department of Justice, 950 Pennsylvania Ave., N.W., Washington, DC 20530-0001. When an agency of the United States that is a party is authorized by law to appear before this Court on its own behalf, or when an officer or employee of the United States is a party, the agency, officer, or employee shall be served in addition to the Solicitor General.

(b) In any proceeding in this Court in which the constitutionality of an Act of Congress is drawn into question, and neither the United States nor any federal department, office, agency, officer, or employee is a party, the initial document filed in this Court shall recite that 28 U.S.C. § 2403(a) may apply and shall be served on the Solicitor General of the United States, Room 5614, Department of Justice, 950 Pennsylvania Ave., N.W., Washington, DC 20530-0001. In such a proceeding from any court of the United States, as defined by 28 U.S.C. § 451, the initial document also shall state whether that court, pursuant to 28 U.S.C. § 2403(a), certified to the Attorney General the fact that the constitutionality of an Act of Congress was drawn into question. See Rule 14.1(e)(v).

(c) In any proceeding in this Court in which the constitutionality of any statute of a State is drawn into question, and neither the State nor any agency, officer, or employee thereof is a party, the initial document filed in this Court shall recite that 28 U.S.C. § 2403(b) may apply and shall be served on the Attorney General of that State. In such a proceeding from any court of the United States, as defined by 28 U.S.C. § 451, the initial document also shall state whether that court, pursuant to 28 U.S.C. § 2403(b), certified to the State Attorney General the fact that the constitutionality of a statute of that State was drawn into question. See Rule 14.1(e)(v).

5. Proof of service, when required by these Rules, shall accompany the document when it is presented to the Clerk for filing and shall be separate from it. Proof of service shall contain, or be accompanied by, a statement that all parties required to be served have been served, together with a list of the names, addresses, and telephone numbers of counsel indicating the name of the party or parties each counsel represents. It is not necessary that service on each party required to be served be made in the same manner or evidenced by the same proof. Proof of service may consist of any one of the following:

(a) an acknowledgment of service, signed by counsel of record for the party served, and bearing the address and telephone number of such counsel;

(b) a certificate of service, reciting the facts and circumstances of service in compliance with the appropriate paragraph or paragraphs of this Rule, and signed by a member of the Bar of this Court representing the party on whose behalf service is made or by an attorney appointed to represent that party under the Criminal Justice Act of 1964, see 18 U.S.C. § 3006A(d)(6), or under any other applicable federal statute; or

(c) a notarized affidavit or declaration in compliance with 28 U.S.C. § 1746, reciting the facts and circumstances of service in accordance with the appropriate paragraph or paragraphs of this Rule, whenever service is made by any person not a member of the Bar of this Court and not an attorney appointed to represent a party under the Criminal Justice Act of 1964, see 18 U.S.C. § 3006A(d)(6), or under any other applicable federal statute.

6. Every document, except a joint appendix or *amicus curiae* brief, filed by or on behalf of one or more corporations shall list all parent companies and nonwholly owned subsidiaries of each of the corporate filers. If there is no parent or subsidiary company to be listed, a notation to this effect shall be included in the document. If a list has been included in a document filed earlier in the case, reference may be made to the earlier document (except when the earlier list appeared in an application for an extension of time or for a stay), and only amendments to the list to make it current need be included in the document being filed.

Rule 30. Computation and Extension of Time

1. In the computation of any period of time prescribed or allowed by these Rules, by order of the Court, or by an applicable statute, the day of the act, event, or default from which the designated period begins to run is not included. The last day of the period shall be included, unless it is a Saturday, Sunday, federal legal holiday listed in 5 U.S.C. § 6103, or day on which the Court building is closed by order of the Court or the Chief Justice, in which event the period shall extend until the end of the next day that is not a Saturday, Sunday, federal legal holiday, or day on which the Court building is closed.

2. Whenever a Justice or the Clerk is empowered by law or these Rules to extend the time to file any document, an application seeking an extension shall be filed within the period sought to be extended. An application to extend the time to file a petition for a writ of certiorari or to file a jurisdictional statement must be received by the Clerk at least 10 days before the specified final filing date as computed under these Rules; if received less than 10 days before the final filing date, such application will not be granted except in the most extraordinary circumstances.

3. An application to extend the time to file a petition for a writ of certiorari, to file a jurisdictional statement, to file a reply brief on the merits, or to file a petition for rehearing shall be made to an individual Justice and presented and served on all other parties as provided by Rule 22. Once denied, such an application may not be renewed.

4. An application to extend the time to file any document or paper other than those specified in paragraph 3 of this Rule may be presented in the form of a letter to the Clerk setting out specific reasons why an extension of time is justified. The letter shall be served on all other parties as required by Rule 29. The application may be acted on by the Clerk in the first instance, and any party aggrieved by the Clerk's action may request that the application be submitted to a Justice or to the Court. The Clerk will report action under this paragraph to the Court as instructed.

Rule 31. Translations

Whenever any record to be transmitted to this Court contains material written in a foreign language without a translation made under the authority of the lower court, or admitted to be correct, the clerk of the court transmitting the record shall advise the Clerk of this Court immediately so that this Court may order that a translation be supplied and, if necessary, printed as part of the joint appendix.

Rule 32. Models, Diagrams, and Exhibits

1. Models, diagrams, and exhibits of material forming part of the evidence taken in a case and brought to this Court for its inspection shall be placed in the custody of the Clerk at least two weeks before the case is to be heard or submitted.

2. All models, diagrams, and exhibits of material placed in the custody of the Clerk shall be removed by the parties no more than 40 days after the case is decided. If this is not done, the Clerk will notify counsel to remove the articles forthwith. If they are not removed within a reasonable time thereafter, the Clerk will destroy them or dispose of them in any other appropriate way.

Rule 33. Document Preparation: Booklet Format; 8½- by 11-inch Paper Format

1. Booklet Format: (a) Except for a document expressly permitted by these Rules to be submitted on 8½- by 11-inch paper, see, e.g., Rules 21, 22, and 39, every document filed with the Court shall be prepared using typesetting (e.g., wordprocessing, electronic publishing, or image setting) and reproduced by offset printing, photocopying, or similar process. The process used must produce a clear, black image on white paper.

(b) The text of every document, including any appendix thereto, except a document permitted to be produced on 8½- by 11-inch paper, shall be typeset in standard 11-point or larger type with 2-point or more leading between lines. The type size and face shall be no smaller than that contained in the United States Reports beginning with Volume 453. Type size and face shall be consistent throughout. No attempt should be made to reduce, compress, or condense the typeface in a manner that would increase the content of a document. Quotations in excess of three lines shall be indented. Footnotes shall appear in print as standard 9-point or larger type with 2-point or more leading between lines. The text of the document must appear on both sides of the page.

(c) Every document, except one permitted to be produced on 8½- by 11-inch paper, shall be produced on paper that is opaque, unglazed, 6⅛ by 9¼ inches in size, and not less than 60 pounds in weight, and shall have margins of at least three-fourths of an inch on all sides. The text field, including footnotes, should be approximately 4⅛ by 7⅛ inches. The document shall be bound firmly in at least two places along the left margin (saddle stitch or perfect binding preferred) so as to permit easy opening, and no part of the text should be obscured by the binding. Spiral, plastic, metal, and string bindings may not be used. Copies of patent documents, except opinions, may be duplicated in such size as is necessary in a separate appendix.

(d) Every document, except one permitted to be produced on 8½- by 11-inch paper, shall comply with the page limits shown on the chart in subparagraph 1(g) of this Rule. The page limits do not include the pages containing the questions presented, the list of parties and corporate affiliates of the filing party, the table of contents, the table of cited authorities, or any appendix. Verbatim quotations required under Rule 14.1(f), if set out in the text of a brief rather than in the appendix, are also excluded. For good cause, the Court or a Justice may grant leave to file a document in excess of the page limits, but application for such leave is not favored. An application to exceed page limits shall comply with Rule 22 and must be received by the Clerk at least 15 days before the filing date of the document in question, except in the most extraordinary circumstances.

(e) Every document, except one permitted to be produced on 8½- by 11-inch paper, shall have a suitable cover consisting of 65-pound weight paper in the color indicated on the chart in subparagraph 1(g) of this Rule. If a separate appendix to any document is filed, the color of its cover shall be the same as that of the cover of the document it supports. The Clerk will furnish a color chart upon request. Counsel shall ensure that there is adequate contrast between the printing and the color of the cover. A document filed by the United States, or by any other federal party represented by the Solicitor General, shall have a gray cover. A joint appendix, answer to a bill of complaint, motion for leave to intervene, and any other document not listed in subparagraph 1(g) of this Rule shall have a tan cover.

(f) Forty copies of a document prepared under this paragraph shall be filed.

(g) Page limits and cover colors for booklet-format documents are as follows:

	Type of Document	Page Limits	Color of Cover
(i)	Petition for a Writ of Certiorari (Rule 14); Motion for Leave to File a Bill of Complaint and Brief in Support (Rule 17.3); Jurisdictional Statement (Rule 18.3); Petition for an Extraordinary Writ (Rule 20.2)	30	white
(ii)	Brief in Opposition (Rule 15.3); Brief in Opposition to Motion for Leave to File an Original Action (Rule 17.5); Motion to Dismiss or Affirm (Rule 18.6);	30	orange

	Type of Document	Page Limits	Color of Cover
	Brief in Opposition to Mandamus or Prohibition (Rule 20.3(b)); Response to a Petition for Habeas Corpus (Rule 20.4)		
(iii)	Reply to Brief in Opposition (Rules 15.6 and 17.5); Brief Opposing a Motion to Dismiss or Affirm (Rule 18.8)	10	tan
(iv)	Supplemental Brief (Rules 15.8, 17, 18.10, and 25.5)	10	tan
(v)	Brief on the Merits for Petitioner or Appellant (Rule 24); Exceptions by Plaintiff to Report of Special Master (Rule 17)	50	light blue
(vi)	Brief on the Merits for Respondent or Appellee (Rule 24.2); Brief on the Merits for Respondent or Appellee Supporting Petitioner or Appellant (Rule 12.6); Exceptions by Party Other Than Plaintiff to Report of Special Master (Rule 17)	50	light red
(vii)	Reply Brief on the Merits (Rule 24.4)	20	yellow
(viii)	Reply to Plaintiff's Exceptions to Report of Special Master (Rule 17)	50	orange
(ix)	Reply to Exceptions by Party Other Than Plaintiff to Report of Special Master (Rule 17)	50	yellow
(x)	Brief for an *Amicus Curiae* at the Petition Stage (Rule 37.2)	20	cream
(xi)	Brief for an *Amicus Curiae* in Support of the Plaintiff, Petitioner, or Appellant, or in Support of Neither Party, on the Merits or in an Original Action at the Exceptions Stage (Rule 37.3)	30	light green
(xii)	Brief for an *Amicus Curiae* in Support of the Defendant, Respondent, or Appellee, on the Merits or in an Original Action at the Exceptions Stage (Rule 37.3)	30	dark green
(xiii)	Petition for Rehearing (Rule 44)	10	tan

2. 8½- by 11-Inch Paper Format: (a) The text of every document, including any appendix thereto, expressly permitted by these Rules to be presented to the Court on 8½- by 11-inch paper shall appear double spaced, except for indented quotations, which shall be single spaced, on opaque, unglazed, white paper. The document shall be stapled or bound at the upper left-hand corner. Copies, if required, shall be produced on the same type of paper and shall be legible. The original of any such document (except a motion to dismiss or affirm under Rule 18.6) shall be signed by the party proceeding pro se or by counsel of record who must be a member of the Bar of this Court or an attorney appointed under the Criminal Justice Act of 1964, see 18 U.S.C. § 3006A(d)(6), or under any other applicable federal statute. Subparagraph 1(g) of this Rule does not apply to documents prepared under this paragraph.

(b) Page limits for documents presented on 8½- by 11-inch paper are: 40 pages for a petition for a writ of certiorari, jurisdictional statement, petition for an extraordinary writ, brief in opposition, or motion to dismiss or affirm; and 15 pages for a reply to a brief in opposition, brief opposing a motion to dismiss or affirm, supplemental brief, or petition for rehearing. The page exclusions specified in subparagraph 1(d) of this Rule apply.

Rule 34. Document Preparation: General Requirements

Every document, whether prepared under Rule 33.1 or Rule 33.2, shall comply with the following provisions:

1. Each document shall bear on its cover, in the order indicated, from the top of the page:

(a) the docket number of the case or, if there is none, a space for one;

(b) the name of this Court;

(c) the October Term in which the document is filed (see Rule 3);

(d) the caption of the case as appropriate in this Court;

(e) the nature of the proceeding and the name of the court from which the action is brought (*e.g.*, "On Petition for Writ of Certiorari to the United States Court of Appeals for the Fifth Circuit"; or, for a merits brief, "On Writ of Certiorari to the United States Court of Appeals for the Fifth Circuit");

(f) the title of the document (*e.g.*, "Petition for Writ of Certiorari," "Brief for Respondent," "Joint Appendix");

(g) the name of the attorney who is counsel of record for the party concerned (who must be a member of the Bar of this Court except as provided in Rule 33.2), and on whom service is to be made, with a notation directly thereunder identifying the attorney as counsel of record and setting out counsel's office address and telephone number. Only one counsel of record may be noted on a single document. The names of other members of the Bar of this Court or of the bar of the highest court of a State acting as counsel, and, if desired, their addresses, may be added, but counsel of record shall be clearly identified. Names of persons other than attorneys admitted to a state bar may not be listed, unless the party is appearing *pro se,* in which case the party's name, address, and telephone number shall appear. The foregoing shall be displayed in an appropriate typographic manner and, except for the identification of counsel, may not be set in type smaller than standard 11–point, if the document is prepared as required by Rule 33.1.

2. Every document exceeding five pages (other than a joint appendix), whether prepared under Rule 33.1 or Rule 33.2, shall contain a table of contents and a table of cited authorities (*i.e.,* cases alphabetically arranged, constitutional provisions, statutes, treatises, and other materials) with references to the pages in the document where such authorities are cited.

3. The body of every document shall bear at its close the name of counsel of record and such other counsel, identified on the cover of the document in conformity with subparagraph 1(g) of this Rule, as may be desired.

Rule 35. Death, Substitution, and Revivor; Public Officers

1. If a party dies after filing a petition for a writ of certiorari to this Court, or after filing a notice of appeal, the authorized representative of the deceased party may appear and, on motion, be substituted as a party. If the representative does not voluntarily become a party, any other party may suggest the death on the record and, on motion, seek an order requiring the representative to become a party within a designated time. If the representative then fails to become a party, the party so moving, if a respondent or appellee, is entitled to have the petition for a writ of certiorari or the appeal dismissed, and if a petitioner or appellant, is entitled to proceed as in any other case of nonappearance by a respondent or appellee. If the substitution of a representative of the deceased is not made within six months after the death of the party, the case shall abate.

2. Whenever a case cannot be revived in the court whose judgment is sought to be reviewed, because the deceased party's authorized representative is not subject to that court's jurisdiction, proceedings will be conducted as this Court may direct.

3. When a public officer who is a party to a proceeding in this Court in an official capacity dies, resigns, or otherwise ceases to hold office, the action does not abate and any successor in office is automatically substituted as a party. The parties shall notify the Clerk in writing of any such successions. Proceedings following the substitution shall be in the name of the substituted party, but any misnomer not affecting substantial rights of the parties will be disregarded.

4. A public officer who is a party to a proceeding in this Court in an official capacity may be described as a party by the officer's official title rather than by name, but the Court may require the name to be added.

Rule 36. Custody of Prisoners in Habeas Corpus Proceedings

1. Pending review in this Court of a decision in a habeas corpus proceeding commenced before a court, Justice, or judge of the United States, the person having custody of the prisoner may not transfer custody to another person unless the transfer is authorized under this Rule.

2. Upon application by a custodian, the court, Justice, or judge who entered the decision under review may authorize transfer and the substitution of a successor custodian as a party.

3. **(a)** Pending review of a decision failing or refusing to release a prisoner, the prisoner may be detained in the custody from which release is sought or in other appropriate custody or may be enlarged on personal recognizance or bail, as may appear appropriate to the court, Justice, or judge who entered the decision, or to the court of appeals, this Court, or a judge or Justice of either court.

(b) Pending review of a decision ordering release, the prisoner shall be enlarged on personal recognizance or bail, unless the court, Justice, or judge who entered the decision, or the court of appeals, this Court, or a judge or Justice of either court, orders otherwise.

4. An initial order respecting the custody or enlargement of the prisoner, and any recognizance or surety taken, shall continue in effect pending review in the court of appeals and in this Court unless for reasons shown to the court of appeals, this Court, or a judge or Justice of either court, the order is modified or an independent order respecting custody, enlargement, or surety is entered.

Rule 37. Brief for an Amicus Curiae

1. An *amicus curiae* brief that brings to the attention of the Court relevant matter not already brought to its attention by the parties may be of considerable help to the Court. An *amicus curiae* brief that does not serve this purpose burdens the Court, and its filing is not favored.

2. **(a)** An *amicus curiae* brief submitted before the Court's consideration of a petition for a writ of certiorari, motion for leave to file a bill of complaint, jurisdictional statement, or petition for an extraordinary writ, may be filed if accompanied by the written consent of all parties, or if the Court grants leave to file under subparagraph 2(b) of this Rule. The brief shall be submitted within the time allowed for filing a brief in opposition or for filing a motion to dismiss or affirm. The *amicus curiae* brief shall specify whether consent was granted, and its cover shall identify the party supported.

(b) When a party to the case has withheld consent, a motion for leave to file an *amicus curiae* brief before the Court's consideration of a petition for a writ of certiorari, motion for leave to file a bill of complaint, jurisdictional statement, or petition for an extraordinary writ may be presented to the Court. The motion, prepared as required by Rule 33.1 and as one document with the brief sought to be filed, shall be submitted within the time allowed for filing an *amicus curiae* brief, and shall indicate the party or parties who have withheld consent and state the nature of the movant's interest. Such a motion is not favored.

3. (a) An *amicus curiae* brief in a case before the Court for oral argument may be filed if accompanied by the written consent of all parties, or if the Court grants leave to file under subparagraph 3(b) of this Rule. The brief shall be submitted within the time allowed for filing the brief for the party supported, or if in support of neither party, within the time allowed for filing the petitioner's or appellant's brief. The *amicus curiae* brief shall specify whether consent was granted, and its cover shall identify the party supported or indicate whether it suggests affirmance or reversal. The Clerk will not file a reply brief for an *amicus curiae*, or a brief for an *amicus curiae* in support of, or in opposition to, a petition for rehearing.

(b) When a party to a case before the Court for oral argument has withheld consent, a motion for leave to file an *amicus curiae* brief may be presented to the Court. The motion, prepared as required by Rule 33.1 and as one document with the brief sought to be filed, shall be submitted within the time allowed for filing an *amicus curiae* brief, and shall indicate the party or parties who have withheld consent and state the nature of the movant's interest.

4. No motion for leave to file an *amicus curiae* brief is necessary if the brief is presented on behalf of the United States by the Solicitor General; on behalf of any agency of the United States allowed by law to appear before this Court when submitted by the agency's authorized legal representative; on behalf of a State, Commonwealth, Territory, or Possession when submitted by its Attorney General; or on behalf of a city, county, town, or similar entity when submitted by its authorized law officer.

5. A brief or motion filed under this Rule shall be accompanied by proof of service as required by Rule 29, and shall comply with the applicable provisions of Rules 21, 24, and 33.1 (except that it suffices to set out in the brief the interest of the *amicus curiae*, the summary of the argument, the argument, and the conclusion). A motion for leave to file may not exceed five pages. A party served with the motion may file an objection thereto, stating concisely the reasons for withholding consent; the objection shall be prepared as required by Rule 33.2.

6. Except for briefs presented on behalf of *amicus curiae* listed in Rule 37.4, a brief filed under this Rule shall indicate whether counsel for a party authored the brief in whole or in part and shall identify every person or entity, other than the *amicus curiae*, its members, or its counsel, who made a monetary contribution to the preparation or submission of the brief. The disclosure shall be made in the first footnote on the first page of text.

Rule 38. Fees

Under 28 U.S.C. § 1911, the fees charged by the Clerk are:

(a) for docketing a case on a petition for a writ of certiorari or on appeal or for docketing any other proceeding, except a certified question or a motion to docket and dismiss an appeal under Rule 18.5, $300;

(b) for filing a petition for rehearing or a motion for leave to file a petition for rehearing, $200;

(c) for reproducing and certifying any record or paper, $1 per page; and for comparing with the original thereof any photographic reproduction of any record or paper, when furnished by the person requesting its certification, $.50 per page;

(d) for a certificate bearing the seal of the Court, $10; and

(e) for a check paid to the Court, Clerk, or Marshal that is returned for lack of funds, $35.

Rule 39. Proceedings *in Forma Pauperis*

1. A party seeking to proceed *in forma pauperis* shall file a motion for leave to do so, together with the party's notarized affidavit or declaration (in compliance with 28 U.S.C. § 1746) in the form prescribed by the Federal Rules of Appellate Procedure, Form 4. The motion shall state whether leave to proceed *in forma pauperis* was sought in any other court and, if so, whether leave was granted. If the United States district court or the United States court of appeals has appointed counsel under the Criminal Justice Act of 1964, 18 U.S.C. § 3006A, or under any other applicable federal statute, no affidavit or declaration is required, but the motion shall cite the statute under which counsel was appointed.

2. If leave to proceed *in forma pauperis* is sought for the purpose of filing a document, the motion, and an affidavit or declaration if required, shall be filed together with that document and shall comply in every respect with Rule 21. As provided in that Rule, it suffices to file an original and 10 copies, unless the party is an inmate confined in an institution and is not represented by counsel, in which case the original, alone, suffices. A copy of the motion shall precede and be attached to each copy of the accompanying document.

3. Except when these Rules expressly provide that a document shall be prepared as required by Rule 33.1, every document presented by a party proceeding under this Rule shall be prepared as required by Rule 33.2 (unless such preparation is impossible). Every document shall be legible. While making due allowance for any case presented under this Rule by a person appearing *pro se*, the Clerk will not file any document if it does not comply with the substance of these Rules or is jurisdictionally out of time.

4. When the documents required by paragraphs 1 and 2 of this Rule are presented to the Clerk, accompanied by proof of service as required by Rule 29, they will be placed on the docket without the payment of a docket fee or any other fee.

5. The respondent or appellee in a case filed *in forma pauperis* shall respond in the same manner and within the same time as in any other case of the same nature, except that the filing of an original and 10 copies of a response prepared as required by Rule 33.2, with proof of service as required by Rule 29, suffices. The respondent or appellee may challenge the grounds for the motion for leave to proceed *in forma pauperis* in a separate document or in the response itself.

6. Whenever the Court appoints counsel for an indigent party in a case set for oral argument, the briefs on the merits submitted by that counsel, unless otherwise requested, shall be prepared under the Clerk's supervision. The Clerk also will reimburse appointed counsel for any necessary travel expenses to Washington, D.C., and return in connection with the argument.

7. In a case in which certiorari has been granted, probable jurisdiction noted, or consideration of jurisdiction postponed, this Court may appoint counsel to represent a party financially unable to afford an attorney to the extent authorized by the Criminal Justice Act of 1964, 18 U.S.C. § 3006A, or by any other applicable federal statute.

8. If satisfied that a petition for a writ of certiorari, jurisdictional statement, or petition for an extraordinary writ is frivolous or malicious, the Court may deny leave to proceed *in forma pauperis.*

Rule 40. Veterans, Seamen, and Military Cases

1. A veteran suing to establish reemployment rights under any provision of law exempting veterans from the payment of fees or court costs, may file a motion for leave to proceed on papers prepared as required by Rule 33.2. The motion shall ask leave to proceed as a veteran and be accompanied by an affidavit or declaration setting out the moving party's veteran status. A copy of the motion shall precede and be attached to each copy of the petition for a writ of certiorari or other substantive document filed by the veteran.

2. A seaman suing under 28 U.S.C. § 1916 may proceed without prepayment of fees or costs or furnishing security therefor, but is not entitled to proceed under Rule 33.2, except as authorized by the Court on separate motion under Rule 39.

3. An accused person petitioning for a writ of certiorari to review a decision of the United States Court of Appeals for the Armed Forces under 28 U.S.C. § 1259 may proceed without prepayment of fees or costs or furnishing security therefor and without filing an affidavit of indigency, but is not entitled to proceed on papers prepared as required by Rule 33.2, except as authorized by the Court on separate motion under Rule 39.

PART VIII. DISPOSITION OF CASES

Rule 41. Opinions of the Court

Opinions of the Court will be released by the Clerk immediately upon their announcement from the bench, or as the Court otherwise directs. Thereafter, the Clerk will cause the opinions to be issued in slip form, and the Reporter of Decisions will prepare them for publication in the preliminary prints and bound volumes of the United States Reports.

Rule 42. Interest and Damages

1. If a judgment for money in a civil case is affirmed, any interest allowed by law is payable from the date the judgment under review was entered. If a judgment is modified or reversed with a direction that a judgment for money be entered below, the mandate will contain instructions with respect to the allowance of interest. Interest in cases arising in a state court is allowed at the same rate that similar judgments bear interest in the courts of the State in which judgment is directed to be entered. Interest in cases arising in a court of the United States is allowed at the interest rate authorized by law.

2. When a petition for a writ of certiorari, an appeal, or an application for other relief is frivolous, the Court may award the respondent or appellee just damages, and single or double costs under Rule 43. Damages or costs may be awarded against the petitioner, appellant, or applicant, against the party's counsel, or against both party and counsel.

Rule 43. Costs

1. If the Court affirms a judgment, the petitioner or appellant shall pay costs unless the Court otherwise orders.

2. If the Court reverses or vacates a judgment, the respondent or appellee shall pay costs unless the Court otherwise orders.

3. The Clerk's fees and the cost of printing the joint appendix are the only taxable items in this Court. The cost of the transcript of the record from the court below is also a taxable item, but shall be taxable in that court as costs in the case. The expenses of printing briefs, motions, petitions, or jurisdictional statements are not taxable.

4. In a case involving a certified question, costs are equally divided unless the Court otherwise orders, except that if the Court decides the whole matter in controversy, as permitted by Rule 19.2, costs are allowed as provided in paragraphs 1 and 2 of this Rule.

5. To the extent permitted by 28 U.S.C. § 2412, costs under this Rule are allowed for or against the United States or an officer or agent thereof, unless expressly waived or unless the Court otherwise orders.

6. When costs are allowed in this Court, the Clerk will insert an itemization of the costs in the body of the mandate or judgment sent to the court below. The prevailing side may not submit a bill of costs.

7. In extraordinary circumstances the Court may adjudge double costs.

Rule 44. Rehearing

1. Any petition for the rehearing of any judgment or decision of the Court on the merits shall be filed within 25 days after entry of the judgment or decision, unless the Court or a Justice shortens or extends the time. The petitioner shall file 40 copies of the rehearing petition and shall pay the filing fee prescribed by Rule 38(b), except that a petitioner proceeding *in forma pauperis* under Rule 39, including an inmate of an institution, shall file the number of copies required for a petition by such a person under Rule 12.2. The petition shall state its grounds briefly and distinctly and shall be served as required by Rule 29. The petition shall be presented together with certification of counsel (or of a party unrepresented by counsel) that it is presented in good faith and not for delay; one copy of the certificate shall bear the signature of counsel (or of a party unrepresented by counsel). A copy of the certificate shall follow and be attached to each copy of the petition. A petition for rehearing is not subject to oral argument and will not be granted except by a majority of the Court, at the instance of a Justice who concurred in the judgment or decision.

2. Any petition for the rehearing of an order denying a petition for a writ of certiorari or extraordinary writ shall be filed within 25 days after the date of the order of denial and shall comply with all the form and filing requirements of paragraph 1 of this Rule, including the payment of the filing fee if required, but its grounds shall be limited to intervening circumstances of a substantial or controlling effect or to other substantial grounds not previously presented. The petition shall be presented together with certification of counsel (or of a party unrepresented by counsel) that it is restricted to the grounds specified in this paragraph and that it is presented in good faith and not for delay; one copy of the certificate shall bear the signature of counsel (or of a party unrepresented by counsel). A copy of the certificate shall follow and be attached to each copy of the petition. The Clerk will not file a petition without a certificate. The petition is not subject to oral argument.

3. The Clerk will not file any response to a petition for rehearing unless the Court requests a response. In the absence of extraordinary circumstances, the Court will not grant a petition for rehearing without first requesting a response.

4. The Clerk will not file consecutive petitions and petitions that are out of time under this Rule.

5. The Clerk will not file any brief for an *amicus curiae* in support of, or in opposition to, a petition for rehearing.

Rule 45. Process; Mandates

1. All process of this Court issues in the name of the President of the United States.

2. In a case on review from a state court, the mandate issues 25 days after entry of the judgment, unless the Court or a Justice shortens or extends the time, or unless the parties stipulate that it issue sooner. The filing of a petition for rehearing stays the mandate until disposition of the petition, unless the Court orders otherwise. If the petition is denied, the mandate issues forthwith.

3. In a case on review from any court of the United States, as defined by 28 U.S.C. § 451, a formal mandate does not issue unless specially directed; instead, the Clerk of this Court will send the clerk of the lower court a copy of the opinion or order of this Court and a certified copy of the judgment. The certified copy of the judgment, prepared and signed by this Court's Clerk, will provide for costs if any are awarded. In all other respects, the provisions of paragraph 2 of this Rule apply.

Rule 46. Dismissing Cases

1. At any stage of the proceedings, whenever all parties file with the Clerk an agreement in writing that a case be dismissed, specifying the terms for payment of costs, and pay to the Clerk any fees then due, the Clerk, without further reference to the Court, will enter an order of dismissal.

2. **(a)** A petitioner or appellant may file a motion to dismiss the case, with proof of service as required by Rule 29, tendering to the Clerk any fees due and costs payable. No more than 15 days after service thereof, an adverse party may file an objection, limited to the amount of damages and costs in this Court alleged to be payable or to showing that the moving party does not represent all petitioners or appellants. The Clerk will not file any objection not so limited.

(b) When the objection asserts that the moving party does not represent all the petitioners or appellants, the party moving for dismissal may file a reply within 10 days, after which time the matter will be submitted to the Court for its determination.

(c) If no objection is filed—or if upon objection going only to the amount of damages and costs in this Court, the party moving for dismissal tenders the additional damages and costs in full within 10 days of the demand therefor—the Clerk, without further reference to the Court, will enter an order of dismissal. If, after objection as to the amount of damages and costs in this Court, the moving party does not respond by a tender within 10 days, the Clerk will report the matter to the Court for its determination.

3. No mandate or other process will issue on a dismissal under this Rule without an order of the Court.

PART IX. DEFINITIONS AND EFFECTIVE DATE

Rule 47. Reference to "State Court" and "State Law"

The term "state court," when used in these Rules, includes the District of Columbia Court of Appeals and the Supreme Court of the Commonwealth of Puerto Rico. See 28 U.S.C. §§ 1257 and 1258. References in these Rule to the common law and statutes of a State include the common law and statutes of the District of Columbia and of the Commonwealth of Puerto Rico.

Rule 48. Effective Date of Rules

1. These Rules, adopted January 16, 1997, will be effective May 1, 1997.

2. The Rules govern all proceedings after their effective date except to the extent that, in the opinion of the Court, their application to a pending matter would not be feasible or would work an injustice, in which event the former procedure applies.

TITLE 28

JUDICIARY AND JUDICIAL PROCEDURE

Act June 25, 1948, c. 646, § 1, 62 Stat. 869
As amended to January 4, 1999

Part		Section
I.	ORGANIZATION OF COURTS	1
II.	DEPARTMENT OF JUSTICE	501
III.	COURT OFFICERS AND EMPLOYEES	601
IV.	JURISDICTION AND VENUE	1251
V.	PROCEDURE	1651
VI.	PARTICULAR PROCEEDINGS	2201

HISTORICAL AND STATUTORY NOTES

Enactment into Law; Citation

Section 1 of Act June 25, 1948, c. 646, 62 Stat. 869, provided in part: "That title 28 of the United States Code, entitled 'Judicial Code and Judiciary' is hereby revised, codified, and enacted into law, and may be cited as 'Title 28, United States Code, section ___.' "

Miscellaneous Provisions

Sections 2 to 32 of Act June 25, 1948, c. 646, 62 Stat. 985 to 991 contained certain executing provisions and conforming amendments to sections in other titles of the United States Code. For text of sections 2 to 32, see "Act June 25, 1948, c. 646, §§ 2 to 39, 62 Stat. 985 to 991," set out following the last section of Title 28.

Section 35 of Act June 25, 1948, c. 646, 62 Stat. 991, was not classified to the United States Code. For text of section 35, see "Act June 25, 1948, c. 646, §§ 2 to 39, 62 Stat. 985 to 991" set out following the last section of Title 28.

Sections 36 and 37 of Act June 25, 1948, c. 646, 62 Stat. 991, 992, contained certain executing provisions and conforming amendments to sections in other titles of the United States Code. For text of sections 36 and 37, see "Act June 25, 1948, c. 646, §§ 2 to 39, 62 Stat. 985 to 991", set out following the last section of Title 28.

Legislative Construction

Section 33 of Act June 25, 1948, c. 646, 62 Stat. 991, provided that: "No inference of a legislative construction is to be drawn by reason of the chapter in Title 28, Judiciary and Judicial Procedure, as set out in section 1 of this Act, in which any section is placed, nor by reason of the catchlines used in such title."

Separability of Provisions

Section 34 of Act June 25, 1948, c. 646, 62 Stat. 991, provided that: "If any part of Title 28, Judiciary and Judicial Procedure, as set out in section 1 of this Act, shall be held invalid, the remainder shall not be affected thereby."

Effective Date

Section 38 of Act June 25, 1948, c. 646, 62 Stat. 992, provided that: "The provisions of this Act shall take effect on Sept. 1, 1948."

Repeals; Rights and Liabilities Saved

Section 39 of Act June 25, 1948, c. 646, 62 Stat. 992, repealed the sections or parts thereof of the Revised Statutes of the United States, Statutes at Large, or the Revised Statutes of the District of Columbia covering provisions codified in this title, but saved any rights or liabilities then existing under said sections or parts thereof.

Writs of Error

Act Jan. 31, 1928, c. 14, § 1, 45 Stat. 54 [section 861a of former Title 28, Judicial Code and Judiciary], provided that: "The writ of error in cases, civil and criminal, is abolished. All relief which heretofore [Jan. 31, 1928] could be obtained by writ of error shall hereafter be obtainable by appeal." This provision was omitted from the 1948 Revised Judicial Code as obsolete, and repealed by Act June 25, 1948, c. 646, § 39, 62 Stat. 992.

R.S. § 1012 as affected by Act Mar. 3, 1911, c. 231, § 291, 36 Stat. 1167 [Section 880 of former Title 28, Judicial Code and Judiciary], provided that appeals from district courts shall be subject to the same rules, regulations, and restrictions as are or may be prescribed in law in cases of writs of error. This provision was repealed by Act June 25, 1948, c. 646, § 39, 62 Stat. 992. Section 2 of Act Jan. 31, 1928, c. 14, 45 Stat. 54, as amended Apr. 26, 1928, c. 440, 45 Stat. 466; June 25, 1948, c. 646, § 23, 62 Stat. 990 [section 861b of former Title 28, Judicial Code and Judiciary], provided that: "All Acts of Congress referring to writs of error shall be construed as amended to the extent necessary to substitute appeal for writ of error."

Title 28 as Continuation of Existing Law; Change of Name of Circuit Courts of Appeals

Section 2(b) of Act June 25, 1948, c. 646, 62 Stat. 985, provided that: "The provisions of Title 28, Judiciary and Judicial Procedure, of the United States Code, set out in section 1 of this Act, with respect to the organization of each of the several courts therein provided for and of the Administrative Office of the United States Courts, shall be construed as continuations of existing law, and the tenure of the judges, officers, and employees thereof and of the United States attorneys and marshals and their deputies and assistants, in office on the effective date of this Act [Sept. 1, 1948], shall not be affected by its enactment, but each of them shall continue to serve in the same capacity under the appropriate provisions of title 28, as set out in section 1 of this Act, pursuant to his prior appointment: *Provided, however,* That each circuit court of appeals shall, as in said title 28 set out, hereafter be known as a United States court of appeals. No loss of rights, interruption of jurisdiction, or prejudice to matters pending in any of such courts on the effective date of this Act shall result from its enactment."

PART I—ORGANIZATION OF COURTS

Chapter		Section
1.	Supreme Court	1
3.	Courts of appeals	41
5.	District courts	81
6.	Bankruptcy judges	151
7.	United States Court of Federal Claims	171
[9.	Repealed]	
11.	Court of International Trade	251
13.	Assignment of judges to other courts	291
15.	Conferences and councils of judges	331
17.	Resignation and retirement of judges [1]	371
19.	Distribution of reports and digests	411
21.	General provisions applicable to courts and judges	451
23.	Civil justice expense and delay reduction plans	471

[1] Chapter heading amended by Pub.L. 92–397 without corresponding amendment of analysis.

HISTORICAL AND STATUTORY NOTES

Codifications

Analysis of chapters comprising Part I was amended by Pub.L. 95–598, Title II, § 201(b), Nov. 6, 1978, 92 Stat. 2660, effective June 28, 1984, pursuant to Pub.L. 95–598, Title IV, § 402(b), Nov. 6, 1978, 92 Stat. 2682, as amended by Pub.L. 98–249, § 1(a), Mar. 31, 1984, 98 Stat. 116; Pub.L. 98–271, § 1(a), Apr. 30, 1984, 98 Stat. 163; Pub.L. 98–299, § 1(a), May 25, 1984, 98 Stat. 214; Pub.L. 98–325, § 1(a), June 20, 1984, 98 Stat. 268, by adding:

"6. Bankruptcy courts .... 151".

Section 402(b) of Pub.L. 95–598 was amended by section 113 of Pub.L. 98–353, Title I, July 10, 1984, 98 Stat. 343, by substituting "shall not be effective" for "shall take effect on June 28, 1984", thereby eliminating the amendment by section 201(b) of Pub.L. 95–598, effective June 27, 1984, pursuant to section 122(c) of Pub.L. 98–353, set out as an Effective Date note under section 151 of the title.

Section 121(a) of Pub.L. 98–353 directed that section 402(b) of Pub.L. 95–598 be amended by substituting "the date of enactment of the Bankruptcy Amendments and Federal Judgeship Act of 1984 [i.e. July 10, 1984]" for "June 28, 1984". This amendment was not executed in view of the prior amendment to section 402(b) of Pub.L. 95–598 by section 113 of Pub.L. 98–353.

CHAPTER 1—SUPREME COURT

Sec.
1. Number of justices; quorum.
2. Terms of court.
3. Vacancy in office of Chief Justice; disability.
4. Precedence of associate justices.
5. Salaries of justices.
6. Records of former court of appeals.

§ 1. Number of justices; quorum

The Supreme Court of the United States shall consist of a Chief Justice of the United States and eight associate justices, any six of whom shall constitute a quorum.

(June 25, 1948, c. 646, 62 Stat. 869.)

HISTORICAL AND STATUTORY NOTES

Short Title

1998 Amendments. Pub.L. 105–315, § 1, Oct. 30, 1998, 112 Stat. 2993, provided that: "This Act [amending sections 651 to 658 of this title, enacting a provision set out as a note under section 651 of this title, and amending a provision set out as a note under section 652 of this title] may be cited as the 'Alternative Dispute Resolution Act of 1998'."

1996 Amendments. Pub.L. 104–317, § 1(a), Oct. 19, 1996, 110 Stat. 3847, provided that: "This Act [enacting sections 258 and 1932 of this title, amending sections 112, 125, 134, 253, 331, 332, 371, 376, 601, 621, 627, 636, 753, 954, 1332, 1404, 1406, 1442, 1446, 1827, 1914, 1931, 1963, and 2511 of this title, sections 3154, 3401, and 3603 of Title 18, Crimes and Criminal Procedure, sections 1983 and 1988 of Title 42, The Public Health and Welfare, and sections 719, 743, 745, 1104, and 1105 of Title 45, Railroads, enacting provisions set out as notes under sections 258, 1332, 1404, 1827, 1914, 1931, and 2412 of this title and section 719 of Title 45, and amending provisions set out as notes under sections 133, 152, 471, and 1913 of this title] may be cited as the 'Federal Courts Improvement Act of 1996'."

1994 Amendments. Pub.L. 103–420, § 1, Oct. 25, 1994, 108 Stat. 4343, provided that: "This Act [amending section 612 of this title, amending provisions set out as notes under sections 471 and 651 of this title, and repealing a provision set out as a note under section 651 of this title] may be cited as the 'Judicial Amendments Act of 1994'."

Pub.L. 103–383, § 1, Oct. 20, 1994, 108 Stat. 4063 provided that: "This Act [enacting section 1738B of this title and a provision set out as a note under section 1738B of this title] may be cited as the 'Full Faith and Credit for Child Support Orders Act'."

Pub.L. 103–270, § 1, June 30, 1994, 108 Stat. 732, provided that: "This Act [amending sections 591 through 596 and 599 of this title and enacting provisions set out as notes under section 591 of this title and section 113 of Title 3, The President] may be cited as the 'Independent Counsel Reauthorization Act of 1994'."

1992 Amendments. Pub.L. 102–572, § 1, Oct. 29, 1992, 106 Stat. 4506, provided that: "This Act [Pub.L. 102–572, Oct. 29, 1992, 106 Stat. 4506, for classifications to which see Tables] may be cited as the 'Federal Courts Administration Act of 1992'."

Pub.L. 102–572, Title IX, § 901, Oct. 29, 1992, 106 Stat. 4516, provided that: "This title [Title IX of Pub.L. 102–572, Oct. 29, 1992, 106 Stat. 4516, for classifications to which see Tables] may be cited as the 'Court of Federal Claims Technical and Procedural Improvements Act of 1992'."

Pub.L. 102–559, § 1, Oct. 28, 1992, 106 Stat. 4227, provided that: "This Act [enacting chapter 178 of this title and provisions set out as a note under section 3701 of this title] may be cited as the 'Professional and Amateur Sports Protection Act'."

Pub.L. 102–417, § 1, Oct. 14, 1992, 106 Stat. 2138, provided that: "This Act [amending section 1821 of this title and enacting provisions set out as a note under section 1821 of this title] may be cited as the 'Incarcerated Witness Fees Act of 1991'."

Pub.L. 102–361, § 1, Aug. 26, 1992, 106 Stat. 965, provided that: "This Act [amending section 152 of this title and enacting provisions set out as a note under section 152 of this title] may be cited as the 'Bankruptcy Judgeship Act of 1992'."

1990 Amendments. Pub.L. 101–650, § 1, Dec. 1, 1990, 104 Stat. 5089, provided: "That this Act [enacting sections 178, 471 to 482, 1367, and 1658 of this title, section 8440b of Title 5, Government Organization and Employees, sections 106A and 120 of Title 17, Copyrights, and section 404c of Title 47, Telegraphs, Telephones, and Radiotelegraphs, amending sections 44, 108, 112, 122, 133, 152, 332, 333, 372, 375, 376, 377, 453, 601, 602, 604, 631, 636, 995, 996, 1334, 1391, 1441, 1452, 1499, 1605, 1610, 1821, 1871, 2072, and 2077 of this title, sections 8331, 8334, 8336, 8339, and 8402 of Title 5, section 104 of Appendix 6 to Title 5, section 502 of Appendix 7 to Title 5, section 305 of Title 11, Bankruptcy, and sections 101, 102, 106, 107, 109, 113, 301, 411, 412, 501, and 506 of Title 17, enacting provisions set out as notes under sections 1, 44, 133, 331, 332, 372, 376, 471, 620, 631, 1367, and 1658 of this title, section 8331 of Title 5, section 307 of Title 11, sections 101, 106A, 109, and 205 of Title 17, and sections 3006A and 3551 of Title 18, Crimes and Criminal Procedure, and amending provisions set out as notes under sections 533 and 581 of this title] may be cited as the 'Judicial Improvements Act of 1990'."

Pub.L. 101–650, Title I, § 101, Dec. 1, 1990, 104 Stat. 5089, provided that: "This title [enacting section 471 to 482 of this title and provisions set out as notes under section 471 of this title] may be cited as the 'Civil Justice Reform Act of 1990'."

Pub.L. 101–650, Title II, § 201, Dec. 1, 1990, 104 Stat. 5098, provided that: "This title [amending sections 44 and 133 of this title and enacting provisions set out as notes under sections 44, 133, and 331 of this title] may be cited as the 'Federal Judgeship Act of 1990'."

Pub.L. 101–650, Title III, § 301, Dec. 1, 1990, 104 Stat. 5104, provided that: "This title [enacting sections 178, 1367, and 1658 of this title and section 8440b of Title 5, Government Organization and Employees, amending sections 108, 112, 122, 133, 152, 158, 332, 333, 375, 376, 377, 601, 602, 604, 631, 636, 995, 996, 1334, 1391, 1441, 1452, 1499, 1605, 1610, 1821, 1871, and 2072 of this title, sections 8331, 8334, 8336, 8339, and 8402 of Title 5, section 502 of Appendix 7 to Title 5, and section 305 of Title 11, Bankruptcy, enacting provisions set out as notes under sections 376, 620, 631, 1367, and 1658 of this title, sections 8331 of Title 5, section 307 of Title 11, and sections 3006A and 3551 of Title 18, Crimes and Criminal Procedure, and amending provisions set out as notes under sections 533 and 581 of this title] may be cited as the 'Federal Courts Study Committee Implementation Act of 1990'."

Pub.L. 101–650, Title IV, § 401, Dec. 1, 1990, 104 Stat. 5122, provided that: "This title [amending sections 332, 372, 453, and 2077 of this title and section 104 of Appendix 6 to Title 5, Government Organization and Employees, and enacting provisions set out as notes under sections 332 and 372 of this title] may be cited as the 'Judicial Discipline and Removal Reform Act of 1990'."

Pub.L. 101–647, Title XXXVI, § 3601, Nov. 29, 1990, 104 Stat. 4933, provided that: "This title [enacting section 2044 and chapter 176 (section 3001 et seq.) of this title, amending sections 550, 1962, 1963 and 2410 of this title, section 523 of Title 11, Bankruptcy, and sections 3142 and 3552 of Title 18, Crimes and Criminal Procedure, and enacting provisions set out as a note under section 3001 of this title] may be cited as the 'Federal Debt Collection Procedures Act of 1990'."

1988 Amendments. Pub. L. 100–702, § 1, Nov. 19, 1988, 102 Stat. 4642, provided that: "This Act [enacting chapter 44 (sections 651–658) and sections 153(d), 297, 332(d)(4), 371(e), 455(f), 604(a)(19) [redesignated (20)], (21), (22), 611(e), 623(a)(7), 627(f), 629, 631(*l*), 1292(d)(4), 1338(c), 1447(e), 1498(e), 1878, 2071(b)–(f), and 2072–2074 of this title and sections 5584(a)(3), (g)(6) of Title 5, Government Organization and Employees, and 15 of Title 9, Arbitration; amending sections 89(b), (c), 156(a), 172(b), 331, 332, 372(c)(11), 376(m), 462(c), 604(a)(2), (7), 611(a), 620(b)(3), 624(1), 626, 627(b), 634(c), 636(c)(7), (d), 712, 752, 794, 1295(a)(1), 1332(a)–(c), 1338, 1391(c), 1400(a), 1441, 1446, 1447(c), 1827(a)–(e), (g)–(k), 1863(b)(5), (6), 1864(a), 1865(a), 1866(c)(1), 1869(a), (f), 1963, 2077(b), and 2520 of this title and sections 5108(c)(1) of Title 5, 460n–8 of Title 16, Conservation, 912 of Title 17, Copyrights, 3402 of Title 18, Crimes and Criminal Procedure, and 10702(f), 10704(d)(2), 10705(c), (d), 10706(a), and 10708 of Title 42, The Public Health and Welfare; redesignating as 604(a)(15)–(20) former section 604(a)(14)–(19) and as 604(a)(23) former section 604(a)(18) and redesignating and amending as 2071(a) former section 2071 of this title; repealing chapter 44 (sections 651–658) and sections 1393, 1963A, 2072, and 2076 of this title and 3771 and 3772 of Title 18; and enacting provisions set out as notes under sections 1, 89, 153, 331, 371, 376, 611, 626, 651, 652, 1292, 1332, 1391, 1393, 1827, 1963, 2071, and 2520 of this title and 5584 of Title 5] may be cited as the 'Judicial Improvements and Access to Justice Act'."

Pub. L. 100–702, Title VII, § 701, Nov. 19, 1988, 102 Stat. 4654, provided that: "This title [amending section 1827(a) to (e), (g) to (k) of this title and enacting provisions set out as notes under section 1827 of this title] may be cited as the 'Court Interpreter Amendments Act of 1988'."

Pub. L. 100–694, § 1, Nov. 18, 1988, 102 Stat. 4563, provided that: "This Act [enacting section 831c–2 of Title 16, Conservation; amending sections 2671, 2674, and 2679(b), (d) of this title; and enacting provisions set out as notes under sections 2671 and 2679 of this title] may be cited as the

'Federal Employees Liability Reform and Tort Compensation Act of 1988'."

Pub. L. 100–659, § 1, Nov. 15, 1988, 102 Stat. 3910, provided that: "This Act [which enacted section 377 of this title and section 8440a of Title 5, Government Organization and Employees, amended sections 155, 375, 376, 604, 631, and 636 of this title and sections 8334 and 8402 of Title 5 and enacted provisions set out as notes under sections 376 and 377 of this title] may be cited as the 'Retirement and Survivors' Annuities for Bankruptcy Judges and Magistrates Act of 1988'."

1987 Amendments. Pub.L. 100–191, § 1, Dec. 15, 1987, 101 Stat. 1293, provided that: "This Act [enacting section 599 of this title, amending sections 49 and 591 to 598 of this title, sections 203 and 205 of the Ethics in Government Act of 1978, set out in Appendix 4 to Title 5, Government Organization and Employees, and section 202 of Title 18, Crimes and Criminal Procedure, and enacting provisions set out as a note under section 591 of this title and amending provisions set out as a note under section 591 of this title] may be cited as the 'Independent Counsel Reauthorization Act of 1987'."

1986 Amendments. Pub.L. 99–657, § 1, Nov. 14, 1986, 100 Stat. 3670, provided that: "This Act [amending sections 90 and 121 of this title, and enacting provisions set out as a note under section 121 of this title] may be cited as the 'Judicial Housekeeping Act of 1986'."

Pub.L. 99–570, Title I, § 1151, Oct. 27, 1986, 100 Stat. 3207–12, provided that: "This subtitle [subtitle b (§§ 1151–1153) of Title 1 of amending section 524 of this title, section 1963 of Title 18, Crimes and Criminal Procedure, section 1613a of Title 19, Customs Duties, and section 853 of Title 21, Food and Drugs, and repealing section 1613b of Title 19] may be cited as the 'Department of Justice Assets Forfeiture Fund Amendments Act of 1986'."

Pub.L. 99–363, § 1, July 11, 1986, 100 Stat. 770, provided that: "This Act [amending section 994 of this title] may be cited as the 'Sentencing Guidelines Act of 1986'."

Pub.L. 99–336, § 1, June 19, 1986, 100 Stat. 633, provided that: "This Act [amending sections 376, 620, 1441, 1914, and 2342 of this title, section 288d of Title 2, The Congress, and sections 8706, 8714a, 8714b, and 8714c of Title 5, Government Organization and Employees, and enacting provisions set out as notes under sections 376, 620, 1441, 1914, and 2342 of this title and section 8706 of Title 5] may be cited as the 'Judicial Improvements Act of 1985'.".

1984 Amendments. Pub.L. 98–620, Title IV, § 404, Nov. 8, 1984, 98 Stat. 3361, provided that: "This subtitle [subtitle B (sections 404 to 411) of Title IV of Pub.L. 98–620, which amended sections 85, 90, 93, 112, 124, and 126 of this title and enacted provisions set out as notes under sections 85, 90, 93 and 124 of this title] may be cited as the 'Federal District Court Organization Act of 1984'."

Pub.L. 98–620, Title IV, preceding § 412, Nov. 8, 1984, 98 Stat. 3362, provided that: "This subtitle [subtitle C (sections 412 to 416) of Title IV of Pub.L. 98–620, enacting section 798 of this title, amending section 1292 of this title, section 1071 of Title 15, Commerce and Trade, section 1337 of Title 19, Customs Duties, and sections 142 to 144 of Title 35, Patents, and enacting provisions set out as notes under section 713 of this title and section 142 of Title 35] may be cited as the 'Technical Amendments to the Federal Courts Improvement Act of 1982'."

For short title of Pub.L. 98–353, July 10, 1984, 98 Stat. 333 as the "Bankruptcy Amendments and Federal Judgeship Act of 1984", see Short Title of 1984 Amendments note set out under section 151 of this title.

1983 Amendments. Pub.L. 97–409, § 1, Jan. 3, 1983, 96 Stat. 2039, provided: "That this Act [amending sections 49, 591 to 598 of this title and amending provisions set out as a note under section 591 of this title] may be cited as the 'Ethics in Government Act Amendments of 1982'."

1982 Amendments. For provisions authorizing the citation of sections 2–6 of Pub.L. 97–394 as the Indian Claims Limitation Act of 1982, see section 1 of Pub.L. 97–394, as amended, set out as a note under section 2415 of this title.

Pub.L. 97–292, § 1, Oct. 12, 1982, 96 Stat. 1259, provided: "That this Act [amending section 534 of this title] may be cited as the 'Missing Children Act'."

Pub.L. 97–164, § 1, Apr. 2, 1982, 96 Stat. 25, provided: "That this Act [enacting sections 176, 177, 462, 463, 714, 715, 1295, 1296, 1631, 2077, and 2522 of this title, amending sections 41, 44, 45, 46, 48, 136, 160, 171 to 175, 256, 291, 292, 293, 331, 372, 451, 456, 460, 518, 520, 605, 610, 713, 753, 791, 794 to 797, 957, 1291, 1292, 1294, 1336, 1346, 1398, 1402, 1406, 1491, 1492, 1494 to 1503, 1505, 1507, 1926, 1961, 2342, 2411, 2501 to 2517, 2519, 2520, and 2645 of this title, section 308 and rule 1101 in the Appendix to this title, section 356 of Title 2, The Congress, sections 7703, 8332, 8334, 8715, and 8912 of Title 5, Government Organization and Employees, section 2461 of Title 7, Agriculture, section 2273 of Title 10, Armed Forces, sections 714b, 1071, 1121, and 2210 of Title 15, Commerce and Trade, section 831s of Title 16, Conservation, sections 204, 3006A, and 6001 of Title 18, Crimes and Criminal Procedure, sections 1337, 1516, 1516a, 1528, and 2395 of Title 19, Customs Duties, sections 1642b and 2356 of Title 22, Foreign Relations and Intercourse, sections 70v–3, 119, 475a, 652, 1401, and 1402 of Title 25, Indians, sections 6110, 7422, 7428, 7456, and 7482 of Title 26, Internal Revenue Code, section 193a of Title 30, Mineral Lands and Mining, sections 72 and 724a of Title 31, Money and Finance, sections 1321 and 1479 of Title 33, Navigation and Navigable Waters, sections 141 to 146, 183, and 282 of Title 35, Patents, section 330 of Title 40, Public Buildings, Property, and Works, sections 113, 114, 607, and 609 of Title 41, Public Contracts, sections 2182, 2221, 2223, and 2475 of Title 42, The Public Health and Welfare, sections 713, 906, and 1103 of Title 44, Public Printing and Documents, section 87 of Title 45, Railroads, and sections 42, 1213, 1215, 1216, 1218, 1218a, 1224, and 1984 of the Appendix to Title 50, War and National Defense, repealing sections 142, 211 to 216, 415, 792, 831 to 834, 1255, 1256, 1504, 1506, 1541 to 1546, 1584, 2110, 2353, 2518, and 2601–2604 of this title, and enacting provisions set out as notes under sections 44, 45, 171, and 753 of this title, section 7456 of Title 26, and section 3006A of Title 18] may be cited as the 'Federal Courts Improvement Act of 1982'."

1980 Amendments. Pub.L. 96–486, § 1, Dec. 1, 1980, 94 Stat. 2369, provided: "That this Act [amending section 1331 of this title and section 2072 of Title 15, Commerce and Trade, and enacting provisions set out as a note under section 1331 of this title] may be cited as the 'Federal Question Jurisdictional Amendments Act of 1980'."

Pub.L. 96–462, § 1, Oct. 15, 1980, 94 Stat. 2053, provided that: "This Act [amending sections 84, 95, 105, 113, and 124 of this title, and enacting provisions set out as notes under sections 84, 95, 105, and 113 of this title] may be cited as the 'Federal District Court Organization Act of 1980'."

Pub.L. 96–458, § 1, Oct. 15, 1980, 94 Stat. 2035, provided that: "This Act [amending sections 331, 332, 372, and 604 of this title, and enacting provisions set out as notes under section 331 of this title] may be cited as the 'Judicial Councils Reform and Judicial Conduct and Disability Act of 1980'."

Pub.L. 96–452, § 1, Oct. 14, 1980, 94 Stat. 1994, provided: "That this Act [amending sections 41, 44 and 48 of this title, and enacting provisions set out as notes under section 41 of this title] may be cited as the 'Fifth Circuit Court of Appeals Reorganization Act of 1980'."

Pub.L. 96–417, § 1, Oct. 10, 1980, 94 Stat. 1727, provided: "That this Act [which enacted sections 1546, 1581 to 1585, 1876, 1963A, 2603, 2604, and 2631 to 2647 of this title and section 2395 of Title 19, Customs Duties; amended sections 251 to 255, 257, 292, 293, 372, 451, 456, 518, 569, 605, 610, 751, 871 to 873, 1337, 1340, 1352, 1355, 1356, 1491, 1541, 1543, 1862, 1919, 2414, 2601, and 2602 of this title and section 308 of Pub.L. 95–521 in the Appendix of this title, section 791 of Title 16, Conservation, section 6001 of Title 18, Crimes and Criminal Procedure, sections 1305, 1337, 1502, 1503, 1514 to 1516a, 1528, 1592, 1604, and 1641 of Title 19, Customs Duties, section 7443 of Title 26, Internal Revenue Code, and section 906 of Title 44, Public Printing and Documents; repealed sections 405a and 2322 of Title 19, Customs Duties; omitted former sections 1581, 1582, and 2631 to 2639 of this title; and enacted provisions set out as notes under section 251 of this title] may be cited as the 'Customs Courts Act of 1980'."

1979 Amendments. For short title of Pub.L. 96–82, as the "Federal Magistrate Act of 1979", see section 1 of Pub.L. 96–82, set out as a note under section 631 of this title.

1978 Amendments. For short title of Pub.L. 95–572 as the "Jury System Improvements Act of 1978", see section 1 of Pub.L. 95–572, set out as a note under section 1861 of this title.

Pub.L. 95–539, § 1, Oct. 28, 1978, 92 Stat. 2040, provided: "That this Act [enacting sections 1827 and 1828 of this title, amending sections 602 to 604 and 1920 of this title, enacting provisions set out as notes under section 602 of this title, and repealing a provision set out as a note under section 602 of this title] may be cited as the 'Court Interpreters Act'."

Pub.L. 95–408, § 1, Oct. 2, 1978, 92 Stat. 883, provided that: "This Act [amending sections 89, 93, 97, 98, 104, 112, 114, 133 of this title and enacting provisions set out as a note under section 89 of this title] may be cited as the 'Federal District Court Organization Act of 1978'."

1976 Amendments. Pub.L. 94–583, § 1, Oct. 21, 1976, 90 Stat. 2891, provided: "That this Act [enacting sections 1330 and 1602 to 1611 of this title, amending sections 1332, 1391, and 1441 of this title, and enacting provisions set out as notes under section 1602 of this title] may be cited as the 'Foreign Sovereign Immunities Act of 1976'."

Pub.L. 94–554, § 1, Oct. 19, 1976, 90 Stat. 2603, provided: "That this Act [amending this section, and enacting provisions set out as notes under section 376 of this title] may be cited as the 'Judicial Survivors' Annuities Reform Act'."

1970 Amendments. Pub.L. 91–271, Title I, § 101, June 2, 1970, 84 Stat. 274, provided that: "This title [enacting sections 256 and 257 of this title, amending sections 253 to 255, 1541, 1582, 2601, 2602, and 2631 to 2639 of this title, repealing sections 1583 and 2640 to 2642 of this title, and enacting provisions set out as notes under sections 1 and 256 of this title] may be cited as 'The Customs Courts Act of 1970'."

1966 Amendments. Pub.L. 89–504, Title II, § 201, July 18, 1966, 80 Stat. 293, provided that: "This title [enacting provisions set out as notes under sections 603, 604, and 753 of this title] may be cited as the 'Federal Judicial Salary Act of 1966'."

1964 Acts. Pub.L. 88–426, Title IV, § 401, Aug. 14, 1964, 78 Stat. 433, provided that: "This title [amending this section and sections 44, 135, 173, 213, 252, 603 and 792 of this title, section 867 of Title 10, Armed Forces, section 68 of former Title 11, Bankruptcy, and section 7443 of Title 26, Internal Revenue Code, and enacting provisions set out as notes under sections 603, 604 and 753 of this title] may be cited as the 'Federal Judicial Salary Act of 1964'."

§ 2. Terms of court

The Supreme Court shall hold at the seat of government a term of court commencing on the first Monday in October of each year and may hold such adjourned or special terms as may be necessary.

(June 25, 1948, c. 646, 62 Stat. 869.)

§ 3. Vacancy in office of Chief Justice; disability

Whenever the Chief Justice is unable to perform the duties of his office or the office is vacant, his powers and duties shall devolve upon the associate justice next in precedence who is able to act, until such disability is removed or another Chief Justice is appointed and duly qualified.

(June 25, 1948, c. 646, 62 Stat. 869.)

§ 4. Precedence of associate justices

Associate justices shall have precedence according to the seniority of their commissions. Justices whose commissions bear the same date shall have precedence according to seniority in age.

(June 25, 1948, c. 646, 62 Stat. 869.)

§ 5. Salaries of justices

The Chief Justice and each associate justice shall each receive a salary at annual rates determined under section 225 of the Federal Salary Act of 1967 (2 U.S.C. 351–361), as adjusted by section 461 of this title.

(June 25, 1948, c. 646, 62 Stat. 870; Mar. 2, 1955, c. 9, § 1(a), 69 Stat. 9; Aug. 14, 1964, Pub.L. 88–426, Title IV, § 403(a), 78 Stat. 434; Aug. 9, 1975, Pub.L. 94–82, Title II, § 205(b)(1), 89 Stat. 422.)

HISTORICAL AND STATUTORY NOTES

References in Text

Section 225 of the Federal Salary Act of 1967, referred to in text, is section 225 of Pub.L. 90–206, Dec. 16, 1967, 81 Stat. 642, as amended, which is classified to chapter 11 (section 351 et seq.) of Title 2, The Congress.

Effective Dates

1964 Acts. Amendment by Pub.L. 88–426 effective on the first day of the first pay period which begins on or after July 1, 1964, except to the extent provided in section 501(c) of Pub.L. 88–426, see section 501 of Pub.L. 88–426.

1955 Acts. Amendment by Act Mar. 2, 1955, effective Mar. 1, 1955, see section 5 of Act Mar. 2, 1955, set out as a note under section 31 of Title 2, The Congress.

Increase in Salaries

1998—Salaries of the Chief Justice and Associate Justices increased to $175,400, and $167,900 per annum, respectively, effective on the first day of the first applicable pay period beginning on or after Jan. 1, 1998, by Ex. Ord. No. 13071, Dec. 29, 1997, 62 F.R. 68521, set out as a note under section 5332 of Title 5, Government Organization and Employees.

1997—Salaries of the Chief Justice and Associate Justices continued at $171,500, and $164,100 per annum, respectively, effective on the first day of the first applicable pay period beginning on or after Jan. 1, 1997, by Ex. Ord. No. 13033, Dec. 27, 1996, 61 F.R. 68987, formerly set out as a note under section 5332 of Title 5, Government Organization and Employees.

1996—Salaries of the Chief Justice and Associate Justices continued at $171,500, and $164,100 per annum, respectively, effective on the first day of the first applicable pay period beginning on or after Jan. 1, 1996, by Ex. Ord. No. 12984, Dec. 28, 1995, 61 F.R. 237, formerly set out as a note under section 5332 of Title 5, Government Organization and Employees.

1995—Salaries of the Chief Justice and Associate Justices continued at $171,500, and $164,100 per annum, respectively, effective on the first day of the first applicable pay period beginning on or after Jan. 1, 1995, by Ex. Ord. No. 12944, Dec. 28, 1994, 60 F.R. 309, formerly set out as a note under section 5332 of Title 5, Government Organization and Employees.

1993—Salaries of the Chief Justice and Associate Justices increased to $171,500, and $164,100 per annum, respectively, effective on the first day of the first applicable pay period beginning on or after Jan. 1, 1993, by Ex. Ord. No. 12826, Dec. 30, 1992, 56 F.R. 62909, formerly set out as a note under section 5332 of Title 5, Government Organization and Employees.

1992—Salaries of the Chief Justice and Associate Justices increased to $166,200, and $159,000 per annum, respectively, effective on the first day of the first applicable pay period beginning on or after Jan. 1, 1992, by Ex. Ord. No. 12786, Dec. 26, 1991, 56 F.R. 67453, formerly set out as a note under section 5332 of Title 5.

1991—Salaries of the Chief Justice and Associate Justices increased to $160,600, and $153,600 per annum, respectively, effective on the first day of the first applicable pay period beginning on or after Jan. 1, 1991, by Ex. Ord. No. 12736, Dec. 12, 1990, 55 F.R. 51385, formerly set out as a note under section 5332 of Title 5.

1990—Salaries of Chief Justice and Associate Justices continued respectively at $115,000 and $110,000 per annum, and increased to $124,000 and $118,600, respectively, effective on first day of first pay period beginning on or after Jan. 31, 1990, by Ex. Ord. No. 12698, Dec. 23, 1989, 54 F.R. 53473, formerly set out as a note under section 5332 of Title 5.

1989—Salaries of Chief Justice and Associate Justices increased in the amount of 25 percent of their respective rates (as last in effect before the increase), effective Jan. 1, 1991, see Pub.L. 101–194, Title VII, § 703(a)(3), Nov. 30, 1989, 103 Stat. 1768, set out as a note under section 5318 of Title 5.

Salaries of Chief Justice and Associate Justices continued respectively at $115,000 and $110,000 per annum by Ex. Ord. No. 12663, Jan. 6, 1989, 54 F.R. 791, formerly set out as a note under section 5332 of Title 5.

1988—Salaries of Chief Justice and Associate Justices continued at $115,000 and $110,000, respectively, effective on the first day of the first applicable pay period beginning on or after Jan. 1, 1988, by Ex. Ord. No. 12622, Dec. 31, 1987, 53 F.R. 222, formerly set out as a note under section 5332 of Title 5.

1987—Salaries of Chief Justice and Associate Justices increased respectively to $115,000 and $110,000 per annum, on recommendation of the President of the United States, see note set out under section 358 of Title 2, The Congress.

Salaries of the Chief Justice and Associate Justices increased to $111,700 and $107,200, respectively, as required by section 406 of the Judiciary Appropriation Act, 1987, as incorporated in section 101(b) of Pub.L. 99–500 and section 101(b) of Pub.L. 99–591, effective on the first day of the first applicable pay period beginning on or after Jan. 1, 1987, by Ex. Ord. No. 12578, Dec. 31, 1986, 52 F.R. 505, formerly set out as a note under section 5332 of Title 5.

1985—Salaries of the Chief Justice and Associate Justices increased to $108,400 and $104,100, respectively, effective on the first day of the first day period beginning on or after Jan. 1, 1985, by Ex. Ord. No. 12496, Dec. 28, 1984, 50 F.R. 211, as amended by Ex. Ord. No. 12540, Dec. 30, 1985, 51 F.R. 577, formerly set out as a note under section 5332 of Title 5, Government Organization and Employees. Prior to its amendment by Ex. Ord. No. 12540, schedule 7 of Ex. Ord. No. 12496 had contained a footnote directing that, pursuant to section 140 of Pub.L. 97–92, set out as a note under section 461 of this title, funds were not available to pay any such salary after Dec. 15, 1981, at a rate exceeding the rate on that date, which was $96,800 for the Chief Justice and $93,000 for the Associate Justices.

See also section 2207 of Pub.L. 98–369, set out as a note under section 461 of this title, which provided for overall percentage adjustment increases in certain rates of pay under the General Schedule.

1984—Salaries of the Chief Justice and Associate Justices increased to $104,700 and $100,600, respectively, effective on the first day of the first pay period beginning on or after Jan. 1, 1984, by Ex. Ord.No. 12456, Dec. 30, 1983, 49 F.R. 347, as amended Ex. Ord. No. 12477, May 23, 1984, 49 F.R. 22041; Ex. Ord. No. 12487, Sept. 14, 1984, 49 F.R. 36493, formerly set out as a note under section 5332 of Title 5.

1982—Salaries of the Chief Justice and Associate Justices increased to $100,700, and $96,700, respectively, effective on the first day of the first pay period beginning on or after Oct. 1, 1982, by Ex. Ord. No. 12387, Oct. 8, 1982, 47 F.R. 44981, formerly set out as a note under section 5332 of Title 5, Government Organization and Employees. Ex. Ord. No. 12387 further provided that pursuant to section 140 of Pub.L. 97–92, funds are not available to pay a salary at a rate which exceeds the rate in effect on Dec. 15, 1981, which was $96,800 for the Chief Justice and $93,000 for the Associate Justices.

Maximum rates payable after Dec. 17, 1982, increased from $96,800 and $93,000 to $100,700 and $96,700, respectively, see Pub.L. 97–377, Title I, § 129(b)–(d), Dec. 21, 1982, 96 Stat. 1941, set out as a note under section 5318 of Title 5.

Limitations on use of funds for fiscal year ending Sept. 30, 1983, appropriated by any Act to pay the salary or pay of any individual in legislative, executive, or judicial branch in position equal to or above level V of the Executive Schedule, see section 101(e) of Pub.L. 97–276, as amended, set out as a note under section 5318 of Title 5.

1981—Salaries of the Chief Justice and Associate Justices increased to $96,800 and $93,000 respectively, effective on the first day of the first pay period beginning on or after Oct. 1, 1981, by Ex. Ord. No. 12330, Oct. 15, 1981, 46 F.R. 50921, formerly set out as a note under section 5332 of Title 5.

Limitations on use of funds for fiscal year ending Sept. 30, 1982, appropriated by any Act to pay the salary or pay of any individual in legislative, executive, or judicial branch in position equal to or above level V of the Executive Schedule, see sections 101(g) and 141 of Pub.L. 97–92, set out as a note under section 5318 of Title 5.

1980—Salaries of the Chief Justice and Associate Justices increased to $92,400 and $88,700, respectively, effective on the first day of the first pay period beginning on or after Oct. 1, 1980, by Ex. Ord. No. 12248, Oct. 16, 1980, 45 F.R. 69199, formerly set out as a note under section 5332 of Title 5. Ex. Ord. No. 12248 further provided that pursuant to Pub.L. 96–369 funds are not available to pay a salary at a rate which exceeds the rate in effect on Sept. 30, 1980, which was $79,125 for the Chief Justice and $75,960 for the Associate Justices.

Limitations on use of funds for fiscal year ending Sept. 30, 1981, appropriated by any Act to pay the salary or pay of any individual in legislative, executive, or judicial branch in position equal to or above level V of the Executive Schedule, see section 101(c) of Pub.L. 96–536, as amended, set out as a note under section 5318 of Title 5.

1979—Salaries of the Chief Justice and Associate Justices increased to $84,700 and $81,300, respectively, effective on the first day of the first applicable pay period beginning on or after Oct. 1, 1979, by Ex. Ord. No. 12165, Oct. 9, 1979, 44 F.R. 58671, as amended by Ex. Ord. No. 12200, Mar. 12, 1980, 45 F.R. 16443, formerly set out as a note under section 5332 of Title 5. Ex. Ord. No. 12165 further provided that pursuant to Pub.L. 96–86 funds appropriated for fiscal year 1980 may not be used to pay a salary at a rate which exceeds an increase of 5.5 percent over the applicable rate payable for such position or office in effect on Sept. 30, 1978, which was $79,125 for the Chief Justice and $75,960 for the Associate Justices.

Applicability to funds appropriated by any Act for fiscal year ending Sept. 30, 1980, of limitation of section 304 of Pub.L. 95–391 on use of funds to pay the salary or pay of any individual in legislative, executive, or judicial branch in position equal to or above level V of the Executive Schedule, see section 101(c) of Pub.L. 96–86, set out as a note under section 5318 of Title 5.

1978—Salaries of the Chief Justice and Associate Justices increased to $79,100 and $76,000, respectively, effective on the first day of the first pay period beginning on or after Oct. 1, 1978, by Ex. Ord. No. 12087, Oct. 7, 1978, 43 F.R. 46823, formerly set out as a note under section 5332 of Title 5. Ex. Ord. No. 12087, further provided that pursuant to the Legislative Branch Appropriation Act, 1979 [Pub.L. 95–391, Title III, § 304, Sept. 30, 1978, 92 Stat. 788, set out as a note under section 5318 of Title 5], funds are not available to pay a salary at a rate which exceeds the rate in effect on Sept. 30, 1978, which was $75,000 for the Chief Justice and $72,000 for the Associate Justices.

1977—Salaries of the Chief Justice and Associate Justices increased respectively to $75,000 and $72,000 per annum, upon recommendation of the President of the United States, see note set out under section 358 of Title 2, The Congress.

1976—Salaries of the Chief Justice and Associate Justices increased to $68,800 and $66,000, respectively, effective on the first day of the first pay period beginning on or after Oct. 1, 1976, by Ex. Ord. No. 11941, Oct. 1, 1976, 41 F.R. 43889, formerly set out as a note under section 5332 of Title 5, Government Organization and Employees. Ex. Ord. No. 11941, further provided that pursuant to the Legislative Branch Appropriation Act, 1977, funds are not available to pay a salary at a rate which exceeds the rate in effect on Sept. 30, 1976, which was $65,600 for the Chief Justice and $63,000 for the Associate Justices.

1975—Salaries of the Chief Justice and Associate Justices increased to $65,600 and $63,000, respectively, effective on the first day of the first pay period beginning on or after Oct. 1, 1975, by Ex. Ord. No. 11883, Oct. 6, 1975, 40 F.R. 47091, formerly set out as a note under section 5332 of Title 5.

1969—Salaries of the Chief Justice and Associate Justices increased respectively from $40,000 and $39,500 to $62,500 and $60,000 per annum, commencing February 14, 1969, upon recommendation of the President of the United States, see note set out under section 358 of Title 2, The Congress.

1946—The salary of the Chief Justice was increased from $20,500 to $25,500 a year, and the salaries of the associate justices were increased from $20,000 to $25,000 per year, by Act July 31, 1946, c. 704, § 1, 60 Stat. 716.

1925—Salary of the Chief Justice was increased from $15,000 for year to $20,500 per year, and the salaries of the associate justices were increased from $14,500 per year to $20,000 per year, by Act Dec. 13, 1926, c. 6, § 1, 44 Stat. 919.

1911—Salary of the Chief Justice was set at $15,000 a year and the salaries of the associate justices were set at $14,500 a year by the Judicial Code of 1911, Act Mar. 3, 1911, c. 231, § 1, 36 Stat. 1152.

§ 6. Records of former court of appeals

The records and proceedings of the court of appeals, appointed previous to the adoption of the Constitution, shall be kept until deposited with the National Archives of the United States in the office of the clerk of the Supreme Court, who shall furnish copies thereof to any person requiring and paying for them, in the manner provided by law for giving copies of the records and proceedings of the Supreme Court. Such copies shall have the same faith and credit as proceedings of the Supreme Court.

(June 25, 1948, c. 646, 62 Stat. 870; Oct. 25, 1951, c. 562, § 4(7), 65 Stat. 640.)

CHAPTER 3—COURTS OF APPEALS

Sec.

41. Number and composition of circuits.
42. Allotment of Supreme Court justices to circuits.
43. Creation and composition of courts.
44. Appointment, tenure, residence and salary of circuit judges.
45. Chief judges; precedence of judges.
46. Assignment of judges; panels; hearings; quorum.
47. Disqualification of trial judge to hear appeal.
48. Terms of court.
49. Assignment of judges to division to appoint independent counsels.

§ 41. Number and composition of circuits

The thirteen judicial circuits of the United States are constituted as follows:

Circuits	*Composition*
District of Columbia	District of Columbia.
First	Maine, Massachusetts, New Hampshire, Puerto Rico, Rhode Island.
Second	Connecticut, New York, Vermont.
Third	Delaware, New Jersey, Pennsylvania, Virgin Islands.
Fourth	Maryland, North Carolina, South Carolina, Virginia, West Virginia.
Fifth	District of the Canal Zone, Louisiana, Mississippi, Texas.
Sixth	Kentucky, Michigan, Ohio, Tennessee.
Seventh	Illinois, Indiana, Wisconsin.
Eighth	Arkansas, Iowa, Minnesota, Missouri, Nebraska, North Dakota, South Dakota.
Ninth	Alaska, Arizona, California, Idaho, Montana, Nevada, Oregon, Washington, Guam, Hawaii.
Tenth	Colorado, Kansas, New Mexico, Oklahoma, Utah, Wyoming.
Eleventh	Alabama, Florida, Georgia.
Federal	All Federal judicial districts.

(June 25, 1948, c. 646, 62 Stat. 870; Oct. 31, 1951, c. 655, § 34, 65 Stat. 723; Oct. 14, 1980, Pub.L. 96–452, § 2, 94 Stat. 1994; Apr. 2, 1982, Pub.L. 97–164, Title I, § 101, 96 Stat. 25.)

HISTORICAL AND STATUTORY NOTES

Effective Dates

1982 Acts. Amendment by Pub.L. 97–164 effective Oct. 1, 1982, see section 402 of Pub.L. 97–164, set out as a note under section 171 of this title.

1980 Acts. Section 12 of Pub.L. 96–452 provided that: "This Act [see Short Title of 1980 Amendments note set out under section 1 of this title] and the amendments made by this Act [amending sections 41, 44, and 48 of this title, and enacting provisions set out as notes under this section] shall take effect on October 1, 1981."

Administrative Action by Fifth Circuit Court of Appeals; Termination of Court

Section 11 of Pub.L. 96–452 provided that: "The court of appeals for the fifth circuit as constituted on the day before the effective date of this Act [Oct. 1, 1981] may take such administrative action as may be required to carry out this Act [see Short Title of 1980 Amendments note set out under section 1 of this title]. Such court shall cease to exist for administrative purposes on July 1, 1984."

Appeals Court Administrative Units

Pub.L. 95–486, § 6, Oct. 20, 1978, 92 Stat. 1633, provided that: "Any court of appeals having more than 15 active judges may constitute itself into administrative units complete with such facilities and staff as may be prescribed by the Administrative Office of the United States Courts, and may perform its en banc function by such number of members of its en banc courts as may be prescribed by rule of the court of appeals."

Assignment of Judges and Procedure For Administration of Pending Cases With Regard to Reorganization of the Fifth Circuit Court of Appeals

Sections 5 to 10 of Pub.L. 96–452 provided that:

"Sec. 5. Each circuit judge in regular active service of the former fifth circuit whose official station on the day before the effective date of this Act [Oct. 1, 1981]—

"(1) is in Louisiana, Mississippi, or Texas is assigned as a circuit judge of the new fifth circuit; and

"(2) is in Alabama, Florida, or Georgia is assigned as a circuit judge of the eleventh circuit.

"Sec. 6. Each judge who is a senior judge of the former fifth circuit on the day before the effective date of this Act [Oct. 1, 1981] may elect to be assigned to the new fifth circuit or to the eleventh circuit and shall notify the Director of the Administrative Office of the United States Courts of such election.

"Sec. 7. The seniority of each judge—

"(1) who is assigned under section 5 of this Act; or

"(2) who elects to be assigned under section 6 of this Act;

shall run from the date of commission of such judge as a judge of the former fifth circuit.

"Sec. 8. The eleventh circuit is authorized to hold terms or sessions of court at New Orleans, Louisiana, until such time as adequate facilities for such court are provided in Atlanta, Georgia.

"Sec. 9. The provisions of the following paragraphs of this section apply to any case in which, on the day before the effective date of this Act [Oct. 1, 1981], an appeal or other proceeding has been filed with the former fifth circuit:

"(1) If the matter has been submitted for decision, further proceedings in respect of the matter shall be had in the same manner and with the same effect as if this Act [see Short Title of 1980 Amendments note under section 1 of this title] had not been enacted.

"(2) If the matter has not been submitted for decision, the appeal or proceeding, together with the original papers, printed records, and record entries duly certified, shall, by appropriate orders, be transferred to the court to which it would have gone had this Act [see Short Title of 1980 Amendments note under section 1 of this title] been in full force and effect at the time such appeal was taken or other proceeding commenced, and further proceedings in respect of the case shall be had in the same manner and with the same effect as if the appeal or other proceeding had been filed in such court.

"(3) A petition for rehearing or a petition for rehearing en banc in a matter decided before the effective date of this Act [Oct. 1, 1981], or submitted before the effective date of this Act and decided on or after the effective date as provided in paragraph (1) of this section, shall be treated in the same manner and with the same effect as though this Act [see Short Title of 1980 Amendments note under section 1 of this title] had not been enacted. If a petition for rehearing en banc is granted, the matter shall be reheard by a court comprised as though this Act [see Short Title of 1980 Amendments note under section 1 of this title] had not been enacted.

"**Sec. 10.** As used in sections 5, 6, 7, 8, and 9 of this Act, the term—

"(1) 'former fifth circuit' means the fifth judicial circuit of the United States as in existence on the day before the effective date of this Act [Oct. 1, 1981];

"(2) the term 'new fifth circuit' means the fifth judicial circuit of the United States established by the amendment made by section 2(2) of this Act [amending this section]; and

"(3) the term 'eleventh circuit' means the eleventh judicial circuit of the United States established by the amendment made by section 2(3) of this Act [amending this section]."

Commission on Revision of the Federal Appellate System

Pub.L. 92–489, Oct. 13, 1972, 86 Stat. 807, as amended by Pub.L. 93–420, Sept. 19, 1974, 88 Stat. 1153, provided for the establishment, membership, travel expenses, personnel, experts and consultants, administrative and research services, cooperation of other governmental agencies, and appropriations of not to exceed $606,000 of a Commission on Revision of the Federal Court Appellate System which Commission was to study the geographical division of the judicial circuits and the structure and internal procedures of the appellate court system and to report to the President, Congress, and the Chief Justice its recommendations for changes in the geographical boundaries of the circuits to expedite disposition of judicial business and for changes in the appellate court structure to expedite disposition of the appellate court structure to expedite disposition of the appellate courts caseload in a manner consistent with fundamental concepts of fairness and due process. The Commission was to cease existence ninety days after submission of its final report, which report was submitted June 20, 1975.

Commission on Structural Alternatives for the Federal Courts of Appeals

Pub.L. 105–119, Title III, § 305, Nov. 26, 1997, 111 Stat. 2491, provided that:

"**(1) Establishment and functions of commission.**—

"**(A) Establishment.**—There is established a Commission on Structural Alternatives for the Federal Courts of Appeals (hereinafter referred to as the 'Commission').

"**(B) Functions.**—The functions of the Commission shall be to—

"(i) study the present division of the United States into the several judicial circuits;

"(ii) study the structure and alignment of the Federal Court of Appeals system, with particular reference to the Ninth Circuit; and

"(iii) report to the President and the Congress its recommendations for such changes in circuit boundaries or structure as may be appropriate for the expeditious and effective disposition of the caseload of the Federal Courts of Appeals, consistent with fundamental concepts of fairness and due process.

"**(2) Membership.**—

"**(A) Composition.**—The Commission shall be composed of five members who shall be appointed by the Chief Justice of the United States.

"**(B) Appointment.**—The members of the Commission shall be appointed within 30 days after the date of enactment of this Act.

"**(C) Vacancy.**—Any vacancy in the Commission shall be filled in the same manner as the original appointment.

"**(D) Chair.**—The Commission shall elect a chair and vice chair from among its members.

"**(E) Quorum.**—Three members of the Commission shall constitute a quorum, but two may conduct hearings.

"**(3) Compensation.**—

"**(A) In general.**—Members of the Commission who are officers, or full-time employees, of the United States shall receive no additional compensation for their services, but shall be reimbursed for travel, subsistence, and other necessary expenses incurred in the performance of duties vested in the Commission, but not in excess of the maximum amounts authorized under section 456 of title 28, United States Code.

"**(B) Private members.**—Members of the Commission from private life shall receive $200 for each day (including travel time) during which the member is engaged in the actual performance of duties, but not in excess of the maximum amounts authorized under section 456 of title 28, United States Code.

"**(4) Personnel.**—

"**(A) Executive Director.**—The Commission may appoint an Executive Director who shall receive compensation at a rate not exceeding the rate prescribed for level V of the Executive Schedule under section 5316 of title 5, United States Code.

"**(B) Staff.**—The Executive Director, with the approval of the Commission, may appoint and fix the compensation of such additional personnel as the Executive Director determines necessary, without regard to the provisions of title 5, United States Code, governing appointments in the competitive service or the provisions of chapter 51 [section 5101 et seq. of Title 5] and subchapter III of chapter 53 of such title [section 5331 et seq. of Title 5] relating to classification and General Schedule pay rates. Compensation under this paragraph shall not exceed the annual maximum rate of basic pay for a position above GS–15 of the General Schedule under section 5108 of title 5, United States Code.

"(C) **Experts and consultants.**—The Executive Director may procure personal services of experts and consultants as authorized by section 3109 of title 5, United States Code, at rates not to exceed the highest level payable under the General Schedule pay rates under section 5332 of title 5, United States Code.

"(D) **Services.**—The Administrative Office of the United States Courts shall provide administrative services, including financial and budgeting services, to the Commission on a reimbursable basis. The Federal Judicial Center shall provide necessary research services to the Commission on a reimbursable basis.

"(5) **Information.**—The Commission is authorized to request from any department, agency, or independent instrumentality of the Government any information and assistance the Commission determines necessary to carry out its functions under this section. Each such department, agency, and independent instrumentality is authorized to provide such information and assistance to the extent permitted by law when requested by the chair of the Commission.

"(6) **Report.**—The Commission shall conduct the studies required in this section during the 10–month period beginning on the date on which a quorum of the Commission has been appointed. Not later than 2 months following the completion of such 10–month period, the Commission shall submit its report to the President and the Congress. The Commission shall terminate 90 days after the date of the submission of its report.

(b) Authorization of appropriations.—There are authorized to be appropriated to the Commission such sums, not to exceed $900,000, as may be necessary to carry out the purposes of this section. Such sums as are appropriated shall remain available until expended."

Continuation of Organization of Court

Section 2(b) of Act June 25, 1948, c. 646, 62 Stat. 985, provided in part that the provisions of this title as set out in section 1 of said Act of June 25, 1948, with respect to the organization of each of the several courts therein provided, shall be construed as a continuation of existing law, and the tenure of the judges, officers, and employees in office on Sept. 1, 1948, and of the United States attorneys and marshals and their deputies and assistants in office on that date, shall not be affected by its enactment but each of them shall continue to serve in the same capacity under the appropriate provisions of this title, pursuant to his prior appointment.

Northern Mariana Islands

Pub.L. 95–157, § 1(a), Nov. 8, 1977, 91 Stat. 1265, provided that the Northern Mariana Islands be part of the same judicial circuit as Guam, i.e., the Ninth Circuit. See section 1694(a) of Title 48, Territories and Insular Possessions.

Puerto Rico

The name of the island of "Porto Rico" was changed to "Puerto Rico" by Act May 17, 1932, c. 190, 47 Stat. 158.

Tenth Judicial Circuit

Act Feb. 28, 1929, c. 363, § 1, 45 Stat. 1346, divided the eight judicial circuit and created the tenth judicial circuit. Prior to such division the eighth judicial circuit included, in addition, the states now constituting the tenth judicial circuit.

Termination of United States District Court for the District of the Canal Zone

For termination of the United States District Court for the District of the Canal Zone at end of the "transition period", being the 30-month period beginning Oct. 1, 1979, and ending midnight Mar. 31, 1982, see Paragraph 5 of Article XI of the Panama Canal Treaty of 1977 and sections 3831 and 3841 to 3843 of Title 22, Foreign Relations and Intercourse.

§ 42. Allotment of Supreme Court justices to circuits

The Chief Justice of the United States and the associate justices of the Supreme Court shall from time to time be allotted as circuit justices among the circuits by order of the Supreme Court. The Chief Justice may make such allotments in vacation.

A justice may be assigned to more than one circuit, and two or more justices may be assigned to the same circuit.

(June 25, 1948, c. 646, 62 Stat. 870.)

§ 43. Creation and composition of courts

(a) There shall be in each circuit a court of appeals, which shall be a court of record, known as the United States Court of Appeals for the circuit.

(b) Each court of appeals shall consist of the circuit judges of the circuit in regular active service. The circuit justice and justices or judges designated or assigned shall also be competent to sit as judges of the court.

(June 25, 1948, c. 646, 62 Stat. 870; Nov. 13, 1963, Pub.L. 88–176, § 1(a), 77 Stat. 331.)

HISTORICAL AND STATUTORY NOTES

Change of Name of Court

Section 2(b) of Act June 25, 1948, c. 646, 62 Stat. 869, provided in part that each circuit court of appeals should, after Sept. 1, 1948, be known as a United States Court of Appeals, but that the enactment of said Act June 25, 1948 should in no way entail any loss of rights, interruption of jurisdiction, or prejudice to matters pending in any such courts on Sept. 1, 1948.

§ 44. Appointment, tenure, residence and salary of circuit judges

(a) The President shall appoint, by and with the advice and consent of the Senate, circuit judges for the several circuits as follows:

Circuits	Number of Judges
District of Columbia	12
First	6
Second	13
Third	14
Fourth	15
Fifth	17
Sixth	16

Complete Annotation Materials, see Title 28 U.S.C.A.

Circuits	Number of Judges
Seventh	11
Eighth	11
Ninth	28
Tenth	12
Eleventh	12
Federal	12.

(b) Circuit judges shall hold office during good behavior.

(c) Except in the District of Columbia, each circuit judge shall be a resident of the circuit for which appointed at the time of his appointment and thereafter while in active service. While in active service, each circuit judge of the Federal judicial circuit appointed after the effective date of the Federal Courts Improvement Act of 1982, and the chief judge of the Federal judicial circuit, whenever appointed, shall reside within fifty miles of the District of Columbia. In each circuit (other than the Federal judicial circuit) there shall be at least one circuit judge in regular active service appointed from the residents of each state in that circuit.

(d) Each circuit judge shall receive a salary at an annual rate determined under section 225 of the Federal Salary Act of 1967 (2 U.S.C. 351–361), as adjusted by section 461 of this title.

(June 25, 1948, c. 646, 62 Stat. 871; Aug. 3, 1949, c. 387, § 1, 63 Stat. 493; Feb. 10, 1954, c. 6, § 1, 68 Stat. 8; Mar. 2, 1955, c. 9, § 1(b), 69 Stat. 10; May 19, 1961, Pub.L. 87–36, § 1(b), 75 Stat. 80; Aug. 14, 1964, Pub.L. 88–426, Title IV, § 403(b), 78 Stat. 434; Mar. 18, 1966, Pub.L. 89–372, § 1(b), 80 Stat. 75; June 18, 1968, Pub.L. 90–347, § 3, 82 Stat. 184; Aug. 9, 1975, Pub.L. 94–82, Title II, § 205(b)(2), 89 Stat. 422; Oct. 20, 1978, Pub.L. 95–486, § 3(b), 92 Stat. 1632; Oct. 14, 1980, Pub.L. 96–452, § 3, 94 Stat. 1994; Apr. 2, 1982, Pub.L. 97–164, Title I, § 102, 96 Stat. 25; July 10, 1984, Pub.L. 98–353, Title II, § 201(b), 98 Stat. 346; Dec. 1, 1990, Pub.L. 101–650, Title II, § 202(b), 104 Stat. 5099; Dec. 9, 1991, Pub.L. 102–198, § 10(c), 105 Stat. 1626; Nov. 26, 1997, Pub.L. 105–119, Title III, § 307, 111 Stat. 2493.)

HISTORICAL AND STATUTORY NOTES

References in Text

The effective date of the Federal Courts Improvement Act of 1982, referred to in subsec. (c), is Oct. 1, 1982. See Effective Dates of 1982 Amendments note set out under section 171 of this title.

Section 225 of the Federal Salary Act of 1967, referred to in subsec. (d), is section 225 of Pub.L. 90–206, Dec. 16, 1967, 81 Stat. 642, as amended, which is classified to chapter 11 (section 351 et seq.) of Title 2, The Congress.

Effective Dates

1990 Acts. Section 206 of Title II of Pub.L. 101–650 provided that: "This title [amending this section and section 133 of this title and enacting provisions set out as notes under this section and sections 133 and 331 of this title] shall take effect on the date of the enactment of this title [Dec. 1, 1990]."

1982 Acts. Amendment by Pub.L. 97–164 effective Oct. 1, 1982, see section 402 of Pub.L. 97–164, set out as a note under section 171 of this title.

1980 Acts. Amendment by Pub.L. 96–452 effective Oct. 1, 1981, see section 12 of Pub.L. 96–452, set out as a note under section 41 of this title.

1964 Acts. Amendment by Pub.L. 88–426 effective on the first day of the first pay period which begins on or after July 1, 1964, except to the extent provided in section 501(c) of Pub.L. 88–426, see section 501 of Pub.L. 88–426.

1955 Acts. Amendment by Act Mar. 2, 1955, effective Mar. 1, 1955, see section 5 of Act Mar. 2, 1955, set out as a note under section 31 of Title 2, The Congress.

Additional Judges

Since 1925, the appointment of additional judges was authorized by the following acts:

Second circuit. Act May 31, 1938, c. 290, § 1, 52 Stat. 584.

Third circuit. Act Aug. 3, 1949, c. 387, § 1, 63 Stat. 493; Act Dec. 7, 1944, c. 521, § 1, 58 Stat. 796; Act June 10, 1930, c. 438, 46 Stat. 538; Act June 24, 1936, c. 735, § 1, 49 Stat. 1903, repealed by Act May 31, 1938, c. 290, § 3, 52 Stat. 585.

Fifth circuit. Act Dec. 14, 1942, c. 731, 56 Stat. 1050; Act May 31, 1938, c. 290, § 1, 52 Stat. 584; Act June 10, 1930, c. 437, 46 Stat. 538.

Sixth circuit. Act May 24, 1940, c. 209, § 1, 54 Stat. 219; Act May 31, 1938, c. 290, § 1, 52 Stat. 584.

Seventh circuit. Act Aug. 3, 1949, c. 387, § 1, 63 Stat. 493; Act May 31, 1938, c. 290, § 1, 52 Stat. 584.

Eighth circuit. Act May 24, 1940, c. 209, § 1, 54 Stat. 219; Act Mar. 3, 1925, c. 437, 43 Stat. 1116.

Ninth circuit. Act Apr. 14, 1937, c. 80, 50 Stat. 64; Act Aug. 2, 1935, c. 425, § 1, 49 Stat. 508; Act June 16, 1933, c. 102, 48, Stat. 310 (removing limitation on filling of vacancy); Act Mar. 1, 1929, c. 413, 45 Stat. 1414.

Tenth circuit. Act Aug. 3, 1949, c. 387, § 1, 63 Stat. 493.

District of Columbia Court of Appeals. Act Aug. 3, 1949, c. 387, § 1, 63 Stat. 493; Act May 31, 1938, c. 290, § 2, 52 Stat. 584; Act June 19, 1930, c. 538, 46 Stat. 785.

Act Feb. 28, 1929, c. 363, § 2, 45 Stat. 1346, 1347 provided that "There shall be in the sixth, seventh, and tenth circuits, respectively, four circuit judges; and in the second and eighth circuits, respectively, five circuit judges; and in each of the other circuits three circuit judges, to be appointed by the President by and with the advice and consent of the Senate."

Another part of section 1 of Act Feb. 10, 1954, which amended subsec. (a) of this section, provided for the appointment by the President, by and with the advice and consent of the Senate, of the additional judges for the Fifth and Ninth Circuits, provided for in such amendment.

Section 1(a) of Pub.L. 87–36 provided that: "The President shall appoint, by and with the advice and consent of the Senate, three additional circuit judges for the second circuit, one additional circuit judge for the third circuit, two additional circuit judges for the fourth circuit, two additional circuit judges for the fifth circuit, one additional circuit judge for the seventh circuit, and one additional circuit judge for the tenth circuit."

Section 1(a) of Pub.L. 89–372 provided that: "The President shall appoint, by and with the advice and consent of the Senate, two additional circuit judges for the fourth circuit, two additional circuit judges for the sixth circuit, one additional circuit judge for the seventh circuit, and one additional circuit judge for the eighth circuit."

Section 1(c) of Pub.L. 89–372, as amended by Pub.L. 90–347, § 2, June 18, 1968, 82 Stat. 183, provided that: "The President shall appoint, by and with the advice and consent of the Senate, four additional circuit judges for the fifth circuit." The second sentence of section 1(c) of Pub.L. 89–372 which provided that the first four vacancies occurring in the office of circuit judge in the fifth circuit shall not be filled was deleted by section 2 of Pub.L. 90–347, which also made those judgeships permanent and further provided that the present incumbents of such judgeships shall henceforth hold their offices under this section.

Section 1 of Pub.L. 90–347 provided: "That the President shall appoint, by and with the advice and consent of the Senate, one additional circuit judge for the third circuit, two additional circuit judges for the fifth circuit, one additional circuit judge for the sixth circuit, four additional circuit judges for the ninth circuit, and one additional circuit judge for the tenth circuit."

Section 3(a) of Pub.L. 95–486 provided that: "The President shall appoint, by and with the advice and consent of the Senate, one additional circuit judgeship for the first circuit, two additional circuit judgeships for the second circuit, one additional circuit judgeship for the third circuit, three additional circuit judgeships for the fourth circuit, eleven additional circuit judgeships for the fifth circuit, two additional circuit judgeships for the sixth circuit, one additional circuit judgeship for the seventh circuit, one additional circuit judgeship for the eighth circuit, ten additional circuit judgeships for the ninth circuit, one additional circuit judgeship for the tenth circuit, and two additional circuit judgeships for the District of Columbia."

Section 201(a) of Pub.L. 98–353 provided that:

"(1) Subject to the provisions of paragraph (2), the President shall appoint, by and with the advice and consent of the Senate, two additional circuit judges for the first circuit court of appeals, two additional circuit judges for the second circuit court of appeals, two additional circuit judges for the third circuit court of appeals, one additional circuit judge for the fourth circuit court of appeals, two additional circuit judges for the fifth circuit court of appeals, four additional circuit judges for the sixth circuit court of appeals, two additional circuit judges for the seventh circuit court of appeals, one additional circuit judge for the eighth circuit court of appeals, five additional circuit judges for the ninth circuit court of appeals, two additional circuit judges for the tenth circuit court of appeals, and one additional circuit judge for the District of Columbia circuit court of appeals.

"(2) The President shall appoint, by and with the advice and consent of the Senate, no more than 11 of such judges prior to January 21, 1985."

Section 202(a) of Pub.L. 101–650 provided that: "The President shall appoint, by and with the advice and consent of the Senate—

"(1) 2 additional circuit judges for the third circuit court of appeals;

"(2) 4 additional circuit judges for the fourth circuit court of appeals;

"(3) 1 additional circuit judge for the fifth circuit court of appeals;

"(4) 1 additional circuit judge for the sixth circuit court of appeals;

"(5) 1 additional circuit judge for the eighth circuit court of appeals; and

"(6) 2 additional circuit judges for the tenth circuit court of appeals."

Congressional Statement Regarding Appointment of Judges of United States Court of Appeals for the Federal Circuit and United States Claims Court

Section 168 of Pub.L. 97–164 provided that: "The Congress—

"(1) takes notice of the fact that the quality of the Federal judiciary is determined by the competence and experience of its judges; and

"(2) suggests that the President, in nominating individuals to judgeships on the United States Court of Appeals for the Federal Circuit and the United States Claims Court [now the United States Court of Federal Claims], select from a broad range of qualified individuals."

Continued Service of Judges of Court of Claims and Court of Customs and Patent Appeals as Judges of Court of Appeals for the Federal Circuit

Section 165 of Pub.L. 97–164 provided that: "The judges of the United States Court of Claims and of the United States Court of Customs and Patent Appeals in regular active service on the effective date of this Act [Oct. 1, 1982] shall continue in office as judges of the United States Court of Appeals for the Federal Circuit. Senior judges of the United States Court of Claims and of the United States Court of Customs and Patent Appeals on the effective date of this Act [Oct. 1, 1982] shall continue in office as senior judges of the United States Court of Appeals for the Federal Circuit."

Increase in Salaries

1998—Salaries of circuit judges increased to $145,000, effective on the first day of the first applicable pay period beginning on or after Jan. 1, 1998, by Ex. Ord. No. 13071, Dec. 29, 1997, 62 F.R. 68521, set out as a note under section 5332 of Title 5, Government Organization and Employees.

1997—Salaries of circuit judges continued at $141,700, effective on the first day of the first applicable pay period beginning on or after Jan. 1, 1997, by Ex. Ord. No. 13033, Dec. 27, 1996, 61 F.R. 68987, formerly set out as a note under section 5332 of Title 5, Government Organization and Employees.

1996—Salaries of circuit judges continued at $141,700, effective on the first day of the first applicable pay period beginning on or after Jan. 1, 1996, by Ex. Ord. No. 12984, Dec. 28, 1995, 61 F.R. 237, formerly set out as a note under section 5332 of Title 5, Government Organization and Employees.

1995—Salaries of circuit judges continued at $141,700, effective on the first day of the first applicable pay period beginning on or after Jan. 1, 1995, by Ex. Ord. No. 12944, Dec. 28, 1994, 60 F.R. 309, formerly set out as a note under section 5332 of Title 5, Government Organization and Employees.

1993—Salaries of circuit judges increased to $141,700, effective on the first day of the first applicable pay period beginning on or after Jan. 1, 1993, by Ex. Ord. No. 12826, Dec. 30, 1992, 57 F.R. 62909, formerly set out as a note under section 5332 of Title 5, Government Organization and Employees.

1992—Salaries of circuit judges increased to $137,300, effective on the first day of the first applicable pay period beginning on or after Jan. 1, 1992, by Ex. Ord. No. 12786, Dec. 26, 1991, 56 F.R. 67453, formerly set out as a note under section 5332 of Title 5.

1991—Salaries of circuit judges increased to $132,700, effective on the first day of the first applicable pay period beginning on or after Jan. 1, 1991, by Ex. Ord. No. 12736, Dec. 12, 1990, 55 F.R. 51385, formerly set out as a note under section 5332 of Title 5.

1990—Salaries of circuit judges continued at $95,000 per annum, and increased to $102,500, effective on first day of first pay period beginning on or after Jan. 31, 1990, by Ex. Ord. No. 12698, Dec. 23, 1989, 54 F.R. 53473, formerly set out as a note under section 5332 of Title 5.

1989—Salaries of circuit judges increased in the amount of 25 percent of their rates (as last in effect before the increase), effective Jan. 1, 1991, see Pub.L. 101–194, Title VII, § 703(a)(3), Nov. 30, 1989, 103 Stat. 1768, set out as a note under section 5318 of Title 5.

Salaries of circuit judges continued at $95,000 per annum, effective on the first day of the first applicable pay period beginning on or after Jan. 1, 1989, by Ex. Ord. No. 12663, Jan. 6, 1989, 54 F.R. 791, formerly set out as a note under section 5332 of Title 5.

1988—Salaries of circuit judges continued at $95,000 per annum, effective on the first day of the first applicable pay period beginning on or after Jan. 1, 1988, by Ex. Ord. No. 12622, Dec. 31, 1987, 53 F.R. 222, formerly set out as a note under section 5332 of Title 5.

1987—Salaries of circuit judges increased to $95,000 per annum, on recommendation of the President of the United States, see note set out under section 358 of Title 2, The Congress.

Salaries of circuit judges increased to $85,700, as required by section 406 of the Judiciary Appropriation Act, 1987, as incorporated in section 101(b) of Pub.L. 99–500 and section 101(b) of Pub.L. 99–591, effective on the first day of the first applicable pay period beginning on or after Jan. 1, 1987, by Ex. Ord. No. 12578, Dec. 31, 1986, 52 F.R. 505, formerly set out as a note under section 5332 of Title 5.

1985—Salaries of circuit judges increased to $83,200 effective on the first day of the first pay period beginning on or after Jan. 1, 1985, by Ex. Ord. No. 12496, Dec. 28, 1984, 50 F.R. 211, as amended by Ex. Ord. No. 12540, Dec. 30, 1985, 51 F.R. 577, formerly set out as a note under section 5332 of Title 5, Government Organization and Employees. Prior to its amendment by Ex. Ord. No. 12540. schedule 7 of Ex. Ord. 12496 had contained a footnote directing that, pursuant to section 140 of Pub.L. 97–92, set out as a note under section 461 of this title, funds were not available to pay a salary at a rate which exceeded the rate in effect on Dec. 15, 1981, which was $74,300.

See also section 2207 of Pub.L. 98–369, set out as a note under section 461 of this title, which provided for overall percentage adjustment increases in certain rates of pay under the General Schedule.

1984—Salaries of circuit judges increased to $80,400 effective on the first day of the first pay period beginning on or after Jan. 1, 1984, by Ex. Ord. No. 12456, Dec. 30, 1983, 49 F.R. 347, as amended Ex. Ord. No. 12477, May 23, 1984, 49 F.R. 22041; Ex. Ord. No. 12487, Sept. 14, 1984, 49 F.R. 36493, formerly set out as a note under section 5332 of Title 5.

1982—Salaries of circuit judges increased to $77,300 effective on the first day of the first pay period beginning on or after Oct. 1, 1982, by Ex. Ord. No. 12387, Oct. 8, 1982, 47 F.R. 44981, formerly set out as a note under section 5332 of Title 5, Government Organization and Employees. Ex. Ord. No. 12387 further provided that pursuant to section 140 of Pub.L. 97–92 funds are not available to pay a salary at a rate which exceeds the rate in effect on Dec. 15, 1981, which was $74,300.

Maximum rate payable after Dec. 17, 1982, increased from $74,300 to $77,300, see Pub.L. 97–377, Title I, § 129(b)–(d), Dec. 21, 1982, 96 Stat. 1914, set out as a note under section 5318 of Title 5.

Limitations on use of funds for fiscal year ending Sept. 30, 1983, appropriated by any Act to pay the salary or pay of any individual in legislative, executive, or judicial branch in position equal to or above level V of the Executive Schedule, see section 101(e) of Pub.L. 97–276, as amended, set out as a note under section 5318 of Title 5.

1981—Salaries of circuit judges increased to $74,300 effective on the first day of the first pay period beginning on or after Oct. 1, 1981, by Ex. Ord. No. 12330, Oct. 15, 1981, 46 F.R. 50921, formerly set out as a note under section 5332 of Title 5.

Limitations on use of funds for fiscal year ending Sept. 30, 1982, appropriated by any Act to pay the salary or pay of any individual in legislative, executive, or judicial branch in position equal to or above level V of the Executive Schedule, see sections 101(g) and 141 of Pub.L. 97–92, set out as a note under section 5318 of Title 5.

1980—Salaries of circuit judges increased to $70,900 effective on the first day of the first pay period beginning on or after Oct. 1, 1980, by Ex. Ord. No. 12248, Oct. 16, 1980, 45 F.R. 69199, formerly set out as a note under section 5332 of Title 5. Ex. Ord. No. 12248 further provided that pursuant to Pub.L. 96–369 funds are not available to pay a salary at a rate which exceeds the rate in effect on Sept. 30, 1980, which was $60,662.50.

Limitations on use of funds for fiscal year ending Sept. 30, 1981, appropriated by any Act to pay the salary or pay of any individual in legislative, executive, or judicial branch in position equal to or above level V of the Executive Schedule, see section 101(c) of Pub.L. 96–536, as amended, set out as a note under section 5318 of Title 5.

1979—Salaries of circuit judges increased to $65,000 effective on the first day of the first applicable pay period beginning on or after Oct. 1, 1979, by Ex. Ord. No. 12165, Oct. 9, 1979, 44 F.R. 58671, as amended by Ex. Ord. No. 12200, Mar. 12, 1980, 45 F.R. 16443, formerly set out as a note under section 5332 of Title 5. Ex. Ord. No. 12165 further provided that pursuant to Pub.L. 96–86 funds appropriated for fiscal year 1980 may not be used to pay a salary at a rate which exceeds an increase of 5.5 percent over the applicable rate payable for such position or office in effect on Sept. 30, 1978, which was $60,662.50 for circuit judges.

Applicability to funds appropriated by any Act for fiscal year ending Sept. 30, 1980, of limitation of section 304 of Pub.L. 95–391 on use of funds to pay the salary or pay of any individual in legislative, executive, or judicial branch in position equal to or above level V of the Executive Schedule, see section 101 of Pub.L. 96–86, set out as a note under section 5318 of Title 5.

1978—Salaries of circuit judges increased to $60,700 effective on the first day of the first pay period beginning on or after Oct. 1, 1978, by Ex. Ord. No. 12087, Oct. 7, 1978, 43 F.R. 46823, formerly set out as a note under section 5332 of Title 5. Ex. Ord. No. 12087 further provided that pursuant to the Legislative Branch Appropriation Act, 1979 [Pub.L. 95–391, Title III, § 304, Sept. 30, 1978, 92 Stat. 788, set out as a note under section 5318 of Title 5], funds are not available to pay a salary at a rate which exceeds the rate in effect on Sept. 30, 1978, which was $57,500.

1977—Salaries of circuit judges increased to $57,500 per annum, upon recommendation of the President of the United States, see note set out under section 358 of Title 2, The Congress.

1976—Salaries of circuit judges increased to $46,800 effective on the first day of the first pay period beginning on or after Oct. 1, 1976, by Ex. Ord. No. 11941, Oct. 1, 1976, 41 F.R. 43889, formerly set out as a note under section 5332 of Title 5, Government Organization and Employees. Ex. Ord. No. 11941 further provided that pursuant to the Legislative Branch Appropriation Act, 1977, funds are not available to pay a salary at a rate which exceeds the rate in effect on Sept. 30, 1976, which was $44,600.

1975—Salaries of circuit judges increased to $44,600 effective on the first day of the first pay period beginning on or after Oct. 1, 1975, by Ex. Ord. No. 11883, Oct. 6, 1975, 40 F.R. 47091, formerly set out as a note under section 5332 of Title 5.

1969—Salary of circuit judges increased from $33,000 to $42,500 per annum, commencing February 14, 1969, upon recommendation of the President of the United States, see note set out under section 358 of Title 2, The Congress.

1946—The salaries of the circuit judges were increased from $12,500 to $17,500 a year by Act July 31, 1946, c. 704, § 1, 60 Stat. 716.

1926—Salaries of the circuit judges were increased from $8,500 to $12,500 a year by Act Dec. 13, 1926, c. 6, § 1, 44 Stat. 919.

1919—Salaries of the circuit judges were increased from $7,000 to $8,500 a year by Act Feb. 25, 1919, c. 29, § 1, 40 Stat. 1156.

1911—Salaries of circuit court judges had been set at $7,000 a year by the Judicial Code of 1911, Act Mar. 3, 1911, c. 231, § 118, 36 Stat. 1131.

Nomination to Federal Judgeship on Nondiscriminatory Basis

Section 211 of Pub.L. 98–353 provided that: "It is the sense of the Congress that the President, in selecting individuals for nomination to the Federal judgeships created by this Act [see Short Title of 1984 Amendments note set out under section 151 of this title], shall give due consideration to qualified individuals without regard to race, color, sex, religion, or national origin."

§ 45. Chief judges; precedence of judges

(a)(1) The chief judge of the circuit shall be the circuit judge in regular active service who is senior in commission of those judges who—

(A) are sixty-four years of age or under;

(B) have served for one year or more as a circuit judge; and

(C) have not served previously as chief judge.

(2)(A) In any case in which no circuit judge meets the qualifications of paragraph (1), the youngest circuit judge in regular active service who is sixty-five years of age or over and who has served as circuit judge for one year or more shall act as the chief judge.

(B) In any case under subparagraph (A) in which there is no circuit judge in regular active service who has served as a circuit judge for one year or more, the circuit judge in regular active service who is senior in commission and who has not served previously as chief judge shall act as the chief judge.

(3)(A) Except as provided in subparagraph (C), the chief judge of the circuit appointed under paragraph (1) shall serve for a term of seven years and shall serve after expiration of such term until another judge is eligible under paragraph (1) to serve as chief judge of the circuit.

(B) Except as provided in subparagraph (C), a circuit judge acting as chief judge under subparagraph (A) or (B) of paragraph (2) shall serve until a judge has been appointed who meets the qualifications under paragraph (1).

(C) No circuit judge may serve or act as chief judge of the circuit after attaining the age of seventy years unless no other circuit judge is qualified to serve as chief judge of the circuit under paragraph (1) or is qualified to act as chief judge under paragraph (2).

(b) The chief judge shall have precedence and preside at any session of the court which he attends. Other circuit judges of the court in regular active service shall have precedence and preside according to the seniority of their commissions. Judges whose commissions bear the same date shall have precedence according to seniority in age. The circuit justice, however, shall have precedence over all the circuit judges and shall preside at any session which he attends.

(c) If the chief judge desires to be relieved of his duties as chief judge while retaining his active status as circuit judge, he may so certify to the Chief Justice of the United States, and thereafter the chief judge of the circuit shall be such other circuit judge who is qualified to serve or act as chief judge under subsection (a).

(d) If a chief judge is temporarily unable to perform his duties as such, they shall be performed by the circuit judge in active service, present in the circuit and able and qualified to act, who is next in precedence.

(June 25, 1948, c. 646, 62 Stat. 871; Oct. 31, 1951, c. 655, § 35, 65 Stat. 723; Aug. 6, 1958, Pub.L. 85–593, § 1, 72 Stat. 497; Apr. 2, 1982, Pub.L. 97–164, Title II, §§ 201, 204, 96 Stat. 51, 53.)

HISTORICAL AND STATUTORY NOTES

Effective Dates

1982 Acts. Amendment by Pub.L. 97–164 effective Oct. 1, 1982, see section 402 of Pub.L. 97–164, set out as a note under section 171 of this title.

1958 Acts. Section 3 of Pub.L. 85–593, as amended by Pub.L. 95–486, § 4, Oct. 20, 1978, 92 Stat. 1632, provided that: "The amendments to sections 45 and 136 of title 28 of the United States Code [this section and section 136 of this title] made by this Act shall take effect at the expiration of one year from the date of enactment of this Act [Aug. 6, 1958]."

Savings Provisions

Section 203 of part A of Title II of Pub.L. 97–164 provided that:

"**(a)** The amendments to section 45 of title 28, United States Code [this section], and to section 136 of such title [section 136 of this title], made by sections 201 and 202 of this Act, shall not apply to or affect any person serving as chief judge on the effective date of this Act [Oct. 1, 1982].

"**(b)** The provisions of section 45(a) of title 28, United States Code [subsec. (a) of this section], as in effect on the day before the effective date of this Act [Oct. 1, 1982], shall apply to the chief judge of a circuit serving on such effective date. The provisions of section 136(a) of title 28, United States Code [section 136(a) of this title], as in effect on the day before the effective date of this part [Oct. 1, 1982], shall apply to the chief judge of a district court serving on such effective date."

Appointment of Chief Judge of Court of Appeals for the Federal Circuit

Section 166 of Pub.L. 97–164 provided that: "Notwithstanding the provisions of section 45(a) of title 28, United States Code [subsec. (a) of this section], the first chief judge of the United States Court of Appeals for the Federal Circuit shall be the Chief Judge of the United States Court of Claims or the Chief Judge of the United States Court of Customs and Patent Appeals, whoever has served longer as chief judge of his court. Notwithstanding section 45 of title 28, United States Code [this section], whichever of the two chief judges does not become the first chief judge of the United States Court of Appeals for the Federal Circuit under the preceding sentence shall, while in active service, have precedence and be deemed senior in commission over all the circuit judges of the United States Court of Appeals for the Federal Circuit (other than the first chief judge of that circuit). When the person who first serves as chief judge of the United States Court of Appeals for the Federal Circuit vacates that position, the position shall be filled in accordance with section 45(a) of title 28, United States Code [subsec. (a) of this section], as modified by the preceding sentence of this section."

Chief Judge of Court of Appeals for District of Columbia

Section 2(a) of Act June 25, 1948, provided in part that the Chief Justice of the Court of Appeals for the District of Columbia in office on Sept. 1, 1948, shall thereafter be known as the Chief Judge.

§ 46. Assignment of judges; panels; hearings; quorum

(a) Circuit judges shall sit on the court and its panels in such order and at such times as the court directs.

(b) In each circuit the court may authorize the hearing and determination of cases and controversies by separate panels, each consisting of three judges, at least a majority of whom shall be judges of that court, unless such judges cannot sit because recused or disqualified, or unless the chief judge of that court certifies that there is an emergency including, but not limited to, the unavailability of a judge of the court because of illness. Such panels shall sit at the times and places and hear the cases and controversies assigned as the court directs. The United States Court of Appeals for the Federal Circuit shall determine by rule a procedure for the rotation of judges from panel to panel to ensure that all of the judges sit on a representative cross section of the cases heard and, notwithstanding the first sentence of this subsection, may determine by rule the number of judges, not less than three, who constitute a panel.

(c) Cases and controversies shall be heard and determined by a court or panel of not more than three judges (except that the United States Court of Appeals for the Federal Circuit may sit in panels of more than three judges if its rules so provide), unless a hearing or rehearing before the court in banc is ordered by a majority of the circuit judges of the circuit who are in regular active service. A court in banc shall consist of all circuit judges in regular active service, or such number of judges as may be prescribed in accordance with section 6 of Public Law 95–486 (92 Stat. 1633), except that any senior circuit judge of the circuit shall be eligible (1) to participate, at his election and upon designation and assignment pursuant to section 294(c) of this title and the rules of the circuit, as a member of an in banc court reviewing a decision of a panel of which such judge was a member, or (2) to continue to participate in the decision of a case or controversy that was heard or reheard by the court in banc at a time when such judge was in regular active service.

(d) A majority of the number of judges authorized to constitute a court or panel thereof, as provided in paragraph (c), shall constitute a quorum.

(June 25, 1948, c. 646, 62 Stat. 871; Nov. 13, 1963, Pub.L. 88–176, § 1(b), 77 Stat. 331; Oct. 20, 1978, Pub.L. 95–486, § 5(a), (b), 92 Stat. 1633; Apr. 2, 1982, Pub.L. 97–164, Title I, § 103, Title II, § 205, 96 Stat. 25, 53; Aug. 6, 1996, Pub.L. 104–175, § 1, 110 Stat. 1556.)

HISTORICAL AND STATUTORY NOTES

References in Text

Section 6 of Public Law 95–486 (92 Stat. 1633), referred to in subsec. (c), is section 6 of Pub.L. 95–486, Oct. 20, 1978, 92 Stat. 1633, which is set out as an Appeals Court Administrative Units note under section 41 of this title.

Effective Dates

1982 Acts. Amendment by Pub.L. 97–164 effective Oct. 1, 1982, see section 402 of Pub.L. 97–164, set out as a note under section 171 of this title.

CHIEF CIRCUIT JUDGE (FOURTH CIRCUIT): ORDER REGARDING PERFORMANCE OF JUDICIAL DUTIES

Pursuant to the authority set forth in 28 U.S.C. § 46(c) and 28 U.S.C. § 294(c), all senior circuit judges in this circuit are hereby assigned to perform all judicial duties in any case, or in the decision of any matter, such as a motion or any other procedural or administrative matter, which has been properly assigned to them, whether in the ordinary course of business or otherwise. Any senior circuit judge who undertakes the performance of any official duties pursuant to this designation consents to participate (except upon absence from duty station or the like) in the consideration of the same until terminated, including, but not exclusively, participation in in banc consideration of the matter.

ENTERED this 31st day of March, 1993.

SAM J. ERVIN, III
CHIEF CIRCUIT JUDGE

CHIEF JUDGE'S ORDER DECLARING AN EMERGENCY UNDER 28 U.S.C. § 46(b)

This court is authorized to have 17 judges in regular active service. Today, the number of judges so serving is 13. Only one nomination has been sent to the Senate for its advice and consent. It is now pending in the Senate. The circuit is experiencing increases in appellate filings greater than those experienced in any other United States court of appeals. Because of the backlog of cases in district courts of the Fifth Circuit, this disproportionate increase in filings is expected to continue. Since the beginning of 1985, except for very brief periods in 1986 and 1990, this court has been at least two judges short of its authorized complement of judges in regular active service. Retirements, a resignation, and the failure of the President to nominate persons to fill vacancies in the court have caused the present increase in the number of vacancies. From all indications, such executive inaction may continue for an indefinite time in the future. Pleas for help have gone unanswered.

Lack of action to fill these vacancies, coupled with filing increases, have caused a judicial emergency in the court. Until such time as the President has nominated and the Congress has advised and consented to the appointment of the number of judges in regular active service provided by law, a judicial emergency exists and will continue which now prevents and will prevent the routine empaneling of three-judge panels consisting of judges at least a majority of whom are judges of this court.

During the continuation of this declared emergency, the hearing and determination of cases and controversies may be conducted by panels of three judges selected without regard to the qualification, set out in 28 U.S.C. § 46(b), that a majority of each panel be composed of judges of this court.

CHARLES CLARK
CHIEF JUDGE

Filed: Oct. 28, 1991

§ 47. Disqualification of trial judge to hear appeal

No judge shall hear or determine an appeal from the decision of a case or issue tried by him.

(June 25, 1948, c. 646, 62 Stat. 872.)

§ 48. Terms of court

(a) The courts of appeals shall hold regular sessions at the places listed below, and at such other places within the respective circuit as each court may designate by rule.

Circuits	*Places*
District of Columbia	Washington.
First	Boston.
Second	New York.
Third	Philadelphia.
Fourth	Richmond, Asheville.
Fifth	New Orleans, Fort Worth, Jackson.
Sixth	Cincinnati.
Seventh	Chicago.
Eighth	St. Louis, Kansas City, Omaha, St. Paul.
Ninth	San Francisco, Los Angeles, Portland, Seattle.
Tenth	Denver, Wichita, Oklahoma City.
Eleventh	Atlanta, Jacksonville, Montgomery.
Federal	District of Columbia, and in any other place listed above as the court by rule directs.

(b) Each court of appeals may hold special sessions at any place within its circuit as the nature of the business may require, and upon such notice as the court orders. The court may transact any business at a special session which it might transact at a regular session.

(c) Any court of appeals may pretermit any regular session of court at any place for insufficient business or other good cause.

(d) The times and places of the sessions of the Court of Appeals for the Federal Circuit shall be prescribed with a view to securing reasonable opportunity to citizens to appear before the court with as little inconvenience and expense to citizens as is practicable.

(June 25, 1948, c. 646, 62 Stat. 872; Oct. 31, 1951, c. 655, § 36, 65 Stat. 723; Oct. 14, 1980, Pub.L. 96–452, § 4, 94 Stat. 1994; Apr. 2, 1982, Pub.L. 97–164, Title I, § 104, 96 Stat. 26; Oct. 29, 1992, Pub.L. 102–572, Title V, § 501, 106 Stat. 4512.)

HISTORICAL AND STATUTORY NOTES

Effective Dates

1992 Acts. Amendment by Pub.L. 102–572 effective Jan. 1, 1993, see section 1101(a) of Pub.L. 102–572, set out as a note under section 905 of Title 2, The Congress.

1982 Acts. Amendment by Pub.L. 97–164 effective Oct. 1, 1982, see section 402 of Pub.L. 97–164, set out as a note under section 171 of this title.

1980 Acts. Amendment by Pub.L. 96–452 effective Oct. 1, 1981, see section 12 of Pub.L. 96–452, set out as a note under section 41 of this title.

Survey of Judicial Business in Alaska

Section 23(a) of Pub.L. 86–70, June 25, 1959, 73 Stat. 147, provided that: "The Judicial Conference of the United States, with the assistance of the Administrative Office of the United States Courts, shall conduct a study, including a field survey, of the Federal judicial business arising in the State of Alaska with a view toward directing the United States Court of Appeals for the Ninth Circuit to hold such terms of court in Anchorage or such other Alaskan cities as may be necessary for the prompt and efficient administration of justice."

§ 49. Assignment of judges to division to appoint independent counsels

(a) Beginning with the two-year period commencing on the date of the enactment of this section, three judges or justices shall be assigned for each successive two-year period to a division of the United States Court of Appeals for the District of Columbia to be the division of the court for the purpose of appointing independent counsels. The Clerk of the United States Court of Appeals for the District of Columbia Circuit shall serve as the clerk of such division of the court and shall provide such services as are needed by such division of the court.

(b) Except as provided under subsection (f) of this section, assignment to such division of the court shall not be a bar to other judicial assignments during the term of such division.

(c) In assigning judges or justices to sit on such division of the court, priority shall be given to senior circuit judges and retired justices.

(d) The Chief Justice of the United States shall designate and assign three circuit court judges or justices, one of whom shall be a judge of the United States Court of Appeals for the District of Columbia, to such division of the court. Not more than one judge or justice or senior or retired judge or justice may be named to such division from a particular court.

(e) Any vacancy in such division of the court shall be filled only for the remainder of the two-year period in which such vacancy occurs and in the same manner as initial assignments to such division were made.

(f) Except as otherwise provided in chapter 40 of this title, no member of such division of the court who participated in a function conferred on the division under chapter 40 of this title involving an independent counsel shall be eligible to participate in any judicial proceeding concerning a matter which involves such independent counsel while such independent counsel is serving in that office or which involves the exercise of such independent counsel's official duties, regardless of whether such independent counsel is still serving in that office.

(Added Pub.L. 95–521, Title VI, § 602(a), Oct. 26, 1978, 92 Stat. 1873, and amended Pub.L. 97–409, § 2(b) (1), Jan. 3, 1983, 96 Stat. 2039; Pub.L. 99–554, Title I, § 144(g)(3), Oct. 27, 1986, 100 Stat. 3097; Pub.L. 100–191, §§ 4, 5(a), Dec. 15, 1987, 101 Stat. 1307.)

HISTORICAL AND STATUTORY NOTES

References in Text

The date of the enactment of this section, referred to in subsec. (a), means Oct. 26, 1978, the date on which Pub.L. 95–521 was approved.

Effective Dates

1987 Acts. Amendment by Pub.L. 100–191 effective on Dec. 15, 1987, see section 6 of Pub.L. 100–191, set out as a note under section 591 of this title.

1986 Acts. Amendment by Pub.L. 99–554 effective 30 days after Oct. 27, 1986, see section 302(a) of Pub.L. 99–554, as amended, set out as a note under section 581 of this title.

1978 Acts. Section effective Oct. 26, 1978, see section 604 of Pub.L. 95–521, set out as a note under section 591 of this title.

Appointment of Regulatory Independent Counsel

Division of the court described in this section authorized to appoint as independent counsel any individual who, on June 30, 1994, is serving as a regulatory independent counsel under parts 600 and 603 of title 28, Code of Federal Regulations, notwithstanding the restriction in section 593(b)(2) of this title, see section 7(h) of Pub.L. 103–270, set out as an Effective Date of 1994 Acts note under section 591 of this title.

CHAPTER 5—DISTRICT COURTS

Sec.
81. Alabama.
81A. Alaska.
82. Arizona.
83. Arkansas.
84. California.
85. Colorado.
86. Connecticut.
87. Delaware.
88. District of Columbia.
89. Florida.
90. Georgia.
91. Hawaii.
92. Idaho.
93. Illinois.
94. Indiana.
95. Iowa.
96. Kansas.
97. Kentucky.
98. Louisiana.
99. Maine.
100. Maryland.
101. Massachusetts.
102. Michigan.
103. Minnesota.
104. Mississippi.
105. Missouri.
106. Montana.
107. Nebraska.
108. Nevada.
109. New Hampshire.
110. New Jersey.
111. New Mexico.
112. New York.
113. North Carolina.
114. North Dakota.
115. Ohio.
116. Oklahoma.
117. Oregon.
118. Pennsylvania.
119. Puerto Rico.
120. Rhode Island.
121. South Carolina.
122. South Dakota.
123. Tennessee.
124. Texas.
125. Utah.
126. Vermont.
127. Virginia.
128. Washington.
129. West Virginia.
130. Wisconsin.
131. Wyoming.
132. Creation and composition of district courts.
133. Appointment and number of district judges.
134. Tenure and residence of district judges.
135. Salaries of district judges.
136. Chief judges; precedence of district judges.
137. Division of business among district judges.
138. Terms abolished.
139. Times for holding regular sessions.

Sec.
140. Adjournment.
141. Special sessions; places; notice.
[142. Repealed.]
143. Vacant judgeship as affecting proceedings.
144. Bias or prejudice of judge.

HISTORICAL AND STATUTORY NOTES

Short Title

1978 Amendments. For short title of Pub.L. 95–408, Oct. 2, 1978, 92 Stat. 883, as "Federal District Court Organization Act of 1978", see note set out under section 1 of this title.

§ 81. Alabama

Alabama is divided into three judicial districts to be known as the Northern, Middle, and Southern Districts of Alabama.

Northern District

(a) The Northern District comprises seven divisions.

(1) The Northwestern Division comprises the counties of Colbert, Franklin, and Lauderdale.

Court for the Northwestern Division shall be held at Florence.

(2) The Northeastern Division comprises the counties of Cullman, Jackson, Lawrence, Limestone, Madison, and Morgan.

Court for the Northeastern Division shall be held at Huntsville and Decatur.

(3) The Southern Division comprises the counties of Blount, Jefferson, and Shelby.

Court for the Southern Division shall be held at Birmingham.

(4) The Eastern Division comprises the counties of Calhoun, Clay, Cleburne, and Talladega.

Court for the Eastern Division shall be held at Anniston.

(5) The Western Division comprises the counties of Bibb, Greene, Pickens, Sumter, and Tuscaloosa.

Court for the Western Division shall be held at Tuscaloosa.

(6) The Middle Division comprises the counties of Cherokee, De Kalb, Etowah, Marshall, and Saint Clair.

Court for the Middle Division shall be held at Gadsden.

(7) The Jasper Division comprises the counties of Fayette, Lamar, Marion, Walker, and Winston.

Court for the Jasper Division shall be held at Jasper.

Middle District

(b) The Middle District comprises three divisions.

(1) The Northern Division comprises the counties of Autauga, Barbour, Bullock, Butler, Chilton, Coosa, Covington, Crenshaw, Elmore, Lowndes, Montgomery, and Pike.

Court for the Northern Division shall be held at Montgomery.

(2) The Southern Division comprises the counties of Coffee, Dale, Geneva, Henry, and Houston.

Court for the Southern Division shall be held at Dothan.

(3) The Eastern Division comprises the counties of Chambers, Lee, Macon, Randolph, Russell, and Tallapoosa.

Court for the Eastern Division shall be held at Opelika.

Southern District

(c) The Southern District comprises two divisions.

(1) The Northern Division comprises the counties of Dallas, Hale, Marengo, Perry, and Wilcox.

Court for the Northern Division shall be held at Selma.

(2) The Southern Division comprises the counties of Baldwin, Choctaw, Clarke, Conecuh, Escambia, Mobile, Monroe, and Washington.

Court for the Southern Division shall be held at Mobile.

(June 25, 1948, c. 646, 62 Stat. 873; May 19, 1961, Pub.L. 87–36, § 3(a), 75 Stat. 83.)

§ 81A. Alaska

Alaska constitutes one judicial district.

Court shall be held at Anchorage, Fairbanks, Juneau, Ketchikan, and Nome.

(Added Pub.L. 85–508, § 12(b), July 7, 1958, 72 Stat. 348, and amended Pub.L. 86–70, § 23(b), June 25, 1959, 73 Stat. 147.)

HISTORICAL AND STATUTORY NOTES

Effective Dates

1958 Acts. Section 12 of Pub.L. 85–508 provided in part that this section, and the amendments to sections 133, 333, 373, 376, 460, 610, 753, 1252, 1291, 1292, 1294, 1346, 1963, 2072, 2201 and 2410 of this title, former section 341b of Title 5, Government Organization and Employees, and sections 3241, 3401, 3771 and 3772 of Title 18, Crimes and Criminal Procedure, shall be effective upon the admission of Alaska into the Union. Admission as a State was accomplished Jan. 3, 1959 upon issuance of Proc. No. 3269, Jan. 3, 1959, 24 F.R. 81, 73 Stat. c16, as required by sections 1 and 8(c) of Pub.L. 85–508. See notes set out preceding section 21 of Title 48, Territories and Insular Possessions.

Appeals

Section 14 of Pub.L. 85–508 provided that: "All appeals taken from the District Court for the Territory of Alaska to the Supreme Court of the United States or the United States Court of Appeals for the Ninth Circuit, previous to the admission of Alaska as a State, shall be prosecuted to final determination as though this Act had not been passed. All cases in which final judgment has been rendered in such district court, and in which appeals might be had except for the admission of such State, may still be sued out, taken, and prosecuted to the Supreme Court of the United States or the United States Court of Appeals for the Ninth Circuit under the provisions of then existing law, and there held and determined in like manner; and in either case, the Supreme Court of the United States, or the United States Court of Appeals, in the event of reversal, shall remand the said cause to either the State supreme court or other final appellate court of said State, or the United States district court for said district, as the case may require: *Provided,* That the time allowed by existing law for appeals from the district court for said Territory shall not be enlarged thereby."

Continuation of Suits

Section 13 of Pub.L. 85–508 provided that: "No writ, action, indictment, cause, or proceeding pending in the District Court for the Territory of Alaska on the date when said Territory shall become a State, and no case pending in an appellate court upon appeal from the District Court for the Territory of Alaska at the time said Territory shall become a State, shall abate by the admission of the State of Alaska into the Union, but the same shall be transferred and proceeded with as hereinafter provided.

"All civil causes of action and all criminal offenses which shall have arisen or been committed prior to the admission of said State, but as to which no suit, action, or prosecution shall be pending at the date of such admission, shall be subject to prosecution in the appropriate State courts or in the United States District Court for the District of Alaska in like manner, to the same extent, and with like right of appellate review, as if said State had been created and said courts had been established prior to the accrual of said causes of action or the commission of such offenses; and such of said criminal offenses as shall have been committed against the laws of the Territory shall be tried and punished by the appropriate courts of said State, and such as shall have been committed against the laws of the United States shall be tried and punished in the United States District Court for the District of Alaska."

Pending Cases

Section 17 of Pub.L. 85–508 provided that: "All cases pending in the District Court for the Territory of Alaska at the time said Territory becomes a State not transferred to the United States District Court for the District of Alaska shall be proceeded with and determined by the courts created by said State with the right to prosecute appeals to the appellate courts created by said State, and also with the same right to prosecute appeals or writs of certiorari from the final determination in said causes made by the court of last resort created by such State to the Supreme Court of the United States, as now provided by law for appeals and writs of certiorari from the court of last resort of a State to the Supreme Court of the United States."

Schedule of Fees, Mileage, or Other Compensation

Section 23(c) of Pub.L. 86–70, June 25, 1959, 73 Stat. 147, provided that: "Such authority as has been exercised by the Attorney General heretofore, with regard to the Federal court system in Alaska, pursuant to section 30 of the Act of June 6, 1900 (48 U.S.C. 25) [omitted], shall continue to be exercised by him after the court created by section 12(b) of the Act of July 7, 1958 (72 Stat. 339, 348) [this section], providing for the admission of the State of Alaska into the Union, is established."

Succession of Courts

Section 16 of Pub.L. 85–508 provided that: "Jurisdiction of all cases pending or determined in the District Court for the Territory of Alaska not transferred to the United States District Court for the District of Alaska shall devolve upon and be exercised by the courts of original jurisdiction created by said State, which shall be deemed to be the successor of the District Court for the Territory of Alaska with respect to cases not so transferred and, as such, shall take and retain custody of all records, dockets, journals, and files of such court pertaining to such cases. The files and papers in all cases so transferred to the United States district court, together with a transcript of all book entries to complete the record in such particular cases so transferred, shall be in like manner transferred to said district court."

Termination of Jurisdiction of District Court for the Territory of Alaska

Section 18 of Pub.L. 85–508 provided that: "The provisions of the preceding sections with respect to the termination of the jurisdiction of the District Court for the Territory of Alaska, the continuation of suits, the succession of courts, and the satisfaction of rights of litigants in suits before such courts, shall not be effective until three years after the effective date of this Act [see section 8(b) of Pub.L. 85–508, set out as a note preceding section 21 of Title 48, Territories and Insular Possessions] unless the President, by Executive order, shall sooner proclaim that the United States District Court for the District of Alaska, established in accordance with the provisions of this Act, is prepared to assume the functions imposed upon it. During such period of three years or until such Executive order is issued, the United States District Court for the Territory of Alaska shall continue to function as heretofore. The tenure of the judges, the United States attorneys, marshals, and other officers of the United States District Court for the Territory of Alaska shall terminate at such time as that court shall cease to function as provided in this section."

Based on Title 28, U.S.C., 1940 ed., § 216, and District of Columbia Code, 1940 ed., § 11–205 (Acts Feb. 9, 1893, c. 74, § 6, 27 Stat. 435; July 30, 1894, c. 172, § 2, 28 Stat. 161; Mar. 3, 1901, c. 854, § 225, 31 Stat. 1225; Mar. 3, 1911, c. 231, § 120, 36 Stat. 1132).

The provision in section 11–205 of the District of Columbia Code, 1940 ed., that a justice of the district court while on the bench of the Court of Appeals in the District of Columbia shall not sit in review of judgment, order, or decree rendered by him below, was consolidated with a similar provision of section 216 of Title 28 U.S.C., 1940 ed. The consolidation simplifies the language without change of substance.

Transfer of Cases

Section 15 of Pub.L. 85–508 provided that: "All causes pending or determined in the District Court for the Territory of Alaska at the time of the admission of Alaska as a State which are of such nature as to be within the jurisdiction of a district court of the United States shall be transferred to the United States District Court for the District of Alaska for final disposition and enforcement in the same manner as is now provided by law with reference to the judgments and decrees in existing United States district courts. All other causes pending or determined in the District Court for the Territory of Alaska at the time of the admission of Alaska as a State shall be transferred to the appropriate State court of Alaska. All final judgments and decrees rendered upon such transferred cases in the United States District Court for the District of Alaska may be reviewed by the Supreme Court of the United States or by the United States Court of Appeals for the Ninth Circuit in the same manner as is now provided by law with reference to the judgments and decrees in existing United States district courts."

EXECUTIVE ORDERS

EXECUTIVE ORDER NO. 10867

ASSUMPTION OF FUNCTIONS BY UNITED STATES DISTRICT COURT FOR DISTRICT OF ALASKA

WHEREAS the act of July 7, 1958, 72 Stat. 339 [set out as a note preceding section 21 of Title 48, Territories and Insular Possessions], relating to the admission of the State of Alaska into the Union, provides that the United States District Court for the Territory of Alaska shall continue to function as theretofore for a period of three years after the effective date of that act, unless the President, by Executive order, shall sooner proclaim that the United States District Court for the District of Alaska, established in accordance with the provisions of that act, is prepared to assume the functions imposed upon it; and

WHEREAS that act further provides that its provisions relating to the termination of the jurisdiction of the District Court for the Territory of Alaska, the continuation of suits, the succession of courts, and the satisfaction of the rights of litigants in suits before such courts shall not be effective until the expiration of the above-mentioned three-year period or until such Executive order is issued; and that the tenure of the judges, the United States Attorneys, Marshals, and other officers of the United States District Court for the Territory of Alaska shall terminate at such time as that court shall cease to function; and

WHEREAS, I have appointed, by and with the advice and consent of the Senate, and commissioned the Honorable Walter N. Hodge to be United States District Judge for the District of Alaska, and he has taken his oath of office; and

WHEREAS Judge Hodge has appointed an acting United States Attorney, an acting United States Marshal, and other court officers; and

WHEREAS the United States District Court for the District of Alaska is now prepared to assume the functions imposed upon it:

NOW, THEREFORE, by virtue of the authority vested in me by section 18 of the said act of July 7, 1958 [set out as a note under this section], I hereby proclaim that the United States District Court for the District of Alaska is prepared to assume the functions imposed upon it. Accordingly, the jurisdiction of the District Court for the Territory of Alaska and the tenure of the judges, the United States Attorneys, Marshals, and other officers of that court are now terminated.

DWIGHT D. EISENHOWER

§ 82. Arizona

Arizona constitutes one judicial district.

Court shall be held at Globe, Phoenix, Prescott, and Tucson.

(June 25, 1948, c. 646, 62 Stat. 874.)

§ 83. Arkansas

Arkansas is divided into two judicial districts to be known as the Eastern and Western Districts of Arkansas.

Eastern District

(a) The Eastern District comprises five divisions.

(1) The Eastern Division comprises the counties of Cross, Lee, Monroe, Phillips, Saint Francis, and Woodruff.

Court for the Eastern Division shall be held at Helena.

(2) The Western Division comprises the counties of Conway, Faulkner, Lonoke, Perry, Pope, Prairie, Pulaski, Saline, Van Buren, White, and Yell.

Court for the Western Division shall be held at Little Rock.

(3) The Pine Bluff Division comprises the counties of Arkansas, Chicot, Cleveland, Dallas, Desha, Drew, Grant, Jefferson, and Lincoln.

Court for the Pine Bluff Division shall be held at Pine Bluff.

(4) The Northern Division comprises the counties of Cleburne, Fulton, Independence, Izard, Jackson, Sharp, and Stone.

Court for the Northern Division shall be held at Batesville.

(5) The Jonesboro Division comprises the counties of Clay, Craighead, Crittenden, Greene, Lawrence, Mississippi, Poinsett, and Randolph.

Court for the Jonesboro Division shall be held at Jonesboro.

Western District

(b) The Western District comprises six divisions.

(1) The Texarkana Division comprises the counties of Hempstead, Howard, Lafayette, Little River, Miller, Nevada, and Sevier.

Court for the Texarkana Division shall be held at Texarkana.

(2) The El Dorado Division comprises the counties of Ashley, Bradley, Calhoun, Columbia, Ouachita, and Union.

Court for the El Dorado Division shall be held at El Dorado.

(3) The Fort Smith Division comprises the counties of Crawford, Franklin, Johnson, Logan, Polk, Scott, and Sebastian.

Court for the Fort Smith Division shall be held at Fort Smith.

(4) The Harrison Division comprises the counties of Baxter, Boone, Carroll, Marion, Newton, and Searcy.

Court for the Harrison Division shall be held at Harrison.

(5) The Fayetteville Division comprises the counties of Benton, Madison, and Washington.

Court for the Fayetteville Division shall be held at Fayetteville.

(6) The Hot Springs Division comprises the counties of Clark, Garland, Hot Springs, Montgomery, and Pike.

Court for the Hot Springs Division shall be held at Hot Springs.

(June 25, 1948, c. 646, 62 Stat. 874; May 19, 1961, Pub.L. 87–36, § 5, 75 Stat. 84.)

§ 84. California

California is divided into four judicial districts to be known as the Northern, Eastern, Central, and Southern Districts of California.

Northern District

(a) The Northern District comprises the counties of Alameda, Contra Costa, Del Norte, Humboldt, Lake, Marin, Mendocino, Monterey, Napa, San Benito, Santa Clara, Santa Cruz, San Francisco, San Mateo, and Sonoma.

Court for the Northern District shall be held at Eureka, Oakland, San Francisco, and San Jose.

Eastern District

(b) The Eastern District comprises the counties of Alpine, Amador, Butte, Calaveras, Colusa, El Dorado, Fresno, Glenn, Inyo, Kern, Kings, Lassen, Madera, Mariposa, Merced, Modoc, Mono, Nevada, Placer, Plumas, Sacramento, San Joaquin, Shasta, Sierra, Siskiyou, Solano, Stanislaus, Sutter, Tehama, Trinity, Tulare, Tuolumne, Yolo, and Yuba.

Court for the Eastern District shall be held at Fresno, Redding, and Sacramento.

Central District

(c) The Central District comprises 3 divisions.

(1) The Eastern Division comprises the counties of Riverside and San Bernardino.

Court for the Eastern Division shall be held at a suitable site in the city of Riverside, the city of San Bernardino, or not more than 5 miles from the boundary of either such city.

(2) The Western Division comprises the counties of Los Angeles, San Luis Obispo, Santa Barbara, and Ventura.

Court for the Western Division shall be held at Los Angeles.

(3) The Southern Division comprises Orange County.

Court for the Southern Division shall be held at Santa Ana.

Southern District

(d) The Southern District comprises the counties of Imperial and San Diego.

Court for the Southern District shall be held at San Diego.

(June 25, 1948, c. 646, 62 Stat. 875; Mar. 18, 1966, Pub.L. 89–372, § 3(a), 80 Stat. 75; Oct. 15, 1980, Pub.L. 96–462, § 2, 94 Stat. 2053; Aug. 26, 1992, Pub.L. 102–357, § 2, 106 Stat. 958.)

HISTORICAL AND STATUTORY NOTES

Effective Dates

1992 Acts. Section 3 of Pub.L. 102–357 provided that:

"(a) In general

"This Act and the amendments made by this Act [amending this section and enacting provisions set out as a note under this section] shall take effect 6 months after the date of the enactment of this Act [Aug. 26, 1992].

"(b) Pending cases not affected

"This Act and the amendments made by this Act [amending this section and enacting provisions set out as a note under this section] shall not affect any action commenced before the effective date of this Act and pending in the United States District Court for the Central District of California on such date.

"(c) Juries not affected

"This Act and the amendments made by this Act [amending this section and enacting provisions set out as a note under this section] shall not affect the composition, or preclude the service, of any grand or petit jury summoned, empaneled, or actually serving in the Central Judicial District of California on the effective date of this Act."

1980 Acts. Section 7 of Pub.L. 96–462 provided that:

"(a) This Act and the amendments made by this Act [amending sections 84, 95, 105, 113, and 124 of this title and enacting provisions set out as notes under sections 95, 105, and 113 of this title] shall take effect on October 1, 1981.

"(b) Nothing in this Act shall affect the composition or preclude the service of any grand or petit juror summoned, empaneled, or actually serving in any judicial district on the effective date of this Act [Oct. 1, 1981]."

1966 Acts. Section 3(i) of Pub.L. 89–372 provided that: "The provisions of this section [amending this section and enacting provisions set out as a note under this section and section 133 of this title] shall become effective six months after the date of enactment of this Act [March 18, 1966]."

Congressional Findings Concerning Creation of Three Divisions in Central District

Section 1 of Pub.L. 102–357 provided that:

"The Congress makes the following findings:

"(1) The Federal Government has the responsibility to provide quality services which are readily accessible to the people it serves.

"(2) The court facilities in the Central Judicial District of California are presently inadequate, and current and projected growth exacerbates the problem.

"(3) The population demographics of southern California have changed dramatically over the last decade, as the center of population shifts inland. Between 1980 and 1990, the population of Riverside County increased 76.5 percent, and San Bernardino County's population increased 58.5 percent, to a combined population of 2,600,000.

"(4) In the next 15 years, the population in Riverside and San Bernardino Counties is expected to increase again by 70 percent, and 67 percent, respectively. By the year 2005, Riverside and San Bernardino Counties will have 4,400,000 residents.

"(5) As a result of the population growth, the freeways connecting the Pacific coast and the inland areas are tremendously overburdened, and Federal offices along the coast are no longer accessible to the residents of Riverside and San Bernardino Counties.

"(6) The creation of 3 divisions in the Central Judicial District of California is urgently needed to provide for the delivery of judicial services to all areas and all residents of the Central Judicial District of California."

Creation of Eastern and Central Districts: Transfer of District Judges; Transfer and Appointment of United States Attorneys and United States Marshals

Section 3(b) to (g) of Pub.L. 89–372 provided that:

"(b) The two district judges for the northern district of California holding office on the day before the effective date of this section [see Effective Dates of 1966 Acts note under this section] and whose official station is Sacramento shall, on and after such date, be district judges for the eastern district of California. All other district judges for the northern district of California holding office on the day before the effective date of this section shall, on and after such date, be district judges for the northern district of California.

"(c) The district judge for the southern district of California, residing in the northern division thereof and holding office on the day before the effective date of this section [see Effective Dates of 1966 Acts note under this section], shall, on and after such date, be a district judge for the eastern district of California. The two district judges for the southern district of California holding office on the day before the effective date of this section, and whose official station is San Diego shall, on and after such date, be the district judges for the southern district of California. All other district judges for the southern district of California holding office on the day before the effective date of this section shall, on and after such date, be district judges for the central district of California.

"(d) Nothing in this Act [amending sections 44, 84, and 133 of this title and enacting provisions set out as notes under sections 44, 84, and 133 of this title] shall in any manner affect the tenure of office of the United States attorney and the United States marshal for the northern district of California who are in office on the effective date of this section [see Effective Dates of 1966 Amendments note under this section], and who shall be during the remainder of their present terms of office the United States attorney and marshal for such district as constituted by this Act.

"(e) Nothing in this Act [amending sections 44, 84, and 133 of this title and enacting provisions set out as notes under sections 44, 84, and 133 of this title] shall in any manner affect the tenure of office of the United States attorney and the United States marshal for the southern district of California who are in office on the effective date of this section, and who shall be during the remainder of their present terms of office the United States attorney and marshal for the central district of California.

"(f) The President shall appoint, by and with the advice and consent of the Senate, a United States attorney and a United States marshal for the southern district of California.

"(g) The President shall appoint, by and with the advice and consent of the Senate, a United States attorney and a United States marshal for the eastern district of California."

Study of Judicial Business in Central District, California and Eastern District, New York and Recommendations for Creation of New Judicial Districts

Pub.L. 95–573, § 5, Nov. 2, 1978, 92 Stat. 2458, required the Director of the Administrative Office of the United States Courts to conduct a study of the judicial business of the Central District of California and the Eastern District of New York, within one year of Nov. 2, 1978, and to make recommendations to Congress with respect to the need for creation of new judicial districts.

§ 85. Colorado

Colorado constitutes one judicial district.

Court shall be held at Boulder, Denver, Durango, Grand Junction, Montrose, Pueblo, and Sterling.

(June 25, 1948, c. 646, 62 Stat. 875; Nov. 8, 1984, Pub.L. 98–620, Title IV, § 409, 98 Stat. 3362.)

HISTORICAL AND STATUTORY NOTES

Effective Dates

1984 Acts. Section 411 of Pub.L. 98–620 provided that:

"(a) The amendments made by this subtitle [amending sections 85, 90, 93, 112, 124 and 126 of this title and enacting provisions set out as notes under sections 1, 90, 93, and 124 of this title] shall take effect on January 1, 1985.

"(b) The amendments made by this subtitle shall not affect the composition, or preclude the service, of any grand or petit jury summoned, impaneled, or actually serving on the effective date of this subtitle [Jan. 1, 1985]."

§ 86. Connecticut

Connecticut constitutes one judicial district.

Court shall be held at Bridgeport, Hartford, New Haven, New London, and Waterbury.

(June 25, 1948, c. 646, 62 Stat. 875; May 19, 1961, Pub.L. 87–36, § 3(b), 75 Stat. 83; Sept. 7, 1966, Pub.L. 89–558, 80 Stat. 705.)

§ 87. Delaware

Delaware constitutes one judicial district.

Court shall be held at Wilmington.

(June 25, 1948, c. 646, 62 Stat. 875.)

§ 88. District of Columbia

The District of Columbia constitutes one judicial district.

Court shall be held at Washington.

(June 25, 1948, c. 646, 62 Stat. 875.)

§ 89. Florida

Florida is divided into three judicial districts to be known as the Northern, Middle, and Southern Districts of Florida.

Northern District

(a) The Northern District comprises the counties of Alachua, Bay, Calhoun, Dixie, Escambia, Franklin, Gadsden, Gilchrist, Gulf, Holmes, Jackson, Jefferson, Lafayette, Leon, Levy, Liberty, Madison, Okaloosa, Santa Rosa, Taylor, Wakulla, Walton, and Washington.

Court for the Northern District shall be held at Gainesville, Marianna, Panama City, Pensacola, and Tallahassee.

Middle District

(b) The Middle District comprises the counties of Baker, Bradford, Brevard, Charlotte, Citrus, Clay, Collier, Columbia, De Soto, Duval, Flagler, Glades, Hamilton, Hardee, Hendry, Hernando, Hillsborough, Lake, Lee, Manatee, Marion, Nassau, Orange, Osceola, Pasco, Pinellas, Polk, Putnam, Saint Johns, Sarasota, Seminole, Sumter, Suwannee, Union, and Volusia.

Court for the Middle District shall be held at Fernandina, Fort Myers, Jacksonville, Live Oak, Ocala, Orlando, Saint Petersburg, and Tampa.

Southern District

(c) The Southern District comprises the counties of Broward, Dade, Highlands, Indian River, Martin, Monroe, Okeechobee, Palm Beach, and Saint Lucie.

Court for the Southern District shall be held at Fort Lauderdale, Fort Pierce, Key West, Miami, and West Palm Beach.

(June 25, 1948, c. 646, 62 Stat. 876; July 17, 1952, c. 929, 66 Stat. 757; May 19, 1961, Pub.L. 87–36, § 3(f), 75 Stat. 83; July 30, 1962, Pub.L. 87–562, § 1, 76 Stat. 247; June 2, 1970, Pub.L. 91–272, § 10, 84 Stat. 298; Oct. 2, 1978, Pub.L. 95–408, § 4(a), 92 Stat. 884; Nov. 19, 1988, Pub.L. 100–702, Title X, § 1021(a), 102 Stat. 4672.)

HISTORICAL AND STATUTORY NOTES

Effective Dates

1988 Acts. Section 1021(b), (c) of Pub. L. 100–702 provided that:

"**(b) Effective Date.—(1)** The amendments made by this section [amending subsecs. (b) and (c) of this section] shall take effect 90 days after the date of enactment of this title [Nov. 19, 1988].

"(2) The amendments made by subsection (a) [amending subsecs. (b) and (c) of this section] shall apply to any action commenced in the United States District Court for the Middle District of Florida, or in the United States District Court for the Southern District of Florida, on or after the effective date of this title [probably should be effective date of this section], and shall not affect any action pending in either such court on such effective date.

"**(c) Juries.**—The amendments made by this section [amending subsecs. (b) and (c) of this section] shall not affect the composition, or preclude the service, of any grand or petit jury summoned, empaneled, or actually serving on the effective date of this title [probably should be effective date of this section]."

1978 Acts. Section 5 of Pub.L. 95–408 provided that:

"**(a)** The amendments made by this Act [amending sections 89, 93, 97, 98, 104, 112, 114, and 133 of this title and enacting provisions set out as a note under section 81 of this title] shall take effect 180 days after the date of enactment of this Act [Oct. 2, 1978].

"**(b)** Nothing in this Act [amending sections 89, 93, 97, 98, 104, 112, 114, and 133 of this title and enacting provisions set out as a note under section 81 of this title] shall affect the composition or preclude the service of any grand or petit juror summoned, empaneled, or actually serving in any judicial district on the effective date of this Act."

1962 Acts. Section 5 of Pub.L. 87–562 provided that: "This Act [amending this section and section 133 of this title, and enacting provisions set out as notes under this section and section 142 of this title] shall become effective ninety days after the date of enactment [July 30, 1962]."

District Judges, United States Attorneys, and United States Marshals; Designations; Tenure; Appointments

Section 2 of Pub.L. 87–562 provided that:

"**(a)** The district judge appointed September 26, 1950, the district judge appointed August 13, 1955, and the district judge appointed March 8, 1961, all for the Southern District of Florida, shall hereafter be designated as district judges for the Middle District of Florida.

"**(b)** The district judge for the Northern and Southern Districts of Florida shall hereafter be designated as the district judge for the Northern, Middle, and Southern Districts of Florida.

"**(c)** Nothing in this Act [amending this section and section 133 of this title, and enacting provisions set out as notes under this section and section 142 of this title] shall in any manner affect the tenure of office of the United States Attorney and the United States Marshal for the Northern District of Florida who are in office at the time of the enactment of this Act [July 30, 1962], and who shall be during the remainder of their present terms of office the United States Attorney and Marshal for such district as constituted by this Act.

"**(d)** Nothing in this Act [amending this section and section 133 of this title, and enacting provisions set out as notes under this section and section 142 of this title] shall in any manner affect the tenure of office of the United States Attorney and the United States Marshal for the Southern District of Florida who are in office at the time of the enactment of this Act [July 30, 1962], and who shall be during the remainder of their present terms of office the United States Attorney and Marshal for the Middle District of Florida as constituted by this Act.

"**(e)** The President is authorized to appoint, by and with the advice and consent of the Senate, a United States Attorney and a United States Marshal for the Southern District of Florida."

Elimination of District Judgeship for Northern, Middle, and Southern Districts of Florida

District judgeship for northern, middle, and southern districts changed to district judgeship for middle district only, see section (b) of Pub.L. 89–372, set out as a note under section 133 of this title.

§ 90. Georgia

Georgia is divided into three judicial districts to be known as the Northern, Middle, and Southern Districts of Georgia.

Northern District

(a) The Northern District comprises four divisions.

(1) The Gainesville Division comprises the counties of Banks, Barrow, Dawson, Fannin, Forsyth, Gilmer, Habersham, Hall, Jackson, Lumpkin, Pickens, Rabun, Stephens, Towns, Union, and White.

Court for the Gainesville Division shall be held at Gainesville.

(2) The Atlanta Division comprises the counties of Cherokee, Clayton, Cobb, De Kalb, Douglas, Fulton, Gwinnett, Henry, Newton, and Rockdale.

Court for the Atlanta Division shall be held at Atlanta.

(3) The Rome Division comprises the counties of Bartow, Catoosa, Chattooga, Dade, Floyd, Gordon, Murray, Paulding, Polk, Walker, and Whitfield.

Court for the Rome Division shall be held at Rome.

(4) The Newnan Division comprises the counties of Carroll, Coweta, Fayette, Haralson, Heard, Meriwether, Pike, Spalding, and Troup.

Court for the Newnan Division shall be held at Newnan.

Middle District

(b) The Middle District comprises seven divisions.

(1) The Athens Division comprises the counties of Clarke, Elbert, Franklin, Greene, Hart, Madison, Morgan, Oconee, Oglethorpe, and Walton.

Court for the Athens Division shall be held at Athens.

(2) The Macon Division comprises the counties of Baldwin, Bibb, Bleckley, Butts, Crawford, Hancock, Houston, Jasper, Jones, Lamar, Monroe, Peach, Pulaski, Putnam, Twiggs, Upson, Washington, and Wilkinson.

Court for the Macon Division shall be held at Macon.

(3) The Columbus Division comprises the counties of Chattahoochee, Clay, Harris, Marion, Muscogee, Quitman, Randolph, Stewart, Talbot, and Taylor.

Court for the Columbus Division shall be held at Columbus.

(4) The Americus Division comprises the counties of Ben Hill, Crisp, Dooly, Lee, Macon, Schley, Sumter, Terrell, Webster, and Wilcox.

Court for the Americus Division shall be held at Americus.

(5) The Albany Division comprises the counties of Baker, Calhoun, Dougherty, Early, Miller, Mitchell, Turner, and Worth.

Court for the Albany Division shall be held at Albany.

(6) The Valdosta Division comprises the counties of Berrien, Clinch, Cook, Echols, Irwin, Lanier, Lowndes, and Tift.

Court for the Valdosta Division shall be held at Valdosta.

(7) The Thomasville Division comprises the counties of Brooks, Colquitt, Decatur, Grady, Seminole, and Thomas.

Court for the Thomasville Division shall be held at Thomasville.

Southern District

(c) The Southern District comprises six divisions.

(1) The Augusta Division comprises the counties of Burke, Columbia, Glascock, Jefferson, Lincoln, McDuffie, Richmond, Taliaferro, Warren, and Wilkes.

Court for the Augusta Division shall be held at Augusta.

(2) The Dublin Division comprises the counties of Dodge, Johnson, Laurens, Montgomery, Telfair, Treutlen, and Wheeler.

Court for the Dublin Division shall be held at Dublin.

(3) The Savannah Division comprises the counties of Bryan, Chatham, Effingham, and Liberty.

Court for the Savannah Division shall be held at Savannah.

(4) The Waycross Division comprises the counties of Atkinson, Bacon, Brantley, Charlton, Coffee, Pierce, and Ware.

Court for the Waycross Division shall be held at Waycross.

(5) The Brunswick Division comprises the counties of Appling, Camden, Glynn, Jeff Davis, Long, McIntosh, and Wayne.

Court for the Brunswick Division shall be held at Brunswick.

(6) The Statesboro Division comprises the counties of Bullock, Candler, Emanuel, Evans, Jenkins, Screven, Tattnall, and Toombs.

Court for the Statesboro Division shall be held at Statesboro.

(June 25, 1948, c. 646, 62 Stat. 876; Aug. 16, 1949, c. 444, 63 Stat. 610; Oct. 31, 1951, c. 655, § 36a, 65 Stat. 723; Nov. 8, 1984, Pub.L. 98–620, Title IV, § 408(a)–(c), 98 Stat. 3362; Nov. 14, 1986, Pub.L. 99–657, § 3, 100 Stat. 3670.)

HISTORICAL AND STATUTORY NOTES

Effective Dates

1986 Acts. Amendment by Pub.L. 99–657 effective 90 days after Nov. 14, 1986, and not to affect any action commenced before and pending on such effective date, or to affect the composition, or preclude the service, of any grand or petit jury summoned, empaneled, or actually serving on such date, see section 4 of Pub.L. 99–657, set out as a note under section 121 of this title.

1984 Acts. Section 408(d) of Pub.L. 98–620 provided that: "The amendments made by this section [amending subsecs. (a) and (c) of this section] shall apply to any action commenced in the United States District Court for the Northern District of Georgia on or after the effective date of this subtitle [Jan. 1, 1985], and shall not affect any action pending in such court on such effective date."

Amendment by Pub.L. 98–620 effective Jan. 1, 1985, and not to affect the composition, or preclude the service, of any grand or petit jury summoned, impaneled, or actually serving on that date, see section 411 of Pub.L. 98–620, set out as a note under section 85 of this title.

§ 91. Hawaii

Hawaii constitutes one judicial district which includes the Midway Islands, Wake Island, Johnston Island, Sand Island, Kingman Reef, Palmyra Island, Baker Island, Howland Island, Jarvis Island, Canton Island, and Enderbury Island: *Provided*, That the inclusion of Canton and Enderbury Islands in such judicial district shall in no way be construed to be prejudicial to the claims of the United Kingdom to said Islands in accordance with the agreement of April 6, 1939, between the Governments of the United States and of the United Kingdom to set up a regime for their use in common.

Court shall be held at Honolulu.

(June 25, 1948, c. 646, 62 Stat. 877; May 24, 1949, c. 139, § 64a, 63 Stat. 99; Mar. 18, 1959, Pub.L. 86–3, § 14(i), 73 Stat. 11; July 12, 1960, Pub.L. 86–624, § 19, 74 Stat. 416.)

HISTORICAL AND STATUTORY NOTES

Effective Dates

1959 Acts. Section 14 of Pub.L. 86–3 provided that the amendments of sections 91, 373, 1252, 1293, and 1294 of this title, sections 3771 and 3772 of Title 18, Crimes and Criminal Procedure, and section 644a of Title 48, Territories and Insular Possessions, the repeal of sections 536, 539, 634, 634a, and 645 of title 48, and notes set out under sections 371 and 373 of this title, are effective on admission of the State of Hawaii into the Union. See Admission of Hawaii as State note under this section.

Admission of Hawaii as State

Admission of Hawaii into the Union was accomplished Aug. 21, 1959, upon issuance of Proc. No. 3309, Aug. 21, 1959, 25 F.R. 6868, 73 Stat. c74, as required by sections 1 and 7(c) of Pub.L. 86–3, Mar. 18, 1959, 73 Stat. 4, set out as notes preceding section 491 of Title 48, Territories and Insular Possessions.

Appeals

Section 13 of Pub.L. 86–3 provided that: "Parties shall have the same rights of appeal from and appellate review of final decisions of the United States District Court for the District of Hawaii or the Supreme Court of the Territory of Hawaii in any case finally decided prior to admission of said State into the Union, whether or not an appeal therefrom shall have been perfected prior to such admission, and the United States Court of Appeals for the Ninth Circuit and the Supreme Court of the United States shall have the same jurisdiction therein, as by law provided prior to admission of said State into the Union, and any mandate issued subsequent to the admission of said State shall be to the United States District Court for the District of Hawaii or a court of the State, as may be appropriate. Parties shall have the same rights of appeal from and appellate review of all orders, judgments, and decrees of the United States District Court for the District of Hawaii and of the Supreme Court of the State of Hawaii as successor to the Supreme Court of the Territory of Hawaii, in any case pending at the time of admission of said State into the Union, and the United States Court of Appeals for the Ninth Circuit and the Supreme Court of the United States shall have the same jurisdiction therein, as by law provided in any case arising subsequent to the admission of said State into the Union."

Canton and Enderbury Islands; Sovereignty of Kiribati

By a treaty of friendship, TIAS 10777, which entered into force Sept. 23, 1983, the United States recognized the sovereignty of Kiribati over Canton Island and Enderbury Island.

Continuation of Suits

Section 12 of Pub.L. 86–3 provided that: "No writ, action, indictment, cause, or proceeding pending in any court of the Territory of Hawaii or in the United States District Court for the District of Hawaii shall abate by reason of the admission of said State into the Union, but the same shall be transferred to and proceeded with in such appropriate State courts as shall be established under the constitution of said State, or shall continue in the United States District Court for the District of Hawaii, as the nature of the case may require. And no writ, action, indictment, cause or proceeding shall abate by reason of any change in the courts, but shall be proceeded with in the State or United States courts according to the laws thereof, respectively. And the appropriate State courts shall be the successors of the courts of the Territory as to all cases arising within the limits embraced within the jurisdiction of such courts, respectively, with full power to proceed with the same, and award mesne or final process therein, and all the files, records, indictments, and proceedings relating to any such writ, action, indictment, cause or proceeding shall be transferred to such appropriate State courts and the same shall be proceeded with therein in due course of law.

"All civil causes of action and all criminal offenses which shall have arisen or been committed prior to the admission of said State, but as to which no writ, action, indictment or proceeding shall be pending at the date of such admission, shall be subject to prosecution in the appropriate State courts or in the United States District Court for the District of Hawaii in like manner, to the same extent, and with like right of appellate review, as if said State had been created and said State courts had been established prior to the accrual of such causes of action or the commission of such offenses. The admission of said State shall effect no change in the substantive or criminal law governing such causes of action and criminal offenses which shall have arisen or been committed; and such of said criminal offenses as shall have been committed against the laws of the Territory shall be tried and punished by the appropriate courts of said State, and such as shall have been committed against the laws of the United States shall be tried and punished in the United States District Court for the District of Hawaii."

Court of the United States; District Judges

Section 9(a) of Pub.L. 86–3 provided that: "The United States District Court for the District of Hawaii established by and existing under title 28 of the United States Code shall thenceforth be a court of the United States with judicial power derived from article III, section 1, of the Constitution of the United States: *Provided, however*, That the terms of office of the district judges for the district of Hawaii then in office shall terminate upon the effective date of this section and the President, pursuant to sections 133 and 134 of title 28, United States Code, as amended by this Act, shall appoint, by and with the advice and consent of the Senate, two district judges for the said district who shall hold office during good behavior."

Section 9 of Pub.L. 86–3 provided in part that subsec. (a) of that section shall be effective upon the admission of the State of Hawaii into the Union.

Extension of Jurisdiction of United States District Court for District of Hawaii and of Civil and Criminal Laws to Midway, Wake, Johnson, Sand, etc., Islands

The jurisdiction of the United States District Court for the District of Hawaii and the laws of the United States relating to civil acts or offenses consummated or committed on the high seas on board a vessel belonging to the United States were extended to the Midway Islands, Wake, Johnson, Sand, etc., Islands by section 644a of Title 48, Territories and Insular Possessions.

§ 92. Idaho

Idaho, exclusive of Yellowstone National Park, constitutes one judicial district.

Court shall be held at Boise, Coeur d'Alene, Moscow, and Pocatello.

(June 25, 1948, c. 646, 62 Stat. 877; June 2, 1970, Pub.L. 91–272, § 5, 84 Stat. 297.)

§ 93. Illinois

Illinois is divided into three judicial districts to be known as the Northern, Central, and Southern Districts of Illinois.

Northern District

(a) The Northern District comprises two divisions.

(1) The Eastern Division comprises the counties of Cook, Du Page, Grundy, Kane, Kendall, Lake, La Salle, and Will.

Court for the Eastern Division shall be held at Chicago.

(2) The Western Division comprises the counties of Boone, Carroll, De Kalb, Jo Daviess, Lee, McHenry, Ogle, Stephenson, Whiteside, and Winnebago.

Court for the Western Division shall be held at Freeport and Rockford.

Central District

(b) The Central District comprises the counties of Adams, Brown, Bureau, Cass, Champaign, Christian, Coles, De Witt, Douglas, Edgar, Ford, Fulton, Greene, Hancock, Henderson, Henry, Iroquois, Kankakee, Knox, Livingston, Logan, McDonough, McLean, Macoupin, Macon, Marshall, Mason, Menard, Mercer, Montgomery, Morgan, Moultrie, Peoria, Piatt, Pike, Putnam, Rock Island, Sangamon, Schuyler, Scott, Shelby, Stark, Tazewell, Vermilion, Warren, and Woodford.

Court for the Central District shall be held at Champaign/Urbana, Danville, Peoria, Quincy, Rock Island, and Springfield.

Southern District

(c) The Southern District comprises the counties of Alexander, Bond, Calhoun, Clark, Clay, Clinton, Crawford, Cumberland, Edwards, Effingham, Fayette, Franklin, Gallatin, Hamilton, Hardin, Jackson, Jasper, Jefferson, Jersey, Johnson, Lawrence, Madison, Marion, Massac, Monroe, Perry, Pope, Pulaski, Randolph, Richland, St. Clair, Saline, Union, Wabash, Washington, Wayne, White, and Williamson.

Court for the Southern District shall be held at Alton, Benton, Cairo, and East Saint Louis.

(June 25, 1948, c. 646, 62 Stat. 878; Aug. 10, 1950, c. 675, § 1, 64 Stat. 438; May 19, 1961, Pub.L. 87–36, § 3(c), 75 Stat. 83; June 2, 1970, Pub.L. 91–272, § 8, 84 Stat. 297; Oct. 2, 1978, Pub.L. 95–408, § 4(b) (1), 92 Stat. 884; Nov. 2, 1978, Pub.L. 95–573, § 1, 92 Stat. 2458; Nov. 8, 1984, Pub.L. 98–620, Title IV, § 406(a), (c), 98 Stat. 3361.)

HISTORICAL AND STATUTORY NOTES

Effective Dates

1984 Acts. Section 406(b) of Pub.L. 98–620 provided that: "The amendments made by subsection (a) of this section [amending subsec. (a) of this section] shall apply to any action commenced in the United States District Court for the Northern District of Illinois on or after the effective date of this subtitle [Jan. 1, 1985], and shall not affect any action pending in such court on such effective date."

Amendment by Pub.L. 98–620 effective Jan. 1, 1985, and not to affect the composition, or preclude the service, of any grand or petit jury summoned, impaneled, or actually serving on that date, see section 411 of Pub.L. 98–620, set out as a note under section 85 of this title.

1978 Acts. Section 6 of Pub.L. 95–573, as amended by Pub.L. 96–4, § 2, Mar. 30, 1979, 93 Stat. 7, provided that:

"**(a)** Except as provided in subsection (b) of this section, the provisions of this Act [amending sections 93, 99, 112 and 118 of this title and enacting provisions set out as a note under section 84 of this title] shall take effect 180 days after the date of enactment of this Act [Nov. 2, 1978].

"**(b)(1)** The provisions of section 5 of this Act [set out as a note under section 84 of this title] shall take effect on the date of enactment of this Act [Nov. 2, 1978].

"**(2)** The provisions of the first section of this Act [amending this section] shall take effect on March 31, 1979.

"**(c)** Nothing in this Act [amending sections 93, 99, 112, and 118 of this title and enacting provisions set out as a note under section 84 of this title] shall affect the composition or preclude the service of any grand or petit juror summoned, empaneled, or actually serving in any judicial district on the effective date of this Act."

Amendment by Pub.L. 95–408 effective 180 days after Oct. 2, 1978, such amendment not to affect the composition or preclude the service of any grand or petit juror summoned, empaneled, or actually serving in any judicial district on the effective date of this Act, see section 5 of Pub.L. 95–408, set out as a note under section 89 of this title.

District Judges, United States Attorneys, Assistant United States Attorneys, and United States Marshals For Central and Southern Districts; Designation; Tenure; Appointment; Grand Jury

Pub.L. 95–408, § 4(b)(2)–(4), as added Pub.L. 96–4, § 1, Mar. 30, 1979, 93 Stat. 6, provided that:

"**(2)** The district judge for the Eastern District of Illinois in office on the effective date of this Act [180 days after Oct. 2, 1978] who is senior in commission shall, on and after the effective date of this Act, be a district judge for the Southern District of Illinois. The remaining district judge for the Eastern District of Illinois who is in office on the effective date of this Act and the district judges for the Southern District of Illinois who are in office on the effective date of this Act shall, on and after the effective date of this Act, be district judges for the Central District of Illinois. The President shall appoint, by and with the advice and consent of the Senate, a second district judge for the Southern District of Illinois.

"**(3)** This section does not in any manner affect the tenure of the United States attorney, the assistant United States attorneys, or the United States marshal for the Eastern District of Illinois or for the Southern District of Illinois who are in office on the effective date of this Act [180 days after Oct. 2, 1978]. The United States attorney, the assistant United States attorneys, and the United States marshal for the Eastern District and for the Southern District of Illinois shall, on the effective date of this Act, become the United States attorney, the assistant United States attorneys, and the United States marshal for the Southern District and for the Central District of Illinois, respectively.

"(4) Notwithstanding section 3240 of title 18, United States Code [section 3240 of Title 18, Crimes and Criminal Procedure], any grand jury impaneled on or after the effective date of this Act [180 days after Oct. 2, 1978] by a district court for the Central District or the Southern District of Illinois may inquire into and return indictments charging offenses against the criminal laws of the United States alleged to have been committed anywhere within the territory of the respective judicial districts as such districts were constituted before or after the effective date of this Act."

§ 94. Indiana

Indiana is divided into two judicial districts to be known as the Northern and Southern Districts of Indiana.

Northern District

(a) The Northern District comprises three divisions.

(1) The Fort Wayne Division comprises the counties of Adams, Allen, Blackford, De Kalb, Grant, Huntington, Jay, Lagrange, Noble, Steuben, Wells, and Whitley.

Court for the Fort Wayne Division shall be held at Fort Wayne.

(2) The South Bend Division comprises the counties of Cass, Elkhart, Fulton, Kosciusko, La Porte, Marshall, Miami, Pulaski, St. Joseph, Starke, and Wabash.

Court for the South Bend Division shall be held at South Bend.

(3) The Hammond Division comprises the counties of Benton, Carroll, Jasper, Lake, Newton, Porter, Tippecanoe, Warren, and White.

Court for the Hammond Division shall be held at Hammond and Lafayette.

Southern District

(b) The Southern District comprises four divisions.

(1) The Indianapolis Division comprises the counties of Bartholomew, Boone, Brown, Clinton, Decatur, Delaware, Fayette, Fountain, Franklin, Hamilton, Hancock, Hendricks, Henry, Howard, Johnson, Madison, Marion, Monroe, Montgomery, Morgan, Randolph, Rush, Shelby, Tipton, Union, and Wayne.

Court for the Indianapolis Division shall be held at Indianapolis and Richmond.

(2) The Terre Haute Division comprises the counties of Clay, Greene, Knox, Owen, Parke, Putnam, Sullivan, Vermilion, and Vigo.

Court for the Terre Haute Division shall be held at Terre Haute.

(3) The Evansville Division comprises the counties of Davies, Dubois, Gibson, Martin, Perry, Pike, Posey, Spencer, Vanderburgh, and Warrick.

Court for the Evansville Division shall be held at Evansville.

(4) The New Albany Division comprises the counties of Clark, Crawford, Dearborn, Floyd, Harrison, Jackson, Jefferson, Jennings, Lawrence, Ohio, Orange, Ripley, Scott, Switzerland, and Washington.

Court for the New Albany Division shall be held at New Albany.

(June 25, 1948, c. 646, 62 Stat. 878; Feb. 10, 1954, c. 6, § 2(b)(7), 68 Stat. 11; June 2, 1970, Pub.L. 91–272, § 9, 84 Stat. 298.)

§ 95. Iowa

Iowa is divided into two judicial districts to be known as the Northern and Southern Districts of Iowa.

Northern District

(a) The Northern District comprises four divisions.

(1) The Cedar Rapids Division comprises the counties of Benton, Cedar, Grundy, Hardin, Iowa, Jones, Linn, and Tama.

Court for the Cedar Rapids Division shall be held at Cedar Rapids.

(2) The Eastern Division comprises the counties of Allamakee, Black Hawk, Bremer, Buchanan, Chickasaw, Clayton, Delaware, Dubuque, Fayette, Floyd, Howard, Jackson, Mitchell, and Winneshiek.

Court for the Eastern Division shall be held at Dubuque and Waterloo.

(3) The Western Division comprises the counties of Buena Vista, Cherokee, Clay, Crawford, Dickinson, Ida, Lyon, Monona, O'Brien, Osceola, Plymouth, Sac, Sioux, and Woodbury.

Court for the Western Division shall be held at Sioux City.

(4) The Central Division comprises the counties of Butler, Calhoun, Carroll, Cerro Gordo, Emmet, Franklin, Hamilton, Hancock, Humboldt, Kossuth, Palo Alto, Pocahontas, Webster, Winnebago, Worth, and Wright.

Court for the Central Division shall be held at Fort Dodge and Mason City.

Southern District

(b) The Southern District comprises six divisions.

(1) The Central Division comprises the counties of Boone, Dallas, Greene, Guthrie, Jasper, Madison, Marion, Marshall, Polk, Poweshiek, Story, and Warren.

Court for the Central Division shall be held at Des Moines.

(2) The Eastern Division comprises the counties of Des Moines, Henry, Lee, Louisa, and Van Buren.

Court for the Eastern Division shall be held at Keokuk.

(3) The Western Division comprises the counties of Audubon, Cass, Fremont, Harrison, Mills, Montgomery, Page, Pottawattamie, and Shelby.

Court for the Western Division shall be held at Council Bluffs.

(4) The Southern Division comprises the counties of Adair, Adams, Clarke, Decatur, Lucas, Ringgold, Taylor, Union, and Wayne.

Court for the Southern Division shall be held at Creston.

(5) The Davenport Division comprises the counties of Clinton, Johnson, Muscatine, Scott, and Washington.

Court for the Davenport Division shall be held at Davenport.

(6) The Ottumwa Division comprises the counties of Appanoose, Davis, Jefferson, Keokuk, Mahaska, Monroe, and Wapello.

Court for the Ottumwa Division shall be held at Ottumwa.

(June 25, 1948, c. 646, 62 Stat. 879; Oct. 15, 1980, Pub.L. 96–462, § 3(a), 94 Stat. 2053.)

HISTORICAL AND STATUTORY NOTES

Effective Dates

1980 Acts. Amendment by Pub.L. 96–462 effective Oct. 1, 1981, but not to affect the composition or preclude the service of any grand or petit juror summoned, empaneled, or actually serving in any judicial district on Oct. 1, 1981, see section 7 of Pub.L. 96–462, set out as a note under section 84 of this title.

Section 3(b) of Pub.L. 96–462 provided that: "The amendments made by subsection (a) [amending subsec. (b)(3), (4) of this section] shall not apply to any action commenced before the effective date of such amendments [Oct. 1, 1981] and pending in the United States District Court for the Southern District of Iowa on such date."

§ 96. Kansas

Kansas constitutes one judicial district.

Court shall be held at Kansas City, Lawrence, Leavenworth, Salina, Topeka, Hutchinson, Wichita, Dodge City, and Fort Scott.

(June 25, 1948, c. 646, 62 Stat. 880; Aug. 27, 1949, c. 516, 63 Stat. 666; Oct. 27, 1986, Pub.L. 99–554, Title I, § 141, 100 Stat. 3096.)

HISTORICAL AND STATUTORY NOTES

Effective Dates

1986 Acts. Amendment by Pub.L. 99–554 effective 30 days after Oct. 27, 1986, see section 302(a) of Pub.L. 99–554, set out as a note under section 581 of this title.

§ 97. Kentucky

Kentucky is divided into two judicial districts to be known as the Eastern and Western Districts of Kentucky.

Eastern District

(a) The Eastern District comprises the counties of Anderson, Bath, Bell, Boone, Bourbon, Boyd, Boyle, Bracken, Breathitt, Campbell, Carroll, Carter, Clark, Clay, Elliott, Estill, Fayette, Fleming, Floyd, Franklin, Gallatin, Garrard, Grant, Greenup, Harlan, Harrison, Henry, Jackson, Jessamine, Johnson, Kenton, Knott, Knox, Laurel, Lawrence, Lee, Leslie, Letcher, Lewis, Lincoln, McCreary, Madison, Magoffin, Martin, Mason, Menifee, Mercer, Montgomery, Morgan, Nicholas, Owen, Owsley, Pendleton, Perry, Pike, Powell, Pulaski, Robertson, Rockcastle, Rowan, Scott, Shelby, Trimble, Wayne, Whitley, Wolfe, and Woodford.

Court for the Eastern District shall be held at Ashland, Catlettsburg, Covington, Frankfort, Jackson, Lexington, London, Pikeville, and Richmond.

Western District

(b) The Western District comprises the counties of Adair, Allen, Ballard, Barren, Breckenridge, Bullitt, Butler, Caldwell, Calloway, Carlisle, Casey, Christian, Clinton, Crittenden, Cumberland, Daviess, Edmonson, Fulton, Graves, Grayson, Green, Hancock, Hardin, Hart, Henderson, Hickman, Hopkins, Jefferson, Larue, Livingston, Logan, Lyon, McCracken, McLean, Marion, Marshall, Meade, Metcalfe, Monroe, Muhlenberg, Nelson, Ohio, Oldham, Russell, Simpson, Spencer, Taylor, Todd, Trigg, Union, Warren, Washington, and Webster.

Court for the Western District shall be held at Bowling Green, Louisville, Owensboro, and Paducah.

(June 25, 1948, c. 646, 62 Stat. 880; Oct. 2, 1978, Pub.L. 95–408, § 2(a), 92 Stat. 883.)

HISTORICAL AND STATUTORY NOTES

Effective Dates

1978 Acts. Amendment by Pub.L. 95–408 effective 180 days after Oct. 2, 1978, such amendment not to affect the composition or preclude the service of any grand or petit juror summoned, empaneled, or actually serving in any judicial district on the effective date of this Act, see section 5 of Pub.L. 95–408, set out as a note under section 89 of this title.

§ 98. Louisiana

Louisiana is divided into three judicial districts to be known as the Eastern, Middle, and Western Districts of Louisiana.

Eastern District

(a) The Eastern District comprises the parishes of Assumption, Jefferson, Lafourche, Orleans, Plaquemines, Saint Bernard, Saint Charles, Saint James, Saint John the Baptist, Saint Tammany, Tangipahoa, Terrebonne, and Washington.

Court for the Eastern District shall be held at New Orleans, and Houma.

Middle District

(b) The Middle District comprises the parishes of Ascension, East Baton Rouge, East Feliciana, Iberville, Livingston, Pointe Coupee, Saint Helena, West Baton Rouge, and West Feliciana.

Court for the Middle District shall be held at Baton Rouge.

Western District

(c) The Western District comprises the parishes of Acadia, Allen, Avoyelles, Beauregard, Bienville, Bossier, Caddo, Calcasieu, Caldwell, Cameron, Catahoula, Claiborne, Concordia, Jefferson Davis, De Soto, East Carroll, Evangeline, Franklin, Grant, Iberia, Jackson, Lafayette, La Salle, Lincoln, Madison, Morehouse, Natchitoches, Ouachita, Rapides, Red River, Richland, Sabine, Saint Landry, Saint Martin, Saint Mary, Tensas, Union, Vermilion, Vernon, Webster, West Carroll, and Winn.

Court for the Western District shall be held at Alexandria, Lafayette, Lake Charles, Monroe, Opelousas, and Shreveport.

(June 25, 1948, c. 646, 62 Stat. 881; May 19, 1961, Pub.L. 87–36, § 4, 75 Stat. 83; Dec. 18, 1971, Pub.L. 92–208, § 3(a), 85 Stat. 741; Oct. 2, 1978, Pub.L. 95–408, § 3(a), 92 Stat. 883; July 10, 1984, Pub.L. 98–353, Title II, § 203(b), 98 Stat. 350.)

HISTORICAL AND STATUTORY NOTES

Effective Dates

1978 Acts. Amendment by Pub.L. 95–408 effective 180 days after Oct. 2, 1978, such amendment not to affect the composition or preclude the service of any grand or petit juror summoned, empaneled, or actually serving in any judicial district on the effective date of this Act, see section 5 of Pub.L. 95–408, set out as a note under section 89 of this title.

1971 Acts. Section 3(f) of Pub.L. 92–208 provided that: "The provisions of this section [amending this section and sections 133 and 134 of this title and enacting provisions set out as a note under this section] shall become effective one hundred and twenty days after the date of enactment of this Act [Dec. 18, 1971]."

District Judge, United States Attorney, and United States Marshal For Middle District; Designation; Tenure; Appointment

Section 3(b), (c) of Pub.L. 92–208 provided that:

"**(b)** The district judge for the Eastern District of Louisiana holding office on the day immediately prior to the effective date of this section [see Effective Dates of 1971 Amendments note under this section], and whose official station on such date is Baton Rouge, shall, on and after such date, be the district judge for the Middle District of Louisiana. All other district judges for the Eastern District of Louisiana holding office on the day immediately prior to the effective date of this section shall be district judges for the Eastern District of Louisiana as constituted by this section.

"**(c)(1)** Nothing in this section [amending this section and sections 133 and 134 of this title] shall in any manner affect the tenure of office of the United States attorney and the United States marshal for the Eastern District of Louisiana who are in office on the effective date of this section [see Effective Dates of 1971 Amendments note under this section], and who shall be during the remainder of their present terms of office the United States attorney and marshal for the Eastern District of Louisiana as constituted by this section.

"**(2)** The President shall appoint, by and with the advice and consent of the Senate, a United States attorney and marshal for the Middle District of Louisiana."

§ 99. Maine

Maine constitutes one judicial district.

Court shall be held at Bangor and Portland.

(June 25, 1948, c. 646, 62 Stat. 881; Nov. 2, 1978, Pub.L. 95–573, § 2, 92 Stat. 2458.)

HISTORICAL AND STATUTORY NOTES

Effective Dates

1978 Acts. Amendment by Pub.L. 95–573 effective 180 days after Nov. 2, 1978, except as otherwise provided, except that nothing in this Act shall affect the composition or preclude the service of any grand or petit juror summoned, empaneled, or actually serving in any judicial district on such effective date, see section 6 of Pub.L. 95–573, set out as a note under section 93 of this title.

§ 100. Maryland

Maryland constitutes one judicial district comprising two divisions.

(1) The Northern Division comprises the counties of Allegany, Anne Arundel, Baltimore, Caroline, Carroll, Cecil, Dorchester, Frederick, Garrett, Harford, Howard, Kent, Queen Anne's, Somerset, Talbot, Washington, Wicomico, and Worcester, and the City of Baltimore.

Court for the Northern Division shall be held at Baltimore, Cumberland, and Denton.

(2) The Southern Division comprises the counties of Calvert, Charles, Montgomery, Prince George's, and St. Mary's.

Court for the Southern Division shall be held at a suitable site in Montgomery or Prince George's County not more than five miles from the boundary of Montgomery and Prince George's Counties.

(June 25, 1948, c. 646, 62 Stat. 882; Dec. 14, 1970, Pub.L. 91–546, § 4, 84 Stat. 1412; Oct. 14, 1988, Pub.L. 100–487, § 1, 102 Stat. 2431.)

HISTORICAL AND STATUTORY NOTES

Effective Dates

1988 Acts. Section 2 of Pub.L. 100–487 provided that:

"**(a) In General.**—This Act [Pub.L. 100–487] and the amendments made by this Act [amending this section] shall take effect 180 days after the date of the enactment of this Act [Oct. 14, 1988].

"**(b) Pending Cases Not Affected.**—This Act [Pub.L. 100–487] and the amendments made by this Act [amending this section] shall not affect any action commenced before the effective date of this Act [180 days after Oct. 14, 1988] and pending in the United States District Court for the District of Maryland on such date.

"**(c) Juries Not Affected.**—This Act [Pub.L. 100–487] and the amendments made by this Act [amending this section] shall not affect the composition, or preclude the service, of any grand or petit jury summoned, empaneled, or actually serving in the Judicial District of Maryland on the effective date of this Act [180 days after Oct. 14, 1988]."

§ 101. Massachusetts

Massachusetts constitutes one judicial district.

Court shall be held at Boston, New Bedford, Springfield, and Worcester.

(June 25, 1948, c. 646, 62 Stat. 882.)

§ 102. Michigan

Michigan is divided into two judicial districts to be known as the Eastern and Western Districts of Michigan.

Eastern District

(a) The Eastern District comprises two divisions.

(1) The Southern Division comprises the counties of Genesee, Jackson, Lapeer, Lenawee, Livingston, Macomb, Monroe, Oakland, Saint Clair, Sanilac, Shiawassee, Washtenaw, and Wayne.

Court for the Southern Division shall be held at Ann Arbor, Detroit, Flint, and Port Huron.

(2) The Northern Division comprises the counties of Alcona, Alpena, Arenac, Bay, Cheboygan, Clare, Crawford, Gladwin, Gratiot, Huron, Iosco, Isabella, Midland, Montmorency, Ogemaw, Oscoda, Otsego, Presque Isle, Roscommon, Saginaw, and Tuscola.

Court for the Northern Division shall be held at Bay City.

Western District

(b) The Western District comprises two divisions.

(1) The Southern Division comprises the counties of Allegan, Antrim, Barry, Benzie, Berrien, Branch, Calhoun, Cass, Charlevoix, Clinton, Eaton, Emmet, Grand Traverse, Hillsdale, Ingham, Ionia, Kalamazoo, Kalkaska, Kent, Lake, Leelanau, Manistee, Mason, Mecosta, Missaukee, Montcalm, Muskegon, Newaygo, Oceana, Osceola, Ottawa, Saint Joseph, Van Buren, and Wexford.

Court for the Southern Division shall be held at Grand Rapids, Kalamazoo, Lansing, and Traverse City.

(2) The Northern Division comprises the counties of Alger, Baraga, Chippewa, Delta, Dickinson, Gogebic, Houghton, Iron, Keweenaw, Luce, Mackinac, Marquette, Menominee, Ontonagon, and Schoolcraft.

Court for the Northern Division shall be held at Marquette and Sault Sainte Marie.

(June 25, 1948, c. 646, 62 Stat. 882; Feb. 10, 1954, c. 6, § 2(b)(8), 68 Stat. 11; May 19, 1961, Pub.L. 87–36, § 3(d), 75 Stat. 83; Oct. 6, 1964, Pub.L. 88–627, 78 Stat. 1003; June 2, 1970, Pub.L. 91–272, § 11, 84 Stat. 298.)

§ 103. Minnesota

Minnesota constitutes one judicial district comprising six divisions.

(1) The First Division comprises the counties of Dodge, Fillmore, Houston, Mower, Olmsted, Steele, Wabasha, and Winona.

Court for the First Division shall be held at Winona.

(2) The Second Division comprises the counties of Blue Earth, Brown, Cottonwood, Faribault, Freeborn, Jackson, Lac qui Parle, Le Sueur, Lincoln, Lyon, Martin, Murray, Nicollet, Nobles, Pipestone, Redwood, Rock, Sibley, Waseca, Watonwan, and Yellow Medicine.

Court for the Second Division shall be held at Mankato.

(3) The Third Division comprises the counties of Chisago, Dakota, Goodhue, Ramsey, Rice, Scott, and Washington.

Court for the Third Division shall be held at Saint Paul.

(4) The Fourth Division comprises the counties of Anoka, Carver, Chippewa, Hennepin, Isanti, Kandiyohi, McLeod, Meeker, Renville, Sherburne, Swift, and Wright.

Court for the Fourth Division shall be held at Minneapolis.

(5) The Fifth Division comprises the counties of Aitkin, Benton, Carlton, Cass, Cook, Crow Wing, Itasca, Kanabec, Koochiching, Lake, Mille Lacs, Morrison, Pine, and Saint Louis.

Court for the Fifth Division shall be held at Duluth.

(6) The Sixth Division comprises the counties of Becker, Beltrami, Big Stone, Clay, Clearwater, Douglas, Grant, Hubbard, Kittson, Lake of the Woods, Mahnomen, Marshall, Norman, Otter Tail, Pennington, Polk, Pope, Red Lake, Roseau, Stearns, Stevens, Todd, Traverse, Wadena, and Wilkin.

Court for the Sixth Division shall be held at Fergus Falls.

(June 25, 1948, c. 646, 62 Stat. 882.)

§ 104. Mississippi

Mississippi is divided into two judicial districts to be known as the northern and southern districts of Mississippi.

Northern District

(a) The northern district comprises four divisions.

(1) Eastern division comprises the counties of Alcorn, Attala, Chickasaw, Choctaw, Clay, Itawamba, Lee, Lowndes, Monroe, Oktibbeha, Prentiss, Tishomingo, and Winston.

Court for the eastern division shall be held at Aberdeen, Ackerman, and Corinth.

(2) The Western Division comprises the counties of Benton, Calhoun, Grenada, Lafayette, Marshall, Montgomery, Pontotoc, Tippah, Union, Webster, and Yalobusha.

Court for the western division shall be held at Oxford.

(3) The Delta Division comprises the counties of Bolivar, Coahoma, De Soto, Panola, Quitman, Tallahatchie, Tate, and Tunica.

Court for the Delta Division shall be held at Clarksdale.

(4) The Greenville Division comprises the counties of Carroll, Humphreys, Leflore, Sunflower, and Washington.

Court for the Greenville Division shall be held at Greenville.

Southern District

(b) The southern district comprises five divisions.

(1) The Jackson Division comprises the counties of Amite, Copiah, Franklin, Hinds, Holmes, Leake, Lincoln, Madison, Pike, Rankin, Scott, Simpson, and Smith.

Court for the Jackson Division shall be held at Jackson.

(2) The Eastern Division comprises the counties of Clarke, Jasper, Kemper, Lauderdale, Neshoba, Newton, Noxubee, and Wayne.

Court for the Eastern Division shall be held at Meridian.

(3) The western division comprises the counties of Adams, Claiborne, Issaquena, Jefferson, Sharkey, Warren, Wilkinson, and Yazoo.

Court for the western division shall be held at Natchez and Vicksburg: *Provided*, That court shall be held at Natchez if suitable quarters and accommodations are furnished at no cost to the United States.

(4) The southern division comprises the counties of George, Hancock, Harrison, Jackson, Pearl River, and Stone.

Court for the southern division shall be held at Biloxi and Gulfport.

(5) The Hattiesburg division comprises the counties of Covington, Forrest, Greene, Jefferson Davis, Jones, Lamar, Lawrence, Marion, Perry, and Walthall.

Court for the Hattiesburg division shall be held at Hattiesburg.

(June 25, 1948, c. 646, 62 Stat. 883; Aug. 7, 1950, c. 601, 64 Stat. 415; Sept. 27, 1967, Pub.L. 90–92, 81 Stat. 229; Dec. 14, 1970, Pub.L. 91–546, §§ 2, 3, 84 Stat. 1412; Oct. 2, 1978, Pub.L. 95–408, § 2(b), 92 Stat. 883.)

HISTORICAL AND STATUTORY NOTES

Effective Dates

1978 Acts. Amendment by Pub.L. 95–408 effective 180 days after Oct. 2, 1978, such amendment not to affect the composition or preclude the service of any grand or petit juror summoned, empaneled, or actually serving in any judicial district on the effective date of this Act, see section 5 of Pub.L. 95–408, set out as a note under section 89 of this title.

§ 105. Missouri

Missouri is divided into two judicial districts to be known as the Eastern and Western Districts of Missouri.

Eastern District

(a) The Eastern District comprises three divisions.

(1) The Eastern Division comprises the counties of Crawford, Dent, Franklin, Gasconade, Iron, Jefferson, Lincoln, Maries, Phelps, Saint Charles, Saint Francois, Saint Genevieve, Saint Louis, Warren, and Washington, and the city of Saint Louis.

Court for the Eastern Division shall be held at Saint Louis.

(2) The Northern Division comprises the counties of Adair, Audrain, Chariton, Clark, Knox, Lewis, Linn, Macon, Marion, Monroe, Montgomery,

Pike, Ralls, Randolph, Schuyler, Scotland, and Shelby.

Court for the Northern Division shall be held at Hannibal.

(3) The Southeastern Division comprises the counties of Bollinger, Butler, Cape Girardeau, Carter, Dunklin, Madison, Mississippi, New Madrid, Pemiscot, Perry, Reynolds, Ripley, Scott, Shannon, Stoddard, and Wayne.

Court for the Southeastern Division shall be held at Cape Girardeau.

Western District

(b) The Western District comprises five divisions.

(1) The Western Division comprises the counties of Bates, Carroll, Cass, Clay, Henry, Jackson, Johnson, Lafayette, Ray, Saint Clair, and Saline.

Court for the Western Division shall be held at Kansas City.

(2) The Southwestern Division comprises the counties of Barton, Barry, Jasper, Lawrence, McDonald, Newton, Stone, and Vernon.

Court for the Southwestern Division shall be held at Joplin.

(3) The Saint Joseph Division comprises the counties of Andrew, Atchison, Buchanan, Caldwell, Clinton, Daviess, De Kalb, Gentry, Grundy, Harrison, Holt, Livingston, Mercer, Nodaway, Platte, Putnam, Sullivan, and Worth.

Court for the Saint Joseph Division shall be held at Saint Joseph.

(4) The Central Division comprises the counties of Benton, Boone, Callaway, Camden, Cole, Cooper, Hickory, Howard, Miller, Moniteau, Morgan, Osage, and Pettis.

Court for the Central Division shall be held at Jefferson City.

(5) The Southern Division comprises the counties of Cedar, Christian, Dade, Dallas, Douglas, Greene, Howell, Laclede, Oregon, Ozark, Polk, Pulaski, Taney, Texas, Webster, and Wright.

Court for the Southern Division shall be held at Springfield.

(June 25, 1948, c. 646, 62 Stat. 884; May 31, 1962, Pub.L. 87–461, 76 Stat. 85; Oct. 15, 1980, Pub.L. 96–462, § 4(a), 94 Stat. 2053.)

HISTORICAL AND STATUTORY NOTES

Effective Dates

1980 Acts. Amendment by Pub.L. 96–462 effective Oct. 1, 1981 with that amendment not to affect the composition or preclude the service of any grand or petit juror summoned, empaneled, or actually serving in any judicial district on Oct. 1, 1981, see section 7 of Pub.L. 96–462, set out as a note under section 84 of this title.

Section 4(b) of Pub.L. 96–462 provided that: "The amendments made by subsection (a) [amending subsec. (a)(1), (2) of this section] shall not apply to any action commenced before the effective date of such amendments [Oct. 1, 1981] and pending in the United States District Court for the Eastern District of Missouri on such date."

§ 106. Montana

Montana, exclusive of Yellowstone National Park, constitutes one judicial district.

Court shall be held at Billings, Butte, Glasgow, Great Falls, Havre, Helena, Kalispell, Lewistown, Livingston, Miles City, and Missoula.

(June 25, 1948, c. 646, 62 Stat. 884.)

§ 107. Nebraska

Nebraska constitutes one judicial district.

Court shall be held at Lincoln, North Platte, and Omaha.

(June 25, 1948, c. 646, 62 Stat. 884; Aug. 9, 1955, c. 627, § 1, 69 Stat. 546.)

HISTORICAL AND STATUTORY NOTES

Effective Dates

1955 Acts. Section 2 of Act Aug. 9, 1955, provided that: "The amendment made by the first section of this Act [amending this section] shall take effect on September 1, 1955."

§ 108. Nevada

Nevada constitutes one judicial district.

Court shall be held at Carson City, Elko, Las Vegas, Reno, Ely, and Lovelock.

(June 25, 1948, c. 646, 62 Stat. 885; Dec. 1, 1990, Pub.L. 101–650, Title III, § 324(a)(1), 104 Stat. 5120.)

§ 109. New Hampshire

New Hampshire constitutes one judicial district.

Court shall be held at Concord and Littleton.

(June 25, 1948, c. 646, 62 Stat. 885.)

§ 110. New Jersey

New Jersey constitutes one judicial district.

Court shall be held at Camden, Newark and Trenton.

(June 25, 1948, c. 646, 62 Stat. 885.)

§ 111. New Mexico

New Mexico constitutes one judicial district.

Court shall be held at Albuquerque, Las Cruces, Las Vegas, Roswell, Santa Fe, and Silver City.

(June 25, 1948, c. 646, 62 Stat. 885.)

§ 112. New York

New York is divided into four judicial districts to be known as the Northern, Southern, Eastern, and Western Districts of New York.

Northern District

(a) The Northern District comprises the counties of Albany, Broome, Cayuga, Chenango, Clinton, Columbia, Cortland, Delaware, Essex, Franklin, Fulton, Greene, Hamilton, Herkimer, Jefferson, Lewis, Madison, Montgomery, Oneida, Onondaga, Oswego, Otsego, Rensselaer, Saint Lawrence, Saratoga, Schenectady, Schoharie, Tioga, Tompkins, Ulster, Warren, and Washington.

Court for the Northern District shall be held at Albany, Auburn, Binghamton, Malone, Syracuse, Utica, and Watertown.

Southern District

(b) The Southern District comprises the counties of Bronx, Dutchess, New York, Orange, Putnam, Rockland, Sullivan, and Westchester and concurrently with the Eastern District, the waters within the Eastern District.

Court for the Southern District shall be held at New York, White Plains, and in the Middletown-Wallkill area of Orange County or such nearby location as may be deemed appropriate.

Eastern District

(c) The Eastern District comprises the counties of Kings, Nassau, Queens, Richmond, and Suffolk and concurrently with the Southern District, the waters within the counties of Bronx and New York.

Court for the Eastern District shall be held at Brooklyn, Hauppauge, and Hempstead (including the village of Uniondale).

Western District

(d) The Western District comprises the counties of Allegany, Cattaraugus, Chautauqua, Chemung, Erie, Genesee, Livingston, Monroe, Niagara, Ontario, Orleans, Schuyler, Seneca, Steuben, Wayne, Wyoming, and Yates.

Court for the Western District shall be held at Buffalo, Canandaigua, Elmira, Jamestown, and Rochester.

(June 25, 1948, c. 646, 62 Stat. 885; Dec. 18, 1967, Pub.L. 90–217, 81 Stat. 662; Dec. 14, 1970, Pub.L. 91–546, § 1, 84 Stat. 1412; Apr. 28, 1978, Pub.L. 95–271, § 1, 92 Stat. 221; Oct. 2, 1978, Pub.L. 95–408, § 4(c), 92 Stat. 885; Nov. 2, 1978, Pub.L. 95–573, § 3, 92 Stat. 2458; Nov. 8, 1984, Pub.L. 98–620, Title IV, § 405, 98 Stat. 3361; Dec. 1, 1990, Pub.L. 101–650, Title III, § 324(a)(2), 104 Stat. 5120; Oct. 19, 1996, Pub.L. 104–317, Title VI, § 609, 110 Stat. 3860.)

HISTORICAL AND STATUTORY NOTES

Effective Dates

1984 Acts. Amendment by Pub.L. 98–620 to take effect on Jan. 1, 1985, and not to affect the composition, or preclude the service, of any grand or petit jury summoned, impaneled, or actually serving on that date, see section 411 of Pub.L. 98–620, set out as a note under section 85 of this title.

1978 Acts. Amendment by Pub.L. 95–573 effective 180 days after Nov. 2, 1978, except as otherwise provided, except that nothing in this Act shall affect the composition or preclude the service of any grand or petit juror summoned, empaneled, or actually serving in any judicial district on such effective date, see section 6 of Pub.L. 95–573, set out as a note under section 93 of this title.

Amendment by Pub.L. 95–408 effective 180 days after Oct. 2, 1978, such amendment not to affect the composition or preclude the service of any grand or petit juror summoned, empaneled, or actually serving in any judicial district on the effective date of this Act, see section 5 of Pub.L. 95–408, set out as a note under section 89 of this title.

Pretermission of Regular Session of Court at Hempstead and Holding of Special Session at Westbury; Procedures Applicable, Appropriations, Etc.

Sections 2 to 5 of Pub.L. 95–271 provided that:

"Sec. 2. The United States District Court for the Eastern District of New York, by order made anywhere within its district, may pretermit the regular session of court at Hempstead until Federal quarters and accommodations are available and ready for occupancy, except that for the entire period and such pretermission, a special session of the court shall be held at Westbury. Pretermission may be ordered without regard to the provisions of section 140(a) of title 28, United States Code [section 140(a) of this title].

"Sec. 3. Notwithstanding the provisions of section 142 of title 28, United States Code [section 142 of this title], the Administrator of General Services, at the request of the Director of the Administrative Office of the United States Courts, shall continue to provide existing quarters and accommodations at Westbury for the duration of the special session held pursuant to section 2 of this Act. Appropriations to the judicial branch of Government shall be available to the Director to make necessary disbursements for such quarters and accommodations, and to pay user charges as required by section 210 of the Federal Property and Administrative Services Act of 1949, as amended (40 U.S.C. 490) [section 490 of Title 40, Public Buildings, Property, and Works], at rates otherwise authorized by law.

"Sec. 4. Notwithstanding the provisions of section 456 of title 28, United States Code [section 456 of this title], any judge, and any officer or employee of the judicial branch, whose official station is, on the day before the date of enactment of this Act [Apr. 28, 1978], Westbury, may maintain that official station for the duration of the special session held pursuant to section 2 of this Act.

"Sec. 5. The Director of the Administrative Office of the United States Courts may pay travel and transportation expenses in accordance with subchapter II, chapter 57 of title 5, United States Code [section 5721 et seq. of Title 5, Government Organization and Employees], to any officer or employee of the judicial branch whose official station changes as a consequence of this Act [amending subsec. (c) of this section] and who relocates his residence incident to such change of official station."

§ 113. North Carolina

North Carolina is divided into three judicial districts to be known as the Eastern, Middle, and Western Districts of North Carolina.

Eastern District

(a) The Eastern District comprises the counties of Beaufort, Bertie, Bladen, Brunswick, Camden, Carteret, Chowan, Columbus, Craven, Cumberland, Currituck, Dare, Duplin, Edgecombe, Franklin, Gates, Granville, Greene, Halifax, Harnett, Hertford, Hyde, Johnston, Jones, Lenoir, Martin, Nash, New Hanover, Northampton, Onslow, Pamlico, Pasquotank, Pender, Perquimans, Pitt, Robeson, Sampson, Tyrrell, Vance, Wake, Warren, Washington, Wayne, and Wilson and that portion of Durham County encompassing the Federal Correctional Institution, Butner, North Carolina.

Court for the Eastern District shall be held at Elizabeth City, Fayetteville, Greenville, New Bern, Raleigh, Wilmington, and Wilson.

Middle District

(b) The Middle District comprises the counties of Alamance, Cabarrus, Caswell, Chatham, Davidson, Davie, Durham (excluding that portion of Durham County encompassing the Federal Correctional Institution, Butner, North Carolina), Forsythe, Guilford, Hoke, Lee, Montgomery, Moore, Orange, Person, Randolph, Richmond, Rockingham, Rowan, Scotland, Stanly, Stokes, Surry, and Yadkin.

Court for the Middle District shall be held at Durham, Greensboro, and Winston-Salem.

Western District

(c) The Western District comprises the counties of Alexander, Alleghany, Anson, Ashe, Avery, Buncombe, Burke, Caldwell, Catawba, Cherokee, Clay, Cleveland, Gaston, Graham, Haywood, Henderson, Iredell, Jackson, Lincoln, McDowell, Macon, Madison, Mecklenburg, Mitchell, Polk, Rutherford, Swain, Transylvania, Union, Watauga, Wilkes, and Yancey.

Court for the Western District shall be held at Asheville, Bryson City, Charlotte, Shelby, and Statesville.

(June 25, 1948, c. 646, 62 Stat. 886; Nov. 2, 1965, Pub.L. 89–319, 79 Stat. 1186; Oct. 15, 1980, Pub.L. 96–462, § 5(a)–(c), 94 Stat. 2053, 2054; Apr. 21, 1992, Pub.L. 102–272, 106 Stat. 112.)

HISTORICAL AND STATUTORY NOTES

Effective Dates

1980 Acts. Amendment by Pub.L. 96–462 effective Oct. 1, 1981, with that amendment not to affect the composition or preclude the service of any grand or petit juror summoned, empaneled, or actually serving in any judicial district on Oct. 1, 1981, see section 7 of Pub.L. 96–462, set out as a note under section 84 of this title.

Section 5(d) of Pub.L. 96–462 provided that: "The amendments made by this section [amending this section] shall not apply to any action commenced before the effective date of such amendments [Oct. 1, 1981] and pending in any judicial district of North Carolina on such date."

§ 114. North Dakota

North Dakota constitutes one judicial district comprising four divisions.

(1) The Southwestern Division comprises the counties of Adams, Billings, Bowman, Burleigh, Dunn, Emmons, Golden Valley, Grant, Hettinger, Kidder, Logan, McIntosh, McLean, Mercer, Morton, Oliver, Sioux, Slope, and Stark.

Court for the Southwestern Division shall be held at Bismarck.

(2) The Southeastern Division comprises the counties of Barnes, Cass, Dickey, Eddy, Foster, Griggs, La Moure, Ransom, Richland, Sargent, Steele, and Stutsman.

Court for the Southeastern Division shall be held at Fargo.

(3) The Northeastern Division comprises the counties of Benson, Cavalier, Grand Forks, Nelson, Pembina, Ramsey, Rolette, Towner, Traill, and Walsh.

Court for the Northeastern Division shall be held at Grand Forks.

(4) The Northwestern Division comprises the counties of Bottineau, Burke, Divide, McHenry, McKenzie, Mountrail, Pierce, Renville, Sheridan, Ward, Wells, and Williams.

Court for the Northwestern Division shall be held at Minot.

(June 25, 1948, c. 646, 62 Stat. 886; Oct. 2, 1978, Pub.L. 95–408, § 3(b), 92 Stat. 883.)

HISTORICAL AND STATUTORY NOTES

Effective Dates

1978 Acts. Amendment by Pub.L. 95–408 effective 180 days after Oct. 2, 1978, such amendment not to affect the composition or preclude the service of any grand or petit juror summoned, empaneled, or actually serving in any judicial district on the effective date of this Act, see section 5 of Pub.L. 95–408, set out as a note under section 89 of this title.

§ 115. Ohio

Ohio is divided into two judicial districts to be known as the Northern and Southern Districts of Ohio.

Northern District

(a) The Northern District comprises two divisions.

(1) The Eastern Division comprises the counties of Ashland, Ashtabula, Carroll, Columbiana, Crawford, Cuyahoga, Geauga, Holmes, Lake, Lorain, Mahoning, Medina, Portage, Richland, Stark, Summit, Trumbull, Tuscarawas, and Wayne.

Court for the Eastern Division shall be held at Cleveland, Youngstown, and Akron.

(2) The Western Division comprises the counties of Allen, Auglaize, Defiance, Erie, Fulton, Hancock, Hardin, Henry, Huron, Lucas, Marion, Mercer, Ottawa, Paulding, Putnam, Sandusky, Seneca, Van Wert, Williams, Woods, and Wyandot.

Court for the Western Division shall be held at Lima and Toledo.

Southern District

(b) The Southern District comprises two divisions.

(1) The Western Division comprises the counties of Adams, Brown, Butler, Champaign, Clark, Clermont, Clinton, Darke, Greene, Hamilton, Highland, Lawrence, Miami, Montgomery, Preble, Scioto, Shelby, and Warren.

Court for the Western Division shall be held at Cincinnati and Dayton.

(2) The Eastern Division comprises the counties of Athens, Belmont, Coshocton, Delaware, Fairfield, Fayette, Franklin, Gallia, Guernsey, Harrison, Hocking, Jackson, Jefferson, Knox, Licking, Logan, Madison, Meigs, Monroe, Morgan, Morrow, Muskingum, Noble, Perry, Pickaway, Pike, Ross, Union, Vinton, and Washington.

Court for the Eastern Division shall be held at Columbus and Steubenville.

(June 25, 1948, c. 646, 62 Stat. 887; Feb. 10, 1954, c. 6, § 2(b)(9), 68 Stat. 11.)

§ 116. Oklahoma

Oklahoma is divided into three judicial districts to be known as the Northern, Eastern, and Western Districts of Oklahoma.

Northern District

(a) The Northern District comprises the counties of Craig, Creek, Delaware, Mayes, Nowata, Osage, Ottawa, Pawnee, Rogers, Tulsa, and Washington.

Court for the Northern District shall be held at Bartlesville, Miami, Pawhuska, Tulsa, and Vinita.

Eastern District

(b) The Eastern District comprises the counties of Adair, Atoka, Bryan, Carter, Cherokee, Choctaw, Coal, Haskell, Hughes, Johnston, Latimer, Le Flore, Love, McCurtain, McIntosh, Marshall, Murray, Muskogee, Okfuskee, Okmulgee, Pittsburg, Pontotoc, Pushmataha, Seminole, Sequoyah, and Wagoner.

Court for the Eastern District shall be held at Ada, Ardmore, Durant, Hugo, Muskogee, Okmulgee, Poteau, and S. McAlester.

Western District

(c) The Western District comprises the counties of Alfalfa, Beaver, Beckham, Blaine, Caddo, Canadian, Cimarron, Cleveland, Comanche, Cotton, Custer, Dewey, Ellis, Garfield, Garvin, Grady, Grant, Greer, Harmon, Harper, Jackson, Jefferson, Kay, Kingfisher, Kiowa, Lincoln, Logan, McClain, Major, Noble, Oklahoma, Payne, Pottawatomie, Roger Mills, Stephens, Texas, Tillman, Washita, Woods, and Woodward.

Court for the Western District shall be held at Chickasha, Enid, Guthrie, Lawton, Mangum, Oklahoma City, Pauls Valley, Ponca City, Shawnee, and Woodward.

(June 25, 1948, c. 646, 62 Stat. 887; Aug. 4, 1966, Pub.L. 89–526, § 1, 80 Stat. 335.)

HISTORICAL AND STATUTORY NOTES

Effective Dates

1966 Acts. Section 2 of Pub.L. 89–526 provided that: "The amendments made by this Act [to subsecs. (b) and (c) of this section] shall take effect on the sixtieth day after the date of enactment of this Act [Aug. 4, 1966]."

§ 117. Oregon

Oregon constitutes one judicial district.

Court shall be held at Coquille, Eugene, Klamath Falls, Medford, Pendleton, and Portland.

(June 25, 1948, c. 646, 62 Stat. 888; Aug. 3, 1950, c. 514, 64 Stat. 393; June 2, 1970, Pub.L. 91–272, § 7, 84 Stat. 297.)

§ 118. Pennsylvania

Pennsylvania is divided into three judicial districts to be known as the Eastern, Middle, and Western Districts of Pennsylvania.

Eastern District

(a) The Eastern District comprises the counties of Berks, Bucks, Chester, Delaware, Lancaster, Lehigh, Montgomery, Northampton, and Philadelphia.

Court for the Eastern District shall be held at Allentown, Easton, Lancaster, Reading, and Philadelphia.

Middle District

(b) The Middle District comprises the counties of Adams, Bradford, Cameron, Carbon, Centre, Clinton, Columbia, Cumberland, Dauphin, Franklin, Fulton, Huntingdon, Juniata, Lackawanna, Lebanon, Luzerne, Lycoming, Mifflin, Monroe, Montour, Northumberland, Perry, Pike, Potter, Schuylkill, Snyder, Sullivan, Susquehanna, Tioga, Union, Wayne, Wyoming, and York.

Court for the Middle District shall be held at Harrisburg, Lewisburg, Scranton, Wilkes-Barre, and Williamsport.

Western District

(c) The Western District comprises the counties of Allegheny, Armstrong, Beaver, Bedford, Blair, Butler, Cambria, Clarion, Clearfield, Crawford, Elk, Erie, Fayette, Forest, Greene, Indiana, Jefferson, Lawrence, McKean, Mercer, Somerset, Venango, Warren, Washington, and Westmoreland.

Court for the Western District shall be held at Erie, Johnstown, and Pittsburgh.

(June 25, 1948, c. 646, 62 Stat. 888; June 2, 1970, Pub.L. 91–272, § 6, 84 Stat. 297; Nov. 2, 1978, Pub.L. 95–573, § 4, 92 Stat. 2458; Oct. 6, 1992, Pub.L. 102–396, Title IX, § 9161, 106 Stat. 1947; Oct. 21, 1998, Pub.L. 105–277, Div. A, § 101(b) [Title VI, § 624(a)], 112 Stat. 2681–___.)

HISTORICAL AND STATUTORY NOTES

Effective Dates

1998 Acts. Pub.L. 105–277, Div. A, § 101(b) [Title VI, § 624(b)], Oct. 21, 1998, 112 Stat. 2681–___, provided that: "**(b)(1)** This section and the amendments made by this section shall take effect 180 days after the date of the enactment of this Act [October 21, 1998].

"(2) This section and the amendments made by this section shall not affect any action commenced before the effective date of this section [October 21, 1998] and pending on such date in the United States District Court for the Eastern District of Pennsylvania.

"(3) This section and the amendments made by this section shall not affect the composition, or preclude the service, of any grand or petit jury summoned, impaneled, or actually serving on the effective date of this session [October 21, 1998]."

1978 Acts. Amendment by Pub.L. 95–573 effective 180 days after Nov. 2, 1978, except as otherwise provided, except that nothing in this Act shall affect the composition or preclude the service of any grand or petit juror summoned, empaneled, or actually serving in any judicial district on such effective date, see section 6 of Pub.L. 95–573, set out as a note under section 93 of this title.

§ 119. Puerto Rico

Puerto Rico constitutes one judicial district.

Court shall be held at Mayaguez, Ponce, and San Juan.

(June 25, 1948, c. 646, 62 Stat. 889.)

§ 120. Rhode Island

Rhode Island constitutes one judicial district.

Court shall be held at Providence.

(June 25, 1948, c. 646, 62 Stat. 889.)

§ 121. South Carolina

South Carolina constitutes one judicial district comprising eleven divisions.

(1) The Charleston Division comprises the counties of Berkeley, Charleston, Clarendon, Colleton, Dorchester, and Georgetown.

Court for the Charleston Division shall be held at Charleston.

(2) The Columbia Division comprises the counties of Kershaw, Lee, Lexington, Richland, and Sumter.

Court for the Columbia Division shall be held at Columbia.

(3) The Florence Division comprises the counties of Chesterfield, Darlington, Dillon, Florence, Horry, Marion, Marlboro, and Williamsburg.

Court for the Florence Division shall be held at Florence.

(4) The Aiken Division comprises the counties of Aiken, Allendale, and Barnwell.

Court for the Aiken Division shall be held at Aiken.

(5) The Orangeburg Division comprises the counties of Bamberg, Calhoun, and Orangeburg.

Court for the Orangeburg Division shall be held at Orangeburg.

(6) The Greenville Division comprises the counties of Greenville and Laurens.

Court for the Greenville Division shall be held at Greenville.

(7) The Rock Hill Division comprises the counties of Chester, Fairfield, Lancaster, and York.

Court for the Rock Hill Division shall be held at Rock Hill.

(8) The Greenwood Division comprises the counties of Abbeville, Edgefield, Greenwood, McCormick, Newberry, and Saluda.

Court for the Greenwood Division shall be held at Greenwood.

(9) The Anderson Division comprises the counties of Anderson, Oconee, and Pickens.

Court for the Anderson Division shall be held at Anderson.

(10) The Spartanburg Division comprises the counties of Cherokee, Spartanburg, and Union.

Court for the Spartanburg Division shall be held at Spartanburg.

(11) The Beaufort Division comprises the counties of Beaufort, Hampton, and Jasper.

Court for the Beaufort Division shall be held at Beaufort.

(June 25, 1948, c. 646, 62 Stat. 889; Oct. 7, 1965, Pub.L. 89–242, § 1(a), 79 Stat. 951; Nov. 14, 1986, Pub.L. 99–657, § 2, 100 Stat. 3670; Oct. 28, 1991, Pub.L. 102–140, Title III, § 304, 105 Stat. 810.)

HISTORICAL AND STATUTORY NOTES

Effective Dates

1986 Acts. Section 4 of Pub.L. 99–657 provided that:

"**(a) Effective date.—(1)** The amendments made by sections 2 and 3 [amending this section and section 90 of this title, respectively] take effect 90 days after the date of the enactment of this Act [Nov. 14, 1986].

"(2) The amendment made by section 4 [enacting this note] takes effect on the date of the enactment of this Act [Nov. 14, 1986].

"**(b) Pending actions.**—The amendments made by this Act [amending this section and section 90 of this title, and enacting provisions set out as a note under section 1 of this title] shall not affect any action commenced before the effective date of such amendments and pending on such date.

"**(c) Juries.**—The amendments made by this Act [amending this section and section 90 of this title, and enacting provisions set out as a note under section 1 of this title] shall not affect the composition, or preclude the service, of any grand or petit jury summoned, empaneled, or actually serving on the effective date of such amendments."

1965 Acts. Section 6 of Pub.L. 89–242 provided that: "The provisions of this Act [amending this section and section 133 of this title and enacting provisions set out as notes under this section] shall become effective on the first day of the month following the date of enactment of this Act [Oct. 7, 1965]."

Consolidation of South Carolina Into a Single Judicial District

Sections 2 to 5 of Pub.L. 89–242 provided that:

"**Sec. 2. [Continuity of Judicial Business; Clerk of Court; Records].** In compliance with section 132 of title 28 of the United States Code [section 132 of this title] the District Courts for the Eastern and Western Districts of South Carolina are hereby consolidated into, and shall henceforth constitute, a single District Court for the District of South Carolina. No loss or interruption of the jurisdiction of the consolidated District Court for the District of South Carolina over cases and controversies heretofore decided by or now pending in the District Courts for the Eastern and Western Districts of South Carolina shall result from such consolidation and prosecutions for offenses committed within the Eastern and Western Districts of South Carolina prior to the effective date of this Act [Nov. 1, 1965] shall be commenced and proceeded with the same as if such consolidation had not occurred. For the purpose of the trial of such offenses, the District Courts for the Eastern and Western Districts of South Carolina are continued in existence and the judges of the District Court for the District of South Carolina shall sit as judges in such courts according to assignment made by the chief judge of the United States District Court for the District of South Carolina or the chief judge of the United States Court of Appeals for the Fourth Circuit. The District Court for the District of South Carolina shall appoint a clerk who shall supersede the clerks of the District Courts for the Eastern and Western Districts of South Carolina and who shall maintain his office at Columbia until the court otherwise directs pursuant to sections 457 and 751(c) of title 28 of the United States Code [sections 457 and 751(c) of this title]. The presently existing records of the District Courts for the Eastern and Western Districts of South Carolina shall be placed in his custody.

"**Sec. 3. [United States Attorney].** When the term of office of either the United States attorney for the Eastern District of South Carolina or the United States attorney for the Western District of South Carolina, holding office on the date of enactment of this Act, has expired, the President is authorized to appoint a United States attorney for the District of South Carolina as provided by section 501 of title 28 of the United States Code [section 501 of this title]. Until the United States attorney for the District of South Carolina has been appointed as herein authorized and has qualified, the United States attorney for the Eastern District of South Carolina holding office on the date of enactment of this Act [Oct. 7, 1965] shall continue to serve as a United States attorney and to perform the duties of such office in the Charleston, Columbia, Orangeburg, Florence, and Aiken divisions of the District of South Carolina, and the United States attorney for the Western District of South Carolina holding office on the date of enactment of this Act [Oct. 7, 1965] shall continue to serve as a United States attorney and to perform the duties of such office in the Greenville, Rock Hill, Greenwood, Spartanburg, and Anderson divisions of the District of South Carolina. In the event a vacancy, other than a vacancy resulting from expiration of term, arises in either of such offices prior to the appointment as herein authorized and qualification, of a United States attorney for the District of South Carolina the incumbent of the other such office shall also perform the duties of the office in which the vacancy occurs until such appointment and qualification.

"**Sec. 4. [United States Marshal].** When the term of office of either the United States marshal for the Eastern District of South Carolina or the United States marshal for the Western District of South Carolina, holding office on the date of enactment of this Act [Oct. 7, 1965], has expired, the President is authorized to appoint a United States marshal for the District of South Carolina as provided by section 541(a) of title 28 of the United States Code [section 541(a) of this title]. Until the United States marshal for the District of South Carolina has been appointed as herein authorized and has qualified, the United States marshal for the Eastern District of South Carolina holding office on the date of enactment of this Act [Oct. 7, 1965] shall continue to serve as a United States marshal and to perform the duties of such office in the Charleston, Columbia, Orangeburg, Florence, and Aiken divisions of the District of South Carolina, and the United States marshal for the Western District of South Carolina holding office on the date of enactment of this Act [Oct. 7, 1965] shall continue to serve as a United States marshal and to perform the duties of such office in the Greenville, Rock Hill, Greenwood, Spartanburg, and Anderson divisions of the District of South Carolina. In the event a vacancy, other than a vacancy resulting from expiration of term, arises in either of such offices prior to the appointment as herein authorized and qualification of a United States marshal for the District of South Carolina the incumbent of the other such office shall also perform the duties of the office in which the vacancy occurs until such appointment and qualification.

"**Sec. 5. [Other Court Personnel].** All deputy clerks, clerical assistants, and other employees of the clerks, all court reporters, all probation officers and their clerical assistants, all referees in bankruptcy and their clerical assistants, all United States commissioners and all other presently serving officers and employees of the United States District Courts for the Eastern and Western Districts of South Carolina shall henceforth be officers or employees, as the case may be, of the United States District Court for the District of South Carolina and shall hold their offices or employment under and perform their duties for that court. All presently serving assistant United States attorneys and clerical assistants of the United States attorneys and all presently serving deputy marshals and clerical assistants of the United States marshals appointed for the Eastern or Western District of South Carolina shall henceforth hold their offices or employment for the District of South Carolina."

§ 122. South Dakota

South Dakota constitutes one judicial district comprising four divisions.

(1) The Northern Division comprises the counties of Brown, Campbell, Clark, Codington, Corson, Day, Deuel, Edmonds, Grant, Hamlin, McPherson, Marshall, Roberts, Spink, and Walworth.

Court for the Northern Division shall be held at Aberdeen.

(2) The Southern Division comprises the counties of Aurora, Beadle, Bon Homme, Brookings, Brule, Charles Mix, Clay, Davison, Douglas, Hanson, Hutchinson, Kingsbury, Lake, Lincoln, McCook, Miner, Minnehaha, Moody, Sanborn, Turner, Union, and Yankton.

Court for the Southern Division shall be held at Sioux Falls.

(3) The central division comprises the counties of Buffalo, Dewey, Faulk, Gregory, Haakon, Hand, Hughes, Hyde, Jerauld, Jones, Lyman, Mellette, Potter, Stanley, Sully, Todd, Tripp, and Ziebach.

Court for the Central Division shall be held at Pierre.

(4) The Western Division comprises the counties of Bennett, Butte, Custer, Fall River, Harding, Jackson, Lawrence, Meade, Pennington, Perkins, and Shannon.

Court for the Western Division shall be held at Deadwood and Rapid City.

(June 25, 1948, c. 646, 62 Stat. 889; Oct. 10, 1966, Pub.L. 89–638, 80 Stat. 883; Aug. 10, 1972, Pub.L. 92–376, 86 Stat. 529; Dec. 1, 1990, Pub.L. 101–650, Title III, § 324(b), 104 Stat. 5120.)

§ 123. Tennessee

Tennessee is divided into three judicial districts to be known as the Eastern, Middle, and Western Districts of Tennessee.

Eastern District

(a) The Eastern District comprises four divisions.

(1) The Northern Division comprises the counties of Anderson, Blount, Campbell, Claiborne, Grainger, Jefferson, Knox, Loudon, Monroe, Morgan, Roane, Scott, Sevier, and Union.

Court for the Northern Division shall be held at Knoxville.

(2) The Northeastern Division comprises the counties of Carter, Cocke, Greene, Hamblen, Hancock, Hawkins, Johnson, Sullivan, Unicoi, and Washington.

Court for the Northeastern Division shall be held at Greenville.

(3) The Southern Division comprises the counties of Bledsoe, Bradley, Hamilton, McMinn, Marion, Meigs, Polk, Rhea, and Sequatchie.

Court for the Southern Division shall be held at Chattanooga.

(4) The Winchester Division comprises the counties of Bedford, Coffee, Franklin, Grundy, Lincoln, Moore, Van Buren, and Warren.

Court for the Winchester Division shall be held at Winchester.

Middle District

(b) The Middle District comprises three divisions.

(1) The Nashville Division comprises the counties of Cannon, Cheatham, Davidson, Dickson, Houston, Humphreys, Montgomery, Robertson, Rutherford, Stewart, Sumner, Trousdale, Williamson, and Wilson.

Court for the Nashville Division shall be held at Nashville.

(2) The Northeastern Division comprises the counties of Clay, Cumberland, De Kalb, Fentress, Jackson, Macon, Overton, Pickett, Putnam, Smith, and White.

Court for the Northeastern Division shall be held at Cookeville.

(3) The Columbia Division comprises the counties of Giles, Hickman, Lawrence, Lewis, Marshall, Maury, and Wayne.

Court for the Columbia Division shall be held at Columbia.

Western District

(c) The Western District comprises two divisions.

(1) The Eastern Division comprises the counties of Benton, Carroll, Chester, Crockett, Decatur, Gibson, Hardeman, Hardin, Haywood, Henderson, Henry, Lake, McNairy, Madison, Obion, Perry, and Weakley.

The Eastern Division also includes the waters of Tennessee River to low-water mark on the eastern shore wherever such river forms the boundary between the western and middle districts from the north line of Alabama north to the point in Henry County, Tennessee, where the south boundary of Kentucky strikes the east bank of the river.

Court for the Eastern Division shall be held at Jackson.

(2) The Western Division comprises the counties of Dyer, Fayette, Lauderdale, Shelby, and Tipton.

Court for the Western Division shall be held at Memphis and Dyersburg.

The district judge for the Eastern District in office on November 27, 1940, shall hold court in the Northern and Northeastern Divisions. The other judge of that district shall hold the terms of court in the Southern and Winchester Divisions. Each may appoint and remove all officers and employees of the court whose official headquarters are located in the divisions within which he holds court and whose appointments are vested by law in a district judge or chief judge of a district.

(June 25, 1948, c. 646, 62 Stat. 890; May 19, 1961, Pub.L. 87–36, § 3(e), 75 Stat. 83; July 11, 1961, Pub.L. 87–86, 75 Stat. 203; June 2, 1970, Pub.L. 91–272, § 12, 84 Stat. 298.)

HISTORICAL AND STATUTORY NOTES

Codifications

Section 3(e) of Pub.L. 87–36 provided that "The second sentence of section 123(c)(2), title 18, United States Code, is amended to read as follows:". Pub.L. 87–86 corrected such reference to "title 18" to "title 28."

§ 124. Texas

Texas is divided into four judicial districts to be known as the Northern, Southern, Eastern, and Western Districts of Texas.

Northern District

(a) The Northern District comprises seven divisions.

(1) The Dallas Division comprises the counties of Dallas, Ellis, Hunt, Johnson, Kaufman, Navarro, and Rockwall.

Court for the Dallas Division shall be held at Dallas.

(2) The Fort Worth Division comprises the counties of Comanche, Erath, Hood, Jack, Palo Pinto, Parker, Tarrant, and Wise.

Court for the Fort Worth Division shall be held at Fort Worth.

(3) The Abilene Division comprises the counties of Callahan, Eastland, Fisher, Haskell, Howard, Jones, Mitchell, Nolan, Shackleford, Stephens, Stonewall, Taylor, and Throckmorton.

Court for the Abilene Division shall be held at Abilene.

(4) The San Angelo Division comprises the counties of Brown, Coke, Coleman, Concho, Crockett, Glasscock, Irion, Menard, Mills, Reagan, Runnels, Schleicher, Sterling, Sutton, and Tom Green.

Court for the San Angelo Division shall be held at San Angelo.

(5) The Amarillo Division comprises the counties of Armstrong, Brisco, Carson, Castro, Childress, Collingsworth, Dallam, Deaf Smith, Donley, Gray, Hall, Hansford, Hartley, Hemphill, Hutchinson, Lipscomb, Moore, Ochiltree, Oldham, Parmer, Potter, Randall, Roberts, Sherman, Swisher, and Wheeler.

Court for the Amarillo Division shall be held at Amarillo.

(6) The Wichita Falls Division comprises the counties of Archer, Baylor, Clay, Cottle, Foard, Hardeman, King, Knox, Montague, Wichita, Wilbarger, and Young.

Court for the Wichita Falls Division shall be held at Wichita Falls.

(7) The Lubbock Division comprises the counties of Bailey, Borden, Cochran, Crosby, Dawson, Dickens, Floyd, Gaines, Garza, Hale, Hockley, Kent, Lamb, Lubbock, Lynn, Motley, Scurry, Terry, and Yoakum.

Court for the Lubbock Division shall be held at Lubbock.

Southern District

(b) The Southern District comprises seven divisions.

(1) The Galveston Division comprises the counties of Brazoria, Chambers, Galveston, and Matagorda.

Court for the Galveston Division shall be held at Galveston.

(2) The Houston Division comprises the counties of Austin, Brazos, Colorado, Fayette, Fort Bend, Grimes, Harris, Madison, Montgomery, San Jacinto, Walker, Waller, and Wharton.

Court for the Houston Division shall be held at Houston.

(3) The Laredo Division comprises the counties of Jim Hogg, La Salle, McMullen, Webb, and Zapata.

Court for the Laredo Division shall be held at Laredo.

(4) The Brownsville Division comprises the counties of Cameron and Willacy.

Court for the Brownsville Division shall be held at Brownsville.

(5) The Victoria Division comprises the counties of Calhoun, DeWitt, Goliad, Jackson, Lavaca, Refugio, and Victoria.

Court for the Victoria Division shall be held at Victoria.

(6) The Corpus Christi Division comprises the counties of Aransas, Bee, Brooks, Duval, Jim Wells, Kenedy, Kleberg, Live Oak, Nueces, and San Patricio.

Court for the Corpus Christi Division shall be held at Corpus Christi.

(7) The McAllen Division comprises the counties of Hidalgo and Starr.

Court for the McAllen Division shall be held at McAllen.

Eastern District

(c) The Eastern District comprises seven divisions.

(1) The Tyler Division comprises the counties of Anderson, Cherokee, Gregg, Henderson, Panola, Rains, Rusk, Smith, Van Zandt, and Wood.

Court for Tyler Division will be held at Tyler.

(2) The Beaumont Division comprises the counties of Hardin, Jasper, Jefferson, Liberty, Newton, and Orange.

Court for the Beaumont Division is to be held at Beaumont.

(3) The Sherman Division comprises the counties of Collin, Cook, Denton, and Grayson.

Court for the Sherman Division shall be held at Sherman.

(4) The Paris Division comprises the counties of Delta, Fannin, Hopkins, Lamar, and Red River.

Court for the Paris Division shall be held at Paris.

(5) The Marshall Division comprises the counties of Camp, Cass, Harrison, Marion, Morris, and Upshur.

Court for the Marshall Division shall be held at Marshall.

(6) The Texarkana Division comprises the counties of Bowie, Franklin, and Titus.

Court for the Texarkana Division shall be held at Texarkana.

(7) The Lufkin Division comprises the counties of Angelina, Houston, Nacogdoches, Polk, Sabine, San Augustine, Shelby, Trinity, and Tyler.

Court for the Lufkin Division shall be held at Lufkin.

Western District

(d) The Western District comprises seven divisions.

(1) The Austin Division comprises the counties of Bastrop, Blanco, Burleson, Burnet, Caldwell, Gillespie, Hays, Kimble, Lampasas, Lee, Llano, Mason, McCulloch, San Saba, Travis, Washington, and Williamson.

Court for the Austin Division shall be held at Austin.

(2) The Waco Division comprises the counties of Bell, Bosque, Coryell, Falls, Freestone, Hamilton, Hill, Leon, Limestone, McLennan, Milam, Robertson, and Somervell.

Court for the Waco Division shall be held at Waco.

(3) The El Paso Division comprises the county of El Paso.

Court for the El Paso Division shall be held at El Paso.

(4) The San Antonio Division comprises the counties of Atascosa, Bandera, Bexar, Comal, Dimmit, Frio, Gonzales, Guadalupe, Karnes, Kendall, Kerr, Medina, Real, and Wilson.

Court for the San Antonio Division shall be held at San Antonio.

(5) The Del Rio Division comprises the counties of Edwards, Kinney, Maverick, Terrell, Uvalde, Val Verde, and Zavalla.

Court for the Del Rio Division shall be held at Del Rio.

(6) The Pecos Division comprises the counties of Brewster, Culberson, Jeff Davis, Hudspeth, Loving, Pecos, Presidio, Reeves, Ward, and Winkler.

Court for the Pecos Division shall be held at Pecos.

(7) The Midland-Odessa Division comprises the counties of Andrews, Crane, Ector, Martin, Midland, and Upton.

Court for the Midland-Odessa Division shall be held at Midland. Court may be held, in the discretion of the court, in Odessa, when courtroom facilities are made available at no expense to the Government.

(June 25, 1948, c. 646, 62 Stat. 891; Feb. 10, 1954, c. 6, § 2(b)(9)(a), (b), 68 Stat. 11; Sept. 4, 1957, Pub.L. 85–298, §§ 1, 2, 71 Stat. 618; Oct. 4, 1961, Pub.L. 87–352, 75 Stat. 772; Mar. 11, 1964, Pub.L. 88–282, 78 Stat. 163; Aug. 30, 1964, Pub.L. 88–512, 78 Stat. 695; Dec. 18, 1967, Pub.L. 90–216, 81 Stat. 661; Oct. 15, 1980, Pub.L. 96–462, § 6, 94 Stat. 2054; Nov. 8, 1984, Pub.L. 98–620, Title IV, § 407(a), 98 Stat. 3362.)

HISTORICAL AND STATUTORY NOTES

Effective Dates

1984 Acts. Section 407(b) of Pub.L. 98–620 provided that: "The amendments made by subsection (a) of this section [amending subsec. (b) of this section] shall apply to any action commenced in the United States District Court for the Southern District of Texas on or after the effective date of this subtitle [Jan. 1, 1985], and shall not affect any action pending in such court on such effective date."

Amendment by Pub.L. 98–620 to take effect Jan. 1, 1985, and not to affect the composition, or preclude the service, of any grand or petit jury summoned, impaneled, or actually serving on that date, see section 411 of Pub.L. 98–620, set out as a note under section 85 of this title.

1980 Acts. Amendment by Pub.L. 96–462 effective Oct. 1, 1981, with that amendment not to affect the composition or preclude the service of any grand or petit juror summoned, empaneled, or actually serving in any judicial district on Oct. 1, 1981, see section 7 of Pub.L. 96–462, set out as a note under section 84 of this title.

§ 125. Utah

Utah constitutes one judicial district comprising two divisions.

(1) The Northern Division comprises the counties of Box Elder, Cache, Davis, Morgan, Rich, and Weber.

Court for the Northern Division shall be held at Salt Lake City and Ogden.

(2) The Central Division comprises the counties of Beaver, Carbon, Daggett, Duchesne, Emery, Garfield, Grand, Iron, Juab, Kane, Millard, Piute, Salt Lake, San Juan, Sanpete, Sevier, Summit, Tooele, Uintah, Utah, Wasatch, Washington, and Wayne.

Court for the Central Division shall be held at Salt Lake City, Provo, and St. George.

(June 25, 1948, c. 646, 62 Stat. 893; Oct. 19, 1996, Pub.L. 104–317, Title VI, § 606, 110 Stat. 3859.)

§ 126. Vermont

Vermont constitutes one judicial district.

Court shall be held at Bennington, Brattleboro, Burlington, Montpelier, Rutland, Saint Johnsbury, and Windsor.

(June 25, 1948, c. 646, 62 Stat. 893; May 28, 1964, Pub.L. 88–312, 78 Stat. 201; Nov. 8, 1984, Pub.L. 98–620, Title IV, § 410, 98 Stat. 3362.)

HISTORICAL AND STATUTORY NOTES

Effective Dates

1984 Acts. Amendment by Pub.L. 98–620 to take effect on Jan. 1, 1985, and not to affect the composition, or preclude the service, of any grand or petit jury summoned, impaneled, or actually serving on that date, see section 411 of Pub.L. 98–620, set out as a note under section 85 of this title.

§ 127. Virginia

Virginia is divided into two judicial districts, to be known as the Eastern and Western Districts of Virginia.

Eastern District

(a) The Eastern District comprises the counties of Accomac, Amelia, Arlington, Brunswick, Caroline, Charles City, Chesterfield, Dinwiddie, Elizabeth City, Essex, Fairfax, Fauquier, Gloucester, Goochland, Greensville, Hanover, Henrico, Isle of Wight, James City, King and Queen, King George, King William, Lancaster, Loudoun, Lunenberg, Mathews, Mecklenburg, Middlesex, Nansemond, New Kent, Norfolk, Northampton, Northumberland, Nottoway, Powhatan, Prince Edward, Prince George, Prince William, Princess Anne, Richmond, Southampton, Spotsylvania, Stafford, Surry, Sussex, Warwick, Westmoreland, and York.

Court for the Eastern District shall be held at Alexandria, Newport News, Norfolk, and Richmond.

Western District

(b) The Western District comprises the counties of Albemarle, Alleghany, Amherst, Appomattox, Augusta, Bath, Bedford, Bland, Botetourt, Buchanan, Buckingham, Campbell, Carroll, Charlotte, Clarke, Craig, Culpeper, Cumberland, Dickenson, Floyd, Fluvanna, Franklin, Frederick, Giles, Grayson, Greene, Halifax, Henry, Highland, Lee, Louisa, Madison, Montgomery, Nelson, Orange, Page, Patrick, Pittsylvania, Pulaski, Rappahannock, Roanoke, Rockbridge, Rockingham, Russell, Scott, Shenandoah, Smyth, Tazewell, Warren, Washington, Wise, and Wythe.

Court for the Western District shall be held at Abingdon, Big Stone Gap, Charlottesville, Danville, Harrisonburg, Lynchburg, and Roanoke.

(c) Cities and incorporated towns are included in that district in which are included the counties within the exterior boundaries of which such cities and incorporated towns are geographically located or out of the territory of which they have been incorporated.

(June 25, 1948, c. 646, 62 Stat. 893; July 5, 1968, Pub.L. 90–383, 82 Stat. 292; Dec. 10, 1991, Pub.L. 102–200, § 1, 105 Stat. 1630.)

HISTORICAL AND STATUTORY NOTES

Effective Dates

1991 Acts. Section 2 of Pub.L 102–200 provided that:

"**(a) Pending Actions.**—The amendments made by section 1 [amending subsecs. (a) and (b) of this section] shall not apply to any action commenced before the date of the enactment of this Act [Dec. 10, 1991] and pending in the United States District Court for the Eastern District of Virginia on such date.

"**(b) Juries.**—The amendments made by section 1 [amending subsecs. (a) and (b) of this section] shall not affect the composition, or preclude the service, of any grand or petit jury summoned, empaneled, or actually serving in the Eastern or Western District of Virginia on the date of the enactment of this Act [Dec. 10, 1991]."

§ 128. Washington

Washington is divided into two judicial districts to be known as the Eastern and Western Districts of Washington.

Eastern District

(a) The Eastern District comprises the counties of Adams, Asotin, Benton, Chelan, Columbia, Douglas, Ferry, Franklin, Garfield, Grant, Kittitas, Klickitat, Lincoln, Okanogan, Pend Oreille, Spokane, Stevens, Walla Walla, Whitman, and Yakima.

Court for the Eastern District shall be held at Spokane, Yakima, Walla Walla, and Richland.

Western District

(b) The Western District comprises the counties of Clallam, Clark, Cowlitz, Grays Harbor, Island, Jefferson, King, Kitsap, Lewis, Mason, Pacific, Pierce, San Juan, Skagit, Skamania, Snohomish, Thurston, Wahkiakum, and Whatcom.

Court for the Western District shall be held at Bellingham, Seattle, and Tacoma.

(June 25, 1948, c. 646, 62 Stat. 894; Sept. 25, 1962, Pub.L. 87–699, 76 Stat. 598; June 2, 1970, Pub.L. 91–272, § 4, 84 Stat. 297.)

§ 129. West Virginia

West Virginia is divided into two judicial districts to be known as the Northern and Southern Districts of West Virginia.

Northern District

(a) The Northern District comprises the counties of Barbour, Berkeley, Braxton, Brooke, Calhoun, Doddridge, Gilmer, Grant, Hampshire, Hancock, Hardy, Harrison, Jefferson, Lewis, Marion, Marshall, Mineral, Monongalia, Morgan, Ohio, Pendleton, Pleasants, Pocahontas, Preston, Randolph, Ritchie, Taylor, Tucker, Tyler, Upshur, Webster, and Wetzel.

Court for the Northern District shall be held at Clarksburg, Elkins, Fairmont, Martinsburg, and Wheeling.

Southern District

(b) The Southern District comprises the counties of Boone, Cabell, Clay, Fayette, Greenbrier, Jackson, Kanawha, Lincoln, Logan, McDowell, Mason, Mercer, Mingo, Monroe, Nicholas, Putnam, Raleigh, Roane, Summers, Wayne, Wirt, Wood, and Wyoming.

Court for the Southern District shall be held at Beckley, Bluefield, Charleston, Huntington, Lewisburg, and Parkersburg.

(June 25, 1948, c. 646, 62 Stat. 894; Jan. 14, 1983, Pub.L. 97–471, § 1, 96 Stat. 2601.)

§ 130. Wisconsin

Wisconsin is divided into two judicial districts to be known as the Eastern and Western districts of Wisconsin.

Eastern District

(a) The Eastern District comprises the counties of Brown, Calumet, Dodge, Door, Florence, Fond du Lac, Forest, Green Lake, Kenosha, Kewaunee, Langlade, Manitowoc, Marinette, Marquette, Menominee, Milwaukee, Oconto, Outagamie, Ozaukee, Racine, Shawano, Sheboygan, Walworth, Washington, Waukesha, Waupaca, Waushara, and Winnebago.

Court for the Eastern District shall be held at Green Bay, Milwaukee, and Oshkosh.

Western District

(b) The Western District comprises the counties of Adams, Ashland, Barron, Bayfield, Buffalo, Burnett, Chippewa, Clark, Columbia, Crawford, Dane, Douglas, Dunn, Eau Claire, Grant, Green, Iowa, Iron, Jackson, Jefferson, Juneau, La Crosse, Lafayette, Lincoln, Marathon, Monroe, Oneida, Pepin, Pierce, Polk, Portage, Price, Richland, Rock, Rusk, Saint Croix, Sauk, Sawyer, Taylor, Trempealeau, Vernon, Vilas, Washburn, and Wood.

Court for the Western District shall be held at Eau Claire, La Crosse, Madison, Superior, and Wausau.

(June 25, 1948, c. 646, 62 Stat. 894; Aug. 6, 1962, Pub.L. 87–573, 76 Stat. 307.)

§ 131. Wyoming

Wyoming and those portions of Yellowstone National Park situated in Montana and Idaho constitute one judicial district.

Court shall be held at Casper, Cheyenne, Evanston, Lander, Jackson, and Sheridan.

(June 25, 1948, c. 646, 62 Stat. 895; July 10, 1984, Pub.L. 98–353, Title II, § 203(a), 98 Stat. 350.)

§ 132. Creation and composition of district courts

(a) There shall be in each judicial district a district court which shall be a court of record known as the United States District Court for the district.

(b) Each district court shall consist of the district judge or judges for the district in regular active service. Justices or judges designated or assigned shall be competent to sit as judges of the court.

(c) Except as otherwise provided by law, or rule or order of court, the judicial power of a district court with respect to any action, suit or proceeding may be exercised by a single judge, who may preside alone and hold a regular or special session of court at the same time other sessions are held by other judges.

(June 25, 1948, c. 646, 62 Stat. 895; Nov. 13, 1963, Pub.L. 88–176, § 2, 77 Stat. 331.)

HISTORICAL AND STATUTORY NOTES

Continuation of Organization of Court

Section 2(b) of Act June 25, 1948, provided in part that the provisions of this title as set out in section 1 of said Act June 25, 1948, with respect to the organization of the court, shall be construed as a continuation of existing law, and the tenure of the judges, officers, and employees thereof, and of the United States attorneys and marshals and their deputies and assistants, in office on Sept. 1, 1948, shall not be affected by its enactment but each of them shall continue to serve in the same capacity under the appropriate provisions of this title pursuant to his prior appointment.

§ 133. Appointment and number of district judges

(a) The President shall appoint, by and with the advice and consent of the Senate, district judges for the several judicial districts, as follows:

DISTRICTS	JUDGES
Alabama:	
Northern	7
Middle	3
Southern	3
Alaska	3
Arizona	8
Arkansas:	
Eastern	5
Western	3
California:	
Northern	14
Eastern	6
Central	27
Southern	8
Colorado	7
Connecticut	8
Delaware	4
District of Columbia	15
Florida:	
Northern	4
Middle	11
Southern	16
Georgia:	
Northern	11
Middle	4
Southern	3
Hawaii	3
Idaho	2
Illinois:	
Northern	22
Central	3
Southern	3
Indiana:	
Northern	5
Southern	5
Iowa:	
Northern	2
Southern	3

DISTRICTS	JUDGES
Kansas	5
Kentucky:	
Eastern	4
Western	4
Eastern and Western	1
Louisiana:	
Eastern	12
Middle	3
Western	7
Maine	3
Maryland	10
Massachusetts	13
Michigan:	
Eastern	15
Western	4
Minnesota	7
Mississippi:	
Northern	3
Southern	6
Missouri:	
Eastern	6
Western	5
Eastern and Western	2
Montana	3
Nebraska	3
Nevada	4
New Hampshire	3
New Jersey	17
New Mexico	5
New York:	
Northern	4
Southern	28
Eastern	15
Western	4
North Carolina:	
Eastern	4
Middle	4
Western	3
North Dakota	2
Ohio:	
Northern	11
Southern	8
Oklahoma:	
Northern	3
Eastern	1
Western	6
Northern, Eastern, and Western	1
Oregon	6
Pennsylvania:	
Eastern	22
Middle	6
Western	10
Puerto Rico	7
Rhode Island	3
South Carolina	9
South Dakota	3
Tennessee:	

Districts	Judges
Eastern	5
Middle	4
Western	5
Texas:	
Northern	12
Southern	18
Eastern	7
Western	10
Utah	5
Vermont	2
Virginia:	
Eastern	9
Western	4
Washington:	
Eastern	4
Western	7
West Virginia:	
Northern	3
Southern	5
Wisconsin:	
Eastern	4
Western	2
Wyoming	3.

(b)(1) In any case in which a judge of the United States (other than a senior judge) assumes the duties of a full-time office of Federal judicial administration, the President shall appoint, by and with the advice and consent of the Senate, an additional judge for the court on which such judge serves. If the judge who assumes the duties of such full-time office leaves that office and resumes the duties as an active judge of the court, then the President shall not appoint a judge to fill the first vacancy which occurs thereafter in that court.

(2) For purposes of paragraph (1), the term "office of Federal judicial administration" means a position as Director of the Federal Judicial Center, Director of the Administrative Office of the United States Courts, or administrative assistant to the Chief Justice.

(June 25, 1948, c. 646, 62 Stat. 895; Aug. 3, 1949, c. 387, § 2(a), 63 Stat. 493; Aug. 14, 1950, c. 708, 64 Stat. 443; Aug. 29, 1950, c. 819, § 1, 64 Stat. 562; Sept. 5, 1950, c. 848, § 1, 64 Stat. 578; Feb. 10, 1954, c. 6, § 2(a)(3), 68 Stat. 9; Sept. 7, 1957, Pub.L. 85–310, 71 Stat. 631; July 7, 1958, Pub.L. 85–508, § 12(c), 72 Stat. 348; Mar. 18, 1959, Pub.L. 86–3, § 9(b), 73 Stat. 8; May 19, 1961, Pub.L. 87–36, § 2(d), 75 Stat. 81; July 30, 1962, Pub.L. 87–562, § 3, 76 Stat. 248; Oct. 7, 1965, Pub.L. 89–242, § 1(c), 79 Stat. 951; Mar. 18, 1966, Pub.L. 89–372, § 4, 80 Stat. 77; June 2, 1970, Pub.L. 91–272, § 1(d), 84 Stat. 295; Dec. 18, 1971, Pub.L. 92–208, § 3(d), 85 Stat. 742; Oct. 2, 1978, Pub.L. 95–408, § 4(b)(2), 92 Stat. 883; Oct. 20, 1978, Pub.L. 95–486, § 1(c), 92 Stat. 1630; Jan. 14, 1983, Pub.L. 97–471, § 3, 96 Stat. 2601; July 10, 1984, Pub.L. 98–353, Title II, § 202(e), 98 Stat. 348; Dec. 1, 1990, Pub.L. 101–650, Title II, § 203(d), Title III, § 303, 104 Stat. 5101, 5105; Oct. 6, 1997, Pub.L. 105–53, § 4, 111 Stat. 1174.)

HISTORICAL AND STATUTORY NOTES

Codifications

Section 4(b)(2) of Pub.L. 95–408, set out in the credit of this section, was stricken by Pub.L. 96–4, § 1, Mar. 30, 1979, 93 Stat. 6, and replaced by section 4(b)(2) to (4) of Pub.L. 95–408, as added by Pub.L. 96–4, § 1, Mar. 30, 1979, 93 Stat. 6, which provisions are now set out as a note under section 93 of this title.

Effective Dates

1990 Acts. Amendment by section 203(d) of Pub.L. 101–650 effective Dec. 1, 1990, see section 206 of Pub.L. 101–650, set out as a note under section 44 of this title.

1978 Acts. Section 7 of Pub.L. 95–486 provided that:

"**(a)** The first section and section 2 of this Act [amending this section and enacting provisions set out as notes under this section] shall take effect immediately upon the President's promulgation and publication of standards and guidelines for the selection, on the basis of merit, of nominees for United States district court judgeships authorized by this Act [amending this section, sections 44, 46, 1337, and 1445 of this title, section 5108 of Title 5, Government Organization and Employees, enacting provisions set out as notes under this section and sections 41 and 44 of this title, and amending provisions set out as a note under section 45 of this title].

"**(b)** The President may waive such standards and guidelines with respect to any nomination by notifying the Senate of the reasons for such waiver.

"**(c)** Following the promulgation and publication of such standards and guidelines, no nomination or appointment to a United States district court judgeship may be invalidated on the basis of the President's failure to comply with this section or with any standards or guidelines promulgated under this section.

"**(d)** This Act, other than the first section and section 2 [amending this section and enacting provisions set out as notes under this section], shall take effect on the date of enactment of this Act [Oct. 20, 1978]."

Section 11 of Pub.L. 95–486 provided that: "Notwithstanding any other provision of this Act [amending this section, sections 44, 46, 1337 and 1445 of this title, section 5108 of Title 5, Government Organization and Employees, enacting provisions set out as notes under this section, sections 41, 44 of this title, and amending provisions set out as notes under section 45 of this title], the first section and section 2 [amending this section and enacting provisions set out as notes under this section] shall not take effect before November 1, 1978."

Amendment by Pub.L. 95–408 effective 180 days after Oct. 2, 1978, such amendment not to affect the composition or preclude the service of any grand or petit juror summoned, empaneled, or actually serving in any judicial district on the effective date of this Act, see section 5 of Pub.L. 95–408, set out as a note under section 89 of this title.

1971 Acts. Amendment by Pub.L. 92–208 effective one hundred and twenty days after Dec. 18, 1971, see section 3(f) of Pub.L. 92–208, set out as a note under section 98 of this title.

1965 Acts. Amendment by Pub.L. 89–242 effective on the first day of the month following the date of enactment of

Pub.L. 89–242, see section 6 of Pub.L. 89–242, set out as a note under section 121 of this title.

1962 Acts. Amendment by Pub.L. 87–562 effective 90 days after July 30, 1962, see section 5 of Pub.L. 87–562, set out as a note under section 89 of this title.

1959 Acts. Section 9 of Pub.L. 86–3 provided in part that the amendment of this section and section 134(a) of this title shall be effective upon the admission of the State of Hawaii into the Union. Admission of Hawaii into the Union was accomplished Aug. 21, 1959, upon issuance of Proc. No. 3309, Aug. 21, 1959, 25 F.R. 6868, 73 Stat. c74, as required by sections 1 and 7(c) of Pub.L. 86–3, Mar. 18, 1959, 73 Stat. 4, set out as notes preceding section 491 of Title 48, Territories and Insular Possessions.

1958 Acts. Amendment by Pub.L. 85–508 effective Jan. 3, 1959, upon admission of Alaska into the Union pursuant to Proc. No. 3269, Jan. 3, 1959, 24 F.R. 81, 73 Stat. c16, as required by sections 1 and 8(c) of Pub.L. 85–508, see notes set out under section 81A of this title and preceding section 21 of Title 48, Territories and Insular Possessions.

Additional Judgeships

Section 203(a) to (c) of Title II of Pub.L. 101–650, as amended Pub.L. 104–60, Nov. 28, 1995, 109 Stat. 635; Pub.L. 104–317, Title III, § 304, Oct. 19, 1996, 110 Stat. 3852; Pub.L. 105–53, § 3, Oct. 6, 1997, 111 Stat. 1173, provided that:

"**(a) In general.**—The President shall appoint, by and with the advice and consent of the Senate—

"(1) 1 additional district judge for the western district of Arkansas;

"(2) 2 additional district judges for the northern district of California;

"(3) 5 additional district judges for the central district of California;

"(4) 1 additional district judge for the southern district of California;

"(5) 2 additional district judges for the district of Connecticut;

"(6) 2 additional district judges for the middle district of Florida;

"(7) 1 additional district judge for the northern district of Florida;

"(8) 1 additional district judge for the southern district of Florida;

"(9) 1 additional district judge for the middle district of Georgia;

"(10) 1 additional district judge for the northern district of Illinois;

"(11) 1 additional district judge for the southern district of Iowa;

"(12) 1 additional district judge for the western district of Louisiana;

"(13) 1 additional district judge for the district of Maine;

"(14) 1 additional district judge for the district of Massachusetts;

"(15) 1 additional district judge for the southern district of Mississippi;

"(16) 1 additional district judge for the eastern district of Missouri;

"(17) 1 additional district judge for the district of New Hampshire;

"(18) 3 additional district judges for the district of New Jersey;

"(19) 1 additional district judge for the district of New Mexico;

"(20) 1 additional district judge for the southern district of New York;

"(21) 3 additional district judges for the eastern district of New York;

"(22) 1 additional district judge for the middle district of North Carolina;

"(23) 1 additional district judge for the southern district of Ohio;

"(24) 1 additional district judge for the northern district of Oklahoma;

"(25) 1 additional district judge for the western district of Oklahoma;

"(26) 1 additional district judge for the district of Oregon;

"(27) 3 additional district judges for the eastern district of Pennsylvania;

"(28) 1 additional district judge for the middle district of Pennsylvania;

"(29) 1 additional district judge for the district of South Carolina;

"(30) 1 additional district judge for the eastern district of Tennessee;

"(31) 1 additional district judge for the western district of Tennessee;

"(32) 1 additional district judge for the middle district of Tennessee;

"(33) 2 additional district judges for the northern district of Texas;

"(34) 1 additional district judge for the eastern district of Texas;

"(35) 5 additional district judges for the southern district of Texas;

"(36) 3 additional district judges for the western district of Texas;

"(37) 1 additional district judge for the district of Utah;

"(38) 1 additional district judge for the eastern district of Washington;

"(39) 1 additional district judge for the northern district of West Virginia;

"(40) 1 additional district judge for the southern district of West Virginia; and

"(41) 1 additional district judge for the district of Wyoming.

"**(b) Existing judgeships.**—(1) The existing district judgeships for the western district of Arkansas, the northern district of Illinois, the northern district of Indiana, the district of Massachusetts, the western district of New York, the eastern district of North Carolina, the northern district of Ohio, and the western district of Washington authorized by section 202(b) of the Bankruptcy Amendments and Federal Judgeship Act of 1984 (Public Law 98–353, 98 Stat. 347–348) [set out as a note under this section] shall, as of the effective date of this title [Dec. 1, 1990], be authorized under section 133 of title 28, United States Code [this section], and the incumbents in those offices shall hold the office under section

133 of title 28, United States Code [this section], as amended by this title.

"(2)(A) The existing 2 district judgeships for the eastern and western districts of Arkansas (provided by section 133 of title 28, United States Code [this section], as in effect on the day before the effective date of this title [Dec. 1, 1990]) shall be district judgeships for the eastern district of Arkansas only, and the incumbents of such judgeships shall hold the offices under section 133 of title 28, United States Code [this section], as amended by this title.

"(B) The existing district judgeship for the northern and southern districts of Iowa (provided by section 133 of title 28, United States Code [this section], as in effect on the day before the effective date of this title [Dec. 1, 1990]) shall be a district judgeship for the northern district of Iowa only, and the incumbent of such judgeship shall hold the office under section 133 of title 28, United States Code [this section], as amended by this title.

"(C) The existing district judgeship for the northern, eastern, and western districts of Oklahoma (provided by section 133 of title 28, United States Code [this section], as in effect on the day before the effective date of this title [Dec. 1, 1990]) and the occupant of which has his or her official duty station at Oklahoma City on the date of the enactment of this title [Dec. 1, 1990], shall be a district judgeship for the western district of Oklahoma only, and the incumbent of such judgeship shall hold the office under section 133 of title 28, United States Code [this section], as amended by this title.

"(c) **Temporary judgeships.**—The President shall appoint, by and with the advice and consent of the Senate—

"(1) 1 additional district judge for the eastern district of California;

"(2) 1 additional district judge for the district of Hawaii;

"(3) 1 additional district judge for the central district of Illinois;

"(4) 1 additional district judge for the southern district of Illinois;

"(5) 1 additional district judge for the district of Kansas;

"(6) 1 additional district judge for the western district of Michigan;

"(7) 1 additional district judge for the eastern district of Missouri;

"(8) 1 additional district judge for the district of Nebraska;

"(9) 1 additional district judge for the northern district of New York;

"(10) 1 additional district judge for the northern district of Ohio;

"(11) 1 additional district judge for the eastern district of Pennsylvania; and

"(12) 1 additional district judge for the eastern district of Virginia.

"[(13) Redesignated (12)]

Except with respect to the western district of Michigan and the eastern district of Pennsylvania, the first vacancy in the office of district judge in each of the judicial districts named in this subsection, occurring 10 years or more after the confirmation date of the judge named to fill the temporary judgeship created by this subsection, shall not be filled. The first vacancy in the office of district judge in the western district of Michigan, occurring after December 1, 1995, shall not be filled. The first vacancy in the office of district judge in the eastern district of Pennsylvania, occurring 5 years or more after the confirmation date of the judge named to fill the temporary judgeship created for such district under this subsection, shall not be filled. For districts named in this subsection for which multiple judgeships are created by this Act, the last of those judgeships filled shall be the judgeships created under this section."

Section 202(a) to (d) of Pub.L. 98–353 provided that:

"(a) Subject to the provisions of subsection (c), the President shall appoint, by and with the advice and consent of the Senate, one additional district judge for the southern district of Alabama, one additional district judge for the district of Alaska, five additional district judges for the central district of California, one additional district judge for the district of Colorado, one additional district judge for the district of Connecticut, one additional district judge for the district of Delaware, three additional district judges for the southern district of Florida, one additional district judge for the middle district of Georgia, one additional district judge for the district of Hawaii, four additional district judges for the northern district of Illinois, one additional district judge for the southern district of Illinois, one additional district judge for the western district of Kentucky, one additional district judge for the western district of Louisiana, one additional district judge for the district of Maryland, one additional district judge for the district of Massachusetts, two additional district judges for the eastern district of Michigan, one additional district judge for the district of Minnesota, one additional district judge for the northern district of Mississippi, two additional district judges for the southern district of Mississippi, one additional district judge for the eastern district of Missouri, one additional district judge for the district of Montana, one additional district judge for the district of Nevada, three additional district judges for the district of New Jersey, one additional district judge for the northern district of New York, two additional district judges for the eastern district of New York, one additional district judge for the southern district of Ohio, one additional district judge for the western district of Oklahoma, one additional district judge for the district of Rhode Island, one additional district judge for the eastern district of Tennessee, one additional district judge for the western district of Tennessee, one additional district judge for the northern district of Texas, two additional district judges for the eastern district of Texas, one additional district judge for the western district of Texas, one additional district judge for the district of Utah, one additional district judge for the eastern district of Virginia, one additional district judge for the eastern district of Washington, one additional district judge for the western district of Washington, and one additional district judge for the district of Wyoming.

"(b) Subject to the provisions of subsection (c) the President shall appoint, by and with the advice and consent of the Senate, one additional district judge for the western district of Arkansas, one additional district judge for the northern district of Illinois, one additional district judge for the northern district of Indiana, one additional district judge for the district of Massachusetts, one additional district judge for the western district of New York, one additional district judge for the eastern district of North Carolina, one additional district judge for the northern district of Ohio, and one additional district judge for the western district of Washington. The first vacancy in each of the offices of district judge authorized by this subsection, occurring five years or more after the effective date of this Act [probably means July 10, 1984], shall not be filled.

"(c) For the judgeships created in subsections (a) and (b), the President shall appoint, by and with the advice and consent of the Senate, no more than twenty-nine of such judges prior to January 21, 1985.

"(d) The existing district judgeship for the district of Minnesota and the existing district judgeship for the northern district of Ohio, heretofore authorized by section 2 of the Act of October 20, 1978 (Public Law 95–486, 92 Stat. 1631) [set out as a note under this section], shall, as of the effective date of this Act [probably means July 10, 1984], be authorized under section 133 of title 28, United States Code [this section], and the incumbents of those offices shall henceforth hold their offices under section 133 [this section], as amended by this Act [Pub.L. 98–353]."

Section 1(a) of Pub.L. 95–486 provided that: "The President shall appoint, by and with the advice and consent of the Senate, three additional district judges for the northern district of Alabama, one additional district judge for the middle district of Alabama, three additional district judges for the district of Arizona, two additional district judges for the eastern district of Arkansas, one additional district judge for the northern district of California, three additional district judges for the eastern district of California, one additional district judge for the central district of California, two additional district judges for the southern district of California, two additional district judges for the district of Colorado, one additional district judge for the district of Connecticut, one additional district judge for the northern district of Florida, three additional district judges for the middle district of Florida, five additional district judges for the southern district of Florida, five additional district judges for the northern district of Georgia, one additional district judge for the southern district of Georgia, three additional district judges for the northern district of Illinois, one additional district judge for the central district of Illinois, one additional district judge for the northern district of Indiana, one additional district judge for the southern district of Indiana, one additional district judge for the southern district of Iowa, one additional district judge for the district of Kansas, two additional district judges for the eastern district of Kentucky, four additional judges for the eastern district of Louisiana, one additional district judge for the middle district of Louisiana, one additional district judge for the western district of Louisiana, one additional district judge for the district of Maine, two additional district judges for the district of Maryland, four additional district judges for the district of Massachusetts, three additional district judges for the eastern district of Michigan, two additional district judges for the western district of Michigan, one additional district judge for the district of Minnesota, one additional district judge for the eastern district of Missouri, two additional district judges for the western district of Missouri, one additional district judge for the district of Nevada, one additional district judge for the district of New Hampshire, two additional district judges for the district of New Jersey, one additional district judge for the district of New Mexico, one additional district judge for the northern district of New York, one additional district judge for the eastern district of New York, one additional district judge for the eastern district of North Carolina, one additional district judge for the middle district of North Carolina, one additional district judge for the western district of North Carolina, one additional district judge for the northern district of Ohio, one additional district judge for the southern district of Ohio, one additional district judge for the western district of Oklahoma, one additional district judge for the northern district of Oklahoma, two additional district judges for the district of Oregon, two additional district judges for the middle district of Pennsylvania, four additional district judges for the district of Puerto Rico, three additional district judges for the district of South Carolina, one additional district judge for the district of South Dakota, one additional district judge for the middle district of Tennessee, three additional district judges for the northern district of Texas, one additional district judge for the eastern district of Texas, five additional district judges for the southern district of Texas, one additional district judge for the western district of Texas, one additional district judge for the district of Utah, two additional district judges for the eastern district of Virginia, two additional district judges for the western district of Virginia, one additional district judge for the eastern district of Washington, one additional district judge for the western district of Washington, one additional district judge for the southern district of West Virginia, one additional district judge for the eastern district of Wisconsin, and one additional district judge for the western district of Wisconsin."

Section 2 of Pub.L. 95–486 provided that: "The President shall appoint, by and with the advice and consent of the Senate, one additional district judge for the eastern district of Kentucky, one additional district judge for the district of Minnesota, one additional district judge for the northern district of Ohio, and one additional district judge for the southern district of West Virginia. The first vacancy in the office of district judge in the judicial districts named in this section occurring five years or more after the effective date of this Act [Oct. 20, 1978] shall not be filled."

Section 1(a) of Pub.L. 91–272 provided that: "The President shall appoint, by and with the advice and consent of the Senate, one additional district judge for the northern district of Alabama, one additional district judge for the middle district of Alabama, one additional district judge for the district of Arizona, two additional district judges for the northern district of California, three additional district judges for the central district of California, three additional district judges for the southern district of California, one additional district judge for the district of Colorado, one additional district judge for the middle district of Florida, two additional district judges for the southern district of Florida, three additional district judges for the northern district of Georgia, one additional district judge for the southern district of Georgia, two additional district judges for the northern district of Illinois, one additional district judge for the eastern district of Kentucky, one additional district judge for the western district of Kentucky, two additional district judges for the eastern district of Louisiana, one additional district judge for the western district of Louisiana, two additional district judges for the district of Maryland, two additional district judges for the eastern district of Michigan, one additional district judge for the eastern district of Missouri, one additional district judge for the district of Nebraska, one additional district judge for the district of New Jersey, one additional district judge for the district of New Mexico, one additional district judge for the eastern district of New York, three additional district judges for the southern district of New York, one additional district judge for the northern district of Ohio, one additional district judge for the southern district of Ohio, six additional district judges for the eastern district of Pennsylvania, two additional district judges for the western district of Pennsylvania, one additional district judge for the district of Puerto Rico, one additional district judge for the district of South Carolina, one additional district judge for the western district of Tennessee, one additional district judge for the northern district of Texas, one additional district judge for the eastern district of Texas, one additional district judge for the southern district of Texas, one additional district judge for the western district of Texas, one additional district judge for the eastern district of Virginia, and one additional district judge for the southern district of West Virginia."

Section 2(a) of Pub.L. 89–372 provided that: "The President shall appoint, by and with the advice and consent of the Senate, one district judge for the middle and southern districts of Alabama, one additional district judge for the district of Arizona, one additional district judge for the northern district of Florida, one additional district judge for the middle district of Florida, two additional district judges for the southern district of Florida, one additional district judge for the northern district of Illinois, one additional district judge for the southern district of Indiana, four additional district judges for the eastern district of Louisiana, one additional district judge for the district of Maryland, one additional district judge for the northern district of Mississippi, one additional district judge for the southern district of Mississippi, one additional district judge for the western district of New York, one additional district judge for the northern district of Ohio, one additional district judge for the southern district of Ohio, one additional district judge for the district of Rhode Island, two additional district judges for the southern district of Texas, one additional district judge for the western district of Texas, two additional district judges for the eastern district of Virginia, and one additional district judge for the district of Vermont."

Section 2(a) of Pub.L. 87–36 provided that: "The President shall appoint, by and with the advice and consent of the Senate, one additional district judge for the northern district of Alabama, one additional district judge for the district of Alaska, one additional district judge for the district of Arizona, one additional district judge for the eastern and western districts of Arkansas, two additional district judges for the northern district of California, two additional district judges for the southern district of California, one additional district judge for the district of Colorado, two additional district judges for the district of Connecticut, two additional district judges for the southern district of Florida, one additional district judge for the northern district of Georgia, two additional district judges for the northern district of Illinois, one additional district judge for the northern district of Indiana, one additional district judge for the southern district of Indiana, one additional district judge for the northern and southern districts of Iowa, one additional district judge for the district of Kansas, two additional district judges for the eastern district of Louisiana, one additional district judge for the western district of Louisiana, two additional district judges for the district of Maryland, one additional district judge for the district of Massachusetts, two additional district judges for the eastern district of Michigan, one additional district judge for the southern district of Mississippi, one additional district judge for the western district of Missouri, one additional district judge for the district of Nevada, one additional district judge for the district of New Jersey, two additional district judges for the eastern district of New York, six additional district judges for the southern district of New York, one additional district judge for the eastern district of North Carolina, one additional district judge for the middle district of North Carolina, one additional district judge for the western district of North Carolina, one additional district judge for the northern district of Ohio, one additional district judge for the northern, eastern, and western districts of Oklahoma, three additional district judges for the eastern district of Pennsylvania, one additional district judge for the middle district of Pennsylvania, two additional district judges for the western district of Pennsylvania, one additional district judge for the district of Puerto Rico, one additional district judge for the eastern and western districts of South Carolina, one additional district judge for the eastern district of Tennessee, one additional district judge for the middle district of Tennessee, one additional district judge for the western district of Tennessee, two additional district judges for the northern district of Texas, one additional district judge for the southern district of Texas, one additional district judge for the western district of Texas, and one additional district judge for the eastern and western districts of Washington."

Subsec. (a)(1) of section 2 of Act Feb. 10, 1954, subsec. (a)(3) of which section amended the table in this section, provided for the appointment by the President, by and with the advice and consent of the Senate, of the additional judges for the districts for which additional permanent judgeships were provided in such amendment.

Alabama.—Section 1(b) of Pub.L. 91–272 provided that: "The existing district judgeship for the middle and southern districts of Alabama, heretofore provided for by section 133 of title 28 of the United States Code [this section], shall hereafter be a district judgeship for the southern district of Alabama only, and the present incumbent of such judgeship shall henceforth hold his office under such section 133, as amended by subsection (d) of this section."

California.—Section 3(h) of Pub.L. 89–372 provided that: "The President shall appoint, by and with the advice and consent of the Senate, three additional district judges for the central district of California, and two additional district judges for the northern district of California."

Delaware.—Act July 24, 1946, c. 602, 60 Stat. 654, which authorized the appointment of an additional judge for the district of Delaware was repealed by section 2 of Act Sept. 5, 1950, cited to text, which by section 1 of said Act Sept. 5, 1950, made the additional judgeship permanent. However, said section 2 also provided that the repeal in no way affected the tenure of the present incumbent.

Florida.—Section 2(b) of Pub.L. 89–372 provided that: "The existing district judgeship for the northern, middle and southern districts of Florida heretofore provided for by section 133 of title 28, United States Code [this section], shall hereafter be a district judgeship for the middle district of Florida only, and the present incumbent of such judgeship shall henceforth hold his office under section 133, as amended by this Act."

Georgia.—Act Mar. 29, 1949, c. 37, 63 Stat. 16, which authorized the appointment of an additional judge for the middle district, was repealed by section 2(b) of Pub.L. 87–36, which made the judgeship permanent and also provided that the incumbent of the judgeship created by Act Mar. 29, 1949, should henceforth hold his office under this section, as amended by Pub.L. 87–36, section 2(d).

Kansas.—Section 5(a) of Pub.L. 89–372, Mar. 18, 1966, 80 Stat. 78, which authorized the appointment of an additional district judge for the eastern district of Kansas and which provided that the first vacancy which occurred in the office of district judge in such district not be filled was repealed by section 1(c) of Pub.L. 91–272, June 2, 1970, 84 Stat. 294, which provided, in part, that such judgeship be a permanent judgeship and that the present incumbent henceforth hold his office under section 133 of title 28, United States Code [this section], as amended by section 1(d) of Pub.L. 91–272.

Missouri.—In connection with the permanent additional judgeship for the Eastern and Western Districts of Missouri, added by section 2(a), (2), (3) of Act Feb. 10, 1954, which previously had been authorized on a temporary basis by Act Dec. 24, 1942, c. 827, 56 Stat. 1083, section 2(b)(10) of Act Feb. 10, 1954, provided: "The present incumbent of the judgeship created by the Act entitled 'An Act to provide for the appointment of an additional district judge for the eastern and western districts of Missouri', approved December 24, 1942 (56 Stat. 1983), shall henceforth hold such office under section 133 of title 28 of the United States Code [this section] as amended by this Act."

Nevada.—Section 2(b)(2) of Act Feb. 10, 1954, provided: "The President shall appoint, by and with the advice and consent of the Senate, one additional district judge for the district of Nevada. The first vacancy occurring in the office of district judge in said district shall not be filled."

New Jersey.—Section 2(a) of Pub.L. 91–272 provided that: "The President shall appoint, by and with the advice and consent of the Senate, one additional district judge for the district of New Jersey. The first vacancy occurring in the office of district judge in that district shall not be filled."

New Mexico.—Act Feb. 10, 1954, c. 6, § 2(b)(1), 68 Stat. 10, which authorized the appointment of an additional judge for the district, was repealed by section 2(b) of Pub.L. 87–36, which made the judgeship permanent and also provided that the incumbent of the judgeship created by Act Feb. 10, 1954, should henceforth hold his office under this section, as amended by Pub.L. 87–36, § 2(d).

North Carolina.—Section 2(c) of Pub.L. 91–272 provided that: "The President shall appoint, by and with the advice and consent of the Senate, one additional district judge for the eastern district of North Carolina. The first vacancy occurring in the office of district judge in that district shall not be filled."

Ohio.—Act May 1, 1941, c. 83, 55 Stat. 148, which provided for the appointment of an additional judge for the northern district was repealed by Act Aug. 3, 1949, c. 387, § 2(e), 63 Stat. 495, which also provided that the incumbent of the judgeship created by said Act May 1, 1941, shall henceforth hold his office under this section, as amended by Act Aug. 3, 1949, § 2(a).

Section 2(e)(1), (2) of Pub.L. 87–36 provided that:

"(1) The President shall appoint, by and with the advice and consent of the Senate, one additional district judge for the southern district of Ohio. The first vacancy occurring in the office of district judge in said district shall not be filled.

"(2) The President shall appoint, by and with the advice and consent of the Senate, one additional district judge for the northern district of Ohio. The first vacancy occurring in the office of district judge in said district shall not be filled."

Oklahoma.—Act May 24, 1940, c. 209, § 2(a), 54 Stat. 219, providing for additional judgeships was amended by Act Aug. 3, 1949, c. 387, 63 Stat. 495, to strike out "western district of Oklahoma", and to make the incumbent of the judgeship created by said Act May 24, 1940, henceforth hold his office under this section, as amended by Act Aug. 3, 1949, § 2(a).

Pennsylvania.—Section 2(b) of Pub.L. 91–272 provided that: "The President shall appoint, by and with the advice and consent of the Senate, one additional district judge for the middle district of Pennsylvania. The first vacancy occurring in the office of district judge in that district shall not be filled."

Section 5(b) of Pub.L. 89–372, Mar. 18, 1966, 80 Stat. 78, as amended by Pub.L. 90–90, Sept. 23, 1967, 81 Stat. 228, which authorized the appointment of three additional district judges for the eastern district of Pennsylvania and which provided that the second, third, and fourth vacancies occurring after Mar. 18, 1966, in the office of district judge in such district not be filled was repealed by section 1(c) of Pub.L. 91–272, June 2, 1970, 84 Stat. 294, which provided, in part, that such judgeships be permanent judgeships and that the present incumbents henceforth hold their offices under section 133 of title 28, United States Code [this section], as amended by section 1(d) of Pub.L. 91–272.

Act Feb. 10, 1954, c. 6, § 2(b)(5), 68 Stat. 10, which authorized the appointment of an additional judge for the western district, was repealed by section 2(b) of Pub.L. 87–36, which made the judgeship permanent and also provided that the incumbent of the judgeship created by Act Feb. 10, 1954, should henceforth hold his office under this section, as amended by Pub.L. 87–36, section 2(d).

Section 2 of Act July 24, 1946, c. 600, 60 Stat. 654, as amended by section 6 of Act Feb. 10, 1954, c. 6, 68 Stat. 14, provided: "The President is authorized to appoint, by and with the advice and consent of the Senate, one additional United States district judge, who shall be an additional district judge for the eastern, middle, and western districts of Pennsylvania. The judge so appointed shall at the time of his appointment be a resident and a citizen of the State of Pennsylvania: *Provided*, That when a vacancy occurs in said office it shall not be filled: *Provided further*, That unless the President shall submit a nomination to the Senate to fill the office hereby created within ninety days after the effective date of this Act [July 24, 1946], then in that event this Act shall be of no force and effect. If a vacancy arises in the office of district judge for the middle district of Pennsylvania while the judge appointed pursuant to this section is holding the office created by this section, such judge shall thereafter be a district judge for the middle district of Pennsylvania."

Section 2(c) of Act Aug. 3, 1949, c. 387, 63 Stat. 495, which provided for an additional temporary judgeship for the western district of Pennsylvania was repealed by section 2 of Act Aug. 29, 1950, which by section 1 of said Act Aug. 29, 1950 made the additional judgeship permanent. However, said section 2 also provided that the repeal in no way affected the tenure of the present incumbent.

South Carolina.—Section 1(b) of Pub.L. 89–242 provided that: "The existing district judgeships for the Eastern District of South Carolina, the Western District of South Carolina, and the Eastern and Western Districts of South Carolina heretofore provided for by section 133 of title 28 of the United States Code [this section] shall hereafter be district judgeships for the District of South Carolina and the present incumbents of such judgeships shall henceforth hold their offices under section 133, as amended by this Act."

South Dakota.—Pub.L. 85–310 provided: "The President is authorized to appoint, by and with the advice and consent of the Senate an additional district judge for the district of South Dakota as authorized by paragraph (3) of section 2(b) of the Act of February 10, 1954 [set out as a note under this section]."

Section 2(b)(3) of Act Feb. 10, 1954, as amended by Pub.L. 85–310, Sept. 7, 1957, 71 Stat. 631, provided: "The President shall appoint, by and with the advice and consent of the Senate, one additional district judge for the district of South Dakota."

Tennessee.—Section 2(b)(4) of Act Feb. 10, 1954, provided: "The President shall appoint, by and with the advice and consent of the Senate, one additional district judge for the middle district of Tennessee. The first vacancy occurring in the office of district judge in said district shall not be filled."

Texas.—In connection with the permanent additional judgeship for the Southern District of Texas, added by section 2(a)(2), (3) of Act Feb. 10, 1954, which previously had been authorized on a temporary basis, section 2(b)(11) of Act Feb. 10, 1954, provided: "The present incumbent of the judgeship for the southern district of Texas created by section 2(d) of the Act entitled 'An Act to provide for the appointment of additional circuit and district judges, and for other purposes', approved August 3, 1949 (63 Stat. 495), shall henceforth hold such office under section 133 of title 28 of the United States Code [this section], as amended by this Act, and section 2(d) of the said Act approved August 3, 1949, is repealed."

Utah.—Act Feb. 10, 1954, c. 6, § 2(b)(6), 68 Stat. 11, which authorized the appointment of an additional judge for the district, was repealed by section 2(b) of Pub.L. 87–36, which made the judgeship permanent and also provided that the incumbent of the judgeship created by Act Feb. 10, 1954, should henceforth hold his office under this section, as amended by Pub.L. 87–36, § 2(d).

Virgin Islands.—Section 3(a) of Pub.L. 91–272 provided that: "The President shall appoint, by and with the advice and consent of the Senate, one additional judge for the District Court of the Virgin Islands, who shall hold office for the term of eight years and until his successor is chosen and qualified, unless sooner removed by the President for cause."

Washington.—Section 1(b) of Pub.L. 95–486 provided that: "The existing district judgeship for the eastern and western districts of Washington, heretofore provided for by section 133 of title 28 of the United States Code [this section], shall hereafter be a district judgeship for the western district of Washington only, and the present incumbent of such judgeship shall henceforth hold his office under section 133 [this section], as amended by this Act [Pub.L. 95–486]."

Section 2(c) of Pub.L. 87–36 provided that: "The existing district judgeship for the eastern and western districts of Washington, heretofore provided for by section 133 of title 28 of the United States Code [this section], shall hereafter be a district judgeship for the western district of Washington only, and the present incumbent of such judgeship shall henceforth hold his office under section 133 [this section], as amended by this Act [Pub.L. 87–36]."

West Virginia.—Section 2 of Pub.L. 97–471 provided that:

"**(a)** The existing district judgeship for the Southern District of West Virginia, authorized by section 2 of the Act entitled 'An Act to provide for the appointment of additional district and circuit judges and for other purposes', approved October 20, 1978 [Pub.L. 95–486] (92 Stat. 1632; 28 U.S.C. 133 note), shall, as of the date of enactment of this Act [Jan. 14, 1983], be authorized under section 133 of title 28 of the United States Code [this section] as a district judgeship for the Northern District of West Virginia, and the incumbent of that office shall henceforth hold office under section 133, as amended by this Act.

"**(b)** The existing district judgeship for the Northern and Southern Districts of West Virginia shall be authorized as the district judgeship for the Southern District."

In connection with the permanent additional judgeship for the Northern and Southern Districts of West Virginia, added by section 2(a)(2), (3) of Act Feb. 10, 1954, which previously had been authorized on a temporary basis by Act June 22, 1936, C. 695, 49 Stat. 1805, section (b)(12) of Act Feb. 10, 1954, provided: "The present incumbent of the judgeship created by the Act entitled 'An Act to provide for the appointment of an additional district judge for the northern and southern districts of West Virginia', approved June 22, 1936 (49 Stat. 1805), shall henceforth hold such office under section 133 of title 28 of the United States Code [this section], as amended by this Act."

Wisconsin.—Section 5(c) of Pub.L. 89–372, Mar. 18, 1966, 80 Stat. 78, which authorized the appointment of an additional district judge for the district of Wisconsin and which provided that the first vacancy occurring in the office of district judge in such district not be filled was repealed by section 1(c) of Pub.L. 91–272, June 2, 1970, 84 Stat. 294, which provided, in part, that such judgeship be a permanent judgeship and that the present incumbent henceforth hold his office under section 133 of title 28, United States Code [this section], as amended by section 1(d) of Pub.L. 91–272.

Nomination of Women and Blacks to Federal Judgeships

Section 8 of Pub.L. 95–486 provided that: "The Congress—

"**(1)** takes notice of the fact that only 1 percent of Federal judges are women and only 4 percent are blacks; and

"**(2)** suggests that the President, in selecting individuals for nomination to the Federal judgeships created by this Act [amending this section, sections 44, 46, 1337, and 1445 of this title, section 5108 of Title 5, Government Organization and Employees, enacting provisions set out as notes under this section, sections 41, 44 of this title, and amending provisions set out as notes under section 45 of this title], give due consideration to qualified individuals regardless of race, color, sex, religion, or national origin."

Residence of Additional Judge for Kansas

Section 2(b)(2) Act Aug. 3, 1949, provided that: "The judge first appointed for the district of Kansas under the authority contained in subsection (a) [amending this section] shall reside at Wichita."

§ 134. Tenure and residence of district judges

(a) The district judges shall hold office during good behavior.

(b) Each district judge, except in the District of Columbia, the Southern District of New York, and the Eastern District of New York, shall reside in the district or one of the districts for which he is appointed. Each district judge of the Southern District of New York and the Eastern District of New York may reside within 20 miles of the district to which he or she is appointed.

(c) If the public interest and the nature of the business of a district court require that a district judge should maintain his abode at or near a particular place for holding court in the district or within a particular part of the district the judicial council of the circuit may so declare and may make an appropriate order. If the district judges of such a district are unable to agree as to which of them shall maintain his abode at or near the place or within the area specified in such an order the judicial council of the circuit may decide which of them shall do so.

(June 25, 1948, c. 646, 62 Stat. 896; Aug. 3, 1949, c. 387, § 2(b)(1), 63 Stat. 495; Feb. 10, 1954, c. 6, § 2(b)(13)(a), 68 Stat. 12; Mar. 18, 1959, Pub.L. 86–3, § 9(c), 73 Stat. 8; May 19, 1961, Pub.L. 87–36, § 2(e)(3), 75 Stat. 83; Sept. 12, 1966, Pub.L. 89–571, § 1, 80 Stat. 764; Dec. 18, 1971, Pub.L. 92–208, § 3(e), 85 Stat. 742; Oct. 19, 1996, Pub.L. 104–317, Title VI, § 607, 110 Stat. 3860.)

HISTORICAL AND STATUTORY NOTES

Effective Dates

1971 Acts. Amendment by Pub.L. 92–208 effective one hundred and twenty days after Dec. 18, 1971, see section 3(f) of Pub.L. 92–208, set out as a note under section 98 of this title.

1959 Acts. Amendment by Pub.L. 86–3 effective upon the admission of Hawaii into the Union, see note set out under Section 133 of this title. Admission of Hawaii into the Union was accomplished Aug. 21, 1959 upon issuance of Proc. No. 3309, Aug. 21, 1959, 25 F.R. 6868, 73 Stat. c74, as required by Sections 1 and 7(c) of Pub.L. 86–3, Mar. 18, 1959, 73 Stat. 4, set out as notes preceding Section 491 of Title 48, Territories and Insular Possessions.

Applicability of Orders under 1954 Amendment

Section 2(b)(13)(b) of Act Feb. 10, 1954, provided: "Orders made by the judicial councils of the circuits under the second sentence of subsection (c) of section 134 of title 28 [this section], as amended by this section, determining that a specified district judge shall maintain his abode at or near a place or within an area which the council has theretofore designated for the abode of a district judge under the first sentence of such subsection, shall be applicable only to district judges appointed after the enactment of this Act [Feb. 10, 1954]."

Tenure and Salary Rights of Judges in Puerto Rico in Office on September 12, 1966

Section 4 of Pub.L. 89–571 provided that: "The amendments made by this section to sections 134 [this section] and 373 of title 28, United States Code [section 373 of this title], shall not affect the tenure of office or right to continue to receive salary after resignation, retirement, or failure of reappointment of any district judge for the district of Puerto Rico who is in office on the date of enactment of this Act [Sept. 12, 1966]."

§ 135. Salaries of district judges

Each judge of a district court of the United States shall receive a salary at an annual rate determined under section 225 of the Federal Salary Act of 1967 (2 U.S.C. 351–361), as adjusted by section 461 of this title.

(June 25, 1948, c. 646, 62 Stat. 897; Mar. 2, 1955, c. 9, § 1(c), 69 Stat. 10; Aug. 14, 1964, Pub.L. 88–426, Title IV, § 403(c), 78 Stat. 434; Aug. 9, 1975, Pub.L. 94–82, Title II, § 205(b)(3), 89 Stat. 422.)

HISTORICAL AND STATUTORY NOTES

References in Text

Section 225 of the Federal Salary Act of 1967, referred to in text, is section 225 of Pub.L. 90–206, Dec. 16, 1967, 81 Stat. 642, as amended, which is classified to Chapter 11 (section 351 et seq.) of Title 2, The Congress.

Effective Dates

1964 Acts. Amendment by Pub.L. 88–426 effective on the first day of the first pay period which begins on or after July 1, 1964, except to the extent provided in section 501(c) of Pub.L. 88–426, see section 501 of Pub.L. 88–426.

1955 Acts. Amendment by Act Mar. 2, 1955, effective Mar. 1, 1955, see section 5 of Act Mar. 2, 1955, set out as a note under section 31 of Title 2, The Congress.

Increase in Salaries

1998—Salaries of district judges increased to $136,700, effective on the first day of the first applicable pay period beginning on or after Jan. 1, 1998, by Ex. Ord. No. 13071, Dec. 29, 1997, 62 F.R. 68521, set out as a note under section 5332 of Title 5, Government Organization and Employees.

1997—Salaries of district judges continued at $133,600 effective on the first day of the first applicable pay period beginning on or after Jan. 1, 1997, by Ex. Ord. No. 13033, Dec. 27, 1996, 61 F.R. 68987, formerly set out as a note under section 5332 of Title 5, Government Organization and Employees.

1996—Salaries of district judges continued at $133,600 effective on the first day of the first applicable pay period beginning on or after Jan. 1, 1996, by Ex. Ord. No. 12984, Dec. 28, 1995, 61 F.R. 237, formerly set out as a note under section 5332 of Title 5, Government Organization and Employees.

1995—Salaries of district judges continued at $133,600 effective on the first day of the first applicable pay period beginning on or after Jan. 1, 1995, by Ex. Ord. No. 12944, Dec. 28, 1994, 60 F.R. 309, formerly set out as a note under section 5332 of Title 5, Government Organization and Employees.

1993—Salaries of district judges increased to $133,600 effective on the first day of the first applicable pay period beginning on or after Jan. 1, 1993, by Ex. Ord. No. 12826, Dec. 30, 1992, 57 F.R. 62909, formerly set out as a note under section 5332 of Title 5, Government Organization and Employees.

1992—Salaries of district judges increased to $129,500 per annum, effective on the first day of the first applicable pay period beginning on or after Jan. 1, 1992, by Ex. Ord. No. 12786, Dec. 26, 1991, 56 F.R. 67453, formerly set out as a note under section 5332 of Title 5.

1991—Salaries of district judges increased to $125,100 per annum, effective on the first day of the first applicable pay period beginning on or after Jan. 1, 1991, by Ex. Ord. No. 12736, Dec. 12, 1990, 55 F.R. 51385, formerly set out as a note under section 5332 of Title 5.

1990—Salaries of district judges continued at $89,500 per annum, and increased to $96,600, effective on first day of first pay period beginning on or after Jan. 31, 1990, by Ex. Ord. No. 12698, Dec. 23, 1989, 54 F.R. 53473, formerly set out as a note under section 5332 of Title 5.

1989—Salaries of district judges increased in the amount of 25 percent of their rates (as last in effect before the increase), effective Jan. 1, 1991, see Pub.L. 101–194, Title VII, § 703(a)(3), Nov. 30, 1989, 103 Stat. 1768, set out as a note under section 5318 of Title 5.

Salaries of district judges continued at $89,500 per annum, effective on the first day of the first applicable pay period beginning on or after Jan. 1, 1989, by Ex. Ord. No. 12663, Jan. 6, 1989, 54 F.R. 791, formerly set out as a note under section 5332 of Title 5.

1988—Salaries of district judges continued at $89,500 per annum, effective on the first day of the first applicable pay period beginning on or after Jan. 1, 1988, by Ex. Ord. No. 12622, Dec. 31, 1987, 53 F.R. 222, formerly set out as a note under section 5332 of Title 5.

1987—Salaries of district judges increased to $89,500 per annum, on recommendation of the President of the United States, see note set out under section 358 of Title 2, The Congress.

Salaries of district judges increased to $81,100, as required by section 406 of the Judiciary Appropriation Act, 1987, as incorporated in section 101(b) of Pub.L. 99–500 and section 101(b) of Pub.L. 99–591, effective on the first day of the first applicable pay period beginning on or after Jan. 1, 1987, by Ex. Ord. No. 12578, Dec. 31, 1986, 52 F.R. 505, formerly set out as a note under section 5332 of Title 5.

1985—Salaries of district judges increased to $78,700 effective on the first day of the first pay period beginning on or after Jan. 1, 1985, by Ex. Ord. No. 12496, Dec. 28, 1984, 50 F.R. 211, as amended by Ex. Ord. No. 12540, Dec. 30, 1985, 51 F.R. 577, formerly set out as a note under section 5332 of Title 5, Government Organization and Employees. Prior to its amendment by Ex. Ord. No. 12540, schedule 7 of Ex. Ord. No. 12496 had contained a footnote directing that, pursuant to section 140 of Pub.L. 97–92, set out as a note under section 461 of this title, funds were not available to pay a salary at a rate which exceeded the rate in effect on Dec. 15, 1981, which was $70,300.

See also section 2207 of Pub.L. 98–369, set out as a note under section 461 of this title, which provided for overall percentage adjustment increases in certain rates of pay under the General Schedule.

1984—Salaries of district judges increased to $76,000 effective on the first day of the first pay period beginning on or after Jan. 1, 1984, by Ex. Ord. No. 12456, Dec. 30, 1983, 49 F.R. 347, as amended Ex. Ord.No. 12477, May 23, 1984, 49 F.R. 22041; Ex. Ord. No. 12487, Sept. 14, 1984, 49 F.R. 36493, formerly set out as a note under section 5332 of Title 5.

1982—Salaries of district judges increased to $73,100 effective on the first day of the first pay period beginning on or after Oct. 1, 1982, by Ex. Ord. No. 12387, Oct. 8, 1982, 47 F.R. 44981, formerly set out as a note under section 5332 of Title 5, Government Organization and Employees. Ex. Ord. No. 12387 further provided that pursuant to section 140 of Pub.L. 97–92 funds are not available to pay a salary at a rate which exceeds the rate in effect on Dec. 15, 1981, which was $70,300.

Maximum rate payable after Dec. 17, 1982, increased from $70,300 to $73,100, see Pub.L. 97–377, Title I, § 129(b)–(d), Dec. 21, 1982, 96 Stat. 1914, set out as a note under section 5318 of Title 5.

Limitations on use of funds for fiscal year ending Sept. 30, 1983, appropriated by any Act to pay the salary or pay of any individual in legislative, executive, or judicial branch in position equal to or above level V of the Executive Schedule, see section 101(e) of Pub.L. 97–276, as amended, set out as a note under section 5318 of Title 5.

1981—Salaries of district judges increased to $70,300 effective on the first day of the first pay period beginning on or after Oct. 1, 1981, by Ex. Ord. No. 12330, Oct. 15, 1981, 46 F.R. 50921, formerly set out as a note under section 5332 of Title 5.

Limitations on use of funds for fiscal year ending Sept. 30, 1982, appropriated by any Act to pay the salary or pay of any individual in legislative, executive, or judicial branch in position equal to or above level V of the Executive Schedule, see sections 101(g) and 141 of Pub.L. 97–92, set out as a note under section 5318 of Title 5.

1980—Salaries of district judges increased to $67,100 effective on the first day of the first pay period beginning on or after Oct. 1, 1980, by Ex. Ord. No. 12248, Oct. 16, 1980, 45 F.R. 69199, formerly set out as a note under section 5332 of Title 5. Ex. Ord. No. 12248 further provided that pursuant to Pub.L. 96–369 funds are not available to pay a salary at a rate which exceeds the rate in effect on Sept. 30, 1980, which was $57,497.50.

Limitations on use of funds for fiscal year ending Sept. 30, 1981, appropriated by any Act to pay the salary or pay of any individual in legislative, executive, or judicial branch in position equal to or above level V of the Executive Schedule, see section 101(c) of Pub.L. 96–536, as amended, set out as a note under section 5318 of Title 5.

1979—Salaries of district judges increased to $61,500 effective on the first day of the first applicable pay period beginning on or after Oct. 1, 1979, by Ex. Ord. No. 12165, Oct. 9, 1979, 44 F.R. 58671, as amended by Ex. Ord. No. 12200, Mar. 12, 1980, 45 F.R. 16443, formerly set out as a note under section 5332 of Title 5. Ex. Ord. No. 12165 further provided that pursuant to Pub.L. 96–86 funds appropriated for fiscal year 1980 may not be used to pay a salary at a rate which exceeds an increase of 5.5 percent over the applicable rate payable for such position or office in effect on Sept. 30, 1978, which was $57,497.50 for district judges.

Applicability to funds appropriated by any Act for fiscal year ending Sept. 30, 1980, of limitation of section 304 of Pub.L. 95–391 on use of funds to pay the salary or pay of any individual in legislative, executive, or judicial branch in position equal to or above level V of the Executive Schedule, see section 101 of Pub.L. 96–86, set out as a note under section 5318 of Title 5.

1978—Salaries of district judges increased to $57,500 effective on the first day of the first pay period beginning on or after Oct. 1, 1978, by Ex. Ord. No. 12087, Oct. 7, 1978, 43 F.R. 46823, formerly set out as a note under section 5332 of Title 5. Ex. Ord. No. 12087, further provided that pursuant to the Legislative Branch Appropriation Act, 1979 [Pub.L. 95–391, Title III, § 304, Sept. 30, 1978, 92 Stat. 788, set out as a note under section 5318 of Title 5], funds are not available to pay a salary at a rate which exceeds the rate in effect on Sept. 30, 1978, which was $54,500.

1977—Salaries of district judges increased to $54,500 per annum, upon recommendation of the President of the United States, see note set out under section 358 of Title 2, The Congress.

1976—Salaries of district judges increased to $44,000 effective on the first day of the first pay period beginning on or after Oct. 1, 1976, by Ex. Ord. No. 11941, Oct. 1, 1976, 41 F.R. 43889, formerly set out as a note under section 5332 of Title 5, Government Organization and Employees. Ex. Ord. No. 11941, further provided that pursuant to the Legislative Branch Appropriation Act, 1977, funds are not available to pay a salary at a rate which exceeds the rate in effect on Sept. 30, 1976, which was $42,000.

1975—Salaries of district judges increased to $42,000 effective on the first day of the first pay period beginning on or after Oct. 1, 1975, by Ex. Ord. No. 11883, Oct. 6, 1975, 40 F.R. 47091, formerly set out as a note under section 5332 of Title 5.

1969—Salary of judge increased from $30,000 to $40,000 per annum, commencing February 14, 1969, upon recommendation of the President of the United States, see note set out under section 358 of Title 2, The Congress.

1946—The salary of the chief judge of District Court for the District of Columbia was increased from $10,500 to $15,500 a year, and the salaries of all other district court judges were increased from $10,000 to $15,000 by Act July 31, 1946, c. 704, § 1, 60 Stat. 716.

1926—Salary of the chief judge of the District Court of the District of Columbia was increased from $7,500 to $10,500 a year, and the salaries of all other district court judges was increased from $7,500 to $10,000 a year by Act Dec. 13, 1926, c. 6, § 1, 44 Stat. 919.

1919—Salaries of district court judges were increased from $6,000 to $7,500 a year by Act Feb. 25, 1919, c. 29, § 1, 40 Stat. 1156.

Salaries of the chief justice and associate justices of the Supreme Court of the District of Columbia, the forerunner of the District Court for the District of Columbia, were set at $5,000 by Act Mar. 3, 1901, c. 854, § 1, 30 Stat. 1199, and increased to $7,500 a year by Act Feb. 25, 1919, c. 29, § 1, 40 Stat. 1156.

1911—Salaries of district court judges had been set at $6,000 a year by the Judicial Code of 1911, Act Mar. 3, 1911, c. 231, § 1, 36 Stat. 1087.

§ 136. Chief judges; precedence of district judges

(a)(1) In any district having more than one district judge, the chief judge of the district shall be the district judge in regular active service who is senior in commission of those judges who—

(A) are sixty-four years of age or under;

(B) have served for one year or more as a district judge; and

(C) have not served previously as chief judge.

(2)(A) In any case in which no district judge meets the qualifications of paragraph (1), the youngest district judge in regular active service who is sixty-five years of age or over and who has served as district judge for one year or more shall act as the chief judge.

(B) In any case under subparagraph (A) in which there is no district judge in regular active service who has served as a district judge for one year or more, the district judge in regular active service who is senior in commission and who has not served previously as chief judge shall act as the chief judge.

(3)(A) Except as provided in subparagraph (C), the chief judge of the district appointed under paragraph (1) shall serve for a term of seven years and shall serve after expiration of such term until another judge is eligible under paragraph (1) to serve as chief judge of the district.

(B) Except as provided in subparagraph (C), a district judge acting as chief judge under subparagraph (A) or (B) of paragraph (2) shall serve until a judge has been appointed who meets the qualifications under paragraph (1).

(C) No district judge may serve or act as chief judge of the district after attaining the age of seventy years unless no other district judge is qualified to serve as chief judge of the district under paragraph (1) or is qualified to act as chief judge under paragraph (2).

(b) The chief judge shall have precedence and preside at any session which he attends.

Other district judges shall have precedence and preside according to the seniority of their commissions. Judges whose commissions bear the same date shall have precedence according to seniority in age.

(c) A judge whose commission extends over more than one district shall be junior to all district judges except in the district in which he resided at the time he entered upon the duties of his office.

(d) If the chief judge desires to be relieved of his duties as chief judge while retaining his active status as district judge, he may so certify to the Chief Justice of the United States, and thereafter, the chief judge of the district shall be such other district judge who is qualified to serve or act as chief judge under subsection (a).

(e) If a chief judge is temporarily unable to perform his duties as such, they shall be performed by the district judge in active service, present in the district and able and qualified to act, who is next in precedence.

(June 25, 1948, c. 646, 62 Stat. 897; Oct. 31, 1951, c. 655, § 37, 65 Stat. 723; Aug. 6, 1958, Pub.L. 85–593, § 2, 72 Stat. 497; Apr. 2, 1982, Pub.L. 97–164, Title II, § 202, 96 Stat. 52.)

HISTORICAL AND STATUTORY NOTES

Effective Dates

1982 Acts. Amendment by Pub.L. 97–164 effective Oct. 1, 1982, see section 402 of Pub.L. 97–164, set out as a note under section 171 of this title.

1958 Acts. Section 3 of Pub.L. 85–593 provided in part that the amendment to this section by Pub.L. 85–593 shall take effect at the expiration of one year from Aug. 6, 1958, see section 3 of Pub.L. 85–593, as amended, set out as a note under section 45 of this title.

Savings Provisions

Amendment of this section by Pub.L. 97–164 not to apply or affect any person serving as chief judge on the effective date of Pub.L. 97–164 [Oct. 1, 1982], and the provisions of subsec. (a) of this section as in effect on the day before the effective date of part A of Title II of Pub.L. 97–164 [Oct. 1, 1982] to apply to the chief judge of a district court serving on Oct. 1, 1982, see section 203 of Pub.L. 97–164, set out as a note under section 45 of this title.

Chief Justice of District Court for the District of Columbia to be known as Chief Judge

Section 2(a) of Act June 25, 1948, provided in part that the Chief Justice of the District Court for the District of Columbia in office on Sept. 1, 1948, shall thereafter be known as the Chief Judge.

§ 137. Division of business among district judges

The business of a court having more than one judge shall be divided among the judges as provided by the rules and orders of the court.

The chief judge of the district court shall be responsible for the observance of such rules and orders, and shall divide the business and assign the cases so far as such rules and orders do not otherwise prescribe.

If the district judges in any district are unable to agree upon the adoption of rules or orders for that purpose the judicial council of the circuit shall make the necessary orders.

(June 25, 1948, c. 646, 62 Stat. 897.)

§ 138. Terms abolished

The district court shall not hold formal terms.

(June 25, 1948, c. 646, 62 Stat. 897; Oct. 16, 1963, Pub.L. 88–139, § 1, 77 Stat. 248.)

§ 139. Times for holding regular sessions

The times for commencing regular sessions of the district court for transacting judicial business at the places fixed by this chapter shall be determined by the rules or orders of the court. Such rules or orders may provide that at one or more of such places the court shall be in continuous session for such purposes on all business days throughout the year. At other places a session of the court shall continue for such purposes until terminated by order of final adjournment or by commencement of the next regular session at the same place.

(June 25, 1948, c. 646, 62 Stat. 897; Oct. 16, 1963, Pub.L. 88–139, § 1, 77 Stat. 248.)

§ 140. Adjournment

(a) Any district court may, by order made anywhere within its district, adjourn or, with the consent of the judicial council of the circuit, pretermit any regular session of court for insufficient business or other good cause.

(b) If the judge of a district court is unable to attend and unable to make an order of adjournment, the clerk may adjourn the court to the next regular session or to any earlier day which he may determine.

(June 25, 1948, c. 646, 62 Stat. 897; Oct. 16, 1963, Pub.L. 88–139, § 1, 77 Stat. 248.)

§ 141. Special sessions; places; notice

Special sessions of the district court may be held at such places in the district as the nature of the business may require, and upon such notice as the court orders.

Any business may be transacted at a special session which might be transacted at a regular session.

(June 25, 1948, c. 646, 62 Stat. 897; Oct. 16, 1963, Pub.L. 88–139, § 1, 77 Stat. 248.)

[§ 142. Repealed. Pub.L. 97–164, Title I, § 115(c)(3), Apr. 2, 1982, 96 Stat. 32]

HISTORICAL AND STATUTORY NOTES

Section, Acts June 25, 1948, c. 646, 62 Stat. 898; Oct. 9, 1962, Pub.L. 87–764, 76 Stat. 762; Nov. 19, 1977, Pub.L. 95–196, 91 Stat. 1420, related to the providing of accommodations at places for holding court. See section 462 of this title.

Effective Date of Repeal

Repeal effective Oct. 1, 1982, see section 402 of Pub.L. 97–164, set out as an Effective Date of 1982 Amendment note under section 171 of this title.

Waiver of Limitations and Restrictions

The limitations and restrictions contained in this section prior to its repeal were waived with respect to the holding of court at certain places by the following Acts:

Pub. L. 87-833, Oct. 15, 1962, 76 Stat. 959, related to Akron, Ohio.

Pub. L. 87-699, Sept. 25, 1962, 76 Stat. 598, related to Richland, Washington.

Pub. L. 87-562, §4, July 30, 1962, 76 Stat. 248, related to Fort Meyers, Saint Petersburg, Fort Pierce, and West Palm Beach, Florida.

Pub. L. 87-560, July 27, 1962, 76 Stat. 247, related to Marshall, Texas.

Pub. L. 87-559, July 27, 1962, 76 Stat. 246, related to Decatur, Alabama.

Pub. L. 87-553, July 27, 1962, 76 Stat. 222, related to Winchester, Tennessee.

Pub. L. 87-551, July 27, 1962, 76 Stat. 221, related to Bridgeport, Connecticut.

Pub. L. 87-337, Oct. 3, 1961, 75 Stat. 750, related to Lafayette, Louisiana.

Pub. L. 87-36, §3(g), May 19, 1961, 75 Stat. 83, related to Kalamazoo, Michigan; Fayetteville, North Carolina; and Dyersburg, Tennessee.

Pub. L. 86-366, Sept. 22, 1959, 73 Stat. 647, related to Durant, Oklahoma.

Act July 20, 1956, c. 657, 70 Stat. 594, related to Bryson City, North Carolina.

Act Sept. 23, 1950, c. 1006, 64 Stat. 982, related to Klamath Falls, Oregon.

Act Aug. 21, 1950, c. 767, 64 Stat. 469, related to Newnan, Georgia.

Act Aug. 10, 1950, c. 675, § 2, 64 Stat. 438, related to Rock Island, Illinois.

Act Oct. 26, 1949, c. 744, 63 Stat. 923, related to Thomasville, Georgia.

Act Oct. 26, 1949, c. 740, 63 Stat. 921, related to Brunswick, Georgia.

§ 143. Vacant judgeship as affecting proceedings

When the office of a district judge becomes vacant, all pending process, pleadings and proceedings shall, when necessary, be continued by the clerk until a judge is appointed or designated to hold such court. (June 25, 1948, c. 646, 62 Stat. 898.)

§ 144. Bias or prejudice of judge

Whenever a party to any proceeding in a district court makes and files a timely and sufficient affidavit that the judge before whom the matter is pending has a personal bias or prejudice either against him or in favor of any adverse party, such judge shall proceed no further therein, but another judge shall be assigned to hear such proceeding.

The affidavit shall state the facts and the reasons for the belief that bias or prejudice exists, and shall be filed not less than ten days before the beginning of the term at which the proceeding is to be heard, or good cause shall be shown for failure to file it within such time. A party may file only one such affidavit in any case. It shall be accompanied by a certificate of counsel of record stating that it is made in good faith. (June 25, 1948, c. 646, 62 Stat. 898; May 24, 1949, c. 139, § 65, 63 Stat. 99.)

CHAPTER 6—BANKRUPTCY JUDGES

Sec.
151. Designation of bankruptcy courts.
152. Appointment of bankruptcy judges.
153. Salaries; character of service.
154. Division of business; chief judge.[1]
155. Temporary transfer of bankruptcy judges.
156. Staff; expenses.
157. Procedures.
158. Appeals.

[1] So in original. Does not conform to section catchline.

HISTORICAL AND STATUTORY NOTES

Codifications

Chapter heading and section analysis of chapter 6, as added by Pub.L. 95–598, Title II, § 201(a), Nov. 6, 1978, 92 Stat. 2657, and amended Pub.L. 97–164, Title I, § 110(d), Apr. 2, 1982, 96 Stat. 29, effective June 28, 1984, pursuant to Pub.L. 95–598, Title IV, § 402(b), Nov. 6, 1978, 92 Stat. 2682, as amended by Pub.L. 98–249, § 1(a), Mar. 31, 1984, 98 Stat. 116; Pub.L. 98–271, § 1(a), Apr. 30, 1984, 98 Stat. 163; Pub.L. 98–299, § 1(a), May 25, 1984, 98 Stat. 214; Pub.L. 98–325, § 1(a), June 20, 1984, 98 Stat. 268, set out as a note preceding section 101 of Title 11, Bankruptcy, read as follows:

CHAPTER 6—BANKRUPTCY COURTS

Sec.
151. Creation and composition of bankruptcy courts.
152. Appointment of bankruptcy judges.
153. Tenure and residence of bankruptcy judges.
154. Salaries of bankruptcy judges.
155. Chief judge; precedence of bankruptcy judges.
156. Division of business among bankruptcy judges.
157. Times of holding court.
158. Accommodations at places for holding court.
159. Vacant judgeship as affecting proceedings.
160. Appellate panels.

Section 402(b) of Pub.L. 95–598 was amended by section 113 of Pub.L. 98–353 by substituting "shall not be effective" for "shall take effect on June 28, 1984", thereby eliminating the addition of the chapter heading and section analysis of chapter 6 by section 201(a) of Pub.L. 95–598, effective June

27, 1984, pursuant to section 122(c) of Pub.L. 98–353, set out as an Effective Dates note under section 151 of this title.

Section 121(a) of Pub.L. 98–353 directed that section 402(b) of Pub.L. 95–598 be amended by substituting "the date of enactment of the Bankruptcy Amendments and Federal Judgeship Act of 1984 [i.e. July 10, 1984]" for "June 28, 1984". This amendment was not executed in view of the prior amendment to section 402(b) of Pub.L. 95–598 by section 113 of Pub.L. 98–353.

Courts During Transition

Pub.L. 95–598, Title IV, § 404, Nov. 6, 1978, 92 Stat. 2683, as amended by Pub.L. 98–249, § 1(b), Mar. 31, 1984, 98 Stat. 116; Pub.L. 98–271, § 1(b), Apr. 30, 1984, 98 Stat. 163; Pub.L. 98–299, § 1(b), May 25, 1984, 98 Stat. 214; Pub.L. 98–325, § 1(b), June 20, 1984, 98 Stat. 268; Pub.L. 98–353, Title I, § 121(b), July 10, 1984, 98 Stat. 345, which provided that, for purposes of Pub.L. 95–598, which enacted Title 11, Bankruptcy, and the amendments made by Pub.L. 95–598, the courts of bankruptcy as defined under section 1(10) of former Title 11, created by section 11(a) of former Title 11, and existing on Sept. 30, 1979, continue to be courts of bankruptcy during the transition period beginning Oct. 1, 1979, and ending June 27, 1984, made provision for extension of the term of office of referees in bankruptcy serving on Nov. 6, 1978, and for such a referee to have the title of United States bankruptcy judge, established for each State a merit screening committee to pass on qualifications of such a referee and determine if the term of such referee should be extended, and set forth the rules and provisions applicable to United States bankruptcy judges during the transition period, was repealed by Pub.L. 98–353, Title I, § 114, 122(a), July 10, 1984, 98 Stat. 343, 346, eff. July 10, 1984.

[Section 121(b) of Pub.L. 98–353 purported to amend section 404 of Pub.L. 95–598 by substituting "the day before the date of enactment of the Bankruptcy Amendments and Federal Judgeship Act of 1984 [i.e. July 9, 1984]" for "June 27, 1984" each place it appeared. This amendment was not executed as the probable intent of Congress in view of the repeal of section 404 of Pub.L. 95–598 by section 114 of Pub.L. 98–353.]

Extension and Termination of Term of Office of Bankruptcy Judge Serving on June 27, 1984

Section 121(e) of Pub.L. 98–353 provided that: "The term of office of any bankruptcy judge who was serving on June 27, 1984, is extended to and shall expire at the end of the day of enactment of this Act [July 10, 1984]."

[Section 121(e) of Pub.L. 98–353 effective June 27, 1984, see section 122(c) of Pub.L. 98–353, set out as an Effective Dates note under section 151 of this title.]

For prior extensions of the term of office of bankruptcy judges see:

Pub.L. 98–325, § 2, June 20, 1984, 98 Stat. 268.

Pub.L. 98–299, § 2, May 25, 1984, 98 Stat. 214.

Pub.L. 98–271, § 2, Apr. 30, 1984, 98 Stat. 163.

Pub.L. 98–249, § 2, Mar. 31, 1984, 98 Stat. 116.

Judicial Administration During Transition

Pub.L. 95–598, Title IV, § 407, Nov. 6, 1978, 92 Stat. 2686, which provided that the Director of the Administrative Office of the United States Courts appoint a committee of not fewer than seven United States bankruptcy judges to advise the Director with respect to matters arising during the transition period, or that are relevant to the purposes of the transition period, and directed that during the transition period, the chief judge of each circuit summon at least one bankruptcy judge from each judicial district within the circuit to the judicial conference of such circuit called and held under section 332 of this title, was repealed by Pub.L. 98–353, Title I, §§ 114, 122(a), July 10, 1984, 98 Stat. 343, 346, eff. July 10, 1984.

Transition Study

Pub.L. 95–598, Title IV, § 406, Nov. 6, 1978, 92 Stat. 2686, as amended by Pub.L. 98–249, § 1(c), Mar. 31, 1984, 98 Stat. 116; Pub.L. 98–271, § 1(c), Apr. 30, 1984, 98 Stat. 163; Pub.L. 98–299, § 1(c), May 25, 1984, 98 Stat. 214; Pub.L. 98–325, § 1(c), June 20, 1984, 98 Stat. 268; Pub.L. 98–353, Title I, § 121(c), July 10, 1984, 98 Stat. 346, which provided that during the transition period, Oct. 1, 1979 to June 27, 1984, the Director of the Administrative Office of the United States Courts make continuing studies and surveys in the judicial districts to determine the number of bankruptcy judges needed after June 27, 1984, to provide for the expeditious and effective administration of justice, their regular places of offices, and the places where the court will be held, and that the Director report to the judicial councils of the circuits and the Judicial Conference of the United States his recommendations, the judicial councils advise the Conference stating their recommendations, and the Conference advise the Congress and the President, before Jan. 3, 1983, the number of bankruptcy judges needed after June 27, 1984, and the locations at which they were to serve, was repealed by Pub.L. 98–353, Title I, §§ 114, 122(a), July 10, 1984, 98 Stat. 343, 346 eff. July 10, 1984.

[Section 121(c) of Pub.L. 98–353 purported to amend section 406 of Pub.L. 95–598 by substituting "the day before the date of enactment of the Bankruptcy Amendments and Federal Judgeship Act of 1984 [i.e. July 9, 1984]" for "June 27, 1984" each place it appeared. This amendment was not executed as the probable intent of Congress in view of the repeal of section 406 of Pub.L. 95–598 by section 114 of Pub.L. 98–353.]

§ 151. Designation of bankruptcy courts

In each judicial district, the bankruptcy judges in regular active service shall constitute a unit of the district court to be known as the bankruptcy court for that district. Each bankruptcy judge, as a judicial officer of the district court, may exercise the authority conferred under this chapter with respect to any action, suit, or proceeding and may preside alone and hold a regular or special session of the court, except as otherwise provided by law or by rule or order of the district court.

(Added Pub.L. 98–353, Title I, § 104(a), July 10, 1984, 98 Stat. 336.)

HISTORICAL AND STATUTORY NOTES

Codifications

This section as added by Pub.L. 95–598, Title II, § 201(a), Nov. 6, 1978, 92 Stat. 2657, effective June 28, 1984, pursuant to Pub.L. 95–598, Title IV, § 402(b), Nov. 6, 1978, 92 Stat. 2682, as amended by Pub.L. 98–249, § 1(a), Mar. 31, 1984, 98

Stat. 116; Pub.L. 98–271, § 1(a), Apr. 30, 1984, 98 Stat. 163; Pub.L. 98–299, § 1(a), May 25, 1984, 98 Stat. 214; Pub.L. 98–325, § 1(a), June 20, 1984, 98 Stat. 268, set out as a note preceding section 101 of Title 11, Bankruptcy, read as follows:

§ 151. Creation and composition of bankruptcy courts

(a) There shall be in each judicial district, as an adjunct to the district court for such district, a bankruptcy court which shall be a court of record known as the United States Bankruptcy Court for the district.

(b) Each bankruptcy court shall consist of the bankruptcy judge or judges for the district in regular active service. Justices or judges designated and assigned shall be competent to sit as judges of the bankruptcy court.

(c) Except as otherwise provided by law, or rule or order of court, the judicial power of a bankruptcy court with respect to any action, suit or proceeding may be exercised by a single bankruptcy judge, who may preside alone and hold a regular or special session of court at the same time other sessions are held by other bankruptcy judges.

Section 402(b) of Pub.L. 95–598 was amended by section 113 of Pub.L. 98–353 by substituting "shall not be effective" for "shall take effect on June 28, 1984", thereby eliminating the addition of section 151 by section 201(a) of Pub.L. 95–598, effective June 27, 1984, pursuant to section 122(c) of Pub.L. 98–353, set out as an Effective Dates note under this section.

Section 121(a) of Pub.L. 98–353 directed that section 402(b) of Pub.L. 95–598 be amended by substituting "the date of enactment of the Bankruptcy Amendments and Federal Judgeship Act of 1984 [i.e. July 10, 1984]" for "June 28, 1984". This amendment was not executed in view of the prior amendment to section 402(b) of Pub.L. 95–598 by section 113 of Pub.L. 98–353.

Effective Dates

1984 Acts. Section 122 of Title I of Pub.L. 98–353 provided that:

"**(a)** Except as otherwise provided in this section, this title and the amendments made by this title [Title I of Pub.L. 98–353, enacting this chapter, and sections 1408 to 1412 and 1452 of this title, amending sections 372, 634, 957, 1334, 1360, and 1930 of this title, sections 8331, 8334, 8336, 8339, 8341, and 8344 of Title 5, Government Organization and Employees, and section 105 of Title 11, Bankruptcy, enacting provisions set out as notes preceding section 151 of this title and under sections 151, 152, 153, 634, and 1334 of this title and section 8331 of Title 5, amending provisions set out as notes preceding sections 151 and 1471 of this title and section 101 of Title 11, and repealing provisions set out as notes preceding this section and section 1471 of this title] shall take effect on the date of the enactment of this Act [July 10, 1984].

"**(b)** Section 1334(c)(2) of title 28, United States Code [section 1334(c)(2) of this title], and section 1411(a) of title 28, United States Code, as added by this Act [section 1411(a) of this title], shall not apply with respect to cases under title 11 of the United States Code [Title 11] that are pending on the date of enactment of this Act [July 10, 1984], or to proceedings arising in or related to such cases.

"**(c)** Sections 108(b) [enacting provisions set out as a note under section 634 of this title], 113 [amending section 402(b) of Pub.L. 95–598, set out as a note preceding section 101 of Title 11], and 121(e) [enacting provisions set out as a note preceding section 151 of this title] shall take effect on June 27, 1984."

Separability of Provisions

Section 119 of Pub.L. 98–353 provided that: "If any provision of this Act [see Short Title of 1984 Amendments note set out under this section] or the application thereof to any person or circumstance is held invalid, the remainder of this Act, or the application of that provision to persons or circumstances other than those as to which it is held invalid, is not affected thereby."

Short Title

1984 Amendments. Section 1 of Pub.L. 98–353 provided: That this Act [enacting this chapter and sections 1408 to 1412 and 1452 of this title and sections 557, 558, 559, and 1113 of Title 11, Bankruptcy, amending sections 44, 98, 131, 133, 371, 372, 634, 957, 1334, 1360, and 1930 of this title, sections 8331, 8334, 8336, 8339, 8341, 8344, 8701, 8706, 8714a, and 8714b of Title 5, Government Organization and Employees, and sections 101, 102, 103, 105, 108, 109, 303, 321, 322, 326, 327, 328, 329, 330, 342, 343, 345, 346, 349, 350, 361, 362, 363, 365, 366, 501, 502, 503, 505, 506, 507, 509, 510, 521, 522, 523, 524, 525, 541, 542, 543, 544, 545, 546, 547, 548, 549, 550, 552, 553, 554, 555, 702, 703, 704, 707, 723, 724, 725, 726, 727, 728, 741, 745, 752, 761, 763, 764, 765, 766, 901, 902, 903, 921, 922, 927, 943, 945, 1102, 1103, 1105, 1106, 1107, 1108, 1112, 1121, 1123, 1124, 1125, 1126, 1127, 1129, 1141, 1142, 1144, 1145, 1146, 1166, 1168, 1169, 1170, 1171, 1173, 1301, 1302, 1304, 1307, 1322, 1324, 1325, 1326, 1328, 1329, 15103, and 151302 of Title 11, Bankruptcy Rules 2002 and 3001, Title 11, and Bankruptcy Form No. 1, Title 11, enacting provisions set out as notes preceding section 151 of this title and under sections 44, 133, 151, 152, 153, 371, 634, 1334, and 2075 of this title, sections 8331 and 8706 of Title 5, and preceding section 101 and sections 101, 365, and 1113 of Title 11, amending provisions set out as notes preceding sections 151, 581 and 1471 of this title and section 101 of Title 11, and repealing provisions set out as notes preceding this section and section 1471 of this title] may be cited as the 'Bankruptcy Amendments and Federal Judgeship Act of 1984'."

§ 152. Appointment of bankruptcy judges

(a)(1) The United States court of appeals for the circuit shall appoint bankruptcy judges for the judicial districts established in paragraph (2) in such numbers as are established in such paragraph. Such appointments shall be made after considering the recommendations of the Judicial Conference submitted pursuant to subsection (b). Each bankruptcy judge shall be appointed for a term of fourteen years, subject to the provisions of subsection (e). However, upon the expiration of the term, a bankruptcy judge may, with the approval of the judicial council of the circuit, continue to perform the duties of the office until the earlier of the date which is 180 days after the expiration of the term or the date of the appointment of a successor. Bankruptcy judges shall serve as judicial officers of the United States district court established under Article III of the Constitution.

(2) The bankruptcy judges appointed pursuant to this section shall be appointed for the several judicial districts as follows:

Districts	Judges
Alabama:	
Northern	5
Middle	2
Southern	2
Alaska	2
Arizona	7
Arkansas:	
Eastern and Western	3
California:	
Northern	9
Eastern	6
Central	21
Southern	4
Colorado	5
Connecticut	3
Delaware	1
District of Columbia	1
Florida:	
Northern	1
Middle	8
Southern	5
Georgia:	
Northern	8
Middle	2
Southern	2
Middle and Southern	1
Hawaii	1
Idaho	2
Illinois:	
Northern	10
Central	3
Southern	1
Indiana:	
Northern	3
Southern	4
Iowa:	
Northern	2
Southern	2
Kansas	4
Kentucky:	
Eastern	2
Western	3
Louisiana:	
Eastern	2
Middle	1
Western	3
Maine	2
Maryland	4
Massachusetts	5
Michigan:	
Eastern	4
Western	3
Minnesota	4
Mississippi:	
Northern	1
Southern	2
Missouri:	
Eastern	3
Western	3
Montana	1
Nebraska	2
Nevada	3
New Hampshire	1
New Jersey	8
New Mexico	2
New York:	
Northern	2
Southern	9
Eastern	6
Western	3
North Carolina:	
Eastern	2
Middle	2
Western	2
North Dakota	1
Ohio:	
Northern	8
Southern	7
Oklahoma:	
Northern	2
Eastern	1
Western	3
Oregon	5
Pennsylvania:	
Eastern	5
Middle	2
Western	4
Puerto Rico	2
Rhode Island	1
South Carolina	2
South Dakota	2
Tennessee:	
Eastern	3
Middle	3
Western	4
Texas:	
Northern	6
Eastern	2
Southern	6
Western	4
Utah	3
Vermont	1
Virginia:	
Eastern	5
Western	3
Washington:	
Eastern	2
Western	5
West Virginia:	
Northern	1

Districts	Judges
Southern	1
Wisconsin:	
Eastern	4
Western	2
Wyoming	1

(3) Whenever a majority of the judges of any court of appeals cannot agree upon the appointment of a bankruptcy judge, the chief judge of such court shall make such appointment.

(4) The judges of the district courts for the territories shall serve as the bankruptcy judges for such courts. The United States court of appeals for the circuit within which such a territorial district court is located may appoint bankruptcy judges under this chapter for such district if authorized to do so by the Congress of the United States under this section.

(b)(1) The Judicial Conference of the United States shall, from time to time, and after considering the recommendations submitted by the Director of the Administrative Office of the United States Courts after such Director has consulted with the judicial council of the circuit involved, determine the official duty stations of bankruptcy judges and places of holding court.

(2) The Judicial Conference shall, from time to time, submit recommendations to the Congress regarding the number of bankruptcy judges needed and the districts in which such judges are needed.

(3) Not later than December 31, 1994, and not later than the end of each 2-year period thereafter, the Judicial Conference of the United States shall conduct a comprehensive review of all judicial districts to assess the continuing need for the bankruptcy judges authorized by this section, and shall report to the Congress its findings and any recommendations for the elimination of any authorized position which can be eliminated when a vacancy exists by reason of resignation, retirement, removal, or death.

(c) Each bankruptcy judge may hold court at such places within the judicial district, in addition to the official duty station of such judge, as the business of the court may require.

(d) With the approval of the Judicial Conference and of each of the judicial councils involved, a bankruptcy judge may be designated to serve in any district adjacent to or near the district for which such bankruptcy judge was appointed.

(e) A bankruptcy judge may be removed during the term for which such bankruptcy judge is appointed, only for incompetence, misconduct, neglect of duty, or physical or mental disability and only by the judicial council of the circuit in which the judge's official duty station is located. Removal may not occur unless a majority of all of the judges of such council concur in the order of removal. Before any order of removal may be entered, a full specification of charges shall be furnished to such bankruptcy judge who shall be accorded an opportunity to be heard on such charges.

(Added Pub.L. 98–353, Title I, § 104(a), July 10, 1984, 98 Stat. 336, and amended Pub.L. 99–554, Title I, § 101, Oct. 27, 1986, 100 Stat. 3088; Pub.L. 100–587, Nov. 3, 1988, 102 Stat. 2982; Pub.L. 101–650, Title III, § 304, Dec. 1, 1990, 104 Stat. 5105; Pub.L. 102–361, §§ 2, 4, Aug. 26, 1992, 106 Stat. 965, 966.)

HISTORICAL AND STATUTORY NOTES

Codifications

This section as added by Pub.L. 95–598, Title II, § 201(a), Nov. 6, 1978, 92 Stat. 2657, effective June 28, 1984, pursuant to Pub.L. 95–598, Title IV, § 402(b), Nov. 6, 1978, 92 Stat. 2682, as amended by Pub.L. 98–249, § 1(a), Mar. 31, 1984, 98 Stat. 116; Pub.L. 98–271, § 1(a), Apr. 30, 1984, 98 Stat. 163; Pub.L. 98–299, § 1(a), May 25, 1984, 98 Stat. 214; Pub.L. 98–325, § 1(a), June 20, 1984, 98 Stat. 268, set out as a note preceding section 101 of Title 11, Bankruptcy, read as follows:

§ 152. Appointment of bankruptcy judges

The President shall appoint, by and with the advice and consent of the Senate, bankruptcy judges for the several judicial districts. In each instance, the President shall give due consideration to the recommended nominee or nominees of the Judicial Council of the Circuit within which an appointment is to be made.

Section 402(b) of Pub.L. 95–598 was amended by section 113 of Pub.L. 98–353 by substituting "shall not be effective" for "shall take effect on June 28, 1984", thereby eliminating the addition of section 152 by section 201(a) of Pub.L. 95–598, effective June 27, 1984, pursuant to section 122(c) of Pub.L. 98–353, set out as an Effective Date note under section 151 of this title.

Section 121(a) of Pub.L. 98–353 directed that section 402(b) of Pub.L. 95–598 be amended by substituting "the date of enactment of the Bankruptcy Amendments and Federal Judgeship Act of 1984 [i.e. July 10, 1984]" for "June 28, 1984". This amendment was not executed in view of the prior amendment to section 402(b) of Pub.L. 95–598 by section 113 of Pub.L. 98–353.

Effective Dates

1986 Acts. Amendment by Pub.L. 99–554 effective on Oct. 27, 1986, see section 302(b) of Pub.L. 99–554, set out as a note under section 581 of this title.

1984 Acts. Section effective July 10, 1984, see section 122(a) of Pub.L. 98–353, set out as a note under section 151 of this title.

Appointment to Fill Vacancies; Nominations; Qualifications

Section 120 of Pub.L. 98–353, as amended by Pub.L. 99–554, Title I, § 102, Oct. 22, 1986, 100 Stat. 3089; Pub.L. 104–317, Title III, § 303, Oct. 19, 1996, 110 Stat. 3852, provided that:

"(a)(1) Whenever a court of appeals is authorized to fill a vacancy that occurs on a bankruptcy court of the United States, such court of appeals shall appoint to fill that vacancy a person whose character, experience, ability, and impartiality qualify such person to serve in the Federal judiciary.

"(2) It is the sense of the Congress that the courts of appeals should consider for appointment under section 152 of title 28, United States Code [this section], to the first vacancy which arises after the date of the enactment of this Act [July 10, 1984] in the office of each bankruptcy judge, the bankruptcy judge who holds such office immediately before such vacancy arises, if such bankruptcy judge requests to be considered for such appointment.

"(3) When filling vacancies, the court of appeals may consider reappointing incumbent bankruptcy judges under procedures prescribed by regulations issued by the Judicial Conference of the United States.

"(b) The judicial council of the circuit involved shall assist the court of appeals by evaluating potential nominees and by recommending to such court for consideration for appointment to each vacancy on the bankruptcy court persons who are qualified to be bankruptcy judges under regulations prescribed by the Judicial Conference of the United States. In the case of the first vacancy which arises after the date of the enactment of this Act [July 10, 1984] in the office of each bankruptcy judge, such potential nominees shall include the bankruptcy judge who holds such office immediately before such vacancy arises, if such bankruptcy judge requests to be considered for such appointment and the judicial council determines that such judge is qualified under subsection (c) of this section to continue to serve. Such potential nominees shall receive consideration equal to that given all other potential nominees for such position. All incumbent nominees seeking reappointment thereafter may be considered for such a reappointment, pursuant to a majority vote of the judges of the appointing court of appeals, under procedures authorized under subsection (a)(3).

"(c) Before transmitting to the court of appeals the names of the persons the judicial council for the circuit deems best qualified to fill any existing vacancy, the judicial council shall have determined that—

"(1) public notice of such vacancy has been given and an effort has been made, in the case of each such vacancy, to identify qualified candidates, without regard to race, color, sex, religion, or national origin,

"(2) such persons are members in good standing of at least one State bar, the District of Columbia bar, or the bar of the Commonwealth of Puerto Rico, and members in good standing of every other bar of which they are members,

"(3) such persons possess, and have a reputation for, integrity and good character,

"(4) such persons are of sound physical and mental health,

"(5) such persons possess and have demonstrated commitment to equal justice under law,

"(6) such persons possess and have demonstrated outstanding legal ability and competence, as evidenced by substantial legal experience, ability to deal with complex legal problems, aptitude for legal scholarship and writing, and familiarity with courts and court processes, and

"(7) such persons [sic] demeanor, character, and personality indicate that they would exhibit judicial temperament if appointed to the position of United States bankruptcy judge."

Extension and Termination of Term of Office of Bankruptcy Judge and Part-Time Bankruptcy Judge Serving on July 10, 1984; Practice of Law by Part-Time Bankruptcy Judge

Section 106 of Pub.L. 98–353 provided that:

"(a) Notwithstanding section 152 of title 28, United States Code, as added by this Act [this section], the term of office of a bankruptcy judge who is serving on the date of enactment of this Act [July 10, 1984] is extended to and expires four years after the date such bankruptcy judge was last appointed to such office or on October 1, 1986, whichever is later.

"(b)(1) Notwithstanding section 153(a) of title 28, United States Code, as added by this Act [section 153(a) of this title], and notwithstanding subsection (a) of this section, a bankruptcy judge serving on a part-time basis on the date of enactment of this Act [July 10, 1984] may continue to serve on such basis for a period not to exceed two years from the date of enactment of this Act [July 10, 1984].

"(2) Notwithstanding the provisions of section 153(b) of title 28, United States Code [section 153(b) of this title], a bankruptcy judge serving on a part-time basis may engage in the practice of law but may not engage in any other practice, business, occupation, or employment inconsistent with the expeditious, proper, and impartial performance of such bankruptcy judge's duties as a judicial officer. The Judicial Conference of the United States may promulgate appropriate rules and regulations to implement this paragraph."

Extension and Termination of Term of Office of Part-Time Bankruptcy Judge Serving on July 2, 1986, In District of Oregon, Western District of Michigan, and Eastern District of Oklahoma

Pub.L. 99–349, Title I, July 2, 1986, 100 Stat. 718, provided that: "Notwithstanding the provisions of section 106(b)(1) of the Bankruptcy Amendments and Federal Judgeship Act of 1984 [section 106(b)(1) of Pub.L. 98–353, set out as a note under this section], a bankruptcy judge serving on a part-time basis on the date of enactment of this Act [July 2, 1986] may continue to serve as a part-time judge for such district until December 31, 1986, or until such time as a full-time bankruptcy judge for such district is appointed, whichever is earlier: *Provided,* That these provisions shall apply only to part-time bankruptcy judges serving in the district of Oregon, the western district of Michigan, and the eastern district of Oklahoma."

Temporary Appointment of Additional Judges

Section 3 of Pub.L. 102–361, as amended Pub.L. 104–317, Title III, § 307, Oct. 19, 1996, 110 Stat. 3852, provided that:

"(a) **Appointments.**—The following bankruptcy judges shall be appointed in the manner prescribed in section 152(a)(1) of title 28, United States Code [subsec. (a)(1) of this section]:

"(1) 1 additional bankruptcy judge for the northern district of Alabama.

"(2) 1 additional bankruptcy judge for the district of Colorado.

"(3) 1 additional bankruptcy judge for the district of Delaware.

"(4) 1 additional bankruptcy judge for the southern district of Illinois.

"(5) 1 additional bankruptcy judge for the district of New Hampshire.

"(6) 1 additional bankruptcy judge for the middle district of North Carolina.

"(7) 1 additional bankruptcy judge for the district of Puerto Rico.

"(8) 1 additional bankruptcy judge for the district of South Carolina.

"(9) 1 additional bankruptcy judge for the eastern district of Tennessee.

"(10) 1 additional bankruptcy judge for the western district of Texas.

"**(b) Vacancies.**—The first vacancy in the office of bankruptcy judge in each of the judicial districts set forth in subsection (a), resulting from the death, retirement, resignation, or removal of a bankruptcy judge, and occurring 5 years or more after the appointment date of the judge named to fill the temporary judgeship position shall not be filled. In the case of a vacancy resulting from the expiration of the term of a bankruptcy judge not described in the preceding sentence, that judge shall be eligible for reappointment as a bankruptcy judge in that district."

§ 153. Salaries; character of service

(a) Each bankruptcy judge shall serve on a full-time basis and shall receive as full compensation for his services, a salary at an annual rate that is equal to 92 percent of the salary of a judge of the district court of the United States as determined pursuant to section 135, to be paid at such times as the Judicial Conference of the United States determines.

(b) A bankruptcy judge may not engage in the practice of law and may not engage in any other practice, business, occupation, or employment inconsistent with the expeditious, proper, and impartial performance of such bankruptcy judge's duties as a judicial officer. The Conference may promulgate appropriate rules and regulations to implement this subsection.

(c) Each individual appointed under this chapter shall take the oath or affirmation prescribed by section 453 of this title before performing the duties of the office of bankruptcy judge.

(d) A bankruptcy judge appointed under this chapter shall be exempt from the provisions of subchapter I of chapter 63 of title 5.

(Added Pub.L. 98–353, Title I, § 104(a), July 10, 1984, 98 Stat. 338, and amended Pub.L. 100–202, § 101(a) [Title IV, § 408(a)], Dec. 22, 1987, 101 Stat. 1329–26; Pub.L. 100–702, Title X, § 1003(a)(1), Nov. 19, 1988, 102 Stat. 4665.)

HISTORICAL AND STATUTORY NOTES

Codifications

This section as added by Pub.L. 95–598, Title II, § 201(a), Nov. 6, 1978, 92 Stat. 2657, effective June 28, 1984, pursuant to Pub.L. 95–598, Title IV, § 402(b), Nov. 6, 1978, 92 Stat. 2682, as amended by Pub.L. 98–249, § 1(a), Mar. 31, 1984, 98 Stat. 116; Pub.L. 98–271, § 1(a), Apr. 30, 1984, 98 Stat. 163; Pub.L. 98–299, § 1(a), May 25, 1984, 98 Stat. 214; Pub.L. 98–325, § 1(a), June 20, 1984, 98 Stat. 268, set out as a note preceding section 101 of Title 11, Bankruptcy, read as follows:

§ 153. Tenure and residence of bankruptcy judges

(a) Each bankruptcy judge shall hold office for a term of 14 years, but may continue to perform the duties of his office until his successor takes office, unless such office has been eliminated.

(b) Removal of a bankruptcy judge during the term for which he is appointed shall be only for incompetency, misconduct, neglect of duty, or physical or mental disability. Removal shall be by the judicial council of the circuit or circuits in which the bankruptcy judge serves, but removal may not occur unless a majority of all the judges of such circuit council or councils concur in the order of removal. Before any order of removal may be entered, a full specification of the charges shall be furnished to the bankruptcy judge, and he shall be accorded an opportunity to be heard on the charges. Any cause for removal of any bankruptcy judge coming to the knowledge of the Director of the Administrative Office of the United States Courts shall be reported by him to the chief judge of the circuit or circuits in which he serves, and a copy of the report shall at the same time be transmitted to the circuit council or councils and to the bankruptcy judge.

(c) Each bankruptcy judge shall reside in the district or one of the districts for which he is appointed, or within 20 miles of his official station.

(d) If the public interest and the nature of the business of a bankruptcy court require that a bankruptcy judge should maintain his abode at or near a particular part of the district the judicial council of the circuit may so declare and may make an appropriate order. If the bankruptcy judges of such a district are unable to agree as to which of them shall maintain his abode at or near the place or within the area specified in such an order the judicial council of the circuit may decide which of them shall do so.

Section 402(b) of Pub.L. 95–598 was amended by section 113 of Pub.L. 98–353 by substituting "shall not be effective" for "shall take effect on June 28, 1984", thereby eliminating the addition of section 153 by section 201(a) of Pub.L. 95–598, effective June 27, 1984, pursuant to section 122(c) of Pub.L. 98–353, set out as an Effective Date note under section 151 of this title.

Section 121(a) of Pub.L. 98–353 directed that section 402(b) of Pub.L. 95–598 be amended by substituting "the date of enactment of the Bankruptcy Amendments and Federal Judgeship Act of 1984 [i.e. July 10, 1984]" for "June 28, 1984". This amendment was not executed in view of the prior amendment to section 402(b) of Pub.L. 95–598 by section 113 of Pub.L. 98–353.

Effective Dates

1987 Acts. Section 101(a) [Title IV, § 408(d)] of Pub.L. 100–202 provided that: "This section [amending this section, section 634 of this title, and section 356 of Title 2, The Congress] shall become effective October 1, 1988, and any salary affected by the provisions of this section shall be adjusted at the beginning of the first applicable pay period commencing on or after such date of enactment [probably should read "such date", meaning Oct. 1, 1988]."

1984 Acts. Section effective July 10, 1984, see section 122(a) of Pub.L. 98–353, set out as a note under section 151 of this title.

Continuation of Salaries of Bankruptcy Judges in Effect on June 27, 1984

Section 105(a) of Pub.L. 98–353 provided that: "The salary of a bankruptcy judge in effect on June 27, 1984, shall remain in effect until changed as a result of a determination or adjustment made pursuant to section 153(a) of title 28, United States Code, as added by this Act [subsec. (a) of this section]."

Increase in Salaries

1988—Salaries of bankruptcy judges continued at $72,500 per annum by Ex. Ord. No. 12622, Dec. 31, 1987, 53 F.R. 222, formerly set out as a note under section 5332 of Title 5, Government Organization and Employees.

1987—Salaries of bankruptcy judges increased to $72,500 per annum, on recommendation of the President of the United States, see note set out under section 358 of Title 2, The Congress.

Salaries of bankruptcy judges increased to $70,500 effective on the first day of the first pay period beginning on or after January 1, 1987, by Ex. Ord. No. 12578, Dec. 31, 1986, 52 F.R. 505, formerly set out as a note under section 5332 of Title 5.

1985—Salaries of bankruptcy judges increased to $68,400 effective on the first day of the first pay period beginning on or after Jan. 1, 1985, by Ex. Ord. No. 12496, Dec. 28, 1984, 50 F.R. 211, as amended by Ex. Ord. No. 12540, Dec. 30, 1985, 51 F.R. 577, formerly set out as a note under section 5332 of Title 5.

1984—Salaries of bankruptcy judges (full-time) and bankruptcy judges (part-time) (maximum rate) increased to $66,100 and $33,100, respectively, effective on the first day of the first pay period beginning on or after Jan. 1, 1984, by Ex. Ord. No. 12456, Dec. 30, 1983, 49 F.R. 347, as amended Ex. Ord. No. 12477, May 23, 1984, 49 F.R. 22041; Ex. Ord. No. 12487, Sept. 14, 1984, 49 F.R. 36493, formerly set out as a note under section 5332 of Title 5.

1982—Salaries of bankruptcy judges and referees in bankruptcy (full-time), or referees in bankruptcy (part-time) (maximum rate) increased to $63,600 and $31,800, respectively, effective on the first day of the first pay period beginning on or after Oct. 1, 1982, by Ex. Ord. No. 12387, Oct. 8, 1982, 47 F.R. 44981, formerly set out as a note under section 5332 of Title 5, Government Organization and Employees. Ex. Ord. No. 12387 further provided that pursuant to section 101(e) of Pub.L. 97–276 funds are not available to pay a salary at a rate which exceeds the rate in effect on Sept. 30, 1982, which was $58,500 for bankruptcy judges and referees in bankruptcy (full-time), and $30,600 for referees in bankruptcy (part-time) (maximum rate).

Maximum rate payable to bankruptcy judges after Dec. 17, 1982, increased from $58,500 to $63,600, see Pub.L. 97–377, Title I, § 129(b)–(d), Dec. 21, 1982, 96 Stat. 1914, set out as a note under section 5318 of Title 5.

1981—Salaries of bankruptcy judges and referees in bankruptcy (full-time), or referees in bankruptcy (part-time) (maximum rate) increased to $61,200 and $30,600, respectively, effective on the first day of the first pay period beginning on or after Oct. 1, 1981, by Ex. Ord. No. 12330, Oct. 15, 1981, 46 F.R. 50921, formerly set out as a note under section 5332 of Title 5. Ex. Ord. No. 12330 further provided that pursuant to section 101(c) of Pub.L. 97–51 funds are not available to pay a salary at a rate which exceeds the rate in effect on Sept. 30, 1981, which was $51,167.50 for bankruptcy judges and referees in bankruptcy (full-time), and $25,583.75 for referees in bankruptcy (part-time) (maximum rate).

1980—Salaries of bankruptcy judges and referees in bankruptcy (full-time), or referees in bankruptcy (part-time) (maximum rate) increased to $58,400 and $29,200, respectively, effective on the first day of the first pay period beginning on or after Oct. 1, 1980, by Ex. Ord. No. 12248, Oct. 16, 1980, 45 F.R. 69199, formerly set out as a note under section 5332 of Title 5. Ex. Ord. No. 12248 further provided that pursuant to section 101(c) of Pub.L. 96–369 funds are not available to pay a salary which exceeds the rate in effect on Sept. 30, 1980, which was $51,167.50 for bankruptcy judges and referees in bankruptcy (full-time), and $25,583.75 for referees in bankruptcy (part-time) (maximum rate).

For limitations on use of funds for period Oct. 1, 1980 through June 5, 1981, appropriated by any Act to pay the salary or pay of any individual in legislative, executive, or judicial branch in position equal to or above level V of the Executive Schedule, see section 101(c) of Pub.L. 96–369 and section 101(c) of Pub.L. 96–536, set out as notes under section 5318 of Title 5.

1979—Salaries of bankruptcy judges increased to $53,500 effective on the first day of the first applicable pay period beginning on or after Oct. 1, 1979, by Ex. Ord. No. 12165, Oct. 9, 1979, 44 F.R. 58671, as amended by Ex. Ord. No. 12200, Mar. 12, 1980, 45 F.R. 16443, formerly set out as a note under section 5332 of Title 5. Ex. Ord. No. 12165 further provided that pursuant to Pub.L. 96–86 funds appropriated for fiscal year 1980 may not be used to pay a salary at a rate which exceeds an increase of 5.5 percent over the applicable rate payable for such position or office in effect on Sept. 30, 1978, which was $51,167.50 for bankruptcy judges.

Part–Time Bankruptcy Judges

For provision that notwithstanding subsecs. (a) and (b) of this section, a bankruptcy judge serving on a part-time basis on July 10, 1984, may continue to serve on such basis for two years from such date, and may engage in the practice of law, see section 106 of Pub.L. 98–353, set out as a note under section 152 of this title.

Transition Provisions

Section 1003(b) of Pub.L. 100–702 provided that:

"(1) If an individual who is exempted from the Leave Act by operation of amendments under this section [amending this section and sections 156, 631, 634, 712, 752, and 794 of this title] and who was previously subject to the provisions of subchapter I of chapter 63 of title 5, United States Code [section 6301 et seq. of Title 5, Government Organization and Employees], without a break in service, again becomes subject to this subchapter on completion of his service as an exempted officer, the unused annual leave and sick leave standing to his credit when he was exempted from this subchapter is deemed to have remained to his credit.

"(2) In computing an annuity under section 8339 of title 5, United States Code [section 8339 of Title 5], the total service of a person specified in paragraph (1) of this subsection who retired on an immediate annuity or dies leaving a survivor or survivors entitled to an annuity includes, without regard to the limitations imposed by subsection (f) of section 8339 of title 5, United States Code [section 8339(f) of Title 5], the days of unused sick leave standing to his credit when he was exempted from subchapter I of chapter 63 of title 5, United States Code [section 6301 et seq. of Title 5], except that these days will not be counted in determining average pay or annuity eligibility."

§ 154. Division of businesses; chief judge

(a) Each bankruptcy court for a district having more than one bankruptcy judge shall by majority vote promulgate rules for the division of business among the bankruptcy judges to the extent that the division of business is not otherwise provided for by the rules of the district court.

(b) In each district court having more than one bankruptcy judge the district court shall designate one judge to serve as chief judge of such bankruptcy court. Whenever a majority of the judges of such district court cannot agree upon the designation as chief judge, the chief judge of such district court shall make such designation. The chief judge of the bankruptcy court shall ensure that the rules of the bankruptcy court and of the district court are observed and that the business of the bankruptcy court is handled effectively and expeditiously.

(Added Pub.L. 98–353, Title I, § 104(a), July 10, 1984, 98 Stat. 339.)

HISTORICAL AND STATUTORY NOTES

Codifications

This section as added by Pub.L. 95–598, Title II, § 201(a), Nov. 6, 1978, 92 Stat. 2657, effective June 28, 1984, pursuant to Pub.L. 95–598, Title IV, § 402(b), Nov. 6, 1978, 92 Stat. 2682, as amended by Pub.L. 98–249, § 1(a), Mar. 31, 1984, 98 Stat. 116; Pub.L. 98–271, § 1(a), Apr. 30, 1984, 98 Stat. 163; Pub.L. 98–299, § 1(a), May 25, 1984, 98 Stat. 214; Pub.L. 98–325, § 1(a), June 20, 1984, 98 Stat. 268, set out as a note preceding section 101 of Title 11, Bankruptcy, read as follows:

§ 154. Salaries of bankruptcy judges

Each judge of a bankruptcy court shall receive a salary at an annual rate of $50,000, subject to adjustment under section 225 of the Federal Salary Act of 1967 (2 U.S.C. 351–361), and section 461 of this title.

Section 402(b) of Pub.L. 95–598 was amended by section 113 of Pub.L. 98–353 by substituting "shall not be effective" for "shall take effect on June 28, 1984", thereby eliminating the addition of section 154 by section 201(a) of Pub.L. 95–598, effective June 27, 1984, pursuant to section 122(c) of Pub.L. 98–353, set out as an Effective Date note under section 151 of this title.

Section 121(a) of Pub.L. 98–353 directed that section 402(b) of Pub.L. 95–598 be amended by substituting "the date of enactment of the Bankruptcy Amendments and Federal Judgeship Act of 1984 [i.e. July 10, 1984]" for "June 28, 1984". This amendment was not executed in view of the prior amendment to section 402(b) of Pub.L. 95–598 by section 113 of Pub.L. 98–353.

Effective Dates

1984 Acts. Section effective July 10, 1984, see section 122(a) of Pub.L. 98–353, set out as a note under section 151 of this title.

§ 155. Temporary transfer of bankruptcy judges

(a) A bankruptcy judge may be transferred to serve temporarily as a bankruptcy judge in any judicial district other than the judicial district for which such bankruptcy judge was appointed upon the approval of the judicial council of each of the circuits involved.

(b) A bankruptcy judge who has retired may, upon consent, be recalled to serve as a bankruptcy judge in any judicial district by the judicial council of the circuit within which such district is located. Upon recall, a bankruptcy judge may receive a salary for such service in accordance with regulations promulgated by the Judicial Conference of the United States, subject to the restrictions on the payment of an annuity in section 377 of this title or in subchapter III of chapter 83, and chapter 84, of title 5 which are applicable to such judge.

(Added Pub.L. 98–353, Title I, § 104(a), July 10, 1984, 98 Stat. 339, and amended Pub.L. 99–651, Title II, § 202(a), Nov. 14, 1986, 100 Stat. 3648; Pub.L. 100–659, § 4(a), Nov. 15, 1988, 102 Stat. 3918.)

HISTORICAL AND STATUTORY NOTES

Codifications

This section as added by Pub.L. 95–598, Title II, § 201(a), Nov. 6, 1978, 92 Stat. 2658, effective June 28, 1984, pursuant to Pub.L. 95–598, Title IV, § 402(b), Nov. 6, 1978, 92 Stat. 2682, as amended by Pub.L. 98–249, § 1(a), Mar. 31, 1984, 98 Stat. 116; Pub.L. 98–271, § 1(a), Apr. 30, 1984, 98 Stat. 163; Pub.L. 98–299, § 1(a), May 25, 1984, 98 Stat. 214; Pub.L. 98–325, § 1(a), June 20, 1984, 98 Stat. 268, set out as a note preceding section 101 of Title 11, Bankruptcy, read as follows:

§ 155. Chief judge; precedence of bankruptcy judges

(a) In each district having more than one judge the bankruptcy judge in regular active service who is senior in commission and under seventy years of age shall be the chief judge of the bankruptcy court. If all the bankruptcy judges in regular active service are 70 years of age or older the youngest shall act as chief judge until a judge has been appointed and qualified who is under 70 years of age, but a judge may not act as chief judge until he has served as a bankruptcy judge for one year.

(b) The chief judge shall have precedence and preside at any session which he attends.

Other bankruptcy judges shall have precedence and preside according to the seniority of their commissions. Judges whose commissions bear the same date shall have precedence according to seniority in age.

(c) A judge whose commission extends over more than one district shall be junior to all bankruptcy judges except in the district in which he resided at the time he entered upon the duties of his office.

(d) If a chief judge desires to be relieved of his duties as chief judge while retaining his active status as a bankruptcy judge, he may so certify to the chief judge of the court of appeals for the circuit in which the bankruptcy judge serves, and thereafter the bankruptcy judge in active service next in precedence and willing to serve shall be designated by the chief judge of the court of appeals as the chief judge of the bankruptcy court.

(e) If a chief judge is temporarily unable to perform his duties as such, they shall be performed by the bankruptcy judge in active service, present in the district and able and qualified to act, who is next in precedence.

(f) Service as a referee in bankruptcy or as a bankruptcy judge under the Bankruptcy Act shall be taken into account in the determination of seniority of commission under this section.

Section 402(b) of Pub.L. 95–598 was amended by section 113 of Pub.L. 98–353 by substituting "shall not be effective" for "shall take effect on June 28, 1984", thereby eliminating the addition of section 155 by section 201(a) of Pub.L. 95–598, effective June 27, 1984, pursuant to section 122(c) of Pub.L. 98–353, set out as an Effective Date note under section 151 of this title.

Section 121(a) of Pub.L. 98–353 directed that section 402(b) of Pub.L. 95–598 be amended by substituting "the date of enactment of the Bankruptcy Amendments and Federal Judgeship Act of 1984 [i.e. July 10, 1984]" for "June 28, 1984". This amendment was not executed in view of the prior amendment to section 402(b) of Pub.L. 95–598 by section 113 of Pub.L. 98–353.

Effective Dates

1988 Acts. Amendment to this section by Pub.L. 100–659 to take effect on Nov. 15, 1988, and shall apply to bankruptcy judges and magistrates who retire on or after Nov. 15, 1988, with special election provisions for bankruptcy judges, etc., who left office on or after July 31, 1987, and before Nov. 15, 1988, see section 9 of Pub.L. 100–659, set out as a note under section 377 of this title.

1986 Acts. Section 203 of Title II of Pub.L. 99–651 provided that: "This title and the amendments made by this title [enacting section 375 of this title, and amending sections 155, 374, 631, 633, 636, and 797 of this title] take effect on January 1, 1987."

1984 Acts. Section effective July 10, 1984, see section 122(a) of Pub.L. 98–353, set out as a note under section 151 of this title.

§ 156. Staff; expenses

(a) Each bankruptcy judge may appoint a secretary, a law clerk, and such additional assistants as the Director of the Administrative Office of the United States Courts determines to be necessary. A law clerk appointed under this section shall be exempt from the provisions of subchapter I of chapter 63 of title 5, unless specifically included by the appointing judge or by local rule of court.

(b) Upon certification to the judicial council of the circuit involved and to the Director of the Administrative Office of the United States Courts that the number of cases and proceedings pending within the jurisdiction under section 1334 of this title within a judicial district so warrants, the bankruptcy judges for such district may appoint an individual to serve as clerk of such bankruptcy court. The clerk may appoint, with the approval of such bankruptcy judges, and in such number as may be approved by the Director, necessary deputies, and may remove such deputies with the approval of such bankruptcy judges.

(c) Any court may utilize facilities or services, either on or off the court's premises, which pertain to the provision of notices, dockets, calendars, and other administrative information to parties in cases filed under the provisions of title 11, United States Code, where the costs of such facilities or services are paid for out of the assets of the estate and are not charged to the United States. The utilization of such facilities or services shall be subject to such conditions and limitations as the pertinent circuit council may prescribe.

(d) No office of the bankruptcy clerk of court may be consolidated with the district clerk of court office without the prior approval of the Judicial Conference and the Congress.

(e) In a judicial district where a bankruptcy clerk has been appointed pursuant to subsection (b), the bankruptcy clerk shall be the official custodian of the records and dockets of the bankruptcy court.

(f) For purposes of financial accountability in a district where a bankruptcy clerk has been certified, such clerk shall be accountable for and pay into the Treasury all fees, costs, and other monies collected by such clerk except uncollected fees not required by an Act of Congress to be prepaid. Such clerk shall make returns thereof to the Director of the Administrative Office of the United States Courts and the Director of the Executive Office For United States Trustees, under regulations prescribed by such Directors.

(Added Pub.L. 98–353, Title I, § 104(a), July 10, 1984, 98 Stat. 339, and amended Pub.L. 99–554, Title I, §§ 103, 142, 144(a), Oct. 27, 1986, 100 Stat. 3090, 3096; Pub.L. 100–702, Title X, § 1003(a)(3), Nov. 19, 1988, 102 Stat. 4665.)

HISTORICAL AND STATUTORY NOTES

Codifications

This section as added by Pub.L. 95–598, Title II, § 201(a), Nov. 6, 1978, 92 Stat. 2659, effective June 28, 1984, pursuant to Pub.L. 95–598, Title IV, § 402(b), Nov. 6, 1978, 92 Stat. 2682, as amended by Pub.L. 98–249, § 1(a), Mar. 31, 1984, 98 Stat. 116; Pub.L. 98–271, § 1(a), Apr. 30, 1984, 98 Stat. 163; Pub.L. 98–299, § 1(a), May 25, 1984, 98 Stat. 214; Pub.L. 98–325, § 1(a), June 20, 1984, 98 Stat. 268, set out as a note preceding section 101 of Title 11, Bankruptcy, read as follows:

§ 156. Division of business among bankruptcy judges

The business of a bankruptcy court having more than one judge shall be divided among the judges as provided by the rules and orders of the court.

The chief judge of the bankruptcy court shall be responsible for the observance of such rules and orders, and shall divide the business and assign the cases so far as such rules and orders do not otherwise prescribe.

If the bankruptcy judges in any district are unable to agree upon the adoption of rules or orders for that purpose the judicial council of the circuit shall make the necessary orders.

Section 402(b) of Pub.L. 95–598 was amended by section 113 of Pub.L. 98–353 by substituting "shall not be effective" for "shall take effect on June 28, 1984", thereby eliminating the addition of section 156 by section 201(a) of Pub.L. 95–598, effective June 27, 1984, pursuant to section 122(c) of Pub.L. 98–353, set out as an Effective Date note under section 151 of this title.

Section 121(a) of Pub.L. 98–353 directed that section 402(b) of Pub.L. 95–598 be amended by substituting "the date of enactment of the Bankruptcy Amendments and Federal Judgeship Act of 1984 [i.e. July 10, 1984]" for "June 28, 1984". This amendment was not executed in view of the prior amendment to section 402(b) of Pub.L. 95–598 by section 113 of Pub.L. 98–353.

Effective Dates

1986 Acts. Amendment of subsec. (d) by section 103 of Pub.L. 99–554 effective on Oct. 27, 1986, see section 302(b) of Pub.L. 99–554, set out as a note under section 581 of this title.

Enactment of subsecs. (e) and (f) by sections 142 and 144(a) of Pub.L. 99–554 effective 30 days after Oct. 27, 1986, except as otherwise provided for, see section 302(a) of Pub.L. 99–554, set out as a note under section 581 of this title.

1984 Acts. Section effective July 10, 1984, see section 122(a) of Pub.L. 98–353, set out as a note under section 151 of this title.

§ 157. Procedures

(a) Each district court may provide that any or all cases under title 11 and any or all proceedings arising under title 11 or arising in or related to a case under title 11 shall be referred to the bankruptcy judges for the district.

(b)(1) Bankruptcy judges may hear and determine all cases under title 11 and all core proceedings arising under title 11, or arising in a case under title 11, referred under subsection (a) of this section, and may enter appropriate orders and judgments, subject to review under section 158 of this title.

(2) Core proceedings include, but are not limited to—

(A) matters concerning the administration of the estate;

(B) allowance or disallowance of claims against the estate or exemptions from property of the estate, and estimation of claims or interests for the purposes of confirming a plan under chapter 11, 12, or 13 of title 11 but not the liquidation or estimation of contingent or unliquidated personal injury tort or wrongful death claims against the estate for purposes of distribution in a case under title 11;

(C) counterclaims by the estate against persons filing claims against the estate;

(D) orders in respect to obtaining credit;

(E) orders to turn over property of the estate;

(F) proceedings to determine, avoid, or recover preferences;

(G) motions to terminate, annul, or modify the automatic stay;

(H) proceedings to determine, avoid, or recover fraudulent conveyances;

(I) determinations as to the dischargeability of particular debts;

(J) objections to discharges;

(K) determinations of the validity, extent, or priority of liens;

(L) confirmations of plans;

(M) orders approving the use or lease of property, including the use of cash collateral;

(N) orders approving the sale of property other than property resulting from claims brought by the estate against persons who have not filed claims against the estate; and

(O) other proceedings affecting the liquidation of the assets of the estate or the adjustment of the debtor-creditor or the equity security holder relationship, except personal injury tort or wrongful death claims.

(3) The bankruptcy judge shall determine, on the judge's own motion or on timely motion of a party, whether a proceeding is a core proceeding under this subsection or is a proceeding that is otherwise related to a case under title 11. A determination that a proceeding is not a core proceeding shall not be made solely on the basis that its resolution may be affected by State law.

(4) Non-core proceedings under section 157(b)(2)(B) of title 28, United States Code, shall not be subject to the mandatory abstention provisions of section 1334(c)(2).

(5) The district court shall order that personal injury tort and wrongful death claims shall be tried in the district court in which the bankruptcy case is pending, or in the district court in the district in which the claim arose, as determined by the district court in which the bankruptcy case is pending.

(c)(1) A bankruptcy judge may hear a proceeding that is not a core proceeding but that is otherwise related to a case under title 11. In such proceeding, the bankruptcy judge shall submit proposed findings of fact and conclusions of law to the district court, and any final order or judgment shall be entered by the district judge after considering the bankruptcy judge's proposed findings and conclusions and after reviewing de novo those matters to which any party has timely and specifically objected.

(2) Notwithstanding the provisions of paragraph (1) of this subsection, the district court, with the consent of all the parties to the proceeding, may refer a proceeding related to a case under title 11 to a bankruptcy judge to hear and determine and to enter appropriate orders and judgments, subject to review under section 158 of this title.

(d) The district court may withdraw, in whole or in part, any case or proceeding referred under this section, on its own motion or on timely motion of any party, for cause shown. The district court shall, on timely motion of a party, so withdraw a proceeding if the court determines that resolution of the proceeding requires consideration of both title 11 and other laws of the United States regulating organizations or activities affecting interstate commerce.

(e) If the right to a jury trial applies in a proceeding that may be heard under this section by a bankruptcy judge, the bankruptcy judge may conduct the jury trial if specially designated to exercise such jurisdiction by the district court and with the express consent of all the parties.

(Added Pub.L. 98–353, Title I, § 104(a), July 10, 1984, 98 Stat. 340, and amended Pub.L. 99–554, Title I, §§ 143, 144(b), Oct. 27, 1986, 100 Stat. 3096; Pub.L. 103–394, Title I, § 112, Oct. 22, 1994, 108 Stat. 4117.)

HISTORICAL AND STATUTORY NOTES

Codifications

This section as added by Pub.L. 95–598, Title II, § 201(a), Nov. 6, 1978, 92 Stat. 2659, effective June 28, 1984, pursuant to Pub.L. 95–598, Title IV, § 402(b), Nov. 6, 1978, 92 Stat. 2682, as amended by Pub.L. 98–249, § 1(a), Mar. 31, 1984, 98 Stat. 116; Pub.L. 98–271, § 1(a), Apr. 30, 1984, 98 Stat. 163; Pub.L. 98–299, § 1(a), May 25, 1984, 98 Stat. 214; Pub.L. 98–325, § 1(a), June 20, 1984, 98 Stat. 268, set out as a note preceding section 101 of Title 11, Bankruptcy, read as follows:

§ 157. Times of holding court

(a) The bankruptcy court at each designated location shall be deemed to be in continuous session on all business days throughout the year.

(b) Each bankruptcy court may establish by local rule or order schedules of court sessions at designated places of holding court other than the headquarters office of the court. Such schedules may be pretermitted by order of the court.

(c) Bankruptcy court may be held at any place within the territory served, in any case, on order of the bankruptcy court, for the convenience of the parties, on such notice as the bankruptcy court orders.

Section 402(b) of Pub.L. 95–598 was amended by section 113 of Pub.L. 98–353 by substituting "shall not be effective" for "shall take effect on June 28, 1984", thereby eliminating the addition of section 157 by section 201(a) of Pub.L. 95–598, effective June 27, 1984, pursuant to section 122(c) of Pub.L. 98–353, set out as an Effective Date note under section 151 of this title.

Section 121(a) of Pub.L. 98–353 directed that section 402(b) of Pub.L. 95–598 be amended by substituting "the date of enactment of the Bankruptcy Amendments and Federal Judgeship Act of 1984 [i.e. July 10, 1984]" for "June 28, 1984". This amendment was not executed in view of the prior amendment to section 402(b) of Pub.L. 95–598 by section 113 of Pub.L. 98–353.

Effective Dates

1994 Acts. Amendment by Pub.L. 103–394 effective on Oct. 22, 1994, and not to apply with respect to cases commenced under Title 11 of the United States Code before Oct. 22, 1994, see section 702 of Pub.L. 103–394, set out as a note under section 101 of Title 11, Bankruptcy.

1986 Acts. Amendment by Pub.L. 99–554 effective 30 days after Oct. 27, 1986, except as otherwise provided for, see section 302(a) of Pub.L. 99–554, set out as a note under section 581 of this title.

1984 Acts. Section effective July 10, 1984, see section 122(a) of Pub.L. 98–353, set out as a note under section 151 of this title.

Separability of Provisions

If any provision of or amendment made by Pub.L. 103–394 or the application of such provision or amendment to any person or circumstance is held to be unconstitutional, the remaining provisions of and amendments made by Pub.L. 103–394 and the application of such provisions and amendments to any person or circumstance shall not be affected thereby, see section 701 of Pub.L. 103–394, set out as a note under section 101 of Title 11, Bankruptcy.

§ 158. Appeals

(a) The district courts of the United States shall have jurisdiction to hear appeals [1]

(1) from final judgments, orders, and decrees;

(2) from interlocutory orders and decrees issued under section 1121(d) of title 11 increasing or reducing the time periods referred to in section 1121 of such title; and

(3) with leave of the court, from other interlocutory orders and decrees;

and, with leave of the court, from interlocutory orders and decrees, of bankruptcy judges entered in cases and proceedings referred to the bankruptcy judges under section 157 of this title. An appeal under this subsection shall be taken only to the district court for the judicial district in which the bankruptcy judge is serving.

(b)(1) The judicial council of a circuit shall establish a bankruptcy appellate panel service composed of bankruptcy judges of the districts in the circuit who are appointed by the judicial council in accordance with paragraph (3), to hear and determine, with the consent of all the parties, appeals under subsection (a) unless the judicial council finds that—

(A) there are insufficient judicial resources available in the circuit; or

(B) establishment of such service would result in undue delay or increased cost to parties in cases under title 11.

Not later than 90 days after making the finding, the judicial council shall submit to the Judicial Conference of the United States a report containing the factual basis of such finding.

(2)(A) A judicial council may reconsider, at any time, the finding described in paragraph (1).

(B) On the request of a majority of the district judges in a circuit for which a bankruptcy appellate panel service is established under paragraph (1), made after the expiration of the 1–year period beginning on the date such service is established, the judicial council of the circuit shall determine whether a circumstance specified in subparagraph (A) or (B) of such paragraph exists.

(C) On its own motion, after the expiration of the 3–year period beginning on the date a bankruptcy appellate panel service is established under paragraph (1), the judicial council of the circuit may determine whether a circumstance specified in subparagraph (A) or (B) of such paragraph exists.

(D) If the judicial council finds that either of such circumstances exists, the judicial council may provide for the completion of the appeals then pending before such service and the orderly termination of such service.

(3) Bankruptcy judges appointed under paragraph (1) shall be appointed and may be reappointed under such paragraph.

(4) If authorized by the Judicial Conference of the United States, the judicial councils of 2 or more circuits may establish a joint bankruptcy appellate panel comprised of bankruptcy judges from the districts within the circuits for which such panel is established, to hear and determine, upon the consent of all the parties, appeals under subsection (a) of this section.

(5) An appeal to be heard under this subsection shall be heard by a panel of 3 members of the bankruptcy appellate panel service, except that a member of such service may not hear an appeal originating in the district for which such member is appointed or designated under section 152 of this title.

(6) Appeals may not be heard under this subsection by a panel of the bankruptcy appellate panel service unless the district judges for the district in which the appeals occur, by majority vote, have authorized such service to hear and determine appeals originating in such district.

(c)(1) Subject to subsection (b), each appeal under subsection (a) shall be heard by a 3–judge panel of the bankruptcy appellate panel service established under subsection (b)(1) unless—

(A) the appellant elects at the time of filing the appeal; or

(B) any other party elects, not later than 30 days after service of notice of the appeal;

to have such appeal heard by the district court.

(2) An appeal under subsections (a) and (b) of this section shall be taken in the same manner as appeals in civil proceedings generally are taken to the courts of appeals from the district courts and in the time provided by Rule 8002 of the Bankruptcy Rules.

(d) The courts of appeals shall have jurisdiction of appeals from all final decisions, judgments, orders, and decrees entered under subsections (a) and (b) of this section.

(Added Pub.L. 98–353, Title I, § 104(a), July 10, 1984, 98 Stat. 341, and amended Pub.L. 101–650, Title III, § 305, Dec. 1, 1990, 104 Stat. 5105; Pub.L. 103–394, Title I, §§ 102, 104(c), (d), Oct. 22, 1994, 108 Stat. 4108–4110.)

[1] So in original.

HISTORICAL AND STATUTORY NOTES

Codifications

Amendment by section 102 of Pub.L. 103–394, which directed amendment of subsec. (a) by striking "from" the first place in appears and all that follows through "decrees," and making a substitution for such language, was executed by striking through "decrees," the first place it appeared, as the probable intent of Congress.

This section (section 158) and section 159 as added by Pub.L. 95–598, Title II, § 201(a), Nov. 6, 1978, 92 Stat. 2659, and section 160, as added by Pub.L. 95–598, Title II, § 201(a), Nov. 6, 1978, 92 Stat. 2659, and amended Pub.L. 97–164, Title I, § 110(d), Apr. 2, 1982, 96 Stat. 29, effective June 28, 1984, pursuant to Pub.L. 95–598, Title IV, § 402(b), Nov. 6, 1978, 92 Stat. 2682, as amended by Pub.L. 98–249, § 1(a), Mar. 31, 1984, 98 Stat. 116; Pub.L. 98–271, § 1(a), Apr. 30, 1984, 98 Stat. 163; Pub.L. 98–299, § 1(a), May 25, 1984, 98 Stat. 214; Pub.L. 98–325, § 1(a), June 20, 1984, 98 Stat. 268, set out as a note preceding section 101 of Title II, Bankruptcy, read as follows:

§ 158. Accommodations at places for holding court

Court shall be held only at places where Federal quarters and accommodations are available, or suitable quarters and accommodations are furnished without cost to the United States. The foregoing restrictions shall not, however, preclude the Administrator of General Services, at the request of the Director of the Administrative Office of the United States Courts, from providing such court quarters and accommodations as the Administrator determines can appropriately be made available at places where court is authorized by law to be held, but only if such court quarters and accommodations have been approved as necessary by the judicial council of the appropriate circuit.

§ 159. Vacant judgeship as affecting proceedings

When the office of a bankruptcy judge becomes vacant, all pending process, pleadings and proceedings shall, when necessary, be continued by the clerk until a judge is appointed or designated to hold such court.

§ 160. Appellate panels

(a) If the circuit council of a circuit orders application of this section to a district within such circuit, the chief judge of each circuit shall designate panels of three bankruptcy judges to hear appeals from judgments, orders, and decrees of the bankruptcy court of the United States for such district. Except as provided in section 293(b) of this title, a panel shall be composed only of bankruptcy judges for districts located in the circuit in which the appeal arises. The chief judge shall designate a sufficient number of such panels so that appeals may be heard and disposed of expeditiously.

(b) A panel designated under subsection (a) of this section may not hear an appeal from a judgment, order, or decree entered by a member of the panel.

(c) When hearing an appeal, a panel designated under subsection (a) of this section shall sit at a place convenient to the parties to the appeal.

Section 402(b) of Pub.L. 95–598 was amended by section 113 of Pub.L. 98–353 by substituting "shall not be effective" for "shall take effect on June 28, 1984", thereby eliminating the additions of sections 158 to 160 by section 201(a) of Pub.L. 95–598, effective June 27, 1984, pursuant to section 122(c) of Pub.L. 98–353, set out as an Effective Date note under section 151 of this title.

Section 121(a) of Pub.L. 98–353 directed that section 402(b) of Pub.L. 95–598 be amended by substituting "the date of enactment of the Bankruptcy Amendments and Federal Judgeship Act of 1984 [i.e. July 10, 1984]" for "June 28, 1984". This amendment was not executed in view of the prior amendment to section 402(b) of Pub.L. 95–598 by section 113 of Pub.L. 98–353.

Effective Dates

1994 Acts. Amendments by Pub.L. 103–394 effective on Oct. 22, 1994, and not to apply with respect to cases commenced under Title 11 of the United States Code before Oct. 22, 1994, see section 702 of Pub.L. 103–394, set out as a note under section 101 of Title 11, Bankruptcy.

1984 Acts. Section effective July 10, 1984, see section 122(a) of Pub.L. 98–353, set out as a note under section 151 of this title.

Separability of Provisions

If any provision of or amendment made by Pub.L. 103–394 or the application of such provision or amendment to any person or circumstance is held to be unconstitutional, the remaining provisions of and amendments made by Pub.L. 103–394 and the application of such provisions and amendments to any person or circumstance shall not be affected thereby, see section 701 of Pub.L. 103–394, set out as a note under section 101 of Title 11, Bankruptcy.

CHAPTER 7—UNITED STATES COURT OF FEDERAL CLAIMS

Sec.
171. Appointment and number of judges; character of court; designation of chief judge.
172. Tenure and salaries of judges.
173. Times and places of holding court.
174. Assignment of judges; decisions.
175. Official duty station; residence.
176. Removal from office.
177. Disbarment of removed judges.
178. Retirement of judges of the Court of Federal Claims.
179.[1] Insurance and annuities programs.
180. Military retirement pay for retired judges.

[1] No text of section 179 has been enacted.

§ 171. Appointment and number of judges; character of court; designation of chief judge

(a) The President shall appoint, by and with the advice and consent of the Senate, sixteen judges who shall constitute a court of record known as the United States Court of Federal Claims. The court is declared to be a court established under article I of the Constitution of the United States.

(b) The President shall designate one of the judges of the Court of Federal Claims who is less than seventy years of age to serve as chief judge. The chief judge may continue to serve as such until he reaches the age of seventy years or until another judge is designated as chief judge by the President. After the designation of another judge to serve as chief judge, the former chief judge may continue to serve as a judge of the court for the balance of the term to which appointed.

(June 25, 1948, c. 646, 62 Stat. 898; July 28, 1953, c. 253, § 1, 67 Stat. 226; Sept. 3, 1954, c. 1263, § 39(a), 68 Stat. 1240; May 11, 1966, Pub.L. 89–425, § 1(b), 80 Stat. 140; Apr. 2, 1982, Pub.L. 97–164, Title I, § 105(a), 96 Stat. 27; Oct. 29, 1992, Pub.L. 102–572, Title IX, § 902(a), 106 Stat. 4516.)

HISTORICAL AND STATUTORY NOTES

Effective Dates

1992 Acts. Section 911 of Pub.L. 102–572 provided that: "This title and the amendments made by this title [Title IX of Pub.L. 102–572, Oct. 29, 1992, 106 Stat. 4516, for classifications to which see Tables] shall take effect on the date of the enactment of this Act [Oct. 29, 1992]."

1982 Acts. Section 402 of Pub.L. 97–164 provided that: "Unless otherwise specified, the provisions of this Act [see Short Title of 1982 Amendments note set out under section 1 of this title] shall take effect on October 1, 1982."

Change of Name

Section 902(b) of Pub.L. 102–572 provided that:

"Reference in any other Federal law [other than chapters 7, 51, 91, and 165 of this title] or any document to—

"(1) the 'United States Claims Court' shall be deemed to refer to the 'United States Court of Federal Claims'; and

"(2) the 'Claims Court' shall be deemed to refer to the 'Court of Federal Claims'."

Additional Judgeships

Section 1(a) of Pub.L. 89–425 provided that: "The President shall appoint, by and with the advice and consent of the Senate, two additional associate judges for the Court of Claims."

Appointment of United States Court of Federal Claims Judges

For Congressional suggestion that the President select judges of the United States Court of Federal Claims and the Court of Appeals for the Federal Circuit from a broad range of qualified individuals, see section 168 of Pub.L. 97–164, set out as a note under section 44 of this title.

Chief Justice to be known as Chief Judge

Section 2(a) of Act June 25, 1948, provided in part that the Chief Justice of the Court of Claims in office on Sept. 1, 1948, shall be thereafter known as the Chief Judge.

Continuation of Organization of Court

Section 2(b) of Act June 25, 1948, provided in part that the provisions of this title as set out in section 1 of Act June 25, 1948, with respect to the organization of the court, shall be construed as a continuation of existing law, and the tenure of the judges, officers, and employees in office on Sept. 1, 1948, shall not be effected by its enactment but each of them shall continue to serve in the same capacity under the appropriate provisions of this title, pursuant to his prior appointment.

Continued Service of Commissioners of Court of Claims as Judges of United States Claims Court

Section 167 of Pub.L. 97–164 provided that:

"**(a)** Notwithstanding the provisions of section 171(a) of title 28, United States Code, as amended by this Act [subsec. (a) of this section], a commissioner of the United States Court of Claims serving immediately prior to the effective date of this Act [Oct. 1, 1982] shall become a judge of the United States Claims Court [now the United States Court of Federal Claims] on the effective date of this Act.

"**(b)** Notwithstanding the provisions of section 172(a) of title 28, United States Code, as amended by this Act [section 172(a) of this title], the initial term of office of a person who becomes a judge of the United States Claims Court under subsection (a) of this section shall expire fifteen years after the date of his or her employment with the United States Court of Claims, or on October 1, 1986, whichever occurs earlier. Any such judge shall continue in office until a successor is sworn or until reappointed. No such individual shall serve as a judge after reaching the age of seventy years.

"**(c)** Notwithstanding the provisions of section 172(b) of title 28, United States Code [section 172(b) of this title], as amended by this Act, until such time as a change in the salary rate of a judge of the United States Claims Court [now the United States Court of Federal Claims] occurs in accordance with such section 172(b), the salary of such judge shall be equal to the salary of a Commissioner of the Court of Claims."

Tennessee Valley Authority Legal Representation

Section 169 of Pub.L. 97–164 provided that: "Nothing in this Act [see Short Title of 1982 Amendments note set out under section 1 of this title] affects the authority of the Tennessee Valley Authority under the Tennessee Valley Authority Act of 1933 [section 831 et seq. of Title 16, Conservation] to represent itself by attorneys of its choosing."

Transition Provisions; Transfer of Pending Cases

Section 403 of Pub.L. 97–164 provided that:

"**(a)** Any case pending before the Court of Claims on the effective date of this Act [Oct. 1, 1982] in which a report on the merits has been filed by a commissioner, or in which there is pending a request for review, and upon which the court has not acted, shall be transferred to the United States Court of Appeals for the Federal Circuit.

"**(b)** Any matter pending before the United States Court of Customs and Patent Appeals on the effective date of this Act [Oct. 1, 1982] shall be transferred to the United States Court of Appeals for the Federal Circuit.

"**(c)** Any petition for rehearing, reconsideration, alteration, modification, or other change in any decision of the United States Court of Claims or the United States Court of Customs and Patent Appeals rendered prior to the effective date of this Act [Oct. 1, 1982] that has not been determined by either of those courts on that date, or that is filed after that date, shall be determined by the United States Court of Appeals for the Federal Circuit.

"**(d)** Any matter pending before a commissioner of the United States Court of Claims on the effective date of this Act [Oct. 1, 1982], or any pending dispositive motion that the United States Court of Claims has not determined on that date, shall be determined by the United States Claims Court [now the United States Court of Federal Claims].

"**(e)** Any case in which a notice of appeal has been filed in a district court of the United States prior to the effective date of this Act [Oct. 1, 1982] shall be decided by the court of appeals to which the appeal was taken."

§ 172. Tenure and salaries of judges

(a) Each judge of the United States Court of Federal Claims shall be appointed for a term of fifteen years.

(b) Each judge shall receive a salary at the rate of pay, and in the same manner, as judges of the district courts of the United States.

(June 25, 1948, c. 646, 62 Stat. 898; Apr. 2, 1982, Pub.L. 97–164, Title I, § 105(a), 96 Stat. 27; Nov. 19, 1988, Pub.L. 100–702, Title X, § 1023, 102 Stat. 4673; Oct. 29, 1992, Pub.L. 102–572, Title IX, § 902(a)(1), 106 Stat. 4516.)

HISTORICAL AND STATUTORY NOTES

Effective Dates

1992 Acts. Amendment by Title IX of Pub.L. 102–572 effective Oct. 29, 1992, see section 911 of Pub.L. 102–572, set out as a note under section 171 of Title 28, Judiciary and Judicial Procedure.

1982 Acts. Amendment by Pub.L. 97–164 effective Oct. 1, 1982, see section 402 of Pub.L. 97–164, set out as a note under section 171 of this title.

Increase in Salaries

1993—Salaries of judges increased to $133,600, effective on the first day of the first applicable pay period beginning on or after Jan. 1, 1993, by Ex. Ord. No. 12826, Dec. 30, 1992, 57 F.R. 62909, set out as a note under section 5332 of Title 5, Government Organization and Employees.

1992—Salaries of judges increased to $129,500, effective on the first day of the first applicable pay period beginning on or after Jan. 1, 1992, by Ex. Ord. No. 12786, Dec. 26, 1991, 56 F.R. 67453, formerly set out as a note under section 5332 of Title 5, Government Organization and Employees.

1991—Salaries of judges increased to $125,100, effective on the first day of the first applicable pay period beginning on or after Jan. 1, 1991, by Ex. Ord. No. 12736, Dec. 12, 1990, 55 F.R. 51385, formerly set out as a note under section 5332 of Title 5, Government Organization and Employees.

1990—Salaries of judges continued at $89,500 per annum, and increased to $96,600, effective on the first day of the first pay period beginning on or after Jan. 31, 1990, by Ex. Ord. No. 12698, Dec. 23, 1989, 54 F.R. 53473, formerly set out as a note under section 5332 of Title 5.

1989—Salaries of judges increased in the amount of 25 percent of their rates (as last in effect before the increase), effective Jan. 1, 1991, see Pub.L. 101–194, Title VII, § 703(a)(3), Nov. 30, 1989, 103 Stat. 1768, set out as a note under section 5318 of Title 5.

Salaries of judges increased to $89,500 per annum by Ex. Ord. No. 12663, Jan. 6, 1989, 54 F.R. 791, formerly set out as a note under section 5332 of Title 5.

1988—Salaries of judges continued at $82,500 per annum by Ex. Ord. No. 12622, Dec. 31, 1987, 53 F.R. 222, formerly set out as a note under section 5332 of Title 5.

1987—Salaries of judges increased to $82,500 per annum, on recommendation of the President of the United States, see note set out under section 358 of Title 2, The Congress.

Salaries of judges increased to $72,300 effective on first day of first pay period beginning on or after January 1, 1987, by Ex. Ord. No. 12578, Dec. 31, 1986, 52 F.R. 505, formerly set out as a note under section 5332 of Title 5.

1985—Salaries of judges increased to $70,200 effective on the first day of the first pay period beginning on or after Jan. 1, 1985, by Ex. Ord. No. 12496, Dec. 28, 1984, 50 F.R. 211, as amended by Ex. Ord. No. 12540, Dec. 30, 1985, 51 F.R. 577, formerly set out as a note under section 5332 of Title 5.

1984—Salaries of judges set at $67,800 effective on the first day of the first pay period beginning on or after Jan. 1, 1984, by Ex. Ord. No. 12456, Dec. 30, 1983, 49 F.R. 347, as amended Ex. Ord. No. 12477, May 23, 1984, 49 F.R. 22041; Ex. Ord. No. 12487, Sept. 14, 1984, 49 F.R. 36493, formerly set out as a note under section 5332 of Title 5.

1982—Salaries of judges set at $65,200 effective on the first day of the first pay period beginning on or after Oct. 1, 1982, by Ex. Ord. No. 12387, Oct. 8, 1982, 47 F.R. 44981, formerly set out as a note under section 5332 of Title 5, Government Organization and Employees. Ex. Ord. No. 12387 further provided that pursuant to section 101(e) of Pub.L. 97–276 funds are not available to pay a salary at a rate which exceeds the rate in effect on Sept. 30, 1982, which was $57,500.

Maximum rate payable after Dec. 17, 1982, increased from $57,500 to $65,200, see Pub.L. 97–377, Title I, § 129(b)–(d), Dec. 21, 1982, 96 Stat. 1914, set out as a note under section 5318 of Title 5.

Limitations on use of funds for fiscal year ending Sept. 30, 1983, appropriated by any Act to pay the salary or pay of any individual in legislative, executive, or judicial branch in position equal to or above level V of the Executive Schedule, see section 101(e) of Pub.L. 97–276, as amended, set out as a note under section 5318 of Title 5.

1981—Salaries of judges increased to $74,300 effective on the first day of the first pay period beginning on or after Oct. 1, 1981, by Ex. Ord. No. 12330, Oct. 15, 1981, 46 F.R. 50921, formerly set out as a note under section 5332 of Title 5.

Limitations on use of funds for fiscal year ending Sept. 30, 1982, appropriated by any Act to pay the salary or pay of any individual in legislative, executive, or judicial branch in position equal to or above level V of the Executive Schedule, see sections 101(g) and 141 of Pub.L. 97–92, set out as a note under section 5318 of Title 5.

1980—Salaries of judges increased to $70,900 effective on the first day of the first pay period beginning on or after Oct. 1, 1980, by Ex. Ord. No. 12248, Oct. 16, 1980, 45 F.R. 69199, formerly set out as a note under section 5332 of Title 5. Ex. Ord. No. 12248 further provided that pursuant to Pub.L. 96–369 funds are not available to pay a salary at a rate which exceeds the rate in effect on Sept. 30, 1980, which was $60,662.50.

Limitations on use of funds for fiscal year ending Sept. 30, 1981, appropriated by any Act to pay the salary or pay of any individual in legislative, executive, or judicial branch in position equal to or above level V of the Executive Schedule, see section 101(c) of Pub.L. 96–536, as amended, set out as a note under section 5318 of Title 5.

1979—Salaries of judges increased to $65,000 effective on the first day of the first applicable pay period beginning on or after Oct. 1, 1979, by Ex. Ord. No. 12165, Oct. 9, 1979, 44 F.R. 58671, as amended by Ex. Ord. No. 12200, Mar. 12, 1980, 45 F.R. 16443, formerly set out as a note under section 5332 of Title 5. Ex. Ord. No. 12165 further provided that pursuant to Pub.L. 96–86 funds appropriated for fiscal year 1980 may not be used to pay a salary at a rate which exceeds an increase of 5.5 percent over the applicable rate payable for such position or office in effect on Sept. 30, 1978, which was $60,662.50.

Applicability to funds appropriated by any Act for fiscal year ending Sept. 30, 1980, of limitation of section 304 of Pub.L. 95–391 on use of funds to pay the salary or pay of any individual in legislative, executive, or judicial branch in position equal to or above level V of the Executive Schedule, see section 101 of Pub.L. 96–86, set out as a note under section 5318 of Title 5.

1978—Salaries of judges increased to $60,700 effective on the first day of the first pay period beginning on or after Oct. 1, 1978, by Ex. Ord. No. 12087, Oct. 7, 1978, 43 F.R. 46823, formerly set out as a note under section 5332 of Title 5. Ex. Ord. No. 12087 further provided that pursuant to the Legislative Branch Appropriation Act, 1979 [Pub.L. 95–391, Title III, § 304, Sept. 30, 1978, 92 Stat. 788, set out as a note under section 5318 of Title 5], funds are not available to pay a salary at a rate which exceeds the rate in effect on Sept. 30, 1978, which was $57,500.

1977—Salaries of judges increased to $57,500 per annum, upon recommendation of the President of the United States, see note set out under section 358 of Title 2, The Congress.

1976—Salaries of judges increased to $46,800 effective on the first day of the first pay period beginning on or after Oct. 1, 1976, see Ex. Ord. No. 11941, Oct. 1, 1976, 41 F.R. 43889, formerly set out as a note under section 5332 of Title 5, Government Organization and Employees. Ex. Ord. No. 11941, further provided that pursuant to the Legislative Branch Appropriation Act, 1977, funds are not available to pay a salary at a rate which exceeds the rate in effect on Sept. 30, 1976, which was $44,600.

1969—Salaries of judges increased from $33,000 to $42,500 per annum, commencing February 14, 1969, on recommendation of the President of the United States, see note set out under section 358 of Title 2, The Congress.

1946—The salaries of the chief judge and associate judges were increased from $12,500 to $17,500 a year by Act July 31, 1946, c. 704, § 1, 60 Stat. 716.

1926—The salary of the Chief Justice, now the chief judge, was increased from $8,000 to $12,500 a year, and the salaries of the associate justices, now judges, were increased from $7,500 to $12,500 a year by Act Dec. 13, 1926, c. 6, § 1, 44 Stat. 919.

1919—The salary of the Chief Justice was increased from $6,500 to $8,000 a year, and the salaries of the associate justices were increased from $6,000 to $7,500 a year by Act Feb. 25, 1919, c. 29, § 1, 40 Stat. 1156.

1911—The salary of the chief justice was set at $6,500, and the salaries of the associate justices were set at $6,000 by the Judicial Code of 1911, Act Mar. 3, 1911, c. 231, § 1, 36 Stat. 1135.

Initial Term of Claims Court Judges; Salaries

For provisions directing that the initial terms of office of former Court of Claims commissioners who become judges of the United States Claims Court [now United States Court of Federal Claims] expire 15 years after the date of his or her employment with the United States Court of Claims or Oct. 1, 1986, whichever occurs earlier, and setting the salary of such judges, see section 167 of Pub.L. 97–164, set out as a note under section 171 of this title.

§ 173. Times and places of holding court

The principal office of the United States Court of Federal Claims shall be in the District of Columbia, but the Court of Federal Claims may hold court at such times and in such places as it may fix by rule of court. The times and places of the sessions of the Court of Federal Claims shall be prescribed with a view to securing reasonable opportunity to citizens to appear before the Court of Federal Claims with as little inconvenience and expense to citizens as is practicable.

(June 25, 1948, c. 646, 62 Stat. 898; Mar. 2, 1955, c. 9, § 1(d), 69 Stat. 10; Aug. 14, 1964, Pub.L. 88–426, Title IV, § 403(d), 78 Stat. 434; Aug. 9, 1975, Pub.L. 94–82, Title II, § 205(b)(4), 89 Stat. 422; Apr. 2, 1982, Pub.L. 97–164, Title I, § 105(a), 96 Stat. 27; Oct. 29, 1992, Pub.L. 102–572, Title IX, § 902(a), 106 Stat. 4516.)

HISTORICAL AND STATUTORY NOTES

Effective Dates

1992 Acts. Amendment by Title IX of Pub.L. 102–572 effective Oct. 29, 1992, see section 911 of Pub.L. 102–572, set out as a note under section 171 of Title 28, Judiciary and Judicial Procedure.

1982 Acts. Amendment by Pub.L. 97–164 effective Oct. 1, 1982, see section 402 of Pub.L. 97–164, set out as a note under section 171 of this title.

1964 Acts. Amendment by Pub.L. 88–426 effective on the first day of the first pay period which begins on or after July 1, 1964, except to the extent provided in section 501(c) of Pub.L. 88–426, see section 501 of Pub.L. 88–426.

1955 Acts. Amendment by Act Mar. 2, 1955, effective Mar. 1, 1955, see section 5 of Act Mar. 2, 1955, set out as a note under section 31 of Title 2, The Congress.

§ 174. Assignment of judges; decisions

(a) The judicial power of the United States Court of Federal Claims with respect to any action, suit, or proceeding, except congressional reference cases, shall be exercised by a single judge, who may preside alone and hold a regular or special session of court at the same time other sessions are held by other judges.

(b) All decisions of the Court of Federal Claims shall be preserved and open to inspection.

(June 25, 1948, c. 646, 62 Stat. 898; Apr. 2, 1982, Pub.L. 97–164, Title I, § 105(a), 96 Stat. 27; Oct. 29, 1992, Pub.L. 102–572, Title IX, § 902(a), 106 Stat. 4516.)

HISTORICAL AND STATUTORY NOTES

Effective Dates

1992 Acts. Amendment by Title IX of Pub.L. 102–572 effective Oct. 29, 1992, see section 911 of Pub.L. 102–572, set out as a note under section 171 of Title 28, Judiciary and Judicial Procedure.

1982 Acts. Amendment by Pub.L. 97–164 effective Oct. 1, 1982, see section 402 of Pub.L. 97–164, set out as a note under section 171 of this title.

§ 175. Official duty station; residence

(a) The official duty station of each judge of the United States Court of Federal Claims is the District of Columbia.

(b) After appointment and while in active service, each judge shall reside within fifty miles of the District of Columbia.

(Added Pub.L. 89–425, § 2, May 11, 1966, 80 Stat. 140, and amended Pub.L. 97–164, Title I, § 105(a), Apr. 2, 1982, 96 Stat. 27; Pub.L. 102–572, Title IX, § 902(a)(1), Oct. 29, 1992, 106 Stat. 4516.)

HISTORICAL AND STATUTORY NOTES

Effective Dates

1992 Acts. Amendment by Title IX of Pub.L. 102–572 effective Oct. 29, 1992, see section 911 of Pub.L. 102–572, set out as a note under section 171 of Title 28, Judiciary and Judicial Procedure.

1982 Acts. Amendment by Pub.L. 97–164 effective Oct. 1, 1982, see section 402 of Pub.L. 97–164, set out as a note under section 171 of this title.

Prior Provisions

A prior section 175, Act June 25, 1948, c. 646, 62 Stat. 898, which required three judges of the Court of Claims to constitute a quorum and the concurrence of three judges for any decision, was struck out by section 2 of Pub.L. 89–425.

§ 176. Removal from office

(a) Removal of a judge of the United States Court of Federal Claims during the term for which he is appointed shall be only for incompetency, misconduct, neglect of duty, engaging in the practice of law, or physical or mental disability. Removal shall be by the United States Court of Appeals for the Federal Circuit, but removal may not occur unless a majority of all the judges of such court of appeals concur in the order of removal.

(b) Before any order of removal may be entered, a full specification of the charges shall be furnished to the judge involved, and such judge shall be accorded an opportunity to be heard on the charges.

(c) Any cause for removal of any judge of the United States Court of Federal Claims coming to the knowledge of the Director of the Administrative Office of the United States Courts shall be reported by him to the chief judge of the United States Court of Appeals for the Federal Circuit, and a copy of the report shall at the same time be transmitted to the judge.

(Added Pub.L. 97–164, Title I, § 105(a), Apr. 2, 1982, 96 Stat. 28, and amended Pub.L. 102–572, Title IX, § 902(a)(1), Oct. 29, 1992, 106 Stat. 4516.)

HISTORICAL AND STATUTORY NOTES

Effective Dates

1992 Acts. Amendment by Title IX of Pub.L. 102–572 effective Oct. 29, 1992, see section 911 of Pub.L. 102–572, set out as a note under section 171 of Title 28, Judiciary and Judicial Procedure.

1982 Acts. Section effective Oct. 1, 1982, see section 402 of Pub.L. 97–164, set out as a note under section 171 of this title.

§ 177. Disbarment of removed judges

A judge of the United States Court of Federal Claims removed from office in accordance with section 176 of this title shall not be permitted at any time to practice before the Court of Federal Claims.

(Added Pub.L. 97–164, Title I, § 105(a), Apr. 2, 1982, 96 Stat. 28, and amended Pub.L. 102–572, Title IX, § 902(a), Oct. 29, 1992, 106 Stat. 4516.)

HISTORICAL AND STATUTORY NOTES

Effective Dates

1992 Acts. Amendment by Title IX of Pub.L. 102–572 effective Oct. 29, 1992, see section 911 of Pub.L. 102–572, set out as a note under section 171 of Title 28, Judiciary and Judicial Procedure.

1982 Acts. Section effective Oct. 1, 1982, see section 402 of Pub.L. 97–164, set out as a note under section 171 of this title.

§ 178. Retirement of judges of the Court of Federal Claims

(a) A judge of the United States Court of Federal Claims who retires from office after attaining the age and meeting the service requirements, whether continuously or otherwise, of this subsection shall, subject to subsection (f), be entitled to receive, during the remainder of the judge's lifetime, an annuity equal to the salary payable to Court of Federal Claims judges in regular active service. The age and service requirements for retirement under this subsection are as follows:

Attained Age:	Years of Service:
65	15
66	14
67	13
68	12
69	11
70	10.

(b) A judge of the Court of Federal Claims who is not reappointed following the expiration of the term of office of such judge, and who retires upon the completion of such term shall, subject to subsection (f), be entitled to receive, during the remainder of such judge's lifetime, an annuity equal to the salary payable to Court of Federal Claims judges in regular active service, if—

(1) such judge has served at least 1 full term as judge of the Court of Federal Claims, and

(2) not earlier than 9 months before the date on which the term of office of such judge expired, and not later than 6 months before such date, such judge advised the President in writing that such judge was willing to accept reappointment as a judge of the Court of Federal Claims.

(c) A judge of the Court of Federal Claims who has served at least 5 years, whether continuously or otherwise, as such a judge, and who retires or is removed from office upon the sole ground of mental or physical disability shall, subject to subsection (f), be entitled to receive, during the remainder of the judge's lifetime—

(1) an annuity equal to 50 percent of the salary payable to Court of Federal Claims judges in regular active service, if before retirement such judge served less than 10 years, or

(2) an annuity equal to the salary payable to Court of Federal Claims judges in regular active

service, if before retirement such judge served at least 10 years.

(d) A judge who retires under subsection (a) or (b) may, at or after such retirement, be called upon by the chief judge of the Court of Federal Claims to perform such judicial duties with the Court of Federal Claims as may be requested of the retired judge for any period or periods specified by the chief judge, except that in the case of any such judge—

(1) the aggregate of such periods in any one calendar year shall not (without his or her consent) exceed 90 calendar days; and

(2) he or she shall be relieved of performing such duties during any period in which illness or disability precludes the performance of such duties.

Any act, or failure to act, by an individual performing judicial duties pursuant to this subsection shall have the same force and effect as if it were the act (or failure to act) of a Court of Federal Claims judge in regular active service. Any individual performing judicial duties pursuant to this subsection shall receive the allowances for official travel and other expenses of a judge in regular active service.

(e)(1) Any judge who retires under the provisions of subsection (a) or (b) of this section shall be designated "senior judge".

(2) Any judge who retires under this section shall not be counted as a judge of the Court of Federal Claims for purposes of the number of judgeships authorized by section 171 of this title.

(f)(1) A judge shall be entitled to an annuity under this section if the judge elects an annuity under this section by notifying the Director of the Administrative Office of the United States Courts in writing. Such an election—

(A) may be made only while an individual is a judge of the Court of Federal Claims (except that in the case of an individual who fails to be reappointed as judge at the expiration of a term of office, such election may be made at any time before the day after the day on which his or her successor takes office); and

(B) once made, shall, subject to subsection (k), be irrevocable.

(2) A judge who elects to receive an annuity under this section shall not be entitled to receive—

(A) any annuity to which such judge would otherwise have been entitled under subchapter III of chapter 83, or under chapter 84 (except for subchapters III and VII), of title 5, for service performed as a judge or otherwise;

(B) an annuity or salary in senior status or retirement under section 371 or 372 of this title;

(C) retired pay under section 7447 of the Internal Revenue Code of 1986; or

(D) retired pay under section 7296 of title 38.

(g) For purposes of calculating the years of service of an individual under subsections (a) and (c), only those years of service as a judge of the Court of Federal Claims or a commissioner of the United States Court of Claims shall be credited, and that portion of the aggregate number of years of such service that is a fractional part of 1 year shall not be credited if it is less than 6 months, and shall be credited if it is 6 months or more.

(h) An annuity under this section shall be payable at the times and in the same manner as the salary of a Court of Federal Claims judge in regular active service. Such annuity shall begin to accrue on the day following the day on which the annuitant's salary as a judge in regular active service ceases to accrue.

(i)(1) Payments under this section which would otherwise be made to a judge of the Court of Federal Claims based upon his or her service shall be paid (in whole or in part) by the Director of the Administrative Office of the United States Courts to another person if and to the extent expressly provided for in the terms of any court decree of divorce, annulment, or legal separation, or the terms of any court order or court-approved property settlement agreement incident to any court decree of divorce, annulment, or legal separation. Any payment under this paragraph to a person bars recovery by any other person.

(2) Paragraph (1) shall apply only to payments made by the Director of the Administrative Office of the United States Courts after the date of receipt by the Director of written notice of such decree, order, or agreement, and such additional information as the Director may prescribe.

(3) As used in this subsection, the term "court" means any court of any State, the District of Columbia, the Commonwealth of Puerto Rico, Guam, the Commonwealth of the Northern Mariana Islands, or the Virgin Islands, and any Indian tribal court or court of Indian offense.

(j)(1) Subject to paragraph (4), any judge of the Court of Federal Claims who retires under this section and who thereafter in the practice of law represents (or supervises or directs the representation of) a client in making any civil claim against the United States or any agency thereof shall forfeit all rights to an annuity under this section for all periods beginning on or after the first day on which he engages in any such activity.

(2) Subject to paragraph (4), if a judge of the Court of Federal Claims who retires under this section fails during any calendar year to perform judicial duties required of such judge by subsection (d), such judge shall forfeit all rights to an annuity under this section for the 1-year period which begins on the first day on which he or she so fails to perform such duties.

(3) If a judge of the Court of Federal Claims who retires under this section accepts compensation for civil office or employment under the Government of the United States (other than for the performance of judicial duties under subsection (d)), such judge shall forfeit all rights to an annuity under this section for the period for which such compensation is received.

(4)(A) If a judge makes an election under this paragraph—

(i) paragraphs (1) and (2) (and subsection (d)) shall not apply to such judge beginning on the date such election takes effect, and

(ii) the annuity payable under this section to such judge, for periods beginning on or after the date such election takes effect, shall be equal to the annuity to which such judge is entitled on the day before such effective date.

(B) An election under subparagraph (A)—

(i) may be made by a judge only if such judge meets the age and service requirements for retirement under subsection (a),

(ii) may be made only during the period during which such judge may make an election to receive an annuity under this section or while the judge is receiving an annuity under this section, and

(iii) shall be filed with the Director of the Administrative Office of the United States Courts.

Such an election, once it takes effect, shall be irrevocable.

(C) Any election under this paragraph shall take effect on the first day of the first month following the month in which the election is made.

(k)(1) Notwithstanding subsection (f)(1)(B), an individual who has filed an election under subsection (f) to receive an annuity may revoke such election at any time before the first day on which such annuity would (but for such revocation) begin to accrue with respect to such individual.

(2) Any revocation under this subsection shall be made by filing a notice thereof in writing with the Director of[1] Administrative Office of the United States Courts.

(3) In the case of any revocation under this subsection—

(A) for purposes of this section, the individual shall be treated as not having filed an election under subsection (f) to receive an annuity,

(B) for purposes of section 376 of this title—

(i) the individual shall be treated as not having filed an election under section 376(a)(1), and

(ii) section 376(g) shall not apply, and the amount credited to such individual's account (together with interest at 3 percent per annum, compounded on December 31 of each year to the date on which the revocation is filed) shall be returned to such individual,

(C) no credit shall be allowed for any service as a judge of the Court of Federal Claims or as a commissioner of the United States Court of Claims unless with respect to such service either there has been deducted and withheld the amount required by chapter 83 or 84 (as the case may be) of title 5 or there has been deposited in the Civil Service Retirement and Disability Fund an amount equal to the amount so required, with interest,

(D) the Court of Federal Claims shall deposit in the Civil Service Retirement and Disability Fund an amount equal to the additional amount it would have contributed to such Fund but for the election under subsection (f), and

(E) if subparagraph (D) is complied with, service on the Court of Federal Claims or as a commissioner of the United States Court of Claims shall be treated as service with respect to which deductions and contributions had been made during the period of service.

(*l*)(1) There is established in the Treasury a fund which shall be known as the "Court of Federal Claims Judges Retirement Fund". The Fund is appropriated for the payment of annuities and other payments under this section.

(2) The Secretary of the Treasury shall invest, in interest bearing securities of the United States, such currently available portions of the Court of Federal Claims Judges Retirement Fund as are not immediately required for payments from the Fund. The income derived from these investments constitutes a part of the Fund.

(3)(A) There are authorized to be appropriated to the Court of Federal Claims Judges Retirement Fund amounts required to reduce to zero the unfunded liability of the Fund.

(B) For purposes of subparagraph (A), the term "unfunded liability" means the estimated excess, determined on an annual basis in accordance with the provisions of section 9503 of title 31, of the present value of all benefits payable from the Court of Federal Claims Judges Retirement Fund, over the balance in the Fund as of the date the unfunded liability is determined. In making any determination under this subparagraph, the Comptroller General shall use the applicable information contained in the reports filed pursuant to section 9503 of title 31, with respect to the retirement annuities provided for in this section.

(C) There are authorized to be appropriated such sums as may be necessary to carry out this paragraph.

(Added Pub.L. 101–650, Title III, § 306(a)(1), Dec. 1, 1990, 104 Stat. 5105, and amended Pub.L. 102–40, Title IV, § 402(d)(2), May 7, 1991, 105 Stat. 239; Pub.L. 102–198, § 7(a), Dec. 9, 1991, 105 Stat. 1624; Pub.L. 102–572, Title IX, § 902(a), Oct. 29, 1992, 106 Stat. 4516.)

[1] So in original. Probably should be "of the".

HISTORICAL AND STATUTORY NOTES

References in Text

Section 7447 of the Internal Revenue Code of 1986, referred to in subsec. (f)(2)(C), is classified to section 7447 of Title 26, Internal Revenue Code.

Effective Dates

1992 Acts. Amendment by Title IX of Pub.L. 102–572 effective Oct. 29, 1992, see section 911 of Pub.L. 102–572, set out as a note under section 171 of Title 28, Judiciary and Judicial Procedure.

1990 Acts. Section applicable to judges of, and senior judges in active service with, the United States Court of Federal Claims on or after Dec. 1, 1990, see section 306(f) of Pub.L. 101–650, set out as a note under section 8331 of Title 5, Government Organization and Employees.

§ 180. Military retirement pay for retired judges

Section 371(e) of this title applies to judges of the United States Court of Federal Claims, and for the purpose of construing section 371(e) of this title, a judge of the United States Court of Federal Claims shall be deemed to be a judge of the United States as defined in section 451 of this title.

(Added Pub.L. 102–572, Title IX, § 903(a), Oct. 29, 1992, 106 Stat. 4517.)

HISTORICAL AND STATUTORY NOTES

Effective Dates

1992 Acts. Amendment by Title IX of Pub.L. 102–572 [enacting this section] effective Oct. 29, 1992, see section 911 of Pub.L. 102–572, set out as a note under section 171 of Title 28, Judiciary and Judicial Procedure.

[CHAPTER 9—REPEALED]

[§§ 211 to 216. Repealed. Pub.L. 97–164, Title I, § 106, Apr. 2, 1982, 96 Stat. 28]

HISTORICAL AND STATUTORY NOTES

Section 211, Acts June 25, 1948, c. 646, 62 Stat. 899; Aug. 25, 1958, Pub.L. 85–755, § 1, 72 Stat. 848, provided for the creation of the United States Court of Customs and Patent Appeals under article III of the United States Constitution and for the appointment of a chief judge and four associate judges for that court.

Section 212, Act June 25, 1948, c. 646, 62 Stat. 899, provided for the order of precedence of the chief judge and associate judges of the Court of Customs and Patent Appeals.

Section 213, Acts June 25, 1948, c. 646, 62 Stat. 899; Mar. 2, 1955, c. 9, § 1(e), 69 Stat. 10; Aug. 14, 1964, Pub.L. 88–426, Title IV, § 403(e), 78 Stat. 434; Aug. 9, 1975, Pub.L. 94–82, Title II, § 205(b) (5), 89 Stat. 422, provided for the tenure and salaries of the judges of the Court of Customs and Patent Appeals.

Section 214, Act June 25, 1948, c. 646, 62 Stat. 899, authorized the Court of Customs and Patent Appeals to hold court at such times and places as it might fix by rule.

Section 215, Act June 25, 1948, c. 646, 62 Stat. 899, provided that three judges of the Court of Customs and Patent Appeals constituted a quorum and that the concurrence of three judges was necessary to any decision.

Section 216, Act June 25, 1948, c. 646, 62 Stat. 899, provided for the filing of written opinions by the Court of Customs and Patent Appeals on appeals from decisions of the Patent Office and the recording of those opinions in the Patent Office.

Effective Date of Repeal

Repeal effective Oct. 1, 1982, see section 402 of Pub.L. 97–164, set out as a note under section 171 of this title.

Transfer of Matters and Petitions Pending in United States Court of Customs and Patent Appeals on October 1, 1982

For provisions that any matter pending before the United States Court of Customs and Patent Appeals on Oct. 1, 1982, and any petition for rehearing, reconsideration, alteration, modification, or other change in any decision of the United States Court of Customs and Patent Appeals rendered prior to Oct. 1, 1982, that has not been determined on that date or that is filed after that date, be determined by the United States Court of Appeals for the Federal Circuit, see section 403(b), (c) of Pub.L. 97–164, set out as a note under section 171 of this title.

CHAPTER 11—COURT OF INTERNATIONAL TRADE

Sec.
251. Appointment and number of judges; offices.
252. Tenure and salaries of judges.
253. Duties of chief judge.
254. Single-judge trial.[1]
255. Three-judge trials.
256. Trials at ports other than New York.
257. Publication of decisions.

258. Chief judges; precedence of judges.

[1] So in original. Does not conform to section catchline.

HISTORICAL AND STATUTORY NOTES

History of Court

The United States Customs Court [now Court of International Trade] as "constituted on June 17, 1930", consisted of nine members as provided by Act Sept. 21, 1922, c. 356, Title IV, § 518, 42 Stat. 972, which established the Board of General Appraisers, designated the "United States Customs Court" by Act May 28, 1926, c. 411, § 1, 44 Stat. 669.

Provisions similar to these were contained in Act Sept. 21, 1922, c. 356, Title IV, § 518, 42 Stat. 972. That section was superseded by section 518 of the Tariff Act of 1930, and was repealed by section 651(a)(1) of said 1930 Act.

The sentence in the former first paragraph as to sitting in a case previously participated in, is from Act Aug. 5, 1909, c. 6, § 28, 36 Stat. 98, which combined and amended Customs Administrative Act June 10, 1890, c. 407, § 12, 26 Stat. 136, and section 31, as added by Act May 27, 1908, c. 205, 35 Stat. 406. Section 12 of the Act of 1890 was expressly saved from repeal by Act Sept. 21, 1922, c. 356, Title IV, § 643, 42 Stat. 989, and prior acts, but its provisions, other than the sentence above mentioned, were omitted from the Code.

Provisions for the review of decisions of Boards of General Appraisers by the Circuit Courts, made by section 15 of the Customs Administrative Act of June 10, 1890, c. 407, were superseded by provisions for such review by the Court of Customs Appeals created by section 29 added to that act by the Payne-Aldrich Tariff Act of Aug. 5, 1909, c. 6. The provisions of said new section 29 were incorporated in and superseded by chapter 8 of the Judicial Code of March 3, 1911, incorporated into the Code as former chapter 8 of Title 28, Judicial Code and Judiciary.

R.S. § 2608 provided for the appointment of four appraisers of merchandise, to be employed in visiting ports of entry under the direction of the Secretary of the Treasury, and to assist in the appraisement of merchandise as might be deemed necessary by the Secretary to protect and insure uniformity in the collection of the revenue from customs. It was repealed by Act June 10, 1890, c. 407, § 29, 26 Stat. 141.

R.S. § 2609 provided for the appointment of merchant appraisers. R.S. § 2610 made every merchant refusing to serve as such appraiser liable to a penalty. Both sections were superseded by the provisions relating to appraisers and appraisements of the Customs Administrative Act of June 10, 1890, c. 407, 26 Stat. 131, and subsequent acts, and were repealed by Act Sept. 21, 1922, c. 356, Title IV, § 642, 42 Stat. 989.

R.S. § 2945, which contained a provision similar to that of R.S. § 2610, was repealed, without mention of section 2610, by said Customs Administrative Act of June 10, 1890, c. 407, § 29, 26 Stat. 141, and was again repealed by section 642 of Act Sept. 21, 1922.

R.S. § 2725, which prescribed the compensation of merchant appraisers, and section 2726, which prescribed the salary of the general appraiser at New York, were superseded by the provisions relating to general appraisers and appraisers made by the Customs Administrative Act of June 10, 1890, c. 407, §§ 12, 13, 26 Stat. 136, as amended by the Payne-Aldrich Act of Aug. 5, 1909, c. 6, § 28.

R.S. § 2727, fixed the salary of the four general appraisers at the sum of $2,500 a year each, and their actual traveling expenses. It was repealed by Act Feb. 27, 1877, c. 69, 19 Stat. 246.

§ 251. Appointment and number of judges; offices

(a) The President shall appoint, by and with the advice and consent of the Senate, nine judges who shall constitute a court of record to be known as the United States Court of International Trade. Not more than five of such judges shall be from the same political party. The court is a court established under article III of the Constitution of the United States.

(b) The offices of the Court of International Trade shall be located in New York, New York.

[(c) Redesignated (b)]

(June 25, 1948, c. 646, 62 Stat. 899; July 14, 1956, c. 589, § 1, 70 Stat. 532; Oct. 10, 1980, Pub.L. 96–417, Title I, § 101, 94 Stat. 1727; Oct. 19, 1996, Pub.L. 104–317, Title V, § 501(b)(1), 110 Stat. 3856.)

HISTORICAL AND STATUTORY NOTES

Effective Dates

1980 Acts. Section 701 of Pub.L. 96–417, as amended Pub.L. 96–542, § 1, Dec. 17, 1980, 94 Stat. 3209, provided that:

"(a) Except as otherwise provided in this section, the provisions of and amendments made by this Act [see section 1 of Pub.L. 96–417, set out as a Short Title of 1980 Amendments note under section 1 of this title] shall take effect on November 1, 1980 and shall apply with respect to civil actions pending on or commenced on or after such date.

"(b)(1) The following sections of title 28, United States Code [this title], shall apply with respect to civil actions commenced on or after the effective date of this Act [Nov. 1, 1980]:

"(A) Sections 1581(d), 1581(g), 1581(h), 1581(i), and 1583, as amended by section 201 of this Act.

"(B) Sections 2631(d), 2631(g), 2631(h), 2631(i), 2631(j), 2632(a), 2635, 2636, 2637(c), 2639(b), 2640(a)(5), 2640(c), 2640(d), 2643(a), 2643(c)(2), 2643(c)(4), and 2644, as amended by section 301 of this Act.

"(C) Section 1876, as added by section 302(a) of this Act.

"(D) Sections 2601 and 2602, as amended by section 403 of this Act.

"(E) Section 1919, as amended by section 510 of this Act.

"(F) Section 1963A, as added by, section 511(a) of this Act.

"(2) Sections 337(c) and 641(b) of the Tariff Act of 1930 [sections 1337(c) and 1641(b) of Title 19, Customs Duties], as amended by sections 604 and 611 of this Act, shall apply with respect to civil actions commenced on or after the effective date of this Act [Nov. 1, 1980].

"(3) Section 284 of the Trade Act of 1974 [section 2395 of Title 19], as added by section 613 of this Act, shall apply with respect to civil actions commenced on or after the effective date of this Act [Nov. 1, 1980].

"(c)(1) The following sections of title 28, United States Code [this title], shall apply with respect to civil actions commenced on or after the 90th day after the effective date of this Act [Nov. 1, 1980]:

"(A) Sections 1582, 2639(a)(2), and 2640(a)(6), as amended by sections 201 and 301 of this Act.

"(B) Sections 1352, 1355, and 1356, as amended by sections 506, 507, and 508 of this Act.

"(2) Section 592(e) of the Tariff Act of 1930 [section 1592(e) of Title 19], as amended by section 609 of this Act, shall apply with respect to civil actions commenced on or after 90th [sic] day after the effective date of this Act [Nov. 1, 1980]."

[Amendment of section 701 of Pub.L. 96–417 by section 1 of Pub.L. 96–542 effective as of Nov. 1, 1980, see section 3 of Pub.L. 96–542, set out as a note under section 1516a of Title 19, Customs Duties.]

Continuation of Organization of Court

Section 2(b) of Act June 25, 1948, provided in part that the provisions of this title as set out in section 1 of Act June 25, 1948, with respect to the organization of the court, shall be construed as continuations of existing law, and the tenure of the judges, officers, and employees, in office on Sept. 1, 1948, shall not be affected by its enactment, but each of them shall continue to serve in the same capacity under the appropriate provisions of this title, pursuant to his prior appointment.

Effect on Customs Court Judges

Section 703 of Pub.L. 96–417 provided that:

"(a) Except as provided in subsection (b) of this section, the amendments made by title I of this Act [amending this section and section 293(b), (d) of this title] shall not affect the status of any individual serving as judge or chief judge of the Customs Court on the date of enactment of this Act [Oct. 10, 1980].

"(b) The requirement that a person may not continue to serve as chief judge of the Court of International Trade after having reached the age of seventy years, as set forth in the amendment made by section 101 of this Act [amending this section], shall apply to any individual serving as chief judge on or after the date of enactment of this Act [Oct. 10, 1980]."

Effect on Pending Cases

Section 704 of Pub.L. 96–417 provided that: "Nothing in this Act [see section 1 of Pub.L. 96–417, set out as a Short Title of 1980 Amendments note under section 1 of this title] shall cause the dismissal of any action commenced prior to the date of enactment of this Act [Oct. 10, 1980] under jurisdictional statutes relating to the Customs Court or the Court of Customs and Patent Appeals as in effect immediately prior to such date of enactment [Oct. 10, 1980]."

Limitation or Alteration of Jurisdiction

Section 4 of Act July 14, 1956, provided that: "Nothing contained in this Act [amending this section and sections 292(f), 293, and 295 of this title] shall be construed in any way to limit or alter the jurisdiction heretofore conferred upon the United States Customs Court by any provision of law."

References to Certain Courts Deemed References to the United States Court of International Trade

Section 702 of Pub.L. 96–417 provided that: "Any reference in any statute or regulation of the United States to the United States Customs Court, the U.S. Customs Court, or the Customs Court shall be deemed to be a reference to the United States Court of International Trade."

Tennessee Valley Authority Legal Representation

Section 705 of Pub.L. 96–417 provided that: "Nothing in this Act [see section 1 of Pub.L. 96–417, set out as a Short Title of 1980 Amendments note under section 1 of this title] affects the authority of the Tennessee Valley Authority under the Tennessee Valley Authority Act of 1933 [section 831 et seq. of Title 16, Conservation] to represent itself by attorneys of its choosing."

§ 252. Tenure and salaries of judges

Judges of the Court of International Trade shall hold office during good behavior. Each shall receive a salary at an annual rate determined under section 225 of the Federal Salary Act of 1967 (2 U.S.C. 351–361), as adjusted by section 461 of this title.

(June 25, 1948, c. 646, 62 Stat. 899; Mar. 2, 1955, c. 9, § 1(f), 69 Stat. 10; Aug. 14, 1964, Pub.L. 88–426, Title IV, § 403(f), 78 Stat. 434; Aug. 9, 1975, Pub.L. 94–82, Title II, § 205(b)(6), 89 Stat. 423; Oct. 10, 1980, Pub.L. 96–417, Title V, § 502, 94 Stat. 1742.)

HISTORICAL AND STATUTORY NOTES

References in Text

Section 225 of the Federal Salary Act of 1967, referred to in text, is section 225 of Pub.L. 90–206, Dec. 16, 1967, 81 Stat. 642, as amended, which is classified to chapter 11 (section 351 et seq.) of Title 2, The Congress.

Effective Dates

1980 Acts. Amendment by Pub.L. 96–417 effective on Nov. 1, 1980, and applicable with respect to civil actions pending on or commenced on or after such date, see section 701(a) of Pub.L. 96–417, as amended, set out as a note under section 251 of this title.

1964 Acts. Amendment by Pub.L. 88–426 effective on the first day of the first pay period which begins on or after July 1, 1964, except to the extent provided in section 501(c) of Pub.L. 88–426, see section 501 of Pub.L. 88–426.

1955 Acts. Amendment by Act Mar. 2, 1955, effective Mar. 1, 1955, see section 5 of Act Mar. 2, 1955, set out as a note under section 31 of Title 2, The Congress.

Increase in Salaries

1998—Salaries of judges increased to $136,700, effective on the first day of the first applicable pay period beginning on or after Jan. 1, 1998, by Ex. Ord. No. 13071, Dec. 29, 1997, 62 F.R. 68521, set out as a note under section 5332 of Title 5, Government Organization and Employees.

1997—Salaries of judges continued at $133,600 effective on the first day of the first applicable pay period beginning on or after Jan. 1, 1997, by Ex. Ord. No. 13033, Dec. 27, 1996, 61 F.R. 68987, formerly set out as a note under section 5332 of Title 5, Government Organization and Employees.

1996—Salaries of judges continued at $133,600 effective on the first day of the first applicable pay period beginning on or after Jan. 1, 1996, by Ex. Ord. No. 12984, Dec. 28, 1995, 61 F.R. 237, formerly set out as a note under section 5332 of Title 5, Government Organization and Employees.

1995—Salaries of judges continued at $133,600 effective on the first day of the first applicable pay period beginning on or after Jan. 1, 1995, by Ex. Ord. No. 12944, Dec. 28, 1994, 60 F.R. 309, formerly set out as a note under section 5332 of Title 5, Government Organization and Employees.

1993—Salaries of judges increased to $133,600 effective on the first day of the first applicable pay period beginning on or after Jan. 1, 1993, by Ex. Ord. No. 12826, Dec. 30, 1992, 57 F.R. 62909, formerly set out as a note under section 5332 of Title 5, Government Organization and Employees.

1992—Salaries of judges increased to $129,500 per annum, effective on the first day of the first pay period beginning on or after Jan. 1, 1992, by Ex. Ord. No. 12786, Dec. 26, 1991, 56 F.R. 67453, formerly set out as a note under section 5332 of Title 5.

1991—Salaries of judges increased to $125,100 per annum, effective on the first day of the first pay period beginning on or after Jan. 1, 1991, by Ex. Ord. No. 12736, Dec. 12, 1990, 55 F.R. 51385, formerly set out as a note under section 5332 of Title 5.

1990—Salaries of judges continued at $89,500 per annum, and increased to $96,600 per annum, effective on the first day of the first pay period beginning on or after Jan. 31, 1990, by Ex. Ord. No. 12698, Dec. 23, 1989, 54 F.R. 53473, formerly set out as a note under section 5332 of Title 5.

1989—Salaries of judges increased in the amount of 25 percent of their rates (as last in effect before the increase), effective Jan. 1, 1991, see Pub.L. 101–194, Title VII, § 703(a)(3), Nov. 30, 1989, set out as a note under section 5318 of Title 5.

Salaries of judges continued at $89,500 per annum by Ex. Ord. No. 12663, Jan. 6, 1989, 54 F.R. 791, formerly set out as a note under section 5332 of Title 5.

1988—Salaries of judges continued at $89,500 per annum by Ex. Ord. No. 12622, Dec. 31, 1987, 53 F.R. 222, formerly set out as a note under section 5332 of Title 5.

1987—Salaries of judges increased to $89,500 per annum, on recommendation of the President of the United States, see note set out under section 358 of Title 2, The Congress.

Salaries of judges increased to $81,100, as required by section 406 of the Judiciary Appropriation Act, 1987, as incorporated in section 101(b) of Pub.L. 99–500 and section 101(b) of Pub.L. 99–591, effective on the first day of the first pay period beginning on or after Jan. 1, 1987, by Ex. Ord. No. 12578, Dec. 31, 1986, 52 F.R. 505, formerly set out as a note under section 5332 of Title 5.

1985—Salaries of judges increased to $78,700 effective on the first day of the first pay period beginning on or after Jan. 1, 1985, by Ex. Ord. No. 12496, Dec. 28, 1984, 50 F.R. 211, as amended by Ex. Ord. No. 12540, Dec. 30, 1985, 51 F.R. 577, formerly set out as a note under section 5332 of Title 5, Government Organization and Employees. Prior to its amendment by Ex. Ord. No. 12540, schedule 7 of Ex. Ord. No. 12496 had contained a footnote directing that, pursuant to section 140 of Pub.L. 97–92, set out as a note under section 461 of this title, funds were not available to pay a salary at a rate which exceeded the rate in effect of Dec. 15, 1981, which was $70,300.

See also section 2207 of Pub.L. 98–369, set out as a note under section 461 of this title, which provided for overall percentage adjustment increases in certain rates of pay under the General Schedule.

1984—Salaries of judges increased to $76,000 effective on the first day of the first pay period beginning on or after Jan. 1, 1984, by Ex. Ord. No. 12456, Dec. 30, 1983, 49 F.R. 347, as amended Ex. Ord. No. 12477, May 23, 1984, 49 F.R. 22041; Ex. Ord. No. 12487, Sept. 14, 1984, 49 F.R. 36493, formerly set out as a note under section 5332 of Title 5.

1982—Salaries of judges increased to $73,100 effective on the first day of the first pay period beginning on or after Oct. 1, 1982, by Ex. Ord. No. 12387, Oct. 8, 1982, 47 F.R. 44981, formerly set out as a note under section 5332 of Title 5. Ex. Ord. No. 12387 further provided that pursuant to section 140 of Pub.L. 97–92 funds are not available to pay a salary at a rate which exceeds the rate in effect on Dec. 15, 1981, which was $70,300.

Maximum rate payable after Dec. 17, 1982, increased from $70,300 to $73,100, see Pub.L. 97–377, Title I, § 129(b)–(d), Dec. 21, 1982, 96 Stat. 1914, set out as a note under section 5318 of Title 5.

Limitations on use of funds for fiscal year ending Sept. 30, 1983, appropriated by any Act to pay the salary or pay of any individual in legislative, executive, or judicial branch in position equal to or above level V of the Executive Schedule, see section 101(e) of Pub.L. 97–276, as amended, set out as a note under section 5318 of Title 5.

1981—Salaries of judges increased to $70,300 effective on the first day of the first pay period beginning on or after Oct. 1, 1981, by Ex. Ord. No. 12330, Oct. 15, 1981, 46 F.R. 50921, formerly set out as a note under section 5332 of Title 5.

Limitations on use of funds for fiscal year ending Sept. 30, 1982, appropriated by any Act to pay the salary or pay of any individual in legislative, executive, or judicial branch in position equal to or above level V of the Executive Schedule, see sections 101(g) and 141 of Pub.L. 97–92, set out as a note under section 5318 of Title 5.

1980—Salaries of judges increased to $67,100 effective on the first day of the first pay period beginning on or after Oct. 1, 1980, by Ex. Ord. No. 12248, Oct. 16, 1980, 45 F.R. 69199, formerly set out as a note under section 5332 of Title 5. Ex. Ord. No. 12248 further provided that pursuant to Pub.L. 96–369 funds are not available to pay a salary at a rate which exceeds the rate in effect on Sept. 30, 1980, which was $57,497.50.

Limitations on use of funds for fiscal year ending Sept. 30, 1981, appropriated by any Act to pay the salary or pay of any individual in legislative, executive, or judicial branch in position equal to or above level V of the Executive Schedule, see section 101(c) of Pub.L. 96–536, as amended, set out as a note under section 5318 of Title 5.

1979—Salaries of judges increased to $61,500 effective on the first day of the first applicable pay period beginning on or after Oct. 1, 1979, by Ex. Ord. No. 12165, Oct. 9, 1979, 44 F.R. 58671, as amended by Ex. Ord. No. 12200, Mar. 12, 1980, 45 F.R. 16443, formerly set out as a note under section 5332 of Title 5. Ex. Ord. No. 12165 further provided that pursuant to Pub.L. 96–86 funds appropriated for fiscal year 1980 may not be used to pay a salary at a rate which exceeds an increase of 5.5 percent over the applicable rate payable for such position or office in effect on Sept. 30, 1978, which was $57,497.50.

Applicability to funds appropriated by any Act for fiscal year ending Sept. 30, 1980, of limitation of section 304 of Pub.L. 95–391 on use of funds to pay the salary or pay of any individual in legislative, executive, or judicial branch in position equal to or above level V of the Executive Schedule, see section 101 of Pub.L. 96–86, set out as a note under section 5318 of Title 5.

1978—Salaries of judges increased to $57,500 effective on the first day of the first pay period beginning on or after Oct. 1, 1978, by Ex. Ord. No. 12087, Oct. 7, 1978, 43 F.R. 46823, formerly set out as a note under section 5332 of Title 5. Ex. Ord. No. 12087, further provided that pursuant to the Legislative Branch Appropriation Act, 1979 [Pub.L. 95–391, Title III, § 304, Sept. 30, 1978, 92 Stat. 788, set out as a note under section 5318 of Title 5], funds are not available to pay a salary at a rate which exceeds the rate in effect on Sept. 30, 1978, which was $54,500.

1977—Salaries of judges increased to $54,500 per annum, on recommendation of the President of the United States, see note set out under section 358 of Title 2, The Congress.

1976—Salaries of judges increased to $44,000 effective on the first day of the first pay period beginning on or after Oct. 1, 1976, see Ex. Ord. No. 11941, Oct. 1, 1976, 41 F.R. 43889, formerly set out as a note under section 5332 of Title 5, Government Organization and Employees. Ex. Ord. No. 11941, further provided that pursuant to the Legislative Branch Appropriation Act, 1977, funds are not available to pay a salary at a rate which exceeds the rate in effect on Sept. 30, 1976, which was $42,000.

1969—Salaries of judges increased from $30,000 to $40,000 per annum, commencing Feb. 14, 1969, upon recommendation of the President of the United States, see note set out under section 358 of Title 2, The Congress.

1946—The salaries of the presiding judge and associate judges were increased from $10,000 to $15,000 a year by Act July 31, 1946, c. 704, § 1, 60 Stat. 716.

1930—The salaries of the presiding judge and associate judges were increased from $9,000 to $10,000 a year by the Tariff Act of 1930, Act June 17, 1930, c. 497, Title IV, § 518, 46 Stat. 737.

§ 253. Duties of chief judge

(a) The chief judge of the Court of International Trade, with the approval of the court, shall supervise the fiscal affairs and clerical force of the court;[1]

(b) The chief judge shall promulgate dockets.

(c) The chief judge, under rules of the court, may designate any judge or judges of the court to try any case and, when the circumstances so warrant, reassign the case to another judge or judges.

[(d), (e) Repealed. Pub.L. 104–317, Title V, § 501(b)(2)(B), Oct. 19, 1996, 110 Stat. 3856]

(June 25, 1948, c. 646, 62 Stat. 900; Sept. 9, 1959, Pub.L. 86–243, § 3, 73 Stat. 474; June 2, 1970, Pub.L. 91–271, Title I, § 105, 84 Stat. 276; Oct. 10, 1980, Pub.L. 96–417, Title V, § 501(3), 94 Stat. 1742; Oct. 19, 1996, Pub.L. 104–317, Title V, § 501(b)(2), 110 Stat. 3856.)

[1] So in original. The semicolon probably should be a period.

HISTORICAL AND STATUTORY NOTES

Effective Dates

1980 Acts. Amendment by Pub.L. 96–417 effective on Nov. 1, 1980, and applicable with respect to civil actions pending on or commenced on or after such date, see section 701(a) of Pub.L. 96–417, as amended, set out as a note under section 251 of this title.

1970 Acts. Amendment by Pub.L. 91–271 effective on Oct. 1, 1970, see section 122 of Pub.L. 91–271, set out as a note under section 256 of this title.

Savings Provisions

Amendment by Pub.L. 86–243 not to deprive Customs Court [now Court of International Trade] officers or employees of any rights, privileges, or civil service status, see section 4 of Pub.L. 86–243, set out as a note under section 871 of this title.

§ 254. Single-judge trials

Except as otherwise provided in section 255 of this title, the judicial power of the Court of International Trade with respect to any action, suit or proceeding shall be exercised by a single judge, who may preside alone and hold a regular or special session of court at the same time other sessions are held by other judges.

(June 25, 1948, c. 646, 62 Stat. 900; May 24, 1949, c. 139, § 66, 63 Stat. 99; June 2, 1970, Pub.L. 91–271, Title I, § 106, 84 Stat. 277; Oct. 10, 1980, Pub.L. 96–417, Title V, § 501(4), 94 Stat. 1742.)

HISTORICAL AND STATUTORY NOTES

Effective Dates

1980 Acts. Amendment by Pub.L. 96–417 effective on Nov. 1, 1980, and applicable with respect to civil actions pending on or commenced on or after such date, see section 701(a) of Pub.L. 96–417, as amended, set out as a note under section 251 of this title.

1970 Acts. Amendment by Pub.L. 91–271 effective on Oct. 1, 1970, see section 122 of Pub.L. 91–271, set out as a note under section 256 of this title.

Transfer of Functions

All offices of collector of customs, comptroller of customs, surveyor of customs, and appraiser of merchandise in the Bureau of Customs of the Department of the Treasury to which appointments were required to be made by the President with the advice and consent of the Senate were ordered abolished, with such offices to be terminated not later than December 31, 1966, by Reorg. Plan No. 1 of 1965, eff. May 25, 1965, 30 F.R. 7035, 79 Stat. 1317, set out in Appendix 1 to Title 5, Government Organization and Employees. All functions of the offices eliminated were already vested in the Secretary of the Treasury by Reorg. Plan No. 26 of 1950, eff. July 31, 1950, 15 F.R. 4935, 64 Stat. 1280, set out in Appendix 1 to Title 5.

Prior Provisions

Provisions similar to those relating to the assignment of judges to hear and determine cases, and provisions similar to those authorizing the chief judge to designate judges to hear and determine cases within the jurisdiction of the United

States, formerly contained in this section, are now covered by sections 255 and 256(a) of this title, respectively.

§ 255. Three-judge trials

(a) Upon application of any party to a civil action, or upon his own initiative, the chief judge of the Court of International Trade shall designate any three judges of the court to hear and determine any civil action which the chief judge finds: (1) raises an issue of the constitutionality of an Act of Congress, a proclamation of the President or an Executive order; or (2) has broad or significant implications in the administration or interpretation of the customs laws.

(b) A majority of the three judges designated may hear and determine the civil action and all questions pending therein.

(Added Pub.L. 91–271, Title I, § 108, June 2, 1970, 84 Stat. 277, and amended Pub.L. 96–417, Title V, § 501(5), Oct. 10, 1980, 94 Stat. 1742.)

HISTORICAL AND STATUTORY NOTES

Effective Dates

1980 Acts. Amendment by Pub.L. 96–417 effective on Nov. 1, 1980, and applicable with respect to civil actions pending on or commenced on or after such date, see section 701(a) of Pub.L. 96–417, as amended, set out as a note under section 251 of this title.

1970 Acts. Section effective on Oct. 1, 1970, see section 122 of Pub.L. 91–271, set out as a note under section 256 of this title.

Prior Provisions

A prior section 255, relating to the publication of decisions of the Customs Court, formerly contained in this section, was renumbered section 257 of this title.

§ 256. Trials at ports other than New York

(a) The chief judge may designate any judge or judges of the court to proceed, together with necessary assistants, to any port or to any place within the jurisdiction of the United States to preside at a trial or hearing at the port or place.

(b) Upon application of a party or upon his own initiative, and upon a showing that the interests of economy, efficiency, and justice will be served, the chief judge may issue an order authorizing a judge of the court to preside in an evidentiary hearing in a foreign country whose laws do not prohibit such a hearing: *Provided, however,* That an interlocutory appeal may be taken from such an order pursuant to the provisions of section 1292(d)(1) of this title, and the United States Court of Appeals for the Federal Circuit may, in its discretion, consider the appeal.

(Added Pub.L. 91–271, Title I, § 109, June 2, 1970, 84 Stat. 277, and amended Pub.L. 97–164, Title I, § 107, Apr. 2, 1982, 96 Stat. 28.)

HISTORICAL AND STATUTORY NOTES

Effective Dates

1982 Acts. Amendment by Pub.L. 97–164 effective Oct. 1, 1982, see section 402 of Pub.L. 97–164, set out as a note under section 171 of this title.

1970 Acts. Section 122 of Title I of Pub.L. 91–271 provided that:

"**(a)** This title [see Short Title of 1970 Amendments note set out under section 1 of this title] shall become effective on October 1, 1970, and shall thereafter apply to all actions and proceedings in the Customs Court and the Court of Customs and Patent Appeals except those involving merchandise entered before the effective date for which trial has commenced by such effective date.

"**(b)** An appeal for reappraisement timely filed with the Bureau of Customs before the effective date, but as to which trial has not commenced by such date, shall be deemed to have had a summons timely and properly filed under this title. When the judgment or order of the United States Customs Court has become final in this appeal, the papers shall be returned to the appropriate customs officer to decide any remaining matters relating to the entry in accordance with section 500 of the Tariff Act of 1930, as amended [section 1500 of Title 19, Customs Duties]. A protest or summons filed after final decision on an appeal for reappraisement shall not include issues which were raised or could have been raised on the appeal for reappraisement.

"**(c)** A protest timely filed with the Bureau of Customs before the effective date of enactment of this Act [June 2, 1970], which is disallowed before that date, and as to which trial has not commenced by such date, shall be deemed to have had a summons timely and properly filed under this title.

"**(d)** All other provisions of this Act [see Short Title notes set out under section 1 of this title and section 1500 of Title 19] shall apply to appeals and disallowed protests deemed to have had summonses timely and properly filed under this section."

§ 257. Publication of decisions

All decisions of the Court of International Trade shall be preserved and open to inspection. The court shall forward copies of each decision to the Secretary of the Treasury or his designee and to the appropriate customs officer for the district in which the case arose. The Secretary shall publish weekly such decisions as he or the court may designate and abstracts of all other decisions.

(June 25, 1948, c. 646, 62 Stat. 900, § 255; renumbered § 257, and amended June 2, 1970, Pub.L. 91–271, Title I, § 107, 84 Stat. 277; Oct. 10, 1980, Pub.L. 96–417, Title V, § 501(6), 94 Stat. 1742.)

HISTORICAL AND STATUTORY NOTES

Effective Dates

1980 Acts. Amendment by Pub.L. 96–417 effective on Nov. 1, 1980, and applicable with respect to civil actions pending on or commenced on or after such date, see section 701(a) of Pub.L. 96–417, as amended, set out as a note under section 251 of this title.

1970 Acts. Amendment by Pub.L. 91–271 effective on Oct. 1, 1970, see section 122 of Pub.L. 91–271, set out as a note under section 256 of this title.

Transfer of Functions

All offices of collector of customs, comptroller of customs, surveyor of customs, and appraiser of merchandise in the Bureau of Customs of the Department of the Treasury to which appointments were required to be made by the President with the advice and consent of the Senate were ordered abolished, with such offices to be terminated not later than December 31, 1966, by Reorg. Plan No. 1 of 1965, eff. May 25, 1965, 30 F.R. 7035, 79 Stat. 1317, set out in the Appendix to Title 5, Government Organization and Employees. All functions of the offices eliminated were already vested in the Secretary of the Treasury by Reorg. Plan No. 26 of 1950, eff. July 31, 1950, 15 F.R. 4935, 64 Stat. 1280, set out in the Appendix to Title 5.

§ 258. Chief judges; precedence of judges

(a)(1) The chief judge of the Court of International Trade shall be the judge of the court in regular active service who is senior in commission of those judges who—

(A) are 64 years of age or under;

(B) have served for 1 year or more as a judge of the court; and

(C) have not served previously as chief judge.

(2)(A) In any case in which no judge of the court meets the qualifications under paragraph (1), the youngest judge in regular active service who is 65 years of age or over and who has served as a judge of the court for 1 year or more shall act as the chief judge.

(B) In any case under subparagraph (A) in which there is no judge of the court in regular active service who has served as a judge of the court for 1 year or more, the judge of the court in regular active service who is senior in commission and who has not served previously as chief judge shall act as the chief judge.

(3)(A) Except as provided under subparagraph (C), the chief judge serving under paragraph (1) shall serve for a term of 7 years and shall serve after expiration of such term until another judge is eligible under paragraph (1) to serve as chief judge.

(B) Except as provided under subparagraph (C), a judge of the court acting as chief judge under subparagraph (A) or (B) of paragraph (2) shall serve until a judge meets the qualifications under paragraph (1).

(C) No judge of the court may serve or act as chief judge of the court after attaining the age of 70 years unless no other judge is qualified to serve as chief judge under paragraph (1) or is qualified to act as chief judge under paragraph (2).

(b) The chief judge shall have precedence and preside at any session of the court which such judge attends. Other judges of the court shall have precedence and preside according to the seniority of their commissions. Judges whose commissions bear the same date shall have precedence according to seniority in age.

(c) If the chief judge desires to be relieved of the duties as chief judge while retaining active status as a judge of the court, the chief judge may so certify to the Chief Justice of the United States, and thereafter the chief judge of the court shall be such other judge of the court who is qualified to serve or act as chief judge under subsection (a).

(d) If a chief judge is temporarily unable to perform the duties as such, such duties shall be performed by the judge of the court in active service, able and qualified to act, who is next in precedence.

(Added Pub.L. 104–317, Title V, § 501(a), Oct. 19, 1996, 110 Stat. 3855.)

HISTORICAL AND STATUTORY NOTES

Continuance of Position of Chief Judge

Section 501(c) of Pub.L. 104–317 provided that:

"(1) Notwithstanding the provisions of section 258(a) of title 28, United States Code (as added by subsection (a) of this section) [subsec. (a) of this section, as added by section 501(a) of Pub.L. 104–317], the chief judge of the United States Court of International Trade who is in office on the day before the date of enactment of this Act [Oct. 19, 1996] shall continue to be such chief judge on or after such date until any one of the following events occurs:

"(A) The chief judge is relieved of his duties under section 258(c) of title 28, United States Code [subsec. (c) of this section].

"(B) The regular active status of the chief judge is terminated.

"(C) The chief judge attains the age of 70 years.

"(D) The chief judge has served for a term of 7 years as chief judge.

"(2) When the chief judge vacates the position of chief judge under paragraph (1), the position of chief judge of the Court of International Trade shall be filled in accordance with section 258(a) of title 28, United States Code [subsec. (a) of this section]."

CHAPTER 13—ASSIGNMENT OF JUDGES TO OTHER COURTS

Sec.
291. Circuit judges.
292. District judges.
293. Judges of the Court of International Trade.
294. Assignment of retired justices or judges to active duty.[1]

Sec.
295. Conditions upon designation and assignment.
296. Powers upon designation and assignment.
297. Assignment of judges to courts of the freely associated compact states.

[1] Section catchline amended by Pub.L. 85–755 without corresponding amendment of analysis.

§ 291. Circuit judges

(a) The Chief Justice of the United States may, in the public interest, designate and assign temporarily any circuit judge to act as circuit judge in another circuit upon request by the chief judge or circuit justice of such circuit.

(b) The chief judge of a circuit or the circuit justice may, in the public interest, designate and assign temporarily any circuit judge within the circuit, including a judge designated and assigned to temporary duty therein, to hold a district court in any district within the circuit.

(June 25, 1948, c. 646, 62 Stat. 900; July 28, 1953, c. 253, § 2, 67 Stat. 226; Sept. 3, 1954, c. 1263, § 39(b), 68 Stat. 1240; July 9, 1956, c. 517, § 1(a), 70 Stat. 497; Aug. 25, 1958, Pub.L. 85–755, § 2, 72 Stat. 848; Nov. 6, 1978, Pub.L. 95–598, Title II, § 202, 92 Stat. 2660; Apr. 2, 1982, Pub.L. 97–164, Title I, § 108, 96 Stat. 28; Oct. 29, 1992, Pub.L. 102–572, Title I, § 104, 106 Stat. 4507.)

HISTORICAL AND STATUTORY NOTES

Codifications

Subsec. (c) of this section was amended by Pub.L. 95–598, Title II, § 202, Nov. 6, 1978, 92 Stat. 2660, effective June 28, 1984, pursuant to Pub.L. 95–598, Title IV, § 402(b), Nov. 6, 1978, 92 Stat. 2682, as amended by Pub.L. 98–249, § 1(a), Mar. 31, 1984, 98 Stat. 116; Pub.L. 98–271, § 1(a), Apr. 30, 1984, 98 Stat. 163; Pub.L. 98–299, § 1(a), May 25, 1984, 98 Stat. 214; Pub.L. 98–325, § 1(a), June 20, 1984, 98 Stat. 268, set out as a note preceding section 101 of Title 11, Bankruptcy, by adding "or bankruptcy" after "to hold a district".

Section 402(b) of Pub.L. 95–598 was amended by section 113 of Pub.L. 98–353, Title I, July 10, 1984, 98 Stat. 343, by substituting "shall not be effective" for "shall take effect on June 28, 1984", thereby eliminating the amendment by section 202 of Pub.L. 95–598, effective June 27, 1984, pursuant to section 122(c) of Pub.L. 98–353, set out as an Effective Date note under section 151 of this title.

Section 121(a) of Pub.L. 98–353 directed that section 402(b) of Pub.L. 95–598 be amended by substituting "the date of enactment of the Bankruptcy Amendments and Federal Judgeship Act of 1984 [i.e. July 10, 1984]" for "June 28, 1984". This amendment was not executed in view of the prior amendment to section 402(b) of Pub.L. 95–598 by section 113 of Pub.L. 98–353.

Effective Dates

1992 Acts. Amendment by Pub.L. 102–572 effective Jan. 1, 1993, see section 1101(a) of Pub.L. 102–572, set out as a note under section 905 of Title 2, The Congress.

1982 Acts. Amendment by Pub.L. 97–164 effective Oct. 1, 1982, see section 402 of Pub.L. 97–164, set out as a note under section 171 of this title.

Jurisdiction of United States Court of Customs and Patent Appeals

Section 7 of Pub.L. 85–755 provided that: "Nothing contained in this Act [amending sections 211 and 291 to 295 of this title] shall be construed in any way to limit or alter the jurisdiction heretofore conferred upon the United States Court of Customs and Patent Appeals [now United States Court of Appeals for the Federal Circuit] by any provision of law."

§ 292. District judges

(a) The chief judge of a circuit may designate and assign one or more district judges within the circuit to sit upon the court of appeals or a division thereof whenever the business of that court so requires. Such designations or assignments shall be in conformity with the rules or orders of the court of appeals of the circuit.

(b) The chief judge of a circuit may, in the public interest, designate and assign temporarily any district judge of the circuit to hold a district court in any district within the circuit.

(c) The chief judge of the United States Court of Appeals for the District of Columbia Circuit may, upon presentation of a certificate of necessity by the chief judge of the Superior Court of the District of Columbia pursuant to section 11–908(c) of the District of Columbia Code, designate and assign temporarily any district judge of the circuit to serve as a judge of such Superior Court, if such assignment (1) is approved by the Attorney General of the United States following a determination by him to the effect that such assignment is necessary to meet the ends of justice, and (2) is approved by the chief judge of the United States District Court for the District of Columbia.

(d) The Chief Justice of the United States may designate and assign temporarily a district judge of one circuit for service in another circuit, either in a district court or court of appeals, upon presentation of a certificate of necessity by the chief judge or circuit justice of the circuit wherein the need arises.

(e) The Chief Justice of the United States may designate and assign temporarily any district judge to serve as a judge of the Court of International Trade upon presentation to him of a certificate of necessity by the chief judge of the court.

(June 25, 1948, c. 646, 62 Stat. 901; July 28, 1953, c. 253, § 3, 67 Stat. 226; Sept. 3, 1954, c. 1263, § 39(c), 68 Stat. 1240; July 9, 1956, c. 517, § 1(b), 70 Stat. 497; July 14, 1956, c. 589, § 2, 70 Stat. 532; Aug. 25, 1958, Pub.L. 85–755, § 3, 72 Stat. 848; July 29, 1970, Pub.L. 91–358, Title I, § 172(e), 84 Stat. 591; Nov. 6, 1978, Pub.L. 95–598, Title II, §§ 203, 204, 92 Stat. 2660; Oct. 10, 1980, Pub.L. 96–417, Title V, § 501(7), 94 Stat. 1742; Apr. 2, 1982, Pub.L. 97–164, Title I, § 109, 96 Stat. 28.)

HISTORICAL AND STATUTORY NOTES

Codifications

This section was amended by Pub.L. 95–598, Title II, §§ 203, 204, Nov. 6, 1978, 92 Stat. 2660, effective June 28, 1984, pursuant to Pub.L. 95–598, Title IV, § 402(b), Nov. 6, 1978, 92 Stat. 2682, as amended by Pub.L. 98–249, § 1(a), Mar. 31, 1984, 98 Stat. 116; Pub.L. 98–271, § 1(a), Apr. 30, 1984, 98 Stat. 163; Pub.L. 98–299, § 1(a), May 25, 1984, 98 Stat. 214; Pub.L. 98–325, § 1(a), June 20, 1984, 98 Stat. 268, set out as a note preceding section 101 of Title II, Bankruptcy, in subsec. (b) by substituting "a district court or a bankruptcy court" for "a district court" and in subsec. (d) by substituting "in a bankruptcy court, district court, or court of appeals" for "either in a district court or court of appeals".

Section 402(b) of Pub.L. 95–598 was amended by section 113 of Pub.L. 98–353, Title I, July 10, 1984, 98 Stat. 343, by substituting "shall not be effective" for "shall take effect on June 28, 1984", thereby eliminating the amendments by sections 203 and 204 of Pub.L. 95–598, effective June 27, 1984, pursuant to section 122(c) of Pub.L. 98–353, set out as an Effective Date note under section 151 of this title.

Section 121(a) of Pub.L. 98–353 directed that section 402(b) of Pub.L. 95–598 be amended by substituting "the date of enactment of the Bankruptcy Amendments and Federal Judgeship Act of 1984 [i.e. July 10, 1984]" for "June 28, 1984". This amendment was not executed in view of the prior amendment to section 402(b) of Pub.L. 95–598 by section 113 of Pub.L. 98–353.

Effective Dates

1982 Acts. Amendment by Pub.L. 97–164 effective Oct. 1, 1982, see section 402 of Pub.L. 97–164, set out as a note under section 171 of this title.

1980 Acts. Amendment by Pub.L. 96–417 effective on Nov. 1, 1980, and applicable with respect to civil actions pending on or commenced on or after such date, see section 701(a) of Pub.L. 96–417, as amended, set out as a note under section 251 of this title.

1970 Acts. Amendment by Pub.L. 91–358 effective the first day of the seventh calendar month which begins after July 29, 1970, see section 199(a) of Pub.L. 91–358, set out as a note under section 1257 of this title.

Jurisdiction of United States Court of Customs and Patent Appeals

Amendment by Pub.L. 85–755 not limiting or altering the jurisdiction of the United States Court of Customs and Patent Appeals [now United States Court of Appeals for the Federal Circuit], see section 7 of Pub.L. 85–755, set out as a note under section 291 of this title.

Limitation or Alteration of Jurisdiction

Amendment by Act July 14, 1956, not to be construed as limiting or altering the jurisdiction heretofore conferred upon the Customs Court [now the United States Court of International Trade], see section 4 of Act July 14, 1956, set out as a note under section 251 of this title.

§ 293. Judges of the Court of International Trade

(a)[1] The Chief Justice of the United States may designate and assign temporarily any judge of the Court of International Trade to perform judicial duties in any circuit, either in a court of appeals or district court, upon presentation of a certificate of necessity by the chief judge or circuit justice of the circuit in which the need arises.

(June 25, 1948, c. 646, 62 Stat. 901; July 14, 1956, c. 589, § 3(a), 70 Stat. 532; Aug. 25, 1958, Pub.L. 85–755, § 4, 72 Stat. 848; Nov. 6, 1978, Pub.L. 95–598, Title II, § 205, 92 Stat. 2660; Oct. 10, 1980, Pub.L. 96–417, Title I, § 102, Title V, § 501(8), 94 Stat. 1727, 1742; Apr. 2, 1982, Pub.L. 97–164, Title I, § 110(a), (b), 96 Stat. 29.)

[1] There is no subsec. (b).

HISTORICAL AND STATUTORY NOTES

Codifications

This section was amended by Pub.L. 95–598, Title II, § 205, Nov. 6, 1978, 92 Stat. 2660; Pub.L. 97–164, Title I, § 110(a)(3), Apr. 2, 1982, 96 Stat. 29, effective June 28, 1984, pursuant to Pub.L. 95–598, Title IV, § 402(b), Nov. 6, 1978, 92 Stat. 2682, as amended by Pub.L. 98–249, § 1(a), Mar. 31, 1984, 98 Stat. 116; Pub.L. 98–271, § 1(a), Apr. 30, 1984, 98 Stat. 163; Pub.L. 98–299, § 1(a), May 25, 1984, 98 Stat. 214; Pub.L. 98–325, § 1(a), June 20, 1984, 98 Stat. 268, set out as a note preceding section 101 of Title II, Bankruptcy, by adding a subsec. (b) to read as follows:

(b)(1) The Chief Justice of the United States may designate and assign temporarily a bankruptcy judge of one circuit for service in a bankruptcy court in another circuit upon presentation of a certificate of necessity by the chief judge or circuit justice of the circuit wherein the need arises.

(2) The chief judge of a circuit may, in the public interest, designate and assign temporarily a bankruptcy judge of the circuit to hold a bankruptcy court in any district within the circuit.

Section 402(b) of Pub.L. 95–598 was amended by section 113 of Pub.L. 98–353, Title I, July 10, 1984, 98 Stat. 343, by substituting "shall not be effective" for "shall take effect on June 28, 1984", thereby eliminating the amendment by section 205 of Pub.L. 95–598, effective June 27, 1984, pursuant to section 122(c) of Pub.L. 98–353, set out as an Effective Date note under section 151 of this title.

Section 121(a) of Pub.L. 98–353 directed that section 402(b) of Pub.L. 95–598 be amended by substituting "the date of enactment of the Bankruptcy Amendments and Federal Judgeship Act of 1984 [i.e. July 10, 1984]" for "June 28, 1984". This amendment was not executed in view of the prior amendment to section 402(b) of Pub.L. 95–598 by section 113 of Pub.L. 98–353.

Effective Dates

1982 Acts. Amendment by Pub.L. 97–164 effective Oct. 1, 1982, see section 402 of Pub.L. 97–164, set out as a note under section 171 of this title.

1980 Acts. Amendment by Pub.L. 96–417 effective on Nov. 1, 1980, and applicable with respect to civil actions pending on or commenced on or after such date, see section 701(a) of Pub.L. 96–417, as amended, set out as a note under section 251 of this title.

Jurisdiction of United States Court of Customs and Patent Appeals

Amendment by Pub.L. 85–755 not limiting or altering the jurisdiction of the United States Court of Customs and Patent Appeals [now United States Court of Appeals for the Federal Circuit], see section 7 of Pub.L. 85–755, set out as a note under section 291 of this title.

Limitation or Alteration of Jurisdiction

Amendment by Act July 14, 1956, not to be construed as limiting or altering the jurisdiction heretofore conferred upon the Customs Court [now United States Court of International Trade], see section 4 of Act July 14, 1956, set out as a note under section 251 of this title.

§ 294. Assignment of retired Justices or judges to active duty

(a) Any retired Chief Justice of the United States or Associate Justice of the Supreme Court may be designated and assigned by the Chief Justice of the United States to perform such judicial duties in any circuit, including those of a circuit justice, as he is willing to undertake.

(b) Any judge of the United States who has retired from regular active service under section 371(b) or 372(a) of this title shall be known and designated as a senior judge and may continue to perform such judicial duties as he is willing and able to undertake, when designated and assigned as provided in subsections (c) and (d).

(c) Any retired circuit or district judge may be designated and assigned by the chief judge or judicial council of his circuit to perform such judicial duties within the circuit as he is willing and able to undertake. Any other retired judge of the United States may be designated and assigned by the chief judge of his court to perform such judicial duties in such court as he is willing and able to undertake.

(d) The Chief Justice of the United States shall maintain a roster of retired judges of the United States who are willing and able to undertake special judicial duties from time to time outside their own circuit, in the case of a retired circuit or district judge, or in a court other than their own, in the case of other retired judges, which roster shall be known as the roster of senior judges. Any such retired judge of the United States may be designated and assigned by the Chief Justice to perform such judicial duties as he is willing and able to undertake in a court outside his own circuit, in the case of a retired circuit or district judge, or in a court other than his own, in the case of any other retired judge of the United States. Such designation and assignment to a court of appeals or district court shall be made upon the presentation of a certificate of necessity by the chief judge or circuit justice of the circuit wherein the need arises and to any other court of the United States upon the presentation of a certificate of necessity by the chief judge of such court. No such designation or assignment shall be made to the Supreme Court.

(e) No retired Justice or judge shall perform judicial duties except when designated and assigned.

(June 25, 1948, c. 646, 62 Stat. 901; July 9, 1956, c. 517, § 1(c), 70 Stat. 497; Aug. 29, 1957, Pub.L. 85–219, 71 Stat. 495; Aug. 25, 1958, Pub.L. 85–755, § 5, 72 Stat. 849; Nov. 6, 1978, Pub.L. 95–598, Title II, § 206, 92 Stat. 2660.)

HISTORICAL AND STATUTORY NOTES

Codifications

This section was amended by Pub.L. 95–598, Title II, § 206, Nov. 6, 1978, 92 Stat. 2660, effective June 28, 1984, pursuant to Pub.L. 95–598, Title IV, § 402(b), Nov. 6, 1978, 92 Stat. 2682, as amended by Pub.L. 98–249, § 1(a), Mar. 31, 1984, 98 Stat. 116; Pub.L. 98–271, § 1(a), Apr. 30, 1984, 98 Stat. 163; Pub.L. 98–299, § 1(a), May 25, 1984, 98 Stat. 214; Pub.L. 98–325, § 1(a), June 20, 1984, 98 Stat. 268, set out as a note preceding section 101 of Title II, Bankruptcy, in subsec. (c) by deleting "or district" and inserting "district or bankruptcy judge" and in subsec. (d) by striking out "or district judge" and inserting in lieu thereof ", district judge or bankruptcy judge".

Section 402(b) of Pub.L. 95–598 was amended by section 113 of Pub.L. 98–353, Title I, July 10, 1984, 98 Stat. 343, by substituting "shall not be effective" for "shall take effect on June 28, 1984", thereby eliminating the amendment by section 206 of Pub.L. 95–598, effective June 27, 1984, pursuant to section 122(c) of Pub.L. 98–353, set out as an Effective Date note under section 151 of this title.

Section 121(a) of Pub.L. 98–353 directed that section 402(b) of Pub.L. 95–598 be amended by substituting "the date of enactment of the Bankruptcy Amendments and Federal Judgeship Act of 1984 [i.e. July 10, 1984]" for "June 28, 1984". This amendment was not executed in view of the prior amendment to section 402(b) of Pub.L. 95–598 by section 113 of Pub.L. 98–353.

Jurisdiction of United States Court of Customs and Patent Appeals

Amendment by Pub.L. 85–755 not limiting or altering the jurisdiction of the United States Court of Customs and Patent Appeals [now United States Court of Appeals for the Federal Circuit], see section 7 of Pub.L. 85–755, set out as a note under section 291 of this title.

§ 295. Conditions upon designation and assignment

No designation and assignment of a circuit or district judge in active service shall be made without the consent of the chief judge or judicial council of the circuit from which the judge is to be designated and assigned. No designation and assignment of a judge of any other court of the United States in active service shall be made without the consent of the chief judge of such court.

All designations and assignments of justices and judges shall be filed with the clerks and entered on the minutes of the courts from and to which made.

The Chief Justice of the United States, a circuit justice or a chief judge of a circuit may make new designation and assignments in accordance with the provisions of this chapter and may revoke those previously made by him.

(June 25, 1948, c. 646, 62 Stat. 901; Sept. 3, 1954, c. 1263, § 39(d), 68 Stat. 1240; July 14, 1956, c. 589, § 3(b), 70 Stat. 532; Aug. 25, 1958, Pub.L. 85–755, § 6, 72 Stat. 850; Nov. 6, 1978, Pub.L. 95–598, Title II, § 207, 92 Stat. 2660.)

HISTORICAL AND STATUTORY NOTES

Codifications

This section was amended by Pub.L. 95–598, Title II, § 207, Nov. 6, 1978, 92 Stat. 2660, effective June 28, 1984, pursuant to Pub.L. 95–598, Title IV, § 402(b), Nov. 6, 1978, 92 Stat. 2682, as amended by Pub.L. 98–249, § 1(a), Mar. 31, 1984, 98 Stat. 116; Pub.L. 98–271, § 1(a), Apr. 30, 1984, 98 Stat. 163; Pub.L. 98–299, § 1(a), May 25, 1984, 98 Stat. 214; Pub.L. 98–325, § 1(a), June 20, 1984, 98 Stat. 268, set out as a note preceding section 101 of Title II, Bankruptcy, by substituting "circuit, district, or bankruptcy judge" for "circuit or district judge".

Section 402(b) of Pub.L. 95–598 was amended by section 113 of Pub.L. 98–353, Title I, July 10, 1984, 98 Stat. 343, by substituting "shall not be effective" for "shall take effect on June 28, 1984", thereby eliminating the amendment by section 207 of Pub.L. 95–598, effective June 27, 1984, pursuant to section 122(c) of Pub.L. 98–353, set out as an Effective Date note under section 151 of this title.

Section 121(a) of Pub.L. 98–353 directed that section 402(b) of Pub.L. 95–598 be amended by substituting "the date of enactment of the Bankruptcy Amendments and Federal Judgeship Act of 1984 [i.e. July 10, 1984]" for "June 28, 1984". This amendment was not executed in view of the prior amendment to section 402(b) of Pub.L. 95–598 by section 113 of Pub.L. 98–353.

Jurisdiction of United States Court of Customs and Patent Appeals

Amendment by Pub.L. 85–755 not limiting or altering the jurisdiction of the United States Court of Customs and Patent Appeals [now United States Court of Appeals for the Federal Circuit], see section 7 of Pub.L. 85–755, set out as a note under section 291 of this title.

Limitation or Alteration of Jurisdiction

Amendment by Act July 14, 1956, not to be construed as limiting or altering the jurisdiction heretofore conferred upon the Customs Court [now United States Court of International Trade], see section 4 of Act July 14, 1956, set out as a note under section 251 of this title.

§ 296. Powers upon designation and assignment

A justice or judge shall discharge, during the period of his designation and assignment, all judicial duties for which he is designated and assigned. He may be required to perform any duty which might be required of a judge of the court or district or circuit to which he is designated and assigned.

Such justice or judge shall have all the powers of a judge of the court, circuit or district to which he is designated and assigned, except the power to appoint any person to a statutory position or to designate permanently a depository of funds or a newspaper for publication of legal notices.

A justice or judge who has sat by designation and assignment in another district or circuit may, notwithstanding his absence from such district or circuit or the expiration of the period of his designation and assignment, decide or join in the decision and final disposition of all matters submitted to him during such period and in the consideration and disposition of applications for rehearing or further proceedings in such matters.

(June 25, 1948, c. 646, 62 Stat. 901.)

§ 297. Assignment of judges to courts of the freely associated compact states

(a) The Chief Justice or the chief judge of the United States Court of Appeals for the Ninth Circuit may assign any circuit or district judge of the Ninth Circuit, with the consent of the judge so assigned, to serve temporarily as a judge of any duly constituted court of the freely associated compact states whenever an official duly authorized by the laws of the respective compact state requests such assignment and such assignment is necessary for the proper dispatch of the business of the respective court.

(b) The Congress consents to the acceptance and retention by any judge so authorized of reimbursement from the countries referred to in subsection (a) of all necessary travel expenses, including transportation, and of subsistence, or of a reasonable per diem allowance in lieu of subsistence. The judge shall report to the Administrative Office of the United States Courts any amount received pursuant to this subsection.

(Added Pub.L. 100–702, Title X, § 1022(1), Nov. 19, 1988, 102 Stat. 4672.)

CHAPTER 15—CONFERENCES AND COUNCILS OF JUDGES

Sec.
331. Judicial Conference of the United States.
332. Judicial councils of circuits.
333. Judicial conferences of circuits.
334. Institutes and joint councils on sentencing.
335. Judicial Conference of the Court of International Trade.

§ 331. Judicial Conference of the United States

The Chief Justice of the United States shall summon annually the chief judge of each judicial circuit, the chief judge of the Court of International Trade, and a district judge from each judicial circuit to a conference at such time and place in the United States as he may designate. He shall preside at such conference which shall be known as the Judicial Conference of the United States. Special sessions of the Conference may be called by the Chief Justice at such times and places as he may designate.

The district judge to be summoned from each judicial circuit shall be chosen by the circuit and district judges of the circuit and shall serve as a member of the Judicial Conference of the United States for a term of not less than 3 successive years nor more than 5 successive years, as established by majority vote of all circuit and district judges of the circuit. A district judge serving as a member of the Judicial Conference may be either a judge in regular active service or a judge retired from regular active service under section 371(b) of this title.

If the chief judge of any circuit, the chief judge of the Court of International Trade, or the district judge chosen by the judges of the circuit is unable to attend, the Chief Justice may summon any other circuit or district judge from such circuit or any other judge of the Court of International Trade, as the case may be. Every judge summoned shall attend and, unless excused by the Chief Justice, shall remain throughout the sessions of the conference and advise as to the needs of his circuit or court and as to any matters in respect of which the administration of justice in the courts of the United States may be improved.

The Conference shall make a comprehensive survey of the condition of business in the courts of the United States and prepare plans for assignment of judges to or from circuits or districts where necessary. It shall also submit suggestions and recommendations to the various courts to promote uniformity of management procedures and the expeditious conduct of court business. The Conference is authorized to exercise the authority provided in section 372(c) of this title as the Conference, or through a standing committee. If the Conference elects to establish a standing committee, it shall be appointed by the Chief Justice and all petitions for review shall be reviewed by that committee. The Conference or the standing committee may hold hearings, take sworn testimony, issue subpoenas and subpoenas duces tecum, and make necessary and appropriate orders in the exercise of its authority. Subpoenas and subpoenas duces tecum shall be issued by the clerk of the Supreme Court or by the clerk of any court of appeals, at the direction of the Chief Justice or his designee and under the seal of the court, and shall be served in the manner provided in rule 45(c) of the Federal Rules of Civil Procedure for subpoenas and subpoenas duces tecum issued on behalf of the United States or an officer or any agency thereof. The Conference may also prescribe and modify rules for the exercise of the authority provided in section 372(c) of this title. All judicial officers and employees of the United States shall promptly carry into effect all orders of the Judicial Conference or the standing committee established pursuant to this section.

The Conference shall also carry on a continuous study of the operation and effect of the general rules of practice and procedure now or hereafter in use as prescribed by the Supreme Court for the other courts of the United States pursuant to law. Such changes in and additions to those rules as the Conference may deem desirable to promote simplicity in procedure, fairness in administration, the just determination of litigation, and the elimination of unjustifiable expense and delay shall be recommended by the Conference from time to time to the Supreme Court for its consideration and adoption, modification or rejection, in accordance with law.

The Judicial Conference shall review rules prescribed under section 2071 of this title by the courts, other than the Supreme Court and the district courts, for consistency with Federal law. The Judicial Conference may modify or abrogate any such rule so reviewed found inconsistent in the course of such a review.

The Attorney General shall, upon request of the Chief Justice, report to such Conference on matters relating to the business of the several courts of the United States, with particular reference to cases to which the United States is a party.

The Chief Justice shall submit to Congress an annual report of the proceedings of the Judicial Conference and its recommendations for legislation.

(June 25, 1948, c. 646, 62 Stat. 902; July 9, 1956, c. 517, § 1(d), 70 Stat. 497; Aug. 28, 1957, Pub.L. 85–202, 71 Stat. 476; July 11, 1958, Pub.L. 85–513, 72 Stat. 356; Sept. 19, 1961, Pub.L. 87–253, §§ 1, 2, 75 Stat. 521; Nov. 6, 1978, Pub.L. 95–598, Title II, § 208, 92 Stat. 2660; Oct. 15, 1980, Pub.L. 96–458, § 4, 94 Stat. 2040; Apr. 2, 1982, Pub.L. 97–164, Title I, § 111, 96 Stat. 29; Oct. 14, 1986, Pub.L. 99–466, § 1, 100 Stat. 1190; Nov. 19, 1988, Pub. L. 100–702, Title IV, § 402(b), 102 Stat. 4650; Oct. 19, 1996, Pub.L. 104–317, Title VI, § 601(a), 110 Stat. 3857.)

HISTORICAL AND STATUTORY NOTES

References in Text

Rule 45(c) of the Federal Rules of Civil Procedure, referred to in fourth undesignated paragraph, means rule 45(c), Federal Rules of Civil Procedure, this title.

Codifications

The first three paragraphs of this section were amended by Pub.L. 95–598, Title II, § 208, Nov. 6, 1978, 92 Stat. 2660, effective June 28, 1984, pursuant to Pub.L. 95–598, Title IV, § 402(b), Nov. 6, 1978, 92 Stat. 2682, as amended by Pub.L.

98–249, § 1(a), Mar. 31, 1984, 98 Stat. 116; Pub.L. 98–271, § 1(a), Apr. 30, 1984, 98 Stat. 163; Pub.L. 98–299, § 1(a), May 25, 1984, 98 Stat. 214; Pub.L. 98–325, § 1(a), June 20, 1984, 98 Stat. 268 set out as a note preceding section 101 of Title II, Bankruptcy, to read as follows:

The Chief Justice of the United States shall summon annually the chief judge of each judicial circuit, a district judge for each judicial circuit, and two bankruptcy judges to a conference at such time and place in the United States as he may designate. He shall preside at such conference which shall be known as the Judicial Conference of the United States. Special sessions of the conference may be called by the Chief Justice at such times and places as he may designate.

The district judge to be summoned from each judicial circuit shall be chosen by the circuit and district judges of the circuit at the annual judicial conference of the circuit held pursuant to section 333 of this title and shall serve as a member of the conference for three successive years, except that in the year following the enactment of this amended section the circuit and district judges of the first, fourth, seventh, and tenth circuits shall choose a district judge to serve for one year, the circuit and district judges in the second, fifth, and eighth circuits shall choose a district judge to serve for two years and the circuit and district judges in the third, sixth, ninth, and District of Columbia circuits shall choose a district judge to serve for three years. The bankruptcy judges to be summoned shall be chosen at large by all the bankruptcy judges. Each bankruptcy judge chosen shall serve as a member of the conference for three successive years, except that in the year following the effective date of this sentence the bankruptcy judges shall choose one bankruptcy judge to serve for two years.

If the chief judge of any circuit or the district judge chosen by the judges of the circuit or a bankruptcy judge chosen by the bankruptcy judges is unable to attend, the Chief Justice may summon any other circuit or district judge from such circuit or any other bankruptcy judge. Every judge summoned shall attend and, unless excused by the Chief Justice, shall remain throughout the sessions of the conference and advise as to the needs of his circuit or court and as to any matters in respect of which the administration of justice in the courts of the United States may be improved.

Section 402(b) of Pub.L. 95–598 was amended by section 113 of Pub.L. 98–353, Title I, July 10, 1984, 98 Stat. 343, by substituting "shall not be effective" for "shall take effect on June 28, 1984", thereby eliminating the amendment by section 208 of Pub.L. 95–598, effective June 27, 1984, pursuant to section 122(c) of Pub.L. 98–353, set out as an Effective Date note under section 151 of this title.

Section 121(a) of Pub.L. 98–353 directed that section 402(b) of Pub.L. 95–598 be amended by substituting "the date of enactment of the Bankruptcy Amendments and Federal Judgeship Act of 1984 [i.e. July 10, 1984]" for "June 28, 1984". This amendment was not executed in view of the prior amendment to section 402(b) of Pub.L. 95–598 by section 113 of Pub.L. 98–353.

Effective Dates

1988 Acts. Amendment by Pub.L. 100–702 effective Dec. 1, 1988, see section 407 of Pub.L. 100–702, set out as a note under section 2071 of this title.

1986 Acts. Section 4 of Pub.L. 99–466 provided that: "This Act and the amendments made by this Act [enacting section 335 of this title, amending this section and section 569 of this title, repealing former section 872 of this title, and redesignating section 873 of this title as 872] shall take effect 60 days after the date of the enactment of this Act [Oct. 14, 1986]."

1982 Acts. Amendment by Pub.L. 97–164 effective Oct. 1, 1982, see section 402 of Pub.L. 97–164, set out as a note under section 171 of this title.

1980 Acts. Section 7 of Pub.L. 96–458 provided that: "This Act [amending this section and sections 332, 372 and 604 of this title, and enacting provisions set out as notes under this section and section 1 of this title] shall become effective on October 1, 1981".

Authorization of Appropriations

Section 6 of Pub.L. 96–458 provided that: "There are authorized to be appropriated such sums as may be necessary to carry out the provisions of this Act [amending this section and sections 332, 372 and 604 of this title, and enacting provisions set out as notes under this section and section 1 of this title]."

Federal Courts Study Committee

Pub.L. 100–702, Title I, Nov. 19, 1988, 102 Stat. 4644, provided that:

"Sec. 101. Short title.

"This title may be cited as the 'Federal Courts Study Act'.

"Sec. 102. Establishment and purposes.

"(a) **Establishment.**—There is hereby established within the Judicial Conference of the United States, a Federal Courts Study Committee on the future of the Federal judiciary (hereafter referred to as the 'Committee').

"(b) **Purposes.**—The purposes of the Committee are to—

"(1) examine problems and issues currently facing the courts of the United States;

"(2) develop a long-range plan for the future of the Federal judiciary, including assessments involving—

"(A) alternative methods of dispute resolution;

"(B) the structure and administration of the Federal court system;

"(C) methods of resolving intracircuit and intercircuit conflicts in the courts of appeals; and

"(D) the types of disputes resolved by the Federal courts; and

"(3) report to the Judicial Conference of the United States, the President, the Congress, the Conference of Chief Justices, and the State Justice Institute on the revisions, if any, in the laws of the United States which the Committee, based on its study and evaluation, deems advisable.

"Sec. 103. Membership of the Committee.

"(a) **Appointments.**—The Committee shall be composed of fifteen members to be appointed by the Chief Justice of the United States, within ten days after the effective date of this title [Jan. 1, 1989].

"(b) **Selection.**—The membership of the Committee shall be selected in such a manner as to be representative of the various interests, needs and concerns which may be affected by the jurisdiction of the Federal courts. The Chief Justice shall designate one of the members of the Committee to serve as Chairman.

"(c) Term of Office.—The Committee members shall serve at the pleasure of the Chief Justice.

"(d) Rules of Procedure.—Rules of procedure shall be promulgated by vote of a majority of the Committee.

"Sec. 104. Powers of the Committee.

"(a) Hearings.—The Committee or, on the authorization of the Committee, any subcommittee thereof may, for the purpose of carrying out its functions and duties, hold such hearings and sit and act at such times and places, as the Committee or any such subcommittee may deem advisable.

"(b) Information and assistance.—The Administrative Office of the United States Courts, the Federal Judicial Center, and each department, agency, and instrumentality of the executive branch of the Government, including the National Institute of Justice and independent agencies, shall furnish to the Committee, upon request made by the Chairman, such information and assistance as the Committee may reasonably deem necessary to carry out its functions under this title [Title I of Pub.L. 100–702], consistent with other applicable provisions of law governing the release of such information.

"(c) Personnel.—(1) Subject to such rules and regulations as may be adopted by the Committee, the Director of the Administrative Office shall furnish to the Committee necessary staff and technical assistance in response to needs specified.

"(2) [Amendment of section 5108(c)(1) of Title 5, Government Organization and Employees.]

"(d) Advisory Panels.—The Committee is authorized, for the purpose of carrying out its functions and duties pursuant to the provisions of this title [Title I of Pub.L. 100–702], to establish advisory panels consisting of Committee members or members of the public. Such panels shall be established to provide expertise and assistance in specific areas, as the Committee deems necessary.

"Sec. 105. Functions and duties.

"The Committee shall—

"(1) make a complete study of the courts of the United States and of the several States and transmit a report to the President, the Chief Justice of the United States, the Congress, the Judicial Conference of the United States, the Conference of Chief Justices, and the State Justice Institute on such study, within fifteen months after the effective date of this title [Jan. 1. 1989];

"(2) recommend revisions to be made to laws of the United States as the Committee, on the basis of such study, deems advisable;

"(3) develop a long-range plan for the judicial system; and

"(4) make such other recommendations and conclusions it deems advisable.

"Sec. 106. Compensation of members.

"(a) Employees of the Government.—A member of the Committee who is an officer or full-time employee of the United States shall receive no additional compensation for his or her services, but shall be reimbursed for travel, subsistence, and other necessary expenses incurred in the performance of duties vested in the Committee, not to exceed the maximum amounts authorized under section 456 of title 28 [section 456 of this title].

"(b) Private Sector.—A member of the Committee who is from the private sector shall receive $200 per diem for each day (including travel time) during which he or she is engaged in the actual performance of duties vested in the Committee, plus reimbursement for travel, subsistence, and other necessary expenses incurred in the performance of such duties, not to exceed the maximum amounts authorized under section 456 of title 28 [section 456 of this title].

"Sec. 107. Expiration of the Committee.

"The Committee shall cease to exist on the date 60 days after it transmits the report pursuant to section 105.

"Sec. 108. Authorization of appropriations.

"To carry out the purposes of this title [Title I of Pub.L. 100–702] there are authorized to be appropriated $300,000 for each of the fiscal years 1989 and 1990.

"Sec. 109. Effective date.

"This title [Title I of Pub.L. 100–702] shall become effective on January 1, 1989."

Policies, Procedures, and Methodologies Used in Recommendation For Creation of Additional Federal Judgeships; Study by General Accounting Office and Report to Congress

Pub.L. 101–650, Title II, § 205, Dec. 1, 1990, 104 Stat. 5103, provided that:

"(a) In general.—The Comptroller General of the United States shall review the policies, procedures, and methodologies used by the Judicial Conference of the United States in recommending to the Congress the creation of additional Federal judgeships. In conducting such review the Comptroller General shall, at a minimum, determine the extent to which such policies, procedures, and methodologies—

"(1) provide an accurate measure of the workload of existing judges;

"(2) are applied consistently to the various circuit courts of appeals and district courts; and

"(3) provide an accurate indicator of the need for additional judgeships.

"(b) Report to Congress.—The Comptroller General shall, not later than 18 months after the date of the enactment of this Act [Dec. 1, 1990], report the results of the review conducted under subsection (a) to the Committees on the Judiciary of the House of Representatives and the Senate. The report shall include such recommendations as the Comptroller General considers appropriate for revisions of the policies, procedures, and methodologies used by the Judicial Conference that were reviewed in the report."

COMMENTARIES

See 28 U.S.C.A. § 331, for Commentary by David D. Siegel.

§ 332. Judicial councils of circuits

(a)(1) The chief judge of each judicial circuit shall call, at least twice in each year and at such places as he or she may designate, a meeting of the judicial council of the circuit, consisting of the chief judge of the circuit, who shall preside, and an equal number of circuit judges and district judges of the circuit, as such number is determined by majority vote of all such judges of the circuit in regular active service.

(2) Members of the council shall serve for terms established by a majority vote of all judges of the circuit in regular active service.

(3) Only circuit and district judges in regular active service shall serve as members of the council.

(4) No more than one district judge from any one district shall serve simultaneously on the council, unless at least one district judge from each district within the circuit is already serving as a member of the council.

(5) In the event of the death, resignation, retirement, or disability of a member of the council, a replacement member shall be designated to serve the remainder of the unexpired term by the chief judge of the circuit.

(6) Each member of the council shall attend each council meeting unless excused by the chief judge of the circuit.

(b) The council shall be known as the Judicial Council of the circuit.

(c) The chief judge shall submit to the council the semiannual reports of the Director of the Administrative Office of the United States Courts. The council shall take such action thereon as may be necessary.

(d)(1) Each judicial council shall make all necessary and appropriate orders for the effective and expeditious administration of justice within its circuit. Any general order relating to practice and procedure shall be made or amended only after giving appropriate public notice and an opportunity for comment. Any such order so relating shall take effect upon the date specified by such judicial council. Copies of such orders so relating shall be furnished to the Judicial Conference and the Administrative Office of the United States Courts and be made available to the public. Each council is authorized to hold hearings, to take sworn testimony, and to issue subpoenas and subpoenas duces tecum. Subpoenas and subpoenas duces tecum shall be issued by the clerk of the court of appeals, at the direction of the chief judge of the circuit or his designee and under the seal of the court, and shall be served in the manner provided in rule 45(c) of the Federal Rules of Civil Procedure for subpoenas and subpoenas duces tecum issued on behalf of the United States or an officer or agency thereof.

(2) All judicial officers and employees of the circuit shall promptly carry into effect all orders of the judicial council. In the case of failure to comply with an order made under this subsection or a subpoena issued under section 372(c) of this title, a judicial council or a special committee appointed under section 372(c)(4) of this title may institute a contempt proceeding in any district court in which the judicial officer or employee of the circuit who fails to comply with the order made under this subsection shall be ordered to show cause before the court why he or she should not be held in contempt of court.

(3) Unless an impediment to the administration of justice is involved, regular business of the courts need not be referred to the council.

(4) Each judicial council shall periodically review the rules which are prescribed under section 2071 of this title by district courts within its circuit for consistency with rules prescribed under section 2072 of this title. Each council may modify or abrogate any such rule found inconsistent in the course of such a review.

(e) The judicial council of each circuit may appoint a circuit executive. In appointing a circuit executive, the judicial council shall take into account experience in administrative and executive positions, familiarity with court procedures, and special training. The circuit executive shall exercise such administrative powers and perform such duties as may be delegated to him by the circuit council. The duties delegated to the circuit executive of each circuit may include but need not be limited to:

(1) Exercising administrative control of all nonjudicial activities of the court of appeals of the circuit in which he is appointed.

(2) Administering the personnel system of the court of appeals of the circuit.

(3) Administering the budget of the court of appeals of the circuit.

(4) Maintaining a modern accounting system.

(5) Establishing and maintaining property control records and undertaking a space management program.

(6) Conducting studies relating to the business and administration of the courts within the circuit and preparing appropriate recommendations and reports to the chief judge, the circuit council, and the Judicial Conference.

(7) Collecting, compiling, and analyzing statistical data with a view to the preparation and presentation of reports based on such data as may be directed by the chief judge, the circuit council, and the Administrative Office of the United States Courts.

(8) Representing the circuit as its liaison to the courts of the various States in which the circuit is located, the marshal's office, State and local bar associations, civic groups, news media, and other private and public groups having a reasonable interest in the administration of the circuit.

(9) Arranging and attending meetings of the judges of the circuit and of the circuit council, including preparing the agenda and serving as secretary in all such meetings.

(10) Preparing an annual report to the circuit and to the Administrative Office of the United States Courts for the preceding calendar year, including recommendations for more expeditious disposition of the business of the circuit.

All duties delegated to the circuit executive shall be subject to the general supervision of the chief judge of the circuit.

(f)(1) Each circuit executive shall be paid at a salary to be established by the Judicial Conference of the United States not to exceed the annual rate of level IV of the Executive Schedule pay rates under section 5315 of title 5.

(2) The circuit executive shall serve at the pleasure of the judicial council of the circuit.

(3) The circuit executive may appoint, with the approval of the council, necessary employees in such number as may be approved by the Director of the Administrative Office of the United States Courts.

(4) The circuit executive and his staff shall be deemed to be officers and employees of the judicial branch of the United States Government within the meaning of subchapter III of chapter 83 (relating to civil service retirement), chapter 87 (relating to Federal employees' life insurance program), and chapter 89 (relating to Federal employees' health benefits program) of title 5, United States Code.

(g) No later than January 31 of each year, each judicial council shall submit a report to the Administrative Office of the United States Courts on the number and nature of orders entered under this section during the preceding calendar year that relate to judicial misconduct or disability.

(June 25, 1948, c. 646, 62 Stat. 902; Nov. 13, 1963, Pub.L. 88–176, § 3, 77 Stat. 331; Jan. 5, 1971, Pub.L. 91–647, 84 Stat. 1907; Nov. 6, 1978, Pub.L. 95–598, Title II, § 209, 92 Stat. 2661; Oct. 15, 1980, Pub.L. 96–458, § 2(a)–(d)(1), 94 Stat. 2035, 2036; Oct. 1, 1988, Pub.L. 100–459, Title IV, § 407, 102 Stat. 2213; Nov. 19, 1988, Pub.L. 100–702, Title IV, § 403(a)(2), (b), Title X, §§ 1018, 1020(a)(1), 102 Stat. 4651, 4670, 4671; Dec. 1, 1990, Pub.L. 101–650, Title III, §§ 323, 325(b)(1), Title IV, § 403, 104 Stat. 5120, 5121, 5124; Dec. 9, 1991, Pub.L. 102–198, § 1, 105 Stat. 1623; Oct. 19, 1996, Pub.L. 104–317, Title II, § 208, 110 Stat. 3851.)

HISTORICAL AND STATUTORY NOTES

References in Text

Rule 45(c) of the Federal Rules of Civil Procedure, referred to in subsec. (d)(1), is rule 45(c) of the Federal Rules of Civil Procedure, this title.

Codifications

Subsec. (d) of this section was amended by Pub.L. 95–598, Title II, § 209, Nov. 6, 1978, 92 Stat. 2661, effective June 28, 1984, pursuant to Pub.L. 95–598, Title IV, § 402(b), Nov. 6, 1978, 92 Stat. 2682, as amended by Pub.L. 98–249, § 1(a), Mar. 31, 1984, 98 Stat. 116; Pub.L. 98–271, § 1(a), Apr. 30, 1984, 98 Stat. 163; Pub.L. 98–299, § 1(a), May 25, 1984, 98 Stat. 214; Pub.L. 98–325, § 1(a), June 20, 1984, 98 Stat. 268, set out as a note preceding section 101 of Title 11, Bankruptcy, by inserting "and bankruptcy judges" following "The district judges".

Section 402(b) of Pub.L. 95–598 was amended by section 113 of Pub.L. 98–353, Title I, July 10, 1984, 98 Stat. 343, by substituting "shall not be effective" for "shall take effect on June 28, 1984", thereby eliminating the amendment by section 209 of Pub.L. 95–598, effective June 27, 1984, pursuant to section 122(c) of Pub.L. 98–353, set out as an Effective Date note under section 151 of this title.

Section 121(a) of Pub.L. 98–353 directed that section 402(b) of Pub.L. 95–598 be amended by substituting "the date of enactment of the Bankruptcy Amendments and Federal Judgeship Act of 1984 [i.e. July 10, 1984]" for "June 28, 1984". This amendment was not executed in view of the prior amendment to section 402(b) of Pub.L. 95–598 by section 113 of Pub.L. 98–353.

Effective Dates

1990 Acts. Section 407 of Pub.L. 101–650 provided that: "The amendments made by this subtitle [subtitle I of Title IV of Pub.L. 101–650, amending this section and sections 372, 453, and 2077 of this title and section 104 of Appendix 6 to Title 5, Government Organization and Employees] shall take effect 90 days after the date of the enactment of this Act [Dec. 1, 1990]."

1988 Acts. Amendment of subsec. (d)(1) and enactment of subsec. (d)(4) by Pub.L. 100–702 effective Dec. 1, 1988, see section 407 of Pub.L. 100–702, set out as a note under section 2071 of this title.

1980 Acts. Amendment by Pub.L. 96–458 effective Oct. 1, 1981, see section 7 of Pub.L. 96–458, set out as a note under section 331 of this title.

COMMENTARIES

See 28 U.S.C.A. § 332, for Commentary by David D. Siegel.

§ 333. Judicial conferences of circuits

The chief judge of each circuit may summon biennially, and may summon annually, the circuit, district, and bankruptcy judges of the circuit, in active service, to a conference at a time and place that he designates, for the purpose of considering the business of the courts and advising means of improving the administration of justice within such circuit. He may preside at such conference, which shall be known as the Judicial Conference of the circuit. The judges of the District Court of Guam, the District Court of the Virgin Islands, and the District Court of the Northern Mariana Islands may also be summoned biennially, and may be summoned annually, to the conferences of their respective circuits.

Every judge summoned may attend.

The court of appeals for each circuit shall provide by its rules for representation and active participation at such conference by members of the bar of such circuit.

(June 25, 1948, c. 646, 62 Stat. 903; Dec. 29, 1950, c. 1185, 64 Stat. 1128; Oct. 31, 1951, c. 655, § 38, 65 Stat. 723; July 7, 1958, Pub.L. 85–508, § 12(e), 72 Stat. 348; Nov. 6, 1978, Pub.L. 95–598, Title II, § 210, 92 Stat. 2661; Dec. 1, 1990, Pub.L. 101–650, Title III, § 320, 104 Stat. 5117; Apr. 26, 1996, Pub.L. 104–134, Title I, § 101[(a)][Title III, § 305], 110 Stat. 1321–36; renumbered Title I May 2, 1996, Pub.L. 104–140, § 1(a), 110 Stat. 1327.)

HISTORICAL AND STATUTORY NOTES

Effective Dates

1978 Acts. Amendment by Pub.L. 95–598 effective Oct. 1, 1979, see section 402(c) of Pub.L. 95–598, as amended, set out as an Effective Date note preceding section 101 of Title 11, Bankruptcy.

1958 Acts. Amendment by Pub.L. 85–508 effective Jan. 3, 1959, upon admission of Alaska into the Union pursuant to Proc. No. 3269, Jan. 31, 1959, 24 F.R. 81, 73 Stat. c16, as required by sections 1 and 8(c) of Pub.L. 85–508, see notes set out under section 81A of this title and preceding section 21 of Title 48, Territories and Insular Possessions.

Termination of United States District Court for the District of the Canal Zone

For termination of the United States District Court for the District of the Canal Zone at end of the "transition period", being the 30–month period beginning Oct. 1, 1979, and ending midnight Mar. 31, 1982, see Paragraph 5 of Article XI of the Panama Canal Treaty of 1977 and sections 3831 and 3841 to 3843 of Title 22, Foreign Relations and Intercourse.

§ 334. Institutes and joint councils on sentencing

(a) In the interest of uniformity in sentencing procedures, there is hereby authorized to be established under the auspices of the Judicial Conference of the United States, institutes and joint councils on sentencing. The Attorney General and/or the chief judge of each circuit may at any time request, through the Director of the Administrative Office of the United States Courts, the Judicial Conference to convene such institutes and joint councils for the purpose of studying, discussing, and formulating the objectives, policies, standards, and criteria for sentencing those convicted of crimes and offenses in the courts of the United States. The agenda of the institutes and joint councils may include but shall not be limited to: (1) The development of standards for the content and utilization of presentence reports; (2) the establishment of factors to be used in selecting cases for special study and observation in prescribed diagnostic clinics; (3) the determination of the importance of psychiatric, emotional, sociological and physiological factors involved in crime and their bearing upon sentences; (4) the discussion of special sentencing problems in unusual cases such as treason, violation of public trust, subversion, or involving abnormal sex behavior, addiction to drugs or alcohol, and mental or physical handicaps; (5) the formulation of sentencing principles and criteria which will assist in promoting the equitable administration of the criminal laws of the United States.

(b) After the Judicial Conference has approved the time, place, participants, agenda, and other arrangements for such institutes and joint councils, the chief judge of each circuit is authorized to invite the attendance of district judges under conditions which he thinks proper and which will not unduly delay the work of the courts.

(c) The Attorney General is authorized to select and direct the attendance at such institutes and meetings of United States attorneys and other officials of the Department of Justice and may invite the participation of other interested Federal officers. He may also invite specialists in sentencing methods, criminologists, psychiatrists, penologists, and others to participate in the proceedings.

(d) The expenses of attendance of judges shall be paid from applicable appropriations for the judiciary of the United States. The expenses connected with the preparation of the plans and agenda for the conference and for the travel and other expenses incident to the attendance of officials and other participants invited by the Attorney General shall be paid from applicable appropriations of the Department of Justice.

(Added Pub.L. 85–752, § 1, Aug. 25, 1958, 72 Stat. 845.)

HISTORICAL AND STATUTORY NOTES

Sentencing Procedures

Section 7 of Pub.L. 85–752 provided that: "This Act [adding this section and sections 4208 and 4209 of Title 18, Crimes and Criminal Procedure, and provisions set out as a note under section 4208 of Title 18] does not apply to any offense for which there is provided a mandatory penalty."

§ 335. Judicial Conference of the Court of International Trade

(a) The chief judge of the Court of International Trade is authorized to summon annually the judges of such court to a judicial conference, at a time and place that such chief judge designates, for the purpose of considering the business of such court and improvements in the administration of justice in such court.

(b) The Court of International Trade shall provide by its rules for representation and active participation at such conference by members of the bar.

(Added Pub.L. 99–466, § 2(a), Oct. 14, 1986, 100 Stat. 1190.)

HISTORICAL AND STATUTORY NOTES

Effective Dates

1986 Acts. Section effective 60 days after Oct. 14, 1986, see section 4 of Pub.L. 99–466, set out as a note under section 331 of this title.

CHAPTER 17—RESIGNATION AND RETIREMENT OF JUSTICES AND JUDGES

Sec.
371. Retirement on salary; retirement in senior status.
372. Retirement for disability; substitute judge on failure to retire; judicial discipline.
373. Judges in Territories and Possessions.[1]
374. Residence of retired judges; official station.
375. Recall of certain judges and magistrates.
376. Annuities for survivors of certain judicial officials of the United States.
377. Retirement of bankruptcy judges and magistrates.

[1] Section catchline amended by Pub.L. 99–396 without corresponding amendment of analysis.

§ 371. Retirement on salary; retirement in senior status

(a) Any justice or judge of the United States appointed to hold office during good behavior may retire from the office after attaining the age and meeting the service requirements, whether continuous or otherwise, of subsection (c) and shall, during the remainder of his lifetime, receive an annuity equal to the salary he was receiving at the time he retired.

(b)(1) Any justice or judge of the United States appointed to hold office during good behavior may retain the office but retire from regular active service after attaining the age and meeting the service requirements, whether continuous or otherwise, of subsection (c) of this section and shall, during the remainder of his or her lifetime, continue to receive the salary of the office if he or she meets the requirements of subsection (f).

(2) In a case in which a justice or judge who retires under paragraph (1) does not meet the requirements of subsection (f), the justice or judge shall continue to receive the salary that he or she was receiving when he or she was last in active service or, if a certification under subsection (f) was made for such justice or judge, when such a certification was last in effect. The salary of such justice or judge shall be adjusted under section 461 of this title.

(c) The age and service requirements for retirement under this section are as follows:

Attained age:	Years of service:
65	15
66	14
67	13
68	12
69	11
70	10

(d) The President shall appoint, by and with the advice and consent of the Senate, a successor to a justice or judge who retires under this section.

(e) Notwithstanding subsection (c) of section 5532 of title 5, if a regular or reserve member or former member of a uniformed service who is receiving retired or retainer pay becomes employed as a justice or judge of the United States, as defined by section 451, or becomes eligible therefor while so employed, such retired or retainer pay shall not be paid during regular active service as a justice or judge, but shall be resumed or commenced without reduction upon retirement from the judicial office or from regular active service (into senior status) as such justice or judge.

(f)(1) In order to continue receiving the salary of the office under subsection (b), a justice must be certified in each calendar year by the Chief Justice, and a judge must be certified by the chief judge of the circuit in which the judge sits, as having met the requirements set forth in at least one of the following subparagraphs:

(A) The justice or judge must have carried in the preceding calendar year a caseload involving courtroom participation which is equal to or greater than the amount of work involving courtroom participation which an average judge in active service would perform in three months. In the instance of a justice or judge who has sat on both district courts and courts of appeals, the caseload of appellate work and trial work shall be determined separately and the results of those determinations added together for purposes of this paragraph.

(B) The justice or judge performed in the preceding calendar year substantial judicial duties not involving courtroom participation under subparagraph (A), including settlement efforts, motion decisions, writing opinions in cases that have not been orally argued, and administrative duties for the court to which the justice or judge is assigned. Any certification under this subparagraph shall include a statement describing in detail the nature and amount of work and certifying that the work done is equal to or greater than the work described in this subparagraph which an average judge in active service would perform in three months.

(C) The justice or judge has, in the preceding calendar year, performed work described in subparagraphs (A) and (B) in an amount which, when calculated in accordance with such subparagraphs, in the aggregate equals at least 3 months work.

(D) The justice or judge has, in the preceding calendar year, performed substantial administrative duties directly related to the operation of the courts, or has performed substantial duties for a Federal or State governmental entity. A certification under this subparagraph shall specify that the work done is equal to the full-time work of an employee of the judicial branch. In any year in which a justice or judge performs work described under this subparagraph for less than the full year, one-half of such work may be aggregated with work described under subparagraph (A), (B), or (C) of this paragraph for the purpose of the justice or judge satisfying the requirements of such subparagraph.

(E) The justice or judge was unable in the preceding calendar year to perform judicial or administrative work to the extent required by any of subparagraphs (A) through (D) because of a temporary or permanent disability. A certification under this subparagraph shall be made to a justice who certifies in writing his or her disability to the Chief Justice, and to a judge who certifies in writing his or her disability to the chief judge of the circuit in which the judge sits. A justice or judge who is certified under this subparagraph as having a permanent disability shall be deemed to have met the requirements of this subsection for each calendar year thereafter.

(2) Determinations of work performed under subparagraphs (A), (B), (C), and (D) of paragraph (1) shall be made pursuant to rules promulgated by the Judicial Conference of the United States. In promulgating such criteria, the Judicial Conference shall take into account existing standards promulgated by the Conference for allocation of space and staff for senior judges.

(3) If in any year a justice or judge who retires under subsection (b) does not receive a certification under this subsection (except as provided in paragraph (1)(E)), he or she may thereafter receive a certification for that year by satisfying the requirements of subparagraph (A), (B), (C), or (D) of paragraph (1) of this subsection in a subsequent year and attributing a sufficient part of the work performed in such subsequent year to the earlier year so that the work so attributed, when added to the work performed during such earlier year, satisfies the requirements for certification for that year. However, a justice or judge may not receive credit for the same work for purposes of certification for more than 1 year.

(4) In the case of any justice or judge who retires under subsection (b) during a calendar year, there shall be included in the determination under this subsection of work performed during that calendar year all work performed by that justice or judge (as described in subparagraphs (A), (B), (C), and (D) of paragraph (1)) during that calendar year before such retirement.

(June 25, 1948, c. 646, 62 Stat. 903; Oct. 31, 1951, c. 655, § 39, 65 Stat. 724; Feb. 10, 1954, c. 6, § 4(a), 68 Stat. 12; July 10, 1984, Pub.L. 98–353, Title II, § 204(a), 98 Stat. 350; Nov. 19, 1988, Pub.L. 100–702, Title X, § 1005(a), 102 Stat. 4666; Nov. 30, 1989, Pub.L. 101–194, Title VII, § 705(a), 103 Stat. 1770; Oct. 19, 1996, Pub.L. 104–317, Title III, § 301, 110 Stat. 3851.)

HISTORICAL AND STATUTORY NOTES

Effective Dates

1989 Acts. Section 705(b) of Pub.L. 101–194 provided that:

"**(1) In general.**—The amendments made by subsection (a) [amending this section] shall first apply with respect to work performed on or after January 1, 1990, by a justice or judge of the United States who has retired under section 371(b) of title 28, United States Code [subsec. (b) of this section].

"**(2) Calendar year 1990.**—In the case certifications required by section 371(f) of title 28, United States Code [subsec. (f) of this section], for calendar year 1990—

"**(A)** such certifications shall be based on the 10-month period beginning on January 1, 1990, and ending on October 31, 1990, and shall be completed not later than December 15, 1990;

"**(B)** determinations of work performed under section 371(f) of title 28, United States Code [subsec. (f) of this section], shall be made pro rata on the basis of such 10-month period; and

"**(C)** such certifications shall be deemed to be certifications made in calendar year 1991."

1988 Acts. Section 1005(b) of Pub.L. 100–702 provided that: "The amendment made by this section [enacting subsec. (e) of this section] shall apply to a justice or judge who retires, or has retired, from the judicial office or from regular active service (into senior status) as such justice or judge of the United States on or after the effective date of section 5532(c) of title 5 [effective 90 days after Oct. 13, 1978 (see Effective Date of 1978 Amendment note under section 5532 of Title 5, Government Organization and Employees)], and to whom section 5532(c) would otherwise be applicable."

1984 Acts. Section 204(c) of Pub.L. 98–353 provided that: "The amendments made by this section [amending this section] shall apply with respect to any justice or judge of the United States appointed to hold office during good behavior who retires on or after the date of enactment of this Act [July 10, 1984]."

Computation of Judicial Service, District of Alaska

Pub.L. 89–70, July 8, 1965, 79 Stat. 213, provided: "That, notwithstanding any other provision of law, any service as a judge of the District Court for the Territory of Alaska shall be included in computing under sections 371 and 372 of title 28, United States Code [this section and section 372 of this title], the aggregate years of judicial service of a United States district judge for the district of Alaska."

Judicial Service in Hawaii Included Within Computation of Aggregate Years of Judicial Service

Pub.L. 86–3, § 14(d), Mar. 18, 1959, 73 Stat. 10, provided in part: "That service as a judge of the District Court for the Territory of Hawaii or as a judge of the United States District Court for the District of Hawaii or as a justice of the Supreme Court of the Territory of Hawaii or as a judge of the circuit courts of the Territory of Hawaii shall be included in computing under section 371, 372, or 373 of title 28, United States Code [this section, section 372, or section 373 of this title], the aggregate years of judicial service of any person who is in office as a district judge for the District of Hawaii on the date of enactment of this Act [Mar. 18, 1959]."

§ 372. Retirement for disability; substitute judge on failure to retire; judicial discipline

(a) Any justice or judge of the United States appointed to hold office during good behavior who becomes permanently disabled from performing his duties may retire from regular active service, and the President shall, by and with the advice and consent of the Senate, appoint a successor.

Any justice or judge of the United States desiring to retire under this section shall certify to the President his disability in writing.

Whenever an associate justice of the Supreme Court, a chief judge of a circuit or the chief judge of the Court of International Trade, desires to retire under this section, he shall furnish to the President a certificate of disability signed by the Chief Justice of the United States.

A circuit or district judge, desiring to retire under this section, shall furnish to the President a certificate of disability signed by the chief judge of his circuit.

A judge of the Court of International Trade desiring to retire under this section, shall furnish to the President a certificate of disability signed by the chief judge of his court.

Each justice or judge retiring under this section after serving ten years continuously or otherwise shall, during the remainder of his lifetime, receive the salary of the office. A justice or judge retiring under this section who has served less than ten years in all shall, during the remainder of his lifetime, receive one-half the salary of the office.

(b) Whenever any judge of the United States appointed to hold office during good behavior who is eligible to retire under this section does not do so and a certificate of his disability signed by a majority of the members of the Judicial Council of his circuit in the case of a circuit or district judge, or by the Chief Justice of the United States in the case of the Chief Judge of the Court of International Trade, or by the chief judge of his court in the case of a judge of the Court of International Trade, is presented to the President and the President finds that such judge is unable to discharge efficiently all the duties of his office by reason of permanent mental or physical disability and that the appointment of an additional judge is necessary for the efficient dispatch of business, the President may make such appointment by and with the advice and consent of the Senate. Whenever any such additional judge is appointed, the vacancy subsequently caused by the death, resignation, or retirement of the disabled judge shall not be filled. Any judge whose disability causes the appointment of an additional judge shall, for purpose of precedence, service as chief judge, or temporary performance of the duties of that office, be treated as junior in commission to the other judges of the circuit, district, or court.

(c)(1) Any person alleging that a circuit, district, or bankruptcy judge, or a magistrate, has engaged in conduct prejudicial to the effective and expeditious administration of the business of the courts, or alleging that such a judge or magistrate is unable to discharge all the duties of office by reason of mental or physical disability, may file with the clerk of the court of appeals for the circuit a written complaint containing a brief statement of the facts constituting such conduct. In the interests of the effective and expeditious administration of the business of the courts and on the basis of information available to the chief judge of the circuit, the chief judge may, by written order stating reasons therefor, identify a complaint for purposes of this subsection and thereby dispense with filing of a written complaint.

(2) Upon receipt of a complaint filed under paragraph (1) of this subsection, the clerk shall promptly transmit such complaint to the chief judge of the circuit, or, if the conduct complained of is that of the chief judge, to that circuit judge in regular active service next senior in date of commission (hereafter, for purposes of this subsection only, included in the term "chief judge"). The clerk shall simultaneously transmit a copy of the complaint to the judge or magistrate whose conduct is the subject of the complaint.

(3) After expeditiously reviewing a complaint, the chief judge, by written order stating his reasons, may—

(A) dismiss the complaint, if he finds it to be (i) not in conformity with paragraph (1) of this subsection, (ii) directly related to the merits of a decision or procedural ruling, or (iii) frivolous; or

(B) conclude the proceeding if he finds that appropriate corrective action has been taken or that action on the complaint is no longer necessary because of intervening events.

The chief judge shall transmit copies of his written order to the complainant and to the judge or magistrate whose conduct is the subject of the complaint.

(4) If the chief judge does not enter an order under paragraph (3) of this subsection, such judge shall promptly—

(A) appoint himself and equal numbers of circuit and district judges of the circuit to a special committee to investigate the facts and allegations contained in the complaint;

(B) certify the complaint and any other documents pertaining thereto to each member of such committee; and

(C) provide written notice to the complainant and the judge or magistrate whose conduct is the subject of the complaint of the action taken under this paragraph.

A judge appointed to a special committee under this paragraph may continue to serve on that committee after becoming a senior judge or, in the case of the chief judge of the circuit, after his or her term as chief judge terminates under subsection (a)(3) or (c) of section 45 of this title. If a judge appointed to a committee under this paragraph dies, or retires from office under section 371(a) of this title, while serving on the committee, the chief judge of the circuit may appoint another circuit or district judge, as the case may be, to the committee.

(5) Each committee appointed under paragraph (4) of this subsection shall conduct an investigation as extensive as it considers necessary, and shall expeditiously file a comprehensive written report thereon with the judicial council of the circuit. Such report shall present both the findings of the investigation and the committee's recommendations for necessary and appropriate action by the judicial council of the circuit.

(6) Upon receipt of a report filed under paragraph (5) of this subsection, the judicial council—

(A) may conduct any additional investigation which it considers to be necessary;

(B) shall take such action as is appropriate to assure the effective and expeditious administration of the business of the courts within the circuit, including, but not limited to, any of the following actions:

(i) directing the chief judge of the district of the magistrate whose conduct is the subject of the complaint to take such action as the judicial council considers appropriate;

(ii) certifying disability of a judge appointed to hold office during good behavior whose conduct is the subject of the complaint, pursuant to the procedures and standards provided under subsection (b) of this section;

(iii) requesting that any such judge appointed to hold office during good behavior voluntarily retire, with the provision that the length of service requirements under section 371 of this title shall not apply;

(iv) ordering that, on a temporary basis for a time certain, no further cases be assigned to any judge or magistrate whose conduct is the subject of a complaint;

(v) censuring or reprimanding such judge or magistrate by means of private communication;

(vi) censuring or reprimanding such judge or magistrate by means of public announcement; or

(vii) ordering such other action as it considers appropriate under the circumstances, except that (I) in no circumstances may the council order removal from office of any judge appointed to hold office during good behavior, and (II) any removal of a magistrate shall be in accordance with section 631 of this title and any removal of a bankruptcy judge shall be in accordance with section 152 of this title;

(C) may dismiss the complaint; and

(D) shall immediately provide written notice to the complainant and to such judge or magistrate of the action taken under this paragraph.

(7)(A) In addition to the authority granted under paragraph (6) of this subsection, the judicial council may, in its discretion, refer any complaint under this subsection, together with the record of any associated proceedings and its recommendations for appropriate action, to the Judicial Conference of the United States.

(B) In any case in which the judicial council determines, on the basis of a complaint and an investigation under this subsection, or on the basis of information otherwise available to the council, that a judge appointed to hold office during good behavior may have engaged in conduct—

(i) which might constitute one or more grounds for impeachment under article II of the Constitution; or

(ii) which, in the interest of justice, is not amenable to resolution by the judicial council,

the judicial council shall promptly certify such determination, together with any complaint and a record of any associated proceedings, to the Judicial Conference of the United States.

(C) A judicial council acting under authority of this paragraph shall, unless contrary to the interests of justice, immediately submit written notice to the complainant and to the judge or magistrate whose conduct is the subject of the action taken under this paragraph.

(8)(A) Upon referral or certification of any matter under paragraph (7) of this subsection, the Judicial Conference, after consideration of the prior proceedings and such additional investigation as it considers appropriate, shall by majority vote take such action, as described in paragraph (6)(B) of this subsection, as it considers appropriate. If the Judicial Conference concurs in the determination of the council, or makes its own determination, that consideration of impeachment may be warranted, it shall so certify and transmit the determination and the record of proceedings to the House of Representatives for whatever action the House of Representatives considers to be necessary. Upon receipt of the determination and record of proceedings in the House of Representatives, the Clerk of the House of Representatives shall make available to the public the determination and any reasons for the determination.

(B) If a judge or magistrate has been convicted of a felony and has exhausted all means of obtaining direct review of the conviction, or the time for seeking further direct review of the conviction has passed and no such review has been sought, the Judicial Conference may, by majority vote and without referral or certification under paragraph (7), transmit to the House of Representatives a determination that consideration of impeachment may be warranted, together with appropriate court records, for whatever action the House of Representatives considers to be necessary.

(9)(A) In conducting any investigation under this subsection, the judicial council, or a special committee appointed under paragraph (4) of this subsection, shall have full subpoena powers as provided in section 332(d) of this title.

(B) In conducting any investigation under this subsection, the Judicial Conference, or a standing committee appointed by the Chief Justice under section 331 of this title, shall have full subpoena powers as provided in that section.

(10) A complainant, judge, or magistrate aggrieved by a final order of the chief judge under paragraph (3) of this subsection may petition the judicial council for review thereof. A complainant, judge, or magistrate aggrieved by an action of the judicial council under paragraph (6) of this subsection may petition the Judicial Conference of the United States for review thereof. The Judicial Conference, or the standing committee established under section 331 of this title, may grant a petition filed by a complainant, judge, or magistrate under this paragraph. Except as expressly provided in this paragraph, all orders and determinations, including denials of petitions for review, shall be final and conclusive and shall not be judicially reviewable on appeal or otherwise.

(11) Each judicial council and the Judicial Conference may prescribe such rules for the conduct of proceedings under this subsection, including the processing of petitions for review, as each considers to be appropriate. Such rules shall contain provisions requiring that—

(A) adequate prior notice of any investigation be given in writing to the judge or magistrate whose conduct is the subject of the complaint;

(B) the judge or magistrate whose conduct is the subject of the complaint be afforded an opportunity to appear (in person or by counsel) at proceedings conducted by the investigating panel, to present oral and documentary evidence, to compel the attendance of witnesses or the production of documents, to cross-examine witnesses, and to present argument orally or in writing; and

(C) the complainant be afforded an opportunity to appear at proceedings conducted by the investigating panel, if the panel concludes that the complainant could offer substantial information.

Any such rule shall be made or amended only after giving appropriate public notice and an opportunity for comment. Any rule promulgated under this subsection shall be a matter of public record, and any such rule promulgated by a judicial council may be modified by the Judicial Conference. No rule promulgated under this subsection may limit the period of time within which a person may file a complaint under this subsection.

(12) No judge or magistrate whose conduct is the subject of an investigation under this subsection shall serve upon a special committee appointed under paragraph (4) of this subsection, upon a judicial council, upon the Judicial Conference, or upon the standing committee established under section 331 of this title, until all related proceedings under this subsection have been finally terminated.

(13) No person shall be granted the right to intervene or to appear as amicus curiae in any proceeding before a judicial council or the Judicial Conference under this subsection.

(14) Except as provided in paragraph (8), all papers, documents, and records of proceedings related to investigations conducted under this subsection shall be confidential and shall not be disclosed by any person in any proceeding except to the extent that—

(A) the judicial council of the circuit in its discretion releases a copy of a report of a special investigative committee under paragraph (5) to the complainant whose complaint initiated the investigation by that special committee and to the judge or magistrate whose conduct is the subject of the complaint;

(B) the judicial council of the circuit, the Judicial Conference of the United States, or the Senate or the House of Representatives by resolution, releases any such material which is believed necessary to an impeachment investigation or trial of a judge under article I of the Constitution; or

(C) such disclosure is authorized in writing by the judge or magistrate who is the subject of the complaint and by the chief judge of the circuit, the Chief Justice, or the chairman of the standing committee established under section 331 of this title.

(15) Each written order to implement any action under paragraph (6)(B) of this subsection, which is issued by a judicial council, the Judicial Conference, or the standing committee established under section 331 of this title, shall be made available to the public through the appropriate clerk's office of the court of appeals for the circuit. Unless contrary to the interests of justice, each such order issued under this paragraph shall be accompanied by written reasons therefor.

(16) Upon the request of a judge or magistrate whose conduct is the subject of a complaint under this subsection, the judicial council may, if the complaint has been finally dismissed under paragraph (6)(C), recommend that the Director of the Administrative Office of the United States Courts award reimbursement, from funds appropriated to the Federal judiciary, for those reasonable expenses, including attorneys' fees, incurred by that judge or magistrate during the investigation which would not have been incurred but for the requirements of this subsection.

(17) Except as expressly provided in this subsection, nothing in this subsection shall be construed to affect any other provision of this title, the Federal Rules of Civil Procedure, the Federal Rules of Criminal Procedure, the Federal Rules of Appellate Procedure, or the Federal Rules of Evidence.

(18) The United States Court of Federal Claims, the Court of International Trade, and the Court of Appeals for the Federal Circuit shall each prescribe rules, consistent with the foregoing provisions of this subsection, establishing procedures for the filing of complaints with respect to the conduct of any judge of such court and for the investigation and resolution of such complaints. In investigating and taking action with respect to any such complaint, each such court shall have the powers granted to a judicial council under this subsection.

(June 25, 1948, c. 646, 62 Stat. 903; May 24, 1949, c. 139, § 67, 63 Stat. 99; Feb. 10, 1954, c. 6, § 4(a), 68 Stat. 12; Sept. 2, 1957, Pub.L. 85–261, 71 Stat. 586; Oct. 10, 1980, Pub.L. 96–417, Title V, § 501(9), 94 Stat. 1742; Oct. 15, 1980, Pub.L. 96–458, § 3(a), (b), 94 Stat. 2036, 2040; Apr. 2, 1982, Pub.L. 97–164, Title I, § 112, 96 Stat. 29; July 10, 1984, Pub.L. 98–353, Title I, § 107, 98 Stat. 342; Nov. 19, 1988, Pub.L. 100–702, Title IV, § 403(c), 102 Stat. 4651; Dec. 1, 1990, Pub.L. 101–650, Title IV, § 402, 104 Stat. 5122; Dec. 1, 1990, Pub.L. 101–650, Title IV, § 402, 104 Stat. 5122; Oct. 29, 1992, Pub.L. 102–572, Title IX, § 902(b)(1), 106 Stat. 4516.)

HISTORICAL AND STATUTORY NOTES

References in Text

The Federal Rules of Civil Procedure, the Federal Rules of Appellate Procedure, and the Federal Rules of Evidence, referred to in subsec. (c)(17) of this section, are, respectively, the Federal Rules of Civil Procedure, this title, the Federal Rules of Appellate Procedure, this title, and the Federal Rules of Evidence, this title.

The Federal Rules of Criminal Procedure, referred to in subsec. (c)(17), are the Federal Rules of Criminal Procedure, Title 18, which are set out in Title 18, Crimes and Criminal Procedure.

Transfer of Functions

Any reference in any provision of law enacted before Jan. 4, 1995, to a function, duty, or authority of the Clerk of the House of Representatives treated as referring, with respect to that function, duty, or authority, to the officer of the House of Representatives exercising that function, duty, or authority, as determined by the Committee on House Oversight of the House of Representatives, see section 2(1) of Pub.L. 104–14, set out as a note preceding section 21 of Title 2, The Congress.

Effective Dates

1992 Acts. Amendment by Pub.L. 102–572 effective Oct. 29, 1992, see section 911 of Pub.L. 102–572, set out as a note under section 171 of this title.

1990 Acts. Amendment by section 402 of Pub.L. 101–650 effective 90 days after Dec. 1, 1990, see section 407 of Pub.L. 101–650, set out as a note under section 332 of this title.

1988 Acts. Amendment by Pub.L. 100–702 effective Dec. 1, 1988, see section 407 of Pub.L. 100–702, set out as a note under section 2071 of this title.

1984 Acts. Amendment by Pub.L. 98–353 effective July 10, 1984, see section 122(a) of Pub.L. 98–353, set out as a note under section 151 of this title.

1982 Acts. Amendment by Pub.L. 97–164 effective Oct. 1, 1982, see section 402 of Pub.L. 97–164, set out as a note under section 171 of this title.

1980 Acts. Amendment by Pub.L. 96–458 effective Oct. 1, 1981, see section 7 of Pub.L. 96–458, set out as a note under section 331 of this title.

Amendment by Pub.L. 96–417 effective on Nov. 1, 1980, and applicable with respect to civil actions pending on or commenced on or after such date, see section 701(a) of Pub.L. 96–417, as amended, set out as a note under section 251 of this title.

Change of Name

References to United States Claims Court deemed to refer to United States Court of Federal Claims and references to Claims Court deemed to refer to Court of Federal Claims, see section 902(b) of Pub.L. 102–572, set out as a note under section 171 of Title 28, Judiciary and Judicial Procedure.

Reference to United States magistrate or to magistrate deemed to refer to United States magistrate judge pursuant to section 321 of Pub.L. 101–650, set out as a note under section 631 of this title.

Computation of Judicial Service, District of Alaska

Inclusion of service as judge of the District Court for the Territory of Alaska in the computation of years of judicial service for judges of the United States District Court for the District of Alaska, see Pub.L. 89–70, July 8, 1965, 79 Stat. 213, set out as a note under section 371 of this title.

Extension of Time For Report by National Commission on Judicial Discipline and Removal

Pub.L. 102–368, Title I, Sept. 23, 1992, 106 Stat. 1118, provided in part that: "Notwithstanding the requirement of section 415 of Public Law 101–650 [set out as a note under this section] to submit the report mandated by said section not later than one year after the date of the Commission's first meeting, the National Commission on Judicial Discipline and Removal shall submit to each House of Congress, the Chief Justice of the United States, and the President, the report mandated in said section no later than August 1, 1993."

Judicial Service in Hawaii

Certain judicial service in Hawaii as included within computation of aggregate years of judicial service, see section 14(d) of Pub.L. 86–3, Mar. 18, 1959, 73 Stat. 10, set out as a note under section 371 of this title.

National Commission on Judicial Discipline and Removal

Subtitle II (sections 408 to 418) of Title IV of Pub.L. 101–650, as amended Pub.L. 102–198, § 8(a),(b)(2), Dec. 9, 1991, 105 Stat. 1625, 1626, provided that:

"Sec. 408. Short Title.

"This subtitle [subtitle II of Title IV of Pub.L. 101–650] may be cited as the 'National Commission on Judicial Discipline and Removal Act'.

"Sec. 409. Establishment.

"There is hereby established a commission to be known as the 'National Commission on Judicial Discipline and Removal' (hereinafter in this subtitle referred to as the 'Commission').

"Sec. 410. Duties of Commission.

"The duties of the Commission are—

"(1) to investigate and study the problems and issues involved in the tenure (including discipline and removal) of an article III judge;

"(2) to evaluate the advisability of proposing alternatives to current arrangements with respect to such problems and issues, including alternatives for discipline or removal of judges that would require amendment to the Constitution; and

"(3) to prepare and submit to the Congress, the Chief Justice of the United States, and the President a report in accordance with section 415.

"Sec. 411. Membership.

"**(a) Number and appointment.**—The Commission shall be composed of 13 members as follows:

"(1) Three appointed by the President pro tempore of the Senate.

"(2) Three appointed by the Speaker of the House of Representatives.

"(3) Three appointed by the Chief Justice of the United States.

"(4) Three appointed by the President.

"(5) One appointed by the Conference of Chief Justices of the States of the United States.

"**(b) Term.**—Members of the Commission shall be appointed for the life of the Commission.

"**(c) Quorum.**—Six members of the Commission shall constitute a quorum, but a lesser number may conduct meetings.

"**(d) Chairman.**—The members of the Commission shall select one of the members to be the Chairman.

"**(e) Vacancy.**—A vacancy on the Commission resulting from the death or resignation of a member shall not affect its powers and shall be filled in the same manner in which the original appointment was made.

"**(f) Continuation of membership.**—If any member of the Commission who was appointed to the Commission as a Member of Congress or as an officer or employee of a government leaves that office, or if any member of the Commission who was appointed from persons who are not officers or employees of a government becomes an officer or employee of a government, the member may continue as a member of the Commission for not longer than the 90–day period beginning on the date the member leaves that office or becomes such an officer or employee, as the case may be.

"Sec. 412. Compensation of the Commission.

"**(a) Pay.**—(1) Except as provided in paragraph (2), each member of the Commission who is not otherwise employed by the United States Government shall be entitled to receive the daily equivalent of the annual rate of basic pay payable for GS–18 of the General Schedule under section 5332 of title 5, United States Code [section 5332 of Title 5, Government Organization and Employees], for each day (including travel time) during which he or she is engaged in the actual performance of duties as a member of the Commission.

"(2) A member of the Commission who is an officer or employee of the United States Government shall serve without additional compensation.

"**(b) Travel.**—All members of the Commission shall be reimbursed for travel, subsistence, and other necessary expenses incurred by them in the performance of their duties.

"Sec. 413. Director and staff of Commission; experts and consultants.

"**(a) Director.**—The Commission shall, without regard to section 5311(b) of title 5, United States Code [section 5311(b) of Title 5], have a Director who shall be appointed by the Chairman and who shall be paid at a rate not to exceed the rate of basic pay payable for level V of the Executive Schedule under section 5316 of such title [section 5316 of Title 5].

"**(b) Staff.**—The Chairman of the Commission may appoint and fix the pay of such additional personnel as the Chairman finds necessary to enable the Commission to carry out its duties. Such personnel may be appointed without regard to the provisions of title 5, United States Code [Title 5], governing appointments in the competitive service, and may be paid without regard to the provisions of chapter 51 and subchapter III of chapter 53 of such title [section 5101 et seq. and section 5331 et seq. of Title 5] relating to classification and General Schedule pay rates, except that the annual rate of pay for any individual so appointed may not exceed a rate equal to the annual rate of basic pay payable for GS–18 of the General Schedule under section 5332 of such title [section 5332 of Title 5].

"**(c) Experts and consultants.**—The Commission may procure temporary and intermittent services of experts and consultants under section 3109(b) of title 5, United States Code [section 3109(b) of Title 5].

"Sec. 414. Powers of Commission.

"**(a) Hearings and sessions.**—The Commission or, on authorization of the Commission, a member of the Commission may, for the purpose of carrying out this subtitle, hold such hearings, sit and act at such times and places, take such testimony, and receive such evidence, as the Commission considers appropriate. The Commission may administer oaths or affirmations to witnesses appearing before it.

"**(b) Obtaining official data.**—The Commission may secure directly from any department, agency, or entity within the executive or judicial branch of the Federal Government information necessary to enable it to carry out this subtitle. Upon request of the Chairman of the Commission, the head of such department or agency shall furnish such information to the Commission.

"(c) Facilities and support services.—The Administrator of General Services shall provide to the Commission on a reimbursable basis such facilities and support services as the Commission may request. Upon request of the Commission, the head of any Federal agency is authorized to make any of the facilities and services of such agency available to the Commission to assist the Commission in carrying out its duties under this subtitle.

"(d) Expenditures and contracts.—The Commission or, on authorization of the Commission, a member of the Commission may make expenditures and enter into contracts for the procurement of such supplies, services, and property as the Commission or member considers appropriate for the purposes of carrying out the duties of the Commission. Such expenditures and contracts may be made only to such extent or in such amounts as are provided in appropriation Acts.

"(e) Mails.—The Commission may use the United States mails in the same manner and under the same conditions as other departments and agencies of the United States.

"(f) Gifts.—The Commission may accept, use, and dispose of gifts or donations of services or property.

"Sec. 415. Report.

"The Commission shall submit to each House of Congress, the Chief Justice of the United States, and the President a report not later than one year after the date of its first meeting. The report shall contain a detailed statement of the findings and conclusions of the Commission, together with its recommendations for such legislative or administrative action as it considers appropriate.

"Sec. 416. Termination.

"The Commission shall cease to exist on the date 30 days after the date it submits its report to the President and the Congress under section 415.

"Sec. 417. Authorization of appropriations.

"There is authorized to be appropriated the sum of $750,000 to carry out the provisions of this subtitle.

"Sec. 418. Effective date.

"This subtitle shall take effect on the date of the enactment of this Act [Dec. 1, 1990]."

[References in laws to the rates of pay for GS–16, 17, or 18, or to maximum rates of pay under the General Schedule, to be considered references to rates payable under specified sections of Title 5, Government Organization and Employees, see section 529 [Title I, § 101(c)(1)] of Pub.L. 101–509, set out in a note under section 5376 of Title 5.]

[For provisions extending the time for submission by the National Commission on Judicial Discipline and Removal of the report required by section 415 of Pub.L. 101–650, see Pub.L. 102–368, Title 1, Sept. 23, 1992, 106 Stat. 1118, set out as a note under this section.]

COMMENTARIES

See 28 U.S.C.A. § 372, for Commentary by David D. Siegel.

§ 373. Judges in territories and possessions

(a) Any judge of the District Court of Guam, the District Court of the Northern Mariana Islands, or the District Court of the Virgin Islands who retires from office after attaining the age and meeting the service requirements whether continuous or otherwise, of subsection (b) shall, during the remainder of his lifetime, receive an annuity equal to the salary he is receiving at the time he retires.

(b) The age and service requirements for retirement under subsection (a) of this section are as follows:

Attained age:	Years of service:
65	15
66	14
67	13
68	12
69	11
70	10

(c)(1) Any judge or former judge who is receiving an annuity pursuant to this section may elect to become a senior judge of the court upon which he served before retiring.

(2) The chief judge of a judicial circuit may recall any such senior judge, with the judge's consent, to perform, for the court from which he retired, such judicial duties for such periods of time as the chief judge may specify.

(3) Any act or failure to act by a senior judge performing judicial duties pursuant to recall under paragraph (2) of this subsection shall have the same force and effect as if it were an act or failure to act of a judge on active duty; but such senior judge shall not be counted as a judge of the court on which he is serving as a recalled annuitant for purposes of the number of judgeships authorized for that court.

(4) Any senior judge performing judicial duties pursuant to recall under paragraph (2) of this subsection shall be paid, while performing such duties, the same compensation (in lieu of the annuity payable under subsection (a) of this section) and the same allowances for travel and other expenses as a judge on active duty with the court being served.

(5) Any senior judge performing judicial duties pursuant to recall under paragraph (2) of this subsection shall at all times be governed by the code of judicial conduct for United States judges approved by the Judicial Conference of the United States.

(d) Any judge who elects to become a senior judge under subsection (c) of this section and who thereafter—

(1) accepts civil office or employment under the Government of the United States (other than the performance of judicial duties pursuant to recall under subsection (c) of this section);

(2) engages in the practice of law; or

(3) materially violates the code of judicial conduct for United States judges,

shall cease to be a senior judge and to be eligible for recall pursuant to subsection (c) of this section.

(e) Any judge of the District Court of Guam, the District Court of the Northern Mariana Islands, or the District Court of the Virgin Islands who is removed by the President of the United States upon the sole ground of mental or physical disability, or who is not reappointed (as judge of such court), shall be entitled, upon attaining the age of sixty-five years or upon relinquishing office if he is then beyond the age of sixty-five years, (1) if his judicial service, continuous or otherwise, aggregates fifteen years or more, to receive during the remainder of his life an annuity equal to the salary he received when he left office, or (2) if his judicial service, continuous or otherwise, aggregated less than fifteen years but not less than ten years, to receive during the remainder of his life an annuity equal to that proportion of such salary which the aggregate number of his years of his judicial service bears to fifteen.

(f) Service at any time as a judge of the courts referred to in subsection (a) or of any other court of the United States, as defined by section 451 of this title, shall be included in the computation of aggregate years of judicial service for purposes of this section.

(g) Any retired judge who is entitled to receive an annuity under subsection (a) shall be entitled to a cost of living adjustment in the amount payable to him computed as specified in section 8340(b) of title 5, except that in no case may the annuity payable to such retired judge, as increased under this subsection, exceed 95 per centum of the salary of a United States district judge in regular active service.

(June 25, 1948, c. 646, 62 Stat. 904; Oct. 31, 1951, c. 655, § 40, 65 Stat. 724; Feb. 10, 1954, c. 6, § 5, 68 Stat. 13; July 7, 1958, Pub.L. 85–508, § 12(d), 72 Stat. 348; Mar. 18, 1959, Pub.L. 86–3, § 14(d), 73 Stat. 10; Sept. 12, 1966, Pub.L. 89–571, § 2, 80 Stat. 764; Oct. 11, 1976, Pub.L. 94–470, 90 Stat. 2052; Aug. 27, 1986, Pub.L. 99–396, § 21(a), 100 Stat. 844.)

HISTORICAL AND STATUTORY NOTES

Effective Dates

1986 Acts. Section 21(c) of Pub.L. 99–396 provided that: "The amendments made by this section [amending this section and section 376 of this title] shall not affect the amount payable to a judge who retired in accordance with the provisions of section 373 of title 28, United States Code [this section], in effect on the day before the date of enactment of this Act [Aug. 27, 1986]."

1959 Acts. Amendment by Pub.L. 86–3 effective upon the admission of the State of Hawaii into the Union, see note set out under section 91 of this title. Admission of Hawaii into the Union was accomplished Aug. 21, 1959 upon issuance of Proc. No. 3309, Aug. 21, 1959, 25 F.R. 6868, 73 Stat. c74, as required by sections 1 and 7(c) of Pub.L. 86–3, Mar. 18, 1959, 73 Stat. 4, set out as notes preceding 491 of Title 48, Territories and Insular Possessions.

1958 Acts. Amendment by Pub.L. 85–508 effective Jan. 3, 1959 upon admission of Alaska into the Union pursuant to Proc. No. 3269, Jan. 5, 1959, 24 F.R. 81, 73 Stat. c16, as required by sections 1 and 8(c) of Pub.L. 85–508, see notes set out under section 81A of this title and preceding section 21 of Title 48, Territories and Insular Possessions.

Election, Recall, Status, Compensation, Conduct, and Termination of Senior Judges

Pub.L. 98–454, Title X, § 1002, Oct. 5, 1984, 98 Stat. 1745, provided that:

"**(a)** Any judge or former judge who is receiving, or will upon attaining the age of sixty-five years be entitled to receive, payments pursuant to section 373 of title 28, United States Code[,] [this section] may elect to become a senior judge of the court on which he served while on active duty.

"**(b)** The chief judge of a judicial circuit may recall any such senior judge of his circuit, with the judge's consent, to perform in the District Court of Guam, the District Court of the Virgin Islands, or the District Court for the Northern Mariana Islands such judicial duties and for such periods of time as the chief judge may specify.

"**(c)** Any act or failure to act by a senior judge performing judicial duties pursuant to this section shall have the same force and effect as if it were the act or failure to act of a judge on active duty; but such senior judge shall not be counted as a judge of the court on which he is serving for purposes of the number of judgeships authorized for that court.

"**(d)** Any senior judge shall be paid, while performing duties pursuant to this section, the same compensation (in lieu of payments pursuant to section 373 of title 28, United States Code) [this section] and the same allowances for travel and other expenses as a judge in active service.

"**(e)** Senior judges under subsection (a) of this section shall at all times be governed by the code of judicial conduct for the United States judges, approved by the Judicial Conference of the United States.

"**(f)** Any person who has elected to be a senior judge under subsection (a) of this section and who thereafter—

"**(1)** accepts civil office or employment under the Government of the United States (other than the performance of judicial duties pursuant to subsection (b) of this section);

"**(2)** engages in the practice of law; or

"**(3)** materially violated the code of judicial conduct for the United States judges,

shall cease to be a senior judge and to be eligible for recall pursuant to subsection (b) of this section."

Judicial Service in Hawaii

Certain judicial service in Hawaii as included within computation of aggregate years of judicial service, see section 14(d) of Pub.L. 86–3, set out as a note under section 371 of this title.

Preservation of Rights of Retired Judges of the District Court for the District of Hawaii and Justices of the Supreme Court of the Territory of Hawaii

Section 14(d) of Pub.L. 86–3 provided in part: "That the amendments made by this subsection shall not affect the rights of any judge or justice who may have retired before the effective date of this subsection". See Effective Dates of 1959 Amendments note set out under this section.

Preservation of Rights of Retired Judges of the District Court for the Territory of Alaska

Section 12(d) of Pub.L. 85–508 provided in part: "That the amendment made by this subsection [amending this section] shall not affect the rights of any judge who may have retired before it takes effect". See Effective Dates of 1958 Amendments note set out under this section.

Tenure and Salary Rights of Judges in Puerto Rico in Office on September 12, 1966

Amendment by Pub.L. 89–571 not to affect tenure of office or right to continue to receive salary after resignation, retirement, or failure of reappointment of any district judge for the district of Puerto Rico in office on September 12, 1966, see section 4 of Pub.L. 89–571, set out as a note under section 134 of this title.

§ 374. Residence of retired judges; official station

Retired judges of the United States are not subject to restrictions as to residence. The place where a retired judge maintains the actual abode in which he customarily lives shall be deemed to be his official station for the purposes of section 456 of this title. The place where a judge or magistrate recalled under section 155, 375, 636, or 797 of this title maintains the actual abode in which the judge or magistrate customarily lives shall be deemed to be the official station of such judge or magistrate for purposes of section 604(a)(7) of this title.

(June 25, 1948, c. 646, 62 Stat. 904; Sept. 21, 1959, Pub.L. 86–312, § 1, 73 Stat. 587; Nov. 14, 1986, Pub.L. 99–651, Title II, § 202(b), 100 Stat. 3648.)

HISTORICAL AND STATUTORY NOTES

Effective Dates

1986 Acts. Amendment by Pub.L. 99–651 effective Jan. 1, 1987, see section 203 of Pub.L. 99–651, set out as a note under section 155 of this title.

§ 375. Recall of certain judges and magistrates

(a)(1) A bankruptcy judge or a United States magistrate appointed under chapter 43 of this title, who has retired under the provisions of section 377 of this title or under the applicable provisions of title 5 upon attaining the age and years of service requirements established in section 371(c) of this title, may agree to be recalled to serve under this section for a period of five years as a bankruptcy judge or magistrate, as the case may be, upon certification that substantial service is expected to be performed by such retired judge or magistrate during such 5-year period. With the agreement of the judge or magistrate involved, a certification under this subsection may be renewed for successive 5-year periods.

(2) For purposes of paragraph (1) of this subsection, a certification may be made, in the case of a bankruptcy judge or a United States magistrate, by the judicial council of the circuit in which the official duty station of the judge or magistrate at the time of retirement was located.

(3) For purposes of this section, the term "bankruptcy judge" means a bankruptcy judge appointed under chapter 6 of this title or serving as a bankruptcy judge on March 31, 1984.

(b) A judge or magistrate recalled under this section may exercise all of the powers and duties of the office of judge or magistrate held at the time of retirement, including the ability to serve in any other judicial district to the extent applicable, but may not engage in the practice of law or engage in any other business, occupation, or employment inconsistent with the expeditious, proper, and impartial performance of duties as a judicial officer.

(c) During the 5-year period in which a certification under subsection (a) is in effect, the judge or magistrate involved shall receive, in addition to the annuity provided under the provisions of section 377 of this title or under the applicable provisions of title 5, an amount equal to the difference between that annuity and the current salary of the office to which the judge or magistrate is recalled. The annuity of a bankruptcy judge or magistrate who completes that 5–year period of service, whose certification is not renewed, and who retired under section 377 of this title shall be equal to the salary in effect, at the end of that 5–year period, for the office from which he or she retired.

(d) A certification under subsection (a) may be terminated in accordance with section 372(c) of this title, and such a certification shall be terminated upon the death of the recalled judge or magistrate involved.

(e) Except as provided in subsection (b), nothing in this section shall affect the right of judges or magistrates who retire under the provisions of chapter 83 or chapter 84 of title 5 to serve as reemployed annuitants in accordance with the provisions of title 5. A judge or magistrate to whom this section applies may be recalled under section 155, 636(h), or 797 of this title, as the case may be, other than during a 5-year period in which a certification under subsection (a) is in effect with respect to that judge or magistrate.

(f) For purposes of determining the years of service requirements in order to be eligible for recall under this section, any service as a bankruptcy judge or a United States magistrate, and any prior service as a referee in bankruptcy or a United States commissioner, may be credited.

(g) Except as provided in subsection (c), a judge or magistrate recalled under this section who retired under the applicable provisions of title 5 shall be considered to be a reemployed annuitant under chapter 83 or chapter 84, as the case may be, of title 5.

(h) The Judicial Conference of the United States may promulgate regulations to implement this section.

(Added Pub.L. 99–651, Title II, § 201(b)(1), Nov. 14, 1986, 100 Stat. 3647, and amended Pub.L. 100–659, § 4(b), Nov. 15, 1988, 102 Stat. 3918; Pub.L. 101–650, Title III, § 325(b)(2), Dec. 1, 1990, 104 Stat. 5121; Pub.L. 102–572, Title IX, § 904(a), Oct. 29, 1992, 106 Stat. 4517.)

HISTORICAL AND STATUTORY NOTES

Effective Dates

1992 Acts. Amendment by Title IX of Pub.L. 102–572 effective Oct. 29, 1992, see section 911 of Pub.L. 102–572, set out as a note under section 171 of Title 28, Judiciary and Judicial Procedure.

1988 Acts. Amendment to this section by Pub.L. 100–659 to take effect on Nov. 15, 1988, and shall apply to bankruptcy judges and magistrates who retire on or after Nov. 15, 1988, with special election provisions for bankruptcy judges, etc., who left office on or after July 31, 1987, and before Nov. 15, 1988, see section 9 of Pub.L. 100–659, set out as a note under section 377 of this title.

1986 Acts. Section effective Jan. 1, 1987, see section 203 of Pub.L. 99–651, set out as an Effective Dates of 1986 Amendments note under section 155 of this title.

Change of Name

References to United States Claims Court deemed to refer to United States Court of Federal Claims and references to Claims Court deemed to refer to Court of Federal Claims, see section 902(b) of Pub.L. 102–572, set out as a note under section 171 of Title 28, Judiciary and Judicial Procedure.

United States magistrate appointed under section 631 of this title to be known as United States magistrate judge after Dec. 1, 1990, with any reference to United States magistrate or magistrate in this title, in any other Federal statute, etc., deemed a reference to United States magistrate judge appointed under section 631 of this title, see section 321 of Pub.L. 101–650, set out as a note under section 631 of this title.

Prior Provisions

A prior section 375, added Aug. 28, 1954, c. 1053, § 1, 68 Stat. 918, and amended Aug. 3, 1956, c. 944, § 1(b), 70 Stat. 1021; Aug. 22, 1972, Pub.L. 92–397, § 1, 86 Stat. 579, which provided for annuities to widows of justices, was repealed by Pub.L. 96–504, § 5, Dec. 5, 1980, 94 Stat. 2742.

§ 376. Annuities for survivors of certain judicial officials of the United States

(a) For the purposes of this section—

(1) "judicial official" means:

(A) a Justice or judge of the United States, as defined by section 451 of this title;

(B) a judge of the District Court of Guam, the District Court of the Northern Mariana Islands, or the District Court of the Virgin Islands;

(C) a Director of the Administrative Office of the United States Courts, after he or she has filed a waiver under subsection (a) of section 611 of this title;

(D) a Director of the Federal Judicial Center, after he or she has filed a waiver under subsection (b) of section 627 of this title;

(E) an administrative assistant to the Chief Justice of the United States, after he or she has filed a waiver in accordance with both subsection (a) of section 677 and subsection (a) of section 611 of this title;

(F) a full-time bankruptcy judge or a full-time United States magistrate; or

(G) a judge of the United States Court of Federal Claims;

who notifies the Director of the Administrative Office of the United States Courts in writing of his or her intention to come within the purview of this section within six months after (i) the date upon which he or she takes office, (ii) the date upon which he or she marries, (iii) January 1, 1977, (iv) October 1, 1986, (v) the date of the enactment of the Retirement and Survivors' Annuities for Bankruptcy Judges and Magistrates Act of 1988, in the case of a full-time bankruptcy judge or United States magistrate in active service on that date, (vi) the date of the enactment of the Federal Courts Study Committee Implementation Act of 1990, in the case of a full-time judge of the Court of Federal Claims in active service on that date, or (vii) the date of the enactment of the Federal Courts Administration Act of 1992;

(2) "retirement salary" means:

(A) in the case of a Justice or judge of the United States, as defined by section 451 of this title, salary paid (i) after retirement from regular active service under subsection (b) of section 371 or subsection (a) of section 372 of this title, or (ii) after retirement from office by resignation on salary under subsection (a) of section 371 of this title;

(B) in the case of a judge of the District Court of Guam, the District Court of the Northern Mariana Islands, or the District Court of the Virgin Islands, (i) an annuity paid under subsection (a) of section 373 of this title or (ii) compensation paid under paragraph (4) of subsection (c) of section 373 of this title;

(C) in the case of a Director of the Administrative Office of the United States Courts, an annuity paid under subsection (b) or (c) of section 611 of this title;

(D) in the case of a Director of the Federal Judicial Center, an annuity paid under subsection (c) or (d) of section 627 of this title;

(E) in the case of an administrative assistant to the Chief Justice of the United States, an annuity paid in accordance with both subsection (a) of section 677 and subsection (a) of section 611 of this title;

(F) in the case of a bankruptcy judge or United States magistrate, an annuity paid under section 377 of this title; and

(G) in the case of a judge of the United States Court of Federal Claims, an annuity paid under section 178 of this title;

(3) "widow" means the surviving wife of a "judicial official", who:

(A) has been married to him for at least one year on the day of his death; or

(B) is the mother of issue by that marriage;

(4) "widower" means the surviving husband of a "judicial official", who:

(A) has been married to her for at least one year on the day of her death; or

(B) is the father of issue by that marriage;

(5) "child" means:

(A) an unmarried child under eighteen years of age, including (i) an adopted child and (ii) a stepchild or recognized natural child who lived with the judicial official in a regular parent-child relationship;

(B) such unmarried child between eighteen and twenty-two years of age who is a student regularly pursuing a full-time course of study or training in residence in a high school, trade school, technical or vocational institute, junior college, college, university, or comparable educational institution. A child whose twenty-second birthday occurs before July 1, or after August 31, of a calendar year, and while he or she is regularly pursuing such a course of study or training, is deemed to have become twenty-two years of age on the first day of July immediately following that birthday. A child who is a student is deemed not to have ceased being a student during an interim period between school years, if that interim period lasts no longer than five consecutive months and if that child shows, to the satisfaction of the Director of the Administrative Office of the United States Courts, that he or she has a bona fide intention of continuing to pursue a course of study or training in the same or a different school during the school semester, or other period into which the school year is divided, immediately following that interim period; or

(C) such unmarried child, regardless of age, who is incapable of self-support because of a mental or physical disability incurred either (i) before age eighteen, or (ii) in the case of a child who is receiving an annuity as a full-time student under paragraph (5)(B) of this subsection, before the termination of that annuity;

(6) "former spouse" means a former spouse of a judicial official if the former spouse was married to such judicial official for at least 9 months; and

(7) "assassinated" and "assassination" mean the killing of a judicial official described in paragraph (1)(A), (B), (F), or (G) of this subsection that is motivated by the performance by that judicial official of his or her official duties.

(b)(1) Every judicial official who files a written notification of his or her intention to come within the purview of this section, in accordance with paragraph (1) of subsection (a) of this section, shall be deemed thereby to consent and agree to having deducted and withheld from his or her salary a sum equal to 2.2 percent of that salary, and a sum equal to 3.5 percent of his or her retirement salary. The deduction from any retirement salary—

(A) of a justice or judge of the United States retired from regular active service under section 371(b) or section 372(a) of this title,

(B) of a judge of the United States Court of Federal Claims retired under section 178 of this title, or

(C) of a judicial official on recall under section 155(b), 373(c)(4), 375, or 636(h) of this title,

shall be an amount equal to 2.2 percent of retirement salary.

(2) A judicial official who is not entitled to receive an immediate retirement salary upon leaving office but who is eligible to receive a deferred retirement salary on a later date shall file, within 90 days before leaving office, a written notification of his or her intention to remain within the purview of this section under such conditions and procedures as may be determined by the Director of the Administrative Office of the United States Courts. Every judicial official who files a written notification in accordance with this paragraph shall be deemed to consent to contribute, during the period before such a judicial official begins to receive his or her retirement salary, a sum equal to 3.5 percent of the deferred retirement salary which that judicial official is entitled to receive. Any judicial official who fails to file a written notification under this paragraph shall be deemed to have revoked his or her election under subsection (a) of this section.

(3) The amounts deducted and withheld from the salary of each judicial official under paragraphs (1) and (2) of this subsection shall, in accordance with such procedures as may be prescribed by the Comptroller General of the United States, be covered into the Treasury of the United States and credited to the "Judicial Survivors' Annuities Fund" established by section 3 of the Judicial Survivors' Annuities Reform Act. Such fund shall be used for the payment of annuities, refunds, and allowances as provided by this section. Payment of such salary less such deductions (and any deductions made under section 178 or 377 of this title or under subchapter III of chapter 83, or chapter 84, of title 5) shall be a full and complete discharge and acquittance of all claims and demands whatsoever for all services rendered by such judicial official during the period covered by such payment, except the rights to those benefits to which such judicial official, or his or her survivors, shall be entitled under the provisions of this section (and under section 178 or 377 of this title or under subchapter III of chapter 83, or chapter 84, of title 5).

(c)(1) There shall also be deposited to the credit of the Judicial Survivors' Annuities Fund, in accordance with such procedures as the Comptroller General of the United States may prescribe, amounts required to reduce to zero the unfunded liability of the Judicial Survivors' Annuities Fund: *Provided*, That such amounts shall not exceed the equivalent of 9 percent of salary or retirement salary. Such deposits shall, subject to appropriations Acts, be taken from the fund used to pay the compensation of the judicial official, and shall immediately become an integrated part of the Judicial Survivors' Annuities Fund for any use required under this section.

(2) For purposes of paragraph (1), the term "unfunded liability" means the estimated excess, determined on an annual basis in accordance with the provisions of section 9503 of title 31, United States Code, of the present value of all benefits payable from the Judicial Survivors' Annuities Fund, over the sum of—

(A) the present value of deductions to be withheld from the future basic pay of judicial officials; plus

(B) the balance in the Fund as of the date the unfunded liability is determined.

In making any determination under this paragraph, the Comptroller General shall use the applicable information contained in the reports filed pursuant to section 9503 of title 31, United States Code, with respect to the judicial survivors' annuities plan established by this section.

(3) There are authorized to be appropriated such sums as may be necessary to carry out this subsection.

(d) Each judicial official shall deposit, with interest at 4 percent per annum to December 31, 1947, and at 3 percent per annum thereafter, compounded on December 31 of each year, to the credit of the "Judicial Survivors' Annuities Fund":

(1) a sum equal to 3.5 percent of that salary, including "retirement salary", which he or she has received for serving in any of the offices designated in paragraph (1) of subsection (a) of this section prior to the date upon which he or she filed notice of an intention to come within the purview of this section with the Director of the Administrative Office of the United States Courts; and

(2) a sum equal to 3.5 percent of the basic salary, pay, or compensation which he or she has received for serving as a Senator, Representative, Delegate, or Resident Commissioner in Congress, or for serving as an "employee", as that term is defined in subsection (1) of section 8331 of title 5, prior to assuming the responsibilities of any of the offices designated in paragraph (1) of subsection (a) of this section.

The interest otherwise required by this subsection shall not be required for any period during which a judicial official was separated from all such service and was not receiving any retirement salary.

Each such judicial official may elect to make such deposits in installments, during the continuance of his or her service in those offices designated in paragraph (1) of subsection (a) of this section, in such amounts and under such conditions as may be determined in each instance by the Director of the Administrative Office of the United States Courts: *Provided*, That, in each instance in which a judicial official does elect to make such deposits in installments, the Director shall require (i) that the first installment payment made shall be in an amount no smaller than that amount necessary to cover at least the last eighteen months of prior creditable civilian service, and (ii) that at least one additional installment payment shall be made every eighteen months thereafter until the total of all such deposits have been made.

Notwithstanding the failure of any such judicial official to make all such deposits or installment payments, credit shall be allowed for the service rendered, but the annuity of that judicial official's widow or widower shall be reduced by an amount equal to 10 percent of the amount of such deposits, computed as of the date of the death of such judicial official, unless such widow or widower shall elect to eliminate such service entirely from credit under subsection (k) of this section: *Provided*, That no deposit shall be required from any such judicial official for any honorable active duty service in the Army, Navy, Air Force, Marine Corps, or Coast Guard of the United States, or for any other creditable service rendered prior to August 1, 1920.

(e) The amounts deducted and withheld in accordance with subsection (b) of this section, and the amounts deposited in accordance with subsection (d) of this section, shall be credited to individual accounts in the name of each judicial official from whom such amounts are received, for credit to the "Judicial Survivors' Annuities Fund."

(f) The Secretary of the Treasury shall invest, from time to time, in interest bearing securities of the United States or Federal farm loan bonds, those portions of the "Judicial Survivors' Annuities Fund" which in his judgment may not be immediately required for the payment of annuities, refunds, and allowances as provided in this section. The income derived from such investments shall constitute a part of such fund for the purposes of paying annuities and carrying out the provisions of subsections (g), (h), (m), (*o*), (p), and (q) of this section.

(g) If any judicial official leaves office and is ineligible to receive a retirement salary or leaves office and is entitled to a deferred retirement salary but fails to make an election under subsection (b)(2) of this section, all amounts credited to his or her account established under subsection (e), together with interest at 4 percent per annum to December 31, 1947, and at 3 percent per annum thereafter, compounded on December 31 of each year, to the date of his or her relinquishment of office, minus a sum equal to 2.2 percent of salary for service while deductions were withheld under subsection (b) or for which a deposit was made by the judicial official under subsection (d), shall be returned to that judicial official in a lump-sum payment within a reasonable period of time following the date of his or her relinquishment of office. For the purposes of this section, a "reasonable period of time" shall be presumed to be no longer than 1 year following the date upon which such judicial official relinquishes his or her office.

(h) Annuities payable under this section shall be paid only in accordance with the following provisions:

(1) In any case in which a judicial official dies while in office, while receiving retirement salary, or after filing an election and otherwise complying with the conditions under subsection (b)(2) of this section (A) after having completed at least eighteen months of creditable civilian service, as computed in accordance with subsection (k) of this section, for the last eighteen months of which the salary deductions provided by subsection (b) of this section or, in lieu thereof, the deposits required by subsection (d) of this section have actually been made, or (B) if the death of such judicial official was by assassination, before having satisfied the requirements of clause (A) if, for the period of such service, the deductions provided by subsection (b) or, in lieu thereof, the deposits required by subsection (d) have actually been made—

(i) if such judicial official is survived by a widow or widower, but not by a child, there shall be paid to such widow or widower an annuity, beginning on the day on which such judicial official died, in an amount computed as provided in subsection (*l*) of this section; or

(ii) if such judicial official is survived by a widow or widower and a child or children, there shall be paid to such widow or widower an annuity, beginning on the day on which such judicial official died, in an amount computed as provided in subsection (*l*) of this section, and there shall also be paid to or on behalf of each such child an immediate annuity equal to:

(I) 10 percent of the average annual salary determined under subsection (*l*)(1) of this section; or

(II) 20 percent of such average annual salary, divided by the number of children;

whichever is smallest; or

(iii) if such judicial official leaves no surviving widow or widower, but does leave a surviving child or children, there shall be paid to or on behalf of each such child an immediate annuity equal to:

(I) the amount of the annuity to which the judicial official's widow or widower would have been entitled under clause (i) of this paragraph, had such widow or widower survived the judicial official, divided by the number of children; or

(II) 20 percent of the average annual salary determined under subsection (*l*)(1) of this section; or

(III) 40 percent of such average annual salary amount, divided by the number of children;

whichever is smallest.

(2) An annuity payable to a widow or widower under clause (i) or (ii) of paragraph (1) of this subsection shall be terminated upon his or her death or remarriage before attaining age 55.

(3) An annuity payable to a child under this subsection shall terminate:

(A) if such child is receiving an annuity based upon his or her status under paragraph (5)(A) of subsection (a) of this section, on the last day of the month during which he or she becomes eighteen years of age;

(B) if such child is receiving an annuity based upon his or her status under paragraph (5)(B) of subsection (a) of this section, either (i) on the first day of July immediately following his or her twenty-second birthday or (ii) on the last day of the month during which he or she ceases to be a full-time student in accordance with paragraph (5)(B) of subsection (a) of this section, whichever occurs first: *Provided*, That if such child is rendered incapable of self-support because of a mental or physical disability incurred while receiving that annuity, that annuity shall not terminate, but shall continue without interruption and shall be deemed to have become, as of the date of disability, an annuity based upon his or her status under clause (ii) of paragraph (5)(C) of subsection (a) of this section;

(C) if such child is receiving an annuity based upon his or her status under paragraph (5)(C) of subsection (a) of this section, on the last day of the month during which he or she ceases to be incapable of self-support because of mental or physical disability; or

(D) on the last day of the month during which such child dies or marries.

(4) An annuity payable to a child or children under paragraph (1)(ii) of this subsection shall be recomputed and paid as provided in paragraph (1)(iii) of this subsection upon the death, but not upon the remarriage, of the widow or widower who is receiving an annuity under paragraph (1)(ii) of this subsection.

(5) In any case in which the annuity of a child is terminated, the annuity of each remaining child which is based upon the service of the same judicial official shall be recomputed and paid as though the child whose annuity has been terminated had not survived that judicial official.

(6) In the case of the survivor or survivors of a judicial official to whom paragraph (1)(B) applies, there shall be deducted from the annuities otherwise payable under this section an amount equal to the amount of salary deductions that would have been made if such deductions had been made for 18 months prior to the judicial official's death.

(i)(1) All questions of dependency and disability arising under this section shall be determined by the Director of the Administrative Office of the United States Courts, subject to review only by the Judicial Conference of the United States, and the decision of the Judicial Conference of the United States shall be final and conclusive. The Director may order or direct at any time such medical or other examinations as he deems necessary to determine the facts relative to the nature and degree of disability of any child who is an annuitant, or an applicant for an annuity, under this section, and may suspend or deny any such annuity for failure to submit to any such examination.

(2) The Director of the Administrative Office of the United States Courts shall determine whether the killing of a judicial official was an assassination, subject to review only by the Judicial Conference of the United States. The head of any Federal agency that investigates the killing of a judicial official shall provide information to the Director that would assist the Director in making such determination.

(j) In any case in which a payment under this section is to be made to a minor, or to a person mentally incompetent or under other legal disability, as determined by a court of competent jurisdiction, such payment may be made to the person who is constituted guardian or other fiduciary of such claimant by the laws of the State of residence of such claimant, or to any other person who is otherwise legally vested with the care of the claimant or of the claimant's estate, and need not be made directly to such claimant. The Director of the Administrative Office of the United States Courts may, at his or her discretion, determine whether such payment is made directly to such claimant or to such guardian, fiduciary, or other person legally vested with the care of such claimant or the claimant's estate. Where no guardian or other fiduciary of such minor or such person under legal disability has been appointed under the laws of the State of residence of such claimant, the Director of the Administrative Office of the United States Courts shall determine the person who is otherwise legally vested with the care of the claimant or of the claimant's estate.

(k) The years of service rendered by a judicial official which may be creditable in calculating the amount of an annuity for such judicial official's widow or widower under subsection (*l*) of this section shall include—

(1) those years during which such judicial official served in any of the offices designated in paragraph (1) of subsection (a) of this section, including in the case of a Justice or judge of the United States those years during which he or she continued to hold office following retirement from regular active service under section 371 or subsection (a) of section 372 of this title;

(2) those years during which such judicial official served as a Senator, Representative, Delegate, or Resident Commissioner in Congress, prior to assuming the responsibilities of any of the offices designated in paragraph (1) of subsection (a) of this section;

(3) those years during which such judicial official honorably served on active duty in the Army, Navy, Air Force, Marine Corps, or Coast Guard of the United States, prior to assuming the responsibilities of any of the offices designated in paragraph (1) of subsection (a) of this section: *Provided*, That those years of such military service for which credit has been allowed for the purposes of retirement or retired pay under any other provision of law shall not be included as allowable years of such service under this section;

(4) those years during which such judicial official served as an "employee", as that term is defined in subsection (1) of section 8331 of title 5, prior to assuming the responsibilities of any of the offices designated in paragraph (1) of subsection (a) of this section,[1] and

(5) those years during which such judicial official had deductions withheld from his or her retirement salary in accordance with subsection (b)(1) or (2) of this section.

For the purposes of this subsection the term "years" shall mean full years and twelfth parts thereof, excluding from the aggregate any fractional part of a month which numbers less than fifteen full days and including, as one full month, any fractional part of a month which numbers fifteen full days or more. Nothing in this subsection shall be interpreted as waiving or canceling that reduction in the annuity of a widow or widower which is required by subsection (d) of this section due to the failure of a judicial official to make those deposits required by subsection (d) of this section.

(*l*) The annuity of a widow or widower of a judicial official shall be an amount equal to the sum of—

(1) 1.5 percent of the average annual salary, including retirement salary, which such judicial official received for serving in any of the offices designated in paragraph (1) of subsection (a) of this section (i) during those three years of such service, or during those three years while receiving a retirement salary, in which his or her annual salary or retirement salary was greatest, or (ii) if such judicial official has so served less than three years, then during the total period of such service prior to his or her death, multiplied by the total of:

(A) the number of years of creditable service tabulated in accordance with paragraph (1) of subsection (k) of this section; plus

(B) the number of years of creditable service tabulated in accordance with paragraph (2) of subsection (k) of this section; plus

(C) the number of years of creditable service tabulated in accordance with paragraph (3) of subsection (k) of this section; plus

(D) the number of years during which the judicial official had deductions withheld from his or her retirement salary under subsection (b)(1) or (2) of this section; plus

(E) the number of years up to, but not exceeding, fifteen of creditable service tabulated in accordance with paragraph (4) of subsection (k) of this section,

plus:

(2) three-fourths of 1 percent of such average annual salary, multiplied by the number of years of any prior creditable service, as tabulated in accordance with subsection (k) of this section, not applied under paragraph (1) of this subsection;

except that such annuity shall not exceed an amount equal to 50 percent of such average annual salary, nor be less than an amount equal to 25 percent of such average annual salary. Any annuity determined in accordance with the provisions of this subsection shall be reduced to the extent required by subsection (d) of this section, and by the amount of any annuity payable to a former spouse under subsection (t).

(m) Each time that an increase is made under section 8340(b) of title 5 in annuities paid under subchapter III of chapter 83 of such title, each annuity payable from the Judicial Survivors' Annuities Fund shall be increased at the same time by the same percentage by which annuities are increased under that section.

(n) Each annuity authorized under this section shall accrue monthly and shall be due and payable in monthly installments on the first business day of the month following the month or other period for which the annuity shall have accrued. No annuity authorized under this section shall be assignable, either in law or in equity, except as provided in subsections (s) and (t), or subject to execution, levy, attachment, garnishment, or other legal process.

(*o*)(1) In any case in which a judicial official dies while in office, while receiving retirement salary, or after filing an election and otherwise complying with the conditions under subsection (b)(2) of this section, and;

(A) subject to paragraph (2) of this subsection, before having completed eighteen months of civilian service, computed in accordance with subsection (k) of this section, during which the salary deductions provided by subsection (b) of this section or the deposit required by subsection (d) of this section have actually been made; or

(B) after having completed eighteen months of civilian service, computed in accordance with subsection (k) of this section, during which all such deductions or deposits have been made, but without a survivor or survivors who are entitled to receive the annuity benefits provided by subsection (h) or (t) of this section; or

(C) the rights of all persons entitled to receive the annuity benefits provided by subsection (h) or (t) of this section terminate before a valid claim therefor has been established;

the total amount credited to the individual account of that judicial official, established under subsection (e) of this section, with interest at 4 percent per annum to December 31, 1947, and at 3 percent per annum thereafter, compounded on December 31, of each year, to the date of that judicial official's death, shall be paid, upon the establishment of a valid claim therefor, to the person or persons surviving at the date title to the payment arises, in the following order of precedence:

First, to the beneficiary or beneficiaries whom that judicial official may have designated in a writing received by the Administrative Office of the United States Courts prior to his or her death;

Second, if there be no such beneficiary, to the widow or widower of such judicial official;

Third, if none of the above, to the child or children of such judicial official and the descendants of any deceased children by representation;

Fourth, if none of the above, to the parents of such judicial official or the survivor of them;

Fifth, if none of the above, to the duly appointed executor, executrix, administrator, or administratrix of the estate of such judicial official;

Sixth, if none of the above, to such other next of kin of such judicial official, as may be determined by the Director of the Administrative Office of the United States Courts to be entitled to such payment, under the laws of the domicile of such judicial official, at the time of his or her death.

Such payment shall be a bar to recovery by any other person. For the purposes of this subsection only, a determination that an individual is a widow, widower, or child of a judicial official may be made by the Director of the Administrative Office of the United States Courts without regard to the definitions of those terms contained in paragraphs (3), (4), and (5) of subsection (a) of this section.

(2) In cases in which a judicial official dies as a result of assassination and leaves a survivor or survivors who are entitled to receive the annuity benefits provided by subsection (h) or (t) of this section, paragraph (1)(A) of this subsection shall not apply.

(p) In any case in which all the annuities which are authorized by this section and based upon the service of a given official terminate before the aggregate amount of annuity payments received by the annuitant or annuitants equals the total amount credited to the individual account of such judicial official, established under subsection (e) of this section with interest at 4 percent per annum to December 31, 1947, and at 3 percent per annum thereafter, compounded on December 31, of each year, to the date of that judicial official's death, the difference between such total amount, with such interest, and such aggregate amount shall be paid, upon establishment of a valid claim therefor, in the order of precedence prescribed in subsection (*o*) of this section.

(q) Any accrued annuity benefits remaining unpaid upon the termination of an annuity, other than by the death of an annuitant, shall be paid to that annuitant. Any accrued annuity benefits remaining unpaid upon the death of an annuitant shall be paid, upon the establishment of a valid claim therefor, in the following order of precedence:

First, to the duly appointed executor, executrix, administrator, or administratrix of the estate of such annuitant;

Second, if there is no such executor, executrix, administrator, or administratrix, payments shall be made, after the expiration of sixty days from the date of death of such annuitant, to such individual or individuals as may appear, in the judgment of the Director of the Administrative Office of the United States Courts, to be legally entitled thereto, and such payment shall be a bar to recovery by any other individual.

(r) Nothing contained in this section shall be interpreted to prevent a widow or widower eligible for an annuity under this section from simultaneously receiving such an annuity while also receiving any other annuity to which such widow or widower may also be entitled under any other law without regard to this section: *Provided*, That service used in the computation of the annuity conferred by this section shall not also be credited in computing any such other annuity.

(s) A judicial official who has a former spouse may elect, under procedures prescribed by the Director of the Administrative Office of the United States Courts, to provide a survivor annuity for such former spouse under subsection (t). An election under this subsection shall be made at the time of retirement, or, if later, within 2 years after the date on which the marriage of the former spouse to the judicial official is dissolved. An election under this subsection—

(1) shall not be effective to the extent that it—

(A) conflicts with—

(i) any court order or decree referred to in subsection (t)(1), which was issued before the date of such election, or

(ii) any agreement referred to in such subsection which was entered into before such date; or

(B) would cause the total of survivor annuities payable under subsections (h) and (t) based on the service of the judicial official to exceed 55 percent of the average annual salary (as such term is used in subsection (*l*)) of such official; and

(2) shall not be effective, in the case of a judicial official who is then married, unless it is made with the spouse's written consent.

The Director of the Administrative Office of the United States Courts shall provide by regulation that paragraph (2) of this subsection may be waived if the judicial official establishes to the satisfaction of the Director that the spouse's whereabouts cannot be determined, or that, due to exceptional circumstances, requiring the judicial official to seek the spouse's consent would otherwise be inappropriate.

(t)(1) Subject to paragraphs (2) through (4) of this subsection, a former spouse of a deceased judicial official is entitled to a survivor annuity under this section if and to the extent expressly provided for in an election under subsection (s), or in the terms of any decree of divorce or annulment or any court order or court-approved property settlement agreement incident to such decree.

(2) The annuity payable to a former spouse under this subsection may not exceed the difference between—

(A) the maximum amount that would be payable as an annuity to a widow or widower under subsection (*l*), determined without taking into account any reduction of such annuity caused by payment of an annuity to a former spouse; and

(B) the amount of any annuity payable under this subsection to any other former spouse of the judicial official, based on an election previously made under subsection (s), or a court order previously issued.

(3) The commencement and termination of an annuity payable under this subsection shall be governed by the terms of the applicable order, decree, agreement, or election, as the case may be, except that any such annuity—

(A) shall not commence before—

(i) the day after the judicial official dies, or

(ii) the first day of the second month beginning after the date on which the Director of the Administrative Office of the United States Courts receives written notice of the order, decree, agreement, or election, as the case may be, together with such additional information or documentation as the Director may prescribe,

whichever is later, and

(B) shall terminate no later than the last day of the month before the former spouse remarries before becoming 55 years of age or dies.

(4) For purposes of this section, a modification in a decree, order, agreement, or election referred to in paragraph (1) of this subsection shall not be effective—

(A) if such modification is made after the retirement of the judicial official concerned, and

(B) to the extent that such modification involves an annuity under this subsection.

(u) In the case of a judicial official who is assassinated, an annuity shall be paid under this section notwithstanding a survivor's eligibility for or receipt of benefits under chapter 81 of title 5, except that the annuity for which a surviving spouse is eligible under this section shall be reduced to the extent that the total benefits paid under this section and chapter 81 of title 5 for any year would exceed the current salary for that year of the office of the judicial official.

(v) Subject to the terms of a decree, court order, or agreement described in subsection (t)(1), if any judicial official ceases to be married after making the election under subsection (a), he or she may revoke such election in writing by notifying the Director of the Administrative Office of the United States Courts. The judicial official shall also notify any spouse or former spouse of the application for revocation in accordance with such requirements as the Director of the Administrative Office of the United States Courts shall by regulation prescribe. The Director may provide under such regulations that the notification requirement may be waived with respect to a spouse or former spouse if the judicial official establishes to the satisfaction of the Director that the whereabouts of such spouse or former spouse cannot be determined.

(w) The Comptroller General of the United States shall, at the end of each 3–fiscal year period, determine whether the contributions by judicial officials under subsection (b) during that 3–year period accounted for 50 percent of the costs of the Judicial Survivors' Annuities Fund and if not, then what adjustments in the contribution rates under subsection (b) should be made to achieve that 50 percent figure. The Comptroller General shall report the results of each determination under this subsection to the Congress.

(Added Aug. 3, 1956, c. 944, § 2, 70 Stat. 1021, and amended July 7, 1958, Pub.L. 85–508, § 12(n), 72 Stat. 348; Dec. 20, 1967, Pub.L. 90–219, Title II, § 202, 81 Stat. 668; Aug. 8, 1968, Pub.L. 90–466, § 1(a), 82 Stat. 662; Aug. 22, 1972, Pub.L. 92–397, §§ 2, 3(c), 86 Stat. 579, 580; Oct. 19, 1976, Pub.L. 94–554, § 2, 90 Stat. 2603; Nov. 6, 1978, Pub.L. 95–598, Title II, § 211, 92 Stat. 2661; June 19, 1986, Pub.L. 99–336, § 2(a), (d)(1) to (3), (e), 100 Stat. 633, 635 to 637; Aug. 27, 1986, Pub.L. 99–396, § 21(b), 100 Stat. 846; Nov. 15, 1988, Pub.L. 100–659, § 3(a), 102 Stat. 3917; Nov. 19, 1988, Pub.L. 100–702, Title X, § 1017(a), 102 Stat. 4670; Dec. 1, 1990, Pub.L. 101–650, Title III, §§ 306(b), 322(a) to (f), (g)[(h)], 104 Stat. 5109, 5117 to 5120; Oct. 29, 1992, Pub.L. 102–572, Title II, § 201(a) to (i), 106 Stat. 4508 to 4510; Dec. 1, 1990, Pub.L. 101–650, Title III, §§ 306(b), 322(a) to (f), (g)[(h)], 104 Stat. 5109, 5117 to 5120; Oct. 29, 1992, Pub.L. 102–572, Title II, § 201(a) to (i), Title IX, § 902(b), 106 Stat. 4508 to 4510, 4516; Oct. 19, 1996, Pub.L. 104–317, Title III, §§ 302, 308, 110 Stat. 3851, 3853.)

[1] So in original. Probably should be a semicolon.

HISTORICAL AND STATUTORY NOTES

References in Text

The date of the enactment of the Retirement and Survivors' Annuities for Bankruptcy Judges and Magistrates Act of 1988, referred to in subsec. (a)(1)(v), is the date of the enactment of Pub.L. 100–659 (which amended this section), which was approved Nov. 15, 1988.

The date of the enactment of the Federal Courts Study Committee Implementation Act of 1990, referred to in subsec. (a)(1)(vi), is the date of enactment of Title III of Pub.L. 101–650, which was approved Dec. 1, 1990.

The date of the enactment of the Federal Courts Administration Act of 1992, referred to in subsec. (a)(1)(vii), means the date of enactment of Pub.L. 102–572, which was approved Oct. 29, 1992.

Section 3 of the Judicial Survivors' Annuities Reform Act, referred to in subsec. (b)(3), is section 3 of Pub.L. 94–554, which is set out as a note under this section.

Codifications

Subsec. (a)(2)(A) of this section was amended by Pub.L. 95–598, Title II, § 211, Nov. 6, 1978, 92 Stat. 2668, effective June 28, 1984, pursuant to Pub.L. 95–598, Title IV, § 402(b), Nov. 6, 1978, 92 Stat. 2682, as amended by Pub.L. 98–249, § 1(a), Mar. 31, 1984, 98 Stat. 116; Pub.L. 98–271, § 1(a), Apr. 30, 1984, 98 Stat. 163; Pub.L. 98–299, § 1(a), May 25, 1984, 98 Stat. 214; Pub.L. 98–325, § 1(a), June 20, 1984, 98 Stat. 268, set out as a note preceding section 101 of Title 11, Bankruptcy, by inserting ", or (iii) in the case of a bankruptcy judge, after retirement under section 337 of this title" following "(ii) after retirement from office by resignation on salary under subsection (a) of section 371 of this title".

Section 402(b) of Pub.L. 95–598 was amended by section 113 of Pub.L. 98–353, Title I, July 10, 1984, 98 Stat. 343, by substituting "shall not be effective" for "shall take effect on June 28, 1984", thereby eliminating the amendment by section 211 of Pub.L. 95–598, effective June 27, 1984, pursuant to section 122(c) of Pub.L. 98–353, set out as an Effective Date note under section 151 of this title.

Section 121(a) of Pub.L. 98–353 directed that section 402(b) of Pub.L. 95–598 be amended by substituting "the date of enactment of the Bankruptcy Amendments and Federal Judgeship Act of 1984 [i.e. July 10, 1984]" for "June 28, 1984". This amendment was not executed in view of the prior amendment to section 402(b) of Pub.L. 95–598 by section 113 of Pub.L. 98–353.

Effective Dates

1992 Acts. Section 202 of Pub.L. 102–572 provided that: "This title [Title II of Pub.L. 102–572, Oct. 29, 1992, 106 Stat. 4508] and the amendments made by this title [amending this section and enacting provisions set out as notes under this section] shall take effect on the date of the enactment of this Act [Oct. 29, 1992]."

Amendment by section 902(b) of Pub.L. 102–572 effective Oct. 29, 1992, see section 911 of Pub.L. 102–572, set out as a note under section 171 of this title.

1988 Acts. Section 1017(c) of Title X of Pub.L. 100–702 provided that: "The amendment made by subsection (a) [enacting subsec. (m) and deleting former subsec. (m) of this section] shall apply with respect to increases in annuities which are made under section 8340(b) of title 5, United States Code [section 8340(b) of Title 5, Government Organization and Employees], on or after the date of enactment of this title [Nov. 19, 1988]."

Amendment to this section by Pub.L. 100–659 to take effect on Nov. 15, 1988, and shall apply to bankruptcy judges and magistrates who retire on or after Nov. 15, 1988, with special election provisions for bankruptcy judges, etc., who left office on or after July 31, 1987, and before Nov. 15, 1988, see section 9 of Pub.L. 100–659, set out as a note under section 377 of this title.

1986 Acts. Amendment by Pub.L. 99–396 not to affect the amount payable to a judge who retired in accordance with the provisions of section 373 of this title in effect on the day before Aug. 27, 1986, see section 21(c) of Pub.L. 99–396, set out as a note under section 373 of this title.

Section 2(f) of Pub.L. 99–336 provided that: "This section [amending this section and enacting provisions set out as notes under this section] shall take effect on October 1, 1986."

1976 Acts. Section 8 of Pub.L. 94–554 provided: "That this Act [amending this section and enacting provisions set out as notes under this section] shall become effective on the first day of the third month following the month in which it is enacted [Jan. 1, 1977], or on October 1, 1976, whichever occurs last."

1958 Acts. Amendment by Pub.L. 85–508 effective Jan. 3, 1959 upon admission of Alaska into the Union pursuant to Proc. No. 3269, Jan. 5, 1959, 24 F.R. 81, 73 Stat. c16, as required by sections 1 and 8(c) of Pub.L. 85–508, see notes set out under section 81A of this title and preceding section 21 of Title 48, Territories and Insular Possessions.

Effective Dates of 1990 Amendments; Transition Provisions

Amendment by section 306(b) of Pub.L. 101–650 applicable to judges of, and senior judges in active service with, the United States Court of Federal Claims on or after Dec. 1, 1990, see section 306(f) of Pub.L. 101–650, set out as a note under section 8331 of Title 5, Government Organization and Employees.

Section 322(g) of Pub.L. 101–650 provided that:

"(1) **Effective date.**—Subject to paragraph (2), the amendments made by this Act [probably means section 322 of Pub.L. 101–650, amending this section] shall apply to all judicial officials assassinated on or after May 28, 1979.

"(2) **Rules for retroactive application.**—(A) In the case of a judicial official who was assassinated on or after May 28, 1979, and before the date of the enactment of this Act [Dec. 1, 1990], if the salary deductions provided by subsection (b) of section 376 of title 28, United States Code [subsec. (b) of this section], or the deposits required by subsection (d) of such section [subsec. (d) of this section], have been withdrawn pursuant to subsection (*o*) of such section [subsec. (*o*) of this section], there shall be deducted from the annuities otherwise payable to the survivor or survivors of such judicial official, and the payment authorized by subparagraph (C) of this paragraph, an amount equal to the amount so withdrawn, with interest on the amount withdrawn at 3 percent per annum compounded on December 31 of each year.

"(B) In the case of the survivor or survivors of a judicial official to whom this paragraph applies who had less than 18 months of service before being assassinated, there shall be deducted from the annuities otherwise payable to the survivor or survivors of such judicial official, and the payment authorized by subparagraph (C) of this paragraph, an amount equal to the amount of salary deductions that would have been made if such deductions [had] been made for 18 months before the judicial official's death, plus interest as described in subparagraph (A).

"(C) Subject to subparagraphs (A) and (B), the survivor or survivors of a judicial official to whom this paragraph applies shall be entitled to the payment of annuities they would have received under section 376 of title 28, United States Code [this section], for the period beginning on the date such judicial official was assassinated and ending the date of the enactment of this Act [Dec. 1, 1990]. The Secretary of the Treasury shall pay into the Judicial Survivors' Annuities fund, out of any money in the Treasury not otherwise appropriated, the amount of the annuities to which the survivor or survivors are entitled under this subparagraph.

"(3) Definition.—For purposes of this subsection, the term—

"(A) 'assassinated' has the meaning given that term in section 376(a)(7) of title 28, United States Code [subsec. (a) of this section], as added by this section; and

"(B) 'judicial official' has the meaning given that term in section 376(a)(1)(A) and (B) of title 28, United States Code [subsec. (a)(1)(A) and (B) of this section]."

Retroactive Effect of 1967 Amendments

The provisions of section 611(a) of this title, the first paragraph of section 611(b) of this title, and subsec. (s) of this section, as added by Pub.L. 90–219, applicable to a Director or former Director of the Administrative Office of the United States Courts who was first appointed prior to Dec. 20, 1967 if at the time such Director or former Director left or leaves such office he had, or shall have, attained the age of sixty-five years and completed fifteen years of service as Director of the Administrative Office of the United States Courts and if, on or before the expiration of six months following Dec. 20, 1967, he makes the election referred to in section 611(a) of this title or subsec. (s) of this section, or both, as the case may be, see section 205(b) of Pub.L. 90–219, set out as a note under section 611 of this title.

Change of Name

References to United States Claims Court deemed to refer to United States Court of Federal Claims and references to Claims Court deemed to refer to Court of Federal Claims, see section 902(b) of Pub.L. 102–572, set out as a note under section 171 of Title 28, Judiciary and Judicial Procedure.

United States magistrate appointed under section 631 of this title to be known as United States magistrate judge after Dec. 1, 1990, with any reference to United States magistrate or magistrate in this title, in any other Federal statute, etc., deemed a reference to United States magistrate judge appointed under section 631 of this title, see section 321 of Pub.L. 101–650, set out as a note under section 631 of this title.

Savings Provisions

Section 6 of Pub.L. 94–554 provided: "That the benefits conferred by this Act shall, on the date upon which this Act becomes effective [see Effective Dates of 1976 Amendments note under this section], immediately become available to any individual then receiving an annuity under section 2 of the Act of August 3, 1956 (70 Stat. 1021) [which enacted this section], as amended: *Provided*, That although the rights of any judicial official electing to come within the purview of section 376 of title 28, United States Code [this section], on or after the date upon which this Act becomes effective, shall be determined exclusively under the provisions of that section as amended by this Act, nothing in this Act shall be interpreted to cancel, abrogate, or diminish any rights to which an individual or his or her survivors may be entitled by virtue of that individuals [sic] having contributed to the judicial survivors annuity fund established by section 2 of the Act of August 3, 1956 (70 Stat. 1021) [which enacted this section], as amended, before the date upon which this Act becomes effective."

Annuity Payment to Surviving Spouses of Judges Who Died Before October 19, 1976

Pub.L. 96–504, § 3, Dec. 5, 1980, 94 Stat. 2741, provided that:

"(a) As of the first pay period beginning after the effective date of this Act [see note set out under section 8344 of Title 5, Government Organization and Employees], a surviving spouse, other than a surviving spouse who has remarried, of any Justice of the United States (as defined by section 451 of title 28, United States Code) [section 451 of this title], who died before October 19, 1976, shall be paid an annuity in accordance with the provisions of section 376 of title 28, United States Code [this section], at a rate of $20,000 per year as if such Justice had elected to come within the provisions of, and having made the full deposit required by, section 376(d) of title 28, United States Code [subsec. (d) of this section].

"(b) Notwithstanding the provisions of section 376(h) of title 28, United States Code [subsec. (h) of this section], such annuity shall be payable as provided in section 376(m) of title 28, United States Code [subsec. (m) of this section], until the date of the death of any such spouse."

Appropriations

Section 5 of Act Aug. 3, 1956, c. 944, 70 Stat. 1026, provided that: "Funds necessary to carry out the provisions of this Act [enacting this section and provisions set out as notes hereunder, and amending sections 375, 604(a)(7), and 605 of this title] may be appropriated out of any money in the Treasury not otherwise appropriated."

Audit by GAO

Section 201(*l*) of Pub.L. 102–572 provided that: "The Comptroller General shall—

"(1) conduct an audit of the judicial survivors annuities program under section 376 of title 28, United States Code [this section], for the 3-year period beginning on the date of the enactment of this Act [Oct. 29, 1992]; and

"(2) report to the Congress, not later than 60 days after the end of that 3-year period, on the results of such audit, comparing such program to other survivors annuities programs within the Federal Government."

Compensation for Actuarial Deficiency in the Annuities Fund

Section 4 of Pub.L. 94–554 provided: "That on the date upon which this Act becomes effective [see Effective Dates of 1976 Amendments note under this section] the Secretary of the Treasury shall ascertain from the Director of the Administrative Office of the United States Courts the amount of the actuarial deficiency in the fund transferred by section 3 of this Act [see Judicial Survivors' Annuities Fund note under this section] on the date of that fund's transfer and, at the earliest time thereafter at which appropriated funds in that amount shall become available, the Secretary shall deposit such funds, in a single payment, into the Judicial Survivors' Annuities Fund established by section 3 of this Act. Such funds as are necessary to carry out this section are hereby authorized to be appropriated."

Covered Beneficiaries under Pub.L. 99–336

Section 2(b) of Pub.L. 99–336 provided that: "The benefits conferred by section 376 of title 28, United States Code [this section], by reason of the amendments made by this section [amending this section] shall apply only to individuals who become eligible for annuities under such section on or after the effective date of this section [Oct. 1, 1986], except that—

"(1) such annuities shall be computed in accordance with the provisions of section 376 of title 28, United States Code, as amended by this section [this section], notwithstanding contributions or deposits made in accordance with applicable law at lower rates; and

"(2) no additional liability shall be created with respect to deposits made in accordance with applicable law before the effective date of this section [October 1, 1986], or after such effective date pursuant to an agreement entered into before such effective date."

Credit for Contributions Prior to 1992 Amendment at Higher Rate

Section 201(j) of Pub.L. 102–572 provided that: "Notwithstanding any other provision of law, the contribution under section 376(b)(1) or (2) of title 28, United States Code (as amended by this section) [subsec. (b)(1) or (2) of this section], of any judicial official who is within the purview of such section 376 on the effective date of this title [Oct. 29, 1992] shall be reduced by 0.5 percent for a period of time equal to the number of years of service for which the judicial official has made contributions or deposits before the enactment of this Act [probably means date of enactment of Pub.L. 102–572, which was approved Oct. 29, 1992] to the credit of the Judicial Survivors' Annuities Fund or for 18 months, whichever is less, if such contributions or deposits were never returned to the judicial official. For purposes of this subsection, the term 'years' shall mean full years and twelfth parts thereof."

Increase for Existing Annuitants

Section 1017(b) of Pub.L. 100–702 provided that: "Each annuity payable from the Judicial Survivors' Annuities Fund under section 376 of title 28, United States Code [this section], on the date of the enactment of this title [Nov. 19, 1988] shall be increased by 10 percent, effective on such date of enactment [Nov. 19, 1988]."

Increases in Widows' Annuities Paid under Section 2 of Act August 3, 1956

Section 5 of Pub.L. 94–554 provided: "That on the date upon which this Act becomes effective [see Effective Dates of 1976 Amendments note under this section] each annuity then being paid to a widow from the judicial survivors annuity fund established by section 2 of the Act of August 3, 1956 (70 Stat. 1021) [which enacted this section], as amended, shall be increased by an amount equal to one-fifth of 1 percent of the amount of such annuity multiplied by the number of months which have passed since the commencement of that annuity. For the purposes of this section, any fractional part of a month which numbers less than fifteen full days shall be excluded from the computation of the number of months and any fractional part of a month which numbers fifteen full days or more shall be included in the computation as one full month. Such funds as are necessary to carry out this section are authorized to be appropriated and, upon appropriation, shall be deposited by the Secretary of the Treasury, in a single payment, to credit of the Judicial Survivors' Annuities Fund established by section 3 of this Act [see Judicial Survivors' Annuities Fund note under this section]."

Judge Taking Office on August 8, 1968

Section 1(b) of Pub.L. 90–466 provided that: "For the purpose of the amendment made by subsection (a) [to subsec. (a) of this section], a judge who is in office on the date of enactment of this Act [Aug. 8, 1968] shall be deemed to have taken office on that date [Aug. 8, 1968]."

Judicial Survivors' Annuities Fund

Section 3 of Pub.L. 94–554 provided: "That on the date upon which this Act becomes effective [see Effective Dates of 1976 Amendments note under this section] there shall be established on the books of the Treasury a fund which shall be known as 'The Judicial Survivors' Annuities Fund,' and all money credited to the judicial survivors annuity fund established by section 2 of the Act of August 3, 1956 (70 Stat. 1021) [which enacted this section], as amended, shall be transferred to the credit of the Judicial Survivors' Annuities Fund established by this section."

Judicial Survivors' Annuity Fund; Authorization of Appropriations

Pub.L. 96–504, § 4, Dec. 5, 1980, 94 Stat. 2742, required the Secretary of the Treasury in consultation with the Director of the Administrative Office of the United States Courts to determine as of Dec. 5, 1980, and deposit as soon as possible thereafter, the amount necessary to offset any actuarial deficiency in the Judicial Survivors Annuities Fund.

Payment of Retirement Salary Pursuant to Court Decree of Divorce, Etc.

Section 2(d)(4) of Pub.L. 99–336 provided that: "Payments of retirement salary as defined in section 376(a)(2) of title 28, United States Code [subsec. (a)(2) of this section], which would otherwise be made to the judicial official upon whose service the retirement salary is based, shall be paid (in whole or in part) to another person if and to the extent expressly provided for in the terms of any court decree of divorce, annulment, or legal separation, or the terms of any court order or court-approved property settlement agreement incident to any court decree of divorce, annulment, or legal separation. Any payment under this paragraph to a person bars recovery by any other person. This paragraph shall apply only to payments made after the date of receipt by the Director of the Administrative Office of [the] United States Courts of written notice of such decree, order, or agreement, and such additional information and documentation as the Director may prescribe. As used in this paragraph, 'court' means any court of any State or the District of Columbia."

Preservation of Rights of Judges of the District Court for the Territory of Alaska

Section 12(n) of Pub.L. 85–508 provided in part that the amendment of subsec. (q) of this section by Pub.L. 85–508 shall not affect the rights under this section of any present or former judge of the District Court for the Territory of Alaska or his survivors.

Prior Death of Judge

Section 7 of Act Aug. 3, 1956, c. 944, 70 Stat. 1021, provided that: "In the case of a living widow of a judge of the United States as defined in section 451 of title 28, United States Code, who died prior to the date of enactment of this Act [Aug. 3, 1956], an annuity shall be paid as provided in section 376 of title 28, United States Code, as added by section 2 of this Act [this section], as if such judge had died on such date and had elected to bring himself within the purview of such section 376 [this section], but had not made the deposit provided for by subsection (c) of the said section: *Provided,* (a) That such widow has not remarried; and (b) that the amount of such annuity and the reduction therein because of such deposit not having been made shall be computed on the basis of the actual length of judicial and other allowable service of such judge: *And provided further,* That notwithstanding the provisions of subsection (g) of such section 376 [this section] such annuity shall be payable even though such judge had not rendered five years of civilian service prior to his death. In the case of a judge of the United States as defined in section 451 of title 28, United States Code, who dies within 6 months after the date of enactment of this Act [August 3, 1956] after having rendered at least 5 years of civilian service computed as prescribed in subsection (*o*) of section 376 of title 28, United States Code, as added by section 2 of this Act, but without having made an election as provided in such section 376 [this section] to bring himself within the purview of that section, an annuity shall be paid to his widow and surviving dependent children as provided in such section 376 [this section] as if such judge had elected on the day of his death to bring himself within the purview of such section 376 [this section] but had not made the deposit provided for by subsection (c) of the said section. An annuity shall be payable under this section computed on the basis of the actual length of judicial and other allowable service of the judge and subject to the reduction required by subsection (c) of such section 376 even though no deposit has been made, as required by subsection (g) of such section 376 [this section], with respect to any of such service."

Redeposit of Contributions Prior to 1992 Amendment

Section 201(k) of Pub.L. 102–572 provided that: "Any judicial official as defined in section 376(a)(1) of title 28, United States Code [subsec. (a)(1) of this section], who makes an election under section 376(b) of title 28, United States Code [subsec. (b) of this section], may make a redeposit, as required by section 7 of Public Law 94–554 [set out as a note under this section] and section 2(c)(2) of Public Law 99–336 [set out as a note under this section], to the credit of the Judicial Survivors' Annuities Fund in installments, in such amounts and under such conditions as may be determined in each instance by the Director of the Administrative Office of the United States Courts. If a judicial official elects to make a redeposit in installments—

"(1) the Director shall require that the first installment payment made shall be in an amount no smaller than the last 18 months of salary deductions or deposits previously returned to that judicial official in a lump-sum payment; and

"(2) the election under section 376(b) of title 28, United States Code [subsec. (b) of this section], shall be effective upon payment of the first such installment."

Resigned, Removed, and Retired Judges

Section 6 of Act Aug. 3, 1956, c. 944, 70 Stat. 1021, provided that: "A judge who resigned prior to the date of enactment of this Act [Aug. 3, 1956] and who on that date is receiving salary under section 371(a) of title 28, United States Code, or who resigned, was removed or failed of reappointment prior to the date of enactment of this Act [Aug. 3, 1956] and who on that date is receiving salary under section 373 of title 28, United States Code, shall be considered a judge within the meaning of section 376 of title 28, United States Code, as added by section 2 of this Act [this section], and as such shall be entitled within six months after the date of enactment of this Act [Aug. 3, 1956] to make the election authorized by and to receive the benefits of that section. A judge who retired from regular active service under section 260 of the Judicial Code of 1911 or the Act of August 5, 1939, chapter 433, and who is living on the date of enactment of this Act shall be deemed for the purposes of this Act to have retired from regular active service under section 371(b) or 372(a), as the case may be, of title 28, United States Code."

Revocation of Election to Participate in Annuities Program

Section 2(c) of Pub.L. 99–336 provided that:

"(1) Within 180 days after the effective date of this section [Oct. 1, 1986], any judicial official who, before such effective date, made an election under section 376 of title 28, United States Code [this section], to come within the purview of that section, shall be entitled to revoke that election. Such revocation shall constitute a complete withdrawal from the judicial survivors' annuities program provided for in such section 376 [this section]. No such revocation shall be effective unless it is submitted in writing to the Director of the Administrative Office of the United States Courts, and until such writing is received by the Director. Upon receipt by the Director of such writing, any rights to survivorship benefits for the survivors of such judicial official shall terminate, and all amounts credited to the individual account of such judicial official under section 376(e) [subsec. (e) of this section], together with interest at 3 percent per annum, compounded on December 31 of each year to such date of revocation, shall be returned to that judicial official in a lump-sum payment.

"(2) Any judicial official who makes a revocation under paragraph (1) of this subsection and who thereafter becomes eligible to make an election under section 376(b) of title 28, United States Code [subsec. (b) of this section], may make such election only if such judicial official redeposits, to the credit of the Judicial Survivors' Annuities Fund, the full amount of the lump-sum payment made to such judicial official under paragraph (1) of this subsection, together with interest at 3 percent per annum, compounded on December 31 of each year from the date of such revocation until the date upon which that amount is so redeposited.

"(3) Any judicial official who fails to revoke an election in accordance with paragraph (1) of this subsection shall be deemed to have irrevocably waived the right to make that revocation."

Section 7 of Pub.L. 94–554 provided: "That, at any time within one hundred and eighty days after the date upon which this Act becomes effective [see Effective Dates of 1976 Amendments note under this section] any judicial official who has, prior to that date, already participated in the judicial survivors annuity program created by the Act of August 3, 1956 (70 Stat. 1021) [which enacted this section] as amended, shall be entitled to revoke his or her earlier election to participate in that program and thereby completely withdraw from participation in the judicial survivors' annuities program created by this Act: *Provided,* That (a) any such revocation may be effected only by means of a writing filed with the Director of the Administrative Office of the United

States Courts, (b) any such writing shall be deemed to have become effective no sooner than the date upon which that writing is received by the Director, (c) upon receipt of such a writing by the Director, any and all rights to survivorship benefits for such judicial official's survivors shall terminate, and all amounts credited to such judicial official's individual account, together with interest at 3 percent per annum, compounded on December 31 of each year to that date of revocation, shall thereafter be returned to that judicial official in a lump-sum refund payment, and (d) any judicial official who effects such a revocation and who subsequently again becomes eligible and elects to join the judicial survivors annuities program created by this Act under the provisions of section 376 of title 28, United States Code [this section] as amended by this Act, shall be permitted to do so only upon the redeposit of the full amount of the refund obtained under this section plus interest at 3 percent per annum, compounded on December 31 of each year from the date of the revocation until the date upon which that amount is redeposited. Any judicial official who fails to effect a revocation in accordance with the right conferred by this section within one hundred and eighty days after the date upon which this Act becomes effective shall be deemed to have irrevocably waived the right to that revocation."

Survivors' Annuities for Incumbents

Section 3(b) of Pub.L. 100–659 provided that: "In the case of a bankruptcy judge or magistrate who elects an annuity under section 2(c) [set out as a note under section 377 of this title], only service for which an annuity under subsection (b) or (c) and subsection (g) of section 377 of title 28, United States Code, as added by section 2 of this Act [section 377(b) or (c) and (g) of this title], is calculated under section 2(c) may be used in the computation of an annuity under section 376 of title 28, United States Code, as amended by subsection (a) of this section."

§ 377. Retirement of bankruptcy judges and magistrates

(a) Retirement based on years of service.—A bankruptcy judge or magistrate to whom this section applies and who retires from office after attaining the age of 65 years and serving at least 14 years, whether continuously or otherwise, as such bankruptcy judge or magistrate shall, subject to subsection (f), be entitled to receive, during the remainder of the judge's or magistrate's lifetime, an annuity equal to the salary being received at the time the judge or magistrate leaves office.

(b) Retirement upon failure of reappointment.—A bankruptcy judge or magistrate to whom this section applies, who is not reappointed following the expiration of the term of office of such judge or magistrate, and who retires upon the completion of the term shall, subject to subsection (f), be entitled to receive, upon attaining the age of 65 years and during the remainder of such bankruptcy judge's or magistrate's lifetime, an annuity equal to that portion of the salary being received at the time the judge or magistrate leaves office which the aggregate number of years of service, not to exceed 14, bears to 14, if—

(1) such judge or magistrate has served at least 1 full term as a bankruptcy judge or magistrate, and

(2) not earlier than 9 months before the date on which the term of office of such judge or magistrate expires, and not later than 6 months before such date, such judge or magistrate notified the appointing authority in writing that such judge or magistrate was willing to accept reappointment to the position in which such judge or magistrate was serving.

For purposes of this subsection, in the case of a bankruptcy judge, the written notice required by paragraph (2) shall be given to the chief judge of the circuit in which such bankruptcy judge is serving and, in the case of a magistrate, such notice shall be given to the chief judge of the district court in which the magistrate is serving.

(c) Service of at least 8 years.—A bankruptcy judge or magistrate to whom this section applies and who retires after serving at least 8 years, whether continuously or otherwise, as such a bankruptcy judge or magistrate shall, subject to subsection (f), be entitled to receive, upon attaining the age of 65 years and during the remainder of the judge's or magistrate's lifetime, an annuity equal to that portion of the salary being received at the time the judge or magistrate leaves office which the aggregate number of years of service, not to exceed 14, bears to 14. Such annuity shall be reduced by ⅙ of 1 percent for each full month such bankruptcy judge or magistrate was under the age of 65 at the time the judge or magistrate left office, except that such reduction shall not exceed 20 percent.

(d) Retirement for disability.—A bankruptcy judge or magistrate to whom this section applies, who has served at least 5 years, whether continuously or otherwise, as such a bankruptcy judge or magistrate, and who retires or is removed from office upon the sole ground of mental or physical disability shall, subject to subsection (f), be entitled to receive, during the remainder of the judge's or magistrate's lifetime, an annuity equal to 40 percent of the salary being received at the time of retirement or removal or, in the case of a judge or magistrate who has served for at least 10 years, an amount equal to that proportion of the salary being received at the time of retirement or removal which the aggregate number of years of service, not to exceed 14, bears to 14.

(e) Cost-of-living adjustments.—A bankruptcy judge or magistrate who is entitled to an annuity under this section is also entitled to a cost-of-living adjustment in such annuity, calculated and payable in the same manner as adjustments under section 8340(b) of title 5, except that any such annuity, as increased under this subsection, may not exceed the salary then payable for the position from which the judge or magistrate retired or was removed.

(f) Election; annuity in lieu of other annuities.—A bankruptcy judge or magistrate shall be entitled to an annuity under this section if the judge or magistrate elects an annuity under this section by notifying the Director of the Administrative Office of the United States Courts. A bankruptcy judge or magistrate who elects to receive an annuity under this section shall not be entitled to receive [1]

(1) any annuity to which such judge or magistrate would otherwise have been entitled under subchapter III of chapter 83, or under chapter 84 (except for subchapters III and VII), of title 5, for service performed as such a judge or magistrate or otherwise;

(2) an annuity or salary in senior status or retirement under section 371 or 372 of this title;

(3) retired pay under section 7447 of the Internal Revenue Code of 1986; or

(4) retired pay under section 7296 of title 38.

(g) Calculation of service.—(1) For purposes of calculating an annuity under this section—

(A) full-time service as a bankruptcy judge or magistrate to whom this section applies may be credited; and

(B) each month of service shall be credited as one-twelfth of a year, and the fractional part of any month shall not be credited.

(2)(A) In the case of an individual who is a bankruptcy judge to whom this section applies and who retires under this section or who is removed from office under subsection (d) upon the sole ground of mental or physical disability, any service of that individual as a United States magistrate to whom this section applies, and any service of that individual as a full-time judicial officer who performed the duties of a magistrate and a bankruptcy judge at the same time, shall be included for purposes of calculating years of service under subsection (a), (b), (c), or (d), as the case may be.

(B) In the case of an individual who is a magistrate to whom this section applies and who retires under this section or who is removed from office under subsection (d) upon the sole ground of mental or physical disability, any service of that individual as a bankruptcy judge to whom this section applies, and any service of that individual as a full-time judicial officer who performed the duties of magistrate and a bankruptcy judge at the same time, shall be included for purposes of calculating years of service under subsection (a), (b), (c), or (d), as the case may be.

(h) Covered positions and service.—This section applies to—

(1) any bankruptcy judge appointed under—

(A) section 152 of this title;

(B) section 34 of the Bankruptcy Act before the repeal of that Act by section 401 of the Act of November 6, 1978 (Public Law 95–598; 92 Stat. 2682); or

(C) section 404 of the Act of November 6, 1978 (Public Law 95–598; 92 Stat. 2549); and

(2) any United States magistrate appointed under section 631 of this title,

only with respect to service on or after October 1, 1979, as such a bankruptcy judge or magistrate.

(i) Payments pursuant to court order.—(1) Payments under this section which would otherwise be made to a bankruptcy judge or magistrate based upon his or her service shall be paid (in whole or in part) by the Director of the Administrative Office of the United States Courts to another person if and to the extent expressly provided for in the terms of any court decree of divorce, annulment, or legal separation, or the terms of any court order or court-approved property settlement agreement incident to any court decree of divorce, annulment, or legal separation. Any payment under this paragraph to a person bars recovery by any other person.

(2) Paragraph (1) shall apply only to payments made by the Director of the Administrative Office of the United States Courts after the date of receipt by the Director of written notice of such decree, order, or agreement, and such additional information as the Director may prescribe.

(3) As used in this subsection, the term "court" means any court of any State, the District of Columbia, the Commonwealth of Puerto Rico, Guam, the Northern Mariana Islands, or the Virgin Islands, and any Indian tribal court or courts of Indian offense.

(j) Deductions, contributions, and deposits.—

(1) **Deductions.**—Beginning with the next pay period after the Director of the Administrative Office of the United States Courts receives a notice under subsection (f) that a bankruptcy judge or magistrate has elected an annuity under this section, the Director shall deduct and withhold 1 percent of the salary of such bankruptcy judge or magistrate. Amounts shall be so deducted and withheld in a manner determined by the Director. Amounts deducted and withheld under this subsection shall be deposited in the Treasury of the United States to the credit of the Judicial Officers' Retirement Fund. Deductions under this subsection from the salary of a bankruptcy judge or magistrate shall terminate upon the retirement of the bankruptcy judge or magistrate or upon completing 14 years of service for which contributions under this section have been made, whether contin-

uously or otherwise, as calculated under subsection (g), whichever occurs first.

(2) Consent to deductions; discharge of claims.—Each bankruptcy judge or magistrate who makes an election under subsection (f) shall be deemed to consent and agree to the deductions from salary which are made under paragraph (1). Payment of such salary less such deductions (and any deductions made under section 376 of this title) is a full and complete discharge and acquittance of all claims and demands for all services rendered by such bankruptcy judge or magistrate during the period covered by such payment, except the right to those benefits to which the bankruptcy judge or magistrate is entitled under this section (and section 376).

(k) Deposits for prior service.—Each bankruptcy judge or magistrate who makes an election under subsection (f) may deposit, for service performed before such election for which contributions may be made under this section, an amount equal to 1 percent of the salary received for that service. Credit for any period covered by that service may not be allowed for purposes of an annuity under this section until a deposit under this subsection has been made for that period.

(*l*) Individual retirement records.—The amounts deducted and withheld under subsection (j), and the amounts deposited under subsection (k), shall be credited to individual accounts in the name of each bankruptcy judge or magistrate from whom such amounts are received, for credit to the Judicial Officers' Retirement Fund.

(m) Annuities affected in certain cases.—

(1) Practicing law after retirement.—

(A) Forfeiture of annuity.—Subject to subparagraph (B), any bankruptcy judge or magistrate who retires under this section and who thereafter practices law shall forfeit all rights to an annuity under this section for all periods beginning on or after the first day on which he or she so practices law.

(B) Forfeiture not to apply where individual elects to freeze amount of annuity.—**(i)** If a bankruptcy judge or magistrate makes an election to practice law after retirement under this section—

(I) subparagraph (A) shall not apply to such bankruptcy judge or magistrate beginning on the date such election takes effect, and

(II) the annuity payable under this section to such bankruptcy judge or magistrate, for periods beginning on or after the date such election takes effect, shall be equal to the annuity to which such bankruptcy judge or magistrate is entitled on the day before such effective date.

(ii) An election under clause (i)—

(I) may be made by a bankruptcy judge or magistrate eligible for retirement under this section, and

(II) shall be filed with the Director of the Administrative Office of the United States Courts.

Such an election, once it takes effect, shall be irrevocable.

(iii) Any election under this subparagraph shall take effect on the first day of the first month following the month in which the election is made.

(2) Recall not permitted.—Any bankruptcy judge or magistrate who retires under this section and who thereafter practices law shall not be eligible for recall under section 155(b), 375, or 636(h) of this title.

(3) Accepting other employment.—Any bankruptcy judge or magistrate who retires under this section and thereafter accepts compensation for civil office or employment under the United States Government (other than for the performance of functions as a bankruptcy judge or magistrate under section 155(b), 375, or 636(h) of this title) shall forfeit all rights to an annuity under this section for the period for which such compensation is received. For purposes of this paragraph, the term "compensation" includes retired pay or salary received in retired status.

(n) Lump-sum payments.—

(1) Eligibility.—**(A)** Subject to paragraph (2), an individual who serves as a bankruptcy judge or magistrate and—

(i) who leaves office and is not reappointed as a bankruptcy judge or magistrate for at least 31 consecutive days;

(ii) who files an application with the Administrative Office of the United States Courts for payment of the lump-sum credit;

(iii) is not serving as a bankruptcy judge or magistrate at the time of filing of the application; and

(iv) will not become eligible to receive an annuity under this section within 31 days after filing the application;

is entitled to be paid the lump-sum credit. Payment of the lump-sum credit voids all rights to an annuity under this section based on the service on which the lump-sum credit is based, until that individual resumes office as a bankruptcy judge or magistrate.

(B) Lump-sum benefits authorized by subparagraphs (C), (D), and (E) of this paragraph shall be paid to the person or persons surviving the bankruptcy judge or magistrate and alive on the date title to the payment arises, in the order of precedence set forth in subsection (*o*) of section 376 of this title, and in accordance with the last two sentences of that subsection. For purposes of the preceding sentence, the term "judicial official" as used in subsection (*o*) of section 376 shall be deemed to mean "bankruptcy judge or magistrate".

(C) If a bankruptcy judge or magistrate dies before receiving an annuity under this section, the lump-sum credit shall be paid.

(D) If all annuity rights under this section based on the service of a deceased bankruptcy judge or magistrate terminate before the total annuity paid equals the lump-sum credit, the difference shall be paid.

(E) If a bankruptcy judge or magistrate who is receiving an annuity under this section dies, annuity accrued and unpaid shall be paid.

(F) Annuity accrued and unpaid on the termination, except by death, of the annuity of a bankruptcy judge or magistrate shall be paid to that individual.

(G) Subject to paragraph (2), a bankruptcy judge or magistrate who forfeits rights to an annuity under subsection (m)(3) before the total annuity paid equals the lump-sum credit, shall be entitled to be paid the difference if the bankruptcy judge or magistrate files an application with the Administrative Office of the United States Courts for payment of that difference. A payment under this subparagraph voids all rights to an annuity on which the payment is based.

(2) Spouses and former spouses.—(A) Payment of the lump-sum credit under paragraph (1)(A) or a payment under paragraph (1)(G)—

(i) may be made only if any current spouse and any former spouse of the bankruptcy judge or magistrate are notified of the bankruptcy judge's or magistrate's application; and

(ii) shall be subject to the terms of a court decree of divorce, annulment, or legal separation or any court or court approved property settlement agreement incident to such decree, if—

(I) the decree, order, or agreement expressly relates to any portion of the lump-sum credit or other payment involved; and

(II) payment of the lump-sum credit or other payment would extinguish entitlement of the bankruptcy judge's or magistrate's spouse or former spouse to any portion of an annuity under subsection (i).

(B) Notification of a spouse or former spouse under this paragraph shall be made in accordance with such requirements as the Director of the Administrative Office of the United States Courts shall by regulation prescribe. The Director may provide under such regulations that subparagraph (A)(i) may be waived with respect to a spouse or former spouse if the bankruptcy judge or magistrate establishes to the satisfaction of the Director that the whereabouts of such spouse or former spouse cannot be determined.

(C) The Director shall prescribe regulations under which this paragraph shall be applied in any case in which the Director receives two or more orders or decrees described in subparagraph (A).

(3) Definition.—For purposes of this subsection, the term "lump-sum credit" means the unrefunded amount consisting of—

(A) retirement deductions made under this section from the salary of a bankruptcy judge or magistrate;

(B) amounts deposited under subsection (k) by a bankruptcy judge or magistrate covering earlier service; and

(C) interest on the deductions and deposits which, for any calendar year, shall be equal to the overall average yield to the Judicial Officers' Retirement Fund during the preceding fiscal year from all obligations purchased by the Secretary of the Treasury during such fiscal year under subsection (*o*);

but does not include interest—

(i) if the service covered thereby aggregates 1 year or less; or

(ii) for the fractional part of a month in the total service.

(*o*) Judicial Officers' Retirement Fund.—

(1) Establishment.—There is established in the Treasury a fund which shall be known as the "Judicial Officers' Retirement Fund". The Fund is appropriated for the payment of annuities, refunds, and other payments under this section.

(2) Investment of Fund.—The Secretary of the Treasury shall invest, in interest bearing securities of the United States, such currently available portions of the Judicial Officers' Retirement Fund as are not immediately required for payments from the Fund. The income derived from these investments constitutes a part of the Fund.

(3) Unfunded liability.—(A) There are authorized to be appropriated to the Judicial Officers' Retirement Fund amounts required to reduce to zero the unfunded liability of the Fund.

(B) For purposes of subparagraph (A), the term "unfunded liability" means the estimated excess, determined on an annual basis in accordance with the provisions of section 9503 of title 31, of the present value of all benefits payable from the Judicial Officers' Retirement Fund over the sum of—

(i) the present value of deductions to be withheld under this section from the future basic pay of bankruptcy judges and magistrates; plus

(ii) the balance in the Fund as of the date the unfunded liability is determined.

In making any determination under this subparagraph, the Comptroller General shall use the applicable information contained in the reports filed pursuant to section 9503 of title 31, with respect to the retirement annuities provided for in this section.

(C) There are authorized to be appropriated such sums as may be necessary to carry out this paragraph.

(Added Pub.L. 100–659, § 2(a), Nov. 15, 1988, 102 Stat. 3910, and amended Pub.L. 101–650, Title III, § 325(b)(3), Dec. 1, 1990, 104 Stat. 5121; Pub.L. 102–40, Title IV, § 402(d)(2), May 7, 1991, 105 Stat. 239.)

1 So in original. Probably should be "receive—"

HISTORICAL AND STATUTORY NOTES

References in Text

Section 7447 of the Internal Revenue Code of 1986, referred to in subsec. (f)(3), is classified to section 7447 of Title 26, Internal Revenue Code.

Section 34 of the Bankruptcy Act, referred to in subsec. (h)(1)(B), was classified to section 62 of former Title 11, Bankruptcy, and was omitted in the enactment of revised Title 11 by Section 101 of Pub.L. 95–598, Nov. 6, 1978, 92 Stat. 2549 the Bankruptcy Act was repealed effective Oct. 1, 1979, by Sections 401(a), 402(a) of Pub.L. 95–598.

Section 404 of the Act of November 6, 1978 (Pub.L. 95–598), referred to in subsec. (h)(1)(C), and formerly set out as a note preceding section 151 of this title, was repealed by Pub.L. 98–353, Title I, § 114, July 10, 1984, 98 Stat. 343.

Effective Dates

1988 Acts. Section 9 of Pub.L. 100–659 provided that:

"**(a) In general.**—Subject to subsection (b), this Act and the amendments made by this Act [enacting this section and section 8440a of Title 5, Government Organization and Employees, amending sections 155, 375, 376, 604, 631, and 636 of this title and sections 8334 and 8402 of Title 5 and enacting provisions set out as notes under this section and sections 1 and 376 of this title] shall take effect on the date of the enactment of this Act [Nov. 15, 1988] and shall apply to bankruptcy judges and magistrates who retire on or after the date of the enactment of this Act.

"**(b) Exception for judges and magistrates retiring on or after July 31, 1987.**—A bankruptcy judge or magistrate who left office on or after July 31, 1987, and before the date of the enactment of this Act [Nov. 15, 1988] may elect to receive an annuity, or to participate in the Judicial Survivors' Annuity System, under the amendments made by this Act if such bankruptcy judge or magistrate, within 60 days after so leaving office, accepted office or employment with the United States Government or a State government or was eligible at the time he or she left office for an immediate annuity under title 5, United States Code. Any election under this subsection shall not be valid unless it is made within 6 months after the date of the enactment of this act [Nov. 15, 1988] and under the same conditions as other persons who may make elections under the amendments made by this Act, except that any such person who makes an election under this subsection shall not receive a lump-sum credit under section 8342 or 8424 of title 5, United States Code [section 8342 or 8424 of Title 5], for prior service and shall not be required to make contributions for prior years of creditable service."

Change of Name

United States magistrate appointed under section 631 of this title to be known as United States magistrate judge after Dec. 1, 1990, with any reference to United States magistrate or magistrate in this title, in any other Federal statute, etc., deemed a reference to United States magistrate judge appointed under section 631 of this title, see section 321 of Pub.L. 101–650, set out as a note under section 631 of this title.

Report to Congress on Financial Operation of Retirement Annuity Program

Section 8 of Pub.L. 100–659 provided that: "The Director of the Administrative Office of the United States Courts shall, not later than 5 years after the date of the enactment of this Act [Nov. 15, 1988], submit a report to the Congress on the financial operation of the retirement annuity program established under this Act and the amendments made by this Act [see Effective Dates of 1988 Amendments note set out under this section]. The report shall, in particular, include a discussion of the deductions from salary and deposits made for contributions to the annuity program and the need for continuing the deductions at the level established under the amendments made by this Act."

Retirement Annuities for Incumbent Bankruptcy Judges and Magistrates

Section 2(c) of Pub.L. 100–659 provided that:

"**(1) Retirement annuity under Title 5 and section 377 of Title 28.**—A bankruptcy judge or United States magistrate in active service on the effective date of this Act [Nov. 15, 1988] shall, subject to paragraph (2), be entitled, in lieu of the annuity otherwise provided under the amendments made by this section [enacting this section], to—

"(A) an annuity under subchapter III of chapter 83, or under chapter 84, of Title 5, United States Code [section 8331 et seq. or section 8401 et seq. of Title 5, Government Organization and Employees], as the case may be, for creditable service before the date on which service would begin to be credited for purposes of subparagraph (B), and

"(B) an annuity calculated under subsection (b) or (c) and subsection (g) of section 377 of title 28, United States Code, as added by this section [subsecs. (b) or (c) and (g) of this section], for any service as a full-time bankruptcy judge or magistrate on or after October 1, 1979 (as specified in the election pursuant to paragraph (2)) for which deductions and deposits are made under subsections (j) and (k) of such section 377 [subsecs. (j) and (k) of this section], as applicable, without regard to the minimum number of years of service as such a bankruptcy judge or magistrate, except that—

"(i) in the case of a judge or a magistrate who retires with less than 8 years of service, the annuity under subsection (c) of section 377 of title 28, United States Code [subsec. (c) of this section], shall be equal to that proportion of the salary being received at the time the judge or magistrate leaves office which the years of service bears to 14, subject to a reduction in accordance with subsection (c) of such section 377 if the bankruptcy judge or magistrate is under age 65 at the time he or she leaves office, and

"**(ii)** the aggregate amount of the annuity initially payable on retirement under this subsection may not exceed the rate of pay for the bankruptcy judge or magistrate which is in effect on the day before the retirement becomes effective.

"**(2) Filing of notice of election.**—A bankruptcy judge or magistrate shall be entitled to an annuity under this subsection only if the judge or magistrate files a notice of that election with the Director of the Administrative Office of the United States Courts specifying the date on which service would begin to be credited under section 377 of title 28, United States Code [this section], in lieu of chapter 83 or chapter 84 of title 5, United States Code [section 8331 et seq. or 8401 et seq. of Title 5].

"**(3) Lump-sum credit under Title 5.**—A bankruptcy judge or magistrate who makes an election under paragraph (2) shall be entitled to a lump-sum credit under section 8342 or 8424 of title 5, United States Code [section 8342 or 8424 of Title 5], as the case may be, for any service which is covered under section 377 of title 28, United States Code [this section], as added by this section, pursuant to that election, and with respect to which any contributions were made by the judge or magistrate under the applicable provisions of title 5, United States Code.

"**(4) Recall.**—With respect to any bankruptcy judge or magistrate receiving an annuity under this subsection who is recalled to serve under section 375 of title 28, United States Code [section 375 of this title]—

"**(A)** the amount of compensation which such recalled judge or magistrate receives under subsection (c) of such section shall be calculated on the basis of the annuity received under this subsection; and

"**(B)** such recalled judge or magistrate may serve as a reemployed annuitant to the extent permitted by subsection (e) of section 375 of such title [section 375(e) of this title].

Section 377(m)(3) of title 28, United States Code, as added by subsection (a) of this section [subsec. (m)(3) of this section], shall not apply with respect to service as a reemployed annuitant described in subparagraph (B)."

CHAPTER 19—DISTRIBUTION OF REPORTS AND DIGESTS

Sec.
411. Supreme Court reports; printing, binding, and distribution.
412. Sale of Supreme Court reports.
413. Publications; distribution to courts.
414. Transmittal of books to successors.
[415. Repealed.]

§ 411. Supreme Court reports; printing, binding, and distribution

(a) The decisions of the Supreme Court of the United States shall be printed, bound, and distributed in the preliminary prints and bound volumes of the United States Reports as soon as practicable after rendition, to be charged to the proper appropriation for the judiciary. The number and distribution of the copies shall be under the control of the Joint Committee on Printing.

(b) Reports printed prior to June 12, 1926, shall not be furnished the Secretary of the Army, the Secretary of the Navy, or the Secretary of the Air Force.

(c) The Public Printer, or other printer designated by the Supreme Court of the United States, upon request, shall furnish to the Superintendent of Documents the reports required to be distributed under the provisions of this section.

(June 25, 1948, c. 646, 62 Stat. 904; May 24, 1949, c. 139, § 68, 63 Stat. 99; Oct. 31, 1951, c. 655, § 41, 65 Stat. 725; July 10, 1952, c. 632, § 4, 66 Stat. 540.)

§ 412. Sale of Supreme Court reports

The Public Printer, or other printer designated by the Supreme Court of the United States shall print such additional bound volumes and preliminary prints of such reports as may be required for sale to the public. Such additional copies shall be sold by the Superintendent of Documents, as provided by law.

(June 25, 1948, c. 646, 62 Stat. 906; July 10, 1952, c. 632, § 5, 66 Stat. 541.)

§ 413. Publications; distribution to courts

Distribution of publications to Federal courts in accordance with the provisions of this chapter shall not be made to any place where such court is held in a building not owned or controlled by the United States unless such publications are committed to the custody of an officer of the United States at such building.

The Attorney General and the Director in the procurement of law books, books of reference or periodicals may exchange or sell similar items and apply the allowance or proceeds to payment in whole or in part of the cost of the items procured.

(June 25, 1948, c. 646, 62 Stat. 906; May 24, 1949, c. 139, § 69, 63 Stat. 100; July 10, 1952, c. 632, § 6, 66 Stat. 541.)

§ 414. Transmittal of books to successors

All government publications and law books furnished to justices, judges, clerks of courts, and United States attorneys of the United States and its territories and possessions, and other officers of the United States or an agency thereof shall be transmitted to their successors in office. All permanent or bound books and publications furnished under this chapter except those books furnished to the Library of Congress for international exchange shall remain the property of the United States and shall be marked plainly, "The Property of the United States".

(June 25, 1948, c. 646, 62 Stat. 906; Oct. 18, 1962, Pub.L. 87–845, § 7, 76A Stat. 699.)

HISTORICAL AND STATUTORY NOTES

Effective Dates

1962 Acts. Amendment by Pub.L. 87–845 effective Jan. 2, 1963, see section 25 of Pub.L. 87–845, set out as a note under Section 14 of Title 18, Crimes and Criminal Procedure.

[§ 415. Repealed. Pub.L. 97–164, Title I, § 113, Apr. 2, 1982, 96 Stat. 29]

HISTORICAL AND STATUTORY NOTES

Section, Acts June 25, 1948, c. 646, 62 Stat. 906; May 24, 1949, c. 139, § 70, 63 Stat. 100, provided for the distribution of copies of the decisions of the Court of Claims. See section 174(b) of this title.

Effective Date of Repeal

Repeal effective Oct. 1, 1982, see section 402 of Pub.L. 97–164, set out as a note under section 171 of this title.

CHAPTER 21—GENERAL PROVISIONS APPLICABLE TO COURTS AND JUDGES

Sec.
451. Definitions.
452. Courts always open; power unrestricted by expiration of sessions.[1]
453. Oath of justices and judges.[1]
454. Practice of law by justices and judges.
455. Disqualification of justice, judge, or magistrate.
456. Traveling expenses of justices and judges; official duty stations.
457. Records; obsolete papers.
458. Relative of justice or judge ineligible to appointment.
459. Administration of oaths and acknowledgments.
460. Application to other courts.
461. Adjustments in certain salaries.
462. Court accommodations.
463. Expenses of litigation.

[1] So in original. Does not conform to section catchline.

§ 451. Definitions

As used in this title:

The term "court of the United States" includes the Supreme Court of the United States, courts of appeals, district courts constituted by chapter 5 of this title, including the Court of International Trade and any court created by Act of Congress the judges of which are entitled to hold office during good behavior.

The terms "district court" and "district court of the United States" mean the courts constituted by chapter 5 of this title.

The term "judge of the United States" includes judges of the courts of appeals, district courts, Court of International Trade and any court created by Act of Congress, the judges of which are entitled to hold office during good behavior.

The term "justice of the United States" includes the Chief Justice of the United States and the associate justices of the Supreme Court.

The term "district" and "judicial district" mean the districts enumerated in Chapter 5 of this title.

The term "department" means one of the executive departments enumerated in section 1 of Title 5, unless the context shows that such term was intended to describe the executive, legislative, or judicial branches of the government.

The term "agency" includes any department, independent establishment, commission, administration, authority, board or bureau of the United States or any corporation in which the United States has a proprietary interest, unless the context shows that such term was intended to be used in a more limited sense.

(June 25, 1948, c. 646, 62 Stat. 907; Mar. 18, 1959, Pub.L. 86–3, § 10, 73 Stat. 9; Sept. 12, 1966, Pub.L. 89–571, § 3, 80 Stat. 764; Nov. 6, 1978, Pub.L. 95–598, Title II, § 213, 92 Stat. 2661; Oct. 10, 1980, Pub.L. 96–417, Title V, § 501(10), 94 Stat. 1742; Apr. 2, 1982, Pub.L. 97–164, Title I, § 114, 96 Stat. 29.)

HISTORICAL AND STATUTORY NOTES

References in Text

Section 1 of Title 5, referred to in text, is section 1 of former Title 5. Executive Departments and Government Officers and Employees, the provisions of which are covered by section 101 of Title 5, Government Organization and Employees.

Codifications

The paragraphs of this section defining the term "court of the United States" and the term "judge of the United States" were amended by Pub.L. 95–598, Title II, § 213, Nov. 6, 1978, 92 Stat. 2668, effective June 28, 1984, pursuant to Pub.L. 95–598, Title IV, § 402(b), Nov. 6, 1978, 92 Stat. 2682, as amended by Pub.L. 98–249, § 1(a), Mar. 31, 1984, 98 Stat. 116; Pub.L. 98–271, § 1(a), Apr. 30, 1984, 98 Stat. 163; Pub.L. 98–299, § 1(a), May 25, 1984, 98 Stat. 214; Pub.L. 98–325, § 1(a), June 20, 1984, 98 Stat. 268, set out as a note preceding section 101 of Title 11, Bankruptcy, to read as follows:

The term "court of the United States" includes the Supreme Court of the United States, courts of appeals, district courts constituted by chapter 5 of this title, including the Court of International Trade and any court created by Act of Congress the judges of which are entitled to hold office during good behavior, and bankruptcy courts, the judges of which are entitled to hold office for a term of 14 years.

The term "judge of the United States" includes judges of the courts of appeals, district courts, Court of International Trade and any court created by Act of Congress, the judges of which are entitled to hold office during good behavior, and judge of the bankruptcy courts, the judges of which are entitled to hold office for a term of 14 years.

Section 402(b) of Pub.L. 95–598 was amended by section 113 of Pub.L. 98–353, Title I, July 10, 1984, 98 Stat. 343, by substituting "shall not be effective" for "shall take effect on June 28, 1984", thereby eliminating the amendment by section 213 of Pub.L. 95–598, effective June 27, 1984, pursuant to section 122(c) of Pub.L. 98–353, set out as an Effective Dates note under section 151 of this title.

Section 121(a) of Pub.L. 98–353 directed that section 402(b) of Pub.L. 95–598 be amended by substituting "the date of enactment of the Bankruptcy Amendments and Federal Judgeship Act of 1984 [i.e. July 10, 1984]" for "June 28, 1984". This amendment was not executed in view of the prior amendment to section 402(b) of Pub.L. 95–598 by section 113 of Pub.L. 98–353.

Effective Dates

1982 Acts. Amendment by Pub.L. 97–164 effective Oct. 1, 1982, see section 402 of Pub.L. 97–164, set out as a note under section 171 of this title.

1980 Acts. Amendment by Pub.L. 96–417 effective on Nov. 1, 1980 and applicable with respect to civil actions pending on or commenced on or after such date, see section 701(a) of Pub.L. 96–417, as amended, set out as a note under section 251 of this title.

1959 Acts. Section 10 of Pub.L. 86–3 provided in part that the amendment of this section shall be effective upon the admission of the State of Hawaii into the Union. Admission of Hawaii into the Union was accomplished Aug. 21, 1959 upon issuance of Proc. No. 3309, Aug. 21, 1959, 25 F.R. 6868, 73 Stat. c74, as required by sections 1 and 7(c) of Pub.L. 86–3, Mar. 18, 1959, 73 Stat. 4, set out as notes preceding Section 491 of Title 48, Territories and Insular Possessions.

"Circuit Court of Appeals;" "Senior Circuit Judge," Etc. Defined

Section 32 of Act June 25, 1948, as amended by Act May 24, 1949, c. 139, § 127, 63 Stat. 107, provided that:

"**(a)** All laws of the United States in force on September 1, 1948, in which reference is made to a 'circuit court of appeals'; 'senior circuit judge'; 'senior district judge'; 'presiding judge'; 'chief justice,' except when reference to the Chief Justice of the United States is intended; or 'justice', except when used with respect to a justice of the Supreme Court of the United States in his capacity as such or as a circuit justice, are hereby amended by substituting 'court of appeals' for 'circuit court of appeals'; 'chief judge of the circuit' for 'senior circuit judge'; 'chief judge of the district court' for 'senior district judge'; 'chief judge' for 'presiding judge'; 'chief judge' for 'chief justice', except when reference to the Chief Justice of the United States is intended; and 'judge' for 'justice', except when the latter term is used with respect to a justice of the Supreme Court of the United States in his capacity as such or as a circuit justice.

"**(b)** All laws of the United States in force on September 1, 1948, in which reference is made to the Supreme Court of the District of Columbia or to the District Court of the United States for the District of Columbia are amended by substituting 'United States District Court for the District of Columbia' for such designations.

"**(c)** All laws of the United States in force on September 1, 1948, in which reference is made to the 'Conference of Senior Circuit Judges', or to the 'Judicial Conference of Senior Circuit Judges' are amended by substituting 'Judicial Conference of the United States' for such designations.

"**(d)** This section shall not be construed to amend historical references to courts or judicial offices which have no present or future application to such courts or offices."

Judges of the United States

Section 2(a) of Act June 25, 1948, c. 646, 62 Stat. 985, amended Sept. 3, 1954, c. 1263, § 51(a), 68 Stat. 1245, provided that: "(a) The Chief Justices of the United States Court of Appeals for the District of Columbia, the District Court of the United States for the District of Columbia, and the Court of Claims [now United States Court of Federal Claims], and the presiding judge of the Court of Customs and Patent Appeals [now United States Court of Appeals for the Federal Circuit], in office on the effective date of this Act shall be the chief judges of their respective courts. The Chief Justice of the United States Court of Appeals for the District of Columbia and the Associate Justices thereof, the Chief Justice of the District Court of the United States for the District of Columbia (formerly named the Supreme Court of the District of Columbia) and the Associate Justices thereof, the Chief Justice of the Court of Claims [now United States Court of Federal Claims], and the presiding judge of the Court of Customs and Patent Appeals [now United States Court of Appeals for the Federal Circuit], in office on the effective date of this Act, shall be judges of the United States within the meaning of Section 451 of Title 28, Judiciary and Judicial Procedure, of the United States Code, set out in Section 1 of this Act. The Chief Justice of the United States Court of Appeals for the District of Columbia and the Associate Justices thereof, in office on the effective date of this Act, shall be circuit judges of the District of Columbia Circuit and vested with all the rights, powers, and duties thereof, and the said Chief Justice of the United States Court of Appeals for the District of Columbia shall be Chief Judge of said Circuit. The Chief Justice of the District Court of the United States for the District of Columbia (formerly named the Supreme Court of the District of Columbia) and the Associate Justices thereof, in office on the effective date of this Act, shall be district judges for the District of Columbia and vested with all the rights, powers, and duties thereof."

Section 51(b) of Act Sept. 3, 1954, provided that this amendment should take effect as of Sept. 1, 1948.

§ 452. Courts always open; powers unrestricted by expiration of sessions

All courts of the United States shall be deemed always open for the purpose of filing proper papers, issuing and returning process, and making motions and orders.

The continued existence or expiration of a session of court in no way affects the power of the court to do any act or take any proceeding.

(June 25, 1948, c. 646, 62 Stat. 907; Oct. 16, 1963, Pub.L. 88–139, § 2, 77 Stat. 248.)

§ 453. Oaths of justices and judges

Each justice or judge of the United States shall take the following oath or affirmation before performing the duties of his office: "I, ______ ______, do solemnly swear (or affirm) that I will administer justice without respect to persons, and do equal right to the poor and to the rich, and that I will faithfully and impartially discharge and perform all the duties incumbent upon me as ______ under the Constitution and laws of the United States. So help me God."

(June 25, 1948, c. 646, 62 Stat. 907; Dec. 1, 1990, Pub.L. 101–650, Title IV, § 404, 104 Stat. 5124.)

HISTORICAL AND STATUTORY NOTES

Effective Dates

1990 Acts. Amendment by section 404 of Pub.L. 101–650 effective 90 days after Dec. 1, 1990, see section 407 of Pub.L. 101–650, set out as a note under section 332 of this title.

§ 454. Practice of law by justices and judges

Any justice or judge appointed under the authority of the United States who engages in the practice of law is guilty of a high misdemeanor.

(June 25, 1948, c. 646, 62 Stat. 908.)

§ 455. Disqualification of justice, judge, or magistrate

(a) Any justice, judge, or magistrate of the United States shall disqualify himself in any proceeding in which his impartiality might reasonably be questioned.

(b) He shall also disqualify himself in the following circumstances:

(1) Where he has a personal bias or prejudice concerning a party, or personal knowledge of disputed evidentiary facts concerning the proceeding;

(2) Where in private practice he served as lawyer in the matter in controversy, or a lawyer with whom he previously practiced law served during such association as a lawyer concerning the matter, or the judge or such lawyer has been a material witness concerning it;

(3) Where he has served in governmental employment and in such capacity participated as counsel, adviser or material witness concerning the proceeding or expressed an opinion concerning the merits of the particular case in controversy;

(4) He knows that he, individually or as a fiduciary, or his spouse or minor child residing in his household, has a financial interest in the subject matter in controversy or in a party to the proceeding, or any other interest that could be substantially affected by the outcome of the proceeding;

(5) He or his spouse, or a person within the third degree of relationship to either of them, or the spouse of such a person:

(i) Is a party to the proceeding, or an officer, director, or trustee of a party;

(ii) Is acting as a lawyer in the proceeding;

(iii) Is known by the judge to have an interest that could be substantially affected by the outcome of the proceeding;

(iv) Is to the judge's knowledge likely to be a material witness in the proceeding.

(c) A judge should inform himself about his personal and fiduciary financial interests, and make a reasonable effort to inform himself about the personal financial interests of his spouse and minor children residing in his household.

(d) For the purposes of this section the following words or phrases shall have the meaning indicated:

(1) "proceeding" includes pretrial, trial, appellate review, or other stages of litigation;

(2) the degree of relationship is calculated according to the civil law system;

(3) "fiduciary" includes such relationships as executor, administrator, trustee, and guardian;

(4) "financial interest" means ownership of a legal or equitable interest, however small, or a relationship as director, adviser, or other active participant in the affairs of a party, except that:

(i) Ownership in a mutual or common investment fund that holds securities is not a "financial interest" in such securities unless the judge participates in the management of the fund;

(ii) An office in an educational, religious, charitable, fraternal, or civic organization is not a "financial interest" in securities held by the organization;

(iii) The proprietary interest of a policyholder in a mutual insurance company, of a depositor in a mutual savings association, or a similar proprietary interest, is a "financial interest" in the organization only if the outcome of the proceeding could substantially affect the value of the interest;

(iv) Ownership of government securities is a "financial interest" in the issuer only if the outcome of the proceeding could substantially affect the value of the securities.

(e) No justice, judge, or magistrate shall accept from the parties to the proceeding a waiver of any ground for disqualification enumerated in subsection (b). Where the ground for disqualification arises only under subsection (a), waiver may be accepted provided it is preceded by a full disclosure on the record of the basis for disqualification.

(f) Notwithstanding the preceding provisions of this section, if any justice, judge, magistrate, or bankruptcy judge to whom a matter has been assigned would be disqualified, after substantial judicial time has been devoted to the matter, because of the appearance or discovery, after the matter was assigned to him or her, that he or she individually or as a fiduciary, or his or her spouse or minor child residing in his or her household, has a financial interest in a party (other than an interest that could be substantially affected by the outcome), disqualification is not required if the justice, judge, magistrate, bankruptcy judge, spouse or minor child, as the case may be, divests himself or herself of the interest that provides the grounds for the disqualification.

(June 25, 1948, c. 646, 62 Stat. 908; Dec. 5, 1974, Pub.L. 93–512, § 1, 88 Stat. 1609; Nov. 6, 1978, Pub.L. 95–598, Title II, § 214(a), (b), 92 Stat. 2661; Nov. 19, 1988, Pub.L. 100–702, Title X, § 1007, 102 Stat. 4667.)

HISTORICAL AND STATUTORY NOTES

Effective Dates

1978 Acts. Amendment by Pub.L. 95–598 effective Oct. 1, 1979, see section 402(c) of Pub.L. 95–598, set out as a note preceding section 101 of Title 11, Bankruptcy. For procedures relating to bankruptcy matters during transition period, see note preceding section 151 of this title.

1974 Acts. Section 3 of Pub.L. 93–512 provided that: "This Act [amending this section] shall not apply to the trial of any proceeding commenced prior to the date of this Act [Dec. 5, 1974], nor to appellate review of any proceeding which was fully submitted to the reviewing court prior to the date of this Act."

§ 456. Traveling expenses of justices and judges; official duty stations

(a) The Director of the Administrative Office of the United States Courts shall pay each justice or judge of the United States, and each retired justice or judge recalled or designated and assigned to active duty, while attending court or transacting official business at a place other than his official duty station for any continuous period of less than thirty calendar days (1) all necessary transportation expenses certified by the justice or judge; and (2) payments for subsistence expenses at rates or in amounts which the Director establishes, in accordance with regulations which the Director shall prescribe with the approval of the Judicial Conference of the United States and after considering the rates or amounts set by the Administrator of General Services and the President pursuant to section 5702 of title 5. The Director of the Administrative Office of the United States Courts shall also pay each justice or judge of the United States, and each retired justice or judge recalled or designated and assigned to active duty, while attending court or transacting official business under an assignment authorized under chapter 13 of this title which exceeds in duration a continuous period of thirty calendar days, all necessary transportation expenses and actual and necessary expenses of subsistence actually incurred, notwithstanding the provisions of section 5702 of title 5, in accordance with regulations which the Director shall prescribe with the approval of the Judicial Conference of the United States.

(b) The official duty station of the Chief Justice of the United States, the Justices of the Supreme Court of the United States, and the judges of the United States Court of Appeals for the District of Columbia Circuit, the United States Court of Appeals for the Federal Circuit, and the United States District Court for the District of Columbia shall be the District of Columbia.

(c) The official duty station of the judges of the United States Court of International Trade shall be New York City.

(d) The official duty station of each district judge shall be that place where a district court holds regular sessions at or near which the judge performs a substantial portion of his judicial work, which is nearest the place where he maintains his actual abode in which he customarily lives.

(e) The official duty station of a circuit judge shall be that place where a circuit or district court holds regular sessions at or near which the judge performs a substantial portion of his judicial work, or that place where the Director provides chambers to the judge where he performs a substantial portion of his judicial work, which is nearest the place where he maintains his actual abode in which he customarily lives.

(f) The official duty station of a retired judge shall be established in accordance with section 374 of this title.

(g) Each circuit or district judge whose official duty station is not fixed expressly by this section shall notify the Director of the Administrative Office of the United States Courts in writing of his actual abode and official duty station upon his appointment and from time to time thereafter as his official duty station may change.

(June 25, 1948, c. 646, 62 Stat. 908; Aug. 8, 1953, c. 376, 67 Stat. 488; Aug. 7, 1959, Pub.L. 86–138, 73 Stat. 285; Nov. 6, 1978, Pub.L. 95–598, Title II, § 215, 92 Stat. 2661; Oct. 10, 1980, Pub.L. 96–417, Title V, § 501(11), 94 Stat. 1742; Apr. 2, 1982, Pub.L. 97–164, Title I, § 115(a) (1), 96 Stat. 30; Jan. 2, 1986, Pub.L. 99–234, Title I, § 107(d), 99 Stat. 1759.)

HISTORICAL AND STATUTORY NOTES

Codifications

The amendment by Pub.L. 95–598 in 1978 to be effective Apr. 1, 1984, was never actually executed to text in view of the later amendment of this section by Pub.L. 97–164, eff. Oct. 1, 1982, which completely revised this section both as it would exist just prior to Oct. 1, 1982, and as it would become effective Apr. 1, 1984. See 1978 and 1982 Amendments notes under this section.

Effective Dates

1986 Acts. Amendment by Pub.L. 99–234 effective on the effective date of regulations to be promulgated not later than

150 days after Jan. 2, 1986, or 180 days after Jan. 2, 1986, whichever occurs first, see section 301(a) of Pub.L. 99–234, set out as a note under section 5701 of Title 5, Government Organization and Employees.

1982 Acts. Amendment by Pub.L. 97–164 effective Oct. 1, 1982, see section 402 of Pub.L. 97–164, set out as a note under section 171 of this title.

1980 Acts. Amendment by Pub.L. 96–417 effective on Nov. 1, 1980 and applicable with respect to civil actions pending on or commenced on or after such date, see section 701(a) of Pub.L. 96–417, as amended, set out as a note under section 251 of this title.

Promulgation of Regulations by Director

Director to promulgate regulations effectuating increases in reimbursement for expenses, see section 6 of Pub.L. 87–139, Aug. 14, 1961, 75 Stat. 340, set out as a note under section 604 of this title.

Report on Transportation Needs

Pub.L. 99–550, § 3, Oct. 27, 1986, 100 Stat. 3070, provided that: "Within one year after the date of enactment of this Act [Oct. 27, 1986], the Director of the Administrative Office of the United States Courts shall prepare, in consultation with the Marshal of the Supreme Court of the United States, the Clerk of the United States Court of Military Appeals [now United States Court of Appeals for the Armed Forces] and the Court Administrator of the United States Tax Court, and transmit to the Congress, appropriate recommendations concerning the transportation needs of the judicial branch and of courts established pursuant to Article I of the Constitution [U.S.C.A. Const. Art. I]."

§ 457. Records; obsolete papers

The records of district courts and of courts of appeals shall be kept at one or more of the places where court is held. Such places shall be designated by the respective courts except when otherwise directed by the judicial council of the circuit.

Papers of any court established by Act of Congress which have become obsolete and are no longer necessary or useful, may be disposed of with the approval of the court concerned in the manner provided by sections 366–380 of Title 44 and in accordance with the rules of the Judicial Conference of the United States.

(June 25, 1948, c. 646, 62 Stat. 908; Nov. 6, 1978, Pub.L. 95–598, Title II, § 216, 92 Stat. 2661.)

HISTORICAL AND STATUTORY NOTES

References in Text

Sections 366–380 of Title 44, referred to in text, were repealed and the provisions thereof reenacted as chapter 33 (Section 3301 et seq.) of Title 44, Public Printing and Documents, by Pub.L. 90–620, Oct. 22, 1968, 82 Stat. 1238.

Codifications

The first paragraph of this section was amended by Pub.L. 95–598, Title II, § 216, Nov. 6, 1978, 92 Stat. 261, effective June 28, 1984, pursuant to Pub.L. 95–598, Title IV, § 402(b), Nov. 6, 1978, 92 Stat. 2682, as amended by Pub.L. 98–249, § 1(a), Mar. 31, 1984, 98 Stat. 116; Pub.L. 98–271, § 1(a), Apr. 30, 1984, 98 Stat. 163; Pub.L. 98–299, § 1(a), May 25, 1984, 98 Stat. 214; Pub.L. 98–325, § 1(a), June 20, 1984, 98 Stat. 268, set out as an Effective Dates note preceding section 101 of Title 11, Bankruptcy by substituting "The records of bankruptcy courts, of district courts, and of courts of appeals" for "The records of district courts and of courts of appeals".

Section 402(b) of Pub.L. 95–598 was amended by section 113 of Pub.L. 98–353, Title I, July 10, 1984, 98 Stat. 343, by substituting "shall not be effective" for "shall take effect on June 28, 1984", thereby eliminating the amendment by section 216 of Pub.L. 95–598, effective June 27, 1984, pursuant to section 122(c) of Pub.L. 98–353, set out as an Effective Dates note under section 151 of this title.

Section 121(a) of Pub.L. 98–353 directed that section 402(b) of Pub.L. 95–598 be amended by substituting "the date of enactment of the Bankruptcy Amendments and Federal Judgeship Act of 1984 [i.e. July 10, 1984]" for "June 28, 1984". This amendment was not executed in view of the prior amendment to section 402(b) of Pub.L. 95–598 by section 113 of Pub.L. 98–353.

§ 458. Relative of justice or judge ineligible to appointment

(a)(1) No person shall be appointed to or employed in any office or duty in any court who is related by affinity or consanguinity within the degree of first cousin to any justice or judge of such court.

(2) With respect to the appointment of a judge of a court exercising judicial power under article III of the United States Constitution [U.S.C.A. Const. Art. III] (other than the Supreme Court), subsection (b) shall apply in lieu of this subsection.

(b)(1) In this subsection, the term—

(A) "same court" means—

(i) in the case of a district court, the court of a single judicial district; and

(ii) in the case of a court of appeals, the court of appeals of a single circuit; and

(B) "member"—

(i) means an active judge or a judge retired in senior status under section 371(b); and

(ii) shall not include a retired judge, except as described under clause (i).

(2) No person may be appointed to the position of judge of a court exercising judicial power under article III of the United States Constitution [U.S.C.A. Const. Art. III] (other than the Supreme Court) who is related by affinity or consanguinity within the degree of first cousin to any judge who is a member of the same court.

(June 25, 1948, c. 646, 62 Stat. 908; as amended Pub.L. 105–300, § 1(a), Oct. 27, 1998, 112 Stat. 2836.)

HISTORICAL AND STATUTORY NOTES

Effective Dates

1998 Acts. Section 1(b) of Pub.L. 105–300 provided that: This Act [amending this section] shall take effect on the date of enactment of this Act [Oct. 27, 1998] and shall apply only to any individual whose nomination is submitted to the Senate on or after such date."

§ 459. Administration of oaths and acknowledgments

Each justice or judge of the United States may administer oaths and affirmations and take acknowledgments.

(June 25, 1948, c. 646, 62 Stat. 908.)

§ 460. Application to other courts

(a) Sections 452 through 459 and section 462 of this chapter shall also apply to the United States Court of Federal Claims, to each court created by Act of Congress in a territory which is invested with any jurisdiction of a district court of the United States, and to the judges thereof.

(b) The official duty station of each judge referred to in subsection (a) which is not otherwise established by law shall be that place where the court holds regular sessions at or near which the judge performs a substantial portion of his judicial work, which is nearest the place where he maintains his actual abode in which he customarily lives.

(June 25, 1948, c. 646, 62 Stat. 908; Oct. 31, 1951, c. 655, § 43(a), 65 Stat. 725; July 7, 1958, Pub.L. 85–508, § 12(e), 72 Stat. 348; Nov. 6, 1978, Pub.L. 95–598, Title II, § 217(a), 92 Stat. 2661; Apr. 2, 1982, Pub.L. 97–164, Title I, § 115(b)(1), 96 Stat. 31; Oct. 29, 1992, Pub.L. 102–572, Title IX, § 902(b)(1), 106 Stat. 4516.)

HISTORICAL AND STATUTORY NOTES

Effective Dates

1992 Acts. Amendment by Pub.L. 102–572 effective Oct. 29, 1992, see section 911 of Pub.L. 102–572, set out as a note under section 171 of this title.

1982 Acts. Amendment by Pub.L. 97–164 effective Oct. 1, 1982, see section 402 of Pub.L. 97–164, set out as a note under section 171 of this title.

1978 Acts. Amendment by Pub.L. 95–598 effective Nov. 6, 1978, see section 402(d) of Pub.L. 95–598, set out as a note preceding section 101 of Title 11, Bankruptcy.

1958 Acts. Amendment by Pub.L. 85–508 effective Jan. 3, 1959 upon admission of Alaska into the Union pursuant to Proc. No. 3269, Jan. 3, 1959, 24 F.R. 81, 73 Stat. c16, as required by section 1 and 8(c) of Pub.L. 85–508, see notes set out under section 81A of this title and preceding section 21 of Title 48, Territories and Insular Possessions.

Change of Name

References to United States Claims Court deemed to refer to United States Court of Federal Claims and references to Claims Court deemed to refer to Court of Federal Claims, see section 902(b) of Pub.L. 102–572, set out as a note under section 171 of Title 28, Judiciary and Judicial Procedure.

§ 461. Adjustments in certain salaries

(a)(1) Subject to paragraph (2), effective at the beginning of the first applicable pay period commencing on or after the first day of the month in which an adjustment takes effect under section 5303 of title 5 in the rates of pay under the General Schedule (except as provided in subsection (b)), each salary rate which is subject to adjustment under this section shall be adjusted by an amount, rounded to the nearest multiple of $100 (or if midway between multiples of $100, to the next higher multiple of $100) equal to the percentage of such salary rate which corresponds to the most recent percentage change in the ECI (relative to the date described in the next sentence), as determined under section 704(a)(1) of the Ethics Reform Act of 1989. The appropriate date under this sentence is the first day of the fiscal year in which such adjustment in the rates of pay under the General Schedule takes effect.

(2) In no event shall the percentage adjustment taking effect under paragraph (1) in any calendar year (before rounding), in any salary rate, exceed the percentage adjustment taking effect in such calendar year under section 5303 of title 5 in the rates of pay under the General Schedule.

(b) Subsection (a) shall not apply to the extent it would reduce the salary of any individual whose compensation may not, under section 1 of article III of the Constitution of the United States, be diminished during such individual's continuance in office.

(Added Pub.L. 94–82, Title II, § 205(a)(1), Aug. 9, 1975, 89 Stat. 422, and amended Pub.L. 101–194, Title VII, § 704(a)(2)(A), Nov. 30, 1989, 103 Stat. 1769; Pub.L. 101–509, Title V, § 529 [Title I, § 101(b)(4)(J)], Nov. 5, 1990, 104 Stat. 1427, 1440; Pub.L. 103–356, Title I, § 101(4), Oct. 13, 1994, 108 Stat. 3411.)

HISTORICAL AND STATUTORY NOTES

References in Text

The General Schedule, referred to in subsec. (a), is set out under section 5332 of Title 5, Government Organization and Employees.

Section 704(a)(1) of the Ethics Reform Act of 1989, referred to in subsec. (a), is section 704(a)(1) of Pub.L. 101–194, which is set out as a note under section 5318 of Title 5, Government Organization and Employees.

Effective Dates

1994 Acts. Amendment to this section by section 101(4) of Pub.L. 103–356 effective Dec. 31, 1994, see section 101 of Pub.L. 103–356 set out as a note under section 31 of Title 2, The Congress.

1990 Acts. Amendment to this section (together with any notes enacted or amended hereunder) by the Federal Employees Pay Comparability Act of 1990, as incorporated in section 529 [Title III, § 305] of Pub.L. 101–509, to take effect on May 4, 1991, except that the Office of Personnel Management may establish an earlier effective date, but not earlier than Feb. 3, 1991, for any such provisions with respect to which the Office determines an earlier effective date to be appropriate, see Ex. Ord. No. 12748, Feb. 1, 1991, 56 F.R. 4521, set out as a note under section 5301 of Title 5, Government Organization and Employees.

1989 Acts. Amendment to this section by section 704(a)(2)(A) of Pub.L. 101–194 to take effect Jan. 1, 1991, see section 704(b) of Pub.L. 101–194, set out as a note under section 5318 of Title 5, Government Organization and Employees.

1977 Comparability Adjustment Not Effective for Justices, Judges, Commissioners, and Referees

Pub.L. 95–66, § 1(3), July 11, 1977, 91 Stat. 270, set out as a note under section 5318 of Title 5, Government Organization and Employees, provided that the first adjustment which, but for the enactment of Pub.L. 95–66, would have been made in the salary and rate of pay of justices, judges, commissioners, and referees under this section after July 11, 1977, would not take effect.

Salary Adjustments

Pub.L. 105–119, Title III, § 306, Nov. 26, 1997, 111 Stat. 2493, provided that: "Pursuant to section 140 of Public Law 97–92 [set out as a note under this section], justices and judges of the United States are authorized during fiscal year 1998, to receive a salary adjustment in accordance with 28 U.S.C. 461 [this section]."

Pub.L. 102–395, Title III, § 304, Oct. 6, 1992, 106 Stat. 1859, provided that: "Pursuant to section 140 of Public Law 97–92 [set out as a note under this section], Justices and judges of the United States are authorized during fiscal year 1993, to receive a salary adjustment in accordance with 28 U.S.C. 461 [this section]."

Pub.L. 102–140, Title III, § 305, Oct. 28, 1991, 105 Stat. 810, provided that: "Pursuant to section 140 of Public Law 97–92 [set out as a note under this section], Justices and judges of the United States are authorized during fiscal year 1992, to receive a salary adjustment in accordance with 28 U.S.C. 461 [this section]."

Pub.L. 101–520, Title III, § 321, Nov. 5, 1990, 104 Stat. 2285, provided that: "Pursuant to section 140 of Public Law 97–92 [set out as a note under this section], Justices and judges of the United States are authorized during calendar year 1991 to receive a salary adjustment in accordance with 28 U.S.C. section 461 [this section]."

For provisions that, effective the first day of the first applicable pay period that begins on or after January 1, 1991, the rate of basic pay for the Chief Justice of the United States, an associate justice of the Supreme Court of the United States, a judge of a United States circuit court, a judge of a district court of the United States, and a judge of the United States Court of International Trade shall be increased in the amount of 25 percent of their respective rates (as last in effect before the increase), rounded to the nearest multiple of $100 (or, if midway between multiples of $100, to the next higher multiple of $100), and related provisions, see Pub.L. 101–194, Title VII, § 703, Nov. 30, 1989, 103 Stat. 1768, set out as a note under section 5318 of Title 5, Government Organization and Employees.

For provisions authorizing, for purposes of section 140 of Pub.L. 97–92 (set out as a note under this section), appropriate salary increases for Federal judges and Justices of the Supreme Court, to be determined, effective for pay periods beginning on or after Nov. 30, 1989, as if the provisions of section 620(b) of Pub.L. 100–440 (5 U.S.C. 5305 note) and section 619(b) of Pub.L. 101–136 (5 U.S.C. 5303 note) had never been enacted, together with related provisions, see section 702 of Pub.L. 101–194, set out as a note under section 5303 of Title 5, Government Organization and Employees.

Pub.L. 100–202, § 101(a) [Title IV, § 406], Dec. 22, 1987, 101 Stat. 1329, 1329–26, provided that:

"Pursuant to section 140 of Public Law 97–92 [set out as a note under this section], during fiscal year 1988, justices and judges of the United States shall receive the same percentage increase in salary accorded to employees paid under the General Schedule (pursuant to 5 U.S.C. 5305)."

Pub.L. 99–500, Title I, § 101(b) [Title IV, § 406], Oct. 18, 1986, 100 Stat. 1783–39, 1783–64; Pub.L. 99–591, Title I, § 101(b), [Title IV, § 406], Oct. 30, 1986, 100 Stat. 3341–39, 3341–64, provided that: "Pursuant to section 140 of Public Law 97–92 [set out as a note under this section], during fiscal year 1987, justices and judges of the United States shall receive the same percentage increase in salary accorded to employees paid under the General Schedule (pursuant to 5 U.S.C. 5305) [5 U.S.C.A. § 5305]."

Pub.L. 99–88, Title I, § 100, Aug. 15, 1985, 99 Stat. 310, provided in part that: "Effective on the first day of the first applicable pay period commencing on or after January 1, 1985, each rate of pay subject to adjustment by section 461 of title 28, United States Code [this section], shall be increased by an amount, rounded to the nearest multiple of $100 (or if midway between multiples of $100, to the next higher multiple of $100), equal to the overall percentage of the adjustment taking effect under section 5305 of title 5, United States Code [section 5305 of Title 5, Government Organization and Employees], in the rates of pay under the General Schedule during fiscal year 1985."

Pub.L. 98–369, Div.B., Title II, § 2207, July 18, 1984, 98 Stat. 1060, provided that: "Effective on the first day of the first applicable pay period commencing on or after January 1, 1984, each rate of pay subject to adjustment by section 461 of title 28, United States Code [this section], shall be increased by an amount, rounded to the nearest multiple of $100 (or if midway between multiples of $100, to the next higher multiple of $100), equal to the overall percentage of the adjustment taking effect under section 5305 of title 5, United States Code [section 5305 of Title 5, Government Organization of Employees], in the rates of pay under the General Schedule during fiscal year 1984."

Salary Rate Limitations or Use of Funds

1982—Limitation on the use of funds appropriated or authority made available for the period Oct. 1, 1982, through Sept. 30, 1983, by any Act to pay the salary or pay of any individual in an office or position in the legislative, executive, or judicial branch, or in the government of the District of Columbia, at a rate equal to or greater than Level V of the Executive Schedule, see section 306(a), (b), and (d) of S.2939, Ninety-seventh Congress, 2nd Session, as reported Sept. 22, 1982, which was incorporated by reference in Pub.L. 97–276, § 101(e), Oct. 2, 1982, 96 Stat. 1189, to be effective as if enacted into law, and which is set out as a note under section 5318 of Title 5, Government Organization and Employees.

1981—Limitation on use of funds appropriated for the fiscal year ending Sept. 30, 1982, by any Act to pay the salary or pay of any individual in the legislative, executive, or judicial branch in a position equal or above Level V of the Executive Schedule, see section 305(a), (b), and (d) of H.R. 4120, as reported July 9, 1981, which was incorporated by reference in Pub.L. 97–92, § 101(g), Dec. 15, 1981, 95 Stat.

1190, to be effective as if enacted into law, and section 141 of Pub.L. 97–92, set out as notes under section 5318 of Title 5, Government Organization and Employees.

1980—Limitations on use of funds for fiscal year ending Sept. 30, 1981, appropriated by any Act to pay the salary or pay of any individual in legislative, executive, or judicial branch in position equal to or above level V of the Executive Schedule, see section 101(c) of Pub.L. 96–536, as amended, set out as a note under section 5318 of Title 5.

1979—Applicability to funds appropriated by any Act for fiscal year ending Sept. 30, 1980, of limitation of section 304 of Pub.L. 95–391 on use of funds to pay the salary or pay of any individual in legislative, executive, or judicial branch in position equal to or above level V of the Executive Schedule, see section 101 of Pub.L. 96–86, set out as a note under section 5318 of Title 5.

1978—Limitations on use of funds for fiscal year ending Sept. 30, 1979, appropriated by any Act to pay the salary or pay of any individual in legislative, executive, or judicial branch in position equal or above level V of the Executive Schedule, see section 304 of Pub.L. 95–391 and section 613 of Pub.L. 95–429, set out as a note under section 5318 of Title 5.

Specific Congressional Authorization Required for Salary Increases for Federal Judges and Justices of the Supreme Court

Pub.L. 97–92, § 140, Dec. 15, 1981, 95 Stat. 1200, provided that: "Notwithstanding any other provision of law or of this joint resolution [Pub.L. 97–92], none of the funds appropriated by this joint resolution or by any other Act shall be obligated or expended to increase, after the date of enactment of this joint resolution [Dec. 15, 1981], any salary of any Federal judge or Justice of the Supreme Court, except as may be specifically authorized by Act of Congress hereafter enacted: Provided, That nothing in this limitation shall be construed to reduce any salary which may be in effect at the time of enactment of this joint resolution [Dec. 15, 1981] nor shall this limitation be construed in any manner to reduce the salary of any Federal judge or of any Justice of the Supreme Court."

§ 462. Court accommodations

(a) Sessions of courts of the United States (except the Supreme Court) shall be held only at places where the Director of the Administrative Office of the United States Courts provides accommodations, or where suitable accommodations are furnished without cost to the judicial branch.

(b) The Director of the Administrative Office of the United States Courts shall provide accommodations, including chambers and courtrooms, only at places where regular sessions of court are authorized by law to be held, but only if the judicial council of the appropriate circuit has approved the accommodations as necessary.

(c) The limitations and restrictions contained in subsection (b) of this section shall not prevent the Director from furnishing chambers to circuit judges at places within the circuit other than where regular sessions of court are authorized by law to be held, when the judicial council of the circuit approves.

(d) The Director of the Administrative Office of the United States Courts shall provide permanent accommodations for the United States Court of Appeals for the Federal Circuit and for the United States Court of Federal Claims only at the District of Columbia. However, each such court may hold regular and special sessions at other places utilizing the accommodations which the Director provides to other courts.

(e) The Director of the Administrative Office of the United States Courts shall provide accommodations for probation officers, pretrial service officers, and Federal Public Defender Organizations at such places as may be approved by the judicial council of the appropriate circuit.

(f) Upon the request of the Director, the Administrator of General Services is authorized and directed to provide the accommodations the Director requests, and to close accommodations which the Director recommends for closure with the approval of the Judicial Conference of the United States.

(Added Pub.L. 97–164, Title I, § 115(c)(1), Apr. 2, 1982, 96 Stat. 31, and amended Pub.L. 100–702, Title X, § 1015, Nov. 19, 1988, 102 Stat. 4669; Pub.L. 102–572, Title IX, § 902(b)(1), Oct. 29, 1992, 106 Stat. 4516.)

HISTORICAL AND STATUTORY NOTES

Effective Dates

1992 Acts. Amendment by Pub.L. 102–572 effective Oct. 29, 1992, see section 911 of Pub.L. 102–572, set out as a note under section 171 of this title.

1982 Acts. Section effective Oct. 1, 1982, see section 402 of Pub.L. 97–164, set out as a note under section 171 of this title.

Change of Name

References to United States Claims Court deemed to refer to United States Court of Federal Claims and references to Claims Court deemed to refer to Court of Federal Claims, see section 902(b) of Pub.L. 102–572, set out as a note under section 171 of Title 28, Judiciary and Judicial Procedure.

§ 463. Expenses of litigation

Whenever a Chief Justice, justice, judge, officer, or employee of any United States court is sued in his official capacity, or is otherwise required to defend acts taken or omissions made in his official capacity, and the services of an attorney for the Government are not reasonably available pursuant to chapter 31 of this title, the Director of the Administrative Office of the United States Courts may pay the costs of his defense. The Director shall prescribe regulations for such payments subject to the approval of the Judicial Conference of the United States.

(Added Pub.L. 97–164, Title I, § 116(a), Apr. 2, 1982, 96 Stat. 32.)

HISTORICAL AND STATUTORY NOTES

Effective Dates

1982 Acts. Section effective Oct. 1, 1982, see section 402 of Pub.L. 97–164, set out as a note under section 171 of this title.

CHAPTER 23—CIVIL JUSTICE EXPENSE AND DELAY REDUCTION PLANS

Sec.
471. Requirement for a district court civil justice expense and delay reduction plan.
472. Development and implementation of a civil justice expense and delay reduction plan.
473. Content of civil justice expense and delay reduction plans.
474. Review of district court action.
475. Periodic district court assessment.
476. Enhancement of judicial information dissemination.
477. Model civil justice expense and delay reduction plan.
478. Advisory groups.
479. Information on litigation management and cost and delay reduction.
480. Training programs.
481. Automated case information.
482. Definitions.

§ 471. Requirement for a district court civil justice expense and delay reduction plan

There shall be implemented by each United States district court, in accordance with this chapter, a civil justice expense and delay reduction plan. The plan may be a plan developed by such district court or a model plan developed by the Judicial Conference of the United States. The purposes of each plan are to facilitate deliberate adjudication of civil cases on the merits, monitor discovery, improve litigation management, and ensure just, speedy, and inexpensive resolutions of civil disputes.

(Added Pub.L. 101–650, Title I, § 103(a), Dec. 1, 1990, 104 Stat. 5090, and amended Pub.L. 102–198, § 2(1), Dec. 9, 1991, 105 Stat. 1623.)

HISTORICAL AND STATUTORY NOTES

Congressional Statement of Findings

Section 102 of Pub.L. 101–650 provided that: "The Congress makes the following findings:

"(1) The problems of cost and delay in civil litigation in any United States district court must be addressed in the context of the full range of demands made on the district court's resources by both civil and criminal matters.

"(2) The courts, the litigants, the litigants' attorneys, and the Congress and the executive branch, share responsibility for cost and delay in civil litigation and its impact on access to the courts, adjudication of cases on the merits, and the ability of the civil justice system to provide proper and timely judicial relief for aggrieved parties.

"(3) The solutions to problems of cost and delay must include significant contributions by the courts, the litigants, the litigants' attorneys, and by the Congress and the executive branch.

"(4) In identifying, developing, and implementing solutions to problems of cost and delay in civil litigation, it is necessary to achieve a method of consultation so that individual judicial officers, litigants, and litigants' attorneys who have developed techniques for litigation management and cost and delay reduction can effectively and promptly communicate those techniques to all participants in the civil justice system.

"(5) Evidence suggests that an effective litigation management and cost and delay reduction program should incorporate several interrelated principles, including—

"(A) the differential treatment of cases that provides for individualized and specific management according to their needs, complexity, duration, and probable litigation careers;

"(B) early involvement of a judicial officer in planning the progress of a case, controlling the discovery process, and scheduling hearings, trials, and other litigation events;

"(C) regular communication between a judicial officer and attorneys during the pretrial process; and

"(D) utilization of alternative dispute resolution programs in appropriate cases.

"(6) Because the increasing volume and complexity of civil and criminal cases imposes increasingly heavy workload burdens on judicial officers, clerks of court, and other court personnel, it is necessary to create an effective administrative structure to ensure ongoing consultation and communication regarding effective litigation management and cost and delay reduction principles and techniques."

Demonstration Program

Section 104 of Pub.L. 101–650, as amended Pub.L. 104–33, § 1, Oct. 3, 1995, 109 Stat. 292; Pub.L. 104–317, Title VI, § 608(a), Oct. 19, 1996, 110 Stat. 3860, provided that:

"(a) **In general.**—(1) During the 5-year period beginning on January 1, 1991, the Judicial Conference of the United States shall conduct a demonstration program in accordance with subsection (b).

"(2) A district court participating in the demonstration program may also be an Early Implementation District Court under section 103(c) [section 103(c) of Pub.L. 101–650, set out as a note under this section].

"(b) **Program requirement.**—(1) The United States District Court for the Western District of Michigan and the United States District Court for the Northern District of Ohio shall experiment with systems of differentiated case management that provide specifically for the assignment of cases to appropriate processing tracks that operate under distinct and explicit rules, procedures, and time frames for the completion of discovery and for trial.

"(2) The United States District Court for the Northern District of California, the United States District Court for the Northern District of West Virginia, and the United States District Court for the Western District of Missouri shall experiment with various methods of reducing cost and delay in civil litigation, including alternative dispute resolution, that such district courts and the Judicial Conference of the United States shall select.

"(c) **Study of results.**—The Judicial Conference of the United States, in consultation with the Director of the Federal Judicial Center and the Director of the Administrative Office of the United States Courts, shall study the experience of the district courts under the demonstration program.

"(d) **Report.**—Not later than June 30, 1997, the Judicial Conference of the United States shall transmit to the Committees on the Judiciary of the Senate and the House of Representatives a report of the results of the demonstration program."

Implementation of Plans

Section 103(b), (c) of Pub.L. 101–650, as amended Pub.L. 102–572, Title V, § 505, Oct. 29, 1992, 106 Stat. 4513; Pub.L. 105–53, § 2, Oct. 6, 1997, 111 Stat. 1173, provided that:

"(b) **Implementation**

"(1) Except as provided in section 105 of this Act [section 105 of Pub.L. 101–650, set out as a note under this section], each United States district court shall, within three years after the date of the enactment of this title [Dec. 1, 1990], implement a civil justice expense and delay reduction plan under section 471 of title 28, United States Code, as added by subsection (a) [this section].

"(2)(A) The requirements set forth in sections 472, 473, 474, 475, 477, and 478 of title 28, United States Code [sections 472, 473, 474, 475, 477, and 478 of this title], as added by subsection (a), shall remain in effect for seven years after the date of the enactment of this title [Dec. 1, 1990].

"(B) The requirements set forth in section 476 of title 28, United States Code, as added by subsection (a), shall remain in effect permanently.

"(c) **Early Implementation District Courts**

"(1) Any United States district court that, no earlier than June 30, 1991, and no later than December 31, 1991, develops and implements a civil justice expense and delay reduction plan under chapter 23 of title 28, United States Code, as added by subsection (a) [this chapter], shall be designated by the Judicial Conference of the United States as an Early Implementation District Court.

"(2) The chief judge of a district so designated may apply to the Judicial Conference for additional resources, including technological and personnel support and information systems, necessary to implement its civil justice expense and delay reduction plan. The Judicial Conference may provide such resources out of funds appropriated pursuant to section 106(a) [section 106(a) of Pub.L. 101–650, not classified to the Code].

"(3) Within 18 months after the date of the enactment of this title [Dec. 1, 1990], the Judicial Conference shall prepare a report on the plans developed and implemented by the Early Implementation District Courts.

"(4) The Director of the Administrative Office of the United States Courts shall transmit to the United States district courts and to the Committees on the Judiciary of the Senate and House of Representatives—

"(A) copies of the plans developed and implemented by the Early Implementation District Courts;

"(B) summaries of the reports submitted by such district courts pursuant to section 472(d) of title 28, United States Code, as added by subsection (a) [section 472(d) of this title]; and

"(C) the report prepared in accordance with paragraph (3) of this subsection."

Pilot Program

Section 105 of Pub.L. 101–650, as amended Pub.L. 103–420, § 4, Oct. 25, 1994, 108 Stat. 4345; Pub.L. 104–317, Title VI, § 608(b), Oct. 19, 1996, 110 Stat. 3860, provided that:

"(a) **In general.**—(1) During the 5-year period beginning on January 1, 1991, the Judicial Conference of the United States shall conduct a pilot program in accordance with subsection (b).

"(2) A district court participating in the pilot program shall be designated as an Early Implementation District Court under section 103(c) [section 103(c) of Pub.L. 101–650, set out as a note under this section].

"(b) **Program requirements.**—(1) Ten district courts (in this section referred to as 'Pilot Districts') designated by the Judicial Conference of the United States shall implement expense and delay reduction plans under chapter 23 of title 28, United States Code (as added by section 103(a)) [this chapter], not later than December 31, 1991. In addition to complying with all other applicable provisions of chapter 23 of title 28, United States Code (as added by section 103(a)) [this chapter], the expense and delay reduction plans implemented by the Pilot Districts shall include the 6 principles and guidelines of litigation management and cost and delay reduction identified in section 473(a) of title 28, United States Code [section 473(a) of this title].

"(2) At least 5 of the Pilot Districts designated by the Judicial Conference shall be judicial districts encompassing metropolitan areas.

"(3) The expense and delay reduction plans implemented by the Pilot Districts shall remain in effect for a period of 4 years. At the end of that 4-year period, the Pilot Districts shall no longer be required to include, in their expense and delay reduction plans, the 6 principles and guidelines of litigation management and cost and delay reduction described in paragraph (1).

"(c) **Program study report.**—(1) Not later than June 30, 1997, the Judicial Conference shall submit to the Committees on the Judiciary of the Senate and House of Representatives a report on the results of the pilot program under this section that includes an assessment of the extent to which costs and delays were reduced as a result of the program. The report shall compare those results to the impact on costs and delays in ten comparable judicial districts for which the application of section 473(a) of title 28, United States Code [section 473(a) of this title], had been discretionary. That comparison shall be based on a study conducted by an independent organization with expertise in the area of Federal court management.

"(2)(A) The Judicial Conference shall include in its report a recommendation as to whether some or all district courts should be required to include, in their expense and delay reduction plans, the 6 principles and guidelines of litigation management and cost and delay reduction identified in section 473(a) of title 28, United States Code [section 473(a) of this title].

"(B) If the Judicial Conference recommends in its report that some or all district courts be required to include such principles and guidelines in their expense and delay reduction plans, the Judicial Conference shall initiate proceedings for the prescription of rules implementing its recommendation, pursuant to chapter 131 of title 28, United States Code [section 2071 et seq. of this title].

"(C) If in its report the Judicial Conference does not recommend an expansion of the pilot program under subparagraph (A), the Judicial Conference shall identify alternative, more effective cost and delay reduction programs that should be implemented in light of the findings of the Judicial Conference in its report, and the Judicial Conference may initiate proceedings for the prescription of rules implementing its recommendation, pursuant to chapter 131 of title 28, United States Code [section 2071 et seq. of this title]."

§ 472. Development and implementation of a civil justice expense and delay reduction plan

(a) The civil justice expense and delay reduction plan implemented by a district court shall be developed or selected, as the case may be, after consideration of the recommendations of an advisory group appointed in accordance with section 478 of this title.

(b) The advisory group of a United States district court shall submit to the court a report, which shall be made available to the public and which shall include—

(1) an assessment of the matters referred to in subsection (c)(1);

(2) the basis for its recommendation that the district court develop a plan or select a model plan;

(3) recommended measures, rules and programs; and

(4) an explanation of the manner in which the recommended plan complies with section 473 of this title.

(c)(1) In developing its recommendations, the advisory group of a district court shall promptly complete a thorough assessment of the state of the court's civil and criminal dockets. In performing the assessment for a district court, the advisory group shall—

(A) determine the condition of the civil and criminal dockets;

(B) identify trends in case filings and in the demands being placed on the court's resources;

(C) identify the principal causes of cost and delay in civil litigation, giving consideration to such potential causes as court procedures and the ways in which litigants and their attorneys approach and conduct litigation; and

(D) examine the extent to which costs and delays could be reduced by a better assessment of the impact of new legislation on the courts.

(2) In developing its recommendations, the advisory group of a district court shall take into account the particular needs and circumstances of the district court, litigants in such court, and the litigants' attorneys.

(3) The advisory group of a district court shall ensure that its recommended actions include significant contributions to be made by the court, the litigants, and the litigants' attorneys toward reducing cost and delay and thereby facilitating access to the courts.

(d) The chief judge of the district court shall transmit a copy of the plan implemented in accordance with subsection (a) and the report prepared in accordance with subsection (b) of this section to—

(1) the Director of the Administrative Office of the United States Courts;

(2) the judicial council of the circuit in which the district court is located; and

(3) the chief judge of each of the other United States district courts located in such circuit.

(Added Pub.L. 101–650, Title I, § 103(a), Dec. 1, 1990, 104 Stat. 5090.)

§ 473. Content of civil justice expense and delay reduction plans

(a) In formulating the provisions of its civil justice expense and delay reduction plan, each United States district court, in consultation with an advisory group appointed under section 478 of this title, shall consider and may include the following principles and guidelines of litigation management and cost and delay reduction:

(1) systematic, differential treatment of civil cases that tailors the level of individualized and case specific management to such criteria as case complexity, the amount of time reasonably needed to prepare the case for trial, and the judicial and other resources required and available for the preparation and disposition of the case;

(2) early and ongoing control of the pretrial process through involvement of a judicial officer in—

(A) assessing and planning the progress of a case;

(B) setting early, firm trial dates, such that the trial is scheduled to occur within eighteen months after the filing of the complaint, unless a judicial officer certifies that—

(i) the demands of the case and its complexity make such a trial date incompatible with serving the ends of justice; or

(ii) the trial cannot reasonably be held within such time because of the complexity of the case or the number or complexity of pending criminal cases;

(C) controlling the extent of discovery and the time for completion of discovery, and ensuring compliance with appropriate requested discovery in a timely fashion; and

(D) setting, at the earliest practicable time, deadlines for filing motions and a time framework for their disposition;

(3) for all cases that the court or an individual judicial officer determines are complex and any other appropriate cases, careful and deliberate monitoring through a discovery-case management conference or a series of such conferences at which the presiding judicial officer—

(A) explores the parties' receptivity to, and the propriety of, settlement or proceeding with the litigation;

(B) identifies or formulates the principal issues in contention and, in appropriate cases, provides for the staged resolution or bifurcation of issues for trial consistent with Rule 42(b) of the Federal Rules of Civil Procedure;

(C) prepares a discovery schedule and plan consistent with any presumptive time limits that a district court may set for the completion of discovery and with any procedures a district court may develop to—

(i) identify and limit the volume of discovery available to avoid unnecessary or unduly burdensome or expensive discovery; and

(ii) phase discovery into two or more stages; and

(D) sets, at the earliest practicable time, deadlines for filing motions and a time framework for their disposition;

(4) encouragement of cost-effective discovery through voluntary exchange of information among litigants and their attorneys and through the use of cooperative discovery devices;

(5) conservation of judicial resources by prohibiting the consideration of discovery motions unless accompanied by a certification that the moving party has made a reasonable and good faith effort to reach agreement with opposing counsel on the matters set forth in the motion; and

(6) authorization to refer appropriate cases to alternative dispute resolution programs that—

(A) have been designated for use in a district court; or

(B) the court may make available, including mediation, minitrial, and summary jury trial.

(b) In formulating the provisions of its civil justice expense and delay reduction plan, each United States district court, in consultation with an advisory group appointed under section 478 of this title, shall consider and may include the following litigation management and cost and delay reduction techniques:

(1) a requirement that counsel for each party to a case jointly present a discovery-case management plan for the case at the initial pretrial conference, or explain the reasons for their failure to do so;

(2) a requirement that each party be represented at each pretrial conference by an attorney who has the authority to bind that party regarding all matters previously identified by the court for discussion at the conference and all reasonably related matters;

(3) a requirement that all requests for extensions of deadlines for completion of discovery or for postponement of the trial be signed by the attorney and the party making the request;

(4) a neutral evaluation program for the presentation of the legal and factual basis of a case to a neutral court representative selected by the court at a nonbinding conference conducted early in the litigation;

(5) a requirement that, upon notice by the court, representatives of the parties with authority to bind them in settlement discussions be present or available by telephone during any settlement conference; and

(6) such other features as the district court considers appropriate after considering the recommendations of the advisory group referred to in section 472(a) of this title.

(c) Nothing in a civil justice expense and delay reduction plan relating to the settlement authority provisions of this section shall alter or conflict with the authority of the Attorney General to conduct litigation on behalf of the United States, or any delegation of the Attorney General.

(Added Pub.L. 101–650, Title I, § 103(a), Dec. 1, 1990, 104 Stat. 5091.)

HISTORICAL AND STATUTORY NOTES

References in Text

The Federal Rules of Civil Procedure, referred to in subsec. (a)(3)(B), are set out in this title.

§ 474. Review of district court action

(a)(1) The chief judge of each district court in a circuit and the chief judge of the circuit shall, as a committee—

(A) review each plan and report submitted pursuant to section 472(d) of this title; and

(B) make such suggestions for additional actions or modified actions of that district court as the committee considers appropriate for reducing cost and delay in civil litigation in the district court.

(2) The chief judge of a circuit may designate another judge of the court of appeals of that circuit, and the chief judge of a district court may designate another judge of such court, to perform that chief judge's responsibilities under paragraph (1) of this subsection.

(b) The Judicial Conference of the United States—

(1) shall review each plan and report submitted by a district court pursuant to section 472(d) of this title; and

(2) may request the district court to take additional action if the Judicial Conference determines that such court has not adequately responded to the conditions relevant to the civil and criminal dockets of the court or to the recommendations of the district court's advisory group.

(Added Pub.L. 101–650, Title I, § 103(a), Dec. 1, 1990, 104 Stat. 5093, and amended Pub.L. 102–198, § 2(2), Dec. 9, 1991, 105 Stat. 1623.)

§ 475. Periodic district court assessment

After developing or selecting a civil justice expense and delay reduction plan, each United States district court shall assess annually the condition of the court's civil and criminal dockets with a view to determining appropriate additional actions that may be taken by the court to reduce cost and delay in civil litigation and to improve the litigation management practices of the court. In performing such assessment, the court shall consult with an advisory group appointed in accordance with section 478 of this title.

(Added Pub.L. 101–650, Title I, § 103(a), Dec. 1, 1990, 104 Stat. 5093.)

§ 476. Enhancement of judicial information dissemination

(a) The Director of the Administrative Office of the United States Courts shall prepare a semiannual report, available to the public, that discloses for each judicial officer—

(1) the number of motions that have been pending for more than six months and the name of each case in which such motion has been pending;

(2) the number of bench trials that have been submitted for more than six months and the name of each case in which such trials are under submission; and

(3) the number and names of cases that have not been terminated within three years after filing.

(b) To ensure uniformity of reporting, the standards for categorization or characterization of judicial actions to be prescribed in accordance with section 481 of this title shall apply to the semiannual report prepared under subsection (a).

(Added Pub.L. 101–650, Title I, § 103(a), Dec. 1, 1990, 104 Stat. 5093.)

§ 477. Model civil justice expense and delay reduction plan

(a)(1) Based on the plans developed and implemented by the United States district courts designated as Early Implementation District Courts pursuant to section 103(c) of the Civil Justice Reform Act of 1990, the Judicial Conference of the United States may develop one or more model civil justice expense and delay reduction plans. Any such model plan shall be accompanied by a report explaining the manner in which the plan complies with section 473 of this title.

(2) The Director of the Federal Judicial Center and the Director of the Administrative Office of the United States Courts may make recommendations to the Judicial Conference regarding the development of any model civil justice expense and delay reduction plan.

(b) The Director of the Administrative Office of the United States Courts shall transmit to the United States district courts and to the Committees on the Judiciary of the Senate and the House of Representatives copies of any model plan and accompanying report.

(Added Pub.L. 101–650, Title I, § 103(a), Dec. 1, 1990, 104 Stat. 5094.)

HISTORICAL AND STATUTORY NOTES

References in Text

Section 103(c) of the Civil Justice Reform Act of 1990, referred to in subsec. (a)(1), is section 103(c) of Pub.L. 101–650, as amended, which is set out as a note under section 471 of this title.

§ 478. Advisory groups

(a) Within ninety days after the date of the enactment of this chapter, the advisory group required in each United States district court in accordance with section 472 of this title shall be appointed by the chief judge of each district court, after consultation with the other judges of such court.

(b) The advisory group of a district court shall be balanced and include attorneys and other persons who are representative of major categories of litigants in such court, as determined by the chief judge of such court.

(c) Subject to subsection (d), in no event shall any member of the advisory group serve longer than four years.

(d) Notwithstanding subsection (c), the United States Attorney for a judicial district, or his or her designee, shall be a permanent member of the advisory group for that district court.

(e) The chief judge of a United States district court may designate a reporter for each advisory group, who may be compensated in accordance with guidelines established by the Judicial Conference of the United States.

(f) The members of an advisory group of a United States district court and any person designated as a reporter for such group shall be considered as independent contractors of such court when in the performance of official duties of the advisory group and may not, solely by reason of service on or for the advisory group, be prohibited from practicing law before such court.

(Added Pub.L. 101–650, Title I, § 103(a), Dec. 1, 1990, 104 Stat. 5094.)

HISTORICAL AND STATUTORY NOTES

References in Text

The date of the enactment of this chapter, referred to in subsec. (a), is the date of enactment of Pub.L. 101–650, which was approved Dec. 1, 1990.

§ 479. Information on litigation management and cost and delay reduction

(a) Within four years after the date of the enactment of this chapter, the Judicial Conference of the United States shall prepare a comprehensive report on all plans received pursuant to section 472(d) of this title. The Director of the Federal Judicial Center and the Director of the Administrative Office of the United States Courts may make recommendations regarding such report to the Judicial Conference during the preparation of the report. The Judicial Conference shall transmit copies of the report to the United States district courts and to the Committees on the Judiciary of the Senate and the House of Representatives.

(b) The Judicial Conference of the United States shall, on a continuing basis—

(1) study ways to improve litigation management and dispute resolution services in the district courts; and

(2) make recommendations to the district courts on ways to improve such services.

(c)(1) The Judicial Conference of the United States shall prepare, periodically revise, and transmit to the United States district courts a Manual for Litigation Management and Cost and Delay Reduction. The Director of the Federal Judicial Center and the Director of the Administrative Office of the United States Courts may make recommendations regarding the preparation of and any subsequent revisions to the Manual.

(2) The Manual shall be developed after careful evaluation of the plans implemented under section 472 of this title, the demonstration program conducted under section 104 of the Civil Justice Reform Act of 1990, and the pilot program conducted under section 105 of the Civil Justice Reform Act of 1990.

(3) The Manual shall contain a description and analysis of the litigation management, cost and delay reduction principles and techniques, and alternative dispute resolution programs considered most effective by the Judicial Conference, the Director of the Federal Judicial Center, and the Director of the Administrative Office of the United States Courts.

(Added Pub.L. 101–650, Title I, § 103(a), Dec. 1, 1990, 104 Stat. 5095.)

HISTORICAL AND STATUTORY NOTES

References in Text

The date of the enactment of this chapter, referred to in subsec. (a), is the date of enactment of Pub.L. 101–650, which was approved Dec. 1, 1990.

Sections 104 and 105 of the Civil Justice Reform Act of 1990, referred to in subsec. (c)(2), are sections 104 and 105 of Pub.L. 101–650, which are set out as notes under section 471 of this title.

§ 480. Training programs

The Director of the Federal Judicial Center and the Director of the Administrative Office of the United States Courts shall develop and conduct comprehensive education and training programs to ensure that all judicial officers, clerks of court, courtroom deputies, and other appropriate court personnel are thoroughly familiar with the most recent available information and analyses about litigation management and other techniques for reducing cost and expediting the resolution of civil litigation. The curriculum of such training programs shall be periodically revised to reflect such information and analyses.

(Added Pub.L. 101–650, Title I, § 103(a), Dec. 1, 1990, 104 Stat. 5095.)

§ 481. Automated case information

(a) The Director of the Administrative Office of the United States Courts shall ensure that each United States district court has the automated capability readily to retrieve information about the status of each case in such court.

(b)(1) In carrying out subsection (a), the Director shall prescribe—

(A) the information to be recorded in district court automated systems; and

(B) standards for uniform categorization or characterization of judicial actions for the purpose of recording information on judicial actions in the district court automated systems.

(2) The uniform standards prescribed under paragraph (1)(B) of this subsection shall include a definition of what constitutes a dismissal of a case and standards for measuring the period for which a motion has been pending.

(c) Each United States district court shall record information as prescribed pursuant to subsection (b) of this section.

(Added Pub.L. 101–650, Title I, § 103(a), Dec. 1, 1990, 104 Stat. 5095.)

§ 482. Definitions

As used in this chapter, the term "judicial officer" means a United States district court judge or a United States magistrate.

(Added Pub.L. 101–650, Title I, § 103(a), Dec. 1, 1990, 104 Stat. 5096.)

HISTORICAL AND STATUTORY NOTES

Change of Name

Reference to United States magistrate or to magistrate deemed to refer to United States magistrate judge pursuant to section 321 of Pub.L. 101–650, set out as a note under section 631 of this title.

PART II—DEPARTMENT OF JUSTICE

Chapter		Section
31.	The Attorney General	501
33.	Federal Bureau of Investigation	531
35.	United States Attorneys	541
37.	United States Marshals[1]	561
39.	United States Trustees	581
40.	Independent Counsel	591

1 So in original. Does not conform to chapter heading.

CHAPTER 31—THE ATTORNEY GENERAL

Sec.
501. Executive department.
502. Seal.
503. Attorney General.
504. Deputy Attorney General.
504a. Associate Attorney General.
505. Solicitor General.
506. Assistant Attorneys General.
507. Assistant Attorney General for Administration.
508. Vacancies.
509. Functions of the Attorney General.
510. Delegation of authority.
511. Attorney General to advise the President.
512. Attorney General to advise heads of executive departments.
513. Attorney General to advise Secretaries of military departments.
514. Legal services on pending claims in departments and agencies.
515. Authority for legal proceedings; commission, oath, and salary for special attorneys.
516. Conduct of litigation reserved to Department of Justice.
517. Interests of United States in pending suits.
518. Conduct and argument of cases.
519. Supervision of litigation.
520. Transmission of petitions in United States Court of Federal Claims or in United States Court of Appeals for the Federal Circuit; statement furnished by departments.
521. Publication and distribution of opinions.
522. Report of business and statistics.
523. Requisitions.
524. Availability of appropriations.
525. Procurement of law books, reference books, and periodicals; sale and exchange.
526. Authority of the Attorney General to investigate United States attorneys, marshals, and trustees, clerks of court, and others.[1]
527. Establishment of working capital fund.
528. Disqualification of officers and employees of the Department of Justice.
529. Annual report of Attorney General.
530. Payment of travel and transportation expenses of newly appointed special agents.
530A. Authorization of appropriations for travel and related expenses and for health care of personnel serving abroad.
530B. Ethical standards for attorneys for the Government.

1 So in original. Does not conform to section catchline.

HISTORICAL AND STATUTORY NOTES

Change of Name

References to United States Claims Court deemed to refer to United States Court of Federal Claims and references to Claims Court deemed to refer to Court of Federal Claims, see section 902(b) of Pub.L. 102–572, set out as a note under section 171 of Title 28, Judiciary and Judicial Procedure.

§ 501. Executive department

The Department of Justice is an executive department of the United States at the seat of Government.

(Added Pub.L. 89–554, § 4(c), Sept. 6, 1966, 80 Stat. 611.)

HISTORICAL AND STATUTORY NOTES

Prior Provisions

A prior section 501, Acts June 25, 1948, c. 646, 62 Stat. 909; Mar. 18, 1959, Pub.L. 86–3, § 11(a), 73 Stat. 9, which related to appointment of United States attorneys, was repealed by Pub.L. 89–554, § 8(a), Sept. 6, 1966, 80 Stat. 632, and reenacted in section 541 of this title by section 4(c) of Pub.L. 89–554.

Specific Authorization of Appropriations Required for Department of Justice

Pub.L. 94–503, Title II, § 204, Oct. 15, 1976, 90 Stat. 2427, provided that: "No sums shall be deemed to be authorized to be appropriated for any fiscal year beginning on or after October 1, 1978, for the Department of Justice (including any bureau, agency, or other similar subdivision thereof) except as specifically authorized by Act of Congress with respect to such fiscal year. Neither the creation of a subdivision in the Department of Justice, nor the authorization of an activity of the Department, any subdivision, or officer thereof, shall be deemed in itself to be an authorization of appropriations for the Department of Justice, such subdivision, or activity, with respect to any fiscal year beginning on or after October 1, 1978."

§ 502. Seal

The Attorney General shall have a seal for the Department of Justice. The design of the seal is subject to the approval of the President.

(Added Pub.L. 89–554, § 4(c), Sept. 6, 1966, 80 Stat. 611.)

HISTORICAL AND STATUTORY NOTES

Prior Provisions

A prior section 502, Act June 25, 1948, c. 646, 62 Stat. 909, which related to appointment of assistant United States attorneys, was repealed by Pub.L. 89–554, § 8(a), Sept. 6, 1966, 80 Stat. 632, and reenacted in section 542 of this title by section 4(c) of Pub.L. 89–554.

§ 503. Attorney General

The President shall appoint, by and with the advice and consent of the Senate, an Attorney General of the United States. The Attorney General is the head of the Department of Justice.

(Added Pub.L. 89–554, § 4(c), Sept. 6, 1966, 80 Stat. 612.)

HISTORICAL AND STATUTORY NOTES

Prior Provisions

A prior section 503, Act June 25, 1948, c. 646, 62 Stat. 909, which related to appointment of attorneys to assist United States attorneys, was repealed by Pub.L. 89–554, § 8(a), Sept. 6, 1966, 80 Stat. 632, and reenacted in section 543 of this title by section 4(c) of Pub.L. 89–554.

Actions Challenging Appointment of Attorney General on Grounds of Violation of Constitutional Provisions Governing Compensation and Other Emoluments

Pub.L. 93–178, § 2, Dec. 10, 1973, 87 Stat. 697, provided that:

"(a) Any person aggrieved by an action of the Attorney General may bring a civil action in the appropriate district court to contest the constitutionality of the appointment and continuance in office of the Attorney General on the ground that such appointment and continuance in office is in violation of article I, section 6, clause 2, of the Constitution. The United States district courts shall have exclusive jurisdiction, without regard to the sum or value of the matter in controversy, to determine the validity of such appointment and continuance in office.

"(b) Any action brought under this section shall be heard and determined by a panel of three judges in accordance with the provisions of section 2284 of title 28, United States Code [this section]. Any appeal from the action of a court convened pursuant to such section shall lie to the Supreme Court.

"(c) Any judge designated to hear any action brought under this section shall cause such action to be in every way expedited."

§ 504. Deputy Attorney General

The President may appoint, by and with the advice and consent of the Senate, a Deputy Attorney General.

(Added Pub.L. 89–554, § 4(c), Sept. 6, 1966, 80 Stat. 612.)

HISTORICAL AND STATUTORY NOTES

Prior Provisions

A prior section 504, Acts June 25, 1948, c. 646, 62 Stat. 909; Mar. 18, 1959, Pub.L. 86–3, § 11(b), 73 Stat. 9, which related to tenure and oath of office of United States attorneys, was repealed by Pub.L. 89–554, § 8(a), Sept. 6, 1966, 80 Stat. 632, and reenacted in sections 541 and 544 of this title by section 4(c) of Pub.L. 89–554.

§ 504a. Associate Attorney General

The President may appoint, by and with the advice and consent of the Senate, an Associate Attorney General.

(Added Pub.L. 95–139, § 1(a), Oct. 19, 1977, 91 Stat. 1171.)

§ 505. Solicitor General

The President shall appoint in the Department of Justice, by and with the advice and consent of the Senate, a Solicitor General, learned in the law, to assist the Attorney General in the performance of his duties.

(Added Pub.L. 89–554, § 4(c), Sept. 6, 1966, 80 Stat. 612.)

HISTORICAL AND STATUTORY NOTES

Prior Provisions

A prior section 505, Act June 25, 1948, c. 646, 62 Stat. 909, which related to residence of United States attorneys, was repealed by Pub.L. 89–554, § 8(a), Sept. 6, 1966, 80 Stat. 632, and reenacted in section 545 of this title by section 4(c) of Pub.L. 89–554.

§ 506. Assistant Attorneys General

The President shall appoint, by and with the advice and consent of the Senate, ten Assistant Attorneys General, who shall assist the Attorney General in the performance of his duties.

(Added Pub.L. 89–554, § 4(c), Sept. 6, 1966, 80 Stat. 612, and amended Pub.L. 95–598, Title II, § 218, Nov. 6, 1978, 92 Stat. 2662.)

HISTORICAL AND STATUTORY NOTES

Effective Dates

1978 Acts. Amendment by Pub.L. 95–598 effective Nov. 6, 1978, see section 402(d) of Pub.L. 95–598, set out as a note preceding section 101 of Title 11, Bankruptcy.

Prior Provisions

A prior section 506, Act June 25, 1948, c. 646, 62 Stat. 909, which related to vacancies in the office of United States attorney, was repealed by Pub.L. 89–554, § 8(a), Sept. 6, 1966, 80 Stat. 632, and reenacted in section 546 of this title by section 4(c) of Pub.L. 89–554.

§ 507. Assistant Attorney General for Administration

(a) The Attorney General shall appoint, with the approval of the President, an Assistant Attorney General for Administration, who shall perform such duties as the Attorney General may prescribe.

(b) The position of Assistant Attorney General for Administration is in the competitive service.

(Added Pub.L. 89–554, § 4(c), Sept. 6, 1966, 80 Stat. 612.)

HISTORICAL AND STATUTORY NOTES

Prior Provisions

A prior section 507, Acts June 25, 1948, c. 646, 62 Stat. 910; May 24, 1949, c. 139, § 71, 63 Stat. 100, which related to duties of United States attorneys, and to supervision by the Attorney General, was repealed by Pub.L. 89–554, § 8(a), Sept. 6, 1966, 80 Stat. 632, and reenacted in sections 509 and 547 of this title by section 4(c) of Pub.L. 89–554.

§ 508. Vacancies

(a) In case of a vacancy in the office of Attorney General, or of his absence or disability, the Deputy Attorney General may exercise all the duties of that office, and for the purpose of section 3345 of title 5 the Deputy Attorney General is the first assistant to the Attorney General.

(b) When by reason of absence, disability, or vacancy in office, neither the Attorney General nor the Deputy Attorney General is available to exercise the duties of the office of Attorney General, the Associate Attorney General shall act as Attorney General. The Attorney General may designate the Solicitor General and the Assistant Attorneys General, in further order of succession, to act as Attorney General.

(Added Pub.L. 89–554, § 4(c), Sept. 6, 1966, 80 Stat. 612, and amended Pub.L. 95–139, § 2, Oct. 19, 1977, 91 Stat. 1171.)

HISTORICAL AND STATUTORY NOTES

Prior Provisions

A prior section 508, Acts June 25, 1948, c. 646, 62 Stat. 910; Mar. 2, 1955, c. 9, § 2(a), 69 Stat. 10; Oct. 11, 1962, Pub.L. 87–793, § 1003(a), 76 Stat. 865; Aug. 14, 1964, Pub.L. 88–426, Title III, § 306(a)(1), 78 Stat. 428; Oct. 6, 1964, Pub.L. 88–631, § 3(b), 78 Stat. 1008, which related to salaries of United States attorneys, assistant United States attorneys, and special attorneys, was repealed by Pub.L. 89–554, § 8(a), Sept. 6, 1966, 80 Stat. 632, and reenacted in section 548 of this title by section 4(c) of Pub.L. 89–554.

§ 509. Functions of the Attorney General

All functions of other officers of the Department of Justice and all functions of agencies and employees of the Department of Justice are vested in the Attorney General except the functions—

(1) vested by subchapter II of chapter 5 of title 5 in administrative law judges employed by the Department of Justice;

(2) of the Federal Prison Industries, Inc.; and

(3) of the Board of Directors and officers of the Federal Prison Industries, Inc..[1]

(Added Pub.L. 89–554, § 4(c), Sept. 6, 1966, 80 Stat. 612, and amended Pub.L. 95–251, § 2(a)(6), Mar. 27, 1978, 92 Stat. 183; Pub.L. 98–473, Title II, § 228(a), Oct. 12, 1984, 98 Stat. 2030.)

[1] So in original.

HISTORICAL AND STATUTORY NOTES

Effective Dates

1984 Acts. Section 235(a)(1)(B)(ii)(IV) of Pub.L. 98–473 had provided that the amendment made by section 228 of Pub.L. 98–473 was to be effective Oct. 12, 1984. Pub.L. 99–646, § 35(2)(D), Nov. 10, 1986, 100 Stat. 3599, amended section 235(a)(1)(B)(ii)(IV) of Pub.L. 98–473 making it inapplicable to section 228. Amendment by Pub.L. 98–473 effective the first day of the first calendar month beginning 36 months after Oct. 12, 1984, see section 235(a)(1) of Pub.L. 98–473, as amended, set out as a note under section 3551 of Title 18, Crimes and Criminal Procedure.

Prior Provisions

A prior section 509, Act June 25, 1948, c. 646, 62 Stat. 910, which related to expenses of United States attorneys, was repealed by Pub.L. 89–554, § 8(a), Sept. 6, 1966, 80 Stat. 632, and reenacted in section 549 of this title by section 4(c) of Pub.L. 89–554.

Abolition of Interstate Commerce Commission and Transfer of Functions

Interstate Commerce Commission abolished and functions of Commission transferred, except as otherwise provided in Pub.L. 104–88, to Surface Transportation Board effective Jan. 1, 1996, by section 702 of Title 49, Transportation, and section 101 of Pub.L. 104–88, set out as a note under section 701 of Title 49. References to Interstate Commerce Commission deemed to refer to Surface Transportation Board, a member or employee of the Board, or Secretary of Transportation, as appropriate, see section 205 of Pub.L. 104–88, set out as a note under section 701 of Title 49.

Authorization of Appropriations for Humanitarian Expenses Incurred by Federal Bureau of Investigation and Drug Enforcement Administration

Pub.L. 101–647, Title XXXII, § 3201, Nov. 29, 1990, 104 Stat. 4916, as amended by Pub.L. 105–277, Div. A, § 101(b) [Title I, § 109(a)], Oct. 21, 1998, 112 Stat. 2681–___, provided that:

"Appropriations in this or any other Act hereafter for the Federal Bureau of Investigation, the Drug Enforcement Administration, or the Immigration and Naturalization Service are available, in an amount of not to exceed $25,000 each per fiscal year, to pay humanitarian expenses incurred by or for any employee thereof (or any member of the employee's immediate family) that results from or is incident to serious illness, serious injury, or death occurring to the employee while on official duty or business."

Emergency Preparedness Functions

For assignment of certain emergency preparedness functions to the Attorney General, see Parts 1, 2, and 11 of Ex. Ord. No. 12656, Nov. 18, 1988, 53 F.R. 47491, set out as a note under section 2251 of Title 50, Appendix, War and National Defense.

Expenses of Legal Defense for Federal Government Employees Performing Official Duties; Fees and Expenses of Witnesses

Pub.L. 101–162, Title II, Nov. 21, 1989, 103 Stat. 997, provided in part: "That for fiscal year 1990 and hereafter the Attorney General may enter into reimbursable agreements with other Federal Government agencies or components within the Department of Justice to pay expenses of private counsel to defend Federal Government employees sued for actions while performing their official duties: *Provided further*, That for fiscal year 1990 and hereafter the Attorney General, upon notification to the Committees on Appropriations of the House of Representatives and the Senate in compliance with provisions set forth in section 606 of this Act [Pub.L. 101–162, Title VI, Nov. 21, 1989, 103 Stat. 1031, not classified to the Code], may authorize litigating components to reimburse this account for expert witness expenses when it appears current allocations will be exhausted for cases scheduled for trial in the current fiscal year."

Federal Environmental or Natural Resource Laws; Investigations Respecting, Etc.

Pub.L. 96–132, § 12, Nov. 30, 1979, 93 Stat. 1048, provided that: "The Attorney General may, with the concurrence of any agency or Department with primary enforcement responsibility for an environmental or natural resource law, investigate any violation, of an environmental or natural resource law of the United States, and bring such actions as are necessary to enforce such laws. This section does not affect the criminal law enforcement authority of the Attorney General."

Impact Analysis of Additional Resources to Certain Components of Federal Criminal Justice System; Study by Comptroller General and Report to Congress

Pub.L. 100–690, Title IX, § 9201, Nov. 18, 1988, 102 Stat. 4535, provided that:

"**(a) Study.**—The Comptroller General of the United States shall conduct a study—

"(1) to determine the impact of additional resources to certain components of the Federal criminal justice system on other components of the system and of enhanced or new Federal criminal penalties or laws on the agencies and offices of the Department of Justice, the Federal courts, and other components of the Federal criminal justice system; and

"(2) use the data derived from the impact analysis to develop a model that can be applied by Congress and Federal agencies and departments to help determine appropriate staff and budget responses in order to maintain balance in the Federal criminal justice system and effectively implement changes in resources, laws, or penalties.

"**(b) Report to Congress.**—The Comptroller General shall report the results and recommendations derived from the study required by subsection (a) no later than 1 year after the date of enactment of this Act [Nov. 18, 1988]."

Investigation of Financial Institutions; Assistance of Government Personnel

Pub.L. 101–509, Title V, § 528, Nov. 5, 1990, 104 Stat. 1427, as amended Pub.L. 103–322, Title XXXII, § 320923, Sept. 13, 1994, 108 Stat. 2131, provided that:

"(a) Notwithstanding any other law and in any fiscal year—

"(1) The Attorney General shall accept, and Federal departments and agencies, including the United States Secret Service, the Internal Revenue Service, the Resolution Trust Corporation, and the appropriate Federal banking agency, may provide, without reimbursement, the services of attorneys, law enforcement personnel, and other employees of any other departments or agencies of the Federal Government to assist the Department of Justice, subject to the supervision of the Attorney General, in the investigation and prosecution of fraud or other criminal or unlawful activity in or against any federally insured financial institution or the Resolution Trust Corporation;

"(2) any attorney of a department or agency whose services are accepted pursuant to paragraph (1) may, subject to the supervision of the Attorney General, conduct any kind of legal proceeding, civil or criminal, including grand jury proceedings and proceedings before committing magistrates, and perform any other investigative or prosecutorial function, which United States attorneys are authorized by law to conduct or perform whether or not the attorney is a resident of the district in which the proceeding is brought; and

"(3) law enforcement personnel of the United States Secret Service are authorized, subject to the supervision of the Attorney General, to conduct or perform any kind of investigation, civil or criminal, related to fraud or other criminal or unlawful activity in or against any federally insured financial institution or the Resolution Trust Corporation, which the Department of Justice law enforcement personnel are authorized by law to conduct or perform: *Provided*, That the Secret Service shall not initiate investigations pursuant to this section independent of the supervision of the Attorney General.

"(b) This section—

"(1) shall not, except as expressly provided herein, alter the authority of any Federal law enforcement agency; and

"(2) shall expire on December 31, 2004.

"(c) This section applies notwithstanding any other provision of law enacted by the 101st Congress after October 15, 1990, that by its terms would grant authority to, or otherwise affect the authority of, the Secret Service or other departments or agencies of the Federal Government to conduct or to assist the Department of Justice in conducting investigations or prosecutions of fraud or other criminal or unlawful activity in or against any federally insured financial institution or the Resolution Trust Corporation, and any other such provision shall not be effective in granting or otherwise affecting any such authority."

Justice Department Organized Crime and Drug Enforcement Enhancement

Pub.L. 100–690, Title I, subtitle B, Nov. 18, 1988, 102 Stat. 4189, provided that:

"Sec. 1051. Short Title.

"This subtitle [this note] may be cited as the 'Justice Department Organized Crime and Drug Enforcement Enhancement Act of 1988'.

"Sec. 1052. Findings.

"The Congress finds that—

"(1) organized criminal activity contributes significantly to the importation, distribution, and sale of illegal and dangerous drugs;

"(2) trends in drug trafficking patterns necessitate a response that gives appropriate weight to—

"(A) the prosecution of drug-related crimes; and

"(B) the forfeiture and seizure of assets and other civil remedies used to strike at the inherent strength of the drug networks and organized crime groups;

"(3) law enforcement components of the Department of Justice should give high priority to the enforcement of civil sanctions against drug networks and organized crime groups; and

"(4) the structure of the Department of Justice Criminal Division needs to be reviewed in order to determine the most effective structure to address such drug-related problems.

"Sec. 1053. Civil Enforcement Report.

"**(a) Report.**—Not later than 1 year after the date of the enactment of this title [Nov. 18, 1988], the Director of National Drug Control Policy (the Director) in consultation with the Attorney General, shall report to the Congress on the necessity to establish a new division or make other organizational changes within the Department of Justice in order to promote better civil and criminal law enforcement. In preparing such report, the Director shall consider restructuring and consolidating one or more of the following divisions and programs—

"(1) the Organized Crime and Racketeering Section of the Criminal Division and all subordinate strike forces therein;

"(2) the Narcotic and Dangerous Drug Section of the Criminal Division;

"(3) the Asset Forfeiture Office of the Criminal Division; and

"(4) the Organized Crime Drug Enforcement Task Force Program;[.]

"**(b) Legislative recommendations.**—The report submitted under subsection (a) shall include appropriate legislative recommendations for the Congress.

"Sec. 1054. Civil Enforcement Enhancement.

"**(a) Duty of Attorney General.**—The Attorney General shall insure that each component of the Department of Justice having criminal law enforcement responsibilities with respect to the prosecution of organized crime and controlled substances violations, including each United States Attorney's Office, attaches a high priority to the enforcement of civil statutes creating ancillary sanctions and remedies for such violations, such as civil penalties and actions, forfeitures, injunctions and restraining orders, and collection of fines.

"**(b) Duty of Associate Attorney General.**—The Associate Attorney General shall be responsible for implementing the policy set forth in this subsection.

"**(c) Authorization of appropriations.**—(1) There are authorized to be appropriated $3,000,000 for salaries and expenses to the Department of Justice General Legal Activities Account and $3,000,000 for salaries and expenses for United States Attorneys for fiscal year 1989.

"(2) Any appropriation of funds authorized under paragraph (1) shall be—

"(A) in addition to any appropriations requested by the President in the 1989 fiscal year budget submitted by the President to the Congress on February 18, 1988, or provided in regular appropriations Acts or continuing resolutions for the fiscal year ending September 30, 1989; and

"(B) used to increase the number of field attorneys and related support staff over such personnel levels employed at the Department of Justice on September 30, 1988.

"(3) Any increase in full-time equivalent positions described under paragraph (2)(B) shall be exclusively used for asset forfeiture and civil enforcement and be assigned to appropriate field offices of the Organized Crime and Racketeering Section and the Organized Crime Drug Enforcement Task Forces.

"**(d) Reporting requirement.**—The Attorney General, at the end of each such fiscal year, shall file a report with the Congress setting forth the extent of such enforcement efforts, as well as the need for any enhancements in resources necessary to carry out this policy.

"Sec. 1055. Expenses of Task Forces.

"**(a) Appropriations and reimbursements procedure.**—Beginning in fiscal year 1990, the Attorney General in his budget shall submit a separate appropriations request for expenses relating to all Federal agencies participating in the Organized Crime Drug Enforcement Task Forces. Such appropriations shall be made to the Department of Justice's Interagency Law Enforcement Appropriation Account for the Attorney General to make reimbursements to the involved agencies as necessary.

"**(b) Enhancement of field activities.**—The appropriations and reimbursements procedure described under subsection (a) shall—

"(1) provide for the flexibility of the Task Forces which is vital to success;

"(2) permit Federal law enforcement resources to be shifted in response to changing patterns of organized criminal drug activities;

"(3) permit the Attorney General to reallocate resources among the organizational components of the Task Forces and between regions without undue delay; and

"(4) ensure that the Task Forces function as a unit, without the competition for resources among the participating agencies that would undermine the overall effort."

Neighborhood Revitalization

Pub.L. 102–395, Title I, Oct. 6, 1992, 106 Stat. 1830, provided in part that: "For fiscal year 1993 and thereafter the Attorney General shall (1) promote neighborhood revitalization by developing a plan for the use of Federal funds appropriated for selected activities in the Departments of Labor, Education, Health and Human Services, Transportation, Agriculture, and Housing and Urban Development; (2) the Attorney General shall solicit from State and local governments plans to revitalize neighborhoods using programs administered by such agencies; and (3) the Attorney General shall review and approve such plans in consultation with the Federal agency to which funds are appropriated."

Overseas Law Enforcement Training Activities

Pub.L. 104–132, Title VIII, § 801, Apr. 24, 1996, 110 Stat. 1304, provided that: "The Attorney General and the Secretary of the Treasury are authorized to support law enforcement training activities in foreign countries, in consultation with the Secretary of State, for the purpose of improving the effectiveness of the United States in investigating and prosecuting transnational offenses."

Positions in Drug Enforcement Administration; Grades Excepted From Competitive Service: Vacancies; Removal, Suspension, or Reduction in Rank or Pay; Rate of Pay

Pub.L. 94–503, Title II, § 201, Oct. 15, 1976, 90 Stat. 2425, provided that:

"**(a)** Effective beginning one year after date of the enactment of this Act [Oct. 15, 1976], the following positions in the Drug Enforcement Administration (and individuals holding such positions) are hereby excepted from the competitive service:

"**(1)** positions at GS–16, 17, and 18 of the General Schedule under section 5332(a) of title 5, United States Code [section 5332(a) of Title 5, Government Organization and Employees], and

"**(2)** positions at GS–15 of the General Schedule which are designated as—

"**(A)** regional directors,

"**(B)** office heads, or

"'**(C)** executive assistants (or equivalent positions) under the immediate supervision of the Administrator (or the Deputy Administrator) of the Drug Enforcement Administration.

"**(b)** Effective during the one year period beginning on the date of the enactment of this Act [Oct. 15, 1976], vacancies in positions in the Drug Enforcement Administration (other than positions described in subsection (a)) at a grade not lower than GS–14 shall be filled—

"**(1)** first, from applicants who have continuously held positions described in subsection (a) since the date of the enactment of this Act and who have applied for, and are qualified to fill, such vacancies, and

"**(2)** then, from other applicants in the order which would have occurred in the absence of this subsection."

Any individual placed in a position under paragraph (1) shall be paid in accordance with subsection (d).

"**(c)(1)** Effective beginning one year after the date of the enactment of this Act [Oct. 15, 1976], an individual in a position described in subsection (a) may be removed, suspended for more than 30 days, furloughed without pay, or reduced in rank or pay by the Administrator of the Drug Enforcement Administration if—

"**(A)** such individual has been employed in the Drug Enforcement Administration for less than the one-year period immediately preceding the date of such action, and

"**(B)** the Administrator determines, in his discretion, that such action would promote the efficiency of the service.

"**(2)** Effective beginning one year after the date of the enactment of this Act [Oct. 15, 1976], an individual in a position described in subsection (a) may be reduced in rank or pay by the Administrator within the Drug Enforcement Administration if—

"**(A)** such individual has been continuously employed in such position since the date of the enactment of this Act, and

"**(B)** the Administrator determines, in his discretion, that such action would promote the efficiency of the service.

Any individual reduced in rank or pay under this paragraph shall be paid in accordance with subsection (d).

"**(3)** The provisions of sections 7512 and 7701 of title 5, United States Code [sections 7512 and 7701 of Title 5], and otherwise applicable Executive orders, shall not apply with respect to actions taken by the Administrator under paragraph (1) or any reduction in rank or pay (under paragraph (2) or otherwise) of any individual in a position described in subsection (a).

"**(d)** Any individual whose pay is to be determined in accordance with this subsection shall be paid basic pay at the rate of basic pay he was receiving immediately before he was placed in a position under subsection (b)(1) or reduced in rank or pay under subsection (c)(2), as the case may be, until such time as the rate of basic pay he would receive in the absence of this subsection exceeds such rate of basic pay. The provisions of section 5337 of title 5, United States Code [section 5337 of Title 5], shall not apply in any case in which this subsection applies."

Processing of Name Checks and Background Records for Noncriminal Employment, Licensing, and Humanitarian Purposes

Pub.L. 101–162, Title II, Nov. 21, 1989, 103 Stat. 995, provided in part: "That for fiscal year 1990 and hereafter the Chief, United States National Central Bureau, INTERPOL, may establish and collect fees to process name checks and background records for noncriminal employment, licensing, and humanitarian purposes and, notwithstanding the provisions of 31 U.S.C. 3302 [section 3302 of Title 31, Money and Finance], credit such fees to this appropriation to be used for salaries and other expenses incurred in providing these services."

Procurement of Expert Witnesses Without Regard to Competitive Procurement Procedures

Pub.L. 102–140, Title VI, § 611(a), Oct. 28, 1991, 105 Stat. 832, provided that, notwithstanding any other provision of law: "For fiscal year 1992 and thereafter, the Department of Justice may procure the services of expert witnesses for use in preparing or prosecuting a civil or criminal action, without regard to competitive procurement procedures, including the Commerce Business Daily publication requirements: *Provided*, That no witness shall be paid more than one attendance fee for any calendar day."

Reimbursement of Employees Traveling on Behalf of United States in Temporary Duty Status

Pub.L. 104–208, Div. A, Title I, § 101(a) [Title I, § 115], Sept. 30, 1996, 110 Stat. 3009–22, provided that: "Effective with the enactment of this Act [Pub.L. 104–208, 110 Stat. 3009, which was approved Sept. 30, 1996] and in any fiscal year hereafter, under policies established by the Attorney General, the Department of Justice may reimburse employees who are paid by an appropriation account within the Department of Justice and are traveling on behalf of the United States in temporary duty status to investigate, prosecute, or litigate (including the provision of support therefor) a criminal or civil matter, or for other similar special circumstances, for Federal, State, and local taxes heretofore and hereafter resulting from any reimbursement of travel expenses from an appropriation account within the Department of Justice: *Provided*, That such reimbursement may include an amount equal to all income taxes for which the employee would be liable due to such reimbursement."

Reimbursement by Other Government Agencies of Department of Justice Salaries and Expenses in High–Cost Litigation

Pub.L. 103–317, Title I, § 109, Aug. 26, 1994, 108 Stat. 1735, provided that: "Notwithstanding 31 U.S.C. 3302 [section 3302 of Title 31, Money and Finance] or any other law, in litigation involving unusually high costs, the Department of Justice may receive and retain reimbursement for salaries and expenses, for fiscal year 1995 and thereafter, from any other governmental component being represented in the litigation."

Structural Reforms to Improve Federal Response to Crimes Affecting Financial Institutions

Pub.L. 101–647, Title XXV, §§ 2536 to 2539, Nov. 29, 1990, 104 Stat. 4883, 4884, provided that:

"Sec. 2536. Establishment of Financial Institutions Crime Unit and Office of Special Counsel for Financial Institutions Crime Unit.

"(a) Establishment.—There is established within the Office of the Deputy Attorney General in the Department of Justice a Financial Institutions Fraud Unit to be headed by a special counsel (hereafter in this title [probably means this subtitle which is subtitle D [sections 2536–2540] of Title XXV of Pub. L. 101–647, which amended section 1441a of Title 12, Banks and Banking, and enacted this note] referred to as the 'Special Counsel').

"(b) Responsibility.—The Financial Institutions Fraud Unit and the Special Counsel shall be responsible to and shall report directly to the Deputy Attorney General.

"(c) Sunset.—The provisions of this section shall cease to apply at the end of the 5–year period beginning on the date of the enactment of this Act [Nov. 29, 1990].

"Sec. 2537. Appointment Responsibilities and Compensation of the Special Counsel.

"(a) Appointment.—The Special Counsel shall be appointed by the President, by and with the advice and consent of the Senate.

"(b) Responsibilities.—The Special Counsel shall—

"(1) supervise and coordinate investigations and prosecutions within the Department of Justice of fraud and other criminal activity in and against the financial services industry, including, to the extent consistent with the independent counsel provision of chapter 40 of title 28, United States Code [section 591 et seq. of this title], any such activity by any current or former elected official or high-level executive branch official or any member of the immediate family of any such official;

"(2) ensure that Federal law relating to civil enforcement, asset seizure and forfeiture, money laundering, and racketeering are used to the fullest extent authorized to recover the proceeds of unlawful activities from persons who have committed crimes in and against the financial services industry; and

"(3) ensure that adequate resources are made available for the investigation and prosecution of fraud and other criminal activity in and against the financial services industry.

"(c) Compensation.—The Special Counsel shall be paid at the basic pay payable for level V of the Executive Schedule [see section 5316 of Title 5, Government Organization and Employees].

"Sec. 2538. Assignment of Personnel.

"There shall be assigned to the Financial Institutions Fraud Unit such personnel as the Attorney General deems necessary to provide an appropriate level of enforcement activity in the area of fraud and other criminal activity in and against the financial services industry.

"Sec. 2539. Financial Institutions Fraud Task Forces.

"(a) Establishment.—The Attorney General shall establish such financial institutions fraud task forces as the Attorney General deems appropriate to ensure that adequate resources are made available to investigate and prosecute crimes in or against financial institutions and to recover the proceeds of unlawful activities from persons who have committed fraud or have engaged in other criminal activity in or against the financial services industry.

"(b) Supervision.—The Attorney General shall determine how each task force shall be supervised and may provide for the supervision of any task force by the Special Counsel.

"(c) Senior interagency group.—

"(1) Establishment.—The Attorney General shall establish a senior interagency group to assist in identifying the most significant financial institution fraud cases and in allocating investigative and prosecutorial resources where they are most needed.

"(2) Membership.—The senior interagency group shall be chaired by the Special Counsel and shall include senior officials from—

"(A) the Department of Justice, including representatives of the Federal Bureau of Investigation, the Advisory Committee of United States Attorneys, and other relevant entities;

"(B) the Department of the Treasury;

"(C) the Office of Thrift Supervision;

"(D) the Resolution Trust Corporation;

"(E) the Federal Deposit Insurance Corporation;

"(F) the Office of the Comptroller of the Currency;

"(G) the Board of Governors of the Federal Reserve System; and

"(H) the National Credit Union Administration.

"(3) Duties.—This senior interagency group shall enhance interagency coordination and assist in accelerating the investigations and prosecution of financial institutions fraud."

Uniforms and Allowances

Pub.L. 101–162, Title II, § 203, Nov. 21, 1989, 103 Stat. 1002, provided that: "For fiscal year 1990 and hereafter, appropriations for 'Salaries and expenses, General Administration', 'Salaries and expenses, United States Marshals Service', 'Salaries and expenses, Federal Bureau of Investigation', 'Salaries and expenses, Drug Enforcement Administration', 'Salaries and expenses, Immigration and Naturalization Service', and 'Salaries and expenses, Federal Prison System', shall be available for uniforms and allowances therefor as authorized by law (5 U.S.C. 5901–5902) [sections 5901 and 5902 of Title 5, Government Organization and Employees]."

EXECUTIVE ORDERS

EXECUTIVE ORDER NO. 12146

MANAGEMENT OF FEDERAL LEGAL RESOURCES

By the authority vested in me as President by the Constitution and statutes of the United States of America, it is hereby ordered as follows:

1–1. Establishment of the Federal Legal Council.

1–101. There is hereby established the Federal Legal Council, which shall be composed of the Attorney General and the representatives of not more than 15 other agencies. The agency representative shall be designated by the head of the agency.

1–102. The initial membership of the Council, in addition to the Attorney General, shall consist of representatives designated by the heads of the following agencies:

(a) The Department of Commerce.

(b) The Department of Defense.

(c) The Department of Energy.

(d) The Environmental Protection Agency.

(e) The Equal Employment Opportunity Commission.

(f) The Federal Trade Commission.

(g) The Department of Health and Human Services.

(h) The Interstate Commerce Commission.

(i) The Department of Labor.

(j) The National Labor Relations Board.

(k) The Securities and Exchange Commission.

(*l*) The Department of State.

(m) The Department of the Treasury.

(n) The United States Postal Service and

(*o*) The Veterans Administration.

1–103. The initial members of the Council shall serve for a term of two years. Thereafter, the agencies which compose the membership shall be designated annually by the Council and at least five positions on the Council, other than that held by the Attorney General, shall rotate annually.

1–104. In addition to the above members, the Directors of the Office of Management and Budget and the Office of Personnel Management, or their designees, shall be advisory members of the Council.

1–105. The Attorney General shall chair the Council and provide staff for its operation. Representatives of agencies that are not members of the Council may serve on or chair subcommittees of the Council.

1–2. Functions of the Council.

1–201. The Council shall promote:

(a) coordination and communication among Federal legal offices;

(b) improved management of Federal lawyers, associated support personnel, and information systems;

(c) improvements in the training provided to Federal lawyers;

(d) the facilitation of the personal donation of pro bono legal services by Federal attorneys;

(e) the use of joint or shared legal facilities in field offices; and

(f) the delegation of legal work to field offices.

1–202. The Council shall study and seek to resolve problems in the efficient and effective management of Federal legal resources that are beyond the capacity or authority of individual agencies to resolve.

1–203. The Council shall develop recommendations for legislation and other actions: (a) to increase the efficient and effective operation and management of Federal legal resources, including those matters specified in Section 1–201, and (b) to avoid inconsistent or unnecessary litigation by agencies.

1–3. Litigation Notice System.

1–301. The Attorney General shall establish and maintain a litigation notice system that provides timely information about all civil litigation pending in the courts in which the Federal Government is a party or has a significant interest.

1–302. The Attorney General shall issue rules to govern operation of the notice system. The rules shall include the following requirement:

(a) All agencies with authority to litigate cases in court shall promptly notify the Attorney General about those cases that fall in classes or categories designated from time to time by the Attorney General.

(b) The Attorney General shall provide all agencies reasonable access to the information collected in the litigation notice system.

1–4. Resolution of Interagency Legal Disputes.

1–401. Whenever two or more Executive agencies are unable to resolve a legal dispute between them, including the question of which has jurisdiction to administer a particular program or to regulate a particular activity, each agency is encouraged to submit the dispute to the Attorney General.

1–402. Whenever two or more Executive agencies whose heads serve at the pleasure of the President are unable to resolve such a legal dispute, the agencies shall submit the dispute to the Attorney General prior to proceeding in any court, except where there is specific statutory vesting of responsibility for a resolution elsewhere.

1–5. Access to Legal Opinions.

1–501. In addition to the disclosure now required by law, all agencies are encouraged to make available for public inspection and copying other opinions of their legal officers that are statements of policy or interpretation that have been adopted by the agency, unless the agency determines that disclosure would result in demonstrable harm.

1–502. All agencies are encouraged to make available on request other legal opinions, when the agency determines that disclosure would not be harmful.

1–6. Automated Legal Research and Information Systems.

1–601. The Attorney General, in coordination with the Secretary of Defense and other agency heads, shall provide for a computerized legal research system that will be available to all Federal law offices on a reimbursable basis. The system may include in its data base such Federal regulations, case briefs, and legal opinions, as the Attorney General deems appropriate.

1–602. The Federal Legal Council shall provide leadership for all Federal legal offices in establishing appropriate word processing and management information systems.

1–7. Responsibilities of the Agencies.

1–701. Each agency shall (a) review the management and operation of its legal activities and report in one year to the Federal Legal Council all steps being taken to improve those operations, and (b) cooperate with the Federal Legal Council and the Attorney General in the performance of the functions provided by this Order.

1–702. To the extent permitted by law, each agency shall furnish the Federal Legal Council and the Attorney General with reports, information and assistance as requested to carry out the provisions of this Order.

JIMMY CARTER

§ 510. Delegation of authority

The Attorney General may from time to time make such provisions as he considers appropriate authorizing the performance by any other officer, employee, or agency of the Department of Justice of any function of the Attorney General.

(Added Pub.L. 89–554, § 4(c), Sept. 6, 1966, 80 Stat. 612.)

HISTORICAL AND STATUTORY NOTES

Prior Provisions

A prior section 510, Act June 25, 1948, c. 646, 62 Stat. 910, which related to clerical assistants and messengers for United States attorneys, was repealed by Pub.L. 89–554, § 8(a), Sept. 6, 1966, 80 Stat. 632, and reenacted in section 550 of this title by section 4(c) of Pub.L. 89–554.

§ 511. Attorney General to advise the President

The Attorney General shall give his advice and opinion on questions of law when required by the President.

(Added Pub.L. 89–554, § 4(c), Sept. 6, 1966, 80 Stat. 612.)

§ 512. Attorney General to advise heads of executive departments

The head of an executive department may require the opinion of the Attorney General on questions of law arising in the administration of his department.

(Added Pub.L. 89–554, § 4(c), Sept. 6, 1966, 80 Stat. 613.)

§ 513. Attorney General to advise Secretaries of military departments

When a question of law arises in the administration of the Department of the Army, the Department of the Navy, or the Department of the Air Force, the cognizance of which is not given by statute to some other officer from whom the Secretary of the military department concerned may require advice, the Secretary of the military department shall send it to the Attorney General for disposition.

(Added Pub.L. 89–554, § 4(c), Sept. 6, 1966, 80 Stat. 613.)

§ 514. Legal services on pending claims in departments and agencies

When the head of an executive department or agency is of the opinion that the interests of the United States require the service of counsel on the examination of any witness concerning any claim, or on the legal investigation of any claim, pending in the department or agency, he shall notify the Attorney General, giving all facts necessary to enable him to furnish proper professional service in attending the examination or making the investigation, and the Attorney General shall provide for the service.

(Added Pub.L. 89–554, § 4(c), Sept. 6, 1966, 80 Stat. 613.)

§ 515. Authority for legal proceedings; commission, oath, and salary for special attorneys

(a) The Attorney General or any other officer of the Department of Justice, or any attorney specially appointed by the Attorney General under law, may, when specifically directed by the Attorney General, conduct any kind of legal proceeding, civil or criminal, including grand jury proceedings and proceedings before committing magistrates, which United States attorneys are authorized by law to conduct, whether or not he is a resident of the district in which the proceeding is brought.

(b) Each attorney specially retained under authority of the Department of Justice shall be commissioned as special assistant to the Attorney General or special attorney, and shall take the oath required by law. Foreign counsel employed in special cases are not required to take the oath. The Attorney General shall fix the annual salary of a special assistant or special attorney at not more than $12,000.

(Added Pub.L. 89–554, § 4(c), Sept. 6, 1966, 80 Stat. 613.)

HISTORICAL AND STATUTORY NOTES

Change of Name

Reference to United States magistrate or to magistrate deemed to refer to United States magistrate judge pursuant to section 321 of Pub.L. 101–650, set out as a note under section 631 of this title.

§ 516. Conduct of litigation reserved to Department of Justice

Except as otherwise authorized by law, the conduct of litigation in which the United States, an agency, or officer thereof is a party, or is interested, and securing evidence therefor, is reserved to officers of the Department of Justice, under the direction of the Attorney General.

(Added Pub.L. 89–554, § 4(c), Sept. 6, 1966, 80 Stat. 613.)

§ 517. Interests of United States in pending suits

The Solicitor General, or any officer of the Department of Justice, may be sent by the Attorney General to any State or district in the United States to attend to the interests of the United States in a suit pending in a court of the United States, or in a court of a State, or to attend to any other interest of the United States.

(Added Pub.L. 89–554, § 4(c), Sept. 6, 1966, 80 Stat. 613.)

§ 518. Conduct and argument of cases

(a) Except when the Attorney General in a particular case directs otherwise, the Attorney General and the Solicitor General shall conduct and argue suits and appeals in the Supreme Court and suits in the United States Court of Federal Claims or in the United States Court of Appeals for the Federal Circuit and in the Court of International Trade in which the United States is interested.

(b) When the Attorney General considers it in the interests of the United States, he may personally conduct and argue any case in a court of the United States in which the United States is interested, or he may direct the Solicitor General or any officer of the Department of Justice to do so.

(Added Pub.L. 89–554, § 4(c), Sept. 6, 1966, 80 Stat. 613, and amended Pub.L. 96–417, Title V, § 503, Oct. 10, 1980, 94 Stat. 1743; Pub.L. 97–164, Title I, § 117, Apr. 2, 1982, 96 Stat. 32; Pub.L. 102–572, Title IX, § 902(b)(1), Oct. 29, 1992, 106 Stat. 4516.)

HISTORICAL AND STATUTORY NOTES

Effective Dates

1992 Acts. Amendment by Pub.L. 102–572 effective Oct. 29, 1992, see section 911 of Pub.L. 102–572, set out as a note under section 171 of this title.

1982 Acts. Amendment by Pub.L. 97–164 effective Oct. 1, 1982, see section 402 of Pub.L. 97–164, set out as a note under section 171 of this title.

1980 Acts. Amendment by Pub.L. 96–417 effective on Nov. 1, 1980 and applicable with respect to civil actions pending on or commenced on or after such date, see section 701(a) of Pub.L. 96–417, as amended, set out as a note under section 251 of this title.

Change of Name

References to United States Claims Court deemed to refer to United States Court of Federal Claims and references to Claims Court deemed to refer to Court of Federal Claims, see section 902(b) of Pub.L. 102–572, set out as a note under section 171 of Title 28, Judiciary and Judicial Procedure.

§ 519. Supervision of litigation

Except as otherwise authorized by law, the Attorney General shall supervise all litigation to which the United States, an agency, or officer thereof is a party, and shall direct all United States attorneys, assistant United States attorneys, and special attorneys appointed under section 543 of this title in the discharge of their respective duties.

(Added Pub.L. 89–554, § 4(c), Sept. 6, 1966, 80 Stat. 614.)

HISTORICAL AND STATUTORY NOTES

Case Management Information and Tracking Systems for Federal Judicial Districts and Divisions of Department; Preparation, Submission, Etc., of Plan

Pub.L. 96–132, § 11, Nov. 30, 1979, 93 Stat. 1047, required the Attorney General, not later than Apr. 15, 1980, after consultation with the Director of the Executive Office of United States Attorneys and such Assistant Attorneys as appropriate, to prepare and submit to the Committees on the Judiciary of the Senate and the House of Representatives a plan for the activation and coordination, within the Department of Justice, of compatible, comprehensive case management information and tracking systems for each of the judicial districts of the United States and for each of the divisions of the Department.

Report to Congress Regarding Provisions of Law Considered Unconstitutional by the Department of Justice; Declaration of Such Position

Pub.L. 96–132, § 21, Nov. 30, 1979, 93 Stat. 1049, required the Attorney General, during the fiscal year ending Sept. 30, 1980, to transmit a report to each House of Congress in any case in which the Attorney General considered the provisions of law enacted by the Congress and at issue to be unconstitutional and in such cases required a representative of the Department of Justice participating in such case to make a declaration that such option of the Attorney General regarding the constitutionality of those provisions of law involved constitutes the opinion of the executive branch of the government with respect to such matter.

Similar provisions were contained in Pub.L. 95–624, § 13, Nov. 9, 1978, 92 Stat. 3464.

Study and Report to Congress on Extent to Which Violations of Federal Criminal Laws Are Not Prosecuted

Pub.L. 95–624, § 17, Nov. 9, 1978, 92 Stat. 3465, provided that the Attorney General undertake a study and make recommendations concerning violations of Federal criminal laws which have not been prosecuted and present such study and recommendations to the Committee on the Judiciary of the Senate and the House of Representatives not later than Oct. 1, 1979.

EXECUTIVE ORDERS

EXECUTIVE ORDER NO. 12778

Ex. Ord. No. 12778, Oct. 23, 1991, 56 F.R. 55195, relating to civil justice reform, was revoked by Ex. Ord. No. 12988, Feb. 5, 1996, 61 F.R. 4729, set out as a note under this section.

§ 520. Transmission of petitions in United States Court of Federal Claims or in United States Court of Appeals for the Federal Circuit; statement furnished by departments

(a) In suits against the United States in the United States Court of Federal Claims or in the United States Court of Appeals for the Federal Circuit founded on a contract, agreement, or transaction with an executive department or military department, or a bureau, officer, or agent thereof, or when the matter or thing on which the claim is based has been passed on and decided by an executive department, military department, bureau, or officer authorized to adjust it, the Attorney General shall send to the department, bureau, or officer a printed copy of the petition filed by the claimant, with a request that the department, bureau, or officer furnish to the Attorney General all facts, circumstances, and evidence concerning the claim in the possession or knowledge of the department, bureau, or officer.

(b) Within a reasonable time after receipt of the request from the Attorney General, the executive department, military department, bureau, or officer shall furnish the Attorney General with a written statement of all facts, information, and proofs. The statement shall contain a reference to or description of all official documents and papers, if any, as may furnish proof of facts referred to in it, or may be necessary and proper for the defense of the United States against the claim, mentioning the department, office, or place where the same is kept or may be secured. If the claim has been passed on and decided by the department, bureau, or officer, the statement shall briefly state the reasons and principles on which the decision was based. When the decision was founded on an Act of Congress it shall be cited specifically, and if any previous interpretation or construction has been given to the Act, section, or clause by the department, bureau, or officer, it shall be set forth briefly in the statement and a copy of the opinion filed, if any, attached to it. When a decision in the case has been based on a regulation of a department or when a regulation has, in the opinion of the department, bureau, or officer sending the statement, any bearing on the claim, it shall be distinctly quoted at length in the statement. When more than one case or class of cases is pending, the defense of which rests on the same facts, circumstances, and proofs, the department, bureau, or officer may certify and send one statement and it shall be held to apply to all cases as if made out, certified, and sent in each case respectively.

(Added Pub.L. 89–554, § 4(c), Sept. 6, 1966, 80 Stat. 614, and amended Pub.L. 97–164, Title I, § 118(a), Apr. 2, 1982, 96 Stat. 32; Pub.L. 102–572, Title IX, § 902(b)(1), Oct. 29, 1992, 106 Stat. 4516.)

HISTORICAL AND STATUTORY NOTES

Effective Dates

1992 Acts. Amendment by Pub.L. 102–572 effective Oct. 29, 1992, see section 911 of Pub.L. 102–572, set out as a note under section 171 of this title.

1982 Acts. Amendment by Pub.L. 97–164 effective Oct. 1, 1982, see section 402 of Pub.L. 97–164, set out as a note under section 171 of this title.

Change of Name

References to United States Claims Court deemed to refer to United States Court of Federal Claims and references to Claims Court deemed to refer to Court of Federal Claims, see section 902(b) of Pub.L. 102–572, set out as a note under section 171 of Title 28, Judiciary and Judicial Procedure.

§ 521. Publication and distribution of opinions

The Attorney General, from time to time—

(1) shall cause to be edited, and printed in the Government Printing Office, such of his opinions as he considers valuable for preservation in volumes; and

(2) may prescribe the manner for the distribution of the volumes.

Each volume shall contain headnotes, an index, and such footnotes as the Attorney General may approve.

(Added Pub.L. 89–554, § 4(c), Sept. 6, 1966, 80 Stat. 614.)

§ 522. Report of business and statistics

The Attorney General, by April 1 of each year, shall report to Congress on the business of the Department of Justice for the last preceding fiscal year, and on any other matters pertaining to the Department that he considers proper, including—

(1) a statement of the several appropriations which are placed under the control of the Department and the amount appropriated;

(2) the statistics of crime under the laws of the United States; and

(3) a statement of the number of causes involving the United States, civil and criminal, pending during the preceding year in each of the several courts of the United States.

(Added Pub.L. 89–554, § 4(c), Sept. 6, 1966, 80 Stat. 615, and amended Pub.L. 94–273, § 19, Apr. 21, 1976, 90 Stat. 379.)

HISTORICAL AND STATUTORY NOTES

Congressional Oversight

Pub.L. 100–700, § 6, Nov. 19, 1988, 102 Stat. 4634, provided that:

"Commencing with the first year after the date of enactment of this section [Nov. 19, 1988], the Attorney General shall annually report to the Congress with respect to—

"(1) the number of referrals of fraud cases by the Department of Defense of defense contractors (with specific statistics with respect to the one hundred largest contractors), the number of open investigation of such contractors, and a breakdown of to which United States Attorney's Office or other component of the Department of Justice each such case was referred;

"(2) the number of referrals of fraud cases from other agencies or sources;

"(3) the number of attorneys and support staff assigned pursuant to this Act [see Short Title of 1988 Amendment note under section 1001 of Title 18, Crimes and Criminal Procedure and Tables];

"(4) the number of investigative agents assigned to each investigation and the period of time each investigation has been opened;

"(5) the number of convictions and acquittals achieved by individuals assigned to positions established by the Act; and

"(6) the sentences, recoveries, and penalties achieved by individuals assigned to positions established by this Act."

Report to Congress on Banking Law Offenses

Pub.L. 101–647, Title XXV, § 2546, Nov. 29, 1990, 104 Stat. 4885, provided that:

"**(a) In general.**—

"**(1) Data collection.**—The Attorney General shall compile and collect data concerning—

"(A) the nature and number of civil and criminal investigations, prosecutions, and related proceedings, and civil enforcement and recovery proceedings, in progress with respect to banking law offenses under sections 981, 1008, 1032, and 3322(d) of title 18, United States Code [sections 981, 1008, 1032, and 3322(d) of Title 18, Crimes and Criminal Procedure], and section 951 of the Financial Institutions Reform, Recovery, and Enforcement Act of 1989 [section 1833a of Title 12, Banks and Banking] and conspiracies to commit any such offense, including inactive investigations of such offenses;

"(B) the number of—

"(i) investigations, prosecutions, and related proceedings described in subparagraph (A) which are inactive as of the close of the reporting period but have not been closed or declined; and

"(ii) unaddressed referrals which allege criminal misconduct involving offenses described in subparagraph (A),

and the reasons such matters are inactive and the referrals unaddressed;

"(C) the nature and number of such matters closed, settled, or litigated to conclusion; and

"(D) the results achieved, including convictions and pretrial diversions, fines and penalties levied, restitution assessed and collected, and damages recovered, in such matters.

"**(2) Analysis and report.**—The Attorney General shall analyze and report to the Congress on the data described in paragraph (1) and its coordination and other related activities named in section 2539(c)(2) [probably means section 2539(c)(3) of Pub.L. 101–647, set out as a note under section 509 of this title] and shall provide such report on the data monthly through December 31, 1991, and quarterly after such date.

"**(b) Specifics of Report.**—The report required by subsection (a) shall—

"(1) categorize data as to various types of financial institutions and appropriate dollar loss categories;

"(2) disclose data for each Federal judicial district;

"(3) describe the activities of the Financial Institution Fraud Unit; and

"(4) list—

"(A) the number of institutions, categorized by failed and open institutions, in which evidence of significant fraud, unlawful activity, insider abuse or serious misconduct has been alleged or detected;

"(B) civil, criminal, and administrative enforcement actions, including those of the Federal financial institutions regulatory agencies, brought against offenders;

"(C) any settlements or judgments obtained against offenders;

"(D) indictments, guilty pleas, or verdicts obtained against offenders; and

"(E) the resources allocated in pursuit of investigations, prosecutions, and sentencings (including indictments, guilty pleas, or verdicts obtained against offenders) and related proceedings."

Report to Congress on Robberies and Burglaries Involving Controlled Substances

Pub.L. 98–305, § 4, May 31, 1984, 98 Stat. 222, provided that: "For each of the first three years after the date of enactment of this Act [May 31, 1984], the Attorney General of the United States shall submit an annual report to the Congress with respect to the enforcement activities of the Attorney General relating to the offenses created by the amendment made by section 2 of this Act [enacting section 2118 of Title 18, Crimes and Criminal Procedure]."

Report to Congress on Sexual Exploitation of Children

Pub.L. 98–292, § 9, May 21, 1984, 98 Stat. 206, provided that: "Beginning one hundred and twenty days after the date of enactment of this Act [May 21, 1984], and every year thereafter, the Attorney General shall report to the Congress on prosecutions, convictions, and forfeitures under chapter 110 of title 18 of the United States Code [section 2251 et seq. of Title 18, Crimes and Criminal Procedure]."

§ 523. Requisitions

The Attorney General shall sign all requisitions for the advance or payment of moneys appropriated for the Department of Justice, out of the Treasury, subject to the same control as is exercised on like estimates or accounts by the General Accounting Office.

(Added Pub.L. 89–554, § 4(c), Sept. 6, 1966, 80 Stat. 615.)

§ 524. Availability of appropriations

(a) Appropriations for the Department of Justice are available for payment of—

(1) notarial fees, including such additional stenographic services as are required in connection

therewith in the taking of depositions, and compensation and expenses of witnesses and informants, all at the rates authorized or approved by the Attorney General or the Assistant Attorney General for Administration; and

(2) when ordered by the court, actual expenses of meals and lodging for marshals, deputy marshals, or criers when acting as bailiffs in attendance on juries.

(b) Except as provided in subsection (a) of this section, a claim of not more than $500 for expenses related to litigation that is beyond the control of the Department may be paid out of appropriations currently available to the Department for expenses related to litigation when the Comptroller General settles the payment.

(c)(1) There is established in the United States Treasury a special fund to be known as the Department of Justice Assets Forfeiture Fund (hereafter in this subsection referred to as the "Fund") which shall be available to the Attorney General without fiscal year limitation for the following law enforcement purposes—

(A) the payment, at the discretion of the Attorney General, of any expenses necessary to seize, detain, inventory, safeguard, maintain, advertise, sell, or dispose of property under seizure, detention, or forfeited pursuant to any law enforced or administered by the Department of Justice, or of any other necessary expense incident to the seizure, detention, forfeiture, or disposal of such property including—

(i) payments for—

(I) contract services;

(II) the employment of outside contractors to operate and manage properties or provide other specialized services necessary to dispose of such properties in an effort to maximize the return from such properties; and

(III) reimbursement of any Federal, State, or local agency for any expenditures made to perform the functions described in this clause;

(ii) payments to reimburse any Federal agency participating in the Fund for investigative costs leading to seizures;

(iii) payments for contracting for the services of experts and consultants needed by the Department of Justice to assist in carrying out duties related to asset seizure and forfeiture; and

(iv) payments made pursuant to guidelines promulgated by the Attorney General if such payments are necessary and directly related to seizure and forfeiture program expenses for—

(I) the purchase or lease of automatic data processing systems (not less than a majority of which use will be related to such program);

(II) training;

(III) printing;

(IV) the storage, protection, and destruction of controlled substances; and

(V) contracting for services directly related to the identification of forfeitable assets, and the processing of and accounting for forfeitures;

(B) the payment of awards for information or assistance directly relating to violations of the criminal drug laws of the United States or of sections 1956 and 1957 of title 18, sections 5313 and 5324 of title 31, and section 6050I of the Internal Revenue Code of 1986;

(C) at the discretion of the Attorney General, the payment of awards for information or assistance leading to a civil or criminal forfeiture involving any Federal agency participating in the Fund;

(D) the compromise and payment of valid liens and mortgages against property that has been forfeited pursuant to any law enforced or administered by the Department of Justice, subject to the discretion of the Attorney General to determine the validity of any such lien or mortgage and the amount of payment to be made, and the employment of attorneys and other personnel skilled in State real estate law as necessary;

(E) disbursements authorized in connection with remission or mitigation procedures relating to property forfeited under any law enforced or administered by the Department of Justice;

(F)(i) for equipping for law enforcement functions of any Government-owned or leased vessel, vehicle, or aircraft available for official use by any Federal agency participating in the Fund;

(ii) for equipping any vessel, vehicle, or aircraft available for official use by a State or local law enforcement agency to enable the vessel, vehicle, or aircraft to assist law enforcement functions if the vessel, vehicle, or aircraft will be used in a joint law enforcement operation with a Federal agency participating in the Fund; and

(iii) payments for other equipment directly related to seizure or forfeiture, including laboratory equipment, protective equipment, communications equipment, and the operation and maintenance costs of such equipment;

(G) for purchase of evidence of any violation of the Controlled Substances Act, the Controlled Substances Import and Export Act, chapter 96 of title 18, or sections 1956 and 1957 of title 18;

(H) the payment of State and local property taxes on forfeited real property that accrued between the date of the violation giving rise to the forfeiture and the date of the forfeiture order; and

(I)[1] payment of overtime salaries, travel, fuel, training, equipment, and other similar costs of State or local law enforcement officers that are incurred in a joint law enforcement operation with a Federal law enforcement agency participating in the Fund;

(I)[1] after all reimbursements and program-related expenses have been met at the end of fiscal year 1989, the Attorney General may transfer deposits from the Fund to the building and facilities account of the Federal prison system for the construction of correctional institutions.

Amounts for paying the expenses authorized by subparagraphs (A)(iv), (B), (F), (G), and (H)[2] shall be specified in appropriations Acts and may be used under authorities available to the organization receiving the funds. Amounts for other authorized expenditures and payments from the Fund, including equitable sharing payments, are not required to be specified in appropriations acts. The Attorney General may exempt the procurement of contract services under subparagraph (A) under the fund[3] from section 3709 of the Revised Statutes of the United States (41 U.S.C. 5), title III of the Federal Property and Administrative Services Act of 1949 (41 U.S.C. 251 and following), and other provisions of law as may be necessary to maintain the security and confidentiality of related criminal investigations.

(2) Any award paid from the Fund for information, as provided in paragraph (1)(B) or (C), shall be paid at the discretion of the Attorney General or his delegate, under existing departmental delegation policies for the payment of awards, except that the authority to pay an award of $250,000 or more shall not be delegated to any person other than the Deputy Attorney General, the Associate Attorney General, the Director of the Federal Bureau of Investigation, or the Administrator of the Drug Enforcement Administration. Any award for information pursuant to paragraph (1)(B) shall not exceed $250,000. Any award for information pursuant to paragraph (1)(C) shall not exceed the lesser of $250,000 or one-fourth of the amount realized by the United States from the property forfeited.

(3) Any amount under subparagraph (F) of paragraph (1) shall be paid at the discretion of the Attorney General or his delegate, except that the authority to pay $100,000 or more may be delegated only to the respective head of the agency involved.

(4) There shall be deposited in the Fund—

(A) all amounts from the forfeiture of property under any law enforced or administered by the Department of Justice, except all proceeds of forfeitures available for use by the Secretary of the Treasury or the Secretary of the Interior pursuant to section 11(d) of the Endangered Species Act (16 U.S.C. 1540(d)) or section 6(d) of the Lacey Act Amendments of 1981 (16 U.S.C. 3375(d)), or the Postmaster General of the United States pursuant to 39 U.S.C. 2003(b)(7);

(B) all amounts representing the Federal equitable share from the forfeiture of property under any Federal, State, local or foreign law, for any Federal agency participating in the Fund; and

(C) all amounts transferred by the Secretary of the Treasury pursuant to section 9703(g)(4)(A)(ii) of title 31.

(5) Amounts in the Fund, and in any holding accounts associated with the Fund which are not currently needed for the purpose of this section[4] shall be kept on deposit or invested in obligations of, or guaranteed by, the United States and all earnings on such investments shall be deposited in the Fund.

(6) The Attorney General shall transmit to the Congress, not later than 4 months after the end of each fiscal year, detailed reports as follows:

(A) a report on—

(i) the estimated total value of property forfeited under any law enforced or administered by the Department of Justice with respect to which funds were not deposited in the Fund; and

(ii) the estimated total value of all such property transferred to any State or local law enforcement agency;

(B) a report on—

(i) the Fund's beginning balance;

(ii) sources of receipts (seized cash, conveyances, and others);

(iii) liens and mortgages paid and amount of money shared with State and local law enforcement agencies;

(iv) the net amount realized from the year's operations, amount of seized cash being held as evidence, and the amount of money legally allowed to be carried over to next year;

(v) any defendant's property, not forfeited at the end of the preceding fiscal year, if the equity in such property is valued at $1,000,000 or more; and

(vi) year-end Fund balance;

(C) a report for such fiscal year, containing audited financial statements, in the form prescribed by the Attorney General, in consultation with the Comptroller General, including profit and loss information with respect to forfeited property (by category), and financial information on forfeited property transactions (by type of disposition).

The report should also contain all annual audit reports from State and local law enforcement agencies required to be reported to the Attorney General under subparagraph (B) of paragraph (7); and

(D) a report for such fiscal year containing a description of the administrative and contracting expenses paid from the Fund under paragraph (1)(A).

(7) The provisions of this subsection relating to deposits in the Fund shall apply to all property in the custody of the Department of Justice on or after the effective date of the Comprehensive Forfeiture Act of 1983.

(8)(A) There are authorized to be appropriated such sums as necessary for the purposes described in subparagraphs (A)(iv), (B), (F), (G), and (H) of paragraph (1).

(B) Subject to subparagraphs (C) and (D), at the end of each of fiscal years 1994, 1995, and 1996, the Attorney General shall transfer from the Fund not more than $100,000,000 to the Special Forfeiture Fund established by section 6073 of the Anti-Drug Abuse Act of 1988.

(C) Transfers under subparagraph (B) may be made only from the excess unobligated balance and may not exceed one-half of the excess unobligated balance for any year. In addition, transfers under subparagraph (B) may be made only to the extent that the sum of the transfers in a fiscal year and one-half of the unobligated balance at the beginning of that fiscal year for the Special Forfeiture Fund does not exceed $100,000,000.

(D) For the purpose of determining amounts available for distribution at year end for any fiscal year, "excess unobligated balance" means the unobligated balance of the Fund generated by that fiscal year's operations, less any amounts that are required to be retained in the Fund to ensure the availability of amounts in the subsequent fiscal year for purposes authorized under paragraph (1).

(E) Subject to the notification procedures contained in section 605 of Public Law 103–121, and after satisfying the transfer requirement in subparagraph (B) of this paragraph, any excess unobligated balance remaining in the Fund on September 30, 1997 and thereafter shall be available to the Attorney General, without fiscal year limitation, for any Federal law enforcement, litigative/prosecutive, and correctional activities, or any other authorized purpose of the Department of Justice. Any amounts provided pursuant to this subparagraph may be used under authorities available to the organization receiving the funds.

(9)(A) Following the completion of procedures for the forfeiture of property pursuant to any law enforced or administered by the Department, the Attorney General is authorized, in her discretion, to warrant clear title to any subsequent purchaser or transferee of such property.

(B) For fiscal year 1997, the Attorney General is authorized to transfer, under such terms and conditions as the Attorney General shall specify, real or personal property of limited or marginal value, to a State or local government agency, or its designated contractor or transferee, for use to support drug abuse treatment, drug and crime prevention and education, housing, job skills, and other community-based public health and safety programs. Such transfer shall not create or confer any private right of action in any person against the United States.

(10) The Attorney General shall transfer from the Fund to the Secretary of the Treasury for deposit in the Department of the Treasury Forfeiture Fund amounts appropriate to reflect the degree of participation of the Department of the Treasury law enforcement organizations (described in section 9703(p) of title 31) in the law enforcement effort resulting in the forfeiture pursuant to laws enforced or administered by the Department of Justice.

(11) For purposes of this subsection and notwithstanding section 9703 of title 31 or any other law, property is forfeited pursuant to a law enforced or administered by the Department of Justice if it is forfeited pursuant to—

(A) a judicial forfeiture proceeding when the underlying seizure was made by an officer of a Federal law enforcement agency participating in the Department of Justice Assets Forfeiture Fund or the property was maintained by the United States Marshals Service; or

(B) a civil administrative forfeiture proceeding conducted by a Department of Justice law enforcement component or pursuant to the authority of the Secretary of Commerce.

[(12) Redesignated (11)]

(d)(1) The Attorney General may accept, hold, administer, and use gifts, devises, and bequests of any property or services for the purpose of aiding or facilitating the work of the Department of Justice.

(2) Gifts, devises, and bequests of money, the proceeds of sale or liquidation of any other property accepted hereunder, and any income accruing from any property accepted hereunder—

(A) shall be deposited in the Treasury in a separate fund and held in trust by the Secretary of the Treasury for the benefit of the Department of Justice; and

(B) are hereby appropriated, without fiscal year limitation, and shall be disbursed on order of the Attorney General.

(3) Upon request of the Attorney General, the Secretary of the Treasury may invest and reinvest the fund described herein in public debt securities with maturities suitable for the needs of the fund and bearing interest at rates determined by the Secretary of the Treasury, taking into consideration the current average market yield on outstanding marketable obligations of the United States or comparable maturities.

(4) Evidences of any intangible personal property (other than money) accepted hereunder shall be deposited with the Secretary of the Treasury, who may hold or liquidate them, except that they shall be liquidated upon the request of the Attorney General.

(5) For purposes of federal income, estate, and gift taxes, property accepted hereunder shall be considered a gift, devise, or bequest to, or for the use of, the United States.

(Added Pub.L. 89–554, § 4(c), Sept. 6, 1966, 80 Stat. 615, and amended Pub.L. 97–258, § 2(g)(1)(B) to (D), Sept. 13, 1982, 96 Stat. 1060; Pub.L. 98–473, Title II, §§ 310, 2303, Oct. 12, 1984, 98 Stat. 2052, 2193; Pub.L. 99–570, Title I, § 1152(a), Oct. 27, 1986, 100 Stat. 3207–12; Pub.L. 99–646, § 27, Nov. 10, 1986, 100 Stat. 3597; Pub.L. 100–202, § 101(a)[Title II, § 210(a)], Dec. 22, 1987, 101 Stat. 1329, 1329–18; Pub.L. 100–690, Title VI, § 6072, Nov. 18, 1988, 102 Stat. 4320; Pub.L. 101–509, Title III, § 1, Nov. 5, 1990, 104 Stat. 1403; Pub.L. 101–647, Title XVI, § 1601, Title XX, §§ 2001(a), 2002, 2005, 2006, Nov. 29, 1990, 104 Stat. 4842, 4854, 4855; Pub.L. 102–27, Title II, § 101, Apr. 10, 1991, 105 Stat. 135; Pub.L. 102–140, Title I, § 112, Oct. 28, 1991, 105 Stat. 795; Pub.L. 102–393, Title VI, § 638(f), Oct. 6, 1992, 106 Stat. 1788; Pub.L. 102–395, Title I, § 114(b), (c), Oct. 6, 1992, 106 Stat. 1845; Pub.L. 102–550, Title XV, § 1529, Oct. 28, 1992, 106 Stat. 4065; Pub.L. 103–121, Title I, § 109, Oct. 27, 1993, 107 Stat. 1164; Pub.L. 103–317, Title I, § 110, Aug. 26, 1994, 108 Stat. 1735; Pub.L. 103–322, Title IX, § 90205(b), Title XXXII, §§ 320301, 320302, 320913(a), Sept. 13, 1994, 108 Stat. 1994, 2114, 2128; Pub.L. 104–66, Title I, § 1091(h), Dec. 21, 1995, 109 Stat. 722; Pub.L. 104–91, Title I, § 101(a), Jan. 6, 1996, 110 Stat. 11; Pub.L. 104–99, Title II, § 211, Jan. 26, 1996, 110 Stat. 37; Pub.L. 104–134, Title I, § 101[(a)][Title I, § 122], Apr. 26, 1996, 110 Stat. 1321–22; renumbered Title I Pub.L. 104–140, § 1(a), May 2, 1996, 110 Stat. 1327, and amended Pub.L. 104–208, Div. A, Title I, § 101(a) [Title I, §§ 108, 114, 116, 117], Sept. 30, 1996, 110 Stat. 3009–18, 3009–22, 3009–23; Pub.L. 105–119, Title I, §§ 108, 124, Title II, § 211(b), Nov. 26, 1997, 111 Stat. 2457, 2471, 2487; Pub.L. 105–272, Title VI, § 605, Oct. 20, 1998, 112 Stat. 2413.)

[1] So in original. Two subpars. (I) were enacted.

[2] See Codifications note set out under this section.

[3] So in original. Probably should be capitalized.

[4] So in original. Probably should be followed by a comma.

HISTORICAL AND STATUTORY NOTES

References in Text

The Controlled Substances Act, referred to in subsec. (c)(1)(G), is Title II of Pub.L. 91–513, Oct. 27, 1970, 84 Stat. 1242, as amended, which is classified principally to subchapter I (section 801 et seq.) of chapter 13 of Title 21, Food and Drugs. For complete classification of this Act to the Code, see Short Title note set out under section 801 of Title 21 and Tables.

The Controlled Substances Import and Export Act, referred to in subsec. (c)(1)(G), is Title III of Pub.L. 91–513, Oct. 27, 1970, 84 Stat. 1285, as amended, which is classified principally to subchapter II (section 951 et seq.) of chapter 13 of Title 21. For complete classification of this Act to the Code, see Short Title note set out under section 951 of Title 21 and Tables.

The Federal Property and Administrative Services Act of 1949, as amended, referred to in subsec. (c)(1), closing provisions, is Act June 30, 1949, c. 288, 63 Stat. 393, as amended. Title III of the Federal Property and Administrative Services Act of 1949 is classified generally to subchapter IV (section 251 et seq.) of chapter 4 of Title 41, Public Contracts. For complete classification of this Act to the Code, see Short Title note set out under section 471 of Title 40, Public Buildings, Property, and Works, and Tables.

The effective date of the Comprehensive Forfeiture Act of 1983, referred to in subsec. (c)(7), probably means the date of enactment of the Comprehensive Forfeiture Act of 1984, chapter III (sections 301 to 323) of title II of Pub.L. 98–473, which was approved Oct. 12, 1984.

Section 6073 of the Anti-Drug Abuse Act of 1988, referred to in subsec. (c)(8)(B), is section 6073 of Pub.L. 100–690, Nov. 18, 1988, 102 Stat. 4323, as amended, which is classified to section 1509 of Title 21, Food and Drugs.

Section 605 of Public Law 103–121, referred to in subsec. (c)(8)(E), was not classified to the Code.

Codifications

Pub.L. 102–393, § 638(f)(1)(C) to (F), which directed that par. (1) of subsec. (c) be amended by adding subpar. (H), by redesignating former subpar. (H) as (I), and substituting "(A)(iv)" for "(A)(ii)" and "(G), and (H)" for "and (G)" in the first sentence of the flush provision following the second of the two subpars. (I), was executed to that flush provision as amended by Pub.L. 102–395, § 114(c), to reflect the probable intent of Congress and the approval of Pub.L. 102–393 and Pub.L. 102–395 on the same day.

Section 101(a) of Pub.L. 104–91, as amended by section 211 of Pub.L. 104–99, provided in part that section 109 of the General Provisions for the Department of Justice in Title I of the Departments of Commerce, Justice, and State, the Judiciary, and Related Agencies Appropriations Act, 1996 (H.R. 2076) as passed by the House of Representatives on Dec. 6, 1995, was enacted into permanent law. Such section 109 of H.R. 2076 directed that subsec. (c)(9) of this section be amended by adding a subpar. (E). However section 110 of Pub.L. 103–317 had previously added a subpar. (E) to former subsec. (c)(9), prior to the redesignation of former subsec. (c)(9) and (10) as subsec. (c)(8) and (9), respectively, by section 1091(h) of Pub.L. 104–66. The subpar. (E) added by section 101(a) of Pub.L. 104–91, as amended, was inserted following the subpar. (E) added by section 110 of Pub.L. 103–317 in subsec. (c)(8), as redesignated, as the probable intent of Congress, because subsec. (c)(9), as redesignated, contained no subpars. (A) through (D). Subpar. (E) as added by Pub.L. 103–317 was subsequently repealed by Pub.L. 104–134, resulting in only one subsec. (c)(8)(E) remaining.

Effective Dates

1994 Acts. Section 320913(b) of Pub.L. 103–322 provided that: "The amendment made by subsection (a) [amending this section] shall apply to all claims pending at the time of or commenced subsequent to the date of enactment of this Act [Sept. 13, 1994]."

1992 Acts. Except as otherwise provided, amendment by Pub.L. 102–550 effective Oct. 28, 1992, see section 2 of Pub.L. 102–550, set out as a note under section 5301 of Title 42, The Public Health and Welfare.

Counterterrorism Fund

Pub.L. 104–19, Title III, July 27, 1995, 109 Stat. 249, provided in part that: "There is hereby established the Counterterrorism Fund which shall remain available without fiscal year limitation. For necessary expenses, as determined by the Attorney General, $34,220,000, to remain available until expended, is appropriated to the Counterterrorism Fund to reimburse any Department of Justice organization for the costs incurred in reestablishing the operational capability of an office or facility which has been damaged or destroyed as the result of the bombing of the Alfred P. Murrah Federal Building in Oklahoma City or any domestic or international terrorism event: *Provided*, That funds from this appropriation also may be used to reimburse the appropriation account of any Department of Justice agency engaged in, or providing support to, countering, investigating or prosecuting domestic or international terrorism, including payment of rewards in connection with these activities, and to conduct a terrorism threat assessment of Federal agencies and their facilities: *Provided further*, That any amount obligated from appropriations under this heading may be used under the authorities available to the organization reimbursed from this appropriation: *Provided further*, That amounts in excess of the $10,555,000 made available for extraordinary expenses incurred in the Oklahoma City bombing for fiscal year 1995, shall be available only after the Attorney General notifies the Committees on Appropriations of the House of Representatives and the Senate in accordance with section 605 of Public Law 103–317 [not classified to the Code]: *Provided further*, That the entire amount is designated by Congress as an emergency requirement pursuant to section 251(b)(2)(D)(i) of the Balanced Budget and Emergency Deficit Control Act of 1985 [section 901(b)(2)(D)(i) of Title 2, The Congress], as amended: *Provided further*, That the amount not previously designated by the President as an emergency requirement shall be available only to the extent an official budget request, for a specific dollar amount that includes designation of the entire amount of the request as an emergency requirement, as defined in the Balanced Budget and Emergency Deficit Control Act of 1985, as amended [Pub.L. 99–177, Dec. 12, 1985, 99 Stat. 1037, for classifications of which to the Code see Tables], is transmitted to Congress."

Notice and Approval of Transfer of Subsec. (c)(1)(H) Deposits

Section 101(a) [Title II, § 210(b)] of Pub.L. 100–202 provided that: "Amounts proposed for transfer pursuant to subsection (a) [amending this section] shall be transferred only upon notification by the Attorney General to the Committees on Appropriations of the House of Representatives and the Senate and approval under said Committees' policies concerning the reprogramming of funds."

Unauthorized Transfers from Department of Justice Accounts; Control of Allocation of Funds by Authority Other Than Office of Management and Budget or Department of Justice

Pub.L. 104–91, Title I, § 101(a), Jan. 6, 1996, 110 Stat. 11, as amended Pub.L. 104–99, Title II, § 211, Jan. 26, 1996, 110 Stat. 37, provided, in part, that: "Hereafter, notwithstanding any other provision of law—

"(1) No transfers may be made from Department of Justice accounts other than those authorized in this Act [probably means H.R. 2076, approved by the House of Representatives on Dec. 6, 1995, see bracketed note following this note], or in previous or subsequent appropriations Acts for the Department of Justice, or in part II of title 28 of the United States Code [section 501 et seq. of this title], or in section 10601 of title 42 of the United States Code [section 10601 of Title 42, The Public Health and Welfare]; and

"(2) No appropriation account within the Department of Justice shall have its allocation of funds controlled by other than an apportionment issued by the Office of Management and Budget or an allotment advice issued by the Department of Justice."

[Section 101(a) of Pub.L. 104–91, as amended by section 211 of Pub.L. 104–99, provided in part that section 110 of the General Provisions for the Department of Justice in Title I of the Departments of Commerce, Justice, and State, the Judiciary, and Related Agencies Appropriations Act, 1996 (H.R. 2076) as passed by the House of Representatives on Dec. 6, 1995, was enacted into permanent law. The text of such section 110 of H.R. 2076 is set out in the above note.]

Similar provisions were contained in the following prior appropriation Act:

Pub.L. 103–317, Title I, § 113, Aug. 26, 1994, 108 Stat. 1736.

Use of Deposits Transferred from Assets Forfeiture Fund to Buildings and Facilities Account of Federal Prison System

Section 106 of Pub.L. 103–121 provided that: "For fiscal year 1994 and thereafter, deposits transferred from the Assets Forfeiture Fund to the Buildings and Facilities account of the Federal Prison System may be used for the construction of correctional institutions, and the construction and renovation of Immigration and Naturalization Service and United States Marshals Service detention facilities, and for the authorized purposes of the Cooperative Agreement Program."

§ 525. Procurement of law books, reference books, and periodicals; sale and exchange

In the procurement of law books, reference books, and periodicals, the Attorney General may exchange or sell similar items and apply the exchange allowances or proceeds of such sales in whole or in part payment therefor.

(Added Pub.L. 89–554, § 4(c), Sept. 6, 1966, 80 Stat. 615.)

§ 526. Authority of Attorney General to investigate United States attorneys, marshals, and trustees, clerks of court, and others

(a) The Attorney General may investigate the official acts, records, and accounts of—

(1) the United States attorneys, marshals,,[1] trustees, including trustees in cases under title 11; and

(2) at the request and on behalf of the Director of the Administrative Office of the United States Courts, the clerks of the United States courts and of the district court of the Virgin Islands, probation officers, United States magistrates, and court reporters;

for which purpose all the official papers, records, dockets, and accounts of these officers, without exception, may be examined by agents of the Attorney General at any time.

(b) Appropriations for the examination of judicial officers are available for carrying out this section.

(Added Pub.L. 89–554, § 4(c), Sept. 6, 1966, 80 Stat. 615, and amended Pub.L. 95–598, Title II, §§ 219(a), (b), 220, Nov. 6, 1978, 92 Stat. 2662; Pub.L. 99–554, Title I, § 144(c), Oct. 27, 1986, 100 Stat. 3096.)

[1] So in original.

HISTORICAL AND STATUTORY NOTES

Codifications

Pub.L. 95–598, Title IV, § 408(c), Nov. 6, 1978, 92 Stat. 2687, as amended by Pub.L. 98–166, Title II, § 200, Nov. 28, 1983, 97 Stat. 1081; Pub.L. 98–353 Title III, § 323, July 10, 1984, 98 Stat. 358; Pub.L. 99–429, Sept. 30, 1986, 100 Stat. 985; Pub.L. 99–500, § 101(b) [Title II, § 200], Oct. 18, 1986, 100 Stat. 1783–39, 1783–45, and Pub.L. 99–591, § 101(b) [Title II, § 200], Oct. 30, 1986, 100 Stat. 3341–39, 3341–45; Pub.L. 99–554, Title III, § 307(a), Oct. 27, 1986, 100 Stat. 3125, which provided for the deletion of any references to United States Trustees in this title at a prospective date, was repealed by Pub.L. 99–554, Title III, § 307(b), Oct. 27, 1986, 100 Stat. 3125.

Effective Dates

1986 Acts. Amendment by Pub.L. 99–554 effective 30 days after Oct. 27, 1986, see section 302(a) of Pub.L. 99–554, set out as a note under section 581 of this title.

1978 Acts. Amendment by Pub.L. 95–598 effective Oct. 1, 1979, see section 402(c) of Pub.L. 95–598, set out as a note preceding section 101 of Title 11, Bankruptcy.

Change of Name

Reference to United States magistrate or to magistrate deemed to refer to United States magistrate judge pursuant to section 321 of Pub.L. 101–650, set out as a note under section 631 of this title.

§ 527. Establishment of working capital fund

There is hereby authorized to be established a working capital fund for the Department of Justice, which shall be available, without fiscal year limitation, for expenses and equipment necessary for maintenance and operations of such administrative services as the Attorney General, with the approval of the Office of Management and Budget, determines may be performed more advantageously as central services. The capital of the fund shall consist of the amount of the fair and reasonable value of such inventories, equipment, and other assets and inventories on order pertaining to the services to be carried on by the fund as the Attorney General may transfer to the fund less related liabilities and unpaid obligations together with any appropriations made for the purpose of providing capital. The fund shall be reimbursed or credited with advance payments from applicable appropriations and funds of the Department of Justice, other Federal agencies, and other sources authorized by law for supplies, materials, and services at rates which will recover the expenses of operations including accrual of annual leave and depreciation of plant and equipment of the fund. The fund shall also be credited with other receipts from sale or exchange of property or in payment for loss or damage to property held by the fund. There shall be transferred into the Treasury as miscellaneous receipts, as of the close of each fiscal year, any net income after making provisions for prior year losses, if any.

(Added Pub.L. 93–613, § 1(1), Jan. 2, 1975, 88 Stat. 1975.)

HISTORICAL AND STATUTORY NOTES

Capital Equipment Acquisition, Etc., by Income Retained from or Transferred to Working Capital Fund; Amounts and Limitations

Pub.L. 102–140, Title I, Oct. 28, 1991, 105 Stat. 784, provided that:

"Of the total income of the Working Capital Fund in fiscal year 1992 and each fiscal year thereafter, not to exceed 4 percent of the total income may be retained, to remain available until expended, for the acquisition of capital equipment and for the improvement and implementation of the Department's financial management and payroll/personnel systems: *Provided,* That in fiscal year 1992, not to exceed $4,000,000 of the total income retained shall be used for improvements to the Department's data processing operation: *Provided further,* That any proposed use of the retained income in fiscal year 1992 and thereafter, except for the $4,000,000 specified above, shall only be made after notification to the Committees on Appropriations of the House of Representatives and the Senate in accordance with section 606 of this Act [not classified to the Code].

"In addition, for fiscal year 1992 and thereafter, at no later than the end of the fifth fiscal year after the fiscal year for which funds are appropriated or otherwise made available, unobligated balances of appropriations available to the Department of Justice during such fiscal year may be transferred into the capital account of the Working Capital Fund to be available for the department wide acquisition of capital equipment, development and implementation of law enforcement or litigation related automated data processing systems, and for the improvement and implementation of the Department's financial management and payroll/personnel systems: *Provided,* That any proposed use of these transferred funds in fiscal year 1992 and thereafter shall only be made after notification to the Committees on Appropriations of the House of Representatives and the Senate in accordance with section 606 of this Act [not classified to the Code]."

Crediting to Working Capital Fund of Amounts Collected Pursuant to Civil Debt Collection Litigation Activities

Pub.L. 103–121, Title I, § 108, Oct. 27, 1993, 107 Stat. 1164, provided that: "Notwithstanding 31 U.S.C. 3302 [section 3302 of Title 31, Money and Finance] or any other statute affecting the crediting of collections, the Attorney General may credit, as an offsetting collection, to the Department of Justice Working Capital Fund, for fiscal year 1994 and thereafter, up to three percent of all amounts collected pursuant to civil debt collection litigation activities of the Department of Justice. Such amounts in the Working Capital Fund shall remain available until expended and shall be subject to the terms and conditions of that fund, and shall be used only for paying the costs of processing and tracking such litigation."

§ 528. Disqualification of officers and employees of the Department of Justice

The Attorney General shall promulgate rules and regulations which require the disqualification of any officer or employee of the Department of Justice, including a United States attorney or a member of such attorney's staff, from participation in a particular investigation or prosecution if such participation may result in a personal, financial, or political conflict of interest, or the appearance thereof. Such rules and regulations may provide that a willful violation of any provision thereof shall result in removal from office.

(Added Pub.L. 95–521, Title VI, § 603(a), Oct. 26, 1978, 92 Stat. 1874.)

HISTORICAL AND STATUTORY NOTES

Effective Dates

1978 Acts. Section effective Oct. 26, 1978, see section 604 of Pub.L. 95–521, set out as a note under section 591 of this title.

§ 529. Annual report of Attorney General

Beginning on June 1, 1979, and at the beginning of each regular session of Congress thereafter, the Attorney General shall report to Congress on the activities and operations of the Public Integrity Section or any other unit of the Department of Justice designated to supervise the investigation and prosecution of—

(1) any violation of Federal criminal law by any individual who holds or who at the time of such violation held a position, whether or not elective, as a Federal Government officer, employee, or special employee, if such violation relates directly or indirectly to such individual's Federal Government position, employment, or compensation;

(2) any violation of any Federal criminal law relating to lobbying, conflict of interest, campaigns, and election to public office committed by any person, except insofar as such violation relates to a matter involving discrimination or intimidation on grounds of race, color, religion, or national origin;

(3) any violation of Federal criminal law by any individual who holds or who at the time of such violation held a position, whether or not elective, as a State or local government officer or employee, if such violation relates directly or indirectly to such individual's State or local government position, employment, or compensation; and

(4) such other matters as the Attorney General may deem appropriate.

Such report shall include the number, type, and disposition of all investigations and prosecutions supervised by such Section or such unit, except that such report shall not disclose information which would interfere with any pending investigation or prosecution or which would improperly infringe upon the privacy rights of any individuals.

(Added Pub.L. 95–521, Title VI, § 603(a), Oct. 26, 1978, 92 Stat. 1874.)

HISTORICAL AND STATUTORY NOTES

Effective Dates

1978 Acts. Section effective Oct. 26, 1978, see section 604 of Pub.L. 95–521, set out as a note under section 591 of this title.

§ 530. Payment of travel and transportation expenses of newly appointed special agents

The Attorney General or the Attorney General's designee is authorized to pay the travel expenses of newly appointed special agents and the transportation expenses of their families and household goods and personal effects from place of residence at time of selection to the first duty station, to the extent such payments are authorized by section 5723 of title 5 for new appointees who may receive payments under that section.

(Added Pub. L. 98–86, § 1, Aug. 26, 1983, 97 Stat. 492.)

§ 530A. Authorization of appropriations for travel and related expenses and for health care of personnel serving abroad

There are authorized to be appropriated, for any fiscal year, for the Department of Justice, such sums as may be necessary—

(1) for travel and related expenses of employees of the Department of Justice serving abroad and their families, to be payable in the same manner as applicable with respect to the Foreign Service under paragraphs (3), (5), (6), (8), (9), (11), and (15) of section 901 of the Foreign Service Act of 1980, and under the regulations issued by the Secretary of State; and

(2) for health care for such employees and families, to be provided under section 904 of that Act.

(Added Pub.L. 100–690, Title VI, § 6281(a), Nov. 18, 1988, 102 Stat. 4368.)

HISTORICAL AND STATUTORY NOTES

References in Text

Section 901 of the Foreign Service Act of 1980, referred to in par. (1), is section 901 of Pub.L. 96–465, Title I, Oct. 17, 1980, 94 Stat. 2124, which is classified to section 4081 of Title 22, Foreign Relations and Intercourse.

Section 904 of the Foreign Service Act of 1980, referred to in par. (2), is section 904 of Pub.L. 96–465, Title I, Oct. 17, 1980, 94 Stat. 2127, which is classified to section 4084 of Title 22, Foreign Relations and Intercourse.

§ 530B. Ethical standards for attorneys for the Government

(a) An attorney for the Government shall be subject to State laws and rules, and local Federal court rules, governing attorneys in each State where such attorney engages in that attorney's duties, to the same extent and in the same manner as other attorneys in that State.

(b) The Attorney General shall make and amend rules of the Department of Justice to assure compliance with this section.

(c) As used in this section, the term "attorney for the Government" includes any attorney described in section 77.2(a) of part 77 of title 28 of the Code of Federal Regulations and also includes any independent counsel, or employee of such a counsel, appointed under chapter 40.

(Added Pub.L. 105–277, Div. A, § 101(b) [Title VIII, § 801(a)], Oct. 21, 1998, 112 Stat. 2681–___.)

HISTORICAL AND STATUTORY NOTES

Effective Dates

1998 Acts. Pub.L. 105–277, Div. A, § 101(b) [Title VIII, § 801(c)], Oct. 21, 1998, 112 Stat. 2681–___, provided that: "The amendments made by this section shall take effect 180 days after the date of the enactment of this Act [October 21, 1998] and shall apply during that portion of fiscal year 1999 that follows that taking effect, and in each succeeding fiscal year."

CHAPTER 33—FEDERAL BUREAU OF INVESTIGATION

Sec.
531. Federal Bureau of Investigation.
532. Director of Federal Bureau of Investigation.[1]
533. Investigative and other officials; appointment.
534. Acquisition, preservation, and exchange of identification records and information; appointment of officials.
535. Investigation of crimes involving Government officers and employees; limitations.
536. Positions in excepted service.
537. Expenses of unforeseen emergencies of a confidential nature.[1]
538. Investigation of aircraft piracy and related violations.
539. Counterintelligence official reception and representation expenses.
540. Investigation of felonious killings of State or local law enforcement officers.
540A. Investigation of violent crimes against travelers.
540B. Investigation of serial killings.

[1] So in original. Does not conform to section catchline.

§ 531. Federal Bureau of Investigation

The Federal Bureau of Investigation is in the Department of Justice.

(Added Pub.L. 89–554, § 4(c), Sept. 6, 1966, 80 Stat. 616.)

HISTORICAL AND STATUTORY NOTES

Federal Bureau of Investigation Funding Authorizations

Pub.L. 104–132, Title VIII, § 811, Apr. 24, 1996, 110 Stat. 1312, provided that:

"(a) In general.—With funds made available pursuant to subsection (c)—

"(1) the Attorney General shall—

"(A) provide support and enhance the technical support center and tactical operations of the Federal Bureau of Investigation;

"(B) create a Federal Bureau of Investigation counterterrorism and counterintelligence fund for costs associated with the investigation of cases involving cases of terrorism;

"(C) expand and improve the instructional, operational support, and construction of the Federal Bureau of Investigation Academy;

"(D) construct a Federal Bureau of Investigation laboratory, provide laboratory examination support, and provide for a command center;

"(E) make grants to States to carry out the activities described in subsection (b); and

"(F) increase personnel to support counterterrorism activities; and

"(2) the Director of the Federal Bureau of Investigation may expand the combined DNA Identification System (CODIS) to include Federal crimes and crimes committed in the District of Columbia.

"(b) State grants.—

"(1) Authorization.—The Attorney General, in consultation with the Director of the Federal Bureau of Investigation, may make grants to each State eligible under paragraph (2) to be used by the chief executive officer of the State, in conjunction with units of local government, other States, or any combination thereof, to carry out all or part of a program to establish, develop, update, or upgrade—

"(A) computerized identification systems that are compatible and integrated with the databases of the

National Crime Information Center of the Federal Bureau of Investigation;

"(B) the capability to analyze deoxyribonucleic acid (DNA) in a forensic laboratory in ways that are compatible and integrated with the combined DNA Identification System (CODIS) of the Federal Bureau of Investigation; and

"(C) automated fingerprint identification systems that are compatible and integrated with the Integrated Automated Fingerprint Identification System (IAFIS) of the Federal Bureau of Investigation.

"(2) **Eligibility.**—To be eligible to receive a grant under this subsection, a State shall require that each person convicted of a felony of a sexual nature shall provide to appropriate State law enforcement officials, as designated by the chief executive officer of the State, a sample of blood, saliva, or other specimen necessary to conduct a DNA analysis consistent with the standards established for DNA testing by the Director of the Federal Bureau of Investigation.

"(3) **Interstate compacts.**—A State may enter into a compact or compacts with another State or States to carry out this subsection.

"(c) **Authorization of appropriations.**—

"(1) **In general.**—There are authorized to be appropriated for the activities of the Federal Bureau of Investigation, to help meet the increased demands for activities to combat terrorism—

"(A) $114,000,000 for fiscal year 1997;

"(B) $166,000,000 for fiscal year 1998;

"(C) $96,000,000 for fiscal year 1999; and

"(D) $92,000,000 for fiscal year 2000.

"(2) **Availability of funds.**—Funds made available pursuant to paragraph (1), in any fiscal year, shall remain available until expended

"(3) **Allocation.**—

"(A) **In general.**—Of the total amount appropriated to carry out subsection (b) in a fiscal year—

"(i) the greater of 0.25 percent of such amount or $500,000 shall be allocated to each eligible State; and

"(ii) of the total funds remaining after the allocation under clause (i), there shall be allocated to each State an amount which bears the same ratio to the amount of remaining funds described in this subparagraph as the population of such State bears to the population of all States.

"(B) **Definition.**—For purposes of this paragraph, the term 'State' means any State of the United States, the District of Columbia, the Commonwealth of Puerto Rico, the Virgin Islands, American Samoa, Guam, and the Commonwealth of the Northern Mariana Islands, except that for purposes of the allocation under this subparagraph, American Samoa and the Commonwealth of the Northern Mariana Islands shall be considered as one State and that for these purposes, 67 percent of the amounts allocated shall be allocated to American Samoa, and 33 percent to the Commonwealth of the Northern Mariana Islands."

"§ 703. Morgan P. Hardiman Child Abduction and Serial Murder Investigative Resources Center

Pub.L. 105–314, Title VII, § 703, Oct. 30, 1998, 112 Stat. 2987, provided:

"(a) **Establishment.**—Not later than 90 days after the date of enactment of this Act [Oct. 30, 1998], the Attorney General shall establish within the Federal Bureau of Investigation a Child Abduction and Serial Murder Investigative Resources Center to be known as the 'Morgan P. Hardiman Child Abduction and Serial Murder Investigative Resources Center' (in this section referred to as the 'CASMIRC').

"(b) **Purpose.**—The CASMIRC shall be managed by the National Center for the Analysis of Violent Crime of the Critical Incident Response Group of the Federal Bureau of Investigation (in this section referred to as the 'NCAVC'), and by multidisciplinary resource teams in Federal Bureau of Investigation field offices, in order to provide investigative support through the coordination and provision of Federal law enforcement resources, training, and application of other multidisciplinary expertise, to assist Federal, State, and local authorities in matters involving child abductions, mysterious disappearances of children, child homicide, and serial murder across the country. The CASMIRC shall be co-located with the NCAVC.

"(c) **Duties of the CASMIRC.**—The CASMIRC shall perform such duties as the Attorney General determines appropriate to carry out the purposes of the CASMIRC, including—

"(1) identifying, developing, researching, acquiring, and refining multidisciplinary information and specialities to provide for the most current expertise available to advance investigative knowledge and practices used in child abduction, mysterious disappearances of children, child homicide, and serial murder investigations;

"(2) providing advice and coordinating the application of current and emerging technical, forensic, and other Federal assistance to Federal, State, and local authorities in child abduction, mysterious disappearances of children, child homicide, and serial murder investigations;

"(3) providing investigative support, research findings, and violent crime analysis to Federal, State, and local authorities in child abduction, mysterious disappearances of children, child homicide, and serial murder investigations;

"(4) providing, if requested by a Federal, State, or local law enforcement agency, on site consultation and advice in child abduction, mysterious disappearances of children, child homicide and serial murder investigations;

"(5) coordinating the application of resources of pertinent Federal law enforcement agencies, and other Federal entities including, but not limited to, the United States Customs Service, the Secret Service, the Postal Inspection Service, and the United States Marshals Service, as appropriate, and with the concurrence of the agency head to support Federal, State, and local law enforcement involved in child abduction, mysterious disappearance of a child, child homicide, and serial murder investigations;

"(6) conducting ongoing research related to child abductions, mysterious disappearances of children, child homicides, and serial murder, including identification and investigative application of current and emerging technologies, identification of investigative searching technologies and methods for physically locating abducted children, investigative use of offender behavioral assessment and analysis concepts, gathering statistics and information necessary for case identification, trend analysis, and case linkages to advance the investigative effectiveness of outstanding abducted children cases, develop investigative systems to identify and track serious serial offenders that repeatedly victimize children for comparison to unsolved cases, and other investigative research pertinent to child abduction, mysterious disappearance of a child, child homicide, and serial murder covered in this section;

"(7) working under the NCAVC in coordination with the National Center For Missing and Exploited Children and the Office of Juvenile Justice and Delinquency Prevention of the Department of Justice to provide appropriate training to Federal, State, and local law enforcement in matters regarding child abductions, mysterious disappearances of children, child homicides; and

"(8) establishing a centralized repository based upon case data reflecting child abductions, mysterious disappearances of children, child homicides and serial murder submitted by State and local agencies, and an automated system for the efficient collection, retrieval, analysis, and reporting of information regarding CASMIRC investigative resources, research, and requests for and provision of investigative support services.

"(d) **Appointment of personnel to the CASMIRC.**—

"(1) **Selection of members of the CASMIRC and participating State and local law enforcement personnel.**—The Director of the Federal Bureau of Investigation shall appoint the members of the CASMIRC. The CASMIRC shall be staffed with Federal Bureau of Investigation personnel and other necessary personnel selected for their expertise that would enable them to assist in the research, data collection, and analysis, and provision of investigative support in child abduction, mysterious disappearances of children, child homicide and serial murder investigations. The Director may, with concurrence of the appropriate State or local agency, also appoint State and local law enforcement personnel to work with the CASMIRC.

"(2) **Status.**—Each member of the CASMIRC (and each individual from any State or local law enforcement agency appointed to work with the CASMIRC) shall remain as an employee of that member's or individual's respective agency for all purposes (including the purpose of performance review), and service with the CASMIRC shall be without interruption or loss of civil service privilege or status and shall be on a nonreimbursable basis, except if appropriate to reimburse State and local law enforcement for overtime costs for an individual appointed to work with the resource team. Additionally, reimbursement of travel and per diem expenses will occur for State and local law enforcement participation in resident fellowship programs at the NCAVC when offered.

"(3) **Training.**—CASMIRC personnel, under the guidance of the Federal Bureau of Investigation's National Center for the Analysis of Violent Crime and in consultation with the National Center For Missing and Exploited Children, shall develop a specialized course of instruction devoted to training members of the CASMIRC consistent with the purpose of this section. The CASMIRC shall also work with the National Center For Missing and Exploited Children and the Office of Juvenile Justice and Delinquency Prevention of the Department of Justice to develop a course of instruction for State and local law enforcement personnel to facilitate the dissemination of the most current multidisciplinary expertise in the investigation of child abductions, mysterious disappearances of children, child homicides, and serial murder of children.

"(e) **Report to Congress.**—One year after the establishment of the CASMIRC, the Attorney General shall submit to Congress a report, which shall include—

"(1) a description of the goals and activities of the CASMIRC; and

"(2) information regarding—

"(A) the number and qualifications of the members appointed to the CASMIRC;

"(B) the provision of equipment, administrative support, and office space for the CASMIRC; and

"(C) the projected resource needs for the CASMIRC.

"(f) **Authorization of appropriations.**—There are authorized to be appropriated to carry out this section such sums as may be necessary for each of fiscal years 1999, 2000, and 2001."

§ 532. Director of the Federal Bureau of Investigation

The Attorney General may appoint a Director of the Federal Bureau of Investigation. The Director of the Federal Bureau of Investigation is the head of the Federal Bureau of Investigation.

(Added Pub.L. 89–554, § 4(c), Sept. 6, 1966, 80 Stat. 616.)

HISTORICAL AND STATUTORY NOTES

Confirmation and Compensation of Director; Term of Service

Pub.L. 90–351, Title VI, § 1101, June 19, 1968, 82 Stat. 236, as amended by Pub.L. 94–503, Title II, § 203, Oct. 15, 1976, 90 Stat. 2427, provided that:

"(a) Effective as of the day following the date on which the present incumbent in the office of Director ceases to serve as such, the Director of the Federal Bureau of Investigation shall be appointed by the President, by and with the advice and consent of the Senate, and shall receive compensation at the rate prescribed for level II of the Federal Executive Salary Schedule [section 5313 of Title 5, Government Organization and Employees].

"(b) Effective with respect to any individual appointment by the President, by and with the advice and consent of the Senate, after June 1, 1973, the term of service of the Director of the Federal Bureau of Investigation shall be ten years. A Director may not serve more than one ten-year term. The provisions of subsections (a) through (c) of section 8335 of title 5, United States Code [section 8335(a) through (c) of

Title 5], shall apply to any individual appointed under this section."

FBI Critical Skills Scholarship Program

Pub.L. 102–183, Title V, § 501, Dec. 4, 1991, 105 Stat. 1268, provided that:

"**(a) Study.**—The Director of the Federal Bureau of Investigation shall conduct a study relative to the establishment of an undergraduate training program with respect to employees of the Federal Bureau of Investigation that is similar in purpose, conditions, content, and administration to undergraduate training programs administered by the Central Intelligence Agency (under section 8 of the Central Intelligence Agency Act of 1949 (50 U.S.C. 403j) [section 403j of Title 50, War and National Defense]), the National Security Agency (under section 16 of the National Security Agency Act of 1959 (50 U.S.C. 402 (note) [set out as a note under section 402 of Title 50])[)], and the Defense Intelligence Agency (under section 1608 of title 10, United States Code [section 1608 of Title 10, Armed Forces]).

"**(b) Implementation.**—Any program proposed under subsection (a) may be implemented only after the Department of Justice and the Office of Management and Budget review and approve the implementation of such program.

"**(c) Availability of funds.**—Any payment made by the Director of the Federal Bureau of Investigation to carry out any program proposed to be established under subsection (a) may be made in any fiscal year only to the extent that appropriated funds are available for that purpose."

§ 533. Investigative and other officials; appointment

The Attorney General may appoint officials—

(1) to detect and prosecute crimes against the United States;

(2) to assist in the protection of the person of the President; and

(3) to conduct such other investigations regarding official matters under the control of the Department of Justice and the Department of State as may be directed by the Attorney General.

This section does not limit the authority of departments and agencies to investigate crimes against the United States when investigative jurisdiction has been assigned by law to such departments and agencies.

(Added Pub.L. 89–554, § 4(c), Sept. 6, 1966, 80 Stat. 616.)

HISTORICAL AND STATUTORY NOTES

Department of Justice Exemption Authority

Pub.L. 104–132, Title VIII, § 815(d), Apr. 24, 1996, 110 Stat. 1315, provided that: "Notwithstanding any other provision of law, section 102(b) of the Department of Justice and Related Agencies Appropriations Act, 1993 (Public Law 102–395) [pars. (5) and (6) of section 102(b) of Pub.L. 102–395, as amended, are set out as a note under this section; pars. (1) to (4) of section 102(b) of such Act were not classified to the Code, see Pub.L. 102–395, Oct. 6, 1992, 106 Stat. 1838], shall remain in effect until specifically repealed, subject to any limitation on appropriations contained in any Department of Justice Appropriation Authorization Act."

FBI Investigations of Espionage by Persons Employed by or Assigned to United States Diplomatic Missions Abroad

Pub.L. 101–193, Title VI, § 603, Nov. 30, 1989, 103 Stat. 1710, provided that: "Subject to the authority of the Attorney General, the FBI shall supervise the conduct of all investigations of violations of the espionage laws of the United States by persons employed by or assigned to United States diplomatic missions abroad. All departments and agencies shall report immediately to the FBI any information concerning such a violation. All departments and agencies shall provide appropriate assistance to the FBI in the conduct of such investigations. Nothing in this provision shall be construed as establishing a defense to any criminal, civil, or administrative action."

Undercover Investigative Operations Conducted by Federal Bureau of Investigation or Drug Enforcement Administration; Annual Report to Congress; Financial Audit

Pub.L. 102–395, Title I, § 102(b)(5), (6), Oct. 6, 1992, 106 Stat. 1840; Pub.L. 104–91, Title I, § 101(a), Jan. 6, 1996, 110 Stat. 11, as amended Pub.L. 104–99, Title II, § 211, Jan. 26, 1996, 110 Stat. 37, provided that:

"(5)(A) The Federal Bureau of Investigation or the Drug Enforcement Administration, as the case may be, shall conduct a detailed financial audit of each undercover investigative operation which is closed in fiscal year 1996—

"(i) submit the results of such audit in writing to the Attorney General, and

"(ii) not later than 180 days after such undercover operation is closed, submit a report to the Congress concerning such audit.

"(B) The Federal Bureau of Investigation and the Drug Enforcement Administration shall each also submit a report annually to the Congress specifying as to their respective undercover investigative operations—

"(i) the number, by programs, of undercover investigative operations pending as of the end of the one-year period for which such report is submitted,

"(ii) the number, by programs, of undercover investigative operations commenced in the one-year period preceding the period for which such report is submitted, and

"(iii) the number, by programs, of undercover investigative operations closed in the one-year period preceding the period for which such report is submitted and, with respect to each such closed undercover operation, the results obtained. With respect to each such closed undercover operation which involves any of the sensitive circumstances specified in the Attorney General's Guidelines on Federal Bureau of Investigation Undercover Operations, such report shall contain a detailed description of the operation and related matters, including information pertaining to—

"(I) the results,

"(II) any civil claims, and

"(III) identification of such sensitive circumstances involved, that arose at any time during the course of such undercover operation.

"(6) For purposes of paragraph (5)—

"(A) the term 'closed' refers to the earliest point in time at which—

"(i) all criminal proceedings (other than appeals) are concluded, or

"(ii) covert activities are concluded, whichever occurs later,

"(B) the term 'employees' means employees, as defined in section 2105 of title 5 of the United States Code [section 2105 of Title 5, Government Organization and Employees], of the Federal Bureau of Investigation, and

"(C) the terms 'undercover investigative operations' and 'undercover operation' mean any undercover investigative operation of the Federal Bureau of Investigation or the Drug Enforcement Administration (other than a foreign counterintelligence undercover investigative operation)—

"(i) in which—

"(I) the gross receipts (excluding interest earned) exceed $50,000, or

"(II) expenditures (other than expenditures for salaries of employees) exceed $150,000, and

"(ii) which is exempt from section 3302 or 9102 of title 31 of the United States Code [section 3302 or 9102 of Title 31, Money and Finance],

except that clauses (i) and (ii) shall not apply with respect to the report required under subparagraph (B) of such paragraph."

[Section 101(a) of Pub.L. 104–91, as amended by section 211 of Pub.L. 104–99, provided in part that section 112(3) of the General Provisions for the Department of Justice in Title I of the Departments of Commerce, Justice, and State, the Judiciary, and Related Agencies Appropriations Act, 1996 (H.R. 2076) as passed by the House of Representatives on Dec. 6, 1995, was enacted into permanent law. Such section 112(3) of H.R. 2076 amended section 102(b)(5)(A) of Pub.L. 102–395, set out above.]

Similar provisions were contained in the following prior appropriation Acts:

Pub.L. 102–140, Title I, § 102(b)(4), (5), Oct. 28, 1991, 105 Stat. 793.

Pub.L. 101–515, Title II, § 202(b)(4), (5), Nov. 5, 1990, 104 Stat. 2118.

Pub.L. 101–162, Title II, § 204(b)(4), (5), Nov. 21, 1989, 103 Stat. 1004.

Pub.L. 100–459, Title II, § 204(b)(4), (5), Oct. 1, 1988, 102 Stat. 2200, 2201, as amended by Pub.L. 101–650, Title III, § 325(c)(2), Dec. 1, 1990, 104 Stat. 5121.

Pub.L. 100–202, § 101(a) [Title II, § 204(b)(4), (5)], Dec. 22, 1987, 101 Stat. 1329–16.

Pub.L. 99–500, Title I, § 101(b) [Title II, § 204(b)(4), (5)], Oct. 18, 1986, 100 Stat. 1783–53 and Pub.L. 99–591, Title I, § 101(b) [Title II, § 204(b)(4), (5)], Oct. 30, 1986, 100 Stat. 3341–53.

Pub.L. 99–180, Title II, § 204(b)(4), (5), Dec. 13, 1985, 99 Stat. 1148.

Pub.L. 98–411, Title II, § 203(b)(4), (5), Aug. 30, 1984, 98 Stat. 1560.

Pub.L. 98–166, Title II, § 205(b)(4), (5), Nov. 28, 1983, 97 Stat. 1087.

Pub.L. 96–132, § 7(d), Nov. 30, 1979, 93 Stat. 1046, provided that:

"(1) The Federal Bureau of Investigation shall conduct detailed financial audits of undercover operations closed on or after October 1, 1979, and—

"(A) report the results of each audit in writing to the Department of Justice, and

"(B) report annually to the Congress concerning these audits.

"(2) For the purposes of paragraph (1), 'undercover operation' means any undercover operation of the Federal Bureau of Investigation, other than a foreign counterintelligence undercover operation—

"(A) in which the gross receipts exceed $50,000, and

"(B) which is exempted from section 3617 of the Revised Statutes (31 U.S.C. 484) [section 3302(b) of Title 31, Money and Finance] or section 304(a) of the Government Corporation Control Act (31 U.S.C. 869(a) [section 9102 of Title 31])."

§ 534. Acquisition, preservation, and exchange of identification records and information; appointment of officials

(a) The Attorney General shall—

(1) acquire, collect, classify, and preserve identification, criminal identification, crime, and other records;

(2) acquire, collect, classify, and preserve any information which would assist in the identification of any deceased individual who has not been identified after the discovery of such deceased individual;

(3) acquire, collect, classify, and preserve any information which would assist in the location of any missing person (including an unemancipated person as defined by the laws of the place of residence of such person) and provide confirmation as to any entry for such a person to the parent, legal guardian, or next of kin of that person (and the Attorney General may acquire, collect, classify, and preserve such information from such parent, guardian, or next of kin);[1]

(4) exchange such records and information with, and for the official use of, authorized officials of the Federal Government, the States, cities, and penal and other institutions.

(b) The exchange of records and information authorized by subsection (a)(4) of this section is subject to cancellation if dissemination is made outside the receiving departments or related agencies.

(c) The Attorney General may appoint officials to perform the functions authorized by this section.

(d) For purposes of this section, the term "other institutions" includes—

(1) railroad police departments which perform the administration of criminal justice and have arrest powers pursuant to a State statute, which allocate a substantial part of their annual budget to the administration of criminal justice, and which

meet training requirements established by law or ordinance for law enforcement officers; and

(2) police departments of private colleges or universities which perform the administration of criminal justice and have arrest powers pursuant to a State statute, which allocate a substantial part of their annual budget to the administration of criminal justice, and which meet training requirements established by law or ordinance for law enforcement officers.

(e)(1) Information from national crime information databases consisting of identification records, criminal history records, protection orders, and wanted person records may be disseminated to civil or criminal courts for use in domestic violence or stalking cases. Nothing in this subsection shall be construed to permit access to such records for any other purpose.

(2) Federal and State criminal justice agencies authorized to enter information into criminal information databases may include—

(A) arrests, convictions, and arrest warrants for stalking or domestic violence or for violations of protection orders for the protection of parties from stalking or domestic violence; and

(B) protection orders for the protection of persons from stalking or domestic violence, provided such orders are subject to periodic verification.

(3) As used in this subsection—

(A) the term "national crime information databases" means the National Crime Information Center and its incorporated criminal history databases, including the Interstate Identification Index; and

(B) the term "protection order" includes an injunction or any other order issued for the purpose of preventing violent or threatening acts or harassment against, or contact or communication with or physical proximity to, another person, including temporary and final orders issued by civil or criminal courts (other than support or child custody orders) whether obtained by filing an independent action or as a pendente lite order in another proceeding so long as any civil order was issued in response to a complaint, petition, or motion filed by or on behalf of a person seeking protection.

(Added Pub.L. 89–554, § 4(c), Sept. 6, 1966, 80 Stat. 616, and amended Pub.L. 97–292, §§ 2, 3(a), Oct. 12, 1982, 96 Stat. 1259; Pub.L. 100–690, Title VII, § 7333, Nov. 18, 1988, 102 Stat. 4469; Pub.L. 103–322, Title IV, § 40601(a), Sept. 13, 1994, 108 Stat. 1950.)

1 So in original. Probably should be followed by "and".

HISTORICAL AND STATUTORY NOTES

Criminal Background Checks for Applicants for Employment in Nursing Facilities and Home Health Care Agencies

Pub.L. 105–277, Div. A, § 101(b) [Title I, § 124], Oct. 21, 1998, 112 Stat. 2681–___, provided that:

"(a)(1) A nursing facility or home health care agency may submit a request to the Attorney General to conduct a search and exchange of records described in subsection (b) regarding an applicant for employment if the employment position is involved in direct patient care.

"(2) A nursing facility or home health care agency requesting a search and exchange of records under this section shall submit to the Attorney General through the appropriate State agency or agency designated by the Attorney General a copy of an employment applicant's fingerprints, a statement signed by the applicant authorizing the nursing facility or home health care agency to request the search and exchange of records, and any other identification information not more than 7 days (excluding Saturdays, Sundays, and legal public holidays under section 6103(a) of title 5, United States Code) after acquiring the fingerprints, signed statement, and information.

"(b) Pursuant to any submission that complies with the requirements of subsection (a), the Attorney General shall search the records of the Criminal Justice Information Services Division of the Federal Bureau of Investigation for any criminal history records corresponding to the fingerprints or other identification information submitted. The Attorney General shall provide any corresponding information resulting from the search to the appropriate State agency or agency designated by the Attorney General to receive such information.

"(c) Information regarding an applicant for employment in a nursing facility or home health care agency obtained pursuant to this section may be used only by the facility or agency requesting the information and only for the purpose of determining the suitability of the applicant for employment by the facility or agency in a position involved in direct patient care.

"(d) The Attorney General may charge a reasonable fee, not to exceed $50 per request, to any nursing facility or home health care agency requesting a search and exchange of records pursuant to this section.

"(e) Not later than 2 years after the date of enactment of this Act [October 21, 1998], the Attorney General shall submit a report to Congress on the number of requests for searches and exchanges of records made under this section by nursing facilities and home health care agencies and the disposition of such requests.

"(f) Whoever knowingly uses any information obtained pursuant to this section for a purpose other than as authorized under subsection (c) shall be fined in accordance with title 18, United States Code, imprisoned for not more than 2 years, or both.

"(g) A nursing facility or home health care agency that, in denying employment for an applicant, reasonably relies upon information provided by the Attorney General pursuant to this section shall not be liable in any action brought by the applicant based on the employment determination resulting from the incompleteness or inaccuracy of the information.

"(h) The Attorney General may promulgate such regulations as are necessary to carry out this section, including regulations regarding the security, confidentiality, accuracy, use, destruction, and dissemination of information, audits and recordkeeping, the imposition of fees, and any necessary modifications to the definitions contained in subsection (i).

"(i) In this section:

"(1) The term 'home health care agency' means an agency that provides home health care or personal care services on a visiting basis in a place of residence.

"(2) The term 'nursing facility' means a facility or institution (or a distinct part of an institution) that is primarily engaged in providing to residents of the facility or institution nursing care, including skilled nursing care, and related services for individuals who require medical or nursing care.

"(j) This section shall apply without fiscal year limitation."

Compilation of Statistics Relating to Intimidation of Government Employees

Pub.L. 104–132, Title VIII, § 808, Apr. 24, 1996, 110 Stat. 1310, provided that:

"**(a) Findings.**—The Congress finds that—

"(1) threats of violence and acts of violence against Federal, State, and local government employees and their families are increasing as the result of attempts to stop public servants from performing their lawful duties;

"(2) these acts are a danger to the constitutional form of government of the United States; and

"(3) more information is needed relating to the extent and nature of the danger to these employees and their families so that actions can be taken to protect public servants at all levels of government in the performance of their duties.

"**(b) Statistics.**—The Attorney General shall collect data, for the calendar year 1990 and each succeeding calendar year thereafter, relating to crimes and incidents of threats of violence and acts of violence against Federal, State, and local government employees and their families in the performance of their lawful duties. Such data shall include—

"(1) in the case of crimes against such employees and their families, the nature of the crime; and

"(2) in the case of incidents of threats of violence and acts of violence, including verbal and implicit threats against such employees and their families, the deterrent effect on the performance of their jobs.

"**(c) Guidelines.**—The Attorney General shall establish guidelines for the collection of the data under subsection (b), including a definition of the sufficiency of evidence of noncriminal incidents required to be reported.

"**(d) Use of data.**—

"**(1) Annual publishing.**—The Attorney General shall publish an annual summary of the data collected under this section [this note].

"**(2) Use of data.**—Except with respect to the summary published under paragraph (1), data collected under this section [this note] shall be used only for research and statistical purposes.

"**(e) Exemption.**—The Attorney General, the Secretary of State, and the United States Secret Service is not required to participate in any statistical reporting activity under this section [this note] with respect to any direct or indirect threat made against any individual for whom that official or Service is authorized to provide protection."

Family and Domestic Violence; Data Collection and Reporting

Section 7609 of Pub.L. 100–690 provided that:

"**(a) Family violence reporting.**—Under the authority of section 534 of title 28, United States Code [this section], the Attorney General shall require, and include in uniform crime reports, data that indicate—

"(1) the age of the victim; and

"(2) the relationship of the victim to the offender, for crimes of murder, aggravated assault, simple assault, rape, sexual offenses, and offenses against children.

"**(b) National Crime Survey.**—The Director of the Bureau of Justice Statistics, through the annual National Crime Survey, shall collect and publish data that more accurately measures the extent of domestic violence in America, especially the physical and sexual abuse of children and the elderly.

"**(c) Authorization of appropriations.**—There are authorized to be appropriated in fiscal years 1989, 1990, 1991, and 1992, such sums as are necessary to carry out the purposes of this section."

FBI Fees to Process Fingerprint Identification Records and Name Checks

Pub.L. 101–515, Title II, Nov. 5, 1990, 104 Stat. 2112; Pub.L. 104–91, Title I, § 101(a), Jan. 6, 1996, 110 Stat. 11, as amended Pub.L. 104–99, Title II, § 211, Jan. 26, 1996, 110 Stat. 37, provided in part that: "For fiscal year 1991 and hereafter the Director of the Federal Bureau of Investigation may establish and collect fees to process fingerprint identification records and name checks for non-criminal justice, non-law enforcement employment and licensing purposes and for certain employees of private sector contractors with classified Government contracts, and notwithstanding the provisions of 31 U.S.C. 3302 [section 3302 of Title 31, Money and Finance], credit such fees to this appropriation to be used for salaries and other expenses incurred in providing these services, and that the Director of the Federal Bureau of Investigation may establish such fees at a level to include an additional amount to establish a fund to remain available until expended to defray expenses for the automation of fingerprint identification and criminal justice information services and associated costs."

[Section 101(a) of Pub.L. 104–91, as amended by section 211 of Pub.L. 104–99, provided in part that section 113 of the General Provisions for the Department of Justice in Title I of the Departments of Commerce, Justice, and State, the Judiciary, and Related Agencies Appropriations Act, 1996 (H.R. 2076) as passed by the House of Representatives on Dec. 6, 1995, was enacted into permanent law. Such section 113 of H.R. 2076 amended Pub.L. 101–515, set out above.]

Funds for Exchange of Identification Records

Pub.L. 92–544, Title II, § 201, Oct. 25, 1972, 86 Stat. 1115, provided that: "The funds provided for Salaries and Expenses, Federal Bureau of Investigation, may be used hereafter, in addition to those uses authorized thereunder, for the exchange of identification records with officials or federally chartered or insured banking institutions to promote or maintain the security of those institutions, and, if authorized by State statute and approved by the Attorney General, to officials of State and local governments for purposes of employment and licensing, any such exchange to be made only for the official use of any such official and subject to the same restriction with respect to dissemination as that provided for under the aforementioned appropriation."

Hate Crime Statistics

Pub.L. 101–275, Apr. 23, 1990, 104 Stat. 140, as amended Pub.L. 103–322, Title XXXII, § 320926, Sept. 13, 1994, 108 Stat. 2131; Pub.L. 104–155, § 7, July 3, 1996, 110 Stat. 1394, provided:

"That (a) this Act [this note] may be cited as the 'Hate Crime Statistics Act'.

"**(b)(1)** Under the authority of section 534 of title 28, United States Code [this section], the Attorney General shall acquire data, for each calendar year, about crimes that manifest evidence of prejudice based on race, religion, disability, sexual orientation, or ethnicity, including where appropriate the crimes of murder, non-negligent manslaughter; forcible rape; aggravated assault, simple assault, intimidation; arson; and destruction, damage or vandalism of property.

"**(2)** The Attorney General shall establish guidelines for the collection of such data including the necessary evidence and criteria that must be present for a finding of manifest prejudice and procedures for carrying out the purposes of this section.

"**(3)** Nothing in this section creates a cause of action or a right to bring an action, including an action based on discrimination due to sexual orientation. As used in this section, the term 'sexual orientation' means consensual homosexuality or heterosexuality. This subsection does not limit any existing cause of action or right to bring an action, including any action under the Administrative Procedure Act [5 U.S.C.A. §§ 551 et seq., 701 et seq.] or the All Writs Act [28 U.S.C.A. § 1651].

"**(4)** Data acquired under this section shall be used only for research or statistical purposes and may not contain any information that may reveal the identity of an individual victim of a crime.

"**(5)** The Attorney General shall publish an annual summary of the data acquired under this section.

"**(c)** There are authorized to be appropriated such sums as may be necessary to carry out the provisions of this section through fiscal year 2002.

"**Sec. 2. (a)** Congress finds that—

"(1) the American family life is the foundation of American Society,

"(2) Federal policy should encourage the well-being, financial security, and health of the American family,

"(3) schools should not de-emphasize the critical value of American family life.

"**(b)** Nothing in this Act [this note] shall be construed, nor shall any funds appropriated to carry out the purpose of the Act [this note] be used, to promote or encourage homosexuality."

National Crime Information Center Project 2000

Pub.L. 101–647, Title VI, Subtitle B, Nov. 29, 1990, 104 Stat. 4823, provided that:

"**Sec. 611. Short title.**

"This section [subtitle] may be cited as the 'National Law Enforcement Cooperation Act of 1990'.

"**Sec. 612. Findings.**

"The Congress finds that—

"(1) cooperation among Federal, State and local law enforcement agencies is critical to an effective national response to the problems of violent crime and drug trafficking in the United States;

"(2) the National Crime Information Center, which links more than 16,000 Federal, State and local law enforcement agencies, is the single most important avenue of cooperation among law enforcement agencies;

"(3) major improvements to the National Crime Information Center are needed because the current system is more than twenty years old; carries much greater volumes of enforcement information; and at this time is unable to incorporate technological advances that would significantly improve its performance; and

"(4) the Federal Bureau of Investigation, working with State and local law enforcement agencies and private organizations, has developed a promising plan, 'NCIC 2000', to make the necessary upgrades to the National Crime Information Center that should meet the needs of United States law enforcement agencies into the next century.

"**Sec. 613. Authorization of appropriations.**

"There are authorized to be appropriated the following sums to implement the 'NCIC 2000' project:

"(1) $17,000,000 for fiscal year 1991;

"(2) $25,000,000 for fiscal year 1992;

"(3) $22,000,000 for fiscal year 1993;

"(4) $9,000,000 for fiscal year 1994; and

"(5) such sums as may be necessary for fiscal year 1995.

"**Sec. 614. Report.**

"By February 1 of each fiscal year for which funds for NCIC 2000 are requested, the Director of the Federal Bureau of Investigation shall submit a report to the Committees on the Judiciary of the Senate and House of Representatives that details the progress that has been made in implementing NCIC 2000 and a complete justification for the funds requested in the following fiscal year for NCIC 2000."

Parimutuel Licensing Simplification.

Pub.L. 100–413, Aug. 22, 1988, 102 Stat. 1101, provided that:

"**Section 1. Short title.**

"This Act [this note] may be cited as the 'Parimutuel Licensing Simplification Act of 1988'.

"**Sec. 2. Submission by association of State regulatory officials.**

"**(a) In general.**—An association of State officials regulating parimutuel wagering, designated for the purpose of this section by the Attorney General, may submit fingerprints to the Attorney General on behalf of any applicant for State license to participate in parimutuel wagering. In response to such a submission, the Attorney General may, to the extent provided by law, exchange, for licensing and employment purposes, identification and criminal history records with the State governmental bodies to which such applicant has applied.

"**(b) Definition.**—As used in this section, the term 'State' means a State of the United States, the District of Columbia, the Commonwealth of Puerto Rico, or any territory or possession of the United States.

"**Sec. 3. Effective date.**

"This Act shall take effect on July 1, 1989."

Rulemaking Relating to Authorization of Access to Federal Criminal Information Databases

Section 40601(b) of Pub.L. 103–322 provided that: "The Attorney General may make rules to carry out the subsection added to section 534 of title 28, United States Code, by subsection (a) [subsec. (e) of this section], after consultation with the officials charged with managing the National Crime Information Center and the Criminal Justice Information Services Advisory Policy Board."

Uniform Federal Crime Reporting Act of 1988

Section 7332 of Pub.L. 100–690 provided that:

"**(a) Short Title.**—This section [this note] may be cited as the 'Uniform Federal Crime Reporting Act of 1988'.

"**(b) Definitions.**—For purposes of this section, the term 'Uniform Crime Reports' means the reports authorized under section 534 of title 28, United States Code [this section], and administered by the Federal Bureau of Investigation which compiles nationwide criminal statistics for use in law enforcement administration, operation, and management and to assess the nature and type of crime in the United States.

"**(c) Establishment of system.**—

"**(1) In general.**—The Attorney General shall acquire, collect, classify, and preserve national data on Federal criminal offenses as part of the Uniform Crime Reports.

"**(2) Reporting by Federal agencies.**—All departments and agencies within the Federal government (including the Department of Defense) which routinely investigate complaints of criminal activity, shall report details about crime within their respective jurisdiction to the Attorney General in a uniform manner and on a form prescribed by the Attorney General. The reporting required by this subsection shall be limited to the reporting of those crimes comprising the Uniform Crime Reports.

"**(3) Distribution of data.**—The Attorney General shall distribute data received pursuant to paragraph (2), in the form of annual Uniform Crime Reports for the United States, to the President, Members of the Congress, State governments, and officials of localities and penal and other institutions participating in the Uniform Crime Reports program.

"**(d) Role of Federal Bureau of Investigation.**—The Attorney General may designate the Federal Bureau of Investigation as the lead agency for purposes of performing the functions authorized by this section and may appoint or establish such advisory and oversight boards as may be necessary to assist the Bureau in ensuring uniformity, quality, and maximum use of the data collected.

"**(e) Inclusion of offenses involving illegal drugs.**—The Director of the Federal Bureau of Investigation is authorized to classify offenses involving illegal drugs and drug trafficking as a part I crime in the Uniform Crime Reports.

"**(f) Authorization of appropriations.**—There are authorized to be appropriated $350,000 for fiscal year 1989 and such sums as may be necessary to carry out the provisions of this section after fiscal year 1989.

"**(g) Effective date.**—The provisions of this section shall be effective on January 1, 1989."

§ 535. Investigation of crimes involving Government officers and employees; limitations

(a) The Attorney General and the Federal Bureau of Investigation may investigate any violation of title 18 involving Government officers and employees—

(1) notwithstanding any other provision of law; and

(2) without limiting the authority to investigate any matter which is conferred on them or on a department or agency of the Government.

(b) Any information, allegation, or complaint received in a department or agency of the executive branch of the Government relating to violations of title 18 involving Government officers and employees shall be expeditiously reported to the Attorney General by the head of the department or agency, unless—

(1) the responsibility to perform an investigation with respect thereto is specifically assigned otherwise by another provision of law; or

(2) as to any department or agency of the Government, the Attorney General directs otherwise with respect to a specified class of information, allegation, or complaint.

(c) This section does not limit—

(1) the authority of the military departments to investigate persons or offenses over which the armed forces have jurisdiction under the Uniform Code of Military Justice (chapter 47 of title 10); or

(2) the primary authority of the Postmaster General to investigate postal offenses.

(Added Pub.L. 89–554, § 4(c), Sept. 6, 1966, 80 Stat. 616.)

HISTORICAL AND STATUTORY NOTES

Transfer of Functions

The office of Postmaster General of the Post Office Department was abolished and all functions, powers, and duties of the Postmaster General were transferred to the United States Postal Service by Pub.L. 91–375, § 4(a), Aug. 12, 1970, 84 Stat. 773, set out as a note under section 201 of Title 39, Postal Service.

§ 536. Positions in excepted service

All positions in the Federal Bureau of Investigation are excepted from the competitive service, and the incumbents of such positions occupy positions in the excepted service.

(Added Pub.L. 89–554, § 4(c), Sept. 6, 1966, 80 Stat. 617.)

§ 537. Expenses of unforeseen emergencies of a confidential character

Appropriations for the Federal Bureau of Investigation are available for expenses of unforeseen emergencies of a confidential character, when so specified in the appropriation concerned, to be spent under the direction of the Attorney General. The Attorney General shall certify the amount spent that he considers advisable not to specify, and his certification is a sufficient voucher for the amount therein expressed to have been spent.

(Added Pub.L. 89–554, § 4(c), Sept. 6, 1966, 80 Stat. 617.)

§ 538. Investigation of aircraft piracy and related violations

The Federal Bureau of Investigation shall investigate any violation of section 46314 or chapter 465 of title 49.

(Added Pub.L. 103–272, § 4(e)(1), July 5, 1994, 108 Stat. 1361.)

§ 539. Counterintelligence official reception and representation expenses

The Director of the Federal Bureau of Investigation may use funds available to the Federal Bureau of Investigation for counterintelligence programs to pay the expenses of hosting foreign officials in the United States under the auspices of the Federal Bureau of Investigation for consultation on counterintelligence matters.

(Added Pub.L. 99–569, Title IV, § 401(a), Oct. 27, 1986, 100 Stat. 3195.)

§ 540. Investigation of felonious killings of State or local law enforcement officers

The Attorney General and the Federal Bureau of Investigation may investigate felonious killings of officials and employees of a State or political subdivision thereof while engaged in or on account of the performance of official duties relating to the prevention, detection, investigation, or prosecution of an offense against the criminal laws of a State or political subdivision, when such investigation is requested by the head of the agency employing the official or employee killed, and under such guidelines as the Attorney General or his designee may establish.

(Added Pub.L. 100–690, Title VII, § 7331(a), Nov. 18, 1988, 102 Stat. 4468.)

§ 540A. Investigation of violent crimes against travelers

(a) In general.—At the request of an appropriate law enforcement official of a State or political subdivision, the Attorney General and Director of the Federal Bureau of Investigation may assist in the investigation of a felony crime of violence in violation of the law of any State in which the victim appears to have been selected because he or she is a traveler.

(b) Foreign travelers.—In a case in which the traveler who is a victim of a crime described in subsection (a) is from a foreign nation, the Attorney General and Director of the Federal Bureau of Investigation, and, when appropriate, the Secretary of State shall assist the prosecuting and law enforcement officials of a State or political subdivision to the fullest extent possible in securing from abroad such evidence or other information as may be needed for the effective investigation and prosecution of the crime.

(c) Definitions.—In this section—

(1) "felony crime of violence" means an offense punishable by more than one year in prison that has as an element the use, attempted use, or threatened use of physical force against the person of another.

(2) "State" means a State, the District of Columbia, and any commonwealth, territory, or possession of the United States.

(3) "traveler" means a victim of a crime of violence who is not a resident of the State in which the crime of violence occurred.

(Added Pub.L. 103–322, Title XXXII, § 320916(a), Sept. 13, 1994, 108 Stat. 2129, and amended Pub.L. 104–294, Title VI, § 604(b)(21), Oct. 11, 1996, 110 Stat. 3507.)

HISTORICAL AND STATUTORY NOTES

Effective Dates

1996 Acts. Amendment by section 604 of Pub.L. 104–294 effective Sept. 13, 1994, see section 604(d) of Pub.L. 104–294, set out as a note under section 13 of Title 18, Crimes and Criminal Procedure.

§ 540B. Investigation of serial killings

(a) In general.—The Attorney General and the Director of the Federal Bureau of Investigation may investigate serial killings in violation of the laws of a State or political subdivision, if such investigation is requested by the head of a law enforcement agency with investigative or prosecutorial jurisdiction over the offense.

(b) Definitions.—In this section:

(1) **Killing.**—The term "killing" means conduct that would constitute an offense under section 1111 of Title 18, if Federal jurisdiction existed.

(2) **Serial killings.**—The term "serial killings" means a series of three or more killings, not less than one of which was committed within the United States, having common characteristics such as to suggest the reasonable possibility that the crimes were committed by the same actor or actors.

(3) **State.**—The term "State" means a State of the United States, the District of Columbia, and any commonwealth, territory, or possession of the United States.

(Added Pub.L. 105–314, Title VII, § 701(a), Oct. 30, 1998, 112 Stat. 2986.)

CHAPTER 35—UNITED STATES ATTORNEYS

Sec.
541. United States attorneys.
542. Assistant United States attorneys.
543. Special attorneys.
544. Oath of office.
545. Residence.
546. Vacancies.
547. Duties.
548. Salaries.
549. Expenses.
550. Clerical assistants, messengers, and private process servers.

§ 541. United States attorneys

(a) The President shall appoint, by and with the advice and consent of the Senate, a United States attorney for each judicial district.

(b) Each United States attorney shall be appointed for a term of four years. On the expiration of his term, a United States attorney shall continue to perform the duties of his office until his successor is appointed and qualifies.

(c) Each United States attorney is subject to removal by the President.

(Added Pub.L. 89–554, § 4(c), Sept. 6, 1966, 80 Stat. 617.)

HISTORICAL AND STATUTORY NOTES

Prior Provisions

A prior Section 541, Acts June 25, 1948, c. 646, 62 Stat. 910; Mar. 18, 1959, Pub.L. 86–3, § 11(c), (d), 73 Stat. 9, which related to appointment, residence and tenure of marshals, was repealed by Pub.L. 89–554, § 8(a), Sept. 6, 1966, 80 Stat. 632, and reenacted in Section 561 of this title by Section 4(c) of Pub.L. 89–554.

§ 542. Assistant United States attorneys

(a) The Attorney General may appoint one or more assistant United States attorneys in any district when the public interest so requires.

(b) Each assistant United States attorney is subject to removal by the Attorney General.

(Added Pub.L. 89–554, § 4(c), Sept. 6, 1966, 80 Stat. 618.)

HISTORICAL AND STATUTORY NOTES

1948 Acts. Prior Section 502.—Based on Title 28, U.S.C., 1940, ed., §§ 483, 594 (May 28, 1896, c. 252, § 8, 29 Stat. 181; July 19, 1919, c. 24, § 1, 41 Stat. 209; Mar. 4, 1923, c. 295, 42 Stat. 1560; June 25, 1936, c. 804, 49 Stat. 1921).

Section consolidates sections 483 and 594 of Title 28, U.S.C., 1940 ed., relating to appointment of assistant United States attorneys.

Words "United States attorneys" were substituted for "district attorneys." (See reviser's note [now Revision Notes and Legislative Reports] under section 501 [now 541] of this title).

The exception of Alaska from the operation of such section 483 was omitted as covered by section 109 of Title 48, U.S.C., 1940 ed., Territories and Insular Possessions, authorizing appointment of assistant United States attorneys in Alaska.

Reference in such section 483 to "District of Columbia" was omitted. (See reviser's note [now Revision Notes and Legislative Reports] under section 501 [now 541] of this title).

The provisions of sections 483 and 594 of Title 28, U.S.C., 1940 ed., requiring the judges and United States attorneys to certify or evidence in writing the necessity for assistant United States attorneys in their respective districts, and specifying that such opinion of the judge shall state to the Attorney General the facts as distinguished from conclusions, showing the necessity therefor, were omitted. The Attorney General, as chief law enforcement officer, is in a better position to determine such necessity.

The salary provisions of such section 594 were omitted as covered by section 508 [now 548] of this title.

Changes were made in phraseology. 80th Congress House Report No. 308.

1966 Acts

Derivation:	United States Code	Revised Statutes and Statutes at Large
(a)	28 U.S.C. 502	[None]
(b)	28 U.S.C. 504(b) (2d sentence, as applicable to assistant United States attorneys)	[None]

In subsection (b), the word "is" is substituted for "shall be".

Prior Provisions

A prior section 542, Act June 25, 1948, c. 646, 62 Stat. 911, which related to appointment and tenure of deputies and assistants for United States marshals, was repealed by Pub.L. 89–554, § 8(a), Sept. 6, 1966, 80 Stat. 632, and reenacted in section 562 of this title by section 4(c) of Pub.L. 89–554.

§ 543. Special attorneys

(a) The Attorney General may appoint attorneys to assist United States attorneys when the public interest so requires.

(b) Each attorney appointed under this section is subject to removal by the Attorney General.

(Added Pub.L. 89–554, § 4(c), Sept. 6, 1966, 80 Stat. 618.)

HISTORICAL AND STATUTORY NOTES

Prior Provisions

A prior section 543, Act June 25, 1948, c. 646, 62 Stat. 911, which related to oath of office for United States Marshals, was repealed by Pub.L. 89–554, § 8(a), Sept. 6, 1966, 80 Stat. 632, and reenacted in section 563 of this title by section 4(c) of Pub.L. 89–554.

§ 544. Oath of office

Each United States attorney, assistant United States attorney, and attorney appointed under section 543 of this title, before taking office, shall take an oath to execute faithfully his duties.

(Added Pub.L. 89–554, § 4(c), Sept. 6, 1966, 80 Stat. 618.)

HISTORICAL AND STATUTORY NOTES

Prior Provisions

A prior section 544, Acts June 25, 1948, c. 646, 62 Stat. 911; Sept. 2, 1958, Pub.L. 85–856, 72 Stat. 1104, which related to bonds of United States marshals, was repealed by Pub.L. 89–554, § 8(a), Sept. 6, 1966, 80 Stat. 632, and reenacted in section 564 of this title by section 4(c) of Pub.L. 89–554.

§ 545. Residence

(a) Each United States attorney shall reside in the district for which he is appointed, except that these officers of the District of Columbia, the Southern District of New York, and the Eastern District of New York may reside within 20 miles thereof. Each assistant United States attorney shall reside in the district for which he or she is appointed or within 25 miles thereof. The provisions of this subsection shall not apply to any United States attorney or assistant United States attorney appointed for the Northern Mariana Islands who at the same time is serving in the same capacity in another district.

(b) The Attorney General may determine the official stations of United States attorneys and assistant United States attorneys within the districts for which they are appointed.

(Added Pub.L. 89–554, § 4(c), Sept. 6, 1966, 80 Stat. 618, and amended Pub.L. 95–530, § 1, Oct. 27, 1978, 92 Stat. 2028; Pub.L. 96–91, Oct. 25, 1979, 93 Stat. 700; Pub.L. 103–322, Title XXXII, § 320932, Sept. 13, 1994, 108 Stat. 2135.)

HISTORICAL AND STATUTORY NOTES

Prior Provisions

A prior section 545, Act June 25, 1948, c. 646, 62 Stat. 911, which related to vacancies in the office of the United States Marshal, was repealed by Pub.L. 89–554, § 8(a), Sept. 6, 1966, 80 Stat. 632, and reenacted in section 565 of this title by section 4(c) of Pub.L. 89–554.

§ 546. Vacancies

(a) Except as provided in subsection (b), the Attorney General may appoint a United States attorney for the district in which the office of United States attorney is vacant.

(b) The Attorney General shall not appoint as United States attorney a person to whose appointment by the President to that office the Senate refused to give advice and consent.

(c) A person appointed as United States attorney under this section may serve until the earlier of—

(1) the qualification of a United States attorney for such district appointed by the President under section 541 of this title; or

(2) the expiration of 120 days after appointment by the Attorney General under this section.

(d) If an appointment expires under subsection (c)(2), the district court for such district may appoint a United States attorney to serve until the vacancy is filled. The order of appointment by the court shall be filed with the clerk of the court.

(Added Pub.L. 89–554, § 4(c), Sept. 6, 1966, 80 Stat. 618, and amended Pub.L. 99–646, § 69, Nov. 10, 1986, 100 Stat. 3616.)

HISTORICAL AND STATUTORY NOTES

Prior Provisions

A prior section 546, Act June 25, 1948, c. 646, 62 Stat. 911, which related to the death of a marshal, was repealed by Pub.L. 89–554, § 8(a), Sept. 6, 1966, 80 Stat. 632, and reenacted in section 566 of this title by section 4(c) of Pub.L. 89–554.

§ 547. Duties

Except as otherwise provided by law, each United States attorney, within his district, shall—

(1) prosecute for all offenses against the United States;

(2) prosecute or defend, for the Government, all civil actions, suits or proceedings in which the United States is concerned;

(3) appear in behalf of the defendants in all civil actions, suits or proceedings pending in his district against collectors, or other officers of the revenue or customs for any act done by them or for the recovery of any money exacted by or paid to these officers, and by them paid into the Treasury;

(4) institute and prosecute proceedings for the collection of fines, penalties, and forfeitures incurred for violation of any revenue law, unless satisfied on investigation that justice does not require the proceedings; and

(5) make such reports as the Attorney General may direct.

(Added Pub.L. 89–554, § 4(c), Sept. 6, 1966, 80 Stat. 618.)

HISTORICAL AND STATUTORY NOTES

Prior Provisions

A prior section 547, Acts June 25, 1948, c. 646, 62 Stat. 912; Oct. 18, 1962, Pub.L. 87–845, § 8, 76A Stat. 699, which related to powers and duties of marshals, was repealed by Pub.L. 89–554, § 8(a), Sept. 6, 1966, 80 Stat. 632, and reenacted in section 569 of this title, by section 4(c) of Pub.L. 89–554.

§ 548. Salaries

Subject to sections 5315 through 5317 of title 5, the Attorney General shall fix the annual salaries of United States attorneys, assistant United States attorneys, and attorneys appointed under section 543 of this title at rates of compensation not in excess of the rate of basic compensation provided for Executive Level IV of the Executive Schedule set forth in section 5315 of title 5, United States Code.

(Added Pub.L. 89–554, § 4(c), Sept. 6, 1966, 80 Stat. 618, and amended Pub.L. 98–473, Title II, § 1701(a), Oct. 12, 1984, 98 Stat. 2184.)

HISTORICAL AND STATUTORY NOTES

Prior Provisions

A prior section 548, Act June 25, 1948, c. 646, 62 Stat. 912, which related to administration of oaths by marshals, was repealed by Pub.L. 89–554, § 8(a), Sept. 6, 1966, 80 Stat. 632.

Alaska, Canal Zone and Virgin Islands

Act Mar. 2, 1955, c. 9, § 2(b), 69 Stat. 10, provided that: "The salaries of United States attorneys and assistant United States attorneys for the districts of Alaska, Canal Zone, and the Virgin Islands are subject to the provisions of section 508 of title 28, United States Code [now this section]."

Compensation of Incumbent United States Attorneys and Assistant United States Attorneys

Pub.L. 88–426, § 306(a)(2), Aug. 14, 1962, 78 Stat. 428, as amended by Pub.L. 88–631, § 3(c), Oct. 6, 1964, 78 Stat. 1008, provided that: "Subject to section 303(f) and (g) of this Act [see sections 5315 to 5317 of Title 5, Government Organization and Employees], each incumbent United States attorney and assistant United States attorney shall be paid compensation at a rate equal to that of attorneys of comparable responsibility and professional qualifications, as determined by the Attorney General, whose compensation is prescribed in the General Schedule of the Classification Act of 1949, as amended [now covered by Chapter 51 and subchapter III of Chapter 53 of Title 5]."

Salary Increases

1969—Increase in the rates of pay of United States Attorneys and Assistant United States Attorneys whose annual salaries are fixed pursuant to this section, effective on the first day of the first pay period which begins on or after Dec. 27, 1969, by amounts equal, as nearly as may be practicable, to the increases provided pursuant to section 2 of Pub.L. 91–231, which raised corresponding rates by 6 percent, see Pub.L. 91–231, set out as a note under section 5332 of Title 5, Government Organization and Employees.

1967—Pub.L. 90–206, Title II, § 211(a), Dec. 16, 1967, 81 Stat. 633, provided that: "The rates of basic pay of United States attorneys and assistant United States attorneys whose annual salaries are fixed pursuant to section 548 of title 28, United States Code [this section] shall be increased, effective on the effective date of section 202 of this title [see Effective Dates of 1967 Amendments note under section 5332 of Title 5], by amounts equal, as nearly as may be practicable, to the increases provided by section 202(a) of this title [see section 5332(a) of Title 5] for corresponding rates of basic pay."

Section 211(a) of Pub.L. 90–206 effective as of the beginning of the first pay period which begins on or after Oct. 1, 1967, see section 220(a)(2) of Pub.L. 90–206, set out as a note under section 5332 of Title 5, Government Organization and Employees.

1966—Pub.L. 89–504, Title I, § 108(a), July 18, 1966, 80 Stat. 293, provided that: "The rates of basic compensation of assistant United States attorneys whose basic salaries are fixed pursuant to section 508 of title 28, United States Code [now this section], shall be increased, effective on the effective date of section 102 of this title [first of the first pay period beginning on or after July 1, 1966], by amounts equal, as nearly as may be practicable, to the increases provided by section 102(a) of this title [see section 5332(a) of Title 5] for corresponding rates of compensation."

Provision effective July 18, 1966, see section 109(1) of Pub.L. 89–504.

1965—Pub.L. 89–301, § 15(a), Oct. 29, 1965, 79 Stat. 1122, provided that: "The rates of basic compensation of assistant United States attorneys whose basic salaries are fixed pursuant to section 508 of title 28, United States Code [now this section], shall be increased by 3.6 per centum effective on the first day of the first pay period which begins on or after October 1, 1965."

1962—Pub.L. 87–793, § 1003(b), Oct. 11, 1962, 76 Stat. 866, provided that: "The rates of basic compensation of assistant United States attorneys whose basic salaries are fixed by section 508 of title 28, United States Code [now this section], shall be increased by 7½ per centum effective on the first day of the first pay period which begins on or after the date of enactment of this Act [Oct. 11, 1962]."

Salary Limitations

Acts Aug. 5, 1953, C. 328, Title II, § 202, 67 Stat. 375; July 2, 1954, C. 456, Title II, § 202, 68 Stat. 421, which prescribed salary limitations, were repealed by Pub.L. 89–554, § 8(a), Sept. 6, 1966, 80 Stat. 657.

§ 549. Expenses

Necessary office expenses of United States attorneys shall be allowed when authorized by the Attorney General.

(Added Pub.L. 89–554, § 4(c), Sept. 6, 1966, 80 Stat. 618.)

HISTORICAL AND STATUTORY NOTES

Prior Provisions

A prior section 549, Act June 25, 1948, c. 646, 62 Stat. 912, which related to the marshal's power as a sheriff, was repealed by Pub.L. 89–554, § 8(a), Sept. 6, 1966, 80 Stat. 632, and reenacted in section 570 of this title by section 4(c) of Pub.L. 89–554.

§ 550. Clerical assistants, messengers, and private process servers

The United States attorneys may employ clerical assistants, messengers, and private process servers on approval of the Attorney General.

(Added Pub.L. 89–554, § 4(c), Sept. 6, 1966, 80 Stat. 619, and amended Pub.L. 101–647, Title XXXVI, § 3626(a), Nov. 29, 1990, 104 Stat. 4965.)

HISTORICAL AND STATUTORY NOTES

Effective Dates

1990 Acts. Amendment by section 3626(a) of Pub.L. 101–647 effective 183 days after Nov. 29, 1990, see section 3631 of Pub.L. 101–647, set out as a note under section 3001 of this title.

Prior Provisions

A prior section 550, Acts June 25, 1948, c. 646, 62 Stat. 912; Sept. 9, 1959, Pub.L. 86–243, § 2, 73 Stat. 474, which related to disbursement of salaries and expenses, was repealed by Pub.L. 89–554, § 8(a), Sept. 6, 1966, 80 Stat. 632, and reenacted in section 571 of this title by section 4(c) of Pub.L. 89–554.

A prior section 551, Act June 25, 1948, c. 646, 62 Stat. 912, which related to the collection of fees by United States marshals, was repealed by Pub.L. 89–554, § 8(a), Sept. 6, 1966, 80 Stat. 632, and reenacted in section 572 of this title by section 4(c) of Pub.L. 89–554.

A prior section 552, Act June 25, 1948, c. 646, 62 Stat. 912, which related to the fixing of salaries of United States marshals, their deputies and assistants, by the Attorney General, was repealed by Pub.L. 89–554, § 8(a), Sept. 6, 1966, 80 Stat. 632, and reenacted in section 571 of this title by section 4(c) of Pub.L. 89–554.

A prior section 553, Acts June 25, 1948, c. 646, 62 Stat. 912; May 24, 1949, c. 139, § 72, 63 Stat. 100; Aug. 4, 1955, c. 550, 69 Stat. 492; Aug. 14, 1961, Pub.L. 87–139, § 5, 75 Stat. 340, which related to expenses of marshal, was repealed by Pub.L. 89–554, § 8(a), Sept. 6, 1966, 80 Stat. 632, and reenacted in section 567 of this title by section 4(c) of Pub.L. 89–554.

A prior section 554, Act June 25, 1948, c. 646, 62 Stat. 913, which related to the delivery of prisoners to the successor marshal, was repealed by Pub.L. 89–554, § 8(a), Sept. 6, 1966, 80 Stat. 632, and reenacted in section 573 of this title by section 4(c) of Pub.L. 89–554.

A prior section 555, Act June 25, 1948, c. 646, 62 Stat. 913, which related to the delivery of all unserved process to the successor marshal or his deputies, was repealed by Pub.L. 89–554, § 8(a), Sept. 6, 1966, 80 Stat. 632, and reenacted in section 574 of this title by section 4(c) of Pub.L. 89–554.

A prior section 556, Act June 25, 1948, c. 646, 62 Stat. 913, which related to the prohibition of the practice of law by a marshal or deputy marshal, was repealed by Pub.L. 89–554, § 8(a), Sept. 6, 1966, 80 Stat. 632, and reenacted in section 575 of this title by section 4(c) of Pub.L. 89–554.

CHAPTER 37—UNITED STATES MARSHALS SERVICE

Sec.
561. United States Marshals Service.
562. Vacancies.
563. Oath of office.
564. Powers as sheriff.
565. Expenses of the Service.
566. Powers and duties.
567. Collection of fees; accounting.
568. Practice of law prohibited.
569. Reemployment rights.
[570, 571. Repealed.]
[572. Renumbered.]
[572a to 574. Repealed.]
[575, 576. Renumbered.]

§ 561. United States Marshals Service

(a) There is hereby established a United States Marshals Service as a bureau within the Department of Justice under the authority and direction of the Attorney General. There shall be at the head of the United States Marshals Service (hereafter in this chapter referred to as the "Service") a Director who shall be appointed by the President, by and with the advice and consent of the Senate.

(b) The Director of the United States Marshals Service (hereafter in this chapter referred to as the "Director") shall, in addition to the powers and duties set forth in this chapter, exercise such other functions as may be delegated by the Attorney General.

(c) The President shall appoint, by and with the advice and consent of the Senate, a United States marshal for each judicial district of the United States and for the Superior Court of the District of Columbia, except that any marshal appointed for the Northern Mariana Islands may at the same time serve as marshal in another judicial district. Each United States marshal shall be an official of the Service and shall serve under the direction of the Director.

(d) Each marshal shall be appointed for a term of four years. A marshal shall, unless that marshal has resigned or been removed by the President, continue to perform the duties of that office after the end of that 4–year term until a successor is appointed and qualifies.

(e) The Director shall designate places within a judicial district for the official station and offices of each marshal. Each marshal shall reside within the district for which such marshal is appointed, except that—

(1) the marshal for the District of Columbia, for the Superior Court of the District of Columbia, and for the Southern District of New York may reside within 20 miles of the district for which the marshal is appointed; and

(2) any marshal appointed for the Northern Mariana Islands who at the same time is serving as marshal in another district may reside in such other district.

(f) The Director is authorized to appoint and fix the compensation of such employees as are necessary to carry out the powers and duties of the Service and may designate such employees as law enforcement officers in accordance with such policies and procedures as the Director shall establish pursuant to the applicable provisions of title 5 and regulations issued thereunder.

(g) The Director shall supervise and direct the United States Marshals Service in the performance of its duties.

(h) The Director may administer oaths and may take affirmations of officials and employees of the Service, but shall not demand or accept any fee or compensation therefor.

(i) There are authorized to be appropriated such sums as may be necessary to carry out the functions of the Service.

(Added Pub.L. 100–690, Title VII, § 7608(a)(1), Nov. 18, 1988, 102 Stat. 4512.)

HISTORICAL AND STATUTORY NOTES

Prior Provisions

A prior section 561, added Pub.L. 89–554, § 4(c), Sept. 6, 1966, 80 Stat. 619, and amended Pub.L. 95–530, § 2, Oct. 27, 1978, 92 Stat. 2028, which related to appointment, term, and residence of United States marshals, was repealed by Pub.L. 100–690, Title VII, § 7608(a)(1), Nov. 18, 1988, 102 Stat. 4512.

§ 562. Vacancies

(a) In the case of a vacancy in the office of a United States marshal, the Attorney General may designate a person to perform the functions of and act as marshal, except that the Attorney General may not designate to act as marshal any person who was appointed by the President to that office but with respect to such appointment the Senate has refused to give its advice and consent.

(b) A person designated by the Attorney General under subsection (a) may serve until the earliest of the following events:

(1) The entry into office of a United States marshal appointed by the President, pursuant to section 561(c).

(2) The expiration of the thirtieth day following the end of the next session of the Senate.

(3) If such designee of the Attorney General is appointed by the President pursuant to section 561(c), but the Senate refuses to give its advice and consent to the appointment, the expiration of the thirtieth day following such refusal.

(Added Pub.L. 100–690, Title VII, § 7608(a)(1), Nov. 18, 1988, 102 Stat. 4513.)

HISTORICAL AND STATUTORY NOTES

Prior Provisions

A prior section 562, added Pub.L. 89–554, § 4(c), Sept. 6, 1966, 80 Stat. 619, which related to appointment of deputy marshals and clerical assistants, was repealed by Pub.L. 100–690, Title VII, § 7608(a)(1), Nov. 18, 1988, 102 Stat. 4512. See section 561(f) of this title.

§ 563. Oath of office

The Director and each United States marshal and law enforcement officer of the Service, before taking office, shall take an oath or affirmation to faithfully execute the duties of that office.

(Added Pub.L. 100–690, Title VII, § 7608(a)(1), Nov. 18, 1988, 102 Stat. 4513.)

HISTORICAL AND STATUTORY NOTES

Prior Provisions

A prior section 563, added Pub.L. 89–554, § 4(c), Sept. 6, 1966, 80 Stat. 619, which specifically stated the oath of office to be taken, was repealed by Pub.L. 100–690, Title VII, § 7608(a)(1), Nov. 18, 1988, 102 Stat. 4512. See section 561(h) of this title.

§ 564. Powers as sheriff

United States marshals, deputy marshals and such other officials of the Service as may be designated by the Director, in executing the laws of the United States within a State, may exercise the same powers which a sheriff of the State may exercise in executing the laws thereof.

(Added Pub.L. 100–690, Title VII, § 7608(a)(1), Nov. 18, 1988, 102 Stat. 4513.)

HISTORICAL AND STATUTORY NOTES

Prior Provisions

A prior section 564, added Pub.L. 89–554, § 4(c), Sept. 6, 1966, 80 Stat. 619, which related to bonds of United States marshals, was repealed by Pub.L. 92–310, Title II, § 206(a)(1), June 6, 1972, 86 Stat. 203.

§ 565. Expenses of the Service

The Director is authorized to use funds appropriated for the Service to make payments for expenses incurred pursuant to personal services contracts and cooperative agreements, authorized by the Attorney General, for security guards and for the service of summons on complaints, subpoenas, and notices in lieu of services by United States marshals and deputy marshals.

(Added Pub.L. 100–690, Title VII, § 7608(a)(1), Nov. 18, 1988, 102 Stat. 4513.)

HISTORICAL AND STATUTORY NOTES

Prior Provisions

A prior section 565, added Pub.L. 89–554, § 4(c), Sept. 6, 1966, 80 Stat. 620, which related to filling vacancies, was repealed by Pub.L. 100–690, Title VII, § 7608(a)(1), Nov. 18, 1988, 102 Stat. 4512. See section 562 of this title.

§ 566. Powers and duties

(a) It is the primary role and mission of the United States Marshals Service to provide for the security and to obey, execute, and enforce all orders of the United States District Courts, the United States Courts of Appeals and the Court of International Trade.

(b) The United States marshal of each district is the marshal of the district court and of the court of appeals when sitting in that district, and of the Court of International Trade holding sessions in that district, and may, in the discretion of the respective courts, be required to attend any session of court.

(c) Except as otherwise provided by law or Rule of Procedure, the United States Marshals Service shall execute all lawful writs, process, and orders issued under the authority of the United States, and shall command all necessary assistance to execute its duties.

(d) Each United States marshal, deputy marshal, and any other official of the Service as may be designated by the Director may carry firearms and make arrests without warrant for any offense against the United States committed in his or her presence, or for any felony cognizable under the laws of the United States if he or she has reasonable grounds to believe that the person to be arrested has committed or is committing such felony.

(e)(1) The United States Marshals Service is authorized to—

(A) provide for the personal protection of Federal jurists, court officers, witnesses, and other threatened persons in the interests of justice where criminal intimidation impedes on the functioning of the judicial process or any other official proceeding; and

(B) investigate such fugitive matters, both within and outside the United States, as directed by the Attorney General.

(2) Nothing in paragraph (1)(B) shall be construed to interfere with or supersede the authority of other Federal agencies or bureaus.

(f) In accordance with procedures established by the Director, and except for public money deposited under section 2041 of this title, each United States marshal shall deposit public moneys that the marshal collects into the Treasury, subject to disbursement by the marshal. At the end of each accounting period, the earned part of public moneys accruing to the United States shall be deposited in the Treasury to the credit of the appropriate receipt accounts.

(g) Prior to resignation, retirement, or removal from office—

(1) a United States marshal shall deliver to the marshal's successor all prisoners in his custody and all unserved process; and

(2) a deputy marshal shall deliver to the marshal all process in the custody of the deputy marshal.

(h) The United States marshals shall pay such office expenses of United States Attorneys as may be directed by the Attorney General.

(Added Pub.L. 100–690, Title VII, § 7608(a)(1), Nov. 18, 1988, 102 Stat. 4514.)

HISTORICAL AND STATUTORY NOTES

Prior Provisions

A prior section 566, added Pub.L. 89–554, § 4(c), Sept. 6, 1966, 80 Stat. 620, and amended Pub.L. 92–310, Title II, § 206(b), June 6, 1972, 86 Stat. 203, which provided that upon death of a marshal his deputy or deputies perform his duties until a successor is appointed and qualifies, was repealed by Pub.L. 100–690, Title VII, § 7608(a)(1), Nov. 18, 1988, 102 Stat. 4512.

§ 567. Collection of fees; accounting

(a) Each United States marshal shall collect, as far as possible, his lawful fees and account for the same as public moneys.

(b) The marshal's accounts of fees and costs paid to a witness or juror on certificate of attendance issued as provided by sections 1825 and 1871 of this title may not be reexamined to charge him for an erroneous payment of the fees or costs.

(Added Pub.L. 89–554, § 4(c), Sept. 6, 1966, 80 Stat. 621, § 572; renumbered, § 567, Pub.L. 100–690, Title VII, § 7608(a)(2)(B), Nov. 18, 1988, 102 Stat. 4514.)

HISTORICAL AND STATUTORY NOTES

Prior Provisions

A prior section 567, added Pub.L. 89–554, § 4(c), Sept. 6, 1966, 80 Stat. 620, which related to expenses of marshals, was repealed by Pub.L. 100–690, Title VII, § 7608(a)(1), Nov. 18, 1988, 102 Stat. 4512. See section 565 of this title.

§ 568. Practice of law prohibited

A United States marshal or deputy marshal may not practice law in any court of the United States.

(Added Pub.L. 89–554, § 4(c), Sept. 6, 1966, 80 Stat. 621, § 575; renumbered § 568, Pub.L. 100–690, Title VII, § 7608(a)(2)(B), Nov. 18, 1988, 102 Stat. 4514.)

HISTORICAL AND STATUTORY NOTES

Prior Provisions

A prior section 568, added Pub.L. 89–554, § 4(c), Sept. 6, 1966, 80 Stat. 620, which related to availability of appropriations for transfer of prisoners to narcotic farms, was repealed by Pub.L. 100–690, Title VII, § 7608(a)(1), Nov. 18, 1988, 102 Stat. 4512.

§ 569. Reemployment rights

(a) A United States marshal for a judicial district who was appointed from a position in the competitive service (as defined in section 2102 of title 5) in the United States Marshals Service and who, for reasons other than misconduct, neglect of duty, or malfeasance, is removed from such office, is entitled to be reemployed in any vacant position in the competitive service in the United States Marshals Service at the same grade or pay level, or lower, as the individual's former position if—

(1) the individual is qualified for the vacant position; and

(2) the individual has made application for the position not later than ninety days after being removed from office as a United States marshal.

Such individual shall be so reemployed within thirty days after making such application or after being removed from office, whichever is later. An individual denied reemployment under this section in a position because the individual is not qualified for that position may appeal that denial to the Merit Systems Protection Board under section 7701 of title 5.

(b) Any United States marshal serving on the effective date of this section shall continue to serve for the remainder of the term for which such marshal was appointed, unless sooner removed by the President.

(Added Pub.L. 98–473, Title II, § 1211(a), Oct. 12, 1984, 98 Stat. 2163, § 576; renumbered § 569, Pub.L. 100–690, Title VII, § 7608(a)(2)(B), Nov. 18, 1988, 102 Stat. 4514.)

HISTORICAL AND STATUTORY NOTES

References in Text

The effective date of this section, referred to in subsec. (b), is Oct. 1, 1984. See Effective Dates note set out under this section.

Effective Dates

1984 Acts. Section 1212 of Pub.L. 98–473 provided that: "The amendments made by this subpart [subpart B (sections 1211, 1212) of part F of chapter XII of Title II of Pub.L. 98–473, which enacted this section] shall take effect on October 1, 1984."

Prior Provisions

A prior section 569, added Pub.L. 89–554, § 4(c), Sept. 6, 1966, 80 Stat. 620, and amended Pub.L. 95–598, Title II, § 221, Nov. 6, 1978, 92 Stat. 2662; Pub.L. 96–417, Title V, § 501(12), Oct. 10, 1980, 94 Stat. 1742; Pub.L. 99–466, § 3(a), Oct. 14, 1986, 100 Stat. 1191, which related to powers and duties generally and supervision by the Attorney General, was repealed by Pub.L. 100–690, Title VII, § 7608(a)(1), Nov. 18, 1988, 102 Stat. 4512. See section 566 of this title.

[§§ 570, 571. Repealed. Pub.L. 100–690, Title VII, § 7608(a)(1), Nov. 18, 1988, 102 Stat. 4512]

HISTORICAL AND STATUTORY NOTES

Section 570, added Pub.L. 89–554, § 4(c), Sept. 6, 1966, 80 Stat. 620, granted United States marshals the power of a sheriff in executing the laws of the United States in a State. See section 564 of this title.

Section 571, added Pub.L. 89–554, § 4(c), Sept. 6, 1966, 80 Stat. 621, and amended Pub.L. 95–598, Title II, §§ 222, 223, Nov. 6, 1978, 92 Stat. 2662; Pub.L. 97–258, § 2(g)(2), Sept. 13, 1982, 96 Stat. 1060, related to disbursement of salaries and moneys.

[§ 572. Renumbered § 567]

[§§ 572a to 574. Repealed. Pub.L. 100–690, Title VII, § 7608(a)(2)(A), Nov. 18, 1988, 102 Stat. 4514]

HISTORICAL AND STATUTORY NOTES

Section 572a, added Pub.L. 97–258, § 2(g)(3)(B), Sept. 13, 1982, 96 Stat. 1060, related to depositing of public moneys. See section 566(f) of this title.

Section 573, added Pub.L. 89–554, § 4(c), Sept. 6, 1966, 80 Stat. 621, related to delivery of prisoners to a successor. See section 566(g)(1) of this title.

Section 574, added Pub.L. 89–554, § 4(c), Sept. 6, 1966, 80 Stat. 621, related to delivery of unserved process to a successor. See section 566(g)(2) of this title.

[§§ 575, 576. Renumbered §§ 568, 569]

CHAPTER 39—UNITED STATES TRUSTEES

Sec.

581. United States trustees.
582. Assistant United States trustees.
583. Oath of office.
584. Official stations.
585. Vacancies.
586. Duties; supervision by Attorney General.
587. Salaries.
588. Expenses.
589. Staff and other employees.
589a. United States Trustee System Fund.

HISTORICAL AND STATUTORY NOTES

United States Trustee Pilot; Repeal of Bankruptcy Provisions Relating to United States Trustees

Pub.L. 95–598, Title IV, § 408, Nov. 6, 1978, 92 Stat. 2686, as amended by Pub.L. 98–166, Title II, § 200, Nov. 28, 1983, 97 Stat. 1081; Pub.L. 98–353, Title III, § 323, July 10, 1984, 98 Stat. 358; Pub.L. 99–429, Sept. 30, 1986, 100 Stat. 985; Pub.L. 99–500, Title I, § 101(b) [Title II, § 200], Oct. 18, 1986, 100 Stat. 1783–39, 1783–45, and Pub.L. 99–591, Title I, § 101(b), [Title II, § 2001, Oct. 30, 1986, 100 Stat. 3341–45; Pub.L. 99–554, Title III, § 307(a), Oct. 27, 1986, 100 Stat. 3125, which provided that the Attorney General conduct such studies and surveys as necessary to evaluate the needs, feasibility, and effectiveness of the United States trustee system, and report the result of such studies and surveys to the Congress, the President, and the Judicial Conference of the United States, beginning on or before January 3, 1980, and annually thereafter during the transition period; that not later than January 3, 1984, the Attorney General report to the Congress, the President, and the Judicial Conference of the United States, as to the feasibility, projected annual cost and effectiveness of the United States trustee system, as determined on the basis of the studies and surveys respecting the operation of the United States trustee system in the districts, together with recommendations as to the desirability and method of proceeding with implementation of the United States trustee system in all judicial districts of the United States; and that chapter 15 of title 11 of the United States Code [section 1501 et seq. of Title 11, Bankruptcy] and chapter 39 of title 28 of the United States Code [this chapter] are repealed, and all references to the United States trustee contained in title 28 of the United States Code [this title] are deleted, as of 30 days after the effective date of the Bankruptcy Judges, United States Trustees, and Family Farmer Bankruptcy Act of 1986 [see section 302 of Pub.L. 99–554, set out as a note under section 581 of this title], with service of any United States trustee, of any assistant United States trustee, and of any employee employed or appointed under the authority of such chapter 39 is terminated on such date, was repealed by Pub.L. 99–554, Title III, § 307(b), Oct. 27, 1986, 100 Stat. 3125 [set out as a note under section 581 of this title].

§ 581. United States trustees

(a) The Attorney General shall appoint one United States trustee for each of the following regions composed of Federal judicial districts (without regard to section 451):

(1) The judicial districts established for the States of Maine, Massachusetts, New Hampshire, and Rhode Island.

(2) The judicial districts established for the States of Connecticut, New York, and Vermont.

(3) The judicial districts established for the States of Delaware, New Jersey, and Pennsylvania.

(4) The judicial districts established for the States of Maryland, North Carolina, South Carolina, Virginia, and West Virginia and for the District of Columbia.

(5) The judicial districts established for the States of Louisiana and Mississippi.

(6) The Northern District of Texas and the Eastern District of Texas.

(7) The Southern District of Texas and the Western District of Texas.

(8) The judicial districts established for the States of Kentucky and Tennessee.

(9) The judicial districts established for the States of Michigan and Ohio.

(10) The Central District of Illinois and the Southern District of Illinois; and the judicial districts established for the State of Indiana.

(11) The Northern District of Illinois; and the judicial districts established for the State of Wisconsin.

(12) The judicial districts established for the States of Minnesota, Iowa, North Dakota, and South Dakota.

(13) The judicial districts established for the States of Arkansas, Nebraska, and Missouri.

(14) The District of Arizona.

(15) The Southern District of California; and the judicial districts established for the State of Hawaii, and for Guam and the Commonwealth of the Northern Mariana Islands.

(16) The Central District of California.

(17) The Eastern District of California and the Northern District of California; and the judicial district established for the State of Nevada.

(18) The judicial districts established for the States of Alaska, Idaho (exclusive of Yellowstone National Park), Montana (exclusive of Yellowstone National Park), Oregon, and Washington.

(19) The judicial districts established for the States of Colorado, Utah, and Wyoming (including those portions of Yellowstone National Park situated in the States of Montana and Idaho).

(20) The judicial districts established for the States of Kansas, New Mexico, and Oklahoma.

(21) The judicial districts established for the States of Alabama, Florida, and Georgia and for the Commonwealth of Puerto Rico and the Virgin Islands of the United States.

(b) Each United States trustee shall be appointed for a term of five years. On the expiration of his term, a United States trustee shall continue to perform the duties of his office until his successor is appointed and qualifies.

(c) Each United States trustee is subject to removal by the Attorney General.

(Added Pub.L. 95–598, Title II, § 224(a), Nov. 6, 1978, 92 Stat. 2662, and amended Pub.L. 99–554, Title I, § 111(a)–(c), Oct. 27, 1986, 100 Stat. 3090, 3091.)

HISTORICAL AND STATUTORY NOTES

Codifications

Section 408(c) of Pub.L. 95–598, as amended, which provided for the repeal of this section and the deletion of any references to United States Trustees in this title at a prospective date, was repealed by section 307(b) of Pub.L. 99–554. See note set out preceding this section.

Effective Dates

1978 Acts. Section effective Oct. 1, 1979, see section 402(c) of Pub.L. 95–598, as amended, set out as a note preceding section 101 of Title 11, Bankruptcy.

Effective Dates of 1986 Amendments; Transition and Administrative Provisions

Title III of Pub.L. 99–554, as amended Pub.L. 101–650, Title III, § 317(a), (c), Dec. 1, 1990, 104 Stat. 5115, 5116; Pub.L. 103–65, § 1, Aug. 6, 1993, 107 Stat. 311, provided that:

"Sec. 301. Incumbent United States Trustees.

"(a) Area for which appointed. Notwithstanding any paragraph of section 581(a) of title 28, United States Code, as in effect before the effective date of this Act, a United States trustee serving in such office on the effective date of this Act shall serve the remaining term of such office as United States trustee for the region specified in a paragraph of such section, as amended by this Act, that includes the site at which the primary official station of the United States trustee is located immediately before the effective date of this Act.

"(b) Term of office. Notwithstanding section 581(b) of title 28, United States Code, as in effect before the effective date of this Act, the term of office of any United States trustee serving in such office on the date of the enactment of this Act [Oct. 27, 1986] shall expire—

"(1) 2 years after the expiration date of such term of office under such section, as so in effect, or

"(2) 4 years after the date of the enactment of this Act [Oct. 27, 1986],

whichever occurs first.

"Sec. 302. Effective dates; Application of Amendments.

"(a) General effective date. Except as provided in subsections (b), (c), (d), (e), and (f), this Act and the amendments made by this Act [see Short Title of 1986 Amendment note set out under this section] shall take effect 30 days after the date of the enactment of this Act [Oct. 27, 1986].

"(b) Amendments relating to bankruptcy judges and incumbent United States trustees. Subtitle A of title I [amending sections 152 and 156 of this title and provisions set out as a note under section 152 of this title], and sections 301 [set out as a note under section 581 of this title] and 307(a) [amending provisions formerly set out as a note preceding section 581 of this title], shall take effect on the date of the enactment of this Act [Oct. 27, 1986].

"(c) Amendments relating to family farmers. (1) The amendments made by subtitle B of title II [enacting sections 1201 to 1231 of Title 11, Bankruptcy, and amending sections 101, 103, 108, 109, 303, 321, 322, 327, 329, 330, 346, 347, 348, 362, 363, 364, 365, 502, 523, 524, 546, 557, 706, 726, 727, 728, 1106, 1112, 1306, and 1307 of Title 11] shall not apply with respect to cases commenced under title 11 of the United States Code before the effective date of this Act.

"(2) Section 1202 of title 11 of the United States Code (as added by the amendment made by section 255 of this Act) [section 1202 of Title 11, Bankruptcy] shall take effect on the effective date of this Act and before the amendment made by section 227 of this Act [amending sections 1202 of Title 11].

"(3) Until the amendments made by subtitle A of title II of this Act [enacting section 307 of Title 11, amending sections 101, 102, 105, 303, 321, 322, 324, 326, 327, 330, 341, 343, 345, 701, 703, 704, 705, 707, 727, 1102, 1104, 1105, 1112, 1129, 1163, 1202, 1302, 1307, and 1326 of Title 11, and repealing sections 1501 to 151326 of Title 11] become effective in a district and apply to a case, for purposes of such case—

"(A)(i) any reference in section 326(b) of title 11 of the United States Code [section 326(b) of Title 11] to chapter 13 of title 11 of the United States Code [section 1301 et seq. of Title 11] shall be deemed to be a reference to chapter 12 or chapter 13 of title 11 of the United States Code [sections 1201 et seq. or 1301 et seq. of Title 11],

"(ii) any reference in such section 326(b) [section 326(b) of Title 11] to section 1302(d) of title 11 of the United States Code [section 1302(d) of Title 11] shall be deemed to be a reference to section 1302(d) of title 11 of the United States Code [section 1302(d) of Title 11] or section 586(b) of title 28 of the United States Code [section 586(b) of this title], and

"(iii) any reference in such section 326(b) [section 326(b) of Title 11] to section 1302(a) of title 11 of the United States Code [section 1302(a) of Title 11] shall be deemed to be a reference to section 1202(a) or section 1302(a) of title 11 of the United States Code [section 1202(a) or 1302(a) of Title 11], and

"(B)(i) the first two references in section 1202(a) of title 11 of the United States Code (as added by the amendment made by section 255 of this Act) [section 1202(a) of Title 11] to the United States trustee shall be deemed to be a reference to the court, and

"(ii) any reference in such section 1202(a) [section 1202(a) of Title 11] to section 586(b) of title 28 of the United States Code [section 586(b) of this title] shall be deemed to be a reference to section 1202(c) of title 11 of the United States Code (as so added) [section 1202(c) of Title 11].

"(d) Application of amendments to judicial districts.

"(1) Certain regions not currently served by United States trustees. (A)The amendments made by subtitle A of title II of this Act [enacting section 307 of Title 11, amending sections 101, 102, 105, 303, 321, 322, 324, 326, 327, 330, 341, 343, 345, 701, 703, 704, 705, 707, 727, 1102, 1104, 1105, 1112, 1129, 1163, 1202, 1302, 1307, and 1326 of Title 11, and repealing sections 1501 to 151326 of Title 11], and section 1930(a)(6) of title 28 of the United States Code (as added by section 117(4) of this Act) [section 1930(a)(6) of this title], shall not—

"(i) become effective in or with respect to a judicial district specified in subparagraph (B) until, or

"(ii) apply to cases while pending in such district before,

the expiration of the 270-day period beginning on the effective date of this Act or of the 30-day period beginning on the date the Attorney General certifies under section 303 of this Act the region specified in a paragraph of section 581(a) of Title 28, United States Code, as amended by section 111(a) of this Act [subsec. (a) of this section], that includes such district, whichever occurs first.

"(B) Subparagraph (A) applies to the following:

"(i) The judicial district established for the Commonwealth of Puerto Rico.

"(ii) The District of Connecticut.

"(iii) The judicial districts established for the State of New York (other than the Southern District of New York).

"(iv) The District of Vermont.

"(v) The judicial districts established for the State of Pennsylvania.

"(vi) The judicial district established for the Virgin Islands of the United States.

"(vii) The District of Maryland.

"(viii) The judicial districts established for the State of North Carolina.

"(ix) The District of South Carolina.

"(x) The judicial districts established for the State of West Virginia.

"(xi) The Western District of Virginia.

"(xii) The Eastern District of Texas.

"(xiii) The judicial districts established for the State of Wisconsin.

"(xiv) The judicial districts established for the State of Iowa.

"(xv) The judicial districts established for the State of New Mexico.

"(xvi) The judicial districts established for the State of Oklahoma.

"(xvii) The District of Utah.

"(xviii) The District of Wyoming (including those portions of Yellowstone National Park situated in the States of Montana and Idaho).

"(xix) The judicial districts established for the State of Alabama.

"(xx) The judicial districts established for the State of Florida.

"(xxi) The judicial districts established for the State of Georgia.

"(2) **Certain remaining judicial districts not currently served by United States trustees.** (A) The amendments made by subtitle A of title II of this Act [enacting section 307 of Title 11, amending sections 101, 102, 105, 303, 321, 322, 324, 326, 327, 330, 341, 343, 345, 701, 703, 704, 705, 707, 727, 1102, 1104, 1105, 1112, 1129, 1163, 1202, 1302, 1307, and 1326 of Title 11, and repealing sections 1501 to 151326 of Title 11], and section 1930(a)(6) of title 28 of the United States Code (as added by section 117(4) of this Act) [section 1930(a)(6) of this title], shall not—

"(i) become effective in or with respect to a judicial district specified in subparagraph (B) until, or

"(ii) apply to cases while pending in such district before,

the expiration of the 2–year period beginning on the effective date of this Act or of the 30–day period beginning on the date the Attorney General certifies under section 303 of this Act the region specified in a paragraph of section 581(a) of title 28, United States Code, as amended by section 111(a) of this Act [subsec. (a) of this section], that includes such district, whichever occurs first.

"(B) Subparagraph (A) applies to the following:

"(i) The judicial districts established for the State of Louisiana.

"(ii) The judicial districts established for the State of Mississippi.

"(iii) The Southern District of Texas and the Western District of Texas.

"(iv) The judicial districts established for the State of Kentucky.

"(v) The judicial districts established for the State of Tennessee.

"(vi) The judicial districts established for the State of Michigan.

"(vii) The judicial districts established for the State of Ohio.

"(viii) The judicial districts established for the State of Illinois (other than the Northern District of Illinois).

"(ix) The judicial districts established for the State of Indiana.

"(x) The judicial districts established for the State of Arkansas.

"(xi) The judicial districts established for the State of Nebraska.

"(xii) The judicial districts established for the State of Missouri.

"(xiii) The District of Arizona.

"(xiv) The District of Hawaii.

"(xv) The judicial district established for Guam.

"(xvi) The judicial district established for the Commonwealth of the Northern Mariana Islands.

"(xvii) The judicial districts established for the State of California (other than the Central District of California).

"(xviii) The District of Nevada.

"(xix) The District of Alaska.

"(xx) The District of Idaho.

"(xxi) The District of Montana.

"(xxii) The District of Oregon.

"(xxiii) The judicial districts established for the State of Washington.

"(3) **Judicial districts for the States of Alabama and North Carolina.** (A) Notwithstanding paragraphs (1) and (2), and any other provision of law, the amendments made by subtitle A of title II of this Act [enacting section 307 of Title 11, amending sections 101, 102, 105, 303, 321, 322, 324, 326, 327, 330, 341, 343, 345, 701, 703, 704, 705, 707, 727, 1102, 1104, 1105, 1112, 1129, 1163, 1202, 1302, 1307, and 1326 of Title 11, and repealing sections 1501 to 151326 of Title 11], and section 1930(a)(6) of title 28 of the United States Code (as added by section 117(4) of this Act) [section 1930(a)(6) of this title], shall not—

"(i) become effective in or with respect to a judicial district specified in subparagraph (E) until, or

"(ii) apply to cases while pending in such district before,

such district elects to be included in a bankruptcy region established in section 581(a) of Title 28, United States Code, as amended by section 111(a) of this Act [subsec. (a) of this section], or October 1, 2002, whichever occurs first, except that the amendment to section 105(a) of title 11, United States Code [section 105(a) of Title 11], shall become effective as of the date of the enactment of the Federal Courts Study Committee Implementation Act of 1990 [Dec. 1, 1990].

"(B) Any election under subparagraph (A) shall be made upon a majority vote of the chief judge of such district and each bankruptcy judge in such judicial district in favor of such election.

"(C) Notice that an election has been made under subparagraph (A) shall be given, not later than 10 days after such election, to the Attorney General and the appropriate Federal Circuit Court of Appeals for such district.

"(D) Any election made under subparagraph (A) shall become effective on the date the amendments made by subtitle A of title II of this Act become effective in the region that includes such district or 30 days after the Attorney General receives the notice required under subparagraph (C), whichever occurs later.

"(E) Subparagraph (A) applies to the following:

"(i) The judicial districts established for the State of Alabama.

"(ii) The judicial districts established for the State of North Carolina.

"(F)(i) Subject to clause (ii), with respect to cases under chapters 7, 11, 12, and 13 of title 11, United States Code [sections 701 et seq., 1101 et seq., 1201 et seq., and 1301 et seq., respectively, of Title 11]—

"(I) commenced before the effective date of this Act, and

"(II) pending in a judicial district in the State of Alabama or the State of North Carolina before any election made under subparagraph (A) by such district becomes effective or October 1, 2002, whichever occurs first,

the amendments made by section 113 [amending section 586 of this title] and subtitle A of title II of this Act, and section 1930(a)(6) of title 28 of the United States Code (as added by section 117(4) of this Act) [section 1930(a)(6) of this title], shall not apply until October 1, 2003, or the expiration of the 1-year period beginning on the date such election becomes effective, whichever occurs first.

"(ii) For purposes of clause (i), the amendments made by section 113 [amending section 586 of this title] and subtitle A of title II of this Act, and section 1930(a)(6) of title 28 of the United States Code (as added by section 117(4) of this Act) [section 1930(a)(6) of this title], shall not apply with respect to a case under chapter 7, 11, 12, or 13 of title 11, United States Code [sections 701 et seq., 1101 et seq., 1201 et seq., and 1301 et seq., respectively, of Title II], if—

"(I) the trustee in the case files the final report and account of administration of the estate, required under section 704 of such title [section 704 of Title 11], or

"(II) a plan is confirmed under section 1129, 1225, or 1325 of such title [section 1129, 1225, or 1325, respectively of Title 11],

before October 1, 2003, or the expiration of the 1-year period beginning on the date such election becomes effective, whichever occurs first.

"(G) Notwithstanding section 589a of title 28, United States Code, as added by section 115 of this Act [section 589a of this title], funds collected as a result of the amendments made by section 117 of this Act [amending section 1930 of this title] in a judicial district in the State of Alabama or the State of North Carolina under section 1930(a) of title 28, United States Code [section 1930(a) of this title], before the date the amendments made by subtitle A of title II of this Act take effect in such district shall be deposited in the general receipts of the Treasury.

"(H) The repeal made by section 231 of this Act [repealing chapter 15 of Title 11] shall not apply in or with respect to the Northern District of Alabama until March 1, 1987, or the effective date of any election made under subparagraph (A) by such district, whichever occurs first.

"(I) In any judicial district in the State of Alabama or the State of North Carolina that has not made the election described in subparagraph (A), any person who is appointed under regulations issued by the Judicial Conference of the United States to administer estates in cases under title 11 of the United States Code may—

"(i) establish, maintain, and supervise a panel of private trustees that are eligible and available to serve as trustees in cases under title 11, United States Code, and

"(ii) supervise the administration of cases and trustees in cases under chapters 7, 11, 12, and 13 of title 11, United States Code [sections 701 et seq., 1101 et seq., 1201 et seq., and 1301 et seq., respectively, of Title II],

until the amendments made by subtitle A of title II take effect in such district.

"(e) **Application of United States Trustee System and quarterly fees to certain cases.**

"(1) **In general.** Subject to paragraph (2), with respect to cases under chapters 7, 11, 12, and 13 of title 11, United States Code [sections 701 et seq., 1101 et seq., 1201 et seq., and 1301 et seq., respectively, of Title 11]—

"(A) commenced before the effective date of this Act, and

"(B) pending in a judicial district referred to in section 581(a)of title 28, United States Code, as amended by section 111(a) of this Act [subsec. (a) of this section], for which a United States trustee is not authorized before the effective date of this Act to be appointed,

the amendments made by section 113 [amending section 586 of this title] and subtitle A of title II of this Act [enacting section 307 of Title 11, amending sections 101, 102, 105, 303, 321, 322, 324, 326, 327, 330, 341, 343, 345, 701, 703, 704, 705, 707, 727, 1102, 1104, 1105, 1112, 1129, 1163, 1202, 1302, 1307, and 1326 of Title 11, and repealing sections 1501 to 151326 of Title 11], and section 1930(a)(6) of title 28 of the United States Code (as added by section 117(4) of this Act) [section 1930(a)(6) of this title], shall not apply until the expiration of the 3-year period beginning on the effective date of this Act, or of the 1-year period beginning on the date the Attorney General certifies under section 303 of this Act the region specified in a paragraph of such section 581(a), as so amended [subsec. (a) of this section], that includes such district, whichever occurs first.

"(2) **Amendments inapplicable.** For purposes of paragraph (1), the amendments made by section 113 [amending section 586 of this title] and subtitle A of title II of this Act, and section 1930(a)(6) of title 28 of the United States Code (as added by section 117(4) of this Act) [section 1930(a)(6) of this title], shall not apply with respect to a case under chapter 7, 11, 12, or 13 of title 11, United States Code [section 701 et seq., 1101 et seq., 1201 et seq., or 1301 et seq., respectively, of Title 11], if—

"(A) the trustee in the case files the final report and account of administration of the estate, required under section 704 of such title [section 704 of Title 11], or

"(B) a plan is confirmed under section 1129, 1225, or 1325 of such title [section 1129, 1225, or 1325, respectively, of Title 11],

before the expiration of the 3-year period, or the expiration of the 1-year period, specified in paragraph (1), whichever occurs first.

"(3) **Rule of construction regarding fees for cases.** This Act [see Short Title of 1986 Amendments note set out under this section] and the amendments made by section 117(4) of this Act [amending section 1930 of this title] shall not be construed to require the payment of a fee under paragraph (6) of section 1930(a) of Title 28, United States Code [section 1930(a) of this title], in a case under Title 11 of the United States Code for any conduct or period occurring before such paragraph becomes effective in the district in which such case is pending.

"(f) **Repeal of Chapter 12 of Title 11.** Chapter 12 of title 11 of the United States Code [section 1201 et seq. of Title 11] is repealed on October 1, 1998. All cases commenced or pending under chapter 12 of title 11, United States Code, and all matters and proceedings in or relating to such cases, shall be conducted and determined under such chapter as if such chapter had not been repealed. The substantive rights of parties in connection with such cases, matters, and proceedings shall continue to be governed under the laws applicable to such cases, matters, and proceedings as if such chapter had not been repealed.

"**Sec. 303.**—Certification of judicial districts; notice and publication of certification.

"(a) **Certification by Attorney General.** The Attorney General may certify in writing a region specified in a paragraph of section 581(a) of title 28, United States Code (other than paragraph (16)), as amended by section 111(a) of this Act [subsec. (a) of this section], to the appropriate court of appeals of the United States, for the purpose of informing such court that certain amendments made by this Act will become effective in accordance with section 302 of this Act.

"(b) **Notice and publication of certification.** Whenever the Attorney General transmits a certification under subsection (a), the Attorney General shall simultaneously—

"(1) transmit a copy of such certification to the Speaker of the House of Representatives and to the President pro tempore of the Senate, and

"(2) publish such certification in the Federal Register.

"**Sec. 304. Administrative provisions.**

"(a) **Cooperative arrangements.** The Attorney General and the Director of the Administrative Office of the United States Courts may enter into agreements under which United States trustees may—

"(1) use—

"(A) the services, equipment, personnel, records, reports, and data compilations, in any form, of the courts of the United States, and

"(B) the facilities of such courts, and

"(2) cooperate in the use by the courts of the United States of—

"(A) the services, equipment, personnel, records, reports, and data compilations, in any form, of United States trustees, and

"(B) the facilities of such trustees,

to prevent duplication during the 2-year period beginning on the effective date of this Act.

"(b) **Information and documents relating to bankruptcy cases and United States trustees.** The Director of the Administrative Office of the United States Courts shall make available to United States trustees, at the request of the Attorney General and on a continuing basis, all records, reports, and data compilations relating to—

"(1) cases and proceedings under title 11 of the United States Code [Title 11, Bankruptcy], and

"(2) the duties of United States trustees under titles 11 and 28 of the United States Code [Title 11 and this title].

"**Sec. 305. Application of certain Bankruptcy Rules.**

"(a) **Rules relating to the United States Trustee System.** If a United States trustee is not authorized, before the effective date of this Act to be appointed for a judicial district referred to in section 581(a) of title 28, United States Code, as amended by section 111(a) of this Act [subsec. (a) of this section], then part X of the Bankruptcy Rules [set out in Title 11, Bankruptcy] shall not apply to cases in such district until the amendments made by subtitle A of title II of this Act [Pub.L. 99–554, Title II, §§ 201 to 231, see tables for classification] become effective under section 302 of this Act in such district.

"(b) **Rules relating to Chapter 12 of Title 11.** The rules prescribed under section 2075 of title 28, United States Code [section 2075 of this title], and in effect on the date of the enactment of this Act [Oct. 27, 1986] shall apply to cases filed under chapter 12 of title 11, United States Code [section 1201 et seq. of Title 11, Bankruptcy], to the extent practicable and not inconsistent with the amendments made by title II of this Act [Pub.L. 99–554, Title II, §§ 201 to 283, see tables for classification].

"**Sec. 306. Salary of incumbent United States trustees.**

"For service as a United States trustee in the period beginning on the effective date of this Act and ending on the expiration under section 301 of this Act of their respective terms of office, the salary payable to United States trustees serving in such offices on the effective date of this Act shall be fixed in accordance with section 587 of title 28, United States Code, as amended by section 114(a) of this Act [section 587 of this title].

"**Sec. 307. Preservation of United States Trustee System during pendency of legislation; repealer.**

"(a) **Temporary delay of Repeal of United States Trustee System.** Effective immediately before November 10, 1986, section 408(c) of the Act of November 6, 1978 (Pub.L. 95–598; 92 Stat. 2687) [formerly set out as a note preceding this section], is amended by striking out 'November 10, 1986' and inserting in lieu thereof '30 days after the effective date of the Bankruptcy Judges, United States Trustees, and Family Farmer Bankruptcy Act of 1986 [Pub.L. 99–554]'.

"(b) **Conforming amendment.** Section 408 of the Act of November 6, 1978 (Pub.L. 95–598; 92 Stat. 2687) [formerly set out as a note preceding this section], is repealed.

[Section 302(b) of Pub.L. 99–554 provided in part that the amendment by subsec. (a) is effective Oct. 27, 1986.]

"**Sec. 308. Consideration of current private trustees for appointment by United States trustees.**

"(a) **Trustees in bankruptcy cases under Chapter 7.** It is the sense of the Congress that individuals who are serving before the effective date of this Act, as trustees in cases under chapter 7 of title 11, United States Code [section 701 et seq. of Title 11, Bankruptcy], should be considered by United States trustees for appointment under section 586(a)(1) of title 28, United States Code [section 586(a)(1) of this title], to the panels of private trustees that are established as a result of the amendments made by this Act [see Short Title of 1986 Amendments note under this section].

"(b) **Standing trustees in bankruptcy cases under Chapter 13.** It is the sense of the Congress that individuals who are serving before the effective date of this Act, as standing trustees in cases under chapter 13 of title 11, United States Code [section 1301 et seq. of Title 11], should be considered by the United States trustees for appointment under section 586(b) of title 28, United States Code [section 586(b) of this title], as standing trustees who are appointed as a result of the amendments made by this Act [see Short Title of 1986 Amendments note set out under this section].

"**Sec. 309. Appointment of United States trustees by the Attorney General.**

"It is the sense of the Congress that individuals otherwise qualified who are serving, before the effective date of this Act, as estate administrators under title 11 of the United States Code [Title 11, Bankruptcy] should be considered by the Attorney General for appointment under sections 581 and 582 of title 28, United States Code [this section and section 582 of this title], to new positions of United States trustee and assistant United States trustee resulting from the amendments made by this Act [see Short Title of 1986 Amendments note set out under this section].

"**Sec. 310. Electronic case management demonstration project.**

"(a) **Establishment of project.** Not later than 1 year after the effective date of this Act, the Director of the Executive Office for United States Trustees, in consultation with the Director of the Administrative Office of the United States Courts, shall establish an electronic case management demonstration project to be carried out in 3 Federal judicial districts that have a sufficiently large and varied bankruptcy caseload so as to provide a meaningful evaluation of the cost and effectiveness of such system. A contract for such project shall be awarded—

"(1) on the basis of competitive bids submitted by qualified nongovernmental entities that are able to design an automated joint information system for use by the United States courts and by United States trustees, and

"(2) in accordance with the Federal Property and Administrative Services Act of 1949 [see Short Title note under 40 U.S.C.A. § 471], the Office of Federal Procurement Policy Act [see Short Title note under 41 U.S.C.A. § 401], and title 31 of the United States Code.

"(b) **Study by General Accounting Office.** Not later than 1 year after the electronic case management system begins to operate in all of the judicial districts participating in the demonstration project carried out under subsection (a), the General Accounting Office shall conduct a study to compare the cost and effectiveness of such system with the cost and effectiveness of case management systems used in Federal judicial districts that are not participating in such project.

"(c) **Term of project.** The demonstration project required by subsection (a) shall be carried out until—

"(1) the expiration of the 2-year period beginning on the date the electronic case management system begins to operate in all of the judicial districts participating in such project, or

"(2) legislation is enacted to extend, expand, modify, or terminate the operation of such project,

whichever occurs first.

"(d) **Use by clerks of the courts.** The electronic case management system demonstrated under the project required by subsection (a) shall provide the clerk of court in each district in which such system is operated, with a means of—

"(1) maintaining a complete electronic case file of all relevant information contained in petitions and schedules (and any amendments thereto) relating to debtors in cases under title 11 of the United States Code [Title 11, Bankruptcy], including—

"(A) a complete list of creditors in each such case, as listed by the debtor,

"(B) a complete list of assets scheduled by the debtor, the value of such asset, and any action taken by the trustee or debtor in possession with regard to such asset during the pendency of such case,

"(C) a complete list of debts and, with respect to each debt—

"(i) any priority of such debt under title 11 of the United States Code,

"(ii) whether such debt is secured or unsecured, and

"(iii) whether such debt is contingent or noncontingent, and

"(D) the debtor's statements of current expenses and income, and

"(2) maintaining all calendars and dockets and producing all notices required to be sent in cases under title 11 of the United States Code.

"(e) **Use by United States trustees.** The electronic case management system demonstrated under the project required by subsection (a) shall provide, at a minimum, the United States trustee in each district in which such system is operated with—

"(1) complete electronic case files which contain, in addition to the information listed in subsection (d), records of case openings, case closings, hearings, and the filing of all motions, trustee appointments, pleadings, and responses, as well as a record of the responses by the United States trustee to those motions, trustee appointments, and pleadings,

"(2) a means to generate standardized forms for motions, appointments, pleadings, and responses,

"(3) a means to generate standard management reports and letters on an exception basis,

"(4) a means to maintain accounting records, reports, and information required to be maintained by debtors in possession and trustees in cases under title 11 of the United States Code,

"(5) a means to calculate and record distribution to creditors, final applications and orders for distribution, and final case closing reports, and

"(6) a means to monitor the payment of filing and other required fees.

"(f) **Availability to certain governmental entities.** Unlimited access to information maintained in the electronic case management system demonstrated under the project required by subsection (a) shall be provided at no charge to the following:

"(1) The Congress.

"(2) The Executive Office for the United States Trustees.

"(3) The Administrative Office of the United States Courts.

"(4) The clerks of the courts in judicial districts in which such system is operated and persons who review case information, in accordance with section 107(a) of title 11, United States Code [section 107(a) of Title 11], in the offices of the clerks.

"(5) The judges on the bankruptcy and district courts in districts in which such system is operated.

"(6) Trustees in cases pending in districts in which such system is operated.

"(g) **Fees for other users.** (1) The entity which is awarded a contract to provide the electronic case management system demonstrated under this project may, under guidelines established by the Director of the Executive Office for the United States Trustees in the provisions of such contract, collect reasonable fees from assets of the estate of the debtor in bankruptcy for providing notices and services to the court and trustees under the demonstration project.

"(2) Access to information maintained in electronic case files pursuant to the demonstration project may be provided to persons other than those specified in subsection (f), but such access shall be limited to viewing such information only. A reasonable charge for such access may be collected by the entity which is awarded a contract under this section, in accordance with the guidelines established by the Director of the Executive Office for the United States Trustees in such contract. A reasonable portion of any charge so collected may be required by the Director to be remitted to the Executive Office for United States Trustees and deposited in the United States Trustee System Fund established in section 589a of title 28, United States Code [section 589a of this title].

"(h) **Security.** Access provided under subsection (f) to an entity or an individual shall be subject to such security limitations as may be imposed by the Congress or the head of the affected entity.

"**Sec. 311. Cases pending under the Bankruptcy Act.**

"At the end of one calendar year following the date the amendments made by subtitle A of title II of this Act [amendments by Pub.L. 99–554, Title II, §§ 201 to 231, which were approved Oct. 27, 1986, see tables for classification] take effect in a district in which any case is still pending under the Bankruptcy Act [section 1 et seq. of former Title 11, Bankruptcy, see notes set out preceding section 101 of Title 11, Bankruptcy], the district court shall withdraw the reference of any such case and, after notice and a hearing, determine the status of the case. Such case shall be remanded to the bankruptcy judge with such instructions as are necessary for the prompt closing of the case and with a requirement that a progress report on the case be provided by the bankruptcy judge after such interval as the district court deems appropriate."

Short Title

1986 Amendments. Section 1 of Pub.L. 99–554 provided: "That this Act [enacting section 589a of this title and sections 307, and 1201 to 1231 of Title 11, Bankruptcy, amending sections 49, 96, 152, 156, 157, 528, 581, 582, 584 to 587, 604, 1334, and 1930 of this title and sections 101 to 103, 105, 108, 109, 303, 321, 322, 324, 326, 327, 329, 330, 341, 343, 345 to 348, 362 to 365, 502, 503, 521 to 524, 546 to 549, 554, 557, 701, 703 to 707, 724, 726 to 728, 743, 1102, 1104 to 1106, 1112, 1121, 1129, 1163, 1202, 1302, 1306, 1307, and 1324 to 1326 of Title 11, Bankruptcy Form No. 1, set out in the Appendix to Title 11, repealing sections 1201 to 1231 and 1501 to 151326 of Title 11, enacting provisions set out as notes under sections 581 and 589 of this title, amending provisions set out as a note under section 152 of this title and preceding section 581 of this title, and repealing provisions set out as notes under preceding section 581 of this title] may be cited as the 'Bankruptcy Judges, United States Trustees, and Family Farmer Bankruptcy Act of 1986'."

§ 582. Assistant United States trustees

(a) The Attorney General may appoint one or more assistant United States trustees in any region when the public interest so requires.

(b) Each assistant United States trustee is subject to removal by the Attorney General.

(Added Pub.L. 95–598, Title II, § 224(a), Nov. 6, 1978, 92 Stat. 2663, and amended Pub.L. 99–554, Title I, § 111(d), Oct. 27, 1986, 100 Stat. 3091.)

HISTORICAL AND STATUTORY NOTES

Codifications

Section 408(c) of Pub.L. 95–598, as amended, which provided for the repeal of this section and the deletion of any references to United States Trustees in this title at a prospective date, was repealed by section 307(b) of Pub.L. 99–554. See note set out preceding section 581 of this title.

Effective Dates

1986 Acts. Amendment by Pub.L. 99–554 effective 30 days after Oct. 27, 1986, except as otherwise provided, see section 302(a) of Pub.L. 99–554, as amended, set out as a note under section 581 of this title.

1978 Acts. Section effective Oct. 1, 1979, see section 402(c) of Pub.L. 95–598, as amended, set out as a note preceding section 101 of Title 11, Bankruptcy.

Appointment of United States Trustees by Attorney General

Appointment of United States Trustees by the Attorney General of individuals otherwise qualified, serving as estate administrators under Title 11, Bankruptcy, before effective date of Pub.L. 99–554, see section 309 of Pub.L. 99–554, as amended; set out as a note under section 581 of this title.

§ 583. Oath of office

Each United States trustee and assistant United States trustee, before taking office, shall take an oath to execute faithfully his duties.

(Added Pub.L. 95–598, Title II, § 224(a), Nov. 6, 1978, 92 Stat. 2663.)

HISTORICAL AND STATUTORY NOTES

Codifications

Section 408(c) of Pub.L. 95–598, as amended, which provided for the repeal of this section and the deletion of any references to United States Trustees in this title at a prospective date, was repealed by section 307(b) of Pub.L. 99–554. See note set out preceding section 581 of this title.

Effective Dates

1978 Acts. Section effective Oct. 1, 1979, see section 402(c) of Pub.L. 95–598, as amended, set out as a note preceding section 101 of Title 11, Bankruptcy.

§ 584. Official stations

The Attorney General may determine the official stations of the United States trustees and assistant United States trustees within the regions for which they were appointed.

(Added Pub.L. 95–598, Title II, § 224(a), Nov. 6, 1978, 92 Stat. 2663, and amended Pub.L. 99–554, Title I, § 144(d), Oct. 27, 1986, 100 Stat. 3096.)

HISTORICAL AND STATUTORY NOTES

Codifications

Section 408(c) of Pub.L. 95–598, as amended, which provided for the repeal of this section and the deletion of any references to United States Trustees in this title at a prospective date, was repealed by section 307(b) of Pub.L. 99–554. See note set out preceding section 581 of this title.

Effective Dates

1986 Acts. Amendment by Pub.L. 99–554 effective 30 days after Oct. 27, 1986, except as otherwise provided, see section 302(a) of Pub.L. 99–554, as amended, set out as a note under section 581 of this title.

1978 Acts. Section effective Oct. 1, 1979, see section 402(c) of Pub.L. 95–598, as amended, set out as a note preceding section 101 of Title 11, Bankruptcy.

§ 585. Vacancies

(a) The Attorney General may appoint an acting United States trustee for a region in which the office of the United States trustee is vacant. The individual so appointed may serve until the date on which the vacancy is filled by appointment under section 581 of this title or by designation under subsection (b) of this section.

(b) The Attorney General may designate a United States trustee to serve in not more than two regions for such time as the public interest requires.

(Added Pub.L. 95–598, Title II, § 224(a), Nov. 6, 1978, 92 Stat. 2663, and amended Pub.L. 99–554, Title I, § 112, Oct. 27, 1986, 100 Stat. 3091.)

HISTORICAL AND STATUTORY NOTES

Codifications

Section 408(c) of Pub.L. 95–598, as amended, which provided for the repeal of this section and the deletion of any references to United States Trustees in this title at a prospective date, was repealed by section 307(b) of Pub.L. 99–554. See note set out preceding section 581 of this title.

Effective Dates

1986 Acts. Amendment by Pub.L. 99–554 effective 30 days after Oct. 27, 1986, except as otherwise provided, see section 302(a) of Pub.L. 99–554, as amended, set out as a note under section 581 of this title.

1978 Acts. Section effective Oct. 1, 1979, see section 402(c) of Pub.L. 95–598, as amended, set out as a note preceding section 101 of Title 11, Bankruptcy.

§ 586. Duties; supervision by Attorney General

(a) Each United States trustee, within the region for which such United States trustee is appointed, shall—

(1) establish, maintain, and supervise a panel of private trustees that are eligible and available to serve as trustees in cases under chapter 7 of title 11;

(2) serve as and perform the duties of a trustee in a case under title 11 when required under title 11 to serve as trustee in such a case;

(3) supervise the administration of cases and trustees in cases under chapter 7, 11, 12, or 13 of title 11 by, whenever the United States trustee considers it to be appropriate—

(A)(i) reviewing, in accordance with procedural guidelines adopted by the Executive Office of the United States Trustee (which guidelines shall be applied uniformly by the United States trustee except when circumstances warrant different treatment), applications filed for compensation and reimbursement under section 330 of title 11; and

(ii) filing with the court comments with respect to such application and, if the United States Trustee considers it to be appropriate, objections to such application.

(B) monitoring plans and disclosure statements filed in cases under chapter 11 of title 11 and filing with the court, in connection with hearings under sections 1125 and 1128 of such title, comments with respect to such plans and disclosure statements;

(C) monitoring plans filed under chapters 12 and 13 of title 11 and filing with the court, in connection with hearings under sections 1224, 1229, 1324, and 1329 of such title, comments with respect to such plans;

(D) taking such action as the United States trustee deems to be appropriate to ensure that all reports, schedules, and fees required to be filed under title 11 and this title by the debtor are properly and timely filed;

(E) monitoring creditors' committees appointed under title 11;

(F) notifying the appropriate United States attorney of matters which relate to the occurrence of any action which may constitute a crime under the laws of the United States and, on the request of the United States attorney, assisting the United States attorney in carrying out prosecutions based on such action;

(G) monitoring the progress of cases under title 11 and taking such actions as the United States trustee deems to be appropriate to prevent undue delay in such progress; and

(H) monitoring applications filed under section 327 of title 11 and, whenever the United States trustee deems it to be appropriate, filing with the court comments with respect to the approval of such applications;

(4) deposit or invest under section 345 of title 11 money received as trustee in cases under title 11;

(5) perform the duties prescribed for the United States trustee under title 11 and this title, and such duties consistent with title 11 and this title as the Attorney General may prescribe; and

(6) make such reports as the Attorney General directs.

(b) If the number of cases under chapter 12 or 13 of title 11 commenced in a particular region so warrants, the United States trustee for such region may, subject to the approval of the Attorney General, appoint one or more individuals to serve as standing trustee, or designate one or more assistant United States trustees to serve in cases under such chapter. The United States trustee for such region shall supervise any such individual appointed as standing trustee in the performance of the duties of standing trustee.

(c) Each United States trustee shall be under the general supervision of the Attorney General, who shall provide general coordination and assistance to the United States trustees.

(d) The Attorney General shall prescribe by rule qualifications for membership on the panels established by United States trustees under paragraph (a)(1) of this section, and qualifications for appointment under subsection (b) of this section to serve as standing trustee in cases under chapter 12 or 13 of title 11. The Attorney General may not require that an individual be an attorney in order to qualify for appointment under subsection (b) of this section to serve as standing trustee in cases under chapter 12 or 13 of title 11.

(e)(1) The Attorney General, after consultation with a United States trustee that has appointed an individual under subsection (b) of this section to serve as standing trustee in cases under chapter 12 or 13 of title 11, shall fix—

(A) a maximum annual compensation for such individual consisting of—

(i) an amount not to exceed the highest annual rate of basic pay in effect for level V of the Executive Schedule; and

(ii) the cash value of employment benefits comparable to the employment benefits provided by the United States to individuals who are employed by the United States at the same rate of basic pay to perform similar services during the same period of time; and

(B) a percentage fee not to exceed—

(i) in the case of a debtor who is not a family farmer, ten percent; or

(ii) in the case of a debtor who is a family farmer, the sum of—

(I) not to exceed ten percent of the payments made under the plan of such debtor, with respect to payments in an aggregate amount not to exceed $450,000; and

(II) three percent of payments made under the plan of such debtor, with respect to payments made after the aggregate amount of payments made under the plan exceeds $450,000;

based on such maximum annual compensation and the actual, necessary expenses incurred by such individual as standing trustee.

(2) Such individual shall collect such percentage fee from all payments received by such individual under plans in the cases under chapter 12 or 13 of title 11 for which such individual serves as standing trustee. Such individual shall pay to the United States trustee, and the United States trustee shall deposit in the United States Trustee System Fund—

(A) any amount by which the actual compensation of such individual exceeds 5 per centum upon all payments received under plans in cases under chapter 12 or 13 of title 11 for which such individual serves as standing trustee; and

(B) any amount by which the percentage for all such cases exceeds—

(i) such individual's actual compensation for such cases, as adjusted under subparagraph (A) of paragraph (1); plus

(ii) the actual, necessary expenses incurred by such individual as standing trustee in such cases. Subject to the approval of the Attorney General, any or all of the interest earned from the deposit of payments under plans by such individual may be utilized to pay actual, necessary expenses without regard to the percentage limitation contained in subparagraph (d)(1)(B) of this section.

(Added Pub.L. 95–598, Title II, § 224(a), Nov. 6, 1978, 92 Stat. 2663, and amended Pub.L. 99–554, Title I, § 113, Oct. 27, 1986, 100 Stat. 3091; Pub.L. 101–509, Title V, § 529 [Title I, § 110(a)], Nov. 5, 1990, 104 Stat. 1427, 1452; Pub.L. 103–394, Title II, § 224(a), Title V, § 502, Oct. 22, 1994, 108 Stat. 4130, 4147.)

HISTORICAL AND STATUTORY NOTES

References in Text

Level V of the Executive Schedule, referred to in subsec. (e)(1)(A)(i), is set out in section 5316 of Title 5, Government Organization and Employees.

Codifications

Section 408(c) of Pub.L. 95–598, as amended, which provided for the repeal of this section and the deletion of any references to United States Trustees in this title at a prospective date, was repealed by section 307(b) of Pub.L. 99–554. See note set out preceding section 581 of this title.

Effective Dates

1994 Acts. Amendments by Pub.L. 103–394 effective on Oct. 22, 1994, and not to apply with respect to cases commenced under Title 11 of the United States Code before Oct. 22, 1994, see section 702 of Pub.L. 103–394, set out as a note under section 101 of Title 11, Bankruptcy.

1990 Acts. Amendment by Pub.L. 101–509 effective on such date as the President shall determine, but not earlier than 90 days, and not later than 180 days, after Nov. 5, 1990, see section 529 [Title III, § 305] of Pub.L. 101–509, set out as a note under section 5301 of Title 5, Government Organization and Employees. [See also related provisions in Ex. Ord. No. 12748, Feb. 1, 1991, 56 F.R. 4521, set out under that section.]

1986 Acts. Effective date and applicability of amendment by Pub.L. 99–554 dependent upon the judicial district involved, see section 302(d), (e) of Pub.L. 99–554, set out as a note under section 581 of this title.

1978 Acts. Section effective Oct. 1, 1979, see section 402(c) of Pub.L. 95–598, as amended, set out as a note preceding section 101 of Title 11, Bankruptcy.

Separability of Provisions

If any provision of or amendment made by Pub.L. 103–394 or the application of such provision or amendment to any person or circumstance is held to be unconstitutional, the remaining provisions of and amendments made by Pub.L. 103–394 and the application of such provisions and amendments to any person or circumstance shall not be affected thereby, see section 701 of Pub.L. 103–394, set out as a note under section 101 of Title 11, Bankruptcy.

Application to All Standing Trustees

Section 529 [Title I, § 110(b)] of Pub.L. 101–509 provided that: "The amendment made by subsection (a) [amending this section] shall apply to any trustee to whom the provisions of section 302(d)(3) of the Bankruptcy Judges, United States Trustees, and Family Farmer Bankruptcy Act of 1986 (Public Law 99–54 [Pub.L. 99–554]; 100 Stat. 3121) [set out in a note under section 581 of this title] apply."

§ 587. Salaries

Subject to sections 5315 through 5317 of title 5, the Attorney General shall fix the annual salaries of United States trustees and assistant United States trustees at rates of compensation not in excess of the rate of basic compensation provided for Executive Level IV of the Executive Schedule set forth in section 5315 of title 5, United States Code.

(Added Pub.L. 95–598, Title II, § 224(a), Nov. 6, 1978, 92 Stat. 2664, and amended Pub.L. 99–554, Title I, § 114(a), Oct. 27, 1986, 100 Stat. 3093.)

HISTORICAL AND STATUTORY NOTES

Codifications

Section 408(c) of Pub.L. 95–598, as amended, which provided for the repeal of this section and the deletion of any references to United States Trustees in this title at a prospective date, was repealed by section 307(b) of Pub.L. 99–554. See note set out preceding section 581 of this title.

Effective Dates

1986 Acts. Amendment by Pub.L. 99–554 effective 30 days after Oct. 27, 1986, except as otherwise provided, see section 302(a) of Pub.L. 99–554, as amended, set out as a note under section 581 of this title.

1978 Acts. Section effective Oct. 1, 1979, see section 402(c) of Pub.L. 95–598, as amended, set out as a note preceding section 101 of Title 11, Bankruptcy.

§ 588. Expenses

Necessary office expenses of the United States trustee shall be allowed when authorized by the Attorney General.

(Added Pub.L. 95–598, Title II, § 224(a), Nov. 6, 1978, 92 Stat. 2664.)

HISTORICAL AND STATUTORY NOTES

Codifications

Section 408(c) of Pub.L. 95–598, as amended, which provided for the repeal of this section and the deletion of any references to United States Trustees in this title at a prospective date, was repealed by section 307(b) of Pub.L. 99–554. See note set out preceding section 581 of this title.

Effective Dates

1978 Acts. Section effective Oct. 1, 1979, see section 402(c) of Pub.L. 95–598, as amended, set out as a note preceding section 101 of Title 11, Bankruptcy.

§ 589. Staff and other employees

The United States trustee may employ staff and other employees on approval of the Attorney General.

(Added Pub.L. 95–598, Title II, § 224(a), Nov. 6, 1978, 92 Stat. 2664.)

HISTORICAL AND STATUTORY NOTES

Codifications

Section 408(c) of Pub.L. 95–598, as amended, which provided for the repeal of this section and the deletion of any references to United States Trustees in this title at a prospective date, was repealed by section 307(b) of Pub.L. 99–554. See note set out preceding section 581 of this title.

Effective Dates

1978 Acts. Section effective Oct. 1, 1979, see section 402(c) of Pub.L. 95–598, as amended, set out as a note preceding section 101 of Title 11, Bankruptcy.

Temporary Suspension of Limitation on Appointments

Pub.L. 99–554, Title I, § 114(b), Oct. 27, 1986, 100 Stat. 3093, provided that: "During the period beginning on the effective date of this Act [see section 302 of Pub.L. 99–554, as amended, set out as a note under section 581 of this title], and ending on October 1, 1989, the provisions of title 5 of the United States Code [Title 5, Government Organization and Employees] governing appointments in the competitive service shall not apply with respect to appointments under section 589 of title 28, United States Code [this section]."

§ 589a. United States Trustee System Fund

(a) There is hereby established in the Treasury of the United States a special fund to be known as the "United States Trustee System Fund" (hereinafter in this section referred to as the "Fund"). Monies in the Fund shall be available to the Attorney General without fiscal year limitation in such amounts as may be specified in appropriations Acts for the following purposes in connection with the operations of United States trustees—

(1) salaries and related employee benefits;

(2) travel and transportation;

(3) rental of space;

(4) communication, utilities, and miscellaneous computer charges;

(5) security investigations and audits;

(6) supplies, books, and other materials for legal research;

(7) furniture and equipment;

(8) miscellaneous services, including those obtained by contract; and

(9) printing.

(b) For the purpose of recovering the cost of services of the United States Trustee System, there shall be deposited as offsetting collections to the appropriation "United States Trustee System Fund", to remain available until expended, the following—

(1) 23.08 percent of the fees collected under section 1930(a)(1) of this title;

(2) one-half of the fees collected under section 1930(a)(3) of this title;

(3) one-half of the fees collected under section 1930(a)(4) of this title;

(4) one-half of the fees collected under section 1930(a)(5) of this title;

(5) 100 percent of the fees collected under section 1930(a)(6) of this title;

(6) three-fourths of the fees collected under the last sentence of section 1930(a) of this title;

(7) the compensation of trustees received under section 330(d) of title 11 by the clerks of the bankruptcy courts; and

(8) excess fees collected under section 586(e)(2) of this title.

(c) Amounts in the Fund which are not currently needed for the purposes specified in subsection (a) shall be kept on deposit or invested in obligations of, or guaranteed by, the United States.

(d) The Attorney General shall transmit to the Congress, not later than 120 days after the end of each fiscal year, a detailed report on the amounts deposited in the Fund and a description of expenditures made under this section.

(e) There are authorized to be appropriated to the Fund for any fiscal year such sums as may be necessary to supplement amounts deposited under subsection (b) for the purposes specified in subsection (a).

(Added Pub.L. 99–554, Title I, § 115(a), Oct. 27, 1986, 100 Stat. 3094, and amended Pub.L. 101–162, Title IV, § 406(c), Nov. 21, 1989, 103 Stat. 1016; Pub.L. 102–140, Title I, § 111(b), (c), Oct. 28, 1991, 105 Stat. 795; Pub.L. 103–121, Title I, § 111(a)(2), (b)(2), (3), Oct. 27, 1993, 107 Stat. 1164; Pub.L. 104–91, Title I, § 101(a), Jan. 6, 1996, 110 Stat. 11, as amended Pub.L. 104–99, Title II, § 211, Jan. 26, 1996, 110 Stat. 37; Pub.L. 104–208, Div. A, Title I, § 101(a) [Title I, § 109(b)], Sept. 30, 1996, 110 Stat. 3009–18.)

HISTORICAL AND STATUTORY NOTES

Codifications

Section 101(a) of Pub.L. 104–91, as amended by section 211 of Pub.L. 104–99, provided in part that section 111(b) and (c) of the General Provisions for the Department of Justice in Title I of the Departments of Commerce, Justice, and State, the Judiciary, and Related Agencies Appropriations Act, 1996 (H.R. 2076) as passed by the House of Representatives on Dec. 6, 1995, was enacted into permanent law. Such section 111(b) and (c) of H.R. 2076 amended subsecs. (b) and (f) of this section. See 1996 Amendments notes set out under this section.

Effective Dates

1996 Acts. Pub.L. 104–208, Div. A, Title I, § 101(a) [Title I, § 109(c)], Sept. 30, 1996, 110 Stat. 3009–19, provided that: "Notwithstanding any other provision of law or of this Act [Pub.L. 104–208, Sept. 30, 1996, 110 Stat. 3009, see Tables for classification] the amendments to 28 U.S.C. 589a [this section] made by subsection (b) of this section shall take effect upon enactment of this Act [probably means the date of enactment of Pub.L. 104–208, 110 Stat. 3009, which was approved Sept. 30, 1996]."

1993 Acts. Section 111(a) of Pub.L. 103–121 provided in part that amendment by section 111(a)(2) of Pub.L. 103–121, amending subsec. (b)(1) of this section, is effective 30 days after Oct. 27, 1993.

Section 111(b) of Pub.L. 103–121 provided in part that amendment by section 111(b)(2) and (3) of Pub.L. 103–121, amending subsecs. (b)(2) and (f)(1) of this section, is effective 30 days after Oct. 27, 1993.

1991 Acts. Section 111 of Pub.L. 102–140 provided that the amendment made by that section is effective 60 days after Oct. 28, 1991.

1986 Acts. Enactment by Pub.L. 99–554 effective 30 days after Oct. 27, 1986, except as otherwise provided, see section 302(a) of Pub.L. 99–554, as amended, set out as a note under section 581 of this title.

CHAPTER 40—INDEPENDENT COUNSEL

Sec.

591. Applicability of provisions of this chapter.
592. Preliminary investigation and application for appointment of an independent counsel.
593. Duties of the division of the court.
594. Authority and duties of an independent counsel.
595. Congressional oversight.
596. Removal of an independent counsel; termination of office.
597. Relationship with Department of Justice.
598. Severability.
599. Termination of effect of chapter.

§ 591. Applicability of provisions of this chapter

(a) Preliminary investigation with respect to certain covered persons.—The Attorney General shall conduct a preliminary investigation in accordance with section 592 whenever the Attorney General receives information sufficient to constitute grounds to investigate whether any person described in subsection (b) may have violated any Federal criminal law other than a violation classified as a Class B or C misdemeanor or an infraction.

(b) Persons to whom subsection (a) applies.—The persons referred to in subsection (a) are—

(1) the President and Vice President;

(2) any individual serving in a position listed in section 5312 of title 5;

(3) any individual working in the Executive Office of the President who is compensated at a rate of pay at or above level II of the Executive Schedule under section 5313 of title 5;

(4) any Assistant Attorney General and any individual working in the Department of Justice who is compensated at a rate of pay at or above level III of the Executive Schedule under section 5314 of title 5;

(5) the Director of Central Intelligence, the Deputy Director of Central Intelligence, and the Commissioner of Internal Revenue;

(6) the chairman and treasurer of the principal national campaign committee seeking the election or reelection of the President, and any officer of that committee exercising authority at the national level, during the incumbency of the President; and

(7) any individual who held an office or position described in paragraph (1), (2), (3), (4), or (5) for 1 year after leaving the office or position.

[(8) Redesignated (6)]

(c) Preliminary investigation with respect to other persons.—

(1) In general.—When the Attorney General determines that an investigation or prosecution of a person by the Department of Justice may result in a personal, financial, or political conflict of interest, the Attorney General may conduct a preliminary investigation of such person in accordance with section 592 if the Attorney General receives information sufficient to constitute grounds to investigate whether that person may have violated Federal criminal law other than a violation classified as a Class B or C misdemeanor or an infraction.

(2) Members of Congress.—When the Attorney General determines that it would be in the public interest, the Attorney General may conduct a preliminary investigation in accordance with section 592 if the Attorney General receives information sufficient to constitute grounds to investigate whether a Member of Congress may have violated any Federal criminal law other than a violation classified as a Class B or C misdemeanor or an infraction.

(d) Examination of information to determine need for preliminary investigation.—

(1) Factors to be considered.—In determining under subsection (a) or (c) (or section 592(c)(2)) whether grounds to investigate exist, the Attorney General shall consider only—

(A) the specificity of the information received; and

(B) the credibility of the source of the information.

(2) Time period for making determination.—The Attorney General shall determine whether grounds to investigate exist not later than 30 days after the information is first received. If within that 30–day period the Attorney General determines that the information is not specific or is not from a credible source, then the Attorney General shall close the matter. If within that 30–day period the Attorney General determines that the information is specific and from a credible source, the Attorney General shall, upon making that determination, commence a preliminary investigation with respect to that information. If the Attorney General is unable to determine, within that 30–day period, whether the information is specific and from a credible source, the Attorney General shall, at the end of that 30-day period, commence a preliminary investigation with respect to that information.

(e) Recusal of Attorney General.—

(1) When recusal is required.—(A) If information received under this chapter involves the Attorney General, the next most senior official in the Department of Justice who is not also recused shall perform the duties assigned under this chapter to the Attorney General.

(B) If information received under this chapter involves a person with whom the Attorney General has a personal or financial relationship, the Attorney General shall recuse himself or herself by designating the next most senior official in the Department of Justice who is not also recused to perform the duties assigned under this chapter to the Attorney General.

(2) Requirements for recusal determination.—Before personally making any other determination under this chapter with respect to information received under this chapter, the Attorney General shall determine under paragraph (1)(B) whether recusal is necessary. The Attorney General shall set forth this determination in writing, identify the facts considered by the Attorney General, and set forth the reasons for the recusal. The Attorney General shall file this determination with any notification or application submitted to the division of the court under this chapter with respect to such information.

(Added Pub.L. 95–521, Title VI, § 601(a), Oct. 26, 1978, 92 Stat. 1867, and amended Pub.L. 97–409, §§ 3, 4(a), Jan. 3, 1983, 96 Stat. 2039, 2040; Pub.L. 98–473, Title II, § 228(b), Oct. 12, 1984, 98 Stat. 2030; Pub.L. 100–191, § 2, Dec. 15, 1987, 101 Stat. 1293; Pub.L. 103–270, §§ 3(j), (k), 4, June 30, 1994, 108 Stat. 735, 736.)

HISTORICAL AND STATUTORY NOTES

Effective Dates

1994 Acts. Section 7 of Pub.L. 103–270 provided that:

"(a) In general.—Except as provided in this section, the amendments made by this Act [amending this section and sections 592 through 596 and 599 of this title and enacting provisions set out as notes under this section and section 113 of Title 3, The President] shall apply with respect to independent counsels appointed before, on, or after the date of enactment of this Act [June 30, 1994].

"(b) Assignment of employee to certify expenditures.—An independent counsel appointed prior to the date of enactment of this Act [June 30, 1994] shall assign to an employee the duty of certifying expenditures, as required by section 594(*l*) of title 28, United States Code, as added by section 3(a) [section 594(*l*) of this title], by the date that is 30 days after the date of enactment of this Act.

"(c) Office space.—The Administrator of General Services, in applying section 594(*l*)(3) of title 28, United States Code, as added by section 3(a) [section 594(*l*)(3) of this title], to determine whether the office of an independent counsel appointed prior to the date of enactment of this Act [June 30, 1994] should be moved to a Federal building, shall take into account the moving, legal, and other expenses that might arise if the office were moved.

"(d) Travel and subsistence expenses.—For purposes of the restrictions on reimbursement of travel and subsistence expenses of an independent counsel and employees of an office of independent counsel contained in paragraph (3) of section 594(b) of title 28, United States Code, as amended by section 3(b) [section 594(b)(3) of this title], as applied to the office of an independent counsel appointed before the date of enactment of this Act [June 30, 1994], the 1-year service period shall begin on the date of enactment of this Act.

"(e) Rates of compensation.—The limitation on rates of compensation of employees of an office of independent counsel contained in the last sentence of section 594(c) of title 28, United States Code, as amended by section 3(c) [section 594(c) of this title], shall not be applied to cause a reduction in the rate of compensation of an employee appointed before the date of enactment of this Act [June 30, 1994].

"(f) Periodic reappointment.—The determinations by the division of the court contained in the last sentence of section 596(b)(2) of title 28, United States Code, as amended by section 3(h) [section 596(b)(2) of this title], shall, for the office of an independent counsel appointed before the date of enactment of this Act [June 30, 1994], be required no later than 1 year after the date of enactment of this Act and at the end of each succeeding 1-year period.

"(g) Reporting requirements.—No amendment made by this Act [amending this section and sections 592 through 596 and 599 of this title and enacting provisions set out as notes under this section and section 113 of Title 3] that establishes or modifies a requirement that any person submit a report to any other person with respect to an activity occurring during any time period shall be construed to require that a report submitted prior to the date of enactment of this Act [June 30, 1994], with respect to that time period be supplemented to include information with respect to such activity.

"(h) Regulatory independent counsel.—Notwithstanding the restriction in section 593(b)(2) of title 28, United States Code [section 593(b)(2) of this title], the division of the court described in section 49 of that title [section 49 of this title] may appoint as an independent counsel any individual who, on the date of enactment of this Act [June 30, 1994], is serving as a regulatory independent counsel under parts 600 and 603 of title 28, Code of Federal Regulations. If such an individual is so appointed, such an independent counsel shall comply with chapter 40 of title 28, United States Code, as amended by this Act [this chapter], in the same manner and to the same extent as an independent counsel appointed before the date of enactment of this Act is required to comply with that chapter, except that subsection (f) of this section shall not apply to such an independent counsel.

"(i) White House personnel report.—Section 6 [enacting provisions set out as a note under section 113 of Title 3] shall take effect on January 1, 1995."

1987 Acts. Section 6 of Pub.L. 100–191 provided that:

"(a) In general.— Subject to subsection (b), the amendments made by this Act [enacting section 599 of this title, amending sections 49 and 591 to 598 of this title, sections 203 and 205 of Pub.L. 95–521 set out in Appendix 4 to Title 5, Government Organization and Employees, and section 202 of

Title 18, Crimes and Criminal Procedure, enacting provisions set out as a note under section 1 of this title, and amending provisions set out as a note under this section] take effect on the date of the enactment of this Act [Dec. 15, 1987].

"(b) Pending proceedings.— With respect to any proceeding under chapter 39 of title 28, United States Code (before the redesignation of such chapter as chapter 40 by section 144(g) of Public Law 99–554) [this chapter], or under chapter 40 of such title (after such redesignation) [this chapter], which is pending on the date of the enactment of this Act [Dec. 15, 1987], the following shall apply:

"(1) Except as provided in paragraphs (2) and (3), the provisions of chapter 40 of such title [this chapter] as in effect on the day before such date of enactment [Dec. 15, 1987] shall, in lieu of the amendments made by this Act, continue to apply on or after such date to such proceeding until such proceeding is terminated in accordance with such chapter.

"(2) The following provisions shall apply to such proceeding on or after such date of enactment:

"(A) Section 593(f) of title 28, United States Code, as amended by section 2 of this Act [section 593(f) of this title] relating to the award of attorneys' fees.

"(B) Section 594(d)(2) of such title, as added by section 2 of this Act [section 594(d)(2) of this title], to the extent that such section 594(d)(2) relates to reports by the Attorney General on expenditures by independent counsel, except that the first such report shall be made only with respect to expenditures on or after the date of the enactment of this Act [Dec. 15, 1987].

"(C) Section 594(h)(1)(A) of such title, as added by section 2 of this Act [section 594(h)(1)(A) of this title], relating to reports by independent counsel, except that the 6–month periods described in such section 594(h)(1)(A) shall be calculated from the date of the enactment of this Act [Dec. 15, 1987].

"(D) Section 594(i) of such title, as added by section 2 of this Act [section 594(i) of this title], relating to the independence of the office of independent counsel for certain purposes.

"(E) Section 594(k) of such title, as added by section 2 of this Act [section 594(u) of this title], relating to custody of records of independent counsel.

"(F) Section 596(a)(3) of such title, as amended by section 2 of this Act [section 596(a)(3) of this title], relating to judicial review of the removal of an independent counsel from office.

"(G) Section 596(c) of such title, as added by section 2 of this Act [section 596(c) of this title], relating to audits of expenditures of independent counsel.

"(H) The amendments made by section 3 of this Act [amending section 202(a) of Title 18, Crimes and Criminal Procedure, and sections 203 and 205 of Pub.L. 95–521, set out in Appendix 4 to Title 5, Government Organization and Employees], relating to the status of independent counsel and their appointees as special government employees and to their financial disclosure requirements.

"(3) Section 594(j) of title 28, United States Code, as added by section 2 of this Act [section 594(j) of this title], relating to certain standards of conduct shall, 90 days after the date of the enactment of this Act [Dec. 15, 1987], apply to a pending proceeding described in this subsection."

1984 Acts. Section 235(a)(1)(B)(ii)(IV) of Pub.L. 98–473 had provided that the amendment made by section 228 of Pub.L. 98–473 was to be effective Oct. 12, 1984. Pub.L. 99–646, § 35(2)(D), Nov. 10, 1986, 100 Stat. 3599, amended section 235(a)(1)(B)(ii)(IV) of Pub.L. 98–473 making it inapplicable to section 228. Amendment by Pub.L. 98–473 effective the first day of the first calendar month beginning 36 months after Oct. 12, 1984, see section 235(a)(1) of Pub.L. 98–473, as amended, set out as a note under section 3551 of Title 18, Crimes and Criminal Procedure.

1978 Acts. Section 604 of Pub.L. 95–521 provided that: "Except as provided in this section, the amendments made by this title [enacting this chapter and sections 49, 528, and 529 of this title] shall take effect on the date of the enactment of this Act [Oct. 26, 1978]. The provisions of chapter 39 of title 28 of the United States Code, as added by section 601 of this Act, shall not apply to specific information received by the Attorney General pursuant to section 591 of such title 28, if the Attorney General determines that—

"(1) such specific information is directly related to a prosecution pending at the time such specific information is received by the Attorney General;

"(2) such specific information is related to a matter which has been presented to a grand jury and is received by the Attorney General within one hundred and eighty days of the date of the enactment of this Act [Oct. 26, 1978]; or

"(3) such specific information is related to an investigation that is pending at the time such specific information is received by the Attorney General, and such specific information is received by the Attorney General within ninety days of the date of the enactment of this Act [Oct. 26, 1978]."

Contingency Fund for Independent Counsels

Section 601(c) of Pub.L. 95–521, as amended Pub.L. 97–409, § 2(c)(2), Jan. 3, 1983, 96 Stat. 2039; Pub.L. 100–191, § 5(b), Dec. 15, 1987, 101 Stat. 1307, provided that: "There are authorized to be appropriated for each fiscal year such sums as may be necessary, to be held by the Department of Justice as a contingent fund for the use of any independent counsels appointed under chapter 40 (relating to independent counsel) of title 28 of the United States Code [this chapter] in the carrying out of functions under such chapter."

Permanent Appropriation for Expenses of Independent Counsels

Pub.L. 100–202, § 101(a) [Title II], Dec. 22, 1987, 101 Stat. 1329–9, provided in part "That a permanent indefinite appropriation is established within the Department of Justice to pay all necessary expenses of investigations and prosecutions by independent counsel appointed pursuant to the provisions of 28 U.S.C. 591 et seq. [this chapter] or other law: *Provided further,* That the Comptroller General shall perform semiannual financial reviews of expenditures from the Independent Counsel permanent indefinite appropriation, and report their findings to the Committees on Appropriations of the House and Senate".

§ 592. Preliminary investigation and application for appointment of an independent counsel

(a) Conduct of preliminary investigation.—

(1) In general.—A preliminary investigation conducted under this chapter shall be of such matters as the Attorney General considers appropriate in order to make a determination, under subsection (b) or (c), on whether further investigation is warranted, with respect to each potential violation, or allegation of a violation, of criminal law. The Attorney General shall make such determination not later than 90 days after the preliminary investigation is commenced, except that, in the case of a preliminary investigation commenced after a congressional request under subsection (g), the Attorney General shall make such determination not later than 90 days after the request is received. The Attorney General shall promptly notify the division of the court specified in section 593(a) of the commencement of such preliminary investigation and the date of such commencement.

(2) Limited authority of Attorney General.—(A) In conducting preliminary investigations under this chapter, the Attorney General shall have no authority to convene grand juries, plea bargain, grant immunity, or issue subpoenas.

(B)(i) The Attorney General shall not base a determination under this chapter that information with respect to a violation of criminal law by a person is not specific and from a credible source upon a determination that such person lacked the state of mind required for the violation of criminal law.

(ii) The Attorney General shall not base a determination under this chapter that there are no reasonable grounds to believe that further investigation is warranted, upon a determination that such person lacked the state of mind required for the violation of criminal law involved, unless there is clear and convincing evidence that the person lacked such state of mind.

(3) Extension of time for preliminary investigation.—The Attorney General may apply to the division of the court for a single extension, for a period of not more than 60 days, of the 90–day period referred to in paragraph (1). The division of the court may, upon a showing of good cause, grant such extension.

(b) Determination that further investigation not warranted.—

(1) Notification of division of the court.—If the Attorney General, upon completion of a preliminary investigation under this chapter, determines that there are no reasonable grounds to believe that further investigation is warranted, the Attorney General shall promptly so notify the division of the court, and the division of the court shall have no power to appoint an independent counsel with respect to the matters involved.

(2) Form of notification.—Such notification shall contain a summary of the information received and a summary of the results of the preliminary investigation.

(c) Determination that further investigation is warranted.—

(1) Application for appointment of independent counsel.—The Attorney General shall apply to the division of the court for the appointment of an independent counsel if—

(A) the Attorney General, upon completion of a preliminary investigation under this chapter, determines that there are reasonable grounds to believe that further investigation is warranted; or

(B) the 90–day period referred to in subsection (a)(1), and any extension granted under subsection (a)(3), have elapsed and the Attorney General has not filed a notification with the division of the court under subsection (b)(1).

In determining under this chapter whether reasonable grounds exist to warrant further investigation, the Attorney General shall comply with the written or other established policies of the Department of Justice with respect to the conduct of criminal investigations.

(2) Receipt of additional information.—If, after submitting a notification under subsection (b)(1), the Attorney General receives additional information sufficient to constitute grounds to investigate the matters to which such notification related, the Attorney General shall—

(A) conduct such additional preliminary investigation as the Attorney General considers appropriate for a period of not more than 90 days after the date on which such additional information is received; and

(B) otherwise comply with the provisions of this section with respect to such additional preliminary investigation to the same extent as any other preliminary investigation under this section.

(d) Contents of application.—Any application for the appointment of an independent counsel under this chapter shall contain sufficient information to assist the division of the court in selecting an independent counsel and in defining that independent counsel's prosecutorial jurisdiction so that the independent counsel has adequate authority to fully investigate and prosecute the subject matter and all matters related to that subject matter.

(e) Disclosure of information.—Except as otherwise provided in this chapter or as is deemed necessary for law enforcement purposes, no officer or employee of the Department of Justice or an office of independent counsel may, without leave of the division of the court, disclose to any individual outside the Department of Justice or such office any notification, application, or any other document, materials, or memorandum supplied to the division of the court under this chapter. Nothing in this chapter shall be construed as authorizing the withholding of information from the Congress.

(f) Limitation on judicial review.—The Attorney General's determination under this chapter to apply to the division of the court for the appointment of an independent counsel shall not be reviewable in any court.

(g) Congressional request.—

(1) By Judiciary Committee or members thereof.—The Committee on the Judiciary of either House of the Congress, or a majority of majority party members or a majority of all nonmajority party members of either such committee, may request in writing that the Attorney General apply for the appointment of an independent counsel.

(2) Report by Attorney General pursuant to request.—Not later than 30 days after the receipt of a request under paragraph (1), the Attorney General shall submit, to the committee making the request, or to the committee on which the persons making the request serve, a report on whether the Attorney General has begun or will begin a preliminary investigation under this chapter of the matters with respect to which the request is made, in accordance with subsection (a) or (c) of section 591, as the case may be. The report shall set forth the reasons for the Attorney General's decision regarding such preliminary investigation as it relates to each of the matters with respect to which the congressional request is made. If there is such a preliminary investigation, the report shall include the date on which the preliminary investigation began or will begin.

(3) Submission of information in response to congressional request.—At the same time as any notification, application, or any other document, material, or memorandum is supplied to the division of the court pursuant to this section with respect to a preliminary investigation of any matter with respect to which a request is made under paragraph (1), such notification, application, or other document, material, or memorandum shall be supplied to the committee making the request, or to the committee on which the persons making the request serve. If no application for the appointment of an independent counsel is made to the division of the court under this section pursuant to such a preliminary investigation, the Attorney General shall submit a report to that committee stating the reasons why such application was not made, addressing each matter with respect to which the congressional request was made.

(4) Disclosure of information.—Any report, notification, application, or other document, material, or memorandum supplied to a committee under this subsection shall not be revealed to any third party, except that the committee may, either on its own initiative or upon the request of the Attorney General, make public such portion or portions of such report, notification, application, document, material, or memorandum as will not in the committee's judgment prejudice the rights of any individual.

(Added Pub.L. 95–521, Title VI, § 601(a), Oct. 26, 1978, 92 Stat. 1868, and amended Pub.L. 97–409, §§ 2(a)(1), 4(b)–(e), Jan. 3, 1983, 96 Stat. 2039–2041; Pub.L. 100–191, § 2, Dec. 15, 1987, 101 Stat. 1295; Pub.L. 103–270, § 3(*l*), June 30, 1994, 108 Stat. 736.)

HISTORICAL AND STATUTORY NOTES

Effective Dates

1994 Acts. Amendment by Pub.L. 103–270 applicable with respect to independent counsels appointed before, on, or after June 30, 1994, see section 7(a) of Pub.L. 103–270, set out as a note under section 591 of this title.

1987 Acts. Amendment by Pub.L. 100–191 to take effect on Dec. 15, 1987, and to apply only to new independent counsel proceedings and to new independent counsels coming into existence on and after Dec. 15, 1987, see section 6 of Pub.L. 100–191, set out as a note under section 591 of this title.

1978 Acts. Section effective Oct. 26, 1978, except for specific information received by the Attorney General pursuant to section 591 of this title based on determinations made by the Attorney General respecting such information, see section 604 of Pub.L. 95–521, set out as a note under section 591 of this title.

§ 593. Duties of the division of the court

(a) Reference to division of the court.—The division of the court to which this chapter refers is the division established under section 49 of this title.

(b) Appointment and jurisdiction of independent counsel.—

(1) Authority.—Upon receipt of an application under section 592(c), the division of the court shall appoint an appropriate independent counsel and shall define that independent counsel's prosecutorial jurisdiction.

(2) Qualifications of independent counsel.—The division of the court shall appoint as independent counsel an individual who has appropriate experience and who will conduct the investigation and any prosecution in a prompt, responsible, and cost-effective manner. The division of the court shall seek to appoint as independent counsel an individual who will serve to the extent necessary to complete the investigation and any prosecution without undue delay. The division of the court may not appoint as an independent counsel any person who holds any office of profit or trust under the United States.

(3) **Scope of prosecutorial jurisdiction.**—In defining the independent counsel's prosecutorial jurisdiction, the division of the court shall assure that the independent counsel has adequate authority to fully investigate and prosecute the subject matter with respect to which the Attorney General has requested the appointment of the independent counsel, and all matters related to that subject matter. Such jurisdiction shall also include the authority to investigate and prosecute Federal crimes, other than those classified as Class B or C misdemeanors or infractions, that may arise out of the investigation or prosecution of the matter with respect to which the Attorney General's request was made, including perjury, obstruction of justice, destruction of evidence, and intimidation of witnesses.

(4) **Disclosure of identity and prosecutorial jurisdiction.**—An independent counsel's identity and prosecutorial jurisdiction (including any expansion under subsection (c)) may not be made public except upon the request of the Attorney General or upon a determination of the division of the court that disclosure of the identity and prosecutorial jurisdiction of such independent counsel would be in the best interests of justice. In any event, the identity and prosecutorial jurisdiction of such independent counsel shall be made public when any indictment is returned, or any criminal information is filed, pursuant to the independent counsel's investigation.

(c) **Expansion of jurisdiction.**—

(1) **In general.**—The division of the court, upon the request of the Attorney General, may expand the prosecutorial jurisdiction of an independent counsel, and such expansion may be in lieu of the appointment of another independent counsel.

(2) **Procedure for request by independent counsel.**—(A) If the independent counsel discovers or receives information about possible violations of criminal law by persons as provided in section 591, which are not covered by the prosecutorial jurisdiction of the independent counsel, the independent counsel may submit such information to the Attorney General. The Attorney General shall then conduct a preliminary investigation of the information in accordance with the provisions of section 592, except that such preliminary investigation shall not exceed 30 days from the date such information is received. In making the determinations required by section 592, the Attorney General shall give great weight to any recommendations of the independent counsel.

(B) If the Attorney General determines, after according great weight to the recommendations of the independent counsel, that there are no reasonable grounds to believe that further investigation is warranted, the Attorney General shall promptly so notify the division of the court and the division of the court shall have no power to expand the jurisdiction of the independent counsel or to appoint another independent counsel with respect to the matters involved.

(C) If—

(i) the Attorney General determines that there are reasonable grounds to believe that further investigation is warranted; or

(ii) the 30-day period referred to in subparagraph (A) elapses without a notification to the division of the court that no further investigation is warranted,

the division of the court shall expand the jurisdiction of the appropriate independent counsel to include the matters involved or shall appoint another independent counsel to investigate such matters.

(d) **Return for further explanation.**—Upon receipt of a notification under section 592 or subsection (c)(2)(B) of this section from the Attorney General that there are no reasonable grounds to believe that further investigation is warranted with respect to information received under this chapter, the division of the court shall have no authority to overrule this determination but may return the matter to the Attorney General for further explanation of the reasons for such determination.

(e) **Vacancies.**—If a vacancy in office arises by reason of the resignation, death, or removal of an independent counsel, the division of the court shall appoint an independent counsel to complete the work of the independent counsel whose resignation, death, or removal caused the vacancy, except that in the case of a vacancy arising by reason of the removal of an independent counsel, the division of the court may appoint an acting independent counsel to serve until any judicial review of such removal is completed.

(f) **Attorneys' fees.**—

(1) **Award of fees.**—Upon the request of an individual who is the subject of an investigation conducted by an independent counsel pursuant to this chapter, the division of the court may, if no indictment is brought against such individual pursuant to that investigation, award reimbursement for those reasonable attorneys' fees incurred by that individual during that investigation which would not have been incurred but for the requirements of this chapter. The division of the court shall notify the the [1] independent counsel who conducted the investigation and Attorney General of any request for attorneys' fees under this subsection.

(2) **Evaluation of fees.**—The division of the court shall direct such independent counsel and the Attorney General to file a written evaluation of any request for attorneys' fees under this subsection, addressing—

(A) the sufficiency of the documentation;

(B) the need or justification for the underlying item;

(C) whether the underlying item would have been incurred but for the requirements of this chapter; and

(D) the reasonableness of the amount of money requested.

(g) **Disclosure of information.**—The division of the court may, subject to section 594(h)(2), allow the disclosure of any notification, application, or any other document, material, or memorandum supplied to the division of the court under this chapter.

(h) **Amicus curiae briefs.**—When presented with significant legal issues, the division of the court may disclose sufficient information about the issues to permit the filing of timely amicus curiae briefs.

(Added Pub.L. 95-521, Title VI, § 601(a), Oct. 26, 1978, 92 Stat. 1869, and amended Pub.L. 97-409, §§ 2(a) (1), 5, Jan. 3, 1983, 96 Stat. 2039, 2041; Pub.L. 100-191, § 2, Dec. 15, 1987, 101 Stat. 1297; Pub.L. 103-270, § 3(n), June 30, 1994, 108 Stat. 736.)

1 So in original.

HISTORICAL AND STATUTORY NOTES

Effective Dates

1994 Acts. Amendment by Pub.L. 103-270 applicable with respect to independent counsels appointed before, on, or after June 30, 1994, with provisions directing that no amendment made by Pub.L. 103-270 establishing or modifying a reporting requirement shall be construed to require that a report submitted prior to June 30, 1994 be supplemented to include information with respect to activity occurring during any time period, and that the division of the court described in section 49 of this title is authorized to appoint as an independent counsel any individual who, on June 30, 1994, is serving as a regulatory independent counsel under parts 600 and 603 of title 28, Code of Federal Regulations, notwithstanding the restriction in subsec. (b)(2) of this section, see section 7(a), (g), (h) of Pub.L. 103-270, set out as a note under section 591 of this title.

1987 Acts. Amendment by Pub.L. 100-191 to take effect on Dec. 15, 1987, and to apply only to new independent counsel proceedings and to new independent counsels coming into existence on and after Dec. 15, 1987, but with subsec. (f) applicable to previously initiated proceedings still pending on Dec. 15, 1987, see section 6 of Pub.L. 100-191, set out as a note under section 591 of this title.

1978 Acts. Section effective Oct. 26, 1978, except for specific information received by the Attorney General pursuant to section 591 of this title based on determinations made by the Attorney General respecting such information, see section 604 of Pub.L. 95-521, set out as a note under section 591 of this title.

§ 594. Authority and duties of an independent counsel

(a) **Authorities.**—Notwithstanding any other provision of law, an independent counsel appointed under this chapter shall have, with respect to all matters in such independent counsel's prosecutorial jurisdiction established under this chapter, full power and independent authority to exercise all investigative and prosecutorial functions and powers of the Department of Justice, the Attorney General, and any other officer or employee of the Department of Justice, except that the Attorney General shall exercise direction or control as to those matters that specifically require the Attorney General's personal action under section 2516 of title 18. Such investigative and prosecutorial functions and powers shall include—

(1) conducting proceedings before grand juries and other investigations;

(2) participating in court proceedings and engaging in any litigation, including civil and criminal matters, that such independent counsel considers necessary;

(3) appealing any decision of a court in any case or proceeding in which such independent counsel participates in an official capacity;

(4) reviewing all documentary evidence available from any source;

(5) determining whether to contest the assertion of any testimonial privilege;

(6) receiving appropriate national security clearances and, if necessary, contesting in court (including, where appropriate, participating in in camera proceedings) any claim of privilege or attempt to withhold evidence on grounds of national security;

(7) making applications to any Federal court for a grant of immunity to any witness, consistent with applicable statutory requirements, or for warrants, subpoenas, or other court orders, and, for purposes of sections 6003, 6004, and 6005 of title 18, exercising the authority vested in a United States attorney or the Attorney General;

(8) inspecting, obtaining, or using the original or a copy of any tax return, in accordance with the applicable statutes and regulations, and, for purposes of section 6103 of the Internal Revenue Code of 1986 and the regulations issued thereunder, exercising the powers vested in a United States attorney or the Attorney General;

(9) initiating and conducting prosecutions in any court of competent jurisdiction, framing and signing indictments, filing informations, and handling all aspects of any case, in the name of the United States; and

(10) consulting with the United States attorney for the district in which any violation of law with respect to which the independent counsel is appointed was alleged to have occurred.

(b) Compensation.—

(1) In general.—An independent counsel appointed under this chapter shall receive compensation at the per diem rate equal to the annual rate of basic pay payable for level IV of the Executive Schedule under section 5315 of title 5.

(2) Travel expenses.—Except as provided in paragraph (3), an independent counsel and persons appointed under subsection (c) shall be entitled to the payment of travel expenses as provided by subchapter I of chapter 57 of title 5, United States Code, including travel, per diem, and subsistence expenses in accordance with section 5703 of title 5.

(3) Travel to primary office.—

(A) In general.—After 1 year of service under this chapter, an independent counsel and persons appointed under subsection (c) shall not be entitled to the payment of travel, per diem, or subsistence expenses under subchapter I of chapter 57 of title 5, United States Code, for the purpose of commuting to or from the city in which the primary office of the independent counsel or person is located. The 1-year period may be extended for successive 6-month periods if the independent counsel and the division of the court certify that the payment is in the public interest to carry out the purposes of this chapter.

(B) Relevant factors.—In making any certification under this paragraph with respect to travel and subsistence expenses of an independent counsel or person appointed under subsection (c), such employee shall consider, among other relevant factors—

(i) the cost to the Government of reimbursing such travel and subsistence expenses;

(ii) the period of time for which the independent counsel anticipates that the activities of the independent counsel or person, as the case may be, will continue;

(iii) the personal and financial burdens on the independent counsel or person, as the case may be, of relocating so that such travel and subsistence expenses would not be incurred; and

(iv) the burdens associated with appointing a new independent counsel, or appointing another person under subsection (c), to replace the individual involved who is unable or unwilling to so relocate.

(c) Additional personnel.—For the purposes of carrying out the duties of an office of independent counsel, such independent counsel may appoint, fix the compensation, and assign the duties of such employees as such independent counsel considers necessary (including investigators, attorneys, and part-time consultants). The positions of all such employees are exempted from the competitive service. Such employees shall be compensated at levels not to exceed those payable for comparable positions in the Office of United States Attorney for the District of Columbia under sections 548 and 550, but in no event shall any such employee be compensated at a rate greater than the rate of basic pay payable for level ES–4 of the Senior Executive Service Schedule under section 5382 of title 5, as adjusted for the District of Columbia under section 5304 of that title regardless of the locality in which an employee is employed.

(d) Assistance of Department of Justice.—

(1) In carrying out functions.—An independent counsel may request assistance from the Department of Justice in carrying out the functions of the independent counsel, and the Department of Justice shall provide that assistance, which may include access to any records, files, or other materials relevant to matters within such independent counsel's prosecutorial jurisdiction, and the use of the resources and personnel necessary to perform such independent counsel's duties. At the request of an independent counsel, prosecutors, administrative personnel, and other employees of the Department of Justice may be detailed to the staff of the independent counsel.

(2) Payment of and reports on expenditures of independent counsel.—The Department of Justice shall pay all costs relating to the establishment and operation of any office of independent counsel. The Attorney General shall submit to the Congress, not later than 30 days after the end of each fiscal year, a report on amounts paid during that fiscal year for expenses of investigations and prosecutions by independent counsel. Each such report shall include a statement of all payments made for activities of independent counsel but may not reveal the identity or prosecutorial jurisdiction of any independent counsel which has not been disclosed under section 593(b)(4).

(e) Referral of other matters to an independent counsel.—An independent counsel may ask the Attorney General or the division of the court to refer to the independent counsel matters related to the independent counsel's prosecutorial jurisdiction, and the Attorney General or the division of the court, as the case may be, may refer such matters. If the Attorney General refers a matter to an independent counsel on the Attorney General's own initiative, the independent counsel may accept such referral if the matter relates to the independent counsel's prosecutorial jurisdiction. If the Attorney General refers any matter to the independent counsel pursuant to the independent counsel's request, or if the independent counsel accepts a referral made by the Attorney General on the Attorney General's own initiative, the independent counsel shall so notify the division of the court.

(f) Compliance with policies of the Department of Justice.—

(1) In general.—An independent counsel shall, except to the extent that to do so would be inconsistent with the purposes of this chapter, comply with the written or other established policies of the Department of Justice respecting enforcement of the criminal laws. To determine these policies and policies under subsection (*l*)(1)(B), the independent counsel shall, except to the extent that doing so would be inconsistent with the purposes of this chapter, consult with the Department of Justice.

(2) National security.—An independent counsel shall comply with guidelines and procedures used by the Department in the handling and use of classified material.

(g) Dismissal of matters.—The independent counsel shall have full authority to dismiss matters within the independent counsel's prosecutorial jurisdiction without conducting an investigation or at any subsequent time before prosecution, if to do so would be consistent with the written or other established policies of the Department of Justice with respect to the enforcement of criminal laws.

(h) Reports by independent counsel.—

(1) Required reports.—An independent counsel shall—

(A) file with the division of the court, with respect to the 6–month period beginning on the date of his or her appointment, and with respect to each 6–month period thereafter until the office of that independent counsel terminates, a report which identifies and explains major expenses, and summarizes all other expenses, incurred by that office during the 6–month period with respect to which the report is filed, and estimates future expenses of that office; and

(B) before the termination of the independent counsel's office under section 596(b), file a final report with the division of the court, setting forth fully and completely a description of the work of the independent counsel, including the disposition of all cases brought.

(2) Disclosure of information in reports.—The division of the court may release to the Congress, the public, or any appropriate person, such portions of a report made under this subsection as the division of the court considers appropriate. The division of the court shall make such orders as are appropriate to protect the rights of any individual named in such report and to prevent undue interference with any pending prosecution. The division of the court may make any portion of a final report filed under paragraph (1)(B) available to any individual named in such report for the purposes of receiving within a time limit set by the division of the court any comments or factual information that such individual may submit. Such comments and factual information, in whole or in part, may, in the discretion of the division of the court, be included as an appendix to such final report.

(3) Publication of reports.—At the request of an independent counsel, the Public Printer shall cause to be printed any report previously released to the public under paragraph (2). The independent counsel shall certify the number of copies necessary for the public, and the Public Printer shall place the cost of the required number to the debit of such independent counsel. Additional copies shall be made available to the public through the depository library program and Superintendent of Documents sales program pursuant to sections 1702 and 1903 of title 44.

(i) Independence from Department of Justice.—Each independent counsel appointed under this chapter, and the persons appointed by that independent counsel under subsection (c), are separate from and independent of the Department of Justice for purposes of sections 202 through 209 of title 18.

(j) Standards of conduct applicable to independent counsel, persons serving in the office of an independent counsel, and their law firms.—

(1) Restrictions on employment while independent counsel and appointees are serving.—(A) During the period in which an independent counsel is serving under this chapter—

(i) such independent counsel, and

(ii) any person associated with a firm with which such independent counsel is associated,

may not represent in any matter any person involved in any investigation or prosecution under this chapter.

(B) During the period in which any person appointed by an independent counsel under subsection (c) is serving in the office of independent counsel, such person may not represent in any matter any person involved in any investigation or prosecution under this chapter.

(2) Post employment restrictions on independent counsel and appointees.—(A) Each independent counsel and each person appointed by that independent counsel under subsection (c) may not, for 3 years following the termination of the service under this chapter of that independent counsel or appointed person, as the case may be, represent any person in any matter if that individual was the subject of an investigation or prosecution under this chapter that was conducted by that independent counsel.

(B) Each independent counsel and each person appointed by that independent counsel under subsection (c) may not, for 1 year following the termination of the service under this chapter of that independent counsel or appointed person, as the case may be, represent any person in any matter involving any investigation or prosecution under this chapter.

(3) One-year ban on representation by members of firms of independent counsel.—Any person who is associated with a firm with which an independent counsel is associated or becomes associated after termination of the service of that independent counsel under this chapter may not, for 1 year following such termination, represent any person in any matter involving any investigation or prosecution under this chapter.

(4) Definitions.—For purposes of this subsection—

(A) the term "firm" means a law firm whether organized as a partnership or corporation; and

(B) a person is "associated" with a firm if that person is an officer, director, partner, or other member or employee of that firm.

(5) Enforcement.—The Attorney General and the Director of the Office of Government Ethics have authority to enforce compliance with this subsection.

(k) Custody of records of an independent counsel.—

(1) Transfer of records.—Upon termination of the office of an independent counsel, that independent counsel shall transfer to the Archivist of the United States all records which have been created or received by that office. Before this transfer, the independent counsel shall clearly identify which of these records are subject to rule 6(e) of the Federal Rules of Criminal Procedure as grand jury materials and which of these records have been classified as national security information. Any records which were compiled by an independent counsel and, upon termination of the independent counsel's office, were stored with the division of the court or elsewhere before the enactment of the Independent Counsel Reauthorization Act of 1987, shall also be transferred to the Archivist of the United States by the division of the court or the person in possession of such records.

(2) Maintenance, use, and disposal of records.—Records transferred to the Archivist under this chapter shall be maintained, used, and disposed of in accordance with chapters 21, 29, and 33 of title 44.

(3) Access to records.—

(A) In general.—Subject to paragraph (4), access to the records transferred to the Archivist under this chapter shall be governed by section 552 of title 5.

(B) Access by Department of Justice.—The Archivist shall, upon written application by the Attorney General, disclose any such records to the Department of Justice for purposes of an ongoing law enforcement investigation or court proceeding, except that, in the case of grand jury materials, such records shall be so disclosed only by order of the court of jurisdiction under rule 6(e) of the Federal Rules of Criminal Procedure.

(C) Exception.—Notwithstanding any restriction on access imposed by law, the Archivist and persons employed by the National Archives and Records Administration who are engaged in the performance of normal archival work shall be permitted access to the records transferred to the Archivist under this chapter.

(4) Records provided by Congress.—Records of an investigation conducted by a committee of the House of Representatives or the Senate which are provided to an independent counsel to assist in an investigation or prosecution conducted by that independent counsel—

(A) shall be maintained as a separate body of records within the records of the independent counsel; and

(B) shall, after the records have been transferred to the Archivist under this chapter, be made available, except as provided in paragraph (3)(B) and (C), in accordance with the rules governing release of the records of the House of Congress that provided the records to the independent counsel.

Subparagraph (B) shall not apply to those records which have been surrendered pursuant to grand jury or court proceedings.

(*l*) Cost controls and administrative support.—

(1) Cost controls.—

(A) In general.—An independent counsel shall—

(i) conduct all activities with due regard for expense;

(ii) authorize only reasonable and lawful expenditures; and

(iii) promptly, upon taking office, assign to a specific employee the duty of certifying that expenditures of the independent counsel are reasonable and made in accordance with law.

(B) Liability for invalid certification.—An employee making a certification under subparagraph (A)(iii) shall be liable for an invalid certification to the same extent as a certifying official certifying a voucher is liable under section 3528 of title 31.

(C) Department of justice policies.—An independent counsel shall comply with the established policies of the Department of Justice respecting expenditures of funds, except to the extent that compliance would be inconsistent with the purposes of this chapter.

(2) Administrative support.—The Director of the Administrative Office of the United States Courts shall provide administrative support and guidance to each independent counsel. No officer or employee of the Administrative Office of the United States Courts shall disclose information related to an independent counsel's expenditures, personnel, or administrative acts or arrangements without the authorization of the independent counsel.

(3) Office space.—The Administrator of General Services, in consultation with the Director of the Administrative Office of the United States Courts, shall promptly provide appropriate office space for each independent counsel. Such office space shall be within a Federal building unless the Administrator of General Services determines that other arrangements would cost less. Until such office space is provided, the Administrative Office of the United States Courts shall provide newly appointed independent counsels immediately upon appointment with appropriate, temporary office space, equipment, and supplies.

(Added Pub.L. 95–521, Title VI, § 601(a), Oct. 26, 1978, 92 Stat. 1869, and amended Pub.L. 97–409, §§ 2(a)(1), 6(a) to (c), Jan. 3, 1983, 96 Stat. 2039, 2041; Pub.L. 99–514, § 2, Oct. 22, 1986, 100 Stat. 2095; Pub.L. 100–191, § 2, Dec. 15, 1987, 101 Stat. 1300; Pub.L. 103–270, § 3(a) to (f), (m), (*o*), June 30, 1994, 108 Stat. 732 to 734, 736; Pub.L. 104–208, Div. A, Title I, § 101(a) [Title I, § 118], Sept. 30, 1996, 110 Stat. 3009–23.)

HISTORICAL AND STATUTORY NOTES

References in Text

Section 6103 of the Internal Revenue Code of 1986, referred to in subsec. (a)(8), is classified to section 6103 of Title 26, Internal Revenue Code.

The Federal Rules of Criminal Procedure, referred to in subsec. (k)(1), (3)(B), are set out in Title 18, Crimes and Criminal Procedure.

The enactment of the Independent Counsel Reauthorization Act of 1987, referred to in subsec. (k)(1), is the enactment of Pub.L. 100–191, which was approved Dec. 15, 1987.

References in Other Laws to GS–16, 17, or 18 Pay Rates

References in laws to the rates of pay for GS–16, 17, or 18, or to maximum rates of pay under the General Schedule, to be considered references to rates payable under specified sections of Title 5, Government Organization and Employees, see section 529 [Title I, § 101(c)(1)] of Pub.L. 101–509, set out in a note under section 5376 of Title 5.

Codifications

Pub.L. 104–208, Div. A, Title I, § 101(a) [Title I, § 118(c)], Sept. 30, 1996, 110 Stat. 3009–23, which directed that the second sentence of subsec. (b)(3)(A) of this section be amended by substituting "the independent counsel" and "the division of the court" for "such employee", could not be executed to text, as second sentence of subsec. (b)(3)(A) did not contain phrase "such employee".

Effective Dates

1994 Acts. Amendment by Pub.L. 103–270 applicable with respect to independent counsels appointed before, on, or after June 30, 1994, with transition provisions relating to assignment of employee to certify expenditures, and relating to office space, travel and subsistence expenses, and rates of compensation under this section, and with provision directing that no amendment made by Pub.L. 103–270 establishing or modifying a reporting requirement be construed to require that a report submitted prior to June 30, 1994 be supplemented to include information with respect to activity occurring during any time period, see section 7(a) to (e), (g) of Pub.L. 103–270, set out as a note under section 591 of this title.

1987 Acts. Amendment by Pub.L. 100–191 effective Dec. 15, 1987, and applicable to proceedings initiated and independent counsels appointed on and after Dec. 15, 1987, but with the following provisions applicable to previously initiated proceedings pending on Dec. 15, 1987: subsec. (d)(2) (relating to reports by Attorney General on expenditures by independent counsel, except that the first such report shall be made only with respect to expenditures on or after Dec. 15, 1987), subsec. (h)(1)(A) except that the 6–month periods described in subsec. (h)(1)(A) of this section shall be calculated from Dec. 15, 1987, subsec. (i), subsec. (k) of this section, and 90 days after Dec. 15, 1987, subsec. (j), see section 6 of Pub.L. 100–191, set out as a note under section 591 of this title.

1978 Acts. Section effective Oct. 26, 1978, except for specific information received by the Attorney General pursuant to section 591 of this title based on determinations made by the Attorney General respecting such information, see section 604 of Pub.L. 95–521, set out as a note under section 591 of this title.

§ 595. Congressional oversight

(a) Oversight of conduct of independent counsel.—

(1) Congressional oversight.—The appropriate committees of the Congress shall have oversight jurisdiction with respect to the official conduct of any independent counsel appointed under this chapter, and such independent counsel shall have the duty to cooperate with the exercise of such oversight jurisdiction.

(2) Reports to Congress.—An independent counsel appointed under this chapter shall submit to the Congress annually a report on the activities of the independent counsel, including a description of the progress of any investigation or prosecution conducted by the independent counsel. Such report may omit any matter that in the judgment of the independent counsel should be kept confidential, but shall provide information adequate to justify the expenditures that the office of the independent counsel has made.

(b) Oversight of conduct of Attorney General.—Within 15 days after receiving an inquiry about a particular case under this chapter, which is a matter of public knowledge, from a committee of the Congress with jurisdiction over this chapter, the Attorney General shall provide the following information to that committee with respect to that case:

(1) When the information about the case was received.

(2) Whether a preliminary investigation is being conducted, and if so, the date it began.

(3) Whether an application for the appointment of an independent counsel or a notification that further investigation is not warranted has been filed with the division of the court, and if so, the date of such filing.

(c) Information relating to impeachment.—An independent counsel shall advise the House of Representatives of any substantial and credible information which such independent counsel receives, in carrying out the independent counsel's responsibilities under this chapter, that may constitute grounds for an impeachment. Nothing in this chapter or section 49 of this title shall prevent the Congress or either House thereof from obtaining information in the course of an impeachment proceeding.

(Added Pub.L. 95–521, Title VI, § 601(a), Oct. 26, 1978, 92 Stat. 1871, and amended Pub.L. 97–409, § 2(a)(1), Jan. 3, 1983, 96 Stat. 2039; Pub.L. 100–191, § 2, Dec. 15, 1987, 101 Stat. 1304; Pub.L. 103–270, § 3(g), June 30, 1994, 108 Stat. 734.)

HISTORICAL AND STATUTORY NOTES

Effective Dates

1994 Acts. Amendment by Pub.L. 103–270 applicable with respect to independent counsels appointed before, on, or after June 30, 1994, with provision directing that no amendment made by Pub.L. 103–270 establishing or modifying a reporting requirement be construed to require that a report submitted prior to June 30, 1994 be supplemented to include information with respect to any time period, see section 7(a), (g) of Pub.L. 103–270, set out as a note under section 591 of this title.

1987 Acts. Amendment by Pub.L. 100–191 effective Dec. 15, 1987, and applicable to proceedings initiated and independent counsels appointed on and after Dec. 15, 1987, see section 6 of Pub.L. 100–191, set out as a note under section 591 of this title.

1978 Acts. Section effective Oct. 26, 1978, except for specific information received by the Attorney General pursuant to section 591 of this title based on determinations made by the Attorney General respecting such information, see section 604 of Pub.L. 95–521, set out as a note under section 591 of this title.

§ 596. Removal of an independent counsel; termination of office

(a) Removal; report on removal.—

(1) Grounds for removal.—An independent counsel appointed under this chapter may be removed from office, other than by impeachment and conviction, only by the personal action of the Attorney General and only for good cause, physical or mental disability (if not prohibited by law protecting persons from discrimination on the basis of such a disability),,[1] or any other condition that substantially impairs the performance of such independent counsel's duties.

(2) Report to division of the court and Congress.—If an independent counsel is removed from office, the Attorney General shall promptly submit to the division of the court and the Committees on the Judiciary of the Senate and the House of Representatives a report specifying the facts found and the ultimate grounds for such removal. The committees shall make available to the public such report, except that each committee may, if necessary to protect the rights of any individual named in the report or to prevent undue interference with any pending prosecution, postpone or refrain from publishing any or all of the report. The division of the court may release any or all of such report in accordance with section 594(h)(2).

(3) Judicial review of removal.—An independent counsel removed from office may obtain judicial review of the removal in a civil action commenced in the United States District Court for the District of Columbia. A member of the division of the court may not hear or determine any such civil action or any appeal of a decision in any such civil action. The independent counsel may be reinstated or granted other appropriate relief by order of the court.

(b) Termination of office.—

(1) Termination by action of independent counsel.—An office of independent counsel shall terminate when—

(A) the independent counsel notifies the Attorney General that the investigation of all matters within the prosecutorial jurisdiction of such independent counsel or accepted by such independent counsel under section 594(e), and any resulting prosecutions, have been completed or so substantially completed that it would be appropriate for the Department of Justice to complete such investigations and prosecutions; and

(B) the independent counsel files a final report in compliance with section 594(h)(1)(B).

(2) Termination by division of the court.—The division of the court, either on its own motion or upon the request of the Attorney General, may terminate an office of independent counsel at any time, on the ground that the investigation of all matters within the prosecutorial jurisdiction of such independent counsel or accepted by such independent counsel under section 594(e), and any resulting prosecutions, have been completed or so substantially completed that it would be appropriate for the Department of Justice to complete such investigations and prosecutions. At the time of such termination, the independent counsel shall file the final report required by section 594(h)(1)(B). If the Attorney General has not made a request under this paragraph, the division of the court shall determine on its own motion whether termination is appropriate under this paragraph no later than 2 years after the appointment of an independent counsel, at the end of the succeeding 2-year period, and thereafter at the end of each succeeding 1-year period.

(c) Audits.—(1) On or before June 30 of each year, an independent counsel shall prepare a statement of expenditures for the 6 months that ended on the immediately preceding March 31. On or before December 31 of each year, an independent counsel shall prepare a statement of expenditures for the fiscal year that ended on the immediately preceding September 30. An independent counsel whose office is terminated prior to the end of the fiscal year shall prepare a statement of expenditures on or before the date that is 90 days after the date on which the office is terminated.

(2) The Comptroller General shall—

(A) conduct a financial review of a mid-year statement and a financial audit of a year-end statement and statement on termination; and

(B) report the results to the Committee on the Judiciary, Committee on Governmental Affairs, and Committee on Appropriations of the Senate and the Committee on the Judiciary, Committee on Government Operations, and Committee on Appropriations of the House of Representatives not later than 90 days following the submission of each such statement.

(Added Pub.L. 95–521, Title VI, § 601(a), Oct. 26, 1978, 92 Stat. 1872, and amended Pub.L. 97–409, §§ 2(a)(1), 6(d), Jan. 3, 1983, 96 Stat. 2039, 2042; Pub.L. 98–620, Title IV, § 402(29)(A), Nov. 8, 1984, 98 Stat. 3359; Pub.L. 100–191, § 2, Dec. 15, 1987, 101 Stat. 1304; Pub.L. 103–270, §§ 3(h), (i), 5, June 30, 1994, 108 Stat. 735, 737.)

[1] So in original.

HISTORICAL AND STATUTORY NOTES

Effective Dates

1994 Acts. Amendment by Pub.L. 103–270 applicable with respect to independent counsels appointed before, on, or after June 30, 1994, with provisions directing that determinations by the division of the court contained in the last sentence of subsec. (b)(2) of this section shall, for the office of an independent counsel appointed before June 30, 1994, be required no later than 1 year after June 30, 1994, and at the end of each succeeding 1-year period, and provisions directing that no amendment made by Pub.L. 103–270 establishing or modifying a reporting requirement be construed to require that a report submitted prior to June 30, 1994 be supplemented to include information with respect to activity occurring during any time period, see section 7(a), (f), (g) of Pub.L. 103–270, set out as a note under section 591 of this title.

1987 Acts. Amendment by Pub.L. 100–191 effective Dec. 15, 1987, and applicable to proceedings initiated and independent counsels appointed on and after Dec. 15, 1987, but with subsecs. (a)(3) and (c) applicable to previously initiated proceedings pending on Dec. 15, 1987, see section 6 of Pub.L. 100–191, set out as a note under section 591 of this title.

1984 Acts. Amendment by Pub.L. 98–620 not to apply to cases pending on Nov. 8, 1984, see section 403 of Pub.L. 98–620, set out as a note under section 1657 of this title.

1978 Acts. Section effective Oct. 26, 1978, except for specific information received by the Attorney General pursuant to section 591 of this title based on determinations made by the Attorney General respecting such information, see section 604 of Pub.L. 95–521, set out as a note under section 591 of this title.

Change of Name

Any reference in any provision of law enacted before Jan. 4, 1995, to the Committee on Government Operations of the House of Representatives treated as referring to the Committee on Government Reform and Oversight of the House of Representatives, except that any reference in any provision of law enacted before Jan. 4, 1995, to the Committee on Government Operations of the House of Representatives treated as referring to the Committee on the Budget of the House of Representatives in the case of a provision of law relating to the establishment, extension, and enforcement of special controls over the Federal budget, see section 1(a)(6) and (c)(2) of Pub.L. 104–14, set out as a note preceding section 21 of Title 2, The Congress.

§ 597. Relationship with Department of Justice

(a) Suspension of other investigations and proceedings.—Whenever a matter is in the prosecutorial jurisdiction of an independent counsel or has been accepted by an independent counsel under section 594(e), the Department of Justice, the Attorney General, and all other officers and employees of the Department of Justice shall suspend all investigations and proceedings regarding such matter, except to the extent required by section 594(d)(1), and except insofar as such independent counsel agrees in writing that such investigation or proceedings may be continued by the Department of Justice.

(b) Presentation as amicus curiae permitted.—Nothing in this chapter shall prevent the Attorney General or the Solicitor General from making a presentation as amicus curiae to any court as to issues of law raised by any case or proceeding in which an independent counsel participates in an official capacity or any appeal of such a case or proceeding.

(Added Pub.L. 95–521, Title VI, § 601(a), Oct. 26, 1978, 92 Stat. 1872, and amended Pub.L. 97–409, § 2(a)(1)(A), Jan. 3, 1983, 96 Stat. 2039; Pub.L. 100–191, § 2, Dec. 15, 1987, 101 Stat. 1306.)

HISTORICAL AND STATUTORY NOTES

Effective Dates

1987 Acts. Amendment by Pub.L. 100–191 effective Dec. 15, 1987, and applicable to proceedings initiated and independent counsels appointed on and after Dec. 15, 1987, section 6 of Pub.L. 100–191, set out as a note under section 591 of this title.

1978 Acts. Section effective Oct. 26, 1978, except for specific information received by the Attorney General pursuant to section 591 of this title based on determinations made by the Attorney General respecting such information, see section 604 of Pub.L. 95–521, set out as a note under section 591 of this title.

§ 598. Severability

If any provision of this chapter or the application thereof to any person or circumstance is held invalid, the remainder of this chapter and the application of such provision to other persons not similarly situated or to other circumstances shall not be affected by such invalidation.

(Added Pub.L. 95–521, Title VI, § 601(a), Oct. 26, 1978, 92 Stat. 1873, and amended Pub.L. 97–409, §§ 2(a)(1)(A), 7, Jan. 3, 1983, 96 Stat. 2039, 2042; Pub.L. 100–191, § 2, Dec. 15, 1987, 101 Stat. 1306.)

HISTORICAL AND STATUTORY NOTES

Effective Dates

1987 Acts. Amendment by Pub.L. 100–191 effective Dec. 15, 1987, and to apply only to new independent counsel proceedings and to new independent counsels coming into existence on and after Dec. 15, 1987, see section 6 of Pub.L. 100–191, set out as a note under section 591 of this title.

1978 Acts. Section effective Oct. 26, 1978, except for specific information received by the Attorney General pursuant to section 591 of this title based on determinations made by the Attorney General respecting such information, see section 604 of Pub.L. 95–521, set out as a note under section 591 of this title.

§ 599. Termination of effect of chapter

This chapter shall cease to be effective five years after the date of the enactment of the Independent Counsel Reauthorization Act of 1994, except that this chapter shall continue in effect with respect to then pending matters before an independent counsel that in the judgment of such counsel require such continuation until that independent counsel determines such matters have been completed.

(Added Pub.L. 100–191, § 2, Dec. 15, 1987, 101 Stat. 1306, and amended Pub.L. 103–270, § 2, June 30, 1994, 108 Stat. 732.)

HISTORICAL AND STATUTORY NOTES

References in Text

The date of the enactment of the Independent Counsel Reauthorization Act of 1994, referred to in text, is the date of the enactment of Pub.L. 103–270, which was approved June 30, 1994.

Effective Dates

1994 Acts. Amendment by Pub.L. 103–270 applicable with respect to independent counsels appointed before, on, or after June 30, 1994, see section 7(a) of Pub.L. 103–270, set out as a note under section 591 of this title.

1987 Acts. Section effective Dec. 15, 1987, see section 6 of Pub.L. 100–191, set out as a note under section 591 of this title.

PART III—COURT OFFICERS AND EMPLOYEES

Chapter		Section
41.	Administrative Office of United States Courts	601
42.	Federal Judicial Center	620
43.	United States Magistrates	631
44.	Alternative Dispute Resolution	651
45.	Supreme Court	671
47.	Courts of Appeals	711
49.	District Courts	751
51.	United States Court of Federal Claims	791
[53.	Repealed]	
55.	Court of International Trade	871
57.	General Provisions Applicable to Court Officers and Employees	951
58.	United States Sentencing Commission	991

HISTORICAL AND STATUTORY NOTES

Codifications

The analysis of chapters comprising Part III was amended by Pub.L. 95–598, Title II, § 233(b) Nov. 6, 1978, 92 Stat. 2667 effective June 28, 1984, pursuant to Pub.L. 95–598, Title IV, § 402(b), Nov. 6, 1978, 92 Stat. 2682, as amended by Pub.L. 98–249, § 1(a), Mar. 31, 1984, 98 Stat. 116; Pub.L. 98–271, § 1(a), Apr. 30, 1984, 98 Stat. 163; Pub.L. 98–299, § 1(a), May 25, 1984, 98 Stat. 214; Pub.L. 98–325, § 1(a), June 20, 1984, 98 Stat. 268, set out as an Effective Dates note preceding section 101 of Title 11, Bankruptcy, by adding:

"50. Bankruptcy Courts .... 771."

Senate Revision Amendment

Chapter 59 was renumbered as Chapter 57 but without change in its section numbers, by Senate amendment. See 80th Congress Senate Report No. 1559.

CHAPTER 41—ADMINISTRATIVE OFFICE OF UNITED STATES COURTS

Sec.	
601.	Creation; Director and Deputy Director.
602.	Employees.
603.	Salaries.
604.	Duties of Director generally.
605.	Budget estimates.
606.	Duties of Deputy Director.
607.	Practice of law prohibited.
608.	Seal.
609.	Courts' appointive power unaffected.
610.	Courts defined.
611.	Retirement of Director.
612.	Judiciary Automation Fund.

HISTORICAL AND STATUTORY NOTES

Codifications

Section 5602(b)(1) of Pub.L. 104–106, Div. E, Title LVI, Feb. 10, 1996, 110 Stat. 699, directed the substitution of "Judiciary Information Technology Fund" for "Judiciary Automation Fund" as the heading of section 612 of this title with no conforming amendment to item 612 of the section analysis. Section 5701 of Pub.L. 104–106, Div. E, Title LVII, Feb. 10, 1996, 110 Stat. 702, provided that the amendment to section 612 of this title is effective 180 days after Feb. 10, 1996.

§ 601. Creation; Director and Deputy Director

The Administrative Office of the United States Courts shall be maintained at the seat of government. It shall be supervised by a Director and a Deputy Director appointed and subject to removal by the Chief Justice of the United States, after consulting with the Judicial Conference. The Director and Deputy Director shall be deemed to be officers for purposes of title 5, United States Code.

(June 25, 1948, c. 646, 62 Stat. 913; Sept. 23, 1959, Pub.L. 86–370, § 5(a)(1), 73 Stat. 652; Dec. 1, 1990, Pub.L. 101–650, Title III, § 307, 104 Stat. 5112; Oct. 19, 1996, Pub.L. 104–317, Title VI, § 602, 110 Stat. 3857.)

HISTORICAL AND STATUTORY NOTES

Effective Dates

1959 Acts. Amendment by Pub.L. 86–370 effective Sept. 23, 1959, see section 7(a) of Pub.L. 86–370.

Judicial Branch Appointments

Pub.L. 105–339, § 4(d), Oct. 31, 1998, 112 Stat. 3186, provided that:

"(1) **In general.**—Subject to paragraphs (2) and (3), the Judicial Conference of the United States shall prescribe procedures to provide for—

"(A) veterans' preference in the consideration of applicants for employment, and in the conduct of any reductions in force, within the judicial branch; and

"(B) redress for alleged violations of any rights provided for under subparagraph (A).

"(2) **Procedures.**—Under the procedures, a preference eligible (as defined by section 2108 of title 5, United States Code) shall be afforded preferences in a manner and to the extent consistent with preferences afforded to preference eligibles in the executive branch.

"(3) **Exclusions.**—Nothing in the procedures shall apply with respect to an applicant or employee—

"(A) whose appointment is made by the President with the advice and consent of the Senate;

"(B) whose appointment is as a judicial officer;

"(C) whose appointment is required by statute to be made by or with the approval of a court or judicial officer; or

"(D) whose appointment is to a position, the duties of which are equivalent to those of a Senior Executive Service position (within the meaning of section 3132(a)(2) of title 5, United States Code).

"(4) **Definitions.**—For purposes of this subsection [this note], the term "judicial officer" means a justice, judge, or magistrate judge listed in subparagraph (A), (B), (F), or (G) of section 376(a)(1) of title 28, United States Code.

"(5) **Submission to Congress; effective date.**—

"(A) **Submission to Congress.**—Not later than 12 months after the date of enactment of this Act [Oct. 31, 1998], the Judicial Conference of the United States shall submit a copy of the procedures prescribed under this subsection [this note] to the Committee on Government Reform and Oversight and the Committee on the Judiciary of the House of Representatives and the Committee on Governmental Affairs and the Committee on the Judiciary of the Senate.

"(B) **Effective date.**—The procedures prescribed under this subsection [this note] shall take effect 13 months after the date of enactment of this Act [Oct. 31, 1998]."

Continuation of Law Existing on Sept. 1, 1948

Section 2(b) of Act June 25, 1948, provided that: "The provisions of Title 28, Judiciary and Judicial Procedure, of the United States Code, set out in section 1 of this Act, with respect to the organization of each of the several courts therein provided for and of the Administrative Office of the United States Courts, shall be construed as continuations of existing law, and the tenure of the judges, officers, and employees thereof and of the United States attorneys and marshals and their deputies and assistants, in office on the effective date of this Act [Sept. 1, 1948], shall not be affected by its enactment, but each of them shall continue to serve in the same capacity under the appropriate provisions of title 28, as set out in section 1 of this Act, pursuant to his prior appointment: *Provided, however,* That each circuit court of appeals shall, as in said title 28 set out, hereafter be known as a United States court of appeals. No loss of rights, interruption of jurisdiction, or prejudice to matters pending in any of such courts on the effective date of this Act shall result from its enactment."

Reference to Assistant Director Deemed Reference to Deputy Director

Section 5(a)(4) of Pub.L. 86-370 provided that: "Whenever the Assistant Director of the Administrative Office of the United States Courts is referred to in any other law, such reference shall be deemed to be to the Deputy Director of the Administrative Office of the United States Courts."

§ 602. Employees

(a) The Director shall appoint and fix the compensation of necessary employees of the Administrative Office in accordance with the Administrative Office of the United States Courts Personnel Act of 1990.

(b) Notwithstanding any other law, the Director may appoint certified interpreters in accordance with section 604(a) (16) (B) of this title without regard to the provisions of chapter 51 and subchapter III of chapter 53 of title 5, relating to classification and General Schedule pay rates, but the compensation of any person appointed under this subsection shall not exceed the appropriate equivalent of the highest rate of pay payable for the highest grade established in the General Schedule, section 5332 of title 5.

(c) The Director may obtain personal services as authorized by section 3109 of title 5, at rates not to exceed the appropriate equivalent of the highest rate of pay payable for the highest grade established in the General Schedule, section 5332 of title 5.

(d) All functions of other officers and employees of the Administrative Office and all functions of organizational units of the Administrative Office are vested in the Director. The Director may delegate any of the Director's functions, powers, duties, and authority (except the authority to promulgate rules and regulations) to such officers and employees of the judicial branch of Government as the Director may designate, and subject to such terms and conditions as the Director may consider appropriate; and may authorize the successive redelegation of such functions, powers, duties, and authority as the Director may deem desirable. All official acts performed by such officers and employees shall have the same force and effect as though performed by the Director in person.

(June 25, 1948, c. 646, 62 Stat. 913; Oct. 28, 1978, Pub.L. 95–539, § 5, 92 Stat. 2044; Oct. 30, 1990, Pub.L. 101–474, § 5(a), (q), 104 Stat. 1099, 1101; Dec. 1, 1990, Pub.L. 101–650, Title III, § 325(b)(4), 104 Stat. 5121.)

HISTORICAL AND STATUTORY NOTES

References in Text

The Administrative Office of the United States Courts Personnel Act of 1990, referred to in subsec. (a), is Pub.L. 101–474, Oct. 30, 1990, 104 Stat. 1097, which is principally classified as a note under this section. For complete classification of this Act to the Code, see Administrative Office of United States Courts Personnel note set out under this section and Tables.

References in Other Laws to GS–16, 17, or 18 Pay Rates

References in laws to the rates of pay for GS–16, 17, or 18, or to maximum rates of pay under the General Schedule, to be considered references to rates payable under specified sections of Title 5, Government Organization and Employees, see section 529 [Title I, § 101 (c)(1)] of Pub.L. 101–509, set out in a note under section 5376 of Title 5.

Effective Dates

1978 Acts. Section 10 of Pub.L. 95–539 provided that:

"(a) Except as provided in subsection (b), this Act [enacting sections 1827 and 1828 of this title, amending sections 602, 603, 604, and 1920 of this title, enacting provisions set out as notes under this section and section 1 of this title, and repealing a provision set out as a note under this section] shall take effect on the date of the enactment of this Act [Oct. 28, 1978].

"(b) Section 2 of this Act [enacting sections 1827 and 1828 of this title] shall take effect ninety days after the date of the enactment of this Act [Oct. 28, 1978]."

Administrative Office of United States Courts Personnel

Sections 1 to 4 and 6 of Pub.L. 101–474 provided that:

"Section 1. Short title.

"This Act [enacting this note and amending sections 602, 603, and 604 of this title and sections 2301, 2302, 4301, 4501, 4701, 5102, 5108, 5349, 5595, 5596, 8331, 8347, 8401, and 8402 of Title 5, Government Organization and Employees] may be cited as the 'Administrative Office of the United States Courts Personnel Act of 1990'.

"Sec. 2. General personnel authority.

"The Director of the Administrative Office of the United States Courts (hereinafter in this Act referred to as the 'Director') may appoint, fix the compensation of, assign, and direct such personnel as the Director determines necessary to discharge the duties and functions of the Administrative Office.

"Sec. 3. Establishment of personnel management system.

"**(a)** The Director shall, by regulation, establish a personnel management system for the Administrative Office which provides for the appointment, pay, promotion, and assignment of all employees on the basis of merit, but without regard to the provisions of title 5, United States Code [Title 5, Government Organization and Employees], governing appointments and other personnel actions in the competitive service, or the provisions of chapter 51 and subchapter III of chapter 53 of such title, relating to classification and General Schedule pay rates. The system shall apply to all Administrative Office employees except those referred to in section 603 of title 28, United States Code [section 603 of this title], and shall, at a minimum—

"**(1)** provide for a schedule of pay rates applicable to all employees; except as provided in paragraph (10), the basic pay of any person appointed under this section shall not exceed the rate of basic pay for level V of the Executive Schedule;

"**(2)** incorporate pay comparability principles as set forth in section 5301(a) of title 5, United States Code [section 5301(a) of Title 5];

"**(3)** provide for the adjustment of the pay of employees at the same time and in the same percentage amount as rates of basic pay are adjusted for General Schedule and prevailing rate employees, as appropriate;

"**(4)** establish procedures for employee evaluations, the granting of periodic pay adjustments, incentive awards, and resolution of employee grievances;

"**(5)** establish procedures for disciplinary actions, including reduction in grade or pay, suspension, and removal, based on unacceptable performance or misconduct, except that—

"**(A)** such procedures shall be consistent with—

"**(i)** section 4303 of title 5, United States Code [section 4303 of Title 5], to the extent that they relate to adverse actions based on unacceptable performance; and

"**(ii)** chapter 75 of title 5, United States Code [section 7501 et seq. of Title 5], to the extent that they relate to adverse actions covered by such chapter; and

"**(B)** the Director may exempt from these procedures positions of a confidential or policy-determining character, not to exceed 4 percent of the authorized positions of the Administrative Office;

"**(6)** establish procedures for premium pay (including overtime), except that the Director may at his discretion implement flexible and compressed work schedules and may exempt the hours constituting such schedules from premium pay to the extent he deems necessary to implement such schedules;

"**(7)** include the principles set forth in section 2301(b) of title 5, United States Code [section 2301(b) of Title 5];

"**(8)** prohibit personnel practices prohibited under section 2302(b) of title 5, United States Code [section 2302(b) of Title 5];

"**(9)** prohibit discrimination on the basis of race, color, religion, age, sex, national origin, political affiliation, marital status, or handicapping condition; the Director must promulgate regulations providing procedures for resolving complaints of discrimination by employees and applicants for employment;

"**(10)** provide for the basic pay of not more than 5 percent of the authorized positions of the Administrative Office (excluding the positions referred to in section 603 of title 28, United States Code [section 603 of this title]) to be set at rates not to exceed the rate of basic pay for positions at level IV of the Executive Schedule; the aggregate pay (including basic pay and incentive awards) of any individual whose basic pay is set under this subsection may not exceed the salary of the Director; and

"**(11)** in the case of any individual who would be a preference eligible in the executive branch, provide preference for that individual in a manner and to an extent consistent with preference accorded to preference eligibles in the executive branch.

"**(b)** The Director may apply the provisions of sections 5723 and 6304(f) of title 5, United State Code [sections 5723 and 6304(f) of Title 5, Government Organization and Employees], to the positions referred to in subsection (a)(10) and in section 603 of title 28, United States Code [section 603 of this title], including the Deputy Director.

"**(c)** The Director may provide for incentive awards for the positions referred to in section 603 of title 28, United States Code [section 603 of this title], including the Deputy Director, subject to the aggregate pay limitation in subsection (a)(10).

"**(d)** The Chief Justice of the United States or the Judicial Conference of the United States may grant incentive awards to the Director, except that the Director's aggregate pay for any fiscal year, including salary and incentive awards, may not exceed the salary of a United States circuit judge. The Chief Justice or the Judicial Conference may authorize application of section 5723 of title 5, United States Code [section 5723 of Title 5, Government Organization and Employees], to the Director.

"**(e)** The Director may develop and conduct programs to meet the short- and long-range training needs of the agency.

"**(f)** Notwithstanding any other provision of law, an individual who is an employee of the Administrative Office on the day before the effective date of this section and who, as of that day, was entitled to—

"(1) appeal a reduction in grade or removal to the Merit Systems Protection Board under chapter 43 of title 5, United States Code [section 4301 et seq. of Title 5],

"(2) appeal an adverse action to the Merit Systems Protection Board under chapter 75 of title 5, United State Code [section 7501 et seq. of Title 5], or

"(3) file an appeal with the Equal Employment Opportunity Commission under part 1613 of title 29 of the Code of Federal Regulations,

shall continue to be entitled to file such appeal so long as the individual remains an employee of the Administrative Office, except that this provision shall not apply to employees in positions referred to in section 603 of title 28, United States Code, or in positions of a confidential or policy-determining character referred to in subsection (a)(10).

"(g) Nothing in this Act shall be construed to abolish or diminish any right or remedy granted to employees of or applicants for employment in the Administrative Office by any law prohibiting discrimination in Federal employment on the basis of race, color, religion, age, sex, national origin, political affiliation, marital status, or handicapping condition, except that, with respect to any such employees and applicants for employment, any authority granted under any such law to the Equal Employment Opportunity Commission, the Office of Personnel Management, the Merit Systems Protection Board, or any other agency in the executive branch, shall be exercised by the Administrative Office.

"Sec. 4. Noncompetitive appointments.

"(a) Notwithstanding any other provision of law, any employee of the Administrative Office who has completed at least 1 year of continuous service under a nontemporary appointment under the personnel system established pursuant to section 3 acquires a competitive status for appointment to any position in the competitive service for which the employee possesses the required qualifications.

"(b) A period of continuous service performed as a nontemporary employee of the Administrative Office immediately before the personnel system under section 3 takes effect shall, for purposes of subsection (a), be treated as if it had been performed under such system.

"Sec. 6. Authorization.

"There are authorized to be appropriated for fiscal year 1990 and for each fiscal year thereafter such sums as may be necessary to carry out the provisions of this Act."

Contract Limitations

Section 11 of Pub.L. 95–539 provided that: "Any contracts entered into under this Act or any of the amendments made by this Act [enacting sections 1827 and 1828 of this title, amending sections 602, 603, 604, and 1920 of this title, enacting provisions set out as notes under this section and section 1 of this title, and repealing a provision set out as a note under this section] shall be limited to such extent or in such amounts as are provided in advance in appropriation Acts."

Employment of Experts or Consultants: Rates

Pub.L. 86–370, § 5(b), Sept. 23, 1959, 73 Stat. 652, which authorized the Director of the Administrative Office of the United States Courts to procure the temporary or intermittent services of experts or consultants, was repealed by Pub.L. 95–539, § 8, Oct. 28, 1978, 92 Stat. 2044.

§ 603. Salaries

The salary of the Director shall be the same as the salary of a district judge. Notwithstanding any other provision of law, the Director shall not be deemed to be an "employee" for the purpose of subchapter I of chapter 63 of title 5. The salary of the Deputy Director shall be 92 percent of the salary of the Director. The salaries of six additional positions shall be fixed by the Director at rates not to exceed the annual rate of basic pay for positions at level IV of the Executive Schedule under section 5315 of title 5. (June 25, 1948, c. 646, 62 Stat. 913; Oct. 15, 1949, c. 695, §§ 5(b), 6(b), 63 Stat. 881; Oct. 31, 1951, c. 655, § 43(b), 65 Stat. 725; Sept. 23, 1959, Pub.L. 86–370, § 5(a)(1), 73 Stat. 652; Aug. 14, 1964, Pub.L. 88–426, Title IV, § 403(g), 78 Stat. 434; Dec. 16, 1967, Pub.L. 90–206, Title II, § 213(d), 81 Stat. 635; Oct. 28, 1978, Pub.L. 95–539, § 6, 92 Stat. 2044; Dec. 22, 1987, Pub.L. 100–202, § 101(a) [Title IV § 409], 101 Stat. 1329–27; Oct. 1, 1988, Pub.L. 100–459, Title IV, § 406, 102 Stat. 2213; Oct. 30, 1990, Pub.L. 101–474, § 5(b), 104 Stat. 1099.)

HISTORICAL AND STATUTORY NOTES

Effective Dates

1978 Acts. Amendment by Pub.L. 95–539 effective Oct. 28, 1978, see section 10(a) of Pub.L. 95–539, set out as a note under section 602 of this title.

1967 Acts. Section 220(a)(3) of Pub.L. 90–206 provided, except as otherwise expressly provided, that: "Sections 213(d) and (e) [which amended this section and section 792 of this title], 214(j), (k), (*l*), (n), and (*o*) [which amended sections 60j and 61–1 of Title 2, The Congress, and section 5533 of Title 5, Government Organization and Employees], 215 [which amended sections 5314 to 5316 of Title 5], 217 [which amended section 5545 of Title 5], 219 [which amended sections 136a and 136a–1 of Title 2, sections 42a and 51a of former Title 31, Money and Finance, sections 162a, 166b, and 166b–1 of Title 40, Public Buildings, Property and Works, and section 39a of Title 44, Public Printing and Documents], and 224(c) [which amended provisions set out as a note under section 102 of Title 2], shall become effective at the beginning of the first pay period which begins on or after the date of enactment of this title [Dec. 16, 1967]."

1964 Acts. Amendment by Pub.L. 88–426 effective on the first day of the first pay period which begins on or after July 1, 1964, except to the extent provided in section 501(c) of Pub.L. 88–426, see section 501(a) of Pub.L. 88–426.

1959 Acts. Amendment by Pub.L. 86–370 effective Sept. 23, 1959, see section 7(a) of Pub.L. 86–370.

1949 Acts. The increased compensation provided for by Act Oct. 15, 1949, took effect on the first day of the first pay period which began after Oct. 15, 1949 by the provisions of section 9 of said Act Oct. 15, 1949 which is set out as a note under section 273 of Title 2, The Congress.

Reference to Assistant Director Deemed Reference to Deputy Director

References in any other law to Assistant Director of the Administrative Office of the United States Courts deemed to be reference to the Deputy Director of the Administrative

Office of the United States Courts, see section 5(a)(4) of Pub.L. 86–370 set out as a note under section 601 of this title.

Salary Increases

1987—Salaries of the Director and Deputy Director increased respectively to $89,500 and $72,500 per annum, on recommendation of the President of the United States, see note set out under section 358 of Title 2, The Congress.

1977—Salaries of the Director and Deputy Director increased respectively to $54,500 and $48,500 per annum, upon recommendation of the President of the United States, see note set out under section 358 of Title 2, The Congress.

1969—Salaries of the Director and Deputy Director increased respectively from $30,000 and $28,000 to $40,000 and $36,000 per annum, commencing February 14, 1969, on recommendation of the President of the United States, see note set out under section 358 of Title 2.

1967—Section 213(a) of Pub.L. 90–206 provided that: "The rates of basic compensation of officers and employees in or under the judicial branch of the Government whose rates of compensation are fixed by or pursuant to paragraph (2) of subdivision a of section 62 of the Bankruptcy Act (11 U.S.C. 102(a)(2) [section 102(a)(2) of Title 11, Bankruptcy]), section 3656 of title 18, United States Code [section 3656 of Title 18, Crimes and Criminal Procedure], the third sentence of section 603, sections 671 to 675, inclusive, or section 604(a)(5), of title 28, United States Code [sections 603, 671 to 675, or 604(a)(5) of this Title], insofar as the latter section applies to graded positions, are hereby increased by amounts reflecting the respective applicable increases provided by section 202(a) of this title [amending section 5332(a) of Title 5, Government Organization and Employees] in corresponding rates of compensation for officers and employees subject to section 5332 of title 5, United States Code [section 5332 of Title 5]. The rates of basic compensation of officers and employees holding ungraded positions and whose salaries are fixed pursuant to such section 604(a)(5) [section 604(a)(5) of this title] may be increased by the amounts reflecting the respective applicable increases provided by section 202(a) of this title [amending section 5332(a) of Title 5] in corresponding rates of compensation for officers and employees subject to section 5332 of title 5, United States Code [section 5332 of Title 5]."

Section 213(a) of Pub.L. 90–206 effective as of the beginning of the first pay period which begins on or after Oct. 1, 1967, see section 220(a)(2) of Pub.L. 90–206, set out as a note under section 5332 of Title 5, Government Organization and Employees.

1966—Pub.L. 89–504, Title II, § 202(a), July 18, 1966, 80 Stat. 293, provided that: "The rates of basic compensation of officers and employees in or under the judicial branch of the Government whose rates of compensations are fixed by or pursuant to paragraph (2) of subdivision a of section 62 of the Bankruptcy Act (11 U.S.C. 102(a)(2) [section 102(a)(2) of Title 11, Bankruptcy]), section 3656 of title 18, United States Code [section 3656 of Title 18, Crimes and Criminal Procedure], the third sentence of section 603, sections 671 to 675, inclusive or section 604(a)(5), of title 28, United States Code [sections 603, 671 to 675, or 604(a)(5) of this title], insofar as the latter section applies to graded positions, are hereby increased by amounts reflecting the respective applicable increases provided by section 102(a) of title I of this Act [amending section 1113(b) of former Title 5, Executive Departments and Government Officers and Employees], in corresponding rates of compensation for officers and employees subject to the Classification Act of 1949, as amended [chapter 51 and subchapter III of chapter 53 of Title 5, Government Organization and Employees]. The rates of basic compensation of officers and employees holding ungraded positions and whose salaries are fixed pursuant to such section 604(a)(5) [section 604(a)(5) of this title] may be increased by the amounts reflecting the respective applicable increases provided by section 102(a) of title I of this Act in corresponding rates of compensation for officers and employees subject to the Classification Act of 1949, as amended [chapter 51 and subchapter III of chapter 53 of Title 5]."

Section 203 of Title II of Pub.L. 89–504 provided that:

"This title [sections 201 to 203 of Pub.L. 89–504] shall become effective as follows:

"(1) This section and section 201 [enacting provisions set out as a note under section 1 of this title] shall become effective on the date of enactment of this Act [July 18, 1966].

"(2) Section 202 [enacting provisions set out as note under this section and sections 604 and 753 of this title] shall become effective on the first day of the first pay period which begins on or after July 1, 1966."

1965—Pub.L. 89–301, § 12(a), Oct. 29, 1965, 79 Stat. 1121, provided that: "The rates of basic compensation of officers and employees in or under the judicial branch of the Government whose rates of compensation are fixed by or pursuant to paragraph (2) of subdivision a of section 62 of the Bankruptcy Act (11 U.S.C. 102(a)(2) [section 102(a)(2) of Title 11, Bankruptcy]), section 3656 of title 18, United States Code [section 3656 of Title 18, Crimes and Criminal Procedure], the third sentence of section 603, sections 671 to 675, inclusive, or section 604(a)(5), of title 28, United States Code [sections 603, 671 to 675, or section 604(a)(5) of this title], insofar as the latter section applies to graded positions, are hereby increased by amounts reflecting the respective applicable increases provided by section 2(a) of this Act [amending section 1113(b) of former Title 5, Executive Departments and Government Officers and Employees] in corresponding rates of compensation for officers and employees subject to the Classification Act of 1949, as amended [chapter 51 and subchapter III of chapter 53 of Title 5, Government Organization and Employees]. The rates of basic compensation of officers and employees holding ungraded positions and whose salaries are fixed pursuant to such section 604(a)(5) [section 604(a)(5) of this title] may be increased by the amounts reflecting the respective applicable increases provided by section 2(a) of this Act in corresponding rates of compensation for officers and employees subject to the Classification Act of 1949, as amended [chapter 51 and subchapter III of chapter 53 of Title 5]."

1964—Section 402(a) of Pub.L. 88–426 provided that: "The rates of basic compensation of officers and employees in or under the judicial branch of the Government whose rates of compensation are fixed by or pursuant to paragraph (2) of subdivision a of section 62 of the Bankruptcy Act (11 U.S.C. 102(a)(2) [section 102(a)(2) of Title 11, Bankruptcy]), section 3656 of title 18, United States Code [section 3656 of Title 18, Crimes and Criminal Procedure], the third sentence of section 603, sections 672 to 675, inclusive, or section 604(a)(5), of title 28, United States Code [sections 603, 672 to 675, or 604(a)(5) of this title], insofar as the latter section applies to graded positions, are hereby increased by amounts reflecting the respective applicable increases provided by title I of this

Act in corresponding rates of compensation for officers and employees subject to the Classification Act of 1949, as amended [chapter 51 and subchapter III of chapter 53 of Title 5, Government Organization and Employees]. The rates of basic compensation of officers and employees holding ungraded positions and whose salaries are fixed pursuant to section 604(a)(5) [section 604(a)(5) of this title] may be increased by the amounts reflecting the respective applicable increases provided by title I of this Act in corresponding rates of compensation for officers and employees subject to the Classification Act of 1949, as amended [chapter 51 and subchapter III of chapter 53 of Title 5]."

1962—Pub.L. 87–793, Title VI, § 1004(a), Oct. 11, 1962, 76 Stat. 866, provided that: "The rates of basic compensation of officers and employees in or under the judicial branch of the Government whose rates of compensation are fixed by or pursuant to paragraph (2) of subdivision a of section 62 of the Bankruptcy Act (11 U.S.C. 102(a)(2) [section 102(a)(2) of Title 11, Bankruptcy]), section 3656 of title 18 of the United States Code [section 3656 of Title 18, Crimes and Criminal Procedure], the third sentence of section 603, section 604(a)(5), or section 672 to 675 inclusive, of title 28 of the United States Code [sections 603, 604(a)(5), or 672 to 675 of this title], or section 107(a)(6) of the Act of July 31, 1956, as amended (5 U.S.C. 2206(a)(6) [section 2206(a)(6) of former Title 5, Executive Departments and Government Officers and Employees]), are hereby increased by two amounts, the first amount to be effective for the period beginning as of the first day of the first pay period which begins on or after the date of enactment of this Act [Oct. 11, 1962], and ending immediately prior to the first day of the first pay period which begins on or after January 1, 1964, and the second amount to be effective on the first day of the first pay period which begins on or after January 1, 1964, and thereafter, which reflect the respective applicable increases provided by title II of this part in corresponding rates of compensation for officers and employees subject to the Classification Act of 1949, as amended [chapter 51 and subchapter III of chapter 53 of Title 5, Government Organization and Employees]."

1960—Pub.L. 86–568, Title I, § 116(a), July 1, 1960, 74 Stat. 303, provided that: "The rates of basic compensation of officers and employees in or under the judicial branch of the Government whose rates of compensation are fixed by or pursuant to paragraph (2) of subdivision a of section 62 of the Bankruptcy Act (11 U.S.C. 102(a)(2) [section 102(a)(2) of Title 11, Bankruptcy]), section 3656 of title 18 of the United States Code [section 3656 of Title 18, Crimes and Criminal Procedure], the third sentence of section 603, section 604(a)(5), or sections 672 to 675, inclusive, of title 28 of the United States Code [sections 603, 604(a)(5), or sections 672 to 675 of this title], or section 107(a)(6) of the Act of July 31, 1956, as amended (5 U.S.C. 2206(a)(6) [section 2206(a)(6) of former Title 5, Executive Departments and Government Officers and Employees]), are hereby increased by amounts equal to the increases provided by section 612 [112] of this part [amending former section 1113(b) of Title 5] in corresponding rates of compensation paid to officers and employees subject to the Classification Act of 1949, as amended [chapter 51 and subchapter III of chapter 53 of Title 5, Government Organization and Employees]."

Pub.L. 87–367, Title III, § 302(d), Oct. 4, 1961, 75 Stat. 793, provided that: "On and after the effective date of this subsection, section 116(a) of the Federal Employees Salary Increase Act of 1960 (Part B of the Act of July 1, 1960; 74 Stat. 303; Public Law 86–568) [set out as a note under this section] shall not be applicable with respect to the Deputy Director of the Administrative Office of the United States Courts."

1958—Pub.L. 85–462, § 3(a), June 20, 1958, 72 Stat. 207, provided that: "The rates of basic compensation of officers and employees in or under the judicial branch of the Government whose rates of compensation are fixed pursuant to paragraph (2) of subdivision a of section 62 of the Bankruptcy Act (11 U.S.C. 102(a)(2) [section 102(a)(2) of Title 11, Bankruptcy]), section 3656 of title 18 of the United States Code [section 3656 of Title 18, Crimes and Criminal Procedure], the third sentence of section 603, section 604(a)(5), or sections 672 to 675, inclusive, of title 28 of the United States Code [sections 603, 604(a)(5), or 672 to 675 of this title] are hereby increased by amounts equal to the increases provided by section 2 of this Act [amending section 1113(b) of former Title 5, Executive Departments and Government Officers and Employees] in corresponding rates of compensation paid to officers and employees subject to the Classification Act of 1949, as amended [chapter 51 and subchapter III of Chapter 33 of Title 5, Government Organization and Employees]."

1955—Act June 28, 1955, c. 189, § 3(a), 69 Stat. 175, provided that: "The rates of basic compensation of officers and employees in or under the judicial branch of the Government whose rates of compensation are fixed pursuant to paragraph (2) of subdivision a of section 62 of the Bankruptcy Act (11 U.S.C., sec. 102(a)(2) [section 102(a)(2) of Title 11, Bankruptcy]), section 3656 of title 18 of the United States Code [section 3656 of Title 18, Crimes and Criminal Procedure], the second and third sentences of section 603, section 604(a)(5), or sections 672 to 675, inclusive, of title 28 of the United States Code [sections 603, 604(a)(5) or 672 to 675 of this title] are hereby increased by amounts equal to the increases provided by section 2 of this Act in corresponding rates of compensation paid to officers and employees subject to the Classification Act of 1949, as amended [chapter 51 and subchapter III of chapter 53 of Title 5, Government Organization and Employees]."

1951—Act Oct. 24, 1951, c. 554, § 1(c), 65 Stat. 613, provided that: "The rates of basic compensation of officers and employees in or under the judicial branch of the Government whose rates of compensation are fixed pursuant to section 62(2) of the Bankruptcy Act (11 U.S.C. 102(a)(2) [section 102(a)(2) of Title 11, Bankruptcy]), section 3656 of Title 18 of the United States Code [section 3656 of Title 18, Crimes and Criminal Procedure], the second and third sentences of section 603, section 604(5), or sections 672 to 675, inclusive, of title 28 of the United States Code [sections 603, 604(a)(5) or 672 to 675 of this title], or who are appointed pursuant to section 792(b) of title 28 of the United States Code [section 792(b) this title], are hereby increased by amounts equal to the increases provided by subsections (a) and (b) in corresponding rates of compensation paid to officers and employees subject to the Classification Act of 1949 [chapter 51 and subchapter III of chapter 53 of Title 5, Government Organization and Employees]."

§ 604. Duties of Director generally

(a) The Director shall be the administrative officer of the courts, and under the supervision and direction of the Judicial Conference of the United States, shall:

(1) Supervise all administrative matters relating to the offices of clerks and other clerical and administrative personnel of the courts;

(2) Examine the state of the dockets of the courts; secure information as to the courts' need of assistance; prepare and transmit semiannually to the chief judges of the circuits, statistical data and reports as to the business of the courts;

(3) Submit to the annual meeting of the Judicial Conference of the United States, at least two weeks prior thereto, a report of the activities of the Administrative Office and the state of the business of the courts, together with the statistical data submitted to the chief judges of the circuits under paragraph (a)(2) of this section, and the Director's recommendations, which report, data and recommendations shall be public documents.

(4) Submit to Congress and the Attorney General copies of the report, data and recommendations required by paragraph (a)(3) of this section;

(5) Fix the compensation of clerks of court, deputies, librarians, criers, messengers, law clerks, secretaries, stenographers, clerical assistants, and other employees of the courts whose compensation is not otherwise fixed by law;

(6) Determine and pay necessary office expenses of courts, judges, and those court officials whose expenses are by law allowable, and the lawful fees of United States Commissioners;

(7) Regulate and pay annuities to widows and surviving dependent children of justices and judges of the United States, judges of the United States Court of Federal Claims, bankruptcy judges, United States magistrates, Directors of the Federal Judicial Center, and Directors of the Administrative Office, and necessary travel and subsistence expenses incurred by judges, court officers and employees, and officers and employees of the Administrative Office, and the Federal Judicial Center, while absent from their official stations on official business, without regard to the per diem allowances and amounts for reimbursement of actual and necessary expenses established by the Administrator of General Services under section 5702 of title 5, except that the reimbursement of subsistence expenses may not exceed that authorized by the Director for judges of the United States under section 456 of this title;

(8) Disburse, directly or through the several United States marshals, moneys appropriated for the maintenance and operation of the courts;

(9) Establish pretrial services pursuant to section 3152 of title 18, United States Code;

(10) **(A)** Purchase, exchange, transfer, distribute, and assign the custody of lawbooks, equipment, supplies, and other personal property for the judicial branch of Government (except the Supreme Court unless otherwise provided pursuant to paragraph (17)); (B) provide or make available readily to each court appropriate equipment for the interpretation of proceedings in accordance with section 1828 of this title; and (C) enter into and perform contracts and other transactions upon such terms as the Director may deem appropriate as may be necessary to the conduct of the work of the judicial branch of Government (except the Supreme Court unless otherwise provided pursuant to paragraph (17)), and contracts for nonpersonal services providing pretrial services, for the interpretation of proceedings, and for the provision of special interpretation services pursuant to section 1828 of this title may be awarded without regard to section 3709 of the Revised Statutes of the United States (41 U.S.C. 5);

(11) Audit vouchers and accounts of the courts, the Federal Judicial Center, the offices providing pretrial services, and their clerical and administrative personnel;

(12) Provide accommodations for the courts, the Federal Judicial Center, the offices providing pretrial services and their clerical and administrative personnel;

(13) Lay before Congress, annually, statistical tables that will accurately reflect the business transacted by the several bankruptcy courts, and all other pertinent data relating to such courts;

(14) Pursuant to section 1827 of this title, establish a program for the certification and utilization of interpreters in courts of the United States;

(15) Pursuant to section 1828 of this title, establish a program for the provision of special interpretation services in courts of the United States;

(16) **(A)** In those districts where the Director considers it advisable based on the need for interpreters, authorize the full-time or part-time employment by the court of certified interpreters; (B) where the Director considers it advisable based on the need for interpreters, appoint certified interpreters on a full-time or part-time basis, for services in various courts when he determines that such appointments will result in the economical provision of interpretation services; and (C) pay out of moneys appropriated for the judiciary interpreters' salaries, fees, and expenses, and other costs which may accrue in accordance with the provisions of sections 1827 and 1828 of this title;

(17) In the Director's discretion, (A) accept and utilize voluntary and uncompensated (gratuitous) services, including services as authorized by section 3102(b) of title 5, United States Code; and (B) accept, hold, administer, and utilize gifts and bequests of personal property for the purpose of aiding or facilitating the work of the judicial branch of Government, but gifts or bequests of money shall be covered into the Treasury;

(18) Establish procedures and mechanisms within the judicial branch for processing fines, restitution, forfeitures of bail bonds or collateral, and assessments;

(19) Regulate and pay annuities to bankruptcy judges and United States magistrates in accordance with section 377 of this title and paragraphs (1)(B) and (2) of section 2(c) of the Retirement and Survivors' Annuities for Bankruptcy Judges and Magistrates Act of 1988;

(20) Periodically compile—

(A) the rules which are prescribed under section 2071 of this title by courts other than the Supreme Court;

(B) the rules which are prescribed under section 372(c)(11) of this title; and

(C) the orders which are required to be publicly available under section 372(c)(15) of this title;

so as to provide a current record of such rules and orders;

(21) Establish a program of incentive awards for employees of the judicial branch of the United States Government, other than any judge who is entitled to hold office during good behavior;

(22) Receive and expend, either directly or by transfer to the United States Marshals Service or other Government agency, funds appropriated for the procurement, installation, and maintenance of security equipment and protective services for the United States Courts in courtrooms and adjacent areas, including building ingress/egress control, inspection of packages, directed security patrols, and other similar activities;

(23) Regulate and pay annuities to judges of the United States Court of Federal Claims in accordance with section 178 of this title; and [1]

(24) [2] Perform such other duties as may be assigned to him by the Supreme Court or the Judicial Conference of the United States.[3]

(24) [2] Lay before Congress, annually, statistical tables that will accurately reflect the business imposed on the Federal courts by the savings and loan crisis.

(b) The clerical and administrative personnel of the courts shall comply with all requests by the Director for information or statistical data as to the state of court dockets.

(c) Inspection of court dockets outside the continental United States may be made through United States officials residing within the jurisdiction where the inspection is made.

(d) The Director, under the supervision and direction of the conference, shall:

(1) supervise all administrative matters relating to the offices of the United States magistrates;

(2) gather, compile, and evaluate all statistical and other information required for the performance of his duties and the duties of the conference with respect to such officers;

(3) lay before Congress annually statistical tables and other information which will accurately reflect the business which has come before the various United States magistrates, including (A) the number of matters in which the parties consented to the exercise of jurisdiction by a magistrate, (B) the number of appeals taken pursuant to the decisions of magistrates and the disposition of such appeals, and (C) the professional background and qualifications of individuals appointed under section 631 of this title to serve as magistrate;

(4) prepare and distribute a manual, with annual supplements and periodic revisions, for the use of such officers, which shall set forth their powers and duties, describe all categories of proceedings that may arise before them, and contain such other information as may be required to enable them to discharge their powers and duties promptly, effectively, and impartially.

(e) The Director may promulgate appropriate rules and regulations approved by the conference and not inconsistent with any provision of law, to assist him in the performance of the duties conferred upon him by subsection (d) of this section. Magistrates shall keep such records and make such reports as are specified in such rules and regulations.

(f) The Director may make, promulgate, issue, rescind, and amend rules and regulations (including regulations prescribing standards of conduct for Administrative Office employees) as may be necessary to carry out the Director's functions, powers, duties, and authority. The Director may publish in the Federal Register such rules, regulations, and notices for the judicial branch of Government as the Director determines to be of public interest; and the Director of the Federal Register hereby is authorized to accept and shall publish such materials.

(g)(1) When authorized to exchange personal property, the Director may exchange or sell similar items and may apply the exchange allowance or proceeds of sale in such cases in whole or in part payment for the property acquired, but any transaction carried out under the authority of this subsection shall be evidenced in writing.

(2) The Director hereby is authorized to enter into contracts for public utility services and related terminal equipment for periods not exceeding ten years.

(3)(A) In order to promote the recycling and reuse of recyclable materials, the Director may provide for the sale or disposal of recyclable scrap materials from paper products and other consumable office supplies held by an entity within the judicial branch.

(B) The sale or disposal of recyclable materials under subparagraph (A) shall be consistent with the procedures provided in section 203 of the Federal Property and Administrative Services Act of 1949 (40 U.S.C. 484) for the sale of surplus property.

(C) Proceeds from the sale of recyclable materials under subparagraph (A) shall be deposited as offsetting collections to the fund established under section 1931 of this title and shall remain available until expended to reimburse any appropriations for the operation and maintenance of the judicial branch.

(h)(1) The Director shall, out of funds appropriated for the operation and maintenance of the courts, provide facilities and pay necessary expenses incurred by the judicial councils of the circuits and the Judicial Conference under section 372 of this title, including mileage allowance and witness fees, at the same rate as provided in section 1821 of this title. Administrative and professional assistance from the Administrative Office of the United States Courts may be requested by each judicial council and the Judicial Conference for purposes of discharging their duties under section 372 of this title.

(2) The Director of the Administrative Office of the United States Courts shall include in his annual report filed with the Congress under this section a summary of the number of complaints filed with each judicial council under section 372(c) of this title, indicating the general nature of such complaints and the disposition of those complaints in which action has been taken.

(June 25, 1948, c. 646, 62 Stat. 914; Aug. 3, 1956, c. 944, § 3, 70 Stat. 1026; Dec. 20, 1967, Pub.L. 90–219, Title II, § 203, 81 Stat. 669; Oct. 17, 1968, Pub.L. 90–578, Title II, § 201, 82 Stat. 1114; Aug. 22, 1972, Pub.L. 92–397, § 4, 86 Stat. 580; Jan. 3, 1975, Pub.L. 93–619, Title II, § 204, 88 Stat. 2089; Oct. 28, 1978, Pub.L. 95–539, §§ 3, 4, 92 Stat. 2043; Nov. 6, 1978, Pub.L. 95–598, Title II, § 225, 92 Stat. 2664; Oct. 10, 1979, Pub.L. 96–82, § 5, 93 Stat. 645; Oct. 15, 1980, Pub.L. 96–458, § 5, 94 Stat. 2040; Dec. 12, 1980, Pub.L. 96–523, § 1(c)(1), 94 Stat. 3040; Sept. 27, 1982, Pub.L. 97–267, § 7, 96 Stat. 1139; Oct. 27, 1986, Pub.L. 99–554, Title I, § 116, 100 Stat. 3095; Dec. 11, 1987, Pub.L. 100–185, § 2, 101 Stat. 1279; Nov. 15, 1988, Pub.L. 100–659, § 6(a), 102 Stat. 3918; Nov. 19, 1988, Pub.L. 100–702, Title IV, § 402(a), Title X, §§ 1008, 1010, 1011, 1020(a)(2), 102 Stat. 4650, 4667, 4668, 4671; Oct. 30, 1990, Pub.L. 101–474, § 5(r), 104 Stat. 1101; Nov. 29, 1990, Pub.L. 101–647, Title XXV, § 2548, 104 Stat. 4888; Dec. 1, 1990, Pub.L. 101–650, Title III, §§ 306(e)(1), 325(c)(1), 104 Stat. 5111, 5121; Oct. 29, 1992, Pub.L. 102–572, Title V, § 503, Title IX, § 902(b)(1), 106 Stat. 4513, 4516.)

[1] So in original. The word "and" probably should not appear.

[2] So in original. Two pars. (24) have been enacted.

[3] So in original. The period probably should be "; and".

HISTORICAL AND STATUTORY NOTES

References in Text

Section 2(c) of the Retirement and Survivors' Annuities for Bankruptcy Judges and Magistrates Act of 1988, referred to in subsec. (a)(19), is section 2(c) of Pub.L. 100–659, Nov. 15, 1988, 102 Stat. 3916, which is set out as a note under section 377 of this title.

Codifications

Pub.L. 101–650, § 306(e)(1)(A), directing amendment of Pub.L. 100–702, § 402(1), probably intended amendment of section 402(a)(1) of pub.L. 100–702, which provided for redesignation of subsec. (a)(19) to be subsec. (a)(23) of this section, redesignated as subsec. (a)(24) by Pub.L. 101–650, § 306(e)(1)(B)(ii).

Effective Dates

1992 Acts. Amendment by section 902(b)(1) of Pub.L. 102–572 effective Oct. 29, 1992, see section 911 of Pub.L. 102–572, set out as a note under section 171 of this title.

Amendment by Pub.L. 102–572 effective Jan. 1, 1993, see section 1101(a) of Pub.L. 102–572, set out as a note under section 905 of Title 2, The Congress.

1990 Acts. Amendment by section 306(e)(1) of Pub.L. 101–650 applicable to judges of, and senior judges in active service with, the United States Court of Federal Claims on or after Dec. 1, 1990, see section 306(f) of Pub.L. 101–650, set out as a note under section 8331 of Title 5, Government Organization and Employees.

1988 Acts. Amendment by section 402(a) of Pub.L. 100–702 effective Dec. 1, 1988, see section 407 of Pub.L. 100–702, set out as a note under section 2071 of this title.

Amendment to this section by Pub.L. 100–659 to take effect on Nov. 15, 1988, and shall apply to bankruptcy judges and magistrates who retire on or after Nov. 15, 1988, with special election provisions for bankruptcy judges, etc., who left office on or after July 31, 1987, and before Nov. 15, 1988, see section 9 of Pub.L. 100–659, set out as a note under section 377 of this title.

1986 Acts. Amendment by Pub.L. 99–554 effective 30 days after Oct. 27, 1986, except as otherwise provided, see section 302(a) of Pub.L. 99–554, as amended, set out as a note under section 581 of this title.

1980 Acts. Amendment by Pub.L. 96–523 effective sixty days after Dec. 12, 1980, see section 3 of Pub.L. 96–523, set out as a note under section 3102 of Title 5, Government Organization and Employees.

Amendment by Pub.L. 96–458 effective Oct. 1, 1981, see section 7 of Pub.L. 96–458, set out as a note under section 331 of this title.

1978 Acts. Amendment by Pub.L. 95–598 effective Oct. 1, 1979, see section 402(c) of Pub.L. 95–598, as amended, set out as a note preceding section 101 of Title 11, Bankruptcy.

Amendment by Pub.L. 95–539 effective Oct. 28, 1978, see section 10(a) of Pub.L. 95–539, set out as a note under section 602 of this title.

1968 Acts. Amendment by Pub.L. 90–578 effective Oct. 17, 1968, except when a later effective date is applicable, which is the earlier of date when implementation of amendment by appointment of magistrates and assumption of office takes place or third anniversary of enactment of Pub.L. 90–578 on

Oct. 17, 1968, see section 403 of Pub.L. 90–578, set out as a note under section 631 of this title.

Change of Name

References to United States Claims Court deemed to refer to United States Court of Federal Claims and references to Claims Court deemed to refer to Court of Federal Claims, see section 902(b) of Pub.L. 102–572, set out as a note under section 171 of Title 28, Judiciary and Judicial Procedure.

Reference to United States magistrate or to magistrate deemed to refer to United States magistrate judge pursuant to section 321 of Pub.L. 101–650, set out as a note under section 631 of this title.

Reference to United States Commissioners deemed to be reference to United States Magistrates pursuant to Pub.L. 90–578. Title IV, § 402(b)(2), Oct. 17, 1968, 82 Stat. 1108. See chapter 43 (section 631 et seq.) of this title.

Compensation and Appointment of Secretaries and Law Clerks

Provisions authorizing the appointment and compensation of secretaries and law clerks to circuit and district judges in such number and at such rates of compensation as may be determined by the Judicial Conference of the United States were contained in the following appropriation acts:

Dec. 12, 1985, Pub.L. 99–180, Title IV, § 400, 99 Stat. 1154.

Aug. 30, 1984, Pub.L. 98–411, Title IV, § 400, 98 Stat. 1571.

Nov. 28, 1983, Pub.L. 98–166, Title IV, § 400, 97 Stat. 1099.

Dec. 21, 1982, Pub.L. 97–377, § 101(d) [S. 2956, Title IV, § 400], 96 Stat. 1866.

Dec. 15, 1981, Pub.L. 97–92, § 101(h) [incorporating Pub.L. 96–536, § 101(*o*); H.R. 7584, Title IV, § 400], 95 Stat. 1190.

Dec. 16, 1980, Pub.L. 96–536, § 101(*o*) [H.R. 7584, Title IV, § 400], 94 Stat. 3169.

Sept. 24, 1979, Pub.L. 96–68, Title IV, § 400, 93 Stat. 428.

Oct. 10, 1978, Pub.L. 95–431, Title IV, § 401, 92 Stat. 1037.

Aug. 2, 1977, Pub.L. 95–86, Title IV, § 401, 91 Stat. 435.

July 14, 1976, Pub.L. 94–362, Title IV, § 401, 90 Stat. 953.

Oct. 21, 1975, Pub.L. 94–121, Title IV, § 401, 89 Stat. 630.

Oct. 5, 1974, Pub.L. 93–433, Title IV, § 401, 88 Stat. 1202.

Nov. 27, 1973, Pub.L. 93–162, Title IV, § 401, 87 Stat. 651.

Oct. 25, 1972, Pub.L. 92–544, Title IV, § 401, 86 Stat. 1126.

Aug. 10, 1971, Pub.L. 92–77, Title IV, § 401, 85 Stat. 262.

Oct. 21, 1970, Pub.L. 91–472, Title IV, § 401, 84 Stat. 1056.

Dec. 24, 1969, Pub.L. 91–153, Title IV, § 401, 83 Stat. 419.

Aug. 9, 1968, Pub.L. 90–470, Title IV, § 401, 82 Stat. 685.

Nov. 8, 1967, Pub.L. 90–133, Title IV, § 401, 81 Stat. 427.

Nov. 8, 1966, Pub.L. 89–797, Title IV, § 401, 80 Stat. 1499.

Sept. 2, 1965, Pub.L. 89–164, Title IV, § 401, 79 Stat. 638.

Aug. 31, 1964, Pub.L. 88–527, Title IV, § 401, 78 Stat. 729.

Dec. 30, 1963, Pub.L. 88–245, Title IV, § 401, 77 Stat. 795.

Oct. 18, 1962, Pub.L. 87–843, Title IV, § 401, 76 Stat. 1099.

Sept. 21, 1961, Pub.L. 87–264, Title III, § 301, 75 Stat. 555.

Aug. 31, 1960, Pub.L. 86–678, Title III, § 301, 74 Stat. 566.

July 13, 1959, Pub.L. 86–84, Title III, § 301, 73 Stat. 192.

June 30, 1958, Pub.L. 85–474, Title III, § 301, 72 Stat. 254.

June 11, 1957, Pub.L. 85–40, Title III, § 301, 70 Stat. 65.

June 20, 1956, c. 414, Title III, § 301, 70 Stat. 310.

July 7, 1955, c. 279, Title III, § 301, 69 Stat. 276.

July 2, 1954, c. 455, Title II, § 201, 68 Stat. 410.

Aug. 1, 1953, c. 304, Title II, § 201, 67 Stat. 334.

July 10, 1952, c. 651, Title IV, § 401, 66 Stat. 569.

Oct. 22, 1951, c. 533, Title IV, § 401, 65 Stat. 596.

Sept. 6, 1950, c. 896, ch. III, Title IV, § 401, 64 Stat. 631.

Increases in Compensation Rates

Increases in rates of basic compensation fixed pursuant to subsec. (a)(5) of this section, see notes under section 603 of this title.

Limitation on Aggregate Salaries of Secretaries and Law Clerks

1967—Pub.L. 90–206, Title II, § 213(b), Dec. 16, 1967, 81 Stat. 635, provided that: "The limitations provided by applicable law on the effective date of this section [see Effective Dates of 1967 amendments note set out under section 5332 of Title 5, Government Organization and Employees] with respect to the aggregate salaries payable to secretaries and law clerks of circuit and district judges are hereby increased by amounts which reflect the respective applicable increases provided by section 202(a) of this title [amending section 5332(a) of Title 5] in corresponding rates of compensation for officers and employees subject to section 5332 of title 5, United States Code [section 5332 of Title 5]."

Section 213(b) of Pub.L. 90–206 effective as of the beginning of the first pay period which begins on or after Oct. 1, 1967, see section 220(a)(2) of Pub.L. 90–206, set out as a note under section 5332 of Title 5, Government Organization and Employees.

1966—Pub.L. 89–504, Title II, § 202(b), July 18, 1966, 80 Stat. 294, provided that: "The limitations provided by applicable law on the effective date of this section with respect to the aggregate salaries payable to secretaries and law clerks of circuit and district judges are hereby increased by amounts which reflect the respective applicable increases provided by section 102(a) of title I of this Act [amending section 1113(b) of former Title 5, Executive Departments and Government Officers and Employees] in corresponding rates of compensation for officers and employees subject to the Classification Act of 1949, as amended [chapter 51 and subchapter III of chapter 53 of Title 5, Government Organization and Employees]."

Provision effective the first day of the first pay period which begins on or after July 1, 1966, see section 203 of Pub.L. 89–504, set out as a note under section 603 of this title.

1965—Pub.L. 89–301, § 12(b), Oct. 29, 1965, 79 Stat. 1122, provided that: "The limitations provided by applicable law on the effective date of this section with respect to the aggregate salaries payable to secretaries and law clerks of circuit and district judges are hereby increased by amounts which reflect the respective applicable increases provided by section 2(a) of this Act [amending section 1113(b) of former Title 5, Executive Departments and Government Officers and Employees] in corresponding rates of compensation for officers and employees subject to the Classification Act of 1949, as amended [chapter 51 and subchapter III of chapter 53 of Title 5, Government Organization and Employees]."

1964—Pub.L. 88–426, Title IV, § 402(b), Aug. 14, 1964, 78 Stat. 433, provided that: "The limitations provided by applicable law on the effective date of this section with respect to the aggregate salaries payable to secretaries and law clerks of circuit and district judges are hereby increased by amounts which reflect the respective applicable increases provided by title I of this Act in corresponding rates of compensation for officers and employees subject to the Classification Act of 1949, as amended [chapter 51 and subchapter III of chapter 53 of Title 5, Government Organization and Employees]."

1962—Pub.L. 87–793, Title VI, § 1004(b), Oct. 11, 1962, 76 Stat. 866, provided that: "The limitations provided by applicable law on the effective date of this section with respect to the aggregate salaries payable to secretaries and law clerks of circuit and district judges are hereby increased by two amounts, the first amount to be effective for the period beginning as of the first day of the first pay period which begins on or after the date of enactment of this Act [Oct. 11, 1962], and ending immediately prior to the first day of the first pay period which begins on or after January 1, 1964, and the second amount to be effective on the first day of the first pay period which begins on or after January 1, 1964, and thereafter, which reflect the respective applicable increases provided by title II of this part in corresponding rates of compensation for officers and employees subject to the Classification Act of 1949, as amended [chapter 51 and subchapter III of chapter 53 of Title 5, Government Organization and Employees]."

1960—Pub.L. 86–568, Title I, § 116(b), July 1, 1960, 74 Stat. 303, provided that: "The limitations provided by applicable law on the effective date of this section with respect to the aggregate salaries payable to secretaries and law clerks of circuit and district judges are hereby increased by the amounts necessary to pay the additional basic compensation provided by this part."

Words "this part", referred to in section 116(b) of Pub.L. 86–568 [this note], means Part B of Pub.L. 86–568, which enacted section 932e of former Title 5, Executive Departments and Government Officers and Employees, amended section 753 of this title, sections 1113, 2091, 2252 and 3002 of former Title 5, sections 867 and 870 of Title 22, Foreign Relations and Intercourse, and sections 4103, 4107 and 4108 of Title 38, Veterans' Benefits and enacted notes set out under sections 603 and 604 of this title, sections 60a and 60f of Title 2, The Congress, sections 1113 and 2252 of former Title 5, section 590h of Title 16, Conservation, and section 867 of Title 22.

1958—Pub.L. 85–462, § 3(b), June 20, 1958, 72 Stat. 207, provided that: "The limitations of $13,485 and $18,010 with respect to the aggregate salaries payable to secretaries and law clerks of circuit and district judges, contained in the paragraph designated "Salaries of supporting personnel" in the Judiciary Appropriation Act, 1958 (71 Stat. 65; Public Law 85–49), or any subsequent appropriation Act, shall be increased by the amounts necessary to pay the additional basic compensation provided by this Act."

1955—Act June 28, 1955, c. 189, § 3(b), 69 Stat. 175, provided that: "The limitations of $10,560 and $14,355 with respect to the aggregate salaries payable to secretaries and law clerks of circuit and district judges, contained in the paragraph under the heading 'SALARIES OF SUPPORTING PERSONNEL' in the Judiciary Appropriation Act, 1955 (Public Law 470, Eighty-third Congress), or in any subsequent appropriation Act, shall be increased by the amounts necessary to pay the additional basic compensation provided by this Act."

1951—Act Oct. 24, 1951, c. 554, § 1(d), 65 Stat. 613, provided that: "The limitations of $9,600 and $13,050 with respect to the aggregate salaries payable to secretaries and law clerks of circuit and district judges, contained in the sixteenth paragraph under the head 'Miscellaneous salaries' in the Judiciary Appropriation Act, 1951 (Public Law 759, Eighty-first Congress), or in any subsequent appropriation Act, shall be increased by the amounts necessary to pay the additional basic compensation provided by this Act."

The particular paragraph of the "Judiciary Appropriation Act, 1951 (Public Law 759, Eighty-first Congress)", referred to in section 1(d) of Act Oct. 24, 1951, c. 554 [this note], is Act Sept. 6, 1950, c. 896, ch. III, Title IV, § 401 (part), 64 Stat. 631. The salary limitations therein, also referred to above, were identical with those in the Judiciary Appropriation Act, 1952 (Act Oct. 22, 1951, c. 533, Title IV, § 401 (part), 65 Stat. 596).

1970 Increase in Pay Rates of Judicial Branch Employees Whose Rates of Pay Are Fixed by Administrative Action

Adjustment of rates of pay of judicial branch employees whose rates of pay are fixed by administrative action by not to exceed the amounts of the adjustment for corresponding rates for employees subject to section 2(a) of Pub.L. 91–231, which raised corresponding rates by 6 percent, effective on the first day of the first pay period which begins on or after Dec. 27, 1969, see Pub.L. 91–231, set out as a note under section 5332 of Title 5, Government Organization and Employees.

Reports by Director of Administrative Office of United States Courts

For requirement that Director of Administrative Office of the United States Courts include statistical information about implementation of chapter 44 of this title in annual report under section 604(a)(3) of this title, see section 903(a) of Pub.L. 100–702, set out as a note under section 651 of this title.

Travel and Subsistence Expenses

Pub.L. 87–139, § 6, Aug. 14, 1961, 75 Stat. 340, provided that: "The Director of the Administrative Office of the United States Courts shall promulgate, in accordance with section 604(a)(7) and section 456 of title 28 of the United States Code [subsec. (a)(7) of this section and section 456 of this title], such regulations as he may deem necessary to effectuate the increases provided by this Act [amending section 553 of this title, section 68b of Title 2, The Congress, sections 73b–2, 836 and 837 of former Title 5, Executive Departments and Government Officers and Employees, and sections 287o, 287q and 1471 of Title 22, Foreign Relations and Intercourse]."

§ 605. Budget estimates

The Director, under the supervision of the Judicial Conference of the United States, shall submit to the Office of Management and Budget annual estimates of the expenditures and appropriations necessary for the maintenance and operation of the courts and the

Administrative Office and the operation of the judicial survivors annuity fund, and such supplemental and deficiency estimates as may be required from time to time for the same purposes, according to law. The Director shall cause periodic examinations of the judicial survivors annuity fund to be made by an actuary, who may be an actuary employed by another department of the Government temporarily assigned for the purpose, and whose findings and recommendations shall be transmitted by the Director to the Judicial Conference.

Such estimates shall be approved, before presentation to the Office of Management and Budget, by the Judicial Conference of the United States, except that the estimate with respect to the Court of International Trade shall be approved by such court and the estimate with respect to the United States Court of Appeals for the Federal Circuit shall be approved by such court.

(June 25, 1948, c. 646, 62 Stat. 915; July 9, 1956, c. 517, § 1(e), 70 Stat. 497; Aug. 3, 1956, c. 944, § 4, 70 Stat. 1026; Sept. 19, 1961, Pub.L. 87–253, § 3, 75 Stat. 521; Oct. 10, 1980, Pub.L. 96–417, Title V, § 501(14), 94 Stat. 1742; Apr. 2, 1982, Pub.L. 97–164, Title I, § 119(a), 96 Stat. 33; Sept. 13, 1982, Pub.L. 97–258, § 5(b), 96 Stat. 1068, 1085.)

HISTORICAL AND STATUTORY NOTES

Effective Dates

1982 Acts. Amendment by Pub.L. 97–164 effective Oct. 1, 1982, see section 402 of Pub.L. 97–164, set out as a note under section 171 of this title.

1980 Acts. Amendment by Pub.L. 96–417 effective on Nov. 1, 1980 and applicable with respect to civil actions pending on or commenced on or after such date, see section 701(a) of Pub.L. 96–417, as amended, set out as a note under section 251 of this title.

§ 606. Duties of Deputy Director

The Deputy Director shall perform the duties assigned to him by the Director, and shall act as Director during the absence or incapacity of the Director or when the Director's office is vacant.

(June 25, 1948, c. 646, 62 Stat. 915; Sept. 23, 1959, Pub.L. 86–370, § 5(a)(1), 73 Stat. 652.)

HISTORICAL AND STATUTORY NOTES

Effective Dates

1959 Acts. Amendment by Pub.L. 86–370 effective Sept. 23, 1959, see section 7(a) of Pub.L. 86–370.

Reference to Assistant Director Deemed Reference to Deputy Director

References in any other law to Assistant Director of the Administrative Office of the United States Courts deemed to be reference to the Deputy Director of the Administrative Office of the United States Courts, see section 5(a)(4) of Pub.L. 86–370, set out as a note under section 601 of this title.

§ 607. Practice of law prohibited

An officer or employee of the Administrative Office shall not engage directly or indirectly in the practice of law in any court of the United States.

(June 25, 1948, c. 646, 62 Stat. 915.)

§ 608. Seal

The Director shall use a seal approved by the Supreme Court. Judicial notice shall be taken of such seal.

(June 25, 1948, c. 646, 62 Stat. 915.)

§ 609. Courts' appointive power unaffected

The authority of the courts to appoint their own administrative or clerical personnel shall not be limited by any provisions of this chapter.

(June 25, 1948, c. 646, 62 Stat. 915.)

§ 610. Courts defined

As used in this chapter the word "courts" includes the courts of appeals and district courts of the United States, the United States District Court for the District of the Canal Zone, the District Court of Guam, the District Court of the Virgin Islands, the United States Court of Federal Claims, and the Court of International Trade.

(June 25, 1948, c. 646, 62 Stat. 915; Oct. 31, 1951, c. 655, § 44, 65 Stat. 725; July 7, 1958, Pub.L. 85–508, § 12(e), 72 Stat. 348; Nov. 6, 1978, Pub.L. 95–598, Title II, § 226, 92 Stat. 2665; Oct. 10, 1980, Pub.L. 96–417, Title V, § 501(15), 94 Stat. 1742; Apr. 2, 1982, Pub.L. 97–164, Title I, § 120(a), 96 Stat. 33; Oct. 29, 1992, Pub.L. 102–572, Title IX, § 902(b)(1), 106 Stat. 4516.)

HISTORICAL AND STATUTORY NOTES

Codifications

This section was amended by Pub.L. 95–598, Title II, § 226, Nov. 6, 1978, 92 Stat. 2665, effective June 28, 1984, pursuant to Pub.L. 95–598, Title IV, § 402(b), Nov. 6, 1978, 92 Stat. 2682, as amended by Pub.L. 98–249, § 1(a), Mar. 31, 1984, 98 Stat. 116; Pub.L. 98–271, § 1(a), Apr. 30, 1984, 98 Stat. 163; Pub.L. 98–299, § 1(a), May 25, 1984, 98 Stat. 214; Pub.L. 98–325, § 1(a), June 20, 1984, 98 Stat. 268, set out as an Effective Dates note preceding section 101 of Title II, Bankruptcy, by substituting ", district courts, and bankruptcy courts" for "and district courts."

Section 402(b) of Pub.L. 95–598 was amended by section 113 of Pub.L. 98–353, Title I, July 10, 1984, 98 Stat. 343, by substituting "shall not be effective" for "shall take effect on June 28, 1984", thereby eliminating the amendment by section 226 of Pub.L. 95–598, effective June 27, 1984, pursuant to section 122(c) of Pub.L. 98–353, set out as an Effective Date, note under section 151 of this title.

Section 121(a) of Pub.L. 98–353 directed that section 402(b) of Pub.L. 95–598 be amended by substituting "the date of enactment of the Bankruptcy Amendments and Federal Judgeship Act of 1984 [i.e. July 10, 1984]" for "June 28, 1984". This amendment was not executed in view of the prior amendment to section 402(b) of Pub.L. 95–598 by section 113 of Pub.L. 98–353.

Effective Dates

1982 Acts. Amendment by Pub.L. 97–164 effective Oct. 1, 1982, see section 402 of Pub.L. 97–164, set out as a note under section 171 of this title.

1980 Acts. Amendment by Pub.L. 96–417 effective on Nov. 1, 1980 and applicable with respect to civil actions pending on or commenced on or after such date, see section 701(a) of Pub.L. 96–417, as amended, set out as a note under section 251 of this title.

1958 Acts. Amendment by Pub.L. 85–508 effective Jan. 3, 1959, upon admission of Alaska into the Union pursuant to Proc. No. 3269, Jan. 3, 1959, 24 F.R. 81, 73 Stat. c16, as required by sections 1 and 8(c) of Pub.L. 85–508, see notes set out under section 81A of this title and preceding section 21 of Title 48, Territories and Insular Possessions.

Termination of United States District Court for the District of the Canal Zone

For termination of the United States District Court for the District of the Canal Zone at end of the "transition period", being the 30–month period beginning Oct. 1, 1979, and ending midnight Mar. 31, 1982, see Paragraph 5 of Article XI of the Panama Canal Treaty of 1977 and sections 3831 and 3841 to 3843 of Title 22, Foreign Relations and Intercourse.

§ 611. Retirement of Director

(a) The Director may, by written election filed with the Chief Justice of the United States within 6 months after the date on which he takes office, waive coverage under chapter 83 of title 5, subchapter III (the Civil Service Retirement System) or chapter 84 of title 5 (the Federal Employees' Retirement System), whichever is applicable, and bring himself within the purview of this section. A Director who elects coverage under this section shall be deemed an "employee" for purposes of chapter 84 of title 5, subchapter III, regardless of whether he has waived the coverage of chapter 83, subchapter III, or chapter 84. Waiver of coverage under chapter 83, subchapter III, and election of this section shall not operate to foreclose to the Director, upon separation from service other than by retirement, such opportunity as the law may provide to secure retirement credit under chapter 83 for service as Director by depositing with interest the amount required by section 8334 of title 5. A Director who waives coverage under chapter 84 and elects this section may secure retirement credit under chapter 84 for service as Director by depositing with interest 1.3 percent of basic pay for service from January 1, 1984, through December 31, 1986, and the amount referred to in section 8422(a) of title 5, for service after December 31, 1986. Interest shall be computed under section 8334(e) of title 5.

(b) Upon the retirement of a Director who has elected coverage under this section and who has served at least fifteen years and attained the age of sixty-five years the Administrative Office of the United States Courts shall pay him an annuity for life equal to 80 per centum of the salary of the office at the time of his retirement.

Upon the retirement of a Director who has elected coverage under this section and who has served at least ten years, but who is not eligible to receive an annuity under the first paragraph of this subsection, the Administrative Office of the United States Courts shall pay him an annuity for life equal to that proportion of 80 per centum of the salary of the office at the time of his retirement that the number of years of his service bears to fifteen, reduced by one-quarter of 1 per centum for each full month, if any, he is under the age of sixty-five at the time of separation from service.

(c) A Director who has elected coverage under this section and who becomes permanently disabled to perform the duties of his office shall be retired and shall receive an annuity for life equal to 80 per centum of the salary of the office at the time of his retirement if he has served at least fifteen years, or equal to that proportion of 80 per centum of such salary that the aggregate number of years of his service bears to fifteen if he has served less than fifteen years, but in no event less than 50 per centum of such salary.

(d) For the purpose of this section, "service" means service, whether or not continuous, as Director of the Administrative Office of the United States Courts, and any service, not to exceed five years, as a judge of the United States, a Senator or Representative in Congress, or a civilian official appointed by the President, by and with the advice and consent of the Senate.

(e) Each annuity payable under this section shall be increased by the same percentage amount and effective on the same date as annuities payable under chapter 83 of title 5, are increased as provided by section 8340 of title 5.

(Added Pub.L. 90–219, Title II, § 201(a), Dec. 20, 1967, 81 Stat. 668, and amended Pub.L. 100–702, Title X, §§ 1004(a), 1006(a)(1), Nov. 19, 1988, 102 Stat. 4665, 4666.)

HISTORICAL AND STATUTORY NOTES

Effective Dates

1988 Acts. Section 1004(b) of Title X of Pub.L. 100–702 provided that: "The amendments made by this section [amending this section and section 627 of this title] shall apply to cost-of-living increases that go into effect on or after the date of enactment of this title [Nov. 19, 1988] with respect to any annuity being paid or becoming payable on or after such date."

Section 1006(b) of Pub.L. 100–702 provided that: "The amendments made by this section [amending this section and section 627 of this title] shall apply to persons holding the offices of Director of the Administrative Office of the United States Courts, Director of the Federal Judicial Center, and Administrative Assistant to the Chief Justice on the date of enactment of this title [Nov. 19, 1988]."

Retroactive Effect

Section 205 of Pub.L. 90–219 provided that:

"(a) Except as provided in subsection (b), the amendments made by this title [enacting this section and amending sections 376 and 604 of this title], insofar as they relate to retirement and survivorship benefits of the Director of the Administrative Office of the United States Courts, shall be applicable only with respect to persons first appointed to such office after the date of enactment of this Act [Dec. 20, 1967].

"(b) The provisions of section 611(a), the first paragraph of section 611(b), and section 376(s), of title 28, United States Code, as added by such amendments [subsecs. (a) and (b) of this section, and section 376(s) of this title], shall be applicable to a Director or former Director of the Administrative Office of the United States Courts who was first appointed prior to the date of enactment of this Act [Dec. 20, 1967] if at the time such Director or former Director left or leaves such office he had, or shall have, attained the age of sixty-five years and completed fifteen years of service as Director of the Administrative Office of the United States Courts and if, on or before the expiration of six months following the date of enactment of this Act [Dec. 20, 1967], he makes the election referred to in section 611(a) or section 376(s) [subsec. (a) of this section or section 376(s) of this title], or both, as the case may be."

§ 612. Judiciary Information Technology Fund

(a) Establishment and availability of Fund.—There is hereby established in the Treasury of the United States a special fund to be known as the "Judiciary Information Technology Fund" (hereafter in this section referred to as the "Fund"). Moneys in the Fund shall be available to the Director without fiscal year limitation for the procurement (by lease, purchase, exchange, transfer, or otherwise) of information technology equipment for program activities included in the court of appeals, district courts, and other judicial services account of the judicial branch of the United States. The Fund shall also be available for expenses, including personal services, support personnel in the courts and in the Administrative Office of the United States Courts, and other costs, for the effective management, coordination, operation, and use of information technology equipment purchased by the Fund. In addition, all agencies of the judiciary may make deposits into the Fund to meet their information technology needs in accordance with subsections (b) and (c)(2).

(b) Plan for meeting information technology needs.—

(1) Development of plan.—The Director shall develop and annually revise, with the approval of the Judicial Conference of the United States, a long range plan for meeting the information technology equipment needs of the activities funded under subsection (a) and shall include an annual estimate of any fees that may be collected under section 404 of the Judiciary Appropriations Act, 1991 (Public Law 101–515; 104 Stat. 2133). Such plan and revisions shall be submitted to Congress.

(2) Expenditures consistent with plan.—The Director may use amounts in the Fund to procure information technology equipment for the activities funded under subsection (a) only in accordance with the plan developed under paragraph (1).

(c) Deposits into Fund.—

(1) Deposits.—There shall be deposited in the Fund—

(A) all proceeds resulting from activities conducted under subsection (a), including net proceeds of disposal of excess or surplus property, all fees collected after the date of the enactment of the Judicial Amendments Act of 1994 by the judiciary under section 404 of the Judiciary Appropriations Act, 1991 (Public Law 101–515; 104 Stat. 2133) and receipts from carriers and others for loss of or damage to property;

(B) amounts available for activities described in subsection (a) from funds appropriated to the judiciary; and

(C) any advances and reimbursements required by paragraph (2).

(2) Advances and reimbursements.—Whenever the Director procures information technology equipment for any entity in the judicial branch other than the courts or the Administrative Office, that entity shall advance or reimburse the Fund, whichever the Director considers appropriate, for the costs of the information technology equipment, from appropriations available to that entity.

(d) Authorization of appropriations.—There are authorized to be appropriated to the Fund for any fiscal year such sums as are required to supplement amounts deposited under subsection (c) in order to conduct activities under subsection (a).

(e) Contract authority.—

(1) For each fiscal year.—In fiscal year 1990, and in each succeeding fiscal year, the Director may enter into contracts for the procurement of information technology equipment in amounts which, in the aggregate, do not exceed amounts estimated to be collected under subsection (c) for that fiscal year in advance of the availability of amounts in the Fund for such contracts.

(2) Multiyear contracts.—In conducting activities under subsection (a), the Director is authorized to enter into multiyear contracts for information technology equipment for periods of not more than five years for any contract, if—

(A) funds are available and adequate for payment of the costs of such contract for the first fiscal year and for payment of any costs of cancellation or termination of the contract;

(B) such contract is awarded on a fully competitive basis; and

(C) the Director determines that—

(i) the need for the information technology equipment being provided will continue over the period of the contract; and

(ii) the use of the multi-year contract will yield substantial cost savings when compared with other methods of providing the necessary resources.

(3) **Cancellation costs of multiyear contract.**—Any cancellation costs incurred with respect to a contract entered into under paragraph (2) shall be paid from currently available amounts in the Fund.

(f) **Applicability of procurement statute.**—The procurement of information technology equipment under this section shall be conducted in compliance with the provisions of law, policies, and regulations applicable to executive agencies under division E of the Clinger-Cohen Act of 1996 (40 U.S.C. 1401 et seq.).

(g) **Authority of Administrator of General Services.**—Nothing in this section shall be construed to limit the authority of the Administrator of General Services under section 201 of the Federal Property and Administrative Services Act of 1949 (40 U.S.C. 481).

(h) **Annual report.**—

(1) **In general.**—The Director shall submit to the Congress an annual report on the operation of the Fund, including on the inventory, use, and acquisition of information technology equipment from the Fund and the consistency of such acquisition with the plan prepared under subsection (b). The report shall set forth the amounts deposited into the Fund under subsection (c).

(2) **Additional contents of report.**—The annual report submitted under this subsection shall include—

(A) the specific actions taken and the progress made to improve the plan developed under subsection (b) and the long range automation plan and strategic business plan developed under subsection (k); and

(B) a comparison of planned Fund expenditures and accomplishments with actual Fund expenditures and accomplishments, and the reasons for any delays in scheduled systems development, or budget overruns.

(3) **Report in year of termination of authority.**—The annual report submitted under this subsection for any year in which the authority for this section is to terminate under subsection (m), shall be submitted no later than 9 months before the date of such termination.

(i) **Reprogramming.**—The Director of the Administrative Office of the United States Courts, under the supervision of the Judicial Conference of the United States, may transfer amounts up to $1,000,000 from the Fund into the account to which the funds were originally appropriated. Any amounts transferred from the Fund in excess of $1,000,000 in any fiscal year may only be transferred by following reprogramming procedures in compliance with section 606 of the Departments of Commerce, Justice, and State, the Judiciary, and Related Agencies Appropriations Act, 1989 (Public Law 100–459; 102 Stat. 2227).

(j) **Appropriations into the Fund.**—If the budget request of the Judiciary [1] is appropriated in full, the amount deposited into the Fund during any fiscal year under the authority of subparagraph (c)(1)(B) will be the same as the amount of funds requested by the Judiciary [1] for activities described in subsection (a). If an amount to be deposited is not specified in statute by Congress and if the full request is not appropriated, the amount to be deposited under (c)(1)(B) [2] will be set by the spending priorities established by the Judicial Conference.

(k) **Long range management and business plans.**—The Director of the Administrative Office of the United States Court shall—

(1) develop an overall strategic business plan which would identify the judiciary's missions, goals, and objectives;

(2) develop a long range automation plan based on the strategic business plan and user needs assessments;

(3) establish effective Administrative Office oversight of court automation efforts to ensure the effective operation of existing systems and control over developments of future systems;

(4) expedite efforts to complete the development and implementation of life cycle management standards;

(5) utilize the standards in developing the next generation of case management and financial systems; and

(6) assess the current utilization and future user requirements of the data communications network.

[(*l*) Repealed. Pub.L. 105–119, Title III, § 304, Nov. 26, 1997, 111 Stat. 2491]

[(m) Redesignated (*l*)]

(Added Pub.L. 101–162, Title IV, § 404(b)(1), Nov. 21, 1989, 103 Stat. 1013, and amended Pub.L. 103–420, § 2, Oct. 25, 1994, 108 Stat. 4343; Pub.L. 104–106, Div. E, Title LVI, § 5602, Feb. 10, 1996, 110 Stat. 699; Pub.L. 104–208, Div. A, Title I, §§ 101(a) [Title III, § 305], 101(f) [Title VIII, § 808(c)], Sept. 30, 1996, 110 Stat. 3009–45, 3009–394; Pub.L. 105–85, Div. A, Title X, § 1073(h)(2), Nov. 18, 1997, 111 Stat. 1907; Pub.L. 105–119, Title III, § 304, Nov. 26, 1997, 111 Stat. 2491.)

1 So in original. Probably should not be capitalized.

2 So in original. Probably should be "subparagraph (c)(1)(B)."

HISTORICAL AND STATUTORY NOTES

References in Text

"Section 404 of the Judiciary Appropriations Act, 1991 (Public Law 101–515; 104 Stat. 2133)", referred to in subsecs. (b)(1) and (c)(1)(A), is Pub.L. 101–515, Title IV, § 404, Nov. 5, 1990, 104 Stat. 2132, which is set out as a note under section 1913 of this title.

The date of the enactment of the Judicial Amendments Act of 1994, referred to in subsec. (c)(1)(A), is the date of enactment of Pub.L. 103–420, 108 Stat. 4343, which was approved Oct. 25, 1994.

The Clinger-Cohen Act of 1996, referred to in subsec. (f), is Pub.L. 104–106, Div. E, §§ 5001 to 5703, Feb. 10, 1996, 110 Stat. 679 et seq., which is classified principally to chapter 25 (section 1401 et seq.) of Title 40, Public Buildings, Property, and Works. For complete classification of this Act to the Code, see Short Title note set out under section 1401 of Title 40 and Tables.

Section 606 of the Departments of Commerce, Justice, and State, the Judiciary, and Related Agencies Appropriations Act, 1989 (Public Law 100–459, 108 Stat. 2227), referred to in subsec. (i), is Pub.L. 100–459, Title VI, § 606, Oct. 1, 1988, 102 Stat. 2227, which is not classified to the Code.

Effective Dates

1996 Acts. Amendment by section 5602 of Pub.L. 104–106 effective 180 days after Feb. 10, 1996, see section 5701 of Pub.L. 104–106, set out as a note under section 1401 of Title 40, Public Buildings, Property, and Works.

Coordination with Other Amendments

Amendments by section 1073 of Pub.L. 105–85 to be treated as having been enacted immediately before the other provisions of Pub.L. 105–85, see section 1073(i) of Pub.L. 105–85, set out as a note under section 5315 of Title 5, Government Organization and Employees.

CHAPTER 42—FEDERAL JUDICIAL CENTER

Sec.

620. Federal Judicial Center.
621. Board; composition, tenure of members, compensation.
622. Meetings; conduct of business.
623. Duties of the Board.
624. Powers of the Board.
625. Director and staff.
626. Compensation of the Director and Deputy Director.
627. Retirement; employee benefits.
628. Appropriations and accounting.
629. Federal Judicial Center Foundation.

§ 620. Federal Judicial Center

(a) There is established within the judicial branch of the Government a Federal Judicial Center, whose purpose it shall be to further the development and adoption of improved judicial administration in the courts of the United States.

(b) The Center shall have the following functions:

(1) to conduct research and study of the operation of the courts of the United States, and to stimulate and coordinate such research and study on the part of other public and private persons and agencies;

(2) to develop and present for consideration by the Judicial Conference of the United States recommendations for improvement of the administration and management of the courts of the United States;

(3) to stimulate, create, develop, and conduct programs of continuing education and training for personnel of the judicial branch of the Government and other persons whose participation in such programs would improve the operation of the judicial branch, including, but not limited to, judges, United States magistrates, clerks of court, probation officers, and persons serving as mediators and arbitrators;

(4) insofar as may be consistent with the performance of the other functions set forth in this section, to provide staff, research, and planning assistance to the Judicial Conference of the United States and its committees;

(5) Insofar[1] as may be consistent with the performance of the other functions set forth in this section, to cooperate with the State Justice Institute in the establishment and coordination of research and programs concerning the administration of justice; and

(6) insofar as may be consistent with the performance of the other functions set forth in this section, to cooperate with and assist agencies of the Federal Government and other appropriate organizations in providing information and advice to further improvement in the administration of justice in the courts of foreign countries and to acquire information about judicial administration in foreign countries that may contribute to performing the other functions set forth in this section.

(Added Pub.L. 90–219, Title I, § 101, Dec. 20, 1967, 81 Stat. 664, and amended Pub.L. 95–598, Title II, § 227, Nov. 6, 1978, 92 Stat. 2665; Pub.L. 98–620, Title II, § 214, Nov. 8, 1984, 98 Stat. 3346; Pub.L. 99–336, § 6(b), June 19, 1986, 100 Stat. 639; Pub.L. 100–702, Title III, § 303, Nov. 19, 1988, 102 Stat. 4648; Pub.L. 102–572, Title VI, § 602(a), Oct. 29, 1992, 106 Stat. 4514.)

[1] So in original. Probably should not be capitalized.

HISTORICAL AND STATUTORY NOTES

Codifications

Subsec. (b)(3) of this section was amended by Pub.L. 95–598, Title II, § 227, Nov. 6, 1978, 92 Stat. 2665, effective June 28, 1984, pursuant to Pub.L. 95–598, Title IV, § 402(b), Nov. 6, 1978, 92 Stat. 2682, as amended by Pub.L. 98–249, § 1(a), Mar. 31, 1984, 98 Stat. 116; Pub.L. 98–271, § 1(a),

Apr. 30, 1984, 98 Stat. 163; Pub.L. 98–299, § 1(a), May 25, 1984, 98 Stat. 214; Pub.L. 98–325, § 1(a), June 20, 1984, 98 Stat. 268, set out as an Effective Date note preceding section 101 of Title 11, Bankruptcy, by substituting "magistrates" for "commissioners" and striking out "referees" following "judges,".

Section 402(b) of Pub.L. 95–598 was amended by section 113 of Pub.L. 98–353, Title I, July 10, 1984, 98 Stat. 343, by substituting "shall not be effective" for "shall take effect on June 28, 1984", thereby eliminating the amendment by section 227 of Pub.L. 95–598, effective June 27, 1984, pursuant to section 122(c) of Pub.L. 98–353, set out as an Effective Date note under section 151 of this title.

Section 121(a) of Pub.L. 98–353 directed that section 402(b) of Pub.L. 95–598 be amended by substituting "the date of enactment of the Bankruptcy Amendments and Federal Judgeship Act of 1984 [i.e. July 10, 1984]" for "June 28, 1984". This amendment was not executed in view of the prior amendment to section 402(b) of Pub.L. 95–598 by section 113 of Pub.L. 98–353.

Effective Dates

1992 Acts. Amendment by Pub.L. 102–572 effective Jan. 1, 1993, see section 1101(a) of Pub.L. 102–572, set out as a note under section 905 of Title 2, The Congress.

1986 Acts. Section 6(c) of Pub.L. 99–336 provided that: "The amendments made by this section [amending this section and section 288d of Title 2, The Congress, and redesignating former section 1364, set out second, and former section 1364, set out third, as sections 1365 and 1366 of this title, respectively] shall take effect on the date of the enactment of this Act [June 19, 1986]."

1984 Acts. Amendment by Pub.L. 98–620 to take effect Oct. 1, 1985, see section 216 of Pub.L. 98–620, set out as a note under section 10701 of Title 42, The Public Health and Welfare.

Change of Name

Reference to United States magistrate or to magistrate deemed to refer to United States magistrate judge pursuant to section 321 of Pub.L. 101–650, set out as a note under section 631 of this title.

Study of Intercircuit Conflicts and Structural Alternatives For Courts of Appeals by Federal Judicial Center

Pub.L. 101–650, Title III, § 302, Dec. 1, 1990, 104 Stat. 5104, as amended Pub.L. 102–572, Title V, § 502(c), Oct. 29, 1992, 106 Stat. 4513, provided that:

"**(a) Intercircuit conflicts.**—The Board of the Federal Judicial Center is requested to conduct a study and submit to the Congress a report by January 1, 1992, on the number and frequency of conflicts among the judicial circuits in interpreting the law that remain unresolved because they are not heard by the Supreme Court.

"**(b) Factors to consider in study.**—In conducting such a study, the Center should consider, to the extent feasible, all relevant factors, such as whether the conflict—

"(1) imposes economic costs or other harm on persons engaging in interstate commerce;

"(2) encourages forum shopping among circuits;

"(3) creates unfairness to litigants in different circuits, as in allowing Federal benefits in one circuit that are denied in other circuits; or

"(4) encourages nonacquiescence by Federal agencies in the holdings of the courts of appeals for different circuits, but is unlikely to be resolved by the Supreme Court.

"**(c) Structural alternatives for the Courts of Appeals.**—The Board of the Federal Judicial Center is requested to study the full range of structural alternatives for the Federal Courts of Appeals and submit a report on the study to the Congress and the Judicial Conference of the United States, no later than 2 years and 9 months after the date of the enactment of this Act [Dec. 1, 1990]."

§ 621. Board; composition, tenure of members, compensation

(a) The activities of the Center shall be supervised by a Board to be composed of—

(1) the Chief Justice of the United States, who shall be the permanent Chairman of the Board;

(2) two circuit judges, three district judges, one bankruptcy judge, and one magistrate judge, elected by vote of the members of the Judicial Conference of the United States, except that any circuit or district judge so elected may be either a judge in regular active service or a judge retired from regular active service under section 371(b) of this title but shall not be a member of the Judicial Conference of the United States; and

(3) the Director of the Administrative Office of the United States Courts, who shall be a permanent member of the Board.

(b) The term of office of each elected member of the Board shall be four years. A member elected to serve for an unexpired term arising by virtue of the death, disability, retirement pursuant to section 371(a) or section 372(a) of this title, or resignation of a member shall be elected only for such unexpired term.

(c) No member elected for a four-year term shall be eligible for reelection to the Board.

(d) Members of the Board shall serve without additional compensation, but shall be reimbursed for actual and necessary expenses incurred in the performance of their official duties.

(Added Pub.L. 90–219, Title I, § 101, Dec. 20, 1967, 81 Stat. 664, and amended Pub.L. 95–598, Title II, §§ 228, 229, Nov. 6, 1978, 92 Stat. 2665; Pub.L. 104–317, Title VI, § 601(b), Oct. 19, 1996, 110 Stat. 3857.)

HISTORICAL AND STATUTORY NOTES

Effective Dates

1978 Acts. Amendment by Pub.L. 95–598 effective Oct. 1, 1979, see section 402(c) of Pub.L. 95–598, set out as a note preceding section 101 of Title 11, Bankruptcy.

§ 622. Meetings; conduct of business

(a) Regular meetings of the Board shall be held quarterly. Special meetings shall be held from time to time upon the call of the Chairman, acting at his own discretion or pursuant to the petition of any four members.

(b) Each member of the Board shall be entitled to one vote. A simple majority of the membership shall constitute a quorum for the conduct of business. The Board shall act upon the concurrence of a simple majority of the members present and voting.

(Added Pub.L. 90–219, Title I, § 101, Dec. 20, 1967, 81 Stat. 665.)

§ 623. Duties of the Board

(a) In its direction and supervision of the activities of the Federal Judicial Center, the Board shall—

(1) establish such policies and develop such programs for the Federal Judicial Center as will further achievement of its purpose and performance of its functions;

(2) formulate recommendations for improvements in the administration of the courts of the United States, in the training of the personnel of those courts, and in the management of their resources;

(3) submit to the Judicial Conference of the United States, at least one month in advance of its annual meeting, a report of the activities of the Center and such recommendations as the Board may propose for the consideration of the Conference;

(4) present to other government departments, agencies, and instrumentalities whose programs or activities relate to the administration of justice in the courts of the United States the recommendations of the Center for the improvement of such programs or activities;

(5) study and determine ways in which automatic data processing and systems procedures may be applied to the administration of the courts of the United States, and include in the annual report required by paragraph (3) of this subsection details of the results of the studies and determinations made pursuant to this paragraph;

(6) consider and recommend to both public and private agencies aspects of the operation of the courts of the United States deemed worthy of special study; and

(7) conduct, coordinate, and encourage programs relating to the history of the judicial branch of the United States Government.

(b) The Board shall transmit to Congress and to the Attorney General of the United States copies of all reports and recommendations submitted to the Judicial Conference of the United States. The Board shall also keep the Committees on the Judiciary of the United States Senate and House of Representatives fully and currently informed with respect to the activities of the Center.

(Added Pub.L. 90–219, Title I, § 101, Dec. 20, 1967, 81 Stat. 665, and amended Pub.L. 100–702, Title III, § 302, Nov. 19, 1988, 102 Stat. 4648.)

§ 624. Powers of the Board

The Board is authorized—

(1) to appoint and fix the duties of the Director and the Deputy Director of the Federal Judicial Center, who shall serve at the pleasure of the Board;

(2) to request from any department, agency, or independent instrumentality of the Government any information it deems necessary to the performance of the functions of the Federal Judicial Center set forth in this chapter, and each such department, agency, or instrumentality is directed to cooperate with the Board and, to the extent permitted by law, to furnish such information to the Center upon request of the Chairman or upon request of the Director when the Board has delegated this authority to him;

(3) to contract with and compensate government and private agencies or persons for research projects and other services, without regard to section 3709 of the Revised Statutes, as amended (41 U.S.C. 5), and to delegate such contract authority to the Director of the Federal Judicial Center, who is hereby empowered to exercise such delegated authority.

(Added Pub.L. 90–219, Title I, § 101, Dec. 20, 1967, 81 Stat. 666, and amended Pub.L. 100–702, Title III, § 304(a), Nov. 19, 1988, 102 Stat. 4648.)

§ 625. Director and staff

(a) The Director shall supervise the activities of persons employed by the Center and perform other duties assigned to him by the Board.

(b) The Director shall appoint and fix the compensation of such additional professional personnel as the Board may deem necessary, without regard to the provisions of title 5, United States Code, governing appointments in competitive service, or the provisions of chapter 51 and subchapter III of chapter 53 of such title, relating to classification and General Schedule pay rates: *Provided, however,* That the compensation of any person appointed under this subsection shall not exceed the annual rate of basic pay of level V of the Executive Schedule pay rates, section 5316, title 5, United States Code: *And provided further,* That the salary of a reemployed annuitant under the Civil Servive [1] Retirement Act shall be adjusted pursuant to the provisions of section 8344, title 5, United States Code.

(c) The Director shall appoint and fix the compensation of such secretarial and clerical personnel as he may deem necessary, subject to the provisions of title 5, United States Code, governing appointments in competitive service without regard to the provisions of chapter 51 and subchapter III of chapter 53 of such title, relating to classification and General Schedule pay rates.

(d) The Director may procure personal services as authorized by section 3109 of title 5, United States Code, at rates not to exceed the daily equivalent of the highest rate payable under General Schedule pay rates, section 5332, title 5, United States Code.

(e) The Director is authorized to incur necessary travel and other miscellaneous expenses incident to the operation of the Center.

(Added Pub.L. 90–219, Title I, § 101, Dec. 20, 1967, 81 Stat. 666, and amended Pub.L. 102–572, Title VI, § 602(b), Oct. 29, 1992, 106 Stat. 4514.)

[1] So in original. Probably should be "Service".

HISTORICAL AND STATUTORY NOTES

References in Text

The General Schedule, referred to in subsec. (b), is set out under section 5332 of Title 5, Government Organization and Employees.

The Civil Service Retirement Act, referred to in subsec. (b), is Act May 29, 1930, c. 349, 46 Stat. 468, as amended by Act July 31, 1956, c. 804, § 401, 70 Stat. 743, which was repealed by Pub.L. 89–554, § 8(a), Sept. 6, 1966, 80 Stat. 632, and reenacted by the first section thereof as subchapter III (section 8331 et seq.) of chapter 83 of Title 5.

References in Other Laws to GS–16, 17, or 18 Pay Rates

References in laws to the rates of pay for GS–16, 17, or 18, or to maximum rates of pay under the General Schedule, to be considered references to rates payable under specified sections of Title 5, Government Organization and Employees, see section 529 [Title I, § 101(c)(1)] of Pub.L. 101–509, set out in a note under section 5376 of Title 5.

Effective Dates

1992 Acts. Amendment by Pub.L. 102–572 effective Jan. 1, 1993, see section 1101 of Pub.L. 102–572, set out as a note under section 905 of Title 2, The Congress.

§ 626. Compensation of the Director and Deputy Director

The compensation of the Director of the Federal Judicial Center shall be the same as that of the Director of the Administrative Office of the United States Courts, and his appointment and salary shall not be subject to the provisions of title 5, United States Code, governing appointments in competitive service, or the provisions of chapter 51 and subchapter III of chapter 53 of such title, relating to classification and General Schedule pay rates: *Provided, however,* That any Director who is a justice or judge of the United States in active or retired status shall serve without additional compensation. The compensation of the Deputy Director of the Federal Judicial Center shall be the same as that of the Deputy Director of the Administrative Office of the United States Courts.

(Added Pub.L. 90–219, Title I, § 101, Dec. 20, 1967, 81 Stat. 666, and amended Pub.L. 100–702, Title III, § 304(b)(1), Nov. 19, 1988, 102 Stat. 4648.)

HISTORICAL AND STATUTORY NOTES

References in Text

The General Schedule, referred to in text, is set out under section 5332 of Title 5, Government Organization and Employees.

Effective Dates

1988 Acts. Section 304(c) of Pub.L. 100–702 provided that: "The amendment made by subsection (b) [amending this section] shall be effective for fiscal years beginning on or after October 1, 1988."

§ 627. Retirement; employee benefits

(a) A Director of the Federal Judicial Center who attains the age of seventy years shall be retired from that office.

(b) The Director, Deputy Director, the professional staff, and the clerical and secretarial employees of the Federal Judicial Center shall be deemed to be officers and employees of the judicial branch of the United States Government within the meaning of subchapter III of chapter 83 (relating to civil service retirement), chapter 84 (relating to the Federal Employees' Retirement System), chapter 87 (relating to Federal employees' life insurance program), and chapter 89 (relating to Federal employees' health benefits program) of title 5, United States Code: *Provided, however,* That the Director, upon written notice filed with the Director of the Administrative Office of the United States Courts within 6 months after the date on which he takes office, may waive coverage under chapter 83 of title 5, subchapter III (the Civil Service Retirement System) or chapter 84 of title 5 (the Federal Employees' Retirement System), whichever is applicable, and elect coverage under the retirement and disability provisions of this section. A Director who elects coverage under this section shall be deemed an "employee" for purposes of chapter 84 of title 5, subchapter III, regardless of whether he has waived the coverage of chapter 83, subchapter III, or chapter 84: *And provided further,* That upon his nonretirement separation from the Federal Judicial Center, waiver of coverage under chapter 83, subchapter III, and election of this section shall not operate to foreclose to the Director such opportunity as the law may provide to secure retirement credit under chapter 83 for service as Director by depositing with interest the amount required by section 8334 of title 5. A Director who waives coverage under chapter 84 and elects this section may secure retirement credit under chapter 84 for service as Director by depositing with interest 1.3 percent of basic pay for service from January 1, 1984, through December 31, 1986, and the amount referred to in section 8422(a) of title 5, for service after December 31, 1986. Interest shall be computed under section 8334(e) of title 5.

(c) Upon the retirement of a Director who has elected coverage under this section and who has served at least fifteen years and attained the age of sixty-five years the Director of the Administrative Office of the United States Courts shall pay him an annuity for life equal to 80 per centum of the salary of the office at the time of his retirement.

Upon the retirement of a Director who has elected coverage under this section and who has served at least ten years, but who is not eligible to receive an annuity under the first paragraph of this subsection, the Administrative Office of the United States Courts shall pay him an annuity for life equal to that proportion of 80 per centum of the salary of the office at the time of his retirement that the number of years of his service bears to fifteen, reduced by one-quarter of 1 per centum for each full month, if any, he is under the age of sixty-five at the time of separation from service.

(d) A Director who has elected coverage under this section and who becomes permanently disabled to perform the duties of his office shall be retired and shall receive an annuity for life equal to 80 per centum of the salary of the office at the time of his retirement if he has served at least fifteen years, or equal to that proportion of 80 per centum of such salary that the aggregate number of years of his service bears to fifteen if he has served less than fifteen years, but in no event less than 50 per centum of such salary.

(e) For the purpose of this section, "service" means service, whether or not continuous, as Director of the Federal Judicial Center, and any service, not to exceed five years, as a judge of the United States, a Senator or Representative in Congress, or a civilian official appointed by the President, by and with the advice and consent of the Senate.

(f) Each annuity payable under this section shall be increased by the same percentage amount and effective on the same date as annuities payable under chapter 83 of title 5, are increased as provided by section 8340 of title 5.

(Added Pub.L. 90–219, Title I, § 101, Dec. 20, 1967, 81 Stat. 666, and amended Pub.L. 100–702, Title X, §§ 1004(a), 1006(a)(2), Nov. 19, 1988, 102 Stat. 4665, 4666; Pub.L. 104–317, Title VI, § 604, Oct. 19, 1996, 110 Stat. 3857.)

HISTORICAL AND STATUTORY NOTES

Effective Dates

1988 Acts. Amendment by section 1004(a) of Pub.L. 100–702 applicable to cost-of-living increases that go into effect on or after Nov. 19, 1988, with respect to any annuity being paid or becoming payable on or after such date, see section 1004(b) of Pub.L. 100–702, set out as a note under section 611 of this title.

Amendment by section 1006(a)(2) of Pub.L. 100–702 applicable to persons holding the offices of Director of the Administrative Office of the United States Courts, Director of the Federal Judicial Center, and Administrative Assistant to the Chief Justice on Nov. 19, 1988, see section 1006(b) of Pub.L. 100–702, set out as a note under section 611 of this title.

§ 628. Appropriations and accounting

There are hereby authorized to be appropriated such sums as may be necessary to carry out the provisions of this chapter. The Administrative Office of the United States Courts shall provide accounting, disbursing, auditing, and other fiscal services for the Federal Judicial Center.

(Added Pub.L. 90–219, Title I, § 101, Dec. 20, 1967, 81 Stat. 667.)

§ 629. Federal Judicial Center Foundation

(a) There is established a private nonprofit corporation which shall be known as the Federal Judicial Center Foundation (hereafter in this section referred to as the "Foundation") and which shall be incorporated in the District of Columbia. The purpose of the Foundation shall be to have sole authority to accept and receive gifts of real and personal property and services made for the purpose of aiding or facilitating the work of the Federal Judicial Center. The Foundation shall not accept conditional or otherwise restricted gifts, except gifts that are designated for the support of specific projects previously approved by the Board of the Center may be accepted. The Foundation shall have no authority to administer or otherwise determine the use of gifts accepted under this section.

(b) The business of the Foundation shall be conducted by a Board that shall have seven members, including a chairman. Three members, including the chairman, shall be appointed by the Chief Justice of the United States, two by the President Pro Tempore of the Senate, and two by the Speaker of the House of Representatives. The term of office of each member of the Board shall be 5 years, except that the initial terms shall be 5 years for the chairman, one member appointed by the President Pro Tempore and one member appointed by the Speaker, 3 years for the other member appointed by the President Pro Tempore and the other member appointed by the Speaker, and two years for the two other members appointed by the Chief Justice. Members of the Board shall serve without compensation but, upon authorization of the Director of the Center, shall be reimbursed by the Federal Judicial Center for actual and necessary expenses incurred in the performance of their official duties. No person who is a Federal or State judge in regular active service or otherwise eligible to perform judicial duties shall be eligible for membership on the

Board. The Center shall provide all administrative support and facilities necessary for the operation of the Board.

(c) The Federal Judicial Center is authorized to administer and use gifts received by the Foundation under this section. The gifts shall be used to further the goals of the Center as determined by the Board of the Center.

(d) Gifts of money and proceeds from sales of other property received as gifts shall be deposited in a separate fund in the Treasury of the United States and disbursed on the order of the Director of the Center, in accordance with policies established by the Board of the Center.

(e) The Board of the Foundation shall, not later than October 1 of each year, submit to the Committees on the Judiciary of the United States Senate and House of Representatives a report with respect to gifts received under this section during the preceding 12–month period, including the source of each such gift, the amount of each gift of cash or cash equivalent, and a description of any other gift. The Center shall include in its annual report of the activities of the Center under section 623(a)(3) a description of the purposes for which gifts were used during the year covered by the report.

(f) For the purpose of Federal income, estate, and gift taxes, property accepted under this section shall be considered as a gift or bequest to or for the use of the United States.

(Added Pub.L. 100–702, Title III, § 301(a), Nov. 19, 1988, 102 Stat. 4647.)

HISTORICAL AND STATUTORY NOTES

Prior Provisions

A prior section 629, added Pub.L. 90–219, Title I, § 101, Dec. 20, 1967, 81 Stat. 667, which related to organization provisions for the Board, was repealed by Pub.L. 95–598, Title II, § 230(1), Nov. 6, 1978, 92 Stat. 2665, effective Nov. 6, 1978, pursuant to section 402(d) of Pub.L. 95–598, as amended, set out as an Effective Dates note preceding section 101 of Title 11, Bankruptcy.

CHAPTER 43—UNITED STATES MAGISTRATES

Sec.
631. Appointment and tenure.
632. Character of service.
633. Determination of number, locations, and salaries of magistrates.
634. Compensation.
635. Expenses.
636. Jurisdiction, powers, and temporary assignment.
637. Training.
638. Dockets and forms; United States Code; seals.
639. Definitions.

§ 631. Appointment and tenure

(a) The judges of each United States district court and the district court of the Virgin Islands shall appoint United States magistrates in such numbers and to serve at such locations within the judicial district as the conference may determine under this chapter. In the case of a magistrate appointed by the district court of the Virgin Islands, this chapter shall apply as though the court appointing such magistrate were a United States district court. Where there is more than one judge of a district court, the appointment, whether an original appointment or a reappointment, shall be by the concurrence of a majority of all the judges of such district court, and when there is no such concurrence, then by the chief judge. Where the conference deems it desirable, a magistrate may be designated to serve in one or more districts adjoining the district for which he is appointed. Such a designation shall be made by the concurrence of a majority of the judges of each of the district courts involved and shall specify the duties to be performed by the magistrate in the adjoining district or districts.

(b) No individual may be appointed or reappointed to serve as a magistrate under this chapter unless:

(1) He has been for at least five years a member in good standing of the bar of the highest court of a State, the District of Columbia, the Commonwealth of Puerto Rico, or the Virgin Islands of the United States, except that an individual who does not meet the bar membership requirements of this paragraph may be appointed and serve as a part-time magistrate if the appointing court or courts and the conference find that no qualified individual who is a member of the bar is available to serve at a specific location;

(2) He is determined by the appointing district court or courts to be competent to perform the duties of the office;

(3) In the case of an individual appointed to serve in a national park, he resides within the exterior boundaries of that park, or at some place reasonably adjacent thereto;

(4) He is not related by blood or marriage to a judge of the appointing court or courts at the time of his initial appointment; and

(5) He is selected pursuant to standards and procedures promulgated by the Judicial Conference of the United States. Such standards and procedures shall contain provision for public notice of all vacancies in magistrate positions and for the estab-

lishment by the district courts of merit selection panels, composed of residents of the individual judicial districts, to assist the courts in identifying and recommending persons who are best qualified to fill such positions.

(c) A magistrate may hold no other civil or military office or employment under the United States: *Provided, however*, That, with the approval of the conference, a part-time referee in bankruptcy or a clerk or deputy clerk of a court of the United States may be appointed and serve as a part-time United States magistrate, but the conference shall fix the aggregate amount of compensation to be received for performing the duties of part-time magistrate and part-time referee in bankruptcy, clerk or deputy clerk: *And provided further*, That retired officers and retired enlisted personnel of the Regular and Reserve components of the Army, Navy, Air Force, Marine Corps, and Coast Guard, members of the Reserve components of the Army, Navy, Air Force, Marine Corps, and Coast Guard, and members of the Army National Guard of the United States, the Air National Guard of the United States, and the Naval Militia and of the National Guard of a State, territory, or the District of Columbia, except the National Guard disbursing officers who are on a full-time salary basis, may be appointed and serve as United States magistrates.

(d) Except as otherwise provided in sections 375 and 636(h) of this title, no individual may serve under this chapter after having attained the age of seventy years: *Provided, however*, That upon a majority vote of all the judges of the appointing court or courts, which is taken upon the magistrate's attaining age seventy and upon each subsequent anniversary thereof, a magistrate who has attained the age of seventy years may continue to serve and may be reappointed under this chapter.

(e) The appointment of any individual as a full-time magistrate shall be for a term of eight years, and the appointment of any individuals as a part-time magistrate shall be for a term of four years, except that the term of a full-time or part-time magistrate appointed under subsection (k) shall expire upon—

(1) the expiration of the absent magistrate's term,

(2) the reinstatement of the absent magistrate in regular service in office as a magistrate,

(3) the failure of the absent magistrate to make timely application under subsection (j) of this section for reinstatement in regular service in office as a magistrate after discharge or release from military service,

(4) the death or resignation of the absent magistrate, or

(5) the removal from office of the absent magistrate pursuant to subsection (i) of this section,

whichever may first occur.

(f) Upon the expiration of his term, a magistrate may, by a majority vote of the judges of the appointing district court or courts and with the approval of the judicial council of the circuit, continue to perform the duties of his office until his successor is appointed, or for 180 days after the date of the expiration of the magistrate's term, whichever is earlier.

(g) Each individual appointed as a magistrate under this section shall take the oath or affirmation prescribed by section 453 of this title before performing the duties of his office.

(h) Each appointment made by a judge or judges of a district court shall be entered of record in such court, and notice of such appointment shall be given at once by the clerk of that court to the Director.

(i) Removal of a magistrate during the term for which he is appointed shall be only for incompetency, misconduct, neglect of duty, or physical or mental disability, but a magistrate's office shall be terminated if the conference determines that the services performed by his office are no longer needed. Removal shall be by the judges of the district court for the judicial district in which the magistrate serves; where there is more than one judge of a district court, removal shall not occur unless a majority of all the judges of such court concur in the order of removal; and when there is a tie vote of the judges of the district court on the question of the removal or retention in office of a magistrate, then removal shall be only by a concurrence of a majority of all the judges of the council. In the case of a magistrate appointed under the third sentence of subsection (a) of this section, removal shall not occur unless a majority of all the judges of the appointing district courts concur in the order of removal; and where there is a tie vote on the question of the removal or retention in office of a magistrate, then removal shall be only by a concurrence of a majority of all the judges of the council or councils. Before any order or removal shall be entered, a full specification of the charges shall be furnished to the magistrate, and he shall be accorded by the judge or judges of the removing court, courts, council, or councils an opportunity to be heard on the charges.

(j) Upon the grant by the appropriate district court or courts of a leave of absence to a magistrate entitled to such relief under chapter 43 of title 38, such court or courts may proceed to appoint, in the manner specified in subsection (a) of this section, another magistrate, qualified for appointment and service under subsections (b), (c), and (d) of this section, who shall serve for the period specified in subsection (e) of this section.

(k) A United States magistrate appointed under this chapter shall be exempt from the provisions of subchapter I of chapter 63 of title 5.

[(*l*) Redesignated (k)]

(June 25, 1948, c. 646, 62 Stat. 915; May 24, 1949, c. 139, § 73, 63 Stat. 100; July 9, 1952, c. 609, § 1, 66 Stat. 509; July 25, 1956, c. 722, 70 Stat. 642; Oct. 17, 1968, Pub.L. 90–578, Title I, § 101, 82 Stat. 1108; Oct. 17, 1976, Pub.L. 94–520, § 2, 90 Stat. 2458; Nov. 6, 1978, Pub.L. 95–598, Title II, § 231, 92 Stat. 2665; Oct. 10, 1979, Pub.L. 96–82, § 3(a)–(d), 93 Stat. 644, 645; Aug. 6, 1982, Pub.L. 97–230, 96 Stat. 255; Nov. 14, 1986, Pub.L. 99–651, Title II, § 201(a)(1), 100 Stat. 3646; Nov. 15, 1988, Pub.L. 100–659, § 5, 102 Stat. 3918; Nov. 19, 1988, Pub.L. 100–702, Title X, § 1003(a)(2), 102 Stat. 4665; June 30, 1989, Pub.L. 101–45, Title II, § 104, 103 Stat. 122; Dec. 1, 1990, Pub.L. 101–650, Title III, § 308(b), 104 Stat. 5112; Oct. 13, 1994, Pub.L. 103–353, § 2(c), 108 Stat. 3169.)

HISTORICAL AND STATUTORY NOTES

Senate Revision Amendment

By Senate amendment, "Big Bend" and "Crater Lake" were inserted in subsection (a) of this section, and section 158a of Title 16 which was derived from Act May 15, 1947, c. 55, § 1, 61 Stat. 91, accordingly became an additional source of this section, such Act being included in the schedule of repeals. See 80th Congress Senate Report No. 1559.

As finally enacted, Act May 15, 1947, c. 57, 61 Stat. 92, which amended section 403c–5 of Title 16 became an additional source of this section and was accordingly included in the schedule of repeals by Senate amendment. See 80th Congress Senate Report No. 1559.

1949 Acts. This amendment conforms the language of section 631(b) to the provisions of section 35 of the Bankruptcy Act, as amended by the Act of June 28, 1946 (§ 3, 60 Stat. 324), that full-time referees in bankruptcy may not be appointed United States Commissioners.

This amendment also removes an ambiguity from section 631(b) by making it clear that the Director of the Administrative Office of the United States Courts has power to establish maximum limits of compensation to be received for performing the combined offices of commissioner and clerk or deputy clerk. This was the intent of sections 631 and 751 of title 28. (See the fifteenth paragraph of the reviser's note to the latter section, H.Rept. No. 308, April 25, 1947, p. A90, to accompany H.R. 3214, 80th Cong.)

1952 Acts. Senate Report No. 1738, see 1952 U.S. Code Cong. and Adm. News, p. 2065.

1956 Acts. House Report No. 2594, see 1956 U.S. Code Cong. and Adm. News, p. 3494.

1968 Acts. House Report No. 1629, see 1968 U.S. Code Cong. and Adm. News, p. 4252.

1976 Acts. House Report No. 94–1607, see 1976 U.S. Code Cong. and Adm. News, p. 5458.

1979 Acts. Senate Report No. 96–74 and House Conference Report No. 96–444, see 1979 U.S. Code Cong. and Adm. News, p. 1469.

1986 Acts. House Report No. 99–417, see 1986 U.S. Code Cong. and Adm. News, p. 6165.

1988 Acts. Senate Report No. 100–293, and House Conference Report No. 100–1072, see 1988 U.S. Code Cong. and Adm. News, p. 5564.

House Report No. 100–889, see 1988 U.S. Code Cong. and Adm. News, p. 5982.

1989 Acts. Statement by President, see 1989 U.S. Code Cong. and Adm. News, p. 27–1.

1990 Acts. Senate Report No. 101–416, related House Reports, and President's Signing Statement, see 1990 U.S. Code Cong. and Adm. News, p. 6802.

1994 Acts. House Report No. 103–65 and Joint Explanatory Statement, see 1994 U.S. Code Cong. and Adm. News, p. 2449.

Codifications

Subsec. (c) of this section was amended by Pub.L. 95–598, Title II, § 231, Nov. 6, 1978, 92 Stat. 2665, effective June 28, 1984, pursuant to Pub.L. 95–598, Title IV, § 402(b), Nov. 6, 1978, 92 Stat. 2682, as amended by Pub.L. 98–249, § 1(a), Mar. 31, 1984, 98 Stat. 116; Pub.L. 98–271, § 1(a), Apr. 30, 1984, 98 Stat. 163; Pub.L. 98–299, § 1(a), May 25, 1984, 98 Stat. 214; Pub.L. 98–325, § 1(a), June 20, 1984, 98 Stat. 268, set out as an Effective Date note preceding section 101 of Title 11, Bankruptcy, by striking out "a part-time referee in bankruptcy or" following "of the conference," and "part-time referee in bankruptcy," following "magistrate and".

Section 402(b) of Pub.L. 95–598 was amended by section 113 of Pub.L. 98–353, Title I, July 10, 1984, 98 Stat. 343, by substituting "shall not be effective" for "shall take effect on June 28, 1984", thereby eliminating the amendment by section 231 of Pub.L. 95–598, effective June 27, 1984, pursuant to section 122(c) of Pub.L. 98–353, set out as an Effective Date note under section 151 of this title.

Section 121(a) of Pub.L. 98–353 directed that section 402(b) of Pub.L. 95–598 be amended by substituting "the date of enactment of the Bankruptcy Amendments and Federal Judgeship Act of 1984 [i.e. July 10, 1984]" for "June 28, 1984". This amendment was not executed in view of the prior amendment to section 402(b) of Pub.L. 95–598 by section 113 of Pub.L. 98–353.

Effective Dates

1994 Acts. Amendment by section 2(c) of Pub.L. 103–353 effective with respect to reemployments initiated on or after the first day after the 60–day period beginning on Oct. 13, 1994, except as otherwise provided, see section 8 of Pub.L. 103–353, set out as a note under section 4301 of Title 38, Veterans' Benefits.

1988 Acts. Amendment by Pub.L. 100–659 effective Nov. 15, 1988, and applicable to bankruptcy judges and magistrates who retire on or after Nov. 15, 1988, with exception for judges and magistrates retiring on or after July 31, 1987, see section 9 of Pub.L. 100–659, set out as an Effective Date note under section 377 of this title.

1986 Acts. Amendment by Pub.L. 99–651 effective Jan. 1, 1987, see section 203 of Pub.L. 99–651, set out as a note under section 155 of this title.

1979 Acts. Section 3(g) of Pub.L. 96–82 provided that: "The amendment made by subsection (c) of this section [enacting subsec. (b)(5) of this section] shall not take effect until 30 days after the meeting of the Judicial Conference of the United States next following the effective date of this Act

[Oct. 10, 1979]." [The meeting of the Judicial Conference took place on Mar. 5 and 6, 1980.]

1968 Acts. Section 403 of Pub.L. 90–578 provided that: "Except as otherwise provided by sections 401 and 402 of this title [set out as Appointment of Magistrate and Applicable Law notes under this section], this Act [which amended this chapter and sections 202, 3006A, 3041, 3043, 3045, 3060, 3102, 3116, 3184, 3191, 3195, 3401, 3402, 3569, and 3771 of Title 18, Crimes and Criminal Procedure, and enacted provisions set out as notes under this section] shall take effect on the date of its enactment [Oct. 17, 1968]."

Change of Name

Section 321 of Pub.L. 101–650 provided that: "After the enactment of this Act [Dec. 1, 1990], each United States magistrate appointed under section 631 of title 28, United States Code [this section], shall be known as a United States magistrate judge, and any reference to any United States magistrate or magistrate that is contained in title 28, United States Code [this title], in any other Federal statute, or in any regulation of any department or agency of the United States in the executive branch that was issued before the enactment of this Act [Dec. 1, 1990], shall be deemed to refer to a United States magistrate judge appointed under section 631 of title 28, United States Code [this section]."

Separability of Provisions

Section 501 of Pub.L. 90–578 provided that: "If any provision of this Act [which amended this chapter and sections 202, 3006A, 3041, 3043, 3045, 3060, 3102, 3116, 3184, 3191, 3195, 3401, 3402, 3569, and 3771 of Title 18, Crimes and Criminal Procedure, and enacted provisions set out as notes under this section] or the application thereof to any person or circumstances is held invalid, the validity of the remainder of the Act [such sections] and of its application to other persons and circumstances shall not be affected."

Short Title

1979 Amendments. Section 1 of Pub.L. 96–82 provided: "That this Act [amending this section, sections 604, 633, 634, 635, 636, and 1915 of this title, and section 3401 of Title 18, Crimes and Criminal Procedure, and enacting provisions set out as notes under this section] may be cited as the 'Federal Magistrate Act of 1979'."

1968 Acts. Section 1 of Pub.L. 90–578 provided: "That this Act [which amended this chapter and sections 202, 3006A, 3041, 3043, 3045, 3060, 3102, 3116, 3184, 3191, 3195, 3401, 3402, 3569, and 3771 of Title 18, Crimes and Criminal Procedure, and enacted provisions set out as notes under this section] may be cited as the 'Federal Magistrates Act'."

Applicable Law

Section 402 of Pub.L. 90–578 provided that:

"(a) All provisions of law relating to the powers, duties, jurisdiction, functions, service, compensation, and facilities of United States commissioners, as such provisions existed on the day preceding the date of enactment of this Act [Oct. 17, 1968], shall continue in effect in each judicial district until but not on or after (1) the date on which the first United States magistrate assumes office within such judicial district pursuant to section 631 of chapter 43, title 28, United States Code, as amended by this Act [this section], or (2) the third anniversary of the date of enactment of this Act [Oct. 17, 1968], whichever date is earlier.

"(b) On and after the date on which the first United States magistrate assumes office within any judicial district pursuant to section 631 of chapter 43, title 28, United States Code, as amended by this Act [this section], or the third anniversary of the date of enactment of this Act [Oct. 17, 1968], whichever date is earlier—

"(1) the provisions of chapter 43, title 28, United States Code, as amended by this Act [this chapter], shall be effective within such judicial district except as otherwise specifically provided by section 401(b) of this title [set out as Appointment of Magistrates note under this section]; and

"(2) within such judicial district every reference to a United States commissioner contained in any previously enacted statute of the United States (other than sections 8331(1)(E), 8332(i), 8701(a) (7), and 8901(1)(G) of title 5), any previously promulgated rule of any court of the United States, or any previously promulgated regulation of any executive department or agency of the United States, shall be deemed to be a reference to a United States magistrate duly appointed under section 631 of chapter 43, title 28, United States Code, as amended by this Act [this section].

"(c) The administrative powers and duties of the Director of the Administrative Office of the United States Courts with respect to United States commissioners under the provisions of chapter 41, title 28, United States Code, as such provisions existed on the day preceding the date of enactment of this Act [Oct. 17, 1968], shall continue in effect until no United States commissioner remains in service."

Appointment of Magistrates

Section 401 of Pub.L. 90–578 provided that:

"(a) No individual may serve as a United States commissioner within any judicial district after the date on which a United States magistrate assumes office in such judicial district.

"(b) An individual serving as a United States commissioner within any judicial district on the date of enactment of this Act [Oct. 17, 1968] who is a member in good standing of the bar of the highest court of any State may be appointed to the office of United States magistrate for an initial term, and may be reappointed to such office for successive terms, notwithstanding his failure to meet the bar membership qualification imposed by section 631(b)(1) of chapter 43, title 28, United States Code [subsec. (b)(1) of this section]: *Provided, however,* That any appointment or reappointment of such an individual must be by unanimous vote of all the judges of the appointing district court or courts."

Authorization of Appropriations

Section 10 of Pub.L. 96–82 provided that: "Such sums as may be necessary to carry out the purposes of this Act [see Short Title of 1979 Amendments note under this section] are hereby authorized to be appropriated for expenditure on or after October 1, 1979."

Due Consideration by Merit Selection Panels of Women, Blacks, Hispanics, and Other Minorities

Section 3(e) of Pub.L. 96–82 provided that: "The merit selection panels established under section 631(b)(5) of title 28, United States Code [subsec. (b)(5) of this section], in recommending persons to the district court, shall give due consideration to all qualified individuals, especially such groups as women, blacks, Hispanics, and other minorities."

Judicial Conference Study of the Future of the Magistrate System

Section 9 of Pub.L. 96–82 provided for a study by the Judicial Conference of the United States to begin within 90 days after the effective date of Pub.L. 96–82, which was approved Oct. 10, 1979, and to be completed and made available to Congress within 24 months thereafter respecting the future of the magistrate system.

Jurisdictional Limitation of Commissioner Holding Office on July 9, 1952

Section 2 of Act July 9, 1952, provided that: "The jurisdiction of the United States commissioner holding office as commissioner of the Great Smoky Mountains National Park on the date of enactment of this Act [July 9, 1952] shall be limited to the portion of the park situated in North Carolina."

Magistrates Serving Prior to Promulgation of Magistrate Selection Standards and Procedures by Judicial Conference; Reappointment; Certification as Qualified

Section 3(f) of Pub.L. 96–82 provided that: "Magistrates serving prior to the promulgation of magistrate selection standards and procedures by the Judicial Conference of the United States may only exercise the jurisdiction conferred under the amendment made by section 2 of this Act [enacting section 636(c) of this title] after having been reappointed under such standards and procedures or after having been certified as qualified to exercise such jurisdiction by the judicial council of the circuit in which the magistrate serves."

Special Commissioner for Grand Canyon National Park; Appointment; Jurisdiction; Compensation

Pub.L. 86–258, Sept. 14, 1959, 73 Stat. 546, provided: "That the United States District Court for the District of Arizona shall appoint a special commissioner for the Grand Canyon National Park, Arizona. The commissioner shall hold office for four years, unless sooner removed by the district court, and he shall be subject to the general laws and requirements applicable to United States commissioners.

"**Sec. 2.** The jurisdiction of the commissioner in adjudicating cases brought before him shall be limited to the trial, and sentencing upon conviction, of persons charged with the commission of those misdemeanors classified as petty offenses (18 U.S.C. 1) [section 1 of Title 18, Crimes and Criminal Procedure] relating to the violation of Federal laws or regulations applicable within the park: *Provided*, That any person charged with a petty offense may elect to be tried in the district court of the United States; and the commissioner shall apprise the defendant of his right to make such election, but shall not proceed to try the case unless the defendant, after being so apprised, signs a written consent to be tried before the commissioner. The exercise of additional functions by the commissioner shall be consistent with and be carried out in accordance with the authority, laws, and regulations of general application to United States commissioners. The rules of procedure set forth in title 18, section 3402, of the United States Code [section 3402 of Title 18], shall be followed in the handling of cases by such commissioner. The probation laws shall be applicable to persons tried by the commissioner and he shall have power to grant probation.

"**Sec. 3.** The commissioner shall receive an annual salary to be fixed by the district court with the approval of the Judicial Conference of the United States and shall account for all fees, fines, and costs collected by him as public moneys. He shall reside within the boundary of the park or at some place reasonably adjacent thereto designated by the Secretary of the Interior with the approval of the district court."

§ 632. Character of service

(a) Full-time United States magistrates may not engage in the practice of law, and may not engage in any other business, occupation, or employment inconsistent with the expeditious, proper, and impartial performance of their duties as judicial officers.

(b) Part-time United States magistrates shall render such service as judicial officers as is required by law. While so serving they may engage in the practice of law, but may not serve as counsel in any criminal action in any court of the United States, nor act in any capacity that is, under such regulations as the conference may establish, inconsistent with the proper discharge of their office. Within such restrictions, they may engage in any other business, occupation, or employment which is not inconsistent with the expeditious, proper, and impartial performance of their duties as judicial officers.

(June 25, 1948, c. 646, 62 Stat. 916; Oct. 17, 1968, Pub.L. 90–578, Title I, § 101, 82 Stat. 1110.)

HISTORICAL AND STATUTORY NOTES

Effective Dates

1968 Acts. Amendment by Pub.L. 90–578 effective Oct. 17, 1968, except when a later effective date is applicable, which is the earlier of date when implementation of amendment by appointment of magistrates and assumption of office takes place or third anniversary of enactment of Pub.L. 90–578 on Oct. 17, 1968, see section 403 of Pub.L. 90–578, set out as a note under section 631 of this title.

Change of Name

United States magistrate appointed under section 631 of this title to be known as United States magistrate judge after Dec. 1, 1990, with any reference to United States magistrate or magistrate in this title, in any other Federal statute, etc., deemed a reference to United States magistrate judge appointed under section 631 of this title, see section 321 of Pub.L. 101–650, set out as a note under section 631 of this title.

§ 633. Determination of number, locations, and salaries of magistrates

(a) Surveys by the Director.—

(1) The Director shall, within one year immediately following the date of the enactment of the Federal Magistrates Act, make a careful survey of conditions in judicial districts to determine (A) the number of appointments of full-time magistrates

and part-time magistrates required to be made under this chapter to provide for the expeditious and effective administration of justice, (B) the locations at which such officers shall serve, and (C) their respective salaries under section 634 of this title. Thereafter, the Director shall, from time to time, make such surveys, general or local, as the conference shall deem expedient.

(2) In the course of any survey, the Director shall take into account local conditions in each judicial district, including the areas and the populations to be served, the transportation and communications facilities available, the amount and distribution of business of the type expected to arise before officers appointed under this chapter (including such matters as may be assigned under section 636(b) of this chapter), and any other material factors. The Director shall give consideration to suggestions from any interested parties, including district judges, United States commissioners or officers appointed under this chapter, United States attorneys, bar associations, and other parties having relevant experience or information.

(3) The surveys shall be made with a view toward creating and maintaining a system of full-time United States magistrates. However, should the Director find, as a result of any such surveys, areas in which the employment of a full-time magistrate would not be feasible or desirable, he shall recommend the appointment of part-time United States magistrates in such numbers and at such locations as may be required to permit prompt and efficient issuance of process and to permit individuals charged with criminal offenses against the United States to be brought before a judicial officer of the United States promptly after arrest.

(b) Determination by the conference.—Upon the completion of the initial surveys required by subsection (a) of this section, the Director shall report to the district courts, the councils, and the conference his recommendations concerning the number of full-time magistrates and part-time magistrates, their respective locations, and the amount of their respective salaries under section 634 of this title. The district courts shall advise their respective councils, stating their recommendations and the reasons therefor; the councils shall advise the conference, stating their recommendations and the reasons therefor, and shall also report to the conference the recommendations of the district courts. The conference shall determine, in the light of the recommendations of the Director, the district courts, and the councils, the number of full-time United States magistrates and part-time United States magistrates, the locations at which they shall serve, and their respective salaries. Such determinations shall take effect in each judicial district at such time as the district court for such judicial district shall determine, but in no event later than one year after they are promulgated.

(c) Changes in number, locations, and salaries.—Except as otherwise provided in this chapter, the conference may, from time to time, in the light of the recommendations of the Director, the district courts, and the councils, change the number, locations, and salaries of full-time and part-time magistrates, as the expeditious administration of justice may require.

(June 25, 1948, c. 646, 62 Stat. 916; Aug. 13, 1954, c. 728, § 1(a), (b), 68 Stat. 703, 704; Sept. 2, 1957, Pub.L. 85–276, §§ 1, 2, 71 Stat. 600; Oct. 17, 1968, Pub.L. 90–578, Title I, § 101, 82 Stat. 1111; Oct. 10, 1979, Pub.L. 96–82, § 4, 93 Stat. 645; Nov. 14, 1986, Pub.L. 99–651, Title II, § 202(d), 100 Stat. 3648.)

HISTORICAL AND STATUTORY NOTES

References in Text

Date of the enactment of the Federal Magistrates Act, referred to in subsec. (a)(1), means Oct. 17, 1968, the date of enactment of Pub.L. 90–578.

Effective Dates

1986 Acts. Amendment by Pub.L. 99–651 effective Jan. 1, 1987, see section 203 of Pub.L. 99–651, set out as a note under section 155 of this title.

1968 Acts. Amendment by Pub.L. 90–578 effective Oct. 17, 1968, except when a later effective date is applicable, which is the earlier of date when implementation of amendment by appointment of magistrates and assumption of office takes place or third anniversary of enactment of Pub.L. 90–578 on Oct. 17, 1968, see section 403 of Pub.L. 90–578, set out as a note under section 631 of this title.

Change of Name

United States magistrate appointed under section 631 of this title to be known as United States magistrate judge after Dec. 1, 1990, with any reference to United States magistrate or magistrate in this title, in any other Federal statute, etc., deemed a reference to United States magistrate judge appointed under section 631 of this title, see section 321 of Pub.L. 101–650, set out as a note under section 631 of this title.

§ 634. Compensation

(a) Officers appointed under this chapter shall receive, as full compensation for their services, salaries to be fixed by the conference pursuant to section 633, at rates for full-time United States magistrates up to an annual rate equal to 92 percent of the salary of a judge of the district court of the United States, as determined pursuant to section 135, and at rates for part-time magistrates of not less than an annual salary of $100, nor more than one-half the maximum salary payable to a full-time magistrate. In fixing the amount of salary to be paid to any officer appointed under this chapter, consideration shall be given to the average number and the nature of matters that have arisen during the immediately preceding period of five years, and that may be expected thereafter to arise, over which such officer would have jurisdiction and to such other factors as may be material. Disbursement of salaries shall be made by or pursuant to the order of the Director.

(b) Except as provided by section 8344, title 5, relating to reductions of the salaries of reemployed annuitants under subchapter III of chapter 83 of such title and unless the office has been terminated as provided in this chapter, the salary of a full-time United States magistrate shall not be reduced, during the term in which he is serving, below the salary fixed for him at the beginning of that term.

(c) All United States magistrates, effective upon their taking the oath or affirmation of office, and all necessary legal, clerical, and secretarial assistants employed in the offices of full-time United States magistrates shall be deemed to be officers and employees in the judicial branch of the United States Government within the meaning of subchapter III (relating to civil service retirement) of chapter 83, chapter 87 (relating to Federal employees' group life insurance), and chapter 89 (relating to Federal employees' health benefits program) of title 5. Part-time magistrates shall not be excluded from coverage under these chapters solely for lack of a prearranged regular tour of duty. A legal assistant appointed under this section shall be exempt from the provisions of subchapter I of chapter 63 of title 5, unless specifically included by the appointing judge or by local rule of court.

(June 25, 1948, c. 646, 62 Stat. 917; Oct. 17, 1968, Pub.L. 90–578, Title I, § 101, 82 Stat. 1112; Sept. 21, 1972, Pub.L. 92–428, 86 Stat. 721; Oct. 17, 1976, Pub.L. 94–520, § 1, 90 Stat. 2458; Nov. 6, 1978, Pub.L. 95–598, Title II, § 232, 92 Stat. 2665; Oct. 10, 1979, Pub.L. 96–82, § 8(b), 93 Stat. 647; July 10, 1984, Pub.L. 98–353, Title I, § 108(a), Title II, § 210, 98 Stat. 342, 351; Dec. 22, 1987, Pub.L. 100–202, § 101(a) [Title IV, § 408 (b)], 101 Stat. 1329, 1329–27; Nov. 19, 1988, Pub.L. 100–702, Title X, § 1003(a)(4), 102 Stat. 4665.)

HISTORICAL AND STATUTORY NOTES

Senate Revision Amendment

As finally enacted, section 158d of Title 16, U.S.C., which was derived from Act May 15, 1947, c. 55, § 4, 61 Stat. 91, 92, was an additional source of this section and was accordingly included by Senate amendment in the schedule of repeals. See 80th Congress Senate Report No. 1559.

1968 Acts. House Report No. 1629, see 1968 U.S.Code Cong. and Adm.News, p. 4252.

1972 Acts. Senate Report No. 92–1065, see 1972 U.S.Code Cong. and Adm.News, p. 3350.

1976 Acts. House Report No. 94–1607, see 1976 U.S.Code Cong. and Adm. News, p. 5458.

1979 Acts. Senate Report No. 96–74 and House Conference Report No. 96–444, see 1979 U.S.Code Cong. and Adm.News, p. 1469.

1984 Acts. Statements by Legislative Leaders, see 1984 U.S.Code Cong. and Adm.News, p. 576.

1988 Acts. House Report No. 100–889, see 1988 U.S.Code Cong. and Adm.News, p. 5982.

Codifications

Subsec. (a) of this section was amended by Pub.L. 95–598, Title II, § 232, Nov. 6, 1978, 92 Stat. 2665, effective June 28, 1984, pursuant to Pub.L. 95–598, Title IV, § 402(b), Nov. 6, 1978, 92 Stat. 2682, as amended by Pub.L. 98–249, § 1(a), Mar. 31, 1984, 98 Stat. 116; Pub.L. 98–271, § 1(a), Apr. 30, 1984, 98 Stat. 163; Pub.L. 98–299, § 1(a), May 25, 1984, 98 Stat. 214; Pub.L. 98–325, § 1(a), June 20, 1984, 98 Stat. 268, set out as an Effective Date note preceding section 101 of Title 11, Bankruptcy, to read as follows:

(a) Officers appointed under this chapter shall receive as full compensation for their services salaries to be fixed by the conference pursuant to section 633 of this title, at rates not to exceed $48,500 per annum, subject to adjustment in accordance with section 225 of the Federal Salary Act of 1967 and section 461 of this title, except that the salary of a part-time United States magistrate shall not be less than $100 nor more than one-half the maximum salary payable to a full-time magistrate. In fixing the amount of salary to be paid to any officer appointed under this chapter, consideration shall be given to the average number and the nature of matters that have arisen during the immediately preceding period of five years, and that may be expected thereafter to arise, over which such officer would have jurisdiction and to such other factors as may be material. Disbursement of salaries shall be made by or pursuant to the order of the Director.

Section 402(b) of Pub.L. 95–598 was amended by section 113 of Pub.L. 98–353, Title I, July 10, 1984, 98 Stat. 343, by substituting "shall not be effective" for "shall take effect on June 28, 1984", thereby eliminating the amendment by section 232 of Pub.L. 95–598, effective June 27, 1984, pursuant to section 122(c) of Pub.L. 98–353, set out as an Effective Date note under section 151 of this title.

Section 121(a) of Pub.L. 98–353 directed that section 402(b) of Pub.L. 95–598 be amended by substituting "the date of enactment of the Bankruptcy Amendments and Federal Judgeship Act of 1984 [i.e. July 10, 1984] " for "June 28, 1984". This amendment was not executed in view of the prior amendment to section 402(b) of Pub.L. 95–598 by section 113 of Pub.L. 98–353.

Effective Dates

1987 Acts. Amendment by section 101(a) [Title IV, § 408(b)] of Pub.L. 100–202 (amending subsec. (a) of this section) effective Oct. 1, 1988, and any salary affected by its provisions to be adjusted at the beginning of the first applicable pay period commencing on or after such date, see section 101(a) [Title IV, § 408(d)] of Pub.L. 100–202, set out as a note under section 153 of this title.

1984 Acts. Amendment by section 108(a) of Pub.L. 98–353 effective July 10, 1984, see section 122(a) of Pub.L. 98–353, set out as a note under section 151 of this title.

1968 Acts. Amendment by Pub.L. 90–578 effective Oct. 17, 1968, except when a later effective date is applicable, which is the earlier of date when implementation of amendment by appointment of magistrates and assumption of office takes place or third anniversary of enactment of Pub.L. 90–578 on Oct. 17, 1968, see section 403 of Pub.L. 90–578, set out as a note under section 631 of this title.

Change of Name

United States magistrate appointed under section 631 of this title to be known as United States magistrate judge after Dec. 1, 1990, with any reference to United States magistrate or magistrate in this title, in any other Federal statute, etc., deemed a reference to United States magistrate judge appointed under section 631 of this title, see section 321 of Pub.L. 101–650, set out as a note under section 631 of this title.

Continuation of Maximum Rates of Salary of Full-Time and Part-Time United States Magistrates in Effect on June 27, 1984

Section 108(b) of Pub.L. 98–353 provided that: "The maximum rates for salary of full-time and part-time United States magistrates in effect on June 27, 1984, shall remain in effect until changed as a result of a determination made under section 634(a) of title 28, United States Code [subsec. (a) of this section], as amended by this Act."

[Section 108(b) of Pub.L. 98–353 effective June 27, 1984, see section 122(c) of Pub.L. 98–353, set out as an Effective Dates note under section 151 of this title.]

Salary Increases of 1987

Maximum salaries of U.S. magistrates (full-time) and U.S. magistrates (part-time) increased respectively to $72,500 and $36,200 per annum, on recommendation of the President of the United States, see note set out under section 358 of Title 2, The Congress.

§ 635. Expenses

(a) Full-time United States magistrates serving under this chapter shall be allowed their actual and necessary expenses incurred in the performance of their duties, including the compensation of such legal assistants as the Judicial Conference, on the basis of the recommendations of the judicial councils of the circuits, considers necessary, and the compensation of necessary clerical and secretarial assistance. Such expenses and compensation shall be determined and paid by the Director under such regulations as the Director shall prescribe with the approval of the conference. The Administrator of General Services shall provide such magistrates with necessary courtrooms, office space, furniture and facilities within United States courthouses or office buildings owned or occupied by departments or agencies of the United States, or should suitable courtroom and office space not be available within any such courthouse or office building, the Administrator of General Services, at the request of the Director, shall procure and pay for suitable courtroom and office space, furniture and facilities for such magistrate in another building, but only if such request has been approved as necessary by the judicial council of the appropriate circuit.

(b) Under such regulations as the Director shall prescribe with the approval of the conference, the Director shall reimburse part-time magistrates for actual expenses necessarily incurred by them in the performance of their duties under this chapter. Such reimbursement may be made, at rates not exceeding those prescribed by such regulations, for expenses incurred by such part-time magistrates for clerical and secretarial assistance, stationery, telephone and other communications services, travel, and such other expenses as may be determined to be necessary for the proper performance of the duties of such officers: *Provided, however,* That no reimbursement shall be made for all or any portion of the expense incurred by such part-time magistrates for the procurement of office space.

(June 25, 1948, c. 646, 62 Stat. 917; Oct. 17, 1968, Pub.L. 90–578, Title I, § 101, 82 Stat. 1112; Oct. 10, 1979, Pub.L. 96–82, § 8(a), 93 Stat. 646.)

HISTORICAL AND STATUTORY NOTES

Effective Dates

1968 Acts. Amendment by Pub.L. 90–578 effective Oct. 17, 1968, except when a later effective date is applicable, which is the earlier of date when implementation of amendment by appointment of magistrates and assumption of office takes place or third anniversary of enactment of Pub.L. 90–578 on Oct. 17, 1968, see section 403 of Pub.L. 90–578, set out as a note under section 631 of this title.

Change of Name

United States magistrate appointed under section 631 of this title to be known as United States magistrate judge after Dec. 1, 1990, with any reference to United States magistrate or magistrate in this title, in any other Federal statute, etc., deemed a reference to United States magistrate judge appointed under section 631 of this title, see section 321 of Pub.L. 101–650, set out as a note under section 631 of this title.

§ 636. Jurisdiction, powers, and temporary assignment

(a) Each United States magistrate serving under this chapter shall have within the territorial jurisdiction prescribed by his appointment—

(1) all powers and duties conferred or imposed upon United States commissioners by law or by the Rules of Criminal Procedure for the United States District Courts;

(2) the power to administer oaths and affirmations, issue orders pursuant to section 3142 of title 18 concerning release or detention of persons pending trial, and take acknowledgements, affidavits, and depositions;

(3) the power to conduct trials under section 3401, title 18, United States Code, in conformity with and subject to the limitations of that section;

(4) the power to enter a sentence for a petty offense that is a class B misdemeanor charging a motor vehicle offense, a class C misdemeanor, or an infraction; and

(5) the power to enter a sentence for a class A misdemeanor, or a class B or C misdemeanor not covered by paragraph (4), in a case in which the parties have consented.

(b)(1) Notwithstanding any provision of law to the contrary—

(A) a judge may designate a magistrate to hear and determine any pretrial matter pending before the court, except a motion for injunctive relief, for judgment on the pleadings, for summary judgment, to dismiss or quash an indictment or information made by the defendant, to suppress evidence in a criminal case, to dismiss or to permit maintenance of a class action, to dismiss for failure to state a claim upon which relief can be granted, and to involuntarily dismiss an action. A judge of the court may reconsider any pretrial matter under this subparagraph (A) where it has been shown that the magistrate's order is clearly erroneous or contrary to law.

(B) a judge may also designate a magistrate to conduct hearings, including evidentiary hearings, and to submit to a judge of the court proposed findings of fact and recommendations for the disposition, by a judge of the court, of any motion excepted in subparagraph (A), of applications for posttrial[1] relief made by individuals convicted of criminal offenses and of prisoner petitions challenging conditions of confinement.

(C) the magistrate shall file his proposed findings and recommendations under subparagraph (B) with the court and a copy shall forthwith be mailed to all parties.

Within ten days after being served with a copy, any party may serve and file written objections to such proposed findings and recommendations as provided by rules of court. A judge of the court shall make a de novo determination of those portions of the report or specified proposed findings or recommendations to which objection is made. A judge of the court may accept, reject, or modify, in whole or in part, the findings or recommendations made by the magistrate. The judge may also receive further evidence or recommit the matter to the magistrate with instructions.

(2) A judge may designate a magistrate to serve as a special master pursuant to the applicable provisions of this title and the Federal Rules of Civil Procedure for the United States district courts. A judge may designate a magistrate to serve as a special master in any civil case, upon consent of the parties, without regard to the provisions of rule 53(b) of the Federal Rules of Civil Procedure for the United States district courts.

(3) A magistrate may be assigned such additional duties as are not inconsistent with the Constitution and laws of the United States.

(4) Each district court shall establish rules pursuant to which the magistrates shall discharge their duties.

(c) Notwithstanding any provision of law to the contrary—

(1) Upon the consent of the parties, a full-time United States magistrate or a part-time United States magistrate who serves as a full-time judicial officer may conduct any or all proceedings in a jury or nonjury civil matter and order the entry of judgment in the case, when specially designated to exercise such jurisdiction by the district court or courts he serves. Upon the consent of the parties, pursuant to their specific written request, any other part-time magistrate may exercise such jurisdiction, if such magistrate meets the bar membership requirements set forth in section 631(b)(1) and the chief judge of the district court certifies that a full-time magistrate is not reasonably available in accordance with guidelines established by the judicial council of the circuit. When there is more than one judge of a district court, designation under this paragraph shall be by the concurrence of a majority of all the judges of such district court, and when there is no such concurrence, then by the chief judge.

(2) If a magistrate is designated to exercise civil jurisdiction under paragraph (1) of this subsection, the clerk of court shall, at the time the action is filed, notify the parties of the availability of a magistrate to exercise such jurisdiction. The decision of the parties shall be communicated to the clerk of court. Thereafter, either the district court judge or the magistrate may again advise the parties of the availability of the magistrate, but in so doing, shall also advise the parties that they are free to withhold consent without adverse substantive consequences. Rules of court for the reference of civil matters to magistrates shall include procedures to protect the voluntariness of the parties' consent.

(3) Upon entry of judgment in any case referred under paragraph (1) of this subsection, an aggrieved party may appeal directly to the appropriate United States court of appeals from the judgment of the magistrate in the same manner as an appeal from any other judgment of a district court. The consent of the parties allows a magistrate designated to exercise civil jurisdiction under paragraph (1) of this subsection to direct the entry of a judgment of the district court in accordance with the Federal Rules of Civil Procedure. Nothing in this paragraph shall be construed as a limitation of any party's right to seek review by the Supreme Court of the United States.

(4) The court may, for good cause shown on its own motion, or under extraordinary circumstances shown by any party, vacate a reference of a civil matter to a magistrate under this subsection.

(5) The magistrate shall, subject to guidelines of the Judicial Conference, determine whether the record taken pursuant to this section shall be taken by electronic sound recording, by a court reporter, or by other means.

[**(6)** and **(7)** Redesignated (4) and (5)]

(d) The practice and procedure for the trial of cases before officers serving under this chapter shall conform to rules promulgated by the Supreme Court pursuant to section 2072 of this title.

(e) In a proceeding before a magistrate, any of the following acts or conduct shall constitute a contempt of the district court for the district wherein the magistrate is sitting: (1) disobedience or resistance to any lawful order, process, or writ; (2) misbehavior at a hearing or other proceeding, or so near the place thereof as to obstruct the same; (3) failure to produce, after having been ordered to do so, any pertinent document; (4) refusal to appear after having been subpenaed or, upon appearing, refusal to take the oath or affirmation as a witness, or, having taken the oath or affirmation, refusal to be examined according to law; or (5) any other act or conduct which if committed before a judge of the district court would constitute contempt of such court. Upon the commission of any such act or conduct, the magistrate shall forthwith certify the facts to a judge of the district court and may serve or cause to be served upon any person whose behavior is brought into question under this section an order requiring such person to appear before a judge of that court upon a day certain to show cause why he should not be adjudged in contempt by reason of the facts so certified. A judge of the district court shall thereupon, in a summary manner, hear the evidence as to the act or conduct complained of and, if it is such as to warrant punishment, punish such person in the same manner and to the same extent as for a contempt committed before a judge of the court, or commit such person upon the conditions applicable in the case of defiance of the process of the district court or misconduct in the presence of a judge of that court.

(f) In an emergency and upon the concurrence of the chief judges of the districts involved, a United States magistrate may be temporarily assigned to perform any of the duties specified in subsection (a), (b), or (c) of this section in a judicial district other than the judicial district for which he has been appointed. No magistrate shall perform any of such duties in a district to which he has been temporarily assigned until an order has been issued by the chief judge of such district specifying (1) the emergency by reason of which he has been transferred, (2) the duration of his assignment, and (3) the duties which he is authorized to perform. A magistrate so assigned shall not be entitled to additional compensation but shall be reimbursed for actual and necessary expenses incurred in the performance of his duties in accordance with section 635.

(g) A United States magistrate may perform the verification function required by section 4107 of title 18, United States Code. A magistrate may be assigned by a judge of any United States district court to perform the verification required by section 4108 and the appointment of counsel authorized by section 4109 of title 18, United States Code, and may perform such functions beyond the territorial limits of the United States. A magistrate assigned such functions shall have no authority to perform any other function within the territory of a foreign country.

(h) A United States magistrate who has retired may, upon the consent of the chief judge of the district involved, be recalled to serve as a magistrate in any judicial district by the judicial council of the circuit within which such district is located. Upon recall, a magistrate may receive a salary for such service in accordance with regulations promulgated by the Judicial Conference, subject to the restrictions on the payment of an annuity set forth in section 377 of this title or in subchapter III of chapter 83, and chapter 84, of title 5 which are applicable to such magistrate. The requirements set forth in subsections (a), (b)(3), and (d) of section 631, and paragraph (1) of subsection (b) of such section to the extent such paragraph requires membership of the bar of the location in which an individual is to serve as a magistrate, shall not apply to the recall of a retired magistrate under this subsection or section 375 of this title. Any other requirement set forth in section 631(b) shall apply to the recall of a retired magistrate under this subsection or section 375 of this title unless such retired magistrate met such requirement upon appointment or reappointment as a magistrate under section 361. (June 25, 1948, c. 646, 62 Stat. 917; Oct. 17, 1968, Pub.L. 90–578, Title I, § 101, 82 Stat. 1113; Mar. 1, 1972, Pub.L. 92–239, §§ 1, 2, 86 Stat. 47; Oct. 21, 1976, Pub.L. 94–577, § 1, 90 Stat. 2729; Oct. 28, 1977, Pub.L. 95–144, § 2, 91 Stat. 1220; Oct. 10, 1979, Pub.L. 96–82, § 2, 93 Stat. 643; Oct. 12, 1984, Pub.L. 98–473, Title II, § 208, 98 Stat. 1986; Nov. 8, 1984, Pub.L. 98–620, Title IV, § 402(29)(B), 98 Stat. 3359; Nov. 14, 1986, Pub.L. 99–651, Title II, § 201(a)(2), 100 Stat. 3647; Nov. 15, 1988, Pub.L. 100–659, § 4(c), 102 Stat. 3918; Nov. 18, 1988, Pub.L. 100–690, Title VII, § 7322, 102 Stat. 4467; Nov. 19, 1988, Pub.L. 100–702, Title IV, § 404(b)(1), Title X, § 1014, 102 Stat. 4651, 4669; Dec. 1, 1990, Pub.L. 101–650, Title III, § 308(a), 104 Stat. 5112; Oct. 19, 1996, Pub.L. 104–317, Title II, §§ 201, 202(b), 207, 110 Stat. 3848, 3849, 3851.)

[1] So in original. Probably should be "post-trial".

HISTORICAL AND STATUTORY NOTES

Senate Revision Amendment

As finally enacted, section 158b of Title 16, U.S.C., which was derived from Act May 15, 1947, c. 55, § 2, 61 Stat. 92, was an additional source of this section, and such Act was accordingly included by Senate amendment in the schedule of repeals. No change in the text of the section was necessary as the result of inclusion of such section 158b. See 80th Congress Senate Report No. 1559.

As finally enacted, Act May 15, 1947, c. 57, 61 Stat. 92, which amended section 403c–5 of Title 16, U.S.C., was an additional source of this section, and such act was accordingly included by Senate amendment in the schedule of repeals. See 80th Congress Senate Report No. 1559.

Prior oaths, acknowledgments, affidavits, and depositions provisions in section 637. Based on Title 28, U.S.C., 1940 ed., §§ 525, 758 (R.S. § 945; May 28, 1896, c. 252, § 19, 29 Stat. 184; Mar. 2, 1901, c. 814, 31 Stat. 956; Mar. 3, 1911, c. 231, § 291, 36 Stat. 1167).

This section consolidates part of section 525 with section 758 of Title 28, U.S.C., 1940 ed. The provision of said section 525 empowering clerks and deputy clerks to administer oaths is incorporated in section 953 of this title. The provision of section 758 that acknowledgments of bail and affidavits should have the same effect as if taken before judges was omitted as surplusage.

The exception as to Alaska, provided in section 591 of Title 28, U.S.C., 1940 ed., and referred to in section 525 of Title 28, U.S.C., 1940 ed., was omitted as unnecessary since section 108 of Title 48, U.S.C., 1940 ed., Territories and Insular Possessions, and section 1119 of the Compiled Laws of Alaska, 1933, give commissioners all powers of notaries public. See also reviser's notes [now Revision Notes and Legislative Reports] to sections 631 and 633 of this title.

Word "acknowledgments" was inserted to make it clear that commissioners, like justices of the peace, can take acknowledgments as well as oaths, affidavits, etc.

The authority to take depositions was included to conform to Federal Rules of Civil Procedure, Rule 28.

Changes were made in phraseology. 80th Congress House Report No. 308.

1968 Acts. House Report No. 1629, see 1968 U.S. Code Cong. and Adm. News, p. 4252.

1972 Acts. Senate Report No. 92–617, see 1972 U.S. Code Cong. and Adm. News, p. 1981.

1976 Acts. House Report No. 94–1609, see 1976 U.S. Code Cong. and Adm. News, p. 6162.

1977 Acts. House Report No. 95–720, see 1977 U.S. Code Cong. and Adm. News, p. 3146.

1979 Acts. Senate Report No. 96–74 and House Conference Report No. 96–444, see 1979 U.S. Code Cong. and Adm. News, p. 1469.

1984 Acts. House Report No. 98–1030 and House Conference Report No. 98–1159, see 1984 U.S. Code Cong. and Adm. News, p. 3182.

House Report No. 98–1062, see 1984 U.S. Code Cong. and Adm. News, p. 5708.

1986 Acts. House Report No. 99–417, see 1986 U.S. Code Cong. and Adm. News, p. 6165.

1988 Acts. Senate Report No. 100–293, and House Conference Report No. 100–1072, see 1988 U.S. Code Cong. and Adm. News, p. 5564.

For Related Reports, see 1988 U.S. Code Cong. and Adm. News, p. 5937.

House Report No. 100–889, see 1988 U.S. Code Cong. and Adm. News, p. 5982.

1990 Acts. Senate Report No. 101–416, related House Reports, and President's Signing Statement, see 1990 U.S. Code Cong. and Adm. News, p. 6802.

References in Text

The Rules of Criminal Procedure for the United States District Courts, referred to in subsec. (a)(1), are classified to Title 18, Crimes and Criminal Procedure.

The Federal Rules of Civil Procedure for the United States district courts, referred to in subsec. (b)(2) and (c)(3), are classified to this title.

Effective Dates

1988 Acts. Amendment by section 404(b)(1) of Pub.L. 100–702 effective Dec. 1, 1988, see section 407 of Pub.L. 100–702, set out as a note under section 2071 of this title.

Amendment to this section by Pub.L. 100–659 to take effect on Nov. 15, 1988, and shall apply to bankruptcy judges and magistrates who retire on or after Nov. 15, 1988, with special election provisions for bankruptcy judges, etc., who left office on or after July 31, 1987, and before Nov. 15, 1988, see section 9 of Pub.L. 100–659, set out as a note under section 377 of this title.

1986 Acts. Amendment by Pub.L. 99–651 effective Jan. 1, 1987, see section 203 of Pub.L. 99–651, set out as a note under section 155 of this title.

1984 Acts. Amendment by Pub.L. 98–620 not to apply to cases pending on Nov. 8, 1984, see section 403 of Pub.L. 98–620, set out as a note under section 1657 of this title.

1968 Acts. Amendment by Pub.L. 90–578 effective Oct. 17, 1968, except when a later effective date is applicable, which is the earlier of date when implementation of amendment by appointment of magistrates and assumption of office takes place or third anniversary of enactment of Pub.L. 90–578 on Oct. 17, 1968, see section 403 of Pub.L. 90–578, set out as a note under section 631 of this title.

Change of Name

United States magistrate appointed under section 631 of this title to be known as United States magistrate judge after Dec. 1, 1990, with any reference to United States magistrate or magistrate in this title, in any other Federal statute, etc., deemed a reference to United States magistrate judge appointed under section 631 of this title, see section 321 of Pub.L. 101–650, set out as a note under section 631 of this title.

§ 637. Training

The Federal Judicial Center shall conduct periodic training programs and seminars for both full-time and part-time United States magistrates, including an introductory training program for new magistrates, to be held within one year after initial appointment. (June 25, 1948, c. 646, 62 Stat. 917; Oct. 17, 1968, Pub.L. 90–578, Title I, § 101, 82 Stat. 1114.)

HISTORICAL AND STATUTORY NOTES

Effective Dates

1968 Acts. Amendment by Pub.L. 90–578 effective Oct. 17, 1968, except when a later effective date is applicable, which is the earlier of date when implementation of amendment by appointment of magistrates and assumption of office takes place or third anniversary of enactment of Pub.L. 90–578 on Oct. 17, 1968, see section 403 of Pub.L. 90–578, set out as a note under section 631 of this title.

Change of Name

United States magistrate appointed under section 631 of this title to be known as United States magistrate judge after Dec. 1, 1990, with any reference to United States magistrate or magistrate in this title, in any other Federal statute, etc., deemed a reference to United States magistrate judge appointed under section 631 of this title, see section 321 of Pub.L. 101–650, set out as a note under section 631 of this title.

§ 638. Dockets and forms; United States Code; seals

(a) The Director shall furnish to United States magistrates adequate docket books and forms prescribed by the Director. The Director shall also furnish to each such officer a copy of the current edition of the United States Code.

(b) All property furnished to any such officer shall remain the property of the United States and, upon the termination of his term of office, shall be transmitted to his successor in office or otherwise disposed of as the Director orders.

(c) The Director shall furnish to each United States magistrate appointed under this chapter an official impression seal in a form prescribed by the conference. Each such officer shall affix his seal to every jurat or certificate of his official acts without fee.

(June 25, 1948, c. 646, 62 Stat. 917; Oct. 17, 1968, Pub.L. 90–578, Title I, § 101, 82 Stat. 1114.)

HISTORICAL AND STATUTORY NOTES

Effective Dates

1968 Acts. Amendment by Pub.L. 90–578 effective Oct. 17, 1968, except when a later effective date is applicable, which is the earlier of date when implementation of amendment by appointment of magistrates and assumption of office takes place or third anniversary of enactment of Pub.L. 90–578 on Oct. 17, 1968, see section 403 of Pub.L. 90–578, set out as a note under section 631 of this title.

Change of Name

United States magistrate appointed under section 631 of this title to be known as United States magistrate judge after Dec. 1, 1990, with any reference to United States magistrate or magistrate in this title, in any other Federal statute, etc., deemed a reference to United States magistrate judge appointed under section 631 of this title, see section 321 of Pub.L. 101–650, set out as a note under section 631 of this title.

§ 639. Definitions

As used in this chapter—

(1) "Conference" shall mean the Judicial Conference of the United States;

(2) "Council" shall mean the Judicial Council of the Circuit;

(3) "Director" shall mean the Director of the Administrative Office of the United States Courts;

(4) "Full-time magistrate" shall mean a full-time United States magistrate;

(5) "Part-time magistrate" shall mean a part-time United States magistrate; and

(6) "United States magistrate" and "magistrate" shall mean both full-time and part-time United States magistrates.

(June 25, 1948, c. 646, 62 Stat. 917; Oct. 17, 1968, Pub.L. 90–578, Title I, § 101, 82 Stat. 1114.)

HISTORICAL AND STATUTORY NOTES

Effective Dates

1968 Acts. Amendment by Pub.L. 90–578 effective Oct. 17, 1968, except when a later effective date is applicable, which is the earlier of date when implementation of amendment by appointment of magistrates and assumption of office takes place or third anniversary of enactment of Pub.L. 90–578 on Oct. 17, 1968, see section 403 of Pub.L. 90–578, set out as a note under section 631 of this title.

Change of Name

United States magistrate appointed under section 631 of this title to be known as United States magistrate judge after Dec. 1, 1990, with any reference to United States magistrate or magistrate in this title, in any other Federal statute, etc., deemed a reference to United States magistrate judge appointed under section 631 of this title, see section 321 of Pub.L. 101–650, set out as a note under section 631 of this title.

CHAPTER 44—ALTERNATIVE DISPUTE RESOLUTION

Sec.
651. Authorization of alternative dispute resolution.
652. Jurisdiction.
653. Neutrals.
654. Arbitration.
655. Arbitrators.
656. Subpoenas.
657. Arbitration award and judgment.
658. Compensation of arbitrators and neutrals.

§ 651. Authorization of alternative dispute resolution

(a) Definition.—For purposes of this chapter, an alternative dispute resolution process includes any process or procedure, other than an adjudication by a presiding judge, in which a neutral third party participates to assist in the resolution of issues in controversy, through processes such as early neutral evaluation, mediation, minitrial, and arbitration as provided in sections 654 through 658.

(b) Authority.—Each United States district court shall authorize, by local rule adopted under section 2071(a), the use of alternative dispute resolution processes in all civil actions, including adversary proceedings in bankruptcy, in accordance with this chapter, except that the use of arbitration may be authorized only as provided in section 654. Each United States district court shall devise and implement its own alternative dispute resolution program, by local rule adopted under section 2071(a), to encourage and promote the use of alternative dispute resolution in its district.

(c) Existing alternative dispute resolution programs.—In those courts where an alternative dispute resolution program is in place on the date of the enactment of the Alternative Dispute Resolution Act of 1998, the court shall examine the effectiveness of that program and adopt such improvements to the program as are consistent with the provisions and purposes of this chapter [28 U.S.C.A. § 651 et seq.].

(d) Administration of alternative dispute resolution programs.—Each United States district court shall designate an employee, or a judicial officer, who is knowledgeable in alternative dispute resolution practices and processes to implement, administer, oversee, and evaluate the court's alternative dispute resolution program. Such person may also be responsible for recruiting, screening, and training attorneys to serve as neutrals and arbitrators in the court's alternative dispute resolution program.

(e) Title 9 not affected.—This chapter [28 U.S.C.A. § 651 et seq.] shall not affect title 9, United States Code.

(f) Program support.—The Federal Judicial Center and the Administrative Office of the United States Courts are authorized to assist the district courts in the establishment and improvement of alternative dispute resolution programs by identifying particular practices employed in successful programs and providing additional assistance as needed and appropriate.

(Added Pub.L. 100–702, Title IX, § 901(a), Nov. 19, 1988, 102 Stat. 4659, and amended Pub.L. 105–315, § 3, Oct. 30, 1998, 112 Stat. 2993.)

HISTORICAL AND STATUTORY NOTES

References in Text

The enactment of the Alternative Dispute Resolution Act of 1998, referred to in subsec. (c), is the enactment of Pub.L. 105–315, 112 Stat. 2993, which was approved Oct. 30, 1998.

Effective and Termination Dates

1988 Acts. Section 906 of Title IX of Pub.L. 100–702, as amended Pub.L. 103–192, § 1(a), Dec. 14, 1993, 107 Stat. 2292, which provided that, effective December 31, 1994, this chapter, as added by section 901 of Pub.L. 100–702, and the item relating to this chapter in the table of chapters at the beginning of part III of this title, were repealed, except that the provisions of this chapter were to continue to apply through final disposition of all actions in which referral to arbitration was made before the date of repeal, was itself repealed by Pub.L. 103–420, § 3(b), Oct. 25, 1994, 108 Stat. 4345.

Section 907 of Title IX of Pub.L. 100–702 provided that: "This title and the amendments made by this title [enacting this chapter, provisions set out as notes under this section and section 652 of this title] shall take effect 180 days after the date of enactment of this Act [Nov. 19, 1988]."

Findings and Declaration of Policy

Pub.L. 105–315, § 2, Oct. 30, 1998, 112 Stat. 2993, provided that:

"Congress finds that—

"(1) alternative dispute resolution, when supported by the bench and bar, and utilizing properly trained neutrals in a program adequately administered by the court, has the potential to provide a variety of benefits, including greater satisfaction of the parties, innovative methods of resolving disputes, and greater efficiency in achieving settlements;

"(2) certain forms of alternative dispute resolution, including mediation, early neutral evaluation, minitrials, and voluntary arbitration, may have potential to reduce the large backlog of cases now pending in some Federal courts throughout the United States, thereby allowing the courts to process their remaining cases more efficiently; and

"(3) the continued growth of Federal appellate court-annexed mediation programs suggests that this form of alternative dispute resolution can be equally effective in resolving disputes in the Federal trial courts; therefore, the district courts should consider including mediation in their local alternative dispute resolution programs."

Authorization of Appropriations

Pub.L. 105–315, § 11, Oct. 30, 1998, 112 Stat. 2998, provided that: "There are authorized to be appropriated for each fiscal year such sums as may be necessary to carry out chapter 44 of title 28, United States Code [28 U.S.C.A. § 651 et seq.], as amended by this Act [Alternative Dispute Resolution Act of 1998, Pub.L. 105–315, Oct. 30, 1998, 112 Stat. 2993, amending sections 651 to 658 of this title, amending a provision set out as a note under section 652 of this title, and enacting notes set out under this section]."

Section 905 of Title IX of Pub.L. 100–702, as amended Pub.L. 103–192, § 1(b), Dec. 14, 1993, 107 Stat. 2292; Pub.L. 103–420, § 3(a), Oct. 25, 1994, 108 Stat. 4345; Pub.L. 105–53, § 1, Oct. 6, 1997, 111 Stat. 1173, provided that: "There are authorized to be appropriated for each fiscal year to the judicial branch such sums as may be necessary to carry out the purposes of chapter 44 [this chapter], as added by section 901 of this Act. Funds appropriated under this section shall be allocated by the Administrative Office of the United States Courts to Federal judicial districts and the Federal Judicial Center. The funds so appropriated are authorized to remain available until expended."

Effect on Judicial Rulemaking Powers

Section 904 of Title IX of Pub.L. 100–702 provided that: "Nothing in this title [enacting this chapter and provisions set out as notes under this section and section 652 of this title], or in chapter 44 [this chapter], as added by section 901 of this Act, is intended to abridge, modify, or enlarge the rule making powers of the Federal judiciary."

Model Procedures

Section 902 of Title IX of Pub.L. 100–702 provided that: "The Judicial Conference of the United States may develop model rules relating to procedures for arbitration under chapter 44 [this chapter], as added by section 901 of this Act. No model rule may supersede any provision of such chapter 44, this title [enacting this chapter and provisions set out as notes under this section and section 652 of this title], or any law of the United States."

Reports by Director of Administrative Office of United States Courts and by Federal Judicial Center

Section 903 of Title IX of Pub.L. 100–702 provided that:

"(a) Annual Report by Director of Administrative Office of the United States Courts.—The Director of the Administrative Office of the United States Courts shall include in the annual report of the activities of the Administrative Office required under section 604(a)(3) [section 604(a)(3) of this title], statistical information about the implementation of chapter 44 [this chapter], as added by section 901 of this Act."

"(b) Report by Federal Judicial Center.—Not later than 5 years after the date of enactment of this Act [Nov. 19, 1988], the Federal Judicial Center, in consultation with the Director of the Administrative Office of the United States Courts, shall submit to the Congress a report on the implementation of chapter 44 [this chapter], as added by section 901 of this Act, which shall include the following:

"(1) A description of the arbitration programs authorized by such chapter, as conceived and as implemented in the judicial districts in which such programs are authorized.

"(2) A determination of the level of satisfaction with the arbitration programs in those judicial districts by a sampling of court personnel, attorneys, and litigants whose cases have been referred to arbitration.

"(3) A summary of those program features that can be identified as being related to program acceptance both within and across judicial districts.

"(4) A description of the levels of satisfaction relative to the cost per hearing of each program.

"(5) Recommendations to the Congress on whether to terminate or continue chapter 44, or alternatively, to enact an arbitration provision in title 28, United States Code [this title], authorizing arbitration in all Federal district courts."

Treatment of Expired Provisions

Pub.L. 103–192, § 2, Dec. 14, 1993, 107 Stat. 2292, provided that: "Chapter 44 of title 28, United States Code [this chapter], and the item relating to that chapter in the table of chapters at the beginning of part III of such title [analysis preceding section 601 of this title], shall be effective on or after the date of the enactment of this Act [Dec. 14, 1993] as if such chapter and item had not been repealed by section 906 of the Judicial Improvements and Access to Justice Act [section 906 of Pub.L. 100–702, set out as an Effective Date of Repeal note under this section] as such section was in effect on the day before the date of the enactment of this Act [Dec. 14, 1993]."

COMMENTARIES

See 28 U.S.C.A. § 651, for Commentary by David D. Siegel.

§ 652. Jurisdiction

(a) Consideration of alternative dispute resolution in appropriate cases.—Notwithstanding any provision of law to the contrary and except as provided in subsections (b) and (c), each district court shall, by local rule adopted under section 2071(a), require that litigants in all civil cases consider the use of an alternative dispute resolution process at an appropriate stage in the litigation. Each district court shall provide litigants in all civil cases with at least one alternative dispute resolution process, including, but not limited to, mediation, early neutral evaluation, minitrial, and arbitration as authorized in sections 654 through 658. Any district court that elects to require the use of alternative dispute resolution in certain cases may do so only with respect to mediation, early neutral evaluation, and, if the parties consent, arbitration.

(b) Actions exempted from consideration of alternative dispute resolution.—Each district court may exempt from the requirements of this section specific cases or categories of cases in which use of alternative dispute resolution would not be appropriate. In defining these exemptions, each district court shall consult with members of the bar, including the United States Attorney for that district.

(c) Authority of the Attorney General.—Nothing in this section shall alter or conflict with the authority of the Attorney General to conduct litigation on behalf of the United States, with the authority of any Federal agency authorized to conduct litigation in the United States courts, or with any delegation of litigation authority by the Attorney General.

(d) Confidentiality provisions.—Until such time as rules are adopted under chapter 131 of this title [28 U.S.C.A. § 2071 et seq.] providing for the confidentiality of alternative dispute resolution processes under this chapter [28 U.S.C.A. § 651 et seq.], each district court shall, by local rule adopted under section 2071(a), provide for the confidentiality of the alternative dispute resolution processes and to prohibit disclosure of confidential dispute resolution communications.

(Added Pub.L. 100–702, Title IX, § 901(a), Nov. 19, 1988, 102 Stat. 4659, and amended Pub.L. 105–315, § 4, Oct. 30, 1998, 112 Stat. 2994.)

HISTORICAL AND STATUTORY NOTES

Effective and Termination Dates

1988 Acts. Section 906 of Pub.L. 100–702, as amended, which provided that, effective Dec. 31, 1994, this section was repealed, with certain exceptions, was itself repealed by Pub.L. 103–420, § 3(b), Oct. 25, 1994, 108 Stat. 4345. See section 906 of Pub.L. 100–702, set out as a note under section 651 of this title.

Section effective 180 days after Nov. 19, 1988, see section 907 of Pub.L. 100–702, set out as a note under section 651 of this title.

Treatment of Expired Provisions

This section to continue to be effective on or after Dec. 14, 1993 as if it had not been repealed by section 906 of Pub.L. 100–702, as such section was in effect on the day before such date, see Treatment of Expired Provisions note set out under section 651 of this title.

Exception to Limitation on Money Damages

Section 901(c) of Pub.L. 100–702, which provided that notwithstanding this section a district court listed in section 658 of this title whose local rule on Nov. 19, 1988 provided for a limitation on money damages with respect to cases referred to arbitration of not more than $150,000 may continue to apply the higher limitation, was repealed by Pub.L. 105–315, § 12(a), Oct. 30, 1998, 112 Stat. 2998.

COMMENTARIES

See 28 U.S.C.A. § 652, for Commentary by David D. Siegel.

§ 653. Neutrals

(a) Panel of neutrals.—Each district court that authorizes the use of alternative dispute resolution processes shall adopt appropriate processes for making neutrals available for use by the parties for each category of process offered. Each district court shall promulgate its own procedures and criteria for the selection of neutrals on its panels.

(b) Qualifications and training.—Each person serving as a neutral in an alternative dispute resolution process should be qualified and trained to serve as a neutral in the appropriate alternative dispute resolution process. For this purpose, the district court may use, among others, magistrate judges who have been trained to serve as neutrals in alternative dispute resolution processes, professional neutrals from the private sector, and persons who have been trained to serve as neutrals in alternative dispute resolution processes. Until such time as rules are adopted under chapter 131 of this title [28 U.S.C.A. § 2071 et seq.] relating to the disqualification of neutrals, each district court shall issue rules under section 2071(a) relating to the disqualification of neutrals (including, where appropriate, disqualification under section 455 of this title, other applicable law, and professional responsibility standards).

(Added Pub.L. 100–702, Title IX, § 901(a), Nov. 19, 1988, 102 Stat. 4660, and amended Pub.L. 105–315, § 5, Oct. 30, 1998, 112 Stat. 2995.)

HISTORICAL AND STATUTORY NOTES

Effective and Termination Dates

1988 Acts. Section 906 of Pub.L. 100–702, as amended, which provided that, effective Dec. 31, 1994, this section was repealed, with certain exceptions, was itself repealed by Pub.L. 103–420, § 3(b), Oct. 25, 1994, 108 Stat. 4345. See section 906 of Pub.L. 100–702, set out as a note under section 651 of this title.

Section effective 180 days after Nov. 19, 1988, see section 907 of Pub.L. 100–702, set out as a note under section 651 of this title.

Treatment of Expired Provisions

This section to continue to be effective on or after Dec. 14, 1993 as if it had not been repealed by section 906 of Pub.L. 100–702 as such section was in effect on the day before such date, see Treatment of Expired Provisions note set out under section 651 of this title.

COMMENTARIES

See 28 U.S.C.A. § 653, for Commentary by David D. Siegel.

§ 654. Arbitration

(a) Referral of actions to arbitration.—Notwithstanding any provision of law to the contrary and except as provided in subsections (a), (b), and (c) of section 652 and subsection (d) of this section, a district court may allow the referral to arbitration of any civil action (including any adversary proceeding in bankruptcy) pending before it when the parties consent, except that referral to arbitration may not be made where—

(1) the action is based on an alleged violation of a right secured by the Constitution of the United States;

(2) jurisdiction is based in whole or in part on section 1343 of this title; or

(3) the relief sought consists of money damages in an amount greater than $150,000.

(b) Safeguards in consent cases.—Until such time as rules are adopted under chapter 131 of this title relating to procedures described in this subsection, the district court shall, by local rule adopted under section 2071(a), establish procedures to ensure that any civil action in which arbitration by consent is allowed under subsection (a)—

(1) consent to arbitration is freely and knowingly obtained; and

(2) no party or attorney is prejudiced for refusing to participate in arbitration.

(c) Presumptions.—For purposes of subsection (a)(3), a district court may presume damages are not in excess of $150,000 unless counsel certifies that damages exceed such amount.

(d) Existing programs.—Nothing in this chapter is deemed to affect any program in which arbitration is conducted pursuant to section title IX of the Judicial Improvements and Access to Justice Act (Public Law 100–702), as amended by section 1 of Public Law 105–53.

(Added Pub.L. 100–702, Title IX, § 901(a), Nov. 19, 1988, 102 Stat. 4660, and amended Pub.L. 105–315, § 6, Oct. 30, 1998, 112 Stat. 2995.)

HISTORICAL AND STATUTORY NOTES

References in Text

Title IX of the Judicial Improvements and Access to Justice Act, referred to in subsec. (d), is Pub.L. 100–702, Title IX, Nov. 19, 1988, 102 Stat. 4663. See Codifications note under this section.

Codifications

Section title IX of the Judicial Improvements and Access to Justice Act, referred to in subsec. (d), probably should read section 905 of title IX of the Judicial Improvements and Access to Justice Act, which is Pub.L. 100–702, Title IX, § 905, Nov. 19, 1988, 102 Stat. 4663, set out as a note under section 651 of this title.

Effective and Termination Dates

1988 Acts. Section 906 of Pub.L. 100–702, as amended, which provided that, effective Dec. 31, 1994, this section was repealed, with certain exceptions, was itself repealed by Pub.L. 103–420, § 3(b), Oct. 25, 1994, 108 Stat. 4345. See section 906 of Pub.L. 100–702, set out as a note under section 651 of this title.

Section effective 180 days after Nov. 19, 1988, see section 907 of Pub.L. 100–702, set out as a note under section 651 of this title.

Treatment of Expired Provisions

This section to continue to be effective on or after Dec. 14, 1993 as if it had not been repealed by section 906 of Pub.L. 100–702 as such section was in effect on the day before such date, see Treatment of Expired Provisions note set out under section 651 of this title.

COMMENTARIES

See 28 U.S.C.A. § 654, for Commentary by David D. Siegel.

§ 655. Arbitrators

(a) Powers of arbitrators.—An arbitrator to whom an action is referred under section 654 shall have the power, within the judicial district of the district court which referred the action to arbitration—

(1) to conduct arbitration hearings;

(2) to administer oaths and affirmations; and

(3) to make awards.

(b) Standards for certification.—Each district court that authorizes arbitration shall establish standards for the certification of arbitrators and shall certify arbitrators to perform services in accordance with such standards and this chapter. The standards shall include provisions requiring that any arbitrator—

(1) shall take the oath or affirmation described in section 453; and

(2) shall be subject to the disqualification rules under section 455.

(c) Immunity.—All individuals serving as arbitrators in an alternative dispute resolution program under this chapter are performing quasi-judicial functions and are entitled to the immunities and protections that the law accords to persons serving in such capacity.

(Added Pub.L. 100–702, Title IX, § 901(a), Nov. 19, 1988, 102 Stat. 4661, and amended Pub.L. 105–315, § 7, Oct. 30, 1998, 112 Stat. 2996.)

HISTORICAL AND STATUTORY NOTES

Effective and Termination Dates

1988 Acts. Section 906 of Pub.L. 100–702, as amended, which provided that, effective Dec. 31, 1994, this section was repealed, with certain exceptions, was itself repealed by Pub.L. 103–420, § 3(b), Oct. 25, 1994, 108 Stat. 4345. See section 906 of Pub.L. 100–702, set out as a note under section 651 of this title.

Section effective 180 days after Nov. 19, 1988, see section 907 of Pub.L. 100–702, set out as a note under section 651 of this title.

Treatment of Expired Provisions

This section to continue to be effective on or after Dec. 14, 1993 as if it had not been repealed by section 906 of Pub.L. 100–702 as such section was in effect on the day before such date, see Treatment of Expired Provisions note set out under section 651 of this title.

COMMENTARIES

See 28 U.S.C.A. § 655, for Commentary by David D. Siegel.

§ 656. Subpoenas

Rule 45 of the Federal Rules of Civil Procedure (relating to subpoenas) applies to subpoenas for the attendance of witnesses and the production of documentary evidence at an arbitration hearing under this chapter.

(Added Pub.L. 100–702, Title IX, § 901(a), Nov. 19, 1988, 102 Stat. 4662, and amended Pub.L. 105–315, § 8, Oct. 30, 1998, 112 Stat. 2996.)

HISTORICAL AND STATUTORY NOTES

Effective and Termination Dates

1988 Acts. Section 906 of Pub.L. 100–702, as amended, which provided that, effective Dec. 31, 1994, this section was repealed, with certain exceptions, was itself repealed by Pub.L. 103–420, § 3(b), Oct. 25, 1994, 108 Stat. 4345. See section 906 of Pub.L. 100–702, set out as a note under section 651 of this title.

Section effective 180 days after Nov. 19, 1988, see section 907 of Pub.L. 100–702, set out as a note under section 651 of this title.

Treatment of Expired Provisions

This section to continue to be effective on or after Dec. 14, 1993 as if it had not been repealed by section 906 of Pub.L. 100–702 as such section was in effect on the day before such date, see Treatment of Expired Provisions note set out under section 651 of this title.

§ 657. Arbitration award and judgment

(a) Filing and effect of arbitration award.—An arbitration award made by an arbitrator under this chapter, along with proof of service of such award on the other party by the prevailing party or by the plaintiff, shall be filed promptly after the arbitration hearing is concluded with the clerk of the district court that referred the case to arbitration. Such award shall be entered as the judgment of the court after the time has expired for requesting a trial de novo. The judgment so entered shall be subject to the same provisions of law and shall have the same force and effect as a judgment of the court in a civil action, except that the judgment shall not be subject to review in any other court by appeal or otherwise.

(b) Sealing of arbitration award.—The district court shall provide, by local rule adopted under section 2071(a), that the contents of any arbitration award made under this chapter shall not be made known to any judge who might be assigned to the case until the district court has entered final judgment in the action or the action has otherwise terminated.

(c) Trial de novo of arbitration awards.—

(1) Time for filing demand.—Within 30 days after the filing of an arbitration award with a district court under subsection (a), any party may file a written demand for a trial de novo in the district court.

(2) Action restored to court docket.—Upon a demand for a trial de novo, the action shall be restored to the docket of the court and treated for all purposes as if it had not been referred to arbitration.

(3) Exclusion of evidence of arbitration.—The court shall not admit at the trial de novo any evidence that there has been an arbitration proceeding, the nature or amount of any award, or any other matter concerning the conduct of the arbitration proceeding, unless—

(A) the evidence would otherwise be admissible in the court under the Federal Rules of Evidence; or

(B) the parties have otherwise stipulated.

(Added Pub.L. 100–702, Title IX, § 901(a), Nov. 19, 1988, 102 Stat. 4662, and amended Pub.L. 105–315, § 9, Oct. 30, 1998, 112 Stat. 2997.)

HISTORICAL AND STATUTORY NOTES

Effective and Termination Dates

1988 Acts. Section 906 of Pub.L. 100–702, as amended, which provided that, effective Dec. 31, 1994, this section was repealed, with certain exceptions, was itself repealed by Pub.L. 103–420, § 3(b), Oct. 25, 1994, 108 Stat. 4345. See section 906 of Pub.L. 100–702, set out as a note under section 651 of this title.

Section effective 180 days after Nov. 19, 1988, see section 907 of Pub.L. 100–702, set out as a note under section 651 of this title.

Treatment of Expired Provisions

This section to continue to be effective on or after Dec. 14, 1993 as if it had not been repealed by section 906 of Pub.L. 100–702 as such section was in effect on the day before such date, see Treatment of Expired Provisions note set out under section 651 of this title.

COMMENTARIES

See 28 U.S.C.A. § 657, for Commentary by David D. Siegel.

§ 658. Compensation of arbitrators and neutrals

(a) Compensation.—The district court shall, subject to regulations approved by the Judicial Conference of the United States, establish the amount of compensation, if any, that each arbitrator or neutral shall receive for services rendered in each case under this chapter.

(b) Transportation allowances.—Under regulations prescribed by the Director of the Administrative Office of the United States Courts, a district court may reimburse arbitrators and other neutrals for actual transportation expenses necessarily incurred in the performance of duties under this chapter.

(Added Pub.L. 100–702, Title IX, § 901(a), Nov. 19, 1988, 102 Stat. 4662, and amended Pub.L. 105–315, § 10, Oct. 30, 1998, 112 Stat. 2997.)

HISTORICAL AND STATUTORY NOTES

Effective and Termination Dates

1988 Acts. Section 906 of Pub.L. 100–702, as amended, which provided that, effective Dec. 31, 1994, this section was repealed, with certain exceptions, was itself repealed by Pub.L. 103–420, § 3(b), Oct. 25, 1994, 108 Stat. 4345. See section 906 of Pub.L. 100–702, set out as a note under section 651 of this title.

Section effective 180 days after Nov. 19, 1988, see section 907 of Pub.L. 100–702, set out as a note under section 651 of this title.

Treatment of Expired Provisions

This section to continue to be effective on or after Dec. 14, 1993 as if it had not been repealed by section 906 of Pub.L. 100–702 as such section was in effect on the day before such date, see Treatment of Expired Provisions note set out under section 651 of this title.

COMMENTARIES

See 28 U.S.C.A. § 658, for Commentary by David D. Siegel.

CHAPTER 45—SUPREME COURT

Sec.
671. Clerk.
672. Marshal.
673. Reporter.
674. Librarian.
675. Law clerks and secretaries.
676. Printing and binding.
677. Administrative Assistant to the Chief Justice.

§ 671. Clerk

(a) The Supreme Court may appoint and fix the compensation of a clerk and one or more deputy clerks. The clerk shall be subject to removal by the Court. Deputy clerks shall be subject to removal by the clerk with the approval of the Court or the Chief Justice of the United States.

[**(b)** Repealed. Pub.L. 92–310, Title II, § 206(c), June 6, 1972, 86 Stat. 203.]

(c) The clerk may appoint and fix the compensation of necessary assistants and messengers with the approval of the Chief Justice of the United States.

(d) The clerk shall pay into the Treasury all fees, costs, and other moneys collected by him. He shall make annual returns thereof to the Court under regulations prescribed by it.

(June 25, 1948, c. 646, 62 Stat. 918; Mar. 10, 1964, Pub.L. 88–279, § 1, 78 Stat. 158; June 6, 1972, Pub.L. 92–310, Title II, § 206(c), 86 Stat. 203.)

HISTORICAL AND STATUTORY NOTES

Effective Dates

1964 Acts. Section 4 of Pub.L. 88–279 provided that: "The amendments proposed in this Act [amending subsecs. (c) and (d) of this section and section 672 of this title] shall become effective only when funds have been appropriated and are available to pay the salaries and other expenses of the clerk's office."

Appropriations

Section 3 of Pub.L. 88–279 provided that: "There are hereby authorized to be appropriated annually such sums as are necessary to carry out the provisions of this Act [amending subsecs. (c) and (d) of this section and section 672 of this title]."

§ 672. Marshal

(a) The Supreme Court may appoint a marshal, who shall be subject to removal by the Court, and may fix his compensation.

(b) The marshal may, with the approval of the Chief Justice of the United States, appoint and fix the compensation of necessary assistants and other employees to attend the Court, and necessary custodial employees.

(c) The marshal shall:

(1) Attend the Court at its sessions;

(2) Serve and execute all process and orders issued by the Court or a member thereof;

(3) Take charge of all property of the United States used by the Court or its members;

(4) Disburse funds appropriated for work upon the Supreme Court building and grounds under the jurisdiction of the Architect of the Capitol upon certified vouchers submitted by the Architect;

(5) Disburse funds appropriated for the purchase of books, pamphlets, periodicals and other publications, and for their repair, binding, and rebinding, upon vouchers certified by the librarian of the Court;

(6) Pay the salaries of the Chief Justice, Associate Justices, and all officers and employees of the Court and disburse other funds appropriated for disbursement, under the direction of the Chief Justice;

(7) Pay the expenses of printing briefs and travel expenses of attorneys in behalf of persons whose motions to appear in forma pauperis in the Supreme Court have been approved and when counsel have been appointed by the Supreme Court, upon vouchers certified by the clerk of the Court;

(8) Oversee the Supreme Court Police.

(June 25, 1948, c. 646, 62 Stat. 918; Mar. 10, 1964, Pub.L. 88–279, § 2, 78 Stat. 158; Dec. 29, 1982, Pub.L. 97–390, § 2, 96 Stat. 1958.)

HISTORICAL AND STATUTORY NOTES

Effective Dates

1964 Acts. Amendment of subsec. (c) of this section by Pub.L. 88–279 effective upon appropriation and availability of funds to pay salaries and other expenses of the clerk's office, see section 4 of Pub.L. 88–279, set out as a note under section 671 of this title.

Appropriations

Annual appropriations to carry out amendment of subsec. (c) of this section by Pub.L. 88–279, see section 3 of Pub.L. 88–279, set out as a note under section 671 of this title.

Increases in Compensation Rates

For increases in rates of basic compensation fixed pursuant to this section, see notes under section 603 of this title.

§ 673. Reporter

(a) The Supreme Court may appoint and fix the compensation of a reporter of its decisions who shall be subject to removal by the Court.

(b) The reporter may appoint and fix the compensation of necessary professional and clerical assistants and other employees, with the approval of the Court or the Chief Justice of the United States.

(c) The reporter shall, under the direction of the Court or the Chief Justice, prepare the decisions of the Court for publication in bound volumes and advance copies in pamphlet installments.

The reporter shall determine the quality and size of the paper, type, format, proofs and binding subject to the approval of the Court or the Chief Justice.

(June 25, 1948, c. 646, 62 Stat. 919.)

HISTORICAL AND STATUTORY NOTES

Increases in Compensation Rates

For increases in rates of basic compensation fixed pursuant to this section, see notes under section 603 of this title.

§ 674. Librarian

(a) The Supreme Court may appoint a librarian, whose salary it shall fix, and who shall be subject to removal by the Court.

(b) The librarian shall, with the approval of the Chief Justice, appoint necessary assistants and fix their compensation and make rules governing the use of the library.

(c) He shall select and acquire by purchase, gift, bequest, or exchange, such books, pamphlets, periodicals, microfilm and other processed copy as may be required by the Court for its official use and for the reasonable needs of its bar.

(d) The librarian shall certify to the marshal for payment vouchers covering expenditures for the purchase of such books and other material, and for binding, rebinding and repairing the same.

(June 25, 1948, c. 646, 62 Stat. 919; June 6, 1972, Pub.L. 92–310, Title II, § 206(d), 86 Stat. 203.)

HISTORICAL AND STATUTORY NOTES

Increases in Compensation Rates

For increases in rates of basic compensation fixed pursuant to this section, see notes under section 603 of this title.

§ 675. Law clerks and secretaries

The Chief Justice of the United States, and the associate justices of the Supreme Court may appoint law clerks and secretaries whose salaries shall be fixed by the Court.

(June 25, 1948, c. 646, 62 Stat. 919.)

HISTORICAL AND STATUTORY NOTES

Increases in Compensation Rates

For increases in rates of basic compensation fixed pursuant to this section, see notes under section 603 of this title.

§ 676. Printing and binding

(a) The printing and binding for the Supreme Court, including the printing and binding of individual copies, advance pamphlet installments, and bound volumes, of its decisions, whether requisitioned or ordered by the Court or any of its officers or by any other office or agency, and whether paid for by, or charged to the appropriation for, the Court or any other office or agency, shall be done by the printer or printers whom the Court or the Chief Justice of the United States may select, unless it shall otherwise order.

(b) Whenever advance pamphlet installments and bound volumes of the Court's decisions are printed by a private printer, an adequate number of copies for distribution in accordance with the requirements of section 411 of this title and for sale to the public shall be provided and made available for these purposes in such manner and at such prices as may be determined from time to time by the Supreme Court or the Chief Justice of the United States, in lieu of compliance by the Public Printer and the Superintendent of Documents with the requirements of sections 411 and 412 of this title with respect to such copies. Pending distribution or sale, such copies shall be the property of the United States and shall be held in the custody of the marshal or such other person, organization, or agency, as the Supreme Court or the Chief Justice of the United States may designate.

(June 25, 1948, c. 646, 62 Stat. 919; May 24, 1949, c. 139, § 74, 63 Stat. 100; Oct. 31, 1951, c. 655, § 45, 65 Stat. 725.)

§ 677. Administrative Assistant to the Chief Justice

(a) The Chief Justice of the United States may appoint an Administrative Assistant who shall serve at the pleasure of the Chief Justice and shall perform such duties as may be assigned to him by the Chief Justice. The salary payable to the Administrative Assistant shall be fixed by the Chief Justice at a rate which shall not exceed the salary payable to the Director of the Administrative Office of the United States Courts. The Administrative Assistant may elect to bring himself within the same retirement program available to the Director of the Administrative Office of the United States Courts, as provided by section 611 of this title, by filing a written election with the Chief Justice within the time and in the manner prescribed by section 611.

(b) The Administrative Assistant, with the approval of the Chief Justice, may appoint and fix the compensation of necessary employees. The Administrative Assistant and his employees shall be deemed employees of the Supreme Court.

(c)(1) Notwithstanding section 1342 of title 31, the Administrative Assistant, with the approval of the Chief Justice, may accept voluntary personal services to assist with public and visitor programs.

(2) No person may volunteer personal services under this subsection unless the person has first agreed, in writing, to waive any claim against the United States arising out of or in connection with such services, other than a claim under chapter 81 of title 5 [5 U.S.C.A. § 8101 et seq.].

(3) No person volunteering personal services under this subsection shall be considered an employee of the United States for any purpose other than for purposes of—

(A) chapter 81 of title 5 [5 U.S.C.A. § 8101 et seq.]; or

(B) chapter 171 of this title [28 U.S.C.A. § 2671 et seq.].

(4) In the administration of this subsection, the Administrative Assistant shall ensure that the acceptance of personal services shall not result in the reduction of pay or displacement of any employee of the Supreme Court.

(Added Pub.L. 92–238, § 1, Mar. 1, 1972, 86 Stat. 46, and amended Pub.L. 105–233, § 1, Aug. 13, 1998, 112 Stat. 1535.)

CHAPTER 47—COURTS OF APPEALS

Sec.

711. Clerks and employees.
712. Law clerks and secretaries.
713. Librarians.
714. Criers and messengers.
715. Staff attorneys and technical assistants.

§ 711. Clerks and employees

(a) Each court of appeals may appoint a clerk who shall be subject to removal by the court.

(b) The clerk, with the approval of the court, may appoint necessary deputies, clerical assistants and employees in such number as may be approved by the Director of the Administrative Office of the United States Courts. Such deputies, clerical assistants and employees shall be subject to removal by the clerk with the approval of the court.

(c) The clerk shall pay into the Treasury all fees, costs and other moneys collected by him and make returns thereof to the Director of the Administrative Office of the United States Courts under regulations prescribed by him.

(June 25, 1948, c. 646, 62 Stat. 920.)

§ 712. Law clerks and secretaries

Circuit judges may appoint necessary law clerks and secretaries. A law clerk appointed under this section shall be exempt from the provisions of subchapter I of chapter 63 of title 5, unless specifically included by the appointing judge or by local rule of court.

(June 25, 1948, c. 646, 62 Stat. 920; Nov. 19, 1988, Pub.L. 100–702, Title X, § 1003(a)(3), 102 Stat. 4665.)

§ 713. Librarians

(a) Each court of appeals may appoint a librarian who shall be subject to removal by the court.

(b) The librarian, with the approval of the court, may appoint necessary library assistants in such numbers as the Director of the Administrative Office of the United States Courts may approve. The librarian may remove such library assistants with the approval of the court.

(June 25, 1948, c. 646, 62 Stat. 920; May 24, 1949, c. 139, § 75, 63 Stat. 100; Apr. 2, 1982, Pub.L. 97–164, Title I, § 120(b) (1), 96 Stat. 33.)

HISTORICAL AND STATUTORY NOTES

Effective Dates

1982 Acts. Amendment by Pub.L. 97–164 effective Oct. 1, 1982, see section 402 of Pub.L. 97–164, set out as a note under section 171 of this title.

Continuation of Service of Marshal for Court of Appeals for District of Columbia; Applicability of Other Law to Court During Such Individual's Service

Pub.L. 98–620, Title IV, § 415, Nov. 8, 1984, 98 Stat. 3364, provided that: "Any individual who, on the date of the enactment of the Federal Courts Improvement Act of 1982 [Pub.L. 97–164, enacted Apr. 2, 1982], was serving as marshal for the Court of Appeals for the District of Columbia under section 713(c) of title 28, United States Code [subsec. (c) of this section], may, after the date of the enactment of this Act [Nov. 8, 1984], so serve under that section as in effect on the date of the enactment of the Federal Courts Improvement Act of 1982. While such individual so serves, the provisions of section 714(a) of title 28, United States Code [section 714(a) of this title], shall not apply to the Court of Appeals for the District of Columbia."

§ 714. Criers and messengers

(a) Each court of appeals may appoint a crier who shall be subject to removal by the court.

(b) The crier, with the approval of the court, may appoint necessary messengers in such number as the Director of the Administrative Office of the United States Courts may approve. The crier may remove such messengers with the approval of the court. The crier shall also perform the duties of bailiff and messenger.

(Added Pub.L. 97–164, Title I, § 120(c)(1), Apr. 2, 1982, 96 Stat. 33.)

HISTORICAL AND STATUTORY NOTES

Effective Dates

1982 Acts. Section effective Oct. 1, 1982, see section 402 of Pub.L. 97–164, set out as a note under section 171 of this title.

Applicability of This Section to Court of Appeals for District of Columbia During Continued Service of Marshal for Court in Office on Apr. 2, 1982

Subsec. (a) of this section not to apply to the Court of Appeals for the District of Columbia during the continued service as Marshal for such Court of any individual who was serving in such office under section 713(c) of this title as of Apr. 2, 1982, see section 415 of Pub.L. 98–620, set out as a note under section 713 of this title.

§ 715. Staff attorneys and technical assistants

(a) The chief judge of each court of appeals, with the approval of the court, may appoint a senior staff attorney, who shall be subject to removal by the chief judge with the approval of the court.

(b) The senior staff attorney, with the approval of the chief judge, may appoint necessary staff attorneys and secretarial and clerical employees in such numbers as the Director of the Administrative Office of the United States Courts may approve, but in no event may the number of staff attorneys exceed the number of positions expressly authorized in an annual appropriation Act. The senior staff attorney may remove such staff attorneys and secretarial and clerical employees with the approval of the chief judge.

(c) The chief judge of the Court of Appeals for the Federal Circuit, with the approval of the court, may appoint a senior technical assistant who shall be subject to removal by the chief judge with the approval of the court.

(d) The senior technical assistant, with the approval of the court, may appoint necessary technical assistants in such number as the Director of the Administrative Office of the United States Courts may approve, but in no event may the number of technical assistants in the Court of Appeals for the Federal Circuit exceed the number of circuit judges in regular active service within such circuit. The senior technical assistant may remove such technical assistants with the approval of the court.

(Added Pub.L. 97–164, Title I, § 120(c)(1), Apr. 2, 1982, 96 Stat. 34.)

HISTORICAL AND STATUTORY NOTES

Effective Dates

1982 Acts. Section effective Oct. 1, 1982, see section 402 of Pub.L. 97–164, set out as a note under section 171 of this title.

CHAPTER 49—DISTRICT COURTS

Sec.

751. Clerks.
752. Law clerks and secretaries.
753. Reporters.
754. Receivers of property in different districts.
755. Criers and bailiffs.
756. Power to appoint.

§ 751. Clerks

(a) Each district court may appoint a clerk who shall be subject to removal by the court.

(b) The clerk may appoint, with the approval of the court, necessary deputies, clerical assistants and employees in such number as may be approved by the Director of the Administrative Office of the United States Courts. Such deputies, clerical assistants and employees shall be subject to removal by the clerk with the approval of the court.

(c) The clerk of each district court shall reside in the district for which he is appointed, except that the clerk of the district court for the District of Columbia and the Southern District of New York may reside within twenty miles thereof. The district court may designate places within the district for the offices of the clerk and his deputies, and their official stations.

(d) A clerk of a district court or his deputy or assistant shall not receive any compensation or emoluments through any office or position to which he is appointed by the court, other than that received as such clerk, deputy or assistant, whether from the United States or from private litigants.

This subsection shall not apply to clerks or deputy clerks appointed as United States commissioners pursuant to section 631 of this title.

(e) The clerk of each district court shall pay into the Treasury all fees, costs and other moneys collected by him, except naturalization fees listed in section 742 of Title 8 and uncollected fees not required by Act of Congress to be prepaid.

He shall make returns thereof to the Director of the Administrative Office of the United States Courts under regulations prescribed by him.

(f) When the Court of International Trade is sitting in a judicial district, other than the Southern District or Eastern District of New York, the clerk of the district court of such judicial district or an authorized deputy clerk, upon the request of the chief judge of the Court of International Trade and with the approval of such district court, shall act in the district as clerk of the Court of International Trade, as prescribed by the rules and orders of the Court of International Trade for all purposes relating to the civil action then pending before such court.

(June 25, 1948, c. 646, 62 Stat. 920; Oct. 10, 1980, Pub.L. 96–417, Title V, § 504, 94 Stat. 1743.)

HISTORICAL AND STATUTORY NOTES

References in Text

Section 742 of Title 8, referred to in subsec. (e), was repealed by Act June 27, 1952, c. 477, Title IV, § 403(a)(42), 66 Stat. 280 eff. Dec. 24, 1952, and is now covered by section 1455 of Title 8, Aliens and Nationality.

Effective Dates

1980 Acts. Amendment by Pub.L. 96–417 effective on Nov. 1, 1980 and applicable with respect to civil actions pending on or commenced on or after such date, see section 701(a) of Pub.L. 96–417, as amended, set out as a note under section 251 of this title.

Change of Name

Reference to United States commissioners deemed to be reference to United States Magistrates pursuant to Pub.L. 90–578, Title IV, § 402(b)(2), Oct. 17, 1968, 82 Stat. 1108. See chapter 43 (section 631 et seq.) of this title.

Reference to United States magistrate or to magistrate deemed to refer to United States magistrate judge pursuant to section 321 of Pub.L. 101–650, set out as a note under section 631 of this title.

§ 752. Law clerks and secretaries

District judges may appoint necessary law clerks and secretaries subject to any limitation on the aggregate salaries of such employees which may be imposed by law. A law clerk appointed under this section shall be exempt from the provisions of subchapter I of chapter 63 of title 5, unless specifically included by the appointing judge or by local rule of court.

(June 25, 1948, c. 646, 62 Stat. 921; Sept. 1, 1959, Pub.L. 86–221, 73 Stat. 452; Nov. 19, 1988, Pub.L. 100–702, Title X, § 1003(a)(3), 102 Stat. 4665.)

HISTORICAL AND STATUTORY NOTES

Senate Revision Amendment

As finally enacted, sections 374c and 374d of Title 28, U.S.C., 1946 ed., which were derived from Act July 23, 1947, ch. 300, §§ 1, 2, 61 Stat. 409, were an additional source of this section. Hence, by Senate amendment, the section was changed to conform with such sections, and such Act was included in the schedule of repeals. See 80th Congress Senate Report No. 1559.

1959 Acts. Senate Report No. 788, see 1959 U.S.Code Cong. and Adm.News, p. 2213.

1988 Acts. House Report No. 100–889, see 1988 U.S.Code Cong. and Adm.News, p. 5982.

§ 753. Reporters

(a) Each district court of the United States, the United States District Court for the District of the Canal Zone, the District Court of Guam, and the District Court of the Virgin Islands shall appoint one or more court reporters.

The number of reporters shall be determined by the Judicial Conference of the United States.

The qualifications of such reporters shall be determined by standards formulated by the Judicial Conference. Each reporter shall take an oath faithfully to perform the duties of his office.

Each such court, with the approval of the Director of the Administrative Office of the United States Courts, may appoint additional reporters for temporary service not exceeding three months, when there is more reporting work in the district than can be performed promptly by the authorized number of reporters and the urgency is so great as to render it impracticable to obtain the approval of the Judicial Conference.

If any such court and the Judicial Conference are of the opinion that it is in the public interest that the duties of reporter should be combined with those of any other employee of the court, the Judicial Conference may authorize such a combination and fix the salary for the performance of the duties combined.

(b) Each session of the court and every other proceeding designated by rule or order of the court or by one of the judges shall be recorded verbatim by shorthand, mechanical means, electronic sound recording, or any other method, subject to regulations promulgated by the Judicial Conference and subject to the discretion and approval of the judge. The regulations promulgated pursuant to the preceding sentence shall prescribe the types of electronic sound recording or other means which may be used. Proceedings to be recorded under this section include (1) all proceedings in criminal cases had in open court; (2) all proceedings in other cases had in open court unless the parties with the approval of the judge shall agree specifically to the contrary; and (3) such other proceedings as a judge of the court may direct or as may be required by rule or order of court as [1] may be requested by any party to the proceeding.

The reporter or other individual designated to produce the record shall attach his official certificate to the original shorthand notes or other original records so taken and promptly file them with the clerk who shall preserve them in the public records of the court for not less than ten years.

The reporter or other individual designated to produce the record shall transcribe and certify such parts of the record of proceedings as may be required by any rule or order of court, including all arraignments, pleas, and proceedings in connection with the imposition of sentence in criminal cases unless they have been recorded by electronic sound recording as provided in this subsection and the original records so taken have been certified by him and filed with the clerk as provided in this subsection. He shall also transcribe and certify such other parts of the record of proceedings as may be required by rule or order of court. Upon the request of any party to any proceeding which has been so recorded who has agreed to pay the fee therefor, or of a judge of the court, the reporter or other individual designated to produce the record shall promptly transcribe the original records of the requested parts of the proceedings and attach to the transcript his official certificate, and deliver the same to the party or judge making the request.

The reporter or other designated individual shall promptly deliver to the clerk for the records of the court a certified copy of any transcript so made.

The transcript in any case certified by the reporter or other individual designated to produce the record shall be deemed prima facie a correct statement of the testimony taken and proceedings had. No transcripts of the proceedings of the court shall be considered as official except those made from the records certified by the reporter or other individual designated to produce the record.

The original notes or other original records and the copy of the transcript in the office of the clerk shall be open during office hours to inspection by any person without charge.

(c) The reporters shall be subject to the supervision of the appointing court and the Judicial Conference in the performance of their duties, including dealings with parties requesting transcripts.

(d) The Judicial Conference shall prescribe records which shall be maintained and reports which shall be filed by the reporters. Such records shall be inspected and audited in the same manner as the records and accounts of clerks of the district courts, and may include records showing:

(1) the quantity of transcripts prepared;

(2) the fees charged and the fees collected for transcripts;

(3) any expenses incurred by the reporters in connection with transcripts;

(4) the amount of time the reporters are in attendance upon the courts for the purpose of recording proceedings; and

(5) such other information as the Judicial Conference may require.

(e) Each reporter shall receive an annual salary to be fixed from time to time by the Judicial Conference of the United States. For the purposes of subchapter III of chapter 83 of title 5 and chapter 84 of such title, a reporter shall be considered a full-time employee during any pay period for which a reporter receives a salary at the annual salary rate fixed for a full-time reporter under the preceding sentence. All supplies shall be furnished by the reporter at his own expense.

(f) Each reporter may charge and collect fees for transcripts requested by the parties, including the United States, at rates prescribed by the court subject to the approval of the Judicial Conference. He shall not charge a fee for any copy of a transcript delivered to the clerk for the records of court. Fees for transcripts furnished in criminal proceedings to persons proceeding under the Criminal Justice Act (18 U.S.C. 3006A), or in habeas corpus proceedings to persons allowed to sue, defend, or appeal in forma pauperis, shall be paid by the United States out of moneys appropriated for those purposes. Fees for transcripts furnished in proceedings brought under section 2255 of this title to persons permitted to sue or appeal in forma pauperis shall be paid by the United States out of money appropriated for that purpose if the trial judge or a circuit judge certifies that the suit or appeal is not frivolous and that the transcript is needed to decide the issue presented by the suit or appeal. Fees for transcripts furnished in other proceedings to persons permitted to appeal in forma pauperis shall also be paid by the United States if the trial judge or a circuit judge certifies that the appeal is not frivolous (but presents a substantial question). The reporter may require any party requesting a transcript to prepay the estimated fee in advance except as to transcripts that are to be paid for by the United States.

(g) If, upon the advice of the chief judge of any district court within the circuit, the judicial council of any circuit determines that the number of court reporters provided such district court pursuant to subsection (a) of this section is insufficient to meet temporary demands and needs and that the services of additional court reporters for such district court should be provided the judges of such district court (including the senior judges thereof when such senior judges are performing substantial judicial services for such court) on a contract basis, rather than by appointment of court reporters as otherwise provided in this section, and such judicial council notifies the Director of the Administrative Office, in writing, of such determination, the Director of the Administrative Office is authorized to and shall contract, without regard to section 3709 of the Revised Statutes of the United States, as amended (41 U.S.C. 5), with any suitable person, firm, association, or corporation for the providing of court reporters to serve such district court under such terms and conditions as the Director of the Administrative Office finds, after consultation with the chief judge of the district court, will best serve the needs of such district court.

(June 25, 1948, c. 646, 62 Stat. 921; Oct. 31, 1951, c. 655, § 46, 65 Stat. 726; June 28, 1955, c. 189, § 3(c), 69 Stat. 176; June 20, 1958, Pub.L. 85–462, § 3(c), 72 Stat. 207; July 7, 1958, Pub.L. 85–508, § 12(e), 72 Stat. 348; July 1, 1960, Pub.L. 86–568, Title I, § 116(c), 74 Stat. 303; Sept. 2, 1965, Pub.L. 89–163, 79 Stat. 619; Sept. 2, 1965, Pub.L. 89–167, 79 Stat. 647; June 2, 1970, Pub.L. 91–272, § 14, 84 Stat. 298; Dec. 11, 1970, Pub.L. 91–545, 84 Stat. 1412; Apr. 2, 1982, Pub.L. 97–164, Title IV, § 401(a), 96 Stat. 56; Oct. 19, 1996, Pub.L. 104–317, Title III, § 305, 110 Stat. 3852.)

[1] So in original. Probably should be "or as".

HISTORICAL AND STATUTORY NOTES

References in Text

The Criminal Justice Act (18 U.S.C. 3006A), referred to in subsec. (f), probably means Pub.L. 88–455, Aug. 20, 1964, 78 Stat. 552, as amended, known as the Criminal Justice Act of 1964, which is classified to section 3006A of Title 18, Crimes and Criminal Procedure, and provisions set out as notes under that section.

Effective Dates

1982 Acts. Amendment by Pub.L. 97–164 effective Oct. 1, 1982, see section 402 of Pub.L. 97–164, set out as a note under section 171 of this title.

1960 Acts. Amendment by Pub.L. 86–568 effective on the first day of the first pay period which begins on or after July 1, 1960, see section 122 of Pub.L. 86–568.

1958 Acts. Amendment by Pub.L. 85–508 effective Jan. 3, 1959, upon admission of Alaska into the Union pursuant to Proc. No. 3269, Jan. 3, 1959, 24 F.R. 81, 73 Stat. c16, as required by sections 1 and 8(c) of Pub.L. 85–508, see notes set out under section 81A of this title and preceding section 21 of Title 48, Territories and Insular Possessions.

Savings Provisions

Section 401(b) of Pub.L. 97–164 provided that: "The regulations promulgated by the Judicial Conference pursuant to subsection (b) of section 753 of title 28 [subsec. (b) of this section], as amended by subsection (a) of this section, shall not take effect before one year after the effective date of this Act [Oct. 1, 1982]. During the one-year period after the date of the enactment of this Act [Apr. 2, 1982], the Judicial Conference shall experiment with the different methods of recording court proceedings. Prior to the effective date of such regulations, the law and regulations in effect the day before the date of enactment of this Act [Apr. 2, 1982] shall remain in full force and effect."

Salary Limitation For Court Reporters

1967—Pub.L. 90–206, Title II, § 213(c), Dec. 16, 1967, 81 Stat. 635, inserted a new salary limitation for court reporters effective the first pay period which begins on or after Oct. 1, 1967, which reflected the respective applicable pay increases provided by section 202(a) of Pub.L. 90–206 in corresponding rates of compensation for particular officers and employees of the government.

1966—Pub.L. 89–504, Title II, § 202(c), July 18, 1966, 80 Stat. 294, inserted a new salary limitation for court reporters effective the first pay period which begins on or after July 1, 1966, which reflected the respective applicable pay increases provided by section 102(a) of title I of Pub.L. 89–504 in corresponding rates of compensation for particular officers and employees of the government.

1965—Pub.L. 89–301, § 12(c), Oct. 29, 1965, 79 Stat. 1122, inserted a new salary limitation for court reporters which reflected the applicable pay increases provided by section 2(a) of Pub.L. 89–301 in corresponding rates of compensation for particular government officers and employees.

1964—Pub.L. 88–426, Title IV, § 402(c), Aug. 14, 1964, 78 Stat. 434, inserted a new salary limitation for court reporters which reflected the applicable pay increases provided by Title I of Pub.L. 88–426 in corresponding rates of compensation for particular government officers and employees.

1962—Pub.L. 87–793, Title VI, § 1004(c), Oct. 11, 1962, 76 Stat. 866, inserted a new salary limitation for court reporters effective for the pay period beginning on or after Oct. 11, 1962, and ending immediately prior to the first pay period beginning on or after Jan. 1, 1964, and provided for a second salary limitation effective for the first pay period beginning on or after Jan. 1, 1964, which reflected applicable pay increases provided by Title II of Pub.L. 87–793 in corresponding rates of compensation for particular government officers and employees.

Termination of United States District Court For The District Of The Canal Zone

For termination of the United States District Court for the District of the Canal Zone at end of the "transition period", being the 30–month period beginning Oct. 1, 1979, and ending midnight Mar. 31, 1982, see Paragraph 5 of Article XI of the Panama Canal Treaty of 1977 and sections 3831 and 3841 to 3843 of Title 22, Foreign Relations and Intercourse.

§ 754. Receivers of property in different districts

A receiver appointed in any civil action or proceeding involving property, real, personal or mixed, situated in different districts shall, upon giving bond as required by the court, be vested with complete jurisdiction and control of all such property with the right to take possession thereof.

He shall have capacity to sue in any district without ancillary appointment, and may be sued with respect thereto as provided in section 959 of this title.

Such receiver shall, within ten days after the entry of his order of appointment, file copies of the complaint and such order of appointment in the district court for each district in which property is located. The failure to file such copies in any district shall divest the receiver of jurisdiction and control over all such property in that district.

(June 25, 1948, c. 646, 62 Stat. 922.)

§ 755. Criers and bailiffs

Each district judge may appoint a crier for the court in which he presides who shall perform also the duties of bailiff and messenger. A crier may perform also the duties of law clerk if he is qualified to do so and the district judge who appointed him designates him to serve as a crier-law clerk. A crier designated to serve as a crier-law clerk shall receive the compensation of a law clerk, but only so much of that compensation as is in excess of the compensation to which he would be entitled as a crier shall be deemed the compensation of a law clerk for the purposes of any limitation imposed by law upon the aggregate salaries of law clerks and secretaries appointed by a district judge.

Each United States marshal may employ, with the approval of the judge, not exceeding four bailiffs as the district judge may determine, to attend the court, maintain order, wait upon the grand and petit juries, and perform such other necessary duties as the judge or marshal may direct.

If the position of crier or bailiff is to be filled by the appointment of a person who has not previously served as either crier or bailiff, preference in the appointment shall be given to a person who has served in the military or naval forces of the United States in time of war and who has been honorably discharged therefrom, if in the opinion of the appointing officer such person is as well qualified as any other available person to perform to the satisfaction of the appointing officer all the duties of the position.

(June 25, 1948, c. 646, 62 Stat. 923; Oct. 21, 1965, Pub.L. 89–281, 79 Stat. 1012; Nov. 18, 1988, Pub.L. 100–690, Title VII, § 7608(b), 102 Stat. 4515.)

§ 756. Power to appoint

Whenever a majority of the district judges of any district court cannot agree upon the appointment of any officer of such court, the chief judge shall make such appointment.

(June 25, 1948, c. 646, 62 Stat. 923.)

HISTORICAL AND STATUTORY NOTES

District of Columbia Register of Wills

Pub.L. 88–241, § 21(b), Dec. 23, 1963, 77 Stat. 628, repealed sections 3 and 4 of Act Aug. 2, 1949, c. 383, 63 Stat. 491, which provided for the appointment and removal of the Register of Wills by the United States District Court for the District of Columbia and made the office of Register of Wills a part of the United States District Court for the District of Columbia. See D.C.Code 1961 Ed., § 11–504(a).

CHAPTER 50—BANKRUPTCY COURTS [OMITTED]

§§ 771 to 775. Omitted.

HISTORICAL AND STATUTORY NOTES

Chapter 50, consisted of sections 771 to 775, as added by Pub.L. 95–598, Title II, § 233(a), Nov. 6, 1978, 92 Stat. 2666, 2667, effective June 28, 1984, pursuant to Pub.L. 95–598, Title IV, § 402(b), Nov. 6, 1978, 92 Stat. 2682, as amended by Pub.L. 98–249, § 1(a), Mar. 31, 1984, 98 Stat. 116; Pub.L. 98–271, § 1(a), Apr. 30, 1984, 98 Stat. 163; Pub.L. 98–299, § 1(a), May 25, 1984, 98 Stat. 214; Pub.L. 98–325, § 1(a), June 20, 1984, 98 Stat. 268.

Section 402(b) of Pub.L. 95–598 was amended by section 113 of Pub.L. 98–353, Title I, July 10, 1984, 98 Stat. 343, by substituting "shall not be effective" for "shall take effect on June 28 1984", thereby eliminating the addition of the chapter heading, section analysis, and sections 771 to 775 by section 233(a) of Pub.L. 95–598, effective June 27, 1984, pursuant to section 122(c) of Pub.L. 98–353, set out as an Effective Date note under section 151 of this title.

Section 121(a) of Pub.L. 98–353 directed that section 402(b) of Pub.L. 95–598 be amended by substituting "the date of enactment of the Bankruptcy Amendments and Federal Judgeship Act of 1984 [i.e. July 10, 1984]" for "June 28, 1984". This amendment was not executed in view of the prior amendment to section 402(b) of Pub.L. 95–598 by section 113 of Pub.L. 98–353.

Sections 771 to 775 read as follows:

CHAPTER 50—BANKRUPTCY COURTS

Sec.
771. Clerks.
772. Other employees.
773. Records of proceedings; reporters.
774. Power to appoint.
775. Salaries of employees.

§ 771. Clerks

(a) Based on need each bankruptcy court may appoint a clerk who shall be subject to removal only by the court.

(b) The clerk may appoint, with the approval of the court, necessary deputies, clerical assistants, and employees in such number as may be approved by the Director of the Administrative Office of the United States Courts. Such deputies, clerical assistants, and employees shall be subject to removal only by the clerk with the approval of the court. If there is no clerk, the Bankruptcy Judge shall perform the duties of this subsection.

(c) The clerk of each bankruptcy court shall reside in the district for which he is appointed. The bankruptcy court may designate places within the district for the offices of the clerk and his deputies, and their official stations.

(d) A clerk of a bankruptcy court or his deputy or assistant shall not receive any compensation or emoluments through any office or position to which he is appointed by the court, other than that received as such clerk, deputy or assistant, whether from the United States or from private litigants.

(e) The clerk of each bankruptcy court shall pay into the Treasury all fees, costs and other moneys collected by him, except uncollected fees not required by Act of Congress to be prepaid.

He shall make returns thereof to the Director of the Administrative Office of the United States Courts under regulations prescribed by him.

§ 772. Other employees

Bankruptcy judges may appoint necessary other employees, including law clerks and secretaries, subject to any limitation on the aggregate salaries of such employees which may be imposed by law.

§ 773. Records of proceedings; reporters

(a) The bankruptcy court shall require a record to be made, whenever practicable, of all proceedings in cases had in open court. The Judicial Conference shall prescribe that the record be taken by electronic sound recording means, by a court reporter appointed or employed by such bankruptcy court to take a verbatim record by shorthand or mechanical means, or by an employee of such court designated by such court to take such a verbatim record.

(b) On the request of a party to a proceeding that has been recorded who has agreed to pay the fee for a transcript, or a judge of the bankruptcy court, a transcript of the original record of the requested parts of such proceeding shall be made and delivered promptly to such party or judge. Any such transcript that is certified shall be deemed prima facie a correct statement of the testimony taken and proceedings had. No transcript of the proceedings of the bankruptcy court shall be considered as official except those made from certified records.

(c) Fees for transcripts furnished in proceedings to persons permitted to appeal in forma pauperis shall be paid by the United States out of money appropriated for that purpose if the trial judge or a circuit judge certifies that the appeal is not frivolous (but presents a substantial question).

§ 774. Power to appoint

Whenever a majority of the bankruptcy judges of any bankruptcy court cannot agree upon the appointment of any officer of such court, the chief judge shall make such appointment.

§ 775. Salaries of employees

The salary of an individual appointed or employed under section 771(a), 772, or 773(a) of this title shall be the same as the salary of an individual appointed or employed under section 751(a), 752, or 753(a) of this title, as the case may be. The salaries of individuals appointed under section 771(b) of this title shall be comparable to the salaries of individuals appointed under section 751(b) of this title.

CHAPTER 51—UNITED STATES COURT OF FEDERAL CLAIMS

Sec.

791. Clerk.
[792, 793. Repealed.]
794. Law clerks and secretaries.
795. Bailiffs and messengers.
796. Reporting of court proceedings.
797. Recall of retired judges.
798. Places of holding court; appointment of special masters.

§ 791. Clerk

(a) The United States Court of Federal Claims may appoint a clerk, who shall be subject to removal by the court. The clerk, with the approval of the court, may appoint necessary deputies and employees in such numbers as may be approved by the Director of the Administrative Office of the United States Courts. Such deputies and employees shall be subject to removal by the clerk with the approval of the court.

(b) The clerk shall pay into the Treasury all fees, costs and other moneys collected by him. He shall make returns thereof to the Director of the Administrative Office of the United States Courts under regulations prescribed by him.

(c) On the first day of every regular session of Congress, the clerk shall transmit to Congress a full and complete statement of all the judgments rendered by the court during the previous year, showing the dates and amounts thereof and the parties in whose favor they were rendered, together with a brief synopsis of the nature of the claims upon which they were rendered, and a statement of the costs taxed in each case.

(June 25, 1948, c. 646, 62 Stat. 923; Apr. 2, 1982, Pub.L. 97–164, Title I, § 121(a), 96 Stat. 34; Oct. 29, 1992, Pub.L. 102–572, Title IX, § 902(a)(1), 106 Stat. 4516.)

HISTORICAL AND STATUTORY NOTES

Effective Dates

1992 Acts. Amendment by Title IX of Pub.L. 102–572 effective Oct. 29, 1992, see section 911 of Pub.L 102–572, set out as a note under section 171 of Title 28, Judiciary and Judicial Procedure.

1982 Acts. Amendment by Pub.L. 97–164 effective Oct. 1, 1982, see section 402 of Pub.L. 97–164, set out as a note under section 171 of this title.

[§ 792. Repealed. Pub.L. 97–164, Title I, § 121(b), Apr. 2, 1982, 96 Stat. 34]

HISTORICAL AND STATUTORY NOTES

Section, Acts June 25, 1948, c. 646, 62 Stat. 923; July 28, 1953, c. 253, § 4(a), 67 Stat. 226; Sept. 3, 1954, c. 1263, § 41, 68 Stat. 1240; Aug. 14, 1964, Pub.L. 88–426, Title IV, § 403(h), 78 Stat. 434; Oct. 15, 1966, Pub.L. 89–681, § 3, 80 Stat. 959; Dec. 16, 1967, Pub.L. 90–206, Title II, § 213(e), 81 Stat. 635; Aug. 9, 1975, Pub.L. 94–82, Title II, § 205(b)(7), 89 Stat. 423; July 20, 1977, Pub.L. 95–69, § 3, 91 Stat. 274, provided for the appointment by the Court of Claims and compensation of sixteen commissioners of the Court of Claims.

Effective Date of Repeal

Repeal effective Oct. 1, 1982, see section 402 of Pub.L. 97–164, set out as an Effective Dates of 1992 Amendments note under section 171 of this title.

[§ 793. Repealed. July 28, 1953, c. 253, § 6, 67 Stat. 226]

HISTORICAL AND STATUTORY NOTES

Section, Act June 25, 1948, c. 646, 62 Stat. 924, related to the appointment of reporter-commissioners by the Court of Claims, and the employment of stenographers therefor.

§ 794. Law clerks and secretaries

The judges of the United States Court of Federal Claims may appoint necessary law clerks and secretaries, in such numbers as the Judicial Conference of the United States may approve for district judges, subject to any limitation of the aggregate salaries of such employees which may be imposed by law. A law clerk appointed under this section shall be exempt from the provisions of subchapter I of chapter 63 of title 5, unless specifically included by the appointing judge or by local rule of court.

(June 25, 1948, c. 646, 62 Stat. 924; Apr. 2, 1982, Pub.L. 97–164, Title I, § 121(c)(1), 96 Stat. 34; Nov. 19, 1988, Pub.L. 100–702, Title X, § 1003(a)(3), 102 Stat. 4665; Oct. 29, 1992, Pub.L. 102–572, Title IX, §§ 902(a)(1), 905, 106 Stat. 4516, 4517.)

HISTORICAL AND STATUTORY NOTES

Effective Dates

1992 Acts. Amendment by Title IX of Pub.L. 102–572 effective Oct. 29, 1992, see section 911 of Pub.L. 102–572, set out as a note under section 171 of Title 28, Judiciary and Judicial Procedure.

1982 Acts. Amendment by Pub.L. 97–164 effective Oct. 1, 1982, see section 402 of Pub.L. 97–164, set out as a note under section 171 of this title.

§ 795. Bailiffs and messengers

The chief judge of[1] United States Court of Federal Claims, with the approval of the court, may appoint necessary bailiffs and messengers, in such numbers as the Director of the Administrative Office of the United States Courts may approve, each of whom shall be subject to removal by the chief judge, with the approval of the court.

(June 25, 1948, c. 646, 62 Stat. 924; Apr. 2, 1982, Pub.L. 97–164, Title I, § 121(d)(1), 96 Stat. 35; Oct. 29, 1992, Pub.L. 102–572, Title IX, § 902(a)(1), 106 Stat. 4516.)

[1] So in original. "The" probably should follow "judge of".

HISTORICAL AND STATUTORY NOTES

Effective Dates

1992 Acts. Amendment by Title IX of Pub.L. 102–572 effective Oct. 29, 1992, see section 911 of Pub.L. 102–572, set out as a note under section 171 of Title 28, Judiciary and Judicial Procedure.

1982 Acts. Amendment by Pub.L. 97–164 effective Oct. 1, 1982, see section 402 of Pub.L. 97–164, set out as a note under section 171 of this title.

§ 796. Reporting of court proceedings

Subject to the approval of the United States Court of Federal Claims, the Director of the Administrative Office of the United States Courts is authorized to contract for the reporting of all proceedings had in open court, and in such contract to fix the terms and conditions under which such reporting services shall be performed, including the terms and conditions under which transcripts shall be supplied by the contractor to the court and to other persons, departments, and agencies.

(Added Pub.L. 91–272, § 15(a), June 2, 1970, 84 Stat. 298, and amended Pub.L. 97–164, Title I, § 121(e), Apr. 2, 1982, 96 Stat. 35; Pub.L. 102–572, Title IX, § 902(a)(1), Oct. 29, 1992, 106 Stat. 4516.)

HISTORICAL AND STATUTORY NOTES

Effective Dates

1992 Acts. Amendment by Title IX of Pub.L. 102–572 effective Oct. 29, 1992, see section 911 of Pub.L. 102–572, set out as a note under section 171 of Title 28, Judiciary and Judicial Procedure.

1982 Acts. Amendment by Pub.L. 97–164 effective Oct. 1, 1982, see section 402 of Pub.L. 97–164, set out as a note under section 171 of this title.

§ 797. Recall of retired judges

(a) Any judge of the United States Court of Federal Claims who has retired from regular active service under subchapter III of chapter 83, or chapter 84, of title 5 shall be known and designated as a senior judge and may perform duties as a judge when recalled pursuant to subsection (b) of this section.

(b) The chief judge of the Court of Federal Claims may, whenever he deems it advisable, recall any senior judge, with such judge's consent, to perform such duties as a judge and for such period of time as the chief judge may specify.

(c) Any senior judge performing duties pursuant to this section shall not be counted as a judge for purposes of the number of judgeships authorized by section 171 of this title.

(d) Any senior judge, while performing duties pursuant to this section, shall be paid the same allowances for travel and other expenses as a judge in active service. Such senior judge shall also receive from the Court of Federal Claims supplemental pay in an amount sufficient, when added to his retirement annuity, to equal the salary of a judge in active service for the same period or periods of time. Such supplemental pay shall be paid in the same manner as the salary of a judge.

(Added Pub.L. 92–375, § 2, Aug. 10, 1972, 86 Stat. 529, and amended Pub.L. 97–164, Title I, § 121(f)(1), Apr. 2, 1982, 96 Stat. 35; Pub.L. 99–651, Title II, § 202(c), Nov. 14, 1986, 100 Stat. 3648; Pub.L. 102–572, Title IX, §§ 902(a), 904(b), Oct. 29, 1992, 106 Stat. 4516, 4517.)

HISTORICAL AND STATUTORY NOTES

Effective Dates

1992 Acts. Amendment by Title IX of Pub.L. 102–572 effective Oct. 29, 1992, see section 911 of Pub.L. 102–572, set out as a note under section 171 of Title 28, Judiciary and Judicial Procedure.

1986 Acts. Amendment by Pub.L. 99–651 effective Jan. 1, 1987, see section 203 of Pub.L. 99–651, set out as a note under section 155 of this title.

1982 Acts. Amendment by Pub.L. 97–164 effective Oct. 1, 1982, see section 402 of Pub.L. 97–164, set out as a note under section 171 of this title.

§ 798. Places of holding court; appointment of special masters

(a) The United States Court of Federal Claims is authorized to use facilities and hold court in Washington, District of Columbia, and throughout the United States (including its territories and possessions) as necessary for compliance with sections 173 and 2503(c) of this title. The facilities of the Federal courts, as well as other comparable facilities administered by the General Services Administration, shall be made available for trials and other proceedings outside of the District of Columbia.

(b) Upon application of a party or upon the judge's own initiative, and upon a showing that the interests of economy, efficiency, and justice will be served, the chief judge of the Court of Federal Claims may issue an order authorizing a judge of the court to conduct proceedings, including evidentiary hearings and trials, in a foreign country whose laws do not prohibit such proceedings, except that an interlocutory appeal may be taken from such an order pursuant to section 1292(d)(2) of this title, and the United States Court of Appeals for the Federal Circuit may, in its discretion, consider the appeal.

(c) The chief judge of the Court of Federal Claims may appoint special masters to assist the court in carrying out its functions. Any special masters so appointed shall carry out their responsibilities and be compensated in accordance with procedures set forth in the rules of the court.

(Added Pub.L. 98–620, Title IV, § 416(a), Nov. 8, 1984, 98 Stat. 3364, and amended Pub.L. 102–572, Title IX, §§ 902(a)(2), 906(a), (b), Oct. 29, 1992, 106 Stat. 4516–4518.)

HISTORICAL AND STATUTORY NOTES

Effective Dates

1992 Acts. Amendment by Title IX of Pub.L. 102–572 effective Oct. 29, 1992, see section 911 of Pub.L. 102–572, set out as a note under section 171 of Title 28, Judiciary and Judicial Procedure.

[CHAPTER 53—REPEALED]

[§§ 831 to 834. Repealed. Pub.L. 97–164, Title I, § 122(a), Apr. 2, 1982, 96 Stat. 36]

HISTORICAL AND STATUTORY NOTES

Section 831, Act June 25, 1948, c. 646, 62 Stat. 924, authorized the Court of Customs and Patent Appeals to appoint a clerk, assistant clerks, stenographic law clerks, clerical assistants, and other necessary employees, and set out duties of clerk.

Section 832, Acts June 25, 1948, c. 646, 62 Stat. 924; May 24, 1949, c. 139, § 76, 63 Stat. 101, authorized the Court of Customs and Patent Appeals to appoint a marshal and set out the duties of that marshal.

Section 833, Act June 25, 1948, c. 646, 62 Stat. 925, authorized the Court of Customs and Patent Appeals to appoint a reporter and set out duties of that reporter.

Section 834, Act June 25, 1948, c. 646, 62 Stat. 925, authorized the Court of Customs and Patent Appeals to appoint necessary bailiffs and messengers and set out the duties of those bailiffs and messengers.

Effective Date of Repeal

Repeal effective Oct. 1, 1982, see section 402 of Pub.L. 97–164, set out as a note under section 171 of this title.

CHAPTER 55—COURT OF INTERNATIONAL TRADE

Sec.
871. Clerk, chief deputy clerk, assistant clerk, deputies, assistants, and other employees.
872. Criers, bailiffs, and messengers.

§ 871. Clerk, chief deputy clerk, assistant clerk, deputies, assistants, and other employees

The Court of International Trade may appoint a clerk, a chief deputy clerk, an assistant clerk, deputy clerks, and such deputies, assistants, and other employees as may be necessary for the effective dispatch of the business of the court, who shall be subject to removal by the court.

(June 25, 1948, c. 646, 62 Stat. 925; Sept. 9, 1959, Pub.L. 86–243, § 1, 73 Stat. 474; Oct. 10, 1980, Pub.L. 96–417, Title V, § 501(17), 94 Stat. 1742.)

HISTORICAL AND STATUTORY NOTES

Effective Dates

1980 Acts. Amendment by Pub.L. 96–417 effective on Nov. 1, 1980 and applicable with respect to civil actions pending on or commenced on or after such date, see section 701(a) of

Pub.L. 96–417, as amended, set out as a note under section 251 of this title.

Savings Provisions

Section 4 of Pub.L. 86–243 provided that: "Nothing contained in the amendments made by this Act [enacting section 873 and amending sections 253, 550, 871 and 872 of this title] shall be construed to deprive any person serving on the date of enactment of this Act [Sept. 9, 1959] as an officer or employee of the Customs Court of any rights, privileges, or civil service status, if any, to which such person is entitled under the laws of the United States or regulations thereunder."

§ 872. Criers, bailiffs, and messengers

The Court of International Trade may appoint such criers as it may require for said court, which criers shall also perform the duties of bailiffs and messengers and such other duties as the court directs and shall be subject to removal by the court.

(Added Pub.L. 86–243, § 1, Sept. 9, 1959, 73 Stat. 474, § 873, and amended Pub.L. 96–417, Title V, § 501(19), Oct. 10, 1980, 94 Stat. 1742; renumbered § 872, Pub.L. 99–466, § 3(b)(2), Oct. 14, 1986, 100 Stat. 1191.)

HISTORICAL AND STATUTORY NOTES

Effective Dates

1980 Acts. Amendment by Pub.L. 96–417 effective on Nov. 1, 1980 and applicable with respect to civil actions pending on or commenced on or after such date, see section 701(a) of Pub.L. 96–417, as amended, set out as a note under section 251 of this title.

Savings Provisions

Enactment of section by Pub.L. 86–243 as not depriving Customs Court officers or employees of any rights, privileges, or civil service status, see section 4 of Pub.L. 86–243, set out as a note under section 871 of this title.

Prior Provisions

A prior section 872, Acts June 25, 1948, c. 646, 62 Stat. 925; May 24, 1949, c. 139, § 78, 63 Stat. 101; Sept. 9, 1959, Pub.L. 86–243, § 1, 73 Stat. 474; Oct. 10, 1980, Pub.L. 96–417, Title V, § 501(18), 94 Stat. 1742, which related to appointment and duties of a marshal and deputy marshals, was repealed by Pub.L. 99–466, § 3(b)(1), Oct. 14, 1986, 100 Stat. 1191, effective 60 days after Oct. 14, 1986, pursuant to section 4 of Pub.L. 99–466, set out as a note under section 331 of this title.

CHAPTER 57—GENERAL PROVISIONS APPLICABLE TO COURT OFFICERS AND EMPLOYEES

Sec.

951. Oath of office of clerks and deputies.
[952. Repealed.]
953. Administration of oaths and acknowledgments.
954. Vacancy in clerk position; absence of clerk.
955. Practice of law restricted.
956. Powers and duties of clerks and deputies.
957. Clerks ineligible for certain offices.
958. Persons ineligible as receivers.
959. Trustees and receivers suable; management; State laws.
960. Tax liability.
961. Office expenses of clerks.
[962. Repealed.]
963. Courts defined.

§ 951. Oath of office of clerks and deputies

Each clerk of court and his deputies shall take the following oath or affirmation before entering upon their duties: "I, __________, having been appointed _____, do solemnly swear (or affirm) that I will truly and faithfully enter and record all orders, decrees, judgments and proceedings of such court, and will faithfully and impartially discharge all other duties of my office according to the best of my abilities and understanding. So help me God."

(June 25, 1948, c. 646, 62 Stat. 925.)

[§ 952. Repealed. Pub.L. 92–310, Title II, § 206(e)(1), June 6, 1972, 86 Stat. 203]

HISTORICAL AND STATUTORY NOTES

Section, Act June 25, 1948, c. 646, 62 Stat. 926, related to bonds of clerks and deputies.

§ 953. Administration of oaths and acknowledgments

Each clerk of court and his deputies may administer oaths and affirmations and take acknowledgments.

(June 25, 1948, c. 646, 62 Stat. 926.)

HISTORICAL AND STATUTORY NOTES

Senate Revision Amendment

Those provisions of this section which related to the Tax Court were eliminated by Senate amendment, therefore section 1114(a) of Title 26, U.S.C., Internal Revenue Code, was not a part of the source of this section upon final enactment. The Senate amendments also eliminated section 1114(a) of the Internal Revenue Code from the schedule of repeals. See 80th Congress Senate Report No. 1559.

§ 954. Vacancy in clerk position; absence of clerk

When the office of clerk is vacant, the deputy clerks shall perform the duties of the clerk in the name of the last person who held that office. When the clerk is incapacitated, absent, or otherwise unavailable to perform official duties, the deputy clerks shall perform the duties of the clerk in the name of the clerk.

The court may designate a deputy clerk to act temporarily as clerk of the court in his or her own name.

(June 25, 1948, c. 646, 62 Stat. 926; June 6, 1972, Pub.L. 92–310, Title II, § 206(f), 86 Stat. 203; Oct. 19, 1996, Pub.L. 104–317, Title II, § 204(a), 110 Stat. 3850.)

§ 955. Practice of law restricted

The clerk of each court and his deputies and assistants shall not practice law in any court of the United States.

(June 25, 1948, c. 646, 62 Stat. 926.)

§ 956. Powers and duties of clerks and deputies

The clerk of each court and his deputies and assistants shall exercise the powers and perform the duties assigned to them by the court.

(June 25, 1948, c. 646, 62 Stat. 926.)

§ 957. Clerks ineligible for certain offices

A clerk of a court or any of his deputies shall not be appointed a commissioner, master, referee or receiver in any case, unless there are special reasons requiring such appointment which are recited in the order of appointment.

(June 25, 1948, c. 646, 62 Stat. 926; Nov. 6, 1978, Pub.L. 95–598, Title II, § 234, 92 Stat. 2667; Apr. 2, 1982, Pub.L. 97–164, Title I, § 122(b), 96 Stat. 36; July 10, 1984, Pub.L. 98–353, Title I, § 109, 98 Stat. 342.)

HISTORICAL AND STATUTORY NOTES

Codifications

Subsec. (a) of this section was amended by Pub.L. 95–598, Title II, § 234, Nov. 6, 1978, 92 Stat. 2667, effective June 28, 1984, pursuant to Pub.L. 95–598, Title IV, § 402(b), Nov. 6, 1978, 92 Stat. 2682, as amended by Pub.L. 98–249, § 1(a), Mar. 31, 1984, 98 Stat. 116; Pub.L. 98–271, § 1(a), Apr. 30, 1984, 98 Stat. 163; Pub.L. 98–299, § 1(a), May 25, 1984, 98 Stat. 214; Pub.L. 98–325, § 1(a), June 20, 1984, 98 Stat. 268, set out as an Effective Dates note preceding section 101 at T. 11, Bankruptcy, by inserting "or bankruptcy court" after "district court".

Section 402(b) of Pub.L. 95–598 was amended by section 113 of Pub.L. 98–353 by substituting "shall not be effective" for "shall take effect on June 28, 1984", thereby eliminating the amendment by section 234 of Pub.L. 95–598, effective June 27, 1984, pursuant to section 122(c) of Pub.L. 98–353, set out as an Effective Dates note under section 151 of this title.

Section 121(a) of Pub.L. 98–353 directed that section 402(b) of Pub.L. 95–598 be amended by substituting "the date of enactment of the Bankruptcy Amendments and Federal Judgeship Act of 1984 [i.e. July 10, 1984]" for "June 28, 1984". This amendment was not executed in view of the prior amendment to section 402(b) of Pub.L. 95–598 by section 113 of Pub.L. 98–353.

Effective Dates

1984 Acts. Amendment by Pub.L. 98–353 effective July 10, 1984, see section 122(a) of Pub.L. 98–353, set out as an Effective Dates note under section 151 of this title.

1982 Acts. Amendment by Pub.L. 97–164 effective Oct. 1, 1982, see section 402 of Pub.L. 97–164, set out as a note under section 171 of this title.

§ 958. Persons ineligible as receivers

A person holding any civil or military office or employment under the United States or employed by any justice or judge of the United States shall not at the same time be appointed a receiver in any case in any court of the United States.

(June 25, 1948, c. 646, 62 Stat. 926.)

§ 959. Trustees and receivers suable; management; State laws

(a) Trustees, receivers or managers of any property, including debtors in possession, may be sued, without leave of the court appointing them, with respect to any of their acts or transactions in carrying on business connected with such property. Such actions shall be subject to the general equity power of such court so far as the same may be necessary to the ends of justice, but this shall not deprive a litigant of his right to trial by jury.

(b) Except as provided in section 1166 of title 11, a trustee, receiver or manager appointed in any cause pending in any court of the United States, including a debtor in possession, shall manage and operate the property in his possession as such trustee, receiver or manager according to the requirements of the valid laws of the State in which such property is situated, in the same manner that the owner or possessor thereof would be bound to do if in possession thereof.

(June 25, 1948, c. 646, 62 Stat. 926; Nov. 6, 1978, Pub.L. 95–598, Title II, § 235, 92 Stat. 2667.)

HISTORICAL AND STATUTORY NOTES

Effective Dates

1978 Acts. Amendment by Pub.L. 95–598 effective Oct. 1, 1979, see section 402(c) of Pub.L. 95–598, as amended, set out as a note preceding section 101 of Title 11, Bankruptcy.

§ 960. Tax liability

Any officers and agents conducting any business under authority of a United States court shall be subject to all Federal, State and local taxes applicable to such business to the same extent as if it were conducted by an individual or corporation.

(June 25, 1948, c. 646, 62 Stat. 927.)

§ 961. Office expenses of clerks

Each clerk of court shall be allowed his necessary office expenses when authorized by the Director of the Administrative Office of the United States Courts.

(June 25, 1948, c. 646, 62 Stat. 927.)

[§ 962. Repealed. Pub.L. 89–554, § 8(a), Sept. 6, 1966, 80 Stat. 663]

HISTORICAL AND STATUTORY NOTES

Section, Act June 25, 1948, c. 646, 62 Stat. 927, related to traveling expenses and subsistence for officers and employees of the courts of the United States and of the Administrative Office of the United States Courts and is now covered by section 5701 et seq. of Title 5, Government Organization and Employees.

§ 963. Courts defined

As used in this chapter, unless the context indicates otherwise, the words "court" and "courts" include the Supreme Court of the United States and the courts enumerated in section 610 of this title.

(June 25, 1948, c. 646, 62 Stat. 927.)

CHAPTER 58—UNITED STATES SENTENCING COMMISSION

Sec.
991. United States Sentencing Commission; establishment and purposes.
992. Terms of office; compensation.
993. Powers and duties of Chair.
994. Duties of the Commission.
995. Powers of the Commission.
996. Director and staff.
997. Annual report.
998. Definitions.

§ 991. United States Sentencing Commission; establishment and purposes

(a) There is established as an independent commission in the judicial branch of the United States a United States Sentencing Commission which shall consist of seven voting members and one nonvoting member. The President, after consultation with representatives of judges, prosecuting attorneys, defense attorneys, law enforcement officials, senior citizens, victims of crime, and others interested in the criminal justice process, shall appoint the voting members of the Commission, by and with the advice and consent of the Senate, one of whom shall be appointed, by and with the advice and consent of the Senate, as the Chair and three of whom shall be designated by the President as Vice Chairs. At least three of the members shall be Federal judges selected after considering a list of six judges recommended to the President by the Judicial Conference of the United States. Not more than four of the members of the Commission shall be members of the same political party, and of the three Vice Chairs, no more than two shall be members of the same political party. The Attorney General, or the Attorney General's designee, shall be an ex officio, nonvoting member of the Commission. The Chair, Vice Chairs, and members of the Commission shall be subject to removal from the Commission by the President only for neglect of duty or malfeasance in office or for other good cause shown.

(b) The purposes of the United States Sentencing Commission are to—

(1) establish sentencing policies and practices for the Federal criminal justice system that—

(A) assure the meeting of the purposes of sentencing as set forth in section 3553(a)(2) of title 18, United States Code;

(B) provide certainty and fairness in meeting the purposes of sentencing, avoiding unwarranted sentencing disparities among defendants with similar records who have been found guilty of similar criminal conduct while maintaining sufficient flexibility to permit individualized sentences when warranted by mitigating or aggravating factors not taken into account in the establishment of general sentencing practices; and

(C) reflect, to the extent practicable, advancement in knowledge of human behavior as it relates to the criminal justice process; and

(2) develop means of measuring the degree to which the sentencing, penal, and correctional practices are effective in meeting the purposes of sentencing as set forth in section 3553(a)(2) of title 18, United States Code.

(Added Pub.L. 98–473, Title II, § 217(a), Oct. 12, 1984, 98 Stat. 2017, and amended Pub.L. 99–22, § 1(1), Apr. 15, 1985, 99 Stat. 46; Pub.L. 103–322, Title XXVIII, § 280005(a), (c)(1), (2), Sept. 13, 1994, 108 Stat. 2096, 2097; Pub.L. 104–294, Title VI, § 604(b)(11), Oct. 11, 1996, 110 Stat. 3507.)

HISTORICAL AND STATUTORY NOTES

Effective Dates

1996 Acts. Amendment by section 604 of Pub.L. 104–294 effective Sept. 13, 1994, see section 604(d) of Pub.L. 104–294, set out as a note under section 13 of Title 18, Crimes and Criminal Procedure.

1984 Acts. Section effective Oct. 12, 1984, see section 235(a)(1)(B)(i) of Pub.L. 98–473, as amended, set out as a note under section 3551 of Title 18, Crimes and Criminal Procedure.

Composition of Members of Commission During First Five-Year Period

For provisions directing that, notwithstanding the provisions of this section, during the five-year period following Oct. 12, 1984, the United States Sentencing Commission shall consist of nine members, including two ex officio, nonvoting members, see section 235(b)(5) of Pub.L. 98–473, set out as an Effective Date note under section 3551 of Title 18, Crimes and Criminal Procedure.

§ 992. Terms of office; compensation

(a) The voting members of the United States Sentencing Commission shall be appointed for six-year terms, except that the initial terms of the first members of the Commission shall be staggered so that—

(1) two members, including the Chair, serve terms of six years;

(2) three members serve terms of four years; and

(3) two members serve terms of two years.

(b)(1) Subject to paragraph (2)—

(A) no voting member of the Commission may serve more than two full terms; and

(B) a voting member appointed to fill a vacancy that occurs before the expiration of the term for which a predecessor was appointed shall be appointed only for the remainder of such term.

(2) A voting member of the Commission whose term has expired may continue to serve until the earlier of—

(A) the date on which a successor has taken office; or

(B) the date on which the Congress adjourns sine die to end the session of Congress that commences after the date on which the member's term expired.

(c) The Chair and Vice Chairs of the Commission shall hold full-time positions and shall be compensated during their terms of office at the annual rate at which judges of the United States courts of appeals are compensated. The voting members of the Commission, other than the Chair and Vice Chairs, shall hold full-time positions until the end of the first six years after the sentencing guidelines go into effect pursuant to section 235(a)(1)(B)(ii) of the Sentencing Reform Act of 1984, and shall be compensated at the annual rate at which judges of the United States courts of appeals are compensated. Thereafter, the voting members of the Commission, other than the Chair and Vice Chairs, shall hold part-time positions and shall be paid at the daily rate at which judges of the United States courts of appeals are compensated. A Federal judge may serve as a member of the Commission without resigning the judge's appointment as a Federal judge.

(d) Sections 44(c) and 134(b) of this title (relating to the residence of judges) do not apply to any judge holding a full-time position on the Commission under subsection (c) of this section.

(Added Pub.L. 98–473, Title II, § 217(a), Oct. 12, 1984, 98 Stat. 2018, and amended Pub.L. 99–646, §§ 4, 6(a), Nov. 10, 1986, 100 Stat. 3592; Pub.L. 102–349, § 1, Aug. 26, 1992, 106 Stat. 933; Pub.L. 103–322, Title XXVIII, § 280005(b), (c)(1), (3), Sept. 13, 1994, 108 Stat. 2096, 2097.)

HISTORICAL AND STATUTORY NOTES

References in Text

Section 235(a)(1)(B)(ii) of the Sentencing Reform Act of 1984, referred to in subsec. (c), is section 235(a)(1)(B)(ii) of Pub.L. 98–473, which is set out as a note under section 3551 of Title 18, Crimes and Criminal Procedure.

Effective Dates

1984 Acts. Section effective Oct. 12, 1984, see section 235(a)(1)(B)(i) of Pub.L. 98–473, as amended, set out as a note under section 3551 of Title 18, Crimes and Criminal Procedure.

Commencement of Terms of First Members of Commission

For provisions directing that, for purposes of subsec. (a) of this section, the terms of the first members of the United States Sentencing Commission shall not begin to run until the sentencing guidelines go into effect pursuant to section 235(a)(1)(B)(ii) of Pub.L. 98–473, set out as an Effective Date note under section 3551 of Title 18, Crimes and Criminal Procedure, see section 235(a)(2) of Pub.L. 98–473, as amended, set out as an Effective Date note under section 3551 of Title 18.

§ 993. Powers and duties of Chair

The Chair shall—

(a) call and preside at meetings of the Commission, which shall be held for at least two weeks in each quarter after the members of the Commission hold part-time positions; and

(b) direct—

(1) the preparation of requests for appropriations for the Commission; and

(2) the use of funds made available to the Commission.

(Added Pub.L. 98–473, Title II, § 217(a), Oct. 12, 1984, 98 Stat. 2019, and amended Pub.L. 99–22, § 1(2), Apr. 15, 1985, 99 Stat. 46; Pub.L. 99–646, § 5, Nov. 10, 1986, 100 Stat. 3592; Pub.L. 103–322, Title XXVIII, § 280005(c)(1), Sept. 13, 1994, 108 Stat. 2097.)

HISTORICAL AND STATUTORY NOTES

Effective Dates

1984 Acts. Section effective Oct. 12, 1984, see section 235(a)(1)(B)(i) of Pub.L. 98–473, as amended, set out as a note under section 3551 of Title 18, Crimes and Criminal Procedure.

§ 994. Duties of the Commission

(a) The Commission, by affirmative vote of at least four members of the Commission, and pursuant to its rules and regulations and consistent with all pertinent provisions of this title and title 18, United States Code, shall promulgate and distribute to all courts of the United States and to the United States Probation System—

(1) guidelines, as described in this section, for use of a sentencing court in determining the sentence to be imposed in a criminal case, including—

(A) a determination whether to impose a sentence to probation, a fine, or a term of imprisonment;

(B) a determination as to the appropriate amount of a fine or the appropriate length of a term of probation or a term of imprisonment;

(C) a determination whether a sentence to a term of imprisonment should include a requirement that the defendant be placed on a term of supervised release after imprisonment, and, if so, the appropriate length of such a term;

(D) a determination whether multiple sentences to terms of imprisonment should be ordered to run concurrently or consecutively; and

(E) a determination under paragraphs (6) and (11) of section 3563(b) of title 18;

(2) general policy statements regarding application of the guidelines or any other aspect of sen-

tencing or sentence implementation that in the view of the Commission would further the purposes set forth in section 3553(a)(2) of title 18, United States Code, including the appropriate use of—

(A) the sanctions set forth in sections 3554, 3555, and 3556 of title 18;

(B) the conditions of probation and supervised release set forth in sections 3563(b) and 3583(d) of title 18;

(C) the sentence modification provisions set forth in sections 3563(c), 3564, 3573, and 3582(c) of title 18;

(D) the fine imposition provisions set forth in section 3572 of title 18;

(E) the authority granted under rule 11(e)(2) of the Federal Rules of Criminal Procedure to accept or reject a plea agreement entered into pursuant to rule 11(e)(1); and

(F) the temporary release provisions set forth in section 3622 of title 18, and the prerelease custody provisions set forth in section 3624(c) of title 18; and

(3) guidelines or general policy statements regarding the appropriate use of the provisions for revocation of probation set forth in section 3565 of title 18, and the provisions for modification of the term or conditions of supervised release and revocation of supervised release set forth in section 3583(e) of title 18.

(b)(1) The Commission, in the guidelines promulgated pursuant to subsection (a)(1), shall, for each category of offense involving each category of defendant, establish a sentencing range that is consistent with all pertinent provisions of title 18, United States Code.

(2) If a sentence specified by the guidelines includes a term of imprisonment, the maximum of the range established for such a term shall not exceed the minimum of that range by more than the greater of 25 percent or 6 months, except that, if the minimum term of the range is 30 years or more, the maximum may be life imprisonment.

(c) The Commission, in establishing categories of offenses for use in the guidelines and policy statements governing the imposition of sentences of probation, a fine, or imprisonment, governing the imposition of other authorized sanctions, governing the size of a fine or the length of a term of probation, imprisonment, or supervised release, and governing the conditions of probation, supervised release, or imprisonment, shall consider whether the following matters, among others, have any relevance to the nature, extent, place of service, or other incidents [1] of an appropriate sentence, and shall take them into account only to the extent that they do have relevance—

(1) the grade of the offense;

(2) the circumstances under which the offense was committed which mitigate or aggravate the seriousness of the offense;

(3) the nature and degree of the harm caused by the offense, including whether it involved property, irreplaceable property, a person, a number of persons, or a breach of public trust;

(4) the community view of the gravity of the offense;

(5) the public concern generated by the offense;

(6) the deterrent effect a particular sentence may have on the commission of the offense by others; and

(7) the current incidence of the offense in the community and in the Nation as a whole.

(d) The Commission in establishing categories of defendants for use in the guidelines and policy statements governing the imposition of sentences of probation, a fine, or imprisonment, governing the imposition of other authorized sanctions, governing the size of a fine or the length of a term of probation, imprisonment, or supervised release, and governing the conditions of probation, supervised release, or imprisonment, shall consider whether the following matters, among others, with respect to a defendant, have any relevance to the nature, extent, place of service, or other incidents [1] of an appropriate sentence, and shall take them into account only to the extent that they do have relevance—

(1) age;

(2) education;

(3) vocational skills;

(4) mental and emotional condition to the extent that such condition mitigates the defendant's culpability or to the extent that such condition is otherwise plainly relevant;

(5) physical condition, including drug dependence;

(6) previous employment record;

(7) family ties and responsibilities;

(8) community ties;

(9) role in the offense;

(10) criminal history; and

(11) degree of dependence upon criminal activity for a livelihood.

The Commission shall assure that the guidelines and policy statements are entirely neutral as to the race, sex, national origin, creed, and socioeconomic status of offenders.

(e) The Commission shall assure that the guidelines and policy statements, in recommending a term of imprisonment or length of a term of imprisonment, reflect the general inappropriateness of considering the education, vocational skills, employment record, family ties and responsibilities, and community ties of the defendant.

(f) The Commission, in promulgating guidelines pursuant to subsection (a)(1), shall promote the purposes set forth in section 991(b)(1), with particular attention to the requirements of subsection 991(b)(1)(B) for providing certainty and fairness in sentencing and reducing unwarranted sentence disparities.

(g) The Commission, in promulgating guidelines pursuant to subsection (a)(1) to meet the purposes of sentencing as set forth in section 3553(a)(2) of title 18, United States Code, shall take into account the nature and capacity of the penal, correctional, and other facilities and services available, and shall make recommendations concerning any change or expansion in the nature or capacity of such facilities and services that might become necessary as a result of the guidelines promulgated pursuant to the provisions of this chapter. The sentencing guidelines prescribed under this chapter shall be formulated to minimize the likelihood that the Federal prison population will exceed the capacity of the Federal prisons, as determined by the Commission.

(h) The Commission shall assure that the guidelines specify a sentence to a term of imprisonment at or near the maximum term authorized for categories of defendants in which the defendant is eighteen years old or older and—

(1) has been convicted of a felony that is—

(A) a crime of violence; or

(B) an offense described in section 401 of the Controlled Substances Act (21 U.S.C. 841), sections 1002(a), 1005, and 1009 of the Controlled Substances Import and Export Act (21 U.S.C. 952(a), 955, and 959), and the Maritime Drug Law Enforcement Act (46 U.S.C. App. 1901 et seq.); and

(2) has previously been convicted of two or more prior felonies, each of which is—

(A) a crime of violence; or

(B) an offense described in section 401 of the Controlled Substances Act (21 U.S.C. 841), sections 1002(a), 1005, and 1009 of the Controlled Substances Import and Export Act (21 U.S.C. 952(a), 955, and 959), and the Maritime Drug Law Enforcement Act (46 U.S.C. App. 1901 et seq.).

(i) The Commission shall assure that the guidelines specify a sentence to a substantial term of imprisonment for categories of defendants in which the defendant—

(1) has a history of two or more prior Federal, State, or local felony convictions for offenses committed on different occasions;

(2) committed the offense as part of a pattern of criminal conduct from which the defendant derived a substantial portion of the defendant's income;

(3) committed the offense in furtherance of a conspiracy with three or more persons engaging in a pattern of racketeering activity in which the defendant participated in a managerial or supervisory capacity;

(4) committed a crime of violence that constitutes a felony while on release pending trial, sentence, or appeal from a Federal, State, or local felony for which he was ultimately convicted; or

(5) committed a felony that is set forth in section 401 or 1010 of the Comprehensive Drug Abuse Prevention and Control Act of 1970 (21 U.S.C. 841 and 960), and that involved trafficking in a substantial quantity of a controlled substance.

(j) The Commission shall insure that the guidelines reflect the general appropriateness of imposing a sentence other than imprisonment in cases in which the defendant is a first offender who has not been convicted of a crime of violence or an otherwise serious offense, and the general appropriateness of imposing a term of imprisonment on a person convicted of a crime of violence that results in serious bodily injury.

(k) The Commission shall insure that the guidelines reflect the inappropriateness of imposing a sentence to a term of imprisonment for the purpose of rehabilitating the defendant or providing the defendant with needed educational or vocational training, medical care, or other correctional treatment.

(*l*) The Commission shall insure that the guidelines promulgated pursuant to subsection (a)(1) reflect—

(1) the appropriateness of imposing an incremental penalty for each offense in a case in which a defendant is convicted of—

(A) multiple offenses committed in the same course of conduct that result in the exercise of ancillary jurisdiction over one or more of the offenses; and

(B) multiple offenses committed at different times, including those cases in which the subsequent offense is a violation of section 3146 (penalty for failure to appear) or is committed while the person is released pursuant to the provisions of section 3147 (penalty for an offense committed while on release) of title 18; and

(2) the general inappropriateness of imposing consecutive terms of imprisonment for an offense of conspiring to commit an offense or soliciting commission of an offense and for an offense that was the sole object of the conspiracy or solicitation.

(m) The Commission shall insure that the guidelines reflect the fact that, in many cases, current sentences do not accurately reflect the seriousness of the offense. This will require that, as a starting point in its development of the initial sets of guidelines for particular categories of cases, the Commission ascertain the average sentences imposed in such categories of cases prior to the creation of the Commission, and in cases involving sentences to terms of imprisonment, the length of such terms actually served. The Commission shall not be bound by such average sentences, and shall independently develop a sentencing range that is consistent with the purposes of sentencing described in section 3553(a)(2) of title 18, United States Code.

(n) The Commission shall assure that the guidelines reflect the general appropriateness of imposing a lower sentence than would otherwise be imposed, including a sentence that is lower than that established by statute as a minimum sentence, to take into account a defendant's substantial assistance in the investigation or prosecution of another person who has committed an offense.

(*o*) The Commission periodically shall review and revise, in consideration of comments and data coming to its attention, the guidelines promulgated pursuant to the provisions of this section. In fulfilling its duties and in exercising its powers, the Commission shall consult with authorities on, and individual and institutional representatives of, various aspects of the Federal criminal justice system. The United States Probation System, the Bureau of Prisons, the Judicial Conference of the United States, the Criminal Division of the United States Department of Justice, and a representative of the Federal Public Defenders shall submit to the Commission any observations, comments, or questions pertinent to the work of the Commission whenever they believe such communication would be useful, and shall, at least annually, submit to the Commission a written report commenting on the operation of the Commission's guidelines, suggesting changes in the guidelines that appear to be warranted, and otherwise assessing the Commission's work.

(p) The Commission, at or after the beginning of a regular session of Congress, but not later than the first day of May, may promulgate under subsection (a) of this section and submit to Congress amendments to the guidelines and modifications to previously submitted amendments that have not taken effect, including modifications to the effective dates of such amendments. Such an amendment or modification shall be accompanied by a statement of the reasons therefor and shall take effect on a date specified by the Commission, which shall be no earlier than 180 days after being so submitted and no later than the first day of November of the calendar year in which the amendment or modification is submitted, except to the extent that the effective date is revised or the amendment is otherwise modified or disapproved by Act of Congress.

(q) The Commission and the Bureau of Prisons shall submit to Congress an analysis and recommendations concerning maximum utilization of resources to deal effectively with the Federal prison population. Such report shall be based upon consideration of a variety of alternatives, including—

(1) modernization of existing facilities;

(2) inmate classification and periodic review of such classification for use in placing inmates in the least restrictive facility necessary to ensure adequate security; and

(3) use of existing Federal facilities, such as those currently within military jurisdiction.

(r) The Commission, not later than two years after the initial set of sentencing guidelines promulgated under subsection (a) goes into effect, and thereafter whenever it finds it advisable, shall recommend to the Congress that it raise or lower the grades, or otherwise modify the maximum penalties, of those offenses for which such an adjustment appears appropriate.

(s) The Commission shall give due consideration to any petition filed by a defendant requesting modification of the guidelines utilized in the sentencing of such defendant, on the basis of changed circumstances unrelated to the defendant, including changes in—

(1) the community view of the gravity of the offense;

(2) the public concern generated by the offense; and

(3) the deterrent effect particular sentences may have on the commission of the offense by others.

(t) The Commission, in promulgating general policy statements regarding the sentencing modification provisions in section 3582(c)(1)(A) of title 18, shall describe what should be considered extraordinary and compelling reasons for sentence reduction, including the criteria to be applied and a list of specific examples. Rehabilitation of the defendant alone shall not be considered an extraordinary and compelling reason.

(u) If the Commission reduces the term of imprisonment recommended in the guidelines applicable to a particular offense or category of offenses, it shall specify in what circumstances and by what amount the sentences of prisoners serving terms of imprisonment for the offense may be reduced.

(v) The Commission shall ensure that the general policy statements promulgated pursuant to subsection (a)(2) include a policy limiting consecutive terms of imprisonment for an offense involving a violation of a general prohibition and for an offense involving a violation of a specific prohibition encompassed within the general prohibition.

(w) The appropriate judge or officer shall submit to the Commission in connection with each sentence imposed (other than a sentence imposed for a petty offense, as defined in title 18, for which there is no applicable sentencing guideline) a written report of the sentence, the offense for which it is imposed, the age, race, and sex of the offender, information regarding factors made relevant by the guidelines, and such other information as the Commission finds appropriate. The Commission shall submit to Congress at least annually an analysis of these reports and any recommendations for legislation that the Commission concludes is warranted by that analysis.

(x) The provisions of section 553 of title 5, relating to publication in the Federal Register and public hearing procedure, shall apply to the promulgation of guidelines pursuant to this section.

(y) The Commission, in promulgating guidelines pursuant to subsection (a)(1), may include, as a component of a fine, the expected costs to the Government of any imprisonment, supervised release, or probation sentence that is ordered.

(Added Pub.L. 98–473, Title II, § 217(a), Oct. 12, 1984, 98 Stat. 2019, and amended Pub.L. 99–217, § 3, Dec. 26, 1985, 99 Stat. 1728; Pub.L. 99–363, § 2, July 11, 1986, 100 Stat. 770; Pub.L. 99–570, Title I, §§ 1006(b), 1008, Oct. 27, 1986, 100 Stat. 3207–7; Pub.L. 99–646, §§ 6(b), 56, Nov. 10, 1986, 100 Stat. 3592, 3611; Pub.L. 100–182, §§ 16(b), 23, Dec. 7, 1987, 101 Stat. 1269, 1271; Pub.L. 100–690, Title VII, §§ 7083, 7103(b), 7109, Nov. 18, 1988, 102 Stat. 4408, 4417, 4419; Pub.L. 103–322, Title II, § 20403(b), Title XXVIII, § 280005(c)(4), Title XXXIII, § 330003(f)(1), Sept. 13, 1994, 108 Stat. 1825, 2097, 2141.)

[1] So in original. Probably should be "incidence".

HISTORICAL AND STATUTORY NOTES

References in Text

The Federal Rules of Criminal Procedure, referred to in subsec. (a)(2)(E), are set out in Title 18, Crimes and Criminal Procedure.

The Maritime Drug Law Enforcement Act (46 U.S.C. App. 1901 et seq.), referred to in subsec. (h), is Pub.L. 96–350, Sept. 15, 1980, 94 Stat. 1159, as amended, which is classified generally to chapter 38 (section 1901 et seq.) of Title 46 Appendix, Shipping. For complete classification of this Act to the Code, see section 1901 of Title 46 Appendix and Tables.

Codifications

Amendment by Pub.L. 99–646 to subsec. (t) of this section has been executed to subsec. (u) as the probable intent of Congress in view of prior redesignation of subsec. (t) as (u) by Pub.L. 99–570.

Effective Dates

1987 Acts. Amendment by Pub.L. 100–182 applicable with respect to offenses committed after Dec. 7, 1987, see section 26 of Pub.L. 100–182, set out as a note under section 3006A of Title 18, Crimes and Criminal Procedure.

1984 Acts. Section effective Oct. 12, 1984, see section 235(a)(1)(B)(i) of Pub.L. 98–473, as amended, set out as a note under section 3551 of Title 18, Crimes and Criminal Procedure.

Short Title

1997 Acts. Pub.L. 105–101, § 1, Nov. 19, 1997, 111 Stat. 2202, provided that: "This Act [enacting a provision set out as a note under this section] may be cited as the 'Veterans' Cemetery Protection Act of 1997'."

1995 Acts. Pub.L. 104–71, § 1, Dec. 23, 1995, 109 Stat. 774, provided that: "This Act [amending section 2423 of Title 18, Crimes and Criminal Procedure, and enacting provisions set out as a note under this section] may be cited as the 'Sex Crimes Against Children Prevention Act of 1995'."

Amendment of Federal Sentencing Guidelines for Offenses Under Section 1028

Pub.L. 105–318, § 4, Oct. 30, 1998, 112 Stat. 3009, provided that:

"(a) In general.—Pursuant to its authority under section 994(p) of title 28, United States Code, the United States Sentencing Commission shall review and amend the Federal sentencing guidelines and the policy statements of the Commission, as appropriate, to provide an appropriate penalty for each offense under section 1028 of title 18, United States Code, as amended by this Act [Identity Theft and Assumption Deterrence Act of 1998, Pub.L. 105–318, Oct. 30, 1998, 112 Stat. 3007, for complete classification of which, see Tables].

"(b) Factors for consideration.—In carrying out subsection (a), the United States Sentencing Commission shall consider, with respect to each offense described in subsection (a)—

"(1) the extent to which the number of victims (as defined in section 3663A(a) of title 18, United States Code) involved in the offense, including harm to reputation, inconvenience, and other difficulties resulting from the offense, is an adequate measure for establishing penalties under the Federal sentencing guidelines;

"(2) the number of means of identification, identification documents, or false identification documents (as those terms are defined in section 1028(d) of title 18, United States Code, as amended by this Act [Pub.L. 105–318, Oct. 30, 1998, 112 Stat. 3007]) involved in the offense, is an adequate measure for establishing penalties under the Federal sentencing guidelines;

"(3) the extent to which the value of the loss to any individual caused by the offense is an adequate measure for establishing penalties under the Federal sentencing guidelines;

"(4) the range of conduct covered by the offense;

"(5) the extent to which sentencing enhancements within the Federal sentencing guidelines and the court's authority to sentence above the applicable guideline range are adequate to ensure punishment at or near the maximum penalty for the most egregious conduct covered by the offense;

"(6) the extent to which Federal sentencing guidelines sentences for the offense have been constrained by statutory maximum penalties;

"(7) the extent to which Federal sentencing guidelines for the offense adequately achieve the purposes of sentencing set forth in section 3553(a)(2) of title 18, United States Code; and

"(8) any other factor that the United States Sentencing Commission considers to be appropriate."

Increased Penalties for Offenses Against Children and for Repeat Offenders

Pub.L. 105–314, Title V, §§ 501 to 507, Oct. 30, 1998, 112 Stat. 2980 to 2982, provided:

"Sec. 501. [Omitted. Amended section 3559(d) of Title 18].

"§ 502. Sentencing Enhancement for Chapter 117 Offenses

"**(a) In general.**—Pursuant to its authority under section 994(p) of title 28, United States Code, the United States Sentencing Commission shall review and amend the Federal Sentencing Guidelines to provide a sentencing enhancement for offenses under chapter 117 [§ 2421 et seq.] of title 18, United States Code.

"**(b) Instruction to Commission.**—In carrying out subsection (a), the United States Sentencing Commission shall ensure that the sentences, guidelines, and policy statements for offenders convicted of offenses described in subsection (a) are appropriately severe and reasonably consistent with other relevant directives and with other Federal Sentencing Guidelines.

"§ 503. Increased Penalties for Use of a Computer in the Sexual Abuse or Exploitation of a Child

"Pursuant to its authority under section 994(p) of title 28, United States Code, the United States Sentencing Commission shall—

"(1) review the Federal Sentencing Guidelines for—

"(A) aggravated sexual abuse under section 2241 of title 18, United States Code;

"(B) sexual abuse under section 2242 of title 18, United States Code;

"(C) sexual abuse of a minor or ward under section 2243 of title 18, United States Code; and

"(D) coercion and enticement of a minor under section 2422(b) of title 18, United States Code, contacting a minor under section 2422(c) of title 18, United States Code, and transportation of minors and travel under section 2423 of title 18, United States Code; and

"(2) upon completion of the review under paragraph (1), promulgate amendments to the Federal Sentencing Guidelines to provide appropriate enhancement if the defendant used a computer with the intent to persuade, induce, entice, coerce, or facilitate the transport of a child of an age specified in the applicable provision of law referred to in paragraph (1) to engage in any prohibited sexual activity.

"§ 504. Increased Penalties for Knowing Misrepresentation in the Sexual Abuse or Exploitation of a Child

"Pursuant to its authority under section 994(p) of title 28, United States Code, the United States Sentencing Commission shall—

"(1) review the Federal Sentencing Guidelines on aggravated sexual abuse under section 2241 of title 18, United States Code, sexual abuse under section 2242 of title 18, United States Code, sexual abuse of a minor or ward under section 2243 of title 18, United States Code, coercion and enticement of a minor under section 2422(b) of title 18, United States Code, contacting a minor under section 2422(c) of title 18, United States Code, and transportation of minors and travel under section 2423 of title 18, United States Code; and

"(2) upon completion of the review under paragraph (1), promulgate amendments to the Federal Sentencing Guidelines to provide appropriate enhancement if the defendant knowingly misrepresented the actual identity of the defendant with the intent to persuade, induce, entice, coerce, or facilitate the transport of a child of an age specified in the applicable provision of law referred to in paragraph (1) to engage in a prohibited sexual activity.

"§ 505. Increased Penalties for Pattern of Activity of Sexual Exploitation of Children

"Pursuant to its authority under section 994(p) of title 28, United States Code, the United States Sentencing Commission shall—

"(1) review the Federal Sentencing Guidelines on aggravated sexual abuse under section 2241 of title 18, United States Code, sexual abuse under section 2242 of title 18, United States Code, sexual abuse of a minor or ward under section 2243 of title 18, United States Code, coercion and enticement of a minor under section 2422(b) of title 18, United States Code, contacting a minor under section 2422(c) of title 18, United States Code, and transportation of minors and travel under section 2423 of title 18, United States Code; and

"(2) upon completion of the review under paragraph (1), promulgate amendments to the Federal Sentencing Guidelines to increase penalties applicable to the offenses referred to in paragraph (1) in any case in which the defendant engaged in a pattern of activity involving the sexual abuse or exploitation of a minor.

"§ 506. Clarification of Definition of Distribution of Pornography

"Pursuant to its authority under section 994(p) of title 28, United States Code, the United States Sentencing Commission shall—

"(1) review the Federal Sentencing Guidelines relating to the distribution of pornography covered under chapter 110 of title 18, United States Code, relating to the sexual exploitation and other abuse of children; and

"(2) upon completion of the review under paragraph (1), promulgate such amendments to the Federal Sentencing Guidelines as are necessary to clarify that the term 'distribution of pornography' applies to the distribution of pornography—

"(A) for monetary remuneration; or

"(B) for a nonpecuniary interest.

"§ 507. Directive to the United States Sentencing Commission

"In carrying out this title, the United States Sentencing Commission shall—

"(1) with respect to any action relating to the Federal Sentencing Guidelines subject to this title, ensure reasonable consistency with other guidelines of the Federal Sentencing Guidelines; and

"(2) with respect to an offense subject to the Federal Sentencing Guidelines, avoid duplicative punishment under the Federal Sentencing Guidelines for substantially the same offense.".

Amendment of Federal Sentencing Guidelines Regarding Telemarketing

Pub.L. 105–184, § 6, June 23, 1998, 112 Stat. 521, provided that:

"**(a) Definition of telemarketing.**—In this section [this note], the term 'telemarketing' has the meaning given that term in section 2326 of title 18, United States Code.

"**(b) Directive to sentencing commission.**—Pursuant to its authority under section 994(p) of title 28, United States Code [subsec. (p) of this section], and in accordance with this section [this note], the United States Sentencing Commission shall—

"(1) promulgate Federal sentencing guidelines or amend existing sentencing guidelines (and policy statements, if appropriate) to provide for substantially increased penalties for persons convicted of offenses described in section 2326 of title 18, United States Code, as amended by this Act [the Telemarketing and Fraud Prevention Act of 1998, Pub.L. 105–184, §§ 3, 4, June 23, 1998, 112 Stat. 520, which amended section 2326 of Title 18], in connection with the conduct of telemarketing; and

"(2) submit to Congress an explanation of each action taken under paragraph (1) and any additional policy recommendations for combating the offenses described in that paragraph.

"**(c) Requirements.**—In carrying out this section [this note], the Commission shall—

"(1) ensure that the guidelines and policy statements promulgated or amended pursuant to subsection (b)(1) [of this note] and any recommendations submitted thereunder reflect the serious nature of the offenses;

"(2) provide an additional appropriate sentencing enhancement, if the offense involved sophisticated means, including but not limited to sophisticated concealment efforts, such as perpetrating the offense from outside the United States;

"(3) provide an additional appropriate sentencing enhancement for cases in which a large number of vulnerable victims, including but not limited to victims described in section 2326(2) of title 18, United States Code, are affected by a fraudulent scheme or schemes;

"(4) ensure that guidelines and policy statements promulgated or amended pursuant to subsection (b)(1) [of this note] are reasonably consistent with other relevant statutory directives to the Commission and with other guidelines;

"(5) account for any aggravating or mitigating circumstances that might justify upward or downward departures;

"(6) ensure that the guidelines adequately meet the purposes of sentencing as set forth in section 3553(a)(2) of title 18, United States Code; and

"(7) take any other action the Commission considers necessary to carry out this section.

"**(d) Emergency authority.**—The Commission shall promulgate the guidelines or amendments provided for under this subsection as soon as practicable, and in any event not later than 120 days after the date of the enactment of the Telemarketing Fraud Prevention Act of 1998 [June 23, 1998], in accordance with the procedures set forth in section 21(a) of the Sentencing Reform Act of 1987 [section 21(a) of Pub.L. 100–182, also known as the Sentencing Act of 1987, set out as a note under this section], as though the authority under that authority had not expired, except that the Commission shall submit to Congress the emergency guidelines or amendments promulgated under this section [this note], and shall set an effective date for those guidelines or amendments not earlier than 30 days after their submission to Congress."

Wireless Telephone Cloning; Sentencing Guidelines

Pub.L. 105–172, § 2(e), Apr. 24, 1998, 112 Stat. 55, provided that:

"**(1) In general.**—Pursuant to its authority under section 994 of title 28, United States Code [this section], the United States Sentencing Commission shall review and amend the Federal sentencing guidelines and the policy statements of the Commission, if appropriate, to provide an appropriate penalty for offenses involving the cloning of wireless telephones (including offenses involving an attempt or conspiracy to clone a wireless telephone).

"**(2) Factors for consideration.**—In carrying out this subsection [this note], the Commission shall consider, with respect to the offenses described in paragraph (1).—

"(A) the range of conduct covered by the offenses;

"(B) the existing sentences for the offenses;

"(C) the extent to which the value of the loss caused by the offenses (as defined in the Federal sentencing guidelines) is an adequate measure for establishing penalties under the Federal sentencing guidelines;

"(D) the extent to which sentencing enhancements within the Federal sentencing guidelines and the court's authority to sentence above the applicable guideline range are adequate to ensure punishment at or near the maximum penalty for the most egregious conduct covered by the offenses;

"(E) the extent to which the Federal sentencing guideline sentences for the offenses have been constrained by statutory maximum penalties;

"(F) the extent to which Federal sentencing guidelines for the offenses adequately achieve the purposes of sentencing set forth in section 3553(a)(2) of title 18, United States Code;

"(G) the relationship of Federal sentencing guidelines for the offenses to the Federal sentencing guidelines for other offenses of comparable seriousness; and

"(H) any other factor that the Commission considers to be appropriate."

Amendment of Sentencing Guidelines Regarding Alien Smuggling

Pub.L. 104–208, Div. C, Title II, § 203(e), Sept. 30, 1996, 110 Stat. 3009–566, provided that:

"**(1) In general.**—Pursuant to its authority under section 994(p) of title 28, United States Code [this section], the United States Sentencing Commission shall promulgate sentencing guidelines or amend existing sentencing guidelines for offenders convicted of offenses related to smuggling, transporting, harboring, or inducing aliens in violation of section 274(a) (1)(A) or (2) of the Immigration and Nationality Act (8 U.S.C. 1324(a)(1)(A), (2)(B)) in accordance with this subsection.

"**(2) Requirements.**—In carrying out this subsection, the Commission shall, with respect to the offenses described in paragraph (1)—

"(A) increase the base offense level for such offenses at least 3 offense levels above the applicable level in effect on the date of the enactment of this Act [Sept. 30, 1996];

"(B) review the sentencing enhancement for the number of aliens involved (U.S.S.G. 2L1.1(b)(2)), and increase the sentencing enhancement by at least 50 percent above the applicable enhancement in effect on the date of the enactment of this Act [Sept. 30, 1996];

"(C) impose an appropriate sentencing enhancement upon an offender with 1 prior felony conviction arising out of a separate and prior prosecution for an offense that involved the same or similar underlying conduct as the current offense, to be applied in addition to any sentencing enhancement that would otherwise apply pursuant to the calculation of the defendant's criminal history category;

"(D) impose an additional appropriate sentencing enhancement upon an offender with 2 or more prior felony convictions arising out of separate and prior prosecutions for offenses that involved the same or similar underling [Sic.] conduct as the current offense, to be applied in addition to any sentencing enhancement that would otherwise apply pursuant to the calculation of the defendant's criminal history category;

"(E) impose an appropriate sentencing enhancement on a defendant who, in the course of committing an offense described in this subsection—

"(i) murders or otherwise causes death, bodily injury, or serious bodily injury to an individual;

"(ii) uses or brandishes a firearm or other dangerous weapon; or

"(iii) engages in conduct that consciously or recklessly places another in serious danger of death or serious bodily injury;

"(F) consider whether a downward adjustment is appropriate if the offense is a first offense and involves the smuggling only of the alien's spouse or child; and

"(G) consider whether any other aggravating or mitigating circumstances warrant upward or downward sentencing adjustments.

"(3) **Emergency authority to Sentencing Commission.**—The Commission shall promulgate the guidelines or amendments provided for under this subsection as soon as practicable in accordance with the procedure set forth in section 21(a) of the Sentencing Act of 1987 [section 21(a) of Pub.L. 100–182, set out as a note under this section], as though the authority under that Act had not expired."

Amendment of Sentencing Guidelines Regarding Fraudulent Use of Government-Issued Documents

Pub.L. 104–208, Div. C, Title II, § 211(b), Sept. 30, 1996, 110 Stat. 3009–569, provided that:

"(b) **Changes to the sentencing levels.**—

"(1) **In general.**—Pursuant to the Commission's authority under section 994(p) of title 28, United States Code [this section], the United States Sentencing Commission shall promulgate sentencing guidelines or amend existing sentencing guidelines for offenders convicted of violating, or conspiring to violate, sections 1028(b)(1), 1425 through 1427, 1541 through 1544, and 1546(a) of title 18, United States Code [18 U.S.C.A. §§ 1028(b)(1), 1425, 1426, 1427, 1541, 1542, 1543, 1544, and 1546(a)], in accordance with this subsection.

"(2) **Requirements.**—In carrying out this subsection, the Commission shall, with respect to the offenses referred to in paragraph (1)—

"(A) increase the base offense level for such offenses at least 2 offense levels above the level in effect on the date of the enactment of this Act [Sept. 30, 1996];

"(B) review the sentencing enhancement for number of documents or passports involved (U.S.S.G. 2L2.1(b)(2)), and increase the upward adjustment by at least 50 percent above the applicable enhancement in effect on the date of the enactment of this Act [Sept. 30, 1996];

"(C) impose an appropriate sentencing enhancement upon an offender with 1 prior felony conviction arising out of a separate and prior prosecution for an offense that involved the same or similar underlying conduct as the current offense, to be applied in addition to any sentencing enhancement that would otherwise apply pursuant to the calculation of the defendant's criminal history category;

"(D) impose an additional appropriate sentencing enhancement upon an offender with 2 or more prior felony convictions arising out of separate and prior prosecutions for offenses that involved the same or similar underlying conduct as the current offense, to be applied in addition to any sentencing enhancement that would otherwise apply pursuant to the calculation of the defendant's criminal history category; and

"(E) consider whether any other aggravating or mitigating circumstances warrant upward or downward sentencing adjustments.

"(3) **Emergency authority to Sentencing Commission.**—The Commission shall promulgate the guidelines or amendments provided for under this subsection as soon as practicable in accordance with the procedure set forth in section 21(a) of the Sentencing Act of 1987 [section 21(a) of Pub.L. 100–182, set out as a note under this section], as though the authority under that Act had not expired."

Amendment of Sentencing Guidelines Regarding Involuntary Servitude

Pub.L. 104–208, Div. C, Title II, § 218(b), (c), Sept. 30, 1996, 110 Stat. 3009–573, 3009–574, provided that:

"(b) **Review of sentencing guidelines.**—The United States Sentencing Commission shall ascertain whether there exists an unwarranted disparity—

"(1) between the sentences for peonage, involuntary servitude, and slave trade offenses, and the sentences for kidnapping offenses in effect on the date of the enactment of this Act [Sept. 30, 1996]; and

"(2) between the sentences for peonage, involuntary servitude, and slave trade offenses, and the sentences for alien smuggling offenses in effect on the date of the enactment of this Act [Sept. 30, 1996] and after the amendment made by subsection (a) [amending sections 1581, 1583, 1584, and 1588 of Title 18, Crimes and Criminal Procedure].

"(c) **Amendment of sentencing guidelines.**—

"(1) **In general.**—Pursuant to its authority under section 994(p) of title 28, United States Code [this section], the United States Sentencing Commission shall review its guidelines on sentencing for peonage, involuntary servitude, and slave trade offenses under sections 1581 through 1588 of title 18, United States Code [18 U.S.C.A. §§ 1581 through 1588], and shall amend such guidelines as necessary to—

"(A) reduce or eliminate any unwarranted disparity found under subsection (b) that exists between the sentences for peonage, involuntary servitude, and slave trade offenses, and the sentences for kidnapping offenses and alien smuggling offenses;

"(B) ensure that the applicable guidelines for defendants convicted of peonage, involuntary servitude, and slave trade offenses are sufficiently stringent to deter such offenses and adequately reflect the heinous nature of such offenses; and

"(C) ensure that the guidelines reflect the general appropriateness of enhanced sentences for defendants whose peonage, involuntary servitude, or slave trade offenses involve—

"(i) a large number of victims;

"(ii) the use or threatened use of a dangerous weapon; or

"(iii) a prolonged period of peonage or involuntary servitude.

"(2) **Emergency authority to Sentencing Commission.**—The Commission shall promulgate the guidelines or amendments provided for under this subsection as soon as practicable in accordance with the procedure set forth in section 21(a) of the Sentencing Act of 1987 [section 21(a) of Pub.L. 100–182, set out as a note under this section], as though the authority under that Act had not expired."

Amendment of Sentencing Guidelines Regarding Manufacture of Methamphetamine

Pub.L. 104–237, Title II, § 203(b), Oct. 3, 1996, 110 Stat. 3102, provided that: "The United States Sentencing Commission shall amend the sentencing guidelines to ensure that the manufacture of methamphetamine in violation of section 403(d)(2) of the Controlled Substances Act, as added by subsection (a) [section 843(d)(2) of Title 21, Food and Drugs], is treated as a significant violation."

Amendment of Sentencing Guidelines Regarding Offenses Involving Flunitrazepam

Pub.L. 104–305, § 2(b)(3), Oct. 13, 1996, 110 Stat. 3808, provided that:

"(A) **Amendment of sentencing guidelines.**—Pursuant to its authority under section 994 of title 28, United States Code [this section], the United States Sentencing Commission shall review and amend, as appropriate, the sentencing guidelines for offenses involving flunitrazepam.

"(B) **Summary.**—The United States Sentencing Commission shall submit to the Congress—

"(i) a summary of its review under subparagraph (A); and

"(ii) an explanation for any amendment to the sentencing guidelines made under subparagraph (A).

"(C) **Serious nature of offenses.**—In carrying out this paragraph, the United States Sentencing Commission shall ensure that the sentencing guidelines for offenses involving flunitrazepam reflect the serious nature of such offenses."

Amendment of Sentencing Guidelines Regarding Repeat Sexual Abuse Offenders

Section 40111(b) of Pub.L. 103–322 provided that: "The Sentencing Commission shall implement the amendment made by subsection (a) [enacting section 2247 of Title 18, Crimes and Criminal Procedure] by promulgating amendments, if appropriate, in the sentencing guidelines applicable to chapter 109A [chapter 109A of Title 18] offenses."

Amendment of Sentencing Guidelines Regarding Sexual Abuse and Aggravated Sexual Abuse; Report

Section 40112 of Pub.L. 103–322 provided that:

"(a) **Amendment of Sentencing Guidelines.**—Pursuant to its authority under section 994(p) of title 28, United States Code [subsec. (p) of this section], the United States Sentencing Commission shall review and amend, where necessary, its sentencing guidelines on aggravated sexual abuse under section 2241 of title 18, United States Code [section 2241 of Title 18, Crimes and Criminal Procedure], or sexual abuse under section 2242 of title 18, United States Code [section 2242 of Title 18], as follows:

"(1) The Commission shall review and promulgate amendments to the guidelines, if appropriate, to enhance penalties if more than 1 offender is involved in the offense.

"(2) The Commission shall review and promulgate amendments to the guidelines, if appropriate, to reduce unwarranted disparities between the sentences for sex offenders who are known to the victim and sentences for sex offenders who are not known to the victim.

"(3) The Commission shall review and promulgate amendments to the guidelines to enhance penalties, if appropriate, to render Federal penalties on Federal territory commensurate with penalties for similar offenses in the States.

"(4) The Commission shall review and promulgate amendments to the guidelines, if appropriate, to account for the general problem of recidivism in cases of sex offenses, the severity of the offense, and its devastating effects on survivors.

"(b) **Report.**—Not later than 180 days after the date of enactment of this Act [Sept. 13, 1994], the United States Sentencing Commission shall review and submit to Congress a report containing an analysis of Federal rape sentencing, accompanied by comment from independent experts in the field, describing—

"(1) comparative Federal sentences for cases in which the rape victim is known to the defendant and cases in which the rape victim is not known to the defendant;

"(2) comparative Federal sentences for cases on Federal territory and sentences in surrounding States; and

"(3) an analysis of the effect of rape sentences on populations residing primarily on Federal territory relative to the impact of other Federal offenses in which the existence of Federal jurisdiction depends upon the offense's being committed on Federal territory."

Amendment of Sentencing Guidelines Regarding Sexual Exploitation of Children

Pub.L. 104–71, §§ 2 to 4, Dec. 23, 1995, 109 Stat. 774, provided that:

"**Sec. 2. Increased Penalties for Certain Conduct Involving the Sexual Exploitation of Children.**

"The United States Sentencing Commission shall amend the sentencing guidelines to—

"(1) increase the base offense level for an offense under section 2251 of title 18, United States Code [18 U.S.C.A. § 2251], by at least 2 levels; and

"(2) increase the base offense level for an offense under section 2252 of title 18, United States Code [18 U.S.C.A. § 2252], by at least 2 levels.

"Sec. 3. Increased Penalties for Use of Computers in Sexual Exploitation of Children.

"The United States Sentencing Commission shall amend the sentencing guidelines to increase the base offense level by at least 2 levels for an offense committed under section 2251(c)(1)(A) or 2252(a) of title 18, United States Code [18 U.S.C.A. § 2251(c)(1)(A) or § 2252(a)], if a computer was used to transmit the notice or advertisement to the intended recipient or to transport or ship the visual depiction.

"Sec. 4. Increased Penalties for Transportation of Children with Intent to Engage in Criminal Sexual Activity.

"The United States Sentencing Commission shall amend the sentencing guidelines to increase the base offense level for an offense under section 2423(a) of title 18, United States Code [18 U.S.C.A. § 2423(a)], by at least 3 levels."

Cocaine and Crack Sentences and Sentences for Money Laundering and Other Unlawful Activity; Reduction of Sentencing Disparities

Pub.L. 104–38, Oct. 30, 1995, 109 Stat. 334, provided that:

"Section 1. Disapproval of Amendments Relating to Lowering of Crack Sentences and Sentences for Money Laundering and Transactions in Property Derived From Unlawful Activity.

"In accordance with section 994(p) of title 28, United States Code [subsec. (p) of this section], amendments numbered 5 and 18 of the 'Amendments to the Sentencing Guidelines, Policy Statements, and Official Commentary', submitted by the United States Sentencing Commission to Congress on May 1, 1995, are hereby disapproved and shall not take effect.

"Sec. 2. Reduction of Sentencing Disparity.

"(a) Recommendations.—

"(1) In general.—The United States Sentencing Commission shall submit to Congress recommendations (and an explanation therefor), regarding changes to the statutes and sentencing guidelines governing sentences for unlawful manufacturing, importing, exporting, and trafficking of cocaine, and like offenses, including unlawful possession, possession with intent to commit any of the forgoing offenses, and attempt and conspiracy to commit any of the forgoing offenses. The recommendations shall reflect the following considerations—

"(A) the sentence imposed for trafficking in a quantity of crack cocaine should generally exceed the sentence imposed for trafficking in a like quantity of powder cocaine;

"(B) high-level wholesale cocaine traffickers, organizers, and leaders, of criminal activities should generally receive longer sentences than low-level retail cocaine traffickers and those who played a minor or minimal role in such criminal activity;

"(C) if the Government establishes that a defendant who traffics in powder cocaine has knowledge that such cocaine will be converted into crack cocaine prior to its distribution to individual users, the defendant should be treated at sentencing as though the defendant had trafficked in crack cocaine; and

"(D) an enhanced sentence should generally be imposed on a defendant who, in the course of an offense described in this subsection—

"(i) murders or causes serious bodily injury to an individual;

"(ii) uses a dangerous weapon;

"(iii) uses or possesses a firearm;

"(iv) involves a juvenile or a woman who the defendant knows or should know to be pregnant;

"(v) engages in a continuing criminal enterprise or commits other criminal offenses in order to facilitate his drug trafficking activities;

"(vi) knows, or should know, that he is involving an unusually vulnerable person;

"(vii) restrains a victim;

"(viii) traffics in cocaine within 500 feet of a school;

"(ix) obstructs justice;

"(x) has a significant prior criminal record; or

"(xi) is an organizer or leader of drug trafficking activities involving five or more persons.

"(2) Ratio.—The recommendations described in the preceding subsection shall propose revision of the drug quantity ratio of crack cocaine to powder cocaine under the relevant statutes and guidelines in a manner consistent with the ratios set for other drugs and consistent with the objectives set forth in section 3553(a) of title 28 United States Code [reference to section 3553(a) of Title 18, Crimes and Criminal Procedure, was probably intended].

"(b) Study.—No later than May 1, 1996, the Department of Justice shall submit to the Judiciary Committees of the Senate and House of Representatives a report on the charging and plea practices of Federal prosecutors with respect to the offense of money laundering. Such study shall include an account of the steps taken or to be taken by the Justice Department to ensure consistency and appropriateness in the use of the money laundering statute. The Sentencing Commission shall submit to the Judiciary Committees comments on the study prepared by the Department of Justice."

Common Carrier Operation Under Influence of Alcohol or Drugs; Sentencing Guidelines

Section 6482(c) of Pub.L. 100–690 provided that:

"(1) Pursuant to its authority under section 994(p) of title 28, United States Code [subsec. (p) of this section], and section 21 of the Sentencing Act of 1987 [section 21 of Pub.L. 100–182, set out as a note under this section], the United States Sentencing Commission shall promulgate guidelines, or shall amend existing guidelines, to provide that—

"(A) a defendant convicted of violating section 342 of title 18, United States Code [section 342 of Title 18, Crimes and Criminal Procedure], under circumstances in which death results, shall be assigned an offense level under chapter 2 of the sentencing guidelines that is not less than level 26; and

"(B) a defendant convicted of violating section 342 of title 18 [section 342 of Title 18, Crimes and Criminal Procedure], United States Code, under circumstances in which serious bodily injury results, shall be assigned an offense level under chapter 2 of the sentencing guidelines that is not less than level 21.

"(2) If the sentencing guidelines are amended after the effective date of this section [probably means date of enactment of this section, Nov. 18, 1988], the Sentencing Commission shall implement the instruction set forth in paragraph (1) so as to achieve a comparable result."

Crimes Against the Elderly; Sentencing Guidelines

Section 240002 of Pub.L. 103–322, as amended Pub.L. 104–294, Title VI, § 604(b)(10), Oct. 11, 1996, 110 Stat. 3507, provided that:

"**(a) In general.**—Pursuant to its authority under the Sentencing Reform Act of 1984 [chapter II of Title II of Pub.L. 98–473, Oct. 12, 1984, 98 Stat. 1987, see Short Title note set out under section 3551 of Title 18, Crimes and Criminal Procedure] and section 21 of the Sentencing Act of 1987 [section 21 of Pub.L. 100–182, set out as a note under this section] (including its authority to amend the sentencing guidelines and policy statements) and its authority to make such amendments on an emergency basis, the United States Sentencing Commission shall ensure that the applicable guideline range for a defendant convicted of a crime of violence against an elderly victim is sufficiently stringent to deter such a crime, to protect the public from additional crimes of such a defendant, and to adequately reflect the heinous nature of such an offense.

"**(b) Criteria.**—In carrying out subsection (a), the United States Sentencing Commission shall ensure that—

"(1) the guidelines provide for increasingly severe punishment for a defendant commensurate with the degree of physical harm caused to the elderly victim;

"(2) the guidelines take appropriate account of the vulnerability of the victim; and

"(3) the guidelines provide enhanced punishment for a defendant convicted of a crime of violence against an elderly victim who has previously been convicted of a crime of violence against an elderly victim, regardless of whether the conviction occurred in Federal or State court.

"**(c) Definitions.**—In this section—

"(1) 'crime of violence' means an offense under section 113, 114, 1111, 1112, 1113, 1117, 2241, 2242, or 2244 of title 18, United States Code [section 113, 114, 1111, 1112, 1113, 1117, 2241, 2242, or 2244 of Title 18].

"(2) 'elderly victim' means a victim who is 65 years of age or older at the time of an offense."

[Amendment by section 604 of Pub.L. 104–294 effective Sept. 13, 1994, see section 604(d) of Pub.L. 104–294, set out as a note under section 13 of Title 18, Crimes and Criminal Procedure.]

Deterrent Against Terrorist Activity Damaging a Federal Interest Computer

Pub.L. 104–132, Title VIII, § 805, Apr. 24, 1996, 110 Stat. 1305, provided that:

"**(a) Review.**—Not later than 60 calendar days after the date of enactment of this Act [Apr. 24, 1996], the United States Sentencing Commission shall review the deterrent effect of existing guideline levels as they apply to paragraphs (4) and (5) of section 1030(a) of title 18, United States Code [pars. (4) and (5) of section 1030(a) of Title 18, Crimes and Criminal Procedure].

"**(b) Report.**—The United States Sentencing Commission shall prepare and transmit a report to the Congress on the findings under the study conducted under subsection (a).

"**(c) Amendment of guidelines.**—Pursuant to its authority under section 994(p) of title 28, United States Code [subsec. (p) of this section], the United States Sentencing Commission shall amend the sentencing guidelines to ensure any individual convicted of a violation of paragraph (4) or (5) of section 1030(a) of title 18, United States Code [par. (4) or (5) of section 1030(a) of Title 18], is imprisoned for not less than 6 months."

Directive to Sentencing Commission

Pub.L. 105–147, § 2(g), Dec. 16, 1997, 111 Stat. 2680, provided that:

"(1) Under the authority of the Sentencing Reform Act of 1984 (Public Law 98–473; 98 Stat.1987) [Pub.L. 98–473, Oct. 12, 1984, 98 Stat. 1987] and section 21 of the Sentencing Act of 1987 (Public Law 100–182; 101 Stat. 1271; 18 U.S.C. 994 note [Pub.L. 100–182, Dec. 7, 1987, 101 Stat. 1271; 18 U.S.C.A. 994 note]) (including the authority to amend the sentencing guidelines and policy statements), the United States Sentencing Commission shall ensure that the applicable guideline range for a defendant convicted of a crime against intellectual property (including offenses set forth at section 506(a) of title 17, United States Code [section 506(a) of Title 17], and sections 2319, 2319A, and 2320 of title 18, United States Code [sections 2319, 2319A, and 2320 of Title 18]) is sufficiently stringent to deter such a crime and to adequately reflect the additional considerations set forth in paragraph (2) of this subsection.

"(2) In implementing paragraph (1), the Sentencing Commission shall ensure that the guidelines provide for consideration of the retail value and quantity of the items with respect to which the crime against intellectual property was committed."

Drug Offenses Within Federal Prisons; Sentencing Guidelines

Section 6468(c), (d) of Pub.L. 100–690 provided that:

"(c) Pursuant to its authority under section 994(p) of title 28, United States Code [subsec. (p) of this section], and section 21 of the Sentencing Act of 1987 [section 21 of Pub.L. 100–182, set out as a note under this section], the United States Sentencing Commission shall promulgate guidelines, or shall amend existing guidelines, to provide that a defendant convicted of violating section 1791(a)(1) of title 18, United States Code [section 1791(a)(1) of Title 18, Crimes and Criminal Procedure], and punishable under section 1791(b)(1) of that title [section 1791(b)(1) of Title 18] as so redesignated, shall be assigned an offense level under chapter 2 of the sentencing guidelines that is—

"(1) two levels greater than the level that would have been assigned had the offense not been committed in prison; and

"(2) in no event less than level 26.

"(d) If the sentencing guidelines are amended after the effective date of this section [probably means the date of enactment of this section, Nov. 18, 1988], the Sentencing Commission shall implement the instruction set forth in subsection (c) so as to achieve a comparable result."

Effective Date of Sentencing Guidelines

For provisions directing that the sentencing guidelines promulgated pursuant to subsec. (a)(1) of this section not go into effect until—

(I) the United States Sentencing Commission has submitted the initial set of sentencing guidelines to the Congress, along with a report stating the reasons for the Commission's recommendations;

(II) the General Accounting Office has undertaken a study of the guidelines, and their potential impact in comparison with the operation of the existing sentencing and parole release system, and has, within one hundred and fifty days of submission of the guidelines, reported to the Congress the results of its study; and

(III) the day after the Congress has had six months after the date described in subclause (I) in which to examine the guidelines and consider the reports, and

(IV) certain other provisions take effect,

see section 235(a)(1)(B)(ii) of Pub.L. 98–473, as amended, set out as a note under section 3551 of Title 18, Crimes and Criminal Procedure.

Emergency Guidelines Promulgation Authority

Section 21 of Pub.L. 100–182 provided that:

"**(a) In general.**—In the case of—

"(1) an invalidated sentencing guideline;

"(2) the creation of a new offense or amendment of an existing offense; or

"(3) any other reason relating to the application of a previously established sentencing guideline, and determined by the United States Sentencing Commission to be urgent and compelling;

the Commission, by affirmative vote of at least four members of the Commission, and pursuant to its rules and regulations and consistent with all pertinent provisions of title 28 and title 18, United States Code, shall promulgate and distribute to all courts of the United States and to the United States Probation System a temporary guideline or amendment to an existing guideline, to remain in effect until and during the pendency of the next report to Congress under section 994(p) of title 28, United States Code [subsec. (p) of this section].

"**(b) Expiration of authority.**—The authority of the Commission under paragraphs (1) and (2) of subsection (a) shall expire on November 1, 1989. The authority of the Commission to promulgate and distribute guidelines under paragraph (3) of subsection (a) shall expire on May 1, 1988."

Enhanced Penalties for Failure to Depart, Illegal Reentry, and Passport and Visa Fraud

Pub.L. 104–208, Div. C, Title III, § 334, Sept. 30, 1996, 110 Stat. 3009–635, provided that:

"**(a) Failing to depart.**—The United States Sentencing Commission shall promptly promulgate, pursuant to section 994 of title 28, United States Code [this section], amendments to the sentencing guidelines to make appropriate increases in the base offense level for offenses under section 242(e) and 276(b) of the Immigration and Nationality Act (8 U.S.C. 1252(e) and 1326(b)) [8 U.S.C.A. §§ 1252(e) and 1326(b) respectively] to reflect the amendments made by section 130001 of the Violent Crime Control and Law Enforcement Act of 1994.

"**(b) Passport and visa offenses.**—The United States Sentencing Commission shall promptly promulgate, pursuant to section 994 of title 28, United States Code [this section], amendments to the sentencing guidelines to make appropriate increases in the base offense level for offenses under chapter 75 of title 18, United States Code [18 U.S.C.A. § 1541 et seq.] to reflect the amendments made by section 130009 of the Violent Crime Control and Law Enforcement Act of 1994."

Enhanced Penalties for Firearms Possession by Violent Felons and Serious Drug Offenders

Section 110513 of Pub.L. 103–322 provided that: "Pursuant to its authority under section 994 of title 28, United States Code [this section], the United States Sentencing Commission shall amend its sentencing guidelines to—

"(1) appropriately enhance penalties in cases in which a defendant convicted under section 922(g) of title 18, United States Code [section 922(g) of Title 18, Crimes and Criminal Procedure], has 1 prior conviction by any court referred to in section 922(g)(1) of title 18 for a violent felony (as defined in section 924(e)(2)(B) of that title [section 924(e)(2)(B) of Title 18]) or a serious drug offense (as defined in section 924(e)(2)(A) of that title [section 924(e)(2)(A) of Title 18]); and

"(2) appropriately enhance penalties in cases in which such a defendant has 2 prior convictions for a violent felony (as so defined) or a serious drug offense (as so defined)."

Enhanced Penalties for Kidnapping Offenses Involving Children; Promulgation of Guidelines

See section 1201(g) of Title 18, Crimes and Criminal Procedure.

Enhanced Penalties for Offenses Involving Certain Listed Chemicals

Pub.L. 104–237, Title III, § 302(c), Oct. 3, 1996, 110 Stat. 3105, provided that:

"**(1) In general.**—The United States Sentencing Commission shall, in accordance with the procedures set forth in section 21(a) of the Sentencing Act of 1987 [section 21(a) of Pub.L. 100–182, set out as a note under this section], as though the authority of that section had not expired, amend the sentencing guidelines to increase by at least two levels the offense level for offenses involving list I chemicals under—

"(A) section 401(d)(1) and (2) of the Controlled Substances Act (21 U.S.C. 841(d)(1) and (2)) [section 841(d)(1) and (2) of Title 21, Food and Drugs]; and

"(B) section 1010(d)(1) and (3) of the Controlled Substance Import and Export Act (21 U.S.C. 960(d)(1) and (3)) [section 960(d)(1), (3) of Title 21].

"**(2) Requirement.**—In carrying out this subsection, the Commission shall ensure that the offense levels for offenses referred to in paragraph (1) are calculated proportionally on the basis of the quantity of controlled substance that reasonably could have been manufactured in a clandestine setting using the quantity of the list I chemical possessed, distributed, imported, or exported."

Enhanced Penalties For Offenses Involving Children

Pub.L. 101–647, Title III, § 321, Nov. 29, 1990, 104 Stat. 4817, provided that: "The United States Sentencing Commission shall amend existing guidelines for sentences involving sexual crimes against children, including offenses contained in chapter 109A of title 18 [section 2241 et seq. of Title 18, Crimes and Criminal Procedure], so that more substantial penalties may be imposed if the Commission determines current penalties are inadequate."

Section 6454 of Pub.L. 100–690 provided that:

"(a) In general.—Pursuant to its authority under section 994(p) of title 28, United States Code [subsec. (p) of this section], and section 21 of the Sentencing Act of 1987 [section 21 of Pub.L. 100–182, set out as a note under this section], the United States Sentencing Commission shall promulgate guidelines, or shall amend existing guidelines, to provide that a defendant convicted of violating sections 405, 405A, or 405B of the Controlled Substances Act (21 U.S.C. 845, 845a or 845b) [sections 845, 845a, and 845b of Title 21, Food and Drugs] involving a person under 18 years of age shall be assigned an offense level under chapter 2 of the sentencing guidelines that is—

"(1) two levels greater than the level that would have been assigned for the underlying controlled substance offense; and

"(2) in no event less than level 26.

"(b) Effects of amendment.—If the sentencing guidelines are amended after the effective date of this section [probably means date of enactment of this section, Nov. 18, 1988], the Sentencing Commission shall implement the instruction set forth in subsection (a) so as to achieve a comparable result.

"(c) Multiple enhancements.—The guidelines referred to in subsection (a), as promulgated or amended under such subsection, shall provide that an offense that could be subject to multiple enhancements pursuant to such subsection is subject to not more than one such enhancement."

Enhanced Penalty for Dangerous Handling of Controlled Substances: Amendment of Sentencing Guidelines

Pub.L. 104–237, Title III, § 303, Oct. 3, 1996, 110 Stat. 3106, provided that:

"(a) In general.—Pursuant to its authority under section 994 of title 28, United States Code [this section], the United States Sentencing Commission shall determine whether the Sentencing Guidelines adequately punish the offenses described in subsection (b) and, if not, promulgate guidelines or amend existing guidelines to provide an appropriate enhancement of the punishment for a defendant convicted of such an offense.

"(b) Offense.—The offense referred to in subsection (a) is a violation of section 401(d), 401(g)(1), 403(a)(6), or 403(a)(7) of the Controlled Substances Act (21 U.S.C. 841(d), 841(g)(1), 843(a)(6), and 843(a)(7)) [sections 841(d), (g)(1), and 843(a)(6), (7) of Title 21, Food and Drugs], in cases in which in the commission of the offense the defendant violated—

"(1) subsection (d) or (e) of section 3008 of the Solid Waste Disposal Act [section 6928(d), (e) of Title 42, The Public Health and Welfare] relating to handling hazardous waste in a manner inconsistent with Federal or applicable State law);

"(2) section 103(b) of the Comprehensive Environmental Response, Compensation and Liability Act (relating to failure to notify as to the release of a reportable quantity of a hazardous substance into the environment) [section 9603(b) of Title 42];

"(3) section 301(a), 307(d), 309(c)(2), 309(c)(3), 311(b)(3), or 311(b)(5) of the Federal Water Pollution Control Act [sections 1311(a), 1317(d), 1319(c)(2), (3), 1321(b)(3) or (5) of Title 33, Navigation and Navigable Waters] (relating to the unlawful discharge of pollutants or hazardous substances, the operation of a source in violation of a pretreatment standard, and the failure to notify as to the release of a reportable quantity of a hazardous substance into the water); or

"(4) section 5124 of title 49, United States Code (relating to violations of laws and regulations enforced by the Department of Transportation with respect to the transportation of hazardous material) [section 5124 of Title 49, Transportation]."

Enhanced Penalty for Second Offense of Using an Explosive to Commit a Felony

Section 110502 of Pub.L. 103–322 provided that: "Pursuant to its authority under section 994 of title 28, United States Code [this section], the United States Sentencing Commission shall promulgate amendments to the sentencing guidelines to appropriately enhance penalties in a case in which a defendant convicted under section 844(h) of title 18, United States Code [section 844(h) of Title 18, Crimes and Criminal Procedure], has previously been convicted under that section."

Enhanced Penalty for Use of a Semiautomatic Firearm During a Crime of Violence or a Drug Trafficking Crime

Section 110501 of Pub.L. 103–322 provided that:

"(a) Amendment to Sentencing Guidelines.—Pursuant to its authority under section 994 of title 28, United States Code [this section], the United States Sentencing Commission shall amend its sentencing guidelines to provide an appropriate enhancement of the punishment for a crime of violence (as defined in section 924(c)(3) of title 18, United States Code [section 924(c)(3) of Title 18, Crimes and Criminal Procedure]) or a drug trafficking crime (as defined in section 924(c)(2) of title 18, United States Code [section 924(c)(2) of Title 18]) if a semiautomatic firearm is involved.

"(b) Semiautomatic firearm.—In subsection (a), 'semiautomatic firearm' means any repeating firearm that utilizes a portion of the energy of a firing cartridge to extract the fired cartridge case and chamber the next round and that requires a separate pull of the trigger to fire each cartridge."

Guidelines Regarding Sentencing Enhancements for Hate Crimes

Section 280003 of Pub.L. 103–322 provided that:

"(a) Definition.—In this section, 'hate crime' means a crime in which the defendant intentionally selects a victim, or in the case of a property crime, the property that is the object of the crime, because of the actual or perceived race, color, religion, national origin, ethnicity, gender, disability, or sexual orientation of any person.

"(b) Sentencing enhancement.—Pursuant to section 994 of title 28, United States Code [this section], the United States Sentencing Commission shall promulgate guidelines or amend existing guidelines to provide sentencing enhancements of not less than 3 offense levels for offenses that the finder of fact at trial determines beyond a reasonable doubt are hate crimes. In carrying out this section [this note], the

United States Sentencing Commission shall ensure that there is reasonable consistency with other guidelines, avoid duplicative punishments for substantially the same offense, and take into account any mitigating circumstances that might justify exceptions."

Guidelines Relating to Methamphetamine Offenses

Pub.L. 101–647, Title XXVII, § 2701, Nov. 29, 1990, 104 Stat. 4912, provided that: "The United States Sentencing Commission is instructed to amend the existing guidelines for offenses involving smokable crystal methamphetamine under section 401(b) of the Controlled Substances Act (21 U.S.C. 841(b) [section 841(b) of Title 21, Food and Drugs]) so that convictions for offenses involving smokable crystal methamphetamine will be assigned an offense level under the guidelines which is two levels above that which would have been assigned to the same offense involving other forms of methamphetamine."

Guidelines Relating to Offenses Substantially Jeopardizing Safety and Soundness of Federally Insured Financial Institutions

Pub.L. 101–73, Title IX, § 961(m), Aug. 9, 1989, 103 Stat. 501, provided that: "Pursuant to section 994 of title 28, United States Code [this section], and section 21 of the Sentencing Act of 1987 [section 21 of Pub.L. 100–182, set out as a note under this section], the United States Sentencing Commission shall promulgate guidelines, or amend existing guidelines, to provide for a substantial period of incarceration for a violation of, or a conspiracy to violate, section 215, 656, 657, 1005, 1006, 1007, 1014, 1341, 1343, or 1344 of title 18, United States Code [section 215, 656, 657, 1005, 1006, 1007, 1014, 1341, 1343, or 1344 of Title 18, Crimes and Criminal Procedure], that substantially jeopardizes the safety and soundness of a federally insured financial institution."

Increased Penalties for Fraud Against Older Victims; Review and Amendment of Guidelines; Report to Congress

Section 250003 of Pub.L. 103–322 provided that:

"**(a) Review.**—The United States Sentencing Commission shall review and, if necessary, amend the sentencing guidelines to ensure that victim related adjustments for fraud offenses against older victims over the age of 55 are adequate.

"**(b) Report.**—Not later than 180 days after the date of enactment of this Act [Sept. 13, 1994], the Sentencing Commission shall report to Congress the result of its review under subsection (a)."

Increased Penalties in Major Bank Crime Cases

Pub.L. 101–647, Title XXV, § 2507, Nov. 29, 1990, 104 Stat. 4862, provided that:

"**(a) Increased penalties.**—Pursuant to section 994 of title 28, United States Code [this section], and section 21 of the Sentencing Act of 1987 [section 21 of Pub.L. 100–182, set out as a note under this section] the United States Sentencing Commission shall promulgate guidelines, or amend existing guidelines, to provide that a defendant convicted of violating, or conspiring to violate, section 215, 656, 657, 1005, 1006, 1007, 1014, 1032, or 1344 of title 18, United States Code [section 215, 656, 657, 1005, 1006, 1007, 1014, 1032, or 1344 of Title 18, Crimes and Criminal Procedure], or section 1341 or 1343 [section 1341 or 1343 of Title 18] affecting a financial institution (as defined in section 20 of title 18, United States Code [section 20 of Title 18]), shall be assigned not less than offense level 24 under chapter 2 of the sentencing guidelines if the defendant derives more than $1,000,000 in gross receipts from the offense.

"**(b) Amendments to sentencing guidelines.**—If the sentencing guidelines are amended after the effective date of this section, the Sentencing Commission shall implement the instruction set forth in subsection (a) so as to achieve a comparable result."

Instruction to Sentencing Commission Regarding Mandatory Victim Restitution

Pub.L. 104–132, Title II, § 208, Apr. 24, 1996, 110 Stat. 1240, provided that: "Pursuant to section 994 of title 28, United States Code [this section], the United States Sentencing Commission shall promulgate guidelines or amend existing guidelines to reflect this subtitle and the amendments made by this subtitle [enacting sections 3613A and 3663A of Title 18, Crimes and Criminal Procedure, amending sections 2248, 2259, 2264, 2327, 3013, 3556, 3563, 3572, 3611, 3612, 3613, 3614, 3663, and 3664 of Title 18 and Rule 32 of the Federal Rules of Criminal Procedure and enacting provisions set out as notes under sections 2248 and 3551 of Title 18]."

[Provisions of section 208 of Pub.L. 104–132 to be effective, to the extent constitutionally permissible, for sentencing proceedings in cases in which the defendant is convicted on or after Apr. 24, 1996, see section 211 of Pub.L. 104–132, set out as a note under section 2248 of this title.]

International Terrorism; Amendment of Sentencing Guidelines

Pub.L. 104–132, Title VII, § 730, Apr. 24, 1996, 110 Stat. 1303, provided that: "The United States Sentencing Commission shall forthwith, in accordance with the procedures set forth in section 21(a) of the Sentencing Act of 1987 [section 21(a) of Pub.L. 100–182, set out as a note under this section], as though the authority under that section had not expired, amend the sentencing guidelines so that the chapter 3 adjustment relating to international terrorism only applies to Federal crimes of terrorism, as defined in section 2332b(g) of title 18, United States Code [section 2332b(g) of Title 18, Crimes and Criminal Procedure]."

Penalties for Conspiring With or Assisting an Alien to Commit an Offense Under the Controlled Substances Import and Export Act

Pub.L. 104–208, Div. C, Title III, § 333, Sept. 30, 1996, 110 Stat. 3009–634, provided that:

"**(a) Review of guidelines.**—Not later than 6 months after the date of the enactment of this Act [Sept. 30, 1996], the United States Sentencing Commission shall conduct a review of the guidelines applicable to an offender who conspires with, or aids or abets, a person who is not a citizen or national of the United States in committing any offense under section 1010 of the Controlled Substance Import and Export Act (21 U.S.C. 960) [21 U.S.C.A. § 960].

"**(b) Revision of guidelines.**—Following such review, pursuant to section 994(p) of title 28, United States Code [subsec. (p) of this section], the Commission shall promulgate sentencing guidelines or amend existing sentencing guidelines to ensure an appropriately stringent sentence for such offenders."

Penalties For Importation of Controlled Substances by Aircraft and Other Vessels

Section 6453 of Pub.L. 100–690 provided that:

"**(a) In general.**—Pursuant to its authority under section 994(p) of title 28, United States Code [subsec. (p) of this section], and section 21 of the Sentencing Act of 1987 [section 21 of Pub.L. 100–182 set out as a note under this section], the United States Sentencing Commission shall promulgate guidelines, or shall amend existing guidelines, to provide that a defendant convicted of violating section 1010(a) of the Controlled Substances Import and Export Act (21 U.S.C. 960(a)) [section 960(a) of Title 21, Food and Drugs] under circumstances in which—

"**(1)** an aircraft other than a regularly scheduled commercial air carrier was used to import the controlled substance; or

"**(2)** the defendant acted as a pilot, copilot, captain, navigator, flight officer, or any other operation officer aboard any craft or vessel carrying a controlled substance,

shall be assigned an offense level under chapter 2 of the sentencing guidelines that is—

"**(A)** two levels greater than the level that would have been assigned had the offense not been committed under circumstances set forth in (A) or (B) [(1) or (2)] above; and

"**(B)** in no event less than level 26.

"**(b) Effect of amendment.**—If the sentencing guidelines are amended after the effective date of this section [probably means date of enactment of this section, Nov. 18, 1988], the Sentencing Commission shall implement the instruction set forth in subsection (a) so as to achieve a comparable result."

Penalty Increases for Trafficking in Methamphetamine

Pub.L. 104–237, Title III, § 301, Oct. 3, 1996, 110 Stat. 3105, provided that:

"**(a) Directive to the United States Sentencing Commission.**—Pursuant to its authority under section 994 of title 28, United States Code [this section], the United States Sentencing Commission shall review and amend its guidelines and its policy statements to provide for increased penalties for unlawful manufacturing, importing, exporting, and trafficking of methamphetamine, and other similar offenses, including unlawful possession with intent to commit any of those offenses, and attempt and conspiracy to commit any of those offenses. The Commission shall submit to Congress explanations therefor and any additional policy recommendations for combating methamphetamine offenses.

"**(b) In general.**—In carrying out this section, the Commission shall ensure that the sentencing guidelines and policy statements for offenders convicted of offenses described in subsection (a) and any recommendations submitted under such subsection reflect the heinous nature of such offenses, the need for aggressive law enforcement action to fight such offenses, and the extreme dangers associated with unlawful activity involving methamphetamine, including—

"**(1)** the rapidly growing incidence of methamphetamine abuse and the threat to public safety such abuse poses;

"**(2)** the high risk of methamphetamine addiction;

"**(3)** the increased risk of violence associated with methamphetamine trafficking and abuse; and

"**(4)** the recent increase in the illegal importation of methamphetamine and precursor chemicals."

Sentencing Commission Authority

Section 80001(b) of Pub.L. 103–322 provided that:

"**(1) In general.**—**(A)** The United States Sentencing Commission (referred to in this subsection as the 'Commission'), under section 994(a)(1) and (p) of title 28 [subsecs. (a)(1) and (p) of this section]—

"**(i)** shall promulgate guidelines, or amendments to guidelines, to carry out the purposes of this section and the amendment made by this section [amending section 3553 of Title 18, Crimes and Criminal Procedure and provisions set out as notes under section 3553 of Title 18]; and

"**(ii)** may promulgate policy statements, or amendments to policy statements, to assist in the application of this section and that amendment.

"**(B)** In the case of a defendant for whom the statutorily required minimum sentence is 5 years, such guidelines and amendments to guidelines issued under subparagraph (A) shall call for a guideline range in which the lowest term of imprisonment is at least 24 months.

"**(2) Procedures.**—If the Commission determines that it is necessary to do so in order that the amendments made under paragraph (1) may take effect on the effective date of the amendment made by subsection (a) [amending section 3553 of Title 18, effective on or after the 10th day beginning after Sept. 13, 1994], the Commission may promulgate the amendments made under paragraph (1) in accordance with the procedures set forth in section 21(a) of the Sentencing Act of 1987 [section 21(a) of Pub.L. 100–182, set out as a note under this section], as though the authority under that section had not expired."

Sentencing for Offenses against Property at National Cemeteries.

Pub.L. 105–101, § 2, Nov. 19, 1997, 111 Stat. 2202, provided that:

"**(a) In General.**—Pursuant to its authority under section 994 of title 28, United States Code [section 994 of Title 28], the United States Sentencing Commission shall review and amend the Federal sentencing guidelines to provide a sentencing enhancement of not less than 2 levels for any offense against the property of a national cemetery.

"**(b) Commission duties.**—In carrying out subsection (a), the Sentencing Commission shall ensure that the sentences, guidelines, and policy statements for offenders convicted of an offense described in that subsection are—

"**(1)** appropriately severe; and

"**(2)** reasonably consistent with other relevant directives and with other Federal sentencing guidelines.

"**(c) Definition of national cemetery.**—In this section, the term 'national cemetery' means a cemetery—

"**(1)** in the National Cemetery System established under section 2400 of title 38, United States Code [section 2400 of Title 38]; or

"**(2)** under the jurisdiction of the Secretary of the Army, the Secretary of the Navy, the Secretary of the Air Force, or the Secretary of the Interior."

[Any reference in a law, map, regulation, document, paper, or other record of the United States to the National Cemetery System shall be deemed to be a reference to the National Cemetery Administration, see section 403(d)(1) of Pub.L. 105–368, set out as a note under section 2400 of Title 38.]

Sentencing Guidelines for Personal Injury from Fraud

See section 2(b) of Pub.L. 100–700, Nov. 19, 1988, 102 Stat. 4632, set out as a note under section 1031 of Title 18, Crimes and Criminal Procedure.

Sentencing Guidelines Increase for Terrorist Crimes

Section 120004 of Pub.L. 103–322 provided that: "The United States Sentencing Commission is directed to amend its sentencing guidelines to provide an appropriate enhancement for any felony, whether committed within or outside the United States, that involves or is intended to promote international terrorism, unless such involvement or intent is itself an element of the crime."

Sexual Abuse and Exploitation of Minors; Amendment of Sentencing Guidelines

Pub.L. 102–141, Title VI, § 632, Oct. 28, 1991, 105 Stat. 876, provided that:

"(1) Pursuant to its authority under section 994 of title 28, United States Code [this section], the Sentencing Commission shall promulgate guidelines, or amend existing or proposed guidelines as follows:

"(A) Guideline 2G2.2 to provide a base offense level of not less than 15 and to provide at least a 5 level increase for offenders who have engaged in a pattern of activity involving the sexual abuse or exploitation of a minor.

"(B) Guideline 2G2.4 to provide that such guideline shall apply only to offense conduct that involves the simple possession of materials proscribed by chapter 110 of title 18, United States Code [section 2251 et seq. of Title 18, Crimes and Criminal Procedure] and guideline 2G2.2 to provide that such guideline shall apply to offense conduct that involves receipt or trafficking (including, but not limited to transportation, distribution, or shipping).

"(C) Guideline 2G2.4 to provide a base offense level of not less than 13, and to provide at least a 2 level increase for possessing 10 or more books, magazines, periodicals, films, video tapes or other items containing a visual depiction involving the sexual exploitation of a minor.

"(D) Section 2G3.1 to provide a base offense level of not less than 10.

"(2)(A) Notwithstanding any other provision of law, the Sentencing Commission shall promulgate the amendments mandated in subsection (1) by November 1, 1991, or within 30 days after enactment [probably means date of enactment of Pub.L. 102–141, which was approved Oct. 28, 1991], whichever is later. The amendments to the guidelines promulgated under subsection (1) shall take effect November 1, 1991, or 30 days after enactment, and shall supersede any amendment to the contrary contained in the amendments to the sentencing guidelines submitted to the Congress by the Sentencing Commission on or about May 1, 1991.

"(B) The provisions of section 944(x) of title 28, United States Code [probably means subsec. (x) of this section], shall not apply to the promulgation or amendment of guidelines under this section."

Solicitation of a Minor to Commit a Crime

Section 140008 of Pub.L. 103–322 provided that:

"**(a) Directive to Sentencing Commission.**—(1) The United States Sentencing Commission shall promulgate guidelines or amend existing guidelines to provide that a defendant 21 years of age or older who has been convicted of an offense shall receive an appropriate sentence enhancement if the defendant involved a minor in the commission of the offense.

"(2) The Commission shall provide that the guideline enhancement promulgated pursuant to paragraph (1) shall apply for any offense in relation to which the defendant has solicited, procured, recruited, counseled, encouraged, trained, directed, commanded, intimidated, or otherwise used or attempted to use any person less than 18 years of age with the intent that the minor would commit a Federal offense.

"**(b) Relevant considerations.**—In implementing the directive in subsection (a), the Sentencing Commission shall consider—

"(1) the severity of the crime that the defendant intended the minor to commit;

"(2) the number of minors that the defendant used or attempted to use in relation to the offense;

"(3) the fact that involving a minor in a crime of violence is frequently of even greater seriousness than involving a minor in a drug trafficking offense, for which the guidelines already provide a two-level enhancement; and

"(4) the possible relevance of the proximity in age between the offender and the minor(s) involved in the offense."

Studies of Impact and Operation of Sentencing Guideline System; Reporting Requirements

Section 236 of Pub.L. 98–473 provided that:

"(a)(1) Four years after the sentencing guidelines promulgated pursuant to section 994(a)(1) [subsec. (a)(1) of this section], and the provisions of sections 3581, 3583, and 3624 of title 18, United States Code, go into effect, the General Accounting Office shall undertake a study of the guidelines in order to determine their impact and compare the guidelines system with the operation of the previous sentencing and parole release system, and, within six months of the undertaking of such study, report to the Congress the results of its study.

"(2) Within one month of the start of the study required under subsection (a), the United States Sentencing Commission shall submit a report to the General Accounting Office, all appropriate courts, the Department of Justice, and the Congress detailing the operation of the sentencing guideline system and discussing any problems with the system or reforms needed. The report shall include an evaluation of the impact of the sentencing guidelines on prosecutorial discretion, plea bargaining, disparities in sentencing, and the use of incarceration, and shall be issued by affirmative vote of a majority of the voting members of the Commission.

"(b) The Congress shall review the study submitted pursuant to subsection (a) in order to determine—

"(1) whether the sentencing guideline system has been effective;

"(2) whether any changes should be made in the sentencing guideline system; and

"(3) whether the parole system should be reinstated in some form and the life of the Parole Commission extended."

Submission to Congress of Initial Sentencing Guidelines

Provisions directing that the United States Sentencing Commission submit to Congress within 30 months of Oct. 12, 1984, the initial sentencing guidelines promulgated pursuant to subsec. (a)(1) of this section, see section 235(a)(1)(B)(i) of Pub.L. 98–473, as amended, set out as an Effective Date note under section 3551 of Title 18, Crimes and Criminal Procedure.

Transportation Safety Offenses

Section 180201(c) of Pub.L. 103–322 provided that: "Pursuant to its authority under section 994 of title 28, United States Code [this section], and section 21 of the Sentencing Act of 1987 (28 U.S.C. 994 note) [section 21 of Pub.L. 100–182, set out as a note under this section], the United States Sentencing Commission shall promulgate guidelines, or shall amend existing guidelines, to provide an appropriate enhancement of punishment for a defendant convicted of violating section 409 of the Controlled Substances Act [section 849 of Title 21, Food and Drugs], as added by subsection (b)."

Using a Firearm in the Commission of Counterfeiting or Forgery

Section 110512 of Pub.L. 103–322 provided that: "Pursuant to its authority under section 994 of title 28, United States Code [this section], the United States Sentencing Commission shall amend its sentencing guidelines to provide an appropriate enhancement of the punishment for a defendant convicted of a felony under chapter 25 of title 18, United States Code [section 471 et seq. of Title 18, Crimes and Criminal Procedure], if the defendant used or carried a firearm (as defined in section 921(a)(3) of title 18, United States Code [section 921(a)(3) of Title 18]) during and in relation to the felony."

§ 995. Powers of the Commission

(a) The Commission, by vote of a majority of the members present and voting, shall have the power to—

(1) establish general policies and promulgate such rules and regulations for the Commission as are necessary to carry out the purposes of this chapter;

(2) appoint and fix the salary and duties of the Staff Director of the Sentencing Commission, who shall serve at the discretion of the Commission and who shall be compensated at a rate not to exceed the highest rate now or hereafter prescribed for Level 6 of the Senior Executive Service Schedule (5 U.S.C. 5382);

(3) deny, revise, or ratify any request for regular, supplemental, or deficiency appropriations prior to any submission of such request to the Office of Management and Budget by the Chair;

(4) procure for the Commission temporary and intermittent services to the same extent as is authorized by section 3109(b) of title 5, United States Code;

(5) utilize, with their consent, the services, equipment, personnel, information, and facilities of other Federal, State, local, and private agencies and instrumentalities with or without reimbursement therefor;

(6) without regard to 31 U.S.C. 3324, enter into and perform such contracts, leases, cooperative agreements, and other transactions as may be necessary in the conduct of the functions of the Commission, with any public agency, or with any person, firm, association, corporation, educational institution, or nonprofit organization;

(7) accept and employ, in carrying out the provisions of this title, voluntary and uncompensated services, notwithstanding the provisions of 31 U.S.C. 1342, however, individuals providing such services shall not be considered Federal employees except for purposes of chapter 81 of title 5, United States Code, with respect to job-incurred disability and title 28, United States Code, with respect to tort claims;

(8) request such information, data, and reports from any Federal agency or judicial officer as the Commission may from time to time require and as may be produced consistent with other law;

(9) monitor the performance of probation officers with regard to sentencing recommendations, including application of the Sentencing Commission guidelines and policy statements;

(10) issue instructions to probation officers concerning the application of Commission guidelines and policy statements;

(11) arrange with the head of any other Federal agency for the performance by such agency of any function of the Commission, with or without reimbursement;

(12) establish a research and development program within the Commission for the purpose of—

(A) serving as a clearinghouse and information center for the collection, preparation, and dissemination of information on Federal sentencing practices; and

(B) assisting and serving in a consulting capacity to Federal courts, departments, and agencies in the development, maintenance, and coordination of sound sentencing practices;

(13) collect systematically the data obtained from studies, research, and the empirical experience of public and private agencies concerning the sentencing process;

(14) publish data concerning the sentencing process;

(15) collect systematically and disseminate information concerning sentences actually imposed, and the relationship of such sentences to the factors set forth in section 3553(a) of title 18, United States Code;

(16) collect systematically and disseminate information regarding effectiveness of sentences imposed;

(17) devise and conduct, in various geographical locations, seminars and workshops providing continuing studies for persons engaged in the sentencing field;

(18) devise and conduct periodic training programs of instruction in sentencing techniques for judicial and probation personnel and other persons connected with the sentencing process;

(19) study the feasibility of developing guidelines for the disposition of juvenile delinquents;

(20) make recommendations to Congress concerning modification or enactment of statutes relating to sentencing, penal, and correctional matters that the Commission finds to be necessary and advisable to carry out an effective, humane and rational sentencing policy;

(21) hold hearings and call witnesses that might assist the Commission in the exercise of its powers or duties;

(22) perform such other functions as are required to permit Federal courts to meet their responsibilities under section 3553(a) of title 18, United States Code, and to permit others involved in the Federal criminal justice system to meet their related responsibilities;

(23) retain private attorneys to provide legal advice to the Commission in the conduct of its work, or to appear for or represent the Commission in any case in which the Commission is authorized by law to represent itself, or in which the Commission is representing itself with the consent of the Department of Justice; and the Commission may in its discretion pay reasonable attorney's fees to private attorneys employed by it out of its appropriated funds. When serving as officers or employees of the United States, such private attorneys shall be considered special government employees as defined in section 202(a) of title 18; and

(24) grant incentive awards to its employees pursuant to chapter 45 of title 5, United States Code.

(b) The Commission shall have such other powers and duties and shall perform such other functions as may be necessary to carry out the purposes of this chapter, and may delegate to any member or designated person such powers as may be appropriate other than the power to establish general policy statements and guidelines pursuant to section 994(a)(1) and (2), the issuance of general policies and promulgation of rules and regulations pursuant to subsection (a)(1) of this section, and the decisions as to the factors to be considered in establishment of categories of offenses and offenders pursuant to section 994(b). The Commission shall, with respect to its activities under subsections (a)(9), (a)(10), (a)(11), (a)(12), (a)(13), (a)(14), (a)(15), (a)(16), (a)(17), and (a)(18), to the extent practicable, utilize existing resources of the Administrative Office of the United States Courts and the Federal Judicial Center for the purpose of avoiding unnecessary duplication.

(c) Upon the request of the Commission, each Federal agency is authorized and directed to make its services, equipment, personnel, facilities, and information available to the greatest practicable extent to the Commission in the execution of its functions.

(d) A simple majority of the membership then serving shall constitute a quorum for the conduct of business. Other than for the promulgation of guidelines and policy statements pursuant to section 994, the Commission may exercise its powers and fulfill its duties by the vote of a simple majority of the members present.

(e) Except as otherwise provided by law, the Commission shall maintain and make available for public inspection a record of the final vote of each member on any action taken by it.

(Added Pub.L. 98–473, Title II, § 217(a), Oct. 12, 1984, 98 Stat. 2024, and amended Pub.L. 100–690, Title VII, §§ 7104, 7105, 7106(b), Nov. 18, 1988, 102 Stat. 4418; Pub.L. 101–650, Title III, § 325(b)(5), Dec. 1, 1990, 104 Stat. 5121; Pub.L. 103–322, Title XXVIII, § 280005(c)(1), Sept. 13, 1994, 108 Stat. 2097.)

HISTORICAL AND STATUTORY NOTES

References in Text

The provisions of title 28, United States Code, with respect to tort claims, referred to in subsec. (a)(7), are classified generally to section 1346(b) and chapter 171 (section 2671 et seq.) of this title.

Effective Dates

1984 Acts. Section effective Oct. 12, 1984, see section 235(a)(1)(B)(i) of Pub.L. 98–473, as amended, set out as a note under section 3551 of Title 18, Crimes and Criminal Procedure.

§ 996. Director and staff

(a) The Staff Director shall supervise the activities of persons employed by the Commission and perform other duties assigned to the Staff Director by the Commission.

(b) The Staff Director shall, subject to the approval of the Commission, appoint such officers and employees as are necessary in the execution of the functions of the Commission. The officers and employees of the Commission shall be exempt from the provisions of part III of title 5, United States Code, except the following chapters: 45 (Incentive Awards), 81 (Compensation for Work Injuries), 83 (Retirement), 85

(Unemployment Compensation), 87 (Life Insurance), and 89 (Health Insurance).

(Added Pub.L. 98–473, Title II, § 217(a), Oct. 12, 1984, 98 Stat. 2026, and amended Pub.L. 100–690, Title VII, § 7106(c), Nov. 18, 1988, 102 Stat. 4418; Pub.L. 101–650, Title III, § 325(b)(6), Dec. 1, 1990, 104 Stat. 5121; Pub.L. 103–322, Title XXVIII, § 280005(c)(5), Sept. 13, 1994, 108 Stat. 2097.)

HISTORICAL AND STATUTORY NOTES

Effective Dates

1984 Acts. Section effective Oct. 12, 1984, see section 235(a)(1)(B)(i) of Pub.L. 98–473, as amended, set out as a note under section 3551 of Title 18, Crimes and Criminal Procedure.

§ 997. Annual report

The Commission shall report annually to the Judicial Conference of the United States, the Congress, and the President of the United States on the activities of the Commission.

(Added Pub.L. 98–473, Title II, § 217(a), Oct. 12, 1984, 98 Stat. 2026.)

HISTORICAL AND STATUTORY NOTES

Effective Dates

1984 Acts. Section effective Oct. 12, 1984, see section 235(a)(1)(B)(i) of Pub.L. 98–473, as amended, set out as a note under section 3551 of Title 18, Crimes and Criminal Procedure.

§ 998. Definitions

As used in this chapter—

(a) "Commission" means the United States Sentencing Commission;

(b) "Commissioner" means a member of the United States Sentencing Commission;

(c) "guidelines" means the guidelines promulgated by the Commission pursuant to section 994(a) of this title; and

(d) "rules and regulations" means rules and regulations promulgated by the Commission pursuant to section 995 of this title.

(Added Pub.L. 98–473, Title II, § 217(a), Oct. 12, 1984, 98 Stat. 2026.)

HISTORICAL AND STATUTORY NOTES

Effective Dates

1984 Acts. Section effective Oct. 12, 1984, see section 235(a)(1)(B)(i) of Pub.L. 98–473, as amended, set out as a note under section 3551 of Title 18, Crimes and Criminal Procedure.

PART IV—JURISDICTION AND VENUE

Chapter		Section
81.	Supreme Court	1251
83.	Courts of Appeals	1291
85.	District Courts; Jurisdiction	1331
87.	District Courts; Venue	1391
89.	District Courts; Removal of Cases from State Courts	1441
[90.	District Courts and Bankruptcy Courts] [Omitted]	1471
91.	United States Court of Federal Claims	1491
[93.	Repealed]	
95.	Court of International Trade	1581
97.	Jurisdictional Immunities of Foreign States	1602
99.	General Provisions	1631

HISTORICAL AND STATUTORY NOTES

Codifications

The analysis of chapters comprising Part IV was amended by Pub.L. 95–598, Title II, § 241(b), Nov. 6, 1978, 92 Stat. 2671, effective June 28, 1984, pursuant to Pub.L. 95–598, Title IV, § 402(b), Nov. 6, 1978, 92 Stat. 2682, as amended by Pub.L. 98–249, § 1(a), Mar. 31, 1984, 98 Stat. 116; Pub.L. 98–271, § 1(a), Apr. 30, 1984, 98 Stat. 163; Pub.L. 98–299, § 1(a), May 25, 1984, 98 Stat. 214; Pub.L. 98–325, § 1(a), June 20, 1984, 98 Stat. 268, set out as an Effective Date note preceding section 101 of Title 11, Bankruptcy, by adding:

Section 402(b) of Pub.L. 95–598 was amended by section 113 of Pub.L. 98–353, Title I, July 10, 1984, 98 Stat. 343, by substituting "shall not be effective" for "shall take effect on June 28, 1984", thereby eliminating the amendment by section 241(b) of Pub.L. 95–598, effective June 27, 1984, pursuant to section 122(c) of Pub.L. 98–353, set out as an Effective Dates note under section 151 of this title.

Section 121(a) of Pub.L. 98–353 directed that section 402(b) of Pub.L. 95–598 be amended by substituting "the date of enactment of the Bankruptcy Amendments and Federal Judgeship Act of 1984 [i.e. July 10, 1984]" for "June 28, 1984". This amendment was not executed in view of the prior amendment to section 402(b) of Pub.L. 95–598 by section 113 of Pub.L. 98–353.

Change of Name

References to United States Claims Court deemed to refer to United States Court of Federal Claims and references to Claims Court deemed to refer to Court of Federal Claims, see section 902(b) of Pub.L. 102–572, set out as a note under section 171 of Title 28, Judiciary and Judicial Procedure.

CHAPTER 81—SUPREME COURT

Sec.
1251. Original jurisdiction.
[1252. Repealed.]
1253. Direct appeals from decisions of three-judge courts.
1254. Courts of appeals; certiorari; certified questions.
[1255, 1256. Repealed.]
1257. State courts; certiorari.
1258. Supreme Court of Puerto Rico; certiorari.
1259. Court of Appeals for the Armed Forces; certiorari.

HISTORICAL AND STATUTORY NOTES

Definitions of Courts and Judges

Section 32 of Act June 25, 1948, as amended by Act May 24, 1949, c. 139, § 127, 63 Stat. 107, provided:

"(a) All laws of the United States in force on September 1, 1948, in which reference is made to a 'circuit court of appeals'; 'senior circuit judge'; 'senior district judge'; 'presiding judge'; 'chief justice', except when reference to the Chief Justice of the United States is intended; or 'justice', except when used with respect to a justice of the Supreme Court of the United States in his capacity as such or as a circuit justice, are hereby amended by substituting 'court of appeals' for 'circuit court of appeals'; 'chief judge of the circuit' for 'senior circuit judge'; 'chief judge of the district court' for 'senior district judge'; 'chief judge' for 'presiding judge'; 'chief judge' for 'chief justice', except when reference to the Chief Justice of the United States is intended; and 'judge' for 'justice', except when the latter term is used with respect to a justice of the Supreme Court of the United States in his capacity as such or as a circuit justice.

"(b) All laws of the United States in force on September 1, 1948, in which reference is made to the Supreme Court of the District of Columbia or to the District Court of the United States for the District of Columbia are amended by substituting 'United States District Court for the District of Columbia' for such designations.

"(c) All laws of the United States in force on September 1, 1948, in which reference is made to the 'Conference of Senior Circuit Judges', or to the 'Judicial Conference of Senior Circuit Judges' are amended by substituting 'Judicial Conference of the United States' for such designations.

"(d) This section shall not be construed to amend historical references to courts or judicial offices which have no present or future application to such courts or offices."

§ 1251. Original jurisdiction

(a) The Supreme Court shall have original and exclusive jurisdiction of all controversies between two or more States.

(b) The Supreme Court shall have original but not exclusive jurisdiction of:

(1) All actions or proceedings to which ambassadors, other public ministers, consuls, or vice consuls of foreign states are parties;

(2) All controversies between the United States and a State;

(3) All actions or proceedings by a State against the citizens of another State or against aliens.

(June 25, 1948, c. 646, 62 Stat. 927; Sept. 30, 1978, Pub.L. 95–393, § 8(b), 92 Stat. 810.)

HISTORICAL AND STATUTORY NOTES

Effective Dates

1978 Acts. Amendment by Pub.L. 95–393 effective at the end of the 90-day period beginning on Sept. 30, 1978, see section 9 of Pub.L. 95–393, set out as a note under section 254a of Title 22, Foreign Relations and Intercourse.

Statutes Governing Writs of Error to Apply to Appeals

Act Jan. 31, 1928, c. 14, § 2, 45 Stat. 54, amended Apr. 26, 1928, c. 440, 45 Stat. 466; June 25, 1948, c. 646, § 23, 62 Stat. 990, provided that: "All Acts of Congress referring to writs of error shall be construed as amended to the extent necessary to substitute appeal for writ of error." See, also, notes preceding section 1 of this title.

[§ 1252. Repealed. Pub.L. 100–352, § 1, June 27, 1988, 102 Stat. 662]

HISTORICAL AND STATUTORY NOTES

Section, Acts June 25, 1948, c. 646, 62 Stat. 928; Oct. 31, 1951, c. 655, § 47, 65 Stat. 726; July 7, 1958, Pub.L. 85–508, § 12(e), (f), 72 Stat. 348; Mar. 18, 1959, Pub.L. 86–3, § 14(a), 73 Stat. 10, provided for direct appeals to Supreme Court from decisions invalidating Acts of Congress.

Effective Date of Repeal

Repeal of section effective ninety days after June 27, 1988, except that such repeal shall not apply to cases pending in the Supreme Court on such effective date or affect the right to review or the manner of reviewing the judgment or decree of a court which was entered before such effective date, see section 7 of Pub.L. 100–352, set out as a note under section 1254 of this title.

COMMENTARIES

See 28 U.S.C.A. § 1252, for Commentary by David D. Siegel.

§ 1253. Direct appeals from decisions of three-judge courts

Except as otherwise provided by law, any party may appeal to the Supreme Court from an order granting or denying, after notice and hearing, an interlocutory or permanent injunction in any civil action, suit or proceeding required by any Act of Congress to be heard and determined by a district court of three judges.

(June 25, 1948, c. 646, 62 Stat. 928.)

§ 1254. Courts of appeals; certiorari; certified questions

Cases in the courts of appeals may be reviewed by the Supreme Court by the following methods:

(1) By writ of certiorari granted upon the petition of any party to any civil or criminal case, before or after rendition of judgment or decree;

(2) By certification at any time by a court of appeals of any question of law in any civil or criminal case as to which instructions are desired, and upon such certification the Supreme Court may give binding instructions or require the entire record to be sent up for decision of the entire matter in controversy.

(June 25, 1948, c. 646, 62 Stat. 928; June 27, 1988, Pub.L. 100–352, § 2(a), (b), 102 Stat. 662.)

HISTORICAL AND STATUTORY NOTES

Effective Dates

1988 Acts. Section 7 of Pub.L. 100–352 provided that: "The amendments made by this Act [amending this section by striking out 'appeal;' in heading and by striking out par. (2) and redesignating former par. (3) as (2), and amending sections 1257, 1258, 2101, 2104, and 2350 of this title, section 437h of Title 2, The Congress, section 136w of Title 7, Agriculture, section 1631e of Title 22, Foreign Relations and Intercourse, section 652 of Title 25, Indians, section 988 of Title 33, Navigation and Navigable Waters, section 1652 of Title 43, Public Lands, and sections 719, 743, and 1105 of Title 45, Railroads, and repealing sections 1252 and 2103 of this title] shall take effect ninety days after the date of the enactment of this Act [June 27, 1988], except that such amendments shall not apply to cases pending in the Supreme Court on the effective date of such amendments or affect the right to review or the manner of reviewing the judgment or decree of a court which was entered before such effective date."

COMMENTARIES

See 28 U.S.C.A. § 1254, for Commentary by David D. Siegel.

[§§ 1255, 1256. Repealed. Pub.L. 97–164, Title I, § 123, Apr. 2, 1982, 96 Stat. 36]

HISTORICAL AND STATUTORY NOTES

Section 1255, Act June 25, 1948, c. 646, 62 Stat. 928, authorized the Supreme Court to review cases in the Court of Claims by writ of certiorari and by certification of questions of law.

Section 1256, Act June 25, 1948, c. 646, 62 Stat. 928, authorized the Supreme Court to review cases in the Court of Customs and Patent Appeals by writ of certiorari.

Effective Date of Repeal

Repeal effective Oct. 1, 1982, see section 402 of Pub.L. 97–164, set out as Effective Dates of 1982 Amendments note under section 171 of this title.

§ 1257. State courts; certiorari

(a) Final judgments or decrees rendered by the highest court of a State in which a decision could be had, may be reviewed by the Supreme Court by writ of certiorari where the validity of a treaty or statute of the United States is drawn in question or where the validity of a statute of any State is drawn in question on the ground of its being repugnant to the Constitution, treaties, or laws of the United States, or where any title, right, privilege, or immunity is specially set up or claimed under the Constitution or the treaties or statutes of, or any commission held or authority exercised under, the United States.

(b) For the purposes of this section, the term "highest court of a State" includes the District of Columbia Court of Appeals.

(June 25, 1948, c. 646, 62 Stat. 929; July 29, 1970, Pub.L. 91–358, Title I, § 172(a)(1), 84 Stat. 590; June 27, 1988, Pub.L. 100–352, § 3, 102 Stat. 662.)

HISTORICAL AND STATUTORY NOTES

Effective Dates

1988 Acts. Amendment by section 3 of Pub.L. 100–352 effective ninety days after June 27, 1988, except that such amendment not to apply to cases pending in the Supreme Court on such effective date or affect the right to review or the manner of reviewing the judgment or decree of a court which was entered before such effective date, see section 7 of Pub.L. 100–352, set out as a note under section 1254 of this title.

1970 Acts. Section 199(a) of Title 1 of Pub.L. 91–358 provided that: "The effective date of this title (and the amendments made by this title) [which enacted sections 1363, 1451, and 2113 of this title, and amended this section and sections 292 and 1869 of this title, section 5102 of Title 5, Government Organization and Employees, and section 260a of Title 42, the Public Health and Welfare] shall be the first day of the seventh calendar month which begins after the date of the enactment of this Act [July 29, 1970]."

COMMENTARIES

See 28 U.S.C.A. § 1257, for Commentary by David D. Siegel.

§ 1258. Supreme Court of Puerto Rico; certiorari

Final judgments or decrees rendered by the Supreme Court of the Commonwealth of Puerto Rico may be reviewed by the Supreme Court by writ of certiorari where the validity of a treaty or statute of the United States is drawn in question or where the validity of a statute of the Commonwealth of Puerto Rico is drawn in question on the ground of its being repugnant to the Constitution, treaties, or laws of the United States, or where any title, right, privilege, or immunity is specially set up or claimed under the Constitution or the treaties or statutes of, or any commission held or authority exercised under, the United States.

(Added Pub.L. 87–189, § 1, Aug. 30, 1961, 75 Stat. 417, and amended, Pub.L. 100–352, § 4, June 27, 1988, 102 Stat. 662.)

HISTORICAL AND STATUTORY NOTES

Effective Dates

1988 Acts. Amendment by section 4 of Pub.L. 100–352 effective ninety days after June 27, 1988, except that such amendment not to apply to cases pending in the Supreme Court on such effective date or affect the right to review or the manner of reviewing the judgment or decree of a court which was entered before such effective date, pursuant to section 7 of Pub.L. 100–352, set out as a note under section 1254 of this title.

COMMENTARIES

See 28 U.S.C.A. § 1258, for Commentary by David D. Siegel.

§ 1259. Court of Appeals for the Armed Forces; certiorari

Decisions of the United States Court of Appeals for the Armed Forces may be reviewed by the Supreme Court by writ of certiorari in the following cases:

(1) Cases reviewed by the Court of Appeals for the Armed Forces under section 867(a)(1) of title 10.

(2) Cases certified to the Court of Appeals for the Armed Forces by the Judge Advocate General under section 867(a)(2) of title 10.

(3) Cases in which the Court of Appeals for the Armed Forces granted a petition for review under section 867(a)(3) of title 10.

(4) Cases, other than those described in paragraphs (1), (2), and (3) of this subsection, in which the Court of Appeals for the Armed Forces granted relief.

(Added Pub.L. 98–209, § 10(a)(1), Dec. 6, 1983, 97 Stat. 1405, and amended Pub.L. 101–189, Div. A, Title XIII, § 1304(b)(3), Nov. 29, 1989, 103 Stat. 1577; Pub.L. 103–337, Div. A, Title IX, § 924(d)(1)(C), (2)(A), Oct. 5, 1994, 108 Stat. 2832.)

HISTORICAL AND STATUTORY NOTES

Effective Dates

1983 Acts. Section effective on the first day of the eighth calendar month beginning after Dec. 6, 1983, see section 12(a)(1) of Pub.L 98–209, set out as a note under section 801 of Title 10, Armed Forces.

CHAPTER 83—COURTS OF APPEALS

Sec.

1291. Final decisions of district courts.
1292. Interlocutory decisions.
[1293. Repealed.]

Sec.
1294. Circuits in which decisions reviewable.
1295. Jurisdiction of the United States Court of Appeals for the Federal Circuit.
1296. Review of certain agency actions.

HISTORICAL AND STATUTORY NOTES

Codifications

The table of sections for chapter 83 was amended by Pub.L. 95–598, Title II, § 236(b), Nov. 6, 1978, 92 Stat. 2667, effective June 28, 1984, pursuant to Pub.L. 95–598, Title IV, § 402(b), Nov. 6, 1978, 92 Stat. 2682, as amended by Pub.L. 98–249, § 1(a), Mar. 31, 1984, 98 Stat. 116; Pub.L. 98–271, § 1(a), Apr. 30, 1984, 98 Stat. 163; Pub.L. 98–299, § 1(a), May 25, 1984, 98 Stat. 214; Pub.L. 98–325, § 1(a), June 20, 1984, 98 Stat. 268, set out as an Effective Dates note preceding section 101 of Title 11, Bankruptcy, by adding:

"1293. Bankruptcy appeals.".

Section 402(b) of Pub.L. 95–598 was amended by section 113 of Pub.L. 98–353, Title I, July 10, 1984, 98 Stat. 343, by substituting "shall not be effective" for "shall take effect on June 28, 1984", thereby eliminating the amendment by section 236(a) of Pub.L. 95–598, effective June 27, 1984, pursuant to section 122(c) of Pub.L. 98–353, set out as an Effective Dates note under section 151 of this title.

Section 121(a) of Pub.L. 98–353 directed that section 402(b) of Pub.L. 95–598 be amended by substituting "the date of enactment of the Bankruptcy Amendments and Federal Judgeship Act of 1984 [i.e. July 10, 1984]" for "June 28, 1984". This amendment was not executed in view of the prior amendment to section 402(b) of Pub.L. 95–598 by section 113 of Pub.L. 98–353.

§ 1291. Final decisions of district courts

The courts of appeals (other than the United States Court of Appeals for the Federal Circuit) shall have jurisdiction of appeals from all final decisions of the district courts of the United States, the United States District Court for the District of the Canal Zone, the District Court of Guam, and the District Court of the Virgin Islands, except where a direct review may be had in the Supreme Court. The jurisdiction of the United States Court of Appeals for the Federal Circuit shall be limited to the jurisdiction described in sections 1292(c) and (d) and 1295 of this title.

(June 25, 1948, c. 646, 62 Stat. 929; Oct. 31, 1951, c. 655, § 48, 65 Stat. 726; July 7, 1958, Pub.L. 85–508, § 12(e), 72 Stat. 348; Apr. 2, 1982, Pub.L. 97–164, Title I, § 124, 96 Stat. 36.)

HISTORICAL AND STATUTORY NOTES

Effective Dates

1982 Acts. Amendment by Pub.L. 97–164 effective Oct. 1, 1982, see section 402 of Pub.L. 97–164, set out as a note under section 171 of this title.

1958 Acts. Amendment of section by Pub.L. 85–508 effective Jan. 3, 1959, upon admission of Alaska into the Union pursuant to Proc. No. 3269, Jan. 3, 1959, 24 F.R. 81, 73 Stat. c16, as required by sections 1 and 8(c) of Pub.L. 85–508, see notes set out under section 81A of this title and preceding section 21 of Title 48, Territories and Insular Possessions.

Termination of United States District Court for the District of the Canal Zone

For termination of the United States District Court for the District of the Canal Zone at end of the "transition period", being the 30–month period beginning Oct. 1, 1979, and ending midnight Mar. 31, 1982, see Paragraph 5 of Article XI of the Panama Canal Treaty of 1977 and sections 3831 and 3841 to 3843 of Title 22, Foreign Relations and Intercourse.

§ 1292. Interlocutory decisions

(a) Except as provided in subsections (c) and (d) of this section, the courts of appeals shall have jurisdiction of appeals from:

(1) Interlocutory orders of the district courts of the United States, the United States District Court for the District of the Canal Zone, the District Court of Guam, and the District Court of the Virgin Islands, or of the judges thereof, granting, continuing, modifying, refusing or dissolving injunctions, or refusing to dissolve or modify injunctions, except where a direct review may be had in the Supreme Court;

(2) Interlocutory orders appointing receivers, or refusing orders to wind up receiverships or to take steps to accomplish the purposes thereof, such as directing sales or other disposals of property;

(3) Interlocutory decrees of such district courts or the judges thereof determining the rights and liabilities of the parties to admiralty cases in which appeals from final decrees are allowed.

(b) When a district judge, in making in a civil action an order not otherwise appealable under this section, shall be of the opinion that such order involves a controlling question of law as to which there is substantial ground for difference of opinion and that an immediate appeal from the order may materially advance the ultimate termination of the litigation, he shall so state in writing in such order. The Court of Appeals which would have jurisdiction of an appeal of such action may thereupon, in its discretion, permit an appeal to be taken from such order, if application is made to it within ten days after the entry of the order: *Provided, however,* That application for an appeal hereunder shall not stay proceedings in the district court unless the district judge or the Court of Appeals or a judge thereof shall so order.

(c) The United States Court of Appeals for the Federal Circuit shall have exclusive jurisdiction—

(1) of an appeal from an interlocutory order or decree described in subsection (a) or (b) of this section in any case over which the court would have jurisdiction of an appeal under section 1295 of this title; and

(2) of an appeal from a judgment in a civil action for patent infringement which would otherwise be appealable to the United States Court of Appeals for the Federal Circuit and is final except for an accounting.

(d)(1) When the chief judge of the Court of International Trade issues an order under the provisions of section 256(b) of this title, or when any judge of the Court of International Trade, in issuing any other interlocutory order, includes in the order a statement that a controlling question of law is involved with respect to which there is a substantial ground for difference of opinion and that an immediate appeal from that order may materially advance the ultimate termination of the litigation, the United States Court of Appeals for the Federal Circuit may, in its discretion, permit an appeal to be taken from such order, if application is made to that Court within ten days after the entry of such order.

(2) When the chief judge of the United States Court of Federal Claims issues an order under section 798(b) of this title, or when any judge of the United States Court of Federal Claims, in issuing an interlocutory order, includes in the order a statement that a controlling question of law is involved with respect to which there is a substantial ground for difference of opinion and that an immediate appeal from that order may materially advance the ultimate termination of the litigation, the United States Court of Appeals for the Federal Circuit may, in its discretion, permit an appeal to be taken from such order, if application is made to that Court within ten days after the entry of such order.

(3) Neither the application for nor the granting of an appeal under this subsection shall stay proceedings in the Court of International Trade or in the Court of Federal Claims, as the case may be, unless a stay is ordered by a judge of the Court of International Trade or of the Court of Federal Claims or by the United States Court of Appeals for the Federal Circuit or a judge of that court.

(4)(A) The United States Court of Appeals for the Federal Circuit shall have exclusive jurisdiction of an appeal from an interlocutory order of a district court of the United States, the District Court of Guam, the District Court of the Virgin Islands, or the District Court for the Northern Mariana Islands, granting or denying, in whole or in part, a motion to transfer an action to the United States Court of Federal Claims under section 1631 of this title.

(B) When a motion to transfer an action to the Court of Federal Claims is filed in a district court, no further proceedings shall be taken in the district court until 60 days after the court has ruled upon the motion. If an appeal is taken from the district court's grant or denial of the motion, proceedings shall be further stayed until the appeal has been decided by the Court of Appeals for the Federal Circuit. The stay of proceedings in the district court shall not bar the granting of preliminary or injunctive relief, where appropriate and where expedition is reasonably necessary. However, during the period in which proceedings are stayed as provided in this subparagraph, no transfer to the Court of Federal Claims pursuant to the motion shall be carried out.

(e) The Supreme Court may prescribe rules, in accordance with section 2072 of this title, to provide for an appeal of an interlocutory decision to the courts of appeals that is not otherwise provided for under subsection (a), (b), (c), or (d).

(June 25, 1948, c. 646, 62 Stat. 929; Oct. 31, 1951, c. 655, § 49, 65 Stat. 726; July 7, 1958, Pub.L. 85–508, § 12(e), 72 Stat. 348; Sept. 2, 1958, Pub.L. 85–919, 72 Stat. 1770; Apr. 2, 1982, Pub.L. 97–164, Title I, § 125, 96 Stat. 36; Nov. 8, 1984, Pub.L. 98–620, Title IV, § 412, 98 Stat. 3362; Nov. 19, 1988, Pub.L. 100–702, Title V, § 501, 102 Stat. 4652; Oct. 29, 1992, Pub.L. 102–572, Title I, § 101, Title IX, §§ 902(b), 906(c), 106 Stat. 4506, 4516, 4518.)

HISTORICAL AND STATUTORY NOTES

Effective Dates

1992 Acts. Amendment by sections 902(b) and 906(c) of Pub.L. 102–572 effective Oct. 29, 1992, see section 911 of Pub.L. 102–572, set out as a note under section 171 of this title.

Amendment by section 906(c) of Pub.L. 102–572 effective Oct. 29, 1992, see section 911 of Pub.L. 102–572, set out as a note under section 171 of Title 28, Judiciary and Judicial Procedure.

Amendment by section 101 of Pub.L. 102–572 effective Jan. 1, 1993, see section 1101(a) of Pub.L. 102–572, set out as a note under section 905 of Title 2, The Congress.

1988 Acts. Section 502 of Title V of Pub.L. 100–702 provided that: "The amendment made by section 501 [enacting subsec. (d)(4) of this section] shall apply to any action commenced in the district court on or after the date of enactment of this title [Nov. 19, 1988]."

1982 Acts. Amendment by Pub.L. 97–164 effective Oct. 1, 1982, see section 402 of Pub.L. 97–164, set out as a note under section 171 of this title.

1958 Acts. Amendment of section by Pub.L. 85–508 effective Jan. 3, 1959, upon admission of Alaska into the Union pursuant to Proc. No. 3269, Jan. 3, 1959, 24 F.R. 81, 73 Stat. c16, as required by Section 1 and 8(c) of Pub.L. 85–508, see notes set out under Section 81A of this title and preceding Section 21 of Title 48, Territories and Insular Possessions.

Change of Name

References to United States Claims Court deemed to refer to United States Court of Federal Claims and references to Claims Court deemed to refer to Court of Federal Claims, see section 902(b) of Pub.L. 102–572, set out as a note under section 171 of Title 28, Judiciary and Judicial Procedure.

Termination of United States District Court for the District of the Canal Zone

For termination of the United States District Court for the District of the Canal Zone at end of the "transition period", being the 30-month period beginning Oct. 1, 1979, and ending midnight Mar. 31, 1982, see Paragraph 5 of Article XI of the Panama Canal Treaty of 1977 and sections 3831 and 3841 to 3843 of Title 22, Foreign Relations and Intercourse.

COMMENTARIES

See 28 U.S.C.A. § 1292, for Commentary by David D. Siegel.

[§ 1293. Repealed. Pub.L. 87–189, § 3, Aug. 30, 1961, 75 Stat. 417]

HISTORICAL AND STATUTORY NOTES

Section, Acts June 25, 1948, c. 646, 62 Stat. 929; Mar. 18, 1959, Pub.L. 86–3, § 14(b), 73 Stat. 10, provided for appeal from supreme court of Puerto Rico to court of appeals for first circuit. See section 1258 of this title.

Codifications

A subsequent section 1293, as added by Pub.L. 95–598, Title II, § 236a, Nov. 6, 1978, 92 Stat. 2667, effective June 28, 1984, pursuant to Pub.L. 95–598, Title IV, § 402(b), Nov. 6, 1978, 92 Stat. 2682, as amended by Pub.L. 98–249, § 1(a), Mar. 31, 1984, 98 Stat. 116; Pub.L. 98–271, § 1(a), Apr. 30, 1984, 98 Stat. 163; Pub.L. 98–299, § 1(a), May 25, 1984, 98 Stat. 214; Pub.L. 98–325, § 1(a), June 20, 1984, 98 Stat. 268, set out as an Effective Dates note preceding section 101 of Title 11, Bankruptcy, read as follows:

§ 1293. Bankruptcy appeals

(a) The courts of appeals shall have jurisdiction of appeals from all final decisions of panels designated under section 160(a) of this title.

(b) Notwithstanding section 1482 of this title, a court of appeals shall have jurisdiction of an appeal from a final judgment, order, or decree of an appellate panel created under section 160 or a District court of the United States or from a final judgment, order, or decree of a bankruptcy court of the United States if the parties to such appeal agree to a direct appeal to the court of appeals.

Section 402(b) of Pub.L. 95–598 was amended by section 113 of Pub.L. 98–353, Title I, July 10, 1984, 98 Stat. 343, by substituting "shall not be effective" for "shall take effect on June 28, 1984", thereby eliminating the addition of subsequent section 1293 by section 236(a) of Pub.L. 95–598, effective June 27, 1984, pursuant to section 122(c) of Pub.L. 98–353, set out as an Effective Dates note under section 151 of this title.

Section 121(a) of Pub.L. 98–353 directed that section 402(b) of Pub.L. 95–598 be amended by substituting "the date of enactment of the Bankruptcy Amendments and Federal Judgeship Act of 1984 [i.e. July 10, 1984]" for "June 28, 1984". This amendment was not executed in view of the prior amendment to section 402(b) of Pub.L. 95–598 by section 113 of Pub.L. 98–353.

§ 1294. Circuits in which decisions reviewable

Except as provided in sections 1292(c), 1292(d), and 1295 of this title, appeals from reviewable decisions of the district and territorial courts shall be taken to the courts of appeals as follows:

(1) From a district court of the United States to the court of appeals for the circuit embracing the district;

(2) From the United States District Court for the District of the Canal Zone, to the Court of Appeals for the Fifth Circuit;

(3) From the District Court of the Virgin Islands, to the Court of Appeals for the Third Circuit;

(4) From the District Court of Guam, to the Court of Appeals for the Ninth Circuit.

(June 25, 1948, c. 646, 62 Stat. 930; Oct. 31, 1951, c. 655, § 50(a), 65 Stat. 727; July 7, 1958, Pub.L. 85–508, § 12(g), 72 Stat. 348; Mar. 18, 1959, Pub.L. 86–3, § 14(c), 73 Stat. 10; Aug. 30, 1961, Pub.L. 87–189, § 5, 75 Stat. 417; Nov. 6, 1978, Pub.L. 95–598, Title II, § 237, 92 Stat. 2667; Apr. 2, 1982, Pub.L. 97–164, Title I, § 126, 96 Stat. 37.)

HISTORICAL AND STATUTORY NOTES

Codifications

This section was amended by Pub.L. 95–598, Title II, § 237, Nov. 6, 1978, 92 Stat. 2667, effective June 28, 1984, pursuant to Pub.L. 95–598, Title IV, § 402(b), Nov. 6, 1978, 92 Stat. 2682, as amended by Pub.L. 98–249, § 1(a), Mar. 31, 1984, 98 Stat. 116; Pub.L. 98–271, § 1(a), Apr. 30, 1984, 98 Stat. 163; Pub.L. 98–299, § 1(a), May 25, 1984, 98 Stat. 214; Pub.L. 98–325, § 1(a), June 20, 1984, 98 Stat. 268, set out as an Effective Dates note preceding section 101 of Title II, Bankruptcy, to read as follows:

§ 1294. Circuits in which decisions reviewable

Except as provided in sections 1292(c), 1292(d), and 1295 of this title, appeals from reviewable decisions of the district, bankruptcy, and territorial courts shall be taken to the courts of appeals as follows:

(1) From a district court of the United States to the court of appeals for the circuit embracing the district;

(2) From the United States District Court for the District of the Canal Zone, to the Court of Appeals for the Fifth Circuit;

(3) From the District Court of the Virgin Islands, to the Court of Appeals for the Third Circuit;

(4) From the District Court of Guam, to the Court of Appeals for the Ninth Circuit;

(5) From a panel designated under section 160(a) of this title to the court of appeals for the circuit in which the panel was so designated;

(6) From a bankruptcy court of the United States to the court of appeals for the circuit embracing the district in which the bankruptcy court is located.

Section 402(b) of Pub.L. 95–598 was amended by section 113 of Pub.L. 98–353, Title I, July 10, 1984, 98 Stat. 343, by substituting "shall not be effective" for "shall take effect on June 28, 1984", thereby eliminating the amendment by section 237 of Pub.L. 95–598, effective June 27, 1984, pursuant to section 122(c) of Pub.L. 98–353, set out as an Effective Dates note under section 151 of this title.

Section 121(a) of Pub.L. 98–353 directed that section 402(b) of Pub.L. 95–598 be amended by substituting "the date of enactment of the Bankruptcy Amendments and Federal Judgeship Act of 1984 [i.e. July 10, 1984]" for "June 28, 1984". This amendment was not executed in view of the prior amendment to section 402(b) of Pub.L. 95–598 by section 113 of Pub.L. 98–353.

Effective Dates

1982 Acts. Amendment by Pub.L. 97–164 effective Oct. 1, 1982, see section 402 of Pub.L. 97–164, set out as a note under section 171 of this title.

1959 Acts. Amendment of section by Pub.L. 86–3 effective upon the admission of the State of Hawaii into the Union, see note set out under section 91 of this title. Admission of Hawaii into the Union was accomplished Aug. 21, 1959 upon issuance of Proc. No. 3309, Aug. 21, 1959, 25 F.R. 6868, 73 Stat. c74, as required by sections 1 and 7(c) of Pub.L. 86–3, Mar. 18, 1959, 73 Stat. 4, set out as notes preceding section 491 of Title 48, Territories and Insular Possessions.

1958 Acts. Amendment of section by Pub.L. 85–508 effective Jan. 3, 1959, upon admission of Alaska into the Union pursuant to Proc. No. 3269, Jan. 3, 1959, 24 F.R. 81, 73 Stat. c16, as required by sections 1 and 8(c) of Pub.L. 85–508, see notes set out under section 81A of this title and preceding section 21 of Title 48, Territories and Insular Possessions.

Termination of United States District Court for the District of the Canal Zone

For termination of the United States District Court for the District of the Canal Zone at end of the "transition period", being the 30–month period beginning Oct. 1, 1979, and ending midnight Mar. 31, 1982, see Paragraph 5 of Article XI of the Panama Canal Treaty of 1977 and sections 3831 and 3841 to 3843 of Title 22, Foreign Relations and Intercourse.

§ 1295. Jurisdiction of the United States Court of Appeals for the Federal Circuit

(a) The United States Court of Appeals for the Federal Circuit shall have exclusive jurisdiction—

(1) of an appeal from a final decision of a district court of the United States, the United States District Court for the District of the Canal Zone, the District Court of Guam, the District Court of the Virgin Islands, or the District Court for the Northern Mariana Islands, if the jurisdiction of that court was based, in whole or in part, on section 1338 of this title, except that a case involving a claim arising under any Act of Congress relating to copyrights, exclusive rights in mask works, or trademarks and no other claims under section 1338(a) shall be governed by sections 1291, 1292, and 1294 of this title;

(2) of an appeal from a final decision of a district court of the United States, the United States District Court for the District of the Canal Zone, the District Court of Guam, the District Court of the Virgin Islands, or the District Court for the Northern Mariana Islands, if the jurisdiction of that court was based, in whole or in part, on section 1346 of this title, except that jurisdiction of an appeal in a case brought in a district court under section 1346(a)(1), 1346(b), 1346(e), or 1346(f) of this title or under section 1346(a)(2) when the claim is founded upon an Act of Congress or a regulation of an executive department providing for internal revenue shall be governed by sections 1291, 1292, and 1294 of this title;

(3) of an appeal from a final decision of the United States Court of Federal Claims;

(4) of an appeal from a decision of—

(A) the Board of Patent Appeals and Interferences of the Patent and Trademark Office with respect to patent applications and interferences, at the instance of an applicant for a patent or any party to a patent interference, and any such appeal shall waive the right of such applicant or party to proceed under section 145 or 146 of title 35;

(B) the Commissioner of Patents and Trademarks or the Trademark Trial and Appeal Board with respect to applications for registration of marks and other proceedings as provided in section 21 of the Trademark Act of 1946 (15 U.S.C. 1071); or

(C) a district court to which a case was directed pursuant to section 145 or 146 of title 35;

(5) of an appeal from a final decision of the United States Court of International Trade;

(6) to review the final determinations of the United States International Trade Commission relating to unfair practices in import trade, made under section 337 of the Tariff Act of 1930 (19 U.S.C. 1337);

(7) to review, by appeal on questions of law only, findings of the Secretary of Commerce under U.S. note 6 to subchapter X of chapter 98 of the Harmonized Tariff Schedule of the United States (relating to importation of instruments or apparatus);

(8) of an appeal under section 71 of the Plant Variety Protection Act (7 U.S.C. 2461);

(9) of an appeal from a final order or final decision of the Merit Systems Protection Board, pursuant to sections 7703(b)(1) and 7703(d) of title 5;

(10) of an appeal from a final decision of an agency board of contract appeals pursuant to section 8(g)(1) of the Contract Disputes Act of 1978 (41 U.S.C. 607(g)(1));

(11) of an appeal under section 211 of the Economic Stabilization Act of 1970;

(12) of an appeal under section 5 of the Emergency Petroleum Allocation Act of 1973;

(13) of an appeal under section 506(c) of the Natural Gas Policy Act of 1978; and

(14) of an appeal under section 523 of the Energy Policy and Conservation Act.

(b) The head of any executive department or agency may, with the approval of the Attorney General, refer to the Court of Appeals for the Federal Circuit for judicial review any final decision rendered by a board of contract appeals pursuant to the terms of any contract with the United States awarded by that department or agency which the head of such department or agency has concluded is not entitled to finality pursuant to the review standards specified in section 10(b) of the Contract Disputes Act of 1978 (41 U.S.C. 609(b)). The head of each executive department or agency shall make any referral under this section within one hundred and twenty days after the receipt of a copy of the final appeal decision.

(c) The Court of Appeals for the Federal Circuit shall review the matter referred in accordance with the standards specified in section 10(b) of the Contract Disputes Act of 1978. The court shall proceed with judicial review on the administrative record made before the board of contract appeals on matters so referred as in other cases pending in such court, shall determine the issue of finality of the appeal decision, and shall, if appropriate, render judgment thereon, or remand the matter to any administrative or executive body or official with such direction as it may deem proper and just.

(Added Pub.L. 97–164, Title I, § 127(a), Apr. 2, 1982, 96 Stat. 37, and amended Pub.L. 98–622, Title II, § 205(a), Nov. 8, 1984, 98 Stat. 3388; Pub.L. 100–418, Title I, § 1214(a)(3), Aug. 23, 1988, 102 Stat. 1156; Pub.L. 100–702, Title X, § 1020(a)(3), Nov. 19, 1988, 102 Stat. 4671; Pub.L. 102–572, Title I, § 102(c), Title IX, § 902(b)(1), Oct. 29, 1992, 106 Stat. 4507, 4516.)

HISTORICAL AND STATUTORY NOTES

References in Text

The Harmonized Tariff Schedule of the United States, referred to in subsec. (a)(7), is not carried in the Code. See Publication of Harmonized Tariff Schedule note set out under section 1202 of Title 19, Customs Duties.

Section 211 of the Economic Stabilization Act of 1970, referred to in subsec. (a)(11), is section 211 of Pub.L. 91–379, Title II, Aug. 15, 1970, as added Pub.L. 92–210, § 2, Dec. 22, 1971, 85 Stat. 743, as amended, which is set out as a note under TECA Rule 3, this title, and in codified form under section 1904 of Title 12, Banks and Banking.

Section 5 of the Emergency Petroleum Allocation Act of 1973, referred to in subsec. (a)(12), is section 5 of Pub.L. 93–159, Nov. 27, 1973, 87 Stat. 633, as amended, which was classified to section 754 of Title 15, Commerce and Trade, prior to the omission of such section pursuant to section 760g of Title 15.

Section 506(c) of the Natural Gas Policy Act of 1978, referred to in subsec. (a)(13), is section 506(c) of Pub.L. 95–621, Title V, Nov. 9, 1978, 92 Stat. 3404, which is classified to section 3416(c) of Title 15, Commerce and Trade.

Section 523 of the Energy Policy and Conservation Act, referred to in subsec. (a)(14), is section 523 of Pub.L. 94–163, Title V, Dec. 22, 1975, 89 Stat. 962, which is classified to section 6393 of Title 42, The Public Health and Welfare.

Effective Dates

1992 Acts. Amendment by section 902(b)(1) of Pub.L. 102–572 effective Oct. 29, 1992, see section 911 of Pub.L. 102–572, set out as a note under section 171 of this title.

Amendment by Pub.L. 102–572 effective Jan. 1, 1993, see section 1101(a) of Pub.L. 102–572, set out as a note under section 905 of Title 2, The Congress.

1988 Acts. Amendment by Pub.L. 100–418 effective Jan. 1, 1989, and applicable with respect to articles entered on or after such date, see section 1217(b)(1) of Pub.L. 100–418, set out as an Effective Dates note under section 3001 of Title 19, Customs Duties.

1984 Acts. Amendment by Pub.L. 98–622 applicable to all United States patents granted before, on, or after Nov. 8, 1984, and to all applications for United States patents pending on or filed after that date, except as otherwise provided, see section 106 of Pub.L. 98–622, set out as a note under section 103 of Title 35, Patents.

Amendment by Pub.L. 98–622, effective three months after Nov. 8, 1984, see section 207 of Pub.L. 98–622, set out as a note under section 7 of Title 35, Patents.

1982 Acts. Section effective Oct. 1, 1982, see section 402 of Pub.L. 97–164, set out as a note under section 171 of this title.

Abolition of Temporary Emergency Court of Appeals

Section 102(d), (e) of Pub.L. 102–572 provided that:

"(d) Abolition of Court.—The Temporary Emergency Court of Appeals created by section 211(b) of the Economic Stabilization Act of 1970 [set out as a note under TECA Rule 3, this title] is abolished, effective 6 months after the date of the enactment of this Act [Oct. 29, 1992].

"(e) Pending cases.—(1) Any appeal which, before the effective date of abolition described in subsection (d), is pending in the Temporary Emergency Court of Appeals but has not been submitted to a panel of such court as of that date shall be assigned to the United States Court of Appeals for the Federal Circuit as though the appeal had originally been filed in that court.

"(2) Any case which, before the effective date of abolition described in subsection (d), has been submitted to a panel of the Temporary Emergency Court of Appeals and as to which the mandate has not been issued as of that date shall remain with that panel for all purposes and, notwithstanding the provisions of sections 291 and 292 of title 28, United States Code [sections 291 and 292 of this title], that panel shall be assigned to the United States Court of Appeals for the Federal Circuit for the purpose of deciding such case."

Termination of United States District Court for the District of the Canal Zone

For termination of the United States District Court for the District of the Canal Zone at end of the "transition period", being the 30–month period beginning Oct. 1, 1979, and ending midnight Mar. 31, 1982, see Paragraph 5 of Article XI of the Panama Canal Treaty of 1977 and sections 3831 and 3841 to 3843 of Title 22, Foreign Relations and Intercourse.

Transfer of Cases and Petitions Pending in Court of Claims and in Court of Customs and Patent Appeals on October 1, 1982

For provisions directing that any case pending before the Court of Claims on Oct. 1, 1982, in which a report on the merits has been filed by a commissioner, or in which there is pending a request for review, and upon which the court has not acted, and any matter pending before the United States Court of Customs and Patent Appeals on Oct. 1, 1982, be transferred to the United States Court of Appeals for the Federal Circuit, and that any petition for rehearing, reconsideration, alteration, modification, or other change in any decision of the United States Court of Claims or the United States Court of Customs and Patent Appeals rendered prior to Oct. 1, 1982, that has not been determined by either of those courts on that date, or that is filed after that date, be determined by the United States Court of Appeals for the Federal Circuit, see section 403(a)–(c) of Pub.L. 97–164, set out as a note under section 171 of this title.

§ 1296. Review of certain agency actions

(a) Jurisdiction.—Subject to the provisions of chapter 179, the United States Court of Appeals for the Federal Circuit shall have jurisdiction over a petition for review of a final decision under chapter 5 of title 3 of—

(1) an appropriate agency (as determined under section 454 of title 3);

(2) the Federal Labor Relations Authority made under part D of subchapter II of chapter 5 of title 3, notwithstanding section 7123 of title 5; or

(3) the Secretary of Labor or the Occupational Safety and Health Review Commission, made under part C of subchapter II of chapter 5 of title 3.

(b) Filing of petition.—Any petition for review under this section must be filed within 30 days after the date the petitioner receives notice of the final decision.

(Added Pub.L. 104–331, § 3(a)(1), Oct. 26, 1996, 110 Stat. 4069.)

HISTORICAL AND STATUTORY NOTES

Effective Dates

1996 Acts. Section 3(d) of Pub.L. 104–331 provided that: "The amendments made by this section [enacting this section, sections 1413, and 3901 to 3908 of this title, and amending sections 1346 and 2402 of this title] shall take effect on October 1, 1997."

Prior Provisions

A prior section 1296, Pub.L. 97–164, Title I, § 127(a), Apr. 2, 1982, 96 Stat. 39, relating to precedence of cases in the United States Court of Appeals for the Federal Circuit, was repealed by Pub.L. 98–620, Title IV, § 402(29)(C), Nov. 8, 1984, 98 Stat. 3359.

CHAPTER 85—DISTRICT COURTS; JURISDICTION

Sec.

1330. Actions against foreign states.
1331. Federal question.
1332. Diversity of citizenship; amount in controversy; costs.
1333. Admiralty, maritime and prize cases.
1334. Bankruptcy cases and proceedings.
1335. Interpleader.
1336. Surface Transportation Board's orders.
1337. Commerce and antitrust regulations; amount in controversy, costs.
1338. Patents, plant variety protection, copyrights, mask works, designs, trade-marks, and unfair competition.
1339. Postal matters.
1340. Internal revenue; customs duties.
1341. Taxes by States.
1342. Rate orders of State agencies.
1343. Civil rights and elective franchise.
1344. Election disputes.
1345. United States as plaintiff.
1346. United States as defendant.
1347. Partition action where United States is joint tenant.
1348. Banking association as party.
1349. Corporation organized under federal law as party.
1350. Alien's action for tort.
1351. Consuls, vice consuls, and members of a diplomatic mission as defendant.
1352. Bonds executed under federal law.
1353. Indian allotments.
1354. Land grants from different states.
1355. Fine, penalty or forfeiture.
1356. Seizures not within admiralty and maritime jurisdiction.
1357. Injuries under Federal laws.
1358. Eminent domain.
1359. Parties collusively joined or made.
1360. State civil jurisdiction in actions to which Indians are parties.
1361. Action to compel an officer of the United States to perform his duty.
1362. Indian tribes.
1363. Jurors' employment rights.
1364. Direct actions against insurers of members of diplomatic missions and their families.
1365. Senate actions.
1366. Construction of references to laws of the United States or Acts of Congress.
1367. Supplemental jurisdiction.
1368. Counterclaims in unfair practices in international trade.

HISTORICAL AND STATUTORY NOTES

Codifications

The table of sections for chapter 85 was amended by Pub.L. 95–598, Title II, § 238(b), Nov. 6, 1978, 92 Stat. 2668, effective June 28, 1984, pursuant to Pub.L. 95–598, Title IV, § 402(b), Nov. 6, 1978, 92 Stat. 2682, as amended by Pub.L.

98-249, § 1(a), Mar. 31, 1984, 98 Stat. 116; Pub.L. 98-271, § 1(a), Apr. 30, 1984, 98 Stat. 163; Pub.L. 98-299, § 1(a), May 25, 1984, 98 Stat. 214; Pub.L. 98-325, § 1(a), June 20, 1984, 98 Stat. 268, by substituting "1334. Bankruptcy appeals." for "1334. Bankruptcy matters and proceedings.".

Section 402(b) of Pub.L. 95-598 was amended by section 113 of Pub.L. 98-353, Title I, July 10, 1984, 98 Stat. 343, by substituting "shall not be effective" for "shall take effect on June 28, 1984", thereby eliminating the amendment by section 238(b) of Pub.L. 95-598, effective June 27, 1984, pursuant to section 122(c) of Pub.L. 98-353, set out as an Effective Date note under section 151 of this title.

Section 121(a) of Pub.L. 98-353 directed that section 402(b) of Pub.L. 95-598 be amended by substituting "the date of enactment of the Bankruptcy Amendments and Federal Judgeship Act of 1984 [i.e. July 10, 1984]" for "June 28, 1984". This amendment was not executed in view of the prior amendment to section 402(b) of Pub.L. 95-598 by section 113 of Pub.L. 98-353.

§ 1330. Actions against foreign states

(a) The district courts shall have original jurisdiction without regard to amount in controversy of any nonjury civil action against a foreign state as defined in section 1603(a) of this title as to any claim for relief in personam with respect to which the foreign state is not entitled to immunity either under sections 1605-1607 of this title or under any applicable international agreement.

(b) Personal jurisdiction over a foreign state shall exist as to every claim for relief over which the district courts have jurisdiction under subsection (a) where service has been made under section 1608 of this title.

(c) For purposes of subsection (b), an appearance by a foreign state does not confer personal jurisdiction with respect to any claim for relief not arising out of any transaction or occurrence enumerated in sections 1605-1607 of this title.

(Added Pub.L. 94-583, § 2(a), Oct. 21, 1976, 90 Stat. 2891.)

HISTORICAL AND STATUTORY NOTES

Effective Dates

1976 Acts. Section effective 90 days after Oct. 21, 1976, see section 8 of Pub.L. 94-583, set out as a note under section 1602 of this title.

§ 1331. Federal question

The district courts shall have original jurisdiction of all civil actions arising under the Constitution, laws, or treaties of the United States.

(June 25, 1948, c. 646, 62 Stat. 930; July 25, 1958, Pub.L. 85-554, § 1, 72 Stat. 415; Oct. 21, 1976, Pub.L. 94-574, § 2, 90 Stat. 2721; Dec. 1, 1980, Pub.L. 96-486, § 2(a), 94 Stat. 2369.)

HISTORICAL AND STATUTORY NOTES

Effective Dates

1980 Acts. Section 4 of Pub.L. 96-486 provided: "This Act [amending this section and section 2072 of Title 15, Commerce and Trade, and enacting provisions set out as a note under section 1 of this title] shall apply to any civil action pending on the date of enactment of this Act [Dec. 1, 1980]."

1958 Acts. Section 3 of Pub.L. 85-554 provided that: "This Act [amending this section and sections 1332 and 1445 of this title] shall apply only in the case of actions commenced after the date of the enactment of this Act [July 25, 1958]."

§ 1332. Diversity of citizenship; amount in controversy; costs

(a) The district courts shall have original jurisdiction of all civil actions where the matter in controversy exceeds the sum or value of $75,000, exclusive of interest and costs, and is between—

(1) citizens of different States;

(2) citizens of a State and citizens or subjects of a foreign state;

(3) citizens of different States and in which citizens or subjects of a foreign state are additional parties; and

(4) a foreign state, defined in section 1603(a) of this title, as plaintiff and citizens of a State or of different States.

For the purposes of this section, section 1335, and section 1441, an alien admitted to the United States for permanent residence shall be deemed a citizen of the State in which such alien is domiciled.

(b) Except when express provision therefor is otherwise made in a statute of the United States, where the plaintiff who files the case originally in the Federal courts is finally adjudged to be entitled to recover less than the sum or value of $75,000, computed without regard to any setoff or counterclaim to which the defendant may be adjudged to be entitled, and exclusive of interest and costs, the district court may deny costs to the plaintiff and, in addition, may impose costs on the plaintiff.

(c) For the purposes of this section and section 1441 of this title—

(1) a corporation shall be deemed to be a citizen of any State by which it has been incorporated and of the State where it has its principal place of business, except that in any direct action against the insurer of a policy or contract of liability insurance, whether incorporated or unincorporated, to which action the insured is not joined as a party-defendant, such insurer shall be deemed a citizen of the State of which the insured is a citizen, as well as of any State by which the insurer has been incorporated and of the State where it has its principal place of business; and

(2) the legal representative of the estate of a decedent shall be deemed to be a citizen only of the same State as the decedent, and the legal representative of an infant or incompetent shall be deemed to be a citizen only of the same State as the infant or incompetent.

(d) The word "States", as used in this section, includes the Territories, the District of Columbia, and the Commonwealth of Puerto Rico.

(June 25, 1948, c. 646, 62 Stat. 930; July 26, 1956, c. 740, 70 Stat. 658; July 25, 1958, Pub.L. 85–554, § 2, 72 Stat. 415; Aug. 14, 1964, Pub.L. 88–439, § 1, 78 Stat. 445; Oct. 21, 1976, Pub.L. 94–583, § 3, 90 Stat. 2891; Nov. 19, 1988, Pub.L. 100–702, Title II, §§ 201(a), 202(a), 203(a), 102 Stat. 4646; Oct. 19, 1996, Pub.L. 104–317, Title II, § 205(a), 110 Stat. 3850.)

HISTORICAL AND STATUTORY NOTES

Effective Dates

1996 Acts. Section 205(b) of Pub.L. 104–317 provided that: "The amendment made by this section [amending this section] shall take effect 90 days after the date of enactment of this Act [Oct. 19, 1996]."

1988 Acts. Section 201(b) of Title II of Pub.L. 100–702 provided that: "The amendments made by this section [amending amount in controversy in subsecs. (a) and (b) of this section] shall apply to any civil action commenced on or after the 180th day after the date of enactment of this title [Nov. 19, 1988]."

Section 202(b) of Title II of Pub.L. 100–702 provided that: "The amendment made by this section [amending subsec. (c) of this section] shall apply to any civil action commenced in or removed to a United States district court on or after the 180th day after the date of enactment of this title [Nov. 19, 1988]."

Section 203(b) of Title II of Pub.L. 100–702 provided that: "The amendment made by this section [amending subsec. (a) of this section by enacting citizenship of permanent resident alien provision] shall apply to claims in civil actions commenced in or removed to the United States district courts on or after the 180th day after the date of enactment of this title [Nov. 19, 1988]."

1976 Acts. Amendment by Pub.L. 94–583 effective 90 days after Oct. 21, 1976, see section 8 of Pub.L. 94–583, set out as a note under section 1602 of this title.

1964 Acts. Section 2 of Pub.L. 88–439 provided that: "The amendment made by this Act to section 1332(c), title 28, United States Code [subsec. (c) of this section], applies only to causes of action arising after the date of enactment of this Act [Aug. 14, 1964]."

1958 Acts. Amendment of section by Pub.L. 85–554 applicable only in the case of actions commenced after July 25, 1958, see section 3 of Pub.L. 85–554, set out as a note under section 1331 of this title.

COMMENTARIES

See 28 U.S.C.A. § 1332, for Commentary by David D. Siegel.

§ 1333. Admiralty, maritime and prize cases

The district courts shall have original jurisdiction, exclusive of the courts of the States, of:

(1) Any civil case of admiralty or maritime jurisdiction, saving to suitors in all cases all other remedies to which they are otherwise entitled.

(2) Any prize brought into the United States and all proceedings for the condemnation of property taken as prize.

(June 25, 1948, c. 646, 62 Stat. 931; May 24, 1949, c. 139, § 79, 63 Stat. 101.)

§ 1334. Bankruptcy cases and proceedings

(a) Except as provided in subsection (b) of this section, the district court shall have original and exclusive jurisdiction of all cases under title 11.

(b) Notwithstanding any Act of Congress that confers exclusive jurisdiction on a court or courts other than the district courts, the district courts shall have original but not exclusive jurisdiction of all civil proceedings arising under title 11, or arising in or related to cases under title 11.

(c)(1) Nothing in this section prevents a district court in the interest of justice, or in the interest of comity with State courts or respect for State law, from abstaining from hearing a particular proceeding arising under title 11 or arising in or related to a case under title 11.

(2) Upon timely motion of a party in a proceeding based upon a State law claim or State law cause of action, related to a case under title 11 but not arising under title 11 or arising in a case under title 11, with respect to which an action could not have been commenced in a court of the United States absent jurisdiction under this section, the district court shall abstain from hearing such proceeding if an action is commenced, and can be timely adjudicated, in a State forum of appropriate jurisdiction.

(d) Any decision to abstain or not to abstain made under this subsection (other than a decision not to abstain in a proceeding described in subsection (c)(2)) is not reviewable by appeal or otherwise by the court of appeals under section 158(d), 1291, or 1292 of this title or by the Supreme Court of the United States under section 1254 of this title. This subsection shall not be construed to limit the applicability of the stay provided for by section 362 of title 11, United States Code, as such section applies to an action affecting the property of the estate in bankruptcy.

(e) The district court in which a case under title 11 is commenced or is pending shall have exclusive jurisdiction of all of the property, wherever located, of the debtor as of the commencement of such case, and of property of the estate.

(June 25, 1948, c. 646, 62 Stat. 931; Nov. 6, 1978, Pub.L. 95–598, Title II, § 238(a), 92 Stat. 2667; July 10, 1984, Pub.L. 98–353, Title I, § 101(a), 98 Stat. 333; Oct. 27, 1986, Pub.L. 99–554, Title I, § 144(e), 100 Stat. 3096; Dec. 1, 1990, Pub.L. 101–650, Title III, § 309(b), 104 Stat. 5113; Oct. 22, 1994, Pub.L. 103–394, Title I, § 104(b), 108 Stat. 4109.)

HISTORICAL AND STATUTORY NOTES

Codifications

This section was amended by Pub.L. 95–598, Title II, § 238(a), Nov. 6, 1978, 92 Stat. 2668, effective June 28, 1984, pursuant to Pub.L. 95–598, Title IV, § 402(b), Nov. 6, 1978, 92 Stat. 2682, as amended by Pub.L. 98–249, § 1(a), Mar. 31, 1984, 98 Stat. 116; Pub.L. 98–271, § 1(a), Apr. 30, 1984, 98 Stat. 163; Pub.L. 98–299, § 1(a), May 25, 1984, 98 Stat. 214; Pub.L. 98–325, § 1(a), June 20, 1984, 98 Stat. 268, set out as an Effective Dates note preceding section 101 of Title 11, Bankruptcy, to read as follows:

§ 1334. Bankruptcy appeals

(a) The district courts for districts for which panels have not been ordered appointed under section 160 of this title shall have jurisdiction of appeals from all final judgments, orders, and decrees of bankruptcy courts.

(b) The district courts for such districts shall have jurisdiction of appeals from interlocutory orders and decrees of bankruptcy courts, but only by leave of the district court to which the appeal is taken.

(c) A district court may not refer an appeal under that section to a magistrate or to a special master.

Section 402(b) of Pub.L. 95–598 was amended by section 113 of Pub.L. 98–353 by substituting "shall not be effective" for "shall take effect on June 28, 1984", thereby eliminating the amendment by section 238(a) of Pub.L. 95–598, effective June 27, 1984, pursuant to section 122(c) of Pub.L. 98–353, set out as an Effective Dates note under section 151 of this title.

Section 121(a) of Pub.L. 98–353 directed that section 402(b) of Pub.L. 95–598 be amended by substituting "the date of enactment of the Bankruptcy Amendments and Federal Judgeship Act of 1984 [i.e. July 10, 1984]" for "June 28, 1984". This amendment was not executed in view of the prior amendment to section 402(b) of Pub.L. 95–598 by section 113 of Pub.L. 98–353.

Effective Dates

1994 Acts. Amendment by Pub.L. 103–394 effective on Oct. 22, 1994, and not to apply with respect to cases commenced under Title 11 of the United States Code before Oct. 22, 1994, see section 702 of Pub.L. 103–394, set out as a note under section 101 of Title 11, Bankruptcy.

1986 Acts. Amendment by Pub.L. 99–554 effective 30 days after Oct. 27, 1986, except as otherwise provided for, see section 302(a) of Pub.L. 99–554, as amended, set out as a note under section 581 of this title.

1984 Acts. Amendment by Pub.L. 98–353, except for subsec. (c)(2), effective July 10, 1984, see section 122(a) of Pub.L. 98–353, set out as a note under section 151 of this title.

Subsec. (c)(2) not applicable with respect to cases under Title 11, Bankruptcy, that are pending on July 10, 1984, or to proceedings arising in or related to such cases, see section 122(b) of Pub.L. 98–353, set out as a note under section 151 of this title.

Separability of Provisions

If any provision of or amendment made by Pub.L. 103–394 or the application of such provision or amendment to any person or circumstance is held to be unconstitutional, the remaining provisions of and amendments made by Pub.L. 103–394 and the application of such provisions and amendments to any person or circumstance shall not be affected thereby, see section 701 of Pub.L. 103–394, set out as a note under section 101 of Title 11, Bankruptcy.

Jurisdiction Over and Transfer of Bankruptcy Cases and Proceedings

Section 115 of Pub.L. 98–353 provided that:

"**(a)** On the date of the enactment of this Act [July 10, 1984] the appropriate district court of the United States shall have jurisdiction of—

"**(1)** cases, and matters and proceedings in cases, under the Bankruptcy Act [former Title 11, Bankruptcy] that are pending immediately before such date in the bankruptcy courts continued by section 404(a) of the Act of November 6, 1978 (Public Law 95–598; 92 Stat. 2687) [Pub.L. 95–598, Title IV, § 404(a), Nov. 6, 1978, 92 Stat. 2683, formerly set out as a note preceding section 151 of this title], and

"**(2)** cases under title 11 of the United States Code [Title 11, Bankruptcy], and proceedings arising under title 11 of the United States Code or arising in or related to cases under title 11 of the United States Code, that are pending immediately before such date in the bankruptcy courts continued by section 404(a) of the Act of November 6, 1978 (Public Law 95–598; 92 Stat. 2687).

"**(b)** On the date of the enactment of this Act [July 10, 1984], there shall be transferred to the appropriate district court of the United States appeals from final judgments, orders, and decrees of the bankruptcy courts pending immediately before such date in the bankruptcy appellate panels appointed under section 405(c) of the Act of November 6, 1978 (Public Law 95–598; 92 Stat. 2685) [formerly set out as a note preceding section 1471 of this title]."

§ 1335. Interpleader

(a) The district courts shall have original jurisdiction of any civil action of interpleader or in the nature of interpleader filed by any person, firm, or corporation, association, or society having in his or its custody or possession money or property of the value of $500 or more, or having issued a note, bond, certificate, policy of insurance, or other instrument of value or amount of $500 or more, or providing for the delivery or payment or the loan of money or property of such amount or value, or being under any obligation written or unwritten to the amount of $500 or more, if

(1) Two or more adverse claimants, of diverse citizenship as defined in section 1332 of this title, are claiming or may claim to be entitled to such money or property, or to any one or more of the benefits arising by virtue of any note, bond, certificate, policy or other instrument, or arising by virtue of any such obligation; and if (2) the plaintiff has deposited such money or

property or has paid the amount of or the loan or other value of such instrument or the amount due under such obligation into the registry of the court, there to abide the judgment of the court, or has given bond payable to the clerk of the court in such amount and with such surety as the court or judge may deem proper, conditioned upon the compliance by the plaintiff with the future order or judgment of the court with respect to the subject matter of the controversy.

(b) Such an action may be entertained although the titles or claims of the conflicting claimants do not have a common origin, or are not identical, but are adverse to and independent of one another.

(June 25, 1948, c. 646, 62 Stat. 931.)

§ 1336. Surface Transportation Board's orders

(a) Except as otherwise provided by Act of Congress, the district courts shall have jurisdiction of any civil action to enforce, in whole or in part, any order of the Surface Transportation Board, and to enjoin or suspend, in whole or in part, any order of the Surface Transportation Board for the payment of money or the collection of fines, penalties, and forfeitures.

(b) When a district court or the United States Court of Federal Claims refers a question or issue to the Surface Transportation Board for determination, the court which referred the question or issue shall have exclusive jurisdiction of a civil action to enforce, enjoin, set aside, annul, or suspend, in whole or in part, any order of the Surface Transportation Board arising out of such referral.

(c) Any action brought under subsection (b) of this section shall be filed within 90 days from the date that the order of the Surface Transportation Board becomes final.

(June 25, 1948, c. 646, 62 Stat. 931; Aug. 30, 1964, Pub.L. 88–513, § 1, 78 Stat. 695; Jan. 2, 1975, Pub.L. 93–584, § 1, 88 Stat. 1917; Apr. 2, 1982, Pub.L. 97–164, Title I, § 128, 96 Stat. 39; Oct. 29, 1992, Pub.L. 102–572, Title IX, § 902(b)(1), 106 Stat. 4516; Dec. 29, 1995, Pub.L. 104–88, Title III, § 305(a)(1), (2), 109 Stat. 944.)

HISTORICAL AND STATUTORY NOTES

Effective Dates

1995 Acts. Amendment by Pub.L. 104–88 effective Jan. 1, 1996, see section 2 of Pub.L. 104–88, set out as a note under section 701 of Title 49, Transportation.

1992 Acts. Amendment by Pub.L. 102–572 effective Oct. 29, 1992, see section 911 of Pub.L. 102–572, set out as a note under section 171 of this title.

1982 Acts. Amendment by Pub.L. 97–164 effective Oct. 1, 1982, see section 402 of Pub.L. 97–164, set out as a note under section 171 of this title.

1975 Acts. Amendment by Pub.L. 93–584 not applicable to actions commenced on or before the last day of the first month beginning after Jan. 2, 1975, and actions to enjoin or suspend orders of the Interstate Commerce Commission which are pending when this amendment becomes effective shall not be affected thereby, but shall proceed to final disposition under the law existing on the date they were commenced, see section 10 of Pub.L. 93–584, set out as a note under section 2321 of this title.

§ 1337. Commerce and antitrust regulations; amount in controversy, costs

(a) The district courts shall have original jurisdiction of any civil action or proceeding arising under any Act of Congress regulating commerce or protecting trade and commerce against restraints and monopolies: *Provided, however,* That the district courts shall have original jurisdiction of an action brought under section 11706 or 14706 of title 49, only if the matter in controversy for each receipt or bill of lading exceeds $10,000, exclusive of interest and costs.

(b) Except when express provision therefor is otherwise made in a statute of the United States, where a plaintiff who files the case under section 11706 or 14706 of title 49, originally in the Federal courts is finally adjudged to be entitled to recover less than the sum or value of $10,000, computed without regard to any setoff or counterclaim to which the defendant may be adjudged to be entitled, and exclusive of any interest and costs, the district court may deny costs to the plaintiff and, in addition, may impose costs on the plaintiff.

(c) The district courts shall not have jurisdiction under this section of any matter within the exclusive jurisdiction of the Court of International Trade under chapter 95 of this title.

(June 25, 1948, c. 646, 62 Stat. 931; Oct. 20, 1978, Pub.L. 95–486, § 9(a), 92 Stat. 1633; Oct. 10, 1980, Pub.L. 96–417, Title V, § 505, 94 Stat. 1743; Jan. 12, 1983, Pub.L. 97–449, § 5(f), 96 Stat. 2442; Dec. 29, 1995, Pub.L. 104–88, Title III, § 305(a)(3), 109 Stat. 944.)

HISTORICAL AND STATUTORY NOTES

Effective Dates

1995 Acts. Amendment by Pub.L. 104–88 effective Jan. 1, 1996, see section 2 of Pub.L. 104–88, set out as a note under section 701 of Title 49, Transportation.

1980 Acts. Amendment by Pub.L. 96–417 effective on Nov. 1, 1980 and applicable with respect to civil actions pending on or commenced on or after such date, see section 701(a) of Pub.L. 96–417, as amended, set out as a note under section 251 of this title.

§ 1338. Patents, plant variety protection, copyrights, mask works, designs, trademarks, and unfair competition

(a) The district courts shall have original jurisdiction of any civil action arising under any Act of Congress relating to patents, plant variety protection, copyrights and trade-marks. Such jurisdiction shall be exclusive of the courts of the states in patent, plant variety protection and copyright cases.

(b) The district courts shall have original jurisdiction of any civil action asserting a claim of unfair competition when joined with a substantial and related claim under the copyright, patent, plant variety protection or trade-mark laws.

(c) Subsections (a) and (b) apply to exclusive rights in mask works under chapter 9 of title 17, and to exclusive rights in designs under chapter 13 of title 17, to the same extent as such subsections apply to copyrights.

(June 25, 1948, c. 646, 62 Stat. 931; Dec. 24, 1970, Pub.L. 91–577, Title III, § 143(b), 84 Stat. 1559; Nov. 19, 1988, Pub.L. 100–702, Title X, § 1020(a)(4), 102 Stat. 4671; Oct. 28, 1998, Pub.L. 105–304, Title V, § 503(b)(1), (2)(A), 112 Stat. 2917.)

HISTORICAL AND STATUTORY NOTES

Effective Dates

1998 Acts. Amendment by Pub.L. 105–304, effective Oct. 28, 1998, and remaining in effect until the end of the 2–year period beginning on such date of enactment, see section 505 of Pub.L. 105–304, set out as a note under section 1301 of Title 17, Copyrights.

1970 Acts. Amendment by Pub.L. 91–577 effective Dec. 24, 1970, see section 141 of Pub.L. 91–577, set out as a note under section 2321 of Title 7, Agriculture.

§ 1339. Postal matters

The district courts shall have original jurisdiction of any civil action arising under any Act of Congress relating to the postal service.

(June 25, 1948, c. 646, 62 Stat. 932.)

§ 1340. Internal revenue; customs duties

The district courts shall have original jurisdiction of any civil action arising under any Act of Congress providing for internal revenue, or revenue from imports or tonnage except matters within the jurisdiction of the Court of International Trade.

(June 25, 1948, c. 646, 62 Stat. 932; Oct. 10, 1980, Pub.L. 96–417, Title V, § 501(21), 94 Stat. 1742.)

HISTORICAL AND STATUTORY NOTES

Effective Dates

1980 Acts. Amendment by Pub.L. 96–417 effective on Nov. 1, 1980 and applicable with respect to civil actions pending on or commenced on or after such date, see section 701(a) of Pub.L. 96–417, as amended, set out as a note under section 251 of this title.

§ 1341. Taxes by States

The district courts shall not enjoin, suspend or restrain the assessment, levy or collection of any tax under State law where a plain, speedy and efficient remedy may be had in the courts of such State.

(June 25, 1948, c. 646, 62 Stat. 932.)

§ 1342. Rate orders of State agencies

The district courts shall not enjoin, suspend or restrain the operation of, or compliance with, any order affecting rates chargeable by a public utility and made by a State administrative agency or a rate-making body of a State political subdivision, where:

(1) Jurisdiction is based solely on diversity of citizenship or repugnance of the order to the Federal Constitution; and,

(2) The order does not interfere with interstate commerce; and,

(3) The order has been made after reasonable notice and hearing; and,

(4) A plain, speedy and efficient remedy may be had in the courts of such State.

(June 25, 1948, c. 646, 62 Stat. 932.)

§ 1343. Civil rights and elective franchise

(a) The district courts shall have original jurisdiction of any civil action authorized by law to be commenced by any person:

(1) To recover damages for injury to his person or property, or because of the deprivation of any right or privilege of a citizen of the United States, by any act done in furtherance of any conspiracy mentioned in section 1985 of Title 42;

(2) To recover damages from any person who fails to prevent or to aid in preventing any wrongs mentioned in section 1985 of Title 42 which he had knowledge were about to occur and power to prevent;

(3) To redress the deprivation, under color of any State law, statute, ordinance, regulation, custom or usage, of any right, privilege or immunity secured by the Constitution of the United States or by any Act of Congress providing for equal rights of citizens or of all persons within the jurisdiction of the United States;

(4) To recover damages or to secure equitable or other relief under any Act of Congress providing for the protection of civil rights, including the right to vote.

(b) For purposes of this section—

(1) the District of Columbia shall be considered to be a State; and

(2) any Act of Congress applicable exclusively to the District of Columbia shall be considered to be a statute of the District of Columbia.

(June 25, 1948, c. 646, 62 Stat. 932; Sept. 3, 1954, c. 1263, § 42, 68 Stat. 1241; Sept. 9, 1957, Pub.L. 85–315, Part III, § 121, 71 Stat. 637; Dec. 29, 1979, Pub.L. 96–170, § 2, 93 Stat. 1284.)

HISTORICAL AND STATUTORY NOTES

Effective Dates

1979 Acts. Section 3 of Pub.L. 96–170 provided that: "The amendments made by this Act [amending this section and section 1983 of Title 42, The Public Health and Welfare] shall apply with respect to any deprivation of rights, privileges, or immunities secured by the Constitution and laws occurring after the date of the enactment of this Act [Dec. 29, 1979]."

§ 1344. Election disputes

The district courts shall have original jurisdiction of any civil action to recover possession of any office, except that of elector of President or Vice President, United States Senator, Representative in or delegate to Congress, or member of a state legislature, authorized by law to be commenced, wherein it appears that the sole question touching the title to office arises out of denial of the right to vote, to any citizen offering to vote, on account of race, color or previous condition of servitude.

The jurisdiction under this section shall extend only so far as to determine the rights of the parties to office by reason of the denial of the right, guaranteed by the Constitution of the United States and secured by any law, to enforce the right of citizens of the United States to vote in all the States.

(June 25, 1948, c. 646, 62 Stat. 932.)

§ 1345. United States as plaintiff

Except as otherwise provided by Act of Congress, the district courts shall have original jurisdiction of all civil actions, suits or proceedings commenced by the United States, or by any agency or officer thereof expressly authorized to sue by Act of Congress.

(June 25, 1948, c. 646, 62 Stat. 933.)

§ 1346. United States as defendant

(a) The district courts shall have original jurisdiction, concurrent with the United States Court of Federal Claims, of:

(1) Any civil action against the United States for the recovery of any internal-revenue tax alleged to have been erroneously or illegally assessed or collected, or any penalty claimed to have been collected without authority or any sum alleged to have been excessive or in any manner wrongfully collected under the internal-revenue laws;

(2) Any other civil action or claim against the United States, not exceeding $10,000 in amount, founded either upon the Constitution, or any Act of Congress, or any regulation of an executive department, or upon any express or implied contract with the United States, or for liquidated or unliquidated damages in cases not sounding in tort, except that the district courts shall not have jurisdiction of any civil action or claim against the United States founded upon any express or implied contract with the United States or for liquidated or unliquidated damages in cases not sounding in tort which are subject to sections 8(g)(1) and 10(a)(1) of the Contract Disputes Act of 1978. For the purpose of this paragraph, an express or implied contract with the Army and Air Force Exchange Service, Navy Exchanges, Marine Corps Exchanges, Coast Guard Exchanges, or Exchange Councils of the National Aeronautics and Space Administration shall be considered an express or implied contract with the United States.

(b)(1) Subject to the provisions of chapter 171 of this title, the district courts, together with the United States District Court for the District of the Canal Zone and the District Court of the Virgin Islands, shall have exclusive jurisdiction of civil actions on claims against the United States, for money damages, accruing on and after January 1, 1945, for injury or loss of property, or personal injury or death caused by the negligent or wrongful act or omission of any employee of the Government while acting within the scope of his office or employment, under circumstances where the United States, if a private person, would be liable to the claimant in accordance with the law of the place where the act or omission occurred.

(2) No person convicted of a felony who is incarcerated while awaiting sentencing or while serving a sentence may bring a civil action against the United States or an agency, officer, or employee of the Government, for mental or emotional injury suffered while in custody without a prior showing of physical injury.

(c) The jurisdiction conferred by this section includes jurisdiction of any set-off, counterclaim, or other claim or demand whatever on the part of the United States against any plaintiff commencing an action under this section.

(d) The district courts shall not have jurisdiction under this section of any civil action or claim for a pension.

(e) The district courts shall have original jurisdiction of any civil action against the United States provided in section 6226, 6228(a), 7426, or 7428 (in the case of the United States district court for the District of Columbia) or section 7429 of the Internal Revenue Code of 1986.

(f) The district courts shall have exclusive original jurisdiction of civil actions under section 2409a to quiet title to an estate or interest in real property in which an interest is claimed by the United States.

(g) Subject to the provisions of chapter 179, the district courts of the United States shall have exclusive jurisdiction over any civil action commenced under section 453(2) of title 3, by a covered employee under chapter 5 of such title.

(June 25, 1948, c. 646, 62 Stat. 933; Apr. 25, 1949, c. 92, § 2(a), 63 Stat. 62; May 24, 1949, c. 139, § 80(a), (b), 63 Stat. 101; Oct. 31, 1951, c. 655, § 50(b), 65 Stat. 727; July 30, 1954, c. 648, § 1, 68 Stat. 589; July 7, 1958, Pub.L. 85–508, § 12(e), 72 Stat. 348; Aug. 30, 1964, Pub.L. 88–519, 78 Stat. 699; Nov. 2, 1966, Pub.L. 89–719, Title II, § 202(a), 80 Stat. 1148; July 23, 1970, Pub.L. 91–350, § 1(a), 84 Stat. 449; Oct. 25, 1972, Pub.L. 92–562, § 1, 86 Stat. 1176; Oct. 4, 1976, Pub.L. 94–455, Title XII, § 1204(c) (1), Title XIII, § 1306(b) (7), 90 Stat. 1697, 1719; Nov. 1, 1978, Pub.L. 95–563, § 14(a), 92 Stat. 2389; Apr. 2, 1982, Pub.L. 97–164, Title I, § 129, 96 Stat. 39; Sept. 3, 1982, Pub.L. 97–248, Title IV, § 402(c) (17), 96 Stat. 669; Oct. 22, 1986, Pub.L. 99–514, § 2, 100 Stat. 2095; Oct. 29, 1992, Pub.L. 102–572, Title IX, § 902(b)(1), 106 Stat. 4516; Apr. 26, 1996, Pub.L. 104–134, Title I, § 101[(a)][Title VIII, § 806], 110 Stat. 1321–75; renumbered Title I May 2, 1996, Pub.L. 104–140, § 1(a), 110 Stat. 1327; Oct. 26, 1996, Pub.L. 104–331, § 3(b)(1), 110 Stat. 4069.)

HISTORICAL AND STATUTORY NOTES

Senate Revision Amendment

The provisions of Title 28, U.S.C., section 932, which related to application of the Federal Rules of Civil Procedure, were originally set out in section 2676 of this revised title, but such section 2676 was eliminated by Senate amendment. See 80th Congress Senate Report No. 1559, amendment No. 61.

1949 Acts. This section corrects typographical errors in section 1346(a)(1) of Title 28, U.S.C., and in section 1346(b) of such title.

House Report No. 276, see 1949 U.S. Code Cong. Service, p. 1226.

Senate Report No. 303 and House Report No. 352, see 1949 U.S.Code Cong.Service, p. 1248.

1951 Acts. Senate Report No. 1020, see 1951 U.S. Code Cong. and Adm. Service, p. 2578.

1954 Acts. House Report No. 659 and Conference Report No. 2276, see 1954 U.S. Code Cong. and Adm. News, p. 2716.

1958 Acts. House Report No. 624, see 1958 U.S. Code Cong. and Adm. News, p. 2933.

1964 Acts. Senate Report No. 1390, see 1964 U.S. Code Cong. and Adm. News, p. 3254.

1966 Acts. Senate Report No. 1708, see 1966 U.S. Code Cong. and Adm. News, p. 3722.

1970 Acts. House Report No. 91–933, see 1970 U.S. Code Cong. and Adm. News, p. 3477.

1972 Acts. House Report No. 92–1559, see 1972 U.S. Code Cong. and Adm. News, p. 4547.

1976 Acts. House Report Nos. 94–658 and 94–1380, Senate Report No. 94–938(Parts I and II), and House Conference Report No. 94–1515, see 1976 U.S. Code Cong. and Adm. News, p. 2897.

1978 Acts. Senate Report No. 95–1118, see 1978 U.S. Code Cong. and Adm. News, p. 5235.

1982 Acts. Senate Report No. 97–275, see 1982 U.S. Code Cong. and Adm. News, p. 11.

Senate Report No. 97–494, House Conference Report No. 97–760 and Statements by Legislative Leaders, see 1982 U.S. Code Cong. and Adm. News, p. 781.

1996 Acts. House Report No. 104–820, see 1996 U.S. Code Cong. and Adm. News, p. 4348.

References in Text

The internal-revenue laws, referred to in subsec. (a)(1), are classified generally to Title 26, Internal Revenue Code.

Sections 8(g)(1) and 10(a)(1) of the Contract Disputes Act of 1978, referred to in subsec. (a)(2), are sections 8(g)(1) and 10(a)(1) of Pub.L. 95–563, Nov. 1, 1978, 92 Stat. 2387, 2388, which are classified to sections 607(g)(1) and 609(a)(1) of Title 41, Public Contracts.

Sections 6226, 6228(a), 7426, 7428, and 7429 of the Internal Revenue Code of 1986, referred to in subsec. (e), are classified to sections 6226, 6228(a), 7426, 7428, and 7429, respectively, of Title 26, Internal Revenue Code.

Effective Dates

1996 Acts. Amendment by Pub.L. 104–331 effective October 1, 1997, see section 3(d) of Pub.L. 104–331, set out as a note under section 1296 of this title.

1992 Acts. Amendment by Pub.L. 102–572 effective Oct. 29, 1992, see section 911 of Pub.L. 102–572, set out as a note under section 171 of this title.

1982 Acts. Amendment by Pub.L. 97–248 applicable to partnership taxable years beginning after Sept. 3, 1982, with provision for the applicability of the amendment to any partnership taxable year ending after Sept. 3, 1982, if the partnership, each partner, and each indirect partner requests such application and the Secretary of the Treasury or his delegate consents to such application, see section 407(a) (1) and (3) of Pub.L. 97–248, as amended, set out as a note under section 6221 of Title 26, Internal Revenue Code.

Amendment by Pub.L. 97–164 effective Oct. 1, 1982, see section 402 of Pub.L. 97–164, set out as a note under section 171 of this title.

1978 Acts. Amendment by Pub.L. 95–563 effective with respect to contracts entered into 120 days after Nov. 1, 1978 and, at the election of the contractor, with respect to any claim pending at such time before the contracting officer or initiated thereafter, see section 16 of Pub.L. 95–563, set out as a note under section 601 of Title 41, Public Contracts.

1970 Acts. Section 2 of Pub.L. 91–350 provided that:

"**(a)** In addition to granting jurisdiction over suits brought after the date of enactment of this Act [July 23, 1970], the provisions of this Act [amending this section and section 1491 of this title and section 724a of former Title 31, Money and Finance], shall also apply to claims and civil actions dismissed before or pending on the date of enactment of this Act if the claim or civil action is based upon a transaction, omission, or breach that occurred not more than six years prior to the date of enactment of this Act [July 23, 1970].

"**(b)** The provisions of subsection (a) of this section shall apply notwithstanding a determination or judgment made prior to the date of enactment of this Act that the United States district courts or the United States Court of Claims [now United States Court of Federal Claims] did not have jurisdiction to entertain a suit on an express or implied contract with a nonappropriated fund instrumentality of the United States described in section 1 of this Act."

1966 Acts. Section 203 of Title II of Pub.L. 89–719 provided that: "The amendments made by this title [amending this section and sections 1402 and 2410 of this title] shall apply after the date of the enactment of this Act [Nov. 2, 1966]."

1958 Acts. Amendment of section by Pub.L. 85–508 effective Jan. 3, 1959, upon admission of Alaska into the Union pursuant to Proc. No. 3269, Jan. 3, 1959, 24 F.R. 81, 73 Stat. c16, as required by sections 1 and 8(c) of Pub.L. 85–508, see notes set out under section 81A of this title and preceding former section 21 of Title 48, Territories and Insular Possessions.

Savings Clause for Act Oct. 31, 1951

Act June 4, 1956, c. 363, 70 Stat. 246, which was formerly set out as a note under this section, and which conferred jurisdiction on district courts of certain actions to recover pay of employees who had been dismissed, was repealed by Pub.L. 89–554, § 8(a), Sept. 6, 1966, 80 Stat. 658.

Severability of Provisions

If any provision of section 101[a] [Title VIII] of Pub.L. 104–134, an amendment made by such Title, or the application of such provision or amendment to any person or circumstance is held to be unconstitutional, the remainder of such Title, the amendments made by such Title, and the application of the provisions of such Title to any person or circumstance not affected thereby, see section 101[a] [Title VIII, § 810] of Pub.L. 104–134, set out as a note under section 3626 of Title 18, Crimes and Criminal Procedure.

Termination of United States District Court for the District of the Canal Zone

For termination of the United States District Court for the District of the Canal Zone at end of the "transition period", being the 30–month period beginning Oct. 1, 1979, and ending midnight Mar. 31, 1982, see Paragraph 5 of Article XI of the Panama Canal Treaty of 1977 and sections 3831 and 3841 to 3843 of Title 22, Foreign Relations and Intercourse.

§ 1347. Partition action where United States is joint tenant

The district courts shall have original jurisdiction of any civil action commenced by any tenant in common or joint tenant for the partition of lands where the United States is one of the tenants in common or joint tenants.

(June 25, 1948, c. 646, 62 Stat. 933.)

§ 1348. Banking association as party

The district courts shall have original jurisdiction of any civil action commenced by the United States, or by direction of any officer thereof, against any national banking association, any civil action to wind up the affairs of any such association, and any action by a banking association established in the district for which the court is held, under chapter 2 of Title 12, to enjoin the Comptroller of the Currency, or any receiver acting under his direction, as provided by such chapter.

All national banking associations shall, for the purposes of all other actions by or against them, be deemed citizens of the States in which they are respectively located.

(June 25, 1948, c. 646, 62 Stat. 933.)

HISTORICAL AND STATUTORY NOTES

Exception as to Transfer of Functions

Functions vested by any provision of law in the Comptroller of the Currency, referred to in this section, were not included in the transfer of functions of officers, agencies and employees of the Department of the Treasury to the Secretary of the Treasury, made by 1950 Reorg. Plan No. 26, § 1, eff. July 31, 1950, 15 F.R. 4935, 64 Stat. 1280, set out in Appendix 1 to Title 5, Government Organization and Employees. See section 321(c)(2) of Title 31 Money and Fiance.

§ 1349. Corporation organized under federal law as party

The district courts shall not have jurisdiction of any civil action by or against any corporation upon the ground that it was incorporated by or under an Act of Congress, unless the United States is the owner of more than one-half of its capital stock.

(June 25, 1948, c. 646, 62 Stat. 934.)

§ 1350. Alien's action for tort

The district courts shall have original jurisdiction of any civil action by an alien for a tort only, committed in violation of the law of nations or a treaty of the United States.

(June 25, 1948, c. 646, 62 Stat. 934.)

HISTORICAL AND STATUTORY NOTES

Torture Victim Protection

Pub.L. 102–256, Mar. 12, 1992, 106 Stat. 73, provided that:

"Section 1. Short Title.

"This Act may be cited as the 'Torture Victim Protection Act of 1991'.

"Sec. 2. Establishment of civil action.

"(a) Liability.—An individual who, under actual or apparent authority, or color of law, of any foreign nation—

"(1) subjects an individual to torture shall, in a civil action, be liable for damages to that individual; or

"(2) subjects an individual to extrajudicial killing shall, in a civil action, be liable for damages to the individual's legal representative, or to any person who may be a claimant in an action for wrongful death.

"(b) Exhaustion of remedies.—A court shall decline to hear a claim under this section if the claimant has not exhausted adequate and available remedies in the place in which the conduct giving rise to the claim occurred.

"(c) Statute of limitations.—No action shall be maintained under this section unless it is commenced within 10 years after the cause of action arose.

"Sec. 3. Definitions.

"(a) Extrajudicial killing.—For the purposes of this Act, the term 'extrajudicial killing' means a deliberated killing not authorized by a previous judgment pronounced by a regularly constituted court affording all the judicial guarantees which are recognized as indispensable by civilized peoples. Such term, however, does not include any such killing that, under international law, is lawfully carried out under the authority of a foreign nation.

"(b) **Torture.**—For the purposes of this Act—

"(1) the term 'torture' means any act, directed against an individual in the offender's custody or physical control, by which severe pain or suffering (other than pain or suffering arising only from or inherent in, or incidental to, lawful sanctions), whether physical or mental, is intentionally inflicted on that individual for such purposes as obtaining from that individual or a third person information or a confession, punishing that individual for an act that individual or a third person has committed or is suspected of having committed, intimidating or coercing that individual or a third person, or for any reason based on discrimination of any kind; and

"(2) mental pain or suffering refers to prolonged mental harm caused by or resulting from—

"(A) the intentional infliction or threatened infliction of severe physical pain or suffering;

"(B) the administration or application, or threatened administration or application, of mind altering substances or other procedures calculated to disrupt profoundly the senses or the personality;

"(C) the threat of imminent death; or

"(D) the threat that another individual will imminently be subjected to death, severe physical pain or suffering, or the administration or application of mind altering substances or other procedures calculated to disrupt profoundly the senses or personality."

§ 1351. Consuls, vice consuls, and members of a diplomatic mission as defendant

The district courts shall have original jurisdiction, exclusive of the courts of the States, of all civil actions and proceedings against—

(1) consuls or vice consuls of foreign states; or

(2) members of a mission or members of their families (as such terms are defined in section 2 of the Diplomatic Relations Act).

(June 25, 1948, c. 646, 62 Stat. 934; May 24, 1949, c. 139, § 80(c), 63 Stat. 101; Sept. 30, 1978, Pub.L. 95–393, § 8(a)(1), 92 Stat. 810.)

HISTORICAL AND STATUTORY NOTES

References in Text

Section 2 of the Diplomatic Relations Act, referred to in par. (2), is section 2 of Pub.L. 95–393, Sept. 30, 1978, 92 Stat. 808, which is classified to section 254a of Title 22, Foreign Relations and Intercourse.

Effective Dates

1978 Acts. Amendment by Pub.L. 95–393 effective at the end of the 90-day period beginning on Sept. 30, 1978, see section 9 of Pub.L. 95–393, set out as a note under section 254a of Title 22, Foreign Relations and Intercourse.

§ 1352. Bonds executed under federal law

The district courts shall have original jurisdiction, concurrent with State courts, of any action on a bond executed under any law of the United States, except matters within the jurisdiction of the Court of International Trade under section 1582 of this title.

(June 25, 1948, c. 646, 62 Stat. 934; Oct. 10, 1980, Pub.L. 96–417, Title V, § 506, 94 Stat. 1743.)

HISTORICAL AND STATUTORY NOTES

Effective Dates

1980 Acts. Amendment by Pub.L. 96–417 applicable with respect to civil actions commenced on or after the 90th day after Nov. 1, 1980, see section 701(c)(1)(B) of Pub.L. 96–417, as amended, set out as a note under section 251 of this title.

§ 1353. Indian allotments

The district courts shall have original jurisdiction of any civil action involving the right of any person, in whole or in part of Indian blood or descent, to any allotment of land under any Act of Congress or treaty.

The judgment in favor of any claimant to an allotment of land shall have the same effect, when properly certified to the Secretary of the Interior, as if such allotment had been allowed and approved by him; but this provision shall not apply to any lands held on or before December 21, 1911, by either of the Five Civilized Tribes, the Osage Nation of Indians, nor to any of the lands within the Quapaw Indian Agency.

(June 25, 1948, c. 646, 62 Stat. 934.)

§ 1354. Land grants from different states

The district courts shall have original jurisdiction of actions between citizens of the same state claiming lands under grants from different states.

(June 25, 1948, c. 646, 62 Stat. 934.)

§ 1355. Fine, penalty or forfeiture

(a) The district courts shall have original jurisdiction, exclusive of the courts of the States, of any action or proceeding for the recovery or enforcement of any fine, penalty, or forfeiture, pecuniary or otherwise, incurred under any Act of Congress, except matters within the jurisdiction of the Court of International Trade under section 1582 of this title.

(b)(1) A forfeiture action or proceeding may be brought in—

(A) the district court for the district in which any of the acts or omissions giving rise to the forfeiture occurred, or

(B) any other district where venue for the forfeiture action or proceeding is specifically provided for in section 1395 of this title or any other statute.

(2) Whenever property subject to forfeiture under the laws of the United States is located in a foreign country, or has been detained or seized pursuant to legal process or competent authority of a foreign government, an action or proceeding for forfeiture may be brought as provided in paragraph (1), or in the United States District court [1] for the District of Columbia.

(c) In any case in which a final order disposing of property in a civil forfeiture action or proceeding is appealed, removal of the property by the prevailing party shall not deprive the court of jurisdiction. Upon motion of the appealing party, the district court or the court of appeals shall issue any order necessary to preserve the right of the appealing party to the full value of the property at issue, including a stay of the judgment of the district court pending appeal or requiring the prevailing party to post an appeal bond.

(d) Any court with jurisdiction over a forfeiture action pursuant to subsection (b) may issue and cause to be served in any other district such process as may be required to bring before the court the property that is the subject of the forfeiture action.

(June 25, 1948, c. 646, 62 Stat. 934; Oct. 10, 1980, Pub.L. 96–417, Title V, § 507, 94 Stat. 1743; Oct. 28, 1992, Pub.L. 102–550, Title XV, § 1521, 106 Stat. 4062.)

1 So in original. Probably should be capitalized.

HISTORICAL AND STATUTORY NOTES

Effective Dates

1992 Acts. Except as otherwise provided, amendment by Pub.L. 102–550 effective Oct. 28, 1992, see section 2 of Pub.L. 102–550, set out as a note under section 5301 of Title 42, The Public Health and Welfare.

1980 Acts. Amendment by Pub.L. 96–417 applicable with respect to civil actions commenced on or after the 90th day after Nov. 1, 1980, see section 701(c)(1)(B) of Pub.L. 96–417, as amended, set out as a note under section 251 of this title.

§ 1356. Seizures not within admiralty and maritime jurisdiction

The district courts shall have original jurisdiction, exclusive of the courts of the States, of any seizure under any law of the United States on land or upon waters not within admiralty and maritime jurisdiction, except matters within the jurisdiction of the Court of International Trade under section 1582 of this title.

(June 25, 1948, c. 646, 62 Stat. 934; Oct. 10, 1980, Pub.L. 96–417, Title V, § 508, 94 Stat. 1743.)

HISTORICAL AND STATUTORY NOTES

Effective Dates

1980 Acts. Amendment by Pub.L. 96–417 applicable with respect to civil actions commenced on or after the 90th day after Nov. 1, 1980, see section 701(c)(1)(B) of Pub.L. 96–417, as amended, set out as a note under section 251 of this title.

§ 1357. Injuries under Federal laws

The district courts shall have original jurisdiction of any civil action commenced by any person to recover damages for any injury to his person or property on account of any act done by him, under any Act of Congress, for the protection or collection of any of the revenues, or to enforce the right of citizens of the United States to vote in any State.

(June 25, 1948, c. 646, 62 Stat. 934.)

§ 1358. Eminent domain

The district courts shall have original jurisdiction of all proceedings to condemn real estate for the use of the United States or its departments or agencies.

(June 25, 1948, c. 646, 62 Stat. 935.)

§ 1359. Parties collusively joined or made

A district court shall not have jurisdiction of a civil action in which any party, by assignment or otherwise, has been improperly or collusively made or joined to invoke the jurisdiction of such court.

(June 25, 1948, c. 646, 62 Stat. 935.)

§ 1360. State civil jurisdiction in actions to which Indians are parties

(a) Each of the States listed in the following table shall have jurisdiction over civil causes of action between Indians or to which Indians are parties which arise in the areas of Indian country listed opposite the name of the State to the same extent that such State has jurisdiction over other civil causes of action, and those civil laws of such State that are of general application to private persons or private property shall have the same force and effect within such Indian country as they have elsewhere within the State:

State of	*Indian country affected*
Alaska	All Indian country within the State
California	All Indian country within the State
Minnesota	All Indian country within the State, except the Red Lake Reservation
Nebraska	All Indian country within the State
Oregon	All Indian country within the State, except the Warm Springs Reservation
Wisconsin	All Indian country within the State

(b) Nothing in this section shall authorize the alienation, encumbrance, or taxation of any real or personal property, including water rights, belonging to any Indian or any Indian tribe, band, or community that is held in trust by the United States or is subject to a restriction against alienation imposed by the United States; or shall authorize regulation of the use of such property in a manner inconsistent with any Federal treaty, agreement, or statute or with any regulation made pursuant thereto; or shall confer jurisdiction upon the State to adjudicate, in probate proceedings or otherwise, the ownership or right to possession of such property or any interest therein.

(c) Any tribal ordinance or custom heretofore or hereafter adopted by an Indian tribe, band, or community in the exercise of any authority which it may possess shall, if not inconsistent with any applicable civil law of the State, be given full force and effect in the determination of civil causes of action pursuant to this section.

(Added Aug. 15, 1953, c. 505, § 4, 67 Stat. 589, and amended Aug. 24, 1954, c. 910, § 2, 68 Stat. 795; Aug. 8, 1958, Pub.L. 85–615, § 2, 72 Stat. 545; Nov. 6, 1978, Pub.L. 95–598, Title II, § 239, 92 Stat. 2668; July 10, 1984, Pub.L. 98–353, Title I, § 110, 98 Stat. 342.)

HISTORICAL AND STATUTORY NOTES

Codifications

Subsec. (a) of this section was amended by Pub.L. 95–598, Title II, § 239, Nov. 6, 1978, 92 Stat. 2668, effective June 28, 1984, pursuant to Pub.L. 95–598, Title IV, § 402(b), Nov. 6, 1978, 92 Stat. 2682, as amended by Pub.L. 98–249, § 1(a), Mar. 31, 1984, 98 Stat. 116; Pub.L. 98–271, § 1(a), Apr. 30, 1984, 98 Stat. 163; Pub.L. 98–299, § 1(a), May 25, 1984, 98 Stat. 214; Pub.L. 98–325, § 1(a), June 20, 1984, 98 Stat. 268, set out as an Effective Dates note preceding section 101 of Title 11, Bankruptcy, by substituting "Alaska ...... All Indian country within the State" for "Alaska ...... All Indian country within the Territory".

Section 402(b) of Pub.L. 95–598 was amended by section 113 of Pub.L. 98–353 by substituting "shall not be effective" for "shall take effect on June 28, 1984", thereby eliminating the amendment by section 239 of Pub.L. 95–598, effective June 27, 1984, pursuant to section 122(c) of Pub.L. 98–353, set out as an Effective Dates note under section 151 of this title.

Section 121(a) of Pub.L. 98–353 directed that section 402(b) of Pub.L. 95–598 be amended by substituting "the date of enactment of the Bankruptcy Amendments and Federal Judgeship Act of 1984 [i.e. July 10, 1984]" for "June 28, 1984". This amendment was not executed in view of the prior amendment to section 402(b) of Pub.L. 95–598 by section 113 of Pub.L. 98–353.

Effective Dates

1984 Acts. Amendment by Pub.L. 98–353 effective July 10, 1984, see section 122(a) of Pub.L. 98–353, set out as a note under section 151 of this title.

Admission of Alaska as State

Admission of Alaska into the Union was accomplished Jan. 3, 1959 upon issuance of Proc. No. 3269, Jan. 3, 1959, 24 F.R. 81, 73 Stat. c16, as required by sections 1 and 8(c) of Pub.L. 85–508, July 7, 1958, 72 Stat. 339, set out as notes preceding former section 21 of Title 48, Territories and Insular Possessions.

Amendment of State Constitutions to Remove Legal Impediment; Effective Date

Section 6 of Act Aug. 15, 1953, provided that: "Notwithstanding the provisions of any Enabling Act for the admission of a State, the consent of the United States is hereby given to the people of any State to amend, where necessary, their State constitution or existing statutes, as the case may be, to remove any legal impediment to the assumption of civil and criminal jurisdiction in accordance with the provisions of this Act [adding section 1360 of this title and section 1162 of Title 18]: *Provided,* That the provisions of this Act shall not become effective with respect to such assumption of jurisdiction by any such State until the people thereof have appropriately amended their State constitution or statutes as the case may be."

Consent of United States to Other States to Assume Jurisdiction

Act Aug. 15, 1953, c. 505, § 7, 67 Stat. 590, which gave consent of the United States to any other State not having jurisdiction with respect to criminal offenses or civil causes of action, or with respect to both, as provided for in this section and section 1162 of Title 18, Crimes and Criminal Procedure, to assume jurisdiction at such time and in such manner as the people of the State shall, by legislative action, obligate and bind the State to assumption thereof, was repealed by section 403(b) of Pub.L. 90–284, Title IV, Apr. 11, 1968, 82 Stat. 79, such repeal not to affect any cession of jurisdiction made pursuant to such section prior to its repeal.

Retrocession by State of jurisdiction acquired by State pursuant to section 7 of Act Aug. 15, 1953, prior to its repeal, see section 1323 of Title 25, Indians.

§ 1361. Action to compel an officer of the United States to perform his duty

The district courts shall have original jurisdiction of any action in the nature of mandamus to compel an officer or employee of the United States or any agency thereof to perform a duty owed to the plaintiff.

(Added Pub.L. 87–748, § 1(a), Oct. 5, 1962, 76 Stat. 744.)

§ 1362. Indian tribes

The district courts shall have original jurisdiction of all civil actions, brought by any Indian tribe or band with a governing body duly recognized by the Secretary of the Interior, wherein the matter in controversy arises under the Constitution, laws, or treaties of the United States.

(Added Pub.L. 89–635, § 1, Oct. 10, 1966, 80 Stat. 880.)

§ 1363. Jurors' employment rights

The district courts shall have original jurisdiction of any civil action brought for the protection of jurors' employment under section 1875 of this title.

(Added Pub.L. 95–572, § 6(b)(1), Nov. 2, 1978, 92 Stat. 2457.)

HISTORICAL AND STATUTORY NOTES

Effective Dates

1978 Acts. Section 7 of Pub.L. 95–572 provided that:

"**(a)** Except as provided in subsection (b) of this section, the amendments made by this Act [enacting sections 1363 and 1875, renumbering as section 1364 prior section 1363, and amending sections 1863, 1865, 1866, 1869, and 1871 of this title] shall apply with respect to any grand or petit juror summoned for service or actually serving on or after the date of enactment of this Act [Nov. 2, 1978].

"**(b)** The amendment made by section 5 of this Act [to section 1871 of this title] shall apply with respect to any grand or petit juror serving on or after the sixtieth day following the date of enactment of this Act [Nov. 2, 1978]."

Prior Provisions

A prior section 1363 was renumbered 1366.

§ 1364. Direct actions against insurers of members of diplomatic missions and their families

(a) The district courts shall have original and exclusive jurisdiction, without regard to the amount in controversy, of any civil action commenced by any person against an insurer who by contract has insured an individual, who is, or was at the time of the tortious act or omission, a member of a mission (within the meaning of section 2(3) of the Diplomatic Relations Act (22 U.S.C. 254a(3))) or a member of the family of such a member of a mission, or an individual described in section 19 of the Convention on Privileges and Immunities of the United Nations of February 13, 1946, against liability for personal injury, death, or damage to property.

(b) Any direct action brought against an insurer under subsection (a) shall be tried without a jury, but shall not be subject to the defense that the insured is immune from suit, that the insured is an indispensable party, or in the absence of fraud or collusion, that the insured has violated a term of the contract, unless the contract was cancelled before the claim arose.

(Added Pub.L. 95–393, § 7(a), Sept. 30, 1978, 92 Stat. 809, and amended Pub.L. 97–241, Title II, § 203(b)(4), Aug. 24, 1982, 96 Stat. 291; Pub.L. 100–204, Title I, § 138(a), Dec. 22, 1987, 101 Stat. 1347.)

HISTORICAL AND STATUTORY NOTES

Codifications

Two other sections 1364 were renumbered sections 1365 and 1366 of this title.

Effective Dates

1987 Acts. Section 138(b) of Pub.L. 100–204 provided that: "The amendment made by subsection (a) [amending subsec. (a) of this section] shall apply to the first tortious act or omission occurring after the date of enactment of this Act [Dec. 22, 1987]."

1982 Acts. Amendment by Pub.L. 97–241 effective Oct. 1, 1982, see section 204 of Pub.L. 97–241, set out as a note under section 4301 of Title 22, Foreign Relations and Intercourse.

1978 Acts. Section effective at the end of the 90 day period beginning on Sept. 30, 1978, see section 9 of Pub.L. 95–393, set out as a note under section 254a of Title 22, Foreign Relations and Intercourse.

§ 1365. Senate actions

(a) The United States District Court for the District of Columbia shall have original jurisdiction, without regard to the amount in controversy, over any civil action brought by the Senate or any authorized committee or subcommittee of the Senate to enforce, to secure a declaratory judgment concerning the validity of, or to prevent a threatened refusal or failure to comply with, any subpena or order issued by the Senate or committee or subcommittee of the Senate to any entity acting or purporting to act under color or authority of State law or to any natural person to secure the production of documents or other materials of any kind or the answering of any deposition or interrogatory or to secure testimony or any combination thereof. This section shall not apply to an action to enforce, to secure a declaratory judgment concerning the validity of, or to prevent a threatened refusal to comply with, any subpena or order issued to an officer or employee of the executive branch of the Federal Government acting within his or her official capacity, except that this section shall apply if the refusal to comply is based on the assertion of a personal privilege or objection and is not based on a governmental privilege or objection the assertion of which has been authorized by the executive branch of the Federal Government.

(b) Upon application by the Senate or any authorized committee or subcommittee of the Senate, the district court shall issue an order to an entity or person refusing, or failing to comply with, or threatening to refuse or not to comply with, a subpena or order of the Senate or committee or subcommittee of the Senate requiring such entity or person to comply forthwith. Any refusal or failure to obey a lawful order of the district court issued pursuant to this section may be held by such court to be a contempt thereof. A contempt proceeding shall be commenced by an order to show cause before the court why the entity or person refusing or failing to obey the court order should not be held in contempt of court. Such contempt proceeding shall be tried by the court and shall be summary in manner. The purpose of sanctions imposed as a result of such contempt proceeding shall be to compel obedience to the order of the court. Process in any such action or contempt proceeding may be served in any judicial district wherein the entity or party refusing, or failing to comply, or threatening to refuse or not to comply, resides, transacts business, or may be found, and subpenas for witnesses who are required to attend such proceeding may run into any other district. Nothing in this section shall confer upon such court jurisdiction to affect by injunction or otherwise the issuance or effect of any subpena or order of the Senate or any committee or subcommittee of the Senate or to review, modify, suspend, terminate, or set aside any such subpena or order. An action, contempt proceeding, or sanction brought or imposed pursuant to this section shall not abate upon adjournment sine die by the Senate at the end of a Congress if the Senate or the committee or subcommittee of the Senate which issued the subpena or order certifies to the court that it maintains its interest in securing the documents, answers, or testimony during such adjournment.

[**(c)** Repealed. Pub.L. 98–620, Title IV, § 402(29)(D), Nov. 8, 1984, 98 Stat. 3359]

(d) The Senate or any committee or subcommittee of the Senate commencing and prosecuting a civil action or contempt proceeding under this section may be represented in such action by such attorneys as the Senate may designate.

(e) A civil action commenced or prosecuted under this section, may not be authorized pursuant to the Standing Order of the Senate "authorizing suits by Senate Committees" (S. Jour. 572, May 28, 1928).

(f) For the purposes of this section the term "committee" includes standing, select, or special committees of the Senate established by law or resolution.

(Added Pub.L. 95–521, Title VII, § 705(f)(1), Oct. 26, 1978, 92 Stat. 1879, § 1364, and amended Pub.L. 98–620, Title IV, § 402(29)(D), Nov. 8, 1984, 98 Stat. 3359; renumbered § 1365, Pub.L. 99–336, § 6(a)(1)(B), June 19, 1986, 100 Stat. 638; Pub.L. 104–292, § 4, Oct. 11, 1996, 110 Stat. 3460.)

HISTORICAL AND STATUTORY NOTES

Effective Dates

1984 Acts. Amendment by Pub.L. 98–620 not to apply to cases pending on Nov. 8, 1984, see section 403 of Pub.L. 98–620, set out as a note under section 1657 of this title.

1978 Acts. Section effective Jan. 3, 1979, see section 717 of Pub.L. 95–521, set out as a note under section 288 of Title 2, The Congress.

§ 1366. Construction of references to laws of the United States or Acts of Congress

For the purposes of this chapter, references to laws of the United States or Acts of Congress do not include laws applicable exclusively to the District of Columbia.

(Added Pub.L. 91–358, Title I, § 172(c)(1), July 29, 1970, 84 Stat. 590, § 1363; renumbered § 1364, Pub.L. 95–572, § 6(b)(1), Nov. 2, 1978, 92 Stat. 2456; renumbered § 1366, Pub.L. 99–336, § 6(a)(1)(C), June 19, 1986, 100 Stat. 639.)

HISTORICAL AND STATUTORY NOTES

Effective Dates

1970 Acts. Section effective first day of seventh calendar month which begins after July 29, 1970, see section 199(a) of Pub.L. 91–358, set out as a note under section 1257 of this title.

§ 1367. Supplemental jurisdiction

(a) Except as provided in subsections (b) and (c) or as expressly provided otherwise by Federal statute, in any civil action of which the district courts have original jurisdiction, the district courts shall have supplemental jurisdiction over all other claims that are so related to claims in the action within such original jurisdiction that they form part of the same case or controversy under Article III of the United States Constitution. Such supplemental jurisdiction shall include claims that involve the joinder or intervention of additional parties.

(b) In any civil action of which the district courts have original jurisdiction founded solely on section 1332 of this title, the district courts shall not have supplemental jurisdiction under subsection (a) over claims by plaintiffs against persons made parties under Rule 14, 19, 20, or 24 of the Federal Rules of Civil Procedure, or over claims by persons proposed to be joined as plaintiffs under Rule 19 of such rules, or seeking to intervene as plaintiffs under Rule 24 of such rules, when exercising supplemental jurisdiction over such claims would be inconsistent with the jurisdictional requirements of section 1332.

(c) The district courts may decline to exercise supplemental jurisdiction over a claim under subsection (a) if—

(1) the claim raises a novel or complex issue of State law,

(2) the claim substantially predominates over the claim or claims over which the district court has original jurisdiction,

(3) the district court has dismissed all claims over which it has original jurisdiction, or

(4) in exceptional circumstances, there are other compelling reasons for declining jurisdiction.

(d) The period of limitations for any claim asserted under subsection (a), and for any other claim in the same action that is voluntarily dismissed at the same time as or after the dismissal of the claim under subsection (a), shall be tolled while the claim is pending and for a period of 30 days after it is dismissed unless State law provides for a longer tolling period.

(e) As used in this section, the term "State" includes the District of Columbia, the Commonwealth of Puerto Rico, and any territory or possession of the United States.

(Added Pub.L. 101–650, Title III, § 310(a), Dec. 1, 1990, 104 Stat. 5113.)

HISTORICAL AND STATUTORY NOTES

References in Text

The Federal Rules of Civil Procedure, referred to in subsec. (b), are set out in this title.

Effective Dates

1990 Acts. Section 310(c) of Pub.L. 101–650 provided that: "The amendments made by this section [enacting this section] shall apply to civil actions commenced on or after the date of the enactment of this Act [Dec. 1, 1990]."

COMMENTARIES

See 28 U.S.C.A. § 1367, for Commentary by David D. Siegel.

§ 1368. Counterclaims in unfair practices in international trade.

The district courts shall have original jurisdiction of any civil action based on a counterclaim raised pursuant to section 337(c) of the Tariff Act of 1930, to the extent that it arises out of the transaction or occurrence that is the subject matter of the opposing party's claim in the proceeding under section 337(a) of that Act.

(Added Pub.L. 103–465, Title III, § 321(b)(3)(A), Dec. 8, 1994, 108 Stat. 4946.)

HISTORICAL AND STATUTORY NOTES

References in Text

Section 337 of the Tariff Act of 1930, referred to in text, is section 337 of Act June 17, 1930, c. 497, Title III, 46 Stat. 703, which is classified to section 1337 of Title 19, Customs Duties.

Effective Dates

1994 Acts. Section applicable with respect to complaints filed under section 1337 of Title 19, Customs Duties, on or after the date on which the WTO Agreement enters into force with respect to the United States, Jan. 1, 1995, or in cases under section 1337 of Title 19 in which no complaint is filed, with respect to investigations initiated under such section on or after such date, see section 322 of Pub.L. 103–465, set out as a note under section 1337 of Title 19.

CHAPTER 87—DISTRICT COURTS; VENUE

Sec.

1391. Venue generally.
1392. Defendants or property in different districts in same State.
[1393. Repealed.]
1394. Banking association's action against Comptroller of Currency.
1395. Fine, penalty or forfeiture.
1396. Internal revenue taxes.
1397. Interpleader.
1398. Interstate Commerce Commission's orders.
1399. Partition action involving United States.
1400. Patents and copyrights, mask works, and designs.
1401. Stockholder's derivative action.
1402. United States as defendant.
1403. Eminent domain.
1404. Change of venue.
1405. Creation or alteration of district or division.
1406. Cure or waiver of defects.
1407. Multidistrict litigation.
1408. Venue of cases under title 11.
1409. Venue of proceedings arising under title 11 or arising in or related to cases under title 11.
1410. Venue of cases ancillary to foreign proceedings.
1411. Jury trials.
1412. Change of venue.
1413. Venue of cases under chapter 5 of title 3.

HISTORICAL AND STATUTORY NOTES

Codifications

Amendment by Pub.L. 104–331, § 3(b)(2)(B), Oct. 26, 1996, 110 Stat. 4069, which directed the addition of item 1413 to the end of chapter 37 of this title, was executed by adding item 1413 to the end of this chapter, as the probable intent of Congress.

The table of sections for chapter 87 was amended by Pub.L. 95–598, Title II, § 240(b), Nov. 6, 1978, 92 Stat. 2668, effective June 28, 1984, pursuant to Pub.L. 95–598, Title IV, § 402(b), Nov. 6, 1978, 92 Stat. 2682, as amended by Pub.L. 98–249, § 1(a), Mar. 31, 1984, 98 Stat. 116; Pub.L. 98–271, § 1(a), Apr. 30, 1984, 98 Stat. 163; Pub.L. 98–299, § 1(a), May 25, 1984, 98 Stat. 214; Pub.L. 98–325, § 1(a), June 20, 1984, 98 Stat. 268, set out as an effective dates note preceding section 101 of Title 11, Bankruptcy, by adding "1408, Bankruptcy appeals."

Section 402(b) of Pub.L. 95–598 was amended by section 113 of Pub.L. 98–353, Title 1, July 10, 1984, 98 Stat. 343, by substituting "shall not be effective" for "shall take effect on June 28, 1984," thereby eliminating the amendment by section 240(b) of Pub.L. 95–598, effective June 27, 1984, pursuant to section 122(e) of Pub.L. 98–353, set out as an Effective Date, note under section 151 of this title.

Section 121(a) of Pub.L. 98–353 directed that section 402(b) of Pub.L. 95–598 be amended by substituting "the date of enactment of the Bankruptcy Amendments and Federal Judgeship Act of 1984 [i.e. July 10, 1984]" for "June 28, 1984". This amendment was not executed in view of the prior amendment to section 402(b) of Pub.L. 95–598 by section 113 of Pub.L. 98–353.

§ 1391. Venue generally

(a) A civil action wherein jurisdiction is founded only on diversity of citizenship may, except as otherwise provided by law, be brought only in (1) a judicial district where any defendant resides, if all defendants reside in the same State, (2) a judicial district in which a substantial part of the events or omissions giving rise to the claim occurred, or a substantial part of property that is the subject of the action is situated, or (3) a judicial district in which any defendant is subject to personal jurisdiction at the time the action is commenced, if there is no district in which the action may otherwise be brought.

(b) A civil action wherein jurisdiction is not founded solely on diversity of citizenship may, except as otherwise provided by law, be brought only in (1) a judicial district where any defendant resides, if all defendants reside in the same State, (2) a judicial district in which a substantial part of the events or omissions giving rise to the claim occurred, or a substantial part of property that is the subject of the action is situated, or (3) a judicial district in which any defendant may be found, if there is no district in which the action may otherwise be brought.

(c) For purposes of venue under this chapter, a defendant that is a corporation shall be deemed to reside in any judicial district in which it is subject to personal jurisdiction at the time the action is commenced. In a State which has more than one judicial district and in which a defendant that is a corporation is subject to personal jurisdiction at the time an action is commenced, such corporation shall be deemed to reside in any district in that State within which its contacts would be sufficient to subject it to personal jurisdiction if that district were a separate State, and, if there is no such district, the corporation shall be deemed to reside in the district within which it has the most significant contacts.

(d) An alien may be sued in any district.

(e) A civil action in which a defendant is an officer or employee of the United States or any agency thereof acting in his official capacity or under color of legal authority, or an agency of the United States, or the United States, may, except as otherwise provided by law, be brought in any judicial district in which (1) a defendant in the action resides, (2) a substantial part of the events or omissions giving rise to the claim occurred, or a substantial part of property that is the subject of the action is situated, or (3) the plaintiff resides if no real property is involved in the action. Additional persons may be joined as parties to any such action in accordance with the Federal Rules of Civil Procedure and with such other venue requirements as would be applicable if the United States or one of its officers, employees, or agencies were not a party.

The summons and complaint in such an action shall be served as provided by the Federal Rules of Civil Procedure except that the delivery of the summons and complaint to the officer or agency as required by the rules may be made by certified mail beyond the territorial limits of the district in which the action is brought.

(f) A civil action against a foreign state as defined in section 1603(a) of this title may be brought—

(1) in any judicial district in which a substantial part of the events or omissions giving rise to the claim occurred, or a substantial part of property that is the subject of the action is situated;

(2) in any judicial district in which the vessel or cargo of a foreign state is situated, if the claim is asserted under section 1605(b) of this title;

(3) in any judicial district in which the agency or instrumentality is licensed to do business or is doing business, if the action is brought against an agency or instrumentality of a foreign state as defined in section 1603(b) of this title; or

(4) in the United States District Court for the District of Columbia if the action is brought against a foreign state or political subdivision thereof.

(June 25, 1948, c. 646, 62 Stat. 935; Oct. 5, 1962, Pub.L. 87–748, § 2, 76 Stat. 744; Dec. 23, 1963, Pub.L. 88–234, 77 Stat. 473; Nov. 2, 1966, Pub.L. 89–714, §§ 1, 2, 80 Stat. 1111; Oct. 21, 1976, Pub.L. 94–574, § 3, 90 Stat. 2721; Oct. 21, 1976, Pub.L. 94–583, § 5, 90 Stat. 2897; Nov. 19, 1988, Pub.L. 100–702, Title X, § 1013(a), 102 Stat. 4669; Dec. 1, 1990, Pub.L. 101–650, Title III, § 311, 104 Stat. 5114; Dec. 9, 1991, Pub.L. 102–198, § 3, 105 Stat. 1623; Oct. 29, 1992, Pub.L. 102–572, Title V, § 504, 106 Stat. 4513; Oct. 3, 1995, Pub.L. 104–34, § 1, 109 Stat. 293.)

HISTORICAL AND STATUTORY NOTES

References in Text

The Federal Rules of Civil Procedure, referred to in subsec. (e), are set out in this title.

Effective Dates

1992 Acts. Amendment by Pub.L. 102–572 effective Jan. 1, 1993, see section 1101(a) of Pub.L. 102–572, set out as a note under section 905 of Title 2, The Congress.

1988 Acts. Section 1013(b) of Title X of Pub.L. 100–702 provided that: "The amendment made by this section [amending this section] takes effect 90 days after the date of enactment of this title [Nov. 19, 1988]."

1976 Acts. Amendment by Pub.L. 94–583 effective 90 days after Oct. 21, 1976, see section 8 of Pub.L. 94–583, set out as a note under section 1602 of this title.

COMMENTARIES

See 28 U.S.C.A. § 1391, for Commentary by David D. Siegel.

§ 1392. Defendants or property in different districts in same State

Any civil action, of a local nature, involving property located in different districts in the same State, may be brought in any of such districts.

(June 25, 1948, c. 646, 62 Stat. 935; Oct. 1, 1996, Pub.L. 104–220, § 1, 110 Stat. 3023.)

[§ 1393. Repealed. Pub.L. 100–702, Title X, § 1001(a), Nov. 19, 1988, 102 Stat. 4664]

HISTORICAL AND STATUTORY NOTES

Section, Act June 25, 1948, c. 646, 62 Stat. 935, related to divisional venue in civil cases of a single defendant or defendants in different divisions.

Effective Date of Repeal

Section 1001(b) of Pub.L. 100–702 provided that "The amendments made by this section [repealing this section] take effect 90 days after the date of enactment of this Act [Nov. 19, 1988]."

COMMENTARIES

See 28 U.S.C.A. § 1393, for Commentary by David D. Siegel.

§ 1394. Banking association's action against Comptroller of Currency

Any civil action by a national banking association to enjoin the Comptroller of the Currency, under the provisions of any Act of Congress relating to such associations, may be prosecuted in the judicial district where such association is located.

(June 25, 1948, c. 646, 62 Stat. 935.)

HISTORICAL AND STATUTORY NOTES

Exception as to Transfer of Functions

Functions vested by any provision of law in the Comptroller of the Currency, referred to in this section, were not included in the transfer of functions of officers, agencies and employees of the Department of the Treasury to the Secretary of the Treasury, made by Reorg. Plan No. 26 of 1950, § 1, eff. July 31, 1950, 15 F.R. 4935, 64 Stat. 1280. See section 321(c)(2) of Title 31, Money and Finance.

§ 1395. Fine, penalty or forfeiture

(a) A civil proceeding for the recovery of a pecuniary fine, penalty or forfeiture may be prosecuted in the district where it accrues or the defendant is found.

(b) A civil proceeding for the forfeiture of property may be prosecuted in any district where such property is found.

(c) A civil proceeding for the forfeiture of property seized outside any judicial district may be prosecuted in any district into which the property is brought.

(d) A proceeding in admiralty for the enforcement of fines, penalties and forfeitures against a vessel may be brought in any district in which the vessel is arrested.

(e) Any proceeding for the forfeiture of a vessel or cargo entering a port of entry closed by the President in pursuance of law, or of goods and chattels coming from a State or section declared by proclamation of the President to be in insurrection, or of any vessel or vehicle conveying persons or property to or from such State or section or belonging in whole or in part to a resident thereof, may be prosecuted in any district into which the property is taken and in which the proceeding is instituted.

(June 25, 1948, c. 646, 62 Stat. 936.)

HISTORICAL AND STATUTORY NOTES

Senate Revision Amendment

While section 3745(c) of Title 26, U.S.C., Internal Revenue Code, is one of the sources of this section, it was eliminated from the schedule of repeals by Senate amendment. Therefore, such section 3745(c) remains in Title 26. See 80th Congress Senate Report No. 1559.

Said section 3745(c) was subsequently repealed by Act May 24, 1949, c. 139, § 142, 63 Stat. 110.

§ 1396. Internal revenue taxes

Any civil action for the collection of internal revenue taxes may be brought in the district where the liability for such tax accrues, in the district of the taxpayer's residence, or in the district where the return was filed.

(June 25, 1948, c. 646, 62 Stat. 936.)

HISTORICAL AND STATUTORY NOTES

Senate Revision Amendment

While section 3744 of Title 26, U.S.C., Internal Revenue Code [1939], is one of the sources of this section, it was eliminated from the schedule of repeals by Senate amendment. Therefore, it remains in Title 26 [I.R.C.1939]. See 80th Congress Senate Report No. 1559.

Said section 3744 was subsequently repealed by Act May 24, 1949, c. 139, § 142, 63 Stat. 110.

§ 1397. Interpleader

Any civil action of interpleader or in the nature of interpleader under section 1335 of this title may be brought in the judicial district in which one or more of the claimants reside.

(June 25, 1948, c. 646, 62 Stat. 936.)

§ 1398. Interstate Commerce Commission's orders

(a) Except as otherwise provided by law, a civil action brought under section 1336(a) of this title shall be brought only in a judicial district in which any of the parties bringing the action resides or has its principal office.

(b) A civil action to enforce, enjoin, set aside, annul, or suspend, in whole or in part, an order of the Interstate Commerce Commission made pursuant to the referral of a question or issue by a district court or by the United States Court of Federal Claims, shall be brought only in the court which referred the question or issue.

(June 25, 1948, c. 646, 62 Stat. 936; Aug. 30, 1964, Pub.L. 88–513, § 2, 78 Stat. 695; Jan. 2, 1975, Pub.L. 93–584, § 2, 88 Stat. 1917; Apr. 2, 1982, Pub.L. 97–164, Title I, § 130, 96 Stat. 39; Oct. 29, 1992, Pub.L. 102–572, Title IX, § 902(b)(1), 106 Stat. 4516.)

HISTORICAL AND STATUTORY NOTES

Effective Dates

1992 Acts. Amendment by Pub.L. 102–572 effective Oct. 29, 1992, see section 911 of Pub.L. 102–572, set out as a note under section 171 of this title.

1982 Acts. Amendment by Pub.L. 97–164 effective Oct. 1, 1982, see section 402 of Pub.L. 97–164, set out as a note under section 171 of this title.

1975 Acts. Amendment by Pub.L. 93–584 not applicable to actions commenced on or before the last day of the first month beginning after Jan. 2, 1975, and actions to enjoin or suspend orders of the Interstate Commerce Commission which are pending when this amendment becomes effective shall not be affected thereby, but shall proceed to final disposition under the law existing on the date they were commenced, see section 10 of Pub.L. 93–584, set out as a note under section 2321 of this title.

Abolition of Interstate Commerce Commission and Transfer of Functions

Interstate Commerce Commission abolished and functions of Commission transferred, except as otherwise provided in Pub.L. 104–88, to Surface Transportation Board effective

Jan. 1, 1996, by sections 702 of Title 49, Transportation, and section 101 of Pub.L. 104–88, set out as a note under section 701 of title 49. References to Interstate Commerce Commission deemed to refer to Surface Transportation Board, a member or employee of the Board, or Secretary of Transportation, as appropriate, see section 205 of Pub.L. 104–88, set out as a note under section 701 of Title 49.

§ 1399. Partition action involving United States

Any civil action by any tenant in common or joint tenant for the partition of lands, where the United States is one of the tenants in common or joint tenants, may be brought only in the judicial district where such lands are located or, if located in different districts in the same State, in any of such districts.

(June 25, 1948, c. 646, 62 Stat. 936.)

§ 1400. Patents and copyrights, mask works, and designs

(a) Civil actions, suits, or proceedings arising under any Act of Congress relating to copyrights or exclusive rights in mask works or designs may be instituted in the district in which the defendant or his agent resides or may be found.

(b) Any civil action for patent infringement may be brought in the judicial district where the defendant resides, or where the defendant has committed acts of infringement and has a regular and established place of business.

(June 25, 1948, c. 646, 62 Stat. 936; Nov. 19, 1988, Pub.L. 100–702, Title X, § 1020(a)(5), 102 Stat. 4671; Oct. 28, 1998, Pub.L. 105–304, Title V, § 503(c)(1), (2), 112 Stat. 2917.)

HISTORICAL AND STATUTORY NOTES

Senate Revision Amendment

Title 17 of the United States Code was enacted into positive law by Act July 30, 1947, c. 391, 61 Stat. 652, and, in such enactment, section 35 of the prior title became section 111 of the new title, and all Acts from which sections of the prior title had been derived, were repealed. Therefore, this paragraph should read: "Based on Title 28, U.S.C., 1940 ed., § 109 (Mar. 3, 1911, c. 231, § 48, 36 Stat. 1100), and section 111 of Title 17, U.S.C., 1946 ed., Copyrights." By Senate amendment, section 111 of Title 17 U.S.C., is included in the schedule of repeals. See 80th Congress Senate Report No. 1559.

1988 Acts. House Report No. 100–889, see 1988 U.S. Code Cong. and Adm. News, p. 5982.

Effective Date

1998 Acts. Amendment by Pub.L. 105–304, effective Oct. 28, 1998, and remaining in effect until the end of the 2–year period beginning on such date of enactment, see section 505 of Pub.L. 105–304, set out as a note under section 1301 of Title 17, Copyrights.

§ 1401. Stockholder's derivative action

Any civil action by a stockholder on behalf of his corporation may be prosecuted in any judicial district where the corporation might have sued the same defendants.

(June 25, 1948, c. 646, 62 Stat. 936.)

§ 1402. United States as defendant

(a) Any civil action in a district court against the United States under subsection (a) of section 1346 of this title may be prosecuted only:

(1) Except as provided in paragraph (2), in the judicial district where the plaintiff resides;

(2) In the case of a civil action by a corporation under paragraph (1) of subsection (a) of section 1346, in the judicial district in which is located the principal place of business or principal office or agency of the corporation; or if it has no principal place of business or principal office or agency in any judicial district (A) in the judicial district in which is located the office to which was made the return of the tax in respect of which the claim is made, or (B) if no return was made, in the judicial district in which lies the District of Columbia. Notwithstanding the foregoing provisions of this paragraph a district court, for the convenience of the parties and witnesses, in the interest of justice, may transfer any such action to any other district or division.

(b) Any civil action on a tort claim against the United States under subsection (b) of section 1346 of this title may be prosecuted only in the judicial district where the plaintiff resides or wherein the act or omission complained of occurred.

(c) Any civil action against the United States under subsection (e) of section 1346 of this title may be prosecuted only in the judicial district where the property is situated at the time of levy, or if no levy is made, in the judicial district in which the event occurred which gave rise to the cause of action.

(d) Any civil action under section 2409a to quiet title to an estate or interest in real property in which an interest is claimed by the United States shall be brought in the district court of the district where the property is located or, if located in different districts, in any of such districts.

(June 25, 1948, c. 646, 62 Stat. 937; Sept. 2, 1958, Pub.L. 85–920, 72 Stat. 1770; Nov. 2, 1966, Pub.L. 89–719, Title II, § 202(b), 80 Stat. 1149; Oct. 25, 1972, Pub.L. 92–562, § 2, 86 Stat. 1176; Apr. 2, 1982, Pub.L. 97–164, Title I, § 131, 96 Stat. 39.)

HISTORICAL AND STATUTORY NOTES

Effective Dates

1982 Acts. Amendment by Pub.L. 97–164 effective Oct. 1, 1982, see section 402 of Pub.L. 97–164, set out as a note under section 171 of this title.

1966 Acts. Subsec. (c) of this section applicable after Nov. 2, 1966, see section 203 of Pub.L. 89–719, set out as a note under section 1346 of this title.

§ 1403. Eminent domain

Proceedings to condemn real estate for the use of the United States or its departments or agencies shall be brought in the district court of the district where the land is located or, if located in different districts in the same State, in any of such districts.

(June 25, 1948, c. 646, 62 Stat. 937.)

§ 1404. Change of venue

(a) For the convenience of parties and witnesses, in the interest of justice, a district court may transfer any civil action to any other district or division where it might have been brought.

(b) Upon motion, consent or stipulation of all parties, any action, suit or proceeding of a civil nature or any motion or hearing thereof, may be transferred, in the discretion of the court, from the division in which pending to any other division in the same district. Transfer of proceedings in rem brought by or on behalf of the United States may be transferred under this section without the consent of the United States where all other parties request transfer.

(c) A district court may order any civil action to be tried at any place within the division in which it is pending.

(d) As used in this section, the term "district court" includes the District Court of Guam, the District Court for the Northern Mariana Islands, and the District Court of the Virgin Islands, and the term "district" includes the territorial jurisdiction of each such court.

(June 25, 1948, c. 646, 62 Stat. 937; Oct. 18, 1962, Pub.L. 87–845, § 9, 76A Stat. 699; Oct. 19, 1996, Pub.L. 104–317, Title VI, § 610(a), 110 Stat. 3860.)

HISTORICAL AND STATUTORY NOTES

Effective Dates

1996 Acts. Section 610(c) of Pub.L. 104–317 provided that: "The amendments made by this section [amending this section and section 1406 of this title] apply to cases pending on the date of the enactment of this Act [Oct. 19, 1996] and to cases commenced on or after such date."

1962 Acts. Amendment of section by Pub.L. 87–845 effective Jan. 2, 1963, see section 25 of Pub.L. 87–845, set out as a note under section 14 of Title 18, Crimes and Criminal Procedure.

Termination of United States District Court for the District of the Canal Zone

For termination of the United States District Court for the District of the Canal Zone at end of the "transition period", being the 30–month period beginning Oct. 1, 1979, and ending midnight Mar. 31, 1982, see Paragraph 5 of Article XI of the Panama Canal Treaty of 1977 and sections 3831 and 3841 to 3843 of Title 22, Foreign Relations and Intercourse.

§ 1405. Creation or alteration of district or division

Actions or proceedings pending at the time of the creation of a new district or division or transfer of a county or territory from one division or district to another may be tried in the district or division as it existed at the institution of the action or proceeding, or in the district or division so created or to which the county or territory is so transferred as the parties shall agree or the court direct.

(June 25, 1948, c. 646, 62 Stat. 937.)

§ 1406. Cure or waiver of defects

(a) The district court of a district in which is filed a case laying venue in the wrong division or district shall dismiss, or if it be in the interest of justice, transfer such case to any district or division in which it could have been brought.

(b) Nothing in this chapter shall impair the jurisdiction of a district court of any matter involving a party who does not interpose timely and sufficient objection to the venue.

(c) As used in this section, the term "district court" includes the District Court of Guam, the District Court for the Northern Mariana Islands, and the District Court of the Virgin Islands, and the term "district" includes the territorial jurisdiction of each such court.

(June 25, 1948, c. 646, 62 Stat. 937; May 24, 1949, c. 139, § 81, 63 Stat. 101; Sept. 13, 1960, Pub.L. 86–770, § 1, 74 Stat. 912; Oct. 18, 1962, Pub.L. 87–845, § 10, 76A Stat. 699; Apr. 2, 1982, Pub.L. 97–164, Title I, § 132, 96 Stat. 39; Oct. 19, 1996, Pub.L. 104–317, Title VI, § 610(b), 110 Stat. 3860.)

HISTORICAL AND STATUTORY NOTES

Effective Dates

1996 Acts. Amendment by section 610(b) of Pub.L. 104–317 to apply to cases pending on Oct. 19, 1996, and to cases commenced on or after such date, see section 610(c) of Pub.L. 104–317, set out as a note under section 1404 of this title.

1982 Acts. Amendment by Pub.L. 97–164 effective Oct. 1, 1982, see section 402 of Pub.L. 97–164, set out as a note under section 171 of this title.

1962 Acts. Amendment of section by Pub.L. 87–845 effective Jan. 2, 1963, see section 25 of Pub.L. 87–845, set out as a note under section 14 of Title 18, Crimes and Criminal Procedure.

1960 Acts. Section 4 of Pub.L. 86–770 provided in part that: "The amendments made by sections 1 and 2 of this Act [adding subsec. (c) of this section and section 1506 of this title] shall apply to any case or proceeding pending on, or brought after, the date of enactment of this Act [Sept. 13, 1960] in the district courts or the Court of Claims."

Termination of United States District Court for the District of the Canal Zone

For termination of the United States District Court for the District of the Canal Zone at end of the "transition period", being the 30–month period beginning Oct. 1, 1979, and ending midnight Mar. 31, 1982, see Paragraph 5 of Article XI of the Panama Canal Treaty of 1977 and sections 3831 and 3841 to 3843 of Title 22, Foreign Relations and Intercourse.

§ 1407. Multidistrict litigation

(a) When civil actions involving one or more common questions of fact are pending in different districts, such actions may be transferred to any district for coordinated or consolidated pretrial proceedings. Such transfers shall be made by the judicial panel on multidistrict litigation authorized by this section upon its determination that transfers for such proceedings will be for the convenience of parties and witnesses and will promote the just and efficient conduct of such actions. Each action so transferred shall be remanded by the panel at or before the conclusion of such pretrial proceedings to the district from which it was transferred unless it shall have been previously terminated: *Provided, however*, That the panel may separate any claim, cross-claim, counter-claim, or third-party claim and remand any of such claims before the remainder of the action is remanded.

(b) Such coordinated or consolidated pretrial proceedings shall be conducted by a judge or judges to whom such actions are assigned by the judicial panel on multidistrict litigation. For this purpose, upon request of the panel, a circuit judge or a district judge may be designated and assigned temporarily for service in the transferee district by the Chief Justice of the United States or the chief judge of the circuit, as may be required, in accordance with the provisions of chapter 13 of this title. With the consent of the transferee district court, such actions may be assigned by the panel to a judge or judges of such district. The judge or judges to whom such actions are assigned, the members of the judicial panel on multidistrict litigation, and other circuit and district judges designated when needed by the panel may exercise the powers of a district judge in any district for the purpose of conducting pretrial depositions in such coordinated or consolidated pretrial proceedings.

(c) Proceedings for the transfer of an action under this section may be initiated by—

(i) the judicial panel on multidistrict litigation upon its own initiative, or

(ii) motion filed with the panel by a party in any action in which transfer for coordinated or consolidated pretrial proceedings under this section may be appropriate. A copy of such motion shall be filed in the district court in which the moving party's action is pending.

The panel shall give notice to the parties in all actions in which transfers for coordinated or consolidated pretrial proceedings are contemplated, and such notice shall specify the time and place of any hearing to determine whether such transfer shall be made. Orders of the panel to set a hearing and other orders of the panel issued prior to the order either directing or denying transfer shall be filed in the office of the clerk of the district court in which a transfer hearing is to be or has been held. The panel's order of transfer shall be based upon a record of such hearing at which material evidence may be offered by any party to an action pending in any district that would be affected by the proceedings under this section, and shall be supported by findings of fact and conclusions of law based upon such record. Orders of transfer and such other orders as the panel may make thereafter shall be filed in the office of the clerk of the district court of the transferee district and shall be effective when thus filed. The clerk of the transferee district court shall forthwith transmit a certified copy of the panel's order to transfer to the clerk of the district court from which the action is being transferred. An order denying transfer shall be filed in each district wherein there is a case pending in which the motion for transfer has been made.

(d) The judicial panel on multidistrict litigation shall consist of seven circuit and district judges designated from time to time by the Chief Justice of the United States, no two of whom shall be from the same circuit. The concurrence of four members shall be necessary to any action by the panel.

(e) No proceedings for review of any order of the panel may be permitted except by extraordinary writ pursuant to the provisions of title 28, section 1651, United States Code. Petitions for an extraordinary writ to review an order of the panel to set a transfer hearing and other orders of the panel issued prior to the order either directing or denying transfer shall be filed only in the court of appeals having jurisdiction over the district in which a hearing is to be or has been held. Petitions for an extraordinary writ to review an order to transfer or orders subsequent to transfer shall be filed only in the court of appeals having jurisdiction over the transferee district. There shall be no appeal or review of an order of the panel denying a motion to transfer for consolidated or coordinated proceedings.

(f) The panel may prescribe rules for the conduct of its business not inconsistent with Acts of Congress and the Federal Rules of Civil Procedure.

(g) Nothing in this section shall apply to any action in which the United States is a complainant arising under the antitrust laws. "Antitrust laws" as used herein include those acts referred to in the Act of October 15, 1914, as amended (38 Stat. 730; 15 U.S.C. 12), and also include the Act of June 19, 1936 (49 Stat. 1526; 15 U.S.C. 13, 13a, and 13b) and the Act of September 26, 1914, as added March 21, 1938 (52 Stat. 116, 117; 15 U.S.C. 56); but shall not include section

4A of the Act of October 15, 1914, as added July 7, 1955 (69 Stat. 282; 15 U.S.C. 15a).

(h) Notwithstanding the provisions of section 1404 or subsection (f) of this section, the judicial panel on multidistrict litigation may consolidate and transfer with or without the consent of the parties, for both pretrial purposes and for trial, any action brought under section 4C of the Clayton Act.

(Added Pub.L. 90–296, § 1, Apr. 29, 1968, 82 Stat. 109, and amended Pub.L. 94–435, Title III, § 303, Sept. 30, 1976, 90 Stat. 1396.)

HISTORICAL AND STATUTORY NOTES

References in Text

The Federal Rules of Civil Procedure, referred to in subsec. (f), are set out in this title.

Section 4C of the Clayton Act, referred to in subsec. (h), is section 4C of Act Oct. 15, 1914, c. 323, as added by Pub.L. 94–435, Title III, § 301, Sept. 30, 1976, 90 Stat. 1394, which is classified to section 15c of Title 15, Commerce and Trade.

CROSS REFERENCES

Rules of Procedure of the Judicial Panel on Multidistrict Litigation are set out ante, following the Federal Rules of Civil Procedure for the United States District Courts.

§ 1408. Venue of cases under title 11

Except as provided in section 1410 of this title, a case under title 11 may be commenced in the district court for the district—

(1) in which the domicile, residence, principal place of business in the United States, or principal assets in the United States, of the person or entity that is the subject of such case have been located for the one hundred and eighty days immediately preceding such commencement, or for a longer portion of such one-hundred-and-eighty-day period than the domicile, residence, or principal place of business, in the United States, or principal assets in the United States, of such person were located in any other district; or

(2) in which there is pending a case under title 11 concerning such person's affiliate, general partner, or partnership.

(Added Pub.L. 98–353, Title I, § 102(a), July 10, 1984, 98 Stat. 334.)

HISTORICAL AND STATUTORY NOTES

Effective Dates

1984 Acts. Section effective July 10, 1984, see section 122(a) of Pub.L. 98–353, set out as a note under section 151 of this title.

Prior Provisions

A prior section 1408, added by Pub.L. 95–598, Title II, § 240(a), Nov. 6, 1978, 92 Stat. 2668, which related to bankruptcy appeals, did not become effective pursuant to section 402(b) of Pub.L. 95–598, as amended, set out as an Effective Dates note preceding section 101 of Title 11, Bankruptcy.

§ 1409. Venue of proceedings arising under title 11 or arising in or related to cases under title 11

(a) Except as otherwise provided in subsections (b) and (d), a proceeding arising under title 11 or arising in or related to a case under title 11 may be commenced in the district court in which such case is pending.

(b) Except as provided in subsection (d) of this section, a trustee in a case under title 11 may commence a proceeding arising in or related to such case to recover a money judgment of or property worth less than $1,000 or a consumer debt of less than $5,000 only in the district court for the district in which the defendant resides.

(c) Except as provided in subsection (b) of this section, a trustee in a case under title 11 may commence a proceeding arising in or related to such case as statutory successor to the debtor or creditors under section 541 or 544(b) of title 11 in the district court for the district where the State or Federal court sits in which, under applicable nonbankruptcy venue provisions, the debtor or creditors, as the case may be, may have commenced an action on which such proceeding is based if the case under title 11 had not been commenced.

(d) A trustee may commence a proceeding arising under title 11 or arising in or related to a case under title 11 based on a claim arising after the commencement of such case from the operation of the business of the debtor only in the district court for the district where a State or Federal court sits in which, under applicable nonbankruptcy venue provisions, an action on such claim may have been brought.

(e) A proceeding arising under title 11 or arising in or related to a case under title 11, based on a claim arising after the commencement of such case from the operation of the business of the debtor, may be commenced against the representative of the estate in such case in the district court for the district where the State or Federal court sits in which the party commencing such proceeding may, under applicable nonbankruptcy venue provisions, have brought an action on such claim, or in the district court in which such case is pending.

(Added Pub.L. 98–353, Title I, § 102(a), July 10, 1984, 98 Stat. 334.)

HISTORICAL AND STATUTORY NOTES

Effective Dates

1984 Acts. Section effective July 10, 1984, see section 122(a) of Pub.L. 98–353, set out as a note under section 151 of this title.

§ 1410. Venue of cases ancillary to foreign proceedings

(a) A case under section 304 of title 11 to enjoin the commencement or continuation of an action or proceeding in a State or Federal court, or the enforcement of a judgment, may be commenced only in the district court for the district where the State or Federal court sits in which is pending the action or proceeding against which the injunction is sought.

(b) A case under section 304 of title 11 to enjoin the enforcement of a lien against a property, or to require the turnover of property of an estate, may be commenced only in the district court for the district in which such property is found.

(c) A case under section 304 of title 11, other than a case specified in subsection (a) or (b) of this section, may be commenced only in the district court for the district in which is located the principal place of business in the United States, or the principal assets in the United States, of the estate that is the subject of such case.

(Added Pub.L. 98–353, Title I, § 102(a), July 10, 1984, 98 Stat. 335.)

HISTORICAL AND STATUTORY NOTES

Effective Dates

1984 Acts. Section effective July 10, 1984, see section 122(a) of Pub.L. 98–353, set out as a note under section 151 of this title.

§ 1411. Jury trials

(a) Except as provided in subsection (b) of this section, this chapter and title 11 do not affect any right to trial by jury that an individual has under applicable nonbankruptcy law with regard to a personal injury or wrongful death tort claim.

(b) The district court may order the issues arising under section 303 of title 11 to be tried without a jury.

(Added Pub.L. 98–353, Title I, § 102(a), July 10, 1984, 98 Stat. 335.)

HISTORICAL AND STATUTORY NOTES

Effective Dates

1984 Acts. Section, except subsec. (a), effective July 10, 1984, see section 122(a) of Pub.L. 98–353, set out as a note under section 151 of this title.

Subsec. (a) not applicable with respect to cases under Title 11, Bankruptcy, that are pending on July 10, 1984, or to proceedings arising in or related to such cases, see section 122(b) of Pub.L. 98–353, set out as a note under section 151 of this title.

§ 1412. Change of venue

A district court may transfer a case or proceeding under title 11 to a district court for another district, in the interest of justice or for the convenience of the parties.

(Added Pub.L. 98–353, Title I, § 102(a), July 10, 1984, 98 Stat. 335.)

HISTORICAL AND STATUTORY NOTES

Effective Dates

1984 Acts. Section effective July 10, 1984, see section 122(a) of Pub.L. 98–353, set out as a note under section 151 of this title.

§ 1413. Venue of cases under chapter 5 of title 3

Notwithstanding the preceding provisions of this chapter, a civil action under section 1346(g) may be brought in the United States district court for the district in which the employee is employed or in the United States District Court for the District of Columbia.

(Added Pub.L. 104–331, § 3(b)(2)(A), Oct. 26, 1996, 110 Stat. 4069.)

HISTORICAL AND STATUTORY NOTES

Codifications

Amendment by Pub.L. 104–331, § 3(b)(2)(A), which directed the addition of this section to the end of chapter 37 of this title, was executed by adding this section to the end of this chapter, as the probable intent of Congress.

Effective Dates

1996 Acts. Amendment by Pub.L. 104–331, § 3(b)(2)(B), effective October 1, 1997, see section 3(d) of Pub.L. 104–331, set out as a note under section 1296 of this title.

CHAPTER 89—DISTRICT COURTS; REMOVAL OF CASES FROM STATE COURTS

Sec.
1441. Actions removable generally.
1442. Federal officers and agencies sued or prosecuted.[1]
1442a. Members of armed forces sued or prosecuted.
1443. Civil rights cases.
1444. Foreclosure action against United States.
1445. Nonremovable actions.
1446. Procedure for removal.
1447. Procedure after removal generally.
1448. Process after removal.
1449. State court record supplied.
1450. Attachment or sequestration; securities.
1451. Definitions.
1452. Removal of claims related to bankruptcy cases.

[1] So in original. Does not conform to section catchline.

§ 1441. Actions removable generally

(a) Except as otherwise expressly provided by Act of Congress, any civil action brought in a State court of which the district courts of the United States have original jurisdiction, may be removed by the defendant or the defendants, to the district court of the United States for the district and division embracing the place where such action is pending. For purposes of removal under this chapter, the citizenship of defendants sued under fictitious names shall be disregarded.

(b) Any civil action of which the district courts have original jurisdiction founded on a claim or right arising under the Constitution, treaties or laws of the United States shall be removable without regard to the citizenship or residence of the parties. Any other such action shall be removable only if none of the parties in interest properly joined and served as defendants is a citizen of the State in which such action is brought.

(c) Whenever a separate and independent claim or cause of action within the jurisdiction conferred by section 1331 of this title is joined with one or more otherwise non-removable claims or causes of action, the entire case may be removed and the district court may determine all issues therein, or, in its discretion, may remand all matters in which State law predominates.

(d) Any civil action brought in a State court against a foreign state as defined in section 1603(a) of this title may be removed by the foreign state to the district court of the United States for the district and division embracing the place where such action is pending. Upon removal the action shall be tried by the court without jury. Where removal is based upon this subsection, the time limitations of section 1446(b) of this chapter may be enlarged at any time for cause shown.

(e) The court to which such civil action is removed is not precluded from hearing and determining any claim in such civil action because the State court from which such civil action is removed did not have jurisdiction over that claim.

(June 25, 1948, c. 646, 62 Stat. 937; Oct. 21, 1976, Pub.L. 94–583, § 6, 90 Stat. 2898; June 19, 1986, Pub.L. 99–336, § 3(a), 100 Stat. 637; Nov. 19, 1988, Pub.L. 100–702, Title X, § 1016(a), 102 Stat. 4669; Dec. 1, 1990, Pub.L. 101–650, Title III, § 312, 104 Stat. 5114; Dec. 9, 1991, Pub.L. 102–198, § 4, 105 Stat. 1623.)

HISTORICAL AND STATUTORY NOTES

Effective Dates

1986 Acts. Section 3(b) of Pub.L. 99–336 provided that: "The amendment made by this section [amending this section] shall apply with respect to claims in civil actions commenced in State courts on or after the date of the enactment of this section [June 19, 1986]."

1976 Acts. Amendment by Pub.L. 94–583 effective 90 days after Oct. 21, 1976, see section 8 of Pub.L. 94–583, set out as a note under section 1602 of this title.

COMMENTARIES

See 28 U.S.C.A. § 1441, for Commentary by David D. Siegel.

§ 1442. Federal officers or agencies sued or prosecuted

(a) A civil action or criminal prosecution commenced in a State court against any of the following may be removed by them to the district court of the United States for the district and division embracing the place wherein it is pending:

(1) The United States or any agency thereof or any officer (or any person acting under that officer) of the United States or of any agency thereof, sued in an official or individual capacity for any act under color of such office or on account of any right, title or authority claimed under any Act of Congress for the apprehension or punishment of criminals or the collection of the revenue.

(2) A property holder whose title is derived from any such officer, where such action or prosecution affects the validity of any law of the United States.

(3) Any officer of the courts of the United States, for any Act [1] under color of office or in the performance of his duties;

(4) Any officer of either House of Congress, for any act in the discharge of his official duty under an order of such House.

(b) A personal action commenced in any State court by an alien against any citizen of a State who is, or at the time the alleged action accrued was, a civil officer of the United States and is a nonresident of such

State, wherein jurisdiction is obtained by the State court by personal service of process, may be removed by the defendant to the district court of the United States for the district and division in which the defendant was served with process.

(June 25, 1948, c. 646, 62 Stat. 938; Oct. 19, 1996, Pub.L. 104–317, Title II, § 206(a), 110 Stat. 3850.)

[1] So in original. Probably should be "act".

§ 1442a. Members of armed forces sued or prosecuted

A civil or criminal prosecution in a court of a State of the United States against a member of the armed forces of the United States on account of an act done under color of his office or status, or in respect to which he claims any right, title, or authority under a law of the United States respecting the armed forces thereof, or under the law of war, may at any time before the trial or final hearing thereof be removed for trial into the district court of the United States for the district where it is pending in the manner prescribed by law, and it shall thereupon be entered on the docket of the district court, which shall proceed as if the cause had been originally commenced therein and shall have full power to hear and determine the cause.

(Added Aug. 10, 1956, c. 1041, § 19(a), 70A Stat. 626.)

HISTORICAL AND STATUTORY NOTES

Codifications

Section was from the Uniform Code of Military Justice, Act May 5, 1950, c. 169, § 9, 64 Stat. 146, which was based on Article 117, Articles of War, Act June 4, 1920, c. 227, subch. II, § 1, 41 Stat. 811, as amended June 24, 1948, c. 625, Title II, § 242, 62 Stat. 642.

§ 1443. Civil rights cases

Any of the following civil actions or criminal prosecutions, commenced in a State court may be removed by the defendant to the district court of the United States for the district and division embracing the place wherein it is pending:

(1) Against any person who is denied or cannot enforce in the courts of such State a right under any law providing for the equal civil rights of citizens of the United States, or of all persons within the jurisdiction thereof;

(2) For any act under color of authority derived from any law providing for equal rights, or for refusing to do any act on the ground that it would be inconsistent with such law.

(June 25, 1948, c. 646, 62 Stat. 938.)

§ 1444. Foreclosure action against United States

Any action brought under section 2410 of this title against the United States in any State court may be removed by the United States to the district court of the United States for the district and division in which the action is pending.

(June 25, 1948, c. 646, 62 Stat. 938; May 24, 1949, c. 139, § 82, 63 Stat. 101.)

§ 1445. Nonremovable actions

(a) A civil action in any State court against a railroad or its receivers or trustees, arising under sections 1–4 and 5–10 of the Act of April 22, 1908 (45 U.S.C. 51–54, 55–60), may not be removed to any district court of the United States.

(b) A civil action in any State court against a carrier or its receivers or trustees to recover damages for delay, loss, or injury of shipments, arising under section 11706 or 14706 of title 49, may not be removed to any district court of the United States unless the matter in controversy exceeds $10,000, exclusive of interest and costs.

(c) A civil action in any State court arising under the workmen's compensation laws of such State may not be removed to any district court of the United States.

(d) A civil action in any State court arising under section 40302 of the Violence Against Women Act of 1994 may not be removed to any district court of the United States.

(June 25, 1948, c. 646, 62 Stat. 939; July 25, 1958, Pub.L. 85–554, § 5, 72 Stat. 415; Oct. 17, 1978, Pub.L. 95–473, § 2(a)(3)(A), 92 Stat. 1465; Oct. 20, 1978, Pub.L. 95–486, § 9(b), 92 Stat. 1634; Sept. 13, 1994, Pub.L. 103–322, Title IV, § 40302(e)(5), 108 Stat. 1942; Dec. 29, 1995, Pub.L. 104–88, Title III, § 305(b), 109 Stat. 944; Oct. 11, 1996, Pub.L. 104–287, § 3, 110 Stat. 3388.)

HISTORICAL AND STATUTORY NOTES

References in Text

The Act of April 22, 1908, referred to in subsec. (a), popularly referred to as the [second] Employers' Liability Act, is Act Apr. 22, 1908, c. 149, 35 Stat. 65, as amended, which is classified generally to chapter 2 (section 51 et seq.) of Title 45, Railroads. For complete classification of this Act to the Code, see Short Title note set out under section 51 of Title 45 and Tables.

Section 40302 of the Violence Against Women Act of 1994, referred to in subsec. (d), means section 40302 of Pub.L. 103–322, the Violent Crime Control and Law Enforcement Act of 1994 (Title IV of such Act is the Violence Against Women Act of 1994), which is classified to section 13981 of Title 42, The Public Health and Welfare.

Effective Dates

1996 Acts. Amendment by section 3 of Pub.L. 104–287 effective on July 5, 1994, see section 8(1) of Pub.L. 104–287, set out as a note under section 5303 of Title 49, Transportation.

1995 Acts. Amendment by Pub.L. 104–88 effective Jan. 1, 1996, see section 2 of Pub.L. 104–88, set out as a note under section 701 of Title 49, Transportation.

1958 Acts. Amendment of section by Pub.L. 85–554 applicable only in the case of actions commenced after July 25, 1958, see section 3 of Pub.L. 85–554, set out as a note under section 1331 of this title.

§ 1446. Procedure for removal

(a) A defendant or defendants desiring to remove any civil action or criminal prosecution from a State court shall file in the district court of the United States for the district and division within which such action is pending a notice of removal signed pursuant to Rule 11 of the Federal Rules of Civil Procedure and containing a short and plain statement of the grounds for removal, together with a copy of all process, pleadings, and orders served upon such defendant or defendants in such action.

(b) The notice of removal of a civil action or proceeding shall be filed within thirty days after the receipt by the defendant, through service or otherwise, of a copy of the initial pleading setting forth the claim for relief upon which such action or proceeding is based, or within thirty days after the service of summons upon the defendant if such initial pleading has then been filed in court and is not required to be served on the defendant, whichever period is shorter.

If the case stated by the initial pleading is not removable, a notice of removal may be filed within thirty days after receipt by the defendant, through service or otherwise, of a copy of an amended pleading, motion, order or other paper from which it may first be ascertained that the case is one which is or has become removable, except that a case may not be removed on the basis of jurisdiction conferred by section 1332 of this title more than 1 year after commencement of the action.

(c)(1) A notice of removal of a criminal prosecution shall be filed not later than thirty days after the arraignment in the State court, or at any time before trial, whichever is earlier, except that for good cause shown the United States district court may enter an order granting the defendant or defendants leave to file the notice at a later time.

(2) A notice of removal of a criminal prosecution shall include all grounds for such removal. A failure to state grounds which exist at the time of the filing of the notice shall constitute a waiver of such grounds, and a second notice may be filed only on grounds not existing at the time of the original notice. For good cause shown, the United States district court may grant relief from the limitations of this paragraph.

(3) The filing of a notice of removal of a criminal prosecution shall not prevent the State court in which such prosecution is pending from proceeding further, except that a judgment of conviction shall not be entered unless the prosecution is first remanded.

(4) The United States district court in which such notice is filed shall examine the notice promptly. If it clearly appears on the face of the notice and any exhibits annexed thereto that removal should not be permitted, the court shall make an order for summary remand.

(5) If the United States district court does not order the summary remand of such prosecution, it shall order an evidentiary hearing to be held promptly and after such hearing shall make such disposition of the prosecution as justice shall require. If the United States district court determines that removal shall be permitted, it shall so notify the State court in which prosecution is pending, which shall proceed no further.

(d) Promptly after the filing of such notice of removal of a civil action the defendant or defendants shall give written notice thereof to all adverse parties and shall file a copy of the notice with the clerk of such State court, which shall effect the removal and the State court shall proceed no further unless and until the case is remanded.

(e) If the defendant or defendants are in actual custody on process issued by the State court, the district court shall issue its writ of habeas corpus, and the marshal shall thereupon take such defendant or defendants into his custody and deliver a copy of the writ to the clerk of such State court.

(f) With respect to any counterclaim removed to a district court pursuant to section 337(c) of the Tariff Act of 1930, the district court shall resolve such counterclaim in the same manner as an original complaint under the Federal Rules of Civil Procedure, except that the payment of a filing fee shall not be required in such cases and the counterclaim shall relate back to the date of the original complaint in the proceeding before the International Trade Commission under section 337 of that Act.

(June 25, 1948, c. 646, 62 Stat. 939; May 24, 1949, c. 139, § 83, 63 Stat. 101; Sept. 29, 1965, Pub.L. 89–215, 79 Stat. 887; July 30, 1977, Pub.L. 95–78, § 3, 91 Stat. 321; Nov. 19, 1988, Pub.L. 100–702, Title X, § 1016(b), 102 Stat. 4669; Dec. 9, 1991, Pub.L. 102–198, § 10(a), 105 Stat. 1626; Dec. 8, 1994, Pub.L. 103–465, Title III, § 321(b)(2), 108 Stat. 4946; Oct. 19, 1996, Pub.L. 104–317, Title VI, § 603, 110 Stat. 3857.)

HISTORICAL AND STATUTORY NOTES

References in Text

The Federal Rules of Civil Procedure, referred to in subsec. (a), are set out in this title.

Codifications

Section 10(a)(5)(A) of Pub.L. 102–198, which directed that subsec. (d) of this section be amended by substituting "removal" for "the removal", was executed by making such substitution at the first appearance of the term "the removal", as the probable intent of Congress.

1994 Acts

House Report No. 103–826 (Parts I and II) and Statement of Administrative Action, see 1994 U.S. Code Cong. and Adm. News, p. 3773.

Effective Dates

1994 Acts. Amendment by section 321(b)(2) of Pub.L. 103–465 applicable with respect to complaints filed under section 1337 of Title 19, Customs Duties, on or after the date on which the WTO Agreement enters into force with respect to the United States, Jan. 1, 1995, or in cases under section 1337 of Title 19 in which no complaint is filed, with respect to investigations initiated under such section on or after such date, see section 322 of Pub.L. 103–465, set out as a note under section 1337 of Title 19.

1977 Acts. Amendment by Pub.L. 95–78 effective Oct. 1, 1977, see section 4 of Pub.L. 95–78, set out as a note under section 3771 of Title 18, Crimes and Criminal Procedure.

COMMENTARIES

See 28 U.S.C.A. § 1446, for Commentary by David D. Siegel.

§ 1447. Procedure after removal generally

(a) In any case removed from a State court, the district court may issue all necessary orders and process to bring before it all proper parties whether served by process issued by the State court or otherwise.

(b) It may require the removing party to file with its clerk copies of all records and proceedings in such State court or may cause the same to be brought before it by writ of certiorari issued to such State court.

(c) A motion to remand the case on the basis of any defect other than lack of subject matter jurisdiction must be made within 30 days after the filing of the notice of removal under section 1446(a). If at any time before final judgment it appears that the district court lacks subject matter jurisdiction, the case shall be remanded. An order remanding the case may require payment of just costs and any actual expenses, including attorney fees, incurred as a result of the removal. A certified copy of the order of remand shall be mailed by the clerk to the clerk of the State court. The State court may thereupon proceed with such case.

(d) An order remanding a case to the State court from which it was removed is not reviewable on appeal or otherwise, except that an order remanding a case to the State court from which it was removed pursuant to section 1443 of this title shall be reviewable by appeal or otherwise.

(e) If after removal the plaintiff seeks to join additional defendants whose joinder would destroy subject matter jurisdiction, the court may deny joinder, or permit joinder and remand the action to the State court.

(June 25, 1948, c. 646, 62 Stat. 939; May 24, 1949, c. 139, § 84, 63 Stat. 102; July 2, 1964, Pub.L. 88–352, Title IX, § 901, 78 Stat. 266; Nov. 19, 1988, Pub.L. 100–702, Title X, § 1016(c), 102 Stat. 4670; Dec. 9, 1991, Pub.L. 102–198, § 10(b), 105 Stat. 1626; Oct. 1, 1996, Pub.L. 104–219, § 1, 110 Stat. 3022.)

HISTORICAL AND STATUTORY NOTES

Exception to Subsection (d)

Section 3(c) of Act Aug. 4, 1947, c. 458, 61 Stat. 732, provided in part that the United States shall have the right to appeal from any order of remand entered in any case removed to a United States district court pursuant to the provisions of Act Apr. 12, 1926, c. 115, 44 Stat. 239. These Acts referred to herein relate to restrictions on land of the Five Civilized Tribes of Oklahoma and are set out as notes under section 355 of Title 25, Indians.

COMMENTARIES

See 28 U.S.C.A. § 1447, for Commentary by David D. Siegel.

§ 1448. Process after removal

In all cases removed from any State court to any district court of the United States in which any one or more of the defendants has not been served with process or in which the service has not been perfected prior to removal, or in which process served proves to be defective, such process or service may be completed or new process issued in the same manner as in cases originally filed in such district court.

This section shall not deprive any defendant upon whom process is served after removal of his right to move to remand the case.

(June 25, 1948, c. 646, 62 Stat. 940.)

§ 1449. State court record supplied

Where a party is entitled to copies of the records and proceedings in any suit or prosecution in a State court, to be used in any district court of the United States, and the clerk of such State court, upon demand, and the payment or tender of the legal fees, fails to deliver certified copies, the district court may, on affidavit reciting such facts, direct such record to be supplied by affidavit or otherwise. Thereupon such proceedings, trial, and judgment may be had in such district court, and all such process awarded, as if certified copies had been filed in the district court.

(June 25, 1948, c. 646, 62 Stat. 940; May 24, 1949, c. 139, § 85, 63 Stat. 102.)

§ 1450. Attachment or sequestration; securities

Whenever any action is removed from a State court to a district court of the United States, any attachment or sequestration of the goods or estate of the defendant in such action in the State court shall hold the goods or estate to answer the final judgment or decree in the same manner as they would have been held to answer final judgment or decree had it been rendered by the State court.

All bonds, undertakings, or security given by either party in such action prior to its removal shall remain valid and effectual notwithstanding such removal.

All injunctions, orders, and other proceedings had in such action prior to its removal shall remain in full force and effect until dissolved or modified by the district court.

(June 25, 1948, c. 646, 62 Stat. 940.)

§ 1451. Definitions

For purposes of this chapter—

(1) The term "State court" includes the Superior Court of the District of Columbia.

(2) The term "State" includes the District of Columbia.

(Added Pub.L. 91–358, Title I, § 172(d)(1), July 29, 1970, 84 Stat. 591.)

HISTORICAL AND STATUTORY NOTES

Effective Dates

1970 Acts. Section effective the first day of the seventh calendar month which begins after July 29, 1970, see section 199(a) of Pub.L. 91–358, set out as a note under section 1257 of this title.

§ 1452. Removal of claims related to bankruptcy cases

(a) A party may remove any claim or cause of action in a civil action other than a proceeding before the United States Tax Court or a civil action by a governmental unit to enforce such governmental unit's police or regulatory power, to the district court for the district where such civil action is pending, if such district court has jurisdiction of such claim or cause of action under section 1334 of this title.

(b) The court to which such claim or cause of action is removed may remand such claim or cause of action on any equitable ground. An order entered under this subsection remanding a claim or cause of action, or a decision to not remand, is not reviewable by appeal or otherwise by the court of appeals under section 158(d), 1291, or 1292 of this title or by the Supreme Court of the United States under section 1254 of this title.

(Added Pub.L. 98–353, Title I, § 103(a), July 10, 1984, 98 Stat. 335, and amended Pub.L. 101–650, Title III, § 309(c), Dec. 1, 1990, 104 Stat. 5113.)

HISTORICAL AND STATUTORY NOTES

Effective Dates

1984 Acts. Section effective July 10, 1984, see section 122(a) of Pub.L. 98–353, set out as a note under section 151 of this title.

[CHAPTER 90—DISTRICT COURTS AND BANKRUPTCY COURTS] [OMITTED]

HISTORICAL AND STATUTORY NOTES

Codifications

Chapter 90, consisting of sections 1471 to 1482, which was added by Pub.L.95–598, Title II, § 241(a), Nov. 6, 1978, 92 Stat. 2668, and which related to district courts and bankruptcy courts, did not become effective pursuant to section 402(b) of Pub.L. 95–598, as amended, set out as an Effective Dates note preceding section 101 of Title 11, Bankruptcy.

Transition to New Court System

Pub.L. 95–598, Title IV, § 409, Nov. 6, 1978, 92 Stat. 2687, as amended by Pub.L. 98–249, § 1(d), Mar. 31, 1984, 98 Stat. 116; Pub.L. 98–271, § 1(d), Apr. 30, 1984, 98 Stat. 163; Pub.L. 98–299, § 1(d), May 25, 1984, 98 Stat. 214; Pub.L. 98–325, § 1(d), June 20, 1984, 98 Stat. 268; Pub.L. 98–353, Title I, § 121(d), July 10, 1984, 98 Stat. 346, was repealed by Pub.L. 98–353, Title I, §§ 114, 122(a), July 10, 1984, 98 Stat. 343, 346, eff. July 10, 1984. The repealed section had provided for transfer to the new court system of 1) cases, and matters and proceedings in cases, under the Bankruptcy Act [former Title 11] pending at the end of Sept. 30, 1983, in the courts of bankruptcy continued under section 404(a) of Pub.L. 95–598, with certain exceptions, and 2) cases and proceedings arising under or related to cases under Title 11 pending at the end of July 9, 1984, in the courts of bankruptcy continued under section 404(a) of Pub.L. 95–598, and directed that civil actions pending on July 9, 1984, over which a bankruptcy court had jurisdiction on July 9, 1984, not abate, that actions not finally determined before Apr. 1, 1985, be removed to a bankruptcy court under this chapter, and that all law books, publications, etc., furnished bankruptcy judges as of July 9, 1984, be transferred to the United States bankruptcy courts under the supervision of the Director of the Administrative Office of the United States Courts.

[§§ 1471 to 1482. Omitted]

CHAPTER 91—UNITED STATES COURT OF FEDERAL CLAIMS

Sec.
1491. Claims against United States generally; actions involving Tennessee Valley Authority.
1492. Congressional reference cases.
[1493. Repealed.]
1494. Accounts of officers, agents or contractors.
1495. Damages for unjust conviction and imprisonment; claim against United States.
1496. Disbursing officers' claims.
1497. Oyster growers' damages from dredging operations.
1498. Patent and copyright cases.
1499. Liquidated damages withheld from contractors under Contract Work Hours and Safety Standards Act.
1500. Pendency of claims in other courts.
1501. Pensions.
1502. Treaty cases.
1503. Set-offs.
[1504. Repealed.]
1505. Indian claims.
[1506. Repealed.]
1507. Jurisdiction for certain declaratory judgments.
1508. Jurisdiction for certain partnership proceedings.
1509. No jurisdiction in cases involving refunds of tax shelter promoter and understatement penalties.

§ 1491. Claims against United States generally; actions involving Tennessee Valley Authority

(a)(1) The United States Court of Federal Claims shall have jurisdiction to render judgment upon any claim against the United States founded either upon the Constitution, or any Act of Congress or any regulation of an executive department, or upon any express or implied contract with the United States, or for liquidated or unliquidated damages in cases not sounding in tort. For the purpose of this paragraph, an express or implied contract with the Army and Air Force Exchange Service, Navy Exchanges, Marine Corps Exchanges, Coast Guard Exchanges, or Exchange Councils of the National Aeronautics and Space Administration shall be considered an express or implied contract with the United States.

(2) To provide an entire remedy and to complete the relief afforded by the judgment, the court may, as an incident of and collateral to any such judgment, issue orders directing restoration to office or position, placement in appropriate duty or retirement status, and correction of applicable records, and such orders may be issued to any appropriate official of the United States. In any case within its jurisdiction, the court shall have the power to remand appropriate matters to any administrative or executive body or official with such direction as it may deem proper and just. The Court of Federal Claims shall have jurisdiction to render judgment upon any claim by or against, or dispute with, a contractor arising under section 10(a)(1) of the Contract Disputes Act of 1978, including a dispute concerning termination of a contract, rights in tangible or intangible property, compliance with cost accounting standards, and other nonmonetary disputes on which a decision of the contracting officer has been issued under section 6 of that Act.

[(3) Repealed. Pub.L. 104–320, § 12(a)(2), Oct. 19, 1996, 110 Stat. 3874]

(b)(1) Both the Unites[1] States Court of Federal Claims and the district courts of the United States shall have jurisdiction to render judgment on an action by an interested party objecting to a solicitation by a Federal agency for bids or proposals for a proposed contract or to a proposed award or the award of a contract or any alleged violation of statute or regulation in connection with a procurement or a proposed procurement. Both the United States Court of Federal Claims and the district courts of the United States shall have jurisdiction to entertain such an action without regard to whether suit is instituted before or after the contract is awarded.

(2) To afford relief in such an action, the courts may award any relief that the court considers proper, including declaratory and injunctive relief except that any monetary relief shall be limited to bid preparation and proposal costs.

(3) In exercising jurisdiction under this subsection, the courts shall give due regard to the interests of national defense and national security and the need for expeditious resolution of the action.

(4) In any action under this subsection, the courts shall review the agency's decision pursuant to the standards set forth in section 706 of title 5.

(c) Nothing herein shall be construed to give the United States Court of Federal Claims jurisdiction of any civil action within the exclusive jurisdiction of the Court of International Trade, or of any action against, or founded on conduct of, the Tennessee Valley Authority, or to amend or modify the provisions of the Tennessee Valley Authority Act of 1933 with respect to actions by or against the Authority.

(June 25, 1948, c. 646, 62 Stat. 940; July 28, 1953, c. 253, § 7, 67 Stat. 226; Sept. 3, 1954, c. 1263, § 44(a), (b), 68 Stat. 1241; July 23, 1970, Pub.L. 91–350, § 1(b), 84 Stat. 449; Aug. 29, 1972, Pub.L. 92–415, § 1, 86 Stat. 652; Nov. 1, 1978, Pub.L. 95–563, § 14(i), 92 Stat. 2391; Oct. 10, 1980, Pub.L. 96–417, Title V, § 509, 94 Stat. 1743; Apr. 2, 1982, Pub.L. 97–164, Title I, § 133(a), 96 Stat. 39; Oct. 29, 1992, Pub.L. 102–572, Title IX, §§ 902(a), 907(b)(1), 106 Stat. 4516, 4519; Oct. 19, 1996, Pub.L. 104–320, § 12(a), 110 Stat. 3874.)

[1] So in original.

HISTORICAL AND STATUTORY NOTES

References in Text

The Contracts Disputes Act of 1978, referred to in subsec. (a)(2), is Pub.L. 95–563, Nov. 1, 1978, 92 Stat. 2383, which is classified principally to chapter 9 (section 601 et seq.) of Title 41, Public Contracts. Sections 6 and 10(a)(1) of such Act are classified to sections 605 and 609(a)(1), respectively, of Title 41. For complete classification of this Act to the Code, see Short Title note set out under section 601 of Title 41 and Tables.

The Tennessee Valley Authority Act of 1933, referred to in subsec. (b), is Act May 18, 1933, c. 32, 48 Stat. 58, as amended, which is classified generally to chapter 12A (section 831 et seq.) of Title 16, Conservation. For complete classification of this Act to the Code, see section 831 of Title 16 and Tables.

Effective Dates

1996 Acts. Section 12(b) of Pub.L. 104–320 provided that: "This section and the amendments made by this section [amending subsecs. (a)(3), (b), and (c) of this section] shall take effect on December 31, 1996 and shall apply to all actions filed on or after that date."

1992 Acts. Amendments by section 902(a) of Pub.L. 102–572 effective Oct. 29, 1992, see section 911 of Pub.L. 102–572, set out as a note under section 171 of this title.

Section 907(b)(2) of Pub.L. 102–572 provided that: "The amendment made by paragraph (1) [amending subsec. (a)(2) of this section] shall be effective with respect to all actions filed before, on, or after the date of the enactment of this Act [Oct. 29, 1992], except for those actions which, before such date of enactment, have been the subject of—

"(A) a final judgment of the United States Claims Court, if the time for appeal of that judgment has expired without an appeal having been filed, or

"(B) a final judgment of the Court of Appeals for the Federal Circuit."

1982 Acts. Amendment by Pub.L. 97–164 effective Oct. 1, 1982, see section 402 of Pub.L. 97–164, set out as a note under section 171 of this title.

1980 Acts. Amendment by Pub.L. 96–417 effective Nov. 1, 1980 and applicable with respect to civil actions pending on or commenced on or after such date, see section 701(a) of Pub.L. 96–417, as amended, set out as a note under section 251 of this title.

1978 Acts. Amendment by Pub.L. 95–563 effective with respect to contracts entered into 120 days after Nov. 1, 1978, and, at the election of the contractor, with respect to any claim pending at such time before the contracting officer or initiated thereafter, see section 16 of Pub.L. 95–563, set out as a note under section 601 of Title 41, Public Contracts.

1972 Acts. Section 2 of Pub.L. 92–415 provided that: "This Act [amending this section] shall be applicable to all judicial proceedings pending on or instituted after the date of its enactment [Aug. 29, 1972]."

1970 Acts. Amendment by Pub.L. 91–350 applicable to claims and civil actions dismissed before or pending on July 23, 1970, if the claim or civil action was based upon a transaction, omission, or breach that occurred not more than six years prior to July 23, 1970, notwithstanding a determination or judgment made prior to July 23, 1970, that the United States district courts or the United States Court of Claims did not have jurisdiction to entertain a suit on an express or implied contract with a nonappropriated fund instrumentality of the United States, see section 2 of Pub.L. 91–350, set out as a note under section 1346 of this title.

Sunset Provisions

Section 12(d) of Pub.L. 104–320 provided that: "The jurisdiction of the district courts of the United States over the actions described in section 1491(b)(1) of title 28, United States Code [subsec. (b)(1) of this section] (as amended by subsection (a) of this section) shall terminate on January 1, 2001 unless extended by Congress. The savings provisions in subsection (e) [section 12(e) of Pub.L. 104–320, set out as a note under this section] shall apply if the bid protest jurisdiction of the district courts of the United States terminates under this subsection [this note]."

Savings Provisions

Section 12(e) of Pub.L. 104–320 provided that:

"(1) **Orders.**—A termination under subsection (d) [section 12(d) of Pub.L. 104–320, set out as a note under this section] shall not terminate the effectiveness of orders that have been issued by a court in connection with an action within the jurisdiction of that court on or before December 31, 2000. Such orders shall continue in effect according to their terms until modified, terminated, superseded, set aside, or revoked by a court of competent jurisdiction or by operation of law.

"(2) **Proceedings and applications.—(A)** a [sic] termination under subsection (d) shall not affect the jurisdiction of a court of the United States to continue with any proceeding that is pending before the court on December 31, 2000.

"**(B)** Orders may be issued in any such proceeding, appeals may be taken therefrom, and payments may be made pursuant to such orders, as if such termination had not occurred. An order issued in any such proceeding shall continue in effect until modified, terminated, superseded, set aside, or revoked by a court of competent jurisdiction or by operation of law.

"**(C)** Nothing in this paragraph prohibits the discontinuance or modification of any such proceeding under the same terms and conditions and to the same extent that proceeding could have been discontinued or modified absent such termination."

Study on Concurrent Jurisdiction

Section 12(c) of Pub.L. 104–320 provided that: "No earlier than 2 years after the effective date of this section [see section 12(b) of Pub.L. 104–320, set out as a note under this section], the United States General Accounting Office shall undertake a study regarding the concurrent jurisdiction of the district courts of the United States and the Court of Federal Claims over bid protests to determine whether concurrent jurisdiction is necessary. Such a study shall be completed no later than December 31, 1999, and shall specifically consider the effect of any proposed change on the ability of small businesses to challenge violations of Federal procurement law."

§ 1492. Congressional reference cases

Any bill, except a bill for a pension, may be referred by either House of Congress to the chief judge of the

United States Court of Federal Claims for a report in conformity with section 2509 of this title.

(June 25, 1948, c. 646, 62 Stat. 941; Oct. 15, 1966, Pub.L. 89–681, § 1, 80 Stat. 958; Apr. 2, 1982, Pub.L. 97–164, Title I, § 133(b), 96 Stat. 40; Oct. 29, 1992, Pub.L. 102–572, Title IX, § 902(a)(1), 106 Stat. 4516.)

HISTORICAL AND STATUTORY NOTES

Effective Dates

1992 Acts. Amendment by Title IX of Pub.L. 102–572 effective Oct. 29, 1992, see section 911 of Pub.L. 102–572, set out as a note under section 171 of this title.

1982 Acts. Amendment by Pub.L. 97–164 effective Oct. 1, 1982, see section 402 of Pub.L. 97–164, set out as a note under section 171 of this title.

[§ 1493. Repealed. July 28, 1953, c. 253, § 8, 67 Stat. 226]

HISTORICAL AND STATUTORY NOTES

Section, Act June 25, 1948, c. 646, 62 Stat. 941, authorized the Court of Claims to give legal advice to the heads of executive departments in matters referred to it by such heads, if the Court had jurisdiction over such matters.

§ 1494. Accounts of officers, agents or contractors

The United States Court of Federal Claims shall have jurisdiction to determine the amount, if any, due to or from the United States by reason of any unsettled account of any officer or agent of, or contractor with, the United States, or a guarantor, surety or personal representative of any such officer, agent or contractor, and to render judgment thereof,[1] where—

(1) claimant or the person he represents has applied to the proper department of the Government for settlement of the account;

(2) three years have elapsed from the date of such application without settlement; and

(3) no suit upon the same has been brought by the United States.

(June 25, 1948, c. 646, 62 Stat. 941; July 28, 1953, c. 253, § 9, 67 Stat. 226; Sept. 3, 1954, c. 1263, § 44(c), 68 Stat. 1242; Apr. 2, 1982, Pub.L. 97–164, Title I, § 133(c) (1), 96 Stat. 40; Oct. 29, 1992, Pub.L. 102–572, Title IX, § 902(a)(1), 106 Stat. 4516.)

[1] So in original. Probably should be "thereon".

HISTORICAL AND STATUTORY NOTES

Effective Dates

1992 Acts. Amendment by Title IX of Pub.L. 102–572 effective Oct. 29, 1992, see section 911 of Pub.L. 102–572, set out as a note under section 171 of this title.

1982 Acts. Amendment by Pub.L. 97–164 effective Oct. 1, 1982, see section 402 of Pub.L. 97–164, set out as a note under section 171 of this title.

§ 1495. Damages for unjust conviction and imprisonment; claim against United States

The United States Court of Federal Claims shall have jurisdiction to render judgment upon any claim for damages by any person unjustly convicted of an offense against the United States and imprisoned.

(June 25, 1948, c. 646, 62 Stat. 941; Apr. 2, 1982, Pub.L. 97–164, Title I, § 133(c) (1), 96 Stat. 40; Oct. 29, 1992, Pub.L. 102–572, Title IX, § 902(a)(1), 106 Stat. 4516.)

HISTORICAL AND STATUTORY NOTES

Effective Dates

1992 Acts. Amendment by Title IX of Pub.L. 102–572 effective Oct. 29, 1992, see section 911 of Pub.L. 102–572, set out as a note under section 171 of this title.

1982 Acts. Amendment by Pub.L. 97–164 effective Oct. 1, 1982, see section 402 of Pub.L. 97–164, set out as a note under section 171 of this title.

§ 1496. Disbursing officers' claims

The United States Court of Federal Claims shall have jurisdiction to render judgment upon any claim by a disbursing officer of the United States or by his administrator or executor for relief from responsibility for loss, in line of duty, of Government funds, vouchers, records or other papers in his charge.

(June 25, 1948, c. 646, 62 Stat. 941; Apr. 2, 1982, Pub.L. 97–164, Title I, § 133(c)(1), 96 Stat. 40; Oct. 29, 1992, Pub.L. 102–572, Title IX, § 902(a)(1), 106 Stat. 4516.)

HISTORICAL AND STATUTORY NOTES

Effective Dates

1992 Acts. Amendment by Title IX of Pub.L. 102–572 effective Oct. 29, 1992, see section 911 of Pub.L. 102–572, set out as a note under section 171 of this title.

1982 Acts. Amendment by Pub.L. 97–164 effective Oct. 1, 1982, see section 402 of Pub.L. 97–164, set out as a note under section 171 of this title.

§ 1497. Oyster growers' damages from dredging operations

The United States Court of Federal Claims shall have jurisdiction to render judgment upon any claim for damages to oyster growers on private or leased lands or bottoms arising from dredging operations or use of other machinery and equipment in making river and harbor improvements authorized by Act of Congress.

(June 25, 1948, c. 646, 62 Stat. 941; Apr. 2, 1982, Pub.L. 97–164, Title I, § 133(c), 96 Stat. 40; Oct. 29, 1992, Pub.L. 102–572, Title IX, § 902(a)(1), 106 Stat. 4516.)

HISTORICAL AND STATUTORY NOTES

Effective Dates

1992 Acts. Amendment by Title IX of Pub.L. 102–572 effective Oct. 29, 1992, see section 911 of Pub.L. 102–572, set out as a note under section 171 of this title.

1982 Acts. Amendment by Pub.L. 97–164 effective Oct. 1, 1982, see section 402 of Pub.L. 97–164, set out as a note under section 171 of this title.

§ 1498. Patent and copyright cases

(a) Whenever an invention described in and covered by a patent of the United States is used or manufactured by or for the United States without license of the owner thereof or lawful right to use or manufacture the same, the owner's remedy shall be by action against the United States in the United States Court of Federal Claims for the recovery of his reasonable and entire compensation for such use and manufacture. Reasonable and entire compensation shall include the owner's reasonable costs, including reasonable fees for expert witnesses and attorneys, in pursuing the action if the owner is an independent inventor, a nonprofit organization, or an entity that had no more than 500 employees at any time during the 5–year period preceding the use or manufacture of the patented invention by or for the United States. Notwithstanding the preceding sentences, unless the action has been pending for more than 10 years from the time of filing to the time that the owner applies for such costs and fees, reasonable and entire compensation shall not include such costs and fees if the court finds that the position of the United States was substantially justified or that special circumstances make an award unjust.

For the purposes of this section, the use or manufacture of an invention described in and covered by a patent of the United States by a contractor, a subcontractor, or any person, firm, or corporation for the Government and with the authorization or consent of the Government, shall be construed as use or manufacture for the United States.

The court shall not award compensation under this section if the claim is based on the use or manufacture by or for the United States of any article owned, leased, used by, or in the possession of the United States prior to July 1, 1918.

A Government employee shall have the right to bring suit against the Government under this section except where he was in a position to order, influence, or induce use of the invention by the Government. This section shall not confer a right of action on any patentee or any assignee of such patentee with respect to any invention discovered or invented by a person while in the employment or service of the United States, where the invention was related to the official functions of the employee, in cases in which such functions included research and development, or in the making of which Government time, materials or facilities were used.

(b) Hereafter, whenever the copyright in any work protected under the copyright laws of the United States shall be infringed by the United States, by a corporation owned or controlled by the United States, or by a contractor, subcontractor, or any person, firm, or corporation acting for the Government and with the authorization or consent of the Government, the exclusive action which may be brought for such infringement shall be an action by the copyright owner against the United States in the Court of Federal Claims for the recovery of his reasonable and entire compensation as damages for such infringement, including the minimum statutory damages as set forth in section 504(c) of title 17, United States Code: *Provided*, That a Government employee shall have a right of action against the Government under this subsection except where he was in a position to order, influence, or induce use of the copyrighted work by the Government: *Provided, however*, That this subsection shall not confer a right of action on any copyright owner or any assignee of such owner with respect to any copyrighted work prepared by a person while in the employment or service of the United States, where the copyrighted work was prepared as a part of the official functions of the employee, or in the preparation of which Government time, material, or facilities were used: *And provided further*, That before such action against the United States has been instituted the appropriate corporation owned or controlled by the United States or the head of the appropriate department or agency of the Government, as the case may be, is authorized to enter into an agreement with the copyright owner in full settlement and compromise for the damages accruing to him by reason of such infringement and to settle the claim administratively out of available appropriations.

Except as otherwise provided by law, no recovery shall be had for any infringement of a copyright covered by this subsection committed more than three years prior to the filing of the complaint or counterclaim for infringement in the action, except that the period between the date of receipt of a written claim for compensation by the Department or agency of the Government or corporation owned or controlled by the United States, as the case may be, having authority to settle such claim and the date of mailing by the Government of a notice to the claimant that his claim has been denied shall not be counted as a part of the three years, unless suit is brought before the last-mentioned date.

(c) The provisions of this section shall not apply to any claim arising in a foreign country.

(d) Hereafter, whenever a plant variety protected by a certificate of plant variety protection under the laws of the United States shall be infringed by the United States, by a corporation owned or controlled by the United States, or by a contractor, subcontractor, or any person, firm, or corporation acting for the Government and with the authorization and consent of the Government, the exclusive remedy of the owner of such certificate shall be by action against the United States in the Court of Federal Claims for the recovery of his reasonable and entire compensation as damages for such infringement: *Provided*, That a Government employee shall have a right of action against the Government under this subsection except where he was in a position to order, influence, or induce use of the protected plant variety by the Government: *Provided, however*, That this subsection shall not confer a right of action on any certificate owner or any assignee of such owner with respect to any protected plant variety made by a person while in the employment or service of the United States, where such variety was prepared as a part of the official functions of the employee, or in the preparation of which Government time, material, or facilities were used: *And provided further*, That before such action against the United States has been instituted, the appropriate corporation owned or controlled by the United States or the head of the appropriate agency of the Government, as the case may be, is authorized to enter into an agreement with the certificate owner in full settlement and compromise, for the damages accrued to him by reason of such infringement and to settle the claim administratively out of available appropriations.

(e) Subsections (b) and (c) of this section apply to exclusive rights in mask works under chapter 9 of title 17, and to exclusive rights in designs under chapter 13 of title 17 [17 U.S.C.A. § 1301 et seq.], to the same extent as such subsections apply to copyrights.

(June 25, 1948, c. 646, 62 Stat. 941; May 24, 1949, c. 139, § 87, 63 Stat. 102; Oct. 31, 1951, c. 655, § 50(c), 65 Stat. 727; July 17, 1952, c. 930, 66 Stat. 757; Sept. 8, 1960, Pub.L. 86–726, §§ 1, 4, 74 Stat. 855, 856; Dec. 24, 1970, Pub.L. 91–577, Title III, § 143(d), 84 Stat. 1559; Oct. 19, 1976, Pub.L. 94–553, Title I, § 105(c), 90 Stat. 2599; Apr. 2, 1982, Pub.L. 97–164, Title I, § 133(d), 96 Stat. 40; Nov. 19, 1988, Pub.L. 100–702, Title X, § 1020(a)(6), 102 Stat. 4671; Oct. 29, 1992, Pub.L. 102–572, Title IX, § 902(a), 106 Stat. 4516; Oct. 19, 1996, Pub.L. 104–308, § 1(a), 110 Stat. 3814; Dec. 16, 1997, Pub.L. 105–147, § 3, 111 Stat. 2680; Oct. 28, 1998, Pub.L. 105–304, Title V, § 503(d), 112 Stat. 2917.)

HISTORICAL AND STATUTORY NOTES

References in Text

Hereafter, referred to in subsec. (b), probably means the date of enactment of Pub. L. 86–726 [which, among other changes, added subsec. (b)], which was approved on Sept. 8, 1960.

The copyright laws of the United States, referred to in subsec. (b), are classified generally to Title 17, Copyrights.

The "hereafter" set out at the beginning of subsec. (d) probably means after Dec. 24, 1970, the date of enactment of Pub.L. 91–577 which added subsec. (d).

Effective Dates

1998 Acts. Amendment by Pub.L. 105–304, effective Oct. 28, 1998, and remaining in effect until the end of the 2–year period beginning on such date of enactment, see section 505 of Pub.L. 105–304, set out as a note under section 1301 of Title 17, Copyrights.

1996 Acts. Section 1(b) of Pub.L. 104–308 provided that: "The amendment made by subsection (a) [amending subsec. (a) of this section] shall apply to actions under section 1498(a) of title 28, United States Code [subsec. (a) of this section], that are pending on, or brought on or after, the date of the enactment of this Act [Oct. 19, 1996]."

1992 Acts. Amendments by Title IX of Pub.L. 102–572 effective Oct. 29, 1992, see section 911 of Pub.L. 102–572, set out as a note under section 171 of Title 28, Judiciary and Judiciary Procedure.

1982 Acts. Amendment by Pub.L. 97–164 effective Oct. 1, 1982, see section 402 of Pub.L. 97–164, set out as a note under section 171 of this title.

1976 Acts. Amendment by Pub.L. 94–553 effective Jan. 1, 1978, see section 102 of Pub.L. 94–553, set out as a note preceding section 101 of Title 17, Copyrights.

1970 Acts. Amendment by Pub.L. 91–577 effective Dec. 24, 1970, see section 141 of Pub.L. 91–577, set out as a note under section 2321 of Title 7, Agriculture.

Waiver of Immunity for Members of Congress

Section 2 of Pub.L. 86–726 provided that: "Nothing in this Act [amending this section and section 2386 of Title 10, Armed Forces] shall be construed to in any way waive any immunity provided for Members of Congress under article I of section 6 of the Constitution of the United States."

§ 1499. Liquidated damages withheld from contractors under Contract Work Hours and Safety Standards Act

The United States Court of Federal Claims shall have jurisdiction to render judgment upon any claim for liquidated damages withheld from a contractor or subcontractor under section 104 of the Contract Work Hours and Safety Standards Act.

(June 25, 1948, c. 646, 62 Stat. 942; Aug. 13, 1962, Pub.L. 87–581, Title II, § 202(a), 76 Stat. 360; Apr. 2, 1982, Pub.L. 97–164, Title I, § 133(e) (1), (2) (A), 96 Stat. 40, 41; Dec. 1, 1990, Pub.L. 101–650, Title III, § 325(b)(7), 104 Stat. 5121; Oct. 29, 1992, Pub.L. 102–572, Title IX, § 902(a)(1), 106 Stat. 4516.)

HISTORICAL AND STATUTORY NOTES

References in Text

Contract Work Hours and Safety Standards Act, referred to in the section catchline and in text, Title I of Pub.L. 87–581, Aug. 13, 1962, 76 Stat. 357, as amended, which is classified generally to subchapter II (section 327 et seq.) of chapter 5 of Title 40, Public Buildings, Property, and Works. Section 104 of the Contract Work Hours and Safety Standards Act is classified to section 330 of Title 40. For complete classification of this Act to the Code, see Short Title note set out under section 327 of Title 40 and Tables.

Effective Dates

1992 Acts. Amendment by Title IX of Pub.L. 102–572 effective Oct. 29, 1992, see section 911 of Pub.L. 102–572, set out as a note under section 171 of Title 28, Judiciary and Judicial Procedure.

1982 Acts. Amendment by Pub.L. 97–164 effective Oct. 1, 1982, see section 402 of Pub.L. 97–164, set out as a note under section 171 of this title.

1962 Acts. Amendment of section by Pub.L. 87–581 effective 60 days after Aug. 13, 1962, but shall not affect contracts existing or thereafter entered into pursuant to invitations for bids outstanding on Aug. 13, 1962, see section 204 of Pub.L. 87–581, set out as a note under section 327 of Title 40, Public Buildings, Property and Works.

Continued Jurisdiction Upon Claims Under Section 324 of Title 40

Section 202(b) of Pub.L. 87–581 provided that: "The Court of Claims [now Court of Federal Claims] shall continue to have jurisdiction to render judgment upon any claim for a penalty withheld from a contractor or subcontractor under section 324 of title 40, United States Code [repealed], in connection with any contract subject to said section existing on the effective date of this Act [see Effective Dates note set out under section 327 of Title 40, Public Buildings, Property and Works], or thereafter entered into pursuant to invitations for bids that are outstanding at the time of the enactment of this Act [Aug. 13, 1962]."

§ 1500. Pendency of claims in other courts

The United States Court of Federal Claims shall not have jurisdiction of any claim for or in respect to which the plaintiff or his assignee has pending in any other court any suit or process against the United States or any person who, at the time when the cause of action alleged in such suit or process arose, was, in respect thereto, acting or professing to act, directly or indirectly under the authority of the United States.

(June 25, 1948, c. 646, 62 Stat. 942; Apr. 2, 1982, Pub.L. 97–164, Title I, § 133(e) (1), 96 Stat. 40; Oct. 29, 1992, Pub.L. 102–572, Title IX, § 902(a)(1), 106 Stat. 4516.)

HISTORICAL AND STATUTORY NOTES

Effective Dates

1992 Acts. Amendment by Title IX of Pub.L. 102–572 effective Oct. 29, 1992, see section 911 of Pub.L. 102–572 , set out as a note under section 171 of this title.

1982 Acts. Amendment by Pub.L. 97–164 effective Oct. 1, 1982, see section 402 of Pub.L. 97–164, set out as a note under section 171 of this title.

§ 1501. Pensions

The United States Court of Federal Claims shall not have jurisdiction of any claim for a pension.

(June 25, 1948, c. 646, 62 Stat. 942; Apr. 2, 1982, Pub.L. 97–164, Title I, § 133(e) (1), 96 Stat. 40; Oct. 29, 1992, Pub.L. 102–572, Title IX, § 902(a)(1), 106 Stat. 4516.)

HISTORICAL AND STATUTORY NOTES

Effective Dates

1992 Acts. Amendment by Title IX of Pub.L. 102–572 effective Oct. 29, 1992, see section 911 of Pub.L. 102–572, set out as a note under section 171 of this title.

1982 Acts. Amendment by Pub.L. 97–164 effective Oct. 1, 1982, see section 402 of Pub.L. 97–164, set out as a note under section 171 of this title.

§ 1502. Treaty cases

Except as otherwise provided by Act of Congress, the United States Court of Federal Claims shall not have jurisdiction of any claim against the United States growing out of or dependent upon any treaty entered into with foreign nations.

(June 25, 1948, c. 646, 62 Stat. 942; May 24, 1949, c. 139, § 88, 63 Stat. 102; Apr. 2, 1982, Pub.L. 97–164, Title I, § 133(e) (1), 96 Stat. 40; Oct. 29, 1992, Pub.L. 102–572, Title IX, § 902(a)(1), 106 Stat. 4516.)

HISTORICAL AND STATUTORY NOTES

Effective Dates

1992 Acts. Amendment by Title IX of Pub.L. 102–572 effective Oct. 29, 1992, see section 911 of Pub.L. 102–572, set out as a note under section 171 of this title.

1982 Acts. Amendment by Pub.L. 97–164 effective Oct. 1, 1982, see section 402 of Pub.L. 97–164, set out as a note under section 171 of this title.

§ 1503. Set-offs

The United States Court of Federal Claims shall have jurisdiction to render judgment upon any set-off or demand by the United States against any plaintiff in such court.

(June 25, 1948, c. 646, 62 Stat. 942; Apr. 2, 1982, Pub.L. 97–164, Title I, § 133(e) (1), 96 Stat. 40; Oct. 29, 1992, Pub.L. 102–572, Title IX, § 902(a)(1), 106 Stat. 4516.)

HISTORICAL AND STATUTORY NOTES

Effective Dates

1992 Acts. Amendment by Title IX of Pub.L. 102–572 effective Oct. 29, 1992, see section 911 of Pub.L. 102–572, set out as a note under section 171 of this title.

1982 Acts. Amendment by Pub.L. 97–164 effective Oct. 1, 1982, see section 402 of Pub.L. 97–164, set out as a note under section 171 of this title.

[§ 1504. Repealed. Pub.L. 97–164, Title I, § 133(f), Apr. 2, 1982, 96 Stat. 41]

HISTORICAL AND STATUTORY NOTES

Section, Act June 25, 1948, c. 646, 62 Stat. 942, directed that the Court of Claims [now Court of Federal Claims] have jurisdiction to review by appeal final judgments in the district courts in civil actions based on tort claims brought under section 1346(b) of this title if the notice of appeal filed in the district court had affixed to it a written consent on behalf of the appellees that the appeal be taken to the Court of Claims.

Effective Date of Repeal

Repeal effective Oct. 1, 1982, see section 402 of Pub.L. 97–164, set out as an Effective Dates of 1982 Amendments note under section 171 of this title.

§ 1505. Indian claims

The United States Court of Federal Claims shall have jurisdiction of any claim against the United States accruing after August 13, 1946, in favor of any tribe, band, or other identifiable group of American Indians residing within the territorial limits of the United States or Alaska whenever such claim is one arising under the Constitution, laws or treaties of the United States, or Executive orders of the President, or is one which otherwise would be cognizable in the Court of Federal Claims if the claimant were not an Indian tribe, band or group.

(Added May 24, 1949, c. 139, § 89(a), 63 Stat. 102, and amended Apr. 2, 1982, Pub.L. 97–164, Title I, § 133(g), 96 Stat. 41; Oct. 29, 1992, Pub.L. 102–572, Title IX, § 902(a), 106 Stat. 4516.)

HISTORICAL AND STATUTORY NOTES

Effective Dates

1992 Acts. Amendment by Title IX of Pub.L. 102–572 effective Oct. 29, 1992, see section 911 of Pub.L. 102–572, set out as a note under section 171 of this title.

1982 Acts. Amendment by Pub.L. 97–164 effective Oct. 1, 1982, see section 402 of Pub.L. 97–164, set out as a note under section 171 of this title.

[§ 1506. Repealed. Pub.L. 97–164, Title I, § 133(h), Apr. 2, 1982, 96 Stat. 41]

HISTORICAL AND STATUTORY NOTES

Section, added Pub.L. 86–770, § 2(a), Sept. 13, 1960, 74 Stat. 912, provided that if a case within the exclusive jurisdiction of the district courts was filed in the Court of Claims [now Court of Federal Claims], the Court of Claims, if it were in the interest of justice, had to transfer such case to any district court in which it could have been brought at the time such case was filed, where the case would proceed as if it had been filed in the district court on the date it was filed in the Court of Claims.

Effective Date of Repeal

Repeal effective Oct. 1, 1982, see section 402 of Pub.L. 97–164, set out as a note under section 171 of this title.

§ 1507. Jurisdiction for certain declaratory judgments

The United States Court of Federal Claims shall have jurisdiction to hear any suit for and issue a declaratory judgment under section 7428 of the Internal Revenue Code of 1986.

(Added Pub.L. 94–455, Title XIII, § 1306(b)(9)(A), Oct. 4, 1976, 90 Stat. 1720, and amended Pub.L. 97–164, Title I, § 133(i), Apr. 2, 1982, 96 Stat. 41; Pub.L. 99–514, § 2, Oct. 22, 1986, 100 Stat. 2095; Pub.L. 102–572, Title IX, § 902(a)(1), Oct. 29, 1992, 106 Stat. 4516.)

HISTORICAL AND STATUTORY NOTES

References in Text

Section 7428 of the Internal Revenue Code of 1986, referred to in text, is classified to section 7428 of Title 26, Internal Revenue Code.

Effective Dates

1992 Acts. Amendment by Title IX of Pub.L. 102–572 effective Oct. 29, 1992, see section 911 of Pub.L. 102–572, set out as a note under section 171 of this title.

1982 Acts. Amendment by Pub.L. 97–164 effective Oct. 1, 1982, see section 402 of Pub.L. 97–164, set out as a note under section 171 of this title.

1976 Acts. Section applicable with respect to pleadings filed with the United States Tax Court, the district court of the United States for the District of Columbia, or the United States Court of Claims more than 6 months after Oct. 4, 1976, but only with respect to determinations (or requests for determinations) made after Jan. 1, 1976, see section 1306(c) of Pub.L. 94–455, set out as a note under section 7428 of Title 26, Internal Revenue Code.

§ 1508. Jurisdiction for certain partnership proceedings

The Court of Federal Claims shall have jurisdiction to hear and to render judgment upon any petition under section 6226 or 6228(a) of the Internal Revenue Code of 1986.

(Added Pub.L. 97–248, Title IV, § 402(c)(18)(A), Sept. 3, 1982, 96 Stat. 669, and amended Pub.L. 99–514, § 2, Oct. 22, 1986, 100 Stat. 2095; Pub.L. 102–572, Title IX, § 902(a)(2), Oct. 29, 1992, 106 Stat. 4516.)

HISTORICAL AND STATUTORY NOTES

References in Text

Sections 6226 and 6228(a) of the Internal Revenue Code of 1986, referred to in text, are classified to sections 6226 and 6228(a) of Title 26, Internal Revenue Code.

Effective Dates

1992 Acts. Amendment by Title IX of Pub.L. 102–572 effective Oct. 29, 1992, see section 911 of Pub.L. 102–572, set out as a note under section 171 of this title.

1982 Acts. Section applicable to partnership taxable years beginning after Sept. 3, 1982, with provision for the applicability of this section to any partnership taxable year ending after Sept. 3, 1982, if the partnership, each partner, and each indirect partner requests such application and the Secretary of the Treasury or his delegate consents to such application, see section 407(a) (1) and (3) of Pub.L. 97–248, set out as a note under section 6221 of Title 26, Internal Revenue Code.

§ 1509. No jurisdiction in cases involving refunds of tax shelter promoter and understatement penalties

The United States Court of Federal Claims shall not have jurisdiction to hear any action or proceeding for any refund or credit of any penalty imposed under section 6700 of the Internal Revenue Code of 1986 (relating to penalty for promoting abusive tax shelters, etc.) or section 6701 of such Code (relating to penalties for aiding and abetting understatement of tax liability).

(Added Pub.L. 98–369, Div. A, Title VII, § 714(g)(2), July 18, 1984, 98 Stat. 962, and amended Pub.L. 99–514, § 2, Oct. 22, 1986, 100 Stat. 2095; Pub.L. 102–572, Title IX, § 902(a)(1), Oct. 29, 1992, 106 Stat. 4516.)

HISTORICAL AND STATUTORY NOTES

References in Text

Sections 6700 and 6701 of the Internal Revenue Code of 1986, referred to in text, are classified to sections 6700 and 6701, respectively, of Title 26, Internal Revenue Code.

Effective Dates

1992 Acts. Amendment by Title IX of Pub.L. 102–572 effective Oct. 29, 1992, see section 911 of Pub.L. 102–572, set out as a note under section 171 of this title.

1984 Acts. Section 714(g)(4) of Pub.L. 98–369 provided that: "The amendments made by this subsection [enacting this section and amending section 7422 of Title 26, Internal Revenue Code] shall apply to any claim for refund or credit filed after the date of the enactment of this Act [July 18, 1984]."

[CHAPTER 93—REPEALED]

[§§ 1541 to 1546. Repealed. Pub.L. 97–164, Title I, § 134, Apr. 2, 1982, 96 Stat. 41]

HISTORICAL AND STATUTORY NOTES

Section 1541, Acts June 25, 1948, c. 646, 62 Stat. 942; June 2, 1970, Pub.L. 91–271, Title I, § 102, 84 Stat. 274; July 26, 1979, Pub.L. 96–39, Title X, § 1001(b) (4) (A), 93 Stat. 305; Oct. 10, 1980, Pub.L. 96–417, Title IV, § 401(a), Title V, § 501(23), (24), 94 Stat. 1740, 1742, gave the Court of Customs and Patent Appeals exclusive jurisdiction of appeals from all final decisions of the Court of International Trade and from interlocutory orders of the Court of International Trade granting, continuing, modifying, refusing, or dissolving injunctions, or refusing to dissolve or modify injunctions, and with discretion to entertain appeals from certain orders of the Court of International Trade. See section 1295(a) (5) of this title.

Section 1542, Acts June 25, 1948, c. 646, 62 Stat. 942; May 24, 1949, c. 139, § 89(b), 63 Stat. 102, gave the Court of Customs and Patent Appeals jurisdiction of appeals from decisions of the Board of Appeals and the Board of Interference Examiners of the Patent Office as to patent applications and interferences, at the instance of an applicant for a patent or any party to a patent interference, with such appeal by an applicant to waive his right to proceed under section 63 of Title 35, and the Commissioner of Patents as to trade-mark applications and proceedings as provided in section 1071 of Title 15. See section 1295(a) (4) of this title.

Section 1543, Acts June 25, 1948, c. 646, 62 Stat. 943; Oct. 10, 1980, Pub.L. 96–417, Title IV, § 401(b) (1), 94 Stat. 1740, gave the Court of Customs and Patent Appeals jurisdiction to review final determinations of the United States International Trade Commission made under section 337 of the Tariff Act of 1930 relating to unfair trade practices in import trade. See section 1295(a) (6) of this title.

Section 1544, added Pub.L. 89–651, § 8(c) (1), Oct. 14, 1966, 80 Stat. 901, gave the Court of Customs and Patent Appeals jurisdiction to review, by appeal on questions of law only, findings of the Secretary of Commerce under headnote 6 to schedule 8, part 4, of the Tariff Schedules of the United States (relating to importation of instruments or apparatus). See section 1295(a) (7) of this title.

Section 1545, added Pub.L. 91–577, Title III, § 143(a), Dec. 24, 1970, 84 Stat. 1558, gave the Court of Customs and Patent Appeals nonexclusive jurisdiction of appeals under section 71 of the Plant Variety Protection Act, classified to section 2461 of Title 7, Agriculture. See section 1295(a) (8) of this title.

Section 1546, added Pub.L. 96–417, Title IV, § 402(a), Oct. 10, 1980, 94 Stat. 1740, gave the Court of Customs and Patent Appeals all of the powers in law and in equity of, or conferred by statute upon, a court of appeals of the United States.

Effective Date of Repeal

Repeal effective Oct. 1, 1982, see section 402 of Pub.L. 97–164, set out as a note under section 171 of this title.

CHAPTER 95—COURT OF INTERNATIONAL TRADE

Sec.
1581. Civil actions against the United States and agencies and officers thereof.
1582. Civil actions commenced by the United States.
1583. Counterclaims, cross-claims, and third-party actions.
1584. Civil actions under the North American Free Trade Agreement or the United States–Canada Free–Trade Agreement.
1585. Powers in law and equity.

HISTORICAL AND STATUTORY NOTES

Prior Provisions

A prior Chapter 95—Customs Court, comprising sections 1581 and 1582, was omitted from the Code upon the general revision of this chapter by Pub.L. 96–417, Title II, § 201, Oct. 10, 1980, 94 Stat. 1728.

§ 1581. Civil actions against the United States and agencies and officers thereof

(a) The Court of International Trade shall have exclusive jurisdiction of any civil action commenced to contest the denial of a protest, in whole or in part, under section 515 of the Tariff Act of 1930.

(b) The Court of International Trade shall have exclusive jurisdiction of any civil action commenced under section 516 of the Tariff Act of 1930.

(c) The Court of International Trade shall have exclusive jurisdiction of any civil action commenced under section 516A of the Tariff Act of 1930.

(d) The Court of International Trade shall have exclusive jurisdiction of any civil action commenced to review—

(1) any final determination of the Secretary of Labor under section 223 of the Trade Act of 1974 with respect to the eligibility of workers for adjustment assistance under such Act;

(2) any final determination of the Secretary of Commerce under section 251 of the Trade Act of 1974 with respect to the eligibility of a firm for adjustment assistance under such Act; and

(3) any final determination of the Secretary of Commerce under section 271 of the Trade Act of 1974 with respect to the eligibility of a community for adjustment assistance under such Act.

(e) The Court of International Trade shall have exclusive jurisdiction of any civil action commenced to review any final determination of the Secretary of the Treasury under section 305(b)(1) of the Trade Agreements Act of 1979.

(f) The Court of International Trade shall have exclusive jurisdiction of any civil action involving an application for an order directing the administering authority or the International Trade Commission to make confidential information available under section 777(c)(2) of the Tariff Act of 1930.

(g) The Court of International Trade shall have exclusive jurisdiction of any civil action commenced to review—

(1) any decision of the Secretary of the Treasury to deny a customs broker's license under section 641(b)(2) or (3) of the Tariff Act of 1930, or to deny a customs broker's permit under section 641(c)(1) of such Act, or to revoke a license or permit under section 641(b)(5) or (c)(2) of such Act;

(2) any decision of the Secretary of the Treasury to revoke or suspend a customs broker's license or permit, or impose a monetary penalty in lieu thereof, under section 641(d)(2)(B) of the Tariff Act of 1930; and

(3) any decision or order of the Customs Service to deny, suspend, or revoke accreditation of a private laboratory under section 499(b) of the Tariff Act of 1930.

(h) The Court of International Trade shall have exclusive jurisdiction of any civil action commenced to review, prior to the importation of the goods involved, a ruling issued by the Secretary of the Treasury, or a refusal to issue or change such a ruling, relating to classification, valuation, rate of duty, marking, restricted merchandise, entry requirements, drawbacks, vessel repairs, or similar matters, but only if the party commencing the civil action demonstrates to the court that he would be irreparably harmed unless given an opportunity to obtain judicial review prior to such importation.

(i) In addition to the jurisdiction conferred upon the Court of International Trade by subsections (a)–(h) of this section and subject to the exception set forth in subsection (j) of this section, the Court of International Trade shall have exclusive jurisdiction of any civil action commenced against the United States, its agencies, or its officers, that arises out of any law of the United States providing for—

(1) revenue from imports or tonnage;

(2) tariffs, duties, fees, or other taxes on the importation of merchandise for reasons other than the raising of revenue;

(3) embargoes or other quantitative restrictions on the importation of merchandise for reasons other than the protection of the public health or safety; or

(4) administration and enforcement with respect to the matters referred to in paragraphs (1)–(3) of this subsection and subsections (a)–(h) of this section.

This subsection shall not confer jurisdiction over an antidumping or countervailing duty determination which is reviewable either by the Court of International Trade under section 516A(a) of the Tariff Act of 1930 or by a binational panel under article 1904 of the North American Free Trade Agreement or the United States–Canada Free–Trade Agreement and section 516A(g) of the Tariff Act of 1930.

(j) The Court of International Trade shall not have jurisdiction of any civil action arising under section 305 of the Tariff Act of 1930.

(Added Pub.L. 96–417, Title II, § 201, Oct. 10, 1980, 94 Stat. 1728, and amended Pub.L. 98–573, Title II, § 212(b)(1), Oct. 30, 1984, 98 Stat. 2983; Pub.L. 99–514, Title XVIII, § 1891(1), Oct. 22, 1986, 100 Stat. 2926; Pub.L. 100–449, Title IV, § 402(a), Sept. 28, 1988, 102 Stat. 1883; Pub.L. 103–182, Title IV, § 414(a)(1), Title VI, § 684(a)(1), Dec. 8, 1993, 107 Stat. 2147, 2219.)

Termination of Amendments

For provisions directing that, except for transition provisions relating to proceedings regarding protective orders and undertakings, and binational panel and extraordinary challenge committee reviews, the amendment to this section by Title IV of Pub.L. 103–182 shall cease to have effect with respect to any country on the date on which such country ceases to be a NAFTA country, see section 3451 of Title 19, Customs Duties.

Termination of United States–Canada Free–Trade Agreement

For provisions directing that the amendments made by Pub.L. 100–449, which amended this section, shall cease to have effect on the date on which the United States–Canada Free–Trade Agreement ceases to be in force, see section 501(c) of Pub.L. 100–449, set out in the note under section 2112 of Title 19, Customs Duties.

Articles 1906 and 2106 of the Agreement authorize either the United States or Canada to terminate the Agreement on 6–month notice if, at the end of the 7–year period following the date of the entry into effect of the Agreement, no agreement has been entered into between the United States and Canada on a substitute system of antidumping and countervailing duties.

HISTORICAL AND STATUTORY NOTES

References in Text

Sections 515 and 516 of the Tariff Act of 1930, referred to in subsecs. (a) and (b), respectively, are classified, respectively, to sections 1515 and 1516 of Title 19, Customs Duties.

The Trade Act of 1974, referred to in subsec. (d)(1) to (3), is Pub.L. 93–618, Jan. 3, 1975, 88 Stat.1978, as amended, which is classified principally to chapter 12 (section 2101 et seq.) of Title 19. Sections 223, 251, and 271 of the Trade Act of 1974 are classified to sections 2273, 2341, and 2371, respectively, of Title 19. For complete classification of this Act to the Code, see References in Text note set out under section 2101 of Title 19 and Tables.

Section 305(b)(1) of the Trade Agreements Act of 1979, referred to in subsec. (e), is classified to section 2515(b)(1) of Title 19, Customs Duties.

Sections 777(c)(2), 641(b), (c), (d), and 305 of the Tariff Act of 1930, referred to in subsecs. (f), (g), and (j), are classified to sections 1677f(c)(2), 1641, (b), (c), (d), and 1305, respectively, of Title 19, Customs Duties.

Section 499(b) of the Tariff Act of 1930, referred to in subsec. (g)(3), is classified to section 1499(b) of Title 19, Customs Duties.

Section 516A of the Tariff Act of 1930, referred to in subsec. (i), is classified to section 1516a of Title 19.

The United States–Canada Free–Trade Agreement, referred to in subsec. (i), was entered into on Jan. 2, 1988. The Agreement is not set out in the Code.

Effective and Termination Dates

1993 Acts. Amendment by section 414 of Pub.L. 103–182 effective on the date the North American Free Trade Agreement enters into force with respect to the United States [Jan. 1, 1994], but not to apply to any final determination described in section 1516a(a)(1)(B) or (2)(B)(i), (ii), or (iii) of Title 19, Customs Duties, notice of which is published in the Federal Register before such date, or to a determination described in section 1516a(a)(2)(B)(vi) of Title 19 notice of which is received by the Government of Canada or Mexico before such date, or to any binational panel review under the United States-Canada Free-Trade Agreement, or to any extraordinary challenge arising out of any such review that was commenced before such date, see section 416 of Pub.L. 103–182, set out as a note under section 3431 of Title 19.

Amendment by section 684(a)(1) of Pub.L. 103–182 effective Dec. 8, 1993, see section 692 of Pub.L. 103–182, set out as a note under section 58c of Title 19, Customs Duties.

1988 Acts. Amendment by Pub.L. 100–449 effective on the date the United States–Canada Free–Trade Agreement enters into force, (Jan. 1, 1989), and to cease to have effect on the date the Agreement ceases to be in force, see section 501(a), (c) of Pub.L. 100–449, set out in a note under section 2112 of Title 19, Customs Duties. [A Presidential Memorandum on the Canada–United States Free–Trade Agreement, dated Dec. 31, 1988, directing the Secretary of State to exchange notes with the Government of Canada to provide for the entry into force of the Agreement on Jan. 1, 1989, is set out in 24 Weekly Compilation of Presidential Documents 1688, Jan. 2, 1989.]

1984 Acts. Amendment by Pub.L. 98–573 to take effect on the close of the 180th day after Oct. 30, 1984, see section 214(d) of Pub.L. 98–573, set out as a note under section 1304 of Title 19, Customs Duties.

1980 Acts. Section effective on Nov. 1, 1980, and applicable with respect to civil actions pending on or commenced on or after such date, see section 701(a) of Pub.L. 96–417, as amended, set out as a note under section 251 of this title.

Subsecs. (d) and (g) to (i) of this section applicable with respect to civil actions commenced on or after Nov. 1, 1980, see section 701(b)(1)(A) of Pub.L. 96–417, as amended, set out as a note under section 251 of this title.

Prior Provisions

A prior section 1581, Act June 25, 1948, c. 646, 62 Stat. 943, related to powers of the Customs Court generally and was omitted in the general revision of this chapter by Pub.L. 96–417. See section 1585 of this title.

Application of Amendments Relating to Accreditation of Private Laboratories

Section 684(b) of Pub.L. 103–182 provided that: "For purposes of applying the amendments made by subsection (a) [amending subsec. (g) of this section, and sections 2631, 2636, 2640 and 2642 of this title], any decision or order of the Customs Service denying, suspending, or revoking the accreditation of a private laboratory on or after the date of the enactment of this Act [Dec. 8, 1993] and before regulations to implement section 499(b) of the Tariff Act of 1930 [section 1499(b) of Title 19, Customs Duties] are issued shall be treated as having been denied, suspended, or revoked under such section 499(b)."

Prior History of Court

The United States Customs Court, the predecessor of the Court of International Trade, was omitted in the general revision of this chapter by Pub.L. 96–417.

The predecessor of the United States Customs Court was the Board of General Appraisers which was created by the Customs Administrative Act of June 10, 1890. The Board was under the administrative supervision of the Secretary of the Treasury.

From 1890 to 1926, the Board of General Appraisers had jurisdiction over all protests from decisions of the collectors of customs and appeals for reappraisement under sections 13 and 14 of the Customs Administrative Act of June 10, 1890, c. 407, 26 Stat. 136.

The Customs Court was established by Act May 28, 1926, c. 411, §§ 1, 2, 44 Stat. 669, sections 405a and 405b of Title 19, Customs Duties, and said act transferred to it all the jurisdiction and powers of the former Board of General Appraisers. The Tariff Act of June 1930, c. 497, Title IV, § 518, 46 Stat. 737, section 1518 of Title 19, continued the Customs Court as constituted on June 17, 1930 with, however, several important changes.

§ 1582. Civil actions commenced by the United States

The Court of International Trade shall have exclusive jurisdiction of any civil action which arises out of an import transaction and which is commenced by the United States—

(1) to recover a civil penalty under section 592, 593A, 641(b)(6), 641(d)(2)(A), 704(i)(2), or 734(i)(2) of the Tariff Act of 1930;

(2) to recover upon a bond relating to the importation of merchandise required by the laws of the United States or by the Secretary of the Treasury; or

(3) to recover customs duties.

(Added Pub.L. 96–417, Title II, § 201, Oct. 10, 1980, 94 Stat. 1729, and amended Pub.L. 98–573, Title II, § 212(b)(2), Oct. 30, 1984, 98 Stat. 2983; Pub.L. 99–514, Title XVIII, § 1891(2), Oct. 22, 1986, 100 Stat. 2926; Pub.L. 103–182, Title VI, § 684(c), Dec. 8, 1993, 107 Stat. 2219.)

HISTORICAL AND STATUTORY NOTES

References in Text

Sections 592, 593A, 641(b)(2), 641(d)(2)(A), 704(i)(2), and 734(i)(2) of the Tariff Act of 1930, referred to in par. (1), are classified to sections 1592, 1593a, 1641(b)(6), 1641(d)(2)(A), 1671c(i)(2), and 1673c(i)(2) of Title 19, Customs Duties.

Effective Dates

1993 Acts. Amendment by section 684(c) of Pub.L. 103–182 effective Dec. 8, 1993, see section 692 of Pub.L. 103–182, set out as a note under section 58c of Title 19, Customs Duties.

1984 Acts. Amendment by Pub.L. 98–573 to take effect on the close of the 180th day after Oct. 30, 1984, see section 214(d) of Pub.L. 98–573, set out as a note under section 1304 of Title 19, Customs Duties.

1980 Acts. Section applicable with respect to civil actions commenced on or after the 90th day after Nov. 1, 1980, see section 701(c)(1)(A) of Pub.L. 96–417, as amended, set out as a note under section 251 of this title.

Prior Provisions

A prior section 1582, Acts June 25, 1948, c. 646, 62 Stat. 943; June 2, 1970, Pub.L. 91–271, Title I, § 110, 84 Stat. 278; July 26, 1979, Pub.L. 96–39, Title X, § 1001(b)(4)(B), 93 Stat. 305, related to the jurisdiction of the Customs Court and was omitted in the general revision of this chapter by Pub.L. 96–417.

§ 1583. Counterclaims, cross-claims, and third-party actions

In any civil action in the Court of International Trade, the court shall have exclusive jurisdiction to render judgment upon any counterclaim, cross-claim, or third-party action of any party, if (1) such claim or action involves the imported merchandise that is the subject matter of such civil action, or (2) such claim or action is to recover upon a bond or customs duties relating to such merchandise.

(Added Pub.L. 96–417, Title II, § 201, Oct. 10, 1980, 94 Stat. 1729.)

HISTORICAL AND STATUTORY NOTES

Effective Dates

1980 Acts. Section applicable with respect to civil actions commenced on or after Nov. 1, 1980, see section 701(b)(1)(A) of Pub.L. 96–417, as amended, set out as a note under section 251 of this title.

Prior Provisions

A prior section 1583, Act June 25, 1948, c. 646, 62 Stat. 943, related to certain cases of exclusive jurisdiction of the Customs Court and was repealed by Pub.L. 91–271, Title I, § 111, June 2, 1970, 84 Stat. 278.

§ 1584. Civil actions under the North American Free Trade Agreement or the United States–Canada Free–Trade Agreement

The United States Court of International Trade shall have exclusive jurisdiction of any civil action which arises under section 777(f) of the Tariff Act of 1930 and is commenced by the United States to enforce administrative sanctions levied for violation of a protective order or an undertaking.

(Added Pub.L. 100–449, Title IV, § 402(d)(1), Sept. 28, 1988, 102 Stat. 1884, and amended Pub.L. 103–182, Title IV, § 414(a)(2), Dec. 8, 1993, 107 Stat. 2147.)

Termination of Amendments

For provisions directing that, except for transition provisions relating to proceedings regarding protective orders and undertakings, and binational panel and extraordinary challenge committee reviews, the amendment to this section by Title IV of Pub.L. 103–182 shall cease to have effect with respect to any country on the date on which such country ceases to be a NAFTA country, see section 3451 of Title 19, Customs Duties.

Termination of United States–Canada Free–Trade Agreement

For provisions directing that the amendments made by Pub.L. 100–449, which enacted this section, shall cease to have effect on the date on which the United States–Canada Free–Trade Agreement ceases to be in force, see section 501(c) of Pub.L. 100–449, set out in the note under section 2112 of Title 19, Customs Duties.

Articles 1906 and 2106 of the Agreement authorize either the United States or Canada to terminate the Agreement on 6–month notice if, at the end of the 7–year period following the date of the entry into effect of the Agreement, no agreement has been entered into between the United States and Canada on a substitute system of antidumping and countervailing duties.

HISTORICAL AND STATUTORY NOTES

References in Text

Section 777(f) of the Tariff Act of 1930, referred to in text, is classified to section 1677f(f) of Title 19, Customs Duties.

Effective and Termination Dates

1993 Acts. Amendment by section 414 of Pub.L. 103–182 effective on the date the North American Free Trade Agreement enters into force with respect to the United States [Jan. 1, 1994], but not to apply to any final determination described in section 1516a(a)(1)(B) or (2)(B)(i), (ii), or (iii) of Title 19, Customs Duties, notice of which is published in the Federal Register before such date, or to a determination described in section 1516a(a)(2)(B)(vi) of Title 19 notice of which is received by the Government of Canada or Mexico before such date, or to any binational panel review under the United States-Canada Free-Trade Agreement, or to any extraordinary challenge arising out of any such review that was commenced before such date, see section 416 of Pub.L. 103–182, set out as a note under section 3431 of Title 19.

1988 Acts. Section effective on the date the United States–Canada Free–Trade Agreement enters into force (Jan. 1, 1989), and to cease to have effect on the date the Agreement ceases to be in force, see section 501(a), (c), of Pub.L. 100–449, set out in a note under section 2112 of Title 19, Customs Duties. [A Presidential Memorandum on the Canada–United States Free–Trade Agreement, dated Dec. 31, 1988, directing the Secretary of State to exchange notes with the Government of Canada to provide for the entry into force of the Agreement on Jan. 1, 1989, is set out in 24 Weekly Compilation of Presidential Documents 1688, Jan. 2, 1989.]

Prior Provisions

A prior section 1584, added Pub.L. 96–417, Title II, § 201, Oct. 10, 1980, 94 Stat. 1729, which provided that if a civil action within the exclusive jurisdiction of the Court of International Trade were commenced in a district court of the United States, the district court, in the interest of justice, would transfer such civil action to the Court of International Trade, where such action proceeded as if it had been commenced in the Court of International Trade in the first instance, and that if a civil action within the exclusive jurisdiction of a district court, a court of appeals, or the Court of Customs and Patent Appeals were commenced in the Court of International Trade, the Court of International Trade, in the interest of justice, would transfer such civil action to the appropriate district court or court of appeals or to the Court of Customs and Patent Appeals where such action proceeded as if it had been commenced in such court in the first instance, was repealed by Pub.L. 97–164, Title I, § 135, Apr. 2, 1982, 96 Stat. 41, eff. Oct. 1, 1982.

§ 1585. Powers in law and equity

The Court of International Trade shall possess all the powers in law and equity of, or as conferred by statute upon, a district court of the United States.

(Added Pub.L. 96–417, Title II, § 201, Oct. 10, 1980, 94 Stat. 1730.)

CHAPTER 97—JURISDICTIONAL IMMUNITIES OF FOREIGN STATES

Sec.
1602. Findings and declaration of purpose.
1603. Definitions.
1604. Immunity of a foreign state from jurisdiction.
1605. General exceptions to the jurisdictional immunity of a foreign state.
1606. Extent of liability.
1607. Counterclaims.
1608. Service; time to answer default.[1]
1609. Immunity from attachment and execution of property of a foreign state.
1610. Exceptions to the immunity from attachment or execution.
1611. Certain types of property immune from execution.

[1] So in original. Does not conform to section catchline.

§ 1602. Findings and declaration of purpose

The Congress finds that the determination by United States courts of the claims of foreign states to immunity from the jurisdiction of such courts would serve the interests of justice and would protect the rights of both foreign states and litigants in United States courts. Under international law, states are not immune from the jurisdiction of foreign courts insofar as their commercial activities are concerned, and their commercial property may be levied upon for the satisfaction of judgments rendered against them in connection with their commercial activities. Claims of foreign states to immunity should henceforth be decided by courts of the United States and of the States in conformity with the principles set forth in this chapter.

(Added Pub.L. 94–583, § 4(a), Oct. 21, 1976, 90 Stat. 2892.)

HISTORICAL AND STATUTORY NOTES

Effective Dates

1976 Acts. Section 8 of Pub.L. 94–583 provided that: "This Act [enacting this chapter and section 1330 of this title, amending sections 1332, 1391, and 1441 of this title, and enacting provisions set out as notes under this section] shall take effect ninety days after the date of its enactment [Oct. 21, 1976]."

Separability of Provisions

Section 7 of Pub.L. 94–583 provided that: "If any provision of this Act [enacting this chapter and section 1330 of this title, amending sections 1332, 1391, and 1441 of this title, and enacting provisions set out as notes under this section and section 1 of this title] or the application thereof to any foreign state is held invalid, the invalidity does not affect other provisions or applications of the Act which can be given effect without the invalid provision or application, and to this end the provisions of this Act are severable."

Short Title

1976 Acts. Authorization to cite Pub.L. 94–583, which enacted this chapter, as the "Foreign Sovereign Immunities Act of 1976", see section 1 of Pub.L. 94–583, set out as a note under section 1 of this title.

§ 1603. Definitions

For purposes of this chapter—

(a) A "foreign state", except as used in section 1608 of this title, includes a political subdivision of a foreign state or an agency or instrumentality of a foreign state as defined in subsection (b).

(b) An "agency or instrumentality of a foreign state" means any entity—

(1) which is a separate legal person, corporate or otherwise, and

(2) which is an organ of a foreign state or political subdivision thereof, or a majority of whose shares or other ownership interest is owned by a foreign state or political subdivision thereof, and

(3) which is neither a citizen of a State of the United States as defined in section 1332(c) and (d) of this title, nor created under the laws of any third country.

(c) The "United States" includes all territory and waters, continental or insular, subject to the jurisdiction of the United States.

(d) A "commercial activity" means either a regular course of commercial conduct or a particular commercial transaction or act. The commercial character of an activity shall be determined by reference to the nature of the course of conduct or particular transaction or act, rather than by reference to its purpose.

(e) A "commercial activity carried on in the United States by a foreign state" means commercial activity carried on by such state and having substantial contact with the United States.

(Added Pub.L. 94–583, § 4(a), Oct. 21, 1976, 90 Stat. 2892.)

HISTORICAL AND STATUTORY NOTES

Effective Dates

1976 Acts. Section effective 90 days after Oct. 21, 1976, see section 8 of Pub.L. 94–583, set out as a note under section 1602 of this title.

§ 1604. Immunity of a foreign state from jurisdiction

Subject to existing international agreements to which the United States is a party at the time of enactment of this Act a foreign state shall be immune from the jurisdiction of the courts of the United States and of the States except as provided in sections 1605 to 1607 of this chapter.

(Added Pub.L. 94–583, § 4(a), Oct. 21, 1976, 90 Stat. 2892.)

HISTORICAL AND STATUTORY NOTES

References in Text

The time of enactment of this Act, referred to in text, probably means the time of enactment of Pub.L. 94–583, which was approved on Oct. 21, 1976.

Effective Dates

1976 Acts. Section effective 90 days after Oct. 21, 1976, see section 8 of Pub.L. 94–583, set out as a note under section 1602 of this title.

§ 1605. General exceptions to the jurisdictional immunity of a foreign state

(a) A foreign state shall not be immune from the jurisdiction of courts of the United States or of the States in any case—

(1) in which the foreign state has waived its immunity either explicitly or by implication, notwithstanding any withdrawal of the waiver which the foreign state may purport to effect except in accordance with the terms of the waiver;

(2) in which the action is based upon a commercial activity carried on in the United States by the foreign state; or upon an act performed in the United States in connection with a commercial activity of the foreign state elsewhere; or upon an act outside the territory of the United States in connection with a commercial activity of the foreign state elsewhere and that act causes a direct effect in the United States;

(3) in which rights in property taken in violation of international law are in issue and that property or any property exchanged for such property is present in the United States in connection with a commercial activity carried on in the United States by the foreign state; or that property or any property exchanged for such property is owned or operated by an agency or instrumentality of the foreign state and that agency or instrumentality is engaged in a commercial activity in the United States;

(4) in which rights in property in the United States acquired by succession or gift or rights in immovable property situated in the United States are in issue;

(5) not otherwise encompassed in paragraph (2) above, in which money damages are sought against a foreign state for personal injury or death, or

damage to or loss of property, occurring in the United States and caused by the tortious act or omission of that foreign state or of any official or employee of that foreign state while acting within the scope of his office or employment; except this paragraph shall not apply to—

(A) any claim based upon the exercise or performance or the failure to exercise or perform a discretionary function regardless of whether the discretion be abused, or

(B) any claim arising out of malicious prosecution, abuse of process, libel, slander, misrepresentation, deceit, or interference with contract rights;

(6) in which the action is brought, either to enforce an agreement made by the foreign state with or for the benefit of a private party to submit to arbitration all or any differences which have arisen or which may arise between the parties with respect to a defined legal relationship, whether contractual or not, concerning a subject matter capable of settlement by arbitration under the laws of the United States, or to confirm an award made pursuant to such an agreement to arbitrate, if (A) the arbitration takes place or is intended to take place in the United States, (B) the agreement or award is or may be governed by a treaty or other international agreement in force for the United States calling for the recognition and enforcement of arbitral awards, (C) the underlying claim, save for the agreement to arbitrate, could have been brought in a United States court under this section or section 1607, or (D) paragraph (1) of this subsection is otherwise applicable; or

(7) not otherwise covered by paragraph (2), in which money damages are sought against a foreign state for personal injury or death that was caused by an act of torture, extrajudicial killing, aircraft sabotage, hostage taking, or the provision of material support or resources (as defined in section 2339A of title 18) for such an act if such act or provision of material support is engaged in by an official, employee, or agent of such foreign state while acting within the scope of his or her office, employment, or agency, except that the court shall decline to hear a claim under this paragraph—

(A) if the foreign state was not designated as a state sponsor of terrorism under section 6(j) of the Export Administration Act of 1979 (50 U.S.C. App. 2405(j)) or section 620A of the Foreign Assistance Act of 1961 (22 U.S.C. 2371) at the time the act occurred, unless later so designated as a result of such act; and

(B) even if the foreign state is or was so designated, if—

(i) the act occurred in the foreign state against which the claim has been brought and the claimant has not afforded the foreign state a reasonable opportunity to arbitrate the claim in accordance with accepted international rules of arbitration; or

(ii) neither the claimant nor the victim was a national of the United States (as that term is defined in section 101(a)(22) of the Immigration and Nationality Act) when the act upon which the claim is based occurred.

(b) A foreign state shall not be immune from the jurisdiction of the courts of the United States in any case in which a suit in admiralty is brought to enforce a maritime lien against a vessel or cargo of the foreign state, which maritime lien is based upon a commercial activity of the foreign state: *Provided*, That—

(1) notice of the suit is given by delivery of a copy of the summons and of the complaint to the person, or his agent, having possession of the vessel or cargo against which the maritime lien is asserted; and if the vessel or cargo is arrested pursuant to process obtained on behalf of the party bringing the suit, the service of process of arrest shall be deemed to constitute valid delivery of such notice, but the party bringing the suit shall be liable for any damages sustained by the foreign state as a result of the arrest if the party bringing the suit had actual or constructive knowledge that the vessel or cargo of a foreign state was involved; and

(2) notice to the foreign state of the commencement of suit as provided in section 1608 of this title is initiated within ten days either of the delivery of notice as provided in paragraph (1) of this subsection or, in the case of a party who was unaware that the vessel or cargo of a foreign state was involved, of the date such party determined the existence of the foreign state's interest.

(c) Whenever notice is delivered under subsection (b)(1), the suit to enforce a maritime lien shall thereafter proceed and shall be heard and determined according to the principles of law and rules of practice of suits in rem whenever it appears that, had the vessel been privately owned and possessed, a suit in rem might have been maintained. A decree against the foreign state may include costs of the suit and, if the decree is for a money judgment, interest as ordered by the court, except that the court may not award judgment against the foreign state in an amount greater than the value of the vessel or cargo upon which the maritime lien arose. Such value shall be determined as of the time notice is served under subsection (b)(1). Decrees shall be subject to appeal and revision as provided in other cases of admiralty and maritime jurisdiction. Nothing shall preclude the plaintiff in any proper case from seeking relief in personam in the same action brought to enforce a maritime lien as provided in this section.

(d) A foreign state shall not be immune from the jurisdiction of the courts of the United States in any action brought to foreclose a preferred mortgage, as defined in the Ship Mortgage Act, 1920 (46 U.S.C. 911 and following). Such action shall be brought, heard, and determined in accordance with the provisions of that Act and in accordance with the principles of law and rules of practice of suits in rem, whenever it appears that had the vessel been privately owned and possessed a suit in rem might have been maintained.

(e) For purposes of paragraph (7) of subsection (a)—

(1) the terms "torture" and "extrajudicial killing" have the meaning given those terms in section 3 of the Torture Victim Protection Act of 1991;

(2) the term "hostage taking" has the meaning given that term in Article 1 of the International Convention Against the Taking of Hostages; and

(3) the term "aircraft sabotage" has the meaning given that term in Article 1 of the Convention for the Suppression of Unlawful Acts Against the Safety of Civil Aviation.

(f) No action shall be maintained under subsection (a)(7) unless the action is commenced not later than 10 years after the date on which the cause of action arose. All principles of equitable tolling, including the period during which the foreign state was immune from suit, shall apply in calculating this limitation period.

(g) Limitation on discovery.—

(1) In general.—(A) Subject to paragraph (2), if an action is filed that would otherwise be barred by section 1604, but for subsection (a)(7), the court, upon request of the Attorney General, shall stay any request, demand, or order for discovery on the United States that the Attorney General certifies would significantly interfere with a criminal investigation or prosecution, or a national security operation, related to the incident that gave rise to the cause of action, until such time as the Attorney General advises the court that such request, demand, or order will no longer so interfere.

(B) A stay under this paragraph shall be in effect during the 12–month period beginning on the date on which the court issues the order to stay discovery. The court shall renew the order to stay discovery for additional 12–month periods upon motion by the United States if the Attorney General certifies that discovery would significantly interfere with a criminal investigation or prosecution, or a national security operation, related to the incident that gave rise to the cause of action.

(2) Sunset.—(A) Subject to subparagraph (B), no stay shall be granted or continued in effect under paragraph (1) after the date that is 10 years after the date on which the incident that gave rise to the cause of action occurred.

(B) After the period referred to in subparagraph (A), the court, upon request of the Attorney General, may stay any request, demand, or order for discovery on the United States that the court finds a substantial likelihood would—

(i) create a serious threat of death or serious bodily injury to any person;

(ii) adversely affect the ability of the United States to work in cooperation with foreign and international law enforcement agencies in investigating violations of United States law; or

(iii) obstruct the criminal case related to the incident that gave rise to the cause of action or undermine the potential for a conviction in such case.

(3) Evaluation of evidence.—The court's evaluation of any request for a stay under this subsection filed by the Attorney General shall be conducted ex parte and in camera.

(4) Bar on motions to dismiss.—A stay of discovery under this subsection shall constitute a bar to the granting of a motion to dismiss under rules 12(b)(6) and 56 of the Federal Rules of Civil Procedure.

(5) Construction.—Nothing in this subsection shall prevent the United States from seeking protective orders or asserting privileges ordinarily available to the United States.

(Added Pub.L. 94–583, § 4(a), Oct. 21, 1976, 90 Stat. 2892, and amended Pub.L. 100–640, § 1, Nov. 9, 1988, 102 Stat. 3333; Pub.L. 100–669, § 2, Nov. 16, 1988, 102 Stat. 3969; Pub.L. 101–650, Title III, § 325(b)(8), Dec. 1, 1990, 104 Stat. 5121; Pub.L. 104–132, Title II, § 221(a), Apr. 24, 1996, 110 Stat. 1241; Pub.L. 105–11, Apr. 25, 1997, 111 Stat. 22.)

HISTORICAL AND STATUTORY NOTES

References in Text

Section 101(a)(22) of the Immigration and Nationality Act, referred to in subsec. (a)(7)(B)(ii), is classified to section 1101(a)(22) of Title 8, Aliens and Nationality.

The Ship Mortgage Act, 1920, referred to in subsec. (d), is section 30 of Act June 5, 1920, c. 250, 41 Stat. 1000, as amended, which was classified generally to chapter 25 (section 911 et seq.) of the Appendix to Title 46, Shipping, and was repealed by Pub.L. 100–710, Title I, § 106(b)(2), Nov. 23, 1988, 102 Stat. 4752, and reenacted by section 102(c) thereof as chapters 301 and 313 of Title 46, Shipping.

Section 3 of the Torture Victim Protection Act of 1991, referred to in subsec. (e)(1), is section 3 of Pub.L. 102–256, Mar. 12, 1992, 106 Stat. 73, set out in a note under section 1350 of this title.

Effective Dates

1997 Acts. Section 1 of Pub.L. 105–11 provided in part that the amendment of subsec. (a)(7)(B)(ii) by Pub.L. 105–11 is effective with respect to any cause of action arising before, on, or after April 25, 1997.

1996 Acts. Section 221(c) of Pub.L. 104–132 provided that: "The amendments made by this subtitle [amending this section and section 1610 of this title] shall apply to any cause of action arising before, on, or after the date of the enactment of this Act [Apr. 24, 1996]."

1988 Acts. Section 3 of Pub.L. 100–640 provided that: "The amendments made by this Act [amending this section and section 1610 of this title] shall apply to actions commenced on or after the date of the enactment of this Act [Nov. 9, 1988]."

1976 Acts. Section effective 90 days after Oct. 21, 1976, see section 8 of Pub.L. 94–583, set out as a note under section 1602 of this title.

Civil Liability for Acts of State Sponsored Terrorism

Pub.L. 104–208, Div. A, Title I, § 101(c) [Title V, § 589], Sept. 30, 1996, 110 Stat. 3009–172, provided that:

"**(a)** An official, employee, or agent of a foreign state designated as a state sponsor of terrorism designated under section 6(j) of the Export Administration Act of 1979 [section 2405(j) of the Appendix to Title 50, War and National Defense] while acting within the scope of his or her office, employment, or agency shall be liable to a United States national or the national's legal representative for personal injury or death caused by acts of that official, employee, or agent for which the courts of the United States may maintain jurisdiction under section 1605(a)(7) of title 28, United States Code [subsec. (a)(7) of this section] for money damages which may include economic damages, solatium, pain, and suffering, and punitive damages if the acts were among those described in section 1605(a)(7) [subsec. (a)(7) of this section].

"**(b)** Provisions related to statute of limitations and limitations on discovery that would apply to an action brought under 28 U.S.C. 1605(f) and (g) [subsecs. (f) and (g) of this section] shall also apply to actions brought under this section. No action shall be maintained under this action [SIC] if an official, employee, or agent of the United States, while acting within the scope of his or her office, employment, or agency would not be liable for such acts if carried out within the United States."

§ 1606. Extent of liability

As to any claim for relief with respect to which a foreign state is not entitled to immunity under section 1605 or 1607 of this chapter, the foreign state shall be liable in the same manner and to the same extent as a private individual under like circumstances; but a foreign state except for an agency or instrumentality thereof shall not be liable for punitive damages, except any action under section 1605(a)(7) or 1610(f); if, however, in any case wherein death was caused, the law of the place where the action or omission occurred provides, or has been construed to provide, for damages only punitive in nature, the foreign state shall be liable for actual or compensatory damages measured by the pecuniary injuries resulting from such death which were incurred by the persons for whose benefit the action was brought.

(Added Pub.L. 94–583, § 4(a), Oct. 21, 1976, 90 Stat. 2894, and amended Pub.L. 105–277, Div. A, § 101(h) [Title I, § 117(b)], Oct. 21, 1998, 112 Stat. 2681–___.)

HISTORICAL AND STATUTORY NOTES

Effective Dates

1976 Acts. Section effective 90 days after Oct. 21, 1976, see section 8 of Pub.L. 94–583, set out as a note under section 1602 of this title.

§ 1607. Counterclaims

In any action brought by a foreign state, or in which a foreign state intervenes, in a court of the United States or of a State, the foreign state shall not be accorded immunity with respect to any counterclaim—

(a) for which a foreign state would not be entitled to immunity under section 1605 of this chapter had such claim been brought in a separate action against the foreign state; or

(b) arising out of the transaction or occurrence that is the subject matter of the claim of the foreign state; or

(c) to the extent that the counterclaim does not seek relief exceeding in amount or differing in kind from that sought by the foreign state.

(Added Pub.L. 94–583, § 4(a), Oct. 21, 1976, 90 Stat. 2894.)

HISTORICAL AND STATUTORY NOTES

Effective Dates

1976 Acts. Section effective 90 days after Oct. 21, 1976, see section 8 of Pub.L. 94–583, set out as a note under section 1602 of this title.

§ 1608. Service; time to answer; default

(a) Service in the courts of the United States and of the States shall be made upon a foreign state or political subdivision of a foreign state:

(1) by delivery of a copy of the summons and complaint in accordance with any special arrangement for service between the plaintiff and the foreign state or political subdivision; or

(2) if no special arrangement exists, by delivery of a copy of the summons and complaint in accordance with an applicable international convention on service of judicial documents; or

(3) if service cannot be made under paragraphs (1) or (2), by sending a copy of the summons and complaint and a notice of suit, together with a translation of each into the official language of the foreign state, by any form of mail requiring a signed receipt, to be addressed and dispatched by the clerk of the court to the head of the ministry of foreign affairs of the foreign state concerned, or

(4) if service cannot be made within 30 days under paragraph (3), by sending two copies of the summons and complaint and a notice of suit, together with a translation of each into the official language of the foreign state, by any form of mail requiring a signed receipt, to be addressed and dispatched by the clerk of the court to the Secretary of State in Washington, District of Columbia, to the attention of the Director of Special Consular Services—and the Secretary shall transmit one copy of the papers through diplomatic channels to the foreign state and shall send to the clerk of the court a certified copy of the diplomatic note indicating when the papers were transmitted.

As used in this subsection, a "notice of suit" shall mean a notice addressed to a foreign state and in a form prescribed by the Secretary of State by regulation.

(b) Service in the courts of the United States and of the States shall be made upon an agency or instrumentality of a foreign state:

(1) by delivery of a copy of the summons and complaint in accordance with any special arrangement for service between the plaintiff and the agency or instrumentality; or

(2) if no special arrangement exists, by delivery of a copy of the summons and complaint either to an officer, a managing or general agent, or to any other agent authorized by appointment or by law to receive service of process in the United States; or in accordance with an applicable international convention on service of judicial documents; or

(3) if service cannot be made under paragraphs (1) or (2), and if reasonably calculated to give actual notice, by delivery of a copy of the summons and complaint, together with a translation of each into the official language of the foreign state—

(A) as directed by an authority of the foreign state or political subdivision in response to a letter rogatory or request or

(B) by any form of mail requiring a signed receipt, to be addressed and dispatched by the clerk of the court to the agency or instrumentality to be served, or

(C) as directed by order of the court consistent with the law of the place where service is to be made.

(c) Service shall be deemed to have been made—

(1) in the case of service under subsection (a)(4), as of the date of transmittal indicated in the certified copy of the diplomatic note; and

(2) in any other case under this section, as of the date of receipt indicated in the certification, signed and returned postal receipt, or other proof of service applicable to the method of service employed.

(d) In any action brought in a court of the United States or of a State, a foreign state, a political subdivision thereof, or an agency or instrumentality of a foreign state shall serve an answer or other responsive pleading to the complaint within sixty days after service has been made under this section.

(e) No judgment by default shall be entered by a court of the United States or of a State against a foreign state, a political subdivision thereof, or an agency or instrumentality of a foreign state, unless the claimant establishes his claim or right to relief by evidence satisfactory to the court. A copy of any such default judgment shall be sent to the foreign state or political subdivision in the manner prescribed for service in this section.

(Added Pub.L. 94–583, § 4(a), Oct. 21, 1976, 90 Stat. 2894.)

HISTORICAL AND STATUTORY NOTES

Effective Dates

1976 Acts. Section effective 90 days after Oct. 21, 1976, see section 8 of Pub.L. 94–583, set out as a note under section 1602 of this title.

§ 1609. Immunity from attachment and execution of property of a foreign state

Subject to existing international agreements to which the United States is a party at the time of enactment of this Act the property in the United States of a foreign state shall be immune from attachment arrest and execution except as provided in sections 1610 and 1611 of this chapter.

(Added Pub.L. 94–583, § 4(a), Oct. 21, 1976, 90 Stat. 2895.)

HISTORICAL AND STATUTORY NOTES

References in Text

The time of enactment of this Act, referred to in text, probably means the time of enactment of Pub.L. 94–583, which was approved on Oct. 21, 1976.

Effective Dates

1976 Acts. Section effective 90 days after Oct. 21, 1976, see section 8 of Pub.L. 94–583, set out as a note under section 1602 of this title.

§ 1610. Exceptions to the immunity from attachment or execution

(a) The property in the United States of a foreign state, as defined in section 1603(a) of this chapter, used for a commercial activity in the United States, shall not be immune from attachment in aid of execution, or from execution, upon a judgment entered by a court of the United States or of a State after the effective date of this Act, if—

(1) the foreign state has waived its immunity from attachment in aid of execution or from execution either explicitly or by implication, notwithstanding any withdrawal of the waiver the foreign state may purport to effect except in accordance with the terms of the waiver, or

(2) the property is or was used for the commercial activity upon which the claim is based, or

(3) the execution relates to a judgment establishing rights in property which has been taken in violation of international law or which has been exchanged for property taken in violation of international law, or

(4) the execution relates to a judgment establishing rights in property—

(A) which is acquired by succession or gift, or

(B) which is immovable and situated in the United States: *Provided*, That such property is not used for purposes of maintaining a diplomatic or consular mission or the residence of the Chief of such mission, or

(5) the property consists of any contractual obligation or any proceeds from such a contractual obligation to indemnify or hold harmless the foreign state or its employees under a policy of automobile or other liability or casualty insurance covering the claim which merged into the judgment, or

(6) the judgment is based on an order confirming an arbitral award rendered against the foreign state, provided that attachment in aid of execution, or execution, would not be inconsistent with any provision in the arbitral agreement, or

(7) the judgment relates to a claim for which the foreign state is not immune under section 1605(a)(7), regardless of whether the property is or was involved with the act upon which the claim is based.

(b) In addition to subsection (a), any property in the United States of an agency or instrumentality of a foreign state engaged in commercial activity in the United States shall not be immune from attachment in aid of execution, or from execution, upon a judgment entered by a court of the United States or of a State after the effective date of this Act, if—

(1) the agency or instrumentality has waived its immunity from attachment in aid of execution or from execution either explicitly or implicitly, notwithstanding any withdrawal of the waiver the agency or instrumentality may purport to effect except in accordance with the terms of the waiver, or

(2) the judgment relates to a claim for which the agency or instrumentality is not immune by virtue of section 1605(a) (2), (3), (5), or (7) or 1605(b) of this chapter, regardless of whether the property is or was involved in the act upon which the claim is based.

(c) No attachment or execution referred to in subsections (a) and (b) of this section shall be permitted until the court has ordered such attachment and execution after having determined that a reasonable period of time has elapsed following the entry of judgment and the giving of any notice required under section 1608(e) of this chapter.

(d) The property of a foreign state, as defined in section 1603(a) of this chapter, used for a commercial activity in the United States, shall not be immune from attachment prior to the entry of judgment in any action brought in a court of the United States or of a State, or prior to the elapse of the period of time provided in subsection (c) of this section, if—

(1) the foreign state has explicitly waived its immunity from attachment prior to judgment, notwithstanding any withdrawal of the waiver the foreign state may purport to effect except in accordance with the terms of the waiver, and

(2) the purpose of the attachment is to secure satisfaction of a judgment that has been or may ultimately be entered against the foreign state, and not to obtain jurisdiction.

(e) The vessels of a foreign state shall not be immune from arrest in rem, interlocutory sale, and execution in actions brought to foreclose a preferred mortgage as provided in section 1605(d).

(f)(1)(A) Notwithstanding any other provision of law, including but not limited to section 208(f) of the Foreign Missions Act (22 U.S.C. 4308(f)), and except as provided in subparagraph (B), any property with respect to which financial transactions are prohibited or regulated pursuant to section 5(b) of the Trading with the Enemy Act (50 U.S.C. App. 5(b)), section 620(a) of the Foreign Assistance Act of 1961 (22 U.S.C. 2370(a)), sections 202 and 203 of the International Emergency Economic Powers Act (50 U.S.C. 1701–1702), or any other proclamation, order, regulation, or license issued pursuant thereto, shall be subject to execution or attachment in aid of execution of any judgment relating to a claim for which a foreign state (including any agency or instrumentality or such state) claiming such property is not immune under section 1605(a)(7).

(B) Subparagraph (A) shall not apply if, at the time the property is expropriated or seized by the foreign state, the property has been held in title by a natural person or, if held in trust, has been held for the benefit of a natural person or persons.

(2)(A) At the request of any party in whose favor a judgment has been issued with respect to a claim for which the foreign state is not immune under section 1605(a)(7), the Secretary of the Treasury and the Secretary of State shall fully, promptly, and effectively assist any judgment creditor or any court that has issued any such judgment in identifying, locating, and executing against the property of that foreign state or any agency or instrumentality of such state.

(B) In providing such assistance, the Secretaries—

(i) may provide such information to the court under seal; and

(ii) shall provide the information in a manner sufficient to allow the court to direct the United

States Marshall's office to promptly and effectively execute against that property.

(Added Pub.L. 94–583, § 4(a), Oct. 21, 1976, 90 Stat. 2896, and amended Pub.L. 100–640, § 2, Nov. 9, 1988, 102 Stat. 3333; Pub.L. 100–669, § 3, Nov. 16, 1988, 102 Stat. 3969; Pub.L. 101–650, Title III, § 325(b)(9), Dec. 1, 1990, 104 Stat. 5121; Pub.L. 104–132, Title II, § 221(b), Apr. 24, 1996, 110 Stat. 1243; Pub.L. 105–277, Div. A § 101(h) [Title I, § 117], Oct. 21, 1998, 112 Stat. 2681–___.)

HISTORICAL AND STATUTORY NOTES

References in Text

The effective date of this Act, referred to in subsecs. (a) and (b), is 90 days after Oct. 21, 1976, see section 8 of Pub.L. 94–583, set out as an Effective Dates note under section 1602 of this title.

Effective Dates

1998 Acts. Pub.L. 105–277, § 101(h) [Title I, § 117(c)], provided that: "The amendments made by subsections (a) and (b) [amending this section and section 1606 of this title] shall apply to any claim for which a foreign state is not immune under section 1605(a)(7) of title 28, United States Code, arising before, on, or after the date of enactment of this Act [Oct. 21, 1998]."

1996 Acts. Amendment by Pub.L. 104–132 to apply to any cause of action arising before, on, or after Apr. 24, 1996, see section 221(c) of Pub.L. 104–132, set out as a note under section 1605 of this title.

1988 Acts. Amendment to this section by section 2 of Pub.L. 100–640, enacting subsec. (e) of this section, to apply to actions commenced on or after Nov. 9, 1988, see section 3 of Pub.L. 100–640, set out as a note under section 1605 of this title.

1976 Acts. Section effective 90 days after Oct. 21, 1976, see section 8 of Pub.L. 94–583, set out as a note under section 1602 of this title.

Waiver of Exception to Immunity from Attachment or Execution

Pub.L. 105–277, Div. A, § 101(h) [Title I, § 117(d)], Oct. 21, 1998, 112 Stat. 2681–___, provided that: "The President may waive the requirements of this section [amending this section and section 1606 of this title and enacting provisions set out as notes under this section] in the interest of national security."

§ 1611. Certain types of property immune from execution

(a) Notwithstanding the provisions of section 1610 of this chapter, the property of those organizations designated by the President as being entitled to enjoy the privileges, exemptions, and immunities provided by the International Organizations Immunities Act shall not be subject to attachment or any other judicial process impeding the disbursement of funds to, or on the order of, a foreign state as the result of an action brought in the courts of the United States or of the States.

(b) Notwithstanding the provisions of section 1610 of this chapter, the property of a foreign state shall be immune from attachment and from execution, if—

(1) the property is that of a foreign central bank or monetary authority held for its own account, unless such bank or authority, or its parent foreign government, has explicitly waived its immunity from attachment in aid of execution, or from execution, notwithstanding any withdrawal of the waiver which the bank, authority or government may purport to effect except in accordance with the terms of the waiver; or

(2) the property is, or is intended to be, used in connection with a military activity and

(A) is of a military character, or

(B) is under the control of a military authority or defense agency.

(c) Notwithstanding the provisions of section 1610 of this chapter, the property of a foreign state shall be immune from attachment and from execution in an action brought under section 302 of the Cuban Liberty and Democratic Solidarity (LIBERTAD) Act of 1996 to the extent that the property is a facility or installation used by an accredited diplomatic mission for official purposes.

(Added Pub.L. 94–583, § 4(a), Oct. 21, 1976, 90 Stat. 2897, and amended Pub.L. 104–114, Title III, § 302(e), Mar. 12, 1996, 110 Stat. 818.)

HISTORICAL AND STATUTORY NOTES

References in Text

The International Organizations Immunities Act, referred to in subsec. (a), is Act Dec. 29, 1945, c. 652, Title I, 59 Stat. 669, as amended, which is classified principally to section 288 et seq. of Title 22, Foreign Relations and Intercourse. For complete classification of this Act to the Code, see Short Title note set out under section 288 of Title 22 and Tables.

Section 302 of the Cuban Liberty and Democratic Solidarity (LIBERTAD) Act of 1996, referred to in subsec. (c), is Pub.L. 104–114, Title III, § 302, Mar. 12, 1996, 110 Stat. 815, which is classified to section 6082 of Title 22, Foreign Relations and Intercourse.

Effective Dates

1996 Acts. Amendment by section 302(e) of Pub.L. 104–114 effective Aug. 1, 1996, except as otherwise provided, see section 6085 of Title 22, Foreign Relations and Intercourse.

1976 Acts. Section effective 90 days after Oct. 21, 1976, see section 8 of Pub.L. 94–583, set out as a note under section 1602 of this title.

CHAPTER 99—GENERAL PROVISIONS

Sec.
1631. Transfer to cure want of jurisdiction.

§ 1631. Transfer to cure want of jurisdiction

Whenever a civil action is filed in a court as defined in section 610 of this title or an appeal, including a petition for review of administrative action, is noticed for or filed with such a court and that court finds that there is a want of jurisdiction, the court shall, if it is in the interest of justice, transfer such action or appeal to any other such court in which the action or appeal could have been brought at the time it was filed or noticed, and the action or appeal shall proceed as if it had been filed in or noticed for the court to which it is transferred on the date upon which it was actually filed in or noticed for the court from which it is transferred.

(Added Pub.L. 97–164, Title III, § 301(a), Apr. 2, 1982, 96 Stat. 55.)

HISTORICAL AND STATUTORY NOTES

Effective Dates

1982 Acts. Section effective Oct. 1, 1982, see section 402 of Pub.L. 97–164, set out as a note under section 171 of this title.

PART V—PROCEDURE

Chapter		Section
111.	General Provisions	1651
113.	Process	1691
115.	Evidence; Documentary	1731
117.	Evidence; Depositions	1781
119.	Evidence; Witnesses	1821
121.	Juries; Trial by Jury	1861
123.	Fees and Costs	1911
125.	Pending Actions and Judgments	1961
127.	Executions and Judicial Sales	2001
129.	Moneys Paid into Court	2041
131.	Rules of Courts	2071
133.	Review—Miscellaneous Provisions	2101

CHAPTER 111—GENERAL PROVISIONS

Sec.
1651. Writs.
1652. State laws as rules of decision.
1653. Amendment of pleadings to show jurisdiction.
1654. Appearance personally or by counsel.
1655. Lien enforcement; absent defendants.
1656. Creation of new district or division or transfer of territory; lien enforcement.
1657. Priority of civil actions.
1658. Time limitations on the commencement of civil actions arising under Acts of Congress.
1659. Stay of certain actions pending disposition of related proceedings before the United States International Trade Commission.

§ 1651. Writs

(a) The Supreme Court and all courts established by Act of Congress may issue all writs necessary or appropriate in aid of their respective jurisdictions and agreeable to the usages and principles of law.

(b) An alternative writ or rule nisi may be issued by a justice or judge of a court which has jurisdiction.

(June 25, 1948, c. 646, 62 Stat. 944; May 24, 1949, c. 139, § 90, 63 Stat. 102.)

HISTORICAL AND STATUTORY NOTES

Writ of Error

Act Jan. 31, 1928, c. 14, § 2, 45 Stat. 54, as amended Apr. 26, 1928, c. 440, 45 Stat. 466; June 25, 1948, c. 646, § 23, 62 Stat. 990, provided that: "All Acts of Congress referring to writs of error shall be construed as amended to the extent necessary to substitute appeal for writ of error."

§ 1652. State laws as rules of decision

The laws of the several states, except where the Constitution or treaties of the United States or Acts of Congress otherwise require or provide, shall be regarded as rules of decision in civil actions in the courts of the United States, in cases where they apply.

(June 25, 1948, c. 646, 62 Stat. 944.)

§ 1653. Amendment of pleadings to show jurisdiction

Defective allegations of jurisdiction may be amended, upon terms, in the trial or appellate courts.

(June 25, 1948, c. 646, 62 Stat. 944.)

§ 1654. Appearance personally or by counsel

In all courts of the United States the parties may plead and conduct their own cases personally or by counsel as, by the rules of such courts, respectively, are permitted to manage and conduct causes therein.

(June 25, 1948, c. 646, 62 Stat. 944; May 24, 1949, c. 139, § 91, 63 Stat. 103.)

§ 1655. Lien enforcement; absent defendants

In an action in a district court to enforce any lien upon or claim to, or to remove any incumbrance or lien or cloud upon the title to, real or personal property within the district, where any defendant can not be served within the State, or does not voluntarily appear, the court may order the absent defendant to appear or plead by a day certain.

Such order shall be served on the absent defendant personally if practicable, wherever found, and also upon the person or persons in possession or charge of such property, if any. Where personal service is not practicable, the order shall be published as the court may direct, not less than once a week for six consecutive weeks.

If an absent defendant does not appear or plead within the time allowed, the court may proceed as if the absent defendant had been served with process within the State, but any adjudication shall, as regards the absent defendant without appearance, affect only the property which is the subject of the action. When a part of the property is within another district, but within the same state, such action may be brought in either district.

Any defendant not so personally notified may, at any time within one year after final judgment, enter his appearance, and thereupon the court shall set aside the judgment and permit such defendant to plead on payment of such costs as the court deems just.

(June 25, 1948, c. 646, 62 Stat. 944.)

§ 1656. Creation of new district or division or transfer of territory; lien enforcement

The creation of a new district or division or the transfer of any territory to another district or division shall not affect or divest any lien theretofore acquired in a district court upon property within such district, division or territory.

To enforce such lien, the clerk of the court in which the same is acquired, upon the request and at the cost of the party desiring the same, shall make a certified copy of the record thereof, which, when filed in the proper court of the district or division in which such property is situated after such creation or transfer shall be evidence in all courts and places equally with the original thereof; and, thereafter like proceedings shall be had thereon, and with the same effect, as though the case or proceeding had been originally instituted in such court.

(June 25, 1948, c. 646, 62 Stat. 944; Nov. 6, 1978, Pub.L. 95–598, Title II, § 242, 92 Stat. 2671.)

HISTORICAL AND STATUTORY NOTES

Codifications

This section, was amended by Pub.L. 95–598, Title II, § 242, Nov. 6, 1978, 92 Stat. 2671, effective June 28, 1984, pursuant to Pub.L. 95–598, Title IV, § 402(b), Nov. 6, 1978, 92 Stat. 2682, as amended by Pub.L. 98–249, § 1(a), Mar. 31, 1984, 98 Stat. 116; Pub.L. 98–271, § 1(a), Apr. 30, 1984, 98 Stat. 163; Pub.L. 98–299, § 1(a), May 25, 1984, 98 Stat. 214; Pub.L. 98–325, § 1(a), June 20, 1984, 98 Stat. 268, set out as an Effective Dates note preceding section 101 of Title 11, Bankruptcy, by inserting "or in a bankruptcy court" following "a district court".

Section 402(b) of Pub.L. 95–598 was amended by section 113 of Pub.L. 98–353, Title I, July 10, 1984, 98 Stat. 343, by substituting "shall not be effective" for "shall take effect on June 28, 1984", thereby eliminating the amendment by section 242 of Pub.L. 95–598, effective June 27, 1984, pursuant to section 122(c) of Pub.L. 98–353, set out as an Effective Dates note under section 151 of this title.

Section 121(a) of Pub.L. 98–353 directed that section 402(b) of Pub.L. 95–598 be amended by substituting "the date of enactment of the Bankruptcy Amendments and Federal Judgeship Act of 1984 [i.e. July 10, 1984]" for "June 28, 1984". This amendment was not executed in view of the prior amendment to section 402(b) of Pub.L. 95–598 by section 113 of Pub.L. 98–353.

§ 1657. Priority of civil actions

(a) Notwithstanding any other provision of law, each court of the United States shall determine the order in which civil actions are heard and determined, except that the court shall expedite the consideration of any action brought under chapter 153 or section 1826 of this title, any action for temporary or preliminary injunctive relief, or any other action if good cause therefor is shown. For purposes of this subsection, "good cause" is shown if a right under the Constitution of the United States or a Federal Statute (including rights under section 552 of title 5) would be maintained in a factual context that indicates that a request for expedited consideration has merit.

(b) The Judicial Conference of the United States may modify the rules adopted by the courts to determine the order in which civil actions are heard and determined, in order to establish consistency among the judicial circuits.

(Added Pub.L. 98–620, Title IV, § 401(a), Nov. 8, 1984, 98 Stat. 3356.)

HISTORICAL AND STATUTORY NOTES

Codifications

Pub.L. 101–647, Title XXV, § 2527(b), Nov. 29, 1990, 104 Stat. 4877, purported to amend section 1657 of Title 18, Crimes and Criminal Procedure, by inserting "section 11, 12, or 13 of the Federal Deposit Insurance Act" after "consideration of any action brought under", which amendment could not be executed to the text of section 1657 of Title 18. Such amendment was probably intended to amend this section.

Effective Dates

1984 Acts. Section 403 of Pub.L. 98–620 provided that: "The amendments made by this subtitle [subtitle A of Title IV of Pub.L. 98–620, enacting this section, amending sections 596, 636, 1364, 2284, and 2349 of this title, sections 437g, 437h and 687 of Title 2, The Congress, section 552 of Title 5, Government Organization and Employees, sections 8, 136d, 136h, 136n, 136w, 194, 1366, 1600 and 1601 of Title 7, Agriculture, section 1464 of Title 12, Banks and Banking, sections 18a, 21, 45, 57a–1, 78k–1, 687a, 687c, 719h, 1415, 2003 and 2622 of Title 15, Commerce and Trade, sections 1463a, 1910, 3117, and 3168 of Title 16, Conservation, sections 1964 and 1966 of Title 18, Crimes and Criminal Procedure, sections 346a and 348 of Title 21, Food and Drugs, section 618 of Title 22, Foreign Relations and Intercourse, section 640d–3 of Title 25, Indians, sections 3310, 6110, 6363, 7609, 9010 and 9011 of Title 26, Internal Revenue Code, sections 110, 160, 660 and 1303 of Title 29, Labor, section 816 of Title 30, Mineral Lands and Mining, section 2022 of Title 38, Veterans' Benefits, section 3628 of Title 39, Postal Service, sections 300j–9, 504, 6508 and 8514 of Title 42, The Public Health and Welfare, sections 1062, 1349, 1652 and 2011 of Title 43, Public Lands, sections 355, 745, 1018 and 1205 of Title 45, Railroads, section 402 of Title 47, Telegraphs, Telephones, and Radiotelegraphs, section 2305 of Title 49 Appendix, Transportation, section 792a of Title 50, War and National Defense, sections 462 and 1984 of the Appendix to Title 50, repealing sections 1296 and 2647 of this title, section 28 of Title 15, Commerce and Trade, and section 3614 of Title 42, The Public Health and Welfare, and amending provisions set out as a note under section 2304 of Title 10, Armed Forces] shall not apply to cases pending on the date of the enactment of this subtitle [Nov. 8, 1984]."

§ 1658. Time limitations on the commencement of civil actions arising under Acts of Congress

Except as otherwise provided by law, a civil action arising under an Act of Congress enacted after the date of the enactment of this section may not be commenced later than 4 years after the cause of action accrues.

(Added Pub.L. 101–650, Title III, § 313(a), Dec. 1, 1990, 104 Stat. 5114.)

HISTORICAL AND STATUTORY NOTES

References in Text

The date of the enactment of this section, referred to in text, is the date of enactment of this section by section 313(a) of Pub.L. 101–650, which was approved Dec. 1, 1990.

Effective Dates

1990 Acts. Section 313(c) of Pub.L. 101–650 provided that: "The amendments made by this section [enacting this section] shall apply with respect to causes of action accruing on or after the date of the enactment of this Act [Dec. 1, 1990]."

COMMENTARIES

See 28 U.S.C.A. § 1658, for Commentary by David D. Siegel.

§ 1659. Stay of certain actions pending disposition of related proceedings before the United States International Trade Commission

(a) Stay.—In a civil action involving parties that are also parties to a proceeding before the United States International Trade Commission under section 337 of the Tariff Act of 1930, at the request of a party to the civil action that is also a respondent in the proceeding before the Commission, the district court shall stay, until the determination of the Commission becomes final, proceedings in the civil action with respect to any claim that involves the same issues involved in the proceeding before the Commission, but only if such request is made within—

(1) 30 days after the party is named as a respondent in the proceeding before the Commission, or

(2) 30 days after the district court action is filed,

whichever is later.

(b) Use of Commission record.—Notwithstanding section 337(n)(1) of the Tariff Act of 1930, after dissolution of a stay under subsection (a), the record of the proceeding before the United States International Trade Commission shall be transmitted to the district court and shall be admissible in the civil action, subject to such protective order as the district court determines necessary, to the extent permitted under the Federal Rules of Evidence and the Federal Rules of Civil Procedure.

(Added Pub.L. 103–465, Title III, § 321(b)(1)(A), Dec. 8, 1994, 108 Stat. 4945.)

HISTORICAL AND STATUTORY NOTES

References in Text

Section 337 of the Tariff Act of 1930, referred to in text, is section 337 of Act June 17, 1930, c. 497, Title III, 46 Stat. 703, which is classified to section 1337 of Title 19, Customs Duties.

Effective Dates

1994 Acts. Section applicable with respect to complaints filed under section 1337 of Title 19, Customs Duties, on or after the date on which the WTO Agreement enters into force with respect to the United States, Jan. 1, 1995, or in cases under section 1337 of Title 19 in which no complaint is filed, with respect to investigations initiated under such section on or after such date, see section 322 of Pub.L. 103–465, set out as a note under section 1337 of Title 19.

CHAPTER 113—PROCESS

Sec.
1691. Seal and teste of process.
1692. Process and orders affecting property in different districts.
1693. Place of arrest in civil action.
1694. Patent infringement action.
1695. Stockholder's derivative action.
1696. Service in foreign and international litigation.

HISTORICAL AND STATUTORY NOTES

Immunity from Seizure under Judicial Process of Cultural Objects Imported for Temporary Exhibition or Display

Presidential determination of cultural significance of objects and exhibition or display thereof in the national interest, see section 2459 of Title 22, Foreign Relations and Intercourse.

§ 1691. Seal and teste of process

All writs and process issuing from a court of the United States shall be under the seal of the court and signed by the clerk thereof.

(June 25, 1948, c. 646, 62 Stat. 945.)

§ 1692. Process and orders affecting property in different districts

In proceedings in a district court where a receiver is appointed for property, real, personal, or mixed, situated in different districts, process may issue and be executed in any such district as if the property lay wholly within one district, but orders affecting the property shall be entered of record in each of such districts.

(June 25, 1948, c. 646, 62 Stat. 945.)

§ 1693. Place of arrest in civil action

Except as otherwise provided by Act of Congress, no person shall be arrested in one district for trial in another in any civil action in a district court.

(June 25, 1948, c. 646, 62 Stat. 945.)

§ 1694. Patent infringement action

In a patent infringement action commenced in a district where the defendant is not a resident but has a regular and established place of business, service of process, summons or subpoena upon such defendant may be made upon his agent or agents conducting such business.

(June 25, 1948, c. 646, 62 Stat. 945.)

§ 1695. Stockholder's derivative action

Process in a stockholder's action in behalf of his corporation may be served upon such corporation in any district where it is organized or licensed to do business or is doing business.

(June 25, 1948, c. 646, 62 Stat. 945.)

§ 1696. Service in foreign and international litigation

(a) The district court of the district in which a person resides or is found may order service upon him of any document issued in connection with a proceeding in a foreign or international tribunal. The order may be made pursuant to a letter rogatory issued, or request made, by a foreign or international tribunal or upon application of any interested person and shall direct the manner of service. Service pursuant to this subsection does not, of itself, require the recognition or enforcement in the United States of a judgment, decree, or order rendered by a foreign or international tribunal.

(b) This section does not preclude service of such a document without an order of court.

(Added Pub.L. 88–619, § 4(a), Oct. 3, 1964, 78 Stat. 995.)

HISTORICAL AND STATUTORY NOTES

Treaties and Conventions; Service Abroad of Judicial and Extrajudicial Documents in Civil or Commercial Matters; Observance On and After Feb. 10, 1969, by United States and Citizens and Persons Subject to Jurisdiction of United States

For text of Convention, see provisions set out as a note under Rule 4, Federal Rules of Civil Procedure, 28 U.S.C.A.

CHAPTER 115—EVIDENCE; DOCUMENTARY

Sec.

1731. Handwriting.
1732. Record made in regular course of business; photographic copies.
1733. Government records and papers; copies.
1734. Court record lost or destroyed generally.[1]
1735. Court record lost or destroyed where United States interested.
1736. Congressional Journals.
1737. Copy of officer's bond.
1738. State and Territorial statutes and judicial proceedings; full faith and credit.
1738A. Full faith and credit given to child custody determinations.
1738B. Full faith and credit for child support orders.
1738C. Certain acts, records, and proceedings and the effect thereof.
1739. State and Territorial nonjudicial records; full faith and credit.
1740. Copies of consular papers.
1741. Foreign official documents.
[1742. Repealed.]
1743. Demand on postmaster.
1744. Copies of patent office documents generally.[1]
1745. Copies of foreign patent documents.
1746. Unsworn declarations under penalty of perjury.

[1] So in original. Does not conform to section catchline.

§ 1731. Handwriting

The admitted or proved handwriting of any person shall be admissible, for purposes of comparison, to determine genuineness of other handwriting attributed to such person.

(June 25, 1948, c. 646, 62 Stat. 945.)

§ 1732. Record made in regular course of business; photographic copies

If any business, institution, member of a profession or calling, or any department or agency of government, in the regular course of business or activity has kept or recorded any memorandum, writing, entry, print, representation or combination thereof, of any act, transaction, occurrence, or event, and in the regular course of business has caused any or all of the same to be recorded, copied, or reproduced by any photographic, photostatic, microfilm, micro-card, miniature photographic, or other process which accurately reproduces or forms a durable medium for so reproducing the original, the original may be destroyed in the regular course of business unless its preservation is required by law. Such reproduction, when satisfactorily identified, is as admissible in evidence as the original itself in any judicial or administrative proceeding whether the original is in existence or not and an enlargement or facsimile of such reproduction is likewise admissible in evidence if the original reproduction is in existence and available for inspection under direction of court. The introduction of a reproduced record, enlargement, or facsimile does not preclude admission of the original. This subsection[1] shall not be construed to exclude from evidence any document or copy thereof which is otherwise admissible under the rules of evidence.

(June 25, 1948, c. 646, 62 Stat. 945; Aug. 28, 1951, c. 351, §§ 1, 3, 65 Stat. 205, 206; Aug. 30, 1961, Pub.L. 87–183, 75 Stat. 413; Jan. 2, 1975, Pub.L. 93–595, § 2(b), 88 Stat. 1949.)

[1] Probably should be read as "section". Section formerly was subsec. (b) of this section.

§ 1733. Government records and papers; copies

(a) Books or records of account or minutes of proceedings of any department or agency of the United States shall be admissible to prove the act, transaction or occurrence as a memorandum of which the same were made or kept.

(b) Properly authenticated copies or transcripts of any books, records, papers or documents of any department or agency of the United States shall be admitted in evidence equally with the originals thereof.

(c) This section does not apply to cases, actions, and proceedings to which the Federal Rules of Evidence apply.

(June 25, 1948, c. 646, 62 Stat. 946; Jan. 2, 1975, Pub.L. 93–595, § 2(c), 88 Stat. 1949.)

HISTORICAL AND STATUTORY NOTES

References in Text

The Federal Rules of Evidence, referred to in subsec. (c), are set out in this title.

§ 1734. Court record lost or destroyed, generally

(a) A lost or destroyed record of any proceeding in any court of the United States may be supplied on application of any interested party not at fault, by substituting a copy certified by the clerk of any court in which an authentic copy is lodged.

(b) Where a certified copy is not available, any interested person not at fault may file in such court a verified application for an order establishing the lost or destroyed record.

Every other interested person shall be served personally with a copy of the application and with notice of hearing on a day stated, not less than sixty days after service. Service may be made on any nonresident of the district anywhere within the jurisdiction of the United States or in any foreign country.

Proof of service in a foreign country shall be certified by a minister or consul of the United States in such country, under his official seal.

If, after the hearing, the court is satisfied that the statements contained in the application are true, it shall enter an order reciting the substance and effect of the lost or destroyed record. Such order, subject to intervening rights of third persons, shall have the same effect as the original record.

(June 25, 1948, c. 646, 62 Stat. 946.)

§ 1735. Court record lost or destroyed where United States interested

(a) When the record of any case or matter in any court of the United States to which the United States is a party, is lost or destroyed, a certified copy of any official paper of a United States attorney, United States marshal or clerk or other certifying or recording officer of any such court, made pursuant to law, on file in any department or agency of the United States and relating to such case or matter, shall, on being filed in the court to which it relates, have the same effect as an original paper filed in such court. If the copy so filed discloses the date and amount of a judgment or decree and the names of the parties thereto, the court may enforce the judgment or decree as though the original record had not been lost or destroyed.

(b) Whenever the United States is interested in any lost or destroyed records or files of a court of the United States, the clerk of such court and the United States attorney for the district shall take the steps necessary to restore such records or files, under the direction of the judges of such court.

(June 25, 1948, c. 646, 62 Stat. 946.)

§ 1736. Congressional Journals

Extracts from the Journals of the Senate and the House of Representatives, and from the Executive Journal of the Senate when the injunction of secrecy is removed, certified by the Secretary of the Senate or the Clerk of the House of Representatives shall be received in evidence with the same effect as the originals would have.

(June 25, 1948, c. 646, 62 Stat. 947.)

HISTORICAL AND STATUTORY NOTES

Transfer of Functions

Any reference in any provision of law enacted before Jan. 4, 1995, to a function, duty, or authority of the Clerk of the House of Representatives treated as referring, with respect to that function, duty, or authority, to the officer of the House of Representatives exercising that function, duty, or authority, as determined by the Committee on House Oversight of the House of Representatives, see section 2(1) of Pub.L. 104–14, set out as a note preceding section 21 of Title 2, The Congress.

§ 1737. Copy of officer's bond

Any person to whose custody the bond of any officer of the United States has been committed shall, on proper request and payment of the fee allowed by any Act of Congress, furnish certified copies thereof, which shall be prima facie evidence in any court of the execution, filing and contents of the bond.

(June 25, 1948, c. 646, 62 Stat. 947.)

§ 1738. State and Territorial statutes and judicial proceedings; full faith and credit

The Acts of the legislature of any State, Territory, or Possession of the United States, or copies thereof, shall be authenticated by affixing the seal of such State, Territory or Possession thereto.

The records and judicial proceedings of any court of any such State, Territory or Possession, or copies thereof, shall be proved or admitted in other courts within the United States and its Territories and Possessions by the attestation of the clerk and seal of the court annexed, if a seal exists, together with a certificate of a judge of the court that the said attestation is in proper form.

Such Acts, records and judicial proceedings or copies thereof, so authenticated, shall have the same full faith and credit in every court within the United States and its Territories and Possessions as they have by law or usage in the courts of such State, Territory or Possession from which they are taken.

(June 25, 1948, c. 646, 62 Stat. 947.)

§ 1738A. Full faith and credit given to child custody determinations

(a) The appropriate authorities of every State shall enforce according to its terms, and shall not modify except as provided in subsections (f), (g), and (h) of this section, any custody determination or visitation determination made consistently with the provisions of this section by a court of another State.

(b) As used in this section, the term—

(1) "child" means a person under the age of eighteen;

(2) "contestant" means a person, including a parent or grandparent, who claims a right to custody or visitation of a child;

(3) "custody determination" means a judgment, decree, or other order of a court providing for the custody of a child, and includes permanent and temporary orders, and initial orders and modifications;

(4) "home State" means the State in which, immediately preceding the time involved, the child lived with his parents, a parent, or a person acting as parent, for at least six consecutive months, and in the case of a child less than six months old, the State in which the child lived from birth with any of such persons. Periods of temporary absence of any of such persons are counted as part of the six-month or other period;

(5) "modification" and "modify" refer to a custody or visitation determination which modifies, replaces, supersedes, or otherwise is made subsequent to, a prior custody or visitation determination concerning the same child, whether made by the same court or not;

(6) "person acting as a parent" means a person, other than a parent, who has physical custody of a child and who has either been awarded custody by a court or claims a right to custody;

(7) "physical custody" means actual possession and control of a child;

(8) "State" means a State of the United States, the District of Columbia, the Commonwealth of Puerto Rico, or a territory or possession of the United States; and

(9) "visitation determination" means a judgment, decree, or other order of a court providing for the visitation of a child and includes permanent and temporary orders and initial orders and modifications.

(c) A child custody or visitation determination made by a court of a State is consistent with the provisions of this section only if—

(1) such court has jurisdiction under the law of such State; and

(2) one of the following conditions is met:

(A) such State (i) is the home State of the child on the date of the commencement of the proceeding, or (ii) had been the child's home State within six months before the date of the commencement of the proceeding and the child is absent from such State because of his removal or retention by a contestant or for other reasons, and a contestant continues to live in such State;

(B) (i) it appears that no other State would have jurisdiction under subparagraph (A), and (ii) it is in the best interest of the child that a court of such State assume jurisdiction because (I) the child and his parents, or the child and at least one contestant, have a significant connection with such State other than mere physical presence in such State, and (II) there is available in such State substantial evidence concerning the child's present or future care, protection, training, and personal relationships;

(C) the child is physically present in such State and (i) the child has been abandoned, or (ii) it is necessary in an emergency to protect the child because he has been subjected to or threatened with mistreatment or abuse;

(D) (i) it appears that no other State would have jurisdiction under subparagraph (A), (B), (C), or (E), or another State has declined to exercise jurisdiction on the ground that the State whose jurisdiction is in issue is the more appropriate forum to determine the custody or visitation of the child, and (ii) it is in the best interest of the child that such court assume jurisdiction; or

(E) the court has continuing jurisdiction pursuant to subsection (d) of this section.

(d) The jurisdiction of a court of a State which has made a child custody or visitation determination consistently with the provisions of this section continues as long as the requirement of subsection (c)(1) of this section continues to be met and such State remains the residence of the child or of any contestant.

(e) Before a child custody or visitation determination is made, reasonable notice and opportunity to be heard shall be given to the contestants, any parent whose parental rights have not been previously terminated and any person who has physical custody of a child.

(f) A court of a State may modify a determination of the custody of the same child made by a court of another State, if—

(1) it has jurisdiction to make such a child custody determination; and

(2) the court of the other State no longer has jurisdiction, or it has declined to exercise such jurisdiction to modify such determination.

(g) A court of a State shall not exercise jurisdiction in any proceeding for a custody or visitation determination commenced during the pendency of a proceeding in a court of another State where such court of that other State is exercising jurisdiction consistently with the provisions of this section to make a custody or visitation determination.

(h) A court of a State may not modify a visitation determination made by a court of another State unless the court of the other State no longer has jurisdiction to modify such determination or has declined to exercise jurisdiction to modify such determination.

(Added Pub.L. 96–611, § 8(a), Dec. 28, 1980, 94 Stat. 3569, and amended Pub.L. 105–374, § 1, Nov. 12, 1998, 112 Stat. 3383.)

HISTORICAL AND STATUTORY NOTES

Congressional Findings and Declaration of Purpose

Section 7 of Pub.L. 96–611 provided that:

"(a) The Congress finds that—

"(1) there is a large and growing number of cases annually involving disputes between persons claiming rights of custody and visitation of children under the laws, and in the courts, of different States, the District of Columbia, the Commonwealth of Puerto Rico, and the territories and possessions of the United States;

"(2) the laws and practices by which the courts of those jurisdictions determine their jurisdiction to decide such disputes, and the effect to be given the decisions of such disputes by the courts of other jurisdictions, are often inconsistent and conflicting;

"(3) those characteristics of the law and practice in such cases, along with the limits imposed by a Federal system on the authority of each such jurisdiction to conduct investigations and take other actions outside its own boundaries, contribute to a tendency of parties involved in such disputes to frequently resort to the seizure, restraint, concealment, and interstate transportation of children, the disregard of court orders, excessive relitigation of cases, obtaining of conflicting orders by the courts of various jurisdictions, and interstate travel and communication that is so expensive and time consuming as to disrupt their occupations and commercial activities; and

"(4) among the results of those conditions and activities are the failure of the courts of such jurisdictions to give full faith and credit to the judicial proceedings of the other jurisdictions, the deprivation of rights of liberty and property without due process of law, burdens on commerce among such jurisdictions and with foreign nations, and harm to the welfare of children and their parents and other custodians.

"(b) For those reasons it is necessary to establish a national system for locating parents and children who travel from one such jurisdiction to another and are concealed in connection with such disputes, and to establish national standards under which the courts of such jurisdictions will determine their jurisdiction to decide such disputes and the effect to be given by each such jurisdiction to such decisions by the courts of other such jurisdictions.

"(c) The general purposes of sections 6 to 10 of this Act [enacting this section and sections 654(17) and 663 of Title 42, The Public Health and Welfare, amending section 655(a) of Title 42, and enacting provisions set out as notes under this section and sections 663 and 1305 of Title 42 and 1073 of Title 18, Crimes and Criminal Procedure] are to—

"(1) promote cooperation between State courts to the end that a determination of custody and visitation is rendered in the State which can best decide the case in the interest of the child;

"(2) promote and expand the exchange of information and other forms of mutual assistance between States which are concerned with the same child;

"(3) facilitate the enforcement of custody and visitation decrees of sister States;

"(4) discourage continuing interstate controversies over child custody in the interest of greater stability of home environment and of secure family relationships for the child;

"(5) avoid jurisdictional competition and conflict between State courts in matters of child custody and visitation which have in the past resulted in the shifting of children from State to State with harmful effects on their well-being; and

"(6) deter interstate abductions and other unilateral removals of children undertaken to obtain custody and visitation awards."

State Court Proceedings for Custody Determinations; Priority Treatment; Fees, Costs, and Other Expenses

Section 8(c) of Pub.L. 96–611 provided that: "In furtherance of the purposes of section 1738A of title 28, United

States Code [this section], as added by subsection (a) of this section, State courts are encouraged to—

"(1) afford priority to proceedings for custody determinations; and

"(2) award to the person entitled to custody or visitation pursuant to a custody determination which is consistent with the provisions of such section 1738A [this section], necessary travel expenses, attorneys' fees, costs of private investigations, witness fees or expenses, and other expenses incurred in connection with such custody determination in any case in which—

"(A) a contestant has, without the consent of the person entitled to custody or visitation pursuant to a custody determination which is consistent with the provisions of such section 1738A [this section], (i) wrongfully removed the child from the physical custody of such person, or (ii) wrongfully retained the child after a visit or other temporary relinquishment of physical custody; or

"(B) the court determines it is appropriate."

§ 1738B. Full faith and credit for child support orders

(a) General rule.—The appropriate authorities of each State—

(1) shall enforce according to its terms a child support order made consistently with this section by a court of another State; and

(2) shall not seek or make a modification of such an order except in accordance with subsections (e), (f), and (i).

(b) Definitions.—In this section:

"child" means—

(A) a person under 18 years of age; and

(B) a person 18 or more years of age with respect to whom a child support order has been issued pursuant to the laws of a State.

"child's State" means the State in which a child resides.

"child's home State" means the State in which a child lived with a parent or a person acting as parent for at least 6 consecutive months immediately preceding the time of filing of a petition or comparable pleading for support and, if a child is less than 6 months old, the State in which the child lived from birth with any of them. A period of temporary absence of any of them is counted as part of the 6-month period.

"child support" means a payment of money, continuing support, or arrearages or the provision of a benefit (including payment of health insurance, child care, and educational expenses) for the support of a child.

"child support order"—

(A) means a judgment, decree, or order of a court requiring the payment of child support in periodic amounts or in a lump sum; and

(B) includes—

(i) a permanent or temporary order; and

(ii) an initial order or a modification of an order.

"contestant" means—

(A) a person (including a parent) who—

(i) claims a right to receive child support;

(ii) is a party to a proceeding that may result in the issuance of a child support order; or

(iii) is under a child support order; and

(B) a State or political subdivision of a State to which the right to obtain child support has been assigned.

"court" means a court or administrative agency of a State that is authorized by State law to establish the amount of child support payable by a contestant or make a modification of a child support order.

"modification" means a change in a child support order that affects the amount, scope, or duration of the order and modifies, replaces, supersedes, or otherwise is made subsequent to the child support order.

"State" means a State of the United States, the District of Columbia, the Commonwealth of Puerto Rico, the territories and possessions of the United States, and Indian country (as defined in section 1151 of title 18).

(c) Requirements of child support orders.—A child support order made by a court of a State is made consistently with this section if—

(1) a court that makes the order, pursuant to the laws of the State in which the court is located and subsections (e), (f), and (g)—

(A) has subject matter jurisdiction to hear the matter and enter such an order; and

(B) has personal jurisdiction over the contestants; and

(2) reasonable notice and opportunity to be heard is given to the contestants.

(d) Continuing jurisdiction.—A court of a State that has made a child support order consistently with this section has continuing, exclusive jurisdiction over the order if the State is the child's State or the residence of any individual contestant unless the court of another State, acting in accordance with subsections (e) and (f), has made a modification of the order.

(e) Authority to modify orders.—A court of a State may modify a child support order issued by a court of another State if—

(1) the court has jurisdiction to make such a child support order pursuant to subsection (i); and

(2)(A) the court of the other State no longer has continuing, exclusive jurisdiction of the child support order because that State no longer is the child's State or the residence of any individual contestant; or

(B) each individual contestant has filed written consent with the State of continuing, exclusive jurisdiction for a court of another State to modify the order and assume continuing, exclusive jurisdiction over the order.

(f) Recognition of child support orders.—If 1 or more child support orders have been issued with regard to an obligor and a child, a court shall apply the following rules in determining which order to recognize for purposes of continuing, exclusive jurisdiction and enforcement:

(1) If only 1 court has issued a child support order, the order of that court must be recognized.

(2) If 2 or more courts have issued child support orders for the same obligor and child, and only 1 of the courts would have continuing, exclusive jurisdiction under this section, the order of that court must be recognized.

(3) If 2 or more courts have issued child support orders for the same obligor and child, and more than 1 of the courts would have continuing, exclusive jurisdiction under this section, an order issued by a court in the current home State of the child must be recognized, but if an order has not been issued in the current home State of the child, the order most recently issued must be recognized.

(4) If 2 or more courts have issued child support orders for the same obligor and child, and none of the courts would have continuing, exclusive jurisdiction under this section, a court having jurisdiction over the parties shall issue a child support order, which must be recognized.

(5) The court that has issued an order recognized under this subsection is the court having continuing, exclusive jurisdiction under subsection (d).

(g) Enforcement of modified orders.—A court of a State that no longer has continuing, exclusive jurisdiction of a child support order may enforce the order with respect to nonmodifiable obligations and unsatisfied obligations that accrued before the date on which a modification of the order is made under subsections (e) and (f).

(h) Choice of law.—

(1) **In general.**—In a proceeding to establish, modify, or enforce a child support order, the forum State's law shall apply except as provided in paragraphs (2) and (3).

(2) **Law of State of issuance of order.**—In interpreting a child support order including the duration of current payments and other obligations of support, a court shall apply the law of the State of the court that issued the order.

(3) **Period of limitation.**—In an action to enforce arrears under a child support order, a court shall apply the statute of limitation of the forum State or the State of the court that issued the order, whichever statute provides the longer period of limitation.

(i) Registration for modification.—If there is no individual contestant or child residing in the issuing State, the party or support enforcement agency seeking to modify, or to modify and enforce, a child support order issued in another State shall register that order in a State with jurisdiction over the nonmovant for the purpose of modification.

(Added Pub.L. 103–383, § 3(a), Oct. 22, 1994, 108 Stat. 4064, and amended Pub.L. 104–193, Title III, § 322, Aug. 22, 1996, 110 Stat. 2221; Pub.L. 105–33, Title V, § 5554, Aug. 5, 1997, 111 Stat. 636.)

HISTORICAL AND STATUTORY NOTES

Effective Dates

1997 Acts. Amendments by Pub.L. 105–33 made by sections 5531 to 5556 to take effect as if included in the enactment of Title III of the Personal Responsibility and Work Opportunity Reconciliation Act of 1996 (Pub.L. 104–193, Aug. 22, 1996, 110 Stat. 2105), except for amendments made by section 5532(b)(2) (amending section 608(a)(3)(A) of Title 42, The Public Health and Welfare), see section 5557 of Pub.L. 105–33, set out as a note under section 608 of Title 42, The Public Health and Welfare.

1996 Acts. For effective date of Title III of Pub.L. 104–193, see section 395(a) to (c) of Pub.L. 104–193, set out as a note under section 654 of Title 42, The Public Health and Welfare.

Congressional Findings and Declaration of Purpose

Section 2 of Pub.L. 103–383 provided that:

"(a) **Findings.**—The Congress finds that—

"(1) there is a large and growing number of child support cases annually involving disputes between parents who reside in different States;

"(2) the laws by which the courts of different jurisdictions determine their authority to establish child support orders are not uniform;

"(3) those laws, along with the limits imposed by the Federal system on the authority of each State to take certain actions outside its own boundaries—

"(A) encourage noncustodial parents to relocate outside the States where their children and the custodial parents reside to avoid the jurisdiction of the courts of such States, resulting in an increase in the amount of interstate travel and communication required to establish and collect on child support orders and a burden on custodial parents that is expensive, time consuming, and disruptive of occupations and commercial activity;

"(B) contribute to the pressing problem of relatively low levels of child support payments in interstate cases and to inequities in child support payments levels that are based solely on the noncustodial parent's choice of residence;

"(C) encourage a disregard of court orders resulting in massive arrearages nationwide;

"(D) allow noncustodial parents to avoid the payment of regularly scheduled child support payments for extensive periods of time, resulting in substantial hardship for the children for whom support is due and for their custodians; and

"(E) lead to the excessive relitigation of cases and to the establishment of conflicting orders by the courts of various jurisdictions, resulting in confusion, waste of judicial resources, disrespect for the courts, and a diminution of public confidence in the rule of law; and

"(4) among the results of the conditions described in this subsection are—

"(A) the failure of the courts of the States to give full faith and credit to the judicial proceedings of the other States;

"(B) the deprivation of rights of liberty and property without due process of law;

"(C) burdens on commerce among the States; and

"(D) harm to the welfare of children and their parents and other custodians.

"**(b) Statement of policy.**—In view of the findings made in subsection (a), it is necessary to establish national standards under which the courts of the various States shall determine their jurisdiction to issue a child support order and the effect to be given by each State to child support orders issued by the courts of other States.

"**(c) Purposes.**—The purposes of this Act [enacting this section and a provision set out as a note under section 1 of this title] are—

"(1) to facilitate the enforcement of child support orders among the States;

"(2) to discourage continuing interstate controversies over child support in the interest of greater financial stability and secure family relationships for the child; and

"(3) to avoid jurisdictional competition and conflict among State courts in the establishment of child support orders."

§ 1738C. Certain acts, records, and proceedings and the effect thereof

No State, territory, or possession of the United States, or Indian tribe, shall be required to give effect to any public act, record, or judicial proceeding of any other State, territory, possession, or tribe respecting a relationship between persons of the same sex that is treated as a marriage under the laws of such other State, territory, possession, or tribe, or a right or claim arising from such relationship.

(Added Pub.L. 104–199, § 2(a), Sept. 21, 1996, 110 Stat. 2419.)

§ 1739. State and Territorial nonjudicial records; full faith and credit

All nonjudicial records or books kept in any public office of any State, Territory, or Possession of the United States, or copies thereof, shall be proved or admitted in any court or office in any other State, Territory, or Possession by the attestation of the custodian of such records or books, and the seal of his office annexed, if there be a seal, together with a certificate of a judge of a court of record of the county, parish, or district in which such office may be kept, or of the Governor, or secretary of state, the chancellor or keeper of the great seal, of the State, Territory, or Possession that the said attestation is in due form and by the proper officers.

If the certificate is given by a judge, it shall be further authenticated by the clerk or prothonotary of the court, who shall certify, under his hand and the seal of his office, that such judge is duly commissioned and qualified; or, if given by such Governor, secretary, chancellor, or keeper of the great seal, it shall be under the great seal of the State, Territory, or Possession in which it is made.

Such records or books, or copies thereof, so authenticated, shall have the same full faith and credit in every court and office within the United States and its Territories and Possessions as they have by law or usage in the courts or offices of the State, Territory, or Possession from which they are taken.

(June 25, 1948, c. 646, 62 Stat. 947.)

§ 1740. Copies of consular papers

Copies of all official documents and papers in the office of any consul or vice consul of the United States, and of all official entries in the books or records of any such office, authenticated by the consul or vice consul, shall be admissible equally with the originals.

(June 25, 1948, c. 646, 62 Stat. 947.)

§ 1741. Foreign official documents

An official record or document of a foreign country may be evidenced by a copy, summary, or excerpt authenticated as provided in the Federal Rules of Civil Procedure.

(June 25, 1948, c. 646, 62 Stat. 948; May 24, 1949, c. 139, § 92(b), 63 Stat. 103; Oct. 3, 1964, Pub.L. 88–619, § 5(a), 78 Stat. 996.)

HISTORICAL AND STATUTORY NOTES

Treaties and Conventions; Taking of Evidence Abroad in Civil or Commercial Matters; Observance On and After Oct. 7, 1972, by United States and Citizens and Persons Subject to Jurisdiction of United States

For text of Convention, see provisions set out as a note under section 1781 of this title.

[§ 1742. Repealed. Pub.L. 88–619, § 6(a), Oct. 3, 1964, 78 Stat. 996]

HISTORICAL AND STATUTORY NOTES

Section, Act June 25, 1948, c. 646, 62 Stat. 948, related to authentication and certification of copies of documents relating to land titles, by persons having custody of such of any foreign government or its agents, certification by an American minister or consul that they be true copies of the originals, the recording of such copies in the office of the General Counsel for the Department of the Treasury, and to the evidentiary value of such copies.

§ 1743. Demand on postmaster

The certificate of the Postmaster General or the General Accounting Office of the mailing to a postmaster of a statement of his account and that payment of the balance stated has not been received shall be sufficient evidence of a demand notwithstanding any allowances or credits subsequently made. A copy of such statement shall be attached to the certificate.

(June 25, 1948, c. 646, 62 Stat. 948.)

HISTORICAL AND STATUTORY NOTES

Transfer of Functions

The office of Postmaster General of the Post Office Department was abolished and all functions, powers, and duties of the Postmaster General were transferred to the United States Postal Service by Pub.L. 91–375, § 4(a), Aug. 12, 1970, 84 Stat. 773, set out as a note under section 201 of Title 39, Postal Service.

§ 1744. Copies of Patent Office documents, generally

Copies of letters patent or of any records, books, papers, or drawings belonging to the Patent Office and relating to patents, authenticated under the seal of the Patent Office and certified by the Commissioner of Patents, or by another officer of the Patent Office authorized to do so by the Commissioner, shall be admissible in evidence with the same effect as the originals.

Any person making application and paying the required fee may obtain such certified copies.

(June 25, 1948, c. 646, 62 Stat. 948; May 24, 1949, c. 139, § 92(c), 63 Stat. 103.)

HISTORICAL AND STATUTORY NOTES

Change of Name

Patent Office and Commissioner of Patents redesignated Patent and Trademark Office and Commissioner of Patents and Trademarks, respectively, by section 3 of Pub.L. 93–596, Jan. 2, 1975, 88 Stat. 1949, set out as a note under section 1 of Title 35, Patents.

Transfer of Functions

The functions of all officers of the Department of Commerce and all functions of all agencies and employees of such Department, were, with a few exceptions, transferred to the Secretary of Commerce, with power vested in him to authorize their performance or the performance of any of his functions by any of such officers, agencies, and employees, by 1950 Reorg. Plan No. 5, §§ 1, 2, eff. May 24, 1950, 15 F.R. 3174, 64 Stat. 1263, set out in Appendix 1 to Title 5, Government Organization and Employees. The Patent Office [now Patent and Trademark Office], referred to in this section, is an agency of the Department of Commerce, and the Commissioner of Patents [now Commissioner of Patents and Trademarks], referred to in this section, is an officer of such Department.

§ 1745. Copies of foreign patent documents

Copies of the specifications and drawings of foreign letters patent, or applications for foreign letters patent, and copies of excerpts of the official journals and other official publications of foreign patent offices belonging to the United States Patent Office, certified in the manner provided by section 1744 of this title are prima facie evidence of their contents and of the dates indicated on their face.

(June 25, 1948, c. 646, 62 Stat. 948, § 1746; renumbered § 1745 and amended May 24, 1949, c. 139, § 92(d), (e), 63 Stat. 103; Oct. 3, 1964, Pub.L. 88–619, § 7(a), 78 Stat. 996.)

HISTORICAL AND STATUTORY NOTES

Change of Name

Patent Office redesignated Patent and Trademark Office by section 3 of Pub.L. 93–596, Jan. 2, 1975, 88 Stat. 1949, set out as a note under section 1 of Title 35, Patents.

Prior Provisions

A prior section 1745, Act June 25, 1948, c. 646, 62 Stat. 948, related to printed copies of patent specifications and drawings, prior to repeal by Act May 24, 1949, c. 139, § 92(d), 63 Stat. 103.

§ 1746. Unsworn declarations under penalty of perjury

Wherever, under any law of the United States or under any rule, regulation, order, or requirement made pursuant to law, any matter is required or permitted to be supported, evidenced, established, or proved by the sworn declaration, verification, certificate, statement, oath, or affidavit, in writing of the person making the same (other than a deposition, or an oath of office, or an oath required to be taken before a specified official other than a notary public), such matter may, with like force and effect, be supported, evidenced, established, or proved by the unsworn declaration, certificate, verification, or statement, in writing of such person which is subscribed by him, as true under penalty of perjury, and dated, in substantially the following form:

(1) If executed without the United States: "I declare (or certify, verify, or state) under penalty of perjury under the laws of the United States of America that the foregoing is true and correct. Executed on (date).

(Signature)".

(2) If executed within the United States, its territories, possessions, or commonwealths: "I declare (or certify, verify, or state) under penalty of perjury that the foregoing is true and correct. Executed on (date).

(Signature)".

(Added Pub.L. 94–550, § 1(a), Oct. 18, 1976, 90 Stat. 2534.)

HISTORICAL AND STATUTORY NOTES

Prior Provisions

A prior section 1746 was renumbered section 1745 of this title by Act May 24, 1949.

CHAPTER 117—EVIDENCE; DEPOSITIONS

Sec.

1781. Transmittal of letter rogatory or request.
1782. Assistance to foreign and international tribunals and to litigants before such tribunals.
1783. Subpoena of person in foreign country.
1784. Contempt.
[1785. Repealed.]

HISTORICAL AND STATUTORY NOTES

Deposition in Admiralty Cases

Prior to the general unification of civil and admiralty procedure and the rescission of the Admiralty Rules on July 1, 1966, Revised Statutes, §§ 863 to 865, as amended, which related to depositions de bene esse, when and how taken, notice, mode of taking, and transmission to court, provided as follows:

"**Sec. 863.** The testimony of any witness may be taken in any civil cause depending in a district court by deposition de bene esse, when the witness lives at a greater distance from the place of trial than one hundred miles, or is bound on a voyage to sea, or is about to go out of the United States, or out of the district in which the case is to be tried, and to a greater distance than one hundred miles from the place of trial, before the time of trial, or when he is ancient and infirm. The deposition may be taken before any judge of any court of the United States, or any clerk of a district court, or any chancellor, justice, or judge of a supreme or superior court, mayor or chief magistrate of a city, judge of a county court or court of common pleas of any of the United States, or any notary public, not being of counsel or attorney to either of the parties, nor interested in the event of the cause. Reasonable notice must first be given in writing by the party or his attorney proposing to take such deposition, to the opposite party or his attorney of record, as either may be nearest, which notice shall state the name of the witness and the time and place of the taking of his deposition; and in all cases in rem, the person having the agency or possession of the property at the time of seizure shall be deemed the adverse party, until a claim shall have been put in; and whenever, by reason of the absence from the district and want of an attorney of record or other reason, the giving of the notice herein required shall be impracticable, it shall be lawful to take such depositions as there shall be urgent necessity for taking, upon such notice as any judge authorized to hold courts in such district shall think reasonable and direct. Any person may be compelled to appear and depose as provided by this section, in the same manner as witnesses may be compelled to appear and testify in court.

"**Sec. 864.** Every person deposing as provided in the preceding section [R.S. § 863] shall be cautioned and sworn to testify the whole truth, and carefully examined.

"His testimony shall be reduced to writing or typewriting by the officer taking the deposition, or by some person under his personal supervision, or by the deponent himself in the officer's presence, and by no other person, and shall, after it has been reduced to writing or typewriting, be subscribed by the deponent. [As amended May 23, 1900, c. 541, 31 Stat. 182.]

"**Sec. 865.** Every deposition taken under the two preceding sections [R.S. §§ 863, 864] shall be retained by the magistrate taking it, until he delivers it with his own hand into the court for which it is taken; or it shall, together with a certificate of the reasons as aforesaid of taking it and of the notice, if any, given to the adverse party, be by him sealed up and directed to such court, and remain under his seal until opened in court. But unless it appears to the satisfaction of the court that the witness is then dead, or gone out of the United States, or to a greater distance than one hundred miles from the place where the court is sitting, or that, by reason of age, sickness, bodily infirmity, or imprisonment, he is unable to travel and appear at court, such deposition shall not be used in the cause."

R.S. §§ 863 to 865, as amended, quoted above, were applicable to admiralty proceedings only. Proceedings in bankruptcy and copyright are governed by Rule 26 et seq. of Federal Rules of Civil Procedure. See also Rules of Bankruptcy Procedure set out in Title 11, Bankruptcy.

§ 1781. Transmittal of letter rogatory or request

(a) The Department of State has power, directly, or through suitable channels—

(1) to receive a letter rogatory issued, or request made, by a foreign or international tribunal, to transmit it to the tribunal, officer, or agency in the United States to whom it is addressed, and to receive and return it after execution; and

(2) to receive a letter rogatory issued, or request made, by a tribunal in the United States, to transmit it to the foreign or international tribunal, officer, or agency to whom it is addressed, and to receive and return it after execution.

(b) This section does not preclude—

(1) the transmittal of a letter rogatory or request directly from a foreign or international tribunal to the tribunal, officer, or agency in the United States to whom it is addressed and its return in the same manner; or

(2) the transmittal of a letter rogatory or request directly from a tribunal in the United States to the foreign or international tribunal, officer, or agency

to whom it is addressed and its return in the same manner.

(June 25, 1948, c. 646, 62 Stat. 949; Oct. 3, 1964, Pub.L. 88–619, § 8(a), 78 Stat. 996.)

CONVENTIONS

CONVENTION ON THE TAKING OF EVIDENCE ABROAD IN CIVIL OR COMMERCIAL MATTERS

The States signatory to the present Convention,

Desiring to facilitate the transmission and execution of Letters of Request and to further the accommodation of the different methods which they use for this purpose.

Desiring to improve mutual judicial co-operation in civil or commercial matters.

Have resolved to conclude a Convention to this effect and have agreed upon the following provisions—

* * * * * * *

CHAPTER I—LETTERS OF REQUEST

Article 1

In civil or commercial matters a judicial authority of a Contracting State may, in accordance with the provisions of the law of that State, request the competent authority of another Contracting State, by means of a Letter of Request, to obtain evidence, or to perform some other judicial act.

A Letter shall not be used to obtain evidence which is not intended for use in judicial proceedings, commenced or contemplated.

The expression "other judicial act" does not cover the service of judicial documents or the issuance of any process by which judgments or orders are executed or enforced, or orders for provisional or protective measures.

Article 2

A Contracting State shall designate a Central Authority which will undertake to receive Letters of Request coming from a judicial authority of another Contracting State and to transmit them to the authority competent to execute them. Each State shall organize the Central Authority in accordance with its own law.

Letters shall be sent to the Central Authority of the State of execution without being transmitted through any other authority of that State.

Article 3

A Letter of Request shall specify—

(a) the authority requesting its execution and the authority requested to execute it, if known to the requesting authority;

(b) the names and addresses of the parties to the proceedings and their representatives, if any;

(c) the nature of the proceedings for which the evidence is required, giving all necessary information in regard thereto;

(d) the evidence to be obtained or other judicial act to be performed.

Where appropriate, the Letter shall specify, inter alia—

(e) the names and addresses of the persons to be examined;

(f) the questions to be put to the persons to be examined or a statement of the subject-matter about which they are to be examined;

(g) the documents or other property, real or personal, to be inspected;

(h) any requirement that the evidence is to be given on oath or affirmation, and any special form to be used;

(i) any special method or procedure to be followed under Article 9.

A Letter may also mention any information necessary for the application of Article 11.

No legalization or other like formality may be required.

Article 4

A Letter of Request shall be in the language of the authority requested to execute it or be accompanied by a translation into that language.

Nevertheless, a Contracting State shall accept a Letter in either English or French, or a translation into one of these languages, unless it has made the reservation authorized by Article 33.

A Contracting State which has more than one official language and cannot, for reasons of internal law, accept Letters in one of these languages for the whole of its territory, shall, by declaration, specify the language in which the Letter or translation thereof shall be expressed for execution in the specified parts of its territory. In case of failure to comply with this declaration, without justifiable excuse, the costs of translation into the required language shall be borne by the State of origin.

A Contracting State may, by declaration, specify the language or languages other than those referred to in the preceding paragraphs, in which a Letter may be sent to its Central Authority.

Any translation accompanying a Letter shall be certified as correct, either by a diplomatic officer or consular agent or by a sworn translator or by any other person so authorized in either State.

Article 5

If the Central Authority considers that the request does not comply with the provisions of the present Convention, it shall promptly inform the authority of the State of origin which transmitted the Letter of Request, specifying the objections to the Letter.

Article 6

If the authority to whom a Letter of Request has been transmitted is not competent to execute it, the Letter shall be sent forthwith to the authority in the same State which is competent to execute it in accordance with the provisions of its own law.

Article 7

The requesting authority shall, if it so desires, be informed of the time when, and the place where, the proceedings will take place, in order that the parties concerned, and their representatives, if any, may be present. This information shall be sent directly to the parties or their representatives when the authority of the State of origin so requests.

Article 8

A Contracting State may declare that members of the judicial personnel of the requesting authority of another Contracting State may be present at the execution of a Letter of Request. Prior authorization by the competent authority designated by the declaring State may be required.

Article 9

The judicial authority which executes a Letter of Request shall apply its own law as to the methods and procedures to be followed.

However, it will follow a request of the requesting authority that a special method or procedure be followed, unless this is incompatible with the internal law of the State of execution or is impossible of performance by reason of its internal practice and procedure or by reason of practical difficulties.

A Letter of Request shall be executed expeditiously.

Article 10

In executing a Letter of Request the requested authority shall apply the appropriate measures of compulsion in the instances and to the same extent as are provided by its internal law for the execution of orders issued by the authorities of its own country or of requests made by parties in internal proceedings.

Article 11

In the execution of a Letter of Request the person concerned may refuse to give evidence in so far as he has a privilege or duty to refuse to give the evidence—

(a) under the law of the State of execution; or

(b) under the law of the State of origin, and the privilege or duty has been specified in the Letter, or, at the instance of the requested authority, has been otherwise confirmed to that authority by the requesting authority.

A Contracting State may declare that, in addition, it will respect privileges and duties existing under the law of States other than the State of origin and the State of execution, to the extent specified in that declaration.

Article 12

The execution of a Letter of Request may be refused only to the extent that—

(a) in the State of execution the execution of the Letter does not fall within the functions of the judiciary; or

(b) the State addressed considers that its sovereignty or security would be prejudiced thereby.

Execution may not be refused solely on the ground that under its internal law the State of execution claims exclusive jurisdiction over the subject-matter of the action or that its internal law would not admit a right of action on it.

Article 13

The documents establishing the execution of the Letter of Request shall be sent by the requested authority to the requesting authority by the same channel which was used by the latter.

In every instance where the Letter is not executed in whole or in part, the requesting authority shall be informed immediately through the same channel and advised of the reasons.

Article 14

The execution of the Letter of Request shall not give rise to any reimbursement of taxes or costs of any nature.

Nevertheless, the State of execution has the right to require the State of origin to reimburse the fees paid to experts and interpreters and the costs occasioned by the use of a special procedure requested by the State of origin under Article 9, paragraph 2.

The requested authority whose law obliges the parties themselves to secure evidence, and which is not able itself to execute the Letter, may, after having obtained the consent of the requesting authority, appoint a suitable person to do so. When seeking this consent the requested authority shall indicate the approximate costs which would result from this procedure. If the requesting authority gives its consent it shall reimburse any costs incurred; without such consent the requesting authority shall not be liable for the costs.

CHAPTER II—TAKING OF EVIDENCE BY DIPLOMATIC OFFICERS, CONSULAR AGENTS AND COMMISSIONERS

Article 15

In a civil or commercial matter, a diplomatic officer or consular agent of a Contracting State may, in the territory of another Contracting State and within the area where he exercises his functions, take the evidence without compulsion of nationals of a State which he represents in aid of proceedings commenced in the courts of a State which he represents.

A Contracting State may declare that evidence may be taken by a diplomatic officer or consular agent only if permission to that effect is given upon application made by him or on his behalf to the appropriate authority designated by the declaring State.

Article 16

A diplomatic officer or consular agent of a Contracting State may, in the territory of another Contracting State and within the area where he exercises his functions, also take the evidence, without compulsion, of nationals of the State in which he exercises his functions or of a third State, in aid of proceedings commenced in the courts of a State which he represents, if—

(a) a competent authority designated by the State in which he exercises his functions has given its permission either generally or in the particular case, and

(b) he complies with the conditions which the competent authority has specified in the permission.

A Contracting State may declare that evidence may be taken under this Article without its prior permission.

Article 17

In a civil or commercial matter, a person duly appointed as a commissioner for the purpose may, without compulsion, take evidence in the territory of a Contracting State in aid of proceedings commenced in the courts of another Contracting State if—

(a) a competent authority designated by the State where the evidence is to be taken has given its permission either generally or in the particular case; and

(b) he complies with the conditions which the competent authority has specified in the permission.

A Contracting State may declare that evidence may be taken under this Article without its prior permission.

Article 18

A Contracting State may declare that a diplomatic officer, consular agent or commissioner authorized to take evidence under Articles 15, 16 or 17, may apply to the competent authority designated by the declaring State for appropriate assistance to obtain the evidence by compulsion. The declaration may contain such conditions as the declaring State may see fit to impose.

If the authority grants the application it shall apply any measures of compulsion which are appropriate and are prescribed by its law for use in internal proceedings.

Article 19

The competent authority, in giving the permission referred to in Articles 15, 16 or 17, or in granting the application referred to in Article 18, may lay down such conditions as it deems fit, *inter alia*, as to the time and place of the taking of the evidence. Similarly it may require that it be given reasonable advance notice of the time, date and place of the taking of the evidence; in such a case a representative of the authority shall be entitled to be present at the taking of the evidence.

Article 20

In the taking of evidence under any Article of this Chapter persons concerned may be legally represented.

Article 21

Where a diplomatic officer, consular agent or commissioner is authorized under Articles 15, 16 or 17 to take evidence—

(a) he may take all kinds of evidence which are not incompatible with the law of the State where the evidence is taken or contrary to any permission granted pursuant to the above Articles, and shall have power within such limits to administer an oath or take an affirmation;

(b) a request to a person to appear or to give evidence shall, unless the recipient is a national of the State where the action is pending, be drawn up in the language of the place where the evidence is taken or be accompanied by a translation into such language;

(c) the request shall inform the person that he may be legally represented and, in any State that has not filed a declaration under Article 18, shall also inform him that he is not compelled to appear or to give evidence;

(d) the evidence may be taken in the manner provided by the law applicable to the court in which the action is pending provided that such manner is not forbidden by the law of the State where the evidence is taken;

(e) a person requested to give evidence may invoke the privileges and duties to refuse to give the evidence contained in Article 11.

Article 22

The fact that an attempt to take evidence under the procedure laid down in this Chapter has failed, owing to the refusal of a person to give evidence, shall not prevent an application being subsequently made to take the evidence in accordance with Chapter I.

CHAPTER III—GENERAL CLAUSES

Article 23

A Contracting State may at the time of signature, ratification or accession, declare that it will not execute Letters of Request issued for the purpose of obtaining pretrial discovery of documents as known in Common Law countries.

Article 24

A Contracting State may designate other authorities in addition to the Central Authority and shall determine the extent of their competence. However, Letters of Request may in all cases be sent to the Central Authority.

Federal States shall be free to designate more than one Central Authority.

Article 25

A Contracting State which has more than one legal system may designate the authorities of one of such systems, which shall have exclusive competence to execute Letters of Request pursuant to this Convention.

Article 26

A Contracting State, if required to do so because of constitutional limitations, may request the reimbursement by the State of origin of fees and costs, in connection with the execution of Letters of Request, for the service of process necessary to compel the appearance of a person to give evidence, the costs of attendance of such persons, and the cost of any transcript of the evidence.

Where a State has made a request pursuant to the above paragraph, any other Contracting State may request from that State the reimbursement of similar fees and costs.

Article 27

The provisions of the present Convention shall not prevent a Contracting State from—

(a) declaring that Letters of Request may be transmitted to its judicial authorities through channels other than those provided for in Article 2;

(b) permitting, by internal law or practice, any act provided for in this Convention to be performed upon less restrictive conditions;

(c) permitting, by internal law or practice, methods of taking evidence other than those provided for in this Convention.

Article 28

The present Convention shall not prevent an agreement between any two or more Contracting States to derogate from—

(a) the provisions of Article 2 with respect to methods of transmitting Letters of Request;

(b) the provisions of Article 4 with respect to the languages which may be used;

(c) the provisions of Article 8 with respect to the presence of judicial personnel at the execution of Letters;

(d) the provisions of Article 11 with respect to the privileges and duties of witnesses to refuse to give evidence;

(e) the provisions of Article 13 with respect to the methods of returning executed Letters to the requesting authority;

(f) the provisions of Article 14 with respect to fees and costs;

(g) the provisions of Chapter II.

Article 29

Between Parties to the present Convention who are also Parties to one or both of the Conventions on Civil Procedure signed at the Hague on the 17th of July 1905 [99 British Foreign and State Papers 990] and the 1st of March 1954 [286 UNTS 265], this Convention shall replace Articles 8–16 of the earlier Conventions.

Article 30

The present Convention shall not affect the application of Article 23 of the Convention of 1905, or of Article 24 of the Convention of 1954.

Article 31

Supplementary Agreements between Parties to the Conventions of 1905 and 1954 shall be considered as equally applicable to the present Convention unless the Parties have otherwise agreed.

Article 32

Without prejudice to the provisions of Articles 29 and 31, the present Convention shall not derogate from conventions containing provisions on the matters covered by this Convention to which the Contracting States are, or shall become Parties.

Article 33

A State may, at the time of signature, ratification or accession exclude, in whole or in part, the application of the provisions of paragraph 2 of Article 4 and of Chapter II. No other reservation shall be permitted.

Each Contracting State may at any time withdraw a reservation it has made; the reservation shall cease to have effect on the sixtieth day after notification of the withdrawal.

When a State has made a reservation, any other State affected thereby may apply the same rule against the reserving State.

Article 34

A State may at any time withdraw or modify a declaration.

Article 35

A Contracting State shall, at the time of the deposit of its instrument of ratification or accession, or at a later date, inform the Ministry of Foreign Affairs of the Netherlands of the designation of authorities, pursuant to Articles 2, 8, 24 and 25.

A Contracting State shall likewise inform the Ministry, where appropriate, of the following—

(a) the designation of the authorities to whom notice must be given, whose permission may be required, and whose assistance may be invoked in the taking of evidence by diplomatic officers and consular agents, pursuant to Articles 15, 16 and 18 respectively;

(b) the designation of the authorities whose permission may be required in the taking of evidence by commissioners pursuant to Article 17 and of those who may grant the assistance provided for in Article 18;

(c) declarations pursuant to Articles 4, 8, 11, 15, 16, 17, 18, 23 and 27;

(d) any withdrawal or modification of the above designations and declarations;

(e) the withdrawal of any reservation.

Article 36

Any difficulties which may arise between Contracting States in connection with the operation of this Convention shall be settled through diplomatic channels.

Article 37

The present Convention shall be open for signature by the States represented at the Eleventh Session of the Hague Conference on Private International Law.

It shall be ratified, and the instruments of ratification shall be deposited with the Ministry of Foreign Affairs of the Netherlands.

Article 38

The present Convention shall enter into force on the sixtieth day after the deposit of the third instrument of ratification referred to in the second paragraph of Article 37.

The Convention shall enter into force for each signatory State which ratifies subsequently on the sixtieth day after the deposit of its instrument of ratification.

Article 39

Any State not represented at the Eleventh Session of the Hague Conference on Private International Law which is a Member of this Conference or of the United Nations or of a specialized agency of that Organization, or a Party to the Statute of the International Court of Justice[1] may accede to the present Convention after it has entered into force in accordance with the first paragraph of Article 38.

The instrument of accession shall be deposited with the Ministry of Foreign Affairs of the Netherlands.

The Convention shall enter into force for a State acceding to it on the sixtieth day after the deposit of its instrument of accession.

The accession will have effect only as regards the relations between the acceding State and such Contracting States as will have declared their acceptance of the accession. Such declaration shall be deposited at the Ministry of Foreign Affairs of the Netherlands; this Ministry shall forward, through diplomatic channels, a certified copy to each of the Contracting States.

The Convention will enter into force as between the acceding State and the State that has declared its acceptance of the accession on the sixtieth day after the deposit of the declaration of acceptance.

Article 40

Any State may, at the time of signature, ratification or accession, declare that the present Convention shall extend to all the territories for the international relations of which it is responsible, or to one or more of them. Such a declaration shall take effect on the date of entry into force of the Convention for the State concerned.

At any time thereafter, such extensions shall be notified to the Ministry of Foreign Affairs of the Netherlands.

The Convention shall enter into force for the territories mentioned in such an extension on the sixtieth day after the notification indicated in the preceding paragraph.

Article 41

The present Convention shall remain in force for five years from the date of its entry into force in accordance with the first paragraph of Article 38, even for States which have ratified it or acceded to it subsequently.

If there has been no denunciation, it shall be renewed tacitly every five years.

Any denunciation shall be notified to the Ministry of Foreign Affairs of the Netherlands at least six months before the end of the five year period.

It may be limited to certain of the territories to which the Convention applies.

The denunciation shall have effect only as regards the State which has notified it. The Convention shall remain in force for the other Contracting States.

Article 42

The Ministry of Foreign Affairs of the Netherlands shall give notice to the States referred to in Article 37, and to the States which have acceded in accordance with Article 39, of the following—

(a) the signatures and ratifications referred to in Article 37;

(b) the date on which the present Convention enters into force in accordance with the first paragraph of Article 38;

(c) the accessions referred to in Article 39 and the dates on which they take effect;

(d) the extensions referred to in Article 40 and the dates on which they take effect;

(e) the designations, reservations and declarations referred to in Articles 33 and 35;

(f) the denunciations referred to in the third paragraph of Article 41.

IN WITNESS WHEREOF the undersigned, being duly authorized thereto, have signed the present Convention.

DONE at The Hague, on the 18th day of March 1970, in the English and French languages, both texts being equally authentic, in a single copy which shall be deposited in the archives of the Government of the Netherlands, and of which a certified copy shall be sent, through the diplomatic channel, to each of the States represented at the Eleventh Session of the Hague Conference on Private International Law. [Signatures omitted.]

Convention on the taking of evidence abroad in civil or commercial matters. Done at The Hague March 18, 1970; entered into force for the United States October 7, 1972. TIAS 7444; 23 UST 2555

States which are parties:

Argentina [1]
Australia [1a]
Barbados [1b]
China, Hong Kong Special Administrative Region only [1c]
Cyprus [1d]
Czech Republic [1e]
Denmark [1f]
Estonia [1g]
Finland [2]
France [2a]
Federal Republic of Germany [2b]
Israel [2c]
Italy [2d]
Latvia [2e]
Luxemburg [2f]
Mexico [2g]
Monaco [2h]
Netherlands [2i]
Norway [3]
Poland [3a]
Portugal [3b]
Singapore [3c]
Slovak Republic [3d]
South Africa [3e]
Spain [3f]
Sweden [3g]
Switzerland [3h]
United Kingdom [3i]
United States [4]
Venezuela [5]

---

[1] *Notification pursuant to Article 42 of the Convention*

In conformity with Article 39, paragraph 2, the instrument of accession by the Argentine Republic to the above-mentioned Convention was deposited with the Ministry of Foreign Affairs of the Kingdom of the Netherlands on 8 May 1987.

The instrument of accession of the Argentine Republic contains the following reservation, referred to in Article 33, first paragraph, of the Convention:

"La República Argentina excluye totalmente la applicación de las disposiciones del pafrafo 2♦ del articulo 4♦, así como las del capítulo II."

(Translation)

"The Argentine Republic totally excludes the application of the provisions of paragraph 2 of Article *4*, as well as those of Chapter II.";

and the following declaration regarding Article 23 of the Convention:

"La República Argentina no cumplirá los exhortos que tengan por objeto un procedimiento conocido en Los Estados del "Common Law", por el nombre de "pre-trial discovery of documents (exhibicion de documentos antes del juicio)."

(Translation)

"The Argentine Republic will not execute Letters of Request issued for the purpose of obtaining pre-trial discovery of documents as known in the Common Law Countries."

Furthermore, the instrument contains the declaration annexed to this notification.

In accordance with paragraph 3 of Article 39, the Convention will enter into force for the Argentine Republic on 7 July 1987.

According to Article 39, paragraph 4 of the Convention, the accession will have effect only as regards the relations between the Argentine Republic and such Contracting States as will have declared their acceptance of the accession. Such declarations shall be deposited at the Ministry of Foreign Affairs of the Kingdom of the Netherlands.

The Hague 20, May 1987

"The Argentine Republic excludes the extension of the application of the Convention on the taking of evidence abroad in civil or commercial matters, adopted at The Hague on March 18, 1970, to the Malvinas, South Georgia, and South Sandwich Islands, which was notified by the United Kingdom of Great Britain and Northern Ireland to the Ministry of Foreign Affairs of the Kingdom of the Netherlands on November 23, 1979, and reaffirms its rights of sovereignty over the Malvinas, South Georgia and South Sandwich Islands, which form an integral part of its national territory."

The General Assembly of the United Nations has adopted resolutions 2065 (XX), 3160 (XXVIII), 31/49, 37/9, 38/12, 39/6, 40/21 and 41/40 in which the existence of a dispute of sovereignty is recognized in reference to the Malvinas Islands, and it urges the Argentine Republic and the United Kingdom of Great Britain and Northern Ireland to maintain negotiations with the purpose of finding a peaceful and definitive solution to the dispute as soon as possible, with the good offices of the Secretary General of the United Nations, who will inform the General Assembly of the progress that has been accomplished.

In like manner, "the Argentine Republic excludes the June 19, 1986 approval formulated by the United Kingdom of Great Britain and Northern Ireland for the Malvinas, South Georgia and South Sandwich Islands with respect to the accession of the Principality of Monaco to the aforementioned Convention." (Translation provided by the Division of Language Services, Department of State)

In accordance with Article 35 of the Convention the Government of the Argentine Republic designated the following competent authority:

Ministerio de Relaciones Exteriores y Culto
Reconquista 1088
Buenos Aires.

In accordance with Article 39 the Convention will enter into force between

Argentina and the United States of America	January 30, 1988
Finland	6 April 1990
Sweden	20 November 1987
Israel	23 November 1987
Denmark	7 December 1987
France	11 January 1988
United Kingdom of Great Britain and Northern Ireland also for Anguilla, the Cayman Islands, the Falklands, Gibraltar, Guernsey, Hong Kong, the Isle of Man, South Georgia and South Sandwich Islands and the Sovereign Base Areas of Akrotiri and Dhekelia in the islands of Cyprus)	11 April 1988
Czechoslovakia	11 April 1988
Federal Republic of Germany	21 June 1988
Jersey	9 September 1988
Spain	28 August 1994
Switzerland	13 January 1995

1a *Notification pursuant to Article 42 of the Convention.*

In conformity with Article 39, paragraph 2, the instrument of accession by Australia to the above-mentioned Convention was deposited with the Ministry of Foreign Affairs of the Kingdom of the Netherlands on 23 October 1992.

The instrument of accession of Australia contains the following reservation and declarations:

Pursuant to Article 33, it excludes the operation of paragraph 2 of Article 4.

The Government of Australia hereby declares, for and on behalf of Australia, that:

—pursuant to Article 2, the Secretary to the Attorney–General's Department of the Commonwealth of Australia will be its Central Authority;

—pursuant to Article 8, members of the judicial personnel of the requesting authority of another Contracting State may be present at the execution of a Letter of Request, subject to prior authorisation by the judicial authority executing the Letter of Request;

—pursuant to Article 15, evidence may be taken by a diplomatic officer or consular agent only if permission to that effect is given upon application to the Secretary of the Attorney–General's Department of the Commonwealth of Australia;

—pursuant to Article 16, the Secretary to the Attorney–General's Department of the Commonwealth of Australia will be its competent authority for the purposes of that Article and is empowered to specify conditions with respect to any permission given under that Article; and

—pursuant to Article 23, it will not execute Letters of Request issued for the purpose of obtaining pre-trial discovery of documents as known in Common Law Countries.

—pursuant to Article 24, it designates the Registrars of the State and Territory Supreme Courts as additional authorities.

—pursuant to Article 40, the Convention extends to all the territories for the international relations of which it is responsible.

In accordance with paragraph 3 of Article 39, the Convention will enter into force for Australia on 22 December 1992.

According to Article 39, paragraph 4, of the Convention the accession will have effect only as regards the relations between Australia and such Contracting States as will have declared their acceptance of the accession. Such declarations shall be deposited at the Ministry of Foreign Affairs of the Kingdom of the Netherlands.

The following States have declared their acceptance of Australia's accession to the Convention: Aruba, Cyprus, Finland, the Federal Republic of Germany, Luxembourg, the Kingdom of the Netherlands (for the Kingdom in Europe), Norway, Switzerland, the United States of America.

In accordance with Article 39 the Convention will enter into force between Australia and

the United States of America	22 August 1993
France	27 March 1993
Denmark	12 April 1993
the United Kingdom of Great Britain and Northern Ireland	20 April 1993
Cyprus	19 June 1993
the Federal Republic of Germany	3 July 1993
Luxembourg	9 February 1993
the Kingdom of the Netherlands (for the Kingdom in Europe)	14 February 1993
Aruba	19 July 1993
Finland	23 July 1993
Sweden	1 March 1994
Norway	18 June 1994
Spain	28 August 1994
Italy	16 January 1996

Slovak Republic .... 20 May 1996
Czech Republic .... 31 May 1996

1b *Notification in conformity with Article 42, sub. e, of the Convention.*

By a Letter of 2 September 1982, received at The Ministry of Foreign Affairs of the Kingdom of the Netherlands on 29 September 1982, Barbados informed the Depositary in accordance with Article 35 of the above-mentioned Convention of the following: ".... for the purpose of the said Convention, the Central Authority is the Registrar of the Supreme Court of Barbados."

In accordance with Article 39 the Convention will enter into force between Barbados and

Spain .... 28 August 1994
Switzerland .... 13 January 1995

1c "The Embassy of the People's Republic of China in the Kingdom of the Netherlands

"No. He Wai Fa(97)–53 .... (Translation)

The Hague, June 10, 1997

"Your Excellency,

"In accordance with the Joint Declaration of the Government of the People's Republic of China and the Government of the United Kingdom of Great Britain and Northern Ireland on the Question of Hong Kong signed on 19 December 1984 (hereinafter referred to as the "Joint Declaration"), the People's Republic of China will resume the exercise of sovereignty over Hong Kong with effect from 1 July 1997. Hong Kong will, with effect from that date, become a Special Administrative Region of the People's Republic of China and will enjoy a high degree of autonomy, except in foreign and defence affairs which are the responsibilities of the Central People's Government of the People's Republic of China.

"It is provided both in Section XI of Annex I to the Joint Declaration, 'Elaboration by the Government of the People's Republic of China of its Basic Policies Regarding Hong Kong', and Article 153 of the Basic Law of the Hong Kong Special Administrative Region of the People's Republic of China, which was adopted on 4 April 1990 by the National People's Congress of the People's Republic of China, that international agreements to which the People's Republic of China is not a party but which are implemented in Hong Kong may continue to be implemented in the Hong Kong Special Administrative Region.

"In accordance with the above provisions, I am instructed by the Minister of Foreign Affairs of the People's Republic of China to make the following notification:

"The Convention on Taking of Evidence Abroad in Civil or Commercial Matters done at the Hague on 18 March 1970 (hereinafter referred to as the 'Convention'), by which the Government of the Kingdom of the Netherlands is designated as the depository, which applies to Hong Kong at present, will continue to apply to the Hong Kong Special Administrative Region with effect from 1 July 1997. The Government of the People's Republic of China also makes the following declarations:

"1. With reference to the provisions of Article 16 of the Convention, the diplomatic officer or consular agent of the other Contracting State will not be permitted to take the evidence of nationals of the People's Republic of China or of a third State in the Hong Kong Special Administrative Region.

"2. It declares, in accordance with Article 23 of the Convention, the Hong Kong Special Administrative Region will not execute the 'Letters of Request issued for the purpose of obtaining pre-trial discovery of documents'. The 'Letters of Request issued for the purpose of obtaining pre-trial discovery of documents' for the purposes of the foregoing Declaration include any Letter of Request which requires a person:

"1) to state what documents relevant to the proceedings to which the Letter of Request relates are, or have been, in his possession, custody or power; or

"2) to produce any documents other than particular documents specified in the Letter of Request as being documents appearing to the requested Court to be, or to be likely to be, in his possession, custody or power.

"3. In accordance with Article 24 of the Convention, it designates the Registrar of the High Court of the Hong Kong Special Administrative Region as an Other Authority competent to receive Letters of Request for execution in the Hong Kong Special Administrative Region; in accordance with Article 17 of the Convention, it designates the Administrative Secretary of the Government of Hong Kong Special Administrative Region as the competent authority for the Hong Kong Special Administrative Region.

"4. In accordance with Article 4 and 33 of the Convention, the Hong Kong Special Administrative Region will not accept a Letter of Request in the French Language.

"Within the above ambit, responsibility for the international rights and obligations of a party to the Convention will be assumed by the Government of the People's Republic of China...."

1d *Notification in conformity with Article 42, sub e. of the Convention.*

After having designated the Central Authority on 3 May 1984 (see Notification No. 2/1984) the Government of Cyprus informed the Ministry of Foreign Affairs of the Kingdom of the Netherlands of the following on 15 May 1984:

"The Republic of Cyprus makes the following declarations:

"**1.** Under Article 2 the Ministry of Justice is designated as the Competent Authority .

"**2.** Under Article 16 the Ministry of Justice is designated as the Competent Authority.

"**3.** Under Article 17 the Ministry of Justice is designated as the Competent Authority.

"**4.** In accordance with Article 18 the Republic of Cyprus declares that a diplomatic officer, consular agent or commissioner authorized to take evidence under Articles 15, 16 or 17 may apply to the Competent Authority for appropriate assistance to obtain such evidence by compulsion as prescribes by the law for internal proceedings, provided that the requesting Contracting State has made a declaration affording reciprocal facilities under Article 18.

"**5.** In accordance with Article 23, the Government of the Republic of Cyprus declares that the Republic of Cyprus will not execute Letters of Request issued for the purpose of obtaining pre-trial discovery of documents. The Government of the Republic of Cyprus further declares that the Republic of Cyprus understands 'Letters of Request issued for the purpose of obtaining pre-trial discovery of documents' for the purposes of the foregoing declaration as including any Letter of Request which requires a person:

"**a.** to state what documents relevant to the proceedings to which the Letter of Request relates are, or have been, in his possession, custody or power; or

"**b.** to produce any documents other than particular documents specified in the Letter of Request as being documents appearing to the requested court to be, or likely to be, in his possession, custody or power.

"The Republic of Cyprus makes the following reservations:

"**1.** In accordance with Article 8 the Republic of Cyprus declares that members of the judicial personnel of the requesting authority may be present at the execution of a Letter of Request.

"**2.** In accordance with the provisions of article 33 the Republic of Cyprus will not accept a Letter of Request in French."

According to the depositary the declaration under 5 and the reservation under 2 should have been made at the time of accession. The States which have declared to accept Cyprus' accession to the Convention, namely: the Federal Republic of Germany, Finland, France, Israel, Italy, the Kingdom of the Netherlands, Luxembourg, Portugal, the United Kingdom of Great Britain and Northern Ireland, Sweden and Czechoslovakia, are requested to inform the Ministry of Foreign Affairs of the Kingdom of the Netherlands whether they accept the declaration and the reservation concerned.

Notification pursuant to Article 42 of the Convention

The following State declared its acceptance of the accession of Cyprus to the above-mentioned Convention:

the United States of America .... 1 December 1987

In accordance with Article 39 the Convention will enter into force between Cyprus and

the United States of America .... 30 January 1988
Spain .... 10 July 1994
Switzerland .... 13 January 1995

1e By notification dated January 28, 1993 the Czech Republic communicated the following: "In accordance with the valid principles of international law and to the extent defined by it, the Czech Republic, as a successor state created as a result of the division of the Czech and Slovak Federal Republic, considers itself bound, as of January 1, 1993, i.e. the date of the division of the Czechoslovak federation, by multilateral international treaties to which the Czech and Slovak Federal Republic was a party on that date, including reservations and declarations to their provisions made earlier by Czechoslovakia", which are as follow:

(Translation)

"The Socialist Republic of Czechoslovakia declares, with reference to Article 16 of the Convention on the taking of evidence abroad in civil or commercial matters, concluded at The Hague on 18 March 1970, that evidence may be taken in accordance with Chapter II without its prior permission provided the principle of reciprocity is applied.

"The Socialist Republic of Czechoslovakia also declares, in connection with Article 18 of the said Convention, that a diplomatic officer, consular agent or commissioner authorized to take evidence under Articles 15, 16 and 17, may request the competent Czechoslovak court or the Czechoslovak state notary to carry out procedural action and that such a diplomatic officer, consular agent or commissioner will transmit the dossier to that court or notary through the intermediary of the Minister of Justice of the Czech Socialist Republic in Prague or the Minister of Justice of the Slovak Socialist Republic in Bratislava, provided the principle of reciprocity is applied.

"The Socialist Republic of Czechoslovakia wishes to state, in connection with Article 40 of the Convention according to all states the right to declare that the convention shall be applicable to all territories for the international relations of which it is responsible, that keeping certain countries in a state of dependence is in its opinion contrary to the spirit and objectives of the United Nations Declaration of 14 December 1960 on the granting of independence to colonial countries and peoples, which declares the necessity for a speedy and unconditional end to colonialism in all its forms."

By notification contained in Note dated May 28, 1978, the Minister of Justice of the Czech Socialist Republic and the Minister of Justice of the Slovak Socialist Republic have been designated as central authorities in accordance with Articles 2 and 24 of the Convention.

1f With the following reservations:

"**1)** Availing itself of the provisions laid down in Article 33, the Danish Government hereby declares, in accordance with Article 4, that Denmark will not accept Letters of Request which are sent in French.

"**2)** Availing itself of the provisions laid down in Article 33, the Danish Government hereby declares, in accordance with Article 17, that Denmark will not accept the taking of evidence by commissioners."

And with the following declarations in accordance with Article 35:

"Article 2

"The Ministry of Justice is hereby designated as Central Authority.

"Article 4

"Letters of Request may be sent in Norwegian and Swedish, and Denmark accepts no obligation to return evidence taken in other languages than Danish.

"Article 8

"Members of the judicial personnel of the requesting authority of another contracting State may be present at the execution of a Letter of Request if they have obtained prior authorization from the competent Danish authority.

"Article 15

"A diplomatic officer or consular agent may take evidence if he has been authorized to do so by the Ministry of Justice.

"Article 16

"The Ministry of Justice will issue authorizations to take evidence.

"Article 23

"Letters of Request issued for the purpose of obtaining pre-trial discovery of documents may not be executed in Denmark.

"Article 27a

"As has been the case hitherto, Letters of Request may be transmitted directly to the competent Danish court by the consular agents of foreign States."

Additional declaration of July 23, 1980:

"The declaration made by the Kingdom of Denmark in accordance with article 23 concerning 'Letters of Request issued for the purpose of obtaining pre-trial discovery of documents' shall apply to any Letter of Request which requires a person:

"**a)** to state what documents relevant to the proceedings to which the Letter of Request relates are, or have been, in his possession, other than particular documents specified in the Letter of Request;

or

"**b)** to produce any documents other than particular documents which are specified in the Letter of Request, and which are likely to be in his possession."

1g The Permanent Bureau of the Hague Conference on private international law presents its compliments to the Diplomatic Missions of the Member States and to the National Organs and has the honour to inform them that, by instrument deposited on 2 February 1996 with the Ministry of Foreign Affairs of the Kingdom of the Netherlands.

the *Republic of Estonia*

acceded to the above-mentioned Convention.

The instrument of accession contains the following declarations:

"1) on the basis of Article 8 the judges of the pursuing state have the right to participate in the process operation subject to the preceding consent of the Ministry of Justice of the Republic of Estonia;

"2) on the basis of Article 11, a person may refuse to participate in the taking of evidence or process operation, in case he has the right or commitment to it in accordance with the laws of his home-state;

"3) on the basis of Article 23 the Republic of Estonia fulfills a requisition where the producing of the documents or its copy is requested if it corresponds to the following requirements:

"a) process has been launched;

"b) documents have been reasonably identified according to the dates, the contents or other information;

"c) circumstances have been indicated giving ground to presume that the documents are in the property, possession of the person or known to him."

According to Articles 16 and 17 of the Convention the competent authority designated to give its permission is the *Ministry of Justice of the Republic of Estonia.*

In accordance with the terms of Article 39, paragraph 3, the Convention will enter into force for the *Republic of Estonia* on *2 April 1996.*

According to Article 39, paragraph 4, of the Convention the accession will have effect only as regards the relations between the Republic of Estonia and such Contracting States as will have declared their acceptance of the accession. Such declaration shall be deposited with the Ministry of Foreign Affairs of the Kingdom of the Netherlands.

In accordance with Article 39 the Convention entered into force between Estonia and

Luxembourg .... 18 June 1996
Denmark .... 22 June 1996

Slovak Republic .... 25 June 1996
Israel .... 30 June 1996
Germany .... 2 July 1996
Italy .... 6 July 1996
Finland .... 5 August 1996
Netherlands (for the Kingdom in Europe and Aruba) .... 16 August 1996
Poland .... 14 September 1996
United Kingdom .... 21 February 1997
(Dependent Territories Anguilla, Cayman Islands, Channel Islands, Sovereign Base Areas of Cyprus, Falkland Islands, Gibraltar, Isle of Man)
Cyprus .... 16 March 1997
Sweden .... 13 April 1997
Singapore .... 4 May 1997
Spain .... 25 May 1997

2 With the following reservation and declaration:

Reservation:

"In conformity with Article 33, Finland enters a reservation to paragraph 2 of Article 4 to the effect that Letters of Request in the English or French languages will not be accepted."

Declaration:

"**1.** In Finland the Ministry of Justice (as of 6/1/82) shall be the Central Authority referred to in Article 2.

"**2.** Swedish is the second official language of Finland. Finland will therefore in accordance with paragraph 1 of Article 4 accept Letters of Request in the Swedish language. The answer shall be given in the Swedish language if in connection with the Letter of Request this has been specifically requested.

"**3.** A member of the judicial personnel of the requesting authority may in accordance with Article 8 be present at the execution of a Letter of Request, provided that the Finnish Ministry of Justice has given its consent.

"**4.** The evidence referred to in Articles 16 and 17 of the Convention may be taken without the prior permission of the Finnish authorities.

"**5.** Finland is not going to execute Letters of Request referred to in Article 23 issued for the purpose of obtaining pre-trial discovery of documents as known in Common Law countries."

Notification in conformity with Article 42, paragraph e, of the Convention

By note dated 11 December 1980 and received at the Ministry of Foreign Affairs of the Kingdom of the Netherlands on 12 December 1980 the Government of Finland informed the Ministry of the withdrawal in part of the reservation to Article 4, paragraph 2, of the above-mentioned Convention made at the time of ratification and declared that it hereafter accepts the Letters of Request done in or translated into the English language. In accordance with Article 35, sub. c, the Government of Finland made the following declaration:

"By accepting Letters of Request in English, the Republic of Finland does not undertake to execute the request, or transmit the evidence thus obtained in the English language; nor to have translated the documents which establish the execution of the Letter of Request.".

Furthermore the Government of Finland modified the declaration concerning Article 23 of the above-mentioned Convention made at the time of ratification. The modified declaration is worded as follows:

"The declaration made by the Republic of Finland in accordance with Article 23 concerning 'Letters of Request issued for the purpose of obtaining pre-trial discovery of documents' shall apply only to Letters of Request which require a person:

"**a)** to state what documents relevant to the proceedings to which the Letter of Request relates are, or have been, in his possession, custody or power;

"**b)** to produce any documents other than particular documents specified in the Letter of Request, which are likely to be in his possession, custody or power.".

2a With the following declarations:

With respect to the first paragraph of Article 40 of the Convention, France declares that the Convention shall apply to all the Territory of the French Republic.

In conformity with the provisions of Article 33, the French Government declares:

That, in application of the second paragraph of Article 4, it will execute only Letters in French or accompanied by a translation in French.

That, in application of Article 23, it will not execute Letters of Request issued for the purpose of obtaining pre-trial discovery of documents as known in Common Law countries;

In conformity with the provisions of Article 2, the Ministry of Justice, Civil Division of International Judicial Assistance, 13 Place Vendôme, Paris (1er), is designated as the Central Authority to the exclusion of any other authority.

In conformity with the provisions of Article 16, the Ministry of Justice, Civil Division of International Judicial Assistance, 13 Place Vendôme, Paris (1er), is designated as the competent authority to give permission to diplomatic officers or consular agents of a Contracting State to take the evidence, without compulsion, of persons other than nationals of that State in aid of proceedings commenced in the courts of a State which they represent.

That permission, which shall be given for each specific case and shall be accompanied by special conditions when appropriate, shall be granted under the following general conditions:

1. Evidence shall be taken only within the confines of the Embassies or Consulates;

2. The date and time of taking the evidence shall be notified in due time to the Civil Division of International Judicial Assistance so that it may have the opportunity to be represented at the proceedings;

3. Evidence shall be taken in premises accessible to the public;

4. Persons requested to give evidence shall be served with an official instrument in French or accompanied by a translation into French, and that instrument shall mention:

a. That evidence is being taken in conformity with the provisions of The Hague Convention of March 18, 1970 on the Taking of Evidence Abroad in Civil or Commercial Matters and relates to legal proceedings pending before a jurisdiction specifically designated by a Contracting State;

b. That appearance is voluntary and failure to appear will not give rise to criminal proceedings in the State of origin;

c. That the parties to the trial are consenting or, if not, the grounds of their objections;

d. That in the taking of evidence the person concerned may be legally represented;

e. That a person requested to give evidence may invoke a privilege or duty to refuse to give evidence.

A copy of these requests shall be transmitted to the Ministry of Justice.

5. The Civil Division of International Judicial Assistance shall be kept informed of any difficulty.

In conformity with the provisions of Article 17, the Ministry of Justice, Civil Division of International Judicial Assistance, 13 Place Vendôme, Paris (1er), is appointed as the competent authority to give permission to persons duly appointed as commissioners to proceed, without compulsion, to take any evidence in aid of proceedings commenced in the courts of a Contracting State.

This permission, which shall be given for each specific case and shall be accompanied by special conditions when appropriate, shall be granted under the following general conditions:

1. Evidence shall be taken only within the Embassy confines;

2. The date and time of taking the evidence shall be notified in due time to the Civil Division of International Judicial Assistance so that it may have the opportunity to be represented at the proceedings;

3. Evidence shall be taken in premises accessible to the public;

4. Persons requested to give evidence shall be served with an official instrument in French or accompanied by a translation in French, and that instrument shall mention:

a. That evidence is being taken in conformity with the provisions of The Hague Convention of March 18, 1970 on the Taking of Evidence Abroad in Civil or Commercial Matters and relates to legal proceedings pending before a jurisdiction specifically designated by a Contracting State;

b. That appearance is voluntary and failure to appear will not give rise to criminal proceedings in the State of origin;

c. That the parties to the trial are consenting and, if not, the grounds of their objections;

d. That in the taking of evidence the person concerned may be legally represented;

e. That a person requested to give evidence may invoke the privilege and duty to refuse to give evidence.

A copy of these requests shall be transmitted to the Ministry of Justice.

5. The Civil Division of International Judicial Assistance shall be kept informed of any difficulty.

The request for permission transmitted by the requesting authority to the Ministry of Justice shall specify:

1. The motives that led to choosing this method of taking evidence in preference to that of a Letter of Request, considering the judiciary costs incurred;

2. The criteria for appointing commissioners when the person appointed does not reside in France.

The French Government declares that, in application of the provisions of Article 8, members of the judicial personnel of the requesting authority of a Contracting State may be present at the execution of a Letter of Request.

The Permanent Bureau of the Hague Conference on private international law presents its compliments to the Diplomatic Missions of the Member States and to the National Organs and has the honour to inform them that, by a letter received at the Ministry of Foreign Affairs of the Kingdom of the Netherlands on 19 January 1987, in accordance with Article 34 of the Convention, *France* has modified its declaration regarding Article 23 as follows:

The declaration made by the French Republic in accordance with Article 23 relating to Letters of Request issued for the purpose of obtaining pre-trial discovery of documents does not apply when the requested documents are enumerated limitatively in the Letter of Request and have a direct and precise link with the object of the procedure. (*Translation*)

The Permanent Bureau avails itself of this opportunity to renew to the Diplomatic Missions of the Member States and to the National Organs an assurance of its highest consideration and esteem.

2b "A. The Government of the Federal Republic of Germany makes the following declarations in accordance with paragraph 1 of Article 33 of the Convention of 18th March 1970:

"The Federal Republic of Germany makes the reservation provided for in the first sentence of paragraph 1 of Article 33 of the Convention excluding the application of the provisions of paragraph 2 of Article 4 of the Convention. Letters of Request to be executed under Chapter 1 of the Convention must, in accordance with paragraphs 1 and 5 of Article 4 of the Convention, be in the German language or be accompanied by a translation into that language.

"The Federal Republic of Germany declares in accordance with the option provided for in the first sentence of paragraph 1 of Article 33 of the Convention to make a reservation excluding the application of the provisions of Chapter II of the Convention that the taking of evidence by diplomatic officers or consular agents is not permissible in its territory if German nationals are involved.

"B. The Government of the Federal Republic of Germany makes the following declarations pursuant to Article 35 of the Convention of 18th of March 1970:

"(1) The authority competent to execute a Letter of Request shall be the local court (Amtsgericht) in whose district the official act is to be performed.

Letters of Request shall be addressed to the Central Authority of the Land in which the respective request is to be executed. Germany has deposited the following revised list of Central Authorities designated in accordance with Article 2 of the Convention:

Baden-Württemberg	Justizministerium Baden-Württemberg Schillerplatz 4 70173 Stuttgart
Bavaria	Bayerisches Staatsministerium der Justiz Justizpalast Prielmayerstrasse 7 80335 München
Berlin	Senatsverwaltung für Justiz von Berlin Salzburger Strasse 21–25 10825 Berlin
Brandenburg	Ministerium der Justiz des Landes Brandenburg Heinrich-Mann-Allee 107 14460 Potsdam
Bremen	der Präsident des Landsgerichts Domsheide 16 28195 Bremen
Hamburg	Präsident des Amtsgerichts Hamburg Sievekingplatz 1 20335 Hamburg
Hesse	Hessisches Ministerium der Justiz Luisenstrasse 13 65185 Wiesbaden
Lower Saxony	der Niedersächsisches Justizministerium Am Waterlooplatz 1 30169 Hannover
Mecklenburg—Western Pomerania	Ministerium für Justiz, Bundes–und Europa-angelegen heiten des Landes Mecklenburg-Vorpommern Demmlerplatz 14 19053 Schwering
Northrhine-Westphalia	Präsident des Oberlandesgerichts Düsseldorf Cecilienallee 3 40474 Düsseldorf
Rhineland-Palatinate	Ministerium der Justiz Ernst-Ludwig Strasse 3

	55116 Mainz
Saarland	Ministerium der Justiz des Saarlandes Zähringerstrasse 12 66119 Saarbrücken
Saxe	Sächsisches Staatsministerium der Justiz Archivstrasse 1 01097 Dresden
Saxe–Anhalt	Ministerium des Justiz des Landes Sachsen –Anhalt Wilhelm-Höpfner-Ring 6 39116 Magdeburg
Schleswig-Holstein	Der Justizminister des Landes Schleswig-Holstein Lorentzdamm 35 24103 Kiel
Thuringe	Thüringer Justizministerium Alfred-Hess-Strasse 8 99094 Erfurt

"(2) Pursuant to Article 8 of the Convention, the Government of the Federal Republic of Germany declares that members of the requesting court of another Contracting State may be present at the execution of a Letter of Request by the local court if prior authorization has been given by the Central Authority of the Land where the request is to be executed.

"(3) The taking of evidence by diplomatic officers or consular agents pursuant to paragraph 1 of Article 16 of the Convention which involves nationals of a third State or stateless persons shall be subject to permission from the Central Authority of the Land where the evidence is to be taken. Pursuant to paragraph 2 of Article 16 of the Convention, permission shall not be required if the national of the third State is also a national of the State of the requesting court.

"(4) A commissioner of the requesting court may not take evidence pursuant to Article 17 of the Convention unless the Central Authority of the Land where the evidence is to be taken has given its permission. Such permission may be made subject to conditions. The local court in whose district official acts would have to be performed by virtue of a Letter of Request in the same matter shall be entitled to control the preparation and the actual taking of the evidence. Under the second sentence of Article 19 of the Convention, a member of the court may be present at the taking of the evidence.

"(5) The Federal Republic of Germany declares in pursuance of Article 23 of the Convention that it will not, in its territory, execute Letters of Request issued for the purpose of obtaining pre-trial discovery of documents as known in Common Law countries."

2c *Notification in conformity with Article 42, paragraph e, of the Convention*

In accordance with Article 35 of the Convention Israel notified by a Note dated April 17, 1980 and received at the Ministry of Foreign Affairs of the Kingdom of the Netherlands on April 25, 1980, that the Central Authority designated by the State of Israel in accordance with Article 2 of the above-mentioned Convention, is the Director of Courts, 19 Jaffa Road, Jerusalem.

2d *Notification in conformity with Article 42, subs. a and e, of the Convention*

The Italian Republic deposited its instrument of ratification of the above-mentioned Convention with the Ministry of Foreign Affairs of the Kingdom of the Netherlands on 22 June 1982, in accordance with Article 37, paragraph 2, of the Convention.

In accordance with Article 38, paragraph 2, the Convention will enter into force for Italy on 21 August 1982.

At the time of the deposit of the instrument of ratification the Italian Government notified the Ministry of Foreign Affairs of the following:

Translation

"(1) The Italian Government declares, in accordance with Article 8, that members of the judicial personnel of the requesting authority of another Contracting State may be present at the execution of a Letter of Request, subject to prior authorization by the competent authority designated by the Italian State under (4) paragraph 2 below.

"(2) The Italian Government declares, in accordance with Article 18, that a diplomatic officer, consular agent or commissioner who is taking evidence under Article 15, 16 or 17, may apply to the Authority designated by the Italian State under (4) paragraph 2 below, for appropriate assistance to obtain the evidence by compulsion.

"(3) The Italian Government declares, in accordance with Article 23, that it will not execute Letters of Request issued for the purpose of obtaining pre-trial discovery of documents as known in Common Law countries.

"(4) In accordance with Article 35 the Italian Government designates the Ministry of Foreign Affairs pursuant to Article 2 as the Central Authority which will undertake to receive Letters of Request coming from a judicial authority of another Contracting State and to transmit them to the authority competent to execute them.

"In accordance with the abovementioned Article the Italian Government designates the Court of Appeal within whose jurisdiction proceedings are to take place as the authority competent to:

"—authorize foreign judicial personnel to be present at the execution of a Letter of Request, pursuant to Article 8;

"—authorize foreign diplomatic officers, consular agents or commissioners to take evidence under Article 16 or 17;

"—grant the judicial assistance provided for in Article 18."

2e In accordance with Article 2 the following Central Authority has been designated by Latvia:

Ministry of Justice

Brivibas Boulevard 34

LV-1536, Riga

Tel: 282607

Fax: 285575

In accordance with Article 39, paragraph 5, the Convention will enter into force between Latvia and

Luxembourg	15 July 1995
Finland	21 August 1995
United Kingdom of Great Britain and Northern Ireland	12 September 1995
United States	24 October 1995
Germany	11 November 1995
Italy	16 January 1996
Australia	20 January 1996
Norway	27 January 1996
Israel	27 February 1996
Slovak Republic	20 May 1996
Denmark	22 June 1996
Netherlands(for the Kingdom in Europe and Aruba)	16 August 1996
Singapore	4 May 1997
Spain	25 May 1997

2f *Notification in accordance with Article 42, subs. a and e, of the Convention*

In accordance with Article 37, paragraph 2, Luxemburg deposited on 26 July 1977 its instrument of ratification of the Convention with the Ministry of Foreign Affairs of the Kingdom of the Netherlands.

In conformity with Article 38, paragraph 2, the Convention shall enter into force for Luxemburg on 24 September 1977.

On the occasion of the deposit of the said instrument of ratification the Government of Luxemburg made the following declarations and reservations (translation):

"—In accordance with Article 2 the Parquet Général is designated as the Central Authority.

"—In pursuance of Article 4, paragraph 4, Letters of Request in German shall also be accepted.

"—In pursuance of Article 23, Letters of Request issued for the purpose of obtaining pre-trial discovery of documents as known in Common Law countries shall not be executed.

"—In accordance with the provisions of Article 16, the Parquet Général is designated as the authority competent to authorise the diplomatic officers or consular agents of a Contracting State to take, without compulsion, the evidence of persons other than the nationals of the State in aid of proceedings commenced in the courts of the State which they represent.

"This authorisation, which is given in each specific case and to which specific conditions, where appropriate, are attached, is granted under the following general conditions:

"**1**—The evidence shall be taken only within the precincts of an Embassy or Consulate.

"**2**—The Parquet Général shall be given reasonable advance notice of the time, date and place of the taking of evidence so that it can, if it wishes, be represented.

"**3**—A request to a person to appear shall, in accordance with the regulations, be in the form of an official document in French or German or accompanied by an [sic] translation into one of these languages stating:

"**a**) that the evidence is to be taken in accordance with the provisions of the Convention on the taking of evidence abroad in civil or commercial matters concluded at The Hague on 18 March 1970, and in the framework of a judicial procedure followed in a jurisdiction designated by a Contracting State;

"**b**) that the appearance is voluntary and that no prosecution in the requesting State will result from failure to appear;

"**c**) that the parties to the action, where appropriate, consent to the taking of the evidence or are opposed to it for reasons to be given;

"**d**) that the person requested to appear may be legally represented;

"**e**) that the person requested to appear may invoke a privilege or a duty to refuse to give evidence.

"—In accordance with the provisions of Article 17, the Parquet Général is designated as the authority competent to authorise persons designated in accordance with the regulations as commissioners to take evidence, without compulsion, in aid of proceedings commenced in the courts of another Contracting State.

"This authorisation, which is given in the particular case and to which specific conditions, where appropriate, are attached, is granted under the following general conditions:

"**1**—The Parquet Général shall be given reasonable advance notice of the time, date and place of the taking of evidence so that it can, if it wishes, be represented.

"**2**—A request to a person to appear shall, in accordance with the regulations, be in the form of an official document in French or German or accompanied by a translation into one of these languages stating:

"**a**) that the evidence is to be taken in accordance with the provisions of the Convention on the taking of evidence abroad in civil or commercial matters concluded at The Hague on 18 March 1970, and in the framework of a judicial procedure followed in a jurisdiction designated by a Contracting State;

"**b**) that the appearance is voluntary and that no prosecution in the requesting State will result from failure to appear;

"**c**) that the parties to the action, where appropriate, consent to the taking of the evidence or are opposed to it for reasons to be given;

"**d**) that the person requested to appear may be legally represented;

"**e**) that the person requested to appear may invoke a privilege or a duty to refuse to give evidence.

"—In pursuance of Article 8, members of the judicial personnel of the requesting authority of a Contracting State may be present at the execution of a Letter of Request."

2g In conformity with Article 39, paragraph 2, the instrument of accession by the United Mexican States to the above-mentioned Convention was deposited with the Ministry of Foreign Affairs of the Kingdom of the Netherlands on 27 July 1989.

The instrument of accession of the United Mexican States contains the declarations and reservations the text of which together with a translation in English is annexed to this notification.

In accordance with paragraph 3 of Article 39, the Convention will enter into force for the United Mexican States on 25 September 1989.

According to Article 39, paragraph 4, of the Convention the accession will have effect only as regards the relations between the United Mexican States and such Contracting States as will have declared their acceptance of the accession. Such declarations shall be deposited at the Ministry of Foreign Affairs of the Kingdom of the Netherlands.

Unofficial translation

A) TRANSMISSION AND EXECUTION OF LETTERS OF REQUEST

1. *Central Authority (Article 2)*

Name: Secretariá de Relaciones Exteriores, Dirección General de Asuntos Jurídicos.
Address: Ricardo Flores Magón No. 1
Telephone: 782-34-40
Telex: 01762090

2. *Language requirements (Article 4)*

2.1 The United Mexican States does hereby make a special reservation related to the provisions of paragraph 2 of Article 4, and declares in accordance with paragraph 4 of the same Article, that letters of request sent to its Central Authority or judicial authorities shall be written in the spanish language or shall otherwise be accompanied by a translation into said language.

B) TAKING OF EVIDENCE ABROAD BY DIPLOMATIC OFFICERS, CONSULAR AGENTS AND COMMISSIONS (CHAPTER II)

3. The United Mexican States makes a special and complete reservation concerning the provisions contained in Articles 17 and 18 of this Chapter in relation to the "commissioners" and the use of measures to compulsion by diplomatic officers and consular agents.

C) FORMULATION OF PRE–TRIAL DISCOVERY OF DOCUMENTS

4. With reference to Article 23 of the Convention, the United Mexican States declares that according to Mexican law, it shall only be able to comply with letters of request issued for the purpose of obtaining the production and transcription of documents when the following requirements are met:

a) that the judicial proceeding has been commenced;

b) that the documents are reasonably identifiable as to date, subject and other relevant information and that the request specifies those facts and circumstances that lead the requesting party to reasonable belief that the requested documents are known to the person from whom they are requested or that they are in his possession or under his control or custody;

c) that the direct relationship between the evidence or information sought and the pending proceeding be identified.

D) OTHER TRANSMISSION CHANNEL TO THE JUDICIAL AUTHORITIES DIFFERENT FROM THOSE PROVIDED FOR IN ARTICLE 2

5. In regard to Article 27, paragraph a) of the Convention, the United Mexican States does hereby declare that the letters of request may be transmitted to its judicial authorities not only through the Central Authority but also through diplomatic or consular channels or through judicial channels (directly sent from the foreign court to the Mexican Court), providing that in the latter case all requirements relating to legalization of signatures are fulfilled.

6. In regard to Article 32 of the Convention, the United Mexican States informs that it is a State Party to the Interamerican Convention on the Taking of Evidence Abroad, signed in Panama on January the thirtieth, nineteen hundred and seventy-five, as well as to its Additional Protocol signed in La Paz, Bolivia, on May the twenty-fourth, nineteen hundred and eighty-four.

In accordance with Article 39 the Convention will enter into force between the United Mexican States and

Norway	20 November 1989
Israel	17 December 1989
the United States of America	24 December 1989
Argentina	25 December 1989
Finland	16 January 1990
Denmark	22 January 1990
the United Kingdom of Great Britain and Northern Ireland (also for Anguilla, the Cayman Islands, the Falkland Islands, Gibraltar, Guernsey, Hong Kong, the Isle of Man, Jersey, South Georgia and the South Sandwich Islands and the Sovereign Base Areas of Akrotiri and Dhekelia in the Island of Cyprus)	16 March 1990
the Federal Republic of Germany	23 March 1990
Czechoslovakia	2 April 1990
the Kingdom of the Netherlands (for the Kingdom in Europe)	16 April 1990
Aruba	18 May 1991
Sweden	17 April 1990
Portugal	14 October 1991
Spain	29 June 1994
Switzerland	13 January 1995
Italy	25 May 1996

2h *Notification in conformity with Article 42, sub c and e, of the Convention*

In accordance with Article 39, paragraph 2, the Principality of Monaco deposited its instrument of accession to the above-mentioned Convention with the Ministry of Foreign Affairs of the Kingdom of the Netherlands on 17 January 1986, with the following declarations and reservations:

Translation

1. In accordance with article 2, the Directorate of Judicial Services, MC 98025 MONACO CEDEX, is designated as the Central Authority.

2. Under article 4, paragraph 2, only Letters of Request drawn up in French or accompanied by a translation in that language shall be accepted.

3. Under article 23, Letters of Request issued for the purpose of obtaining pre-trial discovery of documents shall not be executed.

4. In accordance with articles 16 and 17, the Directorate of Judicial Services is designated as a competent authority for the purpose of authorising, as appropriate:

—the consular authorities of a Contracting State to take the evidence without compulsion of persons other than nationals of that State and in aid of proceedings commenced in a court of the State which they represent, or

—persons duly designated as commissioners to take evidence without compulsion in aid of proceedings commenced in a court of the Contracting State.

Such authorisation, which shall be granted for each particular case and may contain specific conditions, shall be subject to the following general conditions:

a) evidence shall be taken solely on the premises of consulates when the latter are situated within the Principality, and in other cases in the Palais de Justice of Monaco;

b) the Directorate of Judicial Services shall be informed of the date and time of the taking of the evidence in time to permit the Directorate to be represented, and, if necessary, to provide courtroom accommodation at the Palais de Justice of Monaco;

c) the persons concerned in the taking of evidence shall be duly summoned by an official document drawn up in French or accompanied by a translation in that language; this document shall indicate:

—that the taking of the evidence in question is being conducted in accordance with the provisions of the Hague Convention of 18 March 1970 on the Taking of Evidence Abroad in Civil or Commercial Matters, and that the procedure constitutes part of legal proceedings pursued under the specially designated jurisdiction of a Contracting State;

—that appearance is voluntary and non-appearance would not entail legal proceedings in the requesting State;

—that the person concerned in the taking of evidence may be represented by a lawyer or defense counsel;

—that the parties in the proceedings, should they be instituted, give their consent, and if not the document shall state the reasons for their opposition;

—that the person concerned in the taking of evidence may apply to be exempted or barred from testifying.

A copy of the summonses shall be sent to the Directorate of Judicial Services, which is also to be kept informed of any difficulties.

Pursuant to Article 39, paragraph 3, the Convention will enter into force for the Principality of Monaco on 18 March 1986.

The accession will have effect only as regards the relations between Monaco and such Contracting States as will have declared their acceptance of the accession.

Notification pursuant to Article 42 of the Convention

In accordance with Article 39 the Convention will enter into force between Monaco and

the United States of America	January 30, 1988
The Kingdom of the Netherlands (Kingdom in Europe)	14 July 1986
Portugal	14 October 1991
Spain	29 June 1994
Switzerland	13 January 1995

2i *Notification in conformity with Article 42, sub a and e, of the Convention.*

"The Kingdom of the Netherlands deposited on 8 April 1981, in accordance with Article 37, paragraph 2, of the Convention its instrument of ratification for the Kingdom in Europe of the above-mentioned Convention.

"Upon the deposit of the instrument of ratification the Government of the Kingdom of the Netherlands has made the following declarations

Translation

"In the Netherlands the Convention shall be applied as follows:

"Article 2

"The Public Prosecutor at The Hague District Court is designated as the Central Authority.

"Article 4

"Letters of Request will be accepted in Dutch, German, English or French, or if they are accompanied by a translation into one of these languages.

"The Netherlands does not undertake to translate documents for the execution of a Letter of Request.

"Article 8

"Members of the judicial personnel of another Contracting State may be present at the execution of a Letter of Request provided that the court which is responsible for execution authorises this and provided that any conditions which the court may impose are respected.

"Article 11

"Only the court which is responsible for executing the Letter of Request shall be competent to decide whether any person concerned by the execution has a privilege or duty to refuse to give evidence under the law of a State other than the State of origin; no such privilege or duty exists under Dutch law.

"Article 14

"Fees paid to experts and interpreters and costs occasioned by the use of a special procedure requested by the State of origin under Article 9, paragraph 2 of the Convention shall be borne by the State of origin.

"Article 16

"In the Netherlands, no prior permission is required for the taking of evidence as provided for in Article 16.

"Article 17

"The permission referred to in Article 17 must be requested from the President of the District Court in the area in which evidence is to be taken. If evidence is to be taken from witnesses or experts, the area in question will be that in which the witnesses or experts, or the majority of them reside. If the President gives permission, he may impose any conditions which he considers necessary to ensure that the evidence is taken in proper manner. He may decide that the evidence should be taken at the court, under the supervision of a judge designated by him. Permission will only be granted if the following conditions are met:

"**a)** the witness or expert concerned must have been duly summoned; the summons must be in Dutch or must be accompanied by a Dutch translation and must contain:

"—the facts of the case and a summary of the proceedings in connection with which the evidence is to be taken, and details of the court which has requested the evidence;

"—a statement to the effect that there is no obligation for the witness or expert to appear, and that if he refuses to appear, to take an oath, to give his word of honour or to give evidence, he will not incur any penalty or measure of any kind, either in the Netherlands or in the State where the proceedings have been instituted;

"—a statement to the effect that the person concerned may be legally represented;

"—a statement to the effect that in so far as the person concerned has a privilege or duty to refuse to give evidence, he may do so;

"—a statement to the effect that the commissioner will reimburse expenses incurred by the witness or expert in connection with his appearance to give evidence.

"**b)** A copy of the summons must be forwarded to the President.

"**c)** The request for permission must state the reasons why the taking of evidence has been entrusted to a commissioner and it must state the commissioner's official status unless he is a lawyer competent to practise in the Netherlands.

"**d)** The costs of taking the evidence, i.e., the expenses of the witnesses, experts or interpreters, must be reimbursed in full.

"Article 23

"The Netherlands will not execute Letters of Request issued for the purpose of obtaining pre-trial discovery of documents as known in Common Law countries.

"For the purposes of Article 23 of the Convention, "Letters of Request issued for the purpose of obtaining pre-trial discovery of documents as known in Common Law countries", which the Netherlands will not execute, are defined by the Government of the Kingdom of the Netherlands as being any Letters of Request which require a person:

"**a.** to state which of the documents which are of relevance to the proceedings to which the Letter of Request relates have been in his possession, custody or power; or

"**b.** to produce any document other than particular documents specified in the Letter of Request as being documents which the court which is conducting the proceedings believes to be in his possession, custody or power.

"Article 26

"The Netherlands will request that any State of origin which has made a request pursuant to paragraph 1 of Article 26 should reimburse the fees and costs to which this paragraph refers.

"In accordance with Article 38, paragraph 2, the Convention will enter into force for the Kingdom of the Netherlands (the Kingdom in Europe) on 7 June 1981."

In accordance with Article 40, paragraph 2, the Kingdom of the Netherlands declared on 28 May 1986 that the Convention shall extend to Aruba.

In conformity with Article 40, paragraph 3, the Convention will enter into force for Aruba on 27 July 1986.

The Permanent Bureau of the Hague Conference on private international law presents its compliments to the Diplomatic Missions of the Member States and to the National Organs and has the honour to inform them that, in accordance with Article 2 of the above-mentioned Convention, the

Kingdom of the Netherlands

has designated the *"Procureur-Generaal in Aruba van het Gemeenschappelijk Hof van Justitie van de Nederlandse Antillen en Aruba"* (the Attorney-General in Aruba of the joint Court of Justice of the Netherlands Antilles and of Aruba) as Central Authority for *Aruba*.

The Convention is being applied in Aruba subject to the same declarations as made upon ratification of the Convention on 8 April 1981 by the Kingdom of the Netherlands for the Kingdom in Europe. In addition, in conformity with Article 4, paragraphs 3 and 4, Aruba will not accept Letters of Request in French, unless accompanied by a translation into Dutch, English, or Spanish.

The Permanent Bureau avails itself of this opportunity to renew to the Diplomatic Missions of the Members States and to the National Organs an assurance of its highest consideration and esteem.

[3] With the following reservation:

"In conformity with article 33, Norway enters a reservation to paragraph 2 of article 4 to the effect that Letters of Request in the French language will not be accepted."

And with the following declarations:

"I. The Royal Ministry of Justice and Police is designated as the Central Authority with reference to article 2 and as the Competent Authority with reference to articles 15, 16 and 17.

"II. With reference to article 4, paragraph 3, the Kingdom of Norway declares that letters in the Danish or Swedish languages can be sent to the Central Authority.

"III. By accepting Letters of Request in another language than the Norwegian, the Kingdom of Norway does not undertake to execute the request, or transmit the evidence thus obtained in this other language; nor to have translated the documents which establish the execution of the Letter of Request.

"IV. By virtue of article 15, evidence can be taken by diplomatic officers or consular agents only if, upon application, prior permission to that effect has been granted.

"V. By virtue of article 23, the Kingdom of Norway declares that it will not execute Letters of Request issued for the purpose of obtaining pre-trial discovery of documents as known in Common Law countries."

The declaration made by the Kingdom of Norway in accordance with article 23 concerning "Letters of Request issued for the purpose of obtaining pre-trial discovery of documents" shall apply only to Letters of Request which require a person

a) to state what documents relevant to the proceedings to which the Letter of Request relates, are, or have been, in his possession, other than particular documents specified in the Letter of Request; or

b) to produce any documents other than particular documents which are specified in the Letter of Request, and which are likely to be in his possession.

3a The Permanent Bureau of the Hague Conference on private international law presents its compliments to the Diplomatic Missions of the Member States and to the National Organs and has the honour to inform them that, by instrument deposited on 13 February 1996 with the Ministry of Foreign Affairs of the Kingdom of the Netherlands,

the *Republic of Poland*

acceded to the above-mentioned Convention.

./. The instrument of accession contains a reservation, the text of which is attached.

Translation

Articles 23 et 33 will not be applicable within the territory of the Republic of Poland.

./. The instrument of accession was accompanied by the following declarations and reservations, the text of which is also attached.

Translation

Declarations

Article 2, Paragraph I—the Central Authority designated to receive requests for service coming from another Contracting State shall be the Ministry of Justice.

Article 8—the Authority designated to complete a certificate of service in the republic of Poland shall be the Ministry of Justice.

Article 24 and Article 27, sub-paragraph a—other authorities (in addition to the Central Authority) designated to receive requests for service shall be the voivodship courts.

Reservations

Article 23—the Republic of Poland declares, that it will not execute Letters of Request issued for the purpose of obtaining "pre-trial discovery of documents" as known in common law countries.

Article 33—the Republic of Poland excludes the application on its territory:

—the provisions of Article 4, paragraph 2,

—the provisions of Chapter II, excluding provisions of Article 15.

In accordance with paragraph 3 of Article 39, the Convention will enter into force for the *Republic of Poland* on *13 April 1996*.

According to Article 39, paragraph 4, of the Convention the accession will have effect only as regards the relations between the Republic of Poland and such Contracting States as will have declared their acceptance of the accession. Such declarations shall be deposited with the Ministry of Foreign Affairs of the Kingdom of the Netherlands.

In accordance with Article 39, paragraph 5, the Convention will enter into force between Poland and

Luxembourg	2 June 1996
Denmark	22 June 1996
Slovak Republic	25 June 1996
Israel	30 June 1996
Finland	5 August 1996
Netherlands (for the Kingdom in Europe and Aruba)	16 August 1996
Sweden	13 April 1997
Singapore	4 May 1997
Spain	25 May 1997

3b With the following reservations and declarations:

(Translation)

"**a)** In accordance with Article 33 of the Convention, the Portuguese State makes the following reservations:

"**1.** exclusion of the application of paragraph 2 of Article 4;

"**2.** exclusion of the application of Chapter II, with the exception of Article 15.

"**b)** In accordance with Articles 15 and 23 of the Convention, the Portuguese State makes the following declarations:

"**1.** The Portuguese State declares that the evidence as referred to in Article 15, can only be taken if permission to that effect is given by the appropriate authority designated by it upon application made by the diplomatic or consular agent;

"**2.** The Portuguese State declares that it will not execute Letters of Request issued for the purpose of obtaining pre-trial discovery of documents as known in Common Law Countries.

"**c)** With regard to Articles 2 and 15 of the Convention, the competent Portuguese authority will be the Director-General of the Judiciary Department ("Direccào-Geral dos Serviços Judiciários") of the Ministry of Justice.".

3c In accordance with Article 39, paragraph 3, the Convention shall enter into force for the Republic of Singapore on December 26, 1978.

Notification in accordance with Convention Article 42(c) and (e):

On October 27, 1978, the Ministry of Foreign Affairs of the Kingdom of the Netherlands received the instrument of accession of the Republic of Singapore to the Convention on the Taking of Evidence Abroad in Civil and Commercial Matters in accordance with Article 39, Paragraph 2, of the aforesaid Convention.

At the time of its accession the Government of the Republic of Singapore made the following reservations:

"**(i)** The entire Chapter II of the Convention is not applicable to the Republic of Singapore; and

"**(ii)** With regard to Article 4, paragraph 2, the Republic of Singapore will not accept a Letter of Request in a language other than English, since this language is the one used by the judicial personnel in Singapore."

In accordance with Article 23 the Government of the Republic of Singapore has declared that the Republic of Singapore will not execute Letters of Request issued for the purpose of obtaining pre-trial discovery of documents as known in Common Law countries.

The Government of the Republic of Singapore has further declared that it understands "Letters of Request issued for the purpose of obtaining pre-trial discovery of documents" for the purposes of the foregoing declaration as including any Letter of Request which requires a person:

(a) to state what documents relevant to the proceedings to which the Letter of Request relates are, or have been, in his possession, custody or power; or

(b) to produce any documents other than particular documents specified in the Letter of Request as being documents appearing to the requested court to be, or likely to be, in his possession, custody or power. It is also understood that the reference to civil or commercial actions in the Convention does not include tax matters for the Republic of Singapore.

In accordance with Article 39, paragraph 3, the Convention shall enter into force for the Republic of Singapore on December 26, 1978.

The accession shall be effective only for relations between the Republic of Singapore and contracting States that declare that they accept this accession.

Notification in conformity with Article 42, paragraph e, of the Convention:

In accordance with Article 35 of the Convention Singapore notified the Ministry of Foreign Affairs of the Kingdom of the Netherlands by a Note dated August 4, 1979, that the Central Authority which will undertake to receive Letters of Request referred to in Article 2 of the Convention, is the Registrar of the Supreme Court.

In accordance with Article 39, paragraph 5, the Convention will enter into force between Singapore and

Spain ....28 August 1994
Switzerland..........................13 January 1995
United States........................24 October 1995

3d By notification dated March 15, 1993 the Slovak Republic communicated the following: "In accordance with relevant principles and norms of international law and to extent defined by it, the Slovak Republic, as a successor State, born from the division of the Czech and Slovak Federal Republic, considers itself bound, as of January 1, 1993, i.e. the date of the division of the Czechoslovak Federation, by multilateral international treaties to which the Czech and Slovak Federal Republic was a party at that date, including reservations and declarations in respect of provisions made earlier by Czechoslovakia, as well as objections by Czechoslovakia in respect of reservations made by other treaty parties", which are as follows: [Same declarations and reservations, *mutatis mutandis,* under Czech Republic, see footnote 1e].

The Slovak Republic has designated in accordance with Articles 2 and 8 [of the Convention] the following Central Authority:

Ministerstvo spravodlivosti Slovenskej republiky
Zupne namestie 13, 813 11 Bratislava
Slovak Republic
fax: (00427) 5316035

3e The Permanent Bureau of the Hague Conference on private international law presents its compliments to the Diplomatic Missions of the Member States and to the National Organs and has the honour to inform them that, by instrument deposited on 8 July 1997 with the Ministry of Foreign Affairs of the Kingdom of the Netherlands,

the *Republic of South Africa*

acceded to the above-mentioned Convention.

The instrument of accession contains the following reservations, designation of authorities and declarations:

"1. Reservations

"That the Republic of South Africa excludes the following in terms of Article 33 of the Convention, namely—

"(a) the application of the provision of paragraph 2 of Article 4 of the Convention, which provides that a Letter of Request shall be accepted in French; and

"(b) the application of the provisions of Articles 15 and 16 of Chapter II of the Convention.

"2. Designation of authorities

"That the Republic of South Africa designates—

"(a) the Director General of the Department of Justice as Central Authority in terms of Article 2 of the Convention and as the competent authority referred to in Article 8 of the Convention; and

"(b) the division of the High Court of South Africa that has jurisdiction as the competent authority referred to in Articles 17 and 18 of the Convention

"3. Declarations

"That the Republic of South Africa makes the following declarations under the Convention:

"(a) For the purposes of paragraph 4 of Article 4 of the Convention, a Letter of Request, if not in English, may also be sent to the Central Authority in any of the following languages: Sepedi, Sesotho, Setswana, siSwati, Tshivenda, Xitsonga, Afrikaans, isiNdebele, isiXhosa and isiZulu.

"(b) Members of the judicial personnel of the requesting authority of another Contracting State may, after authorisation by the competent authority referred to in Article 8 of the Convention, be present at the execution of a Letter of Request as contemplated in that article.

"(c) Evidence may not be taken in terms of Article 17 of the Convention without the prior permission of the competent authority referred to in that Article.

"(d) A commissioner authorised to take evidence under Article 17 of the Convention may, in terms of Article 18 of the Convention, apply to the competent authority referred to in that Article to obtain the evidence by compulsion, subject to the measures of compulsion which are appropriate and prescribed by South African law for use in internal proceedings.

"(e) Letters of Request issued for the purpose of obtaining pre-trial discovery of documents as known in Common Law countries, will not be executed as provided for in Article 23."

In accordance with the terms of Article 39, paragraph 3, the Convention will enter into force for the *Republic of South Africa* on*6 September 1997.*

According to Article 39, paragraph 4, of the Convention the accession will have effect only as regards the relations between the Republic of South Africa and such Contracting States as will have declared their acceptance of the accession. Such declaration shall be deposited with the Ministry of Foreign Affairs of the Kingdom of the Netherlands.

In accordance with Article 38, paragraph 5, the Convention will enter into force between the United States of America and South Africa on November 1, 1997.

3f *Notification pursuant to Article 42 of the Convention*

In accordance with Article 37, paragraph 2, of the above-mentioned Convention Spain deposited its instrument of ratification with the Ministry of Foreign Affairs of the Kingdom of the Netherlands on 22 May 1987.

The instrument of ratification contains the following reservation:

"De conformidad con el artículo 33 en relacíon con el artículo 4.♦, párrafo 2, España no aceptará comisiones rogatorias que no estén redactadas en español o acompañadas de una traducción.

Translation

In accordance with Article 33 in relation with Article 4, paragraph 2, Spain will not accept Letters of Request which are not drawn up in Spanish or accompanied by a translation.

and the following declarations:

"**a)** La Autoridad Central española a que se refiere el artículo 2 será: El Ministerio de Justicia.-Secretaría General Técnica.-(San Bernardo, 45. 28015 MADRID), con exclusíon de cualquier otra Autoridad.

"**b)** Previa autorización del Ministerio de Justicia español, un Juez del Estado requirente podrá intervenir en el cumplimiento de una comisíon rogatoria, de conformidad con el artículo 8.

"**c)** De conformidad con los artículos 16 y 17, la prueba podrá ser practicada, sin necesidad de autorización previa de la Autoridad española, en los locales de la Representacíon diplomática o consular del Estado requirente.

"**d)** A tenor del artículo 23, España no acepta las comisiones rogatorias derivadas del procedimiento 'pre-trial discovery of documents' conocido en los países del 'Common Law'.".

Translation

"**a)** The Spanish Central Authority is: "La Direccion General de Codificacion y Cooperacion Juridica Internacional, Ministerio de Justicia e Interior", with exclusion of any other Authority.

"**b)** With prior authorization of the Spanish Ministry of Justice, a Judge of the requesting State may intervene in the execution of a Letter of Request, in accordance with Article 8.

"**c)** In accordance with Articles 16 and 17, the evidence may be taken, without prior permission of the Spanish Authority, in the premises of the diplomatic or consular representation of the requesting State.

"**d)** Pursuant to Article 23 Spain does not accept Letters of Request derived from the "pre-trial discovery of documents" procedure known in Common Law countries."

The Convention will enter into force for Spain on 21 July 1987.

3g With the following declarations:

(Translation)

—That, in pursuance of Article 4, para. 4, Letters of Request in the Danish and Norwegian languages will be accepted;

—That, in pursuance of Article 8, members of the judicial personnel of the requesting authority of another Contracting State may be present at the execution of a Letter of Request without prior authorisation;

—That, in pursuance of Article 15, para. 2, a diplomatic officer or consular agent may only take evidence if permission to do so has been granted by the competent Swedish authority;

—That, in pursuance of Article 23, Letters of Request issued for the purpose of obtaining pre-trial discovery of documents as known in Common Law countries will not be executed;

—That documents provided by Sweden which establish that a Letter of Request has been executed will be in the Swedish language only.

Ministry of Foreign Affairs, Stockholm, has been designated as the Central Authority referred to in Article 2 and also as the Competent Authority referred to in Article 15–17.

Additional declaration on July 11, 1980:

"The Swedish Government understands 'Letters of Request issued for the purpose of pre-trial discovery of documents' for the purposes of the foregoing Declaration as including any Letter of Request which requires a person:

"**a)** to state what documents relevant to the proceedings to which the Letter of Request relates are, or have been, in his possession, custody or power; or

"**b)** to produce any documents other than particular documents specified in the Letter of Request, which are likely to be in his possession, custody or power."

3h *Notification pursuant to Article 42 of the Convention*

In accordance with Article 37, paragraph 2, of the above-mentioned Convention *Switzerland* deposited its instrument of ratification with the Ministry of Foreign Affairs of the Kingdom of the Netherlands on 2 November 1994.

The instrument of ratification contains the following reservation and declarations:

Translation

"Re Article 1

"1. With regard to Article 1, Switzerland takes the view that the Convention applies exclusively to the Contracting States. Moreover, regarding the conclusions of the Special Commission which met in The Hague in April 1989, Switzerland believes that, whatever the opinion of the Contracting States on the exclusive application of the Convention, priority should in any event be given to the procedures provided for in the Convention regarding requests for the taking of evidence abroad.

"Re Articles 2 and 24

"2. In accordance with Article 35, first paragraph, Switzerland designates the cantonal authorities listed in the annex as Central Authorities as referred to in Articles 2 and 24 of the Convention. Requests for the taking of evidence or the execution of any other judicial act may also be addressed to the Federal Justice and Police Department in Bern, which will forward them to the appropriate Central Authority.

"Re Article 4, second and third paragraphs

"3. In accordance with Articles 33 and 35, Switzerland declares, with regard to Article 4, second and third paragraphs, that Letters of Request and any accompanying documents must be in the language of the authority requested to execute them, i.e. in German, French or Italian, or accompanied by a translation into one of these languages, depending on the part of Switzerland in which the documents are to be executed. The documents confirming execution will be drawn up in the official language of the requested authority (cf. annex).

"Re Article 8

"In Accordance with Article 35, second paragraph, Switzerland declares, with regard to Article 8, that members of the judicial personnel of the requesting authority of another Contracting State may be present at the execution of a Letter of Request provided they have obtained prior authorization from the executing authority.

"Re Articles 15, 16 and 17

"In accordance with Article 35, Switzerland declares that evidence may be taken according to Articles 15, 16 and 17 subject to prior authorization by the Federal Justice and Police Department. A request for authorization must be addressed to the Central Authority in the canton where the evidence is to be taken.

"Re Article 23

"In accordance with Article 23, Switzerland declares that Letters of Request issued for the purpose of obtaining pre-trial discovery of documents will not be executed if:

"a. the request has no direct and necessary link with the proceedings in question; or

"b. a person is required to indicate what documents relating to the case are or were in his/her possession or keeping or at his/her disposal; or

"c. a person is required to produce documents other than those mentioned in the request for legal assistance, which are probably in his/her possession or keeping or at his/ her disposal; or

"d. interests worthy of protection of the concerned persons are endangered".

The list of Central Authorities for the Cantons is attached.

Autorités centrales cantonales Annexe

Cantons	Langue(s) officielle(s) (a=allemand) (f=français) (i=italien)	Adresses	Numéros de téléphone
Appenzell Ausserrhoden	a	Kantonsgericht Appenzell A.Rh., 9043 Trogen	071/ 94 24 61
Appenzell Innerrhoden	a	Kantonsgericht Appenzell I.Rh., 9050 Appenzell	071/ 87 95 51
Aargau	a	Obergericht des Kantons Aargau,	064/ 21 19 40

Cantons	Langue(s) officielle(s) (a=allemand) (f=français) (i=italien)	Adresses	Numéros de téléphone
		5000 Aarau	
Basel-Landschaft	a	Obergericht des Kantons Basel-Landschaft, 4410 Liestal	061/925 51 11
Basel-Stadt	a	Appellationsgericht Basel-Stadt, 4054 Basel	061/267 81 81
Bern	a/f	Justizdirektion des Kantons Bern, 3011 Bern	031/633 76 76
Fribourg	f/a	Tribunal cantonal, 1700 Fribourg	037/ 25 39 10
Genéve	f	Parquet du Procureur général, 1211Genéve 3	022/319 21 11
Glarus	a	Obergericht des Kantons Glarus, 8750 Glarus	058/ 61 15 32
Graubünden	a	Justiz-, Polizei- und Sanitäts-departement Graubünden, 7001 Chur	081/ 21 21 21
Jura	f	Département de la Justice, 2800 Delémont	066/ 21 51 11
Luzern	a	Obergericht des Kantons Luzern, 6002 Luzern	041/ 24 51 11
Neuchâtel	f	Département de Justice, 2001 Neuchâtel	038/ 22 31 11
Nidwalden	a	Kantonsgericht Nidwalden, 6370 Stans	041/ 63 79 50
Obwalden	a	Kantonsgericht des Kantons Obwalden, 6060 Sarnen	041/ 66 92 22
St. Gallen	a	Kantonsgericht St. Gallen, 9001 St. Gallen	071/ 21 31 11
Schaffhausen	a	Obergericht des Kantons Schaffhausen, 8201 Schaffhausen	053/ 82 74 22
Schwyz	a	Kantonsgericht Schwyz, 6430 Schwyz	043/ 24 11 24
Solothurn	a	Obergericht des Kantons Solothurn, 4500 Solothurn	065/ 21 73 11
Tessin	i	Tribunale di appello, 6901 Lugano	091/ 21 51 11
Thurgau	a	Obergericht des Kantons Thurgau, 8500 Frauenfeld	054/ 22 31 21
Uri	a	Gerichtskanzlei Uri, 6460 Altdorf	044/ 4 22 44
Valais	f/a	Tribunal cantonal, 1950 Sion	027/ 22 93 93
Vaud	f	Tribunal cantonal, 1014 Lausanne	021/313 15 11
Zug	a	Obergericht des Kantons Zug, Rechtshilfe, 6300 Zug	042/ 25 33 11
Zürich	a	Obericht des Kantons Zürich, Rechtshilfe, 8023 Zürich	01/257 91 91

3i *Notification in conformity with Article 42, under a and e, of the Convention:*

In accordance with Article 37, paragraph 2, the United Kingdom of Great Britain and Northern Ireland deposited on July 16, 1976 its instrument of ratification with the Ministry of Foreign Affairs of the Netherlands.

In conformity with Article 38, paragraph 2, the Convention shall enter into force for the United Kingdom on September 14, 1976.

The instrument of ratification mentioned above, contains the following reservation:

". . . in accordance with the provisions of Article 33 the United Kingdom will not accept a Letter of Request in French."

On the occasion of the deposit of the said instrument of ratification the Government of the United Kingdom of Great Britain and Northern Ireland made the following declarations:

"**1.** In accordance with Article 8 Her Majesty's Government declare that members of the judicial personnel of the requesting authority may be present at the execution of a Letter of Request.

"**2.** In accordance with Article 18 Her Majesty's Government declare that a diplomatic officer, consular agent or commissioner authorised to take evidence under Articles 15, 16 and 17 may apply to the competent authority designated hereinbefore for appropriate assistance to obtain such evidence by compulsion provided that the Contracting State whose diplomatic officer, consular agent or commissioner makes the application has made a declaration affording reciprocal facilities under Article 18.

"**3.** In accordance with Article 23 Her Majesty's Government declare that the United Kingdom will not execute Letters of Request issued for the purpose of obtaining pre-trial discovery of documents. Her Majesty's Government further declare that Her Majesty's Government understand "Letters of Request issued for the purpose of obtaining pre-trial discovery of documents" for the purposes of the foregoing Declaration as including any Letter of Request which requires a person:—

"**a.** to state what documents relevant to the proceedings to which the Letter of Request relates are, or have been, in his possession, custody, or power; or

"**b.** to produce any documents other than particular documents specified in the Letter of Request as being documents appearing to the requested court to be, or to be likely to be, in his possession, custody or powers.

"**4.** In accordance with Article 27 Her Majesty's Government declare that by the law and practice of the United Kingdom the prior permission referred to in Articles 16 and 17 is not required in respect of diplomatic officers, consular agents or commissioners of a Contracting State which does not require permission to be obtained for the purposes of taking evidence under Articles 16 and 17."

In accordance with Article 35 of the Convention, the Government of the United Kingdom made the following designations:

1. Under Article 2: the Foreign and Commonwealth Office.

2. Under Article 16: the Foreign and Commonwealth Office.

3. Under Article 17: the Foreign and Commonwealth Office.

4. Under Article 18: the Senior Master of the Supreme Court (Queen's Bench Division) for England and Wales; the Crown Agent for Scotland, for Scotland; the Master (Queen's Bench and Appeals). The address of the Master (Queen's Bench and Appeals) is Royal Courts of Justice, Belfast 1.

5. Under Article 24: the Senior Master of the Supreme Court (Queen's Bench Division) in England and Wales; the Crown Agent for Scotland, for Scotland; the Master (Queen's Bench and Appeals). The address of the Master (Queen's Bench and Appeals) is Royal Courts of Justice, Belfast 1.

Extension to Gibraltar.—

In accordance with Article 40, Paragraph 3, the Convention shall enter into force for Gibraltar on January 20, 1979.

The extension declaration contains the following reservation: "In accordance with the provisions of Article 4 and Article 33 of the Convention, Gibraltar will not accept a Letter of Request in French."

In accordance with Article 35 of the Convention the following designations have been made:

"**(a)** Under Articles 16 and 17 of the Convention, the Deputy Governor is designated as the competent authority for Gibraltar;

"**(b)** Under Article 18 of the Convention, the Registrar of the Supreme Court of Gibraltar is designated as the competent authority;

"**(c)** Under Article 24 of the Convention, the Deputy Governor is designated as an additional authority competent to receive Letters of Request for execution in Gibraltar."

[For declarations see the original note.]

Notification in conformity with Article 42, subs. d and e, of the Convention

By a letter dated November 20, 1978, and received at the Ministry of Foreign Affairs of the Kingdom of the Netherlands on November 21, 1978, the Ambassador of the United Kingdom of Great Britain and Northern Ireland at The Hague, referring to the deposit on July 16, 1976 of the instrument of ratification of the above-mentioned Convention by the United Kingdom of Great Britain and Northern Ireland, declared in accordance with article 40 that the Convention shall extend to Gibraltar. The Convention shall enter into force for Gibraltar on January 20, 1979.

The declaration of extension contains the following reservation:

". . . in accordance with the provisions of Article 4 and Article 33 of the Convention, Gibraltar will not accept a Letter of Request in French."

In accordance with Article 35 of the Convention the following designations have been made:

a) under Articles 16 and 17 of the Convention the Deputy Governor is designated as the competent authority for Gibraltar;

b) under Article 18 of the Convention, the Registrar of the Supreme Court of Gibraltar is designated as the competent authority;

c) under Article 24 of the Convention, the Deputy Governor is designated as an additional authority competent to receive Letters of Request for execution in Gibraltar, and the following declarations:

1. In accordance with Article 8, members of the judicial personnel of the requesting authority may be present at the execution of a Letter of Request in Gibraltar.

2. In accordance with Articles 18, a diplomatic officer, consular agent or commissioner authorised to take evidence under Articles 15, 16 and 17 of the Convention may apply to the competent authority in Gibraltar designated hereinbefore for appropriate assistance to obtain such evidence by compulsion provided that the Contracting State whose diplomatic officer, consular agent or commissioner makes the application has made a declaration affording reciprocal facilities under Article 18.

3. In accordance with Article 23, Gibraltar will not execute Letters of Request issued for the purpose of obtaining pre-trial discovery of documents. The Government of Gibraltar understands "Letters of Request issued for the purpose of obtaining pre-trial discovery of documents" for the purposes of the foregoing Declaration as including any Letter of Request which requires a person:

a) to state what documents relevant to the proceedings to which the Letter of Request relates are, or have been, in his possession, custody or power; or

b) to produce any documents other than particular documents specified in the Letter of Request as being documents appearing to the requested court to be, or likely to be, in his possession, custody or power.

4. In accordance with Article 27, by the law and practice of Gibraltar the prior permission referred to in Articles 16 and 17 of the Convention is not required in respect of diplomatic officers, consular agents or commissioners of a Contracting State which does not require permission to be obtained for the purposes of taking evidence under Articles 16 or 17.

Extension to Sovereign Base Areas of Akrotiri and Dhekelia in the Island of Cyprus.—

"The Convention shall enter into force for the Sovereign Base Areas of Akrotiri and Dhekelia in the Island of Cyprus on August 24, 1979."

The declaration of extension contains the following reservation:

". . . in accordance with the provisions of Article 4 and Article 33 of the Convention, the Sovereign Base Areas will not accept a Letter of Request in French.".

In accordance with Article 35 of the Convention the following designations have been made:

a) under Articles 16 and 17 of the Convention the Chief Officer, Sovereign Base Areas, is designated as the competent authority for the Sovereign Base Areas;

b) under Article 18 of the Convention, the Senior Registrar of the Judge's Court of the Sovereign Base Areas of Akrotiri and Dhekelia is designated as the competent authority;

c) under Article 24 of the Convention, the Senior Registrar of the Judge's Court of the Sovereign Base Areas of Akrotiri and Dhekelia is designated as an additional authority competent to receive Letters of Request for execution in the Sovereign Base Areas.

and the following declarations:

1. In accordance with Article 8, members of the judicial personnel of the requesting authority may be present at the execution of a Letter of Request in the Sovereign Base Areas.

2. In accordance with Article 18, a diplomatic officer, consular agent or commissioner authorised to take evidence under Articles 15, 16 and 17 of the Convention may apply to the competent authority in the Sovereign Base Areas designated hereinbefore for appropriate assistance to obtain such evidence by compulsion provided that the Contracting State whose diplomatic officer, consular agent or commissioner makes the application has made a declaration affording reciprocal facilities under Article 18.

3. In accordance with Article 23, the Sovereign Base Areas will not execute Letters of Request issued for the purpose of obtaining pre-trial discovery of documents. The Administration of the Sovereign Base Areas understands "Letters of Request issued for the purpose of obtaining pre-trial discovery of documents" for the purposes of the foregoing Declaration as including any Letter of Request which requires a person:

a) to state what documents relevant to the proceedings to which the Letter of Request relates are, or have been, in his possession, custody or power; or

b) to produce any documents other than particular documents specified in the Letter of Request as being documents appearing to the requested court to be, or likely to be, in his possession, custody or power.

4. In accordance with Article 27, by the law and practice of the Sovereign Base Areas the prior permission referred to in Articles 16 and 17 of the Convention is not required in respect of diplomatic officers, consular agents or commissioners of a Contracting State which does not require permission to be obtained for the purposes of taking evidence under Articles 16 or 17.

Extension to Falkland Islands and Dependencies.—

Notification in conformity with Article 42, subs. d and e, of the Convention

By a letter dated November 23, 1979, and received at the Ministry of Foreign Affairs of the Kingdom of the Netherlands on November 26, 1979, the Ambassador of the United Kingdom of Great Britain and Northern Ireland at The Hague, referring to the deposit on July 16, 1976 of the instrument of ratification of the above-mentioned Convention by the United Kingdom of Great Britain and Northern Ireland, declared in accordance with Article 40 that the Convention shall extend to the Falkland Islands and Dependencies.

The Convention shall enter into force for the Falkland Islands and Dependencies on January 25, 1980.

The declaration of extension contains the following reservation:

". . . in accordance with the provisions of Article 4 and Article 33 of the Convention, the Falkland Islands and Dependencies will not accept a Letter of Request in French." In accordance with Article 35 of the Convention the following designations have been made:

a) under Articles 16, 17 and 18 of the Convention the Judge of the Supreme Court of the Falkland Islands, is designated as the competent authority for the Falkland Islands and Dependencies;

b) under Article 24 of the Convention, the Governor of the Falkland Islands and its dependencies is designated as an additional authority competent to receive Letters of Request for execution in the Falkland Islands and Dependencies.

and the following declarations:

1. In accordance with Article 8, members of the judicial personnel of the requesting authority may be present at the execution of a Letter of Request in the Falkland Islands and Dependencies.

2. In accordance with Article 18, a diplomatic officer, consular agent or commissioner authorised to take evidence under Articles 15, 16, and 17 of the Convention may apply to the competent authority in the Falkland Islands and Dependencies designated hereinbefore for appropriate assistance to obtain such evidence by compulsion provided that the Contracting State whose diplomatic officer, consular agent or commissioner makes the application has made a declaration affording reciprocal facilities under Article 18.

3. In accordance with Article 23, the Falkland Islands and Dependencies will not execute Letters of Request issued for the purpose of obtaining pre-trial discovery of documents.

The Governor of the Falkland Islands and its Dependencies understands "Letters of Request issued for the purpose of obtaining pre-trial discovery of documents" for the purposes of the foregoing declaration as including any Letter of Request which requires a person:

a) to state what documents relevant to the proceedings to which the Letter of Request relates are, or have been, in his possession, custody or power; or

b) to produce any documents other than particular documents specified in the Letter of Request as being documents appearing to the requested court to be, or likely to be, in his possession, custody or power.

4. In accordance with Article 27, by the law and practice of the Falkland Islands and Dependencies the prior permission referred to in Articles 16 and 17 of the Convention is not required in respect of diplomatic officers, consular agents or commissioners of a Contracting State which does not require permission to be obtained for the purposes of taking evidence under Article 16 or 17.

Extension to Isle of Man.—

Notification in conformity with article 42, subs. d and e, of the Convention

By a letter dated April 16, 1980, and received at the Ministry of Foreign Affairs of the Kingdom of the Netherlands on April 16, 1980, the Ambassador of the United Kingdom of Great Britain and Northern Ireland at The Hague, referring to the deposit on July 16, 1976 of the instrument of ratification of the above-mentioned Convention by the United Kingdom of Great Britain and Northern Ireland, declared in accordance with article 40 that the Convention shall extend to the Isle of Man.

The Convention shall enter into force for the Isle of Man on June 15, 1980.

The declaration of extension contains the following reservation:

". . . in accordance with the provisions of Article 4 and Article 33 of the Convention, the Isle of Man will not accept a Letter of Request in French."

In accordance with Article 35 of the Convention the following designations have been made:

a) under Articles 16, 17 and 18 of the Convention Her Majesty's First Deemster and Clerk of the Rolls is designated as the competent authority for the Isle of Man;

b) under Article 24 of the Convention, Her Majesty's First Deemster and Clerk of the Rolls is designated as an additional authority competent to receive Letters of Request for execution in the Isle of Man.

and the following declarations:

1. In accordance with Article 8, members of the judicial personnel of the requesting authority may be present at the execution of a Letter of Request in the Isle of Man.

2. In accordance with Article 18, a diplomatic officer, consular agent or commissioner authorised to take evidence under Article 15, 16 and 17 of the Convention may apply to the competent authority in the Isle of Man designated hereinbefore for appropriate assistance to obtain such evidence by compulsion provided that the Contracting State whose diplomatic officer, consular agent or commissioner makes the application has made a declaration affording reciprocal facilities under Article 18.

3. In accordance with Article 23, the Isle of Man will not execute Letters of Request issued for the purpose of obtaining pre-trial discovery of documents.

The Government of the Isle of Man understands "Letters of Request issued for the purpose of obtaining pre-trial discovery of documents" for the purposes of the foregoing declaration as including any Letter of Request which requires a person:

a) to state what documents relevant to the proceedings to which the Letter of Request relates are, or have been, in his possession, custody or power; or

b) to produce any documents other than particular documents specified in the Letter of Request as being documents appearing to the requested court to be, or likely to be, in his possession, custody or power.

4. In accordance with Article 27, by the law and practice of the Isle of Man the prior permission referred to in Articles 16 and 17 of the Convention is not required in respect of diplomatic officers, consular agents or commissioners of a Contracting State which does not require permission to be, obtained for the purposes of taking evidence under Article 16 or 17.

Extension to Cayman Islands.—

Notification in conformity with Article 42, subs. d and e, of the Convention

By letter dated 16 September 1980 and received at the Ministry of Foreign Affairs of the Kingdom of the Netherlands on that same date, the Ambassador of the United Kingdom of Great Britain and Northern Ireland at The Hague referring to the deposit on 16 July 1976 of the instrument of ratification of the above-mentioned Convention by the United Kingdom of Great Britain and Northern Ireland declared in accordance with Article 40 that the Convention shall extend to the Cayman Islands.

The Convention will enter into force for the Cayman Islands on 15 November 1980.

The declaration of extension contains the following reservation:

". . . in accordance with the provisions of Article 4 and Article 33 of the Convention, . . . the Cayman Islands will not accept a Letter of Request in French".

In accordance with Article 35 of the Convention the following designations have been made:

a) Under Articles 16 and 17 of the Convention, the Attorney General is designated as the competent authority for the Cayman Islands;

b) Under Article 18 of the Convention, the Clerk of the Grand Court is designated as the competent authority;

c) Under Article 24 of the Convention, His Excellency the Governor is designated as an additional authority competent to receive Letters of Request for execution in the Cayman Islands.

and the following declarations:

1. In accordance with Article 8, members of the judicial personnel of the requesting authority may be present at the execution of a Letter of Request in the Cayman Islands.
2. In accordance with Article 18, a diplomatic officer, consular agent or commissioner authorised to take evidence under Articles 15, 16 and 17 of the Convention may apply to the competent authority in the Cayman Islands designated hereinbefore for appropriate assistance to obtain such evidence by compulsion provided that the Contracting State whose diplomatic officer, consular agent or commissioner makes the application has made a declaration affording reciprocal facilities under Article 18.
3. In accordance with Article 23, the Cayman Islands will not execute Letters of Request issued for the purpose of obtaining pre-trial discovery of documents. The Government of the Cayman Islands understand "Letters of Request issued for the purpose of obtaining pre-trial discovery of documents" for the purposes of the foregoing declaration as including any Letter of Request which requires a person:
   a) to state what documents relevant to the proceedings to which the Letter of Request relates are, or have been, in his possession, custody or power; or
   b) to produce any documents other than particular documents specified in the Letter of Request as being documents appearing to the requested court to be, or likely to be, in his possession, custody or power.
4. In accordance with Article 27, by the law and practice of the Cayman Islands the prior permission referred to in Articles 16 and 17 of the Convention is not required in respect of diplomatic officers, consular agents or commissioners of a Contracting State which does not require permission to be obtained for the purposes of taking evidence under Article 16 or 17.

Extension to Guernsey.—

Notification in accordance with Article 42, subs. d and e, of the Convention

With reference to the deposit of its instrument of ratification of the above-mentioned Convention on 16 July 1985 the Government of the United Kingdom of Great Britain and Northern Ireland declared by letter of 13 November 1985 which was received by the Ministry of Foreign Affairs of the Kingdom of the Netherlands on 19 November 1985, in accordance with Article 40, second paragraph, that the Convention shall extend to Guernsey.

In accordance with Article 35 the Government of the United Kingdom furthermore declared that:

"(a) under Articles 8 and 25 of the Convention, the Bailiff, Deputy Bailiff, any Jurat of the Royal Court of Guernsey, the Chairman or a Jurat of the Court of Alderney and the Seneschal (or Deputy) of the Court of the Seneschal of Sark are designated as the competent authorities for Guernsey;

"(b) under Article 23 of the Convention, Guernsey will not execute Letters of Request issued for the purpose of obtaining pre-trial discovery of documents.".

In accordance with Article 40, third paragraph, the Convention will enter into force for Guernsey on 18 January 1986.

Extension to Anguilla.—

Notification pursuant to Article 42, paragraph c, d and e, of the Convention

In accordance with Article 40, paragraph 2, the Kingdom of Great Britain and Northern Ireland declared, by a Letter dated 1 July 1986, received at the Ministry of Foreign Affairs on 3 July 1986, that the present Convention shall extend to Anguilla.

In accordance with Article 35, of the Convention, the following designations have been made:

"a. Under Articles 16, 17 and 18 of the Convention the Registrar of the East Caribbean Supreme Court is designated as the competent authority for Anguilla.

"b. Under Article 24 of the Convention, the Governor of Anguilla is designated as an additional authority competent to receive Letters of Request for execution in Anguilla."

and the following declarations:

". . . . . . . in accordance with the provisions of Articles 4 and 33 of the Convention, Anguilla will not accept a Letter of Request in French.

"In accordance with Article 8, members of the juridical personnel of the requesting authority may be present at the execution of a Letter Request in Anguilla.

In accordance with Article 18, a diplomatic officer, consular agent or commissioner authorized to take evidence under Articles 15, 16 and 17 of the Convention may apply to the competent authority in Anguilla designated above for appropriate assistance to obtain such evidence by compulsion provided that the contracting State whose diplomatic officer, consular agent or commissioner makes (sic) the application has made a declaration affording reciprocal facilities under Article 18.

In accordance with Article 23, Anguilla will not execute Letters of Request issued for the purpose of obtaining pre-trial discovery of documents. Anguilla understands 'Letters of Request issued for the purpose of obtaining pre-trial discovery of documents' for the purposes of the foregoing declaration as including any Letter of Request which requires a person:

"i. to state what documents relevant to the proceedings to which the Letter of Request relates are, or have been, in his possession, custody or power; or

"ii. to produce any documents other than particular documents specified in the Letter of Request as being documents appearing to the requested court to be, or likely to be, in his possession, custody or power.

In accordance with Article 27, by the law and practice of Anguilla the prior permission referred to in Articles 16 and 17 of the Convention is not required in respect of diplomatic officers, consular agents or commissioners of a Contracting State which does not require permission to be obtained for the purposes of taking evidence under Articles 16 or 17."

4 With the following designations and declarations:

In accordance with Article 40, the Convention entered into force for Anquilla on 1 September 1986.

The United States Department of Justice, Washington, D.C., 20530, is designated as the Central Authority referred to in Article 2 of the Convention.

Under paragraph 2 of Article 4 of the United States has agreed to accept a Letter of Request in or translated into French. The United States wishes to point out that owing to the necessity of translating such documents into English it will take the Central Authority longer to comply with a Letter of Request in or translated into French than with a similar request received in English.

In accordance with paragraph 3 of Article 4 the United States declares that it will also accept Letters of Request in Spanish for execution in the Commonwealth of Puerto Rico.

In accordance with Article 8 the United States declares that subject to prior authorization members of the judicial personnel of the requesting authority of another Contracting State may be present at the execution of a Letter of Request. The Department of Justice is the competent authority for the purposes of this Article.

The United States declares that evidence may be taken in the United States under Articles 16 and 17 without its prior permission.

In accordance with Article 18 the United States declares that a diplomatic or consular officer or a commissioner authorized to take evidence under Articles 15, 16 or 17 may apply for appropriate assistance to obtain the evidence by compulsion. The competent authority for the purposes of Article 18 is the United States district court of the district in which a person resides or is found. Such court may order him to give his testimony or statement or to produce a document or thing for use in a proceeding in a foreign tribunal. The order may direct that the testimony or statement be given, or the document or other thing be produced, before a person appointed by the court.

In accordance with Article 40 the United States declares that the Convention shall extend to Guam, Puerto Rico and the Virgin Islands.

In accordance with the provisions of Article 39 of the Convention, the United States declared its acceptance of the accessions by Argentina, Barbados, Cyprus, Monaco, and Singapore.

[5] In accordance with Article 2 [of the Convention] Venezuela designated the following Central Authority: el ministerio de Relaciones Exteriores.

In accordance with Article 39, paragraph 5, the Convention will enter into force between Venezuela and

Cyprus .... 29 April 1994
United Kingdom of Great Britain
and Northern Ireland .... 15 August 1994*
Sweden .... 3 September 1994
Germany .... 21 October 1994
Denmark .... 27 November 1994
Spain .... 6 February 1995
Finland .... 11 March 1995
Italy .... 16 January 1996
Australia .... 20 January 1996
Israel .... 19 March 1996
Slovakia .... 20 May 1996

* The Permanent Bureau of the Hague Conference on private international law presents its compliments to the Diplomatic Missions of the Member States and to the National Organs and has the honour to inform them that, by a Note dated 9 February 1995 and received on 21 February 1995, the Embassy of the United Kingdom of Great Britain and Northern Ireland informed the Ministry of Foreign Affairs of the Kingdom of the Netherlands that the acceptance of Venezuela's accession to the Convention, set out in the Embassy's Note of 14 June 1994 (see L.c. A No 51/L.c. ON No 47 dated 26 July 1994) was also in respect of the territories for the international relations of which the United Kingdom is responsible and to which the application of the Convention has been extended.

The Embassy also informed that, unless otherwise stated, in future the acceptance by the United Kingdom of the accession of any State to the Convention shall also be acceptance in respect of all the territories for the international relations of which the United Kingdom is responsible and to which the application of the Convention has been extended.

Annotations to the Convention

"Report of the U.S. Delegation on the Evidence Convention", 8 Int'l Legal Materials 804 (1969).

Amram, "Explanatory Report on the Convention on the Taking of Evidence Abroad in Civil and Commercial Matters—Message from the President of the United States", Sen.Exec. A, 92nd Cong., 2d Sess. (Feb. 1, 1972).

Edwards, "Taking of Evidence Abroad in Civil or Commercial Matters", 18 Int'l and Comp.L.Q. 646 (1969).

Amram, "U.S. Ratification of the Hague Convention on the Taking of Evidence Abroad" 67 Am.J. Int'l L. (1973).

Model for Letters of Request Recommended for Use in Applying the Hague Convention of 18 March 1970 on the Taking of Evidence Abroad in Civil or Commercial Matters

Request for International Judicial Assistance Pursuant to the Hague Convention of 18 March 1970 on the Taking of Evidence in Civil or Commercial Matters

N.B. Under the first paragraph of article 4, the Letter of Request shall be in the language of the authority requested to execute it or be accompanied by a translation into that language. However, the provisions of the second and third paragraphs may permit use of other languages.

In order to avoid confusion, please spell out the name of the month in each date.

I. *(Items to be included in all Letters of Request.)*

1. Sender ________*(identity and address)*________

2. Central Authority of the Requested State ________*(identity and address)*________

3. Person to whom the executed request is to be returned __________ *(identity and address)* __________

II. *(Items to be included in all Letters of Request.)*

4. In conformity with article 3 of the Convention, the undersigned applicant has the honour to submit the following request:

5. a. Requesting judicial authority (article 3, a) __________ *(identity and address)* __________

   b. To the competent authority of (article 3, a) __________ *(the requested State)* __________

6. Names and addresses of the parties and their representatives (article 3, b)

   a. Plaintiff __________

   b. Defendant __________

   c. Other parties __________

7. Nature and purpose of the proceedings and summary of the facts (article 3, c) __________

8. Evidence to be obtained or other judicial act to be performed (article 3, d) __________

III. *(Items to be completed where applicable.)*

9. Identity and address of any person to be examined (article 3, e) __________

10. Questions to be put to the persons to be examined or statement of the subject-matter about which they are to be examined (article 3, f) __________ *(or see attached list)* __________

11. Documents or other property to be inspected (article 3, g) __________ *(specify whether it is to be produced, copied, valued, etc.)* __________

12. Any requirement that the evidence be given on oath or affirmation and any special form to be used (article 3, h) __________ *(In the event that the evidence cannot be taken in the manner requested, specify whether it is to be taken in such manner as provided by local law for the formal taking of evidence.)* __________

13. Special methods or procedure to be followed (articles 3, i and 9) ____________
14. Request for notification of the time and place for the execution of the Request and identity and address of any person to be notified (article 7) ____________
15. Request for attendance or participation of judicial personnel of the requesting authority at the execution of the letter of Request ____________
16. Specification of privilege or duty to refuse to give evidence under the law of the State of origin (article 11, b) ____________
17. The fees and costs incurred which are reimbursable under the second paragraph of article 14 or under article 26 of the Convention will be borne by ____________ *(identity and address)* ____________

IV. *(Items to be included in all Letters of Request.)*

18. Date of request ____________
19. Signature and seal of the requesting authority ____________

TREATIES AND CONVENTIONS

INTER-AMERICAN CONVENTION ON LETTERS ROGATORY

The Governments of the Member States of the Organization of American States, desirous of concluding a convention on letters rogatory, have agreed as follows:

I. USE OF TERMS

Article 1

For the purposes of this Convention the terms "exhortos" and "cartas rogatorias" are synonymous in the Spanish text. The terms "letters rogatory", "commissions rogatoires", and "cartas rogatórias" used in the English, French and Portuguese texts, respectively, cover both "exhortos" and "cartas rogatorias".

II. SCOPE OF THE CONVENTION

Article 2

This Convention shall apply to letters rogatory, issued in conjunction with proceedings in civil and commercial matters held before the appropriate judicial or other adjudicatory authority of one of the States Parties to this Convention, that have as their purpose:

a. The performance of procedural acts of a merely formal nature, such as service of process, summonses or subpoenas abroad;

b. The taking of evidence and the obtaining of information abroad, unless a reservation is made in this respect.

Article 3

This Convention shall not apply to letters rogatory relating to procedural acts other than those specified in the preceding article; and in particular it shall not apply to acts involving measures of compulsion.

III. TRANSMISSION OF LETTERS ROGATORY

Article 4

Letters rogatory may be transmitted to the authority to which they are addressed by the interested parties, through judicial channels, diplomatic or consular agents, or the Central Authority of the State of origin or of the State of destination, as the case may be.

Each State Party shall inform the General Secretariat of the Organization of American States of the Central Authority competent to receive and distribute letters rogatory.

IV. REQUIREMENTS FOR EXECUTION

Article 5

Letters rogatory shall be executed in the States Parties provided they meet the following requirements:

a. The letter rogatory is legalized, except as provided for in Articles 6 and 7 of this Convention. The letter rogatory shall be presumed to be duly legalized in the State of origin when legalized by the competent consular or diplomatic agent;

b. The letter rogatory and the appended documentation are duly translated into the official language of the State of destination.

Article 6

Whenever letters rogatory are transmitted through consular or diplomatic channels or through the Central Authority, legalization shall not be required.

Article 7

Courts in border areas of the States Parties may directly execute the letters rogatory contemplated in this Convention and such letters shall not require legalization.

Article 8

Letters rogatory shall be accompanied by the following documents to be delivered to the person on whom process, summons or subpoena is being served:

a. An authenticated copy of the complaint with its supporting documents, and of other exhibits or rulings that serve as the basis for the measure requested;

b. Written information identifying the judicial or other adjudicatory authority issuing the letter, indicating the time-limits allowed the person affected to act upon the request, and warning of the consequences of failure to do so;

c. Where appropriate, information on the existence and address of the court-appointed defense counsel or of competent legal-aid societies in the State of origin.

Article 9

Execution of letters rogatory shall not imply ultimate recognition of the jurisdiction of the judicial or other adjudicatory authority issuing the letter rogatory or a commitment to recognize the validity of the judgment it may render or to execute it.

V. EXECUTION

Article 10

Letters rogatory shall be executed in accordance with the laws and procedural rules of the State of destination.

At the request of the judicial or other adjudicatory authority issuing the letter rogatory, the authority of the State of destination may execute the letter through a special procedure, or accept the observance of additional formalities in performing the act requested, provided this procedure or the observance of those formalities is not contrary to the law of the State of destination.

Article 11

The authority of the State of destination shall have jurisdiction to determine any issue arising as a result of the execution of the measure requested in the letter rogatory.

Should such authority find that it lacks jurisdiction to execute the letter rogatory, it shall ex officio forward the documents and antecedents of the case to the authority of the State which has jurisdiction.

Article 12

The costs and other expenses involved in the processing and execution of letters rogatory shall be borne by the interested parties.

The State of destination may, in its discretion, execute a letter rogatory that does not indicate the person to be held responsible for costs and other expenses when incurred. The identity of the person empowered to represent the applicant for legal purposes may be indicated in the letter rogatory or in the documents relating to its execution.

The effects of a declaration in forma pauperis shall be regulated by the law of the State of destination.

Article 13

Consular or diplomatic agents of the States Parties to this Convention may perform the acts referred to in Article 2 in the State in which they are accredited, provided the performance of such acts is not contrary to the laws of that State. In so doing, they shall not perform any acts involving measures of compulsion.

VI. GENERAL PROVISIONS

Article 14

States Parties belonging to economic integration systems may agree directly between themselves upon special methods and procedures more expeditious than those provided for in this Convention. These agreements may be extended to include other States in the manner in which the parties may agree.

Article 15

This Convention shall not limit any provisions regarding letters rogatory in bilateral or multilateral agreements that may have been signed or may be signed in the future by the States Parties or preclude the continuation of more favorable practices in this regard that may be followed by these States.

Article 16

The States Parties to this Convention may declare that its provisions cover the execution of letters rogatory in criminal, labor, and "contentious-administrative" cases, as well as in arbitrations and other matters within the jurisdiction of special courts. Such declarations shall be transmitted to the General Secretariat of the Organization of American States.

Article 17

The State of destination may refuse to execute a letter rogatory that is manifestly contrary to its public policy ("ordre public").

Article 18

The States Parties shall inform the General Secretariat of the Organization of American States of the requirements stipulated in their laws for the legalization and the translation of letters rogatory.

VII. FINAL PROVISIONS

Article 19

This Convention shall be open for signature by the Member States of the Organization of American States.

Article 20

This Convention is subject to ratification. The instruments of ratification shall be deposited with the General Secretariat of the Organization of American States.

Article 21

This Convention shall remain open for accession by any other State. The instrument of accession shall be deposited with the General Secretariat of the Organization of American States.

Article 22

This Convention shall enter into force on the thirtieth day following the date of deposit of the second instrument of ratification.

For each State ratifying or acceding to the Convention after the deposit of the second instrument of ratification, the Convention shall enter into force on the thirtieth day after deposit by such State of its instrument of ratification or accession.

Article 23

If a State Party has two or more territorial units in which different systems of law apply in relation to the matters dealt with in this Convention, it may, at the time of signature, ratification or accession, declare that this Convention shall extend to all its territorial units or only to one or more of them.

Such declaration may be modified by subsequent declarations, which shall expressly indicate the territorial unit or units to which the Convention applies. Such subsequent declarations shall be transmitted to the General Secretariat of the Organization of American States, and shall become effective thirty days after the date of their receipt.

Article 24

This Convention shall remain in force indefinitely, but any of the States Parties may denounce it. The instrument of denunciation shall be deposited with the General Secretariat of the Organization of American States. After one year from the date of deposit of the instrument of denunciation, the Convention shall no longer be in effect for the denouncing State, but shall remain in effect for the other States Parties.

Article 25

The original instrument of this Convention, the English, French, Portuguese and Spanish texts of which are equally authentic, shall be deposited with the General Secretariat of the Organization of American States. The Secretariat shall notify the Member States of the Organization of American States and the States that have acceded to the Convention of the signatures, deposits of instruments of ratification, accession, and denunciation as well as of reservations, if any. It shall also transmit the information mentioned in the second paragraph of Article 4 and in Article 18 and the declarations referred to in Articles 16 and 23 of this Convention.

IN WITNESS WHEREOF the undersigned Plenipotentiaries, being duly authorized thereto by their respective Governments, have signed this Convention.

DONE AT PANAMA CITY, Republic of Panama, this thirtieth day of January one thousand nine hundred and seventy-five.

[Signatures omitted]

Inter–American Convention on Letters Rogatory.

Done at Panama January 30, 1975; entered into force for the United States August 27, 1988.

States which are parties:

Argentina*
Brazil*
Chile[1],*
Columbia*
Costa Rica
Ecuador[2],*
El Salvador[3]
Guatemala[4],*
Honduras
Mexico[5],*
Panama*
Paraguay*
Peru*
Spain[6]
United States[7]
Uruguay[8],*
Venezuela[9],*

* The United States has a treaty relationship only with those countries which are a party to the Convention and the Additional Protocol.

---

1 (Declaration made at the time of ratification, according to Article 16 of the Convention)

The instrument of ratification corresponding to this Convention contains the declaration "that its provisions cover the execution of letters rogatory in criminal, labor, and contentious-administrative cases, as well as in arbitrations and other matters within the jurisdiction of special courts".

(Provided information in accordance with Article 4)

The Central Authority to receive and distribute letters rogatory is the Ministry of Foreign Affairs of the Republic of Chile (May 7, 1987).

2 On 23 April 1984 sent information (Note No. 89-OEA/84), appointing the Asesoría Técnico-Jurídica of the Ministry of Foreign Affairs of Ecuador as the "Central Authority, to carry out the functions entrusted to it in the Inter-American Convention on Letters Rogatory."

3 Reservation to application of Article 7.

(Provided information in accordance with Articles 4 and 18)

In El Salvador the Supreme Court of Justice is the competent central authority for receiving and distributing Letters Rogatory. The requirements exacted for legalization and translation of Letters Rogatory are those prescribed in Article 261 of the Code of Civil Procedures and Articles 388, 389, 391 and 392 of the Bustamente Code . . . (The text of the articles is omitted).

4 (Provided information in accordance with Article 4)

The Central Authority competent to transmit, receive and distribute letters rogatory is the Supreme Court of Justice (October 21, 1987)

5 With the interpretative declaration made at the time of signature.

"It is the interpretation of the Government of Mexico that Article 9 of this Convention refers to the international validity of foreign judgments."

(Provided information in accordance with Article 4)

The Central Authority competent to receive and distribute letters rogatory is the Secretariat of Foreign Affairs of Mexico.

6 (Provided information in accordance with Article 4)

The Central Authority competent to receive and distribute letters rogatory is the General Technical Secretariat of the Ministry of Justice (Secretaría General Técnica), whose address is: San Bernardo 47, Madrid 28015, Spain (April 14, 1988).

7 (Reservations made at the time of ratification)

"1. Pursuant to Article 2(b) of the Inter–American Convention on Letters Rogatory, letters rogatory that have as their purpose the taking of evidence shall be excluded from the rights, obligations and operation of this Convention between the United States and another State Party.

"2. In ratifying the Inter–American Convention on Letters Rogatory, the United States accepts entry into force and undertakes treaty relations only with respect to States which have ratified or acceded to the Additional Protocol as well as the Inter–American Convention, and not with respect to States which have ratified or acceded to the Inter-American Convention alone."

(Provided information in accordance with Articles 4 and 18)

Pursuant to Article 4 of the Convention and Article 2 of the Additional Protocol, the Government of the United States wishes to inform the Secretary General that the Department of Justice is the Central Authority competent to receive and distribute letters rogatory. The mailing address for these purposes is:

Office of International Judicial Assistance
Civil Division
Department of Justice
Todd Building Room 1234
550 11th Street, N.W.
Washington, D.C. 20530 (*)

Pursuant to Article 18 of the Convention, the Government of the United States wishes to inform the Secretary General that letters rogatory to be executed in the United States must be translated into the English language.

(*) Phone: (202) 724–7455

8 (Provided information in accordance with Article 4)

On 30 August 1985 sent information (Note No. 961/85) appointing the Ministry of Education and Culture "Asesoría Autoridad Central de Cooperación Jurídica Internacional" as the "Central Authority" provided for in Article 4 of the Convention.

9 (Reservation made at the time of ratification)

With reservation to letter b) of Article 2 of the Convention.

(Provided information in accordance with Article 4)

The Central Authority competent to receive and distribute letters rogatory is the Ministry of Foreign Affairs of the Republic of Venezuela (11 December 1984).

ADDITIONAL PROTOCOL TO THE INTER–AMERICAN CONVENTION ON LETTERS ROGATORY

The Governments of the Member States of the Organization of American States, desirous of strengthening and facilitating international cooperation in judicial procedures as provided for in the Inter–American Convention on Letters Rogatory done in Panama on January 30, 1975, have agreed as follows:

I. SCOPE OF PROTOCOL

Article 1

This Protocol shall apply only to those procedural acts set forth in Article 2(a) of the Inter–American Convention on Letters Rogatory, hereinafter referred to as "the Convention". For the purposes of this Protocol, such acts shall be understood to mean procedural acts (pleadings, motions, orders, and subpoenas) that are served and requests for information that are made by a judicial or other adjudicatory authority of a State Party to a judicial or administrative authority of another State Party and are transmitted by a letter rogatory from the Central Authority of the State of origin to the Central Authority of the State of destination.

II. CENTRAL AUTHORITY

Article 2

Each State Party shall designate a central authority that shall perform the functions assigned to it in the Convention and in this Protocol. At the time of deposit of their instruments of ratification or accession to this Protocol, the States Parties shall communicate the designations to the General Secretariat of the Organization of American States, which shall distribute to the States Parties to the Convention a list containing the designations received. The Central Authority designated by a State Party in accordance with Article 4 of the Convention may be changed at any time. The State Party shall inform the above-mentioned Secretariat of such change as promptly as possible.

III. PREPARATION OF LETTERS ROGATORY

Article 3

Letters rogatory shall be prepared on forms that are printed in the four official languages of the Organization of American States or in the languages of the State of origin and of the State of destination and conform to Form A contained in the Annex to this Protocol.

Letters rogatory shall be accompanied by the following:

a. Copy of the complaint or pleading that initiated the action in which the letter rogatory was issued, as well as a translation thereof into the language of the State of destination;

b. Untranslated copy of the documents attached to the complaint or pleading;

c. Untranslated copy of any rulings ordering issuance of the letter rogatory;

d. Form conforming to Form B annexed to this Protocol and containing essential information for the person to be served or the authority to receive the documents; and

e. Certificate conforming to Form C annexed to this Protocol on which the Central Authority of the State of destination shall attest to execution or non-execution of the letter rogatory.

The copies shall be regarded as authenticated for the purposes of Article 8(a) of the Convention if they bear the seal of the judicial or other adjudicatory authority that issued the letter rogatory.

A copy of the letter rogatory together with Form B and the copies referred to in items a, b, and c of this Article shall be delivered to the person notified or to the authority to which the request is addressed. One of the copies of the letter rogatory and the documents attached to it shall remain in the possession of the State of destination; the untranslated original, the certificate of execution and the documents attached to them shall be returned to the Central Authority of the State of origin through appropriate channels.

If a State Party has more than one official language, it shall, at the time of signature, ratification or accession to this Protocol, declare which language or languages shall be considered official for the purposes of the Convention and of this Protocol. If a State Party comprises territorial units that have different official languages, it shall, at the time of signature, ratification or accession to this Protocol, declare which language or languages in each territorial unit shall be considered official for the purposes of the Convention and of this Protocol. The General Secretariat of the Organization of American States shall distribute to the States Parties to this Protocol the information contained in such declarations.

IV. TRANSMISSION AND PROCESSING OF LETTERS ROGATORY

Article 4

Upon receipt of a letter rogatory from the Central Authority in another State Party, the Central Authority in the State of destination shall transmit the letter rogatory to the appropriate judicial or administrative authority for processing in accordance with the applicable local law.

Upon execution of the letter rogatory, the judicial or administrative authority or authorities that processed it shall attest to the execution thereof in the manner prescribed in their local law, and shall transmit it with the relevant documents to the Central Authority. The Central Authority of the State Party of destination shall certify execution of the letter rogatory to the Central Authority of the State Party of origin on a form conforming to Form C of the Annex, which shall not require legalization. In addition, the Central Authority of the State of destination shall return the letter rogatory and attached documents to the Central Authority of the State of origin for delivery to the judicial or other adjudicatory authority that issued it.

V. COSTS AND EXPENSES

Article 5

The processing of letters rogatory by the Central Authority of the State Party of destination and its judicial or administrative authorities shall be free of charge. However, this State Party may seek payment by parties requesting execution of letters rogatory for those services which, in accordance with its local law, are required to be paid for directly by those parties.

The party requesting the execution of a letter rogatory shall, at its election, either select and indicate in the letter rogatory the person who is responsible in the State of destination for the cost of such services or, alternatively, shall attach to the letter rogatory a check for the fixed amount that is specified in Article 6 of this Protocol for its processing by the State of destination and will cover the cost of such services or a document proving that such amount has been transferred by some other means to the Central Authority of the State of destination.

The fact that the cost of such services ultimately exceeds the fixed amount shall not delay or prevent the processing or execution of the letter rogatory by the Central Authority or the judicial or administrative authorities of the State of destination. Should the cost exceed that amount, the Central Authority of the State of destination may, when returning the executed letter rogatory, seek payment of the outstanding amount due from the party requesting execution of the letter rogatory.

Article 6

At the time of deposit of its instrument of ratification or accession to this Protocol with the General Secretariat of the Organization of American States, each State Party shall attach a schedule of the services and the costs and other expenses that, in accordance with its local law, shall be paid directly by the party requesting execution of the letter rogatory. In addition, each State Party shall specify in the above-mentioned schedule the single amount which it considers will reasonably cover the cost of such services, regardless of the number or nature thereof. This amount shall be paid when the person requesting execution of the letter rogatory has not designated a person responsible for the payment of such services in the State of destination but has decided to pay for them directly in the manner provided for in Article 5 of this Protocol.

The General Secretariat of the Organization of American States shall distribute the information received to the States Parties to this Protocol. A State Party may at any time notify the General Secretariat of the Organization of American States of changes in the above-mentioned schedules, which shall be communicated by the General Secretariat to the other States Parties to this Protocol.

Article 7

States Parties may declare in the schedules mentioned in the foregoing articles that, provided there is reciprocity, they will not charge parties requesting execution of letters rogatory for the services necessary for executing them, or will accept in complete satisfaction of the cost of such services either the single fixed amount specified in Article 6 or another specified amount.

Article 8

This Protocol shall be open for signature and subject to ratification or accession by those Member States of the Organization of American States that have signed, ratified, or acceded to the Inter–American Convention on Letters Rogatory signed in Panama on January 30, 1975.

This Protocol shall remain open for accession by any other State that accedes or has acceded to the Inter–American Convention on Letters Rogatory, under the conditions set forth in this article.

The instruments of ratification and accession shall be deposited with the General Secretariat of the Organization of American States.

Article 9

This Protocol shall enter into force on the thirtieth day following the date on which two States Parties to the Convention have deposited their instruments of ratification or accession to this Protocol.

For each State ratifying or acceding to the Protocol after its entry into force, the Protocol shall enter into force on the thirtieth day following deposit by such State of its instrument of ratification or accession, provided that such State is a Party to the Convention.

Article 10

If a State Party has two or more territorial units in which different systems of law apply in relation to matters dealt with in this Protocol, it may, at the time of signature, ratification or accession, declare that this Protocol shall extend to all its territorial units or only to one or more of them.

Such declaration may be modified by subsequent declarations that shall expressly indicate the territorial unit or units to which this Protocol applies. Such subsequent declarations shall be transmitted to the General Secretariat of the Organization of American States, and shall become effective thirty days after the date of their receipt.

Article 11

This Protocol shall remain in force indefinitely, but any of the States Parties may denounce it. The instrument of denunciation shall be deposited with the General Secretariat of the Organization of American States. After one year from the date of deposit of the instrument of denunciation, the Protocol shall no longer be in effect for the denouncing State, but shall remain in effect for the other States Parties.

Article 12

The original instrument of this Protocol and its Annex (Forms A, B and C), the English, French, Portuguese and Spanish texts of which are equally authentic, shall be deposited with the General Secretariat of the Organization of American States, which will forward an authenticated copy of the text to the Secretariat of the United Nations for registration and publication in accordance with Article 102 of its Charter. The General Secretariat of the Organization of American States shall notify the Member States of that Organization and the States that have acceded to the Protocol of the signatures, deposits of instruments of ratification, accession and denunciation, as well as of reservations, if any. It shall also transmit to them the information mentioned in Article 2, the last paragraph of Article 3, and Article 6 and the declarations referred to in Article 10 of this Protocol.

IN WITNESS WHEREOF the undersigned Plenipotentiaries, being duly authorized thereto by their respective Governments, have signed this Protocol.

DONE AT MONTEVIDEO, Republic of Uruguay, this eighth day of May, one thousand nine hundred and seventy-nine.

[Signatures omitted]

ANNEX TO THE ADDITIONAL PROTOCOL
TO THE INTER–AMERICAN CONVENTION ON LETTERS ROGATORY

FORM A

LETTER ROGATORY [1]

1	2
REQUESTING JUDICIAL OR OTHER ADJUDICATORY AUTHORITY Name Address	CASE: DOCKET No.:
3	**4**
CENTRAL AUTHORITY OF THE STATE OF ORIGIN Name Address	CENTRAL AUTHORITY OF THE STATE OF DESTINATION Name Address
5	**6**
REQUESTING PARTY Name Address	COUNSEL TO THE REQUESTING PARTY Name Address

PERSON DESIGNATED TO ACT IN CONNECTION WITH THE LETTER ROGATORY

Name Address	Is this person responsible for costs and expenses? YES ☐ NO ☐ *If not, check in the amount of ________ is attached *Or proof of payment is attached

The Central Authority signing this letter rogatory has the honor to transmit to you in triplicate the documents listed below and, in conformity with the Protocol to the Inter-American Convention on Letters Rogatory:

* A. Requests their prompt service on:

____
____
____

The undersigned authority requests that service be carried out in the following manner:

* (1). In accordance with the special procedure or additional formalities that are described below, as provided for in the second paragraph of Article 10 of the above-mentioned Convention; or

____
____
____

* (2). By service personally on the identified addressee or, in the case of a legal entity, on its authorized agent; or

* (3). If the person or the authorized agent of the entity to be served is not found, service shall be made in accordance with the law of the State of destination.

* B. Requests the delivery of the documents listed below to the following judicial or administrative authority:
Authority ______________________________
____
____

* C. Requests the Central Authority of the State of destination to return to the Central Authority of the State of origin one copy of the documents listed below and attached to this letter rogatory, and an executed Certificate on the attached Form C.
Done at ________ this ________ date of ________, 19___.

______________________________	______________________________
Signature and stamp of the judicial or other adjudicatory authority of the State of origin	Signature and stamp of the Central Authority of the State of origin

Title or other identification of each document to be delivered:

____
____

(Attach additional pages, if necessary.)

1 Complete the original and two copies of this form; if A(1) is applicable, attach the original and two copies of the translation of this item in the language of the State of destination.
* Delete if inapplicable.

ANNEX TO THE ADDITIONAL PROTOCOL
TO THE INTER-AMERICAN CONVENTION ON LETTERS ROGATORY

FORM B

ESSENTIAL INFORMATION FOR THE ADDRESSEE [1]

To (Name and address of the person being served)______________________________
____

You are hereby informed that (Brief statement of nature of service) ______________________________
____
____

A copy of the letter rogatory that gives rise to the service or delivery of these documents is attached to this document. This copy also contains essential information for you. Also attached are copies of the complaint or pleading initiating the action in which the letter rogatory was issued, of the documents attached to the complaint or pleading, and of any rulings that ordered the issuance of the letter rogatory.

ADDITIONAL INFORMATION

I*

FOR SERVICE

A. The document being served on you (original or copy) concerns the following:
____
____

B. The remedies sought or the amount in dispute is as follows:

C. By this service, you are requested:

D. * In case of service on you as a defendant you can answer the complaint before the judicial or other adjudicatory authority specified in Form A, Box 1 (State place, date and hour):

* You are being summoned to appear as:

* If some other action is being requested of the person served, please describe:

E. If you fail to comply, the consequences might be:

F. You are hereby informed that a defense counsel appointed by the Court or the following legal aid societies are available to you at the place where the proceeding is pending.
Name:

Address:

The documents listed in Part III are being furnished to you so that you may better understand and defend your interests.

II *

FOR INFORMATION FROM JUDICIAL OR ADMINISTRATIVE AUTHORITY

To:

(Name and address of the judicial or administrative authority)

You are respectfully requested to furnish the undersigned authority with the following information:

The documents listed in Part III are being furnished to you to facilitate your reply.

III

LIST OF ATTACHED DOCUMENTS

(Attach additional pages if necessary.)

Done at ________ this ________ day of ________, 19___

_______________________ _______________________

Signature and stamp of the judicial or other adjudicatory authority of the State of origin

Signature and stamp of the Central Authority of the State of Origin

[1] Complete the original and two copies of this form in the language of the State of origin and two copies in the language of the State of destination.

* Delete if inapplicable.

ANNEX TO THE ADDITIONAL PROTOCOL
TO THE INTER–AMERICAN CONVENTION ON LETTERS ROGATORY

FORM C

CERTIFICATE OF EXECUTION[1]

To: _______________________

____

(Name and address of judicial or other adjudicatory authority that issued the letter rogatory)

In conformity with the Additional Protocol to the Inter–American Convention on Letters Rogatory, signed at Montevideo on May 8, 1979, and in accordance with the attached original letter rogatory, the undersigned Central Authority has the honor to certify the following:

* A. That one copy of the documents attached to this Certificate has been served or delivered as follows:

Date: _______________________
At (Address) _______________________

By one of the following methods authorized by the Convention.

*(1) In accordance with the special procedure or additional formalities that are described below, as provided for in the second paragraph of Article 10 of the abovementioned Convention, or

____

____

____

*(2) By service personally on the identified addressee or, in the case of a legal entity, on its authorized agent, or

*(3) If the person or the authorized agent of the entity to be served was not found, in accordance with the law of the State of destination: (Specify method used)

____

____

____

____

*B. That the documents referred to in the letter rogatory have been delivered to:

Identity of person _______________________

____

Relationship to the addressee _______________________

(family, business or other)

____

____

*C. That the documents attached to the Certificate have not been served or delivered for the following reason(s):

____

____

____

____

*D. In conformity with the Protocol, the party requesting execution of the letter rogatory is requested to pay the outstanding balance of costs in the amount indicated in the attached statement.

Done at ________ the ______ day of ________ 19___

____

Signature and stamp of Central Authority of the State of destination

Where appropriate, attach originals or copies of any additional documents proving service or delivery, and identify them.

[1] Complete the original and one copy in the language of the State of destination.

* Delete if inapplicable.

Additional Protocol to the Inter–American Convention on Letters Rogatory, with Annex. Done at Montevideo May 8, 1979; entered into force for the United States August 27, 1988.

States which are parties:

Argentina*

Brazil*

Chile*

Columbia*

Ecuador [1]*

Guatemala*

Mexico [2]*

Panama [2a]*

Paraguay*

Peru*

United States [3]

Uruguay [4]*

Venezuela*

* The United States has a treaty relationship only with those countries which are a party to the Convention and the Additional Protocol.

[1] On 23 April 1984 sent information (Note No. 89-OEA/84), appointing the Asesoría-Técnico-Jurídica of the Ministry of Foreign Affairs of Ecuador as the "Central Authority", to carry out the functions entrusted to it in the Additional Protocol to the Inter-American Convention on Letters Rogatory.

[2] In accordance with the provisions stipulated in Article 2 of the Additional Protocol to the Inter-American Convention on Letters Rogatory relative to the designation of a central authority, I notify Your Excellency that this shall be the Secretariat of Foreign Affairs of Mexico (9 March 1983).

[2a] (Provided information in accordance with Article 2 of the Protocol)

On October 4, 1991, Panama designated the Ministry of Foreign Affairs as the Central Authority competent pursuant to the functions of article 2 of the Protocol.

[3] (Reservations made at the time of ratification)

"1. Pursuant to Article 2(b) of the Inter–American Convention on Letters Rogatory, letters rogatory that have as their purpose the taking of evidence shall be excluded from the rights, obligations and operation of this Convention between the United States and another State Party.

"2. In ratifying the Inter–American Convention on Letters Rogatory, the United States accepts entry into force and undertakes treaty relations only with respect to States which have ratified or acceded to the Additional Protocol as well as the Inter–American Convention, and not with respect to States which have ratified or acceded to the Inter-American Convention alone."

(Provided information in accordance with Article 2)

Pursuant to Article 4 of the Convention and Article 2 of the Additional Protocol, the Government of the United States wishes to inform the Secretary General that the Department of Justice is the Central Authority competent to receive and distribute letters rogatory. The mailing address for these purposes is:

Office of International Judicial Assistance
Civil Division
Department of Justice
Todd Building Room 1234
550 11th Street, N.W.
Washington, D.C. 20530
Phone: (202) 724–7455

(Declarations made at the time of ratification)

Pursuant to Article 6 of the Additional Protocol, the Government of the United States declares that the United States reserves the right to charge a total of twenty-five dollars for performance of the services referred to therein.

Pursuant to Article 7 of the Additional Protocol, the Government of the United States declares that the aforementioned charge shall be waived on a reciprocal basis for the execution of a letter rogatory emanating from any State Party to both the Convention and Additional Protocol and may be otherwise waived as appropriate.

[4] (Declaration made at the time of ratification)

With the declaration made at the time of signature.

The scope of public order:

Uruguay wishes to state that it expressly ratifies the line of thought enunciated in Panama at CIDIP–I reaffirming its genuine Pan American spirit and its clear and positive decision to contribute with its ideas and endorsement to the successful development of the legal community.

This line of thinking and conduct has been evidenced in undoubtable form by the unreserved ratification by Uruguay of all the Conventions of Panama, approved by law number 14,534 in 1976.

In line with the foregoing, Uruguay gives its affirmative vote to the formula regarding public order. Nevertheless, Uruguay wishes to state expressly and clearly that, in accordance with the position it maintained in Panama, its interpretation of the aforementioned exception refers to international public order as an individual juridical institution, not necessarily identifiable with the internal public order of each state.

Therefore, in the opinion of Uruguay, the approved formula conveys an exceptional authorization to the various States Parties to declare in a nondiscretionary and well-founded manner that the precepts of foreign law are inapplicable whenever these concretely and in a serious and open manner offend the standards and principles essential to the international public order on which each individual state bases its legal individuality.

(Provided information in accordance with Articles 2, 6 and 7)

For the purposes indicated in articles six and seven of the above-cited Protocol, I wish to state that the single fixed amount of the cost of the services necessary for execution of the letter rogatory will be twenty readjustable units or its equivalent in currency. Also the schedule of the services that must be paid directly by the interested party will be limited to the possibility of resorting to the need for the services of appraisers, experts and other assistants in the case affected.

On 30 August 1985 sent information (Note No. 961/85) appointing the Ministry of Education and Culture "Asesoría Autoridad Central de Cooperación Jurídica Internacional" as the "Central Authority" provided for in Article 2 of the Protocol.

§ 1782. Assistance to foreign and international tribunals and to litigants before such tribunals

(a) The district court of the district in which a person resides or is found may order him to give his testimony or statement or to produce a document or other thing for use in a proceeding in a foreign or international tribunal, including criminal investigations conducted before formal accusation. The order may be made pursuant to a letter rogatory issued, or request made, by a foreign or international tribunal or upon the application of any interested person and may direct that the testimony or statement be given, or the document or other thing be produced, before a person appointed by the court. By virtue of his appointment, the person appointed has power to administer any necessary oath and take the testimony or statement. The order may prescribe the practice and procedure, which may be in whole or part the practice and procedure of the foreign country or the international tribunal, for taking the testimony or statement or producing the document or other thing. To the extent that the order does not prescribe otherwise, the testimony or statement shall be taken, and the document or other thing produced, in accordance with the Federal Rules of Civil Procedure.

A person may not be compelled to give his testimony or statement or to produce a document or other thing in violation of any legally applicable privilege.

(b) This chapter does not preclude a person within the United States from voluntarily giving his testimony or statement, or producing a document or other thing, for use in a proceeding in a foreign or international tribunal before any person and in any manner acceptable to him.

(June 25, 1948, c. 646, 62 Stat. 949; May 24, 1949, c. 139, § 93, 63 Stat. 103; Oct. 3, 1964, Pub.L. 88–619, § 9(a), 78 Stat. 997; Feb. 10, 1996, Pub.L. 104–106, Div. A, Title XIII, § 1342(b), 110 Stat. 486.)

HISTORICAL AND STATUTORY NOTES

References in Text

The Federal Rules of Civil Procedure, referred to in subsec. (a), are set out in this title.

§ 1783. Subpoena of person in foreign country

(a) A court of the United States may order the issuance of a subpoena requiring the appearance as a witness before it, or before a person or body designated by it, of a national or resident of the United States who is in a foreign country, or requiring the production of a specified document or other thing by him, if the court finds that particular testimony or the production of the document or other thing by him is necessary in the interest of justice, and, in other than a criminal action or proceeding, if the court finds, in addition, that it is not possible to obtain his testimony in admissible form without his personal appearance or to obtain the production of the document or other thing in any other manner.

(b) The subpoena shall designate the time and place for the appearance or for the production of the document or other thing. Service of the subpoena and any order to show cause, rule, judgment, or decree authorized by this section or by section 1784 of this title shall be effected in accordance with the provisions of the Federal Rules of Civil Procedure relating to service of process on a person in a foreign country. The person serving the subpoena shall tender to the person to whom the subpoena is addressed his estimated necessary travel and attendance expenses, the amount of which shall be determined by the court and stated in the order directing the issuance of the subpoena.

(June 25, 1948, c. 646, 62 Stat. 949; Oct. 3, 1964, Pub.L. 88–619, § 10(a), 78 Stat. 997.)

HISTORICAL AND STATUTORY NOTES

References in Text

The Federal Rules of Civil Procedure, referred to in subsec. (b), are set out in this title.

§ 1784. Contempt

(a) The court of the United States which has issued a subpoena served in a foreign country may order the person who has failed to appear or who has failed to produce a document or other thing as directed therein to show cause before it at a designated time why he should not be punished for contempt.

(b) The court, in the order to show cause, may direct that any of the person's property within the

United States be levied upon or seized, in the manner provided by law or court rules governing levy or seizure under execution, and held to satisfy any judgment that may be rendered against him pursuant to subsection (d) of this section if adequate security, in such amount as the court may direct in the order, be given for any damage that he might suffer should he not be found in contempt. Security under this subsection may not be required of the United States.

(c) A copy of the order to show cause shall be served on the person in accordance with section 1783(b) of this title.

(d) On the return day of the order to show cause or any later day to which the hearing may be continued, proof shall be taken. If the person is found in contempt, the court, notwithstanding any limitation upon its power generally to punish for contempt, may fine him not more than $100,000 and direct that the fine and costs of the proceedings be satisfied by a sale of the property levied upon or seized, conducted upon the notice required and in the manner provided for sales upon execution.

(June 25, 1948, c. 646, 62 Stat. 949; Oct. 3, 1964, Pub.L. 88–619, § 11, 78 Stat. 998.)

[§ 1785. Repealed. Pub.L. 88–619, § 12(a), Oct. 3, 1964, 78 Stat. 998]

HISTORICAL AND STATUTORY NOTES

Section, Act June 25, 1948, c. 646, 62 Stat. 950, provided a privilege against self-incrimination on examination under letters rogatory. See section 1782(a) of this title.

CHAPTER 119—EVIDENCE; WITNESSES

Sec.
1821. Per diem and mileage generally; subsistence.
1822. Competency of interested persons; share of penalties payable.
[1823. Repealed.]
1824. Mileage fees under summons as both witness and juror.
1825. Payment of fees.
1826. Recalcitrant witnesses.
1827. Interpreters in courts of the United States.
1828. Special interpretation services.

§ 1821. Per diem and mileage generally; subsistence

(a)(1) Except as otherwise provided by law, a witness in attendance at any court of the United States, or before a United States Magistrate, or before any person authorized to take his deposition pursuant to any rule or order of a court of the United States, shall be paid the fees and allowances provided by this section.

(2) As used in this section, the term "court of the United States" includes, in addition to the courts listed in section 451 of this title, any court created by Act of Congress in a territory which is invested with any jurisdiction of a district court of the United States.

(b) A witness shall be paid an attendance fee of $40 per day for each day's attendance. A witness shall also be paid the attendance fee for the time necessarily occupied in going to and returning from the place of attendance at the beginning and end of such attendance or at any time during such attendance.

(c)(1) A witness who travels by common carrier shall be paid for the actual expenses of travel on the basis of the means of transportation reasonably utilized and the distance necessarily traveled to and from such witness's residence by the shortest practical route in going to and returning from the place of attendance. Such a witness shall utilize a common carrier at the most economical rate reasonably available. A receipt or other evidence of actual cost shall be furnished.

(2) A travel allowance equal to the mileage allowance which the Administrator of General Services has prescribed, pursuant to section 5704 of title 5, for official travel of employees of the Federal Government shall be paid to each witness who travels by privately owned vehicle. Computation of mileage under this paragraph shall be made on the basis of a uniformed table of distances adopted by the Administrator of General Services.

(3) Toll charges for toll roads, bridges, tunnels, and ferries, taxicab fares between places of lodging and carrier terminals, and parking fees (upon presentation of a valid parking receipt), shall be paid in full to a witness incurring such expenses.

(4) All normal travel expenses within and outside the judicial district shall be taxable as costs pursuant to section 1920 of this title.

(d)(1) A subsistence allowance shall be paid to a witness when an overnight stay is required at the place of attendance because such place is so far removed from the residence of such witness as to prohibit return thereto from day to day.

(2) A subsistence allowance for a witness shall be paid in an amount not to exceed the maximum per diem allowance prescribed by the Administrator of General Services, pursuant to section 5702(a) of title 5, for official travel in the area of attendance by employees of the Federal Government.

(3) A subsistence allowance for a witness attending in an area designated by the Administrator of General Services as a high-cost area shall be paid in an amount not to exceed the maximum actual subsistence allowance prescribed by the Administrator, pursuant to section 5702(c)(B) of title 5, for official travel in such area by employees of the Federal Government.

(4) When a witness is detained pursuant to section 3144 of title 18 for want of security for his appearance, he shall be entitled for each day of detention when not in attendance at court, in addition to his subsistence, to the daily attendance fee provided by subsection (b) of this section.

(e) An alien who has been paroled into the United States for prosecution, pursuant to section 212(d)(5) of the Immigration and Nationality Act (8 U.S.C. 1182(d)(5)), or an alien who either has admitted belonging to a class of aliens who are deportable or has been determined pursuant to section 240 of such Act (8 U.S.C. 1252(b) [1]) to be deportable, shall be ineligible to receive the fees or allowances provided by this section.

(f) Any witness who is incarcerated at the time that his or her testimony is given (except for a witness to whom the provisions of section 3144 of title 18 apply) may not receive fees or allowances under this section, regardless of whether such a witness is incarcerated at the time he or she makes a claim for fees or allowances under this section.

(June 25, 1948, c. 646, 62 Stat. 950; May 10, 1949, c. 96, 63 Stat. 65; May 24, 1949, c. 139, § 94, 63 Stat. 103; Oct. 31, 1951, c. 655, § 51(a), 65 Stat. 727; Sept. 3, 1954, c. 1263, § 45, 68 Stat. 1242; Aug. 1, 1956, c. 826, 70 Stat. 798; Mar. 27, 1968, Pub.L. 90–274, § 102(b), 82 Stat. 62; Oct. 27, 1978, Pub.L. 95–535, § 1, 92 Stat. 2033; Dec. 1, 1990, Pub.L. 101–650, Title III, § 314(a), 104 Stat. 5115; Oct. 14, 1992, Pub.L. 102–417, § 2(a)-(c), 106 Stat. 2138; Sept. 30, 1996, Pub.L. 104–208, Div. C, Title III, § 308(g)(5)(E), 110 Stat. 3009–623.)

[1] So in original. Reference in parenthesis should probably be "(8 U.S.C. 1229a)".

HISTORICAL AND STATUTORY NOTES

References in Text

Clause (B) of section 5702(c) of title 5, referred to in subsec. (d)(3), was redesignated clause (2) by Pub.L. 96–54, § 2(a)(36), Aug. 14, 1979, 93 Stat. 383. Thereafter subsec. (c) of section 5702 of Title 5, which related to conditions under which an employee could be reimbursed for actual and necessary expenses of official travel when the maximum per diem allowance was less than these expenses, was struck out in its entirety, and subsec. (e) of that section was redesignated as subsec. (c) thereof, by Pub.L. 99–234, Title I, § 102, Jan. 2, 1986, 99 Stat. 1756. Both amendments were made without any conforming amendments to this section.

Effective Dates

1996 Acts. Amendment by section 308(g)(5)(E) of Div. C of Pub.L. 104–208, effective, with certain exceptions and subject to certain transitional rules, on the first day of the first month beginning more than 180 days after Sept. 30, 1996, see section 309 of Pub.L. 104–208, set out as a note under section 1101 of Title, Aliens and Nationality.

1992 Acts. Section 2(d) of Pub.L. 102–417 provided that: "The amendments made by this section [amending this section] shall be effective on and after the date of the enactment of this act [Oct. 14, 1992] and shall apply to any witness who testified before such date and has not received any fee or allowance under section 1821 of title 28, United States Code [this section], relating to such testimony."

1978 Acts. Section 2 of Pub.L. 95–535 provided that: "The amendments made by this Act [amending this section] shall take effect on October 1, 1978, or on the date of enactment [Oct. 27, 1978], whichever occurs later."

1968 Acts. Amendment by Pub.L. 90–274 effective 270 days after Mar. 27, 1968, except as to cases in which an indictment has been returned or a petit jury empaneled prior to such effective date, see section 104 of Pub.L. 90–274, set out as a note under section 1861 of this title.

Change of Name

United States magistrate appointed under section 631 of this title to be known as United States magistrate judge after Dec. 1, 1990, with any reference to United States magistrate or magistrate in this title, in any other Federal statute, etc., deemed a reference to United States magistrate judge appointed under section 631 of this title, see section 321 of Pub.L. 101–650, set out as a note under section 631 of this title.

Severability of Provisions

If any provision of Division C of Pub.L. 104–208 or the application of such provision to any person or circumstances is held to be unconstitutional, the remainder of Division C of Pub.L. 104–208 and the application of the provisions of Division C of Pub.L. 104–208 to any person or circumstance not to be affected thereby, see section 1(e) of Pub.L. 104–208, set out as a note under section 1101 of Title 8, Aliens and Nationality.

Payment of Fact Witness Fee to Incarcerated Person Prohibited

Pub.L. 102–395, Title I, § 108, Oct. 6, 1992, 106 Stat. 1841, provided that: "Notwithstanding 28 U.S.C. 1821 [this section], no funds appropriated to the Department of Justice in fiscal year 1993 or any prior fiscal year, or any other funds available from the Treasury of the United States, shall be obligated or expended to pay a fact witness fee to a person who is incarcerated testifying as a fact witness in a court of the United States, as defined in 28 U.S.C. 1821(a)(2) [subsec. (a)(2) of this section]."

Similar provisions were contained in the following prior appropriations Acts:

Pub.L. 102–140, Title I, § 110, Oct. 28, 1991, 105 Stat. 795.

Pub.L. 102–27, Title II, § 102, Apr. 10, 1991, 105 Stat. 136.

§ 1822. Competency of interested persons; share of penalties payable

Any person interested in a share of any fine, penalty or forfeiture incurred under any Act of Congress, may be examined as a witness in any proceeding for the recovery of such fine, penalty or forfeiture by any party thereto. Such examination shall not deprive the witness of his share.

(June 25, 1948, c. 646, 62 Stat. 950.)

[§ 1823. Repealed. Pub.L. 91–563, § 5(a), Dec. 19, 1970, 84 Stat. 1478]

HISTORICAL AND STATUTORY NOTES

Section, Acts June 25, 1948, c. 646, 62 Stat. 950; May 24, 1949, c. 139, § 95, 63 Stat. 103; Oct. 5, 1949, c. 601, 63 Stat. 704; July 7, 1952, c. 581, 66 Stat. 439; July 28, 1955, c. 424, § 3, 69 Stat. 394, related to payment of witness fees to officers and employees of the United States, and is now covered by sections 5515, 5537, 5751, and 6322 of Title 5, Government Organization and Employees.

§ 1824. Mileage fees under summons as both witness and juror

No constructive or double mileage fees shall be allowed by reason of any person being summoned both as a witness and a juror.

(June 25, 1948, c. 646, 62 Stat. 951.)

§ 1825. Payment of fees

(a) In any case in which the United States or an officer or agency of the United States is a party, the United States marshal for the district shall pay all fees of witnesses on the certificate of the United States attorney or assistant United States attorney, and in the proceedings before a United States magistrate, on the certificate of such magistrate, except that any fees of defense witnesses, other than experts, appearing pursuant to subpoenas issued upon approval of the court, shall be paid by the United States marshal for the district—

(1) on the certificate of a Federal public defender or assistant Federal public defender, in a criminal case in which the defendant is represented by such Federal public defender or assistant Federal public defender, and

(2) on the certificate of the clerk of the court upon the affidavit of such witnesses' attendance given by other counsel appointed pursuant to section 3006A of title 18, in a criminal case in which a defendant is represented by such other counsel.

(b) In proceedings in forma pauperis for a writ of habeas corpus, and in proceedings in forma pauperis under section 2255 of this title, the United States marshal for the district shall pay, on the certificate of the district judge, all fees of witnesses for the party authorized to proceed in forma pauperis, except that any fees of witnesses for such party, other than experts, appearing pursuant to subpoenas issued upon approval of the court, shall be paid by the United States marshal for the district—

(1) on the certificate of a Federal public defender or assistant Federal public defender, in any such proceedings in which a party is represented by such Federal public defender or assistant Federal public defender, and

(2) on the certificate of the clerk of the court upon the affidavit of such witnesses' attendance given by other counsel appointed pursuant to section 3006A of title 18, in any such proceedings in which a party is represented by such other counsel.

(c) Fees and mileage need not be tendered to a witness upon service of a subpoena issued on behalf of the United States or an officer or agency of the United States, upon service of a subpoena issued on behalf of a defendant represented by a Federal public defender, assistant Federal public defender, or other attorney appointed pursuant to section 3006A of title 18, or upon service of a subpoena issued on behalf of a party authorized to proceed in forma pauperis, if the payment of such fees and mileage is to be made by the United States marshal under this section.

(June 25, 1948, c. 646, 62 Stat. 951; Sept. 2, 1965, Pub.L. 89–162, 79 Stat. 618; Nov. 14, 1986, Pub.L. 99–651, Title I, § 104, 100 Stat. 3645.)

HISTORICAL AND STATUTORY NOTES

Effective Dates

1986 Acts. Amendment to this section by section 104 of Pub.L. 99–651 to take effect one hundred and twenty days after Nov. 14, 1986, see section 105 of Pub.L. 99–651, set out as a note under section 3006A of Title 18, Crimes and Criminal Procedure.

Change of Name

United States magistrate appointed under section 631 of this title to be known as United States magistrate judge after Dec. 1, 1990, with any reference to United States magistrate or magistrate in this title, in any other Federal statute, etc., deemed a reference to United States magistrate judge appointed under section 631 of this title, see section 321 of Pub.L. 101–650, set out as a note under section 631 of this title.

§ 1826. Recalcitrant witnesses

(a) Whenever a witness in any proceeding before or ancillary to any court or grand jury of the United States refuses without just cause shown to comply with an order of the court to testify or provide other information, including any book, paper, document, record, recording or other material, the court, upon such refusal, or when such refusal is duly brought to its attention, may summarily order his confinement at a suitable place until such time as the witness is willing to give such testimony or provide such information. No period of such confinement shall exceed the life of—

(1) the court proceeding, or

(2) the term of the grand jury, including extensions,

before which such refusal to comply with the court order occurred, but in no event shall such confinement exceed eighteen months.

(b) No person confined pursuant to subsection (a) of this section shall be admitted to bail pending the determination of an appeal taken by him from the order for his confinement if it appears that the appeal is frivolous or taken for delay. Any appeal from an order of confinement under this section shall be disposed of as soon as practicable, but not later than thirty days from the filing of such appeal.

(c) Whoever escapes or attempts to escape from the custody of any facility or from any place in which or to which he is confined pursuant to this section or section 4243 of title 18, or whoever rescues or attempts to rescue or instigates, aids, or assists the escape or attempt to escape of such a person, shall be subject to imprisonment for not more than three years, or a fine of not more than $10,000, or both.

(Added Pub.L. 91–452, Title III, § 301(a), Oct. 15, 1970, 84 Stat. 932, and amended Pub.L. 98–473, Title II, § 1013, Oct. 12, 1984, 98 Stat. 2142.)

§ 1827. Interpreters in courts of the United States

(a) The Director of the Administrative Office of the United States Courts shall establish a program to facilitate the use of certified and otherwise qualified interpreters in judicial proceedings instituted by the United States.

(b)(1) The Director shall prescribe, determine, and certify the qualifications of persons who may serve as certified interpreters, when the Director considers certification of interpreters to be merited, for the hearing impaired (whether or not also speech impaired) and persons who speak only or primarily a language other than the English language, in judicial proceedings instituted by the United States. The Director may certify interpreters for any language if the Director determines that there is a need for certified interpreters in that language. Upon the request of the Judicial Conference of the United States for certified interpreters in a language, the Director shall certify interpreters in that language. Upon such a request from the judicial council of a circuit and the approval of the Judicial Conference, the Director shall certify interpreters for that circuit in the language requested. The judicial council of a circuit shall identify and evaluate the needs of the districts within a circuit. The Director shall certify interpreters based on the results of criterion-referenced performance examinations. The Director shall issue regulations to carry out this paragraph within 1 year after the date of the enactment of the Judicial Improvements and Access to Justice Act.

(2) Only in a case in which no certified interpreter is reasonably available as provided in subsection (d) of this section, including a case in which certification of interpreters is not provided under paragraph (1) in a particular language, may the services of otherwise qualified interpreters be used. The Director shall provide guidelines to the courts for the selection of otherwise qualified interpreters, in order to ensure that the highest standards of accuracy are maintained in all judicial proceedings subject to the provisions of this chapter.

(3) The Director shall maintain a current master list of all certified interpreters and otherwise qualified interpreters and shall report periodically on the use and performance of both certified and otherwise qualified interpreters in judicial proceedings instituted by the United States and on the languages for which interpreters have been certified. The Director shall prescribe, subject to periodic review, a schedule of reasonable fees for services rendered by interpreters, certified or otherwise, used in proceedings instituted by the United States, and in doing so shall consider the prevailing rate of compensation for comparable service in other governmental entities.

(c)(1) Each United States district court shall maintain on file in the office of the clerk, and each United States attorney shall maintain on file, a list of all persons who have been certified as interpreters by the Director in accordance with subsection (b) of this section. The clerk shall make the list of certified interpreters for judicial proceeding available upon request.

(2) The clerk of the court, or other court employee designated by the chief judge, shall be responsible for securing the services of certified interpreters and otherwise qualified interpreters required for proceedings initiated by the United States, except that the United States attorney is responsible for securing the services of such interpreters for governmental witnesses.

(d)(1) The presiding judicial officer, with the assistance of the Director of the Administrative Office of the United States Courts, shall utilize the services of the most available certified interpreter, or when no certified interpreter is reasonably available, as determined by the presiding judicial officer, the services of an otherwise qualified interpreter, in judicial proceedings instituted by the United States, if the presiding judicial officer determines on such officer's own motion or on the motion of a party that such party (including a defendant in a criminal case), or a witness who may present testimony in such judicial proceedings—

(A) speaks only or primarily a language other than the English language; or

(B) suffers from a hearing impairment (whether or not suffering also from a speech impairment)

so as to inhibit such party's comprehension of the proceedings or communication with counsel or the presiding judicial officer, or so as to inhibit such witness' comprehension of questions and the presentation of such testimony.

(2) Upon the motion of a party, the presiding judicial officer shall determine whether to require the electronic sound recording of a judicial proceeding in which an interpreter is used under this section. In making this determination, the presiding judicial officer shall consider, among other things, the qualifications of the interpreter and prior experience in interpretation of court proceedings; whether the language to be interpreted is not one of the languages for which the Director has certified interpreters, and the complexity or length of the proceeding. In a grand jury proceeding, upon the motion of the accused, the presiding judicial officer shall require the electronic sound recording of the portion of the proceeding in which an interpreter is used.

(e)(1) If any interpreter is unable to communicate effectively with the presiding judicial officer, the United States attorney, a party (including a defendant in a criminal case), or a witness, the presiding judicial officer shall dismiss such interpreter and obtain the services of another interpreter in accordance with this section.

(2) In any judicial proceedings instituted by the United States, if the presiding judicial officer does not appoint an interpreter under subsection (d) of this section, an individual requiring the services of an interpreter may seek assistance of the clerk of court or the Director of the Administrative Office of the United States Courts in obtaining the assistance of a certified interpreter.

(f)(1) Any individual other than a witness who is entitled to interpretation under subsection (d) of this section may waive such interpretation in whole or in part. Such a waiver shall be effective only if approved by the presiding judicial officer and made expressly by such individual on the record after opportunity to consult with counsel and after the presiding judicial officer has explained to such individual, utilizing the services of the most available certified interpreter, or when no certified interpreter is reasonably available, as determined by the presiding judicial officer, the services of an otherwise competent interpreter, the nature and effect of the waiver.

(2) An individual who waives under paragraph (1) of this subsection the right to an interpreter may utilize the services of a noncertified interpreter of such individual's choice whose fees, expenses, and costs shall be paid in the manner provided for the payment of such fees, expenses, and costs of an interpreter appointed under subsection (d) of this section.

(g)(1) There are authorized to be appropriated to the Federal judiciary, and to be paid by the Director of the Administrative Office of the United States Courts, such sums as may be necessary to establish a program to facilitate the use of certified and otherwise qualified interpreters, and otherwise fulfill the provisions of this section and the Judicial Improvements and Access to Justice Act, except as provided in paragraph (3).

(2) Implementation of the provisions of this section is contingent upon the availability of appropriated funds to carry out the purposes of this section.

(3) Such salaries, fees, expenses, and costs that are incurred with respect to Government witnesses (including for grand jury proceedings) shall, unless direction is made under paragraph (4), be paid by the Attorney General from sums appropriated to the Department of Justice.

(4) Upon the request of any person in any action for which interpreting services established pursuant to subsection (d) are not otherwise provided, the clerk of the court, or other court employee designated by the chief judge, upon the request of the presiding judicial officer, shall, where possible, make such services available to that person on a cost-reimbursable basis, but the judicial officer may also require the prepayment of the estimated expenses of providing such services.

(5) If the Director of the Administrative Office of the United States Courts finds it necessary to develop and administer criterion-referenced performance examinations for purposes of certification, or other examinations for the selection of otherwise qualified interpreters, the Director may prescribe for each examination a uniform fee for applicants to take such examination. In determining the rate of the fee for each examination, the Director shall consider the fees charged by other organizations for examinations that are similar in scope or nature. Notwithstanding section 3302(b) of title 31, the Director is authorized to provide in any contract or agreement for the development or administration of examinations and the collection of fees that the contractor may retain all or a portion of the fees in payment for the services. Notwithstanding paragraph (6) of this subsection, all fees collected after the effective date of this paragraph and not retained by a contractor shall be deposited in the fund established under section 1931 of this title and shall remain available until expended.

(6) Any moneys collected under this subsection may be used to reimburse the appropriations obligated and disbursed in payment for such services.

(h) The presiding judicial officer shall approve the compensation and expenses payable to interpreters, pursuant to the schedule of fees prescribed by the Director under subsection (b)(3).

(i) The term "presiding judicial officer" as used in this section refers to any judge of a United States district court, including a bankruptcy judge, a United States magistrate, and in the case of grand jury proceedings conducted under the auspices of the United States attorney, a United States attorney.

(j) The term "judicial proceedings instituted by the United States" as used in this section refers to all proceedings, whether criminal or civil, including pretrial and grand jury proceedings (as well as proceedings upon a petition for a writ of habeas corpus initiated in the name of the United States by a relator) conducted in, or pursuant to the lawful authority and jurisdiction of a United States district court. The term "United States district court" as used in this subsection includes any court which is created by an Act of Congress in a territory and is invested with any jurisdiction of a district court established by chapter 5 of this title.

(k) The interpretation provided by certified or otherwise qualified interpreters pursuant to this section shall be in the simultaneous mode for any party to a judicial proceeding instituted by the United States and in the consecutive mode for witnesses, except that the presiding judicial officer, sua sponte or on the motion of a party, may authorize a simultaneous, or consecutive interpretation when such officer determines after a hearing on the record that such interpretation will aid in the efficient administration of justice. The presiding judicial officer, on such officer's motion or on the motion of a party, may order that special interpretation services as authorized in section 1828 of this title be provided if such officer determines that the provision of such services will aid in the efficient administration of justice.

(*l*) Notwithstanding any other provision of this section or section 1828, the presiding judicial officer may appoint a certified or otherwise qualified sign language interpreter to provide services to a party, witness, or other participant in a judicial proceeding, whether or not the proceeding is instituted by the United States, if the presiding judicial officer determines, on such officer's own motion or on the motion of a party or other participant in the proceeding, that such individual suffers from a hearing impairment. The presiding judicial officer shall, subject to the availability of appropriated funds, approve the compensation and expenses payable to sign language interpreters appointed under this section in accordance with the schedule of fees prescribed by the Director under subsection (b)(3) of this section.

(Added Pub.L. 95–539, § 2(a), Oct. 28, 1978, 92 Stat. 2040, and amended Pub.L. 100–702, Title VII, §§ 702–710, Nov. 19, 1988, 102 Stat. 4654–4657; Pub.L. 104–317, Title III, § 306, Title IV, § 402(a), Oct. 19, 1996, 110 Stat. 3852, 3854.)

HISTORICAL AND STATUTORY NOTES

References in Text

The date of the enactment of the Judicial Improvements and Access to Justice Act, referred to in subsec. (b)(1), is the date of enactment of Pub.L. 100–702, which was approved Nov. 19, 1988.

The Judicial Improvements and Access to Justice Act, referred to in subsec. (g)(1), is Pub.L. 100–702, Nov. 19, 1988, 102 Stat. 4642. For complete classification of this Act to the Code, see Short Title note set out under section 1 of this title and Tables.

The effective date of this paragraph, referred to in subsec. (g)(5), probably means the date of enactment of Pub.L. 104–317, which was approved Oct. 19, 1996.

Effective Dates

1988 Acts. Section 712 of Title VII of Pub.L. 100–702 provided that: "This title [amending subsecs. (a) to (e) and (g) to (k) of this section and enacting provisions set out as notes under this section and section 1 of this title] shall become effective upon the date of enactment [Nov. 19, 1988]."

1978 Acts. Section effective 90 days after Oct. 28, 1978, see section 10(b) of Pub.L. 95–539, set out as a note under section 602 of this title.

Change of Name

United States magistrate appointed under section 631 of this title to be known as United States magistrate judge after Dec. 1, 1990, with any reference to United States magistrate or magistrate in this title, in any other Federal statute, etc., deemed a reference to United States magistrate judge appointed under section 631 of this title, see section 321 of Pub.L. 101–650, set out as a note under section 631 of this title.

Short Title

1978 Acts. For Short title of Pub.L. 95–539 as "Court Interpreters Act", see section 1 of Pub.L. 95–539, set out as a note under section 1 of this title.

Impact on Existing Programs

Section 711 of Title VII of Pub.L. 100–702 provided that: "Nothing in this title [amending subsecs. (a) to (e) and (g) to (k) of this section and enacting provisions set out as notes under this section and section 1 of this title] shall be construed to terminate or diminish existing programs for the certification of interpreters."

Payment for Contractual Services

Section 402(b) of Pub.L. 104–317 provided that: "Notwithstanding sections 3302(b), 1341, and 1517 of title 31, United States Code [sections 3302(b), 1341, and 1517 of Title 31, Money and Finance], the Director of the Administrative Office of the United States Courts may include in any contract for the development or administration of examinations for interpreters (including such a contract entered into before the date of the enactment of this Act [Oct. 19, 1996]) a provision which permits the contractor to collect and retain fees in payment for contractual services in accordance with section 1827(g)(5) of title 28, United States Code [subsec. (g)(5) of this section]."

§ 1828. Special interpretation services

(a) The Director of the Administrative Office of the United States Courts shall establish a program for the provision of special interpretation services in criminal actions and in civil actions initiated by the United States (including petitions for writs of habeas corpus initiated in the name of the United States by relators) in a United States district court. The program shall provide a capacity for simultaneous interpretation services in multidefendant criminal actions and multidefendant civil actions.

(b) Upon the request of any person in any action for which special interpretation services established pursuant to subsection (a) are not otherwise provided, the Director, with the approval of the presiding judicial officer, may make such services available to the person requesting the services on a reimbursable basis at rates established in conformity with section 9701 of title 31, but the Director may require the prepayment of the estimated expenses of providing the services by the person requesting them.

(c) Except as otherwise provided in this subsection, the expenses incident to providing services under subsection (a) of this section shall be paid by the Director from sums appropriated to the Federal judiciary. A presiding judicial officer, in such officer's discretion, may order that all or part of the expenses shall be apportioned between or among the parties or shall be taxed as costs in a civil action, and any moneys collected as a result of such order may be used to reimburse the appropriations obligated and disbursed in payment for such services.

(d) Appropriations available to the Director shall be available to provide services in accordance with subsection (b) of this section, and moneys collected by the Director under that subsection may be used to reimburse the appropriations charged for such services. A presiding judicial officer, in such officer's discretion, may order that all or part of the expenses shall be apportioned between or among the parties or shall be taxed as costs in the action.

(Added Pub.L. 95–539, § 2(a), Oct. 28, 1978, 92 Stat. 2042, and amended Pub.L. 97–258, § 3(g), Sept. 13, 1982, 96 Stat. 1065.)

HISTORICAL AND STATUTORY NOTES

Effective Dates

1978 Acts. Section effective 90 days after Oct. 28, 1978, see section 10(b) of Pub.L. 95–539, set out as a note under section 602 of this title.

CHAPTER 121—JURIES; TRIAL BY JURY

Sec.

1861. Declaration of policy.
1862. Discrimination prohibited.
1863. Plan for random jury selection.
1864. Drawing of names from the master jury wheel; completion of juror qualification form.
1865. Qualifications for jury service.
1866. Selection and summoning of jury panels.
1867. Challenging compliance with selection procedures.
1868. Maintenance and inspection of records.
1869. Definitions.
1870. Challenges.
1871. Fees.
1872. Issues of fact in Supreme Court.
1873. Admiralty and maritime cases.
1874. Actions on bonds and specialties.
1875. Protection of jurors' employment.
1876. Trial by jury in the Court of International Trade.
1877. Protection of jurors.
1878. Optional use of a one-step summoning and qualification procedure.

§ 1861. Declaration of policy

It is the policy of the United States that all litigants in Federal courts entitled to trial by jury shall have the right to grand and petit juries selected at random from a fair cross section of the community in the district or division wherein the court convenes. It is further the policy of the United States that all citizens shall have the opportunity to be considered for service on grand and petit juries in the district courts of the United States, and shall have an obligation to serve as jurors when summoned for that purpose.

(June 25, 1948, c. 646, 62 Stat. 951; Sept. 9, 1957, Pub.L. 85–315, Part V, § 152, 71 Stat. 638; Mar. 27, 1968, Pub.L. 90–274, § 101, 82 Stat. 54.)

HISTORICAL AND STATUTORY NOTES

Effective Dates

1968 Acts. Section 104 of Pub.L. 90–274 provided that: "This Act [amending this section and sections 1821, 1862–1869, and 1871 of this title, repealing section 867 of Title 48, Territories and Insular Possessions, and enacting provisions set out as notes under this section] shall become effective two hundred and seventy days after the date of enactment [Mar. 27, 1968]: *Provided* That this Act shall not apply in any case in which an indictment has been returned or petit jury empaneled prior to such effective date."

Short Title

1978 Acts. Pub.L. 95–572, § 1, Nov. 2, 1978, 92 Stat. 2453, provided that: "This Act [which enacted sections 1363 and 1875 of this title, renumbered as section 1364 prior section 1363 of this title, amended sections 1863, 1865, 1866, 1869, and 1871 of this title, and enacted provisions set out as a note under section 1363 of this title] may be cited as the 'Jury System Improvements Act of 1978'."

1968 Acts. Section 1 of Pub.L. 90–274 provided: "That this Act [amending this section and sections 1821, 1862–1869, and 1871 of this title, repealing section 867 of Title 48, Territories and Insular Possessions, and enacting material set out as notes under this section] may be cited as the 'Jury Selection and Service Act of 1968'."

§ 1862. Discrimination prohibited

No citizen shall be excluded from service as a grand or petit juror in the district courts of the United States or in the Court of International Trade on account of race, color, religion, sex, national origin, or economic status.

(June 25, 1948, c. 646, 62 Stat. 952; Mar. 27, 1968, Pub.L. 90–274, § 101, 82 Stat. 54; Oct. 10, 1980, Pub.L. 96–417, Title III, § 302(c), 94 Stat. 1739.)

HISTORICAL AND STATUTORY NOTES

Effective Dates

1980 Acts. Amendment by Pub.L. 96–417 effective on Nov. 1, 1980 and applicable with respect to civil actions pending on or commenced on or after such date, see section 701(a) of Pub.L. 96–417, as amended, set out as a note under section 251 of this title.

1968 Acts. Amendment by Pub.L. 90–274 effective 270 days after Mar. 27, 1968, except as to cases in which an indictment has been returned or a petit jury empaneled prior to such effective date, see section 104 of Pub.L. 90–274, set out as a note under section 1861 of this title.

§ 1863. Plan for random jury selection

(a) Each United States district court shall devise and place into operation a written plan for random selection of grand and petit jurors that shall be designed to achieve the objectives of sections 1861 and 1862 of this title, and that shall otherwise comply with the provisions of this title. The plan shall be placed into operation after approval by a reviewing panel consisting of the members of the judicial council of the circuit and either the chief judge of the district whose plan is being reviewed or such other active district judge of that district as the chief judge of the district may designate. The panel shall examine the plan to ascertain that it complies with the provisions of this title. If the reviewing panel finds that the plan does not comply, the panel shall state the particulars in which the plan fails to comply and direct the district court to present within a reasonable time an alternative plan remedying the defect or defects. Separate plans may be adopted for each division or combination of divisions within a judicial district. The district court may modify a plan at any time and it shall modify the plan when so directed by the reviewing panel. The district court shall promptly notify the panel, the Administrative Office of the United States Courts, and the Attorney General of the United States, of the initial adoption and future modifications of the plan by filing copies therewith. Modifications of the plan made at the instance of the district court shall become effective after approval by the panel. Each district court shall submit a report on the jury selection process within its jurisdiction to the Administrative Office of the United States Courts in such form and at such times as the Judicial Conference of the United States may specify. The Judicial Conference of the United States may, from time to time, adopt rules and regulations governing the provisions and the operation of the plans formulated under this title.

(b) Among other things, such plan shall—

(1) either establish a jury commission, or authorize the clerk of the court, to manage the jury selection process. If the plan establishes a jury commission, the district court shall appoint one citizen to serve with the clerk of the court as the jury commission: *Provided, however*, That the plan for the District of Columbia may establish a jury commission consisting of three citizens. The citizen jury commissioner shall not belong to the same political party as the clerk serving with him. The clerk or the jury commission, as the case may be, shall act under the supervision and control of the chief judge of the district court or such other judge of the district court as the plan may provide. Each jury commissioner shall, during his tenure in office, reside in the judicial district or division for which he is appointed. Each citizen jury commissioner shall receive compensation to be fixed by the district court plan at a rate not to exceed $50 per day for each day necessarily employed in the performance of his duties, plus reimbursement for travel, subsistence, and other necessary expenses incurred by him in the performance of such duties. The Judicial Conference of the United States may establish standards for allowance of travel, subsistence, and other necessary expenses incurred by jury commissioners.

(2) specify whether the names of prospective jurors shall be selected from the voter registration lists or the lists of actual voters of the political subdivisions within the district or division. The plan shall prescribe some other source or sources of names in addition to voter lists where necessary to foster the policy and protect the rights secured by sections 1861 and 1862 of this title. The plan for the District of Columbia may require the names of prospective jurors to be selected from the city directory rather than from voter lists. The plans for the districts of Puerto Rico and the Canal Zone may prescribe some other source or sources of names of prospective jurors in lieu of voter lists, the use of which shall be consistent with the policies declared and rights secured by sections 1861 and 1862 of this title. The plan for the district of Massachusetts may require the names of prospective jurors to be selected from the resident list provided for in chapter 234A, Massachusetts General Laws, or comparable authority, rather than from voter lists.

(3) specify detailed procedures to be followed by the jury commission or clerk in selecting names from the sources specified in paragraph (2) of this subsection. These procedures shall be designed to ensure the random selection of a fair cross section of the persons residing in the community in the district or division wherein the court convenes. They shall ensure that names of persons residing in each of the counties, parishes, or similar political subdivisions within the judicial district or division are placed in a master jury wheel; and shall ensure that each county, parish, or similar political subdivision within the district or division is substantially proportionally represented in the master jury wheel for that judicial district, division, or combination of divisions. For the purposes of determining proportional representation in the master jury wheel, either the number of actual voters at the last general election in each county, parish, or similar political subdivision, or the number of registered voters if registration of voters is uniformly required throughout the district or division, may be used.

(4) provide for a master jury wheel (or a device similar in purpose and function) into which the names of those randomly selected shall be placed. The plan shall fix a minimum number of names to be placed initially in the master jury wheel, which shall be at least one-half of 1 per centum of the total number of persons on the lists used as a source of names for the district or division; but if this number of names is believed to be cumbersome and unnecessary, the plan may fix a smaller number of names to be placed in the master wheel, but in no event less than one thousand. The chief judge of the district court, or such other district court judge as the plan may provide, may order additional names to be placed in the master jury wheel from time to time as necessary. The plan shall provide for periodic emptying and refilling of the master jury wheel at specified times, the interval for which shall not exceed four years.

(5)(A) except as provided in subparagraph (B), specify those groups of persons or occupational classes whose members shall, on individual request therefor, be excused from jury service. Such groups or classes shall be excused only if the district court finds, and the plan states, that jury service by such class or group would entail undue hardship or extreme inconvenience to the members thereof, and excuse of members thereof would not be inconsistent with sections 1861 and 1862 of this title.

(B) specify that volunteer safety personnel, upon individual request, shall be excused from jury service. For purposes of this subparagraph, the term "volunteer safety personnel" means individuals serving a public agency (as defined in section 1203(6) of title I of the Omnibus Crime Control and Safe Streets Act of 1968) in an official capacity, without compensation, as firefighters or members of a rescue squad or ambulance crew.

(6) specify that the following persons are barred from jury service on the ground that they are exempt: (A) members in active service in the Armed Forces of the United States; (B) members of the fire or police departments of any State, the District of Columbia, any territory or possession of the United States, or any subdivision of a State, the District of Columbia, or such territory or possession; (C) public officers in the executive, legislative, or judicial branches of the Government of the United States, or of any State, the District of Columbia, any territory or possession of the United States, or any subdivision of a State, the District of Columbia, or such territory or possession, who are actively engaged in the performance of official duties.

(7) fix the time when the names drawn from the qualified jury wheel shall be disclosed to parties and to the public. If the plan permits these names to be made public, it may nevertheless permit the chief judge of the district court, or such other district court judge as the plan may provide, to keep these names confidential in any case where the interests of justice so require.

(8) specify the procedures to be followed by the clerk or jury commission in assigning persons whose names have been drawn from the qualified jury wheel to grand and petit jury panels.

(c) The initial plan shall be devised by each district court and transmitted to the reviewing panel specified in subsection (a) of this section within one hundred and twenty days of the date of enactment of the Jury Selection and Service Act of 1968. The panel shall approve or direct the modification of each plan so submitted within sixty days thereafter. Each plan or modification made at the direction of the panel shall become effective after approval at such time thereafter as the panel directs, in no event to exceed ninety days from the date of approval. Modifications made at the instance of the district court under subsection (a) of this section shall be effective at such time thereafter as the panel directs, in no event to exceed ninety days from the date of modification.

(d) State, local, and Federal officials having custody, possession, or control of voter registration lists, lists of actual voters, or other appropriate records shall make such lists and records available to the jury commission or clerks for inspection, reproduction, and copying at all reasonable times as the commission or clerk may deem necessary and proper for the performance of duties under this title. The district courts shall have jurisdiction upon application by the Attorney General of the United States to compel compliance with this subsection by appropriate process.

(June 25, 1948, c. 646, 62 Stat. 952; Mar. 27, 1968, Pub.L. 90–274, § 101, 82 Stat. 54; Apr. 6, 1972, Pub.L. 92–269, § 2, 86 Stat. 117; Nov. 2, 1978, Pub.L. 95–572, § 2(a), 92 Stat. 2453; Nov. 19, 1988, Pub.L. 100–702, Title VIII, § 802(b), (c), 102 Stat. 4657, 4658; Oct. 29, 1992, Pub.L. 102–572, Title IV, § 401, 106 Stat. 4511.)

HISTORICAL AND STATUTORY NOTES

References in Text

Section 1203(6) of title I of the Omnibus Crime Control and Safe Streets Act of 1968, referred to in subsec. (b)(5)(B), is section 1203(6) of Pub.L. 90–351, Title I, as added Pub.L. 96–157, § 2, Dec. 27, 1979, 93 Stat. 1220, which is classified to section 3796b(6) of Title 42, The Public Health and Welfare.

The date of enactment of the Jury Selection and Service Act of 1968, referred to in subsec. (c), is the date of enactment of Pub.L. 90–274, which was approved on Mar. 27, 1968.

Effective Dates

1992 Acts. Amendment by Pub.L. 102–572 effective Jan. 1, 1993, see section 1101(a) of Pub.L. 102–572, set out as a note under section 905 of Title 2, The Congress.

1978 Acts. Amendment by Pub.L. 95–572 applicable with respect to any grand or petit juror summoned for service or actually serving on or after Nov. 2, 1978, see section 7(a) of Pub.L. 95–572, set out as a note under section 1363 of this title.

1968 Acts. Amendment by Pub.L. 90–274 effective 270 days after Mar. 27, 1968, except as to cases in which an indictment has been returned or a petit jury empaneled prior to such effective date, see section 104 of Pub.L. 90–274, set out as a note under section 1861 of this title.

Refilling of Master Jury Wheel Not Later Than September 1, 1973; Refilling of Qualified Jury Wheel Not Later Than October 1, 1973; Retroactive Effect

Sections 3 and 4 of Pub.L. 92–269 provided that:

"**Sec. 3.** **(a)** Each judicial district and each division or combination of divisions within a judicial district, for which a separate plan for random selection of jurors has been adopted pursuant to section 1863 of title 28, United States Code [this section], other than the District of Columbia and the districts of Puerto Rico and the Canal Zone, shall not later than September 1, 1973, refill its master jury wheel with names obtained from the voter registration lists for, or the lists of actual voters in, the 1972 general election.

"**(b)** The District of Columbia and the judicial districts of Puerto Rico and the Canal Zone shall not later than September 1, 1973, refill their master jury wheels from sources which include the names of persons eighteen years of age or older.

"**(c)** The qualified jury wheel in each judicial district, and in each division or combination of divisions in a judicial district for which a separate plan for random selection of jurors has been adopted, shall be refilled from the master jury wheel not later than October 1, 1973.

"**Sec. 4.** **(a)** Nothing in this Act [amending this section and section 1865 of this title] shall affect the composition of any master jury wheel or qualified jury wheel prior to the date on which it is first refilled in compliance with the terms of section 3.

"**(b)** Nothing in this Act shall affect the composition or preclude the service of any jury empaneled on or before the date on which the qualified jury wheel from which the jurors' names were drawn is refilled in compliance with the provisions of section 3."

§ 1864. Drawing of names from the master jury wheel; completion of juror qualification form

(a) From time to time as directed by the district court, the clerk or a district judge shall publicly draw at random from the master jury wheel the names of as many persons as may be required for jury service. The clerk or jury commission may, upon order of the court, prepare an alphabetical list of the names drawn from the master jury wheel. Any list so prepared shall not be disclosed to any person except pursuant to the district court plan or pursuant to section 1867 or 1868 of this title. The clerk or jury commission shall mail to every person whose name is drawn from the master wheel a juror qualification form accompanied by instructions to fill out and return the form, duly signed and sworn, to the clerk or jury commission by mail within ten days. If the person is unable to fill out the form, another shall do it for him, and shall indicate that he has done so and the reason therefor. In any case in which it appears that there is an omission, ambiguity, or error in a form, the clerk or jury commission shall return the form with instructions to the person to make such additions or corrections as may be necessary and to return the form to the clerk or jury commission within ten days. Any person who fails to return a completed juror qualification form as instructed may be summoned by the clerk or jury commission forthwith to appear before the clerk or jury commission to fill out a juror qualification form. A person summoned to appear because of failure to return a juror qualification form as instructed who personally appears and executes a juror qualification form before the clerk or jury commission may, at the discretion of the district court, except where his prior failure to execute and mail such form was willful, be entitled to receive for such appearance the same fees and travel allowances paid to jurors under section 1871 of this title. At the time of his appearance for jury service, any person may be required to fill out another juror qualification form in the presence of the jury commission or the clerk or the court, at which time, in such cases as it appears warranted, the person may be questioned, but only with regard to his responses to questions contained on the form. Any information thus acquired by the clerk or jury commission may be noted on the juror qualification form and transmitted to the chief judge or such district court judge as the plan may provide.

(b) Any person summoned pursuant to subsection (a) of this section who fails to appear as directed shall be ordered by the district court forthwith to appear and show cause for his failure to comply with the summons. Any person who fails to appear pursuant to such order or who fails to show good cause for noncompliance with the summons may be fined not more than $100 or imprisoned not more than three days, or both. Any person who willfully misrepresents a material fact on a juror qualification form for the purpose of avoiding or securing service as a juror may be fined not more than $100 or imprisoned not more than three days, or both.

(June 25, 1948, c. 646, 62 Stat. 952; Mar. 27, 1968, Pub.L. 90–274, § 101, 82 Stat. 57; Nov. 19, 1988, Pub.L. 100–702, Title VIII, § 803(a), 102 Stat. 4658.)

HISTORICAL AND STATUTORY NOTES

Effective Dates

1968 Acts. Amendment by Pub.L. 90–274 effective 270 days after Mar. 27, 1968, except as to cases in which an indictment has been returned or a petit jury empaneled prior to such effective date, see section 104 of Pub.L. 90–274, set out as a note under section 1861 of this title.

§ 1865. Qualifications for jury service

(a) The chief judge of the district court, or such other district court judge as the plan may provide, on his initiative or upon recommendation of the clerk or jury commission, shall determine solely on the basis of information provided on the juror qualification form and other competent evidence whether a person is unqualified for, or exempt, or to be excused from jury service. The clerk shall enter such determination in the space provided on the juror qualification form and in any alphabetical list of names drawn from the master jury wheel. If a person did not appear in response to a summons, such fact shall be noted on said list.

(b) In making such determination the chief judge of the district court, or such other district court judge as the plan may provide, shall deem any person qualified to serve on grand and petit juries in the district court unless he—

(1) is not a citizen of the United States eighteen years old who has resided for a period of one year within the judicial district;

(2) is unable to read, write, and understand the English language with a degree of proficiency sufficient to fill out satisfactorily the juror qualification form;

(3) is unable to speak the English language;

(4) is incapable, by reason of mental or physical infirmity, to render satisfactory jury service; or

(5) has a charge pending against him for the commission of, or has been convicted in a State or Federal court of record of, a crime punishable by imprisonment for more than one year and his civil rights have not been restored.

(June 25, 1948, c. 646, 62 Stat. 952; Mar. 27, 1968, Pub.L. 90–274, § 101, 82 Stat. 58; Apr. 6, 1972, Pub.L. 92–269, § 1, 86 Stat. 117; Nov. 2, 1978, Pub.L. 95–572, § 3(a), 92 Stat. 2453; Nov. 19, 1988, Pub.L. 100–702, Title VIII, § 803(b), 102 Stat. 4658.)

HISTORICAL AND STATUTORY NOTES

Effective Dates

1978 Acts. Amendment by Pub.L. 95–572 applicable with respect to any grand or petit juror summoned for service or actually serving on or after Nov. 2, 1978, see section 7(a) of Pub.L. 95–572, set out as a note under section 1363 of this title.

1968 Acts. Amendment by Pub.L. 90–274 effective 270 days after Mar. 27, 1968, except as to cases in which an indictment has been returned or a petit jury empaneled prior to such effective date, see section 104 of Pub.L. 90–274, set out as a note under section 1861 of this title.

§ 1866. Selection and summoning of jury panels

(a) The jury commission, or in the absence thereof the clerk, shall maintain a qualified jury wheel and shall place in such wheel names of all persons drawn from the master jury wheel who are determined to be qualified as jurors and not exempt or excused pursuant to the district court plan. From time to time, the jury commission or the clerk shall publicly draw at random from the qualified jury wheel such number of names of persons as may be required for assignment to grand and petit jury panels. The jury commission or the clerk shall prepare a separate list of names of persons assigned to each grand and petit jury panel.

(b) When the court orders a grand or petit jury to be drawn, the clerk or jury commission or their duly designated deputies shall issue summonses for the required number of jurors.

Each person drawn for jury service may be served personally, or by registered, certified, or first-class mail addressed to such person at his usual residence or business address.

If such service is made personally, the summons shall be delivered by the clerk or the jury commission or their duly designated deputies to the marshal who shall make such service.

If such service is made by mail, the summons may be served by the marshal or by the clerk, the jury commission or their duly designated deputies, who shall make affidavit of service and shall attach thereto any receipt from the addressee for a registered or certified summons.

(c) Except as provided in section 1865 of this title or in any jury selection plan provision adopted pursuant to paragraph (5) or (6) of section 1863(b) of this title, no person or class of persons shall be disqualified, excluded, excused, or exempt from service as jurors: *Provided*, That any person summoned for jury service may be (1) excused by the court, or by the clerk under supervision of the court if the court's jury selection plan so authorizes, upon a showing of undue hardship or extreme inconvenience, for such period as the court deems necessary, at the conclusion of which such person either shall be summoned again for jury service under subsections (b) and (c) of this section or, if the court's jury selection plan so provides, the name of such person shall be reinserted into the qualified jury wheel for selection pursuant to subsection (a) of this section, or (2) excluded by the court on the ground that such person may be unable to render impartial jury service or that his service as a juror would be likely to disrupt the proceedings, or (3) excluded upon peremptory challenge as provided by law, or (4) excluded pursuant to the procedure specified by law upon a challenge by any party for good cause shown, or (5) excluded upon determination by the court that his service as a juror would be likely to threaten the secrecy of the proceedings, or otherwise adversely affect the integrity of jury deliberations. No person shall be excluded under clause (5) of this subsection unless the judge, in open court, determines that such is warranted and that exclusion of the person will not be inconsistent with sections 1861 and 1862 of this title. The number of persons excluded under clause (5) of this subsection shall not exceed one per centum of the number of persons who return executed jury qualification forms during the period, specified in the plan, between two consecutive fillings of the master jury wheel. The names of persons excluded under clause (5) of this subsection, together with detailed explanations for the exclusions, shall be forwarded immediately to the judicial council of the circuit, which shall have the power to make any appropriate order, prospective or retroactive, to redress any misapplication of clause (5) of this subsection, but otherwise exclusions effectuated under such clause shall not be subject to challenge under the provisions of this title. Any person excluded from a particular jury under clause (2), (3), or (4) of this subsection shall be eligible to sit on another jury if the basis for his initial exclusion would not be relevant to his ability to serve on such other jury.

(d) Whenever a person is disqualified, excused, exempt, or excluded from jury service, the jury commission or clerk shall note in the space provided on his juror qualification form or on the juror's card drawn from the qualified jury wheel the specific reason therefor.

(e) In any two-year period, no person shall be required to (1) serve or attend court for prospective service as a petit juror for a total of more than thirty days, except when necessary to complete service in a particular case, or (2) serve on more than one grand jury, or (3) serve as both a grand and petit juror.

(f) When there is an unanticipated shortage of available petit jurors drawn from the qualified jury wheel, the court may require the marshal to summon a sufficient number of petit jurors selected at random from the voter registration lists, lists of actual voters, or other lists specified in the plan, in a manner ordered by the court consistent with sections 1861 and 1862 of this title.

(g) Any person summoned for jury service who fails to appear as directed shall be ordered by the district court to appear forthwith and show cause for his failure to comply with the summons. Any person who fails to show good cause for noncompliance with a summons may be fined not more than $100 or imprisoned not more than three days, or both.

(June 25, 1948, c. 646, 62 Stat. 952; May 24, 1949, c. 139, § 96, 63 Stat. 103; Mar. 27, 1968, Pub.L. 90–274, § 101, 82 Stat. 58; Dec. 11, 1970, Pub.L. 91–543, 84 Stat. 1408; Nov. 2, 1978, Pub.L. 95–572, § 2(b), 92 Stat. 2453; Jan. 12, 1983, Pub.L. 97–463, § 2, 96 Stat. 2531; Nov. 19, 1988, Pub.L. 100–702, Title VIII, § 801, 102 Stat. 4657.)

HISTORICAL AND STATUTORY NOTES

Effective Dates

1978 Acts. Amendment by Pub.L. 95–572 applicable with respect to any grand or petit juror summoned for service or actually serving on or after Nov. 2, 1978, see section 7(a) of Pub.L. 95–572, set out as a note under section 1363 of this title.

1968 Acts. Amendment by Pub.L. 90–274 effective 270 days after Mar. 27, 1968, except as to cases in which an indictment has been returned or a petit jury empaneled prior to such effective date, see section 104 of Pub.L. 90–274, set out as a note under section 1861 of this title.

§ 1867. Challenging compliance with selection procedures

(a) In criminal cases, before the voir dire examination begins, or within seven days after the defendant discovered or could have discovered, by the exercise of diligence, the grounds therefor, whichever is earlier, the defendant may move to dismiss the indictment or stay the proceedings against him on the ground of substantial failure to comply with the provisions of this title in selecting the grand or petit jury.

(b) In criminal cases, before the voir dire examination begins, or within seven days after the Attorney General of the United States discovered or could have discovered, by the exercise of diligence, the grounds therefor, whichever is earlier, the Attorney General may move to dismiss the indictment or stay the proceedings on the ground of substantial failure to comply with the provisions of this title in selecting the grand or petit jury.

(c) In civil cases, before the voir dire examination begins, or within seven days after the party discovered or could have discovered, by the exercise of diligence, the grounds therefor, whichever is earlier, any party may move to stay the proceedings on the ground of substantial failure to comply with the provisions of this title in selecting the petit jury.

(d) Upon motion filed under subsection (a), (b), or (c) of this section, containing a sworn statement of facts which, if true, would constitute a substantial failure to comply with the provisions of this title, the moving party shall be entitled to present in support of such motion the testimony of the jury commission or clerk, if available, any relevant records and papers not public or otherwise available used by the jury commissioner or clerk, and any other relevant evidence. If the court determines that there has been a substantial failure to comply with the provisions of this title in selecting the grand jury, the court shall stay the proceedings pending the selection of a grand jury in conformity with this title or dismiss the indictment, whichever is appropriate. If the court determines that there has been a substantial failure to comply with the provisions of this title in selecting the petit jury, the court shall stay the proceedings pending the selection of a petit jury in conformity with this title.

(e) The procedures prescribed by this section shall be the exclusive means by which a person accused of a Federal crime, the Attorney General of the United States or a party in a civil case may challenge any jury on the ground that such jury was not selected in conformity with the provisions of this title. Nothing in this section shall preclude any person or the United States from pursuing any other remedy, civil or criminal, which may be available for the vindication or enforcement of any law prohibiting discrimination on account of race, color, religion, sex, national origin or economic status in the selection of persons for service on grand or petit juries.

(f) The contents of records or papers used by the jury commission or clerk in connection with the jury selection process shall not be disclosed, except pursuant to the district court plan or as may be necessary in the preparation or presentation of a motion under subsection (a), (b), or (c) of this section, until after the master jury wheel has been emptied and refilled pursuant to section 1863(b)(4) of this title and all persons selected to serve as jurors before the master wheel was emptied have completed such service. The parties in a case shall be allowed to inspect, reproduce, and copy such records or papers at all reasonable times during the preparation and pendency of such a motion. Any person who discloses the contents of any record or paper in violation of this subsection may be fined not more than $1,000 or imprisoned not more than one year, or both.

(June 25, 1948, c. 646, 62 Stat. 953; Sept. 2, 1957, Pub.L. 85–259, 71 Stat. 583; Mar. 27, 1968, Pub.L. 90–274, § 101, 82 Stat. 59.)

HISTORICAL AND STATUTORY NOTES

Effective Dates

1968 Acts. Amendment by Pub.L. 90–274 effective 270 days after Mar. 27, 1968, except as to cases in which an indictment has been returned or a petit jury empaneled prior to such effective date, see section 104 of Pub.L. 90–274, set out as a note under section 1861 of this title.

§ 1868. Maintenance and inspection of records

After the master jury wheel is emptied and refilled pursuant to section 1863(b)(4) of this title, and after all persons selected to serve as jurors before the master wheel was emptied have completed such service, all records and papers compiled and maintained by the jury commission or clerk before the master wheel was emptied shall be preserved in the custody of the clerk for four years or for such longer period as may be ordered by a court, and shall be available for public inspection for the purpose of determining the validity of the selection of any jury.

(June 25, 1948, c. 646, 62 Stat. 953; Mar. 27, 1968, Pub.L. 90–274, § 101, 82 Stat. 60.)

HISTORICAL AND STATUTORY NOTES

Effective Dates

1968 Acts. Amendment by Pub.L. 90–274 effective 270 days after Mar. 27, 1968, except as to cases in which an indictment has been returned or a petit jury empaneled prior to such effective date, see section 104 of Pub.L. 90–274, set out as a note under section 1861 of this title.

§ 1869. Definitions

For purposes of this chapter—

(a) "clerk" and "clerk of the court" shall mean the clerk of the district court of the United States, any authorized deputy clerk, and any other person authorized by the court to assist the clerk in the performance of functions under this chapter;

(b) "chief judge" shall mean the chief judge of any district court of the United States;

(c) "voter registration lists" shall mean the official records maintained by State or local election officials of persons registered to vote in either the most recent State or the most recent Federal general election, or, in the case of a State or political subdivision thereof that does not require registration as a prerequisite to voting, other official lists of persons qualified to vote in such election. The term shall also include the list of eligible voters maintained by any Federal examiner pursuant to the Voting Rights Act of 1965 where the names on such list have not been included on the official registration lists or other official lists maintained by the appropriate State or local officials. With respect to the districts of Guam and the Virgin Islands, "voter registration lists" shall mean the official records maintained by territorial election officials of persons registered to vote in the most recent territorial general election;

(d) "lists of actual voters" shall mean the official lists of persons actually voting in either the most recent State or the most recent Federal general election;

(e) "division" shall mean: (1) one or more statutory divisions of a judicial district; or (2) in statutory divisions that contain more than one place of holding court, or in judicial districts where there are no statutory divisions, such counties, parishes, or similar political subdivisions surrounding the places where court is held as the district court plan shall determine: *Provided*, That each county, parish, or similar political subdivision shall be included in some such division;

(f) "district court of the United States", "district court", and "court" shall mean any district court established by chapter 5 of this title, and any court which is created by Act of Congress in a territory and is invested with any jurisdiction of a district court established by chapter 5 of this title;

(g) "jury wheel" shall include any device or system similar in purpose or function, such as a properly programmed electronic data processing system or device;

(h) "juror qualification form" shall mean a form prescribed by the Administrative Office of the United States Courts and approved by the Judicial Conference of the United States, which shall elicit the name, address, age, race, occupation, education, length of residence within the judicial district, distance from residence to place of holding court, prior jury service, and citizenship of a potential juror, and whether he should be excused or exempted from jury service, has any physical or mental infirmity impairing his capacity to serve as juror, is able to read, write, speak, and understand the English language, has pending against him any charge for the commission of a State or Federal criminal offense punishable by imprisonment for more than one year, or has been convicted in any State or Federal court of record of a crime punishable by imprisonment for more than one year and has not had his civil rights restored. The form shall request, but not require, any other information not inconsistent with the provisions of this title and required by the district court plan in the interests of the sound administration of justice. The form shall also elicit the sworn statement that his responses are true to the best of his knowledge. Notarization shall not be required. The form shall contain words clearly informing the person that the furnishing of any information with respect to his religion, national origin, or economic status is not a prerequisite to his qualification for jury service, that such information need not be furnished if the person finds it objectionable to do so, and that information concerning race is required solely to enforce nondiscrimination in jury selection and has no bearing on an individual's qualification for jury service.

(i) "public officer" shall mean a person who is either elected to public office or who is directly appointed by a person elected to public office;

(j) "undue hardship or extreme inconvenience", as a basis for excuse from immediate jury service under section 1866(c)(1) of this chapter, shall mean great distance, either in miles or traveltime, from the place of holding court, grave illness in the family or any other emergency which outweighs in immediacy and urgency the obligation to serve as a juror when summoned, or any other factor which the court determines to constitute an undue hardship or to create an extreme inconvenience to the juror; and in addition, in situations where it is anticipated that a trial or grand jury proceeding may require more than thirty days of service, the court may consider, as a further basis for temporary excuse, severe economic hardship to an employer which would result from the absence of a key employee during the period of such service;

(k) "publicly draw", as referred to in sections 1864 and 1866 of this chapter, shall mean a drawing which is conducted within the district after reasonable public notice and which is open to the public at large under the supervision of the clerk or jury commission, except that when a drawing is made by means of electronic data processing, "publicly draw" shall mean a drawing which is conducted at a data processing center located in or out of the district, after reasonable public notice given in the district for which juror names are being drawn, and which is open to the public at large under such supervision of the clerk or jury commission as the Judicial Conference of the United States shall by regulation require; and

(*l*) "jury summons" shall mean a summons issued by a clerk of court, jury commission, or their duly designated deputies, containing either a preprinted or stamped seal of court, and containing the name of the issuing clerk imprinted in preprinted, type, or facsimile manner on the summons or the envelopes transmitting the summons.

(June 25, 1948, c. 646, 62 Stat. 953; Oct. 16, 1963, Pub.L. 88–139, § 2, 77 Stat. 248; Mar. 27, 1968, Pub.L. 90–274, § 101, 82 Stat. 61; July 29, 1970, Pub.L. 91–358, Title I, § 172(b), 84 Stat. 590; Sept. 29, 1972, Pub.L. 92–437, § 1, 86 Stat. 740; Nov. 2, 1978, Pub.L. 95–572, §§ 3(b), (4), 92 Stat. 2453; Nov. 6, 1978, Pub.L. 95–598, Title II, § 243, 92 Stat. 2671; Nov. 14, 1986, Pub.L. 99–650, § 3, 100 Stat. 3641; Nov. 19, 1988, Pub.L. 100–702, Title VIII, §§ 802(a), 804, 102 Stat. 4657, 4658.)

HISTORICAL AND STATUTORY NOTES

References in Text

The Voting Rights Act of 1965, referred to in subsec. (c), is Pub.L. 89–110, Aug. 6, 1965, 79 Stat. 437, as amended, which is classified generally to subchapters I–A (Section 1973 et seq.), I–B (Section 1973aa et seq.), and I–C (Section 1973bb et seq.) of chapter 20 of Title 42, The Public Health and Welfare. For complete classification of this Act to the Code, see Short Title note set out under section 1973 of Title 42 and Tables.

Codifications

Subsec. (f) of this section was amended by Pub.L. 95–598, Title II, § 243, Nov. 6, 1978, 92 Stat. 2671, effective June 28, 1984, pursuant to Pub.L. 95–598, Title IV, § 402(b), Nov. 6, 1978, 92 Stat. 2682, as amended by Pub.L. 98–249, § 1(a), Mar. 31, 1984, 98 Stat. 116; Pub.L. 98–271, § 1(a), Apr. 30, 1984, 98 Stat. 163; Pub.L. 98–299, § 1(a), May 25, 1984, 98 Stat. 214; Pub.L. 98–325, § 1(a), June 20, 1984, 98 Stat. 268, set out as an Effective Dates note preceding section 101 of Title 11, Bankruptcy, by inserting "chapter 6 of title 28, United States Code," following "chapter 5 of title 28, United States Code,".

Section 402(b) of Pub.L. 95–598 was amended by section 113 of Pub.L. 98–353, Title I, July 10, 1984, 98 Stat. 343, by substituting "shall not be effective" for "shall take effect on June 28, 1984", thereby eliminating the amendment by section 243 of Pub.L. 95–598, effective June 27, 1984, pursuant to section 122(c) of Pub.L. 98–353, set out as an Effective Dates note under section 151 of this title.

Section 121(a) of Pub.L. 98–353 directed that section 402(b) of Pub.L. 95–598 be amended by substituting "the date of enactment of the Bankruptcy Amendments and Federal Judgeship Act of 1984 [i.e. July 10, 1984]" for "June 28, 1984". This amendment was not executed in view of the prior amendment to section 402(b) of Pub.L. 95–598 by section 113 of Pub.L. 98–353.

Effective Dates

1986 Acts. Section 4(a) of Pub.L. 99–650 provided in part that: "The provisions of this Act [amending this section] shall take effect 180 days after the date of enactment of this Act [Nov. 14, 1986]".

1978 Acts. Amendment by Pub.L. 95–572 applicable with respect to any grand or petit juror summoned for service or actually serving on or after Nov. 2, 1978, see section 7(a) of Pub.L. 95–572, set out as a note under section 1363 of this title.

1972 Acts. Section 2 of Pub.L. 92–437 provided that: "This Act [amending subsec. (h) of this section] shall take effect on the sixtieth day after the date of its enactment [Sept. 29, 1972]".

1970 Acts. Amendment by Pub.L. 91–358 effective the first day of the seventh calendar month which begins after July 29, 1970, see section 199(a) of Pub.L. 91–358, set out as a note under section 1257 of this title.

1968 Acts. Amendment by Pub.L. 90–274 effective 270 days after Mar. 27, 1968, except as to cases in which an indictment has been returned or a petit jury empaneled prior to such effective date, see section 104 of Pub.L. 90–274, set out as a note under section 1861 of this title.

Termination of United States District Court for the District of the Canal Zone

For termination of the United States District Court for the District of the Canal Zone at end of the "transition period", being the 30-month period beginning Oct. 1, 1979, and ending midnight Mar. 31, 1982, see Paragraph 5 of Article XI of the Panama Canal Treaty of 1977 and sections 3831 and 3841 to 3843 of Title 22, Foreign Relations and Intercourse.

§ 1870. Challenges

In civil cases, each party shall be entitled to three peremptory challenges. Several defendants or several plaintiffs may be considered as a single party for the purposes of making challenges, or the court may allow additional peremptory challenges and permit them to be exercised separately or jointly.

All challenges for cause or favor, whether to the array or panel or to individual jurors, shall be determined by the court.

(June 25, 1948, c. 646, 62 Stat. 953; Sept. 16, 1959, Pub.L. 86–282, 73 Stat. 565.)

§ 1871. Fees

(a) Grand and petit jurors in district courts appearing pursuant to this chapter shall be paid the fees and allowances provided by this section. The requisite fees and allowances shall be disbursed on the certificate of the clerk of court in accordance with the procedure established by the Director of the Administrative Office of the United States Courts. Attendance fees for extended service under subsection (b) of this section shall be certified by the clerk only upon the order of a district judge.

(b)(1) A juror shall be paid an attendance fee of $40 per day for actual attendance at the place of trial or hearing. A juror shall also be paid the attendance fee for the time necessarily occupied in going to and returning from such place at the beginning and end of such service or at any time during such service.

(2) A petit juror required to attend more than thirty days in hearing one case may be paid, in the discretion of the trial judge, an additional fee, not exceeding $10 more than the attendance fee, for each day in excess of thirty days on which he is required to hear such case.

(3) A grand juror required to attend more than forty-five days of actual service may be paid, in the discretion of the district judge in charge of the particular grand jury, an additional fee, not exceeding $10 more than the attendance fee, for each day in excess of forty-five days of actual service.

(4) A grand or petit juror required to attend more than ten days of actual service may be paid, in the discretion of the judge, the appropriate fees at the end of the first ten days and at the end of every ten days of service thereafter.

(5) Certification of additional attendance fees may be ordered by the judge to be made effective commencing on the first day of extended service, without reference to the date of such certification.

(c)(1) A travel allowance not to exceed the maximum rate per mile that the Director of the Administrative Office of the United States Courts has prescribed pursuant to section 604(a)(7) of this title for payment to supporting court personnel in travel status using privately owned automobiles shall be paid to each juror, regardless of the mode of transportation actually employed. The prescribed rate shall be paid for the distance necessarily traveled to and from a juror's residence by the shortest practical route in going to and returning from the place of service. Actual mileage in full at the prescribed rate is payable at the beginning and at the end of a juror's term of service.

(2) The Director shall promulgate rules regulating interim travel allowances to jurors. Distances traveled to and from court should coincide with the shortest practical route.

(3) Toll charges for toll roads, bridges, tunnels, and ferries shall be paid in full to the juror incurring such charges. In the discretion of the court, reasonable parking fees may be paid to the juror incurring such fees upon presentation of a valid parking receipt. Parking fees shall not be included in any tabulation of mileage cost allowances.

(4) Any juror who travels to district court pursuant to summons in an area outside of the contiguous forty-eight States of the United States shall be paid the travel expenses provided under this section, or actual reasonable transportation expenses subject to the discretion of the district judge or clerk of court as circumstances indicate, exercising due regard for the mode of transportation, the availability of alternative modes, and the shortest practical route between residence and court.

(5) A grand juror who travels to district court pursuant to a summons may be paid the travel expenses provided under this section or, under guidelines established by the Judicial Conference, the actual reasonable costs of travel by aircraft when travel by other means is not feasible and when certified by the chief judge of the district court in which the grand juror serves.

(d)(1) A subsistence allowance covering meals and lodging of jurors shall be established from time to time by the Director of the Administrative Office of the United States Courts pursuant to section 604(a)(7) of this title, except that such allowance shall not exceed the allowance for supporting court personnel in travel status in the same geographical area. Claims for such allowance shall not require itemization.

(2) A subsistence allowance shall be paid to a juror when an overnight stay is required at the place of holding court, and for the time necessarily spent in traveling to and from the place of attendance if an overnight stay is required.

(3) A subsistence allowance for jurors serving in district courts outside of the contiguous forty-eight States of the United States shall be allowed at a rate not to exceed that per diem allowance which is paid to supporting court personnel in travel status in those areas where the Director of the Administrative Office of the United States Courts has prescribed an increased per diem fee pursuant to section 604(a)(7) of this title.

(e) During any period in which a jury is ordered to be kept together and not to separate, the actual cost of subsistence shall be paid upon the order of the court in lieu of the subsistence allowances payable under subsection (d) of this section. Such allowance for the jurors ordered to be kept separate or sequestered shall include the cost of meals, lodging, and other expenditures ordered in the discretion of the court for their convenience and comfort.

(f) A juror who must necessarily use public transportation in traveling to and from court, the full cost of which is not met by the transportation expenses allowable under subsection (c) of this section on account of the short distance traveled in miles, may be paid, in the discretion of the court, the actual reasonable expense of such public transportation, pursuant to the methods of payment provided by this section. Jurors who are required to remain at the court beyond the normal business closing hour for deliberation or for any other reason may be transported to their homes, or to temporary lodgings where such lodgings are ordered by the court, in a manner directed by the clerk and paid from funds authorized under this section.

(g) The Director of the Administrative Office of the United States Courts shall promulgate such regulations as may be necessary to carry out his authority under this section.

(June 25, 1948, c. 646, 62 Stat. 953; May 24, 1949, c. 139, § 97, 63 Stat. 103; July 14, 1949, c. 333, 63 Stat. 411; Sept. 7, 1957, Pub.L. 85–299, 71 Stat. 618; Sept. 2, 1965, Pub.L. 89–165, 79 Stat. 645; Mar. 27, 1968, Pub.L. 90–274, § 102(a), 82 Stat. 62; Nov. 2, 1978, Pub.L. 95–572, § 5, 92 Stat. 2454; Dec. 1, 1990, Pub.L. 101–650, Title III, § 314(b), 104 Stat. 5115; Oct. 29, 1992, Pub.L. 102–572, Title IV, § 402, 106 Stat. 4511.)

HISTORICAL AND STATUTORY NOTES

Effective Dates

1992 Acts. Amendment by Pub.L. 102–572 effective Jan. 1, 1993, see section 1101(a) of Pub.L. 102–572, set out as a note under section 905 of Title 2, The Congress.

1978 Acts. Amendment by Pub.L. 95–572 applicable with respect to any grand or petit juror serving on or after the sixtieth day following Nov. 2, 1978, see section 7(b) of Pub.L. 95–572, set out as a note under section 1363 of this title.

1968 Acts. Amendment by Pub.L. 90–274 effective 270 days after Mar. 27, 1968, except as to cases in which an indictment has been returned or a petit jury empaneled prior to such effective date, see section 104 of Pub.L. 90–274, set out as a note under section 1861 of this title.

Refreshment of Jurors

Pub.L. 101–162, Title IV, Nov. 21, 1989, 103 Stat. 1012, provided in part: "That for fiscal year 1990 and hereafter, funds appropriated under this heading [Courts of Appeals, District Courts and Other Judicial Services and Fees of Jurors and Commissioners] shall be available for refreshment of jurors."

§ 1872. Issues of fact in Supreme Court

In all original actions at law in the Supreme Court against citizens of the United States, issues of fact shall be tried by a jury.

(June 25, 1948, c. 646, 62 Stat. 953.)

§ 1873. Admiralty and maritime cases

In any case of admiralty and maritime jurisdiction relating to any matter of contract or tort arising upon or concerning any vessel of twenty tons or upward, enrolled and licensed for the coasting trade, and employed in the business of commerce and navigation between places in different states upon the lakes and navigable waters connecting said lakes, the trial of all issues of fact shall be by jury if either party demands it.

(June 25, 1948, c. 646, 62 Stat. 953.)

§ 1874. Actions on bonds and specialties

In all actions to recover the forfeiture annexed to any articles of agreement, covenant, bond, or other specialty, wherein the forfeiture, breach, or nonperformance appears by default or confession of the defendant, the court shall render judgment for the plaintiff for such amount as is due. If the sum is uncertain, it shall, upon request of either party, be assessed by a jury.

(June 25, 1948, c. 646, 62 Stat. 953.)

§ 1875. Protection of jurors' employment

(a) No employer shall discharge, threaten to discharge, intimidate, or coerce any permanent employee by reason of such employee's jury service, or the attendance or scheduled attendance in connection with such service, in any court of the United States.

(b) Any employer who violates the provisions of this section—

(1) shall be liable for damages for any loss of wages or other benefits suffered by an employee by reason of such violation;

(2) may be enjoined from further violations of this section and ordered to provide other appropriate relief, including but not limited to the reinstatement of any employee discharged by reason of his jury service; and

(3) shall be subject to a civil penalty of not more than $1,000 for each violation as to each employee.

(c) Any individual who is reinstated to a position of employment in accordance with the provisions of this section shall be considered as having been on furlough or leave of absence during his period of jury service, shall be reinstated to his position of employment without loss of seniority, and shall be entitled to participate in insurance or other benefits offered by the employer pursuant to established rules and practices relating to employees on furlough or leave of absence in effect with the employer at the time such individual entered upon jury service.

(d)(1) An individual claiming that his employer has violated the provisions of this section may make application to the district court for the district in which such employer maintains a place of business and the court shall, upon finding probable merit in such claim, appoint counsel to represent such individual in any action in the district court necessary to the resolution of such claim. Such counsel shall be compensated and necessary expenses repaid to the extent provided by section 3006A of title 18, United States Code.

(2) In any action or proceeding under this section, the court may award a prevailing employee who brings such action by retained counsel a reasonable attorney's fee as part of the costs. The court may tax a defendant employer, as costs payable to the court, the attorney fees and expenses incurred on behalf of a prevailing employee, where such costs were expended by the court pursuant to paragraph (1) of this subsection. The court may award a prevailing employer a reasonable attorney's fee as part of the costs only if the court finds that the action is frivolous, vexatious, or brought in bad faith.

(Added Pub.L. 95–572, § 6(a) (1), Nov. 2, 1978, 92 Stat. 2456, and amended Pub.L. 97–463, § 1, Jan. 12, 1983, 96 Stat. 2531.)

HISTORICAL AND STATUTORY NOTES

Effective Dates

1978 Acts. Section applicable with respect to any grand or petit juror summoned for service or actually serving on or after Nov. 2, 1978, see section 7(a) of Pub.L. 95–572, set out as a note under section 1363 of this title.

§ 1876. Trial by jury in the Court of International Trade

(a) In any civil action in the Court of International Trade which is to be tried before a jury, the jury shall be selected in accordance with the provisions of this chapter and under the procedures set forth in the jury selection plan of the district court for the judicial district in which the case is to be tried.

(b) Whenever the Court of International Trade conducts a jury trial—

(1) the clerk of the district court for the judicial district in which the Court of International Trade is sitting, or an authorized deputy clerk, shall act as clerk of the Court of International Trade for the purposes of selecting and summoning the jury;

(2) the qualifications for jurors shall be the same as those established by section 1865(b) of this title for jurors in the district courts of the United States;

(3) each party shall be entitled to challenge jurors in accordance with section 1870 of this title; and

(4) jurors shall be compensated in accordance with section 1871 of this title.

(Added Pub.L. 96–417, Title III, § 302(a), Oct. 10, 1980, 94 Stat. 1739.)

HISTORICAL AND STATUTORY NOTES

Effective Dates

1980 Acts. Section applicable with respect to civil actions commenced on or after Nov. 1, 1980, see section 701(b) (1) (C) of Pub.L. 96–417, as amended, set out as a note under section 251 of this title.

§ 1877. Protection of jurors

(a) Subject to the provisions of this section and title 5 of the United States Code, subchapter 1 of chapter 81, title 5, United States Code, applies to a Federal grand or petit juror, except that entitlement to disability compensation payments does not commence until the day after the date of termination of service as a juror.

(b) In administering this section with respect to a juror covered by this section—

(1) a juror is deemed to receive monthly pay at the minimum rate for grade GS–2 of the General Schedule unless his actual pay as a Government employee while serving on court leave is higher, in which case monthly pay is determined in accordance with section 8114 of title 5, United States Code, and

(2) performance of duty as a juror includes that time when a juror is (A) in attendance at court pursuant to a summons, (B) in deliberation, (C) sequestered by order of a judge, or (D) at a site, by order of the court, for the taking of a view.

(Added Pub.L. 97–463, § 3(1), Jan. 12, 1983, 96 Stat. 2531.)

§ 1878. Optional use of a one-step summoning and qualification procedure

(a) At the option of each district court, jurors may be summoned and qualified in a single procedure, if the court's jury selection plan so authorizes, in lieu of the two separate procedures otherwise provided for by this chapter. Courts shall ensure that a one-step summoning and qualification procedure conducted under this section does not violate the policies and objectives set forth in sections 1861 and 1862 of this title.

(b) Jury selection conducted under this section shall be subject to challenge under section 1867 of this title for substantial failure to comply with the provisions of this title in selecting the jury. However, no challenge under section 1867 of this title shall lie solely on the basis that a jury was selected in accordance with a one-step summoning and qualification procedure authorized by this section.

(Added Pub.L. 100–702, Title VIII, § 805(a), Nov. 19, 1988, 102 Stat. 4658, and amended Pub.L. 102–572, Title IV, § 403(a), Oct. 29, 1992, 106 Stat. 4512.)

HISTORICAL AND STATUTORY NOTES

Effective Dates

1992 Acts. Amendment by Pub.L. 102–572 effective Jan. 1, 1993, see section 1101(a) of Pub.L. 102–572, set out as a note under section 905 of Title 2, The Congress.

Savings Provisions

Section 403(c) of Pub.L. 102–572 provided that: "For courts participating in the experiment authorized under section 1878 of title 28, United States Code [this section] (as in effect before the effective date of this section [see Effective Dates of 1992 Amendments note set out under this section]), the amendment made by subsection (a) of this section [amending this section] shall be effective on and after January 1, 1992."

CHAPTER 123—FEES AND COSTS

Sec.
1911. Supreme Court.
1912. Damages and costs on affirmance.
1913. Courts of appeals.
1914. District court; filing and miscellaneous fees; rules of court.
1915. Proceedings in forma pauperis.
1915A. Screening.
1916. Seamen's suits.
1917. District courts; fee on filing notice of or petition for appeal.
1918. District courts; fines, forfeitures and criminal proceedings.
1919. Dismissal for lack of jurisdiction.
1920. Taxation of costs.
1921. United States marshal's fees.
1922. Witness fees before United States commissioners.

Sec.
1923. Docket fees and costs of briefs.
1924. Verification of bill of costs.
1925. Admiralty and maritime cases.
1926. Court of Federal Claims.
1927. Counsel's liability for excessive costs.
1928. Patent infringement action; disclaimer not filed.
1929. Extraordinary expenses not expressly authorized.
1930. Bankruptcy fees.
1931. Disposition of filing fees.
1932.[1] Judicial Panel on Multidistrict Litigation.
1932.[1] Revocation of earned release credit.

[1] Two sections 1932 have been enacted.

Codifications

Amendment by section 111(c) of Pub.L. 98–353, Title I, July 10, 1984, 98 Stat. 343, purported to amend the table of sections for chapter 125. The amendment was executed to this chapter as the probable intent of Congress. Section 111(c) substituted "Bankruptcy fees" for "Bankruptcy courts" in item 1930.

§ 1911. Supreme Court

The Supreme Court may fix the fees to be charged by its clerk.

The fees of the clerk, cost of serving process, and other necessary disbursements incidental to any case before the court, may be taxed against the litigants as the court directs.

(June 25, 1948, c. 646, 62 Stat. 954.)

§ 1912. Damages and costs on affirmance

Where a judgment is affirmed by the Supreme Court or a court of appeals, the court in its discretion may adjudge to the prevailing party just damages for his delay, and single or double costs.

(June 25, 1948, c. 646, 62 Stat. 954.)

§ 1913. Courts of appeals

The fees and costs to be charged and collected in each court of appeals shall be prescribed from time to time by the Judicial Conference of the United States. Such fees and costs shall be reasonable and uniform in all the circuits.

(June 25, 1948, c. 646, 62 Stat. 954.)

HISTORICAL AND STATUTORY NOTES

Court Fees for Electronic Access to Information

Pub.L. 102–140, Title III, § 303, Oct. 28, 1991, 105 Stat. 810, as amended Pub.L. 104–317, Title IV, § 403(b), Oct. 19, 1996, 110 Stat. 3854, provided that:

"(a) The Judicial Conference shall hereafter prescribe reasonable fees, pursuant to sections 1913, 1914, 1926, 1930, and 1932 of title 28, United States Code [this section and sections 1914, 1926, 1930, and 1932 of this title], for collection by the courts under those sections for access to information available through automatic data processing equipment. These fees may distinguish between classes of persons, and shall provide for exempting persons or classes of persons from the fees, in order to avoid unreasonable burdens and to promote public access to such information. The Director of the Administrative Office of the United States Courts, under the direction of the Judicial Conference of the United States, shall prescribe a schedule of reasonable fees for electronic access to information which the Director is required to maintain and make available to the public.

"(b) The Judicial Conference and the Director shall transmit each schedule of fees prescribed under paragraph (a) to the Congress at least 30 days before the schedule becomes effective. All fees hereafter collected by the Judiciary under paragraph (a) as a charge for services rendered shall be deposited as offsetting collections to the Judiciary Automation Fund pursuant to 28 U.S.C. 612(c)(1)(A) [section 612(c)(1)(A) of this title] to reimburse expenses incurred in providing these services."

Similar provisions were contained in the following prior appropriation Act:

Pub.L. 101–515, Title IV, § 404, Nov. 5, 1990, 104 Stat. 2132.

JUDICIAL CONFERENCE SCHEDULE OF FEES

The Judicial Conference of the United States at its session on March 7–9, 1979, set forth the schedule of fees to be charged in the United States courts of appeals pursuant to this section. That new schedule became effective on October 1, 1979. At its March 1987 meeting, the Judicial Conference, on the recommendation of the Committee on Court Administration, amended the schedule of fees to be effective May 1, 1987. Amendments to this revision of the schedule of fees were adopted at the September, 1988 and March, 1990 meetings of the Judicial Conference. At its 1994 meeting, the Judicial Conference amended its schedule of fees to be effective January 1, 1995. The Judicial Conference at its March 15, 1995 meeting adopted amendments to its fees schedule to be effective April 18, 1995, and at its 1996 meeting adopted amendments to be effective April 1, 1996.

Following are fees to be charged for services to be performed by clerks of the courts of appeals. No fees are to be charged for services rendered on behalf of the United States, with the exception of those specifically prescribed in items 2, 4, and 13. No fees under this schedule shall be charged to federal agencies or programs which are funded from judiciary appropriations, including, but not limited to, agencies, organizations, and individuals providing services authorized by the Criminal Justice Act, 18 U.S.C. § 3006A, and Bankruptcy Administrator programs.

(1) For docketing a case on appeal or review, or docketing any other proceeding, $100. A separate fee shall be paid by each party filing a notice of appeal in the district court, but parties filing a joint notice of appeal in the district court are required to pay only one fee. A docketing fee shall not be charged for the docketing of an application for the allowance of an interlocutory appeal under 28 U.S.C. § 1292(b), unless the appeal is allowed.

(2) For every search of the records of the court and certifying the results thereof, $15.

(3) For certifying any document or paper, whether the certification is made directly on the document, or by separate instrument, $5.

(4) For reproducing any record or paper, 50 cents per page. This fee shall apply to paper copies made from either:

(1) original documents; or (2) microfiche or microfilm reproductions of the original records.

(5) For reproduction of magnetic tape recordings, either cassette or reel-to-reel, $15 including the cost of materials.

(6) For reproduction of the record in any appeal in which the requirement of an appendix is dispensed with by any court of appeals pursuant to Rule 30(f), F.R.A.P., a flat fee of $25.

(7) For each microfiche or microfilm copy of any court record, where available, $3.

(8) For retrieval of a record from a Federal Records Center, National Archives, or other storage location removed from the place of business of the court, $25.

(9) For a check paid into the court which is returned for lack of funds, $25.

(10) Fees to be charged and collected for copies of opinions shall be fixed, from time to time, by each court, commensurate with the cost of printing.

(11) The court may charge and collect fees, commensurate with the cost of printing, for copies of the local rules of court. The court may also distribute copies of the local rules without charge.

(12) The clerk shall assess a charge for the handling of registry funds deposited with the court, to be assessed from interest earnings and in accordance with the detailed fee schedule issued by the Director of the Administrative Office of the United States Courts.

(13) For usage of electronic access to court data, 60 cents per minute of usage [provided the court may, for good cause, exempt persons or classes of persons from the fees, in order to avoid unreasonable burdens and to promote public access to such information]. All such fees collected shall be deposited to the Judiciary Automation Fund. This fee shall apply to the United States. (The Judicial Conference has approved an advisory note clarifying the judiciary's policy with respect to exemptions from this fee. The advisory note is attached to this Fee Schedule as an Appendix.)

APPENDIX

The Judicial Conference has prescribed a fee for electronic access to court data, as set forth above in the Miscellaneous Fee Schedule. The schedule provides that the court may exempt persons or classes of persons from the fees, in order to avoid unreasonable burdens and to promote public access to such information. Exemptions should be granted as the exception, not the rule. The exemption language is intended to accommodate those users who might otherwise not have access to the information in this electronic form. It is not intended to provide a means by which a court would exempt all users.

Examples of persons and classes of persons who may be exempted from electronic public access fees include, but are not limited to: indigents; bankruptcy case trustees; not-for-profit organizations; and voluntary ADR neutrals.

Miscellaneous Fee Schedules

Registry Fund Fees

Effective June 12, 1989, a fee will be assessed for handling funds deposited in noncriminal proceedings with the court and held in interest bearing accounts or instruments pursuant to 28 U.S.C. § 2041 and Federal Rules of Civil Procedure rule 67. For new accounts, i.e., investments made on or after June 12, 1989, the fee will be equal to the first 45 days income earned on the deposit. Each subsequent deposit of new principal in the same case or proceeding will be subject to the fee. Reinvestment of prior deposits will not be subject to the fee. For existing accounts, i.e., investments held by the court prior to June 12, 1989, a fee will be assessed equal to the first 45 days of income earned beginning 30 days after June 12, 1989. Subsequent deposits of new principal in the same account will be subject to the fee. Subsequent reinvestment of existing deposits will not be subject to the fee.

The fee will apply only once to each sum deposited regardless of the length of time deposits are held and will not exceed income actually earned on the account.

The fee does not apply in the District Courts of Guam, Northern Mariana Islands, the Virgin Islands, the United States Claims Court, or other courts whose fees are not set under 28 U.S.C. §§ 1913, 1914, and 1930.

Registry Fund Fees—Item 12
(55 F.R. 42867, October 24, 1990)

Effective December 1, 1990, the registry fee assessment provisions were revised and converted from a one-time charge equal to all income earned in the first 45 days of the investment to a charge of 10 percent of the income earned while funds are held in the court registry. Additionally, the fee was extended to any funds placed in the court's registry and invested regardless of the nature of the action underlying the deposit.

The new method will not be applied on investments in cases from which a fee has been exacted based on the prior method (interest earned in the first 45 days the funds were invested or the first 45 days following July 12, 1989). The new method will also not be applied in cases where the investment instrument has a maturity date greater than one year, but where a fee under the prior method applies but has not been deducted.

The fee does not apply in the District Courts of Guam, the Northern Mariana Islands, the Virgin Islands, the United States Claims Court, or any other federal court whose fees are not set under 28 U.S.C. §§ 1913, 1914, and 1930.

Registry Fund Fees—Item 12
(56 F.R. 56356, November 4, 1991)

Effective February 3, 1992, the registry fee assessment provisions are revised and converted from a charge equal to 10 percent of the income earned while funds are held in the court's registry to a variable rate based on the amount deposited with the court and, in certain cases, the length of time funds are held in the court's registry.

The revised fee will be a fee of 10 percent of the total income received during each income period from investments of less than $100,000,000 of registry funds in income-bearing accounts. On investments exceeding $100,000,000 the 10 percent fee shall be reduced by one percent for each increment of $50,000,000 over the initial $100,000,000. For those deposits where funds are placed in the registry by court order for a time certain, for example, by the terms of an adjudicated trust, the fee will be further reduced. This further reduction will amount to 2.5 percent for each five-year interval or part thereof. The total minimum fee to be charged will be no less than two percent of the income on investments.

The following table sets out the fee schedule promulgated by this notice:

REGISTRY—SCHEDULE OF FEES

[% of income earned]

Amount of deposit *	0–5 yrs.	>5–10 yrs.	>10–15 yrs.	>15 yrs.
less than 100M	10	7.5	5.0	2.5
100M–<150M	9	6.5	4.0	2.0
150M–<200M	8	5.5	3.0	2.0
200M–<250M	7	4.5	2.0	2.0
250M–<300M	6	3.5	2.0	2.0
300M–<350M	5	2.5	2.0	2.0
350M–<400M	4	2.0	2.0	2.0
400M–<450M	3	2.0	2.0	2.0
over 450M	2	2.0	2.0	2.0

* Except where otherwise authorized by the Director, each deposit into any account is treated separately in determining the fee.

The new fee applies to all earnings applied to investments on and after the effective date of this change, except for earnings on investments in cases being administered under the provisions of the May 11, 1989 notice [54 FR 20407], i.e., to which the fee equal to the first 45 days income is applicable.

The fee, as modified herein, will continue to apply to any case where the court has authorized the investment of funds placed in its custody or held by it in trust in its registry regardless of the nature of the underlying action.

The fee does not apply in the District Court of Guam, the Northern Mariana Islands, the Virgin Islands, the United States Claims Court, or any other Federal court whose fees are not set under 28 U.S.C. §§ 1913, 1914, and 1930.

§ 1914. District court; filing and miscellaneous fees; rules of court

(a) The clerk of each district court shall require the parties instituting any civil action, suit or proceeding in such court, whether by original process, removal or otherwise, to pay a filing fee of $150, except that on application for a writ of habeas corpus the filing fee shall be $5.

(b) The clerk shall collect from the parties such additional fees only as are prescribed by the Judicial Conference of the United States.

(c) Each district court by rule or standing order may require advance payment of fees.

(June 25, 1948, c. 646, 62 Stat. 954; Nov. 6, 1978, Pub.L. 95–598, Title II, § 244, 92 Stat. 2671; June 19, 1986, Pub.L. 99–336, § 4(a), 100 Stat. 637; Oct. 18, 1986, Pub.L. 99–500, Title I, § 101(b) [Title IV, § 407(a)], 100 Stat. 1783–39, 1783–64, and Oct. 30, 1986, Pub.L. 99–591, Title I, § 101(b) [Title IV, § 407(a)], 100 Stat. 3341–39, 3341–64; Oct. 19, 1996, Pub.L. 104–317, Title IV, § 401(a), 110 Stat. 3853.)

HISTORICAL AND STATUTORY NOTES

Codifications

Pub.L. 99–591 is a corrected version of Pub.L. 99–500.

Effective Dates

1996 Acts. Section 401(c) of Pub.L. 104–317 provided that: "This section [amending this section and section 1931 of this title] shall take effect 60 days after the date of the enactment of this Act [Oct. 19, 1996]."

1986 Acts. Section 4(c) of Pub.L. 99–336 provided that: "The amendments made by this section [amending this section and provisions of the District of Columbia Code not classified to this Code] shall apply with respect to any civil action, suit, or proceeding instituted on or after the date of the enactment of this Act [June 19, 1986]."

1978 Acts. Amendment by Pub.L. 95–598 effective Oct. 1, 1979, see section 402(c) of Pub.L. 95–598, set out as a note preceding section 101 of Title 11, Bankruptcy.

Court Fees for Electronic Access to Information

Judicial Conference to prescribe reasonable fees for collection by courts under this section for access to information available through automatic data processing equipment and fees to be deposited in Judiciary Automation Fund, see section 303 of Pub.L. 102–140, set out as a note under section 1913 of this title.

JUDICIAL CONFERENCE SCHEDULE OF FEES

The Judicial Conference of the United States, at its session on March 7–9, 1979, set forth the schedule of fees to be charged in the United States district courts pursuant to this section. That new schedule became effective on October 1, 1979. At its March 1987 meeting, the Judicial Conference amended the schedule of fees to be effective May 1, 1987. Amendments to this revision of the schedule of fees were adopted at the September, 1988 and March, 1990 meetings of the Judicial Conference. At its 1991 meeting, the Judicial Conference amended its schedule of fees to be effective Feb. 3, 1992. At its March 1991 meeting, the Judicial Conference amended the schedule of fees to be effective Oct. 19, 1992, with later implementation. At its March, 1993 meeting, the Judicial Conference amended its schedule of fees to be effective May 6, 1993. At its September, 1993 meeting, the Judicial Conference amended its schedule of fees to be effective October 1, 1993. At its 1994 meeting, the Judicial Conference amended its schedule of fees to be effective January 1, 1995. At its March 15, 1995 meeting, the Judicial Conference amended its schedule of fees to be effective April 18, 1995, and at its 1996 meetings it adopted amendments to be effective April 1, 1996 and December 18, 1996. At its 1997 meeting, the Judicial Conference amended its schedule of fees to be effective January 1, 1998.

The Administrative Office of the United States Courts provided for Registry Fund Fees effective June 12, 1989.

District Court Miscellaneous Fee Schedule [1]

Following are fees to be charged for services to be performed by clerks of the district courts. No fees are to be charged for services rendered on behalf of the United States, with the exception of those specifically prescribed in items 2, 4, and 14. No fees under this schedule shall be charged to federal agencies or programs which are funded from judiciary appropriations, including, but not limited to, agencies, organizations, and individuals providing services authorized by the Criminal Justice Act, 18 U.S.C. § 3006A, and Bankruptcy Administrator programs.

(1) For filing or indexing any paper not in a case or proceeding for which a case filing fee has been paid, $20. This fee is applicable to the filing of a petition to perpetuate testimony, Rule 27(a), Federal Rules of Civil Procedure, the filing of papers by trustees under 28 U.S.C.

§ 754, the filing of letters rogatory or letters of request, and registering of a judgment from another district pursuant to 28 U.S.C. § 1963.

(2) For every search of the records of the district court conducted by the clerk of the district court or a deputy clerk, $15 per name or item searched. This fee shall apply to services rendered on behalf of the United States if the information requested is available through electronic access.

(3) For certification of any document or paper, whether the certification is made directly on the document or by separate instrument, $5. For exemplification of any document or paper, twice the amount of the fee for certification.

(4) For reproducing any record or paper, 50 cents per page. This fee shall apply to paper copies made from either: (1) original documents; or (2) microfiche or microfilm reproductions of the original records. This fee shall apply to services rendered on behalf of the United States if the record or paper requested is available through electronic access.

(5) For reproduction of magnetic tape recordings, either cassette or reel-to-reel, $15 including the cost of materials.

(6) Repealed.

(7) For each microfiche sheet of film or microfilm jacket copy of any court record, where available, $3.

(8) For retrieval of a record from a Federal Records Center, National Archives, or other storage location removed from the place of business of the court, $25.

(9) For a check paid into the court which is returned for lack of funds, $25.

(10) For an appeal to a district judge from a judgment of conviction by a magistrate in a misdemeanor case, $25.

(11) For original admission of attorneys to practice, $50 each, including a certificate of admission. For a duplicate certificate of admission or certificate of good standing, $15.

(12) The court may charge and collect fees, commensurate with the cost of printing, for copies of the local rules of court. The court may also distribute copies of the local rules without charge.

(13) The clerk shall assess a charge for the handling of registry funds deposited with the court, to be assessed from interest earnings and in accordance with the detailed fee schedule issued by the Director of the Administrative Office of the United States Courts.

(14) For usage of electronic access to court data, 60 cents per minute of usage [provided the court may, for good cause, exempt persons or classes of persons from the fees, in order to avoid unreasonable burdens and to promote public access to such information]. All such fees collected shall be deposited to the Judiciary Automation Fund. This fee shall apply to the United States. (The Judicial Conference has approved an advisory note clarifying the judiciary's policy with respect to exemptions from this fee. The advisory note is attached to this Fee Schedule as Appendix I.)

(15) For filing an action brought under Title III of the Cuban Liberty and Democratic Solidarity (LIBERTAD) Act of 1996, P.L. 104–114, 110 Stat. § 785 (1996), $4180. (This fee is in addition to the filing fee prescribed in 28 U.S.C. 1914(a) for instituting any civil action other than a writ of habeas corpus.)

APPENDIX I

The Judicial Conference has prescribed a fee for electronic access to court data, as set forth above in the District Court Miscellaneous Fee Schedule. The schedule provides that the court may exempt persons or classes of persons from the fees, in order to avoid unreasonable burdens and to promote public access to such information. Exemptions should be granted as the exception, not the rule. The exemption language is intended to accommodate those users who might otherwise not have access to the information in this electronic form. It is not intended to provide a means by which a court would exempt all users.

Examples of persons and classes of persons who may be exempted from electronic public access fees include, but are not limited to: indigents; bankruptcy case trustees; not-for-profit organizations; and voluntary ADR neutrals.

[1] Issued in accordance with 28 U.S.C. § 1914(b).

Registry Fund Fees—Item 13
(54 F.R 20407, May 11, 1989)

Effective June 12, 1989, a fee will be assessed for handling funds deposited in noncriminal proceedings with the court and held in interest bearing accounts or instruments pursuant to 28 U.S.C. § 2041 and Federal Rules of Civil Procedure rule 67. For new accounts, i.e, investments made on or after June 12, 1989, the fee will be equal to the first 45 days income earned on the deposit. Each subsequent deposit of new principal in the same case or proceeding will be subject to the fee. Reinvestment of prior deposits will not be subject to the fee. For existing accounts, i.e., investments held by the court prior to June 12, 1989, a fee will be assessed equal to the first 45 days of income earned beginning 30 days after June 12, 1989. Subsequent deposits of new principal in the same account will be subject to the fee. Subsequent reinvestment of existing deposits will not be subject to the fee.

The fee will apply only once to each sum deposited regardless of the length of time deposits are held and will not exceed income actually earned on the account.

The fee does not apply in the District Courts of Guam, Northern Mariana Islands, the Virgin Islands, the United States Claims Court, or other courts whose fees are not set under 28 U.S.C. § 1914.

Registry Fund Fees—Item 13
(55 F.R. 42867, October 24, 1990)

Effective December 1, 1990, the registry fee assessment provisions were revised and converted from a one-time charge equal to all income earned in the first 45 days of the investment to a charge of 10 percent of the income earned while funds are held in the court registry. Additionally, the fee was extended to any funds placed in the court's registry and invested regardless of the nature of the action underlying the deposit.

The new method will not be applied on investments in cases from which a fee has been exacted based on the prior method (interest earned in the first 45 days the funds were invested or the first 45 days following July 12, 1989). The new method will also not be applied in cases where the investment instrument has a maturity date greater than one year, but where a fee under the prior method applies but has not been deducted.

The fee does not apply in the District Courts of Guam, the Northern Mariana Islands, the Virgin Islands, the United

States Claims Court, or any other federal court whose fees are not set under 28 U.S.C. §§ 1913, 1914, and 1930.

Registry Fund Fees—Item 13
(56 F.R. 56356, November 4, 1991)

Effective February 3, 1992, the registry fee assessment provisions are revised and converted from a charge equal to 10 percent of the income earned while funds are held in the court's registry to a variable rate based on the amount deposited with the court and, in certain cases, the length of time funds are held in the court's registry.

The revised fee will be a fee of 10 percent of the total income received during each income period from investments of less than $100,000,000 of registry funds in income-bearing accounts. On investments exceeding $100,000,000 the 10 percent fee shall be reduced by one percent for each increment of $50,000,000 over the initial $100,000,000. For those deposits where funds are placed in the registry by court order for a time certain, for example, by the terms of an adjudicated trust, the fee will be further reduced. This further reduction will amount to 2.5 percent for each five-year interval or part thereof. The total minimum fee to be charged will be no less than two percent of the income on investments.

The following table sets out the fee schedule promulgated by this notice:

REGISTRY—SCHEDULE OF FEES

[% of income earned]

Amount of deposit *	0–5 yrs.	>5–10 yrs.	>10–15 yrs.	>15 yrs.
less than 100M	10	7.5	5.0	2.5
100M–<150M	9	6.5	4.0	2.0
150M–<200M	8	5.5	3.0	2.0
200M–<250M	7	4.5	2.0	2.0
250M–<300M	6	3.5	2.0	2.0
300M–<350M	5	2.5	2.0	2.0
350M–<400M	4	2.0	2.0	2.0
400M–<450M	3	2.0	2.0	2.0
over 450M	2	2.0	2.0	2.0

* Except where otherwise authorized by the Director, each deposit into any account is treated separately in determining the fee.

The new fee applies to all earnings applied to investments on and after the effective date of this change, except for earnings on investments in cases being administered under the provisions of the May 11, 1989 notice [54 FR 20407], i.e., to which the fee equal to the first 45 days income is applicable.

The fee, as modified herein, will continue to apply to any case where the court has authorized the investment of funds placed in its custody or held by it in trust in its registry regardless of the nature of the underlying action.

The fee does not apply in the District Court of Guam, the Northern Mariana Islands, the Virgin Islands, the United States Claims Court, or any other Federal court whose fees are not set under 28 U.S.C. §§ 1913, 1914, and 1930.

§ 1915. Proceedings in forma pauperis

(a)(1) Subject to subsection (b), any court of the United States may authorize the commencement, prosecution or defense of any suit, action or proceeding, civil or criminal, or appeal therein, without prepayment of fees or security therefor, by a person who submits an affidavit that includes a statement of all assets such prisoner possesses that the person is unable to pay such fees or give security therefor. Such affidavit shall state the nature of the action, defense or appeal and affiant's belief that the person is entitled to redress.

(2) A prisoner seeking to bring a civil action or appeal a judgment in a civil action or proceeding without prepayment of fees or security therefor, in addition to filing the affidavit filed under paragraph (1), shall submit a certified copy of the trust fund account statement (or institutional equivalent) for the prisoner for the 6-month period immediately preceding the filing of the complaint or notice of appeal, obtained from the appropriate official of each prison at which the prisoner is or was confined.

(3) An appeal may not be taken in forma pauperis if the trial court certifies in writing that it is not taken in good faith.

(b)(1) Notwithstanding subsection (a), if a prisoner brings a civil action or files an appeal in forma pauperis, the prisoner shall be required to pay the full amount of a filing fee. The court shall assess and, when funds exist, collect, as a partial payment of any court fees required by law, an initial partial filing fee of 20 percent of the greater of—

(A) the average monthly deposits to the prisoner's account; or

(B) the average monthly balance in the prisoner's account for the 6-month period immediately preceding the filing of the complaint or notice of appeal.

(2) After payment of the initial partial filing fee, the prisoner shall be required to make monthly payments of 20 percent of the preceding month's income credited to the prisoner's account. The agency having custody of the prisoner shall forward payments from the prisoner's account to the clerk of the court each time the amount in the account exceeds $10 until the filing fees are paid.

(3) In no event shall the filing fee collected exceed the amount of fees permitted by statute for the commencement of a civil action or an appeal of a civil action or criminal judgment.

(4) In no event shall a prisoner be prohibited from bringing a civil action or appealing a civil or criminal judgment for the reason that the prisoner has no assets and no means by which to pay the initial partial filing fee.

(c) Upon the filing of an affidavit in accordance with subsections (a) and (b) and the prepayment of any partial filing fee as may be required under subsection (b), the court may direct payment by the United States of the expenses of (1) printing the record on appeal in any civil or criminal case, if such printing is required by the appellate court; (2) preparing a transcript of proceedings before a United States magistrate in any civil or criminal case, if such transcript is required by the district court, in the case of proceedings conducted under section 636(b) of this title or under section 3401(b) of title 18, United States Code; and (3) printing the record on appeal if such printing is required by the appellate court, in the case of proceedings conducted pursuant to section 636(c) of this title. Such expenses shall be paid when authorized by the Director of the Administrative Office of the United States Courts.

(d) The officers of the court shall issue and serve all process, and perform all duties in such cases. Witnesses shall attend as in other cases, and the same remedies shall be available as are provided for by law in other cases.

(e)(1) The court may request an attorney to represent any person unable to afford counsel.

(2) Notwithstanding any filing fee, or any portion thereof, that may have been paid, the court shall dismiss the case at any time if the court determines that—

(A) the allegation of poverty is untrue; or

(B) the action or appeal—

(i) is frivolous or malicious;

(ii) fails to state a claim on which relief may be granted; or

(iii) seeks monetary relief against a defendant who is immune from such relief.

(f)(1) Judgment may be rendered for costs at the conclusion of the suit or action as in other proceedings, but the United States shall not be liable for any of the costs thus incurred. If the United States has paid the cost of a stenographic transcript or printed record for the prevailing party, the same shall be taxed in favor of the United States.

(2)(A) If the judgment against a prisoner includes the payment of costs under this subsection, the prisoner shall be required to pay the full amount of the costs ordered.

(B) The prisoner shall be required to make payments for costs under this subsection in the same manner as is provided for filing fees under subsection (a)(2).

(C) In no event shall the costs collected exceed the amount of the costs ordered by the court.

(g) In no event shall a prisoner bring a civil action or appeal a judgment in a civil action or proceeding under this section if the prisoner has, on 3 or more prior occasions, while incarcerated or detained in any facility, brought an action or appeal in a court of the United States that was dismissed on the grounds that it is frivolous, malicious, or fails to state a claim upon which relief may be granted, unless the prisoner is under imminent danger of serious physical injury.

(h) As used in this section, the term 'prisoner' means any person incarcerated or detained in any facility who is accused of, convicted of, sentenced for, or adjudicated delinquent for, violations of criminal law or the terms and conditions of parole, probation, pretrial release, or diversionary program.

(June 25, 1948, c. 646, 62 Stat. 954; May 24, 1949, c. 139, § 98, 63 Stat. 104; Oct. 31, 1951, c. 655, § 51(b), (c), 65 Stat. 727; Sept. 21, 1959, Pub.L. 86–320, 73 Stat. 590; Oct. 10, 1979, Pub.L. 96–82, § 6, 93 Stat. 645; Apr. 26, 1996, Pub.L. 104–134, Title I, § 101[(a)][Title VIII, § 804(a), (c) to (e)], 110 Stat. 1321–73, 1321–74, 1321–75; renumbered Title I May 2, 1996, Pub.L. 104–140, § 1(a), 110 Stat. 1327.)

HISTORICAL AND STATUTORY NOTES

Change of Name

United States magistrate appointed under section 631 of this title to be known as United States magistrate judge after Dec. 1, 1990, with any reference to United States magistrate or magistrate in this title, in any other Federal statute, etc., deemed a reference to United States magistrate judge appointed under section 631 of this title, see section 321 of Pub.L. 101–650, set out as a note under section 631 of this title.

Severability of Provisions

If any provision of section 101[a] [Title VIII] of Pub.L. 104–134, an amendment made by such Title, or the application of such provision or amendment to any person or circumstance is held to be unconstitutional, the remainder of such Title, the amendments made by such Title, and the application of the provisions of such Title to any person or circumstance not affected thereby, see section 101[a] [Title VIII, § 810] of Pub.L. 104–134, set out as a note under section 3626 of Title 18, Crimes and Criminal Procedure.

§ 1915A. Screening

(a) Screening.—The court shall review, before docketing, if feasible or, in any event, as soon as practicable after docketing, a complaint in a civil action in which a prisoner seeks redress from a governmental entity or officer or employee of a governmental entity.

(b) Grounds for dismissal.—On review, the court shall identify cognizable claims or dismiss the complaint, or any portion of the complaint, if the complaint—

(1) is frivolous, malicious, or fails to state a claim upon which relief may be granted; or

(2) seeks monetary relief from a defendant who is immune from such relief.

(c) Definition.—As used in this section, the term "prisoner" means any person incarcerated or detained in any facility who is accused of, convicted of, sentenced for, or adjudicated delinquent for, violations of criminal law or the terms and conditions of parole, probation, pretrial release, or diversionary program.

(Added Pub.L. 104–134, Title I, § 101[(a)][Title VIII, § 805(a)], Apr. 26, 1996, 110 Stat. 1321–75; renumbered Title I Pub.L. 104–140, § 1(a), May 2, 1996, 110 Stat. 1327.)

HISTORICAL AND STATUTORY NOTES

Severability of Provisions

If any provision of section 101[a] [Title VIII] of Pub.L. 104–134, an amendment made by such Title, or the application of such provision or amendment to any person or circumstance is held to be unconstitutional, the remainder of such Title, the amendments made by such Title, and the application of the provisions of such Title to any person or circumstance not affected thereby, see section 101[a] [Title VIII, § 810] of Pub.L. 104–134, set out as a note under section 3626 of Title 18, Crimes and Criminal Procedure.

§ 1916. Seamen's suits

In all courts of the United States, seamen may institute and prosecute suits and appeals in their own names and for their own benefit for wages or salvage or the enforcement of laws enacted for their health or safety without prepaying fees or costs or furnishing security therefor.

(June 25, 1948, c. 646, 62 Stat. 955.)

§ 1917. District courts; fee on filing notice of or petition for appeal

Upon the filing of any separate or joint notice of appeal or application for appeal or upon the receipt of any order allowing, or notice of the allowance of, an appeal or of a writ of certiorari $5 shall be paid to the clerk of the district court, by the appellant or petitioner.

(June 25, 1948, c. 646, 62 Stat. 955.)

§ 1918. District courts; fines, forfeitures and criminal proceedings

(a) Costs shall be included in any judgment, order, or decree rendered against any person for the violation of an Act of Congress in which a civil fine or forfeiture of property is provided for.

(b) Whenever any conviction for any offense not capital is obtained in a district court, the court may order that the defendant pay the costs of prosecution.

(June 25, 1948, c. 646, 62 Stat. 955.)

§ 1919. Dismissal for lack of jurisdiction

Whenever any action or suit is dismissed in any district court, the Court of International Trade, or the Court of Federal Claims for want of jurisdiction, such court may order the payment of just costs.

(June 25, 1948, c. 646, 62 Stat. 955; Oct. 10, 1980, Pub.L. 96–417, Title V, § 510, 94 Stat. 1743; Oct. 29, 1992, Pub.L. 102–572, Title IX, § 908(a), (b)(1), 106 Stat. 4519.)

HISTORICAL AND STATUTORY NOTES

Effective Dates

1992 Acts. Amendment by Title IX of Pub.L. 102–572 effective Oct. 29, 1992, see section 911 of Pub.L. 102–572, set out as a note under section 171 of this title.

1980 Acts. Amendment by Pub.L. 96–417 applicable with respect to civil actions commenced on or after Nov. 1, 1980, see section 701(b)(1)(E) of Pub.L. 96–417, as amended, set out as a note under section 251 of this title.

§ 1920. Taxation of costs

A judge or clerk of any court of the United States may tax as costs the following:

(1) Fees of the clerk and marshal;

(2) Fees of the court reporter for all or any part of the stenographic transcript necessarily obtained for use in the case;

(3) Fees and disbursements for printing and witnesses;

(4) Fees for exemplification and copies of papers necessarily obtained for use in the case;

(5) Docket fees under section 1923 of this title;

(6) Compensation of court appointed experts, compensation of interpreters, and salaries, fees, expenses, and costs of special interpretation services under section 1828 of this title.

A bill of costs shall be filed in the case and, upon allowance, included in the judgment or decree.

(June 25, 1948, c. 646, 62 Stat. 955; Oct. 28, 1978, Pub.L. 95–539, § 7, 92 Stat. 2044.)

HISTORICAL AND STATUTORY NOTES

Effective Dates

1978 Acts. Amendment by Pub.L. 95–539 effective Oct. 28, 1978, see section 10(a) of Pub.L. 95–539, set out as a note under section 602 of this title.

§ 1921. United States marshal's fees

(a)(1) The United States marshals or deputy marshals shall routinely collect, and a court may tax as costs, fees for the following:

(A) Serving a writ of possession, partition, execution, attachment in rem, or libel in admiralty, warrant, attachment, summons, complaints, or any other writ, order or process in any case or proceeding.

(B) Serving a subpoena or summons for a witness or appraiser.

(C) Forwarding any writ, order, or process to another judicial district for service.

(D) The preparation of any notice of sale, proclamation in admiralty, or other public notice or bill of sale.

(E) The keeping of attached property (including boats, vessels, or other property attached or libeled), actual expenses incurred, such as storage, moving, boat hire, or other special transportation, watchmen's or keepers' fees, insurance, and an hourly rate, including overtime, for each deputy marshal required for special services, such as guarding, inventorying, and moving.

(F) Copies of writs or other papers furnished at the request of any party.

(G) Necessary travel in serving or endeavoring to serve any process, writ, or order, except in the District of Columbia, with mileage to be computed from the place where service is returnable to the place of service or endeavor.

(H) Overtime expenses incurred by deputy marshals in the course of serving or executing civil process.

(2) The marshals shall collect, in advance, a deposit to cover the initial expenses for special services required under paragraph (1)(E), and periodically thereafter such amounts as may be necessary to pay such expenses until the litigation is concluded. This paragraph applies to all private litigants, including seamen proceeding pursuant to section 1916 of this title.

(3) For purposes of paragraph (1)(G), if two or more services or endeavors, or if an endeavor and a service, are made in behalf of the same party in the same case on the same trip, mileage shall be computed to the place of service or endeavor which is most remote from the place where service is returnable, adding thereto any additional mileage traveled in serving or endeavoring to serve in behalf of the party. If two or more writs of any kind, required to be served in behalf of the same party on the same person in the same case or proceeding, may be served at the same time, mileage on only one such writ shall be collected.

(b) The Attorney General shall from time to time prescribe by regulation the fees to be taxed and collected under subsection (a). Such fees shall, to the extent practicable, reflect the actual and reasonable cost of the service provided.

(c)(1) The United States Marshals Service shall collect a commission of 3 percent of the first $1,000 collected and 1½ percent on the excess of any sum over $1,000, for seizing or levying on property (including seizures in admiralty), disposing of such property by sale, setoff, or otherwise, and receiving and paying over money, except that the amount of commission shall be within the range set by the Attorney General. if[1] the property is not disposed of by marshal's sale, the commission shall be in such amount, within the range set by the Attorney General, as may be allowed by the court. In any case in which the vessel or other property is sold by a public auctioneer, or by some party other than a marshal or deputy marshal, the commission authorized under this subsection shall be reduced by the amount paid to such auctioneer or other party. This subsection applies to any judicially ordered sale or execution sale, without regard to whether the judicial order of sale constitutes a seizure or levy within the meaning of State law. This subsection shall not apply to any seizure, forfeiture, sale, or other disposition of property pursuant to the applicable provisions of law amended by the Comprehensive Forfeiture Act of 1984 (98 Stat. 2040).

(2) The Attorney General shall prescribe from time to time regulations which establish a minimum and maximum amount for the commission collected under paragraph (1).

(d) The United States marshals may require a deposit to cover the fees and expenses prescribed under this section.

(e) Notwithstanding section 3302 of title 31, the United States Marshals Service is authorized, to the extent provided in advance in appropriations Acts—

(1) to credit to such Service's appropriation all fees, commissions, and expenses collected by such Service for—

(A) the service of civil process, including complaints, summonses, subpoenas, and similar process; and

(B) seizures, levies, and sales associated with judicial orders of execution; and

(2) to use such credited amounts for the purpose of carrying out such activities.

(June 25, 1948, c. 646, 62 Stat. 955; Sept. 9, 1950, c. 937, 64 Stat. 824; Aug. 31, 1962, Pub.L. 87–621, § 1, 76 Stat. 417; Nov. 10, 1986, Pub.L. 99–646, § 39(a), 100 Stat. 3600; Nov. 18, 1988, Pub.L. 100–690, Title VII, § 7608(c), 102 Stat. 4515; Nov. 29, 1990, Pub.L. 101–647, Title XII, § 1212, 104 Stat. 4833.)

[1] So in original. Probably should be capitalized.

HISTORICAL AND STATUTORY NOTES

References in Text

The Comprehensive Forfeiture Act of 1984, referred to in subsec. (c)(1), is chapter III (sections 301 to 322) of Title II of Pub.L. 98–473, Oct. 12, 1984, 98 Stat. 2040, as amended. For complete classification of this Act to the Code, see Short Title of 1984 Amendments note set out under section 1961 of Title 18, Crimes and Criminal Procedure, and Tables.

Effective Dates

1986 Acts. Section 39(b) of Pub.L. 99–646 provided that: "The amendments made by this section [amending this section] shall take effect 30 days after the date of enactment of this Act [Nov. 10, 1986]."

1962 Acts. Section 3 of Pub.L. 87–621 provided that: "This Act [amending this section] shall become effective ninety days after enactment [Aug. 31, 1962]."

Collection and Disposition of Fees and Expenses for Services

Pub.L. 101–162, Title II, Nov. 21, 1989, 103 Stat. 997, provided in part: "That notwithstanding the provisions of title 31 U.S.C. 3302 [section 3302 of Title 31, Money and

Finance], for fiscal year 1990 and hereafter the Director of the United States Marshals Service may collect fees and expenses for the services authorized by 28 U.S.C. 1921 as amended by Public Law 100–690 [this section], and credit such fees to this appropriation to be used for salaries and other expenses incurred in providing these services."

§ 1922. Witness fees before United States commissioners

The fees of more than four witnesses shall not be taxed against the United States, in the examination of any criminal case before a United States commissioner, unless their materiality and importance are first approved and certified to by the United States attorney for the district in which the examination is had.

(June 25, 1948, c. 646, 62 Stat. 956.)

HISTORICAL AND STATUTORY NOTES

Change of Name

Reference to United States commissioners deemed to be reference to United States magistrates pursuant to Pub.L. 90–578. Title IV, § 402, Oct. 17, 1968, 32 Stat. 1118. See chapter 43 (section 631 et seq.) of this title.

United States magistrate appointed under section 631 of this title to be known as United States magistrate judge after Dec. 1, 1990, with any reference to United States magistrate or magistrate in this title, in any other Federal statute, etc., deemed a reference to United States magistrate judge appointed under section 631 of this title, see section 321 of Pub.L. 101–650, set out as a note under section 631 of this title.

§ 1923. Docket fees and costs of briefs

(a) Attorney's and proctor's docket fees in courts of the United States may be taxed as costs as follows:

$20 on trial or final hearing (including a default judgment whether entered by the court or by the clerk) in civil, criminal, or admiralty cases, except that in cases of admiralty and maritime jurisdiction where the libellant recovers less than $50 the proctor's docket fee shall be $10;

$20 in admiralty appeals involving not over $1,000;

$50 in admiralty appeals involving not over $5,000;

$100 in admiralty appeals involving more than $5,000;

$5 on discontinuance of a civil action;

$5 on motion for judgment and other proceedings on recognizances;

$2.50 for each deposition admitted in evidence.

(b) The docket fees of United States attorneys and United States trustees shall be paid to the clerk of court and by him paid into the Treasury.

(c) In admiralty appeals the court may allow as costs for printing the briefs of the successful party not more than:

$25 where the amount involved is not over $1,000;

$50 where the amount involved is not over $5,000;

$75 where the amount involved is over $5,000.

(June 25, 1948, c. 646, 62 Stat. 956; June 18, 1954, c. 304, 68 Stat. 253; Nov. 6, 1978, Pub.L. 95–598, Title II, § 245, 92 Stat. 2671.)

HISTORICAL AND STATUTORY NOTES

Codifications

Section 408(c) of Pub.L. 95–598, Nov. 6, 1978, 92 Stat. 2687, as amended by Pub.L. 98–166, Title II, § 200, Nov. 28, 1983, 97 Stat. 1081; Pub.L. 98–353, Title III, § 323, July 10, 1984, 98 Stat. 358; Pub.L. 99–429, Sept. 30, 1986, 100 Stat. 985; Pub.L. 99–500, § 101(b) [title II, § 200], Oct. 18, 1986, 100 Stat. 1783–39, 1783–45, and Pub.L. 99–591, § 101(b) [Title II, § 200], Oct. 30, 1986, 100 Stat. 3341–39, 3341–45; Pub.L. 99–554, Title III, § 307(a), Oct. 27, 1986, 100 Stat. 3125, which provided for the deletion of any references to United States Trustees in this title at a prospective date, was repealed by Pub.L. 99–554, Title III, § 307(b), Oct. 27, 1986, 100 Stat. 3125.

[For effective date of repeal, see section 302 of Pub.L. 99–554, set out as a note under section 581 of Title 28.]

Effective Dates

1978 Acts. Amendment by Pub.L. 95–598 effective Oct. 1, 1979, see section 402(c) of Pub.L. 95–598, set out as a note preceding section 101 of Title 11, Bankruptcy.

§ 1924. Verification of bill of costs

Before any bill of costs is taxed, the party claiming any item of cost or disbursement shall attach thereto an affidavit, made by himself or by his duly authorized attorney or agent having knowledge of the facts, that such item is correct and has been necessarily incurred in the case and that the services for which fees have been charged were actually and necessarily performed.

(June 25, 1948, c. 646, 62 Stat. 957.)

§ 1925. Admiralty and maritime cases

Except as otherwise provided by Act of Congress, the allowance and taxation of costs in admiralty and maritime cases shall be prescribed by rules promulgated by the Supreme Court.

(June 25, 1948, c. 646, 62 Stat. 957.)

§ 1926. Court of Federal Claims

(a) The Judicial Conference of the United States shall prescribe from time to time the fees and costs to be charged and collected in the United States Court of Federal Claims.

(b) The court and its officers shall collect only such fees and costs as the Judicial Conference prescribes.

The court may require advance payment of fees by rule.

(June 25, 1948, c. 646, 62 Stat. 957; Apr. 2, 1982, Pub.L. 97–164, Title I, § 139(p)(1), 96 Stat. 44; Oct. 29, 1992, Pub.L. 102–572, Title IX, § 902(b), 106 Stat. 4516.)

HISTORICAL AND STATUTORY NOTES

Effective Dates

1992 Acts. Amendment by Pub.L. 102–572 effective Oct. 29, 1992, see section 911 of Pub.L. 102–572, set out as a note under section 171 of this title.

1982 Acts. Amendment by Pub.L. 97–164 effective Oct. 1, 1982, see section 402 of Pub.L. 97–164, set out as a note under section 171 of this title.

Court Fees for Electronic Access to Information

Judicial Conference to prescribe reasonable fees for collection by courts under this section for access to information available through automatic data processing equipment and fees to be deposited in Judiciary Automation Fund, see section 303 of Pub.L. 102–140, set out as a note under section 1913 of this title.

JUDICIAL CONFERENCE SCHEDULE OF FEES

The Federal Courts Improvement Act of 1982 [Pub.L. 97–164, Apr. 2, 1982, 96 Stat. 25] added a new Sec. 1926 to Title 28, United States Code [this section], authorizing the Judicial Conference to prescribe from time to time the fees and costs to be charged and collected in the United States Claims Court [now Court of Federal Claims]. A fee schedule was approved, effective October 1, 1982. At its March 1987 meeting, the Judicial Conference amended the schedule of fees to be effective May 1, 1987. Amendments to this revision of the schedule of fees were adopted at the September, 1988 and March, 1990 meetings of the Judicial Conference. At its September, 1992 meeting, the Judicial Conference amended the schedule of fees to be effective Nov. 15, 1992. The Judicial Conference at its March 15, 1995 meeting adopted amendments to the fees schedule to be effective April 18, 1995, and at its 1996 meeting it adopted amendments to be effective April 15, 1996.

Following are fees to be charged for services to be performed by the clerk of the United States Court of Federal Claims. No fees are to be charged for services rendered on behalf of the United States, with the exception of those specifically prescribed in items 2, 8 and 9. No fees under this schedule shall be charged to federal agencies or programs which are funded from judiciary appropriations, including, but not limited to, agencies, organizations, and individuals providing services authorized by the Criminal Justice Act, 18 U.S.C. § 3006A, and Bankruptcy Administrator programs.

(1) For filing a civil action or proceeding, $120.

(2) For reproducing any record or paper, 50 cents per page. This fee shall apply to paper copies made from either: (a) original documents; or (b) microfiche or microfilm reproductions of the original records. This fee shall apply to services rendered on behalf of the United States if the record or paper requested is available through electronic access.

(3) For certification or exemplification of any document or paper, whether the certification is made directly on the document or by separate instrument, $5.

(4) For admission of attorneys to practice, $20 each, including a certificate of admission. For a duplicate certificate of admission or certificate of good standing, $5.

(5) For receipt of a monthly listing of court orders and opinions, $10 per year.

(6) The court may charge and collect fees, commensurate with the cost of printing, for copies of the local rules of court. The court may also distribute copies of the local rules without charge.

(7) For a check paid into the court which is returned for lack of funds, $25.

(8) For usage of electronic access to court data, 60 cents per minute of usage [provided the court may, for good cause, exempt persons or classes of persons from the fees, in order to avoid unreasonable burdens and to promote public access to such information]. All such fees collected shall be deposited to the Judiciary Automation Fund. This fee shall apply to the United States. (The Judicial Conference has approved an advisory note clarifying the judiciary's policy with respect to exemptions from this fee. The advisory note is attached to this fee schedule as an Appendix.)

(9) For every search of the records of the Court of Federal Claims conducted by the clerk of the court or a deputy clerk, $15 per name or item searched. This fee shall apply to services rendered on behalf of the United States if the information requested is available through electronic access. (The Judicial Conference has adopted guidelines to assist courts in the application of this fee. The Guidelines are attached to the District Court Fee Schedule as Appendix I.)

APPENDIX

The Judicial Conference has prescribed a fee for electronic access to court data, as set forth above in the Miscellaneous Fee Schedule. The schedule provides that the court may exempt persons or classes of persons from the fees, in order to avoid unreasonable burdens and to promote public access to such information. Exemptions should be granted as the exception, not the rule. The exemption language is intended to accommodate those users who might otherwise not have access to the information in this electronic form. It is not intended to provide a means by which a court would exempt all users.

Examples of persons and classes of persons who may be exempted from electronic public access fees include, but are not limited to: indigents; bankruptcy case trustees; not-for-profit organizations; and voluntary ADR neutrals.

§ 1927. Counsel's liability for excessive costs

Any attorney or other person admitted to conduct cases in any court of the United States or any Territory thereof who so multiplies the proceedings in any case unreasonably and vexatiously may be required by the court to satisfy personally the excess costs, expenses, and attorneys' fees reasonably incurred because of such conduct.

(June 25, 1948, c. 646, 62 Stat. 957; Sept. 12, 1980, Pub.L. 96–349, § 3, 94 Stat. 1156.)

§ 1928. Patent infringement action; disclaimer not filed

Whenever a judgment is rendered for the plaintiff in any patent infringement action involving a part of a patent and it appears that the patentee, in his specifications, claimed to be, but was not, the original and first inventor or discoverer of any material or substantial part of the thing patented, no costs shall be included in such judgment, unless the proper disclaimer has been filed in the Patent Office prior to the commencement of the action.

(June 25, 1948, c. 646, 62 Stat. 957.)

HISTORICAL AND STATUTORY NOTES

Change of Name

Patent Office redesignated Patent and Trademark Office by section 3 of Pub.L. 93–596, Jan. 2, 1975, 88 Stat. 1949, set out as a note under section 1 of Title 35, Patents.

§ 1929. Extraordinary expenses not expressly authorized

Where the ministerial officers of the United States incur extraordinary expense in executing Acts of Congress, the payment of which is not specifically provided for, the Attorney General may allow the payment thereof.

(June 25, 1948, c. 646, 62 Stat. 957.)

§ 1930. Bankruptcy fees

(a) Notwithstanding section 1915 of this title, the parties commencing a case under title 11 shall pay to the clerk of the district court or the clerk of the bankruptcy court, if one has been certified pursuant to section 156(b) of this title, the following filing fees:

(1) For a case commenced under chapter 7 or 13 of title 11, $130.

(2) For a case commenced under chapter 9 of title 11, $300.

(3) For a case commenced under chapter 11 of title 11 that does not concern a railroad, as defined in section 101 of title 11, $800.

(4) For a case commenced under chapter 11 of title 11 concerning a railroad, as so defined, $1,000.

(5) For a case commenced under chapter 12 of title 11, $200.

(6) In addition to the filing fee paid to the clerk, a quarterly fee shall be paid to the United States trustee, for deposit in the Treasury, in each case under chapter 11 of title 11 for each quarter (including any fraction thereof) until the case is converted or dismissed, whichever occurs first. The fee shall be $250 for each quarter in which disbursements total less than $15,000; $500 for each quarter in which disbursements total $15,000 or more but less than $75,000; $750 for each quarter in which disbursements total $75,000 or more but less than $150,000; $1,250 for each quarter in which disbursements total $150,000 or more but less than $225,000; $1,500 for each quarter in which disbursements total $225,000 or more but less than $300,000; $3,750 for each quarter in which disbursements total $300,000 or more but less than $1,000,000; $5,000 for each quarter in which disbursements total $1,000,000 or more but less than $2,000,000; $7,500 for each quarter in which disbursements total $2,000,000 or more but less than $3,000,000; $8,000 for each quarter in which disbursements total $3,000,000 or more but less than $5,000,000; $10,000 for each quarter in which disbursements total $5,000,000 or more. The fee shall be payable on the last day of the calendar month following the calendar quarter for which the fee is owed.

An individual commencing a voluntary case or a joint case under title 11 may pay such fee in installments. For converting, on request of the debtor, a case under chapter 7, or 13 of title 11, to a case under chapter 11 of title 11, the debtor shall pay to the clerk of the district court or the clerk of the bankruptcy court, if one has been certified pursuant to section 156(b) of this title, a fee of $400.

(b) The Judicial Conference of the United States may prescribe additional fees in cases under title 11 of the same kind as the Judicial Conference prescribes under section 1914(b) of this title.

(c) Upon the filing of any separate or joint notice of appeal or application for appeal or upon the receipt of any order allowing, or notice of the allowance of, an appeal or a writ of certiorari $5 shall be paid to the clerk of the court, by the appellant or petitioner.

(d) Whenever any case or proceeding is dismissed in any bankruptcy court for want of jurisdiction, such court may order the payment of just costs.

(e) The clerk of the court may collect only the fees prescribed under this section.

(Added Pub.L. 95–598, Title II, § 246(a), Nov. 6, 1978, 92 Stat. 2671, and amended Pub.L. 98–353, Title I, § 111(a), (b), July 10, 1984, 98 Stat. 342; Pub.L. 99–500, Title I, § 101(b) [Title IV, § 407(b)], Oct. 18, 1986, 100 Stat. 1783–64; Pub.L. 99–554, Title I, §§ 117, 144(f), Oct. 27, 1986, 100 Stat. 3095, 3097; Pub.L. 99–591, Title I, § 101(b) [Title IV, § 407(b)], Oct. 30, 1986, 100 Stat. 3341–64; Pub.L. 101–162, Title IV, § 406(a), Nov. 21, 1989, 103 Stat. 1016; Pub.L. 102–140, Title I, § 111(a), Oct. 28, 1991, 105 Stat. 795; Pub.L. 103–121, Title I, § 111(a)(1), (b)(1), Oct. 27, 1993, 107 Stat. 1164; Pub.L. 104–91, Title I, § 101(a), Jan. 6, 1996, 110 Stat. 11, as amended Pub.L. 104–99, Title II, § 211, Jan. 26, 1996, 110 Stat. 37; Pub.L. 104–208, Div. A, Title I, § 101(a) [Title I, § 109(a)], Sept. 30, 1996, 110 Stat. 3009–18.)

HISTORICAL AND STATUTORY NOTES

Codifications

Pub.L. 99–591 is a corrected version of Pub.L. 99–500.

Section 101(a) of Pub.L. 104–91, as amended by section 211 of Pub.L. 104–99, provided in part that section 111(a) of the General Provisions for the Department of Justice in Title I of the Departments of Commerce, Justice, and State, the Judiciary, and Related Agencies Appropriations Act, 1996 (H.R. 2076) as passed by the House of Representatives on Dec. 6, 1995, was enacted into permanent law. Such section 111(a) of H.R. 2076 amended subsec. (a)(6) of this section. See 1996 Amendments note set out under this section.

Effective Dates

1993 Acts. Section 111(a) of Pub.L. 103–121 provided in part that amendment by section 111(a)(1) of Pub.L. 103–121, amending subsec. (a)(1) of this section, is effective 30 days after Oct. 27, 1993.

Section 111(b) of Pub.L. 103–121 provided in part that amendment by section 111(b)(1) of Pub.L. 103–121, amending subsec. (a)(3) of this section, is effective 30 days after Oct. 27, 1993.

1991 Acts. Amendment by Pub.L. 102–140 effective 60 days after the date of the enactment of Pub.L. 102–140, which was approved Oct. 28, 1991, see section 111(a) of Pub.L. 102–140, set out as a note under section 589a of this title.

1986 Acts. Amendment by Pub.L. 99–554 effective 30 days after Oct. 27, 1986, except as otherwise provided for, see section 302(a) of Pub.L. 99–554, set out as a note under section 581 of this title.

Amendment by Pub.L. 99–554, § 117(4), not to become effective in or with respect to certain specified judicial districts until, or apply to cases while pending in such district before, the expiration of the 270-day period beginning 30 days after Oct. 27, 1986, or of the 30-day period beginning on the date the Attorney General certifies under section 303 of Pub.L. 99–554 the region specified in a paragraph of section 581(a) of Title 28, as amended by section 111(a) of Pub.L. 99–554, that includes such district, whichever occurs first, see section 302(d)(1) of Pub.L. 99–554, set out as a note under section 581 of this title.

Amendment by Pub.L. 99–554, § 117(4), not to become effective in or with respect to certain specified judicial districts until, or apply to cases while pending in such district before, the expiration of the 2-year period beginning 30 days after Oct. 27, 1986, or of the 30-day period beginning on the date the Attorney General certifies under section 303 of Pub.L. 99–554 the region specified in a paragraph of section 581(a) of Title 28, as amended by section 111(a) of Pub.L. 99–554, that includes such district, whichever occurs first, see section 302(d)(2) of Pub.L. 99–554, set out as a note under section 581 of this title.

Amendment by Pub.L. 99–554, § 117(4), not to become effective in or with respect to judicial districts established for the States of Alabama and North Carolina until, or apply to cases while pending in such district before, such district elects to be included in a bankruptcy region established in section 581(a) of Title 28, as amended by section 111(a) of Pub.L. 99–554, or Oct. 1, 2002, whichever occurs first, and, except as otherwise provided for, with respect to cases under chapters 7, 11, 12, and 13 of Title 11 commenced before 30 days after Oct. 27, 1986, and pending in a judicial district in the States of Alabama or North Carolina before any election made under section 302(d)(3)(A) of Pub.L. 99–554 by such district becomes effective or Oct. 1, 2002, whichever occurs first, amendments by Pub.L. 99–554 not to apply until Oct. 1, 2003, or the expiration of the 1-year period beginning on the date such election becomes effective, whichever occurs first, and further, in any judicial district in Alabama or North Carolina not making the election described in section 302(d)(3)(A) of Pub.L. 99–554, any person appointed under regulations issued by the Judicial Conference to administer estates in cases under Title 11 authorized to establish, etc., a panel of private trustees, and to supervise cases and trustees in cases under chapters 7, 11, 12, and 13 of Title 11, until amendments by sections 201 to 231 of Pub.L. 99–554 effective in such district, see section 302(d)(3)(A) to (F), (H), (I) of Pub.L. 99–554, set out as a note under section 581 of this title.

Deposit in the general receipts of the Treasury of funds collected as a result of the amendments made by section 117 of Pub.L. 99–554 in a judicial district in the States of Alabama or North Carolina under section 1930(a) of Title 28 before the date the amendments made by sections 201 to 231 of Pub.L. 99–554 take effect in such districts, and notwithstanding section 589a of Title 28, see section 302(d)(3)(G) of Pub.L. 99–554, set out as a note under section 581 of this title.

Amendment by Pub.L. 99–554, § 117(4), except as otherwise provided, with respect to cases under chapters 7, 11, 12, and 13 of Title 11 commenced before 30 days after Oct. 27, 1986, and pending in a judicial district referred to in section 581(a) of Title 28, as amended by section 111(a) of Pub.L. 99–554, for which a United States trustee is not authorized before 30 days after Oct. 27, 1986 to be appointed, not applicable until the expiration of the 3-year period beginning on Oct. 27, 1986, or of the 1-year period beginning on the date the Attorney General certifies under section 303 of Pub.L. 99–554 the region specified in a paragraph of such section 581(a) that includes, such district, whichever occurs first, see section 302(e)(1), (2) of Pub.L. 99–554, set out as a note under section 581 of this title.

Rule of construction regarding fees for cases under Title 11 for any conduct or period occurring before section 1930(a)(6) of Title 28 becomes effective in the district in which such case is pending, see section 302(e)(3) of Pub.L. 99–554, set out as a note under section 581 of this title.

1984 Acts. Amendment by Pub.L. 98–353 effective July 10, 1984, see section 122(a) of Pub.L. 98–353, set out as a note under section 151 of this title.

1979 Acts. Section effective Oct. 1, 1979, see section 402(c) of Pub.L. 95–598, set out as a note preceding section 101 of Title 11, Bankruptcy.

Effective Dates of 1989 Amendments; Miscellaneous Fees

Section 406(a) of Pub.L. 101–162 provided in part that: "Pursuant to section 1930(b) of title 28 [subsec. (b) of this section] the Judicial Conference of the United States shall prescribe a fee of $60 on motions seeking relief from the automatic stay under 11 U.S.C. section 362(b) [section 362(b) of Title 11, Bankruptcy] and motions to compel abandonment of property of the estate. The fees established pursuant to the preceding two sentences shall take effect 30 days after the enactment of this Act [Nov. 21, 1989]."

Accrual and Payment of Quarterly Fees in Chapter 11 Cases After Jan. 27, 1996; Confirmation Status of Plans

Section 101(a) of Pub.L. 104-91, as amended Pub.L. 104–99, Title II, § 211, Jan. 26, 1996, 110 Stat. 37; Pub.L. 104–208, Div. A, Title I, § 101(a) [Title I, § 109(d)], Sept. 30, 1996, 110 Stat. 3009–19, provided, in part: "That, notwithstanding any other provision of law, the fees under 28 U.S.C. 1930(a)(6) [subsec. (a)(6) of this section] shall accrue and be payable from and after January 27, 1996, in all cases (including, without limitation, any cases pending as of that date), regardless of confirmation status of their plans."

Collection and Disposition of Fees in Bankruptcy Cases

Section 404(a) of Pub. L. 101–162 provided that: "For fiscal year 1990 and hereafter, such fees as shall be collected for the preparation and mailing of notices in bankruptcy cases as prescribed by the Judicial Conference of the United States pursuant to 28 U.S.C. 1930(b) [subsec. (b) of this section] shall be deposited to the 'Courts of Appeals, District Courts, and Other Judicial Services, Salaries and Expenses' appropriation to be used for salaries and other expenses incurred in providing these services."

Court Fees for Electronic Access to Information

Judicial Conference to prescribe reasonable fees for collection by courts under this section for access to information available through automatic data processing equipment and fees to be deposited in Judiciary Automation Fund, see section 303 of Pub.L. 102–140, set out as a note under section 1913 of this title.

Issuance of Notices to Creditors and Other Interested Parties

Section 403 of Pub.L. 101–162 provided that: "Notwithstanding any other provision of law, for fiscal year 1990 and hereafter, (a) The Administrative Office of the United States Courts, or any other agency or instrumentality of the United States, is prohibited from restricting solely to staff of the Clerks of the United States Bankruptcy Courts the issuance of notices to creditors and other interested parties. (b) The Administrative Office shall permit and encourage the preparation and mailing of such notices to be performed by or at the expense of the debtors, trustees or such other interested parties as the Court may direct and approve. (c) The Director of the Administrative Office of the United States Courts shall make appropriate provisions for the use of and accounting for any postage required pursuant to such directives."

Report on Bankruptcy Fees

Section 111(d) of Pub.L. 103–121 provided that:

"(1) **Report required.**—Not later than March 31, 1998, the Judicial Conference of the United States shall submit to the Committees on the Judiciary of the House of Representatives and the Senate, a report relating to the bankruptcy fee system and the impact of such system on various participants in bankruptcy cases.

"(2) **Contents of report.**—Such report shall include—

"(A)(i) an evaluation of the costs and benefits that would result from waiving bankruptcy fees payable by debtors who are individuals, and

"(ii) recommendations regarding various revenue sources to offset the net cost of waiving such fees; and

"(B)(i) an evaluation of the effects that would result in cases under chapters 11 and 13 of title 11, United States Code [sections 1101 et seq. and 1301 et seq., respectively, of Title 11, Bankruptcy], from using a graduated bankruptcy fee system based on assets, liabilities, or both of the debtor, and

"(ii) recommendations regarding various methods to implement such a graduated bankruptcy fee system.

"(3) **Waiver of fees in selected districts.**—For purposes of carrying out paragraphs (1) and (2), the Judicial Conference of the United States shall carry out in not more than six judicial districts, throughout the 3-year period beginning on October 1, 1994, a program under which fees payable under section 1930 of title 28, United States Code [this section], may be waived in cases under chapter 7 of title 11, United States Code [section 701 et seq. of Title 11], for debtors who are individuals unable to pay such fees in installments.

"(4) **Study of graduated fee system.**—For purposes of carrying out paragraphs (1) and (2), the Judicial Conference of the United States shall carry out, in not fewer than six judicial districts, a study to estimate the results that would occur in cases under chapters 11 and 13 of title 11, United States Code [sections 1101 et seq. and 1301 et seq., respectively, of Title 11], if filing fees payable under section 1930 of title 28, United States Code [this section], were paid on a graduated scale based on assets, liabilities, or both of the debtor."

JUDICIAL CONFERENCE SCHEDULE OF FEES

The Judicial Conference of the United States at its session on March 7-9, 1979, set forth the schedule of fees to be charged in bankruptcy courts pursuant to this section. That schedule became effective on October 1, 1979. At its sessions in March and September 1980, March, 1981, March, 1987, and March and September, 1988, the Judicial Conference amended the schedule of fees. The Administrative Office of the United States Courts provided for Registry Fund Fees effective June 12, 1989. At its September, 1989 meeting, the Judicial Conference again amended the schedule of fees, such amendments effective pursuant to 1989 Judicial Conference Statement. The schedule of fees was again amended by the Judicial Conference at its March, 1990 and September, 1990 meetings. At its 1991 meeting, the Judicial Conference amended the schedule of fees to be effective Feb. 3, 1992. At its March 1991 meeting the Judicial Conference adopted Item 23 to be effective Oct. 19, 1992, with later implementation. At its September, 1992 meeting the Judicial Conference amended Item 8 to be effective Dec. 1, 1992. At its March, 1993 meeting the Judicial Conference amended its fee schedule effective May 6, 1993. At its September, 1993 meeting the Judicial Conference amended its fee schedule to be effective November 8, 1993. At its 1994 meeting, the Judicial Conference amended its fee schedule to be effective January 1, 1995. At its September, 1995 meeting the Judicial Conference amended its fee schedule to be effective November 9, 1995, and at its 1996 meetings it adopted amendments to be effective April 1, 1996 and October 28, 1996. At its 1997 meeting the Judicial Conference amended its fee schedule to be effective January 1, 1998.

Bankruptcy Court Miscellaneous Fee Schedule [1]

Following are fees to be charged for services to be performed by clerks of the bankruptcy courts. No fees are to be charged for services rendered on behalf of the United States, with the exception of those specifically prescribed in items 1, 5, and 23, or to bankruptcy administrators appointed under Public Law No. 99–554, § 302(d)(3)(I). No fees under this schedule shall be charged to federal agencies or programs which are funded from judiciary appropriations, including, but not limited to, agencies, organizations, and individuals providing services authorized by the Criminal Justice Act, 18 U.S.C. § 3006A.

(1) For reproducing any record or paper, 50 cents per page. This fee shall apply to paper copies made from either: (1) original documents; or (2) microfiche or microfilm reproductions of the original records. This fee shall apply to services rendered on behalf of the United States if the record or paper requested is available through electronic access.

(2) For certification of any document or paper, whether the certification is made directly on the document or by separate instrument, $5. For exemplification of any document or paper, twice the amount of the charge for certification.

(3) For reproduction of magnetic tape recordings, either cassette or reel-to-reel, $15 including the cost of materials.

(4) For amendments to a debtor's schedules of creditors or lists of creditors, $20 for each amendment, provided the bankruptcy judge may, for good cause, waive the charge in any case.

(5) For every search of the records of the bankruptcy court conducted by the clerk of the bankruptcy court or a deputy clerk, $15 per name or item searched. This fee shall apply to services rendered on behalf of the United States if the information requested is available through electronic access.

(6) For filing a complaint, a fee shall be collected in the same amount as the filing fee prescribed in 28 U.S.C. § 1914(a) for instituting any civil action other than a writ of habeas corpus. If the United States, other than a United States trustee acting as a trustee in a case under title 11, or a debtor is the plaintiff, no fee is required. If a trustee or debtor in possession is the plaintiff, the fee should be payable only from the estate and to the extent there is any estate realized. If a child support creditor or its representative is the plaintiff, and if such plaintiff files the form required by § 304(g) of the Bankruptcy Reform Act of 1994, no fee is required.

(7) For filing or indexing any paper not in a case or proceeding for which a filing fee has been paid, including registering a judgment from another district, $20.

(8) In all cases filed under Title 11, the clerk shall collect from the debtor or the petitioner a miscellaneous administrative fee of $30. This fee may be paid in installments in the same manner that the filing fee may be paid in installments, consistent with the procedure set forth in Federal Rule of Bankruptcy Procedure 1006.

(8.1) Upon the filing of a petition under chapter 7 of the Bankruptcy Code, the petitioner shall pay $15 to the clerk of the court for payment to trustees serving in cases as provided in 11 U.S.C. § 330(b)(2). An application to pay the fee in installments may be filed in the manner set forth in Federal Rule of Bankruptcy Procedure 1006(b).

(8.2) Upon the filing of a motion to convert a case to chapter 7 of the Bankruptcy Code, the movant shall pay $15 to the clerk of court for payment to trustees serving in cases as provided in 11 U.S.C. § 330(b)(2). Upon the filing of a notice of conversion pursuant to section 1208(a) or section 1307(a) of the Code, $15 shall be paid to the clerk of the court for payment to trustees serving in cases as provided in 11 U.S.C. § 330(b)(2). If the trustee serving in the case before the conversion is the movant, the fee shall be payable only from the estate that exists prior to conversion.

(9) For filing a motion to reopen a Bankruptcy Code case, a fee shall be collected in the same amount as the filing fee prescribed by 28 U.S.C. § 1930(a) for commencing a new case on the date of reopening, unless the reopening is to correct an administrative error or for actions related to the debtor's discharge. The court may waive this fee under appropriate circumstances or may defer payment of the fee from trustees pending discovery of additional assets.

(10) Repealed.

(11) Repealed.

(12) For each microfiche sheet of film or microfilm jacket copy of any court record, where available, $3.

(13) For retrieval of a record from a Federal Records Center, National Archives, or other storage location removed from the place of business of the court, $25.

(14) For a check paid into the court which is returned for lack of funds, $25.

(15) Repealed.

(16) For docketing a proceeding on appeal or review from a final judgment of a bankruptcy judge pursuant to 28 U.S.C. § 158(a) and (b), the fee shall be the same amount as the fee for docketing a case on appeal or review to the appellate court as required by Item 1 of the Courts of Appeals Miscellaneous Fee Schedule. A separate fee shall be paid by each party filing a notice of appeal in the bankruptcy court, but parties filing a joint notice of appeal in the bankruptcy court are required to pay only one fee.

(17) For filing a petition ancillary to a foreign proceeding under 11 U.S.C. § 304, $500.

(18) The court may charge and collect fees, commensurate with the cost of printing, for copies of the local rules of court. The court may also distribute copies of the local rules without charge.

(19) The clerk shall assess a charge for the handling of registry funds deposited with the court, to be assessed from interest earnings and in accordance with the detailed fee schedule issued by the Director of the Administrative Office of the United States Courts.

(20) When a joint case filed under § 302 of title 11 is divided into two separate cases at the request of the debtor(s), a fee shall be charged equal to one-half the current filing fee for the chapter under which the joint case was commenced.

(21) For filing a motion to terminate, annul, modify, or condition the automatic stay provided under § 362(a) of title 11, a motion to compel abandonment of property of the estate pursuant to Rule 6007(b) of the Federal Rules of Bankruptcy Procedure, or a motion to withdraw the reference of a case or proceeding under 28 U.S.C. § 157(d), a fee shall be collected in the amount of one-half the filing fee prescribed in 28 U.S.C. § 1914(a) for instituting any civil action other than a writ of habeas corpus. If a child support creditor or its representative is the movant, and if

such movant files the form required by § 304(g) of the Bankruptcy Reform Act of 1994, no fee is required.

(22) For docketing a cross appeal from a bankruptcy court determination, the fee shall be the same amount as the fee for docketing a case on appeal or review to the appellate court as required by Item 1 of the Courts of Appeals Miscellaneous Fee Schedule.

(23) For usage of electronic access to court data, 60 cents per minute of usage [provided the court may, for good cause, exempt persons or classes of persons from the fees, in order to avoid unreasonable burdens and to promote public access to such information]. All such fees collected shall be deposited to the Judiciary Information Technology Fund. This fee shall apply to the United States. (The Judicial Conference has approved an advisory note clarifying the judiciary's policy with respect to exemptions from this fee. The advisory note is attached to this Fee Schedule as Appendix I.)

APPENDIX I

The Judicial Conference has prescribed a fee for electronic access to court data, as set forth above in the Bankruptcy Court Miscellaneous Fee Schedule. The schedule provides that the court may exempt persons or classes of persons from the fees, in order to avoid unreasonable burdens and to promote public access to such information. Exemptions should be granted as the exception, not the rule. The exemption language is intended to accommodate those users who might otherwise not have access to the information in this electronic form. It is not intended to provide a means by which a court would exempt all users.

Examples of persons and classes of persons who may be exempted from electronic public access fees include, but are not limited to: indigents; bankruptcy case trustees; not-for-profit organizations; and voluntary ADR neutrals.

[1] Issued in accordance with 28 U.S.C. § 1930(b).

Language to Clarify Reopened Bankruptcy Code Cases

Filing fees prescribed by 28 U.S.C. § 1930(a) must be collected when a Bankruptcy Code case is reopened, unless the reopening is to correct an administrative error or for actions related to the debtor's discharge. If a Bankruptcy Code case is reopened for any other purpose, the appropriate fee to be charged is the same as the filing fee in effect for commencing a new case on the date of reopening.

STATEMENT RESPECTING 1988 AMENDMENTS FROM ADMINISTRATIVE OFFICE OF UNITED STATES COURTS

The Director of the Administrative Office of the United States Courts in a memorandum to the Chief Judges of the United States Courts of Appeals, United States District Courts, and United States Bankruptcy Courts, dated April 19, 1988, provided in part that: "The amendment establishing a fee for filing a petition ancillary to a foreign proceeding under § 304 of the Bankruptcy Code will become effective May 1, 1988. The amendment expanding the exemption for services rendered 'to the United States' to include services rendered to bankruptcy administrators simply expresses a policy which has been in effect since the creation of the bankruptcy administrator program by Congress in the Bankruptcy Judges, United States Trustees and Family Farmer Bankruptcy Act of 1986. [Pub.L. No. 99–554, § 302(d)(3)(I).]"

Statement from 1989 Meeting of Judicial Conference

The Judicial Conference, at the September 20, 1989 meeting, provided in part that Item 21 takes effect on December 21, 1989. The Conference further provided that: "The remaining fees, Items 20 and 22, take effect on January 11, 1990, pending approval of the Appropriations Committees."

Registry Fund Fees—Item 19
(54 FR 20407, May 11, 1989)

Effective June 12, 1989, a fee will be assessed for handling funds deposited in noncriminal proceedings with the court and held in interest bearing accounts or instruments pursuant to 28 U.S.C. § 2041 and Federal Rules of Civil Procedure rule 67. For new accounts, i.e., investments made on or after June 12, 1989, the fee will be equal to the first 45 days income earned on the deposit. Each subsequent deposit of new principal in the same case or proceeding will be subject to the fee. Reinvestment of prior deposits will not be subject to the fee. For existing accounts, i.e., investments held by the court prior to June 12, 1989, a fee will be assessed equal to the first 45 days of income earned beginning 30 days after June 12, 1989. Subsequent deposits of new principal in the same account will be subject to the fee. Subsequent reinvestment of existing deposits will not be subject to the fee.

The fee will apply only once to each sum deposited regardless of the length of time deposits are held and will not exceed income actually earned on the account.

The fee does not apply in the District Courts of Guam, Northern Mariana Islands, the Virgin Islands, the United States Claims Court, or other courts whose fees are not set under 28 U.S.C. § 1930.

Registry Fund Fees—Item 19
(55 F.R. 42867, October 24, 1990)

Effective December 1, 1990, the registry fee assessment provisions were revised and converted from a one-time charge equal to all income earned in the first 45 days of the investment to a charge of 10 percent of the income earned while funds are held in the court registry. Additionally, the fee was extended to any funds placed in the court's registry and invested regardless of the nature of the action underlying the deposit.

The new method will not be applied on investments in cases from which a fee has been exacted based on the prior method (interest earned in the first 45 days the funds were invested or the first 45 days following July 12, 1989). The new method will also not be applied in cases where the investment instrument has a maturity date greater than one year, but where a fee under the prior method applies but has not been deducted.

The fee does not apply in the District Courts of Guam, the Northern Mariana Islands, the Virgin Islands, the United States Claims Court, or any other federal court whose fees are not set under 28 U.S.C. §§ 1913, 1914, and 1930.

Registry Fund Fees—Item 19
(56 F.R. 56356, November 4, 1991)

Effective February 3, 1992, the registry fee assessment provisions are revised and converted from a charge equal to 10 percent of the income earned while funds are held in the court's registry to a variable rate based on the amount deposited with the court and, in certain cases, the length of time funds are held in the court's registry.

The revised fee will be a fee of 10 percent of the total income received during each income period from investments of less than $100,000,000 of registry funds in income-bearing accounts. On investments exceeding $100,000,000 the 10 percent fee shall be reduced by one percent for each increment of $50,000,000 over the initial $100,000,000. For those deposits where funds are placed in the registry by court order for a time certain, for example, by the terms of an adjudicated trust, the fee will be further reduced. This further reduction will amount to 2.5 percent for each five-year interval or part thereof. The total minimum fee to be charged will be no less than two percent of the income on investments.

The following table sets out the fee schedule promulgated by this notice:

REGISTRY—SCHEDULE OF FEES

[% of income earned]

Amount of deposit *	0–5 yrs.	>5–10 yrs.	>10–15 yrs.	>15 yrs.
less than 100M	10	7.5	5.0	2.5
100M–<150M	9	6.5	4.0	2.0
150M–<200M	8	5.5	3.0	2.0
200M–<250M	7	4.5	2.0	2.0
250M–<300M	6	3.5	2.0	2.0
300M–<350M	5	2.5	2.0	2.0
350M–<400M	4	2.0	2.0	2.0
400M–<450M	3	2.0	2.0	2.0
over 450M	2	2.0	2.0	2.0

* Except where otherwise authorized by the Director, each deposit into any account is treated separately in determining the fee.

The new fee applies to all earnings applied to investments on and after the effective date of this change, except for earnings on investments in cases being administered under the provisions of the May 11, 1989 notice [54 FR 20407], i.e., to which the fee equal to the first 45 days income is applicable.

The fee, as modified herein, will continue to apply to any case where the court has authorized the investment of funds placed in its custody or held by it in trust in its registry regardless of the nature of the underlying action.

The fee does not apply in the District Court of Guam, the Northern Mariana Islands, the Virgin Islands, the United States Claims Court, or any other Federal court whose fees are not set under 28 U.S.C. §§ 1913, 1914, and 1930.

§ 1931. Disposition of filing fees

(a) Of the amounts paid to the clerk of court as a fee under section 1914(a) or as part of a judgment for costs under section 2412(a)(2) of this title, $90 shall be deposited into a special fund of the Treasury to be available to offset funds appropriated for the operation and maintenance of the courts of the United States.

(b) If the court authorizes a fee under section 1914(a) or an amount included in a judgment for costs under section 2412(a)(2) of this title of less than $150, the entire fee or amount, up to $90, shall be deposited into the special fund provided in this section.

(Added Pub.L. 99–500, Title I, § 101(b) [Title IV, § 407(c)], Oct. 18, 1986, 100 Stat. 1783–64, and Pub.L. 99–591, Title I, § 101(b) [Title IV, § 407(c)], Oct. 30, 1986, 100 Stat. 3341–64, and amended Pub.L. 101–162, Title IV, § 406(d), Nov. 21, 1989, 103 Stat. 1016; Pub.L. 102–572, Title III, § 301(b), Oct. 29, 1992, 106 Stat. 4511; Pub.L. 104–317, Title IV, § 401(b), Oct. 19, 1996, 110 Stat. 3853.)

HISTORICAL AND STATUTORY NOTES

Codifications

Pub.L. 99–591 is a corrected version of Pub.L. 99–500.

Effective Dates

1996 Acts. Amendment by section 401(b) of Pub.L. 104–317 effective 60 days after Oct. 19, 1996, see section 401(c) of Pub.L. 104–317, set out as a note under section 1914 of this title.

1992 Acts. Amendment by Pub.L. 102–572 effective Jan. 1, 1993, see section 1101(a) of Pub.L. 102–572, set out as a note under section 905 of Title 2, The Congress.

Collection and Deposit of Miscellaneous Bankruptcy Fees

Section 406(b) of Pub.L. 101–162, as amended Pub.L. 103–121, Title I, § 111(a)(3), (b)(4), Oct. 27, 1993, 107 Stat. 1164, provided that: "All fees as shall be hereafter collected for any service enumerated after item 18 of the bankruptcy miscellaneous fee schedule prescribed by the Judicial Conference of the United States pursuant to 28 U.S.C. section 1930(b) [section 1930(b) of this title] and 30.76 per centum of the fees hereafter collected under 28 U.S.C. section 1930(a)(1) [section 1930(a)(1) of this title] and 25 percent of the fees hereafter collected under 28 U.S.C. section 1930(a)(3) [section 1930(a)(3) of this title] shall be deposited as offsetting receipts to the fund established under 28 U.S.C. section 1931 [this section] and shall remain available to the Judiciary until expended to reimburse any appropriation for the amount paid out of such appropriation for expenses of the Courts of Appeals, District Courts, and other Judicial Services and the Administrative Office of the United States Courts. The Judicial Conference shall report to the Committees on Appropriations of the House of Representatives and the Senate on a quarterly basis beginning on the first day of each fiscal year regarding the sums deposited in said fund."

[Section 111(a) of Pub.L. 103–121 provided in part that amendment of this note by section 111(a)(3) of Pub.L. 103–121 is effective 30 days after Oct. 27, 1993.]

[Section 111(b) of Pub.L. 103–121 provided in part that amendment of this note by section 111(b)(4) of Pub.L. 103–121 is effective 30 days after Oct. 27, 1993.]

Disposition of Fees

Section 404 of Pub.L. 104–317 provided that:

"(a) Disposition of attorney admission fees.—For each fee collected for admission of an attorney to practice, as prescribed by the Judicial Conference of the United States pursuant to section 1914 of title 28, United States Code [section 1914 of this title], $30 of that portion of the fee exceeding $20 shall be deposited into the special fund of the Treasury established under section 1931 of title 28, United States Code [this section]. Any portion exceeding $5 of the fee for a duplicate certificate of admission or certificate of good standing, as prescribed by the Judicial Conference of the United States pursuant to section 1914 of title 28, United States Code [section 1914 of this title], shall be deposited into the special fund of the Treasury established under section 1931 of title 28, United States Code [this section].

"**(b) Disposition of bankruptcy complaint filing fees.**—For each fee collected for filing an adversary complaint in a bankruptcy proceeding, as established in Item 6 of the Bankruptcy Court Miscellaneous Fee Schedule prescribed by the Judicial Conference of the United States [set out under section 1930 of this title] pursuant to section 1930(b) of title 28, United States Code [section 1930(b) of this title], the portion of the fee exceeding $120 shall be deposited into the special fund of the Treasury established under section 1931 of title 28, United States Code [this section].

"**(c) Effective date.**—This section shall take effect 60 days after the date of the enactment of this Act [Oct. 19, 1996]."

§ 1932.[1] Judicial Panel on Multidistrict Litigation

The Judicial Conference of the United States shall prescribe from time to time the fees and costs to be charged and collected by the Judicial Panel on Multidistrict Litigation.

(Added Pub.L. 104–317, Title IV, § 403(a)(1), Oct. 19, 1996, 110 Stat. 3854.)

1 Another section 1932 is set out post.

§ 1932.[1] Revocation of earned release credit

In any civil action brought by an adult convicted of a crime and confined in a Federal correctional facility, the court may order the revocation of such earned good time credit under section 3624(b) of title 18, United States Code, that has not yet vested, if, on its own motion or the motion of any party, the court finds that—

(1) the claim was filed for a malicious purpose;

(2) the claim was filed solely to harass the party against which it was filed; or

(3) the claimant testifies falsely or otherwise knowingly presents false evidence or information to the court.

(Added Pub.L. 104–134, Title I, § 101[(a)][Title VIII, § 809(a)], Apr. 26, 1996, 110 Stat. 1321–76; renumbered Title I Pub.L. 104–140, § 1(a), May 2, 1996, 110 Stat. 1327.)

1 Another section 1932 is set out ante.

HISTORICAL AND STATUTORY NOTES

Severability of Provisions

If any provision of section 101[a] [Title VIII] of Pub.L. 104–134, an amendment made by such Title, or the application of such provision or amendment to any person or circumstance is held to be unconstitutional, the remainder of such Title, the amendments made by such Title, and the application of the provisions of such Title to any person or circumstance not affected thereby, see section 101[a] [Title VIII, § 810] of Pub.L. 104–134, set out as a note under section 3626 of Title 18, Crimes and Criminal Procedure.

CHAPTER 125—PENDING ACTIONS AND JUDGMENTS

Sec.
1961. Interest.
1962. Lien.
1963. Registration of judgments for enforcement in other districts.
[1963A. Repealed.]
1964. Constructive notice of pending actions.

§ 1961. Interest

(a) Interest shall be allowed on any money judgment in a civil case recovered in a district court. Execution therefor may be levied by the marshal, in any case where, by the law of the State in which such court is held, execution may be levied for interest on judgments recovered in the courts of the State. Such interest shall be calculated from the date of the entry of the judgment, at a rate equal to the coupon issue yield equivalent (as determined by the Secretary of the Treasury) of the average accepted auction price for the last auction of fifty-two week United States Treasury bills settled immediately prior to the date of the judgment. The Director of the Administrative Office of the United States Courts shall distribute notice of that rate and any changes in it to all Federal judges.

(b) Interest shall be computed daily to the date of payment except as provided in section 2516(b) of this title and section 1304(b) of title 31, and shall be compounded annually.

(c)(1) This section shall not apply in any judgment of any court with respect to any internal revenue tax case. Interest shall be allowed in such cases at the underpayment rate or overpayment rate (whichever is appropriate) established under section 6621 of the Internal Revenue Code of 1986.

(2) Except as otherwise provided in paragraph (1) of this subsection, interest shall be allowed on all final judgments against the United States in the United States Court of Appeals for the Federal circuit,[1] at the rate provided in subsection (a) and as provided in subsection (b).

(3) Interest shall be allowed, computed, and paid on judgments of the United States Court of Federal Claims only as provided in paragraph (1) of this subsection or in any other provision of law.

(4) This section shall not be construed to affect the interest on any judgment of any court not specified in this section.

(June 25, 1948, c. 646, 62 Stat. 957; Apr. 2, 1982, Pub.L. 97–164, Title III, § 302(a), 96 Stat. 55; Sept. 13, 1982, Pub.L. 97–258, § 2(m) (1), 96 Stat. 1062; Jan. 12, 1983, Pub.L. 97–452, § 2(d)(1), 96 Stat. 2478; Oct. 22, 1986, Pub.L. 99–514, § 2, Title XV, § 1511(c)(17), 100 Stat. 2095, 2745; Oct. 29, 1992, Pub.L. 102–572, Title IX, § 902(b)(1), 106 Stat. 4516.)

1 So in original. Probably should be "Circuit,".

HISTORICAL AND STATUTORY NOTES

References in Text

Section 6621 of the Internal Revenue Code of 1986, referred to in subsec. (c)(1), is section 6621 of Title 26, Internal Revenue Code.

Codifications

Amendment of subsec. (b) by Pub.L. 97–452, substituting "section 1304(b) of title 31" for "section 1302 of the Act of July 27, 1956 (31 U.S.C. 724a)" was executed without reference to the intervening amendment by Pub.L. 97–258, as the probable intent of Congress.

Effective Dates

1992 Acts. Amendment by Pub.L. 102–572 effective Oct. 29, 1992, see section 911 of Pub.L. 102–572, set out as a note under section 171 of this title.

1986 Acts. Amendment by section 1511(c)(17) of Pub.L. 99–514 applicable for purposes of determining interest for periods after Dec. 31, 1986, see section 1511(d) of Pub.L. 99–514, set out as a note under section 47 of Title 26, Internal Revenue Code.

1982 Acts. Section 2(m) of Pub.L. 97–258 provided in part that the amendment to subsec. (b) would be effective on Oct. 1, 1982.

Amendment by Pub.L. 97–164 effective Oct. 1, 1982, see section 402 of Pub.L. 97–164, set out as a note under section 171 of this title.

52–WEEK T-BILL RATE TABLE OF CHANGES

Date of Auction	Equivalent Coupon Issue Yield
12/11/74	7.07%
01/08/75	6.80%
02/05/75	5.61%
03/05/75	5.99%
04/02/75	6.92%
04/30/75	6.84%
05/28/75	6.17%
06/24/75	6.72%
07/24/75	7.27%
08/20/75	7.89%
09/17/75	7.90%
10/18/75	7.07%
11/13/75	6.40%
12/10/75	6.88%
01/07/76	5.92%
02/04/76	5.92%
03/03/76	6.29%
03/31/76	6.13%
04/29/76	5.98%
05/26/76	6.72%
06/23/76	6.47%
07/21/76	6.25%
08/19/76	5.97%
09/15/76	5.89%
10/13/76	5.41%
11/09/76	5.49%
12/08/76	4.95%
01/05/77	4.97%
02/02/77	5.65%
03/02/77	5.52%
03/30/77	5.44%
04/27/77	5.45%
05/25/77	5.71%
06/22/77	5.72%
07/20/77	5.98%
08/17/77	6.49%
09/14/77	6.55%
10/12/77	7.07%
11/09/77	6.98%
12/07/77	6.99%
01/04/78	6.99%
02/01/78	7.29%
03/01/78	7.34%
03/29/78	7.36%
04/26/78	7.58%
05/24/78	7.97%
06/21/78	8.27%
07/19/78	8.43%
08/16/78	8.50%
09/13/78	8.59%
10/12/78	8.90%
11/08/78	10.17%
12/06/78	10.17%
01/03/79	10.51%
01/31/79	10.21%
02/28/79	10.40%
04/04/79	10.09%
04/25/79	10.10%
05/23/79	10.01%
06/20/79	9.63%
07/18/79	9.70%
08/15/79	10.05%
09/12/79	10.88%
10/10/79	12.83%
11/07/79	13.18%
12/05/79	11.98%
01/02/80	12.25%
01/30/80	12.45%
02/27/80	15.28%
03/26/80	16.46%
04/23/80	11.45%
05/21/80	9.02%
06/18/80	8.08%
07/16/80	8.25%
08/13/80	9.75%
09/10/80	10.93%
10/08/80	13.33%
10/30/80	13.67%
11/26/80	14.97%
12/23/80	13.49%
01/22/81	14.68%

Date of Auction	Equivalent Coupon Issue Yield
02/19/81	14.39%
03/19/81	12.76%
04/16/81	14.63%
05/14/81	16.70%
06/11/81	14.82%
07/09/81	15.57%
08/07/81	16.60%
09/03/81	17.26%
10/01/81	16.55%
10/29/81	14.84%
11/25/81	11.58%
12/23/81	14.02%
01/21/82	14.92%
02/18/82	14.87%
03/18/82	14.03%
04/15/82	14.30%
05/13/82	13.64%
06/10/82	13.61%
07/08/82	13.79%
08/05/82	12.41%
09/02/82	11.32%
09/30/82	10.41%
10/28/82	9.29%
11/24/82	9.07%
12/23/82	8.75%
01/20/83	8.65%
02/17/83	8.99%
03/17/83	9.16%
04/14/83	8.98%
05/12/83	8.72%
06/09/83	9.59%
07/07/83	10.25%
08/09/83	10.74%
09/01/83	10.58%
09/29/83	9.98%
11/01/83	9.86%
11/23/83	9.93%
12/22/83	10.10%
01/19/84	9.87%
02/16/84	10.11%
03/15/84	10.60%
04/12/84	10.81%
05/15/84	11.74%
06/07/84	12.08%
07/10/84	12.17%
08/02/84	11.93%
08/30/84	11.98%
09/27/84	11.36%
10/25/84	10.33%
11/27/84	9.50%
12/20/84	9.08%
01/17/85	9.09%
02/14/85	9.17%
03/14/85	10.08%
04/11/85	9.15%
05/14/85	8.57%
06/06/85	7.70%
07/09/85	7.60%
08/01/85	8.18%
08/29/85	7.91%
09/26/85	7.87%
10/24/85	8.08%

Date of Auction	Equivalent Coupon Issue Yield
11/26/85	7.87%
12/19/85	7.57%
01/16/86	7.85%
02/13/86	7.71%
03/13/86	7.06%
04/10/86	6.31%
05/13/86	6.56%
06/05/86	7.03%
07/08/86	6.35%
07/31/86	6.18%
08/28/86	5.63%
09/25/86	5.79%
10/23/86	5.75%
11/20/86	5.77%
12/23/86	5.93%
01/15/87	5.75%
02/12/87	6.09%
03/12/87	6.04%
04/09/87	6.30%
05/12/87	7.02%
06/04/87	7.00%
07/02/87	6.64%
08/04/87	6.98%
09/01/87	7.22%
09/30/87	7.88%
10/22/87	6.90%
11/19/87	6.93%
12/17/87	7.22%
01/14/88	7.14%
02/11/88	6.59%
03/10/88	6.71%
04/07/88	7.01%
05/05/88	7.20%
06/02/88	7.59%
06/30/88	7.54%
07/28/88	7.95%
08/25/88	8.32%
09/22/88	8.04%
10/20/88	8.15%
11/17/88	8.55%
12/15/88	9.20%
01/12/89	9.16%
02/15/89	9.32%
03/09/89	9.43%
04/06/89	9.31%
05/04/89	9.15%
06/01/89	8.85%
06/29/89	8.16%
07/27/89	7.75%
08/24/89	8.27%
09/21/89	8.19%
10/19/89	7.90%
11/16/89	7.69%
12/14/89	7.66%
01/11/90	7.74%
02/13/90	7.97%
03/08/90	8.36%
04/05/90	8.32%
05/03/90	8.70%
05/31/90	8.24%
06/28/90	8.09%
07/26/90	7.88%

Date of Auction	Equivalent Coupon Issue Yield
08/23/90	7.95%
09/20/90	7.78%
10/26/90	7.51%
11/15/90	7.28%
12/13/90	7.02%
01/10/91	6.62%
02/12/91	6.21%
03/07/91	6.46%
04/04/91	6.26%
05/02/91	6.07%
05/30/91	6.09%
06/27/91	6.39%
07/25/91	6.26%
08/22/91	5.68%
09/19/91	5.57%
10/17/91	5.42%
11/14/91	4.98%
12/12/91	4.41%
01/09/92	4.02%
02/06/92	4.21%
03/05/92	4.58%
04/02/92	4.55%
04/30/92	4.40%
05/28/92	4.26%
06/25/92	4.11%
07/23/92	3.51%
08/20/92	3.41%
09/17/92	3.13%
10/15/92	3.24%
11/17/92	3.76%
12/10/92	3.72%
01/07/93	3.67%
02/04/93	3.45%
03/04/93	3.21%
04/06/93	3.37%
04/30/93	3.25%
05/27/93	3.54%
06/24/93	3.54%
07/22/93	3.58%
08/19/93	3.43%
09/16/93	3.40%
10/14/93	3.38%
11/16/93	3.57%
12/09/93	3.61%
01/06/94	3.67%
02/03/94	3.74%
03/03/94	4.22%
03/31/94	4.51%
04/28/94	5.02%
5/26/94	5.28%
6/23/94	5.31%
7/21/94	5.49%
8/18/94	5.67%
9/15/94	5.69%
10/13/94	6.06%
11/10/94	6.482%
12/08/94	7.22%
1/5/95	7.34%
2/2/95	7.03%
3/2/95	6.57%
3/30/95	6.41%
4/27/95	6.28%
5/25/95	5.88%
6/22/95	5.53%
7/20/95	5.70%
8/17/95	5.89%
9/14/95	5.52%
10/12/95	5.62%
11/15/95	5.45%
12/7/95	5.35%
1/4/96	5.16%
2/1/96	4.89%
2/29/96	5.25%
4/2/96	5.46%
4/25/96	5.60%
5/23/96	5.62%
6/20/96	5.89%
7/18/96	5.81%
8/15/96	5.67%
9/12/96	5.90%
10/10/96	5.64%
11/7/96	5.49%
12/5/96	5.45%
1/2/97	5.61%
1/30/97	5.64%
2/27/97	5.67%
3/26/97	6.00%
4/24/97	6.06%
5/22/97	5.88%
6/19/97	5.65%
7/17/97	5.56%
8/14/97	5.58%
9/11/97	5.60%
10/9/97	5.49%
11/6/97	5.42%
12/4/97	5.468%
1/6/98	5.341%
1/29/98	5.232%
2/26/98	5.407%
3/26/98	5.391%
4/23/98	5.407%
5/21/98	5.434%
6/18/98	5.413%
7/16/98	5.375%
8/18/98	5.271%
9/15/98	4.730%
10/13/98	4.242%
11/9/98	4.616%
12/8/98	4.513%
1/5/99	4.545%

§ 1962. Lien

Every judgment rendered by a district court within a State shall be a lien on the property located in such State in the same manner, to the same extent and under the same conditions as a judgment of a court of general jurisdiction in such State, and shall cease to be a lien in the same manner and time. This section does not apply to judgments entered in favor of the United States. Whenever the law of any State requires a judgment of a State court to be registered, recorded, docketed or indexed, or any other act to be done, in a particular manner, or in a certain office or county or parish before such lien attaches, such requirements shall apply only if the law of such State authorizes the judgment of a court of the United States to be registered, recorded, docketed, indexed or otherwise conformed to rules and requirements relating to judgments of the courts of the State.

(June 25, 1948, c. 646, 62 Stat. 958; Nov. 29, 1990, Pub.L. 101–647, Title XXXVI, § 3627, 104 Stat. 4965.)

HISTORICAL AND STATUTORY NOTES

Effective Dates

1990 Acts. Amendment by section 3627 of Pub.L. 101–647 effective 180 days after Nov. 29, 1990, see section 3631 of Pub.L. 101–647, set out as a note under section 3001 of this title.

§ 1963. Registration of judgments for enforcement in other districts

A judgment in an action for the recovery of money or property entered in any court of appeals, district court, bankruptcy court, or in the Court of International Trade may be registered by filing a certified copy of the judgment in any other district or, with respect to the Court of International Trade, in any judicial district, when the judgment has become final by appeal or expiration of the time for appeal or when ordered by the court that entered the judgment for good cause shown. Such a judgment entered in favor of the United States may be so registered any time after judgment is entered. A judgment so registered shall have the same effect as a judgment of the district court of the district where registered and may be enforced in like manner.

A certified copy of the satisfaction of any judgment in whole or in part may be registered in like manner in any district in which the judgment is a lien.

The procedure prescribed under this section is in addition to other procedures provided by law for the enforcement of judgments.

(June 25, 1948, c. 646, 62 Stat. 958; Aug. 23, 1954, c. 837, 68 Stat. 772; July 7, 1958, Pub.L. 85–508, § 12(*o*), 72 Stat. 349; Nov. 19, 1988, Pub.L. 100–702, Title X, § 1002(a), (b)(1), 102 Stat. 4664; Nov. 29, 1990, Pub.L. 101–647, Title XXXVI, § 3628, 104 Stat. 4965; Oct. 19, 1996, Pub.L. 104–317, Title II, § 203(a), 110 Stat. 3849.)

HISTORICAL AND STATUTORY NOTES

Effective Dates

1990 Acts. Amendment by section 3628 of Pub.L. 101–647 effective 180 days after Nov. 29, 1990, see section 3631 of Pub.L. 101–647, set out as a note under section 3001 of this title.

1988 Acts. Section 1002(c) of Title X of Pub.L. 100–702 provided that: "The amendments made by this section [amending this section and repealing section 1963A of this title] take effect 90 days after the date of enactment of this title [Nov. 19, 1988]."

1958 Acts. Amendment by Pub.L. 85–508 as effective Jan. 3, 1959, upon admission of Alaska into the Union pursuant to Proc. No. 3269, Jan. 3, 1959, 24 F.R. 81, as required by sections 1 and 8(c) of Pub.L. 85–508, see notes set out under section 81A of this title and preceding section 21 of Title 48, Territories and Insular Possessions.

COMMENTARIES

See 28 U.S.C.A. § 1963, for Commentary by David D. Siegel.

[§ 1963A. Repealed. Pub.L. 100–702, Title X, § 1002(b)(2), Nov. 19, 1988, 102 Stat. 4664]

HISTORICAL AND STATUTORY NOTES

Section, added Pub.L. 96–417, Title V, § 511(a), Oct. 10, 1980, 94 Stat. 1743, provided for registration of judgments of the Court of International Trade. See section 1963 of this title.

Effective Date of Repeal

Section repealed 90 days after Nov. 19, 1988, see section 1002(c) of Pub.L. 100–702, set out as a note under section 1963 of this title.

§ 1964. Constructive notice of pending actions

Where the law of a State requires a notice of an action concerning real property pending in a court of the State to be registered, recorded, docketed, or indexed in a particular manner, or in a certain office or county or parish in order to give constructive notice of the action as it relates to the real property, and such law authorizes a notice of an action concerning real property pending in a United States district court to be registered, recorded, docketed, or indexed in the same manner, or in the same place, those requirements of the State law must be complied with in order to give constructive notice of such an action pending in a United States district court as it relates to real property in such State.

(Added Pub.L. 85–689, § 1(a), Aug. 20, 1958, 72 Stat. 683.)

HISTORICAL AND STATUTORY NOTES

Effective Dates

1958 Acts. Section 2 of Pub.L. 85–689 provided that: "The amendments made by this Act [adding this section] shall only be effective with respect to actions commenced in United States district courts more than one hundred and eighty days after the date of enactment of this Act [Aug. 20, 1958]."

CHAPTER 127—EXECUTIONS AND JUDICIAL SALES

Sec.
2001. Sale of realty generally.
2002. Notice of sale of realty.
2003. Marshal's incapacity after levy on or sale of realty.
2004. Sale of personalty generally.
2005. Appraisal of goods taken on execution.
2006. Execution against revenue officer.
2007. Imprisonment for debt.

§ 2001. Sale of realty generally

(a) Any realty or interest therein sold under any order or decree of any court of the United States shall be sold as a whole or in separate parcels at public sale at the courthouse of the county, parish, or city in which the greater part of the property is located, or upon the premises or some parcel thereof located therein, as the court directs. Such sale shall be upon such terms and conditions as the court directs.

Property in the possession of a receiver or receivers appointed by one or more district courts shall be sold at public sale in the district wherein any such receiver was first appointed, at the courthouse of the county, parish, or city situated therein in which the greater part of the property in such district is located, or on the premises or some parcel thereof located in such county, parish, or city, as such court directs, unless the court orders the sale of the property or one or more parcels thereof in one or more ancillary districts.

(b) After a hearing, of which notice to all interested parties shall be given by publication or otherwise as the court directs, the court may order the sale of such realty or interest or any part thereof at private sale for cash or other consideration and upon such terms and conditions as the court approves, if it finds that the best interests of the estate will be conserved thereby. Before confirmation of any private sale, the court shall appoint three disinterested persons to appraise such property or different groups of three appraisers each to appraise properties of different classes or situated in different localities. No private sale shall be confirmed at a price less than two-thirds of the appraised value. Before confirmation of any private sale, the terms thereof shall be published in such newspaper or newspapers of general circulation as the court directs at least ten days before confirmation. The private sale shall not be confirmed if a bona fide offer is made, under conditions prescribed by the court, which guarantees at least a 10 per centum increase over the price offered in the private sale.

(c) This section shall not apply to sales and proceedings under Title 11 or by receivers or conservators of banks appointed by the Comptroller of the Currency.

(June 25, 1948, c. 646, 62 Stat. 958; May 24, 1949, c. 139, § 99, 63 Stat. 104.)

§ 2002. Notice of sale of realty

A public sale of realty or interest therein under any order, judgment or decree of any court of the United States shall not be made without notice published once a week for at least four weeks prior to the sale in at least one newspaper regularly issued and of general circulation in the county, state, or judicial district of the United States wherein the realty is situated.

If such realty is situated in more than one county, state, district or circuit, such notice shall be published in one or more of the counties, states, or districts wherein it is situated, as the court directs. The notice shall be substantially in such form and contain such description of the property by reference or otherwise as the court approves. The court may direct that the publication be made in other newspapers.

This section shall not apply to sales and proceedings under Title 11 or by receivers or conservators of banks appointed by the Comptroller of the Currency.

(June 25, 1948, c. 646, 62 Stat. 959; May 24, 1949, c. 139, § 100, 63 Stat. 104.)

§ 2003. Marshal's incapacity after levy on or sale of realty

Whenever a United States marshal dies, is removed from office, or the term of his commission expires, after levying on realty or any interest therein under a writ of execution issued by a court of the United States, and before sale or other final disposition thereof, like process shall issue to the succeeding marshal and the same proceedings shall be had as if such contingency had not occurred.

Whenever any such contingency arises after a marshal has sold any realty or interest therein and before a deed is executed, the court may, on application by the purchaser, or the plaintiff in whose action the sale was made, setting forth the facts of the case and the reason why the title was not perfected by such marshal, order the succeeding marshal to perfect the title and execute a deed to the purchaser, upon payment of the purchase money and unpaid costs.

(June 25, 1948, c. 646, 62 Stat. 959; May 24, 1949, c. 139, § 101, 63 Stat. 104.)

§ 2004. Sale of personalty generally

Any personalty sold under any order or decree of any court of the United States shall be sold in accordance with section 2001 of this title, unless the court orders otherwise.

This section shall not apply to sales and proceedings under Title 11 or by receivers or conservators of banks appointed by the Comptroller of the Currency.

(June 25, 1948, c. 646, 62 Stat. 959.)

§ 2005. Appraisal of goods taken on execution

Whenever State law requires that goods taken on execution be appraised before sale, goods taken under execution issued from a court of the United States shall be appraised in like manner.

The United States marshal shall summon the appraisers in the same manner as the sheriff is required to summon appraisers under State law.

If the appraisers fail to attend and perform their required duties, the marshal may sell the goods without an appraisal. Appraisers attending and performing their duties, shall receive the fees allowed for appraisals under State law.

(June 25, 1948, c. 646, 62 Stat. 959.)

§ 2006. Execution against revenue officer

Execution shall not issue against a collector or other revenue officer on a final judgment in any proceeding against him for any of his acts, or for the recovery of any money exacted by or paid to him and subsequently paid into the Treasury, in performing his official duties, if the court certifies that:

(1) probable cause existed; or

(2) the officer acted under the directions of the Secretary of the Treasury or other proper Government officer.

When such certificate has been issued, the amount of the judgment shall be paid out of the proper appropriation by the Treasury.

(June 25, 1948, c. 646, 62 Stat. 960.)

§ 2007. Imprisonment for debt

(a) A person shall not be imprisoned for debt on a writ of execution or other process issued from a court of the United States in any State wherein imprisonment for debt has been abolished. All modifications, conditions, and restrictions upon such imprisonment provided by State law shall apply to any writ of execution or process issued from a court of the United States in accordance with the procedure applicable in such State.

(b) Any person arrested or imprisoned in any State on a writ of execution or other process issued from any court of the United States in a civil action shall have the same jail privileges and be governed by the same regulations as persons confined in like cases on process issued from the courts of such State. The same requirements governing discharge as are applicable in such State shall apply. Any proceedings for discharge shall be conducted before a United States commissioner for the judicial district wherein the defendant is held.

(June 25, 1948, c. 646, 62 Stat. 960.)

HISTORICAL AND STATUTORY NOTES

Change of Name

Reference to United States commissioner deemed to be reference to United States magistrate, pursuant to Pub.L. 90–578, Title IV, § 402(b)(2), Oct. 17, 1968, 82 Stat. 1118. See chapter 43 (section 631 et seq.) of this title.

United States magistrate appointed under section 631 of this title to be known as United States magistrate judge after Dec. 1, 1990, with any reference to United States magistrate or magistrate in this title, in any other Federal statute, etc., deemed a reference to United States magistrate judge appointed under section 631 of this title, see section 321 of Pub.L. 101–650, set out as a note under section 631 of this title.

CHAPTER 129—MONEYS PAID INTO COURT

Sec.

2041. Deposit of moneys in pending or adjudicated cases.
2042. Withdrawal.
2043. Deposit of other moneys.
2044. Payment of fine with bond money.

HISTORICAL AND STATUTORY NOTES

Registry Administration Account

Pub.L. 100–459, Title IV, Oct. 1, 1988, 102 Stat. 2211, provided in part: "That any funds hereafter collected by the Judiciary as a charge for services rendered in administering accounts kept in a court's registry shall be deposited into a separate account entitled 'Registry Administration Account' in the Treasury of the United States. Such funds shall remain available to the Judiciary until expended to reimburse any appropriation for the amount paid out of such appropriation for expenses of the Courts of Appeals, District Courts and Other Judicial Services and the Administrative Office of the United States Courts."

§ 2041. Deposit of moneys in pending or adjudicated cases

All moneys paid into any court of the United States, or received by the officers thereof, in any case pending or adjudicated in such court, shall be forthwith deposited with the Treasurer of the United States or a designated depositary, in the name and to the credit of such court.

This section shall not prevent the delivery of any such money to the rightful owners upon security, according to agreement of parties, under the direction of the court.

(June 25, 1948, c. 646, 62 Stat. 960; Sept. 13, 1982, Pub.L. 97–258, § 2(g) (4) (C), 96 Stat. 1061.)

§ 2042. Withdrawal

No money deposited under section 2041 of this title shall be withdrawn except by order of court.

In every case in which the right to withdraw money deposited in court under section 2041 has been adjudicated or is not in dispute and such money has remained so deposited for at least five years unclaimed by the person entitled thereto, such court shall cause such money to be deposited in the Treasury in the name and to the credit of the United States. Any claimant entitled to any such money may, on petition to the court and upon notice to the United States attorney and full proof of the right thereto, obtain an order directing payment to him.

(June 25, 1948, c. 646, 62 Stat. 960; Sept. 13, 1982, Pub.L. 97–258, § 2(g) (4) (D), 96 Stat. 1061.)

§ 2043. Deposit of other moneys

Except for public moneys deposited under section 2041 of this title, each clerk of the United States courts shall deposit public moneys that the clerk collects into a checking account in the Treasury, subject to disbursement by the clerk. At the end of each accounting period, the earned part of public moneys accruing to the United States shall be deposited in the Treasury to the credit of the appropriate receipt accounts.

(Added Pub.L. 97–258, § 2(g) (4) (E), Sept. 13, 1982, 96 Stat. 1061.)

§ 2044. Payment of fine with bond money

On motion of the United States attorney, the court shall order any money belonging to and deposited by or on behalf of the defendant with the court for the purposes of a criminal appearance bail bond (trial or appeal) to be held and paid over to the United States attorney to be applied to the payment of any assessment, fine, restitution, or penalty imposed upon the defendant. The court shall not release any money deposited for bond purposes after a plea or a verdict of the defendant's guilt has been entered and before sentencing except upon a showing that an assessment, fine, restitution or penalty cannot be imposed for the offense the defendant committed or that the defendant would suffer an undue hardship. This section shall not apply to any third party surety.

(Added Pub.L. 101–647, Title XXXVI, § 3629(a), Nov. 29, 1990, 104 Stat. 4966.)

HISTORICAL AND STATUTORY NOTES

Effective Dates

1990 Acts. Section to take effect 180 days after Nov. 29, 1990, see section 3631 of Pub.L. 101–647, set out as a note under section 3001 of this title.

CHAPTER 131—RULES OF COURTS

Sec.
2071. Rule-making power generally.
2072. Rules of procedure and evidence; power to prescribe.
2073. Rules of procedure and evidence; method of prescribing.
2074. Rules of procedure and evidence; submission to Congress; effective date.
2075. Bankruptcy rules.
[2076. Repealed.]
2077. Publication of rules; advisory committees.

§ 2071. Rule-making power generally

(a) The Supreme Court and all courts established by Act of Congress may from time to time prescribe rules for the conduct of their business. Such rules shall be consistent with Acts of Congress and rules of practice and procedure prescribed under section 2072 of this title.

(b) Any rule prescribed by a court, other than the Supreme Court, under subsection (a) shall be prescribed only after giving appropriate public notice and an opportunity for comment. Such rule shall take effect upon the date specified by the prescribing court and shall have such effect on pending proceedings as the prescribing court may order.

(c)(1) A rule of a district court prescribed under subsection (a) shall remain in effect unless modified or abrogated by the judicial council of the relevant circuit.

(2) Any other rule prescribed by a court other than the Supreme Court under subsection (a) shall remain in effect unless modified or abrogated by the Judicial Conference.

(d) Copies of rules prescribed under subsection (a) by a district court shall be furnished to the judicial council, and copies of all rules prescribed by a court other than the Supreme Court under subsection (a) shall be furnished to the Director of the Administrative Office of the United States Courts and made available to the public.

(e) If the prescribing court determines that there is an immediate need for a rule, such court may proceed under this section without public notice and opportunity for comment, but such court shall promptly thereafter afford such notice and opportunity for comment.

(f) No rule may be prescribed by a district court other than under this section.

(June 25, 1948, c. 646, 62 Stat. 961; May 24, 1949, c. 139, § 102, 63 Stat. 104; Nov. 19, 1988, Pub.L. 100–702, Title IV, § 403(a)(1), 102 Stat. 4650.)

HISTORICAL AND STATUTORY NOTES

Senate Revision Amendment

By Senate amendment, all provisions relating to the Tax Court were eliminated. Therefore, section 1111 of Title 26, U.S.C., Internal Revenue Code, was not one of the sources of this section as finally enacted. However, no change in the text of this section was necessary. See 80th Congress Senate Report No. 1559.

1949 Acts. This amendment clarifies section 2071 of Title 28, U.S.C., by giving express recognition to the power of the Supreme Court to prescribe its own rules and by giving a better description of its procedural rules.

1988 Acts. House Report No. 100–889, see 1988 U.S. Code Cong. and Adm. News, p. 5982.

Effective Dates

1988 Acts. Section 407 of Title IV of Pub.L. 100–702 provided that: "This title [enacting sections 332(d)(4), 604(a)(19) [redesignated (a)(20)], 2071(b)–(f), and 2072–2074 of this title; amending sections 331, 332(d)(1), 372(c)(11), 636(d), 2071(a) [formerly designated 2071], and 2077(b) of this title and sections 460n–8 of Title 16, Conservation and 3402 of Title 18, Crimes and Criminal Procedure; redesignating as 604(a)(23) former section 604(a)(18) of this title; repealing former section 2072 and section 2076 of this title and sections 3771 and 3772 of Title 18; and enacting provisions set out as notes under this section] shall take effect on December 1, 1988."

1983 Acts. Pub.L. 97–462, § 4, Jan. 12, 1983, 96 Stat. 2530, provided: "The amendments made by this Act [which amended Rule 4 of the Federal Rules of Civil Procedure, added Form 18–A, Appendix of Forms, enacted provisions set out as notes under this section, and amended section 951 of Title 18, Crimes and Criminal Procedure] shall take effect 45 days after the enactment of this Act [Jan. 12, 1983]."

Savings Provisions

Section 406 of Title IV of Pub.L. 100–702 provided that: "The rules prescribed in accordance with law before the effective date of this title [Dec. 1, 1988] and in effect on the date of such effective date [Dec. 1, 1988] shall remain in force until changed pursuant to the law as amended by this title [see Effective Dates of 1988 Amendments note under this section]."

Short Title

1983 Acts. Pub.L. 97–462, § 1, Jan. 12, 1983, 96 Stat. 2527, provided: "That this Act [which amended Rule 4 of the Federal Rules of Civil Procedure, enacted Form 18–A, Appendix of Forms, enacted provisions set out as notes under this section, and amended section 951 of Title 18, Crimes and Criminal Procedure] may be cited as the 'Federal Rules of Civil Procedure Amendments Act of 1982'."

Admiralty Rules

The Rules of Practice in Admiralty and Maritime Cases, promulgated by the Supreme Court on Dec. 20, 1920, effective Mar. 7, 1921, as revised, amended, and supplemented, were rescinded, effective July 1, 1966, in accordance with the general unification of civil and admiralty procedure which became effective July 1, 1966. Provision for certain distinctively maritime remedies were preserved however in the Supplemental Rules for Certain Admiralty and Maritime Claims, Rules A to F, Federal Rules of Civil Procedure.

Tax Court Rulemaking Not Affected

Section 405 of Title IV of Pub.L. 100–702 provided that: "The amendments made by this title [see Effective Dates of 1988 Amendments note set out under this section] shall not affect the authority of the Tax Court to prescribe rules under section 7453 of the Internal Revenue Code of 1986 [section 7453 of Title 26, Internal Revenue Code]."

COMMENTARIES

See 28 U.S.C.A. § 2071, for Commentary by David D. Siegel.

§ 2072. Rules of procedure and evidence; power to prescribe

(a) The Supreme Court shall have the power to prescribe general rules of practice and procedure and rules of evidence for cases in the United States district courts (including proceedings before magistrates thereof) and courts of appeals.

(b) Such rules shall not abridge, enlarge or modify any substantive right. All laws in conflict with such rules shall be of no further force or effect after such rules have taken effect.

(c) Such rules may define when a ruling of a district court is final for the purposes of appeal under section 1291 of this title.

(Added Pub.L. 100–702, Title IV, § 401(a), Nov. 19, 1988, 102 Stat. 4648, and amended Pub.L. 101–650, Title III, § 315, Dec. 1, 1990, 104 Stat. 5115.)

HISTORICAL AND STATUTORY NOTES

Effective Dates

1988 Acts. Section effective Dec. 1, 1988, see section 407 of Pub.L. 100–702, set out as a note under section 2071 of this title.

Change of Name

United States magistrate appointed under section 631 of this title to be known as United States magistrate judge after Dec. 1, 1990, with any reference to United States magistrate or magistrate in this title, in any other Federal statute, etc., deemed a reference to United States magistrate judge appointed under section 631 of this title, see section 321 of Pub.L. 101–650, set out as a note under section 631 of this title.

Prior Provisions

A prior section 2072, Acts June 25, 1948, c. 646, 62 Stat. 961; May 24, 1949, c. 139, § 103, 63 Stat. 104; July 18, 1949, c. 343, § 2, 63 Stat. 446; May 10, 1950, c. 174, § 2, 64 Stat. 158; July 7, 1958, Pub.L. 85–508, § 12(m), 72 Stat. 348; Nov. 6, 1966, Pub.L. 89–773, § 1, 80 Stat. 1323, which authorized the Supreme Court to prescribe rules of civil procedure, was repealed by Pub.L. 100–702, Title IV, §§ 401(a), 407, Nov. 19, 1988, 102 Stat. 4648, 4652, effective Dec. 1, 1988.

Admiralty Rules

The Rules of Practice in Admiralty and Maritime Cases, promulgated by the Supreme Court on Dec. 20, 1920, effective Mar. 7, 1921, as revised, amended, and supplemented, were rescinded, effective July 1, 1966, in accordance with the general unification of civil and admiralty procedure which became effective July 1, 1966. Provision for certain distinctively maritime remedies were preserved however, in the Supplemental Rules for Certain Admiralty and Maritime

Claims, Rules A to F, Federal Rules of Civil Procedure, this title.

Applicability to Virgin Islands

Rules of civil procedure promulgated under this section as applicable to the District Court of the Virgin Islands, see section 1614 of Title 48, Territories and Insular Possessions.

COMMENTARIES

See 28 U.S.C.A. § 2072, for Commentary by David D. Siegel.

§ 2073. Rules of procedure and evidence; method of prescribing

(a)(1) The Judicial Conference shall prescribe and publish the procedures for the consideration of proposed rules under this section.

(2) The Judicial Conference may authorize the appointment of committees to assist the Conference by recommending rules to be prescribed under sections 2072 and 2075 of this title. Each such committee shall consist of members of the bench and the professional bar, and trial and appellate judges.

(b) The Judicial Conference shall authorize the appointment of a standing committee on rules of practice, procedure, and evidence under subsection (a) of this section. Such standing committee shall review each recommendation of any other committees so appointed and recommend to the Judicial Conference rules of practice, procedure, and evidence and such changes in rules proposed by a committee appointed under subsection (a)(2) of this section as may be necessary to maintain consistency and otherwise promote the interest of justice.

(c)(1) Each meeting for the transaction of business under this chapter by any committee appointed under this section shall be open to the public, except when the committee so meeting, in open session and with a majority present, determines that it is in the public interest that all or part of the remainder of the meeting on that day shall be closed to the public, and states the reason for so closing the meeting. Minutes of each meeting for the transaction of business under this chapter shall be maintained by the committee and made available to the public, except that any portion of such minutes, relating to a closed meeting and made available to the public, may contain such deletions as may be necessary to avoid frustrating the purposes of closing the meeting.

(2) Any meeting for the transaction of business under this chapter, by a committee appointed under this section, shall be preceded by sufficient notice to enable all interested persons to attend.

(d) In making a recommendation under this section or under section 2072 or 2075, the body making that recommendation shall provide a proposed rule, an explanatory note on the rule, and a written report explaining the body's action, including any minority or other separate views.

(e) Failure to comply with this section does not invalidate a rule prescribed under section 2072 or 2075 of this title.

(Added Pub.L. 100–702, Title IV, § 401(a), Nov. 19, 1988, 102 Stat. 4649, and amended Pub.L. 103–394, Title I, § 104(e), Oct. 22, 1994, 108 Stat. 4110.)

HISTORICAL AND STATUTORY NOTES

Effective Dates

1994 Acts. Amendment by Pub.L. 103–394 effective on Oct. 22, 1994, and not to apply with respect to cases commenced under Title 11 of the United States Code before Oct. 22, 1994, see section 702 of Pub.L. 103–394, set out as a note under section 101 of Title 11, Bankruptcy.

1988 Acts. Section effective Dec. 1, 1988, see section 407 of Pub.L. 100–702, set out as a note under section 2071 of this title.

Separability of Provisions

If any provision of or amendment made by Pub.L. 103–394 or the application of such provision or amendment to any person or circumstance is held to be unconstitutional, the remaining provisions of and amendments made by Pub.L. 103–394 and the application of such provisions and amendments to any person or circumstance shall not be affected thereby, see section 701 of Pub.L. 103–394, set out as a note under section 101 of Title 11, Bankruptcy.

Prior Provisions

A prior section 2073, Acts June 25, 1948, c. 646, 62 Stat. 961; May 24, 1949, c. 139, § 104, 63 Stat. 104; May 10, 1950, c. 174, § 3, 64 Stat. 158, which empowered the Supreme Court to prescribe, by general rules, the practice and procedure in admiralty and maritime cases in the district courts, was repealed by Pub.L. 89–773, § 2, Nov. 6, 1966, 80 Stat. 1323, which provided in part that the repeal of section 2073 should not operate to invalidate or repeal rules adopted under the authority of such section prior to the enactment of Pub.L. 89–773, which rules should remain in effect until superseded by rules prescribed under the authority of former section 2072 of this title as amended by Pub.L. 89–773. See sections 2071 to 2074 of this title.

COMMENTARIES

See 28 U.S.C.A. § 2073, for Commentary by David D. Siegel.

§ 2074. Rules of procedure and evidence; submission to Congress; effective date

(a) The Supreme Court shall transmit to the Congress not later than May 1 of the year in which a rule prescribed under section 2072 is to become effective a copy of the proposed rule. Such rule shall take effect no earlier than December 1 of the year in which such rule is so transmitted unless otherwise provided by law. The Supreme Court may fix the extent such rule shall apply to proceedings then pending, except that the Supreme Court shall not require the application of such rule to further proceedings then pending to the extent that, in the opinion of the court in which such proceedings are pending, the application of such rule in such proceedings would not be feasible or would work injustice, in which event the former rule applies.

(b) Any such rule creating, abolishing, or modifying an evidentiary privilege shall have no force or effect unless approved by Act of Congress.

(Added Pub.L. 100–702, Title IV, § 401(a), Nov. 19, 1988, 102 Stat. 4649.)

HISTORICAL AND STATUTORY NOTES

Effective Dates

1988 Acts. Section effective Dec. 1, 1988, see section 407 of Pub.L. 100–702, set out as a note under section 2071 of this title.

Prior Provisions

A prior section 2074, Act July 27, 1954, c. 583, § 1, 68 Stat. 567, which empowered the Supreme Court to prescribe rules for review of decisions of the Tax Court of the United States, was repealed by Pub.L. 89–773, § 2, Nov. 6, 1966, 80 Stat. 1323, which provided in part that the repeal of section 2074 of this title should not operate to invalidate or repeal rules adopted under the authority of such section prior to the enactment of Pub.L. 89–773, which rules should remain in effect until superseded by rules prescribed under the authority of former section 2072 of this title as amended by Pub.L. 89–773. See sections 2071 to 2074 of this title.

Amendments to Criminal Rules Proposed April 29, 1994

Pub.L. 103–322, Title XXIII, § 230101, Sept. 13, 1994, 108 Stat. 2077, provided that:

"(a) Modification of proposed amendments.—The proposed amendments to the Federal Rules of Criminal Procedure which are embraced by an order entered by the Supreme Court of the United States on April 29, 1994, shall take effect on December 1, 1994, as otherwise provided by law, but with the following amendments:

"(b) In general.—Rule 32 of the Federal Rules of Criminal Procedure is amended by—

"(1) striking 'and' following the semicolon in subdivision (c)(3)(C);

"(2) striking the period at the end of subdivision (c)(3)(D) and inserting '; and';

"(3) inserting after subdivision (c)(3)(D) the following:

" '(E) if sentence is to be imposed for a crime of violence or sexual abuse, address the victim personally if the victim is present at the sentencing hearing and determine if the victim wishes to make a statement or present any information in relation to the sentence.';

"(4) in subdivision (c)(3)(D), striking 'equivalent opportunity' and inserting in lieu thereof 'opportunity equivalent to that of the defendant's counsel';

"(5) in the last sentence of subdivision (c)(4), striking 'and (D)' and inserting '(D), and (E)';

"(6) in the last sentence of subdivision (c)(4), inserting 'the victim,' before 'or the attorney for the Government.'; and

"(7) adding at the end the following:

" '(f) **Definitions.**—For purposes of this rule—

" '(1) "victim" means any individual against whom an offense has been committed for which a sentence is to be imposed, but the right of allocution under subdivision (c)(3)(E) may be exercised instead by—

" '(A) a parent or legal guardian if the victim is below the age of eighteen years or incompetent; or

" '(B) one or more family members or relatives designated by the court if the victim is deceased or incapacitated;

if such person or persons are present at the sentencing hearing, regardless of whether the victim is present; and

" '(2) "crime of violence or sexual abuse" means a crime that involved the use or attempted or threatened use of physical force against the person or property of another, or a crime under chapter 109A of title 18, United States Code.'

"(c) Effective date.—The amendments made by subsection (b) [amending Rule 32 of the Federal Rules of Criminal Procedure] shall become effective on December 1, 1994."

Amendments to Civil Rules Proposed April 30, 1991

Pub.L. 102–198, § 11, Dec. 9, 1991, 105 Stat. 1626, provided that:

"(a) Technical amendment.—Rule 15(c)(3) of the Federal Rules of Civil Procedure for the United States Courts, as transmitted to the Congress by the Supreme Court pursuant to section 2074 of title 28, United States Code [this section], to become effective on December 1, 1991, is amended by striking 'Rule 4(m)' and inserting 'Rule 4(j)'.

"(b) Amendment to Forms.—Form 1–A, Notice of Lawsuit and Request for Waiver of Service of Summons, and Form 1–B, Waiver of Service of Summons, included in the transmittal by the Supreme Court described in subsection (a), shall not be effective and Form 18–A, Notice and Acknowledgment for Service by Mail, abrogated by the Supreme Court in such transmittal, effective December 1, 1991, shall continue in effect on or after that date."

Amendments to Civil Rules Proposed April 28, 1982

Pub.L. 97–462, § 5, Jan. 12, 1983, 96 Stat. 2530, provided: "The amendments to the Federal Rules of Civil Procedure [Rule 4], the effective date [Aug. 1, 1982] of which was delayed [to Oct. 1, 1983] by the Act [Pub.L. 97–227] entitled 'An Act to delay the effective date of proposed amendments to rule 4 of the Federal Rules of Civil Procedure', [proposed by the Supreme Court of the United States and transmitted to the Congress by the Chief Justice on Apr. 28, 1982], approved August 2, 1982 (96 Stat. 246), shall not take effect."

Pub.L. 97–227, Aug. 2, 1982, 96 Stat. 246, provided: "That notwithstanding the provisions of section 2072 of title 28, United States Code, [section 2072 of this title] the amendments to rule 4 of the Federal Rules of Civil Procedure as proposed by the Supreme Court of the United States and transmitted to the Congress by the Chief Justice on April 28, 1982, shall take effect on October 1, 1983, unless previously approved, disapproved, or modified by Act of Congress.

"Sec. 2. This Act shall be effective as of August 1, 1982, but shall not apply to the service of process that takes place between August 1, 1982, and the date of enactment of this Act [Aug. 2, 1982]."

Amendments to Criminal Rules and Rules of Evidence Proposed April 30, 1979; Postponement of Effective Date

Pub.L. 96–42, July 31, 1979, 93 Stat. 326, provided: "That notwithstanding any provision of section 3771 or 3772 of title 18 of the United States Code [section 3771 or 3772 of Title 18, Crimes and Criminal Procedure] or of section 2072, 2075, or 2076 of title 28 of the United States Code [sections 2072, 2075 and 2076 of this title] to the contrary—

"(1) the amendments proposed by the United States Supreme Court and transmitted by the Chief Justice on April 30, 1979, to the Federal Rules of Criminal Procedure affecting rules 11(e)(6), 17(h), 32(f), and 44(c), and adding new rules 26.2 and 32.1, and the amendment so proposed and transmitted to the Federal Rules of Evidence affecting rule 410, shall not take effect until December 1, 1980, or until and then only to the extent approved by Act of Congress, whichever is earlier; and

"(2) the amendment proposed by the United States Supreme Court and transmitted by the Chief Justice on April 30, 1979, affecting rule 40 of the Federal Rules of Criminal Procedure shall take effect on August 1, 1979, with the following amendments:

"(A) In the matter designated as paragraph (1) of subdivision (d), strike out 'in accordance with Rule 32.1(a).'

"(B) In the matter designated as paragraph (2) of subdivision (d), strike out 'in accordance with Rule 32.1(a)(1)'."

Approval and Effective Date of Amendments Proposed November 20, 1972 and December 18, 1972

Pub.L. 93–595, § 3, Jan. 2, 1975, 88 Stat. 1949, provided that: "The Congress expressly approves the amendments to the Federal Rules of Civil Procedure [Rules 30(c), 32(c), 43 and 44.1] and the amendments to the Federal Rules of Criminal Procedure [Rules 26, 26.1 and 28], which are embraced by the orders entered by the Supreme Court of the United States on November 20, 1972, and December 18, 1972, and such amendments shall take effect on the one hundred and eightieth day beginning after the date of the enactment of this Act [Jan. 2, 1975]."

Approval and Effective Date of Rules Governing Section 2254 Cases and Section 2255 Proceedings for United States District Courts

Pub.L. 94–426, § 1, Sept. 28, 1976, 90 Stat. 1334, provided: "That the rules governing section 2254 cases in the United States district courts and the rules governing section 2255 proceedings for the United States district courts, as proposed by the United States Supreme Court, which were delayed by the Act entitled 'An Act to delay the effective date of certain proposed amendments to the Federal Rules of Criminal Procedure and certain other rules promulgated by the United States Supreme Court' (Public Law 94–349), are approved with the amendments set forth in section 2 of this Act and shall take effect as so amended, with respect to petitions under section 2254 and motions under section 2255 of title 28 of the United States Code [sections 2254 and 2255 of this title] filed on or after February 1, 1977."

Amendments to Rules of Evidence Proposed on April 29, 1994

Pub.L. 103–322, Title IV, § 40141, Sept. 13, 1994, 108 Stat. 1918, provided that:

"**(a) Modification of proposed amendment.**—The proposed amendments to the Federal Rules of Evidence that are embraced by an order entered by the Supreme Court of the United States on April 29, 1994, shall take effect on December 1, 1994, as otherwise provided by law, but with the amendment made by subsection (b).

"**(b) Rule.**—Rule 412 of the Federal Rules of Evidence is amended to read as follows:

"**'Rule 412. Sex Offense Cases; Relevance of Alleged Victim's Past Sexual Behavior or Alleged Sexual Predisposition**

"'**(a) Evidence generally inadmissible.**—The following evidence is not admissible in any civil or criminal proceeding involving alleged sexual misconduct except as provided in subdivisions (b) and (c):

"'(1) Evidence offered to prove that any alleged victim engaged in her sexual behavior.

"'(2) Evidence offered to prove any alleged victim's sexual predisposition.

"'**(b) Exceptions.**—

"'(1) In a criminal case, the following evidence is admissible, if otherwise admissible under these rules:

"'(A) evidence of specific instances of sexual behavior by the alleged victim offered to prove that a person other than the accused was the source of semen, injury or other physical evidence;

"'(B) evidence of specific instances of sexual behavior by the alleged victim with respect to the person accused of the sexual misconduct offered by the accused to prove consent or by the prosecution; and

"'(C) evidence the exclusion of which would violate the constitutional rights of the defendant.

"'(2) In a civil case, evidence offered to prove the sexual behavior or sexual predisposition of any alleged victim is admissible if it is otherwise admissible under these rules and its probative value substantially outweighs the danger of harm to any victim and of unfair prejudice to any party. Evidence of an alleged victim's reputation is admissible only if it has been placed in controversy by the alleged victim.

"'**(c) Procedure to determine admissibility.**—

"'(1) A party intending to offer evidence under subdivision (b) must—

"'(A) file a written motion at least 14 days before trial specifically describing the evidence and stating the purpose for which it is offered unless the court, for good cause requires a different time for filing or permits filing during trial; and

"'(B) serve the motion on all parties and notify the alleged victim or, when appropriate, the alleged victim's guardian or representative.

"'(2) Before admitting evidence under this rule the court must conduct a hearing in camera and afford the victim and parties a right to attend and be heard. The motion, related papers, and the record of the hearing must be sealed and remain under seal unless the court orders otherwise.'

"**(c) Technical amendment.**—The table of contents for the Federal Rules of Evidence is amended by amending the item relating to rule 412 to read as follows:

"**'412. Sex Offense Cases; Relevance of Alleged Victim's Past Sexual Behavior or Alleged Sexual Predisposition:**

" '(a) Evidence generally inadmissible.

" '(b) Exceptions.

" '(c) Procedure to determine admissibility.' "

Congressional Approval Requirement for Proposed Rules of Evidence for United States Courts and Amendments to Federal Rules of Civil Procedure and Criminal Procedure; Suspension of Effectiveness of Such Rules

Pub.L. 93–12, Mar. 30, 1973, 87 Stat. 9, provided: "That notwithstanding any other provisions of law, the Rules of Evidence for United States Courts and Magistrates, the Amendments to the Federal Rules of Civil Procedure, and the Amendments to the Federal Rules of Criminal Procedure, which are embraced by the orders entered by the Supreme Court of the United States on Monday, November 20, 1972, and Monday, December 18, 1972, shall have no force or effect except to the extent, and with such amendments, as they may be expressly approved by Act of Congress."

Postponement of Effective Date of Proposed Rules and Forms Governing Proceedings Under Sections 2254 and 2255 of this Title

Pub.L. 94–349, § 2, July 8, 1976, 90 Stat. 822, provided: "That, notwithstanding the provisions of section 2072 of title 28 of the United States Code [section 2072 of this title], the rules and forms governing section 2254 [section 2254 of this title] cases in the United States district courts and the rules and forms governing section 2255 [section 2255 of this title] proceedings in the United States district courts which are embraced by the order entered by the United States Supreme Court on April 26, 1976, and which were transmitted to the Congress on or about April 26, 1976, shall not take effect until thirty days after the adjournment sine die of the 94th Congress, or until and to the extent approved by Act of Congress, whichever is earlier."

COMMENTARIES

See 28 U.S.C.A. § 2074, for Commentary by David D. Siegel.

§ 2075. Bankruptcy rules

The Supreme Court shall have the power to prescribe by general rules, the forms of process, writs, pleadings, and motions, and the practice and procedure in cases under title 11.

Such rules shall not abridge, enlarge, or modify any substantive right.

The Supreme Court shall transmit to Congress not later than May 1 of the year in which a rule prescribed under this section is to become effective a copy of the proposed rule. The rule shall take effect no earlier than December 1 of the year in which it is transmitted to Congress unless otherwise provided by law.

(Added Pub.L. 88–623, § 1, Oct. 3, 1964, 78 Stat. 1001, and amended Pub.L. 95–598, Title II, § 247, Nov. 6, 1978, 92 Stat. 2672; Pub.L. 103–394, Title I, § 104(f), Oct. 22, 1994, 108 Stat. 4110.)

HISTORICAL AND STATUTORY NOTES

Effective Dates

1994 Acts. Amendment by Pub.L. 103–394 effective on Oct. 22, 1994, and not to apply with respect to cases commenced under Title 11 of the United States Code before Oct. 22, 1994, see section 702 of Pub.L. 103–394, set out as a note under section 101 of Title 11, Bankruptcy.

1978 Acts. Amendment by Pub.L. 95–598 effective Nov. 6, 1978, see section 402(d) of Pub.L. 95–598, set out as a note preceding section 101 of Title 11, Bankruptcy.

Separability of Provisions

If any provision of or amendment made by Pub.L. 103–394 or the application of such provision or amendment to any person or circumstance is held to be unconstitutional, the remaining provisions of and amendments made by Pub.L. 103–394 and the application of such provisions and amendments to any person or circumstance shall not be affected thereby, see section 701 of Pub.L. 103–394, set out as a note under section 101 of Title 11, Bankruptcy.

Additional Rulemaking Power

Pub.L. 95–598, Title IV, § 410, Nov. 6, 1978, 92 Stat. 2687, provided that: "The Supreme Court may issue such additional rules of procedure, consistent with Acts of Congress, as may be necessary for the orderly transfer of functions and records and the orderly transition to the new bankruptcy court system created by this Act [see Tables for complete classification of Pub.L. 95–598]."

Applicability of Rules to Cases Under Title 11

Pub.L. 95–598, Title IV, § 405(d), Nov. 6, 1978, 92 Stat. 2685, provided that: "The rules prescribed under section 2075 of title 28 of the United States Code and in effect on September 30, 1979, shall apply to cases under title 11, to the extent not inconsistent with the amendments made by this Act, or with this Act [see Tables for complete classification of Pub.L. 95–598], until such rules are repealed or superseded by rules prescribed and effective under such section, as amended by section 248 of this Act."

Rules Promulgated by Supreme Court

Pub.L. 98–353, Title III, § 320, July 10, 1984, 98 Stat. 357, provided that: "The Supreme Court shall prescribe general rules implementing the practice and procedure to be followed under section 707(b) of title 11, United States Code [section 707(b) of Title 11, Bankruptcy]. Section 2075 of title 28, United States Code [this section], shall apply with respect to the general rules prescribed under this section."

[§ 2076. Repealed. Pub.L. 100–702, Title IV, § 401(c), Nov. 19, 1988, 102 Stat. 4650]

HISTORICAL AND STATUTORY NOTES

Section, added Pub.L. 93–595, § 2(a)(1), Jan. 2, 1975, 88 Stat. 1948, and amended Pub.L. 94–149, § 2, Dec. 12, 1975, 89 Stat. 806, related to Federal Rules of Evidence prescribed by the Supreme Court and amendment thereof. See sections 2072 to 2074 of this title.

Effective Date of Repeal

Section repealed effective Dec. 1, 1988, see section 407 of Pub.L. 100–702, set out as a note under section 2071 of this title.

COMMENTARIES

See 28 U.S.C.A. § 2076, for Commentary by David D. Siegel.

§ 2077. Publication of rules; advisory committees

(a) The rules for the conduct of the business of each court of appeals, including the operating procedures of such court, shall be published. Each court of appeals shall print or cause to be printed necessary copies of the rules. The Judicial Conference shall prescribe the fees for sales of copies under section 1913 of this title, but the Judicial Conference may provide for free distribution of copies to members of the bar of each court and to other interested persons.

(b) Each court, except the Supreme Court, that is authorized to prescribe rules of the conduct of such court's business under section 2071 of this title shall appoint an advisory committee for the study of the rules of practice and internal operating procedures of such court and, in the case of an advisory committee appointed by a court of appeals, of the rules of the judicial council of the circuit. The advisory committee shall make recommendations to the court concerning such rules and procedures. Members of the committee shall serve without compensation, but the Director may pay travel and transportation expenses in accordance with section 5703 of title 5.

(Added Pub.L. 97–164, Title II, § 208(a), Apr. 2, 1982, 96 Stat. 54, and amended Pub.L. 100–702, Title IV, § 401(b), Nov. 19, 1988, 102 Stat. 4650; Pub.L. 101–650, Title IV, § 406, Dec. 1, 1990, 104 Stat. 5124.)

HISTORICAL AND STATUTORY NOTES

Effective Dates

1990 Acts. Amendment by section 406 of Pub.L. 101–650 effective 90 days after Dec. 1, 1990, see section 407 of Pub.L. 101–650, set out as a note under section 332 of this title.

1988 Acts. Amendment by Pub.L. 100–702 effective Dec. 1, 1988, see section 407 of Pub.L. 100–702, set out as a note under section 2071 of this title.

1982 Acts. Section effective Oct. 1, 1982, see section 402 of Pub.L. 97–164, set out as a note under section 171 of this title.

COMMENTARIES

See 28 U.S.C.A. § 2077, for Commentary by David D. Siegel.

CHAPTER 133—REVIEW—MISCELLANEOUS PROVISIONS

Sec.

2101. Supreme Court; time for appeal or certiorari; docketing; stay.
2102. Priority of criminal case on appeal from State court.
[2103. Repealed.]
2104. Reviews of State court decisions.
2105. Scope of review; abatement.
2106. Determination.
2107. Time for appeal to court of appeals.
2108. Proof of amount in controversy.
2109. Quorum of Supreme Court justices absent.
[2110. Repealed.]
2111. Harmless error.
2112. Record on review and enforcement of agency orders.
2113. Definition.

§ 2101. Supreme Court; time for appeal or certiorari; docketing; stay

(a) A direct appeal to the Supreme Court from any decision under section 1253 of this title, holding unconstitutional in whole or in part, any Act of Congress, shall be taken within thirty days after the entry of the interlocutory or final order, judgment or decree. The record shall be made up and the case docketed within sixty days from the time such appeal is taken under rules prescribed by the Supreme Court.

(b) Any other direct appeal to the Supreme Court which is authorized by law, from a decision of a district court in any civil action, suit or proceeding, shall be taken within thirty days from the judgment, order or decree, appealed from, if interlocutory, and within sixty days if final.

(c) Any other appeal or any writ of certiorari intended to bring any judgment or decree in a civil action, suit or proceeding before the Supreme Court for review shall be taken or applied for within ninety days after the entry of such judgment or decree. A justice of the Supreme Court, for good cause shown, may extend the time for applying for a writ of certiorari for a period not exceeding sixty days.

(d) The time for appeal or application for a writ of certiorari to review the judgment of a State court in a criminal case shall be as prescribed by rules of the Supreme Court.

(e) An application to the Supreme Court for a writ of certiorari to review a case before judgment has been rendered in the court of appeals may be made at any time before judgment.

(f) In any case in which the final judgment or decree of any court is subject to review by the Supreme Court on writ of certiorari, the execution and enforcement of such judgment or decree may be stayed for a reasonable time to enable the party aggrieved to obtain a writ of certiorari from the Supreme Court. The stay may be granted by a judge of the court rendering the judgment or decree or by a justice of the Supreme Court, and may be conditioned on the giving of security, approved by such judge or justice, that if the aggrieved party fails to make application for such writ within the period allotted therefor, or fails to obtain an order granting his application, or fails to make his plea good in the Supreme Court, he shall answer for all damages and costs which the other party may sustain by reason of the stay.

(g) The time for application for a writ of certiorari to review a decision of the United States Court of Appeals for the Armed Forces shall be as prescribed by rules of the Supreme Court.

(June 25, 1948, c. 646, 62 Stat. 961; May 24, 1949, c. 139, § 106, 63 Stat. 104; Dec. 6, 1983, Pub.L. 98–209, § 10(b), 97 Stat. 1406; June 27, 1988, Pub.L. 100–352, § 5(b), 102 Stat. 663; Oct. 5, 1994, Pub.L. 103–337, Div. A, Title IX, § 924(d)(1)(C), 108 Stat. 2832.)

HISTORICAL AND STATUTORY NOTES

Effective Dates

1988 Acts. Amendment by section 5(b) of Pub.L. 100–352, which substituted "section 1253" for "sections 1252, 1253 and 2282" in subsec. (a), effective ninety days after June 27, 1988, except that such amendment not to apply to cases pending in the Supreme Court on such effective date or affect the right to review or the manner of reviewing the judgment or decree of a court which was entered before such effective date, see section 7 of Pub.L. 100–352, set out as a note under section 1254 of this title.

1983 Acts. Amendment by Pub.L. 98–209 effective on the first day of the eighth calendar month beginning after Dec. 6, 1983, see section 12(a)(1) of Pub.L. 98–209, set out as a note under section 801 of Title 10, Armed Forces.

COMMENTARIES

See 28 U.S.C.A. § 2101, for Commentary by David D. Siegel.

§ 2102. Priority of criminal case on appeal from State court

Criminal cases on review from State courts shall have priority, on the docket of the Supreme Court, over all cases except cases to which the United States is a party and such other cases as the court may decide to be of public importance.

(June 25, 1948, c. 646, 62 Stat. 962.)

[§ 2103. Repealed. Pub.L. 100–352, § 5(c), June 27, 1988, 102 Stat. 663]

HISTORICAL AND STATUTORY NOTES

Section, Acts June 25, 1948, c. 646, 62 Stat. 962; Sept. 19, 1962, Pub.L. 87–669, § 1, 76 Stat. 556, provided that appeal from State court or from a United States court of appeals improvidently taken be regarded as petition for writ of certiorari.

Effective Date of Repeal

Repeal of section effective ninety days after June 27, 1988, except that such repeal not to apply to cases pending in the Supreme Court on such effective date or affect the right to review or the manner of reviewing the judgment or decree of a court which was entered before such effective date, see section 7 of Pub.L. 100–352, set out as a note under section 1254 of this title.

COMMENTARIES

See 28 U.S.C.A. § 2103, for Commentary by David D. Siegel.

§ 2104. Reviews of State court decisions

A review by the Supreme Court of a judgment or decree of a State court shall be conducted in the same manner and under the same regulations, and shall have the same effect, as if the judgment or decree reviewed had been rendered in a court of the United States.

(June 25, 1948, c. 646, 62 Stat. 962; June 27, 1988, Pub.L. 100–352, § 5(d)(1), 102 Stat. 663.)

HISTORICAL AND STATUTORY NOTES

Effective Dates

1988 Acts. Amendment by section 5(d)(1) of Pub.L. 100–352 effective ninety days after June 27, 1988, except that such amendment not to apply to cases pending in the Supreme Court on such effective date or affect the right to review or the manner of reviewing the judgment or decree of a court which was entered before such effective date, see section 7 of Pub.L. 100–352, set out as a note under section 1254 of this title.

§ 2105. Scope of review; abatement

There shall be no reversal in the Supreme Court or a court of appeals for error in ruling upon matters in abatement which do not involve jurisdiction.

(June 25, 1948, c. 646, 62 Stat. 963.)

§ 2106. Determination

The Supreme Court or any other court of appellate jurisdiction may affirm, modify, vacate, set aside or reverse any judgment, decree, or order of a court lawfully brought before it for review, and may remand the cause and direct the entry of such appropriate judgment, decree, or order, or require such further proceedings to be had as may be just under the circumstances.

(June 25, 1948, c. 646, 62 Stat. 963.)

§ 2107. Time for appeal to court of appeals

(a) Except as otherwise provided in this section, no appeal shall bring any judgment, order or decree in an action, suit or proceeding of a civil nature before a court of appeals for review unless notice of appeal is filed, within thirty days after the entry of such judgment, order or decree.

(b) In any such action, suit or proceeding in which the United States or an officer or agency thereof is a party, the time as to all parties shall be sixty days from such entry.

(c) The district court may, upon motion filed not later than 30 days after the expiration of the time otherwise set for bringing appeal, extend the time for appeal upon a showing of excusable neglect or good cause. In addition, if the district court finds—

(1) that a party entitled to notice of the entry of a judgment or order did not receive such notice from the clerk or any party within 21 days of its entry, and

(2) that no party would be prejudiced,

the district court may, upon motion filed within 180 days after entry of the judgment or order or within 7 days after receipt of such notice, whichever is earlier, reopen the time for appeal for a period of 14 days from the date of entry of the order reopening the time for appeal.

(d) This section shall not apply to bankruptcy matters or other proceedings under Title 11.

(June 25, 1948, c. 646, 62 Stat. 963; May 24, 1949, c. 139, §§ 107, 108, 63 Stat. 104; Nov. 6, 1978, Pub.L. 95–598, Title II, § 248, 92 Stat. 2672; Dec. 9, 1991, Pub.L. 102–198, § 12, 105 Stat. 1627.)

HISTORICAL AND STATUTORY NOTES

Senate Revision Amendment

By Senate amendment, all provisions relating to the Tax Court were eliminated. Therefore, section 1142 of Title 26, U.S.C., Internal Revenue Code, was not one of the sources of this section as finally enacted. However, no change in the text of this section was necessary. See 80th Congress Senate Report No. 1559.

1949 Acts. This amendment to section 2107 of Title 28, U.S.C., restores the former 15-day limitation of time within which to appeal from an interlocutory order in admiralty.

This amendment eliminates as surplusage the words "in any such action, suit or proceeding," from the fourth paragraph of section 2107 of Title 28, U.S.C., and corrects a typographical error in the same paragraph.

1991 Acts. House Report No. 102–322, see 1991 U.S. Code Cong. and Adm. News, p. 1303.

Codifications

This section was amended by Pub.L. 95–598, Title II, § 248, Nov. 6, 1978, 92 Stat. 2672, effective June 28, 1984, pursuant to Pub.L. 95–598, Title IV, § 402(b), Nov. 6, 1978, 92 Stat. 2682, as amended by Pub.L. 98–249, § 1(a), Mar. 31, 1984, 98 Stat. 116; Pub.L. 98–271, § 1(a), Apr. 30, 1984, 98 Stat. 163; Pub.L. 98–299, § 1(a), May 25, 1984, 98 Stat. 214; Pub.L. 98–325, § 1(a), June 20, 1984, 98 Stat. 268 [set out as an Effective Dates note preceding section 101 of Title 11, Bankruptcy], by adding "or the bankruptcy court" following "district court" and by striking out the final paragraph relating to nonapplicability to bankruptcy matters or other proceedings under Title 11.

Section 402(b) of Pub.L. 95–598 was amended by section 113 of Pub.L. 98–353, Title I, July 10, 1984, 98 Stat. 343, by substituting "shall not be effective" for "shall take effect on June 28, 1984", thereby eliminating the amendment by section 248 of Pub.L. 95–598, effective June 27, 1984, pursuant to section 122(c) of Pub.L. 98–353, set out as an Effective Date note under section 151 of this title.

Section 121(a) of Pub.L. 98–353 directed that section 402(b) of Pub.L. 95–598 be amended by substituting "the date of enactment of the Bankruptcy Amendments and Federal Judgeship Act of 1984 [i.e. July 10, 1984]" for "June 28, 1984". This amendment was not executed in view of the prior amendment to section 402(b) of Pub.L. 95–598 by section 113 of Pub.L. 98–353.

§ 2108. Proof of amount in controversy

Where the power of any court of appeals to review a case depends upon the amount or value in controversy, such amount or value, if not otherwise satisfactorily disclosed upon the record, may be shown and ascertained by the oath of a party to the case or by other competent evidence.

(June 25, 1948, c. 646, 62 Stat. 963.)

§ 2109. Quorum of Supreme Court justices absent

If a case brought to the Supreme Court by direct appeal from a district court cannot be heard and determined because of the absence of a quorum of qualified justices, the Chief Justice of the United States may order it remitted to the court of appeals for the circuit including the district in which the case arose, to be heard and determined by that court either sitting in banc or specially constituted and composed of the three circuit judges senior in commission who are able to sit, as such order may direct. The decision of such court shall be final and conclusive. In the event of the disqualification or disability of one or more of such circuit judges, such court shall be filled as provided in chapter 15 of this title.

In any other case brought to the Supreme Court for review, which cannot be heard and determined because of the absence of a quorum of qualified justices, if a majority of the qualified justices shall be of opinion that the case cannot be heard and determined at the next ensuing term, the court shall enter its order affirming the judgment of the court from which the case was brought for review with the same effect as upon affirmance by an equally divided court.

(June 25, 1948, c. 646, 62 Stat. 963.)

[§ 2110. Repealed. Pub.L. 97–164, Title I, § 136, Apr. 2, 1982, 96 Stat. 41]

HISTORICAL AND STATUTORY NOTES

Section, Act June 25, 1948, c. 646, 62 Stat. 964; May 24, 1949, c. 139, § 109, 63 Stat. 105, provided that appeals to the

Court of Claims in tort claims cases, as provided in section 1504 of this title, be taken within 90 days after the entry of the final judgment of the district court.

Effective Date of Repeal

Repeal effective Oct. 1, 1982, see section 402 of Pub.L. 97–164, set out as a note under section 171 of this title.

§ 2111. Harmless error

On the hearing of any appeal or writ of certiorari in any case, the court shall give judgment after an examination of the record without regard to errors or defects which do not affect the substantial rights of the parties.

(Added May 24, 1949, c. 139, § 110, 63 Stat. 105.)

§ 2112. Record on review and enforcement of agency orders

(a) The rules prescribed under the authority of section 2072 of this title may provide for the time and manner of filing and the contents of the record in all proceedings instituted in the courts of appeals to enjoin, set aside, suspend, modify, or otherwise review or enforce orders of administrative agencies, boards, commissions, and officers. Such rules may authorize the agency, board, commission, or officer to file in the court a certified list of the materials comprising the record and retain and hold for the court all such materials and transmit the same or any part thereof to the court, when and as required by it, at any time prior to the final determination of the proceeding, and such filing of such certified list of the materials comprising the record and such subsequent transmittal of any such materials when and as required shall be deemed full compliance with any provision of law requiring the filing of the record in the court. The record in such proceedings shall be certified and filed in or held for and transmitted to the court of appeals by the agency, board, commission, or officer concerned within the time and in the manner prescribed by such rules. If proceedings are instituted in two or more courts of appeals with respect to the same order, the following shall apply:

(1) If within ten days after issuance of the order the agency, board, commission, or officer concerned receives, from the persons instituting the proceedings, the petition for review with respect to proceedings in at least two courts of appeals, the agency, board, commission, or officer shall proceed in accordance with paragraph (3) of this subsection. If within ten days after the issuance of the order the agency, board, commission, or officer concerned receives, from the persons instituting the proceedings, the petition for review with respect to proceedings in only one court of appeals, the agency, board, commission, or officer shall file the record in that court notwithstanding the institution in any other court of appeals of proceedings for review of that order. In all other cases in which proceedings have been instituted in two or more courts of appeals with respect to the same order, the agency, board, commission, or officer concerned shall file the record in the court in which proceedings with respect to the order were first instituted.

(2) For purposes of paragraph (1) of this subsection, a copy of the petition or other pleading which institutes proceedings in a court of appeals and which is stamped by the court with the date of filing shall constitute the petition for review. Each agency, board, commission, or officer, as the case may be, shall designate by rule the office and the officer who must receive petitions for review under paragraph (1).

(3) If an agency, board, commission, or officer receives two or more petitions for review of an order in accordance with the first sentence of paragraph (1) of this subsection, the agency, board, commission, or officer shall, promptly after the expiration of the ten-day period specified in that sentence, so notify the judicial panel on multidistrict litigation authorized by section 1407 of this title, in such form as that panel shall prescribe. The judicial panel on multidistrict litigation shall, by means of random selection, designate one court of appeals, from among the courts of appeals in which petitions for review have been filed and received within the ten-day period specified in the first sentence of paragraph (1), in which the record is to be filed, and shall issue an order consolidating the petitions for review in that court of appeals. The judicial panel on multidistrict litigation shall, after providing notice to the public and an opportunity for the submission of comments, prescribe rules with respect to the consolidation of proceedings under this paragraph. The agency, board, commission, or officer concerned shall file the record in the court of appeals designated pursuant to this paragraph.

(4) Any court of appeals in which proceedings with respect to an order of an agency, board, commission, or officer have been instituted may, to the extent authorized by law, stay the effective date of the order. Any such stay may thereafter be modified, revoked, or extended by a court of appeals designated pursuant to paragraph (3) with respect to that order or by any other court of appeals to which the proceedings are transferred.

(5) All courts in which proceedings are instituted with respect to the same order, other than the court in which the record is filed pursuant to this subsection, shall transfer those proceedings to the court in which the record is so filed. For the convenience of the parties in the interest of justice, the court in which the record is filed may thereafter transfer all

the proceedings with respect to that order to any other court of appeals.

(b) The record to be filed in the court of appeals in such a proceeding shall consist of the order sought to be reviewed or enforced, the findings or report upon which it is based, and the pleadings, evidence, and proceedings before the agency, board, commission, or officer concerned, or such portions thereof (1) as the rules prescribed under the authority of section 2072 of this title may require to be included therein, or (2) as the agency, board, commission, or officer concerned, the petitioner for review or respondent in enforcement, as the case may be, and any intervenor in the court proceeding by written stipulation filed with the agency, board, commission, or officer concerned or in the court in any such proceeding may consistently with the rules prescribed under the authority of section 2072 of this title designate to be included therein, or (3) as the court upon motion of a party or, after a prehearing conference, upon its own motion may by order in any such proceeding designate to be included therein. Such a stipulation or order may provide in an appropriate case that no record need be filed in the court of appeals. If, however, the correctness of a finding of fact by the agency, board, commission, or officer is in question all of the evidence before the agency, board, commission, or officer shall be included in the record except such as the agency, board, commission, or officer concerned, the petitioner for review or respondent in enforcement, as the case may be, and any intervenor in the court proceeding by written stipulation filed with the agency, board, commission, or officer concerned or in the court agree to omit as wholly immaterial to the questioned finding. If there is omitted from the record any portion of the proceedings before the agency, board, commission, or officer which the court subsequently determines to be proper for it to consider to enable it to review or enforce the order in question the court may direct that such additional portion of the proceedings be filed as a supplement to the record. The agency, board, commission, or officer concerned may, at its option and without regard to the foregoing provisions of this subsection, and if so requested by the petitioner for review or respondent in enforcement shall, file in the court the entire record of the proceedings before it without abbreviation.

(c) The agency, board, commission, or officer concerned may transmit to the court of appeals the original papers comprising the whole or any part of the record or any supplemental record, otherwise true copies of such papers certified by an authorized officer or deputy of the agency, board, commission, or officer concerned shall be transmitted. Any original papers thus transmitted to the court of appeals shall be returned to the agency, board, commission, or officer concerned upon the final determination of the review or enforcement proceeding. Pending such final determination any such papers may be returned by the court temporarily to the custody of the agency, board, commission, or officer concerned if needed for the transaction of the public business. Certified copies of any papers included in the record or any supplemental record may also be returned to the agency, board, commission, or officer concerned upon the final determination of review or enforcement proceedings.

(d) The provisions of this section are not applicable to proceedings to review decisions of the Tax Court of the United States or to proceedings to review or enforce those orders of administrative agencies, boards, commissions, or officers which are by law reviewable or enforceable by the district courts.

(Added Pub.L. 85–791, § 2, Aug. 28, 1958, 72 Stat. 941, and amended Pub.L. 89–773, § 5(a), (b), Nov. 6, 1966, 80 Stat. 1323; Pub.L. 100–236, § 1, Jan. 8, 1988, 101 Stat. 1731.)

HISTORICAL AND STATUTORY NOTES

Effective Dates

1988 Acts. Section 3 of Pub.L. 100–236 provided that: "The amendments made by this Act [amending subsec. (a) of this section and section 1369(b) of Title 33, Navigation and Navigable Waters] take effect 180 days after the date of the enactment of this Act [Jan. 8, 1988], except that the judicial panel on multidistrict litigation may issue rules pursuant to subsection (a)(3) of section 2112 of title 28, United States Code (as added by section 1) [subsec. (a)(3) of this section], on or after such date of enactment."

Savings Provisions

Section 5(c) of Pub.L. 89–773 provided that: "The amendments of section 2112 of title 28 of the United States Code [this section] made by this Act shall not operate to invalidate or repeal rules adopted under the authority of that section prior to the enactment of this Act [Nov. 6, 1966], which rules shall remain in effect until superseded by rules prescribed under the authority of section 2072 of title 28 of the United States Code [section 2072 of this title] as amended by this Act."

§ 2113. Definition

For purposes of this chapter, the terms "State court", "State courts", and "highest court of a State" include the District of Columbia Court of Appeals.

(Added Pub.L. 91–358, Title I, § 172(a)(2)(A), July 29, 1970, 84 Stat. 590.)

HISTORICAL AND STATUTORY NOTES

Effective Dates

1970 Acts. Section effective the first day of the seventh calendar month which begins after July 29, 1970, see section 199(a) of Pub.L. 91–358, set out as a note under section 1257 of this title.

PART VI—PARTICULAR PROCEEDINGS

Chapter		Section
151.	Declaratory Judgments	2201
153.	Habeas Corpus	2241
154.	Special Habeas Corpus Procedures in Capital Cases	2261
155.	Injunctions; Three-Judge Courts	2281
157.	Surface Transportation Board Orders; Enforcement and Review	2321
158.	Orders of Federal Agencies; Review	2341
159.	Interpleader	2361
161.	United States as Party Generally	2401
163.	Fines, Penalties and Forfeitures	2461
165.	United States Court of Federal Claims Procedure	2501
[167.	Repealed]	
169.	Court of International Trade Procedure	2631
171.	Tort Claims Procedure	2671
173.	Attachment in Postal Suits	2710
175.	Civil Commitment and Rehabilitation of Narcotic Addicts	2901
176.	Federal Debt Collection Procedure	3001
178.	Professional and Amateur Sports Protection	3701
179.	Judicial Review of Certain Actions by Presidential Offices	3901
180.	Assumption of Certain Contractual Obligations	4001

HISTORICAL AND STATUTORY NOTES

Effective Dates

1996 Acts. Amendment of analysis by section 3(e) of Pub.L. 104–331, effective Oct. 1, 1997, see section 3(d) of Pub.L. 104–331, set out as a note under section 1296 of this title.

CHAPTER 151—DECLARATORY JUDGMENTS

Sec.
2201. Creation of remedy.
2202. Further relief.

§ 2201. Creation of remedy

(a) In a case of actual controversy within its jurisdiction, except with respect to Federal taxes other than actions brought under section 7428 of the Internal Revenue Code of 1986, a proceeding under section 505 or 1146 of title 11, or in any civil action involving an antidumping or countervailing duty proceeding regarding a class or kind of merchandise of a free trade area country (as defined in section 516A(f)(10) of the Tariff Act of 1930), as determined by the administering authority, any court of the United States, upon the filing of an appropriate pleading, may declare the rights and other legal relations of any interested party seeking such declaration, whether or not further relief is or could be sought. Any such declaration shall have the force and effect of a final judgment or decree and shall be reviewable as such.

(b) For limitations on actions brought with respect to drug patents see section 505 or 512 of the Federal Food, Drug, and Cosmetic Act.

(June 25, 1948, c. 646, 62 Stat. 964; May 24, 1949, c. 139, § 111, 63 Stat. 105; Aug. 28, 1954, c. 1033, 68 Stat. 890; July 7, 1958, Pub.L. 85–508, § 12(p), 72 Stat. 349; Oct. 4, 1976, Pub.L. 94–455, Title XIII, § 1306(b)(8), 90 Stat. 1719; Nov. 6, 1978, Pub.L. 95–598, Title II, § 249, 92 Stat. 2672; Sept. 24, 1984, Pub.L. 98–417, Title I, § 106, 98 Stat. 1597; Sept. 28, 1988, Pub.L. 100–449, Title IV, § 402(c), 102 Stat. 1884; Nov. 16, 1988, Pub.L. 100–670, Title I, § 107(b), 102 Stat. 3984; Dec. 8, 1993, Pub.L. 103–182, Title IV, § 414(b), 107 Stat. 2147.)

Termination of Amendments

For provisions directing that, except for transition provisions relating to proceedings regarding protective orders and undertakings, and binational panel and extraordinary challenge committee reviews, the amendment to this section by Title IV of Pub.L. 103–182 shall cease to have effect with respect to any country on the date on which such country ceases to be a NAFTA country, see section 3451 of Title 19, Customs Duties.

For provisions directing that the amendments made by Pub.L. 100–449, which amended this section, shall cease to have effect on the date on which the United States-Canada Free-Trade Agreement ceases to be in force, see section 501(c) of Pub.L. 100–449, set out in the note under section 2112 of Title 19, Customs Duties.

Articles 1906 and 2106 of the Agreement authorize either the United States or Canada to terminate the Agreement on 6–month notice if, at the end of the 7–year period following the date of the entry into effect of the Agreement, no agreement has been entered into between the United States and Canada on a substitute system of antidumping and countervailing duties.

HISTORICAL AND STATUTORY NOTES

References in Text

Section 7428 of the Internal Revenue Code of 1986, referred to in subsec. (a), is classified to section 7428 of Title 26, Internal Revenue Code.

Section 516A(f)(10) of the Tariff Act of 1930, referred to in subsec. (a), is classified to section 1516a(f)(10) of Title 19, Customs Duties.

Sections 505 and 512 of the Federal Food, Drug, and Cosmetic Act, referred to in subsec. (b), are classified to sections 355 and 360b, respectively, of Title 21, Food and Drugs.

Effective and Termination Dates

1993 Acts. Amendment of this section by section 414 of Pub.L. 103–182 to take effect on the date the North American Free Trade Agreement enters into force with respect to the United States, but not to apply to any final determination described in section 1516a(a)(1)(B) or (2)(B)(i), (ii), or (iii) of Title 19, Customs Duties, notice of which is published in the Federal Register before such date, or to a determination described in section 1516a(a)(2)(B)(vi) of Title 19 notice of which is received by the Government of Canada or Mexico before such date, or to any binational panel review under the United States-Canada Free-Trade Agreement, or to any extraordinary challenge arising out of any such review that was commenced before such date, see section 416 of Pub.L. 103–182, set out as a note under section 3431 of Title 19.

1988 Acts. Amendment by Pub.L. 100–449 effective on the date the United States-Canada Free-Trade Agreement enters into force (Jan. 1, 1989), and to cease to have effect on the date the Agreement ceases to be in force, see section 501(a), (c) of Pub.L. 100–449, set out in a note under section 2112 of Title 19, Customs Duties. [A Presidential Memorandum on the Canada-United States Free-Trade Agreement, dated Dec. 31, 1988, directing the Secretary of State to exchange notes with the Government of Canada to provide for the entry into force of the Agreement on Jan. 1, 1989, is set out in 24 Weekly Compilation of Presidential Documents 1688, Jan. 2, 1989.]

1978 Acts. Amendment by Pub.L. 95–598 effective Oct. 1, 1979, see section 402(c) of Pub.L. 95–598, set out as a note preceding section 101 of Title 11, Bankruptcy.

1976 Acts. Amendment by Pub.L. 94–455 applicable with respect to pleadings filed with the United States Tax Court, the District Court of the United States for the District of Columbia, or the United States Court of Claims more than 6 months after Oct. 4, 1976, but only with respect to determinations (or requests for determinations) made after Jan. 1, 1976, see section 1306(c) of Pub.L. 94–455, set out as a note under section 7428 of Title 26, Internal Revenue Code.

1958 Acts. Amendment by Pub.L. 85–508 effective Jan. 3, 1959, upon admission of Alaska into the Union pursuant to Proc. No. 3269, Jan. 3, 1959, 24 F.R. 81, 73 Stat. c. 16, as required by sections 1 and 8(c) of Pub.L. 85–508, see notes set out under section 81A of this title and preceding section 21 of Title 48, Territories and Insular Possessions.

Amount in Controversy

Jurisdictional amount increased from $3,000 to $50,000 in diversity of citizenship cases, see section 1332 of this title.

§ 2202. Further relief

Further necessary or proper relief based on a declaratory judgment or decree may be granted, after reasonable notice and hearing, against any adverse party whose rights have been determined by such judgment.

(June 25, 1948, c. 646, 62 Stat. 964.)

CHAPTER 153—HABEAS CORPUS

Sec.
2241. Power to grant writ.
2242. Application.
2243. Issuance of writ; return; hearing; decision.
2244. Finality of determination.
2245. Certificate of trial judge admissible in evidence.
2246. Evidence; depositions; affidavits.
2247. Documentary evidence.
2248. Return or answer; conclusiveness.
2249. Certified copies of indictment, plea and judgment; duty of respondent.
2250. Indigent petitioner entitled to documents without cost.
2251. Stay of State court proceedings.
2252. Notice.
2253. Appeal.
2254. State custody; remedies in Federal courts.
2255. Federal custody; remedies on motion attacking sentence.
[2256. Omitted.]

HISTORICAL AND STATUTORY NOTES

Codifications

The table of sections for chapter 153 was amended by Pub.L. 95–598, Title II, § 250(b), Nov. 6, 1978, 92 Stat. 2672, effective June 28, 1984, pursuant to Pub.L. 95–598, Title IV, § 402(b), Nov. 6, 1978, 92 Stat. 2682, as amended by Pub.L. 98–249, § 1(a), Mar. 31, 1984, 98 Stat. 116; Pub.L. 98–271, § 1(a), Apr. 30, 1984, 98 Stat. 163; Pub.L. 98–299, § 1(a), May 25, 1984, 98 Stat. 214; Pub.L. 98–325, § 1(a), June 20, 1984, 98 Stat. 268, set out as an Effective Dates note preceding section 101 of Title 11, Bankruptcy, by adding: "2256. Habeas corpus from bankruptcy courts.".

Section 402(b) of Pub.L. 95–598 was amended by section 113 of Pub.L. 98–353, Title I, July 10, 1984, 98 Stat. 343, by substituting "shall not be effective" for "shall take effect on June 28, 1984", thereby eliminating the amendment by section 250(b) of Pub.L. 95–598, effective June 27, 1984, pursuant to section 122(c) of Pub.L. 98–353, set out as an Effective Dates note under section 151 of this title.

Section 121(a) of Pub.L. 98–353 directed that section 402(b) of Pub.L. 95–598 be amended by substituting "the date of enactment of the Bankruptcy Amendments and Federal Judgeship Act of 1984 [i.e. July 10, 1984]" for "June 28, 1984". This amendment was not executed in view of the prior amendment to section 402(b) of Pub.L. 95–598 by section 113 of Pub.L. 98–353.

§ 2241. Power to grant writ

(a) Writs of habeas corpus may be granted by the Supreme Court, any justice thereof, the district courts and any circuit judge within their respective jurisdictions. The order of a circuit judge shall be entered in the records of the district court of the district wherein the restraint complained of is had.

(b) The Supreme Court, any justice thereof, and any circuit judge may decline to entertain an application for a writ of habeas corpus and may transfer the application for hearing and determination to the district court having jurisdiction to entertain it.

(c) The writ of habeas corpus shall not extend to a prisoner unless—

(1) He is in custody under or by color of the authority of the United States or is committed for trial before some court thereof; or

(2) He is in custody for an act done or omitted in pursuance of an Act of Congress, or an order, process, judgment or decree of a court or judge of the United States; or

(3) He is in custody in violation of the Constitution or laws or treaties of the United States; or

(4) He, being a citizen of a foreign state and domiciled therein is in custody for an act done or omitted under any alleged right, title, authority, privilege, protection, or exemption claimed under the commission, order or sanction of any foreign state, or under color thereof, the validity and effect of which depend upon the law of nations; or

(5) It is necessary to bring him into court to testify or for trial.

(d) Where an application for a writ of habeas corpus is made by a person in custody under the judgment and sentence of a State court of a State which contains two or more Federal judicial districts, the application may be filed in the district court for the district wherein such person is in custody or in the district court for the district within which the State court was held which convicted and sentenced him and each of such district courts shall have concurrent jurisdiction to entertain the application. The district court for the district wherein such an application is filed in the exercise of its discretion and in furtherance of justice may transfer the application to the other district court for hearing and determination.

(June 25, 1948, c. 646, 62 Stat. 964; May 24, 1949, c. 139, § 112, 63 Stat. 105; Sept. 19, 1966, Pub.L. 89–590, 80 Stat. 811.)

§ 2242. Application

Application for a writ of habeas corpus shall be in writing signed and verified by the person for whose relief it is intended or by someone acting in his behalf.

It shall allege the facts concerning the applicant's commitment or detention, the name of the person who has custody over him and by virtue of what claim or authority, if known.

It may be amended or supplemented as provided in the rules of procedure applicable to civil actions.

If addressed to the Supreme Court, a justice thereof or a circuit judge it shall state the reasons for not making application to the district court of the district in which the applicant is held.

(June 25, 1948, c. 646, 62 Stat. 965.)

§ 2243. Issuance of writ; return; hearing; decision

A court, justice or judge entertaining an application for a writ of habeas corpus shall forthwith award the writ or issue an order directing the respondent to show cause why the writ should not be granted, unless it appears from the application that the applicant or person detained is not entitled thereto.

The writ, or order to show cause shall be directed to the person having custody of the person detained. It shall be returned within three days unless for good cause additional time, not exceeding twenty days, is allowed.

The person to whom the writ or order is directed shall make a return certifying the true cause of the detention.

When the writ or order is returned a day shall be set for hearing, not more than five days after the return unless for good cause additional time is allowed.

Unless the application for the writ and the return present only issues of law the person to whom the writ is directed shall be required to produce at the hearing the body of the person detained.

The applicant or the person detained may, under oath, deny any of the facts set forth in the return or allege any other material facts.

The return and all suggestions made against it may be amended, by leave of court, before or after being filed.

The court shall summarily hear and determine the facts, and dispose of the matter as law and justice require.

(June 25, 1948, c. 646, 62 Stat. 965.)

§ 2244. Finality of determination

(a) No circuit or district judge shall be required to entertain an application for a writ of habeas corpus to inquire into the detention of a person pursuant to a judgment of a court of the United States if it appears that the legality of such detention has been determined by a judge or court of the United States on a prior application for a writ of habeas corpus, except as provided in section 2255.

(b)(1) A claim presented in a second or successive habeas corpus application under section 2254 that was presented in a prior application shall be dismissed.

(2) A claim presented in a second or successive habeas corpus application under section 2254 that was not presented in a prior application shall be dismissed unless—

(A) the applicant shows that the claim relies on a new rule of constitutional law, made retroactive to cases on collateral review by the Supreme Court, that was previously unavailable; or

(B)(i) the factual predicate for the claim could not have been discovered previously through the exercise of due diligence; and

(ii) the facts underlying the claim, if proven and viewed in light of the evidence as a whole, would be sufficient to establish by clear and convincing evidence that, but for constitutional error, no reasonable factfinder would have found the applicant guilty of the underlying offense.

(3)(A) Before a second or successive application permitted by this section is filed in the district court, the applicant shall move in the appropriate court of appeals for an order authorizing the district court to consider the application.

(B) A motion in the court of appeals for an order authorizing the district court to consider a second or successive application shall be determined by a three-judge panel of the court of appeals.

(C) The court of appeals may authorize the filing of a second or successive application only if it determines that the application makes a prima facie showing that the application satisfies the requirements of this subsection.

(D) The court of appeals shall grant or deny the authorization to file a second or successive application not later than 30 days after the filing of the motion.

(E) The grant or denial of an authorization by a court of appeals to file a second or successive application shall not be appealable and shall not be the subject of a petition for rehearing or for a writ of certiorari.

(4) A district court shall dismiss any claim presented in a second or successive application that the court of appeals has authorized to be filed unless the applicant shows that the claim satisfies the requirements of this section.

(c) In a habeas corpus proceeding brought in behalf of a person in custody pursuant to the judgment of a State court, a prior judgment of the Supreme Court of the United States on an appeal or review by a writ of certiorari at the instance of the prisoner of the decision of such State court, shall be conclusive as to all issues of fact or law with respect to an asserted denial of a Federal right which constitutes ground for discharge in a habeas corpus proceeding, actually adjudicated by the Supreme Court therein, unless the applicant for the writ of habeas corpus shall plead and the court shall find the existence of a material and controlling fact which did not appear in the record of the proceeding in the Supreme Court and the court shall further find that the applicant for the writ of habeas corpus could not have caused such fact to appear in such record by the exercise of reasonable diligence.

(d)(1) A 1-year period of limitation shall apply to an application for a writ of habeas corpus by a person in custody pursuant to the judgment of a State court. The limitation period shall run from the latest of—

(A) the date on which the judgment became final by the conclusion of direct review or the expiration of the time for seeking such review;

(B) the date on which the impediment to filing an application created by State action in violation of the Constitution or laws of the United States is removed, if the applicant was prevented from filing by such State action;

(C) the date on which the constitutional right asserted was initially recognized by the Supreme Court, if the right has been newly recognized by the Supreme Court and made retroactively applicable to cases on collateral review; or

(D) the date on which the factual predicate of the claim or claims presented could have been discovered through the exercise of due diligence.

(2) The time during which a properly filed application for State post-conviction or other collateral review with respect to the pertinent judgment or claim is pending shall not be counted toward any period of limitation under this subsection.

(June 25, 1948, c. 646, 62 Stat. 965; Nov. 2, 1966, Pub.L. 89–711, § 1, 80 Stat. 1104; Apr. 24, 1996, Pub.L. 104–132, Title I, §§ 101, 106, 110 Stat. 1217, 1220.)

§ 2245. Certificate of trial judge admissible in evidence

On the hearing of an application for a writ of habeas corpus to inquire into the legality of the detention of a person pursuant to a judgment the certificate of the judge who presided at the trial resulting in the judgment, setting forth the facts occurring at the trial, shall be admissible in evidence. Copies of the certificate shall be filed with the court in which the application is pending and in the court in which the trial took place.

(June 25, 1948, c. 646, 62 Stat. 966.)

§ 2246. Evidence; depositions; affidavits

On application for a writ of habeas corpus, evidence may be taken orally or by deposition, or, in the discretion of the judge, by affidavit. If affidavits are admitted any party shall have the right to propound written interrogatories to the affiants, or to file answering affidavits.

(June 25, 1948, c. 646, 62 Stat. 966.)

§ 2247. Documentary evidence

On application for a writ of habeas corpus documentary evidence, transcripts of proceedings upon arraignment, plea and sentence and a transcript of the oral testimony introduced on any previous similar application by or in behalf of the same petitioner, shall be admissible in evidence.

(June 25, 1948, c. 646, 62 Stat. 966.)

§ 2248. Return or answer; conclusiveness

The allegations of a return to the writ of habeas corpus or of an answer to an order to show cause in a habeas corpus proceeding, if not traversed, shall be accepted as true except to the extent that the judge finds from the evidence that they are not true.

(June 25, 1948, c. 646, 62 Stat. 966.)

§ 2249. Certified copies of indictment, plea and judgment; duty of respondent

On application for a writ of habeas corpus to inquire into the detention of any person pursuant to a judgment of a court of the United States, the respondent shall promptly file with the court certified copies of the indictment, plea of petitioner and the judgment, or such of them as may be material to the questions raised, if the petitioner fails to attach them to his petition, and same shall be attached to the return to the writ, or to the answer to the order to show cause.

(June 25, 1948, c. 646, 62 Stat. 966.)

§ 2250. Indigent petitioner entitled to documents without cost

If on any application for a writ of habeas corpus an order has been made permitting the petitioner to prosecute the application in forma pauperis, the clerk of any court of the United States shall furnish to the petitioner without cost certified copies of such documents or parts of the record on file in his office as may be required by order of the judge before whom the application is pending.

(June 25, 1948, c. 646, 62 Stat. 966.)

§ 2251. Stay of State court proceedings

A justice or judge of the United States before whom a habeas corpus proceeding is pending, may, before final judgment or after final judgment of discharge, or pending appeal, stay any proceeding against the person detained in any State court or by or under the authority of any State for any matter involved in the habeas corpus proceeding.

After the granting of such a stay, any such proceeding in any State court or by or under the authority of any State shall be void. If no stay is granted, any such proceeding shall be as valid as if no habeas corpus proceedings or appeal were pending.

(June 25, 1948, c. 646, 62 Stat. 966.)

§ 2252. Notice

Prior to the hearing of a habeas corpus proceeding in behalf of a person in custody of State officers or by virtue of State laws notice shall be served on the attorney general or other appropriate officer of such State as the justice or judge at the time of issuing the writ shall direct.

(June 25, 1948, c. 646, 62 Stat. 967.)

§ 2253. Appeal

(a) In a habeas corpus proceeding or a proceeding under section 2255 before a district judge, the final order shall be subject to review, on appeal, by the court of appeals for the circuit in which the proceeding is held.

(b) There shall be no right of appeal from a final order in a proceeding to test the validity of a warrant to remove to another district or place for commitment or trial a person charged with a criminal offense against the United States, or to test the validity of such person's detention pending removal proceedings.

(c)(1) Unless a circuit justice or judge issues a certificate of appealability, an appeal may not be taken to the court of appeals from—

(A) the final order in a habeas corpus proceeding in which the detention complained of arises out of process issued by a State court; or

(B) the final order in a proceeding under section 2255.

(2) A certificate of appealability may issue under paragraph (1) only if the applicant has made a substantial showing of the denial of a constitutional right.

(3) The certificate of appealability under paragraph (1) shall indicate which specific issue or issues satisfy the showing required by paragraph (2).

(June 25, 1948, c. 646, 62 Stat. 967; May 24, 1949, c. 139, § 113, 63 Stat. 105; Oct. 31, 1951, c. 655, § 52, 65 Stat. 727; Apr. 24, 1996, Pub.L. 104–132, Title I, § 102, 110 Stat. 1217.)

§ 2254. State custody; remedies in Federal courts

(a) The Supreme Court, a Justice thereof, a circuit judge, or a district court shall entertain an application for a writ of habeas corpus in behalf of a person in custody pursuant to the judgment of a State court only on the ground that he is in custody in violation of the Constitution or laws or treaties of the United States.

(b)(1) An application for a writ of habeas corpus on behalf of a person in custody pursuant to the judgment of a State court shall not be granted unless it appears that—

(A) the applicant has exhausted the remedies available in the courts of the State; or

(B)(i) there is an absence of available State corrective process; or

(ii) circumstances exist that render such process ineffective to protect the rights of the applicant.

(2) An application for a writ of habeas corpus may be denied on the merits, notwithstanding the failure of the applicant to exhaust the remedies available in the courts of the State.

(3) A State shall not be deemed to have waived the exhaustion requirement or be estopped from reliance upon the requirement unless the State, through counsel, expressly waives the requirement.

(c) An applicant shall not be deemed to have exhausted the remedies available in the courts of the State, within the meaning of this section, if he has the right under the law of the State to raise, by any available procedure, the question presented.

(d) An application for a writ of habeas corpus on behalf of a person in custody pursuant to the judgment of a State court shall not be granted with respect to any claim that was adjudicated on the merits in State court proceedings unless the adjudication of the claim—

(1) resulted in a decision that was contrary to, or involved an unreasonable application of, clearly established Federal law, as determined by the Supreme Court of the United States; or

(2) resulted in a decision that was based on an unreasonable determination of the facts in light of the evidence presented in the State court proceeding.

(e)(1) In a proceeding instituted by an application for a writ of habeas corpus by a person in custody pursuant to the judgment of a State court, a determination of a factual issue made by a State court shall be presumed to be correct. The applicant shall have the burden of rebutting the presumption of correctness by clear and convincing evidence.

(2) If the applicant has failed to develop the factual basis of a claim in State court proceedings, the court shall not hold an evidentiary hearing on the claim unless the applicant shows that—

(A) the claim relies on—

(i) a new rule of constitutional law, made retroactive to cases on collateral review by the Supreme Court, that was previously unavailable; or

(ii) a factual predicate that could not have been previously discovered through the exercise of due diligence; and

(B) the facts underlying the claim would be sufficient to establish by clear and convincing evidence that but for constitutional error, no reasonable factfinder would have found the applicant guilty of the underlying offense.

(f) If the applicant challenges the sufficiency of the evidence adduced in such State court proceeding to support the State court's determination of a factual issue made therein, the applicant, if able, shall produce that part of the record pertinent to a determination of the sufficiency of the evidence to support such determination. If the applicant, because of indigency or other reason is unable to produce such part of the record, then the State shall produce such part of the record and the Federal court shall direct the State to do so by order directed to an appropriate State official. If the State cannot provide such pertinent part of the record, then the court shall determine under the existing facts and circumstances what weight shall be given to the State court's factual determination.

(g) A copy of the official records of the State court, duly certified by the clerk of such court to be a true and correct copy of a finding, judicial opinion, or other reliable written indicia showing such a factual determination by the State court shall be admissible in the Federal court proceeding.

(h) Except as provided in section 408 of the Controlled Substances Act, in all proceedings brought under this section, and any subsequent proceedings on review, the court may appoint counsel for an applicant who is or becomes financially unable to afford counsel, except as provided by a rule promulgated by the Supreme Court pursuant to statutory authority. Appointment of counsel under this section shall be governed by section 3006A of title 18.

(i) The ineffectiveness or incompetence of counsel during Federal or State collateral post-conviction proceedings shall not be a ground for relief in a proceeding arising under section 2254.

(June 25, 1948, c. 646, 62 Stat. 967; Nov. 2, 1966, Pub.L. 89–711, § 2, 80 Stat. 1105; Apr. 24, 1996, Pub.L. 104–132, Title I, § 104, 110 Stat. 1218.)

HISTORICAL AND STATUTORY NOTES

Senate Revision Amendments

Senate amendment to this section, Senate Report No. 1559, amendment No. 47, has three declared purposes, set forth as follows:

"The first is to eliminate from the prohibition of the section applications in behalf of prisoners in custody under authority of a State officer but whose custody has not been directed by the judgment of a State court. If the section were applied to applications by persons detained solely under authority of a State officer it would unduly hamper Federal courts in the protection of Federal officers prosecuted for acts committed in the course of official duty.

"The second purpose is to eliminate, as a ground of Federal jurisdiction to review by habeas corpus judgments of State courts, the proposition that the State court has denied a prisoner a 'fair adjudication of the legality of his detention under the Constitution and laws of the United States.' The Judicial Conference believes that this would be an undesirable ground for Federal jurisdiction in addition to exhaustion of State remedies or lack of adequate remedy in the State courts because it would permit proceedings in the Federal court on this ground before the petitioner had exhausted his State remedies. This ground would, of course, always be open to a petitioner to assert in the Federal court after he had exhausted his State remedies or if he had no adequate State remedy.

"The third purpose is to substitute detailed and specific language for the phrase 'no adequate remedy available.' That phrase is not sufficiently specific and precise, and its meaning should, therefore, be spelled out in more detail in the section as is done by the amendment."

1966 Acts. Senate Report No. 1797, see 1966 U.S. Code Cong. and Adm. News, p. 3663.

References in Text

Section 408 of the Controlled Substances Act, referred to in subsec. (h), is classified to section 848 of Title 21, Food and Drugs.

Approval and Effective Date of Rules Governing Section 2254 Cases and Section 2255 Proceedings for United States District Courts

Pub.L. 94–426, § 1, Sept. 28, 1976, 90 Stat. 1334, provided: "That the rules governing section 2254 cases in the United States district courts and the rules governing section 2255 proceedings for the United States district courts, as proposed by the United States Supreme Court, which were delayed by the Act entitled 'An Act to delay the effective date of certain proposed amendments to the Federal Rules of Criminal Procedure and certain other rules promulgated by the United States Supreme Court' (Public Law 94–349), are approved with the amendments set forth in section 2 of this Act and shall take effect as so amended, with respect to petitions under section 2254 and motions under section 2255 of title 28 of the United States Code filed on or after February 1, 1977."

Postponement of Effective Date of Proposed Rules Governing Proceedings Under Sections 2254 and 2255 of this Title

Rules and forms governing proceedings under sections 2254 and 2255 of this title proposed by Supreme Court order of Apr. 26, 1976, effective 30 days after adjournment sine die of 94th Congress, or until and to the extent approved by Act of Congress, whichever is earlier, see section 2 of Pub.L. 94–349, set out as a note under section 2074 of this title.

CROSS REFERENCES

Rules Governing Section 2254 Cases in the United States District Courts are set out ante, following the Rules of Procedure of the Judicial Panel on Multidistrict Litigation.

§ 2255. Federal custody; remedies on motion attacking sentence

A prisoner in custody under sentence of a court established by Act of Congress claiming the right to be released upon the ground that the sentence was imposed in violation of the Constitution or laws of the United States, or that the court was without jurisdiction to impose such sentence, or that the sentence was in excess of the maximum authorized by law, or is otherwise subject to collateral attack, may move the court which imposed the sentence to vacate, set aside or correct the sentence.

Unless the motion and the files and records of the case conclusively show that the prisoner is entitled to no relief, the court shall cause notice thereof to be served upon the United States attorney, grant a prompt hearing thereon, determine the issues and make findings of fact and conclusions of law with respect thereto. If the court finds that the judgment was rendered without jurisdiction, or that the sentence imposed was not authorized by law or otherwise open to collateral attack, or that there has been such a denial or infringement of the constitutional rights of the prisoner as to render the judgment vulnerable to collateral attack, the court shall vacate and set the judgment aside and shall discharge the prisoner or resentence him or grant a new trial or correct the sentence as may appear appropriate.

A court may entertain and determine such motion without requiring the production of the prisoner at the hearing.

An appeal may be taken to the court of appeals from the order entered on the motion as from a final judgment on application for a writ of habeas corpus.

An application for a writ of habeas corpus in behalf of a prisoner who is authorized to apply for relief by motion pursuant to this section, shall not be entertained if it appears that the applicant has failed to apply for relief, by motion, to the court which sentenced him, or that such court has denied him relief, unless it also appears that the remedy by motion is inadequate or ineffective to test the legality of his detention.

A 1-year period of limitation shall apply to a motion under this section. The limitation period shall run from the latest of—

(1) the date on which the judgment of conviction becomes final;

(2) the date on which the impediment to making a motion created by governmental action in violation of the Constitution or laws of the United States is removed, if the movant was prevented from making a motion by such governmental action;

(3) the date on which the right asserted was initially recognized by the Supreme Court, if that right has been newly recognized by the Supreme Court and made retroactively applicable to cases on collateral review; or

(4) the date on which the facts supporting the claim or claims presented could have been discovered through the exercise of due diligence.

Except as provided in section 408 of the Controlled Substances Act, in all proceedings brought under this section, and any subsequent proceedings on review, the court may appoint counsel, except as provided by a rule promulgated by the Supreme Court pursuant to statutory authority. Appointment of counsel under this section shall be governed by section 3006A of title 18.

A second or successive motion must be certified as provided in section 2244 by a panel of the appropriate court of appeals to contain—

(1) newly discovered evidence that, if proven and viewed in light of the evidence as a whole, would be sufficient to establish by clear and convincing evidence that no reasonable factfinder would have found the movant guilty of the offense; or

(2) a new rule of constitutional law, made retroactive to cases on collateral review by the Supreme Court, that was previously unavailable.

(June 25, 1948, c. 646, 62 Stat. 967; May 24, 1949, c. 139, § 114, 63 Stat. 105; Apr. 24, 1996, Pub.L. 104–132, Title I, § 105, 110 Stat. 1220.)

HISTORICAL AND STATUTORY NOTES

References in Text

Section 408 of the Controlled Substances Act, referred to in text, is classified to section 848 of Title 21, Food and Drugs.

Approval and Effective Date of Rules Governing Section 2254 Cases and Section 2255 Proceedings For United States District Courts

Pub.L. 94–426, § 1, Sept. 28, 1976, 90 Stat. 1334, provided: "That the rules governing section 2254 cases in the United States district courts and the rules governing section 2255 proceedings for the United States district courts, as proposed by the United States Supreme Court, which were delayed by the Act entitled 'An Act to delay the effective date of certain proposed amendments to the Federal Rules of Criminal Procedure and certain other rules promulgated by the United States Supreme Court' (Public Law 94–349), are approved with the amendments set forth in section 2 of this Act and shall take effect as so amended, with respect to petitions under section 2254 and motions [sections 2254 and 2255 of this title] under section 2255 of title 28 of the United States Code filed on or after February 1, 1977."

Postponement of Effective Date of Proposed Rules and Forms Governing Proceedings Under Sections 2254 and 2255 of this Title

Rules and forms governing proceedings under this section and section 2254 of this title proposed by Supreme Court order of Apr. 26, 1976, effective 30 days after adjournment sine die of 94th Congress, or until and to the extent approved by Act of Congress, whichever is earlier, see section 2 of Pub.L. 94–349, set out as a note under section 2074 of this title.

CROSS REFERENCES

Rules Governing Section 2255 Proceedings in the United States District Courts are set out ante, following the Rules Governing Section 2254 Cases in the United States District Courts.

[§ 2256. Omitted]

HISTORICAL AND STATUTORY NOTES

Codifications

This section as added by Pub. L. 95–598, Title II, § 250(a), Nov. 6, 1978, 92 Stat. 2672, effective June 28, 1984, pursuant to Pub. L. 95–598, Title IV, § 402(b), Nov. 6, 1978, 92 Stat. 2682, as amended by Pub. L. 98–249, § 1(a), Mar. 31, 1984, 98 Stat. 116; Pub. L. 98–271, § 1(a), Apr. 30, 1984, 98 Stat. 163; Pub. L. 98–299, § 1(a), May 25, 1984, 98 Stat. 214; Pub. L. 98–325, § 1(a), June 20, 1984, 98 Stat. 268 [set out as an Effective Dates note preceding section 101 of Title 11, Bankruptcy], read as follows:

§ 2256. Habeas corpus from bankruptcy courts

A bankruptcy court may issue a writ of habeas corpus—

(1) when appropriate to bring a person before the court—

(A) for examination;

(B) to testify; or

(C) to perform a duty imposed on such person under this title; or

(2) ordering the release of a debtor in a case under title 11 in custody under the judgment of a Federal or State court if—

(A) such debtor was arrested or imprisoned on process in any civil action;

(B) such process was issued for the collection of a debt—

(i) dischargeable under title 11; or

(ii) that is or will be provided for in a plan under chapter 11 or 13 of title 11; and

(C) before the issuance of such writ, notice and a hearing have been afforded the adverse party of such debtor in custody to contest the issuance of such writ.

Section 402(b) of Pub. L. 95–598 was amended by section 113 of Pub. L. 98–353 Title I, July 10, 1984, 98 Stat. 343, by substituting "shall not be effective" for "shall take effect on June 28, 1984", thereby eliminating the amendment by section 250(a) of Pub. L. 95–598, effective June 27, 1984, pursuant to section 122(c) of Pub. L. 98–353, set out as an Effective Dates note under section 151 of this title.

Section 121(a) of Pub. L. 98–353 directed that section 402(b) of Pub. L. 95–598 be amended by substituting "the date of enactment of the Bankruptcy Amendments and Federal Judgeship Act of 1984 [i.e. July 10, 1984]" for "June 28 1984". This amendment was not executed in view of the prior amendment to section 402(b) of Pub. L. 95–598 by section 113 of Pub. L. 98–353.

Prior Provisions

A prior section 2256, added Pub. L. 95–144, § 3, Oct. 28, 1977, 91 Stat. 1220, which related to jurisdiction of proceedings relating to transferred offenders, was transferred to section 3244 of Title 18, Crimes and Criminal Procedure, by Pub. L. 95–598, Title III, § 314(j), Nov. 6, 1978, 92 Stat. 2677.

CHAPTER 154—SPECIAL HABEAS CORPUS PROCEDURES IN CAPITAL CASES

Sec.
2261. Prisoners in State custody subject to capital sentence; appointment of counsel; requirement of rule of court or statute; procedures for appointment.
2262. Mandatory stay of execution; duration; limits on stays of execution; successive petitions.
2263. Filing of habeas corpus application; time requirements; tolling rules.
2264. Scope of Federal review; district court adjudications.
2265. Application to State unitary review procedure.
2266. Limitation periods for determining applications and motions.

§ 2261. Prisoners in State custody subject to capital sentence; appointment of counsel; requirement of rule of court or statute; procedures for appointment

(a) This chapter shall apply to cases arising under section 2254 brought by prisoners in State custody who are subject to a capital sentence. It shall apply only if the provisions of subsections (b) and (c) are satisfied.

(b) This chapter is applicable if a State establishes by statute, rule of its court of last resort, or by another agency authorized by State law, a mechanism for the appointment, compensation, and payment of reasonable litigation expenses of competent counsel in State post-conviction proceedings brought by indigent prisoners whose capital convictions and sentences have been upheld on direct appeal to the court of last resort in the State or have otherwise become final for State law purposes. The rule of court or statute must provide standards of competency for the appointment of such counsel.

(c) Any mechanism for the appointment, compensation, and reimbursement of counsel as provided in subsection (b) must offer counsel to all State prisoners under capital sentence and must provide for the entry of an order by a court of record—

(1) appointing one or more counsels to represent the prisoner upon a finding that the prisoner is indigent and accepted the offer or is unable competently to decide whether to accept or reject the offer;

(2) finding, after a hearing if necessary, that the prisoner rejected the offer of counsel and made the decision with an understanding of its legal consequences; or

(3) denying the appointment of counsel upon a finding that the prisoner is not indigent.

(d) No counsel appointed pursuant to subsections (b) and (c) to represent a State prisoner under capital sentence shall have previously represented the prisoner at trial or on direct appeal in the case for which the appointment is made unless the prisoner and counsel expressly request continued representation.

(e) The ineffectiveness or incompetence of counsel during State or Federal post-conviction proceedings in a capital case shall not be a ground for relief in a proceeding arising under section 2254. This limitation shall not preclude the appointment of different counsel, on the court's own motion or at the request of the prisoner, at any phase of State or Federal post-conviction proceedings on the basis of the ineffectiveness or incompetence of counsel in such proceedings.

(Added Pub.L. 104–132, Title I, § 107(a), Apr. 24, 1996, 110 Stat. 1221.)

HISTORICAL AND STATUTORY NOTES

Effective Dates

1996 Acts. Section 107(c) of Pub.L. 104–132 provided that: "Chapter 154 of title 28, United States Code (as added by subsection (a)) [this chapter] shall apply to cases pending on or after the date of enactment of this Act [Apr. 24, 1996]."

§ 2262. Mandatory stay of execution; duration; limits on stays of execution; successive petitions

(a) Upon the entry in the appropriate State court of record of an order under section 2261(c), a warrant or order setting an execution date for a State prisoner shall be stayed upon application to any court that would have jurisdiction over any proceedings filed under section 2254. The application shall recite that the State has invoked the post-conviction review procedures of this chapter and that the scheduled execution is subject to stay.

(b) A stay of execution granted pursuant to subsection (a) shall expire if—

(1) a State prisoner fails to file a habeas corpus application under section 2254 within the time required in section 2263;

(2) before a court of competent jurisdiction, in the presence of counsel, unless the prisoner has competently and knowingly waived such counsel, and after having been advised of the consequences, a State prisoner under capital sentence waives the right to pursue habeas corpus review under section 2254; or

(3) a State prisoner files a habeas corpus petition under section 2254 within the time required by section 2263 and fails to make a substantial showing of the denial of a Federal right or is denied relief in the district court or at any subsequent stage of review.

(c) If one of the conditions in subsection (b) has occurred, no Federal court thereafter shall have the authority to enter a stay of execution in the case, unless the court of appeals approves the filing of a second or successive application under section 2244(b).

(Added Pub.L. 104–132, Title I, § 107(a), Apr. 24, 1996, 110 Stat. 1222.)

HISTORICAL AND STATUTORY NOTES

Effective Dates

1996 Acts. Section applicable to cases pending on or after Apr. 24, 1996, see section 107(c) of Pub.L. 104–132, set out as a note under section 2261 of this title.

§ 2263. Filing of habeas corpus application; time requirements; tolling rules

(a) Any application under this chapter for habeas corpus relief under section 2254 must be filed in the appropriate district court not later than 180 days after final State court affirmance of the conviction and sentence on direct review or the expiration of the time for seeking such review.

(b) The time requirements established by subsection (a) shall be tolled—

(1) from the date that a petition for certiorari is filed in the Supreme Court until the date of final disposition of the petition if a State prisoner files the petition to secure review by the Supreme Court of the affirmance of a capital sentence on direct review by the court of last resort of the State or other final State court decision on direct review;

(2) from the date on which the first petition for post-conviction review or other collateral relief is filed until the final State court disposition of such petition; and

(3) during an additional period not to exceed 30 days, if—

(A) a motion for an extension of time is filed in the Federal district court that would have jurisdiction over the case upon the filing of a habeas corpus application under section 2254; and

(B) a showing of good cause is made for the failure to file the habeas corpus application within the time period established by this section.

(Added Pub.L. 104–132, Title I, § 107(a), Apr. 24, 1996, 110 Stat. 1223.)

HISTORICAL AND STATUTORY NOTES

Effective Dates

1996 Acts. Section applicable to cases pending on or after Apr. 24, 1996, see section 107(c) of Pub.L. 104–132, set out as a note under section 2261 of this title.

§ 2264. Scope of Federal review; district court adjudications

(a) Whenever a State prisoner under capital sentence files a petition for habeas corpus relief to which this chapter applies, the district court shall only consider a claim or claims that have been raised and decided on the merits in the State courts, unless the failure to raise the claim properly is—

(1) the result of State action in violation of the Constitution or laws of the United States;

(2) the result of the Supreme Court's recognition of a new Federal right that is made retroactively applicable; or

(3) based on a factual predicate that could not have been discovered through the exercise of due diligence in time to present the claim for State or Federal post-conviction review.

(b) Following review subject to subsections (a), (d), and (e) of section 2254, the court shall rule on the claims properly before it.

(Added Pub.L. 104–132, Title I, § 107(a), Apr. 24, 1996, 110 Stat. 1223.)

HISTORICAL AND STATUTORY NOTES

Effective Dates

1996 Acts. Section applicable to cases pending on or after Apr. 24, 1996, see section 107(c) of Pub.L. 104–132, set out as a note under section 2261 of this title.

§ 2265. Application to State unitary review procedure

(a) For purposes of this section, a "unitary review" procedure means a State procedure that authorizes a person under sentence of death to raise, in the course of direct review of the judgment, such claims as could be raised on collateral attack. This chapter shall apply, as provided in this section, in relation to a State unitary review procedure if the State establishes by rule of its court of last resort or by statute a mechanism for the appointment, compensation, and payment of reasonable litigation expenses of competent counsel in the unitary review proceedings, including expenses relating to the litigation of collateral claims in the proceedings. The rule of court or statute must provide standards of competency for the appointment of such counsel.

(b) To qualify under this section, a unitary review procedure must include an offer of counsel following trial for the purpose of representation on unitary review, and entry of an order, as provided in section 2261(c), concerning appointment of counsel or waiver or denial of appointment of counsel for that purpose. No counsel appointed to represent the prisoner in the unitary review proceedings shall have previously represented the prisoner at trial in the case for which the appointment is made unless the prisoner and counsel expressly request continued representation.

(c) Sections 2262, 2263, 2264, and 2266 shall apply in relation to cases involving a sentence of death from any State having a unitary review procedure that qualifies under this section. References to State "post-conviction review" and "direct review" in such sections shall be understood as referring to unitary review under the State procedure. The reference in section 2262(a) to "an order under section 2261(c)" shall be understood as referring to the post-trial order under subsection (b) concerning representation in the unitary review proceedings, but if a transcript of the trial proceedings is unavailable at the time of the filing of such an order in the appropriate State court, then the start of the 180-day limitation period under section 2263 shall be deferred until a transcript is made available to the prisoner or counsel of the prisoner.

(Added Pub.L. 104–132, Title I, § 107(a), Apr. 24, 1996, 110 Stat. 1223.)

HISTORICAL AND STATUTORY NOTES

Effective Dates

1996 Acts. Section applicable to cases pending on or after Apr. 24, 1996, see section 107(c) of Pub.L. 104–132, set out as a note under section 2261 of this title.

§ 2266. Limitation periods for determining applications and motions

(a) The adjudication of any application under section 2254 that is subject to this chapter, and the adjudication of any motion under section 2255 by a person under sentence of death, shall be given priority by the district court and by the court of appeals over all noncapital matters.

(b)(1)(A) A district court shall render a final determination and enter a final judgment on any application for a writ of habeas corpus brought under this chapter in a capital case not later than 180 days after the date on which the application is filed.

(B) A district court shall afford the parties at least 120 days in which to complete all actions, including the preparation of all pleadings and briefs, and if necessary, a hearing, prior to the submission of the case for decision.

(C)(i) A district court may delay for not more than one additional 30–day period beyond the period specified in subparagraph (A), the rendering of a determination of an application for a writ of habeas corpus if the court issues a written order making a finding, and stating the reasons for the finding, that the ends of justice that would be served by allowing the delay outweigh the best interests of the public and the applicant in a speedy disposition of the application.

(ii) The factors, among others, that a court shall consider in determining whether a delay in the disposition of an application is warranted are as follows:

(I) Whether the failure to allow the delay would be likely to result in a miscarriage of justice.

(II) Whether the case is so unusual or so complex, due to the number of defendants, the nature of the prosecution, or the existence of novel questions of fact or law, that it is unreasonable to expect adequate briefing within the time limitations established by subparagraph (A).

(III) Whether the failure to allow a delay in a case that, taken as a whole, is not so unusual or so complex as described in subclause (II), but would otherwise deny the applicant reasonable time to obtain counsel, would unreasonably deny the applicant or the government continuity of counsel, or would deny counsel for the applicant or the government the reasonable time necessary for effective preparation, taking into account the exercise of due diligence.

(iii) No delay in disposition shall be permissible because of general congestion of the court's calendar.

(iv) The court shall transmit a copy of any order issued under clause (i) to the Director of the Administrative Office of the United States Courts for inclusion in the report under paragraph (5).

(2) The time limitations under paragraph (1) shall apply to—

(A) an initial application for a writ of habeas corpus;

(B) any second or successive application for a writ of habeas corpus; and

(C) any redetermination of an application for a writ of habeas corpus following a remand by the court of appeals or the Supreme Court for further proceedings, in which case the limitation period shall run from the date the remand is ordered.

(3)(A) The time limitations under this section shall not be construed to entitle an applicant to a stay of execution, to which the applicant would otherwise not be entitled, for the purpose of litigating any application or appeal.

(B) No amendment to an application for a writ of habeas corpus under this chapter shall be permitted after the filing of the answer to the application, except on the grounds specified in section 2244(b).

(4)(A) The failure of a court to meet or comply with a time limitation under this section shall not be a ground for granting relief from a judgment of conviction or sentence.

(B) The State may enforce a time limitation under this section by petitioning for a writ of mandamus to the court of appeals. The court of appeals shall act on the petition for a writ of mandamus not later than 30 days after the filing of the petition.

(5)(A) The Administrative Office of the United States Courts shall submit to Congress an annual report on the compliance by the district courts with the time limitations under this section.

(B) The report described in subparagraph (A) shall include copies of the orders submitted by the district courts under paragraph (1)(B)(iv).

(c)(1)(A) A court of appeals shall hear and render a final determination of any appeal of an order granting or denying, in whole or in part, an application brought under this chapter in a capital case not later than 120 days after the date on which the reply brief is filed, or if no reply brief is filed, not later than 120 days after the date on which the answering brief is filed.

(B)(i) A court of appeals shall decide whether to grant a petition for rehearing or other request for rehearing en banc not later than 30 days after the date on which the petition for rehearing is filed unless a responsive pleading is required, in which case the court shall decide whether to grant the petition not later than 30 days after the date on which the responsive pleading is filed.

(ii) If a petition for rehearing or rehearing en banc is granted, the court of appeals shall hear and render a final determination of the appeal not later than 120 days after the date on which the order granting rehearing or rehearing en banc is entered.

(2) The time limitations under paragraph (1) shall apply to—

(A) an initial application for a writ of habeas corpus;

(B) any second or successive application for a writ of habeas corpus; and

(C) any redetermination of an application for a writ of habeas corpus or related appeal following a remand by the court of appeals en banc or the Supreme Court for further proceedings, in which case the limitation period shall run from the date the remand is ordered.

(3) The time limitations under this section shall not be construed to entitle an applicant to a stay of execution, to which the applicant would otherwise not be entitled, for the purpose of litigating any application or appeal.

(4)(A) The failure of a court to meet or comply with a time limitation under this section shall not be a ground for granting relief from a judgment of conviction or sentence.

(B) The State may enforce a time limitation under this section by applying for a writ of mandamus to the Supreme Court.

(5) The Administrative Office of the United States Courts shall submit to Congress an annual report on the compliance by the courts of appeals with the time limitations under this section.

(Added Pub.L. 104–132, Title I, § 107(a), Apr. 24, 1996, 110 Stat. 1224.)

HISTORICAL AND STATUTORY NOTES

Effective Dates

1996 Acts. Section applicable to cases pending on or after Apr. 24, 1996, see section 107(c) of Pub.L. 104–132, set out as a note under section 2261 of this title.

CHAPTER 155—INJUNCTIONS; THREE-JUDGE COURTS

Sec.

[2281, 2282. Repealed.]
2283. Stay of State court proceedings.
2284. Three-judge district court; when required; composition; procedure.[1]

[1] So in original. Does not conform to section catchline.

[§ 2281. Repealed. Pub.L. 94–381, § 1, Aug. 12, 1976, 90 Stat. 1119]

HISTORICAL AND STATUTORY NOTES

Section, Act June 25, 1948, c. 646, 62 Stat. 968, provided that an interlocutory or permanent injunction restraining the enforcement, operation or execution of a State statute on grounds of unconstitutionality should not be granted unless the application has been heard and determined by a three-judge district court.

Effective Date of Repeal

Repeal by Pub.L. 94–381 not applicable to any action commenced on or before Aug. 12, 1976, see section 7 of Pub.L. 94–381, set out as an Effective Dates of 1976 Amendments note under section 2284 of this title.

[§ 2282. Repealed. Pub.L. 94–381, § 2, Aug. 12, 1976, 90 Stat. 1119]

HISTORICAL AND STATUTORY NOTES

Section, Act June 25, 1948, c. 646, 62 Stat. 968, provided that an interlocutory or permanent injunction restraining the enforcement, operation or execution of any Act of Congress on grounds of unconstitutionality should not be granted unless the application therefor has been heard and determined by a three-judge district court.

Effective Date of Repeal

Repeal by Pub.L. 94–381 not applicable to any action commenced on or before Aug. 12, 1976, see section 7 of Pub.L. 94–381, set out as an Effective Dates of 1976 Amendments note under section 2284 of this title.

§ 2283. Stay of State court proceedings

A court of the United States may not grant an injunction to stay proceedings in a State court except as expressly authorized by Act of Congress, or where necessary in aid of its jurisdiction, or to protect or effectuate its judgments.

(June 25, 1948, c. 646, 62 Stat. 968.)

§ 2284. Three-judge court; when required; composition; procedure

(a) A district court of three judges shall be convened when otherwise required by Act of Congress, or when an action is filed challenging the constitutionality of the apportionment of congressional districts or the apportionment of any statewide legislative body.

(b) In any action required to be heard and determined by a district court of three judges under subsection (a) of this section, the composition and procedure of the court shall be as follows:

(1) Upon the filing of a request for three judges, the judge to whom the request is presented shall, unless he determines that three judges are not required, immediately notify the chief judge of the circuit, who shall designate two other judges, at least one of whom shall be a circuit judge. The judges so designated, and the judge to whom the request was presented, shall serve as members of the court to hear and determine the action or proceeding.

(2) If the action is against a State, or officer or agency thereof, at least five days' notice of hearing of the action shall be given by registered or certified mail to the Governor and attorney general of the State.

(3) A single judge may conduct all proceedings except the trial, and enter all orders permitted by the rules of civil procedure except as provided in this subsection. He may grant a temporary restraining order on a specific finding, based on evidence submitted, that specified irreparable damage will result if the order is not granted, which order, unless previously revoked by the district judge, shall remain in force only until the hearing and determination by the district court of three judges of an application for a preliminary injunction. A single judge shall not appoint a master, or order a reference, or hear and determine any application for a preliminary or permanent injunction or motion to vacate such an injunction, or enter judgment on the merits. Any action of a single judge may be reviewed by the full court at any time before final judgment.

(June 25, 1948, c. 646, 62 Stat. 968; June 11, 1960, Pub.L. 86–507, § 1(19), 74 Stat. 201; Aug. 12, 1976, Pub.L. 94–381, § 3, 90 Stat. 1119; Nov. 8, 1984, Pub.L. 98–620, Title IV, § 402(29)(E), 98 Stat. 3359.)

HISTORICAL AND STATUTORY NOTES

References in Text

The rules of civil procedure, referred to in subsec. (b)(3), are classified generally to this title.

Effective Dates

1984 Acts. Amendment by Pub.L. 98–620 not to apply to cases pending on Nov. 8, 1984, see section 403 of Pub.L. 98–620, set out as a note under section 1657 of this title.

1976 Acts. Section 7 of Pub.L. 94–381 provided that: "This Act [amending this section and section 2403 of this title and repealing sections 2281 and 2282 of this title] shall not apply to any action commenced on or before the date of enactment [Aug. 12, 1976]."

CHAPTER 157—SURFACE TRANSPORTATION BOARD ORDERS; ENFORCEMENT AND REVIEW

Sec.

2321. Judicial review of Board's orders and decisions; procedure generally; process.
2322. United States as party.
2323. Duties of Attorney General; intervenors.
[2324, 2325. Repealed.]

§ 2321. Judicial review of Board's orders and decisions; procedure generally; process

(a) Except as otherwise provided by an Act of Congress, a proceeding to enjoin or suspend, in whole or in part, a rule, regulation, or order of the Surface Transportation Board shall be brought in the court of appeals as provided by and in the manner prescribed in chapter 158 of this title.

(b) The procedure in the district courts in actions to enforce, in whole or in part, any order of the Surface Transportation Board other than for payment of money or the collection of fines, penalties, and forfeitures, shall be as provided in this chapter.

(c) The orders, writs, and process of the district courts may, in the cases specified in subsection (b) and in enforcement actions and actions to collect civil penalties under subtitle IV of title 49, run, be served and be returnable anywhere in the United States.

(June 25, 1948, c. 646, 62 Stat. 969; May 24, 1949, c. 139, § 115, 63 Stat. 105; Jan. 2, 1975, Pub.L. 93–584, § 5, 88 Stat. 1917; Oct. 17, 1978, Pub.L. 95–473, § 2(a)(3)(B), 92 Stat. 1465; Dec. 29, 1995, Pub.L. 104–88, Title III, § 305(c)(1)(B), (C), 109 Stat. 945.)

HISTORICAL AND STATUTORY NOTES

Effective Dates

1995 Acts. Amendment by Pub.L. 104–88 effective Jan. 1, 1996, see section 2 of Pub.L. 104–88, set out as a note under section 701 of Title 49, Transportation.

1975 Acts. Section 10 of Pub.L. 93–584 provided that: "This Act [amending this section and sections 1336, 1398, 2323, 2341, and 2342 of this title and section 305 of former Title 49, Transportation, and repealing sections 2324 and 2325 of this title] shall not apply to any action commenced on or before the last day of the first month beginning after the date of enactment [Jan. 2, 1975]. However, actions to enjoin or suspend orders of the Interstate Commerce Commission [now Surface Transportation Board] which are pending when this Act becomes effective shall not be affected thereby, but shall proceed to final disposition under the law existing on the date they were commenced."

[Interstate Commerce Commission abolished and functions of Commission transferred, except as otherwise provided in Pub.L. 104–88, to Surface Transportation Board effective Jan. 1, 1996, by sections 702 of Title 49, Transportation, and section 101 of Pub.L. 104–88, set out as a note under section 701 of title 49. References to Interstate Commerce Commission deemed to refer to Surface Transportation Board, a member or employee of the Board, or Secretary of Transportation, as appropriate, see section 205 of Pub.L. 104–88, set out as a note under section 701 of Title 49.]

§ 2322. United States as party

All actions specified in section 2321 of this title shall be brought by or against the United States.

(June 25, 1948, c. 646, 62 Stat. 969.)

§ 2323. Duties of Attorney General; intervenors

The Attorney General shall represent the Government in the actions specified in section 2321 of this title and in enforcement actions and actions to collect civil penalties under subtitle IV of title 49.

The Surface Transportation Board and any party or parties in interest to the proceeding before the Board, in which an order or requirement is made, may appear as parties of their own motion and as of right, and be represented by their counsel, in any action involving the validity of such order or requirement or any part thereof, and the interest of such party.

Communities, associations, corporations, firms, and individuals interested in the controversy or question before the Board, or in any action commenced under the aforesaid sections may intervene in said action at any time after commencement thereof.

The Attorney General shall not dispose of or discontinue said action or proceeding over the objection of such party or intervenor, who may prosecute, defend, or continue said action or proceeding unaffected by the action or nonaction of the Attorney General therein.

(June 25, 1948, c. 646, 62 Stat. 970; May 24, 1949, c. 139, § 116, 63 Stat. 105; Jan. 2, 1975, Pub.L. 93–584, § 6, 88 Stat. 1917; Oct. 17, 1978, Pub.L. 95–473, § 2(a) (3) (C), 92 Stat. 1465; Dec. 29, 1995, Pub.L. 104–88, Title III, § 305(c)(1)(C), (D), 109 Stat. 945.)

HISTORICAL AND STATUTORY NOTES

Effective Dates

1995 Acts. Amendment by Pub.L. 104–88 effective Jan. 1, 1996, see section 2 of Pub.L. 104–88, set out as a note under section 701 of Title 49, Transportation.

1975 Acts. Amendment by Pub.L. 93–584 not applicable to actions commenced on or before the last day of the first month beginning after Jan. 2, 1975, and actions to enjoin or suspend orders of the Interstate Commerce Commission [now Surface Transportation Board] which are pending when this amendment becomes effective shall not be affected thereby, but shall proceed to final disposition under the law existing on the date they were commenced, see section 10 of Pub.L. 93–584, set out as a note under section 2321 of this title.

[Interstate Commerce Commission abolished and functions of Commission transferred, except as otherwise provided in Pub.L. 104–88, to Surface Transportation Board effective Jan. 1, 1996, by sections 702 of Title 49, Transportation, and section 101 of Pub.L. 104–88, set out as a note under section 701 of title 49. References to Interstate Commerce Commission deemed to refer to Surface Transportation Board, a member or employee of the Board, or Secretary of Transportation, as appropriate, see section 205 of Pub.L. 104–88, set out as a note under section 701 of Title 49.]

[§§ 2324, 2325. Repealed. Pub.L. 93–584, § 7, Jan. 2, 1975, 88 Stat. 1918]

HISTORICAL AND STATUTORY NOTES

Section 2324, Act June 25, 1948, c. 646, 62 Stat. 970, related to the power of the court to restrain or suspend the operation of orders of Interstate Commerce Commission pending the final hearing and determination of the action.

Section 2325, Act June 25, 1948, c. 646, 62 Stat. 970, related to the requirement of a three-judge district court to hear and determine interlocutory or permanent injunctions restraining the enforcement, operation or execution of orders of Interstate Commerce Commission.

Effective Date of Repeal

Repeal of sections not applicable to actions commenced on or before the last day of the first month beginning after Jan. 2, 1975, and actions to enjoin or suspend orders of the Interstate Commerce Commission which are pending when this repeal becomes effective shall not be affected thereby, but shall proceed to final disposition under the law existing on the date they were commenced, see section 10 of Pub.L. 93–584, set out as an Effective Dates of 1975 Amendments note under section 2321 of this title.

CHAPTER 158—ORDERS OF FEDERAL AGENCIES; REVIEW

Sec.
2341. Definitions.
2342. Jurisdiction of court of appeals.
2343. Venue.
2344. Review of orders; time; notice; contents of petitions; service.[1]
2345. Prehearing conference.

Sec.
2346. Certification of record on review.
2347. Petitions to review; proceedings.
2348. Representation in proceeding; intervention.
2349. Jurisdiction of the proceeding.
2350. Review in Supreme Court on certiorari or certification.
2351. Enforcement of orders by district courts.
[2352, 2353. Repealed.]

1 So in original. Does not conform to section catchline.

§ 2341. Definitions

As used in this chapter—

(1) "clerk" means the clerk of the court in which the petition for the review of an order, reviewable under this chapter, is filed;

(2) "petitioner" means the party or parties by whom a petition to review an order, reviewable under this chapter, is filed; and

(3) "agency" means—

(A) the Commission, when the order sought to be reviewed was entered by the Federal Communications Commission, the Federal Maritime Commission, or the Atomic Energy Commission, as the case may be;

(B) the Secretary, when the order was entered by the Secretary of Agriculture or the Secretary of Transportation;

(C) the Administration, when the order was entered by the Maritime Administration;

(D) the Secretary, when the order is under section 812 of the Fair Housing Act; and

(E) the Board, when the order was entered by the Surface Transportation Board.

(Added Pub.L. 89–554, § 4(e), Sept. 6, 1966, 80 Stat. 622, and amended Pub.L. 93–584, § 3, Jan. 2, 1975, 88 Stat. 1917; Pub.L. 100–430, § 11(b), Sept. 13, 1988, 102 Stat. 1635; Pub.L. 102–365, § 5(c)(1), Sept. 3, 1992, 106 Stat. 975; Pub.L. 104–88, Title III, § 305(d)(1) to (4), Dec. 29, 1995, 109 Stat. 945.)

HISTORICAL AND STATUTORY NOTES

References in Text

Section 812 of the Fair Housing Act, referred to in par. (3)(D), is classified to section 3612 of Title 42, The Public Health and Welfare.

Effective Dates

1995 Acts. Amendment by Pub.L. 104–88 effective Jan. 1, 1996, see section 2 of Pub.L. 104–88, set out as a note under section 701 of Title 49, Transportation.

1988 Acts. Amendment by Pub.L. 100–430 effective on the 180th day beginning after Sept. 13, 1988, see section 13(a) of Pub.L. 100–430, set out as a note under section 3601 of Title 42, The Public Health and Welfare.

1975 Acts. Amendment by Pub.L. 93–584 not applicable to actions commenced on or before the last day of the first month beginning after Jan. 2, 1975, and actions to enjoin or suspend orders of the Interstate Commerce Commission [now Surface Transportation Board] which are pending when this amendment becomes effective shall not be affected thereby, but shall proceed to final disposition under the law existing on the date they were commenced, see section 10 of Pub.L. 93–584, set out as a note under section 2321 of this title.

[Interstate Commerce Commission abolished and functions of Commission transferred, except as otherwise provided in Pub.L. 104–88, to Surface Transportation Board effective Jan. 1, 1996, by sections 702 of Title 49, Transportation, and section 101 of Pub.L. 104–88, set out as a note under section 701 of title 49. References to Interstate Commerce Commission deemed to refer to Surface Transportation Board, a member or employee of the Board, or Secretary of Transportation, as appropriate, see section 205 of Pub.L. 104–88, set out as a note under section 701 of Title 49.]

Transfer of Functions

The Atomic Energy Commission was abolished and all functions of the Commission, the Chairman, the members of the Commission, and the officers and components of the Commission were transferred to and vested in the Administrator of the Energy Research and Development Administration, with certain exceptions, by Pub.L. 93–438, Oct. 11, 1974, 88 Stat. 1233. See section 5814 of Title 42, The Public Health and Welfare. The Energy Research and Development Administration was terminated and functions vested by law in the Administrator of the Energy Research and Development Administration were transferred to and vested in the Secretary of Energy (unless otherwise specifically provided) by Pub.L. 95–91, Title III, § 301(a), Title VII, § 703, Aug. 4, 1977, 91 Stat. 577, 606. See sections 7151(a), 7293 of Title 42.

§ 2342. Jurisdiction of court of appeals

The court of appeals (other than the United States Court of Appeals for the Federal Circuit) has exclusive jurisdiction to enjoin, set aside, suspend (in whole or in part), or to determine the validity of—

(1) all final orders of the Federal Communications Commission made reviewable by section 402(a) of title 47;

(2) all final orders of the Secretary of Agriculture made under chapters 9 and 20A of title 7, except orders issued under sections 210(e), 217a, and 499g(a) of title 7;

(3) all rules, regulations, or final orders of—

(A) the Secretary of Transportation issued pursuant to section 2, 9, 37, or 41 of the Shipping Act, 1916 (46 U.S.C. App. 802, 803, 808, 835, 839, and 841a) or pursuant to part B or C of subtitle IV of title 49; and

(B) the Federal Maritime Commission issued pursuant to—

(i) section 19 of the Merchant Marine Act, 1920 (46 U.S.C. App. 876);

(ii) section 14 or 17 of the Shipping Act of 1984 (46 U.S.C. App. 1713 or 1716); or

(iii) section 2(d) or 3(d) of the Act of November 6, 1966 (46 U.S.C. App. 817d(d) or 817e(d) [1];

[(iv) and (v) Redesignated (ii) and (iii)]

(4) all final orders of the Atomic Energy Commission made reviewable by section 2239 of title 42;

(5) all rules, regulations, or final orders of the Surface Transportation Board made reviewable by section 2321 of this title;

(6) all final orders under section 812 of the Fair Housing Act; and

(7) all final agency actions described in section 20114(c) of title 49.

Jurisdiction is invoked by filing a petition as provided by section 2344 of this title.

(Added Pub.L. 89–554, § 4(e), Sept. 6, 1966, 80 Stat. 622, and amended Pub.L. 93–584, § 4, Jan. 2, 1975, 88 Stat. 1917; Pub.L. 95–454, Title II, § 206, Oct. 13, 1978, 92 Stat. 1144; Pub.L. 96–454, § 8(b)(2), Oct. 15, 1980, 94 Stat. 2021; Pub.L. 97–164, Title I, § 137, Apr. 2, 1982, 96 Stat. 41; Pub.L. 98–554, Title II, § 227(a)(4), Oct. 30, 1984, 98 Stat. 2852; Pub.L. 99–336, § 5(a), June 19, 1986, 100 Stat. 638; Pub.L. 100–430, § 11(a), Sept. 13, 1988, 102 Stat. 1635; Pub.L. 102–365, § 5(c)(2), Sept. 3, 1992, 106 Stat. 975; Pub.L. 103–272, § 5(h), July 5, 1994, 108 Stat. 1375; Pub.L. 104–88, Title III, § 305(d)(5) to (8), Dec. 29, 1995, 109 Stat. 945; Pub.L. 104–287, § 6(f)(2), Oct. 11, 1996, 110 Stat. 3399.)

1 So in original. Probably should be followed by a closing parenthesis.

HISTORICAL AND STATUTORY NOTES

References in Text

Section 812 of the Fair Housing Act, referred to in par. (6), is classified to section 3612 of Title 42, The Public Health and Welfare.

Effective Dates

1996 Acts. Section 6(f) of Pub.L. 104–287 provided in part that amendments made by such section 6(f) to this section, sections 744 and 797*l* of Title 45, Railroads, and section 30166 of Title 49, Transportation, were effective Dec. 29, 1995.

1995 Acts. Amendment by Pub.L. 104–88 effective Jan. 1, 1996, see section 2 of Pub.L. 104–88, set out as a note under section 701 of Title 49, Transportation.

1988 Acts. Amendment by Pub.L. 100–430 effective on the 180th day beginning after Sept. 13, 1988, see section 13(a) of Pub.L. 100–430, set out as a note under section 3601 of Title 42, The Public Health and Welfare.

1986 Acts. Section 5(b) of Pub.L. 99–336 provided that: "The amendment made by this section [amending this section] shall apply with respect to any rule, regulation, or final order described in such amendment which is issued on or after the date of the enactment of this Act [June 19, 1986]."

1982 Acts. Amendment by Pub.L. 97–164 effective Oct. 1, 1982, see section 402 of Pub.L. 97–164, set out as a note under section 171 of this title.

1978 Acts. Amendment by Pub.L. 95–454 effective 90 days after Oct. 13, 1978, see section 907 of Pub.L. 95–454, set out as a note under section 1101 of Title 5, Government Organization and Employees.

1975 Acts. Amendment by Pub.L. 93–584 not applicable to actions commenced on or before the last day of the first month beginning after Jan. 2, 1975, and actions to enjoin or suspend orders of the Interstate Commerce Commission [now Surface Transportation Board] which are pending when this amendment becomes effective shall not be affected thereby, but shall proceed to final disposition under the law existing on the date they were commenced, see section 10 of Pub.L. 93–584, set out as a note under section 2321 of this title.

[Interstate Commerce Commission abolished and functions of Commission transferred, except as otherwise provided in Pub.L. 104–88, to Surface Transportation Board effective Jan. 1, 1996, by section 702 of Title 49, Transportation, and section 101 of Pub.L. 104–88, set out as a note under section 701 of Title 49. References to Interstate Commerce Commission deemed to refer to Surface Transportation Board, a member or employee of the Board, or Secretary of Transportation, as appropriate, see section 205 of Pub.L. 104–88, set out as a note under section 701 of Title 49.]

Transfer of Functions

The Atomic Energy Commission was abolished and all functions of the Commission, the Chairman, the members of the Commission, and the officers and components of the Commission were transferred to and vested in the Administrator of the Energy Research and Development Administration, with certain exceptions, by Pub.L. 93–438, Oct. 11, 1974, 88 Stat. 1233. See section 5814 of Title 42, The Public Health and Welfare. The Energy Research and Development Administration was terminated and functions vested by law in the Administration of the Energy Research and Development Administration were transferred to and vested in the Secretary of Energy (unless otherwise specifically provided) by Pub.L. 95–91, Title III, § 301(a), Title VII, § 703, Aug. 4, 1977, 91 Stat. 577, 606. See sections 7151(a), 7293 of Title 42.

§ 2343. Venue

The venue of a proceeding under this chapter is in the judicial circuit in which the petitioner resides or has its principal office, or in the United States Court of Appeals for the District of Columbia Circuit.

(Added Pub.L. 89–554, § 4(e), Sept. 6, 1966, 80 Stat. 622.)

§ 2344. Review of orders; time; notice; contents of petition; service

On the entry of a final order reviewable under this chapter, the agency shall promptly give notice thereof by service or publication in accordance with its rules. Any party aggrieved by the final order may, within 60 days after its entry, file a petition to review the order in the court of appeals wherein venue lies. The action shall be against the United States. The petition shall contain a concise statement of—

(1) the nature of the proceedings as to which review is sought;

(2) the facts on which venue is based;

(3) the grounds on which relief is sought; and

(4) the relief prayed.

The petitioner shall attach to the petition, as exhibits, copies of the order, report, or decision of the agency. The clerk shall serve a true copy of the petition on the agency and on the Attorney General by registered mail, with request for a return receipt.

(Added Pub.L. 89–554, § 4(e), Sept. 6, 1966, 80 Stat. 622.)

§ 2345. Prehearing conference

The court of appeals may hold a prehearing conference or direct a judge of the court to hold a prehearing conference.

(Added Pub.L. 89–554, § 4(e), Sept. 6, 1966, 80 Stat. 622.)

§ 2346. Certification of record on review

Unless the proceeding has been terminated on a motion to dismiss the petition, the agency shall file in the office of the clerk the record on review as provided by section 2112 of this title.

(Added Pub.L. 89–554, § 4(e), Sept. 6, 1966, 80 Stat. 623.)

§ 2347. Petitions to review; proceedings

(a) Unless determined on a motion to dismiss, petitions to review orders reviewable under this chapter are heard in the court of appeals on the record of the pleadings, evidence adduced, and proceedings before the agency, when the agency has held a hearing whether or not required to do so by law.

(b) When the agency has not held a hearing before taking the action of which review is sought by the petition, the court of appeals shall determine whether a hearing is required by law. After that determination, the court shall—

(1) remand the proceedings to the agency to hold a hearing, when a hearing is required by law;

(2) pass on the issues presented, when a hearing is not required by law and it appears from the pleadings and affidavits filed by the parties that no genuine issue of material fact is presented; or

(3) transfer the proceedings to a district court for the district in which the petitioner resides or has its principal office for a hearing and determination as if the proceedings were originally initiated in the district court, when a hearing is not required by law and a genuine issue of material fact is presented. The procedure in these cases in the district court is governed by the Federal Rules of Civil Procedure.

(c) If a party to a proceeding to review applies to the court of appeals in which the proceeding is pending for leave to adduce additional evidence and shows to the satisfaction of the court that—

(1) the additional evidence is material; and

(2) there were reasonable grounds for failure to adduce the evidence before the agency;

the court may order the additional evidence and any counterevidence the opposite party desires to offer to be taken by the agency. The agency may modify its findings of fact, or make new findings, by reason of the additional evidence so taken, and may modify or set aside its order, and shall file in the court the additional evidence, the modified findings or new findings, and the modified order or the order setting aside the original order.

(Added Pub.L. 89–554, § 4(e), Sept. 6, 1966, 80 Stat. 623.)

HISTORICAL AND STATUTORY NOTES

References in Text

The Federal Rules of Civil Procedure, referred to in subsec. (b)(3), are classified generally to this title.

§ 2348. Representation in proceeding; intervention

The Attorney General is responsible for and has control of the interests of the Government in all court proceedings under this chapter. The agency, and any party in interest in the proceeding before the agency whose interests will be affected if an order of the agency is or is not enjoined, set aside, or suspended, may appear as parties thereto of their own motion and as of right, and be represented by counsel in any proceeding to review the order. Communities, associations, corporations, firms, and individuals, whose interests are affected by the order of the agency, may intervene in any proceeding to review the order. The Attorney General may not dispose of or discontinue the proceeding to review over the objection of any party or intervenor, but any intervenor may prosecute, defend, or continue the proceeding unaffected by the action or inaction of the Attorney General.

(Added Pub.L. 89–554, § 4(e), Sept. 6, 1966, 80 Stat. 623.)

§ 2349. Jurisdiction of the proceeding

(a) The court of appeals has jurisdiction of the proceeding on the filing and service of a petition to review. The court of appeals in which the record on review is filed, on the filing, has jurisdiction to vacate stay orders or interlocutory injunctions previously granted by any court, and has exclusive jurisdiction to make and enter, on the petition, evidence, and proceedings set forth in the record on review, a judgment determining the validity of, and enjoining, setting aside, or suspending, in whole or in part, the order of the agency.

(b) The filing of the petition to review does not of itself stay or suspend the operation of the order of the agency, but the court of appeals in its discretion may restrain or suspend, in whole or in part, the operation of the order pending the final hearing and determination of the petition. When the petitioner makes application for an interlocutory injunction restraining or suspending the enforcement, operation, or execution of, or setting aside, in whole or in part, any order reviewable under this chapter, at least 5 days' notice of the hearing thereon shall be given to the agency and to the Attorney General. In a case in which irreparable damage would otherwise result to the petitioner, the court of appeals may, on hearing, after reasonable notice to the agency and to the Attorney General, order a temporary stay or suspension, in whole or in part, of the operation of the order of the agency for not more than 60 days from the date of the order pending the hearing on the application for the interlocutory injunction, in which case the order of the court of appeals shall contain a specific finding, based on evidence submitted to the court of appeals, and identified by reference thereto, that irreparable damage would result to the petitioner and specifying the nature of the damage. The court of appeals, at the time of hearing the application for an interlocutory injunction, on a like finding, may continue the temporary stay or suspension, in whole or in part, until decision on the application.

(Added Pub.L. 89–554, § 4(e), Sept. 6, 1966, 80 Stat. 624, and amended Pub.L. 98–620, Title IV, § 402(29)(F), Nov. 8, 1984, 98 Stat. 3359.)

HISTORICAL AND STATUTORY NOTES

Effective Dates

1984 Acts. Amendment by Pub.L. 98–620 not to apply to cases pending on Nov. 8, 1984, see section 403 of Pub.L. 98–620, set out as a note under section 1657 of this title.

§ 2350. Review in Supreme Court on certiorari or certification

(a) An order granting or denying an interlocutory injunction under section 2349(b) of this title and a final judgment of the court of appeals in a proceeding to review under this chapter are subject to review by the Supreme Court on a writ of certiorari as provided by section 1254(1) of this title. Application for the writ shall be made within 45 days after entry of the order and within 90 days after entry of the judgment, as the case may be. The United States, the agency, or an aggrieved party may file a petition for a writ of certiorari.

(b) The provisions of section 1254(2) of this title, regarding certification, and of section 2101(f) of this title, regarding stays, also apply to proceedings under this chapter.

(Added Pub.L. 89–554, § 4(e), Sept. 6, 1966, 80 Stat. 624, and amended Pub.L. 100–352, § 5(e), June 27, 1988, 102 Stat. 663.)

HISTORICAL AND STATUTORY NOTES

Effective Dates

1988 Acts. Amendment by Pub.L. 100–352 effective ninety days after June 27, 1988, except that such amendment not to apply to cases pending in the Supreme Court on such effective date or affect the right to review or the manner of reviewing the judgment or decree of a court which was entered before such effective date, see section 7 of Pub.L. 100–352, set out as a note under section 1254 of this title.

§ 2351. Enforcement of orders by district courts

The several district courts have jurisdiction specifically to enforce, and to enjoin and restrain any person from violating any order issued under section 193 of title 7.

(Added Pub.L. 89–554, § 4(e), Sept. 6, 1966, 80 Stat. 624.)

[§ 2352. Repealed. Pub.L. 89–773, § 4, Nov. 6, 1966, 80 Stat. 1323]

HISTORICAL AND STATUTORY NOTES

Section, Pub.L. 89–554, § 4(e), Sept. 6, 1966, 80 Stat. 624, directed the several courts of appeals to adopt and promulgate rules, subject to the approval of the Judicial Conference of the United States, governing the practice and procedure, including prehearing conference procedure, in proceedings to review orders under this chapter. See section 2072 of this title.

Savings Provisions

Section 4 of Pub.L. 89–773 provided in part that the repeal of this section shall not operate to invalidate or repeal rules adopted under the authority of this section prior to the enactment of Pub.L. 89–773, which rules shall remain in effect until superseded by rules prescribed under authority of section 2072 of this title as amended by Pub.L. 89–773.

[§ 2353. Repealed. Pub.L 97–164, Title I, § 138, Apr. 2, 1982, 96 Stat. 42]

HISTORICAL AND STATUTORY NOTES

Section, added Pub.L. 91–577, Title III, § 143(c), Dec. 24, 1970, 84 Stat. 1559, gave the court of appeals nonexclusive jurisdiction to hear appeals under section 71 of the Plant Variety Protection Act [7 U.S.C.A. § 2461]. See section 1295(a) (8) of this title.

Effective Date of Repeal

Repeal effective Oct. 1, 1982, see section 402 of Pub.L. 97–164, set out as a note under section 171 of this title.

CHAPTER 159—INTERPLEADER

Sec.
2361. Process and procedure.

§ 2361. Process and procedure

In any civil action of interpleader or in the nature of interpleader under section 1335 of this title, a district court may issue its process for all claimants and enter its order restraining them from instituting or prosecuting any proceeding in any State or United States court affecting the property, instrument or obligation involved in the interpleader action until further order of the court. Such process and order shall be returnable at such time as the court or judge thereof directs, and shall be addressed to and served by the United States marshals for the respective districts where the claimants reside or may be found.

Such district court shall hear and determine the case, and may discharge the plaintiff from further liability, make the injunction permanent, and make all appropriate orders to enforce its judgment.

(June 25, 1948, c. 646, 62 Stat. 970; May 24, 1949, c. 139, § 117, 63 Stat. 105.)

CHAPTER 161—UNITED STATES AS PARTY GENERALLY

Sec.
2401. Time for commencing action against United States.
2402. Jury trial in actions against United States.
2403. Intervention by United States or a State; constitutional question.
2404. Death of defendant in damage action.
2405. Garnishment.
2406. Credits in actions by United States; prior disallowance.
2407. Delinquents for public money; judgment at return term; continuance.
2408. Security not required of United States.
2409. Partition actions involving United States.
2409a. Real property quiet title actions.
2410. Actions affecting property on which United States has lien.
2411. Interest.
2412. Costs and fees.
2413. Executions in favor of United States.
2414. Payment of judgments and compromise settlements.
2415. Time for commencing actions brought by the United States.
2416. Time for commencing actions brought by the United States—Exclusions.

§ 2401. Time for commencing action against United States

(a) Except as provided by the Contract Disputes Act of 1978, every civil action commenced against the United States shall be barred unless the complaint is filed within six years after the right of action first accrues. The action of any person under legal disability or beyond the seas at the time the claim accrues may be commenced within three years after the disability ceases.

(b) A tort claim against the United States shall be forever barred unless it is presented in writing to the appropriate Federal agency within two years after such claim accrues or unless action is begun within six months after the date of mailing, by certified or registered mail, of notice of final denial of the claim by the agency to which it was presented.

(June 25, 1948, c. 646, 62 Stat. 971; Apr. 25, 1949, c. 92, § 1, 63 Stat. 62; Sept. 8, 1959, Pub.L. 86–238, § 1(3), 73 Stat. 472; July 18, 1966, Pub.L. 89–506, § 7, 80 Stat. 307; Nov. 1, 1978, Pub.L. 95–563, § 14(b), 92 Stat. 2389.)

HISTORICAL AND STATUTORY NOTES

Senate Revision Amendment

Subsection (b) amended in the Senate to insert the 1 year limitation on the bringing of tort actions and to include the limitation upon the time in which tort claims not exceeding $1000 must be presented to the appropriate Federal agencies for administrative disposition. 80th Congress Senate Report No. 1559, Amendment No. 48.

1949 Acts. House Report No. 276, see 1949 U.S. Code Cong. Service, p. 1226.

1959 Acts. Senate Report No. 797, see 1959 U.S. Code Cong. and Adm. News, p. 2272.

1966 Acts. Senate Report No. 1327, see 1966 U.S. Code Cong. and Adm. News, p. 2515.

1978 Acts. Senate Report No. 95–1118, see 1978 U.S. Code Cong. and Adm. News, p. 5235.

References in Text

The Contract Disputes Act of 1978, referred to in subsec. (a), is Pub.L. 95–563, Nov. 1, 1978, 92 Stat. 2383, as amended, which is classified principally to chapter 9 (section 601 et seq.) of Title 41, Public Contracts. For complete classification of this Act to the Code, see Short Title note set out under section 601 of Title 41 and Tables.

Effective Dates

1978 Acts. Amendment by Pub.L. 95–563 effective with respect to contracts entered into 120 days after Nov. 1, 1978 and, at the election of the contractor, with respect to any claim pending at such time before the contracting officer or initiated thereafter, see section 16 of Pub.L. 95–563, set out as a note under section 601 of Title 41, Public Contracts.

1966 Acts. Amendment by Pub.L. 89–506 applicable to claims accruing six months or more after July 18, 1966, see section 10 of Pub.L. 89–506, set out as a note under section 2672 of this title.

§ 2402. Jury trial in actions against United States

Subject to chapter 179 of this title, any action against the United States under section 1346 shall be tried by the court without a jury, except that any action against the United States under section 1346(a)(1) shall, at the request of either party to such action, be tried by the court with a jury.

(June 25, 1948, c. 646, 62 Stat. 971; July 30, 1954, c. 648, § 2(a), 68 Stat. 589; Oct. 26, 1996, Pub.L. 104–331, § 3(b)(3), 110 Stat. 4069.)

HISTORICAL AND STATUTORY NOTES

Effective Dates

1996 Acts. Amendment by section 3(b)(3) of Pub.L. 104–331, effective Oct. 1, 1997, see section 3(d) of Pub.L. 104–331, set out as a note under section 1296 of this title.

§ 2403. Intervention by United States or a State; constitutional question

(a) In any action, suit or proceeding in a court of the United States to which the United States or any agency, officer or employee thereof is not a party, wherein the constitutionality of any Act of Congress affecting the public interest is drawn in question, the court shall certify such fact to the Attorney General, and shall permit the United States to intervene for presentation of evidence, if evidence is otherwise admissible in the case, and for argument on the question of constitutionality. The United States shall, subject to the applicable provisions of law, have all the rights of a party and be subject to all liabilities of a party as to court costs to the extent necessary for a proper presentation of the facts and law relating to the question of constitutionality.

(b) In any action, suit, or proceeding in a court of the United States to which a State or any agency, officer, or employee thereof is not a party, wherein the constitutionality of any statute of that State affecting the public interest is drawn in question, the court shall certify such fact to the attorney general of the State, and shall permit the State to intervene for presentation of evidence, if evidence is otherwise admissible in the case, and for argument on the question of constitutionality. The State shall, subject to the applicable provisions of law, have all the rights of a party and be subject to all liabilities of a party as to court costs to the extent necessary for a proper presentation of the facts and law relating to the question of constitutionality.

(June 25, 1948, c. 646, 62 Stat. 971; Aug. 12, 1976, Pub.L. 94–381, § 5, 90 Stat. 1120.)

HISTORICAL AND STATUTORY NOTES

Effective Dates

1976 Acts. Amendment by Pub.L. 94–381 not applicable to any action commenced on or before Aug. 12, 1976, see section 7 of Pub.L. 94–381, set out as a note under section 2284 of this title.

§ 2404. Death of defendant in damage action

A civil action for damages commenced by or on behalf of the United States or in which it is interested shall not abate on the death of a defendant but shall survive and be enforceable against his estate as well as against surviving defendants.

(June 25, 1948, c. 646, 62 Stat. 971.)

§ 2405. Garnishment

In any action or suit commenced by the United States against a corporation for the recovery of money upon a bill, note, or other security, the debtors of the corporation may be summoned as garnishees. Any person so summoned shall appear in open court and depose in writing to the amount of his indebtedness to the corporation at the time of the service of the summons and at the time of making the deposition, and judgment may be entered in favor of the United States for the sum admitted by the garnishee to be due the corporation as if it had been due the United States. A judgment shall not be entered against any garnishee until after judgment has been rendered against the corporation, nor until the sum in which the garnishee is indebted is actually due.

When any garnishee deposes in open court that he is not and was not at the time of the service of the summons indebted to the corporation, an issue may be tendered by the United States upon such deposition. If, upon the trial of that issue, a verdict is rendered against the garnishee, judgment shall be entered in favor of the United States, pursuant to such verdict, with costs.

Any garnishee who fails to appear at the term to which he is summoned shall be subject to attachment for contempt.

(June 25, 1948, c. 646, 62 Stat. 971.)

§ 2406. Credits in actions by United States; prior disallowance

In an action by the United States against an individual, evidence supporting the defendant's claim for a credit shall not be admitted unless he first proves that such claim has been disallowed, in whole or in part, by the General Accounting Office, or that he has, at the time of the trial, obtained possession of vouchers not previously procurable and has been prevented from presenting such claim to the General Accounting Office by absence from the United States or unavoidable accident.

(June 25, 1948, c. 646, 62 Stat. 972.)

§ 2407. Delinquents for public money; judgment at return term; continuance

In an action by the United States against any person accountable for public money who fails to pay into the Treasury the sum reported due the United States, upon the adjustment of his account the court shall grant judgment upon motion unless a continuance is granted as specified in this section.

A continuance may be granted if the defendant, in open court and in the presence of the United States attorney, states under oath that he is equitably entitled to credits which have been disallowed by the General Accounting Office prior to the commencement of the action, specifying each particular claim so rejected, and stating that he cannot safely come to trial.

A continuance may also be granted if such an action is commenced on a bond or other sealed instrument and the court requires the original instrument to be produced.

(June 25, 1948, c. 646, 62 Stat. 972.)

§ 2408. Security not required of United States

Security for damages or costs shall not be required of the United States, any department or agency thereof or any party acting under the direction of any such department or agency on the issuance of process or the institution or prosecution of any proceeding.

Costs taxable, under other Acts of Congress, against the United States or any such department, agency or party shall be paid out of the contingent fund of the department or agency which directed the proceedings to be instituted.

(June 25, 1948, c. 646, 62 Stat. 972.)

§ 2409. Partition actions involving United States

Any civil action by any tenant in common or joint tenant owning an undivided interest in lands, where the United States is one of such tenants in common or joint tenants, against the United States alone or against the United States and any other of such owners, shall proceed, and be determined, in the same manner as would a similar action between private persons.

Whenever in such action the court orders a sale of the property or any part thereof the Attorney General may bid for the same in behalf of the United States. If the United States is the purchaser, the amount of the purchase money shall be paid from the Treasury upon a warrant drawn by the Secretary of the Treasury on the requisition of the Attorney General.

(June 25, 1948, c. 646, 62 Stat. 972.)

§ 2409a. Real property quiet title actions

(a) The United States may be named as a party defendant in a civil action under this section to adjudicate a disputed title to real property in which the United States claims an interest, other than a security interest or water rights. This section does not apply to trust or restricted Indian lands, nor does it apply to or affect actions which may be or could have been brought under sections 1346, 1347, 1491, or 2410 of this title, sections 7424, 7425, or 7426 of the Internal Revenue Code of 1986, as amended (26 U.S.C. 7424, 7425, and 7426), or section 208 of the Act of July 10, 1952 (43 U.S.C. 666).

(b) The United States shall not be disturbed in possession or control of any real property involved in any action under this section pending a final judgment or decree, the conclusion of any appeal therefrom, and sixty days; and if the final determination shall be adverse to the United States, the United States nevertheless may retain such possession or control of the real property or of any part thereof as it may elect, upon payment to the person determined to be entitled thereto of an amount which upon such election the district court in the same action shall determine to be just compensation for such possession or control.

(c) No preliminary injunction shall issue in any action brought under this section.

(d) The complaint shall set forth with particularity the nature of the right, title, or interest which the plaintiff claims in the real property, the circumstances under which it was acquired, and the right, title, or interest claimed by the United States.

(e) If the United States disclaims all interest in the real property or interest therein adverse to the plaintiff at any time prior to the actual commencement of the trial, which disclaimer is confirmed by order of the court, the jurisdiction of the district court shall cease unless it has jurisdiction of the civil action or suit on ground other than and independent of the authority conferred by section 1346(f) of this title.

(f) A civil action against the United States under this section shall be tried by the court without a jury.

(g) Any civil action under this section, except for an action brought by a State, shall be barred unless it is commenced within twelve years of the date upon which it accrued. Such action shall be deemed to have accrued on the date the plaintiff or his predecessor in interest knew or should have known of the claim of the United States.

(h) No civil action may be maintained under this section by a State with respect to defense facilities (including land) of the United States so long as the lands at issue are being used or required by the United States for national defense purposes as determined by the head of the Federal agency with jurisdiction over the lands involved, if it is determined that the State action was brought more than twelve years after the State knew or should have known of the claims of the United States. Upon cessation of such use or requirement, the State may dispute title to such lands pursuant to the provisions of this section. The decision of the head of the Federal agency is not subject to judicial review.

(i) Any civil action brought by a State under this section with respect to lands, other than tide or submerged lands, on which the United States or its lessee or right-of-way or easement grantee has made substantial improvements or substantial investments or on which the United States has conducted substantial activities pursuant to a management plan such as range improvement, timber harvest, tree planting, mineral activities, farming, wildlife habitat improvement, or other similar activities, shall be barred unless the action is commenced within twelve years after the date the State received notice of the Federal claims to the lands.

(j) If a final determination in an action brought by a State under this section involving submerged or tide lands on which the United States or its lessee or right-of-way or easement grantee has made substantial improvements or substantial investments is adverse to the United States and it is determined that the State's action was brought more than twelve years after the State received notice of the Federal claim to the lands, the State shall take title to the lands subject to any existing lease, easement, or right-of-way. Any compensation due with respect to such lease, easement, or right-of-way shall be determined under existing law.

(k) Notice for the purposes of the accrual of an action brought by a State under this section shall be—

(1) by public communications with respect to the claimed lands which are sufficiently specific as to be reasonably calculated to put the claimant on notice of the Federal claim to the lands, or

(2) by the use, occupancy, or improvement of the claimed lands which, in the circumstances, is open and notorious.

(*l*) For purposes of this section, the term "tide or submerged lands" means "lands beneath navigable waters" as defined in section 2 of the Submerged Lands Act (43 U.S.C. 1301).

(m) Not less than one hundred and eighty days before bringing any action under this section, a State shall notify the head of the Federal agency with jurisdiction over the lands in question of the State's intention to file suit, the basis therefor, and a description of the lands included in the suit.

(n) Nothing in this section shall be construed to permit suits against the United States based upon adverse possession.

(Added Pub.L. 92–562, § 3(a), Oct. 25, 1972, 86 Stat. 1176, and amended Pub.L. 99–514, § 2, Oct. 22, 1986, 100 Stat. 2095; Pub.L. 99–598, Nov. 4, 1986, 100 Stat. 3351.)

HISTORICAL AND STATUTORY NOTES

References in Text

Section 208 of the Act July 10, 1952, referred to in subsec. (a), is section 208 (a) to (d) of Act July 10, 1952, c. 651, 66 Stat. 560. Section 208 (a) to (c) is classified to section 666 of Title 43, Public Lands. Section 208(d) is not classified to the Code.

§ 2410. Actions affecting property on which United States has lien

(a) Under the conditions prescribed in this section and section 1444 of this title for the protection of the United States, the United States may be named a party in any civil action or suit in any district court, or in any State court having jurisdiction of the subject matter—

(1) to quiet title to,

(2) to foreclose a mortgage or other lien upon,

(3) to partition,

(4) to condemn, or

(5) of interpleader or in the nature of interpleader with respect to,

real or personal property on which the United States has or claims a mortgage or other lien.

(b) The complaint or pleading shall set forth with particularity the nature of the interest or lien of the United States. In actions or suits involving liens arising under the internal revenue laws, the complaint or pleading shall include the name and address of the taxpayer whose liability created the lien and, if a notice of the tax lien was filed, the identity of the internal revenue office which filed the notice, and the date and place such notice of lien was filed. In actions in the State courts service upon the United States shall be made by serving the process of the court with a copy of the complaint upon the United States attorney for the district in which the action is brought or upon an assistant United States attorney or clerical employee designated by the United States attorney in writing filed with the clerk of the court in which the action is brought and by sending copies of the process and complaint, by registered mail, or by certified mail, to the Attorney General of the United States at Washington, District of Columbia. In such actions the United States may appear and answer, plead or demur within sixty days after such service or such further time as the court may allow.

(c) A judgment or decree in such action or suit shall have the same effect respecting the discharge of the property from the mortgage or other lien held by the United States as may be provided with respect to such matters by the local law of the place where the court is situated. However, an action to foreclose a mortgage or other lien, naming the United States as a party under this section, must seek judicial sale. A sale to satisfy a lien inferior to one of the United States shall be made subject to and without disturbing the lien of the United States, unless the United States consents that the property may be sold free of its lien and the proceeds divided as the parties may be entitled. Where a sale of real estate is made to satisfy a lien prior to that of the United States, the United States shall have one year from the date of sale within which to redeem, except that with respect to a lien arising under the internal revenue laws the period shall be 120 days or the period allowable for redemption under State law, whichever is longer, and in any case in which, under the provisions of section 505 of the Housing Act of 1950, as amended (12 U.S.C. 1701k), and subsection (d) of section 3720 of title 38 of the United States Code, the right to redeem does not arise, there shall be no right of redemption. In any case where the debt owing the United States is due, the United States may ask, by way of affirmative relief, for the foreclosure of its own lien and where property is sold to satisfy a first lien held by the United States, the United States may bid at the sale such sum, not exceeding the amount of its claim with expenses of sale, as may be directed by the head (or his delegate) of the department or agency of the United States which has charge of the administration of the laws in respect to which the claim of the United States arises. In any case where the United States is a bidder at the judicial sale, it may credit the amount determined to be due it against the amount it bids at such sales.

(d) In any case in which the United States redeems real property under this section or section 7425 of the Internal Revenue Code of 1986, the amount to be paid for such property shall be the sum of—

(1) the actual amount paid by the purchaser at such sale (which, in the case of a purchaser who is the holder of the lien being foreclosed, shall include the amount of the obligation secured by such lien to the extent satisfied by reason of such sale),

(2) interest on the amount paid (as determined under paragraph (1)) at 6 percent per annum from the date of such sale, and

(3) the amount (if any) equal to the excess of (A) the expenses necessarily incurred in connection with such property, over (B) the income from such property plus (to the extent such property is used by the purchaser) a reasonable rental value of such property.

(e) Whenever any person has a lien upon any real or personal property, duly recorded in the jurisdiction in which the property is located, and a junior lien, other than a tax lien, in favor of the United States attaches to such property, such person may make a written request to the officer charged with the administration of the laws in respect of which the lien of the United States arises, to have the same extinguished. If after appropriate investigation, it appears to such officer that the proceeds from the sale of the property would be insufficient to wholly or partly satisfy the lien of the United States, or that the claim of the United States has been satisfied or by lapse of time or otherwise has become unenforceable, such officer may issue a certificate releasing the property from such lien.

(June 25, 1948, c. 646, 62 Stat. 972; May 24, 1949, c. 139, § 119, 63 Stat. 105; July 7, 1958, Pub.L. 85–508, § 12(h), 72 Stat. 348; June 11, 1960, Pub.L. 86–507, § 1(20), 74 Stat. 201; Nov. 2, 1966, Pub.L. 89–719, Title II, § 201, 80 Stat. 1147; Oct. 22, 1986, Pub.L. 99–514, § 2, 100 Stat. 2095; Nov. 29, 1990, Pub.L. 101–647, Title XXXVI, § 3630, 104 Stat. 4966; Aug. 6, 1991, Pub.L. 102–83, § 5(c)(2), 105 Stat. 406; Oct. 19, 1996, Pub.L. 104–316, Title I, § 114, 110 Stat. 3834.)

HISTORICAL AND STATUTORY NOTES

References in Text

The internal revenue laws, referred to in subsec. (b), are classified generally to Title 26, Internal Revenue Code.

Section 7425 of the Internal Revenue Code of 1986, referred to in subsec. (d), is classified to section 7425 of Title 26, Internal Revenue Code.

Effective Dates

1996 Acts. Amendment by Pub.L. 104–316 effective Oct. 19, 1996, see section 101(e) of Pub.L. 104–316, set out as a note under section 130c of Title 2, The Congress.

1990 Acts. Amendment by section 3630 of Pub.L. 101–647 effective 180 days after Nov. 29, 1990, see section 3631 of Pub.L. 101–647, set out as a note under section 3001 of this title.

1966 Acts. Amendment of section by Pub.L. 89–719 applicable after Nov. 2, 1966, see section 203 of Pub.L. 89–719, set out as a note under section 1346 of this title.

1958 Acts. Amendment of section by Pub.L. 85–508 effective Jan. 3, 1959, upon admission of Alaska into the Union pursuant to Proc. No. 3269, Jan. 3, 1959, 24 F.R. 81, 73 Stat. c16, as required by sections 1 and 8(c) of Pub.L. 85–508, see notes set out under section 81A of this title and preceding section 21 of Title 48, Territories and Insular Possessions.

§ 2411. Interest

In any judgment of any court rendered (whether against the United States, a collector or deputy collector of internal revenue, a former collector or deputy collector, or the personal representative in case of death) for any overpayment in respect of any internal-revenue tax, interest shall be allowed at the overpayment rate established under section 6621 of the Internal Revenue Code of 1986 upon the amount of the overpayment, from the date of the payment or collection thereof to a date preceding the date of the refund check by not more than thirty days, such date to be determined by the Commissioner of Internal Revenue. The Commissioner is authorized to tender by check payment of any such judgment, with interest as herein provided, at any time after such judgment becomes final, whether or not a claim for such payment has been duly filed, and such tender shall stop the running of interest, whether or not such refund check is accepted by the judgment creditor.

(June 25, 1948, c. 646, 62 Stat. 973; May 24, 1949, c. 139, § 120, 63 Stat. 106; Jan. 3, 1975, Pub.L. 93–625, § 7(a)(2), 88 Stat. 2115; Apr. 2, 1982, Pub.L. 97–164, Title III, § 302(b), 96 Stat. 56; Oct. 22, 1986, Pub.L. 99–514, § 2, Title XV, § 1511(c)(18), 100 Stat. 2095, 2746.)

HISTORICAL AND STATUTORY NOTES

References in Text

Section 6621 of the Internal Revenue Code of 1986, referred to in text, is classified to section 6621 of Title 26, Internal Revenue Code.

Effective Dates

1986 Acts. Amendment by section 1511(c)(18) of Pub.L. 99–514 applicable for purposes of determining interest for periods after Dec. 31, 1986, see section 1511(d) of Pub.L. 99–514, set out as a note under section 47 of Title 26, Internal Revenue Code.

1982 Acts. Amendment by Pub.L. 97–164 effective Oct. 1, 1982, see section 402 of Pub.L. 97–164, set out as a note under section 171 of this title.

1975 Acts. Amendment by Pub.L. 93–625 effective July 1, 1975, and applicable to amounts outstanding on such date or arising thereafter, see section 7(e) of Pub.L. 93–625, set out as a note under section 6621 of Title 26, Internal Revenue Code.

§ 2412. Costs and fees

(a)(1) Except as otherwise specifically provided by statute, a judgment for costs, as enumerated in section 1920 of this title, but not including the fees and expenses of attorneys, may be awarded to the prevailing party in any civil action brought by or against the United States or any agency or any official of the United States acting in his or her official capacity in any court having jurisdiction of such action. A judgment for costs when taxed against the United States shall, in an amount established by statute, court rule, or order, be limited to reimbursing in whole or in part the prevailing party for the costs incurred by such party in the litigation.

(2) A judgment for costs, when awarded in favor of the United States in an action brought by the United States, may include an amount equal to the filing fee prescribed under section 1914(a) of this title. The preceding sentence shall not be construed as requiring the United States to pay any filing fee.

(b) Unless expressly prohibited by statute, a court may award reasonable fees and expenses of attorneys, in addition to the costs which may be awarded pursuant to subsection (a), to the prevailing party in any civil action brought by or against the United States or any agency or any official of the United States acting in his or her official capacity in any court having jurisdiction of such action. The United States shall be liable for such fees and expenses to the same extent that any other party would be liable under the common law or under the terms of any statute which specifically provides for such an award.

(c)(1) Any judgment against the United States or any agency and any official of the United States acting in his or her official capacity for costs pursuant to subsection (a) shall be paid as provided in sections 2414 and 2517 of this title and shall be in addition to any relief provided in the judgment.

(2) Any judgment against the United States or any agency and any official of the United States acting in his or her official capacity for fees and expenses of attorneys pursuant to subsection (b) shall be paid as provided in sections 2414 and 2517 of this title, except that if the basis for the award is a finding that the United States acted in bad faith, then the award shall be paid by any agency found to have acted in bad faith and shall be in addition to any relief provided in the judgment.

(d)(1)(A) Except as otherwise specifically provided by statute, a court shall award to a prevailing party other than the United States fees and other expenses, in addition to any costs awarded pursuant to subsection (a), incurred by that party in any civil action (other than cases sounding in tort), including proceedings for judicial review of agency action, brought by or against the United States in any court having jurisdiction of that action, unless the court finds that the position of the United States was substantially justified or that special circumstances make an award unjust.

(B) A party seeking an award of fees and other expenses shall, within thirty days of final judgment in the action, submit to the court an application for fees and other expenses which shows that the party is a prevailing party and is eligible to receive an award under this subsection, and the amount sought, including an itemized statement from any attorney or expert witness representing or appearing in behalf of the party stating the actual time expended and the rate at which fees and other expenses were computed. The party shall also allege that the position of the United States was not substantially justified. Whether or not the position of the United States was substantially justified shall be determined on the basis of the record (including the record with respect to the action or failure to act by the agency upon which the civil action is based) which is made in the civil action for which fees and other expenses are sought.

(C) The court, in its discretion, may reduce the amount to be awarded pursuant to this subsection, or deny an award, to the extent that the prevailing party during the course of the proceedings engaged in conduct which unduly and unreasonably protracted the final resolution of the matter in controversy.

(D) If, in a civil action brought by the United States or a proceeding for judicial review of an adversary adjudication described in section 504(a)(4) of title 5, the demand by the United States is substantially in excess of the judgment finally obtained by the United States and is unreasonable when compared with such judgment, under the facts and circumstances of the case, the court shall award to the party the fees and other expenses related to defending against the excessive demand, unless the party has committed a willful violation of law or otherwise acted in bad faith, or special circumstances make an award unjust. Fees and expenses awarded under this subparagraph shall be paid only as a consequence of appropriations provided in advance.

(2) For the purposes of this subsection—

(A) "fees and other expenses" includes the reasonable expenses of expert witnesses, the reasonable cost of any study, analysis, engineering report, test, or project which is found by the court to be necessary for the preparation of the party's case, and reasonable attorney fees (The amount of fees awarded under this subsection shall be based upon prevailing market rates for the kind and quality of the services furnished, except that (i) no expert witness shall be compensated at a rate in excess of the highest rate of compensation for expert witnesses paid by the United States; and (ii) attorney fees shall not be awarded in excess of $125 per hour unless the court determines that an increase in the cost of living or a special factor, such as the limited availability of qualified attorneys for the proceedings involved, justifies a higher fee.);

(B) "party" means (i) an individual whose net worth did not exceed $2,000,000 at the time the civil action was filed, or (ii) any owner of an unincorporated business, or any partnership, corporation, association, unit of local government, or organization, the net worth of which did not exceed $7,000,000 at the time the civil action was filed, and which had not more than 500 employees at the time the civil action was filed; except that an organization described in section 501(c)(3) of the Internal Revenue Code of 1986 (26 U.S.C. 501(c)(3)) exempt from taxation under section 501(a) of such Code, or a cooperative association as defined in section 15(a) of the Agricultural Marketing Act (12 U.S.C. 1141j(a)), may be a party regardless of the net worth of such organization or cooperative association or for purposes of subsection (d)(1)(D), a small entity as defined in section 601 of Title 5;

(C) "United States" includes any agency and any official of the United States acting in his or her official capacity;

(D) "position of the United States" means, in addition to the position taken by the United States in the civil action, the action or failure to act by the agency upon which the civil action is based; except that fees and expenses may not be awarded to a party for any portion of the litigation in which the party has unreasonably protracted the proceedings;

(E) "civil action brought by or against the United States" includes an appeal by a party, other than the United States, from a decision of a contracting officer rendered pursuant to a disputes clause in a contract with the Government or pursuant to the Contract Disputes Act of 1978;

(F) "court" includes the United States Court of Federal Claims and the United States Court of Appeals for Veterans Claims;

(G) "final judgment" means a judgment that is final and not appealable, and includes an order of settlement;

(H) "prevailing party", in the case of eminent domain proceedings, means a party who obtains a final judgment (other than by settlement), exclusive of interest, the amount of which is at least as close to the highest valuation of the property involved that is attested to at trial on behalf of the property owner as it is to the highest valuation of the property involved that is attested to at trial on behalf of the Government; and

(I) "demand" means the express demand of the United States which led to the adversary adjudication, but shall not include a recitation of the maximum statutory penalty (i) in the complaint, or (ii) elsewhere when accompanied by an express demand for a lesser amount.

(3) In awarding fees and other expenses under this subsection to a prevailing party in any action for judicial review of an adversary adjudication, as defined in subsection (b)(1)(C) of section 504 of title 5, United States Code, or an adversary adjudication subject to the Contract Disputes Act of 1978, the court shall include in that award fees and other expenses to the same extent authorized in subsection (a) of such section, unless the court finds that during such adversary adjudication the position of the United States was substantially justified, or that special circumstances make an award unjust.

(4) Fees and other expenses awarded under this subsection to a party shall be paid by any agency over which the party prevails from any funds made available to the agency by appropriation or otherwise.

[(5) Repealed. Pub.L. 104–66, Title I, § 1091(b), Dec. 21, 1995, 109 Stat. 722]

(e) The provisions of this section shall not apply to any costs, fees, and other expenses in connection with any proceeding to which section 7430 of the Internal Revenue Code of 1986 applies (determined without regard to subsections (b) and (f) of such section). Nothing in the preceding sentence shall prevent the awarding under subsection (a) of section 2412 of title 28, United States Code, of costs enumerated in section 1920 of such title (as in effect on October 1, 1981).

(f) If the United States appeals an award of costs or fees and other expenses made against the United States under this section and the award is affirmed in whole or in part, interest shall be paid on the amount of the award as affirmed. Such interest shall be computed at the rate determined under section 1961(a) of this title, and shall run from the date of the award through the day before the date of the mandate of affirmance.

(June 25, 1948, c. 646, 62 Stat. 973; July 18, 1966, Pub.L. 89–507, § 1, 80 Stat. 308; Oct. 21, 1980, Pub. L. 96–481, Title II, § 204(a), (c), 94 Stat. 2327, 2329; Sept. 3, 1982, Pub. L. 97–248, Title II, § 292(c), 96 Stat. 574; Aug. 5, 1985, Pub. L. 99–80, §§ 2, 6(a), (b)(2), 99 Stat. 184, 186; Oct. 22, 1986, Pub.L. 99–514, § 2, 100 Stat. 2095; Oct. 29, 1992, Pub.L. 102–572, Title III, § 301(a), Title V, §§ 502(b), 506(a), Title IX, § 902(b)(1), 106 Stat. 4511–4513, 4516; Dec. 21, 1995, Pub.L. 104–66, Title I, § 1091(b), 109 Stat. 722; Mar. 29, 1996, Pub.L. 104–121, Title II, § 232, 110 Stat. 863; Pub.L. 105–368, Title V, § 521(b)(1)(B), Nov. 10, 1998, 112 Stat. 3342.)

HISTORICAL AND STATUTORY NOTES

References in Text

The Contract Disputes Act of 1978, referred to in subsec. (d)(2)(E), (3), is Pub. L. 95–563, Nov. 1, 1978, 92 Stat. 2383, as amended, which is classified principally to chapter 9 (section 601 et seq.) of Title 41, Public Contracts. For complete classification of this Act to the Code, see Short Title note set out under section 601 of Title 41 and Tables.

Section 7430 of the Internal Revenue Code of 1986, referred to in subsec. (e), is classified to section 7430 of Title 26, Internal Revenue Code.

Effective Dates

1998 Acts. Amendment by Pub.L. 105–368 effective on the first day of the first month beginning more than 90 days after Nov. 10, 1998, see section 513 of Pub.L. 105–368, set out as a note under section 7251 of Title 38.

1996 Acts. Amendment by Pub.L. 104–121 applicable to civil actions and adversary adjudications commenced on or after March 29, 1996, see section 233 of Pub.L. 104–121, set out as a note under section 504 of Title 5, Government Organization and Employees.

1992 Acts. Section 506(b) of Pub.L. 102–572 provided that: "The amendment made by subsection (a) [amending subsec. (d)(2)(F) of this section] shall apply to any case pending before the United States Court of Veterans Appeals on the date of the enactment of this Act [Oct. 29, 1992], to any appeal filed in that court on or after such date, and to any appeal from that court that is pending on such date in the United States Court of Appeals for the Federal Circuit."

Section 506(d) of Pub.L. 102–572 provided that: "This section, and the amendment made by this section [amending subsec. (d)(2)(F) of this section and enacting provisions set out as notes under this section], shall take effect on the date of the enactment of this Act [Oct. 29, 1992]."

Amendment by section 902(b)(1) of Pub.L. 102–572 effective Oct. 29, 1992, see section 911 of Pub.L. 102–572, set out as a note under section 171 of this title.

Amendments by sections 301(a) and 502(b) of Pub.L. 102–572 effective Jan. 1, 1993, see section 1101(a) of Pub.L. 102–572, set out as a note under section 905 of Title 2, The Congress.

1985 Acts. Amendment by Pub. L. 99–80 applicable to cases pending on or commenced on or after Aug. 5, 1985, but with provision for additional applicability to certain prior cases and to prior board of contracts appeals cases, see section 7 of Pub. L. 99–80, set out as a note under section 504 of Title 5, Government Organization and Employees.

1982 Acts. Amendment by Pub.L. 97–248 applicable to civil actions or proceedings commenced after Feb. 28, 1983, see section 292(e)(1) of Pub.L. 97–248, as amended, set out as a note under section 7430 of Title 26, Internal Revenue Code.

1980 Acts. Amendment by section 204(a) of Pub.L. 96–481 to take effect on Oct. 1, 1981, and applicable to any adversary adjudication, as defined in section 504(b)(1)(C) of Title 5, and to civil actions and adversary adjudications described in this section, which are pending on, or commenced on or after, Oct. 1, 1981, see section 208 of Pub.L. 96–481, as amended, set out as a note under section 504 of Title 5, Government Organization and Employees.

Section 204(c) of Pub.L. 96–481 which provided in part that effective Oct. 1, 1984, subsec. (d) of this section is repealed, except that the provisions of subsec. (d) shall continue to apply through final disposition of any adversary adjudication initiated before the date of repeal, was repealed by Pub.L. 99–80, § 6(b)(2), Aug. 5, 1985, 99 Stat. 186.

1966 Acts. Section 3 of Pub.L. 89–507 provided that: "These amendments [to this section and section 2520 of this title] shall apply only to judgments entered in actions filed subsequent to the date of enactment of this Act [July 18, 1966]. These amendments [to this section and section 2520 of this title] shall not authorize the reopening or modification of judgments entered prior to the enactment of this Act [July 18, 1966]."

Savings Provisions

Section 206 of Pub.L. 96–481, as amended by Pub.L. 99–80, § 3, Aug. 5, 1985, 99 Stat. 186, provided that:

"**(a)** Except as provided in subsection (b), nothing in section 2412(d) of title 28, United States Code, as added by section 204(a) of this title [subsec. (d) of this section], alters, modifies, repeals, invalidates, or supersedes any other provision of Federal law which authorizes an award of such fees and other expenses to any party other than the United States that prevails in any civil action brought by or against the United States.

"**(b)** Section 206(b) of the Social Security Act (42 U.S.C. 406(b)(1)) [section 406(b) of Title 42, The Public Health and Welfare] shall not prevent an award of fees and other expenses under section 2412(d) of title 28, United States Code [subsec. (d) of this section]. Section 206(b)(2) of the Social Security Act [section 406(b)(2) of Title 42] shall not apply with respect to any such award but only if, where the claimant's attorney receives fees for the same work under both section 206(b) of that Act [section 406(b) of Title 42] and section 2412(d) of title 28, United States Code [subsec. (d) of this section], the claimant's attorney refunds to the claimant the amount of the smaller fee."

Congressional Findings and Purposes

For Congressional findings and purposes relating to 1980 amendment of this section, see section 202 of Pub.L. 96–481, set out as a note under section 504 of Title 5, Government Organization and Employees.

Fee Agreements

Section 506(c) of Pub.L. 102–572 provided that: "Section 5904(d) of title 38, United States Code [section 5904(d) of Title 38, Veterans' Benefits], shall not prevent an award of fees and other expenses under section 2412(d) of title 28, United States Code [subsec. (d) of this section]. Section 5904(d) of title 38, United States Code, shall not apply with respect to any such award but only if, where the claimant's attorney receives fees for the same work under both section 5904 of title 38, United States Code, and section 2412(d) of title 28, United States Code, the claimant's attorney refunds to the claimant the amount of the smaller fee."

Nonliability of Judicial Officers for Costs

Pub.L. 104–317, Title III, § 309(a), Oct. 19, 1996, 110 Stat. 3853, provided that: "Notwithstanding any other provision of law, no judicial officer shall be held liable for any costs, including attorney's fees, in any action brought against such officer for an act or omission taken in such officer's judicial capacity, unless such action was clearly in excess of such officer's jurisdiction."

Revival of Previously Repealed Provisions

For revival of subsec. (d) of this section effective on or after Aug. 5, 1985, as if it had not been repealed by section 204(c) of Pub.L. 96–481, and repeal of section 204(c) of Pub.L. 96–481, see section 6 of Pub.L. 99–80, set out as a note under section 504 of Title 5, Government Organization and Employees.

§ 2413. Executions in favor of United States

A writ of execution on a judgment obtained for the use of the United States in any court thereof shall be issued from and made returnable to the court which rendered the judgment, but may be executed in any other State, in any Territory, or in the District of Columbia.

(June 25, 1948, c. 646, 62 Stat. 974.)

§ 2414. Payment of judgments and compromise settlements

Except as provided by the Contract Disputes Act of 1978, payment of final judgments rendered by a district court or the Court of International Trade against the United States shall be made on settlements by the Secretary of the Treasury. Payment of final judgments rendered by a State or foreign court or tribunal against the United States, or against its agencies or officials upon obligations or liabilities of the United States, shall be made on settlements by the Secretary of the Treasury after certification by the Attorney General that it is in the interest of the United States to pay the same.

Whenever the Attorney General determines that no appeal shall be taken from a judgment or that no further review will be sought from a decision affirming the same, he shall so certify and the judgment shall be deemed final.

Except as otherwise provided by law, compromise settlements of claims referred to the Attorney General for defense of imminent litigation or suits against the United States, or against its agencies or officials upon obligations or liabilities of the United States, made by the Attorney General or any person authorized by him, shall be settled and paid in a manner similar to judgments in like causes and appropriations or funds available for the payment of such judgments are hereby made available for the payment of such compromise settlements.

(June 25, 1948, c. 646, 62 Stat. 974; Aug. 30, 1961, Pub.L. 87–187, § 1, 75 Stat. 415; Nov. 1, 1978, Pub.L. 95–563, § 14(d), 92 Stat. 2390; Oct. 10, 1980, Pub.L. 96–417, Title V, § 512, 94 Stat. 1744; Oct. 19, 1996, Pub.L. 104–316, Title II, § 202(k), 110 Stat. 3843.)

HISTORICAL AND STATUTORY NOTES

References in Text

The Contract Disputes Act of 1978, referred to in first paragraph, is Pub.L. 95–563, Nov. 1, 1978, 92 Stat. 2383, as amended, which is classified principally to chapter 9 (section 601 et seq.) of Title 41, Public Contracts. For complete classification of this Act to the Code, see Short Title note set out under section 601 of Title 41 and Tables.

Effective Dates

1980 Acts. Amendment by Pub.L. 96–417 effective on Nov. 1, 1980, and applicable with respect to civil actions pending on or commenced on or after such date, see section 701(a) of Pub.L. 96–417, as amended, set out as a note under section 251 of this title.

1978 Acts. Amendment by Pub.L. 95–563 effective with respect to contracts entered into 120 days after Nov. 1, 1978, and, at the election of the contractor, with respect to any claim pending at such time before the contracting officer or initiated thereafter, see section 16 of Pub.L. 95–563, set out as a note under section 601 of Title 41, Public Contracts.

Transfer of Functions

Effective June 30, 1996, the functions of the Comptroller General under this section to be transferred to the Director of the Office of Management and Budget, contingent upon the additional transfer to the Office of Management and Budget of such personnel, budget authority, records, and property of the General Accounting Office relating to such functions as the Comptroller General and the Director jointly determine to be necessary, see section 211 of Pub.L. 104–53, set out as a note under section 501 of Title 31, Money and Finance.

§ 2415. Time for commencing actions brought by the United States

(a) Subject to the provisions of section 2416 of this title, and except as otherwise provided by Congress, every action for money damages brought by the United States or an officer or agency thereof which is founded upon any contract express or implied in law or fact, shall be barred unless the complaint is filed within six years after the right of action accrues or within one year after final decisions have been rendered in applicable administrative proceedings required by contract or by law, whichever is later: *Provided*, That in the event of later partial payment or written acknowledgment of debt, the right of action shall be deemed to accrue again at the time of each such payment or acknowledgment: *Provided further*, That an action for money damages brought by the United States for or on behalf of a recognized tribe, band or group of American Indians shall not be barred unless the complaint is filed more than six years and ninety days after the right of action accrued: *Provided further*, That an action for money damages which accrued on the date of enactment of this Act in accordance with subsection (g) brought by the United States for or on behalf of a recognized tribe, band, or group of American Indians, or on behalf of an individual Indian whose land is held in trust or restricted status, shall not be barred unless the complaint is filed sixty days after the date of publication of the list required by section 4(c) of the Indian Claims Limitation Act of 1982: *Provided*, That, for those claims that are on either of the two lists published pursuant to the Indian Claims Limitation Act of 1982, any right of action shall be barred unless the complaint is filed within (1) one year after the Secretary of the Interior has published in the Federal Register a notice rejecting such claim or (2) three years after the date the Secretary of the Interior has submitted legislation or legislative report to Congress to resolve such claim or more than two years after a final decision has been rendered in applicable administrative proceedings required by contract or by law, whichever is later.

(b) Subject to the provisions of section 2416 of this title, and except as otherwise provided by Congress, every action for money damages brought by the United States or an officer or agency thereof which is founded upon a tort shall be barred unless the complaint is filed within three years after the right of action first accrues: *Provided*, That an action to recover damages resulting from a trespass on lands of the United States; an action to recover damages resulting from fire to such lands; an action to recover for diversion of money paid under a grant program; and an action for conversion of property of the United States may be brought within six years after the right of action accrues, except that such actions for or on behalf of a recognized tribe, band or group of American Indians, including actions relating to allotted trust or restricted Indian lands, may be brought within six years and ninety days after the right of action accrues, except that such actions for or on behalf of a recognized tribe, band, or group of American Indians, including actions relating to allotted trust or restricted Indian lands, or on behalf of an individual Indian whose land is held in trust or restricted status which accrued on the date of enactment of this Act in accordance with subsection (g) may be brought on or before sixty days after the date of the publication of the list required by section 4(c) of the Indian Claims Limitation Act of 1982: *Provided*, That, for those claims that are on either of the two lists published pursuant to the Indian Claims Limitation Act of 1982, any right of action shall be barred unless the complaint is filed within (1) one year after the Secretary of the Interior has published in the Federal Register a notice rejecting such claim or (2) three years after the Secretary of the Interior has submitted legislation or legislative report to Congress to resolve such claim.

(c) Nothing herein shall be deemed to limit the time for bringing an action to establish the title to, or right of possession of, real or personal property.

(d) Subject to the provisions of section 2416 of this title and except as otherwise provided by Congress, every action for the recovery of money erroneously paid to or on behalf of any civilian employee of any agency of the United States or to or on behalf of any member or dependent of any member of the uniformed services of the United States, incident to the employment or services of such employee or member, shall be barred unless the complaint is filed within six years after the right of action accrues: *Provided*, That in the event of later partial payment or written acknowledgment of debt, the right of action shall be deemed to accrue again at the time of each such payment or acknowledgment.

(e) In the event that any action to which this section applies is timely brought and is thereafter dismissed without prejudice, the action may be recommenced within one year after such dismissal, regardless of whether the action would otherwise then be barred by this section. In any action so recommenced the defendant shall not be barred from interposing any claim which would not have been barred in the original action.

(f) The provisions of this section shall not prevent the assertion, in an action against the United States or an officer or agency thereof, of any claim of the United States or an officer or agency thereof against an opposing party, a co-party, or a third party that arises out of the transaction or occurrence that is the subject matter of the opposing party's claim. A claim of the United States or an officer or agency thereof that does not arise out of the transaction or occurrence that is the subject matter of the opposing party's claim may, if time-barred, be asserted only by way of offset and may be allowed in an amount not to exceed the amount of the opposing party's recovery.

(g) Any right of action subject to the provisions of this section which accrued prior to the date of enactment of this Act shall, for purposes of this section, be deemed to have accrued on the date of enactment of this Act.

(h) Nothing in this Act shall apply to actions brought under the Internal Revenue Code or incidental to the collection of taxes imposed by the United States.

(i) The provisions of this section shall not prevent the United States or an officer or agency thereof from collecting any claim of the United States by means of administrative offset, in accordance with section 3716 of title 31.

(Added Pub.L. 89–505, § 1, July 18, 1966, 80 Stat. 304, and amended Pub.L. 92–353, July 18, 1972, 86 Stat. 499; Pub.L. 92–485, Oct. 13, 1972, 86 Stat. 803; Pub.L. 95–64, July 11, 1977, 91 Stat. 268; Pub.L. 95–103, Aug. 15, 1977, 91 Stat. 842; Pub.L. 96–217, § 1, Mar. 27, 1980, 94 Stat. 126; Pub.L. 97–365, § 9, Oct. 25, 1982, 96 Stat. 1754; Pub.L. 97–394, Title I, § 2, Dec. 30, 1982, 96 Stat. 1976; Pub.L. 97–452, § 2(d) (2), Jan. 12, 1983, 96 Stat. 2478; Pub.L. 98–250, § 4(a), Apr. 3, 1984, 98 Stat. 118.)

HISTORICAL AND STATUTORY NOTES

References in Text

The date of enactment of this Act, referred to in subsecs. (a), (b), and (g), means the date of enactment of Pub.L. 89–505, which was approved on July 18, 1966.

The Indian Claims Limitation Act of 1982, referred to in subsecs. (a) and (b), is Pub.L. 97–394, Title I, §§ 2–6, Dec. 30, 1982, 96 Stat. 1976–1978, which amended this section and enacted provisions set out as notes under this section. For complete classification of this Act to the Code, see Short Title of 1982 Amendments note set out under this section and Tables.

This Act, referred to in subsec. (h), means Pub.L. 89–505, July 18, 1966, 80 Stat. 304, which enacted this section and section 2416 of this title. For complete classification of this Act to the Code see Tables.

Short Title

1982 Amendments. Section 1 of Pub.L. 97–394, as amended by Pub.L. 98–250, § 4(b), Apr. 3, 1984, 98 Stat. 119, provided that: "Sections 2 through 6 of this Act [sections 2–6 of Pub.L. 97–394, which amended this section and enacted provisions set out as a note under this section] may be cited as the 'Indian Claims Limitation Act of 1982'."

Legislative Proposals Respecting Appropriateness of Resolution By Litigation of Unresolved Indian Claims

Section 2 of Pub.L. 96–217 provided that: "Not later than June 30, 1981, the Secretary of the Interior, after consultation with the Attorney General, shall submit to the Congress legislative proposals to resolve those Indian claims subject to the amendments made by the first section of this Act [amending this section] that the Secretary of the Interior or the Attorney General believes are not appropriate to resolve by litigation."

Publication of List of Indian Claims; Additional Claims; Time to Commence Action; Rejection of Claims; Claims Resolved By Legislation

Sections 3 to 6 of Pub.L. 97–394 provided that:

"Sec. 3. (a) Within ninety days after the enactment of this Act [Dec. 30, 1982], the Secretary of the Interior (hereinafter referred to as the 'Secretary') shall publish in the Federal Register a list of all claims accruing to any tribe, band or group of Indians or individual Indian on or before July 18, 1966, which have at any time been identified by or submitted to the Secretary under the 'Statute of Limitation Project' undertaken by the Department of the Interior and which, but for the provisions of this Act [sections 2–6 of Pub.L. 97–394; see Short Title of 1982 Amendments note set out under this section] would be barred by the provisions of section 2415 of title 28, United States Code [this section]: *Provided,* That the Secretary shall have the discretion to exclude from such list any matter which was erroneously identified as a claim and which has no legal merit whatsoever.

"(b) Such list shall group the claims on a reservation-by-reservation, tribe-by-tribe, or State-by-State basis, as appropriate, and shall state the nature and geographic location of each claim and only such other additional information as may be needed to identify specifically such claims.

"(c) Within thirty days after the publication of this list, the Secretary shall provide a copy of the Indian Claims Limitation Act of 1982 [sections 2–6 of Pub.L. 97–394; see short title of 1982 Amendments note under this section] and a copy of the Federal Register containing this list, or such parts as may be pertinent, to each Indian tribe, band or group whose rights or the rights of whose members could be affected by the provisions of section 2415 of title 28, United States Code [this section].

"Sec. 4. (a) Any tribe, band or group of Indians or any individual Indian shall have one hundred and eighty days after the date of the publication in the Federal Register of the list provided for in section 3 of this Act [section 3 of Pub.L. 97–394] to submit to the Secretary any additional specific claim or claims which such tribe, band or group of Indians or individual Indian believes may be affected by section 2415 of title 28, United States Code [this section], and desires to have considered for litigation or legislation by the United States.

"(b) Any such claim submitted to the Secretary shall be accompanied by a statement identifying the nature of the claim, the date when the right of action allegedly accrued, the names of the potential plaintiffs and defendants, if known, and such other information needed to identify and evaluate such claim.

"(c) Not more than thirty days after the expiration of the one hundred and eighty day period provided for in subsection (a) of this section, the Secretary shall publish in the Federal Register a list containing the additional claims submitted during such period: *Provided,* That the Secretary shall have the discretion to exclude from such list any matter which has not been sufficiently identified as a claim.

"Sec. 5. (a) Any right of action shall be barred sixty days after the date of the publication of the list required by section 4(c) of this Act [section 4(c) of Pub.L. 97–394] for those pre-1966 claims which, but for the provisions of this Act [sections 2–6 of Pub.L. 97–394; see Short Title of 1982 Amendments note set out under this section] would have been barred by section 2415 of title 28, United States Code [this section], unless such claims are included on either of the lists required by section 3 or 4(c) of this Act [section 3 or 4(c) of Pub.L. 97–394].

"(b) If the Secretary decides to reject for litigation any of the claims or groups or categories of claims contained on either of the lists required by section 3 or 4(c) of this Act [section 3 or 4(c) of Pub.L. 97–394], he shall send a report to the appropriate tribe, band, or group of Indians, whose rights or the rights of whose members could be affected by such rejection, advising them of his decision. The report shall identify the nature and geographic location of each rejected claim and the name of the potential plaintiffs and defendants if they are known or can be reasonably ascertained and shall, briefly, state the reasons why such claim or claims were rejected for litigation. Where the Secretary knows or can reasonably ascertain the identity of any of the potential individual Indian plaintiffs and their present addresses, he shall provide them with written notice of such rejection. Upon the request of any Indian claimant, the Secretary shall, without undue delay, provide to such claimant any nonprivileged research materials or evidence gathered by the United States in the documentation of such claim.

"(c) The Secretary, as soon as possible, after providing the report required by subsection (b) of this section, shall publish a notice in the Federal Register identifying the claims covered in such report. With respect to any claim covered by such report, any right of action shall be barred unless the complaint is filed within one year after the date of publication in the Federal Register.

"**Sec. 6.** (a) If the Secretary determines that any claim or claims contained in either of the lists as provided in sections 3 or 4(c) of this Act [sections 3 or 4(c) of Pub.L. 97–394] is not appropriate for litigation, but determines that such claims may be appropriately resolved by legislation, he shall submit to the Congress legislation to resolve such claims or shall submit to Congress a report setting out options for legislative resolution of such claims.

"(b) Any right of action on claims covered by such legislation or report shall be barred unless the complaint is filed within 3 years after the date of submission of such legislation or legislative report to Congress."

§ 2416. Time for commencing actions brought by the United States—Exclusions

For the purpose of computing the limitations periods established in section 2415, there shall be excluded all periods during which—

(a) the defendant or the res is outside the United States, its territories and possessions, the District of Columbia, or the Commonwealth of Puerto Rico; or

(b) the defendant is exempt from legal process because of infancy, mental incompetence, diplomatic immunity, or for any other reason; or

(c) facts material to the right of action are not known and reasonably could not be known by an official of the United States charged with the responsibility to act in the circumstances; or

(d) the United States is in a state of war declared pursuant to article I, section 8, of the Constitution of the United States.

(Added Pub.L. 89–505, § 1, July 18, 1966, 80 Stat. 305.)

CHAPTER 163—FINES, PENALTIES AND FORFEITURES

Sec.
2461. Mode of recovery.
2462. Time for commencing proceedings.
2463. Property taken under revenue law not repleviable.
2464. Security; special bond.
2465. Return of property to claimant; certificate of reasonable cause; liability for wrongful seizure.

§ 2461. Mode of recovery

(a) Whenever a civil fine, penalty or pecuniary forfeiture is prescribed for the violation of an Act of Congress without specifying the mode of recovery or enforcement thereof, it may be recovered in a civil action.

(b) Unless otherwise provided by Act of Congress, whenever a forfeiture of property is prescribed as a penalty for violation of an Act of Congress and the seizure takes place on the high seas or on navigable waters within the admiralty and maritime jurisdiction of the United States, such forfeiture may be enforced by libel in admiralty but in cases of seizures on land the forfeiture may be enforced by a proceeding by libel which shall conform as near as may be to proceedings in admiralty.

(June 25, 1948, c. 646, 62 Stat. 974.)

HISTORICAL AND STATUTORY NOTES

Federal Civil Penalties Inflation Adjustment

Pub.L. 101–410, Oct. 5, 1990, 104 Stat. 890; Pub.L. 104–134, Title III, § 31001(s)(1), Apr. 26, 1996, 110 Stat. 1321–373; Pub.L. 105–362, Title XIII, § 1301(a), Nov. 10, 1998, 112 Stat. 3293, provided that:

"SHORT TITLE

"**Section 1.** This Act may be cited as the 'Federal Civil Penalties Inflation Adjustment Act of 1990'.

"FINDINGS AND PURPOSE

"**Sec. 2.** (a) **Findings.**—The Congress finds that—

"(1) the power of Federal agencies to impose civil monetary penalties for violations of Federal law and regulations plays an important role in deterring violations and furthering the policy goals embodied in such laws and regulations;

"(2) the impact of many civil monetary penalties has been and is diminished due to the effect of inflation;

"(3) by reducing the impact of civil monetary penalties, inflation has weakened the deterrent effect of such penalties; and

"(4) the Federal Government does not maintain comprehensive, detailed accounting of the efforts of Federal agencies to assess and collect civil monetary penalties.

"(b) **Purpose.**—The purpose of this Act is to establish a mechanism that shall—

"(1) allow for regular adjustment for inflation of civil monetary penalties;

"(2) maintain the deterrent effect of civil monetary penalties and promote compliance with the law; and

"(3) improve the collection by the Federal Government of civil monetary penalties.

"DEFINITIONS

"**Sec. 3.** For purposes of this Act, the term—

"(1) 'agency' means an Executive agency as defined under section 105 of title 5, United States Code [5 U.S.C.A. § 105], and includes the United States Postal Service;

"(2) 'civil monetary penalty' means any penalty, fine, or other sanction that—

"(A)(i) is for a specific monetary amount as provided by Federal law; or

"(ii) has a maximum amount provided for by Federal law; and

"(B) is assessed or enforced by an agency pursuant to Federal law; and

"(C) is assessed or enforced pursuant to an administrative proceeding or a civil action in the Federal courts; and

"(3) 'Consumer Price Index' means the Consumer Price Index for all-urban consumers published by the Department of Labor.

"CIVIL MONETARY PENALTY INFLATION ADJUSTMENT REPORTS

"**Sec. 4.** The head of each agency shall, not later than 180 days after the date of enactment of the Debt Collection Improvement Act of 1996 [Apr. 26, 1996], and at least once every 4 years thereafter—

"(1) by regulation adjust each civil monetary penalty provided by law within the jurisdiction of the Federal agency, except for any penalty (including any addition to tax and additional amount) under the Internal Revenue Code of 1986 [26 U.S.C.A. § 1 et seq.], the Tariff Act of 1930 [19 U.S.C.A. § 1202 et seq.], the Occupational Safety and Health Act of 1970 [29 U.S.C.A. § 651 et seq.], or the Social Security Act [42 U.S.C.A. § 301 et seq.], by the inflation adjustment described under section 5 of this Act; and

"(2) publish each such regulation in the Federal Register.

"COST-OF-LIVING ADJUSTMENTS OF CIVIL MONETARY PENALTIES

"**Sec. 5.** (a) **Adjustment.**—The inflation adjustment under section 4 shall be determined by increasing the maximum civil monetary penalty or the range of minimum and maximum civil monetary penalties, as applicable, for each civil monetary penalty by the cost-of-living adjustment. Any increase determined under this subsection shall be rounded to the nearest—

"(1) multiple of $10 in the case of penalties less than or equal to $100;

"(2) multiple of $100 in the case of penalties greater than $100 but less than or equal to $1,000;

"(3) multiple of $1,000 in the case of penalties greater than $1,000 but less than or equal to $10,000;

"(4) multiple of $5,000 in the case of penalties greater than $10,000 but less than or equal to $100,000;

"(5) multiple of $10,000 in the case of penalties greater than $100,000 but less than or equal to $200,000; and

"(6) multiple of $25,000 in the case of penalties greater than $200,000.

"(b) **Definition.**—For purposes of subsection (a), the term 'cost-of-living adjustment' means the percentage (if any) for each civil monetary penalty by which—

"(1) the Consumer Price Index for the month of June of the calendar year preceding the adjustment, exceeds

"(2) the Consumer Price Index for the month of June of the calendar year in which the amount of such civil monetary penalty was last set or adjusted pursuant to law.

"ANNUAL REPORT

"**Sec. 6.** Any increase under this Act in a civil monetary penalty shall apply only to violations which occur after the date the increase takes effect."

[Former Sec. 6 repealed by Pub.L. 105–362, Title XIII, § 1301(a)(1), Nov. 10, 1998, 112 Stat. 3293.]

[Pub.L. 104–134, Title III, § 31001(s)(2), Apr. 26, 1996, 110 Stat. 1321–373, provided that: "The first adjustment of a civil monetary penalty made pursuant to the amendment made by paragraph (1) [amending Pub.L. 101–410, set out as a note under this section] may not exceed 10 percent of such penalty."]

[Any reference in any provision of law enacted before Jan. 4, 1995, to the Committee on Government Operations of the House of Representatives treated as referring to the Committee on Government Reform and Oversight of the House of Representatives, except that any reference in any provision of law enacted before Jan. 4, 1995, to the Committee on Government Operations of the House of Representatives treated as referring to the Committee on the Budget of the House of Representatives in the case of a provision of law relating to the establishment, extension, and enforcement of special controls over the Federal budget, see section 1(a)(6) and (c)(2) of Pub.L. 104–14, set out as a note preceding section 21 of Title 2, The Congress.]

Memorandum of President of the United States, May 3, 1991, 56 F.R. 21911, delegated to Director of Office of Management and Budget responsibility of President for submitting reports on civil monetary penalties to Committee on Governmental Affairs of the Senate and Committee on Government Operations of the House of Representatives and to Congress as required by sections 4 and 6 of the Federal Civil Penalties Inflation Adjustment Act of 1990, Pub.L. 101–410, set out as a note under this section.

§ 2462. Time for commencing proceedings

Except as otherwise provided by Act of Congress, an action, suit or proceeding for the enforcement of any civil fine, penalty, or forfeiture, pecuniary or otherwise, shall not be entertained unless commenced within five years from the date when the claim first accrued if, within the same period, the offender or the property is found within the United States in order that proper service may be made thereon.

(June 25, 1948, c. 646, 62 Stat. 974.)

§ 2463. Property taken under revenue law not repleviable

All property taken or detained under any revenue law of the United States shall not be repleviable, but shall be deemed to be in the custody of the law and subject only to the orders and decrees of the courts of the United States having jurisdiction thereof.

(June 25, 1948, c. 646, 62 Stat. 974.)

§ 2464. Security; special bond

(a) Except in cases of seizures for forfeiture under any law of the United States, whenever a warrant of arrest or other process in rem is issued in any admiralty case, the United States marshal shall stay the execution of such process, or discharge the property arrested if the process has been levied, on receiving from the respondent or claimant of the property a bond or stipulation in double the amount claimed by the libellant, with sufficient surety, to be approved by the judge of the district court where the case is pending, or, in his absence, by the collector of the port, conditioned to answer the decree of the court in such case. Such bond or stipulation shall be returned to the court, and judgment or decree thereon, against both the principal and sureties, may be secured at the time of rendering the decree in the original case. The owner of any vessel may deliver to the marshal a bond or stipulation, with sufficient surety, to be approved by the judge of the district court, conditioned to answer the decree of such court in all or any cases that are brought thereafter in such court against the vessel. Thereupon the execution of all such process against such vessel shall be stayed so long as the amount secured by such bond or stipulation is at least double the aggregate amount claimed by libellants in such suits which are begun and pending against such vessel. Similar judgments or decrees and remedies may be had on such bond or stipulation as if a special bond or stipulation had been filed in each of such suits.

(b) The court may make necessary orders to carry this section into effect, particularly in giving proper notice of any such suit. Such bond or stipulation shall be indorsed by the clerk with a minute of the suits wherein process is so stayed. Further security may be required by the court at any time.

(c) If a special bond or stipulation in the particular case is given under this section, the liability as to said case on the general bond or stipulation shall cease. The parties may stipulate the amount of the bond or stipulation for the release of a vessel or other property to be not more than the amount claimed in the libel, with interest, plus an allowance for libellant's costs. In the event of the inability or refusal of the parties to so stipulate, the court shall fix the amount, but if not so fixed then a bond shall be required in the amount prescribed in this section.

(June 25, 1948, c. 646, 62 Stat. 974.)

HISTORICAL AND STATUTORY NOTES

Transfer of Functions

All offices of Collector of Customs, Comptroller of Customs, Surveyor of Customs, and Appraiser of Merchandise in the Bureau of Customs of the Department of the Treasury to which appointments were required to be made by the President with the advice and consent of the Senate were ordered abolished, with such offices to be terminated not later than December 31, 1966, by 1965 Reorg. Plan No. 1, eff. May 25, 1965, 30 F.R. 7035, 79 Stat. 1317, set out in Appendix 1 to Title 5, Government Organization and Employees. All functions of the offices eliminated were already vested in the Secretary of the Treasury by 1950 Reorg. Plan No. 26, eff. July 31, 1950, 15 F.R. 4935, 64 Stat. 1280, set out in Appendix 1 to Title 5.

§ 2465. Return of property to claimant; certificate of reasonable cause; liability for wrongful seizure

Upon the entry of judgment for the claimant in any proceeding to condemn or forfeit property seized under any Act of Congress, such property shall be returned forthwith to the claimant or his agent; but if it appears that there was reasonable cause for the seizure, the court shall cause a proper certificate thereof to be entered and the claimant shall not, in such case, be entitled to costs, nor shall the person who made the seizure, nor the prosecutor, be liable to suit or judgment on account of such suit or prosecution.

(June 25, 1948, c. 646, 62 Stat. 975.)

CHAPTER 165—UNITED STATES COURT OF FEDERAL CLAIMS PROCEDURE

Sec.

2501. Time for filing suit.
2502. Aliens' privilege to sue.
2503. Proceedings generally.
2504. Plaintiff's testimony.
2505. Trial before judges.
2506. Interest of witness.
2507. Calls and discovery.
2508. Counterclaim or set-off.[1]
2509. Congressional reference cases.
2510. Referral of cases by Comptroller General.
2511. Accounts of officers, agents or contractors.
2512. Disbursing officers; relief.
2513. Unjust conviction and imprisonment.
2514. Forfeiture of fraudulent claims.
2515. New trial, stay of judgment.[1]
2516. Interest on claims and judgments.
2517. Payment of judgments.
[2518. Repealed.]
2519. Conclusiveness of judgment.
2520. Fees.
2521. Subpoenas and incidental powers.
2522. Notice of appeal.

[1] So in original. Does not conform to section catchline.

§ 2501. Time for filing suit

Every claim of which the United States Court of Federal Claims has jurisdiction shall be barred unless the petition thereon is filed within six years after such claim first accrues.

Every claim under section 1497 of this title shall be barred unless the petition thereon is filed within two years after the termination of the river and harbor improvements operations on which the claim is based.

A petition on the claim of a person under legal disability or beyond the seas at the time the claim accrues may be filed within three years after the disability ceases.

A suit for the fees of an officer of the United States shall not be filed until his account for such fees has been finally acted upon, unless the General Accounting Office fails to act within six months after receiving the account.

(June 25, 1948, c. 646, 62 Stat. 976; Sept. 3, 1954, c. 1263, § 52, 68 Stat. 1246; Apr. 2, 1982, Pub.L. 97–164, Title I, § 139(a), 96 Stat. 42; Oct. 29, 1992, Pub.L. 102–572, Title IX, § 902(a)(1), 106 Stat. 4516.)

HISTORICAL AND STATUTORY NOTES

Effective Dates

1992 Acts. Amendment by Title IX of Pub.L. 102–572 effective Oct. 29, 1992, see section 911 of Pub.L. 102–572, set out as a note under section 171 of Title 28, Judiciary and Judicial Procedure.

1982 Acts. Amendment by Pub.L. 97–164 effective Oct. 1, 1982, see section 402 of Pub.L. 97–164, set out as a note under section 171 of this title.

§ 2502. Aliens' privilege to sue

(a) Citizens or subjects of any foreign government which accords to citizens of the United States the right to prosecute claims against their government in its courts may sue the United States in the United States Court of Federal Claims if the subject matter of the suit is otherwise within such court's jurisdiction.

(b) See section 7422(f) of the Internal Revenue Code of 1986 for exception with respect to suits involving internal revenue taxes.

(June 25, 1948, c. 646, 62 Stat. 976; Nov. 2, 1966, Pub.L. 89–713, § 3(b), 80 Stat. 1108; Apr. 2, 1982, Pub.L. 97–164, Title I, § 139(a), 96 Stat. 42; Oct. 22, 1986, Pub.L. 99–514, § 2, 100 Stat. 2095; Oct. 29, 1992, Pub.L. 102–572, Title IX, § 902(a)(1), 106 Stat. 4516.)

HISTORICAL AND STATUTORY NOTES

References in Text

Section 7422(f) of the Internal Revenue Code of 1986, referred to in subsec. (b), is classified to section 7422(f) of Title 26, Internal Revenue Code.

Effective Dates

1992 Acts. Amendment by Title IX of Pub.L. 102–572 effective Oct. 29, 1992, see section 911 of Pub.L. 102–572, set out as a note under section 171 of Title 28, Judiciary and Judicial Procedure.

1982 Acts. Amendment by Pub.L. 97–164 effective Oct. 1, 1982, see section 402 of Pub.L. 97–164, set out as a note under section 171 of this title.

1966 Acts. Amendment by Pub.L. 89–713, which added subsec. (b) to this section, applicable to suits brought against officers, employees, or personal representatives instituted 90 days or more after Nov. 2, 1966, see section 3(d) of Pub.L. 89–713, set out as a note under section 7422 of Title 26, Internal Revenue Code.

§ 2503. Proceedings generally

(a) Parties to any suit in the United States Court of Federal Claims may appear before a judge of that court in person or by attorney, produce evidence, and examine witnesses.

(b) The proceedings of the Court of Federal Claims shall be in accordance with such rules of practice and procedure (other than the rules of evidence) as the Court of Federal Claims may prescribe and in accordance with the Federal Rules of Evidence.

(c) The judges of the Court of Federal Claims shall fix times for trials, administer oaths or affirmations, examine witnesses, receive evidence, and enter dispositive judgments. Hearings shall, if convenient, be held in the counties where the witnesses reside.

(d) For the purpose of construing sections 1821, 1915, 1920, and 1927 of this title, the United States Court of Federal Claims shall be deemed to be a court of the United States.

(June 25, 1948, c. 646, 62 Stat. 976; Sept. 3, 1954, c. 1263, § 53, 68 Stat. 1246; Apr. 2, 1982, Pub.L. 97–164, Title I, § 139(b) (1), 96 Stat. 42; Oct. 29, 1992, Pub.L. 102–572, Title IX, §§ 902(a), 909, 106 Stat. 4516, 4519.)

HISTORICAL AND STATUTORY NOTES

References in Text

The Federal Rules of Evidence, referred to in subsec. (b), are set out in this title.

Effective Dates

1992 Acts. Amendment by Title IX of Pub.L. 102–572 effective Oct. 29, 1992, see section 911 of Pub.L. 102–572, set out as a note under section 171 of Title 28, Judiciary and Judicial Procedure.

1982 Acts. Amendment by Pub.L. 97–164 effective Oct. 1, 1982, see section 402 of Pub.L. 97–164, set out as a note under section 171 of this title.

§ 2504. Plaintiff's testimony

The United States Court of Federal Claims may, at the instance of the Attorney General, order any plaintiff to appear, upon reasonable notice, before any judge of the court and be examined on oath as to all matters pertaining to his claim. Such examination shall be reduced to writing by the judge, and shall be returned to and filed in the court, and may, at the discretion of the attorneys for the United States, be read and used as evidence on the trial. If any plaintiff, after such order is made and due and reasonable notice thereof is given to him, fails to appear, or refuses to testify or answer fully as to all material matters within his knowledge, the court may order that the case shall not be tried until he fully complies with such order.

(June 25, 1948, c. 646, 62 Stat. 976; Apr. 2, 1982, Pub.L. 97–164, Title I, § 139(c), 96 Stat. 42; Oct. 29, 1992, Pub.L. 102–572, Title IX, § 902(a)(1), 106 Stat. 4516.)

HISTORICAL AND STATUTORY NOTES

Effective Dates

1992 Acts. Amendment by Title IX of Pub.L. 102–572 effective Oct. 29, 1992, see section 911 of Pub.L. 102–572, set out as a note under section 171 of Title 28, Judiciary and Judicial Procedure.

1982 Acts. Amendment by Pub.L. 97–164 effective Oct. 1, 1982, see section 402 of Pub.L. 97–164, set out as a note under section 171 of this title.

§ 2505. Trial before judges

Any judge of the United States Court of Federal Claims may sit at any place within the United States to take evidence and enter judgment.

(June 25, 1948, c. 646, 62 Stat. 976; Sept. 3, 1954, c. 1263, § 54(a), (b), 68 Stat. 1246; Apr. 2, 1982, Pub.L. 97–164, Title I, § 139(d), 96 Stat. 42; Oct. 29, 1992, Pub.L. 102–572, Title IX, § 902(a)(1), 106 Stat. 4516.)

HISTORICAL AND STATUTORY NOTES

Effective Dates

1992 Acts. Amendment by Title IX of Pub.L. 102–572 effective Oct. 29, 1992, see section 911 of Pub.L. 102–572, set out as a note under section 171 of Title 28, Judiciary and Judicial Procedure.

1982 Acts. Amendment by Pub.L. 97–164 effective Oct. 1, 1982, see section 402 of Pub.L. 97–164, set out as a note under section 171 of this title.

§ 2506. Interest of witness

A witness in a suit in the United States Court of Federal Claims shall not be exempt or disqualified because he is a party to or interested in such suit.

(June 25, 1948, c. 646, 62 Stat. 977; Apr. 2, 1982, Pub.L. 97–164, Title I, § 139(e), 96 Stat. 42; Oct. 29, 1992, Pub.L. 102–572, Title IX, § 902(a)(1), 106 Stat. 4516.)

HISTORICAL AND STATUTORY NOTES

Effective Dates

1992 Acts. Amendment by Title IX of Pub.L. 102–572 effective Oct. 29, 1992, see section 911 of Pub.L. 102–572, set out as a note under section 171 of Title 28, Judiciary and Judicial Procedure.

1982 Acts. Amendment by Pub.L. 97–164 effective Oct. 1, 1982, see section 402 of Pub.L. 97–164, set out as a note under section 171 of this title.

§ 2507. Calls and discovery

(a) The United States Court of Federal Claims may call upon any department or agency of the United States or upon any party for any information or papers, not privileged, for purposes of discovery or for use as evidence. The head of any department or agency may refuse to comply with a call issued pursuant to this subsection when, in his opinion, compliance will be injurious to the public interest.

(b) Without limitation on account of anything contained in subsection (a) of this section, the court may, in accordance with its rules, provide additional means for the discovery of any relevant facts, books, papers, documents or tangible things, not privileged.

(c) The Court of Federal Claims may use all recorded and printed reports made by the committees of the Senate or House of Representatives.

(June 25, 1948, c. 646, 62 Stat. 977; Sept. 3, 1954, c. 1263, § 55(a)–(c), 68 Stat. 1247; Apr. 2, 1982, Pub.L. 97–164, Title I, § 139(f), 96 Stat. 42; Oct. 29, 1992, Pub.L. 102–572, Title IX, § 902(a), 106 Stat. 4516.)

HISTORICAL AND STATUTORY NOTES

Effective Dates

1992 Acts. Amendment by Title IX of Pub.L. 102–572 effective Oct. 29, 1992, see section 911 of Pub.L. 102–572, set out as a note under section 171 of Title 28, Judiciary and Judicial Procedure.

1982 Acts. Amendment by Pub.L. 97–164 effective Oct. 1, 1982, see section 402 of Pub.L. 97–164, set out as a note under section 171 of this title.

§ 2508. Counterclaim or set-off; registration of judgment

Upon the trial of any suit in the United States Court of Federal Claims in which any setoff, counterclaim, claim for damages, or other demand is set up on the part of the United States against any plaintiff making claim against the United States in said court, the court shall hear and determine such claim or demand both for and against the United States and plaintiff.

If upon the whole case it finds that the plaintiff is indebted to the United States it shall render judgment to that effect, and such judgment shall be final and reviewable.

The transcript of such judgment, filed in the clerk's office of any district court, shall be entered upon the records and shall be enforceable as other judgments.

(June 25, 1948, c. 646, 62 Stat. 977; July 28, 1953, c. 253, § 10, 67 Stat. 227; Sept. 3, 1954, c. 1263, § 47(a), 68 Stat. 1243; Apr. 2, 1982, Pub.L. 97–164, Title I, § 139(g), 96 Stat. 42; Oct. 29, 1992, Pub.L. 102–572, Title IX, § 902(a)(1), 106 Stat. 4516.)

HISTORICAL AND STATUTORY NOTES

Effective Dates

1992 Acts. Amendment by Title IX of Pub.L. 102–572 effective Oct. 29, 1992, see section 911 of Pub.L. 102–572, set out as a note under section 171 of Title 28, Judiciary and Judicial Procedure.

1982 Acts. Amendment by Pub.L. 97–164 effective Oct. 1, 1982, see section 402 of Pub.L. 97–164, set out as a note under section 171 of this title.

§ 2509. Congressional reference cases

(a) Whenever a bill, except a bill for a pension, is referred by either House of Congress to the chief judge of the United States Court of Federal Claims pursuant to section 1492 of this title, the chief judge shall designate a judge as hearing officer for the case and a panel of three judges of the court to serve as a reviewing body. One member of the review panel shall be designated as presiding officer of the panel.

(b) Proceedings in a congressional reference case shall be under rules and regulations prescribed for the purpose by the chief judge who is hereby authorized and directed to require the application of the pertinent rules of practice of the Court of Federal Claims insofar as feasible. Each hearing officer and each review panel shall have authority to do and perform any acts which may be necessary or proper for the efficient performance of their duties, including the power of subpena and the power to administer oaths and affirmations. None of the rules, rulings, findings, or conclusions authorized by this section shall be subject to judicial review.

(c) The hearing officer to whom a congressional reference case is assigned by the chief judge shall proceed in accordance with the applicable rules to determine the facts, including facts relating to delay or laches, facts bearing upon the question whether the bar of any statute of limitation should be removed, or facts claimed to excuse the claimant for not having resorted to any established legal remedy. He shall append to his findings of fact conclusions sufficient to inform Congress whether the demand is a legal or equitable claim or a gratuity, and the amount, if any, legally or equitably due from the United States to the claimant.

(d) The findings and conclusions of the hearing officer shall be submitted by him, together with the record in the case, to the review panel for review by it pursuant to such rules as may be provided for the purpose, which shall include provision for submitting the report of the hearing officer to the parties for consideration, exception, and argument before the panel. The panel, by majority vote, shall adopt or modify the findings or the conclusions of the hearing officer.

(e) The panel shall submit its report to the chief judge for transmission to the appropriate House of Congress.

(f) Any act or failure to act or other conduct by a party, a witness, or an attorney which would call for the imposition of sanctions under the rules of practice of the Court of Federal Claims shall be noted by the panel or the hearing officer at the time of occurrence thereof and upon failure of the delinquent or offending party, witness, or attorney to make prompt compliance with the order of the panel or the hearing officer a full statement of the circumstances shall be incorporated in the report of the panel.

(g) The Court of Federal Claims is hereby authorized and directed, under such regulations as it may prescribe, to provide the facilities and services of the office of the clerk of the court for the filing, processing, hearing, and dispatch of congressional reference cases and to include within its annual appropriations the costs thereof and other costs of administration, including (but without limitation to the items herein listed) the salaries and traveling expenses of the judges serving as hearing officers and panel members, mailing and service of process, necessary physical facilities, equipment, and supplies, and personnel (including secretaries and law clerks).

(June 25, 1948, c. 646, 62 Stat. 977; Oct. 15, 1966, Pub.L. 89–681, § 2, 80 Stat. 958; Apr. 2, 1982, Pub.L. 97–164, Title I, § 139(h), 96 Stat. 42; Oct. 29, 1992, Pub.L. 102–572, Title IX, § 902(a), 106 Stat. 4516.)

HISTORICAL AND STATUTORY NOTES

Effective Dates

1992 Acts. Amendment by Title IX of Pub.L. 102–572 effective Oct. 29, 1992, see section 911 of Pub.L. 102–572, set out as a note under section 171 of Title 28, Judiciary and Judicial Procedure.

1982 Acts. Amendment by Pub.L. 97–164 effective Oct. 1, 1982, see section 402 of Pub.L. 97–164, set out as a note under section 171 of this title.

§ 2510. Referral of cases by Comptroller General

(a) The Comptroller General may transmit to the United States Court of Federal Claims for trial and adjudication any claim or matter of which the Court of Federal Claims might take jurisdiction on the voluntary action of the claimant, together with all vouchers, papers, documents, and proofs pertaining thereto.

(b) The Court of Federal Claims shall proceed with the claims or matters so referred as in other cases pending in such Court and shall render judgment thereon.

(June 25, 1948, c. 646, 62 Stat. 977; July 28, 1953, c. 253, § 11, 67 Stat. 227; Sept. 3, 1954, c. 1263, § 47(b), 68 Stat. 1243; Nov. 1, 1978, Pub.L. 95–563, § 14(h)(1), (2)(A), 92 Stat. 2390; Apr. 2, 1982, Pub.L. 97–164, Title I, § 139(i)(1), 96 Stat. 43; Oct. 29, 1992, Pub.L. 102–572, Title IX, § 902(a), 106 Stat. 4516.)

HISTORICAL AND STATUTORY NOTES

Effective Dates

1992 Acts. Amendment by Title IX of Pub.L. 102–572 effective Oct. 29, 1992, see section 911 of Pub.L. 102–572, set out as a note under section 171 of Title 28, Judiciary and Judicial Procedure.

1982 Acts. Amendment by Pub.L. 97–164 effective Oct. 1, 1982, see section 402 of Pub.L. 97–164, set out as a note under section 171 of this title.

1978 Acts. Amendment by Pub.L. 95–563 effective with respect to contracts entered into 120 days after Nov. 1, 1978, and, at the election of the contractor, with respect to any claim pending at such time before the contracting officer or initiated thereafter, see section 16 of Pub.L. 95–563, set out as a note under section 601 of Title 41, Public Contracts.

§ 2511. Accounts of officers, agents or contractors

Notice of suit under section 1494 of this title shall be given to the Attorney General, to the Comptroller General, and to the head of the department requested to settle the account in question.

The judgment of the United States Court of Federal Claims in such suit shall be conclusive upon the parties, and payment of the amount found due shall discharge the obligation.

The transcript of such judgment, filed in the clerk's office of any district court, shall be entered upon the records, and shall be enforceable as other judgments.

(June 25, 1948, c. 646, 62 Stat. 977; July 28, 1953, c. 253, § 12, 67 Stat. 227; Apr. 2, 1982, Pub.L. 97–164, Title I, § 139(j), 96 Stat. 43; Oct. 29, 1992, Pub.L. 102–572, Title IX, § 902(a)(1), 106 Stat. 4516.)

HISTORICAL AND STATUTORY NOTES

Effective Dates

1992 Acts. Amendment by Title IX of Pub. L. 102–572 effective Oct. 29, 1992, see section 911 of Pub.L. 102–572, set out as a note under section 171 of Title 28, Judiciary and Judicial Procedure.

1982 Acts. Amendment by Pub.L. 97–164 effective Oct. 1, 1982, see section 402 of Pub.L. 97–164, set out as a note under section 171 of this title.

§ 2512. Disbursing officers; relief

Whenever the United States Court of Federal Claims finds that any loss by a disbursing officer of the United States was without his fault or negligence, it shall render a judgment setting forth the amount thereof, and the General Accounting Office shall allow the officer such amount as a credit in the settlement of his accounts.

(June 25, 1948, c. 646, 62 Stat. 978; Apr. 2, 1982, Pub.L. 97–164, Title I, § 139(j)(2), 96 Stat. 43; Oct. 29, 1992, Pub.L. 102–572, Title IX, § 902(a)(1), 106 Stat. 4516.)

HISTORICAL AND STATUTORY NOTES

Effective Dates

1992 Acts. Amendment by Title IX of Pub.L. 102–572 effective Oct. 29, 1992, see section 911 of Pub.L. 102–572, set out as a note under section 171 of Title 28, Judiciary and Judicial Procedure.

1982 Acts. Amendment by Pub.L. 97–164 effective Oct. 1, 1982, see section 402 of Pub.L. 97–164, set out as a note under section 171 of this title.

§ 2513. Unjust conviction and imprisonment

(a) Any person suing under section 1495 of this title must allege and prove that:

(1) His conviction has been reversed or set aside on the ground that he is not guilty of the offense of which he was convicted, or on new trial or rehearing he was found not guilty of such offense, as appears from the record or certificate of the court setting aside or reversing such conviction, or that he has been pardoned upon the stated ground of innocence and unjust conviction and

(2) He did not commit any of the acts charged or his acts, deeds, or omissions in connection with such charge constituted no offense against the United States, or any State, Territory or the District of Columbia, and he did not by misconduct or neglect cause or bring about his own prosecution.

(b) Proof of the requisite facts shall be by a certificate of the court or pardon wherein such facts are alleged to appear, and other evidence thereof shall not be received.

(c) No pardon or certified copy of a pardon shall be considered by the United States Court of Federal Claims unless it contains recitals that the pardon was granted after applicant had exhausted all recourse to the courts and that the time for any court to exercise its jurisdiction had expired.

(d) The Court may permit the plaintiff to prosecute such action in forma pauperis.

(e) The amount of damages awarded shall not exceed the sum of $5,000.

(June 25, 1948, c. 646, 62 Stat. 978; Sept. 3, 1954, c. 1263, § 56, 68 Stat. 1247; Apr. 2, 1982, Pub.L. 97–164, Title I, § 139(j)(2), 96 Stat. 43; Oct. 29, 1992, Pub.L. 102–572, Title IX, § 902(a)(1), 106 Stat. 4516.)

HISTORICAL AND STATUTORY NOTES

Effective Dates

1992 Acts. Amendment by Title IX of Pub.L. 102–572 effective Oct. 29, 1992, see section 911 of Pub.L. 102–572, set out as a note under section 171 of Title 28, Judiciary and Judicial Procedure.

1982 Acts. Amendment by Pub.L. 97–164 effective Oct. 1, 1982, see section 402 of Pub.L. 97–164, set out as a note under section 171 of this title.

§ 2514. Forfeiture of fraudulent claims

A claim against the United States shall be forfeited to the United States by any person who corruptly practices or attempts to practice any fraud against the United States in the proof, statement, establishment, or allowance thereof.

In such cases the United States Court of Federal Claims shall specifically find such fraud or attempt and render judgment of forfeiture.

(June 25, 1948, c. 646, 62 Stat. 978; Apr. 2, 1982, Pub.L. 97–164, Title I, § 139(j)(2), 96 Stat. 43; Oct. 29, 1992, Pub.L. 102–572, Title IX, § 902(a)(1), 106 Stat. 4516.)

HISTORICAL AND STATUTORY NOTES

Effective Dates

1992 Acts. Amendment by Title IX of Pub.L. 102–572 effective Oct. 29, 1992, see section 911 of Pub.L. 102–572, set out as a note under section 171 of Title 28, Judiciary and Judicial Procedure.

1982 Acts. Amendment by Pub.L. 97–164 effective Oct. 1, 1982, see section 402 of Pub.L. 97–164, set out as a note under section 171 of this title.

§ 2515. New trial; stay of judgment

(a) The United States Court of Federal Claims may grant a plaintiff a new trial on any ground established by rules of common law or equity applicable as between private parties.

(b) Such court, at any time while any suit is pending before it, or after proceedings for review have been instituted, or within two years after the final disposition of the suit, may grant the United States a new trial and stay the payment of any judgment upon satisfactory evidence, cumulative or otherwise, that any fraud, wrong, or injustice has been done the United States.

(June 25, 1948, c. 646, 62 Stat. 978; Apr. 2, 1982, Pub.L. 97–164, Title I, § 139(j)(2), 96 Stat. 43; Oct. 29, 1992, Pub.L. 102–572, Title IX, § 902(a)(1), 106 Stat. 4516.)

HISTORICAL AND STATUTORY NOTES

Effective Dates

1992 Acts. Amendment by Title IX of Pub.L. 102–572 effective Oct. 29, 1992, see section 911 of Pub.L. 102–572, set out as a note under section 171 of Title 28, Judiciary and Judicial Procedure.

1982 Acts. Amendment by Pub.L. 97–164 effective Oct. 1, 1982, see section 402 of Pub.L. 97–164, set out as a note under section 171 of this title.

§ 2516. Interest on claims and judgments

(a) Interest on a claim against the United States shall be allowed in a judgment of the United States Court of Federal Claims only under a contract or Act of Congress expressly providing for payment thereof.

(b) Interest on a judgment against the United States affirmed by the Supreme Court after review on petition of the United States is paid at a rate equal to the coupon issue yield equivalent (as determined by the Secretary of the Treasury) of the average accepted auction price for the last auction of fifty-two week United States Treasury bills settled immediately before the date of the judgment.

(June 25, 1948, c. 646, 62 Stat. 978; Sept. 3, 1954, c. 1263, § 57, 68 Stat. 1248; Apr. 2, 1982, Pub.L. 97–164, Title I, § 139(j)(2), Title III, § 302(d), 96 Stat. 43, 56; Sept. 13, 1982, Pub.L. 97–258, § 2(g)(5), (m)(3), 96 Stat. 1061, 1062; Oct. 29, 1992, Pub.L. 102–572, Title IX, § 902(a)(1), 106 Stat. 4516.)

HISTORICAL AND STATUTORY NOTES

Effective Dates

1992 Acts. Amendment by Title IX of Pub.L. 102–572 effective Oct. 29, 1992, see section 911 of Pub.L. 102–572, set out as a note under section 171 of Title 28, Judiciary and Judicial Procedure.

1982 Acts. Section 2(g)(5) of Pub.L. 97–258 provided in part that the amendment made to subsec. (b) would become effective on Oct. 1, 1982.

Amendment by Pub.L. 97–164 effective Oct. 1, 1982, see section 402 of Pub.L. 97–164, set out as a note under section 171 of this title.

Repeals

Section 302(d) of Pub.L. 97–164, set out in the credit of this section, was repealed by Pub.L. 97–258, § 2(m)(3), Sept. 13, 1982, 96 Stat. 1062, effective Oct. 1, 1982.

§ 2517. Payment of judgments

(a) Except as provided by the Contract Disputes Act of 1978, every final judgment rendered by the United States Court of Federal Claims against the United States shall be paid out of any general appropriation therefor, on presentation to the Secretary of the Treasury of a certification of the judgment by the clerk and chief judge of the court.

(b) Payment of any such judgment and of interest thereon shall be a full discharge to the United States of all claims and demands arising out of the matters involved in the case or controversy, unless the judgment is designated a partial judgment, in which event only the matters described therein shall be discharged.

(June 25, 1948, c. 646, 62 Stat. 979; Nov. 1, 1978, Pub.L. 95–563, § 14(e), (f), 92 Stat. 2390; Apr. 2, 1982, Pub.L. 97–164, Title I, § 139(k), 96 Stat. 43; Oct. 29, 1992, Pub.L. 102–572, Title IX, § 902(a)(1), 106 Stat. 4516; Oct. 19, 1996, Pub.L. 104–316, Title II, § 202(*l*), 110 Stat. 3843.)

HISTORICAL AND STATUTORY NOTES

References in Text

The Contract Disputes Act of 1978, referred to in subsec. (a), is Pub.L. 95–563, Nov. 1, 1978, 92 Stat. 2383, as amended, which is classified principally to chapter 9 (section 601 et seq.) of Title 41, Public Contracts. For complete classification of this Act to the Code, see Short Title note set out under section 601 of Title 41 and Tables.

Effective Dates

1992 Acts. Amendment by Title IX of Pub.L. 102–572 effective Oct. 29, 1992, see section 911 of Pub.L. 102–572, set out as a note under section 171 of Title 28, Judiciary and Judicial Procedure.

1982 Acts. Amendment by Pub.L. 97–164 effective Oct. 1, 1982, see section 402 of Pub.L. 97–164, set out as a note under section 171 of this title.

1978 Acts. Amendment by Pub.L. 95–563 effective with respect to contracts entered into 120 days after Nov. 1, 1978, and, at the election of the contractor, with respect to any claim pending at such time before the contracting officer or initiated thereafter, see section 16 of Pub.L. 95–563, set out as a note under section 601 of Title 41, Public Contracts.

Transfer of Functions

Effective June 30, 1996, the functions of the Comptroller General under this section to be transferred to the Director of the Office of Management and Budget, contingent upon the additional transfer to the Office of Management and Budget of such personnel, budget authority, records, and property of the General Accounting Office relating to such functions as the Comptroller General and the Director jointly determine to be necessary, see section 211 of Pub.L. 104–53, set out as a note under section 501 of Title 31, Money and Finance.

[§ 2518. Repealed. Pub.L. 97–164, Title I, § 139(*l*), Apr. 2, 1982, 96 Stat. 43]

HISTORICAL AND STATUTORY NOTES

Section, Act June 25, 1948, c. 646, 62 Stat. 979, directed the Secretary of the Treasury to certify to Congress for appropriation only such judgments of the Court of Claims as were not to be reviewed or were entered upon the mandate of the Supreme Court.

Effective Date of Repeal

Repeal effective Oct. 1, 1982, see section 402 of Pub.L. 97–164, set out as an Effective Date of 1982 Amendment note under section 171 of this title.

§ 2519. Conclusiveness of judgment

A final judgment of the United States Court of Federal Claims against any plaintiff shall forever bar any further claim, suit, or demand against the United States arising out of the matters involved in the case or controversy.

(June 25, 1948, c. 646, 62 Stat. 979; Apr. 2, 1982, Pub.L. 97–164, Title I, § 139(m), 96 Stat. 43; Oct. 29, 1992, Pub.L. 102–572, Title IX, § 902(a)(1), 106 Stat. 4516.)

HISTORICAL AND STATUTORY NOTES

Effective Dates

1992 Acts. Amendment by Title IX of Pub.L. 102–572 effective Oct. 29, 1992, see section 911 of Pub.L. 102–572, set out as a note under section 171 of Title 28, Judiciary and Judicial Procedure.

1982 Acts. Amendment by Pub.L. 97–164 effective Oct. 1, 1982, see section 402 of Pub.L. 97–164, set out as a note under section 171 of this title.

§ 2520. Fees

The United States Court of Federal Claims shall by rules impose a fee not exceeding $120, for the filing of any petition.

(June 25, 1948, c. 646, 62 Stat. 979; Sept. 3, 1954, c. 1263, § 58, 68 Stat. 1248; July 18, 1966, Pub.L. 89–507, § 2, 80 Stat. 308; Apr. 2, 1982, Pub.L. 97–164, Title I, § 139(n)(1)–(3), 96 Stat. 43, 44; Nov. 19, 1988, Pub.L. 100–702, Title X, § 1012(a)(1), 102 Stat. 4668; Oct. 29, 1992, Pub.L. 102–572, Title IX, § 902(a)(1), 106 Stat. 4516.)

HISTORICAL AND STATUTORY NOTES

Effective Dates

1992 Acts. Amendment by Title IX of Pub.L. 102–572 effective Oct. 29, 1992, see section 911 of Pub.L. 102–572, set out as a note under section 171 of Title 28, Judiciary and Judicial Procedure.

1988 Acts. Section 1012(a)(2) of Title X of Pub.L. 100–702 provided that: "The amendment made by this subsection [amending this section] shall take effect 30 days after the date of enactment of this title [Nov. 19, 1988]."

1982 Acts. Amendment by Pub.L. 97–164 effective Oct. 1, 1982, see section 402 of Pub.L. 97–164, set out as a note under section 171 of this title.

1966 Acts. Repeal of subsec. (d) of this section by Pub.L. 89–507 applicable only to judgments entered in actions filed subsequent to July 18, 1966, and such repeal not to authorize the reopening or modification of judgments entered prior to July 18, 1966, see section 3 of Pub.L. 89–507, set out as a note under section 2412 of this title.

§ 2521. Subpoenas and incidental powers

(a) Subpoenas requiring the attendance of parties or witnesses and subpoenas requiring the production of books, papers, documents or tangible things by any party or witness having custody or control thereof, may be issued for purposes of discovery or for use of the things produced as evidence in accordance with the rules and orders of the court. Such subpoenas shall be issued and served and compliance therewith shall be compelled as provided in the rules and orders of the court.

(b) The United States Court of Federal Claims shall have power to punish by fine or imprisonment, at its discretion, such contempt of its authority as—

(1) misbehavior of any person in its presence or so near thereto as to obstruct the administration of justice;

(2) misbehavior of any of its officers in their official transactions; or

(3) disobedience or resistance to its lawful writ, process, order, rule, decree, or command.

(c) The United States Court of Federal Claims shall have such assistance in the carrying out of its lawful writ, process, order, rule, decree, or command as is available to a court of the United States. The United States marshal for any district in which the Court of Federal Claims is sitting shall, when requested by the chief judge of the Court of Federal Claims, attend any session of the Court of Federal Claims in such district.

(Added Sept. 3, 1954, c. 1263, § 59(a), 68 Stat. 1248, and amended Oct. 29, 1992, Pub.L. 102–572, Title IX, § 910(a), 106 Stat. 4519.)

HISTORICAL AND STATUTORY NOTES

Effective Dates

1992 Acts. Amendment by Title IX of Pub.L. 102–572 effective Oct. 29, 1992, see section 911 of Pub.L. 102–572, set out as a note under section 171 of Title 28, Judiciary and Judicial Procedure.

§ 2522. Notice of appeal

Review of a decision of the United States Court of Federal Claims shall be obtained by filing a notice of appeal with the clerk of the Court of Federal Claims within the time and in the manner prescribed for appeals to United States courts of appeals from the United States district courts.

(Added Pub.L. 97–164, Title I, § 139(q)(1), Apr. 2, 1982, 96 Stat. 44, and amended Pub.L. 102–572, Title IX, § 902(a), Oct. 29, 1992, 106 Stat. 4516.)

HISTORICAL AND STATUTORY NOTES

Effective Dates

1992 Acts. Amendment by Title IX of Pub.L. 102–572 effective Oct. 29, 1992, see section 911 of Pub.L. 102–572, set out as a note under section 171 of Title 28, Judiciary and Judicial Procedure.

1982 Acts. Section effective Oct. 1, 1982, see section 402 of Pub.L. 97–164, set out as a note under section 171 of this title.

[CHAPTER 167—REPEALED]

[§§ 2601 to 2604. Repealed. Pub.L. 97–164, Title I, § 140, Apr. 2, 1982, 96 Stat. 44]

HISTORICAL AND STATUTORY NOTES

Section 2601, Acts June 25, 1948, c. 646, 62 Stat. 979; June 2, 1970, Pub.L. 91–271, Title I, § 103, 84 Stat. 275; Oct. 10, 1980, Pub.L. 96–417, Title IV, § 403(a)–(d), Title V, § 501(27), (28), 94 Stat. 1740–1742, provided for appeals to the Court of Customs and Patent Appeals from final judgments or orders of the Court of International Trade and for the procedures to be followed in such appeals. See section 1295(a)(5) of this title.

Section 2602, Acts June 25, 1948, c. 646, 62 Stat. 980; Oct. 14, 1966, Pub.L. 89–651, § 8(c)(3), 80 Stat. 902; June 2, 1970, Pub.L. 91–271, Title I, § 104, 84 Stat. 276; Oct. 10, 1980, Pub.L. 96–417, Title IV, § 403(e)(1), 94 Stat. 1741, provided for the precedence of enumerated civil cases in the Court of Customs and Patent Appeals. See note set out under former section 1296 of this title.

Section 2603, added Pub.L. 96–417, Title IV, § 404(a), Oct. 10, 1980, 94 Stat. 1741, provided that, except as provided in section 2639 or 2641(b) of this title or in the rules prescribed by the court, the Federal Rules of Evidence would apply in the Court of Customs and Patent Appeals in any appeal from the Court of International Trade.

Section 2604, added Pub.L. 96–417, Title IV, § 405(a), Oct. 10, 1980, 94 Stat. 1741, authorized the chief judge of the Court of Customs and Patent Appeals to summon annually the judges of the court to a judicial conference for the purpose of considering the business of the court and improvements in the administration of justice of the court.

Effective Date of Repeal

Repeal effective Oct. 1, 1982, see section 402 of Pub.L. 97–164, set out as a note under section 171 of this title.

CHAPTER 169—COURT OF INTERNATIONAL TRADE PROCEDURE

Sec.
2631. Persons entitled to commence a civil action.
2632. Commencement of a civil action.
2633. Procedure and fees.
2634. Notice.
2635. Filing of official documents.
2636. Time for commencement of action.
2637. Exhaustion of administrative remedies.
2638. New grounds in support of a civil action.
2639. Burden of proof; evidence of value.
2640. Scope and standard of review.
2641. Witnesses; inspection of documents.
2642. Analysis of imported merchandise.
2643. Relief.
2644. Interest.
2645. Decisions.
2646. Retrial or rehearing.
[2647. Repealed.]

§ 2631. Persons entitled to commence a civil action

(a) A civil action contesting the denial of a protest, in whole or in part, under section 515 of the Tariff Act of 1930 may be commenced in the Court of International Trade by the person who filed the protest pursuant to section 514 of such Act, or by a surety on the transaction which is the subject of the protest.

(b) A civil action contesting the denial of a petition under section 516 of the Tariff Act of 1930 may be commenced in the Court of International Trade by the person who filed such petition.

(c) A civil action contesting a determination listed in section 516A of the Tariff Act of 1930 may be commenced in the Court of International Trade by any interested party who was a party to the proceeding in connection with which the matter arose.

(d)(1) A civil action to review any final determination of the Secretary of Labor under section 223 of the Trade Act of 1974 with respect to the eligibility of workers for adjustment assistance under such Act may be commenced in the Court of International Trade by a worker, group of workers, certified or recognized union, or authorized representative of such worker or group that applies for assistance under such Act and is aggrieved by such final determination.

(2) A civil action to review any final determination of the Secretary of Commerce under section 251 of the Trade Act of 1974 with respect to the eligibility of a firm for adjustment assistance under such Act may be commenced in the Court of International Trade by a firm or its representative that applies for assistance under such Act and is aggrieved by such final determination, or by any other interested domestic party that is aggrieved by such final determination.

(3) A civil action to review any final determination of the Secretary of Commerce under section 271 of the Trade Act of 1974 with respect to the eligibility of a community for adjustment assistance under such Act may be commenced in the Court of International Trade by a community that applies for assistance under such Act and is aggrieved by such final determination, or by any other interested domestic party that is aggrieved by such final determination.

(e) A civil action to review a final determination made under section 305(b)(1) of the Trade Agreements Act of 1979 may be commenced in the Court of International Trade by any person who was a party-at-interest with respect to such determination.

(f) A civil action involving an application for the issuance of an order directing the administering authority or the International Trade Commission to make confidential information available under section 777(c)(2) of the Tariff Act of 1930 may be commenced in the Court of International Trade by any interested party whose application for disclosure of such confidential information was denied under section 777(c)(1) of such Act.

(g)(1) A civil action to review any decision of the Secretary of the Treasury to deny a customs broker's license under section 641(b)(2) or (3) of the Tariff Act of 1930, or to deny a customs broker's permit under section 641(c)(1) of such Act, or to revoke such license or permit under section 641(b)(5) or (c)(2) of such Act, may be commenced in the Court of International Trade by the person whose license or permit was denied or revoked.

(2) A civil action to review any decision of the Secretary of the Treasury to revoke or suspend a customs broker's license or permit or impose a monetary penalty in lieu thereof under section 641(d)(2)(B) of the Tariff Act of 1930 may be commenced in the Court of International Trade by the person against whom the decision was issued.

(3) A civil action to review any decision or order of the Customs Service to deny, suspend, or revoke accreditation of a private laboratory under section 499(b) of the Tariff Act of 1930 may be commenced in the Court of International Trade by the person whose accreditation was denied, suspended, or revoked.

(h) A civil action described in section 1581(h) of this title may be commenced in the Court of International Trade by the person who would have standing to bring a civil action under section 1581(a) of this title if he imported the goods involved and filed a protest which was denied, in whole or in part, under section 515 of the Tariff Act of 1930.

(i) Any civil action of which the Court of International Trade has jurisdiction, other than an action specified in subsections (a)–(h) of this section, may be commenced in the court by any person adversely affected or aggrieved by agency action within the meaning of section 702 of title 5.

(j)(1) Any person who would be adversely affected or aggrieved by a decision in a civil action pending in the Court of International Trade may, by leave of court, intervene in such action, except that—

(A) no person may intervene in a civil action under section 515 or 516 of the Tariff Act of 1930;

(B) in a civil action under section 516A of the Tariff Act of 1930, only an interested party who was a party to the proceeding in connection with which the matter arose may intervene, and such person may intervene as a matter of right; and

(C) in a civil action under section 777(c)(2) of the Tariff Act of 1930, only a person who was a party to the investigation may intervene, and such person may intervene as a matter of right.

(2) In those civil actions in which intervention is by leave of court, the Court of International Trade shall consider whether the intervention will unduly delay or prejudice the adjudication of the rights of the original parties.

(k) In this section—

(1) "interested party" has the meaning given such term in section 771(9) of the Tariff Act of 1930; and

(2) "party-at-interest" means—

(A) a foreign manufacturer, producer, or exporter, or a United States importer, of merchandise which is the subject of a final determination under section 305(b)(1) of the Trade Agreements Act of 1979;

(B) a manufacturer, producer, or wholesaler in the United States of a like product;

(C) United States members of a labor organization or other association of workers whose members are employed in the manufacture, production, or wholesale in the United States of a like product;

(D) a trade or business association a majority of whose members manufacture, produce, or wholesale a like product in the United States,[1] and

(E) an association composed of members who represent parties-at-interest described in subparagraph (B), (C), or (D).

(Added Pub.L. 96–417, Title III, § 301, Oct. 10, 1980, 94 Stat. 1730, and amended Pub.L. 98–573, Title II, § 212(b)(3), Title VI, § 612(b)(3), Oct. 30, 1984, 98 Stat. 2983, 3034; Pub.L. 103–182, Title VI, § 684(a)(2), Dec. 8, 1993, 107 Stat. 2219.)

[1] So in original. The comma probably should be a semicolon.

HISTORICAL AND STATUTORY NOTES

References in Text

Sections 514, 515, 516, and 516A of the Tariff Act of 1930, referred to in subsecs. (a) and/or (b), (c), (h), and (j)(1)(A), (B), are classified to sections 1514, 1515, 1516, and 1516a of Title 19, Customs Duties.

The Trade Act of 1974, referred to in subsec. (d)(1) to (3), is Pub.L. 93–618, Jan. 3, 1975, 88 Stat. 1978, as amended, which is classified principally to chapter 12 (section 2101 et seq.) of Title 19. Sections 223, 251, and 271 of the Trade Act of 1974 are classified to sections 2273, 2341, and 2371, respectively, of Title 19. For complete classification of this Act to the Code, see References in Text note set out under section 2101 of Title 19 and Tables.

Section 305(b)(1) of the Trade Agreements Act of 1979, referred to in subsecs. (e) and (k)(2)(A), is classified to section 2515(b)(1) of Title 19.

Section 777 of the Tariff Act of 1930, referred to in subsecs. (f) and (j)(1)(C), is classified to section 1677f of Title 19.

Section 641 of the Tariff Act of 1930, referred to in subsec. (g)(1), (2), is classified to section 1641 of Title 19.

Section 499(b) of the Tariff Act of 1930, referred to in subsec. (g)(3), is classified to section 1499(b) of Title 19, Customs Duties.

Section 771(9) of the Tariff Act of 1930, referred to in subsec. (k)(1), is classified to section 1677(9) of Title 19.

Effective Dates

1993 Acts. Amendment by section 684(a)(2) of Pub.L. 103–182 effective Dec. 8, 1993, see section 692 of Pub.L. 103–182, set out as a note under section 58c of Title 19, Customs Duties.

1984 Acts. Amendment by section 212(b)(3) of Pub.L. 98–573 to take effect on the close of the 180th day after Oct. 30, 1984, see section 214(d) of Pub.L. 98–573, set out as a note under section 1304 of Title 19, Customs Duties.

Amendment by section 612(b)(3) of Pub.L. 98–573 applicable with respect to investigations initiated by petition or by the administering authority under subtitle A or B of Title VII of the Tariff Act of 1930 (19 U.S.C. 1671 et seq., 1673 et seq.), and to reviews begun under section 751 of that Act (19 U.S.C. 1675), on or after Oct. 30, 1984, see section 626(b)(1) of Pub.L. 98–573, as amended, set out as a note under section 1671 of Title 19.

1980 Acts. Subsecs. (d) and (g) to (j) of this section applicable with respect to civil actions commenced on or after Nov. 1, 1980, see section 701(b)(1)(B) of Pub.L. 96–417, as amended, set out as a note under section 251 of this title.

Remainder of this section effective on Nov. 1, 1980 and applicable with respect to civil actions pending on or commenced or on after such date, see section 701(a) of Pub.L. 96–417, as amended, set out as a note under section 251 of this title.

Prior Provisions

A prior section 2631, Acts June 25, 1948, c. 646, 62 Stat. 980; May 24, 1949, c. 139, § 122, 63 Stat. 106; June 2, 1970, Pub. L. 91–271, Title I, § 112, 84 Stat. 278; Jan. 3, 1975, Pub. L. 93–618, Title III, § 321(f)(2), 88 Stat. 2048, related to time for commencement of action and was omitted from the Code in the general revision of this chapter by Pub. L. 96–417. See section 2636 of this title.

Application of Amendments Relating to Accreditation of Private Laboratories

For purposes of applying amendments relating to accreditation of private laboratories, any decision or order of the Customs Service denying, suspending, or revoking the accreditation of a private laboratory on or after Dec. 8, 1993 and before regulations to implement section 1499(b) of Title 19, Customs Duties, are issued shall be treated as having been denied, suspended, or revoked under such section 1499(b) of Title 19. See section 684(b) of Pub.L. 103–182 set out as a note under section 1581 of this title.

§ 2632. Commencement of a civil action

(a) Except for civil actions specified in subsections (b) and (c) of this section, a civil action in the Court of International Trade shall be commenced by filing concurrently with the clerk of the court a summons and complaint, with the content and in the form, manner, and style prescribed by the rules of the court.

(b) A civil action in the Court of International Trade under section 515 or section 516 of the Tariff Act of 1930 shall be commenced by filing with the clerk of the court a summons, with the content and in the form, manner, and style prescribed by the rules of the court.

(c) A civil action in the Court of International Trade under section 516A of the Tariff Act of 1930 shall be commenced by filing with the clerk of the court a summons or a summons and a complaint, as prescribed in such section, with the content and in the form, manner, and style prescribed by the rules of the court.

(d) The Court of International Trade may prescribe by rule that any summons, pleading, or other paper mailed by registered or certified mail properly addressed to the clerk of the court with the proper postage affixed and return receipt requested shall be deemed filed as of the date of mailing.

(Added Pub.L. 96–417, Title III, § 301, Oct. 10, 1980, 94 Stat. 1732.)

HISTORICAL AND STATUTORY NOTES

References in Text

Sections 515 and 516 of the Tariff Act of 1930, referred to in subsec. (b), are classified to sections 1515 and 1516 of Title 19, Customs Duties.

Section 516A of the Tariff Act of 1930, referred to in subsec. (c), is classified to section 1516a of Title 19.

Effective Dates

1980 Acts. Subsec. (a) of this section applicable with respect to civil actions commenced on or after Nov. 1, 1980, see section 701(b)(1)(B) of Pub.L. 96–417, as amended, set out as a note under section 251 of this title.

Remainder of this section effective on Nov. 1, 1980 and applicable with respect to civil actions pending on or commenced on or after such date, see section 701(a) of Pub.L. 96–417, as amended, set out as a note under section 251 of this title.

Prior Provisions

A prior section 2632, Acts June 25, 1948, c. 646, 62 Stat. 980; June 2, 1970, Pub. L. 91–271, Title I, § 113, 84 Stat. 279; Jan. 3, 1975, Pub. L. 93–618, Title III, § 321(f)(3), 88 Stat. 2048; July 26, 1979, Pub. L. 96–39, Title X, § 1001(b)(4)(C), 93 Stat. 306, related to Customs Court procedure and fees and was omitted from the Code in the general revision of this chapter by Pub. L. 96–417. See section 2633 of this title.

§ 2633. Procedure and fees

(a) A filing fee shall be payable to the clerk of the Court of International Trade upon the commencement of a civil action in such court. The amount of the fee shall be prescribed by the rules of the court, but shall be not less than $5 nor more than the filing fee for commencing a civil action in a district court of the United States. The court may fix all other fees to be charged by the clerk of the court.

(b) The Court of International Trade shall prescribe rules governing the summons, pleadings, and other papers, for their amendment, service, and filing, for consolidations, severances, suspensions of cases, and for other procedural matters.

(c) All summons, pleadings, and other papers filed in the Court of International Trade shall be served on all parties in accordance with rules prescribed by the court. When the United States, its agencies, or its officers are adverse parties, service of the summons shall be made upon the Attorney General and the head of the Government agency whose action is being contested. When injunctive relief is sought, the summons, pleadings, and other papers shall also be served upon the named officials sought to be enjoined.

(Added Pub.L. 96–417, Title III, § 301, Oct. 10, 1980, 94 Stat. 1732.)

HISTORICAL AND STATUTORY NOTES

Effective Dates

1980 Acts. Section effective on Nov. 1, 1980 and applicable with respect to civil actions pending on or commenced on or after such date, see section 701(a) of Pub.L. 96–417, as amended, set out as a note under section 251 of this title.

Prior Provisions

A prior section 2633, Acts June 25, 1948, c. 646, 62 Stat. 980; June 2, 1970, Pub.L. 91–271, Title I, § 114, 84 Stat. 279; July 26, 1979, Pub.L. 96–39, Title X, § 1001(b)(4)(D), 93 Stat. 306, related to precedence of cases and was omitted from the Code in the general revision of this chapter by Pub.L. 96–417. See note set out under former section 2647 of this title.

SCHEDULE OF FEES

(Effective November 1, 1988, as amended January 24, 1994)

As provided by 28 U.S.C. § 2633(a) and the Rules of the United States Court of International Trade, the clerk of the court shall collect the following fees:

Filing Fees—USCIT R. 3(b)

1. For filing an action other than once commenced under 28 U.S.C. § 1581(d)(1) $120.00
2. For filing an action commenced under 28 U.S.C. § 1581(d)(1) 25.00
3. For filing a complaint in an action commenced under 28 U.S.C. §§ 1581(a) or (b) prior to March 1, 1987 .... 25.00

Attorney Admission Fees—USCIT R. 74(b)(3)

For admission of an attorney to practice, including a certificate of admission .... $ 25.00

Additional Fees—USCIT R. 80(g)

The clerk shall collect in advance from the parties fees for miscellaneous services as are consistent with the "Judicial Conference Schedule of Additional Fees for the United States District Courts." The additional fees that are applicable to this court are as follows:

1. For filing or indexing any paper not in a case or proceeding for which a case filing fee has been paid (e.g., filing a petition to perpetuate testimony, the filing of letters rogatory or letters of request, and the registering of a judgment pursuant to 28 U.S.C. § 1963) ..... $ 20.00
2. For every search of the records of the court for each case searched 15.00
3. For certification or exemplification of any

document or paper, whether the certification is made directly on the document or by separate instrument 5.00

4. For reproducing any record or paper, including paper copies made from either original documents; or microfilm reproductions of the original records 50

5. For reproduction of magnetic tape recordings, either cassette or reel-to-reel (including the cost of materials) 15.00

6. For transcribing a record of any proceeding by a regularly employed member of the court staff who is not entitled by statute to retain the transcript fees for his or her own account, a charge shall be made at the same rate and conditions established by the Judicial Conference for transcripts prepared and sold to parties by official court reporters:

	Original	First Copy to Each Party	Each Add'l Copy to the Same Party
Ordinary	$3.00	$ .75	$ .50
Expedited	4.00	.75	.50
Daily	5.00	1.00	.75
Hourly	6.00	1.00	.75

7. For each microfiche sheet of film or microfilm jacket copy of any court record, where available ....$ 3.00

8. For retrieval of a record from a Federal Records Center, National Archives, or other storage location removed from the place of business of the court 25.00

9. For a check paid into the court which is returned for lack of funds 25.00

10. For a duplicate certificate of admission or certificate of good standing 5.00

11. For handling registry fund, a charge shall be assessed from interest earnings and in accordance with the detailed fee schedule issued by the Director of the Administrative Office of the United States Courts 10%

INTRODUCTION

The following guidelines reflect, to the greatest extent possible, (1) the role of the Clerk's Office in providing information to the public about cases in the court, and (2) the limited amount of resources and personnel available in the Clerk's Office. These guidelines attempt to strike a fair balance between these two competing concerns.

Search Fee Guidelines

Guideline No. 1

A search fee will not be charged for a single request for a "retrieval" of basic information, which is defined as a query for any basic information readily retrievable from a docket sheet. A request of this nature is considered a "retrieval" and is not a "search" under the court's Schedule of Fees, unless the request is written and requires a written response.

Basic information is defined as any information which is easily retrievable from a docket sheet. Basic information which may be retrieved without a search fee may include: (1) the name of a party when the case number is provided; (2) the number of a case when the plaintiff or defendant is known; (3) the date a complaint was filed when the case number is provided; (4) the name of a party's attorney when the case number is provided; (5) the status of the case generally when the case number is provided.

The public is encouraged to come to the court to conduct their own searches for information. Within limits, the Clerk's Office will assist those attempting to use docket sheets.

If the request is made by telephone, and does not require a written response, no charge will be imposed if it is a single request and can be answered easily by examining a docket sheet.

Guideline No. 2

With limited exceptions, the $15 search fee shall be charged for all written search requests.

A written request is defined as any search request made in writing which requires a written response. Because of the time and resources which must be expended in order to respond to a written request, such a request shall be considered a search which is subject to the fee, even if the request is for basic information which may be obtained from a docket sheet. The combination of the search and the written response justify the imposition of the fee.

The search fee should be included with the request, and the court will not process a written request until the search fee is received.

Guideline No. 3

A search fee will be charged for any request which requires a physical search of the court's records.

A request for information which is not easily accessible from a docket sheet (i.e., anything other than "basic" information) and which therefore requires a physical search of the court's records will be considered a "search" which is properly chargeable under the court's Schedule of Fees.

Chargeable searches include, but are certainly not limited to, requests for information whether a certain person has ever been a plaintiff or defendant in any case. In this situation, where the search will take considerable time, the fee will be charged even if the requestor does not ask for a certificate of the search.

Guideline No. 4

The clerk has general authority to refuse to conduct searches which are unreasonable or unduly burdensome.

The Clerk's Office has the responsibility of being responsive to parties in interest to cases pending in the court. However, this does not mean that either the public or government agencies has an unfettered right to make unreasonable or unduly burdensome demands upon the resources and personnel of the Clerk;s Office. The clerk may (and should) refuse to conduct searches which would require a disproportionate expenditure of time and/or resources, and should encourage entities making such requests to conduct their own search of court records.

This procedure applies to federal agencies as well. Although search and copying fees are waived for federal agencies, the clerk is not required to accommodate search requests from such agencies which are unduly burdensome or time-consuming. Because of the volume of requests that often comes from federal agencies, the court may invite or encourage federal agencies (or a local representative), to come into the court to conduct their own searches and will allow them to use court copy facilities.

§ 2634. Notice

Reasonable notice of the time and place of trial or hearing before the Court of International Trade shall be given to all parties to any civil action, as prescribed by the rules of the court.

(Added Pub.L. 96–417, Title III, § 301, Oct. 10, 1980, 94 Stat. 1733.)

HISTORICAL AND STATUTORY NOTES

Effective Dates

1980 Acts. Section effective on Nov. 1, 1980 and applicable with respect to civil actions pending on or commenced on or after such date, see section 701(a) of Pub.L. 96–417, as amended, set out as a note under section 251 of this title.

Prior Provisions

A prior section 2634, Acts June 25, 1948, c. 646, 62 Stat. 981; June 2, 1970, Pub.L. 91–271, Title I, § 115, 84 Stat. 280, related to notice and was omitted from the Code in the general revision of this chapter by Pub.L. 96–417.

§ 2635. Filing of official documents

(a) In any action commenced in the Court of International Trade contesting the denial of a protest under section 515 of the Tariff Act of 1930 or the denial of a petition under section 516 of such Act, the Customs Service, as prescribed by the rules of the court, shall file with the clerk of the court, as part of the official record, any document, paper, information or data relating to the entry of merchandise and the administrative determination that is the subject of the protest or petition.

(b)(1) In any civil action commenced in the Court of International Trade under section 516A of the Tariff Act of 1930, within forty days or within such other period of time as the court may specify, after the date of service of a complaint on the administering authority established to administer title VII of the Tariff Act of 1930 or the United States International Trade Commission, the administering authority or the Commission shall transmit to the clerk of the court the record of such action, as prescribed by the rules of the court. The record shall, unless otherwise stipulated by the parties, consist of—

(A) a copy of all information presented to or obtained by the administering authority or the Commission during the course of the administrative proceedings, including all governmental memoranda pertaining to the case and the record of ex parte meetings required to be maintained by section 777(a)(3) of the Tariff Act of 1930; and

(B) (i) a copy of the determination and the facts and conclusions of law upon which such determination was based, (ii) all transcripts or records of conferences or hearings, and (iii) all notices published in the Federal Register.

(2) The administering authority or the Commission shall identify and transmit under seal to the clerk of the court any document, comment, or information that is accorded confidential or privileged status by the Government agency whose action is being contested and that is required to be transmitted to the clerk under paragraph (1) of this subsection. Any such document, comment, or information shall be accompanied by a nonconfidential description of the nature of the material being transmitted. The confidential or privileged status of such material shall be preserved in the civil action, but the court may examine the confidential or privileged material in camera and may make such material available under such terms and conditions as the court may order.

(c) Within fifteen days, or within such other period of time as the Court of International Trade may specify, after service of a summons and complaint in a civil action involving an application for an order directing the administering authority or the International Trade Commission to make confidential information available under section 777(c)(2) of the Tariff Act of 1930, the administering authority or the Commission shall transmit under seal to the clerk of the Court of International Trade, as prescribed by its rules, the confidential information involved, together with pertinent parts of the record. Such information shall be accompanied by a nonconfidential description of the nature of the information being transmitted. The confidential status of such information shall be preserved in the civil action, but the court may examine the confidential information in camera and may make such information available under a protective order consistent with section 777(c)(2) of the Tariff Act of 1930.

(d)(1) In any other civil action in the Court of International Trade in which judicial review is to proceed upon the basis of the record made before an agency, the agency shall, within forty days or within such other period of time as the court may specify, after the date of service of the summons and complaint upon the agency, transmit to the clerk of the court, as prescribed by its rules—

(A) a copy of the contested determination and the findings or report upon which such determination was based;

(B) a copy of any reported hearings or conferences conducted by the agency; and

(C) any documents, comments, or other papers filed by the public, interested parties, or governments with respect to the agency's action.

(2) The agency shall identify and transmit under seal to the clerk of the court any document, comment, or other information that was obtained on a confidential basis and that is required to be transmitted to the clerk under paragraph (1) of this subsection. Any such document, comment, or information shall include a nonconfidential description of the nature of the material being transmitted. The confidential or privileged status of such material shall be preserved in the civil action, but the court may examine such material in camera and may make such material available under such terms and conditions as the court may order.

(3) The parties may stipulate that fewer documents, comments, or other information than those specified in paragraph (1) of this subsection shall be transmitted to the clerk of the court.

(Added Pub.L. 96–417, Title III, § 301, Oct. 10, 1980, 94 Stat. 1733, and amended Pub.L. 103–182, Title VI, § 684(d), Dec. 8, 1993, 107 Stat. 2219.)

HISTORICAL AND STATUTORY NOTES

References in Text

The Tariff Act of 1930, referred to in subsecs. (a), (b)(1), (b)(1)(A), and (c), is Act June 17, 1930, c. 497, 46 Stat. 590, as amended. Title VII of the Tariff Act of 1930 is classified generally to subtitle IV (section 1671 et seq.) of chapter 4 of Title 19, Customs Duties. Sections 515, 516, 516A and 777 of the Tariff Act of 1930 are classified to sections 1515, 1516, 1516a, and 1677f, respectively, of Title 19. For complete classification of this Act to the Code, see section 1654 of Title 19 and Tables.

Effective Dates

1993 Acts. Amendment by section 684(d) of Pub.L. 103–182 effective Dec. 8, 1993, see section 692 of Pub.L. 103–182, set out as a note under section 58c of Title 19, Customs Duties.

1980 Acts. Section applicable with respect to civil actions commenced on or after Nov. 1, 1980, see section 701(b)(1)(B) of Pub.L. 96–417, as amended, set out as a note under section 251 of this title.

Prior Provisions

A prior section 2635, Acts June 25, 1948, c. 646, 62 Stat. 981; June 2, 1970, Pub. L. 91–271, Title I, § 116, 84 Stat. 280, related to burden of proof and evidence of value and was omitted from the Code in the general revision of this chapter by Pub. L. 96–417. See section 2639 of this title.

§ 2636. Time for commencement of action

(a) A civil action contesting the denial, in whole or in part, of a protest under section 515 of the Tariff Act of 1930 is barred unless commenced in accordance with the rules of the Court of International Trade—

(1) within one hundred and eighty days after the date of mailing of notice of denial of a protest under section 515(a) of such Act; or

(2) within one hundred and eighty days after the date of denial of a protest by operation of law under the provisions of section 515(b) of such Act.

(b) A civil action contesting the denial of a petition under section 516 of the Tariff Act of 1930 is barred unless commenced in accordance with the rules of the Court of International Trade within thirty days after the date of mailing of a notice pursuant to section 516(c) of such Act.

(c) A civil action contesting a reviewable determination listed in section 516A of the Tariff Act of 1930 is barred unless commenced in accordance with the rules of the Court of International Trade within the time specified in such section.

(d) A civil action contesting a final determination of the Secretary of Labor under section 223 of the Trade Act of 1974 or a final determination of the Secretary of Commerce under section 251 or section 271 of such Act is barred unless commenced in accordance with the rules of the Court of International Trade within sixty days after the date of notice of such determination.

(e) A civil action contesting a final determination made under section 305(b)(1) of the Trade Agreements Act of 1979 is barred unless commenced in accordance with the rules of the Court of International Trade within thirty days after the date of the publication of such determination in the Federal Register.

(f) A civil action involving an application for the issuance of an order making confidential information available under section 777(c)(2) of the Tariff Act of 1930 is barred unless commenced in accordance with the rules of the Court of International Trade within ten days after the date of the denial of the request for such confidential information.

(g) A civil action contesting the denial or revocation by the Secretary of the Treasury of a customs broker's license or permit under subsection (b) or (c) of section 641 of the Tariff Act of 1930, or the revocation or suspension of such license or permit or the imposition of a monetary penalty in lieu thereof by such Secretary under section 641(d) of such Act, is barred unless commenced in accordance with the rules of the Court of International Trade within sixty days after the date of the entry of the decision or order of such Secretary.

(h) A civil action contesting the denial, suspension, or revocation by the Customs Service of a private laboratory's accreditation under section 499(b) of the Tariff Act of 1930 is barred unless commenced in accordance with the rules of the Court of International Trade within 60 days after the date of the decision or order of the Customs Service.

(i) A civil action of which the Court of International Trade has jurisdiction under section 1581 of this title, other than an action specified in subsections (a)–(h) of this section, is barred unless commenced in accordance with the rules of the court within two years after the cause of action first accrues.

(Added Pub.L. 96–417, Title III, § 301, Oct. 10, 1980, 94 Stat. 1734, and amended Pub.L. 98–573, Title II, § 212(b)(4), Title VI, § 623(b)(1), Oct. 30, 1984, 98 Stat. 2984, 3041; Pub.L. 103–182, Title VI, § 684(a)(3), Dec. 8, 1993, 107 Stat. 2219.)

HISTORICAL AND STATUTORY NOTES

References in Text

Section 515 of the Tariff Act of 1930, referred to in subsec. (a), is is classified to section 1515 of Title 19, Customs Duties.

Section 516 of the Tariff Act of 1930, referred to in subsec. (b), is classified to section 1516 of Title 19.

Section 516A of the Tariff Act of 1930, referred to in subsec. (c), is classified to section 1516a of Title 19.

Sections 223, 251, and 271 of the Trade Act of 1974, referred to in subsec. (d), are classified to sections 2273, 2341, and 2371 of Title 19.

Section 305(b)(1) of the Trade Agreements Act of 1979, referred to in subsec. (e), is classified to section 2515(b)(1) of Title 19.

Section 777(c)(2) of the Tariff Act of 1930, referred to in subsec. (f), is classified to section 1677f(c)(2) of Title 19.

Section 641 of the Tariff Act of 1930, referred to in subsec. (g), is classified to section 1641 of Title 19.

Section 499(b) of the Tariff Act of 1930, referred to in subsec. (h), is classified to section 1499(b) of Title 19, Customs Duties.

Effective Dates

1993 Acts. Amendment by section 684(a)(3) of Pub.L. 103–182 effective Dec. 8, 1993, see section 692 of Pub.L. 103–182, set out as a note under section 58c of Title 19, Customs Duties.

1984 Acts. Amendment by section 212(b)(4) of Pub.L. 98–573 to take effect on the close of the 180th day after Oct. 30, 1984, see section 214(d) of Pub.L. 98–573, set out as a note under section 1304 of Title 19, Customs Duties.

Amendment by section 623(b)(1) of Pub.L. 98–573 applicable with respect to civil actions pending on, or filed on or after, Oct. 30, 1984, see section 626(b)(2) of Pub.L. 98–573, as amended, set out as a note under section 1671 of Title 19.

1980 Acts. Section applicable with respect to civil actions commenced on or after Nov. 1, 1980, see section 701(b)(1)(B) of Pub.L. 96–417, as amended, set out as a note under section 251 of this title.

Prior Provisions

A prior section 2636, Acts June 25, 1948, c. 646, 62 Stat. 981; June 2, 1970, Pub.L. 91–271, Title I, § 117, 84 Stat. 280, related to analysis of imported merchandise and was omitted from the Code in the general revision of this chapter by Pub.L. 96–417. See section 2642 of this title.

Application of Amendments Relating to Accreditation of Private Laboratories

For purposes of applying amendments relating to accreditation of private laboratories, any decision or order of the Customs Service denying, suspending, or revoking the accreditation of a private laboratory on or after Dec. 8, 1993 and before regulations to implement section 1499(b) of Title 19, Customs Duties, are issued shall be treated as having been denied, suspended, or revoked under such section 1499(b) of Title 19. See section 684(b) of Pub.L. 103–182 set out as a note under section 1581 of this title.

§ 2637. Exhaustion of administrative remedies

(a) A civil action contesting the denial of a protest under section 515 of the Tariff Act of 1930 may be commenced in the Court of International Trade only if all liquidated duties, charges, or exactions have been paid at the time the action is commenced, except that a surety's obligation to pay such liquidated duties, charges, or exactions is limited to the sum of any bond related to each entry included in the denied protest.

(b) A civil action contesting the denial of a petition under section 516 of the Tariff Act of 1930 may be commenced in the Court of International Trade only by a person who has first exhausted the procedures set forth in such section.

(c) A civil action described in section 1581(h) of this title may be commenced in the Court of International Trade prior to the exhaustion of administrative remedies if the person commencing the action makes the demonstration required by such section.

(d) In any civil action not specified in this section, the Court of International Trade shall, where appropriate, require the exhaustion of administrative remedies.

(Added Pub.L. 96–417, Title III, § 301, Oct. 10, 1980, 94 Stat. 1735.)

HISTORICAL AND STATUTORY NOTES

References in Text

Sections 515 and 516 of the Tariff Act of 1930, referred to in subsecs. (a) and (b), respectively, are classified to sections 1515 and 1516, respectively, of Title 19, Customs Duties.

Effective Dates

1980 Acts. Subsec. (c) of this section applicable with respect to civil actions commenced on or after Nov. 1, 1980, see section 701(b)(1)(B) of Pub.L. 96–417, as amended, set out as a note under section 251 of this title.

Remainder of this section effective on Nov. 1, 1980 and applicable with respect to civil actions pending on or commenced on or after such date, see section 701(a) of Pub.L. 96–417, as amended, set out as a note under section 251 of this title.

Prior Provisions

A prior section 2637, Acts June 25, 1948, c. 646, 62 Stat. 982; June 2, 1970, Pub.L. 91–271, Title I, § 118, 84 Stat. 280; July 26, 1979, Pub.L. 96–39, Title X, § 1001(b)(4)(E), 93 Stat. 306, related to witnesses and inspection of documents and was omitted from the Code in the general revision of this chapter by Pub.L. 96–417. See section 2641 of this title.

§ 2638. New grounds in support of a civil action

In any civil action under section 515 of the Tariff Act of 1930 in which the denial, in whole or in part, of a protest is a precondition to the commencement of a civil action in the Court of International Trade, the court, by rule, may consider any new ground in support of the civil action if such new ground—

(1) applies to the same merchandise that was the subject of the protest; and

(2) is related to the same administrative decision listed in section 514 of the Tariff Act of 1930 that was contested in the protest.

(Added Pub.L. 96–417, Title III, § 301, Oct. 10, 1980, 94 Stat. 1736.)

HISTORICAL AND STATUTORY NOTES

References in Text

Sections 515 and 514 of the Tariff Act of 1930, referred to in the introductory text and cl. (2), respectively, are classified to sections 1515 and 1514, respectively, of Title 19, Customs Duties.

Effective Dates

1980 Acts. Section effective on Nov. 1, 1980 and applicable with respect to civil actions pending on or commenced on or after such date, see section 701(a) of Pub.L. 96–417, as amended, set out as a note under section 251 of this title.

Prior Provisions

A prior section 2638, Acts June 25, 1948, c. 646, 62 Stat. 982; June 2, 1970, Pub.L. 91–271, Title I, § 119, 84 Stat. 281, related to decisions, findings of fact and conclusions of law, and effect of opinions and was omitted from the Code in the general revision of this chapter by Pub.L. 96–417. See section 2645(a) and (c) of this title.

§ 2639. Burden of proof; evidence of value

(a)(1) Except as provided in paragraph (2) of this subsection, in any civil action commenced in the Court of International Trade under section 515, 516, or 516A of the Tariff Act of 1930, the decision of the Secretary of the Treasury, the administering authority, or the International Trade Commission is presumed to be correct. The burden of proving otherwise shall rest upon the party challenging such decision.

(2) The provisions of paragraph (1) of this subsection shall not apply to any civil action commenced in the Court of International Trade under section 1582 of this title.

(b) In any civil action described in section 1581(h) of this title, the person commencing the action shall have the burden of making the demonstration required by such section by clear and convincing evidence.

(c) Where the value of merchandise or any of its components is in issue in any civil action in the Court of International Trade—

(1) reports or depositions of consuls, customs officers, and other officers of the United States, and depositions and affidavits of other persons whose attendance cannot reasonably be had, may be admitted into evidence when served upon the opposing party as prescribed by the rules of the court; and

(2) price lists and catalogs may be admitted in evidence when duly authenticated, relevant, and material.

(Added Pub.L. 96–417, Title III, § 301, Oct. 10, 1980, 94 Stat. 1736.)

HISTORICAL AND STATUTORY NOTES

References in Text

Sections 515, 516, and 516A of the Tariff Act of 1930, referred to in subsec. (a)(1), are classified to sections 1515, 1516, and 1516a, respectively, of Title 19, Customs Duties.

Effective Dates

1980 Acts. Subsec. (a)(2) of this section applicable with respect to civil actions commenced on or after the 90th day after Nov. 1, 1980, see section 701(c)(1)(A) of Pub.L. 96–417, as amended, set out as a note under section 251 of this title.

Subsec. (b) of this section applicable with respect to civil actions commenced on or after Nov. 1, 1980, see section 701(b) (1) (B) of Pub.L. 96–417, as amended, set out as a note under section 251 of this title.

Remainder of this section effective on Nov. 1, 1980 and applicable with respect to civil actions pending on or commenced on or after such date, see section 701(a) of Pub.L. 96–417, as amended, set out as a note under section 251 of this title.

Prior Provisions

A prior section 2639, Acts June 25, 1948, c. 646, 62 Stat. 982; June 2, 1970, Pub.L. 91–271, Title I, § 120, 84 Stat. 281, provided for retrial or rehearing and was omitted from the

Code in the general revision of this chapter by Pub.L. 96–417. See section 2646 of this title.

§ 2640. Scope and standard of review

(a) The Court of International Trade shall make its determinations upon the basis of the record made before the court in the following categories of civil actions:

(1) Civil actions contesting the denial of a protest under section 515 of the Tariff Act of 1930.

(2) Civil actions commenced under section 516 of the Tariff Act of 1930.

(3) Civil actions commenced to review a final determination made under section 305(b)(1) of the Trade Agreements Act of 1979.

(4) Civil actions commenced under section 777(c)(2) of the Tariff Act of 1930.

(5) Civil actions commenced to review any decision of the Secretary of the Treasury under section 641 of the Tariff Act of 1930, with the exception of decisions under section 641(d)(2)(B), which shall be governed by subdivision (d) of this section.

(6) Civil actions commenced under section 1582 of this title.

(b) In any civil action commenced in the Court of International Trade under section 516A of the Tariff Act of 1930, the court shall review the matter as specified in subsection (b) of such section.

(c) In any civil action commenced in the Court of International Trade to review any final determination of the Secretary of Labor under section 223 of the Trade Act of 1974 or any final determination of the Secretary of Commerce under section 251 or section 271 of such Act, the court shall review the matter as specified in section 284 of such Act.

(d) In any civil action commenced to review any order or decision of the Customs Service under section 499(b) of the Tariff Act of 1930, the court shall review the action on the basis of the record before the Customs Service at the time of issuing such decision or order.

(e) In any civil action not specified in this section, the Court of International Trade shall review the matter as provided in section 706 of title 5.

(Added Pub.L. 96–417, Title III, § 301, Oct. 10, 1980, 94 Stat. 1736, and amended Pub.L. 98–573, Title II, § 212(b)(5), Oct. 30, 1984, 98 Stat. 2984; Pub.L. 103–182, Title VI, § 684(a)(4), Dec. 8, 1993, 107 Stat. 2219.)

HISTORICAL AND STATUTORY NOTES

References in Text

Sections 515 and 516 of the Tariff Act of 1930, referred to in subsec. (a)(1) and (2), are classified to sections 1515 and 1516, respectively, of Title 19, Customs Duties.

Section 305(b)(1) of the Trade Agreements Act of 1979, referred to in subsec. (a)(3), is classified to section 2515(b)(1) of Title 19.

Section 777(c)(2) of the Tariff Act of 1930, referred to in subsec. (a)(4), is classified to section 1677f(c)(2) of Title 19.

Section 641 of the Tariff Act of 1930, referred to in subsec. (a)(5), is classified to section 1641 of Title 19.

Section 516A of the Tariff Act of 1930, referred to in subsec. (b), is classified to section 1516a of Title 19.

Sections 223, 251, 271, and 284 of the Trade Act of 1974, referred to in subsec. (c), are classified to sections 2273, 2341, 2371, and 2395 of Title 19.

Section 499(b) of the Tariff Act of 1930, referred to in subsec. (d), is classified to section 1499(b) of Title 19, Customs Duties.

Effective Dates

1993 Acts. Amendment by section 684(a)(4) of Pub.L. 103–182 effective Dec. 8, 1993, see section 692 of Pub.L. 103–182, set out as a note under section 58c of Title 19, Customs Duties.

1984 Acts. Amendment by Pub.L. 98–573 to take effect on the close of the 180th day after Oct. 30, 1984, see section 214(d) of Pub.L. 98–573, set out as a note under section 1304 of Title 19, Customs Duties.

1980 Acts. Subsecs. (a)(5), (c), and (d) of this section applicable with respect to civil actions commenced on or after Nov. 1, 1980, see section 701(b)(1)(B) of Pub.L. 96–417, as amended, set out as a note under section 251 of this title.

Subsec. (a)(6) of this section applicable with respect to civil actions commenced on or after the 90th day after Nov. 1, 1980, see section 701(c)(1)(A) of Pub.L. 96–417, as amended, set out as a note under section 251 of this title.

Remainder of this section effective on Nov. 1, 1980 and applicable with respect to civil actions pending on or commenced on or after such date, see section 701(a) of Pub.L. 96–417, as amended, set out as a note under section 251 of this title.

Prior Provisions

A prior section 2640, Act June 25, 1948, c. 646, 62 Stat. 982, authorized the division which had decided a case or the single judge who had decided an appeal for a reappraisement to grant a rehearing or retrial and was repealed by Pub.L. 91–271, Title I, § 121, June 2, 1970, 84 Stat. 281. See section 2646 of this title.

Application of Amendments Relating to Accreditation of Private Laboratories

For purposes of applying amendments relating to accreditation of private laboratories, any decision or order of the Customs Service denying, suspending, or revoking the accreditation of a private laboratory on or after Dec. 8, 1993 and before regulations to implement section 1499(b) of Title 19, Customs Duties, are issued shall be treated as having been denied, suspended, or revoked under such section 1499(b) of Title 19. See section 684(b) of Pub.L. 103–182 set out as a note under section 1581 of this title.

§ 2641. Witnesses; inspection of documents

(a) Except as otherwise provided by law, in any civil action in the Court of International Trade, each party and its counsel shall have an opportunity to introduce evidence, to hear and cross-examine the witnesses of the other party, and to inspect all samples and papers admitted or offered as evidence, as prescribed by the rules of the court. Except as provided in section 2639 of this title, subsection (b) of this section, or the rules of the court, the Federal Rules of Evidence shall apply to all civil actions in the Court of International Trade.

(b) The Court of International Trade may order that trade secrets and commercial or financial information which is privileged and confidential, or any information provided to the United States by any foreign government or foreign person, may be disclosed to a party, its counsel, or any other person under such terms and conditions as the court may order.

(Added Pub.L. 96–417, Title III, § 301, Oct. 10, 1980, 94 Stat. 1737.)

HISTORICAL AND STATUTORY NOTES

References in Text

The Federal Rules of Evidence, referred to in subsec. (a), are set out in this title.

Effective Dates

1980 Acts. Section effective on Nov. 1, 1980 and applicable with respect to civil actions pending on or commenced on or after such date, see section 701(a) of Pub.L. 96–417, as amended, set out as a note under section 251 of this title.

Prior Provisions

A prior section 2641, Act June 25, 1948, c. 646, 62 Stat. 982, authorized the Customs Court to assess a penalty of not less than $5 nor more than $250 against any person filing a frivolous protest or appeal and was repealed by Pub.L. 91–271, Title I, § 121, June 2, 1970, 84 Stat. 281.

§ 2642. Analysis of imported merchandise

The Court of International Trade may order an analysis of imported merchandise and reports thereon by laboratories or agencies of the United States or laboratories accredited by the Customs Service under section 499(b) of the Tariff Act of 1930.

(Added Pub.L. 96–417, Title III, § 301, Oct. 10, 1980, 94 Stat. 1737, and amended Pub.L. 103–182, Title VI, § 684(a)(5), Dec. 8, 1993, 107 Stat. 2219.)

HISTORICAL AND STATUTORY NOTES

References in Text

Section 499(b) of the Tariff Act of 1930, referred to in text, is classified to section 1499(b) of Title 19, Customs Duties.

Effective Dates

1993 Acts. Amendment by section 684(a)(5) of Pub.L. 103–182 effective Dec. 8, 1993, see section 692 of Pub.L. 103–182, set out as a note under section 58c of Title 19, Customs Duties.

1980 Acts. Section effective on Nov. 1, 1980 and applicable with respect to civil actions pending on or commenced on or after such date, see section 701(a) of Pub.L. 96–417, as amended, set out as a note under section 251 of this title.

Prior Provisions

A prior section 2642, Act May 24, 1949, c. 139, § 123, 63 Stat. 106, authorized the Customs Court under its rules and in its discretion to permit the amendment of protests, appeals and pleadings and was repealed by Pub.L. 91–271, Title I, § 121, June 2, 1970, 84 Stat. 281. See section 2633(b) of this title.

Application of Amendments Relating to Accreditation of Private Laboratories

For purposes of applying amendments relating to accreditation of private laboratories, any decision or order of the Customs Service denying, suspending, or revoking the accreditation of a private laboratory on or after Dec. 8, 1993 and before regulations to implement section 1499(b) of Title 19, Customs Duties, are issued shall be treated as having been denied, suspended, or revoked under such section 1499(b) of Title 19. See section 684(b) of Pub.L. 103–182 set out as a note under section 1581 of this title.

§ 2643. Relief

(a) The Court of International Trade may enter a money judgment—

(1) for or against the United States in any civil action commenced under section 1581 or 1582 of this title; and

(2) for or against the United States or any other party in any counterclaim, cross-claim, or third-party action under section 1583 of this title.

(b) If the Court of International Trade is unable to determine the correct decision on the basis of the evidence presented in any civil action, the court may order a retrial or rehearing for all purposes, or may order such further administrative or adjudicative procedures as the court considers necessary to enable it to reach the correct decision.

(c)(1) Except as provided in paragraphs (2), (3), (4), and (5) of this subsection, the Court of International Trade may, in addition to the orders specified in subsections (a) and (b) of this section, order any other form of relief that is appropriate in a civil action, including, but not limited to, declaratory judgments, orders of remand, injunctions, and writs of mandamus and prohibition.

(2) The Court of International Trade may not grant an injunction or issue a writ of mandamus in any civil action commenced to review any final determination of the Secretary of Labor under section 223 of the Trade Act of 1974, or any final determination of the Secretary of Commerce under section 251 or section 271 of such Act.

(3) In any civil action involving an application for the issuance of an order directing the administering authority or the International Trade Commission to make confidential information available under section

777(c)(2) of the Tariff Act of 1930, the Court of International Trade may issue an order of disclosure only with respect to the information specified in such section.

(4) In any civil action described in section 1581(h) of this title, the Court of International Trade may only order the appropriate declaratory relief.

(5) In any civil action involving an antidumping or countervailing duty proceeding regarding a class or kind of merchandise of a free trade area country (as defined in section 516A(f)(10) of the Tariff Act of 1930), as determined by the administering authority, the Court of International Trade may not order declaratory relief.

(d) If a surety commences a civil action in the Court of International Trade, such surety shall recover only the amount of the liquidated duties, charges, or exactions paid on the entries included in such action. The excess amount of any recovery shall be paid to the importer of record.

(e) In any proceeding involving assessment or collection of a monetary penalty under section 641(b)(6) or 641(d)(2)(A) of the Tariff Act of 1930, the court may not render judgment in an amount greater than that sought in the initial pleading of the United States, and may render judgment in such lesser amount as shall seem proper and just to the court.

(Added Pub.L. 96–417, Title III, § 301, Oct. 10, 1980, 94 Stat. 1737, and amended Pub.L. 98–573, Title II, § 212(b)(6), Oct. 30, 1984, 98 Stat. 2984; Pub.L. 100–449, Title IV, § 402(b), Sept. 28, 1988, 102 Stat. 1884; Pub.L. 103–182, Title IV, § 414(b), Dec. 8, 1993, 107 Stat. 2147.)

Termination of Amendments

For provisions directing that, except for transition provisions relating to proceedings regarding protective orders and undertakings, and binational panel and extraordinary challenge committee reviews, the amendment to this section by Title IV of Pub.L. 103–182 shall cease to have effect with respect to any country on the date on which such country ceases to be a NAFTA country, see section 3451 of Title 19, Customs Duties.

For provisions directing that the amendments made by Pub.L. 100–449, which amended this section, shall cease to have effect on the date on which the United States–Canada Free–Trade Agreement ceases to be in force, see section 501(c) of Pub.L. 100–449, set out in a note under section 2112 of Title 19, Customs Duties.

Articles 1906 and 2106 of the Agreement authorize either the United States or Canada to terminate the Agreement on 6–month notice if, at the end of the 7–year period following the date of the entry into effect of the Agreement, no agreement has been entered into between the United States and Canada on a substitute system of antidumping and countervailing duties.

HISTORICAL AND STATUTORY NOTES

References in Text

Section 223 of the Trade Act of 1974 and sections 251, 271 of such Act, referred to in subsec. (c)(2), are classified to sections 2273 and 2341, 2371, respectively, of Title 19, Customs Duties.

Section 777(c)(2) of the Tariff Act of 1930, referred to in subsec. (c)(3), is classified to section 1677f(c)(2) of Title 19.

Section 516A(f)(10) of the Tariff Act of 1930, referred to in subsec. (c)(5), is classified to section 1516a(f)(10) of Title 19, Customs Duties.

Section 641 of the Tariff Act of 1930, referred to in subsec. (e), is classified to section 1641 of Title 19.

Effective and Termination Dates

1993 Acts. Amendment by section by section 414 of Pub.L. 103–182 to take effect on the date the North American Free Trade Agreement enters into force with respect to the United States [Jan. 1, 1994], but not to apply to any final determination described in section 1516a(a)(1)(B) or (2)(B)(i), (ii), or (iii) of Title 19, Customs Duties, notice of which is published in the Federal Register before such date, or to a determination described in section 1516a(a)(2)(B)(vi) of Title 19 notice of which is received by the Government of Canada or Mexico before such date, or to any binational panel review under the United States–Canada Free–Trade Agreement, or to any extraordinary challenge arising out of any such review that was commenced before such date, see section 416 of Pub.L. 103–182, set out as a note under section 3431 of Title 19.

1988 Acts. Amendment by Pub.L. 100–449 effective on the date the United States–Canada Free–Trade Agreement enters into force (Jan. 1, 1989) and to cease to have effect on the date the Agreement ceases to be in force, see section 501(a), (c), of Pub.L. 100–449, set out in a note under section 2112 of Title 19, Customs Duties. [A Presidential Memorandum on the Canada–United States Free–Trade Agreement, dated Dec. 31, 1988, directing the Secretary of State to exchange notes with the Government of Canada to provide for the entry into force of the Agreement on Jan. 1, 1989, is set out in 24 Weekly Compilation of Presidential Documents 1688, Jan. 2, 1989.]

1984 Acts. Amendment by Pub.L. 98–573 to take effect on the close of the 180th day after Oct. 30, 1984, see section 214(d) of Pub.L. 98–573, set out as a note under section 1304 of Title 19, Customs Duties.

1980 Acts. Subsecs. (a) and (c)(2), (4) of this section applicable with respect to civil actions commenced on or after Nov. 1, 1980, see section 701(b)(1)(B) of Pub.L. 96–417, as amended, set out as a note under section 251 of this title.

Remainder of this section effective on Nov. 1, 1980 and applicable with respect to civil actions pending on or commenced on or after such date, see section 701(a) of Pub.L. 96–417, as amended, set out as a note under section 251 of this title.

§ 2644. Interest

If, in a civil action in the Court of International Trade under section 515 of the Tariff Act of 1930, the plaintiff obtains monetary relief by a judgment or under a stipulation agreement, interest shall be allowed at an annual rate established under section 6621 of the Internal Revenue Code of 1986. Such interest shall be calculated from the date of the filing of the summons in such action to the date of the refund.

(Added Pub.L. 96–417, Title III, § 301, Oct. 10, 1980, 94 Stat. 1738, and amended Pub.L. 99–514, § 2, Oct. 22, 1986, 100 Stat. 2095.)

HISTORICAL AND STATUTORY NOTES

References in Text

Section 515 of the Tariff Act of 1930, referred to in text, is classified to section 1515 of Title 19, Customs Duties.

Section 6621 of the Internal Revenue Code of 1986, referred to in the text, refers to section 6621 of Title 26, Internal Revenue Code.

Effective Dates

1980 Acts. Section applicable with respect to civil actions commenced on or after Nov. 1, 1980, see section 701(b)(1)(B) of Pub.L. 96–417, as amended, set out as a note under section 251 of this title.

§ 2645. Decisions

(a) A final decision of the Court of International Trade in a contested civil action or a decision granting or refusing a preliminary injunction shall be supported by—

(1) a statement of findings of fact and conclusions of law; or

(2) an opinion stating the reasons and facts upon which the decision is based.

(b) After the Court of International Trade has rendered a judgment, the court may, upon the motion of a party or upon its own motion, amend its findings or make additional findings and may amend the decision and judgment accordingly. A motion of a party or the court shall be made not later than thirty days after the date of entry of the judgment.

(c) A decision of the Court of International Trade is final and conclusive, unless a retrial or rehearing is granted pursuant to section 2646 of this title or an appeal is taken to the Court of Appeals for the Federal Circuit by filing a notice of appeal with the clerk of the Court of International Trade within the time and in the manner prescribed for appeals to United States courts of appeals from the United States district courts.

(Added Pub.L. 96–417, Title III, § 301, Oct. 10, 1980, 94 Stat. 1738, and amended Pub.L. 97–164, Title I, § 141, Apr. 2, 1982, 96 Stat. 45.)

HISTORICAL AND STATUTORY NOTES

Effective Dates

1982 Acts. Amendment by Pub.L. 97–164 effective Oct. 1, 1982, see section 402 of Pub.L. 97–164, set out as a note under section 171 of this title.

1980 Acts. Section effective on Nov. 1, 1980 and applicable with respect to civil actions pending on or commenced on or after such date, see section 701(a) of Pub.L. 96–417, as amended, set out as a note under section 251 of this title.

§ 2646. Retrial or rehearing

After the Court of International Trade has rendered a judgment or order, the court may, upon the motion of a party or upon its own motion, grant a retrial or rehearing, as the case may be. A motion of a party or the court shall be made not later than thirty days after the date of entry of the judgment or order.

(Added Pub.L. 96–417, Title III, § 301, Oct. 10, 1980, 94 Stat. 1739.)

HISTORICAL AND STATUTORY NOTES

Effective Dates

1980 Acts. Section effective on Nov. 1, 1980 and applicable with respect to civil actions pending on or commenced on or after such date, see section 701(a) of Pub.L. 96–417, as amended, set out as a note under section 251 of this title.

[§ 2647. Repealed. Pub.L. 98–620, Title IV, § 402(29)(G), Nov. 8, 1984, 98 Stat. 3359]

HISTORICAL AND STATUTORY NOTES

Section, added Pub.L. 96–417, Title III, § 301, Oct. 10, 1980, 94 Stat. 1739, and amended Pub.L. 98–573, Title VI, § 623(b)(2), Oct. 30, 1984, 98 Stat. 3041, related to precedence of cases.

Effective Date of Repeal

Repeal not to apply to cases pending on Nov. 8, 1984, see section 403 of Pub.L. 98–620, set out as a note under section 1657 of this title.

CHAPTER 171—TORT CLAIMS PROCEDURE

Sec.
2671. Definitions.
2672. Administrative adjustment of claims.
2673. Reports to Congress.
2674. Liability of United States.
2675. Disposition by federal agency as prerequisite; evidence.
2676. Judgment as bar.
2677. Compromise.
2678. Attorney fees; penalty.
2679. Exclusiveness of remedy.
2680. Exceptions.

§ 2671. Definitions

As used in this chapter and sections 1346(b) and 2401(b) of this title, the term "Federal agency" includes the executive departments, the judicial and legislative branches, the military departments, independent establishments of the United States, and corporations primarily acting as instrumentalities or agencies of the United States, but does not include any contractor with the United States.

"Employee of the government" includes officers or employees of any federal agency, members of the military or naval forces of the United States, members of the National Guard while engaged in training or duty under section 316, 502, 503, 504, or 505 of title 32, and persons acting on behalf of a federal agency in an official capacity, temporarily or permanently in the service of the United States, whether with or without compensation.

"Acting within the scope of his office or employment", in the case of a member of the military or naval forces of the United States or a member of the National Guard as defined in section 101(3) of title 32, means acting in line of duty.

(June 25, 1948, c. 646, 62 Stat. 982; May 24, 1949, c. 139, § 124, 63 Stat. 106; July 18, 1966, Pub.L. 89–506, § 8, 80 Stat. 307; Dec. 29, 1981, Pub.L. 97–124, § 1, 95 Stat. 1666; Nov. 18, 1988, Pub.L. 100–694, § 3, 102 Stat. 4564.)

HISTORICAL AND STATUTORY NOTES

Effective Dates

1988 Acts. Amendment by Pub.L 100–694 effective Nov. 18, 1988, and applicable to all claims, civil actions, and proceedings pending on, or filed on or after, Nov. 18, 1988, see section 8 of Pub.L. 100–694, set out as a note under section 2679 of this title.

1981 Acts. Amendment by Pub.L. 97–124 applicable only with respect to claims arising on or after Dec. 29, 1981, see section 4 of Pub.L. 97–124, set out as a note under section 1089 of Title 10, Armed Forces.

1966 Acts. Amendment of section by Pub.L. 89–506 applicable to claims accruing six months or more after July 18, 1966, see section 10 of Pub.L. 89–506, set out as a note under section 2672 of this title.

Severability

Section 7 of Pub.L. 100–694 provided that: "If any provision of this Act or the amendments made by this Act [enacting section 831c–2 of Title 16, Conservation, amending sections 2671, 2674, and 2679 of this title, and enacting provisions set out as notes under sections 1, 2671, and 2679 of this title] or the application of the provision to any person or circumstance is held invalid, the remainder of this Act and such amendments and the application of the provision to any other person or circumstance shall not be affected by that invalidation."

Congressional Findings and Purposes

Section 2 of Pub.L. 100–694 provided that:

"**(a) Findings.**—the Congress finds and declares the following:

"(1) For more than 40 years the Federal Tort Claims Act [28 U.S.C.A. §§ 1346(b), 2671 et seq.] has been the legal mechanism for compensating persons injured by negligent or wrongful acts of Federal employees committed within the scope of their employment.

"(2) The United States, through the Federal Tort Claims Act, is responsible to injured persons for the common law torts of its employees in the same manner in which the common law historically has recognized the responsibility of an employer for torts committed by its employees within the scope of their employment.

"(3) Because Federal employees for many years have been protected from personal common law tort liability by a broad based immunity, the Federal Tort Claims Act has served as the sole means for compensating persons injured by the tortious conduct of Federal employees.

"(4) Recent judicial decisions, and particularly the decision of the United States Supreme Court in Westfall v. Erwin [1988, 108 S.Ct. 580], have seriously eroded the common law tort immunity previously available to Federal employees.

"(5) This erosion of immunity of Federal employees from common law tort liability has created an immediate crisis involving the prospect of personal liability and the threat of protracted personal tort litigation for the entire Federal workforce.

"(6) The prospect of such liability will seriously undermine the morale and well being of Federal employees, impede the ability of agencies to carry out their missions, and diminish the vitality of the Federal Tort Claims Act as the proper remedy for Federal employee torts.

"(7) In its opinion in Westfall v. Erwin [1988, 108 S.Ct. 580], the Supreme Court indicated that the Congress is in the best position to determine the extent to which Federal employees should be personally liable for common law torts, and that legislative consideration of this matter would be useful.

"**(b) Purpose.**—It is the purpose of this Act [enacting section 831c–2 of Title 16, Conservation, amending sections 2671, 2674, and 2679 of this title, and enacting provisions set out as notes under sections 1, 2671, and 2679 of this title] to protect Federal employees from personal liability for common law torts committed within the scope of their employment, while providing persons injured by the common law torts of Federal employees with an appropriate remedy against the United States."

Actions Taken Within Scope of Law Enforcement Officer's Employment

Pub.L. 105–277, Div. A, § 101(h) [Title I, § 627], Oct. 21, 1998, 112 Stat. 2681–___, provided that:

"**(a) Definitions.**—In this section—

"(1) the term 'crime of violence' has the meaning given that term in section 16 of title 18, United States Code; and

"(2) the term 'law enforcement officer' means any employee described in subparagraph (A), (B), or (C) of section 8401(17) of title 5, United States Code; and any special agent in the Diplomatic Security Service of the Department of State.

"**(b) Rule of construction.**—Notwithstanding any other provision of law, for purposes of chapter 171 of title 28, United States Code [28 U.S.C.A. § 2671 et seq.; this chapter], or any other provision of law relating to tort liability, a law enforcement officer shall be construed to be acting within the scope of his or her office or employment, if the officer takes reasonable action, including the use of force, to—

"(1) protect an individual in the presence of the officer from a crime of violence;

"(2) provide immediate assistance to an individual who has suffered or who is threatened with bodily harm; or

"(3) prevent the escape of any individual who the officer reasonably believes to have committed in the presence of the officer a crime of violence."

§ 2672. Administrative adjustment of claims

The head of each Federal agency or his designee, in accordance with regulations prescribed by the Attorney General, may consider, ascertain, adjust, determine, compromise, and settle any claim for money damages against the United States for injury or loss of property or personal injury or death caused by the negligent or wrongful act or omission of any employee of the agency while acting within the scope of his office or employment, under circumstances where the United States, if a private person, would be liable to the claimant in accordance with the law of the place where the act or omission occurred: *Provided*, That any award, compromise, or settlement in excess of $25,000 shall be effected only with the prior written approval of the Attorney General or his designee. Notwithstanding the proviso contained in the preceding sentence, any award, compromise, or settlement may be effected without the prior written approval of the Attorney General or his or her designee, to the extent that the Attorney General delegates to the head of the agency the authority to make such award, compromise, or settlement. Such delegations may not exceed the authority delegated by the Attorney General to the United States attorneys to settle claims for money damages against the United States. Each Federal agency may use arbitration, or other alternative means of dispute resolution under the provisions of subchapter IV of chapter 5 of title 5, to settle any tort claim against the United States, to the extent of the agency's authority to award, compromise, or settle such claim without the prior written approval of the Attorney General or his or her designee.

Subject to the provisions of this title relating to civil actions on tort claims against the United States, any such award, compromise, settlement, or determination shall be final and conclusive on all officers of the Government, except when procured by means of fraud.

Any award, compromise, or settlement in an amount of $2,500 or less made pursuant to this section shall be paid by the head of the Federal agency concerned out of appropriations available to that agency. Payment of any award, compromise, or settlement in an amount in excess of $2,500 made pursuant to this section or made by the Attorney General in any amount pursuant to section 2677 of this title shall be paid in a manner similar to judgments and compromises in like causes and appropriations or funds available for the payment of such judgments and compromises are hereby made available for the payment of awards, compromises, or settlements under this chapter.

The acceptance by the claimant of any such award, compromise, or settlement shall be final and conclusive on the claimant, and shall constitute a complete release of any claim against the United States and against the employee of the government whose act or omission gave rise to the claim, by reason of the same subject matter.

(June 25, 1948, c. 646, 62 Stat. 983; Apr. 25, 1949, c. 92, § 2(b), 63 Stat. 62; May 24, 1949, c. 139, § 125, 63 Stat. 106; Sept. 23, 1950, c. 1010, § 9, 64 Stat. 987; Sept. 8, 1959, Pub.L. 86–238, § 1(1), 73 Stat. 471; July 18, 1966, Pub.L. 89–506, §§ 1, 9(a), 80 Stat. 306, 308; Nov. 15, 1990, Pub.L. 101–552, § 8(a), 104 Stat. 2746.)

HISTORICAL AND STATUTORY NOTES

Effective and Termination Dates

1990 Acts. The termination of amendments by Pub.L. 101–552 and authority to use dispute resolution proceedings on Oct. 1, 1995, provided by section 11 of Pub.L. 101–552, set out as a note under section 571 of Title 5, Government Organization and Employees, was repealed by section 9 of Pub.L. 104–320.

1966 Acts. Section 10 of Pub.L. 89–506 provided that: "This Act [amending this section and sections 2401(b), 2671, 2675, 2677, 2678, and 2679(b) of this title, section 724a of former Title 31, Money and Finance, and section 4116(a) of Title 38, Veteran's Benefits (see Section 7316 of Title 38)] shall apply to claims accruing six months or more after the date of its enactment [July 18, 1966]."

Laws Unaffected

Section 424(b) of Act Aug. 2, 1946, c. 753, Title IV, 60 Stat. 847, provided that: "Nothing contained herein shall be deemed to repeal any provision of law authorizing any Federal agency to consider, ascertain, adjust, settle, determine, or pay any claim on account of damage to or loss of property or on account of personal injury or death, in cases in which such damage, loss, injury, or death was not caused by any negligent or wrongful act or omission of an employee of the Government while acting within the scope of his office or employment, or any other claim not cognizable under part 2 of this title."

§ 2673. Reports to Congress

The head of each federal agency shall report annually to Congress all claims paid by it under section 2672 of this title, stating the name of each claimant, the amount claimed, the amount awarded, and a brief description of the claim.

(June 25, 1948, c. 646, 62 Stat. 983.)

Repeal

Section 1(1) of Pub.L. 89–348, Nov. 8, 1965, 79 Stat. 1310, repealed the requirement that an annual report to Congress be made of the administrative adjustment of tort claims of $2,500 or less, stating the name of each claimant, the amount claimed, the amount awarded, and a brief description of the claim.

§ 2674. Liability of United States

The United States shall be liable, respecting the provisions of this title relating to tort claims, in the same manner and to the same extent as a private individual under like circumstances, but shall not be liable for interest prior to judgment or for punitive damages.

If, however, in any case wherein death was caused, the law of the place where the act or omission complained of occurred provides, or has been construed to provide, for damages only punitive in nature, the United States shall be liable for actual or compensatory damages, measured by the pecuniary injuries resulting from such death to the persons respectively, for whose benefit the action was brought, in lieu thereof.

With respect to any claim under this chapter, the United States shall be entitled to assert any defense based upon judicial or legislative immunity which otherwise would have been available to the employee of the United States whose act or omission gave rise to the claim, as well as any other defenses to which the United States is entitled.

With respect to any claim to which this section applies, the Tennessee Valley Authority shall be entitled to assert any defense which otherwise would have been available to the employee based upon judicial or legislative immunity, which otherwise would have been available to the employee of the Tennessee Valley Authority whose act or omission gave rise to the claim as well as any other defenses to which the Tennessee Valley Authority is entitled under this chapter.

(June 25, 1948, c. 646, 62 Stat. 983; Nov. 18, 1988, Pub.L. 100–694, §§ 4, 9(c), 102 Stat. 4564, 4567.)

HISTORICAL AND STATUTORY NOTES

Effective Dates

1988 Acts. Amendment by Pub.L. 100–694 effective Nov. 18, 1988, and applicable to all claims, civil actions, and proceedings pending on, or filed on or after, Nov. 18, 1988, see section 8 of Pub.L. 100–694 set out as a note under section 2679 of this title.

§ 2675. Disposition by federal agency as prerequisite; evidence

(a) An action shall not be instituted upon a claim against the United States for money damages for injury or loss of property or personal injury or death caused by the negligent or wrongful act or omission of any employee of the Government while acting within the scope of his office or employment, unless the claimant shall have first presented the claim to the appropriate Federal agency and his claim shall have been finally denied by the agency in writing and sent by certified or registered mail. The failure of an agency to make final disposition of a claim within six months after it is filed shall, at the option of the claimant any time thereafter, be deemed a final denial of the claim for purposes of this section. The provisions of this subsection shall not apply to such claims as may be asserted under the Federal Rules of Civil Procedure by third party complaint, cross-claim, or counterclaim.

(b) Action under this section shall not be instituted for any sum in excess of the amount of the claim presented to the federal agency, except where the increased amount is based upon newly discovered evidence not reasonably discoverable at the time of presenting the claim to the federal agency, or upon allegation and proof of intervening facts, relating to the amount of the claim.

(c) Disposition of any claim by the Attorney General or other head of a federal agency shall not be competent evidence of liability or amount of damages.

(June 25, 1948, c. 646, 62 Stat. 983; May 24, 1949, c. 139, § 126, 63 Stat. 107; July 18, 1966, Pub.L. 89–506, § 2, 80 Stat. 306.)

HISTORICAL AND STATUTORY NOTES

References in Text

The Federal Rules of Civil Procedure, referred to in subsec. (a), are set out in the Appendix to this title.

Effective Dates

1966 Acts. Amendment of section by Pub.L. 89–506 applicable to claims accruing six months or more after July 18, 1966, see section 10 of Pub.L. 89–506, set out as a note under section 2672 of this title.

§ 2676. Judgment as bar

The judgment in an action under section 1346(b) of this title shall constitute a complete bar to any action by the claimant, by reason of the same subject matter, against the employee of the government whose act or omission gave rise to the claim.

(June 25, 1948, c. 646, 62 Stat. 984.)

§ 2677. Compromise

The Attorney General or his designee may arbitrate, compromise, or settle any claim cognizable under section 1346(b) of this title, after the commencement of an action thereon.

(June 25, 1948, c. 646, 62 Stat. 984; July 18, 1966, Pub.L. 89–506, § 3, 80 Stat. 307.)

HISTORICAL AND STATUTORY NOTES

Effective Dates

1966 Acts. Amendment of section by Pub.L. 89–506 applicable to claims accruing six months or more after July 18, 1966, see section 10 of Pub.L. 89–506, set out as a note under section 2672 of this title.

§ 2678. Attorney fees; penalty

No attorney shall charge, demand, receive, or collect for services rendered, fees in excess of 25 per centum of any judgment rendered pursuant to section 1346(b) of this title or any settlement made pursuant to section 2677 of this title, or in excess of 20 per centum of any award, compromise, or settlement made pursuant to section 2672 of this title.

Any attorney who charges, demands, receives, or collects for services rendered in connection with such claim any amount in excess of that allowed under this section, if recovery be had, shall be fined not more than $2,000 or imprisoned not more than one year, or both.

(June 25, 1948, c. 646, 62 Stat. 984; July 18, 1966, Pub.L. 89–506, § 4, 80 Stat. 307.)

HISTORICAL AND STATUTORY NOTES

Effective Dates

1966 Acts. Amendment of section by Pub.L. 89–506 applicable to claims accruing six months or more after July 18, 1966, see section 10 of Pub.L. 89–506, set out as a note under section 2672 of this title.

§ 2679. Exclusiveness of remedy

(a) The authority of any federal agency to sue and be sued in its own name shall not be construed to authorize suits against such federal agency on claims which are cognizable under section 1346(b) of this title, and the remedies provided by this title in such cases shall be exclusive.

(b)(1) The remedy against the United States provided by sections 1346(b) and 2672 of this title for injury or loss of property, or personal injury or death arising or resulting from the negligent or wrongful act or omission of any employee of the Government while acting within the scope of his office or employment is exclusive of any other civil action or proceeding for money damages by reason of the same subject matter against the employee whose act or omission gave rise to the claim or against the estate of such employee. Any other civil action or proceeding for money damages arising out of or relating to the same subject matter against the employee or the employee's estate is precluded without regard to when the act or omission occurred.

(2) Paragraph (1) does not extend or apply to a civil action against an employee of the Government—

(A) which is brought for a violation of the Constitution of the United States, or

(B) which is brought for a violation of a statute of the United States under which such action against an individual is otherwise authorized.

(c) The Attorney General shall defend any civil action or proceeding brought in any court against any employee of the Government or his estate for any such damage or injury. The employee against whom such civil action or proceeding is brought shall deliver within such time after date of service or knowledge of service as determined by the Attorney General, all process served upon him or an attested true copy thereof to his immediate superior or to whomever was designated by the head of his department to receive such papers and such person shall promptly furnish copies of the pleadings and process therein to the United States attorney for the district embracing the place wherein the proceeding is brought, to the Attorney General, and to the head of his employing Federal agency.

(d)(1) Upon certification by the Attorney General that the defendant employee was acting within the scope of his office or employment at the time of the incident out of which the claim arose, any civil action or proceeding commenced upon such claim in a United States district court shall be deemed an action against the United States under the provisions of this title and all references thereto, and the United States shall be substituted as the party defendant.

(2) Upon certification by the Attorney General that the defendant employee was acting within the scope of his office or employment at the time of the incident out of which the claim arose, any civil action or proceeding commenced upon such claim in a State court shall be removed without bond at any time before trial by the Attorney General to the district court of the United States for the district and division embracing the place in which the action or proceeding is pending. Such action or proceeding shall be deemed to be an action or proceeding brought against the United States under the provisions of this title and all references thereto, and the United States shall be substituted as the party defendant. This certification of the Attorney General shall conclusively establish scope of office or employment for purposes of removal.

(3) In the event that the Attorney General has refused to certify scope of office or employment under this section, the employee may at any time before trial petition the court to find and certify that the employee was acting within the scope of his office or employment. Upon such certification by the court, such action or proceeding shall be deemed to be an action or proceeding brought against the United States under the provisions of this title and all references thereto, and the United States shall be substituted as the party defendant. A copy of the petition shall be served upon the United States in accordance with the provisions of Rule 4(d)(4) of the Federal Rules of Civil Procedure. In the event the petition is filed in a civil action or proceeding pending in a State court, the action or proceeding may be removed without bond by the Attorney General to the district court of the United States for the district and division embracing the place in which it is pending. If, in considering the petition, the district court determines that the employee was not acting within the scope of his office or employment, the action or proceeding shall be remanded to the State court.

(4) Upon certification, any action or proceeding subject to paragraph (1), (2), or (3) shall proceed in the same manner as any action against the United States filed pursuant to section 1346(b) of this title and shall be subject to the limitations and exceptions applicable to those actions.

(5) Whenever an action or proceeding in which the United States is substituted as the party defendant under this subsection is dismissed for failure first to present a claim pursuant to section 2675(a) of this title, such a claim shall be deemed to be timely presented under section 2401(b) of this title if—

(A) the claim would have been timely had it been filed on the date the underlying civil action was commenced, and

(B) the claim is presented to the appropriate Federal agency within 60 days after dismissal of the civil action.

(e) The Attorney General may compromise or settle any claim asserted in such civil action or proceeding in the manner provided in section 2677, and with the same effect.

(June 25, 1948, c. 646, 62 Stat. 984; Sept. 21, 1961, Pub.L. 87–258, § 1, 75 Stat. 539; July 18, 1966, Pub.L. 89–506, § 5(a), 80 Stat. 307; Nov. 18, 1988, Pub.L. 100–694, §§ 5, 6, 102 Stat. 4564.)

HISTORICAL AND STATUTORY NOTES

References in Text

The Federal Rules of Civil Procedures referred to in subsec. (d)(3), are set out in this title.

Effective Dates

1988 Acts. Section 8 of Pub.L. 100–694 provided that:

"**(a) General rule.**—This Act and the amendments made by this Act [enacting section 831c–2 of Title 16, Conservation; amending sections 2671, 2674, and 2679(b), (d) of this title, and enacting provisions set out as notes under this section and sections 1 and 2671 of this title] shall take effect on the date of the enactment of this Act [Nov. 18, 1988].

"**(b) Applicability to proceedings.**—The amendments made by this Act [amending sections 2671, 2674, and 2679 of this title] shall apply to all claims, civil actions, and proceedings pending on, or filed on or after, the date of the enactment of this Act [Nov. 18, 1988].

"**(c) Pending State proceedings.**—With respect to any civil action or proceeding pending in a State court to which the amendments made by this Act apply, and as to which the period for removal under section 2679(d) of title 28, United States Code [subsec. (d) of this section] (as amended by section 6 of this Act), has expired, the Attorney General shall have 60 days after the date of the enactment of this Act [Nov. 18, 1988] during which to seek removal under such section 2679(d) [subsec. (d) of this section].

"**(d) Claims accruing before enactment.**—With respect to any civil action or proceeding to which the amendments made by this Act apply in which the claim accrued before the date of the enactment of this Act [Nov. 18, 1988], the period during which the claim shall be deemed to be timely presented under section 2679(d)(5) of title 28, United States Code [subsec. (d)(5) of this section] (as amended by section 6 of this Act) shall be that period within which the claim could have been timely filed under applicable State law, but in no event shall such period exceed two years from the date of the enactment of this Act [Nov. 18, 1988]."

1966 Acts. Amendment of section by Pub.L. 89–506 applicable to claims accruing six months or more after July 18, 1966, see section 10 of Pub.L. 89–506, set out as a note under section 2672 of this title.

1961 Acts. Section 2 of Pub.L. 87–258 provided that: "The amendments made by this Act [adding subsecs. (b)–(e) of this section] shall be deemed to be in effect six months after the enactment hereof [Sept. 21, 1961] but any rights or liabilities then existing shall not be affected."

§ 2680. Exceptions

The provisions of this chapter and section 1346(b) of this title shall not apply to—

(a) Any claim based upon an act or omission of an employee of the Government, exercising due care, in the execution of a statute or regulation, whether or not such statute or regulation be valid, or based upon the exercise or performance or the failure to exercise or perform a discretionary function or duty on the part of a federal agency or an employee of the Government, whether or not the discretion involved be abused.

(b) Any claim arising out of the loss, miscarriage, or negligent transmission of letters or postal matter.

(c) Any claim arising in respect of the assessment or collection of any tax or customs duty, or the detention of any goods or merchandise by any officer of customs or excise or any other law-enforcement officer.

(d) Any claim for which a remedy is provided by sections 741–752, 781–790 of Title 46, relating to claims or suits in admiralty against the United States.

(e) Any claim arising out of an act or omission of any employee of the Government in administering the provisions of sections 1–31 of Title 50, Appendix.

(f) Any claim for damages caused by the imposition or establishment of a quarantine by the United States.

[(g) Repealed. Sept. 26, 1950, c. 1049, § 13(5), 64 Stat. 1043.]

(h) Any claim arising out of assault, battery, false imprisonment, false arrest, malicious prosecution, abuse of process, libel, slander, misrepresentation, deceit, or interference with contract rights: *Provided*, That, with regard to acts or omissions of investigative or law enforcement officers of the

United States Government, the provisions of this chapter and section 1346(b) of this title shall apply to any claim arising, on or after the date of the enactment of this proviso, out of assault, battery, false imprisonment, false arrest, abuse of process, or malicious prosecution. For the purpose of this subsection, "investigative or law enforcement officer" means any officer of the United States who is empowered by law to execute searches, to seize evidence, or to make arrests for violations of Federal law.

(i) Any claim for damages caused by the fiscal operations of the Treasury or by the regulation of the monetary system.

(j) Any claim arising out of the combatant activities of the military or naval forces, or the Coast Guard, during time of war.

(k) Any claim arising in a foreign country.

(*l*) Any claim arising from the activities of the Tennessee Valley Authority.

(m) Any claim arising from the activities of the Panama Canal Company.

(n) Any claim arising from the activities of a Federal land bank, a Federal intermediate credit bank, or a bank for cooperatives.

(June 25, 1948, c. 646, 62 Stat. 984; July 16, 1949, c. 340, 63 Stat. 444; Sept. 26, 1950, c. 1049, §§ 2(a)(2), 13(5), 64 Stat. 1038, 1043; Aug. 18, 1959, Pub.L. 86–168, Title II, § 202(b), 73 Stat. 389; Mar. 16, 1974, Pub.L. 93–253, § 2, 88 Stat. 50.)

HISTORICAL AND STATUTORY NOTES

References in Text

Sections 741–752 of Title 46, referred to in subsec. (d), are popularly known as the "Suits in Admiralty Act" and are classified to Title 46, Appendix, Shipping.

Sections 781–790 of Title 46, referred to in subsec. (d), are popularly known as the "Public Vessels Act" and are classified to Title 46, Appendix.

Sections 1–31 of Title 50, Appendix, referred to in subsec. (e), was in the original source of this section (section 943 [of Title 28, which was section 421] of Act Aug. 2, 1946) a reference to the Trading with the Enemy Act, as amended. The Trading with the Enemy Act is now comprised of sections 1 to 43, which are classified to sections 1 to 6, 7 to 39, and 41 to 44 of Title 50, Appendix, War and National Defense.

Date of the enactment of this proviso, referred to in subsec. (h), means Mar. 16, 1974, the date on which Pub.L. 93–253, enacting the proviso, was approved.

Panama Canal Company, referred to in subsec. (m), deemed to refer to Panama Canal Commission, see section 3602(b)(5) of Title 22, Foreign Relations and Intercourse.

Effective Dates

1959 Acts. Amendment by Pub.L. 86–168 effective Jan. 1, 1960, pursuant to section 203(c) of Pub.L. 86–168.

1950 Acts. Section 14 of Act Sept. 26, 1950, provided that the repeal of subsec. (g) and amendment of subsec. (m) of this section by such Act shall take effect upon the effective date of the transfer to the Panama Canal Company, pursuant to the provisions of section 256 of the Canal Zone Code, as added by section 10 of such Act, of the Panama Canal together with the facilities and appurtenances related thereto.

Transfer of Functions

The Coast Guard was transferred to the Department of Transportation and all functions, powers, and duties, relating to the Coast Guard, of the Secretary of the Treasury and of all other offices and officers of the Department of the Treasury were transferred to the Secretary of Transportation by Pub.L. 89–670, § 6(b)(1), Oct. 15, 1966, 80 Stat. 938. Section 6(b)(2) of Pub.L. 89–670, however, provided that notwithstanding such transfer of functions, the Coast Guard shall operate as part of the Navy in time of war or when the President directs as provided in section 3 of Title 14, Coast Guard. See section 108 of Title 49, Transportation.

For transfer of certain functions relating to claims and litigation, insofar as they pertain to the Air Force, from the Secretary of the Army to the Secretary of the Air Force, see Secretary of Defense Transfer Order No. 34 [§ 1a(2)(4)], eff. July 1, 1949.

Applicability of Subsec. (j)

Section 1(a)(32) of Joint Res. July 3, 1952, c. 570, 66 Stat. 333, as amended by Joint Res. Mar. 31, 1953, c. 13, § 1, 67 Stat. 18 and Joint Res. June 30, 1953, c. 172, 67 Stat. 132, provided that subsec. (j) of this section should continue in force until six months after the termination of the national emergency proclaimed by the President on Dec. 16, 1950, by 1950 Proc. No. 2914, 15 F.R. 9029, set out as a note preceding section 1 of the Appendix to Title 50, War and National Defense, or such earlier date or dates as may be provided for by Congress, but in no event beyond Aug. 1, 1953. Section 7 of Joint Res. July 3, 1952, provided that it should become effective June 16, 1952.

Section 6 of Joint Res. July 3, 1952, c. 570, § 6, 66 Stat. 334, repealed Joint Res. Apr. 14, 1952, c. 204, 66 Stat. 54 as amended by Joint Res. May 28, 1952, c. 339, 66 Stat. 96; Joint Res. June 14, 1952, c. 437, 66 Stat. 137; Joint Res. June 30, 1952, c. 526, 66 Stat. 296, which continued provisions of subsection (j) of this section (see note above) until July 3, 1952. This repeal was made effective June 16, 1952, by section 7 of Joint Res. July 3, 1952.

Northern Mariana Islands as Foreign Country With Respect to Claims Accruing No More than Two Years Prior to Oct. 19, 1982

Pub.L. 97–357, Title II, § 204, Oct. 19, 1982, 96 Stat. 1708, provided: "That the Northern Mariana Islands shall not be considered a foreign country for purposes of subsection (k) of section 2680 of Title 28, United States Code [subsec. (k) of this section], with respect to claims which accrued no more than two years prior to the effective date of this Act [Oct. 19, 1982]."

Termination of National Emergency

Declaration of national emergency in effect on Sept. 14, 1976, was terminated two years from that date by Section 1601 of Title 50, War and National Defense.

CHAPTER 173—ATTACHMENT IN POSTAL SUITS

Sec.
2710. Right of attachment.
2711. Application for warrant.
2712. Issue of warrant.
2713. Trial of ownership of property.
2714. Investment of proceeds of attached property.
2715. Publication.
2716. Personal notice.
2717. Discharge.
2718. Interest on balances due department.

§ 2710. Right of attachment

(a) Where debts are due from a defaulting or delinquent postmaster, contractor, or other officer, agent or employee of the Post Office Department, a warrant of attachment may issue against all property and legal and equitable rights belonging to him, and his sureties, or either of them, where he—

(1) is a nonresident of the district where he was appointed, or has departed from that district for the purpose of permanently residing outside thereof, or of avoiding the service of civil process; and

(2) has conveyed away, or is about to convey away any of his property, or has removed or is about to remove the same from the district wherein it is situated, with intent to defraud the United States.

(b) When the property has been removed, the marshal of the district into which it has been removed, upon receipt of certified copies of the warrant, may seize the property and convey it to a convenient place within the jurisdiction of the court which issued the warrant. Alias warrants may be issued upon due application. The warrant first issued remains valid until the return day thereof.

(Added Pub.L. 86–682, § 9, Sept. 2, 1960, 74 Stat. 706.)

HISTORICAL AND STATUTORY NOTES

Codifications

Section was derived from R.S. § 924, which was originally classified to section 737 of former Title 28. Following the general revision and enactment of Title 28 by Act June 25, 1948, R.S. § 924 was reclassified to section 837 of Title 39. R.S. § 924 was repealed by section 12(c) of Pub.L. 86–682 (section 1 of which revised and enacted Title 39), and reenacted by section 9 thereof as section 2710 of Title 28, Judiciary and Judicial Procedure.

Effective Dates

1960 Acts. Section 11 of Pub.L. 86–682, Sept. 2, 1960, 74 Stat. 708, provided that this chapter shall be effective on Sept. 1, 1960.

Change of Name

References to the Post Office Department, the Postal Service, the Postal Field Service, the Field Postal Service, or the Departmental Service or the Departmental Headquarters of the Post Office Department to be considered references to the United States Postal Service pursuant to Pub.L. 91–375, § 6(*o*), Aug. 12, 1970, 84 Stat. 783, set out as a Cross Reference note preceding section 101 of Title 39, Postal Service.

§ 2711. Application for warrant

A United States attorney or assistant United States attorney or a person authorized by the Attorney General—

(1) upon his own affidavit or that of another credible person, stating the existence of either of the grounds of attachments enumerated in section 2710 of this title and

(2) upon production of legal evidence of the debt

may apply for a warrant of attachment to a judge, or, in his absence, to the clerk of any court of the United States having original jurisdiction of the cause of action.

(Added Pub.L. 86–682, § 9, Sept. 2, 1960, 74 Stat. 707.)

HISTORICAL AND STATUTORY NOTES

Codifications

Section was derived from R.S. § 925, which was originally classified to section 738 of former Title 28. Following the general revision and enactment of Title 28 by Act June 25, 1948, R.S. § 925 was reclassified to section 838 of Title 39. R.S. § 925 was repealed by section 12(c) of Pub.L. 86–682 (section 1 of which revised and enacted Title 39), and reenacted by section 9 thereof as section 2711 of Title 28, Judiciary and Judicial Procedure.

§ 2712. Issue of warrant

Upon an order of a judge of a court, or, in his absence and upon the clerk's own initiative, the clerk shall issue a warrant for the attachment of the property belonging to the person specified in the affidavit. The marshal shall execute the warrant forthwith and take the property attached, if personal, in his custody, subject to the interlocutory or final orders of the court.

(Added Pub.L. 86–682, § 9, Sept. 2, 1960, 74 Stat. 707.)

HISTORICAL AND STATUTORY NOTES

Codifications

Section was derived from R.S. § 926, which was originally classified to section 739 of former Title 28. Following the general revision and enactment of Title 28 by Act June 25, 1948, R.S. § 926 was reclassified to section 839 of Title 39. R.S. § 926 was repealed by section 12(c) of Pub.L. 86–682 (section 1 of which revised and enacted Title 39), and reenacted by section 9 thereof as section 2712 of Title 28. Judiciary and Judicial Procedure.

§ 2713. Trial of ownership of property

Not later than twenty days before the return day of a warrant issued under section 2712 of this title, the party whose property is attached, on notice to the United States Attorney, may file a plea in abatement, denying the allegations of the affidavit, or denying ownership in the defendant of the property attached. The court, upon application of either party, shall order a trial by jury of the issues. Where the parties, by consent, waive a trial by jury, the court shall decide the issues. A party claiming ownership of the property attached and seeking its return is limited to the remedy afforded by this section, but his right to an action of trespass, or other action for damages, is not impaired.

(Added Pub.L. 86–682, § 9, Sept. 2, 1960, 74 Stat. 707.)

HISTORICAL AND STATUTORY NOTES

Codifications

Section was derived from R.S. § 927, which was originally classified to section 740 of former Title 28. Following the general revision and enactment of Title 28 by Act June 25, 1948, R.S. § 927 was reclassified to section 840 of Title 39. R.S. § 927 was repealed by section 12(c) of Pub.L. 86–682 (section 1 of which revised and enacted Title 39), and reenacted by section 9 thereof as section 2713 of Title 28, Judiciary and Judicial Procedure.

§ 2714. Investment of proceeds of attached property

When the property attached is sold on an interlocutory order or is producing revenue, the money arising from the sale or revenue shall be invested, under the order of the court, in securities of the United States. The accretions therefrom are subject to the order of the court.

(Added Pub.L. 86–682, § 9, Sept. 2, 1960, 74 Stat. 707.)

HISTORICAL AND STATUTORY NOTES

Codifications

Section was derived from R.S. § 928, which was originally classified to section 741 of former Title 28. Following the general revision and enactment of Title 28 by Act June 25, 1948, R.S. § 928 was reclassified to section 841 of Title 39. R.S. § 928 was repealed by section 12(c) of Pub.L. 86–682 (section 1 of which revised and enacted Title 39), and reenacted by section 9 thereof as section 2714 of Title 28, Judiciary and Judicial Procedure.

§ 2715. Publication

The marshal shall cause publication of an executed warrant of attachment—

(1) for two months in case of an absconding debtor, and

(2) for four months in case of a nonresident debtor

in a newspaper published in the district where the property is situated pursuant to the details of the order under which the warrant is issued.

(Added Pub.L. 86–682, § 9, Sept. 2, 1960, 74 Stat. 707.)

HISTORICAL AND STATUTORY NOTES

Codifications

Section was derived from R.S. § 929, which was originally classified to section 742 of former Title 28. Following the general revision and enactment of Title 28 by Act June 25, 1948, R.S. § 929 was reclassified to section 842 of Title 39. R.S. § 929 was repealed by section 12(c) of Pub.L. 86–682 (section 1 of which revised and enacted Title 39), and reenacted by section 9 thereof as section 2715 of Title 28, Judiciary and Judicial Procedure.

§ 2716. Personal notice

After the first publication of the notice of attachment, a person indebted to, or having possession of property of a defendant and having knowledge of the notice, shall answer for the amount of his debt or the value of the property. Any disposal or attempted disposal of the property, to the injury of the United States, is unlawful. When the person indebted to, or having possession of the property of a defendant, is known to the United States attorney or marshal, the officer shall cause a personal notice of the attachment to be served upon him, but the lack of the notice does not invalidate the attachment.

(Added Pub.L. 86–682, § 9, Sept. 2, 1960, 74 Stat. 707.)

HISTORICAL AND STATUTORY NOTES

Codifications

Section was derived from R.S. § 930, which was originally classified to section 743 of former Title 28. Following the general revision and enactment of Title 28 by Act June 25, 1948, R.S. § 930 was reclassified to section 843 of Title 39. R.S. § 930 was repealed by section 12(c) of Pub.L. 86–682 (section 1 of which revised and enacted Title 39), and reenacted by section 9 thereof as section 2716 of Title 28, Judiciary and Judicial Procedure.

§ 2717. Discharge

The court, or a judge thereof, upon—

(1) application of the party when property has been attached and

(2) execution to the United States of a penal bond, approved by a judge, in double the value of the property attached and conditioned upon the return of the property or the payment of any judgment rendered by the court

may discharge the warrant of attachment as to the property of the applicant.

(Added Pub.L. 86–682, § 9, Sept. 2, 1960, 74 Stat. 708.)

HISTORICAL AND STATUTORY NOTES

Codifications

Section was derived from R.S. § 931, which was originally classified to section 744 of former Title 28. Following the general revision and enactment of Title 28 by Act June 25, 1948, R.S. § 931 was reclassified to section 844 of Title 39. R.S. § 931 was repealed by section 12(c) of Pub.L. 86–682 (section 1 of which revised and enacted Title 39), and reenacted by section 9 thereof as section 2717 of Title 28, Judiciary and Judicial Procedure.

§ 2718. Interest on balances due department

In suits for balances due the Post Office Department may recover interest at the rate of 6 per centum per year from the time of default.

(Added Pub.L. 86–682, § 9, Sept. 2, 1960, 74 Stat. 708.)

HISTORICAL AND STATUTORY NOTES

Codifications

Section was derived from R.S. § 964, which was originally classified to section 788 of former Title 28. Following the general revision and enactment of Title 28 by Act June 25, 1948, R.S. § 964 was reclassified to section 846 of Title 39. R.S. § 964 was repealed by section 12(c) of Pub.L. 86–682 (section 1 of which revised and enacted Title 39), and reenacted by section 9 thereof as section 2718 of Title 28, Judiciary and Judicial Procedure.

Change of Name

References to the Post Office Department, the Postal Service, the Postal Field Service, the Field Postal Service, or the Departmental Service or the Departmental Headquarters of the Post Office Department to be considered references to the United States Postal Service pursuant to Pub.L. 91–375, § 6(*o*), Aug. 12, 1970, 84 Stat. 783, set out as a Cross References note preceding section 101 of Title 39, Postal Service.

CHAPTER 175—CIVIL COMMITMENT AND REHABILITATION OF NARCOTIC ADDICTS

Sec.
2901. Definitions.
2902. Discretionary authority of court; examination, report, and determination by court; termination of civil commitment.
2903. Authority and responsibilities of the Surgeon General; institutional custody; aftercare; maximum period of civil commitment; credit toward sentence.
2904. Civil commitment not a conviction; use of test results.
2905. Delegation of functions by Surgeon General; use of Federal, State, and private facilities.
2906. Absence of offer by the court to a defendant of an election under section 2902(a) or any determination as to civil commitment, not reviewable on appeal or otherwise.

§ 2901. Definitions

As used in this chapter—

(a) "Addict" means any individual who habitually uses any narcotic drug as defined by section 102(16) of the Controlled Substances Act so as to endanger the public morals, health, safety, or welfare, or who is so far addicted to the use of such narcotic drugs as to have lost the power of self-control with reference to his addiction.

(b) "Surgeon General" means the Surgeon General of the Public Health Service.

(c) "Crime of violence" includes voluntary manslaughter, murder, rape, mayhem, kidnaping, robbery, burglary or housebreaking in the nighttime, extortion accompanied by threats of violence, assault with a dangerous weapon or assault with intent to commit any offense punishable by imprisonment for more than one year, arson punishable as a felony, or an attempt or conspiracy to commit any of the foregoing offenses.

(d) "Treatment" includes confinement and treatment in an institution and under supervised aftercare in the community and includes, but is not limited to, medical, educational, social, psychological, and vocational services, corrective and preventive guidance and training, and other rehabilitative services designed to protect the public and benefit the addict by eliminating his dependence on addicting drugs, or by controlling his dependence, and his susceptibility to addiction.

(e) "Felony" includes any offense in violation of a law of the United States classified as a felony under section 3581 of title 18 of the United States Code, and further includes any offense in violation of a law of any State, any possession or territory of the United States, the District of Columbia, the Canal Zone, or the Commonwealth of Puerto Rico, which at the time of the offense was classified as a felony by the law of the place where that offense was committed.

(f) "Conviction" and "convicted" mean the final judgment on a verdict or finding of guilty, a plea of guilty, or a plea of nolo contendere, but do not include a final judgment which has been expunged by pardon, reversed, set aside or otherwise rendered nugatory.

(g) "Eligible individual" means any individual who is charged with an offense against the United States, but does not include—

(1) an individual charged with a crime of violence.

(2) an individual charged with unlawfully importing, selling, or conspiring to import or sell, a narcotic drug.

(3) an individual against whom there is pending a prior charge of a felony which has not been finally determined or who is on probation or whose sen-

tence following conviction on such a charge, including any time on parole, supervised release, or mandatory release, has not been fully served: *Provided*, That an individual on probation, parole, supervised release, or mandatory release shall be included if the authority authorized to require his return to custody consents to his commitment.

(4) an individual who has been convicted of a felony on two or more occasions.

(5) an individual who has been civilly committed under this Act, under the District of Columbia Code, or any State proceeding because of narcotic addiction on three or more occasions.

(Added Pub.L. 89–793, Title I, § 101, Nov. 8, 1966, 80 Stat. 1438, and amended Pub.L. 91–513, Title III, § 1102(*l*), Oct. 27, 1970, 84 Stat. 1293; Pub.L. 92–420, § 2, Sept. 16, 1972, 86 Stat. 677; Pub.L. 98–473, Title II, § 228(c), Oct. 12, 1984, 98 Stat. 2030.)

HISTORICAL AND STATUTORY NOTES

References in Text

Section 102(16) of the Controlled Substances Act, referred to in subsec. (a), was redesignated section 102(17) of the Controlled Substances Act by Pub.L. 98–473, Title 11, § 507(a), Oct. 12, 1984, 98 Stat. 2071, and is classified to section 802(17) of Title 21, Food and Drugs.

For definition of Canal Zone, referred to in subsec. (e), see section 3602(b) of Title 22, Foreign Relations and Intercourse.

"This Act", referred to in subsec. (g) (5), probably means Pub.L. 89–793, which enacted this chapter, chapter 314 of Title 18, and chapter 42 of Title 42, amended section 7237(d) of Title 26 and section 257 of Title 42, and enacted provisions set out as notes under section 4202 of Title 18 and section 3401 of Title 42. For complete classification of this Act to the Code, see Short Title note set out under section 301 or Title 42 and Tables.

Effective Dates

1984 Acts. Amendment by Pub.L. 98–473 effective the first day of the first calendar month beginning 36 months after Oct. 12, 1984, see section 235(a)(1) of Pub.L. 98–473, as amended, set out as a note under section 3551 of Title 18, Crimes and Criminal Procedure.

1972 Acts. Section 5 of Pub.L. 92–420 provided that: "This Act [amending subsec. (d) of this section, section 4251(c) of Title 18, Crimes and Criminal Procedure, and section 3411(b) of Title 42, The Public Health and Welfare, and enacting provisions set out as note under this section] shall take effect immediately upon enactment [Sept. 16, 1972]. Sections 2 and 3 [amending section 4251(c) of Title 18 and section 3411(b) of Title 42, respectively] shall apply to any case pending in a district court of the United States in which an appearance has not been made prior to the effective date [Sept. 16, 1972]."

1970 Acts. Amendment by Pub.L. 91–513 effective on the first day of the seventh calendar month that begins after the day immediately preceding the date of enactment of Pub.L. 91–513, which was approved on Oct. 27, 1970, see section 1105(a) of Pub.L. 91–513, set out as a note under section 951 of Title 21, Food and Drugs.

1966 Acts. Chapter effective three months after Nov. 8, 1966, and applicable to any case pending in a district court of the United States in which an appearance has not been made prior to such effective date, see section 605 of Pub.L. 89–793, Title VI, Nov. 8, 1966, 80 Stat. 1450, set out as a note under section 3401 of Title 42, The Public Health and Welfare.

Savings Provisions

Prosecutions for any violation of law occurring, and civil seizures or forfeitures and injunctive proceedings commenced, prior to the effective date of amendment of this section by section 1102 of Pub.L. 91–513 not to be affected or abated by reason thereof, see section 1103 of Pub.L. 91–513.

§ 2902. Discretionary authority of court; examination, report, and determination by court; termination of civil commitment

(a) If the United States district court believes that an eligible individual is an addict, the court may advise him at his first appearance or thereafter at the sole discretion of the court that the prosecution of the criminal charge will be held in abeyance if he elects to submit to an immediate examination to determine whether he is an addict and is likely to be rehabilitated through treatment. In offering an individual an election, the court shall advise him that if he elects to be examined, he will be confined during the examination for a period not to exceed sixty days; that if he is determined to be an addict who is likely to be rehabilitated, he will be civilly committed to the Surgeon General for treatment; that he may not voluntarily withdraw from the examination or any treatment which may follow; that the treatment may last for thirty-six months; that during treatment, he will be confined in an institution and, at the discretion of the Surgeon General, he may be conditionally released for supervised aftercare treatment in the community; and that if he successfully completes treatment the charge will be dismissed, but if he does not, prosecution on the charge will be resumed. An individual upon being advised that he may elect to submit to an examination shall be permitted a maximum of five days within which to make his election. Except on a showing that a timely election could not have been made, an individual shall be barred from an election after the prescribed period. An individual who elects civil commitment shall be placed in the custody of the Attorney General or the Surgeon General, as the court directs, for an examination by the Surgeon General during a period not to exceed thirty days. This period may, upon notice to the court and the appropriate United States attorney, be extended by the Surgeon General for an additional thirty days.

(b) The Surgeon General shall report to the court the results of the examination and recommend whether the individual should be civilly committed. A copy of the report shall be made available to the individual and the United States attorney. If the court, acting on the report and other information coming to its attention, determines that the individual is not an addict or is an addict not likely to be rehabilitated through treatment, the individual shall be held to answer the abeyant charge. If the court determines that the individual is an addict and is likely to be rehabilitated through treatment, the court shall commit him to the custody of the Surgeon General for treatment, except that no individual shall be committed under this chapter if the Surgeon General certifies that adequate facilities or personnel for treatment are unavailable.

(c) Whenever an individual is committed to the custody of the Surgeon General for treatment under this chapter the criminal charge against him shall be continued without final disposition and shall be dismissed if the Surgeon General certifies to the court that the individual has successfully completed the treatment program. On receipt of such certification, the court shall discharge the individual from custody and dismiss the charge against him. If prior to such certification the Surgeon General determines that the individual cannot be further treated as a medical problem, he shall advise the court. The court shall thereupon terminate the commitment, and the pending criminal proceeding shall be resumed.

(d) An individual committed for examination or treatment shall not be released on bail or on his own recognizance.

(e) Whoever escapes or attempts to escape while committed to institutional custody for examination or treatment, or whoever rescues or attempts to rescue or instigates, aids, or assists the escape or attempt to escape of such a person, shall be subject to the penalties provided in sections 751 and 752 of title 18, United States Code.

(Added Pub.L. 89–793, Title I, § 101, Nov. 8, 1966, 80 Stat. 1439.)

HISTORICAL AND STATUTORY NOTES

Effective Dates

1966 Acts. Chapter effective three months after Nov. 8, 1966, and applicable to any case pending in a district court of the United States in which an appearance has not been made prior to such effective date, see section 605 of Pub.L. 89–793, Title VI, Nov. 8, 1966, 80 Stat. 1450, set out as a note under section 3401 of Title 42, The Public Health and Welfare.

§ 2903. Authority and responsibilities of the Surgeon General; institutional custody; aftercare; maximum period of civil commitment; credit toward sentence

(a) An individual who is committed to the custody of the Surgeon General for treatment under this chapter shall not be conditionally released from institutional custody until the Surgeon General determines that he has made sufficient progress to warrant release to a supervisory aftercare authority. If the Surgeon General is unable to make such a determination at the expiration of twenty-four months after the commencement of institutional custody, he shall advise the court and the appropriate United States attorney whether treatment should be continued. The court may affirm the commitment or terminate it and resume the pending criminal proceeding.

(b) An individual who is conditionally released from institutional custody shall, while on release, remain in the legal custody of the Surgeon General and shall report for such supervised aftercare treatment as the Surgeon General directs. He shall be subject to home visits and to such physical examination and reasonable regulation of his conduct as the supervisory aftercare authority establishes, subject to the approval of the Surgeon General. The Surgeon General may, at any time, order a conditionally released individual to return for institutional treatment. The Surgeon General's order shall be a sufficient warrant for the supervisory aftercare authority, a probation officer, or any Federal officer authorized to serve criminal process within the United States to apprehend and return the individual to institutional custody as directed. If it is determined that an individual has returned to the use of narcotics, the Surgeon General shall inform the court of the conditions under which the return occurred and make a recommendation as to whether treatment should be continued. The court may affirm the commitment or terminate it and resume the pending criminal proceeding.

(c) The total period of treatment for any individual committed to the custody of the Surgeon General shall not exceed thirty-six months. If, at the expiration of such maximum period, the Surgeon General is unable to certify that the individual has successfully completed his treatment program the pending criminal proceeding shall be resumed.

(d) Whenever a pending criminal proceeding against an individual is resumed under this chapter, he shall receive full credit toward the service of any sentence which may be imposed for any time spent in the institutional custody of the Surgeon General or the Attorney General or any other time spent in institutional custody in connection with the matter for which sentence is imposed.

(Added Pub.L. 89–793, Title I, § 101, Nov. 8, 1966, 80 Stat. 1440.)

HISTORICAL AND STATUTORY NOTES

Effective Dates

1966 Acts. Chapter effective three months after Nov. 8, 1966, and applicable to any case pending in a district court of the United States in which an appearance has not been made prior to such effective date, see section 605 of Pub.L. 89–793, Title VI, Nov. 8, 1966, 80 Stat. 1450, set out as a note under section 3401 of Title 42, The Public Health and Welfare.

§ 2904. Civil commitment not a conviction; use of test results

The determination of narcotic addiction and the subsequent civil commitment under this chapter shall not be deemed a criminal conviction. The results of any tests or procedures conducted by the Surgeon General or the supervisory aftercare authority to determine narcotic addiction may only be used in a further proceeding under this chapter. They shall not be used against the examined individual in any criminal proceeding except that the fact that he is a narcotic addict may be elicited on his cross-examination as bearing on his credibility as a witness.

(Added Pub.L. 89–793, Title I, § 101, Nov. 8, 1966, 80 Stat. 1441.)

HISTORICAL AND STATUTORY NOTES

Effective Dates

1966 Acts. Chapter effective three months after Nov. 8, 1966, and applicable to any case pending in a district court of the United States in which an appearance has not been made prior to such effective date, see section 605 of Pub.L. 89–793, Title VI, Nov. 8, 1966, 80 Stat. 1450, set out as a note under section 3401 of Title 42, The Public Health and Welfare.

§ 2905. Delegation of functions by Surgeon General; use of Federal, State, and private facilities

(a) The Surgeon General may from time to time make such provision as he deems appropriate authorizing the performance of any of his functions under this chapter by any other officer or employee of the Public Health Service, or with the consent of the head of the Department or Agency concerned, by any Federal or other public or private agency or officer or employee thereof.

(b) The Surgeon General is authorized to enter into arrangements with any public or private agency or any person under which appropriate facilities or services of such agency or person will be made available, on a reimbursable basis or otherwise, for the examination or treatment of individuals who elect civil commitment under this chapter.

(Added Pub.L. 89–793, Title I, § 101, Nov. 8, 1966, 80 Stat. 1441.)

HISTORICAL AND STATUTORY NOTES

Effective Dates

1966 Acts. Chapter effective three months after Nov. 8, 1966, and applicable to any case pending in a district court of the United States in which an appearance has not been made prior to such effective date, see section 605 of Pub.L. 89–793, Title VI, Nov. 8, 1966, 80 Stat. 1450, set out as a note under section 3401 of Title 42, The Public Health and Welfare.

§ 2906. Absence of offer by the court to a defendant of an election under section 2902(a) or any determination as to civil commitment, not reviewable on appeal or otherwise

The failure of a court to offer a defendant an election under section 2902(a) of this chapter, or a determination relative to civil commitment under this chapter shall not be reviewable on appeal or otherwise.

(Added Pub.L. 89–793, Title I, § 101, Nov. 8, 1966, 80 Stat. 1441.)

HISTORICAL AND STATUTORY NOTES

Effective Dates

1966 Acts. Chapter effective three months after Nov. 8, 1966, and applicable to any case pending in a district court of the United States in which an appearance has not been made prior to such effective date, see section 605 of Pub.L. 89–793, Title VI, Nov. 8, 1966, 80 Stat. 1450, set out as a note under section 3401 of Title 42, The Public Health and Welfare.

CHAPTER 176—FEDERAL DEBT COLLECTION PROCEDURE

Subchapter		Section[1]
A.	**Definitions and general provisions**	3001
B.	**Prejudgment remedies**	3101
C.	**Postjudgments remedies[2]**	3201
D.	**Fraudulent transfers[2]**	3301

[1]Editorially supplied.

[2]So in original. Does not conform to subchapter heading.

SUBCHAPTER A—DEFINITIONS AND GENERAL PROVISIONS

Sec.
3001. Applicability of chapter.
3002. Definitions.
3003. Rules of construction.
3004. Service of process; enforcement; notice.
3005. Application of chapter to judgments.
3006. Affidavit requirements.
3007. Perishable personal property.
3008. Proceedings before United States magistrates.
3009. United States marshals' authority to designate keeper.
3010. Co-owned property.
3011. Assessment of surcharge on a debt.
3012. Joinder of additional defendant.
3013. Modification or protective order; supervision of enforcement.
3014. Exempt property.
3015. Discovery as to debtor's financial condition.

§ 3001. Applicability of chapter

(a) In general.—Except as provided in subsection (b), the[1] chapter provides the exclusive civil procedures for the United States—

(1) to recover a judgment on a debt; or

(2) to obtain, before judgment on a claim for a debt, a remedy in connection with such claim.

(b) Limitation.—To the extent that another Federal law specifies procedures for recovering on a claim or a judgment for a debt arising under such law, those procedures shall apply to such claim or judgment to the extent those procedures are inconsistent with this chapter.

(c) Amounts owing other than debts.—This chapter shall not apply with respect to an amount owing that is not a debt or to a claim for an amount owing that is not a debt.

(Added Pub.L. 101–647, Title XXXVI, § 3611, Nov. 29, 1990, 104 Stat. 4933.)

[1] So in original. Probably should be "this".

HISTORICAL AND STATUTORY NOTES

Effective Dates

1990 Acts. Section 3631 of Title XXXVI of Pub.L. 101–647 provided that:

"(a) Except as provided in subsection (b), this Act and the amendments made by this Act [Pub.L. 101–647, Title XXXVI, Nov. 29, 1990, 104 Stat. 4933, popularly known as the Federal Debt Collection Procedures Act of 1990. For distribution of this Act to the Code, see Short Title note set out under section 1 of this title and Tables] shall take effect 180 days after the date of the enactment of this Act [Nov. 29, 1990].

"(b)(1) The amendments made by title I of this Act [probably means subtitle A of Title XXXVI of Pub.L. 101–647, which enacted this chapter] shall apply with respect to actions pending on the effective date of this Act [180 days after Nov. 29, 1990] in any court on—

"(A) a claim for a debt; or

"(B) a judgment for a debt.

"(2) All notices, writs, orders, and judgments in effect in such actions shall continue in effect until superseded or modified in an action under chapter 176 of title 28 of the United States Code, as added by title I of this Act [this chapter].

"(3) For purposes of this subsection—

"(A) the term 'court' means a Federal, State, or local court, and

"(B) the term 'debt' has the meaning given such term in section and 3002(3) of such chapter [probably means section 3002(3) of this title]."

§ 3002. Definitions

As used in this chapter:

(1) "Counsel for the United States" means—

(A) a United States attorney, an assistant United States attorney designated to act on behalf of the United States attorney, or an attorney with the United States Department of Justice or with a Federal agency who has litigation authority; and

(B) any private attorney authorized by contract made in accordance with section 3718 of title 31 to conduct litigation for collection of debts on behalf of the United States.

(2) "Court" means any court created by the Congress of the United States, excluding the United States Tax Court.

(3) "Debt" means—

(A) an amount that is owing to the United States on account of a direct loan, or loan insured or guaranteed, by the United States; or

(B) an amount that is owing to the United States on account of a fee, duty, lease, rent, service, sale of real or personal property, overpayment, fine, assessment, penalty, restitution, damages, interest, tax, bail bond forfeiture, reimbursement, recovery of a cost incurred by the United States, or other source of indebtedness to the United States, but that is not owing under the terms of a contract originally entered into by only persons other than the United States;

and includes any amount owing to the United States for the benefit of an Indian tribe or individual Indian, but excludes any amount to which the United States is entitled under section 3011(a).

(4) "Debtor" means a person who is liable for a debt or against whom there is a claim for a debt.

(5) "Disposable earnings" means that part of earnings remaining after all deductions required by law have been withheld.

(6) "Earnings" means compensation paid or payable for personal services, whether denominated as wages, salary, commission, bonus, or otherwise, and includes periodic payments pursuant to a pension or retirement program.

(7) "Garnishee" means a person (other than the debtor) who has, or is reasonably thought to have, possession, custody, or control of any property in which the debtor has a substantial nonexempt interest, including any obligation due the debtor or to become due the debtor, and against whom a garnishment under section 3104 or 3205 is issued by a court.

(8) "Judgment" means a judgment, order, or decree entered in favor of the United States in a court and arising from a civil or criminal proceeding regarding a debt.

(9) "Nonexempt disposable earnings" means 25 percent of disposable earnings, subject to section 303 of the Consumer Credit Protection Act.

(10) "Person" includes a natural person (including an individual Indian), a corporation, a partnership, an unincorporated association, a trust, or an estate, or any other public or private entity, including a State or local government or an Indian tribe.

(11) "Prejudgment remedy" means the remedy of attachment, receivership, garnishment, or sequestration authorized by this chapter to be granted before judgment on the merits of a claim for a debt.

(12) "Property" includes any present or future interest, whether legal or equitable, in real, personal (including choses in action), or mixed property, tangible or intangible, vested or contingent, wherever located and however held (including community property and property held in trust (including spendthrift and pension trusts)), but excludes—

(A) property held in trust by the United States for the benefit of an Indian tribe or individual Indian; and

(B) Indian lands subject to restrictions against alienation imposed by the United States.

(13) "Security agreement" means an agreement that creates or provides for a lien.

(14) "State" means any of the several States, the District of Columbia, the Commonwealth of Puerto Rico, the Commonwealth of the Northern Marianas, or any territory or possession of the United States.

(15) "United States" means—

(A) a Federal corporation;

(B) an agency, department, commission, board, or other entity of the United States; or

(C) an instrumentality of the United States.

(16) "United States marshal" means a United States marshal, a deputy marshal, or an official of the United States Marshals Service designated under section 564.

(Added Pub.L. 101–647, Title XXXVI, § 3611, Nov. 29, 1990, 104 Stat. 4933.)

HISTORICAL AND STATUTORY NOTES

References in Text

Section 303 of the Consumer Credit Protection Act, referred to in par. (9), is classified to section 1673 of Title 15, Commerce and Trade.

Effective Dates

1990 Acts. Section to take effect 180 days after Nov. 29, 1990, except as otherwise provided, see section 3631 of Pub.L. 101–647, set out as a note under section 3001 of this title.

§ 3003. Rules of construction

(a) Terms.—For purposes of this chapter—

(1) the terms "includes" and "including" are not limiting;

(2) the term "or" is not exclusive; and

(3) the singular includes the plural.

(b) Effect on rights of the United States.—This chapter shall not be construed to curtail or limit the right of the United States under any other Federal law or any State law—

(1) to collect taxes or to collect any other amount collectible in the same manner as a tax;

(2) to collect any fine, penalty, assessment, restitution, or forfeiture arising in a criminal case;

(3) to appoint or seek the appointment of a receiver; or

(4) to enforce a security agreement.

(c) Effect on other laws.—This chapter shall not be construed to supersede or modify the operation of—

(1) title 11;

(2) admiralty law;

(3) section 3713 of title 31;

(4) section 303 of the Consumer Credit Protection Act (15 U.S.C. 1673);

(5) a statute of limitation applicable to a criminal proceeding;

(6) the common law or statutory rights to set-off or recoupment;

(7) any Federal law authorizing, or any inherent authority of a court to provide, injunctive relief;

(8) the authority of a court—

(A) to impose a sanction under the Federal Rules of Civil Procedure;

(B) to appoint a receiver to effectuate its order; or

(C) to exercise the power of contempt under any Federal law;

(9) any law authorizing the United States to obtain partition, or to recover possession, of property in which the United States holds title; or

(10) any provision of any other chapter of this title, except to the extent such provision is inconsistent with this chapter.

(d) Preemption.—This chapter shall preempt State law to the extent such law is inconsistent with a provision of this chapter.

(e) Effect on rights of the United States under foreign and international law.—This chapter shall not be construed to curtail or limit the rights of the United States under foreign law, under a treaty or an international agreement, or otherwise under international law.

(f) Applicability of Federal Rules of Civil Procedure.—Except as provided otherwise in this chapter, the Federal Rules of Civil Procedure shall apply with respect to actions and proceedings under this chapter.

(Added Pub.L. 101–647, Title XXXVI, § 3611, Nov. 29, 1990, 104 Stat. 4935.)

HISTORICAL AND STATUTORY NOTES

References in Text

The Federal Rules of Civil Procedure, referred to in subsecs. (c)(8)(A) and (f), are set out in this title.

Effective Dates

1990 Acts. Section to take effect 180 days after Nov. 29, 1990, except as otherwise provided, see section 3631 of Pub.L. 101–647, set out as a note under section 3001 of this title.

§ 3004. Service of process; enforcement; notice

(a) Manner of service.—A complaint, notice, writ, or other process required to be served in an action or proceeding under this chapter shall be served in accordance with the Federal Rules of Civil Procedure unless otherwise provided in this chapter.

(b) Nationwide enforcement.—(1) Except as provided in paragraph (2)—

(A) any writ, order, judgment, or other process, including a summons and complaint, filed under this chapter may be served in any State; and

(B) such writ, order, or judgment may be enforced by the court issuing the writ, order, or process, regardless of where the person is served with the writ, order, or process.

(2) If the debtor so requests, within 20 days after receiving the notice described in section 3101(d) or 3202(b), the action or proceeding in which the writ, order, or judgment was issued shall be transferred to the district court for the district in which the debtor resides.

(c) Notice and other process.—At such time as counsel for the United States considers appropriate, but not later than the time a prejudgment or postjudgment remedy is put into effect under this chapter, counsel for the United States shall exercise reasonable diligence to serve on the debtor and any person who the United States believes, after exercising due diligence, has possession, custody, or control of the property, a copy of the application for such remedy, the order granting such remedy, and the notice required by section 3101(d) or 3202(b).

(Added Pub.L. 101–647, Title XXXVI, § 3611, Nov. 29, 1990, 104 Stat. 4936.)

HISTORICAL AND STATUTORY NOTES

References in Text

The Federal Rules of Civil Procedure, referred to in subsec. (a), are set out in this title.

Effective Dates

1990 Acts. Section to take effect 180 days after Nov. 29, 1990, except as otherwise provided, see section 3631 of Pub.L. 101–647, set out as a note under section 3001 of this title.

§ 3005. Application of chapter to judgments

This chapter shall not apply with respect to a judgment on a debt if such judgment is entered more than 10 years before the effective date of this chapter.

(Added Pub.L. 101–647, Title XXXVI, § 3611, Nov. 29, 1990, 104 Stat. 4936.)

HISTORICAL AND STATUTORY NOTES

References in Text

For effective date of this chapter, referred to in text, see section 3631 of Pub.L. 101–647, set out as an Effective Date note under section 3001 of this title.

Effective Dates

1990 Acts. Section to take effect 180 days after Nov. 29, 1990, except as otherwise provided, see section 3631 of Pub.L. 101–647, set out as a note under section 3001 of this title.

§ 3006. Affidavit requirements

Any affidavit required of the United States by this chapter may be made on information and belief, if reliable and reasonably necessary, establishing with particularity, to the court's satisfaction, facts supporting the claim of the United States.

(Added Pub.L. 101–647, Title XXXVI, § 3611, Nov. 29, 1990, 104 Stat. 4936.)

HISTORICAL AND STATUTORY NOTES

Effective Dates

1990 Acts. Section to take effect 180 days after Nov. 29, 1990, except as otherwise provided, see section 3631 of Pub.L. 101–647, set out as a note under section 3001 of this title.

§ 3007. Perishable personal property

(a) Authority to sell.—If at any time during any action or proceeding under this chapter the court determines on its own initiative or upon motion of any party, that any seized or detained personal property is likely to perish, waste, or be destroyed, or otherwise substantially depreciate in value during the pendency of the proceeding, the court shall order a commercially reasonable sale of such property.

(b) Deposit of sale proceeds.—Within 5 days after such sale, the proceeds shall be deposited with the clerk of the court, accompanied by a statement in writing and signed by the United States marshal, to be filed in the action or proceeding, stating the time and place of sale, the name of the purchaser, the amount received, and an itemized account of expenses.

(c) Presumption.—For purposes of liability on the part of the United States, there shall be a presumption that the price paid at a sale under subsection (a) is the fair market value of the property or portion.

(Added Pub.L. 101–647, Title XXXVI, § 3611, Nov. 29, 1990, 104 Stat. 4937.)

HISTORICAL AND STATUTORY NOTES

Effective Dates

1990 Acts. Section to take effect 180 days after Nov. 29, 1990, except as otherwise provided, see section 3631 of Pub.L. 101–647, set out as a note under section 3001 of this title.

§ 3008. Proceedings before United States magistrates

A district court of the United States may assign its duties in proceedings under this chapter to a United States magistrate to the extent not inconsistent with the Constitution and laws of the United States.

(Added Pub.L. 101–647, Title XXXVI, § 3611, Nov. 29, 1990, 104 Stat. 4937.)

HISTORICAL AND STATUTORY NOTES

Effective Dates

1990 Acts. Section to take effect 180 days after Nov. 29, 1990, except as otherwise provided, see section 3631 of Pub.L. 101–647, set out as a note under section 3001 of this title.

Change of Name of United States Magistrates

United States magistrates appointed under section 631 of this title, to be known as United States magistrate judge after Dec. 1, 1990, with any reference to any United States magistrate or magistrate contained in this title, in any other Federal statute, etc., deemed to refer to a United States magistrate judge appointed under section 631 of this title, see section 321 of Pub.L. 101–650, set out as a note under section 631 of this title.

§ 3009. United States marshals' authority to designate keeper

Whenever a United States marshal is authorized to seize property pursuant to this chapter, the United States marshal may designate another person or Federal agency to hold for safekeeping such property seized.

(Added Pub.L. 101–647, Title XXXVI, § 3611, Nov. 29, 1990, 104 Stat. 4937.)

HISTORICAL AND STATUTORY NOTES

Effective Dates

1990 Acts. Section to take effect 180 days after Nov. 29, 1990, except as otherwise provided, see section 3631 of Pub.L. 101–647, set out as a note under section 3001 of this title.

§ 3010. Co-owned property

(a) Limitation.—The remedies available to the United States under this chapter may be enforced against property which is co-owned by a debtor and any other person only to the extent allowed by the law of the State where the property is located. This section shall not be construed to limit any right or interest of a debtor or co-owner in a retirement system for Federal military or civilian personnel established by the United States or any agency thereof or in a qualified retirement arrangement.

(b) Definitions.—For purposes of subsection (a)—

(1) the term "retirement system for Federal military or civilian personnel" means a pension or annuity system for Federal military or civilian personnel of more than one agency, or for some or all of such personnel of a single agency, established by statute or by regulation pursuant to statutory authority; and

(2) the term "qualified retirement arrangement" means a plan qualified under section 401(a), 403(a), or 409 of the Internal Revenue Code of 1986 or a plan that is subject to the requirements of section 205 of the Employee Retirement Income Security Act of 1974.

(Added Pub.L. 101–647, Title XXXVI, § 3611, Nov. 29, 1990, 104 Stat. 4937.)

HISTORICAL AND STATUTORY NOTES

References in Text

Sections 401(a), 403(a) and 409 of the Internal Revenue Code of 1986, referred to in subsec. (b)(2), are set out in sections 401(a), 403(a) and 409, respectively, of Title 26, Internal Revenue Code.

Section 205 of the Employee Retirement Income Security Act of 1974, referred to in subsec. (b)(2), is classified to section 1055 of Title 29, Labor.

Effective Dates

1990 Acts. Section to take effect 180 days after Nov. 29, 1990, except as otherwise provided, see section 3631 of Pub.L. 101–647, set out as a note under section 3001 of this title.

§ 3011. Assessment of surcharge on a debt

(a) Surcharge authorized.—In an action or proceeding under subchapter B or C, and subject to subsection (b), the United States is entitled to recover a surcharge of 10 percent of the amount of the debt in connection with the recovery of the debt, to cover the cost of processing and handling the litigation and enforcement under this chapter of the claim for such debt.

(b) Limitation.—Subsection (a) shall not apply if—

(1) the United States receives an attorney's fee in connection with the enforcement of the claim; or

(2) the law pursuant to which the action on the claim is based provides any other amount to cover such costs.

(Added Pub.L. 101–647, Title XXXVI, § 3611, Nov. 29, 1990, 104 Stat. 4937.)

HISTORICAL AND STATUTORY NOTES

Effective Dates

1990 Acts. Section to take effect 180 days after Nov. 29, 1990, except as otherwise provided, see section 3631 of Pub.L. 101–647, set out as a note under section 3001 of this title.

§ 3012. Joinder of additional defendant

The United States or the debtor may join as an additional defendant in an action or proceeding under this chapter any person reasonably believed to owe money (including money owed on account of a requirement to provide goods or services pursuant to a loan or loan guarantee extended under Federal law) to the debtor arising out of the transaction or occurrence giving rise to a debt.

(Added Pub.L. 101–647, Title XXXVI, § 3611, Nov. 29, 1990, 104 Stat. 4938.)

HISTORICAL AND STATUTORY NOTES

Effective Dates

1990 Acts. Section to take effect 180 days after Nov. 29, 1990, except as otherwise provided, see section 3631 of Pub.L. 101–647, set out as a note under section 3001 of this title.

§ 3013. Modification or protective order; supervision of enforcement

The court may at any time on its own initiative or the motion of any interested person, and after such notice as it may require, make an order denying, limiting, conditioning, regulating, extending, or modifying the use of any enforcement procedure under this chapter.

(Added Pub.L. 101–647, Title XXXVI, § 3611, Nov. 29, 1990, 104 Stat. 4938.)

HISTORICAL AND STATUTORY NOTES

Effective Dates

1990 Acts. Section to take effect 180 days after Nov. 29, 1990, except as otherwise provided, see section 3631 of Pub.L. 101–647, set out as a note under section 3001 of this title.

§ 3014. Exempt property

(a) Election to exempt property.—An individual debtor may, in an action or proceeding under this chapter, elect to exempt property listed in either paragraph (1) or, in the alternative, paragraph (2). If such action or proceeding is against debtors who are husband and wife, one debtor may not elect to exempt property listed in paragraph (1) and the other debtor elect to exempt property listed in paragraph (2). If the debtors cannot agree on the alternative to be elected, they shall be deemed to elect paragraph (1). Such property is either—

(1) property that is specified in section 522(d) of title 11, as amended from time to time; or

(2)(A) any property that is exempt under Federal law, other than paragraph (1), or State or local law that is applicable on the date of the filing of the application for a remedy under this chapter at the place in which the debtor's domicile has been located for the 180 days immediately preceding the date of the filing of such application, or for a longer portion of such 180–day period than in any other place; and

(B) any interest in property in which the debtor had, immediately before the filing of such application, an interest as a tenant by the entirety or joint tenant, or an interest in a community estate, to the extent that such interest is exempt from process under applicable nonbankruptcy law.

(b) Effect on assertion and manner of determination.—

(1) Statement.—A court may order the debtor to file a statement with regard to any claimed exemption. A copy of such statement shall be served on counsel for the United States. Such statement shall be under oath and shall describe each item of property for which exemption is claimed, the value and the basis for such valuation, and the nature of the debtor's ownership interest.

(2) Hearing.—The United States or the debtor, by application to the court in which an action or proceeding under this chapter is pending, may request a hearing on the applicability of any exemption claimed by the debtor. The court shall determine the extent (if any) to which the exemption applies. Unless it is reasonably evident that the exemption applies, the debtor shall bear the burden of persuasion.

(3) Stay of disposition.—Assertion of an exemption shall prevent the United States from selling or otherwise disposing of the property for which such exemption is claimed until the court determines whether the debtor has a substantial nonexempt interest in such property. The United States may not take possession of, dispose of, sell, or otherwise interfere with the debtor's normal use and enjoyment of an interest in property the United States knows or has reason to know is exempt.

(c) Debtors in joint cases.—Subject to the limitation in subsection (a), this section shall apply separately with respect to each debtor in a joint case.

(Added Pub.L. 101–647, Title XXXVI, § 3611, Nov. 29, 1990, 104 Stat. 4938.)

HISTORICAL AND STATUTORY NOTES

Effective Dates

1990 Acts. Section to take effect 180 days after Nov. 29, 1990, except as otherwise provided, see section 3631 of Pub.L. 101–647, set out as a note under section 3001 of this title.

§ 3015. Discovery as to debtor's financial condition

(a) In general.—Except as provided in subsection (b), in an action or proceeding under subchapter B or C, the United States may have discovery regarding the financial condition of the debtor in the manner in which discovery is authorized by the Federal Rules of Civil Procedure in an action on a claim for a debt.

(b) Limitation.—Subsection (a) shall not apply with respect to an action or proceeding under subchapter B unless there is a reasonable likelihood that the debt involved exceeds $50,000.

(Added Pub.L. 101–647, Title XXXVI, § 3611, Nov. 29, 1990, 104 Stat. 4939.)

HISTORICAL AND STATUTORY NOTES

References in Text

The Federal Rules of Civil Procedure, referred to in subsec. (a), are set out in this title.

Effective Dates

1990 Acts. Section to take effect 180 days after Nov. 29, 1990, except as otherwise provided, see section 3631 of Pub.L. 101–647, set out as a note under section 3001 of this title.

SUBCHAPTER B—PREJUDGMENT REMEDIES

Sec.
3101. Prejudgment remedies.
3102. Attachment.
3103. Receivership.
3104. Garnishment.
3105. Sequestration.

§ 3101. Prejudgment remedies

(a) Application.—(1) The United States may, in a proceeding in conjunction with the complaint or at any time after the filing of a civil action on a claim for a debt, make application under oath to a court to issue any prejudgment remedy.

(2) Such application shall be filed with the court and shall set forth the factual and legal basis for each prejudgment remedy sought.

(3) Such application shall—

(A) state that the debtor against whom the prejudgment remedy is sought shall be afforded an opportunity for a hearing; and

(B) set forth with particularity that all statutory requirements under this chapter for the issuance of the prejudgment remedy sought have been satisfied.

(b) Grounds.—Subject to section 3102, 3103, 3104, or 3105, a prejudgment remedy may be granted by any court if the United States shows reasonable cause to believe that—

(1) the debtor—

(A) is about to leave the jurisdiction of the United States with the effect of hindering, delaying, or defrauding the United States in its effort to recover a debt;

(B) has or is about to assign, dispose, remove, conceal, ill treat, waste, or destroy property with the effect of hindering, delaying, or defrauding the United States;

(C) has or is about to convert the debtor's property into money, securities, or evidence of debt in a manner prejudicial to the United States with the effect of hindering, delaying, or defrauding the United States; or

(D) has evaded service of process by concealing himself or has temporarily withdrawn from the jurisdiction of the United States with the effect of hindering, delaying, or defrauding the United States; or

(2) a prejudgment remedy is required to obtain jurisdiction within the United States and the prejudgment remedy sought will result in obtaining such jurisdiction.

(c) Affidavit.—(1) The application under subsection (a) shall include an affidavit establishing with particularity to the court's satisfaction facts supporting the probable validity of the claim for a debt and the right of the United States to recover what is demanded in the application.

(2) The affidavit shall state—

(A) specifically the amount of the debt claimed by the United States and any interest or costs attributable to such debt;

(B) one or more of the grounds specified in subsection (b); and

(C) the requirements of section 3102(b), 3103(a), 3104(a), or 3105(b), as the case may be.

(3) No bond is required of the United States.

(d) Notice and hearing.—(1) On filing an application by the United States as provided in this section, the counsel for the United States shall prepare, and the clerk shall issue, a notice for service on the debtor against whom the prejudgment remedy is sought and on any other person whom the United States reasonably believes, after exercising due diligence, has possession, custody, or control of property affected by such remedy. Three copies of the notice shall be served on each such person. The form and content of such notice shall be approved jointly by a majority of the chief judges of the Federal districts in the State in which the court is located and shall be in substantially the following form:

"NOTICE

'You are hereby notified that this [property] is being taken by the United States Government ('the Government'), which says that [name of debtor] owes it a debt of $ [amount] for [reason for debt] and has filed a lawsuit to collect this debt. The Government says it must take this property at this time because [recite the pertinent ground or grounds from section 3101(b)]. The Government wants to make sure [name of debtor] will pay if the court determines that this money is owed.

"In addition, you are hereby notified that there are exemptions under the law which may protect some of this property from being taken by the Government if [name of debtor] can show that the exemptions apply. Below is a summary of the major exemptions which apply in most situations in the State of [State where property is located]:

"[A statement summarizing in plain and understandable English the election available with respect to such State under section 3014 and the types of property that may be exempted under each of the alternatives specified in paragraphs (1) and (2) of section 3014(a), and a statement that different property may be so exempted with respect to the State in which the debtor resides.]

"If you are [name of debtor] and you disagree with the reason the Government gives for taking your property now, or if you think you do not owe the money to the Government that it says you do, or if you think the property the Government is taking qualifies under one of the above exemptions, you have a right to ask the court to return your property to you.

"If you want a hearing, you must promptly notify the court. You must make your request in writing, and either mail it or deliver it in person to the clerk of the court at [address]. If you wish, you may use this notice to request the hearing by checking the box below and mailing this notice to the court clerk. You must also send a copy of your request to the Government at [address], so the Government will know you want a hearing. The hearing will take place within 5 days after the clerk receives your request, if you ask for it to take place that quickly, or as soon after that as possible.

"At the hearing you may explain to the judge why you think you do not owe the money to the Government, why you disagree with the reason the Government says it must take your property at this time, or why you believe the property the Government has taken is exempt or belongs to someone else. You may make any or all of these explanations as you see fit.

"If you think you live outside the Federal judicial district in which the court is located, you may request, not later than 20 days after you receive this notice, that this proceeding to take your property be transferred by the court to the Federal judicial district in which you reside. You must make your request in writing, and either mail it or deliver it in person to the clerk of the court at [address]. You must also send a copy of your request to the Government at [address], so the Government will know you want the proceeding to be transferred.

"Be sure to keep a copy of this notice for your own records. If you have any questions about your rights or about this procedure, you should contact a lawyer, an office of public legal assistance, or the clerk of the court. The clerk is not permitted to give legal advice, but can refer you to other sources of information.".

(2) By requesting, at any time before judgment on the claim for a debt, the court to hold a hearing, the debtor may move to quash the order granting such remedy. The court shall hold a hearing on such motion as soon as practicable, or, if requested by the debtor, within 5 days after receiving the request for a hearing or as soon thereafter as possible. The issues at such hearing shall be limited to—

(A) the probable validity of the claim for the debt for which such remedy was granted and of any defense or claim of exemption asserted by such person;

(B) compliance with any statutory requirement for the issuance of the prejudgment remedy granted;

(C) the existence of any ground set forth in subsection (b); and

(D) the inadequacy of alternative remedies (if any) to protect the interests of the United States.

(e) Issuance of writ.—On the court's determination that the requirements of subsections (a), (b), and (c) have been met, the court shall issue all process sufficient to put into effect the prejudgment remedy sought.

(Added Pub.L. 101–647, Title XXXVI, § 3611, Nov. 29, 1990, 104 Stat. 4939.)

HISTORICAL AND STATUTORY NOTES

Effective Dates

1990 Acts. Section to take effect 180 days after Nov. 29, 1990, except as otherwise provided, see section 3631 of Pub.L. 101–647, set out as a note under section 3001 of this title.

§ 3102. Attachment

(a) Property subject to attachment.—(1) Any property in the possession, custody, or control of the debtor and in which the debtor has a substantial nonexempt interest, except earnings, may be attached pursuant to a writ of attachment in an action or proceeding against a debtor on a claim for a debt and may be held as security to satisfy such judgment, and interest and costs, as the United States may recover on such claim.

(2) The value of property attached shall not exceed the amount by which the sum of the amount of the debt claimed by the United States and the amount of interest and costs reasonably likely to be assessed against the debtor by the court exceeds the aggregate value of the nonexempt interest of the debtor in any—

(A) property securing the debt; and

(B) property garnished or in receivership, or income sequestered, under this subchapter.

(b) Availability of attachment.—If the requirements of section 3101 are satisfied, a court shall issue a writ authorizing the United States to attach property in which the debtor has a substantial nonexempt interest, as security for such judgment (and interest and costs) as the United States may recover on a claim for a debt—

(1) in an action on a contract, express or implied, against the debtor for payment of money, only if the United States shows reasonable cause to believe that—

(A) the contract is not fully secured by real or personal property; or

(B) the value of the original security is substantially diminished, without any act of the United States or the person to whom the security was given, below the amount of the debt;

(2) in an action against the debtor for damages in tort;

(3) if the debtor resides outside the jurisdiction of the United States; or

(4) in an action to recover a fine, penalty, or tax.

(c) Issuance of writ; contents.—(1) Subject to subsections (a) and (b), a writ of attachment shall be issued by the court directing the United States marshal of the district where property described in subsection (a) is located to attach the property.

(2) Several writs of attachment may be issued at the same time, or in succession, and sent to different judicial districts until sufficient property is attached.

(3) The writ of attachment shall contain—

(A) the date of the issuance of the writ;

(B) the identity of the court, the docket number of the action, and the identity of the cause of action;

(C) the name and last known address of the debtor;

(D) the amount to be secured by the attachment; and

(E) a reasonable description of the property to be attached.

(d) Levy of attachment.—(1) The United States marshal receiving the writ shall proceed without delay to levy upon the property specified for attachment if found within the district. The marshal may not sell property unless ordered by the court.

(2) In performing the levy, the United States marshal may enter any property owned, occupied, or controlled by the debtor, except that the marshal may not enter a residence or other building unless the writ expressly authorizes the marshal to do so or upon specific order of the court.

(3) Levy on real property is made by entering the property and posting the writ and notice of levy in a conspicuous place upon the property.

(4) Levy on personal property is made by taking possession of it. Levy on personal property not easily taken into possession or which cannot be taken into possession without great inconvenience or expense may be made by affixing a copy of the writ and notice of levy on it or in a conspicuous place in the vicinity of it describing in the notice of levy the property by quantity and with sufficient detail to identify the property levied on.

(5) The United States marshal shall file a copy of the notice of levy in the same manner as provided for judgments in section 3201(a)(1). The United States marshal shall serve a copy of the writ and notice of levy on—

(A) the debtor against whom the writ is issued; and

(B) the person who has possession of the property subject to the writ;

in the same manner that a summons is served in a civil action and make the return thereof.

(e) Return of writ; duties of marshal; further return.—(1) A United States marshal executing a writ of attachment shall return the writ with the marshal's action endorsed thereon or attached thereto and signed by the marshal, to the court from which it was issued, within 5 days after the date of the levy.

(2) The return shall describe the property attached with sufficient certainty to identify it and shall state the location where it was attached, the date and time it was attached, and the disposition made of the property. If no property was attached, the return shall so state.

(3) If the property levied on is claimed, replevied under subsection (j)(2), or sold under section 3007 after the return, the United States marshal shall immediately make a further return to the clerk of the court showing the disposition of the property.

(4) If personal property is replevied, the United States marshal shall deliver the replevin bond to the clerk of the court to be filed in the action.

(f) Levy of attachment as lien on property; satisfaction of lien.—(1) A levy on property under a writ of attachment under this section creates a lien in favor of the United States on the property or, in the case of perishable property sold under section 3007, on the proceeds of the sale.

(2) Such lien shall be ranked ahead of any other security interests perfected after the later of the time of levy and the time a copy of the notice of levy is filed under subsection (d)(5).

(3) Such lien shall arise from the time of levy and shall continue until a judgment in the action is obtained or denied, or the action is otherwise dismissed. The death of the debtor whose property is attached does not terminate the attachment lien. Upon issuance of a judgment in the action and registration under this chapter, the judgment lien so created relates back to the time of levy.

(g) Reduction or dissolution of attachment.—(1) If an excessive or unreasonable attachment is made, the debtor may submit a motion to the court for a reduction of the amount of the attachment or its dissolution. Notice of such motion shall be served on the United States.

(2) The court shall order a part of the property to be released, if after a hearing the court finds that the amount of the attachment is excessive or unreasonable or if the attachment is for an amount larger than the sum of the liquidated or ascertainable amount of the debt and the amount of interest and costs likely to be taxed.

(3) The court shall dissolve the attachment if the amount of the debt is unliquidated and unascertainable by calculation.

(4) If any property claimed to be exempt is levied on, the debtor may, at any time after such levy, request that the court vacate such levy. If it appears to the court that the property so levied upon is exempt, the court shall order the levy vacated and the property returned to the debtor.

(h) Replevin of attached property by debtor; bond.—If attached property is not sold before judgment, the debtor may replevy such property or any part thereof by giving a bond approved by counsel for the United States or the court and payable to the United States in double the reasonable value of the property to be replevied or double the value of the claim, whichever is less.

(i) Preservation of personal property under attachment.—If personal property in custody of the United States marshal under a writ of attachment is not replevied, claimed, or sold, the court may make such order for its preservation or use as appears to be in the interest of the parties.

(j) Judgment and disposition of attached property.—

(1) Judgment for the United States.—On entry of judgment for the United States, the court shall order the proceeds of personal property sold pursuant to section 3007 to be applied to the satisfaction of the judgment, and shall order the sale of any remaining personal property and any real property levied on to the extent necessary to satisfy the judgment.

(2) Judgment for the United States when personal property replevied.—With respect to personal property under attachment that is replevied, the judgment which may be entered shall be against the debtor against whom the writ of attachment is issued and also against the sureties on the debtor's replevin bond for the value of the property.

(3) Restoration of property and exoneration of replevin bond.—If the attachment is vacated or if the judgment on the claim for the debt is for the person against whom the writ attachment is issued, the court shall order the property, or proceeds of perishable property sold under section 3007, restored to the debtor and shall exonerate any replevin bond.

(Added Pub.L. 101–647, Title XXXVI, § 3611, Nov. 29, 1990, 104 Stat. 4942.)

HISTORICAL AND STATUTORY NOTES

Effective Dates

1990 Acts. Section to take effect 180 days after Nov. 29, 1990, except as otherwise provided, see section 3631 of Pub.L. 101–647, set out as a note under section 3001 of this title.

§ 3103. Receivership

(a) Appointment of a receiver.—If the requirements of section 3101 are satisfied, a court may appoint a receiver for property in which the debtor has a substantial nonexempt interest if the United States shows reasonable cause to believe that there is a substantial danger that the property will be removed from the jurisdiction of the court, lost, concealed, materially injured or damaged, or mismanaged.

(b) Powers of receiver.—(1) The appointing court may authorize a receiver—

(A) to take possession of real and personal property and sue for, collect, and sell obligations upon such conditions and for such purposes as the court shall direct; and

(B) to administer, collect, improve, lease, repair or sell pursuant to section 3007 such real and personal property as the court shall direct.

A receiver appointed to manage residential or commercial property shall have demonstrable expertise in the management of these types of property.

(2) Unless expressly authorized by order of the court, a receiver shall have no power to employ attorneys, accountants, appraisers, auctioneers, or other professional persons.

(c) Duration of receivership.—A receivership shall not continue past the entry of judgment, or the conclusion of an appeal of such judgment, unless the court orders it continued under section 3203(e) or unless the court otherwise directs its continuation.

(d) Accounts; requirement to report.—A receiver shall keep written accounts itemizing receipts and expenditures, describing the property and naming the depository of receivership funds. The receiver's accounts shall be open to inspection by any person having an apparent interest in the property. The receiver shall file reports at regular intervals as directed by the court and shall serve the debtor and the United States with a copy thereof.

(e) Modification of powers; removal.—On motion of the receiver or on its own initiative, the court which appointed the receiver may remove the receiver or modify the receiver's powers at any time.

(f) Priority.—If more than one court appoints a receiver for particular property, the receiver first qualifying under law shall be entitled to take possession, control, or custody of the property.

(g) Compensation of receivers.—(1) A receiver is entitled to such commissions, not exceeding 5 percent of the sums received and disbursed by him, as the court allows unless the court otherwise directs.

(2) If, at the termination of a receivership, there are no funds in the hands of a receiver, the court may fix the compensation of the receiver in accordance with the services rendered and may direct the party who moved for the appointment of the receiver to pay such compensation in addition to the necessary expenditures incurred by the receiver which remain unpaid.

(3) At the termination of a receivership, the receiver shall file a final accounting of the receipts and disbursements and apply for compensation setting forth the amount sought and the services rendered by the receiver.

(Added Pub.L. 101–647, Title XXXVI, § 3611, Nov. 29, 1990, 104 Stat. 4944.)

HISTORICAL AND STATUTORY NOTES

Effective Dates

1990 Acts. Section to take effect 180 days after Nov. 29, 1990, except as otherwise provided, see section 3631 of Pub.L. 101–647, set out as a note under section 3001 of this title.

§ 3104. Garnishment

(a) In general.—If the requirements of section 3101 are satisfied, a court may issue a writ of garnishment against property (excluding earnings) in which the debtor has a substantial nonexempt interest and which is in the possession, custody, or control of a person other than the debtor in order to satisfy a claim for a debt. Co-owned property shall be subject to garnishment to the same extent as co-owned property is subject to garnishment under the law of the State in which such property is located. A court may issue simultaneous separate writs of garnishment to several garnishees. A writ of garnishment issued under this subsection shall be continuing and shall terminate only as provided in section 3205(c)(10).

(b) Writ.—(1) Subsections (b)(2) and (c) of section 3205 shall apply with respect to garnishment under this section, except that for purposes of this section—

(A) earnings of the debtor shall not be subject to garnishment; and

(B) a reference in such subsections to a judgment debtor shall be deemed to be a reference to a debtor.

(2) The United States shall include in its application for a writ of garnishment—

(A) the amount of the claim asserted by the United States for a debt; and

(B) the date the writ is issued.

(c) Limitation.—The value of property garnished shall not exceed the amount by which the sum of the amount of the debt claimed by the United States and the amount of interest and costs reasonably likely to be assessed against the debtor by the court exceeds the aggregate value of the nonexempt interest of the debtor in any—

(1) property securing the debt; and

(2) property attached or in receivership, or income sequestered, under this subchapter.

(Added Pub.L. 101–647, Title XXXVI, § 3611, Nov. 29, 1990, 104 Stat. 4945.)

HISTORICAL AND STATUTORY NOTES

Effective Dates

1990 Acts. Section to take effect 180 days after Nov. 29, 1990, except as otherwise provided, see section 3631 of Pub.L. 101–647, set out as a note under section 3001 of this title.

§ 3105. Sequestration

(a) Property subject to sequestration.—(1) Any income from property in which the debtor has a substantial nonexempt interest may be sequestered pursuant to a writ of sequestration in an action or proceeding against a debtor on a claim for a debt and may be held as security to satisfy such judgment, and interest and costs, as the United States may recover on such claim.

(2) The amount of income sequestered shall not exceed the amount by which the sum of the amount of the debt claimed by the United States and the amount of interest and costs reasonably likely to be assessed against the debtor by the court exceeds the aggregate value of the nonexempt interest of the debtor in any—

(A) property securing the debt; and

(B) property attached, garnished, or in receivership under this subchapter.

(b) Availability of sequestration.—If the requirements of section 3101 are satisfied, a court shall issue a writ authorizing the United States to sequester income from property in which the debtor has a substantial nonexempt interest, as security for such judgment (and interest and costs) as the United States may recover on a claim for a debt—

(1) in an action on a contract, express or implied, against the debtor for payment of money, only if the United States shows reasonable cause to believe that—

(A) the contract is not fully secured by real or personal property; or

(B) the value of the original security is substantially diminished, without any act of the United States or the person to whom the security was given, below the amount of the debt;

(2) in an action against the debtor for damages in tort;

(3) if the debtor resides outside the jurisdiction of the United States; or

(4) in an action to recover a fine, penalty, or tax.

(c) Issuance of writ; contents.—(1) Subject to subsections (a) and (b), a writ of sequestration shall be issued by the court directing the United States marshal of the district where income described in subsection (a) is located to sequester the income.

(2) Several writs of sequestration may be issued at the same time, or in succession, and sent to different judicial districts until sufficient income is sequestered.

(3) The writ of sequestration shall contain—

(A) the date of the issuance of the writ;

(B) the identity of the court, the docket number of the action, and the identity of the cause of action;

(C) the name and last known address of the debtor;

(D) the amount to be secured by the sequestration; and

(E) a reasonable description of the income to be sequestered.

(d) Execution of writ.—(1) The United States marshal receiving the writ shall proceed without delay to execute the writ.

(2) The United States marshal shall file a copy of the notice of sequestration in the same manner as provided for judgments in section 3201(a)(1). The United States marshal shall serve a copy of the writ and notice of sequestration on—

(A) the debtor against whom the writ is issued; and

(B) the person who has possession of the income subject to the writ;

in the same manner that a summons is served in a civil action and make the return thereof.

(e) Deposit of sequestered income.—A person who has possession of the income subject to a writ of sequestration shall deposit such income with the clerk of the court, accompanied by a statement in writing stating the person's name, the name of the debtor, the amount of such income, the property from which such income is produced, and the period during which such income is produced.

(f) Return of writ; duties of marshal; further return.—(1) A United States marshal executing a writ of sequestration shall return the writ with the marshal's action endorsed thereon or attached thereto and signed by the marshal, to the court from which it was issued, within 5 days after the date of the execution.

(2) The return shall describe the income sequestered with sufficient certainty to identify it and shall state the location where it was sequestered, and the date and time it was sequestered. If no income was sequestered, the return shall so state.

(3) If sequestered income is claimed after the return, the United States marshal shall immediately make a further return to the clerk of the court showing the disposition of the income.

(g) Reduction or dissolution of sequestration.—(1) If an excessive or unreasonable sequestration is made, the debtor may submit a motion to the court for a reduction of the amount of the sequestration or its dissolution. Notice of such motion shall be served on the United States.

(2) The court shall order a part of the income to be released, if after a hearing the court finds that the amount of the sequestration is excessive or unreasonable or if the sequestration is for an amount larger than the sum of the liquidated or ascertainable amount of the debt and the amount of interest and costs likely to be taxed.

(3) The court shall dissolve the sequestration if the amount of the debt is unliquidated and unascertainable by calculation.

(h) Preservation of income under sequester.—If personal property in custody of the United States marshal under a writ of sequestration is not claimed, the court may make such order for its preservation or use as appears to be in the interest of the parties.

(i) Judgment and disposition of sequestered income.—

(1) Judgment for the United States.—On entry of judgment for the United States, the court shall order the sequestered income to be applied to the satisfaction of the judgment.

(2) **Restoration of income.**—If the sequestration is vacated or if the judgment on the claim for the debt is for the person against whom the writ of sequestration is issued, the court shall order the income restored to the debtor.

(Added Pub.L. 101–647, Title XXXVI, § 3611, Nov. 29, 1990, 104 Stat. 4946.)

HISTORICAL AND STATUTORY NOTES

Effective Dates

Section to take effect 180 days after Nov. 29, 1990, except as otherwise provided, see section 3631 of Pub.L. 101–647, set out as a note under section 3001 of this title.

SUBCHAPTER C—POSTJUDGMENT REMEDIES

Sec.

3201. Judgment liens.
3202. Enforcement of judgments.
3203. Execution.
3204. Installment payment order.
3205. Garnishment.
3206. Discharge.

§ 3201. Judgment liens

(a) Creation.—A judgment in a civil action shall create a lien on all real property of a judgment debtor on filing a certified copy of the abstract of the judgment in the manner in which a notice of tax lien would be filed under paragraphs (1) and (2) of section 6323(f) of the Internal Revenue Code of 1986. A lien created under this paragraph is for the amount necessary to satisfy the judgment, including costs and interest.

(b) Priority of lien.—A lien created under subsection (a) shall have priority over any other lien or encumbrance which is perfected later in time.

(c) Duration of lien; renewal.—(1) Except as provided in paragraph (2), a lien created under subsection (a) is effective, unless satisfied, for a period of 20 years.

(2) Such lien may be renewed for one additional period of 20 years upon filing a notice of renewal in the same manner as the judgment is filed and shall relate back to the date the judgment is filed if—

(A) the notice of renewal is filed before the expiration of the 20–year period to prevent the expiration of the lien; and

(B) the court approves the renewal of such lien under this paragraph.

(d) Release of judgment lien.—A judgment lien shall be released on the filing of a satisfaction of judgment or release of lien in the same manner as the judgment is filed to obtain the lien.

(e) Effect of lien on eligibility for Federal grants, loans or programs.—A debtor who has a judgment lien against the debtor's property for a debt to the United States shall not be eligible to receive any grant or loan which is made, insured, guaranteed, or financed directly or indirectly by the United States or to receive funds directly from the Federal Government in any program, except funds to which the debtor is entitled as beneficiary, until the judgment is paid in full or otherwise satisfied. The agency of the United States that is responsible for such grants and loans may promulgate regulations to allow for waiver of this restriction on eligibility for such grants, loans, and funds.

(f) Sale of property subject to judgment lien.—(1) On proper application to a court, the court may order the United States to sell, in accordance with sections 2001 and 2002, any real property subject to a judgment lien in effect under this section.

(2) This subsection shall not preclude the United States from using an execution sale pursuant to section 3203(g) to sell real property subject to a judgment lien.

(Added Pub.L. 101–647, Title XXXVI, § 3611, Nov. 29, 1990, 104 Stat. 4948.)

HISTORICAL AND STATUTORY NOTES

References in Text

Section 6323(f) of the Internal Revenue Code of 1986, referred to in subsec. (a), is classified to section 6323(f) of Title 26, Internal Revenue Code.

Effective Dates

1990 Acts. Section to take effect 180 days after Nov. 29, 1990, except as otherwise provided, see section 3631 of Pub.L. 101–647, set out as a note under section 3001 of this title.

§ 3202. Enforcement of judgments

(a) Enforcement remedies.—A judgment may be enforced by any of the remedies set forth in this subchapter. A court may issue other writs pursuant to section 1651 of title 28, United States Code, as necessary to support such remedies, subject to rule 81(b) of the Federal Rules of Civil Procedure.

(b) Notice.—On the commencement by the United States of an action or proceeding under this subchapter to obtain a remedy, the counsel for the United States shall prepare, and clerk of the court shall issue, a notice in substantially the following form:

"NOTICE

"You are hereby notified that this [property] is being taken by the United States Government, which has a court judgment in [case docket number and jurisdiction of court] of $[amount] for [reason of debt].

"In addition, you are hereby notified that there are exemptions under the law which may protect some of this property from being taken by the United States Government if [name of judgment debtor] can show that the exemptions apply. Below is a summary of the major exemptions which apply in most situations in the State of [State where property is located]:

"[A statement summarizing in plain and understandable English the election available with respect to such State under section 3014 and the types of property that may be exempted under each of the alternatives specified in paragraphs (1) and (2) of section 3014(a) and a statement that different property may be so exempted with respect to the State in which the debtor resides.]

"If you are [name of judgment debtor], you have a right to ask the court to return your property to you if you think the property the Government is taking qualifies under one of the above exemptions [For a default judgment:] or if you think you do not owe the money to the United States Government that it says you do.

"If you want a hearing, you must notify the court within 20 days after you receive this notice. You must make your request in writing, and either mail it or deliver it in person to the clerk of the court at [address]. If you wish, you may use this notice to request the hearing by checking the box below and mailing this notice to the court clerk. You must also send a copy of your request to the Government at [address], so the Government will know you want a hearing. The hearing will take place within 5 days after the clerk receives your request, if you ask for it to take place that quickly, or as soon after that as possible.

"At the hearing you may explain to the judge why you believe the property the Government has taken is exempt [For a default judgment:] or why you think you do not owe the money to the Government. [For a writ of execution:] If you do not request a hearing within 20 days of receiving this notice, your [property] may be sold at public auction and the payment used toward the money you owe the Government.

"If you think you live outside the Federal judicial district in which the court is located, you may request, not later than 20 days after your[1] receive this notice, that this proceeding to take your property be transferred by the court to the Federal judicial district in which you reside. You must make your request in writing, and either mail it or deliver it in person to the clerk of the court at [address]. You must also send a copy of your request to the Government at [address], so the Government will know you want the proceeding to be transferred.

"Be sure to keep a copy of this notice for your own records. If you have any questions about your rights or about this procedure, you should contact a lawyer, an office of public legal assistance, or the clerk of the court. The clerk is not permitted to give legal advice, but can refer you to other sources of information.".

(c) Service.—A copy of the notice and a copy of the application for granting a remedy under this subchapter shall be served by counsel for the United States on the judgment debtor against whom such remedy is sought and on each person whom the United States, after diligent inquiry, has reasonable cause to believe has an interest in property to which the remedy is directed.

(d) Hearing.—By requesting, within 20 days after receiving the notice described in section 3202(b), the court to hold a hearing, the judgment debtor may move to quash the order granting such remedy. The court that issued such order shall hold a hearing on such motion as soon as practicable, or, if so requested by the judgment debtor, within 5 days after receiving the request or as soon thereafter as possible. The issues at such hearing shall be limited—

(1) to the probable validity of any claim of exemption by the judgment debtor;

(2) to compliance with any statutory requirement for the issuance of the postjudgment remedy granted; and

(3) if the judgment is by default and only to the extent that the Constitution or another law of the United States provides a right to a hearing on the issue, to—

(A) the probable validity of the claim for the debt which is merged in the judgment; and

(B) the existence of good cause for setting aside such judgment.

This subparagraph shall not be construed to afford the judgment debtor the right to more than one such hearing except to the extent that the Constitution or another law of the United States provides a right to more than one such hearing.

(e) Sale of property.—The property of a judgment debtor which is subject to sale to satisfy the judgment may be sold by judicial sale, pursuant to sections 2001, 2002, and 2004 or by execution sale pursuant to section 3203(g). If a hearing is requested pursuant to subsection (d), property with respect to which the request relates shall not be sold before such hearing.

(Added Pub.L. 101–647, Title XXXVI, § 3611, Nov. 29, 1990, 104 Stat. 4949.)

1 So in original. Probably should be "you".

HISTORICAL AND STATUTORY NOTES

Effective Dates

1990 Acts. Section to take effect 180 days after Nov. 29, 1990, except as otherwise provided, see section 3631 of Pub.L. 101–647, set out as a note under section 3001 of this title.

§ 3203. Execution

(a) Property subject to execution.—All property in which the judgment debtor has a substantial nonexempt interest shall be subject to levy pursuant to a writ of execution. The debtor's earnings shall not be subject to execution while in the possession, custody, or control of the debtor's employer. Co-owned property shall be subject to execution to the extent such property is subject to execution under the law of the State in which it is located.

(b) Creation of execution lien.—A lien shall be created in favor of the United States on all property levied on under a writ of execution and shall date from the time of the levy. Such lien shall have priority over all subsequent liens and shall be for the aggregate amount of the judgment, costs, and interest. The execution lien on any real property as to which the United States has a judgment lien shall relate back to the judgment lien date.

(c) Writ of execution.—

(1) Issuance.—On written application of counsel for the United States, the court may issue a writ of execution. Multiple writs may issue simultaneously, and successive writs may issue before the return date of a writ previously issued.

(2) Form of writ.—

(A) General contents.—A writ of execution shall specify the date that the judgment is entered, the court in which it is entered, the amount of the judgment if for money, the amount of the costs, the amount of interest due, the sum due as of the date the writ is issued, the rate of postjudgment interest, the name of the judgment debtor, and the judgment debtor's last known address.

(B) Additional contents.—**(i)** Except as provided in clauses (ii) and (iii), the writ shall direct the United States marshal to satisfy the judgment by levying on and selling property in which the judgment debtor has a substantial nonexempt interest, but not to exceed property reasonably equivalent in value to the aggregate amount of the judgment, costs, and interest.

(ii) A writ of execution issued on a judgment for the delivery to the United States of the possession of personal property, or for the delivery of the possession of real property, shall particularly describe the property, and shall require the marshal to deliver the possession of the property to the United States.

(iii) A writ of execution on a judgment for the recovery of personal property or its value shall direct the marshal, in case a delivery of the specific property cannot be had, to levy and collect such value out of any property in which the judgment debtor has a substantial nonexempt interest.

(d) Levy of execution.—

(1) In general.—Levy on property pursuant to a writ of execution issued under this section shall be made in the same manner as levy on property is made pursuant to a writ of attachment issued under section 3102(d).

(2) Death of judgment debtor.—The death of the judgment debtor after a writ of execution is issued stays the execution proceedings, but any lien acquired by levy of the writ shall be recognized and enforced by the court for the district in which the estate of the deceased is located. The execution lien may be enforced—

(A) against the executor, administrator, or personal representative of the estate of the deceased; or

(B) if there be none, against the deceased's property coming to the heirs or devisees or at their option against cash in their possession, but only to the extent of the value of the property coming to them.

(3) Records of United States marshal.—**(A)** A United States marshal receiving a writ of execution shall endorse thereon the exact hour and date of receipt.

(B) The United States marshal shall make a written record of every levy, specify the property on which levy is made, the date on which levy is made, and the marshal's costs, expenses, and fees.

(C) The United States marshal shall make a written return to the court on each writ of execution stating concisely what is done pursuant to the writ and shall deliver a copy to counsel for the United States who requests the writ. The writ shall be returned not more than—

(i) 90 days after the date of issuance if levy is not made; or

(ii) 10 days after the date of sale of property on which levy is made.

(e) Appointment of receiver.—Pending the levy of execution, the court may appoint a receiver to manage property described in such writ if there is a substantial danger that the property will be removed from the jurisdiction of the court, lost, materially injured or damaged, or mismanaged.

(f) Replevy; redemption.—

(1) Before execution sale.—**(A)** Before execution sale, the United States marshal may return property[1] to the judgment debtor any personal property taken in execution, on—

(i) satisfaction of the judgment, interest, and costs, and any costs incurred in connection with scheduling the sale; or

(ii) receipt from the judgment debtor of a bond—

(I) payable to the United States, with 2 or more good and sufficient sureties to be approved by the marshal, conditioned on the delivery of the property to the marshal at the time and place named in the bond to be sold under subsection (g); or

(II) for the payment to the marshal of a fair value thereof which shall be stated in the bond.

(B) A judgment debtor who sells or disposes of property replevied under subparagraph (A) shall pay the United States marshal the stipulated value of such property.

(C) If the judgment debtor fails to deliver such property to the United States marshal pursuant to the terms of the delivery described in subparagraph (A)(ii)(I) and fails to pay the United States marshal the stipulated value of such property, the United States marshal shall endorse the bond "forfeited" and return it to the court from which the writ of execution issued. If the judgment is not fully satisfied, the court shall issue a writ of execution against the judgment debtor and the sureties on the bond for the amount due, not exceeding the stipulated value of the property, on which execution no delivery bond shall be taken, which instruction shall be endorsed on the writ.

(2) **After execution sale.**—The judgment debtor shall not be entitled to redeem the property after the execution sale.

(g) **Execution sale.**—

(1) **General procedures.**—An execution sale under this section shall be conducted in a commercially reasonable manner—

(A) **Sale of real property.**—

(i) **In general.**—(I) Except as provided in clause (ii), real property, or any interest therein, shall be sold, after the expiration of the 90–day period beginning on the date of levy under subsection (d), for cash at public auction at the courthouse of the county, parish, or city in which the greater part of the property is located or on the premises or some parcel thereof.

(II) The court may order the sale of any real property after the expiration of the 30–day period beginning on the date of levy under subsection (d) if the court determines that such property is likely to perish, waste, be destroyed, or otherwise substantially depreciate in value during the 90–day period beginning on the date of levy.

(III) The time and place of sale of real property, or any interest therein, under execution shall be advertised by the United States marshal, by publication of notice, once a week for at least 3 weeks prior to the sale, in at least one newspaper of general circulation in the county or parish where the property is located. The first publication shall appear not less than 25 days preceding the day of sale. The notice shall contain a statement of the authority by which the sale is to be made, the time of levy, the time and place of sale, and a brief description of the property to be sold, sufficient to identify the property (such as a street address for urban property and the survey identification and location for rural property), but it shall not be necessary for the notice to contain field notes. Such property shall be open for inspection and appraisal, subject to the judgment debtor's reasonable objections, for a reasonable period before the day of sale.

(IV) The United States marshal shall serve written notice of public sale by personal delivery, or certified or registered mail, to each person whom the marshal has reasonable cause to believe, after a title search is conducted by the United States, has an interest in property under execution, including lienholders, co-owners, and tenants, at least 25 days before the day of sale, to the last known address of each such person.

(ii) **Sale of city lots.**—If the real property consists of several lots, tracts, or parcels in a city or town, each lot, tract, or parcel shall be offered for sale separately, unless not susceptible to separate sale because of the character of improvements.

(iii) **Sale of rural property.**—If the real property is not located in a city or town, the judgment debtor may—

(I) divide the property into lots of not less than 50 acres or in such greater or lesser amounts as ordered by the court;

(II) furnish a survey of such prepared by a registered surveyor; and

(III) designate the order in which those lots shall be sold.

When a sufficient number of lots are sold to satisfy the amount of the execution and costs of sale, the marshal shall stop the sale.

(B) **Sale of personal property.**—(i) Personal property levied on shall be offered for sale on the premises where it is located at the time of levy, at the courthouse of the county, parish or city wherein it is located, or at another location if ordered by the court. Personal property susceptible of being exhibited shall not be sold unless it is present and subject to the view of those attending the sale unless—

(I) the property consists of shares of stock in corporations;

(II) by reason of the nature of the property, it is impractical to exhibit it; or

(III) the debtor's interest in the property does not include the right to the exclusive possession.

(ii)(I) Except as provided in subclause (II), personal property, or any interest therein, shall be sold after the expiration of the 30–day period beginning on the date of levy under subsection (d).

(II) The court may order the sale of any personal property before the expiration of such 30–day period if the court determines that such property is likely to perish, waste, be destroyed, or otherwise substantially depreciate in value during such 30–day period.

(iii) Notice of the time and place of the sale of personal property shall be given by the United States marshal by posting notice thereof for not less than 10 days successively immediately before the day of sale at the courthouse of any county, parish, or city, and at the place where the sale is to be made.

(iv) The United States marshal shall serve written notice of public sale by personal delivery, or registered or certified mail at their last known addresses, on the judgment debtor and other persons who the marshal has reasonable cause to believe, after diligent inquiry, have a substantial interest in the property.

(2) Postponement of sale.—The United States marshal may postpone an execution sale from time to time by continuing the required posting or publication of notice until the date to which the sale is postponed, and appending, at the foot of each such notice of a current copy of the following:

"The above sale is postponed until the ________ day of ________, 19___, at ____ o'clock ____.M., ________, United States Marshal for the District of ________, by ________, Deputy, dated ________."

(3) Sale procedures.—

(A) Bidding requirements.—A bidder at an execution sale of property, may be required by the United States marshal to make a cash deposit of as much as 20 percent of the sale price proposed before the bid is accepted.

(B) Resale of property.—If the terms of the sale are not complied with by the successful bidder, the United States marshal shall proceed to sell the property again on the same day if there is sufficient time. If there is insufficient time, the marshal shall schedule and notice a subsequent sale of the property as provided in paragraphs (1) and (2).

(4) Rights and liabilities of purchasers.—

(A) Transfer of title after sale.—

(i) If property is sold under this subsection and the successful bidder complies with the terms of the sale, the United States marshal shall execute and deliver all documents necessary to transfer to the successful bidder, without warranty, all the rights, titles, interests, and claims of the judgment debtor in the property.

(ii) If the successful bidder dies before execution and delivery of the documents needed to transfer ownership, the United States marshal shall execute and deliver them to the successful bidder's estate. Such delivery to the estate shall have the same effect as if accomplished during the lifetime of the purchaser.

(B) Purchaser considered innocent purchaser without notice.—The purchaser of property sold under execution shall be deemed to be an innocent purchaser without notice if the purchaser would have been considered an innocent purchaser without notice had the sale been made voluntarily and in person by the judgment debtor.

(C) Liability of successful bidder who fails to comply.—A successful bidder at an execution sale who fails to comply with the terms of the sale shall forfeit to the United States the cash deposit or, at the election of the United States, shall be liable to the United States, on a subsequent sale of the property, for all net losses incurred by the United States as a result of such failure.

(h) Disposition of proceeds; further levy.—

(1) Distribution of sale proceeds.—(A) The United States marshal shall first deliver to the judgment debtor such amounts to which the judgment debtor is entitled from the sale of partially exempt property.

(B) The United States marshal shall next deduct from the proceeds of an execution sale of property an amount equal to the reasonable expenses incurred in making the levy of execution and in keeping and maintaining the property.

(C) Except as provided in subparagraph (D), the United States marshal shall deliver the balance of the proceeds to the counsel for the United States as soon as practicable.

(D) If more proceeds are received from the execution sale than is necessary to satisfy the executions held by the United States marshal, the marshal shall pay the surplus to the judgment debtor.

(2) Further levy if execution not satisfied.—If the proceeds of the execution sale of the property levied on are insufficient to satisfy the execution, the United States marshal shall proceed on the same writ of execution to levy other property of the judgment debtor.

(Added Pub.L. 101–647, Title XXXVI, § 3611, Nov. 29, 1990, 104 Stat. 4950.)

[1] So in original. The word "property" probably should not appear.

HISTORICAL AND STATUTORY NOTES

Effective Dates

1990 Acts. Section to take effect 180 days after Nov. 29, 1990, except as otherwise provided, see section 3631 of Pub.L. 101–647, set out as a note under section 3001 of this title.

§ 3204. Installment payment order

(a) Authority to issue order.—Subject to subsection (c), if it is shown that the judgment debtor—

(1) is receiving or will receive substantial nonexempt disposable earnings from self employment that are not subject to garnishment; or

(2) is diverting or concealing substantial earnings from any source, or property received in lieu of earnings;

then upon motion of the United States and notice to the judgment debtor, the court may, if appropriate, order that the judgment debtor make specified installment payments to the United States. Notice of the motion shall be served on the judgment debtor in the same manner as a summons or by registered or certified mail, return receipt requested. In fixing the amount of the payments, the court shall take into consideration after a hearing, the income, resources, and reasonable requirements of the judgment debtor and the judgment debtor's dependents, any other payments to be made in satisfaction of judgments against the judgment debtor, and the amount due on the judgment in favor of the United States.

(b) Modification of order.—On motion of the United States or the judgment debtor, and upon a showing that the judgment debtor's financial circumstances have changed or that assets not previously disclosed by the judgment debtor have been discovered, the court may modify the amount of payments, alter their frequency, or require full payment.

(c) Limitation.—(1) An order may not be issued under subsection (a), and if so issued shall have no force or effect, against a judgment debtor with respect to whom there is in effect a writ of garnishment of earnings issued under this chapter and based on the same debt.

(2) An order may not be issued under subsection (a) with respect to any earnings of the debtor except nonexempt disposable earnings.

(Added Pub.L. 101–647, Title XXXVI, § 3611, Nov. 29, 1990, 104 Stat. 4955.)

HISTORICAL AND STATUTORY NOTES

Effective Dates

1990 Acts. Section to take effect 180 days after Nov. 29, 1990, except as otherwise provided, see section 3631 of Pub.L. 101–647, set out as a note under section 3001 of this title.

§ 3205. Garnishment

(a) In general.—A court may issue a writ of garnishment against property (including nonexempt disposable earnings) in which the debtor has a substantial nonexempt interest and which is in the possession, custody, or control of a person other than the debtor, in order to satisfy the judgment against the debtor. Co-owned property shall be subject to garnishment to the same extent as co-owned property is subject to garnishment under the law of the State in which such property is located. A court may issue simultaneous separate writs of garnishment to several garnishees. A writ of garnishment issued under this subsection shall be continuing and shall terminate only as provided in subsection (c)(10).

(b) Writ.—

(1) General requirements.—The United States shall include in its application for a writ of garnishment—

(A) the judgment debtor's name, social security number (if known), and last known address;

(B) the nature and amount of the debt owed and the facts that not less than 30 days has elapsed since demand on the debtor for payment of the debt was made and the judgment debtor has not paid the amount due; and

(C) that the garnishee is believed to have possession of property (including nonexempt disposable earnings) in which the debtor has a substantial nonexempt interest.

(2) Proper garnishee for particular property.—

(A) If the property consists of a right to or share in the stock of an association or corporation, or interests or profits therein, for which a certificate of stock or other negotiable instrument is not outstanding, the corporation, or the president or treasurer of the association shall be the garnishee.

(B) If the property consists of an interest in a partnership interest, any partner other than the debtor shall be the garnishee on behalf of the partnership.

(C) If the property or a debt is evidenced by a negotiable instrument for the payment of money, a negotiable document of title or a certificate of stock of an association or corporation, the instrument, document, or certificate shall be treated as property capable of delivery and the person holding it shall be the garnishee, except that—

(i) subject to clause (ii), in the case of a security which is transferable in the manner set forth in State law, the entity that carries on its books an account in the name of the debtor in which is reflected such security shall be the garnishee; and

(ii) notwithstanding clause (i), the pledgee shall be the garnishee if such security is pledged.

(c) Procedures applicable to writ.—

(1) Court determination.—If the court determines that the requirements of this section are satisfied, the court shall issue an appropriate writ of garnishment.

(2) Form of writ.—The writ shall state—

(A) The nature and amount of the debt, and any cost and interest owed with respect to the debt.

(B) The name and address of the garnishee.

(C) The name and address of counsel for the United States.

(D) The last known address of the judgment debtor.

(E) That the garnishee shall answer the writ within 10 days of service of the writ.

(F) That the garnishee shall withhold and retain any property in which the debtor has a substantial nonexempt interest and for which the garnishee is or may become indebted to the judgment debtor pending further order of the court.

(3) Service of writ.—The United States shall serve the garnishee and the judgment debtor with a copy of the writ of garnishment and shall certify to the court that this service was made. The writ shall be accompanied by—

(A) an instruction explaining the requirement that the garnishee submit a written answer to the writ; and

(B) instructions to the judgment debtor for objecting to the answer of the garnishee and for obtaining a hearing on the objections.

(4) Answer of the garnishee.—In its written answer to the writ of garnishment, the garnishee shall state under oath—

(A) whether the garnishee has custody, control or possession of such property;

(B) a description of such property and the value of such interest;

(C) a description of any previous garnishments to which such property is subject and the extent to which any remaining property is not exempt; and

(D) the amount of the debt the garnishee anticipates owing to the judgment debtor in the future and whether the period for payment will be weekly or another specified period.

The garnishee shall file the original answer with the court issuing the writ and serve a copy on the debtor and counsel for the United States.

(5) Objections to answer.—Within 20 days after receipt of the answer, the judgment debtor or the United States may file a written objection to the answer and request a hearing. The party objecting shall state the grounds for the objection and bear the burden of proving such grounds. A copy of the objection and request for a hearing shall be served on the garnishee and all other parties. The court shall hold a hearing within 10 days after the date the request is received by the court, or as soon thereafter as is practicable, and give notice of the hearing date to all the parties.

(6) Garnishee's failure to answer or pay.—If a garnishee fails to answer the writ of garnishment or to withhold property in accordance with the writ, the United States may petition the court for an order requiring the garnishee to appear before the court to answer the writ and to so withhold property before the appearance date. If the garnishee fails to appear, or appears and fails to show good cause why the garnishee failed to comply with the writ, the court shall enter judgment against the garnishee for the value of the judgment debtor's nonexempt interest in such property (including nonexempt disposable earnings). The court may award a reasonable attorney's fee to the United States and against the garnishee if the writ is not answered within the time specified therein and a petition requiring the garnishee to appear is filed as provided in this section.

(7) Disposition order.—After the garnishee files an answer and if no hearing is requested within the required time period, the court shall promptly enter an order directing the garnishee as to the disposition of the judgment debtor's nonexempt interest in such property. If a hearing is timely requested, the order shall be entered within 5 days after the hearing, or as soon thereafter as is practicable.

(8) Priorities.—Judicial orders and garnishments for the support of a person shall have priority over a writ of garnishment issued under this section. As to any other writ of garnishment or levy, a garnishment issued under this section shall have priority over writs which are issued later in time.

(9) Accounting.—(A) While a writ of garnishment is in effect under this section, the United States shall give an annual accounting on the garnishment to the judgment debtor and the garnishee.

(B) Within 10 days after the garnishment terminates, the United States shall give a cumulative written accounting to the judgment debtor and garnishee of all property it receives under a writ of garnishment. Within 10 days after such accounting is received, the judgment debtor or garnishee may file a written objection to the accounting and a request for hearing. The party objecting shall state grounds for the objection. The court shall hold a hearing on the objection within 10 days after the court receives the request for a hearing, or as soon thereafter as is practicable.

(10) Termination of garnishment.—A garnishment under this chapter is terminated only by—

(A) a court order quashing the writ of garnishment;

(B) exhaustion of property in the possesion,[1] custody, or control of the garnishee in which the debtor has a substantial nonexempt interest (including nonexempt disposable earnings), unless the garnishee reinstates or reemploys the judgment debtor within 90 days after the judgment debtor's dismissal or resignation; or

(C) satisfaction of the debt with respect to which the writ is issued.

(Added Pub.L. 101–647, Title XXXVI, § 3611, Nov. 29, 1990, 104 Stat. 4956.)

[1] So in original. Probably should be "possession,".

HISTORICAL AND STATUTORY NOTES

Effective Dates

1990 Acts. Section to take effect 180 days after Nov. 29, 1990, except as otherwise provided, see section 3631 of Pub.L. 101–647, set out as a note under section 3001 of this title.

§ 3206. Discharge

A person who pursuant to an execution or order issued under this chapter by a court pays or delivers to the United States, a United States marshal, or a receiver, money or other personal property in which a judgment debtor has or will have an interest, or so pays a debt such person owes the judgment debtor, is discharged from such debt to the judgment debtor to the extent of the payment or delivery.

(Added Pub.L. 101–647, Title XXXVI, § 3611, Nov. 29, 1990, 104 Stat. 4959.)

HISTORICAL AND STATUTORY NOTES

Effective Dates

1990 Acts. Section to take effect 180 days after Nov. 29, 1990, except as otherwise provided, see section 3631 of Pub.L. 101–647, set out as a note under section 3001 of this title.

SUBCHAPTER D—FRAUDULENT TRANSFERS INVOLVING DEBTS

Sec.

3301. Definitions.
3302. Insolvency.
3303. Value for a transfer or obligation.[1]
3304. Transfer fraudulent as to a debt to the United States.
3305. When transfer is made or obligation is incurred.
3306. Remedies of the United States.
3307. Defenses, liability and protection of transferee.[1]
3308. Supplementary provision.

[1] So in original. Does not conform to section catchline.

§ 3301. Definitions

As used in this subchapter:

(1) "Affiliate" means—

(A) a person who directly or indirectly owns, controls, or holds with power to vote, 20 percent or more of the outstanding voting securities of the debtor, other than a person who holds the securities—

(i) as a fiduciary or agent without sole discretionary power to vote the securities; or

(ii) solely to secure a debt, if the person has not exercised the power to vote;

(B) a corporation 20 percent or more of whose outstanding voting securities are directly or indirectly owned, controlled, or held with power to vote, by the debtor or a person who directly or indirectly owns, controls, or holds with power to vote, 20 percent or more of the outstanding voting securities of the debtor, other than the person who holds securities—

(i) as a fiduciary or agent without sole power to vote the securities; or

(ii) solely to secure a debt, if the person has not in fact exercised the power to vote;

(C) a person whose business is operated by the debtor under a lease or other agreement, or a person substantially all of whose assets are controlled by the debtor; or

(D) a person who operates the debtor's business under a lease or other agreement or controls substantially all of the debtor's assets.

(2) "Asset" means property of a debtor, but does not include—

(A) property to the extent it is encumbered by a valid lien;

(B) property to the extent it is generally exempt under nonbankruptcy law; or

(C) an interest in real property held in tenancy by the entirety, or as part of a community estate, to extent such interest is not subject to process by the United States holding a claim against only one tenant or co-owner.

(3) "Claim" means a right to payment, whether or not the right is reduced to judgment, liquidated, unliquidated, fixed, contingent, matured, unmatured, disputed, undisputed, legal, equitable, secured, or unsecured.

(4) "Creditor" means a person who has a claim.

(5) "Insider" includes—

(A) if the debtor is an individual—

(i) a relative of the debtor or of a general partner of the debtor;

(ii) a partnership in which the debtor is a general partner;

(iii) a general partner in a partnership described in clause (ii); or

(iv) a corporation of which the debtor is a director, officer, or person in control;

(B) if the debtor is a corporation—

(i) a director of the debtor;

(ii) an officer of the debtor;

(iii) a person in control of the debtor;

(iv) a partnership in which the debtor is a general partner;

(v) a general partner in a partnership described in clause (iv); or

(vi) a relative of a general partner, director, officer, or person in control of the debtor;

(C) if the debtor is a partnership—

(i) a general partner in the debtor;

(ii) a relative of a general partner in, a general partner of, or a person in control of the debtor;

(iii) another partnership in which the debtor is a general partner;

(iv) a general partner in a partnership described in clause (iii); or

(v) a person in control of the debtor.[1]

(D) an affiliate, or an insider of an affiliate as if the affiliate were the debtor; and

(E) a managing agent of the debtor.

(4)[2] "Lien" means a charge against or an interest in property to secure payment of a debt and includes a security interest created by agreement, a judicial lien obtained by legal or equitable process or proceedings, a common law lien, or a statutory lien.

(5)[3] "Relative" means an individual related, by consanguinity or adoption, within the third degree as determined by the common law, a spouse, or an individual so related to a spouse within the third degree as so determined.

(6)[4] "Transfer" means every mode, direct or indirect, absolute or conditional, voluntary or involuntary, of disposing of or parting with an asset or an interest in an asset, and includes payment of money, release, lease, and creation of a lien or other encumbrance.

(7)[5] "Valid lien" means a lien that is effective against the holder of a judicial lien subsequently obtained in legal or equitable proceeding.

(Added Pub.L. 101–647, Title XXXVI, § 3611, Nov. 29, 1990, 104 Stat. 4959.)

[1] So in original. The period probably should be a semicolon.

[2] So in original. Probably should be "(6)".

[3] So in original. Probably should be "(7)".

[4] So in original. Probably should be "(8)".

[5] So in original. Probably should be "(9)".

HISTORICAL AND STATUTORY NOTES

Effective Dates

1990 Acts. Section to take effect 180 days after Nov. 29, 1990, except as otherwise provided, see section 3631 of Pub.L. 101–647, set out as a note under section 3001 of this title.

§ 3302. Insolvency

(a) In general.—Except as provided in subsection (c), a debtor is insolvent if the sum of the debtor's debts is greater than all of the debtor's assets at a fair valuation.

(b) Presumption.—A debtor who is generally not paying debts as they become due is presumed to be insolvent.

(c) Calculation.—A partnership is insolvent under subsection (a) if the sum of the partnership's debts is greater than the aggregate, at a fair valuation, of—

(1) all of the partnership's assets; and

(2) the sum of the excess of the value of each general partner's non-partnership assets over the partner's non-partnership debts.

(d) Assets.—For purposes of this section, assets do not include property that is transferred, concealed, or removed with intent to hinder, delay, or defraud creditors or that has been transferred in a manner making the transfer voidable under this subchapter.

(e) Debts.—For purposes of this section, debts do not include an obligation to the extent such obligation is secured by a valid lien on property of the debtor not included as an asset.

(Added Pub.L. 101–647, Title XXXVI, § 3611, Nov. 29, 1990, 104 Stat. 4961.)

HISTORICAL AND STATUTORY NOTES

Effective Dates

1990 Acts. Section to take effect 180 days after Nov. 29, 1990, except as otherwise provided, see section 3631 of Pub.L. 101–647, set out as a note under section 3001 of this title.

§ 3303. Value for transfer or obligation

(a) Transaction.—Value is given for a transfer or an obligation if, in exchange for the transfer or obligation, property is transferred or an antecedent debt is secured or satisfied, but value does not include an unperformed promise made otherwise than in the ordinary course of the promisor's business to furnish support to the debtor or another person.

(b) Reasonably equivalent value.—For the purposes of sections 3304 and 3307, a person gives a reasonably equivalent value if the person acquires an interest of the debtor in an asset pursuant to a regularly conducted, noncollusive foreclosure sale or execution of a power of sale for the acquisition or disposition of such interest upon default under a mortgage, deed of trust, or security agreement.

(c) Present value.—A transfer is made for present value if the exchange between the debtor and the transferee is intended by them to be contemporaneous and is in fact substantially contemporaneous.

(Added Pub.L. 101–647, Title XXXVI, § 3611, Nov. 29, 1990, 104 Stat. 4961.)

HISTORICAL AND STATUTORY NOTES

Effective Dates

1990 Acts. Section to take effect 180 days after Nov. 29, 1990, except as otherwise provided, see section 3631 of Pub.L. 101–647, set out as a note under section 3001 of this title.

§ 3304. Transfer fraudulent as to a debt to the United States

(a) Debt arising before transfer.—Except as provided in section 3307, a transfer made or obligation incurred by a debtor is fraudulent as to a debt to the United States which arises before the transfer is made or the obligation is incurred if—

(1)(A) the debtor makes the transfer or incurs the obligation without receiving a reasonably equivalent value in exchange for the transfer or obligation; and

(B) the debtor is insolvent at that time or the debtor becomes insolvent as a result of the transfer or obligation; or

(2)(A) the transfer was made to an insider for an antecedent debt, the debtor was insolvent at the time; and

(B) the insider had reasonable cause to believe that the debtor was insolvent.

(b) Transfers without regard to date of judgment.—(1) Except as provided in section 3307, a transfer made or obligation incurred by a debtor is fraudulent as to a debt to the United States, whether such debt arises before or after the transfer is made or the obligation is incurred, if the debtor makes the transfer or incurs the obligation—

(A) with actual intent to hinder, delay, or defraud a creditor; or

(B) without receiving a reasonably equivalent value in exchange for the transfer or obligation if the debtor—

(i) was engaged or was about to engage in a business or a transaction for which the remaining assets of the debtor were unreasonably small in relation to the business or transaction; or

(ii) intended to incur, or believed or reasonably should have believed that he would incur, debts beyond his ability to pay as they became due.

(2) In determining actual intent under paragraph (1), consideration may be given, among other factors, to whether—

(A) the transfer or obligation was to an insider;

(B) the debtor retained possession or control of the property transferred after the transfer;

(C) the transfer or obligation was disclosed or concealed;

(D) before the transfer was made or obligation was incurred, the debtor had been sued or threatened with suit;

(E) the transfer was of substantially all the debtor's assets;

(F) the debtor absconded;

(G) the debtor removed or concealed assets;

(H) the value of the consideration received by the debtor was reasonably equivalent to the value of the asset transferred or the amount of the obligation incurred;

(I) the debtor was insolvent or became insolvent shortly after the transfer was made or the obligation was incurred;

(J) the transfer occurred shortly before or shortly after a substantial debt was incurred; and

(K) the debtor transferred the essential assets of the business to a lienor who transferred the assets to an insider of the debtor.

(Added Pub.L. 101–647, Title XXXVI, § 3611, Nov. 29, 1990, 104 Stat. 4961.)

HISTORICAL AND STATUTORY NOTES

Effective Dates

1990 Acts. Section to take effect 180 days after Nov. 29, 1990, except as otherwise provided, see section 3631 of Pub.L. 101–647, set out as a note under section 3001 of this title.

§ 3305. When transfer is made or obligation is incurred

For the purposes of this subchapter:

(1) A transfer is made—

(A) with respect to an asset that is real property (other than a fixture, but including the interest of a seller or purchaser under a contract for the sale of the asset), when the transfer is so far perfected that a good-faith purchaser of the asset from the debtor against whom applicable law permits the transfer to be perfected cannot acquire an interest in the asset that is superior to the interest of the transferee; and

(B) with respect to an asset that is not real property or that is a fixture, when the transfer is so far perfected that a creditor on a simple contract cannot acquire, otherwise than under this subchapter, a judicial lien that is superior to the interest of the transferee.

(2) If applicable law permits the transfer to be perfected as approved in paragraph (1) and the transfer is not so perfected before the commencement of an action or proceeding for relief under this subchapter, the transfer is deemed made immediately before the commencement of the action or proceeding.

(3) If applicable law does not permit the transfer to be perfected as provided in paragraph (1), the transfer is made when it becomes effective between the debtor and the transferee.

(4) A transfer is not made until the debtor has acquired rights in the asset transferred.

(5) An obligation is incurred—

(A) if oral, when it becomes effective between the parties; or

(B) if evidenced by a writing executed by the obligor, when such writing is delivered to or for the benefit of the obligee.

(Added Pub.L. 101–647, Title XXXVI, § 3611, Nov. 29, 1990, 104 Stat. 4962.)

HISTORICAL AND STATUTORY NOTES

Effective Dates

1990 Acts. Section to take effect 180 days after Nov. 29, 1990, except as otherwise provided, see section 3631 of Pub.L. 101–647, set out as a note under section 3001 of this title.

§ 3306. Remedies of the United States

(a) In general.—In an action or proceeding under this subchapter for relief against a transfer or obligation, the United States, subject to section 3307 and to applicable principles of equity and in accordance with the Federal Rules of Civil Procedure, may obtain—

(1) avoidance of the transfer or obligation to the extent necessary to satisfy the debt to the United States;

(2) a remedy under this chapter against the asset transferred or other property of the transferee; or

(3) any other relief the circumstances may require.

(b) Limitation.—A claim for relief with respect to a fraudulent transfer or obligation under this subchapter is extinguished unless action is brought—

(1) under section 3304(b)(1)(A) within 6 years after the transfer was made or the obligation was incurred or, if later, within 2 years after the transfer or obligation was or could reasonably have been discovered by the claimant;

(2) under subsection (a)(1) or (b)(1)(B) of section 3304 within 6 years after the transfer was made or the obligation was incurred; or

(3) under section 3304(a)(2) within 2 years after the transfer was made or the obligation was incurred.

(Added Pub.L. 101–647, Title XXXVI, § 3611, Nov. 29, 1990, 104 Stat. 4963.)

HISTORICAL AND STATUTORY NOTES

References in Text

The Federal Rules of Civil Procedure, referred to in subsec. (a), are set out in this title.

Effective Dates

1990 Acts. Section to take effect 180 days after Nov. 29, 1990, except as otherwise provided, see section 3631 of Pub.L. 101–647, set out as a note under section 3001 of this title.

§ 3307. Defenses, liability, and protection of transferee

(a) Good faith transfer.—A transfer or obligation is not voidable under section 3304(b) with respect to a person who took in good faith and for a reasonably equivalent value or against any transferee or obligee subsequent to such person.

(b) Limitation.—Except as provided in subsection (d), to the extent a transfer is voidable in an action or proceeding by the United States under section 3306(a)(1), the United States may recover judgment for the value of the asset transferred, but not to exceed the judgment on a debt. The judgment may be entered against—

(1) the first transferee of the asset or the person for whose benefit the transfer was made; or

(2) any subsequent transferee, other than a good faith transferee who took for value or any subsequent transferee of such good-faith transferee.

(c) Value of asset.—For purposes of subsection (b), the value of the asset is the value of the asset at the time of the transfer, subject to adjustment as the equities may require.

(d) Rights of good faith transferees and obligees.—Notwithstanding voidability of a transfer or an obligation under this subchapter, a good-faith transferee or obligee is entitled, to the extent of the value given the debtor for the transfer or obligation, to—

(1) a lien on or a right to retain any interest in the asset transferred;

(2) enforcement of any obligation incurred; or

(3) a reduction in the amount of the liability on the judgment.

(e) **Exceptions.**—A transfer is not voidable under section 3304(a) or section 3304(b)(2) if the transfer results from—

(1) termination of a lease upon default by the debtor when the termination is pursuant to the lease and applicable law; or

(2) enforcement of a security interest in compliance with article 9 of the Uniform Commercial Code or its equivalent in effect in the State where the property is located.

(f) **Limitation of voidability.**—A transfer is not voidable under section 3304(a)(2)—

(1) to the extent the insider gives new value to or for the benefit of the debtor after the transfer is made unless the new value is secured by a valid lien;

(2) if made in the ordinary course of business or financial affairs of the debtor and the insider; or

(3) if made pursuant to a good-faith effort to rehabilitate the debtor and the transfer secured both present value given for that purpose and an antecedent debt of the debtor.

(Added Pub.L. 101–647, Title XXXVI, § 3611, Nov. 29, 1990, 104 Stat. 4963.)

HISTORICAL AND STATUTORY NOTES

Effective Dates

1990 Acts. Section to take effect 180 days after Nov. 29, 1990, except as otherwise provided, see section 3631 of Pub.L. 101–647, set out as a note under section 3001 of this title.

§ 3308. Supplementary provision

Except as provided in this subchapter, the principles of law and equity, including the law merchant and the law relating to principal and agent, estoppel, laches, fraud, misrepresentation, duress, coercion, mistake, insolvency, or other validating or invalidating cause shall apply to actions and proceedings under this subchapter.

(Added Pub.L. 101–647, Title XXXVI, § 3611, Nov. 29, 1990, 104 Stat. 4964.)

HISTORICAL AND STATUTORY NOTES

Effective Dates

1990 Acts. Section to take effect 180 days after Nov. 29, 1990, except as otherwise provided, see section 3631 of Pub.L. 101–647, set out as a note under section 3001 of this title.

CHAPTER 178—PROFESSIONAL AND AMATEUR SPORTS PROTECTION

Sec.

3701. Definitions.
3702. Unlawful sports gambling.
3703. Injunctions.
3704. Applicability.

§ 3701. Definitions

For purposes of this chapter—

(1) the term "amateur sports organization" means—

(A) a person or governmental entity that sponsors, organizes, schedules, or conducts a competitive game in which one or more amateur athletes participate, or

(B) a league or association of persons or governmental entities described in subparagraph (A),

(2) the term "governmental entity" means a State, a political subdivision of a State, or an entity or organization, including an entity or organization described in section 4(5) of the Indian Gaming Regulatory Act (25 U.S.C. 2703(5)), that has governmental authority within the territorial boundaries of the United States, including on lands described in section 4(4) of such Act (25 U.S.C. 2703(4)),

(3) the term "professional sports organization" means—

(A) a person or governmental entity that sponsors, organizes, schedules, or conducts a competitive game in which one or more professional athletes participate, or

(B) a league or association of persons or governmental entities described in subparagraph (A),

(4) the term "person" has the meaning given such term in section 1 of title 1, and

(5) the term "State" means any of the several States, the District of Columbia, the Commonwealth of Puerto Rico, the Commonwealth of the Northern Mariana Islands, Palau, or any territory or possession of the United States.

(Added Pub.L. 102–559, § 2(a), Oct. 28, 1992, 106 Stat. 4227.)

HISTORICAL AND STATUTORY NOTES

Effective Dates

1992 Acts. Section 3 of Pub.L. 102–559 provided that: "This Act [enacting this chapter and enacting provisions set out as a note under section 1 of this title] shall take effect on January 1, 1993."

§ 3702. Unlawful sports gambling

It shall be unlawful for—

(1) a governmental entity to sponsor, operate, advertise, promote, license, or authorize by law or compact, or

(2) a person to sponsor, operate, advertise, or promote, pursuant to the law or compact of a governmental entity,

a lottery, sweepstakes, or other betting, gambling, or wagering scheme based, directly or indirectly (through the use of geographical references or otherwise), on one or more competitive games in which amateur or professional athletes participate, or are intended to participate, or on one or more performances of such athletes in such games.

(Added Pub.L. 102–559, § 2(a), Oct. 28, 1992, 106 Stat. 4228.)

HISTORICAL AND STATUTORY NOTES

Effective Dates

1992 Acts. Section effective Jan. 1, 1993, see section 3 of Pub.L. 102–559, set out as a note under section 3701 of this title.

§ 3703. Injunctions

A civil action to enjoin a violation of section 3702 may be commenced in an appropriate district court of the United States by the Attorney General of the United States, or by a professional sports organization or amateur sports organization whose competitive game is alleged to be the basis of such violation.

(Added Pub.L. 102–559, § 2(a), Oct. 28, 1992, 106 Stat. 4228.)

HISTORICAL AND STATUTORY NOTES

Effective Dates

1992 Acts. Section effective Jan. 1, 1993, see section 3 of Pub.L. 102–559, set out as a note under section 3701 of this title.

§ 3704. Applicability

(a) Section 3702 shall not apply to—

(1) a lottery, sweepstakes, or other betting, gambling, or wagering scheme in operation in a State or other governmental entity, to the extent that the scheme was conducted by that State or other governmental entity at any time during the period beginning January 1, 1976, and ending August 31, 1990;

(2) a lottery, sweepstakes, or other betting, gambling, or wagering scheme in operation in a State or other governmental entity where both—

(A) such scheme was authorized by a statute as in effect on October 2, 1991; and

(B) a scheme described in section 3702 (other than one based on parimutuel animal racing or jai-alai games) actually was conducted in that State or other governmental entity at any time during the period beginning September 1, 1989, and ending October 2, 1991, pursuant to the law of that State or other governmental entity;

(3) a betting, gambling, or wagering scheme, other than a lottery described in paragraph (1), conducted exclusively in casinos located in a municipality, but only to the extent that—

(A) such scheme or a similar scheme was authorized, not later than one year after the effective date of this chapter, to be operated in that municipality; and

(B) any commercial casino gaming scheme was in operation in such municipality throughout the 10–year period ending on such effective date pursuant to a comprehensive system of State regulation authorized by that State's constitution and applicable solely to such municipality; or

(4) parimutuel animal racing or jai-alai games.

(b) Except as provided in subsection (a), section 3702 shall apply on lands described in section 4(4) of the Indian Gaming Regulatory Act (25 U.S.C. 2703(4)).

(Added Pub.L. 102–559, § 2(a), Oct. 28, 1992, 106 Stat. 4228.)

HISTORICAL AND STATUTORY NOTES

References in Text

The effective date of this chapter, referred to in subsec. (a)(3)(A), is Jan. 1, 1993, see section 3 of Pub.L. 102–559, set out as an Effective Dates note under section 3701 of this title.

Effective Dates

1992 Acts. Section effective Jan. 1, 1993, see section 3 of Pub.L. 102–559, set out as a note under section 3701 of this title.

CHAPTER 179—JUDICIAL REVIEW OF CERTAIN ACTIONS BY PRESIDENTIAL OFFICES

Sec.

3901. Civil actions.
3902. Judicial review of regulations.
3903. Effect of failure to issue regulations.
3904. Expedited review of certain appeals.
3905. Attorney's fees and interest.
3906. Payments.
3907. Other judicial review prohibited.
3908. Definitions.

§ 3901. Civil actions

(a) Parties.—In an action under section 1346(g) of this title, the defendant shall be the employing office alleged to have committed the violation involved.

(b) Jury trial.—In an action described in subsection (a), any party may demand a jury trial where a jury trial would be available in an action against a private defendant under the relevant law made applicable by chapter 5 of title 3. In any case in which a violation of section 411 of title 3 is alleged, the court shall not inform the jury of the maximum amount of compensatory damages available under section 411(b)(1) or 411(b)(3) of title 3.

(Added Pub.L. 104–331, § 3(c), Oct. 26, 1996, 110 Stat. 4070.)

HISTORICAL AND STATUTORY NOTES

Effective Dates

1996 Acts. Enactment of this section by section 3(b)(3) of Pub.L. 104–331, effective Oct. 1, 1997, see section 3(d) of Pub.L. 104–331, set out as a note under section 1296 of this title.

§ 3902. Judicial review of regulations

In any proceeding under section 1296 or 1346(g) of this title in which the application of a regulation issued under chapter 5 of title 3 is at issue, the court may review the validity of the regulation in accordance with the provisions of subparagraphs (A) through (D) of section 706(2) of title 5. If the court determines that the regulation is invalid, the court shall apply, to the extent necessary and appropriate, the most relevant substantive executive agency regulation promulgated to implement the statutory provisions with respect to which the invalid regulation was issued. Except as provided in this section, the validity of regulations issued under this chapter is not subject to judicial review.

(Added Pub.L. 104–331, § 3(c), Oct. 26, 1996, 110 Stat. 4070.)

HISTORICAL AND STATUTORY NOTES

Effective Dates

1996 Acts. Enactment of this section by section 3(b)(3) of Pub.L. 104–331, effective Oct. 1, 1997, see section 3(d) of Pub.L. 104–331, set out as a note under section 1296 of this title.

§ 3903. Effect of failure to issue regulations

In any proceeding under section 1296 or 1346(g) of this title, if the President, the designee of the President, or the Federal Labor Relations Authority has not issued a regulation on a matter for which chapter 5 of title 3 requires a regulation to be issued, the court shall apply, to the extent necessary and appropriate, the most relevant substantive executive agency regulation promulgated to implement the statutory provision at issue in the proceeding.

(Added Pub.L. 104–331, § 3(c), Oct. 26, 1996, 110 Stat. 4070.)

HISTORICAL AND STATUTORY NOTES

Effective Dates

1996 Acts. Enactment of this section by section 3(b)(3) of Pub.L. 104–331, effective Oct. 1, 1997, see section 3(d) of Pub.L. 104–331, set out as a note under section 1296 of this title.

§ 3904. Expedited review of certain appeals

(a) In general.—An appeal may be taken directly to the Supreme Court of the United States from any interlocutory or final judgment, decree, or order of a court upon the constitutionality of any provision of chapter 5 of title 3.

(b) Jurisdiction.—The Supreme Court shall, if it has not previously ruled on the question, accept jurisdiction over the appeal referred to in subsection (a), advance the appeal on the docket, and expedite the appeal to the greatest extent possible.

(Added Pub.L. 104–331, § 3(c), Oct. 26, 1996, 110 Stat. 4070.)

HISTORICAL AND STATUTORY NOTES

Effective Dates

1996 Acts. Enactment of this section by section 3(b)(3) of Pub.L. 104–331, effective Oct. 1, 1997, see section 3(d) of Pub.L. 104–331, set out as a note under section 1296 of this title.

§ 3905. Attorney's fees and interest

(a) Attorney's fees.—If a covered employee, with respect to any claim under chapter 5 of title 3, or a qualified person with a disability, with respect to any claim under section 421 of title 3, is a prevailing party in any proceeding under section 1296 or section 1346(g), the court may award attorney's fees, expert fees, and any other costs as would be appropriate if awarded under section 706(k) of the Civil Rights Act of 1964.

(b) Interest.—In any proceeding under section 1296 or section 1346(g), the same interest to compensate for delay in payment shall be made available as would be appropriate if awarded under section 717(d) of the Civil Rights Act of 1964.

(c) Punitive damages.—Except as otherwise provided in chapter 5 of title 3, no punitive damages may be awarded with respect to any claim under chapter 5 of title 3.

(Added Pub.L. 104–331, § 3(c), Oct. 26, 1996, 110 Stat. 4070.)

HISTORICAL AND STATUTORY NOTES

References in Text

The Civil Rights Act of 1964, referred to in subsecs. (a) and (b), is Pub.L. 88–352, July 2, 1964, 78 Stat. 252, as amended. Title VII of such Act is classified generally to subchapter VI (section 2000e et seq.) of chapter 21 of Title 42, The Public Health and Welfare. Sections 706 and 717 of such Act are classified to sections 2000e–5 and 2000e–16, respectively, of Title 42. For complete classification of this Act to the Code, see Short Title note set out under section 2000a of Title 42 and Tables.

Effective Dates

1996 Acts. Enactment of this section by section 3(b)(3) of Pub.L. 104–331, effective Oct. 1, 1997, see section 3(d) of Pub.L. 104–331, set out as a note under section 1296 of this title.

§ 3906. Payments

A judgment, award, or compromise settlement against the United States under this chapter (including any interest and costs) shall be paid—

(1) under section 1304 of title 31, if it arises out of an action commenced in a district court of the United States (or any appeal therefrom); or

(2) out of amounts otherwise appropriated or available to the office involved, if it arises out of an appeal from an administrative proceeding under chapter 5 of title 3.

(Added Pub.L. 104–331, § 3(c), Oct. 26, 1996, 110 Stat. 4071.)

HISTORICAL AND STATUTORY NOTES

Effective Dates

1996 Acts. Enactment of this section by section 3(b)(3) of Pub.L. 104–331, effective Oct. 1, 1997, see section 3(d) of Pub.L. 104–331, set out as a note under section 1296 of this title.

§ 3907. Other judicial review prohibited

Except as expressly authorized by this chapter and chapter 5 of title 3, the compliance or noncompliance with the provisions of chapter 5 of title 3, and any action taken pursuant to chapter 5 of title 3, shall not be subject to judicial review.

(Added Pub.L. 104–331, § 3(c), Oct. 26, 1996, 110 Stat. 4071.)

HISTORICAL AND STATUTORY NOTES

Effective Dates

1996 Acts. Enactment of this section by section 3(b)(3) of Pub.L. 104–331, effective Oct. 1, 1997, see section 3(d) of Pub.L. 104–331, set out as a note under section 1296 of this title.

§ 3908. Definitions

For purposes of applying this chapter, the terms "employing office" and "covered employee" have the meanings given those terms in section 401 of title 3.

(Added Pub.L. 104–331, § 3(c), Oct. 26, 1996, 110 Stat. 4071.)

HISTORICAL AND STATUTORY NOTES

Effective Dates

1996 Acts. Enactment of this section by section 3(b)(3) of Pub.L. 104–331, effective Oct. 1, 1997, see section 3(d) of Pub.L. 104–331, set out as a note under section 1296 of this title.

CHAPTER 180—ASSUMPTION OF CERTAIN CONTRACTUAL OBLIGATIONS

Sec.
4001. Assumption of contractual obligations related to transfers of rights in motion pictures.

§ 4001. Assumption of contractual obligations related to transfers of rights in motion pictures

(a) Assumption of obligations.—(1) In the case of a transfer of copyright ownership under United States law in a motion picture (as the terms "transfer of copyright ownership" and "motion picture" are defined in section 101 of title 17) that is produced subject to 1 or more collective bargaining agreements negotiated under the laws of the United States, if the transfer is executed on or after the effective date of this chapter and is not limited to public performance rights, the transfer instrument shall be deemed to incorporate the assumption agreements applicable to the copyright ownership being transferred that are required by the applicable collective bargaining agreement, and the transferee shall be subject to the obligations under each such assumption agreement to make residual payments and provide related notices, accruing after the effective date of the transfer and applicable to the exploitation of the rights transferred, and any remedies under each such assumption agreement for breach of those obligations, as those obligations and remedies are set forth in the applicable collective bargaining agreement, if—

(A) the transferee knows or has reason to know at the time of the transfer that such collective bargaining agreement was or will be applicable to the motion picture; or

(B) in the event of a court order confirming an arbitration award against the transferor under the collective bargaining agreement, the transferor does not have the financial ability to satisfy the award within 90 days after the order is issued.

(2) For purposes of paragraph (1)(A), "knows or has reason to know" means any of the following:

(A) Actual knowledge that the collective bargaining agreement was or will be applicable to the motion picture.

(B)(i) Constructive knowledge that the collective bargaining agreement was or will be applicable to the motion picture, arising from recordation of a document pertaining to copyright in the motion picture under section 205 of title 17 or from publication, at a site available to the public on-line that is operated by the relevant union, of information that identifies the motion picture as subject to a collective bargaining agreement with that union, if the site permits commercially reasonable verification of the date on which the information was available for access.

(ii) Clause (i) applies only if the transfer referred to in subsection (a)(1) occurs—

(I) after the motion picture is completed, or

(II) before the motion picture is completed and—

(aa) within 18 months before the filing of an application for copyright registration for the motion picture under section 408 of title 17, or

(bb) if no such application is filed, within 18 months before the first publication of the motion picture in the United States.

(C) Awareness of other facts and circumstances pertaining to a particular transfer from which it is apparent that the collective bargaining agreement was or will be applicable to the motion picture.

(b) Scope of exclusion of transfers of public performance rights.—For purposes of this section, the exclusion under subsection (a) of transfers of copyright ownership in a motion picture that are limited to public performance rights includes transfers to a terrestrial broadcast station, cable system, or programmer to the extent that the station, system, or programmer is functioning as an exhibitor of the motion picture, either by exhibiting the motion picture on its own network, system, service, or station, or by initiating the transmission of an exhibition that is carried on another network, system, service, or station. When a terrestrial broadcast station, cable system, or programmer, or other transferee, is also functioning otherwise as a distributor or as a producer of the motion picture, the public performance exclusion does not affect any obligations imposed on the transferee to the extent that it is engaging in such functions.

(c) Exclusion for grants of security interests.—Subsection (a) shall not apply to—

(1) a transfer of copyright ownership consisting solely of a mortgage, hypothecation, or other security interest; or

(2) a subsequent transfer of the copyright ownership secured by the security interest described in paragraph (1) by or under the authority of the secured party, including a transfer through the exercise of the secured party's rights or remedies as a secured party, or by a subsequent transferee.

The exclusion under this subsection shall not affect any rights or remedies under law or contract

(d) Deferral pending resolution of bona fide dispute.—A transferee on which obligations are imposed under subsection (a) by virtue of paragraph (1) of that subsection may elect to defer performance of such obligations that are subject to a bona fide dispute between a union and a prior transferor until that dispute is resolved, except that such deferral shall not stay accrual of any union claims due under an applicable collective bargaining agreement.

(e) Scope of obligations determined by private agreement.—Nothing in this section shall expand or diminish the rights, obligations, or remedies of any person under the collective bargaining agreements or assumption agreements referred to in this section.

(f) Failure to notify.—If the transferor under subsection (a) fails to notify the transferee under subsection (a) of applicable collective bargaining obligations before the execution of the transfer instrument, and subsection (a) is made applicable to the transferee solely by virtue of subsection (a)(1)(B), the transferor shall be liable to the transferee for any damages suffered by the transferee as a result of the failure to notify.

(g) Determination of disputes and claims.—Any dispute concerning the application of subsections (a) through (f) shall be determined by an action in United States district court, and the court in its discretion may allow the recovery of full costs by or against any party and may also award a reasonable attorney's fee to the prevailing party as part of the costs.

(h) Study.—The Comptroller General, in consultation with the Register of Copyrights, shall conduct a study of the conditions in the motion picture industry that gave rise to this section, and the impact of this section on the motion picture industry. The Comptroller General shall report the findings of the study to the Congress within 2 years after the effective date of this chapter.

(Added Pub.L. 105–304, Title IV, § 406(a), Oct. 28, 1998, 112 Stat. 2902.)

HISTORICAL AND STATUTORY NOTES

Effective Dates

1998 Acts. Amendments by Title IV of Pub.L. 105–304 effective Oct. 28, 1998, except as otherwise provided, see section 407 of Pub.L. 105–304, set out as a note under section 108 of Title 17, Copyrights.

MISCELLANEOUS PROVISIONS

Act June 25, 1948, c. 646, §§ 2 to 39, 62 Stat. 985 to 991, as amended

Sec. 2. **(a)** The Chief Justices of the United States Court of Appeals for the District of Columbia, the District Court of the United States for the District of Columbia, and the Court of Claims, and the presiding judge of the Court of Customs and Patent Appeals, in office on the effective date of this Act shall be the chief judges of their respective courts. The Chief Justice of the United States Court of Appeals for the District of Columbia and the Associate Justices thereof, the Chief Justice of the District Court of the United States for the District of Columbia (formerly named the Supreme Court of the District of Columbia) and the Associate Justices thereof, the Chief Justice of the Court of Claims, and the presiding judge of the Court of Customs and Patent Appeals, in office on the effective date of this Act, shall be judges of the United States within the meaning of Section 451 of Title 28, Judiciary and Judicial Procedure, of the United States Code, set out in Section 1 of this Act. The Chief Justice of the United States Court of Appeals for the District of Columbia and the Associate Justices thereof, in office on the effective date of this Act, shall be circuit judges of the District of Columbia Circuit and vested with all the rights, powers, and duties thereof, and the said Chief Justice of the United States Court of Appeals for the District of Columbia shall be Chief Judge of said Circuit. The Chief Justice of the District Court of the United States for the District of Columbia (formerly named the Supreme Court of the District of Columbia) and the Associate Justices thereof, in office on the effective date of this Act shall be district judges for the District of Columbia and vested with all the rights, powers, and duties thereof.

(b) The provisions of title 28, Judiciary and Judicial Procedure, of the United States Code, set out in section 1 of this Act, with respect to the organization of each of the several courts therein provided for and of the Administrative Office of the United States Courts, shall be construed as continuations of existing law, and the tenure of the judges, officers, and employees thereof and of the United States attorneys and marshals and their deputies and assistants, in office on the effective date of this Act, shall not be affected by its enactment, but each of them shall continue to serve in the same capacity under the appropriate provisions of title 28, as set out in section 1 of this Act, pursuant to his prior appointment: *Provided, however,* That each circuit court of appeals shall, as in said title 28 set out, hereafter be known as a United States court of appeals. No loss of rights, interruption of jurisdiction, or prejudice to matters pending in any of such courts on the effective date of this Act shall result from its enactment.

(c) The sum of $7,500 specified in this Act as the salary which the Assistant Director of the Administrative Office of the United States Courts shall receive, and the sum of $7,500 specified in this Act as the salary which each commissioner whom the Court of Claims may appoint shall receive, shall each respectively be that basic compensation on which shall be computed and paid the additional basic compensation mentioned in section 521 of the Act of June 30, 1945 (ch. 212, 59 Stat. 301), as amended by the Act of May 24, 1946 (ch. 270, sec. 6, 60 Stat. 217).

(d) Anything in this Act to the contrary notwithstanding, the provisions of section 14 of the Act of July 1, 1944 (ch. 358, 58 Stat. 663) are not hereby repealed.

Sec. 3. Section 366 of the Revised Statutes (5 U.S.C., section 315), as amended, is amended to read as follows:

"**Sec. 366.** Every attorney specially retained under authority of the Department of Justice shall be commissioned as special assistant to the Attorney General or special attorney and shall take the oath required by law. Foreign counsel employed in special cases shall not be required to take such oath".

Sec. 4. Section 5261 of the Revised Statutes (45 U.S.C., section 87), is amended to read as follows:

"**Sec. 5261.** Any railroad company from whom payments for freight and transportation have been withheld under the provisions of section 5260 may bring suit in the Court of Claims to recover the price of such freight and transportation.".

Sec. 5. Section 3 of the Act approved February 28, 1887 (chapter 210, 24 Stat. 409, 410; 21 U.S.C., section 193) is amended by striking out the present third sentence thereof, and by striking out the final sentence thereof and substituting in lieu of such final sentence the following:

"Every package of opium or package containing opium, either in whole or in part, brought, taken, or transported, trafficked, or dealt in contrary to the provisions of this section, shall be forfeited to the United States, for the benefit of China.".

Sec. 6. Section 1 of the Act approved August 1, 1888 (chapter 728, 25 Stat. 357; 40 U.S.C., sec. 257) is amended to read as follows:

"That in every case in which the Secretary of the Treasury or any other officer of the Government has been, or hereafter shall be, authorized to procure real estate for the erection of a public building or for other public uses, he may acquire the same for the United States by condemnation, under judicial process, whenever in his opinion it is necessary or advantageous to the Government to do so, and the Attorney General of the United States, upon every application of the Secretary of the Treasury, under this Act, or such other officer, shall cause proceedings to be commenced for condemnation within thirty days from receipt of the application at the Department of Justice.".

Sec. 7. Section 13 of the Act approved July 31, 1894 (chapter 174, 28 Stat. 210) is hereby amended by striking out the second paragraph thereof (5 U.S.C., section 321), and by amending the first paragraph thereof (31 U.S.C., section 84) to read as follows:

"**Sec. 13.** Before transmission to the General Accounting Office, the accounts of United States attorneys, assistant attorneys, and marshals, made out and approved as required by law, and accounts relating to prisoners convicted or held for trial in any court of the United States, and all other accounts relating to the Department of Justice, shall be sent with their vouchers to the Attorney General and examined under his supervision. Before transmission to the General Accounting Office, the accounts of United States Commissioners, clerks of court and other officers of the courts of the United States, except the Supreme Court of the United States and consular courts, made out and approved as required by law, shall be sent with their vouchers to the Director of the Administrative Office of the United States Courts and examined under his supervision."

Sec. 8. Section 86 of the Act approved April 30, 1900 (chapter 339, 31 Stat. 158; 48 U.S.C., secs. 641, 642, 643–645), as amended, is amended to read as follows:

"**Sec. 86.** The laws of the United States relating to removal of causes, appeals and other matters and proceedings as between the courts of the United States and the courts of the several States shall govern in such matters and proceedings as between the courts of the United States and the courts of the Territory of Hawaii."

Sec. 9. The first paragraph of section 4 of the Act approved June 6, 1900 (chapter 786, 31 Stat. 322; 48 U.S.C., section 101, first paragraph), as amended, is amended to read as follows:

"**Sec. 4.** There is hereby established a district court for the District of Alaska, with the jurisdiction of district courts of the United States and with general jurisdiction in civil, criminal, equity, and admiralty causes; and four district judges shall be appointed for the district, each at an annual salary of $15,000, who shall during their terms of office reside in the divisions of the district to which they may be respectively assigned by the President. The court shall consist of four divisions, which shall also be recording divisions.".

Sec. 10. Section 7 of the Act approved June 6, 1900 (chapter 786, 31 Stat. 324; 48 U.S.C., section 106), as amended, is amended by striking out the words "Attorney General" wherever such words appear in such section, and substituting in lieu thereof the words "Director of the Administrative Office of the United States Courts"; also by striking out the seventh sentence thereof (such sentence being the third sentence after the proviso in such section) and substituting in lieu of such sentence the following: "He may appoint necessary deputies and employ other necessary clerical assistance to aid him in the expeditious discharge of the duties of his office, with the approval of the court or judge, and, subject to the approval of the Director of the Administrative Office of the United States Courts, fix the compensation of such deputies and the compensation for such clerical assistance."

Sec. 11. Section 8 of the Act approved June 6, 1900 (chapter 786, 31 Stat. 324; 48 U.S.C., section 109), as amended by the Act approved March 3, 1909, ch. 269, § 4, 35 Stat. 841, is amended to read as follows:

"**Sec. 8.** Four district attorneys shall be appointed for the district, one of whom shall be assigned to each division and shall reside at such place in the division as the Attorney General shall direct. They shall each perform the duties required to be performed by United States attorneys in other districts, and such other duties as may be required by law. The Attorney General shall fix the salaries of such district attorneys, and such attorneys shall not while in office accept retainers or engage in any other law business in the district than that pertaining to the duties of their office. The Attorney General may, upon the recommendation of the district attorney, appoint and at pleasure remove one or more assistant district attorneys and one or more clerical assistants, who shall receive such compensation as the Attorney General shall fix, to be paid as assistant United States attorneys and clerical assistants in other districts are paid. In the case of the death or disability of a district attorney the judge may appoint a suitable person to fill the office until his successor is appointed and qualified or until the disability is removed.".

Sec. 12. The first paragraph of section 9 of the Act approved June 6, 1900 (chapter 786, 31 Stat. 324; 48 U.S.C., section 110, part) is amended to read as follows:

"**Sec. 9.** Four United States marshals shall be appointed for the district, at salaries which shall be fixed by the Attorney General, one of whom shall be assigned to each division, and shall reside at such place in the division as the Attorney General shall direct. Each marshal shall have authority and be required to appoint, subject to the approval of the Attorney General, such deputy marshals as he may deem necessary for the efficient execution of the law and the orders of the court and of the commissioners appointed as herein provided.".

Sec. 13. Section 10 of the Act approved June 6, 1900 (chapter 786, 31 Stat. 325; 48 U.S.C., sections 62, 63, 107, 110, 112, 113, 114) is amended to read as follows:

"**Sec. 10.** The governor, attorneys, judges, and the marshals provided for in this Act shall be appointed by the President, by and with the advice and consent of the Senate, and shall hold their respective offices for the term of four years and until their successors are appointed and qualified, unless sooner removed by the President for cause.

"The governor shall receive an annual salary of $10,000, payable from the Treasury of the United States.

"The salaries of the judges, marshals, clerks, and district attorneys shall be payable from the Treasury of the United States, as like officers are paid in other districts.

"Each clerk shall collect all money arising from the fees of his office or on any other account authorized by law to be paid to or collected by him, and shall report the same and the disposition thereof in detail, under oath, quarterly, or more frequently if required, to the court, the Director of the Administrative Office of the United States Courts, and the Secretary of the Treasury, and all public money received by him and his deputies for fees or on any other account shall be paid out by the clerk on the order of the court, duly made and signed by the judge, and any balance remaining in his hands after all payments ordered by the court shall have been made shall be by him covered into the Treasury of the United States at such times and under such rules and regulations as the Secretary of the Treasury may prescribe. The clerk may employ, with the approval of the court, necessary clerical assistants and other employees in such number as may be approved by the Director of the Administrative Office of the United States Courts.

"The governor shall, in addition to his salary, be paid his actual traveling and subsistence expenses when traveling in the discharge of his official duties. The judges shall be entitled to the same travel and subsistence allowances as those of United States District Judges in other districts. The marshals, clerks of court, and district attorneys shall, in addition to their salaries, be paid their actual traveling and subsistence expenses in accordance with the Subsistence Expense Act of 1926 (chapter 457, 44 Stat. 688), as amended, and government travel regulations, when traveling in the discharge of their official duties.

"Accounts for such expenses of judges, marshals, district attorneys, and clerks shall be rendered and paid as are accounts of judges, marshals, district attorneys, and clerks for like expenses in other districts.".

Sec. 14. [Repealed. Pub.L. 88–241, § 21, Dec. 23, 1963, 77 Stat. 628.]

Sec. 15. [Repealed. Pub.L. 88–241, § 21, Dec. 23, 1963, 77 Stat. 628.]

Sec. 16. [Repealed. Pub.L. 88–241, § 21, Dec. 23, 1963, 77 Stat. 628.]

Sec. 17. Section 2 of the Act approved February 11, 1903 (chapter 544, 32 Stat. 823; 15 U.S.C., sec. 29, 49 U.S.C., sec. 45), as amended, is amended to read as follows:

"**Sec. 2.** In every civil action brought in any district court of the United States under any of said Acts, wherein the United States is complainant, an appeal from the final judgment of the district court will lie only to the Supreme Court.".

Sec. 18. The second sentence of the second paragraph of section 6 of the Act approved April 22, 1908 (chapter 149, 35 Stat. 65, 66; 45 U.S.C., section 56), as added by the Act approved April 5, 1910 (chapter 143, section 1, 36 Stat. 291), is amended to read as follows:

"The jurisdiction of the courts of the United States under this Act shall be concurrent with that of the courts of the several States.".

Sec. 19. The final sentence of section 1 of the Act approved June 19, 1912 (chapter 174, 37 Stat. 137; 40 U.S.C., section 324) is amended to read as follows:

"Any contractor or subcontractor aggrieved by the withholding of any penalty as hereinbefore provided shall have the right within six months thereafter to appeal to the head of the department making the contract on behalf of the United States or the Territory, and in the case of a contract made by the District of Columbia to the Commissioners thereof, who shall have power to review the action imposing the penalty, and in all such appeals from such final order whereby a contractor or subcontractor may be aggrieved by the imposition of the penalty hereinbefore provided, such contractor or subcontractor may, within six months after decision by such head of a department or the Commissioners of the District of Columbia, file a claim in the Court of Claims.".

Sec. 20. Section 41 of the Act approved March 2, 1917 (chapter 145, 39 Stat. 965; 48 U.S.C., section 863), as amended, is amended to read as follows:

"**Sec. 41.** The United States District Court for the District of Puerto Rico shall, in addition to its other jurisdiction, have jurisdiction for the naturalization of aliens and Puerto Ricans, and, for this purpose, residence in Puerto Rico shall be counted in the same manner as residence elsewhere in the United States. Said district court shall have jurisdiction of all controversies where all of the parties on either side of the controversy are citizens or subjects of a foreign State or States, or citizens of a State, Territory, or District of the United States not domiciled in Puerto Rico, wherein the matter in dispute exceeds, exclusive of interest or cost, the sum or value of $3,000, and of all controversies in which there is a separable controversy involving such jurisdictional amount and in which all of the parties on either side of such separable controversy are citizens or subjects of the character aforesaid. The salaries of the judge and officials of the United States District Court for the District of Puerto Rico, together with the court expenses, shall be paid from the United States revenues in the same manner as in other United States district courts. In case of vacancy or of the death, absence, or other legal disability on the part of the judge of the said United States District Court for the District of Puerto Rico, the President of the United States is authorized to designate one of the judges of the Supreme Court of Puerto Rico to discharge the duties of judge of said court until such absence or disability shall be removed, and thereupon such judge so designated for said service shall be fully authorized and empowered to perform the duties of said office during such absence or disability of such regular judge, and to sign all necessary papers and records as the acting judge of said court without extra compensation.".

Sec. 21. Section 42 of the Act approved March 2, 1917 (ch. 145, 39 Stat. 966; 48 U.S.C., section 864) is amended to read as follows:

"**Sec. 42.** The laws of the United States relating to appeals, certiorari, removal of causes, and other matters or proceedings as between the courts of the United States and the courts of the several States shall govern in such matters and proceedings as between the United States District Court for the District of Puerto Rico and the courts of Puerto Rico.

"All pleadings and proceedings in the District Court of the United States for Puerto Rico shall be conducted in the English language.".

Sec. 22. Section 1 of the Act approved May 28, 1926 (chapter 411, 44 Stat. 669; 19 U.S.C., section 405a), is amended to read as follows:

"That the Board of General Appraisers shall hereafter be known as the United States Customs Court and the members thereof shall hereafter be known as the judges of the United States Customs Court.".

Sec. 23. Section 2 of the Act approved January 31, 1928 (chapter 14, 45 Stat. 54), as amended, is amended to read as follows:

"**Sec. 2.** All Acts of Congress referring to writs of error shall be construed as amended to the extent necessary to substitute appeal for writ of error.".

Sec. 24. [Repealed. Pub.L. 88–241, § 21, Dec. 23, 1963, 77 Stat. 628.]

Sec. 25. Subsection (a) of section 501 of the Act approved June 17, 1930 (chapter 497, Title IV, 46 Stat. 730; 19 U.S.C., section 1501(a)), as amended, is amended by striking out the fourth sentence thereof and inserting in lieu of such sentence the following: "Every such appeal shall be transmitted with the entry and the accompanying papers by the collector to the United States Customs Court."

Sec. 26. Section 509 of the Act approved June 17, 1930 (chapter 497, Title IV, 46 Stat. 733; 19 U.S.C., section 1509) is amended by striking out the words, "Collectors, appraisers, and judges and divisions of the United States Customs Court" at the beginning of such section, and inserting in lieu thereof the words, "Collectors and appraisers".

Sec. 27. Section 3 of the Act approved May 7, 1934 (chapter 222, 48 Stat. 668; 40 U.S.C., section 13c) is amended to read as follows:

"**Sec. 3.** All other duties and work required for the operation, domestic care, and custody of the building shall be performed under the direction of the Marshal of the Supreme Court of the United States, who shall be superintendent of the United States Supreme Court Building.".

Sec. 28. Section 26 of the Act approved June 22, 1936 (chapter 699, section 26, 49 Stat. 1813), as amended by the Act approved August 5, 1939 (chapter 430, 53 Stat. 1203; U.S.C., 48 U.S.C., section 1405y) is amended by adding to the first paragraph thereof, the following:

"In the case of a vacancy in the office of district attorney, the District Court of the Virgin Islands may appoint a district attorney to serve until the vacancy is filled. The order of appointment by the court shall be filed with the clerk of court".

Sec. 29. Section 5 of the Act approved June 26, 1936 (chapter 831, 49 Stat. 1968; 25 U.S.C., section 505) as amended by striking out the third, fourth, and fifth sentences thereof, and substituting in lieu of such sentences the following sentence: "Within thirty days after such service or within such extended time as the trial court may permit, the Secretary of the Interior may intervene in such action or may remove such action to the United States district court."

Sec. 30. Section 3 of the Act approved May 24, 1940 (chapter 209, 54 Stat. 220; 28 U.S.C., 1940 edition, section 5a) is amended to read as follows:

"**Sec. 3.** The salary of the judge of the District Court of the Virgin Islands of the United States shall be at the rate of $15,000 per year.".

Sec. 31. [Repealed. Pub.L. 87–845, § 26(b), Oct. 18, 1962, 76A Stat. 702.]

Sec. 32. (a) All laws of the United States in force on September 1, 1948, in which reference is made to a 'circuit court of appeals'; 'senior circuit judge'; 'senior district judge'; 'presiding judge'; 'chief justice', except when reference to the Chief Justice of the United States is intended; or 'justice', except when used with respect to a justice of the Supreme Court of the United States in his capacity as such or as a circuit justice, are hereby amended by substituting 'court of appeals' for 'circuit court of appeals'; 'chief judge of the circuit' for 'senior circuit judge'; 'chief judge of the district court' for 'senior district judge'; 'chief judge' for 'presiding judge'; 'chief judge' for 'chief justice', except when reference to the Chief Justice of the United States is intended; and 'judge' for 'justice', except when the latter term is used with respect to a justice of the Supreme Court of the United States in his capacity as such or as a circuit justice. As amended May 24, 1949, c. 139, § 127, 63 Stat. 107.

(b) All laws of the United States in force on September 1, 1948, in which reference is made to the Supreme Court of the District of Columbia or to the District Court of the United States for the District of Columbia are amended by substituting 'United States District Court for the District of Columbia' for such designations.

(c) All laws of the United States in force on September 1, 1948, in which reference is made to the 'Conference of Senior Circuit Judges', or to the 'Judicial Conference of Senior Circuit Judges' are amended by substituting 'Judicial Conference of the United States' for such designations.

(d) This section shall not be construed to amend historical references to courts or judicial offices which have no present or future application to such courts or offices.

Sec. 33. No inference of a legislative construction is to be drawn by reason of the chapter in Title 28, Judiciary and Judicial Procedure, as set out in section 1 of this Act, in which any section is placed, nor by reason of the catchlines used in such title.

Sec. 34. If any part of Title 28, Judiciary and Judicial Procedure, as set out in section 1 of this Act, shall be held invalid, the remainder shall not be affected thereby.

Sec. 35. Sections 61 and 62 of Title 7 of the Canal Zone Code are hereby repealed.

Sec. 36. Section 1141(a) of the Internal Revenue Code is hereby amended to read as follows:

"The circuit courts of appeals and the United States Court of Appeals for the District of Columbia shall have exclusive jurisdiction to review the decisions of the Tax Court, except as provided in section 1254 of title 28 of the United States Code, in the same manner and to the same extent as decisions of the district courts in civil actions tried without a jury; and the judgment of any such court shall be final, except that it shall be subject to review by the Supreme Court of the United States upon certiorari, in the manner provided in section 1254 of title 28 of the United States Code."

Sec. 37. Section 6 of the Act approved August 7, 1946 (ch. 864, 60 Stat. 903), is amended to read as follows:

"**Sec. 6.** Whenever any claimant under this Act is dissatisfied with the action of a department or agency of the Government in either granting or denying his claim, such claimant shall have the right within six months to file a petition with the Court of Claims or, if the claim does not exceed $10,000 in amount or suit has heretofore been brought or is brought within thirty days after the enactment of this amendatory act, with any Federal district court of competent jurisdiction, asking a determination by the court of the equities involved in such claim; and upon the filing of such a petition, the court, sitting as a court of equity, shall have jurisdiction to determine the amount, if any, to which such claimant and petitioner may be equitably entitled (not exceeding the amount which might have been allowed by the department or agency concerned under the terms of this Act) and to enter an order directing such department or agency to settle the claim in accordance with the finding of the court; and thereafter either party may appeal from the decision if it was rendered by a district court or petition the Supreme Court for a writ of certiorari if it was rendered by the court of claims, as in other cases. Any case heretofore brought in a district court under this section may, at the election of the petitioner to be exercised within thirty days after the enactment of this amendatory Act, be transferred to the Court of Claims for original disposition in that court."

Sec. 38. The provisions of this Act shall take effect on September 1, 1948.

Sec. 39. The sections or parts thereof of the Revised Statutes of the District of Columbia, Revised Statutes of the United States or Statutes at Large enumerated in the following schedules* are hereby repealed. Any rights or liabilities now existing under such sections or parts thereof shall not be affected by this repeal.

*For schedules, see the volume of U.S.C.A. covering the end of Title 28, Judiciary and Judicial Procedure.

APPENDIX

JUDICIAL PERSONNEL FINANCIAL DISCLOSURE REQUIREMENTS

Pub.L. 95–521, Title III, §§ 301 to 309, Oct. 26, 1978, 92 Stat. 1851, as amended

[§§ 301 to 309. Transferred]

HISTORICAL AND STATUTORY NOTES

Codifications

Title III (§§ 301 to 309) of Pub.L. 95–521, Oct. 26, 1978, 92 Stat. 1851, as amended Pub.L. 96–19, §§ 2(a)(3), (c)(3), 3(a)(3), (b), 4(c), 6, 7(a) to (c), (d)(2), (e), (f), 8(c), 9(c)(3), (d), (j), (p) to (r), June 13, 1979, 93 Stat. 37 to 43; Pub.L. 96–417, Title VI, § 601(9), Oct. 10, 1980, 94 Stat. 1744; Pub.L. 96–579, § 13(c), Dec. 23, 1980, 94 Stat. 3369; Pub.L. 97–164, Title I, § 163(a)(6), Apr. 2, 1982, 96 Stat. 49; Pub.L. 98–150, § 10, Nov. 11, 1983, 97 Stat. 962; Pub.L. 99–514, § 2, Oct. 22, 1986, 100 Stat. 2095; Pub.L. 99–573, § 6, Oct. 28, 1986, 100 Stat. 3231; Pub.L. 101–237, Title VI, § 602(a)(1), Dec. 18, 1989, 103 Stat. 2094, which related to judicial personnel financial disclosure requirements, was repealed by Pub.L. 101–194, Title II, § 201, Nov. 30, 1989, 103 Stat. 1724. See Title I of the Ethics in Government Act of 1978, Pub.L. 95–521, as amended, relating to financial disclosure requirements of Federal personnel, set out in Appendix 4 to Title 5, Government Organization and Employees.

Effective Date of Repeal

The repeal of Pub.L. 95–521, Title III, by Pub.L. 101–194, Title II, § 201, Nov. 30, 1989, 103 Stat. 1724, as effective Jan. 1, 1991, see Pub.L. 101–194, Title II, § 204, as added Pub.L. 101–280, § 3(10)(B), May 4, 1990, 104 Stat. 157, set out as an Effective Date of 1989 Amendment note under section 101 of Pub.L. 95–521 in Appendix 4 to Title 5, Government Organization and Employees.

Provisions of Title III of Pub.L. 95–521, as in effect prior to Nov. 30, 1989, to be effective until Jan. 1, 1991, as if Pub.L. 101–194 had not been enacted, and nothing in Title III, of Pub.L. 101–194 to be construed to prevent prosecution of civil actions against individuals for violating Title III of Pub.L. 95–521 before Jan. 1, 1991, see section 3(10)(C) and (D) of Pub.L. 101–280, set out as notes under section 101 of Pub.L. 95–521 in Appendix 4 to Title 5, Government Organization and Employees.

*

DEVELOPMENT OF MECHANISMS FOR RESOLVING MINOR DISPUTES

Pub.L. 96–190, Feb. 12, 1980, 94 Stat. 17

HISTORICAL AND STATUTORY NOTES

Codifications

Pub.L. 96–190, Feb. 12, 1980, 94 Stat. 17, known as the Dispute Resolution Act, provided for the establishment and maintenance of mechanisms for resolving minor disputes, established the Dispute Resolution Resource Center and Dispute Resolution Advisory Board, prescribed duties for the Center and Board, authorized appropriations for the Center and Board of $1,000,000 for each of the fiscal years 1980, 1981, 1982, 1983, and 1984, directed that financial assistance to eligible applicants be in the form of grants, prescribed conditions for such grants, authorized appropriations for such grants of $10,000,000 for each of the fiscal years 1981, 1982, 1983, and 1984, and required an annual report by the Attorney General to the President and Congress relating to the administration of Pub.L. 96–190.

*

CONSTITUTION OF THE UNITED STATES

PREAMBLE

WE THE PEOPLE of the United States, in Order to form a more perfect Union, establish Justice, insure domestic Tranquility, provide for the common defence, promote the general Welfare, and secure the Blessings of Liberty to ourselves and our Posterity, do ordain and establish this CONSTITUTION for the United States of America.

ARTICLE I

Section. 1. All legislative Powers herein granted shall be vested in a Congress of the United States, which shall consist of a Senate and House of Representatives.

Section. 2. The House of Representatives shall be composed of Members chosen every second Year by the People of the several States, and the Electors in each State shall have the Qualifications requisite for Electors of the most numerous Branch of the State Legislature.

No Person shall be a Representative who shall not have attained to the Age of twenty five Years, and been seven Years a Citizen of the United States, and who shall not, when elected, be an Inhabitant of that State in which he shall be chosen.

[Representatives and direct Taxes shall be apportioned among the several States which may be included within this Union, according to their respective Numbers, which shall be determined by adding to the whole Number of free Persons, including those bound to Service for a Term of Years, and excluding Indians not taxed, three fifths of all other Persons.] [1] The actual Enumeration shall be made within three Years after the first Meeting of the Congress of the United States, and within every subsequent Term of ten Years, in such Manner as they shall by Law direct. The Number of Representatives shall not exceed one for every thirty Thousand, but each State shall have at Least one Representative; and until such enumeration shall be made, the State of New Hampshire shall be entitled to chuse three, Massachusetts eight, Rhode-Island and Providence Plantations one, Connecticut five, New-York six, New Jersey four, Pennsylvania eight, Delaware one, Maryland six, Virginia ten, North Carolina five, South Carolina five, and Georgia three.

When vacancies happen in the Representation from any State, the Executive Authority thereof shall issue Writs of Election to fill such Vacancies.

The House of Representatives shall chuse their Speaker and other Officers; and shall have the sole Power of Impeachment.

1 The clause of this paragraph inclosed in brackets was amended, as to the mode of apportionment of representatives among the several states, by the Fourteenth Amendment, § 2, and as to taxes on incomes without apportionment, by the Sixteenth Amendment.

Section. 3. [The Senate of the United States shall be composed of two Senators from each State, chosen by the Legislature thereof, for six Years; and each Senator shall have one Vote.] [1]

Immediately after they shall be assembled in Consequence of the first Election, they shall be divided as equally as may be into three Classes. The Seats of the Senators of the first Class shall be vacated at the Expiration of the second Year, of the second Class at the Expiration of the fourth Year, and of the third Class at the Expiration of the sixth Year, so that one third may be chosen every second Year; [and if Vacancies happen by Resignation, or otherwise, during the Recess of the Legislature of any State, the Executive thereof may make temporary Appointments until the next Meeting of the Legislature, which shall then fill such Vacancies.] [2]

No Person shall be a Senator who shall not have attained to the Age of thirty Years, and been nine Years a Citizen of the United States, and who shall not, when elected, be an Inhabitant of that State for which he shall be chosen.

The Vice President of the United States shall be President of the Senate, but shall have no Vote, unless they be equally divided.

The Senate shall chuse their other Officers, and also a President pro tempore, in the Absence of the Vice

President, or when he shall exercise the Office of President of the United States.

The Senate shall have the sole Power to try all Impeachments. When sitting for that Purpose, they shall be on Oath or Affirmation. When the President of the United States is tried, the Chief Justice shall preside: And no Person shall be convicted without the Concurrence of two thirds of the Members present.

Judgment in Cases of Impeachment shall not extend further than to removal from Office, and disqualification to hold and enjoy any Office of honor, Trust or Profit under the United States: but the Party convicted shall nevertheless be liable and subject to Indictment, Trial, Judgment and Punishment, according to Law.

1 This paragraph, inclosed in brackets, was superseded by the Seventeenth Amendment.

2 The clause of this paragraph inclosed in brackets was superseded by the Seventeenth Amendment.

Section. 4. The Times, Places and Manner of holding Elections for Senators and Representatives, shall be prescribed in each State by the Legislature thereof; but the Congress may at any time by Law make or alter such Regulations, except as to the Places of chusing Senators.

The Congress shall assemble at least once in every Year, and such Meeting shall be on the [first Monday in December],[1] unless they shall by Law appoint a different Day.

1 The clause of this paragraph inclosed in brackets was superseded by the Twentieth Amendment.

Section. 5. Each House shall be the Judge of the Elections, Returns and Qualifications of its own Members, and a Majority of each shall constitute a Quorum to do Business; but a smaller Number may adjourn from day to day, and may be authorized to compel the Attendance of absent Members, in such Manner, and under such Penalties as each House may provide.

Each House may determine the Rules of its Proceedings, punish its Members for disorderly Behaviour, and, with the Concurrence of two thirds, expel a Member.

Each House shall keep a Journal of its Proceedings, and from time to time publish the same, excepting such Parts as may in their Judgment require Secrecy; and the Yeas and Nays of the Members of either House on any question shall, at the Desire of one fifth of those Present, be entered on the Journal.

Neither House, during the Session of Congress, shall, without the Consent of the other, adjourn for more than three days, nor to any other Place than that in which the two Houses shall be sitting.

Section. 6. The Senators and Representatives shall receive a Compensation for their Services, to be ascertained by Law, and paid out of the Treasury of the United States. They shall in all Cases, except Treason, Felony and Breach of the Peace, be privileged from Arrest during their Attendance at the Session of their respective Houses, and in going to and returning from the same; and for any Speech or Debate in either House, they shall not be questioned in any other Place.

No Senator or Representative shall, during the Time for which he was elected, be appointed to any civil Office under the Authority of the United States, which shall have been created, or the Emoluments whereof shall have been encreased during such time; and no Person holding any Office under the United States, shall be a Member of either House during his Continuance in Office.

Section. 7. All Bills for raising Revenue shall originate in the House of Representatives; but the Senate may propose or concur with Amendments as on other Bills.

Every Bill which shall have passed the House of Representatives and the Senate, shall, before it becomes a Law, be presented to the President of the United States; If he approve he shall sign it, but if not he shall return it, with his Objections to that House in which it shall have originated, who shall enter the Objections at large on their Journal, and proceed to reconsider it. If after such Reconsideration two thirds of that House shall agree to pass the Bill, it shall be sent, together with the Objections, to the other House, by which it shall likewise be reconsidered, and if approved by two thirds of that House, it shall become a Law. But in all such Cases the Votes of both Houses shall be determined by Yeas and Nays, and the Names of the Persons voting for and against the Bill shall be entered on the Journal of each House respectively. If any Bill shall not be returned by the President within ten Days (Sundays excepted) after it shall have been presented to him, the Same shall be a Law, in like Manner as if he had signed it, unless the Congress by their Adjournment prevent its Return, in which Case it shall not be a Law.

Every Order, Resolution, or Vote to which the Concurrence of the Senate and House of Representatives may be necessary (except on a question of Adjournment) shall be presented to the President of the United States; and before the Same shall take Effect, shall be approved by him, or being disapproved by him, shall be repassed by two thirds of the Senate and House of Representatives, according to the Rules and Limitations prescribed in the Case of a Bill.

Section. 8. The Congress shall have Power To lay and collect Taxes, Duties, Imposts and Excises, to pay the Debts and provide for the common Defence and general Welfare of the United States; but all Duties, Imposts and Excises shall be uniform throughout the United States;

To borrow Money on the credit of the United States;

To regulate Commerce with foreign Nations, and among the several States, and with the Indian Tribes;

To establish an uniform Rule of Naturalization, and uniform Laws on the subject of Bankruptcies throughout the United States;

To coin Money, regulate the Value thereof, and of foreign Coin, and fix the Standard of Weights and Measures;

To provide for the Punishment of counterfeiting the Securities and current Coin of the United States;

To establish Post Offices and post Roads;

To promote the Progress of Science and useful Arts, by securing for limited Times to Authors and Inventors the exclusive Right to their respective Writings and Discoveries;

To constitute Tribunals inferior to the supreme Court;

To define and punish Piracies and Felonies committed on the high Seas, and Offences against the Law of Nations;

To declare War, grant Letters of Marque and Reprisal, and make Rules concerning Captures on Land and Water;

To raise and support Armies, but no Appropriation of Money to that Use shall be for a longer Term than two Years;

To provide and maintain a Navy;

To make Rules for the Government and Regulation of the land and naval Forces;

To provide for calling forth the Militia to execute the Laws of the Union, suppress Insurrections and repel Invasions;

To provide for organizing, arming, and disciplining, the Militia, and for governing such Part of them as may be employed in the Service of the United States, reserving to the States respectively, the Appointment of the Officers, and the Authority of training the Militia according to the discipline prescribed by Congress;

To exercise exclusive Legislation in all Cases whatsoever, over such District (not exceeding ten Miles square) as may, by Cession of particular States, and the Acceptance of Congress, become the Seat of the Government of the United States, and to exercise like Authority over all Places purchased by the Consent of the Legislature of the State in which the Same shall be, for the Erection of Forts, Magazines, Arsenals, dock-Yards, and other needful Buildings;—And

To make all Laws which shall be necessary and proper for carrying into Execution the foregoing Powers, and all other Powers vested by this Constitution in the Government of the United States, or in any Department or Officer thereof.

Section. 9. The Migration or Importation of such Persons as any of the States now existing shall think proper to admit, shall not be prohibited by the Congress prior to the Year one thousand eight hundred and eight, but a Tax or duty may be imposed on such Importation, not exceeding ten dollars for each Person.

The Privilege of the Writ of Habeas Corpus shall not be suspended, unless when in Cases of Rebellion or Invasion the public Safety may require it.

No Bill of Attainder or ex post facto Law shall be passed.

No Capitation, or other direct, Tax shall be laid, unless in Proportion to the Census or Enumeration herein before directed to be taken.[1]

No Tax or Duty shall be laid on Articles exported from any State.

No Preference shall be given by any Regulation of Commerce or Revenue to the Ports of one State over those of another; nor shall Vessels bound to, or from, one State, be obliged to enter, clear, or pay Duties in another.

No Money shall be drawn from the Treasury, but in Consequence of Appropriations made by Law; and a regular Statement and Account of the Receipts and Expenditures of all public Money shall be published from time to time.

No Title of Nobility shall be granted by the United States: And no Person holding any Office of Profit or Trust under them, shall, without the Consent of the Congress, accept of any present, Emolument, Office, or Title, of any kind whatever, from any King, Prince, or foreign State.

[1] This paragraph has been affected by the Sixteenth Amendment.

Section. 10. No State shall enter into any Treaty, Alliance, or Confederation; grant Letters of Marque and Reprisal; coin Money; emit Bills of Credit; make any Thing but gold and silver Coin a Tender in Payment of Debts; pass any Bill of Attainder, ex post facto Law, or Law impairing the Obligation of Contracts, or grant any Title of Nobility.

No State shall, without the Consent of the Congress, lay any Imposts or Duties on Imports or Exports, except what may be absolutely necessary for executing it's inspection Laws: and the net Produce of all Duties and Imposts, laid by any State on Imports or Exports, shall be for the Use of the Treasury of the United States; and all such Laws shall be subject to the Revision and Controul of the Congress.

No State shall, without the Consent of Congress, lay any Duty of Tonnage, keep Troops, or Ships of War in time of Peace, enter into any Agreement or Compact with another State, or with a foreign Power, or engage in War, unless actually invaded, or in such imminent Danger as will not admit of delay.

ARTICLE II

Section. 1. The executive Power shall be vested in a President of the United States of America. He shall hold his Office during the Term of four Years, and, together with the Vice President, chosen for the same Term, be elected, as follows:

Each State shall appoint, in such Manner as the Legislature thereof may direct, a Number of Electors, equal to the whole Number of Senators and Representatives to which the State may be entitled in the Congress: but no Senator or Representative, or Person holding an Office of Trust or Profit under the United States, shall be appointed an Elector.

[The Electors shall meet in their respective States, and vote by Ballot for two Persons, of whom one at least shall not be an Inhabitant of the same State with themselves. And they shall make a List of all the Persons voted for, and of the Number of Votes for each; which List they shall sign and certify, and transmit sealed to the Seat of the Government of the United States, directed to the President of the Senate. The President of the Senate shall, in the Presence of the Senate and House of Representatives, open all the Certificates, and the Votes shall then be counted. The Person having the greatest Number of Votes shall be the President, if such Number be a Majority of the whole Number of Electors appointed; and if there be more than one who have such Majority, and have an equal Number of Votes, then the House of Representatives shall immediately chuse by Ballot one of them for President; and if no Person have a Majority, then from the five highest on the List the said House shall in like Manner chuse the President. But in chusing the President, the Votes shall be taken by States, the Representation from each State having one Vote; A quorum for this Purpose shall consist of a Member or Members from two thirds of the States, and a Majority of all the States shall be necessary to a Choice. In every Case, after the Choice of the President, the Person having the greatest Number of Votes of the Electors shall be the Vice President. But if there should remain two or more who have equal Votes, the Senate shall chuse from them by Ballot the Vice President.] [1]

The Congress may determine the Time of chusing the Electors, and the Day on which they shall give their Votes; which Day shall be the same throughout the United States.

No Person except a natural born Citizen, or a Citizen of the United States, at the time of the Adoption of this Constitution, shall be eligible to the Office of President; neither shall any Person be eligible to that Office who shall not have attained to the Age of thirty five Years, and been fourteen Years a Resident within the United States.

In Case of the Removal of the President from Office, or of his Death, Resignation, or Inability to discharge the Powers and Duties of the said Office, the Same shall devolve on the Vice President, and the Congress may by Law provide for the Case of Removal, Death, Resignation or Inability, both of the President and Vice President, declaring what Officer shall then act as President, and such Officer shall act accordingly, until the Disability be removed, or a President shall be elected.

The President shall, at stated Times, receive for his Services, a Compensation, which shall neither be encreased nor diminished during the Period for which he shall have been elected, and he shall not receive within that Period any other Emolument from the United States, or any of them.

Before he enter on the Execution of his Office, he shall take the following Oath or Affirmation:—"I do solemnly swear (or affirm) that I will faithfully execute the Office of President of the United States, and will to the best of my Ability, preserve, protect and defend the Constitution of the United States."

1 This paragraph, inclosed in brackets, was superseded by the Twelfth Amendment, post.

Section. 2. The President shall be Commander in Chief of the Army and Navy of the United States, and of the Militia of the several States, when called into the actual Service of the United States; he may require the Opinion, in writing, of the principal Officer in each of the executive Departments, upon any Subject relating to the Duties of their respective Offices, and he shall have Power to grant Reprieves and Pardons for Offences against the United States, except in Cases of Impeachment.

He shall have Power, by and with the Advice and Consent of the Senate, to make Treaties, provided two thirds of the Senators present concur; and he shall nominate, and by and with the Advice and Consent of the Senate, shall appoint Ambassadors, other public Ministers and Consuls, Judges of the supreme Court, and all other Officers of the United States, whose Appointments are not herein otherwise provided for, and which shall be established by Law: but the Congress may by Law vest the Appointment of such inferior Officers, as they think proper, in the President alone, in the Courts of Law, or in the Heads of Departments.

The President shall have Power to fill up all Vacancies that may happen during the Recess of the Senate, by granting Commissions which shall expire at the End of their next Session.

Section. 3. He shall from time to time give to the Congress Information of the State of the Union, and recommend to their Consideration such Measures as he shall judge necessary and expedient; he may, on extraordinary Occasions, convene both Houses, or either of them, and in Case of Disagreement between them, with Respect to the Time of Adjournment, he may adjourn them to such Time as he shall think proper; he shall receive Ambassadors and other public Ministers; he shall take Care that the Laws be faithfully executed, and shall Commission all the Officers of the United States.

Section. 4. The President, Vice President and all civil Officers of the United States, shall be removed from Office on Impeachment for, and Conviction of, Treason, Bribery, or other high Crimes and Misdemeanors.

ARTICLE III

Section. 1. The judicial Power of the United States, shall be vested in one supreme Court, and in such inferior Courts as the Congress may from time to time ordain and establish. The Judges, both of the supreme and inferior Courts, shall hold their Offices during good Behaviour, and shall, at stated Times, receive for their Services, a Compensation, which shall not be diminished during their Continuance in Office.

Section. 2. The judicial Power shall extend to all Cases, in Law and Equity, arising under this Constitution, the Laws of the United States, and Treaties made, or which shall be made, under their Authority;—to all Cases affecting Ambassadors, other public Ministers and Consuls;—to all Cases of admiralty and maritime Jurisdiction;—to Controversies to which the United States shall be a Party;—to Controversies between two or more States;—between a State and Citizens of another State;—between citizens of different States;—between Citizens of the same State claiming Lands under Grants of different States, and between a State, or the Citizens thereof, and foreign States, Citizens or Subjects.[1]

In all Cases affecting Ambassadors, other public Ministers and Consuls, and those in which a State shall be Party, the supreme Court shall have original Jurisdiction. In all the other Cases before mentioned, the supreme Court shall have appellate Jurisdiction, both as to Law and Fact, with such Exceptions, and under such Regulations as the Congress shall make.

The Trial of all Crimes, except in Cases of Impeachment, shall be by Jury; and such Trial shall be held in the State where the said Crimes shall have been committed; but when not committed within any State, the Trial shall be at such Place or Places as the Congress may by Law have directed.

1 This section has been affected by the Eleventh Amendment.

Section. 3. Treason against the United States, shall consist only in levying War against them, or in adhering to their Enemies, giving them Aid and Comfort. No Person shall be convicted of Treason unless on the Testimony of two Witnesses to the same overt Act, or on Confession in open Court.

The Congress shall have Power to declare the Punishment of Treason, but no Attainder of Treason shall work Corruption of Blood, or Forfeiture except during the Life of the Person attainted.

ARTICLE IV

Section. 1. Full Faith and Credit shall be given in each State to the public Acts, Records, and judicial Proceedings of every other State. And the Congress may by general Laws prescribe the Manner in which such Acts, Records and Proceedings shall be proved, and the Effect thereof.

Section. 2. The Citizens of each State shall be entitled to all Privileges and Immunities of Citizens in the several States.

A Person charged in any State with Treason, Felony, or other Crime, who shall flee from Justice, and be found in another State, shall on Demand of the executive Authority of the State from which he fled, be delivered up, to be removed to the State having Jurisdiction of the Crime.

No Person held to Service or Labour in one State, under the Laws thereof, escaping into another, shall, in Consequence of any Law or Regulation therein, be discharged from such Service or Labour, but shall be delivered up on Claim of the Party to whom such Service or Labour may be due.[1]

1 This clause was affected by the Thirteenth Amendment.

Section. 3. New States may be admitted by the Congress into this Union; but no new State shall be formed or erected within the Jurisdiction of any other State; nor any State be formed by the Junction of two or more States, or Parts of States, without the Consent of the Legislatures of the States concerned as well as of the Congress.

The Congress shall have Power to dispose of and make all needful Rules and Regulations respecting the Territory or other Property belonging to the United States; and nothing in this Constitution shall be so construed as to Prejudice any Claims of the United States, or of any particular State.

Section. 4. The United States shall guarantee to every State in this Union a Republican Form of Government, and shall protect each of them against Invasion; and on Application of the Legislature, or of the Executive (when the Legislature cannot be convened) against domestic Violence.

ARTICLE V

The Congress, whenever two thirds of both Houses shall deem it necessary, shall propose Amendments to this Constitution, or, on the Application of the Legislatures of two thirds of the several States, shall call a Convention for proposing Amendments, which, in either Case, shall be valid to all Intents and Purposes, as Part of this Constitution, when ratified by the Legislatures of three fourths of the several States, or by Conventions in three fourths thereof, as the one or the other Mode of Ratification may be proposed by the Congress; Provided that no Amendment which may be made prior to the Year One thousand eight hundred and eight shall in any Manner affect the first and fourth Clauses in the Ninth Section of the first Article; and that no State, without its Consent, shall be deprived of its equal Suffrage in the Senate.

ARTICLE VI

All Debts contracted and Engagements entered into, before the Adoption of this Constitution, shall be as valid against the United States under this Constitution, as under the Confederation.

This Constitution, and the Laws of the United States which shall be made in Pursuance thereof; and all Treaties made, or which shall be made, under the Authority of the United States, shall be the supreme Law of the Land; and the Judges in every State shall be bound thereby, any Thing in the Constitution or Laws of any State to the Contrary notwithstanding.

The Senators and Representatives before mentioned, and the Members of the several State Legislatures, and all executive and judicial Officers, both of the United States and of the several States, shall be bound by Oath or Affirmation, to support this Constitution; but no religious Test shall ever be required as a Qualification to any Office or public Trust under the United States.

ARTICLE VII

The Ratification of the Conventions of nine States, shall be sufficient for the Establishment of this Constitution between the States so ratifying the Same.

DONE in Convention by the Unanimous Consent of the States present the Seventeenth Day of September in the Year of Our Lord one thousand seven hundred and Eighty seven and of the Independence of the United States of America the Twelfth. IN WITNESS whereof We have hereunto subscribed our Names.

Go. WASHINGTON—*Presidt. and deputy from Virginia*

Attest WILLIAM JACKSON *Secretary*

New Hampshire

JOHN LANGDON NICHOLAS GILMAN

Massachusetts

NATHANIEL GORHAM RUFUS KING

Connecticut

WM. SAML. JOHNSON ROGER SHERMAN

New York

ALEXANDER HAMILTON

New Jersey

WIL: LIVINGSTON WM. PATERSON.
DAVID BREARLEY. JONA: DAYTON

Pennsylvania

B FRANKLIN THOS. FITZSIMONS
THOMAS MIFFLIN JARED INGERSOLL
ROBT MORRIS JAMES WILSON
GEO. CLYMER GOUV MORRIS

Delaware

GEO: READ RICHARD BASSETT
GUNNING BEDFORD jun JACO: BROOM
JOHN DICKINSON

Maryland

JAMES MCHENRY DANL CARROLL
DAN OF ST THOS. JENIFER

Virginia

JOHN BLAIR— JAMES MADISON JR.

North Carolina

WM. BLOUNT HU WILLIAMSON
RICHD. DOBBS SPAIGHT

South Carolina

J. RUTLEDGE CHARLES PINCKNEY
CHARLES COTESWORTH PINCKNEY PIERCE BUTLER

Georgia

WILLIAM FEW ABR BALDWIN

HISTORICAL NOTES

Proposal and Ratification of Original Articles

In May, 1785, a committee of Congress made a report recommending an alteration in the Articles of Confederation, but no action was taken on it, and it was left to the State Legislatures to proceed in the matter. In January, 1786, the Legislature of Virginia passed a resolution providing for the appointment of five commissioners, who, or any three of them, should meet such commissioners as might be appointed in the other States of the Union, at a time and place to be agreed upon, to take into consideration the trade of the United States; to consider how far a uniform system in their commercial regulations may be necessary to their common interest and their permanent harmony; and to report to the several States such an act, relative to this great object, as, when ratified by them, will enable the United States in Congress effectually to provide for the same. The Virginia commissioners, after some correspondence, fixed the first Monday in September as the time, and the city of Annapolis as the place for the meeting, but only four other States were represented, viz.: Delaware, New York, New Jersey, and Pennsylvania; the commissioners appointed by Massachusetts, New Hampshire, North Carolina, and Rhode Island failed to attend. Under the circumstances of so partial a representation, the commissioners present agreed upon a report, (drawn by Mr. Hamilton, of New York,) expressing their unanimous conviction that it might essentially tend to advance the interests of the Union if the States by which they were respectively delegated would concur, and use their endeavors to procure the concurrence of the other States, in the appointment of commissioners to meet at Philadelphia on the second Monday of May following, to take into consideration the situation of the United States; to devise such further provisions as should appear to them necessary to render the Constitution of the Federal Government adequate to the exigencies of the Union; and to report such an act for that purpose to the United States in Congress assembled as, when agreed to by them, and afterwards confirmed by the Legislatures of every State, would effectually provide for the same.

Congress, on the 21st of February, 1787, adopted a resolution in favor of a convention, and the Legislatures of those States which had not already done so (with the exception of Rhode Island) promptly appointed delegates. On the 25th of May, seven States having convened, George Washington, of Virginia, was unanimously elected President, and the consideration of the proposed constitution was commenced. On the 17th of September, 1787, the Constitution as engrossed and agreed upon was signed by all the members present, except Mr. Gerry, of Massachusetts, and Messrs. Mason and Randolph, of Virginia. The president of the convention transmitted it to Congress, with a resolution stating how the proposed Federal Government should be put in operation, and an explanatory letter. Congress, on the 28th of September, 1787, directed the Constitution so framed, with the resolutions and letter concerning the same, to "be transmitted to the several Legislatures in order to be submitted to a convention of delegates chosen in each State by the people thereof, in conformity to the resolves of the convention."

On the 4th of March, 1789, the day which had been fixed for commencing the operations of Government under the new Constitution, it had been ratified by the conventions chosen in each State to consider it, as follows: Delaware, December 7, 1787; Pennsylvania, December 12, 1787; New Jersey, December 18, 1787; Georgia, January 2, 1788; Connecticut, January 9, 1788; Massachusetts, February 6, 1788; Maryland, April 28, 1788; South Carolina, May 23, 1788; New Hampshire, June 21, 1788; Virginia, June 25, 1788; and New York, July 26, 1788.

The President informed Congress, on the 28th of January, 1790, that North Carolina had ratified the Constitution November 21, 1789; and he informed Congress on the 1st of June, 1790, that Rhode Island had ratified the Constitution May 29, 1790. Vermont, in convention, ratified the Constitution January 10, 1791, and was on March 4, 1791, by an act of Congress approved February 18, 1791, "received and admitted into this Union as a new and entire member of the United States."

Articles in Addition to, and Amendment of, the Constitution of the United States of America, Proposed by Congress, and Ratified by the Legislatures of the Several States Pursuant to the Fifth Article of the Original Constitution

ARTICLE [I]

Congress shall make no law respecting an establishment of religion, or prohibiting the free exercise thereof; or abridging the freedom of speech, or of the press; or the right of the people peaceably to assemble, and to petition the Government for a redress of grievances.

HISTORICAL NOTES

Proposal and Ratification of Amendments 1 to 10

The first ten amendments to the Constitution of the United States, which comprise the Bill of Rights, set out in 1 Stat. 97, were proposed to the Legislatures of the several States by the First Congress, on September 25, 1789. They were ratified by the following States, and the notifications of ratification by the governors or secretaries of state thereof were communicated successively by the President to Congress: New Jersey, November 20, 1789; Maryland, December 19, 1789; North Carolina, December 22, 1789; South Carolina, January 19, 1790; New Hampshire, January 25, 1790; Delaware, January 28, 1790; New York, February 27, 1790; Pennsylvania, March 10, 1790; Rhode Island, June 7, 1790; Vermont, November 3, 1791; and Virginia, December 15, 1791. The Legislatures of Connecticut, Georgia, and Massachusetts ratified them on April 19, 1939, March 18, 1939, and March 2, 1939, respectively.

Twelve articles were proposed on September 25, 1789. The first two, which failed of adoption, read as follows:

"Art. I. After the first enumeration required by the first article of the Constitution, there shall be one representation for every thirty thousand, until the number shall amount to one hundred, after which the proportion shall be so regulated by Congress, that there shall be not less than one hundred representatives, nor less than one representative for every forty thousand persons, until the number of representatives shall amount to two hundred; after which the proportion shall be so regulated by Congress, that there shall not be less than two hundred representatives, nor more than one representative for every fifty thousand persons.

"Art. II. No law varying the compensation for the services of the senators and representatives shall take effect, until an election of representatives shall have intervened."

ARTICLE [II]

A well regulated Militia, being necessary to the security of a free State, the right of the people to keep and bear Arms, shall not be infringed.

ARTICLE [III]

No Soldier shall, in time of peace be quartered in any house, without the consent of the Owner, nor in time of war, but in a manner to be prescribed by law.

ARTICLE [IV]

The right of the people to be secure in their persons, houses, papers, and effects, against unreasonable searches and seizures, shall not be violated, and no Warrants shall issue, but upon probable cause, supported by Oath or affirmation, and particularly describing the place to be searched, and the persons or things to be seized.

ARTICLE [V]

No person shall be held to answer for a capital, or otherwise infamous crime, unless on a presentment or indictment of a Grand Jury, except in cases arising in the land or naval forces, or in the Militia, when in actual service in time of War or public danger; nor shall any person be subject for the same offence to be twice put in jeopardy of life or limb; nor shall be compelled in any criminal case to be a witness against himself, nor be deprived of life, liberty, or property, without due process of law; nor shall private property be taken for public use, without just compensation.

ARTICLE [VI]

In all criminal prosecutions, the accused shall enjoy the right to a speedy and public trial, by an impartial jury of the State and district wherein the crime shall have been committed, which district shall have been previously ascertained by law, and to be informed of the nature and cause of the accusation; to be confronted with the witnesses against him; to have compulsory process for obtaining witnesses in his favor, and to have the Assistance of Counsel for his defence.

ARTICLE [VII]

In Suits at common law, where the value in controversy shall exceed twenty dollars, the right of trial by jury shall be preserved, and no fact tried by a jury, shall be otherwise reexamined in any Court of the United States, than according to the rules of the common law.

ARTICLE [VIII]

Excessive bail shall not be required, nor excessive fines imposed, nor cruel and unusual punishments inflicted.

ARTICLE [IX]

The enumeration in the Constitution, of certain rights, shall not be construed to deny or disparage others retained by the people.

ARTICLE [X]

The powers not delegated to the United States by the Constitution, nor prohibited by it to the States, are reserved to the States respectively, or to the people.

ARTICLE [XI]

The Judicial power of the United States shall not be construed to extend to any suit in law or equity, commenced or prosecuted against one of the United States by Citizens of another State, or by Citizens or Subjects of any Foreign State.

HISTORICAL NOTES

Proposal and Ratification

The eleventh amendment, set out in 1 Stat. 402, was proposed to the legislatures of the several States by the Third Congress, on March 4, 1794, and was declared in a message from the President to Congress, dated January 8, 1798, to have been ratified by the legislatures of three fourths of the States. The States which ratified this amendment, and the dates of ratification are: New York, March 27, 1794; Rhode Island, March 31, 1794; Connecticut, May 8, 1794; New Hampshire, June 16, 1794; Massachusetts, June 26, 1794; Vermont, between October 9 and November 9, 1794; Virginia, November 18, 1794; Georgia, November 29, 1794; Kentucky, December 7, 1794; Maryland, December 26, 1794; Delaware, January 23, 1795; North Carolina, February 7, 1795; and South Carolina, December 4, 1797.

ARTICLE [XII]

The Electors shall meet in their respective states, and vote by ballot for President and Vice-President, one of whom, at least, shall not be an inhabitant of the same state with themselves; they shall name in their ballots the person voted for as President, and in distinct ballots the person voted for as Vice-President, and they shall make distinct lists of all persons voted for as President, and of all persons voted for as Vice-President, and of the number of votes for each, which lists they shall sign and certify, and transmit sealed to the seat of the government of the United States, directed to the President of the Senate;—The President of the Senate shall, in the presence of the Senate and House of Representatives, open all the certificates and the votes shall then be counted;—The person having the greatest number of votes for President, shall be the President, if such number be a majority of the whole number of Electors appointed; and if no person have such majority, then from the persons having the highest numbers not exceeding three on the list of those voted for as President, the House of Representatives shall choose immediately, by ballot, the President. But in choosing the President, the votes shall be taken by states, the representation from each state having one vote; a quorum for this purpose shall consist of a member or members from two-thirds of the states, and a majority of all the states shall be necessary to a choice. And if the House of Representatives shall not choose a President whenever the right of choice shall devolve upon them, before the fourth day of March next following, then the Vice-President shall act as President, as in the case of the death or other constitutional disability of the President.—The person having the greatest number of votes as Vice-President, shall be the Vice-President, if such number be a majority of the whole number of Electors appointed, and if no person have a majority, then from the two highest numbers on the list, the Senate shall choose the Vice-President; a quorum for the purpose shall consist of two-thirds of the whole number of Senators, and a majority of the whole number shall be necessary to a choice. But no person constitutionally ineligible to the office of President shall be eligible to that of Vice-President of the United States.[1]

1 This Amendment was affected by the Twentieth Amendment.

HISTORICAL NOTES

Proposal and Ratification

The Twelfth Amendment, set out in 2 Stat. 306, was proposed to the legislatures of the several States by the Eighth Congress, on December 9, 1803, and was declared in a proclamation of the Secretary of State, dated September 25, 1804, to have been ratified by the legislatures of three-fourths of the States. It supersedes Article 2, section 1, clause 3. Ratification by the States was accomplished as follows: North Carolina, December 22, 1803; Maryland, December 24, 1803; Kentucky, December 27, 1803; Ohio, between December 5 and December 30, 1803; Virginia, between December 20, 1803, and February 3, 1804; Pennsylvania, January 5, 1804; Vermont, January 30, 1804; New York, February 10, 1804; New Jersey, February 22, 1804; Rhode Island, between February 27 and March 12, 1804; South Carolina, May 15, 1804; Georgia, May 19, 1804; New Hampshire, June 15, 1804; and Tennessee, July 27, 1804. The States of Delaware and Connecticut rejected this amendment on January 18, 1804 and May 10, 1804, respectively. Massachusetts rejected this amendment on February 3, 1804 and subsequently ratified it in 1961.

ARTICLE XIII

Section 1. Neither slavery nor involuntary servitude, except as a punishment for crime whereof the party shall have been duly convicted, shall exist within the United States, or any place subject to their jurisdiction.

Section 2. Congress shall have power to enforce this article by appropriate legislation.

HISTORICAL NOTES

Proposal and Ratification

Amendment XIII, set out in 13 Stat. 567, was proposed to the legislatures of the several States by the Thirty-eighth Congress, on January 31, 1865, and was declared, in a proclamation of the Secretary of State, dated December 18, 1865, to have been ratified by the legislatures of twenty-seven of the thirty-six States. The States which ratified this amendment and the dates of ratification are: Illinois, February 1, 1865; Rhode Island, February 2, 1865; Michigan, February 2, 1865; Maryland, February 3, 1865; New York, February 3, 1865; West Virginia, February 3, 1865; Missouri, February 6, 1865; Maine, February 7, 1865; Kansas, February 7, 1865; Massachusetts, February 7, 1865; Pennsylvania, February 8, 1865; Virginia, February 9, 1865; Ohio, February 10, 1865; Louisiana, February 15 or 16, 1865; Indiana, February 16, 1865; Nevada, February 16, 1865; Minnesota, February 23, 1865; Wisconsin, February 24, 1865; Vermont, March 9, 1865; Tennessee, April 7, 1865; Arkansas, April 14, 1865; Connecticut, May 4, 1865; New Hampshire, June 30, 1865; South Carolina, November 13, 1865; Alabama, December 2, 1865; North Carolina, December 4, 1865; and Georgia, December 6, 1865. The Legislatures of the following States ratified this amendment after December 6, 1865: Oregon, December 11, 1865; California, December 15, 1865; Florida, December 28, 1865; Iowa, January 17, 1866; New Jersey, January 23, 1866; Texas, February 18, 1870; Delaware, February 12, 1901; Kentucky, March 18, 1976, and Mississippi, March 16, 1995.

The Thirteenth Amendment was rejected by New Jersey on March 16, 1865; Delaware, February 8, 1865; Kentucky, February 24, 1865, and Mississippi, December 2, 1865. However, New Jersey, Delaware and Kentucky subsequently ratified the amendment on the dates set forth above.

ARTICLE XIV

Section 1. All persons born or naturalized in the United States, and subject to the jurisdiction thereof, are citizens of the United States and of the State wherein they reside. No State shall make or enforce any law which shall abridge the privileges or immunities of citizens of the United States; nor shall any State deprive any person of life, liberty, or property, without due process of law; nor deny to any person within its jurisdiction the equal protection of the laws.

Section 2. Representatives shall be apportioned among the several States according to their respective numbers, counting the whole number of persons in each State, excluding Indians not taxed. But when the right to vote at any election for the choice of electors for President and Vice President of the United States, Representatives in Congress, the Executive and Judicial officers of a State, or the members of the Legislature thereof, is denied to any of the male inhabitants of such State, being twenty-one years of age, and citizens of the United States, or in any way abridged, except for participation in rebellion, or other crime, the basis of representation therein shall be reduced in the proportion which the number of such male citizens shall bear to the whole number of male citizens twenty-one years of age in such State.

Section 3. No person shall be a Senator or Representative in Congress, or elector of President and Vice President, or hold any office, civil or military, under the United States, or under any State, who, having previously taken an oath, as a member of Congress, or as an officer of the United States, or as a member of any State legislature, or as an executive or judicial officer of any State, to support the Constitution of the United States, shall have engaged in insurrection or rebellion against the same, or given aid or comfort to the enemies thereof. But Congress may by a vote of two-thirds of each House, remove such disability.

Section 4. The validity of the public debt of the United States, authorized by law, including debts incurred for payment of pensions and bounties for services in suppressing insurrection or rebellion, shall not be questioned. But neither the United States nor any State shall assume or pay any debt or obligation incurred in aid of insurrection or rebellion against the United States, or any claim for the loss or emancipation of any slave; but all such debts, obligations and claims shall be held illegal and void.

Section 5. The Congress shall have power to enforce, by appropriate legislation, the provisions of this article.

HISTORICAL NOTES

Proposal and Ratification

Amendment XIV, set out in 14 Stat. 358, was proposed to the legislatures of the several States by the Thirty-ninth Congress, on June 13, 1866. On July 21, 1868, Congress adopted and transmitted to the Department of State a concurrent resolution, declaring that "the legislatures of the States of Connecticut, Tennessee, New Jersey, Oregon, Vermont, New York, Ohio, Illinois, West Virginia, Kansas, Maine, Nevada, Missouri, Indiana, Minnesota, New Hampshire, Massachusetts, Nebraska, Iowa, Arkansas, Florida, North Carolina, Alabama, South Carolina, and Louisiana, being three-fourths and more of the several States of the Union, have ratified the fourteenth article of amendment to the Constitution of the United States, duly proposed by two-thirds of each House of the Thirty-ninth Congress: Therefore, Resolved, That said fourteenth article is hereby declared to be a part of the Constitution of the United States, and it shall be duly promulgated as such by the Secretary of State." The Secretary of State accordingly issued a proclamation, dated July 28, 1868, declaring that the proposed fourteenth amendment had been ratified by the legislatures of thirty of the thirty-six States. The amendment was ratified by the State Legislatures on the following dates: Connecticut, June 25, 1866; New Hampshire, July 6, 1866; Tennessee, July 19, 1866; New Jersey, September 11, 1866; Oregon, September 19, 1866; Vermont, October 30, 1866; New York, January 10, 1867; Ohio, January 4, 1867; Illinois, January 15, 1867; West Virginia, January 16, 1867; Michigan, January 16, 1867; Kansas, January 11, 1867; Minnesota, January 16, 1867; Maine, January 19, 1867; Nevada, January 22, 1867; Indiana, January 23, 1867; Missouri, January 25, 1867; Rhode Island, February 7, 1867; Pennsylvania, February 12, 1867; Wisconsin, February 7, 1867; Massachusetts, March 20, 1867; Nebraska, June 15, 1867; Iowa, March 16, 1868; Arkansas, April 6, 1868; Florida, June 9, 1868; North Carolina, July 2, 1868; Louisiana, July 9, 1868; South Carolina, July 9, 1868; Alabama, July 13, 1868; Georgia, July 21, 1868. Subsequent to the proclamation the following States ratified this amendment: Virginia, October 8, 1869; Mississippi, January 17, 1870; Texas, February 18, 1870; Delaware, February 12, 1901; Maryland, April 4, 1959; California, May 6, 1959; and Kentucky, March 18, 1976.

The Fourteenth Amendment originally was rejected by Delaware, Georgia, Kentucky, Louisiana, North Carolina, South Carolina, Texas and Virginia, however, the State Legislatures of the aforesaid States subsequently ratified the amendment on the dates set forth in the preceding paragraph. Maryland rejected this amendment on March 23, 1867.

The States of New Jersey, Ohio and Oregon "withdrew" their consent to the ratification of this amendment on March 24, 1868, January 15, 1868, and October 15, 1868, respectively.

The New Jersey State Assembly Concurrent Resolution No. 128, introduced Apr. 21, 1980, and filed Nov. 12, 1980, expressed the support of the Legislature of the State of New Jersey for the Fourteenth Amendment of the United States Constitution.

ARTICLE XV

Section 1. The right of citizens of the United States to vote shall not be denied or abridged by the United States or by any State on account of race, color, or previous condition of servitude.

Section 2. The Congress shall have power to enforce this article by appropriate legislation.

HISTORICAL NOTES

Proposal and Ratification

Amendment XV, set out in 15 Stat. 346, was proposed to the legislatures of the several States by the Fortieth Congress, on Feb. 26, 1869, and was declared, in a proclamation of the Secretary of State dated March 30, 1870, to have been ratified by the legislatures of twenty-nine of the thirty-seven

States. The dates of ratification are: Nevada, March 1, 1869; West Virginia, March 3, 1869; North Carolina, March 5, 1869; Louisiana, March 5, 1869; Illinois, March 5, 1869; Michigan, March 8, 1869; Wisconsin, March 9, 1869; Maine, March 11, 1869; Massachusetts, March 12, 1869; South Carolina, March 15, 1869; Arkansas, March 15, 1869; Pennsylvania, March 25, 1869; New York, April 14, 1869; Indiana, May 14, 1869; Connecticut, May 19, 1869; Florida, June 14, 1869; New Hampshire, July 1, 1869; Virginia, October 8, 1869; Vermont, October 20, 1869; Alabama, November 16, 1869; Missouri, January 7, 1870; Minnesota, January 13, 1870; Mississippi, January 17, 1870; Rhode Island, January 18, 1870; Kansas, January 19, 1870; Ohio, January 27, 1870; Georgia, February 2, 1870; Iowa, February 3, 1870; Nebraska, February 17, 1870; and Texas, February 18, 1870. Subsequent to the issuance of the proclamation, the Fifteenth Amendment was ratified by New Jersey, February 15, 1871; Delaware, February 12, 1901; Oregon, February 24, 1959; California, April 3, 1962; and Kentucky, March 18, 1976.

The States of California, Delaware, Kentucky, Maryland, New Jersey, and Tennessee rejected the Fifteenth Amendment, however, California, Delaware, Kentucky, and New Jersey ratified it on the dates set forth in the above paragraph.

Consent to ratification of the Fifteenth Amendment was "withdrawn" by New York on January 5, 1870, which action was rescinded on March 30, 1970.

ARTICLE XVI

The Congress shall have power to lay and collect taxes on incomes, from whatever source derived, without apportionment among the several States, and without regard to any census or enumeration.

HISTORICAL NOTES

Proposal and Ratification

The Sixteenth Amendment, set out in 36 Stat. 184, was proposed to the legislatures of the several States by the Sixty-First Congress, on July 12, 1909, and was declared, in a proclamation by the Secretary of State, dated February 25, 1913, to have been ratified. The dates of ratification are as follows: Alabama, August 10, 1909; Kentucky, February 8, 1910; South Carolina, February 19, 1910; Illinois, March 1, 1910; Mississippi, March 7, 1910; Oklahoma, March 10, 1910; Maryland, April 8, 1910; Georgia, August 3, 1910; Texas, August 16, 1910; Ohio, January 19, 1911; Idaho, January 20, 1911; Oregon, January 23, 1911; Washington, January 26, 1911; Montana, January 27, 1911; Indiana, January 30, 1911; California, January 31, 1911; Nevada, January 31, 1911; South Dakota, February 1, 1911; Nebraska, February 9, 1911; North Carolina, February 11, 1911; Colorado, February 15, 1911; North Dakota, February 17, 1911; Michigan, February 23, 1911; Iowa, February 24, 1911; Kansas, March 2, 1911; Missouri, March 16, 1911; Maine, March 31, 1911; Tennessee, April 7, 1911; Arkansas, April 22, 1911; Wisconsin, May 16, 1911; New York, July 12, 1911; Arizona, April 3, 1912; Minnesota, June 11, 1912; Louisiana, June 28, 1912; West Virginia, January 31, 1913; Delaware, February 3, 1913; Wyoming, February 3, 1913; New Mexico, February 3, 1913; New Jersey, February 4, 1913; and Vermont, February 19, 1913. Subsequent to the proclamation, the Sixteenth Amendment was ratified by Massachusetts on March 4, 1913 and by New Hampshire on March 7, 1913.

The States of Arkansas, Connecticut, New Hampshire, Rhode Island and Utah rejected the amendment, but in later years Arkansas and New Hampshire ratified it.

ARTICLE [XVII]

The Senate of the United States shall be composed of two Senators from each state, elected by the people thereof, for six years; and each Senator shall have one vote. The electors in each State shall have the qualifications requisite for electors of the most numerous branch of the State legislatures.

When vacancies happen in the representation of any State in the Senate, the executive authority of such State shall issue writs of election to fill such vacancies: *Provided,* That the legislature of any State may empower the executive thereof to make temporary appointments until the people fill the vacancies by election as the legislature may direct.

This amendment shall not be so construed as to affect the election or term of any Senator chosen before it becomes valid as part of the Constitution.

HISTORICAL NOTES

Proposal and Ratification

Amendment XVII, set out in 37 Stat. 646, was proposed to the legislatures of the several States by the Sixty-Second Congress, on May 13, 1912, and was declared, in a proclamation by the Secretary of State, dated May 31, 1913, to have been ratified. The amendment was ratified on the following dates by the respective States: Massachusetts, May 22, 1912; Arizona, June 3, 1912; Minnesota, June 10, 1912; New York, January 15, 1913; Kansas, January 17, 1913; Oregon, January 23, 1913; North Carolina, January 25, 1913; California, January 28, 1913; Michigan, January 28, 1913; Iowa, January 30, 1913; Montana, January 30, 1913; Idaho, January 31, 1913; West Virginia, February 4, 1913; Colorado, February 5, 1913; Nevada, February 6, 1913; Texas, February 7, 1913; Washington, February 7, 1913; Wyoming, February 8, 1913; Arkansas, February 11, 1913; Illinois, February 13, 1913; North Dakota, February 14, 1913; Wisconsin, February 18, 1913; Indiana, February 19, 1913; New Hampshire, February 19, 1913; Vermont, February 19, 1913; South Dakota, February 19, 1913; Maine, February 20, 1913; Oklahoma,

February 24, 1913; Ohio, February 25, 1913; Missouri, March 7, 1913; New Mexico, March 13, 1913; Nebraska, March 14, 1913; New Jersey, March 17, 1913; Tennessee, April 1, 1913; Pennsylvania, April 2, 1913; and Connecticut, April 8, 1913. The State of Louisiana ratified the amendment on June 5, 1914, after issuance of the proclamation.

The Seventeenth Amendment was rejected by Utah on February 26, 1913.

ARTICLE [XVIII] [Repealed. See Article XXI]

Section 1. After one year from the ratification of this article the manufacture, sale, or transportation of intoxicating liquors within, the importation thereof into, or the exportation thereof from the United States and all territory subject to the jurisdiction thereof for beverage purposes is hereby prohibited.

Section 2. The Congress and the several States shall have concurrent power to enforce this article by appropriate legislation.

Section 3. This article shall be inoperative unless it shall have been ratified as an amendment to the Constitution by the legislatures of the several States, as provided in the Constitution, within seven years from the date of the submission hereof to the States by the Congress.

HISTORICAL NOTES

Proposal and Ratification

The Eighteenth Amendment, set out in 40 Stat. 1050, was proposed to the legislatures of the several States by the Sixty-Fifth Congress, on December 18, 1917, and was declared, in a proclamation by the Acting Secretary of State, dated January 29, 1919, to have been ratified. The State legislatures ratified this amendment on the following dates: Mississippi, January 8, 1918; Virginia, January 11, 1918; Kentucky, January 14, 1918; North Dakota, January 28, 1918; South Carolina, January 29, 1918; Maryland, February 13, 1918; Montana, February 19, 1918; Texas, March 4, 1918; Delaware, March 18, 1918; South Dakota, March 20, 1918; Massachusetts, April 2, 1918; Arizona, May 24, 1918; Georgia, June 26, 1918; Louisiana, August 9, 1918; Florida, November 27, 1918; Michigan, January 2, 1919; Ohio, January 7, 1919; Oklahoma, January 7, 1919; Idaho, January 8, 1919; Maine, January 8, 1919; West Virginia, January 9, 1919; California, January 13, 1919; Tennessee, January 13, 1919; Washington, January 13, 1919; Arkansas, January 14, 1919; Kansas, January 14, 1919; Illinois, January 14, 1919; Indiana, January 14, 1919; Alabama, January 15, 1919; Colorado, January 15, 1919; Iowa, January 15, 1919; New Hampshire, January 15, 1919; Oregon, January 15, 1919; Nebraska, January 16, 1919; North Carolina, January 16, 1919; Utah, January 16, 1919; Missouri, January 16, 1919; Wyoming, January 16, 1919; Minnesota, January 17, 1919; Wisconsin, January 17, 1919; New Mexico, January 20, 1919, and Nevada, January 21, 1919. The amendment was also ratified after issuance of the proclamation by New York, January 29, 1919; Vermont, January 29, 1919; Pennsylvania, February 25, 1919; Connecticut, May 6, 1919; and New Jersey, March 9, 1922.

The amendment was rejected by Rhode Island.

Amendment XVIII was repealed by the Twenty-first Amendment which was ratified on December 5, 1933.

ARTICLE [XIX]

The right of citizens of the United States to vote shall not be denied or abridged by the United States or by any State on account of sex.

Congress shall have power to enforce this article by appropriate legislation.

HISTORICAL NOTES

Proposal and Ratification

The Nineteenth Amendment, set out in 41 Stat. 362, was proposed to the legislatures of the several States by the Sixty-Sixth Congress, on May 4, 1919, and was declared, in a proclamation by the Secretary of State, dated August 26, 1920, to have been ratified. The dates of ratification are as follows: Illinois, June 10, 1919; Michigan, June 10, 1919; Wisconsin, June 10, 1919; Kansas, June 16, 1919; New York, June 16, 1919; Ohio, June 16, 1919; Pennsylvania, June 24, 1919; Massachusetts, June 25, 1919; Texas, June 28, 1919; Iowa, July 2, 1919; Missouri, July 3, 1919; Arkansas, July 28, 1919; Montana, August 2, 1919; Nebraska, August 2, 1919; Minnesota, September 8, 1919; New Hampshire, September 10, 1919; Utah, October 2, 1919; California, November 1, 1919; Maine, November 5, 1919; North Dakota, December 1, 1919; South Dakota, December 4, 1919; Colorado, December 15, 1919; Kentucky, January 6, 1920; Rhode Island, January 6, 1920; Oregon, January 13, 1920; Indiana, January 16, 1920; Wyoming, January 27, 1920; Nevada, February 7, 1920; New Jersey, February 9, 1920; Idaho, February 11, 1920; Arizona, February 12, 1920; New Mexico, February 21, 1920; Oklahoma, February 28, 1920; West Virginia, March 10, 1920; Washington, March 22, 1920; and Tennessee, August 18, 1920. Connecticut and Vermont subsequently ratified the amendment on September 14, 1920 and February 8, 1921, respectively.

This amendment was ratified by Maryland, March 29, 1941 (after having rejected it on February 24, 1920); Virginia, February 21, 1952 (after having rejected it on February 12, 1920); Alabama, September 8, 1953 (after having rejected it on September 22, 1919); Florida, May 13, 1969; South Carolina, July 1, 1969 (after having rejected it on January 28, 1920); Georgia, February 20, 1970 (after having rejected it on July 25, 1919); Louisiana, June 11, 1970 (after having rejected it on July 1, 1920); and North Carolina May 6, 1971.

The amendment was rejected by Mississippi on March 29, 1920 and Delaware on June 2, 1920.

ARTICLE [XX]

Section 1. The terms of the President and Vice President shall end at noon on the 20th day of January, and the terms of Senators and Representatives at noon on the 3d day of January, of the years in which such terms would have ended if this article had not been ratified; and the terms of their successors shall then begin.

Sec. 2. The Congress shall assemble at least once in every year, and such meeting shall begin at noon on the 3d day of January, unless they shall by law appoint a different day.

Sec. 3. If, at the time fixed for the beginning of the term of the President, the President elect shall have died, the Vice President elect shall become President. If a President shall not have been chosen before the time fixed for the beginning of his term, or if the President elect shall have failed to qualify, then the Vice President elect shall act as President until a President shall have qualified; and the Congress may by law provide for the case wherein neither a President elect nor a Vice President elect shall have qualified, declaring who shall then act as President, or the manner in which one who is to act shall be selected, and such person shall act accordingly until a President or Vice President shall have qualified.

Sec. 4. The Congress may by law provide for the case of the death of any of the persons from whom the House of Representatives may choose a President whenever the right of choice shall have devolved upon them, and for the case of the death of any of the persons from whom the Senate may choose a Vice President whenever the right of choice shall have devolved upon them.

Sec. 5. Sections 1 and 2 shall take effect on the 15th day of October following the ratification of this article.

Sec. 6. This article shall be inoperative unless it shall have been ratified as an amendment to the Constitution by the legislatures of three-fourths of the several States within seven years from the date of its submission.

HISTORICAL NOTES

Proposal and Ratification

Amendment XX, set out in 47 Stat. 745, was proposed to the legislatures of the several States by the Seventy-Second Congress, on March 2, 1932, and was declared, in a proclamation by the Secretary of State, dated Feb. 6, 1933, to have been ratified. The State legislatures ratified this Amendment on the following dates: Virginia, March 4, 1932; New York, March 11, 1932; Mississippi, March 16, 1932; Arkansas, March 17, 1932; Kentucky, March 17, 1932; New Jersey, March 21, 1932; South Carolina, March 25, 1932; Michigan, March 31, 1932; Maine, April 1, 1932; Rhode Island, April 14, 1932; Illinois, April 21, 1932; Louisiana, June 22, 1932; West Virginia, July 30, 1932; Pennsylvania, August 11, 1932; Indiana, August 15, 1932; Texas, September 7, 1932; Alabama, September 13, 1932; California, January 4, 1933; North Carolina, January 5, 1933; North Dakota, January 9, 1933; Minnesota, January 12, 1933; Arizona, January 13, 1933; Montana, January 13, 1933; Nebraska, January 13, 1933; Oklahoma, January 13, 1933; Kansas, January 16, 1933; Oregon, January 16, 1933; Delaware, January 19, 1933; Washington, January 19, 1933; Wyoming, January 19, 1933; Iowa, January 20, 1933; South Dakota, January 20, 1933; Tennessee, January 20, 1933; Idaho, January 21, 1933; New Mexico, January 21, 1933; Georgia, January 23, 1933; Missouri, January 23, 1933; Ohio, January 23, 1933; Utah, January 23, 1933; Colorado, January 24, 1933; Massachusetts, January 24, 1933; Wisconsin, January 24, 1933; Nevada, January 26, 1933; Connecticut, January 27, 1933; New Hampshire, January 31, 1933, and Vermont, February 2, 1933. The States of Maryland and Florida later ratified this amendment on March 24, 1933 and April 26, 1933, respectively.

ARTICLE [XXI]

Section 1. The eighteenth article of amendment to the Constitution of the United States is hereby repealed.

Sec. 2. The transportation or importation into any State, Territory, or possession of the United States for delivery or use therein of intoxicating liquors, in violation of the laws thereof, is hereby prohibited.

Sec. 3. This article shall be inoperative unless it shall have been ratified as an amendment to the Constitution by conventions in the several States, as provided in the Constitution, within seven years from the date of the submission hereof to the States by the Congress.

HISTORICAL NOTES

Proposal and Ratification

The Twenty-first Amendment, set out in 47 Stat. 1625, was proposed to the several States by the Seventy-Second Congress, on February 20, 1933, and was declared, in a proclamation by the Secretary of State, dated December 5, 1933, to have been ratified by State Conventions as follows: Michigan, April 10, 1933; Wisconsin, April 25, 1933; Rhode Island, May 8, 1933; Wyoming, May 25, 1933; New Jersey, June 1, 1933; Delaware, June 24, 1933; Indiana, June 26, 1933; Massachusetts, June 26, 1933; New York, June 27, 1933; Illinois, July 10, 1933; Iowa, July 10, 1933; Connecticut, July 11, 1933; New Hampshire, July 11, 1933; California, July 24, 1933; West Virginia, July 25, 1933; Arkansas, August 1, 1933; Oregon, August 7, 1933; Alabama, August 8, 1933; Tennessee, August 11, 1933; Missouri, August 29, 1933; Arizona, September 5, 1933; Nevada, September 5, 1933; Vermont, September 23, 1933; Colorado, September 26, 1933; Washington, October 3, 1933; Minnesota, October 10, 1933; Idaho, October 17, 1933; Maryland, October 18, 1933; Virginia, October 25, 1933; New Mexico, November 2, 1933; Florida, November 14, 1933; Texas, November 24, 1933; Kentucky, November 27, 1933; Ohio, December 5, 1933; Pennsylvania, December 5, 1933; and Utah, December 5, 1933. Conventions held in the State of Maine and in the State of Montana ratified this amendment on December 6, 1933 and August 6, 1934, respectively.

The State of South Carolina rejected this amendment on December 4, 1933, and North Carolina voted on November 7, 1933 against holding a convention.

ARTICLE [XXII]

Section 1. No person shall be elected to the office of the President more than twice, and no person who has held the office of President, or acted as President, for more than two years of a term to which some other person was elected President shall be elected to the office of the President more than once. But this Article shall not apply to any person holding the office of President when this Article was proposed by the Congress, and shall not prevent any person who may be holding the office of President, or acting as President, during the term within which this Article becomes operative from holding the office of President or acting as President during the remainder of such term.

Sec. 2. This Article shall be inoperative unless it shall have been ratified as an amendment to the Constitution by the legislatures of three-fourths of the several States within seven years from the date of its submission to the States by the Congress.

HISTORICAL NOTES

Proposal and Ratification

The Twenty-second Amendment, set out in 61 Stat. 959, was proposed to the legislatures of the several States by the Eightieth Congress on March 21, 1947 and was declared by the Administrator of General Services, in a proclamation dated March 3, 1951, to have been ratified. The legislatures ratified this Amendment on the following dates: Maine, March 31, 1947; Michigan, March 31, 1947; Iowa, April 1, 1947; Kansas, April 1, 1947; New Hampshire, April 1, 1947; Delaware, April 2, 1947; Illinois, April 3, 1947; Oregon, April 3, 1947; Colorado, April 12, 1947; California, April 15, 1947; New Jersey, April 15, 1947; Vermont, April 15, 1947; Ohio, April 16, 1947; Wisconsin, April 16, 1947; Pennsylvania, April 29, 1947; Connecticut, May 21, 1947; Missouri, May 22, 1947; Nebraska, May 23, 1947; Virginia, January 28, 1948; Mississippi, February 12, 1948; New York, March 9, 1948; South Dakota, January 21, 1949; North Dakota, February 25, 1949; Louisiana, May 17, 1950; Montana, January 25, 1951; Indiana, January 29, 1951; Idaho, January 30, 1951; New Mexico, February 12, 1951; Wyoming, February 12, 1951; Arkansas, February 15, 1951; Georgia, February 17, 1951; Tennessee, February 20, 1951; Texas, February 22, 1951; Utah, February 26, 1951; Nevada, February 26, 1951; Minnesota, February 27, 1951; and North Carolina, February 28, 1951.

Subsequent to the proclamation, Amendment XXII was ratified by South Carolina on March 13, 1951; Maryland, March 14, 1951; Florida, April 16, 1951, and Alabama, May 4, 1951.

The amendment was rejected by Oklahoma, June 1947 and Massachusetts, June 9, 1949.

Certification of Validity

Publication of the certifying statement of the Administrator of General Services that the Amendment had become valid was made on Mar. 1, 1951, F.R. Doc. 51–2940, 16 F.R. 2019, 65 Stat. 777.

ARTICLE [XXIII]

Section 1. The District constituting the seat of Government of the United States shall appoint in such manner as the Congress may direct:

A number of electors of President and Vice President equal to the whole number of Senators and Representatives in Congress to which the District would be entitled if it were a State, but in no event more than the least populous State; they shall be in addition to those appointed by the States, but they shall be considered, for the purposes of the election of President and Vice President, to be electors appointed by a State; and they shall meet in the District and perform such duties as provided by the twelfth article of amendment.

Sec. 2. The Congress shall have power to enforce this article by appropriate legislation.

HISTORICAL NOTES

Proposal and Ratification

The Twenty-third Amendment, set out in 74 Stat. 1057, was proposed by the Eighty-sixth Congress on June 17, 1960 and ratification was completed on Apr. 3, 1961, when the thirty-eighth State ratified it.

The amendment was ratified by the following States: Hawaii, June 23, 1960; Massachusetts, Aug. 22, 1960; New Jersey, Dec. 19, 1960; New York, Jan. 17, 1961; California, Jan. 19, 1961; Oregon, Jan. 27, 1961; Maryland, Jan. 30, 1961; Idaho, Jan. 31, 1961; Maine, Jan. 31, 1961; Minnesota, Jan. 31, 1961; New Mexico, Feb. 1, 1961; Nevada, Feb. 2, 1961; Montana, Feb. 6, 1961; Colorado, Feb. 8, 1961; Washington, Feb. 9, 1961; West Virginia, Feb. 9, 1961; Alaska, Feb. 10, 1961; South Dakota, Feb. 14, 1961; Wyoming, Feb. 13, 1961; Delaware, Feb. 20, 1961; Utah, Feb. 21, 1961; Wisconsin, Feb. 21, 1961; Pennsylvania, Feb. 28, 1961; Indiana, Mar. 3, 1961; North Dakota, Mar. 3, 1961; Tennessee, Mar. 6, 1961; Michigan, Mar. 8, 1961; Connecticut, Mar. 9, 1961; Arizona, Mar. 10, 1961; Illinois, Mar. 14, 1961; Nebraska, Mar. 15, 1961; Vermont, Mar. 15, 1961; Iowa, Mar. 16, 1961; Missouri, Mar. 20, 1961; Oklahoma, Mar. 21, 1961; Rhode Island, Mar. 22, 1961; Kansas, Mar. 29, 1961; New Hampshire, Mar. 29, 1961; Ohio, Mar. 29, 1961.

The amendment was rejected by Arkansas on Jan. 24, 1961.

Certification of Validity

Publication of the certifying statement of the Administrator of General Services that the Amendment had become valid was made on Apr. 3, 1961, F.R. Doc. 61–3017, 26 F.R. 2808, 75 Stat. 847.

ARTICLE [XXIV]

Section 1. The right of citizens of the United States to vote in any primary or other election for President or Vice President, for electors for President or Vice President, or for Senator or Representative in Congress, shall not be denied or abridged by the United States or any State by reason of failure to pay any poll tax or other tax.

Sec. 2. The Congress shall have power to enforce this article by appropriate legislation.

HISTORICAL NOTES

Proposal and Ratification

The Twenty-fourth Amendment, set out in 76 Stat. 1259, was proposed by the Eighty-seventh Congress by Senate Joint Resolution No. 29, which was approved by the Senate on Mar. 27, 1962, and by the House of Representatives on Aug. 27, 1962. It was declared by the Administrator of General Services on Feb. 4, 1964, to have been ratified.

The Twenty-fourth Amendment was ratified by the following States: Illinois, Nov. 14, 1962; New Jersey, Dec. 3, 1962; Oregon, Jan. 25, 1963; Montana, Jan. 28, 1963; West Virginia, Feb. 1, 1963; New York, Feb. 4, 1963; Maryland, Feb. 6, 1963; California, Feb. 7, 1963; Alaska, Feb. 11, 1963; Rhode Island, Feb. 14, 1963; Indiana, Feb. 19, 1963; Utah, Feb. 20, 1963; Michigan, Feb. 20, 1963; Colorado, Feb. 21, 1963; Ohio, Feb. 27, 1963; Minnesota, Feb. 27, 1963; New Mexico, Mar. 5, 1963; Hawaii, Mar. 6, 1963; North Dakota, Mar. 7, 1963; Idaho, Mar. 8, 1963; Washington, Mar. 14, 1963; Vermont, Mar. 15, 1963; Nevada, Mar. 19, 1963; Connecticut, Mar. 20, 1963; Tennessee, Mar. 21, 1963; Pennsylvania, Mar. 25, 1963; Wisconsin, Mar. 26, 1963; Kansas, Mar. 28, 1963; Massachusetts, Mar. 28, 1963; Nebraska, Apr. 4, 1963; Florida, Apr. 18, 1963; Iowa, Apr. 24, 1963; Delaware, May 1, 1963; Missouri, May 13, 1963; New Hampshire, June 12, 1963; Kentucky, June 27, 1963; Maine, Jan. 16, 1964; South Dakota, Jan. 23, 1964; and Virginia, Feb. 25, 1977.

The amendment was rejected by Mississippi on Dec. 20, 1962.

Certification of Validity

Publication of the certifying statement of the Administrator of General Services that the Amendment had become valid was made on Feb. 5, 1964, F.R. Doc. 64–1229, 29 F.R. 1715, 78 Stat. 1117.

ARTICLE [XXV]

Section 1. In case of the removal of the President from office or of his death or resignation, the Vice President shall become President.

Sec. 2. Whenever there is a vacancy in the office of the Vice President, the President shall nominate a Vice President who shall take office upon confirmation by a majority vote of both Houses of Congress.

Sec. 3. Whenever the President transmits to the President pro tempore of the Senate and the Speaker of the House of Representatives his written declaration that he is unable to discharge the powers and duties of his office, and until he transmits to them a written declaration to the contrary, such powers and duties shall be discharged by the Vice President as Acting President.

Sec. 4. Whenever the Vice President and a majority of either the principal officers of the executive departments or of such other body as Congress may by law provide, transmit to the President pro tempore of the Senate and the Speaker of the House of Representatives their written declaration that the President is unable to discharge the powers and duties of his office, the Vice President shall immediately assume the powers and duties of the office as Acting President.

Thereafter, when the President transmits to the President pro tempore of the Senate and the Speaker of the House of Representatives his written declaration that no inability exists, he shall resume the powers and duties of his office unless the Vice President and a majority of either the principal officers of the executive department or of such other body as Congress may by law provide, transmit within four days to the President pro tempore of the Senate and the Speaker of the House of Representatives their written declaration that the President is unable to discharge the powers and duties of his office. Thereupon Congress shall decide the issue, assembling within forty-eight hours for that purpose if not in session. If the Congress, within twenty-one days after receipt of the latter written declaration, or, if Congress is not in session, within twenty-one days after Congress is required to assemble, determines by two-thirds vote of both Houses that the President is unable to discharge the powers and duties of his office, the Vice President shall continue to discharge the same as Acting President; otherwise, the President shall resume the powers and duties of his office.

HISTORICAL NOTES

Proposal and Ratification

The Twenty-fifth Amendment, set out in 79 Stat. 1327, was proposed by the Eighty-ninth Congress by Senate Joint Resolution No. 1, which was approved by the Senate on Feb. 19, 1965, and by the House of Representatives, in amended form, on Apr. 13, 1965. The House of Representatives agreed to a Conference Report on June 30, 1965, and the Senate agreed to the Conference Report on July 6, 1965. It was declared by the Administrator of General Services, on Feb. 23, 1967, to have been ratified.

The Twenty-fifth Amendment was ratified by the following States: Nebraska, July 12, 1965; Wisconsin, July 13, 1965; Oklahoma, July 16, 1965; Massachusetts, Aug. 9, 1965; Pennsylvania, Aug. 18, 1965; Kentucky, Sept. 15, 1965; Arizona, Sept. 22, 1965; Michigan, Oct. 5, 1965; Indiana, Oct. 20, 1965; California, Oct. 21, 1965; Arkansas, Nov. 4, 1965; New Jersey, Nov. 29, 1965; Delaware, Dec. 7, 1965; Utah, Jan. 17, 1966; West Virginia, Jan. 20, 1966; Maine, Jan. 24, 1966; Rhode Island, Jan. 28, 1966; Colorado, Feb. 3, 1966; New Mexico, Feb. 3, 1966; Kansas, Feb. 8, 1966; Vermont, Feb. 10, 1966; Alaska, Feb. 18, 1966; Idaho, Mar. 2, 1966; Hawaii, Mar. 3, 1966; Virginia, Mar. 8, 1966; Mississippi, Mar. 10, 1966; New York, Mar. 14, 1966; Maryland, Mar. 23, 1966; Missouri, Mar. 30, 1966; New Hampshire, June 13, 1966; Louisiana, July 5, 1966; Tennessee, Jan. 12, 1967; Wyoming, Jan. 25, 1967; Washington, Jan. 26, 1967; Iowa, Jan. 26, 1967; Oregon, Feb. 2, 1967; Minnesota, Feb. 10, 1967; Nevada, Feb. 10, 1967; Connecticut, Feb. 14, 1967; Montana, Feb. 15, 1967; South Dakota, Mar. 6, 1967; Ohio, Mar. 7, 1967; Alabama, Mar. 14, 1967; North Carolina, Mar. 22, 1967; Illinois, Mar. 22, 1967; Texas, Apr. 25, 1967; and Florida, May 25, 1967.

Certification of Validity

Publication of the certifying statement of the Administrator of General Services that the Amendment had become valid was made on Feb. 25, 1967, F.R.Doc. 67–2208, 32 F.R. 3287, 81 Stat. 983.

ARTICLE [XXVI]

Section 1. The right of citizens of the United States, who are eighteen years of age or older, to vote shall not be denied or abridged by the United States or by any State on account of age.

Sec. 2. The Congress shall have power to enforce this article by appropriate legislation.

HISTORICAL NOTES

Proposal and Ratification

The Twenty-sixth Amendment was proposed by the Ninety-second Congress by Senate Joint Resolution No. 7, which was approved by the Senate on Mar. 10, 1971, and by the House of Representatives on Mar. 23, 1971. It was declared by the Administrator of General Services on July 5, 1971, to have been ratified.

This amendment was ratified by the following States: Connecticut, March 23, 1971; Delaware, March 23, 1971; Minnesota, March 23, 1971; Tennessee, March 23, 1971; Washington, March 23, 1971; Hawaii, March 24, 1971; Massachusetts, March 24, 1971; Montana, March 29, 1971; Arkansas, March 30, 1971; Idaho, March 30, 1971; Iowa, March 30, 1971; Nebraska, April 2, 1971; New Jersey, April 3, 1971; Kansas, April 7, 1971; Michigan, April 7, 1971; Alaska, April 8, 1971; Maryland, April 8, 1971; Indiana, April 8, 1971; Maine, April 9, 1971; Vermont, April 16, 1971; Louisiana, April 17, 1971; California, April 19, 1971; Colorado, April 27, 1971; Pennsylvania, April 27, 1971; Texas, April 27, 1971; South Carolina, April 28, 1971; West Virginia, April 28, 1971; New Hampshire, May 13, 1971; Arizona, May 14, 1971; Rhode Island, May 27, 1971; New York, June 2, 1971; Oregon, June 4, 1971; Missouri, June 14, 1971; Wisconsin, June 22, 1971; Illinois, June 29, 1971; Alabama, June 30, 1971; Ohio, June 30, 1971; North Carolina, July 1, 1971; Oklahoma, July 1, 1971.

The amendment was subsequently ratified by Virginia, July 8, 1971; Wyoming, July 8, 1971; Georgia, October 4, 1971.

Certification of Validity

Publication of the certifying statement of the Administrator of General Services that the Amendment had become valid was made on July 7, 1971, F.R.Doc. 71–9691, 36 F.R. 12725.

ARTICLE [XXVII][1]

[1] "Article [XXVII]" editorially added. Originally read "Article the second".

No law, varying the compensation for the services of the Senators and Representatives, shall take effect, until an election of Representatives shall have intervened.

HISTORICAL NOTES

Proposal and Ratification

The Twenty-seventh Amendment was proposed on September 25, 1789. The State legislatures ratified this Amendment on the following dates: Maryland, North Carolina, South Carolina, Delaware, Vermont, Virginia, 1789–1791; Ohio, May 6, 1873; Wyoming, March 6, 1978; Maine, April 27, 1983; Colorado, April 22, 1984; South Dakota, February 1985; New Hampshire, March 7, 1985; Arizona, April 3, 1985; Tennessee, May 28, 1985; Oklahoma, July 10, 1985; New Mexico, February 14, 1986; Indiana, February 24, 1986; Utah, February 25, 1986; Arkansas, March 13, 1987; Montana, March 17, 1987; Connecticut, May 13, 1987; Wisconsin, July 15, 1987; Georgia, February 2, 1988; West Virginia, March 10, 1988; Louisiana, July 7, 1988; Iowa, February 9, 1989; Idaho, March 23, 1989; Nevada, April 26, 1989; Alaska, May 6, 1989; Oregon, May 19, 1989; Minnesota, May 22, 1989; Texas, May 25, 1989; Kansas, April 5, 1990; Florida, May 31, 1990; North Dakota, March 25, 1991; Alabama, May 5, 1992; Missouri, May 5, 1992; Michigan, May 7, 1992. The State of New Jersey later ratified this amendment on May 7, 1992.

Certification of Validity

Publication of the certifying statement of the Archivist of the United States, pursuant to 1 U.S.C.A. § 106b, that the amendment has become valid was made on May 19, 1992. F.R.Doc. 92–11951, 57 F.R.21187.

TITLE 5

GOVERNMENT ORGANIZATION AND EMPLOYEES

APPENDIX 4

ETHICS IN GOVERNMENT ACT OF 1978[1]

[1] Number and order of Appendixes editorially supplied.

TITLE I—FINANCIAL DISCLOSURE REQUIREMENTS OF FEDERAL PERSONNEL

Sec.

101. Persons required to file.
102. Contents of reports.
103. Filing of reports.
104. Failure to file or filing false reports.
105. Custody of and public access to reports.
106. Review of reports.
107. Confidential reports and other additional requirements.
108. Authority of Comptroller General.
109. Definitions.
110. Notice of actions taken to comply with ethics agreements.
111. Administration of provisions.

[112. Repealed.]

[TITLE II—REPEALED]

[201 to 212. Repealed.]

[TITLE III—REPEALED]

[301 to 309. Repealed.]

TITLE IV—OFFICE OF GOVERNMENT ETHICS

401. Office of Government Ethics.
402. Authority and functions.
403. Administrative provisions.
404. Rules and regulations.
405. Authorization of appropriations.
406. Annual pay.
407. Annual pay of Director.
408. Reports to Congress.

TITLE V—GOVERNMENT-WIDE LIMITATIONS ON OUTSIDE EARNED INCOME AND EMPLOYMENT

501. Outside earned income limitation.
502. Limitations on outside employment.
503. Administration.
504. Civil penalties.
505. Definitions.

TITLE I—FINANCIAL DISCLOSURE REQUIREMENTS OF FEDERAL PERSONNEL

HISTORICAL AND STATUTORY NOTES

Codifications

Title I of Pub.L. 95–521 was classified to chapter 18 (section 701 et seq.) of Title 2, The Congress, prior to general amendment of Title I by Pub.L. 101–194, Title II, § 202, Nov. 30, 1989, 103 Stat. 1724.

§ 101. Persons required to file

(a) Within thirty days of assuming the position of an officer or employee described in subsection (f), an individual shall file a report containing the information described in section 102(b) unless the individual has left another position described in subsection (f) within thirty days prior to assuming such new position or has already filed a report under this title with respect to nomination for the new position or as a candidate for the position.

(b)(1) Within five days of the transmittal by the President to the Senate of the nomination of an individual (other than an individual nominated for appointment to a position as a Foreign Service Officer or a grade or rank in the uniformed services for which the pay grade prescribed by section 201 of title 37, United States Code, is O–6 or below) to a position, appointment to which requires the advice and consent of the Senate, such individual shall file a report containing the information described in section 102(b). Such individual shall, not later than the date of the first hearing to consider the nomination of such individual, make current the report filed pursuant to this paragraph by filing the information required by section 102(a)(1)(A) with respect to income and honoraria received as of the date which occurs five days before the date of such hearing. Nothing in this Act shall prevent any Congressional committee from requesting, as a condition of confirmation, any additional financial information from any Presidential nominee whose nomination has been referred to that committee.

(2) An individual whom the President or the President-elect has publicly announced he intends to nominate to a position may file the report required by paragraph (1) at any time after that public announcement, but not later than is required under the first sentence of such paragraph.

(c) Within thirty days of becoming a candidate as defined in section 301 of the Federal Campaign Act of 1971, in a calendar year for nomination or election to the office of President, Vice President, or Member of Congress, or on or before May 15 of that calendar year, whichever is later, but in no event later than 30 days before the election, and on or before May 15 of each successive year an individual continues to be a candidate, an individual other than an incumbent President, Vice President, or Member of Congress shall file a report containing the information described in section 102(b). Notwithstanding the preceding sentence, in any calendar year in which an individual continues to be a candidate for any office but all elections for such office relating to such candidacy were held in prior calendar years, such individual need not file a report unless he becomes a candidate for another vacancy in that office or another office during that year.

(d) Any individual who is an officer or employee described in subsection (f) during any calendar year and performs the duties of his position or office for a period in excess of sixty days in that calendar year shall file on or before May 15 of the succeeding year a report containing the information described in section 102(a).

(e) Any individual who occupies a position described in subsection (f) shall, on or before the thirtieth day after termination of employment in such position, file a report containing the information described in section 102(a) covering the preceding calendar year if the report required by subsection (d) has not been filed and covering the portion of the calendar year in which such termination occurs up to the date the individual left such office or position, unless such individual has accepted employment in another position described in subsection (f).

(f) The officers and employees referred to in subsections (a), (d), and (e) are—

(1) the President;

(2) the Vice President;

(3) each officer or employee in the executive branch, including a special Government employee as defined in section 202 of title 18, United States Code, who occupies a position classified above GS–15 of the General Schedule or, in the case of positions not under the General Schedule, for which the rate of basic pay is equal to or greater than 120 percent of the minimum rate of basic pay payable for GS–15 of the General Schedule; each member of a uniformed service whose pay grade is at or in excess of O–7 under section 201 of title 37, United States Code; and each officer or employee in any other position determined by the Director of the Office of Government Ethics to be of equal classification;

(4) each employee appointed pursuant to section 3105 of title 5, United States Code;

(5) any employee not described in paragraph (3) who is in a position in the executive branch which is excepted from the competitive service by reason of being of a confidential or policymaking character, except that the Director of the Office of Government Ethics may, by regulation, exclude from the application of this paragraph any individual, or group of individuals, who are in such positions, but only in cases in which the Director determines such exclusion would not affect adversely the integrity of the Government or the public's confidence in the integrity of the Government;

(6) the Postmaster General, the Deputy Postmaster General, each Governor of the Board of Governors of the United States Postal Service and each officer or employee of the United States Postal Service or Postal Rate Commission who occupies a position for which the rate of basic pay is equal to or greater than 120 percent of the minimum rate of basic pay payable for GS–15 of the General Schedule;

(7) the Director of the Office of Government Ethics and each designated agency ethics official;

(8) any civilian employee not described in paragraph (3), employed in the Executive Office of the President (other than a special government employee) who holds a commission of appointment from the President;

(9) a Member of Congress as defined under section 109(12);

(10) an officer or employee of the Congress as defined under section 109(13);

(11) a judicial officer as defined under section 109(10); and

(12) a judicial employee as defined under section 109(8).

(g)(1) Reasonable extensions of time for filing any report may be granted under procedures prescribed by the supervising ethics office for each branch, but the total of such extensions shall not exceed ninety days.

(2)(A) In the case of an individual who is serving in the Armed Forces, or serving in support of the Armed Forces, in an area while that area is designated by the President by Executive order as a combat zone for purposes of section 112 of the Internal Revenue Code of 1986, the date for the filing of any report shall be extended so that the date is 180 days after the later of—

(i) the last day of the individual's service in such area during such designated period; or

(ii) the last day of the individual's hospitalization as a result of injury received or disease contracted while serving in such area.

(B) The Office of Government Ethics, in consultation with the Secretary of Defense, may prescribe procedures under this paragraph.

(h) The provisions of subsections (a), (b), and (e) shall not apply to an individual who, as determined by the designated agency ethics official or Secretary concerned (or in the case of a Presidential appointee under subsection (b), the Director of the Office of Government Ethics), the congressional ethics committees, or the Judicial Conference, is not reasonably expected to perform the duties of his office or position for more than sixty days in a calendar year, except that if such individual performs the duties of his office or position for more than sixty days in a calendar year—

(1) the report required by subsections (a) and (b) shall be filed within fifteen days of the sixtieth day, and

(2) the report required by subsection (e) shall be filed as provided in such subsection.

(i) The supervising ethics office for each branch may grant a publicly available request for a waiver of any reporting requirement under this section for an individual who is expected to perform or has performed the duties of his office or position less than one hundred and thirty days in a calendar year, but only if the supervising ethics office determines that—

(1) such individual is not a full-time employee of the Government,

(2) such individual is able to provide services specially needed by the Government,

(3) it is unlikely that the individual's outside employment or financial interests will create a conflict of interest, and

(4) public financial disclosure by such individual is not necessary in the circumstances.

(Pub.L. 95–521, Title I, § 101, Oct. 26, 1978, 92 Stat. 1824; Pub.L. 96–19, §§ 2(a)(1), (b), (c)(1), 4(b)(1), (d) to (f), 5, June 13, 1979, 93 Stat. 37, 38, 40; Pub.L. 101–194, Title II, § 202, Nov. 30, 1989, 103 Stat. 1725; Pub.L. 101–280, § 3(1), (2), May 4, 1990, 104 Stat. 152; Pub.L. 102–25, Title VI, § 605(a), Apr. 6, 1991, 105 Stat. 110; Pub.L. 102–378, § 4(a)(1), Oct. 2, 1992, 106 Stat. 1356.)

HISTORICAL AND STATUTORY NOTES

References in Text

This Act, referred to in subsec. (b)(1), is Pub.L. 95–521, Oct. 26, 1978, 92 Stat. 1824, as amended, known as the Ethics in Government Act of 1978. For complete classification of this Act to the Code, see Short Title note set out under this section and Tables.

Section 301 of the Federal Campaign Act of 1971, referred to in subsec. (c), probably means section 301 of Pub.L. 92–225, Feb. 7, 1972, 86 Stat. 3, as amended, known as the Federal Election Campaign Act of 1971, which is classified to section 431 of Title 2, The Congress.

The General Schedule, referred to in subsec. (f)(3), (6), is set out under section 5332 of Title 5, Government Organization and Employees.

Section 112 of the Internal Revenue Code, referred to in subsec. (g)(2), is classified to section 112 of Title 26, Internal Revenue Code.

Codifications

Section was formerly classified to section 701 of Title 2, The Congress.

Effective Dates

1992 Acts. Amendment by Pub.L. 102–378 effective Oct. 2, 1992, see section 9(a) of Pub.L. 102–378, set out as a note under section 6303 of this title.

1991 Acts. Section 605(b) of Pub.L. 102–25 provided that: "The amendments made by subsection (a) [amending this section] shall apply with respect to reports required to be filed after January 17, 1991."

1990 Acts. Section 11 of Pub.L. 101–280 provided that: "Except as otherwise provided in this joint resolution, this Act and the amendments made by this joint resolution [amending sections 101 to 106, 109 to 111, former section 202, and sections 501 to 503 of Pub.L. 95–521, set out in this Appendix, sections 3393, 7351, 7353, and 7701 of this title, sections 31–1, 31–2, and 441i of Title 2, The Congress, sections 1601 and 2397a of Title 10, Armed Forces, sections 202, 203, 205, 207, 207 note, 208, 208 note, and 216 of Title 18, Crimes and Criminal Procedure, section 3945 of Title 22, Foreign Relations and Intercourse, section 1043 of Title 26, Internal Revenue Code, and sections 1353, 1344 note, and 3730 of Title 31, Money and Finance, repealing section 112 of Pub.L. 95–521, set out in this Appendix, renumbering section 1352 of Title 31 as section 1353, and enacting provisions set out as notes under sections 101 and 105 of Pub.L. 95–521, set out in this Appendix, and under section 2397a of Title 10 and section 1043 of Title 26] take effect on the date of the enactment of this joint resolution [May 4, 1990]."

1989 Acts. Section 204 of Pub.L. 101–194, as added Pub.L. 101–280, § 3(10)(B), May 4, 1990, 104 Stat. 157, provided that: "The amendments made by this title [enacting sections 110 to 112 of Pub.L. 95–521, set out in this Appendix, amending sections 101 to 109 of Pub.L. 95–521, set out in this Appendix, but formerly classified to sections 701 to 709 of Title 2, The Congress] and the repeal made by section 201 [repealing sections 201 to 212 of Pub.L. 95–521, formerly set out under the heading Executive Personnel Financial Disclosure Requirements in this Appendix, and sections 301 to 309 of Pub.L. 95–521, formerly set out under the heading Judicial Personnel Financial Disclosure Requirements in the Appendix to Title 28, Judiciary and Judicial Procedure] shall take effect on January 1, 1991, except that the provisions of section 102(f)(4)(B) of the Ethics in Government Act of 1978, as amended by this title [section 102(f)(4)(B) of Pub.L.

95–521, set out in this Appendix], shall be effective as of January 1, 1990."

Section 3(10)(C), (D) of Pub.L. 101–280 provided that:

"**(C)** The provisions of titles I [formerly classified to section 701 et seq. of Title 2, The Congress], II [formerly set out under the heading Executive Personnel Financial Disclosure Requirements in this Appendix], and III [formerly set out under the heading Judicial Personnel Financial Disclosure Requirements in the Appendix to Title 28, Judiciary and Judicial Procedure] of the Ethics in Government Act of 1978 [Pub.L. 95–521] as in effect on the day before the date of the enactment of the Ethics Reform Act of 1989 [Nov. 30, 1989], shall be effective for the period beginning on November 30, 1989, and ending on January 1, 1991, as if the Ethics Reform Act of 1989 [Pub.L. 101–194] had not been enacted, except that the provisions of section 202(f)(4)(B) of the Ethics in Government Act of 1978 [section 202(f)(4)(B) of Pub.L. 95–521] shall be repealed as of January 1, 1990.

"**(D)** "Nothing in title II of the Ethics Reform Act of 1989 or the amendments made by such title [title II of Pub.L. 101–194, amending title I of Pub.L. 95–521, set out in this Appendix, but formerly classified to sections 701 to 709 of Title 2, The Congress, and repealing title II of Pub.L. 95–521, formerly set out in this Appendix, and title III of Pub.L. 95–521, formerly set out in the Appendix to Title 28, Judiciary and Judicial Procedure] shall be construed to prevent the prosecution of civil actions against individuals for violations of the Ethics in Government Act of 1978 [Pub.L. 95–521] before January 1, 1991."

Short Title

1996 Amendments. Pub.L. 104–179, § 1, Aug. 6, 1996, 110 Stat. 1566, provided that: "This Act [amending sections 401, 403, 405, and 408 of Pub.L. 95–521, set out in this Appendix, section 1822 of Title 12, Banks and Banking, and section 207 of Title 18, Crimes and Criminal Procedure, and repealing a provision set out as a note under section 7301 of this title] may be cited as the 'Office of Government Ethics Authorization Act of 1996'."

1992 Amendments. Pub.L. 102–506, § 1, Oct. 24, 1992, 106 Stat. 3280, provided that: "This Act [amending section 405 of Pub.L. 95–521, set out in this Appendix] may be cited as the 'Office of Government Ethics Amendment of 1992'."

1990 Amendments. Pub.L. 101–334, § 1, July 16, 1990, 104 Stat. 318, provided that: "This Act [amending section 405 of Pub.L. 95–521, set out in this Appendix] may be cited as the 'Ethics in Government Act Amendment of 1990'."

1989 Amendments. Section 1 of Pub.L. 101–194 provided that: "This Act [see table for classification] may be cited as the 'Ethics Reform Act of 1989'."

1978 Acts. Section 1 of Pub.L. 95–521 provided: "That this Act [enacting provisions set out in this Appendix, sections 118a, 288 to 288m of Title 2, The Congress, sections 49, 528, 529, 591 to 598, 1364 of Title 28, Judiciary and Judicial Procedure, amending section 5316 of this title, section 207 of Title 18, Crimes and Criminal Procedure, and sections 3210, 3216, and 3219 of Title 39, Postal Service, and enacting provisions set out as notes under section 288 of Title 2, section 207 of Title 18, and section 591 of Title 28] may be cited as the 'Ethics in Government Act of 1978'."

Declaration of Purpose of 1990 Amendments

Section 1 of Pub.L. 101–280 provided that: "It is the purpose of this joint resolution to make technical corrections in the Ethics Reform Act of 1989 [Pub.L. 101–194, see Short Title of 1989 Amendments note set out under this section and Tables for classification]."

Rulemaking Power of Congress

Pub.L. 102–90, Title III, § 314(f), Aug. 14, 1991, 105 Stat. 470, provided that: "The provisions of this section [amending sections 102 and 505 of Pub.L. 95–521, set out in this Appendix, section 31–2 of Title 2, The Congress, and section 7701 of Title 26, Internal Revenue Code, and enacting provisions set out as a note under section 31–2 of Title 2] that are applicable to Members, officers, or employees of the legislative branch are enacted by the Congress—

"(1) as an exercise of the rulemaking power of the House of Representatives and the Senate, respectively, and as such they shall be considered as part of the rules of each House, respectively, or of that House to which they specifically apply, and such rules shall supersede other rules only to the extent that they are inconsistent therewith; and

"(2) with full recognition of the constitutional right of either House to change such rules (so far as relating to such House) at any time, in the same manner, and to the same extent as in the case of any other rule of such House."

Section 1001 of Pub.L. 101–194 provided that: "The provisions of this Act [see Short Title of 1989 Amendments note set out under this section] that are applicable to Members, officers, or employees of the legislative branch are enacted by the Congress—

"(1) as an exercise of the rulemaking power of the House of Representatives and the Senate, respectively, and as such they shall be considered as part of the rules of each House, respectively, or of that House to which they specifically apply, and such rules shall supersede other rules only to the extent that they are inconsistent therewith; and

"(2) with full recognition of the constitutional right of either House to change such rules (so far as relating to such House) at any time, in the same manner, and to the same extent as in the case of any other rule of such House."

§ 102. Contents of reports

(a) Each report filed pursuant to section 101(d) and (e) shall include a full and complete statement with respect to the following:

(1)(A) The source, type, and amount or value of income (other than income referred to in subparagraph (B)) from any source (other than from current employment by the United States Government), and the source, date, and amount of honoraria from any source, received during the preceding calendar year, aggregating $200 or more in value and, effective January 1, 1991, the source, date, and amount of payments made to charitable organizations in lieu of honoraria, and the reporting individual shall simultaneously file with the applicable supervising ethics office, on a confidential basis, a corresponding list of recipients of all such payments, together with the dates and amounts of such payments.

(B) The source and type of income which consists of dividends, rents, interest, and capital gains, received during the preceding calendar year which exceeds $200 in amount or value, and an indication of which of the following categories the amount or value of such item of income is within:

(i) not more than $1,000,

(ii) greater than $1,000 but not more than $2,500,

(iii) greater than $2,500 but not more than $5,000,

(iv) greater than $5,000 but not more than $15,000,

(v) greater than $15,000 but not more than $50,000,

(vi) greater than $50,000 but not more than $100,000,

(vii) greater than $100,000 but not more than $1,000,000,

(viii) greater than $1,000,000 but not more than $5,000,000, or

(ix) greater than $5,000,000.

(2)(A) The identity of the source, a brief description, and the value of all gifts aggregating more than the minimal value as established by section 7342(a)(5) of title 5, United States Code, or $250, whichever is greater, received from any source other than a relative of the reporting individual during the preceding calendar year, except that any food, lodging, or entertainment received as personal hospitality of an individual need not be reported, and any gift with a fair market value of $100 or less, as adjusted at the same time and by the same percentage as the minimal value is adjusted, need not be aggregated for purposes of this subparagraph.

(B) The identity of the source and a brief description (including a travel itinerary, dates, and nature of expenses provided) of reimbursements received from any source aggregating more than the minimal value as established by section 7342(a)(5) of title 5, United States Code, or $250, whichever is greater and received during the preceding calendar year.

(C) In an unusual case, a gift need not be aggregated under subparagraph (A) if a publicly available request for a waiver is granted.

(3) The identity and category of value of any interest in property held during the preceding calendar year in a trade or business, or for investment or the production of income, which has a fair market value which exceeds $1,000 as of the close of the preceding calendar year, excluding any personal liability owed to the reporting individual by a spouse,,[1] or by a parent, brother, sister, or child of the reporting individual or of the reporting individual's spouse, or any deposits aggregating $5,000 or less in a personal savings account. For purposes of this paragraph, a personal savings account shall include any certificate of deposit or any other form of deposit in a bank, savings and loan association, credit union, or similar financial institution.

(4) The identity and category of value of the total liabilities owed to any creditor other than a spouse, or a parent, brother, sister, or child of the reporting individual or of the reporting individual's spouse which exceed $10,000 at any time during the preceding calendar year, excluding—

(A) any mortgage secured by real property which is a personal residence of the reporting individual or his spouse; and

(B) any loan secured by a personal motor vehicle, household furniture, or appliances, which loan does not exceed the purchase price of the item which secures it.

With respect to revolving charge accounts, only those with an outstanding liability which exceeds $10,000 as of the close of the preceding calendar year need be reported under this paragraph.

(5) Except as provided in this paragraph, a brief description, the date, and category of value of any purchase, sale or exchange during the preceding calendar year which exceeds $1,000—

(A) in real property, other than property used solely as a personal residence of the reporting individual or his spouse; or

(B) in stocks, bonds, commodities futures, and other forms of securities.

Reporting is not required under this paragraph of any transaction solely by and between the reporting individual, his spouse, or dependent children.

(6)(A) The identity of all positions held on or before the date of filing during the current calendar year (and, for the first report filed by an individual, during the two-year period preceding such calendar year) as an officer, director, trustee, partner, proprietor, representative, employee, or consultant of any corporation, company, firm, partnership, or other business enterprise, any nonprofit organization, any labor organization, or any educational or other institution other than the United States. This subparagraph shall not require the reporting of positions held in any religious, social, fraternal, or political entity and positions solely of an honorary nature.

(B) If any person, other than the United States Government, paid a nonelected reporting individual compensation in excess of $5,000 in any of the two calendar years prior to the calendar year during which the individual files his first report under this title, the individual shall include in the report—

(i) the identity of each source of such compensation; and

(ii) a brief description of the nature of the duties performed or services rendered by the reporting individual for each such source.

The preceding sentence shall not require any individual to include in such report any information which is considered confidential as a result of a privileged relationship, established by law, between such individual and any person nor shall it require an individual to report any information with respect to any person for whom services were provided by any firm or association of which such individual was a member, partner, or employee unless such individual was directly involved in the provision of such services.

(7) A description of the date, parties to, and terms of any agreement or arrangement with respect to (A) future employment; (B) a leave of absence during the period of the reporting individual's Government service; (C) continuation of payments by a former employer other than the United States Government; and (D) continuing participation in an employee welfare or benefit plan maintained by a former employer.

(8) The category of the total cash value of any interest of the reporting individual in a qualified blind trust, unless the trust instrument was executed prior to July 24, 1995 and precludes the beneficiary from receiving information on the total cash value of any interest in the qualified blind trust.

(b)(1) Each report filed pursuant to subsections (a), (b), and (c) of section 101 shall include a full and complete statement with respect to the information required by—

(A) paragraph (1) of subsection (a) for the year of filing and the preceding calendar year,

(B) paragraphs (3) and (4) of subsection (a) as of the date specified in the report but which is less than thirty-one days before the filing date, and

(C) paragraphs (6) and (7) of subsection (a) as of the filing date but for periods described in such paragraphs.

(2)(A) In lieu of filling out one or more schedules of a financial disclosure form, an individual may supply the required information in an alternative format, pursuant to either rules adopted by the supervising ethics office for the branch in which such individual serves or pursuant to a specific written determination by such office for a reporting individual.

(B) In lieu of indicating the category of amount or value of any item contained in any report filed under this title, a reporting individual may indicate the exact dollar amount of such item.

(c) In the case of any individual described in section 101(e), any reference to the preceding calendar year shall be considered also to include that part of the calendar year of filing up to the date of the termination of employment.

(d)(1) The categories for reporting the amount or value of the items covered in paragraphs (3), (4), (5), and (8) of subsection (a) are as follows:

(A) not more than $15,000;

(B) greater than $15,000 but not more than $50,000;

(C) greater than $50,000 but not more than $100,000;

(D) greater than $100,000 but not more than $250,000;

(E) greater than $250,000 but not more than $500,000;

(F) greater than $500,000 but not more than $1,000,000;

(G) greater than $1,000,000 but not more than $5,000,000;

(H) greater than $5,000,000 but not more than $25,000,000;

(I) greater than $25,000,000 but not more than $50,000,000; and

(J) greater than $50,000,000.

(2) For the purposes of paragraph (3) of subsection (a) if the current value of an interest in real property (or an interest in a real estate partnership) is not ascertainable without an appraisal, an individual may list (A) the date of purchase and the purchase price of the interest in the real property, or (B) the assessed value of the real property for tax purposes, adjusted to reflect the market value of the property used for the assessment if the assessed value is computed at less than 100 percent of such market value, but such individual shall include in his report a full and complete description of the method used to determine such assessed value, instead of specifying a category of value pursuant to paragraph (1) of this subsection. If the current value of any other item required to be reported under paragraph (3) of subsection (a) is not ascertainable without an appraisal, such individual may list the book value of a corporation whose stock is not publicly traded, the net worth of a business partnership, the equity value of an individually owned business, or with respect to other holdings, any recognized indication of value, but such individual shall include in his report a full and complete description of the method used in determining such value. In lieu of any value referred to in the preceding sentence, an individual may list the assessed value of the item for tax purposes, adjusted to reflect the market value of the item used for the assessment if the assessed value is computed at less than 100 percent of such market value, but a full and complete description of the method used in determining such assessed value shall be included in the report.

(e)(1) Except as provided in the last sentence of this paragraph, each report required by section 101 shall also contain information listed in paragraphs (1) through (5) of subsection (a) of this section respecting the spouse or dependent child of the reporting individual as follows:

(A) The source of items of earned income earned by a spouse from any person which exceed $1,000 and the source and amount of any honoraria received by a spouse, except that, with respect to earned income (other than honoraria), if the spouse is self-employed in business or a profession, only the nature of such business or profession need be reported.

(B) All information required to be reported in subsection (a)(1)(B) with respect to income derived by a spouse or dependent child from any asset held by the spouse or dependent child and reported pursuant to subsection (a)(3).

(C) In the case of any gifts received by a spouse or dependent child which are not received totally independent of the relationship of the spouse or dependent child to the reporting individual, the identity of the source and a brief description of gifts of transportation, lodging, food, or entertainment and a brief description and the value of other gifts.

(D) In the case of any reimbursements received by a spouse or dependent child which are not received totally independent of the relationship of the spouse or dependent child to the reporting individual, the identity of the source and a brief description of each such reimbursement.

(E) In the case of items described in paragraphs (3) through (5) of subsection (a), all information required to be reported under these paragraphs other than items (i) which the reporting individual certifies represent the spouse's or dependent child's sole financial interest or responsibility and which the reporting individual has no knowledge of, (ii) which are not in any way, past or present, derived from the income, assets, or activities of the reporting individual, and (iii) from which the reporting individual neither derives, nor expects to derive, any financial or economic benefit.

(F) For purposes of this section, categories with amounts or values greater than $1,000,000 set forth in sections 102(a)(1)(B) and 102(d)(1) shall apply to the income, assets, or liabilities of spouses and dependent children only if the income, assets, or liabilities are held jointly with the reporting individual. All other income, assets, or liabilities of the spouse or dependent children required to be reported under this section in an amount or value greater than $1,000,000 shall be categorized only as an amount or value greater than $1,000,000.

Reports required by subsections (a), (b), and (c) of section 101 shall, with respect to the spouse and dependent child of the reporting individual, only contain information listed in paragraphs (1), (3), and (4) of subsection (a), as specified in this paragraph.

(2) No report shall be required with respect to a spouse living separate and apart from the reporting individual with the intention of terminating the marriage or providing for permanent separation; or with respect to any income or obligations of an individual arising from the dissolution of his marriage or the permanent separation from his spouse.

(f)(1) Except as provided in paragraph (2), each reporting individual shall report the information required to be reported pursuant to subsections (a), (b), and (c) of this section with respect to the holdings of and the income from a trust or other financial arrangement from which income is received by, or with respect to which a beneficial interest in principal or income is held by, such individual, his spouse, or any dependent child.

(2) A reporting individual need not report the holdings of or the source of income from any of the holdings of—

(A) any qualified blind trust (as defined in paragraph (3));

(B) a trust—

(i) which was not created directly by such individual, his spouse, or any dependent child, and

(ii) the holdings or sources of income of which such individual, his spouse, and any dependent child have no knowledge of; or

(C) an entity described under the provisions of paragraph (8),

but such individual shall report the category of the amount of income received by him, his spouse, or any dependent child from the trust or other entity under subsection (a)(1)(B) of this section.

(3) For purposes of this subsection, the term "qualified blind trust" includes any trust in which a reporting individual, his spouse, or any minor or dependent child has a beneficial interest in the principal or income, and which meets the following requirements:

(A)(i) The trustee of the trust and any other entity designated in the trust instrument to perform fiduciary duties is a financial institution, an attorney, a certified public accountant, a broker, or an investment advisor who—

(I) is independent of and not associated with any interested party so that the trustee or other person cannot be controlled or influenced in the administration of the trust by any interested party; and

(II) is not and has not been an employee of or affiliated with any interested party and is not a partner of, or involved in any joint venture or other investment with, any interested party; and

(III) is not a relative of any interested party.

(ii) Any officer or employee of a trustee or other entity who is involved in the management or control of the trust—

(I) is independent of and not associated with any interested party so that such officer or employee cannot be controlled or influenced in the administration of the trust by any interested party;

(II) is not a partner of, or involved in any joint venture or other investment with, any interested party; and

(III) is not a relative of any interested party.

(B) Any asset transferred to the trust by an interested party is free of any restriction with respect to its transfer or sale unless such restriction is expressly approved by the supervising ethics office of the reporting individual.

(C) The trust instrument which establishes the trust provides that—

(i) except to the extent provided in subparagraph (B) of this paragraph, the trustee in the exercise of his authority and discretion to manage and control the assets of the trust shall not consult or notify any interested party;

(ii) the trust shall not contain any asset the holding of which by an interested party is prohibited by any law or regulation;

(iii) the trustee shall promptly notify the reporting individual and his supervising ethics office when the holdings of any particular asset transferred to the trust by any interested party are disposed of or when the value of such holding is less than $1,000;

(iv) the trust tax return shall be prepared by the trustee or his designee, and such return and any information relating thereto (other than the trust income summarized in appropriate categories necessary to complete an interested party's tax return), shall not be disclosed to any interested party;

(v) an interested party shall not receive any report on the holdings and sources of income of the trust, except a report at the end of each calendar quarter with respect to the total cash value of the interest of the interested party in the trust or the net income or loss of the trust or any reports necessary to enable the interested party to complete an individual tax return required by law or to provide the information required by subsection (a)(1) of this section, but such report shall not identify any asset or holding;

(vi) except for communications which solely consist of requests for distributions of cash or other unspecified assets of the trust, there shall be no direct or indirect communication between the trustee and an interested party with respect to the trust unless such communication is in writing and unless it relates only (I) to the general financial interest and needs of the interested party (including, but not limited to, an interest in maximizing income or long-term capital gain), (II) to the notification of the trustee of a law or regulation subsequently applicable to the reporting individual which prohibits the interested party from holding an asset, which notification directs that the asset not be held by the trust, or (III) to directions to the trustee to sell all of an asset initially placed in the trust by an interested party which in the determination of the reporting individual creates a conflict of interest or the appearance thereof due to the subsequent assumption of duties by the reporting individual (but nothing herein shall require any such direction); and

(vii) the interested parties shall make no effort to obtain information with respect to the holdings of the trust, including obtaining a copy of any trust tax return filed or any information relating thereto except as otherwise provided in this subsection.

(D) The proposed trust instrument and the proposed trustee is approved by the reporting individual's supervising ethics office.

(E) For purposes of this subsection, "interested party" means a reporting individual, his spouse, and any minor or dependent child; "broker" has the meaning set forth in section 3(a)(4) of the Securities and Exchange Act of 1934 (15 U.S.C. 78c(a)(4)); and "investment adviser" includes any investment adviser who, as determined under regulations prescribed by the supervising ethics office, is generally involved in his role as such an adviser in the management or control of trusts.

(F) Any trust qualified by a supervising ethics office before the effective date of title II of the Ethics Reform Act of 1989 shall continue to be governed by the law and regulations in effect immediately before such effective date.

(4)(A) An asset placed in a trust by an interested party shall be considered a financial interest of the reporting individual, for the purposes of any applicable conflict of interest statutes, regulations, or rules of the Federal Government (including section 208 of title 18, United States Code), until such time as the reporting individual is notified by the trustee that such asset has been disposed of, or has a value of less than $1,000.

(B)(i) The provisions of subparagraph (A) shall not apply with respect to a trust created for the benefit of a reporting individual, or the spouse, dependent child, or minor child of such a person, if the supervising ethics office for such reporting individual finds that—

(I) the assets placed in the trust consist of a well-diversified portfolio of readily marketable securities;

(II) none of the assets consist of securities of entities having substantial activities in the area of the reporting individual's primary area of responsibility;

(III) the trust instrument prohibits the trustee, notwithstanding the provisions of paragraphs (3)(C)(iii) and (iv) of this subsection, from making public or informing any interested party of the sale of any securities;

(IV) the trustee is given power of attorney, notwithstanding the provisions of paragraph (3)(C)(v) of this subsection, to prepare on behalf of any interested party the personal income tax returns and similar returns which may contain information relating to the trust; and

(V) except as otherwise provided in this paragraph, the trust instrument provides (or in the case of a trust established prior to the effective date of this Act which by its terms does not permit amendment, the trustee, the reporting individual, and any other interested party agree in writing) that the trust shall be administered in accordance with the requirements of this subsection and the trustee of such trust meets the requirements of paragraph (3)(A).

(ii) In any instance covered by subparagraph (B) in which the reporting individual is an individual whose nomination is being considered by a congressional committee, the reporting individual shall inform the congressional committee considering his nomination before or during the period of such individual's confirmation hearing of his intention to comply with this paragraph.

(5)(A) The reporting individual shall, within thirty days after a qualified blind trust is approved by his supervising ethics office, file with such office a copy of—

(i) the executed trust instrument of such trust (other than those provisions which relate to the testamentary disposition of the trust assets), and

(ii) a list of the assets which were transferred to such trust, including the category of value of each asset as determined under subsection (d) of this section.

This subparagraph shall not apply with respect to a trust meeting the requirements for being considered a qualified blind trust under paragraph (7) of this subsection.

(B) The reporting individual shall, within thirty days of transferring an asset (other than cash) to a previously established qualified blind trust, notify his supervising ethics office of the identity of each such asset and the category of value of each asset as determined under subsection (d) of this section.

(C) Within thirty days of the dissolution of a qualified blind trust, a reporting individual shall—

(i) notify his supervising ethics office of such dissolution, and

(ii) file with such office a copy of a list of the assets of the trust at the time of such dissolution and the category of value under subsection (d) of this section of each such asset.

(D) Documents filed under subparagraphs (A), (B), and (C) of this paragraph and the lists provided by the trustee of assets placed in the trust by an interested party which have been sold shall be made available to the public in the same manner as a report is made available under section 105 and the provisions of that section shall apply with respect to such documents and lists.

(E) A copy of each written communication with respect to the trust under paragraph (3)(C)(vi) shall be filed by the person initiating the communication with the reporting individual's supervising ethics office within five days of the date of the communication.

(6)(A) A trustee of a qualified blind trust shall not knowingly and willfully, or negligently, (i) disclose any information to an interested party with respect to such trust that may not be disclosed under paragraph (3) of this subsection; (ii) acquire any holding the ownership of which is prohibited by the trust instrument; (iii) solicit advice from any interested party with respect to such trust, which solicitation is prohibited by paragraph (3) of this subsection or the trust agreement; or (iv) fail to file any document required by this subsection.

(B) A reporting individual shall not knowingly and willfully, or negligently, (i) solicit or receive any information with respect to a qualified blind trust of which he is an interested party that may not be disclosed under paragraph (3)(C) of this subsection or (ii) fail to file any document required by this subsection.

(C)(i) The Attorney General may bring a civil action in any appropriate United States district court against any individual who knowingly and willfully violates the provisions of subparagraph (A) or (B) of this paragraph. The court in which such action is brought may assess against such individual a civil penalty in any amount not to exceed $10,000.

(ii) The Attorney General may bring a civil action in any appropriate United States district court against any individual who negligently violates the provisions of subparagraph (A) or (B) of this paragraph. The court in which such action is brought may assess against such individual a civil penalty in any amount not to exceed $5,000.

(7) Any trust may be considered to be a qualified blind trust if—

(A) the trust instrument is amended to comply with the requirements of paragraph (3) or, in the case of a trust instrument which does not by its terms permit amendment, the trustee, the reporting individual, and any other interested party agree in writing that the trust shall be administered in accordance with the requirements of this subsection and the trustee of such trust meets the requirements of paragraph (3)(A); except that in the case of any interested party who is a dependent child, a parent or guardian of such child may execute the agreement referred to in this subparagraph;

(B) a copy of the trust instrument (except testamentary provisions) and a copy of the agreement referred to in subparagraph (A), and a list of the assets held by the trust at the time of approval by the supervising ethics office, including the category of value of each asset as determined under subsection (d) of this section, are filed with such office and made available to the public as provided under paragraph (5)(D) of this subsection; and

(C) the supervising ethics office determines that approval of the trust arrangement as a qualified blind trust is in the particular case appropriate to assure compliance with applicable laws and regulations.

(8) A reporting individual shall not be required to report the financial interests held by a widely held investment fund (whether such fund is a mutual fund, regulated investment company, pension or deferred compensation plan, or other investment fund), if—

(A)(i) the fund is publicly traded; or

(ii) the assets of the fund are widely diversified; and

(B) the reporting individual neither exercises control over nor has the ability to exercise control over the financial interests held by the fund.

(g) Political campaign funds, including campaign receipts and expenditures, need not be included in any report filed pursuant to this title.

(h) A report filed pursuant to subsection (a), (d), or (e) of section 101 need not contain the information described in subparagraphs (A), (B), and (C) of subsection (a)(2) with respect to gifts and reimbursements received in a period when the reporting individual was not an officer or employee of the Federal Government.

(i) A reporting individual shall not be required under this title to report—

(1) financial interests in or income derived from—

(A) any retirement system under title 5, United States Code (including the Thrift Savings Plan under subchapter III of chapter 84 of such title); or

(B) any other retirement system maintained by the United States for officers or employees of the United States, including the President, or for members of the uniformed services; or

(2) benefits received under the Social Security Act [42 U.S.C.A. § 301 et seq.].

(Pub.L. 95–521, Title I, § 102, Oct. 26, 1978, 92 Stat. 1825; Pub.L. 96–19, §§ 3(a)(1), (b), 6(a), 7(a) to (d)(1), (f), 9(b), (c)(1), (j), June 13, 1979, 93 Stat. 39 to 43; Pub.L. 97–51, § 130(b), Oct. 1, 1981, 95 Stat. 966; Pub.L. 98–150, § 10, Nov. 11, 1983, 97 Stat. 962; Pub.L. 101–194, Title II, § 202, Nov. 30, 1989, 103 Stat. 1727; Pub.L. 101–280, § 3(3), May 4, 1990, 104 Stat. 152; Pub.L. 102–90, Title III, § 314(a), Aug. 14, 1991, 105 Stat. 469; Pub.L. 104–65, §§ 20, 22(a), (b), Dec. 19, 1995, 109 Stat. 704, 705.)

[1] So in original.

HISTORICAL AND STATUTORY NOTES

References in Text

The effective date of title II of the Ethics Reform Act of 1989, referred to in subsec. (f)(3)(F) is Jan. 1, 1991. See section 204 of Pub.L. 101–194, set out as an Effective Date of 1989 Acts note under section 101 of this Appendix.

The effective date of this Act, referred to in subsec. (f)(4)(B)(i)(V), probably refers to the effective date of title II of the Ethics Reform Act of 1989, which is Jan. 1, 1991. See section 204 of Pub.L. 101–194, set out as an Effective Date of 1989 Acts note under section 101 of this Appendix.

The Social Security Act, referred to in subsec. (i)(2), is Act Aug. 14, 1935, c. 531, 49 Stat. 620, as amended, which is classified generally to chapter 7 (section 301 et seq.) of Title 42, The Public Health and Welfare. For complete classification of this Act to the Code, see section 1305 of Title 42 and Tables.

Codifications

Section was formerly classified to section 702 of Title 2, The Congress.

Effective Dates

1995 Acts. Amendment by section 20 of Pub.L. 104–65 effective Jan. 1, 1996, see section 24 of Pub.L. 104–65, set out as a note under section 1601 of Title 2, The Congress.

Section 22(c) of Pub.L. 104–65 provided that: "The amendment made by this section [enacting par. (8) of subsec. (a) of this section and amending subsec. (d)(1) of this section] shall apply with respect to reports filed under title I of the Ethics in Government Act of 1978 [Title I of this Appendix] for calendar year 1996 and thereafter."

1991 Acts. Amendment by Pub.L. 102–90 effective Jan. 1, 1993, see section 314(g)(2) of Pub.L. 102–90, as amended, set out as a note under section 31–2 of Title 2, The Congress.

1990 Acts. Amendment of the text of this section by Pub.L. 101–280 effective May 4, 1990, see section 11 of Pub.L. 101–280, set out as a note under section 101 of this

Appendix. The text as thus amended to be effective Jan. 1, 1991, see section 204 of Pub.L. 101–194 set out as a note under section 101 of this Appendix.

1989 Acts. Amendment by Pub.L. 101–194 effective Jan. 1, 1991, except that subsec. (f)(4)(B) of this section as amended by Pub.L. 101–194 is effective Jan. 1, 1990, see section 204 of Pub.L. 101–194, as added Pub.L. 101–280, § 3(10)(B), May 4, 1990, 104 Stat. 157, set out as a note under section 101 of this Appendix.

1983 Acts. Section 13 of Pub.L. 98–150 provided that: "The amendments made by this Act [enacting sections 211 and 407 of Pub.L. 95–521, set out in this Appendix, amending sections 102, 201 to 203, 210, 302, and 401 to 405 of Pub.L. 95–521, set out in this Appendix, and enacting provisions set out as a note under section 402 of this Appendix] shall take effect on October 1, 1983."

§ 103. Filing of reports

(a) Except as otherwise provided in this section, the reports required under this title shall be filed by the reporting individual with the designated agency ethics official at the agency by which he is employed (or in the case of an individual described in section 101(e), was employed) or in which he will serve. The date any report is received (and the date of receipt of any supplemental report) shall be noted on such report by such official.

(b) The President, the Vice President, and independent counsel and persons appointed by independent counsel under chapter 40 of title 28, United States Code, shall file reports required under this title with the Director of the Office of Government Ethics.

(c) Copies of the reports required to be filed under this title by the Postmaster General, the Deputy Postmaster General, the Governors of the Board of Governors of the United States Postal Service, designated agency ethics officials, employees described in section 105(a)(2)(A) or (B), 106(a)(1)(A) or (B), or 107(a)(1)(A) or (b)(1)(A)(i), of title 3, United States Code, candidates for the office of President or Vice President and officers and employees in (and nominees to) offices or positions which require confirmation by the Senate or by both Houses of Congress other than individuals nominated to be judicial officers and those referred to in subsection (f) shall be transmitted to the Director of the Office of Government Ethics. The Director shall forward a copy of the report of each nominee to the congressional committee considering the nomination.

(d) Reports required to be filed under this title by the Director of the Office of Government Ethics shall be filed in the Office of Government Ethics and, immediately after being filed, shall be made available to the public in accordance with this title.

(e) Each individual identified in section 101(c) who is a candidate for nomination or election to the Office of President or Vice President shall file the reports required by this title with the Federal Election Commission.

(f) Reports required of members of the uniformed services shall be filed with the Secretary concerned.

(g) Each supervising ethics office shall develop and make available forms for reporting the information required by this title.

(h)(1) The reports required under this title shall be filed by a reporting individual with—

(A)(i)(I) the Clerk of the House of Representatives, in the case of a Representative in Congress, a Delegate to Congress, the Resident Commissioner from Puerto Rico, an officer or employee of the Congress whose compensation is disbursed by the Chief Administrative Officer of the House of Representatives, an officer or employee of the Architect of the Capitol, the United States Botanic Garden, the Congressional Budget Office, the Government Printing Office, the Library of Congress, or the Copyright Royalty Tribunal (including any individual terminating service, under section 101(e), in any office or position referred to in this subclause), or an individual described in section 101(c) who is a candidate for nomination or election as a Representative in Congress, a Delegate to Congress, or the Resident Commissioner from Puerto Rico; and

(II) the Secretary of the Senate, in the case of a Senator, an officer or employee of the Congress whose compensation is disbursed by the Secretary of the Senate, an officer or employee of the General Accounting Office, the Office of Technology Assessment, or the Office of the Attending Physician (including any individual terminating service, under section 101(e), in any office or position referred to in this subclause), or an individual described in section 101(c) who is a candidate for nomination or election as a Senator; and

(ii) in the case of an officer or employee of the Congress as described under section 101(f)(10) who is employed by an agency or commission established in the legislative branch after the date of the enactment of the Ethics Reform Act of 1989—

(I) the Secretary of the Senate or the Clerk of the House of Representatives, as the case may be, as designated in the statute establishing such agency or commission; or

(II) if such statute does not designate such committee, the Secretary of the Senate for agencies and commissions established in even numbered calendar years, and the Clerk of the House of Representatives for agencies and commissions established in odd numbered calendar years; and

(B) the Judicial Conference with regard to a judicial officer or employee described under paragraphs (11) and (12) of section 101(f) (including individuals terminating service in such office or position under section 101(e) or immediately preceding service in such office or position).

(2) The date any report is received (and the date of receipt of any supplemental report) shall be noted on such report by such committee.

(i) A copy of each report filed under this title by a Member or an individual who is a candidate for the office of Member shall be sent by the Clerk of the House of Representatives or Secretary of the Senate, as the case may be, to the appropriate State officer designated under section 316(a) of the Federal Election Campaign Act of 1971 of the State represented by the Member or in which the individual is a candidate, as the case may be, within the 30–day period beginning on the day the report is filed with the Clerk or Secretary.

(j)(1) A copy of each report filed under this title with the Clerk of the House of Representatives shall be sent by the Clerk to the Committee on Standards of Official Conduct of the House of Representatives within the 7–day period beginning on the day the report is filed.

(2) A copy of each report filed under this title with the Secretary of the Senate shall be sent by the Secretary to the Select Committee on Ethics of the Senate within the 7–day period beginning on the day the report is filed.

(k) In carrying out their responsibilities under this title with respect to candidates for office, the Clerk of the House of Representatives and the Secretary of the Senate shall avail themselves of the assistance of the Federal Election Commission. The Commission shall make available to the Clerk and the Secretary on a regular basis a complete list of names and addresses of all candidates registered with the Commission, and shall cooperate and coordinate its candidate information and notification program with the Clerk and the Secretary to the greatest extent possible.

(Pub.L. 95–521, Title I, § 103, Oct. 26, 1978, 92 Stat. 1831; Pub.L. 96–19, §§ 4(b)(2), 9(a), June 13, 1979, 93 Stat. 40, 42; Pub.L. 101–194, Title II, § 202, Nov. 30, 1989, 103 Stat. 1736; Pub.L. 101–280, § 3(1), (4), May 4, 1990, 104 Stat. 152, 153; Pub.L. 102–90, Title III, § 313(1), Aug. 14, 1991, 105 Stat. 469; Pub.L. 104–186, Title II, § 216(1), Aug. 20, 1996, 110 Stat. 1747.)

HISTORICAL AND STATUTORY NOTES

References in Text

The date of the enactment of the Ethics Reform Act of 1989, referred to in subsec. (h)(1)(A)(ii), is the date of the enactment of Pub.L. 101–194, Nov. 30, 1989, 103 Stat. 1716, which was approved Nov. 30, 1989.

Section 316(a) of the Federal Election Campaign Act of 1971, referred to in subsec. (i), was probably intended to be a reference to section 312(a) of the Federal Election Campaign Act of 1971, Pub.L. 92–225, which is classified to section 439(a) of Title 2, The Congress, which directs the chief executive officer of each State to designate a State officer to receive reports and statements filed by persons under the Federal Election Campaign Act of 1971.

Codifications

Section was formerly classified to section 703 of Title 2, The Congress.

Effective Dates

1990 Acts. Amendment of the text of this section by Pub.L. 101–280 effective May 4, 1990, see section 11 of Pub.L. 101–280, set out as a note under section 101 of this Appendix. The text as thus amended to be effective Jan. 1, 1991, see section 204 of Pub.L. 101–194 set out as a note under section 101 of this Appendix.

1989 Acts. Amendment by Pub.L. 101–194 effective Jan. 1, 1991, see section 204 of Pub.L. 101–194, as added Pub.L. 101–280, § 3(10)(B), May 4, 1990, 104 Stat. 157, set out as a note under section 101 of this Appendix.

Transfer of Functions

Any reference in any provision of law enacted before Jan. 4, 1995, to a function, duty, or authority of the Clerk of the House of Representatives treated as referring, with respect to that function, duty, or authority, to the officer of the House of Representatives exercising that function, duty, or authority, as determined by the Committee on House Oversight of the House of Representatives, see section 2(1) of Pub.L. 104–14, set out as a note preceding section 21 of Title 2, The Congress.

§ 104. Failure to file or filing false reports

(a) The Attorney General may bring a civil action in any appropriate United States district court against any individual who knowingly and willfully falsifies or who knowingly and willfully fails to file or report any information that such individual is required to report pursuant to section 102. The court in which such action is brought may assess against such individual a civil penalty in any amount, not to exceed $10,000.

(b) The head of each agency, each Secretary concerned, the Director of the Office of Government Ethics, each congressional ethics committee, or the Judicial Conference, as the case may be, shall refer to the Attorney General the name of any individual which such official or committee has reasonable cause to believe has willfully failed to file a report or has willfully falsified or willfully failed to file information required to be reported. Whenever the Judicial Conference refers a name to the Attorney General under this subsection, the Judicial Conference also shall notify the judicial council of the circuit in which the named individual serves of the referral.

(c) The President, the Vice President, the Secretary concerned, the head of each agency, the Office of Personnel Management, a congressional ethics committee, and the Judicial Conference, may take any appropriate personnel or other action in accordance with applicable law or regulation against any individual failing to file a report or falsifying or failing to report information required to be reported.

(d)(1) Any individual who files a report required to be filed under this title more than 30 days after the later of—

(A) the date such report is required to be filed pursuant to the provisions of this title and the rules and regulations promulgated thereunder; or

(B) if a filing extension is granted to such individual under section 101(g), the last day of the filing extension period,

shall, at the direction of and pursuant to regulations issued by the supervising ethics office, pay a filing fee of $200. All such fees shall be deposited in the miscellaneous receipts of the Treasury. The authority under this paragraph to direct the payment of a filing fee may be delegated by the supervising ethics office in the executive branch to other agencies in the executive branch..[1]

(2) The supervising ethics office may waive the filing fee under this subsection in extraordinary circumstances.

(Pub.L. 95–521, Title I, § 104, Oct. 26, 1978, 92 Stat. 1832; Pub.L. 96–19, § 8(a), June 13, 1979, 93 Stat. 41; Pub.L. 101–194, Title II, § 202, Nov. 30, 1989, 103 Stat. 1737; Pub.L. 101–280, § 3(1), (5), May 4, 1990, 104 Stat. 152, 154; Pub.L. 101–650, Title IV, § 405, Dec. 1, 1990, 104 Stat. 5124.)

[1] So in original.

HISTORICAL AND STATUTORY NOTES

Codifications

Section was formerly classified to section 704 of Title 2, The Congress.

Effective Date

1990 Acts. Amendment by section 405 of Pub.L. 101–650 effective 90 days after Dec. 1, 1990, see section 407 of Pub.L. 101–650, set out as a note under section 332 of Title 28, Judiciary and Judicial Procedure.

Amendment of the text of this section by Pub.L. 101–280 effective May 4, 1990, see section 11 of Pub.L. 101–280, set out as a note under section 101 of this Appendix. The text as thus amended to be effective Jan. 1, 1991, see section 204 of Pub.L. 101–194 set out as a note under section 101 of this Appendix.

1989 Acts. Amendment by Pub.L. 101–194 effective Jan. 1, 1991, see section 204 of Pub.L. 101–194, as added Pub.L. 101–280, § 3(10)(B), May 4, 1990, 104 Stat. 157, set out as a note under section 101 of this Appendix.

§ 105. Custody of and public access to reports

(a) Each agency, each supervising ethics office in the executive or judicial branch, the Clerk of the House of Representatives, and the Secretary of the Senate shall make available to the public, in accordance with subsection (b), each report filed under this title with such agency or office or with the Clerk or the Secretary of the Senate, except that—

(1) this section does not require public availability of a report filed by any individual in the Central Intelligence Agency, the Defense Intelligence Agency, the National Imagery and Mapping Agency, or the National Security Agency, or any individual engaged in intelligence activities in any agency of the United States, if the President finds or has found that, due to the nature of the office or position occupied by such individual, public disclosure of such report would, be [1] revealing the identity of the individual or other sensitive information, compromise the national interest of the United States; and such individuals may be authorized, notwithstanding section 104(a), to file such additional reports as are necessary to protect their identity from public disclosure if the President first finds or has found that such filing is necessary in the national interest; and

(2) any report filed by an independent counsel whose identity has not been disclosed by the division of the court under chapter 40 of title 28, United States Code, and any report filed by any person appointed by that independent counsel under such chapter, shall not be made available to the public under this title.

(b)(1) Except as provided in the second sentence of this subsection, each agency, each supervising ethics office in the executive or judicial branch, the Clerk of the House of Representatives, and the Secretary of the Senate shall, within thirty days after any report is received under this title by such agency or office or by the Clerk or the Secretary of the Senate, as the case may be,,[2] permit inspection of such report by or furnish a copy of such report to any person requesting such inspection or copy. With respect to any report required to be filed by May 15 of any year, such report shall be made available for public inspection within 30 calendar days after May 15 of such year or within 30 days of the date of filing of such a report for which an extension is granted pursuant to section 101(g). The agency, office, Clerk, or Secretary of the Senate, as the case may be [3] may require a reasonable fee to be paid in any amount which is found necessary to recover the cost of reproduction or mailing of such report excluding any salary of any employee involved in such reproduction or mailing. A copy of such report may be furnished without charge or at a reduced charge if it is determined that waiver or reduction of the fee is in the public interest.

(2) Notwithstanding paragraph (1), a report may not be made available under this section to any person nor may any copy thereof be provided under this section to any person except upon a written application by such person stating—

(A) that person's name, occupation and address;

(B) the name and address of any other person or organization on whose behalf the inspection or copy is requested; and

(C) that such person is aware of the prohibitions on the obtaining or use of the report.

Any such application shall be made available to the public throughout the period during which the report is made available to the public.

(3)(A) This section does not require the immediate and unconditional availability of reports filed by an individual described in section 109(8) or 109(10) of this Act [sections 109(8) or 109(10) of Appendix 4 of this title] if a finding is made by the Judicial Conference, in consultation with United States Marshall Service, that revealing personal and sensitive information could endanger that individual.

(B) A report may be redacted pursuant to this paragraph only—

(i) to the extent necessary to protect the individual who filed the report; and

(ii) for as long as the danger to such individual exists.

(C) The Administrative Office of the United States Courts shall submit to the Committees on the Judiciary of the House of Representatives and of the Senate an annual report with respect to the operation of this paragraph including—

(i) the total number of reports redacted pursuant to this paragraph;

(ii) the total number of individuals whose reports have been redacted pursuant to this paragraph; and

(iii) the types of threats against individuals whose reports are redacted, if appropriate.

(D) The Judicial Conference, in consultation with the Department of Justice, shall issue regulations setting forth the circumstances under which redaction is appropriate under this paragraph and the procedures for redaction.

(E) This paragraph shall expire on December 31, 2001, and apply to filings through calendar year 2001.

(c)(1) It shall be unlawful for any person to obtain or use a report—

(A) for any unlawful purpose;

(B) for any commercial purpose, other than by news and communications media for dissemination to the general public;

(C) for determining or establishing the credit rating of any individual; or

(D) for use, directly or indirectly, in the solicitation of money for any political, charitable, or other purpose.

(2) The Attorney General may bring a civil action against any person who obtains or uses a report for any purpose prohibited in paragraph (1) of this subsection. The court in which such action is brought may assess against such person a penalty in any amount not to exceed $10,000. Such remedy shall be in addition to any other remedy available under statutory or common law.

(d) Any report filed with or transmitted to an agency or supervising ethics office or to the Clerk of the House of Representatives or the Secretary of the Senate pursuant to this title shall be retained by such agency or office or by the Clerk or the Secretary of the Senate, as the case may be. Such report shall be made available to the public for a period of six years after receipt of the report. After such six-year period the report shall be destroyed unless needed in an ongoing investigation, except that in the case of an individual who filed the report pursuant to section 101(b) and was not subsequently confirmed by the Senate, or who filed the report pursuant to section 101(c) and was not subsequently elected, such reports shall be destroyed one year after the individual either is no longer under consideration by the Senate or is no longer a candidate for nomination or election to the Office of President, Vice President, or as a Member of Congress, unless needed in an ongoing investigation.

(Pub.L. 95–521, Title I, § 105, Oct. 26, 1978, 92 Stat. 1833; Pub.L. 101–194, Title II, § 202, Nov. 30, 1989, 103 Stat. 1737; Pub.L. 101–280, § 3(6), May 4, 1990, 104 Stat. 154; Pub.L. 102–90, Title III, § 313(2), Aug. 14, 1991, 105 Stat. 469; Pub.L. 103–359, Title V, § 501(m), Oct. 14, 1994, 108 Stat. 3430; Pub.L. 104–201, Div. A, Title XI, § 1122(b)(2), Sept. 23, 1996, 110 Stat. 2687; Pub.L. 105–318, § 7, Oct. 30, 1998, 112 Stat. 3011.)

[1] So in original. Probably should be "by".

[2] So in original.

[3] So in original. Probably should be followed by a comma.

HISTORICAL AND STATUTORY NOTES

Codifications

Section was formerly classified to section 705 of Title 2, The Congress.

Effective Dates

1990 Acts. Amendment of the text of this section by Pub.L. 101–280 effective May 4, 1990, see section 11 of Pub.L. 101–280, set out as a note under section 101 of this Appendix. The text as thus amended to be effective Jan. 1, 1991, see section 204 of Pub.L. 101–194 set out as a note under section 101 of this Appendix.

1989 Acts. Amendment by Pub.L. 101–194 effective Jan. 1, 1991, see section 204 of Pub.L. 101–194, as added Pub.L. 101–280, § 3(10)(B), May 4, 1990, 104 Stat. 157, set out as a note under section 101 of this Appendix.

Transfer of Functions

Any reference in any provision of law enacted before Jan. 4, 1995, to a function, duty, or authority of the Clerk of the House of Representatives treated as referring, with respect to that function, duty, or authority, to the officer of the House of Representatives exercising that function, duty, or authority, as determined by the Committee on House Oversight of the House of Representatives, see section 2(1) of Pub.L. 104–14, set out as a note preceding section 21 of Title 2, The Congress.

Certain functions of Clerk of House of Representatives transferred to Director of Non-legislative and Financial Services by section 7 of House Resolution No. 423, One Hundred Second Congress, Apr. 9, 1992. Any reference in any provision of law enacted before Jan. 4, 1995, to a function, duty, or authority of the Director of Non-legislative and Financial Services treated as referring, with respect to that function, duty, or authority, to the officer of the House of Representatives exercising that function, duty, or authority, as determined by the Committee on House Oversight of the House of Representatives, see section 2(4) of Pub.L. 104–14, set out as a note preceding section 21 of Title 2, The Congress.

Public Availability of Reports Filed Under Pre–1991 Ethics in Government Act Provisions

Section 9 of Pub.L. 101–280 provided that: "Those reports filed under title I [formerly classified to section 701 et seq. of Title 2, The Congress], II [formerly set out under the heading Executive Personnel Financial Disclosure Requirements in this Appendix], or III [formerly set out under the heading Judicial Personnel Financial Disclosure Requirements in the Appendix to Title 28, Judiciary and Judicial Procedure] of the Ethics in Government Act of 1978 [Pub.L. 95–521], as in effect before January 1, 1991, shall be made available to the public on or after such date in accordance with section 105 of that Act [this section], as amended by the Ethics Reform Act of 1989 [Pub.L. 101–194], and the provisions of such section shall apply with respect to those reports."

§ 106. Review of reports

(a)(1) Each designated agency ethics official or Secretary concerned shall make provisions to ensure that each report filed with him under this title is reviewed within sixty days after the date of such filing, except that the Director of the Office of Government Ethics shall review only those reports required to be transmitted to him under this title within sixty days after the date of transmittal.

(2) Each congressional ethics committee and the Judicial Conference shall make provisions to ensure that each report filed under this title is reviewed within sixty days after the date of such filing.

(b)(1) If after reviewing any report under subsection (a), the Director of the Office of Government Ethics, the Secretary concerned, the designated agency ethics official, a person designated by the congressional ethics committee, or a person designated by the Judicial Conference, as the case may be, is of the opinion that on the basis of information contained in such report the individual submitting such report is in compliance with applicable laws and regulations, he shall state such opinion on the report, and shall sign such report.

(2) If the Director of the Office of Government Ethics, the Secretary concerned, the designated agency ethics official, a person designated by the congressional ethics committee, or a person designated by the Judicial Conference, after reviewing any report under subsection (a)—

(A) believes additional information is required to be submitted, he shall notify the individual submitting such report what additional information is required and the time by which it must be submitted, or

(B) is of the opinion, on the basis of information submitted, that the individual is not in compliance with applicable laws and regulations, he shall notify the individual, afford a reasonable opportunity for a written or oral response, and after consideration of such response, reach an opinion as to whether or not, on the basis of information submitted, the individual is in compliance with such laws and regulations.

(3) If the Director of the Office of Government Ethics, the Secretary concerned, the designated agency ethics official, a person designated by a congressional ethics committee, or a person designated by the Judicial Conference, reaches an opinion under paragraph (2)(B) that an individual is not in compliance with applicable laws and regulations, the official or committee shall notify the individual of that opinion and, after an opportunity for personal consultation (if practicable), determine and notify the individual of which steps, if any, would in the opinion of such official or committee be appropriate for assuring compliance with such laws and regulations and the date by which such steps should be taken. Such steps may include, as appropriate—

(A) divestiture,

(B) restitution,

(C) the establishment of a blind trust,

(D) request for an exemption under section 208(b) of title 18, United States Code, or

(E) voluntary request for transfer, reassignment, limitation of duties, or resignation.

The use of any such steps shall be in accordance with such rules or regulations as the supervising ethics office may prescribe.

(4) If steps for assuring compliance with applicable laws and regulations are not taken by the date set under paragraph (3) by an individual in a position in the executive branch (other than in the Foreign Service or the uniformed services), appointment to which requires the advice and consent of the Senate, the matter shall be referred to the President for appropriate action.

(5) If steps for assuring compliance with applicable laws and regulations are not taken by the date set under paragraph (3) by a member of the Foreign Service or the uniformed services, the Secretary concerned shall take appropriate action.

(6) If steps for assuring compliance with applicable laws and regulations are not taken by the date set under paragraph (3) by any other officer or employee, the matter shall be referred to the head of the appropriate agency, the congressional ethics committee, or the Judicial Conference, for appropriate action; except that in the case of the Postmaster General or Deputy Postmaster General, the Director of the Office of Government Ethics shall recommend to the Governors of the Board of Governors of the United States Postal Service the action to be taken.

(7) Each supervising ethics office may render advisory opinions interpreting this title within its respective jurisdiction. Notwithstanding any other provision of law, the individual to whom a public advisory opinion is rendered in accordance with this paragraph, and any other individual covered by this title who is involved in a fact situation which is indistinguishable in all material aspects, and who acts in good faith in accordance with the provisions and findings of such advisory opinion shall not, as a result of such act, be subject to any penalty or sanction provided by this title.

(Pub.L. 95–521, Title I, § 106, Oct. 26, 1978, 92 Stat. 1833; Pub.L. 101–194, Title II, § 202, Nov. 30, 1989, 103 Stat. 1739; Pub.L. 101–280, § 3(1), (7), May 4, 1990, 104 Stat. 152, 155.)

HISTORICAL AND STATUTORY NOTES

Codifications

Section was formerly classified to section 706 of Title 2, The Congress.

Effective Dates

1990 Acts. Amendment of the text of this section by Pub.L. 101–280 effective May 4, 1990, see section 11 of Pub.L. 101–280, set out as a note under section 101 of this Appendix. The text as thus amended to be effective Jan. 1, 1991, see section 204 of Pub.L. 101–194 set out as a note under section 101 of this Appendix.

1989 Acts. Amendment by Pub.L. 101–194 effective Jan. 1, 1991, see section 204 of Pub.L. 101–194, as added Pub.L. 101–280, § 3(10)(B), May 4, 1990, 104 Stat. 157, set out as a note under section 101 of this Appendix.

§ 107. Confidential reports and other additional requirements

(a)(1) Each supervising ethics office may require officers and employees under its jurisdiction (including special Government employees as defined in section 202 of title 18, United States Code) to file confidential financial disclosure reports, in such form as the supervising ethics office may prescribe. The information required to be reported under this subsection by the officers and employees of any department or agency shall be set forth in rules or regulations prescribed by the supervising ethics office, and may be less extensive than otherwise required by this title, or more extensive when determined by the supervising ethics office to be necessary and appropriate in light of sections 202 through 209 of title 18, United States Code, regulations promulgated thereunder, or the authorized activities of such officers or employees. Any individual required to file a report pursuant to section 101 shall not be required to file a confidential report pursuant to this subsection, except with respect to information which is more extensive than information otherwise required by this title. Subsections (a), (b), and (d) of section 105 shall not apply with respect to any such report.

(2) Any information required to be provided by an individual under this subsection shall be confidential and shall not be disclosed to the public.

(3) Nothing in this subsection exempts any individual otherwise covered by the requirement to file a public financial disclosure report under this title from such requirement.

(b) The provisions of this title requiring the reporting of information shall supersede any general requirement under any other provision of law or regulation with respect to the reporting of information required for purposes of preventing conflicts of interest or apparent conflicts of interest. Such provisions of this title shall not supersede the requirements of section 7342 of title 5, United States Code.

(c) Nothing in this Act requiring reporting of information shall be deemed to authorize the receipt of income, gifts, or reimbursements; the holding of assets, liabilities, or positions; or the participation in transactions that are prohibited by law, Executive order, rule, or regulation.

(Pub.L. 95–521, Title I, § 107, Oct. 26, 1978, 92 Stat. 1834; Pub.L. 96–19, § 9(d), (g), June 13, 1979, 93 Stat. 42, 43; Pub.L. 101–194, Title II, § 202, Nov. 30, 1989, 103 Stat. 1740.)

HISTORICAL AND STATUTORY NOTES

References in Text

This Act, referred to in subsec. (c), is Pub.L. 95–521, Oct. 26, 1978, 92 Stat. 1824, as amended, known as the Ethics in Government Act of 1978. For complete classification of this Act to the Code, see Short Title note set out under section 101 of this Appendix and Tables.

Codifications

Section was formerly classified to section 707 of Title 2, The Congress.

Effective Dates

1989 Acts. Amendment by Pub.L. 101–194 effective Jan. 1, 1991, see section 204 of Pub.L. 101–194, as added Pub.L.

101–280, § 3(10)(B), May 4, 1990, 104 Stat. 157, set out as a note under section 101 of this Appendix.

§ 108. Authority of Comptroller General

(a) The Comptroller General shall have access to financial disclosure reports filed under this title for the purposes of carrying out his statutory responsibilities.

(b) No later than December 31, 1992, and regularly thereafter, the Comptroller General shall conduct a study to determine whether the provisions of this title are being carried out effectively.

(Pub.L. 95–521, Title I, § 108, Oct. 26, 1978, 92 Stat. 1835; Pub.L. 96–19, § 9(t), June 13, 1979, 93 Stat. 44; Pub.L. 101–194, Title II, § 202, Nov. 30, 1989, 103 Stat. 1741.)

HISTORICAL AND STATUTORY NOTES

Codifications

Section was formerly classified to section 708 of Title 2, The Congress.

Effective Dates

1989 Acts. Amendment by Pub.L. 101–194 effective Jan. 1, 1991, see section 204 of Pub.L. 101–194, as added Pub.L. 101–280, § 3(10)(B), May 4, 1990, 104 Stat. 157, set out as a note under section 101 of this Appendix.

§ 109. Definitions

For the purposes of this title, the term—

(1) "congressional ethics committees" means the Select Committee on Ethics of the Senate and the Committee on Standards of Official Conduct of the House of Representatives;

(2) "dependent child" means, when used with respect to any reporting individual, any individual who is a son, daughter, stepson, or stepdaughter and who—

(A) is unmarried and under age 21 and is living in the household of such reporting individual; or

(B) is a dependent of such reporting individual within the meaning of section 152 of the Internal Revenue Code of 1986 [26 U.S.C.A. § 152];

(3) "designated agency ethics official" means an officer or employee who is designated to administer the provisions of this title within an agency;

(4) "executive branch" includes each Executive agency (as defined in section 105 of title 5, United States Code), other than the General Accounting Office, and any other entity or administrative unit in the executive branch;

(5) "gift" means a payment, advance, forbearance, rendering, or deposit of money, or any thing of value, unless consideration of equal or greater value is received by the donor, but does not include—

(A) bequest and other forms of inheritance;

(B) suitable mementos of a function honoring the reporting individual;

(C) food, lodging, transportation, and entertainment provided by a foreign government within a foreign country or by the United States Government, the District of Columbia, or a State or local government or political subdivision thereof;

(D) food and beverages which are not consumed in connection with a gift of overnight lodging;

(E) communications to the offices of a reporting individual, including subscriptions to newspapers and periodicals; or

(F) consumable products provided by home-State businesses to the offices of a reporting individual who is an elected official, if those products are intended for consumption by persons other than such reporting individual;

(6) "honoraria" has the meaning given such term in section 505 of this Act;

(7) "income" means all income from whatever source derived, including but not limited to the following items: compensation for services, including fees, commissions, and similar items; gross income derived from business (and net income if the individual elects to include it); gains derived from dealings in property; interest; rents; royalties; dividends; annuities; income from life insurance and endowment contracts; pensions; income from discharge of indebtedness; distributive share of partnership income; and income from an interest in an estate or trust;

(8) "judicial employee" means any employee of the judicial branch of the Government, of the United States Sentencing Commission, of the Tax Court, of the Court of Federal Claims, of the Court of Appeals for Veterans Claims, or of the United States Court of Appeals for the Armed Forces, who is not a judicial officer and who is authorized to perform adjudicatory functions with respect to proceedings in the judicial branch, or who occupies a position for which the rate of basic pay is equal to or greater than 120 percent of the minimum rate of basic pay payable for GS–15 of the General Schedule;

(9) "Judicial Conference" means the Judicial Conference of the United States;

(10) "judicial officer" means the Chief Justice of the United States, the Associate Justices of the Supreme Court, and the judges of the United States courts of appeals, United States district courts, including the district courts in Guam, the Northern Mariana Islands, and the Virgin Islands, Court of Appeals for the Federal Circuit, Court of International Trade, Tax Court, Court of Federal Claims,

Court of Appeals for Veterans Claims, United States Court of Appeals for the Armed Forces, and any court created by Act of Congress, the judges of which are entitled to hold office during good behavior;

(11) "legislative branch" includes—

(A) the Architect of the Capitol;

(B) the Botanic Gardens;

(C) the Congressional Budget Office;

(D) the General Accounting Office;

(E) the Government Printing Office;

(F) the Library of Congress;

(G) the United States Capitol Police;

(H) the Office of Technology Assessment; and

(I) any other agency, entity, office, or commission established in the legislative branch;

(12) "Member of Congress" means a United States Senator, a Representative in Congress, a Delegate to Congress, or the Resident Commissioner from Puerto Rico;

(13) "officer or employee of the Congress" means—

(A) any individual described under subparagraph (B), other than a Member of Congress or the Vice President, whose compensation is disbursed by the Secretary of the Senate or the Chief Administrative Officer of the House of Representatives;

(B)(i) each officer or employee of the legislative branch who, for at least 60 days, occupies a position for which the rate of basic pay is equal to or greater than 120 percent of the minimum rate of basic pay payable for GS–15 of the General Schedule; and

(ii) at least one principal assistant designated for purposes of this paragraph by each Member who does not have an employee who occupies a position for which the rate of basic pay is equal to or greater than 120 percent of the minimum rate of basic pay payable for GS–15 of the General Schedule;

(14) "personal hospitality of any individual" means hospitality extended for a nonbusiness purpose by an individual, not a corporation or organization, at the personal residence of that individual or his family or on property or facilities owned by that individual or his family;

(15) "reimbursement" means any payment or other thing of value received by the reporting individual, other than gifts, to cover travel-related expenses of such individual other than those which are—

(A) provided by the United States Government, the District of Columbia, or a State or local government or political subdivision thereof;

(B) required to be reported by the reporting individual under section 7342 of title 5, United States Code; or

(C) required to be reported under section 304 of the Federal Election Campaign Act of 1971 (2 U.S.C. 434);

(16) "relative" means an individual who is related to the reporting individual, as father, mother, son, daughter, brother, sister, uncle, aunt, great aunt, great uncle, first cousin, nephew, niece, husband, wife, grandfather, grandmother, grandson, granddaughter, father-in-law, mother-in-law, son-in-law, daughter-in-law, brother-in-law, sister-in-law, stepfather, stepmother, stepson, stepdaughter, stepbrother, stepsister, half brother, half sister, or who is the grandfather or grandmother of the spouse of the reporting individual, and shall be deemed to include the fiance or fiancee of the reporting individual;

(17) "Secretary concerned" has the meaning set forth in section 101(a)(9) of title 10, United States Code, and, in addition, means—

(A) the Secretary of Commerce, with respect to matters concerning the National Oceanic and Atmospheric Administration;

(B) the Secretary of Health and Human Services, with respect to matters concerning the Public Health Service; and

(C) the Secretary of State, with respect to matters concerning the Foreign Service;

(18) "supervising ethics office" means—

(A) the Select Committee on Ethics of the Senate, for Senators, officers and employees of the Senate, and other officers or employees of the legislative branch required to file financial disclosure reports with the Secretary of the Senate pursuant to section 103(h) of this title;

(B) the Committee on Standards of Official Conduct of the House of Representatives, for Members, officers and employees of the House of Representatives and other officers or employees of the legislative branch required to file financial disclosure reports with the Clerk of the House of Representatives pursuant to section 103(h) of this title;

(C) the Judicial Conference for judicial officers and judicial employees; and

(D) the Office of Government Ethics for all executive branch officers and employees; and

(19) "value" means a good faith estimate of the dollar value if the exact value is neither known nor easily obtainable by the reporting individual.

(Pub.L. 95–521, Title I, § 109, Oct. 26, 1978, 92 Stat. 1836; Pub.L. 101–194, Title II, § 202, Nov. 30, 1989, 103 Stat. 1741; Pub.L. 101–280, § 3(1), (8), May 4, 1990, 104 Stat. 152, 155; Pub.L. 102–378, § 4(a)(2), Oct. 2, 1992, 106 Stat. 1357; Pub.L. 102–572, Title IX, § 902(b)(2), Oct. 29, 1992, 106 Stat. 4516; Pub.L. 103–160, Div. A, Title XI, § 1182(d)(3), Nov. 30, 1993, 107 Stat. 1773; Pub.L. 103–337, Div. A, Title IX, § 924(d)(3), Oct. 5, 1994, 108 Stat. 2832; Pub.L. 104–186, Title II, § 216(2), Aug. 20, 1996, 110 Stat. 1747; Pub.L. 105–368, Title V, § 521(b)(1)(D), Nov. 10, 1998, 112 Stat. 3342.)

HISTORICAL AND STATUTORY NOTES

References in Text

The General Schedule, referred to in pars. (8) and (13)(B), is set out under section 5332 of this title.

Codifications

Section was formerly classified to section 709 of Title 2, The Congress.

Effective Dates

1998 Acts. Amendment by Pub.L. 105–368 effective on the first day of the first month beginning more than 90 days after Nov. 10, 1998, see section 513 of Pub.L. 105–368, set out as a note under section 7251 of Title 38.

1992 Acts. Amendment by Pub.L. 102–572 effective Oct. 29, 1992, see section 911 of Pub.L. 102–572, set out as a note under section 171 of Title 28, Judiciary and Judicial Procedure.

Amendment by Pub.L. 102–378 effective Oct. 2, 1992, see section 9(a) of Pub.L. 102–378, set out as a note under section 6303 of this title.

1990 Acts. Amendment of the text of this section by Pub.L. 101–280 effective May 4, 1990, see section 11 of Pub.L. 101–280, set out as a note under section 101 of this Appendix. The text as thus amended to be effective Jan. 1, 1991, see section 204 of Pub.L. 101–194 set out as a note under section 101 of this Appendix.

1989 Acts. Amendment by Pub.L. 101–194 effective Jan. 1, 1991, see section 204 of Pub.L. 101–194, as added Pub.L. 101–280, § 3(10)(B), May 4, 1990, 104 Stat. 157, set out as a note under section 101 of this Appendix.

Transfer of Functions

Any reference in any provision of law enacted before Jan. 4, 1995, to a function, duty, or authority of the Clerk of the House of Representatives treated as referring, with respect to that function, duty, or authority, to the officer of the House of Representatives exercising that function, duty, or authority, as determined by the Committee on House Oversight of the House of Representatives, see section 2(1) of Pub.L. 104–14, set out as a note preceding section 21 of Title 2, The Congress.

Certain functions of Clerk of House of Representatives transferred to Director of Non-legislative and Financial Services by section 7 of House Resolution No. 423, One Hundred Second Congress, Apr. 9, 1992. Any reference in any provision of law enacted before Jan. 4, 1995, to a function, duty, or authority of the Director of Non-legislative and Financial Services treated as referring, with respect to that function, duty, or authority, to the officer of the House of Representatives exercising that function, duty, or authority, as determined by the Committee on House Oversight of the House of Representatives, see section 2(4) of Pub.L. 104–14, set out as a note preceding section 21 of Title 2, The Congress.

Prior Provisions

Provisions similar to those comprising this section were contained in section 107 prior to the general revision of this title by Pub.L. 101–194.

Provision similar to that comprising par. (11) of this section was contained in section 101(e) prior to the general revision of this title by Pub.L. 101–194.

§ 110. Notice of actions taken to comply with ethics agreements

(a) In any case in which an individual agrees with that individual's designated agency ethics official, the Office of Government Ethics, a Senate confirmation committee, a congressional ethics committee, or the Judicial Conference, to take any action to comply with this Act or any other law or regulation governing conflicts of interest of, or establishing standards of conduct applicable with respect to, officers or employees of the Government, that individual shall notify in writing the designated agency ethics official, the Office of Government Ethics, the appropriate committee of the Senate, the congressional ethics committee, or the Judicial Conference, as the case may be, of any action taken by the individual pursuant to that agreement. Such notification shall be made not later than the date specified in the agreement by which action by the individual must be taken, or not later than three months after the date of the agreement, if no date for action is so specified.

(b) If an agreement described in subsection (a) requires that the individual recuse himself or herself from particular categories of agency or other official action, the individual shall reduce to writing those subjects regarding which the recusal agreement will apply and the process by which it will be determined whether the individual must recuse himself or herself in a specific instance. An individual shall be considered to have complied with the requirements of subsection (a) with respect to such recusal agreement if such individual files a copy of the document setting forth the information described in the preceding sentence with such individual's designated agency ethics official or the appropriate supervising ethics office within the time prescribed in the last sentence of subsection (a).

(Pub.L. 95–521, Title I, § 110, as added Pub.L. 101–194, Title II, § 202, Nov. 30, 1989, 103 Stat. 1744, and amended Pub.L. 101–280, § 3(1), May 4, 1990, 104 Stat. 152.)

HISTORICAL AND STATUTORY NOTES

References in Text

This Act, referred to in subsec. (a), is Pub.L. 95–521, Oct. 26, 1978, 92 Stat. 1824, as amended, known as the Ethics in Government Act of 1978. For complete classification of this Act to the Code, see Short Title note set out under section 101 of this Appendix and Tables.

Effective Dates

1990 Acts. Amendment of the text of this section by Pub.L. 101–280 effective May 4, 1990, see section 11 of Pub.L. 101–280, set out as a note under section 101 of this Appendix. The text as thus amended to be effective Jan. 1, 1991, see section 204 of Pub.L. 101–194 set out as a note under section 101 of this Appendix.

1989 Acts. Section effective Jan. 1, 1991, see section 204 of Pub.L. 101–194, set out as a note under section 101 of this Appendix.

§ 111. Administration of provisions

The provisions of this title shall be administered by—

(1) the Director of the Office of Government Ethics, the designated agency ethics official, or the Secretary concerned, as appropriate, with regard to officers and employees described in paragraphs (1) through (8) of section 101(f);

(2) the Select Committee on Ethics of the Senate and the Committee on Standards of Official Conduct of the House of Representatives, as appropriate, with regard to officers and employees described in paragraphs (9) and (10) of section 101(f); and

(3) the Judicial Conference in the case of an officer or employee described in paragraphs (11) and (12) of section 101(f).

The Judicial Conference may delegate any authority it has under this title to an ethics committee established by the Judicial Conference.

(Pub.L. 95–521, Title I, § 111, as added Pub.L. 101–194, Title II, § 202, Nov. 30, 1989, 103 Stat. 1744, and amended Pub.L. 101–280, § 3(1), (9), May 4, 1990, 104 Stat. 152, 157.)

HISTORICAL AND STATUTORY NOTES

Effective Dates

1990 Acts. Amendment of the text of this section by Pub.L. 101–280 effective May 4, 1990, see section 11 of Pub.L. 101–280, set out as a note under section 101 of this Appendix. The text as thus amended to be effective Jan. 1, 1991, see section 204 of Pub.L. 101–194 set out as a note under section 101 of this Appendix.

1989 Acts. Section effective Jan. 1, 1991, see section 204 of Pub.L. 101–194, set out as a note under section 101 of this Appendix.

Transmittal of Financial Disclosure Reports

Section 902 of Pub.L. 101–194 provided that:

"**(a)** The Select Committee on Ethics shall transmit a copy of each report filed with it under title I of the Ethics in Government Act of 1978 [sections 101 to 112 of Pub.L. 95–521, set out in this Appendix] (other than a report filed by a Member of Congress) to the head of the employing office of the individual filing the report.

"**(b)** For purposes of this section, the head of the employing office shall be—

"**(A)** in the case of an employee of a Member, the Member by whom that person is employed;

"**(B)** in the case of an employee of a Committee, the chairman and ranking minority member of such Committee;

"**(C)** in the case of an employee on the leadership staff, the Member of the leadership on whose staff such person serves; and

"**(D)** in the case of any other employee of the legislative branch, the head of the office in which such individual serves."

[§ 112. Repealed. Pub.L. 101–280, § 3(10)(A), May 4, 1990, 104 Stat. 157]

HISTORICAL AND STATUTORY NOTES

Section, Pub.L. 95–521, Title I, § 112, as added Pub.L. 101–194, Title II, § 202, Nov. 30, 1989, 103 Stat. 1744, directed that the provisions made by title I of Pub.L. 95–521 [sections 101 to 112 of Pub.L. 95–521, set out in this Appendix] take effect on January 1, 1990, and be applicable to reports filed under such title after January 1, 1991. See section 3(10)(C) of Pub.L. 101–280 and section 204 of Pub.L. 101–194, as added by section 3(10)(B) of Pub.L. 101–280, set out as notes under section 101 of this Appendix.

Effective Date of Repeal

Repeal effective May 4, 1990, see section 11 of Pub.L. 101–280, set out as a note under section 101 of this Appendix.

[TITLE III—REPEALED]

[§§ 301 to 309. Repealed. Pub.L. 101–194, Title II, § 201, Nov. 30, 1989, 103 Stat. 1724]

HISTORICAL AND STATUTORY NOTES

Sections 301 to 309 of Pub.L. 95–521, Title III, Oct. 26, 1978, 92 Stat. 1851, as amended Pub.L. 96–19, §§ 2(a)(3), (c)(3), 3(a)(3), (b), 4(c), 6, 7(a) to (c), (d)(2), (e), (f), 8(c), 9(c)(3), (d), (j), (p) to (r), June 13, 1979, 93 Stat. 37 to 43; Pub.L. 96–417, Title VI, § 601(9), Oct. 10, 1980, 94 Stat. 1744; Pub.L. 96–579, § 13(c), Dec. 23, 1980, 94 Stat. 3369; Pub.L. 97–164, Title I, § 163(a)(6), Apr. 2, 1982, 96 Stat. 49; Pub.L. 98–150, § 10, Nov. 11, 1983, 97 Stat. 962; Pub.L. 99–573, § 6, Oct. 28, 1986, 100 Stat. 3231; Pub.L. 101–237, Title VI, § 602(a)(1), Dec. 18, 1989, 103 Stat. 2094, related to judicial personnel financial disclosure requirements.

Effective Date of Repeal

Repeal effective Jan. 1, 1991, see section 204 of Pub.L. 101–194, as added Pub.L. 101–280, § 3(10)(B), May 4, 1990, 104 Stat. 157, set out as a Effective Date of 1989 Amendment note under section 101 of this Appendix.

See section 3(10)(C) and (D) of Pub.L. 101–280, May 4, 1990, 104 Stat. 157, set out as notes under section 101 of this Appendix, for provisions directing that the provisions of Title III of Pub.L. 95–521, as in effect prior to Nov. 30, 1989, are effective until Jan. 1, 1991, as if Pub.L. 101–194 had not been enacted, and that nothing in Title III of Pub.L. 101–194 shall be construed to prevent the prosecution of civil actions against individuals for violations of Title III of Pub.L. 95–521 before Jan. 1, 1991.

Prior Provisions

Prior to repeal, sections 301 to 309 of Pub.L. 95–521, Title III, Oct. 26, 1978, 92 Stat. 1851, read as follows:

§ 301. Persons required to file

(a) Within thirty days of assuming the position of a judicial employee, an individual shall file a report containing the information described in section 302(b).

(b) Within five days of the transmittal by the President to the Senate of the nomination of an individual to be a judicial officer, such individual shall file a report containing the information described in section 302(b). Nothing in this Act shall prevent any Congressional committee from requesting, as a condition of confirmation, any additional financial information from any Presidential nominee whose nomination has been referred to that committee.

(c) Any individual who is a judicial officer or employee during any calendar year and performs the duties of his position or office for a period in excess of sixty days in that calendar year shall file on or before May 15 of the succeeding year a report containing the information described in section 302(a).

(d) Any individual who occupies a position as a judicial officer or employee shall, on or before the thirtieth day after termination of employment in such position, file a report containing the information described in section 302(a) covering the preceding calendar year if the report required by subsection (c) of this subsection[1] has not been filed and covering the portion of the calendar year in which such termination occurs up to the date the individual left such office or position, unless such individual has accepted employment in another position as a judicial officer or employee.

(e) Reasonable extensions of time for filing any report may be granted under procedures prescribed by the Judicial Ethics Committee established pursuant to section 303(a) of this title (hereinafter in this title referred to as the "Committee"), but the total of such extensions shall not exceed ninety days.

(f) The provisions of subsections (a) and (d) of this section shall not apply to an individual who, as determined by the Judicial Ethics Committee, is not reasonably expected to perform the duties of his office or position for more than sixty days in a calendar year, except that if such individual performs the duties of his office or position for more than sixty days in a calendar year—

(1) the report required by subsection (a) of this section shall be filed within fifteen days of the sixtieth day, and

(2) the report required by subsection (d) of this section shall be filed as provided in such subsection.

(g) The Committee may grant a publicly available request for a waiver of any reporting requirement under this section for an individual who is expected to perform or has performed the duties of his office or position less than one hundred and thirty days in a calendar year but only if the Committee determines that—

(1) such individual is not a full-time employee of the Government,

(2) such individual is able to provide services specially needed by the Government,

(3) it is unlikely that the individual's outside employment or financial interests will create a conflict of interest, and

(4) public financial disclosure by such individual is not necessary in the circumstances.

(h) The provisions of this Act shall not apply to any judicial officer or employee of the Superior Court of the District of Columbia or the District of Columbia Court of Appeals or any other employee of the District of Columbia court system.

(Pub.L. 95–521, Title III, § 301, Oct. 26, 1978, 92 Stat. 1851; Pub.L. 96–19, §§ 2(a)(3), (c)(3), 9(p), June 13, 1979, 93 Stat. 37, 38, 43; Pub.L. 99–573, § 6(a), Oct. 28, 1986, 100 Stat. 3231.)

[1] So in original. Probably should be "section".

§ 302. Contents of reports

(a) Each report filed pursuant to section 301(c) shall include a full and complete statement with respect to the following:

(1)(A) The source, type, and amount or value of income (other than income referred to in subparagraph (B)) from any source (other than from current employment by the United States Government), and the source, date, and amount of honoraria from any source, received during the preceding calendar year, aggregating $100 or more in value.

(B) The source and type of income which consists of dividends, rent, interest, and capital gains received during the preceding calendar year which exceeds $100 in amount or value, and an indication of which of the following categories the amount or value of such item of income is within—

(i) not more than $1,000,

(ii) greater than $1,000 but not more than $2,500,

(iii) greater than $2,500 but not more than $5,000,

(iv) greater than $5,000 but not more than $15,000,

(v) greater than $15,000 but not more than $50,000,

(vi) greater than $50,000 but not more than $100,000, or

(vii) greater than $100,000.

(2)(A) The identity of the source and a brief description of any gifts of transportation, lodging, food, or entertainment aggregating $250 or more in value received from any source other than a relative of the reporting individual during the preceding calendar year, except that any food, lodging, or entertainment received as personal hospitality of any individual need not be reported, and any gift with a fair market value of $35 or less need not be aggregated for purposes of this subparagraph.

(B) The identity of the source, a brief description, and the value of all gifts other than transportation, lodging, food, or entertainment aggregating $100 or more in value received from any source other than a relative of the reporting individual during the preceding calendar year, except that any gift with a fair market value of $35 or less need not be aggregated for purposes of this subparagraph.

(C) The identity of the source and a brief description of reimbursements received from any source aggregating $250 or more in value and received during the preceding calendar year.

(D) In an unusual case, a gift need not be aggregated under subparagraph (A) or (B) if a publicly available request for a waiver is granted.

(3) The identity and category of value of any interest in property held during the preceding calendar year in a trade or business, or for investment or the production of income, which has a fair market value which exceeds $1,000 as of the close of the preceding calendar year, excluding any personal liability owed to the reporting individual by a relative or any deposits aggregating $5,000 or less in a personal savings account. For purposes of this

paragraph, a personal savings account shall include any certificate of deposit or any other form of deposit in a bank, savings and loan association, credit union, or similar financial institution.

(4) The identity and category of value of the total liabilities owed to any creditor other than a relative which exceed $10,000 at any time during the preceding calendar year, excluding—

(A) any mortgage secured by real property which is a personal residence of the reporting individual or his spouse; and

(B) any loan secured by a personal motor vehicle, household furniture, or appliances, which loan does not exceed the purchase price of the item which secures it.

With respect to revolving charge accounts, only those with an outstanding liability which exceeds $10,000 as of the close of the preceding calendar year need be reported under this paragraph.

(5) Except as provided in this paragraph, a brief description, the date, and category of value of any purchase, sale, or exchange during the preceding calendar year which exceeds $1,000—

(A) in real property, other than property used solely as a personal residence of the reporting individual or his spouse; or

(B) in stocks, bonds, commodities futures, and other forms of securities.

Reporting is not required under this paragraph of any transactions solely by and between the reporting individual, his spouse, or dependent children.

(6) The identity of all positions held on or before the date of filing during the current calendar year as an officer, director, trustee, partner, proprietor, representative, employee, or consultant of any corporation, company, firm, partnership, or other business enterprise, any non-profit organization, any labor organization, or any educational or other institution other than the United States. This paragraph shall not require the reporting of positions held in any religious, social, fraternal, or political entity and positions solely of an honorary nature.

(7) A description of the date, parties to, and terms of any agreement or arrangement with respect to (A) future employment; (B) a leave of absence during the period of the reporting individual's Government service; (C) continuation of payments by a former employer other than the United States Government; and (D) continuing participation in an employee welfare or benefit plan maintained by a former employer.

(b) Each report filed pursuant to subsections (a) and (b) of section 301 shall include a full and complete statement with respect to the information required by—

(1) paragraph (1) of subsection (a) of this section for the year of filing and the preceding calendar year,

(2) paragraphs (3) and (4) of subsection (a) of this section as of the date specified in the report but which is less than thirty-one days before the filing date, and

(3) paragraphs (6) and (7) of subsection (a) of this section as of the filing date but for periods described in such paragraphs.

(c) In the case of any individual described in section 301(d) of this title, any reference to the preceding calendar year shall be considered also to include that part of the calendar year of filing up to the date of the termination of employment.

(d)(1) The categories for reporting the amount or value of the items covered in paragraphs (3), (4), and (5) of subsection (a) of this section are as follows:

(A) not more than $5,000;

(B) greater than $5,000 but not more than $15,000;

(C) greater than $15,000 but not more than $50,000;

(D) greater than $50,000 but not more than $100,000;

(E) greater than $100,000 but not more than $250,000; and

(F) greater than $250,000.

(2) For the purposes of paragraph (3) of subsection (a) of this section if the current value of an interest in real property (or an interest in a real estate partnership) is not ascertainable without an appraisal, an individual may list (A) the date of purchase and the purchase price of the interest in the real property, or (B) the assessed value of the real property for tax purposes, adjusted to reflect the market value of the property used for the assessment if the assessed value is computed at less than 100 percent of such market value, but such individual shall include in his report a full and complete description of the method used to determine such assessed value, instead of specifying a category of value pursuant to paragraph (1) of this subsection. If the current value of any other item required to be reported under paragraph (3) of subsection (a) of this section is not ascertainable without an appraisal, such individual may list the book value of a corporation whose stock is not publicly traded, the net worth of a business partnership, the equity value of an individually owned business, or with respect to other holdings, any recognized indication of value, but such individual shall include in his report a full and complete description of the method used in determining such value. In lieu of any value referred to in the preceding sentence, an individual may list the assessed value of the item for tax purposes, adjusted to reflect the market value of the item used for the assessment if the assessed value is computed at less than 100 percent of such market value, but a full and complete description of the method used in determining such assessed value shall be included in the report.

(e)(1) Except as provided in the last sentence of this paragraph, each report required by subsection (a), (b), or (c) of this section shall also contain information listed in paragraphs (1) through (5) of subsection (a) of this section respecting the spouse or dependent child of the reporting individual as follows:

(A) The source of items of earned income earned by a spouse from any person which exceed $1,000 and, with respect to his spouse or dependent child, all information required to be reported in subsection (a)(1)(B) of this section with respect to income derived from any asset held by the spouse or dependent child and reported pursuant to paragraph (3). With respect to earned income, if the spouse is self-employed in business or a profession, only the nature of such business or profession need be reported.

(B) In the case of any gifts received by a spouse which are not received totally independent of the spouse's relationship to the reporting individual, the identity of the source and a brief description of gifts of transportation, lodging, food, or entertainment or the value of other gifts.

(C) In the case of any reimbursements received by a spouse which are not received totally independent of the spouse's relationship to the reporting individual, the identity of the source and a brief description of each such reimbursement.

(D) In the case of items described in paragraphs (3) through (5), all information required to be reported under these paragraphs other than items (i) which the reporting individual certifies represent the spouse's or dependent child's sole financial interest or responsibility and which the reporting individual has no knowledge of, (ii) which are not in any way, past or present, derived from the income, assets, or activities of the reporting individual, and (iii) from which the reporting individual neither derives, nor expects to derive, any financial or economic benefit.

Each report referred to in subsection (b) of this section shall, with respect to the spouse and dependent child of the reporting individual, only contain information listed in paragraphs (1), (3), and (4) of subsection (a) of this section, as specified in this paragraph.

(2) No report shall be required with respect to a spouse living separate and apart from the reporting individual with the intention of terminating the marriage or providing for permanent separation; or with respect to any income or obligations of an individual arising from the dissolution of his marriage or the permanent separation from his spouse.

(f)(1) Except as provided in paragraph (2), each reporting individual shall report the information required to be reported pursuant to subsections (a), (b), and (c) of this subsection [1] with respect to the holdings of and the income from a trust or other financial arrangement from which income is received by, or with respect to which a beneficial interest in principal or income is held by, such individual, his spouse, or any dependent child.

(2) A reporting individual other than a judicial officer of the United States need not report the holdings of or the source of income from any of the holdings of—

(A) any qualified blind trust (as defined in paragraph (3)); or

(B) a trust—

(i) which was not created directly by such individual, his spouse, or any dependent child, and

(ii) the holding or sources of income of which such individual, his spouse, and any dependent child have no knowledge of,

but such individual shall report the category of the amount of income received by him, his spouse, or any dependent child from the trust under subsection (a)(1)(B) of this section.

(3) For purposes of this subsection, the term "qualified blind trust" includes any trust in which a reporting individual, his spouse, or any dependent child has a beneficial interest in the principal or income, and which meets the following requirements:

(A) The trustee of the trust is a financial institution, an attorney, a certified public accountant, a broker, or an investment adviser, who (in the case of a financial institution or investment company, any officer or employee involved in the management or control of the trust who)—

(i) is independent of and unassociated with any interested party so that the trustee cannot be controlled or influenced in the administration of the trust by any interested party,

(ii) is not or has not been an employee of any interested party, or any organization affiliated with any interested party and is not a partner of, or involved in any joint venture or other investment with, any interested party, and

(iii) is not a relative of any interested party.

(B) Any asset transferred to the trust by an interested party is free of any restriction with respect to its transfer or sale unless such restriction is expressly approved by the supervising ethics office of the reporting individual.

(C) The trust instrument which establishes the trust provides that—

(i) except to the extent provided in subparagraph (B) of this paragraph, the trustee in the exercise of his authority and discretion to manage and control the assets of the trust shall not consult or notify any interested party;

(ii) the trust shall not contain any asset the holding of which by an interested party is prohibited by any law or regulation;

(iii) the trustee shall promptly notify the reporting individual and his supervising ethics office when the holdings of any particular asset transferred to the trust by any interested party are disposed of or when the value of such holding is less than $1,000;

(iv) the trust tax return shall be prepared by the trustee or his designee, and such return and any information relating thereto (other than the trust income summarized in appropriate categories necessary to complete an interested party's tax return), shall not be disclosed to any interested party;

(v) an interested party shall not receive any report on the holdings and sources of income of the trust, except a report at the end of each calendar quarter with respect to the total cash value of the interest of the interested party in the trust or the net income or loss of the trust or any reports necessary to enable the interested party to complete an individual tax return required by law or to provide the information required by subsection (a)(1)(B) of this section, but such report shall not identify any asset or holding;

(vi) except for communications which solely consist of requests for distributions of cash or other unspecified assets of the trust, there shall be no direct or indirect communication between the trustee and an interested party with respect to the trust unless such communication is in writing and unless it relates only (I) to the general financial interest and needs of the interested party (including, but not limited to, an interest in maximizing income or long-term capital gain), (II) to the notification of the trustee of a law or regulation subsequently applicable to the reporting individual which prohibits the interested party from holding an asset, which notification directs that the asset not be held by the trust, or (III) to directions to the trustee to sell all of an asset initially placed in the trust by an interested party which in the determination of the reporting individual creates a conflict of interest or the appearance thereof due to the subsequent assumption of duties by the reporting individual (but nothing herein shall require any such direction); and

(vii) the interested parties shall make no effort to obtain information with respect to the holdings of the trust, including obtaining a copy of any trust tax return filed or any information relating thereto except as otherwise provided in this subsection.

(D) The proposed trust instrument and the proposed trustee is approved by the reporting individual's supervising ethics office.

For purposes of this subsection "interested party" means a reporting individual, his spouse, and any dependent child if the reporting individual, his spouse, or dependent child has a beneficial interest in the principal or income of a qualified blind trust; "broker" has the meaning set forth in section 78c(a)(4) of title 15; "investment adviser" includes any investment adviser who, as determined under regulations prescribed by the supervising ethics office, is generally involved in his role as such an adviser in the management or control of trusts; and "supervising ethics office" means the Judicial Ethics Committee.

(4) An asset placed in a trust by an interested party shall be considered a financial interest of the reporting individual, for the purpose of section 208 of title 28,[2] and any other conflict of interest statutes or regulations of the Federal Government, until such time as the reporting individual is notified by the trustee that such asset has been disposed of, or has a value of less than $1,000.

(5)(A) The reporting individual shall, within thirty days after a qualified blind trust is approved by his supervising ethics office, file with such office a copy of—

(i) the executed trust instrument of such trust (other than those provisions which relate to the testamentary disposition of the trust assets), and

(ii) a list of the assets which were transferred to such trust, including the category of value of each asset as determined under subsection (d) of this section.

This subparagraph shall not apply with respect to a trust meeting the requirements for being considered a qualified blind trust under paragraph (7) of this subsection.

(B) The reporting individual shall, within thirty days of transferring an asset (other than cash) to a previously established qualified blind trust, notify his supervising ethics office of the identity of each such asset and the category of value of each asset as determined under subsection (d) of this section.

(C) Within thirty days of the dissolution of a qualified blind trust, a reporting individual shall—

(i) notify his supervising ethics office of such dissolution, and

(ii) file with such office a copy of a list of the assets of the trust at the time of such dissolution and the category of value under subsection (d) of this section of each such asset.

(D) Documents filed under subparagraphs (A), (B), and (C) of this paragraph and the lists provided by the trustee of assets placed in the trust by an interested party which have been sold shall be made available to the public in the same manner as a report is made available under section 305 and the provisions of that section shall apply with respect to such documents and lists.

(E) A copy of each written communication with respect to the trust under paragraph (3)(C)(vi) shall be filed by the person initiating the communication with the reporting individual's supervising ethics office within five days of the date of the communication.

(6)(A) A trustee of a qualified blind trust shall not knowingly or negligently (i) disclose any information to an interested party with respect to such trust that may not be disclosed under paragraph (3) of this subsection; (ii) acquire any holding the ownership of which is prohibited by the trust instrument; (iii) solicit advice from any interested party with respect to such trust, which solicitation is prohibited by paragraph (3) of this subsection or the trust agreement; or (vi)[3] fail to file any document required by this subsection.

(B) A reporting individual shall not knowingly or negligently (i) solicit or receive any information with respect to a qualified blind trust of which he is an interested party that may not be disclosed under paragraph (3)(C) of this subsection, or (ii) fail to file any document required by this subsection.

(C)(i) The Attorney General may bring a civil action in any appropriate United States District Court against any individual who knowingly and willfully violates the provisions of subparagraph (A) or (B) of this paragraph. The court in which such action is brought may assess against such individual a civil penalty in any amount not to exceed $5,000.

(ii) The Attorney General may bring a civil action in any appropriate United States District Court against any individual who negligently violates the provisions of subparagraph (A) or (B) of this paragraph. The court in which such action is brought may assess against such individual a civil penalty in any amount not to exceed $1,000.

(7) Any trust may be considered to be a qualified blind trust if—

(A) the trust instrument is amended to comply with the requirements of paragraph (3) or, in the case of a trust instrument which does not by its terms permit amendment, the trustee, the reporting individual, and any other interested party agree in writing that the trust shall be administered in accordance with the requirements of this subsection and the trustee of such trust meets the requirements of paragraph (3)(A); except that in the case of any interested party who is a dependent child, a parent or guardian of such child may execute the agreement referred to in this subparagraph;

(B) a copy of the trust instrument (except testamentary provisions) and a copy of the agreement referred to in subparagraph (A), and a list of the assets held by the trust at the time of approval by the supervising ethics office, including the category of value of each asset as determined under subsection (d) of this section, are filed with such office and made available to the public as provided under paragraph (5)(D) of this subsection; and

(C) the supervising ethics office determines that approval of the trust arrangement as a qualified blind trust is in the particular case appropriate to assure compliance with applicable laws and regulations.

(g) Political campaign funds, including campaign receipts and expenditures, need not be included in any report filed pursuant to this title.

(h) A report filed pursuant to subsection (c) or (d) of section 301 need not contain the information described in subparagraphs (A), (B), and (C) of subsection (a)(2) of this section with respect to gifts and reimbursements received in a period when the reporting individual was not an officer or employee of the Federal Government.

(Pub.L. 95–521, Title III, § 302, Oct. 26, 1978, 92 Stat. 851; Pub.L. 96–19, §§ 3(a)(3), (b), 6, 7(a) to (c), (d)(2), (e), (f), 9(c)(3), (j), (q), June 13, 1979, 93 Stat. 39, 40–43; Pub.L. 98–150, § 10, Nov. 11, 1983, 97 Stat. 962.)

[1] So in original. Probably should be "section".

[2] So in original. Probably should be "title 18,".

[3] So in original. Probably should be "(iv)".

§ 303. Filing of reports

(a) The Judicial Conference of the United States shall establish a Judicial Ethics Committee which shall be responsible for developing the forms for reporting the information required by this title and for receiving and making available, in accordance with the provisions of this title, the reports described in section 301.

(b) Each judicial officer and judicial employee shall file the report required by this title with the Committee and shall file a copy of such report as a public document with the clerk of the court on which he sits or serves.

(c) In the performance of its functions under this title, the Committee, with the approval of the Judicial Conference of the United States, shall—

(1) develop the necessary forms and promulgate such rules and regulations as may be necessary;

(2) monitor and investigate compliance with the requirements of this title;

(3) provide for the availability of reports as required by section 305;

(4) conduct, or cause to be conducted, the reviews required by section 306;

(5) cooperate with the Attorney General in enforcing the requirements of this title;

(6) submit to the Congress and the President recommendations for legislative revision of this title; and

(7) perform such other functions as may be assigned by the Judicial Conference of the United States.

(d) The Committee shall, within one hundred and twenty days after October 26, 1978, develop and, with the approval of the Judicial Conference of the United States, promulgate a regulation establishing a method or methods for readily determining, without the necessity for expert appraisal, the fair market value of assets required to be disclosed by this title.

(Pub.L. 95–521, Title III, § 303, Oct. 26, 1978, 92 Stat. 1858; Pub.L. 96–19, § 9(r), June 13, 1979, 93 Stat. 43.)

§ 304. Failure to file or falsifying reports

(a) The Attorney General may bring a civil action in any appropriate United States District Court against any individual who knowingly and willfully falsifies or who knowingly or willfully fails to file or report any information that such individual is required to report pursuant to section 302. The court in which such action is brought may assess against such individual a civil penalty in any amount not to exceed $5,000.

(b) The Committee shall refer to the Attorney General the name of any individual the Committee has reasonable cause to believe has willfully failed to file a report or has willfully falsified or failed to file information required to be reported.

(Pub.L. 95–521, Title III, § 304, Oct. 26, 1978, 92 Stat. 1858.)

§ 305. Custody of and public access to reports

(a) The Committee shall make each report filed with it under this title available to the public in accordance with subsection (b) of this section.

(b)(1) The Committee shall, within fifteen days after any report is received by the Committee under this title, permit inspection by or furnish a copy of such report to any person requesting such inspection or copy. The Committee may require the requesting person to pay a reasonable fee in any amount which is found necessary to recover the cost of reproduction or mailing of such report excluding any salary of any employee involved in such reproduction or mailing. A copy of such report may be furnished without charge or at a reduced charge if it is determined that waiver or reduction of the fee is in the public interest.

(2) Notwithstanding paragraph (1), a report may not be made available under this section to any person nor may any copy thereof be provided under this section to any person except upon a written application by such person stating—

(A) that person's name, occupation and address;

(B) the name and address of any other person or organization on whose behalf the inspection or copy is requested; and

(C) that such person is aware of the prohibitions on the obtaining or use of the report.

Any such application shall be made available to the public throughout the period during which the report is made available to the public.

(c)(1) It shall be unlawful for any person to obtain or use a report—

(A) for any unlawful purpose;

(B) for any commercial purpose other than by news and communications media for dissemination to the general public;

(C) for determining or establishing the credit rating of any individual; or

(D) for use, directly or indirectly, in the solicitation of money for any political, charitable, or other purpose.

(2) The Attorney General may bring a civil action against any person who obtains or uses a report for any purpose prohibited in paragraph (1). The court in which such action is brought may assess against such person a penalty in any amount not to exceed $5,000. Such remedy shall be in addition to any other remedy available under statutory or common law.

(d) Any report received by the Committee shall be held in its custody and be made available to the public for a period of six years after receipt of the report. After such six-year period the report shall be destroyed unless needed in an ongoing investigation, except that in the case of an individual who filed the report pursuant to section 301(b) and was not subsequently confirmed by the Senate, such reports shall be destroyed one year after the individual is no longer under consideration by the Senate unless needed in an ongoing investigation.

(Pub.L. 95–521, Title III, § 305, Oct. 26, 1978, 92 Stat. 1859; Pub.L. 96–19, § 8(c), June 13, 1979, 93 Stat. 41.)

§ 306. Compliance procedures

(a) The Committee shall establish procedures for the review of reports filed with it under this title to determine whether the reports are filed in a timely manner, are complete, and are in proper form. In the event a determination is made that a report is not so filed, the Committee shall so inform the reporting individual and direct him to take all necessary corrective action.

(b) Such procedures shall include provisions for conducting a review each year of financial statements filed in that year by judicial officers and employees to determine whether such statements reveal possible violations of applicable conflict of interest laws or regulations and recommending appropriate action to correct any conflict of interest or ethical problems revealed by such review.

(Pub.L. 95–521, Title III, § 306, Oct. 26, 1978, 92 Stat. 1859.)

§ 307. Additional requirements

(a) Nothing in this title shall be construed to prevent the Committee, with the approval of the Judicial Conference of the United States, from requiring officers or employees of the judicial branch not covered by this title to submit confidential financial statements.

(b) The Committee, with the approval of the Judicial Conference, may require disclosure, in the reports filed pursuant to subsections (a) and (c) of section 302, of gifts received by a dependent child of a reporting individual if the information required to be disclosed does not exceed that which must be reported by a spouse of a reporting individual under this title.

(c) Nothing in this Act requiring reporting of information shall be deemed to authorize the receipt of income, gifts, or reimbursements; the holding of assets, liabilities, or positions; or the participation in transactions that are prohibited by law or regulation.

(d) The provisions of this title requiring the reporting of information shall not supersede the requirements of section 7342 of title 5.

(Pub.L. 95–521, Title III, § 307, Oct. 26, 1978, 92 Stat. 1860.)

§ 308. Definitions

For the purposes of this title, the term—

(1) "income" means all income from whatever source derived, including but not limited to the following items: compensation for services, including fees, commissions, and similar items; gross income derived from business (and net income if the individual elects to include it); gains derived from dealings in property; interest; rents; royalties; dividends; annuities; income from life insurance and endowment contracts; pensions; income from discharge of indebtedness; distributive share of partnership income; and income from an interest in an estate or trust;

(2) "relative" means an individual who is related to the reporting individual, as father, mother, son, daughter, brother, sister, uncle, aunt, great aunt, great uncle, first cousin, nephew, niece, husband, wife, grandfather, grandmother, grandson, granddaughter, father-in-law, mother-in-law, son-in-law, daughter-in-law, brother-in-law, sister-in-law, stepfather, stepmother, stepson, stepdaughter, stepbrother, stepsister, half brother, half sister, or who is the grandfather or grandmother of the spouse of the reporting individual, and shall be deemed to include the fiance or fiancee of the reporting individual;

(3) "gift" means a payment, advance, forebearance, rendering, or deposit of money, or any thing of value, unless consideration of equal or greater value is received by the donor, but does not include—

(A) bequest and other forms of inheritance;

(B) suitable mementos of a function honoring the reporting individual;

(C) food, lodging, transportation, and entertainment provided by a foreign government within a foreign country or by the United States Government;

(D) food and beverages consumed at banquets, receptions, or similar events; or

(E) communications to the offices of a reporting individual including subscriptions to newspapers and periodicals;

(4) "honoraria" has the meaning given such term in the Federal Election Campaign Act of 1971 [2 U.S.C.A. § 431 et seq.].

(5) "value" means a good faith estimate of the dollar value if the exact value is neither known nor easily obtainable by the reporting individual;

(6) "personal hospitality of any individual" means hospitality extended for a nonbusiness purpose by an individual, not a corporation or organization, at the personal residence of that individual or his family or on property or facilities owned by that individual or his family;

(7) "dependent child" means, when used with respect to any reporting individual, any individual who is a son, daughter, stepson, or stepdaughter and who—

(A) is unmarried and under age 21 and is living in the household of such reporting individual; or

(B) is a dependent of such reporting individual within the meaning of section 152 of title 26;

(8) "reimbursement" means any payment or other thing of value received by the reporting individual, other than gifts, to cover travel-related expenses of such individual other than those which are—

(A) provided by the United States Government;

(B) required to be reported by the reporting individual under section 7342 of title 5; or

(C) required to be reported under section 434 of title 2;

(9) "judicial officer" means the Chief Justice of the United States, the Associate Justices of the Supreme Court, and the judges of the United States courts of appeals; United States district courts, including the district courts in the Canal Zone, Guam, and the Virgin Islands; Court of Claims; Court of Appeals for the Federal Circuit; Court of International Trade; Tax Court; United States Court of Military Appeals [now United States Court of Appeals for the Armed Forces]; United States Court of Veterans Appeals; and any court created by Act of Congress, the judges of which are entitled to hold office during good behavior; and

(10) "judicial employee" means any employee of the judicial branch of the Government, of the Tax Court, of the United States Court of Military Appeals [now United States Court of Appeals for the Armed Forces], or of the United States Court of Veterans Appeals who is not a judicial officer and who is authorized to perform adjudicatory functions with respect to proceedings in the judicial branch, or who receives compensation at a rate at or in excess of the minimum rate prescribed for grade 16 of the General Schedule under section 5332 of title 5.

(Pub.L. 95–521, Title III, § 308, Oct. 26, 1978, 92 Stat. 1860; Pub.L. 96–19, §§ 4(c), 9(d), June 13, 1979, 93 Stat. 40, 42; Pub.L. 96–417, title VI, § 601(9), Oct. 10, 1980, 94 Stat. 1744; Pub.L. 96–579, § 12(c), Dec. 23, 1980, 94 Stat. 3369; Pub.L. 97–164, title I, § 163(a)(6), Apr. 2, 1982, 96 Stat. 49; Pub.L. 99–514, § 2, Oct. 22, 1986, 100 Stat. 2095; Pub.L. 99–573,

§ 6(b), Oct. 28, 1986, 100 Stat. 3231; Pub.L. 101–237, title VI, § 602(a)(1), Dec. 18, 1989, 103 Stat. 2094.)

§ 309. Effective Date

This title shall take effect on January 1, 1979, and the reports filed under section 301(c) on May 15, 1979, shall include information for calendar year 1978.

(Pub.L. 95–521, Title III, § 309, Oct. 26, 1978, 92 Stat. 1861.)

Filing of Reports by Judges, Judicial Nominees, and Employees of United States Court of Veterans Appeals

Pub.L. 101–237, Title VI, § 602(a)(2), Dec. 18, 1989, 103 Stat. 2095, provided that: "Not later than 30 days after the date of the enactment of this Act [Dec. 18, 1989], each person who, on that date, is a judge of the United States Court of Veterans Appeals or a judicial employee of such court and each person who, before that date, has been nominated by the President to be a judge on such court shall file a report containing the information described in section 302(b) of the Ethics in Government Act of 1978 (28 U.S.C.App. 302(b)) [former section 302(b) of this Appendix]. Subsections (e), (f), and (g) of section 302 of such Act [former section 302(e), (f) and (g) of this Appendix] shall apply to the requirement in the preceding sentence."

CONSOLIDATED INDEX

Federal Rules and Supplemental Rules of Civil Procedure

Rules of Procedure of the Judicial Panel on Multidistrict Litigation

Rules Governing Section 2254 Cases (Habeas Corpus) and Section 2255 Proceedings (Motion Attacking Sentence)

Federal Rules of Evidence

Federal Rules of Appellate Procedure

Rules of the Supreme Court of the United States

Title 28 U.S. Code, Judiciary and Judicial Procedure

Title 5 U.S. Code, App. 4, Financial Disclosure Requirements

Constitution of the United States (See text following Titles 28 and 5 U.S. Code)

CITATION ABBREVIATIONS

FRCVP	**Federal Rules of Civil Procedure Rule**
FRCVP	**Supplemental Rules to the Federal Rules of Civil Procedure—Admiralty and Maritime Claims**
FRCVP Form	**Federal Rules of Civil Procedure Form**
MDL	**Rules of Procedure of the Judicial Panel on Multidistrict Litigation**
HCR	**Rules Governing Section 2254 Cases (Habeas Corpus)**
MAS	**Rules Governing Section 2255 Proceedings (Motion Attacking Sentence)**
FRE	**Federal Rules of Evidence**
FRAP	**Federal Rules of Appellate Procedure Rule**
FRAP Form	**Federal Rules of Appellate Procedure Form**
SCR	**Rules of the Supreme Court of the United States**
28 §____	**Sections of Title 28 United States Code, Judiciary and Judicial Procedure**
5, Ap 4, §____	**Financial Disclosure Requirements of Federal Personnel**
EON	**Executive Order Number**
nt	**Note**

ABANDONMENT
Bankruptcy, generally, this index

ABATEMENT AND REVIVAL
Death of party,
Defendant in damage action, commenced by or on behalf of U.S., **28 § 2404**
Reversal in Supreme Court or courts of appeals for errors in ruling on matters in abatement not involving jurisdiction, **28 § 2105**

ABDUCTION
Kidnapping, generally, this index
Missing Children, generally, this index

ABUSE OF PROCESS
Tort Claims Act, exception of claim, **28 § 2680**

ABUSIVE SEXUAL CONDUCT
Sexual Abuse, generally, this index

ACCIDENTS
Workers Compensation, generally, this index

ACCOUNTS AND ACCOUNTING
Audits and Auditors, generally, this index
General Accounting Office, generally, this index
Indians,
Tribal trust fund accounts, forest land assistance accounts. Indian Lands and Reservations, generally, this index
Judicial Center, services provided for, **28 § 628**
Officers and Employees of Government, this index
Rules of Civil Procedure, this index

ACKNOWLEDGMENTS
Clerks of courts, power to take, **28 § 953**
Justice or judge of U.S., authorized to take, **28 § 459**

ACTIONS AND PROCEEDINGS
Abatement and Revival, generally, this index
Administrative Law and Procedure, generally, this index
Admiralty, generally, this index
Aliens, this index
Ambassadors, **28 § 1251**
Amount in Controversy, generally, this index
Arbitration, generally, this index
Arrest in one district for trial in another, **28 § 1693**
Attorney General, generally, this index
Bank Fraud Crimes, generally, this index
Bankruptcy, this index
Bankruptcy Rules and Forms, this index
Bonds, this index
Civil justice reform, **28 § 519 nt, EON 12988**

ACTIONS AND PROCEEDINGS
—Cont'd
Civil Rights, this index
Claims, generally, this index
Constitution (U.S.),
Against U.S., trial by court, **28 § 2402**
Continuances, generally, this index
Copyrights, this index
Corporations, this index
Counterclaim. Set-Off and Counterclaim, generally, this index
Court of International Trade. United States Court of International Trade, generally, this index
Crimes and Offenses, generally, this index
Declaratory judgments, **28 § 2201**
Delinquents for public money, action by U.S. against, **28 § 2407**
Derivative Actions, generally, this index
Detention, generally, this index
Dismissal and Nonsuit, generally, this index
Dispute resolution, alternative means of. Administrative Law and Procedure, generally, this index
Disqualification of justice or judge to sit, **28 § 455**
District Courts, generally, this index
Eminent Domain, generally, this index
Equity, generally, this index
Evidence, generally, this index
Execution, generally, this index
Federal Debt Collection, this index
Federal Employers' Liability Act, generally, this index
Federal Legal Council, functions, concerning, **28 § 509 nt, EON 12146**
Fines, Penalties and Forfeitures, generally, this index
Forma Pauperis, generally, this index
Frivolous actions, inmates, **28 § 1915A**
Independent Counsel, generally, this index
Indians, this index
Injunctions, generally, this index
Internal Revenue Service, this index
Interpleader, generally, this index
Intervention, generally, this index
Judgments and Decrees, generally, this index
Judicial review. Appeal and Review, generally, this index
Jurisdiction, generally, this index
Justice, judge, Magistrate Judge, disqualification, **28 § 455**
Limitation of Actions, generally, this index
Managers of property, suit against without leave of court appointing them, **28 § 959**
Ministers of foreign states, **28 § 1251**
Monopolies and Combinations, this index
National Banks, this index
Nonsuit. Dismissal and Nonsuit, generally, this index

ACTIONS AND PROCEEDINGS
—Cont'd
Officers and employees of Government,
Compelling performance of duty, jurisdiction, **28 § 1361**
Violating income and employment limitations, **5, Ap 4, § 504**
Parties, generally, this index
Partition, generally, this index
Patents, this index
Pending actions,
In U.S. courts, number, report by Attorney General, **28 § 522**
Involving real property, registration of notice under State law, as constructive notice, **28 § 1964**
Place of arrest, civil action, **28 § 1693**
Postal Service, this index
Process, generally, this index
Protection of jurors' employment, discharge by employer, **28 § 1875**
Quieting Title, this index
Receivers and Receivership, this index
Release, generally, this index
Removal of Cases or Causes, generally, this index
Seamen,
Prepayment of fees or costs unnecessary, **28 § 1916**
Searches and Seizures, generally, this index
Senate, this index
Set-Off and Counterclaim, generally, this index
States, this index
Stay of Proceedings, generally, this index
Stipulations, generally, this index
Summons, generally, this index
Surface Transportation Board, this index
Torts, generally, this index
Torture victim protection, civil liability, **28 § 1350 nt**
Transfer of Cases or Causes, generally, this index
Trustees, suits against without leave of court appointing them, **28 § 959**
United States, this index
United States attorneys, duties, **28 § 547**
Venue or District of Trial, generally, this index
Witnesses, generally, this index
Writs, generally, this index

ACTS OF CONGRESS
Statutes, generally, this index

ADDICT AND ADDICTS
Drug Abuse Prevention, Control and Treatment, generally, this index
Immigration, generally, this index
Narcotic Drug Addicts, generally, this index
National Drug Policy, generally, this index

ADMINISTRATION OF ESTATES
Decedents' Estates, generally, this index

ADMINISTRATION OF ESTATES—Cont'd
Executors and Administrators, generally, this index

ADMINISTRATIVE CONFERENCE OF UNITED STATES
Administrative adjudications, recommendation implementation, civil justice reform, **28 § 519 nt, EON 12988**
Chairman,
United States Court of Appeals for District of Columbia, generally, this index
Federal agencies and instrumentalities, administrative adjudications, recommendation implementation, civil justice reform, **28 § 519 nt, EON 12988**
United States Court of Appeals for District of Columbia, generally, this index

ADMINISTRATIVE LAW AND PROCEDURE
Adjudications,
Guidelines, civil justice reform, **28 § 519 nt, EON 12988**
Improving quality, civil justice reform, **28 § 519 nt, EON 12988**
Administrative Conference of United States, generally, this index
Alternative dispute resolution. Dispute resolution, alternative means of, generally, post
Bias, administrative adjudications, civil justice reform, **28 § 519 nt, EON 12988**
Civil action or proceeding,
Brought by or against the United States, defined, award of attorneys' fees and other expenses, **28 § 2412**
Civil justice reform, guidelines, filings, **28 § 519 nt, EON 12988**
Civil justice reform, **28 § 519 nt, EON 12988**
Court, defined, award of attorneys' fees and other expenses, **28 § 2412**
Demand, defined, award of costs and fees, **28 § 2412**
Disclosure,
Civil justice reform, guidelines, **28 § 519 nt, EON 12988**
Dispute resolution, alternative means of,
Attorney General, approval, payment of awards after compromise or settlement, **28 § 2672**
Civil justice reform, **28 § 519 nt, EON 12988**
Federal tort claims, compromise or settlement of, payment, approval of Attorney General, **28 § 2672**
Torts, payments of awards, **28 § 2672**
United States,
Guidelines, civil justice reform, **28 § 519 nt, EON 12988**

ADMINISTRATIVE LAW AND PROCEDURE—Cont'd
Document search,
Guidelines, civil justice reform, **28 § 519 nt, EON 12988**
Excessive demands,
United States as party, award of costs and fees, **28 § 2412**
Fees and other expenses,
Defined,
Award of costs and fees, **28 § 2412**
Social security proceedings, applicability of awards, **28 § 2412 nt**
Final judgment, defined, award of attorneys' fees and other expenses, **28 § 2412**
Guidelines, civil justice reform, **28 § 519 nt, EON 12988**
Hearings,
Witness fees and allowances, **28 § 2412**
Interest, appeal by U.S. agency of award of costs and fees, **28 § 2412**
Legislation, civil justice reform, guidelines for proposals, **28 § 519 nt, EON 12988**
Notice,
Complaints, pre-filing requirements, civil justice reform, **28 § 519 nt, EON 12988**
Parties,
Award of attorneys' fees and other expenses, **28 § 2412**
Payment by agency of fees and other expenses awarded to prevailing party in adversary adjudication, **28 § 2412**
Savings provisions, **28 § 2412 nt**
Position of the United States, defined, award of attorneys' fees and other expenses, **28 § 2412**
Prevailing party, defined, award of attorneys' fees and other expenses, **28 § 2412**
Public education, agency benefits, civil justice reform, **28 § 519 nt, EON 12988**
Rules and regulations,
Civil justice reform, promulgation, principals, **28 § 519 nt, EON 12988**
Rules of Appellate Procedure, this index
Settlement, guidelines, civil justice reform, **28 § 519 nt, EON 12988**
Social security benefits, provisions regarding attorneys' fees, inapplicability to award of fees, to party prevailing against U.S., **28 § 2412 nt**
United States, defined, award of costs and fees, **28 § 2412**
Witnesses, fees and allowances, hearings, **28 § 2412**

ADMINISTRATIVE LAW JUDGES
Attorney General, functions, exception, **28 § 509**

ADMINISTRATIVE OFFICE OF UNITED STATES COURTS
Administrative Law and Procedure, generally, this index
Annuity, retirement, Director, **28 §§ 376, 611**
Appropriations, authorization, Judiciary Information Technology Fund, **28 § 612**
Assistant Director, reference to in other laws deemed to be to Deputy Director, **28 § 601 nt**
Bankruptcy, this index
Circuit court executives, direction as to collection, of statistical data by, **28 § 332**
Clerical court assistants,
Accommodations provided by Director, **28 § 604**
Audit of vouchers and accounts by Director, **28 § 604**
Information furnished to Director, **28 § 604**
Compensation and salaries,
Deputy Director, **28 § 603**
Director, **28 § 603**
Additional positions, fixed by, **28 § 603**
Officers and employees, post
Courts,
Defined, **28 § 610**
Interpreters, this index
Courts of appeals, administrative units of, facilities and staff prescribed by, **28 § 41 nt**
Creation, **28 § 601**
Data processing, Judiciary Information Technology Fund, establishment, **28 § 612**
Deputy Director,
Duties, **28 § 606**
Removal, **28 § 601**
Salary, **28 § 603**
Supervision, **28 § 601**
Director,
Accommodations for courts, providing, **28 §§ 462, 604**
Annual leave and sick leave, not employee for purposes of, **28 § 603**
Annuities,
Retirement and pensions, **28 §§ 376, 611**
Cost of living adjustment, **28 § 611**
To widows and dependents of justices and judges, regulation and payment, **28 § 604**
Appeal in forma pauperis, payment of printing expense, **28 § 1915**
Appointment, **28 § 601**
Assistance of courts, securing information as to need, **28 § 604**
Assumption of duties by judge, appointment of additional judge by President, **28 § 133**

ADMINISTRATIVE OFFICE OF UNITED STATES COURTS—Cont'd
Director—Cont'd
Attorney General requested to investigate official acts, of clerks of courts, **28 § 526**
Audit of vouchers and accounts of court, **28 § 604**
Board of Certification, circuit court executives, appointees certified by, membership, **28 § 332**
Books and periodicals, authority to sell and exchange, **28 § 413**
Budget,
Estimates of courts and Administrative Office, **28 § 605**
Chief judges of circuits, statistical data and reports of business, transmission to, **28 § 604**
Clerical court assistants, generally, ante
Clerks of Courts, generally, this index
Compensation, **28 § 603**
Employees, powers, **28 § 602**
Fixing compensation of clerks of courts, deputies, librarians, **28 § 604**
Secretaries and law clerks of circuit and district judges, fixing, **28 § 604 nt**
Court officers and employees, fixing of traveling expenses, **28 § 604**
Deemed judicial official for purposes of annuities to widows and dependent children of justices or judges, **28 § 376**
Delegation of functions and duties, limitation of powers, **28 § 602**
Deputy Director, generally, ante
Disbursements, **28 § 604**
Fees and allowances for jurors, procedure, establishment by, **28 § 1871**
District courts, reporters,
Approval of appointment of additional reporters, **28 § 753**
Contracts for additional reporters, **28 § 753**
Duties, **28 § 604**
Equipment and supplies, purchasing for courts, **28 § 604**
Examination, state of dockets, **28 § 604**
Expenses of litigation, costs of defense of action against judge, justice, when payable by, **28 § 463**
Fees, prescribing schedule, electronic access to information, **28 § 1913 nt**
Fines, penalties and forfeitures,
Forfeitures of bail bonds, establishment of procedures and mechanisms, **28 § 604**
Functions of officers, employees and organizational units vested in, **28 § 602**

ADMINISTRATIVE OFFICE OF UNITED STATES COURTS—Cont'd
Director—Cont'd
Independent Counsel, administrative support and guidance, provision, **28 § 594**
Inspection of dockets outside continental U.S., **28 § 604**
Judgments, district courts, interest on, rates, distribution of notice, **28 § 1961**
Judicial Conference,
Reprogramming of funds, Judiciary Information Technology Fund, **28 § 612**
Supervision and direction of, **28 § 604**
Judicial Survivors Annuity Fund, causing examination to be made, **28 § 605**
Justices or judges, election to participate in survivors annuity system, time, filing with, **28 § 376**
Law Books, generally, this index
Librarians, compensation fixed by, **28 § 604**
Library assistant in courts of appeals, appointment by librarian with approval of, **28 § 713**
Long range management and business plans, development, **28 § 612**
Messengers, appointments by criers in courts of appeals with approval of, **28 § 714**
Notice,
Appointment of United States Magistrate Judges, **28 § 631**
Circuit and district judges, change of residence, **28 § 456**
Office expenses of courts, judges, determination and payment, **28 § 604**
Office of Management and Budget, budget estimates of court submitted to, **28 § 605**
Officers and employees, equal employment opportunity programs for employees in competitive service, litigation, when costs of defense payable by, **28 § 463**
Organizational units, functions vested in Director, **28 § 602**
Payment of traveling expenses to justices and judges, **28 § 456**
Personnel Management System, powers, duties, **28 § 602 nt**
Pretrial Services, generally, this index
Probation officers,
Provisions of accommodations for, **28 § 462**
Questions of dependency and disability decided by, annuities for survivors of judges or justices, **28 § 376**
Recycling and recyclable materials, utilization, sale, or disposal, **28 § 604**
Removal, **28 § 601**

ADMINISTRATIVE OFFICE OF UNITED STATES COURTS—Cont'd
Director—Cont'd
Reports, **28 §§ 332, 604**
Chief judge to submit to judicial councils, **28 § 332**
Congress, annual, progress and functioning of Fund, **28 § 612**
Reprogramming,
Transfer of funds, requirements, **28 § 612**
Utilization of funds, requirements, **28 § 612**
Request for convening of institutes and joint councils on sentencing, **28 § 334**
Restitution,
Procedures and mechanisms for, establishment by, **28 § 604**
Retirement and pensions, **28 §§ 376, 611**
Retroactive effect, **28 § 611 nt**
Service, defined, **28 § 611**
Retroactive effect, retirement and survivorship benefits, **28 § 611 nt**
Rules and regulations, interim travel allowances to jurors, **28 § 1871**
Savings and loan crisis, statistical tables, **28 § 604**
Seal, **28 § 608**
Secretaries, compensation fixed by, **28 § 604**
Secretaries and law clerks of circuit and district court judges, compensation fixed by, **28 § 604 nt**
Securing information, assistance required by courts, **28 § 604**
Service, defined, retirement, **28 § 611**
Staff of attorneys and secretarial and clerical employees in courts of appeals, appointment, approval, **28 § 715**
Statistical data concerning business of courts, preparation and transmission, **28 § 604**
Stenographers, compensation fixed by, **28 § 604**
Submission of required reports, to Congress and Attorney General, **28 § 604**
Supervision, **28 §§ 601, 604**
Technical assistants in courts of appeals, appointment, approval, **28 § 715**
Transportation, appropriations, passenger carrier use, **28 § 456**
Travel allowance for jurors, establishment of minimum rate by, **28 § 1871**
Travel and subsistence expenses, payment to justices and judges, **28 § 456**
Travel reimbursement, **28 § 604**

ADMINISTRATIVE OFFICE OF UNITED STATES COURTS—Cont'd
Director—Cont'd
United States Magistrate Judges,
Compilation, statistical and other information required for performance of duties respecting, **28 § 604**
Copy of U.S. Code, duty to furnish to, **28 § 638**
Director, defined, **28 § 639**
Disbursement of salaries made by or pursuant to order of, **28 § 634**
Docket books and forms, duty to furnish to, **28 § 638**
Expenses and compensation determined and paid by, regulations, **28 § 635**
Notice of appointment given to, **28 § 631**
Payment of office expenses and other compensation, **28 § 635**
Proceedings before magistrate judge specially designated to try persons in district court, authorization, payment of expenses, **28 § 1915**
Purchase, law books, needed for maintenance and operation of officers of, **28 § 604**
Reimbursement of part-time Magistrate Judges for expenses incurred, **28 § 635**
Rules and regulations respecting, promulgation, **28 § 604**
Statistical tables and information reflecting business which has come before Magistrate Judges, duty to lay before Congress, **28 § 604**
Supervision of administrative matters relating to offices of, **28 § 604**
Surveys respecting, **28 § 633**
United States trustees, use of court services, facilities, cooperative arrangements with Attorney General respecting, **28 § 581 nt**
Vacancy in office, performance of duties, **28 § 606**
Waiver, coverage under civil service retirement, **28 §§ 376, 611**
Employees. Officers and employees, generally, post
Exchange of personal property, powers of Director, **28 § 604**
Federal Public Defender Organizations, provisions of accommodations for, **28 § 462**
Habeas corpus, capital cases, reports, **28 § 2266**
Incentive Pay or Awards, generally, this index
Information technology, Judiciary Information Technology Fund, **28 § 612**

ADMINISTRATIVE OFFICE OF UNITED STATES COURTS—Cont'd
Judiciary Information Technology Fund, establishment, **28 § 612**
Juror qualification form, prescribing, **28 § 1869**
Librarians, compensation fixed by Director, **28 § 604**
Notice, plan for,
Random jury selection, adoption or modification, **28 § 1863**
Office of Federal Judicial Administration, defined, effect of appointing judge as director of certain judicial branch agencies, **28 § 133**
Officers and employees, **28 § 602**
Appointments, competitive status, Personnel Management System, **28 § 602 nt**
Compensation and salaries,
Additional positions, fixed by Director, **28 § 603**
Increase in compensation rates, **28 § 603 nt**
Personnel Management System, **28 § 602 nt**
Grievance procedure, Personnel Management System, **28 § 602 nt**
Incentive Pay or Awards, generally, this index
Personnel Management System, **28 § 602 nt**
Practice of law in U.S. courts prohibited, **28 § 607**
Personnel Management System, establishment, functions, **28 § 602 nt**
Pretrial Services, this index
Public utility services, contracts for, powers of director, **28 § 604**
Reports,
Habeas corpus, capital cases, **28 § 2266**
Jury selection process, **28 § 1863**
Rules and regulations,
Payment of expenses of litigation directed against judge or justice, **28 § 463**
Standards of conduct, publication in Federal Register, powers of Director to promulgate, **28 § 604**
Travel and subsistence expenses, promulgation by Director, **28 § 604 nt**
Secretaries, compensation,
Fixed by Director, **28 § 604**
Increase, **28 § 603 nt**
Limitation, **28 § 604 nt**
Stenographers, compensation,
Fixed by Director, **28 § 604**
Increase, **28 § 603 nt**
Terminal equipment, contracts for, powers of Director, **28 § 604**
United States Court of Federal Claims, this index
United States Magistrate Judges. Director, ante

ADMINISTRATIVE OFFICE OF UNITED STATES COURTS—Cont'd
Voluntary and uncompensated services, acceptance and use by Director, **28 § 604**

ADMIRALTY
See, also, Ships and Shipping, generally, this index
Appeals,
Docket fees, taxation as costs, **28 § 1923**
Interlocutory decisions of district courts to courts of appeals, **28 § 1292**
Printing of briefs, taxation as costs, **28 § 1923**
Arrest of,
Property, discharge from arrest, **28 § 2464**
Bonds, stay of execution of process in rem, **28 § 2464**
Briefs, appeals, taxation of printing as costs, **28 § 1923**
Costs,
Docket fees, **28 § 1923**
Fees of U.S. marshal, **28 § 1921**
Taxation prescribed by rules promulgated by Supreme Court, **28 § 1925**
District courts, original jurisdiction, **28 § 1333**
Docket fees, taxation as costs, **28 § 1923**
Fines, penalties and forfeitures, venue of proceedings, **28 § 1395**
Forfeitures, property seized on high seas or navigable waters, **28 § 2461**
Jurisdiction,
District court, **28 § 1333**
Jury trial, **28 § 1873**
Libel,
Fees of U.S. marshal for serving, **28 § 1921**
Forfeiture of property taken on high seas or navigable waters, **28 § 2461**
Maritime lien, suit to enforce, jurisdictional immunities of foreign states, exception, **28 § 1605**
Orders of court, stay of execution of process in rem issued in admiralty, **28 § 2464**
Printing of appeal briefs, taxation as costs, **28 § 1923**
Prize (Vessels), generally, this index
Process, stay of execution of process, **28 § 2464**
Proclamation, preparation, fees of U.S. marshal, **28 § 1921**
Rules of Civil Procedure, this index
Sale of vessels, fees of U.S. marshal, **28 § 1921**
Seizures in admiralty,
High seas or navigable waters, forfeiture of property in admiralty, **28 § 2461**

ADMIRALTY—Cont'd
Seizures in admiralty—Cont'd
Not within admiralty jurisdiction, jurisdiction of district court, **28 § 1356**
Special bond, stay of execution of process in rem, **28 § 2464**
Stipulation, stay of execution of process in rem, **28 § 2464**
Tort Claims Act, exception of claims for which remedy is provided under Suits in Admiralty Act, **28 § 2680**
United States Court of International Trade, this index
United States marshals,
Expenses of keeping boats, vessels, attached or libeled, **28 § 1921**
Fees for serving libel, **28 § 1921**
Venue,
Enforcement of fines, penalties and forfeitures against vessels, **28 § 1395**
Warrant of arrest or other process in rem, stay of execution of process, **28 § 2464**

ADMISSIBILITY IN EVIDENCE
Evidence, generally, this index

ADMISSIONS
Rules of Civil Procedure, this index

ADOPTION
Citizens and Citizenship, generally, this index

ADVANCE PAYMENT
Advances, generally, this index

ADVANCES
Justice Department, payment, moneys appropriated for, requisitions, **28 § 523**

ADVERSE OR PECUNIARY INTEREST
Conflicts of Interest, generally, this index

ADVERSE POSSESSION
Quieting title, actions against U.S., construction of provisions, **28 § 2409a**

ADVISORY COMMITTEES
Courts of appeals, appointment, study of rules of practice, **28 § 2077**

AFFIDAVITS
Attachment against delinquent postmasters and postal officers, employees, application for warrant, **28 § 2711**
Costs, this index
District judges, bias or prejudice, **28 § 144**
Evidence in habeas corpus proceeding, **28 § 2246**
Federal agencies, review of orders, hearings, proceedings in court of appeals, **28 § 2347**
Federal Debt Collection, this index

AFFIDAVITS—Cont'd
Forma pauperis, proceeding in, **28 § 1915**
Jury service, summons for service by registered, certified, or first-class mail, **28 § 1866**
Removal of case, supplying record by affidavit, **28 § 1449**
Rules of Appellate Procedure, this index
Rules of Civil Procedure, this index
United States Court of International Trade, this index

AFFIRMATIONS
Oaths and Affirmations, generally, this index

AFFIRMATIVE ACTION PROGRAMS
Equal employment opportunity, generally. Civil Rights, this index

AFRICAN AMERICANS
Black Persons, generally, this index

AGE
Rules of Civil Procedure, this index

AGED PERSONS
Crimes and offenses against,
Sentencing Commission, guidelines, criteria, violent crime control, **28 § 994 nt**
Fraud, older victims, sentencing guideline adjustments, review and report, **28 § 994 nt**
Health Insurance for Aged and Disabled, generally, this index
Social Security, generally, this index

AGENCIES OR INSTRUMENTALITIES OF UNITED STATES
Federal Agencies and Instrumentalities, generally, this index

AGENTS AND AGENCIES
Bill of costs, affidavit verifying, **28 § 1924**
Court agents conducting business, tax liability, **28 § 960**
Disbursing Officials, Clerks, and Agents, generally, this index
Executive Agencies, generally, this index
Federal Agencies and Instrumentalities, generally, this index
Patent infringement action, defendant not resident of district, service of process, on agent, **28 § 1694**
Service of Process, this index

AGGRAVATED SEXUAL ABUSE
Sexual Abuse, generally, this index

AGREEMENTS
Contracts, generally, this index

AGRICULTURAL ASSOCIATIONS AND ORGANIZATIONS
Attorneys' fees and other costs and expenses, award to party prevailing against U.S. or agency, applicability, **28 § 2412**

AGRICULTURAL ORGANIZATIONS
Agricultural Associations and Organizations, generally, this index

AGRICULTURE DEPARTMENT
Community development, neighborhood revitalization plan, development by Attorney General, use of appropriated funds, **28 § 509 nt**

AGRICULTURE SECRETARY
Secretary of Agriculture, generally, this index

AIR FORCE
See, also,
Armed Forces, generally, this index
Uniformed Services, generally, this index
Air Force Reserve. Reserves, generally, post
Department of the Air Force. Air Force Department, generally, this index
National Cemeteries, generally, this index
Reserves,
Retirement and pensions,
United States Magistrate Judges, eligibility of retired officers and enlisted personnel for appointment and service as, **28 § 631**
United States Magistrate Judges, eligibility of retired officers, enlisted personnel and members for appointment and service as, **28 § 631**
Retirement and pensions,
Enlisted members,
United States Magistrate Judges, eligibility for appointment and service as, **28 § 631**
Reserves, ante
United States Magistrate Judges, appointment and service as, **28 § 631**
Secretary of Air Force, generally, this index
Tort Claims Act, exception of claim arising out of combatant activities, **28 § 2680**
United States Magistrate Judges, eligibility of retired officers and enlisted personnel for appointment and service as, **28 § 631**

AIR FORCE DEPARTMENT
See, also, Military Departments, generally, this index
Attorney General's advice concerning, **28 § 513**

AIR FORCE DEPARTMENT—Cont'd
Secretary of Air Force, generally, this index

AIR FORCE RESERVE
Reserves, generally. Air Force, this index

AIR FORCE SECRETARY
Secretary of Air Force, generally, this index

AIR NATIONAL GUARD
See, also, National Guard, generally, this index
Cemeteries and dead bodies. National Cemeteries, generally, this index
National Cemeteries, generally, this index
Technicians. National Guard, generally, this index

AIRCRAFT
Drug Abuse Prevention, Control and Treatment, this index

ALABAMA
See, also, States, generally, this index
Bankruptcy, judges, appointment, number in judicial district, **28 § 152**
District courts,
Cities, held at, **28 § 81**
Judges,
Additional, **28 § 133 nt**
Existing judgeships for middle and southern districts consolidated as judgeship for southern district, **28 § 133 nt**
Number, **28 § 133**
Temporary judgeships, **28 § 133 nt**
Places of holding, **28 § 81**
Judicial circuit of U.S., **28 § 41**
Judicial districts, **28 § 81**
Bankruptcy provisions, applicability of certain amendments to, **28 § 581 nt**
Judgeships for middle and southern districts combined into southern district only, **28 § 133 nt**
Number of district judges, **28 § 133**
United States trustees of judicial districts, appointment, **28 § 581**

ALASKA
See, also, States, generally, this index
Admission into Union,
Not to affect rights of retired judges of District Court for the Territory, **28 § 373 nt**
Bankruptcy judges, appointment, number in judicial district, **28 § 152**
District Court for Territory,
Appeals to Supreme Court or Court of Appeals for Ninth Circuit prosecuted to final determination, **28 § 81A nt**
Continuation of suits, upon admission into Union, **28 § 81A nt**

ALASKA—Cont'd
District Court for Territory—Cont'd
Jurisdiction of pending cases not transferred to U.S. District Court, exercise by State courts, **28 § 81A nt**
Pending cases not transferred to U.S. District Court, determination by State courts, **28 § 81A nt**
State court as successor court, **28 § 81A nt**
Tenure of judges, termination of, **28 §§ 81A nt, 81A nt, EON 10867**
Termination of jurisdiction, **28 §§ 81A nt, 81A nt, EON 10867**
Transfer of cases to U.S. District Court, **28 § 81A nt**
District courts, **28 § 81A**
Assumption of functions, **28 § 81A nt, EON 10867**
Cities, held at, **28 § 81A**
Final judgments and decrees in transferred cases, review of, **28 § 81A nt**
Places of holding, **28 § 81A**
Prosecution of actions or criminal offenses arising prior to admission into Union, **28 § 81A nt**
Transfer of causes from territorial district court, **28 § 81A nt**
Indians,
Claims of tribe or band against U.S., jurisdiction and procedure of U.S. Court of Federal Claims, **28 § 1505**
Jurisdiction,
Actions to which Indians are parties, **28 § 1360**
Judges, **28 § 133**
Additional, **28 § 133 nt**
Admission into Union not to affect rights of retired judges for the Territory, **28 §§ 373 nt, 376 nt**
Computation, judicial service, **28 § 371 nt**
Inclusion of judicial service in certain courts in computing aggregate years of judicial service for retirement, **28 § 371 nt**
Tenure, termination, **28 § 81A nt, EON 10867**
Judicial circuit of U.S., **28 § 41**
Judicial district, **28 § 81A**
Bankruptcy provisions, applicability of certain amendments to, **28 § 581 nt**
Number of district judges, **28 § 133**
Jurisdiction,
Civil actions to which Indians are parties, **28 § 1360**
Marshals, tenure, termination, **28 § 81A nt, EON 10867**
President of the United States, this index
United States attorneys and assistants, tenure, termination, **28 § 81A nt, EON 10867**

ALASKA—Cont'd
United States trustees of judicial districts, appointment, **28 § 581**

ALCOHOLICS AND ALCOHOLISM
Common carriers, operation under influence, sentencing guidelines,
Authority and duties of Sentencing Commission, **28 § 994 nt**
Drug Abuse Prevention, Control and Treatment, generally, this index

ALIENS
See, also,
Citizens and Citizenship, generally, this index
Immigration, generally, this index
Actions and proceedings,
Court of Federal Claims, privilege to sue, **28 § 2502**
Removal of action by alien against civil officer of U.S. who is non-citizen of State, **28 § 1442**
Supreme Court, jurisdiction of proceedings by State against aliens, **28 § 1251**
Tort action, jurisdiction of district court, **28 § 1350**
Torture victim protection, civil liability, **28 § 1350 nt**
United States Court of Federal Claims, privilege to sue, **28 § 2502**
Venue of action against, **28 § 1391**
Armed Forces, honorable service in, special immigrant status. Immigration, generally, this index
Bringing in and harboring certain aliens, Sentencing guidelines, **28 § 994 nt**
Citizens and Citizenship, generally, this index
Controlled substances, import and export offense, United States Sentencing Commission, guidelines, **28 § 994 nt**
Court of Federal Claims, privilege to sue, **28 § 2502**
District Courts, this index
Foreign countries, transfer of offenders to or from. Transfer of Offenders to or from Foreign Countries, generally, this index
Foreign Service, generally, this index
Foreign terrorist organizations. Terrorists and Terrorism, generally, this index
Harboring,
Certain aliens,
Sentencing guidelines, **28 § 994 nt**
Immigration, this index
Immigration and Naturalization Service, generally, this index
Imprisonment. Sentence and punishment, generally, post
Income tax,
Refund, civil actions for, limitation on right of action, exception, U.S. Court of Federal Claims, **28 § 2502**

ALIENS—Cont'd
Internal Revenue Service. Income tax, generally, ante
International terrorism. Terrorists and Terrorism, generally, this index
Naturalization, generally, this index
Paroled into the U.S.,
For prosecution, witness fees and allowances, ineligibility for, **28 § 1821**
Passport fraud, sentencing guidelines, **28 § 994 nt**
Proceedings. Actions and proceedings, generally, ante
Punishment. Sentence and punishment, generally, post
Residents, permanent, Federal litigation, jurisdiction, diverse citizenship, deemed residents of State of domicile, **28 § 1332**
Sentence and punishment,
Bringing in and harboring certain aliens,
Guidelines, **28 § 994 nt**
Smuggling, alien smuggling-related crimes, RICO-predicate offenses, establishment as,
Unlawful alien,
Sentencing guidelines, **28 § 994 nt**
Supreme Court jurisdiction of proceeding by State against aliens, **28 § 1251**
Terrorists and Terrorism, generally, this index
Tort action, **28 § 1350**
Torture victim protection, civil action for damages, **28 § 1350 nt**
Transfer of Offenders to or from Foreign Countries, generally, this index
United States Court of Federal Claims, privilege to sue, **28 § 2502**
United States Sentencing Commission, guidelines, enhanced penalties, certain offenses, **28 § 994 nt**
Venue of action against, **28 § 1391**
Visa fraud, sentencing guidelines, **28 § 994 nt**

ALLIANCES
Treaties, generally, this index

ALTERATION OF INSTRUMENTS
Counterfeiting, generally, this index

ALTERNATIVE DISPUTE RESOLUTION
District Courts, this index

ALTERNATIVE WRITS
Power to issue, **28 § 1651**

AMATEUR SPORTS AND ATHLETIC ORGANIZATIONS
Amateur sports organization, defined, U.S. Olympic Committee, **28 § 3701**

AMATEUR SPORTS AND ATHLETIC ORGANIZATIONS—Cont'd
Attorneys' fees and other costs, award to party prevailing against U.S. or agency, applicability, **28 §§ 2412, 2412 nt**

AMBASSADORS AND CONSULS
Foreign Diplomatic and Consular Officers, generally, this index

AMNESTY
Pardon, generally, this index

AMOUNT IN CONTROVERSY
District Courts, this index
United States, action against, interest on judgment, trial by court, **28 § 2402**

ANNUITIES
Director of Administrative Office of U.S. Courts, retirement, **28 §§ 376, 611**
Judges or Justices, this index
Judicial Center, Director of, **28 §§ 376, 627**
Judicial Survivors Annuity Fund, generally, this index
Retirement of Civil Service Employees, this index

ANSWER
Plea or Answer, generally, this index
Rules of Appellate Procedure, this index

APPEAL AND REVIEW
Amendment of pleadings to show jurisdiction, **28 § 1653**
Annuities to survivors of justices and judges, determinations concerning dependency and disability, **28 § 376**
Arbitration,
Alternative means of dispute resolution. Administrative Law and Procedure, generally, this index
Bankruptcy, this index
Certificates,
Appeal in good faith, in forma pauperis proceeding, **28 § 1915**
Certification by Attorney General of no appeal from judgment against U.S., **28 § 2414**
Communications Commission,
Telecommunications, this index
Congressional reference cases, **28 § 2509**
Costs,
Forma pauperis, proceedings in, **28 § 1915**
Seamen, prepayment unnecessary, **28 § 1916**
Crimes and offenses,
State courts, priority, **28 § 2102**
Declaratory judgments, **28 § 2201**
Disqualification of justice or judge to sit, **28 § 455**
District Courts, this index
Docket fees, taxation as costs, **28 § 1923**
Extension, time for appeal, **28 § 2107**

APPEAL AND REVIEW—Cont'd
Federal agency action,
Judicial review,
Record on review in courts of appeals of orders of administrative agencies, **28 § 2112**
Venue of proceedings, **28 § 1391**
Fees,
Docket fee, **28 § 1923**
Forma pauperis proceeding, **28 § 1915**
Seamen, prepayment unnecessary, **28 § 1916**
Forma pauperis, **28 § 1915**
Transcripts, fees of district court reporter, **28 § 753**
Habeas Corpus, this index
Harmless error, judgment, **28 § 2111**
In forma pauperis. Forma pauperis, generally, ante
Injunctions,
Direct appeal to Supreme Court from three-judge court decisions, **28 § 1253**
Interlocutory, orders of district courts to courts of appeals, **28 § 1292**
Judicial review. Federal agency action, ante
Merit Systems Protection Board, this index
Modification of judgment, powers of Supreme Court, courts of appeals, **28 § 2106**
Narcotic drug addicts, civil commitment and rehabilitation, election, **28 § 2906**
Notice,
Allowance of appeal, fees in district court, **28 § 1917**
Federal agency orders, **28 § 2344**
Interlocutory injunction, suspension, of orders, **28 § 2349**
Officers and Employees of Government, this index
Orders of Federal agencies, **28 § 2341 et seq.**
Agency, defined, **28 § 2341**
Attorney General, responsibility and control, **28 § 2348**
Certification, record on review, **28 § 2346**
Clerk, defined, **28 § 2341**
Copies of orders, reports, attached to petition, **28 § 2344**
Definitions, **28 § 2341**
Evidence, proceedings in court of appeals, **28 § 2347**
Final judgment, review in Supreme Court on certiorari or certification, **28 § 2350**
Hearings,
Interlocutory injunction restraining, enforcement, of orders, **28 § 2349**
Proceedings in court of appeals, **28 § 2347**

APPEAL AND REVIEW—Cont'd
Orders of Federal agencies—Cont'd
Interlocutory injunction, suspending, orders, **28 § 2349**
Review in Supreme Court on certiorari or certification, **28 § 2350**
Intervention, **28 § 2348**
Jurisdiction, court of appeals, **28 §§ 2342, 2349**
Notice, **28 § 2344**
Interlocutory injunction, suspension, of orders, **28 § 2349**
Packers, enforcement by district court, **28 § 2351**
Petitions, **28 § 2342**
Contents, **28 § 2344**
Filing, effect, **28 § 2349**
Petitioner, defined, **28 § 2341**
Prehearing conference, **28 § 2345**
Proceedings in court of appeals on petition, **28 § 2347**
Representation in proceeding, **28 § 2348**
Rules, courts of appeals, power of Supreme Court to prescribe, **28 § 2072**
Service of petition, **28 § 2344**
Time, **28 § 2344**
Venue, **28 § 2343**
Plant Variety Protection, this index
Presidential and Executive Office Accountability, this index
Real estate, quieting title, retention and control by U.S. in actions for, pending conclusion of, **28 § 2409a**
Receivers and receivership, interlocutory orders of district courts to courts of appeals, **28 § 1292**
Record on Appeal, generally, this index
Registration in other district of judgment becoming final by appeal, **28 § 1963**
Remand of cause, powers of Supreme Court, courts of appeals, **28 § 2106**
Removed cause remanded to State court from which removed, **28 § 1447**
Reopen, time for appeal, **28 § 2107**
Rules of Civil Procedure, this index
Seamen, fees and costs, prepayment unnecessary, **28 § 1916**
Supreme Court, this index
Telecommunications, this index
Territorial courts, review of decisions by courts of appeals, **28 § 1294**
Three-judge court,
Review of action of single judge by full court, **28 § 2284**
Time for taking appeal,
Court of Appeals, **28 § 2107**
Supreme Court, **28 § 2101**
Transfer,
To cure want of jurisdiction, appeals or petitions for review of administrative action, **28 § 1631**
United States, this index
United States Court of Appeals for District of Columbia, this index

APPEAL AND REVIEW—Cont'd
United States Court of Appeals for the Armed Forces, generally, this index
United States Court of Appeals for the Federal Circuit, this index
United States Court of Appeals for Veterans Claims, generally, this index
United States Court of Federal Claims, this index
United States Court of International Trade, this index
United States District Court for District of Columbia, generally, this index
United States Magistrate Judges, this index
United States Tax Court, this index
Vacation or setting aside judgment, powers of Supreme Court, courts of appeals, **28 § 2106**
Want of jurisdiction, transfer to cure, appeals and petitions for review of administrative action, **28 § 1631**

APPEAL BOARD
Trademark Trial and Appeal Board, generally, this index

APPEARANCE
Rules of Appellate Procedure, this index
Rules of Civil Procedure, this index

APPEARANCE BOND
Release, generally, this index

APPELLATE JURISDICTION
Affirmance, reversal, judgment, decree or order, **28 § 2106**
Courts of appeals, **28 § 1291 et seq.**
Determination, **28 § 2106**
Supreme Court, generally, this index

APPRAISAL AND APPRAISERS
Execution, goods taken on, **28 § 2005**
Fees,
Appraisal of goods taken under execution, **28 § 2005**
United States marshals fees for service of summons, **28 § 1921**
Imported merchandise,
Civil actions where protest denied, exclusive jurisdiction of U.S. Court of International Trade, **28 § 1582**
Sale of realty under order of court, **28 § 2001**
United States Court of International Trade, this index
United States marshal, fees for serving of summons, **28 § 1921**

APPREHENSION
Arrest, generally, this index

APPROPRIATIONS
Bureau of Investigation, this index
Compromise settlements against U.S., **28 § 2414**

APPROPRIATIONS—Cont'd
Drugs and medicine, civil enforcement enhancement by Justice Department, authorization, **28 § 509 nt**
Government Ethics, Office of. Personnel Management, Office of, this index
Hate crimes, compilation of data, **28 § 534 nt**
Institutes and joint councils on sentencing, **28 § 334**
Judgments against U.S., **28 § 2414**
Judicial Center, **28 § 628**
Judicial officers, examination, **28 § 526**
Judicial Survivors' Annuity Fund, authorization of, **28 § 376 nt**
Justice Department, this index
National Crime Information Center Project 2000, **28 § 534 nt**

APPROPRIATIONS COMMITTEE (SENATE OR HOUSE OF REPRESENTATIVES)
Congressional Committees, this index

ARBITRATION
Administrative Law and Procedure, generally, this index
Alternative means of dispute resolution. Administrative Law and Procedure, generally, this index
Arbitrators,
Award of arbitrator, generally, post
Certificates and certification, **28 § 655**
Compensation and salaries, **28 § 658**
Disqualification, **28 § 655**
Privileges and immunities, **28 § 655**
Referral from alternative dispute resolution, **28 § 655**
Training, Federal Judicial Center, provision for, **28 § 620**
Attorney General, approval, payment of Federal tort claims, after compromise or settlement, provisions, **28 § 2672**
Award of arbitrator,
Referral from alternative dispute resolution, **28 §§ 655, 657**
Certificates and certification,
Arbitrators, **28 § 655**
Certification,
Copy of foreign judgments, registration, **28 § 1963**
Compensation and salaries,
Arbitrators, neutrals, **28 § 658**
Disqualification,
Arbitrators, **28 § 655**
Dockets and docketing,
Restoration, new trial, **28 § 657**
Federal tort claims, settlements by, **28 § 2672**
Hearings,
Referral from alternative dispute resolution, **28 § 655**
Judgment,
Award of arbitrator, force and effect, **28 § 657**

ARBITRATION—Cont'd
Neutrals,
Compensation and salaries, **28 § 658**
New trial, **28 § 657**
Oaths and affirmations,
Referral from alternative dispute resolution, **28 § 655**
Powers and duties,
Arbitrators,
Referral from alternative dispute resolution, **28 § 655**
Privileges and immunities,
Arbitrators, **28 § 655**
Production of books and papers, **28 § 656**
Referral from alternative dispute resolution, **28 § 654**
Registration, foreign judgments, **28 § 1963**
Sealing, award, **28 § 657**
Service,
Award of arbitrator, referral from alternative dispute resolution, **28 § 657**
Subpoenas, **28 § 656**
Time,
New trial, **28 § 657**
Torts,
Claims against U.S., authority of Attorney General, **28 § 2677**
Payment of awards, **28 § 2672**
Traveling expenses,
Arbitrators, neutrals, **28 § 658**
Trial de novo, **28 § 657**
United States Attorneys, this index

ARCHITECT OF CAPITOL
Supreme Court marshal to disburse funds for work on Supreme Court building and grounds under jurisdiction of, **28 § 672**

ARIZONA
See, also, States, generally, this index
Bankruptcy judges, appointment, number in judicial district, **28 § 152**
District court,
Additional, **28 § 133 nt**
Cities, held at, **28 § 82**
Judges, additional, **28 § 133 nt**
Number, **28 § 133**
Places of holding, **28 § 82**
Judicial circuit of U.S., **28 § 41**
Judicial districts, **28 § 82**
Bankruptcy provisions, applicability of certain amendments to, **28 § 581 nt**
Number of district judges, **28 § 133**
States, generally, this index
United States trustees of judicial districts, appointment, **28 § 581**

ARKANSAS
See, also, States, generally, this index
Bankruptcy judges, appointment, number in judicial district, **28 § 152**

ARKANSAS—Cont'd
District court,
Cities, **28 § 83**
Judges,
Additional, **28 § 133 nt**
Appointment, additional judges, advice and consent, **28 § 133 nt**
Existing judgeships, authorization, treatment, **28 § 133 nt**
Number, **28 § 133**
Places of holding, **28 § 83**
Judicial circuit of U.S., **28 § 41**
Judicial districts, **28 § 83**
Bankruptcy provisions, applicability of certain amendments to, **28 § 581 nt**
Number of district judges, **28 § 133**
United States trustees of judicial districts, appointment, **28 § 581**

ARMED FORCES
See, also,
Uniformed Services, generally, this index
Air Force, generally, this index
Army, generally, this index
Coast Guard, generally, this index
Combat zones,
Tort Claims Act, **28 § 2680**
Commissary stores,
Contracts,
Jurisdiction, **28 §§ 1346, 1491**
Crimes and offenses,
State courts, removal, **28 § 1442a**
District court crier or bailiff, preference, **28 § 755**
Honorable Discharges, generally, this index
Jury service, exemption because of active service, **28 § 1863**
Justices and judges in service, no deposit required for annuities to survivors and dependents, **28 § 376**
Marine Corps, generally, this index
Military Departments, generally, this index
National Cemeteries, generally, this index
National Guard, generally, this index
Navy, generally, this index
Negligence, wrongful acts, of members, claims against U.S., procedure, **28 § 2671 et seq.**
Newly democratic nations, retired members, service in military forces of, **28 § 2671 et seq.**
Removal,
From State to Federal court of action or prosecution against member of, **28 § 1442a**
Reserves,
Air Force, this index
Army, this index
Coast Guard Reserve, generally, this index
Marine Corps, this index

ARMED FORCES—Cont'd
Reserves—Cont'd
National Cemeteries, generally, this index
Navy, this index
Veterans, generally, this index

ARMY
See, also,
Armed Forces, generally, this index
Uniformed Services, generally, this index
Air Force, generally, this index
Department of the Army. Army Department, generally, this index
Honorable Discharges, this index
Marine Corps, generally, this index
National Cemeteries, generally, this index
Reserves,
National Cemeteries, generally, this index
Retired officers and enlisted personnel, United States Magistrate Judges, appointment and service as, **28 § 631**
United States Magistrate Judges, eligibility of retired members of for appointment and service as, **28 § 631**
Retirement and pensions,
United States Magistrate Judge, eligibility of retiree for appointment and service as, **28 § 631**
Secretary of Army, generally, this index
Tort Claims Act, exception of claim arising out of combatant activities, **28 § 2680**
United States Magistrate Judges, eligibility of retired officers and enlisted personnel for appointment and service, as, **28 § 631**
Veterans, generally, this index

ARMY DEPARTMENT
See, also,
Army, generally, this index
Military Departments, generally, this index
Attorney General, advice concerning, **28 § 513**
Secretary of Army, generally, this index

ARMY RESERVE
Reserves, generally. Army, this index

ARMY SECRETARY
Secretary of Army, generally, this index

ARRAIGNMENT
District courts, reporter or other individual designated to produce record, transcribing and certifying parts of record of proceedings, **28 § 753**
Habeas corpus, proceedings, transcript of proceedings upon arraignment as evidence, **28 § 2247**

ARREST
Admiralty, stay of execution of process, **28 § 2464**
Conflicts of Interest, generally, this index
Detention, generally, this index
Removal of actions or prosecution against Federal officer for acts under color of office, **28 § 1442**
Rules of Civil Procedure, this index
United States Magistrate Judges, this index

ARTICLES (WRITTEN)
Government employees, honoraria, prohibited, **5, Ap 4, § 501**

ARTISTS
Copyrights, generally, this index

ASHEVILLE, NC
Court of Appeals for Fourth Circuit, generally, this index

ASSASSINATION
Terrorists and Terrorism, generally, this index

ASSAULT AND BATTERY
Tort Claims Act,
  Exception of claims, **28 § 2680**

ASSESSMENTS
Internal Revenue Service, this index
Moneys paid into court, criminal appearance bail bond, use of to pay, **28 § 2044**

ASSIGNMENTS
Congressional reference cases, **28 § 2509**
Copyrights, this index
Jury panels, names to, **28 § 1866**
United States Court of Federal Claims, this index
United States Magistrate Judges, rules of procedure, trial of misdemeanors before, temporary assignment from one judicial district to another in an emergency, **28 § 636**

ASSOCIATIONS AND SOCIETIES
Agricultural Associations and Organizations, generally, this index
Attorneys' fees and other costs and expenses, award to party prevailing against U.S. or agency, applicability, **28 § 2412**
Carriers, generally, this index
Cooperative Marketing, this index
Federal agencies, review of orders, right to intervene, **28 § 2348**
Fraternal Associations and Societies, generally, this index
Interpleader, filing, district courts, jurisdiction, **28 § 1335**
Intervention, review, orders, certain Federal agencies, **28 § 2348**

ASSOCIATIONS AND SOCIETIES—Cont'd
Limitations, outside employment, certain Government employees, **5, Ap 4, § 502**
Literary Associations and Organizations, generally, this index
Religious Organizations and Societies, generally, this index
Rules of Civil Procedure, this index
Scientific Associations, Institutions or Organizations, generally, this index
Surface Transportation Board, orders, intervention in actions to enforce, **28 § 2323**

ATLANTA, GA
Court of Appeals for Eleventh Circuit, this index
United States Tax Court sessions held for trial at, rules. United States Tax Court, generally, this index

ATOMIC ENERGY
Atomic Energy Commission,
  Courts of appeals, jurisdiction, review, final orders, **28 § 2342**
  Orders, review, **28 § 2341 et seq.**

ATTACHMENT
Clerks of Courts, this index
Coastal suits, **28 § 2710 et seq.**
Contempt,
  Garnishee failing to appear on garnishment by U.S., **28 § 2405**
Deposit, collection by U.S. marshal, expenses for keeping property attached, **28 § 1921**
Federal Debt Collection, generally, this index
Fees of U.S. marshal for serving, **28 § 1921**
Foreign states, jurisdictional immunities, **28 § 1609**
  Exceptions, **28 § 1610**
  Types of property immune under any conditions, **28 § 1611**
  Vessels, preferred mortgage foreclosures, subject to jurisdiction, **28 § 1610**
  Waiver, **28 § 1610 nt**
Justices and judges, annuities to survivors, exemption from, **28 § 376**
Postal suits, **28 § 2710 et seq.**
  Absconding debtors, publication of executed warrant in proceedings against, **28 § 2715**
  Accretions, investment of proceeds of attached property, **28 § 2714**
  Affidavit, application for warrant, **28 § 2711**
  Alias warrants, **28 § 2710**
  Answer, amount of debt or value of property, **28 § 2716**
  Application,
    Discharge on bond, **28 § 2717**

ATTACHMENT—Cont'd
Postal suits—Cont'd
  Application—Cont'd
    Trial of ownership of property, **28 § 2713**
    Warrant, **28 § 2711**
  Attempted disposal of property after attachment, **28 § 2716**
  Attorney General, application for warrant by persons authorized by, **28 § 2711**
  Certified copies of warrant, seizure of property upon receipt, **28 § 2710**
  Clerk of court,
    Application for warrant made to, **28 § 2711**
    Issuance of warrant, **28 § 2712**
  Court trial of ownership of property, **28 § 2713**
  Custody of attached property, **28 § 2712**
  Damages, right of action for unimpaired, **28 § 2713**
  Discharge on bond, **28 § 2717**
  Disposal of property after attachment, **28 § 2716**
  Equitable rights subject to attachment, **28 § 2710**
  Execution of warrant, **28 § 2712**
    Publication, **28 § 2715**
  Fraudulent conveyance or removal of property as grounds, **28 § 2710**
  Grounds for attachment, **28 § 2710**
  Interest on balances due, **28 § 2718**
  Interlocutory order, sale of attached property, **28 § 2714**
  Investment of proceeds of attached property, **28 § 2714**
  Issuance of warrant, **28 §§ 2710, 2712**
  Judges, discharge on bonds, approval, **28 § 2717**
  Judgments and decrees, discharge on bond, payments as ground for, **28 § 2717**
  Jurisdiction of court, **28 §§ 2710, 2711**
  Jury trial, **28 § 2713**
  Legal evidence of debt, production of, application for warrant, **28 § 2711**
  Legal rights subject to attachment, **28 § 2710**
  Nonresidents,
    Ground, **28 § 2710**
    Publication of executed warrant in proceedings against nonresident debtor, **28 § 2715**
  Notice, trial of ownership of property, **28 § 2713**
  Orders of court,
    Investment of proceeds of attached property, **28 § 2714**
    Trial of ownership of property, **28 § 2713**
  Penal bond, discharge, **28 § 2717**
  Personal notice, **28 § 2716**
  Plea of abatement, **28 § 2713**

ATTACHMENT—Cont'd
Postal suits—Cont'd
Property subjected to attachment, **28 § 2710**
Publication, executed warrant, **28 § 2715**
Removal of property from district as ground, **28 § 2710**
Return of property, ground for discharge on bond, **28 § 2717**
Rights, **28 § 2710**
Sale of attached property, disposition of proceeds, **28 § 2714**
Service of notice on debtors or possessors of property, **28 § 2716**
Sureties subject to attachment, **28 § 2710**
Time, plea of abatement, **28 § 2713**
Trespass, right of action unimpaired by trial of ownership of property, **28 § 2713**
Trial of ownership of property, **28 § 2713**
United States Attorneys, this index
United States marshal,
Custody of attached property, **28 § 2712**
Execution of warrant, **28 § 2712**
Personal notice of attachment served by, **28 § 2716**
Publication of executed warrant by, **28 § 2715**
Seizure of property removed to another district, **28 § 2710**
United States securities, investment of proceeds of attached property in, **28 § 2714**
Waiver of jury trial of ownership of property, **28 § 2713**
Warrant,
Application, **28 § 2711**
Discharge, **28 § 2717**
Execution, **28 § 2712**
Publication, **28 § 2715**
Issuance, **28 §§ 2710, 2712**
Removal of case, **28 § 1450**
Rules of Civil Procedure, this index
United States Attorneys, this index
United States marshal, expenses and fees for keeping property attached, **28 § 1921**

ATTACKING SENTENCE
Sentence and Punishment, this index

ATTESTATION
Records of States, territories, or possessions, evidence, **28 §§ 1738, 1739**

ATTORNEY GENERAL
Generally, **28 § 502 et seq.**
Absence, vacancy in office, **28 § 508**
Administrative expenses, Justice Department, rates, appropriations, **28 § 524**

ATTORNEY GENERAL—Cont'd
Administrative Office of United States Courts, cooperative arrangements with Director respecting U.S. trustees, use of services, equipment, **28 § 581 nt**
Advice,
Heads of executive departments, **28 § 512**
President, when required by, **28 § 511**
Secretaries of military departments, **28 § 513**
Agency, defined, civil litigation reform, **28 § 519 nt, EON 12988**
Agreements to pay expenses, private counsel, defense, Federal employees sued for actions while performing official duties, **28 § 509 nt**
Appeal,
Civil action challenging appointment, **28 § 503 nt**
Appointment, **28 § 503**
Assistant Attorneys General, **28 § 506**
Administration, **28 § 507**
Civil action to contest constitutionality of, **28 § 503 nt**
Criminal and other identification records, officials to perform functions concerning, **28 § 534**
Deputy Attorney General, **28 § 504**
Director of FBI, **28 § 532**
Investigative and other officials, **28 § 533**
Special attorney or special assistant, **28 § 515**
Appropriations,
Examination, judicial officers, **28 § 526**
Argument of cases, **28 § 518**
Associate Attorney General,
Appointment, **28 § 504a**
Drugs and medicine, civil enforcement by Justice Department, duties, **28 § 509 nt**
Filling vacancy in office of Attorney General, **28 § 508**
Attachment against delinquent postmasters and postal officers, employees, application for warrant, **28 § 2711**
Automated legal research and information systems, computerization, functions concerning, **28 § 509 nt, EON 12146**
Bankruptcy,
Appointment of U.S. trustees by, **28 § 581 nt**
Books and periodicals, exchange and sale authorized, **28 § 413**
Bureau of Investigation,
Counterterrorism, powers and duties, **28 § 531 nt**
Espionage investigations, persons employed by or assigned to U.S. diplomatic missions abroad, subject to Attorney General's authority, **28 § 533 nt**

ATTORNEY GENERAL—Cont'd
Bureau of Investigation—Cont'd
Undercover investigative operations closed in certain year, submission of results,
Financial audit to, **28 § 533 nt**
Reports, **28 § 533 nt**
Cases, conduct and argument, **28 § 518**
Certificates and certification,
Constitutionality of Act of Congress involved, **28 § 2403**
Contract Disputes Act of 1978,
New appeal from judgment against U.S., exception, **28 § 2414**
Payment of judgment by State or foreign court against U.S., exception, **28 § 2414**
No appeal from judgment against U.S., **28 § 2414**
Payment of judgment by State or foreign court against U.S., **28 § 2414**
United States trustees, certification of judicial districts, notice and publication, **28 § 581 nt**
Chairman, Federal Legal Council, **28 § 509 nt, EON 12146**
Civil actions challenging appointment, grounds, **28 § 503 nt**
Civil justice reform, **28 § 519 nt, EON 12988**
Clerks of court, investigation, official acts, **28 § 526**
Commission,
Special assistants or special attorneys, **28 § 515**
Community Development, this index
Compensation and salaries,
Special assistants or special attorneys, **28 § 515**
Competitive service, Assistant Attorney General for Administration, **28 § 507**
Complaints, pre-filing requirements, civil justice reform, **28 § 519 nt, EON 12988**
Compromise settlements of claims against U.S., **28 § 2414**
Conduct of,
Cases, **28 § 518**
Litigation under direction, **28 § 516**
Conflict of interest, disqualification of officers and employees in case of, penalty for violation, **28 § 528**
Constitution of U.S., civil action to contest constitutionality of appointment and continuance in office of, **28 § 503 nt**
Continuance in office, civil actions to contest constitutionality of, **28 § 503 nt**
Correctional Institutions, this index
Counterterrorism Fund, powers and duties with regard to, **28 § 524 nt**
Court reporters, investigations, official acts, **28 § 526**

ATTORNEY GENERAL—Cont'd
Crimes and offenses,
Federally insured financial institutions, investigation and prosecution powers, use of attorneys and employees of other Federal departments or agencies, **28 § 509 nt**
Statistics, report to Congress, **28 § 522**
Delegation of,
Authority, **28 § 510**
Department of Justice Assets Forfeiture Fund, establishment, functions, **28 § 524**
Deputy and Assistant Attorneys General,
Administration,
Appointment, duties, **28 § 507**
Rates, notarial fees, **28 § 524**
Appointment, and duties, **28 §§ 504, 506**
Filling vacancy in office of Attorney General, order of succession, **28 § 508**
Director,
Administrative Office of U.S. Courts, copies of required reports, submitted to, **28 § 604**
Federal Bureau of Investigation, appointment, **28 § 532**
Disability, vacancy in office, **28 § 508**
Disqualification of officers and employees in case of conflict of interest, penalty for violation, **28 § 528**
Distribution of opinion, **28 § 521**
District Courts, this index
Drug Abuse Prevention, Control and Treatment, this index
Drug Enforcement Administration,
Financial audit of undercover investigative operations closed in certain year, submission of results to, **28 § 533 nt**
Undercover investigative operations closed in certain year, submission of results, reports, **28 § 533 nt**
Drugs and medicine, civil enforcement enhancement by Justice Department, powers, duties, **28 § 509 nt**
Environmental or natural resource law, violations of, investigation action by, **28 § 509 nt**
Examination,
Official papers, of judicial officers, **28 § 526**
Witnesses, pending claims in executive departments and agencies, **28 § 514**
Exchange, procurement, law books, reference books, and periodicals, **28 § 525**
Executive departments or agencies, legal service, pending claims, **28 § 514**
Extraordinary expenses of ministerial officers executing act of Congress, allowance of payment, **28 § 1929**
Federal Agencies and Instrumentalities, this index

ATTORNEY GENERAL—Cont'd
Federal Bureau of Investigation. Bureau of Investigation, generally, ante
Federal environmental and natural resource laws, investigations respecting, **28 § 509 nt**
Federal Legal Council, member of, duties, concerning, **28 § 509 nt, EON 12146**
Felonious killings of State or local law enforcement officers, investigation, **28 § 540**
Financial disclosure, Government Ethics, Office of, cooperation with in developing rules and regulations, **5, Ap 4, § 402**
Financial institutions,
Federally insured, criminal investigation and prosecution powers, use of attorneys and employees of other Federal departments or agencies, **28 § 509 nt**
Fraud task forces, establishment, purpose, duties, **28 § 509 nt**
Fines, penalties and forfeitures,
Awards for information concerning forfeitures, authority, **28 § 524**
Forfeited property, transfer, clear title upon, authority to warrant, **28 § 524**
Forfeitures. Fines, penalties and forfeitures, generally, ante
Functions in general, **28 § 509**
Delegation, **28 § 510**
Government Ethics, Office of, cooperation with in developing rules and regulations relating to conflicts of interest, **5, Ap 4, § 402**
Grand jury proceedings,
Conducting, authority, **28 § 515**
Guidelines,
Civil justice reform, issuance, powers and duties, **28 § 519 nt, EON 12988**
Investigation of felonious killings of State or local law enforcement officers, establishment by, **28 § 540**
Hate crimes statistics, duties, **28 § 534 nt**
Head of department,
Executive departments, advice to, **28 § 512**
Justice Department, **28 § 503**
Homicide, serial killings, investigations and investigators, **28 § 540B**
Identification and criminal identification records,
Acquisition, preservation, and exchange, **28 § 534**
Parimutuel licensing, simplification, requests from State regulatory authorities, **28 § 534 nt**
Independent Counsel, this index
Institutes on sentencing, functions and duties relative to, **28 § 334**
Interagency legal disputes, resolutions by, **28 § 509 nt, EON 12146**

ATTORNEY GENERAL—Cont'd
Intimidation of Government employees, statistics compilation, **28 § 534 nt**
Investigations,
Crimes involving Government officers and employees, **28 § 535**
Government Ethics, Office of, cooperation, conflict of interest, **5, Ap 4, § 402**
Felonious killings of State or local law enforcement officers, **28 § 540**
Official acts, of U.S. attorneys and marshals, clerks of court, **28 § 526**
Pending claims in executive departments and agencies, **28 § 514**
Serial killings, **28 § 540B**
United States trustees, **28 § 526**
Joint councils on sentencing, functions and duties relative to, **28 § 334**
Judicial Center, Board, transmission, copies, reports and recommendations submitted to Judicial Conference of U.S., **28 § 623**
Judicial Conference,
Membership on. Court of Appeals for Second Circuit, generally, this index
Report by Attorney General to, **28 § 331**
Jury selection procedures, noncompliance, grounds for moving to dismiss indictment, **28 § 1867**
Justice Department,
Criminal investigation and prosecution, federally insured financial institutions, use of attorneys and employees of other Federal departments or agencies, **28 § 509 nt**
Drugs and medicine, civil enforcement enhancement, powers, duties, **28 § 509 nt**
Special agents, travel and transportation expenses of new appointees, authorization to pay, **28 § 530**
Law books, sale or exchange, **28 § 525**
Law enforcement,
Training activities, overseas, **28 § 509 nt**
Legal proceedings, conducting, authority, **28 § 515**
Legal services, pending claims in executive departments or agencies, **28 § 514**
Litigation,
Civil justice reform, powers and duties, **28 § 519 nt, EON 12988**
Notice system, establishing, information, civil litigation pending in courts in which Federal Government is party or has significant interest, **28 § 509 nt, EON 12146**
Supervision, **28 § 519**
Litigation counsel, defined, civil litigation reform, **28 § 519 nt, EON 12988**

ATTORNEY GENERAL—Cont'd
Murder,
Serial killings, investigations and investigators, **28 § 540B**
Narcotic drug addicts,
Credit toward sentence, time spent in institutional custody of, **28 § 2903**
Placement in custody of, **28 § 2902**
Notice,
Hearing,
Interlocutory injunction restraining, enforcement, of Federal agency's orders, **28 § 2349**
Three-judge court, actions against State, **28 § 2284**
Plan for random jury selection, adoption or modification, **28 § 1863**
Oath, special assistants or special attorneys, **28 § 515**
Opinions and decisions,
Heads of executive departments, **28 § 512**
President, when required by, **28 § 511**
Publication and distribution, **28 § 521**
Overseas law enforcement training activities, **28 § 509 nt**
Parimutuel licensing, simplification, consolidated requests of State regulatory officials to Federal Government for identification and criminal records of applicants, **28 § 534 nt**
Penalties. Fines, penalties and forfeitures, generally, ante
Periodicals, sale or exchange, **28 § 525**
President of the United States,
Advice and opinions to, **28 § 511**
Appointment, **28 § 503**
Assistant Attorneys General, **28 § 506**
Administration, approval, **28 § 507**
Associate Attorney General, **28 § 504a**
Deputy Attorney General, **28 § 504**
Probation officers,
Investigation, official acts, **28 § 526**
Public contracts, awarded by executive agencies,
Payment of judgments and compromise settlements against U.S., exception, **28 § 2414**
Review of decision of board of contract appeals by U.S. Court of Appeals for the Federal Circuit, approval, **28 § 1295**
Publication of opinions, **28 § 521**
Reference books, sale or exchange, **28 § 525**
Reports,
Banking law offenses, **28 § 522 nt**
Business and statistics of Justice Department, **28 § 522**
Congressional oversight, fraud cases, **28 § 522 nt**
Crimes involving Government officers and employees, **28 § 535**

ATTORNEY GENERAL—Cont'd
Reports—Cont'd
Crimes involving Government officers and employees—Cont'd
Government Ethics, Office of, cooperation, conflict of interest, **5, Ap 4, § 402**
Fraud cases, Congressional oversight, **28 § 522 nt**
Legal activities of Federal agencies, **28 § 509 nt, EON 12146**
Public Integrity Section or other supervisory unit, to Congress, **28 § 529**
Requisitions,
Advance or payment of moneys, signing, **28 § 523**
United States as purchaser in partition action, payment, purchase money, **28 § 2409**
Review, orders, certain Federal agencies,
Responsibility, **28 § 2348**
Service of petition, **28 § 2344**
Rules and regulations,
Disqualification of officers and employees in case of conflict of interest, penalty for violation, **28 § 528**
Salary. Compensation and salaries, generally, ante
Sale, procurement, law books, reference books, and periodicals, **28 § 525**
Seal for Justice Department, custody, **28 § 502**
Secretaries of military departments, advice to, **28 § 513**
Senior interagency group, financial institution fraud, establishment, duties, **28 § 509 nt**
Serial killings, investigations and investigators, **28 § 540B**
Solicitor General to assist, **28 § 505**
Special assistants or special attorneys,
Appointment, commission, oath, and salary, **28 § 515**
Supervision, **28 § 519**
Special prosecutor. Independent Counsel, generally, this index
State court action involving property on which U.S. has lien, service of copies of process and complaint, **28 § 2410**
Statement,
Appropriation and number of pending causes, **28 § 522**
Facts, relating to petitions of U.S. United States Court of Federal Claims or U.S. Court of Appeals for the Federal Circuit, furnishing by executive departments, **28 § 520**
States, this index
Statistics, intimidation of Federal Government employees, compilation, **28 § 534 nt**
Supervision of litigation, **28 § 519**
Civil justice reform, **28 § 519 nt, EON 12988**
Supreme Court, this index

ATTORNEY GENERAL—Cont'd
Surface Transportation Board,
Actions to enforce orders, **28 § 2323**
Duties in actions to enforce, orders of Board, **28 § 2323**
Tax liens, U.S. as party, actions to quiet title, foreclosure, service of process, **28 § 2410**
Tort claims,
Authority to compromise, settle, **28 § 2677**
Award, compromise, approval, **28 § 2672**
Certification, removal of State court case to district court, **28 § 2679**
Compromise or settlement of claim, **28 § 2679**
Defense of actions or proceedings against Government employees for damages or injuries, **28 § 2679**
Disposition of claim, incompetent as evidence of liability for amount of damages, **28 § 2675**
Transmission, petitions in U.S. Court of Federal Claims or in U.S. Court of Appeals for the Federal Circuit, **28 § 520**
Trustees in bankruptcy, investigation, official acts, **28 § 526**
Unemancipated persons, acquire, collect, classify, information concerning missing persons, provide information to parent, guardian, **28 § 534**
United States,
Courts, conduct and argument of cases in, **28 § 518**
Interests of in pending suits, attending to, **28 § 517**
United States Attorneys, this index
United States Court of Appeals for the Federal Circuit, transmission of petitions in, **28 § 520**
United States Court of Federal Claims, this index
United States Court of International Trade, this index
United States Marshals Service, this index
United States Sentencing Commission, member, **28 § 991**
United States trustees. Bankruptcy, this index
Unlawful activities, federally insured financial institutions, investigation and prosecution powers, use of attorneys and employees of other Federal departments or agencies, **28 § 509 nt**
Vacancy in office, **28 § 508**
Wages. Compensation and salaries, generally, ante

ATTORNEYS
Administrative Office of U.S. Courts, practice of law prohibited as to officers and employees in U.S. Courts, **28 § 607**

ATTORNEYS—Cont'd
Admission to practice, disposition of fees, **28 § 1931 nt**
Appearance by,
Courts of U.S., **28 § 1654**
Attorney fees. Fees, generally, post
Attorney General, generally, this index
Bankruptcy, this index
Bill of costs, affidavit verifying, **28 § 1924**
Certificate of counsel as to good faith in filing affidavit of bias or prejudice of district judge, **28 § 144**
Civil justice reform, civil litigation on behalf of U.S., guidelines, **28 § 519 nt, EON 12988**
Claims, this index
Clerks of courts, restrictions against practice of law in courts of the U.S., **28 § 955**
Compensation and salaries. Fees, generally, post
Convention on,
Taking of Evidence Abroad in Civil or Commercial Matters, representation of persons concerned, **28 § 1781 nt**
Costs, docket fees, taxation as costs, **28 § 1923**
Docket fees, taxation as costs, **28 § 1923**
Ethics, attorneys for the government, **28 § 530B**
Federal agencies,
Assisting Justice Department investigations and prosecutions of fraud, criminal or unlawful activity concerning federally insured financial institutions, **28 § 509 nt**
Civil justice reform, **28 § 519 nt, EON 12988**
Federal Legal Council, establishment, composition, functions, **28 § 509 nt, EON 12146**
Fees,
Award to party prevailing against U.S. or agency, **28 § 2412**
Bad faith,
District court, power to award for unreasonable or vexatious conduct, **28 § 1927**
Copyrights,
Motion pictures, transfer of ownership, collective bargaining agreements, **28 § 4001**
Discharge of employee for jury service, award of attorney's fees to prevailing party, **28 § 1875**
District court, unreasonable or vexatious lawsuits or conduct, **28 § 1927**
Federal judges, defending complaints in disciplinary proceedings, **28 § 372**
Federal tort claims, **28 § 2678**
Government employees,
Sued while performing official duties, **28 § 509 nt**

ATTORNEYS—Cont'd
Fees—Cont'd
Independent counsel,
Attorney General requesting, award to subject of investigation, **28 § 593**
Judges, defending disciplinary complaints, **28 § 372**
Parental Kidnapping Prevention Act, award to person entitled to custody or visitation, **28 § 1738A nt**
Presidential and Executive Office Accountability,
Judicial review, **28 § 3905**
Tort claims against U.S., **28 § 2678**
United States,
Civil actions and administrative proceedings,
Payment, limitation, **28 § 2412 nt**
United States Court of Federal Claims, sanctions, unreasonable, vexatious proceedings, **28 § 1927**
United States magistrate judges, defending disciplinary complaints, **28 § 372**
Forma pauperis proceedings, requesting attorney to represent person unable to employ counsel, **28 § 1915**
Habeas Corpus, this index
Independent Counsel, generally, this index
Judicial conference of circuit, participation, **28 § 333**
Justice Department, ethics, **28 § 530B**
Justice or judge,
Disqualification to sit, grounds, **28 § 455**
Practicing as, high misdemeanor, **28 § 454**
Prior private practice in matters in controversy, disqualification, **28 § 455**
Pretrial Services, generally, this index
Public Defenders, generally, this index
Review, orders, certain Federal agencies, representation, **28 § 2348**
Rules of Civil Procedure, this index
Special Counsel, Office of, generally, this index
Supreme Court, this index
Surface Transportation Board, this index
Transfer of Offenders to or from Foreign Countries, this index
United States,
Civil justice reform, litigation on behalf of U.S., guidelines, **28 § 519 nt, EON 12988**
United States Attorneys, generally, this index
United States Court of International Trade, this index
United States Magistrate Judges, practice of law by, **28 § 632**
United States marshals, practice of law prohibited, **28 § 568**

AUCTIONS AND AUCTIONEERS
Sale of vessel by public auctioneer, commissions of U.S. marshal, **28 § 1921**

AUDITS AND AUDITORS
Comptroller General, generally, this index
Director of Administrative Office of U.S. Courts, vouchers and accounts of courts, Judicial Center, **28 § 604**
Drug Enforcement Administration, undercover investigative operations, reports, **28 § 533 nt**
Federal Bureau of Investigation, undercover investigative operations, reports, **28 § 533 nt**
Independent Counsel, generally, this index
Judicial Center,
Accounts and vouchers, **28 § 604**
Services provided for, **28 § 628**
Pretrial services, accounts and vouchers, **28 § 604**

AUTHENTICATION
Acts of legislature of State, territory or possession for evidence, **28 § 1738**
Consul, documents and papers in office for evidence, **28 § 1740**
Foreign patent specifications and drawings, copies, evidence, **28 § 1745**
Foreign records, copies, as evidence, **28 § 1741**
Judicial proceedings and records of courts of States, territories or possessions, full faith and credit, **28 § 1738**
Patent and Trademark Office, documents, evidence, **28 § 1744**
Records or books of State, territory or possession for use as evidence, **28 § 1739**
Vice consul, documents and papers in office for evidence, **28 § 1740**

AUTHORS
Copyrights, generally, this index

AUTOMATED DATA PROCESSING
Computers, generally, this index

AUTOMOBILES
Motor Vehicles, generally, this index

AWARDS
Administrative Law and Procedure, generally, this index
Incentive Pay or Awards, generally, this index

BACKGROUND CHECKS
Criminal Background Checks, generally, this index

BAIL AND RECOGNIZANCES
Bonds, generally, this index

BAIL AND RECOGNIZANCES—Cont'd
Motion for judgment and other proceedings on, docket fees as costs, **28 § 1923**
Narcotic drug addicts,
Civil commitment for examination or treatment, relief, **28 § 2902**
Commitment and rehabilitation, release on, **28 § 2902**
Pretrial Services, generally, this index
Witnesses,
Confinement of recalcitrant witnesses, **28 § 1826**

BAILIFFS
Appropriations, meals and lodging, jury attendance, **28 § 524**
Courts of appeals, crier to perform duties of, **28 § 714**
District courts,
Appointment, **28 § 755**
Crier to perform duties of bailiff, **28 § 755**
United States Court of Federal Claims, appointment and removal, **28 § 795**
United States Court of International Trade, criers to perform duties of, **28 § 872**

BAILMENT
United States Court of Federal Claims, generally, this index

BAKER ISLAND
Judicial district of Hawaii, inclusion in, **28 § 91**

BALTIMORE, MD
United States Tax Court sessions held for trial at, rules. United States Tax Court, generally, this index

BANK FRAUD CRIMES
Senior interagency group, financial institutions fraud task forces, establishment, membership, duties, **28 § 509 nt**
Task force, financial institutions task forces, establishment, **28 § 509 nt**

BANKRUPTCY
Abatement and Revival, generally, this index
Actions and proceedings,
Bankruptcy courts, generally, post
District courts, original jurisdiction of civil proceedings, **28 § 1334**
Foreign proceedings,
Cases ancillary to,
Filing fees, **28 § 1930**
Venue, district courts, cases ancillary to, **28 § 1410**
Individual debt adjustment, generally, post
Referral to bankruptcy judges, **28 § 157**
Removal of cause of action in civil action to district court, **28 § 1452**

BANKRUPTCY—Cont'd
Adjustments,
Debtor-creditor relationship, proceedings affecting, core proceeding, hearing and determination of bankruptcy of bankruptcy judges, **28 § 157**
Individual debt adjustment, generally, post
Municipal debt adjustment, generally, post
Administration,
Cases, post
Estates, post
Individual debt adjustment, generally, post
Liquidation, post
Administrative Office of United States Courts,
Director,
Assistants for judges, appointment, **28 § 156**
Cases, information and documents made available to U.S. trustees by, **28 § 581 nt**
Recommendations of Judicial Conference, determination, official stations of bankruptcy judges, **28 § 152**
Returns by court clerk to, **28 § 156**
Transition study, contents, **28 nt prec § 151**
Use and accounting, postage for notices required, **28 § 1930 nt**
Notices to creditors, issuance, restrictions, **28 § 1930 nt**
Affiliates,
Case under Title 11 concerning, venue of, **28 § 1408**
Affirmations. Oaths and affirmations, generally, post
Airport leases. Leases, generally, post
Alternative dispute resolution, **28 § 651 et seq.**
Appeal and review,
Bankruptcy appellate panels, generally, post
Bankruptcy courts, post
Claims removed relating to bankruptcy cases, **28 § 1452**
Declaratory judgments, determination of tax liability, **28 § 2201**
District courts,
Decision to abstain from hearing proceedings, prohibition, review by appeal, **28 § 1334**
Jurisdiction, hearing appeals from final judgments, orders, of bankruptcy judges, **28 § 158**
Manner of taking appeals from final orders, judgments, of bankruptcy judges, **28 § 158**
Notice of, filing of, fee, **28 § 1930**
Appellate panel. Bankruptcy appellate panels, generally, post

BANKRUPTCY—Cont'd
Appointment,
Standing trustees by U.S. trustees, qualification of person other than attorney, **28 § 586**
Trusts and trustees, generally, post
Arbitration, alternative dispute resolution, referral, **28 § 654**
Attorneys,
Bankruptcy judges,
Prohibition, practice of law, **28 § 153**
Serving on part-time basis, practice of law permitted, **28 § 152 nt**
Avoidance. Transfers, generally, post
Bankruptcy appellate panels, **28 § 158**
Joint panels, **28 § 158**
Judicial Council of circuit, powers and duties, **28 § 158**
Three member panels, hearing and determination of appeals, **28 § 158**
Transfer to district court, appeals from final judgments, orders, of bankruptcy courts pending in panels, **28 § 1334 nt**
Bankruptcy courts, **28 § 151 et seq.**
Actions, transfer to new court system, **28 nt prec § 1471**
Appeal and review,
Final judgments, orders, of judges, jurisdiction, district courts, **28 § 158**
Orders and judgments of judges, **28 § 157**
Venue, **28 § 1408**
Assistants, judges, appointment, **28 § 156**
Cases,
Pending in courts, jurisdiction of district court, **28 § 1334 nt**
Transfer to new court system, **28 nt prec § 1471**
Clerks of courts,
Appointment, **28 § 156**
Fees and charges, **28 § 1930**
Collection and disposition of, **28 § 1930 nt**
Notices to parties in interest,
Creditors, prohibition, exclusive mailing to, **28 § 1930 nt**
Compensation and salaries,
Judges, **28 § 153**
Adjustments, applicable pay periods, **28 § 153 nt**
Retired judge recalled, **28 § 155**
Consolidation,
Offices of bankruptcy and district court clerks, requirement of prior approval, **28 § 156**
Core proceedings arising under Title 11, hearing and determination by judges, **28 § 157**
Courts of appeals, filling vacancies in office of judge, **28 § 152 nt**
Deputy clerks, appointment and removal, **28 § 156**

BANKRUPTCY—Cont'd
Bankruptcy courts—Cont'd
Designation of, **28 § 151**
Chief judge, **28 § 154**
Discharge of debtor. Discharge, generally, post
District of Columbia, judges, appointment, number in judicial district, **28 § 152**
Division of business, **28 § 154**
Dockets,
Clerk official custodian of, **28 § 156**
Expenses and expenditures, utilization of facilities or services, **28 § 156**
Facilities or services, utilization, **28 § 156**
Fees and charges,
Child support creditors or representatives, exemptions, certain instances, **28 § 1930 nt**
Collection and disposition of, provisions, **28 § 1930 nt**
Electronic access to court data, exemptions, **28 § 1930 nt**
Judicial Conference of U.S., prescribing, **28 § 1930**
Exemptions, **28 § 1930 nt**
Schedule, additional fees, **28 § 1930 nt**
Hearings,
Bankruptcy appellate panel, **28 § 158**
Charges, removal of judges, **28 § 152**
Proceedings not core proceedings but related to case under Title 11, **28 § 157**
Holding of court at places within judicial district as business requires, **28 § 152**
Incompetence, misconduct, grounds for removal of judge, **28 § 152**
Judges or justices, **28 § 151 et seq.**
Annual and sick leave, exceptions from provisions of, **28 § 153**
Appeals from final judgments, jurisdiction of district courts, **28 § 158**
Appellate panels, clerk, employees, during transition period, **28 nt prec § 151**
Appointments, judges, **28 § 152**
Bankruptcy appellate panel, membership on, **28 § 158**
Bankruptcy judge, defined, **28 § 375**
Business, occupation, engaging in employment inconsistent with performance of duties, prohibition, **28 § 153**
Character of service, **28 § 153**
Chief judge,
Court of appeals, appointment of judge where other judges cannot agree upon appointment, **28 § 152**
Designation, **28 § 154**

BANKRUPTCY—Cont'd
Bankruptcy courts—Cont'd
Judges or justices—Cont'd
Chief judge—Cont'd
Functions in general, **28 § 154**
Compensation and salaries, **28 § 153**
Continuance in effect, **28 § 153 nt**
Retired judges recalled, **28 §§ 155, 375**
Constituting unit of district court known as bankruptcy court, **28 § 151**
Core proceedings arising under Title 11, hearing and determination, **28 § 157**
Designation to serve in adjacent district, **28 § 152**
Division of business among, **28 § 154**
Entry of orders and judgments, **28 § 157**
Enumeration of number of judges appointed and judicial districts thereof, **28 § 152**
Exercise of authority respecting actions, proceedings, **28 § 151**
Findings of fact and conclusions of law, submission to district courts, **28 § 157**
Hearings, proceedings not core proceedings but relating to cases under Title 11, **28 § 157**
Holding of,
Court at places within judicial district as business requires, **28 § 152**
Regular or special sessions of court, **28 § 151**
Incumbents, appointment to fill vacancies, **28 § 152 nt**
Judicial Center, Board, membership on, **28 § 621**
Judicial conferences of circuits, **28 § 333**
Judicial discipline, complaint, review procedure, **28 § 372**
Judicial districts, appointment of, **28 § 152**
Number needed, recommendations by Judicial Conference, **28 § 152**
Oaths or affirmations, **28 § 153**
Official duty station, determination by Judicial Conference, **28 § 152**
Part-time basis, continuance of service, **28 § 152 nt**
Practice of law,
Engagement in, prohibition, **28 § 153**
Judges serving on part-time basis, permitted, **28 § 152 nt**
President of U.S. not to consider race, color, sex, in selecting nominees for judgeships, **28 § 44 nt**

BANKRUPTCY—Cont'd
Bankruptcy courts—Cont'd
Judges or justices—Cont'd
Race, color, sex, not to be considered by President in selecting nominees for judgeships, **28 § 44 nt**
Referral,
Cases under Title 11 and any proceedings arising under Title 11, **28 § 157**
Proceedings related to case under Title 11, **28 § 157**
Removal,
Action taken by judicial council, **28 § 372**
Grounds for, **28 § 152**
Retired judges, recall to service, **28 § 155**
Secretary, law clerk, appointment, **28 § 156**
Separability of provisions, Bankruptcy Amendments and Federal Judgeship Act of 1984, **28 § 151 nt**
Service,
As judicial officers of U.S. district court, **28 § 152**
Part-time basis, certain districts, extension, **28 § 152 nt**
Single judge may exercise judicial power, **28 § 151**
Temporary transfer of, **28 § 155**
Term of office, **28 § 152**
Expiration of, **28 nt prec § 151**
Extension of, **28 §§ 151 nt, 152 nt**
Territories, judges of district courts to serve as bankruptcy judges, **28 § 152**
Transition provisions, annual and sick leave, **28 § 153 nt**
Filling, **28 § 152 nt**
Vacancy in office, **28 § 152 nt**
Judgments and decrees, **28 § 157**
Judicial administration during transition, **28 nt prec § 151; 28 § 151**
Judicial Conference of the Circuit, judges, **28 § 333**
Judicial Conference of the United States,
Consolidation, offices of bankruptcy and district court clerks, prior approval by, requirement, **28 § 156**
Fees prescribed by, schedule, additional fees, **28 § 1930 nt**
Payment of judges, **28 § 153**
Retired judges recalled, salary, regulations by, **28 § 155**
Rules and regulations,
Character of service of judges, governing, **28 § 153**
Judges serving on part-time basis, conflicts of interest, **28 § 152 nt**

BANKRUPTCY—Cont'd
Bankruptcy courts—Cont'd
Judicial council,
Certification, clerk, appointment of, **28 § 156**
Powers concerning removal of judges, **28 § 152**
Recall of retired judges, **28 § 155**
Certification of substantial service, **28 § 375**
Removal of judges, action taken by, **28 § 372**
Retirement and pensions, civil service, recall, certification of substantial service, **28 § 375**
Vacancy in office of bankruptcy judge, assisting court of appeals in appointment, **28 § 152 nt**
Jurisdiction,
District courts, **28 § 1334**
Procedure during transition period, **28 nt prec § 1471**
Provisions, relating to during transition, **28 nt prec § 1471**
Transfer to cure want of, **28 § 1631**
Jury trials, power to conduct, **28 § 157**
Law clerk, judges,
Annual and sick leave, exceptions from provisions of, **28 § 156**
Appointment, **28 § 156**
Motions,
Determination whether proceeding is a core proceeding, **28 § 157**
Non-core proceedings not subject to mandatory abstention provisions, **28 § 157**
Oaths and affirmations, judges, **28 § 153**
Orders,
Judges, **28 § 157**
Places of holding court, determination, Judicial Conference, **28 § 152**
Procedures, **28 § 157**
Provisions relating to during transition, **28 nt prec § 1471**
Puerto Rico, judges, appointment, number in judicial district, **28 § 152**
Qualifications, filling vacancy in office of bankruptcy judge, **28 § 152 nt**
Records and recordation, clerk official custodian of, **28 § 156**
Referral to judges,
Cases under Title 11, and any proceedings arising under Title 11, **28 § 157**
Proceedings related to cases under Title 11, **28 § 157**
Regular or special sessions, holding of, **28 § 151**
Removal of judge,
Action taken by judicial council, **28 § 372**
Grounds for, **28 § 152**
Retirement and pensions, generally. Judges or Justices, this index

BANKRUPTCY—Cont'd
Bankruptcy courts—Cont'd
Rules and regulations, division of business, **28 § 154**
Secretary, judges, appointment, **28 § 156**
Separability of provisions, Bankruptcy Amendments and Federal Judgeship Act of 1984, **28 § 151 nt**
Staff for judges, appointment, **28 § 156**
Supreme Court, additional rulemaking power to effectuate transfer of functions, to, **28 nt prec § 1471**
Temporary transfer of judges, **28 § 155**
Territories, judges, appointment and service, **28 § 152**
Transfer,
Appeals from final judgments, orders, of courts pending in bankruptcy appellate panels, **28 § 1334 nt**
Cases, civil actions, to new court system, **28 nt prec § 1471**
To cure want of jurisdiction, **28 § 1631**
Transition, provisions relating to,
Courts, **28 nt prec § 151**
Jurisdiction and procedure during, **28 nt prec § 1471**
Vacancy in office of judge, **28 §§ 152, 152 nt**
Withdrawal of case or proceeding from court by district court, **28 § 157**
Books and papers,
United States trustees, availability to, **28 § 581 nt**
Cases,
Administration,
Liquidation, generally, post
Supervision of, U.S. trustees, **28 § 586**
Commencement of cases,
District courts, venue of proceedings arising under Title 11 or arising in or related to cases under Title 11, **28 § 1409**
Joint cases,
Filing fee, payment in installments, **28 § 1930**
Venue of cases, district court, **28 § 1408**
Voluntary cases,
Filing fee, payment in installments, **28 § 1930**
Debtors,
Property of, exclusive jurisdiction in district court, **28 § 1334**
Dismissal,
Costs, **28 § 1930**
District courts,
Jurisdiction, cases, pending in bankruptcy courts, **28 § 1334 nt**
Original and exclusive jurisdiction of, **28 § 1334**

BANKRUPTCY—Cont'd
Cases—Cont'd
Hearings, proceedings not core proceedings but related to cases under Title 11, **28 § 157**
Information and documents made available by Director of Administrative Office of U.S. Courts, **28 § 581 nt**
Installment payment, fees, individual commencing voluntary or joint case, **28 § 1930**
Officers and employees. Trusts and trustees, generally, post
Property of debtor, exclusive jurisdiction in district court, **28 § 1334**
Referral,
Cases to bankruptcy judges, **28 § 157**
Proceedings related to cases under Title 11 to bankruptcy judge, **28 § 157**
Removal of claims related to, **28 § 1452**
Trusts and trustees, generally, post
Venue, district courts,
Commencement of, **28 § 1408**
Proceedings arising under Title 11 or arising in or related to cases under Title 11, **28 § 1409**
Cash collateral,
Orders approving use, core proceeding, hearing and determination by bankruptcy judges, **28 § 157**
Certiorari, writ of, receipt of order allowing, fees, **28 § 1930**
Change of venue, district courts, **28 § 1412**
Chief judge. Bankruptcy courts, generally, ante
Child support creditors or representatives, exemptions, certain motion costs and fees, **28 § 1930 nt**
Claims,
Estates, post
Priorities and preferences, generally, post
Removal, claims related to bankruptcy cases, **28 § 1452**
Clerks of courts,
Bankruptcy courts, ante
Commencement of cases. Cases, ante
Compensation and salaries,
Bankruptcy courts, ante
United States trustees, post
Congress,
Consolidation, offices of bankruptcy and district court clerks, prior approval by, requirement, **28 § 156**
Judicial conference, recommendations,
Number of bankruptcy judges needed, **28 § 152**
Sense of, court of appeals, filling vacancy in office of bankruptcy judge, **28 § 152 nt**

BANKRUPTCY—Cont'd
Consent,
Arbitration, alternative dispute resolution, referral, **28 § 654**
Conversion,
Cases, generally, ante
Individual debt adjustment, post
Liquidation, post
Core proceedings, defined, hearing and determination by bankruptcy judges, **28 § 157**
Costs,
Dismissal of case or proceeding, **28 § 1930**
Counselors. Attorneys, generally, ante
Counterclaims by estate, core proceeding hearing and determination by bankruptcy judges, **28 § 157**
Courts,
Bankruptcy courts, generally, ante
Clerk of district courts and deputies, ineligible to appointment as master, referee, **28 § 957**
Courts of appeals, generally, post
Courts of appeals,
Appointment of bankruptcy judges, **28 § 152**
Chief judge, appointment of bankruptcy judge where judges cannot agree, **28 § 152**
District courts, generally, post
Filling vacancy in office of bankruptcy judge, **28 § 152 nt**
Jurisdiction, appeals from all final decisions, **28 § 158**
Credit (payment of indebtedness),
Creditors, generally, post
Orders respecting, core proceeding, hearing and determination by bankruptcy judges, **28 § 157**
Creditors,
Proceedings arising under Title 11 or arising in or related to cases under Title 11, venue, district courts, **28 § 1409**
Debt adjustment,
Family farmer with regular annual income, debt adjustment, generally, post
Individual debt adjustment, generally, post
Debtors,
Cases, ante
Proceedings arising under Title 11 or arising in or related to cases under Title 11, venue, district courts, **28 § 1409**
Property,
District courts, exclusive jurisdiction of, **28 § 1334**
Debts,
Discharge, generally, post
Individual debt adjustment, generally, post
Municipal debt adjustment, generally, post

BANKRUPTCY—Cont'd
Decrees. Judgments and decrees, generally, post
Designation of bankruptcy courts, **28 § 151**
Director. Administrative Office of United States Courts, ante
Discharge,
Core proceedings, objections to, determinations concerning, hearing and determination by bankruptcy judges, **28 § 157**
Dismissal,
Cases, ante
Costs, **28 § 1930**
Dispute resolution, **28 § 651 et seq.**
District courts,
Abstention from hearing particular proceeding, comity with State courts or respect for State law, **28 § 1334**
Cases, original and exclusive jurisdiction of, **28 § 1334**
Civil proceedings, original jurisdiction of, **28 § 1334**
Clerk of court, fees and charges, **28 § 1930**
Interlocutory orders and decrees, appeals from, jurisdiction, **28 § 158**
Joint appellate panels, **28 § 158**
Judges or justices,
Entry of final orders or judgments after consideration of bankruptcy judge's proposed findings, **28 § 157**
Jurisdiction,
Appeals from final or interlocutory judgments, orders, of bankruptcy judges, **28 § 158**
Cases, pending in bankruptcy courts, **28 § 1334 nt**
During transition period, **28 nt prec § 1471**
Jury trials, designation of bankruptcy judge to conduct, **28 § 157**
Motions based upon State law claim, abstention, hearing of proceeding, **28 § 1334**
Orders of courts,
Bankruptcy judges, holding regular or special sessions, **28 § 151**
Jury trial, certain issues, **28 § 1411**
Personal injury tort and wrongful death claims, trial of, **28 § 157**
Prohibition, review by appeal, decision to abstain, **28 § 1334**
Property of debtor, exclusive jurisdiction of, **28 § 1334**
Referral to bankruptcy judges,
Cases under Title 11 and any proceedings arising under Title 11, **28 § 157**
Proceedings related to case under Title 11, **28 § 157**
Removal of claims related to bankruptcy cases, **28 § 1452**

BANKRUPTCY—Cont'd
District courts—Cont'd
Transfer of appeals from final judgments, orders, of bankruptcy courts pending in bankruptcy appellate panels, **28 § 1334 nt**
Trustees, commencement of proceedings arising in or related to cases under Title 11, venue, **28 § 1409**
Unit of, dealing with bankruptcy matters. Bankruptcy courts, generally, ante
Venue,
Cases,
Ancillary to foreign proceedings, **28 § 1410**
Under Title 11, **28 § 1408**
Change of, **28 § 1412**
Proceedings arising under Title 11 or arising in or related to cases under Title 11, **28 § 1409**
Withdrawal of cases or proceedings from bankruptcy courts, **28 § 157**
Documents. Books and papers, generally, ante
Domicile and residence,
Person or entity subject of case, location, factor, venue of cases under Title 11, **28 § 1408**
Electronic access to court data, fees and exemptions, **28 § 1930 nt**
Equity security holders,
Proceedings effecting relationship, core proceeding, hearing and determination by bankruptcy judges, **28 § 157**
Estates,
Administration,
Matters concerning, core proceeding, hearing and determination by bankruptcy judge, **28 § 157**
Claims,
Allowance or disallowance against, core proceeding, hearing and determination by bankruptcy judge, **28 § 157**
Counterclaims, core proceeding, hearing and determination by bankruptcy judge, **28 § 157**
Priorities and preferences, generally, post
Property,
Exemptions from, core proceeding, hearing and determination by bankruptcy judge, **28 § 157**
Orders to turn over, core proceeding, hearing and determination by bankruptcy judge, **28 § 157**
Representative of, proceeding arising under Title 11 or arising in or related to cases under Title 11, venue district courts, **28 § 1409**
Family farmer with regular annual income, debt adjustment,
Cases, commencement of, filing fee, **28 § 1930**

BANKRUPTCY—Cont'd
Family farmer with regular annual income, debt adjustment—Cont'd
Claims, allowance or disallowance against, court proceeding, hearing and determination by bankruptcy judges, **28 § 157**
Fees, filing, **28 § 1930**
Filing,
Fee, **28 § 1930**
United States trustees, post
Fees, **28 § 1930**
Bankruptcy administrators, exceptions, **28 § 1930**
Child support creditors or representatives, exemptions, **28 § 1930 nt**
Collection and disposition of, provisions, **28 § 1930 nt**
Electronic access to court data, fees and exemptions, **28 § 1930 nt**
Filing fees, commencement of cases, **28 § 1930**
Motions, relief from automatic stay, compel abandonment of estates property, **28 § 1930 nt**
Preparation and mailing of notices, distribution, **28 § 1930 nt**
Quarterly fees, payment to U.S. trustee, commencement of cases, **28 § 1930**
Report, Bankruptcy Fee System, impact on participants, contents, **28 § 1930 nt**
Schedule, **28 § 1930 nt**
Waiver, generally, post
Filing,
Fees, disposition, **28 § 1931 nt**
Forms. Bankruptcy Rules and Forms, generally, this index
Fraud,
Statutes of fraud,
Transfers, generally, post
Transfers, generally, post
Fraudulent conveyances, proceedings to determine, core proceeding, hearing and determination by bankruptcy judge, **28 § 157**
Garnishment, generally, this index
Governmental units,
Civil action to enforce police or regulatory power, exception, removal of claims related to bankruptcy cases, **28 § 1452**
Hearings,
Bankruptcy courts, ante
Incumbrances. Liens and incumbrances, generally, post
Individual debt adjustment,
Commencement of case, filing fee, payment, **28 § 1930**
Conversion,
Case to case under,
Reorganization,
Request of debtor, fee, **28 § 1930**

BANKRUPTCY—Cont'd
Individual debt adjustment—Cont'd
Family farmer with regular annual income, debt adjustment, generally, ante
Plans and specifications,,
Core proceeding, hearing and determination by bankruptcy judge, confirmation of, **28 § 157**
Standing trustees, appointment by U.S. trustees,
Compensation, **28 § 586**
Trustees,
Appointment,
United States trustees, generally, post
Standing trustees,
Consideration for appointment by U.S. trustees, **28 § 581 nt**
United States trustees, generally, post
United States trustees, generally, post
Information made available to U.S. trustees, **28 § 581 nt**
Injunctions,
District courts, venue, cases ancillary to foreign proceedings, **28 § 1410**
Injuries. Personal injuries, generally, post
Installment, payment of fee in, individual commencing voluntary or joint case, **28 § 1930**
Interstate commerce, activities affecting, withdrawal of case from bankruptcy court, **28 § 157**
Joint appellate panels, establishment, **28 § 158**
Judges or justices,
Bankruptcy courts, ante
District courts, ante
Judgments and decrees,
Declaratory judgments, creation of remedy, determination of tax liability, review, **28 § 2201**
District courts, generally, ante
Venue, cases ancillary to foreign proceedings, **28 § 1410**
Judicial Conference of the United States,
Assessment, need for bankruptcy judges, comprehensive review, report, recommendations to Congress, **28 § 152**
Bankruptcy courts, ante
Commencement of case,
Additional fees prescribed by, payment, **28 § 1930**
Filing fees, additional fees, **28 § 1930**
Determination, official duty stations of bankruptcy judges and places of holding court, **28 § 152**
Fees prescribed by, **28 § 1930**
Motions, relief from automatic stay, compel abandonment of estate property, **28 § 1930 nt**

BANKRUPTCY—Cont'd
Judicial Conference of the United States—Cont'd
Fees prescribed by—Cont'd
Schedule, additional fees, **28 § 1930 nt**
Number of bankruptcy judges needed, submission, recommendations to Congress, **28 § 152**
Recommendations,
Appointment of bankruptcy judges, **28 § 152**
Report, Bankruptcy Fee System, impact on participants, contents, **28 § 1930 nt**
Schedule of fees, **28 § 1930 nt**
Judicial Council,
Bankruptcy appellate panel, establishment, **28 § 158**
Bankruptcy courts, ante
Joint appellate panels, establishment, **28 § 158**
Report,
Director of Administrator of Office of the United States Courts, transition study, **28 nt prec § 151**
Judicial Conference of U.S., bankruptcy appellate panel requirements, various circuits, **28 § 158**
Judicial districts,
United States trustees, certification by Attorney General, notice and publication, **28 § 581 nt**
Judicial Panel on Multidistrict Litigation, generally, this index
Judicial review. Appeal and review, generally, ante
Jurisdiction,
Bankruptcy courts, ante
District courts, ante
Lack of, dismissal of case or proceeding, costs, **28 § 1930**
Jury trial,
Conduct in bankruptcy court, **28 § 157**
Right to unaffected, **28 § 1411**
Laws. State or local laws, generally, post
Leases,
Property,
Orders approving, core proceeding, hearing and determination by bankruptcy judges, **28 § 157**
Liens and incumbrances,
Determinations of validity, core proceeding, hearing and determination by bankruptcy judge, **28 § 157**
Injunction,
Enforcement of, venue, district courts, cases ancillary to foreign proceedings, **28 § 1410**
Liquidation,
Administration,
Cases, supervision by U.S. trustees, **28 § 586**

BANKRUPTCY—Cont'd
Liquidation—Cont'd
Commencement of case, filing fees, payment, **28 § 1930**
Consideration, current private trustees for appointment by U.S. trustees, **28 § 581 nt**
Conversion,
Case to case under,
Reorganization,
Request of debtor, fee, **28 § 1930**
Panel of private trustees, **28 § 586**
Proceedings affecting, core proceeding, hearing and determination by bankruptcy judge, **28 § 157**
United States trustees, post
Local laws. State or local laws, generally, post
Motions,
Forms of, rules prescribing, **28 § 2075**
State law claim, proceeding based upon, district court, abstention from hearing proceeding, **28 § 1334**
Withdrawal of proceedings from bankruptcy courts, **28 § 157**
Municipal debt adjustment,
Commencement of case,
Filing fees, payment, **28 § 1930**
Plan,
Core proceeding, hearing and determination by bankruptcy judge, confirmation of, **28 § 157**
Non-core proceedings, not subject to mandatory abstention provisions, **28 § 157**
Notice,
Appeal or application for appeal separate or joint, filing, fee, **28 § 1930**
Oaths and affirmations,
Bankruptcy judges, **28 § 153**
Officers and employees,
Attorneys, generally, ante
Trusts and trustees, generally, post
United States trustees, generally, post
Orders,
Bankruptcy courts, ante
Papers. Books and papers, generally, ante
Partial invalidity of provisions, Bankruptcy Amendments and Federal Judgeship Act of 1984, **28 § 151 nt**
Partnership,
Cases under Title 11 concerning general partner or partnership, venue of, **28 § 1408**
Personal injuries,
Jury trial, right to unaffected, **28 § 1411**
Liquidation, of, exemption from core proceeding, **28 § 157**
Procedures concerning, **28 § 157**

BANKRUPTCY—Cont'd
Plans and specifications,
Confirmations of, core proceeding, hearing and determination by bankruptcy judge, **28 § 157**
Individual debt adjustment, ante
Pleading,
Forms of, rules prescribing, **28 § 2075**
Principal assets in U.S.,
Location, factor, venue of cases under Title 11, **28 § 1408**
Venue, cases ancillary to foreign proceedings, **28 § 1410**
Principal place of business in U.S.,
Location, factor, venue of cases under Title 11, **28 § 1408**
Venue, district courts, cases ancillary to foreign proceedings, **28 § 1410**
Priorities and preferences,
Proceedings to determine, core proceeding, hearing and determination by bankruptcy judge, **28 § 157**
Proceedings. Actions and proceedings, generally, ante
Proof of claim. Claims, generally, ante
Property,
Debtors, ante
Estates, ante
Liens and incumbrances, generally, ante
Orders approving use, core proceeding, hearing and determination by bankruptcy judges, **28 § 157**
Sales, post
Puerto Rico, bankruptcy judges, appointment, number in judicial district, **28 § 152**
Real estate. Property, generally, ante
References and referees,
Appeals from bankruptcy judges, bankruptcy appellate panel, functions, **28 § 158**
Court interpreters, **28 § 1827**
Interpreters, court interpreters, services of, **28 § 1827**
Term of referee in bankruptcy, termination of, transition provisions, **28 nt prec § 151**
Referral to arbitration, alternative dispute resolution, **28 § 654**
Remand, claim or cause of action removed, **28 § 1452**
Removal of cases or causes, claims related to bankruptcy cases, **28 § 1452**
Reports,
Bankruptcy Fee System, impact on participants, contents, **28 § 1930 nt**
Residence. Domicile and residence, generally, ante
Review. Appeal and review, generally, ante

BANKRUPTCY—Cont'd
Sales,
Property,
Orders approving, core proceeding, hearing and determination by bankruptcy judge, **28 § 157**
Trusts and trustees, generally, post
Separability of provisions, Bankruptcy Amendments and Federal Judgeship Act of 1984, **28 § 151 nt**
Standing trustees. United States trustees, post
State courts, district court,
Comity with, abstention from hearing particular proceeding, **28 § 1334**
Venue,
Enjoining commencement or continuation of action or proceeding in, **28 § 1410**
Proceedings arising under Title 11 or arising in or related to cases under Title 11, **28 § 1409**
State or local laws,
Core proceedings, determination that proceeding is or is not, **28 § 157**
District court, abstention from hearing particular proceeding, **28 § 1334**
Stockbroker liquidation,
United States trustees, duties, **28 § 586**
Study, graduated fee system, Judicial Conference, Bankruptcy Fee System, report, **28 § 1930 nt**
Supersedeas,
Motions to terminate, automatic stay, core proceeding, hearing and determination by bankruptcy judges, **28 § 157**
Supreme Court, this index
Taxation,
Determination of liability, declaratory judgments, creation of remedy, review, **28 § 2201**
Time,
Requirements, venue of cases under Title 11, **28 § 1408**
Transfers,
To new court system, **28 nt prec § 1471**
Transition study, **28 nt prec § 151**
Transitional periods under Reform Act of 1978, **28 nt prec §§ 151, 1471**
Treasury of U.S.,
Accountability of clerk to pay fees, costs, into, **28 § 156**
Standing trustees, excess fees paid into, **28 § 586**
United States trustees, generally, post
Trusts and trustees,
Claims,
Arising from operation of debtor's business, venue, district courts, proceeding commenced by trustee arising under Title 11 or arising in or related to cases under Title 11, **28 § 1409**

BANKRUPTCY—Cont'd
Trusts and trustees—Cont'd
Commencement of proceeding arising in or related to cases under Title 11, power of trustee, venue, district courts, **28 § 1409**
Creditors, generally, ante
Estates, generally, ante
Individual debt adjustment, generally, ante
Investigation, official acts, by Attorney General, **28 § 526**
Money judgment or property worth less than certain sum, venue, district courts, proceeding by trustee to recover, **28 § 1409**
Standing trustees. United States trustees, post
Statutory successor to debtor or creditor, commencement of proceeding by trustee, venue, district courts, **28 § 1409**
United States trustees, generally, post
United States Court of Federal Claims, generally, this index
United States Tax Court,
Exception, removal of claims related to bankruptcy cases, **28 § 1452**
United States trustees,
Applications for compensation or reimbursement, filing comments or objections, **28 § 586**
Appointment, **28 § 581**
By Attorney General, **28 § 581 nt**
Judicial districts, **28 § 581**
Standing trustees, assistant U.S. trustees, supervision, **28 § 586**
Appropriations, System Fund, **28 § 589a**
Assistants,
Appointment, **28 § 582**
Official stations within appointed regions, determination, **28 § 584**
Removal, **28 § 582**
Salaries, limitation, **28 § 587**
Attorney General,
Investigations by, **28 § 526**
Powers, duties, functions, **28 § 581 et seq.**
Availability of System Fund to Attorney General, **28 § 589a**
Compensation and salaries,
Assistants, limitation, **28 § 587**
Incumbent trustees, **28 § 581 nt**
Limitation, **28 § 587**
Standing trustees, **28 § 586**
Consideration, current private trustees for appointment by, **28 § 581 nt**
Continuance in office upon expiration of term until successor appointed and qualified, **28 § 581**
Cost of services of System, recovery, deposits, **28 § 589a**

BANKRUPTCY—Cont'd
United States trustees—Cont'd
Court services, equipment, cooperative arrangements by Attorney General and Director of Administrative Office of U.S. Courts respecting, **28 § 581 nt**
Deposit or investment of moneys received, duties, **28 § 586**
Districts composing regions, appointment to, **28 § 581**
Duties, **28 § 586**
Executive Office for, Director, returns by court clerk to, **28 § 156**
Expenses and expenditures, **28 § 588**
Expiration, term of office, **28 § 581 nt**
Family farmer with regular annual income, debt adjustment,
Appointment of or service as trustee,
Compensation, **28 § 586**
Fees, quarterly fee, payment to, **28 § 1930**
Incumbent trustees, salary, **28 § 581 nt**
Individual debt adjustment,
Consideration, current standing trustees for appointment by, **28 § 581 nt**
Duties, **28 § 586**
Information and documents made available by Director of Administrative Office of U.S. Courts, **28 § 581 nt**
Investigations, Attorney General, **28 § 526**
Judicial districts,
Applicability, certain provisions respecting, **28 § 581 nt**
Appointment, **28 § 581**
Certification by Attorney General, notice and publication, **28 § 581 nt**
Liquidation,
Consideration, current private trustees for appointment by, **28 § 581 nt**
Notice, certification of judicial districts by Attorney General, **28 § 581 nt**
Oath of office, **28 § 583**
Official stations within appointed regions, determination, **28 § 584**
Panel, private trustees, establishment, maintenance, **28 § 586**
Percentage fee, standing trustees, determination, **28 § 586**
Publication, certification of judicial districts by Attorney General, **28 § 581 nt**
Qualifications, membership, panels of private trustees, rules and regulations, **28 § 586**
Quarterly fee, payment to, **28 § 1930**
Regions composed of Federal judicial districts, appointment to, **28 § 581**
Removal, **28 § 581**
Reports, **28 § 586**

BANKRUPTCY—Cont'd
United States trustees—Cont'd
Reports—Cont'd
System Fund deposits, **28 § 589a**
Staff and other employees, **28 § 589**
Standing trustees,
Appointment by, **28 § 586**
Compensation, **28 § 586**
Qualifications, **28 § 586**
Supervision, **28 § 586**
System Fund, establishment, deposits, investments, **28 § 589a**
Term of office, **28 §§ 581, 581 nt**
Treasury of U.S.,
Quarterly fee, deposit in, **28 § 1930**
System Fund, **28 § 589a**
Vacancies, **28 § 585**
Venue. District courts, ante
Waiver,
Fees, selected districts, Judicial Conference, Bankruptcy Fee System, report, **28 § 1930 nt**
Writs, forms of, rules prescribing, **28 § 2075**
Wrongful death claims,
Against estate, exemption from core proceeding, **28 § 157**
Jury trial, right to unaffected, **28 § 1411**
Procedures concerning, **28 § 157**

BANKRUPTCY JUDGESHIP ACT OF 1992
Generally, **28 §§ 1, 152**

BANKRUPTCY RULES AND FORMS
Actions and proceedings,
Forms of, rules prescribing, **28 § 2075**
Bankruptcy courts,
Judges,
Holding regular or special sessions of court, **28 § 151**
Cases,
Practice and procedure in, power of Supreme Court, **28 § 2075**
Chief Justice, report of rules to Congress as governing effective date, **28 § 2075**
Congress,
Report of Rules by Chief Justice governing effective date, **28 § 2075**
Courts,
Judges or justices,
Holding regular or special sessions of court, **28 § 151**
Effective date, report of rules to Congress by Chief Justice as governing, **28 § 2075**
Family farmer's debt adjustment,
With regular annual income, applicability, rules relating to, **28 § 581 nt**
Judges or justices,
Courts, ante
Motions,
Forms, general rules prescribing power of Supreme Court, **28 § 2075**

BANKRUPTCY RULES AND FORMS
—Cont'd
Pleading,
Forms, general rules prescribing power of Supreme Court, **28 § 2075**
Practice, cases, general rules prescribing, power of Supreme Court, **28 § 2075**
Procedure,
Cases, general rules prescribing, power of Supreme Court, **28 § 2075**
Proceedings. Actions and proceedings, generally, ante
Process,
Forms, general rules prescribing power of Supreme Court, **28 § 2075**
Service of process, generally, post
Service of process,
Rules prescribing, **28 § 2075**
Substantive rights, rules not to abridge, enlarge, **28 § 2075**
Supreme Court, power to prescribe forms of process, writs, by general rules, **28 § 2075**
United States Trustee System, applicability of rules relating to, **28 § 581 nt**
Writs,
Forms, general rules prescribing power of Supreme Court, **28 § 2075**

BANKS AND BANKING
Bank Fraud Crimes, generally, this index
Banks for Cooperatives, generally, this index
Checks, generally, this index
Comprehensive thrift and bank fraud prosecution and taxpayer recovery,
Resolution Trust Corporation, generally, this index
Sentence and punishment, major bank crime cases, **28 § 994 nt**
Comptroller of Currency, generally, this index
Conservators, this index
Crimes and offenses,
Comprehensive thrift and bank fraud prosecution and taxpayer recovery, generally, ante
Federal Bureau of Investigation, exchange of identification record with officials, use, funds provided for expenses, **28 § 534 nt**
Federal Intermediate Credit Banks, generally, this index
Federal Land Banks, generally, this index
Financial Institutions, generally, this index
National Banks, generally, this index
Parties, original jurisdiction of district court, **28 § 1348**
Receivers and receivership,
Sales,
Personal property, **28 § 2004**
Real estate, **28 §§ 2001, 2002**
Sentence and punishment, major bank crime cases, **28 § 994 nt**

BANKS AND BANKING—Cont'd
Venue, action against Comptroller of Currency, **28 § 1394**

BANKS FOR COOPERATIVES
Tort Claims Act, exception of claim arising from activities of bank, **28 § 2680**

BARBADOS
Conventions,
Taking of Evidence Abroad in Civil or Commercial Matters, party to, **28 § 1781 nt**

BATTERY
Assault and Battery, generally, this index

BENEVOLENT CORPORATIONS OR SOCIETIES
Fraternal Associations and Societies, generally, this index

BEQUESTS
Supreme Court, books, pamphlets, **28 § 674**

BETTING
Gambling, generally, this index

BIAS AND PREJUDICE
District judge, **28 § 144**
Hate Crimes, generally, this index
Justice, judge or Magistrate Judge, disqualification, grounds, **28 § 455**
United States Court of Federal Claims, generally, this index

BILLS AND NOTES (COMMERCIAL PAPER)
Checks, generally, this index
Garnishment by U.S. in action commenced against corporation, **28 § 2405**
Interest, generally, this index
Interpleader, district courts, jurisdiction, **28 § 1335**

BILLS OF EXCHANGE
Bills and Notes (Commercial Paper), generally, this index

BILLS OF LADING
Motor carriers, amount in controversy for district court jurisdiction determined by, **28 § 1337**
Vessels,
Liability for loss or damage determined by, amount in controversy, **28 § 1337**

BLACK PERSONS
See, also, Race, Color, and Previous Condition of Servitude, generally, this index
Civil Rights, generally, this index
Election disputes, district court jurisdiction, **28 § 1344**
Fair Housing, generally, this index

BLACK PERSONS—Cont'd
Federal judgeships, nomination of Blacks to, Congressional recommendations, **28 § 133 nt**
United States Magistrate Judges, merit selection panel to consider, **28 § 631 nt**

BOARD OF PATENT APPEALS AND INTERFERENCES
Patents, this index

BOARD OF VETERANS' APPEALS
United States Court of Appeals for Veterans Claims, generally, this index

BOARDS AND COMMISSIONS
Citizens' Commission on Public Service and Compensation, generally, this index
Clerks of courts, ineligible to appointment as commissioner, **28 § 957**
Equal Employment Opportunity Commission, generally. Civil Rights, this index
Judicial Center, this index
Labor Disputes, this index
Merit Systems Protection Board, generally, this index
Officers and Employees of Government, generally, this index
Patents. Commissioner of Patents and Trademarks, generally, this index
Resident Commissioner, generally, this index
Securities and Exchange Commission, generally, this index
Structural Alternatives for the Federal Courts of Appeals, **28 § 41 nt**
Trademark Trial and Appeal Board, generally, this index
Trademarks. Commissioner of Patents and Trademarks, generally, this index

BOISE, ID
United States Tax Court sessions held for trial at, rules. United States Tax Court, generally, this index

BONDS
Actions and proceedings,
Execution under Federal law, jurisdiction of district court, **28 § 1352**
Stay of execution of process in rem in admiralty, **28 § 2464**
Aliens,
Immigration, generally, this index
Attachment against delinquent postmasters and postal officers, employees, penal bond for discharge, **28 § 2717**
Bail bonds,
Moneys paid into court, payment of fine, assessment, **28 § 2044**
Continuance in action by U.S. against delinquent for public money, **28 § 2407**

BONDS—Cont'd
Copies as evidence, Federal officers, **28 § 1737**
Customs Duties, this index
Disbursing Officials, Clerks, and Agents, generally, this index
District Courts, this index
Evidence, Federal officers, **28 § 1737**
Forfeiture under process in admiralty, stay of execution of process, **28 § 2464**
Interpleader proceedings, district court, **28 § 1335**
Jurisdiction of suits, executed under Federal law, **28 § 1352**
Interpleader, **28 § 1335**
Jury trial in action to recover forfeiture, **28 § 1874**
Proceedings. Actions and proceedings, generally, ante
Receivers and receivership, district court, **28 § 754**
Release, generally, this index
Removal of case, bonds given prior to removal to remain valid and effectual, **28 § 1450**
United States Court of Federal Claims, generally, this index
United States Court of International Trade, this index
Vessel,
Owner to answer decree of court, **28 § 2464**

BOOKS AND PAPERS
Attorney General, authority to sell and exchange, **28 § 413**
Audits and Auditors, generally, this index
Bankruptcy, this index
Consuls, evidence, **28 § 1740**
Department or agency of U.S., admissibility in evidence, **28 § 1733**
Director of Administrative Office of U.S. Courts, authority to sell and exchange, **28 § 413**
Disbursing officers, jurisdiction of U.S. Court of Federal Claims, relief from responsibility for loss, **28 § 1496**
Documentary Evidence, generally, this index
Examinations and Examiners, this index
Executive Departments, this index
Forms. Bankruptcy Rules and Forms, generally, this index
Grand Jury, this index
Identification Documents, generally, this index
Judicial Panel on Multidistrict Litigation, generally, this index
Law Books, generally, this index
Patent and Trademark Office, evidence, **28 § 1744**
Possessions of U.S., evidence, **28 § 1739**
Production of Books and Papers, generally, this index
Rules of Appellate Procedure, this index

BOOKS AND PAPERS—Cont'd
Rules of Civil Procedure, this index
States, evidence, **28 § 1739**
Supreme Court, this index
Territories, evidence, **28 § 1739**
United States Court of Federal Claims, this index
United States Court of International Trade, this index
United States Magistrate Judges, generally, this index
Vice consuls, evidence, **28 § 1740**
Witnesses,
Recalcitrant witnesses refusal to obey court's order to provide books, **28 § 1826**

BORDER CROSSING POINTS
Customs Duties, generally, this index

BOSTON, MA
Court of Appeals for First Circuit, this index

BOUNTIES
Customs Duties, this index

BRANDS, MARKS AND LABELS
Trademarks and Trade Names, generally, this index

BRIEFS
Judicial Panel on Multidistrict Litigation, this index
Rules of Appellate Procedure, this index
Supreme Court, this index

BUDGET
Administrative Office of U.S. Courts, estimates, **28 § 605**
Appropriations, generally, this index
Director, generally. Office of Management and Budget, this index
Estimates,
Administrative Office of U.S. Courts, **28 § 605**
Office of Management and Budget, generally, this index
United States Court of International Trade, estimates, approval of, **28 § 605**

BUGGING
Interception of Wire, Oral, or Electronic Communications, generally, this index

BURDEN OF PROOF
Habeas corpus proceedings in Federal courts, State court factual determination erroneous, **28 § 2254**
United States Court of International Trade, certain civil actions, **28 § 2639**

BUREAU OF INVESTIGATION
Generally, **28 § 531 et seq.**

BUREAU OF INVESTIGATION—Cont'd
Aircraft piracy, related violations, authority to investigate, **28 § 538**
Appointment of Director, **28 § 532**
Appropriations,
Counterterrorism, **28 § 531 nt**
Exchange of identification records with certain officials, use of, **28 § 534 nt**
Humanitarian expenses, **28 § 509 nt**
Unforeseen emergencies, confidential character, **28 § 537**
Uniform Crime Reports, authorization, **28 § 534 nt**
Assets Forfeiture Fund, generally. Justice Department, this index
Attorney General, this index
Audits and auditors, undercover investigative operations closed in certain year, submission of results, report, **28 § 533 nt**
Automation, fingerprints and criminal justice information, funds for, **28 § 534 nt**
Child Abduction and Serial Murder Investigative Resources Center, **28 § 531 nt**
Civil service,
Positions in excepted service, **28 § 536**
Closed, defined, financial audit of undercover investigative operations closed in certain year, **28 § 533 nt**
Compensation and salaries,
Director, **28 § 532 nt**
Confirmation of Director, **28 § 532 nt**
Counterintelligence,
Funding authorizations for law enforcement, **28 § 531 nt**
Official reception and representation expenses, **28 § 539**
Counterterrorism, funding authorizations, **28 § 531 nt**
Critical Skills Scholarship Program, study, implementation, **28 § 532 nt**
Director,
Appointment, **28 § 532**
Compensation, **28 § 532 nt**
Confirmation, **28 § 532 nt**
Counterintelligence,
Official reception and representation expenses, **28 § 539**
Drug abuse prevention, forfeiture of property for violations, award for information, authority to make payment delegated to, **28 § 524**
Fingerprint identification records and name checks, certain categories, processing, establishing and collecting fees for, **28 § 534 nt**
Head of Bureau, **28 § 532**
Racketeer influence and corrupt organizations, forfeiture of property for violations, awards for information concerning, authority to make payment delegated to, **28 § 524**

BUREAU OF INVESTIGATION—Cont'd
Director—Cont'd
Study, undergraduate training program, **28 § 532 nt**
Term of service, **28 § 532 nt**
Employees,
Defined, financial audit of undercover investigative operations closed during certain year, **28 § 533 nt**
Espionage investigations,
Persons employed by or assigned to U.S. diplomatic missions abroad, **28 § 533 nt**
Expenses and expenditures, unforeseen emergencies, confidential character, **28 § 537**
Felonious killings of State or local law enforcement officers, investigation by, **28 § 540**
Felony crime of violence, defined, **28 § 540A**
Fingerprints and fingerprinting,
Identification,
Director, generally, ante
Fund for automation of, **28 § 534 nt**
Government officers and employees, investigation, crimes involving, **28 § 535**
Homicide, serial killings, investigations and investigators, **28 § 540B**
Humanitarian expenses, appropriations, authorization, **28 § 509 nt**
Identification records, exchange with certain officials, use of funds provided for salaries and expenses, **28 § 534 nt**
Illegal drugs, offenses involving, inclusion in Uniform Crime Reports, **28 § 534 nt**
Information, criminal justice and fingerprint, automation, funds for, **28 § 534 nt**
Investigation,
Espionage, persons employed by or assigned to U.S. diplomatic missions abroad, **28 § 533 nt**
Felonious killings of State or local law enforcement officers, **28 § 540**
Violent crimes against travelers, **28 § 540A**
Morgan P. Hardiman Child Abduction and Serial Murder Investigative Resources Center, **28 § 531 nt**
Murder, serial killings, investigations and investigators, **28 § 540B**
Part of Justice Department, **28 § 531**
Pay and allowances. Compensation and salaries, generally, ante
Reports,
Congress,
Financial audit of undercover investigative operations closed in certain year, time, contents, **28 § 533 nt**
Federal agencies, Uniform Crime Reports, **28 § 534 nt**

BUREAU OF INVESTIGATION—Cont'd
Reports—Cont'd
National Crime Information Center Project 2000, progress, **28 § 534 nt**
Serial killings,
Child Abduction and Serial Murder Investigative Resources Center, **28 § 531 nt**
Investigations and investigators, **28 § 540B**
State, defined, **28 § 540A**
Counterterrorism, funding authorizations, **28 § 531 nt**
Term of service of Director, **28 § 532 nt**
Terrorism, funding authorizations for programs to counter, **28 § 531 nt**
Traveler, defined, **28 § 540A**
Undercover investigative operations,
Closed in certain year, financial audit of, submission of results, reports, **28 § 533 nt**
Defined, financial audit of undercover investigative operations closed in certain year, **28 § 533 nt**
Undercover operation, defined, financial audit of undercover investigative operations closed in certain year, **28 § 533 nt**
Undergraduate training program, establishment, study, implementation, **28 § 532 nt**
Uniform Crime Reports, reports, Federal Agencies, **28 § 534 nt**
Uniforms, allowances, appropriations as permitted utilization, **28 § 509 nt**

BURLINGTON, VT
District court, location, holding terms of, **28 § 126**

BUSINESS CORPORATIONS
Corporations, generally, this index

CABLES
Interception of Wire, Oral, or Electronic Communications, generally, this index

CABOTAGE
Coasting Trade, generally, this index

CALIFORNIA
See, also, States, generally, this index
Bankruptcy judges, appointment, number in judicial district, **28 § 152**
District courts,
Cities, held at, **28 § 84**
Congressional findings, **28 § 84 nt**
Judges,
Additional, **28 § 133 nt**
Appointment, additional judges, advice and consent, **28 § 133 nt**
Number, **28 § 133**
Temporary judgeships, **28 § 133 nt**
Transfer of, **28 § 84 nt**
Places of holding, **28 § 84**

CALIFORNIA—Cont'd
Indians,
Civil jurisdiction of actions to which Indians are parties, **28 § 1360**
Judicial circuit of U.S., **28 § 41**
Judicial districts,
Bankruptcy provisions, applicability of certain amendments to, **28 § 581 nt**
Number of district judges, **28 § 133**
United States attorneys, transfer and appointment, **28 § 84 nt**
United States marshals, transfer and appointment, **28 § 84 nt**
United States trustees of judicial districts, **28 § 581**

CANAL ZONE
Court, defined, Jury Selection and Service Act, **28 § 1869**
Drug Abuse Prevention, Control and Treatment, generally, this index
Grand jury, selection and service, **28 § 1861 et seq.**
Judicial circuit of U.S., **28 § 41**
Jurors, fees and allowances, **28 § 1871**
Jury,
Refilling master jury wheel, not later than certain date, from sources which include names of persons 18 years or older, **28 § 1863 nt**
Selection and service, **28 § 1861 et seq.**
Tort Claims Act, exception of claim for injury to vessel or cargo while in Canal Zone waters, **28 § 2680**

CANDIDATES
Disclosure of Federal Campaign Funds, generally, this index
Elections, generally, this index
Political Activities, generally, this index

CANTON ISLAND
Judicial district of Hawaii, inclusion in, **28 § 91**

CAPITOL
Architect of Capitol, generally, this index
District of Columbia, generally, this index

CARRIERS
Accounts, orders for Surface Transportation Board, actions to enforce, **28 § 2321 et seq.**
Common Carriers, generally, this index
Damages,
Amount in controversy for district court jurisdiction, **28 § 1337**
Delay, loss or injuries to shipment, nonremovable action, **28 § 1445**
Nonremovable actions against, **28 § 1445**
Delivery,
Delay in, nonremovable action, **28 § 1445**
Federal Employers' Liability Act, generally, this index

CARRIERS—Cont'd
Hours of Labor, generally, this index
Initial carrier's liability,
Amount in controversy for district court jurisdiction, **28 § 1337**
Orders of Surface Transportation Board, actions to enforce, **28 § 2321 et seq.**
Injuries to shipment, nonremovable action, **28 § 1445**
Loss of shipment or property by carrier,
Amount in controversy for district court jurisdiction, **28 § 1337**
Nonremovable actions, **28 § 1445**
Mandamus, this index
Motor Carriers, generally, this index
Nonremovable actions against carriers, **28 § 1445**
Orders of Surface Transportation Board, actions to enforce, **28 § 2321 et seq.**
Receivers and receivership,
Damages for delay, loss or injuries to shipment, nonremovable actions, **28 § 1445**
Nonremovable actions against, **28 § 1445**
Records and recordation,
Surface Transportation Board orders, actions to enforce, **28 § 2321 et seq.**
Reports,
Orders of Surface Transportation Board, actions to enforce, **28 § 2321 et seq.**
Telecommunications, generally, this index
Trustee of carrier,
Damages for delay, loss or injuries to shipment, nonremovable action, **28 § 1445**
Nonremovable actions against, **28 § 1445**
United States Court of Federal Claims, generally, this index
Vessels, generally, this index

CARRYING AWAY
Kidnapping, generally, this index

CARS (MOTOR VEHICLES)
Motor Vehicles, generally, this index

CASH
Money and Finance, generally, this index

CASINOS
Gambling, generally, this index

CATALOGUES AND CATALOGING
United States Court of International Trade, admissibility in evidence where value of merchandise in issue in certain civil actions, **28 § 2639**

CELLULAR TELEPHONES
Telecommunications, this index

CEMETERIES AND DEAD BODIES
National Cemeteries, generally, this index

CERTIFICATES OF PUBLIC CONVENIENCE AND NECESSITY
Circuit judges, temporary assignment in other courts, **28 § 291**
Courts of appeals, temporary assignment of district judges, **28 § 292**
District judge, designation and assignment for service in another circuit, **28 § 292**
Judges, retired U.S. judges, assignment of duties, **28 § 294**

CERTIFIED COPIES
Attachment against delinquent postmasters and postal officers, employees, seizure of property, receipt of certified copies of warrants, **28 § 2710**
Clerks of Courts, this index
Clerks of District Courts, this index
Court record lost or destroyed, evidence, official paper, U.S. interested, **28 § 1735**
Evidence,
Court record lost or destroyed, **28 § 1734**
Pardon, evidence of damages in U.S. Court of Federal Claims for unjust conviction and imprisonment, **28 § 2513**
Patent and Trademark Office, documents, **28 § 1744**
Record of lien, evidence on creation of new district or division, **28 § 1656**
Trade-marks, certified copies of papers as evidence,
United States interested, **28 § 1735**
Fees,
Officer's bond, evidence, **28 § 1737**
Patent and Trademark Office documents, evidence, **28 § 1744**
Habeas corpus proceedings,
Admissibility of State court records, **28 § 2254**
Filing certified copies of judgment, plea of petitioner and indictment, **28 § 2249**
Furnishing to indigent petitioner without cost, **28 § 2250**
Indictment, filing in habeas corpus proceeding, **28 § 2249**
Judgments and decrees,
Filing in habeas corpus proceeding, **28 § 2249**
Satisfaction, registration, **28 § 1963**
Order of remand, mail to clerk of State court, **28 § 1447**
Papers included in record on review or enforcement in courts of appeals of agency, orders, **28 § 2112**
Plea of petitioner, filing in habeas corpus proceeding, **28 § 2249**
Records and proceedings in State court, failure of clerk to deliver on removal of case, **28 § 1449**

CERTIFIED COPIES—Cont'd
United States Court of International Trade, transcript of hearings, notices, transmission by Secretary, action, foreign merchandise not being sold in U.S. at less than fair value, **28 § 2632**

CERTIFIED LISTS
Materials comprising record on review or enforcement in courts of appeals of agency, orders, **28 § 2112**

CERTIFIED OR REGISTERED MAIL
Claims against U.S., final agency denial sent by, **28 § 2675**
Jury service, service of summons on person drawn, **28 § 1866**
Service of process,
Complaints,
Action against officer or employee of U.S., **28 § 1391**
State court action involving property on which U.S. has lien, **28 § 2410**
State court action involving property on which U.S. has lien, service of process and pleading, **28 § 2410**
Tax liens, U.S. as party, actions to quiet title, foreclose, service of process, **28 § 2410**
Three-judge district court, notice in action involving enforcement, operation, or execution of Federal or State statutes, **28 § 2284**

CERTIFIED QUESTIONS
Certification of constitutionality involved, intervention by U.S. or by State, **28 § 2403**
Courts of appeals, **28 § 1254**
Orders of certain Federal agencies, **28 § 2350**

CERTIORARI
District courts,
Notice of allowance of certiorari, fees, **28 § 1917**
State court, bring up records and proceedings on removal of case, **28 § 1447**
Harmless error, judgment, **28 § 2111**
State Courts, this index
Supreme Court, this index
United States Court of Appeals for the Armed Forces, this index

CHALLENGES
Jury, this index

CHANCELLORS
State, territory or possession, certificate to records or books or use as evidence, **28 § 1739**

CHANCERY
Equity, generally, this index

CHANGE OF VENUE
Venue or District of Trial, this index

CHARGES AND RATES
Customs Duties, this index
Orders of State agencies, district court's jurisdiction, **28 § 1342**

CHARITABLE FOUNDATIONS
Foundations, generally, this index

CHARITIES
Attorneys' fees and other costs and expenses, award to party prevailing against U.S. or agency, applicability, **28 §§ 2412, 2412 nt**
Charitable organizations, defined, limitations on outside income and employment by certain Government employees, **5, Ap 4, § 505**
Justice, judge, or magistrate, holding office in, disqualification, exclusions, **28 § 455**

CHATTEL MORTGAGES
Foreclosure, U.S. as party, **28 § 2410**

CHECKS
Commissioner of Internal Revenue Service, tender of checks in payment of judgment as stopping of interest, **28 § 2411**
Treasurer of United States, generally, this index

CHICAGO, IL
Court of Appeals for Seventh Circuit, generally, this index

CHIEF JUDGE OR JUSTICE
Appointment of judge as administrative assistant, **28 § 133**
Courts of Appeals, this index
Defined, Jury Selection and Service Act, **28 § 1869**
District Judges, this index
Institutes and joint councils on sentencing, **28 § 334**
Office of Federal Judicial Administration, defined, **28 § 133**
Supreme Court, this index
United States Court of Appeals for the Federal Circuit, this index
United States Court of Federal Claims, this index
United States Court of International Trade, this index

CHILD
Children and Minors, generally, this index

CHILD SUPPORT
Court, defined, full faith and credit for orders, **28 § 1738B**
Definitions, full faith and credit for child support orders, **28 § 1738B**

CHILD SUPPORT—Cont'd
Full faith and credit for orders, findings and purposes, **28 § 1738B nt**
Modification, defined, full faith and credit for orders, **28 § 1738B**
Orders, full faith and credit, priority recognition, **28 § 1738B**
Registration, orders, full faith and credit, priority, **28 § 1738B**
State, defined,
Full faith and credit for orders, **28 § 1738B**

CHILDREN AND MINORS
Annuities to surviving dependent children of justices and judges, **28 § 376**
Regulation and payment by Director of Administrative Office of U.S. Courts, **28 § 604**
Child, defined,
Judges or justices, annuities for survivors, **28 § 376**
Child Support, generally, this index
Drug Abuse Prevention, Control and Treatment, this index
Federal litigation, diverse citizenship, jurisdiction, representative deemed resident of State of infant, **28 § 1332**
Justice, judge, Magistrate Judge, minor residing in household, financial interest, disqualification, **28 § 455**
Juvenile Delinquents and Dependents, generally, this index
Kidnapping, generally, this index
Missing Children, generally, this index
Parental Kidnapping Prevention, generally, this index
Rules of Civil Procedure, this index
Sexual Abuse, generally, this index
Sexual exploitation,
Computer,
Sentence enhancement, **28 § 994 nt**
Use of,
Increased penalties, **28 § 994 nt**
Penalties,
Enhancement, authority of U.S. Sentencing Commission to amend existing guidelines, **28 § 994 nt**
Sentence and punishment,
Penalty enhancement, authority of U.S. Sentencing Commission to amend existing guidelines, **28 § 994 nt**
Sentence enhancement, **28 § 994 nt**
Sexual Abuse, generally, this index
Transportation,
Minors for purposes of, penalties,
Increase, **28 § 994 nt**
United States Sentencing Commission, promulgation and amendment of guidelines, **28 § 994 nt**
Solicitation of minor to commit crime, sentence enhancement, **28 § 994 nt**
United States, actions by, period of limitation, exclusion, **28 § 2416**

CHURCHES
See, also, Religious Organizations and Societies, generally, this index
Attorneys' fees and other costs and expenses, award to party prevailing against U.S. or agency, applicability, **28 §§ 2412, 2412 nt**

CINCINNATI, OH
Court of Appeals for Sixth Circuit, this index

CIRCUIT COURT OF APPEALS
Courts of Appeals, this index

CIRCUITS
Semiconductor Chip Products, generally, this index

CITIES
Municipal Corporations, generally, this index

CITIZENS AND CITIZENSHIP
Civil Rights, generally, this index
Juror qualification form, contents concerning, **28 § 1869**
National banks,
For purposes of actions, **28 § 1348**
Naturalization, generally, this index
Removal of cases because of citizenship of party, **28 § 1441**
Subpoena of national or resident of U.S. in foreign country, **28 §§ 1783, 1784**
Supreme Court jurisdiction of proceedings by State against citizen of another State, **28 § 1251**

CITIZENS' COMMISSION ON PUBLIC SERVICE AND COMPENSATION
Judges or justices,
Determination, annual pay rates, **28 §§ 5, 132, 252**

CIVIL ACTIONS
Actions and Proceedings, generally, this index

CIVIL PROCEDURE
Rules of Civil Procedure, generally, this index

CIVIL RIGHTS
Actions and proceedings,
Jurisdiction,
District court, **28 §§ 1343, 1344**
Removal of cases, State to Federal court, **28 § 1443**
Boards and commissions,
Equal employment opportunity, post
Conspiracy,
District court's jurisdiction, **28 § 1343**
District courts,
Jurisdiction, **28 § 1343**
Elective franchise, jurisdiction of district court, **28 § 1343**

CIVIL RIGHTS—Cont'd
Equal employment opportunity,
Commission,
Administrative Office of U.S. Courts, Personnel Management System, right of appeal preserved under, **28 § 602 nt**
Chairman,
Federal Legal Council, representatives designated by, **28 § 509 nt, EON 12146**
Discrimination, generally, this index
Equal Employment Opportunity Commission. Equal employment opportunity, ante
Fair Housing, generally, this index
Human Rights, generally, this index
Jurisdiction,
Actions, **28 § 1343**
Elections disputes, **28 § 1344**
District court, **28 §§ 1343, 1344**
Jury,
Qualification for service, **28 § 1865**
Qualification form, contents concerning, **28 § 1869**
Privileges and immunities, jurisdiction of district court, **28 § 1343**
Removal of actions or proceedings, State to Federal court, **28 § 1443**
Torture victim protection, **28 § 1350 nt**
Voting rights,
Official lists,
Voter registration lists, jury selection, **28 § 1869**

CIVIL SERVICE
Administrative Law Judges, generally, this index
Administrative Office of U.S. Courts, employees appointed subject to laws, **28 § 602**
Competitive service,
Assistant Attorney General for Administration, **28 § 507**
Judicial Center, appointment of secretarial and clerical personnel, **28 § 625**
Employees' Compensation for Work Injuries, generally, this index
Merit Systems Protection Board, generally, this index
Political Activities, generally, this index
United States Court of International Trade, officers and employees, deprivation of civil service status prohibited, **28 § 871 nt**

CLAIMS
Attorneys,
Claims against U.S., fees, **28 § 2678**
Bankruptcy, this index
Banks for cooperatives, Tort Claims Act exception, claim arising from activities of bank, **28 § 2680**
Constitution of United States, this index
Court. United States Court of Federal Claims, generally, this index

CLAIMS—Cont'd
Credits in actions by U.S., **28 § 2406**
Damages,
District court's jurisdiction of claim against U.S., **28 § 1346**
Disbursing Officials, Clerks, and Agents, this index
District courts, jurisdiction, claims against U.S., **28 § 1346**
Employees' Compensation for Work Injuries, generally, this index
False or fraudulent claims against Government,
Forfeiture of fraudulent claims, **28 § 2514**
Federal Debt Collection, generally, this index
Federal intermediate credit banks, Tort Claims Act exception, claim arising from activities of bank, **28 § 2680**
Federal land banks, Tort Claims Act exception, claim arising from activities of bank, **28 § 2680**
General Services Administration, generally, this index
Government employees. Officers and Employees of Government, this index
Indians, this index
Interest, claims against U.S., **28 § 2516**
Officers and Employees of Government, this index
Patents, generally, this index
Time, presentation of claims or commencement of action against U.S., **28 § 2401**
Tort Claims Act, **28 §§ 1346, 1402, 2401, 2402, 2411, 2412, 2671 et seq.**
Certification by Attorney General, offended employee acting within scope of office of employment at time of incidents, representation and removal, **28 § 2679**
Congressional declaration of findings and purposes, liability of Federal employees, exclusive remedy, **28 § 2671 nt**
Death, jurisdiction of actions and claims against U.S., **28 § 1346**
Employee of Government, **28 § 2671**
Exceptions, claims arising from certain activities, **28 § 2680**
Exclusiveness of remedy, **28 § 2679**
Filing and final agency denial of claim against U.S., prerequisite, commencement of action, **28 § 2675**
Investigative or law enforcement officer, defined, **28 § 2680**
Judicial immunity, assertion of defense based on, **28 § 2674**
Legislative immunity, assertion of defense based on, **28 § 2674**
Loss, administrative adjustment of claims, **28 § 2672**

CLAIMS—Cont'd
Tort Claims Act—Cont'd
Option to consider claim denied where agency fails to make final disposition thereof, **28 § 2675**
Prisoners, civil actions against U.S., limitations, conditions, **28 § 1346**
Remedies exclusive, **28 § 2679**
Time, presentation of claims or commencement of action against U.S., **28 § 2401**
Venue of action, **28 § 1402**
United States,
Claims against,
Civil justice reform, guidelines, **28 § 519 nt, EON 12988**
Guidelines, civil justice reform, **28 § 519 nt, EON 12988**
Real estate, quieting title, inapplicability to actions involving claims against U.S., **28 § 2409a**
Claims of,
Civil justice reform, **28 § 519 nt, EON 12988**
Guidelines, civil justice reform, **28 § 519 nt, EON 12988**
Payment, judgments, awards and compromise settlements, appropriations, **28 § 2414**
United States Court of Federal Claims, generally, this index

CLAIMS COURT
United States Court of Federal Claims, generally, this index

CLASS ACTIONS
Rules of Civil Procedure, this index

CLERK OF HOUSE OF REPRESENTATIVES
Journals,
Evidence, certification, **28 § 1736**

CLERKS OF COURTS
Absence, **28 § 954**
Acknowledgment, power to take, **28 § 953**
Administration of oaths, **28 § 953**
Assistants,
Powers, **28 § 956**
Practice of law, restrictions, **28 § 955**
Supreme Court clerk, **28 § 671**
Attachment against postmasters and postal officers, employees,
Application for warrant made before, **28 § 2711**
Issuance of warrant, **28 § 2712**
Attestation of records and judicial proceedings of courts of State, territory or possession for evidence, **28 § 1738**
Authentication,
Certificate of judge to records or books of State, territory or possession for use as evidence, **28 § 1739**

CLERKS OF COURTS—Cont'd
Certified copies,
Copy of court record lost or destroyed, certified copy as evidence, **28 § 1734**
Habeas corpus proceeding, furnishing certified copies to indigent petitioner without cost, **28 § 2250**
Official paper, evidence of court record lost or destroyed, **28 § 1735**
Commissioner, appointment as, ineligibility, **28 § 957**
Compensation and salaries,
Deputies, generally, post
Director of Administrative Office of U.S. Courts to fix, **28 § 604**
Fees, generally, post
Increase, **28 § 603 nt**
Supreme Court, generally, post
Copies,
Certified copies, generally, ante
Court record lost or destroyed, certified copy as evidence, **28 § 1734**
Records and proceedings of former court of appeals furnished by clerk of Supreme Court, **28 § 6**
Supreme Court, post
Costs,
Fees, taxation as costs, **28 § 1920**
Habeas corpus proceeding, furnishing certified copies to indigent petitioner without cost, **28 § 2250**
Supreme Court, post
Courts of Appeals, this index
Defined,
Jury Selection and Service Act, **28 § 1869**
Deposit of other moneys in checking account in Treasury, **28 § 2043**
Deputies,
Administration of oaths and taking of acknowledgments, **28 § 953**
Compensation,
Clerk of Supreme Court, **28 § 671**
Fixed by Director, **28 § 604**
Increase, **28 § 603 nt**
Fixing compensation by Director of Administrative Office of U.S. Courts, **28 § 604**
Ineligibility for certain offices, **28 § 957**
Oaths, **28 § 951**
Part-time United States Magistrate Judge, appointment as, **28 § 631**
Powers, **28 § 956**
Practice of law, restrictions, **28 § 955**
Vacancy in clerks position, powers and duties, **28 § 954**
Designations and appointments of justices and judges to be filed with, **28 § 295**
Director of Administrative Office of U.S. Courts, supervision of administrative matters, **28 § 604**

CLERKS OF COURTS—Cont'd
District courts,
Clerks of District Courts, generally, this index
Docket fees of U.S. attorney or trustees, payment, **28 § 1923**
Evidence,
Attestation of records and judicial proceedings of courts of State, territory or possession for evidence, **28 § 1738**
Authentication of certificate of judge to records or books of State, territory or possession for use as evidence, **28 § 1739**
Certified copies,
Copy of court record lost or destroyed, certified copy as evidence, **28 § 1734**
Official paper, evidence of court record lost or destroyed, **28 § 1735**
Expenses and expenditures, office expenses, **28 § 961**
Fees,
Compensation and salaries, generally, ante
Payment of docket fees of U.S. attorney, **28 § 1923**
State court, demand for records and proceeding on removal of case, **28 § 1449**
Supreme Court, post
Taxation as costs, **28 § 1920**
Financial disclosure of Federal personnel, administration of provisions, duties, **5, Ap 4, § 111**
Habeas corpus proceeding, furnishing certified copies to indigent petitioner without cost, **28 § 2250**
Incentive awards for employees, **28 § 604**
Ineligibility for certain offices, **28 § 957**
Investigation, official acts, by Attorney General, **28 § 526**
Judicial Center, conduct of programs of education and training for, **28 § 620**
Judicial Panel on Multidistrict Litigation, this index
Law books and publications furnished, transmitted to successors, **28 § 414**
Masters, this index
Motions. Supreme Court, generally, post
Naturalization, this index
Oaths, **28 § 951**
Administration, **28 § 953**
Office expenses, **28 § 961**
Part-time Magistrate Judge, appointment as, **28 § 631**
Payment,
Costs and other moneys into Treasury, Supreme Court clerk, **28 § 671**
Docket fees of U.S. attorney or trustees, **28 § 1923**
Fees into Treasury, Supreme Court clerk, **28 § 671**
Powers and duties, **28 § 956**

CLERKS OF COURTS—Cont'd
Practice of law, restrictions, **28 § 955**
Process,
Signature, **28 § 1691**
Receiver, appointment as, ineligibility, **28 § 957**
Records and recordation,
Attestation of records of courts of State, territory or possession for evidence, **28 § 1738**
Authentication of certificate of judge to records of State, territory or possession for use as evidence, **28 § 1739**
Certified copies,
Copy of court record lost or destroyed, certified copy as evidence, **28 § 1734**
Official paper, evidence of court record lost or destroyed, **28 § 1735**
Former court of appeals kept in office of Supreme Court clerk, **28 § 6**
Restoration of court records lost or destroyed, U.S. interested, **28 § 1735**
Referee, appointment as, ineligibility, **28 § 957**
Return of fees, costs, by Supreme Court clerk, **28 § 671**
Rules of Appellate Procedure, this index
Rules of Civil Procedure, this index
Salary. Compensation and salaries, generally, ante
Signature to writs or process, **28 § 1691**
State Courts, this index
Supreme Court, **28 § 671**
Appropriations, **28 § 671 nt**
Assistants and messengers,
Appointment by and compensation fixed by clerk, **28 § 671**
Compensation fixed by, **28 § 671**
Compensation, **28 § 671**
Copies, records and proceedings of former court of appeals furnished by, **28 § 6**
Costs,
Payment into Treasury, **28 § 671**
Return to court by clerk, **28 § 671**
Court of appeals, records and proceedings of former court of appeals kept in office of clerk, **28 § 6**
Deputy clerk, compensation, **28 § 671**
Fees,
Court to fix fees charged, **28 § 1911**
Payment into Treasury, **28 § 671**
Taxation, **28 § 1911**
Moneys collected, payment into Treasury, **28 § 671**
Removal, **28 § 671**
Return to court of fees, costs and other moneys, **28 § 671**
Supreme Court, generally, this index
Treasury,
Payment, fees, costs, into, **28 § 671**
United States Court of Appeals for the Armed Forces, generally, this index

CLERKS OF COURTS—Cont'd
United States Court of Appeals for the Federal Circuit, generally, this index
United States Court of Appeals for Veterans Claims, generally, this index
United States Court of Federal Claims, this index
United States Court of International Trade, this index
United States Magistrate Judges, right to hold office of Magistrate Judge, **28 § 631**
United States Tax Court, this index
Vacancies, **28 § 954**
Wages. Compensation and salaries, generally, ante
Witnesses, subpoenas issued, payment of fees upon certificate of, **28 § 1825**
Writs, signature, **28 § 1691**

CLERKS OF DISTRICT COURTS
See, also, Clerks of Courts, generally, this index
Generally, **28 § 751**
Appointment, **28 § 751**
Orders appointing, United States attorneys to fill vacancy, filed with clerk, **28 § 546**
Assistants. Deputies, assistants and employees, generally, post
Certification of attendance fees for extended service of jurors, order of district judge, **28 § 1871**
Certified copies,
Record of lien, evidence on creation of new district or division, **28 § 1656**
Reporter or other designated individual to deliver for the records of court a certified copy of transcript, **28 § 753**
Compensation and salaries,
Deputies, assistants or employees, **28 § 751**
Fixed by Director of Administrative Office of U.S. Courts, **28 § 604**
Increase, **28 § 603 nt**
Restrictions, **28 § 751**
United States Magistrate Judge, compensation on appointment as, **28 § 751**
Continuance of pending process, on vacancy in office of district judge, **28 § 143**
Costs,
Payment into Treasury, **28 § 751**
Return to Director of Administrative Office of U.S. Courts, **28 § 751**
Deputies, assistants and employees,
Appointment, removal, compensation, **28 § 751**
Director of Administrative Office of U.S. Courts,
Approval by Director of appointment of deputies, assistants and employees, **28 § 751**
Fixing of compensation by, **28 § 604**

CLERKS OF DISTRICT COURTS
—Cont'd
Director of Administrative Office of U.S. Courts—Cont'd
Notice to of appointment of United States Magistrate Judge, **28 § 631**
Return on fees and costs to Director, **28 § 751**
Fees, **28 § 1914**
Allowance of appeal, **28 § 1917**
Filing,
Award to U.S., disposition, **28 § 1931**
Payment to, disposition, **28 § 1931**
Jury, certificate for payment, **28 § 1871**
Payments into Treasury, **28 § 751**
Transcript delivered to clerk for record, fees of reporter, **28 § 753**
Filing,
Fees, payment to, disposition, **28 § 1931**
Removal of cases, copies of records and proceedings in State court filed with clerk, **28 § 1447**
Grand Jury, this index
Incentive awards for employees, **28 § 604**
Jury, certificate for payment of jury fees, travel and subsistence allowance, **28 § 1871**
Moneys collected paid into Treasury, **28 § 751**
Notice to Director of Administrative Office of U.S. Courts of appointment of United States Magistrate Judge, **28 § 631**
Offices, designation, **28 § 751**
Official station, designation, **28 § 751**
Orders,
Adjournment, **28 § 140**
Judicial panel on multidistrict litigation filed with, **28 § 1407**
Original notes or other original records, open for inspection in office of, **28 § 753**
Payment,
Certificate for payment of jury fees, travel and subsistence allowance, **28 § 1871**
Costs, fees and moneys collected into Treasury, **28 § 751**
Practice of law restricted, **28 § 955**
Preservation, original shorthand notes or other original records, reporter or other individual designated to produce record certifying, **28 § 753**
Process, continuance of pending process or vacancy on office of district judge, **28 § 143**
Records and recordation,
Certified copies of record of lien, evidence on creation of new district or division, **28 § 1656**
Delivery to clerk, reporter or other designated individual, certified copy of transcript, **28 § 753**

CLERKS OF DISTRICT COURTS
—Cont'd
Records and recordation—Cont'd
Removal of cases, copies of records in State court filed with clerk, **28 § 1447**
Removal,
Cases, copies of records and proceedings in State court filed with clerk, **28 § 1447**
Clerk of court, **28 § 751**
Deputies, assistants or employees, **28 § 751**
Reporter or other designated individual to deliver records of court, certified copy of transcript, **28 § 753**
Residence requirement, **28 § 751**
Returns,
To Director of Administrative Office of U.S. Courts,
Fees and costs, **28 § 751**
Money collected, **28 § 751**
Salaries. Compensation and salaries, generally, ante
Transcripts,
Copy of in office of clerk, open for inspection, **28 § 753**
Delivered to for record, fees of reporter, **28 § 753**
United States attorneys, orders of appointment filed with, **28 § 546**
United States Court of Federal Claims, judgments, transcript,
Filed in office, **28 § 2508**
Suit by Government officers, contractors, on unsettled accounts, entry, **28 § 2511**
United States Court of International Trade, generally, this index
United States District Court for District of Columbia, this index
United States Magistrate Judges, this index
Wages. Compensation and salaries, generally, ante

CLONING
Wireless telephones, **28 § 994 nt**

CLOUD ON TITLE
Removal, district court order for appearance of absent defendant, **28 § 1655**

COAST GUARD
See, also,
Armed Forces, generally, this index
Uniformed Services, generally, this index
Reserves. Coast Guard Reserve, generally, this index
Retirement and pensions,
United States Magistrate Judges, eligibility of retired officers and enlisted men for appointment and service as, **28 § 631**
Seamen, generally, this index

COAST GUARD—Cont'd
Tort Claims Act, exception of claim arising out of combatant activities, **28 § 2680**
Veterans, generally, this index

COAST GUARD EXCHANGES
Contracts,
Express or implied with,
District courts, concurrent jurisdiction with U.S. Court of Federal Claims, civil action or claim against U.S., **28 § 1346**
United States Court of Federal Claims, jurisdiction, claims founded on, **28 § 1491**

COAST GUARD RESERVE
Retirement and pensions,
United States Magistrate Judges, eligibility of retired officers and enlisted personnel for appointment and service as, **28 § 631**
United States Magistrate Judges, eligibility of retired officers, enlisted personnel and members for appointment and service as, **28 § 631**

COASTAL WATERS
Navigable Waters, generally, this index

COASTING TRADE
Jury trial in cases involving certain vessels, **28 § 1873**

CODE
United States Code, generally, this index

CODE OF FEDERAL REGULATIONS
United States Court of Federal Claims, generally, this index

COERCION AND DURESS
Terrorists and Terrorism, generally, this index
United States Court of Federal Claims, generally, this index

COLLECTIVE BARGAINING
Labor Disputes, this index

COLLECTOR OF CUSTOMS
See, also, Customs Officers, generally, this index
Bond, stay of execution of process in admiralty approval, **28 § 2464**

COLLUSION
Joinder of parties, lack of jurisdiction of district courts, **28 § 1359**

COLOR
Race, Color, and Previous Condition of Servitude, generally, this index

COLORADO
See, also, States, generally, this index
Bankruptcy judges, appointment, number in judicial district, **28 § 152**

COLORADO—Cont'd
District court,
Cities held at, **28 § 85**
Judges,
Additional, **28 § 133 nt**
Number, **28 § 133**
Judicial circuit of U.S., **28 § 41**
Judicial districts, **28 § 85**
Number of district judges, **28 § 133**

COLUMBIA, TN
District court held at, **28 § 123**

COMBAT ZONES
Armed Forces, this index

COMBINATIONS
Monopolies and Combinations, generally, this index

COMMANDER–IN–CHIEF
President of the United States, generally, this index

COMMERCE AND TRADE
Carriers, generally, this index
Coasting Trade, generally, this index
District court jurisdiction, actions under Acts regulating commerce, carrier cases, amount in controversy, **28 § 1337**
Federal Trade Commission, generally, this index
International Trade, generally, this index
Monopolies and Combinations, generally, this index
Secretary of Commerce, generally, this index
Ships and Shipping, generally, this index
Telecommunications, generally, this index
Trademarks and Trade Names, generally, this index
United States Court of International Trade, generally, this index

COMMERCE SECRETARY
Secretary of Commerce, generally, this index

COMMERCIAL PAPER
Bills and Notes (Commercial Paper), generally, this index

COMMISSARY STORES
Armed Forces, this index

COMMISSIONER OF INTERNAL REVENUE
Checks, tender in payment of judgment as stopping of running of interest, **28 § 2411**

COMMISSIONER OF PATENTS AND TRADEMARKS
Certification, patent specifications and drawings, evidence, **28 § 1745**

COMMISSIONER OF PATENTS AND TRADEMARKS—Cont'd
United States Court of Appeals for the Federal Circuit, this index

COMMISSIONERS
Boards and Commissions, generally, this index

COMMISSIONS (COMPENSATION)
Compensation and Salaries, generally, this index

COMMISSIONS OF OFFICERS
Associate justices of the Supreme Court, **28 § 4**
Circuit judges, precedence, **28 § 45**
District judges, seniority affecting precedence, **28 § 136**
Special attorney or special assistant to Attorney General, **28 § 515**

COMMITMENT
Habeas Corpus, generally, this index
Narcotic Drug Addicts, this index
Recalcitrant witnesses, escape from custody, **28 § 1826**
Warrants, generally, this index

COMMITTEES
Advisory Committees, generally, this index
Congressional Committees, generally, this index
Joint Committee on Printing, generally, this index

COMMODITY BROKER LIQUIDATION
United States trustees, duties, **28 § 586**

COMMON CARRIERS
See, also, Motor Carriers, generally, this index
Carriers, generally, this index
Customs Duties, generally, this index
Drug Abuse Prevention, Control and Treatment, this index
Railroads, generally, this index
Ships and Shipping, generally, this index
Telecommunications, generally, this index
Travel expenses of witnesses at U.S. courts, **28 § 1821**

COMMUNICATIONS
Interception of Wire, Oral, or Electronic Communications, generally, this index
Sound Recordings or Reproductions, generally, this index
Telecommunications, generally, this index

COMMUNICATIONS COMMISSION
Telecommunications, this index

COMMUNITIES
Development. Community Development, generally, this index
Federal agencies, review of orders, right to intervene, **28 § 2348**
Intervention, review, orders, certain Federal agencies, **28 § 2348**
Surface Transportation Board, orders, intervention in actions to enforce, **28 § 2323**

COMMUNITY CHESTS
Attorneys fees, **28 § 2412**

COMMUNITY DEVELOPMENT
Attorney General,
Neighborhood revitalization plan, development, solicitation from State and local governments, **28 § 509 nt**
Housing and Urban Development Department, generally, this index
Neighborhood revitalization, promotion, plan development, solicitation from State and local governments, **28 § 509 nt**
Plans and specifications,
Neighborhood revitalization, development by Attorney General, solicitation, **28 § 509 nt**
States,
Neighborhood revitalization plans, solicitation by Attorney General, **28 § 509 nt**
Units of general local government,
Neighborhood revitalization plans, solicitation by Attorney General, **28 § 509 nt**

COMPELLING PRODUCTION OF EVIDENCE OR DOCUMENTS
Production of Books and Papers, generally, this index

COMPENSATION AND SALARIES
Administrative Office of United States Courts, this index
Arbitration, this index
Attorney General, this index
Circuit court executives, **28 § 332**
Court Criers, this index
Court employees,
Director of Administrative Office of U.S. Court to fix, **28 § 602 et seq.**
Increase, **28 § 603 nt**
Courts of Appeals, this index
District Courts, this index
District Judges, this index
Employees' Compensation for Work Injuries, generally, this index
Expenses and Expenditures, generally, this index
Garnishment, generally, this index
Grand jurors, **28 § 1871**
Judges or Justices, this index
Judicial Center, this index
Jurors, **28 § 1871**

COMPENSATION AND SALARIES
—Cont'd
Jury commissioner, **28 § 1863**
Law Clerks, this index
Librarian of Supreme Court, **28 § 674**
Marshals,
Supreme Court, **28 § 672**
United States Marshals Service, this index
Messengers, courts, **28 §§ 603 nt, 604**
Per Diem, generally, this index
Reporters, this index
Secretaries, this index
Special attorney to Attorney General, **28 § 515**
Stenographers, this index
Subsistence, generally, this index
Supreme Court, this index
United States Attorneys, this index
United States Court of Federal Claims, generally, this index
United States Court of International Trade, this index
United States Magistrate Judges, this index
United States trustees. Bankruptcy, this index
Witnesses, this index
Workers Compensation, generally, this index

COMPETITION
Monopolies and Combinations, generally, this index
Unfair Competition, generally, this index

COMPETITIVE SERVICE
Civil Service, this index

COMPLAINTS
Correctional institutions, frivolous complaints, inmates, **28 § 1915A**
Crimes involving Government officers and employees, reports, **28 § 535**
Fees of U.S. Marshals for serving, **28 § 1921**
Indictment and Information, generally, this index
Lien of U.S. on property involved in action, service and contents, **28 § 2410**
Real estate, quieting title, actions involving claims against U.S. provisions, **28 § 2409a**
Service, action against officer or employee of U.S., **28 § 1391**
Tax liens, U.S. as party, actions to quiet title, foreclose, **28 § 2410**
United States, service on, lien of U.S. on property involved in action, **28 § 2410**
United States Court of Federal Claims, this index

COMPROMISE AND SETTLEMENT
Award for negligence, wrongful acts, of employee of Government, **28 § 2672**

COMPROMISE AND SETTLEMENT
—Cont'd
Civil justice reform, **28 § 519 nt, EON 12988**
Copyright cases, damages for infringement, actions against U.S., **28 § 1498**
Dispute resolution, alternative means of. Administrative Law and Procedure, generally, this index
Government officers and employees,
Award for negligence, wrongful acts, of, **28 § 2672**
Rules of Appellate Procedure, this index
Rules of Civil Procedure, this index
Secretary of Treasury, contract disputes, payments of judgments against U.S., exceptions, **28 § 2414**
Torts, this index
United States,
Guidelines, civil justice reform, **28 § 519 nt, EON 12988**
Payment of compromise settlements, appropriations for, **28 § 2414**
United States Court of Federal Claims, settlement of accounts of officers, agents or contractors with U.S., **28 § 1494**
United States Court of International Trade, this index

COMPTROLLER GENERAL
Access to information,
Financial disclosure reports of Federal personnel, **5, Ap 4, § 108**
Federal personnel, financial disclosure reports, access to, **5, Ap 4, § 108**
Independent Counsel, audits, provisions, **28 § 596**
Judicial Survivors Annuities Program, audit, reports, Congress, **28 § 376 nt**
Justices and judges, amounts deducted, from salary for annuities to survivors, procedures prescribed by, **28 § 376**
Reports,
Audits of,
Judicial Survivors Annuities Program, **28 § 376 nt**
Studies,
Financial disclosure requirements of Federal personnel, **5, Ap 4, § 108**
United States Court of Federal Claims,
Notice of suit by Government officer, contractor, **28 § 2511**
Referral of cases to, **28 § 2510**

COMPTROLLER OF CURRENCY
Injunctions,
Jurisdiction of district courts, national banks, **28 § 1348**
Venue of action, national banks, **28 § 1394**
National Banks, this index

COMPUTERS
Children and minors, sexual abuse, sentence enhancement, **28 § 994 nt**
Federal computer systems,
Administrative Office of United States Courts, generally, this index
Sexual abuse,
Children and minors, sentence enhancement, **28 § 994 nt**
Sexual exploitation of children, use of,
Increased penalties, **28 § 994 nt**

CONCURRENT JURISDICTION
District Courts, this index

CONDEMNATION (REAL PROPERTY)
Eminent Domain, generally, this index

CONFERENCES
Administrative Conference of United States, generally, this index
Civil justice reform, litigation on behalf of U.S., guidelines, **28 § 519 nt, EON 12988**
Judicial Conference,
Circuit, **28 § 333**
United States, **28 § 331**
Settlement, litigation on behalf of U.S., guidelines, **28 § 519 nt, EON 12988**

CONFESSION OF JUDGMENT
Forfeiture annexed to any articles of bonds, or other specialties, actions to recover, **28 § 1874**

CONFIDENTIAL OR PRIVILEGED INFORMATION
Alternative dispute resolution, **28 § 652**
Civil justice reform, applicability, **28 § 519 nt, EON 12988**
District courts,
Alternative dispute resolution, **28 § 652**
Home health care and services, criminal background checks, labor and employment, **28 § 534 nt**
Nursing homes, criminal background checks, labor and employment, **28 § 534 nt**
United States Court of International Trade, this index

CONFINEMENT
Kidnapping, generally, this index
Recalcitrant witness, **28 § 1826**
Witnesses, recalcitrant witnesses refusal to obey court's order to provide certain information, **28 § 1826**

CONFLICTS OF INTEREST
Bankruptcy judges,
Part-time basis, prohibitions concerning, **28 § 152 nt**
Provisions concerning, **28 § 153**
Justice Department officers and employees, disqualification in case of, rules and regulations, penalties, penalty for violation, **28 § 528**

CONFLICTS OF INTEREST—Cont'd
Special Government employees,
Financial disclosure requirements of Federal personnel,
Confidential reports, **5, Ap 4, § 107**
Filing report, requirement, **5, Ap 4, § 101**
United States Magistrate Judges, **28 §§ 631, 632**

CONGRESS
Bankruptcy Rules and Forms, this index
Bureau of Investigation,
Undercover operations, financial audit, report to, **28 § 533 nt**
Congressional Committees, generally, this index
Delegate to Congress, generally, this index
Director,
Administrative Offices of U.S. Court, copies of the reports submitted to Congress, **28 § 604**
Districts. Congressional Districts, generally, this index
Drugs and medicine,
Civil enforcement enhancement by Justice Department, **28 § 509 nt**
Employees. Officers and employees, generally, post
Hate crimes statistics, findings, **28 § 534 nt**
House of Representatives, generally, this index
Independent Counsel, this index
Joint Committee on Printing, generally, this index
Journals,
Evidence, **28 § 1736**
Judges,
Federal judgeships, recommendations concerning blacks and women as qualified individuals for selection for nomination to, **28 § 133 nt**
Specific authorization required for salary increases to, **28 § 461 nt**
Judicial Center, Board, transmission, copies, reports and recommendations submitted to Judicial Conference of U.S., **28 § 623**
Justice Department, drugs, civil enforcement enhancement, **28 § 509 nt**
Notice,
Judiciary Information Technology Fund, reprogramming of moneys, **28 § 612**
Officers and employees,
Removal of,
Action or prosecution against, act in discharge of official duty, **28 § 1442**
Outside income and employment, Representatives, officers and employees of Congress, **5, Ap 4, § 501 et seq.**

CONGRESS—Cont'd
Pages,
House of Representatives, generally, this index
Patents, generally, this index
President of the United States, this index
Removal of action or prosecution against officer for discharge of duty under order, **28 § 1442**
Reports,
Administrative Office of U.S. Courts,
Director, statistics, information, relating to business transacted by bankruptcy courts, **28 § 604**
Transportation, needs, **28 § 456 nt**
Attorney General,
Banking offenses, **28 § 522 nt**
Business and statistics of Justice Department, **28 § 522**
Forfeited property transactions, **28 § 524**
Public Integrity Section or other supervisory unit, **28 § 529**
Bureau of Investigation, undercover operations, financial audit, **28 § 533 nt**
Chief Justice of Supreme Court, proceedings and recommendations of judicial conference, **28 § 331**
Community Relations Service,
Audits and auditors,
Independent counsel, **28 § 591 nt**
Judicial survivors annuities program, **28 § 376 nt**
Congressional reference cases, **28 § 2509**
Department of Justice Assets Forfeiture Fund, amounts deposited, expended, transfers, **28 § 524**
Director,
Administrative Office of United States Courts, Judiciary Information Technology Fund, data processing, **28 § 612**
Drug Enforcement Administration, undercover investigative operations closed in certain year, financial audit, contents, time, **28 § 533 nt**
General Services Administrator,
Sentencing guidelines, comparison to previous system, submittal to, **28 § 994 nt**
Government Ethics, Office of, summary of actions taken, **5, Ap 4, § 408**
Judicial Center, copies transmitted to, **28 § 623**
Review panel, Congressional reference cases, **28 § 2509**
Rules of Civil Procedure for district courts and courts of appeals, report to Congress before taking effect, **28 § 2072**

CONGRESS—Cont'd
Reports—Cont'd
Secretary of Interior,
Indian Claims Limitation Act of 1982, recommendations, legislation to resolve claims, **28 § 2415 nt**
United States Sentencing Commission, **28 § 997**
Operation of sentencing guidelines system, problems, **28 § 994 nt**
Rules of Civil Procedure, report to Congress before taking effect, **28 § 2072**
Rules of Evidence, this index
Senate, generally, this index
Speaker of the House of Representatives, generally, this index
United States Court of Federal Claims, this index

CONGRESSIONAL COMMITTEES
Appropriations Committee (Senate or House of Representatives),
Judiciary Information Technology Fund, reprogramming of moneys, **28 § 612**
Reports,
Comptroller General to,
Audit reviews of independent counsel, **28 § 591 nt**
Judicial Conference, bankruptcy fees collection, **28 § 1931 nt**
Independent Counsel, this index
Judiciary Committee, Senate or House,
Judicial Center Board to keep informed of activities of, **28 § 623**
Reports,
Bankruptcy fee system, impact on participants, submittal by Judicial Conference of U.S., **28 § 1930 nt**
Federal Judicial Center Foundation, **28 § 629**
Justice Department, money laundering, charging and plea practices of Federal prosecutors, **28 § 994 nt**
Merit Systems Protection Board, generally, this index
Reports,
Use by U.S. Court of Federal Claims, **28 § 2507**

CONGRESSIONAL DISTRICTS
Three-judge court, action challenging constitutionality of apportionment, **28 § 2284**

CONNECTICUT
See, also, States, generally, this index
Bankruptcy judges, appointment, number in judicial district, **28 § 152**
District court,
Cities, held at, **28 § 86**
Judges,
Additional, **28 § 133 nt**
Number, **28 § 133**

CONNECTICUT—Cont'd
Judicial circuit of U.S., **28 § 41**
Judicial districts,
Bankruptcy provisions, applicability of certain amendments to, **28 § 581 nt**
Number of district judges, **28 § 133**
United States trustees of judicial districts, appointment, **28 § 581**

CONNECTING CARRIERS
Initial carrier, recovery from connecting carrier, amount in controversy for district court jurisdiction, **28 § 1337**

CONSERVATION
Recycling and Resource Recovery, generally, this index

CONSERVATORS
Banks and banking,
Sale of,
Personal property, **28 § 2004**
Real estate, **28 §§ 2001, 2002**
National Banks, this index

CONSOLIDATION OF CAUSES
United States Court of International Trade, this index

CONSPIRACY
Civil Rights, this index

CONSTITUTION OF UNITED STATES
Certificate,
Constitutionality of Act of Congress invoked, intervention in proceeding by U.S., **28 § 2403**
Claims, against U.S.,
Jurisdiction,
District courts, actions founded upon, **28 § 1346**
United States Court of Federal Claims, **28 § 1491**
Venue, **28 § 1402**
Constitutional questions,
Apportionment of Congressional districts or Statewide legislative body, Three-Judge Court required, **28 § 2284**
Intervention by U.S. as party, **28 § 2403**
State court decisions, review by Supreme Court, **28 § 1257**
Supreme Court of Puerto Rico's decisions, review by Supreme Court of U.S., **28 § 1258**
Due Process of Law, generally, this index
Electors. Presidential and Vice Presidential Electors, generally, this index
Full Faith and Credit, generally, this index
Habeas Corpus, this index
Jurisdiction, this index
Motion to vacate, set aside or correct sentence, grounds for, Federal custody, **28 § 2255**

CONSTITUTION OF UNITED STATES—Cont'd
Presidential and Vice Presidential Electors, generally, this index
Race, Color, and Previous Condition of Servitude, generally, this index
Rate orders of State agencies, jurisdiction, district courts, **28 § 1342**
State laws,
As rules of decision, exception, **28 § 1652**
Repugnant to, review of State decision by Supreme Court, **28 § 1257**
States, this index
Statute of Puerto Rico repugnant to, review of Supreme Court of Puerto Rico's decision by Supreme Court of U.S., **28 § 1258**
Suffrage,
Elections, generally, this index
Supreme Court, this index
United States Court of International Trade declared court established under Art. III, **28 § 251**
Venue or District of Trial, this index

CONSTITUTIONAL QUESTIONS
District Courts, this index

CONSULAR AGENTS
Foreign Service, this index

CONSULS AND CONSULAR OFFICERS
Foreign Diplomatic and Consular Officers, generally, this index

CONSULTANTS
Commission on,
Revision of Federal Court Appellate System, employment **28 § 41 nt**

CONSUMER PRICE INDEX
Civil penalties, imposition by Federal agencies, inflation adjustment, **28 § 2461 nt**

CONTAGIOUS AND INFECTIOUS DISEASES
Quarantine, generally, this index

CONTEMPT
Attachment for, garnishee failing to appear on garnishment by U.S., **28 § 2405**
Fines, penalties and forfeitures,
Witness in foreign country failing to respond to subpoena, **28 § 1784**
Judicial councils of circuits, officers and employees, noncompliance, with order, **28 § 332**
National, in foreign country failing to appear, subpoenas, **28 § 1784**
Order to show cause, contempt of national, in foreign country failing to respond to subpoena, service, **28 § 1784**
Rules of Civil Procedure, this index

CONTEMPT—Cont'd
United States Magistrate Judges, proceedings before, acts or conduct constituting, **28 § 636**

CONTESTANTS AND CONTESTEES
Contestant, Parental Kidnapping Prevention Act, **28 § 1738A**

CONTINUANCES
Delinquent for public money, action against, **28 § 2407**
Rules of Civil Procedure, this index

CONTRABAND
Counterfeiting, generally, this index

CONTRACTOR WITH UNITED STATES
Patents and copyrights, actions against U.S., jurisdiction of U.S. Court of Federal Claims, **28 § 1498**

CONTRACTORS
United States Court of Federal Claims,
Settlement of accounts, **28 § 1494**
Unsettled accounts,
Jurisdiction, **28 § 1494**
Notice of suit, **28 § 2511**

CONTRACTS
Actions against U.S., trial by court, **28 § 2402**
Administrative Law and Procedure, generally, this index
Admiralty cases, jury trial, **28 § 1873**
Coast Guard Exchanges, this index
Conflicts of Interest, generally, this index
District Courts, this index
Information technology,
Judiciary Information Technology Fund, **28 § 612**
Installments, generally, this index
Interference with contract rights, exception of claim from Tort Claims Act, **28 § 2680**
Judicial Center Board, research projects and other services, **28 § 624**
Labor Disputes, this index
Maritime matters,
Jury trial, **28 § 1873**
Patents, generally, this index
Public Contracts, generally, this index
United States,
Claims founded on,
Interest, **28 § 2516**
Jurisdiction, district courts, **28 § 1346**
Limitation of actions, **28 §§ 2415, 2416**
Real estate, quieting title, inapplicability to actions involving claims against U.S., **28 § 2409a**
Venue, **28 § 1402**
United States Court of Federal Claims, this index

CONTROLLED SUBSTANCES
Drug Abuse Prevention, Control and Treatment, this index
National Drug Policy, generally, this index

CONTROLLER OF CURRENCY
Comptroller of Currency, generally, this index

CONVENTIONS
See, also,
Treaties, generally, this index
Evidence, Taking of Evidence Abroad in Civil or Commercial Matters, text of, reservations, **28 § 1781 nt**
Israel, this index
Legalization for Foreign Public Documents, **FRCVP 44 nt**
Service Abroad of Judicial and Extrajudicial Documents in Civil or Commercial Matter, **FRCVP 4 nt**
Taking of Evidence Abroad in Civil or Commercial Matters, text of, reservations, **28 § 1781 nt**

CONVERSION
Property of U.S., action by, limitations, **28 §§ 2415, 2416**

CONVEYANCES
Deeds and Conveyances, generally, this index

CONVICTION
Costs in district court, **28 § 1918**
Damages for unjust conviction,
Allegations and proof in U.S. Court of Federal Claims, **28 § 2513**
Jurisdiction of U.S. Court of Federal Claims, **28 § 1495**
Defined, exclusion, rehabilitation, of narcotic addicts, **28 § 2901**
Juror, competency to serve, **28 § 1861**
Form, contents concerning, **28 § 1869**
Sentence and Punishment, generally, this index

CONVICTS
Correctional Institutions, generally, this index

COOPERATIVE ASSOCIATIONS AND ORGANIZATIONS
Banks for Cooperatives, generally, this index
Cooperative Marketing, generally, this index

COOPERATIVE MARKETING
Associations and societies,
Under Agricultural Marketing Act,
Attorneys' fees and other costs and expenses, award to party prevailing against U.S. or agency, applicability, **28 §§ 2412, 2412 nt**

COPYRIGHTS
Actions and proceedings,
Damages for infringement, action against U.S., **28 § 1498**
Infringement, generally, post
Mask work cases, semiconductor chip products, **28 § 1498**
Venue, **28 § 1400**
Assignments,
Government employees, action by assignee against Government in U.S. Court of Federal Claims, **28 § 1498**
Claims,
Foreign countries, **28 § 1498**
Collective bargaining agreements,
Motion pictures, transfer of ownership, **28 § 4001**
Costs,
Motion pictures, transfer of ownership, collective bargaining agreements, **28 § 4001**
District courts, jurisdiction of actions under copyright law, **28 § 1338**
Exemptions,
Motion pictures, transfer of ownership, collective bargaining agreements, **28 § 4001**
Immunity, waiver of by Member of Congress not to be construed from amendment of provisions relating to jurisdiction of U.S. Court of Federal Claims, **28 § 1498 nt**
Infringement,
Damages, claims against U.S., **28 § 1498**
Jurisdiction, suits under copyright law, **28 § 1338**
Mask work cases, semiconductor chip products, **28 § 1498**
District court jurisdiction, **28 § 1338**
Motion pictures,
Transfer of ownership, collective bargaining agreements, **28 § 4001**
Notice,
Motion pictures, transfer of ownership, collective bargaining agreements, **28 § 4001**
Officers and employees of Government, suit by employee against Government in U.S. Court of Federal Claims, **28 § 1498**
Ownership,
Infringement, generally, ante
Transfers,
Motion pictures, collective bargaining agreements, **28 § 4001**
Patents, generally, this index
Proceedings. Actions and proceedings, generally, ante
Reasonable and entire compensation, defined, **28 § 1498**
Security interest,
Motion pictures, transfer of ownership, collective bargaining agreements, **28 § 4001**

COPYRIGHTS—Cont'd
Transfers. Ownership, ante
United States,
Jurisdiction of U.S. Court of Federal Claims, 28 § **1498**
United States Court of Federal Claims, this index
Venue of suits under copyright laws, **28 § 1400**

CORPORATIONS
Actions and proceedings,
Organized under Federal law, jurisdiction of district courts, **28 § 1349**
Stockholder's action, behalf of corporation, service on corporation, **28 § 1695**
Venue of actions, generally, post
Attorneys' fees and other costs and expenses, award to party prevailing against U.S. or agency, applicability, **28 § 2412**
Banks and Banking, generally, this index
Banks for Cooperatives, generally, this index
Federal agencies, review of orders, right to intervene, **28 § 2348**
Federal Corporations, generally, this index
Federal Intermediate Credit Banks, generally, this index
Garnishment by U.S., **28 § 2405**
Interpleader, filing, district courts, jurisdiction, **28 § 1335**
Intervention, review, orders, certain Federal agencies, **28 § 2348**
Jurisdiction of district courts, diverse citizenship, corporation deemed citizen of State of incorporation and of State of principal place of business, **28 § 1332**
Limitations, outside employment, certain Government employees, **5, Ap 4, § 502**
Municipal Corporations, generally, this index
National Banks, generally, this index
Nonprofit Corporations, generally, this index
Process on, stockholder's derivative action, **28 § 1695**
Residence for venue purposes, **28 § 1391**
Resolution Trust Corporation, generally, this index
Rules of Civil Procedure, this index
Stock and Stockholders, generally, this index
Surface Transportation Board orders, intervention in actions to enforce, **28 § 2323**
Tax refund suits against U.S., venue, **28 § 1402**
United States Court of International Trade, generally, this index

CORPORATIONS—Cont'd
Venue of actions, **28 § 1391**
Stockholder's derivative action, **28 § 1401**
Tax refund suits against U.S., **28 § 1402**

CORRECTIONAL INSTITUTIONS
Actions and proceedings,
Civil actions,
Against Government, court screening and review, dismissal, grounds, **28 § 1915A**
Prepayment of fees or security, submission, copy of trust fund account statement, requirement, **28 § 1915**
Federal tort claims, limitations, civil actions against U.S., conditions, **28 § 1346**
Frivolous actions, inmates, **28 § 1915A**
Arrest or imprisonment on writ of execution or other process, privileges, **28 § 2007**
Attorney General,
Building and facilities account, transfer of funds to, from Assets Forfeiture Fund, for construction of correctional institutions, **28 § 524**
Building and facilities account, Federal prison systems, construction of correctional institutions, deposits, transfer from Assets Forfeiture Fund, **28 §§ 524, 524 nt**
Complaints, frivolous complaints, inmates, **28 § 1915A**
Construction, use of deposits transferred from Assets Forfeiture Fund to buildings and facilities account of Federal prison system, **28 §§ 524, 524 nt**
Criminal and other identification records, exchange with authorized officials, **28 § 534**
Dismissal and nonsuit, frivolous actions, inmates, **28 § 1915A**
Drug addicts. Narcotic Drug Addicts, generally, this index
Drug offenses, sentencing guidelines, promulgation by U.S. Sentencing Commission, **28 § 994 nt**
Escape, generally, this index
Extradition, generally, this index
Federal Prison Industries, generally, this index
Fees,
Fact witnesses, payment prohibition, **28 § 1821 nt**
Forma Pauperis, generally, this index
Frivolous actions, **28 § 1915A**
Dismissal, **28 § 1915**
Good time allowances,
Revocation, frivolous, harassing, malicious litigation, perjury, **28 § 1932**
Habeas Corpus, generally, this index

CORRECTIONAL INSTITUTIONS
—Cont'd
Prisoner, defined,
Forma pauperis proceedings, **28 § 1915**
Screening of complaints by court in civil actions, **28 § 1915A**
Probation, generally, this index
Revocation, earned release or good time credits, conditions, **28 § 1932**
Rules of Appellate Procedure, this index
Sentence and Punishment, generally, this index
Transfer of Offenders to or from Foreign Countries, generally, this index
Uniforms, allowances, appropriations as permitted utilization, **28 § 509 nt**
United States Marshals Service, generally, this index
Violent Crime Control and Law Enforcement, generally, this index

COST OF LIVING
Adjustment,
Civil penalties imposed by Federal agencies, **28 § 2461 nt**
District judges in territories and possessions, adjustment, retirement benefits, **28 § 373**

COSTS
Admiralty, this index
Affidavits,
Verification of bill of costs, **28 § 1924**
Agencies of U.S.,
Judgment for costs, prevailing party, actions by or against, **28 § 2412**
Security payment, **28 § 2408**
Amount in controversy,
District courts' jurisdiction, exclusion of, **28 § 1332**
Removal of action against carrier to District Court, exclusion of, **28 § 1445**
Appeal, forma pauperis proceeding, **28 § 1915**
Attorneys, this index
Bankruptcy, this index
Bill of costs, filing and inclusion in judgment or decree, **28 § 1920**
Briefs, admiralty appeals taxation of printing as costs, **28 § 1923**
Claimant in proceedings to condemn or forfeit property seized, **28 § 2465**
Clerks of Courts, this index
Contempt, national, in foreign country failing to respond to subpoena, **28 § 1784**
Convention on the Taking of Evidence Abroad in Civil or Commercial Matters, **28 § 1781 nt**
Copies of papers, fees, taxation as costs, **28 § 1920**
Court clerk's fees, taxation as costs, **28 § 1920**
Court interpreters, services, taxation as, **28 §§ 1827, 1828**

COSTS—Cont'd
Court reporter's fees, taxation as costs, **28 § 1920**
Courts of appeals,
Affirmance, **28 § 1912**
Charges prescribed by Judicial Conference of the U.S., **28 § 1913**
Criminal proceedings, in district court, **28 § 1918**
District Courts, this index
Docket fees, **28 § 1923**
Taxation, **28 §§ 1920, 1923**
Exemplification of papers, fees, taxation as costs, **28 § 1920**
Experts, compensation of court appointed experts, taxation as costs, **28 § 1920**
Fees or other compensation,
Docket fees, **28 §§ 1920, 1923**
Taxation as costs, **28 §§ 1920, 1922**
Fines, penalties and forfeitures, violation of provisions, **28 § 1918**
Forfeiture. Fines, penalties and forfeitures, generally, ante
Garnishment by U.S., **28 § 2405**
Interpreters,
Court interpreters, taxation as, **28 §§ 1827, 1828**
Special interpretation services, taxation as costs, **28 § 1920**
Patent infringement action, **28 § 1928**
Penalties. Fines, penalties and forfeitures, generally, ante
Printing fees, taxation as costs, **28 § 1920**
Removal of cases, remand of case removed, **28 § 1447**
Rules of Appellate Procedure, this index
Rules of Civil Procedure, this index
Seamen, this index
Stay of execution and enforcement of judgment to obtain certiorari, **28 § 2101**
Supreme Court, this index
Taxation, **28 § 1920**
United States marshal's fees, **28 § 1921**
United States, as party, **28 § 2412**
Civil actions and administrative proceedings, award of, Congressional findings, **28 § 2412 nt**
Judgment for costs, prevailing party, actions by or against U.S., **28 § 2412**
Payment, **28 § 2408**
Security not required of, **28 § 2408**
United States Court of Federal Claims, this index
United States Court of International Trade, this index
United States marshals,
Accounts, payments to witnesses or jurors, **28 § 567**
Fees, **28 § 1921**
Taxation as costs, **28 § 1920**
Witness fees,
Taxation as costs, **28 § 1920**

COSTS—Cont'd
Witness fees—Cont'd
Taxation as costs—Cont'd
United States Magistrate Judges, **28 § 1922**

COUNCILS
Federal Legal Council, establishment, composition, functions, **28 § 509 nt, EON 12146**
Judicial Council, generally, this index

COUNSELORS
Attorneys, generally, this index

COUNTERCLAIMS
Set-Off and Counterclaim, generally, this index

COUNTERFEITING
Forgery, generally, this index
Sentence and punishment,
Amendment of sentencing guidelines for crimes involving use of firearm during commission of, **28 § 994 nt**

COUNTERVAILING DUTIES
Customs Duties, this index

COURT CRIERS
Compensation and salaries,
Fixed by Director of Administrative Office of U.S. Courts, **28 § 604**
Increase, **28 § 603 nt**
Courts of appeals,
Appointment and removal, **28 § 714**
Director of Administrative Office of U.S. Courts to fix compensation, **28 § 604**
District courts, crier-law clerks, appointment, **28 § 755**
Meals and lodging when acting as bailiffs, appropriations, **28 § 524**
United States Court of International Trade, appointment, duties, **28 § 872**

COURT INTERPRETERS ACT
Generally, **28 §§ 1 nt, 602 et seq., 1827, 1828, 1920**

COURT OF APPEALS
Courts of Appeals, generally, this index

COURT OF APPEALS FOR DISTRICT OF COLUMBIA
United States Court of Appeals for District of Columbia, generally, this index

COURT OF APPEALS FOR FIRST CIRCUIT
See, also,
Courts of Appeals, generally, this index
Boston, MA,
Place of holding terms or sessions, **28 § 48**

COURT OF APPEALS FOR FIRST CIRCUIT—Cont'd
Chief Judge,
Precedence, **28 § 45**
Composition,
Judicial circuit under jurisdiction of, **28 § 41**
Judges,
Additional circuit judgeships, **28 § 44 nt**
Appointment, tenure, **28 § 44**
Assignment, **28 § 46**
Chief Judge, generally, ante
Number of, **28 § 44**
Appointment, additional judges, **28 § 44 nt**
Trial judge, disqualification to hear appeal, **28 § 47**
Judicial circuit under jurisdiction, composition of, **28 § 41**
Judicial discipline, complaint, review procedure, **28 § 372**
Sessions, **28 § 48**
Special sessions, **28 § 48**
Special terms, **28 § 48**

COURT OF APPEALS FOR SECOND CIRCUIT
See, also,
Courts of Appeals, generally, this index
Chief Judge,
Precedence, **28 § 45**
Composition of judicial circuit under jurisdiction of, **28 § 41**
Judges,
Additional circuit judgeships, **28 § 44 nt**
Appointment, tenure, **28 § 44**
Assignment, **28 § 46**
Chief Judge, generally, ante
Number of, **28 § 44**
Appointment of additional judges, **28 § 44 nt**
Trial judge, disqualification to hear appeal, **28 § 47**
Judicial circuit under jurisdiction, composition, **28 § 41**
Judicial discipline, complaint, review procedure, **28 § 372**
New York City, NY,
Place of holding terms or sessions, **28 § 48**
Sessions, **28 § 48**
Special sessions, **28 § 48**
Special terms, **28 § 48**
Terms, **28 § 48**

COURT OF APPEALS FOR THIRD CIRCUIT
See, also,
Courts of Appeals, generally, this index
Chief Judge,
Precedence, **28 § 45**

COURT OF APPEALS FOR THIRD CIRCUIT—Cont'd
Composition,
Judicial circuit under jurisdiction of, 28 § 41
District court,
Virgin Islands, post
Judges,
Additional circuit judgeships, 28 § 44 nt
Appointment, 28 § 44
Additional judges, 28 § 44 nt
Number, 28 § 44
Appointment of additional judges, 28 § 44 nt
Trial judge, disqualification to hear appeal, 28 § 47
Judicial circuit under jurisdiction, composition of, 28 § 41
Judicial discipline,
Complaint, review procedure, 28 § 372
Number,
Judges, ante
Philadelphia, PA,
Place of, holding terms or sessions, 28 § 48
Special sessions, 28 § 48
Special terms, 28 § 48
Terms of Court, 28 § 48
Virgin Islands,
District court,
Appeals to, 28 § 1294

COURT OF APPEALS FOR FOURTH CIRCUIT
See, also,
Courts of Appeals, generally, this index
Asheville, NC, place of holding terms or sessions, 28 § 48
Certiorari,
Precedence, 28 § 45
Composition,
Judicial circuit under jurisdiction of, 28 § 41
Judges,
Additional circuit judgeships, 28 § 44 nt
Appointment,
Additional judges, 28 § 44 nt
Tenure, 28 § 44
Assignment, 28 § 46
Chief Judge,
Precedence, 28 § 45
Number, 28 § 44
Appointment of additional judges, 28 § 44 nt
Senior judges,
Assignment of duties, participation, 28 § 46 nt
Trial judge, disqualification to hear appeal, 28 § 47
Judicial Council,
Composition of, 28 § 41

COURT OF APPEALS FOR FOURTH CIRCUIT—Cont'd
Judicial discipline,
Complaint,
Review procedure, 28 § 372
Richmond, place of, holding terms or sessions, 28 § 48
Senior judges. Judges, ante
Sessions of Court, 28 § 48
Special sessions, 28 § 48
Special terms, 28 § 48
Terms,
Court, 28 § 48

COURT OF APPEALS FOR FIFTH CIRCUIT
See, also,
Courts of Appeals, generally, this index
Administrative action, termination of court, 28 § 41 nt
Assignment,
Judges, 28 § 46
Procedure for administration of pending cases with regard to reorganization, 28 § 41 nt
Chief Judge,
Order declaring emergency, impaneling three-judge panels, 28 § 46
Precedence, 28 § 45
Composition,
Judicial circuit under jurisdiction of, 28 § 41
Decisions,
Orders, generally, post
Former Fifth Circuit, defined, Reorganization Act of 1980, 28 § 41 nt
Fort Worth, TX, place of holding terms or sessions, 28 § 48
Jackson, MS, place of holding terms or sessions, 28 § 48
Judges,
Additional circuit judgeships, 28 § 44 nt
Appointment, 28 § 44
Additional judges, 28 § 44 nt
Assignment, ante
Chief Judge, generally, ante
Number of, appointment of additional judges, 28 § 44 nt
Orders, generally, post
Panels,
Panels, generally, post
Trial judge, disqualification to hear appeal, 28 § 47
Judicial circuit under jurisdiction, composition, 28 § 41
Judicial discipline, complaint, review procedure, 28 § 372
New Fifth Circuit, defined, Reorganization Act of 1980, 28 § 41 nt
New Orleans, LA,
Place of holding terms or sessions, 28 § 48

COURT OF APPEALS FOR FIFTH CIRCUIT—Cont'd
Orders,
Emergency, declaration by Chief Judge, affecting panel selection, 28 § 46
Panels,
Three-judge panel,
Judicial emergency affecting selection process, 28 § 46
Special sessions and terms, 28 § 48
Terms, 28 § 48

COURT OF APPEALS FOR SIXTH CIRCUIT
See, also,
Courts of Appeals, generally, this index
Chief Judge,
Precedence, 28 § 45
Cincinnati, OH,
Place of holding terms or sessions, 28 § 48
Composition of judicial circuit under jurisdiction of, 28 § 41
Judges,
Additional circuit judgeships, 28 § 44 nt
Appointment, 28 § 44
Additional judges, 28 § 44 nt
Assignment, 28 § 46
Chief Judge, generally, ante
Number, 28 § 44
Appointment of additional judges, 28 § 44 nt
Trial judge, disqualification to hear appeal, 28 § 47
Judicial circuit under jurisdiction, composition of, 28 § 41
Judicial discipline, complaints, review procedure, 28 § 372
Judicial misconduct or disability,
Complaints of, 28 § 372
Sessions, 28 § 48
Special sessions, 28 § 48
Special terms, 28 § 48
Terms, 28 § 48

COURT OF APPEALS FOR SEVENTH CIRCUIT
See, also,
Courts of Appeals, generally, this index
Chicago, IL, place of holding terms or sessions, 28 § 48
Chief Judge. Judges, post
Composition,
Judicial Circuit under jurisdiction of, 28 § 41
Judges,
Additional circuit judgeships, 28 § 44 nt
Appointment, tenure, 28 § 44
Assignment, 28 § 46
Chief Judge,
Precedence, 28 § 45
Number, 28 § 44

COURT OF APPEALS FOR SEVENTH CIRCUIT—Cont'd
Judges—Cont'd
Number—Cont'd
Appointment of additional judges, **28 § 44 nt**
Trial judge, disqualification to hear appeal, **28 § 47**
Judicial Circuit under jurisdiction, composition of, **28 § 41**
Judicial discipline, complaint, review procedure, **28 § 372**
Sessions, **28 § 48**
Special,
Sessions, **28 § 48**
Terms, **28 § 48**
Terms of Court, **28 § 48**

COURT OF APPEALS FOR EIGHTH CIRCUIT
See, also,
Courts of Appeals, generally, this index
Chief Judge,
Precedence, **28 § 45**
Composition, judicial circuit under jurisdiction of, **28 § 41**
Judges,
Additional circuit judgeships, **28 § 44 nt**
Appointment, **28 § 44**
Additional judges, **28 § 44 nt**
Assignment, **28 § 46**
Chief Judge, generally, ante
Number, **28 § 44**
Appointment of additional judges, **28 § 44 nt**
Trial judge, disqualification to hear appeal, **28 § 47**
Judicial circuit under jurisdiction, composition of, **28 § 41**
Judicial discipline, complaints,
Review procedure, **28 § 372**
Kansas City, MO, place of holding terms or sessions, **28 § 48**
Omaha, NB, place of holding terms or sessions, **28 § 48**
Saint Louis, MO,
Place of holding terms or sessions, **28 § 48**
Saint Paul, MN,
Place of holding terms or sessions, **28 § 48**
Sessions, **28 § 48**
Special sessions, **28 § 48**
Special terms, **28 § 48**
Terms, **28 § 48**

COURT OF APPEALS FOR TENTH CIRCUIT
See, also,
Courts of Appeals, generally, this index
Chief Judge,
Precedence, **28 § 45**

COURT OF APPEALS FOR TENTH CIRCUIT—Cont'd
Composition,
Judicial circuit under jurisdiction of, **28 § 41**
Denver, CO,
Place of holding terms or sessions, **28 § 48**
Judges,
Additional circuit judgeships, **28 § 44 nt**
Appointment,
Additional judges, **28 § 44 nt**
Tenure, **28 § 44**
Assignment, **28 § 46**
Chief Judge, generally, ante
Number, **28 § 44**
Appointment of additional judges, **28 § 44 nt**
Trial judge, disqualification to hear appeal, **28 § 47**
Judicial circuit under jurisdiction, composition of, **28 § 41**
Judicial discipline, complaint, review procedure, **28 § 372**
Oklahoma City, OK, place of holding terms or sessions, **28 § 48**
Sessions, **28 § 48**
Special sessions, **28 § 48**
Special sessions, **28 § 48**
Special terms, **28 § 48**
Terms and conditions, **28 § 48**
Wichita, KS, place of holding terms or sessions, **28 § 48**

COURT OF APPEALS FOR ELEVENTH CIRCUIT
See, also,
Courts of Appeals, generally, this index
Atlanta, GA,
Place of holding terms or sessions, **28 § 48**
Chief Judge,
Precedence, **28 § 45**
Composition,
Judicial circuit under jurisdiction of, **28 § 41**
Judges,
Appointment, tenure, **28 § 44**
Assignment, **28 § 46**
Chief Judge, generally, ante
Election of assignments, **28 § 41 nt**
Number of, **28 § 44**
Judicial circuit under jurisdiction, composition of, **28 § 41**
Montgomery, AL,
Place of holding terms or sessions, **28 § 48**
Special sessions, **28 § 48**
Special terms, **28 § 48**
Terms, **28 § 48**

COURT OF APPEALS FOR THE ARMED FORCES
United States Court of Appeals for the Armed Forces, generally, this index

COURT OF APPEALS FOR THE FEDERAL CIRCUIT
United States Court of Appeals for the Federal Circuit, generally, this index

COURT OF CLAIMS
United States Court of Federal Claims, generally, this index

COURT OF INTERNATIONAL TRADE
United States Court of International Trade, generally, this index

COURT OF MILITARY APPEALS
United States Court of Appeals for the Armed Forces, generally, this index

COURT RULES
Rules of Court, generally, this index

COURTHOUSES AND COURTROOMS
Accommodations provided by Director of Administrative Office of U.S. Courts, **28 §§ 462, 604**
Director of Administrative Office of U.S. Courts to provide accommodations, **28 §§ 462, 604**
Judicial sale of realty, **28 § 2001**
United States Court of International Trade, **28 § 251**

COURTS
Accommodations, **28 §§ 462, 604**
Administrative Office of United States Courts, generally, this index
Agency, defined, general provisions applicable to, **28 § 451**
Always open, **28 § 452**
Appeals,
Appeal and Review, generally, this index
Appointment of administrative or clerical personnel, authority, limitations, **28 § 609**
Attorney General, conduct and argument of cases in, **28 § 518**
Attorneys, generally, this index
Audit of vouchers and accounts, **28 § 604**
Bail and Recognizances, generally, this index
Bankruptcy, this index
Bankruptcy Rules and Forms, this index
Budget estimate, **28 § 605**
Certificates, execution against revenue officer, **28 § 2006**
Civil actions, priority of, **28 § 1657**
Clerical assistants,
Accommodations, **28 § 604**
Compensation,
Fixed by Director of Administrative Office of U.S. Courts, **28 § 604**
Increase, **28 § 603 nt**
Clerks of Courts, generally, this index
Construction of Act relating to, **28 nt prec § 1**
Contempt, generally, this index

COURTS—Cont'd
Court of the United States, defined,
Fees, per diem and mileage expenses for witnesses, **28 § 1821**
General provisions applicable to, **28 § 451**
Court security, transfer to U.S. Marshals, **28 § 604**
Courts of Appeals, generally, this index
Criers. Court Criers, generally, this index
Department, defined, general provisions applicable to, **28 § 451**
Deposits in court. Funds and Deposits in Court, generally, this index
Detention, generally, this index
Disbursement of moneys for maintenance and operation through U.S. marshals, **28 § 604**
District Courts, generally, this index
District Judges, generally, this index
Dockets and Docketing, generally, this index
Employees. Officers and employees, generally, post
Equipment and supplies, purchase, **28 § 604**
Evidence. Rules of Evidence, generally, this index
Federal Rules of Evidence. Rules of Evidence, generally, this index
Funds and Deposits in Court, generally, this index
Grand Jury, generally, this index
Incentive awards for employees, **28 § 604**
Independent Counsel, generally, this index
Inspection of dockets outside continental U.S., **28 § 604**
Insular Possessions and Dependencies, this index
International Trade, Court of. United States Court of International Trade, generally, this index
Interpreters, this index
Judges or Justices, generally, this index
Judicial Center, generally, this index
Judicial Conference of the United States, generally, this index
Judicial Districts, generally, this index
Judicial officers,
Circuit judges. Courts of Appeals, generally, this index
District Judges, generally, this index
Judges or Justices, generally, this index
Officers and employees, generally, post
United States Magistrate Judges, generally, this index
Judicial review. Appeal and Review, generally, this index
Judicial Sales, generally, this index
Jurisdiction, generally, this index
Jury, generally, this index
Justice Department officers, conducting and arguing cases in, **28 § 518**
Law Books, generally, this index
Law Clerks, generally, this index
Librarians. Law Libraries, generally, this index
Marshals. United States Marshals Service, generally, this index
Masters, generally, this index
Messengers, this index
Minutes, designations, and assignments of justices and judges to be entered on, **28 § 295**
Money paid into court. Funds and Deposits in Court, generally, this index
Obsolete papers, disposal of, **28 § 457**
Office expenses, payment, **28 § 604**
Officers and employees,
Administrative or clerical personnel, appointed authority, restrictions, **28 § 609**
Citizens' Commission on Public Service and Compensation, generally, this index
Civil Service, generally, this index
Clerical assistants, generally, ante
Court Criers, generally, this index
Forma pauperis proceeding, service of process and performance of duties, **28 § 1915**
Jury service, exemption, **28 § 1863**
Pay,
Fixed by Director of Administrative Office of U.S. Courts, **28 § 602 et seq.**
Increase, **28 § 603 nt**
Receiver, ineligibility to appointment as, **28 § 958**
Removal of actions or prosecution against, **28 § 1442**
Tax liability of officers conducting business, **28 § 960**
United States Marshals Service, generally, this index
Orders of Court, generally, this index
Pending causes, statement of, **28 § 522**
Per Diem, generally, this index
Person or body designated by, subpoena requiring appearance before of national, in foreign country, **28 § 1783**
Personal appearance before, **28 § 1654**
Priority of civil actions, **28 § 1657**
Publications distributed to courts, custodian at places where building is not owned by U.S., **28 § 413**
Records of Court, generally, this index
Release, generally, this index
Removal of Cases or Causes, generally, this index
Reporters, generally, this index
Rules of Civil Procedure, generally, this index
Rules of Court, generally, this index
Seals (Official Seals), this index
Secretaries, compensation,
Fixed by Director of Administrative Office of U.S. Courts, **28 § 604**
Increase, **28 § 603 nt**

COURTS—Cont'd
Secretaries, compensation—Cont'd
Limitation, **28 § 604 nt**
Separability, provisions of Act relating to, **28 nt prec § 1**
Sessions, generally, this index
Solicitor General, conducting and arguing cases in, **28 § 518**
Special Terms, generally, this index
Speedy trial, generally. Trial, this index
State Courts, generally, this index
State laws as rules of decision, **28 § 1652**
Stenographers, compensation,
Fixed by Director of Administrative Office of U.S. Courts, **28 § 604**
Increase, **28 § 603 nt**
Subpoena of national or resident of U.S. in foreign country, **28 § 1783**
Supreme Court, generally, this index
Tax court. United States Tax Court, generally, this index
Tax liability of officers and agents conducting business, **28 § 960**
United States Court of Appeals for the Armed Forces, generally, this index
United States Court of Appeals for the Federal Circuit, generally, this index
United States Court of Appeals for Veterans Claims, generally, this index
United States Court of Federal Claims, generally, this index
United States Court of International Trade, generally, this index
United States Courts of Appeals. Courts of Appeals, generally, this index
United States District Court for District of Columbia, generally, this index
United States Magistrate Judges, generally, this index
United States Marshals Service, generally, this index
United States Tax Court, generally, this index
Virgin Islands, this index
Witnesses, generally, this index

COURTS–MARTIAL
Appeals. United States Court of Appeals for the Armed Forces, generally, this index

COURTS OF APPEALS
See, also,
Courts, generally, this index
Adjustment in annual salary rates of judges, **28 § 44**
Administrative Office of U.S. Courts, facilities and staff of administrative units of courts of appeals prescribed by, **28 § 41 nt**
Administrative units, constitution of, facilities and staff, **28 § 41 nt**
Admiralty, appeals from district courts, **28 § 1292**
Advisory committees, appointment, study of rules of practice, **28 § 2077**

COURTS OF APPEALS—Cont'd
Affirmance,
Damages and costs, **28 § 1912**
Always open for certain purposes, **28 § 452**
Amount in controversy, right to review, proof, **28 § 2108**
Appeal and review,
Agency, orders, record on review and enforcement of, **28 § 2112**
Certification, record on review, Federal agencies, orders, **28 § 2346**
Determinations respecting judgments, orders, **28 § 2106**
District courts, generally, post
Jurisdiction, generally, post
Motion to vacate, set aside or correct sentence, Federal custody, **28 § 2255**
Notice, generally, post
Orders of,
Certain Federal agencies, **28 § 2342 et seq.**
Judicial panel on multidistrict litigation, **28 § 1407**
Remand, generally, post
Surface Transportation Board, rules, regulations, final orders, **28 § 2342**
United States Magistrate Judges, appeals from decision of magistrate judge designated to exercise civil jurisdiction, statistics reported to Congress, **28 § 604**
Appearance personally or by counsel, **28 § 1654**
Appointment,
Additional circuit judgeships, by President, **28 § 44 nt**
Chief judges, **28 § 45**
Structural Alternatives for the Federal Courts of Appeals Commission, **28 § 41 nt**
Atomic Energy Commission, final orders, jurisdiction, review, **28 § 2342**
Bailiffs, crier to perform duties of, **28 § 714**
Bankruptcy, this index
Black persons, selection of qualified individuals for nomination to judgeships, Congressional recommendations, **28 § 133 nt**
Business in special sessions, transacting, **28 § 48**
Cases and controversies, hearing and determination by a court or panel, **28 § 46**
Certificates and certification,
Habeas corpus, certificate of appealability, issuance, **28 § 2253**
Record on review or enforcement of agency, orders, **28 § 2112**
Certified,
Copies of papers included in record on review or enforcement of agency, orders, **28 § 2112**

COURTS OF APPEALS—Cont'd
Certified—Cont'd
List of materials comprising record on review or enforcement of agency, orders, **28 § 2112**
Certified Questions, this index
Certiorari. Supreme Court, this index
Chief judge or justice, **28 § 45**
Age restrictions, **28 § 45**
Appointment of, **28 § 45**
Certificate of,
Disability to be furnished President in behalf of retirement, **28 § 372**
Necessity for assignment of, district judge from another circuit, **28 § 292**
Retired judges or justices, substantial judicial duties, salary adjustments, **28 § 371**
Certification,
Emergency, illness of judge, unavailable to sit on panel, **28 § 46**
To Chief Justice of U.S., relief from duties as chief judge, retention of active status as circuit judge, **28 § 45**
Circuit judge to perform duties of chief judge temporarily unable to perform duties, **28 § 45**
Designation and assignment of judges,
Circuit or district judges, consolidated, pretrial proceedings on multidistrict litigation, **28 § 1407**
Consent, **28 § 295**
District judge to sit upon court of appeals or division thereof within circuit, **28 § 292**
New designations and assignments, **28 § 295**
Retired judge, **28 § 294**
Revocation, **28 § 295**
Three-judge court, **28 § 2284**
Director of Administrative Office of the U.S. Courts to report, **28 § 604**
Disability, **28 § 45**
Institutes and joint councils on sentencing, functions and powers relative to, **28 § 334**
Judicial conference, **28 § 331**
Summoning, **28 § 333**
Judicial council of circuit, calling, **28 § 332**
Law clerks and secretaries. Compensation and salaries, post
Precedence, **28 § 45**
Presiding at,
Judicial conference of circuit, **28 § 333**
Judicial council, **28 § 332**
Relief from duties as chief judge while retaining active status as circuit judge, **28 § 45**

COURTS OF APPEALS—Cont'd
Chief judge or justice—Cont'd
Reports of Director of Administrative Office of U.S. Courts submitted to judicial council, **28 § 332**
Retired judge, designation and assignment for duty, **28 § 294**
Savings provisions, Federal Courts Improvement Act of 1982 Amendments relating to, **28 § 45 nt**
Senior circuit judge known as, **28 § 451 nt**
Senior staff attorney, appointment and removal, **28 §§ 604 nt, 715**
Senior technical assistant, appointment and removal, **28 § 715**
Temporary assignment of district judges, **28 § 292**
Terms of, **28 § 45**
Three-judge court, designation of judges to sit, **28 § 2284**
Circuit court executives, functions, respecting, **28 § 332**
Circuit Court of Appeals,
Known as, **28 § 451 nt**
Circuit judges. Judges or justices, post
Circuits,
Allotment of Supreme Court justices to circuits, **28 § 42**
Chief judge, **28 § 45**
Decisions reviewable, **28 § 1294**
Number and composition, **28 §§ 41, 44**
Judges, **28 § 44**
Terms or sessions of court, **28 § 48**
Clerks of courts,
Appointment, removal, duties, **28 § 711**
Compensation and salaries, law clerks and secretaries, limitation on aggregate amount, **28 § 604 nt**
Costs, payment in Treasury, **28 § 711**
Deputies and assistants, **28 § 711**
Record on review, orders, certain Federal agencies, filing, **28 § 2346**
Return of fees and costs to Director of Administrative Office of U.S. Courts, **28 § 711**
Commissions and commissioners, Structural Alternatives for the Federal Courts of Appeals, **28 § 41 nt**
Compensation and salaries,
Judges or justices, post
Law clerks and secretaries, **28 § 604 nt**
Fixed by Director of Administrative Office of U.S. Courts, **28 § 604**
Increase, **28 § 603 nt**
Structural Alternatives for the Federal Courts of Appeals Commission, **28 § 41 nt**
Composition of panels, **28 § 46**
Costs,
Affirmance, **28 § 1912**
Judicial Conference of U.S. to prescribe charges, **28 § 1913**
Creation and composition, **28 § 43**

COURTS OF APPEALS—Cont'd
Criers, appointment and removal, **28 § 714**
Damages, affirmance, **28 § 1912**
Decisions reviewable, **28 § 1291 et seq.**
Deputy clerks of court, **28 § 711**
Designation. Judges or justices, post
Disqualification,
Panels, quorum, effect upon, **28 § 46**
Trial judge to hear appeal, **28 § 47**
District courts,
Decisions reviewable, **28 § 1291 et seq.**
Court to which appeal is taken, **28 § 1294**
Final decisions, **28 § 1291**
Interlocutory orders, **28 § 1292**
Notice of appeal filed in district court prior to effective date of Federal Courts Improvement Act of 1982, decision by court of appeals to which appeal taken, **28 § 171 nt**
District of Columbia. United States Court of Appeals for District of Columbia, generally, this index
Divisions, designation and assignment of district judge to sit, **28 § 292**
Elections,
Senior circuit judge, eligibility to participate as member of en banc court reviewing decision of panel, **28 § 46**
Employees, **28 § 711**
En banc courts,
Composition, **28 § 46**
Performance by en banc functions by administrative units, number of members of courts as prescribed by rules of, **28 § 41 nt**
Review, decision of panel, senior circuit judge, eligibility to participate in, **28 § 46**
En banc functions, performance by administrative units, number of members of en banc courts, prescribing by rules of, **28 § 41 nt**
Evidence, **28 § 1731 et seq.**
Amount in controversy for purpose of review by, **28 § 2108**
Inclusion in record on review or enforcement of agency, orders, **28 § 2112**
Extension of time for appeal to court of appeals, **28 § 2107**
Extradition proceeding, right of appeal, habeas corpus proceedings, **28 § 2253**
Federal Circuit. United States Court of Appeals for the Federal Circuit, generally, this index
Federal Communications Commission, review, final orders, jurisdiction, **28 § 2342**
Federal Maritime Commission, rules, regulations and final orders, jurisdiction, **28 § 2342**

COURTS OF APPEALS—Cont'd
Federal Rules of Evidence. Rules of Evidence, generally, this index
Fees, Judicial Conference of U.S., prescribing, Judiciary Automation Fund, fees deposited into, **28 § 1913 nt**
Schedule, additional fees, **28 § 1913 nt**
Final judgment, review, orders, certain Federal agencies, Supreme Court, **28 § 2350**
Habeas corpus,
Appeals, **28 § 2253**
Application, **28 § 2242**
Capital cases, motions and applications, limitation periods, **28 § 2266**
Finality of determination of judge, **28 § 2244**
Power of judge to grant writ, **28 § 2241**
State custody, grounds for remedies in Federal court, **28 § 2254**
Hearings, **28 § 46**
Interlocutory injunction, suspension, orders, certain Federal agencies, **28 § 2349**
Review, orders, certain Federal agencies, **28 § 2347**
In banc courts. En banc courts, generally, ante
Incentive awards for employees, **28 § 604**
Injunctions,
Appeals from district courts, **28 § 1292**
Orders of certain Federal agencies, **28 §§ 2342, 2349**
Record in proceedings to enjoin agency, orders, **28 § 2112**
Interlocutory injunction,
Review, orders, certain Federal agencies, **28 § 2349**
Suspension, orders, certain Federal agencies, **28 § 2349**
Review in Supreme Court, **28 § 2350**
Interlocutory orders, district courts, jurisdiction on appeal, **28 § 1292**
Interstate Commerce Commission, rules, regulations and final orders, jurisdiction, **28 § 2342**
Judges or justices, **28 § 43**
Acknowledgments, authority to take, **28 § 459**
Active service, judge senior in commission to be chief judge of circuit, **28 § 45**
Additional circuit judgeships, **28 § 44 nt**
Additional judges, appointment, when judge eligible to retire is unable to discharge duties, **28 § 372**
Age, precedence according to seniority, **28 § 45**
Allotment of Supreme Court justices as circuit justices, **28 § 42**
Annuities to survivors, **28 § 376**

COURTS OF APPEALS—Cont'd
Judges or justices—Cont'd
Appointment,
By President, **28 § 44**
Additional judges, **28 § 44 nt**
Tenure and residence, **28 § 44**
Certificate of disability furnished to President in behalf of retirement, **28 § 372**
Chambers, provision by Director of Administrative Office of U.S. Courts, **28 § 462**
Chief judge or justice, generally, ante
Circuit judges,
Competent to sit as, **28 § 43**
Compensation and salaries,
Annual rate, determination and adjustment of, **28 § 44**
Deduction and withholding for purposes of annuities, to survivors, **28 § 376**
Retirement for disability, **28 § 372**
Competency of circuit justice to sit as, **28 § 43**
Composition of court, **28 § 43**
Court in banc, composition, **28 § 46**
Designation and assignment, **28 § 46**
Act in another circuit, **28 § 291**
Conditions on designation and assignment of circuit judge, **28 § 295**
Filed with clerk, **28 § 295**
Judicial Conference of U.S. to prepare plans for, **28 § 331**
Multidistrict litigation, consolidated, pretrial proceedings, **28 § 1407**
Powers and duties, **28 § 296**
Retired judge to perform judicial duties, **28 § 294**
Senior circuit judge, eligibility to participate as member of in banc court reviewing decision of panel, **28 § 46**
Disability,
Appointment of additional judge, **28 § 372**
Retirement for, **28 § 372**
Disqualification,
Hearing appeal of case tried same judge, **28 § 47**
Panels, **28 § 46**
Domicile and residence, **28 § 44**
Official duty station to be that nearest residence, **28 § 456**
Retired judges, **28 § 374**
Habeas corpus,
Appeals, certificates, **28 § 2253**
Finality of determination, **28 § 2244**
Power to grant, **28 § 2241**
State custody, grounds for remedies by, **28 § 2254**
Inability to perform duties when eligible to retire, appointment of additional judge, **28 § 372**

COURTS OF APPEALS—Cont'd
Judges or justices—Cont'd
Increase in limitations, compensation for law clerks and secretaries, **28 § 604 nt**
Judicial Center, Board, membership on, **28 § 621**
Judicial Conference of the United States, this index
Judicial council, attendance, **28 § 332**
Judicial panel on multidistrict litigation, membership on, **28 § 1407**
Jurisdiction, **28 § 1291 et seq.**
Law books and Government publications furnished transmitted to successor, **28 § 414**
Law clerks,
Annual and sick leave, exceptions from provisions of, **28 § 712**
Appointment, **28 § 712**
Compensation and salaries, generally, ante
Number, **28 § 44**
Appointment of additional judges, **28 § 44 nt**
Cases and controversies, hearing and determination, **28 § 46**
Hearing and determination of cases, **28 § 46**
Case remitted from Supreme Court, because of absence of quorum of justices, **28 § 2109**
Oaths and affirmations, **28 § 453**
Authority to administer, **28 § 459**
Office expenses, payment, retired judges, **28 § 374**
Official duty station, **28 § 456**
Order and times of sitting on court and panels, **28 § 46**
Orders of court, generally, post
Panels of court, composition, **28 § 46**
Practice of law as high misdemeanor, **28 § 454**
Precedence, disability causing appointment of additional judge, **28 § 372**
Prehearing conference, review, orders, certain Federal agencies, **28 § 2345**
President of U.S. not to consider race, color, sex, in selecting nominees for judgeships, **28 § 44 nt**
Quorum, **28 § 46**
Race, color, sex, not to be considered by President in selecting nominees for judgeships, **28 § 44 nt**
Regular active service,
Court as consisting of circuit judges in, **28 § 43**
Court en banc as consisting of judges in, **28 § 46**
Relatives ineligible to appointment to any office or duty in court, **28 § 458**
Retired justices, division to appoint special prosecutor, priority in assignment to, **28 § 49**

COURTS OF APPEALS—Cont'd
Judges or justices—Cont'd
Retired justices, division to appoint special prosecutor, priority in assignment to—Cont'd
Designation and assignment to perform judicial duties, **28 § 294**
Disability, **28 § 372**
Secretaries,
Appointment, **28 § 712**
Compensation and salaries, generally, ante
Selection for nomination, Congressional recommendations regarding blacks and women as qualified individuals for, **28 § 133 nt**
Senior circuit judges,
Division to appoint special prosecutors, preference in assignment to, **28 § 49**
Eligibility to participate as member of in banc court reviewing decision of panel, **28 § 46**
Supreme Court justices allotted as circuit justices, **28 § 42**
Temporary assignment to other courts, **28 § 291**
Three-judge court, membership, **28 § 2284**
Traveling expenses, **28 § 456**
Vacancy caused by death, resignation, after additional judge appointed not to be filled, **28 § 372**
Judicial circuits. Circuits, generally, ante
Judicial Conference of the United States, this index
Judicial Council, generally, this index
Judicial districts, defined, general provisions applicable to courts and judges, **28 § 451**
Judicial Sales, generally, this index
Jurisdiction, **28 § 1291 et seq.**
Certain Federal agencies, orders, review, **28 § 2342**
Transfer to cure want of jurisdiction, **28 § 1631**
Justices. Judges or justices, generally, ante
Law clerks,
Annual and sick leave, exceptions from provisions of, **28 § 712**
Appointment, **28 § 712**
Compensation, **28 § 604 nt**
Librarian and library assistants, appointment and removal, **28 § 713**
Marshals. Supreme Court Marshal, generally, this index
Messengers, appointment and removal, **28 § 714**
Military Appeals. United States Court of Appeals for the Armed Forces, generally, this index
Name changed from Circuit Court of Appeals, **28 nt prec § 1**

COURTS OF APPEALS—Cont'd
Nominations, Congressional recommendations regarding blacks and women as qualified individuals for selection for nomination to judgeships, **28 § 133 nt**
Notice,
Appeal, **28 § 2107**
Special sessions, holding, **28 § 48**
Number of judges, **28 § 44**
Hearing and determination, cases and controversies, **28 § 46**
Oath of party, proof of amount in controversy for purpose of review, **28 § 2108**
Obsolete papers, disposition, **28 § 457**
Officers and employees. Supreme Court Marshal, generally, this index
Omission from record on review or enforcement of agency, orders, **28 § 2112**
Orders of court,
Record on review or enforcement of agency, orders, **28 § 2112**
Special sessions, holding, **28 § 48**
Panels, senior circuit judge eligible to participate as member of in banc court reviewing decision of panel, **28 § 46**
Per diem, Structural Alternatives for the Federal Courts of Appeals Commission, **28 § 41 nt**
Pleadings, inclusion in record on review or enforcement of agency, orders, **28 § 2112**
Prehearing conference, review, orders, certain Federal agencies, **28 § 2345**
President of the United States,
Additional circuit judgeships, **28 § 44 nt**
Judges, **28 § 44**
Procedure, **28 § 1651 et seq.**
Quorum, **28 § 46**
Realty sold under orders or decrees. Judicial Sales, generally, this index
Receivers and receivership, appeals from decisions of district court, **28 § 1292**
Records and recordation, **28 § 457**
Former court of appeals kept in office of clerk of Supreme Court, **28 § 6**
Recusal, panels, quorum, effect upon, **28 § 46**
Rehearing, number of judges, **28 § 46**
Remand,
Review, orders, certain Federal agencies, **28 § 2347**
Reports,
Business, Director of Administrative Office of U.S. Courts, **28 § 604**
Structural Alternatives for the Federal Courts of Appeals Commission, **28 § 41 nt**
Reversal,
Ruling on matters in abatement not involving jurisdiction, **28 § 2105**

COURTS OF APPEALS—Cont'd
Review. Appeal and review, generally, ante
Rules of Appellate Procedure, this index
Rules of court,
Administrative units, performing en banc functions as prescribed by, **28 § 41 nt**
Advisory committees, appointment, study of rules, **28 § 2077**
Designation and assignments of district court judge to sit on court of appeals, **28 § 292**
Designation of places for terms or sessions of court, **28 § 48**
Fees, sales, copies of published rules, **28 § 2077**
Free distribution of copies of published rules, **28 § 2077**
Participation by members of bar at Judicial Conference of Circuit, **28 § 333**
Power,
Savings provision, **28 § 2071**
Supreme Court, prescription, **28 § 2072**
To prescribe, public notice and comment, **28 § 2071**
Publication of, **28 § 2077**
Review, orders, certain Federal agencies,
Power of Supreme Court to prescribe, **28 § 2072**
Savings provision, **28 §§ 2073 nt, 2352 nt**
Secretarial and clerical employees, appointment by senior staff attorney, **28 § 715**
Secretaries,
Appointment, **28 §§ 712, 715**
Compensation, **28 § 604 nt**
Secretary of Agriculture,
Review, orders of,
Jurisdiction, **28 § 2342**
Senate, appointment of judges,
Additional circuit judgeships, advice and consent, **28 § 44 nt**
By President, advice and consent, **28 § 44**
Senior staff attorney, appointment by chief judge, **28 § 715**
Senior technical assistant, appointment and removal, powers, **28 § 715**
Sessions, **28 § 48**
Commissioner of Education, actions, public powers unrestricted by, **28 § 452**
Consent of Judicial Conference of the U.S. to pretermit any regular session, **28 § 48**
Setting aside,
Orders of certain Federal agencies, **28 §§ 2342, 2349**
Special sessions, **28 § 48**
Staff attorneys, appointment by senior staff attorneys, **28 § 715**

COURTS OF APPEALS—Cont'd
Stipulation, concerning record on review or enforcement of agency, orders, **28 § 2112**
Studies, Structural Alternatives for the Federal Courts of Appeals Commission, **28 § 41 nt**
Supplement to record on review or enforcement of agency, orders, **28 § 2112**
Supreme Court, this index
Suspension, orders of certain Federal agencies, **28 §§ 2342, 2349**
Table, number of judges, **28 § 44**
Technical assistants, appointment and removal, **28 § 715**
Temporary Emergency Court of Appeals of United States, generally, this index
Terms of chief judges, **28 § 45**
Territorial courts, review of decisions of, **28 § 1294**
Time,
Appeal, **28 § 2107**
Certiorari application for review by Supreme Court, **28 § 2101**
Filing record on review or enforcement of agency, orders, **28 § 2112**
Judges sitting on court and panels, **28 § 46**
Transfer,
Proceedings to review or enforce agency, orders to court in which record had been filed, **28 § 2112**
Review of orders proceedings, to district court, certain Federal agencies, **28 § 2347**
To cure want of jurisdiction, **28 § 1631**
United States Court of Appeals for District of Columbia, generally, this index
United States Court of Appeals for Veterans Claims, generally, this index
United States Court of International Trade,
Designation and assignment, judge to perform judicial duties in court of appeals, **28 § 293**
Judges of, designation and temporary assignment to perform judicial duties in court of appeals, **28 § 293**
United States Magistrate Judges,
Appeal from decision of magistrate judge designated to exercise civil jurisdiction, statistics reported to Congress, **28 § 604**
United States Tax Court, this index
Vacating stay orders or interlocutory injunctions, review, orders, certain Federal agencies, **28 § 2349**
Veterans Appeals. United States Court of Appeals for Veterans Claims, generally, this index

COURTS OF APPEALS—Cont'd
Women, selection of qualified individuals for nomination to judgeships, Congressional recommendations, **28 § 133 nt**
Writs, review, orders of judicial panel on multidistrict litigation, **28 § 1407**

COVA
United States Court of Appeals for Veterans Claims, generally, this index

COVENANTS
Jury trial in action to recover forfeiture, **28 § 1874**

CREDIT (PAYMENT OF INDEBTEDNESS)
Bankruptcy, this index
Federal Intermediate Credit Banks, generally, this index
Federal Land Banks, generally, this index
Garnishment, generally, this index

CREDIT BANKS
Federal Intermediate Credit Banks, generally, this index

CREDITS
United States, action by, **28 §§ 2406, 2407**

CREW
Seamen, generally, this index

CRIERS OF COURTS
Court Criers, generally, this index

CRIME VICTIMS FUND
Victim Compensation and Assistance, generally, this index

CRIMES AND OFFENSES
See, also,
Fines, Penalties and Forfeitures, generally, this index
Sentence and Punishment, generally, this index
Violent Crime Control and Law Enforcement, generally, this index
Aged crime victims. Elderly victims, generally, post
Appeal and Review, this index
Apprehension of criminals, removal of action or prosecution against Federal officer for acts under color of office, **28 § 1442**
Armed Forces, this index
Arrest, generally, this index
Assault and Battery, generally, this index
Attorney General,
Conducting criminal proceedings, authority, **28 § 515**
Background checks. Criminal Background Checks, generally, this index
Bail and Recognizances, generally, this index
Bank Fraud Crimes, generally, this index

CRIMES AND OFFENSES—Cont'd
Certiorari, Supreme Court review of cases in court of appeals, **28 § 1254**
Civil justice reform, applicability, **28 § 519 nt, EON 12988**
Conflicts of Interest, generally, this index
Contempt, generally, this index
Conviction, generally, this index
Counterfeiting, generally, this index
Crime of violence, defined,
- Exclusion, rehabilitation, of narcotic addicts, **28 § 2901**
- Violent crime control, protection for the elderly, **28 § 994 nt**

Criminal Background Checks, generally, this index
Criminal process. Process, generally, this index
Detention, generally, this index
District Courts, this index
Drug Abuse Prevention, Control and Treatment, generally, this index
Elderly victims, violent crime control, Sentencing Commission, guidelines, criteria, **28 § 994 nt**
Environmental or natural resource laws, violation of, investigation and action by Attorney General, **28 § 509 nt**
Escape, generally, this index
Espionage, generally, this index
Extradition, generally, this index
False swearing. Perjury, generally, this index
Felonies, generally, this index
Financial institutions,
- Financial Institutions Fraud Unit, structural reforms to improve Federal response to crimes affecting financial institutions, **28 § 509 nt**

Foreign countries,
- Transfer of Offenders to or from Foreign Countries, generally, this index

Forfeitures. Fines, Penalties and Forfeitures, generally, this index
Forgery, generally, this index
Forma pauperis, proceedings in, **28 § 1915**
Fraud, generally, this index
Fugitives from justice,
- Extradition, generally, this index

Gambling, professional and amateur sports protection, **28 § 3702**
Grand Jury, generally, this index
Hate Crimes, generally, this index
History record information. Criminal Background Checks, generally, this index
Homicide,
- Manslaughter, generally, this index
- Murder, generally, this index

Identification. Criminal Background Checks, generally, this index
Imprisonment. Sentence and Punishment, generally, this index

CRIMES AND OFFENSES—Cont'd
Independent Counsel, generally, this index
Indictment and Information, generally, this index
Informations. Indictment and Information, generally, this index
Infringement, generally. Copyrights, this index
Interception of Wire, Oral, or Electronic Communications, generally, this index
International terrorism. Terrorists and Terrorism, generally, this index
Involuntary Servitude, generally, this index
Judges or Justices, this index
Judgment, on conviction. Sentence and Punishment, generally, this index
Jurors,
- Freedom from charge, qualification for service, **28 § 1865**
- Qualification form, contents concerning, **28 § 1869**

Juvenile Delinquents and Dependents, generally, this index
Kidnapping, generally, this index
Manslaughter, generally, this index
Minor or Petty Offenses, generally, this index
Misdemeanors, generally, this index
Murder, generally, this index
Murder-for-hire. Racketeering, generally, this index
Narcotic Drug Addicts, generally, this index
National Drug Policy, generally, this index
Officers and Employees of Government, this index
Officials to detect and prosecute, appointment, **28 § 533**
Penal institutions,
- Correctional Institutions, generally, this index

Pending actions in U.S. courts, number, report by Attorney General, **28 § 522**
Perjury, generally, this index
Petty offenses. Minor or Petty Offenses, generally, this index
Pretrial Services, generally, this index
Priority, criminal cases on appeal from State court, **28 § 2102**
Prisons,
- Correctional Institutions, generally, this index

Probation, generally, this index
Punishment. Sentence and Punishment, generally, this index
Racketeering,
- Racketeering, generally, this index

Recognizances. Bail and Recognizances, generally, this index
Record on Appeal, generally, this index

CRIMES AND OFFENSES—Cont'd
Records and Recordation, generally, this index
Release, generally, this index
Removal of,
- Prosecution, Armed Forces member prosecuted, **28 § 1442a**

Removal of Cases or Causes, generally, this index
Reports,
- Banking law offenses, Attorney General, **28 § 522 nt**
- Statistics, Attorney General, **28 § 522**

Rules of Appellate Procedure, this index
Rules of Criminal Procedure, generally, this index
Rules of Evidence, this index
Sentence and Punishment, generally, this index
Service in criminal cases, fee of U.S. marshal, **28 § 1921**
Sexual Abuse, generally, this index
Speedy trial, generally. Trial, this index
Subornation of perjury. Perjury, generally, this index
Supreme Court, generally, this index
Telecommunications, this index
Terrorists and Terrorism, generally, this index
United States attorneys, duties, **28 § 547**
United States marshals,
- Fees, service of papers, **28 § 1921**

United States Sentencing Commission, generally. Sentence and Punishment, this index
Unjust conviction and imprisonment, damages in U.S. Court of Federal Claims, allegations and proof concerning, **28 § 2513**
Verdict, generally, this index
Victim Compensation and Assistance, generally, this index
Victims of crime,
- Victim Compensation and Assistance, generally, this index

Witnesses,
- Witnesses, generally, this index

CRIMINAL BACKGROUND CHECKS
Exchange, **28 § 534**
Home health care and services, labor and employment, **28 § 534 nt**
Nursing homes, labor and employment, **28 § 534 nt**
Parimutuel licensing applicants, **28 § 534 nt**

CRIMINAL CODE
Crimes and Offenses, generally, this index
Rules of Criminal Procedure, generally, this index

CRIMINAL INVESTIGATIONS
Investigations, generally, this index

CRIMINAL SEXUAL ABUSE
Sexual Abuse, generally, this index

CRIMINOLOGISTS
Participation in institutes and joint councils on sentencing, **28 § 334**

CROSS CLAIMS
United States Court of International Trade, this index

CROSS EXAMINATION
Narcotic drug addicts, civil commitment, use, test results, credibility as witness, **28 § 2904**
United States Court of International Trade, this index

CRUELTY
Attorneys' fees and other costs and expenses, award to party prevailing against U.S. or agency, corporation for preventing, applicability, **28 § 2412**

CURRENCY
Comptroller of Currency, generally, this index

CUSTODY
Detention, generally, this index
Habeas Corpus, generally, this index
Missing Children, generally, this index
Parental Kidnapping Prevention, generally, this index
Release, generally, this index

CUSTOM HOUSE
Customs Houses, generally, this index

CUSTOMS BROKERS
Customs Duties, generally, this index
United States Court of International Trade, this index

CUSTOMS COURT
United States Court of International Trade, this index

CUSTOMS COURTS ACTS
Generally, **28 §§ 253 et seq., 1582, 2631 et seq.**
United States Court of International Trade, generally, this index

CUSTOMS DUTIES
See, also, International Trade, generally, this index
Actions. Civil actions, generally, post
Admissibility in evidence, value of merchandise issue in civil action, reports or depositions of consuls, customs officers, **28 § 2639**
Affidavits,
Admissibility in evidence, value of merchandise issue in civil action, **28 § 2639**
False affidavits as offense, **28 § 2639**

CUSTOMS DUTIES—Cont'd
American manufacturers', producers', or wholesalers' cases,
Civil actions. United States Court of International Trade, generally, this index
Exclusive jurisdiction of U.S. Court of International Trade, **28 § 1582**
Persons entitled to commence civil action contesting denial of petition, **28 § 2631**
Rules of U.S. Court of International Trade concerning. United States Court of International Trade, generally, this index
Analysis of imported merchandise, **28 § 2642**
Antidumping duties,
Burden of proof in civil actions, **28 § 2639**
Information,
Confidential information,
Disclosure under court order,
U.S. Court of International Trade, exclusive jurisdiction, application for, **28 § 1581**
Disclosure, civil actions under NAFTA or United States-Canada Free-Trade Agreement, exclusive jurisdiction, **28 § 1584**
NAFTA,
Civil actions, disclosure of information, exclusive jurisdiction, **28 § 1584**
Orders,
Protective order,
Limited disclosure of certain confidential information under,
Customs Court jurisdiction of application for order, **28 § 1582**
Persons entitled to commence civil action contesting determination, **28 § 2631**
Protective order,
Disclosure of information under,
U.S. Court of International Trade, exclusive jurisdiction, application for order, **28 § 1581**
Limited disclosure of search and confidential information under,
U.S. Court of International Trade, exclusive jurisdiction, application for order, **28 § 1581**
Scope and standard of review in civil actions, **28 § 2640**
Time for commencement of civil action contesting a reviewable determination, **28 § 2636**
United States-Canada Free-Trade Agreement, civil actions, disclosure of information, exclusive jurisdiction, **28 § 1584**

CUSTOMS DUTIES—Cont'd
Antidumping duties—Cont'd
United States Court of Appeals for the Federal Circuit, generally, this index
United States Court of International Trade, generally, this index
Bonds,
Importation of merchandise, recovery upon, civil action commenced by U.S., exclusive jurisdiction of Court of International Trade, **28 § 1582**
Bounties,
Payments, upon foreign articles, contest of Secretary's determination that bounty not being paid,
Time for commencement of action, **28 § 2631**
Catalogs, admissibility in evidence, value of merchandise issue in civil action, **28 § 2639**
Charges and rates,
Within Secretary's jurisdiction,
Civil actions where protest denied,
Exclusive jurisdiction of U.S. Court of International Trade, **28 § 1582**
Time for commencement of action, **28 § 2631**
Civil actions,
Accreditation of private laboratories, **28 § 2631**
Contesting denial, revocation or suspension by Secretary of customs brokers license, time for commencement of action, **28 § 2636**
Jurisdiction, generally, post
Protests, post
Reliquidation, generally, post
Review,
Actions prior to implementation of regulations, **28 § 1581 nt**
Decision of Secretary to deny, revoke or suspend customs brokers license, decision entitled to commence civil action, **28 § 2631**
Classification,
Merchandise,
Civil actions where protest denied,
Exclusive jurisdiction of U.S. Court of International Trade, **28 § 1582**
Time for commencement of action, **28 § 2631**
Collector of Customs, generally, this index
Contest of Secretary's determination,
Foreign merchandise not being sold in U.S. at less than fair value or that bounty or grant not being paid,
Civil action in U.S. Court of International Trade, procedure, **28 § 2632**

CUSTOMS DUTIES—Cont'd
Contest of Secretary's determination
—Cont'd
Foreign merchandise not being sold in U.S. at less than fair value or that bounty or grant not being paid
—Cont'd
Time for commencement of action, **28 § 2631**
Countervailing duties,
Burden of proof in civil actions, **28 § 2639**
Confidential information, disclosure under court order, application for, exclusive jurisdiction, U.S. Court of International Trade, **28 § 1581**
Contest of Secretary's determination,
Bounty or grant not being paid,
Civil action in Customs Court, procedure, **28 § 2632**
Time for commencement of action, **28 § 2631**
Information,
Confidential information,
Disclosure,
Civil actions under NAFTA or United States-Canada Free-Trade Agreement, exclusive jurisdiction, **28 § 1584**
NAFTA, post
Persons entitled to commence civil action contesting determination, **28 § 2631**
Protective order,
Disclosure of information under,
Application for order, exclusive jurisdiction, U.S. Court of International Trade, **28 § 1581**
Limited disclosure of certain confidential information under,
Application for order, exclusive jurisdiction, U.S. Court of International Trade, **28 § 1581**
Scope and standard of review in civil actions, **28 § 2640**
Time,
Commencement of civil action contesting a reviewable determination, **28 § 2636**
United States-Canada Agreement,
Civil actions under, disclosure of information, exclusive jurisdiction, **28 § 1584**
Customs Houses, generally, this index
Customs Officers, generally, this index
Declaratory judgments and decrees, customs duties, antidumping and countervailing duty determinations, free trade area country merchandise, **28 § 2201**
Depositions of consuls, customs officers, admissibility in evidence where value of merchandise is in issue in civil action, **28 § 2639**

CUSTOMS DUTIES—Cont'd
District courts,
Jurisdiction, **28 § 1340**
Drawbacks, generally, this index
Dumping. Antidumping duties, generally, ante
Exclusion of,
Merchandise, from entry or delivery, civil actions where protest denied,
Exclusive jurisdiction of U.S. Court of International Trade, **28 § 1582**
Time for commencement of action, **28 § 2631**
False,
Drawback claims, penalties. Drawbacks, generally, this index
Federal Register,
Publication in,
Antidumping duties, generally, ante
Countervailing duties, generally, ante
Filing,
Fees, commencement of civil actions, **28 § 2632**
Fines, penalties and forfeitures,
Recovery of civil penalty, civil action commenced by U.S., exclusive jurisdiction, U.S. Court of International Trade, **28 § 1582**
Foreign manufacturer, review, final determination of country of origin, exclusive jurisdiction, U.S. Court of International Trade, action brought by, **28 § 1581**
Fraud,
Customs brokers, recovery of civil penalty for violations, **28 § 1582**
Grants, payments, upon foreign articles, contest of Secretary's determination that grant not being paid,
Civil action in Customs Court, procedure, **28 § 2632**
Time for commencement of action, **28 § 2631**
Gross negligence,
Customs brokers, recovery of civil penalty for violations, **28 § 1582**
Imported goods or merchandise,
Analysis, **28 § 2636**
Importer of record,
Review, final determination as to country of origin, U.S. Court of International Trade, jurisdiction, action brought by, **28 § 1581**
International Trade, generally, this index
Jurisdiction,
Court of International Trade, accreditation of private laboratories, **28 §§ 1581, 1581 nt**
Customs brokers license, suspension or revocation, exclusive jurisdiction of civil action commenced to review, **28 § 1581**

CUSTOMS DUTIES—Cont'd
Jurisdiction—Cont'd
Exclusive jurisdiction, civil action to renew decision of Secretary to deny, revoke or suspend customs brokers license, **28 § 1581**
Review, accreditation of private laboratories, **28 § 2631**
Licenses and permits,
Civil action to review decision of Secretary to deny, revoke or suspend persons entitled to commence action, **28 § 2631**
Revocation or suspension, exclusive jurisdiction of civil action commenced to review, **28 § 1581**
Limitation of actions, **28 § 2631**
Antidumping and countervailing duty proceeding regarding class of free trade area country merchandise, declaratory judgment action, **28 § 2201**
Liquidation,
Entry,
Civil actions where protest denied,
Exclusive jurisdiction of U.S. Court of International Trade, **28 § 1582**
Time for commencement of action, **28 § 2631**
Manufacturers and manufacturing,
American manufacturers', producers', or wholesalers' cases, generally, ante
Review, final determination as to country of origin, exclusive jurisdiction, U.S. Court of International Trade, action brought by, **28 § 1581**
Modification,
Entry, civil actions where protest denied,
Exclusive jurisdiction of U.S. Court of International Trade, **28 § 1582**
Time for commencement of action, **28 § 2631**
NAFTA,
Antidumping duties, ante
Countervailing duties,
Disclosure, exclusive jurisdiction, **28 § 1584**
Negligence,
Customs brokers, recovery of civil penalty for violations, **28 § 1582**
Officers and employees. Customs Officers, generally, this index
Penalties. Fines, penalties and forfeitures, generally, ante
Petitions,
Domestic interested persons,
Burden of proof in civil actions, **28 § 2639**
Civil action contesting denial of petition, exhaustion of administrative remedies, **28 § 2637**

CUSTOMS DUTIES—Cont'd
Petitions—Cont'd
Domestic interested persons—Cont'd
Scope and standard of review in civil actions, **28 § 2640**
Time for commencement of action, civil action contesting denial of, **28 § 2636**
Port of Entry, generally, this index
Presumption, correctness, decisions of Secretary of Treasury or administering authority, **28 § 2639**
Price lists, admissibility in evidence, value of merchandise issue in civil action, **28 § 2639**
Private laboratories, accreditation, time for commencement of civil actions, review, **28 § 2636**
Producers,
American manufacturers', producers', or wholesalers' cases, generally, ante
Review, final determination as to country of origin, exclusive jurisdiction, U.S. Court of International Trade, action brought by, **28 § 1581**
Prohibited acts,
Monetary penalty, relief, customs brokers, **28 § 2643**
Protests,
Civil actions,
Burden of proof in civil actions, **28 § 2639**
Exhaustion of administrative remedies, **28 § 2637**
New grounds in support of civil action, **28 § 2638**
Persons entitled to commence civil action contesting, **28 § 2631**
Scope and standard of review in civil actions, **28 § 2640**
Time for commencement of action, **28 § 2636**
Exclusive jurisdiction, civil action by person where denial of, **28 § 1582**
Provisional relief,
Antidumping duties, generally, ante
Countervailing duties, generally, ante
Rates,
Civil actions where protest denied,
Exclusive jurisdiction of U.S. Court of International Trade, **28 § 1582**
Time for commencement of action, **28 § 2631**
Recovery of, civil action commenced by U.S., exclusive jurisdiction, U.S. Court of International Trade, **28 § 1583**
Refusal to liquidate entry,
Civil actions where protest denied,
Exclusive jurisdiction of U.S. Court of International Trade, **28 § 1582**

CUSTOMS DUTIES—Cont'd
Refusal to liquidate entry—Cont'd
Civil actions where protest denied —Cont'd
Time for commencement of action, **28 § 2631**
Reliquidation,
Entry,
Civil actions where protest denied,
Exclusive jurisdiction of Court of International Trade, **28 § 1582**
Time for commencement of action, **28 § 2631**
Reports,
Consuls, customs officers, admissibility in evidence where value of merchandise is in issue in civil action, **28 § 2639**
Revocation,
Accreditation of private laboratories, exclusive jurisdiction, **28 §§ 1581, 1581 nt**
Customs brokers license,
Exclusive jurisdiction of civil action commenced to review, **28 § 1581**
Rules and regulations,
Special rules,
Antidumping duties, generally, ante
Countervailing duties, generally, ante
Scope and standard of review, civil actions concerning customs brokers, **28 § 2640**
Secretary of Commerce,
Instruments or apparatus, importation of, U.S. Court of Appeals for the Federal Circuit, review of determination on questions of law, **28 § 1295**
Secretary of Treasury,
Civil action to review prior to importation of goods involved, rulings respecting classification, valuation, rate of duty,
Burden of proof in civil actions, **28 § 2639**
Exhaustion of administration remedies, **28 § 2637**
Ordering appropriate declaratory relief, **28 § 2643**
Customs brokers, license, suspension or revocation,
Exclusive jurisdiction of civil action commenced to review, **28 § 1581**
Foreign merchandise not being sold in U.S. at less than fair value or that bounty or grant not being paid, contest,
Civil action in Customs Court, procedure, **28 § 2632**
Determination by,
Time for commencement of action, **28 § 2631**

CUSTOMS DUTIES—Cont'd
Secretary of Treasury—Cont'd
Presumption and burden of proof concerning decisions of, **28 § 2639**
Statute of limitations. Limitation of actions, generally, ante
Suspension,
Customs brokers license, exclusive jurisdiction of civil action commenced to review, **28 § 1581**
Time,
Commencement of certain actions, **28 § 2631**
Tort Claims Act, exception, **28 § 2680**
Trade associations,
Final determination as to country of origin, exclusive jurisdiction, U.S. Court of International Trade, action brought by, **28 § 1581**
Unions,
Final determination as to country of origin, exclusive jurisdiction, U.S. Court of International Trade, action brought by, **28 § 1581**
United States attorneys,
Duties, involving civil actions, **28 § 547**
United States Court of International Trade, generally, this index
Value,
Merchandise, issue in,
Civil action, reports or depositions of consuls, customs officers, admissibility in evidence, **28 § 2639**
Court, reports, determination from evidence, **28 § 2635**
Wholesale dealers. American manufacturers', producers', or wholesalers' cases, generally, ante

CUSTOMS HOUSES
Brokers,
Civil actions, review, decision of Secretary of Treasury to deny, revoke or suspend license, scope and standard of review, **28 § 2640**

CUSTOMS LAWS
Customs Duties, generally, this index

CUSTOMS OFFICERS
Protest against decisions,
Civil action, contesting denial of,
Jurisdiction of U.S. Court of International Trade, **28 § 1582**
United States Court of International Trade, this index

CZECHOSLOVAKIA
Convention on the Taking of Evidence Abroad in Civil or Commercial Matters, party to, **28 § 1781 nt**

DAMAGES
Affirmance by Supreme Court or court of appeals, adjudication to prevailing party, **28 § 1912**

DAMAGES—Cont'd
Agencies, of the U.S., security not required, **28 § 2408**
Attachment against delinquent postmasters and postal officers, employees, right of action unimpaired, **28 § 2713**
Carriers, this index
Conspiracy to interfere with civil rights, jurisdiction of district court, **28 § 1343**
Court of appeals, affirmance of judgment, **28 § 1912**
Death,
  Defendant in damage action, commencement by or on behalf of U.S., **28 § 2404**
  Officers or employees of Government causing, jurisdiction of district court, claim against U.S., **28 § 1346**
District courts,
  Jurisdiction,
    Claim against U.S., **28 § 1346**
    Injury to person or property in protection or collection of revenues, **28 § 1357**
  Liquidated or unliquidated, civil action or claim against U.S., **28 § 1346**
  Venue, claim against U.S., **28 § 1402**
Federal agencies, orders, interlocutory injunction suspending, **28 § 2349**
Federal Employers' Liability Act, nonremovable action, **28 § 1445**
Foreign states, jurisdictional immunities, liability, **28 § 1606**
Indians,
  Time, actions brought by U.S. for money damages, **28 §§ 2415, 2415 nt**
Internal Revenue Service, this index
Liquidated Damages, generally, this index
Plant variety protection, infringement,
  Action against U.S. for infringement, **28 § 1498**
Punitive Damages, generally, this index
Real estate, quieting title, applicability to actions against U.S., **28 § 2409a**
Rules of Civil Procedure, this index
Supreme Court, this index
United States,
  Actions,
    Against U.S., trial by court, **28 §§ 2402, 2416**
    By U.S., limitation, **28 §§ 2415, 2416**
    Exclusion, **28 § 2416**
  Security not required, **28 § 2408**
United States Court of Federal Claims, this index
Voting, injury to person or property enforcing right of citizen to vote, jurisdiction of district court, **28 § 1357**

DATA PROCESSING
Administrative Office of United States Courts, this index
Computers, generally, this index

DEATH
Defendant in damage action, commenced by or on behalf of U.S., **28 § 2404**
Foreign states, jurisdictional immunities, exceptions, **28 § 1605**
Judicial Center Board members, election for unexpired term caused by, **28 § 621**
Justices or judges,
  Annuities to widows, termination upon, **28 § 376**
  Vacancy not filled where additional judge appointed, **28 § 372**
Officers and Employees of Government, this index
Rules of Appellate Procedure, this index
Rules of Civil Procedure, this index
Tort claims against U.S.,
  Administrative adjustment of claims, **28 § 2672**
  Jurisdiction, **28 § 1346**
United States, claims against, real property, quieting title, applicability to actions, **28 § 2409a**
United States marshals, after levying on or sale of real estate, **28 § 2003**

DEATH BENEFITS
Federal old-age, survivors and disability insurance benefits, generally. Social Security, this index

DEBT COLLECTION
Federal Debt Collection, generally, this index

DECEDENTS' ESTATES
Death of defendant in damage action commenced by or on behalf of U.S., enforcement against estate, **28 § 2404**
Estates and Trusts, generally, this index
Executors and Administrators, generally, this index

DECEIT
Fraud, generally, this index

DECLARATORY JUDGMENTS AND DECREES
Bankruptcy, tax liability, review, **28 § 2201**
Creation of remedies, **28 § 2201**
Drugs and medicine,
  Patents, limitations on actions, **28 § 2201**
Further relief based on, **28 § 2202**
Reorganization, special tax provisions, review, **28 § 2201**
Senate orders or subpoenas, validity, District Court for DC, jurisdiction, **28 § 1365**

DECLARATORY JUDGMENTS AND DECREES—Cont'd
United States Court of Federal Claims, this index
United States Court of International Trade, this index

DECREES
Judgments and Decrees, generally, this index

DEEDS AND CONVEYANCES
Judicial sale of realty, death, of marshal before execution, **28 § 2003**
Mortgages, generally, this index

DEFAMATION OF CHARACTER
Libel and Slander, generally, this index

DEFAULT
Bankruptcy, generally, this index

DEFAULT JUDGMENT
Docket fees, taxation as costs, **28 § 1923**
Foreign states, jurisdictional immunities, **28 § 1608**
Forfeiture annexed to any articles of bonds, or other specialties, actions to recover, **28 § 1874**
Rules of Civil Procedure, this index

DEFENSE OF MARRIAGE ACT
  Generally, **28 § 1738C**
Marriage, generally, this index

DEFENSE SECRETARY
Secretary of Defense, generally, this index

DEFINITIONS
Acting within the scope of his office or employment, tort claims against U.S., **28 § 2671**
Addicts,
  Narcotic addicts, rehabilitation, **28 § 2901**
Affiliates,
  Federal debt collection procedures, fraudulent transfers involving debts, **28 § 3301**
Agency or agencies,
  Attorney General, civil litigation reform, **28 § 519 nt, EON 12988**
  Civil penalty, Federal agencies, inflation adjustment, **28 § 2461 nt**
  General provisions applicable to courts and judges, **28 § 451**
  Review,
    Orders of Federal agencies, **28 § 2341**
Agency or instrumentality of a foreign state,
  Jurisdictional immunities of foreign states, **28 § 1603**
Aircraft sabotage, terrorists and terrorism, jurisdictional immunities of foreign states, **28 § 1605**

DEFINITIONS—Cont'd
Alternative dispute resolution,
District courts, **28 § 651**
Amateur sports organization,
Professional and amateur sports protection, **28 § 3701**
An order under section 2261(c), habeas corpus, capital cases, **28 § 2265**
Antitrust laws,
Judicial panel on multidistrict litigation, **28 § 1407**
Assassinated, judges or justices, annuities for survivors, **28 § 376**
Retroactive application, **28 § 376 nt**
Assassination, judges or justices, annuities, to surviving spouses, **28 § 376**
Asset or assets,
Federal debt collection procedures, fraudulent transfers involving debts, **28 § 3301**
Associated, independent counsel, ban on representation by members of firms of, **28 § 594**
Attorney for the government,
Ethics, **28 § 530B**
Bankruptcy judge,
Recall, **28 § 375**
Brokers,
Financial disclosure requirements of Federal personnel, **5, Ap 4, § 102**
Charitable organization,
Government wide limitations on outside income and employment, **5, Ap 4, § 505**
Chief judge,
Jury selection and service, **28 § 1869**
Child or children,
Full faith and credit for child support orders, **28 § 1738B**
Judges or justices, annuities for survivors, **28 § 376**
Parental kidnapping prevention, **28 § 1738A**
Child support,
Full faith and credit for child support orders, **28 § 1738B**
Child support order, full faith and credit for child support orders, **28 § 1738B**
Child's home State, child support, full faith and credit, **28 § 1738B**
Child's State, full faith and credit for child support orders, **28 § 1738B**
Civil action brought by or against the United States, administrative proceedings, award of attorneys' fees and other expenses, **28 § 2412**
Civil monetary penalty, civil penalty, Federal agencies, inflation adjustment, **28 § 2461 nt**
Claim,
Federal debt collection procedures, fraudulent transfers involving debts, **28 § 3301**
Clerk,
Jury selection and service, **28 § 1869**

DEFINITIONS—Cont'd
Clerk—Cont'd
Review, orders of Federal agencies, **28 § 2341**
Clerk of court,
Jury selection and service, **28 § 1869**
Closed,
Drug Enforcement Administration, FBI, financial audit of undercover investigative operations closed in certain year, **28 § 533 nt**
Commercial activities or activity,
Jurisdictional immunities of foreign states, **28 § 1603**
Commercial activity carried on in the United States by a foreign state, jurisdictional immunities of foreign states, **28 § 1603**
Commission,
United States Sentencing Commission, **28 § 998**
Commissioner or commissioners,
United States Sentencing Commission, **28 § 998**
Committee or committees,
Jurisdiction in Senate actions, **28 § 1365**
Compensation,
Retirement of bankruptcy judges and Magistrate Judges, acceptance of employment, **28 § 377**
Conference,
United States Magistrate Judges, **28 § 639**
Congressional ethics committees, financial disclosure requirements of Federal personnel, **5, Ap 4, § 109**
Consumer Price Index,
Civil penalty, Federal agencies, inflation adjustment, **28 § 2461 nt**
Contestant,
Parental kidnapping prevention, **28 § 1738A**
Convicted,
Narcotic addict, rehabilitation, **28 § 2901**
Core proceedings, bankruptcy, hearing and determination by bankruptcy judges, **28 § 157**
Cost-of-living adjustment,
Civil penalty, Federal agencies, **28 § 2461 nt**
Councils,
United States Magistrate Judges, **28 § 639**
Counsel for the United States, Federal debt collection procedures, general provisions, **28 § 3002**
Court of the United States,
General provisions applicable to courts and judges, **28 § 451**
Court or courts,
Administrative Office of U.S. Courts, **28 § 610**

DEFINITIONS—Cont'd
Court or courts—Cont'd
Administrative proceedings, award of attorneys' fees and other expenses, **28 § 2412**
Federal debt collection procedures, general provisions, **28 § 3002**
Full faith and credit for child support orders, **28 § 1738B**
General provisions, applicable to officers and employees, **28 § 963**
Judges or justices, retirement salary, payment pursuant to court decree of divorce, **28 § 376 nt**
Jury selection and service, **28 § 1869**
Retirement of bankruptcy judges and Magistrate Judges, **28 § 377**
United States Court of Federal Claims, retirement of judges, **28 § 178**
Covered employee,
Presidential and executive office accountability,
Judicial review, **28 § 3908**
Creditor,
Federal debt collection procedures, fraudulent transfers involving debts, **28 § 3301**
Crime of violence,
Narcotic addicts, rehabilitation, **28 § 2901**
Sentence and punishment, violent crime control, protection for the elderly, **28 § 994 nt**
Custody determination, parental kidnapping prevention, **28 § 1738A**
Debt,
Federal debt collection procedures, general provisions, **28 § 3002**
Debtor,
Federal debt collection procedures, general provisions, **28 § 3002**
Degree of relationship, justice, judge, Magistrate Judge, disqualification, **28 § 455**
Demand,
Administrative law and procedure, awards of costs and fees, **28 § 2412**
Department,
General provisions applicable to courts and judges, **28 § 451**
Dependent child,
Financial disclosure requirements of Federal personnel, **5, Ap 4, § 109**
Designated agency ethics official, financial disclosure requirements of Federal personnel, **5, Ap 4, § 109**
Direct review, habeas corpus, capital cases, **28 § 2265**
Director,
United States Magistrate Judges, **28 § 639**
Disposable earnings,
Federal debt collection procedures, general provisions, **28 § 3002**

DEFINITIONS—Cont'd
District,
Change of venue, **28 § 1404**
General provisions applicable to courts and judges, **28 § 451**
Venue or district of trial, cure or waiver of defects, **28 § 1406**
District courts,
General provisions, applicable to courts and judges, **28 § 451**
Jury Selection and Service Act, **28 § 1869**
Venue,
Change, **28 § 1404**
Cure or waiver of defects, **28 § 1406**
District courts of the United States,
General provisions applicable to courts and judges, **28 § 451**
Jury Selection and Service Act, **28 § 1869**
Division,
Jury Selection and Service Act, **28 § 1869**
Earnings,
Federal debt collection procedures, general provisions, **28 § 3002**
Eleventh circuit, Fifth Circuit Court of Appeals Reorganization Act of 1980, **28 § 41 nt**
Eligible individuals,
Narcotic addict rehabilitation, **28 § 2901**
Employee of the Government, tort claims against, **28 § 2671**
Employee or employees,
Bureau of Investigation, financial audit of undercover investigative operations closed in certain year, **28 § 533 nt**
Drug Enforcement Administration, financial audit of undercover investigative operations closed in certain year, **28 § 533 nt**
Financial audit of undercover investigative operations closed in certain year, **28 § 533 nt**
Tort claim against U.S., officers and employees of Government, **28 § 2671**
Employing office,
Presidential and executive office accountability,
Judicial review, **28 § 3908**
Excess unobligated balance, Justice Department Assets Forfeiture Fund, appropriations, **28 § 524**
Executive branch,
Financial disclosure requirements of Federal personnel, **5, Ap 4, § 109**
Extrajudicial killing,
Terrorists and terrorism, jurisdictional immunities of foreign states, **28 § 1605**
Torture victim protection, **28 § 1350 nt**
Federal agency or instrumentality,
Tort claims against U.S., **28 § 2671**

DEFINITIONS—Cont'd
Fees and other expenses, administrative procedure, costs and fees of parties, **28 § 2412**
Felony,
Narcotic addicts, rehabilitation, **28 § 2901**
Felony crime of violence, FBI, investigations, **28 § 540A**
Fiduciary,
Justice, judge or Magistrate Judge, disqualification, **28 § 455**
Final judgment,
Administrative proceedings, award of attorneys' fees and other expenses, **28 § 2412**
Financial interest, justice, judge or Magistrate Judge, disqualification, **28 § 455**
Firm,
Independent counsel, ban on representation by members of firms of, **28 § 594**
Foreign state,
Jurisdictional immunities of foreign states, **28 § 1603**
Former fifth circuit, Fifth Circuit Court of Appeals Reorganization Act of 1980, **28 § 41 nt**
Former spouse,
Judges or justices, annuities for survivors, **28 § 376**
Full-time Magistrate Judge, United States Magistrate Judges, **28 § 639**
Garnishee, Federal debt collection procedures, general provisions, **28 § 3002**
Gifts,
Financial disclosure requirements of Federal personnel, **5, Ap 4, § 109**
Governmental entity,
Professional and amateur sports protection, **28 § 3701**
Guidelines, United States Sentencing Commission, **28 § 998**
Hate crime,
Sentencing enhancements, guidelines, promulgation, Sentencing Commission, **28 § 994 nt**
Highest court of a State,
Review, miscellaneous provisions, **28 § 2113**
Supreme Court jurisdiction, **28 § 1257**
Home health care agency,
Criminal background checks, labor and employment, **28 § 534 nt**
Home State,
Parental Kidnapping Prevention, **28 § 1738A**
Honoraria,
Financial disclosure requirements of Federal personnel, **5, Ap 4, § 109**
Government wide limitations on outside income and employment, **5, Ap 4, § 505**

DEFINITIONS—Cont'd
Hostage taking, terrorists and terrorism, jurisdictional immunities of foreign states, **28 § 1605**
Income,
Financial disclosure requirements of Federal personnel, **5, Ap 4, § 109**
Insider,
Federal debt collection procedures, fraudulent transfers involving debts, **28 § 3301**
Interested party,
Financial disclosure requirements of Federal personnel, **5, Ap 4, § 102**
Persons entitled to commence civil action in U.S. Court of International Trade, **28 § 2631**
Investigative or law enforcement officer, Tort Claims Act, **28 § 2680**
Investment adviser,
Financial disclosure requirements of Federal personnel, **5, Ap 4, § 102**
Judge of the United States,
General provisions applicable to courts and judges, **28 § 451**
Judge of the United States Court of Federal Claims, recall, **28 § 375**
Judgment,
Federal debt collection procedures, general provisions, **28 § 3002**
Judicial Conference, financial disclosure requirements of Federal personnel, **5, Ap 4, § 109**
Judicial district,
General provisions applicable to courts and judges, **28 § 451**
Judicial employee, financial disclosure requirements of Federal personnel, **5, Ap 4, § 109**
Judicial officer,
District courts, civil justice expense and delay reduction plans, **28 § 481**
Expense and delay reduction plans, **28 § 482**
Financial disclosure requirements of Federal personnel, **5, Ap 4, § 109**
Veterans, preference, **28 § 601 nt**
Judicial official,
Judges or justices, annuities for survivor, **28 § 376**
Retirement of bankruptcy judges and Magistrate Judges, lump-sum payments, **28 § 377**
Judicial proceedings instituted by the United States, court interpreters, use of services, **28 § 1827**
Juror qualification form, Jury Selection and Service Act, **28 § 1869**
Jury summons, Jury System Improvements Act, **28 § 1869**
Jury wheel, Jury Selection and Service Act, **28 § 1869**
Justice of the United States, general provisions applicable to courts and judges, **28 § 451**

DEFINITIONS—Cont'd
Killing,
Serial killings, investigations and investigators, **28 § 540B**
Knows or has reason to know,
Copyrights, motion pictures, transfer of ownership, collective bargaining agreements, **28 § 4001**
Law enforcement officers,
Torts, **28 § 2671 nt**
Legislative branch,
Financial disclosure requirements of Federal personnel, **5, Ap 4, § 109**
Lien,
Federal debt collection procedures, fraudulent transfers involving debts, **28 § 3301**
Lists of actual voters, Jury Selection and Service Act, **28 § 1869**
Litigation counsel,
Attorney General, civil justice reform, **28 § 519 nt, EON 12988**
Defined, civil litigation reform, **28 § 519 nt, EON 12988**
Lump-sum credit,
Retirement of bankruptcy judges and Magistrate Judges, **28 § 377**
Member or members,
Government wide limitations on outside income and employment, **5, Ap 4, § 505**
Judges, relatives, appointments, **28 § 458**
Members of Congress,
Financial disclosure requirements of Federal personnel, **5, Ap 4, § 109**
Modification,
Full faith and credit for child support orders, **28 § 1738B**
Parental Kidnapping Prevention Act, **28 § 1738A**
Modify, Parental Kidnapping Prevention Act, **28 § 1738A**
National cemetery, veterans' cemetery protection, **28 § 994 nt**
National crime information databases, violence against women, national stalker and domestic violence reduction, **28 § 534**
New fifth circuit, Fifth Circuit Court of Appeals Reorganization Act of 1980, **28 § 41 nt**
Nonexempt disposable earnings, Federal debt collection procedures, general provisions, **28 § 3002**
Notice of suit, jurisdictional immunities of foreign States, **28 § 1608**
Nursing facility,
Criminal background checks, labor and employment, **28 § 534 nt**
Office of Federal Judicial Administration, judges or justices, effect of appointment as director of certain judicial branch agencies, **28 § 133**

DEFINITIONS—Cont'd
Officer or employee,
Government wide limitations on outside income and employment, **5, Ap 4, § 505**
Officer or employee of the Congress, financial disclosure requirements of Federal personnel, **5, Ap 4, § 109**
Other institutions, acquisition, preservation, of identification records, **28 § 534**
Other judicial act, Convention on the Taking of Evidence Abroad in Civil or Commercial Matters, **28 § 1781 nt**
Part time Magistrate Judge, United States Magistrate Judges, **28 § 639**
Party-at-interest, persons entitled to commence civil action in U.S. Court of International Trade, **28 § 2631**
Party or parties,
Administrative law and procedure, Costs and fees of parties, **28 § 2412**
Award of costs and fees of party prevailing in action against U.S., **28 § 2412**
Person,
Federal debt collection procedures, general provisions, **28 § 3002**
Professional and amateur sports protection, **28 § 3701**
Person acting as a parent, Parental Kidnapping Prevention Act, **28 § 1738A**
Petitioner,
Review, orders of Federal agencies, **28 § 2341**
Physical custody, Parental Kidnapping Prevention Act, **28 § 1738A**
Position of the United States,
Administrative proceedings, award of attorneys' fees and other expenses, **28 § 2412**
Post-conviction review, habeas corpus, capital cases, **28 § 2265**
Prejudgment remedy, Federal debt collection procedures, general provisions, **28 § 3002**
Presiding judicial officer, court interpreters, use of services of, **28 § 1827**
Prevailing party,
Administrative proceedings, award of attorneys' fees and other expenses, **28 § 2412**
Prisoner,
Civil actions by, against Government, screening and dismissal, **28 § 1915A**
Forma pauperis proceedings, **28 § 1915**
Proceeding,
Justice, judge or Magistrate Judge, disqualification, **28 § 455**
Professional sports organization, professional and amateur sports protection, **28 § 3701**

DEFINITIONS—Cont'd
Property,
Federal debt collection procedures, general provisions, **28 § 3002**
Protection order,
National stalker and domestic violence reduction, **28 § 534**
Public officer,
Jury Selection and Service Act, **28 § 1869**
Publicly draw, Jury System Improvements Act, **28 § 1869**
Qualified blind trust, financial disclosure requirements of Federal personnel, **5, Ap 4, § 102**
Qualified retirement arrangement, Federal debt collection procedures, co-owned property, general provisions, **28 § 3010**
Reasonable and entire compensation, copyright actions, independent inventors, **28 § 1498**
Reasonable period of time,
Annuities for survivors of judicial officials, **28 § 376**
Return of contributions, retirement of judicial official, **28 § 376**
Reimbursement, financial disclosure requirements of Federal personnel, **5, Ap 4, § 109**
Relative,
Federal debt collection procedures, fraudulent transfers involving debts, **28 § 3301**
Financial disclosure requirements of Federal personnel, **5, Ap 4, § 109**
Retirement salary, judges or justices, annuities for survivors, **28 § 376**
Retirement system for Federal military or civilian personnel, Federal debt collection procedures, co-owned property, general provisions, **28 § 3010**
Rules or regulations,
United States Sentencing Commission, **28 § 998**
Same court,
Judges, relatives, appointments, **28 § 458**
Secretary concerned,
Financial disclosure requirements of Federal personnel, **5, Ap 4, § 109**
Security agreement,
Federal debt collection procedures, general provisions, **28 § 3002**
Semiautomatic firearm, Sentencing Commission, amendment of guidelines for crimes involving use of, **28 § 994 nt**
Serial killings, investigations and investigators, **28 § 540B**
Service,
Administrative Office of United States Courts, Director, retirement, **28 § 611**

DEFINITIONS—Cont'd
Service—Cont'd
Judicial Center, Director, professional staff, retirement, **28 § 627**
Sexual orientation, hate crimes, **28 § 534 nt**
State,
Bureau of Investigation, counterterrorism, **28 § 531 nt**
District courts jurisdiction, **28 § 1332**
FBI, investigations, **28 § 540A**
Federal debt collection procedures, general provisions, **28 § 3002**
Full faith and credit for child support orders, **28 § 1738B**
Parental Kidnapping Prevention Act, **28 § 1738A**
Parimutuel licensing, simplification, **28 § 534 nt**
Professional and amateur sports protection, **28 § 3701**
Removal of cases from State courts to district courts, **28 § 1451**
Serial killings, investigations and investigators, **28 § 540B**
Supplemental jurisdiction, district courts, **28 § 1367**
State court,
District courts, removal of cases, **28 § 1451**
Review, miscellaneous provisions, **28 § 2113**
Supervising ethics office,
Financial disclosure requirements of Federal personnel, **5, Ap 4, § 109**
Surgeon General,
Narcotic addict rehabilitation, **28 § 2901**
Tide or submerged lands, real property quiet title actions against U.S., **28 § 2409a**
Torture,
Terrorists and terrorism, jurisdictional immunities of foreign states, **28 § 1605**
Torture victim protection, **28 § 1350 nt**
Transfer,
Federal debt collection procedures, fraudulent transfers involving debts, **28 § 3301**
Travel, FBI, investigations, **28 § 540A**
Travel expenses,
Government wide limitations on outside income and employment, **5, Ap 4, § 505**
Treatment,
Narcotic addicts, rehabilitation, **28 § 2901**
Undercover investigative operation,
Financial audit of undercover investigative operations closed in certain year, **28 § 533 nt**
Undercover operations,
Drug Enforcement Agency, FBI, **28 § 533 nt**

DEFINITIONS—Cont'd
Undercover operations—Cont'd
Federal Bureau of Investigation, **28 § 533 nt**
Financial audit of undercover investigative operations closed in certain year, **28 § 533 nt**
Undue hardship or extreme inconvenience, Jury System Improvements Act, **28 § 1869**
Unfunded liability,
Judicial Survivors' Annuities Fund, reduction of unfunded liability, **28 § 376**
United States Court of Federal Claims Judges Retirement Fund, **28 § 178**
Uniform Crime Reports, Bureau of Investigation, uniform Federal crime reporting, **28 § 534 nt**
Unitary review, habeas corpus, State procedures, **28 § 2265**
United States,
Administrative proceedings, award of costs and fees, **28 § 2412**
Jurisdictional immunities of foreign states, **28 § 1603**
United States district courts, court interpreters services, use, **28 § 1827**
United States marshal, Federal debt collection procedures, general provisions, **28 § 3002**
Valid lien, Federal debt collection procedures, fraudulent transfers involving debts, **28 § 3301**
Value,
Financial disclosure requirements of Federal personnel, **5, Ap 4, § 109**
Visitation determination,
Parental kidnapping prevention, **28 § 1738A**
Volunteer safety personnel, exemption from jury duty, **28 § 1863**
Voter registration lists, Jury Selection and Service Act, **28 § 1869**
Widow or widower,
Judges or justices, annuities for survivors, **28 § 376**
Year,
Judges or justices, annuities for survivors, **28 § 376**

DELAWARE
See, also, States, generally, this index
Bankruptcy judges, appointment, number and judicial district, **28 § 152**
District courts,
Judges,
Additional, **28 § 133 nt**
Number, **28 § 133**
Places of holding, **28 § 87**
Judicial circuit of U.S., **28 § 41**
Judicial districts, number of district judges, **28 § 133**
United States trustees of judicial districts, appointment, **28 § 581**

DELEGATE TO CONGRESS
District courts, jurisdiction, action to recover possession of office, exception, **28 § 1344**
Justices and judges, deposit of salary and credit for service as, judicial survivors annuity fund, **28 § 376**

DELINQUENCY
Public money, action by U.S. against person accountable, **28 § 2407**

DELINQUENTS
Juvenile Delinquents and Dependents, generally, this index

DELIVERING CARRIER
Amount in controversy for district court jurisdiction of cases, **28 § 1337**

DEMURRER
United States, action affecting property on which it has lien, **28 § 2410**

DENMARK
Conventions on, taking of Evidence Abroad in Civil or Commercial Matters, party to, **28 § 1781 nt**

DENVER, CO
Court of Appeals for Tenth Circuit, generally, this index

DEPENDENCIES OF UNITED STATES
Insular Possessions and Dependencies, generally, this index

DEPOSITARIES
Clerk of U.S. courts, deposits of other moneys into checking account in Treasury, **28 § 2043**
Pending or adjudicated cases, moneys paid into court, deposit, **28 § 2041**
Payment of fine, with bond money, **28 § 2044**

DEPOSITIONS
Docket fees on admission in evidence, taxation as costs, **28 § 1923**
Foreign Service, this index
Garnishment by U.S. against corporation, **28 § 2405**
Habeas corpus proceeding, **28 § 2246**
Justice Department appropriations available for taking of, **28 § 524**
Letters Rogatory, generally, this index
Rules of Civil Procedure, this index
Senate action to secure, District Court for D.C., jurisdiction, **28 § 1365**
United States Court of International Trade, this index
Witnesses,
Per diem, mileage and subsistence expenses, **28 § 1821**

DEPOSITS
Courts. Funds and Deposits in Court, generally, this index

DEPOSITS—Cont'd
Justices and judges, to judicial survivors annuity fund, **28 § 376**
Treasury of United States, this index
United States marshal, covering fees and expenses of, **28 § 1921**

DERIVATIVE ACTIONS
Stockholder,
Process on corporation, **28 § 1695**
Venue, **28 § 1401**

DESCENT AND DISTRIBUTION
Decedents' Estates, generally, this index
Executors and Administrators, generally, this index

DESIGNS
Justice Department seal, approval, **28 § 502**

DESTITUTE PERSONS
Indigent Persons, generally, this index

DESTROYED RECORDS AND DOCUMENTS
Courts, evidence, **28 §§ 1734, 1735**

DETENTION
Correctional Institutions, generally, this index
Habeas Corpus, generally, this index
Pending judicial proceedings,
Orders,
Issuance by magistrate judges, **28 § 636**
United States magistrate judges, power to issue orders, pending trial, **28 § 636**
Witnesses, want of security for appearance, compensation, **28 § 1821**

DEVELOPMENTALLY DISABLED INDIVIDUALS OR PERSONS
Mental Health, generally, this index

DEVICES
Interception of Wire, Oral, or Electronic Communications, generally, this index

DEVISES
Estates and Trusts, generally, this index

DIPLOMATIC MISSIONS
Foreign Service, this index

DIPLOMATIC OFFICERS
Foreign Diplomatic and Consular Officers, generally, this index
Foreign Missions, generally, this index
Foreign Service, generally, this index

DIRECT APPEALS
Supreme Court, this index

DISABILITY
Attorney General, vacancy in office, **28 § 508**

DISABILITY—Cont'd
Bankruptcy judges, grounds for removal, **28 § 152**
Certificates, disability of judge, retirement, **28 § 372**
Contract Disputes Act of 1978, time for commencement of actions against U.S., exception, legal disability, **28 § 2401**
Director of Administrative Office of U.S. Courts, annuity retirement, **28 § 611**
Employees' Compensation for Work Injuries, this index
Fair Housing, generally, this index
Handicapped Persons, generally, this index
Health Insurance for Aged and Disabled, generally, this index
Judges or Justices, this index
Judicial Center,
Board members, election for unexpired term caused by, **28 § 621**
Director of, retirement annuity, **28 § 627**
Legal disability,
Party,
Contract Disputes Act of 1978, time for commencement of actions against U.S., exception, **28 § 2401**
United States Court of Federal Claims, time for filing suit, **28 § 2501**
Party,
Contract Disputes Act of 1978, time for commencement of actions against U.S., exception, **28 § 2401**
United States Court of Federal Claims, time for filing suit, **28 § 2501**
Speech Loss or Disability, generally, this index

DISABLED PERSONS
Handicapped Persons, generally, this index

DISBURSING OFFICIALS, CLERKS, AND AGENTS
Claims,
Against U.S.,
Jurisdiction of U.S. Court of Federal Claims, **28 § 1496**
Comptroller General, generally, this index
Director of,
Administrative Office of U.S. Courts, **28 § 604**
Loss,
Relief,
From responsibility for loss in line of duty, jurisdiction of U.S. United States Court of Federal Claims, **28 § 1496**
In U.S. Court of Federal Claims, **28 § 2512**
Supreme Court marshal, **28 § 672**

DISBURSING OFFICIALS, CLERKS, AND AGENTS—Cont'd
United States Court of Federal Claims,
Jurisdiction,
Claims against U.S., **28 § 1496**
Relief from responsibility for loss in line of duty, **28 § 1496**
Loss, relief in, **28 § 2512**

DISCLAIMER
Patents, this index
Real estate, actions quieting title, prior to trial by U.S., termination, jurisdiction of district court, **28 § 2409a**

DISCLOSURE
Financial disclosure requirements of Federal personnel. Financial Disclosure, generally, this index
United States Court of International Trade, this index

DISCLOSURE OF FEDERAL CAMPAIGN FUNDS
Federal officers and employees, violations of Federal criminal law relating to, report to Congress, **28 § 529**
Traveling expenses,
Financial disclosure requirements of Federal personnel, applicability of provisions, **5, Ap 4, § 109**

DISCOVERY
Civil justice reform, litigation on behalf of U.S., guidelines, **28 § 519 nt, EON 12988**
Convention on the Taking of Evidence Abroad in Civil or Commercial Matters, pretrial discovery of documents, **28 § 1781 nt**
Rules of Civil Procedure, this index
Subpoenas for purposes of discovery, **28 § 2521**
United States Court of Federal Claims, this index

DISCRIMINATION
Fair Housing, generally, this index
Federal employees,
Judicial review, decisions of Merit Systems Protection Board,
United States Court of Appeals for the Federal Circuit, jurisdiction, **28 § 1295**
Jurors,
Exclusion from service, discrimination prohibited, **28 § 1862**
Selection of persons for service, prohibition, remedies, **28 § 1867**
Merit Systems Protection Board, this index
United States Court of International Trade, jurors, exclusion from service because of race, color, prohibition, **28 § 1862**

DISMISSAL AND NONSUIT
Correctional institutions, frivolous actions, inmates, **28 § 1915A**
Criminal charges, narcotic drug addicts, civil commitment and rehabilitation, **28 § 2902**
District courts, lack of jurisdiction, costs, **28 § 1919**
In forma pauperis proceeding, appeals, **28 § 1915**
Indictment, noncompliance with jury selection procedures, grounds for, **28 § 1867**
Recommencement of action by U.S. after dismissal without prejudice, limitation, **28 § 2415**
Rules of Civil Procedure, this index
Single judge of three-judge court not to entertain motion to dismiss action, **28 § 2284**
Venue laid in wrong division or district, **28 § 1406**

DISSEMINATION OF INFORMATION
Identification and criminal identification records, **28 § 534**
National Crime Information Center Project 2000, **28 § 534 nt**

DISTRICT ATTORNEYS
United States Attorneys, generally, this index

DISTRICT COURT OF UNITED STATES FOR DISTRICT OF COLUMBIA
United States District Court for District of Columbia, generally, this index

DISTRICT COURTS
See, also, Courts, generally, this index
Generally, **28 § 81 et seq.**
Abolition of terms, **28 § 138**
Act of Congress, civil action or claim against U.S., concurrent jurisdiction with U.S. Court of Federal Claims, **28 § 1346**
Adjournment, **28 § 140**
Session to continue until order of final adjournment, **28 § 139**
Administration,
Alternative dispute resolution, **28 § 651**
Affidavit of bias or prejudice of judge, **28 § 144**
Agencies of U.S., plaintiff, jurisdiction, **28 § 1345**
Agent, service of process, on agent in patent infringement action where defendant is not resident, **28 § 1694**
Aliens,
Jurisdiction of tort action, **28 § 1350**
Torture victim protection, civil action for damages, **28 § 1350 nt**

DISTRICT COURTS—Cont'd
Alternative dispute resolution, **28 § 651 et seq.**
Administration, **28 § 651**
Confidential or privileged information, **28 § 652**
Consent, arbitration referral, **28 § 654**
Damages, arbitration referral, **28 § 654**
Definitions, **28 § 651**
Exemptions, **28 § 652**
Jurisdiction, **28 § 652**
Neutrals, **28 § 653**
Referral to arbitration, **28 § 654**
Always open for certain purposes, **28 § 452**
Amount in controversy,
Carrier cases determined by receipt or bill of lading, **28 § 1337**
Diversity of citizenship, **28 § 1332**
Jurisdiction, **28 § 1330 et seq.**
Diversity of citizenship, **28 § 1332**
Interpleader, **28 § 1335**
Original jurisdiction, **28 § 1331 et seq.**
Antitrust laws or regulations,
Jurisdiction, **28 § 1337**
Appeal and review,
From district courts,
Allowance of appeal, fees, **28 § 1917**
Courts of Appeals, generally, this index
Supreme Court, generally, this index
Appearance,
Absent defendants, order for, **28 § 1655**
Personally or by counsel, **28 § 1654**
Appellate jurisdiction, circuit court of appeals,
Statistics reported to Congress, **28 § 604**
Application, discharge of employee by employer for jury service, **28 § 1875**
Appointment,
Crier or bailiff, **28 § 755**
Officers and employees, **28 § 756**
Receivers and receivership, copies of complaint and order of appointment to be filed in each district in which property is located, **28 § 754**
Reporters, **28 § 753**
Army and Air Force Exchange Service, express or implied contract with, civil action or claim against U.S., concurrent jurisdiction with U.S. Court of Federal Claims, **28 § 1346**
Arrest in one district for trial in another in civil action, **28 § 1693**
Assignment of cases by chief judge, **28 § 137**
Assistance to foreign and international tribunals and to litigants before such tribunals, **28 § 1782**

DISTRICT COURTS—Cont'd
Attorney General,
Civil actions,
Challenging appointment, jurisdiction, **28 § 503 nt**
Financial disclosure of Federal personnel,
Failure to file or filing false reports, civil action, **5, Ap 4, § 104**
Trust provisions, violation, jurisdiction, **5, Ap 4, § 102**
Attorneys' fees, employer or employee, protection of jurors' employment, **28 § 1875**
Bailiffs, **28 § 755**
Banking association as party, jurisdiction, **28 § 1348**
Bankruptcy, this index
Bid protests jurisdiction, concurrent with Court of Federal Claims, **28 § 1491**
Bonds,
Interpleader proceeding, **28 § 1335**
Jurisdiction of action on bond, executed under Federal law, **28 § 1352**
Carriers, jurisdiction, amount in controversy determined by receipt or bill of lading, **28 § 1337**
Certificates, and certification,
Counsel as to good faith in filing affidavit of bias or prejudice, **28 § 144**
Court's jurisdiction, interpleader, **28 § 1335**
Reporter or other individual designated to produce record, attachment, official certificate to original shorthand notes or other original records, **28 § 753**
Certiorari, this index
Chief Judge or Justice, generally. District Judges, this index
Circuit court judges, temporary assignment to hold, **28 § 291**
Citizens and citizenship,
Corporation deemed citizen of State of incorporation and of principal place of business, **28 § 1332**
States, territories, jurisdiction, **28 § 1332**
Civil action,
Pensions, U.S. as defendant, jurisdiction, exception, **28 § 1346**
Civil justice expense and delay reduction plans, **28 § 471 et seq.**
Advisory groups, appointment, term, **28 § 478**
Automated case information, **28 § 476**
Congressional, findings, **28 § 471 nt**
Content, **28 § 473**
Demonstration Program, **28 § 471 nt**
Development and implementation, **28 § 472**
Early implementation courts, **28 § 471 nt**
Implementation, requirements, **28 § 471 nt**

DISTRICT COURTS—Cont'd
Civil justice expense and delay reduction plans—Cont'd
Information,
Automated case information, 28 **§ 481**
Dissemination, enhancement, 28 **§ 476**
Litigation management and cost and delay reduction, **28 § 479**
Judicial officer, defined, **28 § 482**
Litigation management and cost and delay reduction, information on, **28 § 479**
Model, **28 § 477**
Periodic court assessment, **28 § 475**
Pilot Program, **28 § 471 nt**
Requirements,
Demonstration Program, requirements, **28 § 471 nt**
Pilot Program, **28 § 471 nt**
Review of court action, **28 § 474**
Study,
Report, Pilot Program, **28 § 471 nt**
Results, Demonstration Program, **28 § 471 nt**
Training programs, **28 § 480**
Claims against U.S.,
Jurisdiction, **28 § 1346**
Clerks of District Courts, generally, this index
Coast Guard Exchanges, express or implied contracts with civil action or claim against U.S., concurrent jurisdiction with U.S. Court of Federal Claims, **28 § 1346**
Collusive joinder of parties, lack of jurisdiction, **28 § 1359**
Commerce regulations, jurisdiction, carrier cases, amount in controversy, **28 § 1337**
Compensation and salaries,
Crier-law clerks, **28 § 755**
Reporters, **28 § 753**
Increase in salary limitation, **28 § 753 nt**
Comptroller of Currency, injunction against national banks, jurisdiction, **28 § 1348**
Concurrent jurisdiction,
State courts,
Bonds executed under Federal law, **28 § 1352**
United States Court of Federal Claims, U.S. as defendant, **28 § 1346**
Condemnation,
Property as prize, jurisdiction, **28 § 1333**
Real estate for use of U.S., jurisdiction of District Court, **28 § 1358**
Confidential or privileged information,
Alternative dispute resolution, **28 § 652**
Consent, alternative dispute resolution, arbitration referral, **28 § 654**

DISTRICT COURTS—Cont'd
Conspiracy,
Interference with civil rights, jurisdiction, **28 § 1343**
Constitutional questions,
Original jurisdiction of cases involving, **28 § 1331**
Three Judge Court, generally, this index
Constructive notice, pending actions concerning real property, **28 § 1964**
Consuls,
Jurisdiction of action against, **28 § 1351**
Contempt, generally, this index
Continuation of existing law by Judiciary and Judicial Procedure Code, **28 § 132 nt**
Contracts,
Express or implied with U.S., civil action or claims against U.S., concurrent jurisdiction with U.S. Court of Federal Claims, **28 § 1346**
Public contracts, disputes and claims of contracts awarded by executive agencies,
Claims against U.S., jurisdiction, cases sounding in tort, **28 § 1346**
Reporters, need for providing additional reporters, **28 § 753**
United States, judgments against, payment, **28 § 2414**
With U.S., jurisdiction, **28 § 1346**
Corporations,
Deemed citizens of any State by which incorporated and where it has principal place of business, jurisdiction of, **28 § 1332**
Organized under Federal law as party, jurisdiction, **28 § 1349**
Stockholder's derivative action, service on corporation, **28 § 1695**
Costs,
Amount in controversy, jurisdiction, exclusion of, **28 § 1332**
Carrier cases where award below jurisdictional limit, powers of court, **28 § 1337**
Civil justice expense and delay reduction plans, generally, ante
Criminal proceedings, **28 § 1918**
Denial where recovery less than jurisdictional amount, Federal question, **28 § 1331**
Diversity of citizenship, **28 § 1332**
Dismissal for lack of jurisdiction, **28 § 1919**
Protection of jurors' employment, award, **28 § 1875**
Counterclaims, U.S. as defendant, jurisdiction, **28 § 1346**
Court interpreters, generally. Interpreters, this index

DISTRICT COURTS—Cont'd
Court security, transfer to U.S. Marshals, **28 § 604**
Courts of Appeals, this index
Creation and composition, **28 § 132**
Crier-law clerks, appointment, compensation, **28 § 755**
Criers, appointment, duties, **28 § 755**
Crimes and offenses,
Reporter or other individual designated to produce record, transcribing and certifying parts of record of proceedings, **28 § 753**
Transcript of proceedings involving indigent defendants, fees of reporter, **28 § 753**
Customs duties, jurisdiction, **28 § 1340**
Damages,
Alternative dispute resolution, arbitration referral, **28 § 654**
Injury to person or property in violation of civil rights, jurisdiction, **28 § 1343**
Liquidated or unliquidated, civil action or claim against U.S., cases sounding in tort, Contract Disputes Act of 1978, concurrent jurisdiction with U.S. Court of Federal Claims, **28 § 1346**
Person or property in enforcing right of citizen to vote, jurisdiction, **28 § 1357**
Decisions, three-judge court, direct appeal to Supreme Court, **28 § 1253**
Definitions,
Alternative dispute resolution, **28 § 651**
Delay. Civil justice expense and delay reduction plans, generally, ante
Delay reduction plans. Civil justice expense and delay reduction plans, generally, ante
Deposits or payments into court, interpleader, requirement, **28 § 1335**
Deputies, assistants and employees, generally. Clerks of District Courts, this index
Disposition, filing fees, **28 § 1931**
Dispute resolution. Alternative dispute resolution, generally, ante
District Judges, generally, this index
District of Columbia,
Act of Congress, civil rights and elective franchises, applicability, **28 § 1343**
United States District Court for District of Columbia, generally, this index
Diverse citizenship,
Amount in controversy, **28 § 1332**
Jurisdiction, **28 §§ 1332, 1335, 1342**
Corporation deemed citizen of State of incorporation and of principal place of business, **28 § 1332**

DISTRICT COURTS—Cont'd
Diverse citizenship—Cont'd
Jurisdiction—Cont'd
Estates, legal representatives of, deemed resident of State of decedent, **28 § 1332**
Infants and incompetents, representatives of, deemed resident of State of infant or incompetent, **28 § 1332**
Insurers, liability insurance, direct action against, State citizenship of insurer, **28 § 1332**
Interpleader, **28 § 1335**
Permanent resident aliens, deemed residents of State of domicile, **28 § 1332**
Rate orders of State agencies, **28 § 1342**
Representative parties, requirements, **28 § 1332**
Division of business among judges, **28 § 137**
Early neutral evaluation. Alternative dispute resolution, generally, ante
Elections,
Disputes, jurisdiction, **28 § 1344**
Damages to person or property in enforcing right of citizens to vote, **28 § 1357**
Elective franchise and civil rights cases, jurisdiction, **28 § 1343**
Electric utility companies, jurisdiction of prosecutions for violations of law,
Sound recordings, sessions of court and other proceedings recorded by, **28 § 753**
Eminent domain, jurisdiction, **28 § 1358**
Evidence, **28 § 1731 et seq.**
International Trade Commission record, admissibility, **28 § 1659**
Exclusive jurisdiction,
Admiralty, maritime and prize cases, **28 § 1333**
Fines, penalties or forfeitures incurred under act of Congress, **28 § 1355**
Mask work cases, **28 § 1338**
Patents and copyright cases, **28 § 1338**
Seizures not within admiralty and maritime jurisdiction, **28 § 1356**
Surface Transportation Board's order, civil actions to enforce, upon referrals, **28 § 1336**
Tort claims against U.S., **28 § 1346**
Executive department regulations, action founded upon jurisdiction, **28 § 1346**
Exemptions,
Alternative dispute resolution, **28 § 652**
Expense plans. Civil justice expense and delay reduction plans, generally, ante
Extension of time for appeal to court of appeals, **28 § 2107**
Extrajudicial killing, defined, torture victim protection, **28 § 1350 nt**

DISTRICT COURTS—Cont'd
Federal question, jurisdiction, **28 § 1331**
Federal Rules of Civil Procedure. Rules of Civil Procedure, generally, this index
Federal Rules of Criminal Procedure. Rules of Criminal Procedure, generally, this index
Federal Rules of Evidence. Rules of Evidence, generally, this index
Fees, **28 § 1914**
Certiorari, notice of allowance, **28 § 1917**
Electronic access to court data, exemptions, **28 § 1914 nt**
Filing, disposition, **28 § 1931**
Habeas corpus,
Filing fees, **28 § 1914**
Transcripts, fees of reporter, **28 § 753**
Judicial Conference of U.S., prescribing, **28 § 1914**
Electronic access to court data exemptions, **28 § 1914 nt**
Schedule, additional fees, **28 § 1914 nt**
Notice of, petition for, or allowance of appeal, **28 § 1917**
Schedule, **28 § 1914 nt**
Transcribing records by reporter, **28 § 753**
Transcripts, **28 § 753**
Financial Disclosure, generally, this index
Fines, penalties and forfeitures,
Incurred under Act of Congress, jurisdiction, **28 § 1355**
Foreign and international litigation, service of documents issued in connection with, order, **28 § 1696**
Foreign diplomatic mission,
Direct actions against insurers of members and their families, jurisdiction, **28 § 1364**
Members of a mission or members of their families, jurisdiction, civil actions and proceedings, **28 § 1351**
Foreign states and citizens of a State, jurisdiction, **28 §§ 1330, 1332**
Forfeitures. Fines, penalties and forfeitures, generally, ante
Formal terms, court not to hold, **28 § 138**
Forms, Habeas corpus, Rules Governing Section 2254 Cases in U.S. District Courts. Habeas corpus, generally, post
Grand Jury, this index
Habeas corpus,
Capital cases, application filing, **28 § 2263**
Filing fees, **28 § 1914**
Issuance to get custody of defendant in district court, **28 § 1446**

DISTRICT COURTS—Cont'd
Habeas corpus—Cont'd
Persons in custody under judgment, State court, venue and jurisdiction, State containing 2 or more Federal judicial districts, **28 § 2241**
Power to grant, **28 § 2241**
Proceedings, applications and motions, capital cases, limitation periods, **28 § 2266**
Removal of case, issuance of writ to obtain custody of defendant, **28 § 1446**
Rules Governing Section 2254 Cases, **28 § 2254; HCR 1 et seq.**
Answer, contents, **HCR 5**
Approval and effective date, **28 § 2071 nt**
Civil procedure, federal rules, application, **HCR 11**
Delayed or successive petitions, **HCR 9**
Discovery, **HCR 6**
Evidentiary hearing, **HCR 8**
Expansion of record, **HCR 7**
Filing petition, **HCR 3**
Forms, **Foll. HCR 11**
Judges, preliminary consideration, **HCR 4**
Magistrate judges, powers, **HCR 10**
Petitions, **HCR 2**
Delayed or successive petitions, **HCR 9**
Filing, **HCR 3**
Powers of magistrate judges, **HCR 10**
Preliminary consideration by judge, **HCR 4**
Production of statements at evidentiary hearings, **HCR 8**
Records, expansion, **HCR 7**
Scope of rules, **HCR 1**
Scope of Federal review, capital cases, **28 § 2264**
State courts, grounds for remedies in Federal court, postponement, effective date, proposed rules and forms governing proceedings respecting, **28 § 2071 nt**
State custody,
Grounds for remedies in Federal court, **28 § 2254**
Transcripts, fees of reporter, **28 § 753**
Transfer of application by Supreme Court and court of appeals to district court, **28 § 2241**
Hearing, rate orders of State agencies, jurisdiction, **28 § 1342**
Improper joinder of party, lack of jurisdiction, **28 § 1359**
Increase in salary limitation for court reporters, **28 § 753 nt**
Indian allotments, jurisdiction, **28 § 1353**
Indian tribes or bands, jurisdiction, civil actions, **28 § 1362**

DISTRICT COURTS—Cont'd
Injunctions,
  Appeals to courts of appeals, **28 § 1292**
  Constitutional questions. Three Judge Court, generally, this index
  Federal statute, three-judge court, procedure, **28 § 2284**
  Jurisdiction, post
  National banks, receivers, jurisdiction, **28 § 1348**
  Packers and Stockyards Act, jurisdiction, enjoining violation of Secretary's orders, **28 § 2351**
  Rate orders of State agencies, **28 § 1342**
  State statute, procedure, **28 § 2284**
  Taxes by States, **28 § 1341**
  Three Judge Court, generally, this index
Inspection of records, **28 § 753**
Insular Possessions and Dependencies, this index
Insurance, interpleader, jurisdiction, **28 § 1335**
Insurer, liability insurance, direct action against, citizenship of insurer, **28 § 1332**
Interest,
  Judgment, **28 § 1961**
Interlocutory,
  Decisions, appeals to courts of appeals, **28 § 1292**
  Orders, relief, jurisdiction of courts of appeals, **28 § 1292**
Internal Revenue Service, this index
International Trade Commission,
  Stay of civil action pending related determination, **28 § 1659**
Interpleader,
  Bonds, **28 § 1335**
  Jurisdiction, **28 § 1335**
Interpreters, generally, this index
Interstate commerce, rate orders of State agencies, jurisdiction, **28 § 1342**
Judges. District Judges, generally, this index
Judgments and Decrees, this index
Judicial Conference of the United States, this index
Judicial Council, this index
Judicial districts, **28 § 133**
  Alabama, **28 § 81**
  Alaska, **28 § 81A**
  Arizona, **28 § 82**
  Arkansas, **28 § 83**
  California, **28 § 84**
  Colorado, **28 § 85**
  Connecticut, **28 § 86**
  Delaware, **28 § 87**
  District of Columbia, **28 § 88**
  Florida, **28 § 89**
  Georgia, **28 § 90**
  Hawaii, **28 § 91**
  Idaho, **28 § 92**
  Illinois, **28 § 93**

DISTRICT COURTS—Cont'd
Judicial districts—Cont'd
  Indiana, **28 § 94**
  Iowa, **28 § 95**
  Kansas, **28 § 96**
  Kentucky, **28 § 97**
  Louisiana, **28 § 98**
  Maine, **28 § 99**
  Maryland, **28 § 100**
  Massachusetts, **28 § 101**
  Michigan, **28 § 102**
  Minnesota, **28 § 103**
  Mississippi, **28 § 104**
  Missouri, **28 § 105**
  Montana, **28 § 106**
  Nebraska, **28 § 107**
  Nevada, **28 § 108**
  New Hampshire, **28 § 109**
  New Jersey, **28 § 110**
  New Mexico, **28 § 111**
  New York, **28 § 112**
  North Carolina, **28 § 113**
  North Dakota, **28 § 114**
  Ohio, **28 § 115**
  Oklahoma, **28 § 116**
  Oregon, **28 § 117**
  Pennsylvania, **28 § 118**
  Puerto Rico, **28 § 119**
  Rhode Island, **28 § 120**
  South Carolina, **28 § 121**
  South Dakota, **28 § 122**
  Tennessee, **28 § 123**
  Texas, **28 § 124**
  United States Magistrate Judges, generally, this index
  Utah, **28 § 125**
  Vermont, **28 § 126**
  Virginia, **28 § 127**
  Washington, **28 § 128**
  West Virginia, **28 § 129**
  Wisconsin, **28 § 130**
  Wyoming, **28 § 131**
Judicial Panel on Multidistrict Litigation, generally, this index
Judicial power may be exercised by single judge, **28 § 132**
Judicial Sales, generally, this index
Jurisdiction, **28 § 1330 et seq.**
  Action to compel officer or employee of U.S. to perform duty, **28 § 1361**
  Agencies of U.S., plaintiff, **28 § 1345**
  Aliens, tort action, **28 § 1350**
  Alternative dispute resolution, **28 § 652**
  Amount in controversy, ante
  Antitrust,
    Regulations, **28 § 1337**
  Banking association as party, **28 § 1348**
  Bonds, executed under Federal laws, actions on, **28 § 1352**
  Citizens of different States, territories, **28 § 1332**

DISTRICT COURTS—Cont'd
Jurisdiction—Cont'd
  Civil actions,
    Challenging appointment of Attorney General, **28 § 503 nt**
  Claims against U.S., **28 § 1346**
  Collusive joinder of parties, lack of, **28 § 1359**
  Commerce and antitrust regulations, amount in controversy governing carrier cases, **28 § 1337**
  Commerce regulations, **28 § 1337**
  Comptroller of Currency, injunction against national banks, **28 § 1348**
  Concurrent jurisdiction, generally, ante
  Condemnation,
    Property as prize, **28 § 1333**
    Realty for use of U.S., **28 § 1358**
  Congressional Acts,
    Actions founded upon, **28 § 1346**
    References to, construction, **28 § 1366**
  Conspiracy,
    Interference with civil rights, **28 § 1343**
  Construction, reference to U.S. laws or Congressional Acts, **28 § 1366**
  Consuls, action against, **28 § 1351**
  Contracts with U.S., **28 § 1346**
  Corporations organized under Federal law, as party, **28 § 1349**
  Counterclaims, U.S. as defendant, **28 § 1346**
  Customs duties, **28 § 1340**
  Damages to person or property in,
    Enforcing right of citizens to vote, **28 § 1357**
    Protection or collection of revenues, **28 § 1357**
  Dismissal for want of jurisdiction, costs, **28 § 1919**
  Diverse citizenship, ante
  Election disputes, **28 § 1344**
  Elective franchise, protection, civil rights, **28 § 1343**
  Eminent domain, **28 § 1358**
  Exclusive jurisdiction, generally, ante
  Executive department regulation, action founded upon, **28 § 1346**
  Federal question, **28 § 1331**
  Fines, penalties or forfeitures incurred under Act of Congress, **28 § 1355**
  Foreign diplomatic relations, members of a mission or members of their families, civil actions and proceedings against, **28 § 1351**
  Foreign States,
    Citizens of a State, **28 § 1332**
      Actions against foreign States, **28 § 1330**
  Improper joinder of party, lack of, **28 § 1359**
  Indian allotments, **28 § 1353**
  Indian tribes or bands, civil actions, **28 § 1362**

DISTRICT COURTS—Cont'd
Jurisdiction—Cont'd
Injunctions,
Rate orders of State agencies, **28 § 1342**
Surface Transportation Board's order, **28 § 1336**
Taxes by States, **28 § 1341**
Internal Revenue Service, **28 § 1340**
Laws, actions against U.S. for recovery of taxes, **28 § 1346**
International trade, unfair practices, counterclaims, **28 § 1368**
Interpleader, **28 § 1335**
Interstate commerce, rate orders of State agencies, **28 § 1342**
Land grants from different States, actions between citizens of same State claiming, **28 § 1354**
Liquidated or unliquidated damages, action founded upon, **28 § 1346**
Maritime cases, **28 § 1333**
Mask work cases, **28 § 1338**
Officers and employees of Government, plaintiffs in actions or proceedings, **28 § 1345**
Original jurisdiction, generally, post
Packers and Stockyards Act, enforcement, Secretary's orders, **28 § 2351**
Partition action where U.S. is joint tenant or tenant in common, **28 § 1347**
Patents, **28 § 1338**
Personal injuries, violation of civil rights, **28 § 1343**
Possession of office, action to recover, **28 § 1344**
Postal matters, **28 § 1339**
Prize cases, **28 § 1333**
Rate orders of State agencies, **28 § 1342**
Receivers and receivership, injunction against, **28 § 1348**
References to U.S. laws or Congressional Acts, construction, **28 § 1366**
Remand of cases removed improvidently, other than subject matter jurisdiction, **28 § 1447**
Restraints of trade, **28 § 1337**
Revenues, protection or collection, **28 § 1357**
Set-off, U.S. as defendant, **28 § 1346**
Supplemental jurisdiction, **28 § 1367**
Surface Transportation Board's orders, **28 § 1336**
Taxes by States, **28 § 1341**
Tort claims against U.S., **28 § 1346**
Trade-mark cases, **28 § 1338**
Transfer to cure want of jurisdiction, **28 § 1631**
Unfair competition, **28 § 1338**
United States,
Condemnation of realty for use of U.S., **28 § 1358**

DISTRICT COURTS—Cont'd
Jurisdiction—Cont'd
United States—Cont'd
Construction, references to laws of, **28 § 1366**
Defendant, **28 § 1346**
Plaintiff, **28 § 1345**
Vice consuls, action against, **28 § 1351**
Voting, enforcement of right of citizens, **28 § 1357**
Jurisdictional amount. Amount in controversy, generally, ante
Jury, this index
Justices, designated or assigned justices, competency to sit as judges of court, **28 § 132**
Land grants from different States, jurisdiction of actions between citizens of same State claiming, **28 § 1354**
Liens and incumbrances,
Enforcement,
Absent defendants, **28 § 1655**
Creation of new district or division or transfer of territory, effect, **28 § 1656**
Of U.S. on property as affected by action, **28 § 2410**
Loans, interpleader, jurisdiction, **28 § 1335**
Mandamus,
Action to compel officer or employee of U.S. to perform duty, **28 § 1361**
Marine Corps Exchanges, express or implied contract with, action or claim against U.S., concurrent jurisdiction with U.S. Court of Federal Claims, **28 § 1346**
Maritime cases. Admiralty, generally, this index
Mask work cases, semiconductor chip products, jurisdiction, **28 § 1338**
Mechanical means, sessions of court and other proceedings recorded by, **28 § 753**
Mediation and mediators. Alternative dispute resolution, generally, ante
Messenger, crier to perform duties of, **28 § 755**
Military or naval service, preference in appointment as crier or bailiff, **28 § 755**
Minitrial. Alternative dispute resolution, generally, ante
Money, interpleader, jurisdiction, **28 § 1335**
Monopolies and combinations,
Jurisdiction, **28 § 1337**
Motions, multidistrict litigation, proceedings for transfer to single district, **28 § 1407**

DISTRICT COURTS—Cont'd
National Aeronautics and Space Administration,
Exchange Councils of, express or implied contract with, civil action or claim against U.S., concurrent jurisdiction with U.S. Court of Federal Claims, **28 § 1346**
Navy exchanges, express or implied contract with, civil action or claim against U.S., concurrent jurisdiction with U.S. Court of Federal Claims, **28 § 1346**
Neutrals,
Alternative dispute resolution, **28 § 653**
Notes, interpleader, jurisdiction, **28 § 1335**
Notice of,
Appeals, filed prior to effective date of Federal Courts Improvement Act of 1982, decided by court of appeals to which appeal taken, **28 § 171 nt**
Rate orders of State agencies, jurisdiction, **28 § 1342**
Special sessions, **28 § 141**
Obsolete papers, disposition, **28 § 457**
Officers and employees, power to appoint, **28 § 756**
Officers and employees of Government,
Conflicts of Interest, generally, this index
Jurisdiction, plaintiffs in action or proceedings, **28 § 1345**
Open court, proceedings in, recording verbatim by shorthand, or other methods, **28 § 753**
Orders of court,
Adjournment, **28 § 140**
Advanced payment of fees, **28 § 1914**
Appearance by absent defendant, lien enforcement, **28 § 1655**
Assistance to foreign and international tribunals and to litigants before such tribunals, **28 § 1782**
Contempt, generally, this index
Copies of complaint and order of appointment of receiver to be filed in each district in which property is located, **28 § 754**
Division of business, **28 § 137**
Enforcement, of Surface Transportation Board orders, **28 § 2321 et seq.**
Foreign and international litigation, service of documents issued in connection with, **28 § 1696**
Interpleader action, restraining proceedings involved in, **28 § 2361**
Judicial council, district judges to carry into effect, **28 § 332**
Real estate, actions quieting title, disclaimer by U.S. prior to trial, **28 § 2409a**

DISTRICT COURTS—Cont'd
Orders of court—Cont'd
Record, order affecting property in different districts, 28 § **1692**
Sessions,
Of court and other proceedings designated by order, recording verbatim by shorthand, or other methods, 28 § **753**
To continue until terminated by order, 28 § **139**
Transcription and certification of parts of records of proceedings, reporter or other individual designated to produce record, 28 § **753**
Original jurisdiction, 28 § **1330 et seq.**
Action to compel Government officers to perform duty, 28 § **1361**
Admiralty cases, 28 § **1333**
Alien's action for tort, 28 § **1350**
Amount in controversy, 28 § **1332**
Civil action brought for protection of jurors' employment, 28 § **1363**
Conspiracy, interference with civil rights, 28 § **1343**
Contracts with U.S., 28 § **1346**
Customs duties, 28 § **1340**
Diversity of citizenship, 28 § **1332**
Election disputes, 28 § **1344**
Elective franchise, protection, civil rights, 28 § **1343**
Eminent domain, use of U.S., 28 § **1358**
Executive department regulations, actions founded upon, 28 § **1346**
Federal question, 28 § **1331**
Fines, penalties or forfeitures, recovery, 28 § **1355**
Indian,
Allotments, 28 § **1353**
Tribes, 28 § **1362**
Injuries under Federal laws, 28 § **1357**
Internal Revenue Service, 28 § **1340**
Laws, actions against U.S. for recovery of taxes, 28 § **1346**
Interpleader, 28 § **1335**
Land grants from different States, 28 § **1354**
Maritime jurisdiction, 28 § **1333**
Mask works, 28 § **1338**
Partition action, U.S. as joint tenant or tenant in common, 28 § **1347**
Patents, copyrights and trade-marks, 28 § **1338**
Personal injuries or property damage, violation of civil rights, 28 § **1343**
Possession of office, action to recover, 28 § **1344**
Postal matters, 28 § **1339**
Prize cases, 28 § **1333**
Real estate, actions to quiet title where U.S. is party defendant, 28 § **1346**
Removal of Cases or Causes, generally, this index
Seizures not within admiralty and maritime jurisdiction, 28 § **1356**

DISTRICT COURTS—Cont'd
Original jurisdiction—Cont'd
Treaties, actions involving, 28 § **1331**
Unfair competition, 28 § **1338**
United States,
Agencies or officers thereof, plaintiffs, 28 § **1345**
Defendant, 28 § **1346**
Laws, 28 § **1331**
Packers and Stockyards Act,
Jurisdiction, enforcement, Secretary's orders, 28 § **2351**
Partition action where U.S. is joint tenant or tenant in common, jurisdiction, 28 § **1347**
Patents,
Infringement cases,
Appeals to U.S. Court of Appeals for the Federal Circuit, 28 § **1292**
Defendant non-residents, service of process, 28 § **1694**
Jurisdiction, 28 § **1338**
Payment, judgments against U.S., 28 § **2414**
Penalties. Fines, penalties and forfeitures, generally, ante
Pensions, civil actions or claims for, U.S. as defendant, jurisdiction, exception, 28 § **1346**
Personal injuries, violation of civil rights, jurisdiction, 28 § **1343**
Places of special sessions, 28 § **141**
Plans. Civil justice expense and delay reduction plans, generally, ante
Plant variety protection,
Original jurisdiction of actions relating to, 28 § **1338**
Possession of office, jurisdiction of actions to recover, 28 § **1344**
Postal matters, jurisdiction, 28 § **1339**
Preservation, original shorthand notes or other original records certified by reporter or other individual designated to produce record, 28 § **753**
Priority of civil actions, 28 § **1657**
Prize (Vessels), this index
Procedure, 28 § **1651 et seq.**
Process, this index
Property, interpleader, jurisdiction, 28 § **1335**
Property damage, violation of civil rights, jurisdiction, 28 § **1343**
Rate orders of State agencies, jurisdiction, 28 § **1342**
Receivers and receivership, 28 § **457**
Appeals to courts of appeals, 28 § **1292**
Copies of complaint and order of appointment to be filed in each district in which property is located, 28 § **754**
Judicial sale of property in possession of, 28 § **2001**
Property in different district, 28 § **754**
Process, 28 § **1692**

DISTRICT COURTS—Cont'd
Records and recordation, 28 § **457**
Appointment of United States Magistrate Judges, 28 § **631**
Court of record, 28 § **132**
Duties of reporter or other individual designated to produce record, 28 § **753**
Entry of order of circuit judge as to habeas corpus, 28 § **2241**
Inspection, 28 § **753**
Order affecting property in different districts, 28 § **1692**
Referral to arbitration, alternative dispute resolution, 28 § **654**
Regular sessions,
Single judge may preside and hold, 28 § **132**
Times for holding, 28 § **139**
Release, generally, this index
Remand of cases removed improvidently, other than subject matter jurisdiction, 28 § **1447**
Removal of Cases or Causes, generally, this index
Reporters,
Appointment, qualifications, 28 § **753**
Increase in salary limitation, 28 § **753 nt**
Request of party to proceeding, reporter or other individual designated to produce record, transcription of original records, 28 § **753**
Restraints of trade, jurisdiction, 28 § **1337**
Revenue,
Damages to person or property in protection or collection of revenues, jurisdiction, 28 § **1357**
Review of decisions,
Certain Federal agencies, proceedings transferred from court of appeals, 28 § **2347**
Courts of Appeals, generally, this index
Inapplication to proceedings to review administrative agency orders, provisions concerning record in courts of appeals, 28 § **2112**
Supreme Court, generally, this index
Rules and regulations,
Advance payment of fees may be required, 28 § **1914**
Contempt, generally, this index
Division of business, 28 § **137**
Habeas corpus,
Rules Governing Section 2254 Cases. Habeas corpus, ante
Power to prescribe, public notice and comment, 28 §§ **2071, 2072**
Savings provision, 28 § **2071**
Sessions of court and other proceedings designated by order, recording verbatim by shorthand, or other methods, 28 § **753**
Times for holding regular sessions, 28 § **139**

DISTRICT COURTS—Cont'd
Rules and regulations—Cont'd
Transcription and certification of parts of records of proceedings, reporter or other individual designated to produce record, **28 § 753**
Rules Governing Section 2254 Cases. Habeas corpus, ante
Rules of Civil Procedure, this index
Rules of Evidence, generally, this index
Seizures not within admiralty and maritime jurisdiction, **28 § 1356**
Sentence and Punishment, this index
Sessions,
Adjournment, **28 § 140**
Chief Judge to preside at session which he attends, **28 § 136**
Powers unrestricted by, **28 § 452**
Pretermitting with consent of judicial council, **28 § 140**
Recording of sessions verbatim by shorthand, or other methods, **28 § 753**
Single judge may preside and hold, **28 § 132**
Special sessions, places, notice, **28 § 141**
Time for,
Filing affidavit of bias or prejudice of judge, **28 § 144**
Holding regular sessions, **28 § 139**
Set-off, U.S. as defendant, jurisdiction, **28 § 1346**
Shorthand, sessions of court and other proceedings recorded by, **28 § 753**
Special sessions, **28 § 141**
Standing order, advance payment of fees, **28 § 1914**
State, defined, supplemental jurisdiction, **28 § 1367**
Stay of execution of process in rem, indorsement with minute of suits where in rem process stayed, **28 § 2464**
Stipulation for stay of execution of process in rem issued in admiralty case, **28 § 2464**
Stockholder's derivative action, service on corporation, **28 § 1695**
Studies, concurrent jurisdiction for bid protests with Court of Federal Claims, time, contents, **28 § 1491 nt**
Supervision of reporters, **28 § 753**
Supplemental jurisdiction, **28 § 1367**
Supreme Court, this index
Taxes by States, jurisdiction, **28 § 1341**
Terms of Court,
Abolishment, **28 § 138**
Formal terms, court not to hold, **28 § 138**
Sessions, generally, ante
Testimony or production of documents, assistance to foreign and international tribunals and to litigants before such tribunals, **28 § 1782**
Three Judge Court, generally, this index

DISTRICT COURTS—Cont'd
Times for holding regular sessions, **28 § 139**
Tort claims,
Against U.S., jurisdiction, **28 § 1346**
Removal of State case to, **28 § 2679**
Torture, defined, torture victim protection, **28 § 1350 nt**
Torture victim protection, civil action for damages, **28 § 1350 nt**
Trade-mark cases, jurisdiction, **28 § 1338**
Transcripts, duties of reporter, **28 § 753**
Transfer of case, habeas corpus, persons in custody under judgment, of State court, State containing two or more Federal judicial districts, **28 § 2241**
Transfer to cure want of jurisdiction, **28 § 1631**
Treaties, original jurisdiction of actions involving, **28 § 1331**
Unfair competition,
Jurisdiction, **28 § 1338**
United States,
Defendant, jurisdiction, real property actions to quiet title, **28 § 1346**
Jurisdiction,
Condemnation of realty for use of U.S., **28 § 1358**
United States as,
Defendant, **28 § 1346**
Plaintiff, **28 § 1345**
Lien on property affected by action, **28 § 2410**
Partition action where U.S. is joint tenant or tenant in common, jurisdiction, **28 § 1347**
Payment of judgments against, **28 § 2414**
United States Court of Federal Claims judgment finding plaintiff indebted to U.S., enforcement, **28 § 2508**
United States attorneys, vacancies, filling, **28 § 546**
United States Court of Appeals for the Federal Circuit, this index
United States Court of Federal Claims,
Concurrent jurisdiction, **28 § 1346**
Finding plaintiff indebted to U.S., enforcement, **28 § 2508**
Judgment, suit by Government officers, contractors, on unsettled accounts, entry and enforcement, **28 § 2511**
United States Court of International Trade, this index
United States District Court for District of Columbia, generally, this index
United States laws, original jurisdiction, **28 § 1331**
United States Magistrate Judges, this index
United States marshals, employment of bailiffs to attend court, **28 § 755**
Venue of suits. Venue or District of Trial, generally, this index

DISTRICT COURTS—Cont'd
Venue or District of Trial, generally, this index
Vice consuls, jurisdiction of action against, **28 § 1351**
Voting,
Damages,
Equitable relief for protection of civil rights, jurisdiction, **28 § 1343**
Person or property in enforcing right of citizen to vote, jurisdiction, **28 § 1357**
Writs,
Contempt, generally, this index
Habeas corpus, generally, ante

DISTRICT JUDGES
See, also, Judges or Justices, generally, this index
Acknowledgments, authority to take, **28 § 459**
Active service, senior judge in commission to be Chief Judge, **28 § 136**
Adjustment in annual salary rate, **28 § 135**
Affidavits of bias or prejudice, **28 § 144**
Annuities to survivors, **28 § 376**
Appointment, **28 § 133**
Additional judges, **28 § 133 nt**
Chief judges, **28 § 136**
Crier, **28 § 755**
Disability, appointment of additional judge, **28 § 372**
Disagreement as to appointment of officer, **28 § 756**
Invalidation on President's failure to comply with standards and guidelines for merit selection of nominees, prohibition, **28 § 133 nt**
Law clerks, annual and sick leave, exceptions from provisions of, **28 § 752**
Relatives ineligible to appointment to any office or duty in court, **28 § 458**
Assignment. Designation and assignment, generally, post
Attendance,
At institutes and joint councils on sentencing, **28 § 334**
Fees for extended service of jurors, certification by clerk upon order of, **28 § 1871**
Bailiffs, determination of number, **28 § 755**
Bias and prejudice, **28 § 144**
Black persons, selection of qualified individuals for nomination to judgeships, Congressional recommendations, **28 § 133 nt**
Certificates and certification,
Appeal not frivolous, payment of fees of reporter, **28 § 753**
Disability furnished to President in behalf of retirement, **28 § 372**

DISTRICT JUDGES—Cont'd
Certificates and certification—Cont'd
Habeas corpus, proceedings in forma pauperis, payment, witness fees and mileage, **28 § 1825**
Necessity for assignment for service in another circuit, **28 § 292**
Payment of jurors' fees in excess of certain amount, **28 § 1871**
Chief Judge or justice,
Age restrictions, qualifications, **28 § 136**
Appointment, **28 § 136**
Officers and employees, **28 § 756**
Assignment of cases, **28 § 137**
Determination of availability of full-time United States Magistrate Judge, conduct of civil proceedings in district court by part-time Magistrate Judge, **28 § 636**
Division of business and assignment of cases, **28 § 137**
Inability to perform duties, successor, **28 § 136**
Relief from duties while retaining status as district judge, **28 § 136**
Retired judge, designation and assignment for duty within circuit, **28 § 294**
Senior district judge known as, **28 § 451 nt**
Senior judge in commission to be chief judge, **28 § 136**
Term of, **28 § 136**
Circuit judge, designation and assignment to hold district court, **28 § 291**
Commencement date, temporary judgeships, **28 § 133 nt**
Commissions, affecting precedence, **28 § 136**
Compensation and salaries,
Annual rate, determination and adjustment of, **28 § 135**
Deduction and withholding for purposes of annuities, to widows, **28 § 376**
Increase in limitation on compensation of secretaries and law clerks, **28 § 604 nt**
Law clerks and secretaries,
Fixed by Director of Administrative Office of U.S. Courts, **28 § 604**
Increase, **28 § 603 nt**
Limitation, **28 § 603 nt**
Retirement for disability, **28 § 372**
Territories and possessions on resignation, removal, **28 § 373**
Crier, appointment, **28 § 755**
Designation and assignment,
Another judge on filing of affidavit of bias or prejudice, **28 § 144**
Assigned or designated judges competent to sit as judges of court, **28 § 132**
Conditions on designation and assignment of district judge, **28 § 295**

DISTRICT JUDGES—Cont'd
Designation and assignment—Cont'd
Cost-of-living adjustment, territories and possessions, **28 § 373**
Judicial conference to prepare plans for, **28 § 331**
Multidistrict litigation, consolidated, pretrial proceedings, **28 § 1407**
9th circuit, assignment to Compact States, provisions, **28 § 297**
Powers and duties, **28 § 296**
Retired judge to perform duties, **28 § 294**
Temporary assignment to other courts, **28 § 292**
To hold district court in any district within the circuit, **28 § 292**
Disability,
Appointment of additional judge, **28 §§ 371, 372**
Retirement for, **28 § 372**
Disagreement as to appointment of officer, **28 § 756**
Division of business among judges, **28 § 137**
Domicile and residence, **28 § 134**
Applicability of orders under 1954 Amendment relating to, **28 § 134 nt**
Official duty station to be that nearest residence, **28 § 456**
Retired judges, **28 § 374**
Existing judgeships authorized, **28 § 133 nt**
Expenses and expenditures,
Attendance at institutes and joint council on sentencing, **28 § 334**
Habeas corpus,
Finality of determination, **28 § 2244**
Proceeding, final order, review, **28 § 2253**
Inability to perform duties when eligible to retire, appointment of additional judge, **28 § 372**
Judgments, interest on, rates, distribution, notice of, **28 § 1961**
Judicial Center, Board, membership on, **28 § 621**
Judicial conference,
Attendance, **28 §§ 331, 333**
Summoning to by Chief Justice, **28 § 331**
Judicial Council, generally, this index
Judicial discipline, complaint, review procedure, **28 § 372**
Judicial panel on multidistrict litigation, membership on, **28 § 1407**
Junior judges, commission extending over more than one district, **28 § 136**
Justices, designated or assigned justices, competency to sit as judges of court, **28 § 132**
Law books and Government publications furnished, transmitted to successor, **28 § 414**

DISTRICT JUDGES—Cont'd
Law clerks,
Annual and sick leave, exceptions from provisions of, **28 § 752**
Appointment, **28 § 752**
Compensation and salaries, ante
Merit selection of nominees,
Appointment of additional judges to take effect on publication of, **28 § 133 nt**
Magistrate Judges designated to exercise civil jurisdiction in district court, **28 § 631**
Nominations,
Congressional recommendations regarding blacks and women as qualified individuals for selection for nomination to judgeships, **28 § 133 nt**
Invalidation on President's failure to comply with standards and guidelines for merit selection of nominees, prohibition, **28 § 133 nt**
Nominees, standards and guidelines for merit selection of, appointment of additional judges to take effect on publication of, **28 § 133 nt**
Number, **28 § 133**
Appointment of additional judges, **28 § 133 nt**
Oaths and affirmations, **28 § 453**
Authority to administer, **28 § 459**
Office expenses, payment, retired judges, **28 § 374**
Official duty station, **28 § 456**
Orders,
Judicial council, carrying into effect, **28 § 332**
Pay. Compensation and salaries, generally, ante
Power, **28 § 132**
Practice of law as high misdemeanor, **28 § 454**
Precedence, **28 § 136**
Disability causing appointment of additional judge, **28 § 372**
President of the United States,
Appointment, **28 § 133**
Additional judges, **28 § 133 nt**
Not to consider race, color, sex, in selecting nominees for judgeships, **28 § 44 nt**
Standards and guidelines for merit selection of nominees, promulgation and publication of, **28 § 133 nt**
Presiding judge, **28 § 136**
Promulgation, standards and guidelines for merit selection of nominees, **28 § 133 nt**
Publication, standards and guidelines for merit selection of nominees, **28 § 133 nt**
Race, color, sex, not to be considered by President in selecting nominees for judgeships, **28 § 44 nt**

DISTRICT JUDGES—Cont'd
Record of proceedings, directions to reporter, **28 § 753**
Recording verbatim by shorthand, or other methods, proceedings, duties, concerning, **28 § 753**
Regular active service, court to consist of district judge or judges for district in, **28 § 132**
Regular sessions, single judge may preside and hold, **28 § 132**
Relatives ineligible to appointment to any office or duty in court, **28 § 458**
Request for reporter or other individual designated to produce record to transcribe original records, **28 § 753**
Resignation, retirement,
Disability, **28 § 372**
Salary in territories and possessions, **28 § 373**
Secretaries,
Appointment subject to limitation on salaries, **28 § 752**
Compensation and salaries, ante
Senate,
Appointment, additional judges, advice and consent, **28 § 133 nt**
Notification, waiver of standards and guidelines for merit selection of nominees, **28 § 133 nt**
Seniority affecting precedence, **28 § 136**
Sessions,
Chief Judge to preside at session which he attends, **28 § 136**
Single judge may preside and hold, **28 § 132**
Standards and guidelines for merit selection of nominees, appointment of additional judges to take effect on publication of, **28 § 133 nt**
Supreme Court, generally, this index
Table concerning number of, **28 § 133**
Temporary assignment to other courts, **28 § 292**
Temporary judgeships, **28 § 133 nt**
Tenure, **28 § 134**
Terms of chief judges, **28 § 136**
Territories and possessions, salaries on resignation, removal, **28 § 373**
Three Judge Court, generally, this index
Time for filing affidavit of bias or prejudice of judge, **28 § 144**
Traveling expenses, **28 § 456**
Unable to attend or make order of adjournment, clerk to make adjournment, **28 § 140**
United States Magistrate Judges,
Appointment and removal, **28 § 631**
Assistance to in conduct of pretrial or discovery proceedings in civil or criminal actions, **28 § 636**
Contempt of, punishment for, **28 § 636**
Designation to conduct civil proceedings in district court, **28 § 636**

DISTRICT JUDGES—Cont'd
United States Magistrate Judges—Cont'd
Designation to conduct civil proceedings in district court—Cont'd
Appointment or reappointment after promulgation of selection standards by Judicial Conference or certification as qualified, requirement, **28 § 631 nt**
Professional background and qualifications, statistics reported to Congress, **28 § 604**
Statistics reported to Congress, **28 § 604**
Vacancy,
Affecting pending proceedings, **28 § 143**
Caused by death, resignation, after additional judge appointed not to be filled, **28 § 372**
Waiver, standards and guidelines for merit selection of nominees, notice to Senate, **28 § 133 nt**
Women, selection of qualified individuals for nomination to judgeships, Congressional recommendations, **28 § 133 nt**

DISTRICT OF COLUMBIA
Act of Congress, civil rights and elective franchises, applicability, **28 § 1343**
Civil Rights, generally, this index
Clerk of District Court. United States District Court for District of Columbia, generally, this index
Congress,
Delegate to Congress, generally, this index
Court of Appeals for District. United States Court of Appeals for District of Columbia, generally, this index
Crime victims. Victim Compensation and Assistance, generally, this index
Defendant or res outside of, actions by U.S., time limitation, exclusion, **28 § 2416**
Delegate to Congress, generally, this index
District Court. United States District Court for District of Columbia, generally, this index
Diversity of citizenship, district courts, jurisdiction, **28 § 1332**
Drug Abuse Prevention, Control and Treatment, generally, this index
Executions in favor of U.S., **28 § 2413**
Federal Judicial Center Foundation, incorporation within, **28 § 629**
Foreign countries, transfer of offenders to or from. Transfer of Offenders to or from Foreign Countries, generally, this index
Foreign Missions, generally, this index
Grand jury, selection and service, **28 § 1861 et seq.**

DISTRICT OF COLUMBIA—Cont'd
House of Representatives,
Delegate to. Delegate to Congress, generally, this index
Judicial circuit, **28 § 41**
Judicial districts, **28 § 88**
Number of district judges, **28 § 133**
Jurisdiction,
Diversity of citizenship, district courts, **28 § 1332**
Jury,
Refilling master jury wheel, not later than certain date, from sources which include names of persons 18 years or older, **28 § 1863 nt**
Selection and service, **28 § 1861 et seq.**
National Guard, this index
Parimutuel Licensing, simplification, **28 § 534 nt**
United States Attorney,
Domicile and residence, **28 § 545**
United States Court of Appeals for District of Columbia, generally, this index
United States Court of Appeals for the Federal Circuit, generally, this index
United States Court of Appeals for Veterans Claims, generally, this index
United States Court of Federal Claims,
Official duty station of judges, **28 § 175**
Place of holding, **28 § 798**
Principal office, **28 § 173**
Rules of. United States Court of Federal Claims, generally, this index
United States District Court for District of Columbia, generally, this index
United States Magistrate Judges, appointment, qualifications, **28 § 631**
United States marshal,
Domicile and residence, **28 § 561**
Mileage fees for services in, prohibition, **28 § 1921**
United States trustees of judicial districts, appointment, **28 § 581**
Unjust conviction and imprisonment, damages in U.S. Court of Federal Claims, allegations, concerning acts, in, **28 § 2513**

DISTRICTS
Columbia. District of Columbia, generally, this index
District Courts, generally, this index
Firemen, exemption from jury service, **28 § 1863**
Judicial Districts, generally, this index
Officers and employees,
Exemption from jury service, executive, branches, **28 § 1863**
Pending suits, attending to interests of U.S. in, **28 § 517**
Police, exemption from jury service, **28 § 1863**

DIVERSE CITIZENSHIP
District Courts, this index

DIVISIONS
Designation and assignment of district judge to sit, **28 § 292**

DIVORCE
Parental Kidnapping Prevention, generally, this index

DOCKETS AND DOCKETING
Arbitration,
Restoration, new trial, **28 § 657**
Armed Forces, entry of docket of action or prosecution against member removed from State court to Federal court, **28 § 1442a**
Attorneys' and proctors' docket fees, taxation as costs, **28 § 1923**
Examination by Director of Administrative Office of U.S. Courts, **28 § 604**
Fees,
Taxation as costs, **28 § 1920**
United States attorneys, payment, **28 § 1923**
United States trustees, payment, **28 § 1923**
Information furnished by clerical personnel to Director of Administrative Office of U.S. Courts, **28 § 604**
Judgment,
Lien, **28 § 1962**
Pending action concerning realty, district courts, constructive notice, **28 § 1964**
Rules of Appellate Procedure, this index
Rules of Civil Procedure, this index
Supreme Court, direct appeal, **28 § 2101**
United States Magistrate Judges, Director of Administrative Office of U.S. Courts to furnish, **28 § 638**

DOCUMENTARY EVIDENCE
Book entries, **28 § 1732**
Business records, **28 § 1732**
Congressional journals, **28 § 1736**
Consular papers, **28 § 1740**
Convention on the Taking of Evidence Abroad in Civil or Commercial Matters, pretrial discovery, **28 § 1781 nt**
Copies,
Acts of legislature, territory or possession, **28 § 1738**
Books, records,
Business records, **28 § 1732**
Courts of States, territories or possessions, **28 § 1738**
Department or agency of U.S., inapplicability to cases, to which Federal Rules of Evidence apply, **28 § 1733**
States, territories or possessions, **28 §§ 1738, 1739**
Consular papers, **28 § 1740**
Court record lost or destroyed, **28 § 1734**
Foreign documents, **28 § 1741**
Foreign patent specifications and drawings, **28 § 1745**

DOCUMENTARY EVIDENCE—Cont'd
Copies—Cont'd
Judicial proceedings, records in, States, territories or possessions, **28 § 1738**
Officer's bond, **28 § 1737**
Official documents, office of consul or vice consul, **28 § 1740**
Patent and Trademark Office, documents, evidence, **28 §§ 1744, 1745**
State laws or judicial proceedings, **28 § 1738**
Territorial laws or judicial proceedings, **28 § 1738**
Court records lost or destroyed, **28 § 1734**
Foreign official records, **28 § 1741**
Foreign patent specifications and drawings, **28 § 1745**
Government records and papers, **28 § 1733**
Habeas corpus proceeding, **28 § 2247**
Handwriting, **28 § 1731**
Independent Counsel, this index
Officer's bond, copy, **28 § 1737**
Patent and Trademark Office documents, **28 §§ 1744, 1745**
Photographic, copies of business records, **28 § 1732**
Possessions of U.S.,
Acts of legislature, **28 § 1738**
Judicial proceedings, **28 § 1738**
Records or books, **28 §§ 1738, 1739**
Production of Books and Papers, generally, this index
Reproductions or originals, admissibility, **28 § 1732**
State,
Books and records, **28 §§ 1738, 1739**
Judicial proceedings, **28 § 1738**
Statutes of States, territories, **28 § 1738**
Territories,
Acts of legislature, **28 § 1738**
Judicial proceedings, **28 § 1738**
Records or books, **28 §§ 1738, 1739**
Transcripts of books, records, department or agency of U.S., inapplicability to cases, actions, to which Federal Rules of Evidence apply, **28 § 1733**
United States interested, court records lost or destroyed, **28 § 1735**
Vice consuls, copies of official documents and papers in office, **28 § 1740**

DOCUMENTS
Books and Papers, generally, this index

DOG RACES
Professional and amateur sports protection, applicability, **28 § 3704**

DOMESTIC COMMERCE
Commerce and Trade, generally, this index

DOMESTIC CORPORATIONS
Corporations, generally, this index

DOMESTIC PARTNERSHIPS
Partnership, generally, this index

DOMESTIC VIOLENCE
Insurrection and Sedition, generally, this index
International parental kidnapping, affirmative defense. Parental Kidnapping Prevention, generally, this index
Violent Crime Control and Law Enforcement, generally, this index

DOMICILE AND RESIDENCE
Bankruptcy, this index
Circuit judges, **28 § 44**
Clerk of district court, **28 § 751**
District Judges, this index
Judges or Justices, this index
Jurors,
Qualification for service, **28 § 1865**
Qualification form, contents concerning, **28 § 1869**
Jury commissioner, **28 § 1863**
Nonresidents, generally, this index
United States attorneys, **28 § 545**
United States Court of Appeals for the Federal Circuit, judges and chief judge, **28 § 44**
United States Court of Federal Claims, this index
United States Marshals, **28 § 561**

DONATIONS
Gifts, generally, this index

DOUBLE MILEAGE FEES
Summons as both witness and juror, **28 § 1824**

DRAWBACKS
Refusal to pay claim for,
Civil actions where protest denied, exclusive jurisdiction of U.S. Court of International Trade, **28 § 1582**

DRAWINGS
Copyrights, generally, this index
Foreign letters patent, copies, evidence, **28 § 1745**
Patent and Trademark Office, evidence, **28 § 1744**

DREDGES AND DREDGING
Oyster growers, damage by operations, suit in U.S. Court of Federal Claims, **28 § 1497**

DRUG ABUSE PREVENTION, CONTROL AND TREATMENT
Aircraft,
Importation of controlled substances by, penalties, **28 § 994 nt**
Aliens, U.S. Sentencing Commission, guidelines, controlled substances, **28 § 994 nt**

DRUG ABUSE PREVENTION, CONTROL AND TREATMENT—Cont'd
Attorney General,
Awards for information concerning forfeitures, delegation of authority to Deputy Attorney General or Associate Attorney General, authority, **28 § 524**
Department of Justice Assets Forfeiture Fund, awards for information paid from, delegation of authority to Deputy Attorney General or Associate Attorney General, **28 § 524**
Awards for information or assistance leading to forfeiture paid from Department of Justice Assets Forfeiture Fund, provisions, transfers, **28 § 524**
Children and minors,
Controlled substance offenses involving, enhanced penalties, **28 § 994 nt**
Common carriers,
Sentencing guidelines, operation under influence, **28 § 994 nt**
Controlled substances,
Aircraft, importation by, penalties, **28 § 994 nt**
Children and minors, offenses involving, enhanced penalties, **28 § 994 nt**
Fines, penalties and forfeitures, post
Violations, purchase of evidence, by Justice Department, appropriations, **28 § 524**
Department of Justice Assets Forfeiture Fund to pay awards for information or assistance leading to forfeiture, **28 § 524**
Drug Enforcement Administration, generally, this index
Exports and imports,
Controlled substance, importation by aircraft, penalties, **28 § 994 nt**
Violations,
Purchase of evidence,
Appropriations, paid by Attorney General or delegate, limitations, **28 § 524**
By Justice Department, appropriations, **28 § 524**
Federal agencies,
Justice Department Assets Forfeiture Fund, equipping, procuring, forfeited vehicles, for use by and awards to, agencies participating in Fund, **28 § 524**
Fines, penalties and forfeitures,
Aircraft, importation of controlled substances by, penalties, **28 § 994 nt**
Children and minors, controlled substances offenses involving, enhanced penalties, **28 § 994 nt**

DRUG ABUSE PREVENTION, CONTROL AND TREATMENT—Cont'd
Fines, penalties and forfeitures—Cont'd
Controlled substances,
Importation by aircraft and other vessels, **28 § 994 nt**
Offenses involving children, enhanced penalties, **28 § 994 nt**
Forfeitures. Fines, penalties and forfeitures, generally, ante
Guidelines. United States Sentencing Commission, generally, post
Methamphetamine,
Smokeable crystal methamphetamine, offenses involving, amendment of guidelines by U.S. Sentencing Commission, **28 § 994 nt**
Methamphetamine Interagency Task Force, establishment, membership, responsibilities,
Trafficking, increased penalties, **28 § 994 nt**
National Drug Policy, generally, this index
Penalties. Fines, penalties and forfeitures, generally, ante
Trafficking in,
Methamphetamines, increased penalties, **28 § 994 nt**
Transportation safety offenses,
Sentencing guidelines, **28 § 994 nt**
United States Sentencing Commission,
Controlled substances, **28 § 994 nt**
Transportation safety offenses, **28 § 994 nt**
Violent Crime Control and Law Enforcement, generally, this index

DRUG ENFORCEMENT ADMINISTRATION
Administrative, forfeiture of property for certain violation, award paid for information concerning, delegation of authority to make payment, **28 § 524**
Assets Forfeiture Fund, generally. Justice Department, this index
Attorney General, undercover investigative operations closed in certain year, financial audit, submission of results to, **28 § 533 nt**
Closed, defined, financial audit of undercover investigative operations closed in certain year, **28 § 533 nt**
Compensation,
Rate of, **28 § 509 nt**
Employees,
Defined, financial audit of undercover investigative operations closed in certain year, **28 § 533 nt**
Financial audit, undercover investigative operations closed in certain year, submission of results, reports, **28 § 533 nt**
Grades excepted from competitive service, positions in, **28 § 509 nt**

DRUG ENFORCEMENT ADMINISTRATION—Cont'd
Humanitarian expenses, appropriations, authorization, **28 § 509 nt**
Positions in, grades,
Vacancies, **28 § 509 nt**
Reduction in rank or pay, **28 § 509 nt**
Removal, positions in, **28 § 509 nt**
Reports, undercover investigative operations closed in certain year, financial audit, contents, time, **28 § 533 nt**
Suspension, positions in, **28 § 509 nt**
Undercover investigative operations,
Closed in certain year, financial audit, submission of results, reports, **28 § 533 nt**
Defined, financial audit of undercover investigative operations closed in certain year, **28 § 533 nt**
Undercover operation, defined, financial audit of undercover investigative operations closed in certain year, **28 § 533 nt**
Uniforms, allowances, appropriations as permitted utilization, **28 § 509 nt**
Vacancies, positions in, **28 § 509 nt**

DRUNKENNESS
Alcoholics and Alcoholism, generally, this index

DUE PROCESS OF LAW
Parental Kidnapping Prevention Act,
Congressional findings, **28 § 1738A nt**

DUMPING
Antidumping duties, generally. Customs Duties, this index
Ocean Dumping, generally, this index

EARNINGS
Compensation and Salaries, generally, this index

EAST GERMANY
Germany, generally, this index

EAVESDROPPING
Interception of Wire, Oral, or Electronic Communications, generally, this index

ECONOMIC STATUS
Jurors,
Exclusion from service of, discrimination prohibited, **28 § 1862**
Qualification form, contents concerning, **28 § 1869**
Service, discrimination in selecting persons for prohibited, remedies, **28 § 1867**

EDUCATION
Education Department, generally, this index
Educational Institutions or Organizations, generally, this index

EDUCATION—Cont'd
Judicial Center,
Personnel of judicial branch, function respecting, **28 § 620**
Juror qualification form, contents concerning, **28 § 1869**
National Drug Policy, generally, this index
Secretary of Education, generally, this index
Students, generally, this index

EDUCATION DEPARTMENT
Community development, neighborhood revitalization plan, development by Attorney General, use of appropriated funds, **28 § 509 nt**
Secretary of Education, generally, this index

EDUCATIONAL INSTITUTIONS OR ORGANIZATIONS
Attorneys' fees and other costs and expenses, award to party prevailing against U.S. or agency, applicability, **28 § 2412**
Justice, judge or Magistrate Judge, holding office in, disqualification, exclusions, **28 § 455**

ELDERLY PERSONS
Aged Persons, generally, this index

ELECTIONS
Damages to person or property in enforcing right of citizens to vote, jurisdiction of district court, **28 § 1357**
Denial of right to vote,
District court jurisdiction, **28 § 1344**
Disclosure of Federal Campaign Funds, generally, this index
District Courts, this index
Judicial Center Board, **28 § 621**
Narcotic drug addicts, submission to examination to determine question of addiction and rehabilitation, **28 § 2902**
Political Activities, generally, this index
Political Parties, generally, this index
Presidential and Vice Presidential Electors, generally, this index
Real estate, quieting title, retention and control by U.S. pending filing of judgments, appeals, payments to persons entitled, **28 § 2409a**
Vice President of U.S. Presidential and Vice Presidential Electors, generally, this index

ELECTRONIC COMMUNICATIONS
Interception of Wire, Oral, or Electronic Communications, generally, this index

ELECTRONIC DATA PROCESSING
Computers, generally, this index

EMBASSIES
Foreign Diplomatic and Consular Officers, generally, this index
Foreign Service, generally, this index

EMBEZZLEMENT
Bank Fraud Crimes, generally, this index

EMERGENCIES
Bureau of Investigation, expenses, unforeseen emergencies, confidential character, **28 § 537**
Emergency Federal Law Enforcement Assistance, generally, this index
Temporary Emergency Court of Appeals of United States, generally, this index
United States Magistrate Judges, temporary assignment from one judicial district to another in an emergency, **28 § 636**

EMERGENCY FEDERAL LAW ENFORCEMENT ASSISTANCE
Federal law enforcement assistance, **28 § 509 nt**
Investigations,
Federally insured financial institutions, **28 § 509 nt**

EMIGRATION
Immigration, generally, this index

EMINENT DOMAIN
Jurisdiction,
District court, **28 § 1358**
Liens and incumbrances, property on which U.S. has lien, condemnation proceedings, **28 § 2410**
United States, jurisdiction of district court, **28 § 1358**
Venue, proceeding by U.S., **28 § 1403**

EMPLOYEES' COMPENSATION FOR WORK INJURIES
Disability,
Juror, entitlement, termination of service as, **28 § 1877**
Federal Employers' Liability Act, generally, this index
Jurors, protection of, applicability of provisions, **28 § 1877**

EMPLOYMENT
Labor and Employment, generally, this index

ENCUMBRANCES
Liens and Incumbrances, generally, this index

ENDERBURY ISLANDS
Judicial district of Hawaii, inclusion in, **28 § 91**

ENEMY
Trading with the Enemy, generally, this index

ENEMY—Cont'd
War, generally, this index

ENERGY
Atomic Energy, generally, this index
Recycling and Resource Recovery, generally, this index
Secretary of Energy, generally, this index

ENGLAND
Great Britain, generally, this index

ENGLISH LANGUAGE
Jurors,
Qualification for service, **28 § 1865**
Qualification form, contents concerning, **28 § 1869**
Naturalization, generally, this index

ENVIRONMENT
Community Development, generally, this index
Laws relating to, violations, investigation and action by Attorney General, **28 § 509 nt**

ENVIRONMENTAL PROTECTION AGENCY
Administrator,
Federal Legal Council, representative designated by, **28 § 509 nt, EON 12146**

EQUAL EMPLOYMENT OPPORTUNITY
Administrative Office of U.S. Courts, personnel management system, discrimination prohibited, **28 § 602 nt**
Civil Rights, this index

EQUITY
Bankruptcy, generally, this index
Receivers and receivership, suit against without leave of court appointing them, **28 § 959**
Trustees, suit against without leave of court appointing them, **28 § 959**
United States Court of International Trade, possession of powers in equity as conferred upon district court, **28 § 1585**

ESCAPE
From custody, **28 § 2902**
Narcotic addicts,
Commitment for examination or treatment, penalties, **28 § 2902**

ESPIONAGE
Bureau of Investigation,
Investigations, persons employed by or assigned to U.S. diplomatic missions abroad, **28 § 533 nt**
Trade Secrets, generally, this index

ESTATES AND TRUSTS
Bankruptcy, generally, this index

ESTATES AND TRUSTS—Cont'd
Combinations in restraint of trade. Monopolies and Combinations, generally, this index
Federal Judicial Center Foundation, bequests to, as gifts to U.S., **28 § 629**

ETHICS
Attorneys for the government, **28 § 530B**
Independent Counsel, this index

EVIDENCE
Generally, **28 § 1731 et seq.**
Amount in controversy for review by court of appeals, proof, **28 § 2108**
Authentication, generally, this index
Books,
Department or agency of U.S., **28 § 1733**
Patent and Trademark Office, **28 § 1744**
Burden of Proof, generally, this index
Certificates,
Trial judge as evidence in habeas corpus proceeding, **28 § 2245**
Certified Copies, this index
Clerks of Courts, this index
Compelling production. Production of Books and Papers, generally, this index
Congressional Journals, **28 § 1736**
Consular papers, **28 § 1740**
Contempt of resident, in foreign country failing to respond to subpoena, **28 § 1784**
Convention on the Taking of Evidence Abroad in Civil or Commercial Matters, text of, reservations, **28 § 1781 nt**
Copies of books, records, of department or agency of U.S., admissibility, **28 § 1733**
Courts of Appeals, this index
Cross Examination, generally, this index
Depositions, generally, this index
Deposits in court, proof of right to, **28 § 2042**
Discovery, generally, this index
Documentary Evidence, generally, this index
Federal agencies,
Orders, interlocutory injunction suspending, **28 § 2349**
Federal Rules of Evidence. Rules of Evidence, generally, this index
Foreign Documents, generally, this index
Habeas Corpus, this index
Handwriting, **28 § 1731**
Intervention by U.S. or State in proceeding where constitutional question involved, **28 § 2403**
Judicial Notice, generally, this index
Jury,
Selection procedures, challenging compliance with, **28 § 1867**
Service, qualifications for, **28 § 1865**

EVIDENCE—Cont'd
Justice Department officers, securing, **28 § 516**
Microfilm of records, **28 § 1732**
Multidistrict litigation, transfer to single district for consolidated, pretrial proceedings, **28 § 1407**
Newly Discovered Evidence, generally, this index
Notice of application for order establishing lost or destroyed records, **28 § 1734**
Officer's bond, copy, **28 § 1737**
Patents, this index
Perjury, unsworn declarations under penalty of perjury as evidence in Federal proceedings, **28 § 1746**
Photographs of records, **28 § 1732**
Photostatic copies of business records, **28 § 1732**
Possessions of U.S., nonjudicial records, **28 § 1739**
Postmaster, demand on, **28 § 1743**
Presumptions, generally, this index
Prima Facie Evidence, generally, this index
Production of Books and Papers, generally, this index
Records and recordation,
Business records, **28 § 1732**
Consuls, **28 § 1740**
Court records,
Lost or destroyed, **28 § 1734**
United States interested, **28 § 1735**
States, territories or possessions, **28 § 1738**
Department or agency of U.S., **28 § 1733**
Foreign countries,
Authenticated copy, summary or excerpt as, **28 § 1741**
Lien, creation of new district or division, **28 § 1656**
Made in regular course of business, **28 § 1732**
Microfilm, photographs, or photostatic copies of records, **28 § 1732**
On review or enforcement in courts of appeals of agency, orders, inclusion of evidence, **28 § 2112**
Patent and Trademark Office, **28 § 1744**
Possessions of U.S., **28 § 1739**
States, **28 §§ 1738, 1739**
Territories, **28 § 1739**
Vice consuls, **28 § 1740**
Rules of Civil Procedure, this index
Rules of Evidence, generally, this index
State laws and judicial proceedings, **28 § 1738**
State nonjudicial records, **28 § 1739**
Supreme Court, power to prescribe rules of, for district courts, **28 § 2072**
Territorial laws and judicial proceedings, **28 § 1738**

EVIDENCE—Cont'd
Territorial nonjudicial records, **28 § 1739**
Three-judge court, hearing by, **28 § 2284**
United States, defendant's claim for credit, **28 § 2406**
United States Court of Federal Claims, this index
United States Court of International Trade, this index
Verified application for order establishing lost or destroyed court record, **28 § 1734**
Witnesses, generally, this index

EXAMINATIONS AND EXAMINERS
Books and papers,
Person interested in share of fines, penalties, **28 § 1822**
Judicial officers, appropriations, **28 § 526**
Judicial survivors annuity fund, **28 § 605**
Jurors, plan for random selection, **28 § 1863**
Rules of Civil Procedure, this index

EXCHANGE OF PROPERTY
Attorney General, procurement, law books, reference books, and periodicals, **28 § 525**
Identification and criminal identification records, **28 § 534**
Supreme Court, books, pamphlets, **28 § 674**

EXECUTION
Appraisal of goods taken on, **28 § 2005**
Certificates, execution not to issue against collector or other revenue officer, **28 § 2006**
Federal Debt Collection, generally, this index
Foreign states, immunity from execution of property, **28 § 1609**
Exceptions, **28 § 1610**
Types of property immune under any conditions, **28 § 1611**
Vessels, foreclosure of preferred mortgages, subject to jurisdiction, **28 § 1610**
Waiver, **28 § 1610 nt**
Imprisonment for debts, **28 § 2007**
Interest on money judgment, **28 § 1961**
Justices and judges, annuities to survivors, exemption from, **28 § 376**
Revenue officer, execution against, **28 § 2006**
Rules of Civil Procedure, this index
Sale, goods taken under without appraisal, **28 § 2005**
United States, execution in favor of, **28 § 2413**
United States marshal,
Fee for serving writ, **28 § 1921**
Incapacity after levy on or sale of realty, **28 § 2003**

EXECUTIVE AGENCIES

See, also,
Federal Agencies and Instrumentalities, generally, this index
Attorney General,
Legal services, pending claims in, **28 § 514**
Resolution of interagency legal disputes, **28 § 509 nt, EON 12146**
Attorneys, reasonable fees and expenses, award, prevailing party, actions by or against, **28 § 2412**
Budget, generally, this index
Civil justice reform, **28 § 519 nt, EON 12988**
Civil Service, generally, this index
Conflicts of Interest, generally, this index
Contractor with United States, generally, this index
Costs, judgment for, prevailing party, actions by or against, **28 § 2412**
Crimes involving officers and employees, report to Attorney General, **28 § 535**
Government Ethics, Office of, cooperation, conflict of interest, **5, Ap 4, § 402**
Disbursing Officials, Clerks, and Agents, generally, this index
Espionage laws, violations, report of and assistance to FBI, investigations of persons employed by U.S. diplomatic missions abroad, **28 § 533 nt**
Executive Departments, generally, this index
Government Ethics, Office of. Personnel Management, Office of, this index
Hearings,
Witness fees and allowances, **28 § 2412**
Incentive Pay or Awards, generally, this index
Investigation,
Crimes against U.S., **28 § 533**
Legal activities, resolution of interagency disputes by Attorney General, **28 § 509 nt, EON 12146**
Per Diem, generally, this index
Statement, facts, relating to petition in U.S. Court of Federal Claims or in U.S. Court of Appeals for the Federal Circuit, furnishing Attorney General, **28 § 520**

EXECUTIVE DEPARTMENTS

See, also, Executive Agencies, generally, this index
Accounts. General Accounting Office, generally, this index
Agriculture Department, generally, this index
Air Force Department, generally, this index
Army Department, generally, this index

EXECUTIVE DEPARTMENTS—Cont'd

Attorney General,
Legal services, pending claims in, **28 § 514**
Attorneys, reasonable fees and expenses, award, prevailing party, actions by or against, **28 § 2412**
Books and papers,
Evidence, inapplicability to cases, to which Federal Rules of Evidence apply, **28 § 1733**
Made in regular course of business, admissibility in evidence, **28 § 1732**
Budget, generally, this index
Civil Service, generally, this index
Commissions of Officers, generally, this index
Comptroller General, generally, this index
Condemnation of real estate,
Jurisdiction of district court, **28 § 1358**
Venue, **28 § 1403**
Costs,
Judgment for, prevailing party, actions by or against, **28 § 2412**
Payment and security, **28 § 2408**
Crimes involving officers and employees, report to Attorney General, **28 § 535**
Government Ethics, Office of, cooperation, conflict of interest, **5, Ap 4, § 402**
Damages, security not required of, **28 § 2408**
Employees. Officers and employees, generally, post
Espionage laws, violations, report of and assistance to FBI, investigations of persons employed by or assigned to U.S. diplomatic missions abroad, **28 § 533 nt**
Foreign Service, generally, this index
General Accounting Office, generally, this index
Housing and Urban Development Department, generally, this index
Investigation,
Crimes against U.S., **28 § 533**
Justice Department, generally, this index
Labor Department, generally, this index
National budget. Budget, generally, this index
Navy Department, generally, this index
Officers and employees,
Exemption from jury service, **28 § 1863**
Papers. Books and papers, generally, ante
President of the United States, generally, this index
Rules and regulations,
Actions against U.S., trial by court, **28 § 2402**
District court's jurisdiction, action founded upon, **28 § 1346**

EXECUTIVE DEPARTMENTS—Cont'd

Rules and regulations—Cont'd
Venue, action founded upon, **28 § 1402**
Secretary of Agriculture, generally, this index
Secretary of Army, generally, this index
Secretary of Commerce, generally, this index
Secretary of Labor, generally, this index
Secretary of Navy, generally, this index
Secretary of State, generally, this index
Secretary of Treasury, generally, this index
State Department, generally, this index
Tort claims against U.S. for negligence, of officers or employees, **28 § 2671 et seq.**
Transportation Department, generally, this index
United States Court of Appeals for the Federal Circuit, this index
United States Court of Federal Claims, this index

EXECUTIVE OFFICE

President of the United States, generally, this index

EXECUTIVE ORDERS

Indian claims, jurisdiction of U.S. Court of Federal Claims, **28 § 1505**
United States Court of International Trade, civil action raising constitutionality issue, three-judge trials, **28 § 255**

EXECUTIVE SECRETARIES

Secretaries, generally, this index

EXECUTORS AND ADMINISTRATORS

Annuities unable to be paid to survivors of justices and judges, payment to, **28 § 376**
Disbursing officers, claims against U.S., jurisdiction of U.S. Court of Federal Claims, **28 § 1496**
Income tax,
Justice, judge, magistrate judge or referee in bankruptcy, disqualification, **28 § 455**
Justice, judge or Magistrate Judge, disqualification, **28 § 455**

EXEMPLIFICATION

Fees, taxation as costs, **28 § 1920**

EXEMPTIONS

Jurors, **28 § 1866**
Determination, **28 § 1865**
Qualification form, contents, **28 § 1869**
Service, **28 § 1863**
Multidistrict litigation, exemption, antitrust laws, **28 § 1407**
Witnesses, U.S. Court of Federal Claims, **28 § 2506**

EXHIBITS
Review, orders, certain Federal agencies, attaching to petition, **28 § 2344**
Rules of Civil Procedure, this index

EXPENSES AND EXPENDITURES
Administrative Office of U.S. Courts, **28 § 604**
Bureau of Investigation, unforeseen emergencies, confidential character, **28 § 537**
Clerks of Courts, this index
Court officers and employees, payment by Director, Administrative Office of U.S. Courts, **28 § 604**
Disclosure of Federal Campaign Funds, generally, this index
District court reporter in connection with transcript, **28 § 753**
Extraordinary expenses of ministerial officers executing Act of Congress, allowance for payment, Attorney General, **28 § 1929**
Institutes and joint councils on sentencing, **28 § 334**
Judges or Justices, this index
Judicial Center,
Boards and commissions, members, **28 § 621**
Director, **28 § 625**
Jury commissioners, **28 § 1863**
Ministerial officers executing Acts of Congress, extraordinary expenses, allowance, payment, **28 § 1929**
Rules of Civil Procedure, this index
Subpoena of national or resident of U.S. in foreign country, **28 § 1783**
Subsistence, generally, this index
Traveling Expenses, generally, this index
United States, civil actions and administrative proceedings, payment, limitation, **28 § 2412 nt**
United States attorneys, **28 § 549**
United States Court of Federal Claims, this index
United States Magistrate Judges, reimbursement, temporary assignment in an emergency from one judicial district to another, **28 § 636**
United States marshal, keeping of property attached or libeled, **28 § 1921**

EXPLOSIVES
Atomic Energy, generally, this index
Sentence and Punishment, this index

EX-SERVICEMEN
Veterans, generally, this index

EXTRADITION
Habeas corpus, appeal and proceeding to test validity of warrant of removal, **28 § 2253**
Transfer of Offenders to or from Foreign Countries, generally, this index

EXTRATERRITORIAL JURISDICTION
Jurisdiction, generally, this index

FACULTY
Teachers, generally, this index

FAIR HOUSING
Enforcement,
Private persons,
Agency, defined, review of orders by Secretary, **28 § 2341**
Jurisdiction, courts of appeals, review of rules, regulations or final orders, **28 § 2342**
Orders, review, **28 § 2341 et seq.**
Review, orders, **28 § 2341 et seq.**

FAIR LABOR STANDARDS
Labor and Employment, generally, this index

FALSE ARREST
Tort Claims Act, exception of claim, **28 § 2680**

FALSE OR FRAUDULENT CLAIMS AGAINST GOVERNMENT
Claims, this index

FALSE IMPRISONMENT
Tort Claims Act, exception of claim, **28 § 2680**

FALSE INFORMATION
Identification Documents, generally, this index

FALSE REPRESENTATIONS
Fraud, generally, this index

FARM CREDIT
Federal Land Banks, generally, this index

FARM CREDIT ADMINISTRATION
Land banks. Federal Land Banks, generally, this index

FARMERS ASSOCIATIONS
Agricultural Associations and Organizations, generally, this index

FATHERS
Parent and Child, generally, this index

FBI
Bureau of Investigation, generally, this index

FEDERAL AGENCIES AND INSTRUMENTALITIES
Actions,
Civil justice reform, **28 § 519 nt, EON 12988**
Exclusiveness of remedy for negligence, wrongful acts, **28 § 2679**
Judicial review. Appeal and Review, generally, this index
Administrative adjudications, civil justice reform, **28 § 519 nt, EON 12988**

FEDERAL AGENCIES AND INSTRUMENTALITIES—Cont'd
Administrative adjustment of certain claims,
Negligence, of employees, **28 § 2672**
Administrative Conference of United States, generally, this index
Administrative Law and Procedure, generally, this index
Alternative dispute resolution, civil justice reform, guidelines, **28 § 519 nt, EON 12988**
Appeal and Review, generally, this index
Assets Forfeiture Fund, Justice Department, equipping, procuring, vehicles, for use by and award to, appropriations, **28 § 524**
Attorney General,
Investigative and prosecutorial powers involving fraud, criminal or unlawful activity concerning federally insured financial institutions, **28 § 509 nt**
Legal services, pending claims in, **28 § 514**
Litigation, guidelines, civil justice reform, **28 § 519 nt, EON 12988**
Reimbursable agreements, payment, private counsel, defense of Federal employees sued for actions while performing official duties, **28 § 509 nt**
Attorneys,
Guidelines, civil justice reform, conduct, pro bono service, **28 § 519 nt, EON 12988**
Reasonable fees and expenses, award, prevailing party, actions by or against, **28 § 2412**
Books or records as evidence, **28 § 1733**
Civil justice reform, guidelines, litigation, **28 § 519 nt, EON 12988**
Civil Service, generally, this index
Compelling performance of duty, action for purpose of, jurisdiction, **28 § 1361**
Condemnation of real estate,
Jurisdiction of district court, **28 § 1358**
Venue, **28 § 1403**
Conflicts of Interest, generally, this index
Contractor with United States, generally, this index
Contracts. Public Contracts, generally, this index
Cooperation,
Judicial Center, **28 § 624**
Costs, **28 § 2408**
Actions by or against, award of attorneys' fees and other expenses, **28 § 2412**
Judgment for, prevailing party, actions by or against, **28 § 2412**
Damages, security not required of, **28 § 2408**
Discovery, civil justice reform, guidelines, **28 § 519 nt, EON 12988**

FEDERAL AGENCIES AND INSTRUMENTALITIES—Cont'd
Documents,
Civil justice reform, guidelines, litigation on behalf of U.S., **28 § 519 nt, EON 12988**
Drug Enforcement Administration, generally, this index
Employees. Officers or employees, generally, post
Environmental or natural resource laws, violations, investigation and action by Attorney General with concurrence of, **28 § 509 nt**
Equal employment opportunity. Civil Rights, generally, this index
Espionage laws, violations, report of and assistance to FBI, investigations of persons employed by or assigned to U.S. diplomatic missions abroad, **28 § 533 nt**
Executive Agencies, generally, this index
Foreign Service, generally, this index
General Accounting Office, generally, this index
Government employee rights. Officers and Employees of Government, generally, this index
Hours of Labor, generally, this index
Incentive Pay or Awards, generally, this index
Investigation,
Crimes against U.S., **28 § 533**
Judgments rendered by State or foreign courts, payment, **28 § 2414**
Judicial Center Board,
Contracts for research projects and other services, **28 § 624**
Information requested by, **28 § 624**
Recommendations presented to for improvement of programs for activities, **28 § 623**
Justice Department, Assets Forfeiture Fund, equipping, procuring, forfeited vehicles, for use by and award to, appropriations, **28 § 524**
Law books and Government publications, transmittal to successors, **28 § 414**
Legal disputes, resolution of interagency disputes by Attorney General, **28 § 509 nt, EON 12146**
Legislation,
Civil justice reform, guidelines for proposals, **28 § 519 nt, EON 12988**
Limitation,
Actions brought by, **28 §§ 2415, 2416**
Litigation,
Notice system, agencies with authority to litigate cases, notice to Attorney General, civil litigation in which Federal Government is party, **28 § 509 nt, EON 12146**
Reimbursement, Justice Department, salaries and expenses, **28 § 509 nt**
Where a party, conducting reserved to Justice Department, **28 § 516**
Mileage, generally, this index
Motions, civil justice reform, discovery guidelines, **28 § 519 nt, EON 12988**
Notice,
Complaints, pre-filing requirements, civil justice reform, **28 § 519 nt, EON 12988**
Creditors, other interested parties, issuance, solely to Clerks, of U.S. Bankruptcy Courts, prohibition, **28 § 1930 nt**
Office of,
Government Ethics, **5, Ap 4, § 401 et seq.**
Officers or employees,
Civil Service, generally, this index
Incentive Pay or Awards, generally, this index
Venue, actions against, **28 § 1391**
Open meetings. Administrative Law and Procedure, generally, this index
Parties to action, plaintiff, original jurisdiction of District Court, **28 § 1345**
Payment of awards for negligence, of employees, **28 § 2672**
Per Diem, generally, this index
Pro bono services, civil justice reform, guidelines, **28 § 519 nt, EON 12988**
Public education, agency benefits, civil justice reform, **28 § 519 nt, EON 12988**
Records and Recordation, this index
Regulations. Rules and regulations, generally, post
Removal of actions or prosecution against, agencies or officers of, **28 § 1442**
Review. Appeal and Review, generally, this index
Rules and regulations,
Administrative Law and Procedure, generally, this index
Civil justice reform, guidelines for promulgation, **28 § 519 nt, EON 12988**
Rules of Evidence, this index
Sanctions, civil justice reform, guidelines, **28 § 519 nt, EON 12988**
Settlements, civil justice reform, conferences, attempts, **28 § 519 nt, EON 12988**
Special Counsel, Office of, generally, this index
Subpoena issued in behalf of, tender of fees and mileage, **28 § 1825**
Supervision of litigation where a party, **28 § 519**
Tort claims against U.S.,
Compromise and settlement, **28 § 2672**
Time for presenting claim or commencing action against U.S., **28 § 2401**
Transmittal of letter rogatory or request to, **28 § 1781**
Uniformed Services, generally, this index
United States Magistrate Judges, appointment and qualifications, areas under administration of, **28 § 631**
Volunteers, civil justice reform, **28 § 519 nt, EON 12988**
Witnesses,
Fees, payment, **28 § 1825**

FEDERAL AID
Diversion of money under programs, action by U.S. for recovery, limitations, **28 §§ 2415, 2416**
Federal debt collection, postjudgment remedies, eligibility for grants, loans or programs, effect of judgment lien, **28 § 3201**
Grants, generally, this index

FEDERAL BUREAU OF INVESTIGATION
Bureau of Investigation, generally, this index

FEDERAL CIVIL PENALTIES INFLATION ADJUSTMENT ACT OF 1990
Generally, **28 § 2461 nt**

FEDERAL CORPORATIONS
See, also, Executive Agencies, generally, this index
Jurisdiction of district courts, **28 § 1349**
Patents and copyrights, actions against U.S., jurisdiction of U.S. Court of Federal Claims, **28 § 1498**
Tort claims against U.S. for negligence, of officers or employees, **28 § 2671 et seq.**

FEDERAL DEBT COLLECTION
Generally, **28 § 3001 et seq.**
Actions and proceedings,
Joinder of additional defendant, **28 § 3012**
Service of process, enforcement, notice, manner, **28 § 3004**
Surcharge on debt, assessment, authorization, limitation, **28 § 3011**
United States magistrates, assignment to, **28 § 3008**
Affidavits,
Prejudgment remedies, requirements, contents, **28 § 3101**
Requirements, general provisions, **28 § 3006**
Applicability of law, **28 § 3001**
Judgments, **28 § 3005**
Assessment, surcharge on debt, authorization, limitation, **28 § 3011**
Attachment. Prejudgment remedies, generally, post

FEDERAL DEBT COLLECTION
—Cont'd
Co-owned property,
Prejudgment remedies, garnishment, authority, 28 § **3104**
Remedies available to U.S., limitation, 28 § **3010**
Counsel for the United States,
Defined, general provisions, 28 § **3002**
Prejudgment remedies, notice, preparation, issuance to debtor, 28 § **3101**
Service of process, notice, 28 § **3004**
Court, defined, general provisions, 28 § **3002**
Debt, defined, general provisions, 28 § **3002**
Debtor,
Defined, general provisions, 28 § **3002**
Election to exempt property, effect on assertion and manner of determination, 28 § **3014**
Financial condition of, discovery, limitation, 28 § **3015**
Definitions, 28 § **3002**
Deposit, sale proceeds, perishable personal property, authority, presumption, 28 § **3007**
Discovery, debtor's financial condition, authority, limitation, 28 § **3015**
Disposable earnings, defined, general provisions, 28 § **3002**
Earnings, defined, general provisions, 28 § **3002**
Election to exempt property, debtor, 28 § **3014**
Enforcement,
Nationwide, service of process, notice, manner, 28 § **3004**
Procedures, modification, authority, 28 § **3013**
Exempt property, election by debtor, 28 § **3014**
Federal Rules of Civil Procedure,
Applicability, rules of construction, 28 § **3003**
Service of process in accordance with, 28 § **3004**
Financial condition, debtor, discovery, limitation, 28 § **3015**
Foreign and international law, effect on rights of U.S. under, rules of construction, 28 § **3003**
Fraudulent transfers involving debts, 28 § **3301 et seq.**
Affiliates, defined, 28 § **3301**
Applicability, certain areas of law, supplementary provision, 28 § **3308**
Arising before transfer made or obligation incurred, debt to U.S., when fraudulent, 28 § **3304**
Assets,
Defined, 28 § **3301**
Valuation, 28 § **3307**
Calculation, insolvency, assets and debts, 28 § **3302**

FEDERAL DEBT COLLECTION
—Cont'd
Fraudulent transfers involving debts
—Cont'd
Claim, defined, 28 § **3301**
Creditor, defined, 28 § **3301**
Definitions, 28 § **3301**
Exceptions, voidability of transfer, 28 § **3307**
Federal Rules of Civil Procedure, remedies of U.S. available in accordance with, 28 § **3306**
Good faith transfers for reasonably equivalent value, validity, rights of participants, 28 § **3307**
Insider, defined, 28 § **3301**
Insolvency, presumption, calculation, assets and debts, 28 § **3302**
Intent, actual, determination, transfer made or obligation incurred without regard to judgment date, debt to U.S., when fraudulent, 28 § **3304**
Judgment date, transfers made or obligations incurred without regard to, debt to U.S., when fraudulent, 28 § **3304**
Lien, defined, 28 § **3301**
Limitation,
Recovery by U.S., judgment for value of asset transferred not to exceed judgment on debt, 28 § **3307**
Remedies of U.S., 28 § **3306**
Voidability, 28 § **3307**
Obligation, when incurred, 28 § **3305**
Present value, when given, transfer or obligation, 28 § **3303**
Presumption, insolvency, debtor not paying debts as they become due, 28 § **3302**
Reasonably equivalent value, when given, transfer or obligation, 28 § **3303**
Relative, defined, 28 § **3301**
Remedies, U.S., limitations, 28 § **3306**
Rights, good faith transferees and obligees, limitation, 28 § **3307**
Supplementary provision, 28 § **3308**
Transactions, value, when given, transfer or obligation, 28 § **3303**
Transfer,
Defined, 28 § **3301**
When made, 28 § **3305**
Transferee, liability, defenses, and protection of, 28 § **3307**
United States,
Debt owed to arising before transfer made or obligation incurred, when fraudulent, 28 § **3304**
Remedies of, limitations, 28 § **3306**
Valid lien, defined, 28 § **3301**
Valuation, assets, 28 § **3307**
Value, when given, transfer or obligation, 28 § **3303**
Voidability, limitation, 28 § **3307**

FEDERAL DEBT COLLECTION
—Cont'd
Fraudulent transfers involving debts
—Cont'd
When transfer made or obligation incurred, 28 § **3305**
Garnishee, defined, general provisions, 28 § **3002**
Hearings,
Exempt property, applicability of claim, U.S. or debtor, 28 § **3014**
Prejudgment remedies, post
Joinder, additional defendant, action or proceeding, 28 § **3012**
Joint cases, debtors in, exempt property, 28 § **3014**
Judgments and decrees,
Application of provisions to, 28 § **3005**
Defined, general provisions, 28 § **3002**
Limitation,
Applicability of provisions, 28 § **3001**
Assessment, surcharge on debt, 28 § **3011**
Co-owned property, remedies available to U.S. related to, 28 § **3010**
Debtor's financial condition, discovery, 28 § **3015**
Fraudulent transfers involving debts, ante
Modification, enforcement procedures, authority, 28 § **3013**
Nonexempt disposable earnings, defined, general provisions, 28 § **3002**
Notice,
Prejudgment remedies, post
Service of process, enforcement, manner, 28 § **3004**
Person, defined, general provisions, 28 § **3002**
Personal property, perishable, authority to sell, deposit of proceeds, presumption, 28 § **3007**
Postjudgment remedies, 28 § **3201 et seq.**
Accounting, garnishment, U.S. to conduct and supply to judgment debtor and garnishee, 28 § **3205**
Answer, garnishee, response to writ of garnishment, contents, 28 § **3205**
Appointment, receiver, management of property pending levy of execution, 28 § **3203**
Bidding requirements, execution sale, general procedures, 28 § **3203**
City lots, execution sale, general procedures, 28 § **3203**
Commencement, action or proceeding to obtain remedy, U.S. counsel, notice, form and content, 28 § **3202**
Co-owned property,
Garnishment, subject to, 28 § **3205**
Subject to execution, 28 § **3203**
Counsel for U.S., notice, commencement of action or proceeding to obtain remedy, preparation, form and content, 28 § **3202**

FEDERAL DEBT COLLECTION —Cont'd
Postjudgment remedies—Cont'd
Creation,
Execution lien, priority, 28 § **3203**
Judgment liens, real property, amount, 28 § **3201**
Discharge, 28 § **3206**
Disposition,
Order directing garnishee concerning judgment debtor's nonexempt interest in property, 28 § **3205**
Proceeds, execution sale, 28 § **3203**
Eligibility, Federal grants, loans or programs, effect of judgment lien, 28 § **3201**
Enforcement of judgments, notice, service of process, hearing, sale of property, 28 § **3202**
Execution, property subject to, creation of lien, writ, levy, appointment of receiver, sale, 28 § **3203**
Execution sale, procedures, real or personal property, postponement, rights and liabilities of purchasers, 28 § **3203**
Federal grants, loans or programs, eligibility, effect of judgment lien, 28 § **3201**
Garnishee, failure to answer writ or pay in accordance with, appearance requirement, 28 § **3205**
Garnishment, writ, issuance, requirements, procedures, 28 § **3205**
Hearings, action or proceeding commenced by U.S. to obtain remedy, availability, 28 § **3202**
Installment payment order, authority to issue, modification, limitation, 28 § **3204**
Issuance, writ of execution, form, contents, 28 § **3203**
Judgment debtor, discharge, 28 § **3206**
Levy, additional, proceeds from execution sale insufficient to satisfy execution, 28 § **3203**
Liens and incumbrances, creation, priority, duration, release, 28 § **3201**
Limitation, installment payment order, 28 § **3204**
Modification, installment payment order, 28 § **3204**
Notice,
Action or proceeding commenced by U.S. to obtain a remedy, form and content, 28 § **3202**
Execution sale, real and personal property, general procedures, 28 § **3203**
Payment of debt, discharge, 28 § **3206**
Payment order, installment, authority to issue, modification, limitation, 28 § **3204**

FEDERAL DEBT COLLECTION —Cont'd
Postjudgment remedies—Cont'd
Postponement, execution sale, notice, publication by U.S. marshal, 28 § **3203**
Priorities,
Garnishment, procedures applicable to writ, 28 § **3205**
Judgment liens, 28 § **3201**
Procedures,
Execution sale, real or personal property, rights and liabilities of purchasers, 28 § **3203**
Writ of garnishment, court determination, form, service, answer, objections, 28 § **3205**
Proceeds, execution sale, disposition, 28 § **3203**
Property,
Execution sale,
Real and personal property, general procedures, 28 § **3203**
Subject to levy pursuant to writ, 28 § **3203**
Garnishment, writ, issuance against, requirements, procedures, 28 § **3205**
Purchasers, property, execution sale, rights and liabilities, 28 § **3203**
Receiver, appointment, manage property pending levy of execution, 28 § **3203**
Records and recordation, U.S. marshal, writ of execution, maintenance requirements, 28 § **3203**
Redemption, property, before execution sale, bond submitted by judgment debtor, 28 § **3203**
Release, judgment lien, filing of satisfaction of judgment or release, 28 § **3201**
Renewal, judgment liens, 28 § **3201**
Replevy, property, before execution sale, bond submitted by judgment debtor, 28 § **3203**
Requirements, writ of garnishment, issuance, procedures, 28 § **3205**
Rights and liabilities, purchasers of property, execution sale, 28 § **3203**
Rural property, execution sale, general procedures, 28 § **3203**
Sales, property,
Execution or judicial sale, satisfaction of judgment, enforcement remedy, 28 § **3202**
Subject to judgment lien, 28 § **3201**
Service of process,
Commencement of action or proceeding by U.S. to obtain remedy, 28 § **3202**
Writ of garnishment, 28 § **3205**
Stay of proceedings, death of judgment debtor, after issuance of execution writ, 28 § **3203**

FEDERAL DEBT COLLECTION —Cont'd
Postjudgment remedies—Cont'd
Termination, garnishment, conditions, 28 § **3205**
United States marshals,
Execution sale, real and personal property, procedures, notice, publication by, 28 § **3203**
Writ of execution, duties, 28 § **3203**
Waiver, restriction on eligibility for Federal grants, loans, and funds, effect of judgment liens, regulations promulgated by responsible U.S. agency, 28 § **3201**
Writs,
Execution, issuance, form, contents, 28 § **3203**
Garnishment, issuance, requirements, procedures, form, service, 28 § **3205**
Preemption of provisions over State law, rules of construction, 28 § **3003**
Prejudgment remedies, 28 § **3101 et seq.**
Accounts, receivers required to maintain written records of receipts and expenditures, reports, 28 § **3103**
Affidavits, requirement, contents, 28 § **3101**
Application,
Contents, affidavit, 28 § **3101**
Writ of garnishment, contents, limitation, 28 § **3104**
Appointment, receiver, powers, duration, compensation, 28 § **3103**
Attachment, property subject to, availability, issuance of writ, contents, levy, 28 § **3102**
Availability,
Attachment, 28 § **3102**
Sequestration, 28 § **3105**
Bond, requirement, debtor, replevin of attached property, 28 § **3102**
Compensation, receivers, 28 § **3103**
Co-owned property, garnishment, authority, 28 § **3104**
Counsel for U.S., notice, preparation, issuance to debtor against whom remedy is sought, 28 § **3101**
Debtor, replevin of attached property, bond, 28 § **3102**
Defined, general provisions, 28 § **3002**
Deposit, sequestered income, 28 § **3105**
Disposition,
Attached property, judgment for U.S., 28 § **3102**
Sequestered income, judgment for U.S., 28 § **3105**
Dissolution,
Attachment, 28 § **3102**
Sequestration order, notice, motion, 28 § **3105**

FEDERAL DEBT COLLECTION
—Cont'd
Prejudgment remedies—Cont'd
Excessive or unreasonable attachment, reduction or dissolution, motion, notice, **28 § 3102**
Execution, sequestration writ, U.S. marshal, duties, **28 § 3105**
Exoneration, replevin bond, attached property, **28 § 3102**
Garnishment, writ, issuance, limitation, applicability, **28 § 3104**
Grounds for obtaining, hindering, delaying, or defrauding U.S. debt recovery efforts, **28 § 3101**
Hearings,
Availability to debtor against whom remedy is sought, notice from U.S. counsel, **28 § 3101**
Income sequestration, excessive or unreasonable amount, determination, **28 § 3105**
Hindering, delaying, or defrauding U.S. debt recovery efforts, grounds for obtaining, **28 § 3101**
Issuance of writs,
Attachment, contents, **28 § 3102**
Court determination, **28 § 3101**
Garnishment, limitation, **28 § 3104**
Sequestration, contents, **28 § 3105**
Judgment for U.S.,
Attached property, disposition of, **28 § 3102**
Sequestered income, disposition of, **28 § 3105**
Levy of attachment, U.S. marshal, authority, duties, writ, **28 § 3102**
Lien on property, levy of attachment as, satisfaction, ranking, **28 § 3102**
Limitation, garnishment, **28 § 3104**
Modification, powers, receivers, **28 § 3103**
Notice,
Form and content, issuance to debtor against whom remedy is sought, **28 § 3101**
Income sequestration, reduction or dissolution, motion, **28 § 3105**
Levy of attachment, U.S. marshal to file, **28 § 3102**
Motion, attachment, reduction or dissolution, **28 § 3102**
Sequestration, U.S. marshal to file, **28 § 3105**
Personal property replevied, judgment for U.S., disposition, **28 § 3102**
Powers, receivers, **28 § 3103**
Preservation,
Personal property under attachment, **28 § 3102**
Sequestered income, **28 § 3105**
Priorities, receivers, control of property, **28 § 3103**
Property,
Attachment, availability, **28 § 3102**
Sequestration, **28 § 3105**

FEDERAL DEBT COLLECTION
—Cont'd
Prejudgment remedies—Cont'd
Receiver, appointment, powers, duration, compensation, **28 § 3103**
Receivership, **28 § 3103**
Reduction,
Attachment, **28 § 3102**
Income sequestration, motion, notice, **28 § 3105**
Removal, receiver, **28 § 3103**
Replevin, attached property, debtor, bond, **28 § 3102**
Reports, receivers, requirement, accounts, receipts and expenditures, **28 § 3103**
Restoration,
Attached property, vacated writ, **28 § 3102**
Sequestered income, vacated sequestration order, **28 § 3105**
Return, writs of,
Attachment, duties, of U.S. marshal, **28 § 3102**
Sequestration, U.S. marshal, execution, duties, **28 § 3105**
Sequestration, property subject to, availability, issuance of writ, contents, **28 § 3105**
Termination, receivership, final accounting, receipts and expenditures, **28 § 3103**
United States marshals,
Attachment, execution of writ, return, duties, **28 § 3102**
Writ of sequestration, execution, return, additional duties, **28 § 3105**
Presumption, sale price, perishable personal property, U.S. liability, **28 § 3007**
Property,
Co-owned, remedies available to U.S., limitation, **28 § 3010**
Defined, general provisions, **28 § 3002**
Exempt, election by debtor, **28 § 3014**
Postjudgment remedies, ante
Prejudgment remedies, ante
Seized, authority of U.S. marshal to designate keeper, **28 § 3009**
Qualified retirement arrangement, defined, co-owned property, general provisions, **28 § 3010**
Remedies,
Fraudulent transfers involving debts, generally, ante
Postjudgment remedies, generally, ante
Prejudgment remedies, generally, ante
Requirements, affidavits, general provisions, **28 § 3006**
Retirement system for Federal military or civilian personnel, defined, co-owned property, general provisions, **28 § 3010**
Rules of construction, general provisions, **28 § 3003**

FEDERAL DEBT COLLECTION
—Cont'd
Sales, perishable personal property, authority, deposit of proceeds, presumption, **28 § 3007**
Security agreement, defined, general provisions, **28 § 3002**
Seized property, authority of U.S. marshal to designate keeper, **28 § 3009**
Service of process, enforcement, notice, manner, **28 § 3004**
State, defined, general provisions, **28 § 3002**
Stay of disposition, exempt property, pending determination, applicability of claim, **28 § 3014**
Surcharge, assessment on debt, authorization, limitation, **28 § 3011**
Transfers. Fraudulent transfers involving debts, generally, ante
United States,
Defined, general provisions, **28 § 3002**
Rights of, effect of provisions on, rules of construction, **28 § 3003**
United States magistrates, proceedings before, **28 § 3008**
United States marshal,
Defined, general provisions, **28 § 3002**
Postjudgment remedies, ante
Prejudgment remedies, ante
Seized property, authority to designate keeper, **28 § 3009**
Writs,
Postjudgment remedies, ante
Prejudgment remedies, generally, ante

FEDERAL EMPLOYEES
Officers and Employees of Government, generally, this index

FEDERAL EMPLOYEES' GROUP LIFE INSURANCE
Life Insurance, this index

FEDERAL EMPLOYERS' LIABILITY ACT
Nonremovable action, **28 § 1445**
Removal of cause, **28 § 1445**

FEDERAL GOVERNMENT
United States, generally, this index

FEDERAL INTERMEDIATE CREDIT BANKS
Tort Claims Act, exception of claim arising from activities of Bank, **28 § 2680**

FEDERAL LAND BANKS
Tort Claims Act, exception of claim arising from activities of bank, **28 § 2680**

FEDERAL LANDS
Public Lands, generally, this index

FEDERAL LEGAL COUNCIL
Generally, **28 § 509 nt, EON 12146**

FEDERAL MAGISTRATES ACT
Generally, **28 § 631 et seq.**

FEDERAL MARITIME COMMISSION
Jurisdiction,
Court of appeals, review of rules, regulations, or final orders, **28 § 2342**
Orders, review, **28 § 2341 et seq.**
Review,
Orders, **28 § 2341 et seq.**

FEDERAL OFFICERS AND EMPLOYEES
Officers and Employees of Government, generally, this index

FEDERAL OLD–AGE, SURVIVORS AND DISABILITY INSURANCE BENEFITS
Social Security, this index

FEDERAL PRISON INDUSTRIES
Attorney General,
Exception, certain functions, **28 § 509**
Directors,
Attorney General, exception, certain functions, **28 § 509**

FEDERAL PRISONS
Correctional Institutions, generally, this index

FEDERAL QUESTION JURISDICTIONAL AMENDMENTS ACT OF 1980
Generally, **28 §§ 1 nt, 1331**

FEDERAL REGISTER
Administrative Office of United States Courts, Director, rules and regulations, standards for conduct, **28 § 604**
Indians,
Indian Claims Limitation Act of 1982, list of claims accruing under, **28 § 2415 nt**
Patents, generally, this index
President of the United States, generally, this index
Trademarks and Trade Names, generally, this index
United States Court of Federal Claims, generally, this index

FEDERAL REPUBLIC OF GERMANY
Germany, generally, this index

FEDERAL TRADE COMMISSION
Chairman,
Federal Legal Council, representatives designated by, **28 § 509 nt, EON 12146**
Telecommunications, generally, this index

FELONIES
Crimes and Offenses, generally, this index

FELONIES—Cont'd
United States marshals,
Fees for services in criminal cases, conviction for, **28 § 1921**

FEMALES
Husband and Wife, generally, this index
Women, generally, this index

FERRIES
Jurors, payment of toll, **28 § 1871**

FIDELITY BONDS
Bonds, generally, this index

FIDUCIARIES
Annuities payable to minors or mentally incompetent dependents of justices or judges, payment to, **28 § 376**
Executors and Administrators, generally, this index
Guardian and Ward, generally, this index
Justice, judge or Magistrate Judge, financial interest in subject matter in controversy, disqualification, **28 § 455**
Receivers and Receivership, generally, this index
Trusts. Estates and Trusts, generally, this index

FIFTH CIRCUIT COURT OF APPEALS REORGANIZATION ACT OF 1980
Generally, **28 §§ 1 nt, 41, 44, 48**
Court of Appeals for Fifth Circuit, generally, this index

FINANCE
Money and Finance, generally, this index

FINANCIAL ASSISTANCE
See, also,
Federal Aid, generally, this index
Grants, generally, this index
Loans, generally, this index
Banks for Cooperatives, generally, this index
Federal Intermediate Credit Banks, generally, this index
Federal Land Banks, generally, this index

FINANCIAL DISCLOSURE
Federal personnel,
Actions and proceedings, civil action, obtaining or using report for unlawful or commercial purpose, **5, Ap 4, § 105**
Administrative law judges, persons required to file, **5, Ap 4, § 101**
Advisory opinions by supervising ethics office, **5, Ap 4, § 106**
Agency,
Custody of and public access to reports, **5, Ap 4, § 105**
Permitting inspection or furnishing copy of reports, **5, Ap 4, § 105**
Agency head,
Noncompliance, steps for assuring compliance, **5, Ap 4, § 106**

FINANCIAL DISCLOSURE—Cont'd
Federal personnel—Cont'd
Agency head—Cont'd
Reference to Attorney General, failure to file or filing false reports, personnel action, **5, Ap 4, § 104**
Attorney General,
Civil action, trust provisions violation, **5, Ap 4, § 102**
Failure to file or filing false reports, civil action, **5, Ap 4, § 104**
Obtaining or using reports for unlawful or commercial purpose, civil action, **5, Ap 4, § 105**
Broker, defined, qualified blind trust, **5, Ap 4, § 102**
Candidate, office of President, Vice President, or Member of Congress, persons required to file, **5, Ap 4, § 101**
Central Intelligence Agency, access to reports, exception, **5, Ap 4, § 105**
Clerk of House of Representatives,
Custody of and public access to reports, **5, Ap 4, § 105**
Permitting inspection or furnishing of copy of report, **5, Ap 4, § 105**
Committee on Standards of Official Conduct of House of Representatives,
Administration of provisions with regard to Congress, **5, Ap 4, § 111**
Congressional ethics committees, defined, **5, Ap 4, § 109**
Reports sent to, **5, Ap 4, § 103**
Supervising ethics office, defined, **5, Ap 4, § 109**
Comptroller General, access to financial disclosure reports, study, **5, Ap 4, § 108**
Confidential financial disclosure reports, filing, **5, Ap 4, § 107**
Congress,
Member of,
Candidate for office of, reports to Federal Elections Commission, **5, Ap 4, § 103**
Reports filed with Congressional Ethics Committee, **5, Ap 4, § 103**
Nominees for offices requiring confirmation by, report to Director of Office of Government Ethics, **5, Ap 4, § 103**
Officer or employee of,
Congressional Ethics Committee, reports filed with, **5, Ap 4, § 103**
Persons required to file, **5, Ap 4, § 101**
Congressional committees,
Considering nomination, notice, nominee's compliance with trust requirements, **5, Ap 4, § 102**
Disclosure requirements, limitation on powers of, **5, Ap 4, § 101**

FINANCIAL DISCLOSURE—Cont'd
Federal personnel—Cont'd
Congressional Ethics Committee,
Defined, general provisions, **5, Ap 4, § 109**
Exemption from filing, short term of employment, determination, **5, Ap 4, § 101**
Individual not in compliance, actions taken, **5, Ap 4, § 106**
Notice of actions taken to comply with ethics agreements, **5, Ap 4, § 110**
Reference to Attorney General, failure to file or filing false reports, personnel action, **5, Ap 4, § 104**
Reports filed with, **5, Ap 4, § 103**
Review of reports, **5, Ap 4, § 106**
Defense Intelligence Agency, access to reports, exception, **5, Ap 4, § 105**
Definitions, **5, Ap 4, § 109**
Dependent child,
Contents of report, **5, Ap 4, § 102**
Defined, general provisions, **5, Ap 4, § 109**
Inclusion of assets reported, requirement, **5, Ap 4, § 102**
Designated agency ethics individual, reports filed with, **5, Ap 4, § 103**
Designated agency ethics official,
Administration of provisions with regard to executive branch, **5, Ap 4, § 111**
Defined, general provisions, **5, Ap 4, § 109**
Exemption from filing, short term of employment, determination, **5, Ap 4, § 101**
Filing report with Director of Office of Government Ethics, **5, Ap 4, § 103**
Individual not in compliance, actions taken, **5, Ap 4, § 106**
Notice of actions taken to comply with ethics agreements, **5, Ap 4, § 110**
Persons required to file, **5, Ap 4, § 101**
Review of reports, **5, Ap 4, § 106**
Domestic Policy Staff of President, reports to Director of Office of Government Ethics, **5, Ap 4, § 103**
Executive branch,
Defined, general provisions, **5, Ap 4, § 109**
Officers or employees, persons required to file, **5, Ap 4, § 101**
Executive Office of President, persons required to file, **5, Ap 4, § 101**
Financial disclosure form,
Alternative format, powers of supervising ethics office, **5, Ap 4, § 102**
Office of Government Ethics, powers, **5, Ap 4, § 103**

FINANCIAL DISCLOSURE—Cont'd
Federal personnel—Cont'd
Fines, penalties and forfeitures,
Civil penalty, failure to file or filing false reports, **5, Ap 4, § 104**
Reports, obtaining or using for unlawful or commercial purpose, **5, Ap 4, § 105**
Gifts,
Contents of reports, identity and source, description, **5, Ap 4, § 102**
Defined, general provisions, **5, Ap 4, § 109**
Foreign gifts and decorations, applicability of provisions, **5, Ap 4, § 107**
Honoraria,
Contents of reports, identity and source, description, **5, Ap 4, § 102**
Defined, general provisions, **5, Ap 4, § 109**
House of Representatives, enactment of provisions regulating legislative branch, exercise of rulemaking power, **5, Ap 4, § 101 nt**
Income,
Contents of reports, **5, Ap 4, § 102**
Defined, general provisions, **5, Ap 4, § 109**
Independent counsel or appointee,
Access to reports, exception, **5, Ap 4, § 105**
Reports, filing with Director of Office of Government Ethics, **5, Ap 4, § 103**
Intelligence activities, individuals engaged in, access to reports, exception, **5, Ap 4, § 105**
Interested party, defined, qualified blind trust, **5, Ap 4, § 102**
Investment adviser, defined, qualified blind trust, **5, Ap 4, § 102**
Investment fund, holdings, exemption from reporting requirement, **5, Ap 4, § 102**
Judicial Conference,
Administration of provisions with regard to judiciary, **5, Ap 4, § 111**
Defined, general provisions, **5, Ap 4, § 109**
Exemption from filing, short term of employment, determination, **5, Ap 4, § 101**
Individual not in compliance, actions taken, **5, Ap 4, § 106**
Notice of actions taken to comply with ethics agreements, **5, Ap 4, § 110**
Reference to Attorney General, failure to file or filing false report, personnel action, **5, Ap 4, § 104**
Reports filed with, **5, Ap 4, § 103**
Review of reports, **5, Ap 4, § 106**

FINANCIAL DISCLOSURE—Cont'd
Federal personnel—Cont'd
Judicial Conference—Cont'd
Supervising ethics office, defined, **5, Ap 4, § 109**
Judicial employee,
Defined, general provisions, **5, Ap 4, § 109**
Persons required to file, **5, Ap 4, § 101**
Judicial officer,
Defined, general provisions, **5, Ap 4, § 109**
Persons required to file, **5, Ap 4, § 101**
Legislative branch,
Defined, general provisions, **5, Ap 4, § 109**
Provisions applicable to Members, rulemaking power, **5, Ap 4, § 101 nt**
Liabilities, contents of reports, **5, Ap 4, § 102**
Member of Congress,
Candidate for office of, persons required to file, **5, Ap 4, § 101**
Defined, general provisions, **5, Ap 4, § 109**
Persons required to file, **5, Ap 4, § 101**
National Imagery and Mapping Agency, acts to reports, exception, **5, Ap 4, § 105**
National Security Agency, access to reports, exception, **5, Ap 4, § 105**
Office of Administration of President, reports to Director of Office of Government Ethics, **5, Ap 4, § 103**
Office of Government Ethics,
Director,
Administration of provisions with regard to executive branch, **5, Ap 4, § 111**
Executive branch officers or employees, determination, persons required to file, **5, Ap 4, § 101**
Exemption from filing, short term of employment, determination, **5, Ap 4, § 101**
Noncompliance, actions taken, **5, Ap 4, § 106**
Persons required to file, **5, Ap 4, § 101**
Postal Service, recommendations of actions to assure compliance, **5, Ap 4, § 106**
Reference to Attorney General, failure to file or filing false reports, **5, Ap 4, § 104**
Reports,
Filing with, **5, Ap 4, § 103**
Review, **5, Ap 4, § 106**
To Director, **5, Ap 4, § 103**

FINANCIAL DISCLOSURE—Cont'd
Federal personnel—Cont'd
Office of Government Ethics—Cont'd
Notice, actions taken to comply with ethics agreements, **5, Ap 4, § 110**
Supervising ethics office, defined, **5, Ap 4, § 109**
Officer or employee of the Congress, defined, general provisions, **5, Ap 4, § 109**
Personal hospitality of any individual, defined, general provisions, **5, Ap 4, § 109**
Positions, officer, director, contents of reports, **5, Ap 4, § 102**
Postal Rate Commission, persons required to file, **5, Ap 4, § 101**
Postal Service,
Persons required to file, **5, Ap 4, § 101**
Reports filed with Director, Office of Government Ethics, **5, Ap 4, § 103**
Postmaster General and Deputy Postmaster General,
Noncompliance, steps to assure compliance, **5, Ap 4, § 106**
Persons required to file, **5, Ap 4, § 101**
Reports, filing with Director of Office of Government Ethics, **5, Ap 4, § 103**
President,
Candidate for office of,
Persons required to file, **5, Ap 4, § 101**
Reports,
To Director of Office of Government Ethics, **5, Ap 4, § 103**
To Federal Elections Commission, **5, Ap 4, § 103**
Employees of, reports to Director of Office of Government Ethics, **5, Ap 4, § 103**
Noncompliance by appointees, reference to, **5, Ap 4, § 106**
Persons required to file, **5, Ap 4, § 101**
Reports, filing with Director of Office of Government Ethics, **5, Ap 4, § 103**
Qualified blind trust,
Defined, contents of report, **5, Ap 4, § 102**
Disclosure of interest provisions, **5, Ap 4, § 102**
Recusal agreement, contents, filing, **5, Ap 4, § 110**
Reimbursement,
Contents of reports, **5, Ap 4, § 102**
Defined, general provisions, **5, Ap 4, § 109**
Relative, defined, general provisions, **5, Ap 4, § 109**

FINANCIAL DISCLOSURE—Cont'd
Federal personnel—Cont'd
Reports,
Comptroller General, access to, **5, Ap 4, § 108**
Confidential financial disclosure reports, filing, by special Government employees, **5, Ap 4, § 107**
Contents, **5, Ap 4, § 102**
Custody of and public access to, **5, Ap 4, § 105**
Filing, **5, Ap 4, § 103**
Extensions of time, **5, Ap 4, § 101**
Failure to file or falsification, **5, Ap 4, § 104**
Fee, late filing, **5, Ap 4, § 104**
Persons required to file, **5, Ap 4, § 101**
Time, **5, Ap 4, § 103**
Inspection or furnishing copy of, **5, Ap 4, § 105**
Review of, **5, Ap 4, § 106**
Savings provisions, **5, Ap 4, § 105 nt**
Transmittal by Select Committee on Ethics of the Senate to head of employing office, **5, Ap 4, § 111 nt**
Rulemaking power of Congress, **5, Ap 4, § 101 nt**
Savings provisions, **5, Ap 4, § 105 nt**
Secretary concerned,
Administration of provisions with regard to executive branch, **5, Ap 4, § 111**
Defined, general provisions, **5, Ap 4, § 109**
Exemption from filing, short term of employment, determination, **5, Ap 4, § 101**
Individual not in compliance, actions taken, **5, Ap 4, § 106**
Members of uniformed services, reports filed with Secretary, **5, Ap 4, § 103**
Reference to Attorney General, failure to file or filing false reports, personnel action, **5, Ap 4, § 104**
Review of reports, **5, Ap 4, § 106**
Secretary of Senate,
Custody of and public access to reports, **5, Ap 4, § 105**
Permitting inspection or furnishing copy of report, **5, Ap 4, § 105**
Select Committee on Ethics of the Senate,
Administration of provisions with regard to Congress, **5, Ap 4, § 111**
Congressional ethics committees, defined, **5, Ap 4, § 109**
Head of employing office, transmittal of financial disclosure reports to, **5, Ap 4, § 111 nt**
Reports sent to, **5, Ap 4, § 103**

FINANCIAL DISCLOSURE—Cont'd
Federal personnel—Cont'd
Senate,
Enactment of provisions regulating legislative branch, exercise of rulemaking power, **5, Ap 4, § 101**
Head of employing office, defined, transmittal of financial disclosure reports to, **5, Ap 4, § 111 nt**
Nominees for offices requiring confirmation by, report to Director of Office of Government Ethics, **5, Ap 4, § 103**
Senate Confirmation Committee,
Notice of actions taken to comply with ethics agreements, **5, Ap 4, § 110**
Persons appointed to positions requiring advice and consent of, filing requirement, **5, Ap 4, § 101**
Supervising ethics committee, defined, **5, Ap 4, § 109**
Special Government employees,
Confidential financial disclosure reports, filing, **5, Ap 4, § 107**
Persons required to file, **5, Ap 4, § 101**
Spouse of reporting individual,
Contents of report, **5, Ap 4, § 102**
Inclusion of assets required, **5, Ap 4, § 102**
Supervising ethics office,
Advisory opinions, **5, Ap 4, § 106**
Alternative format for financial disclosure form, powers, **5, Ap 4, § 102**
Confidential financial disclosure reports, requirement for certain officers and employees, **5, Ap 4, § 107**
Custody of and public access to reports, **5, Ap 4, § 105**
Defined, general provisions, **5, Ap 4, § 109**
Extensions of time for filing, procedures for granting, **5, Ap 4, § 101**
Individual not in compliance, steps for assuring compliance, rules and regulations, **5, Ap 4, § 106**
Permitting inspection or furnishing copy of report, **5, Ap 4, § 105**
Qualified blind trust, approval, **5, Ap 4, § 102**
Trust instrument and list of assets filed with, **5, Ap 4, § 102**
Waiver of reporting requirements, part-time employee, **5, Ap 4, § 101**
Transportation, entertainment, contents of reports, **5, Ap 4, § 102**
Trusts, of reporting individual, contents of report, **5, Ap 4, § 102**

FINANCIAL DISCLOSURE—Cont'd
Federal personnel—Cont'd
Uniformed services,
Persons required to file report, **5, Ap 4, § 101**
Reports filed with Secretary concerned, **5, Ap 4, § 103**
Unlawful or commercial purpose, obtaining or use of report for, penalty, **5, Ap 4, § 105**
Value, defined, general provisions, **5, Ap 4, § 109**
Vice President,
Candidates for office of,
Persons required to file, **5, Ap 4, § 101**
Reports,
To Director of Office of Government Ethics, **5, Ap 4, § 103**
To Federal Elections Commission, **5, Ap 4, § 103**
Employees of, reports to Director of Office of Government Ethics, **5, Ap 4, § 103**
Persons required to file, **5, Ap 4, § 101**
Reports, filing with Director of Office of Government Ethics, **5, Ap 4, § 103**

FINANCIAL INSTITUTIONS
Bank Fraud Crimes, generally, this index
Banks for Cooperatives, generally, this index
Federal Intermediate Credit Banks, generally, this index
Federal Land Banks, generally, this index
Securities and Exchange Commission, generally, this index
Sentence and punishment, guidelines, promulgation or amendment of, certain offenses jeopardizing safety, of federally insured institution, **28 § 994 nt**

FINANCIAL INTEREST
Defined, justice, judge or Magistrate Judge, disqualification, **28 § 455**
Justice, judge or Magistrate Judge, subject matter in controversy, disqualification, **28 § 455**

FINES, PENALTIES AND FORFEITURES
See, also, Crimes and Offenses, generally, this index
Attorney General, this index
Bond,
Respondent or claimant of property, admiralty cases, **28 § 2464**
Certificate of reasonable cause for seizure, liability for wrongful seizure, **28 § 2465**
Civil and criminal forfeiture,
Jurisdiction, **28 § 1355**

FINES, PENALTIES AND FORFEITURES—Cont'd
Civil and criminal forfeiture—Cont'd
Order of criminal forfeiture,
Sentence,
Guidelines, **28 § 994**
Civil penalty,
Federal agencies,
Agency, defined, **28 § 2461 nt**
Civil monetary penalty, defined, **28 § 2461 nt**
Consumer Price Index, defined, **28 § 2461 nt**
Cost-of-living adjustment, defined, **28 § 2461 nt**
Inflation adjustment, Congressional findings and purpose, **28 § 2461 nt**
Contempt, this index
Customs Duties, this index
Discharge,
Employee because of jury service, civil penalty, **28 § 1875**
District Courts, this index
Drug Abuse Prevention, Control and Treatment, this index
Escape,
Custody, civil commitment, **28 § 1826**
Forgery, this index
Fraudulent claims against U.S., **28 § 2514**
Grand Jury, this index
Home health care and services, criminal background checks, labor and employment, **28 § 534 nt**
Insurrection and Sedition, this index
Interested persons, examination as witness, **28 § 1822**
Internal Revenue Service, this index
Jury, this index
Limitation of Actions, this index
Limitations,
Outside income and employment, certain Government employees, **5, Ap 4, § 504**
Mode of recovery, **28 § 2461**
Modification, remission, of fine,
Sentencing guidelines, **28 § 994**
Moneys paid into court, criminal appearance bail bond, use to pay, **28 § 2044**
Narcotic Drug Addicts, this index
Nursing homes, criminal background checks, labor and employment, **28 § 534 nt**
Release, generally, this index
Return of property to claimant, liability for wrongful seizure, **28 § 2465**
Revenue law, property taken or detained under as not repleviable, **28 § 2463**
Rules of Civil Procedure, this index
Sentence and Punishment, generally, this index
Sexual Abuse, generally, this index
Special bond, respondent or claimant, admiralty cases, **28 § 2464**

FINES, PENALTIES AND FORFEITURES—Cont'd
Stay,
Execution of process in admiralty, **28 § 2464**
Telecommunications, this index
Time,
Commencement of proceedings to enforce, **28 § 2462**
Tort claims against U.S., excessive attorney's fees, **28 § 2678**
United States Court of International Trade, this index
Venue of action, **28 § 1395**
Vessels, this index

FINGERPRINTS AND FINGERPRINTING
Bureau of Investigation, generally, this index
Criminal Background Checks, generally, this index

FINLAND
Convention on the Taking of Evidence Abroad in Civil or Commercial Matters, party to, **28 § 1781 nt**

FIRE
Fires and Fire Protection, generally, this index

FIREARMS
Sentence and punishment,
Amendment of sentencing guidelines for certain crimes involving use of, **28 § 994 nt**
Semiautomatic firearm, defined, amendment of sentencing guidelines for crimes involving use of, Commission, **28 § 994 nt**
Use by violent felons and serious drug offenders, amendment of guidelines by Sentencing Commission, **28 § 994 nt**
Use in commission of counterfeiting or forgery crimes, amendment of guidelines by Sentencing Commission, **28 § 994 nt**

FIREFIGHTERS AND FIREFIGHTING
Jury service, exemption, **28 § 1863**

FIRES AND FIRE PROTECTION
Public lands,
Action by U.S. for damages, limitations, **28 §§ 2415, 2416**

FISH AND WILDLIFE SERVICE
United States Magistrate Judges, appointment and qualification in bi-State area under administration of, **28 § 631**

FIVE CIVILIZED TRIBES
Judgment in favor of claimant to allotment, exception, **28 § 1353**

FLORIDA
See, also, States, generally, this index
Bankruptcy judges, appointment, number in judicial district, 28 § 152
District court,
Cities, held at, 28 § 89
Judges,
Additional, 28 § 133 nt
Appointment, additional judges, advice and consent, 28 § 133 nt
Designation of, 28 § 89 nt
Number, 28 § 133
Juries, composition, service of, 28 § 89 nt
Places of holding, 28 § 89
Judicial circuit of U.S., 28 § 41
Number of district judges, 28 § 133
Judicial districts,
Bankruptcy provisions, applicability of certain amendments to, 28 § 581 nt
Number of district judges, 28 § 133
States, generally, this index
United States,
Attorneys, tenure and appointment, 28 § 89 nt
Marshals, tenure and appointment, 28 § 89 nt
Trustees of judicial districts, appointment, 28 § 581

FORCES
Armed Forces, generally, this index

FORECLOSURE
Tax liens, 28 § 2410
United States, this index

FOREIGN CONVENTIONS
Conventions, generally, this index

FOREIGN COUNTRIES
Actions against,
District court jurisdiction, 28 § 1330
Jurisdiction, 28 § 1330
Jurisdictional immunities of foreign states, generally, post
Removal of action, 28 § 1441
Venue, 28 § 1391
Aliens, generally, this index
Assistance,
Foreign tribunals and to litigants before such tribunals, 28 § 1782
Conventions, generally, this index
Denmark, generally, this index
District court, jurisdiction,
Actions against, 28 § 1330
Diversity of citizenship, 28 § 1332
Documents. Foreign Documents, generally, this index
Embassies. Foreign Diplomatic and Consular Officers, generally, this index
Foreign Missions, generally, this index
Foreign Service, generally, this index

FOREIGN COUNTRIES—Cont'd
Forfeiture, civil or criminal,
Federal equitable share of, deposit in Justice Department Assets Forfeiture Fund, 28 § 524
Habeas corpus, citizen in custody, condition for granting writ, 28 § 2241
International Trade, generally, this index
Judgments and decrees, payment of final judgment against U.S., exception, 28 § 2414
Jurisdictional immunities of foreign states,
Agency or instrumentality of a foreign state, defined, 28 § 1603
Attachment, 28 § 1609
Exceptions, 28 § 1610
Types of property immune under any conditions, 28 § 1611
Vessels, foreclosure of preferred mortgages, subject to jurisdiction, 28 § 1610
Waiver, 28 § 1610 nt
Attorney General, discovery limitations, general exceptions, 28 § 1605
Commercial activity, defined, 28 § 1603
Commercial activity carried on in the U.S. by a foreign state,
Defined, 28 § 1603
Exception under certain conditions, 28 § 1605
Counterclaims, 28 § 1607
Cuban liberty and democratic solidarity, certain property immune from attachment and execution, 28 § 1611
Death, exception under certain conditions, 28 § 1605
Declaration of purpose, 28 § 1602
Default, 28 § 1608
Definitions, 28 § 1603
Discovery, limitation, general exceptions, 28 § 1605
District court jurisdiction, 28 § 1330
Enforcement of maritime lien, admiralty suit, exception, inclusions, 28 § 1605
Execution of property, 28 § 1609
Exceptions, vessels, foreclosure of preferred mortgages, subject to jurisdiction, 28 § 1610
Types of property immune under any conditions, 28 § 1611
Waiver, 28 § 1610 nt
Extent of liability, 28 § 1606
Findings, 28 § 1602
Foreign state, defined, 28 § 1603
General exceptions, 28 § 1605
General provisions, 28 § 1604
International agreements, immunity subject to, 28 § 1604
Liability, extent of, 28 § 1606
Notice of suit, defined, 28 § 1608

FOREIGN COUNTRIES—Cont'd
Jurisdictional immunities of foreign states—Cont'd
Personal injuries, exception under certain conditions, inclusions, 28 § 1605
Property damage, exception under certain conditions, inclusions, 28 § 1605
Punitive damages, liability for, 28 § 1606
Removal of actions against, 28 § 1441
Service of process, 28 § 1608
Severability of provisions, 28 § 1602 nt
Stays, discovery, general exceptions, 28 § 1605
Terrorist states, 28 § 1605
Time to answer, 28 § 1608
United States, defined, 28 § 1603
Venue of actions against, 28 § 1391
Waiver, 28 § 1605
Letters rogatory or request, transmittal to foreign tribunal, 28 § 1781
Missions. Foreign Missions, generally, this index
National Banks, generally, this index
Nationals of,
Aliens, generally, this index
Official records, authenticated copy, summary or excerpt of as evidence, 28 § 1741
Patents,
Foreign Patents, generally, this index
Patents, generally, this index
Persons in, subpoena of, contempt, 28 § 1784
Protection of,
Trade secrets, generally, this index
Rules of Civil Procedure, this index
Service,
Document issued in connection with proceeding in foreign and international litigation, 28 § 1696
Service Abroad of Judicial and Extrajudicial Documents in Civil or Commercial Matter Convention, FRCVP 4 nt
Subpoena of national or resident of U.S. in foreign country, 28 §§ 1783, 1784
Supreme Court, jurisdiction of actions involving ambassadors, ministers, 28 § 1251
Terrorists and Terrorism, generally, this index
Tort Claims Act, exception of claim arising in foreign countries, 28 § 2680
Northern Mariana Islands not considered foreign country, 28 § 2680 nt
Trade Secrets, generally, this index
Transfer of Offenders to or from Foreign Countries, generally, this index
Treaties, generally, this index
Tribunals, service of document issued in connection with proceeding in, 28 § 1696

FOREIGN COUNTRIES—Cont'd
United States Court of Federal Claims, generally, this index
United States Court of International Trade, this index
Voluntarily giving testimony or producing documents in proceeding in foreign tribunal, **28 § 1782**
Waiver, jurisdictional immunities of foreign states, **28 § 1605**

FOREIGN COURTS OR TRIBUNALS
Civil justice reform, applicability, **28 § 519 nt, EON 12988**
Judgments against U.S., payment, **28 § 2414**

FOREIGN DIPLOMATIC AND CONSULAR OFFICERS
Convention on the Taking of Evidence Abroad in Civil or Commercial Matters, powers, under, **28 § 1781 nt**
District court's jurisdiction of action against, **28 § 1351**
Missions. Foreign Missions, generally, this index
Supreme Court, jurisdiction of action by or against, **28 § 1251**

FOREIGN DOCUMENTS
Authenticated copy, summary or excerpt as evidence of official document, **28 § 1741**
Books and papers, Legalization for Foreign Public Documents Convention, **FRCVP 44 nt**
Evidence,
Authenticated copy, summary or excerpt, **28 § 1741**
Official records or documents, authenticated copy, summary or excerpt as evidence, **28 § 1741**
Service in foreign and international litigation, **28 § 1696**

FOREIGN MISSIONS
Diplomatic relations,
Diplomatic immunity, applicability of defense to direct actions against insurers, **28 § 1364**
Direct action against insurers of members of diplomatic missions and their families, **28 § 1364**
District courts, jurisdiction, direct actions against insurers of members of foreign diplomatic missions and their families, **28 § 1364**
Family,
Direct actions against insurers of, **28 § 1364**
Members of a mission,
Direct actions against insurers of, **28 § 1364**
United Nations, direct actions against insurers of members of diplomatic missions and their families, **28 § 1364**

FOREIGN MISSIONS—Cont'd
Insurance, direct action against insurers, applicability of defense of diplomatic immunity, **28 § 1364**

FOREIGN PATENTS
Application for patent,
Copy as evidence, **28 § 1745**
Copies of specifications and drawings, as evidence, **28 § 1745**
Documents, copies of as evidence, **28 § 1745**
Official journals and publications, copies of excerpts of as evidence, **28 § 1745**
Specifications and drawings,
Evidence, **28 § 1745**

FOREIGN POLICY
Foreign Relations of U.S. historical series. State Department, generally, this index

FOREIGN SERVICE
Consular agents,
Convention on the Taking of Evidence Abroad in Civil or Commercial Matters, powers, under, **28 § 1781 nt**
Consular officers,
Documents and papers in office as evidence, **28 § 1740**
Vice Consuls, generally, post
Depositions,
United States Court of International Trade, admissibility in evidence where value of merchandise in issue in certain civil actions, **28 § 2639**
Diplomatic immunity, defendant exempt from legal process because of, actions by U.S., limitation period, exclusion, **28 § 2416**
Diplomatic missions,
Foreign Missions, generally, this index
United States missions,
Abroad, espionage investigations by FBI of persons employed by or assigned to, **28 § 533 nt**
Foreign Diplomatic and Consular Officers, generally, this index
Foreign Documents, generally, this index
Foreign Missions, generally, this index
Reports,
United States Court of International Trade, admissibility in evidence where value of merchandise in issue in certain civil actions, **28 § 2639**
United Nations, generally, this index
Vice consuls,
Documents and papers in office as evidence, **28 § 1740**

FOREIGN SOVEREIGN IMMUNITIES ACT OF 1976
Generally, **28 §§ 1 nt, 1330, 1332, 1391, 1441, 1602 et seq.**

FOREIGN SOVEREIGN IMMUNITIES ACT OF 1976—Cont'd
Foreign Countries, generally, this index

FOREIGN TRADE
International Trade, generally, this index

FOREIGNERS
Aliens, generally, this index

FORFEITURES
Fines, Penalties and Forfeitures, generally, this index

FORGERY
Fines, penalties and forfeitures,
Amendment of sentencing guidelines for crimes involving use of firearm during commission of, **28 § 994 nt**

FORMA PAUPERIS
Generally, **28 § 1915**
Affidavit, prisoner, statement of assets, required filing, **28 § 1915**
Appeals, **28 § 1915**
Fees, district courts, transcripts of reporter, **28 § 753**
Criminal proceedings, indigent defendants, district courts, fees, reporter's transcripts, **28 § 753**
Frivolous action, appeal prohibited, **28 § 1915**
Habeas corpus proceeding, **28 § 2250**
Appeal, district courts, fees, reporter's transcripts, **28 § 753**
Witness fees and mileage, payment, **28 § 1825**
Indigency, prisoners, may not prohibit bringing civil actions or criminal appeals, **28 § 1915**
Judgments,
Against prisoners, collection, **28 § 1915**
Proceedings, costs assessed against prisoners, collection, **28 § 1915**
Malicious pleadings, dismissal by court, **28 § 1915**
Persons who may institute proceedings, **28 § 1915**
Prepayment of fees or security, civil actions, certified copies of prison trust fund account statement, submission, requirement, **28 § 1915**
Prisoners, defined, fees, **28 § 1915**
Requirement, prisoners, payment of full filing fee, assessments, **28 § 1915**
Successive claims, prisoners, prohibition, conditions, **28 § 1915**
Supreme Court, proceedings in, payment, expenses, printing briefs and traveling of attorneys, **28 § 672**
Transcripts, fees of district court reporters, **28 § 753**
United States Court of Federal Claims, action for unjust conviction and imprisonment, **28 § 2513**

FORMS
See specific index headings

FORT WORTH, TX
Court of Appeals for Fifth Circuit, generally, this index

FORUM NON CONVENIENS
Venue or District of Trial, generally, this index

FOUNDATIONS
Federal Judicial Center, establishment, **28 § 629**

FRANCE
Conventions, taking of Evidence Abroad in Civil or Commercial Matters, party to, **28 § 1781 nt**

FRATERNAL ASSOCIATIONS AND SOCIETIES
Justice, judge, or Magistrate Judge, holding office in, disqualification, exclusions, **28 § 455**

FRAUD
Against U.S. United States, generally, post
Bank Fraud Crimes, generally, this index
Customs Duties, this index
Drawbacks, generally, this index
Federally insured financial institutions, Attorney General, investigation and prosecution, **28 § 509 nt**
Tort Claims Act, exception of claims, **28 § 2680**
United States, fraud against,
Forfeiture of claims against U.S., **28 § 2514**
United States Court of Federal Claims, this index
Visa, this index

FRAUDULENT CONVEYANCES
Attachment against, delinquent postmasters and postal employees, officers, on ground of, **28 § 2710**
Federal Debt Collection, generally, this index

FRAUDULENT REPRESENTATION OR STATEMENTS
Fraud, generally, this index

FREEDOM OF INFORMATION
Administrative Law and Procedure, generally, this index

FRIVOLOUS ACTIONS
Correctional institutions, inmates, **28 § 1915A**

FUGITIVES FROM JUSTICE
Extradition, generally, this index

FULL FAITH AND CREDIT
Child support orders, **28 § 1738B**

FULL FAITH AND CREDIT—Cont'd
Judicial proceedings and records of courts of states, territories or possessions, full faith and credit, **28 § 1738**
Orders for child support, authority, requirements, **28 § 1738B**
Parental Kidnapping Prevention Act, Congressional findings, **28 § 1738A nt**
Records and books of State, territory or possession as evidence, **28 §§ 1738, 1739**

FULL FAITH AND CREDIT FOR CHILD SUPPORT ORDERS ACT
Generally, **28 § 1738B**

FUNDS
Attending Physician Revolving Fund. House of Representatives, generally, this index
Counterterrorism Fund, establishment, provisions, **28 § 524 nt**
Crime victims fund. Victim Compensation and Assistance, generally, this index
Department of Justice Assets Forfeiture Fund, establishment, functions, **28 § 524**
Disbursing officer, jurisdiction of U.S. Court of Federal Claims, relief from responsibility, **28 § 1496**
Disclosure of Federal Campaign Funds, generally, this index
Judicial Survivors' Annuities Fund, **28 § 376**
Judiciary Automation Fund, fees deposited into, **28 § 1913 nt**
Judiciary Information Technology Fund, establishment, **28 § 612**
Solicitation, generally, this index

FUNDS AND DEPOSITS IN COURT
Deposits of other moneys by clerks into checking account in Treasury, **28 § 2043**
Designation by an assigned justice or judge of depositary of funds, exception, **28 § 296**
District courts, interpleader, requirements, **28 § 1335**
Fine, criminal proceedings,
Payment of with bond money, **28 § 2044**
Pending or adjudicated cases, deposit with Treasury of U.S. or designated depository, **28 § 2041**
Withdrawals, **28 § 2042**

GAMBLING
Amateur sports organization, defined, professional and amateur sports protection, **28 § 3701**
Dog races, professional and amateur sports protection, applicability, **28 § 3704**

GAMBLING—Cont'd
Governmental entity, defined, professional and amateur sports protection, **28 § 3701**
Horse Races, generally, this index
Jai-alai, professional and amateur sports protection, applicability, **28 § 3704**
Person, defined, professional and amateur sports protection, **28 § 3701**
Professional and amateur sports protection,
Applicability, **28 § 3704**
Definitions, **28 § 3701**
Unlawful sports gambling, **28 § 3702**
Violations, injunctions, **28 § 3703**
Professional sports organization, defined, professional and amateur sports protection, **28 § 3701**
State,
Defined,
Professional and amateur sports protection, **28 § 3701**

GARNISHMENT
Federal Debt Collection, generally, this index
Justices and judges, annuities to survivors, exemption from, **28 § 376**
United States,
Proceeding by, **28 § 2405**

GENERAL ACCOUNTING OFFICE
Certificate of mailing postmaster statement of his account, as evidence of demand, **28 § 1743**
Civil Rights, generally, this index
Credits,
In actions by U.S. on claim disallowed by GAO, **28 § 2406**
Disallowance of claim, credit in action by U.S., against delinquent for public money, **28 § 2407**
Disbursing officers, relief, from loss, U.S. Court of Federal Claims, allowances, **28 § 2512**
Fees of Federal officer, failure to act on account, time for filing suit in U.S. Court of Federal Claims, **28 § 2501**
Head of Office. Comptroller General, generally, this index
Reports,
United States Sentencing Commission, operation of sentencing guidelines system, problems, **28 § 994 nt**
Sentencing guidelines, study of, report to Congress, time limitation, **28 § 994 nt**
Transcripts,
Judgment, Court of Federal Claims, filing, factor in payment of interest on judgments against U.S. affirmed by Supreme Court, **28 § 2516**

GENERAL ELECTIONS
Elections, generally, this index

GENERAL SERVICES ADMINISTRATION
Administrators,
Administrative Office of U.S. Courts, Director, requests for provision or closing of court accommodations, **28 § 462**
High-cost area, subsistence allowance for witnesses attending in, **28 § 1821**
Independent Counsel, provision of office space, equipment, supplies, **28 § 594**
Subsistence allowance for witnesses, **28 § 1821**
United States Magistrate Judges, providing courtrooms, office space, for, **28 § 635**
Witnesses, computation of mileage, uniform table of distances, **28 § 1821**
Patents, generally, this index

GEORGIA
See, also, States, generally, this index
Bankruptcy judges, appointment, number in judicial district, **28 § 152**
District court,
Cities, held at, **28 § 90**
Judges,
Appointment, additional judges, advice and consent, **28 § 133 nt**
Number, **28 § 133**
Places of holding, **28 § 90**
Judicial Circuit of U.S., **28 § 41**
Judicial districts, **28 § 90**
Bankruptcy provisions, applicability of certain amendments to, **28 § 581 nt**
Number of district judges, **28 § 133**

GERMAN DEMOCRATIC REPUBLIC (EAST GERMANY)
Germany, generally, this index

GERMANY
Conventions, taking of Evidence Abroad in Civil or Commercial Matters, party to, **28 § 1781 nt**

GERMANY, FEDERAL REPUBLIC OF
Germany, generally, this index

GI
Armed Forces, generally, this index
Veterans, generally, this index

GIFT TAX
Federal Judicial Center Foundation, gifts to, considered gifts to U.S., **28 § 629**
Rules of practice and procedure and forms. United States Tax Court, generally, this index
United States Tax Court,
Rules of practice and procedure and forms. United States Tax Court, generally, this index

GIFTS
Charities, generally, this index
Disclosure of Federal Campaign Funds, generally, this index
Federal Judicial Center Foundation, provisions for, administration of, **28 § 629**
Gift Tax, generally, this index
Supreme Court, books, pamphlets, **28 § 674**
Taxation. Gift Tax, generally, this index

GOOD FAITH
Affidavit of bias or prejudice of district judge, certificate as to good faith in filing, **28 § 144**

GOVERNMENT AGENCIES OR INSTRUMENTALITIES
Federal Government. Federal Agencies and Instrumentalities, generally, this index

GOVERNMENT CORPORATIONS
Federal Corporations, generally, this index

GOVERNMENT EMPLOYEES
Officers and Employees of Government, generally, this index

GOVERNMENT ETHICS, OFFICE OF
Personnel Management, Office of, this index

GOVERNMENT LANDS
Public Lands, generally, this index

GOVERNMENT PRINTING OFFICE
Attorney General's opinions, printing, **28 § 521**
Federal Register, generally, this index
Public Printer, generally, this index
Public Printing and Documents, generally, this index

GOVERNMENT SECURITIES
United States Obligations, generally, this index

GOVERNOR
Certificate to records or books of State, territory or possession, evidence, **28 § 1739**
Notice,
Hearing by three-judge court, **28 § 2284**

GRAND JURY
Generally, **28 § 1861 et seq.**
Additional attendance fee, certification, time for payment, **28 § 1871**
Adverse effect upon deliberations, exclusion from service, **28 § 1866**
Affidavits, service of summons for jury service by registered or certified mail, **28 § 1866**
Age requirement for service, **28 § 1865**

GRAND JURY—Cont'd
Alphabetical list, names drawn from master jury wheel, **28 § 1864**
Entry, determination, qualifications for service, **28 § 1865**
Assignment,
Names to panels, **28 § 1866**
Persons drawn, **28 § 1863**
Attendance fees, time for payment, **28 § 1871**
Attorney General, conducting, authority, **28 § 515**
Attorneys,
Fees, award, protection of juror's employment, **28 § 1875**
Bailiffs, employment to wait upon, **28 § 755**
Books and papers,
Maintenance and inspection, **28 § 1868**
Nondisclosure, **28 § 1867**
Voter registration lists and records, generally, post
Certificate for payment of fees, travel and subsistence allowances, **28 § 1871**
Chief judge of district court,
Chief judge, as meaning, **28 § 1869**
Duties, **28 § 1863 et seq.**
Citizenship requirement for service, **28 § 1865**
Civil penalty, discharge of employee for jury service, **28 § 1875**
Clerks of district courts,
Clerk and clerk of the court, as meaning, **28 § 1869**
Duties, **28 § 1863 et seq.**
Commission. Jury Commission, generally, this index
Conditions, ineligibility for service, **28 § 1865**
Court, defined, **28 § 1869**
Court interpreters, use of electronic sound recordings, in addition to, **28 § 1827**
Criminal charge, pending or conviction, freedom from, requirement for service, **28 § 1865**
Declaration of policy, **28 § 1861**
Definitions, **28 § 1869**
Deputy clerks of district courts, summons for jury service, duties concerning, **28 § 1866**
Disclosure,
Names drawn,
Master jury wheel, **28 § 1864**
Time, **28 § 1863**
Discrimination,
Prohibited, **28 § 1862**
Selection of persons for service prohibited, remedies, **28 § 1867**
Dismissal,
Indictment or information,
Noncompliance with selection procedures, **28 § 1867**

GRAND JURY—Cont'd
Disqualification from service, 28 **§§ 1863, 1865, 1866**
Disruption of proceedings, exclusion from service, **28 § 1866**
District courts,
  Contiguous 48 States, jurors serving outside of, amount, subsistence allowance, **28 § 1871**
  Defined, **28 § 1869**
Division, defined, **28 § 1869**
Drawing, names from master jury wheel, **28 §§ 1864, 1866**
Effective date, plan for random selection, **28 § 1863**
Electronic sound recordings, where interpreters are used, **28 § 1827**
Evidence,
  Challenging compliance with selection procedures, **28 § 1867**
  Qualifications for service, **28 § 1865**
Examination, plan for random selection, **28 § 1863**
Exclusion, from service, **28 §§ 1863, 1865, 1866**
  Prohibition on account of race, color, religion, **28 § 1862**
Excuse or exemption from service, **28 §§ 1863, 1866**
  Determination, **28 § 1865**
Exemption from service, juror qualification form contents, **28 § 1869**
Federal employees, forfeiture, annuities and retired pay,
  Compensation for work injuries, applicability of provisions, **28 § 1877**
Fees, **28 § 1871**
  Attendance in excess of 45 days, additional payment in discretion of district judge, **28 § 1871**
  Qualification form, completion, **28 § 1864**
Ferries, payment of toll charges for, **28 § 1871**
Fines, penalties and forfeitures,
  Failure to appear pursuant to summons to complete qualification form, **28 § 1864**
  Noncompliance with summons for service, **28 § 1866**
  Willful misrepresentation of facts on qualification form, **28 § 1864**
First-class mail, service of summons for jury service, **28 § 1866**
Grounds for excuse or exemption from service, **28 § 1863**
Groups of persons or occupational classes excused or exempt from service, **28 § 1863**
Illinois, Central and Southern Districts, inquiry into and return of indictments, **28 § 93 nt**
Impartial service, inability to render, exclusion from service, **28 § 1866**
Imprisonment. Sentence and punishment, generally, post

GRAND JURY—Cont'd
Independent Counsel, generally, this index
Indictment or information,
  Dismissal, ante
Inspection of records and papers, **28 § 1868**
Interim travel allowances to jurors, rules regulating, promulgation by Director of Administrative Office of U.S. Courts, **28 § 1871**
Jurisdiction,
  District court, compelling availability of voter registration lists and records, **28 § 1863**
Juror qualification form,
  Completion, **28 § 1864**
  Contents, **28 § 1869**
  Defined, **28 § 1869**
  Entry, determination of qualifications, **28 § 1865**
  Information, determination of qualifications, **28 § 1865**
  Reasons for exclusion from service, notations on, **28 § 1866**
Jury summons, defined, **28 § 1869**
Jury wheel,
  Defined, **28 § 1869**
  Master jury wheel, generally, post
Limitation, number of persons excluded from service, **28 § 1866**
List,
  Names assigned to panels, **28 § 1866**
  Voter registration lists and records, generally, post
Lists of actual voters, defined, **28 § 1869**
Literacy requirement for service, **28 § 1865**
Mail,
  Qualification form, **28 § 1864**
  Service of summons for jury service, **28 § 1866**
Maintenance of records and papers, **28 § 1868**
Master jury wheel,
  Determination, proportional representation in, **28 § 1863**
  Drawing of names from, **28 § 1864**
  Nondisclosure, records or papers, until after emptying and refilling, **28 § 1867**
  Providing for and placing names in, **28 § 1863**
Meals and lodging,
  Refreshment of jurors, **28 § 1871 nt**
  Subsistence allowance, itemization not required, **28 § 1871**
Mental or physical capacity requirement for service, **28 § 1865**
Mileage, **28 § 1871**
Modification, plan for random selection, **28 § 1863**
Motions, challenging compliance with selection procedures, **28 § 1867**

GRAND JURY—Cont'd
Noncompliance of recalcitrant witness to court's order to provide information, **28 § 1826**
Nondisclosure, records or papers, selection process, **28 § 1867**
Notice, adoption or modification of plan for random selection, **28 § 1863**
Obligation for service on, declaration of policy, **28 § 1861**
Opportunity for service on, declaration of policy, **28 § 1861**
Order of district court,
  Appearance upon failure to appear after being summoned, **28 § 1866**
  Failure to appear pursuant to summons to complete qualification form, penalties, **28 § 1864**
  Noncompliance of recalcitrant witness in testifying or providing information, **28 § 1826**
Original jurisdiction of district courts, jurors' employment rights, **28 § 1363**
Overnight stay, subsistence allowance paid to juror, **28 § 1871**
Papers. Books and papers, generally, ante
Parking fees, payment to juror, presentation of valid parking receipt, **28 § 1871**
Penalties. Fines, penalties and forfeitures, generally, ante
Period of service, **28 § 1866**
Personal service, summons for jury service, **28 § 1866**
Preservation of records and papers, **28 § 1868**
Procedure for selection of names, **28 § 1863**
Prohibition, payment, fees for interim or daily travel exceeding subsistence allowance, **28 § 1871**
Protection,
  Compensation for work injuries, Federal employees, **28 § 1877**
  Employment, **28 § 1875**
  Federal employees' compensation for work injuries, applicability of provisions, **28 § 1877**
Public officer, defined, **28 § 1869**
Publicly draw, defined, **28 § 1869**
Punishment. Sentence and punishment, generally, post
Qualifications for service, **28 § 1865**
Qualified jury wheel, drawing names from, assignment to panels, **28 § 1866**
Random drawing of names from master jury wheel, **28 §§ 1864, 1866**
Random selection,
  Challenging compliance with procedures, **28 § 1867**
  Declaration of policy, **28 § 1861**
  Plan for, **28 § 1863**
Recalcitrant witnesses, **28 § 1826**

GRAND JURY—Cont'd
Registered or certified mail, service of summons for jury service, **28 § 1866**
Reinstatement, discharge by employer for employee's jury service, **28 § 1875**
Reports,
Selection process, **28 § 1863**
Residence requirement for service, **28 § 1865**
Restoration of civil rights, qualifications for service, **28 § 1865**
Return, qualification form, error, **28 § 1864**
Reviewing panel, plan for random selection, approval, **28 § 1863**
Secrecy of proceedings threatened, exclusion from service, **28 § 1866**
Selection, panels, **28 § 1866**
Challenging compliance with procedures, **28 § 1867**
Random selection, generally, ante
Sentence and punishment,
Disclosure, records or papers, violations, **28 § 1867**
Failure to appear pursuant to summons to complete qualification form, **28 § 1864**
Noncompliance with summons for service, **28 § 1866**
Willful misrepresentation of facts on qualification form, **28 § 1864**
Separation of jurors, orders, payment, actual cost of subsistence, **28 § 1871**
Sequestration of jurors, orders, payment, actual cost of subsistence, **28 § 1871**
Service of summons for jury service, **28 § 1866**
Sources of names for selection, specification in plan, **28 § 1863**
Stay of proceedings, noncompliance with selection procedures, **28 § 1867**
Subsistence allowance, meals and lodging, itemization not required, **28 § 1871**
Summons,
Failure to return completed qualification form, **28 § 1864**
Panels, **28 § 1866**
Time,
Challenging compliance with selection procedures, **28 § 1867**
Preservation, records and papers, **28 § 1868**
Tolls for roads, tunnels, and bridges, fees, **28 § 1871**
Transmittal of plan for random selection, time, **28 § 1863**
Traveling expenses,
Air travel, reimbursement, certain cases, **28 § 1871**
Jurors, minimum rate established by Director of Administrative Office of U.S. Courts, **28 § 1871**
Qualification form, completion, **28 § 1864**

GRAND JURY—Cont'd
Traveling expenses—Cont'd
Summons in area outside contiguous 48 States, **28 § 1871**
Undue hardship or extreme inconvenience, defined, **28 § 1869**
United States marshal, payment of fees, **28 § 1871**
Voter registration lists and records,
Availability for inspection, **28 § 1863**
Defined, **28 § 1869**
Random selection where shortage, **28 § 1866**
Witnesses,
Recalcitrant witness, **28 § 1826**

GRANTS
See, also, Federal Aid, generally, this index
Customs Duties, this index
Diversion of money under programs, action by U.S. for recovery, limitations, **28 §§ 2415, 2416**
Federal Aid, generally, this index

GRATUITIES
Gifts, generally, this index

GREAT BRITAIN
Conventions, Taking of Evidence Abroad in Civil or Commercial Matters, party to, **28 § 1781 nt**
Judicial District of Hawaii, inclusion of certain islands not to be prejudicial to claims of United Kingdom, **28 § 91**

GREAT SEAL
Seals (Official Seals), generally, this index

GSA
General Services Administration, generally, this index

GUAM
Bankruptcy court,
"Courts" as including, Administrative Office of U.S. Courts, **28 § 610**
Courts,
Defined, Jury Selection and Service Act, **28 § 1869**
District courts,
Appeals,
Courts of appeals, circuit to which appeal is taken, **28 § 1294**
From final decision in certain cases, jurisdiction of U.S. Court of Appeals for the Federal Circuit, **28 § 1295**
Circuits in which decision is reviewable, **28 § 1294**
"Courts" as including, administrative Office of U.S. Courts, **28 § 610**
Defined, Jury Selection and Service Act, **28 § 1869**
Evidence, **28 § 1731 et seq.**

GUAM—Cont'd
District courts—Cont'd
Interlocutory orders, relief, jurisdiction of courts of appeals, **28 § 1292**
Judges or justices,
Annuities to survivors, **28 § 376**
Relative ineligible to appointment, **28 § 458**
Salary on resignation, removal, **28 § 373**
Effect on amount payable to judge retired before enactment of provisions, **28 § 373 nt**
Senior judge of the court, qualifications, **28 § 373 nt**
Summoned to judicial conference of the circuit, **28 § 333**
Judicial Sales, generally, this index
Jurisdiction,
Court of appeals,
Appeal from, **28 § 1291**
Interlocutory orders of district court, **28 § 1292**
Transfer to cure want of, **28 § 1631**
Obsolete papers, dispositions, **28 § 457**
Procedure, **28 § 1651 et seq.**
Records and recordation, **28 § 457**
Reporter, **28 § 753**
Rules,
Power to prescribe, public notice and comment, **28 § 2071**
Savings provision, **28 § 2071**
Grand jury, selection and service, **28 § 1861 et seq.**
Judges or justices,
District courts, ante
Judicial circuit of U.S., **28 § 41**
Judicial district, bankruptcy provisions, applicability of certain amendments to, **28 § 581 nt**
Jurors,
Fees and allowances, **28 § 1871**
Selection and service, **28 § 1861 et seq.**
United States Court of Appeals for the Federal Circuit, jurisdiction of appeals in certain cases, **28 § 1295**
United States trustees of judicial districts, appointment, **28 § 581**

GUARANTY
Accounts of guarantor, settlement by U.S. Court of Federal Claims, **28 § 1494**
Officers and employees, of U.S., settlement of accounts by U.S. Court of Federal Claims, **28 § 1494**

GUARDIAN AND WARD
Annuities payable to minors or mentally incompetent dependents of justices and judges, payment to guardian, **28 § 376**
Children and minors,
Missing persons, Attorney General to acquire, collect, classify, information, provide to, **28 § 534**

GUARDIAN AND WARD—Cont'd
Justice, judge, or Magistrate Judge, disqualification, **28 § 455**

GUILTY
Sentence and Punishment, generally, this index

GUNS
Firearms, generally, this index

HABEAS CORPUS
Act of Congress, prisoner in custody for act done or omitted in pursuance of Act, conditions for granting, **28 § 2241**
Ad prosequendum, **28 § 2241**
Ad testificandum, **28 § 2241**
Administrative Office of the United States Courts, capital cases, report to Congress, time limitations, **28 § 2266**
Affidavits as evidence, **28 § 2246**
Amendment of return and suggestions made, **28 § 2243**
Answer to order to show cause, **28 § 2248**
Appeal and review, **28 § 2253**
  Final order, **28 § 2253**
  Stay of State court proceedings pending appeal, **28 § 2251**
Application for writ, **28 § 2242**
  Capital cases,
    Filing, **28 § 2263**
    Limitation periods, **28 § 2266**
Attorneys,
  Appointment, effectiveness, **28 § 2254**
  Capital cases, appointment, standards, **28 § 2261**
  Unitary review, State procedure, application, **28 § 2265**
Authority of U.S., prisoner under custody under or by color of, conditions for granting, **28 § 2241**
Burden of proof, Federal court proceedings, State court factual determination erroneous, **28 § 2254**
Capital cases, **28 § 2261 et seq.**
  An order under section 2261(c), defined, State unitary review procedure, **28 § 2265**
  Application for writ, ante
  Attorneys, appointment, standards, competency, provision, **28 § 2261**
  Direct review, defined, State unitary review procedure, **28 § 2265**
  Motions, limitation periods, **28 § 2266**
  Post-conviction review, defined, State unitary review procedure, **28 § 2265**
  Scope of Federal review, **28 § 2264**
  State unitary review procedure, application, **28 § 2265**
  Stay of execution, limits, **28 § 2262**
  Unitary review, defined, **28 § 2265**

HABEAS CORPUS—Cont'd
Certificate of,
  Appealability to courts of appeals, **28 § 2253**
Certified copies of indictment, pleas, filing, **28 § 2249**
Citizen of foreign state, in custody for act done, under any alleged right, title, claimed under commission, of foreign state, conditions for granting, **28 § 2241**
Commitment,
  Appeal from order to test validating of warrant to remove to another place, for, **28 § 2253**
  For trial before U.S. court, prisoner in custody for, conditions for granting, **28 § 2241**
Conditions for granting writ, **28 § 2241**
Constitution, laws, of U.S., prisoner in custody in violation of, conditions for granting, **28 § 2241**
Constitution of United States,
  State custody, violations as grounds for remedies in Federal courts, **28 § 2254**
  Violation, custody, condition for granting writ, **28 § 2241**
Constitutional violations, grounds for remedies in Federal courts where State custody, **28 § 2254**
Copies of indictment, plea of petitioner, attachment to return or answer to order to show cause, **28 § 2249**
Costs, furnishing copies of orders to indigent petitioner without cost, **28 § 2250**
Court interpreters, use of services in action for petition for, **28 §§ 1827, 1828**
Courts of Appeals, this index
Death penalty. Capital cases, generally, ante
Depositions, **28 § 2246**
District Courts, this index
Evidence, **28 § 2246**
  Certificate of trial judge, **28 § 2245**
  Conclusiveness of return or answer, **28 § 2248**
  Documentary evidence, **28 § 2247**
  Proceedings in Federal courts, State court proceedings, sufficiency and admissibility, **28 § 2254**
Execution, mandatory stay, capital cases, **28 § 2262**
Exhaustion of State court remedies, **28 § 2254**
Expedite hearing and determination, priority of civil actions, **28 § 1657**
Extradition proceeding, appeal, proceedings to test validity of warrant for removal, **28 § 2253**

HABEAS CORPUS—Cont'd
Federal custody,
  Motion to vacate, set aside or correct sentence,
    Postponement, effective date, proposed rules and forms governing proceedings respecting, **28 § 2074 nt**
Federal laws or treaties, violations, grounds for remedies in Federal courts where State custody, **28 § 2254**
Filing fees, **28 § 1914**
Final order,
  Review, **28 § 2253**
Finality of prior determination, **28 § 2244**
Hearing, **28 § 2243**
Indigent petitioner,
  Capital cases, appointment of counsel, standards, **28 § 2261**
  Certified copies of documents furnished without cost, **28 § 2250**
Issuance of writ, **28 § 2243**
Limitation of action, State court judgments, **28 § 2244**
Merits, State custody, decision on, remedies, **28 § 2254**
Motions,
  Capital cases, limitation periods, **28 § 2266**
New ground, **28 § 2244**
Notice prior to hearing as to person in custody of State officers, **28 § 2252**
Order to show cause for issuance of writ, **28 § 2243**
  Answer to, **28 §§ 2248, 2249**
Orders of court,
  Furnishing copies of documents or parts of record to indigent petitioner without cost, **28 § 2250**
  Judgment, of U.S. court, prisoner in custody for act done or omitted in pursuance of, conditions for granting, **28 § 2241**
Persons in custody under judgment, of State court, venue and jurisdiction, State containing 2 or more Federal judicial districts, **28 § 2241**
Power,
  To grant writs, **28 § 2241**
Presumption, correctness of State court findings, proceedings in Federal courts, exceptions, **28 § 2254**
Record of State court, production and admissibility in Federal court proceeding, **28 § 2254**
Removal of case, issuance of writ to take custody of defendant in district court, **28 § 1446**
Returns, **28 § 2248**
  Attachment of certified copies of indictment, plea, **28 § 2249**
  Order to show cause, **28 § 2243**
Right to writ, **28 § 2241**

HABEAS CORPUS—Cont'd
Rules Governing, 28 §§ **2254, 2255**
Section 2254 Cases. District Courts, this index
Rules of Appellate Procedure, this index
Rules of Civil Procedure, this index
Sentence and Punishment, this index
State Courts, this index
State custody,
Capital cases, generally, ante
Exhaustion of State court remedies, **28 § 2254**
Remedies in Federal courts, **28 §§ 2244, 2254**
Postponement, effective date, proposed rules and forms governing proceedings respecting, **28 § 2074 nt**
Stay,
Execution, capital cases, duration, limits, **28 § 2262**
State court proceedings, **28 § 2251**
Subsequent application after denial, new ground requirement, **28 § 2244**
Supreme Court, this index
Testify or for trial, necessary to bring prisoner into court for, conditions for granting, **28 § 2241**
Time,
Filing application, capital cases, **28 § 2263**
Return of writ or order to show cause, **28 § 2243**
Transcripts, fees of district court reporter, **28 § 753**
Unitary review, State procedure, capital cases, application, **28 § 2265**
Warrant for removal of offender, appeal in habeas corpus proceeding to test validity of warrant, **28 § 2253**
Witness fees and mileage, payment, proceedings in forma pauperis, **28 § 1825**

HABITUAL DRUNKARDS AND DRUNKENNESS
Alcoholics and Alcoholism, generally, this index

HALFWAY HOUSES
Correctional Institutions, generally, this index

HANDGUNS
Firearms, generally, this index

HANDICAPPED PERSONS
Disability, generally, this index
Fair Housing, generally, this index
Judges or justices, annuities for survivors, **28 § 376**
Mental Health, generally, this index

HANDWRITING
Evidence, **28 § 1731**

HARASSMENT
Civil Rights, generally, this index

HARDSHIP
Jury service, excuse from, **28 § 1866**
Grounds, **28 § 1863**

HARMLESS ERROR
Judgment on hearing on appeal or certiorari, **28 § 2111**

HATE CRIMES
Generally, **28 § 534 nt**
Defined, sentencing enhancements, guidelines, promulgation, Sentencing Commission, **28 § 994 nt**
Sentencing enhancement, guidelines, promulgation, Sentencing Commission, **28 § 994 nt**

HAWAII
See, also, States, generally, this index
Admission into Union,
Not to affect rights of retired judges of the District Court of Hawaii and justices of the Supreme Court of the Territory of Hawaii, **28 § 373 nt**
Admission to statehood,
Appeals and pending appeals, **28 § 91 nt**
Continuation of suits, **28 § 91 nt**
Bankruptcy judges, appointment, number in judicial district, **28 § 152**
Circuit court judges, inclusion of service in computing aggregate years of judicial service, **28 § 371 nt**
District courts,
Judges or justices,
Additional, **28 § 133 nt**
Admission into Union not to affect rights of retired judges for the Territory, **28 § 373 nt**
Inclusion of service in computing aggregate years of judicial service, **28 § 371 nt**
Number, **28 § 133**
Retirement and pensions, inclusion of service in computing aggregate years of judicial service, **28 § 371 nt**
Temporary judgeships, **28 § 133 nt**
Places of holding, **28 § 91**
Powers, **28 § 91 nt**
Judges or justices. District courts, ante
Judicial circuit of U.S., **28 § 41**
Judicial district, **28 § 91**
Bankruptcy provisions, applicability of certain amendments to, **28 § 581 nt**
Number of district judges, **28 § 133**
Supreme Court Justices,
Admission into Union not to affect rights of, **28 § 373 nt**
Inclusion of service in computing aggregate years of judicial service, **28 § 371 nt**
United States,
Trustees of judicial districts, appointment, **28 § 581**

HEALTH AND HUMAN SERVICES DEPARTMENT
See, also, Executive Departments, generally, this index
Community development, neighborhood revitalization plan, development by Attorney General, use of appropriated funds, **28 § 509 nt**

HEALTH CARE FACILITIES AND SERVICES
Justice Department employees serving abroad, authorization of appropriations, **28 § 530A**

HEALTH INSURANCE
Aged persons. Health Insurance for Aged and Disabled, generally, this index
Federal employees' group insurance,
Circuit court executives and staff deemed officers and employees of judicial branch for purposes of, **28 § 332**
Judicial Center, Director, professional staff, as officers and employees within meaning of provisions, **28 § 627**

HEALTH INSURANCE FOR AGED AND DISABLED
Physicians and surgeons,
Judicial Center, proposed rules of practice, procedure, and evidence, **28 § 2073**

HEARINGS
Administrative Law and Procedure, this index
Arbitration, generally, this index
Courts of Appeals, this index
Declaratory judgments and decrees, further relief based on, **28 § 2202**
Federal Debt Collection, this index
Habeas corpus, **28 §§ 2243, 2244**
Interpleader action in district court, **28 § 2361**
Judicial Panel on Multidistrict Litigation, generally, this index
Judicial sale of realty, **28 § 2001**
Lost or destroyed court records, application for order establishing, **28 § 1734**
Motion to vacate, set aside or correct sentence, Federal custody, **28 § 2255**
Multidistrict litigation, transfer to single district for consolidated, pretrial proceedings, **28 § 1407**
Orders, certain Federal agencies. Appeal and Review, this index
Rate orders of State agencies, jurisdiction, district courts, **28 § 1342**
Three-judge court, **28 § 2284**
United States Court of Appeals for the Armed Forces, generally, this index
United States Court of Appeals for the Federal Circuit, generally, this index

HEARINGS—Cont'd
United States Court of Federal Claims, this index
United States Court of International Trade, this index

HEARSAY
Rules of Evidence, this index

HIGH SEAS
Admiralty, generally, this index
Forfeiture of property seized on high seas, **28 § 2461**

HIGHWAYS AND ROADS
Toll Bridges, generally, this index
Toll Roads, generally, this index

HISPANIC AMERICANS
Fair Housing, generally, this index

HISTORY
Rules of Evidence, this index

HOBBS ADMINISTRATIVE ORDERS REVIEW ACT
Generally, **28 §§ 41 et seq., 2341 et seq.**

HOLLAND
Netherlands, generally, this index

HOME HEALTH CARE AND SERVICES
Confidential or privileged information, criminal background checks, labor and employment, **28 § 534 nt**
Criminal background checks, labor and employment, **28 § 534 nt**
Fees, criminal background checks, labor and employment, **28 § 534 nt**
Labor and employment, criminal background checks, **28 § 534 nt**

HOME MORTGAGES
Mortgages, generally, this index

HOME STATE
Defined, Parental Kidnapping Prevention Act, **28 § 1738A**

HOMICIDE
Manslaughter, generally, this index
Murder, generally, this index

HOMOSEXUALS AND HOMOSEXUALITY
Hate Crimes, generally, this index

HONORABLE DISCHARGES
Army,
Preference in appointment as district court criers and bailiffs, **28 § 755**
Navy,
Preference in appointment as district court criers and bailiffs, **28 § 755**

HONORARIA
Financial Disclosure, generally, this index

HORSE RACES
Professional and amateur sports protection, applicability, **28 § 3704**

HOSTILE FORCE OR PERSON
Employees' Compensation For Work Injuries, generally, this index

HOURS OF LABOR
Labor Disputes, generally, this index
Public works,
United States Court of Federal Claims,
Jurisdiction, to render judgment, claim for liquidated damages withheld from contractors or subcontractors, **28 § 1499**
United States Court of Federal Claims. Public works, ante

HOUSE OF REPRESENTATIVES
See, also, Congress, generally, this index
Bill referred to chief judge of U.S. Court of Federal Claims, jurisdiction, **28 § 1492**
Clerk of House of Representatives, generally, this index
Conflicts of Interest, generally, this index
Congressional Committees, generally, this index
Disclosure of Federal Campaign Funds, generally, this index
District courts, jurisdiction, action to recover possession of office, exception, **28 § 1344**
Elections,
Apportionment of Congressional districts, three-judge court required, **28 § 2284**
Employees,
Officers and employees, generally, post
Equal Employment Opportunity, generally, this index
Federal agency rulemaking, Congressional rulemaking review. Administrative Law and Procedure, generally, this index
Financial Disclosure, generally, this index
Journals of Congress,
Evidence, **28 § 1736**
Judicial Center, "service" as meaning service as Representative, retirement of Director, **28 § 627**
Justices and judges, deposit of salary and credit for service in, judicial survivors annuity fund, **28 § 376**
Member, defined,
Limitations on outside income and employment, **5, Ap 4, § 505**
Officers and employees,
Outside income and employment, **5, Ap 4, § 501 et seq.**
Removal of actions or prosecutions against for act in discharge of duty, **28 § 1442**

HOUSE OF REPRESENTATIVES—Cont'd
Outside income and employment, Representatives, officers and employees, Congress, **5, Ap 4, § 501 et seq.**
Political Activities, generally, this index
Presidential and Vice Presidential Electors, generally, this index
Rulemaking powers,
Financial disclosure requirements of Federal personnel, enactment as exercise of power, **5, Ap 4, § 101 nt**
Speaker of the House of Representatives, generally, this index

HOUSING
Fair Housing, generally, this index
Housing and Urban Development Department, generally, this index
Mortgages, generally, this index

HOUSING AND URBAN DEVELOPMENT DEPARTMENT
See, also, Executive Departments, generally, this index
Community development, neighborhood revitalization plan, development by Attorney General, use of appropriated funds, **28 § 509 nt**

HOWLAND ISLAND
Judicial district of Hawaii, inclusion in, **28 § 91**

HUMAN RIGHTS
See, also, Civil Rights, generally, this index
Torture,
Victim protection, civil action for damages, **28 § 1350 nt**

HUSBAND AND WIFE
See, also, Marriage, generally, this index
Justice, judge, or Magistrate Judge, spouse or minor child of, financial interest in subject matter in controversy, disqualification, **28 § 455**

IDAHO
See, also, States, generally, this index
Bankruptcy judges, appointment, number in judicial district, **28 § 152**
District courts,
Cities, held at, **28 § 92**
Judges, number, **28 § 133**
Places of holding, **28 § 92**
Judicial circuit of U.S., **28 § 41**
Judicial districts,
Bankruptcy provisions, applicability of certain amendments to, **28 § 581 nt**
Number of district judges, **28 § 133**
States, generally, this index
United States trustees of judicial districts, appointment, **28 § 581**

IDENTIFICATION DOCUMENTS
Criminal Background Checks, generally, this index
Sentence and punishment,
Theft and assumption deterrence, **28 § 994 nt**

IDENTITY AND IDENTIFICATION
See, also, Identification Documents, generally, this index
Attorney General to collect, classify and preserve information concerning missing persons, including unemancipated persons, **28 § 534**
Criminal and other identification records,
Acquisition, **28 § 534**
Parimutuel licensing, simplification, requests from State regulatory officers, **28 § 534 nt**
Criminal Background Checks, generally, this index
Federal Bureau of Investigation, use, funds provided for expenses, exchange of identification records with certain officials, **28 § 534 nt**
Interstate Identification Index, national crime information databases as including, national stalker and domestic violence reduction, violence against women, **28 § 534**
Other institutions, defined, acquisition, preservation, and exchange of identification records, **28 § 534**
Parents, guardian, Attorney General to collect, classify, information concerning missing persons, unemancipated persons, **28 § 534**
Sentence and punishment,
Theft and assumption deterrence, **28 § 994 nt**
Unemancipated persons, collect, classify, preserve, information assisting in location of, provide information to parent, guardian, **28 § 534**

ILLINOIS
See, also, States, generally, this index
Bankruptcy, judges, appointment, number in judicial district, **28 § 152**
District courts,
Cities, held at, **28 § 93**
Judges,
Additional, **28 § 133 nt**
Appointment, additional judges, advice and consent, **28 § 133 nt**
Designation for Central and Southern Districts and appointment of additional judges, **28 § 93 nt**
Existing judgeships authorized, **28 § 133 nt**
Number, **28 § 133**
Temporary judgeships, **28 § 133 nt**
Places of holding, **28 § 93**
Grand jury impaneled by district court for Central and Southern Districts, inquiry into and return of indictments, **28 § 93 nt**

ILLINOIS—Cont'd
Judicial circuit of U.S., **28 § 41**
Judicial districts, **28 § 93**
Bankruptcy provisions, applicability of certain amendments to, **28 § 581 nt**
Designation of judges for Central and Southern Districts and appointment of additional judge, **28 § 93 nt**
Number of district judges, **28 § 133**
Northern District of, U.S. trustees, appointment of, **28 § 581**
United States attorneys, assistant U.S. attorneys for Central and Southern Districts, designation, tenure, **28 § 93 nt**
United States marshals for Central and Southern Districts, designation, tenure, **28 § 93 nt**
United States trustees of judicial districts, appointment, **28 § 581**

ILLITERATE PERSONS
Jurors, qualification for service, **28 § 1865**

IMMIGRANT VISA
Visa, this index

IMMIGRANTS
Immigration, generally, this index

IMMIGRATION
Aliens,
Paroled into U.S. for prosecution, witness fees or allowances, ineligibility for, **28 § 1821**
Bringing in certain aliens,
Sentencing guidelines, **28 § 994 nt**
Bureau of Immigration. Immigration and Naturalization Service, generally, this index
Harboring certain aliens,
Sentencing guidelines, **28 § 994 nt**
Immigrant visa, generally. Visa, this index
Immigration and Naturalization Service, generally, this index
International terrorism. Terrorists and Terrorism, generally, this index
Naturalization, generally, this index
Smugglers,
Sentencing guidelines, **28 § 994 nt**
Terrorists and Terrorism, generally, this index
Visa, this index

IMMIGRATION AND NATURALIZATION SERVICE
Detention facilities, construction and renovation, use of deposits transferred from Assets Forfeiture Fund, **28 § 524 nt**
Uniforms, allowances, appropriations as permitted utilization, **28 § 509 nt**

IMMUNITIES
Privileges and Immunities, generally, this index

IMPAIRED SPEECH
Speech Loss or Disability, generally, this index

IMPRISONMENT
Sentence and Punishment, this index

IN FORMA PAUPERIS
Generally, **28 § 1915**
Forma Pauperis, generally, this index

IN REM
Attachment, fees of U.S. marshal for serving, **28 § 1921**
United States, proceedings by or on behalf of, change of venue, consent unnecessary, **28 § 1404**
Warrant of arrest or other process in admiralty, stay of execution of process, **28 § 2464**

INCENTIVE PAY OR AWARDS
Administrative Office of United States Courts, incentive awards for employees, **28 §§ 602 nt, 604**

INCOME TAX
Aliens, this index
Distributable net income. Estates and Trusts, generally, this index
Estates,
Executors and Administrators, this index
Executors and Administrators, this index
Federal Judicial Center Foundation, gifts to, as bequests to U.S., **28 § 629**
Partnership, this index
Returns,
Inspection and inspectors,
Independent counsel, powers, limitations, **28 § 594**
United States Court of Federal Claims, this index

INCOMPETENCY
See, also, Mental Health, generally, this index
Bankruptcy judges, grounds for removal, **28 § 152**
Jurisdiction, Federal litigation, diverse citizenship, representative deemed resident of State of incompetent, **28 § 1332**
Rules of Civil Procedure, this index
United States, actions by, period of limitation, exclusion, **28 § 2416**

INCONVENIENCE
Jury service, excuse from, **28 § 1866**
Grounds, **28 § 1863**

INCUMBRANCES
Liens and Incumbrances, generally, this index

INDEBTEDNESS
Bankruptcy, generally, this index
Garnishment, generally, this index

INDEMNITY COMPENSATION
Veterans, generally, this index

INDENTURES
Bankruptcy, generally, this index

INDEPENDENT COUNSEL
Access to records by Justice Department, exception, 28 § 594
Administrative support, 28 § 594
Amicus curiae,
Briefs, disclosure of sufficient information by division of the court to permit filing of, 28 § 593
Presentation by AG or Solicitor General as, 28 § 597
Applicability of provisions, 28 § 591
Appointment,
Application for, 28 § 592
By division of the court, 28 § 593
Appropriations, authorization, 28 § 591 nt
Assistant Attorney General, preliminary investigation by AG prior to appointment of, 28 § 591
Associated, defined, ban on representation by members of firms of independent counsel, 28 § 594
Attorney General,
Appropriations, permanent indefinite, authorization of, 28 § 591 nt
Conduct of preliminary investigation, limited authority, 28 § 592
Conflicts of interest, preliminary investigations, 28 § 591
Congress, members of, preliminary investigation by, 28 § 591
Division of court to appoint, establishment, 28 § 593
Exercise of authority vested in, authority and duties, 28 § 594
Preliminary investigation by AG prior to appointment of, 28 § 591
Presentation as amicus curiae permitted, 28 § 597
Reappointment, periodic review, judicial intervention, 28 § 596
Recusal, generally, post
Report, to Congress, semiannual financial reviews, 28 § 591 nt
Review, removal, 28 §§ 593, 596
Attorneys' fees, division of the court to award, request written evaluation, 28 § 593
Audits, Comptroller General, periodic, determination, 28 § 596
Authorities of, 28 § 594
Central Intelligence Agency, Director, preliminary investigation by AG prior to appointment of, 28 § 591
Certification, expenditures, liabilities, compliance with Justice Department policies, 28 § 594

INDEPENDENT COUNSEL—Cont'd
Compensation and salaries, 28 § 594
Conduct,
Congressional oversight, 28 § 595
Preliminary investigation, 28 § 592
Conflict of interest, preliminary investigation by AG prior to appointment of, 28 § 591
Congress,
Members of, preliminary investigation by AG, 28 § 591
Oversight, conduct of, 28 § 595
Records provided by, maintenance, 28 § 594
Congressional committees, request to AG for appointment of, 28 § 592
Contents, application for appointment of, 28 § 592
Contingency fund for, 28 § 591 nt
Cost controls and administrative support, 28 § 594
Covered persons, preliminary investigations by AG, applicability to, 28 § 591
Custody, records of, 28 § 594
Determination of preliminary investigation, notice, 28 § 592
Disclosure,
Identity and prosecutorial jurisdiction by division of the court, 28 § 593
Information,
Allowance by division of the court, 28 § 593
Prohibition, 28 § 592
Dismissal of matters by, authority, 28 § 594
Division of the court, duties of, 28 § 593
Documentary evidence, review by, authority and duties, 28 § 594
Duties of, 28 § 594
Effect of provisions, termination, 28 § 599
Employees, compensation or wages, comparability, 28 § 594
Ethics, 28 § 530B
Enforcement, 28 § 594
Examination of information to determine need for preliminary investigation, 28 § 591
Expansion of,
Investigations and proceedings by Justice Department, 28 § 597
Prosecutorial jurisdiction by division of the court, 28 § 593
Extension, time, preliminary investigation, application for, 28 § 592
Factors to be considered, examination of information to determine need for preliminary investigation, 28 § 591
Firm, defined, ban on representation by members of firms of independent counsel, 28 § 594
Functions assistance of Justice Department in carrying out, 28 § 594
Grand juries,
Conduct of pleadings before, 28 § 594

INDEPENDENT COUNSEL—Cont'd
Grand juries—Cont'd
Proceedings before, duties, 28 § 594
Grounds, removal, 28 § 596
Impeachment, information to, Congressional oversight, 28 § 595
Income tax, powers, limitations, 28 § 594
Independent from Justice Department, 28 § 594
Indictment and information, framing and signing, authority and duties, 28 § 594
Information,
Disclosure, ante
Examination to determine need for preliminary investigation, 28 § 591
Relating to impeachment, Congressional oversight, 28 § 595
Internal Revenue Service, Commissioner, preliminary investigation by AG prior to appointment of, 28 § 591
Judicial review,
Determination of AG, limitation, 28 § 592
Removal of, 28 § 596
Jurisdiction defined by division of the court, 28 § 593
Justice Department,
Assistance of, 28 § 594
Compliance, guidelines and procedures of, classified material, 28 § 594
Personnel, utilization of, 28 § 594
Preliminary investigation by AG prior to appointment of, 28 § 591
Relationship with, 28 § 597
Maintenance, use, and disposal of records, 28 § 594
National campaign committee, chairman, treasurer, preliminary investigation by AG prior to appointment of, 28 § 591
National security, receipt of appropriate clearances, withholding of evidence on grounds of, authority, 28 § 594
Notice, return by division of the court for further explanation, 28 § 593
Office of, termination, 28 § 596
Payment by Justice Department, 28 § 594
Personnel, appointment, assignment of duties, 28 § 594
Policies of Justice Department, compliance with, 28 § 594
Post-employment restrictions, 28 § 594
Preliminary investigation, conduct of, 28 § 592
President of U.S., preliminary investigation by AG prior to appointment of, 28 § 591
Prosecutions, initiation and conduct of, authority and duties, 28 § 594
Prosecutorial jurisdiction,
Scope determined by division of the court, 28 § 593

INDEPENDENT COUNSEL—Cont'd
Prosecutorial jurisdiction—Cont'd
Suspension of other investigations and proceedings on matters within, **28 § 597**
Publication, reports, **28 § 594**
Qualifications, division of the court to determine, **28 § 593**
Reappointment, counsel, provisions, **28 § 596**
Recusal,
Attorney General, requirements **28 § 591**
Requirements for, determination by AG, **28 § 591**
Reference to the division of the court, **28 § 593**
Referral of matters to, **28 § 594**
Removal of, **28 § 596**
Reports,
Attorney General, request by Congressional committees for appointment of independent counsel, **28 § 592**
Audit after termination of office of, **28 § 596**
Congress, Congressional oversight, **28 § 595**
Expenditures of independent counsel, time, contents, **28 § 594**
Publication, generally, ante
Removal of, **28 § 596**
Requirements, disclosure of information, **28 § 594**
Representation by members of firm of independent counsel, ban, **28 § 594**
Request for expansion of jurisdiction by, procedure, **28 § 593**
Requirements, recusal determination by AG, **28 § 591**
Restrictions, employment, independent counsel and appointees, **28 § 594**
Secretary of Energy, appointment, jurisdiction, powers to investigate and prosecute Federal crimes by, **28 § 592 et seq.**
Severability of provisions, **28 § 598**
Solicitor General, presentation as amicus curiae permitted, **28 § 597**
Standards of conduct applicable to, **28 § 594**
Submission of information in response to Congressional request, **28 § 592**
Tax return, inspecting, obtaining, authority and duties, **28 § 594**
Termination,
Effect of provisions, **28 § 599**
Office of, **28 § 596**
Testimonial privilege, contest of assertion, determination, **28 § 594**
Time,
Period for making determination of need for preliminary investigation, **28 § 591**
Preliminary investigation, application for extension of, **28 § 592**

INDEPENDENT COUNSEL—Cont'd
Transfer, records of, **28 § 594**
Transition provisions, prior counsel, **28 § 591 nt**
Traveling expenses, **28 § 594**
United States Attorney, exercise of authority vested in, authority and duties, **28 § 594**
Vacancies, division of the court to fill, **28 § 593**
Vice President, preliminary investigation by AG prior to appointment of, **28 § 591**
Violation of law, authority and duties respecting, **28 § 594**
Warrants, subpoenas, applications to Federal court for, authority and duties, **28 § 594**
Witnesses, immunity, applications to Federal court for, authority and duties, **28 § 594**

INDEPENDENT ESTABLISHMENTS
See, also, Executive Agencies, generally, this index
Tort claims against U.S. for negligence, of officers or employees, **28 § 2671 et seq.**

INDEPENDENT PROSECUTOR
Independent Counsel, generally, this index

INDEXES
Consumer Price Index, generally, this index
Interstate Identification Index, national crime information databases, as including, national stalker and domestic violence reduction, violent crime control, **28 § 534**
Judgment liens, **28 § 1962**
Pending action concerning realty, district courts, constructive notice, **28 § 1964**

INDIAN LANDS AND RESERVATIONS
Actions,
Money damages, brought by U.S. on behalf of individual whose land held in trust or restricted status, limitation of, **28 §§ 2415, 2415 nt**
State civil jurisdiction in actions to which Indians are parties, **28 § 1360**
Allotments,
District court's jurisdiction, **28 § 1353**
Trusts,
Time limitation, actions brought by U.S. within certain time after right of action accrues, **28 §§ 2415, 2415 nt**
Fires and fire protection,
Action by U.S. for damages, limitations, **28 §§ 2415, 2416**
Five Civilized Tribes, generally, this index

INDIAN LANDS AND RESERVATIONS—Cont'd
Jurisdiction,
Amendment of State constitutions to remove legal impediment for assumption by State, **28 § 1360 nt**
Civil jurisdiction by certain States in actions to which Indians are parties, **28 § 1360**
Limitation,
Action by U.S. on behalf of individual whose land held in trust or restricted status, **28 §§ 2415, 2415 nt**
Osage Indians, generally, this index
Real estate, quieting title, trust or restrictive lands, inapplicability to actions involving claims against U.S., **28 § 2409a**
Restricted lands, action for money damages brought by U.S. on behalf of individual whose land held in restricted status, limitation of, **28 §§ 2415, 2415 nt**
States,
Civil jurisdiction in actions to which Indians are parties, **28 § 1360**
Trespass, action by U.S. for damages, limitations, **28 §§ 2415, 2416**
Trusts,
Action for money damages brought by U.S. on behalf of individual whose land held in trust, limitation of, **28 §§ 2415, 2415 nt**
Taxation, alienation, of property held under prohibited, **28 § 1360**
United States, holding certain lands,
In trust or restricted status, action for money damages, limitation, **28 §§ 2415, 2415 nt**

INDIANA
See, also, States, generally, this index
Bankruptcy judges, appointment, number in judicial district, **28 § 152**
District courts,
Cities, held at, **28 § 94**
Judges,
Additional, **28 § 133 nt**
Existing judgeships authorized, **28 § 133 nt**
Number, **28 § 133**
Places of holding, **28 § 94**
Judicial circuit of U.S., **28 § 41**
Judicial districts, **28 § 94**
Bankruptcy provisions, applicability of certain amendments to, **28 § 581 nt**
Number of district judges, **28 § 133**
United States trustees of judicial districts, appointment, **28 § 581**

INDIANS
Actions and proceedings,
Money damages, brought by U.S. on behalf of tribes, limitation on, **28 §§ 2415, 2415 nt**

INDIANS—Cont'd
Actions and proceedings—Cont'd
State civil jurisdiction in actions to which Indians are parties, **28 § 1360**
Alaska, this index
California, this index
Claims,
Jurisdiction of Court of Federal Claims, Constitution of U.S., **28 § 1505**
Federal Register, this index
Five Civilized Tribes, generally, this index
Jurisdiction,
Actions to which Indians are parties, State civil jurisdiction, **28 § 1360**
Amendment of State constitutions to remove legal impediment for assumption by State, **28 § 1360 nt**
Civil jurisdiction of State in actions to which Indians are parties, **28 § 1360**
Criminal and civil actions,
District courts, **28 § 1362**
District courts, actions, **28 § 1362**
Lands. Indian Lands and Reservations, generally, this index
Limitation of Actions, this index
Osage Indians, generally, this index
Quapaw Indian Agency, judgment in favor of claimant to allotment, exception, **28 § 1353**
Reservations. Indian Lands and Reservations, generally, this index
Secretary of Interior,
Claims limitation provisions, legislation to resolve claims of submission to Congress, **28 § 2415 nt**
States, this index
Treaties,
Allotments, jurisdiction of district court, **28 § 1353**
Civil actions, jurisdiction, district courts, **28 § 1362**
Tribal ordinance or customs, force and effect in civil actions, **28 § 1360**
United States Court of Federal Claims, this index

INDICTMENT AND INFORMATION
Dismissal,
Jury selection procedures, noncompliance, grounds for, **28 § 1867**
Habeas corpus proceeding, filing of certified copy, **28 § 2249**
Independent Counsel, generally, this index

INDIGENT PERSONS
Forma Pauperis, generally, this index
Rules of Appellate Procedure, this index
Transcript in criminal proceedings involving indigent persons or habeas corpus proceedings, fees, district court reporter, **28 § 753**

INDIVIDUAL DEBT ADJUSTMENT
Bankruptcy, this index

INFANTS
Children and Minors, generally, this index

INFORMERS
Justice Department appropriations available for expenses, of, **28 § 524**

INFRINGEMENT
Copyrights, this index
Patents, this index
Plant Variety Protection, this index

INJUNCTIONS
Appeals from district courts to courts of appeals, **28 § 1292**
Bankruptcy, this index
Comptroller of Currency, this index
Courts of Appeals, this index
District Courts, this index
Federal statute, restraining enforcement, three-judge court required, procedure, **28 § 2284**
Interlocutory injunctions. Preliminary or interlocutory injunctions, generally, post
Interpleader, restraining proceedings involved in interpleader action, **28 § 2361**
National Banks, this index
Preliminary or interlocutory injunctions,
Direct appeals to Supreme Court from three-judge court decisions, **28 § 1253**
Order to prevent irreparable damage on application for preliminary injunction, **28 § 2284**
State statutes, restraining enforcement, three-judge court, procedure, **28 § 2284**
Temporary restraining order on application to prevent irreparable damage, **28 § 2284**
Vacate, single judge not to determine, **28 § 2284**
Professional and amateur sports protection, **28 § 3703**
Rate orders of State agencies, district court jurisdiction, **28 § 1342**
Record in proceedings in courts of appeals to enjoin orders of administrative agencies, commissions, **28 § 2112**
Removal of cases, injunction prior to removal to remain in force and effect, **28 § 1450**
Rules of Civil Procedure, this index
State statute, restraining enforcement, three-judge court required, procedure, **28 § 2284**
Stay of State court proceedings, **28 § 2283**
Surface Transportation Board, this index

INJUNCTIONS—Cont'd
Temporary injunctions. Preliminary or interlocutory injunctions, generally, ante
Three-judge court,
Composition, **28 § 2284**
Direct appeals from decisions of Supreme Court, **28 § 1253**
United States Court of International Trade, this index

INJURIES
Employees' Compensation for Work Injuries, generally, this index
International Trade, this index
Personal Injuries, generally, this index

INMATES
Correctional Institutions, generally, this index

INSPECTION AND INSPECTORS
See, also, Examinations and Examiners, generally, this index
Court dockets outside continental U.S., **28 § 604**
District court records, **28 § 753**
Jury,
Commission or clerk of district court, records and papers, **28 § 1868**
Selection procedures, challenging compliance with, records or papers, **28 § 1867**
Legal opinions, access to, executive agencies, **28 § 509 nt, EON 12146**
Rules of Civil Procedure, this index
United States Court of International Trade, this index

INSTALLMENTS
Annuities to survivors of justices and judges, payment, **28 § 376**

INSTITUTES
State Justice Institute, generally, this index

INSTITUTIONS
Civil Rights, generally, this index

INSTRUCTIONS
Juror qualification form, **28 § 1864**
Supreme Court, certification of questions by court of appeals, **28 § 1254**

INSTRUMENTALITIES OF THE UNITED STATES
Federal Agencies and Instrumentalities, generally, this index

INSULAR POSSESSIONS AND DEPENDENCIES
Courts,
Judicial proceedings, proving or admitting in other courts, authentication, entitlement to full faith and credit, **28 § 1738**

INSULAR POSSESSIONS AND DEPENDENCIES—Cont'd
Courts—Cont'd
Officers and employees, exemption from jury service, **28 § 1863**
Records and recordation, proving or admitting in other courts, authentication, entitlement to full faith and credit, **28 § 1738**
Defendant or res outside of, actions by U.S., time limitation, exclusion, **28 § 2416**
District courts,
Admiralty rules, power of Supreme Court to prescribe, savings provision, **28 §§ 2071 nt, 2073**
Firemen, exemption from jury service, **28 § 1863**
Government publications and law books furnished to justices, judges, clerks of courts, transmitted to successors, **28 § 414**
Inspection of dockets outside continental U.S., **28 § 604**
Judicial review, Federal agency action, exclusion,
Official station, **28 § 456**
Salaries on resignation, removal, **28 § 373**
Legislature, officers, exemption from jury service, **28 § 1863**
Officers and employees,
Executive, branches, exemption from jury service, **28 § 1863**
Parimutuel Licensing, simplification, **28 § 534 nt**
Police, exemption from jury service, **28 § 1863**
Records and recordation, evidence, **28 § 1738**
Seal, certificate to records or books for use as evidence, **28 § 1739**

INSURANCE
Health Insurance, generally, this index
Health Insurance for Aged and Disabled, generally, this index
Liability Insurance, generally, this index
Life Insurance, generally, this index

INSURRECTION AND SEDITION
Fines, penalties and forfeitures,
Venue of proceeding for forfeiture of goods from State or section, **28 § 1395**
Proclamations,
Insurrection and sedition,
Venue of proceeding for forfeiture of goods from State or section, **28 § 1395**

INTELLECTUAL PROPERTY
Bankruptcy, generally, this index
Copyrights, generally, this index
Trademarks and Trade Names, generally, this index

INTELLIGENCE
See, also, Espionage, generally, this index
Bureau of Investigation, generally, this index
Counterintelligence,
Bureau of Investigation, this index
Secretary of Defense, generally, this index
Interception of Wire, Oral, or Electronic Communications, generally, this index
Select Committee on Intelligence, House or Senate. Congressional Committees, generally, this index

INTERCEPTION OF WIRE, ORAL, OR ELECTRONIC COMMUNICATIONS
Attorney General,
Special prosecutor, control over actions of, **28 § 594**

INTEREST
Administrative proceedings, appeal by agency of award of costs or fees, **28 § 2412**
Judgments and decrees, **28 § 1961**
Internal Revenue Service tax cases, **28 § 1961**
T-bill rate table of changes, **28 § 1961 nt**
United States as party, **28 § 2674**
United States Court of Appeals for the Federal Circuit, **28 § 1961**
United States Court of Federal Claims, **28 §§ 1961, 2516**
Jurisdiction of District Court, amount in controversy, exclusion of, **28 § 1332**
Taxation,
Internal Revenue Service tax cases, judgments, rate of, **28 § 1961**
Overpayments,
Judgment against U.S., collector of internal revenue, **28 § 2411**
United States,
Judgments against, **28 § 2411**
Liability for interest prior to judgment on tort claims, **28 § 2674**
United States Court of Federal Claims, this index
United States Court of International Trade, monetary relief by judgment or stipulation agreement, civil actions, allowance, rate, **28 § 2644**
Witnesses, this index

INTERGOVERNMENTAL AGREEMENTS
Treaties, generally, this index

INTERLOCUTORY DECISIONS
Court of Appeals, Federal Circuit, exclusive jurisdiction, certain courts, **28 § 1292**
District court, appeals to courts of appeals, **28 § 1292**

INTERMEDIATE CREDIT BANKS
Federal Intermediate Credit Banks, generally, this index

INTERNAL REVENUE SERVICE
Actions and proceedings,
Civil actions by persons other than taxpayers,
Jurisdiction, **28 § 1346**
Venue, **28 § 1402**
District court's jurisdiction, **28 §§ 1340, 1346**
Execution against collecting officer or other revenue officer not to issue, **28 § 2006**
Judgment against collecting officer or other revenue officer, execution not to issue, **28 § 2006**
Jury trial in action for recovery of taxes erroneously paid, **28 § 2402**
Limitation of actions by U.S., applicability, **28 § 2415**
Penalties, collected without authority, actions against U.S., **28 §§ 1346, 2411**
Interest on judgment, **28 § 2411**
Venue, **28 § 1402**
Real estate, actions to quiet title involving claims against U.S., inapplicability, **28 § 2409a**
United States as defendant, venue, **28 § 1402**
Venue, **28 § 1402**
Action for collection, **28 § 1396**
Assessments,
Erroneous or illegal assessment, action against U.S.,
Interest on judgment, **28 § 2411**
Jurisdiction of district court of, **28 § 1346**
Trial by jury, **28 § 2402**
Venue, **28 § 1402**
Tort Claim Act, exception, **28 § 2680**
Civil actions by persons other than taxpayers, real property, quieting title, inapplicability to actions involving claims against U.S., **28 § 2409a**
Collection and collecting officers,
Actions,
To recover taxes illegally or erroneously collected, **28 § 2402**
Interest on judgment, **28 § 2411**
Excessive collection,
Jurisdiction of district court, action against U.S., **28 § 1346**
Venue, action against U.S., **28 § 1402**
Jurisdiction of district court, action against U.S., erroneous or wrongful collection, **28 § 1346**
Removal of action or prosecution against officer for acts under color of office, **28 § 1442**

INTERNAL REVENUE SERVICE
—Cont'd
Collection and collecting officers
—Cont'd
Searches and seizures,
Civil actions by persons other than taxpayers for wrongful levy,
Jurisdiction, **28 § 1346**
Venue, **28 § 1402**
Venue, action against U.S., erroneous or wrongful collection, **28 § 1402**
Tort Claims Act, exception, **28 § 2680**
Venue of action, **28 § 1396**
Damages,
Person or property under laws for protection of collection of revenue, jurisdiction of district court, **28 § 1357**
District courts,
Jurisdiction, **28 §§ 1340, 1346**
Civil actions by persons other than taxpayers,
Real estate, quieting title, inapplicability to actions involving claims against U.S., **28 § 2409a**
Removal of actions or prosecutions against officers, **28 § 1442**
Erroneous or illegal assessment or collection,
Actions to recover tax erroneously or illegally collected, **28 § 2402**
Financial institutions,
Federally insured, fraud, criminal or unlawful activity, investigation and prosecution of, **28 § 509 nt**
Fines, penalties and forfeitures,
Action,
Against U.S. for penalties collected without authority,
District court's jurisdiction of, **28 § 1346**
Interest on,
Judgment, **28 § 2411**
Venue, **28 § 1402**
United States attorneys, duties involving collection proceedings, **28 § 547**
Forfeitures. Fines, penalties and forfeitures, generally, ante
Judgments and decrees,
Interest on money judgment,
Against U.S., **28 § 2411**
Rates of, **28 § 1961**
Payment of judgment against officer on certification of certain facts by court, **28 § 2006**
T-bill rate table of changes, **28 § 1961 nt**
Jury trial in action for recovery of taxes erroneously paid, **28 § 2402**
Officers and employees,
Removal of actions or prosecutions against, **28 § 1442**

INTERNAL REVENUE SERVICE
—Cont'd
Overpayments,
Interest,
On judgment, **28 § 2411**
Payment,
Execution not to issue on judgment against revenue officer for money paid to him, **28 § 2006**
Judgment, against officer on certification of certain facts by court, **28 § 2006**
Penalties. Fines, penalties and forfeitures, generally, ante
Personal representative of revenue officers, interest on judgment against, **28 § 2411**
Real estate,
Penalties collected without authority, action against U.S., jury trial, **28 § 2402**
Quieting title, inapplicability to actions involving claims against U.S., **28 § 2409a**
Refunds,
Action for,
Refund,
Alien's privilege to sue in U.S. Court of Federal Claims, exception, limitation on right of, **28 § 2502**
Execution on or payment of judgment against revenue officer, **28 § 2006**
Judgment against collector or other revenue officer, execution not to issue, **28 § 2006**
Recovery, taxes erroneously paid, venue, **28 § 1402**
Taxes erroneously paid, district courts' jurisdiction, **28 § 1346**
Sales,
Civil actions by persons other than taxpayers for wrongful levy,
Jurisdiction, **28 § 1346**
Venue, **28 § 1402**
Searches and seizures,
Collection and collecting officers, ante
Sentence and punishment. Fines, penalties and forfeitures, generally, ante
Statute of limitations,
Actions by U.S., applicability, **28 § 2415**
Substituted sale proceeds, civil actions by persons other than taxpayers,
Jurisdiction, **28 § 1346**
Venue, **28 § 1402**
Surplus proceeds,
Civil actions by persons other than taxpayers,
Jurisdiction, **28 § 1346**
Venue, **28 § 1402**
Tax sales. Sales, generally, ante
Third parties,
Jurisdiction of district court, **28 § 1346**
Venue, **28 § 1402**
Tort Claims Act, exception, **28 § 2680**

INTERNAL REVENUE SERVICE
—Cont'd
United States,
Attorneys,
Duties involving civil actions, **28 § 547**
United States Tax Court, generally, this index
Venue,
Action for collection, **28 § 1396**
Suits for taxes, **28 § 1396**
Wrongful levy,
Jurisdiction, **28 § 1346**
Venue, **28 § 1402**

INTERNATIONAL CRIMINAL POLICE ORGANIZATION
Chief, United States National Central Bureau, name checks, background records, fees, establishment and collection, **28 § 509 nt**

INTERNATIONAL LAW
Alien's action for tort, jurisdiction of district court, **28 § 1350**
Torture victim protection, civil action for damages, **28 § 1350 nt**
Torture victim protection, civil liability, **28 § 1350 nt**

INTERNATIONAL TERRORISM
Terrorists and Terrorism, this index

INTERNATIONAL TRADE
Actions and proceedings,
Counterclaims, unfair practices in import trade,
District court,
Original jurisdiction, **28 § 1368**
Removal to district court, **28 § 1446**
Stay of civil action pending related Commission determination, **28 § 1659**
Commission,
Counterclaims, removal to district court, **28 § 1446**
Decision of, presumption, correctness, **28 § 2639**
Person,
Entitled to commence civil action involving application for issuance of order directing Commission to make confidential information available, **28 § 2631**
Communities. Injuries, post
Customs Duties, generally, this index
Firms. Injuries, post
Government procedure, scope and standard of review in civil actions, **28 § 2640**
Government procurement,
Civil action contesting final determination, time for commencement of action, **28 § 2636**

INTERNATIONAL TRADE—Cont'd
Government procurement—Cont'd
Persons entitled to commence civil action to review final determinations respecting, **28 § 2631**
Rules of origin,
Exclusive jurisdiction, U.S. Court of International Trade, review, final determination, **28 § 1582**
Review, final determination, exclusive jurisdiction, U.S. Court of International Trade, **28 § 1581**
Secretary of Treasury,
Advisory rulings and final determination on origin of products of foreign country,
Review, final determination, exclusive jurisdiction, U.S. Court of International Trade, **28 § 1581**
Injuries,
Communities, adjustment assistance for,
Commencement of action, time for, **28 § 2636**
Injunctions or issuance of writ of mandamus in civil actions commenced to review final determination of Secretary, exception, **28 § 2643**
Persons entitled to commence civil action to review final determination of Commerce Secretary respecting, **28 § 2631**
Scope and standard of review in civil actions commenced to review final determinations of Secretary, **28 § 2640**
Firms,
Commencement of action, time for, **28 § 2636**
Injunctions or issuance of writ of mandamus in civil actions commenced to review final determination of Secretary, exception, **28 § 2643**
Persons entitled to commence civil action to review final determination of Secretary of Commerce respecting, **28 § 2631**
Scope and standard of review in civil actions to review final determination of Secretary, **28 § 2640**
Workers,
Commencement of action, time for, **28 § 2636**
Injunctions or issuance of writ of mandamus in civil actions commenced to review final determination of Secretary, exception, **28 § 2643**
Persons entitled to commence civil action to review final determination of Labor Secretary respecting, **28 § 2631**

INTERNATIONAL TRADE—Cont'd
Injuries—Cont'd
Workers—Cont'd
Scope and standard of review in civil actions commenced to review determinations of Secretary, **28 § 2640**
International Trade Commission,
Commission, generally, ante
Records and recordation,
Commission proceedings, admissibility in district court civil actions, **28 § 1659**
Secretary of Treasury,
Government procurement, ante
Trade Representative,
Independent counsel, appointment, jurisdiction, power to investigate and prosecute Federal crimes by, **28 § 592 et seq.**
Special prosecutor,
Appointment, jurisdiction, power to investigate and prosecute Federal crimes by, **28 § 592 et seq.**
Investigation by Attorney General of allegations of crime by before appointment, **28 § 591**
United States Court of Appeals for the Federal Circuit, generally, this index
United States Court of Federal Claims, generally, this index
United States Court of International Trade, generally, this index
United States Trade Representative. Trade Representative, generally, ante
Workers. Injuries, ante

INTERNATIONAL TRADE COMMISSION
International Trade, this index

INTERNATIONAL TRIBUNALS
Assistance to and to litigants before such tribunals, **28 § 1782**
Letters rogatory or request, transmittal to, **28 § 1781**
Service of document issued in connection with proceedings in, **28 § 1696**
Voluntarily giving testimony or producing documents for use in proceeding, **28 § 1782**

INTERNET
Computers, generally, this index

INTERPLEADER
District Courts, this index
Process and procedure, **28 § 2361**
Tax lien, property on which U.S. has lien, **28 § 2410**
Venue, **28 § 1397**

INTERPOL
International Criminal Police Organization, generally, this index

INTERPRETERS
Court interpreters,
Administrative Office of U.S. Courts, Director,
Assistance to individual requiring services of interpreter, duties, **28 § 1827**
Deaf persons, establishment of program, **28 § 1827**
Special interpretation services, establishment of programs for, duties, **28 § 1828**
Appropriations, authorization, **28 §§ 602 nt, 1827**
Certification, **28 § 1827**
Impact on existing programs, **28 § 1827 nt**
Clerk of district court,
Assistance to individual requiring services of interpreter, duties, **28 § 1827**
List of certified interpreters, duty to maintain, **28 § 1827**
Securing services of interpreters, duties regarding, **28 § 1827**
Compensation and expenses payable to, **28 § 1827**
Contractual services, payment, **28 § 1827 nt**
Costs, compensation, taxation as cost, **28 § 1920**
Deaf persons, certification program, qualifications, training, **28 § 1827**
Electronic sound recordings of proceedings, determination, **28 § 1827**
Fees, **28 § 1827**
Judicial proceedings instituted by the United States, use of services, **28 § 1827**
Master list, requirement to maintain, **28 § 1827**
Multidefendant criminal and civil actions, special interpretation services, **28 § 1828**
Party to civil or criminal action, motion for services of interpreter, **28 § 1827**
Presiding judicial officer,
Defined, determination whether to use services of interpreter, grounds, **28 § 1827**
Special interpretation services, provision for on motion, **28 §§ 1827, 1828**
Qualifications, certification of, **28 § 1827**
Simultaneous interpretation, proceedings instituted by U.S., **28 § 1827**
Special interpretation services,
Costs, taxation as cost, **28 § 1920**
Provision on motion by presiding judicial officer, **28 § 1827**
United States district court, defined as including courts in territories, uses of services of, **28 § 1827**

INTERPRETERS—Cont'd
Court interpreters—Cont'd
Waiver of right, approval and consultation, **28 § 1827**
Witness, civil or criminal action, motion for services of interpreter, **28 § 1827**
Deaf persons. Court interpreters, generally, ante
Electronic sound recordings, in addition to, **28 § 1827**
Examinations, court interpreters, **28 § 1827**
Fees,
Contractual services, court interpreters, **28 § 1827 nt**
Courts, performance examinations, **28 § 1827**

INTERROGATORIES
Rules of Civil Procedure, this index
Senate action to secure, District Court for District of Columbia, jurisdiction, **28 § 1365**

INTERVENTION
Certificate, constitutionality of Act of Congress involved, intervention in proceeding by U.S., **28 § 2403**
Parties, this index
Real estate, quieting title, tax lien, actions by U.S., inapplicability to actions involving claims against U.S., **28 § 2409a**
Review, orders, certain Federal agencies, **28 § 2348**
State in action or proceeding involving constitutionality of State statute, **28 § 2403**
Surface Transportation Board, this index
United States Court of International Trade, persons adversely affected or aggrieved by decision in civil action pending in, exceptions, **28 § 2631**
United States in,
Action or proceeding, **28 § 2403**

INTOXICATED PERSONS
Alcoholics and Alcoholism, generally, this index

INTOXICATION
Alcoholics and Alcoholism, generally, this index

INVEIGLE AND INVEIGLING
Kidnapping, generally, this index

INVESTIGATIONS
Bureau of Investigation, generally, this index
Criminal Background Checks, generally, this index
Independent Counsel, generally, this index
Officials to conduct, appointment, **28 § 533**

INVESTMENTS
Attached property in actions against delinquent postmasters and postal officers, employees, investment of proceeds, **28 § 2714**
Judicial survivors annuity fund, **28 § 376**

INVOLUNTARY BANKRUPTCY
Bankruptcy, generally, this index

INVOLUNTARY MANSLAUGHTER
Manslaughter, generally, this index

INVOLUNTARY SERVITUDE
Election disputes, original jurisdiction of district court, **28 § 1344**

IOWA
See, also, States, generally, this index
Bankruptcy judges, appointment, number in judicial district, **28 § 152**
District courts,
Judges,
Additional, **28 § 133 nt**
Appointment, additional judges, advice and consent, **28 § 133 nt**
Cities, held at, **28 § 95**
Existing judgeships, treatment, **28 § 133 nt**
Number, **28 § 133**
Judicial districts, **28 § 95**
Places of holding, **28 § 95**
Judicial circuit of U.S., **28 § 41**
Judicial districts, **28 § 95**
Bankruptcy provisions, applicability of certain amendments to, **28 § 581 nt**
Number of district judges, **28 § 133**
United States trustees of judicial districts, appointment, **28 § 581**

IRS
Internal Revenue Service, generally, this index

ISLANDS
Insular Possessions and Dependencies, generally, this index

ISRAEL
Conventions, Taking of Evidence Abroad in Civil or Commercial Matters, party to, **28 § 1781 nt**

ITALY
Conventions, Taking of Evidence Abroad in Civil or Commercial Matters, party to, **28 § 1781 nt**

JACKSON, MS
Court of Appeals for Fifth Circuit, generally, this index

JACKSONVILLE, FL
Court of Appeals for Eleventh Circuit, generally, this index

JAI ALAI
Professional and amateur sports protection, applicability, **28 § 3704**

JAILS
Correctional Institutions, generally, this index

JARVIS ISLAND
Judicial district of Hawaii, inclusion in, **28 § 91**

JOBS
Labor and Employment, generally, this index

JOHNSTON ISLAND
Judicial district of Hawaii, inclusion in, **28 § 91**

JOINDER OF CAUSES
Removal of case to district court, **28 § 1441**

JOINDER OF PARTIES
Civil action against U.S., or an agency or employee, joinder of additional parties subject to rules of venue, **28 § 1391**
Collusive or improper joinder, lack of jurisdiction of district court, **28 § 1359**

JOINT COMMITTEE ON PRINTING
Supreme Court reports, powers and duties of Committee, **28 § 411**

JOINT CONGRESSIONAL COMMITTEES
Joint Committee on Printing, generally, this index

JOINT COUNCILS
Sentencing, councils on, **28 § 334**
Offenses provided with mandatory penalties, applicability to, **28 § 334 nt**

JOINT TENANTS
United States as joint tenant, partition action,
Jurisdiction of district court, **28 § 1347**
Venue, **28 §§ 1399, 2409**

JOURNALS
Foreign patent offices, copies of excerpts as evidence, **28 § 1745**

JOURNALS OF CONGRESS
House of Representatives, this index
Senate, this index

JUDGES OR JUSTICES
Absence from district or circuit to which assigned, powers, **28 § 296**
Acknowledgment, authority to take, **28 § 459**

JUDGES OR JUSTICES—Cont'd
Active duty or service, designation and assignment of retired judge to, **28 § 294**
Adjustments, certain salaries, **28 § 461**
Administrative Law Judges, generally, this index
Age,
  Annuities to surviving dependent children, termination, **28 § 376**
  Retirement for,
    Entitlement to annuity equal to salary, **28 § 371**
    Substantial judicial duties in retirement, certification, **28 § 371**
Agency, defined, general provisions applicable to, **28 § 451**
Alternative writs, power to issue, **28 § 1651**
Annuities,
  Bankruptcy judges and Magistrate Judges. Retirement and pensions, post
  Retirement and pensions, **28 § 371**
    Bankruptcy judges and Magistrate Judges, "retirement salary" as meaning, **28 § 376**
    Calculation of service, bankruptcy judges and Magistrate Judges, **28 § 377**
    Compensation, defined, bankruptcy judges and Magistrate Judges, **28 § 377**
    Effect of certain situations, bankruptcy judges and Magistrate Judges, **28 § 377**
    Election of annuity in lieu of other annuities, bankruptcy judges and Magistrate Judges, **28 § 377**
    Employment, acceptance of, effect, bankruptcy judges and Magistrate Judges, **28 § 377**
    Filing notice of election, requirement, bankruptcy judges and Magistrate Judges, **28 § 377 nt**
    Incumbent bankruptcy judges and Magistrate Judges, **28 § 377 nt**
      Election, **28 § 376 nt**
    Judges in territories and possessions, **28 § 373**
    Judicial Officers' Retirement Fund, establishment, investment, **28 § 377**
    Judicial official, defined, bankruptcy judges and Magistrate Judges, lump-sum payments, **28 § 377**
    Judicial Survivors' Annuity Fund, **28 § 376 nt**
    Law, practicing after retirement, effect, bankruptcy judges and Magistrate Judges, **28 § 377**
    Lump-sum credit,
      Defined, bankruptcy judges and Magistrate Judges, **28 § 377**

JUDGES OR JUSTICES—Cont'd
Annuities—Cont'd
  Retirement and pensions—Cont'd
    Lump-sum credit—Cont'd
      Entitlement, bankruptcy judges and Magistrate Judges, **28 § 377 nt**
    Lump-sum payments, bankruptcy judges and Magistrate Judges, **28 § 377**
    Recall, generally, post
    Receipt equal to salary, retirement after attaining age and meeting service requirements, **28 § 371**
    Survivor annuity, increases, incumbents, **28 § 376 nt**
  To surviving spouses, **28 § 376**
Appointment,
  As judicial branch agency director, effect, **28 § 133**
  Disability, appointment of additional circuit or district judge, **28 § 372**
  Judge, to Office of Federal Judicial Administration, effect, **28 § 133**
  Relatives ineligible to appointment to office or duty in any court, **28 § 458**
Assassinated, defined, annuities for survivors, **28 §§ 376, 376 nt**
Assassination,
  Annuities for survivors, retroactive application, **28 § 376 nt**
  Defined, annuities for survivors, **28 §§ 376, 376 nt**
Assignments. Designation and assignment, generally, post
Attorney General, civil action challenging appointment, expedition of action by, **28 § 503 nt**
Beneficiaries, survivors' annuities, eligibility, computation, **28 § 376 nt**
Black persons, selection of qualified individuals for nomination to judgeships, Congressional recommendations, **28 § 133 nt**
Books and publications, transmittal to successors, **28 § 414**
Certificates,
  Books, or records of State, territory or possession, evidence, **28 § 1739**
  Disability of judge, retirement, **28 § 372**
  Evidence in habeas corpus proceeding, **28 § 2245**
  Records or books of territory, State or possession as evidence, **28 § 1739**
Chief justice known as chief judge, **28 § 451 nt**
Child, defined, annuities for survivors, **28 § 376**
Civil Service retirement. Retirement and pensions, generally, post
Commissions. Commissions of Officers, generally, this index

JUDGES OR JUSTICES—Cont'd
Compensation, defined, retirement of bankruptcy judges and Magistrate Judges, **28 § 377**
Compensation and salaries,
  Adjustments,
    Increase, effective pay periods commencing on or after certain date, **28 § 461 nt**
  Appropriations, judicial salaries, **28 § 461 nt**
  Deductions and withholdings for purpose of annuities, to survivors, **28 § 376**
  Former members of uniformed services, receiving retired or retainer pay, exception, **28 § 371**
  Increases,
    Congressional authorization required, **28 § 461 nt**
    Percentage increase during certain fiscal year, **28 § 461 nt**
    Proportionate increase in annuities for survivors, **28 § 376**
  Reduction,
    Individual's salary whose compensation may not be diminished under provisions of Constitution, inapplicability of adjustment provisions, **28 § 461**
  Resignation or retirement, **28 § 372**
  Retirement and pensions, substantial judicial duties in retirement, certification, **28 § 371**
Conditions upon designation and assignment,**28 § 295**
Contributions, Judicial Survivors' annuity fund, credit, redeposit, prior to certain date, **28 § 376 nt**
Cost-of-living adjustments, retirement, bankruptcy judges and Magistrate Judges, **28 § 377**
Counsel,
  Disqualification by having been of counsel, **28 § 455**
Court, defined,
  Bankruptcy judges and Magistrate Judges, retirement, **28 § 377**
  Retirement salary, payment pursuant to court decree of divorce, **28 § 376 nt**
Court decree, divorce, payment of retirement salary pursuant to, **28 §§ 376, 376 nt**
Court orders, retirement, payments pursuant to, bankruptcy judges and Magistrate Judges, **28 § 377**
Courts of Appeals, this index,
Creditable service, computation, annuities for survivors, **28 § 376**
Crimes and offenses,
  Practice of law, **28 § 454**
Death while in office, return of payments, **28 § 376**

JUDGES OR JUSTICES—Cont'd
Deceased official, former spouse of, entitlement to survivor annuity, terms, **28 § 376**
Decision, joinder in determination after expiration of period of his designation and assignment in another district, **28 § 296**
Defense of action against, when costs payable by Director of Administrative Office of U.S. Courts, **28 § 463**
Degree of relationship, defined, disqualification, **28 § 455**
Department, defined, general provisions applicable to, **28 § 451**
Dependents' annuities. Annuities, generally, ante
Designation and assignment,
Absence from district or circuit to which assigned, powers, **28 § 296**
Annuities for survivors, prohibition, **28 § 376**
Conditions, **28 § 295**
Expiration of designation and assignment to other district or circuit, **28 § 296**
Judicial conference of U.S. to prepare plans for, **28 § 331**
New designations and assignments, **28 § 295**
Ninth Circuit, district judges, to Compact States, **28 § 297**
Other courts, **28 § 291 et seq.**
Retired judge to active duty, **28 § 294**
Revocation of, **28 § 295**
Disability,
Annuities to surviving dependent children, termination upon recovery, **28 § 376**
Appointment of additional circuit or district judge, **28 § 372**
Bankruptcy judges and Magistrate Judges, retirement, **28 § 377**
Retired, unable to perform judicial or administrative work in retirement, certificate for, **28 § 371**
Retirement for, **28 § 372**
Disqualification, **28 § 455**
District, defined, general provisions applicable to, **28 § 451**
District courts,
District Judges, generally, this index
District Judges, generally, this index
Divorce, court decree of, **28 §§ 376, 376 nt**
Domicile and residence,
Certain judges, official duty station to be that nearest residence, **28 § 456**
District Judges, this index
Notice to Director of the Administrative Office of U.S. Courts of change residence, **28 § 456**
Retired judges, **28 § 374**

JUDGES OR JUSTICES—Cont'd
Election,
Annuities, bankruptcy judges and Magistrate Judges, **28 § 377**
Survivors annuities, **28 § 376**
Incumbents, revocation, **28 § 376 nt**
Employees, ineligibility to appointment as receivers, **28 § 958**
Employment, retired bankruptcy judges and Magistrate Judges, effect, **28 § 377**
Expenses and expenditures,
Litigation, when costs of defense payable by Director of Administrative Office of U.S. Courts, **28 § 463**
Payment, Director of Administrative Office of U.S. Courts, **28 § 604**
Traveling expenses, **28 §§ 456, 604**
Increase, rules and regulations, promulgation by Director, **28 § 604 nt**
Expiration of designation and assignment to other district or circuit, **28 § 296**
Fees,
Taxation of costs, **28 § 1920**
Fiduciary, defined, disqualification, **28 § 455**
Financial interest,
Defined, disqualification, **28 § 455**
Subject matter in controversy, personal and fiduciary, duties of, applicability, disqualification, **28 § 455**
Former spouse,
Defined, annuities for survivors, **28 § 376**
Survivor annuity, election, conditions, **28 § 376**
Funds,
Judicial Officers' Retirement, establishment, bankruptcy judges and Magistrate Judges, **28 § 377**
Judicial Survivors' Annuity Fund, establishment, appropriations, **28 § 376 nt**
Habeas Corpus, generally, this index
Incumbent bankruptcy judges and Magistrate Judges,
Retirement and pensions, **28 § 377 nt**
Survivors annuities, election, **28 § 376 nt**
Judge of the United States, defined, general provisions applicable to, **28 § 451**
Judgments, district courts, interest on, rates, distribution, notice to, **28 § 1961**
Judicial Center,
Compensation of Director where active or retired judge or justice, **28 § 626**
Conduct of programs of continuing education and training, **28 § 620**
Judicial conference of the circuit, attendance, **28 § 333**
Judicial Conference of the U.S., **28 § 331**

JUDGES OR JUSTICES—Cont'd
Judicial discipline, complaint, review procedure, **28 § 372**
Judicial Discipline and Removal, National Commission on, establishment, composition, report, **28 § 372 nt**
Judicial Officers' Retirement Fund, establishment, bankruptcy judges and Magistrate Judges, **28 § 377**
Judicial official,
Annuities for survivors, **28 § 376**
Defined, **28 § 376**
Annuities for survivors, **28 § 376**
Retroactive application, **28 § 376 nt**
Retirement of bankruptcy judges and Magistrate Judges, **28 § 377**
Judicial Panel on Multidistrict Litigation, generally, this index
Judicial Survivors Annuity Fund, generally, this index
Labor and employment,
Veterans, preference, **28 § 601 nt**
Law, practice, retired bankruptcy judges and Magistrate Judges, **28 § 377**
Law books and publications furnished to, transmission to successor, **28 § 414**
Lump-sum credit,
Defined, bankruptcy judges and Magistrate Judges, retirement, **28 § 377**
Entitlement, retired bankruptcy judges and Magistrate Judges, **28 § 377 nt**
Lump-sum payments,
Bankruptcy judges and Magistrate Judges, **28 § 377**
Survivors' annuities, **28 § 376**
Magistrate Judges. United States Magistrate Judges, generally, this index
Military service, deposits in Judicial Survivors' Annuities Fund for prior service, exemption, **28 § 376**
New designations and assignments, **28 § 295**
Newspaper for publication of legal notices, designation by assigned justice or judge, exception, **28 § 296**
Nominations, Congressional recommendations regarding blacks and women as qualified individuals for selection for nomination to judgeships, **28 § 133 nt**
Notice, annuity election, bankruptcy judges and Magistrate Judges, effect, **28 § 377 nt**
Oaths and affirmations, **28 § 453**
Authority to administer, **28 § 459**
Offenses. Crimes and offenses, generally, ante
Office expenses, Director of Administrative Office of U.S. Courts to pay, **28 § 604**
Office of Federal Judicial Administration, defined, effect of appointment of judge as Director, **28 § 133**

JUDGES OR JUSTICES—Cont'd
Officers and employees,
Veterans, preference, **28 § 601 nt**
Official station of retired judges, **28 § 374**
Payment,
Expenses and expenditures, ante
Lump sum, bankruptcy judges or Magistrate Judges, retirement, **28 § 377**
Percentage increase, salaries, certain fiscal year, **28 § 461 nt**
Powers,
Alternative writs, issuance, **28 § 1651**
During period of designation and assignment, **28 § 296**
Expiration of designation and assignment to other district or circuit, **28 § 296**
Rule nisi, issuance, **28 § 1651**
Practice of law,
As high misdemeanor, **28 § 454**
Retired bankruptcy judges and Magistrate Judges, effect, **28 § 377**
Proceeding, defined, disqualification, **28 § 455**
Reappointment, bankruptcy judges and Magistrate Judges, failure to attain, retirement, **28 § 377**
Reasonable period of time, defined, annuities for survivors, **28 § 376**
Recall,
Certain retired judges and Magistrate Judges, **28 § 375**
Retired bankruptcy judges and Magistrate Judges, **28 § 375**
Effect, **28 § 377 nt**
Prohibition, **28 § 377**
Records and recordation, individual retirement records, bankruptcy judges and Magistrate Judges, **28 § 377**
Reduction, Judicial Survivors' Annuities Fund unfunded liability, deposits, amount limitation, **28 § 376**
Rehearing, joinder in determination after expiration of period of assignment to another district or circuit, **28 § 296**
Relationship, disqualification, **28 § 455**
Relatives ineligible to appointment to office or duty in any court, **28 § 458**
Release, generally, this index
Removal, territories, and possessions of U.S., salary, **28 § 373**
Resignation. Retirement and pensions, generally, post
Retired judges. Retirement and pensions, generally, post
Retirement and pensions,
Annuities, ante
Bankruptcy judges and Magistrate Judges, **28 § 377**
Chief judge of court, may designate and assign retired judge to perform judicial duties, **28 § 294**
Compensation, **28 § 371 et seq.**

JUDGES OR JUSTICES—Cont'd
Retirement and pensions—Cont'd
Compensation—Cont'd
Substantial judicial duties in retirement, certification, **28 § 371**
Teaching, treatment, outside earned income for limitation purposes, **5, Ap 4, § 502**
Cost-of-living adjustments, bankruptcy judges and Magistrate Judges, **28 § 377**
Court, defined, bankruptcy judges and Magistrate Judges, **28 § 377**
Court orders, payments pursuant to, bankruptcy judges and Magistrate Judges, **28 § 377**
Deductions,
Contributions and deposits, bankruptcy judges and Magistrate Judges, **28 § 377**
Deposits for prior service, bankruptcy judges and Magistrate Judges, **28 § 377**
Designation and assignment of retired judge to active duty, **28 § 294**
Disability, **28 § 372**
Bankruptcy judges and Magistrate Judges, **28 § 377**
Domicile and residence, **28 § 374**
Failure of reappointment, bankruptcy judges and Magistrate Judges, **28 § 377**
Incumbent bankruptcy judges and Magistrate Judges, **28 § 377 nt**
Election, **28 § 376 nt**
Individual retirement records, bankruptcy judges and Magistrate Judges, **28 § 377**
Judicial Officers' Retirement Fund, establishment, investment, bankruptcy judges and Magistrate Judges, **28 § 377**
Judicial official, defined, bankruptcy judges and Magistrate Judges, lump-sum payments, **28 § 377**
Lump-sum credit, defined, bankruptcy judges and Magistrate Judges, **28 § 377**
Lump-sum payments, bankruptcy judges and Magistrate Judges, **28 § 377**
Official duty station, **28 § 456**
Positions covered, bankruptcy judges and Magistrate Judges, **28 § 377**
Recall, generally, ante
Records and recordation, individual retirement records, bankruptcy judges and Magistrate Judges, **28 § 377**
Roster of senior judges able to undertake special judicial duties, **28 § 294**
Senior status, entitlement to salary, **28 § 371**

JUDGES OR JUSTICES—Cont'd
Retirement and pensions—Cont'd
Service,
Covered, bankruptcy judges and Magistrate Judges, **28 § 377**
For certain number of years, bankruptcy judges and Magistrate Judges, **28 § 377**
Traveling and subsistence expenses where recalled or designated and assigned to active duty, **28 § 456**
Unfunded liability, defined, Judicial Officers' Retirement Fund, bankruptcy judges and Magistrate Judges, **28 § 377**
Years of service, basis, bankruptcy judges and Magistrate Judges, **28 § 377**
Retirement salary, defined, annuities for survivors, **28 § 376**
Revocation,
Designations and assignments, **28 § 295**
Election, annuities for survivors, **28 § 376 nt**
Survivors' annuities, eligibility, **28 § 376 nt**
Roster of senior judges, **28 § 294**
Rule nisi, power to issue, **28 § 1651**
Rules of Civil Procedure, this index
Salary. Compensation and salaries, generally, ante
Senior status, retirement, entitlement to salary, **28 § 371**
Service, years of, retirement after meeting requirements,
Annuity and salary, **28 § 371**
Bankruptcy judges and Magistrate Judges, **28 § 377**
Special judicial duties by retired judges, **28 § 294**
Spouses, annuity payments to survivors of judges who died prior to certain date, **28 § 376 nt**
Substitute judge on failure to retire, **28 § 372**
Surviving spouses,
Annuities, generally, ante
Survivor annuity, increases, **28 § 376 nt**
Table, age and service requirements, retirement, annuity and salary, **28 § 371**
Territories, this index
Three Judge Court, generally, this index
Transfer of Offenders to or from Foreign Countries, this index
Traveling expenses, **28 § 456**
Trial of proceeding or appellate review of proceeding, disqualification, applicability, submission prior to date of Act, **28 § 455**
Unfunded liability, defined,
Bankruptcy judges and Magistrate Judges, retirement, **28 § 377**

JUDGES OR JUSTICES—Cont'd
Unfunded liability, defined—Cont'd
Reduction, Judicial Survivors' Annuities Fund, unfunded liability, **28 § 376**
United States Court of Appeals for the Federal Circuit, this index
United States Court of Federal Claims, this index
United States Court of International Trade, this index
United States Magistrate Judges, generally, this index
United States Tax Court, this index
Vacancy caused by death of disabled judge, not to be filled, **28 § 372**
Veterans,
Officers and employees, preference, **28 § 601 nt**
Wages. Compensation and salaries, generally, ante
Waivers of disqualification, applicability, **28 § 455**
Widow, defined, annuities for survivors, **28 § 376**
Widower, defined, annuities for survivors, **28 § 376**
Widows' and widowers' annuities. Annuities, generally, ante
Witnesses, disqualification, **28 § 455**
Women, selection of qualified individuals for nomination to judgeships, Congressional recommendations, **28 § 133 nt**
Years of service,
Bankruptcy judges or Magistrate Judges, retirement, **28 § 377**
Computation, annuities for survivors, **28 § 376**

JUDGMENTS AND DECREES
Generally, **28 § 1961 et seq.**
Absent defendant, lien enforcement, **28 § 1655**
Affirmance, appellate courts, **28 § 2106**
Appeal and review,
Appeal and Review, generally, this index
Appellate court directing entry, **28 § 2106**
Bankruptcy, this index
Bill of costs included in, **28 § 1920**
Certified Copies, this index
Computation, interest on money judgments, district courts, **28 § 1961**
Court record lost or destroyed, enforcement where U.S. is interested, **28 § 1735**
Declaratory Judgments and Decrees, generally, this index
District courts, **28 § 1961 et seq.**
Absent defendant, lien enforcement, **28 § 1655**
Computation, interest on, **28 § 1961**
Interest, **28 § 1961**

JUDGMENTS AND DECREES—Cont'd
District courts—Cont'd
Payment of judgments against U.S., **28 § 2414**
Rate, calculation, interest, **28 § 1961**
Docketing, lien, **28 § 1962**
Entry, appellate court directing entry, **28 § 2106**
Execution, generally, this index
Federal Debt Collection, this index
Foreign courts or tribunals, payment of final judgments against U.S., exception, **28 § 2414**
Foreign judgments, registration of, **28 § 1963**
Forma pauperis, proceedings in, **28 § 1915**
Forms. Bankruptcy Rules and Forms, generally, this index
Garnishment by U.S. against corporation, **28 § 2405**
Habeas Corpus, generally, this index
Index, lien, **28 § 1962**
Interest, this index
Internal Revenue Service, this index
Judicial Panel on Multidistrict Litigation, generally, this index
Judicial Sales, generally, this index
Lien, enforcement where defendant absent, **28 § 1655**
Judgment, **28 §§ 1962, 1963**
Registration in other district, **28 §§ 1962, 1963**
Motions, action by U.S. against delinquents for public money, **28 § 2407**
Payment,
Attachment against,
Delinquent postmasters and postal officers, employees, ground for discharge on penal bond, **28 § 2717**
Internal Revenue Service officer, certification of certain facts by court, **28 § 2006**
Judgments against U.S., exception, **28 § 2414**
Recognizances, motion for judgment on, docket fees as costs, **28 § 1923**
Recording, lien, **28 § 1962**
Registration, this index
Removal of cases, attachment or sequestration to hold goods or estate of defendant to answer judgment, **28 § 1450**
Retention and control of real property by U.S., actions for quieting title, pending final judgment or decree, **28 § 2409a**
Revenue laws property taken under subject to, **28 § 2463**
Rules of Appellate Procedure, this index
Rules of Civil Procedure, this index
Setting aside, appellate courts, power to set aside judgment, decree, **28 § 2106**

JUDGMENTS AND DECREES—Cont'd
Single judge of three judge court not to enter, **28 § 2284**
States, this index
Subpoena of witness in foreign country, service, **28 § 1783**
Tort claims, against U.S., bar to action against employees, **28 § 2676**
United States, this index
United States Court of Appeals for the Federal Circuit, this index
United States Court of Federal Claims, this index
United States Court of International Trade, this index

JUDICIAL AGENCIES
Appointment of judge as director of certain agency, effect, **28 § 133**
Office of Federal Judicial Administration, defined, effective appointment of judge as director of certain judicial branch agencies, **28 § 133**

JUDICIAL AMENDMENTS ACT OF 1994
Generally, **28 §§ 1 nt, 471 nt, 612**
Administrative Office of United States Courts, generally, this index

JUDICIAL CENTER
Generally, **28 § 620**
Accommodations for, **28 § 604**
Accounting and other fiscal services provided for, **28 § 628**
Administrative Office of U.S. Courts,
Accounting, auditing, and other fiscal services, providing, **28 § 628**
Director,
Accommodations, providing, **28 § 604**
Audit of vouchers and accounts, **28 § 604**
Law books, purchase by, **28 § 604**
Membership on Board of, **28 § 621**
Notice, election by Director of Center respecting retirement coverage, **28 §§ 376, 627**
Payment of retirement annuity to Director of Center, **28 §§ 376, 627**
Purchase of equipment and supplies by, **28 § 604**
Regulation and payment of annuities to widows and dependent children of Director of Center, **28 § 604**
Retroactive effect, retirement and survivorship benefits, **28 § 611 nt**
Salary of Director of Center to be same as, **28 § 626**
Travel and subsistence expenses incurred by officers and employees, regulation and payment, **28 § 604**

JUDICIAL CENTER—Cont'd
Annuities, retirement, Director of, **28 §§ 376, 627**
Appropriations, **28 § 628**
Audit of vouchers and accounts, **28 § 604**
Boards and commissions,
  Chairman,
    Chief Justice of U.S. as, **28 § 621**
    Request of Federal agencies, to furnish information, **28 § 624**
    Special meeting held on call of, **28 § 622**
  Composition, **28 § 621**
  Conduct of business, **28 § 622**
  Congressional committees, informing, **28 § 623**
  Contracts, research projects and other services, **28 § 624**
  Direction of activities, **28 § 623**
  Director of Center, duties concerning, **28 § 624**
  Duties, **28 § 623**
  Expenses and expenditures, reimbursement, **28 § 621**
  Meetings, **28 § 622**
  Policies, establishment, **28 § 623**
  Powers, **28 § 624**
  Programs, development, **28 § 623**
  Quorum, **28 § 622**
  Recommendations, **28 § 623**
  Reelection to, eligibility for, **28 § 621**
  Report, **28 § 623**
  Resignation of member, election for unexpired term caused by, **28 § 621**
  Studies, automatic data processing and systems procedures, **28 § 623**
  Supervision of activities, **28 §§ 621, 623**
  Terms of office of members, **28 § 621**
Clerical and secretarial employees,
  Appointment and compensation, **28 § 625**
  Federal employees' life insurance and health benefits programs, applicability, **28 § 627**
  Retirement and pensions, **28 § 627**
Compensation and salaries,
  Board members, **28 § 621**
  Deputy Director, **28 § 626**
  Director, **28 § 626**
  Government and private agencies for research projects, **28 § 624**
  Professional personnel, **28 § 625**
Deputy Director,
  Appointment, duties, **28 § 624**
  Compensation, **28 § 626**
  Retirement and pensions, employee benefits, **28 § 627**
Director,
  Administrative Office of U.S. Courts, ante
  Annuities,
    Retirement and pensions, **28 §§ 376, 627**

JUDICIAL CENTER—Cont'd
Director—Cont'd
  Annuities—Cont'd
    Retirement and pensions—Cont'd
      Cost of living adjustment, **28 § 627 nt**
    Widows and dependent children, regulation and payment, **28 § 604**
  Appointment and duties, **28 §§ 624, 625**
  Assumption of duties by judge, appointment of additional judge by President, **28 § 133**
  Compensation and salary, **28 § 626**
  Deemed judicial official, for purposes of annuities to widows and dependent children of justices or judges, **28 § 376**
  Delegation of Board's contract authority, **28 § 624**
  Disability, retirement annuity, **28 § 627**
  Election, coming within provisions for annuities to survivors of justices and judges, filing, **28 § 376**
  Federal employees' life insurance and health benefit programs, applicability, **28 § 627**
  Judge or justice as, service without additional compensation, **28 § 626**
  Personal services, procurement, **28 § 625**
  Professional personnel, appointment and fixing compensation, **28 § 625**
  Regulation and payment of annuities to widows and dependent children, **28 § 604**
  Request of Federal agencies, to furnish information, **28 § 624**
  Retirement and pensions, **28 §§ 376, 627**
  Secretarial and clerical personnel, appointment and compensation, **28 § 625**
  Supervision of activities of employed persons, **28 § 625**
  Traveling expenses, **28 § 625**
Equipment and supplies, purchase, **28 § 604**
Federal Foundation, establishment, members, powers, duties, **28 § 629**
Judicial Conference of U.S.,
  Assistance to, **28 § 620**
  Election of members to Board of, **28 § 621**
  Submission by Board of report to, **28 § 623**
Law books, purchase for, **28 § 604**
Office of Federal Judicial Administration,
  Effect of appointment of judge as director of certain judicial branch agencies, **28 § 133**
  Federal Courts Study Committee implementation, **28 § 133**

JUDICIAL CENTER—Cont'd
Officers and employees,
  Traveling and subsistence expense, **28 § 604**
Policies, establishment by Board, **28 § 623**
Professional staff,
  Employment, **28 § 625**
  Federal employees' life insurance and health benefits programs, applicability, **28 § 627**
  Retirement benefits, **28 § 627**
Programs, development by Board, **28 § 623**
Recommendations, **28 §§ 620, 623**
Research, conduct of, **28 § 620**
Service, defined, retirement, Director, professional staff, **28 § 627**
Staff, research and planning assistance provided by, **28 § 620**
Studies, functions respecting, **28 §§ 620, 623**
Subsistence, officers and employees, **28 § 604**
Supervision of, **28 § 621**
Training, court personnel, recommendations by Board, **28 § 623**
Traveling expenses,
  Director, **28 § 625**
  Officers and employees, **28 § 604**
United States Magistrate Judges, generally, this index
Wages. Compensation and salaries, generally, ante
Waiver, director of, coverage under civil service retirement, **28 §§ 376, 627**

JUDICIAL CIRCUITS
Circuit court executives, appointment, powers, duties, **28 § 332**
Civil justice expense and delay reduction plans, generally. District Courts, this index
Compensation, circuit court executives, **28 § 332**
Composition, **28 § 41**
Courts of Appeals, generally, this index
Designation and assignment, district judges to hold district court in any district within the circuit, **28 § 292**
Judicial Council, generally, this index
Number, **28 § 41**
Retired justices or judges, assignment to active duty to another circuit, **28 § 294**
Review, orders, certain Federal agencies, venue, **28 § 2343**

JUDICIAL CONFERENCE (CIRCUIT COURTS OF APPEALS)
Generally, **28 § 333**

JUDICIAL CONFERENCE OF THE UNITED STATES
Generally, **28 § 331**

JUDICIAL CONFERENCE OF THE UNITED STATES—Cont'd
Administrative Office of U.S. Courts, Personnel Management System, 28 **§ 602 nt**
Annuities to survivors of justices and judges, review, determination concerning dependency and disability, **28 § 376**
Bankruptcy, this index
Budget for courts and Administrative Office of U.S. Courts, supervision, 28 **§ 605**
Chief judges of judicial circuits, **28 § 331**
Civil justice expense and delay reduction plans, generally. District Courts, this index
Committees, appointment of, proposed rules of practice, procedure, and evidence, **28 § 2073**
Conference of Senior Circuit Judges known as, **28 § 451 nt**
Court of International Trade, representation, **28 § 331**
Courts of appeals,
Fees prescribed by, **28 § 1913**
Electronic access to court data, exemptions, **28 § 1913 nt**
Schedule, additional fees, **28 § 1913 nt**
Judges or justices,
Attendance and participation, **28 § 333**
Summoning by Chief Justice, **28 § 331**
Judiciary Automation Fund, fees prescribed deposited into, **28 § 1913 nt**
Prescribing fees and costs, **28 § 1913**
Rules of practice, fees for sales of copies, **28 § 2077**
Dependency and disability arising as to annuities, determination, **28 § 376**
Director of Administrative Office of the U.S. Courts,
Certification of court interpreters, **28 § 1827**
Court interpreters, maintaining master list of, **28 § 1827**
Duties under supervision and direction of Conference, **28 § 604**
District courts,
Fees prescribed by, **28 § 1914**
Schedule, additional fees, **28 § 1914 nt**
Regulations, sessions of court and other proceedings, recording by certain methods, **28 §§ 753, 753 nt**
Reporters, determination of number and qualifications, fixing compensation of, **28 § 753**
Reports, **28 § 753**
Institutes and joint councils on sentencing, **28 § 334**

JUDICIAL CONFERENCE OF THE UNITED STATES—Cont'd
Judicial Panel on Multidistrict Litigation, fees and costs, prescription, **28 § 1932**
Juror qualification form, approval, **28 § 1869**
Jury,
Commissioners, standards, allowance of expenses, **28 § 1863**
Selection, one-step summoning and qualification procedure, **28 § 1878**
Law clerks and secretaries of U.S. Court of Federal Claims, appointment, approval of numbers, **28 § 794**
Obsolete papers, rules for disposition, **28 § 457**
Powers and functions in general, **28 § 331**
Pretrial Services, this index
Priority of civil actions, authority to modify rules adopted by courts, **28 § 1657**
Procedure, study of, **28 § 331**
Recommendations by Administrative Conference of U.S., Director, activities of the Administrative Office of the U.S. Courts, **28 § 604**
Reports,
Congress, proposed rules of practice, procedure, and evidence, **28 § 2073**
Jury selection process, specification of form and time, **28 § 1863**
Retired judges or justices, substantial judicial duties, determination, **28 § 371**
Review, orders, certain Federal agencies, rules, approval, savings provision, **28 § 2352 nt**
Rules and regulations,
Appointment of committee to recommend rules of practice, procedure, and evidence, **28 § 2073**
District court, sessions of court and other proceedings, recording by certain methods, **28 §§ 753, 753 nt**
Plan for random jury selection, **28 § 1863**
Review of, consistency with Federal law, **28 § 331**
Secretaries and law clerks of circuit and district judges, salaries,
Fixed by Director of Administrative Office of U.S. Courts, **28 § 604**
Increase, **28 § 603 nt**
Limitation on aggregate amount, **28 § 604 nt**
Study of court procedure, **28 § 331**
Transportation and subsistence expenses for judges, regulations prescribed with approval of, **28 § 456**
United States Court of Appeals for Veterans Claims, generally, this index

JUDICIAL CONFERENCE OF THE UNITED STATES—Cont'd
United States Magistrate Judges,
Approval, rules and regulation, **28 § 604**
Determination and payment of expenses and compensation of, **28 § 635**
Compensation, fixing, **28 § 634**
Compilation and evaluation of statistical and other information required for performance of duties of respecting, **28 § 604**
Conference, defined, **28 § 639**
Determination respecting number of full-time and part-time Magistrate Judges and locations of service, **28 § 633**
Seal, form prescribed by, **28 § 638**
Selection of Magistrate Judges pursuant to standards of, **28 § 631**
Exercise of civil jurisdiction in district court dependent on certification or reappointment under, **28 § 631 nt**
Service and locations determined by, **28 § 631**
United States Sentencing Commission. Sentence and Punishment, this index

JUDICIAL COUNCIL
Generally, **28 § 332**
Accommodations for courts, provision by Director of Administrative Office U.S. Courts, approval, **28 § 462**
Bankruptcy, this index
Carrying orders into effect, district judges, **28 § 332**
Chief judge of each circuit, calling, **28 § 332**
Circuit court executives, appointment, **28 § 332**
Circuit judges in regular active service, **28 § 332**
Civil justice expense and delay reduction plans, generally. District Courts, this index
Consent,
Designation and assignment of judge, **28 § 295**
Pretermitting session of district court, **28 § 140**
District courts,
Additional reporters needed, determination, **28 § 753**
Pretermit session of court, consent to, **28 § 140**
Judges,
Failing to retire when eligible, signing certificate of disability, **28 § 372**
Judicial discipline, complaint procedure, **28 § 372**
To carry into effect orders of, **28 § 332**
Jurors,
Plan for random selection, duties as part of reviewing panel, **28 § 1863**

JUDICIAL COUNCIL—Cont'd
Jurors—Cont'd
Service, names of persons excluded from, **28 § 1866**
Orders,
Administration of business of courts within circuit, **28 § 332**
Division of business among district judges, **28 § 137**
Pretrial Services, generally, this index
Records of court, designation of place for keeping, **28 § 457**
Reports, submission to and by, **28 § 332**
Residence requirement for district judges, **28 § 134**
Retired judge, designation and assignment for duty within circuit, **28 § 294**
United States Magistrate Judges,
Council, defined, **28 § 639**
Removal on concurrence of judges of, **28 § 631**
Reports to, recommendations concerning number of full-time and part-time Magistrate Judges, locations and compensation, **28 § 633**

JUDICIAL DISTRICTS
Bankruptcy, this index
Civil justice expense and delay reduction plans, generally. District Courts, this index
District Courts, this index
Division,
Defined, Jury Selection and Service Act, **28 § 1869**
Separate random plan for selection of jurors, refilling master jury wheel not later than certain date, **28 § 1863 nt**
Illinois, this index
Jury wheel, refilling master jury wheel not later than specified date, **28 § 1863 nt**
Multidistrict litigation, **28 § 1407**
Place of trial. Venue or District of Trial, generally, this index

JUDICIAL NOTICE
Seals (official seals),
Director of Administrative Office of U.S. Courts, **28 § 608**

JUDICIAL OFFICIAL
Defined, judges or justices, annuities for survivors, **28 § 376**
Judges or Justices, generally, this index

JUDICIAL PANEL ON MULTIDISTRICT LITIGATION
Generally, **28 § 1407**
Actions by State Attorneys General as parens patriae, monopolies and combinations, consolidation and transfer for pretrial purposes or for trial, **28 § 1407**

JUDICIAL PANEL ON MULTIDISTRICT LITIGATION—Cont'd
Antitrust laws, defined, pretrial proceedings, consolidation and transfer, actions under, **28 § 1407**
Briefs. Rules, post
Clerk. Rules, post
Composition, **28 § 1407**
Costs. Fees and costs, generally, post
Fees and costs, prescription, **28 § 1932**
Judges, assignment to coordinated or consolidated pretrial proceedings, **28 § 1407**
Judicial Conference of the U.S., fees and costs, prescription, **28 § 1932**
Motions, proceedings for transfer of action for coordinated, pretrial proceedings, **28 § 1407**
Notice,
Actions contemplated for transfer for coordinated, pretrial proceedings, **28 § 1407**
Rules, post
Orders, transfer of actions for coordinated, pretrial proceedings, **28 § 1407**
Petitions, extraordinary writ, review, orders of, **28 § 1407**
Process. Rules, post
Remand,
Rules, post
Transferred actions to original district, **28 § 1407**
Review, orders of, petitions for extraordinary writ, **28 § 1407**
Rules,
Accompaniments to notice, **MDL 25.2**
Admission to practice, attorneys, **MDL 1.4**
Affidavits, **MDL 7.6**
Appeal and review, **MDL 1.6**
Applications, extension of time, **MDL 6.2**
Attorneys, representation in transferred actions, **MDL 1.4**
Averments, **MDL 7.1**
Briefs, **MDL 7.1**
Matters submitted on briefs, **MDL 16.2**
Motions, **MDL 7.2**
Remand of cases, **MDL 7.6**
Chairman, defined, **MDL 1.1**
Clerk,
Defined, **MDL 1.1**
Filing,
Manner, **MDL 5.12**
Place, **MDL 5.11**
Motion practice, **MDL 7.2**
Multi-circuit petitions for review, notice, **MDL 25.1 et seq.**
Records and files, retention, **MDL 5.1**
Refusal to file papers, noncompliance with rules, **MDL 1.3**
Service of filed papers, **MDL 5.2**
Tag-along actions, **MDL 7.4**
Transfer of files, **MDL 1.6**

JUDICIAL PANEL ON MULTIDISTRICT LITIGATION—Cont'd
Rules—Cont'd
Conditional orders,
Remand orders, **MDL 7.6**
Transfer orders, tag-along actions, **MDL 5.2, 7.4, 7.5**
Copies and duplicates, **MDL 5.12, 25.1 et seq.**
Counterclaims, **MDL 1.6, 7.6**
Cross-claims, **MDL 1.6, 7.6**
Definitions, **MDL 1.1**
Dismissal, **MDL 7.6**
Extension of time, **MDL 5.12, 5.2, 6.2**
Federal records center, **MDL 5.1**
Fees, duplicating records and files, **MDL 5.1**
Forms,
Notice, **MDL 25.4**
Papers filed, **MDL 7.1**
Government Services Administraton, authority to dispose of records, **MDL 5.1**
Hearings, **MDL 16.1**
Joinder of actions, **MDL 7.2**
Judicial review, **MDL 1.6**
Mail and mailing, papers to clerk, **MDL 5.11**
Motions, **MDL 5.12 et seq.**
Remand, **MDL 7.6**
Multi-circuit petitions for review, notices, **MDL 25.1 et seq.**
Noncompliance with rules, **MDL 1.3**
Notice,
Manner of filing papers, **MDL 5.12**
Motion practice, **MDL 7.2**
Multi-circuit petitions for review, **MDL 25.1 et seq.**
Oral argument, presentation and waiver, **MDL 5.12, 16.2**
Show cause orders, **MDL 7.3**
Tag-along actions, **MDL 7.4**
Transfer of files, **MDL 1.6**
Oral argument, **MDL 5.12, 16.1, 16.2**
Panels, defined, **MDL 1.1**
Pendency of actions, **MDL 1.5**
Tag-along actions, **MDL 7.4**
Petitions for review,
Multicircuit, **MDL 17.1 et seq.**
Notices, **MDL 25.1 et seq.**
Place,
Filing of papers, **MDL 5.11**
Keeping records and files, **MDL 5.1**
Pleadings, **MDL 7.1**
Motion practice, **MDL 7.2**
Practice of panel, **MDL 1.2**
Prescribing, **28 § 1407**
Process, **MDL 5.12, 5.2**
Notices, **MDL 25.3**
Panel consolidation orders, **MDL 25.5**
Proof of service, **MDL 5.2, 25.3**
Tag-along actions, **MDL 7.5**
Questions of fact, **MDL 7.5**
Random selection, multi-circuit petition for review, **MDL 17.1**

JUDICIAL PANEL ON MULTIDISTRICT LITIGATION—Cont'd
Rules—Cont'd
Remand, **MDL 7.6, 16.1**
Tag-along actions, **MDL 7.5**
Transfer of files, **MDL 1.6**
Responsive pleadings, **MDL 7.1, 7.2**
Review and appeal, **MDL 1.6**
Selection of court of appeals, **MDL 17.1**
Show cause orders, **MDL 7.3, 7.6**
Stipulations, **MDL 7.6**
Summary judgment, **MDL 7.6**
Tag-along actions, **MDL 7.5, 16.1**
Conditional transfer orders, **MDL 7.4**
Defined, **MDL 1.1**
Termination of actions, **MDL 7.6**
Third-party claims, **MDL 1.6, 7.6**
Time,
Extension of time, **MDL 5.12, 5.2, 6.2**
Manner of filing papers, **MDL 5.12**
Motion practice, **MDL 7.2**
Service of papers filed, **MDL 5.2**
Show cause orders, **MDL 7.3**
Tag-along actions, **MDL 7.4**
Transfers,
Actions, **MDL 1.4, 5.2**
Records and files, **MDL 1.6, 5.1**
Vacation of orders, **MDL 7.4**
Waiver, oral argument, **MDL 5.12, 16.2**
Words and phrases, **MDL 1.1**
Separation of claims, cross-claims, before remand of action, **28 § 1407**
Tag-along actions. Rules, ante
Time. Rules, ante
Transfer of civil actions for coordinated or consolidated pretrial proceedings, **28 § 1407**

JUDICIAL PROCEDURE
Judiciary and Judicial Procedure, generally, this index

JUDICIAL REVIEW
Appeal and Review, generally, this index

JUDICIAL SALES
Generally, **28 § 2001 et seq.**
Appraisal of goods taken on execution, **28 § 2005**
Bids, actions affecting property on which U.S. has lien, credit amount determined due against amount bid, **28 § 2410**
Bona fide offer exceeding private sale price, **28 § 2001**
Goods, taken on execution, appraisal before sale, **28 § 2005**
Notice of sale of realty, **28 §§ 2001, 2002**
Partition actions involving U.S., **28 § 2409**
Personalty, **28 § 2004**
Place of sale of realty, **28 § 2001**
Private sale of realty, **28 § 2001**

JUDICIAL SALES—Cont'd
Publication of notice of sale of realty, **28 §§ 2001, 2002**
Realty, **28 § 2001 et seq.**
Separate parcels, **28 § 2001**
Terms and conditions, **28 § 2001**
United States having lien on property, **28 § 2410**
United States marshal,
Fees, **28 § 1921**
Incapacity after levy on or sale of real estate, **28 § 2003**
Summoning appraisers of goods taken under execution, **28 § 2005**

JUDICIAL SURVIVORS ANNUITY FUND
Generally, **28 §§ 376, 376 nt**
Examination of, **28 § 605**

JUDICIARY AND JUDICIAL PROCEDURE
Generally, **28 § 1 et seq.**
Bankruptcy complete filing fees, disposition, **28 § 1931 nt**
Fees, disposition, **28 § 1931 nt**
Separability of provisions, Title 28, Judiciary and Judicial Procedure, **28 nt prec § 1**

JUDICIARY COMMITTEE
Congressional Committees, this index

JURATS
United States Magistrate Judges, seal affixed without fee, **28 § 638**

JURISDICTION
Admiralty cases,
District court, **28 § 1333**
Alaska, this index
Ambassadors, Supreme Court, **28 § 1251**
Amendment of pleadings to show, **28 § 1653**
Antitrust, laws, preventing and restraining violations, regulations, district courts, **28 § 1337**
Bankruptcy, this index
Certificates, district court's jurisdiction, interpleader, **28 § 1335**
Civil action, removal, **28 § 1441**
Civil Rights, this index
Commerce regulations, district court, carrier cases, amount in controversy, **28 § 1337**
Constitution of United States,
District courts, **28 § 1331**
Civil rights, **28 § 1343**
Claim against U.S., **28 § 1346**
Civil actions by Indian bands or tribes, **28 § 1362**
Courts of Appeals, this index
Customs duties, district courts, **28 § 1340**
District Courts, this index
District of Columbia, this index
Diverse citizenship. District Courts, this index

JURISDICTION—Cont'd
Foreign ministers, Supreme Court, **28 § 1251**
Indian Lands and Reservations, this index
Indians, this index
Interpleader proceedings, **28 § 1335**
Maritime cases, **28 § 1333**
Mask work cases, semiconductor chip products, **28 § 1338**
Monopolies, **28 § 1337**
Parental Kidnapping Prevention, this index
Patent cases, **28 § 1338**
Plant Variety Protection, this index
Postal matters, **28 § 1339**
Removal, civil action, **28 § 1441**
Restraints of trade, **28 § 1337**
Reversal in Supreme Court or a court of appeals for matters in abatement not involving jurisdiction, **28 § 2105**
Rules of Civil Procedure, this index
Set-Off and Counterclaim, this index
States, this index
Supplemental jurisdiction, generally. District Courts, this index
Taxes by States, **28 § 1341**
Terrorists and Terrorism, this index
Trade-marks, **28 § 1338**
Unfair competition, **28 § 1338**
United States Court of Appeals for the Federal Circuit, this index
United States Court of Federal Claims, this index
United States Court of International Trade, this index
United States District Court for District of Columbia, this index
Venue or District of Trial, generally, this index
Want of jurisdiction, transfer to cure, **28 § 1631**

JUROR QUALIFICATION FORM
Grand Jury, this index
Jury, this index

JURY
Generally, **28 § 1861 et seq.**
Additional,
Attendance fee, certification, time for payment, **28 § 1871**
Peremptory challenges, separate or joint, **28 § 1870**
Admiralty cases, **28 § 1873**
Adverse affect upon deliberations, exclusion from service, **28 § 1866**
Affidavits, service of summons for jury service by registered, certified, or first-class mail, **28 § 1866**
Age requirement for service, **28 § 1865**
Alphabetical list, names drawn from master jury wheel, **28 § 1864**
Entry, determination, qualifications for service, **28 § 1865**
Appropriations, available for refreshment of jurors, **28 § 1871 nt**

JURY—Cont'd
Assignment of,
Names to panels, **28 § 1866**
Persons drawn, **28 § 1863**
Attachment against delinquent postmasters and postal officers, employees, trial of ownership of property, **28 § 2713**
Attendance fees, time for payment, **28 § 1871**
Attorneys' fees, award, protection of jurors' employment, **28 § 1875**
Bailiffs,
Appropriations, meals and lodging, **28 § 524**
Employment to wait upon, **28 § 755**
Bankruptcy, this index
Certificates, payment of fees, travel and subsistence allowances, **28 § 1871**
Challenges, **28 § 1870**
Good cause shown, exclusion from service, **28 § 1866**
Selection procedures, **28 § 1867**
Chief judge of district court, duties, **28 § 1863 et seq.**
Citizenship requirement for service, **28 § 1865**
Civil penalty, discharge of employee for jury service, **28 § 1875**
Civil Rights, this index
Clerk of district court,
Certificate of attendance for payment of fees, **28 § 1871**
Duties, **28 § 1863 et seq.**
Commission. Jury Commission, generally, this index
Composition, affecting composition on or before refilled compliance of master jury wheel, **28 § 1863 nt**
Conditions, ineligibility for service, **28 § 1865**
Court, defined, **28 § 1869**
Criminal charge, pending or conviction, freedom from, requirement for service, **28 § 1865**
Declaration of policy, **28 § 1861**
Definitions, **28 § 1869**
Deputy clerks of district courts, summons for jury service, duties concerning, **28 § 1866**
Disclosure, names drawn,
From master jury wheel, **28 § 1864**
Time, **28 § 1863**
Discrimination,
Prohibited, **28 § 1862**
Selection of persons for service prohibited, remedies, **28 § 1867**
Dismissal of indictment, noncompliance with selection procedures, **28 § 1867**
Disqualification from service, **28 §§ 1863, 1865, 1866**
Disruption of proceedings, exclusion from service, **28 § 1866**
District court of the United States, defined, **28 § 1869**

JURY—Cont'd
District courts,
Contiguous 48 States, jurors serving outside of, amount, subsistence allowance, **28 § 1871**
Defined, **28 § 1869**
Division, defined, **28 § 1869**
Drawing, names from master jury wheel, **28 §§ 1864, 1866**
Effective date, plan for random selection, **28 § 1863**
Evidence,
Challenging compliance with selection procedures, **28 § 1867**
Qualifications for service, **28 § 1865**
Examination, plan for random selection, **28 § 1863**
Exclusion or excuse from service, **28 §§ 1863, 1865, 1866**
Juror qualification form, contents, **28 § 1869**
Prohibition on account of race, color, religion, **28 § 1862**
Exemption from service, **28 §§ 1863, 1866**
Determination, **28 § 1865**
Juror qualification form, contents, **28 § 1869**
Fees, **28 § 1871**
Mileage fees under summons as both witness and juror, **28 § 1824**
Qualification form, completion, **28 § 1864**
Ferries, payment of toll charges, **28 § 1871**
Fines, penalties and forfeitures,
Disclosure, records or papers, violations, **28 § 1867**
Failure to appear pursuant to summons to complete qualification form, **28 § 1864**
Jury trial in action to recover, **28 § 1874**
Noncompliance with summons for service, **28 § 1866**
Willful misrepresentation of facts on qualification form, **28 § 1864**
First-class mail, service of summons for jury service, **28 § 1866**
Grand Jury, generally, this index
Grounds for excuse or exemption from service, **28 § 1863**
Groups of persons or occupational classes excused or exempt from service, **28 § 1863**
Impartial service, inability to render, exclusion from service, **28 § 1866**
Imprisonment. Sentence and punishment, generally, post
Inspection of records and papers, **28 § 1868**
Interim travel allowances to jurors, establishment by Director of Administrative Office of the United States Courts, **28 § 1871**

JURY—Cont'd
Internal Revenue Service taxes, recovery of taxes erroneously paid, **28 § 2402**
Jurisdiction, district court, compelling availability of voter registration lists and records, **28 § 1863**
Juror qualification form,
Completion, **28 § 1864**
Contents, **28 § 1869**
Defined, **28 § 1869**
Entry, determination of qualifications, **28 § 1865**
Information, determination of qualifications, **28 § 1865**
Reasons for exclusion from service, notations on, **28 § 1866**
Jury summons, defined, **28 § 1869**
Jury wheel,
Defined, **28 § 1869**
Master jury wheel, generally, post
Limitation, number of persons excluded from service, **28 § 1866**
Lists,
Actual voters, defined, **28 § 1869**
Drawn from master jury wheels, **28 § 1864**
Names assigned to panels, **28 § 1866**
Voter registration lists and records, generally, post
Literacy requirement for service, **28 § 1865**
Mail,
Qualification form, **28 § 1864**
Service of summons for jury service, **28 § 1866**
Maintenance of records and papers, **28 § 1868**
Managers of property, suit against them without leave of court appointing them, **28 § 959**
Maritime cases, **28 § 1873**
Master jury wheel,
Determination, proportional representation in, **28 § 1863**
Drawing of names from, **28 § 1864**
Emptying and refilling, not exceeding four year interval, **28 § 1863**
Nondisclosure, records or papers, until after emptying and refilling, **28 § 1867**
Providing for and placing names in, **28 § 1863**
Meals and lodging,
Refreshment of jurors, **28 § 1871 nt**
Subsistence allowance, itemization not required, **28 § 1871**
Mental or physical capacity requirement for service, **28 § 1865**
Mileage, fees, summons as both witness and juror, **28 § 1871**
Modification, plan for random selection, **28 § 1863**
Motions, challenging compliance with selection procedures, **28 § 1867**
Names, juror qualification form, contents concerning, **28 § 1869**

JURY—Cont'd
Nondisclosure, records or papers, selection process, 28 § **1867**
Notice,
Adoption or modification of plan for random selection, 28 § **1863**
Obligation for service on, declaration of policy, 28 § **1861**
Officers and Employees of Government, this index
One-step summoning and qualification procedure, 28 § **1878**
Opportunity for service on, declaration of policy, 28 § **1861**
Order of district court,
Appearance upon failure to appear after being summoned, 28 § **1866**
Failure to appear pursuant to summons to complete qualification form, penalties, 28 § **1864**
Original jurisdiction of district courts, jurors' employment rights, 28 § **1363**
Overnight stay, subsistence allowance paid to juror, 28 § **1871**
Parking fees, payment to juror, presentation of valid parking receipt, 28 § **1871**
Penalties. Fines, penalties and forfeitures, generally, ante
Peremptory challenges, 28 § **1870**
Exclusion from service, 28 § **1866**
Period of service, 28 § **1866**
Preservation of records and papers, 28 § **1868**
Procedure for selection of names, 28 § **1863**
Prohibition, payment, fees for interim or daily travel exceeding subsistence allowance, 28 § **1871**
Protection of jurors' employment, 28 § **1875**
Public officer, defined, 28 § **1869**
Publicly draw, defined, 28 § **1869**
Punishment. Sentence and punishment, generally, post
Qualifications for service, 28 § **1865**
Qualified jury wheel, drawing names from, assignment to panels, 28 § **1866**
Random drawing of names from master jury wheel, 28 §§ **1864, 1866**
Random selection,
Challenging compliance with procedures, 28 § **1867**
Declaration of policy, 28 § **1861**
Plan for, 28 § **1863**
Refilling master jury wheel not later than certain specified date, 28 § **1863 nt**
Receivers and receivership, jury trial in suit against receivers without leave of court, 28 § **959**
Records and recordation,
Maintenance and inspection, 28 § **1868**
Nondisclosure, 28 § **1867**

JURY—Cont'd
Records and recordation—Cont'd
Selection,
Procedures, evidence in challenging compliance with, 28 § **1867**
Process, nondisclosure, 28 § **1867**
Voter registration lists and records, generally, post
Registered, certified, or first-class mail, service of summons for jury service, 28 § **1866**
Reinstatement of employee, discharge by employer for employee's jury service, 28 § **1875**
Release, generally, this index
Reports, selection process, 28 § **1863**
Residence requirement for service, 28 § **1865**
Restoration of civil rights, qualifications for service, 28 § **1865**
Return, qualification form, error, 28 § **1864**
Reviewing panel, plan for random selection, approval, 28 § **1863**
Rules of Civil Procedure, this index
Rules of Evidence, this index
Secrecy of proceedings threatened, exclusion from service, 28 § **1866**
Selection,
Challenging compliance with procedures, 28 § **1867**
Panels, 28 § **1866**
Random selection, generally, ante
Sentence and punishment,
Disclosure, records or papers, violations, 28 § **1867**
Failure to appear pursuant to summons to complete qualification form, 28 § **1864**
Juror qualification form, contents concerning, 28 § **1869**
Noncompliance with summons for service, 28 § **1866**
Willful misrepresentation of facts on qualification form, 28 § **1864**
Separation of jurors, orders, payment, actual cost of subsistence, 28 § **1871**
Sequestration of jurors, orders, payment, actual cost of subsistence, 28 § **1871**
Service,
Minimum age qualification, 28 § **1865**
Precluding service of impanelled jury on or before refilled compliance of master jury wheel, 28 § **1863 nt**
Summons for jury service, 28 § **1866**
Sources of names for selection, specification in plan, 28 § **1863**
Stay of proceedings, noncompliance with selection procedures, 28 § **1867**
Subsistence allowance, 28 § **1871**
Summons,
Failure to return completed qualification form, 28 § **1864**
Panels, 28 § **1866**
Preservation, records and papers, 28 § **1868**

JURY—Cont'd
Summons—Cont'd
Qualification procedure, one-step system, implementation, 28 § **1878**
Supreme Court, original actions at law, 28 § **1872**
Time challenging compliance with selection procedures, 28 § **1867**
Tolls for roads, tunnels and bridges, fees, 28 § **1871**
Transmittal of plan for random selection, time, 28 § **1863**
Travel allowance for jurors, minimum rate established by Director of Administrative Office of the U.S. Courts, 28 § **1871**
Travel expenses,
Air travel, reimbursement, certain cases, 28 § **1871**
Qualification form, completion, 28 § **1864**
Summons in area outside contiguous 48 States, 28 § **1871**
Trustees, jury trial in suit against without leave of court appointing them, 28 § **959**
Undue hardship or extreme inconvenience, defined, 28 § **1869**
United States, jury trial in actions against, 28 § **2402**
United States Court of International Trade, this index
United States Marshals Service, this index
Volunteer safety personnel, defined, exemption from duty, 28 § **1863**
Voter registration lists and records,
Availability for inspection, 28 § **1863**
Defined, 28 § **1869**
Random selection where shortage, 28 § **1866**
Waiver, attachment against delinquent postmasters and postal officers, employees, jury trial of ownership of property, 28 § **2713**
Wheels. Jury wheel, generally, ante

JURY COMMISSION
Generally, 28 § **1863**
Alphabetical list, names drawn from master jury wheel, preparation, 28 § **1864**
Appointment of members, 28 § **1863**
Challenging compliance with selection procedures, nondisclosure, papers or records, 28 § **1867**
Compensation and expenses, 28 § **1863**
Deputies, summons for jury service duties concerning, 28 § **1866**
Domicile and residence, 28 § **1863**
Jury,
Panels, duties concerning, 28 § **1866**
Qualification form, duties concerning, 28 § **1864**
Plan for random jury selection, duties, 28 § **1863**

JURY COMMISSION—Cont'd
Qualified jury wheel, maintenance, **28 § 1866**
Recommendations, qualifications for jury service, **28 § 1865**
Records and papers, preservation and availability for public inspection, **28 § 1868**
Reimbursement, Commissioner, expenses, **28 § 1863**

JURY SELECTION AND SERVICE ACT OF 1968
Generally, **28 § 1861 et seq.**

JUSTICE DEPARTMENT
See, also, Executive Departments, generally, this index
Generally, **28 § 501 et seq.**
Accounts,
Transfers from, **28 § 524 nt**
Activities, authorization, effect on authorization of appropriations, **28 § 501 nt**
Administrative expenses, appropriations, **28 § 524**
Agencies or agency,
Delegation,
Attorney General's authority, **28 § 510**
Functions vested in Attorney General, **28 § 509**
Appropriations,
Administrative expenses, **28 § 524**
Allocation of funds, **28 § 524 nt**
Authorization for Department and subdivisions thereof, **28 § 501 nt**
Drugs and medicine, civil enforcement enhancement, authorization, **28 § 509 nt**
Fact witness fees, incarcerated persons, payment, prohibition, **28 § 1821 nt**
Travel and health care expenses, personnel serving abroad, authorization, **28 § 530A**
Assets Forfeiture Fund, **28 § 524**
Appropriations, **28 § 524**
Availability of, **28 § 524**
Deposits in, **28 § 524**
Transfer to Buildings and Facilities account of Federal Prison System, use, **28 § 524 nt**
Excess unobligated balance, defined, appropriations, **28 § 524**
Payment of awards for information or assistance leading to forfeiture, **28 § 524**
Attorney General, generally, this index
Attorneys, ethics, **28 § 530B**
Authorization of appropriations, **28 § 501 nt**
Awards for information or assistance leading to forfeiture, **28 § 524**

JUSTICE DEPARTMENT—Cont'd
Civil debt collection litigation activities, amounts collected pursuant to, credit as offsetting collection to working capital fund, **28 § 527 nt**
Civil justice reform, **28 § 519 nt, EON 12988**
Conduct of litigation reserved to, **28 § 516**
Conflict of interest,
Disqualification of officers and employees in case of, penalty for violation, **28 § 528**
Violations of Federal criminal law by Department personnel relating to, reports to Congress, **28 § 529**
Correctional, activities, Assets Forfeiture Fund, **28 § 524**
Counterterrorism Fund, establishment, provisions, **28 § 524 nt**
Criminal division,
United States Sentencing Commission, consultation with on sentencing guidelines, **28 § 994**
Definitions,
Attorney for the government, ethics, **28 § 530B**
Designation as executive department, **28 § 501**
Disbursing Officials, Clerks, and Agents, generally, this index
Disqualification of officers and employees in case of conflict of interest, penalty for violation, **28 § 528**
Drug Enforcement Administration, generally, this index
Drugs and medicine, civil enforcement enhancement, **28 § 509 nt**
Elections, violations of Federal criminal law by Department personnel relating to, report to Congress, **28 § 529**
Employees. Personnel, generally, post
Enforcement,
Related activities, Assets Forfeiture Fund, **28 § 524**
Ethics, attorneys, **28 § 530B**
Executive Office of United States Attorneys. United States Attorneys, generally, this index
Federal agencies, participation in Assets Forfeiture Fund, equipping, procuring, forfeited vehicles, for use by and awards to, **28 § 524**
Federal equitable share of forfeited property under State, local or foreign law, deposit in Assets Forfeiture Fund, **28 § 524**
Federally insured financial institutions, fraud, criminal or unlawful activity, investigation and prosecution of, **28 § 509 nt**
Forfeited vessels, retention, use by DEA or other Federal agencies, appropriations for equipping, **28 § 524**
Funds,
Assets Forfeiture Fund, generally, ante

JUSTICE DEPARTMENT—Cont'd
Funds—Cont'd
Working capital funds, generally, post
Gifts, bequests and devises, acceptance, use, Attorney General, **28 § 524**
Head of. Attorney General, generally, this index
Health care expenses, personnel serving abroad, authorization of appropriations, **28 § 530A**
Immigration and Naturalization Service,
Immigration and Naturalization Service, generally, this index
Naturalization, generally, this index
Independent Counsel, this index
Institutes and joint councils on sentencing, attendance by Department officials, **28 § 334**
Investigations, official matters, appointment, officials, **28 § 533**
Litigation,
Civil justice reform, **28 § 519 nt, EON 12988**
Expenses less than certain amounts related to, availability of appropriations, **28 § 524**
Reimbursement, salaries and expenses, **28 § 509 nt**
Lobbying, violations of Federal criminal law by Department personnel relating to, report to Congress, **28 § 529**
Marshals. United States Marshals Service, generally, this index
Meals and lodging for bailiffs, appropriations, **28 § 524**
Money, gifts, devises, and bequests, acceptance, use, **28 § 524**
National Crime Information Center, generally, this index
Notarial fees, appropriations, **28 § 524**
Office for Victims of Crime,
Victim Compensation and Assistance, generally, this index
Officers and employees. Personnel, generally, post
Payment, travel and transportation expenses of newly appointed special agents, authorization of Attorney General or designee, **28 § 530**.
Personnel,
Conduct of litigation reserved to officers, **28 § 516**
Delegation of,
Attorney General's authority, **28 § 510**
Disqualification in case of conflict of interest, penalty for violation, **28 § 528**
Functions vested in Attorney General, **28 § 509**
Interests of U.S. in pending suits, attending to, **28 § 517**
Legal proceedings, conducting, authority, **28 § 515**
Reimbursement, certain travel expenses, **28 § 509 nt**

JUSTICE DEPARTMENT—Cont'd
Personnel—Cont'd
Report by Public Integrity Section on violations of Federal criminal law by, **28 § 529**
Service abroad, travel and health care expenses, authorization of appropriations, **28 § 530A**
Special agents, travel and transportation expenses of new appointees, authorization of Attorney General or designee to pay, **28 § 530**
United States courts, conduct and argument of cases in, **28 § 518**
President, appointment, Solicitor General, **28 § 505**
Property taxes, State, local, Assets Forfeiture Fund, availability, **28 § 524**
Public Integrity Section, report to Congress on activities of, **28 § 529**
Removal from office, violation of conflict of interest rules, penalty, **28 § 528**
Refusal to enforce or defend certain provisions of law believed unconstitutional, **28 § 519 nt**
Reports,
Banking law offenses, **28 § 522 nt**
Business and statistics, **28 § 522**
Congressional committees, charging and plea practices of Federal prosecutors, money laundering offenses, **28 § 994 nt**
Drugs and medicine, civil enforcement enhancement, **28 § 509 nt**
United States Sentencing Commission, operation of sentencing guidelines system, problems, **28 § 994 nt**
Requisitions, advance or payment of moneys, **28 § 523**
Rules and regulations, disqualification of officers and employees in case of conflict of interest, penalty for violation, **28 § 528**
Seal, **28 § 502**
Seat of Government, location, **28 § 501**
Solicitor General,
Appointment and duties, **28 § 505**
Conduct and argument of cases, **28 § 518**
Filling vacancy in office of Attorney General, order of succession, **28 § 508**
Interests of U.S. in pending suits, attending to, **28 § 517**
United States courts, conduct and argument of cases in, **28 § 518**
Special agents, payment of travel and transportation expenses of new appointees, authorization of Attorney General, **28 § 530**
Stenographic services, appropriations, **28 § 524**
Subdivisions,
Creation, effect on authorization of appropriations, **28 § 501 nt**

JUSTICE DEPARTMENT—Cont'd
Travel and transportation expenses,
Newly appointed special agents, authorization of Attorney General or designee to pay, **28 § 530**
Personnel serving abroad, authorization of appropriations, **28 § 530A**
Undercover operations, financial audit, reports, **28 § 533 nt**
United States Court of Federal Claims, generally, this index
United States Marshals Service, generally, this index
Violation of Controlled Substances Act or Controlled Substances Import and Export Act, purchase of evidence, appropriations, **28 § 524**
Witnesses,
Fact witness fee, incarcerated persons, payment, prohibition, **28 § 1821 nt**
Services, procurement without regard to competitive procurement procedures, **28 § 509 nt**
Working capital funds, **28 § 527**
Credit as offsetting collection, civil debt collection litigation activities, amounts collected pursuant to, **28 § 527 nt**
Retention of income in, limitation, uses, **28 § 527 nt**
Transfer, unobligated balances of appropriations to, **28 § 527 nt**

JUSTICES
Judges or Justices, generally, this index

JUVENILE DELINQUENTS AND DEPENDENTS
United States Sentencing Commission, study, guidelines relating to, **28 § 995**

KANSAS
See, also, States, generally, this index
Bankruptcy judges, appointment, number in judicial district, **28 § 152**
District court,
Cities, held at, **28 § 96**
Judges,
Additional, **28 § 133 nt**
First appointee, residence, **28 § 133 nt**
Number, **28 § 133**
Temporary judgeships, **28 § 133 nt**
Places of holding, **28 § 96**
Judicial circuit of U.S., **28 § 41**
Judicial district, **28 § 96**
Number of district judges, **28 § 133**
States, generally, this index
United States trustees of judicial districts, appointment, **28 § 581**

KEEPER OF THE GREAT SEAL
Certificate to records or books of State, territory or possession for use as evidence, **28 § 1739**

KENTUCKY
See, also, States, generally, this index
Bankruptcy judges, appointment, number in judicial district, **28 § 152**
District court,
Cities, held at, **28 § 97**
Judges,
Additional, **28 § 133 nt**
Number, **28 § 133**
Places of holding, **28 § 97**
Judicial circuit of U.S., **28 § 41**
Judicial districts,
Bankruptcy provisions, applicability of certain amendments to, **28 § 581 nt**
Number of district judges, **28 § 133**
States, generally, this index
United States trustees of judicial districts, appointment, **28 § 581**

KIDNAPPING
Child Abduction and Serial Murder Investigative Resources Center, **28 § 531 nt**
Missing Children, generally, this index
Morgan P. Hardiman Child Abduction and Serial Murder Investigative Resources Center, **28 § 531 nt**
Parental Kidnapping Prevention, generally, this index

KINGMAN REEF
Judicial district of Hawaii, inclusion in, **28 § 91**

LABOR AND EMPLOYMENT
Civil Service, generally, this index
Compensation and Salaries, generally, this index
Employee's jury service, protection of, **28 § 1875**
Equal employment opportunity, generally. Civil Rights, this index
Government officers and employees, restrictions on, **5, Ap 4, § 501 et seq.**
Hours of Labor, generally, this index
International Trade, generally, this index
Labor Department, generally, this index
Labor Disputes, generally, this index
Secretary of Labor, generally, this index
Workers Compensation, generally, this index

LABOR DEPARTMENT
See, also, Executive Departments, generally, this index
Community development, neighborhood revitalization plan, development by Attorney General, use of appropriated funds, **28 § 509 nt**
Secretary of Labor, generally, this index

LABOR DISPUTES
Boards and commissions,
Chairman,
Federal Legal Council, representatives designated by, **28 § 509 nt, EON 12146**
Collective bargaining,
Copyrights, agreements, motion pictures, transfer of ownership, **28 § 4001**
Contracts,
Between labor organization and employer in construction industry, **28 § 158**
Personnel Management, Office of, generally, this index

LABOR SECRETARY
Secretary of Labor, generally, this index

LABORATORIES
United States Court of International Trade, ordering analysis of imported merchandise and reports from, **28 § 2642**

LABORERS
Hours of Labor, generally, this index

LACHES
Congressional reference cases, hearing officer, determinations concerning, **28 § 2509**

LAND BANKS
Federal Land Banks, generally, this index

LAND GRANTS
Different States, district court, jurisdiction of actions between citizens claiming lands, **28 § 1354**

LAND TITLES
Title to Property, generally, this index

LANDS
Eminent Domain, generally, this index
Indian Lands and Reservations, generally, this index
Mortgages, generally, this index
Public Lands, generally, this index
Real Estate, generally, this index

LANGUAGE
Interpreters, generally, this index

LARCENY
Bank Fraud Crimes, generally, this index

LAW BOOKS
See, also, Law Reports, generally, this index
Attorney General, authority to sell and exchange, **28 § 413**
Procurement, **28 § 525**
Director of Administrative Office of U.S. Courts,
Authority to sell and exchange, **28 § 413**

LAW BOOKS—Cont'd
Director of Administrative Office of U.S. Courts—Cont'd
Purchase for courts, **28 § 604**
Property of U.S., **28 § 414**
Transmittal to successors in office, **28 § 414**
United States Magistrate Judges, purchase, where needed for, **28 § 604**

LAW CLERKS
Annual and sick leave, clerks to district court judges, exceptions from provisions of, **28 § 752**
Bankruptcy judges,
Annual and sick leave, exceptions from provisions of, **28 § 156**
Appointment, **28 § 156**
Consolidation of office with office of clerk of district court, prior approval required, **28 § 156**
Compensation and salaries,
Director of Administrative Office of U.S. Courts to fix, **28 § 604**
District court judges, appointment subject to limitation on, **28 § 752**
Incentive awards, **28 § 604**
Increase, **28 § 603 nt**
Limitation on aggregate salaries, increase, **28 § 604 nt**
Supreme Court, **28 § 675**
Courts of Appeals, this index
Director of Administrative Office of U.S. Courts to fix compensation, **28 § 604**
District Judges, this index

LAW ENFORCEMENT
Assets Forfeiture Fund, availability, equipping Government-owned or leased vessel, vehicle, for law enforcement functions, **28 § 524**
Drug Abuse Prevention, Control and Treatment, generally, this index
Interception of Wire, Oral, or Electronic Communications, generally, this index
Missing Children, generally, this index
National Drug Policy, generally, this index

LAW ENFORCEMENT AGENCIES OR INSTRUMENTALITIES
Bureau of Investigation, generally, this index
Emergency Federal Law Enforcement Assistance, generally, this index
National Crime Information Center Project 2000, **28 § 534 nt**

LAW ENFORCEMENT OFFICERS
Automated legal research and information system, availability to all Federal law offices, **28 § 509 nt, EON 12146**
Drug Abuse Prevention, Control and Treatment, generally, this index

LAW ENFORCEMENT OFFICERS—Cont'd
Felonious killings of, investigation by Attorney General and FBI, **28 § 540**
National Drug Policy, generally, this index

LAW LIBRARIES
Librarians,
Courts, compensation,
Fixed by Director of Administrative Office of U.S. Courts, **28 § 604**
Increase, **28 § 603 nt**
Courts of appeals, librarian and library assistants, appointment and removal, **28 § 713**
Supreme Court, **28 § 674**
Marshal to disburse funds on vouchers certified by librarian, **28 § 672**

LAW OF NATIONS
International Law, generally, this index

LAW REPORTS
See, also, Law Books, generally, this index
Supreme Court reports, printing additional copies, **28 § 412**

LAWYERS
Attorneys, generally, this index

LEASES
Bankruptcy, this index

LEAVE OF COURT
Trustees, receivers or managers of property, suit against without leave of court, **28 § 959**
United States Court of International Trade, this index

LEGAL DISABILITY
Disability, this index

LEGAL DISPUTES
Dispute resolution, alternative means of, generally. Administrative Law and Procedure, this index
Resolution of interagency legal disputes, Attorney General, **28 § 509 nt, EON 12146**

LEGAL RESEARCH
Automated legal research and information systems, providing computerized legal research system to all Federal law offices, **28 § 509 nt, EON 12146**

LEGISLATION
Civil justice reform, enactment principals, **28 § 519 nt, EON 12988**

LEGISLATURE
Officers and employees, exemption from jury service, **28 § 1863**

LEGISLATURE—Cont'd
State legislatures,
Apportionment of statewide legislative body, constitutionality of, three-judge court required, **28 § 2284**
Officers and employees, exemption from jury service, **28 § 1863**
Territories, this index

LENDER
Loans, generally, this index

LETTERS
See, also, Mail and Mailing, generally, this index
Loss, exception from Tort Claims Act, **28 § 2680**

LETTERS PATENT
Patents, generally, this index

LETTERS ROGATORY
Assistance to foreign and international tribunals and to litigants before such tribunals, **28 § 1782**
Convention on the Taking of Evidence Abroad in Civil or Commercial Matters, **28 § 1781 nt**
Foreign and international litigation, service of documents issued in connection with, order made pursuant to, **28 § 1696**
Transmittal, **28 § 1781**

LEVY
Federal Debt Collection, generally, this index
Justices and judges, annuities to survivors, exemption from, **28 § 376**

LIABILITY INSURANCE
District courts, jurisdiction, diversity of citizenship, direct action against insurer, State citizenship of insurer, **28 § 1332**
Foreign diplomatic missions to U.S.,
Direct actions against insurers of members of diplomatic missions and their families, **28 § 1364**

LIBEL AND SLANDER
Tort Claims Act, exception of claims, **28 § 2680**

LIBRARIES
Law Libraries, generally, this index

LICENSES AND PERMITS
Customs Duties, this index
Parimutuel licensing simplification, consolidated request of State regulatory officials to for identification and criminal records of applicants, **28 § 534 nt**
Patents, generally, this index

LIENS AND INCUMBRANCES
Absent defendant, order for appearance of, enforcement by district court, **28 § 1655**
Bankruptcy, this index
Creation of new judicial district or division, **28 § 1656**
District Courts, this index
Income tax. Tax liens, generally, post
Internal Revenue Service. Tax liens, generally, post
Maritime Liens, generally, this index
Mortgages, generally, this index
Real estate,
Quieting title, actions, inapplicability to actions involving claims against U.S., **28 § 2409a**
Removal, district court order for appearance of absent defendant, **28 § 1655**
Sale to satisfy, lien of U.S. on property, **28 § 2410**
Tax liens,
Actions,
Jurisdiction, district courts, **28 § 1346**
Venue, **28 § 1402**
Intervention by U.S., real property, quieting title, inapplicability to actions involving claims against U.S., **28 § 2409a**
United States as party in actions to quiet title, foreclose, **28 § 2410**
Appearance, U.S. as party, actions to quiet title, foreclose, **28 § 2410**
Complaint or pleading in actions to quiet title, where U.S. is party, **28 § 2410**
Condemnation, U.S. as party, **28 § 2410**
Discharge,
Property,
Judgments or decrees in civil actions where U.S. is party, **28 § 2410**
Foreclosure, U.S. as party, **28 § 2410**
Interpleader, U.S. as party, **28 § 2410**
Partition, U.S. as party, **28 § 2410**
Redemption of real property, **28 § 2410**
Release of lien, **28 § 2410**
Sales,
Real estate to satisfy lien prior to that of U.S., **28 § 2410**
Transfer of territory to another district or division, **28 § 1656**
United States, this index

LIFE INSURANCE
Federal employees' group life insurance,
Circuit court executives and staff deemed officers and employees of judicial branch for purposes of, **28 § 332**

LIFE INSURANCE—Cont'd
Federal employees' group life insurance —Cont'd
Judicial Center, Director, professional staff, as officers and employees' within meaning of provisions, **28 § 627**

LIFE SAVING
Coast Guard, generally, this index

LIMITATION OF ACTIONS
Acts of Congress, civil actions, **28 § 1658**
Civil action,
Acts of Congress, **28 § 1658**
Stay pending International Trade Commission determination, **28 § 1659**
Claims against U.S., **28 § 2401**
Congressional reference cases, hearing officer, determinations concerning, **28 § 2509**
Contract Disputes Act of 1978, claims against U.S., exceptions, **28 § 2401**
Copyrights,
Cases, damages for infringement, actions against U.S., **28 § 1498**
Customs Duties, this index
Drug patents, declaratory judgment action, **28 § 2201**
Fines, penalties and forfeitures,
Enforcement, **28 § 2462**
Indians,
Time for commencing actions brought by U.S. for money damages, **28 §§ 2415, 2415 nt**
Tribes, bands, actions for money damages, **28 §§ 2415, 2415 nt**
Oyster growers damaged by dredging operations, suit in U.S. Court of Federal Claims, **28 § 2501**
Penalties. Fines, penalties and forfeitures, generally, ante
Real estate,
Quieting title, actions against U.S., **28 § 2409a**
Torture victim protection, civil liability, **28 § 1350 nt**
United States, this index
United States Court of Federal Claims, this index
United States Court of International Trade, this index

LIQUIDATED DAMAGES
United States Court of Federal Claims, jurisdiction,
Claims not sounding in tort, **28 § 1491**
Liquidated damages withheld from contractors under Contract Work Hours Standards Act, **28 § 1499**

LIQUIDATIONS
Bankruptcy, generally, this index

LITERACY
Illiterate Persons, generally, this index

LITERARY ASSOCIATIONS AND ORGANIZATIONS
Attorneys' fees and other costs and expenses, award to party prevailing against U.S. or agency, applicability, **28 § 2412**

LITERATURE
Copyrights, generally, this index

LOANS
Interpleader, district court, jurisdiction, **28 § 1335**
Mortgages, generally, this index

LOCAL GOVERNMENT
See, also,
Political Subdivisions, generally, this index
Federal Bureau of Investigation, exchange of identification records with officials, use, funds provided for expenses, **28 § 534 nt**
Officers and employees,
Report to Congress, violations of Federal criminal laws by, **28 § 529**

LOCAL LAWS
Forfeitures, Federal equitable share, deposit in Justice Department Assets Forfeiture Fund, **28 § 524**

LOCAL TAXES
Court officers and agents, conducting business liability, **28 § 960**

LODGING
Bailiffs, attending juries, appropriations, **28 § 524**

LOST INSTRUMENTS
Records and recordation. Lost Records, generally, this index

LOST RECORDS
Courts, evidence, **28 § 1734**
United States interested, **28 § 1735**

LOTTERIES
Professional and amateur sports protection. Gambling, generally, this index

LOUISIANA
See, also, States, generally, this index
Bankruptcy judges, appointment, number in judicial district, **28 § 152**
District courts,
Cities, held at, **28 § 98**
Judges,
Appointment, additional judges, advice and consent, **28 § 133 nt**
Eastern and Middle Districts, **28 § 98 nt**
Number, **28 § 133**
Places of holding, **28 § 98**
Judicial circuit of U.S., **28 § 41**

LOUISIANA—Cont'd
Judicial districts, **28 § 98**
Bankruptcy provisions, applicability of certain amendments to, **28 § 581 nt**
Number of district judges, **28 § 133**
United States marshals and attorneys for Eastern and Middle Districts, tenure and appointment, **28 § 98 nt**
United States trustees of judicial districts, appointment, **28 § 581**

LUXEMBOURG
Conventions, Taking of Evidence Abroad in Civil or Commercial Matters, party to, **28 § 1781 nt**

MAGAZINES
Periodicals, generally, this index

MAGISTRATE JUDGES
United States Magistrate Judges, generally, this index

MAGISTRATES
United States Magistrate Judges, generally, this index

MAIL AND MAILING
See, also, Postal Service, generally, this index
Certified or Registered Mail, generally, this index
First-class mail, service of summons for jury service, **28 § 1866**
Juror qualification form, **28 § 1864**
Orders,
Remand, mailed to clerk of State court, **28 § 1447**
Rules of Appellate Procedure, this index
Rules of Civil Procedure, this index
Tort Claims Act, claims arising out of loss, exception, **28 § 2680**

MAINE
See, also, States, generally, this index
Court of Appeals for First Circuit, generally, this index
District courts,
Cities, held at, **28 § 99**
Judges,
Appointment, additional judges, advice and consent, **28 § 133 nt**
Number, **28 § 133**
Places of holding, **28 § 99**
Judicial circuit of U.S., **28 § 41**
Judicial districts, **28 § 99**
Number of district judges, **28 § 133**
United States trustees of judicial districts, appointment, **28 § 581**

MALICIOUS PROSECUTION
Tort Claims Act, exception, claim arising from, **28 § 2680**

MANAGEMENT AND BUDGET, OFFICE OF
Office Of Management And Budget, generally, this index

MANAGERS AND MANAGEMENT
Property, this index

MANDAMUS
Carriers, equal facilities for shippers, procedure in district court, **28 § 2321 et seq.**
District Courts, this index
United States Court of Appeals for the Federal Circuit, generally, this index
United States Court of International Trade, generally, this index

MANIFESTS
Coasting Trade, generally, this index

MANSLAUGHTER
Voluntary manslaughter,
Violent crime, **28 § 2901**

MANUFACTURERS AND MANUFACTURING
Customs Duties, this index

MARINE CORPS
See, also,
Armed Forces, generally, this index
Uniformed Services, generally, this index
National Cemeteries, generally, this index
Reserves,
Retirement and pensions,
United States Magistrate Judges, eligibility of retired officers and enlisted personnel to appointment and service as, **28 § 631**
United States Magistrate Judges, eligibility of members, retired officers and enlisted personnel to appointment and service as, **28 § 631**
Retirement and pensions,
Enlisted members,
United States Magistrate Judges, eligibility for appointment and service as, **28 § 631**
Reserves, ante
Tort Claims Act, exception of claim arising out of combatant activities, **28 § 2680**
Veterans, generally, this index

MARINE CORPS RESERVE
Reserves, generally. Marine Corps, this index

MARINERS
Seamen, generally, this index

MARINES
Marine Corps, generally, this index

MARITIME ADMINISTRATION
Orders, review, **28 § 2341 et seq.**

MARITIME ADMINISTRATION—Cont'd
Review of orders, **28 § 2341 et seq.**

MARITIME COMMISSION
Federal Maritime Commission, generally, this index

MARITIME JURISDICTION
Admiralty, generally, this index

MARITIME LIENS
Jurisdictional immunities of foreign states, enforcement, exception, inclusions, **28 § 1605**

MARITIME TRANSACTIONS
Costs, docket fees, **28 § 1923**
Jury trial, **28 § 1873**

MARKETS AND MARKETING
Cooperative Marketing, generally, this index

MARRIAGE
See, also, Remarriage, generally, this index
Justices and judges, annuities to surviving dependent children, termination, **28 § 376**
Same sex marriages, States, not required to recognize, **28 § 1738C**

MARSHALS
Supreme Court Marshal, generally, this index
United States Marshals Service, generally, this index

MARYLAND
See, also, States, generally, this index
Bankruptcy judges, appointment, number and judicial district, **28 § 152**
District courts,
Cities, held at, **28 § 100**
Judges,
Additional, **28 § 133 nt**
Number, **28 § 133**
Places of holding, **28 § 100**
District of Columbia, generally, this index
Judicial circuit of U.S., **28 § 41**
Judicial districts, **28 § 100**
Bankruptcy provisions, applicability of certain amendments to, **28 § 581 nt**
Number of district judges, **28 § 133**
United States trustees of judicial districts, appointment, **28 § 581**

MASSACHUSETTS
See, also, States, generally, this index
Bankruptcy judges, appointment, number in judicial district, **28 § 152**
Court of Appeals for First Circuit, generally, this index
District courts,
Cities, held at, **28 § 101**
Judges,
Additional, **28 § 133 nt**

MASSACHUSETTS—Cont'd
District courts—Cont'd
Judges—Cont'd
Appointment, additional judges, advice and consent, **28 § 133 nt**
Existing judgeships authorized, **28 § 133 nt**
Number, **28 § 133**
Places of holding, **28 § 101**
Judicial circuit of U.S., **28 § 41**
Judicial districts, **28 § 101**
Number of district judges, **28 § 133**
Jury selection, Federal courts, utilization, resident list, **28 § 1863**
United States trustees of judicial districts, appointment, **28 § 581**

MASTERS
Clerks of courts, ineligible to appointment as master, **28 § 957**
Rules of Civil Procedure, this index
Three-judge court, appointment by single judge prohibited, **28 § 2284**
United States Court of International Trade, generally, this index

MATERIALS
Confidential or Privileged Information, generally, this index

MEALS
Bailiffs, attending juries, appropriations, **28 § 524**

MEDIATION AND MEDIATORS
Alternative dispute resolution, generally. District Courts, this index
Federal Judicial Center, training, of, **28 § 620**

MEDICAL CARE AND TREATMENT
Federal employees,
Group health insurance. Health Insurance, generally, this index

MEDICAL EXAMINATION
Judges or justices, annuities for survivors, power of Director of Administrative Office of U.S. Courts to order, **28 § 376**
Narcotic drug addicts, commitment and rehabilitation, **28 § 2902 et seq.**

MEETINGS
Judicial Center Board, **28 § 622**

MENTAL CAPACITY
Jury,
For service, **28 § 1865**
Form, contents, concerning, **28 § 1869**

MENTAL HEALTH
Annuities payable to mentally incompetent dependents of justices and judges, payment to fiduciaries, **28 § 376**

MERIT SYSTEM
Civil Service, generally, this index

MERIT SYSTEMS PROTECTION BOARD
Administrative Office of U.S. Courts, Personnel Management System, appeal rights preserved, **28 § 602 nt**
Appeal and review,
Final decisions or orders, U.S. Court of Appeals for the Federal Circuit, **28 § 1295**
Reemployment rights, United States Marshals, **28 § 569**
Decisions,
Final decisions, judicial review of by U.S. Court of Appeals for the Federal Circuit, **28 § 1295**
Disciplinary actions against employees, United States Court of Appeals for the Federal Circuit, jurisdiction, **28 § 1295**
Discrimination,
Actions involving,
Judicial review, decisions of,
United States Court of Appeals for the Federal Circuit, jurisdiction, **28 § 1295**
United States Court of Appeals for the Federal Circuit, this index
United States Marshals, reemployment rights, **28 § 569**

MESSENGERS
Courts, compensation,
Fixed by Director of Administrative Office of U.S. Courts, **28 § 604**
Increase, **28 § 603 nt**
Courts of appeals, appointment and removal, **28 § 714**
District courts, crier to perform duties of messenger, **28 § 755**
United States attorneys, employment, **28 § 550**
United States Court of Federal Claims, appointment and removal, **28 § 795**
United States Court of International Trade, criers to perform duties of, **28 § 872**

MICHIGAN
See, also, States, generally, this index
Bankruptcy judges,
Appointment, number in judicial district, **28 § 152**
Serving on part-time basis on certain date, extension, **28 § 152 nt**
District courts,
Cities, held at, **28 § 102**
Judges,
Additional, **28 § 133 nt**
Number, **28 § 133**
Temporary judgeships, **28 § 133 nt**
Places of holding, **28 § 102**
Western district, temporary judgeships, commencement date, **28 § 133 nt**
Judicial circuit of U.S., **28 § 41**

MICHIGAN—Cont'd
Judicial districts, **28 § 102**
Bankruptcy provisions, applicability of certain amendments to, **28 § 581 nt**
Number of district judges, **28 § 133**
United States trustees of judicial districts, appointment, **28 § 581**

MICROFILMS AND MICROPHOTOGRAPHS
Business records, evidence, **28 § 1732**
Records and recordation,
Business records, evidence, **28 § 1732**
Supreme Court, purchase, by librarian, **28 § 674**

MIDWAY ISLANDS
Judicial district of Hawaii, inclusion in, **28 § 91**

MILEAGE
See, also, Traveling Expenses, generally, this index
Grand jurors, **28 § 1871**
Jurors, **28 § 1871**
Grand jurors, generally, ante
Summons as both witness and juror, **28 § 1824**
United States marshals, **28 § 1921**
Witnesses, this index

MILITARY APPEALS COURT
United States Court of Appeals for the Armed Forces, generally, this index

MILITARY COURTS
United States Court of Appeals for the Armed Forces, generally, this index

MILITARY DEPARTMENTS
See, also,
Air Force Department, generally, this index
Army Department, generally, this index
Navy Department, generally, this index
Air Force Department, generally, this index
Army Department, generally, this index
Attorneys, reasonable fees and expenses, award, prevailing party, actions by or against, **28 § 2412**
Civil Service, generally, this index
Costs, judgment for, prevailing party, actions by or against, **28 § 2412**
Foreign Service, generally, this index
Hearings, witness fees and allowances, **28 § 2412**
Investigation,
Persons or offenses not limited, **28 § 535**
Navy Department, generally, this index
Secretaries,
Attorney General to advise, **28 § 513**

MILITARY DEPARTMENTS—Cont'd
Statement, facts, relating to petition in U.S. Court of Federal Claims or in U.S. Court of Appeals for the Federal Circuit, furnishing Attorney General, **28 § 520**
Tort claims against U.S. for negligence, of officers or employees, **28 § 2671 et seq.**
United States Court of Appeals for the Federal Circuit, transmission of petition to Attorney General, **28 § 520**
United States Court of Federal Claims, transmission of petition to Attorney General, **28 § 520**

MILITARY JUSTICE CODE
United States Court of Appeals for the Armed Forces, generally, this index

MINNESOTA
See, also, States, generally, this index
Bankruptcy judges, appointment, number in judicial district, **28 § 152**
District court,
Cities, held at, **28 § 103**
Judges,
Additional, **28 § 133 nt**
Number, **28 § 133**
Places of holding, **28 § 103**
Indians,
Civil jurisdiction in actions to which Indians are parties, **28 § 1360**
Judicial circuit of U.S., **28 § 41**
Judicial districts, **28 § 103**
Number of district judges, **28 § 133**
United States trustees of judicial districts, appointment, **28 § 581**

MINOR OR PETTY OFFENSES
United States Magistrate Judges, this index
United States Sentencing Commission, report, judge to, sentence information, exception, sentence imposed for petty offense, **28 § 994**

MINORITY GROUPS
Discrimination, generally, this index
United States Magistrate Judges, merit selection panel to consider, **28 § 631 nt**

MINORS
Children and Minors, generally, this index

MISDEMEANORS
United States marshal, fees for services in criminal cases, conviction for, **28 § 1921**

MISREPRESENTATION
Fraud, generally, this index

MISSING CHILDREN
Generally, **28 §§ 1 nt, 534**

MISSING CHILDREN—Cont'd
Unemancipated person, Attorney General to acquire, collect, classify, information, provide to parent, guardian, **28 § 534**

MISSIONS
Foreign Missions, generally, this index

MISSISSIPPI
See, also, States, generally, this index
Bankruptcy judges, appointment, number in judicial district, **28 § 152**
District courts,
Cities, held at, **28 § 104**
Judges,
Additional, **28 § 133 nt**
Appointment, additional judges, advice and consent, **28 § 133 nt**
Number, **28 § 133**
Places of holding, **28 § 104**
Judicial Circuit of U.S., **28 § 41**
Judicial districts, **28 § 104**
Bankruptcy provisions, applicability of certain amendments to, **28 § 581 nt**
Number of district judges, **28 § 133**
United States trustees of judicial districts, appointment, **28 § 581**

MISSOURI
See, also, States, generally, this index
Bankruptcy judges, appointment, number in judicial district, **28 § 152**
District courts,
Cities, held at, **28 § 105**
Judges,
Appointment, additional judges, advice and consent, **28 § 133 nt**
Number, **28 § 133**
Temporary judgeships, **28 § 133 nt**
Judicial districts, **28 § 105**
Places of holding, **28 § 105**
Judicial circuit of U.S., **28 § 41**
Judicial districts, **28 § 105**
Bankruptcy provisions, applicability of certain amendments to, **28 § 581 nt**
Number of district judges, **28 § 133**
United States trustees of judicial districts, appointment, **28 § 581**

MONEY AND FINANCE
Interpleader, district court, jurisdiction, **28 § 1335**

MONEY LAUNDERING
Racketeering, this index
Reports,
Justice Department to Congressional committees, charging and plea practices of Federal prosecutors, **28 § 994 nt**

MONOPOLIES AND COMBINATIONS
Actions and proceedings,
State Attorneys General as parens patriae,
Judicial panel on multidistrict litigation, consolidation and transfer pretrial purposes or for trial, **28 § 1407**
District court jurisdiction, **28 § 1337**
Multidistrict litigation, exemption, antitrust laws, **28 § 1407**
Patents, generally, this index

MONTANA
See, also, States, generally, this index
Bankruptcy judges, appointment, number in judicial district, **28 § 152**
District courts,
Cities, held at, **28 § 106**
Judges, number, **28 § 133**
Additional, **28 § 133 nt**
Places of holding, **28 § 106**
Judicial circuit of U.S., **28 § 41**
Judicial districts, **28 § 106**
Bankruptcy provisions, applicability of certain amendments to, **28 § 581 nt**
Number of district judges, **28 § 133**
United States trustees of judicial districts, appointment, **28 § 581**

MONTGOMERY, AL
Court of Appeals for Eleventh Circuit, generally, this index

MORGAN P. HARDIMAN CHILD ABDUCTION AND SERIAL MURDER INVESTIGATIVE RESOURCES CENTER
Generally, **28 § 531 nt**

MORTGAGES
Chattel Mortgages, generally, this index
Civil actions respecting, U.S. as party, **28 § 2410**
Discharge of property, judgments or decrees in civil actions where U.S. is party, **28 § 2410**
Housing and Urban Development Department, generally, this index
United States, actions affecting property on which U.S. has mortgage, **28 § 2410**

MOTION PICTURES
Copyrights, this index

MOTIONS
Bankruptcy, this index
Change of venue, **28 § 1404**
Courts always open for making motions, **28 § 452**
Dismiss action, single judge of three judge court not to entertain, **28 § 2284**
Judgment on, action by U.S. against delinquents for public money, **28 § 2407**

MOTIONS—Cont'd
Judicial Panel on Multidistrict Litigation, generally, this index
Jury selection procedures, challenging compliance with, **28 § 1867**
Multidistrict litigation, proceedings for transfer to single district, **28 § 1407**
Remand after removal of case, **28 § 1448**
Rules of Appellate Procedure, this index
Rules of Civil Procedure, this index
Supreme Court, this index
Surface Transportation Board orders, appearance by parties of their own motion, actions to enforce orders, **28 § 2323**
United States Court of Appeals for the Armed Forces, generally, this index
United States Court of Federal Claims, generally, this index
United States Court of International Trade, this index
United States Magistrate Judges, trial of misdemeanors before. United States Magistrate Judges, generally, this index

MOTOR CARRIERS
See, also, Common Carriers, generally, this index
Connecting carriers, recovery by initial carrier from, amount in controversy for district court jurisdiction of cases involving, **28 § 1337**
Initial carrier, recovery from connecting carrier, amount in controversy for district court jurisdiction, **28 § 1337**
Receipts or bills of lading, amount in controversy for district court jurisdiction of cases involving, **28 § 1337**
Surface Transportation Board, generally, this index

MOTOR VEHICLES
Federal employees,
Defense of suits against employees arising out of operation of motor vehicles in scope of employment, **28 § 2679**
Officers and Employees of Government, this index

MULTIDISTRICT LITIGATION
Generally, **28 § 1407**
District courts, transfer to single district for consolidated, pretrial proceedings, **28 § 1407**
Judicial Panel on Multidistrict Litigation, generally, this index

MULTIPLE CLAIMS
United States Court of Federal Claims, generally, this index

MUNICIPAL CORPORATIONS
Criminal and other identification records, exchange with authorized officials,. **28 § 534**

MUNICIPAL DEBT ADJUSTMENT
Bankruptcy, this index

MURDER
Attorney general, serial killings, investigations and investigators, **28 § 540B**
Bureau of Investigation, serial killings, investigations and investigators, **28 § 540B**
Child Abduction and Serial Murder Investigative Resources Center, **28 § 531 nt**
Federal Bureau of Investigation, serial killings, investigations and investigators, **28 § 540B**
Foreign country,
Conspiracy to commit in, **28 § 956**
Morgan P. Hardiman Child Abduction and Serial Murder Investigative Resources Center, **28 § 531 nt**
Serial killings,
Child Abduction and Serial Murder Investigative Resources Center, **28 § 531 nt**
Investigations and investigators, **28 § 540B**

MUSIC
Sound Recordings or Reproductions, generally, this index

MUTUAL FUNDS
Justice, judge or Magistrate Judge, ownership in, disqualification, **28 § 455**

MUTUAL INSURANCE
Justice, judge or Magistrate Judge, proprietary interest of policyholder, disqualification, **28 § 455**

MUTUAL SAVINGS AND LOAN ASSOCIATIONS
Justice, judge or Magistrate Judge, proprietary interest of depositor, disqualification, **28 § 455**

NAFTA
Customs Duties, this index

NAMES
Rules of Civil Procedure, this index
Trademarks and Trade Names, generally, this index
United States Bankruptcy Court, **28 § 151**

NARCOTIC DRUG ADDICTS
See, also,
Drug Abuse Prevention, Control and Treatment, generally, this index
Attorney General, this index
Care and treatment,
Commitment and rehabilitation, generally, post

NARCOTIC DRUG ADDICTS—Cont'd
Commitment and rehabilitation,
Absence of offer by court of election for examination or determination as to civil commitment review, **28 § 2906**
Addict, defined, **28 § 2901**
Advisement of eligible individuals, **28 § 2902**
Affirmation or termination of commitment by court, **28 § 2903**
Aftercare treatment, **28 § 2902 et seq.**
Answering criminal charges, **28 § 2902**
Conditional release for supervised aftercare treatment, **28 §§ 2902, 2903**
Convicted, defined, **28 § 2901**
Conviction, defined, **28 § 2901**
Credibility as witness, fact of addiction as bearing on, **28 § 2904**
Credit for sentence, time spent in institutional custody, **28 § 2903**
Crime of violence, defined, **28 § 2901**
Definitions, **28 § 2901**
Determination of,
Addiction and subsequent commitment not deemed criminal conviction, **28 § 2904**
Court as to addiction or likely rehabilitation, **28 § 2902**
Discharge from custody and dismissal of criminal charges, **28 § 2902**
Discretionary authority of court, **28 § 2902**
Election to submit to examination to determine addiction and likely rehabilitation, **28 § 2902**
Eligible individual, defined, **28 § 2901**
Elimination or control of drug dependence, inclusion in term "treatment", **28 § 2901**
Federal or private agencies or officers, delegation of functions from Surgeon General, **28 § 2905**
Felony, defined, **28 § 2901**
Home visits and physical examination, conditionally released individual, **28 § 2903**
Institutional treatment, return of conditionally released individual for, **28 § 2903**
Maximum period of civil commitment, **28 § 2903**
Officers or employees of PHS, functions delegated from Surgeon General, **28 § 2905**
Penalties, escape or rescue from custody, **28 § 2902**
Pending criminal proceedings, dismissal or resumption, **28 §§ 2902, 2903**
Period of treatment, **28 § 2902**
Placement in custody, **28 § 2902**
Release on bail or recognizance, **28 § 2902**

NARCOTIC DRUG ADDICTS—Cont'd
Commitment and rehabilitation—Cont'd
Return of individual to use of narcotics, recommendation, continued treatment, **28 § 2903**
Supervised aftercare in community, inclusion in term "treatment", **28 § 2901**
Surgeon General,
Advising court as to further or continued treatment, **28 §§ 2902, 2903**
Authority and responsibility, **28 § 2903**
Confinement in institution at discretion of, **28 § 2902**
Defined, **28 § 2901**
Delegation of functions, **28 § 2905**
Examination by, **28 § 2902**
Order, return of conditionally released individual for institutional treatment, **28 § 2903**
Reports of results of examination and recommendations, **28 § 2902**
Termination of commitment, **28 § 2902**
Treatment, defined, **28 § 2901**
Use of,
Federal, State and private facilities, **28 § 2905**
Test results in criminal proceedings against the examined individual, **28 § 2904**
Withdrawal from examination or treatment, **28 § 2902**
Confinement. Commitment and rehabilitation, generally, ante
Crime of violence, defined, **28 § 2901**
District courts, civil commitment and rehabilitation, authority, duties, **28 §§ 2902, 2903, 2906**
Fines, penalties and forfeitures,
Escape or rescue from custody, **28 § 2902**
National Drug Policy, generally, this index
Penalties. Fines, penalties and forfeitures, generally, ante
Rehabilitation. Commitment and rehabilitation, generally, ante
Surgeon General,
Commitment and rehabilitation, ante
United States Attorneys, this index

NARCOTICS
National Drug Policy, generally, this index

NATIONAL BANKS
Actions and proceedings,
Jurisdiction, **28 § 1348**
National bank against Comptroller of Currency, venue, **28 § 1394**
Citizenship of associations for purposes of actions, **28 § 1348**

NATIONAL BANKS—Cont'd
Comptroller of Currency,
Injunction against,
Jurisdiction of district court, **28 § 1348**
Venue, **28 § 1394**
Conservators,
District court's jurisdiction, sales, **28 § 1348**
Sale of,
Personal property, **28 § 2004**
Real estate, **28 §§ 2001, 2002**
Injunctions,
Jurisdiction of district court, **28 § 1348**
Venue, **28 § 1394**
Receivers and receivership,
Injunction, jurisdiction of district court, **28 § 1348**
Sale of,
Personal property, **28 § 2004**
Real estate, **28 §§ 2001, 2002**
Winding up business,
District court jurisdiction, **28 § 1348**

NATIONAL CEMETERIES
Crimes and offenses,
Property offenses, enhanced penalties, veterans' cemetery protection, **28 § 994 nt**
Protection, property offenses, enhanced penalties, **28 § 994 nt**

NATIONAL COMMISSION ON JUDICIAL DISCIPLINE AND REMOVAL
Generally, **28 § 372 nt**

NATIONAL CRIME INFORMATION CENTER
Appropriations, authorization, national law enforcement cooperation, **28 § 534 nt**
National crime information databases, defined, violence against women, national stalker and domestic violence reduction, **28 § 534**
National law enforcement cooperation, Congressional findings, **28 § 534 nt**
National stalker and domestic violence reduction, rulemaking, consultation with Attorney General, violence against women, **28 § 534 nt**

NATIONAL DRUG POLICY
Civil enforcement enhancement, Justice Department, **28 § 509 nt**
National Drug Control,
Justice Department,
Civil enforcement enhancement, **28 § 509 nt**

NATIONAL GUARD
Disbursing officers, United States Magistrate Judges, eligibility for appointment and service as, **28 § 631**

NATIONAL GUARD—Cont'd
District of Columbia,
United States Magistrate Judges, eligibility of members for employment and service as, **28 § 631**
States,
United States Magistrate Judges, eligibility of members for appointment and service as, **28 § 631**
Tort claims against U.S. for negligence, officers or employees, **28 § 2671 et seq.**

NATIONAL ORIGIN
Civil Rights, generally, this index
Courts of appeals, district court and bankruptcy court judges, nominees for appointment, selection not affected by, **28 § 44 nt**
Discrimination, generally, this index
Federal judgeships, nomination of individuals for without regard to, Congressional recommendations, **28 § 133 nt**
Jurors,
Exclusion from service of, discrimination prohibited, **28 § 1862**
Qualification form, contents, concerning, **28 § 1869**
Service, discrimination in selecting persons for jury prohibited, remedies, **28 § 1867**

NATIONAL PARK SERVICE
United States Magistrate Judges, appointment and qualification in bi-State area under administration of, **28 § 631**

NATIONALS AND NATIONALITY
Aliens, generally, this index
Naturalization, generally, this index

NATIVE AMERICANS
Indian Lands and Reservations, generally, this index
Indians, generally, this index

NATURAL RESOURCES
Laws relating to, violations, investigation and action by Attorney General, **28 § 509 nt**

NATURALIZATION
Citizens and Citizenship, generally, this index
Clerks of courts,
Payment of fees into Treasury, exceptions, **28 § 751**
Immigration and Naturalization Service, generally, this index

NAVAL MILITIA
United States Magistrate Judges, eligibility of members for appointment and service as, **28 § 631**

NAVAL RESERVE
Reserves, generally. Navy, this index

NAVIGABLE WATERS
Property, forfeitures, **28 § 2461**

NAVY
See, also,
Armed Forces, generally, this index
Navy Department, generally, this index
Uniformed Services, generally, this index
Coast Guard, generally, this index
Department. Navy Department, generally, this index
District court crier or bailiff, preference in appointment, because of naval service, **28 § 755**
Exchanges,
Express or implied contracts with,
District courts, concurrent jurisdiction with U.S. Court of Federal Claims, civil action or claim against U.S., **28 § 1346**
United States Court of Federal Claims, jurisdiction, claims founded on, **28 § 1491**
Foreign Service, generally, this index
Honorable Discharges, this index
Marine Corps, generally, this index
National Cemeteries, generally, this index
Navy Department, generally, this index
Prize (Vessels), generally, this index
Reserves,
National Cemeteries, generally, this index
United States Magistrate Judges, eligibility of members, retired officers and enlisted personnel to appointment and service as, **28 § 631**
Retirement and pensions,
United States Magistrate Judges, eligibility of retirees for appointment and service as, **28 § 631**
Secretary of Navy, generally, this index
Tort Claims Act, exception of claim arising out of combatant activities, **28 § 2680**
United States Magistrate Judges, eligibility of retired officers and enlisted personnel for appointment and service as, **28 § 631**
Veterans, generally, this index
Women's Reserve. Reserves, generally, ante

NAVY DEPARTMENT
See, also,
Military Departments, generally, this index
Navy, generally, this index
Attorney General, advice concerning, **28 § 513**
Secretary of Navy, generally, this index

NEBRASKA
See, also, States, generally, this index
Bankruptcy judges, appointment, number in judicial district, **28 § 152**
District courts,
Cities, held at, **28 § 107**
Judges,
Additional, **28 § 133 nt**
Number, **28 § 133**
Temporary judgeships, **28 § 133 nt**
Places of holding, **28 § 107**
Indians,
State civil jurisdiction in actions to which Indians parties, **28 § 1360**
Judicial circuit of U.S., **28 § 41**
Judicial districts, **28 § 107**
Bankruptcy provisions, applicability of certain amendments to, **28 § 581 nt**
Number of district judges, **28 § 133**
United States trustees of judicial districts, appointment, **28 § 581**

NEEDY PERSONS
Indigent Persons, generally, this index

NEGLIGENCE
Federal Employers' Liability Act, generally, this index
Federal Tort Claims Act, **28 §§ 1346, 1402, 2401, 2402, 2411, 2412, 2671 et seq.**
Officers and Employees of Government, this index
Rules of Civil Procedure, this index
United States, claims against, real property, quieting title, inapplicability to actions involving claims against U.S., **28 § 2409a**
United States Court of Appeals for District of Columbia, generally, this index

NEGOTIABLE INSTRUMENTS
Bills and Notes (Commercial Paper), generally, this index
Racketeering, generally, this index

NETHERLANDS
Convention, taking of Evidence Abroad in Civil or Commercial Matters, party to, **28 § 1781 nt**

NEUTRALS
Alternative dispute resolution, district courts, **28 § 653**

NEVADA
See, also, States, generally, this index
Bankruptcy judges, appointment, number in judicial district, **28 § 152**
District court,
Cities, held at, **28 § 108**
Judges,
Additional, **28 § 133 nt**
Number, **28 § 133**
Places of holding, **28 § 108**
Judicial circuit of U.S., **28 § 41**

NEVADA—Cont'd
Judicial districts, **28 § 108**
  Bankruptcy provisions, applicability of certain amendments to, **28 § 581 nt**
  Number of district judges, **28 § 133**
United States trustees of judicial districts, appointment, **28 § 581**

NEW HAMPSHIRE
  See, also, States, generally, this index
Bankruptcy judges, appointment, number in judicial district, **28 § 152**
Court of Appeals for First Circuit, generally, this index
District courts,
  Cities, held at, **28 § 109**
  Judges,
    Appointment, additional judges, advice and consent, **28 § 133 nt**
    Number, **28 § 133**
  Places of holding, **28 § 109**
Judicial circuit of U.S., **28 § 41**
Judicial districts, **28 § 109**
  Number of district judges, **28 § 133**
United States trustees of judicial districts, appointment, **28 § 581**

NEW JERSEY
  See, also, States, generally, this index
Bankruptcy judges, appointment, number in judicial district, **28 § 152**
District courts,
  Cities, held at, **28 § 110**
  Judges,
    Appointment, additional judges, advice and consent, **28 § 133 nt**
    Number, **28 § 133**
  Places of holding, **28 § 110**
Judicial circuit of U.S., **28 § 41**
Judicial districts, **28 § 110**
  Number of district judges, **28 § 133**
United States trustees of judicial districts, appointment, **28 § 581**

NEW MEXICO
  See, also, States, generally, this index
Bankruptcy judges, appointment, number in judicial district, **28 § 152**
District courts,
  Cities, held at, **28 § 111**
  Judges,
    Appointment, additional judges, advice and consent, **28 § 133 nt**
    Number, **28 § 133**
  Places of holding, **28 § 111**
Judicial circuit of U.S., **28 § 41**
Judicial districts,
  Bankruptcy provisions, applicability of certain amendments to, **28 § 581 nt**
  Number of district judges, **28 § 133**
United States trustees of judicial districts, appointment, **28 § 581**

NEW ORLEANS, LA
Court of Appeals for Fifth Circuit, this index

NEW TRIAL
Arbitration, **28 § 657**
Rules of Civil Procedure, this index
United States Court of Federal Claims, this index

NEW YORK
  See, also, States, generally, this index
Bankruptcy judges, appointment, number in judicial district, **28 § 152**
Court of International Trade. United States Court of International Trade, generally, this index
District courts,
  Cities, held at, **28 § 112**
  Eastern District, pretermission, special session at Westbury, **28 § 112 nt**
  Judges,
    Additional, **28 § 133 nt**
    Appointment, additional judges, advice and consent, **28 § 133 nt**
    Existing judgeships authorized, **28 § 133 nt**
    Number, **28 § 133**
    Residency requirements, **28 § 134**
    Temporary judgeships, **28 § 133 nt**
  Places of holding, **28 § 112**
Eastern district, U.S. Attorneys, residents, **28 § 545**
Judicial districts, **28 § 112**
  Bankruptcy provisions, applicability of certain amendments to, **28 § 581 nt**
  Number of district judges, **28 § 133**
  Southern district, clerk of district court, residence, **28 § 751**
  United States, **28 § 41**
Southern district,
  United States attorneys, residence, **28 § 545**
  United States marshals, residence, **28 § 561**
United States Court of International Trade, generally, this index
United States trustees of judicial districts, appointment, **28 § 581**

NEW YORK CITY, NY
Court of Appeals for Second Circuit, this index
United States Court of International Trade, generally, this index

NEWLY DISCOVERED EVIDENCE
Tort claim against U.S., amount of claim, **28 § 2675**

NEWS MEDIA
Copyrights, generally, this index

NEWSPAPERS
Attachment against delinquent postmasters and postal officers, employees, publication of executed warrant, **28 § 2715**
Copyrights, generally, this index
Legal notices, designation by assigned justices or judges, exception, **28 § 296**

NEXT FRIEND
United States Court of Federal Claims, generally, this index

NEXT OF KIN
  See, also, Relatives, generally, this index
Annuities unable to be paid to survivors, of justices and judges, payment to, **28 § 376**
Missing persons, children, Attorney General to acquire, collect, classify, information, provide to, **28 § 534**

NOMINATIONS
District Judges, this index
Judges, Federal judgeships, recommendations concerning blacks and women as qualified individuals for selection for nomination to, **28 § 133 nt**

NONPROFIT CORPORATIONS
Federal Judicial Center Foundation, establishment, **28 § 629**

NONRESIDENTS
Aliens, generally, this index
Application for order establishing lost or destroyed court record, service, **28 § 1734**
Attachment against delinquent postmasters, and postal employees, officers, on ground of, **28 §§ 2710, 2715**
Income tax, generally. Aliens, this index
Officer of U.S., removal of action or prosecution against, **28 § 1442**
Patent infringement action where defendant is nonresident, service of process, **28 § 1694**

NONSUIT
Dismissal and Nonsuit, generally, this index

NORTH CAROLINA
  See, also, States, generally, this index
Bankruptcy judges, appointment, number in judicial district, **28 § 152**
District courts,
  Additional, **28 § 133 nt**
  Cities, held at, **28 § 113**
  Judges,
    Additional, **28 § 133 nt**
    Appointment, additional judges, advice and consent, **28 § 133 nt**
    Existing judgeships authorized, **28 § 133 nt**
    Number, **28 § 133**

NORTH CAROLINA—Cont'd
District courts—Cont'd
Number, **28 § 133**
Places of holding, **28 § 113**
Judicial districts, **28 § 113**
Bankruptcy provisions, applicability of certain amendments to, **28 § 581 nt**
Number of district judges, **28 § 133**
United States trustees of judicial districts, appointment, **28 § 581**

NORTH DAKOTA
See, also, States, generally, this index
Bankruptcy judges, appointment, number in judicial district, **28 § 152**
District courts,
Cities, held at, **28 § 114**
Judges, number, **28 § 133**
Places of holding, **28 § 114**
Judicial circuit of U.S., **28 § 41**
Judicial districts, **28 § 114**
Number of district judges, **28 § 133**
United States trustees of judicial districts, appointment, **28 § 581**

NORTHERN MARIANA ISLANDS
District Court,
Appeals,
Final decision in certain cases, jurisdiction of U.S. Court of Appeals for the Federal Circuit, **28 § 1295**
Judge,
Annuities to survivors, **28 § 376**
Salary and resignation, removal, effect on amount payable to judge retired before enactment of provisions, **28 § 373 nt**
Senior judge of the court, qualifications, **28 § 373 nt**
Judicial district, bankruptcy provisions, applicability of certain amendments to, **28 § 581 nt**
Resident U.S. attorney and marshal residing in appointed district, applicability of requirement, **28 § 545**
Tort Claims Act, exceptions, not considered foreign country for purposes of, **28 § 2680 nt**
United States attorney,
Residency requirement in district appointed to, applicability, **28 § 545**
United States Court of Appeals for the Federal Circuit, jurisdiction of appeals in certain cases, **28 § 1295**
United States marshal,
Residency requirement in appointed district, applicability, **28 § 545**
Service in more than one judicial district, **28 § 561**
United States trustees of judicial districts, appointment, **28 § 581**

NORTHERN MARIANAS, COMMONWEALTH OF
Northern Mariana Islands, generally, this index

NORWAY
Convention on the Taking of Evidence Abroad in Civil or Commercial Matters, party to, **28 § 1781 nt**

NOTES
Bankruptcy, generally, this index
Bills and Notes (Commercial Paper), generally, this index
Federal Intermediate Credit Banks, generally, this index
Federal Land Banks, generally, this index

NOTICE
Administrative Law and Procedure, this index
Appeal and Review, this index
Application,
Order establishing lost or destroyed court records, **28 § 1734**
Attachment against delinquent postmasters and postal officers, employees, personal notice to debtors or possessors of property, **28 § 2716**
Attorney General, this index
Bankruptcy, this index
Congress, this index
Constructive notice, pending action in Federal district court as to realty, recording under State law as constructive notice, **28 § 1964**
Copyrights, this index
Courts of Appeals, this index
Deposits in courts, claimant of fund, **28 § 2042**
District Courts, this index
Federal Agencies and Instrumentalities, this index
Federal Debt Collection, this index
Foreign States, jurisdictional immunities, "notice of suit", defined, **28 § 1608**
Habeas corpus proceedings, prior to hearing as to person in custody of State officer, **28 § 2252**
Interlocutory injunction restraining, enforcement, of Federal agency, orders, **28 § 2349**
Judicial Center, Director of, election of retirement coverage, **28 §§ 376, 627**
Judicial Notice, generally, this index
Judicial Panel on Multidistrict Litigation, this index
Judicial sale of realty, **28 §§ 2001, 2002**
Jurors, plan for random selection, adoption or modification, **28 § 1863**
Justices and judges, change of residence, **28 § 456**
Litigation notice system, **28 § 509 nt, EON 12146**
Lost or destroyed court records, application for order establishing, **28 § 1734**

NOTICE—Cont'd
Maritime lien, suit in admiralty to enforce, jurisdictional immunities of foreign States, exception, inclusions, **28 § 1605**
Multidistrict litigation, transfer to single district for consolidated, pretrial proceedings, **28 § 1407**
Publication, this index
Rate orders of State agencies, jurisdiction of district courts, **28 § 1342**
Recording of pending action before Federal district court under State law as constructive notice, **28 § 1964**
Removal of case, filing, contents, **28 § 1446**
Review. Appeal and Review, this index
Rules of Appellate Procedure, this index
Rules of Civil Procedure, this index
Service of Process, generally, this index
Special sessions of district courts, **28 § 141**
Three-judge court, hearing by, **28 § 2284**
United States Attorneys, this index
United States Court of Federal Claims, this index
United States Court of International Trade, this index
United States Magistrate Judges,
Appointment of, **28 § 631**
United States marshal, fee for preparing public notice, **28 § 1921**
United States trustees, certification of judicial districts by Attorney General, **28 § 581 nt**

NUCLEAR ENERGY
Atomic Energy, generally, this index

NURSING HOMES
Confidential or privileged information, criminal background checks, labor and employment, **28 § 534 nt**
Criminal background checks, labor and employment, **28 § 534 nt**
Fees, criminal background checks, labor and employment, **28 § 534 nt**
Fines, penalties and forfeitures, criminal background checks, labor and employment, **28 § 534 nt**
Labor and employment,
Criminal background checks, **28 § 534 nt**

OATHS AND AFFIRMATIONS
Arbitration,
Referral from alternative dispute resolution, **28 § 655**
Bankruptcy, this index
Clerks of court, **28 § 951**
Administration of, **28 § 953**
Congressional reference cases, **28 § 2509**
Convention on the Taking of Evidence Abroad in Civil or Commercial Matters, power of diplomatic officer, consular agent or commissioner to administer, **28 § 1781 nt**

OATHS AND AFFIRMATIONS—Cont'd
Delinquents for public money, continuance of action by U.S. against, **28 § 2407**
District court reporters, **28 § 753**
Habeas corpus, denial of facts set forth in return, **28 § 2243**
Judges or Justices, this index
Party, proof of amount in controversy for review by court of appeals, **28 § 2108**
Refusal to take as contempt, **28 § 636**
Reporters, this index
Special assistant to Attorney General or special attorney, **28 § 515**
United States attorneys, **28 § 544**
United States Court of Federal Claims, this index
United States Magistrate Judges, **28 § 631**

OBSOLETE PAPERS
Courts, disposition, **28 § 457**

OCCUPATIONS
Professions and Occupations, generally, this index

OCEAN DUMPING
United States Marshals, appointment, advice and consent, **28 § 561**

OFFENSES
Crimes and Offenses, generally, this index

OFFICE OF MANAGEMENT AND BUDGET
Apportionment, Justice Department, appropriations, **28 § 524 nt**
Budget,
Courts, submission to, **28 § 605**
Courts, budget estimates submitted to, **28 § 605**
Director,
Federal Legal Council, advisory members, **28 § 509 nt, EON 12146**

OFFICERS AND EMPLOYEES
See, also, Officers and Employees of Government, generally, this index
Administrative Office of U.S. Courts,
Appointment, **28 § 602**
Personnel Management System, **28 § 602 nt**
Courts,
Authority to appoint unaffected by law concerning Administrative Office of U.S. Courts, **28 § 609**
Compensation,
Fixed by Director of Administrative Office of U.S. Courts, **28 § 604**
Increase, **28 § 603 nt**
Incentive awards, **28 § 604**
Courts of appeals, **28 § 711 et seq.**
District court, power to appoint, **28 § 756**

OFFICERS AND EMPLOYEES—Cont'd
Equal employment opportunity. Civil Rights, generally, this index
Federal employees. Officers and Employees of Government, generally, this index
Judges or Justices, generally, this index
Labor and Employment, generally, this index
Labor Disputes, generally, this index
Law enforcement officers, generally, this index
Officers and Employees of Government, generally, this index
Probation, this index
Rules of Appellate Procedure, this index
Rules of Civil Procedure, this index
States, this index
Supreme Court, reporter may appoint and fix compensation, **28 § 673**
Territories, this index
United States. Officers and Employees of Government, generally, this index

OFFICERS AND EMPLOYEES OF GOVERNMENT
Accounts and accounting,
Fees, time for filing suit in U.S. Court of Federal Claims, **28 § 2501**
Settlement by U.S. Court of Federal Claims, **28 § 1494**
Allowances,
Pay and allowances, generally, post
Appeal and review,
Record on review in court of appeals of orders of administrative officers, **28 § 2112**
Attorneys, reasonable fees and expenses,
Award, prevailing party, actions by or against, **28 § 2412**
Civil actions by or against U.S. officials, award of, **28 § 2412**
Civil Service, generally, this index
Claims,
Personal injuries by, administrative adjustment of claims, **28 § 2672**
Commissions of Officers, generally, this index
Compelling performance of duty, action for purpose of, jurisdiction, **28 § 1361**
Comptroller General, generally, this index
Comptroller of Currency, generally, this index
Conflicts of Interest, generally, this index
Costs,
Actions by or against, **28 § 2412**
Award of,
Attorneys' fees and other expenses, **28 § 2412**
Civil actions by or against U.S. officials, award of, **28 § 2412**
Judgment for, prevailing party, actions by or against, **28 § 2412**

OFFICERS AND EMPLOYEES OF GOVERNMENT—Cont'd
Crimes and offenses,
Investigation, **28 § 535**
Government Ethics, Office of, cooperation, conflict of interest, **5, Ap 4, § 402**
Investigation and prosecution, assistance to Justice Department, **28 § 509 nt**
Removal of action or prosecution against for acts under color of office, **28 § 1442**
Criminal and other identification records,
Exchange with authorized officials, **28 § 534**
Parimutuel licensing, simplification, requests from State regulatory officials, **28 § 534 nt**
Damages, district court's jurisdiction of claim against U.S., **28 § 1346**
Death,
Caused by Government personnel,
Action against U.S., trial by court, **28 § 2402**
Administrative adjustment of claims for damages, **28 § 2672**
Disposition of case by agency prerequisite to action against U.S., **28 § 2675**
District court's jurisdiction of claim against U.S., **28 § 1346**
Punitive damages, liability of U.S., **28 § 2674**
Disbursing Officials, Clerks, and Agents, generally, this index
Discrimination, generally, this index
Extraordinary expense in executing Act of Congress, allowance of payment by Attorney General, **28 § 1929**
Facts material to action by U.S. unknown, time limitation, exclusion, **28 § 2416**
Fees,
Claims in U.S. Court of Federal Claims, time for filing suit, **28 § 2501**
Frauds, investigation,
Assistance to Justice Department, **28 § 509 nt**
General Services Administration, generally, this index
Government Ethics, Office of, preventing conflicts of interest. Personnel Management, Office of, generally, this index
Government Printing Office, generally, this index
Heads of executive departments, military departments,
Judicial sales, actions affecting property in which U.S. has lien, bidding, **28 § 2410**
Legal services, on pending claims in executive departments or agencies, **28 § 514**

OFFICERS AND EMPLOYEES OF GOVERNMENT—Cont'd
Heads of executive departments, military departments—Cont'd
Notice,
Legal services required on pending claims in departments and agencies, **28 § 514**
Questions of law, opinion by Attorney General, **28 § 512**
Refusal to comply with call for information or papers by U.S. Court of Federal Claims, **28 § 2507**
Reports,
Crimes involving officers and employees, **28 § 535**
United States Court of Federal Claims, notice of suit on unsettled accounts by Government officers, contractors, **28 § 2511**
Witness fees and allowances, **28 § 2412**
Hours of Labor, generally, this index
Incentive Pay or Awards, generally, this index
Independent Counsel, generally, this index
Inspection,
Dockets outside continental U.S., **28 § 604**
Institutes and joint councils on sentencing, attendance by Federal officers, **28 § 334**
Intimidation,
Statistics compilation, **28 § 534 nt**
Investigations,
Crimes involving, **28 § 535**
Government Ethics, Office of, cooperation, conflict of interest, **5, Ap 4, § 402**
Judgments rendered by State or foreign courts, payment, **28 § 2414**
Jury service,
Compensation for work injuries, applicability of provisions, **28 § 1877**
Exemptions from, **28 § 1863**
Justice, judge or Magistrate Judge, prior participation as counsel, matter in controversy, disqualification, **28 § 455**
Law books and publications furnished transmitted to successors, **28 § 414**
Limitation,
Actions brought by, **28 §§ 2415, 2416**
Litigation where a party, conducting reserved to Justice Department, **28 § 516**
Motor vehicles,
Defense of suits against employees in scope of employment arising from operation of, **28 § 2679**
Mileage, generally, this index
Narcotic drug addicts, civil commitment and rehabilitation, delegation of functions and use of facilities, **28 § 2905**

OFFICERS AND EMPLOYEES OF GOVERNMENT—Cont'd
Negligence,
Administration, adjustment of claim, **28 § 2672**
Arbitration, compromise or settlement of claims, **28 § 2677**
Attorney General authorized to arbitrate, compromise or settle claim, **28 § 2677**
Attorney's fees, **28 § 2678**
Claims against U.S., administrative adjustment, **28 § 2672**
Disposition by agency as prerequisite to action on claim against U.S., **28 § 2675**
District courts, jurisdiction of claim against U.S., **28 § 1346**
Exceptions as to obligation of actions, **28 § 2680**
Exclusiveness of remedy, **28 § 2679**
Judgment as bar to action against employee, **28 § 2676**
Penalty for excessive attorneys' fees, **28 § 2678**
Real estate, quieting title, inapplicability to actions involving claims against U.S., **28 § 2409a**
Trial by court, **28 § 2402**
Oaths and Affirmations, generally, this index
Parties,
Plaintiff, original jurisdiction of district court, **28 § 1345**
Time for appeal to court of appeals, **28 § 2107**
Pay and allowances,
Basic pay,
Judicial branch,
Increase, **28 § 603 nt**
Congressional authorization required for increases to, **28 § 461 nt**
Per Diem, generally, this index
Postmaster General, generally, this index
President of the United States, generally, this index
Presidential appointment, prohibition of cash awards. Incentive Pay or Awards, generally, this index
Public officer,
Defined, Jury Selection and Service Act, **28 § 1869**
Publications distributed to Federal courts at places where building not owned by U.S., officer as custodian, **28 § 413**
Receivers and receivership, ineligibility to appointment as receivers, **28 § 958**
Recovery of money erroneously paid to, action by U.S., limitation, **28 §§ 2415, 2416**
Removal,
Action or prosecution against, **28 § 1442**
Reports,
Crimes involving, **28 § 535**

OFFICERS AND EMPLOYEES OF GOVERNMENT—Cont'd
Reports—Cont'd
Crimes involving—Cont'd
Government Ethics, Office of, cooperation, conflict of interest, **5, Ap 4, § 402**
Review. Appeal and review, generally, ante
Secretary of Agriculture, generally, this index
Secretary of Army, generally, this index
Secretary of Commerce, generally, this index
Secretary of Defense, generally, this index
Secretary of Housing and Urban Development, generally, this index
Secretary of Labor, generally, this index
Secretary of State, generally, this index
Secretary of Transportation, generally, this index
Secretary of Treasury, generally, this index
Secretary of Veterans Affairs, generally, this index
Separation pay. Pay and allowances, generally, ante
Special Counsel, Office of, generally, this index
Statement concerning facts, relating to petitions in U.S. Court of Federal Claims or U.S. Court of Appeals for Federal Circuit, furnishing, **28 § 520**
Subpoena issued in behalf of, tender of fees and mileage, **28 § 1825**
Supervision of litigation where a party, **28 § 519**
Transmittal of letter rogatory or request to, **28 § 1781**
Treasurer of United States, generally, this index
United States Attorneys, generally, this index
United States Magistrate Judges, generally, this index
United States Marshals Service, generally, this index
Venue, actions against, **28 § 1391**
Wages for services. Pay and allowances, generally, ante
Witnesses, payment, **28 § 1825**
Wrongful acts. Negligence, generally, ante

OFFICES
Review, orders, certain Federal agencies, venue, **28 § 2343**
United States Court of International Trade, location, **28 § 251**
United States Marshals, **28 § 561**

OFFICIAL BONDS
Bonds, generally, this index

OFFICIAL DUTY STATION
Justices and judges, **28 § 456**

OFFICIAL MARK
Trademarks and Trade Names, generally, this index

OFFICIAL NOTICE
Notice, generally, this index

OFFICIAL SEALS
Seals (Official Seals), generally, this index

OFFICIAL STATIONS
Bankruptcy courts, judges, **28 § 152**
Clerks of district court, designation, **28 § 751**
United States attorneys, **28 § 545**
United States Marshals, **28 § 561**

OGDEN, UT
United States District Court, location, **28 § 125**

OHIO
See, also, States, generally, this index
Bankruptcy judges, appointment, number in judicial district, **28 § 152**
District courts,
Cities, held at, **28 § 115**
Judges,
Additional, **28 § 133 nt**
Appointment, additional judges, advice and consent, **28 § 133 nt**
Existing judgeships authorized, **28 § 133 nt**
Number, **28 § 133**
Temporary judgeships, **28 § 133 nt**
Places of holding, **28 § 115**
Judicial circuit of U.S., **28 § 41**
Judicial districts, **28 § 115**
Bankruptcy provisions, applicability of certain amendments to, **28 § 581 nt**
Number of district judges, **28 § 133**
United States trustees of judicial districts, appointment, **28 § 581**

OKLAHOMA
See, also, States, generally, this index
Bankruptcy judges,
Appointment, number in judicial district, **28 § 152**
Serving on part-time basis on certain date, extension, **28 § 152 nt**
District courts,
Cities, held at, **28 § 116**
Judges,
Existing judgeships, treatment, **28 § 133 nt**
Number, additional, **28 §§ 133, 133 nt**
Places of holding, **28 § 116**
Judicial circuit of U.S., **28 § 41**
Judicial districts,
Bankruptcy provisions, applicability of certain amendments to, **28 § 581 nt**
Number of district judges, **28 § 133**

OKLAHOMA—Cont'd
United States trustees of judicial districts, appointment, **28 § 581**

OKLAHOMA CITY, OK
Counterterrorism Fund, establishment, to restore operational capability of facility destroyed in bombing, **28 § 524 nt**
Court of Appeals for Tenth Circuit, generally, this index

OLYMPIC GAMES
Amateur Sports and Athletic Organizations, generally, this index

OPINIONS AND DECISIONS
Attorney General, this index
Law Reports, generally, this index
United States Court of Federal Claims, this index
United States Court of International Trade, this index

ORAL COMMUNICATIONS
Interception of Wire, Oral, or Electronic Communications, generally, this index

ORAL TESTIMONY
Evidence, generally, this index

ORDERS OF COURT
Appellate court directing entry, **28 § 2106**
Change of venue, **28 § 1404**
Court always open for making, **28 § 452**
Courts of Appeals, this index
District Courts, this index
Habeas Corpus, this index
Lost or destroyed record, verified application for order establishing record, **28 § 1734**
Moneys paid into court, criminal appearance bail bond, use to pay fine, assessment, **28 § 2044**
Property in different districts affected, **28 § 1692**
Real estate, actions quieting title, disclaimer by U.S. prior to trial, termination, jurisdiction of district court, **28 § 2409a**
Removal of Cases or Causes, this index
Revenue laws, property taken under subject to, **28 § 2463**
Rules of Appellate Procedure, this index
Rules of Civil Procedure, this index
Sentence and Punishment, this index
Supreme Court,
Allotment of justices as circuit justices, **28 § 42**
Marshal to serve and execute, **28 § 672**
United States Court of Federal Claims, this index
United States Court of International Trade, this index
Withdrawal of money deposited in court, **28 § 2042**

ORDERS OF COURT—Cont'd
Witnesses, recalcitrant witnesses refusal to comply with order to testify or provide information, **28 § 1826**

ORDERS TO SHOW CAUSE
Habeas corpus,
Answer to, **28 § 2248**
Issuance of writ, **28 § 2243**
Persons in foreign country failing to respond to subpoena, **28 § 1784**
Resident or U.S. national in foreign country failing to respond to subpoena, **28 § 1784**
Subpoena of national or resident of U.S. in foreign country, service, **28 §§ 1783, 1784**
United States Magistrate Judges, contempt in proceedings before, **28 § 636**

OREGON
See, also, States, generally, this index
Bankruptcy judges,
Appointment, number in judicial district, **28 § 152**
Serving on part-time basis on certain date, extension, **28 § 152 nt**
District courts,
Cities, held at, **28 § 117**
Judges, number, additional, **28 §§ 133, 133 nt**
Places of holding, **28 § 117**
Indians,
State civil jurisdiction in actions to which Indians are parties, **28 § 1360**
Judicial circuit of U.S., **28 § 41**
Judicial districts, **28 § 117**
Bankruptcy provisions, applicability of certain amendments to, **28 § 581 nt**
Number of district judges, **28 § 133**
United States trustees of judicial districts, appointment, **28 § 581**

ORIGINAL JURISDICTION
District Courts, this index
Supreme Court, **28 § 1251**

OSAGE INDIANS
Judgment in favor of claimant to allotment of land, exceptions, **28 § 1353**

OUTLYING POSSESSIONS
Insular Possessions and Dependencies, generally, this index

OYSTERS
Dredging operations damaging,
Jurisdiction of U.S. Court of Federal Claims, **28 § 1497**
Time for filing suit in U.S. Court of Federal Claims, **28 § 2501**

PACKERS
Secretary of Agriculture,
Orders,
Enforcement by district courts, 28 § 2351

PAINTINGS (WORKS OF ART)
Copyrights, generally, this index

PALMYRA ISLAND
Judicial district of Hawaii, inclusion in, 28 § 91

PAMPHLETS
Supreme Court, this index

PAN AMERICAN GAMES
Amateur Sports and Athletic Organizations, generally, this index

PANAMA CANAL
Canal Zone, generally, this index
Panama Canal Company, generally, this index
Zone. Canal Zone, generally, this index

PANAMA CANAL COMPANY
Tort Claims Act, exception of claim arising from activities of company, 28 § 2680

PANELS
Courts of Appeals, senior circuit judge eligible to participate as member of in banc court reviewing decision of panel, 28 § 46
Judicial Panel on Multidistrict Litigation, generally, this index
Jury panels,
Challenging compliance with selection procedures, 28 § 1867
Selection and summoning, 28 § 1866
United States Court of Appeals for the Federal Circuit, this index

PAPERS
Books and Papers, generally, this index

PARDON
Jurors, qualifications for service, form, contents concerning, 28 § 1869
United States Court of Federal Claims, this index

PARENT AND CHILD
See, also, Children and Minors, generally, this index
Annuities unable to be paid to survivors of justices and judges, payments to parents, 28 § 376
Missing persons, Attorney General to acquire, collect, classify, information concerning, provide information to parent, 28 § 534

PARENTAL KIDNAPPING PREVENTION
Generally, 28 § 1738A

PARENTAL KIDNAPPING PREVENTION—Cont'd
Congressional findings and purposes, 28 § 1738A nt
Contestant,
Notice and hearing before custody determination, 28 § 1738A
Custody determination,
Consistent with provisions of Act, requirements, 28 § 1738A
Custody disputes, consequences, Congressional findings and purposes, 28 § 1738A nt
Definitions, 28 § 1738A
Full faith and credit given to child custody determinations of other States, 28 § 1738A
Home State,
Presence of child in or other relationship of child to, requirement for custody determination consistent with Act, 28 § 1738A
Jurisdiction, continuation while custody determination is consistent with Act, 28 § 1738A
National system of locating parents, establishment, 28 § 1738A
Physical custody,
Person having, notice and hearing before custody determination, 28 § 1738A
State courts, jurisdiction, conditions for exercise, 28 § 1738A
Visitation determination, 28 § 1738A

PARIMUTUEL LICENSING SIMPLIFICATION ACT OF 1988
Generally, 28 § 534 nt
Parimutuel licensing, simplification, consolidated related request to Federal Government for identification and criminal records of applicants, 28 § 534 nt
State, defined, 28 § 534 nt

PARKING
Fees for, payment to juror, presentation of valid parking receipt, 28 § 1871

PARKS
National Park Service, generally, this index

PARTIES
Absent defendant, district court, order for appearance, lien enforcement, 28 § 1655
Administrative Law and Procedure, this index
Change of venue for convenience of, 28 § 1404
Collusive joinder, lack of jurisdiction of district courts, 28 § 1359
Disability, time for commencing action against U.S., 28 § 2401
Improper joinder, lack of jurisdiction of district court, 28 § 1359

PARTIES—Cont'd
Intervention,
State, proceeding involving constitutionality of State statute, 28 § 2403
Surface Transportation Board orders, actions to enforce, 28 § 2323
United States in proceeding where constitutional question involved, 28 § 2403
Jury, number of challenges permitted, 28 § 1870
Justice, judge or Magistrate Judge, relationship in affairs of, disqualification, 28 § 455
Multidistrict litigation, transfer to single district for consolidated, pretrial proceedings, 28 § 1407
Peremptory challenges in civil cases, additional, multiple plaintiffs and defendants, 28 § 1870
Personal conduct of case in court, 28 § 1654
Review, orders, certain Federal agencies, 28 § 2348
Rules of Appellate Procedure, this index
Rules of Civil Procedure, this index
Supreme Court, this index
Surface Transportation Board, proceedings to enforce orders of Board, 28 § 2323
Tax liens, U.S., actions to quiet title, foreclose, 28 § 2410
United States Court of Federal Claims, this index
United States Court of International Trade, this index
Venue or District of Trial, generally, this index

PARTIES TO ACTIONS
Parties, generally, this index

PARTITION
Liens and incumbrances, property on which U.S. has lien, 28 § 2410
Marshal's fees for serving writ, 28 § 1921
United States,
As tenant in common or joint tenant, venue, 28 § 1399
Jurisdiction of district court, 28 § 1347
Inapplicability to actions involving claims against, real property, quieting title, 28 § 2409a

PARTNERSHIP
Attorneys' fees and other costs and expenses, award to party prevailing against U.S. or agency, applicability, 28 § 2412
Bankruptcy, this index
Income tax,
Final partnership administrative adjustments, jurisdiction of district court, 28 § 1346

PARTNERSHIP—Cont'd
Internal Revenue Service,
Income tax, generally, ante
Limitations, outside employment, certain Government employees, **5, Ap 4, § 502**
Rules of Civil Procedure, this index

PATENT AND TRADEMARK OFFICE
Commissioner of Patents and Trademarks, generally, this index
Disclaimer, filing, inclusion of costs in judgment, infringement action, **28 § 1928**
Patents, generally, this index
Records and recordation,
Evidence, **28 § 1744**
Seals (official seals),
Copies of Patent and Trademark documents as evidence, **28 § 1744**
Trademarks and Trade Names, generally, this index
United States Court of Appeals for the Federal Circuit, this index

PATENTS
Actions and proceedings,
Infringement,
Service of process, where defendant is not resident of district, **28 § 1694**
Jurisdiction of district court, **28 § 1338**
Venue, **28 § 1400**
Board of Patent Appeals and Interferences,
United States Court of Appeals for the Federal Circuit, jurisdiction of appeals from decision of, **28 § 1295**
Claims,
Foreign countries, **28 § 1498**
Commissioner of Patents and Trademarks, generally, this index
Copies, letters patent as evidence, **28 § 1744**
Costs, infringement action, **28 § 1928**
Disclaimer,
Inclusion of costs in judgment, **28 § 1928**
District Courts, this index
Evidence, **28 § 1744**
Foreign Patents, generally, this index
Infringement,
Cost in action for, **28 § 1928**
Defendant not resident of district, service of process, **28 § 1694**
Notice,
Infringement, generally, ante
Patent and Trademark Office, generally, this index
Proceedings. Actions and proceedings, generally, ante
Process,
Defendant not resident of district, service of process, **28 § 1694**
Rules of Civil Procedure, this index
Trademarks and Trade Names, generally, this index

PATENTS—Cont'd
United States Court of Appeals for the Federal Circuit, this index
United States Court of Federal Claims, this index
Venue of action, **28 § 1400**

PAUPERS
Indigent Persons, generally, this index

PAY AND ALLOWANCES
Compensation and Salaries, generally, this index

PECUNIARY INTEREST
Conflicts of Interest, generally, this index

PENAL CODE
Crimes and Offenses, generally, this index

PENAL INSTITUTIONS
Correctional Institutions, generally, this index

PENALTIES
Fines, Penalties and Forfeitures, generally, this index

PENNSYLVANIA
See, also, States, generally, this index
Bankruptcy judges, appointment, number in judicial district, **28 § 152**
District court,
Cities, held at, **28 § 118**
Judges,
Appointment, additional judges, advice and consent, **28 § 133 nt**
Number, **28 § 133**
Additional, **28 § 133 nt**
Temporary judgeships, **28 § 133 nt**
Places of holding, **28 § 118**
Judicial circuit of U.S., **28 § 41**
Judicial districts, **28 § 118**
Bankruptcy provisions, applicability of certain amendments to, **28 § 581 nt**
Number of district judges, **28 § 133**
National Cemeteries, generally, this index
United States trustees of judicial districts, appointment, **28 § 581**

PENOLOGISTS
Participation in institutes and joint councils on sentencing, **28 § 334**

PENSIONS
Retirement and Pensions, generally, this index

PER DIEM
See, also, Traveling Expenses, generally, this index
Citizens' Commission on Public Service and Compensation, generally, this index

PER DIEM—Cont'd
Courts of Appeals, Structural Alternatives for the Federal Courts of Appeals Commission, **28 § 41 nt**
Judges, Ninth Circuit, temporarily assigned to Compact States, **28 § 297**
Structural Alternatives for the Federal Courts of Appeals Commission, **28 § 41 nt**
Witnesses, **28 § 1821**

PEREMPTORY CHALLENGES
Jury, this index

PERFORMING ARTS
Copyrights, generally, this index

PERIODICALS
Attorney General, authority to sell and exchange, procurement, **28 §§ 413, 525**
Director of Administrative Office of U.S. Courts, authority to sell and exchange in procurement of periodicals, **28 § 413**
Foreign patent offices, copies of excerpts as evidence, **28 § 1745**
Newspapers, generally, this index
Supreme Court,
Disbursement of funds for by marshal, **28 § 672**
Purchase, by librarian, **28 § 674**

PERJURY
Federal proceedings, evidence, unsworn declarations under penalty of perjury, **28 § 1746**
Unsworn declaration under penalty of perjury as evidence in Federal proceedings, **28 § 1746**

PERMITS
Licenses and Permits, generally, this index

PERSONAL INJURIES
Bankruptcy, this index
District courts, jurisdiction,
Civil rights, interference with, **28 § 1343**
Damages in enforcing right of citizens to vote, **28 § 1357**
Employees' Compensation for Work Injuries, generally, this index
Federal Employers' Liability Act, generally, this index
Foreign states, jurisdictional immunity, exception under certain conditions, **28 § 1605**
Workers Compensation, generally, this index

PERSONAL PROPERTY
Federal Debt Collection, this index
Judicial sales, **28 § 2004**

PERSONAL REPRESENTATIVES
Executors and Administrators, generally, this index
Fiduciaries, generally, this index
Guardian and Ward, generally, this index

PERSONAL SERVICE
Service of Process, generally, this index

PERSONNEL
Officers and Employees of Government, generally, this index

PERSONNEL MANAGEMENT, OFFICE OF
Administrative Office of United States Courts, generally, this index
Director,
Federal Legal Council, advisory members of, **28 § 509 nt, EON 12146**
Government Ethics, Office of, post
Discrimination, generally, this index
Government Ethics, Office of, **5, Ap 4, § 401**
Actions and proceedings against Government employees violating income and employment limitations, **5, Ap 4, § 504**
Administration, limitations on outside income and employment, **5, Ap 4, § 503**
Administrative provisions, **5, Ap 4, § 403**
Advisory opinion service, powers, **5, Ap 4, § 402**
Advisory opinions, limitations on outside income and employment, **5, Ap 4, § 504**
Agency ethics counselors, consultation with, **5, Ap 4, § 402**
Appropriations, authorization, **5, Ap 4, § 405**
Attorney General,
Civil actions for violations,
Government employees violating income and employment limitations, **5, Ap 4, § 504**
Limitation on outside income and employment, **5, Ap 4, § 504**
Cooperation in developing rules and regulations, **5, Ap 4, § 402**
Authority and functions, **5, Ap 4, § 402**
Charitable contributions in lieu of honoraria, treatment, **5, Ap 4, § 501**
Charitable organization, defined, limitations on outside income and employment, **5, Ap 4, § 505**
Civil penalties, violation of limitations on outside income and employment, Representatives, officers and employees of Congress, **5, Ap 4, § 504**
Conflicts of interest,
Executive agency officers and employees, overall direction of policies preventing, **5, Ap 4, § 402**

PERSONNEL MANAGEMENT, OFFICE OF—Cont'd
Government Ethics, Office of—Cont'd
Conflicts of interest—Cont'd
Rules and regulations,
Issuance, **5, Ap 4, § 404**
Promulgation, **5, Ap 4, § 402**
Corrective action, agencies, individuals, provisions for, **5, Ap 4, § 402**
Definitions, limitations on outside income and employment, **5, Ap 4, § 505**
Director,
Appointment, **5, Ap 4, § 401**
Attorneys, appointment of, **5, Ap 4, § 401**
Authority and functions, **5, Ap 4, § 402**
Contracting authority, financial and administrative services, **5, Ap 4, § 401**
Corrective action, provisions, **5, Ap 4, § 402**
Officers and employees, appointment of, powers regarding, **5, Ap 4, § 401**
Reports, Congress, summary of actions taken, **5, Ap 4, § 408**
Request,
Assistance from inspector general of an agency to conduct investigations, authority, **5, Ap 4, § 403**
To executive agencies for cooperation, **5, Ap 4, § 403**
Rules and regulations,
Conflicts of interest, promulgation, **5, Ap 4, § 402**
Issuance, **5, Ap 4, § 404**
Responsibilities of, effect of Act, **5, Ap 4, § 402 nt**
Term of service, **5, Ap 4, § 401**
Employment, outside employment, limitations on, Representatives, officers and employees of Congress, **5, Ap 4, § 502**
Ethical standards in executive agencies, providing information, **5, Ap 4, § 402**
Ethics,
Executive branch, rules and regulations, issuance, **5, Ap 4, § 404**
Evaluation of items required to be reported, development of rules and regulations relating to, **5, Ap 4, § 402**
Executive agencies,
Authority of Director with relation to, **5, Ap 4, § 402**
Cooperate with, **5, Ap 4, § 403**
Information to be reported by, **5, Ap 4, § 402**
Financial statements, filing, by executive branch officers and employees, rules and regulations relating to, **5, Ap 4, § 402**

PERSONNEL MANAGEMENT, OFFICE OF—Cont'd
Government Ethics, Office of—Cont'd
Fines, penalties and forfeitures, Government employees, violating outside income and employment limitations, **5, Ap 4, § 504**
Gifts, bequests, authorization of Director to accept, conditions, **5, Ap 4, § 403**
Honoraria prohibition, Representatives, officers and employees of Congress, **5, Ap 4, § 501**
Honorarium, defined, limitations on outside income and employment, **5, Ap 4, § 505**
Information, reported by executive agencies, provisions, **5, Ap 4, § 402**
Inspector general of an agency, Director, requesting assistance from to conduct investigations, **5, Ap 4, § 403**
Investigations,
Crimes involving Government officers and employees, cooperation with Attorney General, **5, Ap 4, § 402**
Director, authority to request assistance from inspector general of an agency to conduct, **5, Ap 4, § 403**
Judicial review of rules or regulations, **5, Ap 4, § 404**
Limitations on outside earned income and employment, **5, Ap 4, § 501 et seq.**
Member, defined, limitations on outside income and employment, Representatives, officers and employees of Congress, **5, Ap 4, § 505**
Officer or employee, defined, limitations on outside income and employment, **5, Ap 4, § 505**
Outside earned income limitation, **5, Ap 4, § 501**
President of U.S.,
Appointment of Director, **5, Ap 4, § 402**
Rules and regulations relating to conflicts of interest, **5, Ap 4, § 402**
Reports, executive agencies, **5, Ap 4, § 402**
Rules and regulations,
Conflicts of interest, promulgation, **5, Ap 4, § 402**
In effect before certain date, remaining in effect until modified, **5, Ap 4, § 402 nt**
Issuance, **5, Ap 4, § 404**
Travel expenses, defined, limitations on outside income and employment, **5, Ap 4, § 505**

PERSONNEL MANAGEMENT, OFFICE OF—Cont'd
House of Representatives, limitations, outside earned income and employment. Government Ethics, Office of, generally, ante
Incentive Pay or Awards, generally, this index
Limitations, outside earned income and employment. Government Ethics, Office of, generally, ante

PETIT JURY
Jury, generally, this index

PETITIONS
Customs Duties, this index
Judicial Center Board, special meetings, **28 § 622**
Multidistrict Litigation Judicial Panel, review, orders, **28 § 1407**
Petitioner, defined, review, orders of Federal agencies, **28 § 2341**
Rules of Appellate Procedure, this index
Supreme Court, this index
United States Court of Appeals for the Federal Circuit, this index
United States Court of Federal Claims, this index

PETTY OFFENSES
Minor or Petty Offenses, generally, this index

PHILADELPHIA, PA
Court of Appeals for Third Circuit, this index

PHOTOGRAPHS AND PHOTOGRAPHY
Business records, evidence, **28 § 1732**
Copyrights, generally, this index

PHOTOSTATIC COPIES
Business records, evidence, **28 § 1732**

PHYSICAL INFIRMITIES
Jurors, qualification for service, **28 § 1865**
Form, contents concerning, **28 § 1869**

PHYSICAL INJURIES
Personal Injuries, generally, this index

PHYSICALLY HANDICAPPED PERSONS
Handicapped Persons, generally, this index

PICTURES
Photographs and Photography, generally, this index

PLACE OF TRIAL
Venue or District of Trial, generally, this index

PLANS AND SPECIFICATIONS
Bankruptcy, this index

PLANS AND SPECIFICATIONS
—Cont'd
Community Development, this index
Judicial Conference of the U.S., preparation of plans for assignment of judges, **28 § 331**
Jurors, plan for random selection, **28 § 1863**

PLANT VARIETY PROTECTION
Generally, **28 § 1498**
Appeal and review,
Refusal, application for protection of variety, jurisdiction, U.S. Court of Appeals for the Federal Circuit, **28 § 1295**
United States Court of Appeals for the Federal Circuit and other review, **28 § 1295**
Applications,
Protection of varieties,
Appeals from refusal, jurisdiction, U.S. Court of Appeals for the Federal Circuit, **28 § 1295**
Cease and desist orders, false marking,
Appeals from decisions respecting, jurisdiction, U.S. Court of Appeals for the Federal Circuit, **28 § 1295**
Certificate recognizing variety rights,
Reexamination after issue,
Appeals, decisions respecting, jurisdiction, U.S. Court of Appeals for the Federal Circuit, **28 § 1295**
Damages,
Infringement cases,
Action against U.S. for infringement, **28 § 1498**
District courts, original jurisdiction of actions relating to, **28 § 1338**
False marking,
Cease and desist orders, appeals from decisions respecting, jurisdiction, U.S. Court of Appeals for the Federal Circuit, **28 § 1295**
Infringement,
By U.S., or federally owned or controlled corporation, exclusive remedy by action in U.S. Court of Federal Claims for recovery of damages, **28 § 1498**
Jurisdiction, United States Court of Appeals for the Federal Circuit, appeals from decisions, **28 § 1295**
Priorities and preferences, appeals, from decision respecting, jurisdiction, U.S. Court of Appeals for the Federal Circuit, **28 § 1295**
Public interest in wide usage,
Appeals from decisions respecting, jurisdiction, U.S. Court of Appeals for the Federal Circuit, **28 § 1295**

PLANT VARIETY PROTECTION
—Cont'd
Reexamination after issue of certificate of variety protection,
Appeals from decisions respecting, jurisdiction, U.S. Court of Appeals for the Federal Circuit, **28 § 1295**
United States Court of Appeals for the Federal Circuit, jurisdiction, appeals from decisions, **28 § 1295**
United States Court of Federal Claims, exclusive remedy of owner of certificate by action against U.S. for damages for infringement, **28 § 1498**

PLEA IN ABATEMENT
Attachment against delinquent postmasters and postal officers, employees, trial of ownership of property, **28 § 2713**

PLEA OF NOLO CONTENDERE
Rules of Evidence, this index

PLEA OR ANSWER
District courts, reporter or other individual designated to produce record, transcribing and certifying parts of record of proceedings, **28 § 753**
Foreign states, jurisdictional immunities, **28 § 1608**
Habeas corpus proceedings,
Evidence, **28 § 2247**
Filing of certified copy, **28 § 2249**
Order to show cause in, **28 § 2248**
Tax liens, U.S. as party, actions to quiet title, foreclose, **28 § 2410**
United States, action affecting property on which it has liens, **28 § 2410**

PLEADING
Absent defendant, district court order to plead, lien enforcement, **28 § 1655**
Amendment of pleadings, jurisdiction, amendment to show jurisdiction, **28 § 1653**
Answer. Plea or Answer, generally, this index
Bankruptcy, this index
Bankruptcy Rules and Forms, this index
Complaints, generally, this index
Declaratory judgments, **28 § 2201**
District courts,
Continuance of pending pleadings on vacancy in office of district judge, **28 § 143**
Federal agencies,
Review of orders, hearings, proceedings in court of appeals, **28 § 2347**
Habeas corpus, **28 § 2244**
Record on review or enforcement in courts of appeals of agency, orders, inclusion of pleadings, **28 § 2112**
Removal of cases, filing of copy with notice of, **28 § 1446**
Rules of Civil Procedure, this index

PLEADING—Cont'd
Set-off or counterclaim, jurisdiction of district court, U.S. as defendant, **28 § 1346**
Tax liens, U.S. as party, actions to quiet title, foreclose, **28 § 2410**
Tort claims against U.S., **28 § 2679**
United States, action affecting property on which it has lien, **28 § 2410**
United States Court of Federal Claims, this index
United States Court of International Trade, this index

POLICE
See, also, Law Enforcement Officers, generally, this index
Jury service, exemption, **28 § 1863**

POLITICAL ACTIVITIES
Disclosure of Federal Campaign Funds, generally, this index
Federal employees,
Violations of Federal criminal law relating to, report to Congress, **28 § 529**

POLITICAL PARTIES
Disclosure of Federal Campaign Funds, generally, this index
Jury commission, prohibition on membership, **28 § 1863**
United States Court of International Trade judges, restrictions on appointment, **28 § 251**

POLITICAL SUBDIVISIONS
See, also,
Local Government, generally, this index
Municipal Corporations, generally, this index
Community Development, generally, this index
Firemen, exemption from jury service, **28 § 1863**
Officers and employees,
Executive, branches, exemption from jury service, **28 § 1863**
Police, exemption from jury service, **28 § 1863**
Rate orders, jurisdiction of district courts, **28 § 1342**

POLLUTION
Ocean Dumping, generally, this index

POOR PERSONS
Indigent Persons, generally, this index

PORT OF ENTRY
Forfeiture of vessel or cargo entering closed port of entry, venue, **28 § 1395**

PORTUGAL
Conventions, on the taking of Evidence Abroad in Civil or Commercial Matters, party to, **28 § 1781 nt**

POSSESSION, WRIT OF
Marshal's fees for serving, **28 § 1921**

POSSESSIONS OF UNITED STATES
Insular Possessions and Dependencies, generally, this index

POST OFFICE DEPARTMENT
See, also, Postal Service, generally, this index
Interest, suits for balances due, former Department, **28 § 2718**
Suits, former Department, balances due, interest, **28 § 2718**

POSTAL SERVICE
See, also, Mail and Mailing, generally, this index
Actions and proceedings,
Jurisdiction of district court, **28 § 1339**
District courts, jurisdiction, **28 § 1339**
Postmaster General, generally, this index
Postmasters, generally, this index
Tort claims, applicability, **28 § 2680**

POSTMASTER GENERAL
Certificate,
Mailing to postmaster statement of his account, as evidence of demand, **28 § 1743**
Federal Legal Council, representatives designated by, **28 § 509 nt, EON 12146**
Mail and Mailing, generally, this index

POSTMASTERS
Certificates, mailing to postmaster statement of his account, as evidence of demand, **28 § 1743**
Demand on, evidence, **28 § 1743**

POVERTY
Indigent Persons, generally, this index

PRECEDENCE
United States Court of International Trade, this index

PREEMPTION
Federal debt collection procedures, preemption of State law, rules of construction, **28 § 3003**

PREFERENCES
Priorities and Preferences, generally, this index

PREFERENCES AND PRIORITIES
Priorities and Preferences, generally, this index

PREJUDICE
Bias and Prejudice, generally, this index

PRELIMINARY OR INTERLOCUTORY INJUNCTIONS
Injunctions, this index

PRESENTS
Gifts, generally, this index

PRESERVATION
Identification and criminal identification records, **28 § 534**
Jury commission or clerk of district court, records and papers, **28 § 1868**
United States Court of International Trade decisions, **28 § 257**

PRESIDENT OF SENATE PRO TEMPORE
Federal Judicial Center Foundation, appointment of members to, **28 § 629**

PRESIDENT OF THE UNITED STATES
Accountability, Presidential and executive offices. Presidential and Executive Office Accountability, generally, this index
Alaska,
United States District Court for District of Alaska proclaimed ready to assume functions, **28 § 81A nt, EON 10867**
Bankruptcy judges, nominees for appointment, race, color, sex, not to be considered in selecting, **28 § 44 nt**
Budget, generally, this index
Closing of port of entry, venue of proceeding for forfeiture of vessel or cargo entering port, **28 § 1395**
Conflicts of Interest, generally, this index
Congress,
Statement, appointment of judges, **28 § 44 nt**
Courts of appeals,
Appointment of additional circuit judgeships, **28 § 44 nt**
Judges, appointment, **28 § 44**
Additional judges, **28 § 44 nt**
Nominees for appointment, race, color, sex, not to be considered in selecting, **28 § 44 nt**
Disclosure of Federal Campaign Funds, generally, this index
Discrimination,
Nominees for appointment, race, color, sex, not to be considered in selecting, **28 § 44 nt**
District Judges, this index
Executive Orders, generally, this index
Government Ethics, Office of,
Director, appointment, **5, Ap 4, § 401**
Rules and regulations relating to conflicts of interest, **5, Ap 4, § 402**
Illinois, Southern District, appointment of district judge, **28 § 93 nt**
Independent Counsel, generally, this index

PRESIDENT OF THE UNITED STATES —Cont'd
Judges or justices appointed by President,
Congressional statement, **28 § 44 nt**
District court, **28 § 133**
Retirement for disability, appointment of successor, **28 § 372**
Territories and possessions, removal for disability, salary, **28 § 373**
Judicial Center, "service" as meaning service as Presidential appointee, retirement of Director, **28 § 627**
Justice Department seals, approval, **28 § 502**
National budget. Budget, generally, this index
Officials to assist in protecting, appointment, **28 § 533**
Pardon, generally, this index
Political Activities, generally, this index
Presidential and Vice Presidential Electors, generally, this index
Proclamations, generally, this index
Public Printing and Documents, generally, this index
Reports,
To President,
Personnel Management, Office of, generally, this index
United States Sentencing Commission, **28 § 997**
Seals (Official Seals), generally, this index
Solicitor General, appointment, **28 § 505**
Special Counsel, Office of, generally, this index
Special prosecutor, appointment, jurisdiction, powers to investigate and prosecute Federal crimes by, **28 § 592 et seq.**
United States attorneys, appointment and removal, **28 § 541**
United States Court of Appeals for Federal Circuit, appointment of judges, **28 § 44 nt**
United States Court of Federal Claims, judges, appointments, **28 § 171**
United States Court of International Trade, judges, appointment, **28 § 251**
United States marshals, appointment and removal, **28 § 561**
United States Sentencing Commission, appointment of members, **28 § 991**
Virgin Islands, this index

PRESIDENT PRO TEMPORE OF SENATE
President of Senate Pro Tempore, generally, this index

PRESIDENTIAL AND EXECUTIVE OFFICE ACCOUNTABILITY
Appeal and review, **28 § 3901 et seq.**
Attorney's fees, **28 § 3905**
Civil actions, **28 § 3901**

PRESIDENTIAL AND EXECUTIVE OFFICE ACCOUNTABILITY—Cont'd
Appeal and review—Cont'd
Definitions, **28 § 3908**
Exclusivity of remedy, **28 § 3907**
Expedited appeals, **28 § 3904**
Interest, **28 § 3905**
Jurisdiction, expedited review of certain appeals, **28 § 3904**
Jury trial, civil actions, **28 § 3901**
Payments, **28 § 3906**
Regulations, **28 § 3902**
Failure to issue, effect, **28 § 3903**
Supreme Court of the U.S., expedited review, **28 § 3904**
United States Court of Appeals for the Federal Circuit, jurisdiction, filings, **28 § 1296**
Attorneys, fees,
Judicial review, **28 § 3905**
Awards, judicial review, payments, **28 § 3906**
Compromise settlements, judicial review, payments, **28 § 3906**
Covered employee, defined,
Judicial review, **28 § 3908**
Damages,
Punitive, judicial review, **28 § 3905**
District courts, venue, **28 § 1413**
Employing office,
Defined,
Judicial review, **28 § 3908**
Interest,
Judicial review, **28 § 3905**
Judgments, judicial review, payments, **28 § 3906**
Jurisdiction, expedited review of certain appeals, **28 § 3904**
Jury trial, civil actions, **28 § 3901**
Rules and regulations,
Failure to issue, effect, judicial review, **28 § 3903**
Judicial review, **28 § 3902**
Supreme Court of the U.S., expedited review of certain appeals, **28 § 3904**
United States Court of Appeals for the Federal Circuit, review of certain agency actions, **28 § 1296**
United States District Court for the District of Columbia, venue, **28 § 1413**
Venue, **28 § 1413**

PRESIDENTIAL AND VICE PRESIDENTIAL ELECTORS
District courts, jurisdiction, action to recover possession of office, exception, **28 § 1344**

PRESIDING JUDICIAL OFFICER
Defined, court interpreters, **28 § 1827**
Electronic sound recordings of judicial proceedings, when court interpreters used, determinations, **28 § 1827**

PRESUMPTIONS
Habeas corpus proceedings in Federal courts, correctness of State court findings, exceptions, **28 § 2254**
United States Court of International Trade, decisions of Secretary of Treasury, administering authority, in certain civil actions presumed correct, **28 § 2639**

PRETRIAL PROCEEDINGS AND PROCEDURE
District courts, multidistrict litigation,
Transfer to single district for consolidated, pretrial proceedings, **28 § 1407**
Justice, judge or Magistrate Judge, disqualification, **28 § 455**

PRETRIAL SERVICES
Accommodations, Director of Administrative Office of U.S. Courts to provide, **28 § 604**
Administrative Office of United States Courts,
Director, **28 § 604**
Provisions of accommodations for, **28 § 462**
Division of Probation, provision of accommodations, **28 § 462**
Audit of vouchers and accounts of agencies and clerical and administrative personnel, **28 § 604**
Clerical and administrative personnel, accommodations, provided by Director of Administrative Office of U.S. Courts, **28 § 604**
Equipment and supplies, Director of Administrative Office of U.S. Courts to purchase, **28 § 604**
Federal public defender,
Provision of accommodations by Director of Administrative Office of U.S. Courts, **28 § 462**
Judicial Conference of the United States, **28 § 604**
Law books, Director of Administrative Office of U.S. Courts to purchase, **28 § 604**
Pretrial service officer, provision of accommodations by Director of Administrative Office of U.S. Courts, **28 § 462**

PRIMA FACIE EVIDENCE
District courts, transcript, case certified by reporter or other individual designated to produce record certificate deemed prima facie correct statement of testimony **28 § 753**

PRINCIPAL AND AGENT
Agents and Agencies, generally, this index

PRINCIPAL AND SURETY
Bonds, generally, this index

PRINCIPAL AND SURETY—Cont'd
Officers and employees, of U.S., settlement of accounts by U.S. Court of Federal Claims, **28 § 1494**

PRINTERS
Public Printer, generally, this index

PRINTING
Briefs in admiralty appeals, taxation as costs, **28 § 1923**
Fees, taxation as costs, **28 § 1920**
Public Printing and Documents, generally, this index
Record on appeal, in forma pauperis proceeding, expenses, **28 § 1915**

PRINTING OFFICE
Government Printing Office, generally, this index

PRINTS
Copyrights, generally, this index

PRIORITIES AND PREFERENCES
Bankruptcy, this index
Civil actions, determination of priority by court, exception, **28 § 1657**
Criminal cases on appeal from State court, **28 § 2102**
Lien of U.S. on property, **28 § 2410**
Plant Variety Protection, this index
Rules of Civil Procedure, this index

PRISONS AND PRISONERS
Correctional Institutions, generally, this index

PRIVATE AGENCIES
Judicial Center,
Boards and commissions, contracts for research projects and other services, **28 § 624**
Coordination, research and study, operation of courts, **28 § 620**
Operations of courts worthy of special study, recommendation, **28 § 623**
Narcotic drug addicts, civil commitment and rehabilitation, delegation of functions and use of facilities, **28 § 2905**

PRIVATE CORPORATIONS
Corporations, generally, this index

PRIVATE FOUNDATIONS
Foundations, generally, this index

PRIVILEGED INFORMATION
Confidential or Privileged Information, generally, this index

PRIVILEGES AND IMMUNITIES
Arbitrators, **28 § 655**
Civil Rights, this index
Diplomatic, limitation of actions by U.S. exclusion, **28 § 2416**
Rules of Evidence, this index

PRIVILEGES AND IMMUNITIES—Cont'd
Testimonial privilege, generally. Independent Counsel, this index
Trademarks and Trade Names, generally, this index

PRIZE (VESSELS)
District courts,
Jurisdiction, **28 § 1333**

PROBATION
Conditions of probation,
Modification of conditions,
Sentencing guidelines, **28 § 994**
Sentencing guidelines,
Duties of Commission, **28 § 994**
Officers and employees,
Accommodations provided by Director of Administrative Office of U.S. Courts, **28 § 462**
Investigations,
Official acts, by Attorney General, **28 § 526**
Judicial Center, conduct of programs of continuing education and training, **28 § 620**
Revocation or modification,
Sentencing guidelines, **28 § 994**
Transfer of Offenders to or from Foreign Countries, generally, this index
United States Sentencing Commission,
Consultation with Probation System on sentencing guidelines, **28 § 994**
Emergency guidelines promulgation authority, distribution to, System, expiration date, **28 § 994 nt**

PROCEEDINGS
Actions and Proceedings, generally, this index

PROCESS
Absent defendant, enforcement of lien, district courts, **28 § 1655**
Abuse of process, exception of claim from Tort Claims Act, **28 § 2680**
Admiralty, this index
Bankruptcy Rules and Forms, this index
Clerks of Courts, this index
Clerks of District Courts, this index
Courts always open for issuing and returning, **28 § 452**
District courts,
Continuance of pending process on vacancy in office of district judge, **28 § 143**
Enforcement, of ICC orders, **28 § 2321**
Receivers and receivership, property in different States, **28 § 1692**
Habeas corpus, prisoner in custody for act done, condition for granting writ, **28 § 2241**
Imprisonment for debt, **28 § 2007**
Interpleader,
District court, **28 § 2361**

PROCESS—Cont'd
Judicial Panel on Multidistrict Litigation, this index
Justices and judges, annuities to survivors, exemption from, **28 § 376**
New process, removal of case from state court, **28 § 1448**
Patents, this index
Place of arrest and civil action, **28 § 1693**
Property in different districts affected, **28 § 1692**
Removal of Cases or Causes, this index
Rules of Appellate Procedure, this index
Rules of Civil Procedure, this index
Seal of court, **28 § 1691**
Service of Process, generally, this index
Signature by clerk of court, **28 § 1691**
State court,
Action involving property on which U.S. has lien, **28 § 2410**
Habeas corpus to obtain custody of defendant on removal of case, **28 § 1446**
Subpoenas, generally, this index
Summons, generally, this index
Supreme Court, this index
Surface Transportation Board, enforcement or annulment of orders, **28 § 2321**
Tort claims against U.S., **28 § 2679**
United States, security for damages or cost not required on issuance of process, **28 § 2408**
United States attorney, action in State court involving property on which U.S. has lien, **28 § 2410**
United States Marshals Service, this index

PROCLAMATIONS
Admiralty, fees of U.S. marshal, preparation, **28 § 1921**
Insurrection and sedition,
Venue of proceedings for forfeiture of goods when State declared in insurrection, **28 § 1395**
United States Court of International Trade, civil action raising constitutionality issue, three-judge trials, **28 § 255**

PROCTORS
Docket fees, taxation as costs, **28 § 1923**

PROCUREMENT
Attorney General,
Law books, reference books, authority, **28 § 525**
Information technology,
Judiciary Information Technology Fund, establishment, **28 § 612**
Law books, books of reference or periodicals, **28 § 413**

PRODUCTION OF BOOKS AND PAPERS
Arbitration, **28 § 656**

PRODUCTION OF BOOKS AND PAPERS—Cont'd
Assistance to foreign and international tribunals and to litigants before such tribunals, **28 § 1782**
Contempt, failure of person in foreign country to produce, **28 § 1784**
Continuance in action by U.S. against delinquents for public moneys, original instrument required to be produced, **28 § 2407**
Person not to be compelled to produce document for use in proceeding in foreign or international tribunal, **28 § 1782**
Rules of Civil Procedure, this index
Senate action to secure, District Court for District of Columbia, jurisdiction, **28 § 1365**
Subpoena for,
National or resident of U.S. in foreign country, **28 § 1783**
United States Court of Federal Claims, **28 § 2521**

PROFESSIONS AND OCCUPATIONS
Juror qualification form, contents concerning, **28 § 1869**

PROMISSORY NOTES
Bills and Notes (Commercial Paper), generally, this index

PROOF
Evidence, generally, this index

PROPERTY
Bankruptcy, this index
Damages,
Foreign states, jurisdictional immunity, exception under certain conditions, **28 § 1605**
Federal Debt Collection, this index
Internal Revenue Service, generally, this index
Interpleader, district court, jurisdiction, **28 § 1335**
Liens and Incumbrances, generally, this index
Loss,
Tort claims against U.S., adjustment of claims, **28 § 2672**
Managers and management,
Actions and proceedings, leave of court, appointments, **28 § 959**
Application of state law, **28 § 959**
Personal Property, generally, this index
Real Estate, generally, this index
Searches and Seizures, generally, this index
Tax liens, generally. Liens and Incumbrances, this index
United States marshals, commissions, sales, **28 § 1921**

PROSECUTING ATTORNEY
Independent Counsel, generally, this index

PROTESTS
Customs Duties, this index

PROTHONOTARIES
Authentication of certificate of judge to records or books of State, territory or possession for use as evidence, **28 § 1739**

PSYCHIATRY AND PSYCHIATRISTS
Participation in institutes and joint councils on sentencing, **28 § 334**

PUBLIC AGENCIES
Federal Agencies and Instrumentalities, generally, this index
Judicial Center,
Coordination, research and study, operation of courts, **28 § 620**
Operations of courts worthy of special study, recommendation, **28 § 623**
Narcotic drug addicts, civil commitment and rehabilitation, delegation of functions and use of facilities, **28 § 2905**

PUBLIC ASSISTANCE
Social Security, generally, this index

PUBLIC CONTRACTS
See, also, Contracts, generally, this index
Aeronautics and Space Administration, Exchange Councils, express or implied contract with,
Civil action or claim against U.S., concurrent jurisdiction with U.S. Court of Federal Claims, **28 § 1346**
Court of Federal Claims, jurisdiction, claims founded on, **28 § 1491**
District courts, concurrent jurisdiction with Court of Federal Claims, civil action or claim against U.S., **28 § 1346**
Civil Rights, generally, this index
Disputes and claims, contracts awarded by executive agencies,
Agency boards of contract appeals,
Appeal and review, judicial review, cases sounding in tort, jurisdiction, claims against U.S., **28 § 1346**
Judicial review of,
Court of Appeals for the Federal Circuit, jurisdiction, **28 § 1295**
Appeal and review,
Certification by Attorney General of no appeal from judgment against U.S., exception, **28 § 2414**

PUBLIC CONTRACTS—Cont'd
Disputes and claims, contracts awarded by executive agencies—Cont'd
Appeal and review—Cont'd
Judicial review,
Decision of agency boards of contract appeals,
Court of Appeals for the Federal Circuit, jurisdiction, **28 § 1295**
Attorney General,
Payment of judgments and compromised settlements against U.S., exception, **28 § 2414**
Chairman, agency boards of contract appeals,
Against the U.S., jurisdiction, **28 § 1491**
Court of Federal Claims, payment by Treasury Secretary, **28 § 2517**
Claims, by contractor,
Over certain amount,
Court of Federal Claims, payment by Treasury Secretary, **28 § 2517**
Court of Federal Claims, judgment upon claim by or against the dispute with contract arising, claims against U.S., **28 § 1491**
Judgments,
Written by State or foreign courts, payment, exception, **28 § 2414**
Legal disability, time for commencement of actions against U.S., exception, **28 § 2401**
Limitation of actions,
Claims against U.S., exception, **28 § 2401**
Payment of,
Judgments and compromise settlements, exception, **28 § 2414**
Secretary of Treasury,
Compromise and settlement, payment of judgments against U.S., exceptions, **28 § 2414**
State courts, judgments against U.S., payment, exception, **28 § 2414**
Time,
Presenting claim commencing action against U.S., exception, **28 § 2401**
Tort claims against U.S., time for presenting claims or commencing action against U.S., exceptions, **28 § 2401**
Torts,
Cases sounding in, claims against U.S., **28 § 1346**
Time for presentation of claims or commencement of action against U.S., exception, **28 § 2401**
United States,
Claims against, jurisdiction, cases sounding in tort, **28 § 1346**

PUBLIC CONTRACTS—Cont'd
Disputes and claims, contracts awarded by executive agencies—Cont'd
United States—Cont'd
Judgments,
Payment, exception, State courts, **28 § 2414**
Payment, exception, **28 § 2414**
Tort claims, time for commencement of action or presentation of claims against, exception, **28 § 2401**
United States Court of Federal Claims,
Certification of judgment, payment by Treasury Secretary, exception, **28 § 2517**
Clerks, certification of judgment, payment by Treasury Secretary, **28 § 2517**
Judgment, **28 § 2517**

PUBLIC DEFENDERS
See, also, Pretrial Services, this index
Federal public defender,
United States Sentencing Commission, consultation with on sentencing guidelines, **28 § 994**
Witnesses, subpoenas issued, payment of fees on certificate of, **28 § 1825**

PUBLIC DOCUMENTS
Public Printing and Documents, generally, this index

PUBLIC LANDS
Fires and fire protection,
Action by U.S. for damages, limitations, **28 §§ 2415, 2416**
Trespass, action by U.S. for damages, limitations, **28 §§ 2415, 2416**
Water rights,
Suits for adjudication, real property, quieting title, inapplicability to actions involving claims against U.S., **28 § 2409a**

PUBLIC MONEYS
Delinquents for, action by U.S. against, **28 § 2407**
Disbursing Officials, Clerks, and Agents, generally, this index
Treasury of United States, generally, this index
Warrants, generally, this index

PUBLIC PRINTER
See, also, Public Printing and Documents, generally, this index
Supreme Court reports,
Furnished for distribution, **28 § 411**
Printing additional reports by, **28 § 412**

PUBLIC PRINTING AND DOCUMENTS
Attorney General's opinions, **28 § 521**
Courts of appeals, rules of practice, **28 § 2077**

PUBLIC PRINTING AND DOCUMENTS—Cont'd
Federal Register, generally, this index
Supreme Court reports, **28 §§ 411, 412**
Transmittal of government publications to successors in office of justices, judges, **28 § 414**

PUBLIC SAFETY
Corporation testing for,
Attorneys' fees and other costs and expenses, award to party prevailing against U.S. or agency, **28 § 2412**

PUBLIC UTILITIES
Rate orders of State agencies, district court's jurisdiction, **28 § 1342**

PUBLIC UTILITIES REVIEW ACTS
Generally, **28 § 1342**

PUBLICATION
Attachment against delinquent postmasters and postal officers, employees, **28 § 2715**
Attorney General's opinions, **28 § 521**
Courts of appeals, rules of practice, **28 § 2077**
Judicial sale of realty, **28 §§ 2001, 2002**
Newspapers, generally, this index
Notice,
Review, orders, certain Federal agencies, **28 § 2344**
Periodicals, generally, this index
Private sale under order of court, terms of, **28 § 2001**
Service of district court order for appearance by absent defendant, lien enforcement, **28 § 1655**
Transmittal of publications and books to successor in office, **28 § 414**
United States Court of International Trade, decisions and abstracts thereof, **28 § 257**
United States trustees, certification of judicial districts by Attorney General, **28 § 581 nt**

PUERTO RICO
Appeals to Supreme Court of U.S. from final judgments or decrees by Supreme Court of Puerto Rico, certiorari, **28 § 1258**
Certiorari to, Supreme Court of U.S., review of final judgments or decrees of Supreme Court of Puerto Rico, **28 § 1258**
Courts,
District courts, generally, post
Defendant or res outside of, actions by U.S., time limitation, exclusion, **28 § 2416**
District courts,
Cities, held at, **28 § 119**
Judges,
Additional, **28 § 133 nt**

PUERTO RICO—Cont'd
District courts—Cont'd
Judges—Cont'd
Number, **28 § 133**
Tenure and salary rights of judges in office on certain date, **28 § 134 nt**
Jurors. Jury, generally, post
Places of holding, **28 § 119**
Diversity of citizenship, district courts, jurisdiction, **28 § 1332**
Grand jury, selection and service, **28 § 1861 et seq.**
Judicial circuit of U.S., **28 § 41**
Judicial districts, **28 § 119**
Bankruptcy provisions, applicability of certain amendments to, **28 § 581 nt**
Number of district judges, **28 § 133**
Jurisdiction, diversity of citizenship, district courts, **28 § 1332**
Jury,
Refilling master jury wheel, not later than certain date, from sources which include names of persons 18 years or older, **28 § 1863 nt**
Selection and service, **28 § 1861 et seq.**
Laws,
Certiorari to Supreme Court of U.S. from decisions of Supreme Court of Puerto Rico, **28 § 1258**
Legislature,
Laws, generally, ante
Parimutuel Licensing, simplification, **28 § 534 nt**
Supreme Court of Puerto Rico,
Review of final judgments or decrees by writ of certiorari, **28 § 1258**
Supreme Court of U.S.,
Review of final judgments or decrees of Supreme Court of Puerto Rico by writ of certiorari, **28 § 1258**
United States Magistrate Judges, appointment and qualifications, **28 § 631**
United States trustees of judicial districts, appointment, **28 § 581**

PUNISHMENT
Sentence and Punishment, generally, this index

PUNITIVE DAMAGES
Foreign states, jurisdictional immunities, liability for, **28 § 1606**
United States, liability on tort claims, **28 § 2674**

PUPILS
Students, generally, this index

PURCHASERS AND PURCHASING
Supreme Court, books, pamphlets, **28 § 674**

QUALIFIED BLIND TRUST
Defined, financial disclosure requirements of Federal personnel, **5, Ap 4, § 102**

QUAPAW INDIAN AGENCY
Judgment in favor of claimant to allotment of land, exception, **28 § 1353**

QUARANTINE
Tort Claims Act, exception, claim for damages caused by quarantine, **28 § 2680**

QUESTIONS OF LAW OR FACT
Attorney General,
  Advice to Secretaries of military departments, **28 § 513**
  Opinion to,
    Heads of executive departments, **28 § 512**
    President, **28 § 511**
District courts, multidistrict litigation, transfer to single district, consolidated, pretrial proceedings, **28 § 1407**

QUIETING TITLE
Actions and proceedings,
  District courts, exclusive original jurisdiction, **28 § 1346**
  States against U.S., **28 § 2409a**
Tax liens,
  United States as party, **28 § 2410**
United States, lien on property affected by action, **28 § 2410**

RACE, COLOR, AND PREVIOUS CONDITION OF SERVITUDE
  See, also, Black Persons, generally, this index
Civil Rights, generally, this index
Court of appeals, district court and bankruptcy court judges, nominees for appointment, selection not affected by, **28 § 44 nt**
Discrimination, generally, this index
Election disputes, jurisdiction of district court, **28 § 1344**
Equal employment opportunity, generally. Civil Rights, this index
Federal judgeships, nomination of individuals for without regard to, Congressional recommendation, **28 § 133 nt**
Hate Crimes, generally, this index
Jury service,
  Discrimination in selecting persons for service prohibited, remedies, **28 § 1867**
  Exclusion,
    From service, discrimination prohibited, **28 § 1862**
  Qualification form, contents concerning, **28 § 1869**

RACE TRACKS
Horse Races, generally, this index

RACKETEERING
Money laundering,
  Special counsel, powers, duties, **28 § 509 nt**

RAILROADS
  See, also, Carriers, generally, this index
Federal Employers' Liability Act, generally, this index
Receivers and receivership,
  Federal Employers' Liability Act,
    Non-removable, **28 § 1445**
Safety,
  Judicial review of final agency action taken, **28 § 2342**
Trustees, Federal Employer's Liability Act, nonremovable actions, **28 § 1445**

RATES
Charges and Rates, generally, this index

REAL ESTATE
Adverse Possession, generally, this index
Appraisal and Appraisers, generally, this index
Community Development, generally, this index
Constructive notice of pending actions affecting in Federal court, registration, notice under State law, **28 § 1964**
Eminent Domain, generally, this index
Indian Lands and Reservations, generally, this index
Internal Revenue Service, this index
Judicial sales, **28 § 2001 et seq.**
  Capacity of U.S. marshal after levy on or sale, **28 § 2003**
Public Lands, generally, this index
Security Interest, this index
State registration, recording, of notice of pending action in Federal district court affecting, **28 § 1964**
Tax liens. Liens and Incumbrances, generally, this index

REAPPORTIONMENT
Three-judge court, action challenging constitutionality of apportionment of Congressional or statewide legislative body, **28 § 2284**

REASONABLE CAUSE
Certificate of reasonable cause for seizure, costs of claimant of property, **28 § 2465**

REBELLION
Insurrection and Sedition, generally, this index

RECALL
Bankruptcy judges, retired, recall to service, **28 § 155**

RECEIPTS
District court jurisdiction of cases involving interstate carriers, amount in controversy, **28 § 1337**
Motor carriers, amount of controversy for district court jurisdiction determined by, **28 § 1337**

RECEIVERS AND RECEIVERSHIP
Actions and proceedings,
  National bank, jurisdiction of district court, **28 § 1348**
  Property in different district, **28 § 754**
  Suit against without leave of court appointing them, **28 § 959**
Ancillary districts, order for sale of property in possession of, **28 § 2001**
Appeals to courts of appeals from interlocutory orders appointing, refusing, **28 § 1292**
Bankruptcy, generally, this index
Banks and Banking, this index
Carriers, this index
Clerks of courts, ineligible to appointment as receiver, **28 § 957**
District Courts, this index
Federal Debt Collection, generally, this index
Ineligibility to appointment as receivers, **28 § 958**
Judicial sale of property in possession of, **28 § 2001**
Management and operation of property according to the laws of the State in which property is situated, **28 § 959**
National Banks, this index
Property in different districts, **28 § 754**

RECORD ON APPEAL
Printing,
  In forma pauperis proceeding, expenses, **28 § 1915**
  Payment of expenses, proceeding before Magistrate Judge designated to exercise jurisdiction in civil court, **28 § 1915**
Supreme Court, direct appeal, **28 § 2101**

RECORDS AND RECORDATION
Audits and Auditors, generally, this index
Carriers, this index
Classification, criminal identification records, **28 § 534**
Clerks of Courts, this index
Clerks of District Courts, this index
Consuls, evidence, **28 § 1740**
Copies, lien, certified copy as evidence on creation of new district or division, **28 § 1656**
Courts of Appeals, this index
Criminal Background Checks, generally, this index
Department, of U.S., evidence, **28 § 1733**
Disbursing officers, relief from responsibility for loss, jurisdiction of U.S. Court of Federal Claims, **28 § 1496**
District Courts, this index

RECORDS AND RECORDATION
—Cont'd
Documentary Evidence, generally, this index
Evidence, this index
Federal agencies and instrumentalities,
Evidence, applicability to cases, **28 § 1733**
Made in regular course of business, admissibility in evidence, **28 § 1732**
Federal Bureau of Investigation, use, funds provided for expenses, exchange of identification records with certain officials, **28 § 534 nt**
Federal records,
Admissibility in evidence, **28 § 1733**
Documentary evidence, admissibility, **28 § 1733**
Standards for selective retention,
Admissibility, **28 § 1733**
Foreign countries, authenticated copy, summary or excerpt as evidence of official record, **28 § 1741**
Habeas corpus proceedings in Federal courts, admissibility of State court records, **28 § 2254**
House of Representatives, committees of, use by U.S. Court of Federal Claims, **28 § 2507**
Jury, this index
Justice, judge or Magistrate Judge, waiver of disqualification, full disclosure, basis for, **28 § 455**
Lien,
Certified copy as evidence on creation of new district or decision, **28 § 1656**
Judgment, **28 § 1962**
Microfilms and Microphotographs, this index
Patent and Trademark Office, this index
Pending action concerning realty, district courts, constructive notice, **28 § 1964**
Possessions of U.S., evidence, **28 §§ 1738, 1739**
Production of Books and Papers, generally, this index
Rules of Appellate Procedure, this index
Rules of Civil Procedure, this index
Rules of Evidence, this index
Senate committees, use by U.S. Court of Federal Claims, **28 § 2507**
State courts, this index
States, this index
Supreme Court, this index
Territories, evidence, **28 § 1739**
United States Court of Federal Claims, this index
United States Magistrate Judges, this index
Vice consuls, evidence, **28 § 1740**

RECORDS OF COURT
Copies, former court of appeals, furnished by clerk of Supreme Court, **28 § 6**
Courts of appeals,
Records of former court kept in office of clerk of Supreme Court, **28 § 6**
Habeas corpus,
Entry of order of circuit judge in records of district court, **28 § 2241**
Furnishing to indigent petitioner without cost, **28 § 2250**
Justice, judge or Magistrate Judge, waiver of disqualification, full disclosure, basis for, **28 § 455**
Lost or destroyed, U.S. interested, evidence, **28 § 1735**
Order affecting property situated in different districts, **28 § 1692**

RECUSAL
Judges or justices, disqualification of, **28 § 455**
United States Magistrate Judges, disqualification of, **28 § 455**

RECYCLING AND RESOURCE RECOVERY
Courts of U.S., sale, disposal, reuse, **28 § 604**

REDEMPTION
Judicial sale, U.S., **28 § 2410**

REFEREE
References, generally, this index

REFERENCE BOOKS
Attorney General, authority to sell and exchange, procurement, **28 § 525**

REFERENCES
Bankruptcy, this index
Clerks of court, ineligibility to appointment as referee, **28 § 957**
Federal agencies, orders, interlocutory injunction suspending, **28 § 2349**
Pending action concerning realty, district courts, constructive notice, **28 § 1964**
Three-judge court, order by single judge prohibited, **28 § 2284**

REFERRALS
References, generally, this index

REFORMATORIES
Correctional Institutions, generally, this index

REFUNDS
Internal Revenue Service, this index
Judicial survivors annuity fund, **28 § 376**
Taxation,
Venue, action by corporation against U.S., **28 § 1402**

REGISTERED MAIL
Certified or Registered Mail, generally, this index

REGISTRATION
Certified copy of satisfaction of judgment, **28 § 1963**
Child support, orders, full faith and credit, **28 § 1738B**
Judgments and decrees,
Lien, **28 § 1962**
Other districts, **28 § 1963**
Pending action concerning realty, district courts, constructive notice, **28 § 1964**

REHEARING
Courts of appeals,
Number of judges, **28 § 46**
Designation and assignment of judge to another district or circuit, joinder in final disposition upon expiration of assignment, **28 § 296**
United States Court of International Trade, this index

RELATIVES
See, also, Next of Kin, generally, this index
Degree of relationship, defined, justice, judge or Magistrate Judge, disqualification, **28 § 455**
Justice, judge or Magistrate Judge,
Grounds for disqualification, **28 § 455**
Ineligible to appointment to office or duty in any court, **28 § 458**

RELEASE
Lien of U.S. on property, **28 § 2410**
Negligence, wrongful act, of employee of Government, claim against U.S. and employee, **28 § 2672**
Pending judicial proceedings,
Orders,
Issuance by Magistrate Judges, **28 § 636**
United States Magistrate Judges, power to issue orders, pending trial, **28 § 636**
Supervised release after imprisonment, generally. Sentence and Punishment, this index
Vessel or property arrested in admiralty, **28 § 2464**

RELIGION
Civil Rights, generally, this index
Court of appeals, district court and bankruptcy court judges, nominees for appointment, selection not affected by, **28 § 44 nt**
Federal judgeships, nomination of individuals for without regard to, Congressional recommendations, **28 § 133 nt**
Hate Crimes, generally, this index

RELIGION—Cont'd
Jury service,
Discrimination in selecting persons for prohibited, remedies, **28 § 1867**
Exclusion from service of, discrimination prohibited, **28 § 1862**
Qualification form, contents concerning, **28 § 1869**

RELIGIOUS ORGANIZATIONS AND SOCIETIES
See, also, Churches, generally, this index
Attorneys' fees and other costs and expenses, award to party prevailing against U.S. or agency, applicability, **28 § 2412**
Justice, judge or Magistrate Judge, holding office in, disqualification, exclusions, **28 § 455**

REMAND
Appellate court, **28 § 2106**
Judicial Panel on Multidistrict Litigation, this index
State courts,
Motion to remand after removal to Federal court, **28 § 1448**
Order for remand, **28 § 1447**
Suits against Federal employees arising out of operation of motor vehicles in scope of employment, **28 § 2679**

REMARRIAGE
See, also, Marriage, generally, this index
Justices and judges, annuities to widows, termination upon, **28 § 376**

REMOVAL OF CASES OR CAUSES
Generally, **28 § 1441 et seq.**
Actions removable, **28 § 1441**
Affidavit to supply record, **28 § 1449**
Aliens, removal of actions by aliens against officers of U.S., **28 § 1442**
Amount in controversy, carriers, removal of actions against, **28 § 1445**
Appeal from order remanding case to State court from which removed, **28 § 1447**
Armed Forces,
Actions or prosecutions against members of, **28 § 1442a**
Attachment of goods or estate of defendant, **28 § 1450**
Bankruptcy, this index
Bonds, undertakings or security given prior to removal to remain valid and effectual, **28 § 1450**
Carriers, nonremovable actions against, **28 § 1445**
Civil rights cases, **28 § 1443**
Violence against women, limitation, violent crime control, **28 § 1445**

REMOVAL OF CASES OR CAUSES—Cont'd
Congress,
Actions or prosecutions against officers for acts in discharge of duty, **28 § 1442**
Constitutional questions, **28 § 1441**
Costs, order for payment on remand, **28 § 1447**
Court officers, actions or prosecutions against, **28 § 1442**
Custody of defendant, **28 § 1446**
Discretion of court, matters not within original jurisdiction, **28 § 1441**
Evidentiary hearing, **28 § 1446**
Federal agencies, actions or prosecutions against, **28 § 1442**
Federal Employers' Liability Act, nonremovable action, **28 § 1445**
Federal officer prosecuted, **28 § 1442**
Filing notice of removal, **28 § 1446**
Foreclosure action against U.S., **28 § 1444**
Foreign States, actions against, **28 § 1441**
Injunction prior to removal to remain in force and effect, **28 § 1450**
Internal Revenue Service officers, removal of actions or prosecutions against, **28 § 1442**
International Trade Commission, counterclaims, removal to district court, **28 § 1446**
Joinder of causes, **28 § 1441**
Judgment, attachment or sequestration to hold goods or estate to answer judgment, **28 § 1450**
Jurisdiction, **28 § 1441**
Liens and incumbrances, foreclosure, action against U.S., **28 § 1444**
Marshal, custody of defendant, **28 § 1446**
Mortgages, foreclosure, action against U.S., **28 § 1444**
Motion by defendant to remand after removal, **28 § 1448**
Notice of removal, action or prosecution, **28 § 1446**
Officers of U.S. sued or prosecuted, **28 § 1442**
Orders of court,
Filing of copy with notice of removal, **28 § 1446**
Improvidently removed, other than subject matter jurisdiction, district court, **28 § 1447**
Issuance by district court after removal, **28 § 1447**
Prior to removal, to remain in force and effect, **28 § 1450**
Remand of cause, **28 § 1447**
Original jurisdiction of district court, removal of cause from State court, **28 § 1441**
Pleadings, filing of copy with petition, **28 § 1446**
Procedure, **28 § 1446**
After removal, **28 § 1447 et seq.**

REMOVAL OF CASES OR CAUSES—Cont'd
Process,
After removal, **28 § 1448**
Failure of clerk of State court to supply records and proceedings, **28 § 1449**
Filing of copy with notice of removal, **28 § 1446**
Issuance by district court after removal, **28 § 1447**
Property holder whose title is derived from Federal officer, action of prosecution affecting validity of U.S. laws, **28 § 1442**
Record, supplied by affidavit or otherwise, **28 § 1449**
Remand of cause removed improvidently, other than subject matter jurisdiction, district court, **28 § 1447**
Review of order remanding case to State court from which removed, **28 § 1447**
Sequestration of goods or estate of defendant, **28 § 1450**
State, defined, **28 § 1451**
State court, defined, **28 § 1451**
Time for for filing notice of removal, **28 § 1446**
United States, foreclosure action against, **28 § 1444**
Workmen's compensation cases under State laws, nonremovable, **28 § 1445**

REORGANIZATION OF CORPORATIONS
Cases,
Commencement of,
Filing fee, payment, **28 § 1930**
Railroad reorganization,
Commencement of case,
Filing fee, payment, **28 § 1930**
State or local laws,
Trustees, receivers, and managers subject to, **28 § 959**
Trusts and trustees,
Managers, liability under State law, exception, **28 § 959**
United States trustees,
Duties, **28 § 586**
Special tax provisions,
Declaratory judgments, review, **28 § 2201**
State or local laws,
Railroad reorganization, ante
Trusts and trustees,
Railroad reorganization, ante
United States trustees,
Duties, **28 § 586**
Railroad reorganization, ante

REPEAL
Rules of court, rules of civil procedure for district courts and courts of appeals, **28 § 2072**

REPLEVIN
Revenue law, property taken or detained under, 28 § 2463

REPORTERS
Compensation and salaries,
District court reporters, 28 § 753
Increase in salary limitation, 28 § 753 nt
Supreme Court reporter, 28 § 673
District Courts, this index
Fees, taxation as costs, 28 § 1920
Investigation, court reporters, official acts, by Attorney General, 28 § 526
Oaths and affirmations, district court, 28 § 753
Supreme Court, this index

REPORTING SERVICES
United States Court of Federal Claims, contracts for, 28 § 796

REPORTS
Administrative Office of United States Courts, this index
Attorney General, this index
Bankruptcy, this index
Carriers, this index
Chief Justice of the Supreme Court to Congress of proceedings and recommendations of Judicial Conference, 28 § 331
Comptroller General, this index
Congress, this index
Congressional Committees, this index
Customs Duties, this index
Federal Legal Council, legal activities of Federal agencies, 28 § 509 nt, EON 12146
Foreign Service, this index
General Accounting Office, this index
Independent Counsel, this index
Judicial Center, 28 § 623
Judicial Conference of the United States, this index
Justice Department, this index
Law Reports, generally, this index
Narcotic drug addicts, civil commitment and rehabilitation, examination results and recommendations, 28 § 2902
Officers and Employees of Government, this index
President of the United States, this index
Rules of Civil Procedure, this index
Supreme Court, this index
United States Attorneys, this index
United States Court of Federal Claims, this index
United States Court of International Trade, this index
United States Sentencing Commission, evaluation of sentencing guidelines, time limitation, 28 § 994 nt

REPORTS OF JUDICIAL DECISIONS
Law Reports, generally, this index

REQUISITIONS
Justice Department, moneys appropriated for, 28 § 523

RESEARCH
Judicial Center,
Boards and commissions, contracts for research projects, 28 § 624
Functions, 28 § 620

RESERVATIONS (LANDS)
Indian Lands and Reservations, generally, this index

RESERVE FORCES
Army, this index
Coast Guard Reserve, generally, this index
National Guard, generally, this index

RESERVES
Army, this index
Marine Corps, this index
Navy, this index

RESIDENCE
Domicile and Residence, generally, this index

RESIDENT COMMISSIONER
Justices and judges, deposit of salary and credit for service as, judicial survivors annuity fund, 28 § 376

RESIDENTS
Domicile and Residence, generally, this index

RESOLUTION TRUST CORPORATION
Attorney General, investigation and prosecution of fraud, criminal or unlawful activity, 28 § 509 nt
Justice Department, investigation and prosecution of fraud, criminal or unlawful activity, 28 § 509 nt

RESOURCES
Natural Resources, generally, this index

RESTITUTION
Crime victims. Victim Compensation and Assistance, generally, this index
Director of Administrative Office of U.S. Courts to establish procedures, within judicial branch, 28 § 604
Moneys paid into court, use to pay criminal appearance bail bond, 28 § 2044

RESTRAINT OF TRADE
Monopolies and Combinations, generally, this index

RETIREMENT AND PENSIONS
Air Force, this index
Annuities, generally, this index
Army, this index
Bills, exception, reference to Chief Judge of U.S. Court of Federal Claims, 28 §§ 1492, 2509

RETIREMENT AND PENSIONS
—Cont'd
Chief Justice of U.S., Administrative Assistant to, election, coverage under retirement program, 28 § 677
Civil actions or claims for, U.S. as defendant, jurisdiction of district court, exception, 28 § 1346
Coast Guard, this index
Congressional reference to Chief Judge of U.S. Court of Federal Claims, 28 §§ 1492, 2509
District court not to have jurisdiction of action or claim for, 28 § 1346
Judges or Justices, this index
Marine Corps, this index
Navy, this index
Social Security, generally, this index
United States Court of Federal Claims,
Congressional reference of bills to Chief Judge, exception, 28 §§ 1492, 2509
Jurisdiction, 28 § 1501

RETIREMENT OF CIVIL SERVICE EMPLOYEES
Annuities,
Administrative Office of U.S. Courts, Director, 28 § 611
Judicial Center,
Director, 28 § 627
Reemployed annuitant, adjustment of salary, 28 § 625
Circuit court executives and staff deemed officers and employees of judicial branch for purposes of, 28 § 332
Director of Administrative Office of U.S. Courts, 28 § 611
Waiver of coverage, 28 §§ 376, 611
Employee, defined,
Deposit in Judicial Survivors' Annuities Fund by judicial official, amount governed by length of service as, 28 § 376
Judges or Justices, generally, this index
Judicial Center,
Director, professional staff, 28 § 627
Reemployed annuitant, adjustment, 28 § 625
Magistrate Judges. United States Magistrate Judges, generally, post
United States Court of Federal Claims,
Recall of retired judges, 28 § 797
United States Magistrate Judges,
Recall, compensation, 28 § 636

RETRIALS
United States Court of International Trade, this index

RETURNS
Clerks of District Courts, this index
Habeas Corpus, this index
Income Tax, this index

REVENUE OFFICERS
Internal Revenue Service, this index

REVIEW
Appeal and Review, generally, this index

REVIVAL OF ACTION
Abatement and Revival, generally, this index

RHODE ISLAND
See, also, States, generally, this index
Bankruptcy judges, appointment, number in judicial district, **28 § 152**
Court of Appeals for First Circuit, generally, this index
District courts,
Judges,
Additional, **28 § 133 nt**
Number, **28 § 133**
Places of holding, **28 § 120**
Judicial Circuit of U.S., **28 § 41**
Judicial district, **28 § 120**
Number of district judges, **28 § 133**
United States trustees of judicial districts, appointment, **28 § 581**

RIVER AND HARBOR IMPROVEMENTS
Oyster growers damaged by dredging operations,
Jurisdiction of U.S. United States Court of Federal Claims, **28 § 1497**
Time for filing suit in U.S. Court of Federal Claims, **28 § 2501**

RULE NISI
Power to issue, **28 § 1651**

RULES GOVERNING SECTION 2254 CASES
District Courts, this index

RULES OF APPELLATE PROCEDURE
Administrative law and procedure, **FRAP 15 et seq.**
Agency, defined, **FRAP 15**
Amendments, omissions or misstatements in record, **FRAP 16**
Amicus curiae briefs, **FRAP 29**
Answer, enforcement of orders, **FRAP 15**
Appeal conferences, **FRAP 33**
Appellant, defined, **FRAP 20**
Appellee, defined, **FRAP 20**
Appendix. Briefs, post
Applicability of rules, **FRAP 1, 2**
Applications,
Enforcement of orders, **FRAP 15**
Review, service, **FRAP 15**
Stay pending review, **FRAP 18**
Argument, **FRAP 34**
Attorneys, **FRAP 46**
Banc, determination of causes by court, **FRAP 35**
Books and papers, filing of record, **FRAP 17**
Briefs, generally, post
Certified lists,
Documents, **FRAP 17**

RULES OF APPELLATE PROCEDURE
—Cont'd
Administrative law and procedure —Cont'd
Certified lists—Cont'd
Filing of record, **FRAP 17**
Clerks of court, duties, **FRAP 45**
Composition of record, **FRAP 16**
Computation of time, **FRAP 26**
Conferences, appeal conferences, **FRAP 33**
Constitutional law, cases involving constitutional questions where United States is not a party, **FRAP 44**
Costs, **FRAP 39**
Frivolous appeals, **FRAP 38**
Court in banc, determination of causes, **FRAP 35**
Cross-applications, enforcement of order, **FRAP 15**
Damages, frivolous appeals, **FRAP 38**
Default, application for enforcement, **FRAP 15**
Determination of causes, court in banc, **FRAP 35**
Dismissal, voluntary dismissal, **FRAP 42**
Duties of clerks, **FRAP 45**
Enforcement of agency orders, **FRAP 15**
Record, **FRAP 16**
Enlargement of time, motion for review, **FRAP 26**
Entry of judgments, **FRAP 36**
Exhibits, reproduction in briefs, **FRAP 30**
Extension of time, **FRAP 26**
Fees, petition for review, **FRAP 15**
Filing, **FRAP 25**
Briefs, **FRAP 31**
Petition for review of orders, **FRAP 15**
Record on review or enforcement, **FRAP 17**
Stay pending review, notice, **FRAP 18**
Forma pauperis proceedings, **FRAP 24**
Friend of court, briefs, **FRAP 29**
Frivolous appeals, damages and costs, **FRAP 38**
In banc, determination of causes, **FRAP 35**
In forma pauperis proceedings, **FRAP 24**
Indigent persons, generally, post
Interest, judgments, **FRAP 37**
Intervention, **FRAP 15**
Joint petition for review of order, **FRAP 15**
Judgments and decrees,
Entry, **FRAP 36**
Interest, **FRAP 37**
Settlement, judgments enforcing orders, **FRAP 19**
Lists, certified lists, filing of record, **FRAP 17**

RULES OF APPELLATE PROCEDURE
—Cont'd
Administrative law and procedure —Cont'd
Mandate, **FRAP 41**
Misstatements in record, **FRAP 16**
Motions, **FRAP 27**
Stay pending review, **FRAP 18**
National labor relation board, briefs and oral arguments in proceedings, **FRAP 15.1**
Notice,
Filing of record, **FRAP 17**
Stay pending review, **FRAP 18**
Omissions in record, **FRAP 16**
Oral argument, **FRAP 34**
Parties,
Cases involving constitutional questions where United States is not a party, **FRAP 44**
Petition for review, **FRAP 15**
Substitution, **FRAP 43**
Pending review, stay, **FRAP 18**
Petition for rehearing, **FRAP 40**
Petition for review,
Orders, **FRAP 15, FRAP Form 3**
Proceedings in forma pauperis, **FRAP 24**
Proposed judgments enforcing orders, **FRAP 19**
Record, review or enforcement, **FRAP 16**
Record on review, filing, **FRAP 17**
Rehearing petition, **FRAP 40**
Review of agency orders, record, **FRAP 16**
Rules of court, applicability of other rules to review or enforcement, **FRAP 20**
Service,
Petition or application for review, **FRAP 15**
Process, **FRAP 25**
Briefs, **FRAP 31**
Settlement of judgments enforcing orders, **FRAP 19**
Stay,
Mandate, **FRAP 41**
Pending review, **FRAP 18**
Stipulation, filing of record, **FRAP 17**
Substitution of parties, **FRAP 43**
Supersedeas or stay, **FRAP 18**
Mandate, **FRAP 41**
Time,
Computation and extension, **FRAP 26**
Filing of record, **FRAP 17**
Transcript, briefs, reproduction of exhibits, **FRAP 30**
United States, cases involving constitutional questions where United States is not a party, **FRAP 44**
Voluntary dismissal, **FRAP 42**
Administrative office of the United States courts, duties of clerks of courts of appeals, **FRAP 45**

RULES OF APPELLATE PROCEDURE
—Cont'd

Admission to bar, court of appeals, **FRAP 46**
Affidavits,
District courts, motion for stay or injunction pending appeal, **FRAP 8**
Indigent persons,
Affidavit accompanying motion for permission to appeal in forma pauperis, **FRAP Form 4**
Proceedings in forma pauperis, **FRAP 24**
Motions, service with, **FRAP 27**
Affirmations. Oaths and affirmations, generally, post
Agents and agencies. Administrative law and procedure, generally, ante
Agreed statement, record on appeal, district courts, **FRAP 10**
Alternative methods of designating contents, appendix to briefs, **FRAP 30**
Amendments,
Administrative law and procedure, record on review or enforcement, **FRAP 16**
Habeas corpus, order respecting custody, **FRAP 23**
Judgments and decrees,
Interest on judgments, **FRAP 37**
Motion, effect on time for appeal, **FRAP 4**
Record on appeal, district courts, **FRAP 10**
Amicus curiae,
Briefs, **FRAP 29**
Extraordinary writs, **FRAP 21**
Oral argument participation, **FRAP 29**
Answer,
Administrative law and procedure, application for enforcement of order, **FRAP 15**
Appeals by permission, **FRAP 5**
Corporate disclosure statements, **FRAP 26.1**
District courts, appeals by permission, **FRAP 5**
Petition for,
Extraordinary writs, **FRAP 21**
Rehearing, **FRAP 40**
Review of order of administrative body, **FRAP 15**
Rehearing, petition, **FRAP 40**
Appeal and review,
Administrative law and procedure, generally, ante
District courts. Appeals From district courts, generally, post
Appeal as of right,
District courts,
Judgments and orders, **FRAP 3**
Time, **FRAP 4**
When taken, **FRAP 4**
Appeal conferences, **FRAP 33**
Appealability, habeas corpus, necessity of certificate, **FRAP 22**

RULES OF APPELLATE PROCEDURE
—Cont'd

Appeals by permission, petition, **FRAP 5**
Appeals from district courts, **FRAP 3 et seq.**
Agreed statement, record on appeal, **FRAP 10**
Amendments, record on appeal, **FRAP 10**
Amicus curiae briefs, **FRAP 29**
Appeal as of right, **FRAP 3**
Time, **FRAP 4**
Appeal conferences, **FRAP 33**
Appeals by permission, **FRAP 5**
Appendix. Briefs, post
Applicability of rules, **FRAP 1, 2**
Argument, **FRAP 34**
Attorney fees, motion for, time for appeal, **FRAP 4**
Attorneys, **FRAP 46**
Representation statements, **FRAP 12**
Banc, determination of causes by court, **FRAP 35**
Bankruptcy cases, **FRAP 6**
Bonds, district courts, generally. Supersedeas or stay, post
Briefs, generally, post
Clerks of court, duties, **FRAP 45**
Composition of record on appeal, **FRAP 10**
Computation of time, **FRAP 26**
Conferences, appeal conferences, **FRAP 33**
Consolidated appeals as of right, **FRAP 3**
Constitutional law, cases involving constitutional questions where United States is not a party, **FRAP 44**
Corporate disclosure statements, **FRAP 26.1**
Correction of record on appeal, **FRAP 10**
Costs, **FRAP 39**
Frivolous appeals, **FRAP 38**
Court in banc, determination of causes, **FRAP 35**
Crimes and offenses, generally, post
Damages, frivolous appeals, **FRAP 38**
Determination of causes, court in banc, **FRAP 35**
Dismissal, voluntary dismissal, **FRAP 42**
Docketing, **FRAP 12**
Duties of clerks, **FRAP 45**
Entry of judgments, **FRAP 36**
Evidence, statement in absence of report or transcript, **FRAP 10**
Extension of time, **FRAP 26**
Transmission of record, **FRAP 11**
Filing, **FRAP 25**
Briefs, **FRAP 31**
Notice of appeal, **FRAP 3**
Record, **FRAP 12**
Stay or injunction pending appeal, **FRAP 8**
Forma pauperis proceedings, **FRAP 24**

RULES OF APPELLATE PROCEDURE
—Cont'd

Appeals from district courts—Cont'd
Forms, briefs, appendices and other papers, **FRAP 32**
Friend of court, briefs, **FRAP 29**
Frivolous appeals, damages and costs, **FRAP 38**
In banc, determination of causes, **FRAP 35**
In forma pauperis proceedings, **FRAP 24**
Indigent persons, generally, post
Injunctions, pending appeal, **FRAP 8**
Interest, judgments, **FRAP 37**
Joint appeals as of right, **FRAP 3**
Judgments,
Entry, **FRAP 36**
Interest, **FRAP 37**
Magistrate judges decisions, **FRAP 3**
Mandate, **FRAP 41**
Modification of record on appeal, **FRAP 10**
Motions, post
Notice, post
Oral argument, **FRAP 34**
Order of court, retention of record, **FRAP 11**
Partial transcript, notice to appellee, **FRAP 10**
Parties, cases involving constitutional questions where United States is not a party, **FRAP 44**
Pending appeal, injunction or stay, **FRAP 8**
Permission, appeals by, **FRAP 5**
Petition for rehearing, **FRAP 40**
Preliminary hearing, record for hearing in court of appeals, **FRAP 11**
Preliminary or interlocutory injunctions, **FRAP 8**
Proceedings in forma pauperis, **FRAP 24**
Process, service, **FRAP 25**
Briefs, **FRAP 31**
Records, **FRAP 10**
Appeal by permission, **FRAP 5**
Docketing, **FRAP 12**
Filing, **FRAP 12**
Preliminary hearing in court of appeals, **FRAP 11**
Transmission, **FRAP 11**
Rehearing petition, **FRAP 40**
Release in criminal cases, **FRAP 9**
Representation statements, attorneys, **FRAP 12**
Retention of record, temporary retention in preparing papers, **FRAP 11**
Right to appeal, **FRAP 3**
Time, **FRAP 4**
Service,
Notice of appeal as of right, **FRAP 3**
Process, **FRAP 25**
Briefs, **FRAP 31**
Statement of evidence in absence of report or transcript, **FRAP 10**

RULES OF APPELLATE PROCEDURE —Cont'd

Appeals from district courts—Cont'd
  Stay. Supersedeas or stay, generally, post
  Stipulations,
    Retention of record, **FRAP 11**
    Voluntary dismissal, **FRAP 42**
  Substitution, **FRAP 43**
  Substitution of parties, **FRAP 43**
  Supersedeas or stay, generally, post
  Temporary injunctions, **FRAP 8**
  Temporary retention of record, **FRAP 11**
  Time,
    Appeal as of right, **FRAP 4**
    Computation and extension, **FRAP 26**
    Transmission of record, **FRAP 11**
  Transcript of proceedings, **FRAP 10**
  Transmission of record, **FRAP 11**
  United States, cases involving constitutional questions where United States is not a party, **FRAP 44**
  Voluntary dismissal, **FRAP 42**
Appearance,
  Arguments, non-appearance of parties, **FRAP 34**
  Mandamus, judges, **FRAP 21**
  Prohibition, judges, **FRAP 21**
Appellants,
  Appendix to briefs, **FRAP 30**
  Briefs, **FRAP 28**
  Defined, administrative bodies and proceedings, **FRAP 20**
Appellees,
  Briefs, **FRAP 28**
  Damages and costs, award for frivolous appeals, **FRAP 38**
  Defined, administrative bodies and proceedings, **FRAP 20**
Appendices,
  Briefs, **FRAP 30**
  Form, **FRAP 32**
  Costs, copies and duplicates, **FRAP 39**
  Filing, **FRAP 25**
Applicability of rules, **FRAP 1, 2**
Applications,
  Administrative law and procedure, ante
  Attorneys, admission to bar of court of appeals, **FRAP 46**
  Extraordinary writs, **FRAP 21**
  Habeas corpus, application for original writ, **FRAP 22**
  Indigent persons, proceedings in forma pauperis, **FRAP 24**
  Mandate, stay, **FRAP 41**
Arguments. Oral argument, generally, post
Attorney fees,
  Appeals from district courts, time, motion for attorney fees, **FRAP 4**

RULES OF APPELLATE PROCEDURE —Cont'd

Attorney general,
  Cases involving constitutional questions where United States is not a party, **FRAP 44**
Attorneys, **FRAP 46**
  Admission to bar of court of appeals, **FRAP 46**
  Appeal conferences, **FRAP 33**
  Appeals from district courts, service of notice of appeal, **FRAP 3**
  Conferences, appeal conferences, **FRAP 33**
  Costs, increase, sanctions, **FRAP 30**
  Crimes and offenses, disbarment, **FRAP 46**
  Disbarment, **FRAP 46**
  Disciplinary powers of court, **FRAP 46**
  Representation statement, **FRAP 12**
  Service of,
    Notice of appeal, judgments and orders of district courts, **FRAP 3**
    Papers required, **FRAP 25**
  Suspension, **FRAP 46**
Banc, determination of causes by court in banc, **FRAP 35**
Bankruptcy,
  Corporate disclosure statements, **FRAP 26.1**
  Final judgments and orders, appeals from, **FRAP 6**
Bankruptcy appellate panels,
  Final judgments and orders, appeal from, **FRAP 6**
  Notice of appeal from, **FRAP Form 5**
Bar, attorneys, admission to court of appeals, **FRAP 46**
Bill of costs, verification, **FRAP 39**
Binding, briefs, form of briefs and appendices, **FRAP 32**
Boards and commissions. Administrative law and procedure, generally, ante
Bonds (officers and fiduciaries),
  Appeals by permission, **FRAP 5**
  Clerks of courts of appeals, **FRAP 45**
  Cost bonds, generally, post
  Indigent persons, proceedings in forma pauperis, **FRAP 24**
  Mandate, stay, **FRAP 41**
  Supersedeas or stay, post
Books and papers,
  Administrative law and procedure, filing of record, **FRAP 17**
  Briefs, generally, post
  Clerk of court of appeals, office hours, **FRAP 45**
  Filing, generally, post
  Form of briefs, appendix and other papers, **FRAP 32**
  Motions, service with, **FRAP 27**
Briefs, **FRAP 28**
  Alternative method of designating contents of appendix, **FRAP 30**
  Amicus curiae, **FRAP 29**

RULES OF APPELLATE PROCEDURE —Cont'd

Briefs—Cont'd
  Appellants, **FRAP 28**
    Appendices, duty to prepare and file, **FRAP 30**
  Appellees, **FRAP 28**
  Appendix, **FRAP 30**
    Costs, copies and duplicates, **FRAP 39**
    Form of briefs, appendix and other papers, **FRAP 32**
  Arguments, submission on briefs, **FRAP 34**
  Arrangement of appendix, **FRAP 30**
  Certificates of compliance, length, **FRAP 32**
  Contents of appendices, **FRAP 30**
  Copies and duplicates,
    Appendices, **FRAP 30**
    Exhibits, **FRAP 30**
    Form of briefs, appendices and other papers, **FRAP 32**
    Number filed and served, **FRAP 31**
  Corporate disclosure statement, **FRAP 26.1**
  Cost of producing, appendices, **FRAP 30**
  Costs, **FRAP 39**
    Printing, **FRAP 39**
  Cross-appeals, **FRAP 28**
    Appendix, **FRAP 30**
  Deferred appendix, **FRAP 30**
  Designation of parties, **FRAP 28**
  Dismissal of appeal, failure to file briefs, **FRAP 31**
  Exhibits, reproduction, **FRAP 30**
  Extraordinary writs, **FRAP 21**
  Failure to file, **FRAP 31**
  Filing and service, **FRAP 25, 31**
    Amicus curiae, **FRAP 29**
    Appendix to briefs, **FRAP 30**
    Time, **FRAP 31**
  Form, **FRAP 32**
  Friend of court, briefs, **FRAP 29**
  Jurisdiction, statement, **FRAP 28**
  Length, **FRAP 28**
  Lists, arrangement of appendix, **FRAP 30**
  Mandamus, **FRAP 21**
  Motion for filing, amicus curiae, **FRAP 29**
  Multiple appellants or appellees, **FRAP 28**
  National Labor Relations Board proceedings, **FRAP 15.1**
  Number of copies to be filed and served, **FRAP 31**
  Omissions, arrangement of appendix, **FRAP 30**
  Original record, hearing without necessity of appendix, **FRAP 30**
  Printing, costs, **FRAP 39**
  Prohibition, **FRAP 21**
  Records, references to, **FRAP 28, 30**
  Reply briefs, **FRAP 28**

RULES OF APPELLATE PROCEDURE —Cont'd

Briefs—Cont'd
  Reply briefs—Cont'd
    Time for serving and filing, **FRAP 31**
  Reproduction of exhibits, **FRAP 30**
  Rules and regulations, reproduction, **FRAP 28**
  Service, **FRAP 31**
  Standard of review, **FRAP 28**
  Statutes, reproduction, **FRAP 28**
  Submission on briefs, **FRAP 34**
  Time,
    Amicus curiae, **FRAP 29**
    Appendices, filing and service, **FRAP 30**
    Briefs, filing and service, **FRAP 31**
Calendar, clerk of court of appeals, office hours, **FRAP 45**
Cases involving constitutional questions, United States not a party, **FRAP 44**
Certificates,
  Briefs, compliance with length limitation, **FRAP 32**
  Habeas corpus, certificate of appealability, **FRAP 22**
  Indigent persons, leave to proceed in forma pauperis, **FRAP 24**
Certified lists, administrative bodies and proceedings, filing of record, **FRAP 17**
Certiorari, mandate, stay pending application, **FRAP 41**
Circuit judges. Judges, generally, post
Class actions, notice of appeal, contents, **FRAP 3**
Clerks of court,
  Appeals from district courts,
    Filing notice of appeal, **FRAP 3**
    Transmission of record, **FRAP 11**
  Attorneys, admission to bar of court of appeals, **FRAP 46**
  Dockets, **FRAP 45**
  Exhibits used at argument, removal, **FRAP 34**
  Filing, generally, post
  Office hours, **FRAP 45**
  Powers and duties, **FRAP 45**
  Transmission of records, appeals from district courts, **FRAP 11**
Commercial carriers, service of process, **FRAP 25**
Compromise and settlement,
  Appeal conferences, **FRAP 33**
  Dismissal, voluntary dismissal, **FRAP 42**
  Voluntary dismissal, **FRAP 42**
Computation of time, **FRAP 26**
Conferences,
  Appeal conferences, **FRAP 33**
  Prehearing conferences, **FRAP 33**
Congressional acts, cases involving constitutional questions where United States is not a party, **FRAP 44**
Consolidated appeals, district court, appeals as of rights, **FRAP 3**

RULES OF APPELLATE PROCEDURE —Cont'd

Constitutional questions,
  Courts of appeals, **FRAP 44**
  United States is not a party, **FRAP 44**
Contracts,
  Dismissal, voluntary dismissal, **FRAP 42**
  Voluntary dismissal, **FRAP 42**
Convicts. Correctional institutions, generally, post
Copies and duplicates,
  Briefs, ante
  Clerk of court of appeals, office hours, **FRAP 45**
  Corporate disclosure statements, **FRAP 26.1**
  Costs, copies of records, **FRAP 39**
  District courts,
    Appeals as of right, notice of appeal, **FRAP 3**
    Appeals by permission, **FRAP 5**
  Extraordinary writs, **FRAP 21**
  Filing and service, **FRAP 25**
  Indigent persons, proceedings in forma pauperis, **FRAP 24**
  Judgments and decrees, mailing parties, **FRAP 36**
  Mandamus, **FRAP 21**
  Mandate, issuance, **FRAP 41**
  Motions, **FRAP 27**
  Opinions, mailing parties, **FRAP 36**
  Petition for rehearing, **FRAP 40**
  Prohibition, **FRAP 21**
  Rehearing petition, **FRAP 40**
  Rules by courts of appeals, **FRAP 47**
  Tax court decisions, review, notice of appeal, **FRAP 13**
Corporate disclosure statements, **FRAP 26.1**
Correctional institutions,
  District courts, release in criminal cases, **FRAP 9**
  Filing of papers, inmates, **FRAP 25**
  Habeas corpus proceedings, **FRAP 22**
    Custody of prisoners, **FRAP 23**
  Notice of appeal, filing, inmate confined in institution, **FRAP 4**
  Release in criminal cases, appeals from district court, **FRAP 9**
Corrections. Amendments, generally, ante
Cost bonds,
  Appeals from district courts,
    Civil cases, **FRAP 7**
    Permission, **FRAP 5**
    Record for preliminary hearing in court of appeals, **FRAP 11**
    Stay or injunction pending appeal, **FRAP 8**
Costs, **FRAP 39**
  Appeals by permission, **FRAP 5**
  Appendices, **FRAP 39**
    Briefs, cost of producing, **FRAP 30**
  Attorneys, increase, sanctions, **FRAP 30**

RULES OF APPELLATE PROCEDURE —Cont'd

Costs—Cont'd
  Briefs, **FRAP 39**
  Copies of records, **FRAP 39**
  Cost bonds, generally, ante
  Dismissal in court of appeals, **FRAP 42**
  District courts, **FRAP 39**
  Frivolous appeals, **FRAP 38**
  Mandate,
    Clerk inserting costs, **FRAP 39**
    Issuance, **FRAP 41**
  Masters, compensation, **FRAP 48**
  Parties, **FRAP 39**
  Printing, **FRAP 39**
  United States, costs for and against, **FRAP 39**
Counsel. Attorneys, generally, ante
Court in banc, determination of causes, **FRAP 35**
Courts of appeals, **FRAP 1 et seq.**
  Administrative law and procedure, generally, ante
  Admission to bar, **FRAP 46**
  Amicus curiae, briefs, **FRAP 29**
  Appeal conferences, **FRAP 33**
  Appeals from district courts, generally, ante
  Appendix to briefs, **FRAP 30**
    Form, **FRAP 32**
  Applicability of rules, **FRAP 1, 2**
  Arguments, **FRAP 34**
  Attorneys, powers and duties, **FRAP 46**
  Briefs, generally, ante
  Clerks of court, duties, **FRAP 45**
  Computation of time, **FRAP 26**
  Conferences, **FRAP 33**
  Constitutional questions, **FRAP 44**
  Corporate disclosure statements, **FRAP 26.1**
  Correctional institution inmates, filing of papers, **FRAP 25**
  Costs, **FRAP 39**
    Frivolous appeals, **FRAP 38**
  Crimes and offenses, generally, post
  Damages, frivolous appeals, **FRAP 38**
  Dismissal of causes, **FRAP 42**
  District courts. Appeals From district courts, generally, ante
  Entry of judgment, **FRAP 36**
  Extension of time, **FRAP 26**
  Extraordinary writs, **FRAP 21**
  Filing papers, **FRAP 25**
    Briefs, **FRAP 31**
  Forms, briefs, **FRAP 32**
  Frivolous appeals, damages and costs, **FRAP 38**
  Habeas corpus, **FRAP 22, 23**
  In banc, determination of causes, **FRAP 35**
  In forma pauperis, proceedings, **FRAP 24**
  Interest, judgment and decrees, **FRAP 37**
  Judges, generally, post

RULES OF APPELLATE PROCEDURE
—Cont'd
Courts of appeals—Cont'd
Judgments and decrees,
Entry, **FRAP 36**
Interest, **FRAP 37**
Mandamus, **FRAP 21**
Mandate, issuance, **FRAP 41**
Masters, **FRAP 48**
Motions, **FRAP 27**
Oral argument, **FRAP 34**
Parties, substitution, **FRAP 43**
Petitions, rehearings, **FRAP 40**
Prohibition, **FRAP 21**
Rehearing, petitions, **FRAP 40**
Rules by, **FRAP 47**
Scope of rules, **FRAP 1**
Service of papers, **FRAP 25**
Briefs, **FRAP 31**
Stay of mandate, **FRAP 41**
Substitution of parties, **FRAP 43**
Suspension of rules, **FRAP 2**
Time, computation and extension, **FRAP 26**
United States Tax Court, generally, post
Voluntary dismissal, **FRAP 42**
Writ, extraordinary writs, **FRAP 21**
Crimes and offenses,
Appeal as of right, time, **FRAP 4**
Attorneys, suspension or disbarment, **FRAP 46**
Corporate disclosure statements, **FRAP 26.1**
Habeas corpus, generally, post
Indigent persons, generally, post
Release in criminal cases, appeals from district court, **FRAP 9**
Service of notice of appeal, judgments and orders of district court, **FRAP 3**
Supersedeas or stay, district courts, **FRAP 8**
Cross-appeals,
Appendix to briefs, **FRAP 30**
Arguments, **FRAP 34**
Briefs in cases involving, **FRAP 28**
Oral arguments, **FRAP 34**
Cross-applications,
Administrative law and procedure, application for enforcement of order, **FRAP 15**
Appeals by permission, **FRAP 5**
Custody of prisoners, habeas corpus proceedings, **FRAP 23**
Damages, frivolous appeals, **FRAP 38**
Death,
Parties, substitution of parties, **FRAP 43**
Service of notice of appeal, sufficiency, appeals from district courts, **FRAP 3**
Substitution of parties, **FRAP 43**
Decrees. Judgments and decrees, generally, post

RULES OF APPELLATE PROCEDURE
—Cont'd
Default, administrative bodies and proceedings, application for enforcement of order, **FRAP 15**
Denial,
Extraordinary writs, **FRAP 21**
Indigent persons, leave to proceed in forma pauperis, **FRAP 24**
Destitute persons. Indigent persons, generally, post
Destruction, physical exhibits used at argument, **FRAP 34**
Detention of prisoners, habeas corpus, custody pending review, **FRAP 23**
Determination of causes, court in banc, **FRAP 35**
Disbarment, attorneys, **FRAP 46**
Discipline of attorneys, power of court, **FRAP 46**
Disclosure statements, corporations, **FRAP 26.1**
Dismissal of appeal,
Briefs, consequence of failure to file, **FRAP 31**
Voluntary dismissal, **FRAP 42**
District courts,
Appeals from district courts, generally, ante
Notice, post
Dockets and docketing,
Appeals from district court, **FRAP 12**
Clerk of court of appeals, office hours, **FRAP 45**
District courts, appeals, **FRAP 12**
Entry of judgment, **FRAP 36**
Tax court, record on appeal, **FRAP 13**
Documents. Books and papers, generally, ante
Duplicates. Copies and duplicates, generally, ante
Electronic filing, **FRAP 25**
Employees. Officers and employees, generally, post
En banc, determination of causes by court, **FRAP 35**
Enlargement of time, **FRAP 26**
Entry of judgment, **FRAP 36**
Escape,
Habeas corpus proceedings, **FRAP 22**
Custody of prisoners, **FRAP 23**
Evidence,
Statement of evidence, district court appeals, absence of report or transcript, **FRAP 10**
Excusable neglect, district court, appeals as of right, civil cases, time, **FRAP 4**
Exhibits,
Briefs, reproduction, **FRAP 30**
Use at argument, **FRAP 34**
Extension of time, **FRAP 26**
District courts,
Appeals as of right, **FRAP 4**
Transmission of record, **FRAP 11**
Extraordinary questions, determination of causes by court in banc, **FRAP 35**

RULES OF APPELLATE PROCEDURE
—Cont'd
Extraordinary writs, **FRAP 21**
Applicability of rules, **FRAP 1, 2**
Mandamus, generally, post
Prohibition, generally, post
Facsimile transmission, filing, **FRAP 25**
Fees,
Administrative law and procedure, petition for review, **FRAP 15**
Appeals by permission, **FRAP 5**
Attorneys, admission to bar of court of appeals, **FRAP 46**
Dismissal in court of appeals, **FRAP 42**
Felonies. Crimes and offenses, generally, ante
Fidelity bonds. Bonds (officers and fiduciaries), generally, ante
Fiduciaries. Bonds (officers and fiduciaries), generally, ante
Filing, **FRAP 25**
Administrative law and procedure, ante
Amicus curiae briefs, **FRAP 29**
Appeal as of right, notice of appeal, **FRAP 3**
Appeals from district courts, ante
Appendix to briefs, **FRAP 30**
Attorneys, admission to bar of court of appeals, **FRAP 46**
Briefs, ante
Clerk of court of appeals, duties, **FRAP 45**
Electronic filing, **FRAP 25**
Indigent persons, leave to proceed in forma pauperis, **FRAP 24**
Mail and mailing, **FRAP 25**
Notice of appeal, Tax Court of the United States, **FRAP 13**
Tax court,
Notice of appeal, **FRAP 13**
Record on appeal, **FRAP 13**
Finality of judgments and decrees, determination of causes by court in banc, **FRAP 35**
Findings, indigent persons, leave to proceed in forma pauperis, **FRAP 24**
Forms,
Administrative law and procedure, petition for review of orders, **FRAP Form 3**
Affidavit, motion for permission to appeal in forma pauperis, **FRAP Form4**
Attorneys, admission to bar of court of appeals, **FRAP 46**
Indigent persons, proceedings in forma pauperis, **FRAP 24**
Notice of appeal,
Court of appeals from district court or bankruptcy appellate panel, **FRAP Form 5**
Court of appeals from judgment or order of district court, **FRAP Form 1**

RULES OF APPELLATE PROCEDURE
—Cont'd
Forms—Cont'd
Notice of appeal—Cont'd
Court of appeals from Tax Court of the United States, **FRAP Form 2**
Petition for,
Administrative body or officer, review of order, **FRAP Form orm 3**
Prescribing, powers and duties, **28 § 2072**
Friend of court briefs, **FRAP 29**
Frivolous appeals, damages and costs, **FRAP 38**
Grant of permission, district courts, appeals by permission, **FRAP 5**
Habeas corpus, **FRAP 22, 23**
Amendment, order respecting custody, **FRAP 23**
Applicability of rules, **FRAP 1, 2**
Application for original writ, **FRAP 22**
Certificate of appealability, **FRAP 22**
Courts of appeals, **FRAP 22, 23**
Custody of prisoners, **FRAP 23**
Detention of prisoner when pending review, **FRAP 23**
In forma pauperis proceedings, **FRAP 24**
Modification, order respecting custody, **FRAP 23**
Original writ, application, **FRAP 22**
Release of prisoner pending review, **FRAP 23**
Transfer of custody pending review, **FRAP 23**
Hearings,
Determination of causes by court in banc, **FRAP 35**
In banc, determination of causes, **FRAP 35**
Oral argument, **FRAP 34**
Petition for rehearing, **FRAP 40**
Rehearing petition, **FRAP 40**
Holidays. Legal holidays, generally, post
Hours of business, clerk of court of appeals, **FRAP 45**
Important questions, determination of causes by court in banc, **FRAP 35**
Imprisonment,
Correctional institutions, generally, ante
Crimes and offenses, generally, ante
In banc, determination of causes by court in banc, **FRAP 35**
In forma pauperis, **FRAP 24**
Index, clerk of court of appeals, office hours, **FRAP 45**
Indigent persons,
Affidavit accompanying motion for permission to appeal in forma pauperis, **FRAP Form 4**
Forms, affidavit accompanying motion for permission to appeal, **FRAP Form 4**

RULES OF APPELLATE PROCEDURE
—Cont'd
Indigent persons—Cont'd
In forma pauperis, **FRAP 24**
Proceedings in forma pauperis, **FRAP 24**
Industrial schools and reformatories. Correctional institutions, generally, ante
Injunctions, district court appeals, pending appeal, **FRAP 8**
Instructions, mandates, interest on judgments modified or reversed, **FRAP 37**
Interest, judgments and decrees, **FRAP 37**
Interlocutory injunctions, appeals from district courts, **FRAP 8**
Intervention, administrative bodies and proceedings, enforcement or review of orders, **FRAP 15**
Jails. Correctional institutions, generally, ante
Joint appeals, district court, appeals as of right, **FRAP 3**
Joint petitions, administrative bodies and proceedings, review of order, **FRAP 15**
Judges,
Determination of causes by court in banc, **FRAP 35**
Habeas corpus, certificate of appealability, **FRAP 22**
In banc, determination of causes, **FRAP 35**
Judgment as a matter of law, motion, renewal, effect on time for appeal, **FRAP 4**
Judgments and decrees,
Alteration or amendment, motion, effect on time for appeal, **FRAP 4**
Bankruptcy cases, appeal from, **FRAP 6**
Clerk of court of appeals, office hours, **FRAP 45**
Copies and duplicates, mailing parties, **FRAP 36**
Criminal cases, release pending appeal from judgment of conviction, **FRAP 9**
Determination of causes by court in banc, **FRAP 35**
Entry of judgment, **FRAP 36**
Interest on judgments, **FRAP 37**
Magistrate judges in civil cases, appeals, **FRAP 3**
Notice of entry, **FRAP 36**
Untimely notice, reopening of time to appeal, **FRAP 4**
Petition for rehearing, **FRAP 40**
Rehearing, petition for, **FRAP 40**
Release pending appeal from judgment of conviction, **FRAP 9**
Relief from, motion, effect on time for appeal, **FRAP 4**

RULES OF APPELLATE PROCEDURE
—Cont'd
Jurisdiction,
Briefs, statement of jurisdiction, **FRAP 28**
Scope of rules, **FRAP 1**
Lawyers. Attorneys, generally, ante
Leave to proceed, appeal in forma pauperis, **FRAP 24**
Legal holidays,
Clerk of court of appeals, office hours, **FRAP 45**
Defined, computation and extension of time, **FRAP 26**
Time, computation and extension, **FRAP 26**
Length, briefs, **FRAP 28**
Limitation of actions, district courts, appeals as of right, time, **FRAP 4**
Lists,
Administrative law and procedure, certified list, filing of record, **FRAP 17**
Briefs, arrangement of appendix, **FRAP 30**
Local rules and procedure, **FRAP 47**
Magistrate judges,
Appeals by permission, **FRAP 5**
Appeals from judgments in civil cases, **FRAP 3**
Mail and mailing,
Clerk of court of appeals, office hours, **FRAP 45**
District courts, appeals from, service of notice of appeal, **FRAP 3**
Filing, **FRAP 25**
Judgments and decrees, copies, **FRAP 36**
Opinions, copies, **FRAP 36**
Service of notice of appeal, judgments and orders of district courts, **FRAP 3**
Time, additional time after service by mail, **FRAP 26**
Mandamus,
Applicability of rules, **FRAP 1, 2**
Extraordinary writs, **FRAP 21**
Mandate,
Certiorari, stay of mandate pending application, **FRAP 41**
Costs, clerk inserting costs, **FRAP 39**
Dismissal in court of appeals, **FRAP 42**
Interest on judgments, **FRAP 37**
Issuance and stay, **FRAP 41**
Rehearing, stay of mandate pending petition, **FRAP 41**
Suggestion for rehearing in banc, **FRAP 35**
Supersedeas or stay, **FRAP 41**
Suggestion for rehearing in banc, **FRAP 35**
Masters, **FRAP 48**
Misdemeanors. Crimes and offenses, generally, ante

RULES OF APPELLATE PROCEDURE —Cont'd

Misstatements, administrative bodies and proceedings, record on review or enforcement, **FRAP 16**
Modification. Amendments, generally, ante
Motions, **FRAP 27**
  Administrative law and procedure, stay pending review, **FRAP 18**
  Admiralty or maritime claims, **28 § 2072**
  Amicus curiae brief, filing, **FRAP 29**
  Appeal as of right, district courts, when taken, **FRAP 4**
  Appeals from district courts. District courts, generally, post
  Arguments, postponement, **FRAP 34**
  Brief of amicus curiae, filing, **FRAP 29**
  Clerk of court of appeals, duties, **FRAP 45**
  Content of motions, **FRAP 27**
  Corporate disclosure statements, **FRAP 26.1**
  Death of party, substitution of parties, **FRAP 43**
  Dismissal in,
    Court of appeals, **FRAP 42**
    District court, **FRAP 42**
  District courts,
    Appeal as of right, time, **FRAP 4**
    Dismissal, **FRAP 42**
    Stay or injunction pending appeal, **FRAP 8**
  Enlargement of time, **FRAP 26**
  Filing, **FRAP 25**
  Forms,
    Affidavit accompanying motion for permission to appeal in forma pauperis, **FRAP Form 4**
    Briefs, appendices and other papers, **FRAP 32**
  In forma pauperis appeals, affidavit accompanying motion, **FRAP Form 4**
  Indigent persons, proceedings in forma pauperis, **FRAP 24**
  Oral argument, postponement, **FRAP 34**
  Postponement, oral argument, **FRAP 34**
  Power of single judge to entertain, **FRAP 27**
  Procedural orders, determination of motions, **FRAP 27**
  Reply to response, **FRAP 27**
  Response, **FRAP 27**
  Single judge, powers and duties, **FRAP 27**
  Statement of grounds, **FRAP 27**
  Stay of mandate, **FRAP 41**
  Stay pending review, administrative bodies and proceedings, **FRAP 18**
  Substitution of parties, death of party, **FRAP 43**
  Suspension of rules, **FRAP 2**

RULES OF APPELLATE PROCEDURE —Cont'd

Motions—Cont'd
  Time, response, **FRAP 27**
Multiple parties, briefs, cases involving multiple appellants or appellees, **FRAP 28**
National labor relations board, briefs and oral arguments in proceedings, **FRAP 15.1**
New trial, notice of appeal, filing, **FRAP 4**
Non-appearance of parties, arguments, **FRAP 34**
Notice,
  Administrative law and procedure,
    Filing of record, **FRAP 17**
    Stay pending review, **FRAP 18**
  Appeals from district courts. District courts, generally, post
  Argument, oral argument, **FRAP 34**
  Attorneys, disciplinary actions, **FRAP 46**
  Clerk of court of appeals, office hours, **FRAP 45**
  Constitutional questions, cases involving, United States not a party, **FRAP 44**
  Death of party, substitution of party, **FRAP 43**
  District courts,
    Appeal as of right, **FRAP 3**
    Dismissal in, **FRAP 42**
    Magistrate judges decisions, **FRAP 3**
    Notice of appeal to court of appeals from judgment or order, **FRAP Form 1**
    Partial transcript ordered, **FRAP 10**
    Release in criminal cases, notice of appeal, **FRAP 9**
    Stay or injunction pending appeal, **FRAP 8**
  Entry of judgment, **FRAP 36**
  Exhibits used at argument, removal, **FRAP 34**
  Filing notice of appeal,
    Appeal as of right, **FRAP 3**
    Tax court of the United States, **FRAP 13**
  Filing of record, administrative bodies and proceedings, **FRAP 17**
  Forms, appeal to court of appeals from,
    District court or bankruptcy appellate panel, final decisions, **FRAP Form 5**
    Judgment or order of district court, **FRAP Form 1**
    Tax court decision, **FRAP Form 2**
  Judgments and decrees, entry of judgment, **FRAP 36**
  Oral argument, **FRAP 34**
  Partial transcripts, appeals from district courts, record on appeal, **FRAP 10**

RULES OF APPELLATE PROCEDURE —Cont'd

Notice—Cont'd
  Stay pending review, administrative bodies and proceedings, **FRAP 18**
  Tax court,
    Filing notice of appeal, **FRAP 13**
    Notice of appeal to court of appeals from decision, **FRAP Form 2**
Oaths and affirmations,
  Attorneys, admission to bar of court of appeals, **FRAP 46**
  Clerks of court of appeals, **FRAP 45**
Offenses. Crimes and offenses, generally, ante
Officers and employees,
  Administrative law and procedure, generally, ante
  Attorneys, admission to bar, discipline, **FRAP 46**
  Bonds (officers and fiduciaries), generally, ante
  Cases involving constitutional questions where United States is not a party, **FRAP 44**
  Clerk of court of appeals, duties, **FRAP 45**
  Separation from office, substitution of parties, **FRAP 43**
  Substitution of parties, death or separation from office, **FRAP 43**
Offices, clerk of court of appeals, **FRAP 45**
Official bonds. Bonds (officers and fiduciaries), generally, ante
Omissions,
  Administrative law and procedure, record on review or enforcement, **FRAP 16**
  Briefs, arrangement of appendices, **FRAP 30**
Opinions, mailing copies, parties, **FRAP 36**
Oral argument, **FRAP 34**
  Amicus curiae participation, **FRAP 29**
  Appeal by permission, **FRAP 5**
  Extraordinary writs, **FRAP 21**
  Mandamus, **FRAP 21**
  National Labor Relations Board hearings, **FRAP 15.1**
  Petition for rehearing, **FRAP 40**
  Prohibition, **FRAP 21**
  Rehearing, petition for, **FRAP 40**
Orders of court,
  Appeal conferences, **FRAP 33**
  Attorneys, suspension or disbarment, **FRAP 46**
  Bankruptcy cases, appeal from, **FRAP 6**
  Clerk of court of appeals,
    Duties, **FRAP 45**
    Office hours, **FRAP 45**
  Conferences, appeal conferences, **FRAP 33**
  Determination of motions for procedural orders, **FRAP 27**

RULES OF APPELLATE PROCEDURE —Cont'd

Orders of court—Cont'd
Dismissal in court of appeals, **FRAP 42**
District courts, retention of record, **FRAP 11**
Extraordinary writs, directing answer, **FRAP 21**
Hearings in banc, **FRAP 35**
Mandamus, directing answer, **FRAP 21**
Prohibition, directing answer, **FRAP 21**
Rehearing in banc, **FRAP 35**
Relief from, motion, effect on time for appeal, **FRAP 4**
Substitution of parties, **FRAP 43**
Original writ, habeas corpus, application, **FRAP 22**
Papers. Books and papers, generally, ante
Partial transcript, district courts, record on appeal, notice, **FRAP 10**
Parties,
Administrative law and procedure, ante
Appeal conference, **FRAP 33**
Briefs, references to parties, **FRAP 28**
Cases involving constitutional questions where United States is not a party, **FRAP 44**
Conferences, appeal conferences, **FRAP 33**
Costs, persons entitled, **FRAP 39**
Judgments and decrees, mailing copies, **FRAP 36**
Non-appearance, arguments, **FRAP 34**
Opinions, mailing, **FRAP 36**
References in briefs, **FRAP 28**
Representation statement, attorneys, **FRAP 12**
Substitution of parties, **FRAP 43**
Paupers. Indigent persons, generally, ante
Penitentiaries. Correctional institutions, generally, ante
Permission. Appeals by permission, district courts, **FRAP 5**
Personal representatives, death of party, substitution, **FRAP 43**
Petitions,
Administrative law and procedure, review of order, **FRAP 15**
Petition for, **FRAP Form 3**
Appeals by permission, **FRAP 5**
Corporate disclosure statements, **FRAP 26.1**
District courts, appeals by permission, **FRAP 5**
Extraordinary writs, **FRAP 21**
Forms, briefs, appendices and other papers, **FRAP 32**
Mandamus, **FRAP 21**
Permission to appeal, **FRAP 5**
Prohibition writs, **FRAP 21**
Rehearing, **FRAP 40**

RULES OF APPELLATE PROCEDURE —Cont'd

Petitions—Cont'd
Writs, extraordinary writs, **FRAP 21**
Plea or answer. Answer, generally, ante
Pleadings,
Prescribing, powers and duties, **28 § 2072**
Poor persons. Indigent persons, generally, ante
Postponement, arguments, **FRAP 34**
Preliminary hearings,
Court of appeals, transmission of record from district court, **FRAP 11**
Record for preliminary hearing in court of appeals, district courts, transmission of record, **FRAP 11**
Printing,
Briefs,
Costs, **FRAP 39**
Form of briefs and appendices, **FRAP 32**
Prisons and prisoners. Correctional institutions, generally, ante
Pro se appeals, notice of appeal, contents, **FRAP 3**
Process,
Acknowledgments, proof of service, **FRAP 25**
Briefs, service, **FRAP 31**
Extraordinary writs, **FRAP 21**
Mandamus, proof of service, **FRAP 21**
Manner of service, **FRAP 25**
Prohibition, proof of service, **FRAP 21**
Service, **FRAP 25**
Acknowledgment, **FRAP 25**
Administrative law and procedure, ante
Briefs, **FRAP 31**
Commercial carriers, **FRAP 25**
Copies of papers filed, **FRAP 25**
District court, notice of appeal, **FRAP 3**
Extraordinary writs, **FRAP 21**
Mandamus, **FRAP 21**
Manner of service, **FRAP 25**
Motions, service of briefs, **FRAP 27**
Notice of appeal, tax court, **FRAP 13**
Prohibition, **FRAP 21**
Proof, **FRAP 25**
Extraordinary writs, **FRAP 21**
Tax court, notice of appeal, **FRAP 13**
Time, additional time after service by mail, **FRAP 26**
Tax court, notice of appeal, **FRAP 13**
Time, additional time after service by mail, **FRAP 26**
Prohibition,
Applicability of rules, **FRAP 1, 2**
Extraordinary writs, **FRAP 21**
Proof of service,
Mandamus, **FRAP 21**
Process, **FRAP 25**
Prohibition, **FRAP 21**

RULES OF APPELLATE PROCEDURE —Cont'd

Proposed judgments, administrative bodies and proceedings, enforcing orders, **FRAP 19**
Public officers. Officers and employees, generally, ante
Punishment. Crimes and offenses, generally, ante
Records,
Administrative law and procedure,
Filing of record, **FRAP 17**
Review or enforcement of orders, **FRAP 16**
Amendment, record on review or enforcement, administrative bodies and proceedings, **FRAP 16**
Appeals from district courts, ante
Bankruptcy appeals, **FRAP 6**
Briefs,
Hearing appeals without necessity of appendix, **FRAP 30**
References to record, **FRAP 28, 30**
Clerk of court of appeals, office hours, **FRAP 45**
Composition of record, administrative bodies and proceedings, **FRAP 16**
Costs, copies of records, **FRAP 39**
District courts, generally. Appeals from district courts, ante
Enforcement of administrative orders, **FRAP 16**
Filing of record, **FRAP 17**
Filing of record,
Administrative law and procedure, review and enforcement of orders, **FRAP 17**
Tax court, **FRAP 13**
Review of administrative orders, **FRAP 16**
Filing record, **FRAP 17**
Tax court, record on appeal, **FRAP 13**
Transmission of records,
Bankruptcy cases, **FRAP 6**
Tax court, **FRAP 13**
Records on appeal,
Administrative orders, enforcement, **28 § 2112**
Defined, appeal from district court, **FRAP 10**
Reformatories. Correctional institutions, generally, ante
Rehearing,
Bankruptcy, effect on time for appeal, **FRAP 6**
Determination of causes by court in banc, **FRAP 35**
In banc, determination of causes, **FRAP 35**
Petitions, **FRAP 40**
Stay of mandate pending petition, **FRAP 41**
Release, habeas corpus, custody of prisoner pending review, **FRAP 23**
Removal, exhibits used at argument, **FRAP 34**

RULES OF APPELLATE PROCEDURE —Cont'd

Reply briefs,
  Amicus curiae, **FRAP 29**
  Contents, **FRAP 28**
  Time for serving and filing, **FRAP 31**
Reports,
  District court, record on appeal, statement of evidence or proceedings when report and transcript are unavailable, **FRAP 10**
Representation statements, attorneys, **FRAP 12**
Response,
  Corporate disclosure statements, **FRAP 26.1**
  Motions, **FRAP 27**
Retention of record,
  Administrative law and procedure, filing of record, **FRAP 17**
  Appeals from district courts, transmission of record, **FRAP 11**
Reversal of judgments,
  Costs, **FRAP 39**
  Interest on judgments, **FRAP 37**
Revival of actions, substitution of parties, death or separation from office, **FRAP 43**
Right to appeal, district court judgments and orders, **FRAP 3**
Rules and regulations, briefs, reproduction, **FRAP 28**
Rules of court,
  Administrative law and procedure, applicability of other rules to review or enforcement, **FRAP 20**
  Courts of appeals, **FRAP 47**
  Tax court, applicability of other rules, **FRAP 14**
Saturdays,
  Clerk of court of appeals, office hours, **FRAP 45**
  Time, computation and extension, **FRAP 26**
Scope of rules, **FRAP 1**
Security, mandate, stay of mandate, **FRAP 41**
Separate appeals, oral arguments, **FRAP 34**
Service, **FRAP 25**
  Administrative law and procedure, ante
  Appeals from district courts, ante
  Briefs, **FRAP 31**
  Process, ante
Single judge, motions, powers and duties, **FRAP 27**
Standard of review, statement, briefs, **FRAP 28**
State courts,
  Certificate of appealability, habeas corpus, **FRAP 22**
  Habeas corpus, **FRAP 22**
    Custody of prisoners, **FRAP 23**

RULES OF APPELLATE PROCEDURE —Cont'd

Statement of evidence, appeals from district courts, absence of report or transcript, **FRAP 10**
Statements,
  Agreed statement, record on appeal, district courts, **FRAP 10**
  Misconduct, attorneys, suspension or disbarment, **FRAP 46**
  Representation statements, attorneys, **FRAP 12**
Statements of issues, extraordinary writs, petitions, **FRAP 21**
Statute of limitations. Limitation of actions, generally, ante
Statutes,
  Briefs, reproductions, **FRAP 28**
  Cases involving constitutional questions where United States is not a party, **FRAP 44**
  Time, computation and extension, **FRAP 26**
Stay of proceedings. Supersedeas or stay, generally, post
Stipulations,
  Administrative law and procedure, filing of record, **FRAP 17**
  District courts,
    Dismissal, voluntary dismissal, **FRAP 42**
    Transmission of record, **FRAP 11**
Substitution of parties, **FRAP 43**
Suggestions, parties for hearing or rehearing in banc, **FRAP 35**
Sundays,
  Clerk of court of appeals, office hours, **FRAP 45**
  Time, computation and extension, **FRAP 26**
Supersedeas or stay,
  Administrative law and procedure, ante
  Bonds (officers and fiduciaries),
    Cost bonds in civil cases, **FRAP 7**
    Record for preliminary hearing in court of appeals, **FRAP 11**
    Stay or injunction pending appeals, **FRAP 8**
  Mandate, **FRAP 41**
  Pending appeals, district court appeals, **FRAP 8**
Supreme Court of the United States, attorneys, admission to bar of courts of appeals, **FRAP 46**
Sureties. Cost bonds, generally, ante
Suspension, attorneys, **FRAP 46**
Suspension of rules, **FRAP 2**
Tax Court of the United States. United States Tax Court, generally, post
Taxation of costs, **FRAP 39**
Temporary injunctions, appeals from district courts, **FRAP 8**
Temporary retention of record, appeals from district courts, **FRAP 11**

RULES OF APPELLATE PROCEDURE —Cont'd

Time,
  Additional time after service by mail, **FRAP 26**
  Administrative law and procedure, ante
  Appeals from district courts, ante
  Appendices to briefs, filing, **FRAP 30**
  Arguments, **FRAP 34**
    Postponement, **FRAP 34**
  Briefs, ante
  Certiorari, stay of mandate pending application, **FRAP 41**
  Clerk of court of appeals, office hours, **FRAP 45**
  Computation and extension, **FRAP 26**
  Court in banc, hearing or rehearing, **FRAP 35**
  Enlargement of time, motions, **FRAP 26**
  Extension, **FRAP 26**
  Filing, administrative orders, enforcement, **28 § 2112**
  Hearing in banc, **FRAP 35**
  In banc, hearing or rehearing, **FRAP 35**
  Issuance of mandate, **FRAP 41**
  Legal holidays, defined, **FRAP 26**
  Mandate, issuance, **FRAP 41**
  Motions, response, **FRAP 27**
  Oral arguments, notice, **FRAP 34**
  Petition for rehearing, **FRAP 40**
  Rehearing,
    In banc, **FRAP 35**
    Petition, **FRAP 40**
  Reply to response, motions, **FRAP 27**
  Response, motions, **FRAP 27**
  Service of process, additional time after service by mail, **FRAP 26**
  Stay of mandate, **FRAP 41**
  Tax court, filing notice of appeal, **FRAP 13**
Title of rules, **FRAP 1**
Transcripts,
  Administrative law and procedure, filing of record, **FRAP 17**
  Appeals from district courts, record on appeal, **FRAP 10**
  Briefs, references to record, **FRAP 28**
  District courts,
    Record on appeal, **FRAP 10**
    Statement of evidence or proceedings in absence of report or transcript, **FRAP 10**
  Partial transcript, district courts, record on appeal, **FRAP 10**
  Statement of evidence or proceedings in absence of report or transcript, district courts, **FRAP 10**
Transfers, habeas corpus, custody of prisoner pending review, **FRAP 23**
Transmission of record,
  Appeals from district court, **FRAP 11**
  Tax court, **FRAP 13**

RULES OF APPELLATE PROCEDURE —Cont'd

Typewriting, form of briefs and appendices, **FRAP 32**
United States,
Cases involving constitutional questions where United States is not a party, **FRAP 44**
Costs for and against, **FRAP 39**
Rehearing petition, time, **FRAP 40**
United States Agencies. Administrative law and procedure, generally, ante
United States Tax Court,
Applicability of rules, **FRAP 1, 2**
Application of other rules, review of tax court decisions, **FRAP14**
Decision of tax court, **FRAP Form 2**
Docketing of appeal, **FRAP 13**
Filing and service of notice of appeal, **FRAP 13**
Forms, notice of appeal to court of appeals from tax court decision, **FRAP Form 2**
Notice of appeal, **FRAP 13**
Review of decisions, **FRAP 13**
Application of other rules, **FRAP 14**
Time, filing notice of appeal, **FRAP 13**
Vacating and setting aside judgments and decrees, costs, **FRAP 39**
Voluntary dismissal, **FRAP 42**
Weather delays, computation of time, **FRAP 26**
Words and phrases,
Agency, administrative bodies and proceedings, **FRAP 15**
Appellant, administrative bodies or proceedings, **FRAP 20**
Appellee, administrative bodies and proceedings, **FRAP 20**
Legal holidays, time, **FRAP 26**
Record on appeal, appeals from district courts, **FRAP 10**
Writs,
Extraordinary writs, generally, ante
Habeas corpus, generally, ante
Prescribing, powers and duties, **28 § 2072**

RULES OF BANKRUPTCY

Bankruptcy Rules and Forms, generally, this index

RULES OF CIVIL PROCEDURE

Abatement of actions, substitution of parties where public officer was party, **FRCVP 25(d)**
Absence, joinder, persons needed for just adjudication, **FRCVP 19(a)**
Abstracts, business records, interrogatories, **FRCVP 33**
Accord and satisfaction, affirmative defense, **FRCVP 8(c)**
Accounts and accounting,
Complaint in action on, form, **FRCVP Form 4**
Default judgment, necessity of taking account, **FRCVP 55(b)**

RULES OF CIVIL PROCEDURE —Cont'd

Accounts and accounting—Cont'd
Masters, statement of accounts, **FRCVP 53(d)**
Reference to master, **FRCVP 53(b)**
Stay of judgment, accounting for infringement, **FRCVP 62(a)**
Address, plaintiffs address to appear in summons, **FRCVP 4(a)**
Adjournment, masters proceeding, failure of party to appear at time and place appointed, **FRCVP 53(d)**
Administrative Office of the United States Courts,
Clerk to keep records required by director, **FRCVP 79(d)**
Director to prescribe form of civil docket, **FRCVP 79(a)**
Administrators, prosecution of action, **FRCVP 17(a)**
Admiralty and maritime claims,
Applicability of rules, **FRCVP 1; FRCVP A**
Costs,
Actions in rem and quasi in rem,
Release, property, **FRCVP E(5)**
Security, **FRCVP E(2)**
Limitation of liability, security, **FRCVP F(1)**
Deposits,
Actions in rem and quasi in rem, seizing property, **FRCVP E(4)**
Limitation of liability, **FRCVP F(1)**
Distribution, **FRCVP F(8)**
Increase or decrease, **FRCVP F(7)**
Expenses and expenditures,
Actions in rem and quasi in rem,
Directions respecting custody, **FRCVP E(4)**
Security, **FRCVP E(2)**
Seizing property, **FRCVP E(4)**
Filing,
Actions in rem, **FRCVP C(6)**
Limitation of liability, **FRCVP F(4, 5)**
Garnishment,
Actions in rem and quasi in rem, applicability, **FRCVP E(1)**
Applicability, supplemental rules, **FRCVP A**
Special provisions, **FRCVP B**
General provisions, actions in rem and quasi in rem, **FRCVP E**
Joinder, **FRCVP 18(a)**
Judgments and decrees,
Actions in rem, **FRCVP C(5)**
Actions in rem and quasi in rem,
Release, property, bonds, **FRCVP E(5)**
Security, **FRCVP E(2)**
Jurisdiction, form of allegation, **FRCVP Form 2**
Complaint under Merchant Marine Act, **FRCVP Form 15**
Jury trial of right, **FRCVP 38(e)**

RULES OF CIVIL PROCEDURE —Cont'd

Admiralty and maritime claims—Cont'd
Limitation of liability, **FRCVP F**
Applicability, supplemental rules, **FRCVP A**
Marshals,
Actions in rem,
Process, service, **FRCVP 4.1, FRCVP C(3)**
Property delivered to, **FRCVP C(5)**
Actions in rem and quasi in rem,
Disposition, property, duties, **FRCVP E(9)**
Process, execution, **FRCVP E(4)**
Motions,
Actions in rem, property, payment into court, **FRCVP C(5)**
Actions in rem and quasi in rem,
Sale, property, **FRCVP E(9)**
Security, reduction, **FRCVP E(5, 6)**
Limitation of liability, increase, funds, **FRCVP F(7)**
Power of Supreme Court to prescribe rules, **28 § 2072**
Notice,
Actions in rem and quasi in rem,
Clearance of vessel, **FRCVP E(4)**
Directions respecting custody, **FRCVP E(4)**
Release, property, **FRCVP E(5)**
Attachment and garnishment, **FRCVP B(2)**
In rem actions, release, property, **FRCVP C(4)**
Limitation of liability, **FRCVP F(4)**
Insufficiency, funds, **FRCVP F(7)**
Possessory or petitory actions, **FRCVP D**
Oaths and affirmations,
Actions in rem, **FRCVP C(6)**
Verified complaint, **FRCVP C(2)**
Affirmation in lieu of oath, **FRCVP 43(d)**
Answer by garnishee, **FRCVP B(3)**
Deponent, power to administer, **FRCVP 28(a)**
Foreign countries, depositions, taking by person authorized to administer oath in place in which examination is held, **FRCVP 28(b)**
Witnesses, powers of master, **FRCVP 53(c)**
Orders,
Actions in rem, public notice, **FRCVP C(4)**
Actions in rem and quasi in rem,
Release, property, **FRCVP E(5)**
Sale, property, **FRCVP E(9)**
Limitation of liability, insufficiency of funds, **FRCVP F(7)**

RULES OF CIVIL PROCEDURE —Cont'd
Admiralty and maritime claims—Cont'd
Partition, petitory and possessory actions,
Actions in rem and quasi in rem, applicability, **FRCVP E(1)**
Applicability, supplemental rules, **FRCVP A**
Process and notice, **FRCVP D**
Release, property, **FRCVP E(5)**
Payment into court,
Actions in rem, **FRCVP C(5)**
Actions in rem and quasi in rem, **FRCVP E(4)**
Sale, proceeds, **FRCVP E(9)**
Permissive joinder of vessels or cargo, **FRCVP 20(a)**
Pleadings, **FRCVP 9(h)**
Power of Supreme Court to prescribe rules for, **28 § 2072**
Power of Supreme Court to prescribe rules for, **28 § 2072**
Savings provision, **28 § 2073 nt**
Prize proceedings, nonapplicability of rules, **FRCVP 81(a)**
Process,
Actions in rem, **FRCVP C(3)**
Actions in rem and quasi in rem, **FRCVP E(3, 4)**
Stay, **FRCVP E(5)**
Attachment and garnishment, **FRCVP B(1)**
Possessory or petitory actions, **FRCVP D**
Power of Supreme Court to prescribe rules for, **28 § 2072**
Savings provision, **28 § 2073 nt**
Remedies, applicability, supplemental rules, **FRCVP A**
Scope, supplemental rules, **FRCVP A**
Security,
Actions in rem and quasi in rem, **FRCVP E(2)**
Counterclaim, **FRCVP E(7)**
Reduction or impairment, **FRCVP E(6)**
Release, property, **FRCVP E(5)**
Sales, property, **FRCVP E(9)**
Limitation of liability, **FRCVP F(1)**
Distribution, **FRCVP F(8)**
Increase or decrease, **FRCVP F(7)**
Service of process,
Actions in rem, answer, **FRCVP C(6)**
Attachment and garnishment, process, **FRCVP B(2)**
Limitation of liability, **FRCVP F(4, 5)**
Special provisions,
Actions in rem, **FRCVP C**
Attachment and garnishment, **FRCVP B**
Statutory condemnation proceedings, applicability, supplemental rules, **FRCVP A**
Third-party practice, **FRCVP 14(a, c)**

RULES OF CIVIL PROCEDURE —Cont'd
Admiralty and maritime claims—Cont'd
Time,
Actions in rem,
Filing, **FRCVP C(6)**
Notice, **FRCVP C(4)**
Limitation of liability,
Filing complaint, **FRCVP F(1)**
Information for claimants, **FRCVP F(6)**
Treatment as civil action, venue purposes, **FRCVP 82**
Trusts and trustees,
Limitation of liability,
Security, **FRCVP F(1)**
Transfer, interest in vessel, **FRCVP F(1, 2)**
Admissibility of evidence,
Depositions, use in court proceedings, **FRCVP 32(a)**
Objections to, **FRCVP 32(b)**
Official foreign record, attested copy, **FRCVP 44(a)**
Admissions,
Effect, **FRCVP 36(b)**
Pending action only, **FRCVP 36(b)**
Pleading, failure to deny, **FRCVP 8(d)**
Prohibition against use in other proceedings, **FRCVP 36(b)**
Requests, **FRCVP 36**
Answer, service, requirements, **FRCVP 36(a)**
Copies of documents served with, **FRCVP 36(a)**
Effect of admission, **FRCVP 36(b)**
Expenses,
Award of, **FRCVP 36(a)**
Failure to admit genuineness of document or truth of matter requested, **FRCVP 37(c)**
Form of, **FRCVP Form 25**
Motion to determine sufficiency of answers or objections, **FRCVP 36(a)**
Objections, service, requirements, **FRCVP 36(a)**
Orders, sufficiency of answers or objections, **FRCVP 36(a)**
Pretrial conference or prior to trial, final disposition, **FRCVP 36(a)**
Scope, **FRCVP 36(a)**
Service, time of, **FRCVP 36(a)**
Stipulations, extension of time for responses, approval of court, **FRCVP 29**
Supplementation of responses, **FRCVP 26**
Summary judgment, admissions show no genuine issue, **FRCVP 56(c)**
Withdrawal or amendment, **FRCVP 36(b)**
Advancement, causes on docket, **FRCVP 78**

RULES OF CIVIL PROCEDURE —Cont'd
Adverse or pecuniary interest, depositions, person taking, disqualification, **FRCVP 28(c)**
Advisory juries, trial by court with advisory jury, **FRCVP 52(a)**
Affidavits,
Admiralty and maritime claims, attachment and garnishment, **FRCVP B(1)**
Contempt, filing summary judgment affidavit in bad faith, **FRCVP 56(g)**
Default judgment, **FRCVP 55**
Motion based on facts appearing of record, hearing on affidavits, **FRCVP 43(e)**
New trial, time for serving no motion for, **FRCVP 59(c)**
Opposing affidavits,
Made in bad faith, **FRCVP 56(g)**
Time for service, **FRCVP 6(d)**
Proof of service, **FRCVP 4(*l*)**
Service, affidavit supporting motion, **FRCVP 6(d)**
Summary judgment, **FRCVP 56**
Temporary restraining order, notice, **FRCVP 65(b)**
Affirmative defenses,
Pleading, **FRCVP 8(c)**
Service of pleadings, numerous defendants, **FRCVP 5(c)**
Age,
Service of process, **FRCVP 4(c)**
Witness, inability to attend or testify, depositions, use in court proceedings, **FRCVP 32(a)**
Agencies of United States,
Answer or reply, time, service, **FRCVP 12(a)**
Appeal and review, stay without bond or security, **FRCVP 62(e)**
Depositions,
Introduction in evidence, making deponent witness of introducing party, applicability, **FRCVP 32(c)**
Oral examination,
Failure of officer to attend at own deposition, sanctions, **FRCVP 37(d)**
Failure to comply with order compelling designation, sanctions, **FRCVP 37(b)**
Motion for order compelling designation, **FRCVP 37(a)**
Use in court proceedings, **FRCVP 32(a)**
Written questions,
Failure of officer to attend at own deposition, sanctions, **FRCVP 37(d)**
Failure to comply with order compelling answer, sanctions, **FRCVP 37(b)**

RULES OF CIVIL PROCEDURE —Cont'd

Agencies of United States—Cont'd
Depositions—Cont'd
Introduction in evidence, making deponent witness of introducing party, applicability—Cont'd
Written questions—Cont'd
Motion for order compelling answer, **FRCVP 37(a)**
Interrogatories, service of, **FRCVP 33(a)**
Process, pleading, amendment, change of party, **FRCVP 15(c)**
Restraining order or preliminary injunction, security, **FRCVP 65(c)**
Review of orders, **28 § 2347**
Subpoena,
Application of rules, **FRCVP 81(a)**
Tender of fees and mileage, **FRCVP 45(b)**
Agents and agency,
Consular agent, authentication of official record, **FRCVP 44(a)**
Service,
Process, admiralty and maritime claims, actions in rem and quasi in rem, **FRCVP E(4)**
Agreements, parties, physical and mental examinations, **FRCVP 35(b)**
Alteration,
Class actions, orders, **FRCVP 23(d)**
Judgments and decrees,
Stay of proceedings pending motion for, **FRCVP 62(b)**
Time for service of motion for, **FRCVP 59(e)**
Order, class action maintainable, determination, **FRCVP 23(c)**
Amendment,
Admission, **FRCVP 36(b)**
Class actions, orders, **FRCVP 23(d)**
Conclusions of law on motion for new trial, **FRCVP 59(a)**
Effective date of amendments to rules, **FRCVP 86**
Findings of court, **FRCVP 52(b)**
Extension of time, **FRCVP 6(b)**
Motion for new trial, **FRCVP 59(a)**
Stay of proceedings to enforce judgment, pending disposition of motion to amend, **FRCVP 62(b)**
Judgments and decrees,
Stay of proceedings pending motion for, **FRCVP 62(b)**
Time for service of motion, **FRCVP 59(e)**
Order, class action maintainable, determination, **FRCVP 23(c)**
Proof of service, **FRCVP 4(*l*)**
Rules by district courts, **FRCVP 83**
Summons, **FRCVP 4(a)**
Ancillary process, admiralty and maritime claims, actions in rem, **FRCVP C(5)**
Answers. Pleadings, post

RULES OF CIVIL PROCEDURE —Cont'd

Appeal and review,
Admiralty and maritime claims,
Actions in rem and quasi in rem, security, **FRCVP E(2)**
Power of Supreme Court to prescribe rules for, **28 § 2072**
Application of rules, **FRCVP 81(a)**
Class action certification, **FRCVP 23(f)**
Correction of clerical errors, judgments, orders and record, pendency of appeal, **FRCVP 60(a)**
Court of appeals, notice, form, **FRCVP Form 27**
Depositions pending appeal, **FRCVP 27(b)**
District of Columbia courts, application of rules to appeals, **FRCVP 81(a)**
Extension of time, taking appeal to court of appeals, **FRCVP 6(b)**
Filing, power of Supreme Court to prescribe rules for, **28 § 2072**
Findings by court, requests for purpose of review, **FRCVP 52(a)**
Habeas corpus cases, certification of probable cause, **FRCVP 81(a)**
Injunctions, post
Judgments and decrees, copy, clerk to keep correct copy of final judgment, **FRCVP 79(b)**
Longshoremens and Harbor Workers Compensation Act, review, application of rules, **FRCVP 81(a)**
Magistrate judges,
Judgment entered upon direction of, **FRCVP 73(c, d)**
Notice of appeal, form on appeal, **FRCVP Form 27**
Record on appeal, service, **FRCVP 5(a)**
Relief from failure to appeal within time, lack of notice of entry of judgment, **FRCVP 77(d)**
Status quo, order preserving pending appeal, **FRCVP 62(g)**
Stay pending appeal, **FRCVP 62**
Supersedeas bond, **FRCVP 62(d)**
Taxation of costs by clerk, **FRCVP 54(d)**
Time,
Appeal to court of appeals, **FRCVP 6(b)**
Extension of time for taking, **FRCVP 6(b)**
Lack of notice of entry of judgment, **FRCVP 77(d)**
Supersedeas bond, giving, **FRCVP 62(d)**
Taxation of costs by clerk, **FRCVP 54(d)**
Appearance,
Admiralty and maritime claims, actions in rem and quasi in rem, restricted, **FRCVP E(8)**

RULES OF CIVIL PROCEDURE —Cont'd

Appearance—Cont'd
Civil docket entry in, **FRCVP 79(a)**
Condemnation proceedings, **FRCVP 71A(e)**
Service, **FRCVP 5(a)**
Application of rules, **FRCVP 1, 81**
Personal property, rules governing procedure for condemnation, **FRCVP 71A(a)**
Applications,
Intervention, **FRCVP 24**
Preliminary injunction, consolidation, hearing with trial on merits, **FRCVP 65(a)**
Appointment,
Interpreters, **FRCVP 43(f)**
Master, **FRCVP 53(a)**
Process servers, **FRCVP 4(c)**
Arbitration and award,
Affirmative defenses, **FRCVP 8(c)**
Applicability of rules to, **FRCVP 81(a)**
Arrest,
Admiralty and maritime claims, actions in rem, notice, **FRCVP C(4)**
Satisfaction of judgment ultimately to be entered, **FRCVP 64**
Third-party complaint, admiralty and maritime claims, **FRCVP 14(a)**
United States vessels, exemptions, supplemental rules inapplicable, **FRCVP C(1)**
Warrant for arrest,
Admiralty and maritime claims,
Actions in rem, **FRCVP C(3)**
Possessory or petitory actions, **FRCVP D**
Assessor, master, inclusion in term, **FRCVP 53(a)**
Assignment of errors on appeal, instructions, giving or failure to give, **FRCVP 51**
Assistance,
To foreign tribunals and to litigants before such tribunals, testimony taken and document produced in accordance with, **28 § 1782**
Writ of, delivery of possession, **FRCVP 70**
Associations and societies,
Capacity to sue or be sued, **FRCVP 17(b)**
Depositions,
Introduction in evidence, making deponent witness of introducing party, applicability, **FRCVP 32(c)**
Oral examination,
Failure of officer or director to attend at own deposition, sanctions, **FRCVP 37(d)**
Failure to comply with order compelling designation, sanctions, **FRCVP 37(b)**

RULES OF CIVIL PROCEDURE
—Cont'd
Associations and societies—Cont'd
Depositions—Cont'd
Oral examination—Cont'd
Motion for order compelling designation, **FRCVP 37(a)**
Use in court proceedings, **FRCVP 32(a)**
Written questions,
Failure of officer or director to attend at own deposition, sanctions, **FRCVP 37(d)**
Motion for order compelling answer, **FRCVP 37(a)**
Interrogatories, service, **FRCVP 33(a)**
Officer, director or managing agent of adverse party, examination and cross examination, **FRCVP 43(b)**
Pleading, capacity to sue or be sued, **FRCVP 9(a)**
Service of summons, **FRCVP 4(h)**
Witnesses, interrogation, **FRCVP 43(b)**
Assumption of risk, affirmative defense, **FRCVP 8(c)**
Attachment,
Admiralty and maritime claims,
Actions in rem and quasi in rem, applicability, **FRCVP E(1)**
Applicability, supplemental rules, **FRCVP A**
Special provisions, **FRCVP B**
Compulsory counterclaims, **FRCVP 13(a)**
Property of person disobeying judgment directing performance of specific acts, **FRCVP 70**
Seizure of person or property, availability of remedy, **FRCVP 64**
Attestation, official records, authentication, **FRCVP 44(a)**
Attorney general,
Notice of intervention, **FRCVP 24(c)**
Process, pleading, amendment, change of party, **FRCVP 15(c)**
Attorneys,
Admiralty and maritime claims, limitation of liability, information for claimants, **FRCVP F(6)**
Depositions upon oral examination,
Use against parties not represented by counsel, **FRCVP 32**
Fees. Attorneys fees, generally, post
Interrogatories, signing answers to, **FRCVP 33**
Master, submission of draft of report for suggestions, **FRCVP 53(e)**
Motions, signature, **FRCVP 11**
Notice,
Court of proposed action upon requests for instructions, **FRCVP 51**
Meeting on order of reference, **FRCVP 53(d)**
Temporary restraining order, **FRCVP 65(b)**

RULES OF CIVIL PROCEDURE
—Cont'd
Attorneys—Cont'd
Pleadings, signature, **FRCVP 11**
Pretrial conference, **FRCVP 16**
Representations to court, signatures, **FRCVP 11**
Sanctions, **FRCVP 11**
Service,
Admiralty and maritime claims, limitation of liability, **FRCVP F(4)**
Pleadings, **FRCVP 5(b)**
Signature,
Answers or objections to requests for admission, **FRCVP 36(a)**
Discovery disclosure, **FRCVP 26**
Submission, forms of judgment, **FRCVP 58**
Summons, stating name and address of plaintiffs attorney, **FRCVP 4(a)**
Attorneys fees,
Delay of entry of judgment for taxing, **FRCVP 58**
Depositions,
Failure of party to attend at own deposition, **FRCVP 37(d)**
Oral examination, sanctions, **FRCVP 30**
Disclosure by parties, refusal, **FRCVP 37**
Discovery, failure to comply with order compelling, **FRCVP 37(b)**
Documents, failure to admit genuineness, **FRCVP 37(c)**
Entry upon land for inspection and other purposes, failure of party to respond to request, **FRCVP 37(d)**
Interrogatories, failure of party to serve answers to, **FRCVP 37(d)**
Motions, **FRCVP 54**
Orders, compelling discovery, **FRCVP 37(a)**
Sanctions, **FRCVP 11**
Pleadings, sanctions, **FRCVP 11**
Pretrial conferences, sanctions, **FRCVP 16(f)**
Pretrial orders, sanctions, **FRCVP 16(f)**
Production of documents or things, failure of party to respond to request for inspection, **FRCVP 37(d)**
Scheduling conferences, sanctions, **FRCVP 16(f)**
Scheduling orders, sanctions, **FRCVP 16(f)**
Summary judgment, fees imposed on person filing affidavit in bad faith, **FRCVP 56(g)**
Summons, waiver of service, refusal, **FRCVP 4(d)**
Truth of matter, failure to admit, **FRCVP 37(c)**
United States, discovery proceedings, **FRCVP 37(f)**
Waiver, service of summons, refusal, **FRCVP 4(d)**

RULES OF CIVIL PROCEDURE
—Cont'd
Audita querela, abolition of writ, **FRCVP 60(b)**
Audits and auditors,
Business records, interrogatories, **FRCVP 33**
Inclusion in term "master", **FRCVP 53(a)**
Authentication, official record, **FRCVP 44(a)**
Availability,
Admiralty and maritime claims
Actions in rem, **FRCVP C(1)**
Attachment and garnishment, **FRCVP B(1)**
Avoidance,
Pleading, matters constituting, **FRCVP 8(c)**
Service of pleadings, numerous defendants, **FRCVP 5(c)**
Award,
Attorneys fees, generally, ante
Expenses, generally, post
Bad faith, depositions upon oral examination, sanctions, **FRCVP 30**
Bailees, prosecution of action, **FRCVP 17(a)**
Bankruptcy, pleading, discharge, affirmative defenses, **FRCVP 8(c)**
Bills of review, abolition, **FRCVP 60(b)**
Boards and commissions, pleading decision, **FRCVP 9(e)**
Bonds (officers and fiduciaries),
General bond, admiralty and maritime claims, actions in rem and quasi in rem, release, **FRCVP E(5)**
Injunction pending appeal, **FRCVP 62(c)**
Proceedings against sureties, **FRCVP 65.1**
Special bond, admiralty and maritime claims, actions in rem and quasi in rem, release, **FRCVP E(5)**
Supersedeas or stay, post
Books and papers,
Clerk to keep, **FRCVP 79(d)**
Documents, generally, post
Master, compelling production, **FRCVP 53(c)**
Subpoena for production, **FRCVP 45(a)**
Business associations, service of summons on, **FRCVP 4(h)**
Business records, interrogatories, option to produce, **FRCVP 33**
Calendars,
Assignment of cases for trial, **FRCVP 40**
Clerk to prepare, **FRCVP 79(c)**
Declaratory judgment case advanced on calendar, **FRCVP 57**
Pretrial calendar, **FRCVP 16(b)**
Capacity, pleading, **FRCVP 9(a)**

RULES OF CIVIL PROCEDURE —Cont'd

Captions,
  Motions and other papers, **FRCVP 7(b)**
  Pleading, **FRCVP 10(a)**
Certificates and certification,
  Attorneys,
    Discovery materials, **FRCVP 26**
    Temporary restraining order, notice, **FRCVP 65(b)**
  Authentication of official record, **FRCVP 44(a)**
  Class actions, appeal and review, **FRCVP 23(f)**
  Depositions,
    Oral examination, officer taking, **FRCVP 30**
  Probable cause, appeals in habeas corpus cases, **FRCVP 81(a)**
  Service of process, filing, **FRCVP 5(d)**
Certified copies, summary judgment, copies attached to affidavit supporting or opposing, **FRCVP 56(e)**
Certified public accountants, statement of accounts, evidence before master, **FRCVP 53(d)**
Challenges, jury, **FRCVP 47(b)**
Chambers, business which may be conducted at, **FRCVP 77(b)**
Charts. Production of documents or things, generally, post
Chief Justice of Supreme Court to report to Congress, **28 § 2072**
Children and minors,
  Default judgment entered against, **FRCVP 55(b)**
  Depositions, taking before action, **FRCVP 27(a)**
  Parties, **FRCVP 17(c)**
  Service of summons upon, **FRCVP 4(g)**
Citation,
  Federal Rules of Civil Procedure, **FRCVP 85**
  Local district rules, **FRCVP 83**
Citizens and citizenship,
  Diversity, jurisdiction, form of allegation, **FRCVP Form 2**
  Proceedings for admission to citizenship, applicability of rules to, **FRCVP 81(a)**
Civil commitment, service of order, **FRCVP 4.1**
Civil docket, entry, **FRCVP 79(a)**
Civil justice reform, applicability, **28 § 519 nt, EON 12988**
Claimant, third-party practice, admiralty and maritime claims, **FRCVP 14(a)**
Claims, discovery, sanctions for failure to comply with order compelling, refusal to allow support or opposition to, **FRCVP 37(b)**
Class actions, **FRCVP 23**
  Joinder, persons needed for just adjudication, **FRCVP 19(d)**

RULES OF CIVIL PROCEDURE —Cont'd

Class actions—Cont'd
  Separate actions, risk created, class actions maintainable, **FRCVP 23(b)**
  Shareholders, derivative actions, **FRCVP 23.1**
  Unincorporated associations, actions relating to, **FRCVP 23.2**
Clerical mistakes, correction, **FRCVP 60(a)**
Clerks of courts,
  Agent for service of process, proceedings against sureties, **FRCVP 65.1**
  Appeal and review, taxation of costs, **FRCVP 54(d)**
  Books and papers, **FRCVP 79**
  Business hours, **FRCVP 77(c)**
  Calendar preparation, **FRCVP 79(c)**
  Chambers, attendance of clerk, **FRCVP 77(b)**
  Copies,
    Final judgment or appealable order, **FRCVP 79(b)**
    Order of reference to be furnished to master, **FRCVP 53(d)**
  Costs, taxation, **FRCVP 54(d)**
  Default judgment, entry, **FRCVP 55(a, b(1))**
  Entries in books kept by clerk of district court, **FRCVP 79**
  Execution to enforce judgment directing delivery of possession, issuance, **FRCVP 70**
  Filing pleadings and papers with court, **FRCVP 5(e)**
  Indexes for civil docket and civil judgments and orders, **FRCVP 79(c)**
  Judgments and decrees,
    Entry, **FRCVP 58**
    Indices, **FRCVP 79(c)**
  Local rule or order of district court, office hours on Saturdays or particular legal holidays, **FRCVP 77(c)**
  Masters, filing report with clerk, **FRCVP 53(e)**
  Notice,
    Filing of report by master, **FRCVP 53(e)**
    Orders or judgments given by clerk, **FRCVP 77(d)**
  Office, **FRCVP 77(c)**
  Orders grantable by clerk, **FRCVP 77(c)**
  Records and recordation, **FRCVP 79(d)**
  Release of property, admiralty and maritime claims, actions in rem and quasi in rem, **FRCVP E(5)**
  Saturdays, Sundays and legal holidays, exception, business hours, **FRCVP 77(c)**
  Service, pleading or other papers, leaving copy with clerk of court, **FRCVP 5(b)**

RULES OF CIVIL PROCEDURE —Cont'd

Clerks of courts—Cont'd
  Summons, issuance, signature, and delivery for service on filing of complaint, **FRCVP 4(b)**
  Writ of assistance, issuance, **FRCVP 70**
Collector of customs, clearance of vessels, admiralty and maritime claims, actions in rem and quasi in rem, **FRCVP E(4)**
Collector of internal revenue, judgment against, satisfaction of, **FRCVP 69(b)**
Commencement of action, filing of complaint, **FRCVP 3**
Commission by court, foreign countries, persons authorized to take deposition, **FRCVP 28(b)**
Commissioners, inclusion in term "master", **FRCVP 53(a)**
Committees, incompetent person, action or defense, **FRCVP 17(c)**
Commonwealth, official record, authentication, **FRCVP 44(a)**
Compensation and salaries,
  Interpreters, **FRCVP 43(f)**
  Master, **FRCVP 53(a)**
Complaints. Pleadings, post
Complicated issues, reference to master, **FRCVP 53(b)**
Compromise and settlement,
  Class actions, **FRCVP 23(e)**
  Derivative actions by shareholders, **FRCVP 23.1**
  Unincorporated associations, actions relating to, **FRCVP 23.2**
Compulsory counterclaims, pleading, **FRCVP 13(a)**
Compulsory process, admiralty and maritime claims, refusal by garnishee to answer, **FRCVP B(3)**
Conciseness, pleading, **FRCVP 8(e)**
Conclusions of law,
  Amendment on motion for new trial, **FRCVP 59(a)**
  Findings by court, **FRCVP 52(a)**
  Master, setting forth in report, **FRCVP 53(e)**
Condemnation of property, **FRCVP 71A**
  Commission, **FRCVP 71A**
  Complaint, **FRCVP Form 29**
  Notice, **FRCVP Form 28**
Conditional rulings, grant of motion, judgment as a matter of law, **FRCVP 50**
Conditions, pleading, **FRCVP 9(c)**
Conferences, pretrial, **FRCVP 16**
Confidential or privileged information, discovery, protective orders, **FRCVP 26**
Conflict of interest, depositions, person taking, disqualification, **FRCVP 28(c)**
Conflict of laws, capacity to sue or be sued, **FRCVP 17(b)**

RULES OF CIVIL PROCEDURE
—Cont'd
Consent,
Parties,
Order for trial by jury, **FRCVP 39(c)**
Trial by court, **FRCVP 39(a)**
Withdrawal of demand for jury trial, **FRCVP 38(d)**
Release, property, admiralty and maritime claims, actions in rem and quasi in rem, **FRCVP E(5)**
Conservators and conservatorship, infants or incompetents, action or defense, **FRCVP 17(c)**
Consideration, pleading, failure of consideration, defenses, **FRCVP 8(c)**
Consolidation. Merger and consolidation, generally, post
Consuls and consular agents,
Authentication of official record, **FRCVP 44(a)**
Depositions, taking, **FRCVP 28(b)**
Contempt,
Depositions, refusal to answer, **FRCVP 37(b)**
Discovery, sanction for failure to comply with order compelling, **FRCVP 37(b)**
Service of order, **FRCVP 4.1**
Persons required to respond to order of commitment, places outside state but within United States, **FRCVP 4.1**
Subpoena, disobedience, **FRCVP 45(e)**
Summary judgment, filing affidavit in bad faith, **FRCVP 56(g)**
Witnesses, failure to appear before master, **FRCVP 53(d)**
Continuances,
Pleading, amendment, conforming to evidence, **FRCVP 15(b)**
Summary judgment, continuance to procure opposing affidavit, **FRCVP 56(f)**
Contradicting testimony, deponents, use of deposition in court proceedings, **FRCVP 32(a)**
Contribution, liability, third-party practice, admiralty and maritime claims, **FRCVP 14(c)**
Contributory negligence, affirmative defenses, **FRCVP 8(c)**
Conversion, complaint in action for, form, **FRCVP Form 11**
Copies,
Business records, interrogatories, **FRCVP 33**
Documents, service with requests for admission, **FRCVP 36(a)**
Foreign official records, authentication, **FRCVP 44(a)**
Order for copying, **FRCVP 27(a, b)**
Order of reference, clerk to furnish to master, **FRCVP 53(d)**

RULES OF CIVIL PROCEDURE
—Cont'd
Copies—Cont'd
Process, execution, admiralty and maritime claims, actions in rem and quasi in rem, **FRCVP E(4)**
Production of documents or things, generally, post
Written instruments, exhibit as part of pleading, **FRCVP 10(c)**
Copyright,
Complaint in action for infringement, form of, **FRCVP Form 17**
Inapplicability of rules to proceedings relating to, **FRCVP 81(a)**
Coram nobis, writ abolished, **FRCVP 60(b)**
Coram vobis, writ abolished, **FRCVP 60(b)**
Corporations,
Admiralty and maritime claims, actions in rem and quasi in rem, security, **FRCVP E(7)**
Capacity to sue or be sued, determination, **FRCVP 17(b)**
Depositions,
Introduction in evidence, making deponent witness of introducing party, applicability, **FRCVP 32(c)**
Oral examination,
Failure of officer or director to attend at own deposition, sanctions, **FRCVP 37(d)**
Failure to comply with order compelling designation, sanctions, **FRCVP 37(b)**
Motion for order compelling designation, **FRCVP 37(a)**
Use in court proceedings, **FRCVP 32(a)**
Written questions,
Failure of officer or director to attend at own deposition, sanctions, **FRCVP 37(d)**
Failure to comply with order compelling answer, sanctions, **FRCVP 37(b)**
Motion for order compelling answer, **FRCVP 37(a)**
Interrogatories, service, **FRCVP 33(a)**
Service of summons, **FRCVP 4(h)**
Shares and shareholders, derivative actions, **FRCVP 23.1**
Corrections, clerical errors in judgments or orders, pendency of appeal, **FRCVP 60(a)**
Costs,
Admiralty and maritime claims, ante
Condemnation of property, **FRCVP 71A**
Default judgment including costs, **FRCVP 55(b)**
Delay of entry of judgment for taxing of costs, **FRCVP 58**

RULES OF CIVIL PROCEDURE
—Cont'd
Costs—Cont'd
Depositions upon oral examination,
Recordation, **FRCVP 30**
Sanctions, **FRCVP 30**
Disclosure by parties, refusal, **FRCVP 37**
Discovery requests, signing, sanctions, **FRCVP 26(g)**
Evidence of offer of judgment, proceeding to determine costs, **FRCVP 68**
Offer of judgment affecting, **FRCVP 68**
Pretrial conferences, sanctions, **FRCVP 16(f)**
Pretrial orders, sanctions, **FRCVP 16(f)**
Previously dismissed action, **FRCVP 41(d)**
Refusal to waive service of process, **FRCVP 4(d)**
Restraining order or preliminary injunction, security, **FRCVP 65(c)**
Scheduling conferences, sanctions, **FRCVP 16(f)**
Scheduling orders, sanctions, **FRCVP 16(f)**
Service of summons, avoiding unnecessary costs, **FRCVP 4(d)**
Signatures, pleadings and motions, sanctions, **FRCVP 11**
Summary judgment, affidavits presented in bad faith, **FRCVP 56(g)**
Taxation,
Entry of judgment, delay for, **FRCVP 58**
Interpreters compensation, **FRCVP 43(f)**
Unnecessary costs, service of summons, avoidance, **FRCVP 4(d)**
Counterclaims. Setoff and counterclaim, generally, post
Court,
Discovery,
Failure to comply with order compelling, sanctions, **FRCVP 37(b)**
Motion for order to compel, **FRCVP 37(a)**
District courts, generally, post
Filing of papers with court after complaint, **FRCVP 5(d)**
Judges, generally, post
Official record, authentication, **FRCVP 44(a)**
Supreme court, generally, post
Courts of appeals, appeal to,
Extension of time, **FRCVP 6(b)**
Notice of appeal, form, **FRCVP Form 27**
Cross-claims, **FRCVP 13(g)**
Answers, **FRCVP 7(a)**
Time, **FRCVP 12(a)**
Default judgment against cross-claimant, **FRCVP 55(d)**
Dismissal, **FRCVP 41(c)**

RULES OF CIVIL PROCEDURE
—Cont'd
Cross-claims—Cont'd
Entry of judgment disposing of, **FRCVP 54(b)**
Form, **FRCVP Form 20**
Joinder, **FRCVP 18(a)**
Judgments and decrees, one or more but fewer than all the claims, **FRCVP 54(b)**
Requisites, **FRCVP 8(a)**
Separate trial, **FRCVP 42(b)**
Service of pleadings, numerous defendants, **FRCVP 5(c)**
Summary judgment, **FRCVP 56**
Third party practice, **FRCVP 14(a)**
Time, answers, United States, **FRCVP 12(a)**
Cross-examination, depositions upon oral examination, **FRCVP 30**
Cross-questions, depositions upon written questions, **FRCVP 31**
Custody, property, admiralty and maritime claims, actions in rem and quasi in rem, **FRCVP E(4)**
Damages,
Admiralty and maritime claims, actions in rem and quasi in rem, security, **FRCVP E(7)**
Computation, reference to master, **FRCVP 53(b)**
Default judgment, determination of amount of damages, **FRCVP 55(b)**
Discovery, computation information, **FRCVP 26**
Pleading, special damages, **FRCVP 9(g)**
Restraining order or preliminary injunction, security, **FRCVP 65(c)**
Summary judgment, **FRCVP 56(c)**
Data compilations. Production of documents or things, generally, post
Death,
Admiralty and maritime claims, limitation of liability, notice, **FRCVP F(4)**
Party, substitution, **FRCVP 25(a)**
Suggestion of death upon the record under rule concerning, form, **FRCVP Form 30**
Public officers, substitution of party, **FRCVP 25(d)**
Witness, depositions, use in court proceedings, **FRCVP 32(a)**
Debtors and creditors, complaint in action for debt, form of, **FRCVP Form 13**
Decisions,
Formal exceptions unnecessary, **FRCVP 46**
Judgment on decision by the court, form of, **FRCVP Form 32**
Pleading, **FRCVP 9(e)**
Declaratory judgments, **FRCVP 57**
Summary judgment, **FRCVP 56**

RULES OF CIVIL PROCEDURE
—Cont'd
Declaratory relief, class actions, **FRCVP 23(b)**
Decrees. Judgments and decrees, generally, post
Default judgments, **FRCVP 55**
Admiralty and maritime claims, attachment and garnishment, **FRCVP B(2)**
Demand for judgment, **FRCVP 54(c)**
Discovery, sanction for failure to comply with order compelling, **FRCVP 37(b)**
Pleading,
Failure to plead, grounds for entering default, **FRCVP 55(a)**
Relief demanded by, **FRCVP 54(c)**
Relief awarded, **FRCVP 54(c)**
Summons, failure to appear and defend, **FRCVP 4(a)**
Defendants. Parties, post
Defenses. Pleadings, post
Delays,
Depositions upon oral examination, sanctions, **FRCVP 30**
Discovery, prohibition, **FRCVP 26(d)**
Entry of judgment, taxing of costs and attorney fees, **FRCVP 58**
Delivery,
Copy of pleadings, meaning of term, **FRCVP 5(b)**
Process,
Admiralty and maritime claims, actions in rem and quasi in rem, **FRCVP E(3)**
United States, pleading, amendment, change of party, **FRCVP 15(c)**
Report of examiner, physical and mental examinations, **FRCVP 35(b)**
Demands,
Judgment, demand for, **FRCVP 54(c)**
Jury trial, **FRCVP 38(b)**
Removed action, **FRCVP 81(c)**
Service, **FRCVP 5(a)**
Demurrers, abolition, **FRCVP 7(c)**
Denials, form, **FRCVP 8(b)**
Depositions,
Admissibility under rules of evidence, use in court proceedings, **FRCVP 32(a)**
Adverse or pecuniary interest, person taking deposition, disqualification, **FRCVP 28(c)**
Affidavits for summary judgment, supplemented or opposed by depositions, **FRCVP 56(e)**
Agencies of United States, ante
Associations and societies, ante
Before action, **FRCVP 27(a)**
Certification, oral deposition, **FRCVP 30**
Changes in form or substance, oral examination, **FRCVP 30**

RULES OF CIVIL PROCEDURE
—Cont'd
Depositions—Cont'd
Competency, relevancy, or materiality of testimony, objections, **FRCVP 32(d)**
Competency of witness, objections, **FRCVP 32(d)**
Completion, errors and irregularities, effect, **FRCVP 32(d)**
Conflict of interest, person taking deposition, disqualification, **FRCVP 28(c)**
Contradicting or impeaching testimony of deponent, use, **FRCVP 32(a)**
Corporations, ante
Costs, recordation, deposition upon oral examination, **FRCVP 30**
Cross-examination of deponent, taking depositions before action, **FRCVP 27(a)**
Cross-questions, written questions, **FRCVP 31**
Death of witness, use in court proceedings, **FRCVP 32(a)**
Delay, oral examination, sanctions, **FRCVP 30**
Disqualification,
Officer, objections, **FRCVP 32(d)**
Person taking, adverse or pecuniary interest, **FRCVP 28(c)**
Examination of deponent, **FRCVP 27(a), 30**
Exceptional circumstances requiring use in court proceedings, **FRCVP 32(a)**
Exhibits, **FRCVP 30**
Expenses and expenditures,
Failure of party to attend at own deposition, **FRCVP 37(d)**
Expert witnesses, **FRCVP 26**
Foreign countries, persons before whom taken, **FRCVP 28(b)**
Form of presentation, **FRCVP 32**
Hearing, motions, use, **FRCVP 32(a)**
Inability of witness to attend or testify because of age or illness, use in court proceedings, **FRCVP 32(a)**
Interlocutory proceedings, use, **FRCVP 32(a)**
Interrogatories, **FRCVP 31, 33**
Introduction,
Other parts, use in court proceedings, **FRCVP 32(a)**
Letters of request, foreign countries, persons before whom depositions may be taken, **FRCVP 28**
Limitation,
Alteration, **FRCVP 26**
Oral examination, **FRCVP 30**
Multiple depositions, leave of court, **FRCVP 30**
Written questions, **FRCVP 31**
Notice,
Effect, errors and irregularities, **FRCVP 32(d)**

RULES OF CIVIL PROCEDURE
—Cont'd
Depositions—Cont'd
Notice—Cont'd
Oral examination, **FRCVP 30**
Taking,
In foreign country, **FRCVP 28(b)**
Stipulations, **FRCVP 29**
Written questions, **FRCVP 31**
Oath or affirmation,
Oral examination, **FRCVP 30**
Power to administer oaths, **FRCVP 28(a)**
Objections and exceptions, **FRCVP 26, 30**
Errors and irregularities, **FRCVP 32(d)**
Oral examination depositions, **FRCVP 30**
Subpoena for taking, **FRCVP 45(c)**
To admissibility in court proceedings, **FRCVP 32(b)**
Officers, persons before whom taken, **FRCVP 28, 30**
Oral examination, **FRCVP 30**
Completion or adjournment of examination before applying for order to compel answer, **FRCVP 37(a)**
Errors and irregularities, effect, **FRCVP 32(d)**
Evasive or incomplete answer, defined, motion for order to compel, **FRCVP 37(a)**
Failure of party to attend at own depositions, sanctions, **FRCVP 37(d)**
Failure to comply with order compelling answer, sanctions, **FRCVP 37(b)**
Motion for order to compel answer, **FRCVP 37(a)**
Objections, errors and irregularities, **FRCVP 32(d)**
Subpoena, **FRCVP 45(a)**
Orders, post
Outside United States, witness, use in court proceedings, **FRCVP 32(a)**
Partnerships, post
Pending appeal, **FRCVP 27(b)**
Persons before whom taken, **FRCVP 28**
Petition for depositions before action, **FRCVP 27(a)**
Physical and mental examinations, examiners agreement not precluding, **FRCVP 35(b)**
Place,
Trial or hearing, witness more than 100 miles from, use in court proceedings, **FRCVP 32(a)**
Prior actions or proceedings in United States or State courts, effect on use, **FRCVP 32(a)**

RULES OF CIVIL PROCEDURE
—Cont'd
Depositions—Cont'd
Protective orders, parties requesting, use of deposition against, **FRCVP 32**
Recordation, oral examination, **FRCVP 30**
Recross-questions, written questions, **FRCVP 31**
Redirect questions, written questions, **FRCVP 31**
Return, errors and irregularities, effect, **FRCVP 32(d)**
Sanctions, oral examination, **FRCVP 30**
Service, notice of taking before action, **FRCVP 27(a)**
Stipulations as to taking, **FRCVP 29**
Subpoenas,
Attendance at deposition, **FRCVP 45(a)**
Failure to procure attendance of witness, use in court proceedings, **FRCVP 32(a)**
Use in court proceedings upon failure of witness to attend, **FRCVP 32(a)**
Written questions, compelling attendance of witness, **FRCVP 31**
Substitution of parties, effect on use, **FRCVP 32(a)**
Summary judgments,
Continuance to procure depositions opposing, **FRCVP 56(f)**
No genuine shown in depositions, **FRCVP 56(e)**
Supplementation of responses, **FRCVP 26**
Termination, **FRCVP 30**
Time, written questions, **FRCVP 31**
Trial, use at, **FRCVP 32(a)**
Use of in court proceedings, **FRCVP 32**
Venue, post
Written questions, **FRCVP 31**
Evasive or incomplete answer, defined, motion for order to compel, **FRCVP 37(a)**
Failure of party to attend at own deposition, sanctions, **FRCVP 37(d)**
Failure to comply with order compelling answer, sanctions, **FRCVP 37(b)**
Motion for order to compel answer, **FRCVP 37(a)**
Objections to form, **FRCVP 32(d)**
Place of examination, **FRCVP 45(d)**
Subpoena, **FRCVP 45(a)**
Deposits,
Admiralty and maritime claims, ante
Condemnation proceedings, **FRCVP 71A(j)**
Eminent domain, condition to exercise of power, **FRCVP 71A(j)**
In court, **FRCVP 67**

RULES OF CIVIL PROCEDURE
—Cont'd
Deposits—Cont'd
Security, appeal to court of appeals, **FRCVP 73(c)**
Derivative actions by shareholders, **FRCVP 23.1**
Descriptive title, notice or commission may designate persons before whom deposition to be taken, **FRCVP 28(b)**
Diagnoses, examiners report, physical and mental examinations, **FRCVP 35(b)**
Directed verdict. Judgment as a matter of law, generally, post
Disclosure by parties, motion to compel, **FRCVP 37**
Discovery, **FRCVP 26**
Attorneys fees, generally, ante
Depositions, generally, ante
Entry upon land, generally, post
Expenses and expenditures, post
Failure to make, sanctions, **FRCVP 37**
Foreign country, subpoena of person in, **FRCVP 37(e)**
Initial disclosures, **FRCVP 26**
Interrogatories, generally, post
Judgment or execution, obtaining in aid of, **FRCVP 69(a)**
Meeting of parties, **FRCVP 26**
Methods, **FRCVP 26**
Modification of procedures,
Stipulations, **FRCVP 29**
Time, disclosure, **FRCVP 16**
Orders,
Compelling, **FRCVP 37(a, b)**
Failure to comply with order compelling sanctions, **FRCVP 37(b)**
Sanctions upon failure to comply with order compelling, **FRCVP 37(b)**
Stipulations regarding procedure, **FRCVP 29**
Physical and mental examinations, generally, post
Plans, **FRCVP 26**
Pretrial conferences, control and scheduling, **FRCVP 16(b)**
Pretrial disclosures, **FRCVP 26**
Production of documents or things, generally, post
Protective orders, post
Request for, responses to,
Extension of time, stipulations, approval of court, **FRCVP 29**
Requests for admissions,
Admissions, generally, ante
Scope and limits, **FRCVP 26**
Service, papers relating to, **FRCVP 5(a)**
Signature, disclosures, **FRCVP 26**
State practice, applicability, proceedings in aid of judgment or execution, **FRCVP 69(a)**

RULES OF CIVIL PROCEDURE
—Cont'd
Discovery—Cont'd
Stipulations regarding procedure, **FRCVP 29**
Summary judgment, continuance to procure discovery opposing, **FRCVP 56(f)**
Supplementation of responses, **FRCVP 26**
Time,
Methods, use of, **FRCVP 26(d)**
Modification, **FRCVP 16(b)**
Pretrial disclosures, **FRCVP 26**
Trial preparation material, exemption, **FRCVP 26**
Witnesses, **FRCVP 26 et seq.**
Discretion,
Interpreters, compensation, taxation as costs, **FRCVP 43(f)**
Jury trial, court to order, **FRCVP 39(b)**
Master, adjournment of proceedings, **FRCVP 53(d)**
Dismissal and nonsuit, **FRCVP 41**
Action for condemnation of property, **FRCVP 71A(i)**
Admiralty and maritime claims, limitation of liability, **FRCVP F(9)**
Class actions, **FRCVP 23(e)**
Derivative actions by shareholders, **FRCVP 23.1**
Determination by court when joinder not feasible, **FRCVP 19(b)**
Discovery, sanction for failure to comply with order compelling, **FRCVP 37(b)**
Joined party, **FRCVP 19(a)**
Jurisdiction, lack of subject matter, **FRCVP 12(h)**
Motions, post
Prosecution not in name of real party in interest, **FRCVP 17(a)**
Receivers, order of court for dismissal of action wherein receiver has been appointed, **FRCVP 66**
Service of summons, failure, **FRCVP 4(m)**
Substitution of parties, failure to serve motion for within certain time after death, **FRCVP 25(a)**
Third party claim, **FRCVP 41(c)**
Unincorporated associations, actions and proceedings, **FRCVP 23.2**
Disposition of property, admiralty and maritime claims, actions in rem and quasi in rem, **FRCVP E(9)**
Distribution of funds, admiralty and maritime claims, limitation of liability, **FRCVP F(8)**
District courts,
Depositions, sanctions by court where taken, failure to comply with order compelling answer, **FRCVP 37(b)**
Hearings conducted outside district, **FRCVP 77(b)**

RULES OF CIVIL PROCEDURE
—Cont'd
District courts—Cont'd
Local rules, **FRCVP 83**
Computation of time, **FRCVP 6(a)**
Motion day, **FRCVP 78**
Official record, authentication, **FRCVP 44(a)**
Open, court to remain open, **FRCVP 77(a)**
Open court, trial conducted in, **FRCVP 77(b)**
District director of internal revenue, **FRCVP 81(f)**
District of Columbia courts, applicability of rules, **FRCVP 81(a, e)**
Dockets and docketing,
Appeal and review,
Correction, clerical mistakes in judgments and orders before docketing appeal, **FRCVP 60(a)**
Court of appeals, extension of time for docketing, **FRCVP 6(b)**
Civil docket, **FRCVP 79(a)**
Jury trial, designation, **FRCVP 39(a)**
Note of mailing notice of entry of order or judgment, **FRCVP 77(d)**
Documents,
Admission of genuineness. Admissions, generally, ante
Discovery, pretrial disclosure, **FRCVP 26**
Disobedience to judgment directing delivery, **FRCVP 70**
Masters, compelling production, **FRCVP 53(c)**
Order for production, **FRCVP 27(a, b)**
Pleading, official document, **FRCVP 9(d)**
Production of documents or things, generally, post
Subpoenas, response, **FRCVP 45(d)**
Domestic official records, authentication, **FRCVP 44(a)**
Domicile and residence, parties, capacity to sue or be sued, **FRCVP 17(b)**
Drawings. Production of documents or things, generally, post
Duress, pleading, affirmative defenses, **FRCVP 8(c)**
Dwelling houses,
Service of pleading, **FRCVP 5(b)**
Service of summons, **FRCVP 4(e)**
Effective date, original rules and amendments, **FRCVP 86**
Electronic filing, **FRCVP 5(e)**
Electronic means, depositions upon oral examination, **FRCVP 30**
Eminent domain. Condemnation of property, generally, ante
Employees. Officers and employees, generally, post
Enlargement of time. Extension of time, generally, post

RULES OF CIVIL PROCEDURE
—Cont'd
Entry,
Answers to interrogatories where harmonious with general verdict, **FRCVP 49(b)**
Judgments and decrees, post
Entry upon land,
Failure of party to respond to request for inspection, sanctions, **FRCVP 37(d)**
Failure to comply with order compelling inspection, sanctions, **FRCVP 37(b)**
Motion for order to compel inspection, **FRCVP 37(a)**
Objections, **FRCVP 34(b)**
Procedure, **FRCVP 34(b)**
Requests, **FRCVP 34(a, b)**
Responses to requests, **FRCVP 34(b)**
Scope, **FRCVP 34(a)**
Service, requests, **FRCVP 34(a, b)**
Stipulations, extension of time for responses, approval of court, **FRCVP 29**
Equity,
Application of rules, **FRCVP 1**
Determination by court whenever joinder not feasible, **FRCVP 19(b)**
Joinder of claims, **FRCVP 18(a)**
Pleading, separate claims or defenses, **FRCVP 8(e)**
Errors. Mistakes and errors, generally, post
Estoppel, pleading, affirmative defenses, **FRCVP 8(c)**
Evidence,
Action to perpetuate testimony, **FRCVP 27(c)**
Affidavits, hearing of motion based on facts appearing of record, **FRCVP 43(e)**
Affirmation in lieu of oath, **FRCVP 43(d)**
Compelling giving of testimony, application of rules, **FRCVP 81(a)**
Costs, evidence of offer of judgment in proceeding to determine costs, **FRCVP 68**
Depositions, generally, ante
Discovery, generally, ante
Documents, generally, ante
Findings of fact by court, objection, **FRCVP 52(b)**
Foreign law, determination, **FRCVP 44.1**
Form and admissibility, **FRCVP 43(a)**
Harmless error in admitting or excluding, **FRCVP 61**
Interpreters, **FRCVP 43(f)**
Letters of request, exclusion, **FRCVP 28**
Master, **FRCVP 53**
Motions, **FRCVP 43(e)**
Official record, **FRCVP 44**
Perpetuation by action, **FRCVP 27(c)**

RULES OF CIVIL PROCEDURE
—Cont'd
Evidence—Cont'd
Pleading, amendments, conforming, **FRCVP 15(b)**
Preliminary injunction hearing, admissibility upon trial, **FRCVP 65(a)**
Pretrial procedure, **FRCVP 16(c)**
Production of documents or things, generally, post
Record,
Evidence by master, **FRCVP 53(c)**
Stenographic report or transcript as evidence, **FRCVP 80(c)**
Subpoena for production, **FRCVP 45**
Transcript of evidence, filing by master with report, **FRCVP 53(e)**
United States, establishing claim on default, **FRCVP 55(e)**
Voluntary dismissal before introduction of evidence at trial, **FRCVP 41(c)**
Ex parte proceedings, master, failure of party to appear at time and place appointed, **FRCVP 53(b)**
Examinations and examiners,
Accounting parties before master, **FRCVP 53(d)**
Business records, interrogatories, **FRCVP 33**
Deponent, order for examination, **FRCVP 27(a)**
Depositions upon oral examination, **FRCVP 30**
Included in term "master," **FRCVP 53(a)**
Jurors, **FRCVP 47(a)**
Physical and mental examinations, generally, post
Witnesses, master, **FRCVP 53(c)**
Exceptional circumstances, depositions use in court proceedings, **FRCVP 32(a)**
Exceptions. Objections and exceptions, generally, post
Excessive funds or security, admiralty and maritime claims, limitation of liability, **FRCVP F(7)**
Excusable neglect,
Extension of time, **FRCVP 6(b)**
Relief from judgment on ground of, **FRCVP 60(b)**
Execution,
Civil docket, entry, **FRCVP 79(a)**
Compensation of master against delinquent party, **FRCVP 53(a)**
Discovery in aid of, **FRCVP 69(a)**
Possession, execution to enforce judgment directing delivery of possession, **FRCVP 70**
Process, admiralty and maritime claims, actions in rem and quasi in rem, **FRCVP E(4)**
Stay, **FRCVP 62**
Time for issuing, **FRCVP 62(a)**

RULES OF CIVIL PROCEDURE
—Cont'd
Executors and administrators, prosecution of action, **FRCVP 17(a)**
Exemptions, U.S. vessels, arrest, supplemental rules inapplicable, **FRCVP C(1)**
Exhibits,
Depositions upon oral examination, **FRCVP 30**
Discovery, pretrial disclosure, **FRCVP 26**
Masters, filing with report, **FRCVP 53(e)**
Motion, bringing in third-party defendant, form, **FRCVP Form 22–B**
Pleadings, written instruments, **FRCVP 10(c)**
Exoneration from liability,
Admiralty and maritime claims, **FRCVP F**
Applicability, supplemental rules, **FRCVP A**
Expenses and expenditures,
Admiralty and maritime claims, ante
Depositions, ante
Discovery, failure to comply with order compelling, **FRCVP 37(b)**
Documents, failure to admit genuineness, **FRCVP 37(c)**
Entry upon land, failure of party to respond to request for inspection, **FRCVP 37(d)**
Interrogatories, failure of party to serve answers, **FRCVP 37(d)**
Motion, order to compel discovery, **FRCVP 37(a)**
Production of documents or things, failure of party to respond to request for inspection, **FRCVP 37(d)**
Requests for admission, **FRCVP 36(a)**
United States, discovery proceedings, **FRCVP 37(f)**
Expert witnesses. Opinion and expert testimony, generally, post
Extension of time, **FRCVP 6(b)**
Admiralty and maritime claims, limitation of liability, **FRCVP F(4)**
Affidavits opposing new trial, service, **FRCVP 59(c)**
Answers or objections to requests for admission, **FRCVP 36(a)**
Discovery responses, approval of court, stipulations, **FRCVP 29**
Interrogatories, service, copies of answers and objections, **FRCVP 33**
Responses to request for production of documents or things and entry upon land, **FRCVP 34(b)**
Service of summons, **FRCVP 4(m)**
Temporary restraining order, **FRCVP 65(b)**
Facsimile transmission, filing, **FRCVP 5(e)**

RULES OF CIVIL PROCEDURE
—Cont'd
Facts,
Statements or opinions of. Admissions, generally, ante
Taken to be established, discovery, sanctions for failure to comply with order compelling, **FRCVP 37(b)**
Fair conduct, class actions, orders, **FRCVP 23(d)**
Federal agencies. Agencies of United States, generally, ante
Federal Employers Liability Act, complaint for negligence under, form of, **FRCVP Form 14**
Federal question, existence, jurisdiction, form of allegation, **FRCVP Form 2**
Fees. Attorneys Fees, generally, ante
Fellow servant, pleading, injury by, affirmative defenses, **FRCVP 8(c)**
File numbers, actions entered in civil docket, assignment, **FRCVP 79(a)**
Filing,
Admiralty and maritime claims, ante
Complaint, admiralty and maritime claims, limitation of liability, **FRCVP F(1)**
Depositions upon oral examination, officer taking, **FRCVP 30**
Electronic means, **FRCVP 5(e)**
Facsimile transmission, **FRCVP 5(e)**
Masters reports, **FRCVP 53(e)**
Papers after complaint, **FRCVP 5(d)**
Pleading,
Complaint,
Commencement of civil action, **FRCVP 3**
Issuance of summons, **FRCVP 4(b)**
Numerous defendants, **FRCVP 5(c)**
Temporary restraining order, **FRCVP 65(b)**
With the court, defined, **FRCVP 5(e)**
Findings,
Additional findings by court, **FRCVP 52(b)**
Admiralty and maritime claims, limitation of liability, insufficiency of funds, **FRCVP F(7)**
Amendment of findings, **FRCVP 52(b)**
Extension of time, **FRCVP 6(b)**
Motion for new trial, **FRCVP 59(a)**
Stay of proceedings, enforcement of judgment pending disposition of motion to amend, **FRCVP 62(b)**
Class actions maintainable, **FRCVP 23(b)**
Court, **FRCVP 52**
Master, **FRCVP 53(e)**
Findings by court, **FRCVP 52(a)**
Motion for amendment of findings by court, **FRCVP 52(b)**
Partial findings, judgment on, **FRCVP 52**
Special verdict, **FRCVP 49(a)**

RULES OF CIVIL PROCEDURE —Cont'd

Findings—Cont'd
- Stay of proceedings to enforce judgment, pending disposition of motion to amend, **FRCVP 62(b)**
- Unanimity of jurors, **FRCVP 48**

Fines, penalties and forfeitures,
- Depositions upon oral examination, **FRCVP 30**
- Disclosure by parties, refusal, **FRCVP 37**
- Discovery, failure to make, **FRCVP 37**
- Motions, representations to court, **FRCVP 11**
- Pleadings, representations to court, **FRCVP 11**
- Pretrial conferences, **FRCVP 16(f)**
- Pretrial orders, **FRCVP 16(f)**
- Scheduling conferences, **FRCVP 16(f)**
- Scheduling orders, **FRCVP 16(f)**
- Subpoenas, excessive burden, **FRCVP 45(c)**
- Witnesses, failure to appear before master, **FRCVP 53(d)**

Foreign countries,
- Authentication of official records or documents, **28 § 1741**
- Depositions, persons before whom taken, **FRCVP 28(b)**
- Discovery, subpoena of person in, **FRCVP 37(e)**
- Service of summons, **FRCVP 4(f)**
- Subpoena directed to witness in foreign country, **FRCVP 45(b)**

Foreign judgments, pleading, **FRCVP 9(e)**

Foreign law, determination, **FRCVP 44.1**

Foreign official records, authentication, **FRCVP 44(a)**

Foreign states, service of summons on, **FRCVP 4(j)**

Forfeitures, disposition of property, admiralty and maritime claims, actions in rem and quasi in rem, **FRCVP E(9)**

Former district director or collector of internal revenue, **FRCVP 81(f)**

Forms,
- Answer, **FRCVP Form 21**
  - Intervener, **FRCVP Form 23**
  - Presenting defenses, **FRCVP Form 20**
- Appendix forms, intent to indicate simplicity and brevity of statement contemplated, **FRCVP 84**
- Complaint. Pleading, post
- Counterclaims, **FRCVP Form 20**
  - Interpleader, **FRCVP Form 21**
- Cross-claims, **FRCVP Form 20**
- Depositions, presentation, **FRCVP 32**
- Evidence, **FRCVP 43(a)**
- Exhibit accompanying motion, bringing in third-party defendant, **FRCVP Form 22–B**
- Failure to use, effect, **FRCVP 83**

RULES OF CIVIL PROCEDURE —Cont'd

Forms—Cont'd
- Judgment on,
  - Decision by the court, **FRCVP Form 32**
  - Jury verdict, **FRCVP Form 31**
- Jurisdiction, allegation of, **FRCVP Form 2**
- Magistrate judges,
  - Consent to exercise of jurisdiction, **FRCVP Form 34**
  - Notice of availability to exercise jurisdiction, **FRCVP Form 33**
  - Order of reference, **FRCVP Form 34A**
- Motions,
  - Bringing in third-party defendant, **FRCVP Form 22–B**
  - Dismissal of complaint, **FRCVP Form 19**
  - Intervention as defendant, **FRCVP Form 23**
  - Production of documents, form, **FRCVP Form 24**
  - Technical forms not required, **FRCVP 8(e)**
- Notice,
  - Appeal to court of appeals, **FRCVP Form 27**
  - Bringing in third-party defendant, **FRCVP Form 22–B**
  - Condemnation of property, **FRCVP Form 28**
  - Intervention as defendant, **FRCVP Form 23**
  - Lawsuit, **FRCVP Form 1A**
  - Motion,
    - Dismiss complaint, **FRCVP Form 19**
    - Production of documents, **FRCVP Form 24**
- Parties planning meeting, report, **FRCVP Form 35**
- Pleading, post
- Process, writs, power of Supreme Court to prescribe, **28 § 2072**
- Purpose, **FRCVP 84**
- Request,
  - For admission, **FRCVP Form 25**
  - Production of documents or things, **FRCVP Form 24**
- Statement of accounts before master, **FRCVP 53(d)**
- Subpoenas, **FRCVP 45(a)**
- Suggestion of death upon the record under rule concerning substitution of parties, **FRCVP Form 30**
- Summons, **FRCVP Form 1**
  - Third-party defendant, summons against, **FRCVP Form 22–A**
  - Waiver of service, **FRCVP Form 1B**
    - Request for, **FRCVP Form 1A**

Fraud,
- Pleading, **FRCVP 9(b)**
- Relief from judgment, **FRCVP 60(b)**

RULES OF CIVIL PROCEDURE —Cont'd

Fraudulent conveyances,
- Complaint in action to set aside, form, **FRCVP Form 13**
- Joinder of remedy, **FRCVP 18(b)**

Garnishment,
- Admiralty and maritime claims, ante
- Availability, **FRCVP 64**

Good cause, physical and mental examinations, order for, **FRCVP 35(a)**

Goods sold and delivered, complaints, **FRCVP Form 5**

Governmental agency. Agencies of United States, generally, ante

Graphs. Production of documents or things, generally, post

Grounds,
- Class actions maintainable, **FRCVP 23(b)**
- New trial, **FRCVP 59(d)**

Guardian and ward, action or defense by representative, **FRCVP 17(a, c)**

Habeas corpus,
- Application of rules to, **FRCVP 81(a)**
- Direction of writ or show cause order to person having custody, **FRCVP 81(a)**
- Return of writ or show cause order, time, **FRCVP 81(a)**

Harmless error, disregard of error not affecting substantial rights, **FRCVP 61**

Hearings,
- Admiralty and maritime claims,
  - Actions in rem and quasi in rem, security, reduction, **FRCVP E(5, 6)**
  - Limitation of liability, insufficiency, funds, **FRCVP F(7)**
- Conducted outside district, **FRCVP 77(b)**
- Consolidation of actions for hearing, **FRCVP 42(a)**
- Discovery, order to compel, award of expenses, **FRCVP 37(a)**
- Inability of judge to proceed, **FRCVP 63**
- Motions,
  - Depositions, use, **FRCVP 32(a)**
  - Without oral hearing, determination, **FRCVP 78**
- New trial, **FRCVP 59(d)**
- Preliminary hearings, pleadings, **FRCVP 12(d)**
- Preliminary injunction, consolidation with trial on merits, **FRCVP 65(a)**
- Service of notice, **FRCVP 6(d)**
- Subpoena for attendance, **FRCVP 45(a)**
- Successor judges, **FRCVP 63**
- Temporary restraining order, **FRCVP 65(b)**
- Voluntary dismissal before introduction of evidence, **FRCVP 41(c)**

RULES OF CIVIL PROCEDURE
—Cont'd
Holidays,
Clerks of court, business hours for office, exceptions concerning opening, **FRCVP 77(c)**
Legal holidays, generally, post
Illegality, pleading, affirmative defenses, **FRCVP 8(c)**
Illness of witness, inability to attend or testify, depositions, use in court proceedings, **FRCVP 32(a)**
Impairment of security, admiralty and maritime claims, actions in rem and quasi in rem, **FRCVP E(6)**
Impeachment, deposition in court proceedings, use of, **FRCVP 32(a)**
Imprisonment of witness, inability to attend or testify, depositions, use in court proceedings, **FRCVP 32(a)**
In forma pauperis, process, service, **FRCVP 4(c)**
In personam actions, admiralty and maritime claims, **FRCVP B, C, E**
In rem actions,
Admiralty and maritime claims, generally, ante
Applicability, supplemental rules, **FRCVP A**
Inadvertence, relief from judgment on ground of, **FRCVP 60(b)**
Incompetent persons, **FRCVP 17(c)**
Default judgments, entry against, **FRCVP 55(b)**
Depositions, taking before action, **FRCVP 27(a)**
Service of summons upon, **FRCVP 4(g)**
Substitution, **FRCVP 25(b)**
Indices, civil docket and civil judgments and orders, **FRCVP 79(c)**
Indispensable party, determination by court, **FRCVP 19(b)**
Indorsement,
Admiralty and maritime claims, actions in rem and quasi in rem, bond or stipulation, **FRCVP E(5)**
Temporary restraining order, **FRCVP 65(b)**
Infants. Children and minors, generally, ante
Infirmity of witness, inability to attend or testify, depositions, use in court proceedings, **FRCVP 32(a)**
Infringement,
Complaint in action for infringement of,
Copyright, **FRCVP Form 17**
Patent, **FRCVP Form 16**
Stay of judgment for accounting for infringement, **FRCVP 62(a)**
Initial discovery disclosure, **FRCVP 26**
Injunctions, **FRCVP 65**
Admiralty and maritime claims, limitation of liability, **FRCVP F(3)**
Appeal and review,
Pending appeal, **FRCVP 62(c)**

RULES OF CIVIL PROCEDURE
—Cont'd
Injunctions—Cont'd
Appeal and review—Cont'd
Suspending, modifying or granting by appellate court pending appeal, **FRCVP 62(g)**
Class actions, **FRCVP 23(b)**
Preliminary or temporary injunction, **FRCVP 65**
Insane persons. Incompetent persons, generally, ante
Inspection and inspectors,
Business records, interrogatories, **FRCVP 33**
Entry upon land, generally, ante
Order for, **FRCVP 27**
Production of documents or things, generally, post
Instructions to jury, **FRCVP 51**
Answers to interrogatories and rendering general verdict, instruction to enable, **FRCVP 49(b)**
Special verdict, **FRCVP 49(a)**
Insufficiency of fund or security, admiralty and maritime claims, limitation of liability, **FRCVP F(7)**
Insular possessions, official record, authentication, **FRCVP 44(a)**
Insurance agreements, discovery, initial disclosure, **FRCVP 26**
Intangible property,
Admiralty and maritime claims, actions in rem, ancillary process, **FRCVP C(5)**
Custody, admiralty and maritime claims, action in rem and quasi in rem, **FRCVP E(4)**
Intent, pleading, **FRCVP 9(b)**
Interest, admiralty and maritime claims, limitation of liability, security, **FRCVP F(1)**
Interested parties,
Adverse or pecuniary interest, person taking deposition, disqualification, **FRCVP 28(c)**
Class actions, protection of interests, **FRCVP 23(a)**
Intervention, inability to protect interest in property, **FRCVP 24(a)**
Subject of action, interest in, joinder of persons needed for just adjudication, **FRCVP 19(a)**
Interlocutory proceedings,
Depositions, use, **FRCVP 32(a)**
Injunctions, findings of facts and conclusions of law, **FRCVP 52(a)**
Orders, admiralty and maritime claims, actions in rem and quasi in rem, security, **FRCVP E(9)**
Sales, admiralty and maritime claims, actions in rem and quasi in rem, **FRCVP E(9)**
Internal revenue officers, execution against, **FRCVP 69(b)**

RULES OF CIVIL PROCEDURE
—Cont'd
International agreements, service of summons, foreign countries, **FRCVP 4(f)**
Interpleader, **FRCVP 22**
Complaint for interpleader and declaratory relief, form, **FRCVP Form 18**
Counterclaim for interpleader, form, **FRCVP Form 21**
Injunction, **FRCVP 65(e)**
Service of summons, establishing jurisdiction, **FRCVP 4(k)**
Interpreters, appointment and compensation, **FRCVP 43(f)**
Interrogatories, **FRCVP 33**
Admiralty and maritime claims,
Actions in rem, **FRCVP C(6)**
Attachment and garnishment, **FRCVP B(3)**
Answers. Pleadings, post
Business records, option to produce, **FRCVP 33**
Evasive or incomplete answer, defined, motion for order to compel, **FRCVP 37(a)**
Examination of accounting parties before master, **FRCVP 53(d)**
Expert witnesses, use at trial, **FRCVP 26**
Failure of party to serve answers or objections, sanctions, **FRCVP 37(b)**
Failure to comply with order compelling answer, sanction, **FRCVP 37(d)**
General verdict accompanied by answer to interrogatories, **FRCVP 49(b)**
Limitations, alteration, **FRCVP 26**
Motion for order to compel answer, **FRCVP 37(a)**
Objections, **FRCVP 33**
Orders, post
Scope, **FRCVP 33**
Service, **FRCVP 33(a)**
Stipulations, extension of time for responses, approval of court, **FRCVP 29**
Submission to jury with forms for a general verdict, **FRCVP 49(b)**
Summary judgment,
Affidavits, supplemented or opposed by answers, **FRCVP 56(e)**
No genuine issue shown in answers, **FRCVP 56(c)**
Supplementation of responses, **FRCVP 26**
Time of service, **FRCVP 33(a)**
Trial, use, **FRCVP 33**
Intervention, **FRCVP 24**
Form, **FRCVP Form 23**
Introduction of designated evidence, prohibition, sanction for failure to comply with order compelling discovery, **FRCVP 37(b)**

RULES OF CIVIL PROCEDURE
—Cont'd
Investigations,
Admiralty and maritime claims, actions in rem and quasi in rem, complaints, **FRCVP E(3)**
Foreign official records, **FRCVP 44(a)**
Involuntary plaintiff, refusal to join, **FRCVP 19(a)**
Issuance of process, admiralty and maritime claims, actions in rem and quasi in rem, **FRCVP E(3)**
Issues,
Jury trial,
Specification of issues in demand, **FRCVP 38(c)**
Trial of issues, **FRCVP 39(a)**
Pretrial procedure, **FRCVP 16**
Separate trial, **FRCVP 42(b)**
Trial by court, **FRCVP 39(b)**
Joinder,
Claims, **FRCVP 18(a)**
Parties, post
Property in condemnation proceeding, **FRCVP 71A(b)**
Remedies, **FRCVP 18(b)**
Joint hearing, order of court, **FRCVP 42(a)**
Judges,
Appointment of masters, **FRCVP 53(a)**
Inability to proceed, **FRCVP 63**
Magistrate Judges, generally, post
Official record, authentication, **FRCVP 44(a)**
Permit for filing pleading and papers with judge, **FRCVP 5(e)**
Successor judges, **FRCVP 63**
Judgment as a matter of law, **FRCVP 50**
Extension of time, **FRCVP 6(b)**
Stay of proceedings to enforce judgment pending disposition of motion, **FRCVP 62(b)**
Judgments and decrees,
Admiralty and maritime claims, ante
Amendment or alteration,
Additional or amended findings, **FRCVP 52(b)**
Stay of proceedings pending disposition of motion, **FRCVP 62(b)**
Time for filing of motion, **FRCVP 59(e)**
Attachment of property, person disobeying judgment for specific acts, **FRCVP 70**
Attorneys, submission of forms, **FRCVP 58**
Bills of review abolished, **FRCVP 60(b)**
Civil docket, entry, **FRCVP 79(a)**
Class actions, **FRCVP 23(c)**
Clerical mistakes, correction, **FRCVP 60(a)**
Clerk to enter, **FRCVP 58**
Compulsory counterclaims, **FRCVP 13(a)**

RULES OF CIVIL PROCEDURE
—Cont'd
Judgments and decrees—Cont'd
Contempt, disobeying judgment directing specific performance, **FRCVP 70**
Copies, retention of correct copies, final judgments, **FRCVP 79(b)**
Counterclaim or cross-claim, **FRCVP 13(i)**
Entry of judgment, **FRCVP 54(b)**
Decision by the court, form, **FRCVP Form 32**
Declaratory judgments, **FRCVP 56, 57**
Decree included in judgment, **FRCVP 54(a)**
Default judgments, generally, ante
Defined, **FRCVP 54(a)**
Demand for judgment, **FRCVP 54(c)**
Pleading, **FRCVP 8(a)**
Determination by court whenever joinder not feasible, **FRCVP 19(b)**
Discovery to aid, **FRCVP 69(a)**
Effective when set forth on separate document and entered, **FRCVP 58**
Entry of judgment, **FRCVP 58**
Actions tried upon facts without jury or with an advisory jury, findings by court, **FRCVP 52(a)**
Disposing of multiple claims or multiple parties, **FRCVP 54(b)**
General verdict and answers to interrogatories harmonious with each other, **FRCVP 49(b)**
New judgment on motion for new trial, **FRCVP 59(a)**
Partial findings, **FRCVP 52**
Excusable neglect, ground for relief, **FRCVP 60(b)**
Execution, generally, ante
Finality, unaffected by motion for relief on ground of mistake, inadvertence, surprise or excusable neglect, **FRCVP 60(b)**
Fraud, relief from judgment, **FRCVP 60(b)**
General verdict accompanied by answers to interrogatories, entry of judgment, **FRCVP 58**
Inadvertence, ground for relief, **FRCVP 60(b)**
Indices, retention by clerk, **FRCVP 79(c)**
Inequitable prospective application, relief from judgment, **FRCVP 60(b)**
Judges, approval of form, special verdict or general verdict accompanied by answers to interrogatories, **FRCVP 58**
Jury verdict, form, **FRCVP Form 31**
Misconduct, relief from judgment, **FRCVP 60(b)**
Mistake, ground for relief, **FRCVP 60(b)**
Modification, errors not affecting substantial rights, **FRCVP 61**

RULES OF CIVIL PROCEDURE
—Cont'd
Judgments and decrees—Cont'd
Motions,
Alteration or amendment,
Extension of time, **FRCVP 6(b)**
Time for filing, **FRCVP 59(e)**
Correction of clerical mistakes, **FRCVP 60(a)**
Findings of fact and conclusions of law, **FRCVP 52(a)**
Judgment on the pleading, **FRCVP 12(c)**
Multiple claims or parties, **FRCVP 54(b)**
Raising objections to evidence to sustain findings by court, **FRCVP 52(b)**
Relief on ground of mistake, inadvertence, surprise or excusable neglect, **FRCVP 60(b)**
Stay of enforcement, **FRCVP 62(h)**
Stay of proceedings to enforce judgment pending motion to alter or amend, **FRCVP 62(b)**
New trial, stay of proceedings to enforce on motion for new trial, **FRCVP 62(b)**
Newly discovered evidence, relief from judgment, **FRCVP 60(b)**
Notice of entry, **FRCVP 58**
Notice of motion for correction of clerical mistakes, **FRCVP 60(a)**
Notwithstanding the verdict, judgment as a matter of law, **FRCVP 50**
Offer of judgment, **FRCVP 68**
Service, **FRCVP 5(a)**
Opening judgment on motion for new trial, **FRCVP 59(a)**
Order included in meaning of "judgment," **FRCVP 54(a)**
Partial findings, **FRCVP 52**
Personal jurisdiction lacking, opposing party bringing suit upon claim by attachment, counterclaims, **FRCVP 13(a)**
Pleadings, post
Possession, enforcement of judgment directing delivery, **FRCVP 70**
Recitals, **FRCVP 54(a)**
Record of prior proceedings, recitals of record not required, **FRCVP 54(a)**
Recovery by party only of sum certain or costs or that relief shall be denied, entry of judgment, **FRCVP 58**
Relief from judgment, **FRCVP 60**
Extension of time, **FRCVP 6(b)**
Stay of proceedings to enforce judgment pending disposition of motion, **FRCVP 62(b)**
Report of master, recitals of report not required, **FRCVP 54(a)**
Reversal, relief, **FRCVP 60(b)**

RULES OF CIVIL PROCEDURE
—Cont'd
Judgments and decrees—Cont'd
Satisfaction, admiralty and maritime claims, actions in rem or quasi in rem, sales, **FRCVP E(9)**
Satisfied, released or discharged, relief, **FRCVP 60(b)**
Security on stay of proceedings to enforce, **FRCVP 62(b)**
Separate document setting forth, **FRCVP 58**
Separate judgment, one or more but fewer than all claims, **FRCVP 54(b)**
Sequestration of property, person disobeying judgment for specific acts, **FRCVP 70**
Setting aside judgment,
Power unaffected by motion for relief on ground of mistake, inadvertence, surprise or excusable neglect, **FRCVP 60(b)**
Special verdict, entry of judgment, **FRCVP 58**
Specific acts, performance of judgment directing specific acts, **FRCVP 70**
State law, staying enforcement in accordance to state law, **FRCVP 62(f)**
Summary judgment, generally, post
Supersedeas or stay,
Judgment on one or more but fewer than all of the claims or parties, **FRCVP 62(h)**
Proceedings to enforce, **FRCVP 62**
Separate judgment as to one or more but fewer than all claims, **FRCVP 62(h)**
Surprise, ground for relief, **FRCVP 60(b)**
Suspension by motion for relief on ground of mistake, inadvertence, surprise or excusable neglect, **FRCVP 60(b)**
Termination of action as to claim disposed of, **FRCVP 54(b)**
Third-party claim, **FRCVP 54(b)**
Third-party practice, admiralty and maritime claims, **FRCVP 14(c)**
Time,
Extension of time for relief from judgment, **FRCVP 6(b)**
Motion,
Alter or amend judgment, extension of time, **FRCVP 6(b)**
Relief on ground of mistake, inadvertence, surprise or excusable neglect, **FRCVP 60(b)**
Proceedings to enforce, **FRCVP 62(a)**
Title, judgment vesting title in another, **FRCVP 70**
United States, stay of judgment against, **FRCVP 62(e)**

RULES OF CIVIL PROCEDURE
—Cont'd
Judgments and decrees—Cont'd
Vacation, errors not affecting substantial rights, **FRCVP 61**
Verdict submitted on written interrogatories to jury, **FRCVP 49(b)**
Void judgment, relief, **FRCVP 60(b)**
Writs of coram nobis, coram vobis and audita querela abolished, **FRCVP 60(b)**
Judicial Conference,
Power to recommend, **28 § 2073**
Judicial Panel on Multidistrict Litigation, generally, this index
Jurisdiction,
Dismissal for lack, operation and effect, **FRCVP 41(b)**
Establishment, service of summons, **FRCVP 4(k)**
Lack, defense, **FRCVP 12(b, h)**
Magistrate Judges, post
Motion to dismiss complaint for lack of jurisdiction, form, **FRCVP Form 19**
Objection, waiver due to waiver of service of summons, **FRCVP 4(d)**
Personal jurisdiction, establishment by service of summons, **FRCVP 4(k)**
Pleading,
Judgment or decision, necessity of setting forth matter showing jurisdiction, **FRCVP 9(e)**
Jurisdiction, form of allegations, **FRCVP Form 2**
Property seizure, service of summons not feasible, **FRCVP 4(n)**
Rules not to extend or limit, **FRCVP 82**
Sureties, proceedings against, **FRCVP 65.1**
Jury,
Admiralty and maritime claims, **FRCVP 38(e)**
Advisory jury, **FRCVP 39(c), 52(a)**
Calendar, designating cases as jury actions, **FRCVP 79(c)**
Complicated issues, reference to master, **FRCVP 53(b)**
Declaratory judgments, **FRCVP 57**
Default judgment, determination of amount of damages, **FRCVP 55(b)**
Demand for, **FRCVP 38(b)**
Removed action, **FRCVP 81(c)**
Right of court to order in absence of demand, **FRCVP 39(b)**
Disclosure by parties, failure to make, informing jury, **FRCVP 37**
Entry of demand in civil docket, **FRCVP 79(a)**
Examination of jurors, **FRCVP 47(a)**
Excusing juror, **FRCVP 47(c)**
Findings, unanimity, **FRCVP 48**
Instructions to jury, generally, ante
Judgment as a matter of law, **FRCVP 50**

RULES OF CIVIL PROCEDURE
—Cont'd
Jury—Cont'd
Peremptory challenges, **FRCVP 47(b)**
Preliminary injunction, **FRCVP 65(a)**
Reference to master, **FRCVP 53(b)**
Removed action, **FRCVP 81(c)**
Reports of master, **FRCVP 53(e)**
Right preserved, **FRCVP 38(a); 28 § 2072**
Separate trials, **FRCVP 42(b)**
Size of jury, **FRCVP 48**
Specification of issues, **FRCVP 38(c)**
Stipulations for trial by court, **FRCVP 39(a)**
Waiver, **FRCVP 38(d)**
Failure of party to make demand for jury trial upon removal of action from state court, **FRCVP 81(c)**
Omission of instruction on issue of fact raised by evidence or pleading, **FRCVP 49(a)**
Withdrawal of demand, **FRCVP 38(d)**
Knowledge, pleading, **FRCVP 9(b)**
Laches, pleading, affirmative defenses, **FRCVP 8(c)**
Land. Entry upon land, generally, ante
Law,
Application of rules, **FRCVP 1**
Governing, capacity to sue or be sued, **FRCVP 17(b)**
Leave of court,
Depositions upon oral examination, **FRCVP 30**
Requests for admission, **FRCVP 36(a)**
Legal holidays,
Clerks of court, business hours, **FRCVP 77(c)**
Computation of time, **FRCVP 6(a)**
Defined, **FRCVP 6(a)**
Legal representatives, judgment against, relief on ground of mistake, inadvertence, surprise or excusable neglect, **FRCVP 60(b)**
Letters of request, foreign countries, taking depositions, **FRCVP 28**
Licenses and permits, pleading, affirmative defenses, **FRCVP 8(c)**
Liens and incumbrances, maritime, enforcement, action in rem, **FRCVP C(1)**
Limitation of actions, pleading, affirmative defenses, **FRCVP 8(c)**
Limitation of liability. Admiralty and maritime claims, ante
Longshoremens and Harbor Workers Compensation Act, applicability of rules, review proceedings under, **FRCVP 81(a)**
Magistrate Judges, **FRCVP 72 et seq.**
Appeal after trial, **FRCVP 73**
Attorney fees, deciding motions, **FRCVP 54**

RULES OF CIVIL PROCEDURE
—Cont'd
Magistrate Judges—Cont'd
Civil proceedings, designation to conduct in district court with consent of parties, **28 § 636**
Consent,
Jurisdiction, **FRCVP Form 33, 34**
Parties, conduct of civil proceedings in district court by, **28 § 636**
Designation of magistrate judge to conduct civil proceedings in district court, **28 § 636**
Jurisdiction,
Powers of magistrate judge designated to conduct civil proceedings in district court, **28 § 636**
Order of reference, **FRCVP Form 34A**
Part-time Magistrate Judges, conduct of civil proceedings in district court, **28 § 636**
Pretrial matters, **FRCVP 72**
Rule governing masters, application, **FRCVP 53(f)**
Trial by consent, **FRCVP 73**
Mail and mailing,
Admiralty and maritime claims, limitation of liability, information for claimants, **FRCVP F(6)**
Corporations and business associations, service of summons, **FRCVP 4(h)**
Notice,
Admiralty and maritime claims, limitation of liability, **FRCVP F(4)**
Entry of orders or judgments by clerk, **FRCVP 77(d)**
Filing of report by master, **FRCVP 53(e)**
Service of process,
Additional time after service by mail, **FRCVP 6(e)**
Admiralty and maritime claims, attachment and garnishment, process, **FRCVP B(2)**
Foreign countries, summons, **FRCVP 4(f)**
Pleading and other papers, **FRCVP 5(b)**
Summons and complaint on defendant, **FRCVP 4**
Sureties, proceedings against, **FRCVP 65.1**
United States, **FRCVP 4(i)**
United States agencies and officers, service of summons, **FRCVP 4(i)**
Malice, pleading, **FRCVP 9(b)**
Mandamus, abolition of writ, **FRCVP 81(b)**
Maritime claims. Admiralty and maritime claims, generally, ante
Marshals,
Admiralty and maritime claims, ante
Process, service, **FRCVP 4, 4.1**

RULES OF CIVIL PROCEDURE
—Cont'd
Master and servant,
Complaint for negligence under Federal Employers Liability Act, form, **FRCVP Form 14**
Injunctions in proceedings affecting, **FRCVP 65(e)**
Masters, **FRCVP 53**
Attorney fees, deciding motion, **FRCVP 54**
Defined, **FRCVP 53(a)**
Findings,
Acceptance by court, action tried without jury or with advisory jury, **FRCVP 52(a), 53(e)**
Court, **FRCVP 52(a)**
Magistrate judges, application of rule, **FRCVP 53**
Reports, **FRCVP 53**
Judgment not required to recite, **FRCVP 54(a)**
Matter of law. Judgment as a matter of law, generally, ante
Measuring of property or objects. Entry upon land, generally, ante
Mental examinations. Physical and mental examinations, generally, post
Mental health proceedings, applicability of rules in U.S. District Court for District of Columbia, **FRCVP 81(a)**
Merchant Marine Act, complaint for damages, form, **FRCVP Form 15**
Merger and consolidation,
Actions for trial or hearing, **FRCVP 42(a)**
Defenses, motions, **FRCVP 12(g)**
Preliminary injunction hearing with trial on merits, **FRCVP 65(a)**
Mileage, tender on delivery of copy of subpoena, **FRCVP 45(b)**
Minors. Children and minors, generally, ante
Misconduct, relief from judgment, order or proceeding, **FRCVP 60(b)**
Misjoinder, parties, **FRCVP 21**
Misnomers, substitution proceedings involving public officers, disregarding when not substantial, **FRCVP 25(d)**
Mistakes and errors,
Correction of clerical mistakes, **FRCVP 60(a)**
Depositions, use in court proceedings, effect, **FRCVP 32(d)**
Judgments and decrees, relief from judgment on ground of mistake, **FRCVP 60(b)**
Pleadings, post
Modification,
Discovery procedures, stipulations, **FRCVP 29**
Masters report by court, **FRCVP 53(e)**
Money,
Had and received, complaint, form, **FRCVP Form 8**
Lent, complaint, form, **FRCVP Form 6**

RULES OF CIVIL PROCEDURE
—Cont'd
Money—Cont'd
Paid, complaint in action for money paid by mistake, form, **FRCVP Form 7**
Motion day, **FRCVP 78**
Motions,
Additional findings by court, **FRCVP 52(b)**
Admiralty and maritime claims, ante
Admission, withdrawal or amendment, **FRCVP 36(b)**
Adoption by reference, **FRCVP 10(c)**
Advisory jury, **FRCVP 39(c)**
Amendment of findings of court, **FRCVP 52(b)**
Application to court for,
Action on report of master, **FRCVP 53(e)**
Order, **FRCVP 7(b)**
Attorneys fees, **FRCVP 54**
Bringing in third-party defendant, form, **FRCVP Form 22–B**
Consolidation of defenses, **FRCVP 12(g)**
Correction of clerical mistakes, **FRCVP 60(a)**
Depositions, use, hearings on, **FRCVP 32(a)**
Disclosure by parties, motion to compel, **FRCVP 37**
Dismissal and nonsuit,
Findings of fact and conclusions of law, **FRCVP 52(a)**
Form, **FRCVP Form 19**
Pleadings, defects, **FRCVP 12(b)**
Extension of time, **FRCVP 6(b)**
Filing, new trial, **FRCVP 59(b)**
Findings of fact and conclusions of law, necessity on decision of motion, **FRCVP 52(a)**
Forms, ante
Interrogatories, objections to or failure to answer, **FRCVP 33**
Intervention, **FRCVP 24(c)**
Defendant, form, **FRCVP Form 23**
Judgment as a matter of law, **FRCVP 50**
Judgments and decrees, ante
Jury trial, order by court, **FRCVP 39(b)**
More definite statement, pleadings, **FRCVP 12(e)**
New trial, post
Notice of motion,
Bringing in third-party defendant, form, **FRCVP Form 22–B**
Correction of clerical mistakes, **FRCVP 60(a)**
Dismissal of complaint, form, **FRCVP Form 19**
Intervention as defendant, form, **FRCVP Form 23**
Order compelling discovery, **FRCVP 37(a)**

RULES OF CIVIL PROCEDURE
—Cont'd
Motions—Cont'd
Notice of motion—Cont'd
Sureties, proceedings against, **FRCVP 65.1**
Oral hearing, **FRCVP 78**
Orders,
Compelling discovery, **FRCVP 37(a)**
Depositions,
Failure of party to attend at own deposition, sanctions, **FRCVP 37(d)**
Entry upon land, failure of party to respond to request for inspection, sanctions, **FRCVP 37(d)**
Examiners report, physical and mental examinations, delivery, **FRCVP 35(b)**
Interrogatories,
Failure of party to respond to request for inspection, sanctions, **FRCVP 37(d)**
Failure of party to serve answers, sanctions, **FRCVP 37(d)**
Objections to or failure to answer, **FRCVP 33(a)**
Physical and mental examinations, **FRCVP 35(a)**
Production of documents or things and entry upon land, **FRCVP 34(b)**
Particularity, **FRCVP 7(b)**
Pleadings, post
Power of Supreme Court to prescribe for district courts and courts of appeals, **28 § 2072**
Sanctions, inappropriate use, **FRCVP 11**
Service of process, **FRCVP 5(a), 6(d)**
Alteration or amendment of judgment, **FRCVP 59(e)**
Dismiss action for lack, form, **FRCVP Form 19**
Intervention, **FRCVP 24(c)**
Substitution of parties, **FRCVP 25**
Summary judgment, **FRCVP 56(c)**
Severance or separate trial, third-party claim, **FRCVP 14(a)**
Signature,
Application of rules to motions and other papers, **FRCVP 7(b, c)**
Sanctions, **FRCVP 11**
Striking,
Pleading, **FRCVP 12(f)**
Third-party claim, **FRCVP 14(a)**
Substitution of parties, **FRCVP 25**
Sufficiency, determination of answers or objections to requests for admission, **FRCVP 36(a)**
Summary judgment, **FRCVP 12(b), 56**
Suppression, depositions, errors and irregularities in completion and return of, **FRCVP 32(d)**
Sureties, liability, enforcement, **FRCVP 65.1**

RULES OF CIVIL PROCEDURE
—Cont'd
Motions—Cont'd
Technical forms not required, **FRCVP 8(e)**
Temporary restraining order, **FRCVP 65(b)**
Third-party complaint, service, leave to make, **FRCVP 14(a)**
Time,
Enlargement, **FRCVP 6(b)**
Judgment on the pleadings, **FRCVP 12(c)**
New trial, **FRCVP 59(b)**
Person defending for summary judgment, **FRCVP 56(b)**
Pleading, responsive, effect, **FRCVP 12(a)**
Relief from judgment on ground of mistake, inadvertence, surprise or excusable neglect, **FRCVP 60(b)**
Service, **FRCVP 6(d)**
Summary judgment by claimant, **FRCVP 56(a)**
Writing, **FRCVP 7(b)**
Multiple claims or parties,
Judgments and decrees, **FRCVP 54(b)**
Stay of enforcement, **FRCVP 62(h)**
Multiple defendants, summons, **FRCVP 4(b)**
Municipal corporations, foreign states, service of summons on, **FRCVP 4(j)**
Names,
Depositions, notice or commission may designate persons before whom to be taken, **FRCVP 28(b)**
Discovery, initial disclosure, **FRCVP 26**
Nonjoinder, persons, needed for just adjudication, pleading, **FRCVP 19(c)**
Pleading, captions, **FRCVP 10(a)**
National Labor Relations Board, applicability of rules to enforcement proceedings, **FRCVP 81(a)**
Naturalization, applicability of rules to proceedings, **FRCVP 81(a)**
Negligence,
Complaint, **FRCVP Form 9**
Federal Employers Liability Act, form, **FRCVP Form 14**
Plaintiff unable to determine person responsible, form, **FRCVP Form 10**
New trial, **FRCVP 59**
Affidavits, time for serving, **FRCVP 59(c)**
Alternative motion, judgment as a matter of law, **FRCVP 50**
Answers to written interrogatories inconsistent with general verdict, **FRCVP 49(b)**
Courts own initiative, **FRCVP 59(d)**
Harmless error, grounds, **FRCVP 61**

RULES OF CIVIL PROCEDURE
—Cont'd
New trial—Cont'd
Judgment as a matter of law, alternative motion accompanying, **FRCVP 50**
Motions, **FRCVP 59(d)**
Additional or amended findings, motion accompanying, **FRCVP 52(b)**
Extension of time, **FRCVP 6(b)**
Judgment as a matter of law motion, alternative, **FRCVP 50**
Time, **FRCVP 59(b)**
Order, **FRCVP 59(d)**
Extension of time, **FRCVP 6(b)**
Stay of execution or proceedings to enforce judgment, motion for new trial, **FRCVP 62(b)**
Newly discovered evidence, relief from judgment, order or proceeding, **FRCVP 60(b)**
Newspapers,
Admiralty and maritime claims, notice,
Actions in rem, **FRCVP C(4)**
Limitation of liability, **FRCVP F(4)**
Next friend, action by infant or incompetent person, **FRCVP 17(c)**
Nonjoinder, persons needed for just adjudication, pleading, reasons, **FRCVP 19(c)**
Nonresidents, subpoena requiring attendance for taking deposition, **FRCVP 45(b)**
Notice,
Acceptance, offer of judgment, **FRCVP 68**
Adjournment, proceedings before master, **FRCVP 53(d)**
Admiralty and maritime claims, ante
Amendment of pleading, change of party, relation back, **FRCVP 15(c)**
Appeal and review, ante
Application, order of court to speed proceedings of master, **FRCVP 53(d)**
Attorneys, ante
Class actions, **FRCVP 23(c)**
Commencement of action, request for waiver of service, **FRCVP 4(d)**
Condemnation of property, form, **FRCVP Form 28**
Default judgments,
Applications, **FRCVP 55(b)**
Failure to appear and defend, summons as notice, **FRCVP 4(a)**
Depositions, ante
Derivative actions by shareholders, dismissal or compromise, **FRCVP 23.1**
Dismissal, **FRCVP 41(a)**
Extension of time, **FRCVP 6(b)**
Filing,
Pleading, **FRCVP 5(c)**
Report by master, **FRCVP 53(e)**

RULES OF CIVIL PROCEDURE
—Cont'd
Notice—Cont'd
Foreign law, determination, pleadings, **FRCVP 44.1**
Hearing of motion, writing requirement, **FRCVP 7(b)**
Judgments and decrees, entry, **FRCVP 58**
Lawsuit, form, **FRCVP Form 1A**
Magistrate judge jurisdiction, consent, **FRCVP 73**
Meeting on order of reference, **FRCVP 53(d)**
Motions, ante
New trial, **FRCVP 59(d)**
Orders, notice of entry, **FRCVP 77(d)**
Physical and mental examinations, **FRCVP 35(a)**
Placing of actions on trial calendar, **FRCVP 40**
Preliminary injunction, **FRCVP 65(a)**
Rules, amendments, **FRCVP 83**
Service of process, **FRCVP 5**
Application for default judgment, **FRCVP 55(b)**
Condemnation proceedings, **FRCVP 71A(d)**
Entry of order or judgment, **FRCVP 77(d)**
Hearing, **FRCVP 6(d)**
Taking depositions before action, **FRCVP 27(a)**
Third-party complaint, **FRCVP 14(a)**
Taxation of costs by clerk, **FRCVP 54(d)**
Temporary restraining order, **FRCVP 65(b)**
Time,
Admiralty and maritime claims, limitation of liability, **FRCVP F(4)**
Enlargement, **FRCVP 6(b)**
Hearing, service, **FRCVP 6(d)**
Taxation of cost, **FRCVP 54(d)**
Numbers and numbering,
Claims, cross-claims, separate trial, **FRCVP 42(b)**
Expert witnesses, pretrial conferences, limitation, **FRCVP 16**
Oaths and affirmations,
Admiralty and maritime claims, ante
Depositions upon oral examination, **FRCVP 30**
Objections and exceptions,
Admiralty and maritime claims, limitation of liability, **FRCVP F(8)**
Depositions, ante
Failure of party to serve, sanctions, **FRCVP 37(d)**
Findings of fact by court, **FRCVP 52(b)**
Formal exceptions to rulings unnecessary, **FRCVP 46**
Instructions, **FRCVP 51**
Insufficiency of pleadings, abolished, **FRCVP 7(c)**
Interrogatories, **FRCVP 33**

RULES OF CIVIL PROCEDURE
—Cont'd
Objections and exceptions—Cont'd
Magistrate judges, recommended disposition, **FRCVP 72**
Masters report, **FRCVP 53(e)**
Motions, omission, effect, **FRCVP 12(g)**
Pleading, **FRCVP 12**
Production of documents or things and entry upon land, **FRCVP 34(b)**
Requests for admission, service, **FRCVP 36(a)**
Rulings, absence of objection as not prejudicial, **FRCVP 46**
Sufficiency, motion for determination on request for admission, **FRCVP 36(a)**
Offer of judgment, **FRCVP 68**
Officers and employees,
Depositions, generally, ante
Parties, termination of office, substitution, **FRCVP 25(d)**
Pleading decision, **FRCVP 9(e)**
Proof of record, **FRCVP 44**
Public officers in official capacity, description as party by, **FRCVP 25(d)**
United States, post
Official acts, pleading, **FRCVP 9(d)**
Open court, trial conducted in, **FRCVP 77(b)**
Opinion and expert testimony,
Depositions, **FRCVP 26**
Discovery, **FRCVP 26**
Numbers and numbering, pretrial conference, limitation, **FRCVP 16(c)**
Opinions,
Facts. Admissions, generally, ante
Trial by court, **FRCVP 52(a)**
Opposing party, actions by, class actions maintainable, **FRCVP 23(b)**
Oral examination. Depositions, ante
Orders,
Admiralty and Maritime Claims, ante
Admissions, requests for, expenses on failure to admit, **FRCVP 37(c)**
Civil docket, entry, **FRCVP 79(a)**
Class actions, determination whether maintainable, **FRCVP 23(c)**
Clerical mistakes, correction, **FRCVP 60(a)**
Clerk,
Copies, appealable orders or orders affecting title, **FRCVP 79(b)**
Indexes, maintenance, **FRCVP 79(c)**
Power to grant, **FRCVP 77(c)**
Computation, time, **FRCVP 6(a)**
Conduct, class actions, **FRCVP 23(d)**
Consolidation, preliminary injunction hearing with trial on merits, **FRCVP 65(a)**
Depositions, **FRCVP 27(a)**
Failure of party to attend at own deposition, sanctions, **FRCVP 37(d)**

RULES OF CIVIL PROCEDURE
—Cont'd
Orders—Cont'd
Discovery, ante
Dismissal of action,
Condemnation of property, **FRCVP 71A(i)**
Receivers appointment, **FRCVP 66**
Documents, failure to admit genuineness, award of expenses, **FRCVP 37(c)**
Entry upon land, failure of party to respond to request for inspection, sanctions, **FRCVP 37(d)**
Examiners report, physical and mental examinations, delivery, **FRCVP 35(b)**
Exceptions unnecessary, **FRCVP 46**
Fraud, relief from order, **FRCVP 60(b)**
Interrogatories,
Answers, **FRCVP 33**
Failure of party to serve answers, sanctions, **FRCVP 37(d)**
Objections or failure to answer, **FRCVP 33**
Joinder, persons needed for just adjudication, **FRCVP 19(a)**
Judgment includes order, **FRCVP 54(a)**
Magistrate judges, referral of cases, **FRCVP Form 34A**
Mental examination, **FRCVP 27(a, b)**
Misconduct of party, relief from order, **FRCVP 60(b)**
Motions, ante
Multiple claims or involving multiple parties, termination of action, **FRCVP 54(b)**
New trial, **FRCVP 59(d)**
Newly discovered evidence, relief from order, **FRCVP 60(b)**
Notice of entry given by clerk, **FRCVP 77(d)**
Physical and mental examinations, **FRCVP 35(a)**
Pretrial order, after conference, **FRCVP 16(e)**
Production of documents or things, failure of party to respond to request for inspection, sanctions, **FRCVP 37(d)**
Protective Orders, generally, post
Reference to master, **FRCVP 53(c, d)**
Sanctions,
Representations to court, **FRCVP 11**
Scheduling or pretrial orders, **FRCVP 16(f)**
Scheduling, pretrial conference, **FRCVP 16(b)**
Service, **FRCVP 5(a)**
Pleading, numerous defendants, **FRCVP 5(c)**
Speed proceedings of master, **FRCVP 53(d)**

RULES OF CIVIL PROCEDURE
—Cont'd
Orders—Cont'd
Substitution of parties, public officers ceasing to hold office, **FRCVP 25(d)**
Sufficiency of answers or objections to requests for admission, **FRCVP 36(a)**
Truth of matter, failure to admit, award of expenses, **FRCVP 37(c)**
Unincorporated associations, actions relating to, **FRCVP 23.2**
Voluntary dismissal, **FRCVP 41(a)**
Owners, admiralty and maritime claims against limitation of liability, **FRCVP F(3)**
Papers. Books and Papers, generally, ante
Paragraphs, pleading, **FRCVP 10(b)**
Partial findings, judgment on, **FRCVP 52**
Parties,
Additional parties, joinder, counterclaim or cross-claim, **FRCVP 13(h)**
Admissions, generally, ante
Capacity to sue or be sued, determination, **FRCVP 17(b)**
Change of, pleadings, amendments, relation back, **FRCVP 15(c)**
Class actions, **FRCVP 23(a)**
Compensation of master, payment, **FRCVP 53(a)**
Consent, withdrawal of demand for jury trial, **FRCVP 38(d)**
Corporation, capacity to sue or be sued, **FRCVP 17(b)**
Cross-claim against coparty, **FRCVP 13(g)**
Death, substitution, **FRCVP 25(a)**
Defendants, bringing in third party, **FRCVP 14(a)**
Depositions, generally, ante
Disclosure, motion to compel, **FRCVP 37**
Discovery, **FRCVP 26 et seq.**
Dismissal for lack of an indispensable party, **FRCVP 41(b)**
Failure to join, **FRCVP 12(b)**
Inability to protect property interest, intervention, **FRCVP 24(a)**
Incompetency, **FRCVP 17(c)**
Substitution, **FRCVP 25(b)**
Indispensable party, dismissal for lack of, **FRCVP 41(b)**
Infants, **FRCVP 17(c)**
Interpleader, generally, ante
Interrogatories, generally, ante
Intervention, **FRCVP 24**
Form, **FRCVP Form 23**
Joinder, **FRCVP 19 et seq.**
Additional parties, counterclaim or cross-claim, **FRCVP 13(h)**
Class actions, impracticability, **FRCVP 23(a)**

RULES OF CIVIL PROCEDURE
—Cont'd
Parties—Cont'd
Joinder—Cont'd
Dismissal for failure to join, **FRCVP 41(d)**
Misjoinder or nonjoinder, **FRCVP 12(b, h), 21**
Service of summons, establishing personal jurisdiction, **FRCVP 4(k)**
Meeting, discovery matters, **FRCVP 26**
Misjoinder or nonjoinder, **FRCVP 12(b, h), 21**
Motions,
Bringing in third-party defendant, form, **FRCVP Form 22–B**
Defenses, pleadings, defects, **FRCVP 12(b)**
Multiple parties, judgment, **FRCVP 54(b)**
Stay of enforcement, **FRCVP 62(h)**
Needed for just adjudication,
Defense, failure to join, **FRCVP 12(b, h)**
Joinder, **FRCVP 19**
Notice, generally, ante
Partnership, capacity to sue or to be sued, **FRCVP 17(b)**
Physical and mental examinations, generally, post
Plaintiffs,
Bringing in third party, **FRCVP 14(b)**
Default judgment against, **FRCVP 55(d)**
Real party in interest, **FRCVP 17(a)**
Voluntary dismissal, **FRCVP 41(a)**
Planning meeting, report, **FRCVP Form 35**
Pleadings,
Captions, names, **FRCVP 10(a)**
Reason for omitting, form, **FRCVP Form 26**
Process in behalf of and against persons not parties, **FRCVP 71**
Public officer, substitution, **FRCVP 25(d)**
Real party in interest, prosecution of action, **FRCVP 17(a)**
Receiver, law governing capacity to sue or be sued, **FRCVP 17(b)**
Representations to court, **FRCVP 11**
Representative capacity, capacity to sue or be sued, **FRCVP 17(b)**
Representative parties, class actions, **FRCVP 23(a)**
Service of pleadings and papers, **FRCVP 5(b, c)**
Substitution, **FRCVP 25**
Condemnation proceedings, **FRCVP 71A(g)**
Depositions, effect on use, **FRCVP 32(a)**

RULES OF CIVIL PROCEDURE
—Cont'd
Parties—Cont'd
Substitution—Cont'd
Suggestion of death upon the record under rule concerning, form, **FRCVP Form 30**
Suggestion, lack of jurisdiction, **FRCVP 12(h)**
Third-party practice, generally, post
Transfer of interest, substitution, **FRCVP 25(c)**
United States, action for use or benefit of another, **FRCVP 17(a)**
Partition, petitory and possessory actions. Admiralty and maritime claims, ante
Partnerships,
Capacity to sue or be sued, **FRCVP 17(b)**
Depositions,
Introduction in evidence, making deponent witness of introducing party, applicability, **FRCVP 32(c)**
Oral examination,
Failure of officer or director to attend at own deposition, sanctions, **FRCVP 37(d)**
Failure to comply with order compelling designation, sanctions, **FRCVP 37(b)**
Motion for order to compel designation, **FRCVP 37(a)**
Use in court proceedings, **FRCVP 32(a)**
Written questions,
Failure of officer or director to attend at own deposition, sanctions, **FRCVP 37(d)**
Failure to comply with order compelling answer, sanctions, **FRCVP 37(b)**
Motion for order compelling answer, **FRCVP 37(a)**
Interrogatories, service, **FRCVP 33(a)**
Service of summons, **FRCVP 4(h)**
Patents,
Complaint in action for infringement, form of, **FRCVP Form 16**
Stay of judgment for accounting for infringement, **FRCVP 62(a)**
Payment,
Complaint for money paid by mistake, form of, **FRCVP Form 7**
Pleading, affirmative defenses, **FRCVP 8(c)**
Payment into court, **FRCVP 67**
Admiralty and maritime claims, ante
Pending actions,
Counterclaims, **FRCVP 13(a)**
Discovery, failure to comply with order compelling, sanctions by court, **FRCVP 37(b)**
Peremptory challenges, jury, **FRCVP 47(b)**

RULES OF CIVIL PROCEDURE
—Cont'd
Permissive counterclaims, pleading, **FRCVP 13(b)**
Permissive intervention, parties, **FRCVP 24(b)**
Permissive joinder, parties, **FRCVP 20**
Perpetuation of testimony, proceedings for, **FRCVP 27**
Personal jurisdiction lacking, defense, **FRCVP 12(b, h)**
Personal property, application of rules governing procedure for condemnation, **FRCVP 71A(a)**
Personal representatives, officers, deceased district director or collector of internal revenue, **FRCVP 81(f)**
Personal service,
Notice, condemnation proceedings, **FRCVP 71A(d)**
Summons, **FRCVP 4(e)**
Petroleum control boards, applicability of rules, review orders of boards, **FRCVP 81(a)**
Phono-records. Production of documents or things, generally, post
Photographs and pictures,
Entry upon land, generally, ante
Orders, **FRCVP 27(a, b)**
Production of documents or things, generally, ante
Physical and mental examinations, **FRCVP 35**
Agreement of parties, **FRCVP 35(b)**
Deposition of examiner, **FRCVP 35(b)**
Discovery, examiners report, **FRCVP 35(b)**
Effect, failure or refusal to make report, **FRCVP 35(b)**
Examiners report, **FRCVP 35(b)**
Failure to comply with order compelling, sanctions, **FRCVP 37(b)**
Notice, **FRCVP 35(a)**
Order, **FRCVP 35(a)**
Prior or future reports by examiner, requesting, **FRCVP 35(b)**
Psychologists, **FRCVP 35**
Waiver, privilege of prior examination reports, **FRCVP 35(b)**
Place,
Deposition, taking, stipulations, **FRCVP 29**
Physical and mental examinations, **FRCVP 35(a)**
Pleading, averments, **FRCVP 9(f)**
Trial. Venue, generally, post
Plaintiffs. Parties, ante
Plans and specifications,
Discovery plans, **FRCVP 26**
Parties planning meeting, report, **FRCVP Form 35**
Pleadings,
Account, form of complaint in action on, **FRCVP Form 4**

RULES OF CIVIL PROCEDURE
—Cont'd
Pleadings—Cont'd
Additional claims for relief, service, **FRCVP 5(a)**
Admiralty and maritime claims, **FRCVP 9(h)**
Admissions, failure to deny, **FRCVP 8(d)**
Affirmative defenses, **FRCVP 8(c)**
Allowed, **FRCVP 7(a)**
Alternative statements, claims or defenses, **FRCVP 8(a, e)**
Ambiguity, motions, more definite statement, **FRCVP 12(e)**
Amendment, **FRCVP 15**
Admiralty and maritime claims, identifying statement, **FRCVP 9(h)**
Class actions, orders, **FRCVP 23(d)**
Condemnation proceedings, **FRCVP 71A(f)**
Evidence, conforming, **FRCVP 15(b)**
Omission, defense, waiver, **FRCVP 12(h)**
Pretrial procedure, **FRCVP 16(c)**
Relation back, **FRCVP 15(c)**
Answers,
Admiralty and maritime claims,
Actions in rem, service, **FRCVP C(6)**
Actions in rem and quasi in rem, **FRCVP E(4)**
Garnishee or defendant, **FRCVP B(3)**
Limitation of liability, **FRCVP F(5)**
Allowed, **FRCVP 7(a)**
Condemnation proceedings, **FRCVP 71A(e)**
Depositions,
Motion for order to compel, **FRCVP 37(a)**
Sanctions for failure to comply with order compelling answer, **FRCVP 37(b)**
Evasive or incomplete answer, defined, motion for order to compel discovery, **FRCVP 37(a)**
Form, **FRCVP Form 20, 21, 23**
General verdict accompanied by answer to interrogatory, **FRCVP 49(b)**
Interrogatories, **FRCVP 33**
Affidavits for summary judgments, supplementation or opposition, **FRCVP 56(e)**
Failure of party to serve, sanctions, **FRCVP 37(d)**
Motion for order to compel, **FRCVP 37(a)**
Summary judgment, answers show no genuine issue, **FRCVP 56(c)**
Use, **FRCVP 33**

RULES OF CIVIL PROCEDURE
—Cont'd
Pleadings—Cont'd
Answers—Cont'd
Interrogatories—Cont'd
Written, submission to jury with form in general verdict, **FRCVP 49(b)**
Intervener, form, **FRCVP Form 23**
Removed action, **FRCVP 81(c)**
Requirements, after requests for admission, service, **FRCVP 36(a)**
Sufficiency, motion for determination on request for admission, **FRCVP 36(a)**
Time, service and reply, **FRCVP 12(a)**
Associations, capacity to sue or be sued, **FRCVP 9(a)**
Authority, **FRCVP 9(a)**
Boards, decisions, **FRCVP 9(e)**
Capacity, **FRCVP 9(a)**
Caption, **FRCVP 10(a)**
Signature, motions and other papers, **FRCVP 7(b)**
Claims for relief, requirements, **FRCVP 8(a)**
Complaints,
Account, form of complaint in action on, **FRCVP Form 4**
Admiralty and maritime claims,
Actions in rem and quasi in rem, **FRCVP E(2)**
Execution, **FRCVP E(4)**
Limitation of liability, **FRCVP F(1, 2)**
Commencement of action by filing, **FRCVP 3**
Condemnation of property, **FRCVP 71A(c); Form 29**
Conversion action, form of complaint, **FRCVP Form 11**
Debt action, form of complaint, **FRCVP Form 13**
Fraudulent conveyances, form of complaint in action to set aside, **FRCVP Form 13**
Goods sold and delivered, form of complaint, **FRCVP Form 5**
Infringement,
Copyright, form of complaint, **FRCVP Form 17**
Patent, form of complaint, **FRCVP Form 16**
Interpleader and declaratory relief, form of complaint, **FRCVP Form 18**
Jurisdiction, form of allegation, **FRCVP Form 2**
Merchant Marine Act, form of complaint in action for damages, **FRCVP Form 15**
Money,
Had and received, form of complaint, **FRCVP Form 8**

RULES OF CIVIL PROCEDURE
—Cont'd
Pleadings—Cont'd
Complaints—Cont'd
Money—Cont'd
Lent, form of complaint, **FRCVP Form 6**
Paid by mistake, form of complaint, **FRCVP Form 7**
Motion to dismiss, form, **FRCVP Form 19**
Negligence, form of complaint, **FRCVP Form 9**
Federal Employers Liability Act, **FRCVP Form 14**
Plaintiff unable to determine person responsible, **FRCVP Form 10**
Pleadings allowed, **FRCVP 7(a)**
Promissory note, form of complaint, **FRCVP Form 3**
Service,
Act against officer or employee of U.S., **28 § 1391**
Specific performance, contract to convey land, form of complaint **FRCVP Form 12**
Summons,
Notice to defendant, default judgment for failure to appear, **FRCVP 4(a)**
Service together with complaint, **FRCVP 4(c)**
Third-party defendant, complaint against, form, **FRCVP Form 22–A**
Third-party practice, **FRCVP 14(a, b)**
Title of action, **FRCVP 10(a)**
Unfair competition, form of complaint, **FRCVP Form 17**
Verification,
Admiralty and maritime claims,
Actions in rem, **FRCVP C(2)**
Attachment and garnishment, **FRCVP B(1)**
Derivative actions by shareholders, **FRCVP 23.1**
Injunction, **FRCVP 65(b)**
Temporary restraining order, notice, **FRCVP 65(b)**
Compulsory counterclaim, **FRCVP 13(a)**
Conciseness, requirement, **FRCVP 8(e)**
Condemnation proceedings, **FRCVP 71A**
Condition of the mind, **FRCVP 9(b)**
Conditions precedent, **FRCVP 9(c)**
Consistency, **FRCVP 8(e)**
Consolidation, defenses in motion, **FRCVP 12(g)**
Construction, **FRCVP 8(f)**
Conversion, form of complaint, **FRCVP Form 11**
Counterclaims, generally, ante
Cross-claims, generally, ante

RULES OF CIVIL PROCEDURE
—Cont'd
Pleadings—Cont'd
Damages, special damages, **FRCVP 9(g)**
Debt, form of complaint, **FRCVP Form 13**
Default judgments,
Entered on failure to plead, **FRCVP 55(a)**
Relief demanded by pleading, **FRCVP 54(c)**
Defective, supplemental pleading, **FRCVP 15(d)**
Defenses, **FRCVP 8(b, c), 12**
Alternative allegation, **FRCVP 8(e)**
Answer presenting, form, **FRCVP Form 20**
Consolidation in motion, **FRCVP 12(g)**
Discovery, sanctions for failure to comply with order compelling, refusal to allow support or opposition, **FRCVP 37(b)**
Hypothetical statement, **FRCVP 8(e)**
Motion to strike, insufficient defense, **FRCVP 12(f)**
Omission from motion, **FRCVP 12(h)**
Effect, **FRCVP 12(g)**
Paragraphs, **FRCVP 10(b)**
Removed action, **FRCVP 81(c)**
Summary judgment, **FRCVP 56(e)**
Third-party practice, **FRCVP 14(a, b)**
Admiralty and maritime claims, **FRCVP 14(c)**
Waiver or preservation, **FRCVP 12(h)**
Demurrers, abolition, **FRCVP 7(c)**
Denial,
Conditions precedent, performance or occurrence, **FRCVP 9(c)**
Form, **FRCVP 8(b)**
Directness, requirement, **FRCVP 8(e)**
Dismissal before responsive pleading is served, **FRCVP 41(c)**
Evidence, amendments, conforming, **FRCVP 15(b)**
Exceptions, insufficiency of pleading, abolition, **FRCVP 7(c)**
Exhibits, written instruments, pleadings, **FRCVP 10(c)**
Existence, capacity, **FRCVP 9(a)**
Filing with the court, defined, **FRCVP 5(e)**
Foreign judgments, **FRCVP 9(e)**
Foreign law, determination, notice, **FRCVP 44.1**
Forms, **FRCVP 10**
Account, action on, **FRCVP Form 4**
Answer, **FRCVP Form 20, 21**
Conversion, action for, **FRCVP Form 11**
Debt, action for, **FRCVP Form 13**

RULES OF CIVIL PROCEDURE
—Cont'd
Pleadings—Cont'd
Forms—Cont'd
Fraudulent conveyances, action to set aside, **FRCVP Form 13**
Goods sold and delivered, **FRCVP Form 5**
Infringement,
Copyright, **FRCVP Form 17**
Patent, **FRCVP Form 16**
Interpleader and declaratory relief, **FRCVP Form 18**
Jurisdiction, form of allegation, **FRCVP Form 2**
Merchant Marine Act, action for damages, **FRCVP Form 15**
Money,
Had and received, **FRCVP Form 8**
Lent, **FRCVP Form 6**
Paid by mistake, **FRCVP Form 7**
Negligence, **FRCVP Form 9**
Federal Employers Liability Act, **FRCVP Form 14**
Plaintiff is unable to determine person responsible, **FRCVP Form 10**
Promissory note, **FRCVP Form 3**
Reason for omitting party, **FRCVP Form 26**
Specific performance, contract to convey land, **FRCVP Form 12**
Technical forms not required, **FRCVP 8(e)**
Unfair competition, **FRCVP Form 17**
Fraud, **FRCVP 9(b)**
Affirmative defense, **FRCVP 8(c)**
Fraudulent conveyance,
Form of complaint in action to set aside, **FRCVP Form 13**
Joinder of remedies, **FRCVP 18(b)**
General denial, **FRCVP 8(b)**
General rules, **FRCVP 8**
Goods sold and delivered, form of complaint, **FRCVP Form 5**
Hypothetical statements, claims or defenses, **FRCVP 8(e)**
Infringement,
Copyright, form of complaint, **FRCVP Form 17**
Patent, form of complaint, **FRCVP Form 16**
Intent, **FRCVP 9(b)**
Interpleader and declaratory relief, form of complaint, **FRCVP Form 18**
Joinder of claims and remedies, **FRCVP 18**
Judgments and decrees, **FRCVP 9(e)**
Demand for judgment, **FRCVP 8(a)**
Not to contain recitals of pleadings, **FRCVP 54(a)**
Jurisdiction, form of allegation, **FRCVP Form 2**
Knowledge, **FRCVP 9(b)**

RULES OF CIVIL PROCEDURE
—Cont'd
Pleadings—Cont'd
Mail, service, **FRCVP 5(b)**
Malice, **FRCVP 9(b)**
Merchant Marine Act, form of complaint in action for damages, **FRCVP Form 15**
Mistakes and errors, **FRCVP 9(b)**
Amendment, relation back, **FRCVP 15(c)**
Counterclaim, defense, designation, **FRCVP 8(c)**
Money,
Had and received, form of complaint, **FRCVP Form 8**
Lent, form of complaint, **FRCVP Form 6**
Paid by mistake, form of complaint, **FRCVP Form 7**
Motions,
Consolidation, defenses, **FRCVP 12(g)**
Dismiss, form, **FRCVP Form 19**
Judgment on the pleading, **FRCVP 12(c)**
More definite statement, **FRCVP 12(e)**
Strike, **FRCVP 12(f)**
Summary judgment, **FRCVP 12(b, c)**
Supplemental pleading, **FRCVP 15(d)**
Time, responsive pleading, **FRCVP 12(a)**
Names, title of action, **FRCVP 10(a)**
Negative averments, capacity, existence or authority, **FRCVP 9(a)**
Negligence, form of complaint, **FRCVP Form 9**
Federal Employers Liability Act, **FRCVP Form 14**
Plaintiff unable to determine person responsible, **FRCVP Form 10**
New claims for relief, service, **FRCVP 5(a)**
Numerous defendants, service of pleading of defendants, **FRCVP 5(c)**
Objections, **FRCVP 12**
Officers, decisions, **FRCVP 9(e)**
Official document or act, **FRCVP 9(d)**
Omitted,
Counterclaim, **FRCVP 13(f)**
Persons, setting forth names, **FRCVP 19(c)**
Paragraphs, numbers and numbering, **FRCVP 10(b)**
Particularity, conditions precedent, **FRCVP 9(c)**
Party,
Defense, failure to join party needed for just adjudication, **FRCVP 12(b, h)**
Form, allegation of reason for omitting party, **FRCVP Form 26**
Title of action, **FRCVP 10(a)**

RULES OF CIVIL PROCEDURE
—Cont'd
Pleadings—Cont'd
Permissive counterclaims, **FRCVP 13(b)**
Place, **FRCVP 9(f)**
Pleas for insufficiency, pleading, abolition, **FRCVP 7(c)**
Power of Supreme Court to prescribe rules for, **28 § 2072**
Savings provision, **28 § 2073 nt**
Preliminary hearings, defenses, **FRCVP 12(d)**
Presentation of matters outside the pleading, **FRCVP 12(b, c)**
Promissory note, form of complaint, **FRCVP Form 3**
Quasi-judicial tribunals, decisions, **FRCVP 9(e)**
Reasons for nonjoinder of persons needed for just adjudication, **FRCVP 12(b, h)**
Reference, adoption by, **FRCVP 10(c)**
Removed cases, repleading after removal, **FRCVP 81(c)**
Reply, **FRCVP 7(a)**
Time, **FRCVP 12(a)**
Responsive pleadings,
Admission by failure to deny, **FRCVP 8(d)**
Omission, defenses, waiver, **FRCVP 12(h)**
Service, supplemental pleading, **FRCVP 15(d)**
Time, **FRCVP 12(a)**
Signatures,
Motions and other papers, **FRCVP 7(b)**
Sanctions, **FRCVP 11**
Statements, **FRCVP 8(e)**
Special matters, **FRCVP 9**
Specific performance, contract to convey land, form of complaint, **FRCVP Form 12**
Striking of pleadings, generally, post
Summary judgment, **FRCVP 12(b, c)**
Rendered where pleadings show no genuine issue, **FRCVP 56(c)**
Supplemental pleading, **FRCVP 15(d)**
Third-party practice, generally, post
Time, **FRCVP 9(f)**
Amendment, **FRCVP 15**
Dismissal of action, **FRCVP 41(a)**
Service, **FRCVP 12(a)**
Summary judgment, **FRCVP 56(a)**
Title of action, caption, **FRCVP 10(a)**
Unfair competition, form of complaint in action for, **FRCVP Form 17**
United States,
Counterclaim against, **FRCVP 13(d)**
Time, answer or reply, **FRCVP 12(a)**
Waiver, defenses and objections, **FRCVP 8(c)**
Pleas, abolition, **FRCVP 7(c)**
Political subdivisions, foreign states, service of summons on, **FRCVP 4(j)**

RULES OF CIVIL PROCEDURE
—Cont'd
Possession,
Judgment directing delivery of possession, **FRCVP 70**
Vessel, admiralty and maritime claims, process and notice, **FRCVP D**
Prayer, default judgments, relief prayed for, **FRCVP 54(c)**
Preferred ship mortgage, foreclosure, actions in rem, application, **FRCVP C(4)**
Preliminary hearing, pleading, **FRCVP 12(d)**
Preliminary injunctions, **FRCVP 65**
Preservation of defenses, **FRCVP 12(h)**
Pretrial conference, **FRCVP 16**
Pretrial disclosures, discovery, **FRCVP 26**
Prevailing party, costs, **FRCVP 54(d)**
Priorities and preferences,
Cases on trial calendar, **FRCVP 40**
Declaratory judgments, **FRCVP 57**
Interrogatories, answers, orders, **FRCVP 33**
Requests for admission, final disposition, **FRCVP 36(a)**
Prisoners, depositions,
Oral examination, leave of court, **FRCVP 30**
Use in court proceedings, **FRCVP 32(a)**
Written questions, leave of court, **FRCVP 31**
Private corporations. Corporations, generally, ante
Privileges and immunities, subpoenas, response, **FRCVP 45(d)**
Prize proceedings in admiralty, nonapplicability of rules, **FRCVP 81(a)**
Process, **FRCVP 4**
Admiralty and maritime claims, ante
Behalf of and against persons not parties, **FRCVP 71**
Civil docket, entry, **FRCVP 79(a)**
Compulsory counterclaims, **FRCVP 13(a)**
Condemnation of property, **FRCVP 71A(d)**
Defense of insufficiency, **FRCVP 12(b, h)**
Motion to dismiss complaint for failure to serve, form, **FRCVP Form 19**
Power of Supreme Court to prescribe rules for, **28 § 2072**
Service of process, generally, post
Summons, generally, post
Third-party practice, **FRCVP 14(a)**
Production of documents or things,
Application of rules, **FRCVP 81(a)**
Compelling production, **FRCVP 45(c)**
Failure to,
Comply with order compelling inspection, sanctions, **FRCVP 37(b)**

RULES OF CIVIL PROCEDURE
—Cont'd
Production of documents or things
—Cont'd
Failure to—Cont'd
Respond to request for inspection, sanctions, **FRCVP 37(d)**
Motion for order to compel inspection, **FRCVP 37(a)**
Objections, **FRCVP 34(b)**
Persons not parties, independent action against, **FRCVP 34(c)**
Procedure, **FRCVP 34(b)**
Requests, **FRCVP 34(a, b)**
Form, **FRCVP Form 24**
Responses to requests, **FRCVP 34(b)**
Scope, **FRCVP 34(a)**
Service, requests, **FRCVP 34(a, b)**
Stipulations, extension of time, responses to approval of court, **FRCVP 29**
Subpoenas, **FRCVP 45**
Supplementation, **FRCVP 26**
Promissory notes, complaint in action on form of, **FRCVP Form 3**
Proof,
Default judgments, admiralty and maritime claims, attachment and garnishment, **FRCVP B(2)**
Evidence, generally, ante
Official record, **FRCVP 44**
Service, **FRCVP 4(*l*)**
Subpoenas, **FRCVP 45(b)**
Property disposition, admiralty and maritime claims, actions in rem and quasi in rem, **FRCVP E(9)**
Protective orders,
Depositions, use against party requesting order, **FRCVP 32**
Discovery, **FRCVP 26**
Denial of motion for order compelling, **FRCVP 37(a)**
Failure of parties to take certain actions, excuse discovery objectionable, **FRCVP 37(d)**
Psychologists and psychology, mental examination of persons, **FRCVP 35**
Public corporations. Corporations, generally, ante
Publication, official records, evidence, **FRCVP 44(a)**
Purpose of rules, **FRCVP 1**
Quasi in rem actions, admiralty and maritime claims, general provisions, **FRCVP E**
Quasi-judicial tribunals, pleading, judgments or decisions, **FRCVP 9(e)**
Questions of law or fact,
Common to class, actions, **FRCVP 23(a, b)**
Foreign law, determination, **FRCVP 44.1**
Quo warranto, application of rules, **FRCVP 81(a)**
Railroad labor disputes, application of rules, **FRCVP 81(a)**

RULES OF CIVIL PROCEDURE
—Cont'd
Real party in interest, prosecution in name of, **FRCVP 17(a)**
Receipts, proof of service, **FRCVP 4(*l*)**
Receivers and receivership, **FRCVP 66**
Law governing capacity to sue or be sued, **FRCVP 17(b)**
Stay of judgment, **FRCVP 62(a)**
Recitals, judgments and decrees, **FRCVP 54(a)**
Records and recordation,
Authentication, **FRCVP 44(a)**
Business records, option to produce, interrogatories, **FRCVP 33**
Clerical mistakes, correction, **FRCVP 60(a)**
Clerks retention, **FRCVP 79(d)**
Depositions upon oral examination, order, manner, **FRCVP 30**
Discovery,
Initial disclosure, **FRCVP 26,**
Pretrial disclosure, **FRCVP 26**
Findings by the court, **FRCVP 52(a)**
Judgment not required to recite record of prior proceedings, **FRCVP 54(a)**
Magistrate judges, proceedings before, **FRCVP 72, 73**
Master, record of evidence, **FRCVP 53(c)**
Service, **FRCVP 5(a)**
Preliminary injunction hearing, evidence, **FRCVP 65(a)**
Proof, **FRCVP 44**
Recross questions, depositions upon written questions, **FRCVP 31**
Redirect questions, depositions upon written questions, **FRCVP 31**
Reduction of security, admiralty and maritime claims, actions in rem and quasi in rem, **FRCVP E(6)**
Redundancy, pleading, motion to strike, **FRCVP 12(f)**
Reference,
Default judgments, reference to determine account or amount of damages, **FRCVP 55(b)**
Magistrate judges, **FRCVP 73**
Master, **FRCVP 53(b, d)**
Notice of meeting, **FRCVP 53(d)**
Pleading, adoption by, **FRCVP 10(c)**
Referee included in term master, **FRCVP 53(a)**
Release,
Pleading, affirmative defenses, **FRCVP 8(c)**
Property, admiralty and maritime claims,
Actions in rem, notice, **FRCVP C(4)**
Actions in rem and quasi in rem, **FRCVP E(4, 5)**
Removal of property, admiralty and maritime claims, actions in rem, ancillary process, **FRCVP C(5)**

RULES OF CIVIL PROCEDURE
—Cont'd
Removed cases, application of rules, **FRCVP 81(c)**
Repleading, removed cases, **FRCVP 81(c)**
Replevin, availability of remedy, **FRCVP 64**
Reply, **FRCVP 7(a)**
Affidavits, motion for new trial, **FRCVP 59(c)**
Time, **FRCVP 12(a)**
Reports,
Discovery meeting, **FRCVP 26**
Masters, ante
Mental examinations, psychologists, **FRCVP 35**
Parties planning meeting, **FRCVP Form 35**
Physical and mental examinations, **FRCVP 35(b)**
Representative capacity,
Action on behalf of infant or incompetent, **FRCVP 17(c)**
Capacity to sue or be sued, determination, **FRCVP 17(b)**
Representatives, deceased party, making motion for substitution, **FRCVP 25(a)**
Requests,
Admissions, ante
Findings by court, **FRCVP 52(a)**
Instruction, **FRCVP 51**
Physical and mental examinations, prior to future reports of examiner, **FRCVP 35(b)**
Production of documents or things and entry upon land, **FRCVP 34(a, b)**
Form, **FRCVP Form 24**
Record of evidence by master, **FRCVP 53(c)**
Res judicata, pleading, affirmative defenses, **FRCVP 8(c)**
Responses,
Request for,
Discovery,
Extension of time, stipulations, approval of court, **FRCVP 29**
Production of documents or things and entry upon land, **FRCVP 34(b)**
Form, **FRCVP Form 24**
Restraining orders,
Form and scope, **FRCVP 65(d)**
Security, **FRCVP 65(c)**
Return,
Habeas corpus, writ or show cause order, time, **FRCVP 81(a)**
Marshal, admiralty and maritime claims, actions in rem and quasi in rem, execution, process, **FRCVP E(4)**
Reversal, judgment as a matter of law, alternative new trial motion, **FRCVP 50**

RULES OF CIVIL PROCEDURE
—Cont'd
Review. Appeal and review, generally, ante
Rules of evidence,
Amendments concerning, effectiveness, Congressional approval required and suspension of effectiveness, **28 § 2074 nt**
Sales,
Complaint in action for goods sold and delivered, form, **FRCVP Form 5**
Property, admiralty and maritime claims,
Actions in rem, ancillary process, **FRCVP C(5)**
Actions in rem and quasi in rem, **FRCVP E(9)**
Samples,
Entry upon land, generally, ante
Production of documents or things, generally, ante
Sanctions. Fines, penalties and forfeitures, generally, ante
Saturday,
Clerks of court, business hours, **FRCVP 77(c)**
Computation of time, **FRCVP 6(a)**
Scandalous matter, motion to strike, **FRCVP 12(f)**
Scire facias, abolition of writ, **FRCVP 81(b)**
Scope of rules, **FRCVP 1**
Seal,
Authentication of official record, **FRCVP 44(a)**
Summons, **FRCVP 4(a)**
Seamen, process, service, **FRCVP 4(c)**
Secretary of agriculture, applicability of rules, proceedings to review orders, **FRCVP 81(a)**
Secretary of embassy or legation, authentication of official record, **FRCVP 44(a)**
Secretary of interior, applicability of rules, proceedings to review orders, **FRCVP 81(a)**
Security,
Admiralty and maritime claims, ante
Injunctions, **FRCVP 65(c)**
Pending appeal, **FRCVP 62(c)**
Master not to retain report as security for compensation, **FRCVP 53(a)**
Proceedings against sureties, **FRCVP 65.1**
Return of vessel, admiralty and maritime claims, process and notice, **FRCVP D**
Stay of proceedings to enforce judgment, **FRCVP 62(b)**
Seizures,
Person or property, **FRCVP 64**
Property,
Admiralty and maritime claims, actions in rem and quasi in rem, expenses, **FRCVP E(4)**

RULES OF CIVIL PROCEDURE
—Cont'd
Seizures—Cont'd
Property—Cont'd
Service in action begun by seizure, **FRCVP 5(a)**
Service of summons not feasible, **FRCVP 4(n)**
United States vessels, exemptions, supplemental rules inapplicable, **FRCVP C(1)**
Sequestration, property of person disobeying judgment directing performance of specific acts, **FRCVP 70**
Service of process, **FRCVP 4 et seq.**
Admiralty and maritime claims, ante
Age, person serving, **FRCVP 4(c)**
Answer, time, **FRCVP 12(a)**
Answers or objections to requests for admission, **FRCVP 36(a)**
Appearance, **FRCVP 5(a)**
Attorney, pleading and other papers, **FRCVP 5(b)**
Certificate of service, filing, **FRCVP 5(d)**
Clerk of court, agent, proceeding against sureties, **FRCVP 65.1**
Contempt, subpoena of persons in foreign country, order to show cause, effecting in accordance with rules, **28 § 1783**
Defense, insufficiency, **FRCVP 12(b, h)**
Demand, **FRCVP 5(a)**
Jury trial, failure to serve as waiver, **FRCVP 38(d)**
Discovery, related papers, **FRCVP 5(a)**
How made, **FRCVP 5(b)**
In forma pauperis cases, **FRCVP 4(c)**
Interrogatories, **FRCVP 33(a)**
Failure of party to serve answers or objections, sanctions, **FRCVP 37(d)**
Joinder, persons needed for just adjudication, **FRCVP 19(a)**
Mail and mailing, ante
Motions, ante
Notice, ante
Numerous defendants, **FRCVP 5(c)**
Objections, depositions,
Errors and irregularities in notice, **FRCVP 32(d)**
Written questions, form, **FRCVP 32(d)**
Offer of judgment, **FRCVP 5(a), 68**
Orders of court, **FRCVP 5(a)**
Papers other than pleading and process, **FRCVP 5**
Personal service, notice, condemnation proceedings, **FRCVP 71A(d)**
Pleadings, **FRCVP 5**
Sanctions, **FRCVP 11**
Supplemental pleadings, **FRCVP 15(d)**
Time, **FRCVP 12(a)**
Proof of service, **FRCVP 4, 4.1**

RULES OF CIVIL PROCEDURE
—Cont'd
Service of process—Cont'd
Publication,
Condemnation proceedings, **FRCVP 71A(d)**
Depositions, taking before action, **FRCVP 27(a)**
Qualifications of servers, **FRCVP 4(c)**
Record on appeal, **FRCVP 5(a)**
Requests for,
Admission, **FRCVP 36(a)**
Production of documents or things and entry upon land, **FRCVP 34(a, b)**
Responses to requests for production of documents or things and entry upon land, **FRCVP 34(b)**
Seizure of property in action begun by, **FRCVP 5(a)**
Subpoena, **FRCVP 45**
Discovery, person in foreign country, **FRCVP 37(e)**
Substitution of parties, motion, **FRCVP 25**
Summons, post
Third-party practice, **FRCVP 14(a)**
Time,
Admiralty and maritime claims, garnishee or defendant, answer, **FRCVP B(3)**
Affidavits for new trial, **FRCVP 59(c)**
Answer, **FRCVP 12(a)**
Answers or objections to requests for admission, **FRCVP 36(a)**
Copies, answers and objections to interrogatories, **FRCVP 33**
Interrogatories, **FRCVP 33(a)**
Motion, **FRCVP 6(d)**
Summary judgment, **FRCVP 56(c)**
Notice,
Application for default judgment, **FRCVP 55(b)**
Hearing, **FRCVP 6(d)**
Objections to subpoenas, **FRCVP 45(c)**
Offer of judgment, **FRCVP 68**
Reply to counterclaim, **FRCVP 12(a)**
Requests for,
Admission, **FRCVP 36(a)**
Production of documents or things and entry upon land, **FRCVP 34(b)**
Responses to requests for production of documents or things and entry upon land, **FRCVP 34(b)**
Substitution of parties, motions, **FRCVP 25(a)**
United States marshals, service, **FRCVP 4(c)**
Warrant for arrest, admiralty and maritime claims, actions in rem, **FRCVP C(3)**
When required, **FRCVP 5(a)**

RULES OF CIVIL PROCEDURE
—Cont'd
Setoff and counterclaim, **FRCVP 7(a), 13**
Acquisitions after pleading, **FRCVP 13(e)**
Admiralty and maritime claims, actions in rem and quasi in rem, security, **FRCVP E(7)**
Compulsory counterclaims, **FRCVP 13(a)**
Default judgment against counterclaimants, **FRCVP 55(d)**
Dismissal, **FRCVP 41(a, c)**
Entry of judgment disposing of, **FRCVP 54(b)**
Exceeding opposing claim, **FRCVP 13(c)**
Form, **FRCVP Form 20**
Counterclaim for interpleader, **FRCVP Form 21**
Joinder, **FRCVP 18(a)**
Judgments and decrees, **FRCVP 13(i), 54(b)**
Maturing after pleading, **FRCVP 13(e)**
Mistake, defense, designation, **FRCVP 8(c)**
Omissions, **FRCVP 13(f)**
Permissive counterclaims, **FRCVP 13(b)**
Reply, **FRCVP 7(a)**
Time, service, **FRCVP 12(a)**
Requisites, **FRCVP 8(a)**
Separate trial, **FRCVP 42(b)**
Service of pleadings, numerous defendants, **FRCVP 5(c)**
Summary judgment, **FRCVP 56**
Third party practice, **FRCVP 14(a, b)**
Time, reply, United States, **FRCVP 12(a)**
United States, claim against, **FRCVP 13(d)**
Voluntary dismissal, **FRCVP 41(a)**
Setting aside,
Default judgments, **FRCVP 55(c)**
Findings of fact by court, **FRCVP 52(a)**
Judgments and decrees, ante
Verdict,
Errors not affecting substantial rights, grounds, **FRCVP 61**
Settlement. Compromise and settlement, generally, ante
Shareholders derivative actions, **FRCVP 23.1**
Show cause orders,
Admiralty and maritime claims, actions in rem, property, payment into court, **FRCVP C(5)**
Habeas corpus, generally, ante
Signatures,
Admiralty and maritime claims,
Actions in rem and quasi in rem, release, property, **FRCVP E(5)**
Affidavits, attachment and garnishment, **FRCVP B(1)**
Answer or objection to requests for admission, **FRCVP 36(a)**

RULES OF CIVIL PROCEDURE
—Cont'd
Signatures—Cont'd
Discovery disclosures, **FRCVP 26**
Electronic means, **FRCVP 5(e)**
Foreign official records, authentication, **FRCVP 44(a)**
Interrogatories, answers, **FRCVP 33**
Motions and other papers, **FRCVP 7(b), 11**
Objections, answers to interrogatories, **FRCVP 33**
Pleadings, ante
Summons by clerk, **FRCVP 4(a)**
Special,
Damages, pleading, **FRCVP 9(g)**
Masters, generally, ante
Matters, pleading, **FRCVP 9**
Verdict,
Entry of judgment, **FRCVP 58**
Requirement of return, **FRCVP 49(a)**
Specific performance, contract to convey land,
Complaint in action for, form, **FRCVP Form 12**
Disobedience to judgment directing execution of conveyance, **FRCVP 70**
State,
Official record, authentication, **FRCVP 44(a)**
Practice, execution and discovery in aid of, applicability, **FRCVP 69(a)**
State courts,
Prior actions or proceedings, depositions, effect on use, **FRCVP 32(a)**
State law,
Admiralty and maritime claims, attachment and garnishment, **FRCVP B(1)**
Condemnation under state law, application, **FRCVP 71A(k)**
Demand for jury trial made in accordance with, demand not needed after removal to district court, **FRCVP 81(c)**
Statement,
Claim, failure, defense, **FRCVP 12(b, h)**
Facts. Admissions, generally, ante
Lack of official record, admissibility, **FRCVP 44(b)**
Statute of frauds, pleading, affirmative defenses, **FRCVP 8(c)**
Statute of limitations, pleading, affirmative defenses, **FRCVP 8(c)**
Statutes,
Computation, time, **FRCVP 6(a)**
Maritime action in rem, **FRCVP C(1)**
Question arising under, jurisdiction, form of allegation, **FRCVP Form 2**
Right to intervene, conferring, **FRCVP 24(a)**

RULES OF CIVIL PROCEDURE
—Cont'd
Statutory condemnation proceedings, admiralty claims, applicability of supplemental rules, **FRCVP A**
Stay of proceedings. Supersedeas or stay, generally, post
Stenographers, report or transcript as evidence, **FRCVP 80(c)**
Stipulations,
Admiralty and maritime claims, actions in rem and quasi in rem, release, property, **FRCVP E(5)**
Depositions,
Taking, **FRCVP 29**
Upon oral examination, recordation, **FRCVP 30**
Discovery procedure, **FRCVP 29**
Dismissal, **FRCVP 41(a)**
Action for condemnation of property, **FRCVP 71A(i)**
Findings of master, **FRCVP 53(e)**
Jury verdict, unanimity and size of jury, **FRCVP 48**
New trial, stipulations extending time for filing, **FRCVP 59(c)**
Proceedings against sureties, **FRCVP 65.1**
Trial by court, **FRCVP 39(a)**
Striking of pleadings, **FRCVP 12(f)**
Discovery, sanction for failure to comply with order compelling, **FRCVP 37(b)**
Motions, more definite statement, **FRCVP 12(e)**
Third-party claim, **FRCVP 14(a)**
Subclasses, treatment, class actions, **FRCVP 23(c)**
Subject matter, lack of jurisdiction, defense, **FRCVP 12(b, h)**
Subpoena duces tecum,
Designation of materials in notice, taking deposition upon oral examination, **FRCVP 30**
Subpoenas, **FRCVP 45**
Depositions, ante
Discovery, person in foreign country, **FRCVP 37(e)**
Form, **FRCVP 45(a)**
Master, procuring attendance of witnesses, **FRCVP 53(d)**
Objections, **FRCVP 45(c)**
Production of documents, application of rules, **FRCVP 81(a)**
Protection of persons subject to, **FRCVP 45**
Substantial rights, disregard of error not affecting, **FRCVP 61**
Substitution. Parties, ante
Successors of deceased party, motion for substitution made by, **FRCVP 25(a)**
Summaries,
Business records, interrogatories, **FRCVP 33**
Foreign official records, evidence, **FRCVP 44(a)**

RULES OF CIVIL PROCEDURE
—Cont'd
Summary judgment, **FRCVP 56**
Motions, **FRCVP 12(b, c), 56**
Findings of fact and conclusions of law, **FRCVP 52(a)**
Pretrial conference, appropriateness and timing, **FRCVP 16(c)**
Time, dismissal of action, **FRCVP 41(a)**
Summons, **FRCVP 4**
Admiralty and maritime claims, actions in rem, **FRCVP C(3)**
Attachment and garnishment, **FRCVP B(1)**
Form, **FRCVP 4; Form 1**
Service of process, **FRCVP 4**
Action against officer or employee of U.S., **28 § 1391**
Application of rule to service of pleading, **FRCVP 5(a)**
Copy of complaint to accompany, **FRCVP 4(b)**
Third-party practice, **FRCVP 14(a, b)**
Time, limit for service, **FRCVP 4(m)**
Waiver, **FRCVP Form 1B**
Request for, **FRCVP Form 1A**
Third-party defendant, **FRCVP Form 22–A**
Sunday,
Clerks of court, business hours, **FRCVP 77(c)**
Computation of time, **FRCVP 6(a)**
Supersedeas or stay,
Accounting in action for infringement of patent, **FRCVP 62(a)**
Admiralty and maritime claims, actions in rem and quasi in rem, **FRCVP E(7)**
Process, **FRCVP E(5)**
Appeal without bond, United States or officer or agency thereof, **FRCVP 62(e)**
Appellate courts powers, **FRCVP 62(g)**
Approval of supersedeas bond by court, **FRCVP 62(d)**
Bonds (officers and fiduciaries),
Appeal and review, **FRCVP 62(d)**
United States, bonds in favor of, **FRCVP 62(e)**
Class action certification, stay pending appeal, **FRCVP 23(f)**
Discovery, failure to comply with order compelling, sanctions, **FRCVP 37(b)**
Execution, **FRCVP 62(b)**
Injunction judgment, **FRCVP 62(a)**
Judgments and decrees, proceedings to enforce, **FRCVP 62**
Payment of costs, previously dismissed action, **FRCVP 41(d)**
Receivership judgment, **FRCVP 62(a)**
State law, stay according to, **FRCVP 62(f)**

RULES OF CIVIL PROCEDURE
—Cont'd
Supersedeas or stay—Cont'd
Supersedeas bond, stay on appeal, **FRCVP 62(d)**
United States or agency thereof, stay in favor of, **FRCVP 62(e)**
Supplemental pleadings, **FRCVP 15(d)**
Supplemental process, actions in rem, **FRCVP C(3)**
Supplemental rules. Admiralty and maritime claims, generally, ante
Supplementary proceedings, execution, **FRCVP 69(a)**
Supplementation of responses, discovery, **FRCVP 26**
Supreme Court,
Power to prescribe, **28 § 2072**
Submission to Congress, effectiveness, **28 § 2074**
Sureties and suretyship,
Admiralty and maritime claims, actions in rem and quasi in rem, security, reduction, **FRCVP E(5, 6)**
Proceedings against, **FRCVP 65.1**
Surprise, relief from judgment on ground of, **FRCVP 60(b)**
Surveys of property or objects. Entry upon land, generally, ante
Tangible property, custody, admiralty and maritime claims, actions in rem and quasi in rem, **FRCVP E(4)**
Telecommunications, depositions upon oral examination, **FRCVP 30**
Temporary restraining orders, **FRCVP 65(b, c, e)**
Territorial limits, service, process, admiralty and maritime claims, actions in rem and quasi in rem, **FRCVP E(3)**
Territories, official record, authentication, **FRCVP 44(a)**
Testimony, taking, **FRCVP 43**
Tests,
Entry upon land, generally, ante
Production of documents or things, generally, ante
Results, report of examiner, physical and mental examinations, **FRCVP 35(b)**
Third-party practice, **FRCVP 14**
Admiralty and maritime claims, **FRCVP 14(a, c)**
Answer, service of third-party complaint, **FRCVP 7(a)**
Claim,
Dismissal, **FRCVP 41(c)**
Entry of judgment disposing of claim, **FRCVP 54(b)**
Joinder, **FRCVP 18(a)**
Judgment on one or more but fewer than all claims, **FRCVP 54(b)**
Requirements, **FRCVP 8(a)**
Separate trial, **FRCVP 42(b)**
Complaint,
Form, **FRCVP Form 22–A**

RULES OF CIVIL PROCEDURE
—Cont'd
Third-party practice—Cont'd
Complaint—Cont'd
Summoning person not an original party, **FRCVP 7(a)**
Third-party defendant,
Motion to bring in, form, **FRCVP Form 22–B**
Summons and complaint against, form, **FRCVP Form 22–A**
Third-party plaintiff, default judgment against, **FRCVP 55(d)**
Three-judge courts,
Conducting of proceedings, permitted by, **28 § 2284**
Injunction pending appeal, **FRCVP 62(c)**
Time, **FRCVP 6**
Acceptance, offer of judgment, **FRCVP 68**
Additional time for proceeding or act after service by mail, **FRCVP 6(e)**
Admiralty and maritime claims, ante
Admissions, request for, answers or objections, **FRCVP 36(a)**
Appeal and review, ante
Appearance by defendant, statement in summons, **FRCVP 4(a)**
Computation, **FRCVP 6(a)**
Third-party practice, **FRCVP 14(a, b)**
Depositions,
Taking, stipulations, **FRCVP 29**
Written questions, **FRCVP 31**
Discovery, **FRCVP 26**
Dismissal of action, prosecution not in name of real party in interest, **FRCVP 17(a)**
Effective date of amendment, **FRCVP 86**
Execution, time for issuing, **FRCVP 62(a)**
Extension of time, generally, ante
Filing papers after complaint, **FRCVP 5(d)**
Initial disclosures, discovery, **FRCVP 26**
Involuntary dismissal, **FRCVP 41(b)**
Meeting of parties on order of reference, **FRCVP 53(d)**
Motions, ante
Notice, ante
Objections, masters report, **FRCVP 53(e)**
Offer of judgment, **FRCVP 68**
Opposing affidavits, motion for new trial, **FRCVP 59(c)**
Physical and mental examinations, **FRCVP 35(a)**
Pleadings, ante
Return, habeas corpus, writ of or show cause order, **FRCVP 81(a)**
Rules, effective date, **FRCVP 86**
Service of process, ante
Summary judgment, **FRCVP 56(a)**

RULES OF CIVIL PROCEDURE —Cont'd
Time—Cont'd
Summons, time limit for service, **FRCVP 4(m)**
Supersedeas bond, time for giving, **FRCVP 62(d)**
Temporary restraining order, **FRCVP 65(b)**
United States agencies and officers, service, **FRCVP 4(i)**
Voluntary dismissal, **FRCVP 41(c)**
Waiver, service of summons, **FRCVP 4(d)**
Title,
Actions, pleading captions, **FRCVP 10(a)**
Judgment vesting title in another, **FRCVP 70**
Rules, **FRCVP 85**
Trade secrets,
Disclosure, subpoenas requiring, relief from, **FRCVP 45(c)**
Discovery, protective orders, **FRCVP 26**
Transcription, depositions upon oral examination, recording by non-stenographic means, **FRCVP 30**
Transcripts,
Master, filing of transcript of proceedings with report, **FRCVP 53(e)**
Stenographic transcript as evidence, **FRCVP 80(c)**
Treaties, depositions in foreign countries, **FRCVP 28**
Trial,
Assignment of cases for trial, **FRCVP 40**
Condemnation proceedings, **FRCVP 71A(h)**
Consolidation,
Actions for trial, **FRCVP 42(a)**
With preliminary injunction hearing, **FRCVP 65(a)**
Continuances, generally, ante
Depositions, use, **FRCVP 32(a)**
Inability of judge to proceed, **FRCVP 63**
Instructions to jury, generally, ante
Interrogatories, use, **FRCVP 33**
Jury, generally, ante
Magistrate judge, trial by consent, **FRCVP 73**
New trial, generally, ante
Open court, trial conducted in, **FRCVP 77(b)**
Preparation material, discovery exemption, **FRCVP 26**
Pretrial procedure, **FRCVP 16**
Separate trials,
Joinder of parties, **FRCVP 20(b)**
Judgment, counterclaim or cross-claim, **FRCVP 13(i)**
Order of court, **FRCVP 42(b)**

RULES OF CIVIL PROCEDURE —Cont'd
Trial—Cont'd
Separate trials—Cont'd
Pretrial conference, discussion of order, **FRCVP 16**
Third-party claim, **FRCVP 14(a, b)**
Subpoena for attendance, **FRCVP 45(a)**
Successor judges, **FRCVP 63**
Venue, generally, post
Verdict, generally, post
Voluntary dismissal before introduction of evidence, **FRCVP 41(c)**
Trial by court,
Advisory jury, **FRCVP 52(a)**
Dismissal motion by defendant, **FRCVP 41(b)**
Finding, **FRCVP 52**
Issues, **FRCVP 39(b)**
Motion by defendant for dismissal, **FRCVP 41(b)**
Opinion or memorandum of decision, **FRCVP 52(a)**
Partial findings, judgment on, **FRCVP 52**
Reference to magistrate judge, **FRCVP 72**
Reference to master, **FRCVP 53(b)**
Reports of master, **FRCVP 53(e)**
Stipulations, **FRCVP 39(a)**
Trusts and trustees,
Admiralty and maritime claims, ante
Prosecution of action, **FRCVP 17(a)**
Undertakings. Bonds (officers and fiduciaries), generally, ante
Unfair competition, complaint, form, **FRCVP Form 17**
Uniform numbering system, local rules, conformity, **FRCVP 83**
Unincorporated associations, **FRCVP 23.2**
Service of summons, **FRCVP 4(h)**
Shareholders, derivative actions, **FRCVP 23.1**
United States,
Action for benefit of another, bringing in name of United States, **FRCVP 17(a)**
Admiralty and maritime claims, actions in rem and quasi in rem, security, **FRCVP E(7)**
Answers, time, **FRCVP 12(a)**
Appeal, stay without bond or security, **FRCVP 62(e)**
Bond for stay of judgment against, **FRCVP 62(e)**
Claims against, final agency denial, applicability, counterclaims, **28 § 2675**
Costs imposed against, **FRCVP 54(d)**
Counterclaims,
Against, **FRCVP 13(d)**
Reply, time, **FRCVP 12(a)**
Depositions, **FRCVP 55(e)**

RULES OF CIVIL PROCEDURE —Cont'd
United States—Cont'd
Depositions—Cont'd
Oral examination, leave of court not required where person about to leave, **FRCVP 30**
Persons before whom taken, **FRCVP 28(a)**
Use in court proceedings, witness outside country, **FRCVP 32(a)**
Discovery, expenses and fees allowable, **FRCVP 37(f)**
Officers and employees,
Appeal, stay without bond or security, **FRCVP 62(e)**
Compelling giving of testimony, application of rules, **FRCVP 81(a)**
Definition, **FRCVP 81(f)**
Process, pleading, amendments, change of party, **FRCVP 15(c)**
Restraining order or preliminary injunction, security, **FRCVP 65(c)**
Tender of fees and mileage, delivery of copy of subpoena, **FRCVP 45(b)**
Time, service of answer or reply, **FRCVP 12(a)**
Official record, authentication, **FRCVP 44(a)**
Process, amendment of pleading, change of party, **FRCVP 15(c)**
Service of summons,
On United States, **FRCVP 4(i)**
Within United States, **FRCVP 4(e)**
Stay in favor of, **FRCVP 62(e)**
Subpoena,
Compelling giving of testimony, application of rules, **FRCVP 81(a)**
Tender of fees and mileage, **FRCVP 45(b)**
United States attorneys,
Process, amendment of pleading, change of party, **FRCVP 15(c)**
Service on, **FRCVP 4, 12(a)**
United States laws, preference of actions on trial calendar, **FRCVP 40**
United States Magistrate Judges. Magistrate Judges, generally, ante
United States marshals. Marshals, generally, ante
Vacation of judgments, judgment as a matter of law, alternative new trial motion, **FRCVP 50**
Venue,
Admiralty and maritime claims,
Limitation of liability, **FRCVP F(9)**
Treatment as civil action, **FRCVP 82**
Defense, improper venue, **FRCVP 12(b, h)**
Depositions,
Failure to comply with order compelling answer, sanctions in district where deposition taken, **FRCVP 37(b)**

RULES OF CIVIL PROCEDURE —Cont'd
Venue—Cont'd
Depositions—Cont'd
Use in court proceedings, witness outside of area, **FRCVP 32(a)**
Discovery, motion for order compelling, **FRCVP 37(a)**
Dismissal for improper venue, **FRCVP 41(b)**
Motion, form, **FRCVP Form 19**
Joinder of party, improper venue, **FRCVP 19(a)**
Objections, waiver due to waiver of service of summons, **FRCVP 4(d)**
Rules, effect, **FRCVP 82**
Verdict,
Civil docket, entry, **FRCVP 79(a)**
Directed verdict, generally, ante
General verdict,
Accompanied by answer to interrogatory, **FRCVP 49(b)**
Entry of judgment on, **FRCVP 58**
Judgment on jury verdict, form, **FRCVP Form 31**
Setting aside, harmless error, **FRCVP 61**
Special verdicts, **FRCVP 49(a)**
Unanimity of jurors, **FRCVP 48**
Verification,
Admiralty and maritime claims, actions in rem, **FRCVP C(6)**
Electronic means, **FRCVP 5(e)**
Vice consul, authentication of official record, **FRCVP 44(a)**
Voluntary dismissal, **FRCVP 41(b)**
Effect, **FRCVP 41(a)**
Time, **FRCVP 41(c)**
Waiver,
Defenses, **FRCVP 12(h)**
Jury, ante
Objections to depositions, errors and irregularities, **FRCVP 32(d)**
Physical and mental examination report, prior reports, privilege, effect, **FRCVP 35(b)**
Pleading, affirmative defenses, **FRCVP 8(c)**
Service of summons, **FRCVP 4, Form 1B**
Request, **FRCVP Form 1A**
Warrant for arrest. Arrest, ante
Withdrawal,
Admission, **FRCVP 36(b)**
Demand for jury trial, **FRCVP 38(d)**
Deposits in court, **FRCVP 67**
Offer of judgment, **FRCVP 68**
Witnesses,
Certified public accountant before master, statement of accounts as evidence, **FRCVP 53(d)**
Compelling testimony, application of rules, **FRCVP 81(a)**
Depositions, generally, ante
Discovery, generally, ante
Examination, master, **FRCVP 53(c)**

RULES OF CIVIL PROCEDURE —Cont'd
Witnesses—Cont'd
Master, proceedings before, **FRCVP 53**
Oaths and affirmations,
Affirmation in lieu of oath, **FRCVP 43(d)**
Powers of master, **FRCVP 53(c)**
Pretrial conference, number, limitation, **FRCVP 16(c)**
Recalling, successor judges, **FRCVP 63**
Writings,
Answer or objection, requests for admission, **FRCVP 36(a)**
Discovery procedure, stipulations, **FRCVP 29**
Motions, **FRCVP 7(b)**
Objections,
Depositions upon written questions, form, **FRCVP 32(d)**
Subpoena for inspection, **FRCVP 45(c)**
Physical and mental examinations, report of examiner, **FRCVP 35(b)**
Production of documents or things, generally, ante
Writs,
Abolished writs, **FRCVP 60(b)**
Admiralty and maritime claims, power of Supreme Court to prescribe rules for, **28 § 2072**
Applicability of rules, **FRCVP 81(a, b)**
Assistance, judgment directing delivery of possession, **FRCVP 70**
Execution, generally, ante
Habeas corpus, generally, ante
Power of Supreme Court to prescribe rules for, **28 § 2072**
Written interrogatories. Interrogatories, generally, ante
Written questions. Depositions, ante

RULES OF COURT
Advisory committees, appointment, functions relating to study of rules of practice, **28 § 2077**
Appearance personally or by counsel in U.S. Courts, **28 § 1654**
Bankruptcy Rules and Forms, generally, this index
Civil procedure for district courts. Rules of Civil Procedure, generally, this index
Courts of Appeals, this index
Criminal procedure for district courts. Rules of Criminal Procedure, generally, this index
District Courts, this index
Evidence. Rules of Evidence, generally, this index
Fees, sales, copies of published rules, **28 § 2077**
Free distribution, copies of rules, **28 § 2077**
Publication of, **28 § 2077**

RULES OF COURT—Cont'd
Rulemaking power of courts,
Public notice and comment, **28 § 2071**
Savings provision, **28 § 2071**
Rules of Civil Procedure, generally, this index
Rules of Criminal Procedure, generally, this index
Rules of Evidence, generally, this index
United States Court of Appeals for the Federal Circuit, this index
United States Court of Federal Claims, this index
United States Court of International Trade, this index
United States Tax Court, this index

RULES OF CRIMINAL PROCEDURE
Agreements, plea agreement procedure,
Sentencing guidelines, **28 § 994**
Federal Magistrate Judge. Magistrate Judges, generally, post
Judicial Conference of U.S.,
Power to recommend, **28 § 2073**
Magistrate judges,
Seal, **28 § 638**
Selection pursuant to standards of Judicial Conference of U.S., **28 § 631**
Separability of provisions respecting, **28 § 631 nt**
Supervision of administrative matters relating to, **28 § 604**
Surveys respecting number of appointments, locations of service and compensation, **28 § 633**
Temporary assignment from one judicial district to another in an emergency, **28 § 636**
Tenure, **28 § 631**
Training, function of Federal Judicial Center, **28 § 620**
Transcripts, civil or criminal proceedings, preparation where required by district court as in forma pauperis proceeding, **28 § 1915**
Trials, **28 § 636**
Proceeding or appellate review of proceeding, disqualification, applicability, submission prior to date of act, **28 § 455**
United States magistrates' name changed to, **28 § 631 nt**
Virgin Islands, district courts, appointment of, **28 § 631**
Waiver,
Disqualification, applicability, applicability, **28 § 455**
Rules of Evidence,
Amendments concerning, effectiveness, Congressional approval required and suspension of effectiveness, **28 § 2074 nt**
Searches and seizures,
Magistrate Judges, generally, ante

RULES OF CRIMINAL PROCEDURE
—Cont'd
Supreme Court,
Power to prescribe, submission to Congress, effectiveness, **28 § 2074**
United States Magistrate Judges. Magistrate judges, generally, ante

RULES OF EVIDENCE
Absence,
Declarant, hearsay rule exceptions, **FRE 804**
Mistake or accident, evidence of other crimes or wrongs showing, **FRE 404**
Accidents, absence of, evidence of other crimes or wrongs showing, **FRE 404**
Actions and proceedings, sexual assault or child molestation, relevancy of similar cases, **FRE 415**
Acts of Congress, self-authentication, **FRE 902**
Admiralty and maritime cases, application of rules, **FRE 1101**
Agencies,
Federal agencies and instrumentalities, generally, post
Amendments to rules, **FRE 1102**
Ancient documents or data compilations,
Authentication, **FRE 901**
Hearsay rule exception, **FRE 803**
Annulment, conviction of crime, impeachment of witnesses, effect, **FRE 609**
Appeal of criminal conviction, impeachment of witnesses, effect of pending appeal, **FRE 609**
Application of rules, **FRE 101, 1101**
Arrest warrants, application of rules, **FRE 1101**
Authentication of evidence, **FRE 901 et seq.**
Bail, application of rules, **FRE 1101**
Baptismal certificates, hearsay rule exception, **FRE 803**
Bases of opinions, opinion and expert testimony, **FRE 703**
Best evidence, **FRE 1001 et seq.**
Bias or prejudice, exclusion, prejudicial evidence, **FRE 403**
Books and papers,
Best evidence, **FRE 1001 et seq.**
Department or agency of U.S., inapplicability to cases, to which Rules apply, **28 § 1733**
Boundaries,
Judgment concerning, hearsay rule exception, **FRE 803**
Reputation, hearsay rule exception, **FRE 803**
Burden of proof, effect of presumptions, **FRE 301**
Character,
Methods of proving, **FRE 405**
Relevancy, **FRE 404**

RULES OF EVIDENCE—Cont'd
Character—Cont'd
Reputation concerning, hearsay rule exception, **FRE 803**
Witnesses, character of, **FRE 608**
Children and minors, molestation, relevancy of similar crimes, **FRE 414, 415**
Citation of rules, **FRE 1102**
Collateral matters, writing, recording or photograph concerning, extrinsic evidence of contents, **FRE 1004**
Commercial paper, self-authentication, **FRE 902**
Commercial publications, hearsay rule exception, **FRE 803**
Compensation and salaries, court-appointed experts, **FRE 706**
Competency. Witnesses, post
Compromise and settlement, relevancy, **FRE 408**
Confessions, determination of admissibility, hearing of jury, **FRE 104**
Confusing evidence, exclusion, **FRE 403**
Congress,
Approval required for effectiveness, **28 § 2074 nt**
Construction of rules, **FRE 102**
Contempt, application of rules, **FRE 1101**
Conviction of crime,
Judgment, hearsay rule exception, **FRE 803**
Witnesses, attacking credibility, **FRE 609**
Copies and duplicates,
Admissibility, **FRE 1003**
Books, records, of department or agency of U.S., admissibility, **28 § 1733**
Certified copies, public records, self-authentication, **FRE 902**
Credibility, preliminary determinations, evidence relevant to credibility, **FRE 104**
Crimes and offenses,
Conviction, attacking credibility of witness, **FRE 609**
Judgment of conviction, facts essential to sustain, hearsay rule exception, **FRE 803**
Other crimes or wrongs, relevancy, **FRE 404**
Cross-examination,
Preliminary matters, testimony by accused, **FRE 104**
Scope, **FRE 611**
Cumulative evidence, exclusion, **FRE 403**
Definitions. Words and phrases, generally, post
Domestic public documents, self-authentication, **FRE 902**
Duplicates and copies, admissibility, **FRE 1003**
Emotional condition then existing, hearsay rule exception, **FRE 803**
Errors and mistakes, rulings, effect, **FRE 103**

RULES OF EVIDENCE—Cont'd
Excited utterances, hearsay rule exception, **FRE 803**
Exclusion of witnesses, **FRE 615**
Expert witnesses. Opinion and expert testimony, generally, post
Extradition, application of rules, **FRE 1101**
Family history,
Judgment concerning, hearsay rule exception, **FRE 803**
Statements, hearsay rule exception, **FRE 804**
Family records, hearsay rule exception, **FRE 803**
Federal agencies and instrumentalities,
Books or records, admissibility, **28 §§ 1732, 1733**
Foreign public documents, self-authentication, **FRE 902**
Forfeiture by wrongdoing, hearsay rule, right to claim, **FRE 804**
Former testimony, hearsay rule exception, **FRE 804**
General history,
Judgment concerning, hearsay rule exception, **FRE 803**
Reputation, hearsay rule exception, **FRE 803**
Grand jury, application of rules, **FRE 1101**
Habits, relevancy, **FRE 406**
Handwriting, authentication, **FRE 901**
Hearsay, **FRE 801 et seq.**
Admissibility, **FRE 802**
Credibility of declarant, attacking and supporting, **FRE 806**
Definitions, **FRE 801**
Exceptions to rule,
Declarant availability immaterial, **FRE 803**
Declarant unavailable, **FRE 804**
Hearsay within hearsay, **FRE 805**
Residual exception, **FRE 807**
History,
Family history, statements, hearsay rule exception, **FRE 804**
Judgment concerning, hearsay rule exception, **FRE 803**
Reputation, hearsay rule exception, **FRE 803**
Identity and identification,
Authentication of evidence, **FRE 901 et seq.**
Other crimes or wrongs, introduction to show, **FRE 404**
Impeachment. Witnesses, post
Impending death, statement made under belief, hearsay rule exception, **FRE 804**
Indictment and information, inquiry into validity, jurors as witnesses, **FRE 606**
Instructions to jury,
Judicial notice, **FRE 201**
Limited admissibility of evidence, **FRE 105**

RULES OF EVIDENCE—Cont'd
Insurance, liability insurance, relevancy, **FRE 411**
Intent, evidence of other crimes or wrongs showing, **FRE 404**
Interpreters, witnesses, **FRE 603**
Judges, competency as witness, **FRE 605**
Judgments and decrees, conviction of crime, facts essential to sustain, hearsay rule exception, **FRE 803**
Judicial Conference,
  Power to recommend, **28 § 2073**
Judicial notice, **FRE 201**
Jury,
  Competency as witness, jurors, **FRE 606**
  Instructions,
    Judicial notice, **FRE 201**
    Limited admissibility of evidence, **FRE 105**
  Preliminary determinations, outside hearing of jury, **FRE 104**
  Rulings, outside hearing of jury, **FRE 103**
  Writings, recordings and photographs, proving contents, function, **FRE 1008**
Juvenile delinquents and dependents, conviction of crime, impeachment of witnesses, **FRE 609**
Knowledge, evidence of other crimes or wrongs showing, **FRE 404**
Leading questions, witnesses, **FRE 611**
Learned treatises, hearsay rule exception, **FRE 803**
Liability insurance, relevancy, **FRE 411**
Limited admissibility, instructions to jury, **FRE 105**
Lost or destroyed originals, other proof of contents, admissibility, **FRE 1004**
Market reports, hearsay rule exception, **FRE 803**
Marriage certificates, hearsay rule exception, **FRE 803**
Medical care and treatment,
  Payment of expenses, relevancy, **FRE 409**
  Statements concerning, hearsay rule exception, **FRE 803**
Mental condition then existing, hearsay rule exception, **FRE 803**
Mistakes and errors,
  Absence of, evidence of other crimes or wrongs showing, **FRE 404**
  Rulings, effect, **FRE 103**
Motive, evidence of other crimes or wrongs showing, **FRE 404**
Newspapers, self-authentication, **FRE 902**
Nolo contendere. Plea of nolo contendere, generally, post
Notice, evidence of other crimes or wrongs, intent to introduce, **FRE 404**
Offenses. Crimes and offenses, generally, ante

RULES OF EVIDENCE—Cont'd
Opinion and expert testimony, **FRE 701 et seq.**
  Bases of opinion, **FRE 703**
  Character evidence, methods of proving, **FRE 405**
  Court-appointed experts, **FRE 706**
  Facts or data underlying expert opinion, disclosure, **FRE 705**
  Lay witnesses, **FRE 702**
  Ultimate issue, opinion on, **FRE 704**
  Witnesses, evidence concerning, **FRE 608**
Opportunity, evidence of other crimes or wrongs showing, **FRE 404**
Original writing, recording or photograph, requirement, **FRE 1002**
Other crimes or wrongs, relevancy, **FRE 404**
Pardons, impeachment of witnesses, effect, **FRE 609**
Party opponents,
  Admissions or testimony, proof of contents of writings, recordings or photographs, **FRE 1007**
  Original writing or photograph in possession, extrinsic evidence of contents, **FRE 1004**
Past sexual history or predisposition, victims of sex offenses, relevancy, **FRE 412**
Periodicals, self-authentication, **FRE 902**
Personal history,
  Judgment concerning, hearsay rule exception, **FRE 803**
  Statements, hearsay rule exception, **FRE 804**
Personal knowledge, witnesses, competency, **FRE 602**
Personal or family history, reputation, hearsay rule exception, **FRE 803**
Photographs and pictures, best evidence, **FRE 1001 et seq.**
Physical condition then existing, hearsay rule exception, **FRE 803**
Plain error, notice by court, **FRE 103**
Plans and specifications, evidence of other crimes or wrongs showing, **FRE 404**
Plea of nolo contendere,
  Admissibility,
    Postponement of effective date of amendment, **28 § 2074 nt**
  Offer of, admissibility,
    Postponement of effective date of amendment, **28 § 2074 nt**
Pleas, relevancy, **FRE 410**
Prejudice or bias, exclusion of prejudicial evidence, **FRE 403**
Preliminary examinations, criminal cases, application of rules, **FRE 1101**
Preliminary questions,
  Evidence, **FRE 104**
  Facts, application of rules, **FRE 1101**
Preparation, evidence of other crimes or wrongs showing, **FRE 404**

RULES OF EVIDENCE—Cont'd
Present sense impressions, hearsay rule exception, **FRE 803**
Presumptions, **FRE 301**
  State law, application, **FRE 302**
Previous conviction of crime, hearsay rule exception, **FRE 803**
Prior inconsistent statements of witnesses, **FRE 613**
Privileges and immunities, **FRE 501**
  Application of rules, **FRE 1101**
  Existence, preliminary determination, **FRE 104**
Probation and parole, application of rules, **FRE 1101**
Procuring unavailability of witness, hearsay rule exception, **FRE 804**
Property interests, records and statements concerning, hearsay rule exception, **FRE 803**
Public records. Records and recordation, generally, post
Purpose of rules, **FRE 102**
Rape shield, victims of crime, past sexual history or predisposition, **FRE 412**
Recorded recollections, hearsay rule exception, **FRE 803**
Records and recordation,
  Absence of entry, hearsay rule exception, **FRE 803**
  Authentication, **FRE 901**
  Best evidence, **FRE 1001 et seq.**
  Copies and duplicates, admissibility, **FRE 1005**
  Department or agency of U.S., nonapplicability to cases, to which rules apply, **28 § 1733**
  Extrinsic evidence of contents, **FRE 1005**
  Hearsay rule exception, **FRE 803**
  Offers of evidence and rulings, **FRE 103**
  Self-authentication, **FRE 902**
Regularly conducted activities, records and recordation, hearsay rule exception, **FRE 803**
Rehabilitation certificate, witness convicted of crime, impeachment, **FRE 609**
Related writings, required introduction, **FRE 106**
Relevancy, **FRE 401 et seq.**
  Admissibility, **FRE 402**
  Character evidence, **FRE 404, 405**
  Compromise and settlement, **FRE 408**
  Conditioned on fact, preliminary determination, **FRE 104**
  Definition, **FRE 401**
  Habit, **FRE 406**
  Liability insurance, **FRE 411**
  Medical care and treatment, payment of expenses, **FRE 409**
  Pleas and plea discussions, **FRE 410**
  Prejudicial, confusing or cumulative evidence, **FRE 403**
  Routine practice, **FRE 406**

RULES OF EVIDENCE—Cont'd
Relevancy—Cont'd
Sex offenses, post
Subsequent remedial measures, **FRE 407**
Religion, impeachment of witnesses, **FRE 610**
Religious organizations and societies, records and recordation, hearsay rule exception, **FRE 803**
Remainder of writings, required introduction, **FRE 106**
Rendition, application of rules, **FRE 1101**
Reports,
Authentication, **FRE 901**
Public records and reports, hearsay rule exception, **FRE 803**
Reputation,
Character evidence, methods of proving, **FRE 405**
Witnesses, evidence concerning, **FRE 608**
Routine, relevancy, **FRE 406**
Rules of Civil Procedure, this index
Rules of Criminal Procedure, this index
Rulings on evidence, **FRE 103**
Scope of rules, **FRE 101**
Searches and seizures, warrants, application of rules, **FRE 1101**
Self-authentication of evidence, **FRE 902**
Sentence and punishment, application of rules, **FRE 1101**
Settlement and compromise, relevancy, **FRE 408**
Sex offenses,
Relevancy,
Child molestation, similar crimes, **FRE 414**
Civil cases, sexual assault or child molestation, similar crimes, **FRE 415**
Sexual assault, similar crimes, **FRE 413**
Victims past sexual behavior or predisposition, **FRE 412**
Specific instances of conduct,
Character evidence, methods of proving, **FRE 405**
Witnesses, evidence concerning, **FRE 608**
Statements against interest, hearsay rule exception, **FRE 804**
Subsequent remedial measures, relevancy, **FRE 407**
Summaries, writings, recordings and photographs, admissibility, **FRE 1006**
Summons, criminal cases, application of rules, **FRE 1101**
Supreme Court,
Power to prescribe, submission to Congress, effectiveness, **28 § 2074**
Suspension of effectiveness, **28 § 2071 nt**
Telecommunications, authentication, **FRE 901**

RULES OF EVIDENCE—Cont'd
Time,
Conviction of crime, impeachment of witnesses, limitation, **FRE 609**
Judicial notice, **FRE 201**
Title of rules, **FRE 1102**
Trade inscriptions, self-authentication, **FRE 902**
Ultimate issues, opinion and expert testimony, **FRE 704**
United States Court of International Trade, applicability to civil actions in, **28 § 2641**
Unobtainable originals, other proof of contents, admissibility, **FRE 1004**
Verdicts, inquiry into validity, jurors as witnesses, **FRE 606**
Victims of crime,
Character evidence, **FRE 404**
Sex offenses, past sexual behavior or predisposition, relevancy, **FRE 412**
Vital statistics, records and recordation, hearsay rule exception, **FRE 803**
Voices, authentication, **FRE 901**
Weight of evidence, preliminary determinations, evidence relevant to weight, **FRE 104**
Witnesses,
Calling and interrogation by court, **FRE 614**
Character evidence concerning, **FRE 404, 608**
Competency, **FRE 601 et seq.**
Judges, **FRE 605**
Jurors, **FRE 606**
Personal knowledge lacking, **FRE 602**
Conviction of crime, attacking credibility, **FRE 609**
Cross-examination, scope, **FRE 611**
Exclusion, **FRE 615**
Experts. Opinion and expert testimony, generally, ante
Hearsay, generally, ante
Impeachment,
Character evidence, **FRE 608**
Conviction of crime, **FRE 609**
Religious beliefs or opinions, **FRE 610**
Specific instances of conduct, **FRE 608**
Who may impeach, **FRE 607**
Interpreters, **FRE 603**
Leading questions, **FRE 611**
Mode, interrogation and presentation, **FRE 611**
Opinion and expert testimony, generally, ante
Opinion and reputation evidence concerning, **FRE 608**
Order, interrogation and presentation, **FRE 611**
Prior statements, examination concerning, **FRE 613**
Qualifications, preliminary determination, **FRE 104**

RULES OF EVIDENCE—Cont'd
Witnesses—Cont'd
Specific instances of witness conduct, **FRE 608**
Writing used to refresh memory, **FRE 612**
Words and phrases,
Court, application of rules, **FRE 1101**
Declarant, hearsay, **FRE 801**
Duplicate, best evidence, **FRE 1001**
Hearsay, **FRE 801**
Judge, application of rules, **FRE 1101**
Original, best evidence, **FRE 1001**
Photograph, best evidence, **FRE 1001**
Recording, best evidence, **FRE 1001**
Relevant evidence, **FRE 401**
Statement, hearsay, **FRE 801**
Unavailability as a witness, hearsay, **FRE 804**
Writing, best evidence, **FRE 1001**
Writings used to refresh memory, witnesses, **FRE 612**

RUTLAND, VT
District court, location, holding terms of, **28 § 126**

SAFETY
Railroads, this index

SAINT LOUIS, MO
Court of Appeals for Eighth Circuit, this index

SAINT PAUL, MN
Court of Appeals for Eighth Circuit, this index

SALARIES
Compensation and Salaries, generally, this index

SALES
Attached property in actions against delinquent postmasters and postal officers, employees, **28 § 2714**
Attorney General, procurement of law books, reference books, and periodicals, **28 § 525**
Bankruptcy, this index
Courts of appeals, rules of practice, **28 § 2077**
Customs Duties, generally, this index
Execution, goods taken on, without appraisal, **28 § 2005**
Internal Revenue Service, this index
International Trade, generally, this index
Judicial Sales, generally, this index
Notice, preparation, fee of U.S. marshal, **28 § 1921**
Real estate, private sale, order of court, **28 § 2001**
Rules of Civil Procedure, this index
Supreme Court decisions on reports, **28 §§ 412, 676**
United States marshal, fees, commissions, for property seized, levied on or attached, **28 § 1921**

SALT LAKE CITY, UT
United States District Court, location, **28 § 125**

SAMPLES
United States Court of International Trade, inspection by parties and counselors in civil actions, **28 § 2641**

SAND ISLAND
Judicial district of Hawaii, inclusion in, **28 § 91**

SAULT SAINTE MARIE, MI
District court held at, **28 § 102**

SAVINGS BONDS
United States Obligations, generally, this index

SCIENTIFIC ASSOCIATIONS, INSTITUTIONS OR ORGANIZATIONS
Attorneys' fees, award to party prevailing against U.S. or agency, applicability, **28 § 2412**

SCRANTON, PA
District court held at, **28 § 118**

SEALS (OFFICIAL SEALS)
Books of States, territories or possessions, evidence, **28 § 1739**
Continuance in action by U.S. against delinquents for public money, **28 § 2407**
Courts,
  Records and judicial proceedings of States, territories or possessions for evidence, **28 § 1738**
Director of Administrative Office of U.S. Court, **28 § 608**
Judicial Notice, this index
Justice Department, **28 § 502**
Patent and Trademark Office, this index
Possession of U.S.,
  Authentication of acts of legislature for evidence, **28 § 1738**
  Books or records of, evidence, **28 §§ 1738, 1739**
Process, **28 § 1691**
Record of States, territories or possessions, evidence, **28 §§ 1738, 1739**
State,
  Authentication of acts of legislature for evidence, **28 § 1738**
  Books or records of, evidence, **28 §§ 1738, 1739**
Territories,
  Authentication of acts of legislature for evidence, **28 § 1738**
  Books or records of territories, evidence, **28 §§ 1738, 1739**
United States Magistrate Judges, **28 § 638**
Writs, **28 § 1691**

SEAMEN
Appeal and review, fees and costs, prepayment unnecessary, **28 § 1916**
Costs,
  Court, prepayment unnecessary, **28 § 1916**
Fees, court, prepayment unnecessary, **28 § 1916**

SEARCHES AND SEIZURES
Attachment against delinquent postmasters and postal employees, officers, property removed from district, **28 § 2710**
Fees, U.S. marshal, **28 § 1921**
Interception of Wire, Oral, or Electronic Communications, generally, this index
Jurisdiction of district court, seizures not within admiralty or maritime jurisdiction, **28 § 1356**
Land, enforcement of forfeiture by libel proceedings, **28 § 2461**
Liability of person making, **28 § 2465**
Navigable waters, or high seas, forfeitures enforced in admiralty, **28 § 2461**
Return of seized property,
  To claimant, liability for wrongful seizure, **28 § 2465**
Rules of Civil Procedure, this index
United States Court of International Trade, this index
United States marshal,
  Fees, **28 § 1921**
Witness' property held, contempt for failure to respond to subpoena in foreign country, **28 § 1784**
Wrongful seizure, liability of officer, **28 § 2465**

SECOND AND SUBSEQUENT OFFENSES
Sentence and Punishment, this index

SECRET SERVICE
Counterfeiting, generally, this index
Federally insured financial institutions, fraud, criminal or unlawful activity, investigation and prosecution of, **28 § 509 nt**

SECRETARIAT OF UNITED NATIONS
United Nations, generally, this index

SECRETARIES
Circuit judges, appointment, **28 § 712**
Compensation and salaries,
  Court secretaries,
    Fixed by Director of Administrative Office of U.S. Courts, **28 § 604**
    Increase, **28 § 603 nt**
    Limitation, **28 § 604 nt**
  Director of Administrative Office of U.S. Courts to fix, **28 § 604**
  Supreme Court justices, **28 § 675**
District Judges, this index

SECRETARIES—Cont'd
Increase in limitations, compensation for secretaries of circuit and district court judges, **28 § 604 nt**
Judges,
  Bankruptcy courts, appointment, **28 § 156**
  Compensation, **28 § 604 nt**
Military Departments, this index

SECRETARY OF AGRICULTURE
Courts of Appeals, this index
Orders,
  Review, **28 § 2341 et seq.**
Packers, this index
Review,
  Orders, **28 § 2341 et seq.**
Special prosecutor, appointment, jurisdiction, powers to investigate and prosecute Federal crimes by, **28 § 592 et seq.**

SECRETARY OF AIR FORCE
Attorney General to advise, **28 § 513**

SECRETARY OF ARMY
Attorney General to advise, **28 § 513**

SECRETARY OF COMMERCE
Customs Duties, this index
Federal Legal Council, representatives designated by, **28 § 509 nt, EON 12146**
Special prosecutor, appointment, jurisdiction, powers to investigate and prosecute Federal crimes by, **28 § 592 et seq.**
United States Court of International Trade, this index

SECRETARY OF DEFENSE
See, also,
  Military Departments, generally, this index
Automated legal research and information system, coordination with Attorney General, availability to all Federal law offices, **28 § 509 nt, EON 12146**
Consultation,
  Office of Government Ethics, extension, time for filing financial reports for Armed Forces personnel in combat zones, **5, Ap 4, § 101**
Federal Legal Council, representatives designated by, **28 § 509 nt, EON 12146**
Special prosecutor, appointment, jurisdiction, powers to investigate and prosecute Federal crimes by, **28 § 592 et seq.**

SECRETARY OF EDUCATION
Special prosecutor, investigation and prosecution of Federal crimes by, appointment, powers, **28 § 592 et seq.**

SECRETARY OF ENERGY

Alaska Federal-Civilian Energy Efficiency Swap Act of 1980. Alaska, generally, this index

Federal Legal Council, representative designated by, **28 § 509 nt, EON 12146**

Special prosecutor, appointment, jurisdiction, powers to investigate and prosecute Federal crimes by, **28 § 592 et seq.**

SECRETARY OF HOUSING AND URBAN DEVELOPMENT

Special prosecutor, investigation by Attorney General of allegations of crime by before appointment, **28 § 591**

SECRETARY OF INTERIOR

Indians, this index

SECRETARY OF LABOR

Federal Legal Council, representatives designated by, **28 § 509 nt, EON 12146**

Special prosecutor, investigation by Attorney General of allegations of crime by before appointment, **28 § 591**

United States Court of International Trade, this index

SECRETARY OF NAVY

Attorney General to advise, **28 § 513**

SECRETARY OF SENATE

Journals,
- Evidence, certification, **28 § 1736**

SECRETARY OF STATE

Certification,
- Records or books of State, territory or possession, evidence, **28 § 1739**

Federal Legal Council, representatives designated by, **28 § 509 nt, EON 12146**

Special prosecutor,
- Appointment, jurisdiction, powers to investigate and prosecute Federal crimes by, **28 § 592 et seq.**
- Investigation by Attorney General of allegations of crime by before appointment, **28 § 591**

SECRETARY OF TRANSPORTATION

Orders, Maritime Act of 1981, orders in exercise of functions transferred under, subject to judicial review,
- Review, **28 § 2341**

SECRETARY OF TREASURY

District courts, judgment, interest on, calculation, rate, determinations concerning, **28 § 1961**

Federal Legal Council, representatives designated by, **28 § 509 nt, EON 12146**

SECRETARY OF TREASURY—Cont'd

Law enforcement,
- Training activities, overseas, **28 § 509 nt**

Overseas law enforcement training activities, **28 § 509 nt**

Payment,
- Judgment against U.S., exception, **28 § 2414**

United States Court of International Trade, this index

United States Obligations, generally, this index

SECRETARY OF VETERANS AFFAIRS

Federal Legal Council, representatives designated by, **28 § 509 nt, EON 12146**

SECRETARY OF WAR

Secretary of Army, generally, this index

SECRETS AFFECTING NATIONAL DEFENSE

Espionage, generally, this index

SECURITIES AND EXCHANGE COMMISSION

Chairman,
- Federal Legal Council, representatives designated by, **28 § 509 nt, EON 12146**

SECURITY

Action or proceeding by U.S., **28 § 2408**

Contempt of witness in foreign country failing to appear pursuant to subpoena, **28 § 1784**

Garnishment by U.S. in action commenced against corporation on security, **28 § 2405**

Pending or adjudicated cases, moneys paid into court, delivery to rightful owners upon security, **28 § 2041**

Removal of cases, security given prior to removal to remain valid and effectual, **28 § 1450**

Rules of Civil Procedure, this index

Seamen's suits, **28 § 1916**

Social Security, generally, this index

Stay of Proceedings, this index

Witnesses, want of security for appearances, compensation, **28 § 1821**

SECURITY INTEREST

Copyrights, motion pictures, transfer of ownership, collective bargaining agreements, **28 § 4001**

Real estate,
- Quieting title, inapplicability to actions involving claims against U.S., **28 § 2409a**

SEDITION

Insurrection and Sedition, generally, this index

SEEDS AND PLANTS

Plant Variety Protection, generally, this index

SEGREGATION

Civil Rights, generally, this index

Fair Housing, generally, this index

SEIZURES

Searches and Seizures, generally, this index

SEMICONDUCTOR CHIP PRODUCTS

District court, jurisdiction, mask work cases, **28 § 1338**

Jurisdiction, mask work disputes, **28 § 1498**

Protection of,
- Mask works,
  - Actions and proceedings involving, district court jurisdiction, **28 §§ 1338, 1400, 1498**

SEMINARS

United States Magistrate Judges, Judicial Center to conduct seminars for, **28 § 637**

SENATE

See, also, Congress, generally, this index

Actions and proceedings,
- Subpoena or order, enforcement or validity, jurisdiction, **28 § 1365**

Assistant Attorneys General, appointment, advice, **28 § 506**

Attorney General, appointment, advice, **28 § 503**

Bill referred to chief judge of U.S. Court of Federal Claims, jurisdiction, **28 § 1492**

Chief clerk of Senate succeeded by Assistant Secretary of Senate. Secretary of Senate, generally, this index

Committees,
- Defined, jurisdiction in Senate actions, **28 § 1365**

Conflicts of Interest, generally, this index

Congressional Committees, generally, this index

Courts of appeals,
- Additional judges, **28 § 44 nt**
- Appointment, additional circuit judgeships, advice and consent, **28 § 44 nt**
- Judges, appointment, advice and consent, **28 §§ 44, 44 nt**

Deposition, District Court for District of Columbia, jurisdiction, Senate action to require, **28 § 1365**

Deputies,
- Attorney General, appointment, advice, **28 § 504**

SENATE—Cont'd
Directors,
Offices of,
Government Ethics, appointment, advice and consent, **5, Ap 4, § 401**
Disclosure of Federal Campaign Funds, generally, this index
District court judges,
Additional judges, appointment, advice and consent, **28 § 133 nt**
Appointment, advice and consent, **28 § 133**
Standards and guidelines for merit selection of nominees for, notice of waiver, **28 § 133 nt**
District courts, jurisdiction, action to recover possession of office, exception, **28 § 1344**
Employees. Officers and employees, generally, post
Financial disclosure requirements of Federal personnel. Financial Disclosure, generally, this index
Government Ethics, Office of,
Director, appointment with advice and consent of, **5, Ap 4, § 401**
Outside income and employment, prohibition, applicability, **5, Ap 4, § 505**
Illinois, Southern District of, appointment of additional judge, advice and consent of, **28 § 93 nt**
Interrogatory, District Court for the District of Columbia, jurisdiction, Senate action to require, **28 § 1365**
Journals of Congress,
Evidence, **28 § 1736**
Judges or justices,
Deposit of salary and credit for service in, judicial survivors annuity fund, **28 § 376**
Retirement and pensions, disability, appointment of successor, advice and consent, **28 § 372**
Judicial Center, "service" as meaning service as Senator, retirement of Director, **28 § 627**
Notice,
Standards and guidelines for merit selection of nominees for district court judgeships, waiver, **28 § 133 nt**
Officers and employees,
Removal of action or prosecution against for act in discharge of duty, **28 § 1442**
Orders,
Enforcement, jurisdiction of District Court for District of Columbia, **28 § 1365**
Political Activities, generally, this index
Political contributions and expenditures. Political Activities, generally, this index

SENATE—Cont'd
President of Senate Pro Tempore, generally, this index
Presidential and Vice Presidential Electors, generally, this index
Production of documents, District Court for District of Columbia, jurisdiction, Senate action to secure, **28 § 1365**
Rulemaking power,
Financial disclosure requirements of Federal personnel, enactment as exercise of power, **5, Ap 4, § 101 nt**
Solicitor General, appointment, advice, **28 § 505**
Staff. Officers and employees, generally, ante
Subpoenas,
Enforcement,
Jurisdiction, District Court for District of Columbia, **28 § 1365**
United States attorneys, appointment, advice, **28 § 541**
Attorney General not to fill vacancy with person for whom senate has refused advice and consent, **28 § 546**
United States Court of Federal Claims, judges, appointment, advice and consent, **28 § 171**
United States Court of International Trade judges, appointment, advice and consent, **28 § 251**
United States Sentencing Commission, appointment of members, advice and consent, **28 § 991**
Virgin Islands, this index
Witnesses,
Testimony of, District Court for District of Columbia, jurisdiction, Senate action to secure testimony of, **28 § 1365**

SENIOR CITIZENS
Aged Persons, generally, this index

SENIORITY
Associate justices of the Supreme Court, **28 § 4**
Circuit judges, precedence and presiding at court, **28 § 45**
Courts of appeals judges, hearing of appeal remitted from Supreme Court because of absence of quorum of justices, **28 § 2109**
District judges, precedence, **28 § 136**
United States Court of International Trade judges, **28 § 253**
Chief judge, **28 § 258**

SENTENCE AND PUNISHMENT
See, also,
Crimes and Offenses, generally, this index
Fines, Penalties and Forfeitures, generally, this index

SENTENCE AND PUNISHMENT
—Cont'd
Aliens, this index
Attacking sentence, **28 § 2255; MAS 1 et seq.**
Answer, contents, **MAS 5**
Appeal and review, time, **MAS 11**
Civil procedure, federal rules, application, **MAS 12**
Criminal procedure, federal rules, application, **MAS 12**
Delayed or successive motions, **MAS 9**
Discovery, **MAS 6**
Evidentiary hearings, **MAS 8**
Expansion of record, **MAS 7**
Filing motions, **MAS 3**
Forms, **Foll. MAS 12**
Judges, preliminary consideration of motion, **MAS 4**
Magistrate judges, powers, **MAS 10**
Motions, **MAS 2**
Preliminary consideration by judge, **MAS 4**
Record, expansion, **MAS 7**
Scope of rules, **MAS 1**
Time for appeal, **MAS 11**
Attorneys,
Appointment, motion to vacate, set aside or correct sentence, Federal custody, **28 § 2255**
Excessive charges in tort claims against U.S., **28 § 2678**
Bank crime, major cases, **28 § 994 nt**
Children and minors,
United States Sentencing Commission, post
Cloning, wireless telephones, **28 § 994 nt**
Commitment, generally, this index
Congress,
Report, maximum utilization of resources, Federal prison population, Bureau of Prisons, **28 § 994**
United States Sentencing Commission, post
Counterfeiting, this index
Crime of violence, defined, violent crime control, protection for the elderly, **28 § 994 nt**
Crimes against the elderly, Sentencing Commission, guidelines, criteria, violent crime control, **28 § 994 nt**
Criminal Background Checks, generally, this index
Damages for unjust imprisonment, jurisdiction of U.S. Court of Federal Claims, **28 § 1495**
Detention, generally, this index
District court reporter or other individual designated to produce record, transcribing pleas, proceedings, in connection with sentence, **28 § 753**
District courts,
Rules governing Section 2255 proceedings (motion attacking sentence). Attacking sentence, generally, ante

SENTENCE AND PUNISHMENT
—Cont'd
Enhancement, child victims, second and subsequent offenses, **28 § 994 nt**
Escape, custody, civil commitment, **28 § 1826**
Explosives,
Use of to commit a felony, second offenses, amendment of guidelines by Sentencing Commission, **28 § 994 nt**
False,
Imprisonment, Tort Claims Act, exception of claim, **28 § 2680**
Fines, penalties and forfeitures,
Additional penalties, dangerous handling of controlled substances, **28 § 994 nt**
Controlled substances, dangerous handling, enhanced penalties, **28 § 994 nt**
Firearms, this index
Foreign countries,
Transfer of Offenders to or from Foreign Countries, generally, this index
Forgery, generally, this index
Fraud,
Older victims, sentencing guideline adjustments, review and report, **28 § 994 nt**
Telemarketing,
Guidelines, **28 § 994 nt**
Grand Jury, this index
Guidelines,
Fraud,
Telemarketing, **28 § 994 nt**
Telemarketing,
Fraud, **28 § 994 nt**
United States Sentencing Commission, post
Wireless telephones, cloning, **28 § 994 nt**
Habeas corpus,
Persons in custody under judgment, of State court, venue and jurisdiction, State containing 2 or more Federal judicial districts, **28 § 2241**
Proceeding, evidence, **28 § 2247**
Identification Documents, this index
Identity and identification,
Theft and assumption deterrence, **28 § 994 nt**
Imprisonment,
For debt,
Writ of execution, **28 § 2007**
Postsentence administration, generally, post
Institutes and joint councils on sentencing, **28 § 334**
Offenses provided with mandatory penalties, applicability to, **28 § 334 nt**

SENTENCE AND PUNISHMENT
—Cont'd
Interception of Wire, Oral, or Electronic Communications, generally, this index
Judicial conference of United States, consultation with on sentencing guidelines, **28 § 994**
Jury, this index
Limitation of action, motion to vacate, set aside or correct sentence, Federal custody, **28 § 2255**
Modification,
Term or condition of imprisonment, Sentencing guidelines, **28 § 994**
Motions,
Attacking sentence under 28 § 2255. Attacking sentence, generally, ante
To vacate, set aside or correct sentence, Federal custody, **28 § 2255**
Orders of court,
Restitution,
United States Sentencing Commission guidelines, instruction for promulgation, **28 § 994 nt**
Policy statements. United States Sentencing Commission, post
Postsentence administration,
Temporary release of prisoner, Sentencing guidelines, **28 § 994**
Pre-release custody,
Sentencing guidelines, **28 § 994**
Probation, generally, this index
Racketeering, generally, this index
Release, generally, this index
Restitution,
Orders of court, ante
Revocation,
Earned release credits, prisoners bringing malicious law suits, provisions, **28 § 1932**
Rules governing motions to attack sentence under 28 § 2255. Attacking sentence, generally, ante
Second and subsequent offenses,
Enhancement, **28 § 994 nt**
Second or successive application to vacate, set aside or correct sentence, Federal custody, **28 § 2255**
Sentencing Commission. United States Sentencing Commission, generally, post
Solicitation,
Minors to commit crime, Sentencing Commission, enhanced penalties, **28 § 994 nt**
Staff Director, United States Sentencing Commission, **28 § 995**
Standards, **28 § 334**
Statutory minimum,
Sentencing Commission, guidelines, **28 § 994 nt**

SENTENCE AND PUNISHMENT
—Cont'd
Supervised release after imprisonment,
Guidelines and policy statements of Sentencing Commission, applicability, **28 § 994**
Term,
Determination in sentencing guidelines, **28 § 994**
Telecommunications, this index
Telemarketing,
Fraud,
Guidelines, **28 § 994 nt**
Terrorists and Terrorism, this index
Time,
Motion to vacate, set aside or correct sentence, Federal custody, **28 § 2255**
United States Court of Federal Claims, this index
United States Sentencing Commission, **28 § 991**
Administrative Office of U.S. Courts, utilization of existing resources of, **28 § 995**
Annual report, Judicial Conference of the United States, Congress, President, **28 § 997**
Appropriateness, sentences other than imprisonment, recommendations, **28 § 994**
Attorney General, as member of commission, **28 § 991**
Bureau of Prisons, Congress, submission of analysis and recommendations, maximum utilization of resources, Federal prison population, **28 § 994**
Categories of offenses, establishment of, **28 § 994**
Chair, **28 § 991**
Compensation, **28 § 992**
Powers, duties, **28 § 993**
Children and minors,
Sexual abuse, exploitation, promulgation and amendment of guidelines, **28 § 994 nt**
Sexual crimes against, amendment of existing guidelines, penalty enhancement, **28 § 994 nt**
Solicitation to commit crime, **28 § 994 nt**
Commission, defined, **28 § 998**
Commissioner, defined, **28 § 998**
Compensation and salaries,
Members, **28 § 992**
Staff Director, **28 § 995**
Computers, use in sexual exploitation of children, increased penalties, **28 § 994 nt**
Congress,
Analysis, recommendation for legislation, **28 § 994**
Annual report to, **28 § 997**

SENTENCE AND PUNISHMENT
—Cont'd
United States Sentencing Commission
—Cont'd
Congress—Cont'd
Recommendations,
Raising or lowering grades, modification of penalties, **28 § 994**
Statutes, sentencing, penal, and correctional matters, **28 § 995**
Report, guidelines, **28 § 994**
Review study of guidelines to determine effectiveness, **28 § 994 nt**
Consecutive terms, imprisonment, policy limiting, **28 § 994**
Consultation, other Federal criminal justice representatives, **28 § 994**
Contracts, power to make, **28 § 995**
Cooperative agreements, power to enter into, **28 § 995**
Correctional or penal institutions, recommendations for changes in, **28 § 994**
Defendants, petitions, **28 § 994**
Elderly crime victims, applicable guideline range, criteria, violent crime control, protection for the elderly, **28 § 994 nt**
Emergency guidelines promulgation authority, expiration date, **28 § 994 nt**
Employment, power to, **28 § 995**
Federal agencies and instrumentalities, power to request information, data, and reports from, **28 § 995**
Federal interest computer, damage deterrent, guideline amendment, **28 § 994 nt**
Federal Judicial Center, utilization of existing resources of, **28 § 995**
Fine, component, Government cost, **28 § 994**
General Accounting Office to study guidelines, report to Congress, time limitation, **28 § 994 nt**
Guidelines,
Aliens, smuggling, transporting, harboring or inducing, **28 § 994 nt**
Amendment,
Certain offenses jeopardizing safety, of federally insured financial institution, **28 § 994 nt**
Children and minors,
Sexual abuse, exploitation, **28 § 994 nt**
Sexual crimes against, penalty enhancement, **28 § 994 nt**
Explosives used to commit a felony, second offenses, **28 § 994 nt**
Firearms, use by,
Counterfeiters and forgers, **28 § 994 nt**
Violent felons and serious drug offenders, **28 § 994 nt**

SENTENCE AND PUNISHMENT
—Cont'd
United States Sentencing Commission
—Cont'd
Guidelines—Cont'd
Amendment—Cont'd
Methamphetamines, trafficking, increased penalties, **28 § 994 nt**
Offenses involving smokeable crystal methamphetamine, **28 § 994 nt**
Sex offenses, safe streets for women, **28 § 994 nt**
Terrorist crimes, **28 § 994 nt**
Violent crimes and drug trafficking crimes involving use of semiautomatic firearms, **28 § 994 nt**
Changes needed, Congress to determine, **28 § 994 nt**
Common carriers, operation under influence of alcohol or drugs, **28 § 994 nt**
Computers, use in sexual exploitation of children, increased penalties, **28 § 994 nt**
Congress, report on operation of system, problems, submittal to, **28 § 994 nt**
Courts and probation system, distribution to, **28 § 994**
Crack cocaine, enhanced sentences, provisions, **28 § 994 nt**
Crimes against the elderly, applicable range, criteria, violent crime control, **28 § 994 nt**
Defined, **28 § 998**
Disparity, **28 § 994**
Drug free truck stops and safety rest areas, **28 § 994 nt**
Duties, **28 § 994**
Effectiveness, Congress to determine, **28 § 994 nt**
Emergency guidelines promulgation authority, expiration date, **28 § 994 nt**
Fraud, older victims, adjustments, review and report, **28 § 994 nt**
General Accounting Office, report on operation of system, problems, submittal to, **28 § 994 nt**
Identity theft and assumption deterrence, **28 § 994 nt**
Justice Department, report on operation of system, problems, submittal to, **28 § 994 nt**
Petition filed by defendant, requesting modification of, **28 § 994**
Promulgation and distribution, **28 § 994**
Offenses jeopardizing safety, of federally insured financial institution, **28 § 994 nt**
Sentencing enhancements, hate crimes, **28 § 994 nt**

SENTENCE AND PUNISHMENT
—Cont'd
United States Sentencing Commission
—Cont'd
Guidelines—Cont'd
Reinstatement of parole system and Parole Commission extended, Congress to determine, **28 § 994 nt**
Reports, **28 §§ 994, 994 nt**
Sexual abuse, exploitation, of children, promulgation and amendment of guidelines, **28 § 994 nt**
Solicitation of minor to commit crime, **28 § 994 nt**
Statutory minimum application limitations, authority, **28 § 994 nt**
Study of, General Accounting Office shall undertake, report to Congress, **28 § 994 nt**
Transportation of children, intent to engage in criminal sexual activity, increased penalties, **28 § 994 nt**
Use of controlled substance with intent to commit crime of violence or rape, submission of sentencing guidelines to Congress, **28 § 994 nt**
Victim restitution, **28 § 994 nt**
Hearings, power to hold, **28 § 995**
Identity theft and assumption deterrence,
Guidelines, **28 § 994 nt**
Imprisonment, length or term of, factors, **28 § 994**
Incremental penalties, guidelines, **28 § 994**
Judicial Conference of the United States,
Annual report to, **28 § 997**
Recommendation of judges, **28 § 991**
Juvenile delinquents, study, feasibility of developing guidelines for disposition of, **28 § 995**
Leases, power to enter into, **28 § 995**
Legal advice, retention of private attorneys to provide, power respecting, **28 § 995**
Maximum and substantial terms of imprisonment, certain offenses, **28 § 994**
National cemetery, defined, veterans' cemetery protection, **28 § 994 nt**
Offenses, categories of, establishment, **28 § 994**
Officers and employees,
Exemptions, from provisions of law, **28 § 996**
Penal or correctional facilities, changes in, **28 § 994**
Petitions, filing by defendant, requesting modification of guidelines, **28 § 994**

SENTENCE AND PUNISHMENT
—Cont'd
United States Sentencing Commission
—Cont'd
Petty offenses, sentences imposed for, exceptions, report, judge, sentence information, **28 § 994**
Policy statements,
Courts and probation system, distribution to, **28 § 994**
Offenses, **28 § 994**
Statutory minimum application limitations, authority, **28 § 994 nt**
Powers of, **28 § 995**
President of U.S.,
Appointment, members, **28 § 991**
Report to, **28 § 997**
Probation officers, power to monitor performance of, **28 § 995**
Publication, data, **28 § 995**
Quorum, **28 § 995**
Removal, members, **28 § 991**
Reports,
Annual report, **28 § 995**
Congress,
Amendment, guidelines, **28 § 994**
Emergency guidelines promulgation authority, expiration date, **28 § 994 nt**
Guideline system, time limitation, **28 § 994 nt**
Judges, submission to, **28 § 994**
Research and development program, establishment of, **28 § 995**
Residence requirement waived for members, **28 § 992**
Rules and regulations,
Defined, **28 § 998**
Duties, guidelines relating to, **28 § 994**
Emergency guidelines promulgation authority, expiration date, **28 § 994 nt**
Power to promulgate, **28 § 995**
Semiautomatic firearm, defined, amendment of guidelines for crimes involving use of, **28 § 994 nt**
Seminars, workshops, conduct of, **28 § 995**
Senate, advice and consent of members, **28 § 991**
Sentence reduction, extraordinary and compelling reasons, **28 § 994**
Service,
Continuation by voting member with expired term, **28 § 992**
Temporary and intermittent, procure for, **28 § 995**
Sexual abuse, amendment of existing guidelines, penalty enhancement, safe streets for women, violent crime control, **28 § 994 nt**
Sexual crimes against children, amendment of existing guidelines, penalty enhancement, **28 § 994 nt**

SENTENCE AND PUNISHMENT
—Cont'd
United States Sentencing Commission
—Cont'd
Solicitation of minor to commit crime, **28 § 994 nt**
Staff, **28 § 996**
Staff Director,
Compensation and salary, **28 § 995**
Powers, duties, **28 § 996**
Substantial or maximum terms of imprisonment, certain offenses, **28 § 994**
Terms of office, members, **28 § 992**
Veterans' cemetery protection, property offenses, enhanced penalties, **28 § 994 nt**
Vice chairs,
Appointment, members, **28 § 991**
Compensation, **28 § 992**
Victim impact statements, intellectual property crimes, submission, **28 § 994**
Witnesses, power to call, **28 § 995**
Veterans' cemetery protection, amendment of guidelines by Sentencing Commission, **28 § 994 nt**
Victim impact statements, intellectual property crimes, submission, **28 § 994**
Violent Crime Control and Law Enforcement, generally, this index
Wireless telephones, cloning, **28 § 994 nt**

SENTENCING GUIDELINES ACT OF 1986
Generally, **28 §§ 1 nt, 994**

SENTENCING REFORM ACTS AND AMENDMENTS
Generally, **28 § 994**
Sentence and Punishment, generally, this index

SERIAL KILLINGS
Child Abduction and Serial Murder Investigative Resources Center, **28 § 531 nt**
Investigations and investigators, **28 § 540B**

SERVICE OF PROCESS
Agents,
Patent infringement action with defendant not resident, **28 § 1694**
Attachment,
Delinquent postmasters and postal officers, employees, **28 § 2716**
Fees of U.S. marshal, **28 § 1921**
Bankruptcy Rules and Forms, this index
Capias, fees of U.S. marshal for serving, **28 § 1921**
Complaint,
Action against officer or employee of U.S., **28 § 1391**

SERVICE OF PROCESS—Cont'd
Convention,
Service Abroad of Judicial and Extrajudicial Documents in Civil or Commercial Matter, **FRCVP 4 nt**
Taking of Evidence Abroad in Civil or Commercial Matters, **28 § 1781 nt**
Corporations, stockholders, derivative action, **28 § 1695**
Federal Debt Collection, this index
Foreign states, jurisdictional immunities, **28 § 1608**
Forma pauperis, proceedings in, **28 § 1915**
Interpleader action, **28 § 2361**
Process servers, private, employment by U.S. attorneys, **28 § 550**
Review, orders, certain Federal agencies, petition, **28 § 2344**
Rules of Civil Procedure, this index
Stockholder's derivative action, **28 § 1695**
Subpoena,
Fees of U.S. marshal, **28 § 1921**
National or resident of U.S. in foreign country, **28 § 1783**
Patent infringement action, **28 § 1694**
Summons, generally, this index
Tax liens,
United States as party, actions to quiet title, foreclose, **28 § 2410**
Tort claims against U.S., **28 § 2679**
United States attorney, State court action involving property in which U.S. has lien, **28 § 2410**
United States Court of International Trade, this index
United States Marshals Service, this index
Warrant fees of U.S. marshal, **28 § 1921**
Writs, fees of U.S. marshal, **28 § 1921**

SESSIONS
Courts of appeals, **28 §§ 46, 48**
District Courts, this index
Powers of courts unrestricted by, **28 § 452**

SET-OFF AND COUNTERCLAIM
Claims by U.S. against opposing or third parties where time barred, **28 § 2415**
Foreign states, jurisdictional immunities, **28 § 1607**
Jurisdiction, district court, U.S. as defendant, **28 § 1346**
Rules of Civil Procedure, this index
United States, this index
United States Court of Federal Claims, this index

SETTLEMENT
Compromise and Settlement, generally, this index

SEVERANCE OF CASES
United States Court of International Trade, prescribing rules governing, **28 § 2633**

SEX
Court of appeals, district court and bankruptcy court judges, nominees for appointment, selection not affected by, **28 § 44 nt**
Federal judgeships, nomination of individuals for without regard to, Congressional recommendations, **28 § 133 nt**
Jurors, exclusion from service of, discrimination prohibited, **28 § 1862**
Jury service, discrimination in selecting persons for prohibited, remedies, **28 § 1867**

SEX OFFENSES
Rules of Evidence, this index

SEXUAL ABUSE
Children and minors,
Penalty enhancement, authority of U.S. Sentencing Commission to amend existing guidelines, **28 § 994 nt**
Promulgation and amendment of sentencing guidelines, U.S. Sentencing Commission, **28 § 994 nt**
Victims, enhancement, **28 § 994 nt**
Computers,
Children and minors,
Sentence enhancement, **28 § 994 nt**
Harassment. Sex, generally, this index
Repeat offenders, enhanced penalties,
Sentencing guidelines, amendment, authority of Sentencing Commission, **28 § 994 nt**
Sentence and punishment,
Children and minors,
Victims, enhancement, **28 § 994 nt**
Victims,
Children and minors,
Sentence enhancement, **28 § 994 nt**

SEXUAL EXPLOITATION
Children and Minors, this index

SEXUAL ORIENTATION
Defined, hate crimes, **28 § 534 nt**

SHARES AND SHAREHOLDERS
Stock and Stockholders, generally, this index

SHELLFISH
Oysters, generally, this index

SHIPS AND SHIPPING
See, also, Vessels, generally, this index
Admiralty, generally, this index
Coast Guard, generally, this index
Coasting Trade, generally, this index
Customs Duties, generally, this index
Ferries, generally, this index

SHIPS AND SHIPPING—Cont'd
Liability,
Loss or damage to property determined by bill of lading or receipt, amount in controversy for district court jurisdiction, **28 § 1337**
Liens and incumbrances. Maritime Liens, generally, this index
Manning,
Vessels. Seamen, generally, this index
Maritime Liens, generally, this index
Maritime Transactions, generally, this index
Port of Entry, generally, this index
Seamen, generally, this index
Stay of execution of process in rem issued in admiralty, **28 § 2464**

SHORTHAND RECORDING
District courts, sessions of court and other proceedings, recording by, **28 § 753**

SHOW CAUSE ORDERS
Orders to Show Cause, generally, this index

SICKNESS INSURANCE
Health Insurance, generally, this index

SIGNATURES
Attorney General, requisitions for advance or payment of moneys, **28 § 523**
Clerks of courts, writs and process issuing from court, **28 § 1691**
Convention on the Taking of Evidence Abroad in Civil or Commercial Matters, party to, **28 § 1781 nt**
Copyrights, generally, this index
Habeas corpus, application for writ, **28 § 2242**
Rules of Civil Procedure, this index

SITES
National Cemeteries, generally, this index

SLAVERY
Involuntary Servitude, generally, this index
Race, Color, And Previous Condition Of Servitude, generally, this index

SLOVAKIA
Czechoslovakia, generally, this index

SMALL BUSINESS ADMINISTRATION
Patents, generally, this index

SMALL BUSINESSES
Loans,
Veterans, generally, this index

SOCIAL SECURITY
Child's home State, defined, full faith and credit for child support order, **28 § 1738B**

SOCIAL SECURITY—Cont'd
Federal old-age, survivors and disability insurance benefits,
Attorneys,
Fees,
Applicability to awards under certain other administrative proceedings, **28 § 2412 nt**
Court proceedings, determination, attorneys' fees, representation of claimants,
Applicability to awards under certain other administrative proceedings, **28 § 2412 nt**
Fees,
Attorneys, representation of claimants,
Applicability to awards in certain other administrative proceedings, **28 § 2412 nt**
Health Insurance for Aged and Disabled, generally, this index

SOCIETIES
Associations and Societies, generally, this index

SOLICITATION
Children and minors, commission of crime, sentence enhancement, **28 § 994 nt**

SOLICITOR GENERAL
Justice Department, this index

SOUND RECORDINGS OR REPRODUCTIONS
Copyrights, generally, this index
District courts, sessions and other proceedings recorded by, **28 § 753**

SOUTH CAROLINA
See, also, States, generally, this index
Bankruptcy judges, appointment, number in judicial district, **28 § 152**
District courts,
Cities, held at, **28 § 121**
Judges,
Additional, **28 § 133 nt**
Appointment, additional judges, advice and consent, **28 § 133 nt**
Number, **28 § 133**
Places of holding, **28 § 121**
Judicial circuit of U.S., **28 § 41**
Judicial districts, **28 § 121**
Bankruptcy provisions, applicability of certain amendments to, **28 § 581 nt**
Number of district judges, **28 § 133**
United States trustees of judicial districts, appointment, **28 § 581**

SOUTH DAKOTA
See, also, States, generally, this index
Bankruptcy judges, appointment, number in judicial district, **28 § 152**
District courts,
Cities, held at, **28 § 122**

SOUTH DAKOTA—Cont'd
District courts—Cont'd
Judges,
Additional, **28 § 133 nt**
Number, **28 § 133**
Places of holding, **28 § 122**
Judicial circuit of U.S., **28 § 41**
Judicial districts, **28 § 122**
Number of district judges, **28 § 133**
United States trustees of judicial districts, appointment, **28 § 581**

SOVEREIGN IMMUNITY
Indians, generally, this index

SPEAKER OF THE HOUSE OF REPRESENTATIVES
Federal Judicial Center Foundation, appointment of members to, **28 § 629**

SPECIAL COUNSEL, OFFICE OF
Senior interagency group Chairman, **28 § 509 nt**

SPECIAL GOVERNMENT EMPLOYEES
Conflicts of Interest, this index

SPECIAL PROSECUTOR
Independent Counsel, generally, this index

SPECIAL TERMS
Supreme Court, **28 § 2**

SPECIALTIES
Jury trial in actions to recover forfeiture, **28 § 1874**

SPECIFICATIONS
Plans and Specifications, generally, this index

SPEECH LOSS OR DISABILITY
Court Interpreters Act, applicability of provisions to hearing impaired persons also suffering from, **28 § 1827**

SPEECHES
Government officers and employees, honorarium, prohibited, **5, Ap 4, § 501**

SPEEDY TRIAL
Trial, this index

SPIES
Espionage, generally, this index

SPOUSE
Husband and Wife, generally, this index

SPYING
Espionage, generally, this index

STATE, SECRETARY OF
Secretary of State, generally, this index

STATE COURTS
Appeals to Supreme Court,
Criminal cases, **28 § 2101**
Priority of criminal cases, **28 § 2102**
Bankruptcy, this index
Certified or registered mail, service of process on U.S. in proceedings in which it has lien on property, **28 § 2410**
Certiorari,
Records and proceedings on removal of case, **28 § 1447**
Review by Supreme Court, decision involving validity of State statute, **28 § 1257**
State courts,
Decision involving validity of State statute, **28 § 1257**
Time, **28 § 2101**
Clerks of courts,
Copy of order of remand mailed to clerk, **28 § 1447**
Removal of case,
Duties, **28 §§ 1446, 1447**
Failure of clerk to supply records and proceedings, **28 § 1449**
Procedure on, **28 § 1446**
Contract Disputes Act of 1978, judgments against U.S., payment, exception, **28 § 2414**
Defined, to include Superior Court of the District of Columbia, removal of cases from State courts to district courts, **28 § 1451**
Habeas corpus proceedings,
Exhaustion of State court remedies, **28 § 2254**
Factual determinations and records, Federal court proceedings, **28 § 2254**
Persons in custody under judgment, venue and jurisdiction, State containing two or more Federal judicial districts, **28 § 2241**
State custody, remedies in Federal courts, **28 §§ 2244, 2254**
Stay of proceedings on pendency of, **28 § 2251**
Judgments, against U.S., payment, **28 § 2414**
Judicial proceedings, proving or admitting in other courts, authentication, entitlement to full faith and credit, **28 § 1738**
Marshal, removal of case, custody of defendant, **28 § 1446**
Officers and employees,
Exemption from jury service, **28 § 1863**
Priority of criminal cases on appeal from, **28 § 2102**
Process, service on U.S. in proceeding in which it has lien on property, **28 § 2410**
Records and recordation,
Evidence, **28 § 1738**

STATE COURTS—Cont'd
Records and recordation—Cont'd
Failure of court to supply records and proceedings on removal of case, **28 § 1449**
Proving or admitting in other courts, authentication, entitlement to full faith and credit, **28 § 1738**
Supplied by affidavit or otherwise on removal, **28 § 1449**
Removal of cases to Federal courts. Removal of Cases or Causes, generally, this index
Review by Supreme Court, **28 § 1257**
Manner of taking, **28 § 2104**
Stay of proceedings,
Injunction, **28 § 2283**
Pendency of habeas corpus proceedings, **28 § 2251**
Tax liens, U.S. as party, actions to quiet title, foreclose, service of process, **28 § 2410**
United States,
Interests in pending suits, attending to, **28 § 517**
Lien on property affected by action, **28 § 2410**

STATE DEPARTMENT
See, also, Executive Departments, generally, this index
Consuls. Foreign Service, generally, this index
Espionage laws, violations, report of and assistance to FBI, investigations of persons employed by or assigned to U.S. diplomatic missions abroad, **28 § 533 nt**
Investigations,
Regarding official matters, appointment, officials, **28 § 533**
Letter rogatory or request, transmittal of, **28 § 1781**

STATE JUSTICE INSTITUTE
Generally, **28 § 620**
Judicial Center to establish, research and programs concerning administration of justice, functions, **28 § 620**

STATE LAWS
Appeal to Supreme Court, state court decisions, **28 § 1257**
District courts, judgments, execution levied for interest on, **28 § 1961**
Evidence, **28 § 1738**
Federal Bureau of Investigation, exchange of identification records with State, officials, use, funds provided for expenses, **28 § 534 nt**
Forfeitures, Federal equitable share of, deposit in Justice Department Assets Forfeiture Fund, **28 § 524**
Injunction against enforcement, three-judge court, procedure, **28 § 2284**

STATE LAWS—Cont'd
Repugnant to treaty, constitution or U.S. laws, review of State decision by Supreme Court, 28 § **1257**
Review by Supreme Court of State decision involving validity, 28 § **1257**
Rules of decision, exception, 28 § **1652**
Senate subpoena or order to entity acting under color of, enforcement in District Court for District of Columbia, 28 § **1365**
Trustees, receivers, appointed in U.S. courts, management, of property according to State laws in which property situated, 28 § **959**

STATE OFFICERS AND EMPLOYEES
States, this index

STATES
Actions and proceedings,
 Agencies, rate orders by, jurisdiction of district court, 28 § **1342**
 Original and exclusive jurisdiction of Supreme Court,
  Action against citizens of another State or aliens, 28 § **1251**
  Controversies between U.S. and State, 28 § **1251**
 Quieting title, against United States, 28 § **2409a**
 State laws as rules of decision, 28 § **1652**
 Taxation, jurisdiction of district court, 28 § **1341**
Aliens,
 Supreme Court jurisdiction of proceedings against, 28 § **1251**
Apportionment,
 Three-judge court, action challenging constitutionality of apportionment of statewide legislative body, 28 § **2284**
Attorney General,
 Certification, constitutionality of State statute, intervention, 28 § **2403**
 Habeas corpus proceedings, notice to prior to hearing of habeas corpus as to person in custody of State, 28 § **2252**
 Three-judge court, notice of hearing by, 28 § **2284**
Citizens of another State, Supreme Court jurisdiction of actions or proceedings against, 28 § **1251**
Claims,
 Against U.S., founded on Act of Congress, jurisdiction of U.S. Court of Federal Claims, 28 § **1491**
Community Development, this index
Constitution of United States,
 Certification, constitutionality of State statute, intervention, 28 § **2403**
Courts. State Courts, generally, this index

STATES—Cont'd
Criminal and other identification records, exchange with authorized officials, 28 § **534**
Decrees. Judgments and decrees, generally, post
District court jurisdiction, diversity of citizenship, 28 § **1332**
Election officials, "voter registration lists" as meaning official records maintained by, jury selection, 28 § **1869**
Executions in favor of U.S., 28 § **2413**
Federal Aid, generally, this index
Federal Bureau of Investigation, exchange of identification records with officials, use, funds provided for expenses, 28 § **534 nt**
Firemen, exemption from jury service, 28 § **1863**
Indian Lands and Reservations, this index
Indians,
 Civil jurisdiction in actions to which Indians are parties, 28 § **1360**
 Reservations, jurisdiction of offenses,
  Amendment of State constitutions to remove legal impediment for States to assume, 28 § **1360 nt**
Intervention in action where constitutionality of State statute is in question, 28 § **2403**
Judgments and decrees,
 Contract Disputes Act of 1978, payment of final judgments against U.S., exception, 28 § **2414**
 Payment of final judgments against U.S., 28 § **2414**
Judicial proceedings, evidence, 28 § **1738**
Jurisdiction,
 Offenses,
  By or against Indians in Indian country,
   Amendment of State constitutions to remove legal impediment for States to assume, 28 § **1360 nt**
 Original and exclusive jurisdiction of Supreme Court,
  Actions or proceedings by State against citizens of another State or against aliens, 28 § **1251**
  Controversies between U.S. and a State, 28 § **1251**
Land grants, district courts jurisdiction of actions between citizens claiming, 28 § **1354**
National Guard, this index
Nonjudicial records, evidence, 28 § **1739**
Officers and employees,
 Exemption of officers from jury service, executive, branches, 28 § **1863**
 Habeas corpus proceeding, notice to officer prior to hearing as to person in custody of, 28 § **2252**

STATES—Cont'd
Officers and employees—Cont'd
 Report to Congress, violations of Federal criminal laws by, 28 § **529**
Parimutuel licensing, simplification, 28 § **534 nt**
Pending suits, attending to interests of U.S. in, 28 § **517**
Police, exemption from jury service, 28 § **1863**
Proceedings. Actions and proceedings, generally, ante
Quieting title, real property, claims against United States, 28 § **2409a**
Rate orders of agencies, jurisdiction of district courts, 28 § **1342**
Real property of U.S.,
 Quieting title, claims, proceedings, 28 § **2409a**
Records and recordation,
 Evidence, 28 § **1739**
Regulatory officials, association of, parimutuel licensing, simplification, consolidated reports to Federal Government for identification and criminal records of applicants, 28 § **534 nt**
Seal, certificate to records or books for use as evidence, 28 § **1739**
Secretary of,
 State,
  Certificate to records or books for use as evidence, 28 § **1739**
Supreme Court,
 Action and proceedings by State against citizens of another State or aliens, 28 § **1251**
 Controversies between,
  States, 28 § **1251**
  United States and a State, 28 § **1251**
Taxation,
 Court officers and agents, conducting business, liability, 28 § **960**
 Jurisdiction of district courts, 28 § **1341**
Unjust conviction and imprisonment, damages in U.S. Court of Federal Claims, allegations, concerning acts, in, 28 § **2513**

STATISTICS
Attorney General,
 Maintaining, hate crimes, 28 § **534 nt**
 Report, crime, 28 § **522**
Hate crimes, acquisition of data, guidelines, 28 § **534 nt**
Savings and loan crisis, preparation by Director of Administrative Office of United States Courts, 28 § **604**

STATUTE OF LIMITATIONS
Limitation of Actions, generally, this index

STATUTES
Actions against U.S., trial by court, 28 § **2402**

STATUTES—Cont'd
Administrative Conference of United States, generally, this index
Civil rights, jurisdiction of district court, **28 § 1343**
Claims,
Against U.S.,
Jurisdiction, district courts, actions founded upon, **28 § 1346**
Real estate, quieting title, not applicable to actions founded upon, **28 § 2409a**
Venue, **28 § 1402**
Founded on Act of Congress, jurisdiction of U.S. Court of Federal Claims, **28 § 1491**
Code,
District of Columbia, generally, this index
United States Code, generally, this index
Conflict with rules for district courts and courts of appeals, civil procedure, **28 § 2072**
District courts, jurisdiction,
Fines, penalties or forfeitures incurred under, recovery, **28 § 1355**
Indian tribes or bands, civil actions by, **28 § 1362**
Extraordinary expenses, ministerial officers executing, allowance, payment, **28 § 1929**
Fines or forfeitures, violations, costs, **28 § 1918**
Habeas corpus,
Procedure, **28 § 2284**
State custody, violations as grounds for remedies in Federal courts, **28 § 2254**
Violation, custody, condition for granting writ, **28 § 2241**
Indian claims, jurisdiction of U.S. Court of Federal Claims, **28 § 1505**
Judicial panel on multidistrict litigation, rules for conduct, **28 § 1407**
Limitation of Actions, generally, this index
Motion to vacate, set aside or correct sentence, violations, grounds for, Federal custody, **28 § 2255**
Original jurisdiction of district courts, **28 § 1331**
Removal of causes to district court, **28 § 1441**
Repugnancy of,
Puerto Rican law to laws of U.S., review of Supreme Court of Puerto Rico's decisions by U.S. Supreme Court, **28 § 1258**
State law to laws of U.S., review of State court decisions by Supreme Court, **28 § 1257**
Review by Supreme Court, decision by Supreme Court of Puerto Rico involving validity, **28 § 1258**

STATUTES—Cont'd
Rules, consistency of rules prescribed by courts, **28 § 2071**
Rules of Appellate Procedure, this index
Rules of Civil Procedure, this index
State court case involving validity, review by Supreme Court, **28 § 1257**
State Laws, generally, this index
United States, claims founded on, interest, **28 § 2516**
United States Court of International Trade, civil action raising constitutionality of, three-judge trials, **28 § 255**
Violations, recovery of fines, penalties or forfeitures for, **28 § 2461 et seq.**

STATUTORY LIEN
Liens and Incumbrances, generally, this index

STAY OF PROCEEDINGS
Arrest or process in rem issued in admiralty case, **28 § 2464**
Execution of process, in rem issued in admiralty, **28 § 2464**
Execution or enforcement of judgment or decree, to obtain certiorari from Supreme Court, **28 § 2101**
Federal agency action,
Review of orders, **28 § 2350**
Forfeiture under warrant of arrest or other process in rem in admiralty, **28 § 2464**
International Trade Commission, stay of civil action pending related Commission determination, **28 § 1659**
Jury selection procedures, noncompliance, grounds for, **28 § 1867**
Rules of Appellate Procedure, this index
Rules of Civil Procedure, this index
Security,
Execution and enforcement of judgment to obtain certiorari from Supreme Court, **28 § 2101**
Execution of process in rem issued in admiralty case, **28 § 2464**
State Courts, this index
United States Court of Federal Claims, this index

STENOGRAPHERS
Compensation and salaries,
Courts, increase, **28 § 603 nt**
Fixed by Director of Administrative Office of U.S. Courts, **28 § 604**
Reporters, generally, this index

STENOGRAPHIC TRANSCRIPT
Transcripts, generally, this index

STIPENDS
Compensation and Salaries, generally, this index

STIPULATIONS
Admiralty case, stay of process in rem, **28 § 2464**

STIPULATIONS—Cont'd
Change of venue, **28 § 1404**
Record on review or enforcement in courts of appeals of agency, orders, **28 § 2112**
Rules of Appellate Procedure, this index
Rules of Civil Procedure, this index
Stay of execution of process under warrant of arrest or other process in admiralty, **28 § 2464**
Vessel owner to answer decree of court, **28 § 2464**

STOCK AND STOCKHOLDERS
Derivative Actions, generally, this index
Service of process on corporation in stockholder's derivative action, **28 § 1695**
United States ownership of capital stock, jurisdiction of district court of action involving corporation, **28 § 1349**
Venue in stockholder's derivative action, **28 § 1401**

STRUCTURAL ALTERNATIVES FOR THE FEDERAL COURTS OF APPEALS COMMISSION
Generally, **28 § 41 nt**

STUDENTS
Judges or justices, annuities for survivors, continued status as child, **28 § 376**

STUDIES
Comptroller General, this index
Courts of appeals, Structural Alternatives for the Federal Courts of Appeals Commission, **28 § 41 nt**
Judicial Center, functions respecting, **28 §§ 620, 623**
Sentencing guidelines, General Accounting Office shall undertake, report to Congress, **28 § 994 nt**
Structural Alternatives for the Federal Courts of Appeals Commission, **28 § 41 nt**

SUBORNATION OF PERJURY
Perjury, generally, this index

SUBPOENAS
Arbitration, this index
Congressional reference cases, **28 § 2509**
Foreign country, national or resident of U.S. in, **28 §§ 1783, 1784**
Issuance, by court of U.S., to U.S. national or resident in foreign country, **28 § 1783**
Patent infringement action, defendant not resident of district, service of, **28 § 1694**
Rules of Civil Procedure, this index
Senate, this index
Tender of fees and mileage, witnesses, **28 § 1825**
United States marshal, fees for serving, **28 § 1921**

SUBSISTENCE
See, also, Traveling Expenses, generally, this index
Administrative Office of U.S. Courts, expenses, **28 § 604**
Court officers and employees, payment of subsistence expenses by Director of Administrative Office of U.S. Courts, **28 § 604**
Director of Administrative Office of U.S. Courts, rules and regulations, **28 § 604 nt**
Grand jurors, allowance, **28 § 1871**
Judges, payment, subsistence expenses by Director of Administrative Offices of U.S. Courts, **28 § 604**
Judicial Center, officers and employees, payment by Director of Administrative Office of U.S. Courts, **28 § 604**
Jury, **28 § 1871**
Jury commissioners, **28 § 1863**
Justices and judges, **28 § 456**
Ninth Circuit, temporarily assigned to Compact States, **28 § 297**
Witnesses of U.S. courts, allowance, **28 § 1821**

SUBSTANCE ABUSE
Alcoholics and Alcoholism, generally, this index
Drug Abuse Prevention, Control and Treatment, generally, this index
Narcotic Drug Addicts, generally, this index
National Drug Policy, generally, this index

SUFFRAGE
Elections, generally, this index

SUITS
Actions and Proceedings, generally, this index

SUMMONS
Appraisers,
Fees of U.S. marshal for serving, **28 § 1921**
Goods taken under execution, **28 § 2005**
Garnishment by U.S., **28 § 2405**
Grand Jury, this index
Jury, this index
Patent interference action,
Defendant not resident of district, **28 § 1694**
Rules of Civil Procedure, this index
Service,
Action against officer or employee of U.S., **28 § 1391**
Fees of U.S. marshal, **28 § 1921**
Jury service, **28 §§ 1866, 1867**
Patent infringement action with defendant not resident, **28 § 1694**
United States Court of International Trade, this index

SUMMONS—Cont'd
United States marshal, fee for serving, **28 § 1921**
Witnesses,
Fees of U.S. marshal for serving, **28 § 1921**

SUPERINTENDENT OF DOCUMENTS
Supreme Court reports,
Copies furnished to, **28 § 411**
Sale, **28 § 412**

SUPERSEDEAS
Bankruptcy, this index
Stay of Proceedings, generally, this index

SUPPLIES
Director of Administrative Office of U.S. Courts,
Purchase, for courts, Judicial Center, **28 § 604**

SUPREME COURT
Absence of quorum of qualified justices, **28 § 2109**
Adjourned terms, **28 § 2**
Adjustment in annual rates of salaries of Chief Justice and associate justices, **28 § 5**
Administrative Assistant to Chief Justice,
Appointment, duties, compensation, **28 § 677**
Deemed,
Employee of Court, **28 § 677**
Judicial official, annuities for survivors of judges or justices, **28 § 376**
Election, coverage, retirement program available to Director of Administrative Office of U.S. Courts, **28 § 677**
Volunteers, **28 § 677**
Affirmance, judgments, **28 § 2106**
Absence of quorum of qualified justices, **28 § 2109**
Damages and costs, **28 § 1912**
Always open for certain purposes, **28 § 452**
Ambassadors, jurisdiction of actions or proceedings by or against, **28 § 1251**
Appeal and review,
Absence of quorum of justices, **28 § 2109**
Attorney General, civil actions challenging appointment, **28 § 503 nt**
Attorney General and Solicitor General, conduct and argument in, **28 § 518**
Courts of appeals, generally, post
Criminal cases, time for appeal from State courts, **28 § 2101**
Determination, **28 § 2106**
Direct appeals, generally, post
District courts, post
Priority of criminal cases, **28 § 2102**
Record on direct appeal, **28 § 2101**

SUPREME COURT—Cont'd
Appeal and review—Cont'd
State court cases,
Certiorari, **28 § 1257**
Criminal cases, time for appeal, **28 § 2101**
Manner of taking, **28 § 2104**
Priority of criminal cases from State court, **28 § 2102**
Supreme Court of Puerto Rico, final judgments or decrees, **28 § 1258**
Time for taking, **28 § 2101**
United States Court of Federal Claims cases, interest on judgments affirmed by Supreme Court after review on petition, **28 § 2516**
United States Magistrate Judge, designation to exercise civil jurisdiction, no limitation on right to seek review by Supreme Court, **28 § 636**
Appearance,
Personally or by counsel, **28 § 1654**
Appointment, Administrative Assistant to Chief Justice and employees thereof, **28 § 677**
Assistant librarians, **28 § 674**
Assistants, reporter, apportionment and compensation, **28 § 673**
Associate justices. Justices, generally, post
Attorney General,
Civil actions challenging appointment, appeal, **28 § 503 nt**
Conduct, and argument of cases in, **28 § 518**
Report to Judicial Conference on request of Chief Justice, **28 § 331**
Surface Transportation Board orders, representation of Government on appeal and action to enforce orders, **28 § 2323**
Attorneys,
Forma pauperis proceedings, payment, traveling expenses, **28 § 672**
Rules, post
Bankruptcy, forms of process, writs, rules prescribing, **28 § 2075**
Binding. Printing and binding, generally, post
Books and papers,
Cost and sale of reports, **28 § 676**
Disbursement of funds for by marshal, **28 § 672**
Printing, binding, and distribution of decisions, **28 §§ 411, 676**
Purchase and acquisition by librarian, **28 § 674**
Transmittal of justice's books to successor, **28 § 414**
Vouchers covering expenditures certified to marshal for payment, **28 § 674**
Briefs,
Forma pauperis proceedings, payment, expenses, printing, **28 § 672**
Rules, post

SUPREME COURT—Cont'd
Building. Supreme Court Building, generally, this index
Certiorari,
Additional time, **28 § 2101**
Costs, stay of execution and enforcement of judgment to obtain writ, **28 § 2101**
Court of Claims cases, review of, **28 § 2101**
Courts of appeals, **28 § 1254**
Criminal case, time for review of judgment of State court, **28 § 2101**
Damages, stay of execution and enforcement of judgment to obtain writ, **28 § 2101**
Federal agencies, orders, review, **28 § 2350**
Habeas corpus proceedings, finality of determination, **28 § 2244**
Review of case before judgment rendered in courts of appeals, time for application, **28 § 2101**
Rules, post
State courts,
Criminal cases, time for, **28 § 2101**
Decision involving validity of treaty, statute or State law, **28 § 1257**
Supreme Court of Puerto Rico's decisions involving validity of treaties, statutes, **28 § 1258**
Time, **28 § 2101**
United States Court of Appeals for the Armed Forces, review in certain circumstances, **28 § 1259**
Chief Justice, **28 § 1**
Administrative Office of U.S. Courts, Personnel Management System, incentive awards to Director, **28 § 602 nt**
Allotment,
As circuit justice, **28 § 42**
Of Supreme Court justices to circuits, **28 § 42**
Approval,
Appointments and compensation of employees and assistants of reporter, **28 § 673**
Compensation, clerk and clerk's assistants and messengers, **28 § 671**
Attorney General to report to judicial conference on request of, **28 § 331**
Chief judge of,
Court of appeals, relief from duties as chief judge while retaining status as circuit judge, **28 § 45**
District court, relief from duties as chief judge while retaining status as district judge, **28 § 136**
Circuit judges, temporary assignment to other court, **28 § 291**
Compensation, generally, post
Decisions,
Determination of price, **28 § 676**

SUPREME COURT—Cont'd
Chief Justice—Cont'd
Decisions—Cont'd
Preparation by reporter for publication under direction of Chief Justice, **28 § 673**
Designation and assignment,
Circuit judge,
Act in another circuit, **28 § 291**
District judge,
Consolidated, pretrial proceedings on multidistrict litigation, **28 § 1407**
One circuit for service in another circuit, **28 § 292**
Serve as U.S. Court of International Trade judge, **28 § 292**
Temporary assignments,
To Compact States, **28 § 297**
To other courts, **28 § 292**
Division to appoint special prosecutor, **28 § 49**
New designations and assignments, **28 § 295**
Retired justices or judges to active duty, **28 § 294**
Revocation, **28 § 295**
Senior Judges, **28 § 294**
Director of Administrative Office of U.S. Courts,
Appointment and removal, **28 § 601**
Filing election to waive coverage under civil service retirement, **28 §§ 376, 611**
Incentive awards, **28 § 602 nt**
Disability, **28 § 3**
District judges,
Relief from duties as chief judge, certification to, **28 § 136**
Temporary assignments to other courts, **28 § 292**
Division to appoint special prosecutor, assignment by, **28 § 49**
Expenses of litigation, when costs of defense payable by Director of Administrative Office of U.S. Courts, **28 § 463**
Federal Judicial Center Foundation, appointment of Chairman, **28 § 629**
Judicial conference, summoning and presiding at, **28 § 331**
Judicial panel on multidistrict litigation, designation of members to, **28 § 1407**
Law clerks, appointment and compensation, **28 § 675**
Official duty station, **28 § 456**
Printers, selection, **28 § 676**
Report to Congress of proceedings and recommendations of judicial conference, **28 § 331**
Retired Chief Justice, designation and assignment to perform judicial duties in any circuit, **28 § 294**

SUPREME COURT—Cont'd
Chief Justice—Cont'd
Retired justices or judges,
Designation and assignment to active duty, **28 § 294**
Substantial judicial duties, certification by, **28 § 371**
Roster of Senior Judges, maintenance, **28 § 294**
Rules of Civil Procedure, report to Congress, **28 § 2072**
Signing certificate of disability for retirement of chief judges of certain courts, **28 § 372**
United States Court of International Trade judge,
Designation and assignment of district judge to serve as, **28 § 292**
Designation and temporary assignment to perform judicial duties in other courts, **28 § 293**
Vacancy in office, **28 § 3**
Circuit justices,
Allotment of Supreme Court justices, **28 § 42**
Competency to sit as judges of court of appeals, **28 § 43**
Temporary assignment to other courts, **28 § 291**
Compensation and salaries,
Administrative Assistant to Chief Justice and employees thereof, **28 § 677**
Chief Justice, **28 § 672**
Annual rate, determination and adjustment of, **28 § 5**
Payment by marshal, **28 § 672**
Justices, **28 §§ 371, 372, 672**
Annual rate, determination and adjustment of, **28 § 5**
Retirement for disability, **28 § 372**
Law clerks and secretaries, **28 § 675**
Librarian and assistants, **28 § 674**
Marshal and assistants, **28 § 672**
Reporter and assistants, **28 § 673**
Constitution of United States,
Appeals from,
Courts of appeals, **28 § 1254**
State court decisions, certiorari, **28 § 1257**
Supreme Court of Puerto Rico's final judgments or decrees, certiorari, **28 § 1258**
Constitutionality,
Acts of Congress, review,
State court decisions, certiorari, **28 § 1257**
Supreme Court of Puerto Rico's decisions, **28 § 1258**
State statute, review of decision of,
State court, certiorari, **28 § 1257**
Statute of Puerto Rico, review of decision of Supreme Court of Puerto Rico, **28 § 1258**
Consuls of foreign States as parties, jurisdiction of proceedings, **28 § 1251**

SUPREME COURT—Cont'd
Copies of records and proceedings of court of appeals furnished by clerk of Supreme Court, **28 § 6**
Costs,
Affirmance, **28 § 1912**
Rules, post
Serving process, taxation of, **28 § 1911**
Stay of execution and enforcement of judgment to obtain writ of certiorari, **28 § 2101**
Taxation, **28 § 1911**
Courts of appeals,
Appeal to, **28 § 1254**
Certiorari, ante
Chief judge of, relief by Chief Justice from duties as chief judge while retaining status as circuit judge, **28 § 45**
Copies of records and proceedings of court of appeals furnished by clerk of Supreme Court, **28 § 6**
General provisions applicable to courts and judges, **28 § 451**
Interlocutory decisions, lower courts, promulgation, rules permitting appeal, **28 § 1292**
Power of Supreme Court to prescribe rules for court of appeals, **28 § 2072**
Records kept in clerk's office, **28 § 6**
Remission of direct appeal to courts of appeals because of absence of quorum, **28 § 2109**
Review of, **28 § 1254**
Damages,
Affirmance, **28 § 1912**
Stay of execution and enforcement of judgment to obtain writ of certiorari, **28 § 2101**
Decisions,
Pamphlets, reporter to prepare for publication, **28 § 673**
Preparation for publication, **28 § 673**
Price of, determination, **28 § 676**
Printing, binding, and distribution, **28 §§ 411, 676**
Reporter, **28 § 673**
Definition of courts, judges, **28 nt prec § 1251**
Designation and assignment,
Chief Justice, ante
District judges, post
Justices, post
Determination on review, **28 § 2106**
Direct appeals,
Absence of quorum of justices, **28 § 2109**
Docket, **28 § 2101**
Record on direct appeal, **28 § 2101**
Remission to courts of appeals because of absence of quorum of justices, **28 § 2109**
Time for taking, **28 § 2101**

SUPREME COURT—Cont'd
Director of Administrative Office of U.S. Courts,
Approval, seal of director, **28 § 608**
Incentive awards granted by Chief Justice, **28 § 602 nt**
Performance of duties assigned by Court, **28 § 604**
Retirement program, coverage, availability to Administrative Assistant to Chief Justice upon election of, **28 § 677**
Disability,
Chief Justice, **28 § 3**
Retirement of justices, **28 § 372**
Disbursements,
Incidental to case, taxation, **28 § 1911**
Marshal, **28 § 672**
Discretion,
Costs on affirmance, **28 § 1912**
Damages for delay, **28 § 1912**
District courts,
Appeal and review,
Remission to court of appeals because of absence of quorum of justices, **28 § 2109**
Three-judge courts, **28 § 1253**
Chief judge of, relief by Chief Justice from duties as chief judge while retaining status as district judge, **28 § 136**
Power to prescribe rules,
Admiralty rules, **28 § 2072**
Civil procedure, **28 § 2072**
Power to prescribe rules of evidence for, **28 § 2072**
Rules of Civil Procedure for, report to Congress, **28 § 2072**
District judges,
Chief Justice, ante
Designation and assignment, judge of one circuit for service in another circuit, **28 § 292**
Dockets and docketing,
Direct appeal, **28 § 2101**
Priority of criminal cases from State court, **28 § 2102**
Election, by Administrative Assistant to Chief Justice, coverage under retirement program available to Director of Administrative Office of U.S. Courts, **28 § 677**
Evidence, **28 § 1731 et seq.**
Exclusive jurisdiction, **28 § 1251**
Filing. Rules, post
Habeas corpus,
Application, **28 § 2242**
Power to grant, **28 § 2241**
Prior judgment on appeal or review, conclusiveness, exception, **28 § 2244**
State custody, grounds for remedies in Federal court, **28 § 2254**
Highest court of a State, defined, jurisdiction, **28 § 1257**

SUPREME COURT—Cont'd
Instructions, courts of appeals on certification of questions, **28 § 1254**
Judges or justices. Justices, generally, post
Jurisdiction, **28 § 1251 et seq.**
Rules, post
Jury trial, issues of fact, original actions at law in, **28 § 1872**
Justices,
Absence of quorum of qualified justices, **28 § 2109**
Acknowledgments, authority to take, **28 § 459**
Allotment to circuits, **28 § 42**
Books and publications, transmitted to successor, **28 § 414**
Certificate of disability to be furnished President in behalf of retirement, **28 § 372**
Circuit justices, competency to sit as judges of courts of appeals, **28 § 43**
Compensation and salaries, ante
Designation and assignment,
Circuits, **28 § 42**
Retired justice to perform judicial duties in circuit, **28 § 294**
Disability,
Chief Justice, performance of duties by associate justice, **28 § 3**
Retirement and pensions, **28 § 372**
Expenses of litigation, costs of defense, when payable by Director of Administrative Office of U.S. Courts, **28 § 463**
Habeas corpus,
Power to grant, **28 § 2241**
State custody, grounds for remedies by, **28 § 2254**
Number composing court or constituting quorum, **28 § 1**
Oaths and affirmations, **28 § 453**
Official duty station, **28 § 456**
Practice of law as high misdemeanor, **28 § 454**
Precedence, **28 § 4**
Performance of duties as Chief Justice in case of vacancy or disability, **28 § 3**
Quorum, **28 § 1**
Relatives ineligible to appointment to any office or duty in court, **28 § 458**
Retired justice, designation and assignment to perform judicial duties in any circuit, **28 § 294**
Retirement for disability, **28 § 372**
Secretaries, appointment and compensation, **28 § 675**
Seniority, precedence according to, **28 § 4**
Transfer of application for habeas corpus to district court, **28 § 2241**
Traveling expenses, **28 § 456**

SUPREME COURT—Cont'd
Librarian, **28 § 674**
Marshal to disburse funds upon vouchers certified by librarian, **28 § 672**
Marshal. Supreme Court Marshal, generally, this index
Microfilm, purchase, by librarian, **28 § 674**
Ministers of foreign states, jurisdiction of actions or proceedings by or against, **28 § 1251**
Modification of judgment, decree, or order, **28 § 2106**
Motions,
Rules, post
Officers and employees,
Law clerks and secretaries, **28 § 675**
Payment of salaries of, **28 § 672**
Orders,
Allotment of justices of Supreme Court as circuit justices, **28 § 42**
Marshal to serve and execute, **28 § 672**
Original jurisdiction, **28 § 1251**
Pamphlets,
Decisions, reporter to prepare for publication, **28 § 673**
Disbursement of funds for by marshal, **28 § 672**
Printing and binding, **28 § 676**
Purchase, by librarian, **28 § 674**
Parties,
Rules, post
Periodicals, purchase, by librarian, **28 § 674**
Petitions,
Rules, post
Place of holding, **28 § 2**
Police,
Marshal's duty to oversee, **28 § 672**
Power to,
Grant writ of habeas corpus, **28 § 2241**
Issue writs, **28 § 1651**
Prescribe,
Admiralty and maritime rules for district courts, **28 § 2072**
Rules of evidence for district courts, **28 § 2072**
Rules of procedure,
Civil procedure for district courts and courts of appeals, **28 § 2072**
Submission to Congress, effectiveness, **28 § 2074**
Printing and binding, **28 § 676**
Decisions and reports, **28 § 411**
Reports, power to publish, **28 § 412**
Procedure, **28 § 1651 et seq.**
Process,
Marshal to serve and execute, **28 § 672**
Taxation of cost of serving, **28 § 1911**
Property of U.S. used by court, marshal to take charge, **28 § 672**
Publications, disbursement of funds for by marshal, **28 § 672**
Quorum, **28 §§ 1, 2109**

SUPREME COURT—Cont'd
Records and recordation,
Former court of appeals, kept in office of clerk, **28 § 6**
On direct appeal, **28 § 2101**
Rules, post
Remand, cause, **28 § 2106**
Remission of direct appeal to courts of appeals because of absence of quorum, **28 § 2109**
Reporters, **28 § 673**
Reports,
Additional bound volume and preliminary prints, **28 § 412**
Cost and sale, **28 § 676**
Cost of printing and binding charged to appropriation for judiciary, **28 § 411**
Preliminary prints, **28 §§ 411, 412**
Printing, binding, and distribution, **28 §§ 411, 676**
Reporter to prepare for publication, **28 § 673**
Sale, **28 § 412**
Retirement program available to Director of Administrative Office of U.S. Courts, availability, coverage upon election by Administrative Assistant to Chief Justice, **28 § 677**
Reversal,
Judgment, decree or orders, **28 § 2106**
Ruling on matters in abatement not involving jurisdiction, **28 § 2105**
Review. Appeal and review, generally, ante
Rules,
Admission to bar, **SCR 5**
Adverse or pecuniary interest, practice of law, court officers and employees, **SCR 7**
Affirmations and oaths, admission to bar, **SCR 5**
Amicus curiae,
Briefs, **SCR 37**
Oral argument by, **SCR 28**
Appeals from district courts, **SCR 18**
Appearances, attorneys, **SCR 9**
Applications to individual justices, **SCR 22**
Attorneys, **SCR 5 et seq.**
Admission to bar, **SCR 5**
Appearance, **SCR 9**
Appointment, in forma pauperis proceedings, **SCR 39**
Court officers and employees, conflict of interest, **SCR 7**
Disciplinary action, **SCR 8**
Pro hac vice argument, **SCR 6**
Bonds (officers and fiduciaries), supersedeas or stay, **SCR 23**
Briefs, **SCR 24 et seq.**
Amicus curiae, **SCR 37**
Appeals from district courts, **SCR 18**
Certified questions, **SCR 19**
Certiorari, **SCR 15**
Copies, **SCR 25**

SUPREME COURT—Cont'd
Rules—Cont'd
Briefs—Cont'd
Extraordinary writs, petitions, **SCR 20**
Joint appendix, **SCR 26**
Original actions, **SCR 17**
Printing, **SCR 33**
Time, **SCR 25**
Calendar of cases, **SCR 27**
Certificates and certification, admission to bar, **SCR 5**
Certified questions, **SCR 19**
Certiorari, **SCR 10 et seq.**
Before judgment of Court of Appeals, **SCR 11**
Briefs, **SCR 15**
Considerations governing review, **SCR 10**
Contents of petition, **SCR 14**
Disposition of petition, **SCR 16**
Method of seeking, **SCR 12**
Parties, **SCR 12**
Time, **SCR 13**
Clerk of court, **SCR 1**
Fees, **SCR 38**
Conditional cross-appeals from district courts, **SCR 18**
Conditional cross-petitions, certiorari, **SCR 12**
Conflict of interest, practice of law, court officers and employees, **SCR 7**
Copies and duplicates, briefs, **SCR 25**
Corporate disclosure statements, **SCR 29**
Correctional institutions, custody of prisoners, habeas corpus proceedings, **SCR 36**
Costs, **SCR 43**
Frivolous cases, **SCR 42**
Veterans, seamen and military cases, **SCR 40**
Court officers and employees, conflict of interest, practice of law, **SCR 7**
Cross-appeals from district courts, **SCR 18**
Cross-petitions, certiorari, **SCR 12**
Damages, **SCR 42**
Death, parties, **SCR 35**
Definitions,
State court, **SCR 47**
State law, **SCR 47**
Diagrams, evidence, **SCR 32**
Disbarment, attorneys, **SCR 8**
Disciplinary action, attorneys, **SCR 8**
Dismissal, **SCR 46**
Appeals from district courts, **SCR 18**
Duplicates and copies, briefs, **SCR 25**
Effective date of rules, **SCR 47**
Employees and officers, substitution of parties, **SCR 35**
Evidence, models, diagrams and exhibits, **SCR 32**
Exhibits, evidence, **SCR 32**
Extension of time, **SCR 30**

SUPREME COURT—Cont'd
Rules—Cont'd
Extension of time—Cont'd
Certiorari, **SCR 13**
Extraordinary writs, petitions for, **SCR 20**
Fees,
Clerk of court, **SCR 38**
Veterans, seamen and military cases, **SCR 40**
Filing, **SCR 29**
Applications to individual justices, **SCR 22**
Form of filed documents, **SCR 34**
Motions, **SCR 21**
Printing requirements, **SCR 33**
Rejection or withdrawal, **SCR 1**
Foreign languages, translations of records, **SCR 31**
Frivolous cases, damages and costs, **SCR 42**
Habeas corpus writ,
Custody of prisoners pending, **SCR 36**
Petitions, **SCR 20**
In forma pauperis proceedings, **SCR 39**
Certiorari, **SCR 12**
Indigent persons, in forma pauperis proceedings, **SCR 39**
Individual justices, applications to, **SCR 22**
Interest, **SCR 42**
Joint appendix, briefs, **SCR 26**
Jurisdiction,
Appeals from district courts, **SCR 18**
Certified questions, **SCR 19**
Certiorari, generally, ante
Extraordinary writs, petitions for, **SCR 20**
Original actions, **SCR 17**
Statements of, appeals from district courts, **SCR 18**
Library, **SCR 2**
Mail and mailing, filing and service of process, **SCR 29**
Mandamus writ, petitions, **SCR 20**
Mandate, **SCR 45**
Military court cases, fees and costs, **SCR 40**
Models, evidence, **SCR 32**
Motions, **SCR 21**
Amicus curiae briefs, leave to file, **SCR 37**
Certiorari, **SCR 12**
Dismissal of case, **SCR 46**
Notice,
Appeal from district courts, **SCR 18**
Appearance, **SCR 9**
Oaths and affirmations, admission to bar, **SCR 5**
Objections, dismissal motions, **SCR 46**
Officers and employees, substitution of parties, **SCR 35**
Opinions of court, **SCR 41**
Oral argument, **SCR 28**

SUPREME COURT—Cont'd
Rules—Cont'd
Oral argument—Cont'd
Motions, **SCR 21**
Pro hac vice argument, **SCR 6**
Original actions, **SCR 17**
Parties,
Appeals from district courts, **SCR 18**
Certiorari, **SCR 12**
Death, **SCR 35**
Petitions,
Certiorari, generally, ante
Extraordinary writs, **SCR 20**
Rehearing, **SCR 44**
Printing, filed documents, **SCR 33**
Prisons and prisoners, custody of prisoners, habeas corpus proceedings, **SCR 36**
Pro hac vice argument, attorneys, **SCR 6**
Process, **SCR 45**
Prohibition writ, petitions, **SCR 20**
Proof of service, **SCR 29**
Motions, **SCR 21**
Public officers and employees, substitution of parties, **SCR 35**
Quorum of court, **SCR 4**
Records and recordation,
Appeals from district courts, **SCR 18**
Certified questions, **SCR 19**
Certiorari, **SCR 12**
Court records, **SCR 1**
Translations, **SCR 31**
Rehearing, petitions, **SCR 44**
Reply briefs, **SCR 24**
Certiorari, **SCR 15**
Original actions, **SCR 17**
Responses, motions, **SCR 21**
Revivor, death of parties, **SCR 35**
Seamens cases, fees and costs, **SCR 40**
Service of process, **SCR 29**
Sessions of court, **SCR 4**
State court, defined, **SCR 47**
State law, defined, **SCR 47**
Substitution of parties, **SCR 35**
Supersedeas or stay, **SCR 23**
Mandate pending rehearing petition, **SCR 45**
Supplemental briefs, certiorari, **SCR 15**
Term of court, **SCR 3**
Time,
Briefs, **SCR 25**
Certiorari, **SCR 13**
Clerks office, hours, **SCR 1**
Computation and extension, **SCR 30**
Translations, records in foreign languages, **SCR 31**
Unconstitutionality of statutes, notice of claim, **SCR 29**
United States, service on, **SCR 29**
Veterans cases, fees and costs, **SCR 40**
Words and phrases,
State court, **SCR 47**
State law, **SCR 47**
Writs,
Certiorari, generally, ante

SUPREME COURT—Cont'd
Rules—Cont'd
Writs—Cont'd
Extraordinary writs, petitions for, **SCR 20**
Rules of Civil Procedure, this index
Rules of Criminal Procedure, this index
Rules of Evidence, this index
Salaries. Compensation, generally, ante
Secretaries to justices, appointment and compensation, **28 § 675**
Sessions,
Marshal to attend, **28 § 672**
Powers unrestricted by, **28 § 452**
Solicitor General,
Conduct and argument of cases in, **28 § 518**
Special terms, **28 § 2**
State Courts, generally, this index
Statutes, generally, this index
Terms, **28 § 2**
Interest on judgment against U.S. in Court of Federal Claims, affirmance by, **28 § 2516**
Time,
Appeal or certiorari, **28 § 2101**
Rules, ante
Treaties, review of decisions of State courts, certiorari, **28 § 1257**
United States Court of Appeals for the Armed Forces, this index
United States judges. Justices, generally, ante
United States Magistrate Judges, designation to exercise civil jurisdiction in district court, no limitation on right to seek review by Supreme Court, **28 § 636**
United States Tax Court, this index
Vacancy in office of Chief Justice, **28 § 3**
Vacation of courts,
Allotment of justices as circuit justices, **28 § 42**
Setting aside judgment, decree or order, **28 § 2106**
Volunteers,
Administrative Assistant to Chief Justice, **28 § 677**
Wages. Compensation, generally, ante
Widows and widowers of justices, annuities, **28 § 376**
Writs,
Power to issue, **28 § 1651**

SUPREME COURT BUILDING
Disbursement of funds by marshal, **28 § 672**

SUPREME COURT MARSHAL
Generally, **28 § 672**
Appropriations, **28 § 671 nt**
Compensation, **28 § 672**
Disbursements by, **28 § 672**
Forma pauperis proceedings, payment, expenses, printing briefs and traveling of attorneys, **28 § 672**

SUPREME COURT MARSHAL—Cont'd
Librarian to certify vouchers for payment covering expenditures, **28 § 674**
Salaries of Chief Justice, associate justices and court officers and employees, payment, **28 § 672**
Transportation needs, judicial branch, recommendations to Congress, **28 § 456 nt**

SURETY COMPANIES
Bonds, generally, this index

SURETYSHIP
Principal and Surety, generally, this index

SURFACE TRANSPORTATION BOARD
Actions and proceedings,
District courts, **28 § 1398**
United States as party, **28 § 2322**
Appeal and review. Review, generally, post
Attorney General, this index
Attorneys,
Orders, representation to enforce, **28 § 2323**
District courts,
Enforcement, judicial review of orders and decisions, procedures, **28 § 2321 et seq.**
Jurisdiction,
Civil actions to, enforce, orders of Board, **28 § 1336**
Orders, **28 § 1398**
Orders, proceedings to enforce or set aside orders, **28 § 2321 et seq.**
Enforce, enjoin or set aside orders, **28 § 2321 et seq.**
Federal Legal Council, representation, **28 § 509 nt, EON 12146**
Fines, penalties and forfeitures,
District courts, cases and proceedings other than collection of fines, procedures, **28 § 2321 et seq.**
Jurisdiction, district courts in civil actions to enjoin or suspend collection, **28 § 1336**
Injunctions,
Jurisdiction,
Courts of appeals, proceedings to enjoin or suspend rule, regulation or order, procedures, **28 § 2321 et seq.**
District courts, civil actions to enjoin or suspend orders for payment of money or collection of fines, **28 § 1336**
Orders,
Jurisdiction of district court or U.S. Court of Federal Claims, **28 § 1336**
Procedure in district court, **28 § 2321 et seq.**
Intervention,
Actions to enforce orders, **28 § 2323**

SURFACE TRANSPORTATION BOARD—Cont'd
Jurisdiction, district courts or U.S. Court of Federal Claims relating to orders, **28 § 1336**
Orders,
Action to enforce, jurisdiction of district court or U.S. Court of Federal Claims, **28 § 1336**
Jurisdiction and venue, **28 § 1398**
Review, **28 § 2321 et seq.**
Rates,
Equity proceeding to enforce law, actions to enforce, orders, procedure in, district courts, **28 § 2321 et seq.**
Referral of questions or issues to board, civil actions to enforce, orders, jurisdiction, **28 § 1336**
Reports and records,
Liability for loss, judicial review, procedures, **28 § 2321 et seq.**
Review,
Courts of appeals, jurisdiction, rules, regulations, final orders, **28 § 2342**
Jurisdiction of district courts, civil actions to,
Enforce orders of Board, **28 § 1336**
Enjoin or suspend payment of money or collection of fines, **28 § 1336**
Orders, **28 § 2341 et seq.**
Tariffs, proceedings in equity to enforce, procedures, **28 § 2321 et seq.**
United States,
Party to actions, **28 § 2322**
Venue, district courts, **28 § 1398**
Writs and process, cases and proceedings,
Mandamus to obtain equal facilities for shippers, procedures, **28 § 2321 et seq.**
Other than payment of money or collection of fines, procedures, **28 § 2321 et seq.**

SURGEON GENERAL
Defined,
Narcotic addict rehabilitation, **28 § 2901**
Deputies. Public Health Service, generally, post
Public Health Service,
Narcotic drug addicts, powers relating to, commitment and rehabilitation, **28 § 2901 et seq.**

SURVEYS
Judicial Conference of the U.S., **28 § 331**

SURVIVORS' INSURANCE
Federal old-age, survivors and disability insurance benefits, generally. Social Security, this index

SWEDEN
Convention on the Taking of Evidence Abroad in Civil or Commercial Matters, party to, **28 § 1781 nt**

SWINDLING
Fraud, generally, this index

SWORN
Oaths and Affirmations, generally, this index

SYNDICATES
Income tax, generally. Partnership, this index

TAG–ALONG ACTIONS
Judicial Panel on Multidistrict Litigation, this index

TAIWAN
Naturalization, generally, this index

TALLAHASSEE, FL
Court of Appeals for Eleventh Circuit, generally, this index

TAMPA, FL
Court of Appeals for Eleventh Circuit, generally, this index

TARIFFS
Customs Duties, generally, this index

TASK FORCES
Bank fraud, Attorney General, authority to establish financial institutions task forces, **28 § 509 nt**
Drugs and medicine, civil enforcement enhancement by Justice Department, expenses, **28 § 509 nt**

TAX COURT OF THE UNITED STATES
United States Tax Court, generally, this index

TAX EXEMPT ORGANIZATIONS
Charities, generally, this index

TAX LIENS
Liens and Incumbrances, this index

TAXATION
Bankruptcy, this index
Court officers and agents conducting business, liability, **28 § 960**
Gift Tax, generally, this index
Income Tax, generally, this index
Interest, this index
Internal Revenue Service, generally, this index
Liens and Incumbrances, this index
Local Taxes, generally, this index
Refunds, this index
States, this index
United States Tax Court, generally, this index

TEACHERS
Limitations, outside employment, certain Government employees, **5, Ap 4, § 502**

TECHNICAL INFORMATION AND DATA
Patents, generally, this index

TELECOMMUNICATIONS
Appeal and review,
Communications Commission,
Orders, review, **28 § 2341 et seq.**
Assistance for planning and construction of facilities,
Communications Commission, generally, post
Cellular telephones,
Cloning, sentence and punishment, **28 § 994 nt**
Cloning, wireless telephones, sentence and punishment, **28 § 994 nt**
Communications Commission,
Orders, review, **28 § 2341 et seq.**
Copyrights, generally, this index
Crimes and offenses,
Cloning, wireless telephones, **28 § 994 nt**
Wireless telephones, cloning, **28 § 994 nt**
Fines, penalties and forfeitures,
Cloning, wireless telephones, **28 § 994 nt**
Crimes and offenses, generally, ante
Interception of Wire, Oral, or Electronic Communications, generally, this index
Sentence and punishment,
Cloning, wireless telephones, **28 § 994 nt**
Wireless telephones, cloning, **28 § 994 nt**
Telephones,
Sentencing guidelines, fraud enhancement, older victims, review and report, **28 § 994**
Wireless telephones, cloning, **28 § 994 nt**
Wiretapping. Interception of Wire, Oral, or Electronic Communications, generally, this index

TELEPHONES
Telecommunications, this index

TEMPORARY EMERGENCY COURT OF APPEALS OF UNITED STATES
Savings provision, **28 § 1295 nt**

TENANTS IN COMMON
Generally, **28 § 2409**
United States as tenant, partition action,
Jurisdiction, **28 § 1347**
Venue, **28 § 1399**

TENNESSEE
See, also, States, generally, this index

TENNESSEE—Cont'd
Bankruptcy judges, appointment, number in judicial district, **28 § 152**
District courts,
Cities, held at, **28 § 123**
Judges, appointment,
Additional, advice and consent, **28 § 133 nt**
Number, **28 § 133**
Places of holding, **28 § 123**
Judicial circuit of U.S., **28 § 41**
Judicial districts, **28 § 123**
Bankruptcy provisions, applicability of certain amendments to, **28 § 581 nt**
Number of district judges, **28 § 133**
United States trustees of judicial districts, appointment, **28 § 581**

TENNESSEE VALLEY AUTHORITY
Attorneys,
Federal Courts Improvement Act of 1982, provisions concerning not to affect authority to choose attorneys, **28 § 171 nt**
Legal representation,
Choice of, effect of provisions of Customs Courts Act of 1980, **28 § 251 nt**
Federal Courts Improvement Act of 1982, provisions of not to affect authority to choose, **28 § 171 nt**
Tort Claims Act, exception of claim arising from activities of authority, **28 § 2680**

TERMS OF COURT
Courts of appeals, **28 § 48**
District Courts, this index
Special Terms, generally, this index

TERRITORIES
Costs, council's liability for excessive costs, expenses, and attorneys fees reasonably incurred of multiplication of proceedings, **28 § 1927**
Courts,
Appeals to courts of appeals, circuit to which appeal is taken, **28 § 1294**
Applicability of general provisions relating to, **28 § 460**
Judicial proceedings, proving or admitting in other courts, authentication, entitlement to full faith and credit, **28 § 1738**
Officers and employees, exemption from jury service, **28 § 1863**
Records and recordation, proving or admitting in other courts, authentication, entitlement to full faith and credit, **28 § 1738**
Defendant or res outside of, actions by U.S., time limitation, exclusion, **28 § 2416**
Delegate to Congress, generally, this index

TERRITORIES—Cont'd
District courts,
Admiralty case, power of Supreme Court to prescribe, savings provision, **28 § 2073 nt**
Diversity of citizenship, jurisdiction, **28 § 1332**
Judges, service as bankruptcy judges, **28 § 152**
Diversity of citizenship, district courts, jurisdiction, **28 § 1332**
Documentary Evidence, this index
Executions in favor of U.S., **28 § 2413**
Firemen, exemption from jury service, **28 § 1863**
Government publications and lawbooks furnished to justices, judges, clerks of courts, transmitted to successors, **28 § 414**
Insular Possessions and Dependencies, generally, this index
Judges or justices,
Applicability of general provisions relating to, **28 § 460**
Official duty station, location, **28 § 460**
Salaries on resignation, removal, **28 § 373**
Judicial,
Proceedings, evidence, **28 § 1738**
Jurisdiction,
Diversity of citizenship, district courts, **28 § 1332**
Laws,
Evidence, **28 § 1738**
Legislature,
Laws, generally, ante
Officers and employees, exemption from jury service, **28 § 1863**
Nonjudicial records, evidence, **28 § 1739**
Officers and employees,
Executive, branches, exemption from jury service, **28 § 1863**
Parimutuel licensing, simplification, **28 § 534 nt**
Police, exemption from jury service, **28 § 1863**
Possessions,
Insular Possessions and Dependencies, generally, this index
Puerto Rico, generally, this index
Records and recordation,
Evidence, **28 § 1739**
Unjust conviction and imprisonment, damages in U.S. Court of Federal Claims, allegations, concerning acts, in, **28 § 2513**
Virgin Islands, generally, this index

TERRORISTS AND TERRORISM
Fraud, older victims, sentencing guideline adjustments, review and report, **28 § 994 nt**
Immunities, foreign states, jurisdictional, **28 § 1605**

TERRORISTS AND TERRORISM
—Cont'd
International terrorism,
Aircraft sabotage, defined, jurisdictional immunities of foreign states, **28 § 1605**
Extrajudicial killing, defined, jurisdictional immunities of foreign states, **28 § 1605**
Hostage taking, defined, jurisdictional immunities of foreign states, **28 § 1605**
Jurisdiction,
Immunities of foreign states, **28 § 1605**
Sentence and punishment, post
State sponsor of terrorism, foreign state designated as, official or employee, civil liability, **28 § 1605 nt**
Torture, defined, jurisdictional immunities of foreign states, **28 § 1605**
Jurisdiction,
Immunities of foreign states, **28 § 1605**
International terrorism, ante
Sentence and punishment,
Amendment of sentencing guidelines,
By United States Sentencing Commission, **28 § 994 nt**
For terrorist crimes, **28 § 994 nt**
International terrorism,
Sentencing guidelines,
Directions to Commission, **28 § 994 nt**
State sponsored terrorism, acts of, civil liability, **28 § 1605 nt**

TESTIMONY
Evidence, generally, this index

TESTS
Narcotic drug addicts, civil commitment, use of results in criminal proceedings against examined individual, **28 § 2904**
Rules of Civil Procedure, this index

TEXAS
See, also, States, generally, this index
Bankruptcy judges, appointment, number in judicial district, **28 § 152**
District courts,
Cities, held at, **28 § 124**
Judges, appointment,
Additional, advice and consent, **28 § 133 nt**
Number, **28 § 133**
Judicial districts, **28 § 124**
Places of holding, **28 § 124**
Judicial circuit of U.S., **28 § 41**
Judicial districts, **28 § 124**
Bankruptcy provisions, applicability of certain amendments to, **28 § 581 nt**
Number of district judges, **28 § 133**
United States trustees of judicial districts, appointment, **28 § 581**

THIRD PARTIES
Claims by U.S. against unaffected by time limitations, **28 § 2415**
Internal Revenue Service, this index
United States Court of International Trade, this index

THREE JUDGE COURT
Appeals, direct to Supreme Court, **28 § 1253**
Apportionment of Congressional or statewide legislative districts, court convened, **28 § 2284**
Composition, **28 § 2284**
Injunction,
Enforcement of State statute, procedure, **28 § 2284**
Preliminary injunction, single judge not to hear and determine application for, **28 § 2284**
Temporary restraining order pending hearing by three-judge court, **28 § 2284**
Orders, **28 § 2284**
Performance of functions, **28 § 2284**

TITLE TO PROPERTY
Action by U.S. to establish, limitations, inapplicable, **28 § 2415**
Claim to, enforcement, of liens, district court, order for appearance of absent defendant, **28 § 1655**
Quieting Title, generally, this index
Removal of action or prosecution against Federal officers to affect validity of laws of U.S., **28 § 1442**
United States,
Marshal, successor, perfecting title, judicial sale of realty, **28 § 2003**

TOLL BRIDGES
Jurors, tolls, fees, **28 § 1871**

TOLL ROADS
Jurors, tolls, fees, **28 § 1871**

TOLLS
Jurors, fees, **28 § 1871**
Tunnels, this index
Witnesses of U.S. courts, allowance, **28 § 1821**

TORTS
See, also, Claims, generally, this index
Generally, **28 §§ 1346, 2671 et seq.**
Acting within scope of his office or employment, defined, **28 § 2671**
Actions by U.S. founded on, limitation, **28 §§ 2415, 2416**
Administrative adjustment of claims, **28 § 2672**
Aliens,
District court's jurisdiction of action for, **28 § 1350**
Torture victim protection, civil action for damages, **28 § 1350 nt**

TORTS—Cont'd
Attorneys' fees, claims against U.S., **28 § 2678**
Availability, funds, payment, judgments and compromises for payment of awards, **28 § 2672**
Compromise and settlement, **28 § 2677**
Approval, **28 § 2672**
Head of Federal agency, **28 § 2672**
Payment of award, **28 § 2672**
Definitions, **28 § 2671**
Dispute resolution, alternative means of, generally. Administrative Law and Procedure, this index
District courts, jurisdiction,
Alien's action for tort, **28 § 1350**
Claims against U.S., **28 § 1346**
Employee of the Government, defined, **28 § 2671**
Federal agency, defined, **28 § 2671**
Filing and final agency denial of claim against U.S., prerequisite to commencement of action, **28 § 2675**
Law enforcement officers,
Defined, **28 § 2671 nt**
Military departments,
Federal agency as including, **28 § 2671**
Option to consider claim denied where agency fails to make final disposition thereof, **28 § 2675**
Payment of award, compromise or settlement, **28 § 2672**
Release of claim by acceptance of award, compromise or settlement, **28 § 2672**
Time for presentation of claims or commencement of action against U.S., **28 § 2401**
United States, claims against,
Real estate, quieting title, inapplicability to actions involving claims against U.S., **28 § 2409a**
Venue of action against U.S., **28 § 1402**

TORTURE VICTIM PROTECTION ACT OF 1991
Generally, **28 § 1350 nt**

TRADE
Commerce and Trade, generally, this index
International Trade, generally, this index

TRADE REPRESENTATIVE
International Trade, this index

TRADE SECRETS
United States Court of International Trade, disclosure of trade secrets which are privileged, ordering of, **28 § 2641**

TRADEMARK TRIAL AND APPEAL BOARD
United States Court of Appeals for the Federal Circuit, jurisdiction of appeals from decisions, **28 § 1295**

TRADEMARKS AND TRADE NAMES
Commissioner of Patents and Trademarks, generally, this index
District courts, jurisdiction, **28 § 1338**
Trademark Trial and Appeal Board, generally, this index
United States Court of Appeals for the Federal Circuit,
  Appeals to,
    From final decision in district court involving, jurisdiction, **28 § 1295**
  Patent and Trademark Office, Board of Appeals or Board of Patent Interferences, appeals from, jurisdiction, **28 § 1295**

TRADING WITH THE ENEMY
Tort Claims Act, exception of claim arising out of administration of Trading With the Enemy Act, **28 § 2680**

TRAINING
Judicial Center, functions respecting, **28 §§ 620, 623**
United States Magistrate Judges, programs for, **28 § 637**

TRAINS
Railroads, generally, this index

TRANSCRIPTS
Costs, **28 § 1920**
  In forma pauperis proceeding, taxation, **28 § 1915**
District court reporter or other designated individual, certification, of, **28 § 753**
Federal departments, agencies,
  Evidence, **28 § 1733**
Habeas corpus proceedings, evidence on application for writ, **28 § 2247**
Printing, payment of expenses, proceeding before magistrate judge designated to exercise jurisdiction in civil court, **28 § 1915**
Rules of Appellate Procedure, this index
United States Court of Federal Claims, this index
United States Magistrate Judges, this index

TRANSFER OF CASES OR CAUSES
See, also, Removal of Cases or Causes, generally, this index
Courts, want of jurisdiction, transfer to cure, **28 § 1631**
District courts,
  Transfer to single district, consolidated, pretrial proceedings, **28 § 1407**
Federal agencies, review of orders, **28 § 2347**

TRANSFER OF CASES OR CAUSES—Cont'd
United States Court of Claims (former court), case pending before where report on merits filed by commissioner, transfer to U.S. Court of Appeals for the Federal Circuit, **28 § 171 nt**
United States Court of Customs and Patent Appeals (former court), transfer of pending matters to U.S. Court of Appeals for the Federal Circuit, **28 § 171 nt**
United States Court of Federal Claims, this index

TRANSFER OF OFFENDERS TO OR FROM FOREIGN COUNTRIES
See, also, Extradition, generally, this index
Attorneys,
  Right to consult with before consenting to transfer,
    Appointment of counsel, **28 § 636**
      Powers of Magistrate Judge, **28 § 636**
Consent to transfer, from U.S.,
  Verification, **28 § 636**
Judges or justices,
  Appointment of Magistrate Judge, **28 § 636**
Magistrate Judge, powers and duties, verification of consent to transfer from U.S., **28 § 636**

TRANSPORTATION DEPARTMENT
Community development, neighborhood revitalization plan, development by Attorney General, use of appropriated funds, **28 § 509 nt**
Secretary of Transportation, generally, this index

TRAVELING EXPENSES
Administrative Office of U.S. Courts, **28 § 604**
Arbitration, this index
Court officers and employees, payment by Director of Administrative Office of U.S. Courts, **28 § 604**
Courts of appeals, advisory committees appointed to study rules of practice, members of, **28 § 2077**
Director,
  Administrative Office of U.S. Courts, rules and regulations, **28 § 604 nt**
Espionage, generally, this index
Federal officers and employees,
  Travel expenses, defined, limitations on outside income and employment, **5, Ap 4, § 505**
Government officers and employees. Federal officers and employees, generally, ante
Independent Counsel, **28 § 594**
Institutes and joint councils on sentencing, participants, **28 § 334**

TRAVELING EXPENSES—Cont'd
Judges, Ninth Circuit, temporarily assigned to Compact States, **28 § 297**
Judicial Center,
  Director, **28 § 625**
  Officers and employees, **28 § 604**
Jurors, summoning to appear to complete qualification form, **28 § 1864**
Jury commissioner, **28 § 1863**
Justice Department,
  Employees serving abroad, authorization of appropriations, **28 § 530A**
  Newly appointed special agents, authorization of Attorney General or designee to pay, **28 § 530**
Justices and judges, **28 § 456**
Mileage, generally, this index
Officers and employees of Government. Federal officers and employees, generally, ante
Parental Kidnapping Prevention Act, award to person entitled to custody or visitation, **28 § 1738A nt**
Part-time United States Magistrate Judges, **28 § 635**
Per Diem, generally, this index
Subsistence, generally, this index
Supreme Court, forma pauperis proceedings, attorneys, **28 § 672**
United States marshals, **28 § 1921**
Witnesses,
  Allowance in lieu of mileage in certain cases, **28 § 1821**
  Foreign country, subpoena in, **28 § 1783**

TREASON
Espionage, generally, this index

TREASURER OF UNITED STATES
Tort Claims Act, exception of claim caused by fiscal operations, **28 § 2680**

TREASURY BILLS
District courts, judgments, interest, rate, calculation, price as determining factor, **28 § 1961**
Interest on judgments against U.S. paid at rate equal to coupons issue yield equivalent of average auction price, **28 § 2516**
United States Court of Federal Claims, payment, interest on judgments against U.S. affirmed by Supreme Court, rates, auction price as determining factor, **28 § 2516**

TREASURY OF UNITED STATES
Bills of. Treasury Bills, generally, this index
Clerk,
  Deposit of other moneys in checking account in, **28 § 2043**
  Payment of fees and costs into Treasury,
    Courts of appeals, **28 § 711**

TREASURY OF UNITED STATES
—Cont'd
Clerk—Cont'd
Payment of fees and costs into Treasury—Cont'd
District court, **28 § 751**
Supreme Court, **28 § 671**
Court of Federal Claims Judges Retirement Fund established in, **28 § 178**
Department of Justice Assets Forfeiture Fund, established, contents, payments, **28 § 524**
Deposits,
Court, unclaimed funds, **28 § 2042**
Docket fees of U.S. trustees and U.S. Attorneys, paid into, **28 § 1923**
Information technology,
Judiciary Information Technology Fund, establishment, **28 § 612**
Internal Revenue Service,
Payment of judgment against collector or other revenue officer on certification of certain facts, **28 § 2006**
Judicial Officers' Retirement Fund, investment of available portions by, bankruptcy judges and Magistrate Judges, **28 § 377**
Judicial survivors annuity fund, deposits to credit of, **28 § 376**
Justice Department, moneys appropriated for, requisitions, **28 § 523**
Partition actions involving U.S., purchase money, payment from, **28 § 2409**
Pending or adjudicated cases, moneys paid into court, deposit in Registry Administration Account, deposit with, **28 §§ 2041, 2041 nt**
Public moneys, action by U.S. against person failing to pay into, **28 § 2407**
Registry Administration Account, funds collected by Judiciary as charge for services, deposit in, availability, **28 § 2041 nt**
Secretary of Treasury, generally, this index
Special fund,
Filing fee awards, actions commenced by U.S., operation and maintenance of courts, **28 § 1931**
Witnesses, fact witness fees, payment, prohibition, **28 § 1821 nt**

TREATIES
See, also,
Conventions, generally, this index
Alien,
Action for tort, jurisdiction of district court, **28 § 1350**
District courts, original jurisdiction, **28 § 1331**
Extradition, generally, this index
Habeas corpus,
State custody, violations as grounds for remedies in Federal courts, **28 § 2254**

TREATIES—Cont'd
Habeas corpus—Cont'd
Violation, custody, condition for granting writ, **28 § 2241**
Indians, this index
Removal of cases to district court, **28 § 1441**
State court case involving validity, appeal to Supreme Court, certiorari, **28 § 1257**
State laws, as rules of decision, exception, **28 § 1652**
Suits against U.S., jurisdiction of U.S. Court of Federal Claims, **28 § 1502**
Supreme Court, appeals from, Supreme Court of Puerto Rico's final judgments or decrees, **28 § 1258**
Validity, Supreme Court of Puerto Rico's decisions questioning, review by, **28 § 1258**

TRESPASS
Attachment against delinquent postmasters and postal officers, employees, right of action unimpaired, **28 § 2713**
Indian Lands and Reservations, this index
Public and Indian lands, action by U.S. for damages, limitations, **28 §§ 2415, 2416**

TRIAL
By court, actions against U.S., **28 § 2402**
Real estate, quieting title, **28 § 2409a**
Disqualification of justice or judge to sit, **28 § 455**
Evidence, generally, this index
Habeas corpus, condition for granting writ, **28 § 2241**
Jury, generally, this index
Justice, judge, or Magistrate Judge, disqualification, **28 § 455**
Misdemeanors, rules of procedure for trial before United States Magistrate Judges. United States Magistrate Judges, generally, this index
New Trial, generally, this index
Real estate, quieting title, actions against U.S., tried by court, **28 § 2409a**
Release, generally, this index
Rules of Civil Procedure, this index
Speedy trial, **28 § 604**
United States Court of Federal Claims, this index
United States Court of International Trade, this index
Venue or District of Trial, generally, this index

TRIAL DE NOVO
New Trial, generally, this index

TRUSTS AND TRUSTEES
Estates and Trusts, generally, this index

TUNNELS
Tolls,
Jurors, fees, **28 § 1871**

TVA
Tennessee Valley Authority, generally, this index

UNAVOIDABLE ACCIDENT
Credits for claims in actions by U.S., **28 § 2406**

UNCLAIMED FUNDS
Deposits in court, **28 § 2042**

UNDERTAKINGS
Bonds, generally, this index

UNFAIR COMPETITION
District courts, jurisdiction, **28 § 1338**

UNIFORM FEDERAL CRIME REPORTING ACT OF 1988
Generally, **28 § 534 nt**
Bureau of Investigation, generally, this index

UNIFORMED SERVICES
See, also, Armed Forces, generally, this index
Air Force, generally, this index
Armed Forces, generally, this index
Army, generally, this index
Cemeteries and dead bodies. National Cemeteries, generally, this index
Coast Guard, generally, this index
Marine Corps, generally, this index
Money erroneously paid to members, actions by U.S. for recovery, limitation, **28 §§ 2415, 2416**
National Cemeteries, generally, this index
Navy, generally, this index

UNIFORMS
Allowances,
Appropriations to certain Federal agencies, permitted utilization, **28 § 509 nt**

UNINCORPORATED BUSINESS ENTERPRISES
Attorneys' fees and other costs and expenses, award to party prevailing against U.S. or agency, applicability, **28 § 2412**

UNITED KINGDOM
Great Britain, generally, this index

UNITED NATIONS
Diplomatic immunity,
Direct action against insurers of persons entitled to, **28 § 1364**
Members of foreign missions,
Direct actions against insurers of members of diplomatic missions and their families, no defense, **28 § 1364**

UNITED STATES

Actions and proceedings,
- Award, fees, prevailing party, 28 **§ 2412**
- Civil justice reform, guidelines, 28 **§ 519 nt, EON 12988**
- Controversy with State, original jurisdiction with Supreme Court, 28 **§ 1251**
- Costs, 28 **§ 2412**
- Credits in actions by U.S., 28 **§ 2406**
- Death of defendant in damage action, 28 **§ 2404**
- Delinquents for public money, 28 **§ 2407**
- Executions, 28 **§ 2413**
- Foreclosure of mortgages or other liens, generally, post
- Guidelines, civil justice reform, 28 **§ 519 nt, EON 12988**
- Judgments, generally, post
- Judicial officers, liability for costs, 28 **§ 2412 nt**
- Jurisdiction, district court, 28 **§§ 1345, 1346**
- Jury trial, 28 **§ 2402**
- Liens and incumbrances, 28 **§ 2410**
- Limitation of actions, generally, post
- Partition, 28 **§ 2409**
- Payment, judgments and compromise settlements, 28 **§ 2414**
- Prevailing party, costs, judgment, 28 **§ 2412**
- Recommencement after dismissal without prejudice, 28 **§ 2415**
- Security not required of U.S., 28 **§ 2408**
- Set-off and counterclaim, generally, post

Appeal and review,
- Judgments, certification, 28 **§ 2414**

Appearance, lien actions, 28 **§ 2410**

Attorney General, this index

Bids, judicial sales, actions affecting property on which U.S. has lien, 28 **§ 2410**

Civil justice reform, guidelines, legislation, 28 **§ 519 nt, EON 12988**

Claims, this index

Compromise,
- Settlements, payment, appropriations for, 28 **§ 2414**

Condemnation, property on which U.S. has lien, 28 **§ 2410**

Constitution of United States, generally, this index

Contracts, this index

Costs, this index

Court of Veterans Appeals, awards of costs and fees, disposition, 28 **§ 2412 nt**

Court records lost or destroyed, evidence where U.S. interested, 28 **§ 1735**

Death of defendant in damage action, 28 **§ 2404**

UNITED STATES—Cont'd

Defendant or res outside of, actions by, period of limitations, exclusion, 28 **§ 2416**

District Courts, this index

Eminent domain,
- Jurisdiction of district court, 28 **§ 1358**
- Venue, 28 **§ 1403**

Executions in favor of, 28 **§ 2413**

Fees, district court reporter, payment, 28 **§ 753**

Foreclosure of mortgages or other liens, 28 **§ 2410**

Forma pauperis, proceedings in, costs, payment, 28 **§ 1915**

Fraud against,
- Forfeiture of claims against U.S., 28 **§ 2514**

Garnishment proceedings by, 28 **§ 2405**

In rem proceedings, change of venue, consent unnecessary, 28 **§ 1404**

Interest, this index

Internal Revenue Service, this index

Interpleader, property on which U.S. has lien, 28 **§ 2410**

Intervention in action or proceedings, constitutional question, 28 **§ 2403**

Joint tenant, partition actions involving, 28 **§ 2409**
- Jurisdiction of district court, 28 **§ 1347**
- Venue, 28 **§ 1399**

Judgments and decrees,
- Appropriation for payment of judgment against, 28 **§ 2414**
- Civil actions and administrative proceedings, payment, limitation, 28 **§ 2412 nt**
- Costs, actions by or against, 28 **§ 2412**
- Discharge of property from mortgage or lien held by, 28 **§ 2410**
- Liens and incumbrances, entered in favor of U.S., applicability of provisions, 28 **§ 1962**
- Payment of judgments, 28 **§ 2414**
  - Exception, 28 **§ 2414**
  - Limitation, 28 **§ 2412 nt**
- Registration in other districts after judgment in favor of U.S. is entered, 28 **§ 1963**

Judicial and executive officers,
- Liability for costs, actions and proceedings, 28 **§ 2412 nt**

Judicial sales, lien of U.S. on property, 28 **§ 2410**

Jury trial, actions against U.S., 28 **§ 2402**

Liens and incumbrances,
- Actions affecting property on which U.S. has lien, 28 **§ 2410**
- Judgments entered in favor of U.S., applicability of provisions, 28 **§ 1962**

Limitation of actions, 28 **§ 2401**
- Actions brought by, 28 **§ 2415**
- Exclusions, 28 **§ 2416**

UNITED STATES—Cont'd

Litigation where a party, conducting reserved to Justice Department, 28 **§ 516**

Mortgages, action affecting property on which U.S. has mortgage, 28 **§ 2410**

Partition,
- Property on which U.S. has lien, 28 **§ 2410**
- Tenant in common, jurisdiction, district court, 28 **§ 1347**
- Venue of action, 28 **§ 1399**

Party in actions, 28 **§ 2401 et seq.**
- Awards, 28 **§ 2412**
- Banking association, jurisdiction of district court, 28 **§ 1348**
- Concurrent jurisdiction of district court with U.S. Court of Federal Claims, 28 **§ 1346**
- Controversy between U.S. and State, original jurisdiction of Supreme Court, 28 **§ 1251**
- Costs, 28 **§ 2412**
- Credits in actions by U.S., 28 **§ 2406**
  - Delinquents for public money, 28 **§ 2407**
- Death of defendant in damage action, 28 **§ 2404**
- Delinquents for public money, 28 **§ 2407**
- Execution in favor of U.S., 28 **§ 2413**
- Garnishment, 28 **§ 2405**
- Lien on property affected by action, 28 **§ 2410**
- Original jurisdiction of district courts, 28 **§§ 1345, 1346**
- Partition, 28 **§ 2409**
  - Venue, 28 **§ 1399**
- Report on cases by Attorney General to Judicial Conference, 28 **§ 331**
- Security not required, 28 **§ 2408**
- Time for,
  - Appeal to court of appeals, 28 **§ 2107**
  - Commencement of action against, 28 **§ 2401**
- Venue, 28 **§ 1402**
- Witness fees, payment, 28 **§ 1825**

Payment,
- Costs, 28 **§ 2408**

Pending suits, interests of, attending to, 28 **§ 517**

Punitive damages, liability on tort claims, 28 **§ 2674**

Quieting title to property on which U.S. has lien, 28 **§ 2410**

Removal of action against, foreclosure action, 28 **§ 1444**

Rules of Appellate Procedure, this index

Rules of Civil Procedure, this index

Savings provision, limitation of actions, 28 **§ 2415**

Set-off and counterclaim,
- United States as defendant, jurisdiction of district court, 28 **§ 1346**

UNITED STATES—Cont'd
Subpoena issued in behalf of, tender of fees and mileage, **28 § 1825**
Supervision of litigation where a party, **28 § 519**
Tax refund suits by corporations, venue, **28 § 1402**
Tenant in common, partition actions involving, venue, **28 §§ 1399, 2409**
Jurisdiction of district court, **28 § 1347**
Transcripts requested by, fees of district court reporter, **28 § 753**
United States Court of International Trade, this index
Venue,
Partition, **28 § 1399**
Tax refund suits, corporations, **28 § 1402**
Tort claims, **28 § 1402**
Witnesses,
Fees, payment, **28 § 1825**

UNITED STATES AIR FORCE
Air Force, generally, this index

UNITED STATES ARMED FORCES
Armed Forces, generally, this index

UNITED STATES ARMY
Army, generally, this index

UNITED STATES ATTORNEYS
Generally, **28 § 541 et seq.**
Alaska, tenure, termination, **28 § 81A nt, EON 10867**
Alternative means of dispute resolution, authority, **28 § 2672**
Appearance for defense in civil actions, against revenue, officers, **28 § 547**
Appointments, **28 § 541**
Assistants, **28 § 542**
Special attorneys, **28 § 543**
Vacancies, filling, **28 § 546**
Arbitration, authority to compromise or settle claims utilizing, **28 § 2672**
Assistants,
Appointment and removal, **28 § 542**
Certificate for payment of witness fees, **28 § 1825**
Domicile and residence, **28 § 545**
Oath of office, **28 § 544**
Official stations, determination, **28 § 545**
Salaries, **28 § 548**
Attachment,
Postal suits,
Application for warrant, **28 § 2711**
Notice of trial of ownership of property, **28 § 2713**
Personal notice of attachment served by, **28 § 2716**
Attorney General,
Appointment and removal,
Assistants, **28 § 542**
Special attorneys, **28 § 543**

UNITED STATES ATTORNEYS
—Cont'd
Attorney General—Cont'd
Approval, employment, clerical assistants, messengers, and private process servers, **28 § 550**
Commitment proceedings, authority, **28 § 515**
Direction of, **28 § 519**
Expenses and expenditures, authorization, **28 § 549**
Filling vacancies, powers, **28 § 546**
Fixing salaries, **28 § 548**
Investigation of official acts, **28 § 526**
Official stations, determination, **28 § 545**
Reports to, **28 § 547**
California, transfer and appointment, **28 § 84 nt**
Certificate, payment of witness fees, **28 § 1825**
Certified copy of official paper, evidence of court record lost or destroyed, **28 § 1735**
Civil actions, prosecuting or defending, **28 § 547**
Civil justice reform, litigation guidelines, **28 § 519 nt, EON 12988**
Clerical assistants, employment, **28 § 550**
Compensation and salaries, **28 § 548**
Conflict of interest, disqualification in case of, rules and regulations, penalty for violation, **28 § 528**
Court interpreters, duties to secure for governmental witnesses, **28 § 1827**
Crimes and Offenses, this index
Customs Duties, this index
Delinquents for public money, action by U.S. against, continuance in presence of, **28 § 2407**
Dispute resolution, alternative means of, authority to settle claims, **28 § 2672**
Domicile and residence, **28 § 545**
Duties, **28 § 547**
Employment, clerical assistants, messengers, and private process servers, **28 § 550**
Expenses and expenditures, **28 § 549**
Fines, penalties, and forfeitures, revenue law violations, instituting, proceedings, **28 § 547**
Florida, tenure and appointment, **28 § 89 nt**
Guidelines, litigation, civil justice reform, **28 § 519 nt, EON 12988**
Illinois, Central and Southern Districts of, designation, tenure, **28 § 93 nt**
Investigations,
Official acts, by Attorney General, **28 § 526**
Law books and publications furnished, transmission to successor, **28 § 414**
Lien of U.S. on property involved in State courts, service on, **28 § 2410**
Louisiana, Eastern and Middle Districts, tenure and appointment, **28 § 98 nt**

UNITED STATES ATTORNEYS
—Cont'd
Messengers, employment, **28 § 550**
Moneys paid into court, criminal appearance bail bond, use to pay fine, assessment, **28 § 2044**
Narcotic drug addicts,
Advising whether treatment should be continued, **28 § 2903**
Commitment,
Report of examination available to, **28 § 2902**
Northern Mariana Islands,
Residency requirements in district so appointed, applicability, **28 § 545**
Notice,
Claimant of money deposited in court, **28 § 2042**
Hearing by three-judge court, **28 § 2284**
Motion to vacate, set aside or correct sentence, Federal custody, **28 § 2255**
Oath of office, **28 § 544**
Offenses,
Against U.S., prosecution, **28 § 547**
Official stations, determination, **28 § 545**
President,
Appointment and removal, **28 § 541**
Process servers, private, employment, **28 § 550**
Removal, **28 § 541 et seq.**
Reports, **28 § 547**
Restoration of court records lost or destroyed, U.S. interested, **28 § 1735**
Senate,
Person refused advice and consent by, Attorney General not to fill vacancy with, **28 § 546**
Service, process in State court in action involving property on which U.S. has lien, **28 § 2410**
Special attorneys,
Appointment and removal, **28 § 543**
Oaths of office, **28 § 544**
Salaries, **28 § 548**
Staff, disqualification in case of conflict of interest, rules and regulations, penalty for violation, **28 § 528**
Subsistence expenses, **28 § 509**
Tax liens, U.S. as party, actions to quiet title, foreclose, service of process, **28 § 2410**
Term of office, **28 § 541**
Tort claims against U.S., copies of pleadings and process furnished to, **28 § 2679**
Vacancies, filling, **28 § 546**
Wages. Compensation and salaries, generally, ante
Witnesses,
United States Magistrate Judges, approval and certification of fees, **28 § 1922**

UNITED STATES COAST GUARD
Coast Guard, generally, this index

UNITED STATES CODE
Director of Administrative Office of U.S. Courts to furnish to United States Magistrate Judges, **28 § 638**
United States Magistrate Judge furnished copy, **28 § 638**

UNITED STATES COMMISSIONER
See, also, United States Magistrate Judges, generally, this index
Applicability of provisions relating to powers, duties, not to continue after United States Magistrate Judges assumes office, **28 § 631 nt**
Appointment to office of United States Magistrate Judges, qualifications, **28 § 631 nt**
Reference to commissioner deemed reference to United States Magistrate Judge, **28 § 631 nt**
Rules of procedure and practice, United States Magistrate Judges to have powers and duties conferred or imposed upon commissioners by Rules of Criminal Procedure, **28 § 636**
Service as after date on which United States Magistrate Judge assumes office in judicial district, prohibition, **28 § 631 nt**

UNITED STATES COURT OF APPEALS FOR DISTRICT OF COLUMBIA
Appeal and review,
Orders, certain Federal agencies, venue, **28 § 2343**
Chief Judge,
Chief justice known as, **28 § 451 nt**
Designation of chief justice to be known as, **28 § 45 nt**
Judge of the U.S., **28 § 451 nt**
Precedence, **28 § 45**
Clerk of court,
Independent counsel, service as clerk of division of court to appoint, **28 § 49**
Composition of judicial district under jurisdiction of, **28 § 41**
Division of court to appoint independent counsel, clerk of court to serve as division clerk, establishment, vacancy, filling, **28 § 49**
Evidence, **28 § 1731 et seq.**
Judges,
Additional circuit judgeships, **28 § 44 nt**
Appointment, tenure, **28 § 44**
Assignment, **28 § 46**
Chief Judge, generally, ante
Chief Justice and Associate Justices as judges of the U.S., **28 § 451 nt**
Circuit judges, exception as to residence requirement, number, **28 § 44**

UNITED STATES COURT OF APPEALS FOR DISTRICT OF COLUMBIA—Cont'd
Judges—Cont'd
Number of, **28 § 44**
Appointment of additional judges, **28 § 44 nt**
Official duty station, **28 § 456**
Trial judge, disqualification to hear appeal, **28 § 47**
Judicial circuit under jurisdiction, composition of, **28 § 41**
Marshal, serving as on certain date, applicability of other provisions, **28 § 713 nt**
Number of judges, **28 § 44**
Official duty station of judges, **28 § 456**
Place of holding sessions, **28 § 48**
Procedure, **28 § 1651 et seq.**
Retired justices, division to appoint special prosecutor, priority in assignment to, **28 § 49**
Review. Appeal and review, generally, ante
Senior circuit judges, division to appoint special prosecutor, priority in assignment to, **28 § 49**
Sessions, **28 § 48**
Special sessions, **28 § 48**
Special terms, **28 § 48**
Terms, **28 § 48**
Traveling expenses of judges, **28 § 456**
Washington, City of, place of holding terms or sessions, **28 § 48**

UNITED STATES COURT OF APPEALS FOR THE ARMED FORCES
Certiorari, writ of, Supreme Court, **28 § 1259**
Supreme Court,
Writ of certiorari, review in certain circumstances, **28 § 1259**
Time,
Certiorari application for review by Supreme Court, prescribed by Supreme Court rules, **28 § 2101**
Transportation needs, recommendations to Congress, **28 § 456 nt**

UNITED STATES COURT OF APPEALS FOR THE FEDERAL CIRCUIT
See, also,
Courts of Appeals, generally, this index
Appeal and review,
Economic stabilization, decisions respecting, **28 § 1295**
Emergency petroleum allocations, decisions respecting, **28 § 1295**
Energy policy and conservation, decisions respecting, **28 § 1295**
Executive offices, certain actions, **28 § 1296**

UNITED STATES COURT OF APPEALS FOR THE FEDERAL CIRCUIT—Cont'd
Appeal and review—Cont'd
Interlocutory appeal from order of Chief Judge of U.S. Court of International Trade authorizing judge to preside in evidentiary hearing in foreign country, **28 § 256**
Interlocutory order, controlling question of law involved, U.S. Court of Federal Claims, **28 § 1292**
Judicial discipline, complaint, review procedure, **28 § 372**
Natural gas policy decisions, **28 § 1295**
Patents, post
Plant variety protection, decisions respecting, **28 § 1295**
Presidential offices, certain actions, **28 § 1296**
United States Court of International Trade, appeal to, effect on finality, of decision, **28 § 2645**
Appointment, chief judge, **28 § 45 nt**
Attorney General,
Conduct and argument of cases in, **28 § 518**
Transmission of petitions to, **28 § 520**
Black persons, selection of qualified individuals for nomination to judgeships, Congressional recommendations, **28 § 133 nt**
Board of Patent Appeals and Interferences,
Jurisdiction, appeals from decision of, **28 § 1295**
Budget, approval of estimate, **28 § 605**
Chief judge,
Appointment of, **28 § 45 nt**
Former chief judge of former U.S. Court of Claims or U.S. Court of Customs and Patents Appeals, appointment as chief judge with long time service, **28 § 45 nt**
Precedence, **28 § 45**
Report from Director of Administrative Office of U.S. Courts, cause for removal of judge of U.S. Court of Federal Claims, report, **28 § 176**
Residence requirement, **28 § 44**
Vacancy in position, filling of, **28 § 45 nt**
Circuits in which decisions are reviewable, exceptions, **28 § 1294**
Civil action or claim against U.S., jurisdiction of appeals from final decisions of district courts, exception, **28 § 1295**
Commissioner of Patents and Trademarks,
Appeals from,
Decisions of, jurisdiction, **28 § 1295**
Jurisdiction of appeals from decisions of, **28 § 1295**

UNITED STATES COURT OF APPEALS FOR THE FEDERAL CIRCUIT—Cont'd
Complaint, judicial discipline, review procedure, **28 § 372**
Composition of judicial district under jurisdiction of, **28 § 41**
Conduct and argument of cases in by Attorney General or Solicitor General, **28 § 518**
Copyright, appeal from final decision in district court involving, jurisdiction, **28 § 1295**
Court accommodations, provisions by Director of Administrative Office of U.S. Courts, **28 § 462**
Decisions,
  Judgments and decrees, generally, post
Decrees. Judgments and decrees, generally, post
Discipline, judicial, complaint, review procedure, **28 § 372**
District courts,
  Appeals from decisions of, jurisdiction, **28 § 1295**
  Interlocutory appeals, **28 § 1292**
District of Columbia, place of holding terms or sessions, **28 § 48**
Executive departments,
  Final decisions rendered by board of contract appeals, review, jurisdiction, **28 § 1295**
  Furnishing statement concerning facts, relating to petitions, **28 § 520**
  Transmission of petition to Attorney General, **28 § 520**
Foreign country, order of Chief Judge of U.S. Court of International Trade authorizing judge to preside in evidentiary hearing in, interlocutory appeal from, **28 § 256**
Guam, District Court of, jurisdiction of certain appeals from, **28 § 1295**
Harmonized Tariff Schedules of the United States, importation of instruments or apparatus, questions of law relating to, jurisdiction over appeal, **28 § 1295**
Instruments and apparatus, importation of, review, questions of law relating to, **28 § 1295**
Interest, final judgments against U.S., rate of, **28 § 1961**
Interlocutory decisions, appeals from, jurisdiction, **28 § 1292**
Interlocutory order, controlling question of law involved, jurisdiction, discretionary appeal from U.S. Court of Federal Claims, **28 § 1292**
International Trade Commission, determinations,
  Unfair practices, appeal, jurisdiction, **28 § 1295**
Judges,
  Appointment, tenure, **28 § 44**
  Assignment, **28 § 46**

UNITED STATES COURT OF APPEALS FOR THE FEDERAL CIRCUIT—Cont'd
Judges—Cont'd
  Chief judge, generally, ante
  Continued service as, judges of former U.S. Court of Claims and U.S. Court of Customs Patent and Appeals, **28 § 44 nt**
  Number of, **28 § 44**
    Quorum, panel, **28 § 46**
  Official duty station, **28 § 456**
  Panels, generally, post
  Residence requirement, **28 § 44**
  Resignation or retirement for age, **28 § 371**
  Rotation of, panels, **28 § 46**
  Salary, resignation or retirement for age, **28 § 371**
  Selection for nomination, Congressional recommendations regarding blacks and women as qualified individuals for, **28 § 133 nt**
  Senior judges, continued service as, senior judges of former U.S. Court of Claims and U.S. Court of Customs and Patent Appeals, **28 § 44 nt**
  Successor, appointment upon retirement of predecessor, **28 § 371**
  Trial judge, disqualification to hear appeal, **28 § 47**
Judgments and decrees,
  Interest allowable on final money judgments against U.S., rate of, **28 § 1961**
Judicial circuit under jurisdiction, composition of, **28 § 41**
Judicial discipline, complaint, review procedure, **28 § 372**
Jurisdiction,
  Appeals from interlocutory decisions, **28 § 1292**
  Construction of provisions regarding, **28 § 291 nt**
  Courts of appeals, exclusions of U.S. Court of Appeals for the Federal Circuit, **28 § 2342**
  Exclusive, appeals from certain courts, interlocutory decisions, **28 § 1292**
  Limitation, **28 §§ 1291, 1292**
  Presidential and executive offices, certain actions, **28 § 1296**
Merit Systems Protection Board,
  Judicial review, decisions or orders of, **28 § 1295**
Nominations, Congressional recommendations regarding blacks and women as qualified individuals for selection for nomination to judgeships, **28 § 133 nt**
Northern Mariana Islands, District Court for, jurisdiction of certain appeals from, **28 § 1295**
Number of judges, **28 § 44**
  Quorum, panels, **28 § 46**

UNITED STATES COURT OF APPEALS FOR THE FEDERAL CIRCUIT—Cont'd
Official duty station of judges, **28 § 456**
Orders,
  United States Court of Federal Claims, removal of judges, **28 § 176**
Panels,
  Quorum, number of judges, **28 § 46**
  Rotation of judges, **28 § 46**
  Rules, post
Patent and Trademark Office,
  Board of Patent Appeals and Interferences, jurisdiction, appeals from, decisions of, **28 § 1295**
Patents,
  Actions and proceedings,
    Case of interference, review by, **28 § 1295**
  Appeal and review,
    District court to this Court, **28 § 1292**
    Infringement cases, district courts to this Court, **28 § 1292**
  Infringement cases,
    Appeals from district courts, **28 § 1292**
    Judgment, final except for accounting, jurisdiction of appeal, **28 § 1292**
  Interference, action in case of, review by, **28 § 1295**
  Issuance of patent, judgment, interference action authorizing issuance, review by, **28 § 1295**
  Jurisdiction from appeals in district courts involving, **28 § 1295**
Petitions,
  Attorney General, transmission to, **28 § 520**
  Rehearing, reconsideration, or other changes in decisions of former U.S. Court of Claims or U.S. Court of Customs and Patent Appeals, determination by, **28 § 171 nt**
Places for holding terms or sessions, **28 § 48**
Plant variety protection, appeals from decisions respecting, **28 § 1295**
Presidential offices, certain actions, review, **28 § 1296**
Quorum, panels, number of judges, **28 § 46**
Residence requirement for judges and chief judge, **28 § 44**
Review. Appeal and review, generally, ante
Rules, **Title 28 (Rules Volume)**
  Judicial Conference,
    Chief Judge, Judicial Conference, generally, ante
  Panels,
    Rotation, judges, from panel to panel, **28 § 46**

UNITED STATES COURT OF APPEALS FOR THE FEDERAL CIRCUIT—Cont'd
Rules—Cont'd
Rotation of judges from panel to panel, **28 § 46**
Sessions, **28 § 48**
Solicitor General, conduct and argument of cases in, **28 § 518**
Special sessions, **28 § 48**
Special terms, **28 § 48**
Stay of proceedings in interlocutory appeal, **28 § 1292**
Temporary Emergency Court of Appeals, abolition, assignment of cases from, **28 § 1295 nt**
Terms, **28 § 48**
Time,
Sessions, **28 § 48**
Trademarks and Trade Names, this index
Transfer of,
Case pending before former Court of Claims in which report on merits has been filed by Commissioner, **28 § 171 nt**
Matters pending before former U.S. Court of Customs and Patent Appeals to, **28 § 171 nt**
Transmission, Attorney General, petitions in, **28 § 520**
Unfair competition, appeal from final decision in district court involving patent, copyright, jurisdiction, **28 § 1295**
United States as defendant, certain cases involving, jurisdiction of appeals, **28 § 1295**
United States Court of Claims (former court),
Cases pending before, in which report on merits had been filed by Commissioner, transfer to, **28 § 171 nt**
Chief Judge to be appointed as Chief Judge of Court, **28 § 45 nt**
Judges of, in regular active service, continued service as judge of Court, **28 § 44 nt**
Petition for rehearing, reconsideration, or other changes in any decision, determination by, **28 § 171 nt**
Senior judges of, continued service as senior judges of Court, **28 § 44 nt**
United States Court of Customs and Patent Appeals (former court),
Chief Judge to be appointed as Chief Judge of Court, **28 § 45 nt**
Judges of, in regular active service, continued service as judge of Court, **28 § 44 nt**
Matters pending before, transfer to, **28 § 171 nt**
Pending cases, effect of provisions of Customs Courts Act of 1980 upon, **28 § 251 nt**

UNITED STATES COURT OF APPEALS FOR THE FEDERAL CIRCUIT—Cont'd
United States Court of Customs and Patent Appeals (former court)—Cont'd
Petition for rehearing, reconsideration, or other changes in any decision, determination by, **28 § 171 nt**
Senior judges of, continued service as senior judges of Court, **28 § 44 nt**
Vacancy in office of Chief Judge, filling of, **28 § 45 nt**
Virgin Islands, District Court of, jurisdiction, appeals, **28 § 1295**
Women, selection of qualified individuals for nominations to judgeships, **28 § 133 nt**

UNITED STATES COURT OF APPEALS FOR VETERANS CLAIMS
Attorney fees,
United States or federal agencies and instrumentalities, **28 § 2412**
Federal agencies and instrumentalities,
Attorney fees, **28 § 2412**
United States,
Attorney fees, **28 § 2412**

UNITED STATES COURT OF FEDERAL CLAIMS
Generally, **28 § 2501 et seq.**
Act of Congress, jurisdiction of claims founded on, **28 § 1491**
Adjustment, annual salary rates of judges, **28 § 172**
Administrative bodies, employment or retirement status or records, power of court to remand matters involving, **28 § 1491**
Administrative Office of United States Courts,
Director,
Annuities, regulation and payment by, **28 § 604**
Bailiffs and messengers approval of appointment, **28 § 795**
Deputies, clerks and employees, appointment, approval, **28 § 791**
Reporting, court proceedings, contracts, authorization, **28 § 176**
Judges, cause for removal of report to Chief Judge of U.S. Court of Appeals for the Federal Circuit and to judge, **28 § 176**
Affirmations. Oaths and affirmations, generally, post
Age limitation on service as judge, **28 § 171 nt**
Agreements. Contracts, generally, post
Aliens, privilege to sue, **28 § 2502**
Appeal and review,
Decisions,
Obtained by filing notice of appeal, **28 § 2522**
Discretionary appeal of interlocutory order where controlling question of law is involved, **28 § 1292**

UNITED STATES COURT OF FEDERAL CLAIMS—Cont'd
Appeal and review—Cont'd
Interest on judgments against U.S. after affirmance by Supreme Court, **28 § 2516**
Interlocutory order, controlling question of law involved, U.S. Court of Appeals for the Federal Circuit, **28 § 1292**
Judgment finding plaintiff indebted to U.S., **28 § 2508**
Judicial discipline, complaint, review procedure, **28 § 372**
Jurisdiction, U.S. Court of Appeals for the Federal Circuit, **28 § 1295**
New trial after proceeding for review instituted, **28 § 2515**
Panel, Congressional reference cases, **28 § 2509**
Appearance,
Failure of plaintiff to appear for examination before judges, **28 § 2504**
Judge, plaintiff's failure to appear after order for examination before, **28 § 2504**
Proceedings before judge, **28 § 2503**
Applicability, general provisions relating to, **28 § 460**
Appointment,
Bailiffs and messengers, **28 § 795**
Clerks, deputy clerks and employees, **28 § 791**
Judges, by President, **28 § 171**
Law clerks and secretaries, **28 § 794**
Appropriations,
Costs of Congressional reference cases, **28 § 2509**
Army and Air Force Exchange Service, express or implied contract with, jurisdiction of claims founded on, **28 § 1491**
Assignments,
Government employee, action by assignee against Government, patent cases, jurisdiction, **28 § 1498**
Hearing officer, Congressional reference cases, **28 § 2509**
Judges, **28 § 174**
Attorney General,
Conduct and argument of cases in, **28 § 518**
Transmission of petitions to, **28 § 520**
Attorneys,
Admission to practice, certificates, fee schedule, **28 § 1926 nt**
Fees or other compensation, awarded as liability for creating unreasonable, vexatious procedures, **28 § 1927**
Bailiffs, appointment and removal, **28 § 795**
Black persons, selection of qualified individuals for nomination to judgeships, Congressional recommendations, **28 § 133 nt**

UNITED STATES COURT OF FEDERAL CLAIMS—Cont'd
Books and papers,
Call on Federal departments or agencies for discovery purposes, **28 § 2507**
Certification of documents or papers, fee schedule, **28 § 1926 nt**
Referral of cases by Comptroller General, **28 § 2510**
Reproduction, fee schedule, **28 § 1926 nt**
Calls,
On Federal departments or agencies for information or papers, **28 § 2507**
Certificates and certification,
Admission to practice, fee schedule, **28 § 1926 nt**
Documents or papers, fee schedule, **28 § 1926 nt**
Judgment, payment by Treasury Secretary, **28 § 2517**
Unjust conviction and imprisonment, evidence in, **28 § 2513**
Certified copy of pardon, consideration, **28 § 2513**
Chief judge,
Bailiffs, appointment and removal, **28 § 795**
Certification of judgment, payment by Treasury Secretary, **28 § 2517**
Congress, reference of bills to, **28 §§ 1492, 2509**
Assignment of judges, **28 § 174**
Designation, **28 § 171**
Hearings and trials in foreign countries, provisions authorizing, **28 § 798**
Messengers, appointment and removal, **28 § 795**
Special masters appointed by, **28 § 798**
United States Marshals Service, request for attendance at sessions, **28 § 2521**
Clerks of courts,
Appointment and removal, **28 § 791**
Certification of judgment, payment by Treasury Secretary, **28 § 2517**
Costs, payment into Treasury, **28 § 791**
Fee, **28 § 2520**
Payment into Treasury, **28 § 791**
Schedule, services performed by, **28 § 1926 nt**
Moneys collected paid into Treasury, **28 § 791**
Notice of appeal filed with, **28 § 2522**
Returns of money collected to Director of Administrative Office of U.S. Courts, **28 § 791**
Statement of judgments rendered, to every regular session of Congress, **28 § 791**
Coast Guard Exchanges, express or implied contract with, jurisdiction of claims founded on, **28 § 1491**

UNITED STATES COURT OF FEDERAL CLAIMS—Cont'd
Commissioners,
Former Court of Claims, continued service as judges, **28 § 171 nt**
Compensation and salaries,
Judges, post
Complaints,
Judicial discipline, review procedure, **28 § 372**
Conclusions,
Hearing officer, Congressional reference cases, **28 § 2509**
Concurrent jurisdiction with district court, U.S. as defendant, **28 § 1346**
Conduct and argument of cases in by Attorney General or Solicitor General, **28 § 518**
Congress,
Acts of interest on claims against U.S., allowance in judgment, **28 § 2516**
Clerk, transmission of statement of judgments rendered to Congress, **28 § 791**
Jurisdiction, patent and copyright cases, immunity, waiver of not to be construed from amendment of provisions relating to, **28 § 1498 nt**
Reference of bills to chief judge, **28 §§ 1492, 2509**
Congressional reference,
Bills to chief judge, assignment of judges, **28 § 174**
Cases, facilities, providing, **28 § 2509**
Constitution, jurisdiction of claims founded on, **28 § 1491**
Contempt. Rules, post
Contracts,
Express or implied with U.S., jurisdiction of claims founded on, **28 § 1491**
Interest on claims against U.S., allowance in judgment, **28 § 2516**
United States, claims founded on, jurisdiction, **28 § 1491**
Copyrights,
Immunity, waiver of by Member of Congress not to be construed from amendment of provisions relating to, **28 § 1498 nt**
Owner's action against U.S. for infringement, **28 § 1498**
Proceedings against U.S. for infringement, **28 § 1498**
Costs,
Congressional reference cases, **28 § 2509**
Excess, expenses, liability for creating, **28 § 1927**
Lack of jurisdiction, dismissal of suit or action, **28 § 1919**
Payment by clerk into Treasury, **28 § 791**
Prescribed by Judicial Conference, **28 § 1926**

UNITED STATES COURT OF FEDERAL CLAIMS—Cont'd
Costs—Cont'd
Statement by clerk of costs taxed, to Congress, **28 § 791**
Taxation, **28 § 2503**
Counterclaim. Set-off and counterclaim, generally, post
Court accommodations, provision by Director of Administrative Office of U.S. Courts, at District of Columbia, **28 § 462**
Court of the U.S., deemed to be, **28 § 1927**
Damages,
Claim for damages by U.S., against plaintiff making claim, **28 § 2508**
Liquidated or unliquidated, jurisdiction of claims founded on, **28 § 1491**
Not in tort, jurisdiction, **28 § 1491**
Oyster growers, damages from dredging, **28 § 1497**
Unjust conviction and imprisonment, allegations and proof, **28 § 2513**
Decisions. Opinions and decisions, generally, post
Declaratory judgments and decrees,
Relating to status and classification of exempt organizations under section 501(c)(3), income tax, jurisdiction, **28 § 1507**
Decrees. Judgments and decrees, generally, post
Demand set up by U.S. against plaintiff making claim, **28 § 2508**
Deputy clerks, appointment and removal, **28 § 791**
Director. Administrative Office of United States Courts, ante
Discipline, judicial, complaint, review procedure, **28 § 372**
Discovery, **28 § 2507**
Subpoenas for purposes of discovery, **28 § 2521**
District of Columbia, principal office at, **28 § 173**
Domicile and residence,
Judges, **28 § 175**
Electronic access to court data exemptions, **28 § 1926 nt**
Employees. Officers and employees, generally, post
Employment status or records, power of court to fashion remedy involving, **28 § 1491**
Evidence,
Call on Federal departments, agencies, for information or papers, **28 § 2507**
Proceedings to be in accordance with, **28 § 2503**
Fraud,
Forfeiture of claims against U.S., **28 § 2514**
New trial, **28 § 2515**
Place of taking, **28 § 2505**

UNITED STATES COURT OF FEDERAL CLAIMS—Cont'd
Evidence—Cont'd
Rules, post
Unjust conviction and imprisonment, **28 § 2513**
Executive departments,
Call on departments for information or papers, **28 § 2507**
Employment or retirement status or records, remand, **28 § 1491**
Furnishing statement concerning facts, petitions, **28 § 520**
Regulations, claims founded on, jurisdiction, **28 § 1491**
Transmission of petition to Attorney General, **28 § 520**
Expenses and expenditures,
Recalled retired judges, **28 § 797**
Failure to act by party, witness, notation by review panel, Congressional reference cases, **28 § 2509**
Fees, **28 § 2520**
Payment into Treasury, **28 § 791**
Prescribed by Judicial Conference, **28 § 1926**
Rules, post
Filing,
Civil action or proceeding, fee schedule, **28 § 1926 nt**
Findings,
Fraud, forfeiture of claims, **28 § 2514**
Hearing officer, Congressional reference cases, **28 § 2509**
Fines, penalties and forfeitures, contempt proceedings, punishment, **28 § 2521**
Forma pauperis proceedings, **28 § 2503**
Fraud,
Evidence, ante
Findings and forfeiture, **28 § 2514**
New trial, fraud against U.S., **28 § 2515**
Hearings,
Held in counties where witnesses reside, **28 § 2503**
Immunity, waiver of by Member of Congress not to be construed from amendment of provisions relating to patent and copyright cases, **28 § 1498 nt**
In forma pauperis, damages for unjust conviction and imprisonment, **28 § 2513**
Income tax,
Declaratory judgments relating to status and classification of certain exempt organizations,
Jurisdiction over, **28 § 1507**
Partnership and partnership items,
Administrative adjustment request not allowed in full, request on behalf of partnership, review, jurisdiction, **28 § 1508**
Indians,
Jurisdiction, claims arising under Constitution of U.S., **28 § 1505**

UNITED STATES COURT OF FEDERAL CLAIMS—Cont'd
Indians—Cont'd
Treaties, jurisdiction, claims arising under, **28 § 1505**
Interest,
Claims and judgments against U.S., **28 § 2516**
Final money judgment against U.S., rate of, **28 § 1961**
Judgments of money, allowance, computation, **28 § 1961**
Interlocutory order, controlling question of law involved, discretionary appeal to U.S. Court of Appeals for the Federal Circuit, **28 § 1292**
Internal Revenue Service,
Refunds, civil actions for, limitations on right of action, aliens, exception, **28 § 2502**
Judges,
Age limitation on service, **28 § 171 nt**
Appointment, **28 § 171**
Law clerks and secretaries, **28 § 794**
Assignment of, **28 § 174**
Certification of substantial service, recall, **28 § 375**
Chief judge, generally, ante
Commissioner of former U.S. Court of Claims, continued service as, **28 § 171 nt**
Compensation and salaries, **28 § 171 nt**
Adjustments in certain salaries, **28 § 172**
Annual rate, determination and adjustment, of, **28 § 172**
Recall of retired judges, supplemental pay, **28 §§ 375, 797**
Resignation or retirement for age, **28 § 371**
Congressional reference of bills to chief judge, **28 § 2509**
Deemed judges of U.S., **28 § 180**
Director of Administrative Office of U.S. Courts, report on cause for removal, copy transmitted to judge, **28 § 176**
Domicile and residence, **28 § 175**
Duties with regard to trial, **28 § 2503**
Entry of judgment, **28 § 2505**
Hearing officers, Congressional reference cases, powers and duties, **28 § 2509**
Judge of the United States Court of Federal Claims, defined, recall, **28 § 375**
Law books and Government publications furnished transmitted to successor, **28 § 414**
Law clerks,
Annual and sick leave, exceptions from provisions of, **28 § 794**
Appointment by, **28 § 794**
Number, **28 § 171**

UNITED STATES COURT OF FEDERAL CLAIMS—Cont'd
Judges—Cont'd
Official duty station, District of Columbia, **28 § 175**
Recall, retired judges, **28 § 375**
Removal from office, **28 § 176**
Disbarment of removed judges, **28 § 177**
Resignation or retirement for age, **28 § 371**
Retired, military retirement pay, **28 § 180**
Retirement and pensions,
Age, requirement, **28 § 178**
Annuities, **28 § 178**
Regulation and payment by Director of Administrative Office of U.S. Courts, **28 § 604**
Survivors, **28 § 376**
Court, defined, **28 § 178**
Payments, **28 § 178**
Recall, **28 §§ 375, 797**
Requirements, **28 § 178**
Retirement Fund, establishment in Treasury, **28 § 178**
Service, requirement, **28 § 178**
Unfunded liability, defined, Retirement Fund, **28 § 178**
Review panel, Congressional reference cases, **28 § 2509**
Secretaries, appointment by, **28 § 794**
Selection for nomination, Congressional recommendations regarding Blacks and women as qualified individuals, **28 § 133 nt**
Senior retired judge recalled to perform duties as judge, **28 § 797**
Successor, appointment upon retirement of predecessor, **28 § 371**
Tenure, **28 § 172**
Term of office, **28 § 171 nt**
Judgments and decrees,
Conclusiveness, **28 § 2519**
Decisions, preserved and open to inspection, **28 § 174**
Disbursing officers, relief from liability from loss, **28 § 2512**
Employment or retirement status or records, power of court to fashion remedy involving, **28 § 1491**
Entry, **28 § 2505**
Indebtedness of plaintiff to U.S., **28 § 2508**
Interest,
Allowance, computation, **28 § 1961**
Judgments against U.S., **28 § 2516**
Powers and duties of judges, **28 § 2503**
Referral of cases by Comptroller General, **28 § 2510**
Statement to Congress by clerk, **28 § 791**
Transcripts, post
Unsettled accounts of Government officers, contractors, suit by, conclusiveness and payment, **28 § 2511**

UNITED STATES COURT OF FEDERAL CLAIMS—Cont'd
Judicial Conference,
Fees and costs prescribed by, **28 § 1926**
Schedule of fees, **28 § 1926 nt**
Judicial discipline, complaint, review procedure, **28 § 372**
Judicial review. Appeal and review, generally, ante
Jurisdiction,
Accounts of officer or agent of, or contractor with, U.S., **28 § 1494**
Appeal from decision of, **28 § 1295**
Concurrent jurisdiction with District Court, U.S. as defendant, **28 § 1346**
Contracts, claims founded on, **28 § 1491**
Copyright cases, **28 § 1498**
Disbursing officers claims, **28 § 1496**
Income tax,
Declaratory judgments relating to status and classification of exempt organizations under section 501(c)(3), **28 § 1507**
Partnership and partnership items,
Administrative adjustment request not allowed in full, judicial review, **28 § 1508**
Judicial review of final partnership administrative adjustments, **28 § 1508**
Refunds of tax shelter promoter and understatement penalties, **28 § 1509**
Indian claims, **28 § 1505**
Lack of, dismissal, **28 § 1919**
Liquidated damages withheld from contractors under Contract Work Hours Standards Act, **28 § 1499**
Mask work cases, semiconductor chip products, **28 § 1498**
Oyster growers, damages from dredging operation, **28 § 1497**
Penalties withheld from contractor, **28 § 1499 nt**
Pendency, claims in other courts, **28 § 1500**
Pensions, **28 § 1501**
Set-offs or demands by U.S., **28 § 1503**
Transfer to cure want of jurisdiction, **28 § 1631**
Treaty cases, **28 § 1502**
United States as defendant, concurrent jurisdiction with district court, **28 § 1346**
Unjust conviction and imprisonment, damages for, **28 § 1495**
Law clerks,
Annual and sick leave, exceptions from provisions of, **28 § 794**
Appointment by judges, **28 § 794**
Limitation of actions, **28 § 2501**
New trial by U.S., **28 § 2515**

UNITED STATES COURT OF FEDERAL CLAIMS—Cont'd
Liquidated damages withheld from contractors under Contract Work Hours Standards provisions, jurisdiction, **28 § 1499**
Lists,
Monthly listing of opinions and orders, **28 § 1926 nt**
Marine Corps Exchanges, express or implied contract with, jurisdiction of claims founded on, **28 § 1491**
Mask work cases, semiconductor chip products, jurisdiction, **28 § 1498**
Messengers, appointment and removal, **28 § 795**
Military retirement pay, judges, **28 § 180**
Motions. Rules, post
National Aeronautics and Space Administration, Exchange Councils of, express or implied contract, jurisdiction, **28 § 1491**
Navy,
Exchanges, express or implied contract with, jurisdiction of claims founded on, **28 § 1491**
New trial, **28 § 2515**
Nominations, Congressional recommendations regarding Blacks and women as qualified individuals for selection for nomination to judgeships, **28 § 133 nt**
Notice,
Appeal, review of decision obtained by, **28 § 2522**
Attorney General, suit by Government officers, contractors, **28 § 2511**
Plaintiff to appear and be examined on oath, **28 § 2504**
Suit by Government officers, contractors, on unsettled accounts, **28 § 2511**
Number of judges, **28 § 171**
Oaths and affirmations,
Examination of plaintiff on oath, **28 § 2504**
Judges, administration, **28 § 2503**
Officers and employees,
Appointment and removal by clerk of court, **28 § 791**
Jurisdiction of accounts, **28 § 1494**
Refusal to comply with call for information or papers, **28 § 2507**
Remand of matters involving employment or retirement status or records to, power of court, **28 § 1491**
Suit by employee against Government, patent cases, jurisdiction, **28 § 1498**
Unsettled accounts, notice of suit, **28 § 2511**
Opinions and decisions,
Monthly listing, fee schedule, **28 § 1926 nt**

UNITED STATES COURT OF FEDERAL CLAIMS—Cont'd
Orders of court,
Employment or retirement status or records, power of court to fashion remedy involving, **28 § 1491**
Examination of plaintiff on oath before judges, **28 § 2504**
Issuance and service of subpoenas, **28 § 2521**
Monthly listing, fee schedule, **28 § 1926 nt**
Postponement of trial until plaintiff appears for examination before judge, **28 § 2504**
Oyster growers, damages from dredging operations, **28 § 1497**
Papers. Books and papers, generally, ante
Pardon,
Consideration, **28 § 2513**
Evidence of unjust conviction and imprisonment, **28 § 2513**
Parties,
Call on party for information or papers, **28 § 2507**
Examination of plaintiff on oath before judge, **28 § 2504**
Exemption or disqualification as witness, **28 § 2506**
Subpoena for attendance, **28 § 2521**
Partnership,
Income tax, ante
Patents,
Actions,
Immunity of Member of Congress, waiver of not to be construed from amendment of provisions relating to, **28 § 1498 nt**
Jurisdiction, **28 § 1498**
Payment,
Interest on judgment against U.S. affirmed by Supreme Court, **28 § 2516**
Judgments against U.S., **28 § 2517**
Pendency of claims in other courts, **28 § 1500**
Pension bills, exception, reference to chief judge, **28 §§ 1492, 2509**
Pensions, jurisdiction, **28 § 1501**
Petitions,
Attorney General, transmission to, **28 § 520**
Fee for filing, **28 § 2520**
Places, **28 § 798**
Plaintiff,
Appear for examination at instance of Attorney General, **28 § 2504**
Plant variety protection, infringement by U.S., corporation owned or controlled by U.S., exclusive remedy by action against U.S. in, **28 § 1498**
Pleading,
Unjust conviction and imprisonment, **28 § 2513**

UNITED STATES COURT OF FEDERAL CLAIMS—Cont'd
President, appointment of judges, 28 **§ 171**
Reasonable and entire compensation, defined, copyright cases, **28 § 1498**
Records and recordation, **28 § 171**
Employment, power of court to fashion remedy involving, **28 § 1491**
Reproduction, fee schedule, **28 § 1926 nt**
Referral, cases, Comptroller General, **28 § 2510**
Refusal,
Plaintiff to testify or answer at examination before judge, **28 § 2504**
Remand, remedy involving employment or retirement status or records, powers of court, **28 § 1491**
Removal,
Bailiffs and messengers, **28 § 795**
Clerk, deputy clerks and employees, **28 § 791**
Judges, **28 §§ 176, 177**
Reporting services, proceedings in open court, contracts by Director of Administrative Office of U.S. Courts, **28 § 796**
Reports,
Reference of bill by Congress, **28 §§ 1492, 2509**
Review panel, Congressional reference cases, **28 § 2509**
Reproduction, records or papers, fee schedule, **28 § 1926 nt**
Retirement and pensions,
Judges, ante
Status, power of court to fashion remedy involving, **28 § 1491**
Review. Appeal and review, generally, ante
Rules, Title 28 (Rules Volume)
Contempt,
Power to impose, **28 § 2521**
Evidence,
Proceedings in accordance with, **28 § 2503**
Fees,
Advance payment, requirements, **28 § 1926**
Motions,
Stay of proceedings,
Motions to transfer action, **28 § 1292**
Sanctions,
Unreasonable or vexatious conduct, liability for excess costs, expenses, attorneys fees, **28 § 1927**
Schedule,
Fees prescribed by Judicial Conference, **28 § 1926 nt**
Secretaries, appointment by judges, **28 § 794**

UNITED STATES COURT OF FEDERAL CLAIMS—Cont'd
Secretary of Treasury,
Contract disputes, judgment of U.S., payment, exception, **28 § 2517**
Sentence and punishment,
Imprisonment, contempt proceedings, **28 § 2521**
Unjust imprisonment,
Damages in Court, allegations and proof, **28 § 2513**
Jurisdiction, claim for damages, **28 § 1495**
Set-off and counterclaim, **28 § 2508**
Jurisdiction, **28 § 1503**
Solicitor General, conduct and argument of cases in, **28 § 518**
Special masters,
Appointment, **28 § 798**
Stay of proceedings,
Interlocutory appeal, proceedings in, **28 § 1292**
Judgment, **28 § 2515**
Studies, concurrent jurisdiction with district courts, time, contents, **28 § 1491 nt**
Subpoenas,
Issuance for attendance of parties, production of books, **28 § 2521**
Supreme Court,
Interest on judgments against U.S. affirmed by after review on petition, **28 § 2516**
Surface Transportation Board,
Orders, judicial referral cases, civil actions to enforce,
Jurisdiction, **28 § 1336**
Venue, **28 § 1398**
Rules, generally, ante
Tax refund cases, jurisdiction in cases involving tax shelter promoter and understatement penalties, **28 § 1509**
Tax shelter promoter cases involving refunds, no jurisdiction, **28 § 1509**
Tenure of judges, **28 § 171**
Term of office of judge, **28 § 171 nt**
Time,
Filing suit, limitation of action, claim of which Court has jurisdiction, **28 § 2501**
Holding court, **28 § 173**
Tort claims, jurisdiction of claims for damages not sounding in tort, **28 § 1491**
Transcripts,
Judgments and decrees, **28 § 2508**
Filing in GAO, factor, payment, interest on judgment against U.S. affirmed by Supreme Court, **28 § 2516**
Suits by Government officers, contractors, on unsettled accounts, entry and enforcement, **28 § 2511**

UNITED STATES COURT OF FEDERAL CLAIMS—Cont'd
Transcripts—Cont'd
Supplying to court, contract for reporting of proceedings, terms and condition for, **28 § 796**
Transfer of cases or causes,
To cure want of jurisdiction, **28 § 1631**
Transmission,
Attorney General, petitions in, **28 § 520**
Treaties,
Jurisdiction of claims, **28 § 1502**
Trial,
Before judges, **28 § 2505**
Fixing times, **28 § 2503**
Judge, Congressional reference cases, **28 § 2509**
Understatement penalties, cases involving refunds, no jurisdiction, **28 § 1509**
United States Court of Appeals for the Federal Circuit,
Chief Judge, report by Director of Administrative Office of U.S. Courts to, cause for removal of judge of, **28 § 176**
Discretionary appeal of interlocutory order where controlling question of law is involved, **28 § 1292**
Jurisdiction, appeals from U.S. United States Court of Federal Claims, **28 § 1295**
Removal of judges by order of, **28 § 176**
United States Court of Claims (former court),
Cases pending before, in which report on merits filed by commissioner, transfer to U.S. Court of Appeals for the Federal Circuit, **28 § 171 nt**
Chief judge of, appointment as chief judge of U.S. Court of Appeals for the Federal Circuit, **28 § 45 nt**
Commissioners of,
Continued service as judge of Court, **28 § 171 nt**
Matters pending before, determination by U.S. United States Court of Federal Claims, **28 § 171 nt**
Judges of, continued service as judges of U.S. Court of Appeals for the Federal Circuit, **28 § 44 nt**
Pending dispositive motions, determination by, **28 § 171 nt**
Petition for rehearing, reconsideration, or other changes in decisions, determination by U.S. Court of Appeals for the Federal Circuit, **28 § 171 nt**
United States Marshals Service, attendance at sessions, **28 § 2521**

UNITED STATES COURT OF FEDERAL CLAIMS—Cont'd
Unjust conviction and imprisonment,
Allegations and proof of claims, 28 § 2513
Damages for, 28 § 1495
Vouchers,
Disbursing officers, jurisdiction to relieve from responsibility, 28 § 1496
Papers, referral of cases by Comptroller General, 28 § 2510
Witnesses,
Administration of oaths or affirmations, examination by judges, 28 § 2503
Exemption or disqualification, party or interested in suit, 28 § 2506
Interest as disqualification, 28 § 2506
Per diem and mileage allowances, 28 § 1821
Subpoenas,
Attendance, 28 § 2521
Subsistence allowance, 28 § 1821
Women, selection of qualified individuals for nomination to judgeships, Congressional recommendations, 28 § 133 nt

UNITED STATES COURT OF INTERNATIONAL TRADE
Abstracts of decisions, publication, 28 § 257
Accredited laboratories, reports from, analysis of imported merchandise, 28 § 1581 nt
Additional findings of court, 28 § 2645
Adjustment in annual salary rate of judges, 28 § 252
Administering authority,
Identification and transmission to clerk of court, documents, comments, that are accorded confidential or privileged status, 28 § 2635
Administrative remedies, exhaustion of, 28 § 2637
Admiralty, seizures in, jurisdiction, 28 § 1356
Admissibility in evidence, value of merchandise issue in civil action, reports or depositions of consuls, customs officers, 28 § 2639
Affidavits,
Admissibility in evidence, value of merchandise issue in civil action, 28 § 2639
Affirmative statement, transmission to clerk of court certain items not existing in particular civil action, filing of official documents, 28 § 2635
Age,
Chief judge, 28 § 258
Judges, precedence according to seniority in, 28 § 253
Amendments,
Decisions and judgments, 28 § 2645

UNITED STATES COURT OF INTERNATIONAL TRADE—Cont'd
Amendments—Cont'd
Findings of court, 28 § 2645
Summons, pleadings and other papers, 28 § 2633
American manufacturers', producers', or wholesalers' cases,
Exclusive jurisdiction, 28 § 1582
Persons entitled to commence civil action contesting denial of protest, 28 § 2631
Analysis of imported merchandise, 28 § 2642
Antidumping duties,
Burden of proof in civil actions, 28 § 2639
Civil actions,
Free trade area country merchandise, authority, 28 § 2643
Transmission by administering authority or International Trade Commission to Clerk, record of civil action, 28 § 2635
Exclusive jurisdiction,
Civil actions under NAFTA or United States-Canada Free-Trade Agreement, disclosure of information, 28 § 1584
Proceedings concerning, 28 § 1581
Persons entitled to commence civil action contesting determination, 28 § 2631
Protective order, disclosure of information under, exclusive jurisdiction, application for order, 28 § 1581
Scope and standard of review in civil actions, 28 § 2640
Time for commencement of civil action contesting a reviewable determination, 28 § 2636
Appeal and review,
Effect on finality, of decision, 28 § 2645
Exclusive jurisdiction, final determination of Secretary of Commerce respecting eligibility of a firm for adjustment assistance, civil action, 28 § 1581
Interlocutory appeal from order authorizing judge to preside in evidentiary hearing in foreign country, 28 § 256
Judicial discipline, complaint, review procedure, 28 § 372
Rules, post
Scope and standard of, 28 § 2640
Transmission to clerk of court, official documents, 28 § 2635
Application,
Issuance of order,
Directing administering authority or International Trade Commission to make confidential information available, disclosure, limitations, 28 § 2643

UNITED STATES COURT OF INTERNATIONAL TRADE—Cont'd
Application—Cont'd
Issuance of order—Cont'd
Making confidential information available, time for commencement of action, 28 § 2636
Order directing administering authority or International Trade Commission to make confidential information available, 28 § 2635
Three-judge trial, 28 § 255
Appointment and performance of duties of bailiffs and messengers, 28 § 872
Appraisal and appraisers,
Value of,
Merchandise, exclusive jurisdiction, civil action by person whose protest denied, 28 § 1582
Assistant clerk of court, appointment and removal, 28 § 871
Attorney General,
Conduct and argument of cases in, 28 § 518
Service, summons upon, where U.S. or its agencies or officers are adverse parties, 28 § 2633
Attorneys,
Civil actions, opportunity to introduce evidence, hear and cross-examine witnesses, in, 28 § 2641
Bailiffs, criers to perform duties of, 28 § 872
Black persons, selection of qualified individuals for nomination to judgeships, Congressional recommendations, 28 § 133 nt
Bonds,
Civil action to recover on bond relating to importation of merchandise, exclusive jurisdiction, action commenced by U.S., 28 § 1582
Executed under Federal law, 28 § 1352
Recovery upon, claim or action, counterclaims, exclusive jurisdiction to render judgment upon, 28 § 1583
Books and papers,
Amendment, service, of papers, 28 § 2633
Injunctions, service upon named officials, 28 § 2633
Inspection, civil actions, 28 § 2641
Mailing by registered or certified mail, deemed filed as of date of mailing, 28 § 2632
Official documents, filing of, 28 § 2635
Rules, post
Budget, approval of estimate, 28 § 605
Burden of proof in civil actions, 28 § 2639
Catalogs, admissibility in evidence, value of merchandise issue in civil action, 28 § 2639

UNITED STATES COURT OF INTERNATIONAL TRADE—Cont'd
Certified copies, transcript of hearings, notices, transmission by Secretary, action, foreign merchandise not being sold in U.S. at less than fair value, **28 § 2632**
Charges, within jurisdiction of Secretary of Treasury, exclusive jurisdiction, civil action by person whose protest denied, **28 § 1582**
Chief deputy clerk of court, appointment and removal, **28 § 871**
Chief judge,
Certificate of disability furnished to President in behalf of retirement, **28 § 372**
Designation,
Judges to preside at trial or hearing at ports other than New York, **28 § 256**
Judges to try cases, **28 § 253**
Three-judge trials, **28 § 255**
District court clerk to act as clerk of, request to judicial district, **28 § 751**
Dockets, promulgation of, **28 § 253**
Duties, **28 § 253**
Fiscal affairs and clerical force of court, supervision of, approval of court, **28 § 253**
Inability to perform duties, **28 § 253**
Judicial Conference of U.S., representation, **28 § 331**
Mandatory retirement age, **28 § 251 nt**
Powers and duties devolving upon inability to perform duties or vacancy in office, **28 § 253**
Precedence and to preside at any session which he attends, **28 § 253**
Qualifications, precedence of judges, **28 § 258**
Application, **28 § 258 nt**
Reassignment of cases to other judges, **28 § 253**
Vacancy in office, **28 § 253**
Civil penalties, civil actions commenced by U.S. to recover, exclusive jurisdiction, **28 § 1582**
Claims,
United States, payment, judgment and compromise settlement, **28 § 2414**
Classification,
Exclusive jurisdiction, civil action commenced to review prior to importation of goods, rulings issued by Secretary of Treasury respecting, **28 § 1581**
Rates, of duties chargeable, exclusive jurisdiction, civil action by person whose protest denied, **28 § 1582**
Clerical force of court, supervision by chief judge, approval of court, **28 § 253**

UNITED STATES COURT OF INTERNATIONAL TRADE—Cont'd
Clerks of courts,
Administering authority or International Trade Commission to transmit to clerk confidential information, **28 § 2635**
Appointment and removal, **28 § 871**
Customs officers to transmit official documents to in certain civil actions, **28 § 2635**
District court clerk for judicial district to act as clerk of,
Purposes of selecting and summoning jury, **28 § 1876**
Request by chief judge, approval, **28 § 751**
Fees, generally, post
Filing, generally, post
Commencement,
Action, time for, **28 § 2636**
Civil action, **28 § 2632**
Persons entitled to, **28 § 2631**
Communities, eligibility for adjustment assistance,
Civil action commenced to review final determination of Secretary of Commerce respecting,
Exception, granting injunction or issuing writ of mandamus, **28 § 2643**
Persons entitled to commence civil action, **28 § 2631**
Scope and standard of review, **28 § 2640**
Time for commencement of action, **28 § 2636**
Final determination of Secretary of Commerce respecting, exclusive jurisdiction, civil action commenced to review, **28 § 1581**
Compensation and salaries,
Judges, post
Jurors, **28 § 1876**
Complaints,
Commencement of civil action by filing with clerk, **28 § 2632**
Content, form, style, **28 § 2632**
Judicial discipline,
Review procedure, **28 § 372**
Compromise and settlement, claims against U.S., payment, **28 § 2414**
Conclusions of law,
Final decision in contested civil action, support by statement of, **28 § 2645**
Conduct and argument of cases in by Attorney General, **28 § 518**
Confidential or privileged information,
Availability, exclusive jurisdiction, civil action involving application for order directing administering authority or International Trade Commission to make, **28 § 1581**

UNITED STATES COURT OF INTERNATIONAL TRADE—Cont'd
Confidential or privileged information —Cont'd
Order directing administering authority or International Trade Commission to make available, civil action involving, application for, persons entitled to commence civil action, **28 § 2631**
Trade secrets, order and disclosure of, **28 § 2641**
Confidential or privileged status of certain documents, in certain civil actions, **28 § 2635**
Congressional Acts, constitutionality, three-judge trials, **28 § 255**
Consolidation of causes, **28 § 2633**
Rules, post
Constitution of U.S., establishment under Art. III, **28 § 251**
Constitutionality of Congressional Acts or Presidential proclamations or Executive orders, three-judge trials, **28 § 255**
Consuls, reports or depositions admissible in evidence, value of merchandise in issue in certain civil actions, **28 § 2646**
Contents, summons and complaint, **28 § 2632**
Contested civil action, final decision, support by statement of findings or fact, **28 § 2645**
Continuation of existing law by Judiciary and Judicial Procedure Code, **28 §§ 251, 251 nt**
Copies,
Decisions, forwarding to Secretary of Treasury, **28 § 257**
Costs,
Lack of jurisdiction, dismissal of suit or action, **28 § 1919**
Counterclaims,
Civil action, exclusive jurisdiction, judgment upon respecting claims involving imported merchandise or to recover upon bond or customs duties, **28 § 1583**
Entry of money judgment for or against U.S. or any other party in civil actions, **28 § 2643**
Countervailing duties,
Burden of proof in civil actions, **28 § 2639**
Civil actions,
Free trade area country merchandise, authority, **28 § 2643**
Transmission by administering authority or ITC to Clerk, record of civil action, **28 § 2635**
Exclusive jurisdiction,
Civil actions under NAFTA or United States-Canada Free-Trade Agreement, disclosure of information, **28 § 1584**

UNITED STATES COURT OF INTERNATIONAL TRADE—Cont'd
Countervailing duties—Cont'd
Exclusive jurisdiction—Cont'd
Proceedings involving, **28 § 1581**
Persons entitled to commence civil action contesting determination, **28 § 2631**
Protective order, disclosure of information under, exclusive jurisdiction, application for order, **28 § 1581**
Scope and standard of review in civil actions, **28 § 2640**
Time for commencement of civil action contesting a reviewable determination, **28 § 2636**
Criers, appointment and performance of duties of bailiffs and messengers, **28 § 872**
Cross claims,
Civil action, exclusive jurisdiction, judgment upon respecting claims involving imported merchandise or to recover upon bond or customs duties, **28 § 1583**
Entry of money judgment for or against U.S. or any other party in civil actions, **28 § 2643**
Cross examination,
Witnesses, civil actions, **28 § 2641**
Customs brokers,
Civil actions, contesting denial, revocation or suspension by Secretary of license, time for commencement of action, **28 § 2636**
Exclusive jurisdiction civil action to review decision of Secretary of Treasury to deny, revoke or suspend, **28 § 1581**
License,
Civil action to review decision of Secretary to deny, revoke, or suspend,
Persons entitled to commence civil action, **28 § 2631**
Scope and standard of review, **28 § 2640**
Suspension, revocation, exclusive jurisdiction of civil action commenced to review, **28 § 1581**
Permit, recovery of civil penalty for violation, **28 § 1582**
Prohibited acts, monetary penalty, relief, **28 § 2643**
Scope and standard of review of civil actions concerning, **28 § 2640**
Customs Court,
Judges, provisions of 1980 Act not to affect status of judge or chief judge, **28 § 251 nt**
Pending cases, effect of provisions upon, **28 § 251 nt**
References in statutes or regulations of U.S. to deemed references to, **28 § 251 nt**

UNITED STATES COURT OF INTERNATIONAL TRADE—Cont'd
Customs laws, civil actions having significant, implications in administration, three-judge trials, **28 § 255**
Customs officers,
Forwarding copies of decisions to, **28 § 257**
Reports or depositions admissible in evidence, value of merchandise in issue in certain civil action, **28 § 2639**
Transmission to clerk, filing of documents in certain civil actions, **28 § 2635**
Death, judge, vacancy caused by, after additional judge appointed, not to be filled, **28 § 372**
Decisions, **28 § 2645**
Final and conclusive, **28 § 2645**
Inability to determine correct decision on basis of evidence, order, retrial or rehearing, **28 § 2643**
Motion to amend, **28 § 2645**
Preservation and inspection, **28 § 257**
Publication, **28 § 257**
Support of final decision by statement of findings of fact, in contested civil action, **28 § 2645**
Declaratory judgments and decrees,
Order for, civil actions, **28 § 2643**
Depositions,
Consuls, customs officers, admissibility in evidence where value of merchandise is in issue in civil action, **28 § 2639**
Deputy clerks of court, appointment and removal, **28 § 871**
Disability. Judges, post
Discipline, judicial, complaint, review procedure, **28 § 372**
Disclosure,
Information, civil action involving application for issuance of order directing administering authority or International Trade Commission to make confidential information available, **28 § 2643**
Trade secrets and commercial or financial information which is privileged, ordering, disclosure of, **28 § 2641**
Discrimination prohibited, exclusion from service as grand or petit juror on account of race, color, **28 § 1862**
Dismissal,
Action or suit for lack of jurisdiction, **28 § 1919**
District courts,
Bonds executed under Federal law, exclusion of international trade matters, **28 § 1352**
Designation and assignment,
District judge to serve as judge of, **28 § 292**

UNITED STATES COURT OF INTERNATIONAL TRADE—Cont'd
District courts—Cont'd
Designation and assignment—Cont'd
Judge to perform judicial duties in district court, **28 § 293**
Exclusion of international trade matters from jurisdiction of, **28 § 1337**
Fines, penalties or forfeitures, recovery of, exclusion of international trade matters, **28 § 1355**
Judges of, designation and temporary assignment to perform judicial duties in district court, **28 § 293**
Jurisdiction over civil actions concerning customs duties, exception, matters within jurisdiction of, **28 § 1340**
Jurors in, qualifications as applicable to jurors in, **28 § 1876**
Jury selection plan, selection of jury in civil action in, conformity to, **28 § 1876**
Powers of Court of International Trade, same as powers in law and equity of, **28 § 1585**
Docket,
Promulgation by chief judge, **28 § 253**
Drawbacks,
Exclusive jurisdiction, civil action commenced to review prior to importation of goods, rulings issued by Secretary of Treasury respecting, **28 § 1581**
Refusal to pay claim for, exclusive jurisdiction, civil action by person whose protest denied, **28 § 1582**
Embargoes or other restrictions on importation of merchandise, exclusive jurisdiction, civil action commenced against U.S. or its agencies or officers, **28 § 1581**
Employees and officers,
Appointment and removal, **28 § 871**
Deprivation of any rights, privileges, or civil service status, **28 § 871 nt**
Exclusive jurisdiction, civil action commenced against respecting revenue from imports or tonnage, tariffs, duties, **28 § 1581**
Reports or depositions admissible in evidence, value of merchandise in issue in certain civil actions, **28 § 2646**
Service of summons upon Attorney General where adverse party, **28 § 2633**
Entry,
Money judgments in certain civil actions, **28 § 2643**
Requirements, exclusive jurisdiction, civil action commenced to review prior to importation of goods, rulings issued by Secretary of Treasury respecting, **28 § 1581**

UNITED STATES COURT OF INTERNATIONAL TRADE—Cont'd
Equity, powers in equity same as district court, **28 § 1585**
Estimate, budget, approval of, **28 § 605**
Evidence,
Inability to determine correct decision on basis of, order, retrial or rehearing, **28 § 2643**
Opportunity introduced, civil actions, **28 § 2641**
Rules, post
Exclusion, merchandise from entry or delivery, exclusive jurisdiction, civil action by person whose protest denies, **28 § 1582**
Exclusive jurisdiction. Jurisdiction, generally, post
Exhaustion,
Administrative remedies, **28 § 2637**
Remedies, requirement, exclusive jurisdiction, civil action by person whose protest denied, **28 § 1582**
Federal Register, publication in, time for commencement of civil action contesting determinations by administering authorities, **28 § 2636**
Federal Rules of Evidence, applicability to all civil actions, **28 § 2641**
Fees,
Court may fix fees charged by clerk, **28 § 2633**
Filing fee, payment to clerk of court upon commencement of civil action, **28 § 2633**
Rules, post
Schedule of, **28 § 2633 nt**
Filing,
Commencement of civil action by filing summons and complaint with clerk, **28 § 2632**
Fee, payment to clerk of court upon commencement of civil action, **28 § 2633**
Official documents, **28 § 2635**
Protest, requirement, exclusive jurisdiction, civil action instituted by person whose protest denied, **28 § 1582**
Rules, post
Summons,
Pleadings, and other papers, **28 § 2633**
Findings of fact, final decision in contested civil action, support by statement of, **28 § 2645**
Fines, penalties and forfeitures,
Customs broker's permit, recovery of civil penalty for violation, **28 § 1582**
Recovery of, **28 § 1355**

UNITED STATES COURT OF INTERNATIONAL TRADE—Cont'd
Firms, eligibility for adjustment assistance,
Civil action commenced to review final determination of Secretary of Commerce respecting,
Exception granting injunction or issuing writ of mandamus, **28 § 2643**
Persons entitled to commence civil action, **28 § 2631**
Scope and standard of review, **28 § 2640**
Time for commencement of action, **28 § 2636**
Final determination of Secretary of Commerce respecting, exclusive jurisdiction, civil action commenced to review, **28 § 1581**
Fiscal affairs, supervision by chief judge, **28 § 253**
Foreign countries,
Order authorizing judge to preside in evidentiary hearing in,
Interlocutory appeal from, **28 § 256**
United States Court of Appeals for the Federal Circuit, jurisdiction of discretionary appeal, **28 § 1292**
Foreign manufacturers, producers, or exporters, "party-at-interest" as meaning, persons entitled to commence civil action, **28 § 2631**
Forms,
Rules, post
Summons and complaint, **28 § 2632**
Government agencies,
Persons adversely affected or aggrieved by agency action, persons entitled to commence civil action, **28 § 2631**
Reports from, analysis of imported merchandise, **28 § 2642**
Service of summons upon Attorney General where adverse party, **28 § 2633**
Government procurement,
Civil action contesting final determination, time for commencement of action, **28 § 2636**
Persons entitled to commence civil action to review final determinations respecting, **28 § 2631**
Scope and standard of review in civil actions, **28 § 2640**
Secretary of Treasury, exclusive jurisdiction of civil action commenced to review final determination of concerning, **28 § 1581**
Grand jury, exclusion from service as because of race, color, discrimination prohibited, **28 § 1862**
Hearings,
Civil action, three-judge trials, **28 § 255**

UNITED STATES COURT OF INTERNATIONAL TRADE—Cont'd
Hearings—Cont'd
Foreign countries, orders authorizing judges to preside in, **28 § 256**
Ports other than New York, **28 § 256**
Rehearing, generally, post
Rules, post
Time and place of, notice of, **28 § 2634**
Witnesses, civil actions, **28 § 2641**
Immoral articles, importation prohibited, exception to exclusive jurisdiction of civil action concerning, **28 § 1581**
Imported merchandise,
Analysis of, **28 § 2642**
Exclusive jurisdiction, judgment, claim or action involving, **28 § 1583**
Importers of merchandise, "party-at-interest" as meaning, persons entitled to commence civil action, **28 § 2631**
Inability of chief judge to perform duties, **28 § 253**
Injunctions,
Inapplicability in civil actions commenced to review final determinations of Secretaries of Labor and Commerce relating to adjustment assistance for workers, **28 § 2643**
Orders of, civil actions, **28 § 2643**
Preliminary injunctions, decision granting or refusing, support by statement of findings or fact, **28 § 2645**
Summons, pleadings, and other papers, service upon named officials, **28 § 2633**
Inspection and inspectors,
Decisions, **28 § 257**
Rules, post
Samples and papers, civil actions, **28 § 2641**
Interest, monetary relief by judgment or stipulation agreement, civil actions, allowance, rate, **28 § 2644**
Interested party, defined, persons entitled to commence civil actions, **28 § 2631**
Interlocutory order, controlling question of law involved, U.S. Court of Appeals for the Federal Circuit, jurisdiction of discretionary appeal, **28 § 1292**
International Trade Commission,
Decision of, presumption, correctness, **28 § 2639**
Identification and transmission to clerk of court, documents, comments, that are accorded confidential or privileged status, **28 § 2635**
International trade matters, exclusive jurisdiction of, **28 § 1337**
Intervention, leave of court, persons adversely affected or aggrieved by decisions in civil actions pending in, **28 § 2631**

UNITED STATES COURT OF INTERNATIONAL TRADE—Cont'd
Judges,
Additional judge, appointment when judge eligible to retire is unable to discharge duties, **28 § 372**
Age, precedence according to seniority in, **28 § 253**
Annuities to survivors, **28 § 376**
Appointment and number, **28 § 251**
Certificate of disability furnished to President in behalf of retirement, **28 § 372**
Chief judge, generally, ante
Compensation and salaries,
Annual rate, determination and adjustment of, **28 § 252**
Deduction and withholding for purposes of annuities, to survivors, **28 § 376**
Retirement for disability, **28 § 372**
Decisions, generally, ante
Designation,
Assignment, district judge, to serve as judge of, **28 § 292**
Judges to preside at trail or hearing at port other than New York, **28 § 256**
Temporary assignment to perform judicial duties in court of appeals or district court, **28 § 293**
Try cases, **28 § 253**
Disability,
Appointment of additional judge, **28 § 372**
Retirement for, **28 § 372**
District judge to serve as judge of, **28 § 292**
Evidentiary hearing in foreign country, authorization to preside in, **28 § 256**
Inability to perform duties when eligible to retire, appointment of additional judge, **28 § 372**
Judgments and decrees, generally, post
Judicial Conference of Court, attendance, **28 § 335**
Law books and Government publications furnished transmitted to successor, **28 § 414**
Number, **28 § 251**
Official duty station, **28 § 456**
Orders of court, generally, post
Political affiliations, restrictions on appointment, **28 § 251**
Powers and duties of chief judge devolving upon judge, conditions, **28 § 253**
Precedence, **28 § 253**
Presiding judge, **28 § 253**
Reassignment of cases to other judges, **28 § 253**
Selection for nomination, Congressional recommendation regarding blacks and women as qualified individuals for, **28 § 133 nt**

UNITED STATES COURT OF INTERNATIONAL TRADE—Cont'd
Judges—Cont'd
Seniority, **28 § 253**
Single-judge trials, **28 § 254**
Tenure, **28 § 252**
Three-judge trials, **28 § 255**
Traveling expenses, **28 § 456**
Vacancy caused by death, resignation, after additional judge appointed, not to be filled, **28 § 372**
Judgments and decrees,
Against U.S., payment of, **28 § 2414**
Monetary relief, interest, allowance, rate, **28 § 2644**
Money judgments, entry in certain civil actions, **28 § 2643**
Judicial Conference of Court, **28 § 335**
Judicial Conference of U.S., representation, **28 § 331**
Judicial discipline, complaint, review procedure, **28 § 372**
Judicial district, request by Chief Judge to, clerk of district court to act as clerk of, **28 § 751**
Judicial review. Appeal and review, generally, ante
Jurisdiction,
Accreditation of private laboratories, **28 §§ 1581, 1581 nt**
Application for order directing administering authority or International Trade Commission to make confidential information available, exclusive jurisdiction, **28 § 1581**
Counterclaims, cross-claims, and third-party actions involving imported merchandise or action to recover upon bond or customs duties, **28 § 1583**
Countervailing duty and antidumping duty proceedings, **28 § 1581**
District courts, jurisdiction over civil actions concerning customs duties, exception, matters within jurisdiction of, **28 § 1340**
Government procurement, exclusive jurisdiction, civil action to review final determination of Secretary of Treasury respecting, **28 § 1581**
Immoral articles, importation of, exception to exclusive jurisdiction of civil action concerning, **28 § 1581**
International trade matters, **28 § 1337**
Lack of, dismissal, **28 § 1919**
Petitions by domestic interested parties, **28 § 1581**
Prohibition, construction of act concerning judges to limit or alter court's jurisdiction, **28 § 251 nt**
Protective orders, limited disclosure of information relating to antidumping duties or countervailing duties, exclusive jurisdiction, application for order, **28 § 1581**

UNITED STATES COURT OF INTERNATIONAL TRADE—Cont'd
Jurisdiction—Cont'd
Protest, contesting denial of, civil actions, **28 § 1581**
Secretary of Commerce, final determination of, exclusive jurisdiction of civil action commenced to review, respecting eligibility of a community for adjustment assistance, **28 § 1581**
Secretary of Labor, final determination of, exclusive jurisdiction of civil action commenced to review, respecting eligibility of firm for adjustment assistance, **28 § 1581**
Secretary of Treasury,
Civil action commenced to review decision to deny, revoke or suspend customhouse broker's license, **28 § 1581**
Exclusive jurisdiction, civil action commenced to review prior to importation of goods involved, rulings issued, relating to classification, valuation, rate of duty, **28 § 1581**
Transfer to cure want of jurisdiction, **28 § 1631**
United States, civil actions commenced by, respecting import transactions, **28 § 1582**
United States or its agencies or officers, exclusive jurisdiction, civil action commenced against relating to tariffs, duties, revenue from imports or tonnage, **28 § 1581**
Jury,
Exclusion from service as because of race, color, discrimination prohibited, **28 § 1862**
Trial by,
Challenging jurors, **28 § 1876**
Compensation of jurors, **28 § 1876**
District court clerk to sit as clerk of court for purposes of selecting and summoning jury, **28 § 1876**
Qualifications for jurors to be same as qualifications for jurors of district courts, **28 § 1876**
Selection under procedures in jury selection plan of district court, **28 § 1876**
Labor organizations, manufacture, in U.S. of like products, U.S. members of, "party-at-interest" as meaning persons entitled to commence civil action, **28 § 2631**
Laboratories,
Private, jurisdiction over accreditation, **28 §§ 1581, 1581 nt**
Reports from, analysis of imported merchandise, **28 § 2642**

UNITED STATES COURT OF INTERNATIONAL TRADE—Cont'd
Leave of court, intervention in civil actions by persons adversely affected or aggrieved by decision, exceptions, **28 § 2631**
Limitation of actions,
Civil action brought to contest denial of protest, **28 § 1582**
Liquidated duties, charges, amount of recovery, civil action, action by surety, **28 § 2643**
Liquidation or reliquidation of an entry, exclusive jurisdiction, civil action by person whose protest denied, **28 § 1582**
Majority, three-judge trials, hearing and determination of civil actions, **28 § 255**
Mandamus,
Exception, issuance of writ in civil actions commenced to review final determinations of Secretaries of Labor and Commerce respecting adjustment assistance for workers, **28 § 2643**
Writs of, orders of, **28 § 2643**
Manner, summons and complaint, **28 § 2632**
Marking, exclusive jurisdiction, civil action commenced to review prior to importation of goods, rulings issued by Secretary of Treasury respecting, **28 § 1581**
Messengers, criers to perform duties of, **28 § 872**
Motions,
Amendments of findings or making additional findings, **28 § 2645**
Retrial or rehearing, **28 § 2646**
New grounds in support of civil action, **28 § 2638**
New York City,
Location of offices, **28 § 251**
Official station of judges, **28 § 456**
Nomination, Congressional recommendations regarding blacks and women as qualified individuals for selection for nomination to judgeships, **28 § 133 nt**
Notice,
Rules, post
Trial or hearing, time and place of, **28 § 2634**
Number, entries of merchandise involving common issues, inclusion in civil action by person whose protest denied, **28 § 1582**
Office, location, **28 § 251**
Officers and employees. Employees and officers, generally, ante
Official station of judges, **28 § 456**
Opinions and decisions,
Final decision in contested civil action, supported by, **28 § 2645**

UNITED STATES COURT OF INTERNATIONAL TRADE—Cont'd
Orders of court,
Analysis of imported merchandise, **28 § 2642**
Availability of confidential or privileged material in certain civil actions, **28 § 2635**
Declaratory judgments and decrees, orders of remand, injunctions, **28 § 2643**
Interlocutory appeal from, **28 § 256**
Relief, **28 § 2643**
Retrial or rehearing, upon failure to determine correct decision on basis of evidence, **28 § 2643**
Trade secrets and commercial or financial information, disclosure, **28 § 2641**
Papers. Books and papers, generally, ante
Parties,
Application,
Order authorizing judge to preside in evidentiary hearing in foreign country, **28 § 256**
Three-judge trial, **28 § 255**
Opportunity to introduce evidence, hear and cross-examine witnesses, in civil actions, **28 § 2641**
Party-at-interest, defined, persons entitled to commence civil action, **28 § 2631**
Petitions by domestic interested persons,
Burden of proof in civil actions, **28 § 2639**
Civil action,
Contesting denial of petition, exhaustion of administrative remedies, **28 § 2637**
Denial of petition, filing of official documents, **28 § 2635**
Exclusive jurisdiction, **28 § 1581**
Persons entitled to commence civil action contesting denial of, **28 § 2631**
Scope and standard of review in civil actions, **28 § 2640**
Time for commencement of action, civil action contesting denial of, **28 § 2636**
Place,
Rules, post
Trial or hearing, notice of, **28 § 2634**
Pleading,
Amendment, service, **28 § 2633**
Injunctions, service upon named officials, **28 § 2633**
Mailing by registered or certified mail, deemed filed as of date of mailing, **28 § 2632**
Rules, post
Powers and duties in general, powers in law and equity same as district court, **28 § 1585**

UNITED STATES COURT OF INTERNATIONAL TRADE—Cont'd
Precedence, chief judge and judges, **28 §§ 253, 258**
Preservation, decisions, **28 § 257**
Presidential proclamations or Executive orders, constitutionality of, three-judge trials, **28 § 255**
Presumption, correctness, decisions of Secretary of Treasury or administering authority, **28 § 2639**
Price lists, admissibility in evidence, value of merchandise issue in civil action, **28 § 2639**
Procedure, **28 § 2631 et seq.**
Procedure and fees, schedule, **28 § 2633 nt**
Prohibition, writ of, orders of, **28 § 2643**
Protective orders, limited disclosure, information relating to antidumping duties or countervailing duties, exclusive jurisdiction, application for order, **28 § 1581**
Protest,
Civil actions,
Contesting denial of,
Burden of proof in civil actions, **28 § 2639**
Exclusive jurisdiction, **28 § 1581**
Exhaustion of administrative remedies, **28 § 2637**
New grounds in support of civil action, **28 § 2638**
Official documents, filing of, **28 § 2635**
Persons entitled to commence civil action, **28 § 2631**
Scope and standard of review in civil actions, **28 § 2640**
Time for commencement of action, **28 § 2636**
Exclusive jurisdiction, civil actions, **28 § 1582**
Contesting denial of, **28 § 1581**
Rules, post
Publication of decisions, **28 § 257**
Race, color, religion, exclusion from service as grand or petit juror on account of, discrimination prohibited, **28 § 1862**
Rate of duty, exclusive jurisdiction, civil action commenced to review prior to importation of goods, rulings issued by Secretary of Treasury respecting, **28 § 1581**
Reassignment, cases to other judges by chief judge, **28 § 253**
Records and recordation,
Court of, **28 § 251**
Determinations upon basis of, **28 § 2640**
Official records, transmittal from Customs Service to clerk, entry of merchandise, administrative determination, **28 § 2635**

UNITED STATES COURT OF INTERNATIONAL TRADE—Cont'd
Recovery of customs duties, exclusive jurisdiction,
Civil action commenced by U.S., **28 § 1582**
Refusal to reliquidate entry, civil action by person whose protest denied, exclusive jurisdiction, **28 § 1582**
Rehearing,
Effect on finality of decision, **28 § 2645**
Order of, inability to determine correct decision on basis of evidence, **28 § 2643**
Relief, **28 § 2643**
Remand, order of, civil actions, **28 § 2643**
Removal,
Criers, **28 § 872**
Reports,
Consuls, customs officers, admissibility in evidence where value of merchandise is in issue in civil action, **28 § 2639**
Laboratories or Government agencies, analysis of imported merchandise, **28 § 2642**
Resignation, judge, vacancy caused by, after additional judge appointed, not to be filled, **28 § 372**
Restricted merchandise, exclusive jurisdiction, civil action commenced to review prior to importation of goods, rulings issued by Secretary of Treasury respecting, **28 § 1581**
Retirement and pensions, judge, for disability, **28 § 372**
Retrials,
Effect on finality, of decision, **28 § 2645**
Order of, inability to determine correct decision on basis of evidence, **28 § 2643**
Revenue from imports or tonnage, exclusive jurisdiction, civil action commenced against U.S. or its agencies or employees, **28 § 1581**
Rules, **Title 28 (Rules Volume)**
Amendments,
Summons,
Pleadings, and other papers, prescribing, **28 § 2633**
Antidumping duties, administering authority or International Trade Commission to transmit to clerk, record of civil action, prescribing, **28 § 2635**
Appeal and review,
Transmission of official documents to clerk of court in certain civil actions, prescribing, **28 § 2635**
Books and papers,
Inspection,
Civil actions, prescribing, **28 § 2641**

UNITED STATES COURT OF INTERNATIONAL TRADE—Cont'd
Rules—Cont'd
Books and papers—Cont'd
Mailing by registered or certified mail, deemed filed as of date of mailing, prescribing, **28 § 2632**
Official documents,
Filing,
Prescribing, **28 § 2635**
Commencement of action,
Time for, prescribing, **28 § 2636**
Confidential or privileged information,
Transmission by administering authority or International Trade Commission to clerk, certain civil actions, prescribing, **28 § 2635**
Consolidation of causes,
Cases, prescribing, **28 § 2633**
Contents,
Summons and complaint, prescribing, **28 § 2632**
Countervailing duties, administering authority or International Trade Commission to transmit to clerk, record of civil action, prescribing, **28 § 2635**
Cross examination,
Witnesses, civil actions, prescribing, **28 § 2641**
Customs duties, antidumping and countervailing duty proceedings, elimination of interlocutory appeals, commencement of action, prescribing, **28 § 2636**
Evidence,
Civil actions, opportunity to introduce evidence, prescribing, **28 § 2641**
Fees,
Filing,
Amount prescribed by, **28 § 2633**
Filing,
Official documents,
Prescribing, **28 § 2635**
Forms,
Summons,
Complaint, prescribing, **28 § 2632**
Hearings,
Time and place of, notice of, prescribing, **28 § 2634**
Witnesses, civil actions, prescribing, **28 § 2641**
Inspection and inspectors,
Samples and papers, civil actions, prescribing, **28 § 2641**
Manner, summons and complaint, prescribing, **28 § 2632**
Notice,
Trial or hearing, time and place of, prescribing, **28 § 2634**
Place,
Trial or hearings,
Notice of, prescribing, **28 § 2634**

UNITED STATES COURT OF INTERNATIONAL TRADE—Cont'd
Rules—Cont'd
Pleading,
Mailing by certified or registered mail,
Deemed filed as of date of mailing, prescribing, **28 § 2632**
Protest,
Protesting denial of, customs officers, transmission to Clerk, official documents as part of official record, prescribing, **28 § 2635**
Registered or certified mail, summons, pleading, or other paper mailed by, deemed filed as of date of mailing, prescribing, **28 § 2632**
Samples,
Inspection, civil actions, prescribing, **28 § 2641**
Service of process,
Summons, **CIT R3, Prac nt; R4, Prac nt**
Pleadings and other papers, prescribing, **28 § 2633**
Severance of cases, prescribing, **28 § 2633**
Stay of proceedings,
Interlocutory appeal, **28 § 1292**
Style, summons and complaint, prescribing, **28 § 2632**
Summons,
Mailing by registered or certified mail, deemed filed as of date of mailing, prescribing, **28 § 2632**
Suspension of cases, prescribing, **28 § 2633**
Time,
Commencement of action, prescribing, judicial review, countervailing and antidumping duty proceedings, **28 § 2636**
Trial or hearing, notice of, prescribing, **28 § 2634**
Trial,
Time and place of, notice of, prescribing, **28 § 2634**
Witnesses,
Civil actions, opportunity to hear and cross-examine, prescribing, **28 § 2641**
Salaries. Compensation and salaries, generally, ante
Samples, inspection, civil actions, **28 § 2641**
Schedule of fees, **28 § 2633 nt**
Scope of review, **28 § 2640**
Seal of court, identification and transmission under seal to clerk of court, documents, contents, that were obtained on confidential basis, **28 § 2635**
Searches and seizures,
Not within admiralty or maritime jurisdiction, **28 § 1356**

UNITED STATES COURT OF INTERNATIONAL TRADE—Cont'd
Secretary of Commerce,
Civil action commenced to review final determination respecting eligibility of a community for adjustment assistance,
Exception, granting injunction or issuing writ of mandamus, **28 § 2643**
Persons entitled to commence civil action, **28 § 2631**
Scope and standard of review, **28 § 2640**
Time for commencement of action, **28 § 2636**
Final determination of,
Civil action commenced to review, exclusive jurisdiction, eligibility of a community for adjustment assistance, **28 § 1581**
Exclusive jurisdiction, civil action commenced to review eligibility of a firm for adjustment assistance, **28 § 1581**
Secretary of Labor,
Civil action commenced to review final determination respecting eligibility of workers for adjustment assistance,
Exception, granting injunction or issuing writ of mandamus, **28 § 2643**
Persons entitled to commence civil action, **28 § 2631**
Scope and standard of review, **28 § 2640**
Time for commencement of action, **28 § 2636**
Final determination respecting eligibility of workers for adjustment assistance, exclusive jurisdiction of civil action commenced to review, **28 § 1581**
Secretary of Treasury,
Civil actions,
Commenced to review prior to importation of goods, rulings respecting classification, valuation, rate of duty, persons entitled to commence civil action, **28 § 2631**
Contesting denial, revocation or suspension of customhouse broker's license, time for commencement of action, **28 § 2636**
Review decision to deny, revoke or suspend customhouse broker's license,
Persons entitled to commence civil action, **28 § 2631**
Scope and standard of review, **28 § 2640**

UNITED STATES COURT OF INTERNATIONAL TRADE—Cont'd
Secretary of Treasury—Cont'd
Civil actions—Cont'd
Review prior to importation of goods involved, rulings respecting classification, valuation, rate of duty,
Burden of proof in civil actions, **28 § 2639**
Exhaustion of administration remedies, **28 § 2637**
Ordering appropriate declaratory relief, **28 § 2643**
Decisions of, presumption and burden of proof concerning, **28 § 2639**
Exclusive jurisdiction, civil action commenced to review prior to importation of goods involved, rulings relating to classification, valuation, rate of duty, **28 § 1581**
Payment of judgments and compromise settlements against U.S., **28 § 2414**
Publication, decisions and abstracts thereof, **28 § 257**
Seniority, chief judge, **28 § 258**
Service of process,
Rules, ante
Summons, pleadings, and other papers, **28 § 2633**
Sessions, single judges holding regular or special session, **28 § 254**
Severance of cases, **28 § 2633**
Solicitor General, conduct and argument of cases in, **28 § 518**
Standards, review, **28 § 2640**
Stay of proceedings. Rules, ante
Stipulations,
Agreement, monetary relief, interest, allowance, rate, **28 § 2644**
Documents, comments, transmission to clerk of court, **28 § 2635**
Style, summons and complaint, **28 § 2632**
Summons,
Amendment, service, **28 § 2633**
Commencement of civil action by filing with clerk, **28 § 2632**
Content, form, style, **28 § 2632**
Injunctions, service upon named officials, **28 § 2633**
Mailing by registered or certified mail, deemed filed as of date of mailing, **28 § 2632**
Rules, ante
Surety,
Commencement of civil action, amount of recovery, **28 § 2643**
Suspension,
Cases, **28 § 2633**
Tariffs, duties, importation of merchandise, exclusive jurisdiction, civil action commenced against U.S. or its agencies, or employees, **28 § 1581**

UNITED STATES COURT OF INTERNATIONAL TRADE—Cont'd
Third parties,
Civil action, exclusive jurisdiction, judgment upon respecting claims involving imported merchandise or to recover upon bond or customs duties, **28 § 1583**
Entry of money judgment for or against U.S. or any other party in civil actions, **28 § 2643**
Time,
Amendments of findings of court, **28 § 2645**
Commencement of action, **28 § 2636**
Motions,
Amendment of findings or making additional findings, **28 § 2645**
Retrial or rehearing, **28 § 2646**
Retrial or rehearing, **28 § 2646**
Rules, ante
Trial or hearing, notice of, **28 § 2634**
Trade or business association manufacturing, producing, like products in U.S., "party-at-interest" as meaning, **28 § 2631**
Trade secrets and commercial or financial information which is privileged, disclosure of, ordering, **28 § 2641**
Transfer to cure want of jurisdiction, **28 § 1631**
Traveling expenses, judges, **28 § 456**
Trial,
Notice, time and place of, **28 § 2634**
Ports other than New York, **28 § 256**
Retrials, generally, ante
Rules, ante
Single-judge trials, **28 § 254**
Three-judge trials, **28 § 255**
Undue delay or prejudice, intervention, leave of court, civil actions, considerations concerning, **28 § 2631**
United States,
Civil actions commenced by,
Burden of proof provisions inapplicable to, **28 § 2639**
Scope and standard of review, **28 § 2640**
Claims against,
Payment, judgments and compromise settlements, **28 § 2414**
Entry of money judgment in civil actions for or against, **28 § 2643**
Exclusive jurisdiction, civil action,
Arising out of import transactions commenced by, **28 § 1582**
Commenced against respecting revenue from imports or tonnage, tariffs, duties, **28 § 1581**
Service of summons upon Attorney General where adverse party, **28 § 2633**

UNITED STATES COURT OF INTERNATIONAL TRADE—Cont'd
United States Court of Appeals for the Federal Circuit,
Appeal and review,
Effect on finality, of decisions, **28 § 2645**
Interlocutory appeal from order of Chief Judge authorizing judge to preside in evidentiary hearing in foreign country, **28 § 256**
Foreign country, order authorizing judge to preside at evidentiary hearing in,
Controlling question of law involved, jurisdiction of discretionary appeal, **28 § 1292**
Interlocutory appeal from, **28 § 256**
Interlocutory order, controlling question of law involved, jurisdiction of appeal, **28 § 1292**
Jurisdiction of appeals from final decisions of, **28 § 1295**
Rules of practice. United States Court of Appeals for the Federal Circuit, generally, this index
Vacancy in office of chief judge, **28 § 253**
Valuation, exclusive jurisdiction, civil action commenced to review prior to importation of goods, rulings issued by Secretary of Treasury respecting, **28 § 1581**
Value of merchandise, issue in civil action, reports or depositions of consuls, customs officers, admissibility in evidence, **28 § 2639**
Vessel repairs, exclusive jurisdiction, civil action commenced to review prior to importation of goods, rulings issued by Secretary of Treasury respecting, **28 § 1581**
Wages. Compensation and salaries, generally, ante
Witnesses,
Civil action, **28 § 2641**
Rules, ante
Women, selection of qualified individuals for nomination to judgeships, Congressional recommendations, **28 § 133 nt**
Workers, eligibility for adjustment assistance,
Civil action commenced to review final determination of Secretary respecting,
Exception, granting injunction or issuing writ of mandamus, **28 § 2643**
Persons entitled to civil action, **28 § 2631**
Scope and standard of review, **28 § 2640**
Time for commencement of action, **28 § 2636**

UNITED STATES COURT OF INTERNATIONAL TRADE—Cont'd
Workers, eligibility for adjustment assistance—Cont'd
Final determination of Secretary of Labor respecting, exclusive jurisdiction, civil action commenced to review, **28 § 1581**

UNITED STATES COURT OF MILITARY APPEALS
United States Court of Appeals for the Armed Forces, generally, this index

UNITED STATES COURTS OF APPEALS
Courts of Appeals, generally, this index

UNITED STATES DISTRICT COURT FOR DISTRICT OF COLUMBIA
Chief Judge,
Chief Justice, known as, **28 § 451 nt**
Civil rights and elective franchises, State for purpose of this section, **28 § 1343**
Clerks of district courts,
Domicile and residence, **28 § 751**
Contempt, Senate order or subpoena, enforcement, **28 § 1365**
Declaratory judgments,
Senate subpoena or order, validity, jurisdiction, **28 § 1365**
District Court of the U.S. for the District of Columbia known as, **28 § 451 nt**
Evidence, **28 § 1731 et seq.**
Fees, applicability of provisions, **28 § 1914**
Judges,
Acknowledgments, authority to take, **28 § 459**
Chief Judge, generally, ante
Domicile and residence, exemption from requirements, **28 § 134**
Number, **28 § 133**
Oaths and affirmations, authority to administer, **28 § 459**
Official duty station, **28 § 456**
Relatives ineligible to appointment to any office or duty in court, **28 § 458**
Jurisdiction,
Senate actions to enforce subpoena or order, **28 § 1365**
Obsolete papers, disposition, **28 § 457**
Official duty station of judges, **28 § 456**
Places of holding, **28 § 88**
Procedure, **28 § 1651 et seq.**
Process, Senate action to enforce subpoena, **28 § 1365**
Rules,
Power to prescribe, public notice and comment, **28 § 2071**
Savings provision, **28 § 2071**
Supreme Court of District of Columbia known as, **28 § 451 nt**
Traveling expenses of judges, **28 § 456**

UNITED STATES DISTRICT COURTS
District Courts, generally, this index

UNITED STATES DUTY
Customs Duties, generally, this index

UNITED STATES GOVERNMENT
United States, generally, this index

UNITED STATES INSTRUMENTALITY
Federal Agencies and Instrumentalities, generally, this index

UNITED STATES JUDGES OR JUSTICES
Judges or Justices, generally, this index

UNITED STATES MAGISTRATE JUDGES
Additional duties, assignment, rules, **28 § 636**
Adjoining districts, designation to serve in, district judges, **28 § 631**
Age, continuation of service and reappointment after age 70, **28 § 631**
Annual and sick leave, exceptions from provisions of, **28 § 631**
Appeal and review,
Disqualification, **28 § 455**
Appointment, **28 §§ 631, 631 nt**
United States commissioners to office of, **28 § 631 nt**
Virgin Islands, **28 § 631**
Arrest or imprisonment or writ of execution or other process, proceedings for discharge before, **28 § 2007**
Assistance to district judge in conduct of pretrial or discovery proceedings in civil or criminal actions, **28 § 636**
Black persons, selection of qualified individuals for nomination to judgeships,
Congressional recommendations, **28 § 133 nt**
Merit selection panels to consider, **28 § 631 nt**
Certificate of,
Official acts, seal affixed without fee, **28 § 638**
Payment of witness fees, **28 § 1825**
Changes in number, locations and salaries, **28 § 633**
Character of service, **28 § 631**
Civil jurisdiction in district court exercise dependent on certification or reappointment under Judicial Conference of U.S., **28 § 631 nt**
Civil office, restrictions on holding, **28 § 631**
Civil proceedings, designation to conduct in district court with consent of parties, **28 § 636**
Clerical, legal and secretarial assistants,
Annual and sick leave, exceptions from provision of, **28 § 634**
As officers and employees in judicial branch of U.S. Government, **28 § 634**

UNITED STATES MAGISTRATE JUDGES—Cont'd
Clerical, legal and secretarial assistants —Cont'd
Compensation, **28 § 635**
Clerks of district courts,
Compensation on appointment as, **28 § 751**
Magistrate judge designated to conduct civil proceedings, notice to parties, right to consent to exercise of jurisdiction, **28 § 636**
Notice to Director of Administrative Office of U.S. of appointment of, **28 § 631**
Compensation and salaries, **28 § 634**
Clerical, legal and secretarial assistants, **28 § 635**
Clerks of district courts appointed as, **28 § 751**
Determination respecting, **28 § 633**
Full-time and part-time magistrate judges,
Maximum rates, continuation of, **28 § 634 nt**
Compilation and evaluation of statistical and other information required for performance of duties, **28 § 604**
Conflicts of interest provisions, **28 §§ 631, 632**
Consent,
Parties, conduct of civil proceedings in district court by, **28 § 636**
Contempt, proceedings before, acts or conduct constituting, **28 § 636**
Continuing education, function of Federal Judicial Center, **28 § 620**
Court interpreters. Interpreters, generally, this index
Court security, transfer to U.S. marshals, **28 § 604**
Courtrooms, office space, furniture and facilities, providing, **28 § 635**
Deemed to be officers and employees in judicial branch of U.S. Government, **28 § 634**
Definitions, **28 § 639**
Degree of relationship, defined, disqualification, **28 § 455**
Designation of Magistrate Judge to conduct,
Civil proceedings in district court, **28 § 636**
Appointment or reappointment after promulgation of selection standards by Judicial Conference or certification as qualified, requirement, **28 § 631 nt**
Professional background and qualifications, statistics reported to Congress, **28 § 604**
Statistics reported to Congress, **28 § 604**
Misdemeanors, trial of in district court, **28 § 636**

UNITED STATES MAGISTRATE JUDGES—Cont'd
Determination respecting number of full-time and part-time Magistrate Judges, locations of service and compensation, **28 § 633**
Disqualification, personal grounds, **28 § 455**
District courts,
Chief judges, temporary assignment of Magistrate Judge in emergency from one judicial district to another, approval and orders concerning, **28 § 636**
Merit selection panels, establishment to fill vacancies, **28 § 631**
Virgin Islands, appointment of, **28 § 631**
District Judges, this index
Dockets, furnishing of, **28 § 639**
Emergencies, temporary assignment from one judicial district to another, **28 § 636**
Engaging in business, occupation or employment inconsistent with performance of duties as judicial officers, **28 § 632**
Equipment and supplies, purchase, for, **28 § 604**
Expenses and expenditures, **28 § 635**
Printing of record on appeal or preparation of transcript, payment as in forma pauperis proceedings, **28 § 1915**
Temporary assignment in an emergency from one judicial district to another, reimbursement of, **28 § 636**
Expiration of term, performance of duties until appointment of successor, Judicial Council approval required, **28 § 631**
Federal employment, restrictions, **28 § 631**
Fees,
Jurors, **28 § 1871**
Seal to be affixed to jurat or certificate without fee, **28 § 638**
Taxation as costs, **28 § 1920**
Witnesses, **28 § 1922**
Fiduciary, defined, disqualification, **28 § 455**
Financial interest, defined, disqualification, **28 § 455**
Forms, furnishing of, **28 § 638**
Full-time Magistrate Judges,
Appointment, **28 § 631**
Compensation, **28 § 634**
Continuation of maximum rates, **28 § 634 nt**
Defined, **28 § 639**
Fixing maximum limits of compensation, **28 § 634**
Practice of law by, **28 § 632**
Term of office, **28 § 631**

UNITED STATES MAGISTRATE JUDGES—Cont'd
Government officers and employees, restrictions on holding office of, **28 § 631**
Hearings,
Conducting, **28 § 636**
Hispanics, selection of qualified individuals to be Magistrate Judges, merit selection panels to consider, **28 § 631 nt**
Infractions,
Powers and duties, **28 § 636**
Investigation, official acts, by Attorney General, **28 § 526**
Judicial Center,
Boards and commissions, membership on, **28 § 621**
Conduct of,
Periodic training programs and seminars, **28 § 637**
Programs, continuing education and training, **28 § 620**
Judicial Conference of the United States, this index
Judicial Council, this index
Judicial discipline, complaint, review procedure, **28 § 372**
Jurat, seal to be affixed without fee, **28 § 638**
Jurisdiction, powers of Magistrate Judge designated to conduct civil proceedings in district court, **28 § 636**
Jurors, fees, **28 § 1871**
Labor and employment,
Veterans, preference, **28 § 601 nt**
Law books, purchase, for, **28 § 604**
Legal assistants, payment of expenses for, **28 § 635**
Manuals with supplements and revisions, preparation and distribution for use of, **28 § 604**
Merit selection panels,
Consideration of women, blacks, Hispanics, and other minorities, **28 § 631 nt**
Standards of Judicial Conference, **28 § 631**
Military office, restrictions on holding, **28 § 631**
Minor or petty offenses,
Powers, **28 § 636**
Minorities, selection of qualified individuals to serve as Magistrate Judges, merit selection panels to consider, **28 § 631 nt**
Misdemeanors,
Powers and duties, **28 § 636**
Nominations, Congressional recommendations regarding blacks and women as qualified individuals for selection for nomination to judgeships, **28 § 133 nt**
Notice,
Appointment, **28 § 631**

UNITED STATES MAGISTRATE JUDGES—Cont'd
Notice—Cont'd
Vacancies in magistrate judge positions, standards and procedures of Judicial Conference, **28 § 631**
Oaths and affirmations, **28 § 631**
Office space, procurement, reimbursement for expense incurred for, **28 § 635**
Officers and employees,
Veterans, preference, **28 § 601 nt**
Other office, restrictions on holding, **28 § 631**
Part-time Magistrate Judges, **28 § 631**
Compensation, **28 § 634**
Continuation of maximum rates, **28 § 634 nt**
Conduct of, civil proceedings in district court, **28 § 636**
Appointment or reappointment after promulgation of selection standards by Judicial Conference or certification as qualified, requirement, **28 § 631 nt**
Professional background and qualifications, statistics reported to Congress, **28 § 604**
Statistics reported to Congress, **28 § 604**
Defined, **28 § 639**
Fixing maximum limits of compensation, **28 § 634**
Practice of law by, **28 § 632**
Recommendation concerning appointment, surveys, **28 § 633**
Reimbursement for expenses incurred, **28 § 635**
Surveys respecting, **28 § 633**
Term of office, **28 § 631**
Periodic training programs and seminars for, Judicial Center to conduct, **28 § 637**
Petty offenses. Minor or petty offenses, generally, ante
Powers, **28 § 636**
Preliminary review, applications for post-trial relief, individuals convicted of criminal offenses, report and recommendations, submission, **28 § 636**
Pretrial matter pending, hearing and determining, **28 § 636**
Proceeding, defined, disqualification, **28 § 455**
Property furnished to remain property of U.S., **28 § 638**
Provisions applicable to powers, duties, of U.S. commissioners not to continue after Magistrate Judge assumes office, **28 § 631 nt**
Qualifications, **28 § 631**
Recall of retired Magistrate Judge, compensation, **28 § 636**
Records and recordation,
Appointment, **28 § 631**

UNITED STATES MAGISTRATE JUDGES—Cont'd
Records and recordation—Cont'd
Determination of manner of taking, Magistrate Judge designated to exercise civil jurisdiction in district court, **28 § 636**
Duty to keep, **28 § 604**
On appeal, payment of expenses of printing as in forma pauperis proceeding, appeal from decision of Magistrate Judge designated to exercise civil jurisdiction in district court, **28 § 1915**
Reduction of compensation, prohibition, **28 § 634**
Reference to United States magistrate deemed reference to United States Magistrate Judge, **28 § 631 nt**
References to United States commissioner deemed reference to, **28 § 631 nt**
Reinstatement after release from service or training, in Armed Forces, **28 § 631**
Removal, **28 § 631**
Reporters,
Transcription of civil proceeding in district court heard by Magistrate Judge designated to exercise civil jurisdiction, transfer for temporary service, **28 § 636**
Reports, duty to make, **28 § 604**
Restrictions on holding office of, **28 § 631**
Seal, **28 § 638**
Selection pursuant to standards of Judicial Conference of U.S., **28 § 631**
Separability of provisions respecting, **28 § 631 nt**
Service as U.S. commissioner after date on which Magistrate Judge assumes office, prohibition, **28 § 631 nt**
Special master, service as in civil action, **28 § 636**
Supervision of administrative matters relating to, **28 § 604**
Surveys respecting number of appointments, locations of service and compensation, **28 § 633**
Temporary assignment from one judicial district to another in an emergency, **28 § 636**
Tenure, **28 § 631**
Training, function of Federal Judicial Center, **28 § 620**
Transcripts, civil or criminal proceedings, preparation where required by district court as in forma pauperis proceeding, **28 § 1915**
Trial, **28 § 636**
Proceeding or appellate review of proceeding, disqualification, applicability, submission prior to date of act, **28 § 455**
United States magistrates' name changed to, **28 § 631 nt**

UNITED STATES MAGISTRATE JUDGES—Cont'd
Veterans,
Labor and employment, preference, **28 § 601 nt**
Virgin Islands, district courts, appointment of, **28 § 631**
Waiver,
Disqualification, applicability, **28 § 455**
Witnesses,
Fees, **28 § 1922**
Per diem, mileage and subsistence expenses, **28 § 1821**
Women, selection of qualified individuals for nomination to judgeships,
Congressional recommendations, **28 § 133 nt**
Merit selection panels to consider, **28 § 631 nt**

UNITED STATES MAGISTRATES
United States Magistrate Judges, generally, this index

UNITED STATES MARINE CORPS
Marine Corps, generally, this index

UNITED STATES MARSHALS SERVICE
Generally, **28 § 561 et seq.**
Accounts and accounting, public monies, **28 § 566**
Appointment of marshals, **28 § 561**
Appropriations, **28 § 561**
Arrest,
Property in admiralty, discharge of property from, **28 § 2464**
Without warrant, authority to make, **28 § 566**
Attorney General,
Appointment of persons to fill vacancies, **28 § 562**
Fees for services, establishment, **28 § 1921**
Bailiffs, employment to attend district court, **28 § 755**
California, transfer and appointment, **28 § 84 nt**
Certified copy of official paper, evidence of court record lost or destroyed, **28 § 1735**
Collection of lawful fees, accounting as public moneys, **28 § 567**
Commissions,
Sale of property seized, **28 § 1921**
Compensation and salaries,
Commissions, **28 § 1921**
Determination by Director, **28 § 561**
Fees, generally, post
Utilization of fees collected, **28 §§ 1921, 1921 nt**
Court security, responsibility for, transfer to, **28 § 604**
Criminal cases, services in, fees, **28 § 1921**
Death, after levy on or sale of realty, **28 § 2003**

UNITED STATES MARSHALS SERVICE—Cont'd
Deposits required to cover fees and expenses, **28 § 1921**
Deputies,
  Keeping of property attached, special services, fee, **28 § 1921**
  Practice of law prohibited, **28 § 568**
Deputy Marshals,
  Designation by Director, **28 § 564**
  Oath of office, **28 § 563**
  Power as sheriff, **28 § 564**
  Practice of law prohibited, **28 § 568**
Detention facilities, construction and renovation, use of deposits transferred from Assets Forfeiture Fund, **28 § 524 nt**
Director,
  Administrative Office of U.S. Courts, disbursements through marshals, **28 § 604**
  Appointment, duties, **28 § 561 et seq.**
  Fees and expenses, collection, utilization for salaries, **28 § 1921 nt**
District of Columbia, services in, mileage fees prohibited, **28 § 1921**
Execution, interest on money judgment, levying, **28 § 1961**
Expenses and expenditures, **28 § 565**
  Property, keeping attached, **28 § 1921**
  Traveling, **28 § 1921**
Expiration of term, performance of duties until successor is appointed and qualified, **28 § 541**
Fees, **28 § 1921**
  Collection and disposition of, expenses for services, **28 § 1921 nt**
  Collection and taxation as costs, **28 § 1921**
  Forwarding writ, to another district for service, **28 § 1921**
  Subpoena, summons, serving, **28 § 1921**
Firearms,
  Authority to carry, **28 § 566**
Florida, tenure and appointment, **28 § 89 nt**
Forwarding writ, order, or process to another judicial district, fee, **28 § 1921**
Grand jury, service of summons for service, **28 § 1866**
Habeas corpus, proceedings in forma pauperis, witness fees and mileage, payment, **28 § 1825**
Illinois, Central and Southern Districts of, designation, tenure, **28 § 93 nt**
Interpleader actions, service of process and orders restraining proceedings involving matters, in, **28 § 2361**
Investigation, official acts, by Attorney General, **28 § 526**
Judicial sales, summoning appraisers of goods taken under execution, **28 § 2005**
Jury,
  Payment of fees, **28 § 1871**

UNITED STATES MARSHALS SERVICE—Cont'd
Jury—Cont'd
  Service of summons, service on, **28 § 1866**
Justice Department, equipping forfeited vehicles, for use by, appropriations, **28 § 524**
Louisiana, Eastern and Middle Districts, tenure and appointment, **28 § 98 nt**
Meals and lodging when acting as bailiffs, appropriations, **28 § 524**
Mileage, **28 § 1921**
Northern Mariana Islands,
  Residency requirements in appointed district, applicability, **28 § 545**
Notices, preparation of, sales, fee, **28 § 1921**
Oaths and affirmations,
  Director, Marshals, of Service, oath of office, **28 § 563**
  Power of Director to administer, **28 § 561**
Official station and offices, designation, **28 § 561**
Pay. Compensation and salaries, generally, ante
Payment,
  Certain office expenses of U.S. Attorneys, **28 § 566**
Powers and duties, **28 § 566**
Powers as sheriff, **28 § 564**
Practice of law prohibited, **28 § 568**
President of U.S., appointment of marshals, **28 § 561**
Process,
  Execution, **28 § 566**
  Fees for serving, **28 § 1921**
  Interpleader, service of process in proceedings, **28 § 2361**
  Stay of execution of process in admiralty, **28 § 2464**
  Traveling expenses in serving, **28 § 1921**
Property, fee for seizing, levying on or keeping attached, **28 § 1921**
Public monies collected, deposit and disbursements, **28 § 566**
Reemployment rights, **28 § 569**
Removal, after levy on or sale of realty, **28 § 2003**
Removal of marshals, **28 § 561**
Residence of marshals, **28 § 561**
Resignation, retirement, of marshal, procedure, **28 § 566**
Salaries. Compensation and salaries, generally, ante
Sale of property, incapacity after levy on or sale, **28 § 2003**
Service of process,
  Fees, writs, orders, or process, **28 § 1921**
  Subpoenas,
    Use of appropriations to cover expenses incurred, **28 § 565**

UNITED STATES MARSHALS SERVICE—Cont'd
Stay of execution of process under warrant of arrest or other process in rem in admiralty case, **28 § 2464**
Successor, sale of realty not completed by predecessor, **28 § 2003**
Supreme Court Marshal, generally, this index
Term of office of marshals, **28 § 561**
Traveling expenses, **28 § 1921**
Uniforms, allowances, appropriations as permitted utilization, **28 § 509 nt**
United States Court of Federal Claims, attendance at sessions, **28 § 2521**
Vacancies, **28 § 562**

UNITED STATES NAVY
Navy, generally, this index

UNITED STATES OBLIGATIONS
Attached property in actions against delinquent postmasters and postal officers, employees, investment of proceeds in, **28 § 2714**

UNITED STATES POSSESSIONS
Insular Possessions and Dependencies, generally, this index

UNITED STATES SENTENCING COMMISSION
Sentence and Punishment, this index

UNITED STATES TAX COURT
Appeal and review,
  Courts of appeals,
    Rules prescribed by Supreme Court, **28 § 2072**
  Rules,
    Prescribing by Supreme Court, **28 § 2072**
    Savings provision, **28 § 2073 nt**
Appearance,
  Personally or by counsel, **28 § 1654**
Bankruptcy,
  Removal of claims related to bankruptcy cases to district courts, exception, **28 § 1452**
Black persons, selection of qualified individuals for nomination to judgeships, Congressional recommendations, **28 § 133 nt**
Clerks of courts,
  Transportation needs, judicial branch, recommendations to Congress, **28 § 456 nt**
Courts of appeals, review of Tax Court decisions,
  Provisions concerning record on review of agency, orders, inapplicability, **28 § 2112**
  Rules to be prescribed by Supreme Court, **28 §§ 2072, 2073 nt**

UNITED STATES TAX COURT—Cont'd
Judges,
Selection for nomination, Congressional recommendations regarding blacks and women as qualified individuals for, **28 § 133 nt**
Judicial review of decisions. Appeal and review, generally, ante
Nominations, Congressional recommendations regarding blacks and women as qualified individuals for selection for nomination to judgeships, **28 § 133 nt**
Rules of Appellate Procedure, this index
Rules of practice and procedure and forms,
Civil justice reform, applicability, **28 § 519 nt, EON 12988**
Supreme Court,
Rules for review of decisions, **28 § 2072**
Savings provision, **28 § 2073 nt**
Women, selection of qualified individuals for nomination to judgeships, Congressional recommendations, **28 § 133 nt**

UNITED STATES TREASURER
Treasurer of United States, generally, this index

UNITED STATES TREASURY
Treasury of United States, generally, this index

UNLAWFUL COMBINATIONS
Monopolies and Combinations, generally, this index

UNLAWFUL RESTRAINT
Kidnapping, generally, this index

UNOBLIGATED BALANCES
Appropriations, generally, this index

URBAN AREAS
Community Development, generally, this index

URBAN HOMESTEADS AND HOMESTEADING
Resolution Trust Corporation, generally, this index

UTAH
See, also, States, generally, this index
Bankruptcy judges, appointment, number in judicial district, **28 § 152**
District courts,
Cities, held at, **28 § 125**
Judges,
Additional, **28 § 133 nt**
Number, **28 § 133**
Places of holding, **28 § 125**
Judicial circuit of U.S., **28 § 41**

UTAH—Cont'd
Judicial districts, **28 § 125**
Bankruptcy provisions, applicability of certain amendments to, **28 § 581 nt**
Number of district judges, **28 § 133**
United States trustees of judicial districts, appointment, **28 § 581**

VACATION OF COURTS
Supreme Court, this index

VENUE OR DISTRICT OF TRIAL
See, also, Jurisdiction, generally, this index
Generally, **28 § 1391 et seq.**
Acts of Congress, claims against U.S., **28 § 1402**
Admiralty, enforcement of fines, penalties and forfeiture, **28 § 1395**
Aliens, suit against, **28 § 1391**
Alteration of district or division, **28 § 1405**
Arrest in one district for trial in another in civil action, **28 § 1693**
Banking associations, actions against Comptroller of Currency, **28 § 1394**
Cargo, forfeiture, **28 § 1395**
Change of venue, **28 § 1404**
Creation or alteration of district or division, **28 § 1405**
Cure or waiver of defects, **28 § 1406**
Transfer of case to district or division in which it could have been brought, **28 § 1406**
Common questions of fact, multidistrict litigation, transfer to single district, **28 § 1407**
Comptroller of Currency, banking association action against, **28 § 1394**
Constitution of United States,
Claims against U.S., **28 § 1402**
Contracts with U.S., claims founded on, **28 § 1402**
Creation or alteration of district or division, **28 § 1405**
Damages, claim against U.S., **28 § 1402**
Dismissal of action where venue laid in wrong division or district, **28 § 1406**
District,
Defined, change of venue, **28 §§ 1404, 1406**
In which claim arose, bringing action in, **28 § 1391**
District courts, defined, change of venue, **28 §§ 1404, 1406**
Diversity of citizenship, **28 § 1391**
Eminent domain, proceedings by U.S. **28 § 1403**
Excessive taxes, recovery, action against U.S., **28 § 1402**
Executive departments, regulations, actions founded upon, **28 § 1402**

VENUE OR DISTRICT OF TRIAL—Cont'd
Fines, penalties and forfeitures, **28 § 1395**
Collected without authority, internal revenue, recovery, action against U.S., **28 § 1402**
Foreign states, actions against, **28 § 1391**
Habeas corpus, persons in custody under judgment, of State court, State containing 2 or more Federal judicial districts, **28 § 2241**
Injunction, against Comptroller of Currency by national bank, **28 § 1394**
Interpleader, **28 § 1397**
Joinder of additional parties in accordance with other venue requirements, **28 § 1391**
Laying venue in wrong division or district, cure or waiver of defects, **28 § 1406**
Lien, enforcement, district courts, absence of defendant, **28 § 1655**
Mask works, **28 § 1400**
Objections, waiver of defects, **28 § 1406**
Officers or employees of U.S., actions against, **28 § 1391**
Order for trial at any place in division, **28 § 1404**
Partition action involving U.S., **28 § 1399**
Patents, **28 § 1400**
Presidential and executive office accountability, **28 § 1413**
Pretrial proceedings, coordinated or consolidated, multidistrict litigation, **28 § 1407**
Property located in different districts in same State, **28 § 1392**
Quieting title to real property, actions where U.S. party defendant, **28 § 1402**
Recovery of taxes erroneously or illegally assessed or collected, action against U.S., **28 § 1402**
Review, orders, certain Federal agencies, **28 § 2343**
Rules of Civil Procedure, this index
Stockholders,
Derivative action by, **28 § 1401**
Surface Transportation Board orders, enforcement, suspension, **28 § 1398**
Tax refund action, corporation against U.S., **28 § 1402**
United States,
As party defendant, actions to quiet title to real property, **28 § 1402**
Partition action involving, **28 § 1399**
Suit against, **28 § 1402**
Vessels, enforcement of fines, penalties and forfeitures against, venue, **28 § 1395**

VERDICT
Garnishment proceedings by U.S., **28 § 2405**

VERMONT
See, also, States, generally, this index
Bankruptcy judges, appointment, number in judicial district, **28 § 152**
District courts,
Cities, held at, **28 § 126**
Judges, number, **28 § 133**
Places of holding, **28 § 126**
Judicial circuit of U.S., **28 § 41**
Judicial districts, **28 § 126**
Bankruptcy provisions, applicability, certain amendments to, **28 § 581 nt**
Number of district judges, **28 § 133**
United States trustees of judicial districts, appointment, **28 § 581**

VESSELS
See, also, Ships and Shipping, generally, this index
Fines, penalties and forfeitures,
Cargo, venue, **28 § 1395**
Enforcement against vessels, venue, **28 § 1395**
Jury trial in matters involving certain vessels in coasting trade, **28 § 1873**
United States marshal, fees for keeping attached or libeled vessel, **28 § 1921**

VETERANS
Colleges, approval for benefit payments, **28 § 104**
National Cemeteries, generally, this index
Secretary of Veterans Affairs, generally, this index
United States Court of Appeals for Veterans Claims, generally, this index

VETERANS AFFAIRS, SECRETARY OF
Secretary of Veterans Affairs, generally, this index

VETERANS APPEALS, UNITED STATES COURT OF
United States Court of Appeals for Veterans Claims, generally, this index

VETERANS' CEMETERY PROTECTION ACT OF 1997
Generally, **28 § 994 nt**

VICE PRESIDENT
Disclosure of Federal Campaign Funds, generally, this index
Presidential and Vice Presidential Electors, generally, this index
Seals (Official Seals), generally, this index

VICTIM COMPENSATION AND ASSISTANCE
Crime victims,
United States Sentencing Commission, guidelines, instruction for promulgation, **28 § 994 nt**

VICTIMS
Torture victim protection, **28 § 1350 nt**
Victim Compensation and Assistance, generally, this index
Violent Crime Control and Law Enforcement, generally, this index

VIETNAM
Veterans, generally, this index

VIOLENT CRIME CONTROL AND LAW ENFORCEMENT
Foreign travelers, violent crimes, FBI, investigation, **28 § 540A**
Missing Children, generally, this index
National Drug Policy, generally, this index
Travelers, violent crimes, FBI, investigation, **28 § 540A**
Violence against women,
National stalker and domestic violence reduction,
Attorney General, powers, duties, functions, **28 § 534 nt**
Authorization of access, Federal criminal information databases, **28 § 534**
Databases, Federal criminal information, authorization of access, **28 § 534**
Information, Federal criminal databases, authorization of access, **28 § 534**
National crime information databases, defined, **28 § 534**
Protection order, defined, **28 § 534**
Records and recordation, Federal criminal information databases, authorization of access, **28 § 534**
Rules and regulations, promulgation, consultation, Attorney General, **28 § 534 nt**
Stalkers and stalking, reduction, authorization of access, Federal criminal information databases, **28 § 534**
Safe streets,
Reports,
Federal rape sentencing analysis, sex crimes, **28 § 994 nt**
Sex crimes,
Federal penalties, amendment of sentencing guidelines, authority of Sentencing Commission, **28 § 994 nt**
Women's civil rights,
Removal of actions or proceedings, limitation, removal prohibited, district court, gender-motivated violent crimes, **28 § 1445**

VIRGIN ISLANDS
Courts,
Defined, Jury Selection and Service Act, **28 § 1869**

VIRGIN ISLANDS—Cont'd
District courts,
Appeal,
From final decision in certain cases, jurisdiction of U.S. Court of Appeals for the Federal Circuit, **28 § 1295**
Appeals from district court, courts of appeals,
Circuit to which appeal is taken, **28 § 1294**
Final decisions, **28 § 1291**
Interlocutory decisions, **28 § 1292**
Cities, held, **28 § 127**
Claims against U.S., jurisdiction, **28 § 1346**
Clerk of court,
Investigation, official acts, by Attorney General, **28 § 526**
Defined,
Jury Selection and Service Act, **28 § 1869**
Evidence, **28 § 1731 et seq.**
Interlocutory orders, relief, jurisdiction of courts of appeals, **28 § 1292**
Judges or justices,
Acknowledgments, authority to take, **28 § 459**
Additional, appointment and term of office, **28 § 133 nt**
Annuities to survivors, **28 § 376**
Judicial conference, summoning judge to attend, **28 § 333**
Oaths and affirmations, authority to administer, **28 §§ 459, 460**
Relative ineligible to appointment to office or duty in court, **28 § 458**
Salary,
On resignation, removal, **28 § 373**
Effect on amount payable to judge retired before enactment of provisions, **28 § 373 nt**
Senior judge of the court, qualifications, **28 § 373 nt**
Jurisdiction,
Claims against U.S., **28 § 1346**
Transfer to cure want of, **28 § 1631**
Obsolete papers, disposition, **28 § 457**
Procedure, **28 § 1651 et seq.**
Records and recordation, **28 § 457**
Reporter, **28 § 753**
Rules,
Power to prescribe, public notice and comment, **28 § 2071**
Savings provision, **28 § 2071 nt**
United States Magistrate Judges, appointment, **28 § 631**
Grand jury, selection and service, **28 § 1861 et seq.**
Judges or justices,
District courts, ante
Judicial Circuit of U.S., **28 § 41**
Judicial district, bankruptcy provisions, applicability of certain amendments to, **28 § 581 nt**

VIRGIN ISLANDS—Cont'd
Jurisdiction. District courts, ante
Jury selection and service, **28 § 1861 et seq.**
President of the United States,
Judges for district court, appointment, Additional, **28 § 133 nt**
Senate,
District court judges, appointment, advice and consent, **28 § 133 nt**
United States Magistrate Judges, appointment, **28 § 631**
United States trustees of judicial districts, appointment, **28 § 581**

VIRGINIA
See, also, States, generally, this index
Bankruptcy judges, appointment, number in judicial district, **28 § 152**
District courts,
Judges,
Additional, **28 § 133 nt**
Number, **28 § 133**
Temporary judgeships, **28 § 133 nt**
Places of holding, **28 § 127**
Judicial Circuit of U.S., **28 § 41**
Judicial districts, **28 § 127**
Bankruptcy provisions, applicability of certain amendments to, **28 § 581 nt**
Number of district judges, **28 § 133**
United States trustees of judicial districts, appointment, **28 § 581**

VISA
Fraud,
Sentencing guidelines, **28 § 994 nt**
Immigrant visa,
Fraud in obtaining,
Sentencing guidelines, **28 § 994 nt**

VOLUNTARY MANSLAUGHTER
Manslaughter, generally, this index

VOLUNTEERS
Federal agencies and instrumentalities, civil justice reform, **28 § 519 nt, EON 12988**
Supreme Court,
Administrative Assistant to Chief Justice, **28 § 677**

VOUCHERS
Disbursing officers,
Jurisdiction of U.S. Court of Federal Claims to relieve from responsibility, **28 § 1496**
United States, credit in actions by, **28 § 2406**
United States Court of Federal Claims, referral of cases by Comptroller General, **28 § 2510**

WAGERS AND WAGERING
Gambling, generally, this index

WAGES
Compensation and Salaries, generally, this index

WAKE ISLAND
Judicial district of Hawaii, inclusion in, **28 § 91**

WAR
Actions by U.S., period of limitation, exclusion, **28 § 2416**
Insurrection and Sedition, generally, this index
Prize (Vessels), generally, this index
Secretary of Army, generally, this index
Tort Claims Act, exception of claim arising out of combatant activities of military forces, **28 § 2680**

WARD
Guardian and Ward, generally, this index

WARRANTS
Fees, U.S. marshal for serving, **28 § 1921**
Independent Counsel, this index

WASHINGTON (STATE)
See, also, States, generally, this index
Bankruptcy judges, appointment, number in judicial district, **28 § 152**
District court,
Cities, where held, **28 § 128**
Judges, **28 § 133 nt**
Places of holding, **28 § 128**
Judicial circuit of U.S., **28 § 41**
Judicial districts, **28 § 128**
Bankruptcy provisions, applicability of certain amendments to, **28 § 581 nt**
Judgeships for Eastern and Western districts combined into Western district only, **28 § 133 nt**
Number of district judges, **28 § 133**
States, generally, this index
United States trustees of judicial districts, appointment, **28 § 581**

WASHINGTON, DC
District of Columbia, generally, this index

WATER RIGHTS
Public lands, suits for adjudication, real property, quieting title, inapplicability to actions involving claims against U.S., **28 § 2409a**
Real estate, quieting title, inapplicability to actions involving claims against U.S., **28 § 2409a**

WATERS AND WATER COURSES
Navigable Waters, generally, this index

WEST GERMANY
Germany, generally, this index

WEST VIRGINIA
See, also, States, generally, this index

WEST VIRGINIA—Cont'd
Bankruptcy judges, appointment, number in judicial district, **28 § 152**
District courts,
Cities, held at, **28 § 129**
Judges,
Additional, **28 § 133 nt**
Appointment, additional judges, advice and consent, **28 § 133 nt**
Modification as to distribution of judges to districts, **28 § 133 nt**
Number, **28 § 133**
Places of holding, **28 § 129**
Judicial circuit of U.S., **28 § 41**
Judicial districts, **28 § 129**
Bankruptcy provisions, applicability of certain amendments to, **28 § 581 nt**
Modification as to distribution of judges in, **28 § 133 nt**
Number of district judges, **28 § 133**
United States trustees of judicial districts, appointment, **28 § 581**

WICHITA, KS
Court of Appeals for Tenth Circuit, generally, this index

WIFE
Husband and Wife, generally, this index

WIRE TAPPING
Interception of Wire, Oral, or Electronic Communications, generally, this index

WIRELESS TELEPHONE PROTECTION ACT
Generally, **28 § 994 nt**

WISCONSIN
See, also, States, generally, this index
Bankruptcy judges, appointment, number in judicial district, **28 § 152**
District courts,
Cities, held at, **28 § 130**
Judges,
Additional, **28 § 133 nt**
Number, **28 § 133**
Places of holding, **28 § 130**
Indians, State civil jurisdiction in actions to which Indians are parties, **28 § 1360**
Judicial circuit of U.S., **28 § 41**
Judicial districts, **28 § 130**
Bankruptcy provisions, applicability of certain amendments to, **28 § 581 nt**
Number of district judges, **28 § 133**
United States trustees of judicial districts, appointment, **28 § 581**

WITNESSES
Administrative Law and Procedure, this index
Allowances, incarcerated persons, prohibition, **28 § 1821**

WITNESSES—Cont'd
Appearance, detention for want of security of appearance, **28 § 1821**
Assistance to foreign and international tribunals, and to litigants before such tribunals, **28 § 1782**
Bail and recognizances, confinement of recalcitrant witnesses, **28 § 1826**
Books and papers, recalcitrant witnesses refusal to obey court's order to provide books, **28 § 1826**
Certificates,
  United States attorney for payment of witness fees, **28 § 1825**
Change of venue for convenience, **28 § 1404**
Compensation and salaries, **28 § 1821**
  Fees, generally, post
Competency,
  Interested persons, **28 § 1822**
  United States Court of Federal Claims, party or interested in suit, **28 § 2506**
Confinement, recalcitrant witnesses refusal to obey court's order to provide certain information, **28 § 1826**
Contempt of witness. Contempt, generally, this index
Cross Examination, generally, this index
Depositions, this index
Examinations and Examiners, generally, this index
Expenses and expenditures. Fees, generally, post
Experts. Fees, generally, post
Federal agency hearings, award of attorneys' fees and other expenses, **28 § 2412**
Fees, **28 § 1821**
  Fact witness fee for testifying, incarcerated person, prohibition, **28 § 1821 nt**
  Federal agency hearings,
    Award of attorneys' fees and other expenses, **28 § 2412**
  Foreign country, subpoena, **28 § 1783**
  Habeas corpus, proceedings in forma pauperis, payment, **28 § 1825**
  Incarcerated persons, prohibition, **28 § 1821**
  Parental Kidnapping Prevention Act, award to person entitled to custody or visitation, **28 § 1738A nt**
  Payment, **28 § 1825**
  Taxation as costs, **28 § 1920**
  Tender on service of subpoena, **28 § 1825**
  United States Magistrate Judge, proceeding before, **28 § 1922**
  United States marshal, service of subpoena, **28 § 1921**
Forma pauperis, proceedings in, **28 § 1915**
Grand Jury, this index

WITNESSES—Cont'd
Immunity,
  Foreign and international tribunals, person not to be compelled to give testimony or produce document for use in proceeding in, **28 § 1782**
Incarcerated persons, fees or allowances, prohibition, **28 § 1821**
Independent Counsel, this index
Information, refusal of recalcitrant witness to provide, **28 § 1826**
Interested persons,
  Competency, **28 § 1822**
  United States Court of Federal Claims, exemption or disqualification, **28 § 2506**
Justice Department,
  Appropriations available for expenses, of, **28 § 524**
  Competitive procurement procedures, procure services without regard to, **28 § 509 nt**
Justice or judge of U.S., disqualification by being or having been witness, **28 § 455**
Letters rogatory, transmittal, **28 § 1781**
Mileage, **28 § 1821**
  Habeas corpus, proceedings in forma pauperis, payment, **28 § 1825**
  Subpoena in behalf of U.S., forma pauperis proceedings, tender, **28 § 1825**
  Summons as both witness and juror, **28 § 1824**
  Tender on service of subpoena, **28 § 1825**
Multidistrict litigation, transfer to single district for consolidated, pretrial proceedings, **28 § 1407**
Noncompliance of recalcitrant witness to court's order to testify, **28 § 1826**
Order of court, noncompliance of recalcitrant witness in testifying or providing information, **28 § 1826**
Per diem, **28 § 1821**
Privileges and immunities. Immunity, generally, ante
Recalcitrant witnesses, **28 § 1826**
  Expedite proceeding to hear and determine, **28 § 1657**
Release, generally, this index
Rules of Civil Procedure, this index
Rules of Evidence, this index
Security for appearance, compensation of witness detained for want of, **28 § 1821**
Senate, this index
Subpoenas, generally, this index
Subsistence expenses, **28 § 1821**
Summons, this index
Traveling Expenses, this index
United States, this index
United States Attorneys, this index
United States Court of Federal Claims, this index

WITNESSES—Cont'd
United States Court of International Trade, this index
Voluntarily giving testimony or statement for use in proceeding in foreign or international tribunal, **28 § 1782**

WIVES
Husband and Wife, generally, this index

WOMEN
Federal judgeships, nomination of women to, Congressional recommendations, **28 § 133 nt**
Husband and Wife, generally, this index
United States Magistrate Judges, merit selection panel to consider, **28 § 631 nt**

WORDS AND PHRASES
Definitions, generally, this index

WORK FARMS
Correctional Institutions, generally, this index

WORK HOURS AND SAFETY ACT OF 1962
  Generally, **28 § 1499**
Hours of Labor, generally, this index

WORKERS COMPENSATION
Employees' Compensation for Work Injuries, generally, this index
Federal Employers' Liability Act, generally, this index
Removability from action under State compensation laws to Federal court, **28 § 1445**

WORKING CAPITAL FUNDS
Justice Department, this index

WORKING HOURS
Hours of Labor, generally, this index

WORKMEN
Labor and Employment, generally, this index

WORKMENS COMPENSATION
Workers Compensation, generally, this index

WORLD WAR I
Veterans, generally, this index

WORLD WAR II
Trading With the Enemy, generally, this index
Veterans, generally, this index

WRITINGS
Habeas corpus,
  Application for writ, **28 § 2242**
  Written interrogatories, affidavits admitted as evidence, **28 § 2246**
Handwriting, evidence, **28 § 1731**

WRITINGS—Cont'd
Interrogatories,
Habeas corpus proceeding, affidavits admitted as evidence, **28 § 2246**
Public Contracts, generally, this index
Regular course of business, evidence, **28 § 1732**

WRITS
Admiralty rules for district courts and courts of appeals, power of Supreme Court to prescribe, **28 § 2072**
Savings provision, **28 § 2073 nt**
Alternative writs, power to issue, **28 § 1651**
Appeal and Review, generally, this index
Bankruptcy, forms, rules prescribing, **28 § 2075**
Certiorari, generally, this index
Error, construction of writ of error to mean appeal, **28 § 1651 nt**
Habeas Corpus, generally, this index
Judicial Panel on Multidistrict Litigation, review, orders of, **28 § 1407**

WRITS—Cont'd
Mandamus, generally, this index
Power to issue, **28 § 1651**
Process, generally, this index
Rules of Appellate Procedure, this index
Rules of Civil Procedure, this index
Seal of court, **28 § 1691**
Supreme Court, this index
Surface Transportation Board orders, procedure in district court, **28 § 2321**
United States marshals, fees for serving, **28 § 1921**

WRITS OF ERROR
Abolished, **28 nt prec § 1**
Appeal substituted for, **28 nt prec § 1**
Construction of Acts of Congress referring to, **28 nt prec § 1**

WRITTEN INTERROGATORIES
Interrogatories, generally, this index

WYOMING
See, also, States, generally, this index
District courts,
Judges,
Additional, **28 § 133 nt**
Appointment,
Additional judges, advice and consent, **28 § 133 nt**
Number in judicial district, **28 § 152**
Number, **28 § 133**
Places of holding, **28 § 131**
Judicial circuit of U.S., **28 § 41**
Judicial districts, **28 § 131**
Bankruptcy provisions, applicability of certain amendments to, **28 § 581 nt**
Number of district judges, **28 § 133**
United States trustees of judicial districts, appointment, **28 § 581**

YOUTH
Children and Minors, generally, this index